Merriam-Webster's Dictionary of English Usage

A Merriam-Webster®

Merriam-Webster, Incorporated, *Publishers*
Springfield, Massachusetts

Library of Congress Cataloging in Publication Data
Main entry under title:

Merriam-Webster's dictionary of English usage.
     p.   cm.
    Includes bibliographical references.
    ISBN 0-87779-132-5
    1. English language—Usage—Dictionaries. I. Merriam-
Webster, Inc. II. Title: Dictionary of English usage
PE1460.M45   1994
428′.003—dc20   94-12822
                                CIP

9101112HP0201009998

Contents

Preface

Merriam-Webster's Dictionary of English Usage examines and evaluates common problems of confused or disputed English usage from two perspectives: that of historical background, especially as shown in the great historical dictionaries, and that of present-day usage, chiefly as shown by evidence in the Merriam-Webster files. Most of the topics treated have been selected from existing books on usage, primarily those published in the second half of the 20th century; a few have emerged too recently to have yet become part of the tradition of usage commentary. We have also ranged freely over much earlier books, many of which contain the seeds of current concerns. Most of our topics have been commented on by numerous writers; the pet peeves of individual commentators have in the main been passed over. During the course of writing this book, new books on usage were published, and they find mention in entries written after they were received, but no systematic attempt has been made to incorporate mention of them in entries written before they were received.

Besides articles dealing with the traditional concerns of usage, we have included many illustrating idiomatic English usage, chiefly in the area of which prepositions go with which nouns, verbs, and adjectives. In our selection of these we have simply included those that have come readily to our attention and have not tried to make an exhaustive search for them. A thorough treatment of English idioms would require an entire book at least as large as this one. We think our selection is fairly generous—there are about 500 entries—and we have been careful to illustrate instances of varying usage. A number of common spelling problems are also discussed briefly. While the emphasis of this work is properly on usage in writing, a small group of articles has been devoted to problems of pronunciation.

Insofar as we could, we have generously supplied the articles with illustrative quotations on the theory that examples of actual usage are more valuable to one who is actually grappling with a problem in usage than are the made-up examples many commentators rely on. The bulk of these quotations have been taken from the Merriam-Webster files. We have supplemented our own resources, as necessary, with quotations taken from other published sources, such as the historical dictionaries and Otto Jespersen's seven-volume *Modern English Grammar.* We have tried to identify parenthetically every citation taken from these publications.

This preface is followed in the front matter by two sections which we recommend to all users of this work. A Brief History of English Usage will provide useful orientation for readers who wonder how questions involving no more than a tiny portion of the huge vocabulary of English and a handful of grammatical constructions came to take on so much importance to teachers, writers, and others. The Explanatory Notes attempt to anticipate users' questions with information about the conventions employed within the dictionary itself. Following the last entry is a Bibliography, which serves the dual purpose of recording those commentaries on usage, dictionaries, grammars, and other works frequently consulted during the writing of this book and being a source of suggestions for further reading.

It is the fate of most of the harmless drudges in the lexicographical world to receive their most material tribute in the unread front matter of a book. This time-honored tradition will be continued here. By rights the entire Merriam-Webster editorial staff could be listed, since almost everyone has contributed at least indirectly, but instead we will list only those who worked directly on the book. Staff members are grouped according to their several tasks. The conspicuous avoidance of alphabetical order in listing names is intended only to provide a temporary escape from the tyranny of the alphabet.

The articles were written by Stephen J. Perrault, Kathleen M. Doherty, David B. Justice, Madeline L. Novak, and E. Ward Gilman. They were taken in hand for copyediting by James G. Lowe, Madeline L. Novak, John M. Morse, and Stephen J. Perrault. The quotations have been verified by Kathleen M. Doherty, who also compiled the bibliography. Eileen M. Haraty has connected all the loose wires of cross-reference. The bothersome business of proofreading has been carried out by Daniel J. Hopkins, Paul F. Cappellano, Peter D. Haraty, Julie A. Collier, Kelly L. Tierney, and Robert D. Copeland, as well as some of the aforementioned. The manuscript was deciphered and turned into readable typescript for the compositor by Georgette B. Boucher, Barbara A. Winkler, and Helene Gingold; other kinds of invaluable clerical assistance have been performed by Ruth W. Gaines and Gloria J. Afflitto. Madeline L. Novak directed the book through its typesetting stages. Francine A. Roberts cajoled copies of rare books from various college and university libraries. The entire manuscript has been reviewed by Frederick C. Mish, Editorial Director.

James Thurber once referred in a letter to "the perils of typo and garble." No reference work is immune from these perils in spite of the diligent efforts of copy editors and proofreaders. We can only hope that if you encounter a typo or garble that has slipped through, you are not misled or confused. We would be glad to know of any that are found.

We believe that Merriam-Webster's Dictionary of English Usage contains a wealth of information, along with some quite practical advice, and that you will find it a useful, interesting, and occasionally entertaining work of reference.

E. Ward Gilman
Editor

4a

Explanatory Notes

Articles

Each article in this dictionary, like the entries in a general dictionary, is introduced by one or more boldface words indicating the subject for discussion:

media
glimpse, glance
reason is because
agreement: indefinite pronouns

Words that are homographs are distinguished by italic labels indicating part of speech:

hold, *verb*
hold, *noun*

An article that treats more than one aspect of its subject may be divided into sections, each section introduced by a boldface arabic numeral. Where it seems useful, the topic of the section is indicated with an introductory word or phrase:

locate . . .
1. *Locate* "settle." . . .
2. *Located* "situated." . . .
3. *Locate* "find." . . .

The articles in this dictionary are too diverse and many are too complex for all to be treated according to a single uniform pattern. The longer ones, however, usually contain all or most of the following elements: origin and development of the usage with examples, origin and development of criticism of the usage, the contemporary status of the usage with examples, review of alternatives, summary and recommendation. The order and proportion of the elements vary with the requirements of the topic, of course.

Citation of Sources

Sources cited within the text of an article—as distinct from illustrative quotations, discussed below—are handled in two different ways. Works cited infrequently are identified at each appearance by author, title, and date of publication. Works cited frequently are treated in a different way, in order to conserve space. References to these works—chiefly books of commentary on English usage, handbooks for writers of various kinds, grammars, and dictionaries—take a shortened form, most often the author's last name and the date of the book's publication (as Fowler 1926 or Bolinger 1980). This form of attribution has conveniently allowed us to refer either to author or to work as the discourse requires. The context will always make clear which reference is intended.

Handbooks and dictionaries cited as sources of usage opinion may instead be identified by an element of the title combined with the date (as Prentice Hall 1978 or Heritage 1969).

A dictionary referred to as a record of usage is usually given its title without a date on its first appearance in an article (as Dictionary of American Regional English) but is thereafter referred to by a customary abbreviation (as DARE). The exception to this last rule is the Oxford English Dictionary, which is consistently cited by the well-known abbreviation OED. Noah Webster's An American Dictionary of the English Language and its successor editions are cited in this way: editions from 1828 to 1909 appear as Webster and the year of publication. The two most recent (and most familiar) editions are simply called Webster's Second and Webster's Third, for the most part, but a date is sometimes added when it seems to be helpful in the context.

Full references to all works cited in these ways appear in the Bibliography at the end of this volume.

Illustrative Quotations

This book includes thousands of illustrative quotations intended to clarify and to test the discussion. These may very occasionally be run in with the text but are usually indented and are always followed by an attribution, typically consisting of the author's name (if known), the title of the book or serial, and the date of publication. When the sources discussed in the last section are quoted, however, the usual shortened form of attribution is used.

We have not italicized the word or construction being illustrated in a quotation, so that the typographic conventions of each passage as we found it can be reproduced with reasonable accuracy. We have tried not to interfere with spelling. If the editor of an old work cited in a modern edition modernized the spelling, we have used it; if the editor preserved the old spelling, we have used that. We have only very rarely modernized spelling on our own and then only to make old words more easily recognizable. We have, however, silently corrected a few typographical errors irrelevant to the matter under discussion.

Quotations have been dated, insofar as possible, in order to establish the antiquity of a locution or its currency at some particular time or to show when an unfamiliar writer was working. As a reader you can generally assume that any quotation from the last fifty years or so represents current usage—editors have frequently preferred a clear older quotation to an ambiguous or unhelpful newer one.

The date given for a work that has passed through several editions is, in general, the date of the edition actually seen by us. Exceptions are made for famous works of earlier periods, for which the date is usually that of original publication, even though we may have consulted a modern edition. This policy has inevitably led to some inconsistencies that the observant reader may notice between our dates and those given by other sources. These are most likely with old works (as the poems of Chaucer or the plays of Shakespeare) for which we may have used one conventional set of dates while an older reference work, such as the Dictionary of Americanisms or the Oxford English Dictionary, may have used a different one. Similar problems are created by different editions of a work. Henry Alford's *A Plea for the Queen's English,* for instance, originally appeared in 1864. Our copy is the American edition of 1866. Some usage commentators may refer to the earlier edition and others to the later; you may thus find his name with 1864 in one place and 1866 in another.

We have taken a few liberties with the sources of quotations, generally omitting initial *the* when it is part of the title of a periodical, and abbreviating *supplement, magazine, journal,* and *review.* Short titles like *Robinson Crusoe* and *Tom Sawyer* are used for a few well-known works.

Cross-Reference

Directional cross-references to articles where relevant discussion may be found are employed liberally throughout the book. These may take any of several forms. If the term where the discussion is located is mentioned within the text, a parenthetical "(which see)" is placed immediately after the term. All other cross-references are in small capital letters; they may appear at the end of an article or section of an article, or they may receive separate entry:

> **good 1.** *Feel good, feel well.* . . .
> See also FEEL BAD, FEEL BADLY.

> **under the circumstances** See CIRCUMSTANCES.

No separate entry is made, however, if it would fall immediately before or after the article where the discussion is located. Thus, the misspelling *quandry* is discussed at **quandary**, but no entry for the former appears.

Pronunciation

Articles on problems of pronunciation necessarily include pronunciation respellings. The symbols used in these respellings are essentially those of Webster's Ninth New Collegiate Dictionary and are explained on the Pronunciation Symbols page, which faces the first page of the dictionary.

A Brief History of English Usage

English usage today is an area of discourse—sometimes it seems more like dispute—about the way words are used and ought to be used. This discourse makes up the subject matter of a large number of books that put the word *usage* in their titles. Behind usage as a subject lies a collection of opinions about what English grammar is or should be, about the propriety of using certain words and phrases, and about the social status of those who use certain words and constructions. A fairly large number of these opinions have been with us long enough to be regarded as rules or at least to be referred to as rules. In fact they are often regarded as rules of grammar, even if they concern only matters of social status or vocabulary selection. And many of these rules are widely believed to have universal application, even though they are far from universally observed.

To understand how these opinions and rules developed, we have to go back in history, at least as far back as the year 1417, when the official correspondence of Henry V suddenly and almost entirely stopped being written in French and started being written in English. By mid-century many government documents and even private letters were in English, and before 1500 even statutes were being recorded in the mother tongue. This restoration of English as the official language of the royal bureaucracy was one very important influence on the gradual emergence of a single standard dialect of English out of the many varied regional dialects that already existed. English now had to serve the functions formerly served by Latin and French, languages which had already assumed standard forms, and this new reality was a powerful spur to the formation of a standard in writing English that could be quite independent of variable speech. The process was certainly not completed within the 15th century, but increasingly the written form of the language that modern scholars call Chancery English had its effect, in combination with other influences such as the newfangled process of printing from movable type.

But the rise of Standard English did not by itself generate concern over usage. There was no special interest in language as such at that time. Indeed, the English historian G. M. Trevelyan called the 15th century, until its last fifteen or twenty years, the most intellectually barren epoch in English history since the Norman conquest. Not until Henry VII had established himself on the throne near the end of the century did the intellectual ferment of the European Renaissance begin to be felt in England. By the middle of the 16th century the English Renaissance was in full flower, and the revival of learning and letters brought with it a conscious interest in the English language as a medium for literature and learned discourse. There were those who had their doubts about its suitability. Still, the desire to use the vernacular rather than Latin was strong, and some of the doubters sought to put flesh on the bare bones of English by importing words from Latin, Italian, and French—the European languages of learned and graceful discourse. Among those who enriched English from the word stock of Europe were Sir Thomas Elyot and Sir Thomas More. Opposed to these enrichers of the language were purists such as Roger Ascham and Sir John Cheke, who preferred their English, rude as it might be, untainted by foreign imports. The imported learned terms became known as *inkhorn terms,* and their use and misuse by the imperfectly educated became the subject of much lively satire—some of it written by Shakespeare, among many others.

In addition to the controversy over imported words there were other concerns, such as the state of English spelling. In those days people mostly spelled things the way they sounded, and there was little uniformity indeed. A number of people consequently became interested in spelling reform. Among these was the schoolmaster Richard Mulcaster, who may have served as the model for Shakespeare's pedant Holofernes. Mulcaster and the somewhat later Edmund Coote were interested in regularizing spelling as best they could. There were more radical reformers, too—John Hart, Sir Thomas Smith, and William Bullokar are examples—who devised phonetic alphabets to better represent English speech sounds. Bullokar is worthy of note for another reason: in 1586 he published *Bref Grammar for English*—the first English grammar book. It was probably intended as an introduction to the subsequent study of Latin grammar.

So 16th-century interest in language produced two of the basic tools of the writer on usage. Bullokar, out of his interest in regularizing and reforming, had been moved to write a grammar of English. And the vocabulary controversy—the introduction of inkhorn terms by the enrichers and the revival of English archaisms by the purists (of whom the poet Edmund Spenser was one)—led another schoolmaster, Robert Cawdrey, to produce the first English dictionary in 1604.

The 17th century provides several more signposts on the way to the treatment of usage as we know it. One of these is the expression of a desire for regulation of the language by an academy similar to the ones established in Italy in the 16th century and in France in 1635. Calls for the establishment of an English academy came as early as 1617; among the writers to urge one were John Dryden in 1664, John Evelyn in 1665, and Daniel Defoe in 1697.

More grammar books were also published at this time. Ben Jonson's appeared posthumously in 1640. It is short and sketchy and is intended for the use of foreigners. Its grammar is descriptive, but Jonson hung his observations on a Latin grammatical framework. It also seems to be the first English grammar book to quote the

Roman rhetorician Quintilian's dictum "Custom is the most certain mistress of language."

John Wallis, a mathematician and member of the Royal Society, published in 1653 a grammar, written in Latin, for the use of foreigners who wanted to learn English. Wallis, according to George H. McKnight, abandoned much of the method of Latin grammar. Wallis's grammar is perhaps best remembered for being the source of the much discussed distinction between *shall* and *will*. Wallis's grammar is also the one referred to by Samuel Johnson in the front matter of his 1755 dictionary.

John Dryden deserves mention too. He defended the English of his time as an improvement over the English of Shakespeare and Jonson. He is the first person we know of who worried about the preposition at the end of a sentence. He eliminated many such from his own writings when revising his works for a collected edition. He seems to have decided the practice was wrong because it could not happen in Latin.

C. C. Fries tells us that 17th-century grammars in general were designed either for foreigners or for school use, in order to lead to the study of Latin. In the 18th century, however, grammars were written predominantly for English speakers, and although they were written for the purpose of instructing, they seem to find more fun in correcting. A change in the underlying philosophy of grammar had occurred, and it is made explicit in perhaps the first 18th-century grammar, *A Key to the Art of Letters . . .* , published in 1700 by a schoolmaster named A. Lane. He thought it a mistake to view grammar simply as a means to learn a foreign language and asserted that "the true End and Use of *Grammar* is to teach how to speak and write well and learnedly in a language already known, according to the unalterable Rules of right Reason." Gone was Ben Jonson's appeal to custom.

There was evidently a considerable amount of general interest in things grammatical among men of letters, for Addison, Steele, and Swift all treated grammar in one way or another in *The Tatler* and *The Spectator* in 1710, 1711, and 1712. In 1712 Swift published yet another proposal for an English academy (it came within a whisker of succeeding); John Oldmixon attacked Swift's proposal in the same year. Public interest must have helped create a market for the grammar books which began appearing with some frequency about this same time. And if controversy fuels sales, grammarians knew it; they were perfectly willing to emphasize their own advantages by denigrating their predecessors, sometimes in abusive terms.

We need mention only a few of these productions here. Pride of place must go to Bishop Robert Lowth's *A Short Introduction to English Grammar*, 1762. Lowth's book is both brief and logical. Lowth was influenced by the theories of James Harris's *Hermes*, 1751, a curious disquisition about universal grammar. Lowth apparently derived his notions about the perfectibility of English grammar from Harris, and he did not doubt that he could reduce the language to a system of uniform rules. Lowth's approach was strictly prescriptive; he meant to improve and correct, not describe. He judged correctness by his own rules—mostly derived from Latin grammar—which frequently went against established usage. His favorite mode of illustration is what was known as "false syntax": examples of linguistic wrongdoing from the King James Bible, Shakespeare, Sidney, Donne, Milton, Swift, Addison, Pope—the most respected names in English literature. He was so sure of himself that he could permit himself a little joke;

discussing the construction where a preposition comes at the end of a clause or sentence, he says, "This is an idiom, which our language is strongly inclined to."

Lowth's grammar was not written for children. But he did what he intended to so well that subsequent grammarians fairly fell over themselves in haste to get out versions of Lowth suitable for school use, and most subsequent grammars—including Noah Webster's first—were to some extent based upon Lowth's.

The older descriptive tradition of Jonson and Wallis was not quite dead, however. Joseph Priestley, whose grammar was first published in 1761, added a supplementary section in 1768 that used false syntax too. In the main Priestley was more tolerant of established usages than Lowth, and he disagreed with Lowth on specific points. Priestley's grammar enjoyed some success and his opinions were treated with respect, but he was not imitated like Lowth.

The most successful of the Lowth adapters was Lindley Murray. Murray was an American living in England—Dennis Baron informs us that he had made a considerable fortune trading with the Loyalists during the American Revolution and had moved to England ostensibly for reasons of health. Friends asked him to write a grammar for use in an English girls' school, and he obliged. Murray considered himself only a compiler, and that he was. He took over verbatim large patches from Lowth and teased them out with pieces taken from Priestley and a few other grammarians and rhetoricians. He removed the authors' names from the false syntax and stirred in a heavy dose of piety. He silently and primly corrected Lowth's jocular little clause to "to which our language is strongly inclined." The resulting mixture was one of the most successful grammar books ever, remaining a standard text in American schools for a half century.

George Campbell's *The Philosophy of Rhetoric*, 1776, is not a grammar book proper, but it contains a long discussion of grammatical proprieties. Campbell starts out sensibly enough; he says that grammar is based on usage, and he rejects notions of an abstract or universal grammar. But he then proceeds to examine usage, concluding that the usage that counts is reputable, national, and present use. He goes on to present nine canons of verbal criticism, by one or another of which he can reject any usage he chooses to. By the time all the discussions of barbarisms, solecisms, and improprieties are finished—the discussions are well supplied with examples from many of Bishop Lowth's favorite whipping boys—it is quite apparent that the reputable, national, and present use that passes all tests is simply whatever suits the taste of George Campbell.

Books of grammar and rhetoric had existed in English from the 16th and 17th centuries. The 18th century's new contribution was the book of unvarnished usage opinion, best exemplified by Robert Baker's anonymously published *Reflections on the English Language*, 1770. (Baker was apparently anticipated in this genre by *Observations upon the English Language*, 1752, another anonymous publication, ascribed by Sterling A. Leonard to one George Harris.) We know nothing of Baker except what he put down about himself in his preface. He says that he left school at fifteen, that he learned no Greek and only the easiest Latin, that he has never seen the folio edition of Johnson's Dictionary, and that he owns no books. He fancies he has good taste, however, and he clearly understands French. His book is patterned on *Remarques sur la langue françoise*, 1659, written by Claude Faure de Vaugelas, a leading member of the French Academy.

Baker's *Reflections* is a random collection of comments, mostly about what he considers misuses, based chiefly on books that he has borrowed or read. He brings forward no authorities to support his *ipse dixit* pronouncements, many of which are on the order of "This is not good English" or "This does not make sense." Yet a surprising number of the locutions he questioned are still to be found as topics of discussion in current books on usage. It is less surprising, perhaps, that the moderns are still repeating Baker's conclusions.

The 19th century is so rich in usage lore that it is hard to summarize. We find something new in the entrance of journalists into the usage field. Reviews had commented on grammatical matters throughout the 18th century, it is true, but in the 19th newspapers and magazines with wider popular appeal began to pronounce. One result of this activity was the usage book that consists of pieces first written for a newspaper or magazine and then collected into a book along with selected comments and suggestions by readers (this type of book is still common today). Perhaps the first of these was *A Plea for the Queen's English,* 1864, by Henry Alford, dean of Canterbury. Alford was vigorously attacked by George Washington Moon, a writer born in London of American parents, in a work that eventually became titled *The Dean's English.* The controversy fueled several editions of both books and seems to have entertained readers on both sides of the Atlantic.

On the American side of the Atlantic the puristic strictures of Edward S. Gould, originally newspaper and magazine contributions, were collected as *Good English* in 1867. Gould was apparently annoyed to find that Alford had anticipated him on several points, and devoted a section to belaboring the Dean, only to discover that Moon had anticipated him there. He acknowledged the justness of Moon's criticisms and then appended a few parting shots at Moon's English, before tacking on an assault on the spelling reforms of Noah Webster and a series of lectures on pulpit oratory. Moon replied with *The Bad English of Lindley Murray and Other Writers on the English Language,* 1868, listed by H. L. Mencken as being in its eighth edition in 1882, under the title *Bad English Exposed.* (Gould was one of the "other writers.") Language controversy sold books in America as well as in England.

The most popular of American 19th-century commentators was Richard Grant White, whose *Words and Their Uses,* 1870, was also compiled from previously published articles. He did not deign to mention earlier commentators except to take a solitary whack at Dean Alford for his sneer at American English. His chapters on "misused words" and "words that are not words" hit many of the same targets as Gould's chapters on "misused words" and "spurious words," but White's chapters are longer. Perhaps his most entertaining sections deal with his denial that English has a grammar, which is introduced by a Dickensian account of having been rapped over the knuckles at age five and a half for not understanding his grammar lesson. White, who was not without intellectual attainments—he had edited Shakespeare—was nevertheless given to frequent faulty etymologizing, and for some reason he was so upset by the progressive passive *is being built* that he devoted a whole chapter to excoriating it. These last two features caught the attention of the peppery Fitzedward Hall, an American teacher of Sanskrit living in England. Hall produced a whole book—*Recent Exemplifications of False Philology,* 1872—exposing White's errors, and returned to the attack again with *Modern English* in 1873. Hall was a new breed of commentator, bringing a

wealth of illustrative material from his collection of examples to bear on the various points of contention. Hall's evidence should have been more than enough to overwhelm White's unsupported assertions, but it was not. Partly to blame is the public's disdain of the scholarly, and partly to blame is Hall's style—he never makes a point succinctly, but lets his most trenchant observations dissipate in a cloud of sesquipedalian afterthoughts. White's books, Mencken tells us, remained in print until the 1930s; Hall's collection of examples became part of the foundations of the *Oxford English Dictionary.*

Two other 19th-century innovations deserve mention. William Cullen Bryant's *Index Expurgatorius,* 1877, is the start of the American newspaper tradition in usage—works written by newspaper editors. Bryant was editor-in-chief and part owner of the *New York Evening Post.* His *Index* is simply a list of words not to be used in the *Post;* there was no explanatory matter. Lists of forbidden words were popular for a time afterward, but the fashion passed. The newspaper editor as usage arbiter has continued to the present, however. The pseudonymous Alfred Ayres in *The Verbalist,* 1881, seems to have been the first, or one of the first, of these to arrange his comments in alphabetical order, creating a sort of dictionary of usage.

In the early decades of the Republic, many Americans patriotically supported the home-grown version of the language against the language of the vanquished British oppressors. There were proposals for a Federal English—Noah Webster was in the forefront of the movement—and for the establishment of an American academy to promote and regulate the language—John Adams made one such proposal.

The British, for their part, were not amused by the presumption of former colonials. Americanisms had been viewed askance as early as 1735, but the frequency and the ferocity of denunciation markedly increased in the 19th century, as British travelers, some of them literary folk like Captain Marryat, Mrs. Frances Trollope, and Charles Dickens, visited the United States and returned to England to publish books of their travels, almost always disparaging in tone. They seldom failed to work in a few criticisms of the language as well as the uncouth character and manners of Americans. British reviewers, too, were outspoken in their denunciation of things American, and especially Americanisms.

American writers put up a spirited defense for a time, but the writing class eventually began to wear down under the onslaught. By 1860, in an article crying up Joseph Worcester's dictionary, the *Atlantic Monthly* could call American English "provincial." The general attitude after the Civil War seems to have been one of diffidence rather than defiance. The diffident attitude is of interest here because it was in the second half of the 19th century that Americanisms began to make their way silently into American usage books as errors. Many of these, such as *balance* for *remainder* and *loan* for *lend,* are still denigrated by American usage writers and their native origin passed over in silence.

We have said nothing about 19th-century grammars, and not much needs to be said about them. If those grammars were computers, the most successful could be called clones of Lindley Murray. Some dissatisfaction with the older English traditions existed, especially in the first half of the 19th century in this country, but little seems to have resulted from it. Books with innovative systems met with little success. Goold Brown, in his *Grammar of English Grammars,* first published in 1851, collected most of the grammars published up to his own time, and used them for his examples of false grammar. He also exhibited at length their inconsistencies and disagreements. Goold Brown permitted himself one mild observation (most were rather tart): "Grammarians would perhaps differ less, if they read more."

By the end of the 19th century, differences had developed between the ways usage issues were being treated in England and in the United States. Except for the fruits of the Alford–Moon controversy, there seem to be very few British books concerned exclusively with usage problems. The most frequently reprinted of these few was one written by a Scot: William B. Hodgson's *Errors in the Use of English,* 1881. British literati were not indifferent to such issues, but they seem mainly to have put their comments in reviews and letters and works directed primarily to other subjects. Walter Savage Landor, for instance, delivered himself of a number of idiosyncratic views about language and usage in one or two of his *Imaginary Conversations.* John Stuart Mill put a few of his opinions into *A System of Logic.*

America, on the other hand, saw the growth of a small industry devoted to the cultivation of the linguistically insecure, who were being produced in increasing numbers by American public schools using the grammar of Lindley Murray combined with the opinions of Richard Grant White. After the Civil War little handbooks for the guidance of the perplexed appeared with some frequency. We have mentioned one of these, Alfred Ayres's *The Verbalist.* Others bear such titles as *Vulgarisms and Other Errors of Speech, Words: Their Use and Abuse, Some Common Errors of Speech,* and *Slips of Tongue and Pen.* The production of popular books on usage topics continues to be common in the 20th-century United States.

The different approaches of the British and Americans to usage questions have continued along the lines evident in the last half of the 19th century. Fewer books devoted to usage issues have been produced in England, and the arena there has been dominated by two names: Fowler and Gowers. H. W. Fowler's best-known work is *Modern English Usage,* 1926, an expanded, updated, and alphabetized version of *The King's English,* which he had produced with one of his brothers in 1906. This book gained ready acceptance as an authority, and it is usually treated with considerable deference on both sides of the Atlantic. It is a thick book in small print, packed with a combination of good sense, traditional attitudes, pretension-pricking, minute distinctions, and a good deal of what Otto Jespersen, the Danish scholarly grammarian of the English language, called "language moralizing." Fowler, in the tradition of Alford and Richard Grant White, found much to dislike in the prose of contemporary newspapers. He had no gadfly like George Washington Moon to challenge his authority, although he did dispute a few constructions with Otto Jespersen in the pages of the tracts issued by the Society for Pure English. In some of these disputes a characteristic pattern emerges: the historical grammarian finds a construction in literature and wonders how it came to be; Fowler finds the same construction in the newspapers and condemns it.

Sir Ernest Gowers came into usage commentary from a different direction: he was asked to prepare a book for British civil servants to help them avoid the usual bureaucratic jargon of British official prose. The result was *Plain Words,* 1941. This slender book has gone through several editions, growing a bit each time. In 1965 a new edition of Fowler appeared, edited by Gowers, to which Gowers added a number of his own favorite topics. In addition to Fowler and Gowers, the work

of Eric Partridge, particularly *Usage and Abusage,* 1942, has been influential.

In recent years, while some English books about usage have concerned themselves with traditional questions of propriety, others have taken a different path, explaining the peculiarities of English idiom to learners of English.

The treatment of usage in 20th-century America, however, hews steadfastly to the traditional line of linguistic etiquette. School grammars are elaborately graded and decked out with color printing, but the most successful are still solidly based on Lowth and Murray. College handbooks have proliferated since 1907, the date of the earliest one of which we've heard. The contents of these works have not changed greatly, however; the essential sameness of the "Glossaries of Usage" attached to them suggests that their contents are to some extent determined by a desire to carry over from the previous edition as much as possible and to cover what the competition covers. General-purpose guides for those whose schooling is complete are still produced regularly, and in a wider variety of shapes and sizes than in the 19th century. These have developed offshoots in the form of books aimed at business writers and others aimed at technical and scientific writers.

The newspaper tradition has also continued strong. Some usage questions are dealt with in house stylebooks (now often published for outsiders, as well), and newspaper editors have written usage guides for the general public, though these usually have a strong newspaper slant. Especially prominent among these are the several books of Theodore Bernstein, particularly *The Careful Writer,* 1965.

A characteristic of writing on usage has been, right from the beginning, disagreement among the writers on specific points. Various attempts at reconciling these differences have been made, especially in the 20th century. One of the earliest dates from 1883. C. W. Bardeen, a schoolbook publisher, put out a little book in which he tried to discover a consensus by examining some thirty sources, including a number of current usage books, some grammars, some works on philology, some on synonymy, and Webster's and Worcester's dictionaries. Roy Copperud has produced books on the same general plan in 1970 and 1980.

Another approach to the problem of varying opinion has been the survey of opinion. Sterling A. Leonard made the first in 1931. Leonard's survey was replicated in 1971 by Raymond D. Crisp, and a similar survey was conducted in England by G. H. Mittins and three colleagues and published in 1970. The results of these surveys are quantified, so that interested readers can discover the relative acceptability or obloquy of each tested item. Somewhat the same idea has also been tried with the usage panel, an assembled panel of experts to whom each individual item is submitted for approval or disapproval. Again, quantification of relative approval or disapproval is the aim.

The 20th century is the first in which usage has been studied from a scholarly or historical point of view, although Fitzedward Hall's *Modern English* of 1873 should probably be acknowledged as a precursor. Thomas R. Lounsbury collected a number of his magazine articles into *The Standard of Usage in English,* 1908, which examined the background of attitudes and issues. J. Lesslie Hall's *English Usage,* 1917, checked 141 issues drawn from the work of Richard Grant White and from several college-level grammars and rhetorics against evidence from English and American literature. Sterling A. Leonard in *The Doctrine of Correctness in*

English Usage 1700–1800, 1929, provided the first thorough examination of the origins of many attitudes about usage in the 18th century.

Looking back from the late 1980s we find that the 1920s and 1930s were a time of considerable interest in the examination and testing of attitudes and beliefs about usage and in a rationalization of the matter and methods of school grammar. Various publications written by Charles C. Fries and Robert C. Pooley, for example, seemed to point the way. They had relatively little influence in the following decades, however; the schoolbooks by and large follow the traditional lines, and the popular books of usage treat the traditional subjects. A notable exception is Bergen and Cornelia Evans's *A Dictionary of Contemporary American Usage,* 1957. The book takes the traditional view of many specific issues, but it is strong in insisting that actual usage, both historical and contemporary, must be weighed carefully in reaching usage opinions.

If the mainstream of usage commentary has continued to run in the same old channels, there have nonetheless been some undercurrents of importance. Serious examination of the received truths has continued. Margaret M. Bryant's *Current American Usage,* 1962, reported the results of the testing of many specific items against actual use as shown in current books, magazines, and newspapers. Articles in scholarly books and journals (like *American Speech*) evince continuing interest in real language and real usage in spite of a strong tendency in modern linguistics toward the study of language in more abstract ways. If the popular idea of usage is represented by the continuing series of books produced by the journalists Philip Howard (in England) and William Safire (in the United States) and by the continuing publication of traditionally oriented handbooks, there is also some countervailing critical opinion, as shown by such books as Dwight Bolinger's *Language—the Loaded Weapon,* Jim Quinn's *American Tongue and Cheek,* Dennis Baron's *Grammar and Good Taste,* and Harvey Daniels's *Famous Last Words,* all published in the early 1980s.

A historical sketch of this length necessarily must omit many deserving names and titles and pass over many interesting observers and observations. This we regret, but do not apologize for, as the need to omit what we would prefer to include seems almost omnipresent in our work as lexicographers. Much of the historical information herein draws heavily on materials available in Leonard's *Doctrine of Correctness;* Charles Carpenter Fries's *The Teaching of the English Language,* 1927; George H. McKnight's *Modern English in the Making,* 1928; H. L. Mencken's *The American Language,* 4th edition, 1936, and Supplement 1, 1945; Baron's *Grammar and Good Taste,* 1982; Daniels's *Famous Last Words,* 1983; and Sundby et al.'s *Dictionary of English Normative Grammar,* 1991. These books constitute a rich mine of information for the serious student of English usage and its history, to whom we also recommend a perusal of our bibliography.

Pronunciation Symbols

ə . . . . banana, collide, abut

'ə, ˌə . . . . humdrum, abut

ᵊ . . . . immediately preceding \l\, \n\, \m\, \ŋ\, as in battle, mitten, eaten, and sometimes open \'ōp-ᵊm\, lock and key \-ᵊŋ-\; immediately following \l\, \m\, \r\, as often in French table, prisme, titre

ər . . . . further, merger, bird

'ər-⎫
   ⎬ . . . . as in two different pronunciations
'ə-r⎭   of hurry \'hər-ē, 'hə-rē\

a . . . . mat, map, mad, gag, snap, patch

ā . . . . day, fade, date, aorta, drape, cape

ä . . . . bother, cot, and, with most American speakers, father, cart

ȧ . . . . father as pronounced by speakers who do not rhyme it with bother; French patte

au̇ . . . . now, loud, out

b . . . . baby, rib

ch . . . . chin, nature \'nā-chər\ (actually, this sound is \t\ + \sh\)

d . . . . did, adder

e . . . . bet, bed, peck

'ē, ˌē . . . . beat, nosebleed, evenly, easy

ē . . . . easy, mealy

f . . . . fifty, cuff

g . . . . go, big, gift

h . . . . hat, ahead

hw . . . . whale as pronounced by those who do not have the same pronunciation for both whale and wail

i . . . . tip, banish, active

ī . . . . site, side, buy, tripe (actually, this sound is \ä\ + \i\, or \ȧ\ + \i\)

j . . . . job, gem, edge, join, judge (actually, this sound is \d\ + \zh\)

k . . . . kin, cook, ache

k̠ . . . . German ich, Buch; one pronunciation of loch

l . . . . lily, pool

m . . . . murmur, dim, nymph

n . . . . no, own

ⁿ . . . . indicates that a preceding vowel or diphthong is pronounced with the nasal passages open, as in French un bon vin blanc \œⁿ-bōⁿ-vaⁿ-bläⁿ\

ŋ . . . . sing \'siŋ\, singer \'siŋ-ər\, finger \'fiŋ-gər\, ink \'iŋk\

ō . . . . bone, know, beau

ȯ . . . . saw, all, gnaw, caught

œ . . . . French boeuf, German Hölle

œ̄ . . . . French feu, German Höhle

ȯi . . . . coin, destroy

p . . . . pepper, lip

r . . . . red, car, rarity

s . . . . source, less

sh . . . . as in shy, mission, machine, special (actually, this is a single sound, not two); with a hyphen between, two sounds as in grasshopper \'gras-ˌhäp-ər\

t . . . . tie, attack, late, later, latter

th . . . . as in thin, ether (actually, this is a single sound, not two); with a hyphen between, two sounds as in knighthood \'nīt-ˌhu̇d\

t̠h̠ . . . . then, either, this (actually, this is a single sound, not two)

ü . . . . rule, youth, union \'yün-yən\, few \'fyü\

u̇ . . . . pull, wood, book, curable \'kyu̇r-ə-bəl\, fury \'fyu̇(ə)r-ē\

ue . . . . German füllen, hübsch

ūe . . . . French rue, German fühlen

v . . . . vivid, give

w . . . . we, away; in some words having final \(ˌ)ō\, \(ˌ)yü\, or \(ˌ)ü\ a variant \ə-w\ occurs before vowels, as in \'fäl-ə-wiŋ\, covered by the variant \ə-(w)\ or \yə-(w)\ at the entry word

y . . . . yard, young, cue \'kyü\, mute \'myüt\, union \'yün-yən\

ʸ . . . . indicates that during the articulation of the sound represented by the preceding character the front of the tongue has substantially the position it has for the articulation of the first sound of yard, as in French digne \dēnʸ\

z . . . . zone, raise

zh . . . . as in vision, azure \'azhər\ (actually, this is a single sound, not two); with a hyphen between, two sounds as in hogshead \'hȯgz-ˌhed, 'hägz-\

\ . . . . slant line used in pairs to mark the beginning and end of a transcription: \'pen\

' . . . . mark preceding a syllable with primary (strongest) stress: \'pen-mən-ˌship\

ˌ . . . . mark preceding a syllable with secondary (medium) stress: \'pen-mən-ˌship\

- . . . . mark of syllable division

( ) . . . . indicate that what is symbolized between is present in some utterances but not in others: factory \'fak-t(ə-)rē\

A

a, an   There is an article on the proper use of *a* and *an* in almost every usage book ever written, although hardly a native speaker of English has any difficulty with them—in fact one seldom thinks about them at all in speech.

The difficulty, when there is any, is to be found in writing. The basic rules are these: use *a* before a consonant sound; use *an* before a vowel sound. Before a letter or an acronym or before numerals, choose *a* or *an* according to the way the letter or numeral is pronounced: *an* FDA directive, *a* U.N. resolution, *a* $5.00 bill.

Actual usage, of course, is more complex than the simple rules would lead you to expect. Here is what actual usage shows:

1. Before words with an initial consonant sound, *a* is usual in speech and writing. This is in line with the basic rule.

2. Before *h* in an unstressed or weakly stressed syllable, *a* and *an* are both used in writing (*an* historic, *a* historic) but *an* is more usual in speech, whether the *h* is pronounced or not. This variation is the result of historical development; in unstressed and weakly stressed syllables, *h* was formerly not pronounced in many words where it is pronounced at the present time. A few words, such as *historic* and (especially in England) *hotel,* are in transition, and may be found with either *a* or *an.* You choose the article that suits your own pronunciation.

3. Occasionally in modern writing and speech and regularly in the King James Version of the Bible, *an* is used before *h* in a stressed syllable, as in *an* hundred. Again, we have the same historical change: many more words were pronounced with a silent initial *h* in the past than are at present. A few words, such as *heir, hour,* and *honest,* generally have silent initial *h;* some others, like *herb* or *humble* are pronounced both ways. Use *a* or *an* according to your own pronunciation.

4. Before words beginning with a consonant sound but an orthographic vowel, *an* is sometimes used in speech and writing (*an* unique, such *an* one). This use is less frequent now than in the past.

5. Before words with an initial vowel sound, *an* is usual in speech and writing. This is in line with the basic rule.

6. Occasionally, and more often in some dialects than others, *a* is used in speech before words beginning with a vowel sound. The Dictionary of American Regional English reports this to be frequent in the United States; the evidence suggests it may have been somewhat more common in the past.

7. *A* is normally unstressed, and pronounced \ə\. When stressed, as in "He's *a* vice president, not *the* vice president," it is pronounced \ˈā\ in the United States, but often \ˈa\ in Canada.

abbreviations   Abbreviations have been receiving bad notices since the 18th century. Such writers as Addison and Swift satirized the fashionable practice of the time of using truncated or clipped forms of long words—such as *pozz, phizz, plenipo,* and *hippo* for *positively, physiognomy, plenipotentiary,* and *hypochondria*—in conversation. Ordinary contractions—*can't, haven't, shan't, isn't,* for instance—were likewise satirized. Campbell 1776 took notice of the practice, class-

ing the clipped forms as barbarisms, but commenting that he thought the practice had fallen into general disgrace because of the attacks of the satirists and that it never showed itself in books.

Perhaps Dr. Campbell was premature in announcing the abandonment of the practice of abbreviating, for usage books down to the present day wag their fingers at the practice. MacCracken & Sandison 1917, for instance, lists several truncations disapprovingly—among them *auto, phone, photo, exam,* and *gym.* Guth 1985 continues the critical tradition but changes the truncations:

> Avoid informal abbreviations. Avoid clipped forms like *bike, prof, doc, fan mag, exec, econ.* (Other shortened forms, like *phone, ad,* and *exam* are now commonly used in serious writing.)

Aside from the social acceptability of clipped forms (Emily Post in 1927 disapproved *phone* and *photo*), there are other considerations to be taken into account. Handbooks in general recommend avoiding abbreviations in "formal" writing. Flesch 1964 disagrees, however:

> It's a superstition that abbreviations shouldn't be used in serious writing and that it's good style to spell everything out. Nonsense: use abbreviations whenever they are customary and won't attract the attention of the reader.

Flesch's advice seems sound; but care should be taken to observe what in fact is customary. It is obvious that what is customary in technical writing will be different from what is customary in journalism or in scholarly articles. If you are uncertain, you should consult an appropriate style manual or handbook. General advice can be found in any of a number of composition handbooks and in general style manuals, such as *Webster's Standard American Style Manual.*

See also ETC.; I.E., E.G.

abdomen   This word may be pronounced with the main stress on the first syllable or on the second: \ˈab-də-mən\ or \ab-ˈdō-mən\. The former version predominates among laypeople; physicians are more evenly divided.

abhorrence   Bernstein 1965 notes that *abhorrence,* when followed by a preposition, takes *of.* This is true in a large majority of cases.

> . . . an abhorrence of draughts —*Times Literary Supp.,* 14 Nov. 1968

> . . . my natural abhorrence of its sickening inhumanity —George Bernard Shaw, *Back to Methuselah,* 1921

The word has also been used with a few other prepositions, however, such as *to* (an instance of which was corrected to *of* by Lindley Murray in 1795), *against,* and *for.* These are less frequent by far, and are in the main to be found in older literature.

> He recognized her as "Goldy," famous in Hsi-Yu for her abhorrence to sleeping alone —*Sericana Quarterly,* April 1952

... abhorrence against relationship with Wickham —Jane Austen, *Pride and Prejudice,* 1813

... my unbounded abhorrence for this miserable wretch —P. B. Shelley, quoted by Matthew Arnold, *Essays in Criticism, Second Series,* 1888

abhorrent When used with a preposition, *abhorrent* is almost always followed by *to:*

Not only was success abhorrent to their ethical prejudices —Lewis H. Lapham, *Harper's,* May 1971

... words like "unfair" whose very sound is abhorrent to him —Joseph Conrad, *Chance,* 1913

abide 1. The original principal parts of *abide* are *abode,* past, and *abidden,* past participle. The OED notes that in time the past and past participle coalesced in *abode,* and *abidden* fell into disuse, although a few 19th-century writers tried to revive it. During the 19th century a regular past and past participle *abided* came into use. It is more likely to be used now than *abode* is. *Abode,* while not very much used by modern writers, is kept alive by its use in such familiar literary works as "The Legend of Sleepy Hollow," and in works referring to an earlier era, as Samuel Hopkins Adams's *Grandfather Stories* (1955).
2. Except for *can't abide* and *abide by,* which are in continuing vigorous use, most senses of *abide* have a rather literary or old-fashioned flavor. They do, however, continue in reputable, if somewhat infrequent, use.
3. Evans 1957 comments that *can't abide* is "commonly disparaged." One source of the disparagement is Partridge 1942, who calls the expression "a low-class colloquialism"—he does allow that in American use it might be "homely or half-humorous," an opinion he may have derived from Krapp 1927, who commented on the expression's "somewhat archaic and rustic character." Evans defends *can't abide* as having force and flavor. Indeed it is hard to see what the objection was. The expression goes back to the 16th century; Shakespeare uses it several times in his plays:

She could not abide Master Shallow —*2 Henry IV,* 1598

It is true that Shakespeare puts it into the mouths of commoners—those who speak prose rather than blank verse. Modern evidence, however, shows that the usage is perfectly proper:

... which may have been intended to prove how open-minded and aesthetically susceptible Canaday is even to work he cannot abide —Harold Rosenburg, *New Yorker,* 1 Jan. 1972

This sense of *abide* is usually used in a negative construction or in one with negative implications:

My inability when I was young to abide most males of my own age disguised loneliness that no amount of variety assuaged —Donald Hall, *N.Y. Times Book Rev.,* 16 Jan. 1983

abject Nickles 1974 and Safire (*N.Y. Times,* 2 Sept. 1984) call the phrase *abject poverty* a cliché. Our evidence shows that *abject* is frequently used to modify *poverty;* in this use *abject* is not much more than an intensifier:

... the Place Maubert, still at the end of the nineteenth century the area of the most abject poverty — *Times Literary Supp.,* 14 Nov. 1968

Our earliest evidence for the phrase, however, does not refer to economic circumstances:

... while they profess to build upon Naturalism an edifying and attractive philosophy of life, they disguise from themselves and others the bare and abject poverty of the scheme —W. R. Inge, *The Church in the World,* 1928

Nickles strikes further at *abject* by claiming it "tends to generate clichés in clusters, vitiating any noun it accompanies." This is a patent overstatement. *Abject* connotes two kinds of low degree: one of low circumstances—abasement—and one of servility or spinelessness—debasement. It can be applied directly to persons:

Farmers who have to work 16 hours a day to pay rent and interest on mortgages in addition to buying necessities for their families are not free: they are abject slaves —George Bernard Shaw, *New Republic,* 22 Nov. 1954

... the time would come that no human being should be humiliated or be made abject —Katherine Anne Porter, *The Never-Ending Wrong,* 1977

... Bloom beholds himself, in a hideous vision, looking on at Blazes Boylan and Molly, an abject cuckold —Edmund Wilson, *Axel's Castle,* 1931

He was abject before Wolf Larsen and almost grovelled to Johansen —Jack London, *The Sea-Wolf,* 1904

... a sinner, and a repentant prostrate abject sinner —George Meredith, *The Ordeal of Richard Feverel,* 1859

More often it is applied to the actions and conditions of such persons:

... my critical intelligence sometimes shrivels to an abject nodding of the head —Lewis H. Lapham, *Harper's,* May 1971

... the aversion my person inspired even in its most abject and obsequious attitudes —Samuel Beckett, *Evergreen,* June 1967

The possibility of humiliation ... touched a vein of abject cowardice in his composition —H. G. Wells, *Joan and Peter,* 1918

Then, what submission, what cringing and fawning, what servility, what abject humiliation —Charles Dickens, *A Tale of Two Cities,* 1859

... when the least sickness attacked her, under the most abject depression and terror of death —W. M. Thackeray, *Vanity Fair,* 1848

The sensation of nameless terror and abject fear ... overmastered me completely —Rudyard Kipling, "The Strange Ride of Morrowbie Jukes," 1888

... having dictated to our enemies the terms of a most abject surrender —Archibald MacLeish, *Saturday Rev.,* 9 Feb. 1946

... without fear, but with the most abject awe of the aristocracy —T. S. Eliot, "Philip Massinger," *Selected Essays,* 1932

Conway survived and penned an abject apology to Washington —*American Guide Series: Maryland,* 1940

These examples are typical uses of *abject*. The most frequently modified nouns, after *poverty*, are *fear, terror, surrender,* and *apology.* It seems unlikely that any of the writers cited considered *abject* to have a vitiating effect.

abjure, adjure A number of commentators (such as Harper 1985, Shaw 1975, Bremner 1980, the Oxford American Dictionary 1980, Bernstein 1965, Evans 1957) warn that these words are confused with some frequency. Evidence of such confusion is not to be found in the Merriam-Webster files; if it does exist, it is apparently corrected in manuscript. *Abjure* means "to renounce, reject, avoid"; *adjure* "to urge or advise earnestly." Besides differing in meaning, the two words take different grammatical constructions. *Abjure* regularly takes a noun as direct object. The noun often is, but need not be, abstract; it is rarely a personal noun.

> Galileo was summoned before the Inquisition at Rome, and there he was made to abjure the Copernican theory —S. F. Mason, *Main Currents of Scientific Thought,* 1953

> Just one whiff of that vast butchery . . . is enough to make a sensitive person abjure meat forever —Ian Fleming, *Thrilling Cities,* 1963

Adjure, on the other hand, typically takes a personal noun or pronoun followed by *to* and an infinitive:

> The wives and daughters of the Germans rushed about the camp . . . adjuring their countrymen to save them from slavery —J. A. Froude, *Caesar,* 1879

> There is no use adjuring them to take part in it or warning them to keep out of it —Malcolm Cowley, *Exile's Return,* 1934

Adjure, incidentally, is used quite a bit less frequently than *abjure.*

ablative See INCOMPARABLE.

able to In constructions where *able* is followed by *to* and the infinitive, the infinitive is nearly always in the active voice, whether the subject is human or nonhuman. Human subjects are more common:

> . . . people have traditionally been able to walk into museums free —Huntington Hartford, *The Public Be Damned,* 1955

> So far, I have been able to keep my enthusiasm . . . under control —John Fischer, *Harper's,* November 1970

> But the City that lay between was not his ground, and Richard II was no more able than Charles I to dictate to its militia —G. M. Trevelyan, *English Social History,* 1942

> She hopes to find Somebody able and willing to buy her freedom —Lafcadio Hearn, *Glimpses of Unfamiliar Japan,* 1894

> There are those from whom not even death has been able to disconnect me —George P. Elliott, *Harper's,* September 1970

The passive infinitive is much less common. Some commentators (Longman 1984, Perrin & Ebbitt 1972) opine that the construction sounds awkward; perhaps it often does, and awkwardness may account for its being fairly uncommon. Here are three examples to show that it is used on occasion:

> . . . Mr. Doddington, from whose disapproval the story of Gavin and the Concannons' party had not been able to be kept —Elizabeth Bowen, *Horizon,* September 1945

> . . . so social and religious life would be able to be carried out on a normal basis —L. S. B. Leakey, *Mau Mau and the Kikuyu,* 1952

> . . . a simple experiment able to be performed by anyone —*Monsanto Mag.,* December 1953

Using the last example for illustrative purposes, we can avoid the passive infinitive by revising it to include *can* or *could:*

> . . . a simple experiment that anyone could (can) perform;
> *or*
> . . . a simple experiment that can (could) be performed by anyone.

abortive A love of etymology and the consequent dismembering of English words into their presumed constituent parts has led many a usage commentator down the primrose path of error (see ETYMOLOGICAL FALLACY). Safire 1982 seconds a correspondent's objection to the use of *abortive* to describe a failed mission to rescue U.S. hostages in Iran in 1979. Safire claims to see in the suffix *-ive* an implication of continuation or permanence, and he maintains that *abortive* must therefore "suggest a continuous process of aborting." This is, of course, a conclusion that could only be reached by ignoring the use of the whole word in English in favor of speculating about what it might mean. No "continuous process of aborting" is suggested by Shakespeare's line

> Why should I joy in any abortive birth? —*Love's Labour's Lost,* 1595

Safire further asserts that "'abortive efforts' should be used only when the emphasis is on a series of past failures." In actuality the word is often used to modify a plural noun, but emphasis on past failures may or may not be present:

> . . . a magazine existed,—after so many abortive attempts —Van Wyck Brooks, *The Flowering of New England, 1815–1865,* rev. ed., 1946

> . . . and forget that abortive efforts from want of heart are as possible to revenge as to generosity — Thomas Hardy, *The Mayor of Casterbridge,* 1886

> He knew it was like feeling over a chilling motor for loose wires, and after two or three abortive motions he gave it up —Wallace Stegner, "The Traveler," in *Perspectives USA,* Summer 1953

Moreover, many a writer from Shakespeare to the present has used the word of a single incident with no hint of recurrence or permanence:

> The power that had proved too strong for this abortive restoration —Arnold J. Toynbee, *Center Mag.,* March 1968

> After the abortive Decembrist insurrection in 1825 —George F. Kennan, *New Yorker,* 1 May 1971

In describing her abortive visit —Margery Sharp, *Britannia Mews,* 1946

In September, 1938, came the Munich crisis. . . . The result was only an abortive armistice —Franklin D. Roosevelt, campaign address, 28 Oct. 1940, in *Nothing to Fear,* ed. B. D. Zevin, 1946

There was an abortive conspiracy against the life of the Princeps —John Buchan, *Augustus,* 1937

Only at the third did our visit prove abortive —Sir Arthur Conan Doyle, *The Return of Sherlock Holmes,* 1904

. . . Mr. Pickwick expressed a strong desire to recollect a song which he had heard in his infancy, and the attempt proving abortive, sought to stimulate his memory with more glasses of punch —Charles Dickens, *Pickwick Papers,* 1836–37

Two slips of ground, half arable, half overrun with an abortive attempt at shrubbery —Sir Walter Scott, *The Surgeon's Daughter,* 1827 (OED)

Our first design, my friend, has prov'd abortive — Joseph Addison, *Cato,* 1713 (OED)

abound When a person, place, or thing abounds— that is, is copiously supplied—it usually abounds *in* or abounds *with.*

Literary men indulge in humbug only at a price, and Bancroft abounded in humbug —Van Wyck Brooks, *The Flowering of New England, 1815–1865,* rev. ed. 1946

. . . London abounds in public monuments —Max Beerbohm, *And Even Now,* 1920

Yet if life abounded in mysteries —Norman Mailer, *Harper's,* March 1971

. . . buoyed by the most personal of human hopes, he abounded with good nature —Francis Hackett, *Henry the Eighth,* 1929

. . . a school ostensibly abounding with fair-sized drips —J. D. Salinger, *Nine Stories,* 1953

Both prepositions are in frequent use; when the object is a relative pronoun, *with* appears to be more common:

. . . those ironies with which history abounds —John Dewey, *Freedom and Culture,* 1939

The pictures with which it abounds —Charles Lamb, *Essays of Elia,* 1823

about 1. Vizetelly 1906 noted that *about* was commonly interchangeable with *almost* and "formerly, such was condemned." MacCracken & Sandison 1917 still had some doubts about the use, except in connection with numbers. This issue has seldom been mentioned since, though Perrin & Ebbitt 1972 note it, calling *about* "Standard but mainly Informal." Shaw 1970, however, maintains the old position, recommending that *about* in the sense of "almost" or "all but" be avoided in formal English. He is more moderate in 1975. If there was no reason to avoid it in 1906, there is no reason to avoid it now.
2. Perrin & Ebbitt 1972 say *around* is more common than *about* in reference to physical position; the assertion cannot be confirmed from the Merriam-Webster files. Both are exceedingly common. See AROUND 1.

3. Copperud 1970, Johnson 1982, Bernstein 1958, Bryson 1984, and Janis 1984 point out that *about* can be used redundantly with figures when other signs of approximation, such as the mention of a span (150 to 200) or the verb *estimate,* are present. Bernstein quotes a couple of instances from the *New York Times.* If the evidence in the Merriam-Webster files is representative, this is a minor problem—we have nearly no evidence of its occurrence in edited prose. Perhaps sharp-eyed copy editors catch it regularly, or perhaps the phenomenon occurs in other contexts, such as student writing.

Bernstein also mentions the use of a round number as an implicit indication of approximation, but shows no example that involves redundancy. The use of *about* with round numbers is extremely common, and is for the obvious purpose of indicating that the number is not exact. *About* is also frequently used with nearly exact and less than round numbers for the same purpose:

The edges of the base of the great pyramid are about 756 feet long; and the lengths of these four edges agree, with an error of only about two-thirds of an inch —School Mathematics Study Group, *Geometry,* Part 1, 1965

. . . weighs about 172 pounds —*Current Biography,* February 1966

. . . were producing 108 million net cubic feet of gas and about 1,270 net barrels of crude oil —*Annual Report, Atlantic Richfield Co.,* 1970

4. Bernstein 1958, 1965 objects to the expression "about the head" as "police-blotter lingo." This is perhaps an expression that has gone out of date. Here is a typical example, from a story in the *Saturday Evening Post* in 1954:

He slapped Mr. Norris heavily about the head several times —Harold H. Martin

Bernstein's objection was originally made in 1953. We have little evidence of the use since. At one time it had some facetious, as well as more serious use, but it seems simply to have dropped out of currency now. Copperud 1970 says it is (or was) standard, anyway.
5. Johnson 1982 dislikes the *about* construction shown in this example:

. . . does not know what the Sixties were all about — Garry Wills, *Harper's,* January 1972

He opines that the construction appeared about two decades earlier and may now be going out of fashion. The expression, usually in the form "what . . . is (all) about," seems to have reached a high tide of popularity in the late 1960s and early 1970s and is slowly receding, but it is still found from time to time, as in this quotation attributed to actress Shari Belafonte-Harper:

My father has a tough time with what Hollywood's about —*US,* 2 Jan. 1984

Here are some earlier examples:

What the p.-o.-w. hold-up in Korea was really all about —*The Bulletin* (Sydney, Australia), 30 Dec. 1953

Many all over the country know very well what ballet is about —Edwin Denby, in *The Dance Encyclopedia,* ed. Anatole Chujoy, 1949

. . . Europeans have only the vaguest conception of what American music is about —Virgil Thomson, *The Musical Scene,* 1947

Reader's Digest 1983 says that the construction is standard; its frequency of use, however, does appear to be declining.

6. For two further current idiomatic uses of *about,* see AT ABOUT and NOT ABOUT TO.

above **1.** Sometime during the later part of the 19th century, a number of critics began objecting to the use of *above* as an adjective and as a noun, presumably on the grounds that *above* is an adverb. The earliest objection we have found seems to have been directed at Dean Alford in the 1860s; at least in *A Plea for the Queen's English* (1866) he defends his use of *above* as an adjective, saying that while it was not elegant, it was not uncommon. The critics, except for being generally unhappy about both uses, are a bit uncertain of just what is so bad. Vizetelly 1906 says that *above* is "inelegantly used as a noun" but finds the adjective use more objectionable; the Heritage 1969 usage panel, on the other hand, found the adjective acceptable, but the noun unacceptable. Some commentators object that such uses of *above* smack too much of commercial or legal lingo; on the other hand, Whipple 1924 and other writers on business writing recommend against its use.

The issue appears to be more long-lived than substantial. More than a century ago, the adjective was adjudged legitimate (Bardeen 1883); MacCracken & Sandison 1917 call both adjective and noun "allowable," although "The most careful speakers ... prefer *preceding* or *foregoing.*" Copperud's 1970 consensus finds both acceptable; Perrin & Ebbitt 1972 find them standard; Bernstein 1971 calls them "legitimate and above-board." Yet Harper 1985 and Freeman 1983 are still objecting.

Utter 1916 says that the adjectival use of *above* (as in "the above address") "has been idiomatic in English since Anglo-Saxon times." He does not, however, provide examples. The OED shows no citation earlier than 1873, but many earlier ones, from Dickens, Thackeray, Scott, and Hawthorne, among others, have been cited by other investigators. The oldest we have found is from Campbell 1776:

> Guided by the above reflections. ...

The adjective *above* is not uncommon in writers on language and usage:

> The facts of the case being now sufficiently supplied by the above list —Robert Bridges, *S.P.E. Tract 2,* 1919
>
> ... a few remarks on some of the above words may perhaps instil caution —Fowler 1926
>
> ... for a comment on the above use of the word "claims," consult Chapter 1 —Bernstein 1958
>
> The above discussion gives us some idea about the complexity —Braj B. Kachru, in Greenbaum 1985

Other writers also have used it:

> I don't for a moment doubt that for daily purposes he feels to me as a friend—as certainly I do to him and without the above reserve —Oliver Wendell Holmes d. 1935, letter, 12 Jan. 1921
>
> "Fear God, Honour the Queen" ... I was brought up on the above words —Sir Bernard Law Montgomery, *This Week Mag.,* 1 June 1952

The use of *above* as a noun is somewhat more lightly attested in our files. It too has been around at least since the 18th century; the first OED citation is dated 1779.

> ... the above is Theseus's opinion —William Blake, *Annotations to Swedenborg's Of Heaven and Hell,* 2d ed., 1784
>
> It is not of pictures like the above that galleries, in Rome or elsewhere, are made up —Nathaniel Hawthorne (cited in Hall 1917)
>
> Let us pretend that the above is the original plot — Ring W. Lardner, Preface, *How to Write Short Stories,* 1924

We judge that both adjective and noun uses of *above* are standard, notwithstanding the objections of a few holdouts for 19th-century opinion. Gowers's revision of Fowler 1965 sums the matter up:

> There is ample authority, going back several centuries, for this use of *a[bove]* as adverb, adjective, or noun, and no solid ground for the pedantic criticism of it sometimes heard.

2. "*Above* should not be used for 'more than.'" This curious statement from Vizetelly 1906 may have had its origin in William Cullen Bryant's 19th-century *Index Expurgatorius* for the *New York Evening Post,* which he edited. Bryant objected to the use of either *above* or *over* in this sense. It is an odd usage for any critic to pick on; it goes back to the 16th century and has good literary credentials:

> It was never acted; or, if it was, not above once — Shakespeare, *Hamlet,* 1601
>
> After that, he was seen of above five hundred brethren at once —1 Corinthians 15:6 (AV), 1611
>
> ... added that he had not made above three or four [words] in his Dictionary —James Boswell, *Journal of a Tour to the Hebrides,* 1785
>
> "It is above a week since I saw Miss Crawford." — Jane Austen, *Mansfield Park,* 1814
>
> I know that place well, having spent six weeks there above twenty years ago —William Cowper, letter, 28 July 1784
>
> ... telling Aubrey that he cannot remember being drunk above a hundred times —Harold J. Laski, letter, 19 Mar. 1928
>
> He doesn't look above forty —*The Journals of Arnold Bennett,* ed. Frank Swinnerton, 1954
>
> ... and it took above 10 minutes to get the police — Edward Dahlberg, *Prose,* Spring 1972

We have no record of the stricture on this sense of *above* having persisted beyond Whipple 1924; the objection to *over* in the same sense has been longer-lived (see OVER).

absent Bernstein 1977 and Copperud 1980 both comment on the appearance of *absent* as a preposition in constructions such as this:

> Absent such a direct threat, Mr. Carter professes to feel no pressure —William Safire, *N.Y. Times,* 20 Dec. 1976

Both of these commentators note that the preposition is entered in Webster's Third, and neither condemns it. Copperud concludes by saying, "Whether *absent* as a preposition will win any wide acceptance only time will tell."

Such evidence as we have accumulated since Copperud wrote his remark indicates that the prepositional use is gaining acceptance, though perhaps grudgingly. Safire 1984 discusses it; unsurprisingly, he approves it but notes some opposition. Harper 1985 puts the prepositional use, which the editors ascribe to "a few rather pretentious columnists," to a vote of their usage panel; unsurprisingly the panel rejects it by a thumping 92 percent in writing, and 95 percent in speech. (Three panelists use the preposition in their quoted rejections.)

What is the background of this use? It is not quite as new as our commentators think. The earliest citation in the Merriam-Webster files is from 1945; it is used in paraphrasing a decision of the Supreme Court of South Dakota:

> We think it clear, continued the Supreme Court, that under this definition, absent any other facts, there arises an implied contract —*JAMA,* 24 Feb. 1945

The origin of the preposition is clearly in legal writing. Here are a couple more examples:

> Absent a general usage or custom, the importance of particular treaty provisions becomes apparent —in Edwin D. Dickinson, *Cases and Materials on International Law,* 1950

> Absent such a reservation, only the Court of Claims has jurisdiction —*Bare* v. *United States,* 107 F. Supp. 551, 17 Nov. 1952

It seems likely that someone reading extensively in judicial American English would be able to discover even earlier examples of the use.

Up until the early 1970s all of our evidence for it came from published judicial decisions or reports of such decisions. In the 70s we began to see a spread of the preposition into quasi-legal contexts and into the reported speech of lawyers and politicians:

> A program of unconditional amnesty, absent some accommodation on the part of the beneficiaries would be a disservice to the memory of those who fought and died in Vietnam —Hubert H. Humphrey, quoted by James A. Wechsler, *N.Y. Post* (undated citation received from a correspondent 15 Dec. 1975)

But by the late 1970s and the 1980s, the use of the prepositional *absent* had broadened somewhat, appearing in such publications as *Saturday Review, Newsweek, New York Times, Wall Street Journal, College English,* and *New Yorker.* Most of the time now it is used to begin an introductory phrase:

> Moreover, absent either huge further spending reductions or major tax increases, ... the government's budget deficit is as likely to grow as to shrink —Benjamin M. Friedman, *Wall Street Jour.,* 13 Jan. 1982

> Absent baseball's antitrust exemption, this agreement ... would be illegal —John F. Seiberling, *N.Y. Times,* 29 May 1983

> Absent a hyphen, the epithet must be taken at face value —Maxwell R. D. Vos, letter, in Safire 1984

> What I want is a clear blue sky, fresh sparkling waters, a handsome log house not made from a kit but put up for me by friends. Absent that, I want success in lawsuits —George W. S. Trow, *New Yorker,* 12 Mar. 1984

It also appears in phrases elsewhere in the sentence:

> In a world absent politics and biology, they'd be chasing Tammy Mercer to do Kool-Aid commercials in a couple of years —Jonathan Evan Maslow, *Saturday Rev.,* 26 Nov. 1977

absolute adjectives *Absolute adjective* is one of the terms used by usage writers to refer to adjectives that are not, or (more often) should not in the view of the writer, be compared or intensified (other terms applied to these words include *incomparables* and *uncomparable adjectives*).

How many words belong to this class? Here is one commentator's answer:

> Our language contains perhaps a score of words that may be described as *absolute words.* These are words that properly admit of no comparison or intensification —Kilpatrick 1984

A score, perhaps? In the first column of page 1280 of Webster's Ninth New Collegiate Dictionary, a page chosen at random, we find *ultrashort, ultrasonic, ultrasonographic, ultrastructural, ultraviolet, ululant, umbellate, umbelliferous, umber, umbilical, umbilicate, umbonal, umbral*—a baker's dozen of adjectives most persons would be hard put to use in the comparative or superlative. It should take no great effort to fill out our score—how about *ancillary, residual, aliphatic, Triassic, epoxy, diocesan, diphthongal?* The plain fact is that a majority of adjectives in English admit of no comparison—they are of too narrow an application, or too technical, to be so used, or they simply name a quality that cannot exist in degrees.

Then why, you may ask, is there a question at all? The reason is simple: the absolute adjectives that concern the usage writers have, almost without exception, actually been used in the comparative, in the superlative, or with an intensifier. Partridge 1942 includes a list of some eighty uncomparable adjectives; Bernstein 1971 gently derides this selection by using some of them, in a quite normal manner, with modifiers such as *more* and *less.* But Bernstein has his own treasured list, and so do many other usage writers. It seems to be traditional to list as words not susceptible of comparison words that have, in fact, been compared.

The tradition seems to have originated in the 18th century. Lowth 1763 says, "So likewise adjectives, that have in themselves a superlative signification, admit not properly the superlative form superadded," and he cites as examples *chiefest* and *extremest.* Lowth found these in poetry, and is inclined to be tolerant of them in that medium. Priestley, revised ed., 1798 also comments on the subject: " ... yet it is not uncommon to see the comparative or superlative of such words; being used, either through inadvertency, or for the sake of emphasis." Priestley's approach also seems tolerant.

But Lindley Murray 1795 is not tolerant. Murray, who compiled his grammar from many earlier works including those of Lowth, Priestley, and Campbell, and here uses examples from all three, takes Lowth's remarks from their original position in a footnote and elevates them to the status of a rule; he also adds "or comparative" to Lowth's "superlative form." He labels all the examples "incorrect."

Murray's *Grammar* was widely popular and widely imitated. As Murray had elaborated on the rules he took over from Lowth and Priestley, so later grammarians elaborated on Murray. Where Lowth mentioned two adjectives, Murray lists six (plus an *etc.*); Goold Brown

1851 reproduces the list of Samuel Kirkham, *English Grammar in Familiar Lectures* (1825), which contains 22 adjectives and concludes with "and many others" and mentions Joseph W. Wright, *A Philosophical Grammar of the English Language* (1838) as listing 72.

Goold Brown, however, does not share the usual view of these adjectives. He begins his discussion by saying, "Our grammarians deny the comparison of many adjectives, from a false notion that they are already superlatives." He goes on to demonstrate, using Kirkham's 22, that they are not superlatives; his method is to show—to use modern terminology—that Kirkham (and all the rest) have confused semantics with morphology.

Goold Brown's criticisms do not seem to have affected the issue much, unless they were somehow responsible for the shift in terminology from "superlative" meaning to "absolute" meaning. Usage writers have continued the lists of the pre-Goold Brown grammarians, our modern commentators perhaps having inherited some of the material from late 19th-century handbooks such as those written by William Matthews, *Words: their Use and their Abuse* (1880), Edward S. Gould 1870, and Alfred Ayres 1881 (all cited in Bardeen 1883).

The reason for the mismatch between actual usage and the writers' expressed preference is simple: the lists are wish lists. The reason such words are compared was succinctly summed up as long ago as 1946:

Adjectives expressing some quality that does not admit of degrees are not compared when used in their strict or full sense; as, *square, perpendicular, circular, absolute, eternal, illimitable, complete, perfect,* etc.

But such adjectives are often used in a modified or approximate sense, and when so used admit of comparison.

If we say, "This is *more perfect* than that," we do not mean that either is perfect without limitation, but that "this" has "more" of the qualities that go to make up perfection than "that"; it is *more nearly* perfect. Such usage has high literary authority —Fernald 1946

To summarize, a majority of adjectives, perhaps a substantial majority, do not admit of comparison simply because they are too technical or have a meaning that truly does not allow such modification. Most of the adjectives called uncomparable by usage writers have, in fact, been compared or modified by adverbs of degree other than *more* and *most,* for two reasons. First, they tend to be common words with more than one meaning and are liable to comparison in some senses, if not all. Second, the comparative degree is commonly used to mean "more nearly," as Fernald explains.

See also COMPLETE, COMPLETELY; CORRECT; EQUAL 2; ESSENTIAL, *adjective;* PARAMOUNT; PERFECT; PREFERABLE; UNIQUE.

absolute comparative

The absolute comparative is the comparative form of an adjective used where the positive might be expected; either no comparison at all is implied, or no comparison is overtly stated although it may be inferred by the reader or hearer. The second of these types is also called *incomplete comparison.*

Except for a few familiar fixed phrases that are clearly of the first type—higher education, higher learning, the greater Boston area, better stores everywhere, the younger generation, the finer things in life—the two varieties of the absolute comparative are difficult to distinguish, and perhaps need not be distinguished for practical purposes. The following examples of *older* should suffice to make the point:

... the way to teach rhetoric to older young people —Ruth G. Strickland, in *The Range of English,* 1968

... when even the older girls are new to the organization —Mabel A. Hammersmith, *Girl Scout Leader,* January 1968

Starting independent study for older students, who are most prepared for it —Arno Karlen, *Change,* July–August 1969

The age of the counselors is another factor in controlling applicants, especially older, professionally-trained ones —Thomas M. Martinez, *Trans-Action,* March 1968

The constant counterpoint of this search has been an awareness of the older traditions of Europe —*Current Biography,* December 1964

... disciplinary notions and forms were taken over from the past and from the most prestigious of the older universities —Norman Birnbaum, *Change,* July–August 1969

The absolute comparative is a favorite device of advertisers, who for various reasons prefer to leave the comparisons implied in "a brighter smile," "a new lovelier you," or "higher mileage" up to the perceptions of the consumer.

With terms relating to age, the comparative form is often more polite than the positive:

... a book dealer who is loved by an older woman —*Current Biography,* June 1966

... an Institute for Retired Professionals, allowing older people to putter around in their own courses —J. Kirk Sale, *Change,* July–August 1969

For some reason "an older woman" or "an older man" seems younger than "an old woman" or "an old man."

Bryant 1962 concludes that both forms of the absolute comparative are used in informal standard English, but a number of the fixed phrases and other conventional forms occur in English of any level of formality:

... what physiologists term a consensus, similar to that existing among the various organs and functions of the physical frame of man and the more perfect animals —John Stuart Mill, *A System of Logic,* 1843

absolute constructions, absolute clauses

See ABSOLUTE PHRASES.

absolutely

Usage commentators have taken up a couple of points about *absolutely.*

1. Howard 1978 notes the emergence of *absolutely* in England as a vogue word for *yes;* he thinks it fairly recent. The usage appears, from dictionary evidence, to have been originally American: the earliest citation in the OED Supplement is from Mark Twain's *The American Claimant,* 1892. It appeared in British English somewhat earlier than Howard thinks; the OED Supplement lists it from Alec Waugh in 1917 and James Joyce's *Ulysses,* 1922. Harper 1985 labels it entirely acceptable in both speech and writing. It appears to be more common in speech.

2. At least since the 1920s commentators have been disparaging the intensive use of *absolutely*. Thus Ball 1923:

> *Absolutely* is a favorite word nowadays; like *positively, quite, literally,* and some other words, it is much used, but seldom needed.

I. A. Richards, in *Basic English and Its Uses,* 1943, says

> In all but a few contexts *absolutely* is an absolutely (completely) meaningless intensifier. . . .

There are two separate uses here. The first is use as what Quirk et al. 1985 terms a "maximizer"—it indicates the greatest degree of something. Here are a few typical instances:

> Unwilling to make myself disagreeable . . . , I absolutely refused —Benjamin Franklin, *Autobiography,* 1788

> She was no longer absolutely bent on winning him —George Meredith, *The Ordeal of Richard Feverel,* 1859

> Constance was absolutely in the wrong —Arnold Bennett, *The Old Wives' Tale,* 1908

> And where else but in England can one find three expensive but flourishing weeklies devoted to absolutely nothing but the life of the rich and the titled? —Aldous Huxley, *The Olive Tree,* 1937

> . . . its legitimacy, if not absolutely assured, is certainly strengthened —Thurgood Marshall, *Center Mag.,* September 1969

> . . . while Ralph Fox avoided doctrinal cant absolutely —*Times Literary Supp.,* 19 Feb. 1971

> . . . neither disavowal nor avowal seemed absolutely essential —John Kenneth Galbraith, *Harper's,* February 1971

> . . . these letters should be rewritten until they are absolutely perfect —Amy Vanderbilt, *Ladies' Home Jour.,* September 1971

Although it can be argued that the adverb might have been omitted in some of these instances without great loss, its intensifying or maximizing purpose is clear. We have another set of instances, however, in which the intensity of the adverb is much diminished. Such use is not especially modern:

> She grew absolutely ashamed of herself —Jane Austen, *Pride and Prejudice,* 1813

> . . . so absolutely flooded by the Hawkesbury and its tributaries, that the farmers are forced to fly for their lives —Anthony Trollope, from *Australia and New Zealand,* 1873, in *Wanderers in Australia,* ed. Colin Roderick, 1949

> John McClain of the New York *Journal-American* (March 19, 1965) described the sets as "absolutely magnificent beige and pastel etchings" —*Current Biography,* December 1967

> Markel had been absolutely shattered when he had not been invited —Gay Talese, *Harper's,* February 1969

> . . . my piano playing was absolutely terrible —Rosemary Brown, *Ladies' Home Jour.,* September 1971

> I washed my hair and it was absolutely glorious — Abby Darer, in *Ladies' Home Jour.,* January 1971

This second use, as you can see, is more open to criticism as unnecessary or meaningless than the first; there is a considerable difference between the use of *absolutely* in "no drug can be proved absolutely harmless" and that in "he was absolutely shattered when he was not invited." The weakened use, however, does have literary authority. If it is a fault, it is, to paraphrase the 18th-century grammarian Joseph Priestley, but a venial fault.

absolute phrases A participial phrase that is not overtly connected to the rest of the sentence is called an *absolute phrase* or *absolute construction.* Quirk et al. 1985 uses the term *absolute clause* but extends the class to include constructions from which the participle has been omitted. Absolute phrases may contain either a past or present participle. An absolute phrase has a head, usually a noun or pronoun, which the participle modifies. We may think of it as the subject of the phrase.

The subject of the absolute phrase and that of the sentence are always different:

> The scholars increasing fast, the house was soon found too small —Benjamin Franklin, *Autobiography,* 1788

> Miss Ward's match, indeed . . . was not contemptible, Sir Thomas being happily able to give his friend an income —Jane Austen, *Mansfield Park,* 1814

> But I don't believe that any writer under thirty— geniuses excepted—can stay writing in the attic forever without drying up —Joan Aiken, *The Writer,* May 1968

If the subject of what would otherwise be an absolute phrase is suppressed as though it were the same as that of the main clause, a dangling participle results. Here are two excerpts from a speech of Richard M. Nixon (quoted by William Safire, *N.Y. Times Mag.,* 19 June 1983) that illustrate the problem. In the first example, both subjects are the same—*I*—and the phrase is properly attached to the clause; in the second, they are different—*I* and *tendency*—and connection is not made: the phrase dangles:

> Speaking candidly, I believe some of our Chinese friends have misunderstood and misjudged President Reagan's position on the Taiwan issue.

> Speaking as an old friend, there has been a disturbing tendency in statements emanating from Peking to question the good faith of President Reagan. . . .

See DANGLING MODIFIERS.

Perrin & Ebbitt 1972 point out that absolute phrases, when short, are direct and economical; and that when they follow the main clause, they are a convenient way to add details. Reader's Digest 1983 warns that absolute phrases with a pronoun subject (as "he having gone on ahead") are often felt to be awkward or old-fashioned.

A number of absolute phrases have been so frequently used that they are now fixed phrases:

> No, my friends, I go (always, other things being equal) for the man who inherits family traditions — Oliver Wendell Holmes d. 1894, *The Autocrat of the Breakfast-Table,* 1858

> I suggest that the university's most feasible function, all things considered, is essentially what it has been

for nearly a millennium now —Robert A. Nisbet, *Psychology Today,* March 1971

So, beyond the damage to the front end, the valves had to be reground. It came to $350 all told —Garrison Keillor, *Lake Wobegon Days,* 1985

absolutist See PURIST.

absolve Bernstein 1965 observes that when *absolve* is followed by a preposition, the choice is *from* or sometimes *of.* Before 1965 *from* was certainly more frequent than *of,* but since then the proportion of *of* to *from* has increased noticeably. Both prepositions are in current good use.

By this device I am absolved from reading much of what is published in a given year —Lewis H. Lapham, *Harper's,* May 1984

... his subjects were absolved from their allegiance to him —Arnold J. Toynbee, *Center Mag.,* March 1968

Having thus absolved himself from the duty of making the essential discriminations —F. R. Leavis, *The Common Pursuit,* 1952

... to absolve you from your promise —Willa Cather, *Death Comes for the Archbishop,* 1927

... in order to establish their independence and absolve the guide of any responsibility —Jeremy Bernstein, *New Yorker,* 30 Oct. 1971

... the 1965 pronouncement by Vatican II absolving Jews, as a people, of guilt in the death of Christ — Cyril E. Bryant, *Christian Herald,* December 1969

... arrested but later absolved of any complicity in the plot —*Current Biography 1953*

... in return, Dollar was absolved of personal liability for the line's debts —*Time,* 27 Nov. 1950

A less frequent, but still current, construction uses *for:*

... the manner in which Chicago police were absolved for the brutality they visited on the young —Donald McDonald, *Center Mag.,* July/August 1970

We may perhaps absolve Ford for the language of the article—it seems somewhat too academic for his unassisted pen —Roger Burlingame, *Backgrounds of Power,* 1949

abstain When abstain is followed by a preposition, it is regularly *from.*

They seemed careful to abstain from rich, extravagant, or passionate language —Norman Mailer, *Harper's,* November 1968

... an act of renunciation, his decision to abstain from meat —William L. Shirer, *The Rise and Fall of the Third Reich,* 1960

... now of course he would have to abstain from his allusions to the "son of the poet—you know" — Joseph Conrad, *Chance,* 1913

... was abstaining from her customary work simply from an excess of prudence —Arnold Bennett, *The Old Wives' Tale,* 1908

In reference to voting, *abstain* usually takes no preposition. *From* may be used, and rarely *in* appears:

No less than 213 Diet members abstained in the final vote —*Collier's Year Book,* 1949

abstract The verb *abstract,* in most of its senses, takes the preposition *from,* if it takes one at all. The usual pattern is to "abstract a thing from something else." Occasionally we find that "something is abstracted by something else" or "something is abstracted into something else." These last two patterns are much less frequent than constructions with *from.* Here are some examples of the usual construction:

With the nail of his right forefinger he abstracted a string of meat from between two teeth —Liam O'Flaherty, *The Informer,* 1925

Immediately afterwards he was abstracted from the scene, and has not been heard from since —H. J. Muller, *Saturday Rev.,* 4 Dec. 1948

... the logical impossibility ... of wholly abstracting this knowledge from all reference to the matter contained in the form —Bertrand Russell, *Foundations of Geometry,* 1897

... an apparition, rather insubstantial and eerie, abstracted from time and space —Edmund Wilson, *New Yorker,* 22 Nov. 1952

... the Romantic project was to abstract from religion its essential "feeling" and leave contemptuously behind its traditional formulations —Theodore Roszak, *The Making of a Counter Culture,* 1969

... basic esthetic criteria and standards he has abstracted from long intimacy with time-tested masterpieces —Aline B. Saarinen, *N.Y. Times Book Rev.,* 7 Nov. 1954

Nor can it be doubted that some kind of social picture can be abstracted from literature —René Wellek & Austin Warren, *Theory of Literature,* 1949

... the large illustrated Rabelais which she had abstracted from the library —Robertson Davies, *Tempest-tost,* 1951

And an example of each of the rarer constructions:

... these together do not supply more material to the soil than is annually abstracted by the extensive roots of trees, of bushes, and by the fern —Richard Jefferies, *The Open Air,* 1885

... conscientiously and with great purity made the uncompromising effort to abstract his view of life into an art work —Norman Mailer, *Advertisements for Myself,* 1959

abusage Nickles 1974 labels *abusage* "an obsolete and needless form of *abuse.*" Needless it may be, but it is not obsolete. The OED has only 16th- and 17th-century citations, but Eric Partridge revived the word in the title of his 1942 book: *Usage and Abusage.* Since Partridge revived it the word has been limited in use to commentators on English usage:

... Edwin Newman was called on to open the proceedings on the strength of his two books on English abusage —John Simon, *Esquire,* June 1977

There is a limit to the propriety of rejecting new usage, or abusage —Anthony Burgess, *Saturday Rev.,* 2 Sept. 1978

According to recent reports . . . the dictionary "lays down the law" about word usage and abusage —Ken Kister, *Library Jour.,* 15 Nov. 1979

abut Bernstein 1965 opines that the intransitive verb *abut* takes *against* for a wall and *on* for a line; Krapp 1927 allows *upon* or *against* for Bernstein's walls and *upon* for his line. Both of these commentators are partly right. Evidence in the Merriam-Webster files shows that *on* is the preposition of choice when something conceived of as having chiefly lateral extension is in mind:

The England of the later Middle Ages . . . abutted on Scotland —G. M. Trevelyan, *A Shortened History of England,* 1942

. . . important and populous states that abut on the Great Lakes —Harold L. Ickes, *New Republic,* 12 Feb. 1951

The northeast and southeast arms of this cross abut on Ninth Avenue —Lewis Mumford, *New Yorker,* 19 Apr. 1952

Upon is occasionally used:

. . . a lot which abuts upon a public or private alley —*Zoning for Truck-Loading Facilities,* 1952

When the thing abutted is conceived of as having a vertical as well as lateral extension, *against* and *on* are both used:

. . . a partition abutted against a window —Hugh Morrison, *Early American Architecture,* 1952

. . . the Nechako Plateau, which abuts against the Rocky Mountains —*Canadian Geographical Jour.,* September 1952

The Whitney abuts at right angles on the Modern Museum —Lewis Mumford, *New Yorker,* 15 Oct. 1955

Other prepositions are occasionally used:

Here a retaining wall is to abut into a rocky hillside —Clarence W. Dunham, *Foundations of Structures,* 1950

On the Soviet side of Potsdamer Platz, which abuts on to West Berlin —*Time,* 29 June 1953

The transitive *abut* sometimes admits of a prepositional phrase after the direct object; various prepositions are used:

Sparks, abutting Reno on I-80 east —*Dodge News Mag.,* February 1972

This Caroline Ridge province abuts the Philippine Sea along the southern side of the Mariana Trench —Alfred G. Fischer et al., *Science,* 5 June 1970

Owners with two-story brick houses were permitted to abut their piazzas to the sea wall —Hugh Morrison, *Early American Architecture,* 1952

A good diagnostician abuts the whole of himself against the whole of the patient —*Encore,* January 1947

abysm Reader's Digest 1983 adverts to *abysm* as an old variant of *abyss* that is now archaic or obsolete. This is not quite correct, though it is close. Both *abysm* and *abyss* were in use in the 14th century for the void believed in the old cosmography to exist below the earth. *Abyss* has continued in vigorous use; *abysm* might well have become obsolete except for Shakespeare. In *The Tempest* (1612) he wrote this line:

What seest thou else
In the dark backward and abysm of time?

This line has continued to echo in later writers:

. . . the surviving memory, signalling out of the dark backward and abysm of time the images of perished things —Robert Louis Stevenson, *Memories and Portraits,* 1887

. . . the mind grows dizzy at contemplating the abysm of time between —Norman Douglas, *Siren Land,* 1911

To advocate . . . appeared in English in the dark backward and abysm of time, but during the eighteenth century it seems to have dropped out of general use —H. L. Mencken, "The American Language" (1936), in *Yale Rev. Anthology,* 1942

. . . the illumination, through people, of the dark backward and abysm of American time —Carlos Baker, *Saturday Rev.,* 20 Aug. 1955

. . . the Cherry Lane Theatre, which is located somewhere in the dark backward and abysm of Greenwich Village —Wolcott Gibbs, *New Yorker,* 19 Feb. 1955

Other modern use of *abysm* also exists but is rare.

Pleasantly and with delicacy he picks his way among some of the less quoted lyrics, avoiding such abysms as "The Vampire" and some of the more purple . . . pieces —*New Republic,* 21 Oct. 1940

. . . those other forces to whom he gave his love and loyalty, which were taking his administration down to an abysm of political dishonor —*The Autobiography of William Allen White,* 1946

abysmal, abyssal Oddly enough, *abysmal,* derived from *abysm,* a relatively little used word, is the more commonly used adjective of this pair; *abyssal,* derived from *abyss,* which continues in vigorous use, is limited mostly to technical contexts. *Abysmal* is used for the most part figuratively, but it has some use of actual depths:

. . . he tosses off the abysmal Royal Gorge of the Arkansas with the phrase "perpendicular precipices" —David Lavender, *N.Y. Times Book Rev.,* 25 Sept. 1966

. . . driven at a good speed, often it appeared to me within a few inches of abysmal precipices —W. R. Arnold, *The Postmark,* May–June 1955

. . . only a few miles from the beach the bottom breaks off into the abysmal depths of the ocean — Thomas Barbour, *That Vanishing Eden,* 1944

. . . not much happens to star-light in its long passage through the abysmal depths of interstellar space — Paul W. Merrill, *The Nature of Variable Stars,* 1938

Or the depths may be figurative:

> Geology gives one the same abysmal extent of Time that Astronomy does of Space —Thomas Carlyle, *The Life of John Sterling,* 1851

> ... two octaves below the standard bassoon, with the phenomenal bottom note B,,, flat, though whether that abysmal pitch can be directly audible to the human ear is more than doubtful —Robert Donington, *The Instruments of Music,* 2d ed. rev., 1951

> ... the great head reared up, mouth open in a slack, savage grin, eyes black and abysmal —Peter Benchley, in *Cosmopolitan,* July 1974

Sometimes there is an allusion to the original abysm:

> ... as if the spirit were steeped in abysmal blackness —George Meredith, *The Ordeal of Richard Feverel,* 1859

Often figurative use suggests a sense of immensity or profundity:

> Such staggering smugness, such abysmal ignorance leave one breathless —William L. Shirer, *The Rise and Fall of the Third Reich,* 1960

> ... he had known the abysmal depletions that follow intellectual excess —Edmund Wilson, *A Piece of My Mind,* 1956

> ... the abysmal solitude of aging —Maya Angelou, *N.Y. Times,* 4 Feb. 1973

But perhaps most often *abysmal* denotes wretchedness or low quality or sometimes quantity:

> ... exploiting the just political grievances and the abysmal living conditions of the people there —*New Republic,* 6 Sept. 1954

> The weather, even by London standards, was abysmal —Frank Deford, *Sports Illustrated,* 12 July 1982

> ... I have suffered abysmal baseball luck when watching the Yankees —Roger Angell, *New Yorker,* 16 July 1973

> Earnings of the whole textile industry, traditionally low, were an abysmal 1 per cent of sales —*Newsweek,* 1 Aug. 1955

Abyssal is found chiefly in contexts referring to the bottom of the sea:

> ... to where the continental slope meets the abyssal ocean floor —Neil H. Jacoby, "Pacem in Maribus," *A Center Occasional Paper,* 1970

> The creatures appear to limit their habitat to the dark, cold, high-pressure abyssal plains below depths of 10,000 feet —*N.Y. Times,* 2 Apr. 1970

academe, academia   Copperud 1970 reports that both Fowler 1926, 1965 and Evans 1957 disapprove of *academe* as applied to a place of learning, an academy. Fowler maintains that *Academe* properly means *Academus,* a hero of Greek mythology: an olive grove in Athens sacred to his memory was near the place where Plato established his philosophical school, and it gave the name, Academy, to Plato's school. Fowler therefore opines that the "grove of Academe," mentioned by Milton, is correct in reference to Plato's Academy, and that the use of the phrase in Shakespeare, Tennyson, and

James Russell Lowell (quoted in the OED) to mean "a seat of learning" is wrong. Evans says that *Academe* properly refers to Plato's academy; he censures its use otherwise as a pomposity, instancing the title of Mary McCarthy's novel *Groves of Academe* (1952). Reader's Digest 1983 essentially agrees with Evans; they find in Mary McCarthy's "ironic" title the origin of modern journalistic use, of which they disapprove, recommending the use of *academia* instead.

These notions need to be disentangled and examined. First, we have *academe* used to mean a place of learning. As far as we can tell, this use was invented by Shakespeare, who needed a three-syllable word for *academy:*

> From women's eyes this doctrine I derive:
> They are the ground, the books, the academes,
> From whence doth spring the true Promethean fire.
> —*Love's Labour's Lost,* 1595

What Shakespeare has done here is to establish a literary expression—he used it both literally and figuratively in the same play—that would be echoed by later writers, Tennyson and Lowell among them. Fowler's objection came 330 years too late.

A 17th-century writer named Peacham cited in the OED also used the word, suggesting to someone that "thy solitary Academe should be some shady grove upon the Thames' fair side." This is the earliest attachment of *grove* in English, but it took Milton to firmly unite the two words. In the fourth book of *Paradise Regained* (1671) Satan is lecturing the Son of God on the literature and culture of the gentiles. He mentions Athens:

> See there the olive-grove of Academe,
> Plato's retirement, where the Attic bird
> Trills ...

Here *Academe* means *Academus;* like Shakespeare before him, Milton changed the usual word for the sake of his meter. No one seems to have followed Milton's spelling of the hero's name, but the phrase *grove of Academe* has stayed with us, eventually becoming plural by the mid-19th century.

So we have Shakespeare's *academe,* both literal and figurative, and Milton's *grove of Academe,* referring to Plato's Academy. Our evidence suggests, not surprisingly, that the phrase occurred chiefly in poetry. Being a literary allusion, its reference was not necessarily precise. Sometimes it might pretty clearly indicate the Platonic surrounds:

> Fulfilment of his boyhood's dream,
>   Greece welcomes now the freedman's son;
> He haunts the groves of Academe,
>   And quaffs the springs of Helicon
> —John Osborne Sargent, *Horatian Echoes,* 1893

And other times it might suggest a wider reference:

> And whether in the groves of Academe,
> Or where contending factions strive and strain
> In the mid-current of life's turbid stream,
> His honour knew no stain
>   —Charles L. Graves, "Samuel
>   Henry Butcher," 1856

The same characteristics of the phrase also are evident in prose. Sometimes the reference is clearly to Plato:

> ... his studious frequentation of that Hercynian forest, which takes the place of the groves of Academe

in German philosophical writing —George Saints-bury, *A History of Nineteenth Century Literature,* 1896

And sometimes not:

> Out of the groves of Academe comes a voice of lamentation for the political sins of New York. It is that of Arthur Twining Hadley, president of Yale University —*N.Y. Herald,* 24 Jan. 1904

Here the reference is clearly to the academic world or the academic community. This sense can also be found without the groves:

> He lived within a stone's throw of Academe, and he threw the stone —*American Mercury,* November 1928

As the sense relating to the academic world or community grew in use (with and without *groves*), specific reference to Plato's Academy receded. By the time that Evans 1957 was trying to restrict *Academe* to Platonic reference, such use had all but disappeared. Loss of specific reference is further demonstrated by the diminishing use of the capital *A*. Lowell had used Shakespeare's *academe* with a lowercase *a* in 1870; the newer sense began to appear lowercase in American publications in the mid-1920s, and by the 1950s lowercase prevailed, although capitalized examples may still be found from time to time.

We do not know exactly what Mary McCarthy had in mind when she chose *Groves of Academe* as a title, but we do know the phrase was well established by 1952, even in its widest reference (the Graves poem cited above is dated 1856). Her novel may well have added to the popularity of both the phrase and the word *academe.*

Here are some examples of how *academe* is actually used. Shakespeare's original figurative sense is still alive, although the contexts are not so elevated:

> Out of the groves of a ragtime academe . . . came Fats Waller's stride-style piano —Barry Ulanov, *A Handbook of Jazz,* 1957

> . . . splendid new texts from two doyennes of Manhattan's Chinese cooking academe —Ellen Stern, *New York,* 9 June 1975

It is also used to mean an academic:

> Young academes who have not read the works listed say my choice is capricious —Ezra Pound, *Polite Essays,* 1937

But by far the most common use is to indicate the academic environment, community, or world:

> Here is the essence of *academe:* the trials and tribulations of midnight oil —*The Bookman,* March 1925

> . . . it is clear that he speaks of the publishing scene from the remoteness of the groves of academe — Charles J. Rolo, *Atlantic,* July 1956

> . . . out of the sweat of the schoolroom where it belongs into the Groves of Academe —*Times Literary Supp.,* 14 Nov. 1968

> . . . because the most influential men in business, labor and academe appeared ready to help him — Max Frankel, *N.Y. Times,* 8 Jan. 1968

He deliberately lived outside Detroit and away from the other auto people, in the Ann Arbor groves of academe —David Halberstam, *Harper's,* February 1971

> It is some years since I've been in an American university, but I can't believe that activist corruption there has hit the very decor of academe as it has in Italy —Anthony Burgess, *Saturday Rev.,* 13 May 1978

> . . . pleasant cafes are being opened by enthusiastic refugees from the theater, the arts, academe, and the professions —John L. Hess & Karen Hess, *The Taste of America,* 1977

> . . . deep in the thickets of academe where feminism trysts with sociology —Anne Crutcher, *Wall Street Jour.,* 3 Feb. 1982

> The writer in the tower of Academe looks out upon the world like a god —Earl Shorris, *N.Y. Times Book Rev.,* 1 July 1984

Academia is a more recent word. It has been filtered through Latin from the Greek. Its earliest appearance in our files is as a synonym for Plato's Academy:

> From the Acropolis to the gardens of the Academia —C. M. Thompson, translation of Georges Clemenceau, *Demosthenes,* 1926

This use appears not to have caught on. In 1946 it turned up as a synonym for the most popular sense of *academe:*

> . . . beyond the complacent paddocks of academia, clubdom, or social status —Lucien Price, *Atlantic,* June 1946

It has stuck:

> . . . the self-directed scholar who investigates items about which he is from time to time curious, without concern for the shaping of policy, the government of tribes, or the fashions of academia —David Riesman, *New Republic,* 12 Jan. 1953

> He was intent on carving a career of public service, not within the halls of academia but on the national and international stage —*Times Literary Supp.,* 16 Jan. 1964

> . . . where the mandarins of academia dine with top Pentagon officials and Senators —Robert Reinhold, *N.Y. Times,* 18 Aug. 1974

> Like the homosexual professors who are rising fast in American academia —Pauline Kael, in *The Film,* 1968

> . . . students . . . itchy to close their notebooks and break out of the halls of academia —Susan McDonald, *Hampshire Life,* 7 Feb. 1986

> . . . the Potential Gas Committee, whose members represent all branches of the industry, as well as the government and academia —David Osborne, *Atlantic,* March 1984

> The modern traffic from academia to public life can show nothing to its medieval counterpart —Gordon Leff, *Times Literary Supp.,* 20 Nov. 1981

Conclusion: The use of *Academe* to refer to Plato's Academy seems to be moribund: we have no evidence of its use since the 1920s. *Academe* for *Academus* was used only by Milton, and survives only in the fixed phrase *groves of Academe,* where its origin is in general forgotten, as the prevalent lowercasing of the phrase attests. People who insist that these are the only correct uses are living in the past.

Both *academe* and *academia* are in current good usage in American and British English meaning "academic life, environment, community, world." When these words begin to steal each other's metaphors and insinuate themselves into other hoary metaphors of academic life—when we find groves of academia, halls not of ivy but academia, towers not of ivory but of Academe, and thickets rather than groves of academe—it is clear that they have firmly established themselves in the language. They appear to be used with about equal frequency at the present.

accede   Janis 1984 points out that this word is spelled *-cede* not *-ceed.* The Oxford American Dictionary notes that it is also a homophone of *exceed* and so subject to being confused. We do not happen to have run across examples of either mistake, and while they seem not unlikely in some kinds of writing, they do not find their way into print.

Accede is regularly followed by *to:*

> . . . for the purpose of forcing employers to accede to their demands —Eugene J. McCarthy, *Dictionary of American Politics,* 1968

> I don't want to accede to persistent demands to repeat myself —Susan Sontag, in *Vogue,* 1 Aug. 1971

> Pacifism acceded to the place of belligerency in the British heart —Michael Straight, *New Republic,* 18 Apr. 1955

accent, accentuate   *Accentuate* is what Fowler 1926 would call a "long variant" of *accent.* In this case instead of condemnation, there is approval. Fowler notes that *accentuate* is being used for figurative senses and *accent* for literal and technical ones; this is differentiation (a favorite process of Fowler and other members of the Society for Pure English), and Fowler approves and encourages it. Fowler would be pleased to learn that in the years since his writing the differentiation has continued. *Accent* has more meanings, mainly technical, but *accentuate* has more usage.

The Merriam-Webster files show that when *accent* is used in a nontechnical way, it may be used to mean "to give prominence or emphasis to":

> . . . skirts, pants, culottes and shorts that zero in on the fanny—and accent the belly —*Women's Wear Daily,* 27 Oct. 1975

> The problem of tying so far-flung a nation together . . . is accented by the population's uneven distribution —J. Hervie Haufler, *General Electric Investor,* Winter 1972

> . . . the cheapness and potency of tequila, which helped accent his paranoid and manic moods —Sy Kahn, *Jour. of Modern Literature,* 1970

Accentuate, however, is considerably more common in such use:

> Intimacy breeds rivalry, accentuates the meaning of moods —Thomas J. Cottle, *Change,* January–February 1971

> Sleek, modern design accentuates shining simulated stone —*Sears, Roebuck Catalogue,* Fall and Winter 1955

> Grayish daylight seeping into the tunnel accentuated the rough texture of the walls —Joseph Wechsberg, *New Yorker,* 12 May 1956

> . . . a slender, small-breasted girl, with an erect carriage, which she accentuated by throwing her body backward at the shoulders —F. Scott Fitzgerald, *The Great Gatsby,* 1925

> The scolding of the New England woman, that had but accentuated his awkwardness and stupidity — Sherwood Anderson, *Poor White,* 1920

Accent may emphasize a setting off by contrast; *accentuate* is seldom used thus:

> The corners of the towers are accented by brick quoins —*American Guide Series: Maryland,* 1940

> . . . had traces of Castilian beauty which she accented with pendulous amethyst earrings —Ludwig Bemelmans, *Now I Lay Me Down to Sleep,* 1943

> . . . retain the 1952 basic body styling, but the lines have been accented with additional chrome —*Newsweek,* 20 Oct. 1952

> A Sauternes . . . finished off the meal, agreeably accenting the dessert —Jane Nickerson, *N.Y. Times Mag.,* 20 June 1954

> . . . patch pockets accented with buttons —*Women's Wear Daily,* 3 June 1953

> . . . a pasty complexion and a wide, even smile accented by a rather pointy nose —Jack Falla, *Sports Illustrated,* 23 Jan. 1984

Accent is also used when the writer wants to single out or stress some particular:

> Gunther's account of his record at SHAPE accents the General's deep belief in working toward a European Federation —Charles J. Rolo, *Atlantic,* March 1952

> Although Dr. Heller in the past has made suggestions in this vein, he hardly accents them in his book — Leon H. Keyserling, *New Republic,* 25 Mar. 1967

> . . . thirty regional dramas, the more recent ones accenting Texas —Richard L. Coe, *Holiday,* May/ June 1973

Accentuate is seldom used in this way, except in the phrase *accentuate the positive,* which has been reinforced by a popular song with that title. *Accent* is also sometimes used in the phrase:

> An occasionally negative pronouncement tends to be mild and regretful; then it quickly accents the positive —Alfred Kazin, *N.Y. Times Book Rev.,* 29 Jan. 1984

> We would rather accentuate the positive —Gerard Onisa, *Media & Methods,* March 1969

> In the course of some missionary work . . . Whitehead stoutly accentuated the positive —Russell Watson, *Newsweek,* 15 Jan. 1973

Accentuate has developed an additional meaning, approximately "to intensify or increase" that is not shared by *accent:*

> ... the frail health she experienced as a result may have accentuated her natural tendency to meditate —*Dictionary of American Biography,* 1944

> ... the Bank's operations would tend to accentuate rather than to moderate the cycle —*Proceedings of the Academy of Political Science,* January 1947

> ... needs which are accentuated or created by the culture —Abram Kardiner, *The Individual and His Society,* 1939

> The 1959 crisis in Tibet accentuated, though it by no means initiated, strains in relations —*Times Literary Supp.,* 9 Apr. 1970

> ... they certainly accentuate rather than attenuate the divisiveness in the faculty —T. R. McConnell, *AAUP Bulletin,* September 1969

> Milwaukee's precipitous decline in the American League East was accentuated by a 10-game losing streak —Herm Weiskopf, *Sports Illustrated,* 3 Oct. 1983

So the differentiation between *accent* and *accentuate* noticed and encouraged by Fowler 1926 has continued, although it cannot be called complete. Except for the two general uses mentioned above where *accent* still predominates, *accentuate* holds the field for most general and figurative uses, and has developed a use of its own not shared by *accent.*

accept, except Nearly every handbook published between 1917 and the present carries a warning against confusing *accept* and *except.* A good half of these unnecessarily distinguish the preposition or conjunction *except* from *accept,* which is only a verb. The verb *except* is, however, sometimes written in place of *accept:*

> Still excepting bookings for 1984 —advt., *Morgan Horse,* December 1983

This confusion must be due entirely to similarity of sound, for the meanings of the two verbs are so dissimilar as to obviate confusion on that score. Even though Queen Elizabeth I wrote *except* for *accept* in one of her own letters (noted in McKnight 1928), the 1983 use must be accounted an error. Queen Elizabeth I spelled as she pronounced, and she spelled before there were such amenities as spelling books and dictionaries for reference.

acceptance, acceptation Fowler 1926 proclaims *acceptance* and *acceptation* "fully differentiated" in meaning. The differentiation is not quite complete even now, however, although it characterizes most use of these words. *Acceptation* is the less frequently used word, and its usual meaning is "a generally understood meaning of a word or understanding of a concept":

> ... are never supposed to be understood in the literal acceptation of the words —Tobias Smollett, *Travels Through France and Italy,* 1766

> In its technical acceptation as a term of psychology —Arthur Pap, *Elements of Analytic Philosophy,* 1949

> And it is in this spirit that they [authors of a work on French grammar] make use of such terms as punctual in their usual acceptation —Howard B. Garey, *Language,* April–June 1957

Occasionally it is used like *acceptance:*

> His record is plainly true and worthy of all acceptation —*Times Literary Supp.,* 16 Nov. 1951

> "All right, then!" he cried bitterly, with sudden acceptation of the other's story —Thomas Wolfe, *Of Time and the River,* 1935

Acceptance is much the more frequent word. It occasionally is used much like *acceptation:*

> There is also a common acceptance among far too many teachers that the field trip is a device for exposing youngsters to museum facilities without any particular preparation or use of their experience upon return to the classroom —Gilbert Hagerty, *New-England Galaxy,* Fall 1970

But mostly it does duty as the noun for *accept* in its common and specialized senses:

> ... uncritical acceptance of sense experience —Iris Murdoch, *The Fire and the Sun,* 1977

> ... that expression of mildly cynical regret and acceptance that one often notices in people who have seen much of life —Thomas Wolfe, *You Can't Go Home Again,* 1940

> ... a general uncritical acceptance of novelty as advance —Howard Mumford Jones, *Saturday Rev.,* 23 Apr. 1955

> ... a fine indifference to things that did not interest him, and an acceptance of those that did —Osbert Sitwell, *Noble Essences,* 1950

> ... the acceptance of English as the language of North America —I. A. Richards, *Basic English and Its Uses,* 1943

> ... in spite of their acceptance into the new structure —Martin Bernal, *N.Y. Rev. of Books,* 23 Oct. 1969

> ... high product acceptance in the extensive agricultural ... industrial and logging markets —*Annual Report, Caterpillar Tractor Co.,* 1952

> Through its acceptance corporation it helps surmount problems of home financing —Frederick Gutheim, *New Republic,* 26 July 1954

access 1. *Access, excess.* The Oxford American Dictionary 1980 and Shaw 1962 warn against the confusion of these two words, which sound very much alike. The OED notes that *access* was used quite a bit in the past for *excess;* it also notes that the sense "addition, increase" approaches *excess* in meaning.

We have no clear-cut evidence of confusion, and confusion would seem possible only in those senses of *access*—"outburst, fit" and "an increase by addition"— that are used in constructions with *of* similar to those in which *excess* is also used. For instance:

> Adrian's report accused his pupil of an extraordinary access of cynicism —George Meredith, *The Ordeal of Richard Feverel,* 1859

An excess of zeal in that direction entangled them in difficulties with their bishops —Oscar Handlin, *The American People in the Twentieth Century,* 1954

. . . until the chiefs, in a sudden access of wickedness, took it from them —G. M. Trevelyan, *English Social History,* 1942

. . . for the teeth the government wanted were never there (in a legislative act) until other judges in an excess of patriotism put in false ones —Zechariah Chafee, Jr., *Free Speech in the United States,* 1941

Mr. Cruncher, in an access of loyalty, growlingly repeated the words after Miss Pross —Charles Dickens, *A Tale of Two Cities,* 1859

. . . he had gotten his little pants so filthy, by crawling extensively under houses in some excess of industry —Peggy Bennett, *The Varmints,* 1947

. . . the momentary rise in us of that curious access of tenderness which may bring tears to the eyes —C. E. Montague, *A Writer's Notes on His Trade,* 1930

It is possible for the words to be exchanged in a few of these examples, but real confusion on the part of the authors seems unlikely. *Access* is most frequently used of emotions, and is not infrequently modified by *sudden;* when *excess* is used of emotions, it is frequently pluralized.

2. The most commonly used senses of *access,* when followed by a preposition, take *to:*

"Will that restrict your access to information?" —Upton Sinclair, *A World to Win,* 1946

. . . a man with access to the President —David Halberstam, *Harper's,* July 1969

. . . to provide poor citizens with access to the nation's courts —Donald McDonald, *Center Mag.,* March/April 1971

. . . the difficulty of gaining access to complete copies of such vital sources —*Times Literary Supp.,* 19 Feb. 1971

accessorize Popular writers on language enjoy lampooning advertising copy, which tends to make a target about as elusive as the proverbial side of a barn. Here is a typical instance:

As it happened, I did not have time to sparkle my table because I was busy following instructions given in another advertisement and was accessorizing my spacious master bedroom with oil paintings — Edwin Newman, *Esquire,* December 1975

One object of Newman's scorn here is the verb *accessorize,* which seems to have been discovered by usage commentators in 1975. Here is Harper 1975 on the subject:

Accessorize is a bastard offshoot of the noun *accessory.* It has appeared in advertising copy like the following: "The new kitchen range is *accessorized* with stainless steel." This says nothing that "trimmed" doesn't say better and more simply. Avoid *accessorize.*

The advice implied here—that *trim* is preferable to *accessorize*—shows the weakness of relying on a single example. Try using *trim* in place of *accessorize* in these examples and see what the effect is in each case:

We'd love to get into making accessories, because if a woman isn't accessorized properly, the whole thing goes down the drain —Edith Head, *Holiday,* November/December 1973

We've selected a suit dress, accessorized it with a hat and bag —*American Girl,* February 1953

A quaint old Early American clock and a pair of antique porcelain flower pots filled with green foliage which ties in with the wallpaper pattern nicely accessorize the narrow mantel shelf —Betty Lenahan, *Sunday Republican* (Springfield, Mass.), 20 Apr. 1958

And even toy horses are now accessorized. Among the additional items you are at liberty to buy for them is a blacksmith set —*New Yorker,* 11 Dec. 1965

. . . herringbone jackets accessorized with long silk aviator scarves —Richard Natale, *Cosmopolitan,* April 1975

Accessorize is a relatively new word—it has been around since 1939—and it is found almost entirely in contexts dealing with fashion and interior decoration, where it is well established. It is undoubtedly a handy word in such writing. If you are writing on something else, however—philosophy, geometry, grammar, art history—you will probably never need *accessorize.*

See -IZE 2.

accident See MISHAP.

accidently, accidentally Shaw 1962 and Watt 1967 disparage the spelling *accidently* as a misspelling or an illiteracy. Copperud 1970 notes that "although Webster now sanctions the second spelling, it is unusual enough so that it is likely to be considered an error."

If the OED is right, *accidently* was formed in the early 16th century, in a sense now obsolete, from the obsolete adjective *accident;* by the 17th century it was in occasional use as a variant of *accidentally.* In the latter use it has continued to appear sporadically up until the present time. Its continued use is undoubtedly encouraged by its more closely representing the usual pronunciation of *accidentally* than the predominant spelling does. Here are a few 20th-century examples:

. . . when the millet stalks which Robin looked upon as breakfast were accidently rustled by a passing foot —Freya Stark, *A Winter in Arabia,* 1940

"He asked me if it were true that it was accidently that you were locked up in the museum. . . ." —Oliver St. John Gogarty, *Mourning Became Mrs. Spendlove,* 1948

A conniving ranch foreman . . . accidently kills the drunken chief —Oscar Lewis, *N.Y. Herald Tribune Book Rev.,* 6 Jan. 1952

During childhood a brother had accidently shot an arrow into his right eye —*Australian Dictionary of Biography,* 1966

. . . they promoted him to vice president before accidently discovering the mythical account —Bill Surface, *Saturday Rev.,* 13 July 1968

One policeman accidently shot another last night — *N.Y. Times,* 6 July 1971

... the lightweight lambskin jacket, very soft and textured (as the young woman behind me in the bank line kept "accidently" confirming) —Gary B. Trudeau, in a clothing catalog, Summer 1984

The spelling *accidently* is not an illiteracy, but it is much less frequent than *accidentally,* and even though it has some reputable use, it may be thought a misspelling.

accommodate **1.** Copperud 1970, Holt 1976, Phythian 1979, and Janis 1984 all warn that this word is often misspelled with one *m: accomodate.* It certainly is. And it has been so misspelled for some time:

We were accomodated in Henrietta St. —Jane Austen, letter, 25 Sept. 1813

It even sneaks into schoolbooks:

The lens in your eye changes quickly (a doctor would say it *accomodates*) — *You and Science* (9th grade text), Paul F. Brandwein et al., 1960 ed.

The example of Jane Austen and many hundreds of others (including a few dictionary editors) notwithstanding, you should remember to double that *m.* The same warning goes for *accommodation.*
2. Bernstein 1965 says that *accommodate* can take either *to* or *with* as a preposition. Our files show that when a preposition is used, *to* predominates. It is used with the intransitive:

... she accommodated quickly to the traditional bisexuality of the British theatre and the British upper classes —Brendan Gill, *Harper's Bazaar,* November 1972

... presupposed a certain stable element in American life that you learned ... to accommodate to — Edward Grossman, *Harper's,* February 1970

... learn how to live together and to accommodate to each other —Ramsey Clark, *Center Mag.,* July/August 1970

The transitive verb may take *to* after a reflexive pronoun or after another direct object:

... the musician who seems mad to a bourgeois world because he cannot accommodate himself to its demands —*Times Literary Supp.,* 21 May 1970

... a secular morality ... that accommodates itself to what man will actually do —Daniel P. Moynihan, *American Scholar,* Autumn 1969

A bride, to help take care of such a creature,
And accommodate her young life to his
        —Robert Frost, *North of Boston,* 1914

... he had to accommodate his step to hers — Michael Arlen, *These Charming People,* 1924

With is much less frequently used, though not rare:

I wish I might accommodate you with a supper of pemmican —Elinor Wylie, *The Orphan Angel,* 1926

... to accommodate them with valuable jobs — James Gould Cozzens, *Guard of Honor,* 1948

... we were determined to accommodate our basic interests with those of other powers —Dean Acheson, in *The Pattern of Responsibility,* ed. McGeorge Bundy, 1951

When the transitive *accommodate* is used in the passive, it is used with whatever preposition seems most appropriate according to sense. Here, again, *to* is the most frequent.

It was completely accommodated to their culture — John Kenneth Galbraith, *The Scotch,* 1964

... while the latter is covertly accommodated to events —John Dewey, *Freedom and Culture,* 1939

... then congratulates himself on being accommodated with a machine —Thomas Love Peacock, *Headlong Hall,* 1816

... careers of the "movie brats," each of whom is accommodated by a full chapter —Robert F. Moss, *Saturday Rev.,* 23 June 1979

... I looked in the mirror and saw that though my nose was still long and sharp, it was newly accommodated by a softened cheek —Lore Segal, *New Yorker,* 25 July 1964

Brummell's cravat was twelve inches broad, and had to be accommodated between his chin and his shoulders —*English Digest,* December 1952

The girl was accommodated at the station for the night —*Springfield* (Mass.) *Union,* 22 Aug. 1953

About seventy of them were accommodated in wards —Nevil Shute, *Most Secret,* 1945

It is not easily accommodated among the peculiarities of our constitutional system —Dean Rusk, in *Fifty Years of Foreign Affairs,* ed. Hamilton Fish Armstrong, 1972

accompanist See PIANIST.

accompany When *accompany* is used in the passive voice, notes Whitford & Foster 1937, "*by* is nearly always used unless the idea is that of combining or supplementing." Shaw 1962 repeats their view. Bernstein 1965 specifies "*with* (things), *by* (persons)" and several later commentators echo him. None of these statements are quite right. *Accompanied by* is the usual form, regardless of the situation; *by* is always used with persons and is usual with things. *Accompanied with* is limited to things, but citations of it are both markedly less frequent and older; most recent use shows *by* in all cases. Here are some typical examples:

... children should be accompanied by an adult — Karla Kuskin, *N.Y. Times Book Rev.,* 11 Nov. 1979

... sudden arguments would flare up accompanied by much cussing and finger jabbing —Richard M. Levine, *Harper's,* April 1971

The use of violence is accompanied by anger, hatred and fear, or by exultant malice and conscious cruelty —Aldous Huxley, *Ends and Means,* 1937

Any inflammation or infection of the diaphragm will be accompanied by a shortness of breath —Morris Fishbein, *The Popular Medical Encyclopedia,* 1946

Just how far the fact of uniformity is accompanied by a sense of equality —John Dewey, *Freedom and Culture,* 1939

... a lofty mountain ... from the top of which a sulphurous vapour, accompanied sometimes by smoke and flames —Sir James G. Frazer, *Aftermath,* 1937

... has accompanied her appealing, precise, pastel-colored drawings with some equally sprightly verse —George A. Woods, *N.Y. Times Book Rev.,* 19 Sept. 1954

... his delivery is impassioned and accompanied with emphatic gestures —*Current Biography 1947*

Putting up the ridge-pole was accompanied with a swig of rum —*American Guide Series: New Hampshire,* 1938

account, *noun* See ON ACCOUNT OF.

account, *verb* When *account* is used as an intransitive verb, it is regularly followed by the preposition *for:*

... arms and space programs account for seventy per cent of available federal expenditures —Donald McDonald, *Center Mag.,* July/August 1970

... won twenty-seven games while losing ten, thereby accounting for nearly half of his team's total victories for the year —Roger Angell, *New Yorker,* 11 Nov. 1972

... still incapable of accounting for facts that are obvious to introspection —Noam Chomsky, *Columbia Forum,* Spring 1968

... the Humour definition quite fails to account for the total effect produced —T. S. Eliot, "Ben Jonson," in *Selected Essays,* 1932

accountable One is accountable *to* someone who is due an explanation *for* something done or not done.

... public officials are agents of the people and accountable to them for their public acts —Hyman G. Rickover, *Center Mag.,* September 1969

The F.B.I. has not been forced to address such issues in public because it has never been accountable to the public —Victor S. Navasky, *N.Y. Times Book Rev.,* 14 Mar. 1976

They would, finally, make the schools accountable for results —Peter Janssen, *Saturday Rev.,* 5 Feb. 1972

accrue Copperud 1970 advises us that two commentators recommend leaving *accrue* to legal and financial contexts; Bryson 1984 offers the same message. This being the case, we will largely ignore legal and financial uses and concentrate on those more general and literary contexts that tend to provoke criticism.

Bryson 1984 begins by telling us that the word must mean to be added to bit by bit. The source of his notion is obscure; it is not to be found in the OED definitions (or in Merriam-Webster's) nor is it supported by etymology, since *accrue* comes ultimately from a Latin verb meaning "to grow." Perhaps Bryson had *accrete* in mind. Anyway, he illustrates his assertion with this example: "A balloon, for instance, cannot accrue." That is certainly true.

Accrue has been used in contexts other than the legal and financial kind since the 16th century. Indeed, it appears that the usual financial uses grew out of a more general sense. The typical examples below show the word in its various constructions and also make clear which prepositions are idiomatic with *accrue.* Bernstein 1965 says *accrue* takes *to,* but in fact *to* is used only to indicate the recipient of the accruing; *from, through,* and *for* are usual for indicating its source:

... the gain which accrues to his poetry ... from his superiority, and the loss which accrues to it from his defects —Matthew Arnold, *Essays in Criticism, Second Series,* 1888

I have addressed the navvies on the advantages that would accrue to them if they married wealthy ladies of rank —W. S. Gilbert, *The Sorcerer,* 1877

... and some good repute accrues to him from his increased wealth —Thorstein Veblen, *The Theory of the Leisure Class,* 1899, in *Outside Readings in Economics,* Arleigh P. Hess, Jr., et al., 1951

... a good deal accrued eventually to my benefit through these visits —Osbert Sitwell, *Noble Essences,* 1950

... the *réclame* that would accrue to everyone concerned —S. J. Perelman, *New Yorker,* 1 Jan. 1972

... Macbeth, surrounded by disasters which have accrued from his evil ambition —Clyde S. Kilby, *Poetry and Life,* 1953

However, to make any such study and analysis of the savings which may accrue through the use of electronic equipment —John W. Mauchly, *Systems,* September–October, 1954

... whatever credit or blame accrues for easing the way of the People's Republic into the United Nations —Richard H. Rovere, *New Yorker,* 18 Sept. 1971

The intransitive verb can, of course, be used without prepositions:

Though Florence's flood was an incalculable disaster, certain unexpected advantages accrued —Katharine Kuh, *Saturday Rev.,* 22 July 1967

... the thesis that there is a threshold dose below which no harm accrues —*The Economist,* quoted in *Atlas,* March 1970

My hatred has no consequences. It accrues only in my mind —Renata Adler, *New Yorker,* 24 Apr. 1971

Accrue also has transitive use:

It's been around five years now, accruing readers, even disciples, in snowball fashion —Robert Lambert, *Media & Methods,* March 1969

While participating ..., a student would accrue benefits on a monthly basis —Frank Newman, *Change,* May 1972

People changed through the arithmetic of birth, marriage, and death, but not by going away. So families just accrued stories, which through the fullness of time, in those times, their own lives made —Eudora Welty, *Esquire,* December 1975

The foregoing examples show that *accrue* can be used unexceptionably in contexts having nothing to do with law or finance. The two following suggest that it can also be used when the author has been fishing for a word, and has apparently not caught the right one:

> ... as the film goes along, some of Buck's dignity accrues to the Preacher, who becomes an engagingly childlike figure, and some of the Preacher's anarchism rubs off on Buck —Joseph McBride, *Rolling Stone,* 20 July 1972

> It is hard to say why, but some of the reasons accrue from overzealous building, when concrete was poured over the top of the greenery, the palms were blighted, and the beaches cut away —Horace Sutton, *Saturday Rev.,* 10 Dec. 1977

You can use *accrue* in contexts neither financial nor legal, if you take care to use it clearly in one of its accepted meanings. Your dictionary will show you what those are.

accuse The usual preposition used with *accuse,* to indicate the charge, is *of;* it has been the usual one at least since John Gower in the late 14th century. But from time to time other prepositions have come into use with *accuse,* and grammarians and commentators have been at pains to correct them. In 1762 Bishop Lowth corrected these two well-known writers for using *for:*

> Ovid, whom you accuse for luxuriancy of verse —John Dryden, "Essay on Dramatic Poesy," 1668

> Accused the ministers for betraying the Dutch —Jonathan Swift, *The History of the Four Last Years of the Queen,* 1758

Evidence in the OED shows *for* with *accuse* to have come in around the middle of the 17th century; the latest citation with *for* is dated 1809; the OED calls it obsolete, along with *in* and *upon* (of which no examples are shown).

The occasional use of *with* seems to have originated in the 20th century. Our earliest evidence is from Lurie 1927, who corrects this example from an unnamed newspaper:

> Jeremiah Jenks, having sold butter for more than the market price, was accused with being a profiteer.

Lurie supposes *with* to have come from confusion of *charged with* and *accused of* (see SYNTACTIC BLEND). Bernstein 1965, 1977 also criticizes the use of *with,* and concurs in Lurie's theory of its origin. Aside from the examples provided by Lurie and Bernstein, Merriam-Webster editors have gathered only one additional citation:

> In 1947, the FTC accused Monarch and Stolkin with "misrepresentation...." —*Newsweek,* 3 Nov. 1952

Most examples are from journalistic sources (one is quoted speech, however, and Reader's Digest 1983 cites Louis Nizer's autobiography). *Accuse with* seems to appear seldom and sporadically.

The usual constructions are *accuse* + object (noun or pronoun) + *of* + noun, which is the older one, and *accuse* + object + *of* + gerund. The first goes all the way back to Gower's *Confessio Amantis* (1393). The construction with the gerund turns up in Swift's sentence with *for;* the OED shows none earlier. Evidence in the Merriam-Webster files suggests that the gerund construction is somewhat more common in current use.

Here are a couple of examples of each:

> ... two Negroes who had been accused by a federal grand jury in Jackson, Mississippi of perjury —*Current Biography,* July 1965

> Niebuhr accuses secular social thinkers of these erroneous beliefs —Ralph Gilbert Ross, *Partisan Rev.,* January–February 1954

> If you accuse me of being a gross optimist —Melvin M. Belli, *Los Angeles Times Book Rev.,* 23 May 1971

> Carlyle has been accused of making a habit of this shifting of the phrase modifier in his writings —Margaret M. Bryant, *Modern English and Its Heritage,* 1948

accused No one quibbles over uses of the adjective *accused* like this:

> ... the accused teacher should be informed before the hearing ... of the charges —*AAUP Bulletin,* December 1967

But several commentators—Copperud 1970, Bernstein 1971, Reader's Digest 1983—note that *accused* is also used in such combinations as *the accused spy, the accused assassin, the accused murderer:*

> Previously, accused shoplifters had been disciplined by an administration committee —Glynn Mapes, *Security World,* May 1968

Copperud advises avoiding these because they imply guilt before it is established; Reader's Digest calls the use an error; *Winners & Sinners* (19 Apr. 1985) finds it "journalese"; Bernstein finds the meaning of *accused* "distorted" but "accepted" and advises avoiding it as ambiguous. A combination like *the accused murderer* actually is journalistic shorthand for "the person accused of the murder"; it is probably not often misunderstood as "the murderer who has been unlucky enough to be caught and charged." While many commentators say such uses of *accused* are quite common, our files hold few examples other than those held up as bad examples. Reader's Digest prefers and approves *alleged* in place of *accused* in such combinations. See ALLEGED, which has had its share of detractors, too.

This is, perhaps, more of a problem for journalists than for other writers.

See also SUSPECTED 1.

Achilles' heel Although the story of Achilles' vulnerable heel is ancient, the phrase *Achilles' heel* meaning "a vulnerable point" seems to have been used in English only since the middle of the 19th century. Before that century was out, it had developed a spelling without the apostrophe—perhaps thanks to George Bernard Shaw, who seems to have been the first to write it that way.

Our most recent evidence on the question of whether the apostrophe should appear or not is split exactly 50-50. For what it's worth, publications like the *New York Times* and *Saturday Review* can be found on both sides of the aisle. British journals—*Times Literary Supplement, The Guardian, New Scientist, The Listener*—tend to use the spelling without the apostrophe. Reader's Digest 1983 likes to see the apostrophe kept. Either way you choose to write it, you will find yourself in decent company.

acid test   Back in 1920 when H. W. Fowler was compiling his magnum opus (Fowler 1926), he noted that *acid test* had the greatest vogue of all the popularized technicalities he was listing. He attributed the popularity of the phrase to Woodrow Wilson's conspicuous use of it during World War I. The OED Supplement cites Wilson:

> The treatment accorded Russia by her sister nations in the months to come will be the acid test of their good will —*The Times,* 9 Jan. 1918

The same statement was paraphrased just a couple of weeks later:

> He said the attitude of other nations toward revolutionary Russia was the acid test of their democracy and good faith —*Saturday Evening Post,* 25 Jan. 1918

The OED Supplement shows that the figurative sense of acid test—"a crucial test"—had actually been in use as early as 1912, but Fowler was probably right in attributing its sudden popularity to Wilson. The *Saturday Evening Post* report is the earliest citation in the Merriam-Webster files. It was soon followed by more evidence from 1918, 1919, and the early 1920s, and the term was entered in the 1923 Addenda section of Webster 1909.

As is often the case with a phrase that has become popular in a relatively short time, *acid test* was soon disparaged as a cliché—as early as 1929 by one John Y. T. Greig in *Breaking Priscian's Head; or, English as She Will Be Spoke and Wrote.* A number of subsequent commentators—some as recent as Shaw 1975 and Bremner 1980—have repeated that judgment. Howard 1983 gives a somewhat different opinion, calling the term "old-fashioned," which it may be in British English. Our files do not have enough evidence to confirm or refute his opinion; we do have evidence, however, that *acid test* is still flourishing on this side of the Atlantic.

The expression is a metaphor derived from the practice of testing gold with acid. The use of *acid test* in print for the chemical operation is rare; and even though we have evidence of other technical uses of *acid test,* the figurative use is by far the dominant one in 20th-century English.

The question of what constitutes a cliché is not simple (see the discussion at CLICHÉ), so we will leave you to judge *acid test* from these examples, drawn from eight decades of use. We do note that the phrase seems not to be much used in literary contexts.

> Every banking institution in this country to-day applies an acid test to applications for loans. Is the note which it will receive capable of discount with the Federal Reserve Bank? —*The Nation,* 28 Mar. 1918

> . . . the scientist is content to hold them up to the acid test of present-day efficiency —*World's Work,* November 1928

> The peculiar drudgery . . . of reading papers is the acid test of the teacher —*English Jour.,* December 1935

> . . . should say something about selling textbooks, for in the American economic system that is the acid test of any product —*Textbooks in Education,* 1949

> . . . rationally testing our hypothesis by the acid test of seeing how it works in experience —Gardner Murphy, in *Feelings and Emotions,* ed. Martin L. Reymert, 1950

> The acid test will be whether the members of the United Nations, in it and through it, will be able to stop an aggressor —Sir Leslie Munro, *United Nations: Hope for a Divided World,* 1960

> . . . he has avoided the acid test of declaring himself in detail on Vietnam —Thomas P. Murphy, *Trans-Action,* March 1968

> Even when all these acid tests are ruthlessly applied, however, the inventory of probable Scandinavian phonic and lexical influences in English remains impressive —John Geipel, *The Viking Legacy,* 1971

> Deciding to put Patria Mia to the acid test without beating about the bush, I ordered *calamari luciana* as my entrée the first time I set foot in the place — Jay Jacobs, *Gourmet,* February 1979

> . . . Sawyer has devised an acid test for friendship: take a job that requires getting up at 5:30 in the afternoon —Margo Howard, *People,* 5 Nov. 1984

acoustics   *Acoustics* takes a singular verb when it refers to the science, and a plural verb when it applies to the characteristics (as of an auditorium) that enable distinct hearing.

> Acoustics is the science of sound —*Acoustical Terminology,* 1951

> The acoustics of the place are not very good —Virgil Thomson, *The Musical Scene,* 1947

acquaint   **1.** Two sources—Bernstein 1965 and Chambers 1985—remind us that *acquaint* should be followed by *with.* It was not always so. Johnson's Dictionary (1798 ed.) for the sense Johnson defined "To inform" carries this note: "*With* is more in use before the object, than *of.*" He includes a quotation from Shakespeare using *of.* Actually, the construction *acquaint someone* could also be used with a clause introduced by *that* or even a contact clause. Shakespeare uses all four possibilities, but even with him *with* is the most common. The OED shows the construction with *that* from Fielding and Sir Walter Scott but calls the construction with *of* obsolete. The *of* construction is not quite obsolete, but it is certainly of very low frequency:

> I'll presently acquaint the Queen of your most noble offer —Shakespeare, *The Winter's Tale,* 1611

> . . . acquainted him formally of the honour which Providence and Sr. Azaña had in store for him —E. Allison Peers, *Spanish Tragedy 1930–1936,* 1936

Here are examples of *acquaint* with a *that* clause and a contact clause:

> I must acquaint you that I have received new-dated letters —Shakespeare, *2 Henry IV,* 1598

> May I be bold to acquaint his Grace you are gone about it? —Shakespeare, *All's Well That Ends Well,* 1603

But *with* predominates, from Shakespeare's time to our own:

> Misery acquaints a man with strange bedfellows —Shakespeare, *The Tempest,* 1612

> ... his near relation to you makes you more particularly acquainted with his merits —Edmund Burke, speech, 1780, in *Burke's Speeches at Bristol,* ed. Edward Bergin, 1916

> Any young gentlemen and ladies, who wish to acquaint themselves with the English language —Noah Webster, quoted in Horace E. Scudder, *Noah Webster,* 1882

> ... you expect to be informed of the secret with which I am acquainted —Mary Shelley, *Frankenstein,* 1818

> ... not very well acquainted with our Parliamentary or political affairs —Sir Winston Churchill, *The Unrelenting Struggle,* 1942

> ... music-lovers who are thoroughly acquainted with Bruckner —Winthrop Sargeant, *Saturday Rev.,* 28 Aug. 1954

> ... to acquaint a boy with how to use tools and handle materials —James B. Conant, *Slums and Suburbs,* 1961

> His interest in modern writers acquainted him with such philosophers as Pascal, Voltaire and Rousseau —Edmund White, *N.Y. Times Book Rev.,* 19 June 1983

2. *Acquaint* is one of the terms Gowers 1948 found overworked in British governmental prose; Chambers 1985 seems to take a similar line in suggesting *acquaint with* is rather formal for *tell* or *inform* and reporting that some people think *acquaint someone with the facts* is a cliché. British and American usage may differ in this regard, for Merriam-Webster files have little evidence of the supposed cliché. Many of our citations do, however, come from educational sources, in which there is often a tendency to bureaucratic prose. Gowers suggests *tell* or *inform* as substitutes, but *acquaint,* with its overtones of familiarity, cannot always be felicitously replaced.

acquaintanceship Characterized as "a needless variant" by Fowler 1926 and "unnecessary" by Evans 1957, *acquaintanceship* was formed in the early 19th century, apparently to distinguish the meaning "state of being acquainted" from *acquaintance* "a person with whom one is acquainted." It does serve to make the distinction, but most people have continued to use *acquaintance* for both meanings. Curiously, Long 1888 writes: "Prefer: ... Acquaintanceship *to* acquaintance, as an abstract noun. Reserve *acquaintance* for persons or things one is acquainted with." The word evidently had some status as a carrier of the distinction before it was condemned by Fowler.
  Acquaintanceship is not widely used, but is not rare. It tends to show up in literary contexts.

> They struck up an acquaintanceship —Samuel Hopkins Adams, *Incredible Era,* 1939

> ... found an acquaintanceship with alcohol easy enough, but one with women formidably difficult —William Styron, *Lie Down in Darkness,* 1951

> At intervals I was able to renew my acquaintanceship with this room —Lucien Price, *Dialogues of Alfred North Whitehead,* 1954

> ... both Hawthorne and Thoreau profited more from their acquaintanceship than has been generally allowed —Earle Labor, *CEA Critic,* January 1971

> It also reveals the width of his acquaintanceship —Graham Reynolds, *Times Literary Supp.,* 6 June 1980

acquiesce Around the turn of the century *acquiesce* began to receive attention from usage commentators. Vizetelly 1906 seems to have begun things with a prohibition of *with* after the word; he prescribes *in.* Krapp 1927 prescribes *in* and censures *to;* so does Carr & Clark, *An ABC of Idiom and Diction,* 1937. Similar views are expressed in Follett 1966, Bernstein 1965, Harper 1975, 1985, Macmillan 1982, Ebbitt & Ebbitt 1982, Reader's Digest 1983, and Chambers 1985. Dictionaries are less dogmatic; Webster's Third states "often used with *in,* sometimes with *to,* and formerly with *with*"; Heritage 1982 concurs in this assessment.
  The OED shows that *acquiesce* has been used with several prepositions—*from* and *under* in senses now obsolete, and *in, to,* and *with* in the current sense. *In* and *to* are of equal antiquity, both having been used by Thomas Hobbes 1651, who is the earliest user of the modern sense cited in the dictionary. The OED marks *to* and *with* obsolete, but in fact *to* has continued in use, although *in* is used considerably more often. Here are a few samples of the construction with *to:*

> ... to have Carrie acquiesce to an arrangement —Theodore Dreiser, *Sister Carrie,* 1900

> Some abundance within herself would not let Theodosia acquiesce completely to the hour, to any hour or to any experience, as being sufficient —Elizabeth Madox Roberts, *My Heart and My Flesh,* 1927

> ... had, just before Kalgan's fall, acquiesced to Marshall's proposal for a ten-day truce —*Time,* 21 Oct. 1946

> ... political sociologists today are often reluctant to acquiesce to Michels' law —Lewis S. Feuer, *Jour. of Philosophy,* 11 Nov. 1954

> Man's freedom *must* at last acquiesce to the inhibiting claims of his fellows and to the melancholy necessity of death —Theodore Roszak, *The Making of a Counter Culture,* 1969

None of these examples is incorrect or nonstandard. But *acquiesce in* is the predominant construction:

> ... no organism acquiesces in its own destruction —H. L. Mencken, *Prejudices: Second Series,* 1920

> ... it was wrong to acquiesce in the opinion that there was nothing to be done —Compton Mackenzie, *The Parson's Progress,* 1923

> He discreetly acquiesced in the election of one of the principal assassins —John Buchan, *Augustus,* 1937

> To acquiesce in discrepancy is destructive of candour —Alfred North Whitehead, *Science and the Modern World,* 1925

> ... a pose which was accepted and acquiesced in by Delacroix —Sacheverell Sitwell, *The Dance of the Quick and the Dead,* 1936

. . . the general intellectual tendency is to acquiesce in what one no longer feels able to change —Irving Howe, *Partisan Rev.,* January–February 1954

. . . one should not on that account acquiesce in it —Bertrand Russell, *London Calling,* 7 Apr. 1955

Dr. Brown's refreshing refusal to acquiesce in certain current fashions —*Times Literary Supp.,* 10 July 1969

acquit When *acquit* means "to discharge completely," it is often used in the construction *acquit* (a person) *of* (something charged):

. . . was acquitted of robbery on an alibi —*Time,* 30 Oct. 1950

. . . cannot therefore be acquitted of being out of touch in some respects —*Times Literary Supp.,* 23 Apr. 1971

. . . neither pamphlet nor book could acquit him of indecency —Henry Seidel Canby, *Walt Whitman,* 1943

For may substitute for *of* in this construction but is rare:

In the end, Mary Todd Lincoln stands acquitted for any evil intent —Gerald W. Johnson, *New Republic,* 23 Feb. 1953

From was formerly in use, but is no longer:

If I sin, then thou markest me, and thou wilt not acquit me from mine iniquity —Job 10:14 (AV), 1611

When the person is not present in the sentence, other constructions may be found:

The military "jury" . . . voted 3-1 to acquit on the charges of failure to report for duty and resisting arrest —Steve Wise, *Great Speckled Bird,* 24 Jan. 1972

acronyms A number of commentators (as Copperud 1970, Janis 1984, Howard 1984) believe that acronyms can be differentiated from other abbreviations in being pronounceable as words. Dictionaries, however, do not make this distinction because writers in general do not:

The powder metallurgy industry has officially adopted the acronym "P/M Parts" —*Precision Metal Molding,* January 1966

Users of the term *acronym* make no distinction between those which are pronounced as words . . . and those which are pronounced as a series of characters —Jean Praninskas, *Trade Name Creation,* 1968

It is not J.C.B.'s fault that its name, let alone its acronym, is not a household word among European scholars —*Times Literary Supp.,* 5 Feb. 1970

. . . the confusion in the Pentagon about abbreviations and acronyms—words formed from the first letters of other words —Bernard Weinraub, *N.Y. Times,* 11 Dec. 1978

Pyles & Algeo 1970 divide acronyms into "initialisms," which consist of initial letters pronounced with the letter names, and "word acronyms," which are pronounced as words. *Initialism,* an older word than *acro-*

nym, seems to be too little known to the general public to serve as the customary term standing in contrast with *acronym* in a narrow sense. Such burning issues among etymologists of a few decades ago as whether *minicam* and *motel* were allowable as acronyms seem to have faded into the past—we have no current evidence that such blends are referred to as acronyms any more.

A number of commentators warn against the indiscriminate use of acronyms that may not be familiar to the reader of general text—sound common sense. Of course, if one is writing for a technical audience, one has more leeway in the use of acronyms. But even in technical articles, many authors gloss new acronyms for their readers' information at least upon their first appearance in the text.

Many a seemingly catchy acronym has proven to have a short life, as the list of disapproved acronyms in Nickles 1974 illustrates: only two or three of his pageful are still easily recognized. Pyles & Algeo point out other examples: the spate of offsprings patterned on World War II's *snafu* are mostly forgotten, although *fubar* has had at least a temporary revival among computer hackers.

act, action Both *act* and *action* can be similarly used to denote something done. In theory, an act is conceived of as individual and momentary or instantaneous; an action involves discrete stages or steps and is conceived of as occupying more time than an act. However, even though many writers and speakers give little thought to the theory, in most cases, as we shall see, the two words tend to fall into different patterns of use.

Sometimes, it is true, either word might have been used:

. . . deGaulle made public his proposal on December 28. This action brought a reply from Algiers —Arthur L. Funk, *Current History,* November 1952

. . . one of the first acts of President Buchanan was to appoint him —*Dictionary of American Biography,* 1928

So far as we can tell from these extracts, deGaulle's action might just as well have been Buchanan's act, and vice versa.

Nevertheless, differences in usage are usually apparent. When *act* is modified by something descriptive, for example, it tends to be followed by *of* and a noun:

. . . performing numerous acts of kindness to those in need —*Times Literary Supp.,* 8 Feb. 1968

. . . engaged in an act of arson, or an act of revolutionary heroism, depending on his view —Jerome H. Skolnick, *Trans-Action,* November 1968

. . . they could never catch Reston in an act of arrogance or selfishness —Gay Talese, *Harper's,* January 1969

. . . sit down to commit an act of literature —William Zinsser, 1975

The physical act of moving is even worse—the sheer awfulness of facing that jammed and cluttered attic —Anna Fisher Rush, *McCall's,* March 1971

Once the act of reading has begun —Joe Flaherty, *N.Y. Times Book Rev.,* 27 Mar. 1977

One phrase is a notable exception:

> The sex act has to do more for humans than for other creatures —Robert Jay Lifton, *N.Y. Times Book Rev.,* 19 Aug. 1979

Action tends to be preceded by its modifier:

> . . . a similar CNVA protest action —*Current Biography,* October 1965

> . . . his bungling unilateral actions during the Corsican campaign —Arthur L. Funk, *Current History,* November 1952

> . . . his occasional political actions . . . seem unrelated to any other aspect of his character —*Times Literary Supp.,* 14 Mar. 1968

> There are squatter actions going on all the time — Philip St. George, quoted in *N.Y. Times,* 23 Mar. 1980

When a prepositional phrase introduced by *of* follows *action,* it usually functions as a genitive:

> It is the actions of men and not their sentiments which make history —Norman Mailer, *Advertisements for Myself,* 1959

> . . . the future of our children depends in great measure on the actions of our political leaders —Lena L. Gitter, *Children's House,* Fall 1968

Action has a collective use that *act* does not:

> . . . the only time in which it took decisive action — *Times Literary Supp.,* 16 Jan. 1969

> . . . immediately pressed for Congressional action — *Current Biography,* December 1965

> . . . after the Socialists' April triumph, action against them was indicated —John Paton Davies, *N.Y. Times Mag.,* 13 July 1975

Action is also used attributively, while *act* is not:

> . . . scrutiny by . . . environmental action groups — *Annual Report, Owens-Illinois,* 1970

> . . . lots of exciting action photographs —C. H. Simonds, *National Rev.,* 17 Dec. 1971

In addition, both *act* and *action* fit into characteristic idiomatic constructions where no native speaker of English would be tempted to interchange them: for instance, *caught in the act, a piece of the action.* (Those involving *act* often invoke the performance sense of that word.) Here is a sampling:

> "She had a class act going there." —Cyra McFadden, *The Serial,* 1977 (*class action* is a legal term)

> . . . Washington must get its act together —Wassily Leontief, *N.Y. Times Mag.,* 30 Dec. 1979

> ". . . to try to clean up his act." —John Maher, quoted in *Harper's Weekly,* 20 Oct. 1975

> . . . a bulletin on how the hairdressers are getting into the act —Lois Long, *New Yorker,* 8 Sept. 1956

> . . . no action has yet been taken —Hugh Thomas, *Times Literary Supp.,* 11 Apr. 1968

> ". . . tomorrow they swing into action. . . ." — unnamed announcer, WTIC radio, 23 Feb. 1975

> . . . a general program that . . . was not put into action at first —*Current Biography,* May 1965

> Its editorial offices are in Manhattan, near the action —Herbert Mitgang, *N.Y. Times Book Rev.,* 13 Jan. 1980

activate, actuate Gowers in Fowler 1965 disparages *activate* as a popularized technicality replacing *actuate;* Shaw 1975, 1987 considers the meanings of the two words to be "confused when used to refer to persons" and both he and Evans 1957 attempt to discriminate between them. Here is what evidence in the Merriam-Webster files shows.

Both words are currently much used in technical contexts, although *activate* seems to be used more frequently and widely. Technical uses are not disputed, so we pass them over, except to note that when a person sets some mechanism in motion, either word might be used, but *activate* is more frequent in our more recent citations:

> Then he actuated the mechanism, and the mass of metal fell with a muffled, reverberating thud — Arnold Bennett, *The Old Wives' Tale,* 1908

> . . . the throttle being actuated by hand —Priscilla Hughes, *Now There's No Excuse,* 1952

> Whenever Dr. Kelman activates a switch, the wall . . . begins to slide away —Brian Vachon, *Saturday Rev.,* 15 Apr. 1972

> . . . small sonic pingers that could be activated in an emergency —John Devany & Sylvia Earle, "My Two Weeks Under the Sea," in *Networks,* ed. Marjorie Seddon Johnson et al., 1977

When the words are used in reference to persons, they are usually distinguished. *Actuate,* which has a long background of literary use, almost always indicates an interior cause for the action:

> Notwithstanding the high veneration which I entertained for Dr. Johnson, I was sensible that he was sometimes a little actuated by the spirit of contradiction —James Boswell, *Life of Samuel Johnson,* 1791

> . . . men, who . . . are always actuated by the hope of personal advantage, or by the dread of personal punishment —Thomas Love Peacock, *Headlong Hall,* 1816

> Individuals may be actuated by a sense of justice — William Ellery Channing, *Discourses on War,* 1903

> . . . the spirit that actuated the grandfather having lain fallow in the son —Samuel Butler, *The Way of All Flesh,* 1903

> Still, as he is actuated by a sense of duty —W. S. Gilbert, *The Pirates of Penzance,* 1879

> . . . that very British spirit of freedom which has actuated them throughout —Osbert Sitwell, *Triple Fugue,* 1924

> . . . the man who is actuated by love of power is more apt to inflict pain than to permit pleasure —Bertrand Russell, *Atlantic,* March 1952

When *activate* is applied to individuals, it almost always implies an external force:

> . . . her life in art is closely related to the places where she has lived and visited, to the natural phenomena

that have activated her —Katharine Kuh, *Saturday Rev.,* 22 Jan. 1977

He was rarely seen by day, but the feast of St. Patrick had altered his habits and activated him this noon —Herman Wouk, *Aurora Dawn,* 1947

... he lacked the force to control his party and the personality and leadership to activate the public —Sidney Warren, *Current History,* May 1952

Infrequently *actuate* is used of an external stimulus and *activate* of an internal one:

... a society too ill-organized to actuate the generosity of decent human beings —*Times Literary Supp.,* 4 Mar. 1939

... many persons, hitherto vaguely sympathetic, become ... energized and activated out of indignation —Richard Hofstadter, *Harper's,* April 1970

Activate is, in general, the more likely word to be used of something that is compared to or conceived of as machinery:

The federal government finally was activated —Donald Canty, *City,* March–April 1972

Economists are accordingly much more interested in societies activated by command than in those run by tradition —Robert L. Heilbroner, *The World of Economics,* 1963

... exhortations ... fail to activate the more costly self-sacrificing behaviors —James H. Bryan, *Psychology Today,* December 1969

Those who have activated the evil forces loose in the world today —*JAMA,* 26 June 1954

"I ain't a vegetarian, and Garbo does *not* have big feet," he said, activating knowing titters —*New Yorker,* 1 July 1950

To summarize, *actuate* has a long history of literary use; it is applied to people who act for internal reasons. *Activate* is more often used of things thought of as mechanical in their operation; when applied to people, it almost always indicates the working of some external spur to action.

active voice   See PASSIVE VOICE.

actual, actually   Both words are tarred with the brush of meaninglessness by Copperud 1970, who cites Fowler 1965 and Evans 1957 in support of his view, although Evans and Fowler (actually Gowers, since Fowler 1926 does not mention it) condemn only *actually.* We will examine the words separately.
Copperud's objection to *actual* lies in a single quoted sentence: "The stocks were sold at prices above actual market prices." The trouble with this example is that it lacks its preceding context. In a majority of instances of the use of *actual* in our files, it contrasts with some other adjective, either stated or implied. Combined with *price, actual* is usually so contrasted:

... actual prices received (as opposed to posted prices) have not kept pace —Fred L. Hartley, *Annual Report, Union Oil Co. of California,* 1970

In Copperud's example, the contrasting price may have been mentioned or implied in an earlier sentence in such a way as to make the use of *actual* entirely appo-

site. Here are some other examples of *actual* in its contrastive use:

I had enjoyed my actual sins, those I had committed rather than those I had been accused of —Ernest Hemingway, "Miss Mary's Lion," 1956

... I'm no judge of the feelings of actual or prospective parents —Rose Macaulay, *Potterism,* 1920

... how would he set out to make any actual person a character in a novel? —Bernard DeVoto, *The World of Fiction,* 1950

... the services it provides ... to actual and potential publics —Jerome H. Skolnick, *AAUP Bulletin,* September 1969

... a very popular subject indeed among intending and actual undergraduates —Malcolm Bradbury, *Times Literary Supp.,* 25 July 1968

... his wonderful dramatic monologues ... are written in verse that uses, sometimes with absolute mastery, the rhythms of actual speech —Randall Jarrell, *N.Y. Times Book Rev.,* 21 Mar. 1954

Phythian 1979 mentions *actual,* too, objecting to "the common phrase *in actual fact.*" The phrase is probably more common in speech than in print, for it is not abundantly attested in our files.

In actual fact, Fishpond Lake is not the beautiful paradise that Bethlehem's camera makes it out to be. Whereas it looks large, serene, and lush in the ad, it is actually cramped and barely covered with scrub brush —Peter Harnik, *Environmental Action,* 15 May 1971

The phrase seems justified in this instance by contrast with the pseudo-factuality of what the camera shows. The phrase has appeared in somewhat altered forms:

He did, as an actual fact, miss Cards terribly —Hugh Walpole, *Fortitude,* 1913

Actual has, besides its use in pointing up a contrast, an intensive function sometimes meant to stress authenticity:

... she demanded that the soldiers' uniforms in "Fatinitza" be trimmed with actual sable! —Carl Van Vechten, *Saturday Rev.,* 29 May 1954

... some of his suits have actual whalebone up the ribs —Lois Long, *New Yorker,* 27 Mar. 1954

It is also used as a simple intensive:

It would be an actual benefit to the town if a few men owned the factory —Sherwood Anderson, *Poor White,* 1920

But whatever the actual human and physical cost, the political shock was devastating —Allen S. Whiting, *Life,* 21 Feb. 1969

... many heavy leatherites will think twice about confronting an actual well-dressed lady —Blair Sabol, *Vogue,* November 1976

The intensive *actual* can reasonably be challenged as unnecessary in many instances. In the following quotations, it could probably have been omitted if the author so chose. The choice is a matter of style and taste. It might be a useful exercise to try to determine whether the sentences sound better with or without *actual.*

... there ensued a long conversation as they walked as to whether waiters made more in actual wages than in tips —F. Scott Fitzgerald, "May Day," in *The Portable F. Scott Fitzgerald,* 1945

A doctrine that identifies what ought to be with the lowest elements of actual reality cannot remain acceptable for long —Aldous Huxley, *The Olive Tree,* 1937

I have rounded the figures to make the arithmetic easy, but the orders of magnitude are not far from the actual facts —Robert M. Solow, *Think,* May–June 1967

On the other hand, Auden is steadily increasing his mastery over the actual craft of verse —G. S. Fraser, in *Little Reviews Anthology 1949,* ed. Denys Val Baker, 1949

... a delightful rendition that awed the audience especially when they learned that both Glee Clubs had but an hour's combined rehearsal time before the actual concert —Duncan Dobie III, *Dartmouth Alumni Mag.,* May 1954

Actually is a more difficult subject. It is the more widely disparaged word, and disparagement of it is somewhat diffuse. In addition, the usages that seem to have excited the criticism are primarily spoken rather than written usages, so that printed evidence of the disputed usages is not as abundant as one would like it to be and as it would be if a primarily written use were in question. We will first examine typical written usage before passing on to the spoken.

It should not be surprising to find *actually* used in adverbial functions corresponding to the adjective functions of *actual.* It is used to point up a contrast:

Whereas it looks large, serene and lush in the ad, it is actually cramped and barely covered with scrub brush —Peter Harnik, *Environmental Action,* 15 May 1971

But actually there is a pattern which underlies these contradictory orders —Margaret Mead, *And Keep Your Powder Dry,* 1942

Sea anemones may resemble pretty flowers, but actually they are deadly animals —Murray T. Pringle, *Boy's Life,* April 1968

But the most common use is to stress the reality or factuality of something. In this use, *actually* is not necessarily emphatic:

... could not even find out how many airplanes there actually were —David Halberstam, *Harper's,* February 1971

... nobody actually knows ... whether fewer books are being read —J. Donald Adams, *N.Y. Times Book Rev.,* 11 Apr. 1954

... showing the picture that was actually on the air —Denis Johnston, *Irish Digest,* June 1954

Rose really meant what she said. She was actually beginning to forget —C. S. Forester, *The African Queen,* 1935

"... but as I have actually paid the visit, we cannot escape the acquaintance now." —Jane Austen, *Pride and Prejudice,* 1813

Actually he was less angry than perplexed —Jean Stafford, *The Mountain Lion,* 1947

... how to obtain a cooperative apartment without actually cheating —Richard Schickel, *Harper's,* February 1971

It may be used to suggest something unexpected:

Now they were off ... , leaving Jason standing and actually waving —Rita Madocs, *Ladies' Home Jour.,* September 1971

I had been actually invited —F. Scott Fitzgerald, *The Great Gatsby,* 1925

... Mother Goose (a real person actually named Mary Goose) —*American Guide Series: Massachusetts,* 1937

Of course any of these uses would be normal in speech, too. But in conversation the sense may be weakened or even absent, and it is presumably this use that has occasioned censure of *actually* as unnecessary. When its semantic content is low, *actually* may be serving a special purpose in conversation—that of a filler (see FILLERS)—as Phythian 1979 and Bremner 1980 observe (in different terms). "*Actually* is usually used to give the speaker a moment in which to think," says Phythian. The filler *actually* is likely to be syntactically a sentence adverb, and it is probably this use that Evans 1957 characterizes as "a worn-out import from England." There is no strong evidence on which to base the supposition that it is an import. As a sentence adverb, *actually* is typically found at the beginning or sometimes in the middle of an utterance in American use, and at the end of an utterance in British use:

Actually, if we weren't so worried about forcing independence on them, they would be less likely to beat us over the head with it —Bruno Bettelheim, *Ladies' Home Jour.,* January 1971

Actually, the people who truly are Mrs. Lieberman's dearest friends are a great deal like her —John Corry, *Harper's,* February 1971

Because I've seen some of the recent criticisms—the continuing criticism, actually—of the statistics — William Ruckelshaus, quoted in *N.Y. Times Mag.,* 19 Aug. 1973

... he didn't fall about laughing, he helped me a lot actually —Saffron Summerfield, quoted in *Spare Rib* (London), December 1974

As much a Wykeham Diary as a Langham Diary, actually —Alan Ryan, *The Listener,* 28 Mar. 1974

Conclusion: criticism of *actual* and *actually* as unnecessary is of very limited value in a usage handbook. The usages criticized are primarily spoken, and few people trouble to chasten their speech in accordance with the pronouncements found in usage books addressed to writers. Both *actual* and *actually* have legitimate uses in writing, which have been illustrated here. It can be argued that in many instances they can be omitted from sentences in which they appear without changing the sense; but if you will read the sentences quoted without the *actual* or *actually,* you will find in very many cases that something is missing, that *actual* or *actually* is far from useless in context. Where these words do not add much to meaning, they often improve the rhythm of a sentence and help set off the more important words effectively. Judicious use of these and many words of similar function can be a mark of a smooth and understandable style. The tersest message is not always the most readily understood.

actuate See ACTIVATE, ACTUATE.

ad "Standard for *advertisement*" says Copperud 1970 of this word. Several later commentators (Harper 1985, Perrin & Ebbitt 1972, Ebbitt & Ebbitt 1982, Colter 1981) agree in the main, excluding it only from the most formal of contexts. But lest you think that at last there is one item of usage comment on which everyone agrees, we must record the fact that there are dissenters.

Colloquial shortening of *advertisement*. Prefer the full word —Bell & Cohn 1981

This clipped form and others like it (such as *math, exam, bike*) are appropriate in informal speech, but in formal writing the words usually appear in full —Macmillan 1982

These nay-sayers have their predecessors, being part of a tradition:

Ad. and Advertising—Do not use the abbreviation —Whipple 1924

Ad: unauthorized abbreviation for *advertisement* —MacCracken & Sandison 1917

Whipple 1924 is a handbook on business writing; MacCracken & Sandison 1917 is the earliest college handbook in our collection. These represent two streams of opposition to *ad*. Of the college-handbook opposition we do not know the origin, other than a general disapproval of clipped forms (see ABBREVIATIONS). The business opposition seems to have arisen in the advertising fraternity itself. H. L. Mencken, *The American Language, Supplement I*, 1945, gives its history:

The American advertising men, in the glorious days when the more forward-looking of them hoped to lift their art and mystery to the level of dogmatic theology, astronomy, ophthalmology and military science, carried on a crusade against the clipped form *ad*, but it came, alas, to nothing.

Mencken traces the beginning of this campaign to 1918, and says that nothing has been heard of it since 4 Mar. 1933. If the admen have given up the campaign themselves, a few writers of college handbooks are still carrying the old banner. Even so, a large majority find *ad* acceptable in general and informal writing:

It [the word *better*] can even sound unpleasantly snobbish, as in those ads that end with "At better stores everywhere" —Simon 1980

Janis 1984 and Ebbitt & Ebbitt 1982, among others, point out that *ad* is a clipped form rather than an abbreviation, and is not terminated by a period. This is certainly true in American practice. British practice seems mixed; when used alone, it seems to be often treated like an abbreviation and given the period:

... marked on the ad. dummy as it goes to the editorial department —Allen Hutt, *Newspaper Design*, 2d ed., 1971

... when a non-publishing ad. had been removed —Quentin Oates, *The Bookseller*, 6 Apr. 1974

But in attributive combinations (such as *ad-man, ad-writer*) the period is generally omitted in the presence of a hyphen (the OED Supplement does have a citation for an unhyphenated *ad. man*).

The most frequently used British equivalent of the originally American *ad* appears to be *advert* (with no period):

... when I come up about the advert, I specially said no mornings —Alan Coren, *Punch*, 23 Dec. 1975

In one of the Sunday papers I saw an advert in capitals —John Fowles, *The Collector*, 1963

... the adverts on the telly —Alan Sillitoe, *The Loneliness of the Long Distance Runner*, 1959

... certain crucial terms are used in a highly ambiguous way (hardly a good advert for linguistics) — David Crystal, *Linguistics*, 1971

Advert pops up occasionally in American sources:

... despite an advert implying there were —Thomas Plate, *N.Y. Times Book Rev.*, 23 Mar. 1975

A.D., B.C. *B.C.* is here for the record—there is no dispute about it and never has been. *B.C.* follows the year and follows the word century:

... sometime before 2000 B.C., corn was introduced —Katherine Hinds, *Brown Alumni Monthly*, October 1982

We have Panini's analysis of Sanskrit from the fourth century B.C. —Edward Finegan, *Attitudes Toward English Usage*, 1980

A.D. is a different story. It presents three problems: Does it go before or after the year? Can it be used with *in?* Can it be used after *century?*

The traditional and still most frequently used styling places A.D. before the year:

A.D. 1942 was the year —*Time*, 28 Dec. 1942

... objects, which date from A.D. 200 —*Newsweek*, 10 July 1944

Until A.D. 1200 the Great Plains were virtually unpopulated —Albert H. Johnston, *Publishers Weekly*, 29 Dec. 1975

Some writers and publishers, however, place *A.D.* after the date like *B.C.:*

Strictly speaking, we should use *A.D.* only with numbers indicating particular years (43 *A.D.*, 8–10 *A.D.*) —MacCracken & Sandison 1917

Lucian flourished approximately 125–190 A.D. — *Insect Enemies of Books*, 1937

... the vast platform that before 70 A.D. had supported the Temple —John Updike, *Bech is Back*, 1982

MacCracken & Sandison 1917 finds that usage justifies placing *A.D.* either before or after the year (they chose after); Reader's Digest 1983 also finds placement after the date acceptable, especially in writing in which such dates are frequent.

MacCracken & Sandison brings up the question of *in:*

"Though purists insist on 'He died 48 A.D.' [not *in* 48 A.D.], usage allows *in*. . . ." The objection to *in* is based on insistence on the literal translation of the Latin *anno Domini* "in the year of the Lord." Bremner 1980 is still defending the position of the 1917 purists, but no other commentators mention it.

Insistence on the literal "in the year of the Lord" is also the basis for the objection to using *A.D.* after *century;* the use is illogical if you insist on the literal interpretation. Bremner 1980 does. But many people will agree with Johnson 1982 when he terms the etymological objection to *A.D.* after century "rather a fussy point" and adds "there is little to be gained by binding A.D. forever to its original exact meaning." There is plenty of evidence that writers and publishers have found *A.D.* convenient to use after *century:*

> . . . fourth century A.D. —Leonard Bloomfield, *Language,* 1933

> Arabians borrowed coffee from the Abyssinians about the twelfth century A.D. —Science News Letter, 28 July 1945

> . . . came over from Ireland in the second century A.D. —Thomas F. O'Rahilly, *Early Irish History and Mythology,* 1946

> . . . built in the first half of the third century, A.D. —*Current Biography,* October 1967

> . . . the first century A.D. —John P. Dessauer, *Book Publishing,* 2d ed., 1981

Bremner 1980, on the side of the literalists, suggests that only *B.C.* be used with *century;* any century without *B.C.* could then be assumed to be *A.D.,* and there would be no need for the illogical designation. His solution would work were the use of *A.D.* not already established, but as matters stand it hardly seems a realistic goal. Ebbitt & Ebbitt 1982 report that some sophisticated stylists and Latinists analyze both *A.D.* and *B.C.* as nontranslated adverbials, applying to both years and centuries; their interpretation sidesteps all controversy.

In summary, *B.C.* goes after the year and after *century; A.D.* is more often placed before the year than after; it is widely used after *century.* Some commentators attempt to rate these stylings on a basis of formality, but our evidence tends to undercut that argument. The question is most likely to be decided as a matter of individual or house style; in other words, consistency of application is more important than which styling is selected.

adage   See OLD ADAGE.

adapt, adopt, adept   Under the heading *Adapt/Adopt* Kilpatrick 1984 says, "No good reason suggests itself for the two words ever to be confused. . . ." And even less reason for *adept,* which is not even a verb like the other two, to be confused. Yet many handbooks, from the elementary-school to the college level are at pains to distinguish them. Let us hope someone actually benefits from all this help. We have evidence of an error or two among our citations, but they may easily be typographical in origin and not from any confusion in the writer:

> The next Kraft show, adopted from Hemingway's *Fifty Grand* —*Current Biography,* September 1967

It is possible to use one or the other of the verbs in a context vague enough that only the author knows which verb is intended:

> . . . the Café des Artistes, which Lang will turn into what he calls a neighborhood restaurant. It will adapt the concept of the English ordinary that became popular in early New York taverns —Horace Sutton, *Saturday Rev.,* 15 Nov. 1975

It is hard to feel certain whether the concept will be used with or without modifications, though in this instance it doesn't seem to matter much. But such hermaphrodite constructions are rare. Usually the two verbs are easily distinguished both by meaning and typical construction. Here are a few typical examples of *adapt:*

> . . . the principle by which the Law was adapted to changing conditions —Edmund Wilson, *A Piece of My Mind,* 1956

> . . . a method the writer can adapt to his material —Ted Morgan, *Saturday Rev.,* August 1979

> . . . to adapt what was already known about them to television —Richard Poirier, *Saturday Rev.,* 22 Apr. 1972

> . . . where huge mammals were skinned, boned, and adapted for use —Julia Howard, *Science 80,* March/April 1980

> . . . a script that he himself adapted from the original by Euripides —*Current Biography,* May 1966

Here are some typical examples of *adopt:*

> . . . those who adopt this course must at least be clear about the likely dynamics of the process —Noam Chomsky, *Columbia Forum,* Winter 1969

> . . . as was the custom, he was adopted into his future wife's family —*Current Biography,* December 1965

> Common policies were to be adopted for foreign trade, agriculture, and transport —*Current Biography,* May 1966

> . . . has been adopted as prospective Liberal parliamentary candidate for the Garston division of the city —*The Times* (London), 15 Nov. 1973

> . . . I was adopted almost at once by a townsman —Richard Joseph, *Your Trip to Britain,* 1954

The two verbs can even be used with complete clarity in the same sentence:

> . . . had been slow to adapt to a changing world or to adopt modern education —Rosanne Klass, *Saturday Rev.,* 5 Feb. 1972

Adept is both a noun and an adjective. Some examples of the noun:

> She has . . . become an adept in ambiguities —John Leonard, *N.Y. Times Book Rev.,* 13 May 1973

> Blake may be regarded as an adept of ancient mystical doctrine —W. L. Renwick, *English Literature 1789–1815,* 1963

> Luigi was an adept at understatement —John Buchan, *The House of the Four Winds,* 1935

Evans 1957 thinks *in* preferable to *at* after the adjective. But *at* appears to be used more often, and other prepositions are used as well:

> The Swede is adept at the gentle pastime of fishing in troubled waters —W. Somerset Maugham, *The Moon and Sixpence,* 1919

... so adept at the lovely polishing of every grave and lucent phrase —Stella Gibbons, *Cold Comfort Farm,* 1932

... were far from adept at lobbying —Emily Hahn, *New Yorker,* 24 Apr. 1971

There is no intrinsic reason why a lawyer should not be adept in grammar and logic —Scott Buchanan, "So Reason Can Rule," 1967

... is so adept in extracting himself plausibly from the most compromising situations —Victor Heiser, *An American Doctor's Odyssey,* 1936

... the only surprise is that he is so adept with both instruments —Don Heckman, *Stereo Rev.,* September 1971

... as you become more and more adept as a ham —Arthur Henley, *Boy's Life,* May 1968

... is a working ranch-dog and is equally adept on all kinds of stock —*Dog World,* June 1976

adapter, adaptor Phythian 1979 wants us to distinguish *adaptor* "an electrical device" from *adapter* "a person who adapts." Even for British English he is only partly right. Both *adapter* and *adaptor* are used in British English for devices (and not only electrical ones), and *adapter* is used for a person, while *adaptor* is not. In American English *adapter* is usual for both persons and devices; *adaptor* is relatively infrequent.

addicted Copperud 1970 tells us that Bernstein 1965 and Evans 1957 advise reserving the participial adjective *addicted* for what is harmful; Bernstein dislikes its facetious use for what is not harmful. Partridge 1942 also finds *addicted to* pejorative and recommends not using it neutrally unless one is being facetious. But evidence in the OED shows neutral use to have existed from the 17th century at least:

He was much addicted to civil Affairs —Thomas Stanley, *The History of Philosophy,* 1660 (OED)

His majesty is much addicted to useful reading — 'Junius,' *Letters,* 1771 (OED)

Neutral and mildly humorous use has continued undiminished:

Dear Sir, that is an excellent example
Of an old school of stately compliment
To which I have, through life, been much addicted
—W. S. Gilbert, *The Sorcerer,* 1877

... those addicted to late dinner and those who still revelled in the primitive simplicity of high-tea — Osbert Sitwell, *Triple Fugue,* 1924

They were addicted to travel, and spent only a month or so of each year in England —Stella Gibbons, *Cold Comfort Farm,* 1932

... as a man, addicted to pleasure, to work, and to fresh air —John Galsworthy, quoted in *Correct English,* January–February 1939

... he himself, addicted to books and too blind to participate in games —Edmund Wilson, *The Wound and the Bow,* 1941

... rich sportsmen addicted to deer shooting — George Bernard Shaw, *Everybody's Political What's What,* 1944

She was addicted to gaudy shawls and the most God-awful hats —*The Autobiography of William Allen White,* 1946

... he was neither stupid, simple-minded, nor addicted to strait-jackets and pigeonholes —Stanley Edgar Hyman, *The Armed Vision,* 1948

In appearance, Herbert Morrison is short, chunky, addicted to colorful ties and boutonnières —Mollie Panter-Downes, *New Yorker,* 31 Mar. 1951

Catherine Morland, having become addicted to novels of terror —Lionel Trilling, *Encounter,* September 1954

He must have been as addicted to clear thinking as Larkey Waldron —Oliver St. John Gogarty, *It Isn't This Time of Year At All!* 1954

I've mentioned before how I feel about the use of football as a metaphor for national policy.
President Ford is evidently addicted to it — Thomas H. Middleton, *Saturday Rev.,* 14 June 1975

... you can become addicted to losing fights with any society you're in —William Stafford, *Writing the Australian Crawl,* 1978

He was hopelessly addicted to the Senators, a team of monumental incompetence on the baseball diamond —Russell Baker, *Growing Up,* 1982

There is a British tradition (Fowler 1926, Treble & Vallins 1937, Longman 1984) of warning writers not to follow *addicted* by an infinitive, although the regular preposition is *to.* OED remarks that the infinitive was formerly used in this way but shows no example of it later than the 16th century.

additionally Copperud 1964, 1970 does not like *additionally* used as a sentence adverb; clumsy, he thinks, for *also.* The sentence he gives as an example does seem somewhat awkward. The word, however, seems to be used primarily as an alternative to *in addition* or *besides.* Although our examples are not notably awkward, the word has a fairly low frequency of occurrence—perhaps many writers do find that it has more syllables than they usually want in an adverb.

Additionally, we witnessed last April the senseless murder of a night watchman at a university campus in Santa Barbara —Ronald Reagan, *Change,* July–August 1969

Additionally, it held that its doctrines were so perfectly formulated that it was impossible to improve on them —*Times Literary Supp.,* 29 Jan. 1971

Additionally, the student is being encouraged to survey this material to learn about basic reference sources —Susan P. Miller, in Greenbaum 1985

And additionally, working in this new, fictional approach, I followed Hemingway's grand method — Gertrude Samuels, *The Writer,* May 1968

address Flesch 1964 warns against using *address* as a pompous substitute for *speech.* Since an address by definition is "a formal prepared speech delivered to a special audience or on a special occasion," it is hard to see what the point of the warning is. *Address* is frequently used in combinations that indicate the occasion—inaugural address, commencement address. It is not used for an impromptu speech.

> . . . the President attempted to reassure the nation on this point in his television address —*New Yorker,* 12 May 1973

> In his first public address as an FCC member —*Current Biography,* July 1967

adept   See ADAPT, ADOPT, ADEPT.

adequate   Follett 1966 touches on most of the points about *adequate* that others (Copperud 1964, 1970, 1980, Evans 1957, Partridge 1942) comment upon. He deals with idiom, first noting that *adequate* is normally followed by *to:*

> . . . occasions when school textbooks are not adequate to the purpose —Albert H. Marckwardt, *Linguistics and the Teaching of English,* 1966

> . . . his resources weren't adequate to the ambition —F. R. Leavis, *Revaluation,* 1947

> This supply of literature was long found adequate to the demand —T. B. Macaulay, *The History of England,* vol. I, 1849

> The materials at present within my command hardly appeared adequate to so arduous an undertaking — Mary Shelley, *Frankenstein,* 1818

However, he does not note that it is also followed by *for:*

> Biggest casting problem: an actress adequate for the double role —*Time,* 24 Apr. 1944

> But projective coordinates . . . though perfectly adequate for all projective properties —Bertrand Russell, *Foundations of Geometry,* 1897

> And the nobility was not much more adequate for the role attributed to it by Montesquieu —*Times Literary Supp.,* 21 Sept. 1951

Follett says that idiom requires the gerund rather than the infinitive after *to:*

> . . . mind . . . is not always adequate to mastering the forms of rage, horror, and disgust —Norman Mailer, *Advertisements for Myself,* 1959

However, the construction with the infinitive is more common in actual use:

> . . . attain the perfect music of their style under the stress of a stimulus adequate to arouse it —Havelock Ellis, *The Dance of Life,* 1923

> . . . tolls and concession rentals . . . will be more than adequate to cover the principal and interest on all the bonds —*Wall Street Jour.,* 5 Nov. 1954

> Psychological explanations alone are not adequate to understand today's student radicals —Kenneth Kenniston, *Change,* November–December 1969

Follett does acknowledge use without any complement, and in the Merriam-Webster files, *adequate* appears most frequently without a complement:

> A rat has to have a protected home and an adequate food supply —Victor Heiser, *An American Doctor's Odyssey,* 1936

> . . . simple causes which did not seem to him adequate —Joseph Conrad, *Chance,* 1913

> . . . could be relied on to be socially adequate, in spite of a dangerous distaste for fools —Rose Macaulay, *Told by an Idiot,* 1923

> It may be that there is nothing more demoralizing than a small but adequate income —Edmund Wilson, *Memoirs of Hecate County,* 1946

Follett calls *adequate enough* "too familiar" and "nonsense" (Evans, Partridge, and Bremner 1980 also find it redundant), but our files have no examples of it.

Along with *adequate enough,* Follett mentions *more adequate, less adequate, insufficiently adequate* with disapproval; he believes *adequate* "resistant to comparison." Oddly enough, *adequate* escaped Partridge's lengthy list of adjectives that he thought should not be compared. Like other adjectives usage commentators call "uncomparable" or "absolute," *adequate* is an adjective with which *more* patently means "more nearly":

> If a more adequate return is to be achieved —Augustus C. Long et al., *Annual Report, Texaco Inc.,* 1970

> . . . would regret the lack of a more adequate formal education —*Current Biography,* September 1966

> The future of civilization depends on our having a more adequate supply of both —Robert M. Hutchins, *Center Mag.,* September 1968

> The convention asked for a more adequate Indian policy —Ray Allen Billington, *Westward Expansion,* 1949

> . . . continued to champion the poem as the most adequate expression of the complex ambiguity of experience —*Current Biography,* July 1964

> . . . not only is he the most ignorant and provincial of all the Marxist critics . . . but probably the least adequate Marxist —Stanley Edgar Hyman, *Antioch Rev.,* Winter 1947–1948

The intensifier *very* is occasionally found:

> . . . some very adequate salaries are given to a few — *American Guide Series: New Jersey,* 1939

> . . . a very adequate summary of it was made by T. E. Hulme in a lecture —Herbert Read, *The Philosophy of Modern Art,* 1952

Copperud and Follett both observe that *adequate* is used in a conventional way by reviewers to convey faint praise or faint derogation. The sense (OED Supplement dates it from 1900) is generally recorded in dictionaries.

> . . . not particularly inspired. An adequate performance —Henry Barnard Stafford, *Saturday Rev.,* 30 Mar. 1940

> . . . is at best adequate as the slight, brooding producer and moonstruck lover —Judith Crist, *Saturday Rev.,* 11 Dec. 1976

The sense is not limited to use by reviewers:

> ". . . After all, in any other walk in life it doesn't matter if you're not very good; you can get along quite comfortably if you're just adequate. . . ." —W. Somerset Maugham, *The Moon and Sixpence,* 1919

adhere Copperud 1964 finds his risibilities tickled by such expressions as "adhere to a plan," but in his 1970 book he admits he is alone—nearly everyone else finds such use perfectly standard and normal. Little wonder: the OED traces this sort of use back to the 17th century and even quotes "adhere to a plan" from an 1897 book. The regular preposition is *to:*

> I adhere to my resolution of not going there at all — Thomas Love Peacock, letter, 29 Nov. 1818

> ... how firmly they adhere to their own delusions — *Times Literary Supp.,* 9 Apr. 1970

> ... causes all the fruit to rot, so that in digging up the plant nothing is found but foul matter adhering to the leaves —Sir James G. Frazer, *Aftermath,* 1937

Follett 1966 is dubious about the transitive use of *adhere,* even though it was to be found in the dictionary. It is in reputable use, and the use is most often both literal and technical:

> The crystal was adhered to a prism of known index —*Technical Highlights 1967,* November 1967

> The hairs to which the fly is adhered begin to bend, and pass their prey to hairs nearer to the center of the leaf —*The Sciences,* September 1964

Occasionally figurative use of the transitive verb may be found:

> The economic principles to which Mr. Simon and Mr. Greenspan adhere, and to which they adhered the unwitting Mr. Ford —John Kenneth Galbraith, *Esquire,* May 1977

adherence, adhesion A number of theorists comment on the distinction between *adherence* and *adhesion* from Vizetelly 1906 through Follett 1966 and on to Chambers 1985. The thrust of all three is the same: *adherence* is generally used figuratively, *adhesion* literally. This analysis is not far wrong, but it needs some elaboration in detail. *Adherence* is mostly used figuratively:

> ... a religious adherence to what appears to me truth and reason —Edmund Burke, (Speech on) *Conciliation with the Colonies,* 1775

> ... mask their intentions of continuing the struggle for world mastery by a superficial adherence to the ideals of human brotherhood —Oscar Handlin, *The American People in the Twentieth Century,* 1954

> Donald's adherence to the firm of Middleton was now the topic —Angus Wilson, *Anglo-Saxon Attitudes,* 1956

But it is also used literally:

> ... results in imperfect adherence of rubber to the fabric —*Industrial Improvement,* January 1946

> The tremendous adherence achieved through stickyback, a double sided adhesive fabric —*Bookbinding and Book Production,* January 1952

Adhesion is a bit more complex. Its various technical and literal senses account for half, or perhaps a bit more than half, of the citations in our files. But figurative use is not at all uncommon. It falls into two varieties—political-diplomatic and general. President Harding's use of "adhesion to a treaty" was criticized by Frederick

Lewis Allen in *Only Yesterday* (1931), but Harding's use seems to have been technically impeccable:

> ... the terms of this Convention which is open to adhesion by all countries of the world —*UNESCO Copyright Bulletin,* No. 3, 1951

> Adhesion of some, if not all, of the Little Entente Governments to the Rome protocols of 1934 and 1936 —Arnaldo Cortesi, *N.Y. Times,* 10 Nov. 1936

> ... the Communist International won at first the adhesion of several powerful and well-established labor organizations —H. B. Parkes, *Marxism—an Autopsy,* 1939

> ... his ardent attachment to Washington, and his adhesion generally to the federal party —Horace E. Scudder, *Noah Webster,* 1882

Follett ascribes the political use of *adhesion* to translations from the French, and French may indeed have had some influence on the diplomatic usage, at least, though we have no clear evidence of that. He also says it "has begun to make its way into English and American writings on politics," but the OED shows it began to do so in the 17th century. General figurative use seems somewhat less frequent than the political:

> ... a too strict adhesion to those so-called 'laws' — Eric Partridge, "Imagination and Good Sense in Etymology," 1952

> ... marital breakups ... are usually regarded by counselors as a failure of adhesion —Vance Packard, *The Sexual Wilderness,* 1968

Our files, then, show that this is not a simple matter of "one word, one sense." *Adherence* is more often figurative than literal; *adhesion* is somewhat more often used literally and technically, and its chief figurative use is in the general area of politics and diplomacy.

adjacent *Adjacent* is often followed by *to:*

> ... the border region below the Bolovens Plateau and adjacent to the Highlands —Robert Shaplen, *New Yorker,* 24 Apr. 1971

> All I knew was the state—one adjacent to the state Beardsley was in —Vladimir Nabokov, *Lolita,* 1958

> "... something adjacent to your talents and interests—commercial art, perhaps." —Lore Segal, *New Yorker,* 25 July 1964

Copperud 1970 reports some concern over the meaning of *adjacent,* emphasizing that it means "near but not necessarily touching." This information is readily available in dictionaries. Clearly *adjacent*—excluding its mathematical uses—sometimes means touching and sometimes not:

> ... the academic speaker's strings of adjacent nouns —Stringfellow Barr, *Center Mag.,* May 1968

> ... it is not likely that pure accident caused three adjacent windows to take a Spanish tone —Henry Adams, *Mont-Saint-Michel and Chartres,* 1904

> ... a line of separation between adjacent warm and cold masses of air —*Dictionary of American Biography,* 1929

> Adjacent events need not be contiguous —James Jeans, *The New Background of Science,* 1934

On Cape Cod, on the adjacent islands of Nantucket and Martha's Vineyard —*American Guide Series: Massachusetts,* 1937

He despised the six field officers at the adjacent table —Norman Mailer, *The Naked and the Dead,* 1948

. . . through the piazza of St. Peter's and the adjacent streets —Nathaniel Hawthorne, *The Marble Faun,* 1860

Other commentators (such as Flesch 1964 and Gowers in Fowler 1965) make various comments on *adjacent,* but there seems to be no serious problem in the use of this word.

adjectives   1. Under the heading *adjective* most commentators on usage place a miscellaneous collection of faults they are intent on exposing and eradicating. Some include general observations on matters of grammar and rhetoric, as well. In this book, most of the usage issues that adjectives are involved in are treated under separate headings. See, for instance, ABSOLUTE ADJECTIVES; ABSOLUTE COMPARATIVE; DOUBLE COMPARISON; FLAT ADVERBS; IMPLICIT COMPARATIVE; PARTICIPLE 2; SENTENCE ADJECTIVE; SUPERLATIVE OF TWO.

2. For those to whom some of the descriptive terminology of adjectives may be unfamiliar, we will mention here that there are two kinds of adjectives, from the standpoint of their position in the sentence. Their conventional names are used from time to time in articles in this book. Adjectives that stand in front of the nouns they modify are *attributive* adjectives:

The *full* and *careful* report was published.

When the adjectives follow a form of *be* or a linking verb (or copula), they are *predicate* adjectives:

The report that was published was *full* and *careful.*

Appositive adjectives may follow their noun, or they may precede it and its other modifiers (such as an article or possessive), often as part of a longer phrase:

The report, *full* and *careful,* was published.

Full and *careful* in its attention to detail, the report was published in a national magazine.

3. *Idiomatic placement of adjectives.* Harper 1975, 1985 points out that some precisians—"nit-pickers" is Harper's word—object to the illogical placement of adjectives in such expressions as "a hot cup of coffee,""a brand-new pair of shoes." The argument is that it's the coffee that's hot, the shoes that are brand-new. Similarly objectionable is your leisurely cup of coffee after dinner. Harper points out that the placement of these adjectives is idiomatically correct, so the nitpickers may be ignored. Partridge 1942 cites an authority who points out the absurdity of "stylish gentlemen's suits." In his zeal for logic, the critic has lost sight of both sense and idiom. *Gentlemen's suits* is for all practical purposes a unit. To try to separate it with a modifier—"gentlemen's stylish suits"—is to violate normal English word order and so create an utterly unnecessary bump in the road down which your thought and your readers' attention are supposed to be traveling together.

4. *Adjectives as nouns.* Adjectives are used as nouns essentially in two ways: as noncount nouns to indicate a quality or a number of a group having a quality—the *beautiful,* the *sublime,* the *just,* the *unemployed*—and as count nouns—*moderns,* an all-time *high,* the *ancients,*

big-city *dailies.* Evans 1957 has a long article discussing these. The noncount use, which some grammarians refer to as "the absolute use of the adjective," seems to have excited little discussion in usage books. The count nouns, however, have drawn the attention of Harper 1985, which devotes a usage panel question to the propriety of a handful of advertising uses such as a toothpaste that leaves a "clean in your mouth" and a washing machine with a special device for washing "your delicates." There is no principle involved in this sort of discussion; the strained syntax of advertising is used solely to catch attention and evoke a predictable response. Whether *delicates* will join *unmentionables* in the dictionary only time will tell.

adjectives as nouns   See ADJECTIVES 4.

adjure   See ABJURE, ADJURE.

adjust, adjusted   1. Copperud 1970 notes that prices are "adjusted"—upwards, as a rule—in his discussion of euphemisms. See EUPHEMISMS.
2. Bernstein 1965 says *adjusted* takes *to.* This is true, as far as it goes, but the participial adjective is more often used without a complement than with one. When there is a complement, *to* is the most common preposition:

. . . a program . . . as dramatic and as sound and as adjusted to today and tomorrow as the programs of 1933 —Leon H. Keyserling, *New Republic,* 8 Feb. 1954

. . . factory in which the workers are perfectly adjusted to the machines —Aldous Huxley, *Brave New World Revisited,* 1958

This characteristic of the participial adjective merely reflects the behavior of the verb:

. . . account of one man's addled efforts to adjust to his own obsolescence —Jane Clapperton, *Cosmopolitan,* March 1976

. . . a delightful girl who could adjust to any confusion —James A. Michener, *Report of the County Chairman,* 1961

. . . was trying to adjust to being the head of my family —Mrs. Medgar Evers, *Ladies' Home Jour.,* September 1971

. . . had no difficulty in adjusting to more than a million dollars —Hamilton Basso, *The View from Pompey's Head,* 1954

Adjust is also used with *for.*

. . . is altered when we adjust for the predisposition —Stanley L. Payne, *The Art of Asking Questions,* 1951

Adjust for tends to occur in financial contexts. Thus it would not be out of the ordinary to read of figures "adjusted for inflation."

administer   1. As late as 1942 Eric Partridge was expressing disapproval of *administer* when used of a blow; he cites with approval Weseen 1928 on the question. Several earlier handbooks also censured the use, beginning perhaps with Utter 1916 who termed it "humorous" (as did the OED), but Vizetelly 1920 was not amused and neither were several subsequent commentators. Bernstein 1971, calling the objectors "driven-snow purists," cites Webster's Second in defense of the use and asks, "What more is needed to administer a fatal blow to those purists?" Not much, apparently; no writer since Partridge seems to have objected. The use may have developed from the administering of medicine, which is not always pleasant. If the earliest uses were humorous, current use is neutral, straightforward, and standard:

> The spider descends, embraces its victim while administering a paralyzing bite, then slowly wraps it securely in silk —William G. Eberhard, *Natural History,* January 1980

> . . . administered an overwhelming defeat to her Republican opponent —*Current Biography,* September 1967

2. The Oxford American Dictionary tells us that "nurses do not administer to the wounded," echoing a sentiment expressed in Follett 1966 and F. K. Ball's *Constructive English,* 1923. Longman 1984 also notes that some disapprove of this intransitive use of *administer.* The OED traces the sense to *The Spectator* in 1712. No definite reason seems to be adduced by objectors as a basis of their objection, although there is an underlying feeling that *administer* should forever be a transitive verb and that, in this use, it is usurping the place of *minister.* Perhaps it is also the relative infrequency of this use that makes them feel it to be improper. It is entirely standard:

> Dr. Binder had often traveled with his wife into the Peruvian jungles to administer to the Indians —*Current Biography,* September 1964

> . . . the church was erected over a period of years, 1906–36, to administer to the largest French parish in Lewiston —*American Guide Series: Maine,* 1937

> . . . to prevent him from administering to the last wants of Pulaski —*Dictionary of American Biography,* 1928

3. See ADMINISTRATE.

administrate Usage writers will sometimes pass along misinformation because they have not used important resources such as the historical dictionaries. Copperud 1970, 1980 tells us *administrate* is an Americanism. It is not; it was first used in British English in the 17th century. Nickles 1974 calls it a back-formation; it is not, having been coined out of pure Latin. Nickles further informs us it is overused. That is a matter of judgment, of course, but as a matter of fact it is a much less frequ用ly used word than its synonym *administer.* Jerry Adler, writing in *Newsweek* (8 Dec. 1980), quotes William Safire to the effect that administrators no longer administer, but administrate. Our files contain abundant evidence that they administer. Sometimes they do both:

> I'm a good administrator when I have something to administer. I mean, I really think I administered the Civil Aeronautics Board very effectively, and the Public Service Commission. But I don't have anything to administrate here —Alfred E. Kahn, quoted in *N.Y. Times,* 9 Nov. 1980

Administrate is an unstigmatized entry in OED, Webster's Second, and Webster's Third. It might not have been noticed at all had not H. W. Fowler put it in his list of long variants in 1926. It is not used nearly as often

as *administer,* although our citations of its use have increased somewhat in recent years. It appears to be developing an intransitive as well as a transitive use. William Safire (*N.Y. Times Mag.,* 6 Oct. 1985) quotes a linguist, William Kretzschmer, Jr., as finding that *administrate* is becoming differentiated from *administer.* Our evidence is too sparse at the present to confirm any differentiation.

admission, admittance "*Admittance* is usu[ally] applied to mere physical entrance to a locality or a building: *admission* applies to entrance or formal acceptance (as into a club) that carries with it rights, privileges, standing, or membership." This discrimination appears in Webster's Ninth New Collegiate Dictionary, and others like it can be found in usage books from Vizetelly 1906 to Harper 1985. Ambrose Bierce 1909 stands alone: he refuses to sanction *admission* for *admittance* in "The price of admission is one dollar."

The distinction is one you can certainly make in your writing if you want to. Copperud 1970 reports some commentators as feeling that the distinction is disappearing and others as feeling that the two words are simply synonyms. Certainly there have been writers of repute who have not observed the distinction.

Physical entrance:

> . . . somebody must gain admittance to his cell — George Meredith, *The Ordeal of Richard Feverel,* 1859

> Tom lifted him in his arms, and got admission to the Inn —George Meredith, *The Ordeal of Richard Feverel,* 1859

Permission to enter an academic institution:

> . . . the parental demand that their offspring obtain admittance to a four-year college —James B. Conant, *Slums and Suburbs,* 1961

> . . . the attempt of James Meredith, a Negro, to obtain admission to the University of Mississippi — *Current Biography,* July 1965

Permission to join the union as a state:

> . . . a constitutional provision . . . it had to eliminate from its constitution as a condition of admittance in 1912 —Thomas P. Neill, *The Common Good* (12th-grade text), 1956

> . . . until the size of the population warranted the territory's admission as a state —John H. Haefner et al., *Our Living Government* (12th-grade text), 1960

Permission to join the United Nations:

> . . . the demand from overseas for the immediate admittance of Communist China to the United Nations —Richard H. Rovere, *New Yorker,* 8 Aug. 1953

> . . . celebrating Japan's admission to the United Nations —*Current Biography,* December 1965

Entrance to society:

> . . . a very accessible and, at the same time, highly enviable society. Whatever the quality that gained you admittance —Virginia Woolf, *The Death of the Moth,* 1942

> . . . all the nice men she knew of moved in circles into which an obscure governess had no chance of

admission —George Bernard Shaw, *Cashel Byron's Profession,* 1886

Or to some other institution:

. . . admittance to the academy is a coveted honor — *Current Biography,* March 1964

. . . insisting now on stricter standards of admission to the church —Edmund S. Morgan, *N.Y. Times Book Rev.,* 13 July 1980

For a fee paid to gain entrance, *admission* is much more common, but *admittance* is not unknown:

. . . open to anyone with 500 yuan to spare, which at 3,000 yuan to the dollar, is not a ruinous admittance —James Cameron, *N.Y. Times Mag.,* 9 Jan. 1955

. . . there is no admission fee — *Village Voice,* 28 Feb. 1968

. . . the price of admission is starkly prohibitive — Norman Cousins, *Saturday Rev.,* 21 Feb. 1976

These last two examples show contexts in which *admittance* is no longer used—in the attributive position, and in the phrase "price of ____."

There is a distinction between the two words when preceded by *no.* The sign "No Admittance" refers to physical entrance, but *no admission* is likely to mean no admission fee:

ALL FREE—NO ADMISSION —advt., *Ochiltree County* (Tex.) *Herald,* 15 Jan. 1967

Documentary film . . . shown several times daily. No admission —*Where Mag.,* 15 Mar. 1975

The persons who deal with the entrance of students to educational institutions regularly use *admission,* often in the plural:

. . . college admissions officers —Robert L. Foose, *NEA Jour.,* January 1965

. . . an open admissions policy —Theodore L. Gross, *Saturday Rev.,* 4 Feb. 1978

Admission is the usual word for the granting of something not proven or an acknowledgment that something is true:

To ask for a pardon was, he said, an admission of guilt —Robert Penn Warren, *Jefferson Davis Gets His Citizenship Back,* 1980

Fifty-four percent of the Harper 1985 usage panel, however, confesses to not distinguishing in speech between "admittance to the theater" and "admission of guilt." Perhaps they did not think out the implications of their statement. *Admittance* in the sense it would have in "admittance of guilt" is labeled obsolete in the OED, which shows no citations since the 17th century. It appears, rather, to be very rare; Merriam-Webster editors have unearthed a couple of 20th-century instances. One was an oral use by Johnny Pesky, a former Boston Red Sox shortstop:

. . . by his own admittance yesterday, said that he always hated to . . . —2 May 1971

The other was in print by a distinguished historian:

This is splendid until one is brought up sharply by this naïve admittance —J. H. Plumb, *Saturday Rev.,* 29 July 1967

Although many authors have used *admission* and *admittance* synonymously, there is no harm in your making the distinction outlined in the Collegiate if you want to. Except for the sign "No Admittance" and the use of *admittance* as a technical term in electricity, *admission* is the more frequent word in all uses in current English.

admit 1. *Admit to.* Copperud 1970 records himself 1964, Follett 1966, Fowler 1965, and Heritage 1969 as objecting to the use of *admit to* in a sense approximating *confess.* Bremner 1980, Colter 1981, and Bryson 1984 concur in finding fault with it; Chambers 1985 does not object. Bernstein 1965 merely notes its use with *to* (perhaps thinking of other meanings of *admit* that are used with *to*), but in 1977 he notes objections to *admit to* by "the idiom watchdogs."

This objection seems to have its origin in some edition of Fowler published after World War II; it is not in Fowler 1926 nor in the corrected editions of the 1930s and early 1940s; it is in Gowers's 1965 revision but is cited by Copperud as early as 1960. The basis for the objection is the assertion that *confess* can be followed idiomatically by *to,* but *admit* cannot. But the assertion is wrong. When *admit* is used as an intransitive verb meaning "to make acknowledgment," it is regularly followed by *to:*

The acquaintance of a lady very much misjudged and ill used by the world, Richard admitted to — George Meredith, *The Ordeal of Richard Feverel,* 1859

While he does not admit to being a member of the Gestapo neither does he deny it —*N.Y. Herald Tribune Book Rev.,* 21 May 1939

But no one could be found who would admit to seeing an attack on Duboko —MacKinlay Kantor, in *Best American Short Stories,* ed. Martha Foley, 1942

"I admit to a touch of grey above the ears, such as you might expect in a man of my years . . ." —Eric Linklater, *Private Angelo,* 1946

Stokowski, who admits to 66 —*Time,* 5 Oct. 1953

. . . he might incriminate himself if he should admit to membership —Curtis Bok, *Saturday Rev.,* 13 Feb. 1954

The lady had some records, but she was wary about admitting to having any specific ones —Rexford G. Tugwell, *Center Mag.,* September 1968

. . . most of us cannot admit to intellectual fashions or political passions we have discarded —Naomi Bliven, *New Yorker,* 17 July 1971

. . . the one-sided relationship that Proust . . . seeks to secure from the world around him, but seldom admits to —Angus Wilson, *N.Y. Times Book Rev.,* 11 Apr. 1976

. . . we are less consciously familiar with its rules. We have admitted to them less, but they are there notwithstanding —Margaret Drabble, *Saturday Rev.,* 27 May 1978

. . . though Canada admits to no Middle West, the nerve he touches runs all the way down Middle North America —Ronald Bryden, *N.Y. Times Book Rev.,* 3 June 1984

This idiom appears to be well-established indeed. The uses referring to gray hair and age cannot be replaced by *admit* alone without rephrasing—surely a sign of an established idiom. To say with Colter 1981 that *admit* is never followed by *to* or with Follett 1966 that it is archaic in tone is to exhibit a certain unfamiliarity with the language writers use.

2. Other uses of *admit* with *to* (and *into*). There is one other intransitive use of *admit* that takes *to:*

> ... tickets which admit to the famous Chelsea Flower Show —*Popular Gardening,* 11 Apr. 1976

> ... reached the door admitting to the kitchen —John Morrison, *The Creeping City,* 1949

It appears to be chiefly British.

As a transitive verb *admit* takes *to* in several common uses:

> The maid admitted him to the living room —Irving Stone, *McCall's,* March 1971

> ... one of the first non-Communist journalists admitted to China —*Harper's,* February 1969

> ... they have admitted to their pages execrable examples of English prose —J. Donald Adams, *N.Y. Times Book Rev.,* 7 Mar. 1954

> In 1962 Trinidad and Tobago was admitted to the United Nations —*Current Biography,* February 1966

> ... was subsequently admitted to practice both before the New York bar and the U.S. Supreme Court —*Psychology Today,* February 1969

Admit is also used with *into:*

> ... the process of admitting a new state into the Union —Stanley E. Dimond & Elmer F. Pflieger, *Our American Government,* 1961

> ... she regretted admitting sorrow into their lives — Jean Stafford, *Children Are Bored on Sunday,* 1953

> ... he is prepared to admit into history the irrational and the unconscious —Peter Stansky, *N.Y. Times Book Rev.,* 25 July 1976

None of these uses is the subject of criticism.

3. *Admit of.* Fowler 1926 points out that the combination *admit of* is more limited in application than it once was and that it usually takes a nonhuman subject. Numerous later commentators echo the same sentiment; for instance, Chambers 1985: "The subject of the verb ... must always be impersonal or abstract." The commentators are, in the main, correct.

> ... his eyes ... would not admit of their being strained upon any definite object without ... risk — Thomas Hardy, *The Return of the Native,* 1878

> ... the banqueting-hall, always vast enough to admit of many more guests —Lafcadio Hearn, *Glimpses of Unfamiliar Japan,* 1894

> ... many crucial dilemmas simply do not admit of analysis on one page —Dorothy Fosdick, *N.Y. Times Mag.,* 23 Jan. 1955

> The problems of ecology ... admit of a rational solution —Aldous Huxley, *Center Mag.,* September 1969

> ... evidence for the way in which Renaissance artists really thought is insufficient to admit of dogmatism —John Pope-Hennessy, *N.Y. Times Book Rev.,* 8 May 1977

Jane Austen was even able to use a clause as subject:

> That Edmund must be for ever divided from Miss Crawford did not admit of a doubt with Fanny — *Mansfield Park,* 1814

Use with a personal subject in modern prose is rare:

> ... we admit of creatures who are transitions from one kingdom to another —René Wellek & Austin Warren, *Theory of Literature,* 1949

The sense "allow, permit" is also used as a transitive without *of:*

> To Garfield ... and to all of the men of his generation educated under the old academic system, it admitted no debate —*The Nation,* 18 July 1923

> ... this procedural logic does not admit more than minute changes —Paul Henry Lang, *Saturday Rev.,* 26 June 1954

> ... a situation as wretched as Rhodesia's may admit no right solutions —Carll Tucker, *Saturday Rev.,* 3 Mar. 1979

See also ALLOW 2; PERMIT OF.

admittance See ADMISSION, ADMITTANCE.

ad nauseam This phrase from the Latin has been at work in English since the 17th century, when writers regularly learned to read and write Latin. Writers today are less familiar with Latin, and more likely to spell the phrase wrong when they trot it out to show off with. "If you are determined to use this poor old thing," says Kilpatrick 1984, "at least spell it right." Somebody goofed in these examples:

> Again Dobler has researched his subject *ad nauseum* and again he has created a veritable horde of stereotyped characters —*N.Y. Times Book Rev.,* 12 Sept. 1976

> As Brendan becomes the Horatio Alger of porn, we trace, ad nauseum, his rise to wealth and power — *Publishers Weekly,* 5 Sept. 1977

Even if these particular examples are typos, as they may well be, it behooves the writer to be careful.

adopt See ADAPT, ADOPT, ADEPT.

adopted, adoptive Usage writers since Fowler 1926 and Krapp 1927 have been telling us that the rule is *adopted* children, *adoptive* parents. And it usually is so in practice. Formerly *adopted* had a fair amount of use applied to parents, as Fowler, Krapp, and Evans 1957 observe:

> ... the estate of the last of Janice's adopted parents —Erle Stanley Gardner, *The Case of the Stuttering Bishop,* 1936

> ... worked upon her adopted father with his threats of the wrath to come —Max Peacock, *King's Rogue* 1947

We have no recent evidence of this use in print, although it may still persist in spoken English.

Adoptive, too, crosses the usage boundary and is sometimes applied to children (Johnson's 1755 Dictionary has a citation from Francis Bacon for "adoptive son"):

> The Stein menage also included Mme. Gabrielle Osorio and her adoptive daughter —Edward T. Cone, *American Scholar,* Summer 1973

But most writers follow the pattern suggested in the usage books:

> First, let's consider the risks to adoptive parents — Claude Forell, *The Age* (Melbourne), 17 Apr. 1975

> Claire Kellerman, 18, adopted daughter of Sally Kellerman —Peter Carlson, *People,* 9 Aug. 1982

The usage writers are silent about other relationships *adopted* and *adoptive* are used for. *Adoptive* is used not only for parents but for homes, families, and other relatives:

> ... the agency refused to return Lenore because she was already in an adoptive home —Eileen Hughes, *Ladies' Home Jour.,* September 1971

> ... expect adoptive families to be easily found — Catherine Calvert, *Town & Country,* December 1982

> He falls in love with his adoptive sister —*Time,* 31 Mar. 1947

Both words are used for a new country, city, or state and for people who have them:

> And naturally they discussed their adopted home. America came in for both good and bad marks — Paule Marshall, *N.Y. Times Book Rev.,* 9 Jan. 1983

> ... foreign-born Americans who were loyal, dedicated defenders of their adopted country —William S. Garmon, *Averett Jour.,* Autumn 1970

> ... who was knighted in his adoptive England in 1980 —Diane McWhorter, *N.Y. Times Book Rev.,* 1 May 1983

> ... a heterogeneous cross section of New Yorkers, born and adopted —Carey Winfrey, *N.Y. Times,* 1 Jan. 1980

> ... written by an adoptive Californian —Darrell Berrigan, *Saturday Evening Post,* 3 July 1954

adult   **1.** Both the end-stressed pronunciation, \ə-ˈdəlt\, and the fore-stressed version, \ˈad-ˌəlt\, are perfectly acceptable, whether the word is used as an adjective or as a noun. \ə-ˈdəlt\ seems somewhat more prevalent in the U.S., and especially so as an adjective; \ˈad-ˌəlt\ is the form currently recommended in England.
2. Copperud 1980 describes *adult* as "the current euphemism for *pornographic.*" Howard 1977 writes "what seedy cinemas and pornographic publishers describe as 'adult' is in fact childishly prurient." The sense has been recognized in dictionaries.

adumbrate   *Adumbrate* is a hard word, a learned word, frequently found in works of literary and art criticism. Around the time of World War II it came in for some disparagement by the British commentators Sir Ernest Gowers and Eric Partridge (Gowers 1948, Partridge 1942) when it began to surface in British government writing. Copperud 1970 finds in addition a couple of American commentators who discourage its use; the consensus, says Copperud, is that *adumbrate* is "formal, literary, and unsuitable for ordinary contexts." The problem, of course, is knowing just what contexts are ordinary. To be sure, the word is not found in children's stories or on the sports pages. It is, however, occasionally found in political writing—mostly British:

> ... if the policy of milk direction adumbrated by the Ministry is not balanced with reason —*The Economist,* 20 Dec. 1947

> Such attitudes are only faintly adumbrated in the Conservative manifesto —Henry Fairlie, *Observer Rev.,* 20 Mar. 1966

> ... the famous "Mr. X" article that adumbrated the Cold War policy of "firm containment...." — Patrick J. Buchanan, *TV Guide,* 19 Apr. 1980

But mostly it is a word found in criticism and in other writings of learned people:

> ... he was much better at adumbrating his doctrine through rhetorical devices —William Empson, *Sewanee Rev.,* Spring 1948

> ... to overcome student self-protectiveness is a terribly ambitious enterprise, which can only be adumbrated even in the best institutions —David Riesman, *American Scholar,* Summer 1969

> ... ideas first adumbrated in the work of these and other modern masters —Hilton Kramer, *N.Y. Times Mag.,* 4 Nov. 1979

advance   **1.** *Advance, advanced.* As adjectives these words are rarely, if ever, used of the same things, and why usage writers, who treat them frequently, believe they are a problem is not clear. Any good dictionary will show you the differences. Here are a few typical examples:

> ... with a little advance warning plus tip, the principal steward was always ready to prepare his own special recipe of crêpes Suzette —Caleb Pirtle III, *Southern Living,* November 1971

> ... you could show up on registration day without advance notice —Tom Wicker, *Change,* September 1971

> ... advisors had already reviewed advance copies of Northeast's plan —Homer Page, *Not Man Apart,* July 1971

> ... modernizing their building regulations to allow the advanced systems of construction —Harold Howe II, *Saturday Rev.,* 20 Nov. 1971

> ... the education of those less gifted or less advanced —Jerome S. Bruner, *Saturday Rev.,* 15 Jan. 1972

> ... employees with bachelor's as well as advanced degrees —Lucia Mouat, *Christian Science Monitor,* 19 Aug. 1980

> Advanced age ended Dr. Schweitzer's practice as a surgeon —*Current Biography,* July 1965

2. The phrases *advance warning, advance planning,* and *advance preparations* are sometimes censured as redundant (see REDUNDANCY). We have little evidence of their use in print. In the first example in section 1 above, *advance warning* is roughly synonymous with *advance notice,* which has not been called redundant. Janis 1984 defends *advance planning,* judging that it is not redundant when *advance* means "early."

3. *Advance, advancement.* These nouns overlap occasionally in meaning, but we have little evidence that they cause difficulty for writers. A few commentators insist that *advance* means "progress," *advancement* "promotion," but the words have more senses than that, as a check of your dictionary will show. Here are a few examples:

> . . . a great advance in the ability of moviemakers to render physical reality more accurately —Richard Schickel, *Harper's,* March 1971

> . . . the fruits of research and scientific advances — *Carnegie Quarterly,* Summer 1970

> . . . the peculiar role assigned his hero in the advance of civilization —Richard Poirier, *A World Elsewhere,* 1966

> . . . had come to feel it almost an emancipation from the conventional feminine freedoms, certainly an advance over the starved lives that so many of her friends gained from their independent, mutual sharing marriages —Angus Wilson, *The Middle Age of Mrs. Eliot,* 1958

> . . . an authentic advance upon traditional Marxism —Theodore Roszak, *The Making of a Counter Culture,* 1969

> . . . failed to obtain an advance of salary from the lycée —*Times Literary Supp.,* 16 Apr. 1970

> The program of the Corporation included the advancement of education through support of specific undertakings —*Collier's Year Book,* 1949

> . . . for university students at every stage of their advancement —E. Adelaide Hahn, *Language,* April-June 1954

> Middle-aged executives, bureaucrats, and salaried professionals favor mandatory retirement for reasons related to their own advancement —Paul Woodring, *Saturday Rev.,* 7 Aug. 1976

4. *Advance feedback* is noted as business jargon by Janis 1984. We have no evidence of it (so far) in our files.

advancement   See ADVANCE 3.

advantage   In the sense of "superiority of position or condition," *advantage* was formerly followed by *of:*

> Lest Satan should get an advantage of us —2 Corinthians 2:11 (AV), 1611

> We undoubtedly have the advantage of England, in promoting a comparative purity in language among the entire mass of our population —William S. Cardell, circular issued in the name of The American Academy of Language and Belles Lettres, 1821 (in Baron 1982)

The phrase "have the advantage of" with personal subject and object at one time was used in polite conversation to admit not remembering having been introduced before:

> "You have the advantage of me; I don't remember ever to have had the honour." —Richard Brinsley Sheridan, *The Rivals,* 1775

The usual preposition in modern use is *over:*

> The exacting life of the sea has this advantage over the life of the earth, that its claims are simple and cannot be evaded —Joseph Conrad, *Chance,* 1913

> . . . it is generally conceded that Soviet chess players hold an advantage over competitors of other nationalities —*Current Biography,* July 1967

Of still prevails in *take advantage of:*

> . . . bullying or taking an unfair advantage of the other person —Margaret Mead, *And Keep Your Powder Dry,* 1942

In modern use *of* most often denotes a simple genitive relationship:

> . . . personal favoritism or the advantage of a family name —Charles Frankel, *Columbia Forum,* Summer 1970

> The author of the second poem has the advantage of dealing with a more unusual death —Florence Trefethen, *The Writer,* May 1968

> The advantages to an economy of this sort of literacy are apparent —Robert Pattison, *On Literacy,* 1982

Here are a few other idiomatic phrases with *advantage:*

> . . . restaurateurs are more and more finding it in their advantage to tinker with menus —Dave Rank, *Cooking for Profit,* July 1982

> She wears clothes from them all—and wears them to advantage —Gail Cameron, *Ladies' Home Jour.,* August 1971

> A miner will learn . . . to use his body to best advantage —Laurence Leamer, *Harper's,* December 1971

> What we should do is make it to everyone's advantage to reach environmental goals —Peter F. Drucker, *Harper's,* January 1972

adverbial disjunct   See SENTENCE ADVERB.

adverbial genitive   Bryant 1962 and Evans 1957 tell us that in Old English the genitive of some nouns could be used adverbially. For instance, the genitive of the Old English word for *day* could be used to mean "by day." Evans notes that many of our adverbs that end in an \s\ or \z\ sound—*nowadays, always*—are survivals of this form. But, says he, "Today there is no feeling that this is a genitive relationship and an apostrophe is never used in words of this kind."

One survival of the old adverbial genitive is in certain adverbs of time: "He never works *evenings* or *Sundays*" (test sentence from Leonard 1929). The propriety of this construction seems to have been questioned at some time in the past, although we have not encountered the questioning in our reading of the commentators. Utter 1916 calls these adverbs "sometimes condemned." He defends them as an "old idiomatic usage," as do most other commentators. Leonard's 1929 survey found the construction acceptable to about 75 percent of his respondents. Here are a few typical examples:

> During his college days at Harvard he taught days and studied nights —*Dictionary of American Biography,* 1929

. . . he sold cars, mowed lawns, sang nights and week-ends whenever he could get bookings —*Current Biography,* July 1967

. . . waking up mornings in my own vomit —Conrad Rooks, quoted in *Evergreen,* December 1967

I got to thinking that I went to work nights and Saturdays in a paper mill when I was a boy —Bergen Evans, address at Marshall University, June 1968

Many commentators (Evans 1957, Fowler 1926, Mittins et al. 1970, Quirk et al. 1985, for example) observe that this adverbial genitive of time is better established in American English than in British English. It is not, however, dead in British English, as Evans thought in 1957. The new OED Supplement under *nights* lists Australian and Canadian examples. It may be rather more common in spoken than in written British English:

. . . but I don't stay up nights worrying —John Lennon, quoted in *Current Biography,* December 1965

Bryant finds the use firmly established in informed standard speech and writing in the U.S. Jespersen 1909–49 (vol. 7) gives a few citations from American literature:

. . . their cats were pretty sociable around her nights —Mark Twain, *The Stolen White Elephant,* 1882

I've got to work evenings! —Sinclair Lewis, *Arrowsmith,* 1925

Summers I used to cover Missouri —Thornton Wilder, *Heaven's My Destination,* 1934

I went over there afternoons —Ernest Hemingway, *A Farewell to Arms,* 1929

adverbial nouns   One of the charming and infuriating aspects of English is that English nouns may upon occasion function as adverbs. Some handbooks and other textbooks refer to these as *adverbial nouns.* A couple of examples:

Every night she runs four *miles.* (Clark et al. 1981)

The tie cost a *dollar.* (Roberts 1954)

Other grammarians would analyze the examples above as noun phrases *(every night, four miles, a dollar)* used as adverbs. Adverbial nouns are one member of the larger class of *adverbials.*

See ADVERBIAL GENITIVE for another kind of adverbial noun.

adverbials   A noun, noun phrase, prepositional phrase, verbal phrase, or clause that functions in a sentence in the same way an adverb would is called by many grammarians an *adverbial.* A few typical examples might include:

They arrived *Monday.*

I finished the book *last week.*

We left *on a chartered bus.*

She entered the competition *hoping to set a new record.*

You must make a greater effort *to achieve your goals.*

His house was broken into *while he was away on vacation.*

It is only fair to warn you that different grammarians may put different limitations on the class of adverbials. If you are interested in learning more about the adverbial, you will find considerable detail in Sledd 1959 or Quirk et al. 1985 (nearly 175 pages in the latter). Adverbials are not mentioned very often in this book, but the term is frequently used in discussing matters of usage by the authors of composition handbooks.

adverbs   **1.** An adverb is a member of one of the traditional part-of-speech classes. The class of adverbs is highly useful to grammarians and lexicographers, for into it they toss many terms otherwise resistant to classification. Adverbs modify verbs, adjectives, other adverbs, verbals, phrases, clauses, and sentences. They probably even modify nouns on occasion—at least they commonly modify adjectives used as nouns ("the very wealthy").

Some interesting aspects of the usage of adverbs can be found under these headings: FLAT ADVERBS; SENTENCE ADVERB.

2. Copperud 1970, 1980 talks about an erroneous idea widespread among newspaper journalists that adverbs should not separate auxiliaries from their main verbs (as in "you can easily see" or "they must be heartily congratulated"). This bugaboo, commentators agree, seems to have sprung from fear of the dread split infinitive (see SPLIT INFINITIVE). Copperud cites five commentators on the subject, all of whom see no harm in placing an adverb between the parts of a verb, and one of whom (Fowler 1965) prescribes such placement. Fowler (under *position of adverbs*) has a long and detailed discussion, complete with numerous examples in which the adverb has been improperly (to his mind) shifted so as to avoid the split. Since dividing the auxiliary from the verb with an adverb has been approved at least since Lindley Murray 1795, it would seem that Fowler is justified in calling the avoidance a superstition.

Comments in the 18th-century grammars of Priestley, Lowth, and Murray indicate a considerable interest in the placement of adverbs. Murray, for instance, rejects "We always find them ready when we want them," correcting the placement to "We find them always ready. . . ." For more discussion of this sort of adverb placement, see EVEN and ONLY 1.

3. Copperud 1970, 1980 states flatly that "an adverb should not intervene between a verb and its object," citing Fowler, himself, Evans, and Follett as being of that opinion. The statement is oversimplified. For instance, the sentence

He claimed quickly the victory

is certainly more awkward than

He claimed the victory quickly.

But if we change the object to a clause,

He claimed quickly that he had won

means one thing, and

He claimed that he had won quickly

something else. Thus, you as writer have to think the problem of meaning through for yourself in each case, and not just rely on a simple rule of thumb. (Here, for instance, "He quickly claimed . . ." might be the best possible solution in both cases.)

Another exception can occur with those phrasal verbs—verbs followed by particles—where the close connection of the adverbial particle to the verb may keep it comfortably before the direct object:

> Clemens struck out the side in the seventh inning.

This question, then, is partly a matter of grammar, partly of style, and partly of idiom. You will need to rely on your common sense and your ear for the language rather than on a rule.

adverse, averse 1. Many commentators, British and American, warn us against confusing *adverse* and *averse* in such sentences as

> He is not adverse to an occasional brandy —*The Observer,* cited in Bryson 1984

The word in such a sentence should be *averse,* we are told. Beyond that specific judgment, little help is given us, for the most part. Here is some information we think will be more helpful.

The two words are only close in meaning in the combination *adverse/averse to. Adverse,* however, is usually used attributively:

> . . . 18 to 30 percent of all hospitalized patients have an adverse reaction to one or more of the drugs they are given —David Zimmerman, *Ladies' Home Jour.,* October 1971

> Are any of us . . . certain that an adverse wind will not sweep away our possessions —Henry Miller, *The Air-Conditioned Nightmare,* 1945

> . . . her own conduct must be carefully regulated so as not to give rise to a breath of adverse comment —Stella Gibbons, *Cold Comfort Farm,* 1932

> We do not face an adverse balance of trade —Paul A. Samuelson, *New Republic,* 26 Mar. 1945

> . . . maintaining a cheerful countenance under adverse circumstances —George Bernard Shaw, *Cashel Byron's Profession,* 1886

Averse, on the other hand, is rare as an attributive adjective:

> . . . he was on his way to fame despite the averse crew —Jane Ross, *Early American Life,* April 1977

It is most often a thing, rather than a person, that is said to be adverse, even when *adverse* is followed by *to:*

> . . . Johnson firmly and resolutely opposed any restraint whatever, as adverse to a free investigation of the characters of mankind —James Boswell, *Life of Samuel Johnson,* 1791

> . . . was able to hear all testimony adverse to her — *AAUP Bulletin,* December 1967

> But it is really almost completely adverse to the very interests which it pretends to protect —Leland Olds, *New Republic,* 14 Sept. 1953

> His own written enunciations were adverse to his chances of escape —George Meredith, *The Ordeal of Richard Feverel,* 1859

> . . . the whole Parliamentary tradition as built up in this country . . . is adverse to it —Sir Winston Churchill, *The Unrelenting Struggle,* 1942

When used of people, *adverse* and *averse* are essentially synonymous, but *adverse* chiefly refers to opinion or intention, *averse* to feeling or inclination. Or, as it was put in the *Literary Digest* of 10 Feb. 1934, "We are *adverse* to that which we disapprove, but *averse* to that which we dislike."

> I . . . hope that our periodical judges will not be very adverse to me —William Cowper (in Webster 1909)

> Mr. Richards . . . was adverse to his union with this young lady —George Meredith, *The Ordeal of Richard Feverel,* 1859

> Protestants . . . adverse to all implicit submission of mind and opinion —Edmund Burke (in Webster 1909)

> The Roosevelts are, as you may suspect, not averse to travel; we thrive on it —Franklin D. Roosevelt, address to Congress, 1 Mar. 1945, in *Nothing to Fear,* ed. B. D. Zevin, 1946

> . . . he was never averse to another encounter. All the devil that was in him challenged the devil in Wolf Larsen —Jack London, *The Sea-Wolf,* 1904

> Under certain circumstances, to be explained later, I am not averse to pillorying the innocent —John Barth, *The Floating Opera,* 1956

> Miss Carew, averse to the anomalous relations of courtship, made as little delay as possible in getting married —George Bernard Shaw, *Cashel Byron's Profession,* 1886

But the distinction is a subtle one and not observed universally, even by respected writers:

> . . . for Leonora Penderton was a person who liked to settle herself and was adverse to complications — Carson McCullers, *Reflections in a Golden Eye,* 1941

> Her Majesty, as I have said, was by no means averse to reforms —Edith Sitwell, *Victoria of England,* 1936

The criticized uses of *adverse to* all occur in negative sentences. It is in such contexts that it is most difficult to distinguish opinion or intention from feeling or inclination. In the sentence about brandy at the beginning of this discussion, one suspects inclination, as one does in this:

> . . . and he is not adverse to reading about himself — *N.Y. Times,* cited in Bernstein 1962

But either nuance may be plausibly inferred in these instances:

> Aside from his desire to see the natives come out on top, Jarel was not at all adverse to the idea of a trick being played on Dulard —Sylvia Louise Engdahl, "Enchantress from the Stars," 1970 in *Literature,* Carl B. Smith et al., 1980

> . . . Holbrook would not be adverse to a regular TV series —*N.Y. Times,* cited in Bernstein 1977

In summary, *adverse* and *averse* are only synonymous when used of persons and with *to. Adverse* is most often used as an attributive adjective and of things; *averse* is extremely rare as an attributive and is regularly used of persons. When used with *to* and of persons a subtle distinction can be drawn, but it is not universally observed, and in negative contexts it is hard to make out whether the distinction is being observed or ignored.
2. See AVERSE TO, FROM.

advert, *verb* Fowler 1965 and Flesch 1964 are reported in Copperud 1970 to consider *advert to* as obsolete for *refer to.* Sir Ernest Gowers, editor of Fowler 1965, considers it an archaism, and he remarks on it elsewhere as one of the words he considers overworked in British official prose. *Advert to,* however, is not obsolete; it is still in use, chiefly as a learned alternative to *refer to* or to *turn the mind or attention to.* Here are a few typical examples:

So let us escape from all this for a while and advert to a fascinating subject —Simon 1980

. . . it will not be enough to advert to the dignity of man, the connectedness among things —A. Bartlett Giamatti, *Profession 79,* 1979

Webster set out to correct Pickering's views on the American corruption of the English language, adverting only briefly to the oblique personal reference —Ronald A. Wells, *Dictionaries and the Authoritarian Tradition,* 1973

The point which I think needs comment is the distinction, adverted to by William James —Mortimer J. Adler, *The Conditions of Philosophy,* 1965

However, the type of cooperation I advert to can be brought about in any of America's institutions of higher learning —Charles E. Wilson, *Think,* June 1957

advert, *noun* See AD.

advice See ADVISE 1.

advise 1. *Advise, advice.* Numerous commentators and handbooks, from grade school on up, warn us not to confuse *advise* and *advice: advise* is a verb, *advice* is a noun. If this advice seems like old stuff to you, we have some citations to show you:

She can spot creative genius in a stick-figure drawing, pack a mean lunch and give great advise — advt., *N.Y. Times Mag.,* 27 Apr. 1980

. . . honor bound to advice prospective students of the dismal prospects for employment —*Biographical Dictionary of the Phonetic Sciences,* 1977

The U.S. Constitution spells the noun *advice* when it speaks of the Senate's role in relation to treaties made by the President. So does this distinguished modern writer:

Its Board of Pardons, established in 1883, consists of five responsible citizens appointed by the governor with the advice and consent of the state Senate — William Styron, *This Quiet Dust and Other Writings,* 1982

So should you.
2. Copperud 1970 cites a considerable number of commentators who object to the use of *advise* to mean "inform." They chiefly object to its use in business correspondence. The objectors, it should be noted, are neither in business nor writing for those who are; Janis 1984, who is addressing business people, finds it only "sometimes stilted" and thinks the phrase "Please be advised" is often deadwood—it is, in fact, only a polite formula. Reader's Digest 1983 notes that the sense is

fully established "in its own sphere." As you can see from the examples, it is not limited to business correspondence. It sometimes carries the sense of "to inform officially":

The Immigration and Naturalization Service advised Krips that he must either depart voluntarily or be detained —*Current Biography,* June 1965

But more often it simply means "inform":

. . . which prompted our inquiring lawyer to write thus: " . . . If it does deal with said subject will you kindly advise where I can buy said book." —John Barkham, *Saturday Rev.,* 13 Feb. 1954

Jiro Tokuyama . . . advised me that today 80 percent of young Japanese husbands in urban communities turn over their pay envelopes, unopened, to their wives —Vance Packard, *The Sexual Wilderness,* 1968

He had not advised his friends of his marriage — Willa Cather, *The Old Beauty and Others,* 1948

. . . a stone guide-post advised him that Gaza was still eight miles distant —Lloyd C. Douglas, *The Big Fisherman,* 1948

advisedly Cranky old Ambrose Bierce in 1909 objected to the use of *advisedly* to mean "intentionally." He said it "should mean that it was done after advice." Bernstein 1971 dismantles Bierce's ill-founded opinion: "when you do something advisedly your counsel is self-contained." Phythian 1979 agrees with Bernstein. They are right and Bierce wrong:

I am working as a judge at the Los Angeles County Fair, and I use the word "working" advisedly — Frank J. Prial, *N.Y. Times,* 15 Aug. 1979

. . . and strictly "educationally" speaking (inverted commas are used advisedly) —*Times Literary Supp.,* 2 Apr. 1971

I often say that one must permit oneself, and that quite advisedly and deliberately, a certain margin of misstatement —Benjamin N. Cardozo, "Law and Literature," 1925, in *Selected Writings of Benjamin N. Cardozo,* ed. Margaret E. Hall, 1947

The constituent principles of the modern point of view, as accepted advisedly or by oversight by Adam Smith and his generation —Thorstein Veblen, *The Vested Interests,* 1919

adviser, advisor Both of these spellings are in current good use. Copperud 1970 and Reader's Digest 1983 note *adviser* as being the spelling preferred by journalists; Copperud cites one of Porter Perrin's works as saying *advisor* is probably predominant, but it is not, at least in the Merriam-Webster files—we have more evidence for *adviser.* For what it's worth, Reader's Digest tells us that *advisor* is the preferred spelling of fortune tellers.

. . . appointed to the five-man panel of advisers — *Current Biography,* July 1965

A chief advisor in the administrations of Franklin D. Roosevelt and of succeeding presidents —*Current Biography,* February 1966

The military euphemism of the Vietnam war era was spelled *adviser:*

> . . . though the Marines are "advisers," a Vietnamese seldom questions a U.S. sergeant's advice —Sherwood Dickerman, *The Reporter,* 6 Apr. 1967

advocate   **1.** Bernstein 1965 tells us the noun *advocate* takes the preposition *of,* the verb *for.* Both these generalizations are off the mark.

Advocate the verb is used almost entirely as a transitive verb and usually takes no preposition at all. When a prepositional phrase does happen to follow the direct object, the preposition can be *for* but can just as easily be *in, on,* or *by,* among others:

> While Henry advocates federal loan programs for individual needy students —*Current Biography,* June 1966

The use of *for* is seen when *advocate* is intransitive, but the intransitive is fairly rare. The OED (which marks it obsolete) does show citations with *for:* three from the 17th century and one from the 19th:

> I am not going to advocate for this sense of *actual* —Fitzedward Hall, *Recent Exemplifications of False Philology,* 1872

The noun *advocate* most usually takes *of* to show what is being advocated:

> . . . advocates of our disastrous military-oriented policies in Asia —Chester Bowles, *Saturday Rev.,* 6 Nov. 1971

> . . . wrong if he takes me as an advocate of amorality in the conduct of foreign policy —Arthur M. Schlesinger, Jr., *Harper's,* October 1971

> . . . as an advocate of probity and thrift he could be seen splitting wood in front of his house each morning —John Cheever, *The Wapshot Chronicle,* 1957

For is also used sometimes to indicate what is being advocated:

> . . . is an advocate for the extended use of psychiatry in the field of law —Morris L. Ernst, *New Republic,* 8 June 1953

> I am certainly not an advocate for frequent and untried changes in laws and constitutions —John Morley, in *The Practical Cogitator,* ed. Charles P. Curtis, Jr. & Ferris Greenslet, 1945

More often, though, *for* indicates on whose behalf one advocates:

> Let them . . . be advocates for their organizations — Leslie H. Gelb & Morton H. Halperin, *Harper's,* June 1972

> . . . the responsibility of acting as a personal advocate for his chief —McGeorge Bundy, in Preface to *The Pattern of Responsibility,* 1951

> Young Heinrich became a sort of advocate for his people before the tribunal of Mr. Britling's mind — H. G. Wells, *Mr. Britling Sees It Through,* 1916

With may be used for the authority to whom one advocates a cause:

> And if any man sin, we have an advocate with the Father, Jesus Christ the righteous: And he is the propitiation for our sins —1 John 2:1–2 (AV), 1611

> . . . promising to act as his advocate with Katherine —James Sutherland, *English Literature of the Late Seventeenth Century,* 1969

> We are their advocate with the credit company — unidentified spokesperson, NBC Radio News, 9 June 1974

2. A couple of issues of some historical interest adhere to *advocate.* In the late 18th century the verb *advocate* was supposed to be an American innovation. Benjamin Franklin in a letter to Noah Webster in December 1798 described *to advocate* as an innovation he had encountered only upon his return from France; he asked Webster to reprobate the word (along with several other innovations—*to notice, to progress, to oppose*—that are perfectly standard today). An English traveler named Henry Wamsey in 1794 also noted *to advocate* as a novelty. The verb was not entered in Johnson's Dictionary of 1755, but H. J. Todd added it in his expanded version of Johnson published early in the 19th century. Todd remarks that a Mr. Boucher gave credit to Americans for this particular enrichment of English; Todd says they do not deserve the credit, since the word was used by Milton and Burke. But Mencken 1963 (abridged) notes it was attacked as an Americanism by Robert Southey as late as 1838. All this and more can be found, more entertainingly recounted, in Mencken.

Fowler 1926, 1965 asserts that *advocate,* unlike *recommend, propose, urge,* is not idiomatically followed by a *that*-clause. In fact, although clauses are considerably less common than nouns and gerunds as direct objects, they are not in the least unidiomatic:

> . . . he used the occasion to join Walter Reuther in advocating that organized labor in the United States work within the Democratic party —*Current Biography,* November 1966

> The officers advocate that the large, unwieldy units be replaced by smaller ARVN mobile brigades — Robert Shaplen, *New Yorker,* 24 Apr. 1971

aegis   Back in 1939 the editors of Webster's Second (1934) added a new sense of *aegis* in the New Words Section: "Patronage; sponsorship; auspices; as, under the *aegis* of the Liberal Club." Bernstein 1965 criticizes this sense of *aegis.* The new definition had been occasioned by uses like this one:

> It is improper to pass from the questions of Seneca's influence upon the Tragedy of Blood and upon the language of the Elizabethans without mentioning the group of "Senecal" plays, largely produced under the aegis of the Countess of Pembroke —T. S. Eliot, "Seneca in Elizabethan Translation," in *Selected Essays,* 1932

The history of *aegis* up to the development of the 1939 sense is fairly straightforward. Its earliest meaning was a shield or breastplate originally associated in classical mythology with Zeus and Athena. This meaning has had some use in literary English:

> Where was thine Ægis, Pallas, that appalled Stern Alaric? —Lord Byron, *Childe Harold's Pilgrimage,* 1812 (OED)

> The purposes of Ægis-bearing Jove —William Cullen Bryant, *The Odyssey of Homer,* 1877 (OED)

From the shield or breastplate, the transition to a sense meaning "protection" is plain enough:

> They were sheltered by the ægis of the laws —Connop Thirlwall, *A History of Greece*, 1836 (OED)

> ... behind the aegis of a big and bright and newly forged telephone-inspector badge —Albert Payson Terhune, *Further Adventures of Lad*, 1922

> "... now that the Imperial ægis protects me...." —Raphael Sabatini, *The Strolling Saint*, 1924

> Had they come to Philippi to preach the tidings of the Messiah under the aegis of their Roman citizenship? Their aegis was God —Sholem Asch, *The Apostle*, 1943

> It is urged that motion pictures do not fall within the First Amendment's aegis —*Joseph Burstyn, Inc.* v. *Wilson*, 72 S. Ct. 777, 1952

> ... we witnessed the power of the people, and even now our bodies are wrapped in the magic aegis of their love —William Crain, *East Village Other*, 10 Nov. 1970

You should observe that this sense of *aegis* does not necessarily come in the phrase *under the aegis of*. That phrase is not attested until 1910. A sharp-eyed reader for the OED Supplement found this example in the 11th edition of the *Encyclopaedia Britannica* in the article on billiards:

> Under the aegis of the Billiard Association a tacit understanding was arrived at. . . .

The sense here is neither of the first two, of course, but rather the new sense "patronage, sponsorship, auspices" recorded in Webster's Second; it is easy enough to see how this meaning developed from that of "protection." It is this meaning, especially used with *under,* that has produced, in its various subsenses, the predominant uses in 20th-century English. Reader's Digest 1983 thinks these are secondary uses, but they are not. Copperud 1970 could not find them in dictionaries, but he must have skipped Webster's Third and the 1963 Collegiate Dictionary abridged from it.

In addition to T. S. Eliot and the encyclopedia, here are some examples of "sponsorship, patronage, auspices":

> So why not a series of rock concerts, produced under the aegis of the Fillmore —Richard Goldstein, *New York*, 24 May 1971

> It was written (and published) under the aegis of the Council on Foreign Relations —Willard L. Thorp, *Yale Rev.*, Summer 1954

> ... it was under the aegis of Sir Barry Jackson . . . that many of the later Shaw plays saw the light —W. Bridges-Adams, *The British Theatre*, rev. ed., 1946

> ... under the aegis of London University, university colleges have been started . . . in the Sudan and East Africa —Eric Ashby, *London Calling*, 20 May 1954

Often the word carries the notion of direction, supervision, guidance, or control:

> ... the Central Office for South Vietnam, which runs the war in the South under Hanoi's aegis —Robert Shaplen, *New Yorker*, 24 Apr. 1971

> Before the brief era of reform came to Philadelphia's schools ... under the aegis of Mark R. Shedd and Richardson Dilworth —Peter Binzen, *Saturday Rev.*, 5 Feb. 1972

> ... urging his government to send troops—to include his son—under the aegis of the United Nations —Sir Leslie Munro, *United Nations: Hope for a Divided World*, 1960

> That was not our fault, however, but that of the Holy Alliance under the aegis of Metternich —A. L. Rowse, *Britain To-Day*, September 1944

This sense is sometimes used in the context of the theater and films to connote the functions of producer, director, or distributor:

> Her first Hollywood picture as a free-lance star, no longer under the aegis of Selznick —*Current Biography*, September 1965

> ... last done on film so satisfyingly by Joe Mankiewicz in 1953 under the star-studded aegis of M-G-M —Judith Crist, *New York*, 8 Feb. 1971

When used of individuals, the meaning may sometimes be close to "leadership":

> He joined the Fabian Society, which under the intellectual aegis of Sidney and Beatrice Webb had repudiated the violent revolutionary doctrines of Karl Marx —*Time*, 6 Aug. 1945

> ... the nontonalists, relatively weak, but united under the aegis of Schoenberg —Robert Evett, *Atlantic*, July 1971

Aegis is also used in a sense of "a strong or guiding influence":

> Gide was unable even to approach this goal at first, all the more so because he began his literary activities under the aegis of symbolism —Carlos Lynes, Jr., in *Forms of Modern Fiction*, ed. William Van O'Connor, 1948

> ... little was added to the requirements of notice and hearing developed by the courts under the aegis of the due process clause —Nathaniel L. Nathanson, *American Political Science Rev.*, June 1951

> The feminine dramas of *Little Women* unfold under the ægis of a father deified by absence —H. M. Parshley, Translator's Preface to Simone de Beauvoir, *The Second Sex*, 1952

> Without realizing it, many American mothers, under the aegis of benevolent permissiveness ... actually neglect their children —*Time*, 28 Dec. 1970

Further senses of *aegis* appear to be developing, but they are not readily or fully identifiable yet. One of these carries a notion of an identifying name or label:

> The new publication ... will appear under the aegis of Breskin Publications —*Plastics Newsfront*, January 1951

> The disc is issued under the aegis of Middlebury College —Bertrand H. Bronson, *Western Folklore*, October 1954

> ... Fawcett Crest reports that nearly 19 million softcover copies of 16 Taylor Caldwell novels are in print under its aegis alone —Nan Robertson, *N.Y. Times*, 11 Dec. 1976

These examples show the main areas of expansion that *aegis* is occupying in 20th-century English prose. It is a word that has developed largely within this century, and it shows no sign at present of settling down.

aerate Bryson 1984 reminds us not to misspell this word *aereate,* as is sometimes done:

> . . . kept the water aereated —*Scouting,* April 1953

This is a case of minding your *a*'s and *e*'s.

affect, effect There are two verbs *affect.* The first means, among other things, "to make a show of liking; to put on a pretense of," and the second, "to produce an effect in or on, influence." *Effect* has been used for the second of these since at least 1494 and for the first since 1652. Clearly, we are talking about a long-term confusion here. It happens that *effect* is a verb, too, with a meaning roughly "to bring about." And, to complete the picture, both *affect* and *effect* are nouns. Even though *effect* is the only one in common use (*affect* is a technical term in psychology), *affect* is sometimes put in its place.

All of this history of befuddlement has left us with a fat collection of warning notices. Nearly every handbook published in the 20th century—from Vizetelly 1906 to Chambers 1985—contains one. Does anybody pay attention? Our evidence suggests that nearly everyone who gets published does, although we have substantial evidence for mistaken usage too. Although the verb *affect* and the noun *effect* are a semantic pair—if you affect something, the result is an effect—and this fact alone is bound to create some uncertainty, confusion is probably not the whole problem. More likely it is often simply inattention to spelling. When, for instance, a professional basketball player named Darryl Dawkins commented upon some electrodes attached to his shoulder during a game for therapeutic purposes, and a wire service sent the comment out as "It effected my interplanetary funksmanship," it was not Dawkins who used the wrong verb but a careless professional journalist. Many other of our examples of the mistake probably attest to poor proofreading, or no proofreading; a few—such as dictionary manuscript errors and mistakes in business letters—suggest ordinary inattention in writing.

Here is a handful of correct usages of the several verbs:

> . . . the luxury of contemporary London, which he affected to find nauseating —Paul Fussell, *Samuel Johnson and the Life of Writing,* 1971

> That is all I have, I said, affecting a pathos in my voice —Flann O'Brien, *At Swim-Two-Birds,* 1939

> This was the last age in which writers were seriously affected by the doctrines associated with the traditional literary 'kinds' —John Butt, *English Literature in the Mid-Eighteenth Century,* edited & completed by Geoffrey Carnall, 1979

> No one at AAI measured how day care affects the company —Andrea Fooner, *Inc. Mag.,* 5 May 1981

> . . . drop them a card and tell them your release has been effected —Flannery O'Connor, letter, 19 Apr. 1963

> . . . this President has a mandate to effect some serious changes —Andrew Hacker, *N.Y. Times Book Rev.,* 24 Oct. 1982

And of *effect,* noun (we will omit *affect,* noun):

> . . . prose which essays effects beyond the mere conveying of basic information —Anthony Burgess, *N.Y. Times Book Rev.,* 5 Feb. 1984

> An unimaginative crescendo of stage effects —Jon Pareles, *N.Y. Times,* 16 Jan. 1984

The verbs *affect* and *effect* and the nouns *affect* and *effect* are clearly enough differentiated in meaning that it is unlikely that you will go wrong if you pay attention to your intended meaning. If you entertain any nagging doubts, a dictionary will settle them.

affiliate 1. *Affiliate* is used with both *with* and *to. Affiliate with* is usually but not always American; *affiliate to* is usually but not always British. We have Canadian evidence for both combinations:

> . . . which will be affiliated with the University of Alaska —Michael A. Pollock, *Change,* October 1971

> We finally affiliated with the Newhope Baptist Church —Mrs. Medgar Evars, *Ladies' Home Jour.,* September 1971

> . . . it was affiliated with the University of Glasgow —Sir James Mountford, *British Universities,* 1966

> . . . to affiliate it with a prevailing approach to the lyric stage —Irving Kolodin, *Saturday Rev.,* 26 Sept. 1964

> . . . loose national federations with which the local bodies affiliated —Oscar Handlin, *The American People in the Twentieth Century,* 1954

> . . . which is not affiliated with a university —John E. Robbins, *Institutions of Higher Education in Canada,* ca. 1944

> . . . it was affiliated to the University of Edinburgh in 1933 —Sir James Mountford, *British Universities,* 1966

> . . . said his organisation was affiliated to a worldwide body —*The Guardian,* 28 Nov. 1973

> . . . socially it was advisable that everyone should be affiliated to the religious customs prevalent in his country —George Santayana, *Persons and Places,* 1944

> The urban imagery that affiliates Mr. Eliot to Baudelaire —F. R. Leavis, *New Bearings in English Poetry,* new ed., 1950

> . . . 150 colleges, many affiliated to the universities —*Canada Today,* 1953

2. There is some evidence that in the middle of the 19th century *affiliate* was used in the U.S. in the sense of "associate, fraternize." Thornton 1939 defines it as "Erroneously used instead of *fraternize.*" Perhaps Thornton considered the use a bit below the salt, but the Dictionary of American English did not stigmatize it. The use was also noted in H. W. Horwill's *An Anglo-American Interpreter* (1939). The sense does not appear to be current, at least in print.

affinity Fowler 1926 declared that *between* and *with* are the normal prepositions with *affinity* and that *to* and *for* should not be used. This assertion appears to be based on his analysis of the word as indicating a reciprocal relationship only, while *to* and *for* suggest a more one-sided relationship. Unfortunately for the analysis, the use of *affinity* for a one-sided relationship was already three centuries old, attested as early as 1616 in the OED (sense 8). Follett 1966 elaborates Fowler's treatment by basing his assertion that the meaning is a strong mutual attraction on the word's original meaning, "relationship by marriage." Of course, observation suggests that many relationships by marriage are not based on strong mutual attraction; in-laws are often related solely by the happenstance of marriage. But the real weakness of Follett's argument lies in its assumption that a word's earliest meaning must restrict its later semantic development to some favored pattern. A little time spent with a dictionary that places senses in historical order will persuade you that development of new meaning often does not take place in that way and that, moreover, there is usually no good reason why it should.

In modern use, *affinity* is used with *for* and *with* most often, with *to* and *between* somewhat less often, and with a few other prepositions occasionally. Perhaps it will be most helpful to show a few illustrations of the important general meanings of *affinity* and the prepositions used with each.

The original meaning:

> In a few months it was announced that he was closely related by affinity to the royal house. His daughter had become, by a secret marriage, Duchess of York —T. B. Macaulay, *The History of England,* vol. I, 1849

It is also used of family relationships:

> Every creature that bears any affinity to my mother is dear to me, and you, the daughter of her brother —William Cowper, letter, 27 Feb. 1790

The family relationship may be figurative:

> . . . its degree of affinity with any other language or dialect —Mario Pei, *Word,* August 1949

> The period of ten years that follows is full of experimental variation, but there is a recognizable stylistic affinity between the extremes —Herbert Read, *The Philosophy of Modern Art,* 1952

> ". . . Whatever bears affinity to cunning is despicable." —Jane Austen, *Pride and Prejudice,* 1813

This use is often close in meaning to "resemblance" or "similarity":

> . . . it is likely his Elvish language shows some affinities with Finnish —*Current Biography,* October 1967

> . . . affirms a general affinity between the police and the military—both refer to outsiders as 'civilians' — Allen Young, quoted in *Playboy,* September 1968

> . . . something in the English character, something mystical, tough and fierce, has a special affinity to Hebrew —Edmund Wilson, *A Piece of My Mind,* 1956

A common figurative sense is "a feeling of kinship, sympathy, rapport":

> . . . I feel a certain affinity to the situation and to the institution —Keith M. Cottam, *Library Jour.,* 1 Feb. 1967

> . . . the mysterious affinity between them —Zane Grey, *The Mysterious Rider,* 1921

> . . . there is an affinity between them and their African friends —Michael Blundell, *London Calling,* 3 Feb. 1955

> . . . I have always felt a real affinity with Havel's point of view —Tom Stoppard, quoted in *N.Y. Times,* 25 Oct. 1979

> . . . a true rabbit dog . . . which it took but one glance to see had an affinity a rapport with rabbits —William Faulkner, *Intruder in the Dust,* 1948

> . . . the passion of Giovanni and Annabella is not shown as an affinity of temperament —T. S. Eliot, "John Ford," in *Selected Essays,* 1932

> . . . racism therefore did obeisance to the affinities of the Celtic soul and the Slavic soul —Ruth Benedict, *Race: Science and Politics,* 1945

> . . . the man who on the out-of-town hustings makes much of his affinity for "the street people, *my* people, the workers of my city" —Andy Logan, *New Yorker,* 30 Oct. 1971

The sympathy is sometimes extended to foods to suggest that things go well together:

> . . . new crackers that have a true affinity for cheese —*New Yorker,* 12 Dec. 1953

> Rum also has an amazing affinity for foods we love —Marilyn Kayter, *American Way,* December 1971

A frequent use of *affinity* is to denote an attraction to or liking for something:

> What an affinity for Christianity had this persecutor of the Christians! —Matthew Arnold, *Essays in Criticism, First Series,* 1865

> . . . revels in Macaulay, who has a special affinity for the eternal schoolboy —W. R. Inge, *The Church in the World,* 1928

> . . . they punish themselves, by their natural affinity for the defective —C. S. Peirce, "Evolutionary Love," 1893, in *The Philosophy of Peirce,* ed. Justus Buchler, 1940

> If you have no affinity for verse, better skip this — Oliver St. John Gogarty, *It Isn't This Time of Year At All!* 1954

> I think you have an affinity for aging British ladies of unimpeachable integrity —Flannery O'Connor, letter, 11 May 1963

> His affinity for controversy got him into further trouble —Michael & Sheila Cole, *Psychology Today,* March 1971

> . . . this affinity for exotica made itself felt in St. Denis's repertory —Anna Kisselgoff, *N.Y. Times Book Rev.,* 10 Oct. 1976

Sometimes affinity suggests a natural or sympathetic aptitude or liking for something, a natural talent, a flair:

> . . . Weingartner had a close affinity with this style, and I recall some Haydn symphonies . . . that are well-nigh unsurpassable —Paul Henry Lang, *Saturday Rev.,* 26 June 1954

Gifted with an affinity for the art song —*Current Biography,* November 1966

... Irishmen, who seem to have an affinity for politics —Green Peyton, *San Antonio: City in the Sun,* 1946

... early displayed an affinity for finance and bookkeeping —*Current Biography,* April 1966

The attempt to limit the prepositions *affinity* can be used with has never had any basis in other than artificial notions and thus has achieved no striking success. In addition to the examples shown above, there are many technical uses of *affinity* (as in chemistry and botany) that usually go with *for* (but sometimes *to* or another preposition). You can use *affinity* with any preposition that seems natural.

affirmative, negative An objection is sometimes made to the use of *affirmative* and *negative* in such sentences as "The witness answered in the negative." Copperud 1964, 1970, Flesch 1964, Watt 1967, and Heritage 1982 may be recorded among the objectors; Gowers (in Fowler 1965) objects to it as pompous; he sees it as a Parliamentary convention that has been satirized to such an extent that it is now seldom used in Britain. He has also found it in American use, however, and he quotes an effusion of self-evident pomposity.

Copperud 1970 also notes a magazine report that secretaries at NASA headquarters in Houston were then saying "negative" rather than "no." The practice presumably derives from military aviation use, where *affirmative* and *negative* replace *yes* and *no* in radio communications as less likely to be garbled by static:

... the squawk box rasped, "Admiral, 1591 says he will have to ditch."
"Can he ditch near the destroyers?"
"Negative."
"Is his wingman still with him?"
"Affirmative."
—James A. Michener, *The Bridges at Toko-Ri,* 1953

It should be further noted that *affirmative* and *negative* can be used with *answer* in sentences where simple replacement with *yes* or *no* is not desirable:

... a question that can't be answered in the affirmative—for if it could, there would be no need to ask it —Jon Landau, *Rolling Stone,* 2 Mar. 1972

A final note: usage writers are apt to disparage usages like this as modern barbarisms. But this expression was around long before the courtroom reportage rejected by Copperud, Flesch, and Watt developed:

... I met an old woman in the street, who accosting me, asked, if I were a physician. When I answered in the affirmative ... —Tobias Smollett, translation of René Le Sage, *Gil Blas,* 1749

afflict See INFLICT, AFFLICT.

affluent There are several reasons for preferring the pronunciation with main stress on the initial syllable: \ˈaf-ˌlü-ənt\. The variant with main stress on the second syllable, \a-ˈflü-ənt\, is disapproved by usage writers, is less common among educated speakers (though certainly in respectable use), and could be confused with

effluent, which is also sometimes pronounced with main stress on the second syllable. Confusion is far less likely when main stress falls on the contrasting initial vowels.

aforementioned, aforesaid Copperud 1970 cites himself and Flesch as finding these words unsuitable for ordinary contexts; Strunk & White 1959 finds *aforesaid* "damaging in standard prose"; Nickles 1974 labels both words "legal lingo" to be avoided. Although these two words are used in legal contexts, they also appear in general contexts, where they are not used in quite the same way as in documents.

Aforementioned seems to be somewhat the more common word. It is widely employed as part of a standard auditor's statement:

In our opinion, the aforementioned financial statements present fairly the consolidated financial position of ... —*Annual Report, Atlantic Richfield Co.,* 1970

It also appears in rather ordinary contexts, many of which—perhaps surprisingly—are written in an informal style:

... in the aforementioned times when not just natural-shoulder but all suits were eschewed in favor of jeans —David Platt, *Playboy,* April 1980

The first of the six, the aforementioned Oberhoffer, remained at the helm until 1922 —Roland Gelatt, *Saturday Rev.,* 29 Oct. 1977

Grandaddy of them all, the aforementioned Bonanza International —Charles Biderman, *Barron's,* 8 May 1972

In 1966 the aforementioned Mr. Jenkins, in one of his earlier though not wiser pronouncements — "Albion," *Security World,* May 1968

... the aforementioned impartial and incorruptible chance —Frank Stockton, "The Lady or the Tiger?" 1882, in *Worlds of People* (textbook), 1951

The word is used at times for humorous effect:

"Four gin-and-tonics is whose idea of healthful sport?" said the aforementioned spouse of aforesaid with a snarl that so incensed the snarlee that I—I mean, the snarlee—did spitefully consume the four and then two more —John Ciardi, *Saturday Rev.,* 22 Jan. 1972

Margaret is, I regret to say, called Mopsy and she burns genteely [sic] for the unworthy Luke. In the end she gets him but not before everybody gets entangled in the aforementioned plot devices — Edward Fitzgerald, *Saturday Rev.,* 26 July 1952

... the height of its forehead being lost in the still more perilous height of the aforementioned hat — *Irish Statesman,* 22 Nov. 1924

We have less evidence for *aforesaid* than for *aforementioned.* It does not appear regularly in any formulaic statements that we are aware of. Like *aforementioned* it often appears in contexts of a light or humorous nature:

I had just finished "sottin'" 48 tender celery plants in a neat row in my tillage when a large, yellow Thomas Cat hastened in a generally south-north direction and placed a foot precisely on each plant aforesaid *en passant.* The reason for this intrusion was immediately clear—four large and excited hounds in full cry —John Gould, *Christian Science Monitor,* 18 July 1980

Aforementioned and *aforesaid* furnish one convenient way to refer back to something mentioned earlier, perhaps on occasion to avoid the often sullied *above* (see ABOVE 1). They come from legal lingo and are used in legal contexts. In ordinary contexts they seem to be often used informally and for humorous effect.

afraid 1. Chambers 1985 and Evans 1957 discuss the constructions *afraid* is found in. It is derived from a past participle in Middle English and is used now as a predicate adjective, not as an attributive adjective. *Afraid* can be followed by a clause:

Afraid that any precipitous action on his part might well cost him his position —*NEA Jour.,* January 1965

He seemed afraid, if he were kind, he might be ridiculed —Edwin A. Peeples, *Saturday Evening Post,* 25 Dec. 1954

It can be followed by an infinitive:

... ready to say bluntly what every one else is afraid to say —T. S. Eliot, "Charles Whibley," in *Selected Essays,* 1932

... is not afraid to go out and ask a playwright or a director just what he thinks he's doing —Richard Schickel, *Harper's,* November 1970

The usual preposition after *afraid* is *of,* which can be followed by a noun or a gerund:

We have been much too much afraid of the Russians —Edmund Wilson, *A Piece of My Mind,* 1956

"... She told me she was afraid of him. He had threatened to kill her." —Dashiell Hammett, *Red Harvest,* 1929

"... were you so afraid of a man like Keegan, you wouldn't step forward ... ?" —Anthony Trollope, *The Macdermots of Ballycloran,* 1847

Some of us are afraid of dying —Thomas Pynchon, *V.,* 1963

But I am now as much afraid of drinking as of bathing —Tobias Smollett, *Humphry Clinker,* 1771

Afraid is also followed by *for;* in this construction the object is not the source of the threat but rather what is threatened:

... clerks, who had come early because they were afraid for their jobs —Wirt Williams, *The Enemy,* 1951

The men aren't afraid for their jobs, either, because unemployment is negligible —John Fischer, *Harper's,* January 1969

... once or twice she is in real physical danger and genuinely afraid for herself —*Times Literary Supp.,* February 1969

2. Bierce 1909 directs us flatly, "Do not say 'I am afraid it will rain.' Say, I fear that it will rain." End of direction. Vizetelly 1920 cannot find any reason for this proscription; Utter 1916 opines that the objection seems to be based on the theory that an adjective cannot take a

dependent clause. Utter says that this "construction has long been good English," even though the censorious condemn it as colloquial. Among the censorious must be listed Krapp 1927, who calls it colloquial.

The element of fear in Bierce's example is not strong, a fact that makes his revision seem less than sensible. In Utter's (I'm afraid I can't go) and Krapp's (I'm afraid you'll have to wait for the next train) examples, it is even weaker. This aspect of the expression is picked on by our next two commentators, Bremner 1980 and Freeman 1983. Here is what Bremner says:

Try to avoid *afraid* unless the context calls for fear, fright, terror, alarm. Don't use it casually, as in "I'm afraid not"....

And Freeman:

The expression "She's *afraid* he's right" is an informal—and incorrect—way of saying "She *fears* that he's right." And "I'm afraid not" is folksy for "I *think* not." The use of *afraid* should be restricted to reflect a real cause for fear, fright, or alarm.

As noted above, Utter mentions the long history of this construction. Shakespeare certainly used it:

I am afraid, sir, Do what you can, yours will not be entreated —*The Taming of the Shrew,* 1594

I am afraid this great lubber, the world, will prove a cockney —*Twelfth Night,* 1602

I am half afraid he will have need of washing —*The Merry Wives of Windsor,* 1601

And it has been used in impeccable literary sources ever since:

Disagreeable enough (as most necessities are) but, I am afraid, unavoidable —Thomas Gray, letter, 16 July 1740 (OED Supplement)

I am afraid you do not like your pen. Let me mend it for you —Jane Austen, *Pride and Prejudice,* 1813 (OED Supplement)

... though even that is more, I am afraid, than my powers are up to —Henry Adams, letter, 9 Feb. 1859

But when I use it now, I am afraid, it will usually be a dignified way of circling round the more indefinable aspects of a novelist's skill —Bernard De Voto, *The World of Fiction,* 1950

... I am afraid that often in reading the *Cantos* I feel as if what is being said were not much better than nothing —F. R. Leavis, *New Bearings in English Poetry,* new ed., 1950

I am afraid that it is a feeling that I share —William Styron, *This Quiet Dust and Other Writings,* 1982

The expression may at times suggest informality, but it is in no way incorrect.

after 1. In Irish dialect *after* is used in a construction *to be after doing something* about whose meaning there seems to have been some confusion. P. W. Joyce in *English As We Speak It in Ireland* (1910) explains it as an idiom by which the Irish get round the perfect tense—instead of "I have finished my work" they use "I am after finishing my work." Some older American dictionaries seem to have thought it to mean "to be about to" rather than "to have just done"; Gowers (in Fowler

1965) notes that some English novelists have made the same mistake. Here are a few genuine Irish examples:

> 'Listen to me,' says I, 'do you think I did this on purpose? I'm after having two punctures. . . ." —Rex MacGall, *Irish Digest*, November 1955

> Cracked Mary it is, that is after coming back this day from the asylum —Lady Gregory, *The Full Moon*, 1910

> I'm after thinking of something good, something very good unless I'm very much mistaken, said Furriskey —Flann O'Brien, *At Swim-Two-Birds*, 1939

2. Longman 1984 thinks *after* meaning "afterwards" is not suitable for formal writing unless accompanied by an adverb like *soon* or *shortly*. The OED shows this construction used by Shakespeare, Thomas Fuller, Edmund Burke, and Horace Walpole, among others. Modern examples are standard but not of the highest formality:

> . . . during your trip through Britain (and . . . across the Channel if you're touring the Continent after) —Richard Joseph, *Your Trip to Britain*, 1954

> . . . walking to church with them on a Sunday, and going home after to a roast —Mary Deasy, *The Hour of Spring*, 1948

> During those periods when Thomas, and after, Butler, were occupied elsewhere —*Current Biography 1947*

It quite commonly goes with expressions of time:

> . . . Latin was the language of international scholarship in his day, as for centuries before and after —W. F. Bolton, *A Short History of Literary English*, 1967

> For years after, when Sallie and I went to the National Arts Club, Mary Austin was there —*The Autobiography of William Allen White*, 1946

> He kept telling me for a week after, that those dancing girls wore . . . the prettiest dresses —Eudora Welty, *The Ponder Heart*, 1954

And, of course, it is used with adverbs:

> Not long after, a trio of friends . . . came in to see her —Robert M. Coates, *New Yorker*, 25 May 1963

> . . . some of them not long after converted to fascism —*Times Literary Supp.*, 5 June 1969

> . . . the name "Georgy," having once been mispronounced "Doody" in childhood, may take on the latter form forever after —*Selected Writings of Edward Sapir*, ed. David G. Mandelbaum, 1949

> Soon after, in November 1947 —*Current Biography*, June 1965

> . . . lightning again ripped the world apart and the thunder came tumbling right after —Rita Madocs, *Ladies' Home Jour.*, September 1971

> . . . and disappeared shortly after —*Dictionary of American Biography*, 1928

3. Jensen 1935 considered *after* redundant with a perfect participial phrase. Jensen seems to have stood alone. The use is entirely standard in biographical writing, where the order of events is emphasized, and is found

in many other sources using standard English. A few samples:

> Returning to Liverpool after having attained some popularity in Hamburg, they were booked for several months in the Cavern —*Current Biography*, December 1965

> My impression, after having excavated in several of the sites —Edward P. Lanning, *Peru Before the Incas*, 1967

> She died in 1947 after having launched some hundreds of boys on their course in life —*Times Literary Supp.*, 17 Feb. 1950

African-American, Afro-American   See BLACK.

aftermath   Let us begin by demonstrating how the figurative senses of *aftermath* are used. In one sense it is applied to something that follows from something else: a result or consequence. This following or resulting thing is very often unpleasant, but need not necessarily be so:

> How could he know she would arrive an hour later alone, that there would be a snowstorm in which she wandered about in slippers, too confused to find a taxi? Then the aftermath, her escaping pneumonia by a miracle, and all the attendant horror —F. Scott Fitzgerald, "Babylon Revisited," in *The Portable F. Scott Fitzgerald*, 1945

> . . . perhaps it is a mistake to resuscitate his theory, with all its melancholy aftermath of 'art for art's sake' —Herbert Read, *The Philosophy of Modern Art*, 1952

> In pioneer days, when an editor could term a fellow citizen a "low-born loon" with no fear of legal aftermath —*American Guide Series: Tennessee*, 1939

> Deep pessimism is perhaps a natural aftermath of the shock of recognizing that the vaunted "progress" of modern civilization is only a thin cloak for global catastrophe —Barry Commoner, *New Yorker*, 2 Oct. 1971

> . . . the feigned death of Juliet and its aftermath of grief —Winthrop Sargeant, *New Yorker*, 1 May 1971

> One of the truly dramatic aftermaths of the World War has been the awakening and expansion of commercial life in the Latin-American countries —*The Nation*, 16 Jan. 1929

> As a gratifying aftermath of the recent aeronautical exposition manufacturers of aircraft have received orders —*N.Y. Times*, 30 Mar. 1919

It is worth remarking that there is a tendency toward more unpleasant aftermaths in recent use of the word.

The other main figurative use of *aftermath* is for a period immediately following some event. Usually the event is an important and ruinous one, such as a war. In this sense *aftermath* is often found in the phrase *in the aftermath of*.

> Perhaps the greatest crime of the war and its aftermath —*Manchester Guardian Weekly*, 17 Feb. 1922

It bodes ill for a future in which the life and strength of Britain, compared to the other Powers, will be tested to the full, not only in war but in its aftermath —Sir Winston Churchill, address in Commons, 18 Jan. 1945, in *Voices of History 1945–1946,* ed. Nathan Ausubel, 1946

... salutary effect of Eliot's earlier criticism in curbing the carelessness and gush of the aftermath of Romanticism —Edmund Wilson, *Axel's Castle,* 1931

It is just as well that there was no competitive piano or violin playing in the immediate aftermath of theirs —Irving Kolodin, *Saturday Rev.,* 2 Jan. 1954

In the aftermath of the Coronation —*Punch,* 2 Sept. 1954

When old William Jennings Bryan, the advocate of the Bible, died in the exhausted aftermath of that trial —*Time,* 6 Feb. 1956

... in the melancholy aftermath of Vietnam —Arthur M. Schlesinger, Jr., *Harper's,* March 1969

... the ice ages—in the aftermath of which we are now living —*Times Literary Supp.,* 1 Jan. 1971

With that background we may turn now to the usage writers. The earliest in our files is Vizetelly 1920, who tells us that *aftermath* is "a word persistently misused." His adverb should have alerted him to the fact that he had missed the direction of usage. But it did not, and he goes on to entangle himself in the etymology and agricultural senses of the word. *Math* is an old word for "mowing"; *after* is simply *after.* Literally, then, *aftermath* means "after mowing." The citations in the OED, from the 17th century on, show the word being used to refer to the herbage that grows in a field after the first crop—of hay, for instance—has been mowed. But Vizetelly thinks the word means "second mowing"—with stress on *second*—and so refers to an event. He then draws conclusions about what figurative extensions are allowable based on his misconception of the original meaning. No wonder the world does not go along with him.

Evans 1957, 1962 follows a similar line of argument, basing conclusions on a supposed right relationship of extended meanings to the original. Evans feels the word should be restricted to real consequences, not just subsequent events; he notes that the consequences are usually unpleasant but does not insist that they must be. Gowers in Fowler 1965 sees extended use as "firmly established" and thinks it pedantry to object to the unpleasant aspect of the meaning on etymological grounds (as it would be, if anyone did so). Copperud 1970 thinks they both favor restriction to unpleasant results, which is not quite the case, and he agrees. Clearly a tangle of opinion surrounds this word, but as the examples above show, the opinion really does not matter. Both figurative senses are well established in standard writing.

Since *aftermath* originally referred to a crop that grows after a first crop is cut, it is easy to see how it came to be used figuratively for one thing that happened after another. How it came to acquire its generally unpleasant connotations is not so clear. Here are two hints. The OED cites the poet Robert Southey as writing "No aftermath has the ... sweetness of the first crop" and the poet Coventry Patmore as using the phrase "the bloomless aftermath." Beyond these suggestions of disappointment, we have evidence from veterinary sources that aftermath might be considered bad for sheep or horses to graze on because of possible infestation with parasites. Perhaps the unpleasant connotations came from farmers with sick livestock.

afterward, afterwards   Copperud 1970 says that both forms are used in the U.S. while *afterwards* prevails in British English; Watt 1967 opines that *afterward* is more common in the U.S. Standard reference works and our evidence confirm these observations.

against   1. *Conjunction.* Hodgson 1889 censured the conjunction *against* ("Have it ready *against* I come") as a vulgar usage; Bardeen 1883 considered it disputable. Reader's Digest 1983 mentions regional use. The conjunction *against* was created by functional shift from the preposition back in the 14th century. It had perfectly acceptable literary use for several centuries:

> And they made ready the present against Joseph came at noon —Genesis 43:25 (AV), 1611

> "I will be prepared, *says he,* against you come again." —Daniel Defoe, *Moll Flanders,* 1722

> Throw on another log of wood against father comes home —Charles Dickens, *Pickwick Papers,* 1837 (OED)

As a standard locution, the conjunction is now archaic; it survives only in dialect (the Dictionary of American Regional English has examples) and in fiction representing archaic or dialectal speech:

> One of the men ... called out, "Let 'em come on. They'll drive just like hogs against they get out on the pike." —Elizabeth Madox Roberts, *The Time of Man,* 1926

See also WITHOUT.

2. The pronunciation \ə-ˈgin\ represented by the spelling *agin* is generally treated as dialectal or rural (the Dictionary of American Regional English covers it generously under *again*). Lounsbury 1908 points out that this form, like others that survive among the less educated, represents the original form of the preposition in Middle English.

ageism   Simon 1980 asperses *ageism* as an illiteracy. He also purports, ironically, not to understand its meaning. *Ageism* is a product of that new use of *-ism* to mean "prejudice, discrimination," which seems to derive from *racism* and earlier gave the language *sexism.* At worst, the word might be judged rather trendy (it originated around 1970):

> "... Don't leave anything valuable lying around, like your stash. She's one heavy old lady, and we let her move in because we wanted to make a statement about ageism in America, but she's got these sticky fingers...." —Cyra McFadden, *The Serial,* 1977

> ... Granny Jump is a living warning against ageism —Joy Chant, *Times Literary Supp.,* 28 Mar. 1980

> ... few gerontologists ... have taken up arms against one of the most insidious forms of ageism—the myth of senility —Robin M. Henig, *N.Y. Times Mag.,* 3 Dec. 1978

> Such ageism may well be a major reason many people age poorly in this society —Ann E. Gerike, letter, *Newsweek,* 17 Nov. 1986

Our files show that the word has even reached Australia, so it may be with us for a while. Some writers will find it a conveniently brief way of putting a notion that otherwise requires a phrase; others may well prefer to leave it alone.

agenda Everybody agrees, according to Copperud 1970, 1980, that *agenda* is standard in English as a singular, with *agendas* as its plural. We have about a dozen commentators—both English and American—who are also in agreement in addition to Copperud's group of experts. Against this formidable array stands the OED Supplement:

> **agenda** . . . treated as a singular (a use now increasingly found but avoided by careful writers).

The OED Supplement is supported by a couple of letter writers: the novelist Upton Sinclair objecting to the appearance of "a broad agenda" in the *New Republic* in 1951 and a correspondent to William Safire in the *New York Times* in 1984 objecting to "a hidden agenda."

Everyone further agrees that *agenda* is the plural of *agendum* in Latin. The use of *agendum* in English to mean "a list or program" is considered a slip by Evans 1961 and pedantic by a few other commentators. It is considerably less frequent than *agenda,* but it has been in use since 1898 and is entered as standard in dictionaries.

> Each instructor or student leader receives an agendum of suggested "overhead" or general discussion questions —Major James L. Jackson, Ph.D., *College English,* March 1954

Many commentators say that *agendum* means "something to be done." This is more a direct translation of the Latin word than a well-established meaning in English. In fact, it is so rare in English that it is not recognized in Webster's Third. But it does exist:

> Principal agendum of the pages standing at the rostrum steps was to lift the train of each ascending delegate with combined dexterity, good timing and discretion —*Time,* 2 May 1938

The present use of *agenda* did not arise until the end of the 19th century. It barely made the OED, which included a single italicized example from 1882 under the entry *agend,* a spelling no longer used. It appears to have caught on quickly enough—*agenda-paper* appearing in 1887, *agendum* in 1898. The use of *agenda* for the list was such a rapid development that dictionaries had not yet caught up with it when this Kansas journalist felt it necessary to explain details of usage in 1928:

> An "agendum" is "something to be done." In the plural—"agenda"—it means a "memorandum book." In diplomatic speech it comes nearer to signifying a "program." In this sense it's most conveniently mentioned in the singular, rather than the plural—one "agenda," not a whole flock of "agendums." —Charles P. Stewart, *Emporia* (Kans.) *Gazette,* 11 Feb. 1928

The feeling that *agenda* referred to a single entity was developed early:

> . . . it was resolved that "items 1 to 4 on the agenda need not be discussed" —*The Strand,* September 1900

> The agenda drawn up for the Congress contains the following items —*Soviet Union Rev.,* 31 Jan. 1925

This singular *agenda* has continued in standard use:

> There was an agenda or program of the conference —*The Autobiography of William Allen White,* 1946

> The original agenda, which was to have covered many motions —Mollie Panter-Downes, *New Yorker,* 13 Oct. 1951

> It's a vast agenda —Prime Minister Harold Wilson, BBC radio broadcast, 1 June 1967

> President Carter's agenda for America is too important to be jeopardized by a defense of the indefensible —Norman Cousins, *Saturday Rev.,* 2 Apr. 1977

> But many have another agenda as well —Elizabeth Drew, *New Yorker,* 6 Dec. 1982

In those instances where a plural is necessary, *agendas* is the standard form. The OED Supplement shows *agendas* as early as 1907. Our evidence suggests that the plural is relatively uncommon.

> The two agendas, which were not as far apart as the draft agendas of some past East-West conferences — *Time,* 12 Mar. 1951

> But the agendas of faculty meetings rarely include such issues —Ruth R. Hawkins, *Change,* November–December 1969

> . . . a Trojan horse filled full of all kinds of budget-busting measures and secondary agendas —David A. Stockman, quoted by William Greider, *Atlantic,* December 1981

Agendum, usually in the form *agenda,* has some relatively infrequent use to mean "an item on the agenda":

> They should have the right to initiate agenda, to discuss the entire range of university concerns —William M. Roth, *Saturday Rev.,* 10 Jan. 1970

This use may be curtailed by the use of the wordier but self-explanatory *agenda item* to convey the same sense:

> . . . it may be useful to survey some of the agenda items and problem areas he will confront —Samuel Halperin, *Change,* January–February 1971

> . . . the President moved on to other agenda items without asking for reactions —Irving Janis, *Psychology Today,* November 1971

William Safire (*N.Y. Times Mag.,* 16 Sept. 1984) tries to trace the development of the expression *hidden agenda.* He finds its roots in the use of *agenda* for a political program, a use that has been around since at least the 1950s:

> It now appeared that military aggression was most definitely on the agenda of international Communism —Edgar S. Furniss, Jr., *Yale Rev.,* Autumn 1954

Our earliest citation for *hidden agenda* suggests that the term was already familiar when the author used it:

> The schooling process has a hidden agenda—an invisible curriculum—that sorts knowledge into packages . . . ; that categorizes persons as successes or failures with a fixed criterion; that mistakes conformity for allegiance —John Gagnon, *Change,* October 1971

The collection had indeed a hidden agenda—it was a running argument with Stalinism —Steven Marcus, *N.Y. Times Book Rev.,* 8 Feb. 1976

The phrase continues to be popular:

In a field where polemics and ideology are the norm, Walker's book is a refreshing exception. It has no hidden agenda —Stephen Stich, *Times Literary Supp.,* 29 Apr. 1983

This credibility could not be long sustained if readers come to believe that our articles are tainted by some hidden agenda —*Wall Street Jour.,* 3 Apr. 1984

In the last two examples, *hidden agenda* is beginning to come close in meaning to *ulterior motive.*

Agenda, then, is fully established as a singular in standard English, with a plural *agendas* available, if you need it. *Agendum,* with a plural *agenda,* has infrequent use as "something to be done," slightly greater use as "an item in an agenda," and some use as an equivalent to *agenda. Agenda* and *agendum* also have a few other uses; for them we recommend an unabridged dictionary.

For other foreign plurals, see LATIN PLURALS.

aggravate, aggravation, aggravating There is a body of opinion with a long tradition holding that *aggravate* should only be used to mean "make worse" and that its use to mean "irritate, exasperate, annoy" is wrong, incorrect, childish, vulgar, colloquial, or (at best) informal. A good deal of expressed opinion on this topic has accumulated since Richard Grant White condemned it in 1870 and John Stuart Mill labeled it "a vulgarism of the nursery" in one of the later editions of his *A System of Logic* (1872), but it is by no means unanimous. Here is a sampling:

Richard Grant White 1870: . . . misused by many persons ignorantly . . . by many others thoughtlessly, in the sense of provoke, irritate, anger.

Hodgson 1889: Its employment as a synonym for 'irritate' or 'vex,' being quite superfluous, cannot be defended. . . .

Bierce 1909: But a person cannot be aggravated, even if disagreeable or bad. Women are singularly prone to misuse of this word.

Utter 1916: . . . we may *aggravate* a man's ill temper . . . but not the man himself.

Whipple 1924: *Aggravate* means to *make worse* and never should be used as a synonym for *annoy, exasperate,* or *vex.*

Fowler 1926: . . . should be left to the uneducated. It is for the most part a feminine or childish colloquialism. . . .

Treble & Vallins 1937: The use of *aggravate* with a personal object . . . is purely colloquial. . . . It should never appear in written English.

Bernstein 1958: . . . it should not be used to mean "irritate" or "exasperate."

Shaw 1970: Standard usage: Sneezing *aggravated* his wound. The mosquito *annoyed*—not *aggravated*—me.

Fowler 1965 (Gowers's revision): It is time to recognize that usage has beaten the grammarians, as it

so often does, and that the condemnation of this use of *aggravate* has become a fetish.

Copperud 1970: The consensus is that the struggle to limit *aggravate* to the traditional sense has been lost.

Sellers 1975: *Aggravate* and *annoy* are not synonymous.

Bander 1978: This word is incorrect in the sense of *irritate* or *annoy.*

Little, Brown 1980: . . . in writing it should not be used in its colloquial meaning of "irritate" or "exasperate."

Reader's Digest 1983: The use of *aggravate* to mean 'irritate, anger' . . . is standard and correct.

Einstein 1985: To *aggravate* is to take something that *irritates* and make it worse.

There are many more commentators, but by now the general idea is clear: in recent years opinion has begun to swing away from the White-Mill condemnation, but there are still holdouts.

Aggravate was introduced into English in the 16th century, straight from the past participle of the Latin verb *aggravare,* "to make heavier." It replaced an earlier word *aggrege,* used by Chaucer and earlier writers, which had dropped out of use around 1500. It was first used in several senses now obsolete but by 1597 was being used in its "make worse" sense. Only fourteen years later, in 1611, it appeared in the "annoy" sense. The 1611 use is by one Randle Cotgrave, who used it (along with *exasperate*) to gloss a word in his French-English dictionary. Clearly Cotgrave considered the meaning familiar enough to make *aggravate* useful as a gloss.

The evidence suggests, however, that the "annoy" sense was primarily in spoken use. The OED, which labels the sense *familiar,* shows only a 17th-century book of travels and Samuel Richardson's epistolary novel *Clarissa* (1748) before the 19th century. Samuel Pegge, a Londoner interested in dialect, included the "annoy" sense in a list of Cockneyisms he published in 1807—further evidence that the sense was current in speech. Some of our earlier American citations also come from the realm of speech—even though fictional:

. . . for writin' only aggravates your opponents, and never convinces them —Thomas C. Haliburton, *The Clockmaker,* 1837

"O, go 'long with you, Tom, before you aggravate me again. . . ." —Mark Twain, *Tom Sawyer,* 1876

It seems likely that during the 19th century the usage of the "annoy" sense increased, especially in writing or printing. Mill complains that it "has crept into almost all newspapers, and into many books"; White's dislike may have been similarly inspired, as many of his complaints about language are based on journalistic examples. White's objection, however, seems to center primarily on etymology—he insists on the literalness of "make heavier" and conveniently ignores the extension of meaning to "make worse." (The etymology of this word still comes in for mention—as recently as Freeman 1983 and Kilpatrick 1984.) One of the earlier expositors of etymology, Hodgson (1889), rather undermines his own argument, in the course of showing off his knowledge of Latin, by revealing that the secondary sense of *aggravare* is "to bear down upon or annoy."

Sir Ernest Gowers in *Plain Words* (1947) credits Dickens with giving "powerful encouragement" to the usage, and, if appearance in novels counts for a bit more than newspaper use, then Dickens and Thackeray probably were influential. They are cited, at least, as evidence for the sense in numerous dictionaries. Gowers further observes (in Fowler 1965) that "writers have shown no less persistence in refusing to be trammeled by this admonition [to avoid the use]." Here are a few examples from a number of writers (and the speech of one U.S. President) in a variety of settings:

'I'm very much obliged to you, Misses Brown,' said the unfortunate youth, greatly aggravated —Charles Dickens, *Dombey and Son,* 1848 (OED)

... no doubt our two countries *aggravate* each other from time to time —Oliver Wendell Holmes d. 1935, letter to Sir Frederick Pollock, 27 Dec. 1895

There are times when the French get aggravated and displeased by us —Jimmy Carter, quoted in *N.Y. Times,* 14 Feb. 1980

She noticed his pleasant and contented manner ... and it merely aggravated her the more —Theodore Dreiser, *Sister Carrie,* 1900

The mere sight of her twisted mouth ... seemed to aggravate him to further abuse —John Cowper Powys, *Ducdame,* 1925

... he aggravated 'em a lot by making 'em think he would —Will James, *Smoky,* 1926

The man's lack of friends amazed and then began to aggravate and trouble Clancy —John Cheever, *New Yorker,* 24 Mar. 1951

Nothing so aggravates an earnest person as a passive resistance —Herman Melville, "Bartleby the Scrivener," 1856

... the celebrated incident of Mr. Yarborough's declining to participate directly in the motorcade, ... greatly aggravating the President —William F. Buckley, Jr., *National Rev.,* 19 Nov. 1971

Keitel ... was aggravated at the delay —William L. Shirer, *The Rise and Fall of the Third Reich,* 1960

... when his silly conceit and his youthful pomposity about his not-very-good early work has begun to aggravate us —William Styron, *This Quiet Dust and Other Writings,* 1982

John Stuart Mill's comments contained the complaint that when the word is used in its proper sense, the meaning "it is probable, is already misunderstood." Jespersen 1905, who reprinted Mill's comments, remarked that he "exaggerated." This is surely true: the "make worse" sense of *aggravate* is by far the more common in edited prose, and there never seems to have been a problem of misunderstanding. Dickens certainly used the sense as well as the "annoy" sense:

'I have a long series of insults to avenge,' said Nicholas, flushed with passion; 'and my indignation is aggravated by the dastardly cruelties practiced on helpless infancy in this foul den.' —Charles Dickens, *Nicholas Nickleby,* 1839

The "make worse" sense continues in vigorous use today and remains the primary meaning of the verb. The case with the derivatives *aggravation* and *aggravating* is somewhat different, however.

The noun *aggravation* has been used in the sense "irritation" at least since the end of the 17th century:

In this respect the stage is faulty to a scandalous degree of nauseousness and aggravation —Jeremy Collier, *A Short View of the Immorality and Profaneness of the English Stage,* 1698

... and to have Miss Crawford's liveliness repeated to her at such a moment, and on such a subject, was a bigger aggravation —Jane Austen, *Mansfield Park,* 1814

Aggravations between people South and North were getting worse —Carl Sandburg, *Abraham Lincoln,* 1926

The "irritation" sense divides usage with earlier senses about evenly, but our most recent evidence shows that it is beginning to predominate.

The participial adjective *aggravating* has seldom been used to mean anything except "annoying" since the middle third of the 19th century; it may have been, in fact, what set the critics off (it is the form cited by Mill). It is certainly well attested:

... its grievances had become so numerous and aggravating —Diedrich Knickerbocker (Washington Irving), *A History of New York,* 1832

... kicking pupils with his nailed boots, pulling the hair of some of the smaller boys, pinching the others in aggravating places —Charles Dickens, *Nicholas Nickleby,* 1839

... the summons had to be taken out at Stratford-le-Bow (that is where this aggravating man is living) —Lewis Carroll, letter, 11 Nov. 1886

Among the many boys ... was one more aggravating than the rest —Rudyard Kipling, "Baa Baa, Black Sheep," 1888

... only it is aggravating to have you talking about so small a business —George Bernard Shaw, letter to Ellen Terry, 16 Sept. 1896

But Archbishop Tenison, though much out of favour with the Queen, outlived her in a most aggravating manner —G. M. Trevelyan, *Blenheim,* 1930 (Gowers 1948)

The final effect is interesting, but aggravating — Irwin Shaw, *New Republic,* 29 Dec. 1947

... he can be extremely aggravating and silly —Cyril Connolly, *The Condemned Playground,* 1946

... all the funny papers and Coca-Cola pictures plastering the walls were, he complained, crooked and aggravating —Truman Capote, *Other Voices, Other Rooms,* 1948

... blow hot, blow cold, the most aggravating man —Herman Wouk, *Marjorie Morningstar,* 1955

... this most stimulating, original, aggravating writer —*Times Literary Supp.,* 28 Sept. 1967

Aggravating as they were to Flaubert —William Styron, *This Quiet Dust and Other Writings,* 1982

Conclusion: the senses of *aggravate, aggravation,* and *aggravating* involving annoyance were strongly established well before John Stuart Mill and Richard Grant White found fault with them. They seem never to have been entirely vulgarisms, as some early commentators asserted, and there is no doubt that they continue well established in speech and writing today. They are standard. *Aggravate* in this sense is considerably less frequent in edited prose than in the "make worse" sense; *aggravation* is somewhat more likely to mean "irritation" than not; *aggravating* is seldom used except to express annoyance.

aggress   Heritage 1982 notes some current objection to *aggress* as psychology jargon even though the verb has long been in use. We have but slight evidence of the verb's questionable status:

> I asked him [Harvey Kurzman] if women could be funny in print. "Absolutely not," he said, "they don't aggress as well as men. (Author's note: his verb). . . ." —Janie T. Gaynor, *Harper's Weekly,* 14 June 1976

Our evidence shows that *aggress* has been more or less confined to contexts dealing with behavior and psychology during the past twenty years or so, but from the time of World War II well into the 1950s it was used primarily in political contexts. Here is a sample of the older usage; the last citation is probably partly psychological:

> [Von Ribbentrop] said it was not Germany who had aggressed against Poland —Sir Nevile Henderson, *Life,* 16 Oct. 1939

> The Peiping Politburo may decide neither to aggress further nor to negotiate —*N.Y. Times,* 4 Feb. 1951

> Westerners even aggressed against one another — Adlai E. Stevenson, *Call to Greatness,* 1954

> Yet it would appear from recent events that the users of force rarely think they are aggressing, and never admit they are —E. B. White, *New Yorker,* 15 Dec. 1956

> . . . stay away from those of lesser rank, for fear of being aggressed against —Norman Podhoretz, *Making It,* 1967

ago   See SINCE 2.

agree   1. Numerous handbooks from as long ago as 1917 to the 1980s tell us that *agree* takes various prepositions idiomatically in various senses. The prepositions *to, on,* and *with* are most frequently mentioned, but some sources—chiefly older ones—mention others. Here is a selection of typical constructions with various prepositions; of all these only *in* seems to be showing signs of age.

> . . . the company agreed to mediation —*Current Biography,* June 1953

> . . . members of the Swedish Academy failed to agree on a candidate —*Current Biography 1951*

> . . . they were always agreed on what movie they should see —Katherine Anne Porter, *Ladies' Home Jour.,* August 1971

> In 1831 the payment by France of outstanding claims . . . was agreed upon by treaty —Francis D. Wormuth, "The Vietnam War: The President versus the Constitution," 1968

> Christ, the boondocks of Oregon must agree with you, Stan —Lee Marvin, quoted in *Rolling Stone,* 21 Dec. 1972

> . . . it is difficult not to agree with Byron that Pope was profoundly moved when he wrote this poem — Bonamy Dobrée, *English Literature in the Early Eighteenth Century, 1700–1740,* 1959

> . . . he agreed with Lowell's opposition to the war — Eric F. Goldman, *Harper's,* January 1969

> Latin has a much better-developed system of adjective-noun concord. Every adjective must agree with its noun in three categories: number, gender, and case —H. A. Gleason, Jr., *An Introduction to Descriptive Linguistics,* rev. ed., 1961

> This agrees with seismic evidence —C. A. Cotton, *Geographical Jour.,* June 1953

> Four of the nation's leading white urbanologists . . . were agreed about the nature of the urban crisis — Allen B. Ballard, *Change,* March 1973

> . . . they agreed as to the unreadiness of Italian Somaliland for political independence —*Collier's Year Book,* 1949

> . . . no two of his admirers would be likely to agree in their selection —Bliss Perry, *The Pocket University,* 1924

> We agreed in our estimate of Beecham —*The Journals of Arnold Bennett,* ed. Frank Swinnerton, 1954

> . . . as so often in morals and in motivation, the upper and lower classes agree against the middle — Basil Cottle, in Michaels & Ricks 1980

Evans 1957 reminds us that *agree* is also commonly followed by a clause or an infinitive phrase:

> Traditional theories of esthetics agreed that coherent form emerges from the basic principle of fused elements —Frederick Goldman & Linda R. Burnett, *Need Johnny Read?,* 1971

> . . . Deerslayer agrees to surrender his claims —Richard Poirier, *A World Elsewhere,* 1966

2. In British use, the transitive *agree* often replaces the *agree on* or *agree to* of American English. Longman 1984, Chambers 1985, and Burchfield 1981 find these uses acceptable; Gowers (in Fowler 1965) accepts *agree* "agree on" but not *agree* "agree to." Frederick T. Wood, *English Verbal Idioms* (1964), thinks the use exists only in the passive; it is, however, also active. Here are some examples. Note that you can substitute either *agree on* or *agree to* in some of them, a fact which may suggest that Gowers's distinction is a bit overcareful.

> ". . . since this has to be, in its small way, a combined operation, we should want to agree the commander with you people." —Nevil Shute, *Most Secret,* 1945

> . . . and after much discussion the following articles were agreed —Sir Winston Churchill, *Closing the Ring,* 1951

> This no doubt was what Lord Salisbury agreed at the Little Bermuda conference —*New Statesman & Nation,* 17 Oct. 1953

> The price has yet to be agreed —*Times Literary Supp.,* 21 May 1970

> Some of the invaders returned to the Continent but others, after agreeing peace terms, twice raided the country south of the Thames —D. J. V. Fisher, *The Anglo-Saxon Age,* 1973

On a small job you will probably have to agree a set fee with your architect —John Bath, *Australian Home Beautiful,* June 1975

As the awaited seed catalogues arrive there are long discussions . . . with the housekeeper to agree vegetable and herb varieties —*This England,* Winter 1983

This use is rare but not unknown in the U.S.:

But as happens so often with U.S.-Japan conversations, the parties departed with different impressions of what had been agreed —Sol W. Sanders, *Business Week,* 23 Mar. 1981

agreement In this book *agreement* usually refers to either the agreement in number between the subject and verb of a sentence, or to the agreement in number between a pronoun and its antecedent. The term *concord,* used by some American and many British writers, can be considered a synonym; it turns up here and there in various articles, especially in the terms *notional concord* and *formal* (or *grammatical*) *concord.* There are, in fact, two kinds of agreement in English:

There are two kinds of concord: *formal concord,* in which there is harmony of form, and *notional concord,* in which there is harmony of meaning. In such a sentence as "Two boys were in the room," we have both formal and notional concord, the subject and the verb both being plural in both form and meaning. But sometimes we have notional concord only, as "None were left," where the subject, though singular in form, takes a plural verb because it is plural in meaning; and sometimes we have formal concord only, as "Everybody was late," where the subject, though plural in meaning, takes a singular verb because it is singular in form —Paul Roberts, *Understanding Grammar,* 1954

It appears that in early modern English the pull of notional agreement (or concord) was very strong. McKnight 1928, after quoting sentences from the 17th-century writers Francis Bacon, Thomas Browne, and John Milton, says:

The grammatical number in pronoun or verb is determined by the number, plural or singular, of the idea rather than by the grammatical number of the subject. . . . Obviously the earlier Elizabethan freedom had not yet been reduced to formal grammatical regularity.

The tug-of-war between notional and formal agreement underlies most of the agreement problems we deal with. There is one additional contributor to these problems. It is what Quirk et al. 1985 calls the *principle of proximity* (it is also called *attraction* and *blind agreement*)—the agreement of the verb with a noun or pronoun intervening between it and the subject. No doubt it likewise was in operation at an early time. Here is an instance written by Swift and cited by Strang 1970:

The common weight of these Halfpence are . . .

The verb *are* here matches *Halfpence* rather than *weight;* it appears in the sentence as printed in 1724. Strang tells us that in 1725 *are* was corrected to *is.* Quirk remarks that conflict between formal concord and attraction through proximity tends to increase with the distance between the noun head (true subject) and the

verb, and that proximity agreement is more often found in unplanned discourse than in writing.

Fries 1940 notes that gross violations of concord—use of a number-distinctive form that matches neither the formal nor the notional number of the subject—are found only in uneducated English. Sentences like

And them bass fiddles that's electrified, they're so loud, and the average man that plays 'em don't know how to turn 'em down —Birch Monroe, quoted in *Bluegrass Unlimited,* September 1982

that are typical of the speech of uneducated people, are seldom treated in books on usage and grammar, simply because everyone recognizes them as nonstandard. They will not receive much attention in this book either.

In the articles immediately following, we have broken the large subject of agreement into several smaller sections, which we hope you will find easier to refer to than one long treatment would be. In addition, many specific problems that usage writers treat separately have been put at their own places. See, for instance, AS WELL AS; EACH; MANY A; NONE; ONE OF THOSE WHO; THERE IS, THERE ARE; THEY, THEIR, THEM.

agreement: collective nouns See COLLECTIVE NOUNS.

agreement: indefinite pronouns The indefinite pronouns *anybody, anyone, each, either, everybody, everyone, neither, nobody, somebody, someone* share an interesting and often perplexing characteristic: they are usually grammatically singular and often notionally plural. The result is mixed usage with respect to number agreement with verbs and pronouns.

Bryant 1962 reports 25 studies of verb agreement with indefinite pronouns and finds both singular and plural verbs in use, but with the singular outnumbering the plural in the ratio of six to one. Curme 1931 and Quirk et al. 1985 both say the singular verb is usual; the singular verb also predominates in the Merriam-Webster files. Curme associates the occurrence of a plural verb after any of the indefinite pronouns (except *neither*) with older English (he cites *Tom Jones,* for instance). You are safe in assuming that the singular verb will be right.

Pronoun agreement has been more problematical. Conflict here revolves around the use of the pronouns *they, their, them, themselves* to refer to the indefinite pronouns. Such use, OED evidence shows, goes back to the 14th century. It has been disparaged as improper since the 18th century, however, when such grammarians as Lowth and Lindley Murray decreed the indefinite pronouns singular. Two considerations have strengthened the use of the plural pronoun in reference to a preceding indefinite. The first is notional concord; the indefinite pronouns are often notionally plural—some, indeed, more often than others—and in early modern English (before the 18th century) agreement is largely governed by notional concord. The other is the much-touted lack of a common-gender third person singular pronoun in English. How early *they, their, them* begins to be used as a common-gender singular is uncertain; perhaps Sir Kenelm Digby's use of *their* referring back to *one* in the middle of the 17th century (cited in the OED) represents such a use.

Let us look at a few examples from the letters of Thomas Gray, written in the second quarter of the 18th century, nearly a quarter century before Lowth and a half century before Murray. In the first he speaks of

"People of high quality" in Paris and of their devotion to gambling:

> Another thing is, there is not a House where they don't play, nor is any one at all acceptable, unless they do so too —21 Apr. 1739

Notional agreement seems to explain *they* in this instance, as it does in the next:

> ... if any body don't like their Commons, they send down into the Kitchen —31 Oct. 1734

In this letter Gray is complaining of not being written to; *them* might be interpreted here as a common-gender singular:

> What! to let any body reside three months at Rheims, and write but once to them? —18 Sept. 1739

At any rate the plural pronouns, whether through notional agreement or through being used as common-gender singulars, were well entrenched when Lowth issued his opinion, as his footnote attests; in it he corrects the translators of the King James Bible, Addison in *The Spectator,* and Richard Bentley, the scholar and critic. Lindley Murray has even more passages to correct, but their authors are unidentified. Lowth's tradition continued deep into the 19th century. Hodgson 1889, for instance, corrects the grammar of such seasoned practitioners as Elizabeth Gaskell, Jane Austen, Sydney Smith, John Ruskin, Charles Reade, and Leslie Stephen. (Our latter-day critics satisfy themselves with smaller game, reproving anonymous journalists, media personalities, and a mixed bag of educators and bureaucrats.) Hodgson also notes the problem of the common-gender singular; he cites a 19th-century grammarian named Bain, who approved the plural use. "Grammarians," writes Bain, "frequently call this construction an error, not reflecting that it is equally an error to apply 'his' to feminine subjects. The best writers (Defoe, Paley, Byron, Miss Austen, &c.) furnish examples of the use of the plural as a mode of getting out of the difficulty." The professor's tolerant attitude toward the plural did not satisfy Hodgson, however; he insisted that the gender difficulty should be removed by revision (the same advice set forth in such 20th-century sources as Bernstein 1962 and Bremner 1980).

Curme 1931 found the use of the plural to be typical of older literature and to have survived in popular speech; Bryant 1962 considers *they, their, them* established as the third person common-gender singular in all but the most formal usage.

The howls of the spiritual descendents of Lowth and Lindley Murray notwithstanding, the plural *they, their, them* with an indefinite pronoun as referent is in common standard use, both as common-gender singular and to reflect notional agreement. We give you a few examples below. Since many of the individual indefinite pronouns have received considerable comment, they have been treated separately (see ANYBODY, ANYONE; EACH; EVERYBODY, EVERYONE, for instance), and more examples of each will appear at those entries.

> ... nothing was done without a clatter, nobody sat still, and nobody could command attention when they spoke —Jane Austen, *Mansfield Park,* 1814

> Someone told me last night that they.... —Eleanor Roosevelt, "My Day," 1941, cited in H. L. Mencken, *The American Language, Supplement II,* 1948

> ... always look around ... to see if any of the girls playing in the street was her, but they never were — Bernard Malamud, *The Magic Barrel,* 1958

> Whenever anyone uses the pressure of usage to force you to accept the nonsensical and swallow the solecism, here's what to tell them —Safire 1984

agreement, notional   See NOTIONAL AGREEMENT, NOTIONAL CONCORD.

agreement: organizations considered as collective nouns   Quirk et al. 1985 says that collective nouns "differ from other nouns in taking as pronoun coreferents either singular *it* and relative *which* or plural *they* and relative *who* without change of number in the noun...." Copperud 1970 (under *collective nouns*) asserts, "Ordinarily, nouns for organizations considered as an entity, like *company,* are referred to by *it,* not *they....*"

Copperud is too dogmatic. Our evidence shows that names of companies and other organizations function like other collective nouns, being sometimes singular and sometimes plural (see also COLLECTIVE NOUNS). A few examples of the singular construction:

> And Harvard may consider itself very fortunate — *President's Report, Harvard University,* 1950–1951

> ... until GM was tooling up for its 1940 models — *American Mercury,* May 1953

Some examples of the plural:

> The D.A.R. are going to do another pageant —Sinclair Lewis, *Dodsworth,* 1929

> The NBS now admit that they can confirm —*New Republic,* 11 May 1953

> The announcement by the University of Oklahoma Press that they are reissuing —*The Pleasures of Publishing,* August–September 1954

> I wrote to the Pinkerton Tobacco Company.... Mr. E. D. Wanamaker, their president —Curtis I. Kohn, in Safire 1982

And like other collective nouns, organizations sometimes appear with a singular verb but a plural pronoun in reference:

> ... M-G-M ... hopes to sell their records in 5,000 key stores —*Time,* 24 Feb. 1947

> ... the National Bureau of Standards has not been sufficiently objective, because they discount entirely the play of the market place —*New Republic,* 13 Apr. 1953

> Chrysler is the only American car maker who builds their convertible from start to finish —cited by William Safire, *N.Y. Times Mag.,* 15 June 1986

It seems reasonable to expect that use of the plural pronoun, even after the singular verb, will continue to flourish as large corporations, through their advertising and public-relations releases, try to present a more human and less monolithic face to the public.

agreement, pronoun: nouns joined by *and, or*
When the 18th-century grammarians were laying down the law of grammatical agreement, Lowth 1775—in a footnote—made the statement that the "conjunction

disjunctive," *or,* requires agreement in the singular number. To illustrate his point, he reprinted this sentence:

> A man may see a metaphor, or an allegory, in a picture, as well as read them (it) in a description — Joseph Addison, *Dialogues upon the Usefulness of Ancient Medals,* 1702

Lowth, of course, was correcting Addison's *them* to *it.* It was a general practice of the 18th-century grammarians to give examples that contravened their rules, for purposes of correction; the practice has for us moderns the weakness of leaving us wondering whether anybody did, in fact, follow the rules the grammarians laid down. Addison, one of the master stylists of English prose who died in 1719 and never knew that grammarians a half century later would make frequent use of him as a bad example, was simply following notional agreement, as everyone did before the middle of the 18th century. Notional agreement did not disappear with the preachments of Lowth and his contemporaries, moreover, as a perusal of articles in this book will demonstrate.

When singular nouns are joined by *and,* notional agreement will not often clash with grammatical agreement (but see some of the examples at EACH):

> One goaded professor once denied that two & two make four, merely because a pro-Adler student said they did — *Time,* 17 Feb. 1952

> ... in a gentle stupefaction of mind, & very tolerable health of body hitherto. If they last, I shall not much complain — Thomas Gray, letter, 5 Mar. 1766

But singular nouns joined by *or* are more likely to be affected by notional agreement at the expense of grammatical agreement (as Lowth well knew but could not accept):

> We shall be pleased to send a free specimen copy ... to a friend or relative on receipt of their address — advt., *London Calling,* 22 July 1954

> ... no lady or gentleman would so far forget themselves — George Bernard Shaw, *Plays Pleasant and Unpleasant,* 1898 (in Jespersen)

> How quickly the American student makes friends with a book or a man and treats them as if they were his contemporaries — *Time,* 2 Aug. 1954

> We would soon become a nation of sleepless neurotics if the average man or woman was not endowed with courage, some common sense, and the ability to resist the continual assaults against their peace of mind — Harrison Smith, *Saturday Rev.,* 30 Jan. 1954

> ... a man or a woman would come in here, glance around, find smiles and pleasant looks waiting for them, then wave and sit down by themselves — Doris Lessing (in Reader's Digest 1983)

In the next example the author starts out with the *him or her* prescribed by grammatical agreement, but then abandons it for the less unwieldy plural pronouns of notional agreement:

> If you have a young brother or sister of, say, fifteen years old or so, think that you have him or her before you and that you are trying to explain the point of your article to them and at the same time to prevent them from thinking what an ass you are to be wast-

ing their time — R. B. McKerrow, *Rev. of English Studies,* XVI, 1940

> No man or woman can hesitate to give what they have — Woodrow Wilson, speech, 17 Sept. 1918 (in H. L. Mencken, *The American Language,* abridged, 1963)

Mencken notes that this is the line as Wilson spoke it, according to the papers reporting it. But when it was published in his *Selected ... Addresses,* the professional Wilson emended "they have" to "he or she has."

In our view, singular nouns joined by *and* will seldom present a problem; notional and grammatical agreement will join to call for a plural pronoun. When singular nouns are joined by *or,* notional and grammatical agreement will likely conflict. It would appear that the farther the pronoun is from the set of nouns referred to, the more likely it is to be plural in accordance with notional agreement. And the farther the pronoun is from its referent, the less likely it is to be noticed by some zealous spiritual descendant of Bishop Lowth. You should feel free to use a plural pronoun where it sounds right and natural to you, even though some stickler for grammatical agreement may spot it. Where it does not seem natural, stick to the singular. Ask yourself who was the greater writer—Addison or Lowth?

agreement, pronoun: singular nouns with plural pronouns   See THEY, THEIR, THEM.

agreement, subject-verb: a bunch of the boys

> A bunch of the boys were whooping it up in the Malamute saloon — Robert W. Service, "The Shooting of Dan McGrew," 1907

The usage question is this: should the verb be *were* or *was* whooping it up? The answer, say the experts (Kilpatrick in *Pittsburgh Press,* 11 Aug. 1985, Jacques Barzun in Safire 1982, *Winners & Sinners,* 5 Aug. 1983), is *were.* Why? There are several reasons. First, we can see two of the three forces that chiefly determine agreement—proximity and notional agreement—pulling in the direction of the plural. Second, we have the plain sense of the subject-verb relation: the boys whoop, not the bunch. And if *boys* is the real subject of the sentence, then the phrase *a bunch of* is functioning essentially as a modifier—it is, in fact, very similar to what many modern grammarians call a *predeterminer.* Here are a few more examples:

> A rash of stories in the Chicago media have reported —cited by James J. Kilpatrick, *Pittsburgh Press Sunday Mag.,* 11 Aug. 1985

> Yet the flock of acolytes surrounding each *jefe* are not expected to justify their servility — Alan Riding, *Distant Neighbors: A Portrait of the Mexicans,* 1985

> A crew of Pyrates are driven — Jonathan Swift, *Gulliver's Travels,* 1726 (in McKnight 1928)

> A set of writers have lately sprung up in England — *Columbia Mag.,* March 1787 (in Shopen & Williams 1980)

> ... a host of people who are interested in language — Charlton Laird, Foreword to Finegan 1980

> A trio of genies are — Bryant Gumble, cited from a television broadcast in *Counterforce,* June 1983

... a class of sentences which are superficially parallel —Brian Joseph, *Language,* June 1980

Thus, only a fraction of such deposits are actually insured —*Consumer Reports,* January 1983

Moreover, the preponderance of users view transparency as blue-sky technology —Eugene Lowenthal, *Datamation,* August 1982

Though experts and common sense agree that the plural verb is natural and correct, actual usage still shows a few holdouts for the singular verb. Except for the first—Lindley Murray perhaps was too conscious of the grammatical subject—the examples below may be the result of nervous copy editors or indecision on the part of the writers:

... many errors have been committed: a number of which is subjoined, as a further caution —Lindley Murray 1795 (but the errors are subjoined, not a number)

... a set of numbered rods, developed by John Napier, which was used for calculating —Ellen Richman, *Spotlight on Computer Literacy,* 1982

... a neat, little package of words that describes Bird's play —Gerry Finn, *Morning Union* (Springfield, Mass.), 29 Jan. 1985 (but the words describe, not the package)

... are run through a set of computer algorithms that rearranges them —*The Economist,* 17 May 1986 (the algorithms rearrange)

When you have a collecting noun phrase *(a bunch of)* before a plural noun *(the boys),* the sense will normally be plural and so should the verb.

See also NUMBER 1; ONE OF THOSE WHO.

agreement, subject-verb: compound subjects 1. *Joined by "and."* Before the 18th-century grammarians undertook to prune the exuberant growth of English, no one seems to have worried whether two or more singular nouns joined by a copulative conjunction *(and)* took a plural or a singular verb. Writers of the 16th and 17th centuries used whatever verb sounded best and did not trouble themselves about grammatical agreement. "Scoffing and girding is their daily bread," wrote Gabriel Harvey in his 16th-century dispute with Thomas Nashe and Robert Greene (cited in McKnight 1928). Shakespeare could write "art and practice hath enriched" in *Measure for Measure* and in *Much Ado About Nothing* "All disquiet, horror, and perturbation follows her" (both cited in McKnight). The King James Bible at Daniel 5:14 has "light and understanding and excellent wisdom is found in thee" (cited in Hall 1917).

So when Lowth 1763 set his rule down, he was well aware of mixed usage. He favored the plural but allowed for the singular "sometimes," using James Greenwood's earlier analysis that the singular verb "is understood as applied to each of the preceding terms"; thus, we find in the Bible:

Sand, and salt, and a mass of iron, is easier to bear, than a man without understanding —Ecclesiasticus 22:18 (Douay), 1609

Priestley 1798 takes a different approach but reaches a similar conclusion:

It is a rule, that two distinct subjects of an affirmation require the verb to be in the plural number. . . .

But, notwithstanding this, if the subject of the affirmation be nearly related, the verb is rather better in the singular number. *Nothing but the* marvellous and supernatural hath *any charms for them.*

Priestley's approach is reflected in some 20th-century commentators (Vizetelly 1906, Barzun 1975, Freeman 1983, who quotes Fowler), but where our moderns allow the singular verb with compound singular nouns close in thought, Priestley rather insisted on it, quoting David Hume's "His politeness and obliging behaviour were changed" and saying "*was* would have read better."

The insistence that only the plural verb is correct seems to have begun with a writer named Philip Withers in 1788 (cited in Leonard 1929); his attack on the singular verb was based entirely on logic. He appears to have influenced several later grammarians including Lindley Murray 1795. Murray assembled his grammar largely from Lowth and Priestley, but in this instance he insists on the plural verb, mentioning Lowth's exceptions but finding them "evidently contrary to the first principles of grammar."

Modern grammarians are not so insistent. Curme 1931 and Quirk et al. 1985 agree that in modern practice the plural verb prevails after coordinate singular nouns with *and:*

While Keats and Chapman were at Heidelberg —Myles na gCopaleen (Flann O'Brien), *The Best of Myles,* 1968

... Trixie La Monte, Margie White, Florence Leeper, Donna Rogers, Doris Hudson, Sandra Lee and Rita Green, who even at the moment you are fascinatedly reading this are probably catching their deaths of colds by denuding themselves hourly somewhere —George Jean Nathan, *The Entertainment of a Nation,* 1942

... the streak of sentimentality and the lack of true originality which mark much of his creative writing —*New Yorker,* 18 Nov. 1985

... the bitterness and heartache that fill the world —Frank Sullivan, *A Rock in Every Snowball,* 1946

If the Arab and Israeli left are to develop a common program —Noam Chomsky, *Columbia Forum,* Winter 1969

But both recognize that when the nouns form "a collective idea" or "a oneness of idea" (the terms are Curme's), the singular verb is appropriate—notional agreement prevails in such cases.

... the end of all the privacy and propriety which was talked about at first —Jane Austen, *Mansfield Park,* 1814

I think the time involved and the red tape is one of the biggest problems —Richard L. DeChant, *Modern Industry,* February 1967

Brinsley, whose education and maintenance was a charge on the rates of his native county —Flann O'Brien, *At Swim-Two-Birds,* 1939

The name and address of the grocery was painted on the slats —E. L. Doctorow, *Loon Lake,* 1979

Time and patience is necessary —*Cats Mag.,* December 1981

The News Service's depth and scope represents the best in American journalism —advt., cited by William Safire, *N.Y. Times Mag.*, 1 May 1983

Curme also notes an exception to the required plural verb in a way that sounds much like Greenwood and Lowth: "when each of a number of singular noun subjects is considered separately, the verb is in the singular." He cites Emerson:

A fever, a mutilation, a cruel disappointment, a loss of wealth, a loss of friends, seems at the moment untold loss.

The same principle appears to operate in these cases:

Every legislator, every doctor, and every citizen needs to recognize —Ronald Reagan, *Abortion and the Conscience of the Nation,* 1984

The power of the algorithm, and the phonological approach to spelling, is strengthened when the error list is examined —Richard E. Hodges & E. Hugh Rudorf, *Elementary English,* May 1965

We have seen so far that in present-day English coordinate singular nouns compounded by *and* (or *and* understood) usually are followed by a plural verb. The singular verb is appropriate when the nouns form a unitary notion or when they refer to a single person (as in "My friend and colleague says"). It is also possible to intend that the singular verb be construed with each noun separately; when such a construction is intended, it should perhaps be accentuated by distributive adjectives (as *each, every*) or punctuation. You should not forget that some people who evaluate other people's language have no idea the singular verb can ever be used, and even those whose understanding does encompass this possibility can disagree over what is a single idea—Baker 1770 did not like "what your Justice and Honour require" and Safire in 1983 did not like "The News Service's depth and scope represents. . . ." Readers might well be divided on the acceptability of this example:

The consultant and evaluation team has by this time converted the application task list —*Datamation,* February 1982

2. *Joined by "or" (or "nor").* Lowth 1762 says that singular nouns joined by *or* take the singular verb; Priestley 1761 agrees; Leonard 1929 notes that Philip Withers in *Aristarchus* (1788) raked the Scottish rhetorician Hugh Blair over the coals for using a plural verb with nouns joined by *or.* Quirk et al. 1985 notes that *or* is notionally disjunctive and that the singular verb is the rule.

. . . if the average man or woman was not endowed with courage —Harrison Smith, *Saturday Rev.,* 30 Jan. 1954

. . . neither she nor any other of the book's characters has endurance —E. L. Doctorow, *N.Y. Times Book Rev.,* 25 Aug. 1985

In English, neither chicken nor beef nor soup has formal gender —William Safire, *N.Y. Times Mag.,* 10 Aug. 1986

Quirk further notes that when plural nouns are so joined, the plural verb is used, and when nouns of different number are so joined, the principle of proximity tends to be called in, and the verb usually agrees with the nearest noun. Freeman 1983 makes the same point.

However strong the disjunctive notion that Quirk finds attached to *or* (and *nor*) may be, there is abundant evidence from the past—and some from modern writers—that the notion of plurality of the subjects can at times overbalance that of disjunctiveness. Not only did Withers roast Blair for using plural, but Lindley Murray 1795 accompanied his rule with several counterexamples using the plural, their authors tastefully suppressed. Curme 1931 notes that the negative *neither . . . nor* often contains a plural idea under the negative; he cites several instances from the 15th century to the 20th, including these:

Neither search nor labor are necessary —Samuel Johnson, *The Idler,* No. 44

Neither he nor his lady were at home —George Washington, diary, 2 Dec. 1789

. . . neither the friendship nor the sorrow seem so profound —Robert Bridges, *Forum,* May 1923

More recently we have some unattributed examples collected by Kilpatrick 1984 for censure: "Neither price nor menu description are a fair guide" and "Neither Johnny nor his teacher have mastered the art of writing."

Curme also finds examples with *or* with no negative attached; these, he opines, probably come from the author's feeling that the statement applies in all cases, even though applicable to only one or two at a time. He instances these extracts:

My life or death are equal both to me —John Dryden

A drama or an epic fill the mind —Matthew Arnold, *Essays in Criticism*

Acting, singing, or reciting are forbidden them —H. G. Wells

What are honor or dishonor to her? —Henry James

The notion determining the agreement in these examples often seems to be "this or that or both (or all)." We have similar instances among our citations:

But it's when sex or scurrility are used for their own sakes that they are in bad taste —Flannery O'Connor, letter, 10 Mar. 1956

In summary, compound singular nouns with *or* or *nor* are supposed to take a singular verb and in current use usually do. The plural verb is most likely to appear where the notion of plurality is suggested by negative construction or when the writer is thinking of "this or that or both."

3. *Quasi-coordination by words like "with," "along with," "together with" or by punctuation.* Quirk et al. 1985 points out that when a singular noun is joined to another by a quasi-coordinator (the term is Quirk's) like *with, rather than, as well as,* etc., grammatical concord calls for the singular verb. Murray 1795 implies the same view of things through his examples but does not attempt to articulate a rule. Here are some examples:

. . . that tale in prose . . . which was published at Christmas, with nine others, by us, has reached a second edition —Charles Lamb, letter, 7 June 1809

. . . the Petterell with the rest of the Egyptian Squadron was off the Isle of Cyprus —Jane Austen, letter, 1 Nov. 1800

Quasi-coordinators are semantically equivalent to coordinators (as *and*), notes Quirk, and thus notional concord can interfere with grammatical concord:

> This word, with all those of the same race, are of uncertain etymology —Samuel Johnson, *A Dictionary of the English Language,* 1755

> ... *A piece of cake,* along with *cakewalk,* were expressions used by Royal Air Force Pilots —Safire 1984

Parenthetical insertions are also separate in theory and should not affect grammatical agreement. Parenthetical insertions may be set off by commas, dashes, or parentheses:

> ... their management—and their companies' balance sheets—has suffered —Margaret Yao, *Wall Street Jour.,* 11 June 1980

Commas are the weakest way of setting off a parenthetical element that is not otherwise signaled; consequently, they may be thought not to be setting off a parenthesis at all:

> They suggest that it is not just the world, and civilization as we know it, that are going to the dogs —Howard 1984

You would think, however, that actual parentheses () would clearly remind a writer that the material included is not to affect the number agreement of the sentence. But real writers forget—even writers on language and grammar.

> Southern Black English (and some white dialects influenced by it) have *bossman* as an elaboration on *boss* —J. L. Dillard, *American Talk,* 1976

> The occurrence of *phenomena, criteria, strata* with *is* or *was* shows up the careless writer, even though *agenda* (and *data* for some) have achieved the singular number —Barzun 1975

> The very complex gravity field of Mars (and the simple one of Venus) have been mapped —John S. Lewis, in *The New Solar System,* ed. J. Kelly Beatty et al., 1982

See also AS WELL AS.

agreement, subject-verb: miscellaneous problems

1. *Titles.* Curme 1931 notes that titles of written works are treated as singular even if the title is plural. Our evidence generally confirms this:

> ... Shakespeare's *Sonnets* has remained the exception —A. Kent Hieatt, *PMLA,* October 1983

Pronoun reference, however, may be plural in notional agreement:

> I have been reading the *Lives of the Poets* for thirty years, and can testify that in all that time I have never known the day or the hour when I failed to find interest, instruction, amusement, somewhere in their pages —John Wain, *Samuel Johnson,* 1974

2. *Amounts of money, periods of time, etc.* "The principle of notional concord accounts for the common use of a singular with subjects that are plural noun phrases of quantity or measure. The entity expressed by the noun phrase is viewed as a single unit ... ," says Quirk et al. 1985. Quirk appends such examples as

> Ten dollars is all I have left.

> Two miles is as far as they can walk.

> Two thirds of the area is under water.

Quirk's observations are consistent with the evidence in Curme 1931. Much earlier Fitzedward Hall, in an article excoriating William Cullen Bryant (published in 1880 and reprinted in Bolton & Crystal 1969), had taken time in a footnote to prefer Bryant's "Eight dollars a month is the common rate" to T. B. Macaulay's "Four shillings a week, therefore, were ... fair agricultural wages." Hall notes that Macaulay was not consistent—he also used the singular verb: "The ambassador told his master that six thousand guineas was the smallest gratification that could be offered to so important a minister."

Copperud 1970, 1980 also recommends the singular verb.

3. *Subject and complement of different number.* People are often uncertain about the number of a linking verb in sentences like "Potatoes are a vegetable." The uncertainty lies, says Curme 1931, in the uncertainty a copula (linking verb) creates about whether the noun before or the noun after is the true subject. Curme goes on to say, "The present tendency is to avoid a decision on this perplexing point by regulating the number of the copula by a mere formal principle—namely, as the nominative before the copula is often the subject, it has become the rule to place the copula in accord with it, whether it be a subject or a predicate." Copperud 1970, 1980 cites several of his sources as agreeing to what Curme observes to have become customary—to treat the first noun as the subject. The custom seems not to have changed over the last 50 years and more: the noun before the verb governs it.

agreement, subject-verb: one or more, one in (out of)_____.

1. Bernstein 1962, 1977, Freeman 1983, and Bryson 1984 remind us that the phrase *one or more* is plural in meaning and should take a plural verb; Bernstein 1958 asserts the same of *one or two.* What relevant evidence of these constructions we have in our files agrees with the commentators:

> One or two of the red brick and green copper pavilions ... still remain —Gerald Weissman, *The Woods Hole Cantata,* 1975

> ... one or more of whose members have seen fit to order the removal —Mark Van Doren, *American Scholar,* Autumn 1951

In a majority of our instances, however, those phrases do not govern a verb.

2. Chambers 1985, Heritage 1969, 1982, Longman 1984, and Simon 1980 agree that the phrase *one in* (a larger number) or *one out of* (a larger number) should take the singular verb. Our evidence for this construction is not plentiful, but most of the modern examples we have found are either being held up as items to be corrected because they occur with a plural verb, or they simply occur with a plural verb and are not noticed. This appears to be a case where actual usage is more often governed by notional agreement than by grammatical agreement: the writers who use the construction realize that it represents a statistical proportion and thus stands for a multitude of individuals. A few examples of the plural verb:

> One out of ten soldiers, he reported, are unable to recognize an enemy on a dark starlit night at a distance of only ten yards —*Science News Letter,* 14 Oct. 1944

> Nationwide, an estimated one in four adults are functionally illiterate —Gannett Foundation news release, cited in *New Yorker,* 22 July 1985

> ONE IN THREE PUPILS GET POOR EDUCA-TION —headline in *The Times* (London), cited in *New Yorker,* 28 Jan. 1985

Our earliest example with a singular verb is from Jane Austen; in it the singular notion is probably reinforced by the negative:

> . . . there is not one in a hundred of either sex who is not taken in when they marry —*Mansfield Park,* 1814

Jespersen 1909–49 cites a different passage from *Mansfield Park* without a preceding negative and a bit of John Ruskin's *Fors Clavigera,* 1871–84 with a negative. It may appear from our citations that the singular is the minority usage in the modern era, but the citations are really too few to permit an assured judgment on the matter. Clearly, at the very least, the singular is still in respectable use:

> One in four in our labor force is organized —*New Republic,* 15 Dec. 1952

> . . . 1 in 4 teachers in the Southeast was undecided compared with only 1 in 8 in the Northeast —*NEA Jour.,* December 1964

agreement, subject-verb: the principle of proximity Quirk et al. 1985 describes the principle of proximity (also called *attraction* and *blind agreement*) as the tendency of a verb to agree with a closely preceding noun or noun phrase rather than with the subject. Quirk further observes:

> Conflict between grammatical concord and attraction through proximity tends to increase with the distance between the noun phrase head of the subject and the verb, for example when the postmodifier is lengthy or when an adverbial or a parenthesis intervenes between the subject and the verb. Proximity concord occurs mainly in unplanned discourse. In writing it will be corrected to grammatical concord if it is noticed.

A couple of instances collected from the 1954 Army-McCarthy hearings in Pyles 1979 will serve as examples:

> The filing of the false, fraudulent charges are a complete contradiction —Joseph McCarthy

> . . . as far as coddling Communists are concerned — Roy Cohn

And more recently:

> The reaction that I have taken to these steps are appropriate —Jimmy Carter, quoted in *N.Y. Times,* 14 Feb. 1980

Our evidence for proximity agreement suggests that Quirk's observations are correct; we find it operating

mostly in unplanned discourse, such as speech or personal letters. Instances do, however, sneak past the eyes of copy editors and proofreaders and reach print. Bernstein 1962 and Simon 1980 cite a few examples. We have even found a few in the works of those who write on usage:

> . . . the word *regards* have no Nominative —Baker 1770

> His system of citing examples of the best authorities, of indicating etymology, and pronunciation, are still followed by lexicographers —Howard 1984

It should be noted that proximity does not always influence a singular verb to be plural; sometimes the proximate noun is singular and the subject plural:

> And the words that close the last story in the book has the music of a requiem —Padraic Colum, Introduction to James Joyce, *Dubliners* (Modern Library edition), 1926

> You, the educated consumer, is our best customer — advt., cited in Bernstein 1977

Proximity agreement may pass in speech and other forms of unplanned discourse; in print it will be considered an error. And it is one that is probably easier to fall into than you might expect—let the examples above be a warning.

agreement, subject-verb: *what*-clauses

> What is frightening is to discover how easily we can be misled —Alden Whitman, *Harper's,* April 1972

> What officials have done is essentially this —Frederick N. Robinson, *General Electric Investor,* Summer 1971

The two clauses beginning with *what* in the examples are the subjects of their sentences. The pronoun *what* in the first example is the subject of the clause; in the second, it is the object. The usage problem with these *what*-clauses is primarily the number of the verb in the main sentence, and, when *what* is the subject of the clause, the number of the verb in the clause. Copperud 1970, 1980 reports various long discussions of the subject, mostly from different perspectives. From the welter of analysis and opinions he discerns one clear point of agreement: *what* is not necessarily singular in construction but can be plural. Commentators not covered by Copperud tend to agree, except Simon 1980, who has to go back to Partridge 1942 for support in requiring the singular. The best discussion of this question is in Bryant 1962; the citations in the Merriam-Webster files gathered since 1962 generally confirm the findings of the studies she reports.

The first point to observe is that mixed usage occurs in only a limited number of cases, namely when the complement of the verb of the main sentence is plural. In the great majority of *what*-clause sentences in our files, everything is singular, and there are no problems.

When the *what* in the *what*-clause is the object of the clause and when the predicate noun following the main verb is plural, it tends to pull the verb with it. Bryant reports the plural verb favored by about three to one over the singular. Here are examples of both kinds:

> What we need and crave are shows as handsomely preposterous as . . . the kind George Edwards used to

put on at Max's Gaiety —George Jean Nathan, *The Theatre Book of the Year, 1946–1947*

What we need in government, in education, in business . . . are men who seek to understand issues in all their complexity —J. W. McSwiney, *Annual Report, The Mead Corp.*, 1970

What we are getting is old answers to old questions —Daniel Boorstin, *Look,* 20 Aug. 1968 (Perrin & Ebbitt 1972)

When *what* is the subject of the clause, and the *what*-clause is the subject of the sentence, things get a bit more complicated. Perrin & Ebbitt 1972 points out that usage is consistent when the *what*-clause, linking verb, and predicate nominative agree in number—being either all singular or all plural. Bernstein 1958, 1962, 1965 and Johnson 1982 concur and urge writers to try for such a consistency. Simon 1980, however, wants only the singular and reproduces the following sentence for criticism, though it illustrates the consistent plural:

What *have* [Rubins's italics] surfaced are similes, viscous streams of them —Josh Rubins, *Harvard Mag.*

The consistent singular is actually the most common case:

What is absent from the present book is any attempt to think in terms of practical problems —*Times Literary Supp.,* 22 Oct. 1971

Mixed usage occurs when the subject *what* in the clause is singular but the predicate nominative is plural. In such cases the main verb tends to be plural:

What bothers Professor Teeter most are the guesses, hunches, speculations, and fancies in which many language shamans like me indulge —Safire 1984

What is needed from the left wing of university reform are programs that begin to specify the steps of change —John Gagnon, *Change,* October 1971

Bryant further points out that when the complement consists of two or more predicate nouns, the verb is plural if the nouns are plural and singular if the nouns are singular:

What impresses them are planes and divisions and ships —Harry S. Truman, radio address, 26 June 1953 (in Bryant)

What is most striking about Johnson is the vigor of his ideas, the variety of his knowledge, the forcefulness of his conversation —J. C. Mendenhall, *English Literature, 1650–1800,* 1940 (in Bryant)

When the complement of the main verb is a *that*-clause the verb is singular:

What does follow is that the issue is susceptible to rational methods —Phillip H. Scribner, *AAUP Bulletin,* September 1971

Clearly usage is mixed in these complex sentences, but you need not regard *what* as inflexibly singular. Dwight Bolinger notes in a letter reprinted in Safire 1984 that in the influence of the plural predicate noun over the main verb English is similar to French and Spanish. It is desirable to be consistent, but, in an area where notional agreement appears to hold absolute sway, it is perhaps even more desirable to be natural.

a half, a half a See HALF 2.

ahold Copperud 1970 and Bernstein 1958 both label *ahold* dialectal (as do several dictionaries) and discourage its use in standard prose (Bernstein found it in a *New York Times* article). The Dictionary of American Regional English lists it, with attestations from several states: Florida, Arkansas, Georgia, Maryland, West Virginia, Kentucky, Missouri, New York, New Jersey, Ohio, Illinois. Citations in Merriam-Webster files suggest Michigan, Wisconsin, Massachusetts, Alabama, Texas, and California as well. If it is indeed dialectal, it is well spread around (we have it in a few British sources also).

The idiom we are discussing here most often follows *get* (*catch, have, seize, take, lay,* and *grasp* as well) and is regularly followed by *of.* When *hold* is followed by a different preposition—*on, upon, over*—it always takes the indefinite article; only with *of* is the article idiomatically omitted. The majority idiom, then, is (to take the most common verb) *get hold of;* the minority or dialectal idiom is *get ahold of,* with the article separate from or attached to *hold.* The OED (under *get* 13b) shows the idiom as *to get (a) hold of;* no nonstandard label is appended. Its earliest citations, however, lack the article.

Part of the difficulty with *ahold* is simply the way it is styled in writing or print. When the article is separated from *hold,* the expression is not especially noticeable, as in these examples (the first two British):

. . . signal-towers improved the east coast defences; a stronger hold was taken of Wales —Jacquetta & Christopher Hawkes, *Prehistoric Britain,* 1949

. . . until you can get a hold of the splinter —Peter Heaton, *Cruising,* 1952

A reporter got a hold of this tax business —Sally Rand, quoted in Studs Terkel, *Hard Times,* 1970

But when *a* is attached to *hold,* with or without a hyphen, the expression calls more attention to itself:

If you can't get ahold of a voltmeter —Len Feldman, *Rolling Stone,* 6 June 1974

I got ahold of the dean at Miles College —E. D. Nixon, quoted in Studs Terkel, *Hard Times,* 1970

We found this export control business was a nasty nettle to grasp ahold of —Gerald C. Smith, quoted in *Wall Street Jour.,* 30 Nov. 1984

The pronunciation spelling *aholt* is also used:

I swum to de stern uv it, en tuck aholt —Mark Twain, *Huckleberry Finn,* 1884 (Dictionary of American Regional English)

I must admit some of the birds tried to get aholt of me —Colin MacInnes, *Absolute Beginners,* 1959

Shot said that when he died, he grabbed aholt of him . . . and he like to have never got away —Flannery O'Connor, letter, 11 Jan. 1958

Bremner 1980 thinks *ahold* does not exist except as "an illiterate provincialism." Recent evidence suggests otherwise; although it still appears primarily in transcriptions of speech, it does turn up in edited prose:

Sometimes, if you could get ahold of a representative who was a regular guy —Norman Mailer, *The Naked and the Dead,* 1948

The words [*good stuff*] suggest something gratifyingly material, whereas in baseball they describe that which, ideally, one cannot get ahold of —Roy Blount, Jr., *Sports Illustrated,* 18 May 1970

The expression is frequently used in the sense of "get in touch with":

"I'll get ahold of Blatty to put his nomination on the agenda tomorrow." —Leon Uris, *Saturday Evening Post,* 30 May 1964

I got ahold of General Cushman —Richard Helms, 2 Aug. 1973 (U.S. Senate Watergate hearings)

Although *ahold* usually has a literal meaning, it does occasionally appear in figurative uses:

I'm most happy when I'm three and a half or four months into a picture. . . . I'm over the worst hurdle of it. I feel I've got ahold of it; I'm the boss —Carolyn Wyeth, quoted by Richard Meryman, *N.Y. Times Mag.,* 7 Jan. 1970

Okay, girl, get ahold of yourself —Christina Ferrare De Lorean, *People,* 29 Nov. 1982

But it is primarily a spoken construction, and its most frequent appearance is in the transcription of speech:

As soon as Lyndon got ahold of the damn thang — Sam Houston Johnson, quoted by Larry L. King, *Harper's,* April 1970

When Rosalynn gets ahold of you, it's going to be even worse —Jimmy Carter, quoted by B. Drummond Ayres, Jr., *N.Y. Times Mag.,* 3 June 1979

. . . success is not such a fabulous goal. It's like air— you can't get ahold of it —Tammy Grimes, quoted by Kristin McMurran, *People,* 2 Feb. 1981

It felt good getting ahold of it —Darryl Strawberry, quoted by William Nack, *Sports Illustrated,* 23 Apr. 1984

In summary, *hold* when followed by *of* and preceded by *get* or another verb in the idiom of the majority of English speakers and writers from Shakespeare to the present is not accompanied by *a: get hold of.* Since the late 19th century, the minority idiom with *a* seems to have been gaining in respectability, but it is still primarily a spoken rather than a written form. When transcribed from speech, it is generally styled as one word, *ahold.*

aim   **1.** *Aim to, aim at.* Copperud 1970, 1980 reports some uncertainty about the status of *aim* followed by *to* and the infinitive. Fowler 1926 plumps for the *aim at* construction, but does not disparage *aim to,* calling it good American (he notes that Emerson was fond of it) even though not good English. Fowler's reviser, Sir Ernest Gowers, notes (in Fowler 1965) that *aim to* has become established in British English, citing an MP. In America, Bernstein 1965 fears that some think *aim to* has too much of "the dust of the frontier" about it, but Shaw 1970 inexplicably relegates the *aim at* expression to "colloquial or dialectal" status. The following discussion should clarify the present situation.
Dialectal status: the Dictionary of American Regional English finds *aim to* formerly widespread in American speech but now chiefly limited to the Southern and south Midland areas; in print, however, it does not appear to be receding. The construction appears to

have originated in England—the OED Supplement cites John Marston in 1602 and John Selden in 1649; it is attested in America from Anne Bradstreet in 1650 (Dictionary of American English). Foster 1968 says the expression was current in England in the 18th century, instancing Samuel Johnson:

They pleas'd their Age, and did not aim to mend — *Prologue Spoken by Mr. Garrick, at the Opening of the Theatre in Drury Lane,* 1747

He also quotes an old rhyme:

Gamesters and puss alike doe watch,
And plaie with those they aim to catch.

Foster opines that the construction survived in the U.S. after declining in British use, and was then reintroduced from the U.S. in the 20th century. It is clearly flourishing on both sides of the Atlantic now:

. . . Mr. Trudeau aims for the jugular as often as he aims to please —Herbert Mitgang, *N.Y. Times Book Rev.,* 12 July 1981

The communes aim to supply these —Margaret Mead, *Barnard Alumnae,* Winter 1971

. . . a format aimed to give pleasure to hand and eye —*Times Literary Supp.,* 19 Feb. 1971

. . . this provision aims to ensure on all future occasions the kind of independent reporting which the United Nations got —Dean Acheson in *The Pattern of Responsibility,* ed. McGeorge Bundy, 1951

. . . we aimed to be absolutely ready from May 15 onwards —Sir John Hunt & Sir Edmund Hillary, *Geographical Jour.,* December 1953

The stringent sedition laws thus aimed to mobilize a completely united population —Oscar Handlin, *The American People in the Twentieth Century,* 1954

"I want to know if you aim to use steel spurs." — Burl Ives, *Wayfaring Stranger,* 1952

It aims to drive the Europeans and all other foreigners out —L. S. B. Leakey, *Mau Mau and the Kikuyu,* 1952

. . . aiming to say something about the soul —C. Day Lewis, *The Grand Manner,* 1952

. . . aimed to link the fortunes of an individual family with actual text-book events —Leslie Rees, *Towards An Australian Drama,* 1953

Aim at, however, has not dropped out of use:

. . . a recent story aimed at helping French youths to see the U.S.A. —David Butwin, *Saturday Rev.,* 26 Feb. 1972

. . . aimed at helping motorists to understand the truck driver's point of view —Julie Candler, *Ford Truck Times,* Summer 1970

. . . research activities aimed at developing man's capability to work in the sea —*Annual Report, Union Carbide Corp.,* 1970

. . . proposals aimed at correcting the deficiencies — Eileen Hughes, *Ladies' Home Jour.,* September 1971

. . . a new television series aimed at helping high school students —*American Labor,* December 1969

... has aimed at wooing back women audiences — *Current Biography,* December 1967

2. *Aim at, aim for* with a noun. Colter 1981 thinks only *at* and not *for* should be used with *aim,* but he is alone in his belief; Chambers 1985 and Janis 1984 say either may be used, and in fact both are widely used:

... Mr. Trudeau aims for the jugular —Herbert Mitgang, *N.Y. Times Book Rev.,* 12 July 1981

... climbed down a bank, aiming for a promontory —Edward Hoagland, *Harper's,* February 1971

... when Mr. Causley neglects this rare gift and aims specifically for children —*Times Literary Supp.,* 2 Apr. 1971

The thing to aim for in posture —James Hewitt, *Irish Digest,* April 1955

... the highway aims straight for Lake Champlain — *American Guide Series: Vermont,* 1937

... to keep the antennas aimed at the earth —Henry S. F. Cooper, Jr., *New Yorker,* 11 Nov. 1972

... one sometimes wonders what effect their creator is aiming at —Edmund Wilson, *New Yorker,* 18 Sept. 1971

... we cannot even be sure what Hamlet is aiming at —William Empson, *Sewanee Rev.,* January–March 1953

... aim at results which the other sciences can neither prove nor disprove —Bertrand Russell, *Selected Papers,* 1927

In the long run men hit only what they aim at — Henry David Thoreau, *Walden,* 1854

Occasionally *toward(s)* may be used:

... products, systems and services aimed toward better living —*Annual Report, American Home Products Corp.,* 1970

It is towards London that touring companies aim — Peter Forster, *London Calling,* 11 Nov. 1954

ain't The history of *ain't* is both complicated and obscure, and the amount of real historical investigation devoted to it has been very small compared to the reams of paper that have been written to condemn it. Much of what has been written is not informative, and some of it is misinformative. We will try here to lay out what is known about *ain't* and how it came to be in its present disesteem, and then examine the ways in which it has been and still is used.

The grammarians Jespersen 1909–49 and Curme 1931 made brief examinations of the origin of *ain't;* but, as far as we know, a short study by Professor Harold H. Bender of Princeton (also the chief etymologist for Webster's Second) in *Word Study,* March 1936, is the first devoted entirely to an examination of the subject. (Two later ones—among many—that you may find of interest are Martin Stevens, "The Derivation of 'Ain't'," *American Speech,* October 1954, and Archibald A. Hill, "The Tainted *Ain't* Once More," *College English,* June 1965.)

One of the things that makes *ain't* stand out is its apparent lack of direct connection to any of the inflected forms of *be: am, is, are, were, was,* etc. The reason is ultimately a shift in the way we perceive words. When *ain't* was first used in writing in the early 18th century,

the spelling represented a way of pronouncing the word. Nowadays we tend to pronounce a word according to the way we see it spelled. Thus, *ain't* looks stranger to us than it did to those who spoke and wrote it two or three centuries ago.

Another complication is that we cannot be entirely certain whether *ain't* began as a shortening of *are not* or *am not.* We do know that it had an earlier spelling *an't* (or sometimes *a'n't*), which you can see would not be difficult to derive phonologically from *are* or *am;* the spelling *ain't* seems originally to have represented one particular way of pronouncing the contraction more often spelled *an't.* Bender found that *an't* arose almost simultaneously from both *am not* and *are not.* The phonology of these derivations is discussed in Jespersen (vol. 5) and in Hill's article mentioned above. Our present evidence—and there is doubtless more to be found—shows *am not* the earliest:

MISS PRUE. You need not sit so near one, if you have any thing to say, I can hear you farther off, I a'n't deaf —William Congreve, *Love for Love,* 1695

The earliest evidence for *are not* is from 1696:

LORD FOPPINGTON. ...these shoes a'n't ugly, but they don't fit me —Sir John Vanbrugh, *The Relapse*

Evidence in Jespersen shows that Jonathan Swift, in his *Journal to Stella,* was using *an't* for *am not, are not,* and *is not* around 1710: "I a'n't vexed," "an't you an impudent slut," "Presto is plaguy silly tonight, an't he?" It would thus appear that either *an't* also developed from *isn't* somehow or that it was extended in use to the third person singular. Jespersen advances (somewhat tentatively) this third derivation, which Strang 1970 represents as *isn't → i'n't → e'n't → ain't.* Bender, on the other hand, supposes *an't = isn't* is simply an extension of the form to the third person. To complicate matters, we have here the curious fact that *an't = isn't* is attested earlier than *i'n't.* E'n't, however, is old enough; it was noticed as early as 1685. Until more and clearer evidence is turned up, we cannot be sure which route led to third person singular *a(i)n't.*

We also have to take account of a fourth line of derivation in which *an't* and *ain't* are used for *has not* and *have not.* The derivation of *ain't* from *has* or *have not* is a favorite of a couple of investigators (see Stevens, above, for instance), but such evidence as we have suggests that this is a later development, apparently in the 19th century. The earliest citation for it in the Dictionary of American Regional English is dated 1838. It is not, however, an Americanism, being recorded also in the English Dialect Dictionary. The derivation itself is fairly straightforward: 18th-century *ha'n't,* for both *has not* and *have not,* becomes *an't* by loss of the *h* (in American English the *h* will sometimes be restored to produce *hain't*).

Let us pause to recapitulate. *Ain't* comes from *an't* which in turn comes from *am not* (perhaps by way of *amn't,* which still survives in Irish English and—according to Gowers in Fowler 1965—in Scots English too), from *are not* (one common pronunciation of *are* was close to that of *air;* Baron 1982 cites a 1791 American spelling reformer named Chambers whose system spelled *are* as *er*), from *is not* (perhaps through *i'n't* and *en't*), and later from *have not* and *has not* (through *ha'n't*). So the connection of *ain't* with *be* (and *have*) is not quite as obscure as it might appear on the surface.

How *ain't* came to the widely disparaged status it now occupies is scarcely more obvious than its origin. Strang

1970 notes that several negative contractions—among them *don't, shan't, won't,* as well as *an't*—seem to have developed around 1600; they begin to show up in literary sources, especially the Restoration dramatists, toward the end of the century (Mario Pei in *The Story of Language,* 1949 asserts *ain't* was established in usage by King Charles II). But in the early 18th century, some of these abbreviated forms begin to be criticized; Addison (*The Spectator* 135, 1711) and Swift (*The Tatler* 230, 1710 and *Polite Conversations,* 1738) are among the earliest to disparage them, although (as we have seen) Swift used them himself. The earliest mentions of *an't* specifically are in lists of condemned contractions. The Reverend John Witherspoon, as "The Druid," contributed a number of papers to the *Pennsylvania Journal* on things he didn't care for in American English; his No. VI (16 May 1781) says:

> I will mention the vulgar abbreviations in general, as an't, can't, han't, don't, should'nt, would'nt, could'nt, &c. (in Mathews 1931)

The Dictionary of American English mentions a similar listing in B. Dearborn's *Columbian Grammar* of 1795, and Leonard 1929 mentions the English grammarian Philip Withers in 1788 as offering similar criticism. *Ain't* is lumped with other contractions for condemnation in 1825 by the American grammarian Samuel Kirkham. The first to single out *ain't* specifically seems to have been Alford 1866. While he notes that *ain't* is very frequently used "even by highly educated persons," he does not approve, partly because he thinks *ain't* bears no resemblance to *am not* and *are not.* Oddly enough, Bardeen 1883 lists only Alford (from among his list of two dozen commentators) as opposed to *ain't,* but he does mention that the dictionaries of Webster and Worcester consider it indefensible.

Hill in the *College English* article mentioned above quotes the linguist Raven I. McDavid, Jr. to the effect that *ain't* lost status as a pronunciation while the broader of the two pronunciations probably represented by *an't* gained status (a shift which would eventually lead to the appearance in British books of *aren't I*—with the *r* not pronounced; see AREN'T I). Jespersen tells us that in the 19th and 20th centuries authors put *ain't* "is not" in the speech of vulgar or uneducated characters. Thus Jane Austen has a vulgar woman say:

> ". . . I'm sure I don't pretend to say that there an't" —*Sense and Sensibility,* 1811

Charles Dickens puts it in the mouth of his detestable Yorkshire schoolmaster:

> 'So it is,' said Squeers. 'Ain't it, Nickleby?' —*Nicholas Nickleby,* 1839

And George Bernard Shaw has a prizefighter say:

> "Oh, no," said Skeene, soothingly; ". . . sparring ain't the real thing. . . ." —*Cashel Byron's Profession,* 1886

American pedagogues of the 19th century were willing to take Witherspoon's 1781 observations (based in turn on Addison's *Spectator* strictures of 1711) and make them part of the teaching of English. But some discrimination seems to have been attempted at times, at least in the advice given to graduates of the Newburyport Female High School in 1846 by a man named Peabody. He advises great care and discretion in the employment of the negative contractions, working his way through

can't, don't, haven't, isn't, hasn't, didn't, couldn't, wouldn't and *shouldn't* in a sort of descending scale of acceptability. He saves the worst for last:

> *Won't* for *will not,* and *ain't* for *is not* or *are not* are absolutely vulgar; and *ain't* for *has not* or *have not,* is utterly intolerable —quoted by Shirley Brice Heath, in Shopen & Williams 1980

It is to be noted that Peabody was attempting to discriminate among not only the various contractions, but also the different uses of *ain't.* A few early 20th-century commentators also discriminate:

> **ain't.** Avoid as inelegant. In such a phrase as "he ain't," it is both vulgar and ungrammatical —Vizetelly 1906

Baron 1982 cites John Bechtel in *Slips of Speech* (1903) as making a similar discrimination. By 1926 H. W. Fowler could view first-person use of *ain't* quite differently from other uses:

> *A(i)n't* is merely colloquial, & as used for *isn't* is an uneducated blunder & serves no useful purpose. But it is a pity that *a(i)n't* for *am not,* being a natural contraction & supplying a real want, should shock us as though tarred with the same brush. Though *I'm not* serves well enough in statements, there is no abbreviation but *a(i)n't I?* for *am I not?. . . .*

Fowler's defense of *ain't I?* was repeated on this side of the Atlantic:

> What is the matter with *ain't I?* for *am not I?* Nothing whatever, save that a number of minor grammarians object to it —*American Mercury,* August 1927 (probably H. L. Mencken)

But such nice differences have generally been abandoned by the minor grammarians, both British and American, and they have held the whip hand. Here is Josephine Turck Baker 1927:

> *I ain't* and *Ain't I* are always incorrect, *I'm not* and *Am I not* being the correct forms. As a contraction in place of *isn't, ain't* is a vulgarism.

And her single-minded view has become a tradition:

> **ain't** is a vulgarism altogether too frequently used for *am not, aren't, isn't, hasn't, haven't,* and still other verbal negatives. It is, if possible, worse for *am not, has not, have not,* than for *is not* and *are not.* But there is really no such word. Don't use it —Opdyke 1939

> **ain't.** Nonstandard for *am not, isn't, aren't,* or *hasn't* —Guth 1985

It will be seen that whatever discrimination was earlier made among different uses of *ain't* has been lost; and in Opdyke's remark about nonexistence the historical connection of *ain't* to *am not, are not,* etc., is entirely unrecognized, possibly because the earlier form *an't* had dropped out of use around the end of the 19th century.

We cannot be sure why *an't* vanished, but it did. The loss probably had something to do with its most prestigious pronunciation being more frequently spelled *aren't* in the 19th century and the less prestigious pronunciations being spelled *ain't. Ain't* appears to have become the regular spelling in American English at a fairly early date.

Now that we have traced the history of the word from

the ordinary conversational English of educated 17th- and 18th-century English men and women through its transformation into the bugbear of the American school-teacher of the 20th century, we can turn our attention to how this much vilified word is actually used. When the entry for *ain't* in Webster's Third tried in 1961 to describe actual use based on the information then available, it caused a great deal of controversy in the press, especially the portion of the usage note that allowed that *ain't* was "used orally in most parts of the U.S. by many cultivated speakers esp. in the phrase *ain't I.*" And only a couple of years ago a correspondent in a remote corner of the Southwest troubled himself to tear off a piece of paper bag, inscribe on it his opinion that no one in his town would stoop so low as to use *ain't,* and mail it to Merriam-Webster. Such outbursts remind us that the statement of James H. Sledd that "any red-blooded American would prefer incest to *Ain't*" (cited by Raven I. McDavid, Jr., *PADS,* April 1967) is only slightly exaggerated.

The use of *ain't* in present-day spoken English is hard for dictionary editors to assess accurately, since most dictionary evidence is from print. We do know that it is common among the less educated and among children, especially when talking to their peers. We do have evidence that educated persons whose regular vocabulary still includes *ain't* use the term in talking to relatives and to peers with whom they are both friendly and on a first-name basis (there is an intelligent discussion of this in Hill).

While we have little evidence of unguarded, friendly, peer-to-peer conversation in our files, we do have letters. From the old days to the present, the use of *ain't* in a letter marks a close and warm relationship.

Ain't you mightily moped on the banks of the Cam! —Charles Lamb, letter, February 1801

Where is Moore? Why an't he out? —Lord Byron, letter, 29 July 1816

Thence to Dresden. Ain't I glad, though the weather is no better —Henry Adams, letter, 6 Apr. 1859

Nurse doesn't know I'm writing. Aint I lawless! —Ellen Terry, letter, 4 Mar. 1897

Ain't it hell to have a head of the State in the family? —Harry S. Truman, letter, 11 May 1952

I trust you find my handwriting as bad as yr own. I ain't strong enough to hit a key tonight —Flannery O'Connor, letter, 26 Mar. 1957

Ain't is also used in what Professor Hill calls a "congruently informal style." This may be spoken—as in an interview or even in a talk—or written—as in an article. If *ain't* has a special function in these examples, it is to emphasize their informality.

Like, they had these three heavies coming down the street and me walking toward them. Now right away that ain't right. Three guys coming at me, I run, right ... ? —Steve McQueen, *Newsweek* (6 Jan. 1964); interview reproduced in *Current Biography,* October 1966

He ain't too interested in what the contemporary world thinks about him —William Faulkner, talk to students at University of Virginia, quoted in Barnard 1979

I'm from my generation, you know, if you ain't working you're doing something wrong —Lena Horne, quoted in *Northeast Mag.,* 3 Feb. 1985

She's the doctor from Australia who goes around telling everybody we're all gonna die, that if we keep these politicians in there, they're going to blow up the world. I ain't buying it —Arlo Guthrie, quoted in *Yankee,* August 1986

Well, I have my doubts, folks. I recently saw the first 1980s graffiti exhibition ... and, let me tell you, these artists ain't —Gerald Peary, *Flare,* April 1984

But that was before I learned one of my favorite speakers can be purchased in only one city in Texas, and it ain't Houston, folks —Henry Hunt, *Houston Post,* 26 Aug. 1984

The congruently informal *ain't,* if we may call it that, can also be used for characterizing purposes. In the next example we see Will Rogers projecting his stage personality in print:

Just imagine, if you can, if the flesh of this Country were allowed to wander around promiscuously! Why, there ain't no telling where it would wind up —Will Rogers, *The Illiterate Digest,* 1924

The characterizing *ain't* in writing is often meant to mark the speaker as belonging to a lower class or being poorly educated or being black or being countrified. This use is common in fiction:

'What! he ain't rich then?' Foker asked —W. M. Thackeray, *The History of Pendennis,* 1850

"Oh, Lord!" exclaimed Cashel, "don't say that. You're joking, ain't you?" —George Bernard Shaw, *Cashel Byron's Profession,* 1886

When he returned he said, "What have I got that I can pay? Ain't I been a poor man every day of my life?" —Bernard Malamud, *The Magic Barrel,* 1958

The Jews, Ford said. They ain't like anyone else I know —E. L. Doctorow, *Ragtime,* 1975

". . . You ain't do nothing like that, did you Mitch, huh?" —Vern E. Smith, *The Jones Men,* 1974

Although most common in fiction, the characterizing *ain't* can also be found in other forms of writing. The first example describes an unpromising family of white farm helpers, the second a Southern sheriff.

. . . these . . . look like they've been joined up with the human race for only a couple of months now. Mrs. W. says she went to school for one day and didn't loin ... nothin and ain't went back —Flannery O'Connor, letter, 25 Jan. 1953

. . . the country people's ignorance he found irresistible and I think it tickled him to perplex their foolish heads, white or black, with the same old leading question: "You heard about old Nat Turner, ain't you?" —William Styron, *This Quiet Dust and Other Writings,* 1982

An editorial in the *Boston Globe* (5 Sept. 1983) also notes that the characterizing *ain't* can be used in reportage:

It may well quote the person accurately, but it may also be a code word, used in a sly way to tip off the reader to the fact that the person being quoted is poor, illiterate, or black.

It is a moot point whether accuracy or characterization is the purpose here:

> The grocery store ain't got no limits on how many groceries they sell. I ought to be able to sell all the guns I want —Blake Roberts, a Greenville, S.C., gun dealer, quoted by Wayne King, *N.Y. Times,* 13 Mar. 1975

Another of the most common public uses of *ain't* makes use of the word's ability to attract attention. This use pops up unsurprisingly in advertising and in political slogans. It is also used in otherwise rather straightforward prose for purposes of contrast.

> ... Reagan ... continued to use the line he had used when he kicked off his campaign on Labor Day: "You ain't seen nothin' yet." —Elizabeth Drew, *New Yorker,* 3 Dec. 1984

> You ain't seen nothin' until you've seen ... —television advt., 16 Feb. 1980

> ... and that ain't hay —singing commercial, 24 Feb. 1981

> ... firms who can make things smell like what they ain't —Bennett Cerf, *Saturday Rev.,* 7 Mar. 1953

> So what? Jack Dempsey isn't; Babe Ruth isn't; Joe Louis and Douglas MacArthur ain't —George Jean Nathan, *Beware of Parents: A Bachelor's Book for Children,* 1943

> Louise ain't what she used to be in voice —*Metronome,* January 1952

> The old pervading desire to show the schoolmarm that the cultured ain't so cultured —Sheridan Baker, *College English,* November 1964 (in Hill)

> I ain't referring to strip-mining, scoop-shovel operators —Malcolm S. Forbes, *Forbes,* 1 Feb. 1974

> ... misprint, catachresis, misspelling, solecism, barbarism, and other evidence that English ain't what it used to be. It never was —Howard 1980

> To look at the objects you wouldn't think they were worth very much. The Hope Diamond they ain't — Edwards Park, *Smithsonian,* August 1983

> This is an infuriating misuse by an ignoramus who thinks 'authoring' three books is somehow a grander achievement than writing them. It ain't —Charles Kuralt, in *Harper* 1975, 1985

You will probably have noticed by now that many of these attention-getting uses of *ain't* occur in familiar phrases. Such catch phrases and variations on them make up a goodly portion of the word's use, both orally and in writing. We add a few more samples:

> This show might be described as a working-class comedy, but although it works pretty hard, well—class it ain't —Cleveland Amory, *TV Guide,* 20 Mar. 1976

> The wackiness of movies, once so deliciously amusing, ain't funny anymore —Richard Schickel, *Harper's,* March 1971

What is wrong with all this, of course, is that it just ain't so —Archibald MacLeish, quoted in *English Jour.,* November 1968

> No, no, cried the America of World War II—"Say it ain't so, Lyndon." —Philip Roth, *Reading Myself and Others,* 1975

> It ain't over till it's over —Mike Williams, stock-market analyst, in news telecast, 16 Dec. 1985

> ... doomsayers ... have been warning us that we ain't seen nothing yet —Louis Rukeyser, "Wall Street Week" (PBS television), 13 Mar. 1981

> Leftovers ain't what they used to be —*Apartment Life,* January 1980

> Davies has the Order of Lenin—just conferred. He's an economic royalist—"ain't that sompin?" — Harry S. Truman, diary entry, 22 May 1945

> But, overall, to borrow Burt Lance's phrase, the system ain't broke —Albert R. Hunt, Jr., *Wall Street Jour.,* 5 July 1979

Another use of *ain't,* seldom mentioned though often heard, is in popular music. You have only to recall songs with lines like "It ain't necessarily so," "The old gray mare, she ain't what she used to be," "Ain't she sweet?" to realize that the medium of popular music alone could have kept *ain't* alive without much help from other sources. The function of *ain't* in the lyrics of songs is obvious: it has only one syllable, and it is more clearly heard and more easily enunciated than the *isn't* it usually replaces.

Now we come to the famous tag question "ain't I?" We have seen earlier that Fowler 1926 regretted its being considered indicative of low breeding and that *The American Mercury* wondered what is the matter with it. The tag question was used by the linguistic geographers to elicit oral uses of *ain't;* their results influenced the statement in Webster's Third that caused so much controversy. Hill's article discusses the tag question; so do Einstein 1985 and others. A few hardy souls approve the locution:

> Only in the first-person-negative interrogative of the verb "to be" is the contraction "ain't" acceptable in standard speech —William Safire, *N.Y. Times Mag.,* 23 May 1982

> I'll accept 'ain't I?' instead of 'am I not?' That's useful —Abe Burrows, in Harper 1985

Even Bernstein 1977 admits the utility of the tag:

> There can be no doubt that *ain't I* is easier to say than *aren't I* or *amn't I* and sounds less stilted than *am I not.* Nevertheless. ...

Bernstein nevertheless rejects the tag and questions the validity of the usage note in Webster's Third. There may be legitimate reasons for a certain skepticism about the use of *ain't I.* One is that much of Linguistic Atlas material was gathered about a half century ago; it is hard to know if the information is still valid. The Dictionary of American Regional English does not mention the tag specifically, although the editors do reprint E. Bagby Atwood's summary of its distribution in *A Survey of Verb Forms in the Eastern United States* (1953). But even if the tag is logical, is grammatically sound, is approved by some, and is desired by others, does it actually come up very often in real speech? Although, as conceded above, we do not have enough direct evidence to answer that question conclusively, we do have a fair amount of indirect evidence from letters and such showing that *ain't* occurs frequently in inverted expressions, such as questions.

> As for the Fraülein, ain't she a one-er, that's all — Henry Adams, letter, 8 Nov. 1859

> Ain't I a beast for not answering you before? — Alfred, Lord Tennyson, letter (in Jespersen 1909–49)

> Oh aint it a dark day —Ellen Terry, letter, 2 Oct. 1896

> My cousin thought this a remarkable coincidence, illustrating how remarkable coincidences can be. Now ain't it? —Flannery O'Connor, letter, 24 Apr. 1951

(Other examples may be found above.) So all we can say for sure is that when the tag is necessary, *ain't* will probably occur in it in some people's speech.

One use of *ain't* that many handbooks agree is common is facetious or jocular or humorous use. We do not have much evidence for such use. Here is an obvious case:

> We like to make jokes, for instance, about the language of tax forms. Heh heh, we chuckle, ain't them bureaucrats a caution? —Mitchell 1979

Don't be surprised if you're not chuckling. *Ain't* in itself ain't funny. It is a fact, of course, that *ain't* can commonly be found in humorous writers from Bill Arp to Artemus Ward to Mark Twain to Ring Lardner and Will Rogers. But its use is generally appropriate to the character (sometimes the narrator) using it; the humor does not reside in the use of *ain't*. What the handbooks probably mean is that many educated people, when they use *ain't*, try to use it in such a way as to show that it is not part of their serious day-to-day vocabulary. Such disinfecting of the word seems most frequently to be accomplished by the use of the familiar fixed phrases we illustrated earlier. An old chestnut like "things ain't what they used to be" or its wry contemporary cousin "nostalgia ain't what it used to be" is the verbal equivalent of a wink or nudge intended to show that you are not so ill-bred as to really use *ain't*. It's not really an attempt at jocularity or humor—it's an attempt at distancing.

We have saved till last a clutch of citations—from speech—for *ain't* as used by various public figures. Several are U.S. presidents or others active in the political life, but few of these uses sound like self-conscious attempts by the educated to affect the speech of the general electorate. Most sound perfectly natural and untouched by irony:

> . . . education means moving a man from where he is to where he ain't —Robert Frost, cited by Calvin H. Plimpton, *Amherst College Bulletin,* January 1967

> . . . Harry Truman would not say. To one probing reporter he quipped: "You just want to find out something and you ain't going to do it." —*Time,* 25 July 1949

> You think it's going to be done, but it ain't —Julia Child, television show, 3 Mar. 1971

> Sir Winston . . . said the portrait of him seated and wearing his characteristic bow tie "makes me look

half-witted, which I ain't." —Sir Winston Churchill, in *N.Y. Times,* 12 Jan. 1978

> John ain't been worth a damn since he started wearing $300 suits —Lyndon B. Johnson, quoted by Larry L. King, *New Times,* 20 Aug. 1976

> Eleven-thirty at night ain't a time to read up on this very complicated higher-education problem —Gerald R. Ford, quoted by John Hersey, *N.Y. Times Mag.,* 20 Apr. 1975

> Reagan dodged a question about the Hodel report Wednesday night at his nationally televised news conference.
> "I ain't talking," he said —Ronald R. Reagan, in *Morning Union* (Springfield, Mass.), 10 Jan. 1985

> You're looking at a man what ain't straining — George C. Wallace, quoted by B. Drummond Ayres, Jr., *N.Y. Times,* 30 Mar. 1975

> "If at the end of four years they want to throw me out, it's O.K. with me," the Mayor responds, adding: "I like my job very much, but it ain't the end of the world if I don't have it." —Edward Koch, quoted by Richard Haitch, *N.Y. Times,* 6 July 1980

Conclusion: We have seen that *ain't* is a stigmatized word in general use; in ordinary speaking and writing it tends to mark the speaker and writer as socially or educationally inferior. We have also seen that it is in widespread use but usually in particular circumscribed ways that tend to remove the stigma from its use. Study the examples here. Then decide when and how you will use the word, if at all. Though you may choose—indeed, be well advised—to forgo making sentences like "I ain't had dinner yet" a regular feature of your conversation or writing, at times you will probably find *ain't* a very useful word despite (or even because of) the controversy that surrounds its use.

air Copperud 1970, 1980 finds the verb *air* "broadcast" unexceptional, and Janis 1984 agrees. Earlier the term had been objected to as jargon by Bernstein 1958; Harper 1975, 1985 agrees with Bernstein. Bernstein had condemned the word in a 1955 *Winners & Sinners;* the Morrises seem to have had this "new" verb called to their attention by a correspondent in 1971. But the verb had been appearing in print for at least 15 years when Bernstein spotted it in a *New York Times* headline. Our earliest citations are essentially technical, but by 1943 *air* had appeared in fiction:

> "Now, now, boys!" said the account executive genially. "The program isn't aired until three o'clock!" —Marguerite Lyon, *And So to Bedlam,* 1943

By 1945 it was appearing in the weekly news magazines:

> The *Post, Times, Daily Mirror,* and *Journal-American* all aired special news programs —*Time,* 16 July 1945

And it had become quite common by the end of the 1940s:

> . . . which has been aired at one time or another on the four major radio networks —*Current Biography 1948*

> . . . the local radio station was going to air it —Christopher Morley, *The Man Who Made Friends with Himself,* 1949

Henry Morgan and Herb Sheldon each air at 6:30 p.m. —*The Billboard,* 15 Apr. 1950

Our evidence shows no diminution of use. You may safely follow Copperud and Janis, whose judgment on the word is sound for this late in the second half of the 20th century. But you can always use *broadcast* if you happen not to like *air.*

à la This imported preposition has its grave accent over the *a* printed often enough, even in American use, that the unaccented form is considered a secondary variant. And although it has been used in English contexts since the end of the 16th century, some writers still feel that it is French and italicize it. It is widely used in English outside the field of cookery as well as within. Longman 1984 and Fowler 1965 note that its form is fixed in English (as it is in French for reasons of the underlying grammar). In English the preposition is often followed by a proper name, and even when the name is clearly masculine the feminine article *la* is retained. Here is a selection of fairly recent examples of its use:

. . . going on to other things, whether à la David Frost or à la Jonathan Miller —*Times Literary Supp.,* 26 Nov. 1971

. . . chomping on a large cigar à la Castro —Alan Riding, *Saturday Rev.,* 24 July 1976

. . . eating up the keyboard *à la* Horowitz —Harold C. Schonberg, *Harper's,* April 1971

. . . the camera does a semicircular track à la *Vertigo* —John Simon, *New York,* 6 Dec. 1976

. . . a division-sized posse prepared to go in à la Entebbe —*Pine Bluff* (Ark.) *Commercial,* quoted in *N.Y. Times,* 13 Nov. 1979

I was filling in with my drumsticks all kinds of complicated rhythmical riffs *a la* castanet parts — Michael Tilson Thomas, quoted in *Rolling Stone,* 14 Sept. 1972

. . . will now try to ignore the flap and get the renominations over with, a la politics-as-usual —*Wall Street Jour.,* 3 June 1980

albeit Copperud 1970, 1980 observes that "a generation ago" *albeit* was considered archaic but is "now being revived." The source of the notice of revival is Gowers (in Fowler 1965). This is a most curious business, since *albeit* seems never to have gone out of use, though it may have faded somewhat in the later 19th century. If it did, the revival began decades before the commentators noticed.

Johnson's Dictionary of 1755 had the word with three illustrations, one from Shakespeare's Othello (1605):

Of one, whose . . . eyes,
Albeit unused to the melting mood,
Drop tears, as fast as the Arabian trees
Their medicinal gum.

The OED quotes from 18th- and 19th-century sources including Southey, Thackeray, and the Irish novelist Charles Lever. Poutsma 1904–26 quotes from Kipling, and we have found *albeit* in the verse of the elder Holmes and of Yeats. Nonetheless, the brothers Fowler 1907 found it to be an archaism, citing two contemporary sources for censure. The opinion of 1907 was car-

ried over to Fowler 1926, from whence it came to Krapp 1927. It does not seem to have been called archaic by any other commentators, although a *Dictionary of Unusual Words* published in 1948 included it with the *Othello* quotation above, and Janis 1984, who may have looked only into Fowler, thinks that it is "considered archaic by many."

Since the word seems to have continued in use all along, Gowers's comment that it had been "picked up and dusted" is not especially apt; it has, however, considerably increased in use since the 1930s, to judge by evidence in the Merriam-Webster files. A selection of examples:

We have lived and we have learned, albeit the lesson was a costly one —*Vanity Fair,* January 1920

. . . through a hundred channels where waters flowed with steady force, albeit under a glassy surface —Sir Winston Churchill, *Great Contemporaries,* 1937

It took that pause to make him realize
The mountain he was climbing had the slant
As of a book held up before his eyes
(And was a text albeit done in plant)
—Robert Frost, *A Witness Tree,* 1942

The wind was new albeit it was the same that had blown before the time of man came to the hillside — Elizabeth Madox Roberts, *The Time of Man,* 1926

That these ties, albeit the deepest, should have left me so remarkably free was a happy circumstance for my philosophy —George Santayana, *Persons and Places,* 1944

. . . the glamorous, albeit fast, colors of modern journalism —Vladimir Nabokov, *New Republic,* 13 Jan. 1941

. . . betraying clearly what the relationship between them was, albeit a fleeting one —Vita Sackville-West, *The Easter Party,* 1953

. . . I watched the trees and the rain with increasing interest albeit with no radio support —E. B. White, *New Yorker,* 25 Sept. 1954

. . . conversation might have found its natural level, albeit low —Mary McCarthy, *Atlantic,* August 1970

. . . I should doubt very much that a literary manner of this sort was a matter of instinct. It is purely preconscious, and learned, albeit imperfectly —Donald Hall, *Goatfoot, Milktongue, Twinbird,* 1978

. . . they had treated me as a pal, albeit a junior one —Anthony Bailey, *New Yorker,* 29 July 1985

alibi The extended sense of *alibi* meaning any excuse is an Americanism; although it was overlooked by the Dictionary of American English, the Dictionary of Americanisms recorded the noun, citing a 1912 story in *Collier's.* "The rot started in the United States," says Howard 1980. He cites Big Bill Tilden (as does OED Supplement):

Don't offer alibis for losing —*Lawn Tennis,* 1922

This sense was apparently popular in spoken American English from around the time just before World War I. That it already had a good foothold is attested by Ring Lardner's use of the word in the title of one of his best-known stories, "Alibi Ike" (first published in 1915). The story begins:

His right name was Frank X. Farrell, and I guess the X stood for "Excuse me." Because he never pulled a play, good or bad, on or off the field, without apologizin' for it.
"Alibi Ike" was the name Carey wished on him the first day he reported down South.

A bit further on Lardner writes:

"He's got the world beat," says Carey to Jack and I. "I've knew lots o' guys that had an alibi for every mistake they made.... But this baby can't even go to bed without apologizin'...." —Ring Lardner, "Alibi Ike," in *How to Write Short Stories,* 1924

Lardner's association of *alibi* with baseball is appropriate; sports contexts are among the earliest for the word in this sense. Besides Big Bill Tilden, we have these examples:

Among the countless alibis that go hand in hand with bad golf —*Vanity Fair,* December 1919

... "I dropped it because the sun was in my eyes." Sport's oldest alibi —*N.Y. Times,* 16 May 1928

No room is left for alibis in the pre-battle statements of Gene Tunney, Jack Dempsey, and their two managers —*Emporia* (Kans.) *Gazette,* 22 Sept. 1927

But writers for American newspapers and magazines used it in other contexts, too—especially politics.

After putting through his program, the governor must face the people at the polls without alibis — *Emporia* (Kans.) *Gazette,* 3 Feb. 1927

Leaders of the Labor Party are quite willing to allow the Liberals to hold a check rein over them if they can only obtain office. It would give them a perfect alibi —*N.Y. Times,* 21 Oct. 1928

They want an alibi to gouge the public —*Time,* 18 Jan. 1926

It even began to crop up in the fiction of others than Ring Lardner:

And the meaning Aline had to jump at, knowing nothing, get instinctively or not at all. Esther would be one to leave herself always a clear alibi —Sherwood Anderson, *Dark Laughter,* 1925

As soon as any new expression becomes widespread and popular enough, it will draw critical attention. The extended sense of *alibi* had only to wait until 1925 for disapproval: John A. Powell in *How to Write Business Letters* (1925) said it should not be used, and M. V. P. Yeaman in *American Speech,* November 1925, noticed it unfavorably—his examples are from conversation. In Australia, *The Bulletin* (New South Wales) for 14 Apr. 1927 answered a letter from a lawyer complaining about the new *alibi:*

The Yanks have corrupted it to signify any sort of defence, explanation or excuse. Thus a man arriving with a black eye offers his "alibi" that he got it chopping wood. It may be only vernacular American as yet, but it has got into the newspapers and fiction, and hence is probably beyond eradication.

Krapp 1927 also notes the new sense "In careless colloquial speech," and Weseen 1928 calls it a misuse. Fow-

ler 1926 seems not to have noticed it, so the earliest British disapproval we have found is in Partridge 1942. Subsequent British commentators followed Partridge— a complaining letter to the *Picture Post* in 1949, an editorial in the *Manchester Guardian* in 1950, Lord Conesford in the *Saturday Evening Post* in 1957. Gowers in Fowler 1965 gives it a fairly long disapproval, quoting two unnamed English politicians. Others sustain the tradition: Sellers 1975, Phythian 1979, Bryson 1980, Longman 1984, and Chambers 1985 record widespread disapproval. Howard 1980 doesn't like it either but considers it established.

There is a bit of a British-American split here. While some American handbooks and commentators follow the early condemnation (for instance Shaw 1962, Bell & Cohn 1980, Oxford American Dictionary 1980), more are neutral (for instance Nickles 1974, Reader's Digest 1983, Janis 1984, Bremner 1980, Kilpatrick 1984), and both Bernstein 1971 and William Safire (*New York Magazine,* 24 July 1983) defend it; in Bernstein's words:

The hand-wringers suppose that it is merely a synonym for *excuse,* but it is more than that. It carries a connotation of slight or outright dishonesty and it represents a plea to get out from under.

Even the usage panels of Heritage 1969, 1982 and Harper 1975, 1985 split nearly evenly on it. The use, therefore, seems to be regarded with considerably less disfavor in the U.S. than in the U.K. The sense itself, however, to judge from the examples in the British handbooks, is now established on both sides of the Atlantic. Here are a few examples more recent than the ones given above:

... we lie to ourselves, in order that we may still have the excuse of ignorance, the alibi of stupidity and incomprehension —Aldous Huxley, *The Olive Tree,* 1937

Partly, they are the new alibi of great wealth —Harold J. Laski, *New Republic,* 5 Aug. 1946

Direct treachery by friends in publishing a private manuscript was one alibi a poet could plead —J. W. Saunders, *Essays in Criticism,* April 1951

... I intend to let everyone know about them, even if I am depriving reluctant hosts of an excellent alibi —*New Yorker,* 20 Mar. 1954

... given the noise of a helicopter ride there may have been some misunderstanding. But I do not use this as an alibi —Henry J. Kissinger, quoted in *N.Y. Times,* 12 June 1974

It is, on the other hand, a wonderful alibi for refusing to attempt anything less —Hilton Kramer, *N.Y. Times Book Rev.,* 19 Feb. 1984

The American Heritage usage panel, almost half of which accepted the extended sense of *alibi* as a noun, rejected intransitive use of the verb in writing by a wide margin. The OED Supplement shows that the verb has been in use since 1909. It too was establishing itself by the 1920s and is now fully established, in general prose, in both transitive and intransitive uses:

He let the men alibi away to their heart's content — *Printer's Ink,* 23 Aug. 1923

... haughtily refuse to alibi themselves when suspected —*Emporia* (Kans.) *Gazette,* 25 Oct. 1926

... a belief that is very much in the service of moral alibi-ing —Weston La Barre, *The Human Animal*, 1954

... wherein he endeavors to alibi reversal, surprise, and defeat —S. L. A. Marshall, *Saturday Rev.*, 9 Oct. 1954

They cannot point to the basest elements of their public and say, "They wanted chaff and slops," and thus alibi their failures —Frank Luther Mott, *The News in America*, 1952

... this secretary asked if she mightn't take the message, and alibied. "You see, the delegates are all in the meeting now," she said —*New Yorker*, 23 Sept. 1950

They might enter with a rather rough admonition of, "What do youse guys think you're up to anyhow?" This, however, was merely to alibi the fact that they were crashing —Anita Loos, *Gourmet*, January 1970

... he didn't alibi. He took the blame for his four interceptions —Dave Anderson, *N.Y. Times*, 8 Sept. 1980

The extended senses of *alibi* have been around for about three quarters of a century, and they have been upwardly mobile in status—the noun perhaps more than the verb. The usage is more controversial in British English than American English but is established in both.

alien In 20th-century English, when *alien* is used with a preposition, the choice is most often *to:*

... the contempt he felt for a quality so alien to the traditions of his calling —W. Somerset Maugham, *The Moon and Sixpence*, 1919

Are such relationships alien to the principles of UNO? —Sir Winston Churchill, quoted in *Time*, 18 Mar. 1946

... an acrid empty home with everyone growing alien to one another —Norman Mailer, *The Naked and the Dead*, 1948

At one time, *alien* was also commonly used with *from*, especially in literary contexts. While still found occasionally, *alien from* is much less frequent now than *alien to:*

　　　　　　　... soon discerned his looks
Alien from Heaven, with passions foul obscured
　　　　　　　　—John Milton, *Paradise Lost*, 1667

　　Here, oft the Curious Trav'ller finds,
The Combat of *opposing Winds:*
And seeks to learn the secret Cause,
Which alien seems from Nature's Laws
　　　　　　　　—Jonathan Swift, "The Gulph of
　　　　　　　　　all human Possessions," 1724

... to become a moral nihilist was to papa unthinkable, so alien was it from all his habits —Rose Macaulay, *Told by an Idiot*, 1923

I felt somewhat alien from this company because of my experience with would-be Communists —Katherine Anne Porter, *The Never-Ending Wrong*, 1977

all 1. See ALL OF; ALL THAT; ALL READY, ALREADY; ALL TOGETHER, ALTOGETHER.
2. In the worrisome world of pronoun agreement with indefinite pronoun referents (see, for instance: EACH; EVERY; EVERYBODY, EVERYONE; THEY, THEIR, THEM), some textbooks have recommended substituting constructions with *all* in place of constructions with *each* or *every* in order to make both pronoun and referent grammatically and notionally plural. *All* is unquestionably plural in such constructions as these:

... all of us have our part —Wyllis E. Wright, *Williams Alumni Rev.*, November 1953

No one is held in higher esteem by all here, no matter what their faith, than the American monsignor —John Cogley, *Commonweal*, 25 Dec. 1953

Some textbooks, therefore, advise taking such sentences as

Every child should brush his/his or her/their teeth.

and converting it to

All children should brush their teeth.

in order to avoid the difficult pronoun-referent choice presented by the first sentence. If you are uncomfortable with using *his or her* or the generic *his* or *their*, you may well want to consider using a construction with *all* to avoid the problem.
3. *All ... not.* Nickles 1974 and Kilpatrick 1984 note that in a conversational style of sentence with *all* and a negative *(not)*, the negative element is often postponed so that it follows the verb, instead of preceding *all.*
Copperud 1970, 1980 mentions several other commentators on the subject, including Fowler 1926. Fowler points out that the *all ... not* form is old, and instances this well-known example:

All that glisters is not gold —Shakespeare, *The Merchant of Venice*, 1597

Kilpatrick 1984 gives some more modern examples:

... all of the people who supported Ronald Reagan in California were not opposed to him on this tax bill —Lyn Nofziger

... indicates that all places are not undercounted to the same extent —James Trussell

... all seventy-four hospitals did not report every month —*Washington Post*

The point Kilpatrick is making with these examples is that in conversation these constructions are not ambiguous, but that they can be in print. In the last example did none of the hospitals report? Or did only some fail to report? In writing it would be entirely unambiguous put this way: "not all seventy-four hospitals report every month." Kilpatrick's examples also show this potentially ambiguous construction with *every, everyone,* and *everything.* He quotes Ann Landers:

Everyone in San Francisco is not gay.

Putting the *not* first will remove the ambiguity:

Not everyone in San Francisco is gay.

This is a point worth keeping in mind when you write.

all-around, all-round Copperud 1970, 1980 cites a few commentators as worrying about which of these synonyms is more logical or otherwise preferable. What all the discussion omits is the only thing of real interest: *all-around* is American and has no British use; *all-round* has both British and American use. Here are a few examples of each:

> ... unbeatable as all-around satisfying entertainment —Judith Crist, *Saturday Rev.,* 17 Apr. 1976

> ... his exceptional all-around athletic performance —*Current Biography,* February 1966

> The new ideal is the all-around boy —Malcolm Cowley, *New Republic,* 22 Nov. 1954

> ... such a strange thing as an all-around left-handed man —Mark Twain, "How to Make Hist. Dates Stick," written 1899 (*A Mark Twain Lexicon,* 1938)

> ... a fearless, self-confident swimmer, surfer, all-round athlete —Lyn Tornabene, *Ladies' Home Jour.,* January 1971

> ... the all-round incompetence revealed by the Crimean War —*Times Literary Supp.,* 16 July 1970

> ... but Antigua has an all-round climate —Alec Waugh, *Love and the Caribbean,* 1958

> ... one of the best all-round men in surgery —*Dictionary of American Biography,* 1929

alleged   **1.** As long ago as 1909 Ambrose Bierce was grousing about the use of *allege* in "the alleged murderer." "One can allege a murder, but not a murderer," says Bierce, basing his criticism on the meaning of the verb. But even then *alleged* was already leading an independent existence as an adjective, not necessarily to be trammeled by the meanings of the verb.

The adjective is attested as early as the 16th century (as *allegit*) in Scots law; it perhaps came into mainstream English from this source, as the earliest attributive *alleged* (in this meaning) cited in the OED is from Sir Walter Scott's *The Fair Maid of Perth* (1828). None of the OED citations shows *alleged* applied to a person, as in "the alleged murderer." This particular use may have originated in American journalism—as Bierce's complaint suggests—but if it is an Americanism, none of the standard compendia of Americanisms have taken note of it. And since Bierce was apparently the first to notice the use, it probably arose around the turn of the century.

Alleged has become a fixture of both print and broadcast journalism. Its use is approved by Reader's Digest 1983 (in preference to *accused*). Other commentators accept its inevitability but point out that it is sometimes carelessly applied; they warn against such examples as "the alleged suspect."

> ... is seeking three quarters of a million dollars in alleged libel damages —"Morning Edition," National Public Radio, 22 May 1986

Occasional careless use occurs outside straight reporting, too:

> ... alleging that the Company's underground electric service plans violated antitrust laws and claiming alleged treble damages of $4.5 million —*Annual Report, Virginia Electric & Power Co.,* 1970

> This alleged account of sexual ambidexterity in high life —*Times Literary Supp.,* 18 Dec. 1969

Our evidence is not sufficient to tell whether *alleged* is more often applied to persons or to actions and things in straight reporting. In contexts that are not reportorial we find it much more commonly applied to actions and things—even Ambrose Bierce would not have been displeased by most of our evidence.

> ... the Watergate affair and other alleged malpractices by members of his campaign staff —Richard H. Rovere, *New Yorker,* 18 Nov. 1972

> ... a controversial segment dealing with alleged FBI undercover operations —Robert Lewis Shayon, *Saturday Rev.,* 4 Dec. 1971

One result of the frequency of the word in journalistic use has been the development of a humorous application:

> The only thing we could find was a bottle of alleged brandy —George S. Patton, Jr., *War as I Knew It,* 1947

> ... a round tin of alleged pork and egg, ground up together and worked to a consistency like the inside of a sick lobster's claw —A. J. Liebling, *New Yorker,* 19 May 1956

A spelling reminder may not come amiss: *alleged* is no longer spelled, as it once was, with a *-dge-*.
2. When *alleged* is used as an adjective (as in "the alleged arsonist"), it is often pronounced as three syllables, though not as often as the adjective *learned* meaning "erudite" (as in "learned counsel") is pronounced as two. In the case of *learned,* the extra syllable helps to underscore the sharp difference in meaning between *learned* in "learned counsel" and *learned* in "learned and innate behavior patterns." By comparison, the semantic split between the adjective *alleged* and past participial uses of the verb *allege* is not so sharp, and the extra syllable is not as consistently used. Both pronunciations are acceptable, however.

allergic   Usage commentators often fail to discover a new use until it is too late for their opinion to have any influence on whether or not it becomes established. Copperud 1970 reports Bernstein 1965, Evans 1957, and Follett 1966 all in disapproval of the nonmedical extended sense of *allergic,* "having an aversion." Phythian 1979 dislikes it too. The sense found its way into Webster's Second in the 1950 Addenda section, albeit with a *slang* label (about which some of the editors were doubtful). The new sense was first called to public attention by Dwight L. Bolinger in *Words,* October 1937, the very year in which it is first attested. The OED Supplement cites as its earliest evidence a *New Yorker* cartoon printed in January 1938. A sample of early uses from our files:

> For St. Louis shoppers allergic to holiday crowds —*Time,* 19 Dec. 1938

> Newspapermen, on the whole, are allergic to him —*Life,* 31 Oct. 1938

> ... for some strange and yet unexplained reason, women continue to be allergic to the charms of Mr. Wodehouse's tales —*Times Literary Supp.,* 13 May 1939

By the late 1940s the sense was fully established, and it continues so despite the belated censure:

> The twins were at all times entirely allergic to good influences —Elizabeth Goudge, *Pilgrim's Inn,* 1948

If he was allergic to Scott, Byron, and Shelley, he was among the first to recognize Coleridge, Burns, and Wordsworth —John Mason Brown, *Saturday Rev.,* 31 July 1948

The majority abandoned their cars and set out to walk. I, who am allergic to rain, remained like a snail in its shell —S. P. B. Mais, *The English Scene Today,* 2d ed., 1949

. . . for the sensitive who are allergic to social sheen and waste —Cyril Connolly, *Encounter,* January 1955

He is allergic to facts —William W. Watt, Ph.D., *Famous Writers Mag.,* Spring 1968

. . . I was allergic not only to things British, but to English literature as well —Oscar Cargill, *CEA Critic,* March 1972

. . . says he is allergic to chain-link fencing and barbed wire —John McPhee, *New Yorker,* 11 Sept. 1971

all of   Copperud 1970, 1980 reports "a morass of conflicting opinion" about the propriety of whether *all* should be followed by *of* where *of* is unnecessary, as in "All (of) the percussion instruments" (*American Mercury,* January 1935, where *of* is included). Copperud goes on to say, "The point is hardly an important one, since the choice has no effect on meaning and is unlikely to be noticed by the reader."

Copperud is right. But much has been written about this unimportant point, all the same. Let's begin with Bernstein 1971, who says, "The use of the word *of* after *all* has for some time offended certain authoritarians. . . ." These authoritarians seem to have included one named Quackenbos (*Practical Rhetoric,* 1896, cited by Hall 1917), Bierce 1909, and Vizetelly 1906. Hall 1917 reports Alford 1864 as defending the locution, so there were perhaps earlier objectors in England. The phrase singled out by Vizetelly for particular censure, oddly enough, was *all of them.* He does not seem to have been aware that this phrase dated all the way back to Shakespeare:

I do forgive thy rankest fault—all of them —*The Tempest,* 1612

. . . so shall the Prince, and all of them —*Much Ado About Nothing,* 1599

Ay, all of them at Bristow lost their heads —*Richard II,* 1596

Evidence in the Middle English Dictionary shows that at least as early as the 13th century *all* could modify a following pronoun. Thus, the King James Bible (1611) has in Isaiah 53:6

All we like sheep have gone astray

—a locution picked up directly from Wycliffe's 1382 translation. By Shakespeare's time idiom required *all of us;* the King James Bible in following Wycliffe had used an archaic form. *All* followed by a personal pronoun has nearly disappeared from modern English; we have only a few examples:

We have been, all we Americans, strangely complacent —*Ecclesiastical Rev.,* April 1939

What all we of the general public have learned — Dorothy Canfield Fisher, *ALA Bulletin,* April 1943

Most modern handbooks (and there are many) expect *all of* before a pronoun:

We all of us complain —Joseph Addison, *The Spectator,* No. 93, 1711 (OED)

We all of us, from our own feelings, can understand —Lionel Trilling, *Partisan Rev.,* September–October 1940

King, like most all of us —Dan Wakefield, *Los Angeles Times Book Rev.,* 25 Apr. 1971

The students, almost all of whom live at home — James B. Conant, *Slums and Suburbs,* 1961

. . . has written some twenty books, almost all of which have been published —*Current Biography,* January 1964

Your letter gave pleasure to all of us —Jane Austen, letter, 11 Oct. 1813

Vizetelly (and his followers) recommended that *all of them* be replaced by *they all* or *them all; all* can always follow the pronoun:

Fought you with them all? —Shakespeare, *I Henry IV,* 1598

And they all dead did lie —Samuel Taylor Coleridge, "The Rime of the Ancient Mariner," 1798 (OED)

"Your patron saint, such as we all have." —Henry James, *The American,* 1877

. . . solidarity between Gatsby and me against them all —F. Scott Fitzgerald, *The Great Gatsby,* 1925

They all played "Body and Soul" —radio broadcast program title, 1986

Bierce took out after *all of* followed by a noun; "all of his property" was the phrase he found to be "contradictory." Some other early commentator must have found such phrases redundant too—Utter 1916 mentions redundancy in his puzzled comment on the objection to *all of them*—for redundancy, not contradiction is the basis of remarks about *all of* down to the present time. Here, in fact, we do have mixed usage, but (as Copperud and Bernstein suggest) it is not an issue of great importance. Whether you use the pronoun *all,* with *of,* or the adjective *all,* without *of,* is a matter of style, not of right or wrong. Here are some examples, first of the adjective followed by nouns:

All my pretty ones? —Shakespeare, *Macbeth,* 1606

. . . with all his feet off the ground —Ford Madox Ford, *It Was The Nightingale,* 1933

All his long struggle proves —Stanislaus Joyce, *Interim,* vol. 4, 1954

Perhaps the most unique of all these hills —Donald A. Whiting, *Ford Times,* February 1968

. . . bringing all these old stories together —*Times Literary Supp.,* 9 Apr. 1970

Just record on cards all those terms from this book —Robert Burchfield, in *U.S. News & World Report,* 11 Aug. 1986

The adjective is often used before an indefinite pronoun:

> ... all these become the subjects —Theodore Roszak, *The Making of a Counter Culture,* 1969

And here are some examples of the pronoun:

> ... during Nehru's last illness, Mrs. Gandhi handled all of his affairs —*Current Biography,* June 1966

> ... all of this happens in a flash —William G. Moulton, *NEA Jour.,* January 1965

> You can fool some of the people all of the time, and all of the people some of the time, but you can't fool all of the people all of the time —ascribed to Abraham Lincoln by A. K. McClure, *Lincoln's Yarns and Stories,* 1904 (in Bergen Evans, *A Dictionary of Quotations,* 1968)

> ... a face-to-face talk, with all of its give and take —Edward P. Bailey, Jr., *Writing Clearly,* 1984

The pronoun, like the adjective, can be used before an indefinite pronoun:

> All of this, and much more —Will Herberg, *National Rev.,* 25 Aug. 1970

One additional point: a few handbooks (as Prentice-Hall 1978 and Little, Brown 1980, 1986) call for *all of* before a proper noun, by which, their examples show, they mean geographical names. Our evidence, however, is that both *all* and *all of* are used before such terms:

> ... the best-equipped kitchen in all Boston —*Current Biography,* February 1967

> ... all Alexandria turned out —Lawrence Durrell, *Mountolive,* 1958

> ... the artlessness of all Ohio —Kay Boyle, *Saturday Evening Post,* 11 Dec. 1954

> ... the most fishable river banks in all New England —Edward Weeks, *New England Journeys,* no. 3, 1955

> ... the largest and most receptive audiences for new music in all of Europe —*Current Biography,* December 1964

> ... the most rugged country in all of Colombia — Preston E. James, *Latin America,* rev. ed., 1950

We can conclude that *all of* is usual before personal pronouns, both *all* and *all of* are used before nouns—the *all* users seem to be a bit stronger on the literary side. The choice is a matter of style and it is likely to turn on the rhythm and emphasis of your sentence. It is unlikely that most of your readers will even notice which construction you have chosen.

See also BOTH 4.

allow 1. Vizetelly 1906 and Bierce 1909 make an issue of distinguishing between *allow* and *permit;* they both insist that *permit* is better for the giving of express consent or authorization and would restrict *allow* to uses where no objection or prevention is attempted. Shaw 1975 follows Vizetelly's interpretation, and the Oxford American Dictionary assures us that careful writers observe the distinction. Good writers, however, do as seems best to them, and while some observe the distinction, others do not. Here are some examples of *allow* in its senses that are close to *permit.*

With a personal subject, in the active voice:

> Whether his relationship with the Duchess was anything more than the last platonic imbroglio of an eccentric and slightly senile old codger Mr. Hough does not allow himself to contemplate —*Times Literary Supp.,* 18 Dec. 1969

> I tried to leave, but they wouldn't allow it —E. L. Doctorow, *Loon Lake,* 1979

> The trial judge allowed testimony by the ... officer —*Security World,* November 1969

> Having promised the government ... to stay off the streets, they did not allow a single incident —Tad Szulc, *N.Y. Times,* 9 Jan. 1969

> ... he allowed everyone to believe ... that American participation in the war was not inevitable —*Times Literary Supp.,* 9 Apr. 1970

In the passive voice:

> This they must not be allowed to do! —Joseph Miller, *Not Man Apart,* July 1971

> ... how rapidly the economy can be allowed to expand —Robert M. Solow, *Think,* May–June 1967

> After Eisenhower pleaded with him, Roosevelt said De Gaulle could be brought from Algiers to London and allowed to broadcast —Stephen E. Ambrose, *Johns Hopkins Mag.,* April 1966

With an impersonal subject:

> ... the menu, which allowed each astronaut 2,500 calories a day —*Current Biography,* November 1965

> The catwalk was too narrow to allow them to step back from the tank at all —Paul Horgan, *Ladies' Home Jour.,* January 1971

> ... a routine surgical procedure to unblock his esophagus and allow him to eat —Ronald Reagan, *Abortion and the Conscience of the Nation,* 1984

2. *Allow of.* The intransitive *allow,* used with *of,* has excited the disapproval of Copperud 1964, but it is perfectly reputable. Reader's Digest 1983 accepts *allow of* with an impersonal subject, but not with a personal one. Our evidence for use with a personal subject is old; impersonal subjects predominate in current usage.

> ... I consented at the request of Lyell and Hooker to allow of an abstract from my manuscript ... to be published —Charles Darwin, reprinted in *The Practical Cogitator,* ed. Charles P. Curtis, Jr. & Ferris Greenslet, 1945

> ... the real charm of the 1930's bushwah Communism was the set of fine amateur theatricals it allowed of later —G. Legman, *The Fake Revolt,* 1967

> It takes a very sophisticated man to admit that the world is run by forces that do not always allow of rational analysis —G. R. Urban, *Center Mag.,* January 1969

> The past is the proper study of autobiography, for it allows of tranquil recollection —John Simon, in *The Film,* 1968

See also ADMIT 3; PERMIT OF.

3. The Dictionary of American Regional English lists four senses of *allow* with regional connections, some of which have come under attack as misuses, village idioms, vulgarisms, or provincialisms. We will take them up in order of increasing complexity.

"To plan, intend" (DARE sense 4). The DARE labels this sense chiefly Southern and Midland. They cite examples from Mark Twain, Bret Harte, Edward Eggleston. In this sense, *allow* is regularly followed by *to* and the infinitive:

> "I allowed to go back and help," Ellen said —Elizabeth Madox Roberts (born in Kentucky), *The Time of Man,* 1926

"To admit, concede" (DARE sense 3). This sense is mostly mainstream; it is not labeled in Webster's Third or in the OED. It has a considerable literary background:

> You'll allow, that nothing receives infection sooner, or retains it longer, than blankets, feather-beds, and mattresses —Tobias Smollett, reprinted in *Encore,* November 1944

> Those were your words. . . . it was some time, I confess, before I was reasonable enough to allow their justice —Jane Austen, *Pride and Prejudice,* 1813

> "Slay him not, Sir Knight," cried the Grand Master, "We allow him vanquished." —Sir Walter Scott, *Ivanhoe,* 1819

> . . . I flatter myself, that it will be allowed that I, at least, am a moral man —W. M. Thackeray, *The Book of Snobs,* 1846

> . . . one must allow that Pierre's promise of allegiance was kept —Henry Adams, *Mont-Saint-Michel and Chartres,* 1904

This sense continues to be used in mainstream English, usually, as earlier, followed by a clause:

> . . . asked if "Time and Time Again" would have a sequel, as rumored, he allowed it might —John K. Hutchens, *N.Y. Herald Tribune Book Rev.,* 27 Sept. 1953

> Epstein allows that the priest was on the right track —*Time,* 14 Mar. 1955

> Do ordinary people have more sense than professionals ordinarily allow? —*Nature,* 20 Sept. 1969

> We must . . . allow that economic pressure in itself can be generally disruptive —Elizabeth Janeway, *Atlantic,* March 1970

The DARE remarks that its senses 1 ("to suppose, think, consider") and 2 ("to assert, remark, opine, declare") are often hard to distinguish; some books, like the OED and Reader's Digest 1983, do not try to distinguish them. Sense 1 is marked chiefly Southern and Midland; 2 is not labeled, indicating widespread dialectal use.

When someone holds an opinion and expresses it, you cannot with certainty assign the use to either sense—it is a blend of the two. It is this blended use that is the most common in our files, and it sometimes takes most peculiar turns. First, we show a couple of examples that mean merely "say." These are both from the cor-respondence of Flannery O'Connor, a Georgian who used many regional expressions in her letters:

> My uncle Louis allowed he saw you the other day but you didn't see him —letter, 1 June 1957

> . . . she allowed that they were going to query Rodgers and Hammerstein —letter, 9 Mar. 1957

She also used *allow* in the blended sense:

> . . . heard Willard Thorpe read a paper on "The Grotesque in Southern Literature." He (Thorpe) allowed as how the roots of it were in antebellum Southern writings —letter, 10 Dec. 1957

> . . . she allowed as how she liked the book —letter, 24 Jan. 1962

We have evidence of Canadian use too—or at least use by Canadian-born authors:

> They all allowed it was the most splendid thing in the world —Thomas C. Haliburton, *The Clockmaker,* 1837

> "That," he allowed, beaming, "is my favorite city in the United States." —Mordecai Richler, *Saturday Rev.,* 8 Jan. 1977

And by an Indiana native, not noted for his use of regional terms:

> . . . the meritorious critic, P. P. Howe, thinks otherwise and allows it was Wilde's utter disinterest — George Jean Nathan, *The Theatre Book of the Year, 1946–1947*

But it is the use in widely distributed newspapers and magazines with no smack of the regional about them that is puzzling. *Winners & Sinners* disapproves this use:

> While he never disparaged Mr. Hoover, he allowed that the late founder of the Federal Bureau of Investigation "was a man of the old school." —*N.Y. Times,* 20 May 1975

But many similar uses appear in the *Times* and elsewhere, and they seem to be deliberate rather than inadvertant:

> Brunot allowed as how a certain number of sets could be sold by mail —Bennett Cerf, *Saturday Rev.,* 21 Mar. 1953

> Harry Truman met the press, felt the cloth of a reporter's cord suit and allowed as how he had one just like it —*Time,* 29 June 1953

> Renée Simmons, a 7-year-old . . . , shyly allowed that the roller skates were the best thing she had come across —Lisa Hammel, *N.Y. Times,* 7 July 1967

> . . . my faculty critic allowed as how the topic of drug use was a timely one —Robert J. Armbruster, *Johns Hopkins Mag.,* Spring 1971

> Premier Chou expressed cordiality toward the United States but allowed as how neither he nor . . . Mao Tse-tung, who is studying English, are planning American visits —John Hughes, *Christian Science Monitor,* 10 Oct. 1972

> All allowed that they liked it all right —John Fischer, *Harper's,* November 1972

Sounding like Polonius, Papp went on to allow that anything the British can do, we can do better —Karl E. Meyer, *Saturday Rev.,* 22 July 1978

... and Imogene Glover allowed as how she was intending to buy her son a sleeveless sweater —Enid Nemy, *N.Y. Times,* 12 Aug. 1980

Any hardwood will do, Henry allows, but hop hornbeam ... is preferable —Nancy Means Wright, *Blair & Ketchum's Country Jour.,* November 1980

Reader's Digest 1983 quotes William Safire:

Nixon allowed as how the best way to knock Romney down in the polls was to remove his winner status by beating him in New Hampshire —*Before the Fall*

with the observation that *allow as how* is being used for a mildly satirical effect. But there has to be more to it than that in our examples above—what would be the point, for instance, of satirizing, no matter how mildly, a 7-year-old girl on roller skates?

The picture is further complicated when the "concede, admit" sense is combined with "say," as it is rather frequently:

Riots conceivably are a good thing, Banfield allows, but we can't be very sure of that —Richard Todd, *Atlantic,* September 1970

... admits that the $5,000-per-couple tariff is fairly steep, and stands to net First Metropolitan a neat profit. "It's priced to reflect the uniqueness of the tour," he allows —Bruce McEwen, quoted by Robert Levy in *Dun's,* October 1971

The official cleared his throat and allowed as how that was so —William H. Honan, *Saturday Rev.,* May 1973

... a chastened Beutel allowed as how he wanted to return —Gary Paul Gates, *TV Guide,* 24 Aug. 1979

... admitted he had been scared up there. But then he allowed as how he is always scared in the wind —Jim Doherty, *Sports Illustrated,* 11 Aug. 1980

Conclusion: *Allow* "intend" (I allowed to help) is chiefly Southern and Midland; *allow* "concede" (You must allow that ...) has dialectal use but also much mainstream use, of which there is a long tradition; *allow* "say" (Uncle Louis allows he saw you) is dialectal; *allow* "suppose, think" (We allowed you wasn't coming) is chiefly Southern and Midland and somewhat old-fashioned. But when *allow* "say" combines with *allow* "think" or *allow* "concede," we seem to have something different. *Allow that* and *allow as how* have escaped from the bottle of regionalisms into general prose; they seem to be used, especially by journalists, as leavening to help in the creation of a light, informal style. While *allow* "concede" can be found in very serious writing—

It is allowed that Hegel may have propounded individual doctrines which could be of some interest: in aesthetics, in political philosophy, perhaps even in philosophy of religion —*Times Literary Supp.,* 19 June 1969

—*allow* "state as an opinion or concession" especially with *as how* cannot. The current use of *allow as how* is somewhat similar to the use of *ain't* in some of its fixed phrases, for both are signs of a style that aims not to impress but to charm with just-plain-folksiness. If you are unsure of how to use these expressions through unfamiliarity, or are simply not comfortable with them, we suggest you avoid them. But they are available to be used for the purposes described and in contexts like those quoted above.

See also AS HOW.

all ready, already In the closing decades of the 20th century the distinction between *all ready* and *already* no longer needs explanation except perhaps for school children. It is primarily a spelling problem now, one only rarely muffed by grown-ups:

A few of these have been sold for breeding purposes all ready —*Holstein-Friesian World,* 1 Mar. 1952

All ready is two words. When they occur together as a fixed phrase rather than a coincidence (as in "We are all ready to leave"), they mean *ready; all* is merely an intensive. The phrase exists chiefly in speech, and is seldom to be found in edited prose except transcribed speech. It is therefore seldom a problem.

Already is an adverb. It is used in sentences like this:

The train had already left when we got to the station —Corder 1981

all right   See ALRIGHT, ALL RIGHT.

all-round   See ALL-AROUND, ALL-ROUND.

all that The usage in question here is simply the adverbial *that* (see THAT 5) with the intensifier *all* added to it; it is almost always found in negative constructions:

... Durham City ... had not changed all that much since medieval times —Sam Pollock, *London Calling,* 10 June 1954

They are not all that worried now. They took Taft more seriously than Goldwater —C. L. Sulzberger, *N.Y. Times,* 9 Oct. 1963

Copperud 1970 cites himself, Bernstein 1965, and Heritage 1969 in disapproval, although he concedes that Fowler 1965 says it is approaching literary acceptance. Copperud claims the expression is a Briticism that sounds affected in the U.S. Mittins et al. 1970, on the other hand, cite a British usage book that says it is an Americanism. As you might expect from such contradictory statements, *not all that* is common on both sides of the Atlantic.

A large tomcat came along the gutter and found a fish head; he spurred it once or twice with his claws and then moved on: he wasn't all that hungry —Graham Greene, *The Confidential Agent,* 1939

He likes to act country, but he don't have all that far to go—he *is* country —Eudora Welty, *The Ponder Heart,* 1954

Piggy rebuked him with dignity.
"I haven't said anything all that funny." —William Golding, *Lord of the Flies,* 1954

... took a look at the cemetery designed by the great Sir Joseph, but didn't think it all that impressive —Clemence Dane, *The Flower Girls,* 1954

... asking at the wrong time why they did not go back to their Banks and Braes, if they were all that fashed about the lack of them —Wilson Neill, *Scots Mag.,* October 1957

Slowly he becomes aware that the world isn't all that easy to conquer —Hollis Alpert, *Saturday Rev.,* 3 Oct. 1964

By itself, the temporary walkout was not all that important —*Newsweek,* 27 June 1966

. . . anything that it takes a computer to work out is not gong to be checked all that quickly —*Times Literary Supp.,* 8 Sept. 1966

Even here Johnson is not being all that original: wishes of exactly this sort are a well established eighteenth-century satiric convention —Paul Fussell, *Samuel Johnson and the Life of Writing,* 1971

It was not that he would find life there dangerous or even, at the time, all that expensive —John Kenneth Galbraith, *New York,* 15 Nov. 1971

Farmers are not used to theatre and they're not all that polite —Rick Salutin, in *Canadian Theatre Rev.,* Spring 1975

Separate diseases, even though they were recognized as distinct clinical entities and given different names, were not regarded as all that separate in their underlying mechanisms —Lewis Thomas, *Atlantic,* April 1981

. . . incredibly rich and tasty and not all that difficult to prepare —Craig Claiborne et al., *N.Y. Times Mag.,* 24 Apr. 1983

Ebbitt & Ebbitt 1982 calls the construction "informal and imprecise"—complaining, as it were, about its primary virtues. It is used for understatement, sometimes with ironic intent. Harper 1975, 1985 and the survey of Mittins et al. agree in finding it unobjectionable in speech. Some of the foregoing examples are from real or fictional speech, but many are not. It has been used in fiction, in reportage, and occasionally in more serious writing. It appears to be established as standard.

all the   1. *All the* plus a comparative adverb (or sometimes adjective) is an English idiom that occurs in standard written English; in it *all the* functions as a simple intensifier:

. . . the omission found by me was an all the deadlier record of poor Soames' failure to impress himself on his decade —Max Beerbohm, *Seven Men,* 1920

. . . hating their clean white shiny faces and loving the Johnsons all the more —Morley Callaghan, *The Loved and the Lost,* 1951

They will like you all the better for not filling their minds with any nonsense about jurisprudence — Robert M. Hutchins, *Center Mag.,* January 1969

. . . from Soviet sources and therefore all the more revealing —*Geographical Jour.* June 1954

. . . and when this is the case the humanist is all the farther from revealing the relevance of the humanities to the contemporary concerns of most living men —*American Council of Learned Societies, Agenda,* 27-28 Oct. 1950

2. *All the* plus an adjective or adverb in the positive or comparative degree replaces the written *as . . . as* con-

struction in speech in many areas of the United States. Surveys made for the Dictionary of American Regional English found the construction in 40 of the 50 states, but it is especially common in Southern and South Midland speech with a positive adjective and in inland Northern and North Midland speech with a comparative adjective. Informants on all educational levels use the construction. For example,

That's all the fast this horse can run. (DARE)

is the spoken equivalent of the written

That's as fast as this horse can run.

Or

That is all the tighter I can tie it. (*American Speech,* December 1953)

is the spoken equivalent of

That's as tight as I can tie it.

If the handbooks are to be trusted, *all the farther* (or *further*) for the written *as far as* is particularly common. We have no evidence of the expression in written English, except in reports of speech. The *as . . . as* construction prevails in written English.

all-time   Copperud 1970, 1980 and Kilpatrick 1984 object to *all-time record* as redundant; Bernstein 1971 defends *all-time high* (aspersed by an editor of his acquaintance) as well as other uses of *all-time* in contexts where it is not superfluous. In these days of rampant record-keeping, *all-time* is not necessarily out of place as an intensifier. Records are reported by the day, month, quarter, year, decade, and many other units of time. Modification of *record* is often essential for clarity. *All-time* has been used with *record* since the 1930s:

Gehrig ties all-time record with four straight home runs —*N.Y. Times,* 4 June 1932

. . . 1936 was an all-time record year for the commercial producers —*Harper's,* February 1938

. . . flew from England to South Africa in 45 hours, an all-time record —*Time,* 4 Apr. 1938

It is still in use:

. . . who has set an all-time major-league record for saves during the season —Roger Angell, *New Yorker,* 11 Nov. 1972

. . . must set an all-time record for boredom in televised sports —Jonathan Evan Maslow, *Saturday Rev.,* 10 Dec. 1977

Most of the use of *all-time* is taken up in modifying a relatively few nouns. Among the most common are *high, low* (more common with *all-time* than *record* is), and *great.*

Betting also hit an all-time high —Audax Minor, *New Yorker,* 12 May 1973

. . . the power of traditionally shocking words to shock is at an all-time low —Thomas H. Middleton, *Saturday Rev.,* 11 Dec. 1976

. . . Dame Alicia Markova, an all-time ballet great — Walter Terry, *Saturday Rev.,* 12 Feb. 1972

Time has been writing *all-time* as one word without a hyphen since the 1940s, but most publications use the hyphenated form.

all together, altogether 1. Copperud 1970, 1980 warns us that these expressions are often confused; a score of books or more from 1907 to the present warn us not to confuse them. Evidence in the OED suggests, in fact, that *all together* "in a group"—actually an intensified form of *all*—was up until the late 16th or early 17th century spelled *altogether*. Thus, what the modern handbooks call confusion would appear to be simply a substitution of an obsolete spelling for what is now the usual form.

The problem is perhaps exacerbated by the sense of the adverb *altogether* that means "in all, in sum, in toto":

Altogether, about 1,500 insects died in the Harvard laboratories —Isaac Asimov, *Think,* May–June 1967

. . . altogether she has recorded twelve discs for this label —*Current Biography,* June 1967

This sense was at least once converted to *all together,* perhaps by someone who was trying too hard not to confuse the two:

Kazanski batted in five runs all together —*N.Y. Times,* 9 Aug. 1956 (cited in *Winners & Sinners* 15 Aug. 1956)

It is, however, the opposite error that the handbooks seem mostly interested in. It is first spotted in Fowler & Fowler 1907, where an example from something John Ruskin wrote is cited. Fowler 1926 adds a few more examples. The OED Supplement takes notice, with examples from 1765 to 1930. The Merriam-Webster files contain a few examples too:

Put it altogether, and it added up to a tragic Labor Day weekend —*Deerfield* (Wisc.) *Independent,* 2 Sept. 1954

. . . designs these three pieces with enough panache to be worn with basic black, or altogether as an ensemble —*Boston Proper Catalog,* Spring/Summer 1982

Here are a few examples of *all together:*

. . . life . . . is wider than science or art or philosophy or all together —Jacques Barzun, quoted in *Current Biography,* September 1964

. . . the crowd rose to them, clapping all together in time —William Hunter, *Glasgow* (Scotland) *Herald,* 14 June 1974

All together can be divided by intervening words, as those know who remember the satirist Tom Lehrer's line "We'll all go together when we go":

We must all be there together —Cleveland Amory, *Saturday Rev.,* 28 June 1969

There is a modern use of *together* as an adjective—a use sometimes associated with psychobabble—that is occasionally given emphasis by the addition of *all:*

Does he look nervous? Does he have it all together? —V. Lance Tarrance, quoted in *N.Y. Times Mag.,* 15 June 1980

The trouble was, however, that it was so concerned and involved and relevant and all together and right-on —Cleveland Amory, *TV Guide,* 13 Mar. 1971

. . . records for us Boswell-like the public all-together Angels —*Times Literary Supp.,* 11 Jan. 1968

This use too can turn up with the spelling of the adverb:

. . . just a nice, warm altogether sort of a family — Walter Schackenbach, quoted in *N.Y. Times,* 5 Mar. 1984

In spite of the instances from 1765 to 1984 of the adverbial spelling in place of the usually adjectival phrase, *all together* does not appear to be in danger of being replaced by the old one-word form. Still, you will want to take care in your choice of spelling, case by case.

2. We are assured by Copperud that when *altogether* means "nude" in the phrase *in the altogether,* it is spelled as one word. Why this warning is necessary is not clear, for no evidence of a two-word spelling has been brought forward since the expression first appeared in the novel *Trilby* by George du Maurier in 1894, and we have none. Perhaps the possibility of punning worries the pundits:

. . . these kids continually indulged in swimming all together in the "altogether" —*The Bulletin* (Sydney, Australia), 9 May 1903

A more interesting question is how du Maurier's "for the 'altogether'" became *in the altogether,* as it had by 1903. No one offers a guess.

all told Bernstein 1965, who is perhaps more aware of etymology than most of us, is alone in objecting to the use of this phrase when enumeration is not involved. The phrase is derived from the sense of *tell* that means "count." But the phrase is used in general summation too, perhaps because many people are unaware of the "count" meaning of the verb. Here are a couple of examples of each kind of summation. The numerical is more frequent.

All told, he figures, the government next year will borrow about $800 billion —Lindley H. Clark, Jr., *Wall Street Jour.,* 30 Dec. 1981

All told, some 63 species of birds breed in the Falklands —Tui De Roy Moore, *International Wildlife,* September–October 1982

All told, the "natural" granolas are not nearly as good for you —Jane E. Brody, *N.Y. Times,* 12 Dec. 1979

All told, a bad and boring book —Joseph W. Bishop, *Trans-Action,* February 1970

allude 1. *Allude* has been the subject of much commentary since sometime around the middle of the nineteenth century. Richard Grant White 1870 is the earliest critic in our library to discuss the subject, but Bardeen 1883 lists two sources from the 1860s, so White was not the originator. The gist of the 19th-century argument is that *allude* has a certain subtle meaning—"delicate" is White's term—involving indirection and wordplay that has been sullied if not entirely spoiled by the unlettered and unwashed, who cannot tell the difference between *allude* and *say, mention, name, speak of.* Around the turn of the century there is a slight shift in the wind: the new commentators (Vizetelly 1906, Bierce 1909, Utter 1916, for instance) abandon the lament for what is being lost and turn to straightforward prescription. "One can *allude* to a thing only indirectly," says Utter 1916; "What is alluded to is not mentioned, but referred to indirectly," says Bierce 1909. And so it goes, down to the present: "To *allude to* is to refer to indirectly" (Prentice Hall 1978); "To *allude* is to make indirect mention of something" (Corder 1981); "*Allude* means to refer to a person or thing indirectly or by suggestion" (Macmillan 1982). "*Allude* is often misused for *refer*," says Copperud 1970, 1980.

What is most important for you as a modern reader or writer to realize about these commentators—the distant and the recent alike—is that their whole argument is based on a set of false assumptions. First is the assumption of the primacy of the etymology. White insists that *allude* must involve wordplay because the word is derived from the Latin *alludere* "to play with." Vizetelly 1906 also talks at length about the etymology, but Bierce 1909 dismisses it: "That meaning is gone out of it." And indeed it had. The OED shows 1607 as the date of the latest example of *allude* used for wordplay.

The second false assumption is that the ignorant and uneducated are responsible for the "direct" sense (as opposed to the prescribed "indirect" sense). Even the OED subscribes to this view. Only Lounsbury 1908 has looked carefully enough to recognize that the sense has "been employed not simply by ordinary men, but by speakers and writers of high cultivation, and in a few instances of high authority." Examples of this class of use are given below in the course of the discussion.

The third false assumption is that the new "direct" use has driven or will drive the old subtle sense out of the language. The fact is that it has done no such thing in well over 100 years. You can use the "indirect" sense just as well today as you could two centuries ago:

You can disguise its aggressiveness all you want with veils of subordinate clauses and qualifiers and tentative subjunctives, with ellipses and evasions—with the whole manner of intimating rather than claiming, of alluding rather than stating —Joan Didion, *N.Y. Times Book Rev.,* 5 Dec. 1976

The fourth false assumption is that the "direct" use is a misuse. It is not. It is simply a logical extension from the indirect use, and indeed is an inevitable development from the surviving senses of *allude*—inevitable from the very indirectness of the earlier use.

Why inevitable? you may ask. Most readers, even those who later become authors, learn the use of words from the contexts in which they find them. *Allude* is often found in contexts in which it is not possible to know for certain whether the word is to be taken in its "indirect" sense or not. Some examples are offered here. In the first, those readers familiar with what Dr. Johnson said of Goldsmith will know if *allude* here is indirect or direct; others will not:

He had . . . none of that charm of style to which Dr. Johnson alluded when he wrote of Goldsmith, that he touched nothing he did not adorn —Thomas Seccombe, Introduction to Everyman edition of George Borrow's *Lavengro,* 1906

I wonder if you and Mrs. Aubrey Moore will ever allude to your acceptance of an invitation which she declined —Lewis Carroll, letter, 16 Nov. 1896

. . . it was against all the rules of their code that the mother and son should ever allude to what was uppermost in their thoughts —Edith Wharton, *The Age of Innocence,* 1920

Never once did he allude to the reason for her visit —Daphne du Maurier, *Ladies' Home Jour.,* September 1971

. . . but Boswell never heard Johnson allude to the matter —John Wain, *Samuel Johnson,* 1974

The resemblance between the two was strong, except that Dolly had a bust—a difference she alluded to several times —Jay McInerney, *Bright Lights, Big City,* 1984

In these contexts—which are of common occurrence— the reader is not given enough clues to identify one meaning or the other. These passages are not in the least incorrect or carelessly written—they are simply too general to help discriminate fine shades of meaning.

Then too, the very indirectness of reference of *allude* has contributed to the development of the direct sense. We will illustrate this with a passage written by John Adams; his use of *allude* is a textbook example— indeed, he probably could not have chosen a different word. But please notice where the actual allusion occurs with respect to where *allude* appears:

I concluded with a motion, in form, that Congress would adopt the army at Cambridge, and appoint a General; that though this was not the proper time to nominate a General, yet, as I had reason to believe this was a point of the greatest difficulty, I had no hesitation to declare that I had but one gentleman in my mind for that important command, and that was a gentleman from Virginia who was among us and very well known to all of us, a gentleman whose skill and experience as an officer, whose independent fortune, great talents, and excellent universal character, would command the approbation of all America, and unite the cordial exertions of all the Colonies better than any other person in the Union. Mr. Washington, who happened to sit near the door, as soon as he heard me allude to him, from his usual modesty, darted into the library-room —reprinted in *The Practical Cogitator,* ed. Charles P. Curtis, Jr. & Ferris Greenslet, 1945

This passage demonstrates that when the indirect sense of *allude* is clearly the one being used, the indirect reference itself is very likely to occur well ahead of the word. And if you begin reading in the middle, or if part of the passage is excerpted, you may never realize the care with which *allude* was selected.

Allude to has another sense—approximately "to mention in passing"—that the handbooks (but not the large dictionaries) tend to overlook. Here is a classic example of the use from George Jean Nathan:

If, suffering from a selfish conviction that I was doing too great a share of the work, I wrote him somewhat acrimoniously to that effect, instead of making matters worse by replying directly to the idiotic contention all that he would do would be to send me a lengthy list of his ailments, thus breaking my heart, together with some such irrelevant footnote as, "I hope you put aside a case of that Roederer against my birthday, which occurs on September 12th. In general, as you know, I detest birthday presents, but mature reflection has led me to conclude that I should make an exception of wines and liquors of high tone."

I have alluded to his maladies. —*The Intimate Notebooks of George Jean Nathan,* 1932

Nathan, having mentioned the maladies in passing, goes on then to expand upon the subject considerably. This use of *allude* is not rare—it is accounted for by definitions in the OED and Webster's Third. Again we find the allusion itself placed at some distance from *allude.*

In our next example, from Thackeray, the actual allusion (in the edition at hand) is on the preceding page:

It is not snobbish of persons of rank of any other nation to employ their knife in the manner alluded to —*The Book of Snobs,* 1846

The manner alluded to involves the use of the knife to eat peas with. Between the description of the act and Thackeray's resumption of the subject on the next page there is interposed a considerable bit of matter devoted to Thackeray's social relationship with the man who so used his knife. But the allusion is not, in fact, merely mentioned in passing—it is the chief motivating action of the essay. Thackeray's allusion is at once more remote—physically—and less casual than Nathan's. (And even Nathan's reference has been purposely planted to supply a bridge to the further discussion of maladies.)

From a variety of rhetorical strategies or unintended effects, then, the "indirect" sense can shade into the "direct" sense; they are, so to speak, simply different parts of a continuum. There does not appear to be anything out of the ordinary in the development, and, given the number of ambiguous examples likely to be encountered, it hardly seems possible that *allude* could have continued pure in the narrow stream of signification the commentators had laid out for it. What we have in reality is a word with three interrelated uses—indirect, casual, direct—that can shade into one another imperceptibly. We conclude this exegesis with a selection of examples from this century and the last—most of them considerably shorter than the preceding examples— some of which will fit obviously into one or another of the three categories of use, and some of which will not. They are all impeccably standard.

She alluded once or twice to her husband but her tone was not such as to make the allusion a warning —James Joyce, *Dubliners,* 1914

He ascribed the poverty of her attire to the attempts to keep herself respectable, which Ellen during supper had more than once alluded to —Samuel Butler, *The Way of All Flesh,* 1903

Hazlitt has written a *grammar* for Godwin; Godwin sells it bound up with a treatise of his own on language, but the *grey mare is the better horse.* I don't allude to Mrs. Godwin, but to the word *grammar* — Charles Lamb, letter, 2 Jan. 1810

Never once did she allude to anything that had occurred since her marriage —Ellen Glasgow, *Barren Ground,* 1925

He never alluded so directly to his story again —E. E. Hale, *The Man Without A Country,* 1863

. . . that intense mental collectedness and concentration to which I have previously alluded as observ-

able only in particular moments —Edgar Allan Poe, "The Fall of the House of Usher," 1839

He writhes when anyone so much as hints at a reference to his work, and actually groans aloud today when V. alludes to a dramatization of *Brave New World* —Robert Craft, *Stravinsky,* 1972

She remembered what a sweet, lovely, polite girl my sister was, and was shocked that I should be so thoughtless as to write as I had about her intimate life, especially to make jokes about her unfortunate tendency to gain weight. Since unlike Alexander Portnoy, I happen never to have had a sister, I assumed it was some other Jewish Athena with a tendency to gain weight to whom my correspondent was alluding —Philip Roth, *Reading Myself and Others,* 1975

At one of the plenary sessions, Churchill alluded obliquely to his idea —*New Statesman & Nation,* 19 Dec. 1953

. . . sexual matters only obliquely alluded to —Howard Kissel, *Women's Wear Daily,* 25 Oct. 1976

. . . proposals, which were never called proposals, but always alluded to slightingly as innovations — Compton Mackenzie, *The Parson's Progress,* 1923

". . . The trouble with fruit, though, is that it gives him that intestinal condition I alluded to." —Jean Stafford, *Children Are Bored on Sunday,* 1945

To be such a master of the inward richness of words is to take visionary possession of the things to which the words allude —Richard Poirier, *A World Elsewhere,* 1966

. . . the records of the colony allude to beer as one of its commodities —*Dictionary of American History,* 1940

This theory is alluded to in the title; it is explicitly stated, by my count, at least thirty times in the book —David Littlejohn, *Commonweal,* 30 Jan. 1970

. . . serves as a kind of fable, to which the rest of the novel will repeatedly allude in one way or another — *Times Literary Supp.,* 7 Nov. 1968

I'm bound to allude to some classic of literature whether it's Pindar or Homer or Virgil —Erich Segal, quoted in *Vogue,* 1 Aug. 1971

By now you will have a good enough sense of how *allude* is actually used to be able to ignore with safety the blinkered directions of the handbooks.

2. *Allude, elude.* MacCracken & Sandison 1917 warn against confusing *allude* and *elude.* The verbs sound about the same, but differ considerably in meaning, as a glance at your dictionary will demonstrate. We do have evidence that they are occasionally confused:

. . . widespread recognition has alluded Larry Sparks —*Bluegrass Unlimited,* February 1982

If you are doubtful, get out that dictionary.

allusion Fowler 1926 and a few other commentators (as Bryson 1984) discuss their disapproval of the sense development of *allude* under this heading. See the discussion at ALLUDE 1.

ally *Ally* is used about equally with *to* or *with* when it requires a preposition:

Closely allied to his pride was his very strict sense of justice —Robert A. Hall, Jr., *A Short History of Italian Literature,* 1951

Allied to this general problem is the need in many cases to retrain teachers —James B. Conant, *Slums and Suburbs,* 1961

It is to ally you with the events of the page —Bernard DeVoto, *The World of Fiction,* 1950

John Dewey and Thorstein Veblen were allied in his mind with the Chicago sociologist George Herbert Mead —Alfred Kazin, *N.Y. Times Book Rev.,* 16 Sept. 1979

Our files show that when *ally* is used with *to,* the verb is usually in the past tense or in the past participle; when *ally* is used with *with,* a greater variety of tenses appears. *Ally* is also used with *against* sometimes:

... the great resources and wealth of the Arab states should be allied against the temptations ... of godless communism —David L. Lawrence, *Land Reborn,* November–December 1953

almost 1. See MOST, ALMOST.
2. Copperud 1970, 1980 tells us that *almost* as an adjective modifying a noun is standard and well established, but that in the U.S. this use is likely to be considered a mistake. Who considers it a mistake now we do not know, but around the turn of the century there seems to have been some controversy about it. Vizetelly 1906 considers that the adjective use "has not received the sanction of general usage." Hall 1917 reports the textbooks of three rhetoricians—A. S. Hill, Quackenbos, Genung—as condemning the construction, but he cites examples of its use by Thackeray, Hawthorne, Coleridge and others. Evidence in the Merriam-Webster files shows the adjective use to be standard, but not especially frequent. Here is a sampling, including many American sources:

At Barking, in the almost solitude of which so large a portion of my life was passed —Jeremy Bentham, "Reminiscences of Childhood," 1843

The contrast between Harding's zest for physical exercise and his almost torpor when in repose — Mark Sullivan, *Our Times,* vol. 6, 1935

... the car skidded, plowing sideways to an almost stop —Ernest Hemingway, "The Short Happy Life of Francis Macomber," in *The Short Stories,* 1938

... a potential, an almost Prime Minister —*Times Literary Supp.,* 12 Feb. 1938

There was a flash of almost admiration —Christopher Morley, *The Man Who Made Friends with Himself,* 1949

... a little fellow whom only an almost miracle can set on his feet —Henry Seidel Canby, *Saturday Rev.,* 13 Sept. 1952

... the present limits and the future possibilities of the almost science of economics —Robert Lekachman, *New Republic,* 10 Aug. 1953

So the U.S. embraces an *almost* imperialism — Michael Harrington, *American Power in the Twentieth Century,* 1967

The adjective is sometimes hyphenated to its noun:

... the blond with the almost-beard —Ned Hoopes, *Media & Methods,* November 1968

... and an almost-doctorate from Harvard —*Business Week,* 22 July 1972

Almost also has some uses as an adverb that look much like adjective uses:

Almost everybody should be happy —*Forbes,* 1 Dec. 1970

... he was almost a virgin —David J. Pittman, *Trans-Action,* March–April 1971

... the students, almost all of whom live at home — James B. Conant, *Slums and Suburbs,* 1961

... how young an animal—a baby almost —Stephen Jay Gould, *Natural History,* December 1983

3. The use of *almost* before *never* (and other negatives such as *no* and *nothing*) comes in for passing mention in Harper 1975, 1985 and Copperud 1980. Harper believes that some people still object to this combination, but the issue is an old one, dating back to the 18th century, and seems to draw little attention now. Copperud and Jespersen 1917 both mention James Boswell, who was prevailed upon to change such sentences as "I suppose there is almost no language" to "we scarcely know of a language" by the argument that *almost no* or *almost nothing* was not English. Boswell apparently had his doubts, but revised all the same. Jespersen adduces examples from British, Scottish, and American English to demonstrate that the construction was not especially rare. Among the English writers Jespersen quotes are Bacon, Cowper, and Jane Austen:

... she has found almost nothing —Jane Austen, *Mansfield Park,* 1814

The same phrase occurs in Ford Madox Ford:

... if he wants to find Louis Treize stuff ... for almost nothing —*The Last Post,* 1928

Jespersen cites Henry James, too:

He himself was almost never bored —*The American,* 1877

These are a couple of more recent examples from our files:

... has accomplished almost nothing —Joseph P. Lyford, *Center Mag.,* May 1968

... you could almost never get him in so far that he couldn't get out and beat you —R. C. Padden, *Harper's,* February 1971

It is hard to imagine anyone objecting to them.
4. Copperud 1970, 1980 and Johnson 1982 object to *almost* before comparatives like *more, less,* and *better* on the grounds that it violates logic. Although both seem to feel the construction is common, we have no examples of it in the Merriam-Webster files. It may be chiefly or exclusively an oral use.

alone From Ayres 1881 to Jensen 1935 a modest amount of objection was entered to *alone* meaning "only," as in

It is written, That man shall not live by bread alone —Luke 4:4 (AV), 1611

Jensen explains that the sense is not current; but in fact the sense was current in the 19th century when Ayres wrote, and is still current in carefully edited standard prose:

He alone lynches in cold blood —G. Legman, *Love and Death,* 1949

. . . not all of whom had their minds on baseball alone —Al Hirshberg, quoted in *Current Biography,* March 1965

. . . decided that fur trading alone would never make New Netherland a proper colony —Samuel Eliot Morison, *Oxford History of the American People,* 1965

Follett 1966 and Barzun 1975 try to tease some ambiguity out of sentences like those above in order to justify a preference for *only* that Ayres simply states. But when *alone* means "only", it regularly follows the noun it modifies. One can argue that

Davis now alone unites them —Henry Adams, letter, 23 Apr. 1863

is ambiguous, since it is not certain whether *alone* means "only" or "all by himself," but the ambiguity is really created by the intervention of *now* between the name and *alone.* Reverse the adjective and adverb, and presto—no more ambiguity. In any case, worrying about ambiguity here is worth little, because the sentence says essentially the same thing no matter which interpretation you give *alone.* When an author wants to emphasize "by oneself," *alone* is usually placed after a verb or copula:

She wished only to be alone —Stella Gibbons, *Cold Comfort Farm,* 1932

alongside of, alongside Longman 1984 tells us *alongside of* is widely disliked, but little evidence of widespread dislike has reached our files. The Oxford American Dictionary, Shaw 1962, and Harper 1975, 1985 mention it. It is, of course, perfectly proper, and historically antecedent to the single word preposition, *alongside,* recommended by our four commentators. The adverb *alongside* came first, was then used as a preposition with *of,* and later the *of* was dropped. (For a counter case where the commentators object to dropping *of,* see COUPLE, *adjective.*) The OED shows that *alongside of* was used by Thomas Jefferson and Nathaniel Hawthorne in the 19th century.

Our files show that *alongside* has been more frequently used in the modern era than *alongside of,* and that *alongside* is much more common in our most recent evidence; use of the two-word form may be beginning to recede. Our evidence also suggests that the nautical origin of these words is no longer a major factor in their use and that figurative use is at least as common as the literal use that refers to physical position. We will give you a sampling of 20th-century use of *alongside of* and then a few, mostly recent, examples of the single-word preposition.

Alongside of your last letter a day or two ago came a dear little note from your daughter —Oliver Wendell Holmes d. 1935, letter, 5 Nov. 1923

. . . Tacitus really has the spirit of great drama and alongside of him the medieval chroniclers . . . seem dull and tame —Harold J. Laski, letter, 15 Aug. 1925

. . . airplanes that will stand up fairly well alongside of the best in the world —*Yale Rev.,* 1936

. . . now engaged alongside of us in the battle —Dwight D. Eisenhower, *Britain To-Day,* September 1944

They also use them alongside of the ideograms —Mario Pei, *The Story of Language,* 1949

. . . postulate a second substance whose essence is thought, alongside of body —Noam Chomsky, *Columbia Forum,* Spring 1968

This work had to be carried forward alongside the first —Harry S. Truman, State of the Union Address, 7 Jan. 1953

Should it, in a draft . . . , have been published alongside the flawless final writing of *The Great Gatsby?* —James Thurber, *New Republic,* 22 Nov. 1954

. . . bring the launch alongside the Lamb Island dock —Daphne du Maurier, *Ladies' Home Jour.,* September 1971

Did the novel grow out of the critical study, or alongside it . . . ? —J. M. Cocking, *Times Literary Supp.,* 21 May 1982

. . . ever since she graduated (alongside Nancy Davis Reagan) from Smith College —William F. Buckley, Jr., *New Yorker,* 31 Jan. 1983

aloof The usual preposition following *aloof* is *from:*

. . . the Peels were always quite aloof from the ordinary social life of the town —Arnold Bennett, *The Old Wives' Tale,* 1908

He stood aloof from worldly success —John Buchan, *Pilgrim's Way,* 1940

. . . remain aloof from the war —Irwin Shaw, *The Young Lions,* 1948

. . . morbidly aloof from reality —William Styron, *Lie Down in Darkness,* 1951

I felt curiously aloof from my own self —Vladimir Nabokov, *Lolita,* 1958

. . . remain resolutely aloof from the Vietnam war —Norman Cousins, *Saturday Rev.,* 28 June 1975

Occasionally *to* is used:

. . . the United States remained coldly aloof to the suggestion —*Collier's Year Book,* 1949

. . . respectful but aloof to Marx, Engels, and Lenin —Lucien Price, *Dialogues of Alfred North Whitehead,* 1954

Other prepositions may be used to indicate somewhat different relationships:

He is terse, cool-headed in a crisis, inclined to be aloof with strangers —Tris Coffin, *Nation's Business,* April 1954

. . . holding herself aloof in chosen loneliness of passion —Paul Elmer More, *Selected Shelburne Essays,* 1921

alot, a lot *A lot* is apparently often written as one word—perhaps by people in a hurry—for we have an even dozen handbooks reminding their readers to write it as two words, and presumably there are others. Two words is the accepted norm:

> Each of these writers had plainly worried about my Nat Turner a lot —William Styron, *This Quiet Dust and Other Writings,* 1982

> The Kremlin must be a lot like this —Jay McInerney, *Bright Lights, Big City,* 1984

Our evidence for the one-word spelling *alot* comes mostly from memos, drafts, private letters. It occasionally sees the light of day in newspapers where proofreading has not been careful enough:

> "When I was in junior, I was on the power-play alot," Turgeon said —*Morning Union* (Springfield, Mass.), 3 Nov. 1983

See also LOTS, A LOT.

aloud See OUT LOUD.

already See ALL READY, ALREADY.

alright, all right Is *alright* all right? The answer is a qualified yes, with these cautions. First, *all right* is much more common in print than *alright.* Second, many people, including the authors of just about every writer's handbook, think *alright* is all wrong. Third, *alright* is more likely to be found in print in comic strips (like "Doonesbury"), trade journals, and newspapers and magazines (*Rolling Stone, Cosmopolitan, Punch,* or *The American Rifleman,* for instance) than in more literary sources, although it does appear from time to time in literature as well.

How did *alright* come to be in this situation? It has a complex and somewhat mysterious history. It seems to have been formed in Old English as *ealriht,* but was used in senses that are now obsolete. In those days before printing, the spelling and compounding of a word depended entirely on scribal practice, which varied considerably. Early citations for the word in the OED and Middle English Dictionary show such variant forms as *eall right, alrihtes, al riht, alriht, all rihht, al rizt,* and *al right.* It is not until Chaucer's "Criseyde was this lady name, al right" (ca. 1385) that we find an early citation for what sounds like a modern use.

After Chaucer, however, there is a long gap in the record, and we have no examples of *all right* until the late seventeenth and early eighteenth centuries, where it appears as part of a longer phrase, *all right as my leg,* in which *all* is a pronoun.

> STAND. Five guineas. [*Gives her money.*]
> PAR. Are they right? [*Examines them.*] No Gray's-Inn pieces amongst 'em.
> All right as my leg.
> —George Farquhar, *Sir Harry Wildair,* 1701 (quoted from *S.P.E. Tract* 18, 1924)

In *Robinson Crusoe* (1719) we find "desir'd him to . . . keep all right in the Ship" (OED), with *all* still a pronoun. Uses of the two words as a fixed phrase begin to turn up only in the first half of the nineteenth century.

> That was all right, my friend. —Percy Bysshe Shelley, *Scenes from Goethe's Faust,* 1822 (OED)

> 'Stand firm, Sam,' said Mr. Pickwick, looking down. 'All right, sir,' replied Mr. Weller. —Charles Dickens, *Pickwick Papers,* 1837 (*S.P.E. Tract* 18)

> I got your letter all right. —Edward FitzGerald, letter, 1844 (*S.P.E. Tract* 18)

What happened to the phrase between Chaucer and Shelley we simply don't know. It may have continued in oral use all along but have been seldom used in works that have survived. Or it may have been re-formed in modern English. At any rate, before the nineteenth century ended, *alright* had appeared in print.

> I think I shall pass alright —*Durham University Jour.,* November 1893 (OED Supplement)

Alright did not appear in a Merriam-Webster dictionary until 1934, but several dictionary users had spotted its omission earlier and had written to us to urge its inclusion. The earliest of these was a New York businessman named William E. Scott:

> I wish you would submit to your experts the feasibility of putting the word *alright* into use. As a matter of fact it is used quite extensively without the authority of dictionaries because it is the quick common-sense way of doing. The cable and telegraph companies are the ones who profit by the lack of an authoritative ruling that *alright* is synonymous with *all right* —25 Sept. 1913

Scott's letter suggests some of the influences that kept *alright* in use. A still stronger force is that of analogy: words like *altogether, already,* and *although* were similarly formed in Old or Middle English, and had come into modern English as solid words. When *alright* came to be a matter of dispute, many commentators recognized the force of analogy and then had to devise reasons to deny its applicability.

The controversy over the appropriateness of *alright* seems to have begun in the early 20th century. In August 1909, this answer to a letter from a reader appeared in the *Literary Digest.* It was probably written by Frank Vizetelly; his *A Desk Book of Errors in English* (1906) carries the same message.

> The correct form is "all right"; this is the commonly accepted form to-day. Formerly "alright" had some vogue and like "already" was formed of two words, but altho "all ready" was displaced early in our literature (1380) by "already" "all right" did not meet with the same fate.

There was reaction against *alright* in Great Britain too. In 1924 the Society for Pure English published a symposium on *alright* (Tract 18), and here H. W. Fowler took up the cudgels against it. He appears to have been irritated by *alright* primarily because he considered it bad spelling. His *Modern English Usage* of 1926 condensed his 1924 denunciation; from that point on nearly all usage commentators fall into line. We have recorded thirty-five to forty commentators, both British and American, expressing disapproval; only one or two dissent. It should be noted, however, that the usual way of disapproving *alright* is to append a pejorative label (as *illiterate* or *colloquial*) to it or to deny it exists; no very cogent reasons are presented for its being considered wrong.

Even the critics of *alright* admit it is found more often in manuscript than in print; undoubtedly it would be even more frequent in print than it is if copy editors were less hostile. (Theodore Dreiser used it repeatedly in the manuscript of *The 'Genius'* in 1914; H. L. Mencken had him change it to *all right.*) Our evidence shows that it is used in letters, real and fictional:

> I hope that this procedure is alright with you —editor, N.Y. publishing house, letter received at Merriam-Webster, 1964

> I had intended to ask you to give a lecture much like you have in the past. I hope that is alright with you —director, technical writing institute, letter received at Merriam-Webster, 1984

> Yes, I did get your letter alright —Margaret Kennedy, *The Feast,* 1950

> He told Regina that he had told me and she said that was alright —Flannery O'Connor, letter, July 1952

Miss O'Connor used both spellings:

> . . . but if so I can do without it all right —letter, 1 Jan. 1956

One of the points involved in the discussion of the propriety of *alright* hinges on the assertion that *all right* represents one stress pattern in speech, and *alright* another. Evans 1962 alludes to this point when he says, "My own—dissenting—opinion is that most people who write *alright* instead of *all right* (when they mean "alright" and not "all right") are not slovenly. They are simply asking for the privilege of making a distinction in writing which is accepted in speech." This argument is difficult to evaluate because stress patterns are observable only in speech, whereas *alright* is purely a spelling variant. But it is a fact of some relevance, perhaps, that when *alright* is used in fiction, it is very often used in representing the speech of the characters:

> "My briefing alright, First Sergeant?" —Josiah Bunting, *The Lionheads,* 1972

> 'Alright. O.K. I'll write him a cheque right now.' —Mordecai Richler, *The Apprenticeship of Duddy Kravitz,* 1959

> ". . . It's goin' to be alright. . . ." —Waldo Frank, *Not Heaven,* 1953

> "Alright, wait a minute," —Langston Hughes, *Laughing to Keep from Crying,* 1952

> "Well, alright, but you're going to miss your golf. . . ." —Pat Frank, *Hold Back the Night,* 1952

> Alright, already! I'll turn on the grill! —Gary B. Trudeau, *Guilty, Guilty, Guilty,* 1973

It appears in Molly Bloom's soliloquy:

> . . . however alright well seen then let him go to her —James Joyce, *Ulysses,* 1922

It is also used in other transcribed speech.

> "Alright, darling. I was wrong. I apologise." —Eamonn Andrews, *Punch,* 1 May 1974

> Mom said, "Yes, it's lonely here alright. It's lonely." —John Allan May, *Christian Science Monitor,* 1 Aug. 1953

> . . . so let's look at Bittman. Bittman says he is trying to blackmail the White House. Alright you called Bittman —Richard M. Nixon, in *The White House Transcripts,* 1974

> "Okay honey, I've ironed your blue ensemble if that's alright. . . ." —Jim Guzzo, *Springfield* (Mass.) *Republican,* 30 Dec. 1984

From the beginning *alright* seems to have reached print primarily in journalistic and business publications. We have plenty of evidence that it continues to appear in these publications:

> There's plenty of luxury here alright —*Variety,* 28 Jan. 1942

> The first batch of aquatic ovines will get by alright —T. J. McManus, *Tasmanian Jour. of Agriculture,* May 1962

> War is there alright —Richard Gilman, *New Republic,* 25 Nov. 1967

> . . . came out alright in the end —*National Jeweler,* January 1942

> Berkeley is a weird city, alright —Ralph J. Gleason, *Rolling Stone,* 13 May 1971

> Alright, alright—I know, it was all the fault of those confounded British colonialists! —Brian Walker, *Bicycling!,* January 1971

> We got through it alright —Avery Corman, *Cosmopolitan,* October 1974

> . . . the movie tells us it's alright for him to cheat his customers —David Sterritt, *Christian Science Monitor,* 11 Sept. 1980

> Gutenberg's movable type was alright for the middle ages —*British Printer,* February 1976

> They will see him alright for food and female company —Jonathan Sale, *Punch,* 7 Oct. 1975

Finally, we have a little evidence from books where speech is not being re-created.

> Men don't want a woman to wilt on them. That was alright in Mother's time —Vivian Ellis, *Faint Harmony,* 1934

> The first two years of the medical school were alright —Gertrude Stein, *The Autobiography of Alice B. Toklas,* 1933

> Trying to decide if it is alright to say *anxious* when you mean *eager* —Quinn 1980

Summary: in its modern use *alright* has reached print primarily through journalistic and business publication and is still to be found in those sources. It has appeared now and again in literature, at least from the mid-twenties, though mostly in fictional dialogue. Its critics acknowledge that it is more often to be found in manuscript than in print; it would likely be much more nearly as frequent as *all right* if it were not so regularly suppressed by copy editors. It seems to have some acceptance in British English—in spite of disapproval in British handbooks: it is the standard spelling in *Punch* and the King's Printer at Ottawa officially sanctioned its use as far back as 1928. The OED Supplement calls it simply "a frequent spelling of *all right.*" It remains a commonly written but less often printed variant of *all right.* It is clearly standard in general prose, but is widely condemned nonetheless by writers on usage.

also This word raises two related problems for usage commentators, and we will take them one at a time.

First we have the matter of *also* used as a loose connective roughly equivalent to *and.* Some of the commentators call this *also* a conjunction, but in the language of traditional grammar it is a conjunctive adverb. The palm for discovering this problem goes to the brothers Fowler (Fowler 1907), who showed Richard Grant White using the conjunctive *also:*

> 'Special' is a much overworked word, it being used to mean great in degree, also peculiar in kind — *Words and their Uses,* 1870

The Fowlers added two more examples, both from *The* (London) *Times.* Since 1907 this construction has picked up considerable unfavorable notice, especially in handbooks, right into the 1980s. Criticism is strongest when the elements joined by *also* are words or phrases (as in the example from White), but some commentators extend it to the joining of clauses. The curious thing is that no one but the Fowlers has an attributed example to bring forward. The question becomes, then, who uses this construction, and where? The coverage in college handbooks suggests it turns up in student papers, and it apparently occurs in speech—Reader's Digest 1983 finds it acceptable in speech and most of the handbooks disapprove it only in writing. Margaret M. Bryant says in *English in the Law Courts* (1930) that it is common in speech. Her examples show it to have been common also in 19th-century American wills. Here is an example, much abridged:

> I give, devise, and bequeath to my beloved wife . . . my homestead . . . with the buildings thereon . . . ; also all my farming tools and utensils . . . ; also one thousand dollars.

This use continues common in wills, and judges are still having to decide what *also* means in disputed cases.

Wills are rather a special kind of writing, however. More apt for your guidance are literature and contemporary general published prose, and our files yield examples of conjunctive *also* in both categories:

> . . . these are the only eels I have heard of here;— also, I have a faint recollection of a little fish some five inches long, with silvery sides and a greenish back —Henry David Thoreau, *Walden,* 1854

> Accompanying it were two accessories, also bits of pottery —Herman Melville, *The Confidence Man,* 1857

> . . . tends to obscure the new affiliations of psychology with the sciences of biology, sociology, and anthropology; also its claim to be considered as a natural science itself —Thomas Munro, *The Arts and Their Interrelations,* 1949

> . . . and they occasionally go to galleries together; also Mitterand fancies old books, and occasionally they browse together in bookshops —John Newhouse, *New Yorker,* 30 Dec. 1985

Our examples are not numerous, however, and concordances of major authors often omit *also,* so it is hard to be sure just how common this use is in published writing.

The handbooks' approach to the conjunctive *also* is to recommend conversion to *and* or *and also.* (The commentators who prescribe *and also* are presumably not the same ones Nickles 1974 notes as condemning *and also* as a redundant phrase.) *And also* is common in all kinds of writing:

> By October of 1983, the CNN Headline News Service . . . was going out to six hundred and seventy-five cable systems, . . . and also to a hundred and forty-three commercial television stations — Thomas Whiteside, *New Yorker,* 3 June 1985

> . . . a lifelong favorite of Borges and also frequently alluded to —Ambrose Gordon, Jr., *Jour. of Modern Literature,* 1st issue, 1970

> Like Izzy, Moe was a natural comedian, and also like Izzy, he was corpulent —Herbert Asbury, in *The Aspirin Age 1919–1941,* ed. Isabel Leighton, 1949

> . . . slices of liver and also of kidney —*Annual Rev. of Biochemistry,* 1946

As mentioned earlier, Reader's Digest 1983 finds the conjunctive *also* acceptable in speech and informal writing, but would avoid it in formal writing. The rest tend to disapprove it in writing, period, although Fowler 1926 will allow it when the writer needs to emphasize that what follows is an afterthought. The relative dearth of evidence for its use strongly suggests that we have here much ado over very little. *Also* is a much less frequently used word than *and;* apparently most people make do with *and* in writing as their additive conjunction.

The second problem involves beginning a sentence with *also.* Follett 1966, Janis 1984, Harper 1985, Bander 1978, and Perrin & Ebbitt 1972 suggest avoiding *also* at the beginning of a sentence. Bernstein 1971 allows some sentences to begin with *also;* his example turns out to be an inverted sentence of a kind also approved by Follett, Perrin & Ebbitt, and Janis. This type of inverted sentence does exist:

> Also created was a Governor's Commission for Efficiency and Improvement in Government —*Current Biography,* December 1964

> Also old are the words from Old English and Middle English —W. F. Bolton, *A Short History of Literary English,* 1967

But the evidence in our files shows it to be of relatively infrequent occurrence. Most of the sentences beginning with *also* in our files are of the straightforward type the commentators seem to disapprove:

> Also, at the mouth of the Nile, fish in the Mediterranean used to feed on organisms conveyed by the silt —William Styron, *This Quiet Dust and Other Writings,* 1982

> Also, certain even-numbered groups of protons and neutrons are particularly stable —*Current Biography,* June 1964

> Also, it was in itself, as I have said, a period of depressed spirits —Sacheverell Sitwell, *All Summer in a Day,* 1926

> Also, he was not in the Congresses which debated the danger of war —Jonathan Daniels, in *The Aspirin Age 1919–1941,* ed. Isabel Leighton, 1949

> Also, Latin seems to have been used for cultural purposes much more exclusively than in western countries —Gilbert Highet, *The Classical Tradition,* 1949

> Also, during the summer, so-called interim disciplinary rules were promulgated —Sylvan Fox, *N.Y. Times,* 9 Jan. 1969

The objections to this use of *also* are not usually stated clearly; it is simply described as "weak." Bernstein 1971, one of the few books to elaborate on the topic, sees it as essentially just an aspect of the problematic conjunctive use of *also.* Beginning a sentence, it suggests that what follows is an afterthought and thus that the writer is disorganized and self-indulgent. Despite occasional references by other critics to functional classes like conjunction, adverb, conjunctive adverb, it is difficult to escape the conclusion that this is entirely a matter of style, and has nothing to do with grammar. The objection seems about as soundly based as the widely believed notion that you should never begin a sentence with *and.* Our evidence agrees with the statement in Perrin & Ebbitt that *also* usually stands within the sentence. But some writers of high repute do use it as an opener, and you can too, when you think it appropriate.

alternate, *verb*   Bernstein 1965 tells us this verb takes *with,* but that is only half the story. One person or one thing may alternate *with* another or others; one person or one thing may alternate *between* (usually) two things.

Some examples of *with:*

> . . . the popluation has in fact pressed close upon the food supply, and security has alternated with famine —Lewis Mumford, *Technics and Civilization,* 1934

> The plan enabled Robertson to alternate seven weeks of study with seven weeks of work —*Current Biography,* January 1966

> Basso Norman Scott, who this season alternates with Moscona and three others in the part —*Time,* 28 Mar. 1955

> . . . dark green alternating with light green stripes, bluish green, bluish or yellowish gray, light cream, yellowish brown, etc. —Jane Nickerson, *N.Y. Times Mag.,* 4 July 1954

Some examples of *between:*

> Alternating between sensuous and explosive styles —*Look,* 2 Feb. 1960, in *Current Biography,* June 1965

> The reader alternates between admiration . . . and irritation —*Times Literary Supp.,* 5 Mar. 1970

> . . . alternating perpetually between physical and mental activity —Agnes Repplier, *The Fireside Sphinx,* 1901

> The weather alternated between blinding sandstorms and brilliant sunlight —Willa Cather, *Death Comes for the Archbishop,* 1927

> . . . the rest of the spectators continued to alternate between maddening immobility and creeping movement —Irving Wallace, *The Plot,* 1967

We have one citation with *among,* which may be a copy editor's doing:

> . . . the author alternates among mod slang, clichés and quotes from literary giants —Albert H. Johnston, *Publishers Weekly,* 24 July 1978

alternate, alternative, *adjectives*   The adjectives *alternate* and *alternative,* say many commentators, are often confused; they advise keeping them separate. The senses recommended are "occurring or succeeding by

turns" for *alternate,* and "offering or expressing a choice" for *alternative.* But not much light is shed on how these words are confused, if indeed they are, nor on what actual use is. We will begin our examination with Fowler 1926.

Fowler says that *alternative* (and *alternatively*) "had formerly, besides their present senses, those now belonging" to *alternate* (and *alternately*). He claims that the two words are now (in 1926) completely differentiated, a claim somewhat vitiated by his following it immediately with an example, presumably from some British newspaper, of *alternatively* meaning "by turns." This violation of his dictum he terms "confusion."

There are two separate considerations here. The first is the use of *alternative* where *alternate* might be expected; the second, *alternate* where *alternative* might be expected.

The first use is, so far as we know, the oldest sense of the adjective *alternative,* attested in 1540. Johnson missed it in his 1755 dictionary, but Todd added it in his expanded edition at the beginning of the 19th century. Robert Herrick used it in a poem:

> That Happines do's still the longest thrive
> Where Joye and Griefs have Turns Alternative.
> —*Hesperides,* 1648

This sense of the adjective is now quite rare, and it survives chiefly in the form of its derived adverb:

> . . . the door-knob, wherein oil and rust alternatively soothed and retarded the scrape of metal upon metal —Elinor Wylie, *Jennifer Lorn,* 1923

> In one hand she held a peeled hard-boiled egg and a thick slice of bread and butter in the other, and between her sentences she bit at them alternatively —Aldous Huxley, *Antic Hay,* 1923

> There are two courses open to them, which can be taken alternatively, sequentially or together —Margaret Mead, *Saturday Evening Post,* 3 Mar. 1962

The second use—that of *alternate* where *alternative* might be expected—is a more vexatious one to trace. The OED marks the sense obsolete, citing only Robert Greene (1590). But it seems to have had a revival in the second third of the 20th century. Our earliest citations for this revival do not, unfortunately, include much in the way of context; they supply more in the way of opinion than information. In 1933 a column in the *Literary Digest* termed the phrase "an alternate bill of goods" incorrect, but did not provide enough context to show just what was being referred to, spending most of its space on the explication of the difference between *alternate* and *alternative.* A letter from linguist Dwight L. Bolinger to this company in 1943 mentions *alternate* as a euphemism for *substitute* in *alternate goods:* again not much actual context is supplied but such information as is given suggests that both phrases may have been commercial terms used in retail advertising at the time. The revival was not strictly an American phenomenon, however; Gowers 1948 complains of its occurrence in official British writing.

American citations begin to show up in some numbers in the 1940s and early 1950s. Among these there are three new categories of use where *alternative* had not been (and would not be) used—book clubs:

> His *Collected Stories,* a Book-of-the-Month Club alternate selection —*Time,* 18 Dec. 1950

politics:

> ... was named alternate United States delegate to the fifth General Assembly of the United Nations — *Current Biography 1950*

and highways:

> ... an alternate route, built by the Federal Government in 1932 —*American Guide Series: Virginia, 1941*

These three uses continue to the present, with no competition from *alternative*.

More general uses also appeared about the same time:

> Right now, the U.N. weighs the advantage of having Russia at its conference table against the alternate advantage of having a set of basic principles on which members are agreed —*New Yorker,* 31 Mar. 1951

> Early copper shortages stimulated manufacturers to investigate alumnium as an alternate material — *Bulletin, American Institute of Architects,* March 1952

> The book also contains the complete alternate lyrics —*Saturday Rev.,* 29 Nov. 1952

> But they found an alternate, and very free-trade, way of expressing themselves—the smuggling of opium —Christopher Rand, *New Yorker,* 29 Mar. 1952

> ... certain forms have considerable prestige as compared with alternate forms for practically the same meaning —C. C. Fries, cited by Harry R. Warfel, in *Who Killed Grammar?,* 1952

Such uses as these, from much the same kinds of sources, continue unabated in current use, at least in the U.S. In addition, the antiestablishment use of the 1960s—alternative journalism, alternative schools, and the like—is expressed by both adjectives, with *alternative* somewhat more common.

The evidence in the Merriam-Webster files shows this curious tendency: *alternative* is becoming more and more a noun, and the adjective appears to be in the process of being replaced (at least in American English) by *alternate*. Except in botany, the adjective *alternate* in its sense "by turns" is giving way to the verb *alternate* and its participle *alternating*. We cannot be sure that this trend will continue, but if it does, differentiation, far from having been complete in 1926, will have continued along markedly different lines from those announced by Fowler.

alternative, *noun* Harper 1975, in a question to its usage panel about *dilemma,* uses the phrase "one of two equal alternatives." Panelist Heywood Hale Broun took this notice (excised from the 1985 edition): "This is a tautology, since these alternatives, like the horns of a dilemma, come only in pairs." Do alternatives come only in pairs? The writing of recent usage commentators suggests that they do not:

> ... two or more alternatives —Longman 1984

> ... the number of alternatives should be definite — Bryson 1984

> ... anyone who doesn't like the other alternatives — Reader's Digest 1983

> ... choice between two unpleasant alternatives — Freeman 1983

> ... involving two equally unsatisfactory alternatives —Kilpatrick 1984

Copperud 1970, 1980 says "The idea that *alternative* may apply to a choice between two and no more is a pedantry." Howard 1980 and Gowers in Fowler 1965 call it "a fetish." Most other recent commentators, however, take note of the existence of a "traditionalist" or "purist" position—a position that insists on restriction to two.

The development of this "traditionalist" position is curious indeed, for it involves the overlooking of the original objection to the use of the noun in favor of what was then essentially a side issue, brought in to reinforce the original objection. To trace this development, we must go back to 1870.

The earliest commentary on *alternative* that we have found is that of Gould 1870. Here is what he says:

> This word means a choice—*one* choice—between two things. Yet popular usage has so corrupted it, that it is now commonly applied to the things themselves, and not to the choice between them; as thus, "You may take *either* alternative"; "I was forced to choose between *two* alternatives." And, indeed, some people go so far as to say "*several* alternatives were presented to him."
>
> Nevertheless, if the primary meaning is respected, there can be but *one* alternative in any one case. *Two* alternatives is a contradiction in terms.

Why would Gould emphasize *one* choice, rather than *two* things? The reason seems to lie in dictionary definitions. Gould was a vociferous proponent of Joseph Worcester's Dictionary in the late 19th-century war between the dictionaries of Webster and Worcester. The definition of *alternative* in Worcester's 1860 edition reads "The choice given of two things." A quotation from 18th-century poet Edward Young is added. Worcester's definition was taken directly from Samuel Johnson's Dictionary of 1755: "The choice given of two things; so that if one be rejected, the other must be taken," with the same quotation from Young. Each of these lexicographers had a reason for the definition. Johnson had to depend on Young's usage for his definition—Young was apparently the earliest literary figure in English to use the term (the OED shows only a 1624 letter earlier). Worcester had to depend on Johnson— although he unfortunately pruned off the helpful second half of Johnson's definition—because in his position as the chief competitor of Webster's successors, he could not use Webster's definition. Webster in 1828 had noticed the application of the term to the thing to be chosen: "That which may be chosen or omitted; a choice of two things, so that if one is taken, the other must be left. Thus when *two* things offer a choice of *one* only, the two things are called *alternatives*." Noah thus recognized two uses—the choice and the thing chosen; if Worcester recognized them, he presumably felt he could not admit it lest he be accused of plagiarizing his former employer.

To return to Gould: his objection, then, depended entirely upon Johnson's definition via Worcester. Ayres 1881 agreed with Gould's view. But they had no foundation for their objection—the extension of meaning to the thing or things to be chosen had taken place long before. The OED cites Sterne's *Tristram Shandy* (1760):

> There was no alternative in my Uncle Toby's wardrobe.

This citation is, as the OED points out, ambiguous; it might but probably does not mean "choice." There are other early uses, however:

> ... forced to take the other alternative —Henry Fielding, *Journal of a Voyage to Lisbon,* 1755

> ... while another alternative remains —Jane Austen, *Lady Susan,* 1814 (OED)

> Poor Rip was at last reduced almost to despair; and his only alternative, to escape from the labor of the farm and clamor of his wife, was to take gun in hand and stroll away into the woods —Washington Irving, "Rip Van Winkle," 1820

> Between these alternatives there is no middle ground —William Cranch (cited in Webster 1828)

The OED (*A* appeared in 1884) defines four senses (as do most modern dictionaries) and notes that except for Johnson's sense, the others were unknown to dictionaries until "very recently."

Hodgson 1889, while following the current objection to the application to the thing or course chosen, brings in etymology; after a disquisition upon Latin *alter* and its derivatives and congeners, he cites with approbation a definition from Whatley's *Synonyms* (1851): "a choice between *two* courses" (the italics are Hodgson's). In his emphasis on *two,* Hodgson joins Noah Webster, who concluded his definition with

> In strictness, then, the word can not be applied to more than *two* things, and when one thing only is offered for choice, it is said there is no *alternative.*

Evidence in the OED shows that if the word had not been extended to a choice of more than two in Noah's time—and his "in strictness" suggests that indeed it already had—it would soon be. The OED's earliest citation for extension to three is from the logician John Stuart Mill:

> The alternative seemed to be either death, or to be permanently supported by other people, or a radical change in the economical arrangements —*Principles of Political Economy,* 1848

The editors also quote Gladstone in 1857 extending the number to four. Hodgson supplies evidence of three alternatives from 1853 and 1857. Our files have this from a letter of Henry Adams to his brother:

> ... and if your three alternatives are right, I acknowledge I'm wrong —22 Apr. 1859

The traditionalists after Hodgson tend to follow the etymological argument and ignore the original, although Vizetelly 1906 quotes Gould, and some of his later pronouncements mention that theme. But both schools of objectors were too late: the horse was long out of the barn before they arrived to lock the door. All four senses given in the OED are in current reputable use—even Fowler 1926 examines them minutely without objecting to any.

Harper 1975, 1985 draws attention to "a certain imperative connotation" that *alternative* carries but *choice* does not. They say that a person faced with three

alternatives must choose one of the three. This is not quite right, for it applies only part of the time. In a use like this:

> The three basic funeral alternatives are ... —*Homemaking: Skills for Everyday Living,* 1981 (school text)

the imperative notion obtains, enforced by a death in the family. But in other instances:

> ... I feel bound to offer you the alternative of coming alone, or coming with Edy some other Sunday, or letting us send a trap to Witley to bring you both to lunch or tea next Sunday week, or, in short, anything you please —George Bernard Shaw, letter to Ellen Terry, 20 Apr. 1899

none of the alternatives need be taken—indeed, Miss Terry never made the suggested vacation visit. The subtle imperative that *alternative* contains but *choice* does not is the one first put down by Samuel Johnson—if you take one, you must forgo the other or others. *Choice* does not necessarily carry the same implication.

While the history of this objection is rather complex, the actual status of the word in usage is not. The extension of *alternative* from a choice between two to the things or courses to be chosen and then to a choice of more than two has been long established in reputable usage.

alternatively, alternately   See ALTERNATE, ALTERNATIVE, *adjectives.*

altho   *Altho* is one of the simplified spellings whose adoption was urged by the Simplified Spelling Board and other bodies concerned with spelling reform around the end of the 19th century (see SPELLING REFORM). Krapp 1927 says *altho* is to be found here and there through all the modern period of English, but that it did not have much widespread use until the movement for spelling reform had reached its peak. Baron 1982 notes that *altho* was one of a dozen reformed spellings adopted by the National Educational Association in 1898. Our evidence shows that by the 1920s quite a few authors and publishers were using at least some of the reformed spellings in print, including this one:

> ... Bryant's list remains a significant document, altho its impressiveness has departed —Brander Matthews, *Essays on English,* 1921

> And altho in this country —*Publishers Weekly,* 2 Nov. 1918

> Altho forced to resign —*Literary Digest,* 20 Nov. 1926

Some authors and publishers continued up into the 1950s:

> Altho Nida speaks of native tutors —Morris Swadesh, *Word,* April 1954

Our most recent evidence suggests, however, that *altho* is dropping out of use in print, altho it may well continue to thrive in personal writing.

although, though   Although these conjunctions have been essentially interchangeable since about 1400 (according to the OED), usage books seldom fail to include them, apparently because people keep wondering whether one or the other is preferable. And no matter how much detail a study might contain, the results always come out the same: the conjunctions are interchangeable. (Bryant 1962 has a detailed examination, for instance.)

> Although the lake was by now black, though the sky still dimly reflected white, turning from time to time to peer ahead, he guided himself by the flickering lights of the Stresa shore —Bernard Malamud, *The Magic Barrel,* 1958

Though is more frequently used than *although,* perhaps because it is shorter. Assertions of delicate shades of difference in formality made by some commentators cannot be confirmed by the citations in Merriam-Webster files. The difference seems merely to be a matter of personal choice.

Though is used as an adverb; *although* is not.

> A fine book though —W. H. Auden, *N.Y. Rev. of Books,* 27 Jan. 1972

altogether   See ALL TOGETHER, ALTOGETHER.

alum   See ALUMNUS, ALUMNA.

alumnus, alumna   **1.** As any dictionary will tell you, *alumna* is pluralized *alumnae; alumnus* is pluralized *alumni.* These words have not developed English plurals. *Alumna* is used for female graduates and *alumnus* for males, although it is sometimes used also of women. *Alumni* is the form usually used for a mixed bag of graduates of both sexes. Janis 1984 points out that the clipped form *alum* (not to be confused with the chemical compound of the same spelling) is available to those who feel that *alumni* is not sufficiently asexual or those who have trouble spelling Latin:

> . . . second-guessing from undergrads and die-hard alums —Edwin McDowell, *Wall Street Jour.,* 5 Dec. 1972

> . . . join the 951 alums who have put, or are planning to put, Randolph-Macon in their wills —Carolyn Morrison Barton, *Randolph-Macon Woman's College Alumnae Bulletin,* Winter 1971

Alumnus is also used for a former member, employee, inmate, or contributor of any of a number of institutions:

> In fact, I still get the 69th Division alumni bulletin or whatever it's called —Frank Mankiewicz, quoted in *The Washingtonian,* October 1978

> . . . the Liverpool Repertory Company, whose alumni include Sir Michael Redgrave and Rex Harrison —*Current Biography,* October 1965

> . . . *Saturday Night Live* alumnus Michael O'Donoghue —Timothy White, *Rolling Stone,* 24 July 1980

Alumna is not unknown in this use, but is fairly rare:

> . . . another debutante, albeit a Lee Strasberg alumna, whose Cecilia is teary-eyed vapidity —Judith Crist, *Saturday Rev.,* 11 Dec. 1976

> . . . widowed, loaded, an alumna of analysis and a veteran of A.A. —Martin Levin, *N.Y. Times Book Rev.,* 16 Mar. 1975

2. The use of *alumni* as a singular is called substandard by Copperud. Our only genuine evidence of straightforward use is from speech:

> . . . another UCLA alumni —Frank Gifford, football telecast, 12 Nov. 1984

It has also been used facetiously:

> As a loyal alumni, you'll be aghast to know that the head football coach has to get by on just $96,000 a year —Jeff Millar & Bill Hinds, "Tank McNamara" (cartoon), *Boston Globe,* 24 Jan. 1982

a.m., p.m.   These abbreviations are usually used with the hour as a short substitute for "before noon" and "after noon" (or whatever phrase you may use for the same idea). Copperud 1970 tells us that he and Evans 1957 agree that expressions like "6 a.m. in the morning" are redundant; our files show precious little evidence of such expressions, a fact which may indicate that they exist mainly in speech.

The abbreviations are occasionally used as an informal substitute for *morning* and *afternoon* or *evening:*

> I flew in from Vienna this a.m. —Irving Wallace, *The Plot,* 1967

> "Judith? No—that is, yes—I saw her this a.m." —Josephine Pinckney, *Three O'Clock Dinner,* 1945

> Last Thursday, at one in the p.m. —*New Yorker,* 19 Aug. 1972

> . . . my wife suggests that we can see a Charlie Chaplin movie tomorrow p.m. —Oliver Wendell Holmes d. 1935, letter, 30 Oct. 1921

amalgam   *Amalgam* in its nontechnical senses takes *of* when it needs a preposition:

> . . . synthetic new genres that are amalgams of the old —Peter Winn, *N.Y. Times Book Rev.,* 10 June 1979

> The average reader imagines him as a rather Byronic, darkly brooding individual, an amalgam of Baudelaire, Robinson Jeffers, and MacKinlay Kantor —S. J. Perelman, *New Yorker,* 1 Jan. 1972

> . . . the British Walker Cup team, traditionally an amalgam of the top amateurs from England, Scotland, Wales, and Ireland —Herbert Warren Wind, *New Yorker,* 10 Apr. 1971

amalgamate   When *amalgamate,* in its nontechnical uses, requires a preposition, *into* and *with* are used:

> Indian, African, and Portuguese ingredients and cooking techniques began to amalgamate into the rich Brazilian cuisine of today —Elizabeth Lambert Ortiz, *Gourmet,* October 1975

> Dirac amalgamated the varied equations into one —*Current Biography,* October 1967

> . . . the Workers' Union was amalgamated with it —*Current Biography 1948*

> . . . a chance to size me up, test me out by my reaction to his sallies, amalgamate me with his previous audience —Edmund Wilson, *Memoirs of Hecate County,* 1946

amateur Bernstein 1965 presents us with the choice of *of, in,* or (sometimes) *at* for a preposition with which to follow the noun *amateur.* Although all of them can be used without violating English idiom, our files show that only *of* has much in the way of current use. *Of*'s preeminence is partly due to its being the only preposition used when *amateur* is used in its earliest sense— "devotee, admirer"—or in a use close to that meaning:

> "No, seriously," he said, in his quality of an amateur of dogs —Arnold Bennett, *The Old Wives' Tale,* 1908

> They are *amateurs* of Horace in the best sense of that word —Edward Townsend Booth, *Saturday Rev.,* 4 Oct. 1947

> As all amateurs of marzipan must agree —*New Yorker,* 8 Dec. 1956

> He was an amateur of gadgets, but he was not even an engineer on the model of Watt or Fulton —O. B. Hardison, Jr., *Entering the Maze,* 1981

When used in the sense of "one not a professional," *amateur* followed by *of* tends to have a bookish tang that probably favors its selection in such contexts:

> . . . edition of Donne is intended, I expect, for the university student and the advanced amateur of English letters —D. C. Allen, *Modern Language Notes,* May 1957

> . . . I must co-opt for our profession one or two amateurs of the discipline —John Kenneth Galbraith, *Esquire,* May 1977

> . . . a simplistic amateur of letters, boring students with one's own enthusiasm —John Bayley, *N.Y. Times Book Rev.,* 27 Feb. 1983

The prepositions *of, in,* or *at* serve to connect *amateur* with the name of some activity, profession, discipline, or field of study or interest. Our citations show that in recent time the indication of such a relationship has been more and more taken over by the adjective *amateur:* when in the past you might have been an amateur of, in, or at photography, nowadays you are much more likely to be an amateur photographer. The prepositions, of course, are still likely to be used where no fully appropriate agent noun is available, or where the writer simply chooses not to use the agent noun.

ambiguous See AMBIVALENT, AMBIGUOUS; EQUIVOCAL, AMBIGUOUS, AMBIVALENT.

ambition Both the prepositions *for* and *of* are in use with *ambition,* but the most common construction (in our evidence) is *to* and the infinitive. Here's a sample:

> . . . developed an ambition to become a writer — *Current Biography,* February 1967

> . . . carrying out his ambition to reform the map of the world —Benjamin Farrington, *Greek Science,* 1953

> Dvořák had a great ambition for special success in his D minor symphony —John Burk, *Boston Symphony Orchestra Program,* 5 Feb. 1972

> He had nursed the ambition of becoming a foreign correspondent —*Times Literary Supp.,* 29 Feb. 1968

With *in* a somewhat different relationship is suggested:

> . . . my brother Philip, who had ambitions in this direction —C. P. Snow, *The Conscience of the Rich,* 1958

ambivalent, ambiguous *Ambivalent* is a much newer word than *ambiguous;* while the latter has been in the language since the 16th century, *ambivalent* is not attested until 1916, and its earliest citations are from translations of Jung and Freud. Its first use in English, then, was as a technical term in psychology, but it seems to have found itself a niche in popular usage fairly quickly as a descriptive word for a state in which one holds simultaneous contradictory feelings or in which one wavers between two polar opposites. *Ambiguous* had earlier been used for analogous situations; consequently, the words sometimes are used in similar contexts.

> My attitude toward the plan . . . will be called by some of my friends ambiguous, or perhaps—since the word is now in fashion—"ambivalent." —Albert Guérard, *Education of a Humanist,* 1949

> Keats confused, confounded two centuries
> By ambivalent, ambiguous
> Mating of truth with beauty
>   —Richard Eberhart, *Accent,* Spring 1947

> . . . her frustrating and ambiguous role—acknowledged neither as wife nor as mistress —William L. Shirer, *The Rise and Fall of the Third Reich,* 1960

> In all matters Blum's ambivalent position was motivated by a desire to preserve unity —Joel Colton, *Yale Rev.,* March 1954

Both *ambivalent* and *ambiguous* may connote duality:

> To adopt the Committee's own ambivalent phrasing, that may or may not be the result —*Wall Street Jour.,* 1 Apr. 1955

> But, like the bearded lady of the fair ground, it wears an ambiguous appearance —Iain Colquhoun, *New Republic,* 18 Oct. 1954

But they are seldom really confused, because *ambiguous* tends to stress uncertainty and is usually applied to external things while *ambivalent* tends to stress duality and is usually applied to internal things:

> English fleets and armies forced the ambiguous benefits of modern civilization on the reluctant Chinese —D. W. Brogan, *The English People,* 1943

> . . . in the matter of Miss Thompson's ambiguous femininity —Diana Trilling, *N.Y. Times Book Rev.,* 22 Apr. 1973

> . . . the complaint is commonplace that spoken language is too ambiguous and conceptually fuzzy — Nehemiah Jordan, *Themes in Speculative Phychology,* 1968

> . . . only partially excavated but illuminating for the new light they throw on the ambiguous world of the Maya —Katharine Kuh, *Saturday Rev.,* 28 June 1969

> His intensely ambivalent attitude to his father—of admiration for his positive qualities and bitter hatred for his insensitivity and brutality —Anne Fremantle, *Commonweal,* 6 Dec. 1946

He has Thackeray's fruitfully ambivalent attitude toward his own class —Clifton Fadiman, *Holiday*, October 1954

He spoke of the number of people . . . who had urged him to withdraw from the festival, and of his own ambivalent feelings —Eric F. Goldman, *Harper's*, January 1969

Ambivalent may be followed by the prepositions *toward(s)* and *about*:

In an era when Americans were not yet ambivalent about the fruits of science —Harriet Zuckerman, *Trans-Action*, March 1968

. . . if its author had been a little less ambivalent about its potential audience —*Times Literary Supp.*, 9 Dec. 1965

. . . I'm a trifle ambivalent toward "Room Service" —John McCarten, *New Yorker*, 18 Apr. 1953

American woman, ambivalent towards fighting — Margaret Mead, *And Keep Your Powder Dry*, 1942

The handful of commentators who object to *ambivalent* used other than in its original narrow sense are out-of-date. The extended uses are well established.

See also EQUIVOCAL, AMBIGUOUS, AMBIVALENT.

amenable   *Amenable* is regularly followed by *to*:

As an idea "circle" is amenable to punning applications —Roger Greenspun, in *The Film*, 1968

I am both submissive to facts and amenable to argument —Virgil Thomson, *The Musical Scene*, 1947

Ever amenable to party demands, the President responded —Samuel Hopkins Adams, *Incredible Era*, 1939

amend, emend   When was the last time you needed to use the verb *emend*? Our evidence suggests that writers usually feel little need for this bookish and technical word. Yet a number of usage commentators feel the need to distinguish the seldom-used *emend* from the much more common *amend*. Kilpatrick 1984, for instance, objects to the use of *amend* meaning "to make emendations." His assertion about use is wrong, however, as Chambers 1985 and Shaw 1975 show. In fact, *amend* has been used in the sense of "make emendations" since Caxton in the 15th century. But it has a wider use as well, which Kilpatrick recognizes:

. . . the Commission hopes to amend its rules — *Forbes*, 15 May 1967

Laws that are not repealed are amended and amended and amended like a child's knickers — George Bernard Shaw, *The Intelligent Woman's Guide To Socialism and Capitalism*, 1928

Then there are these uses:

. . . I honestly thought Goldwater would also amend the error of his ways —Karl Hess, quoted in *Playboy*, July 1976

. . . inflamed with a desire to amend the lives of themselves and others —C. S. Peirce, reprinted in *Encore*, March 1947

Afterwards he amended his discourtesy, and I forgot the offence —Rudyard Kipling, *Kim*, 1901

. . . these, like the other faults of the book, are too well diffused throughout to be amended —T. S. Eliot, Preface to 1928 edition of *The Sacred Wood*

These two uses are quite a bit more common than the "make emendations" sense. Here are a few examples of the last:

The new seal followed exactly the old one in design, except that "F.D. IND. IMP." was amended to "FIDEI DEF" —*82d Annual Report of the Controller of the Royal Mint, 1951*, 1953

The translation was amended here and there by his own pen —Lucien Price, *Dialogues of Alfred North Whitehead*, 1954

Arthur Wilmart's translation has been shortened and amended —*Saturday Rev.*, 29 Jan. 1955

Emend is much the less common word and is usually applied only to the correction of a text:

The decision to keep the original arrangement of the poems, but print the final corrected text, emended only in some instances —*Times Literary Supp.*, 19 Feb. 1971

It is rarely used with a somewhat broader application:

Not especially gifted with literary originality, the Roman Paul borrowed Plato's image and emended it to suit his needs —Henry Silverstein, *Accent*, Winter 1947

. . . the more serious objection that my criterion, as it stands, allows meaning to any indicative statement whatsoever. To meet this, I shall emend it as follows —Alfred Jules Ayer, *Language, Truth and Logic*, 2d ed., 1946

In summary, *amend* is the more common word, sometimes applied to the emendation of text but much more often used in extended and figurative senses. *Emend* is much less often used, is usually applied to the correction of text, and is rare in extended use.

America, American   From 1791 to the present people have questioned the propriety or accuracy of using *America* to mean the United States and *American* to mean an inhabitant or citizen of the United States.

America is used very generally both by writers and public speakers, when they only intend the territory of the United States. . . . It may have first come into use as being much shorter to say *Americans*, than citizens of the United States —*Gazette of the United States*, 16 Feb. 1791 (Dictionary of American English)

Every once in a while someone comes along who is perturbed about Americans calling themselves Americans, feeling that we have no right to use this term exclusively, that citizens of all the nations of the American continents are Americans —letter to editor, *Christian Science Monitor*, 1 Aug. 1967

It is becoming presumptuous and inaccurate to refer to North Americans as "Americans," especially in the context of defending or upsetting Central Americans, South Americans and Latin Americans —William Safire, *N.Y. Times Mag.*, 3 June 1984

Safire followed his remark with a call for his readers to suggest "new monickers for United States citizens," but his call seems to have brought in few suggestions, since no mention of them was contained in Safire 1986. H. L. Mencken in *American Speech,* December 1947, had quite a long list of suggested replacements for *American.* The list contains (in approximate historical order from 1789 to 1939) such terms as *Columbian, Columbard, Fredonian, Frede, Unisian, United Statesian, Colonican, Appalacian, Usian, Washingtonian, Usonian, Uessian, U-S-ian, Uesican.* None of these proposed substitutes has caught on.

Despite the perceived difficulty with *America* and *American* in this use, the terms are fully established. Cotton Mather seems to have been the first writer to use *American* for a colonist, back before the dawn of the 18th century. It became established during the course of that century. The historian Samuel Eliot Morison cites a naval expedition of 1741 as being the first time the English referred to colonial troops as *Americans* rather than *provincials.* Benjamin Franklin used both *America* and *American* in this sense. The Dictionary of American English also cites George Washington:

> The name of American, which belongs to you in your national capacity, must always exalt the just pride of patriotism, more than appellatives derived from local discriminations —*Farewell Address,* 1796

Here are two other commenators:

> The general term *American* is now commonly understood (at least in all places where the English language is spoken) to mean an inhabitant of the United States, and is so employed except where unusual precision is required —John Pickering, *An American Glossary,* 1816

> The use of *America* for *the United States & American* for *(citizen) of the U.S. . . .* will continue to be protested against by purists & patriots, & will doubtless survive the protests —Fowler 1926

If you feel diffident about these words like Safire, or require "unusual precision," the equivalent phrases are readily available. In other cases, *America* and *American* will do.

American Indian See NATIVE AMERICAN.

amid, amidst 1. Copperud 1970, 1980 tells us that *amid* and *amidst* are criticized as bookish, literary, or quaint by four commentators; Harper 1985 finds them out of fashion—formerly common but now "literary words" to be stricken in favor of *among* or *in.* This notion seems to have originated with Fowler 1926. There was probably little basis for Fowler's opinion in 1926; there is no basis whatsoever for its repetition by later commentators. The words are in frequent current use, as you will see from the examples given in section 3 below.

2. Fowler opines that *amidst* is more common than *amid;* Evans 1957 finds *amid* more common in American use and *amidst* in British use; Reader's Digest 1983 says *amid* is the more usual choice. Our evidence—mostly American—supports none of these generalizations. We find *amidst* somewhat more frequent before 1960, *amid* somewhat more frequent 1960–1980, and since 1980 the two words of about equal frequency. Both forms are in frequent use; you can use whichever sounds better to you.

3. *Amid, amidst, among.* A curious belief is expressed in variant terms by Evans 1957, Copperud 1970, Bernstein 1962, Bryson 1984, and Simon 1980 that *amid* and *amidst* should go with singular nouns (there is some disagreement whether the singular noun can be a collective noun or a mass noun or not) and *among* with plural nouns (or separable, enumerable, or countable items). The origin of this belief is obscure; it does not appear in Fowler's discussion of the words and does not seem to have concerned the 19th-century commentators. There may be some hint of an origin in Campbell 1776 and Murray 1795, who both object to *among* with indefinite pronouns that they deem singular. Yet, neither *amid* nor *amidst* is mentioned in their discussions.

Simon's version of the distinction is this: "*Among* clearly pre-supposes a number of surrounding but separate entities . . . ; whereas *amid* denotes a position in the middle of something larger but of a piece and not divisible. . . ." Bernstein takes about the same tack: "'Among' means in the midst of countable things. When the things are not separable the word is 'amid' or 'amidst.'" Bryson is in essential agreement. Evans, however, makes the distinction on a different basis, saying that *amid* is more likely to be followed by a singular word and *among* by a plural. Copperud prefers *amid* with singular nouns that are not collectives. Thus, we may note some uncertainty among the commentators about just what it is they would have us observe. The feeling of uncertainty is heightened by Simon, who criticizes (at the instance of a correspondent) his own sentence beginning "Among richly homoerotic overtones"); he should have used *amid,* he says, but we are aware that his plural *overtones* would satisfy Evan's criterion. Simon is presumably basing his *mea culpa* on the notion of the inseparability of the overtones.

You may suspect that a distinction based on criteria so elusive is not founded on actual usage—and indeed it is not. *Amid* and *amidst* are followed by both singular and plural nouns as well as by nouns that denote separable or countable items.

Singular nouns with *amid:*

> Amid such a world . . . our ideals henceforth must find a home —*Selected Papers of Bertrand Russell,* 1927

> . . . to reconcile, amid his womanizing, with his wife —Judith Crist, *Saturday Rev.,* 2 Apr. 1977

> . . . and amid a babble of goodnights the ladies came forward —Allen Tate, *Prose,* Fall 1971

> . . . there is amid the garbage a steady supply of good writing —Jacques Barzun, *Atlantic,* December 1953

> Amid a snowstorm of press gossip —Penina Spiegel, *US,* 13 Aug. 1984

> . . . worked on the steaming docks, amid the coal-dust —Van Wyck Brooks, *The Flowering of New England, 1815–1865,* rev. ed., 1946

Amidst with singular nouns:

> . . . she fled Cambodia amidst gunfire —Cable Neuhaus, *People,* 11 Mar. 1985

> Amidst the junk mail and the hate mail and the crank mail —Aristides, *American Scholar,* Autumn 1979

> He was merely walking amidst an inferior form of life —Richard Wright, *Negro Digest,* January 1947

> . . . amidst an unlimited magnificence —Edmund Wilson, "The Ambiguity of Henry James," in *Amer-*

ican Harvest, ed. Allen Tate & John Peale Bishop, 1942

... where the last czar and his family had lived, uncomfortably, amidst too much furniture —John Steinbeck, *Russian Journal,* 1948

Those eyes of his, that mouth amidst a stubble of beard —Ion L. Idriess, *Madman's Island,* 1938

Amid with plural nouns:

... my plight amid complex issues —William Stafford, *Writing the Australian Crawl,* 1978

Amid the partygoers at Luchow's restaurant —*People,* 20 Sept. 1982

... resigned amid charges of misconduct —Elizabeth Drew, *N.Y. Times Mag.,* 7 Oct. 1973

Amid bulging wicker and pasteboard suitcases and bundles done up in cloth sat elderly men —Andy Logan, *New Yorker,* 12 May 1951

... amid scenes of riot and debauch —*Times Literary Supp.,* 27 Feb. 1953

There they all fell, amid yells and hissing curses and shrieks of pain —Liam O'Flaherty, *The Informer,* 1925

Amidst with plural nouns:

... floating amidst the planets and stars —Evan Thomas, *Time,* 26 Nov. 1984

Amidst visitors, orderlies and chatter, we listened gravely —T.R.B., *New Republic,* 19 Apr. 1954

... which still endure amidst the soulless ruins —Henry Miller, *The Air-Conditioned Nightmare,* 1945

... situated in palaces, amidst beautiful parks —Janet Flanner, *New Yorker,* 27 Oct. 1951

... amidst the cries of *"Mazeltov! Mazeltov!"* —Alfred Kazin, *New Republic,* 5 Feb. 1945

... amidst the lifeless personages who surround her —Robert Pick, *Saturday Rev.,* 31 Mar. 1945

... amidst all the proposed new subsidies —Michael Kinsley, *Harper's,* January 1983

Another frequent construction finds *amid* or *amidst* with a collective noun or indefinite pronoun followed by a preposition having a plural noun as its object:

... amidst a crackle of blue sparks —A. J. Cronin, *The Green Years,* 1944

... amid some of the richest and most detailed period sets —Judith Crist, *The Washingtonian,* November 1970

... amidst an astonishing variety of other pandemics —John Wilkinson, *A Center Occasional Paper,* December 1970

Amid such a welter of uncertainties —Sir James Mountford, *British Universities,* 1966

... amid a pandemonium of cheers —John Buchan, *Castle Gay,* 1930

We can thus see that actual usage does not follow the varying distinctions about *amid* and *amidst* the com-

mentators make, and that their use is not restricted to "literary" or "quaint" publications. You will also note that *among* can be substituted for *amid* or *amidst* in very few of the examples. The fact is that *among* and *amid (amidst)* tend to seek different contexts anyway, and so the distinction the commentators are trying to urge is not only factitious but largely superfluous.

The invocation of *among* by commentators on *amid* and *amidst* seems to be related to the use of *among* with certain singular nouns and indefinite pronouns. This subject is treated at AMONG 2.

amidst See AMID, AMIDST.

amn't See AIN'T; AREN'T I.

amok See AMUCK, AMOK.

among 1. See BETWEEN 1.
2. Several commentators have brought *among* into a discussion that involves distinguishing between *among* and *amid* or *amidst* on somewhat questionable grounds (see AMID, AMIDST 3). These commentators restrict *among* to use with plural or countable or separable nouns. The question of the propriety of using *among* with a singular noun or an indefinite pronoun is an old one, going back at least to Priestley in his 1768 edition:

The preposition *among* always implies a number of things; and, therefore, cannot be used in conjunction with the word *every,* which is in the singular number. *Which is found* among every *species of liberty.* Hume's Essays, p. 92. *The opinion of the advance of riches in the island seems to gain ground* among every body. Hume's Political Essays, p. 71.

This opinion apparently originated with a grammarian named James Elphinstone in 1765, but Murray 1795 picked it up from Priestley and transmitted it down the ages. Somewhere along the way the specific reference to *every* was lost, and the question became simply whether *among* could be used with a singular noun. When a correspondent wrote to this company about the problem in 1939, an editor sent this reply:

We regret that ... you are still uncertain of the propriety of *among* used with a collective noun. This usage has the authority lent by examples from the earliest English, from Chaucer, from Steele, and from more modern writers. Longfellow wrote "We were among the crowd that gathered there." When the collective noun obviously means the members of something, *among* may properly precede the singular collective noun in many contexts, as "to circulate among the audience."

Our editor's letter was in harmony with the evidence shown at the appropriate sense in the OED. The OED notes that this sense of *among* is used with collectives and singular nouns of substances. The latter use is still alive, but now much less common than use with collectives. Two examples:

A hagfish will get right in among the muscle of the fish it is parasitising, dissolving the muscle and killing the fish —David Wilson, *Body and Antibody,* 1971

Among the smoke and fog of a December afternoon —T. S. Eliot, "Portrait of a Lady," 1917

Probably *in* is more common with such nouns, as the OED also observes. *Among* is used with nouns that are collective and also denote a substance:

> Often, I think, he slept in our barn among the hay — Adrian Bell, *The Cherry Tree,* 1932
>
> . . . it slipped off the stone and down among the gorse —Arthur Loveridge, *Many Happy Days I've Squandered,* 1944
>
> . . . some land animals hibernate among the vegetation —W. H. Dowdeswell, *Animal Ecology,* 2d ed., 1959

Other collective nouns are more frequent:

> Among the plunder from the church was a large silver image —*American Guide Series: New Hampshire,* 1938
>
> . . . Henry James is, among a large part of our reading public, held to be to blame —Lionel Trilling, *Kenyon Rev.,* Winter 1948
>
> Among the luggage which I take on board —William Beebe, *Jungle Peace,* 1918
>
> These are lost among a vast bulk of verse interesting only by its oddity —F. R. Leavis, *New Bearings in English Poetry,* new ed., 1950
>
> Among her evidence was a report —*Time,* 6 Feb. 1956
>
> . . . nothing could happen, among a certain class of society, without the cognizance of some philanthropic agency —Arnold Bennett, 1899, in *The Journals of Arnold Bennett,* ed. Frank Swinnerton, 1954
>
> One may hazard that the *Economic History Review* is not among his bedside reading —*Times Literary Supp.,* 24 Apr. 1969
>
> . . . he is not really a politician and lacks any organised political backing among the public —Ian Stephens, *London Calling,* 29 Apr. 1954

Collective nouns are notionally plural, which is why they fit with *among.* Differences in time and place can have an effect on the way such a noun is apprehended. Leonard in his 1932 usage survey included a sentence from De Quincey that seemed to puzzle many of the Americans tested:

> I enjoy wandering among a library.

To many Americans *library* connotes an institution rather than a collection, and hence the *among* seemed strange. A similar use is this:

> He thought of the Australian gold and how those who lived among it had never seen it though it abounded all around them —Samuel Butler, *The Way of All Flesh,* 1903

Among may certainly be used before a singular noun, especially when it is a collective noun. Our evidence suggests such use may be slightly more common in British English than it is in American, but it is not rare in either.
3. A related use of *among* involves its combination with the indefinite pronouns *one another* and *each other.* The original objection seems to have been raised by Campbell 1776, who quoted this sentence from *The Spectator,* No. 321 for correction:

> The greatest masters of critical learning differ among one another.

Campbell recommends *themselves* for *one another;* in fact, Addison in an earlier *Spectator* (cited in the OED) had written "quarrelled among themselves." Evans 1957 also mentions the construction. We cannot tell much about it. It is probably not wrong—the indefinite pronouns are notionally plural—but it is exceedingly rare, and may well sound odd to many ears on that account. We have only this one example:

> . . . the trio of directors . . . also share among each other the credits for production, writing, photographing, and editing —Arthur Knight, *Saturday Rev.,* 7 Nov. 1953

Themselves is far more common in such contexts.
4. *Among, amongst.* Most of the commentators who mention these words note that *amongst* is less common but both are correct. Our evidence confirms this; it also shows *amongst* a bit more common in British use than American. The few commentators who call *amongst* quaint or overrefined are off target. Here is a selection of mostly recent and unquaint examples:

> We would sell the raft . . . and go way up the Ohio amongst the free states —Mark Twain, *Huckleberry Finn,* 1884
>
> . . . a dead spot amongst the maze of microwave beams —John W. Verity, *Datamation,* July 1982
>
> Amongst the evidence were verbal slams from such network luminaries . . . —John Weisman, *TV Guide,* 11 Sept. 1981
>
> Amongst other things, it is about the horrible family —Twyla Tharp, quoted in *Horizon,* September 1981
>
> One or two of the red brick and green copper pavilions . . . still remain amongst the rubble —Gerald Weissman, *The Woods Hole Cantata,* 1975
>
> . . . this impulse almost universal amongst scholars and teachers —William Stafford, *Writing The Australian Crawl,* 1978
>
> . . . in divided usage amongst adults —Strang 1970
>
> . . . alcohol use and drinking problems amongst women —*Times Literary Supp.,* December 1980

amongst See AMONG 4.

amount 1. *Amount, number.* Many 20th-century commentators explain the difference between *amount* and *number.* The general rule seems first to have been stated in more or less contemporary terms by Vizetelly 1906:

> *Amount* is used of substances in mass; *number* refers to the individuals of which such mass is constituted.

(Our only earlier commentator is Raub 1897, who handles the matter a little differently by discriminating *amount, quantity,* and *number* in a short synonymy paragraph.) Almost all modern commentators echo Vizetelly. They are partly right, but the flat distinction does not account for all standard usage.

Number is regularly used with plural count nouns to indicate an indefinite number of individuals or items:

> There were a number of serious (heavy) journalists —Michael Herr, *Esquire,* April 1970

There is a number of misprints —Albert H. Smith, *Notes and Queries,* October 1966

. . . a number of forces in Western life —Vance Packard, *The Sexual Wilderness,* 1968

. . . a number of other schools —James B. Conant, *Slums and Suburbs,* 1961

. . . a number of activities government undertakes —*New Republic,* 21 June 1954

There are . . . a number of Arabic dialects —James T. Maher, *The Lamp,* Summer 1963

Amount is most frequently used with singular mass nouns:

Given a reasonable amount of prosperity —Aldous Huxley, *The Olive Tree,* 1937

. . . the doctrine requires a ridiculous amount of erudition —T. S. Eliot, "Tradition and the Individual Talent," 1917

. . . it took a certain amount of faith —Hollis Alpert, *Saturday Rev.,* 13 Nov. 1971

. . . the amount of independence they would like to have —Eulah C. Laucks, *Center Mag.,* January 1968

A considerable amount of misinformation exists regarding the temperatures of tropical countries —Preston E. James, *Latin America,* rev. ed., 1950

. . . losing . . . a fair amount of their accent —*N.Y. Times,* 30 Nov. 1976

Lincoln Library 1924 insisted that *amount* could be used only of substances or material; the six examples above all demonstrate that the criticism was invalid. It seems to have arisen in Ayres 1881, who was offended by the phrase *amount of perfection.* The insistence on substance or material is now a dead issue. Of course, *amount* is used of material mass nouns too:

But the lion would certainly come down to the plain with the amount of game that was here now —Ernest Hemingway, "Miss Mary's Lion," 1956

. . . spent any amount of money on him —*Times Literary Supp.,* 20 Feb. 1969

. . . the amount of snow that we usually have —Richard Joseph, *Your Trip to Britain,* 1954

Alexander added to his heavy troops archers, slingers, and javelin men, and a certain amount of cavalry —Tom Wintringham, *The Story of Weapons and Tactics,* 1943

Amount is also used with plural count nouns when they are thought of as an aggregate:

. . . who wrote the U.N. that he'd be glad to furnish any amount of black pebbles —*New Yorker,* 20 Sept. 1952

. . . the high amount of taxes —*Harper's Weekly,* 29 Sept. 1975

Surely twelve men, whose eyes were opened, having the knowledge of the Most High, were better than any amount of lecturers —Richard M. Benson, *An Exposition of the Epistle of St. Paul to the Romans,* 1898

There have been 110,000 American casualties—one third the amount in World War I —*N.Y. Times,* 22 June 1952

. . . we could absorb a vast amount of South American products —Thurman W. Arnold, *The Bottlenecks of Business,* 1940

One of the minor mysteries of modern life is the large amount of police cars with flashing lights and sirens —Alan Coren, *Punch,* 15 July 1975

. . . an Eighth Avenue saloon that had become known affectionately as the Tavern of the Bite, in deference to the unique amount of worthless IOUs collected during each day's business —Robert Lewis Taylor, *New Yorker,* 12 Nov. 1955

. . . brunets possess a great amount of the substances required for the production of pigment —Ashley Montagu, *Man's Most Dangerous Myth: The Fallacy of Race,* 2d ed., 1945

. . . every professional activity requires a fixed amount of calories —*Psychological Abstracts,* April 1947

This less common use of *amount* is sometimes criticized, but the critics bring forward no cogent reason for condemning it, only the condemnation itself. Colter 1981 says this: "When 'amount' is used with plurals—the amount of people—it sounds plain dumb." Most other commentators, such as Bernstein 1965, Shaw 1970, and many handbooks, merely state the distinction. The use is well established in general prose.

2. Flesch 1964 finds the phrase *in the amount of* wordy and suggests replacing it with *of* or *for.* Such a revision may work in some contexts, but in the example below such a substitution would make nonsense.

The Cuban trade balance with the United States for the first three quarters of 1943 was favourable in the amount of $103,518,000 —*Britannica Book of the Year 1944*

The phrases *in the amount of* and more often *to the amount of* are used with large amounts of money and are not always easily omissible or replaceable:

. . . had supported the Choral Masterworks Series of 1952 to the amount of $40,000 —*Current Biography,* July 1966

3. The verb *amount* is regularly followed by *to:*

Probably the population never amounted to more than a few hundred souls —Jacquetta & Christopher Hawkes, *Prehistoric Britain,* 1949

. . . a cumulative cheerfulness, which soon amounted to delight —Thomas Hardy, *The Return of the Native,* 1878

And according to my uncle, the scrapes he was always getting into didn't really amount to much —Peter Taylor, *The Old Forest and Other Stories,* 1985

amuck, amok The notice in Copperud 1970 that *amuck* is the preferred spelling is now out of date; the disparaging remarks about the spelling *amok* in Evans 1957, Fowler 1965, and Bremner 1980 have apparently not influenced writers to reject it. *Amok* is currently the more common spelling in the U.S. Reader's Digest 1983 agrees.

amuse The verb *amuse* (and its past participle *amused* used adjectivally) commonly occurs with the prepositions *at, by,* and *with. At* is somewhat less common than the others, in part because it follows no form of the verb but the past participle.

> . . . at first surprised, then cynical, and eventually amused at this procession —David Halberstam, *Harper's,* January 1969

> . . . it was a private satisfaction . . . to see people occupied and amused at this pecuniary expense —Henry James, *The American,* 1877

> To be amused by what you read —C. E. Montague, *A Writer's Notes on His Trade,* 1930

> A small mob . . . amused itself by cheering —Joseph Conrad, *Chance,* 1913

> . . . amused the citizens by issuing a series of fancy proclamations —Green Peyton, *San Antonio: City in the Sun,* 1946

> . . . no one will have the slightest difficulty in being amused by it —Daniel George, *London Calling,* 19 Aug. 1954

> A King may be pardoned for amusing his leisure with wine, wit, and beauty —T. B. Macaulay, *The History of England,* vol I, 1849

> . . . a witness who was seen amusing himself with a lady on a haycock —Oliver Wendell Holmes d. 1935, letter, 20 May 1920

> . . . adult thumb-suckers, amusing themselves with comic strips, TV, cars —Elmer V. McCollum, *Johns Hopkins Mag.,* Winter 1966

> . . . would begin to amuse himself with some other woman —Marcia Davenport, *My Brother's Keeper,* 1954

Amuse can also be followed by *to* and an infinitive:

> . . . I had been amused to note that . . . —O. S. Nock, *The Railways of Britain,* 1947

analogous When it is followed by a complementary prepositional phrase, *analogous* almost always takes *to:*

> . . . suggesting that both sound and light were wave vibrations, colours being analogous to notes of different frequencies —S. F. Mason, *Main Currents of Scientific Thought,* 1953

> . . . the binucleate mycelium of the Basidiomycetes . . . is certainly analogous to the ascogenous hyphae from which the asci arise —Constantine John Alexopoulos, *Introductory Mycology,* 2d ed., 1962

> . . . the doctrines of Symbolism were in some ways closely analogous to the doctrines of Romanticism —Edmund Wilson, *Axel's Castle,* 1931

> Faulkner's style makes the reader's experience analogous to the hero's —Richard Poirier, *A World Elsewhere,* 1966

> . . . developing in a manner analogous to that of the literary review —Annette Michelson, *Evergreen,* August 1967

With is also idiomatic but seems always to have been much less frequent than *to.* We have no evidence for it more recent than the first example here:

> This is usually silicon tetrafluoride or silicon tetrachloride, analogous with carbon tetrachloride —*Science News Letter,* 16 Sept. 1944

> Russia's present economic situation is analogous with the situation of the United States after the Civil War —*Struggling Russia,* 5 Apr. 1919

> . . . not by means superior to, though analogous with, human reason —Charles Darwin, *On the Origin of Species by Means of Natural Selection,* 1859

analogy Bernstein 1965 mentions only *between* or *with* as being used with this noun; Follett 1966, only *with.* They seem to have missed such other prepositions as *to, of,* and *among.* The examples below also incidentally illustrate many of the typical constructions in which *analogy* may be found.

> . . . tracing the analogies between star and metal or herb and element —Maurice Evans, *Essays in Criticism,* July 1953

> . . . those who would draw any kind of facile analogy between the situation in Vietnam today and Munich —Arthur M. Schlesinger, Jr., *N.Y. Times Mag.,* 6 Feb. 1966

> Analogies between sex manuals and cookbooks are being made in all literary quarters —Marcia Seligson, *McCall's,* March 1971

> Then *k* is said to determine or to measure the state of analogy among the things —Georg Henrik Von Wright, *A Treatise on Induction and Probability,* 1951

> . . . the sash, door, sheathing, chimney-top, and pendills are restored on analogy with examples elsewhere —Fiske Kimball, *Domestic Architecture of the American Colonies and of the Early Republic,* 1922

> A certain analogy with spherical Geometry . . . is also proved —Bertrand Russell, *Foundations of Geometry,* 1897

> Like other popular views, this one follows the analogy of the most usual experience —William James, *Pragmatism,* 1907

> . . . an impatience with all distinctions of kind created on the analogy of a class-structured society —Leslie A. Fiedler, *Los Angeles Times Book Rev.,* 23 May 1971

> . . . utters them *on the analogy* of similar forms which he has heard —Leonard Bloomfield, *Language,* 1933

> He preferred a more solemn analogy of himself as a *medico politico* —Irving Kristol, *Encounter,* December 1954

> . . . uses the image of intensive husbandry as an analogy of the human situation —*Times Literary Supp.,* 9 Mar. 1951

> . . . he went on, thoroughly mesmerized, it seemed, by the analogy he was drawing to his experiences —Joseph Lelyveld, *N.Y. Times Mag.,* 26 Feb. 1967

... the analogy of these societies to human and insect communities is quite superficial —Alexis Carrel, *Man, the Unknown,* 1935

... women in prison build a society on an analogy to the family —Paul Bohannan, *Science 80,* May/June 1980

analysis The phrase *in the final* (or *last* or *ultimate*) *analysis* is disparaged by a few commentators—Flesch 1964 calls it "beloved by pompous writers," Gowers in Fowler 1965 "a popularized technicality," Strunk & White 1959 "a bankrupt expression," and Nickles 1974 a cliché. It seems not to bother anyone else.

The OED Supplement shows the original form to have been *in the ultimate analysis,* which it dates back to 1791. This form of the phrase has been essentially replaced by the shorter forms with *last* and *final* since about the last third of the 19th century. The phrase is not often found in informal contexts. The form with *final* is occasionally used without *the.* Here are a few examples from respected writers; we see nothing amiss in them.

In final analysis the minority that we respect is first and foremost the smallest minority of all—the individual conscience —William O. Douglas, *Being an American,* 1948

... as also, in the final analysis, nations will act to limit national sovereignty —Margaret Mead, *Saturday Rev.,* 10 Jan. 1970

In the final analysis ... ways must be found to produce the greatest good for the greatest number in the shortest period of time —Carl Marcy, *N.Y. Times Book Rev.,* 21 Aug. 1983

In the last analysis, we will not sit by and do nothing when a chronic slump is developing —Paul A. Samuelson, quoted in *Current Biography,* May 1965

I can, in the last analysis, talk only about my own work —Shirley Jackson, *The Writer,* January 1969

Forgive me for speaking personally, but in the last analysis no one can speak for any person except himself —John Mason Brown, *Saturday Rev.,* 3 July 1954

... whether she could, in the last analysis, be absolutely counted on —Louis Auchincloss, *A Law for the Lion,* 1953

analyzation Although Macmillan 1982 thinks this word does not exist, it does, and has since the 18th century. It is formed, perfectly regularly, from the verb *analyze.* It is a rarely used alternative to *analysis*—so rare that it is scarcely worth the space taken to disparage it in Macmillan, McMahan & Day 1980, and Janis 1984. You need not use it if you find it clumsy or sesquipedalian, of course. Few writers do use it, in fact.

anchorperson See PERSON 2.

and 1. Everybody agrees that it's all right to begin a sentence with *and,* and nearly everybody admits to having been taught at some past time that the practice was wrong. Most of us think the prohibition goes back to our early school days. Bailey 1984 points out that the prohibition is probably meant to correct the tendency of children to string together independent clauses or simple declarative sentences with *and*s: "We got in the car and we went to the movie and I bought some popcorn and. . . ." As children grow older and master the more sophisticated technique of subordinating clauses, the prohibition of *and* becomes unnecessary. But apparently our teachers fail to tell us when we may forget about the prohibition. Consequently, many of us go through life thinking it wrong to begin a sentence with *and.*

Few commentators have actually put the prohibition in print; the only one we have found is George Washington Moon:

It is not scholarly to begin a sentence with the conjunction *and* —*The Bad English of Lindley Murray and Other Writers on the English Language,* 1868 (in Baron 1982)

Phythian 1979 does advise following the "old rule," but he recommends it not as a rule but as a general guideline. Many commentators advise not overusing *and* at the beginning of a sentence. It is perhaps overuse that led to this criticism:

The book has another distinction in that practically every other sentence begins with one of those suspended, capital-letter "Ands" which are becoming so popular —*Saturday Rev.,* 12 Feb. 1927

The *Literary Digest* seems to have had so many inquiries about the propriety of beginning a sentence with *and* throughout the 1920s that its editors came up with a stock answer. Here is the version of 5 April 1930:

The practise of beginning sentences with the conjunction "and" dates from 855, and can be verified from *The Old English Chronicle* (Parker M. S.). The use may be found also in Shakespeare's *King John* (act iv, scene 1), the *Gospel of St. John,* xxi:21; Grote's "History of Greece," and Kingsley's "Hypatia."

Here are two contemporary examples of initial *and.* In the second example, it even begins a paragraph:

He didn't believe I found the cart abandoned at a tilt in an alley. And then I turned over into his hands the cash receipts. To the penny —E. L. Doctorow, *Loon Lake,* 1979

"Now, boys," he said, "I want to read you an essay. This is titled 'The Art of Eating Spaghetti.'"

And he started to read. My words! He was reading *my words* out loud to the entire class —Russell Baker, *Growing Up,* 1982

2. There are several other usage problems involving *and.* These are covered at such entries as AND SO; AND WHICH, AND WHO; AGREEMENT, SUBJECT-VERB: COMPOUND SUBJECTS 1; FAULTY PARALLELISM; GOOD AND; and TRY AND.

and etc. See ETC.

and/or *And/or,* says Janis 1984, is "a formal expression used in law and commerce. . . ." It is, in fact, more widely used than that, but Janis has aptly described its origin. David Mellinkoff shows us in *The Language of the Law* (1963), that *and/or* was used first in maritime shipping contracts (of a kind called *charter party*) in the middle of the 19th century. Who first used the device—it was then written $\dfrac{and}{or}$ or $\left\{\begin{matrix} and \\ or \end{matrix}\right\}$—we do not know, but no doubt the first user thought it a convenient way to indicate some limited variability in the contract. The trouble was, however, that one party to the contract might take one view of the matter and the other party a different view. So the interpretation of *and/or* became a matter of litigation in 1854.

English judges had long practice in interpreting English conjunctions in contracts. Not only were there residual problems from translating Latin into English—three Latin conjunctions, *ant, vel,* and *sive,* of different functions in Latin, were all translated into English as *or*—but judicial interpretation had already allowed for *and* = *or* and *or* = *and*. (There is further information on American judicial interpretation of *and* and *or* in Margaret M. Bryant, *English in the Law Courts,* 1930.) And into these shifting tides of legal opinion came *and/or.*

There were three judges involved in the first *and/or* case; they reached three different conclusions as to what it meant. Mellinkoff cites a later case involving *and/or* in a shipping contract. Again there were three judges and three differing opinions. This time none of the three opinions agreed with any of the first three opinions. *And/or* thus began in a cloud of legal ambiguity, but such an inauspicious infancy proved no deterrent in its use.

And/or seems to have established itself with some rapidity both in legal and business contexts. In the 1920s it attracted the vigorous opposition of Samuel Hardin Church, then president of Carnegie Institute in Pittsburgh, who seems to have been grievously offended by its occurrence in some correspondence with the Interstate Commerce Commission. Church peppered publishers and lexicographers with letters of protest, terming *and/or* an atrocious barbarism and "a hideous invention." Church's objection seems to have been aesthetic; he proposed replacing the hideous invention with its unsightly virgule by a new word (are you ready for this?): *andor.*

Most of the more recent criticism in our files is likewise aesthetic—*ugly* is the usual epithet—although a few consider it confusing or ambiguous, and a few (Johnson 1982, Shaw 1970, 1975, Reader's Digest 1983) find it compact and convenient. Opdyke 1939 interestingly says that defenders of *and/or* claim Daniel Defoe used it, perhaps in *The Compleat English Tradesman* (1725, 1727), but no actual citations are produced. Mellinkoff says the term has both defenders and disparagers in the legal profession. A number of commentators recommend replacing "A and/or B" with "A or B or both."

A note on form: *and/or* is nowadays usually found with the virgule. It has been written from time to time with a hyphen *(and-or)* and infrequently with only a space *(and or).* The one-word form advocated by Church seems entirely disused, although we had one notification of its adoption by the Georgia legislature in 1954.

While most of the handbooks refer to legal, commercial, technical, or bureaucratic contexts, none of them provides much in the way of illustrative material. Our evidence shows that it has a wider use; we present some examples of that here.

> . . . and read aloud extracts therefrom for the general benefit and or diversion of the company —Flann O'Brien, *At Swim-Two-Birds,* 1939

> . . . will deduce that the speaker is poorly educated and/or stupid —Robert Claiborne, *Our Marvelous Native Tongue,* 1983

> The award . . . goes to a trade-book editor under 40 who has shown special talent in discovering and/or getting the best work out of his authors —Victor S. Navasky, *N.Y. Times Book Rev.,* 15 Apr. 1973

> . . . discriminatory laws were passed almost everywhere to make certain women were treated as slaves and/or children —Pete Hamill, *Cosmopolitan,* April 1976

> In the public mind it is generally considered to be carried out by priests and/or ministers —*Times Literary Supp.,* 19 Mar. 1970

> The book containing (1) the rites and ceremonies for the services, and/or (2) the rules and customs of discipline —*Oxford Dictionary of the Christian Church,* 1957

> . . . attempts to dramatize the presumably hectic and/or nefarious goings-on in the newsrooms of big-city tabloids —Harrison Smith, *Saturday Rev.,* 21 Aug. 1954

> As Brando hummed and/or drummed in some secluded hideaway —*Time,* 13 Oct. 1958

> . . . and a bow or belt in the back, depending on the size and/or sophistication of the girl who gets it —*New Yorker,* 24 Nov. 1956

These examples are fairly typical of the general uses of *and/or;* we do have some, of course, that are vaguer than these. You may have observed that in each of these *and/or* is used between only two options and that it can readily be understood in the sense "A or B or both." But if the number of options is increased, the number of possibilities multiplies, and the chance for ambiguity likewise increases. In "A, B, and/or C" lie "A or B or C," "A and B or C," "A or B and C," "A and B and C." The knotty problems of maritime law mentioned above were in fact of "A, B, and/or C" type. Little wonder the judges could reach so many conclusions.

Most of the examples in our files use *and/or* between two alternatives. We have only a few examples of the "A, B, and/or C" type, two of which we give you here:

> . . . someone who feels he has been the victim of negligence by physicians, nurses, and/or hospitals —*Center Mag.,* November/December 1971

> All you will end up with will be a set of platitudes, truisms, and/or trivialities —Nehemiah Jordan, *Themes in Speculative Psychology,* 1968

In these instances the multiplicity of possible combinations seems not to matter. Which might suggest, to some, that *and/or* serves no purpose in them and might well have been avoided.

If you have a need to use *and/or,* we recommend that you use it only between two alternatives, where the meaning will obviously be "A or B or both." In longer series *and/or* will likely be either vague or unnecessary.

and so   Bierce 1909 objected to the use of *and so* as wordy, but modern books generally ignore it. It is, of course, in perfectly good use:

> To my intense disappointment I was turned down, and so I went to another Presbyterian college —Wil-

liam Styron, *This Quiet Dust and Other Writings,* 1982

And so the methods will be settled, and then I shall be returning —Jonathan Swift, *Journal to Stella,* 27 Nov. 1710

According to rumor, they did not like each other and so the arrangement might be termed a feudal partnership —Heywood Broun, *New Republic,* 8 Mar. 1939

He had never confided in them or shared his hopes or feelings and so they saw no marked change in his behavior —E. L. Doctorow, *Ragtime,* 1975

. . . smiled broadly at Coverly all during the pause and so it was not an anxious silence —John Cheever, *The Wapshot Chronicle,* 1957

and which, and who These headings, sometimes compounded (as in Copperud 1970, 1980) with *but,* cover a number of constructions marked by faulty parallelism (which see) in the use of conjunctions and relative pronouns (and sometimes other connectives). The problem is better exemplified than described:

. . . a lady very learned in stones, ferns, plants, and vermin, and who had written a book about petals — Anthony Trollope, *Barchester Towers,* 1857 (in A. S. Hill 1895)

In the example *and* joins a clause ("who had written a book . . .") with an adjective phrase ("learned in stones . . .") not structurally parallel to it. The usual corrective measure would be to insert *who was* after *lady* and, perhaps, then omit the *who* after *and.*

Copperud gives this a fairly long entry, Fowler 1926, 1965 devotes about five pages to it, and several other handbooks discuss the question. There is no doubt that this construction is a fault; A. S. Hill, in *Principles of Rhetoric* (1895), calls it "an offence against ease." It is more accurately an offense against elegance or precision. It is a minor offense, however; the examples we have are readily understandable notwithstanding the fault; one third of the Heritage 1969 usage panel even found it acceptable. Here are a few samples:

. . . Stephen, with a glance serious but which indicated intimacy, caught the eye of a comely lady — Benjamin Disraeli, *Sybil,* 1845 (in Hill)

. . . preserve for him his Highland garb and accoutrements, particularly the arms, curious in themselves, and to which the friendship of the donors gave additional value —Sir Walter Scott, *Waverly,* 1814 (in Hill)

. . . the hold he exerted over the friend of his youth, and which lasted until her death, is here, rather tragically, revealed —*Times Literary Supp.,* 31 Aug. 1951

Declarations made under Article 36 of the Statute of the Permanent Court of International Justice and which are still in force shall be deemed . . . to be acceptances —*Charter of the United Nations,* 1945

The *and which* construction, in its various guises, is a fault that can be found, at least occasionally, in the work of good writers. It is most likely simply an inadvertency. Since it generally does not seem to interfere with the reader's understanding of the passage it appears in, it

probably goes unnoticed for the most part. It is therefore a venial sin. We suggest that you try to avoid it, however, for when it is spotted, it distracts the reader's attention from more important matters—namely, what you are saying.

anent The old preposition *anent* "concerning, about" appears to have undergone a revival during the 19th century. The OED notes the sense as being "common in Scotch law phraseology, and affected by many English writers." The OED evidence suggests little use of the word in the 17th and 18th centuries; an early 19th-century citation is from Sir Walter Scott; he may have helped spread the use among English men of letters. The OED's comment about affectation was not taken up by usage commentators until the 20th century, beginning with Utter 1913, Vizetelly 1922, Fowler 1926, and Krapp 1927. Their two chief words of disapproval are *affected* and *archaic.* Later commentators continue in essentially the same vein, right up to Janis 1984 who is still calling *anent* archaic. Copperud, 1970, 1980 notes that dictionaries list it as standard.

Anent is an odd word. It has a bookish air about it— you rarely (or perhaps never) hear it used in ordinary conversation—but it seems to pop up in contexts that are not at all bookish (along with some that are). Fowler notes the frequency with which it is met in letters to the press. It is still found in letters to the editor:

Anent your editorial with its "Go ahead and gripe" message —letter to the editor, *InfoWorld,* 19 Sept. 1983

Anent your allusion to the military predilection for the noun-comma-adjective format —letter reprinted in Safire 1982

The combined usage of letter-to-the-editor writers and literary as well as nonliterary people has brought *anent* back to life. Here is a healthy sample of such usage. It is clearly not archaic, nor in most cases does the level of affectation seem especially high. Dead words do sometimes rise from the grave, and this is one of them.

I find another remark anent "pupils"—a bold speculation that my 1,000 pupils may really "go on" in the future life —Lewis Carroll, letter, 14 Feb. 1886

. . . a remark anent the advancement of the spring — George Moore, *The Brook Kerith,* 1916

. . . was writing anent the suggestion that Colonel House's trip to Europe . . . was for the purpose of adjusting certain alleged squabbles —Arthur D. Howden Smith, *The Real Colonel House,* 1918

. . . a brief note from Felix anent some hostile review in the *New Republic* of my last book —Harold J. Laski, letter, 28 Nov. 1920

. . . but he wrote letters telling of his progress and his thoughts anent the proper dissemination of religion —F. Tennyson Jesse, *The Lacquer Lady,* 1930

Anent the origin of sweet corn —*Biological Abstracts,* January 1943

. . . dispute over the dying wartime President's remarks anent the League of Nations —*Newsweek,* 11 June 1944

There is another marvelously wacky correspondence between Mr. Thurber and both customs officials and the Connecticut State Tax Commission, anent a small bottle of wine sent as a gift —Irwin Edman, *N.Y. Herald Tribune Book Rev.,* 1 Nov. 1953

Anent this, a report from Sweden on establishment of the nation's fourth dental school —*Dental Survey,* March 1966

... and saying, anent the rumors of my going to India, that perhaps a word might go to Ellsworth Bunker —John Kenneth Galbraith, *Ambassador's Journal,* 1969

The nattering nabobs of negativism on the national networks will no longer natter negatively anent Nixon —Richard H. Rovere, *New Yorker,* 1 May 1971

"A middle-class white son-of-a-bitch without goals will usually break your heart," a trainer remarks, anent fighters —Judith Crist, *New York,* 29 Oct. 1973

Anent the practice of snaring ptarmigan with brass wires —Henry Tegner, *Scottish Field,* February 1975

A line from his 'Prologue to *Macbeth',* anent the apparition of Banquo —D. J. Enright, *The Listener,* 22 May 1975

angle   *Angle,* "the viewpoint from which something is considered," is described by Copperud 1970, 1980 as "mildly criticized" and "under a faint shadow that is fast disappearing." Since many of the books that criticize this sense of *angle* are school or college handbooks, it may be used more often in student papers than instructors like. The Merriam-Webster files do not show evidence of the overuse asserted in the handbooks; *attitude, point of view, position*—the words Guth 1985 calls *angle* an overused synonym for—are used with considerably more frequency than *angle. Angle* appears most frequently in reviews. Here are some examples:

A solidly good, offbeat Bicentennial book idea that cries out for a wider angle and a richer sense of the American cartoonists' diversity —Albert H. Johnston, *Publishers Weekly,* 27 Oct. 1975

It is a special angle of vision granted to certain writers who already write good English —William Zinsser, *N.Y. Times Mag.,* 2 Dec. 1979

Roughly speaking, there are three main angles from which a novel can be criticized —*Times Literary Supp.,* 25 July 1968

And the angle of vision here is very different — Arthur M. Schlesinger, Jr., *Saturday Rev.,* 2 Sept. 1978

... a travel article, like any good article, must have an angle or approach, a peg or slant, that will make it interesting to the audience —John J. Chalmers, *The Writer,* July 1968

The verb *angle,* in the past participle, is used in a similar sense:

It was all on paper, all of it, angled from Matthew Brennan's point of view —Irving Wallace, *The Plot,* 1967

Admirers of Churchill may well be angered or saddened or both by this harsh but freshly angled and

trenchant portrait —Albert A. Johnston, *Publishers Weekly,* 11 Mar. 1974

An analysis of the headlines taken from all the papers in any country, on the same day, will show that many are angled politically —David Kimball, *The Machinery of Self-Government,* 1953

Anglo   *Anglo* is an ethnic term of relatively recent vintage used to distinguish those of English ethnic or English-speaking background from others. The Dictionary of Canadianisms dates Canadian use from 1800; U.S. use is much more recent, dating from the mid-1930s.

There are at present two chief uses. The first is Canadian; it distinguishes the Canadian of English ethnic and language background from one whose background is French.

... the language we Anglos have all been speaking unwittingly—*Canajan* —Val Clery, *Books in Canada,* July–September 1973

We all know Quebec isn't entirely French. ... there are still nearly a million Anglos in the province — Sonia Day, letter to the editor, *Word Watching,* June 1983

The second arose in the southwestern U.S. and originally distinguished the American of English-speaking background from one of Spanish-speaking background.

But as far as the newcomer can see, the ordinary Anglo is little more civilized, less blatant, or less confident of his own noisy progress because of his contact with the two more gracious cultures —Dudley Wynn, *New Mexico Quarterly,* February 1935

The Spanish-speaking also are still about. They dress for the most part like Anglos now —Conrad Richter, *Holiday,* December 1953

But *Anglo* has been extended to other kinds of distinctions. In the 1980s these have not yet sorted themselves out into uses that are both discrete and fixed enough to be recognized as separate meanings. Here is a sample:

Unless you happen to be Spanish, Mexican, or Indian, when you go to Santa Fe you are casually classed as an "Anglo," even if you are Greek, Chinese, or British —Edith Moore Jarrett & Beryl J. M. McManus, *El Camino Real,* 3d ed., 1960

... a rate of depression midway between that of Jewish women with European-born mothers on the one hand and Anglo women on the other —Pauline Bart, *Trans-Action,* November–December 1970

In Miami, if you are not Cuban and not black, you are, by local definition, an Anglo —Herbert Burkholz, *N.Y. Times Mag.,* 21 Sept. 1980

... third graders in Denver—some Hispanic kids, some Indochinese, with half the class Anglo —Lawrence Fuchs, *People,* 6 Dec. 1982

To Anglo minds, Latins often seem to typify the macho ethos; how then does Puerto Rico happen to have women in many of its top jobs? —Lorraine Davis, *Vogue,* January 1984

How far these terms are disparaging, it is hard to tell. We have some evidence that the U.S. *Anglo* has been considered a derogatory term, but evidence in print suggests that it is apparently not so apprehended a great majority of the time. If the term was in origin disparaging, its usefulness as a classifying term has obscured that intent. Most of our current evidence—and there is a lot—appears neutral.

There is also use of *Anglo* in British English. Our evidence for it is somewhat thin, but at least sometimes it refers to one who is English, as distinguished from Irish, Scottish, or Welsh—and perhaps others. This term may be used disparagingly:

> From the start Scotland produced brilliant players, saw them bribed away to play in England and spat after them the contemptuous term "Anglos" —Brian James, *Sunday Times Mag.* (London), 2 June 1974

angry From Vizetelly 1906 to Chambers 1985 much advice and prescription has been written about the prepositions that can be used with *angry*. Much of the discussion deals with whether the object of the anger is human, animal, or inanimate; often particular prepositions are prescribed for particular objects. Much of the prescription is plainly in conflict with actual usage, such as Shaw 1970's "Idiomatically, one is angry *with*, not *at*, a person." *Angry at* (a person) has been around since Shakespeare's time (the OED cites *Timon of Athens*, 1607) and is still in use.

The chief prepositions are *with*, *at*, and *about*. *With* is the most frequently used preposition when the object is a person:

> Indeed, be not angry with her, bud —William Wycherly, *The Country Wife*, 1675

> I fancy I shall have reason to be angry with him very soon —Jonathan Swift, *Journal to Stella*, 9 Aug. 1711

> I am sorry to be angry with you —Samuel Johnson (1776), in James Boswell, *Life of Samuel Johnson*, 1791

> Be not angry with me, Coleridge —Charles Lamb, letter, 24 Oct. 1796

> She wanted somebody to be angry with —George Meredith, *The Ordeal of Richard Feverel*, 1859

> . . . I hope she isn't angry with me for talking nonsense about her name —Lewis Carroll, letter, 28 Nov. 1867

> You have often made me angry with you, poor little innocent —George Bernard Shaw, *Cashel Byron's Profession*, 1886

> . . . angry with herself for having suffered from it so much —Joseph Conrad, *Chance*, 1913

> She was angry with Clare for crying —Rose Macaulay, *Potterism*, 1920

> The author is very angry with anyone who dislikes the cockney manner of speech —*Times Literary Supp.*, 20 Feb. 1953

> On this day Mary was angry with me —Ernest Hemingway, "Miss Mary's Lion," 1956

> He was angry with himself, still more angry with Rose —C. P. Snow, *The New Men*, 1954

> ". . . I get that it's okay to be angry with you." —R. D. Rosen, *Psychobabble*, 1977

With is sometimes used with inanimate or abstract objects:

> . . . angry also with the change of fortune which was reshaping the world about him —James Joyce, *A Portrait of the Artist as a Young Man*, 1916

> I think I was all the angrier with my own ineffectiveness because I knew the streets —*The Autobiography of Malcolm X*, 1966

At is used with objects that are persons and objects that are actions or things:

> I have heard some people so extravagantly angry at this play —George Farquhar, Preface to *The Inconstant*, 1702

> Yet I am angry at some bad Rhymes and Triplets —Jonathan Swift, letter, 28 June 1715

> I find no considerable Man angry at the Book —Alexander Pope, letter, 16 Nov. 1726

> "I do not see, Sir, that it is reasonable for a man to be angry at another. . . ." —Samuel Johnson (1775), in James Boswell, *Life of Samuel Johnson*, 1791

> . . . there is nothing which makes us so angry at the people we love as their way of letting themselves be imposed upon —Margaret Deland, *Old Chester Tales*, 1898

> Jealous of the smallest cover,
> Angry at the simplest door;
> —D. H. Lawrence, *Collected Poems*, 1928

> I became angry at him and I went after him —Henry Clark, quoted in *Sports Illustrated*, 15 July 1968

> They might be angry at him —Gay Talese, *Harper's*, January 1969

About is used of persons or actions or things:

> . . . they are so angry about the affair of Duke Hamilton —Jonathan Swift, *Journal to Stella*, 2 Feb. 1712

> Still it's better to have Mr. L. angry about her than about other topics —C. P. Snow, *The Conscience of the Rich*, 1958

> Mr. Reed is angry about what he perceives to be negative characterizations of black men in fiction and drama —Brent Staples, *N.Y. Times Book Rev.*, 23 Mar. 1986

Other prepositions are also possible:

> . . . he feels angry towards your community —Fred Sharpe, *6th Annual Report, Peace Officers Training School*, 1952

> She said, 'I was only angry for my sweet little baby.' —Angus Wilson, *Anglo-Saxon Attitudes*, 1956

It does not seem reasonable, on the basis of the evidence here and in the OED, to make rigid distinctions about which prepositions are proper in which uses.

animadversion, animadvert 1. Of these hard words Bernstein 1965 observes that the verb takes *upon*. Actually, both the noun and verb are followed by *on* or *upon*, as Simon 1980 says. The instance of *animadver-*

sion to that he detected probably resulted from the writer's confusing *animadversion* with *aversion,* which usually takes *to* (but see section 2 below). A few examples of the usual prepositions:

> There are quite a few animadversions, for example, on the plight of women —Anatole Broyard, *N.Y. Times,* 28 Aug. 1980

> I refrain from further animadversions on the quality of tone —Richard Franko Goldman, *The Concert Band,* 1946

> ... animadversions upon the shortcomings of his fellow biographers —*Times Literary Supp.,* 21 Dec. 1973

> ... the justice of his animadversion upon his old acquaintance and pupil —James Boswell, *Life of Samuel Johnson,* 1791

> ... let us notice and animadvert on the vogue use of *reiterate* —Howard 1977

> ... had wearied of animadverting upon the late King's devotion to duty —Malcolm Muggeridge, *Saturday Evening Post,* 19 Oct. 1957

> ... to the extent of our animadverting upon his economics or his politics —John Crowe Ransom, *Sewanee Rev.,* Spring 1953

2. The *animadversion to* detected by Simon 1980 may just possibly have been more than a casual confusion of *aversion to* with *animadversion (up)on.* We have some slight evidence of the use of *animadversion* as a longer and perhaps more impressive or emphatic form of *aversion.* Our evidence for this use is sparse, and so far as we know, it is recognized by only two dictionaries, *Macmillan Dictionary* (1973)—a high-school dictionary—and one of its derivatives for lower grades. William D. Halsey and his editors give as sense 2 of *animadversion:* "dislike or antipathy; aversion: *He became a vegetarian because of his animadversion toward meat.*" We have no evidence of *animadversion* used with *toward,* but we do have one example with *to:*

> It embarrasses me now that I ever could have questioned the ingenuousness of her Polish sentiments and suspected her animadversion to the U.S.S.R. of being simulated —Robert Craft, *Stravinsky,* 1972

It is possible that this sense is more common than our evidence suggests. If evidence continues to accumulate to the point that the meaning seems to have established itself in the language, it will have to go into dictionaries, so the puzzled can look it up. Then, if tradition prevails, usage experts will begin to lament the destruction of another splendid word and the decline of literacy. For now our judgment has to be that this sense is still nonstandard.

anniversary   Kilpatrick 1984 animadverts on the use of *anniversary* to mark the recurrence of a period other than a year. He cites among his examples a *Wall Street Journal* report of Poland's "six-month anniversary" of a military crackdown.

This use seems to be chiefly an oral one that is found very infrequently in print. A correspondent wrote to ask us about it in 1967, claiming it to be "not uncommon in speech." At that time we had but a single example in print:

> On the 15-month anniversary of Defense he had at last accepted a way to get everything done that must be done —*Time,* 8 Sept. 1941

Our evidence since then is scant. Our correspondent of 1967 seems to have been right: it is probably not uncommon in speech (we do have some confirming evidence), but it remains uncommon in print. The extension to a period of time other than a year does not seem especially irrational, however, in the absence of an alternative word for the idea.

annoint   See ANOINT.

annoy   Since early in this century, some commentators have been trying to help us with the prepositions that go with *annoyed,* the past participle of this verb. Their distinctions are various and are based on such considerations as whether one *is* or *feels* annoyed, whether the annoyer is an action, thing, or person, and whether *annoyed* means "pestered." As is usual with such attempts, actual usage proves more complex than the proffered distinctions. Here are some examples of the common prepositions, *with, at,* and *by,* and the less common *about:*

> ... annoyed the British in Philadelphia with a satirical ballad —*American Guide Series: Pennsylvania,* 1940

> ... if she annoys him with her watchfulness —H. M. Parshley, translation of Simone de Beauvoir, *The Second Sex,* 1952

> ... get greatly annoyed with anything in it that happens to interfere —Elmer Davis, *But We Were Born Free,* 1954

> ... annoyed about a trembling hand —*Current Biography,* December 1964

> ... annoyed at the waste of it all —Alan Rich, *New York,* 8 Feb. 1971

> ... became annoyed at newspaper reports —John Barkham, *Saturday Rev.,* 13 Feb. 1954

> My hostess was annoyed at me —Maude Phelps Hutchins, *Epoch,* Fall 1947

> ... are often puzzled and sometimes annoyed by the ways of other peoples —William A. Parker, *Understanding Other Cultures,* 1954

> ... she was disturbed and next annoyed by the silence —Jean Stafford, *Children Are Bored on Sunday,* 1953

> ... much annoyed by the wolves that still existed in Florida then —Marjory Stoneman Douglas, *The Everglades: River of Grass,* 1947

> He was annoyed by the cold, the starvation, and chiefly by the coarseness of the dying soldiers — Morris Bishop, *Saturday Rev.,* 11 Dec. 1954

> Though annoyed by the tone of the Tringsbys' letters —Elizabeth Bowen, *The Heat of the Day,* 1949

> ... he was distinctly annoyed by Clara's advent — Elinor Wylie, *Mr. Hodge and Mr. Hazard,* 1928

Annoy and *annoyed* are followed by constructions other than those consisting of preposition and noun. A sample:

> It annoys me to have smokers blow smoke in my face —H. Thompson Fillmer et al., *Patterns of Language,* Level F (textbook), 1977

> ... I was annoyed to lose it —Nora Waln, *The House of Exile,* 1933

> Some of his friends were annoyed to recognize themselves in the latter book —*Dictionary of American Biography,* 1929

> Annoyed that the university administrators had publicly aired their views —*Current Biography,* January 1966

> "It's annoying that we have to rush. . . ." —*Adventures Here and There* (5th grade textbook), 1950

anoint Often misspelled *annoint,* says Copperud 1970, 1980. The spelling *annoint* is already recognized as a standard variant in the sense of anointing as a sacred rite. But our evidence confirms Copperud: the *ann-* spelling is spreading to the other sense of *anoint:*

> ... former times when no boy would annoint himself below his navel —*Prose,* Fall 1971

> ... his views and his new power have served to annoint him as the spiritual leader of the new bloc of ultraconservatives —*N.Y. Times Mag.,* 8 Feb. 1981

> ... oysters poached in white wine and annointed with beurre blanc —*Town & Country,* June 1980

We also have a couple of *annointments.* None of these spellings is yet recognized in dictionaries.

an't, a'n't This is the original contraction that eventually gave us *ain't.* It may possibly have originated as an Irishism; at least the earliest evidence we have found so far occurs in the writing of Congreve, Farquhar, and Swift. The contraction seems to have dropped out of use in the U.S. around the middle of the 19th century and in England a bit later. In America it was replaced by *ain't;* in England it seems to have been replaced by *aren't,* although a few writers use *ain't.* See AIN'T; AREN'T I. Here are a few examples from the past:

> MISS PRUE. You need not sit so near one, if you have any thing to say, I can hear you farther off, I an't deaf —William Congreve, *Love for Love,* 1695

> CHERRY. ... I hope, Sir, you an't affronted — George Farquhar, *The Beaux Stratagem,* 1707

> ... an't I a reasonable creature? —Jonathan Swift, *Journal to Stella,* 18 Feb. 1711

> SIR PETER. Two hundred pounds! what, a'n't I to be in a good humor without paying for it? —Richard Brinsley Sheridan, *A School for Scandal,* 1783

> It is thought he has gone sick upon them. He a'n't well, that's certain —Charles Lamb, letter, 26 Feb. 1808

> An a'n't I a woman? —Sojourner Truth, recorded by Frances D. Gage, May 1851 (in J. L. Dillard, *American Talk,* 1976)

ante-, anti- Several handbooks warn against confusing these prefixes. *Ante-* means "earlier, before," and *anti-* (sometimes found as *ant-* or *anth-*) "opposite, opposed, against." See a good dictionary for fuller definitions. There was an *anti-* in use as a variant of *ante-* at one time, but it seems to have become disused because of the possibility of confusion with the "against" *anti-.* So there is now no excuse for a mistake with these prefixes.

antecedent The adjective *antecedent* is less attested in our files than the noun; as an adjective it is not usually placed in a construction requiring a preposition, but when it is, the preposition is *to.*

> For him, character and society are antecedent to talk —Richard Poirier, *A World Elsewhere,* 1966

> If we believe that we have rights antecedent to government —*Time,* 26 Sept. 1955

anterior Our evidence of *anterior* as an attributive adjective runs pretty heavily to technical contexts. As a predicate adjective it usually takes *to.* It tends to be found in rather learned or at least elevated styles.

> In political theory, even a constitutional system entails powers anterior to those specified in the Constitution —*National Rev.,* 17 Nov. 1970

> ... the Babylonian epic *Gilgamesh,* which is a genuine epic by any definition and is not only anterior to the Bible but may also have influenced both the Greek and the Indian epics —Moses Hadas, *Commentary,* October 1957

> ... a parallel liberation which Croce seeks in his presentation of Art as ideally anterior to Thought — Cecil Sprigge, *Benedetto Croce,* 1952

anti- See ANTE-, ANTI-.

anticipate "The verb *anticipate* is often used with the meaning 'to foresee (something) and take action to prevent it, counter it, meet its requirements, etc.'. . . . Some people consider this to be the only correct meaning of *anticipate,* but for most speakers of English this verb has another meaning, equivalent simply to 'foresee' or 'expect'. . . ." Thus Chambers 1985. While this statement is reasonable as far as it goes, it is based on the mistaken assumption that *anticipate* has but two senses. The OED identifies nine senses, most of which are still active; even Webster's Ninth New Collegiate offers six transitive and one intransitive. When the Chambers editors go on to observe that "it is perhaps unfortunate that *anticipate* has taken on this wider meaning," they are nodding in the direction of many earlier commentators—Reader's Digest 1983, Copperud 1970, 1980, Bryson 1984, Phythian 1979, Burchfield 1981, Sellers 1975, Gowers 1948, to name some—who condemn the "expect" use.

The original objection seems to have been made by Ayres 1881. Ayres decided that certain examples he had collected meant "expect" and were wrong. To prove his contention, he points to the etymology of the word and a number of different definitions presumably taken from an unnamed dictionary, none of which is "expect." This is merely a game being played with the words that have been used to define *anticipate;* nothing whatsoever has been proved. But no matter. Along comes Bierce 1909 to take the same position; Bierce, however, discards all but one approved sense of *anticipate,* which has made life much simpler for later commentators. Copperud 1980, for instance, refers to the word's "pristine sense," although several of the OED's senses are from the sixteenth century and the "forestall" sense is not among them.

The plain fact of the matter is that in some instances *anticipate* comes close in meaning to some meanings of *expect.* And in some instances it comes close to *predict, foresee, look forward to, forestall, foreshadow.* But none of these words are precise synonyms for *anticipate;* they serve only to suggest meaning. It is therefore vain to erect a whole edifice of lexical right and wrong on the shifting sands of occasional near synonyms.

Here are some examples of *anticipate* that do not mean "forestall." Some of them do not mean "expect" either. All of them are perfectly standard.

Always she was restlessly anticipating the day when they would leave —Arnold Bennett, *The Old Wives' Tale,* 1908

Pleasure not known beforehand is half wasted; to anticipate it is to double it —Thomas Hardy, *The Return of the Native,* 1878

He became more dependent on her; and she anticipated that he would become more exacting in his demands on her time —George Bernard Shaw, *Cashel Byron's Profession,* 1886

... said she would give me her tickets to the anticipated celebration at party headquarters —Elsa Maxwell, *Woman's Home Companion,* April 1954

... which the beau monde of the Cambrian mountains was in the habit of remembering with the greatest pleasure, and anticipating with the most lively satisfaction —Thomas Love Peacock, *Headlong Hall,* 1816

She certainly had not anticipated taking a whole day to get through a belt of reeds a mile wide —C. S. Forester, *The African Queen,* 1935

"I can tell you that our overall bomber losses are proving light. Only a fraction of what we anticipated, what we were prepared for." —James Gould Cozzens, *Guard of Honor,* 1948

No obstacles were anticipated —Eileen Hughes, *Ladies' Home Jour.,* September 1971

Both had anticipated and foretold a bit of rain before night —George Meredith, *The Ordeal of Richard Feverel,* 1859

Each side anticipates that the other will add to its armament —Jerome D. Frank, *Psychology Today,* November 1968

Some marketers anticipate that by Labor Day motorists will be paying as much as 50 to 60 cents for a gallon of gasoline —August Gribbin, *National Observer,* 28 Apr. 1973

All of these examples fall within the range of the OED's sense 9. You will see that no single word, like *expect* or *predict,* and no phrase, like *look forward to,* quite comprehends every one. The usage of actual writers can be much subtler than commentators are often willing to recognize.

antidote **1.** The OED and other dictionaries note that *antidote* can be followed by *against, for,* or *to.* Evidence in our files shows that all three are in use for both literal and figurative senses. Of the three, *to* is the most commonly used at the present time, *for* next, and *against* the least. A few examples:

An antidote against nerve gases —*Time,* 19 Mar. 1956

... no surer antidote against the dull monotony of travel —Douglas Carruthers, *Beyond the Caspian,* 1949

... the first effective antidote for PCP —*N.Y. Times,* 11 Feb. 1980

... hate may be the only antidote for despair —David Black, *New Times,* 11 July 1975

... an antidote to the arsenical blister gases —Russell L. Cecil & Robert F. Loeb, *Textbook of Medicine,* 8th ed., 1951

... the grim reality of life in Kiev acted as a strong antidote to romantic notions —Glenn Plaskin, *N.Y. Times,* 6 Feb. 1983

2. A few commentators warn against confusing *antidote* with *anecdote.* The likelihood of this malapropism would seem to be low, but it has happened:

... if I could tell an antidote about self-incrimination —*Police,* September–October 1967

If you have *tell* before or *about* after, *antidote* is clearly not the word you want.

antipathy Bernstein 1965 says that *antipathy* takes *to, toward,* or *against;* Lincoln Library 1924 says *to,* sometimes *for* or *against,* and *between;* Krapp 1927 says *to* but not *for* or *against;* Webster 1909 says *to, against, between,* sometimes *for.* We had better straighten this out.

Construction with *against* seems to be archaic. We have no recent evidence for it, although it was once current:

What a strange antipathy I have taken against these creatures! —George Farquhar, *The Inconstant,* 1702

... nothing is more essential than that permanent inveterate antipathies against particular nations ... should be excluded —George Washington, *Farewell Address,* 1796

The use of *between* (two persons or things), while not common, is still current:

... there was a marked antipathy between their radicalism or liberalism and the conservative peasant ideas of the mass of Italian immigrants —Oscar Handlin, *The American People in the Twentieth Century,* 1954

The antipathy between Mr. Barbieri and Mr. Lee has grown —William Borders, *N.Y. Times,* 15 Oct. 1967

The antipathy between the groups is deep —Renata Adler, *Pitch Dark,* 1983

To has been and continues to be the most common preposition:

> Whose peering eye and wrinkled front declare
> A fixed antipathy to young and fair
> —Richard Brinsley Sheridan,
> *The School for Scandal,* 1783

... perceived above a dozen large bugs. You must know I have the same kind of antipathy to these vermin —Tobias Smollett, *Travels Through France and Italy,* 1766

Hogarth's antipathy to France —Agnes Repplier, *In Pursuit of Laughter,* 1936

... who shares this antipathy to the indefiniteness of aesthetic morality —Havelock Ellis, *The Dance of Life,* 1923

... a definite antipathy to permitting outside doctors to come into their home communities and take over their practice —*JAMA,* 3 Apr. 1943

... Grandmother's belief that the medical profession needed informed lay augmentation was the basis for her implacable antipathy to hospitals —James A. Maxwell, *New Yorker,* 24 Nov. 1951

... the growing sensibility cult with its antipathy to the generic explicitness of the novel —Anthony J. Hassall, *Novel,* Spring 1972

While *for* and *toward* appear somewhat less frequently than *to,* both are in regular use, and they are about equally common:

The antipathy Lessing felt for the French wit — Irving Babbitt, *The New Laokoon,* 1910

... both species knew instinctively of his pronounced antipathy for them —Osbert Sitwell, *Noble Essences,* 1950

Her one antipathy is for Schrader, whose work she has never liked —Robert F. Moss, *Saturday Rev.,* October 1980

Little remains of the Puritanical antipathy toward them as immoral —Thomas Munro, *The Arts and Their Interrelations,* 1949

And the American antipathy toward a preventive nuclear strike —Stephen A. Garrett, *Center Mag.,* July–August 1971

anxious The discovery that *anxious* must not be used to mean "eager" seems to have been made in the U.S. in the early 20th century. Bierce 1909 is the earliest usage book we have found that prohibits the usage, but apparently Alfred Ayres beat him to the punch. A correspondent reading the Chattanooga, Tennessee, *Times* in 1901 sent us a clipping from that paper with the following quotation:

> Only a few days ago, I heard a learned man, an LL.D., a dictionary-maker, an expert in English, say that he was anxious to finish the moving of his belongings from one room to another.
>   "No, you are not," said I.
>   "Yes, I am. How do you know?"
>   "I know you are not."
>   "Why, what do you mean?"
>   "There is no anxiety about it. You are simply desirous." —Alfred Ayres, *Harper's,* July 1901

The learned dictionary-maker, of course, collapsed completely at this shrewd observation, and Mr. Ayres presumably went on his merry way, illuminating other learned men. This particular learned dictionary-maker seems not to have looked at *anxious* in the OED (*A* appeared in 1884); if he had, he would have discovered that his use of *anxious* had already existed for some 160 years when he was corrected. Even lexicographers can be taken unawares.

From its modest beginnings in the Ayres anecdote and Bierce's prescription, the *anxious-eager* question rapidly became a shibboleth in American usage. It appears in Utter 1916, MacCracken & Sandison 1917, Vizetelly 1922, Ball 1923, Whipple 1924, Powell 1925, and others down to Bernstein 1965, 1977, Shaw 1970, 1975, Bremner 1980, Bell & Cohn 1981, Janis 1984, Kilpatrick 1984, and Harper 1975, 1985. Fowler 1926 pooh-poohed the whole matter with the result that *anxious-eager* has not found much of a place in English usage books, being noticed only in Partridge 1942 and Bryson 1984 among those we have seen.

There are two aspects to the question, both touched upon by Bierce. The first is semantic—do not use *anxious* for *eager*—and the second is idiomatic: "*Anxious* should not be followed by an infinitive." Let's begin with meaning.

Bierce's semantic equation, *anxious = eager* in this use, is an oversimplification subscribed to by most, but not all, of the commentators who disapprove it. Utter 1916, for instance, admits *anxious to* (do something) when the eagerness is qualified by a troubled mind about the endeavor. Partridge 1942 seems to be thinking along similar lines when he rules out *anxious* meaning "eager" or "desirous," but permits it for "solicitous" and "earnestly desirous" (which might in practice be difficult to distinguish from plain "desirous" but must be passed because it is the OED definition). The word, in fact, fairly often has the notion of anxiety mingled with that of eagerness; it is not unreasonable to suppose that this is how the use developed. Here is Dr. Johnson holding forth:

> ... there must always be some degree of care and anxiety. The master of the house is anxious to entertain his guests; the guests are anxious to be agreeable —in James Boswell, *Life of Samuel Johnson,* 1791

Without Johnson's mention of *anxiety,* a reader might take *anxious* to mean "eager" here. A few more examples that suggest a mixture of eagerness and anxiety are these:

Even without his books, Don Quixote set forth once again, anxious as before not to lose any time, "for he could not but blame himself for what the world was losing by his delay...." —Malcolm Muggeridge, *Punch,* 8 Apr. 1953

The Court may be anxious to dispose of this potentially troublesome affair —Arthur E. Wise, *Saturday Rev.,* 20 Nov. 1971

Most spiders are shy and far more anxious to avoid than to attack man —Katherine W. Moseley, *Massachusetts Audubon,* June 1971

... all the Christian churches in Africa are anxious to escape from "the foreignness of Christianity" — *Times Literary Supp.,* 2 Oct. 1969

Bierce's association of the "eager" sense with the construction with *to* and the infinitive is probably a clue to the way in which the sense developed in the 18th century. A few books—Scott-Foresman 1981, Swan 1980—distinguish the senses of *anxious* by their typical constructions. *Anxious about* and *anxious at* are associated with the "worried, troubled" sense, and *anxious to* and *anxious for* with the "eager, desirous" sense. A. S. Hornby, in *A Guide to Patterns and Usage in English* (1954), also places *anxious that* in the "eager, desirous" column. The examples that follow show that actual usage is not quite as neat as they suggest.

The *anxious at* construction does not show up in our files, nor in the OED. We do have an *anxious lest:*

> He was anxious lest they were broken and thus make an evil omen —Pearl Buck, *The Good Earth,* 1931

Anxious about is well attested. The examples are for the "worried" sense, but a couple are equivocal and the source of anxiety can often be trivial:

> "We want to make a table [at cards] for Mrs. Rushworth, you know. Your mother is quite anxious about it, but cannot very well spare time to sit down herself, because of her fringe." —Jane Austen, *Mansfield Park,* 1814

> As an American, I hope we shall. As a moralist and occasional sermonizer, I am not so anxious about it —Oliver Wendell Holmes d. 1894, *The Autocrat of the Breakfast-Table,* 1858

> "So you're anxious about my reputation." —George Meredith, *The Ordeal of Richard Feverel,* 1859

> The male is hilarious and demonstrative, the female serious and anxious about her charge —John Burroughs, *Wake-Robin,* 1871

> ... will ease the professor's mind on a point that he seemed anxious about —George Bernard Shaw, *Cashel Byron's Profession,* 1886

> He would be too anxious about his son, I thought, he would care too much —C. P. Snow, *The New Men,* 1954

Partridge and one or two other British sources object to *anxious of;* why, they do not tell. The OED has a little evidence of its use from the 18th century; they mark it obsolete, but it is in fact only rare:

> The Arizona statesman's practice has since been to seem anxious of an election outcome so as to stir his supporters to greater campaign activity —*Current Biography 1951*

But the most common constructions in which the "worried" senses of *anxious* are found are those of the attributive adjective and the plain predicate adjective without any following prepositional phrase:

> 'Tie a rope round him—it is dangerous!' cried a soft and anxious voice somewhere above them — Thomas Hardy, *The Return of the Native,* 1878

> Two anxious days followed while the ship was being loaded —Thomas B. Costain, *The Black Rose,* 1945

> ... avoid envy; anxious fears; anger fretting inwards —Francis Bacon, *Essays,* 1625

> The household income cannot be large, yet there is no sign of want, or even of anxious thrift —Rebecca West, *New Yorker,* 14 Feb. 1953

> ... he smiled broadly at Coverly all during the pause and so it was not an anxious silence —John Cheever, *The Wapshot Chronicle,* 1957

> ... her sister ... for whose happiness she grew daily more anxious —Jane Austen, *Pride and Prejudice,* 1813

> ... a little tired, and more than a little anxious and nervous —Arnold Bennett, *The Old Wives' Tale,* 1908

> ... he who had once been oily and unctuous, a man of plenty and of ease, was now become anxious and harried —Pearl Buck, *The Good Earth,* 1931

> Allen Dulles would not have been impressed by the risk involved, though a modestly competent lawyer would, one imagines, have been anxious —John Kenneth Galbraith, *New York,* 30 July 1973

The "eager" sense is said to be found in the *anxious for, anxious that,* and *anxious to* constructions. While this is true in the main, the first of these constructions is used for both the "worried" and "eager" senses:

> ... Cicero, anxious for his own safety —J. A. Froude, *Caesar,* 1879

> She was wounded by the disapproval of many of her friends, and anxious for the future of Hull House — Robert Morss Lovett, *All Our Years,* 1948

> Distraction display very rarely occurs except when a bird is anxious for its nest and eggs or young — Edward A. Armstrong, *Bird Display and Behaviour,* 2d ed., 1947

> His sisters were very anxious for his having an estate —Jane Austen, *Pride and Prejudice,* 1813

> All seemed pleased with the performance and anxious for another of the same sort —Kingsley Amis, *Lucky Jim,* 1954

> ... unlike many idealistic spokesmen for the left ... Bevan was always anxious for power —Kenneth O. Morgan, *Times Literary Supp.,* 14 Nov. 1980

Anxious that is found with the "eager" sense, although some of these examples carry connotations of concern as well:

> ... is anxious for the sake of both that there sh^d not be a disappointment —Jane Austen, letter, 7 Oct. 1808

> ... Constance insisted, anxious that he should live up to his reputation for Sophia's benefit —Arnold Bennett, *The Old Wives' Tale,* 1908

> ... and visibly anxious that his wife should be on easy terms with us all —Agnes Repplier, *Eight Decades,* 1937

> Don Juan was anxious that his son be given a specific role in Spanish public life —*Current Biography,* October 1964

> ... Japan's chiefs felt certain Germany would win. This being so they were anxious that they, and not the Germans, should seize the Dutch, British and French possessions in the Far East —L. E. Snellgrove, *The Modern World Since 1870,* 1968

The most prominently represented construction of *anxious* in our files is the one reprehended by Bierce: *anxious* with *to* and an infinitive. The construction occurs in spoken English. Here we have Sir Winston Churchill in a debate in the House of Commons, sometime after World War II:

> ... intellectual highbrows who are naturally anxious to impress British labor with the fact that they learned Latin at Winchester —quoted by William Safire, *N.Y. Times Mag.*, 10 Oct. 1982

(Safire could not refrain from adding "Churchill meant to say *eager*, not *anxious*," but *anxious/eager* is not a shibboleth in British English, and if Churchill had meant to say *eager* he no doubt would have said *eager*.) We find it also in letters:

> I feel no hesitation in saying, I was more anxious to hear your critique, however severe, than the praises of the *million* —Lord Byron, letter, 6 Mar. 1807

> I *hope* I should be ready to go, if He called me now, but I'm not the least anxious to be called yet —Lewis Carroll, letter, 12 Feb. 1887

> Mr. Cameron is anxious to have us come down, but Hay pleads his beautiful treaties —Henry Adams, letter, 1 Feb. 1900

> My book came out yesterday officially, though no copies are yet to hand; I am more anxious than I can say to know how it strikes your eminence —Harold J. Laski, letter, 28 Mar. 1919

> Thanks so much for the comments which I'll always be anxious to get, good or bad —Flannery O'Connor, letter, 30 Apr. 1952

And we have evidence from other kinds of writing:

> His manner was perhaps the more seductive,
>   Because he ne'er seem'd anxious to seduce
>   —Lord Byron, *Don Juan*, Canto xv, 1824

> ... the men looked hard at him, anxious to see what sort of a looking "cove" he was —Herman Melville, *Omoo*, 1847

> ... ever anxious to ameliorate the condition of the poor —Anthony Trollope, *The Macdermots of Ballycloran*, 1847

> In any weather, at any hour of the day or night, I have been anxious to improve the nick of time — Henry David Thoreau, *Walden*, 1854

> I could give many facts, showing how anxious bees are to save time —Charles Darwin, *On the Origin of Species by Means of Natural Selection*, 1859

> Miss Manette ... was extremely anxious to see the gentleman from Tellson's —Charles Dickens, *A Tale of Two Cities*, 1859

> Sir Austin ... appeared so scrupulously anxious to hear the exact extent of injury sustained by the farmer —George Meredith, *The Ordeal of Richard Feverel*, 1859

> The male is very active in hunting out a place and exploring the boxes and cavities, but seems to have no choice in the matter and is anxious only to please and encourage his mate —John Burroughs, *Wake-Robin*, 1871

> He was willing, perhaps anxious, to take the Eastern command —J. A. Froude, *Caesar*, 1879

> ... anxious as I was to tell them my story, I durst not interrupt —Robert Louis Stevenson, *Treasure Island*, 1883

> Punch was always anxious to oblige everybody — Rudyard Kipling, *Wee Willie Winkie and Other Child Stories*, 1888

> He was so anxious to do what was right —Samuel Butler, *The Way of All Flesh*, 1903

> ... schoolmasters may be pathetically anxious to guide boys right —A. C. Benson, *From A College Window*, 1906

> ... city bankers anxious to furnish him capital — Sherwood Anderson, *Poor White*, 1920

> I am particularly anxious in this lecture not to assume the role of a Christian apologist —W. R. Inge, *The Church in the World*, 1928

> ... the gravely courteous air of a dog who is anxious to show himself interested in what interests his master —Mary Austin, *Starry Adventure*, 1931

> ... I am not anxious to appraise the good or evil in the Soviet system —Bertrand Russell, *The Scientific Outlook*, 1931

> ... many firms are anxious to employ their cash profitably —*Manchester Guardian Weekly*, 19 Jan. 1940

> ... information which our enemies are desperately anxious to obtain —Franklin D. Roosevelt, fireside chat, 9 Dec. 1941, in *Nothing to Fear*, ed. B. D. Zevin, 1946

> The average immigrant was pathetically anxious to become an American —Allan Nevins & Henry Steele Commager, *The Pocket History of the U.S.*, 1942

> ... more ready to sell other things besides drink, less anxious to send their customers away tipsy —G. M. Trevelyan, *English Social History*, 1942

> ... Paris, where there are a great many young writers anxious to experiment in literary form —Cyril Connolly, *The Condemned Playground*, 1946

> ... poets like Auden and Milton are more anxious to persuade than poets, like Herbert, or Vaughan, or Crashaw, of actual religious experience —G. S. Fraser, in *Little Reviews Anthology 1949*, ed. Denys Val Baker

> ... the Japanese themselves are anxious to assume their proper international role —Dean Acheson, in *The Pattern of Responsibility*, ed. McGeorge Bundy, 1951

> He was so anxious to get a fly into the water that he had to reproach himself for haste —John Cheever, *The Wapshot Chronicle*, 1957

> I know nothing of this democracy ... but I am anxious to learn —Myles na gCopaleen (Flann O'Brien), *The Best of Myles*, 1968

> ... Elizabeth was initially anxious to improve the conditions of the peasants —*Times Literary Supp.*, 2 Oct. 1970

This couple seemed anxious to avoid Philip's four friends, or at least spoke as little as possible —Doris Lessing, *The Good Terrorist*, 1985

We believe these examples show clearly and amply the major patterns in which *anxious* occurs. Anyone who says that careful writers do not use *anxious* in its "eager" sense has simply not examined the available evidence.

any   **1.** The pronoun *any* can be either singular or plural in construction—even Harper 1985 and Bernstein 1977 agree. Bernstein believes the plural construction to be more common, but we cannot confirm his belief from the evidence in our files, in which the two constructions are roughly equal:

> ... had reached its final shape before any of his volumes of poems were published —*The Tiger's Eye*, December 1947

> ... nor is any of his novels purely a novel of ideas —Frederick J. Hoffman, in *Forms of Modern Fiction*, ed. William Van O'Connor, 1948

2. Longman 1984 notes that *any* with a singular noun may be referred to by a plural pronoun.

> ... he would at no time be a willing party to any artist breaking their contract —*The Times* (in Longman)

> ... he kept his door wide open so that any one of his 12,000 employees could walk in and spill their troubles —*Time*, 17 Nov. 1952

Lurie 1927 thought this construction a "transgression against good form in grammar." He quotes an unidentified newspaper:

> ... it is a wonderful thing for any person to be so imaginative that they think they are still attractive.

What Lurie did not understand, and the Longman editors do, is that notional agreement is the principle in operation here. It is a long-established construction:

> Any man that has a Humour is under no restraint or fear of giving it a vent; they have a proverb among them which, maybe, will show the bent and genius of the people as well as a longer discourse —William Congreve, "Concerning Humour in Comedy," 1695

Congreve's use shows the typical singular-verb-plural-pronoun agreement of many indefinite pronouns and adjectives.
  See THEY, THEIR, THEM and the articles under AGREEMENT.

3. *Of any, than any* (illogical comparison). In 1705 Joseph Addison, in the preface to a book of travels in Italy written by someone else, noted that the author

> ... has wrote a more correct Account of Italy than any before him. (OED)

Two centuries later Vizetelly 1906 calls the construction incorrect, objecting to "the finest of any I have seen." Bryant 1962 reports that the construction with a superlative (or, less often, a comparative) and *of* or *than* has been in use since the time of Chaucer. The handbooks and commentators following Vizetelly's lead are engaged in the ex post facto application of logical analysis to a long-established idiom—with entirely predictable results.

Here are a few examples of the idiom from writers more recent than Addison:

> We boast that we belong to the nineteenth century and are making the most rapid strides of any nation —Henry David Thoreau, *Walden*, 1854 (in Reader's Digest 1983)

> Its population would have remained the most carefully screened of any body of settlers ever to have come to America —*N.Y. Times Book Rev.*, 20 Apr. 1947 (in Bryant)

> Although its coverage of the government, Capitol Hill and the world is more complete than any paper in the city —*Time*, 29 Dec. 1952

> ... the price deflator for construction has risen by far the most of any —Garfield V. Cox, *Jour. of Business*, January 1954

> Why does Jennifer House sell more convertible sofabeds in Manhattan than the convertible department in any Manhattan department store? —advt., *N.Y. Times Mag.*, 18 Apr. 1982

The studies cited in Bryant suggest that the more logical constructions—"of any other" and "of all"—prescribed by the handbooks are more commonly met in print nowadays than the older *any* idiom. The rewriting of *any* as *any other* or *all* is a simple enough correction, and it may be that more recent writers have tended to use the prescribed forms. If this is the case—and the evidence is not conclusive—the older idiom may be on the wane. Perrin & Ebbitt 1972, for instance, finds *any other* not just more logical but more idiomatic. A couple of examples:

> The tobacco industry has funded more scientific research on smoking and health problems than has any other source —*Annual Report, R. J. Reynolds Industries, Inc.*, 1970

> ... obtained for New Haven more renewal money per capita than that received by any other city —*Current Biography*, December 1967

In conclusion, we must agree with Reader's Digest 1983: you can revise *any* in such a construction to *any other* or *all* easily if you want to, but the *any* idiom is old, well-established, and standard.

4. *Any* as an adverb. When *any* is used as an adverb it usually modifies an adjective, but it sometimes also occurs by itself after a verb in the sense "at all." This use was disparaged by American usage writers (Bache 1869, Ayres 1881, Compton 1898) toward the end of the 19th century; their comments were repeated in the early 20th (MacCracken & Sandison 1917, Utter 1916, Lincoln Library 1924). Utter noted it had long been in use but thought it did not have "the sanction of the best writers." It appears in the journals of Lewis and Clark (in 1805 Clark wrote, "the three horses with me do not detain me any") and in Mark Twain: "It is a good tune—you can't improve it any" (*Innocents Abroad*, 1869—in OED Supplement). Here are a few more examples:

> ... Fat and Red didn't let that worry them any —Fred Gipson, *Cowhand: The Story of a Working Cowboy*, 1953

> And prices have not fallen any —*Commonweal*, 19 Oct. 1945

. . . to eat our dinner under the shade and rest . . . before we dug any —J. Frank Dobie, *Coronado's Children,* 1931

"You're not helping it any," I said —Robert Clark, in *Coast to Coast: Australian Stories 1946*

As a usage issue this one is pretty cold now. Longman 1984 mentions some dislike of the use in Britain as an Americanism. The OED Supplement, however, shows it in such British sources as Kipling, Agatha Christie, and *Punch.*

any and all   This phrase, an emphatic form of *any* intended to cover all possibilities, has its chief use in legal documents such as contracts and official regulations:

He shall have the power to suspend any and all members so offending —*Rules and Regulations of the Fire Department,* Springfield, Mass., 1949

Bernstein 1958, 1965, Copperud 1964, and Shaw 1975 disparage its use in ordinary prose; the one epithet they agree on is "trite." Whether writers have yielded to authority on this point or whether the phrase is just not very appealing, our evidence shows it rather uncommon in extralegal use. A few examples:

. . . over a thousand being arrested in one night and the fact of any and all arrests being kept an official secret —A. Morgan Young, *The Rise of a Pagan State,* 1939

. . . he had not realized how completely mistrusted and feared were any and all Indians here in Eastern Pennsylvania —F. Van Wyck Mason, *The Winter at Valley Forge,* 1953

There is, then, prior to any and all principles of logic a principle of metaphysics declaring for this self-consistency —*Modern Schoolman,* January 1954

It is perhaps sometimes unavoidable in text relating to legal matters:

The company contends that the grant of immunity from further prosecution which was part of the bargain disposes of any and all federal criminal charges —*The Economist,* 1 Feb. 1975

You will probably have little need of it.

anybody, anyone   **1.** These indefinite pronouns share with other indefinite pronouns the characteristic of taking a singular verb and, more often than not, a plural pronoun in reference. See AGREEMENT: INDEFINITE PRONOUNS; THEY, THEIR, THEM; NOTIONAL AGREEMENT, NOTIONAL CONCORD. This use of the plural pronoun— *they, their, them*—has traditionally been disapproved by grammarians who do not recognize the existence of notional agreement, but the use is winning greater acceptance. Copperud 1970 records Bryant, Evans, and Flesch as finding the plural pronoun acceptable, and the four commentators he cites as disapproving it in writing are said to be "indulgent" of it in speech. Reader's Digest 1983 finds it acceptable.

Usage is, of course, not uniform; some occurrences follow notional agreement, and others formal agreement. Here are a few samples of each.

Formal agreement:

. . . before releasing a child to anyone except his parents —J. Edgar Hoover, *NEA Jour.,* January 1965

Anyone who thinks he's pure is surely not —Flannery O'Connor, letter, 1 Jan. 1956

. . . a cheap way for a well-heeled anyone to see his name in the company of bookish folk —Bernard Kalb, *Saturday Rev.,* 20 Mar. 1954

Any one who tries to discuss this problem candidly is at once met with the suggestion that he is unaware —Wendell L. Willkie, *N.Y. Herald Tribune,* 21 Nov. 1943

Anyone who wishes to find his bearings —H. B. Parkes, *Marxism—An Autopsy,* 1939

. . . when anybody was condemned to be impaled, or knouted, or beheaded, he or she promptly retained the Empress as intercessor at a handsome fee — George Bernard Shaw, letter, 31 Dec. 1897

Notional agreement:

But if I did say or do an ill thing to anybody, it should be sure to be behind their backs, out of pure good manners —William Wycherly, *The Plain Dealer,* 1676

. . . as anybody in their senses would have done — Jane Austen, *Mansfield Park,* 1814

It is fatal to anyone who writes to think of their sex —Virginia Woolf, *A Room of One's Own,* 1929

. . . it will then be open for anyone to take up the quarrel, if they think there is any public advantage in so doing —Sir Winston Churchill, *The Unrelenting Struggle,* 1942

He is afraid to have anyone mention sin without having them add "Nuts with that sin bunk" —*New Republic,* 4 Aug. 1952

"Anyone can think what they please," she said rather grimly —Louis Auchincloss, *A Law for the Lion,* 1953

. . . anyone may progress to these better posts if they have the required qualifications —*Employment Opportunities in the Civil Service* (Canada), 1953

. . . it may be difficult for anyone to find their path through what may be a sort of maze —Ford Madox Ford, quoted in Graham Greene, *Collected Essays,* 1969

. . . anyone in your office can be generating their own reports within 15 minutes —advt., *InfoWorld,* 27 Feb. 1984

You haven't told anyone at work. When they ask about Amanda you say she's fine —Jay McInerney, *Bright Lights, Big City,* 1984

2. Both *anybody* and *anyone* were formerly spelled as two words, but the open styling is now reserved for instances in which *any* is a separate adjective.
3. *Anybody else's.* See ELSE.

anymore   **1.** Both *anymore* and *any more* are found in current written use. Although usage prescribers disagree about which form to use—"preferably spelled as one word" (Shaw 1975); "two words" (Bremner 1980)—the one-word styling is the more common. Feel free to write it as two words, if you prefer.
2. *Anymore* is regularly used in negative contexts ("we

never go there anymore"), in questions ("do you listen to the radio anymore?"), and in conditional contexts ("if you do that anymore, I'll leave"). It is used in a number of positive statements in which the implication is negative:

There's only one woman for him any more —Owen Wister, *The Virginian*, 1902

Damn few people take the time to read anymore —William Du Bois, *The Island in the Square*, 1947

The Washingtonian is too sophisticated to believe any more in solutions —Russell Baker, *N.Y. Times Mag.*, 14 Feb. 1965

... thought about whether such a profession as merely *pork* butcher exists any more —*Times Literary Supp.*, 13 Mar. 1969

... she found it harder and harder to sort out anymore what was worth saving and how best to save it —Russell Baker, *Growing Up*, 1982

Few private owners have worthwhile collections anymore —Spencer Davidson, *Avenue*, March 1984

None of these uses draws comment. But *anymore* is also used in contexts with no negative implication, much to the consternation and perplexity of some usage writers:

Every time I even smile at a man any more the papers have me practically married to him —Betty Grable, quoted in *Time*, 25 Nov. 1940

Useta be I had to go down to the still and carry my own whisky outa the Hollow, but anymore I'm such a good customer they tote it up here ... for me —Charley Robertson, *Shadow of a Cloud*, 1950

In a way he almost felt sorry for him, any more —James Jones, *From Here to Eternity*, 1951

Listening is a rare art anymore —Alma Holland, *Writer's Digest*, March 1970

Who I would vote for anymore is the stronger learner, of whatever party —Stewart Brand, *Esquire*, July 1970

It sometimes seems to me that all I do anymore is go to funerals —Harry S. Truman, quoted in Merle Miller, *Plain Speaking*, 1973

Every time we leave the house anymore, I play a game called "Stump the Housebreaker" —Erma Bombeck, syndicated column, 24 Jan. 1973

"There's a funny thing about women any more," said author and humorist Peg Bracken, "and that's that there isn't much funny about women any more." —Bob Curtright, *Chicago Tribune*, 24 Apr. 1977

... everybody's cool anymore —Bill White, N.Y. Yankees baseball telecast, 26 Mar. 1984

This usage is dialectal. It has been discovered anew almost every year since 1931 and has been abundantly documented. The Dictionary of American Regional English reports it to be widespread in all dialect areas of the U.S. except New England. It appears to have been of Midland origin—the states where it is most common appear to be Kentucky, West Virginia, Indiana, and Oklahoma—and has spread considerably to such other states as New York, New Jersey, Iowa, Minnesota, California, and Oregon. It is still predominantly a spoken feature, although, as the citations above show, it does appear in fiction and occasionally in journalistic sources. Both the older American Dialect Dictionary and the new DARE note that it is used by persons of all educational levels; it is not substandard, and it is not a feature of speech that is considered indicative of social standing.

Bryant 1962 conjectures that the positive *anymore* may have come to the U.S. with Scotch-Irish immigrants in the 18th century. There is an *any more* listed in the English Dialect Dictionary that occurs in both positive and negative contexts, but its meaning is different from that of the American usage. D. H. Lawrence, however, did put it into the mouth of the character named Rupert Birkin in his novel *Women in Love*, published in 1920:

"Quite absurd," he said. "Suffering bores me, any more."

And P. W. Joyce, in *English As We Speak It in Ireland* (1910), notes the existence of a positive *any more* in the West and Northwest of Ireland. It is also used in Canada. *Modern Canadian English Usage* (1974) reports 8 or 9 percent of its respondents using the positive *anymore* with the highest incidences found in Ontario and Newfoundland.

Although many who encounter the usage for the first time think it is new, it is not: the earliest attestation cited in the DARE is dated 1859.

3. Some handbooks and dictionaries caution against confusing the adverb *anymore* ("we don't go there anymore") with the phrase *any more* where *more* is a pronoun or adjective, as in "we don't have any more" or "I can't eat any more pizza." The adverb may be written either closed or open, as noted in section 1 above, but the phrase should certainly be written open.

anyone **1.** See ANYBODY, ANYONE.
2. The usage panel of Heritage 1969, 1982 objects to the use of *anyone* in the sentence "She is the most thrifty person of anyone I know." This is the same construction as the one discussed at ANY 3, with *anyone* in place of *any*.

any other See ANY 3.

anyplace For a word as recent as *anyplace*, it might seem a bit surprising that we know so little of its origins. It first came to the attention of Merriam-Webster editors through handbooks warning their readers not to use it—Utter 1916, MacCracken & Sandison 1917, Whipple 1924, Lincoln Library 1924, Krapp 1927, and several others. The editors of Webster's Second had all of this comment in the early 1930s, but no printed evidence of its use; they assumed it must be an oral use and entered it with the label *Colloq.*

The adverb seems to be American in origin—Phythian 1979 assures us that it is both American and wrong—and probably cropped up sometime around the turn of the century. But we did not begin to find it in print with any frequency until the 1940s:

U-turn allowed any place except at traffic light —*American Guide Series: Pennsylvania*, 1940

... the minister never went any place in the house but the parlor and the diningroom —*New Republic*, 29 July 1940

. . . doubted whether there would be much sympathy in America for fascism any place —Irwin Shaw, *Yale Rev.,* Summer 1944

. . . if you just quit, you found yourself on a sort of a black list and they wouldn't let you work anyplace else —Edmund Wilson, *Memoirs of Hecate County,* 1946

Although the early objectors give no reason for their objections, Evans 1957 and Bernstein 1971 say that the objection is based on the replacement of the adverb *where* in the compound with the noun *place.* Bernstein points out that *place* has other adverbial uses and that other nouns, too, have been used with adverbial force. *Anyplace* seems to have been gaining slightly in frequency of use in print since the 1940s, and is long since established as standard. The one-word form has gradually replaced the two-word form that was earliest attested. Here is a sample of use from the past four decades:

Italian women dress more elaborately during the Venice season than they do anyplace else any time in the year —Janet Flanner, *New Yorker,* 23 Sept. 1950

Anyplace would be better than these taverns —Richard Bissell, *A Stretch on the River,* 1950

. . . the worthiest effort in musical scholarship to be produced anyplace in the world —Irving Kolodin, *Saturday Rev.,* 26 July 1952

Men could get the call anyplace, but it always happened to them when they were alone —St. Clair McKelway, *New Yorker,* 18 May 1957

. . . it was worse in Poland than anyplace else —William L. Shirer, *The Rise and Fall of the Third Reich,* 1960

He wants us to look at what we can see everyday, anyplace, here —Robert Coles, *Trans-Action,* May 1968

. . . never *quite* at home anywhere in this world, never quite the citizens of anyplace this side of Heaven —Leslie A. Fiedler, *Jour. of Modern Literature,* 1st issue, 1970

Now there just aren't that many men among us who could go anyplace, never mind to work, after five pints —Malcolm S. Forbes, *Forbes,* 15 Sept. 1970

Anyplace north of the Potomac was unthinkable —William Styron, *This Quiet Dust and Other Writings,* 1982

See also EVERYPLACE; NOPLACE; SOMEPLACE.

anytime   This adverb is generally spelled as one word. Johnson 1982 tells us that the one-word spelling is all right when it can be replaced by the phrase "at any time" but when it cannot be so replaced, it should be spelled as two words. Johnson's rule of thumb is a sensible one, though occasionally it is not observed:

This is dressing that's fun, never a burden for anytime of day —advt., *N.Y. Times,* 28 Apr. 1980

Evans 1957 and Phythian 1979 agree *anytime* is not in British use—Phythian in fact insists it does not exist.

We have no British evidence since 1945. Here are a few adverbial examples:

. . . have entered the city from a state in the deep South anytime within the last month —James B. Conant, *Slums and Suburbs,* 1961

If you run short of money . . . feel free to put the bite on me anytime —Leon Uris, *Battle Cry,* 1953

. . . I can get a job anywhere anytime —Jack Kerouac, *The Town and The City,* 1950

Things won't improve anytime soon —Robert L. Simison, *Wall Street Jour.,* 30 May 1980

anyways   None of the senses of *anyways* are standard contemporary English, but you should not conclude that they are substandard, as Copperud 1970 does. When *anyways* means "anywise," it is archaic:

And if the people of the land do any ways hide their eyes —Leviticus 20:4 (AV), 1611

. . . who have no places, nor are anyways dependent on the King —Thomas Gray, letter, 24 May 1742

The other uses—"to any degree at all" and "in any case, anyway, anyhow"—are dialectal. The Dictionary of American Regional English marks both senses now chiefly South and South Midland, though some of the earliest evidence for "to any degree at all" is from New England. A few examples:

Then the trial began, and, as you might expect, it didn't look anyways good for the defense —Stephen Vincent Benét, "The Devil and Daniel Webster," 1937, in *American Harvest,* ed. Allen Tate & John Peale Bishop, 1942

"Anyways," said Jackie, "better late than never. . . ." —John Dos Passos, *Number One,* 1943

. . . I think I will go to New York anyways sometime next summer —Flannery O'Connor, letter, 25 Jan. 1953

The "anyway" use exists in some British dialects, too. The OED notes Dickens, and our files contain this:

Anyways, it could not be found there —Joseph Conrad, *Youth,* 1902

anywheres   *Anywheres* is an Americanism (not recorded in the OED or the Supplement) that has been censured as nonexistent, illiterate, or nonstandard ever since MacCracken & Sandison put out their handbook of language etiquette for Vassar girls in 1917. Subsequent handbooks treat it much like a social disease. Bryant 1962 believes it to be a receding form; our evidence would tend to bear her out, but the Dictionary of American Regional English has evidence as recent as 1981. The word is not dead yet. Here are a few samples from our less fastidious past (remember that *anywheres* is primarily a speech form and seldom appears in print outside of fiction):

"Anywheres in this country, sir?" —Herman Melville, *Pierre,* 1852

. . . if you are anywheres where it won't do for you to scratch, why you will itch all over in upwards of a thousand places —Mark Twain, *Huckleberry Finn,* 1884

... I would rather live in Detroit than anywheres else —Ring Lardner, *You Know Me Al*, 1916

... it looked impossible that I'd ever be anywheres else —Joseph C. Lincoln, *Galusha the Magnificent*, 1921

From this beginning, a skilled writer could go most anywheres —Ring Lardner, Preface, *How to Write Short Stories*, 1924

Now instead of trees we have parking meters on Main Street ... and very few trees anywheres else —John O'Hara, *Collier's*, 2 Mar. 1956

Anywheres is attested in the U.S. from the late 18th century. It appears to have been originally a New England term that spread.

See also NOWHERES; SOMEWHERES.

apart from *Apart from* is a fixed two-word preposition in English. Some commentators believe it to be the British equivalent of American *aside from*, but in fact it is used on both sides of the Atlantic:

But 'ain't' will always be facetious in British English, apart from cockney —Anthony Burgess, in Harper 1985

Apart from being a brother of the Secretary of State —*Atlantic*, April 1953

So, apart from minor discontents ... Americans were satisfied —Samuel Eliot Morison, *Oxford History of the American People*, 1965

Apart from that, the British and U.S. viewpoints coalesce —William O. Douglas, *Center Mag.*, March 1969

... very much as before apart from some mildly gloomy talk —*Times Literary Supp.*, 2 Oct. 1970

Apart from ceremonial performances of Handel's "Messiah," we are in the Christmas doldrums —Winthrop Sargeant, *New Yorker*, 1 Jan. 1972

See also ASIDE FROM.

apathy *Apathy* is not very frequently used in a context in which a preposition connects it to its object. When it is, *toward* and *towards* are most common.

Individuals maintained their sanity by developing an apathy toward their experiences —George Robert Carlsen, *English Jour.*, March 1949

... the American apathy toward the struggles of colonial peoples —*New Republic*, 28 Mar. 1955

Their apathy toward course designing borders on ignorance —William Johnson, *Sports Illustrated*, 15 July 1968

... apathy towards the Hindu-Moslem question —*Manchester Guardian Weekly*, 21 May 1937

About, to, and *regarding* are also in use:

... a general apathy about this whole business of reading —Mortimer J. Adler, *How to Read a Book*, 1940

... professional and public apathy about Australian drama —Leslie Rees, *Towards an Australian Drama*, 1953

Apathy of audience to all the good things —*The Journals of Arnold Bennett*, ed. Frank Swinnerton, 1954

... general apathy still prevailed regarding the potential of conventional agriculture —*Rockefeller Foundation: President's Five-Year Rev. & Annual Report*, 1968

apostrophe **1.** The original use of the apostrophe in English appears to have been as a mark of elision used to indicate in writing and printing the omission of a letter—usually a vowel—that was not pronounced. Ben Jonson's *Grammar* (1640) lists such examples as these:

| Th' outward man | If y' utter | If thou'rt |
| is time t' awake | A man t' have | |

The plays of Restoration dramatists such as Etherege, Wycherley, Congreve, and Farquhar abound in such contractions. A great many of them are still familiar: *she'll, I'll, 'em, can't, 'tis, e'en, e'er, he's, I've,* among others. And some are no longer familiar: *i'fac, 'ygad, to't, in't, an't, on't, i'faith, 'zbud, wo't, dar'st,* for example. (One can't help noticing that the pronoun *it* was reduced to *'t* in a great many spoken environments.)

In his own writings Ben Jonson frequently used the apostrophe to mark omission of silent *e* in the *-ed* ending of verbs. *Timber: or, Discoveries* (written before 1637) shows *borrow'd, deform'd, refus'd, expung'd, banish'd, squar'd,* among others. The convention of spelling *-ed* as *-'d* when the *e* was not pronounced was more common in verse than in prose for the purpose of emphasizing scansion. It seems, however, to have become more frequent in prose during the early 18th century. In Defoe, for instance, can be found many an *arriv'd* and *order'd*. The practice provoked some curious remarks by Swift and Addison in the *Tatler* and *Spectator* objecting to the practice. It is not overly clear today what their objection was. Here, for instance, is Addison in *The Spectator*, No. 135 (4 Aug. 1711):

... by closing in one Syllable the Termination of our Præterperfect Tense, as in the Words *drown'd, walk'd, arriv'd,* for *drowned, walked, arrived,* which has very much disfigured the Tongue, and turn'd a tenth part of our smoothest Words into so many Clusters of Consonants.

Addison seems to be writing about speech, but his own inconsistency is curious; not only do we have *turn'd* in the same sentence in which he decries the practice, he has earlier used *observ'd, us'd,* and *deriv'd*. It is hard to tell what he is driving at. At any rate, the convention of marking the unpronounced *e* of the *-ed* ending by an apostrophe gradually died out.

Also gone are such early 18th-century apostrophized spellings as Defoe's *cou'd, shou'd, wou'd*—showing that the *l* was not pronounced. *Cou'd* is a most curious case; Strang 1970 notes that "the native word *coud* was altered to *could* on the model of *should, would.*" Defoe's apostrophe thus indicates the omission of a letter that didn't belong there in the first place. Strang also notes the occasional use of the apostrophe to mark imaginary omissions, for instance *ha's,* as if it were contracted from *haves*.

The chief modern uses of the apostrophe are about the same as those of the late 17th century, with certain old conventions having been discarded. We still use the apostrophe to show contractions *(didn't, I'll)* and to mark features of speech *(singin', N'Orleans)*. In addition, the apostrophe is used to mark the omission of numerals:

class of '86   politics during the '60s

Some words or their variants are consistently spelled with apostrophes:

fo'c'sle   bos'n   rock 'n' roll

2. The apostrophe is used to mark the possessive case of nouns and indefinite pronouns. The *Grammar* of Joseph Priestley (rev. ed., 1798) contains the basic modern system:

> The GENITIVE case is that which denotes property or possession; and is formed by adding *(s)* with an apostrophe before it to the nominative; as *Solomon's Wisdom; The Men's wit; Venus's beauty;* or the apostrophe only in the plural number, when the nominative ends in *(s)* as the *Stationers' arms.*

Current usage deviates very little from the general system described by Priestley. The chief variation in current use is in the case of nouns ending in an \s\ or \z\ sound, such as *audience, waitress, index.* Even with these *-'s* is usual: *audience's, waitress's, index's.* Some writers prefer the apostrophe alone, especially if the word is followed immediately by a word beginning with the same sound: for *convenience'* sake (see SAKE).

For other questions relating to the use of the possessive, see GENITIVE.

3. The apostrophe is sometimes used with *-s* to form the plural of letters, numerals, abbreviations, symbols, and words used as words.

Letters are usually pluralized with *-'s*

mind your p's and q's

although capital letters are sometimes pluralized with *-s* alone.

The use of *-'s* to form the plurals of numerals, abbreviations and symbols is not now as common as pluralization with simple *-s;* 1970s, CPUs, &s are more likely to be found than their apostrophized counterparts. A dissent can be found in Safire 1980; he prefers *1980's,* and the *80's* to the *'80s.*

Words used as words—such as might be given as examples from a text: too many *howsoever's*—are usually pluralized with *-'s.* But words representing sounds or words used as words in common phrases are pluralized with *-s* alone:

the oohs and aahs of the crowd
the whys and wherefores of the issue
Theodore Bernstein's *Dos, Don'ts & Maybes of English Usage*

4. *Her's, our's, your's, their's.* Lowth 1762 notes that these pronouns "have evidently the form of the possessive case"; Baker 1770 likewise spells them with the apostrophe. But even then usage was mixed: Lowth on the preceding page in his paradigm spells all of them without the apostrophe, even *its.* Priestley 1798 spells them without the apostrophe but later comments, "Sometimes these possessives have an apostrophe before the *s,* when they are found without their substantives, which gives them more the appearance of a genitive case." He gives as an example "That you may call her your's" from a novel. Jonathan Swift writes "better to be in your hands than her's" in his *Journal to Stella* (21 Nov. 1710). Priestley regularly spells *it's* with the apostrophe, as does Jane Austen later (see ITS, IT'S).

Today all these pronouns are regularly written without the apostrophe: *hers, ours, yours, theirs, its.*

5. Simon 1980 speaks of " . . . the Great Apostrophe Plague: the newfangled insertion of apostrophes in ordinary plurals." It can be pointed out that Joseph Addison in *The Spectator,* 4 Aug. 1711, pluralized *Genius* into *Genius's,* but it is far from certain what Addison meant by his apostrophe. It marks the omission of *e,* but in Addison's time such an omission usually meant that the syncopated syllable was not pronounced; perhaps Addison pronounced the plural of *genius* the same way as he did the singular.

The phenomenon is not as recent as many writers think, but older evidence is scarce. Robert Baker in 1770 censured the use in his time of *'s* after nouns ending in vowels (as *idea's, opera's, virtuoso's*) and *-s* (as the *Genius's* of Addison). But we do not have enough evidence to assume with confidence that this late 18th-century practice has led to the present one. At any rate it has certainly become more noticed in recent years by writers of English texts and writers on usage. Bernstein 1977, Simon 1980, Harper 1975, 1985, and Janis 1984 all notice *'s* plurals in the U.S.; Howard 1984 and Longman 1984 note them in Britain. No one has an explanation for the practice, but it is widely assumed to be practiced chiefly by the less well educated—handwritten signs offering "Fresh Strawberry's" or "Auto Repair's" are often cited. Such plurals also turn up in handwritten letters sent to this office: " . . . these type of dictionary's." Bernstein and Janis mention their appearing in ads; several such have been noticed here too:

> . . . the finest Tibetan Mastiff's —*Dog World,* May 1984

> The floating mover judge's look for —*Chronicle of the Horse,* 25 May 1984

Apostrophized plurals also turn up in other text:

> . . . by using *he* to refer to all people, she's and he's alike —Carol Tavris, *Vogue,* June 1984

> The buyback's included Texaco's purchase —*N.Y. Times,* 13 June 1984

> I thought we kept the weirdo's locked up —"Brock" cartoon, *Morning Union* (Springfield, Mass.), 25 July 1984

No apostrophe is necessary or wanted in any of the above examples.

6. Words formed from abnormal elements, such as numerals, abbreviations, and the like, are often provided with an apostrophe before the addition of a suffix:

OD'd on heroin
86'd our party
4-H'ers

7. If you need any further evidence that the apostrophe has not been universally understood, a correspondent of Simon's sent in as an example a sign reading "Larr'y 66 Service." To this gem we can add only

> T'was not always so —*Southwest Art,* May 1984

Commenting on the apostrophe, Robert Burchfield, editor of the newest OED Supplement, has said:

> The apostrophe was only a moderately successful device, and it is probably coming to the end of its usefulness, certainly for forming plurals and marking possession. It may only be retained for contractions —quoted in *Boston Sunday Globe,* 12 May 1985

apparently, evidently Entries in Kilpatrick 1984 and Bremner 1980 at the adjective *apparent* express concern about the contradictory senses of the word and about the problem of distinguishing it from *evident*. These problems are, as a matter of fact, fully treated in good desk dictionaries and synonymy books. But Kilpatrick's underlying concern seems really to be with the adverbs, and here, at least in the case of *apparently*, dictionary treatment tends to be less than full, dictionary editors having the habit of tucking *-ly* adverb derivatives at the end of adjective entries without definitions in order to conserve space.

A. S. Hill 1895 distinguishes between *apparently* and *evidently* in this way:

> *Apparently* is properly used of that which seems, but may not be, real; *evidently,* of that which both seems and is real.

Hill's observation is still essentially right. *Evidently* regularly suggests that there is some overt reason for drawing an inference:

> It evidently didn't want to share its ocean with us, because it hauled off for about a hundred yards — Patrick Ellam, "The Dangerous Deep," in *Networks,* ed. Marjorie Seddon Johnson et al., 1977

> ... went off, evidently satisfied that he had upheld private-property rights —Roy Bongartz, *N.Y. Times Mag.,* 13 July 1975

> His father was evidently a man of means, for in 1782 he presented his son with a farm of 220 acres —*Dictionary of American Biography,* 1929

Apparently is used as a disclaimer, as if the author were telling us, "This is what it seems to be, but I won't vouch for it."

> There is a difference, apparently, between the aims of Leningrad and Moscow —John Tebbel, *Saturday Rev.,* 8 Jan. 1972

> ... beginning and then putting aside several manuscripts, apparently dissatisfied with all of them — Irving Howe, *Harper's,* October 1970

> There was apparently no investigation into the child's welfare and the mother's fitness —Eileen Hughes, *Ladies' Home Jour.,* September 1971

> The explanation for this apparently abject sell-out — *Times Literary Supp.,* 26 Mar. 1970

> ... gives an artistic effect apparently closer to a possible original than the scenes from Dante —T. S. Eliot, "Tradition and the Individual Talent," 1917, in *American Harvest,* ed. Allen Tate & John Peale Bishop, 1942

Evidently is sometimes used in contexts where *apparently* could also be used:

> Mr. Dahl evidently believes that others will in the long run follow the same course, even where recent history reads as a record of backsliding —*Times Literary Supp.,* 30 July 1971

Still, it always connotes some evidence in corroboration; *apparently* may connote that, if there is evidence, it does not necessarily corroborate.

Our evidence and that in Kučera & Francis 1967 show *apparently* to be much more frequently used than is *evidently.*

append *Append* regularly takes *to:*

> ... failed to append the sticker to the windshield — *Springfield* (Mass.) *Republican,* 3 Jan. 1954

> This entitles him to append the letters "S.C." ... to his name —*Current Biography 1950*

> To this is appended a calendar —Benjamin Farrington, *Greek Science,* 1953

> ... stories, orderly set down, with the objection appended to each story —Charles Lamb, *Essays of Elia,* 1823

appendix A generous number of commentators, buttressed by the evidence in various dictionaries, assure us that both *appendixes* and *appendices* are standard and acceptable plurals for *appendix*. A couple of British books find *appendices* more common in the U.K., and a few American ones find *appendixes* more common in the U.S. The Merriam-Webster files do not lack evidence in this matter, and we believe that both plurals may be found with almost equal frequency on both sides of the Atlantic. A correspondent in 1977 informed us that in the U.K. *appendixes* is preferred in medical contexts; *appendices* in publishing contexts. Our evidence gives the lie to the second half of the assertion, but we cannot prove or disprove the medical contention. We have evidence for both plurals in American medical contexts. As for publishing contexts:

> ... 100 pages of exceedingly miscellaneous appendixes —*N.Y. Times Book Rev.,* 5 Aug. 1984

> The appendixes are particularly valuable —*Times Literary Supp.,* 21 May 1982

> ... 30 pages of appendices —*N.Y. Times Book Rev.,* 9 Aug. 1981

> ... study of the appendices to the working timetables —*Times Literary Supp.,* 15 July 1983

Take your pick.

apportion The verb *apportion* may idiomatically take the prepositions *among, to,* and *between* when a complementary prepositional phrase is required.

Among has a certain cachet in writings on American government because of its use in the U.S. Constitution:

> Representatives and direct taxes shall be apportioned among the several States —Article I, Section 2

> ... apportion the expenses among the member states —Frank Abbott Magruder, *National Governments and International Relations,* 1950

> It is left to the reader to apportion compassion ... among those who suffer in the novel —Frances Gaither, *N.Y. Times Book Rev.,* 2 May 1954

To is about as frequent as *among, between* somewhat less frequent:

> ... the roles are apportioned rather to episodes than to character —Richard Ellmann, *Times Literary Supp.,* 21 May 1971

> ... the apportioning to each producer his share in goods and services —Kennard E. Goodman & William L. Moore, *Today's Economics,* 1960

Nietzsche ... urges that the law should apportion special privileges to a cultural elite —Arthur Pap, *Elements of Analytic Philosophy,* 1949

But he will be a brave man who will apportion responsibility for Britain's attitude between parties and classes —Roy Lewis & Angus Maude, *The English Middle Classes,* 1950

... difficult to apportion the responsibility between the two —Joseph Conrad, reprinted in *Correct English,* April 1939

... to apportion the judicial power between the supreme and inferior courts —John Marshall, *Marbury* v. *Madison,* 1803

appositive genitive   See GENITIVE 1.

appositives   Since Copperud 1970, 1980, Janis 1984, and Safire (*N.Y. Times Mag.,* 16 Feb. 1986) (along with many handbooks) are at some pains to distinguish restrictive and nonrestrictive appositives for purposes of punctuation and they connect the distinction with somewhat dubious inferences about meaning, it may be helpful if we say something here about the behavior of appositives. These comments are based on Quirk et al. 1985, wherein the subject is dealt with in considerable detail and with admirable clarity.

An appositive is defined in school grammar books as

> ... a noun or pronoun—often with modifiers—set beside another noun or pronoun to explain or identify it —*Warriner's English Grammar and Composition, Complete Course,* 1986

Quirk distinguishes three sets of characteristics of appositives. First, there is full and partial apposition. In full apposition, either of the nouns can be omitted from the sentence, and what remains will still be an acceptable English sentence. In the resultant sentence, each noun will have the same grammatical function, such as the subject or direct object. In addition, the sentences made by omitting one or other of the nouns will have the same meaning in the real world—"in extralinguistic reference," to use Quirk's term. Thus, in this sentence

A cousin of mine, Leonard Davis, has been elected to Congress.

we can omit either noun

A cousin of mine has been elected to Congress.

Leonard Davis has been elected to Congress.

and still have acceptable English sentences with the remaining noun as subject. And the nouns are coreferential—they both stand for Leonard Davis, the new congressman, in the extralinguistic world. Appositives that do not meet all three criteria are said to be in partial apposition.

Quirk next notes strict and weak apposition. In strict apposition the appositives belong to the same syntactic class:

Journalism, her choice of a career, has brought her great happiness.

In the example sentence, both *journalism* and *her choice of a career* fall into the class of noun phrases.

In weak apposition, they are from different syntactic classes:

Her choice of a career, reporting the news, has brought her great happiness.

Here we have a noun phrase in apposition with a gerund phrase (or "-ing-clause" in Quirk's terminology); they are members of different syntactic classes.

Then Quirk discusses restrictive and nonrestrictive apposition. In nonrestrictive apposition (our examples so far are all nonrestrictive) the appositives are in different units of information which in speech are signaled by different stress and intonation and often a pause, and in writing are signaled by punctuation—usually commas. The two nonrestrictive appositive units contribute relatively independent information, with the first unit usually acting as the defined expression and the second as the defining expression. Because the appositives are distinctly separate units, the defining and defined roles can be switched by merely reversing their order:

Sally Williams, the coach of the visiting team, predicted victory.

The coach of the visiting team, Sally Williams, predicted victory.

In restrictive apposition the two units are not separated in speech or by punctuation in writing:

I wish I could shimmy like my sister Kate.

Of course, these characteristics can be combined in various ways. Here, for instance, we have partial, strict, nonrestrictive apposition:

Mr. Holohan, assistant secretary of the *Eire Abu* Society, had been walking up and down Dublin for nearly a month —James Joyce, *Dubliners,* 1914

Quirk has many more examples and much more detail.

One thing Quirk does not mention is the rule-of-thumb inference that Copperud, Safire, and Janis expound upon about the number of items in the class to which the appositives refer based on the restrictive or nonrestrictive status of the appositives. Their theory is that a nonrestrictive appositive signals but a single one of the items in the extralinguistic world, while a restrictive appositive means that one out of a group of more than one in the extralinguistic world is being identified. Thus, "His wife, Helen, attended the ceremony" would mean but one wife, and "He sent his daughter Cicely to college" would suggest more than one daughter. The inference will be valid in most cases but can be untrustworthy if drawn too casually. From "Springfield, a city in Massachusetts, ... " no reasonable inference about the number of Springfields is possible, though the appositive is plainly nonrestrictive. The particular Springfield has either been identified in earlier context or isolated in the writer's mind. And then we have this nonrestrictive example:

He sent the older daughter, Kathleen, to a good convent —James Joyce, *Dubliners,* 1914

Older signals two daughters, in spite of the nonrestrictive appositive. If it is argued that there is but one older daughter, we will concede that to be most likely. Still, we have no trouble in conceiving of a context where two older daughters are being contrasted with a younger one, and in that context the appositive in Joyce's sentence would suddenly become restrictive and need to lose its commas. Quirk says only that "restrictiveness . . . indicates a limitation on the possible reference of the head"; no numbers are given. It seems safest to identify restrictive and nonrestrictive appositives as Quirk does, by informational relationship and by differing rhythm, stress, and tone.

appraise, apprise No fewer than ten sources warn us against using *appraise* for *apprise*. The examples given suggest that the confusion occurs chiefly in speech; our files yield but a single example of the mistake in print:

> . . . had not properly appraised herself of Mrs. Macduff's nature —Rex Ingamells, *Of Us Now Living,* 1952

Even if you did not know the difference in meaning between these two words, you could tell them apart by their typical constructions. *Apprise,* which means "give notice to," usually occurs in the construction *apprise one of:*

> . . . Hitler . . . had not bothered to apprise them of his thoughts —William L. Shirer, *The Rise and Fall of the Third Reich,* 1960

> . . . had kept him apprised of the high regard in which he is held —Hollis Alpert, in *The Film,* 1968

Sometimes the *of* phrase is replaced by a *that* clause:

> . . . in a guarded way which apprised him that she had been in touch with Renata —Marcia Davenport, *My Brother's Keeper,* 1954

Appraise, which means "evaluate," is used in neither of those constructions. The object of *appraise* is usually inanimate or abstract:

> . . . made it difficult for friends and foes alike to appraise his performance —Ronald P. Kriss, *Saturday Rev.,* 11 Mar. 1972

Less often the object is a person:

> John was conscious that Jabez Winkleman had been studying him with shrewd eyes, appraising him — Clarence Budington Kelland, *Saturday Evening Post,* 25 Dec. 1954

There is a verb *apprize* which means "appraise, value." It is quite rare.

appreciate Ever since Ayres 1881 various critics have felt it necessary to find fault with one sense or another of *appreciate.* Not infrequently one critic approves the very sense another disparages. Bierce 1909 and Vizetelly 1906, for instance, specifically approve a meaning that Ayres disapproves: "to increase in value." Bernstein 1971 approves "be grateful" while Evans 1957 dislikes it. Bierce and Follett 1966 set up a primary sense and decry the decay of the word from it. Other commentators have various other points to make. One century of criticism has produced no clear, consistent, and legitimate concern. Reader's Digest 1983 lists the senses found in most dictionaries and declares them all acceptable. So they are. Trust your dictionary.

apprehensive When the object of concern is a person, *apprehensive* takes *for:*

> Watching these contests, I could not help feeling apprehensive for Fitzgerald, whose physical condition was precarious at best —Andrew W. Turnbull, *New Yorker,* 7 Apr. 1956

More frequently the preposition links *apprehensive* to a usually impersonal cause of concern. In such cases, a selection of prepositions is available. *Of* is the most common:

> . . . whole troops of hungry and affrighted provincials, less apprehensive of servitude than of famine —Edward Gibbon, *The Decline and Fall of the Roman Empire,* 1788

> . . . no sooner would they stow themselves away . . . than they would rush out again, as if apprehensive of some approaching danger —John Burroughs, *Wake-Robin,* 1871

> The violence of his temper and his reputation for cruelty had made the City apprehensive of what would happen if he succeeded his father —Robert Graves, *I, Claudius,* 1934

> . . . made a great many people apprehensive of aggregations of more than one or two birds —Deborah Howard, *Massachusetts Audubon Newsletter,* December 1970

About is also quite common:

> "Then she didn't seem apprehensive about what might happen here while she was away?" — S. S. Van Dine, *The Greene Murder Case,* 1927

> The child with an infection of the bone will probably refuse to have the arm or leg examined and will be apprehensive about having it touched —Morris Fishbein, *The Popular Medical Encyclopedia,* 1946

> He was apprehensive about the increase of China's influence inside the Communist world —Norman Cousins, *Saturday Rev.,* 30 Oct. 1971

Regarding is sometimes chosen:

> . . . were outspokenly apprehensive regarding its full significance —*Collier's Year Book,* 1949

> . . . was perhaps apprehensive regarding the ultimate effect in Japan —Rodger Swearingen, *Current History,* July 1952

Sometimes a clause will be used instead of a phrase:

> As I stood aside to let that carriage pass, apprehensive that it might otherwise run me down —Charles Dickens, *A Tale of Two Cities,* 1859

> . . . apprehensive lest this evacuation inspire the extreme Left to become even bolder —*Collier's Year Book,* 1949

apprise See APPRAISE, APPRISE.

approve 1. When used as an intransitive verb with the meaning "to take a favorable view," *approve* takes the preposition *of:*

> . . . she doesn't approve of fighting —Margaret Mead, *And Keep Your Powder Dry,* 1942

> . . . does not mean that it favors it or even always approves of it —Roger Angell, *Holiday,* November 1953

> The New York critics generally approved of the way she handled the part —*Current Biography,* June 1964

When used as a transitive verb—usually in the sense of "to sanction officially"—it can take *by* to indicate the agent of approval:

> ... magic hath been publicly professed in former times, ... maintained and excused, and so far approved by some princes —Robert Burton, *The Anatomy of Melancholy,* 1621

> ... the plan must be approved by state legislators — Peter Janssen, *Saturday Rev.,* 5 Feb. 1972

2. Foster 1968 discusses a British concern of the earlier 20th century to restrict the transitive verb to the "official sanction" sense, and the "favorable view" sense to the intransitive. The transitive verb, however, had been in use in the "favorable view" sense earlier than in the "official sanction" sense, so it is not surprising that the urged distinction failed to make much headway. These examples provide some evidence of its failure:

> Jane secretly approved his discernment —Rose Macaulay, *Potterism,* 1920

> ... a friend, whom he liked, but whose conduct he could not approve —Osbert Sitwell, *Noble Essences,* 1950

> Along with George Orwell, whom he never knew and did not always approve, Lewis now looks like the finest British polemicist of the mid-century —George Watson, *Times Literary Supp.,* 24 Sept. 1982

approximate   As an intransitive verb, *approximate* can take *to:*

> The desire to approximate to a certain pattern has been evoked in him from without —Van Wyck Brooks, in *A Century of the Essay,* ed. David Daiches, 1951

> ... the result approximates more to fantasy than to science fiction —John Christopher, *The Writer,* November 1968

> A study of medieval delinquency that rests principally on gaol delivery records can only approximate to veracity —R. B. Pugh, *Times Literary Supp.,* 15 Feb. 1980

> ... its guying of upper class English must have approximated to the real thing —Howard 1984

approximately   The view of *approximately* originating in Flesch 1964 and Follett 1966, reported in Copperud 1970 and seconded by Nickles 1974, is that this adverb should be replaced by *about* or *nearly* or *almost* when it can be. These opinions appear to have been issued with little regard for how the word is actually used. It is in frequent use but is found most often in such contexts as corporate annual reports, technical works, and reference works. Our evidence shows it also appears in general prose of a serious cast but almost never in casual or informal contexts, where such substitutions as those suggested would be particularly suitable. Its most common single application in our files is to numerical quantities. Some examples of typical use:

> Humble's share of ... reserves of crude oil and natural gas liquids currently is estimated to be approximately 2 billion barrels —*Annual Report, Standard Oil Co.* (New Jersey), 1970

> ... a rational number which is approximately equal to the given irrational number —Edwina Deans et al., *Extending Mathematics,* 2d ed., 1968

> ... along a corridor approximately 200 miles long — *Times Literary Supp.,* 14 Nov. 1968

A few examples without numbers:

> ... a quadrangle running approximately east and west —*Johns Hopkins Mag.,* April 1966

> ... have approximately the same feeling for it that the Black Panthers have for the Urban League — John Corry, *Harper's,* October 1970

> ... pills which never had a taste but whose brand names are approximately remembered —Anthony Burgess, *N.Y. Times Mag.,* 4 Dec. 1977

These uses are typical, and to judge from them there seems to be no very strong reason to avoid *approximately.*

approximation   Follett 1966 says that *approximate* (presumably the verb) takes no preposition (see APPROXIMATE, where its use with *to* is illustrated) and that *approximation* takes *to.* This latter statement is partly true, but will not fully bear comparison with actual usage.

In mathematics we find *approximation* used with *to, of,* and *for:*

> ... successively better approximations to L — School Mathematics Study Group, *Calculus, Part I,* 1965

> To get a better approximation of the mathematical idea of a point —School Mathematics Study Group, *Geometry, Part I,* 1965

> ... rational approximations for irrational numbers —Chuan C. Feng et al., *A Course in Algebra and Trigonometry with Computer Programming,* 1969

In other contexts we find both *to* and *of,* with more recent nontechnical writing favoring *of:*

> ... the second approximation to the vertical pressure gradient —E. V. Laitone, *Bulletin of the American Physical Society,* 2 Sept. 1965

> ... a first approximation to the data which would be thus obtained —James B. Conant, *Slums and Suburbs,* 1961

> ... an extremely simple mechanism requiring only an approximation to accuracy —Roger Burlingame, *Backgrounds of Power,* 1949

> ... a close approximation of reality —Ralph Linton, *The Cultural Background of Personality,* 1945

> ... a terrifyingly close approximation of her own situation —Richard Poirier, *A World Elsewhere,* 1966

> ... in which the common language will be English, or some approximation of it —Herbert A. Simon, *Think,* May–June 1967

> ... the early accounts and estimates ... are often cruelly inadequate approximations of the historic truth —Max Lerner, *Saturday Rev.,* 29 May 1976

> ... every effort should be made to achieve the closest approximation of it that is possible —Robert M. Hutchins, *Center Mag.,* January 1968

apropos, apropos of, apropos to *Apropos* is a word taken into English from the French phrase *à propos* in the second half of the 17th century. It has functioned variously as an adjective, adverb, noun, and preposition. No one would have given it a second thought, perhaps, had not Fowler 1926 written

> **apropos** is so clearly marked by its pronunciation as French, & the French construction is, owing to *à propos de bottes,* so familiar, that it is better always to use *of* rather than *to* after it. . . .

Fowler gives no further elucidation, but presumably he felt *of* to be better because it translates the French *de* of the longer phrase. At any rate, such later commentators as Copperud 1970, 1980 and Bernstein 1965 take Fowler's recommendation to be a virtual commandment to use *of* and not to use *to.*

Apropos of functions in English as a compound preposition; it has been functioning as a compound preposition in English since the middle of the 18th century. Some dictionaries—for instance, Webster's Ninth New Collegiate—recognize it as such. Some examples follow:

> . . . tell you a story apropos of two noble instances of fidelity and generosity —Horace Walpole, letter, 1750 (in *Stanford Dictionary of Anglicised Words and Phrases,* 1892)

> It was such an odd expression, coming *apropos* of nothing, that it quite startled me —Bram Stoker, *Dracula,* 1897

> . . . apropos of the election of 1900, when McKinley ran against Bryan —Edmund Wilson, *New Yorker,* 20 Oct. 1951

> Apropos of the Congressional vote to terminate action in Cambodia . . . he writes —Barbara W. Tuchman, *N.Y. Times Book Rev.,* 11 Nov. 1979

Early in the 20th century it began to be used without *of* as a preposition having the same meaning:

> . . . remarked the other day, apropos the formal ending of the censorship —Dorothy Thompson, *Saturday Rev.,* 20 May 1939

> One of Oscar Wilde's characters made, apropos another character, the famous remark, "He always behaves like a gentleman—a thing no gentleman ever does" —Joseph Wood Krutch, *Saturday Rev.,* 30 Jan. 1954

> "The subject is unpleasant to dwell on," he writes primly, apropos the "life-denying nihilism" in Conrad's "Heart of Darkness" —Dwight Macdonald, *New Yorker,* 13 Oct. 1956

> A propos the exclusively female consciousness — John Bayley, *Times Literary Supp.,* 22 Aug. 1980

The use of *to* with *apropos* is not so much wrong (even Fowler did not call it wrong) as rare. The combination is used in two ways. First, we find *to* used when *apropos* is a predicate adjective meaning "appropriate":

> . . . the remark was particularly apropos to the large wisdom of the stranger's tone and air —Nathaniel Hawthorne, *American Notebooks,* 1838 (in *Stanford Dictionary of Anglicised Words and Phrases,* 1892)

This indicates that *Nuclear Science Abstracts* source documents are more apropos to this particular group

than *Science Citation Index* source documents —C. R. Sage, *American Documentation,* October 1966

> Mudrick quotes a fan letter apropos of the *Life,* and apropos to his argument —D. J. Enright, *Times Literary Supp.,* January 1980

The combination is also used, though less often, as a preposition equivalent to *apropos of:*

> . . . it was, I think, apropos to some zoological discussion —John Gibson Lockhart, *Memoirs of the Life of Sir Walter Scott,* 1838

> Apropos to this, you ask me what my plans are — Henry Adams, letter, 3 Nov. 1858

> . . . the excellent and uplifted of all lands would write me, *apropos* to each new piece of broad-minded folly —Rudyard Kipling, excerpt from his *Autobiography,* reprinted in *N.Y. Times,* 10 Feb. 1937

As prepositions, *apropos of* and *apropos* are usual. *Apropos to* is in occasional use; it is rare but not wrong.

apt See LIABLE 2.

Arab See ETHNIC DESIGNATIONS: PRONUNCIATION.

archive, archives The singular and plural forms of *archive* have existed side by side since the word first came into the language in the 17th century. Montgomery & Stratton 1981 assures us that "an archives" is preferred by archivists. We cannot confirm or deny that statement, but our evidence does show greater use of the plural than the singular in the names of institutions. For instance:

> From 1954 the National Archives has carried out training programmes for its serving archivists — *Library Science Abstracts* (London), 1956

> An act to establish a National Archives of the United States Government —*U.S. Code,* 1948

In unofficial use, however, the plural *archives* more often than not is used with a plural verb:

> . . . until the Russian archives are opened —*Times Literary Supp.,* 14 Nov. 1968

> The archives contain some of Jefferson's correspondence —*American Guide Series: Virginia,* 1941

> The archives in the European capitals were searched —Van Wyck Brooks, *The Flowering of New England, 1815–1865,* rev. ed., 1946

At the time the section of the OED containing *archive* was published (1885), the plural form had taken over in the sense of "a place housing documents," and preponderated in the sense of "a collection of documents." In more recent usage, however, the pendulum has begun to swing back, and the singular use is now about as common as the plural in both senses:

> He has had access to the whole of Lady Astor's archive, including her draft of an autobiography — *British Book News,* December 1972

> Miss Carroll's reconverted farmhouse has become something of a Steinian archive —Michiko Kakutani, *N.Y. Times,* 1 Aug. 1979

Both singular and plural are in figurative use:

> ... memorizing practically every line, thus making herself a living archive —Hedrick Smith, *Saturday Rev.,* 24 Jan. 1976

> But we must have more than an intellectual desire, filed away in the archives of idea —Charles A. Lindbergh, *Saturday Rev.,* 27 Feb. 1954

area Copperud 1970, 1980 reports a few members of his consensus as objecting in a rather general way to *area* used as a vague or faddish term in place of *field, problem, issue,* or *question*—themselves no great shakes in respect to specific application. Copperud's critics are echoed by Nickles 1974 and Janis 1984.

The objection to vagueness is not compelling—you use *area* (or *field* or *problem,* etc.) in a vague and imprecise way when you do not want a more precise term, or when there is no such term. The vagueness is not inadvertent. The extension of *area* from spatial reference to a more figurative sense is neither illogical nor far-fetched. It is hard, therefore, to find any sound basis for objection.

What probably brought forth the complaint was the relatively recent and apparently sudden onset of the usage (the sudden popularity of an expression or construction always seems to excite negative comment—for some examples see ARGUABLY; AS; HOPEFULLY; LIKE, AS, AS IF; SPLIT INFINITIVE). Most of our evidence for this figurative extension of *area* comes after World War II. In addition, much of the early evidence comes from education—a discipline frequently reproved for its use of jargon—and some from law, similarly the object of reproof. Here are a few typical examples from our early evidence:

> ... one course in each of the three Areas: Natural Sciences (including Mathematics); Social Studies; and Arts, Letters and Philosophy —*Official Register of Harvard University,* 1947

> The work in the Area of the Holy Scriptures is coordinated to present the study of the Bible as an essential unity —*San Francisco Theological Seminary, 1948 Catalog*

> ... the appointment of principal bibliographers in the areas of the humanities and the social sciences —*Current Biography 1947*

> ... all measures affecting a particular area of the law —Charles J. Zinn, "How Our Laws Are Made," in *U.S. Code,* 1952

Extension to more general areas (or fields or realms or domains), though not well attested in our files, came fairly early:

> You have limited the area of illusion and you have set conditions which the novelist must meet —Bernard DeVoto, *The World of Fiction,* 1950

When we move to more recent evidence, we find a considerable spread in application and the addition of another specific locus of frequent use—annual reports of corporations. Some examples of the spread:

> ... the Company's development in the area of consumer products and services —Thomas E. Hanigan, Jr., in *Annual Report, W. R. Grace & Co.,* 1970

> ... one of those statements that fall within the twilight area of being neither right nor wrong —*Times Literary Supp.,* 22 Jan. 1970

The confrontation model pervades every area of international politics —Richard Barnet, *Harper's,* November 1971

> ... TV news is another area in which being female is somewhat analogous to being black —Harvey Aronson, *Cosmopolitan,* April 1973

> ... the unusually large number of salable titles this year—most of them in the fantasy area —Richard R. Lingeman, *N.Y. Times Book Rev.,* 11 Dec. 1977

> Any form, insofar as we can name it ... associates itself with an area of thought —Donald Hall, *Goatfoot Milktongue Twinbird,* 1978

The spread, and perhaps the increasing frequency, of use has contributed to the establishment of two phrases in which *area* figures: "in the area of X" and "in the X area." Janis takes note of "in the area of"—he terms it informal for *about.* His example relates to money; we likewise have evidence for this use from business contexts:

> Sylvania earns in the area of 15% pretax —*Forbes,* 1 Dec. 1970

In other contexts the meaning of the phrase comes closer to "with respect to":

> In the area of plotters, Hewlett-Packard, Tektronix, or Houston Instruments can sell you ... —Eric Teicholz, *Datamation,* 4 Mar. 1980

> In the area of international relations he has upheld military assistance —*Current Biography,* January 1966

> In the areas of race relations, student protesters and anti-war protesters ... he has the approval of ... —Peter Steinfels, *Commonweal,* 9 Oct. 1970

"In the X area" has a similar financial application:

> Most of the disbursements have been in the $1000 area —Jay Merritt, *Rolling Stone,* 12 June 1980

It also has some vogue among those who speak for public officials, when they are interviewed on radio or television and wish to avoid, for whatever reason, being too specific:

> ... shot in the stomach area ... the knee area ... the chest area —Springfield, Mass., police spokesman, television news, 13 Aug. 1984

Even this intentional vagueness can be put to use by a clever writer:

> ... she insisted that Bond's do something about the voluminous excesses of the pants, which in the seat area could have accommodated both me and a watermelon —Russell Baker, *Growing Up,* 1982

All of the uses of *area* illustrated here are in fact from standard English, and a few are even from literary English. You need not be afraid of using a vague word when a vague word is what you need.

aren't I *Aren't I* has been a bugbear of American commentators since about the beginning of the 20th century. Frank H. Vizetelly in his many guises is one of the earliest. In *Mend Your Speech* (1920) he terms it erroneous, and in the *Literary Digest* (5 June 1926) a solecism; in the same magazine in February 1927 he says, "It is to be hoped that American editors will curb this undesirable alien. It has no authoritative standing anywhere, not even in England, and its usage is marked evidence of illiteracy." Strong words. What occasioned such vehemence?

It is a widely noted phenomenon of modern English that there is no satisfactory filler for the blank in sentences like this: "I'm a little late,_____I?" Perhaps the most logical filler, *ain't,* has been cried down successfully by the pedagogues (see AIN'T), leaving only *amn't, a'n't* or *an't,* and *aren't.* Now, strange as it may seem, these three boil down to the same thing. *Amn't,* which Gowers in Fowler 1965 says is still in use in Scottish and Irish English, in Southern English speech loses the sound of the *m* and becomes *a'n't,* or *an't,* which are attested in print from the late 17th century. *Aren't* is a fairly recent contraction; we have little evidence of its existence before the 20th century. (We do have a Boswellian transcription "I ar'n't" from the speech of "a poor boy from the country" in 1775, but it probably is only Boswell's way of transcribing the sound other writers spelled *an't* or *a'n't.*) In Southern English speech it is pronounced the same, or nearly the same, as *an't.* Thus the same spoken word could be realized in writing by either *an't* or *aren't.* For reasons that we do not understand, the spelling *aren't* began to replace *an't* in *aren't I* in British drama and fiction early in this century. This *aren't I,* then, is a curious hybrid: its meaning comes from *am* and its spelling from *are.*

Aren't I on paper looks incongruous, and in those American dialects that pronounce the *r,* it sounds incongruous. Thus the early outrage of American commentators. Many later commentators have also disparaged the expression, though the bases for objection have grown more diverse. Several point out its ungrammaticality; Krapp 1927 found it "sometimes employed in a kind of kittenish feminine English" (an opinion recorded by Evans 1957 and paraphrased by Copperud 1964); Shaw 1975 calls it pompous and affected; Red Smith, a Harper 1975 panelist, termed it a "Nice Nelly usage."

But the acceptability of the phrase has been growing. There never seems to have been much fuss about it in England; Fowler 1926 doesn't mention it at all, nor do Treble & Vallins 1937; Partridge 1942 notes that the spelling is common but disapproves of it (he favors *a'n't*); Gowers in Fowler 1965 terms it "colloquially respectable." American commentators have begun to soften their opposition; Bremner 1980 plumps for its acceptance; Reader's Digest 1983 finds it perfectly reasonable for those who dislike the other alternatives. Both the Heritage and Harper usage panels find it acceptable in speech, although they reject it in writing in favor, presumably, of uncontracted *am I not?* (What point the distinction between speech and writing has in this instance is unclear, since the form is unlikely to appear in writing except in recorded speech, actual or fictional, or in very informal writing that is close to speech.) Safire (*N.Y. Times Mag.,* 23 May 1982) prefers *ain't I,* however.

Given the continuing hostility to *ain't I,* it looks as though *aren't I* will win its way to respectability on both sides of the Atlantic.

argot   *Argot* is a vocabulary and idiom that is peculiar to a certain group. It is sometimes more or less secret, but perhaps its most important function is to identify the user as a member of the group. Fowler 1965 discusses *argot* and other similar language terms under *jargon;* Bernstein 1965 under *Inside Talk.* See also JARGON.

arguably   You will notice as you browse around in this book that the sudden—or seemingly sudden—popularity of an expression or construction will almost invariably attract the negative comment of people concerned with usage. The split infinitive and the adverb *hopefully* are two well-documented cases. *Arguably* is another such. The British seem to have been first to discover it: Howard 1977 calls it "modish" and "grossly overused"; Phythian 1979 calls it "fashionable and unnecessary." Longman 1984 also notes some objection to it and to its base adjective *arguable.* On the American side, William Safire commented on it in his newspaper column in 1983 and James J. Kilpatrick in 1985. Now that it has been noticed, it may reasonably be supposed that other commentators will take up the cudgels against it.

Both *arguable* and *arguably* are of relatively recent vintage, even though *arguable* turned up as a gloss on a French word in a glossary of 1611. Contextual citations do not appear until 1860 for *arguable* and 1890 for *arguably.* Our evidence shows occasional use of the adjective during the first half of the 20th century, and very little of the adverb. Usage of both begins to pick up noticeably in the 1960s. An editorial in the *Boston Globe* in late 1984 notes the increasing frequency with which *arguably* has been appearing in that newspaper. And our most recent evidence—from the past 10 years or so— shows the adverb beginning to outstrip the adjective.

Safire 1986 contains a discussion of the *arguably* problem. He finds the root of the American objection in the fact that the adverb is regularly used in a positive way—from the idea of "argue in favor of"—but the adjective is regularly used in a negative way—from "argue against." Safire thinks it strange to have such a semantic switch from the adjective to the adverb.

Actually he is overstating the case somewhat. *Arguable* has been and is used with both positive and negative implications. Here are some examples of the use Safire is referring to (though a few are not especially negative):

> Sixth-formers might enjoy the book tremendously; whether they would thereby have been introduced to philosophy proper is arguable —*Times Literary Supp.,* 11 Sept. 1969

> . . . often offering incentives of arguable legality — *N.Y. Times,* 24 Apr. 1977

> Even if every word they wrote were objective truth, the applicability of their work to human behavior would remain arguable —GraceAnne Andreassi DeCandido, *N.Y. Times Book Rev.,* 13 Feb. 1983

> . . . at least one hardly arguable truth—that men and women are different —*Atlantic,* March 1970

> . . . the dictum that foreign relations were supreme among the influences that shape the history of nations. This may be arguable, but for the immediate past it is certainly maintainable —Barbara W. Tuchman, *N.Y. Times Book Rev.,* 11 Nov. 1979

These are completely neutral examples:

> . . . like a doctrine in mediaeval theology, arguable almost indefinitely —Marquis W. Childs, *Yale Rev.,* Summer 1949

> . . . an arguable issue that he does not pause to argue —Walter Goodman, *N.Y. Times Book Rev.,* 31 Oct. 1982

And these are positive examples:

> There is no saying what he might have done. It is arguable that he exhausted himself in "The House with the Green Shutters" —George Blake, Introduction (1927) to Modern Library edition of George Douglas Brown, *The House with the Green Shutters*

> ... an explanation is offered that if not self-evident is at least arguable —Gerald W. Johnson, *N.Y. Herald Tribune Book Rev.*, 20 Sept. 1953

> It is arguable that the wounds left by these political traumas of the 1950s have not yet healed sufficiently for an objective appraisal of Evatt's later career —*Times Literary Supp.*, 30 July 1971

> ... it's perfectly arguable that letting down all the barriers of "decency" ... will pose more problems for the really creative artist than it solves —Robert M. Adams, *Bad Mouth*, 1977

The adverb, then, does not show a complete reversal of attitude from the adjective; rather it springs from just one side of the adjective's usage, which may be curious but is not alarming.

The adverb functions as a hedge against too absolute a statement. Early citations show no particular pattern of use:

> ... a lawyer who urges a defense which he believes to be false may be held, arguably enough, to be ... a disingenuous man —*Atlantic*, April 1927

> ... opposite values each arguably good for the nation —Henry Seidel Canby, *Saturday Rev.*, 13 July 1946

> ... arguably, Mount Morris was inauspicious —Elizabeth Bowen, *The Heat of the Day*, 1949

Many of the weaknesses of the Middle Eastern states are arguably the result of their failure to recognize and meet adequately the problems of a prolonged social crisis —Sir Hamilton A. R. Gibb, *Atlantic*, October 1956

Fairly early on (as early as 1920, according to the OED Supplement), *arguably* was used to modify a comparative adjective:

> But the theatre, behind the scenes, has an emotional freemasonry of its own, certainly franker and arguably wholesomer than the stiffnesses of suburban society outside —George Bernard Shaw, Preface, *The Shaw-Terry Letters*, 1931

> ... a better film critic than almost anybody else: arguably better than anybody else writing for non-specialist magazines —*Times Literary Supp.*, 12 Mar. 1970

And, most recently, it is used to qualify a superlative:

> This is, arguably, the best Shakespeare film to date —Eric Bentley, *New Republic*, 3 Aug. 1953

> ... Yeats, arguably the latest great poet in English —*Times Literary Supp.*, 23 Apr. 1964

> ... arguably still the best introduction to the world that underlies and surrounds the works of art —John E. C. T. White, *Johns Hopkins Mag.*, Spring 1967

> ... when monarchy was arguably the single most important factor in politics —Peter Stansky, *Saturday Rev.*, 20 Jan. 1973

> Richard Savage was, arguably, the most hopeless case among all Johnson's acquaintances at this time —John Wain, *Samuel Johnson*, 1974

> ... described as arguably Britain's greatest living bard —Kingsley Amis, *Antaeus*, Spring 1975

Sportswriters have been blamed for the popularity of this use. As the foregoing examples show, sportswriters had nothing to do with its beginnings—the credit or blame belongs to reviewers, critics, and writers on a variety of subjects. Sportswriters do use it, however:

> Arguably the greatest European sprinter of all time —*The Oxford Companion to Sports and Games*, ed. John Arlott, 1975

> ... arguably the greatest skate racer ever —Chip Greenwood, *Rolling Stone*, 7 Feb. 1980

> ... arguably the two finest forwards in history —Joe Klein, *Inside Sports*, May 1982

> ... arguably the country's leading authority on college football —Jill Lieber, *Sports Illustrated*, 1 Sept. 1982

In summary we may say that *arguably* is used in a positive sense and that it is primarily a qualifier or hedge against too strong a statement. It derives from one side of its parent adjective *arguable*. It is of fairly recent popularity, but did not originate with sportswriters.

Safire does not find the usage objectionable and the *Boston Globe* editorialist concludes that it fills a need in the language. The objection of the British commentators that it is merely a faddish replacement for *perhaps* or *probably* is off-target; *arguably* may be close in meaning to those two, but it carries its own connotation. Unless you are a person who habitually avoids what happens to be in fashion, there seems to be no reason to avoid *arguably*.

argument from etymology See ETYMOLOGICAL FALLACY.

aroma In the world of the usage writer *aroma* always suggests a pleasant odor—Copperud 1980, Bernstein 1965, and Bryson 1984 tell us so. Evans 1957 is a bit more cagey; he says that our forefathers, much given to euphemism and jocularity, tended to use it otherwise, but recommends hewing to the pleasant smell line. Copperud also notes the existence of facetious use.

Perhaps the sense of smell is the most plebeian of the senses, or perhaps the nose is sooner aware of unpleasant odors than pleasant ones, but in any case the words associated with olfactory sensations tend to acquire less pleasant connotations over time. *Aroma* has pretty well resisted this tendency; it is most often used of pleasant smells:

> ... spiced among these odors was the sultry aroma of strong boiling coffee —Thomas Wolfe, *You Can't Go Home Again*, 1940

> ... the pleasing aroma of fresh produce —*The Lamp*, Summer 1971

It may have, in technical contexts, an entirely neutral use:

> The aroma of a loaf should not be strong, sour, or gassy as a result of underbaking —Frank J. Gruber, *Baker's Digest*, February 1955

The euphemistic and humorous uses also continue; they are not as frequent as the pleasant smell uses:

> . . . the critical scene in the comedy is set off by the gruesomely strong aroma of the old dog, who has eaten . . . too much fish —Christopher Morley, *Book-of-the-Month Club News,* May 1948

> . . . the particular meadows smell for which Secaucus is celebrated—a blend dominated by the pungent aroma of pigs —John Brooks, *New Yorker,* 16 Mar. 1957

The foregoing examples all refer to real odors. Unremarked by the commentators is the considerable figurative use of *aroma* for a distinctive quality or atmosphere. In this use *aroma* is pleasant, unpleasant, or neutral as the context dictates:

> . . . an atmosphere, impalpable as a perfume yet as real, rose above the heads of the laughing guests. It was the aroma of enjoyment and gaiety —Stella Gibbons, *Cold Comfort Farm,* 1932

> " . . . And by now it is all beginning to lose its eccentric charm, Nathan, and is taking on a decidedly paranoic aroma. . . ." —Philip Roth, *Atlantic,* April 1981

> The aroma of the continental tradition hangs about the sayings —John Dewey, *Freedom and Culture,* 1939

Figurative use is at least as common as use for an actual smell.

Aroma in its current meanings is a relatively recent word, not attested until the early 19th century. It first meant "spice" and then "the distinctive odor of a spice." When it connotes a pleasant smell, *aroma* is more often associated with food than any other single source of odor.

around 1. *Around, about.* The propriety of using *around* in senses it shares with *about* seems first to have been questioned by M. Schele De Vere in his *Americanisms* of 1872. He modestly defers to John Russell Bartlett, whose 1859 edition of his *Dictionary of Americanisms* gave a couple of examples, but Bartlett merely listed the examples rather than censuring them. Bardeen 1883 notes only Schele De Vere's stricture and the fact that the sense is recorded in Webster 1864 with this quotation:

> I was standing around when the fight took place — *N.Y. Police Gazette*

Such a source in the dictionary seems to surprise Bardeen, but it was a well-traveled quotation, having first appeared in Bartlett and having been used by Schele De Vere too. Bardeen describes the use as "in dispute." Other usage writers of the time ignored the issue, although it did surface upon occasion in the newspapers:

> How regularly "around" is used and abused when "about" is the right word! Thus: "I guess we will be able to go around Noo York with you this afternoon." —letter to editor, *Springfield* (Mass.) *Republican,* 18 Dec. 1902

Ambrose Bierce picked the subject up in 1909, objecting to "The débris of battle lay around them" and "The huckster went around, crying his wares." Bierce brought something new to the subject—a reason for objecting:

"Around carries the concept of circularity." From Bierce on, the subject becomes a regular feature of usage books and handbooks.

An interesting aspect of the *around–about* issue is its ability to migrate from sense to sense of *around* and from one construction to another, as if the commentators were not quite sure of what they should be advising people to avoid. Bierce added a prepositional use to the adverb criticized by Schele De Vere; Jensen 1935 criticizes adverbial uses, which also figure in Watt 1967 and Prentice-Hall 1978. Somewhere along the line the sense of *around* meaning "approximately" or "near" is picked up, and for Bernstein 1965, Shaw 1970, Nickles 1974, and Janis 1984 it has become the chief focus of criticism. This sense had not even been recorded when Schele De Vere made the original comment.

And there is another aspect of the use of *around* to consider: the difference between British and American usage. All of the various usages criticized by American commentators are predominantly American in use and some are American in origin. Why American commentators are so persistently diffident about our native usages is somewhat of a mystery. Recent British commentators (Longman 1984, Burchfield 1981) do not disparage the "approximately" use, for instance; they merely say it is more usual in the U.S. than in Britain; Chambers 1985 even finds it in informal British use.

Since the "approximately" or "near" sense of *around* is at present the one most often objected to, we will give here some examples of its use by American authors:

> . . . looking forty instead of what she was, around twenty-two —*American Mercury,* March 1928

> The idea of becoming a composer seems gradually to have dawned upon me some time around 1916 — Aaron Copland, *Our New Music,* 1941

> Around ten o'clock the little five-piece band got tired of messing around with a rhumba —Raymond Chandler, *The Simple Art of Murder,* 1950

> It was around two bells. The starboard watch had just gone below —Captain Harry Allen Chippendale, *Sails and Whales,* 1951

> He was a bullet-headed man of around sixty —John Cheever, *The Reporter,* 29 Dec. 1955

> . . . overhung the rim of the bench at an angle of around thirty degrees —John Updike, *New Yorker,* 3 Dec. 1955

> Around six thousand years ago —Lewis Mumford, *New Yorker,* 3 Mar. 1956

> My father, for around half a century, was the leading Liberal of the community —John Kenneth Galbraith, *The Scotch,* 1964

> Around the turn of the century, grammarians adjured writers not to use *people* for persons individually —Bernstein 1971

> . . . a word that would have been unprintable until around 1960 —John Gross, *N.Y. Times Book Rev.,* 15 July 1984

Although the OED marks this sense *U.S.,* other British commentators recognize its existence in British English; everybody agrees that *about* is much more common.

Here are a few samples from writers of British English:

> ... a rate of natural increase for Quebec of around 17 per thousand —B. K. Sandwell, *The Canadian Peoples,* 1941

> If the land be in need of lime, this should be applied around November —Henry Wynmalen, *Horse Breeding and Stud Management,* 1950

> Leopoldina Terminal debentures were also better at 86 and the ordinary units changed hands around 1s. 6d. —*Railway Gazette,* 15 Dec. 1950

> ... at around the same price —*The Bulletin* (Sydney, Australia), 10 Feb. 1954

> ... around and before the beginning of the Christian era —Stuart Piggot, *London Calling,* 10 June 1954

> Around fourteen per cent. of students —Sir James Mountford, *British Universities,* 1966

> ... around that time, many of the halls built for dancing came to be converted into skating-rinks — Frances Rust, *Dance in Society,* 1969

In sum, you can use *around* in senses it shares with *about* without apologizing or feeling diffident—especially if you are an American. A handful of surveys made back around 1954 showed *about* more common than *around* even in American use; nothing seems to have been done recently to estimate relative frequency. See also ABOUT.

2. *Around, round.* Everybody knows that *around* is more common in American English and *round* more common in British English. "More common" does not imply exclusiveness, however; both words are in use on both sides of the Atlantic and have been for a good while—even though the OED notes that *around* was rare before 1600.

A number of commentators say, and evidence in the OED Supplement shows, that some originally American uses of *around* have become established to some extent in British English. In addition to the "about, approximately" sense documented above, there is the phrase *have been around:*

> I'd been around long enough to find out that ... — Len Deighton, *Spy Story,* 1974

> ... was a friend of some of the really big wheels south of the border.... Moar had been around — Ronald A. Keith, *Bush Pilot With a Briefcase,* 1972

These next examples show the perhaps unexpected cross-national use of *around* and *round:*

> ... he has not got around to this conundrum —John V. Kelleher, *Irish Digest,* December 1954

> ... destined to be finally extinguished when we got around to it —*Manchester Guardian Weekly,* 10 Nov. 1944

> ... all explanations must accommodate to them, not the other way round —William Stafford, *Writing the Australian Crawl,* 1978

In these examples we have British evidence for both words in similar constructions:

> A look around Krefeld —*Manchester Guardian Weekly,* 9 Mar. 1945

> An English friend whom he took round California — Foster 1968

> It was Wood who should have gone to Australia, and Luckhurst to India, not the other way around — Tony Lewis, *Cricketer International,* August 1976

> ... these days it is usually the other way round — *Times Literary Supp.,* 22 Oct. 1971

> "... Actually, I shall be in all evening, if you would like to call around" —Michael Ryan, *Irish Digest,* December 1955

> "... I just got your letter and came straight round ..." —Iris Murdoch, *A Fairly Honourable Defeat,* 1970

> It was visiting day and there were a lot of women around to see their husbands —Graham Greene, *Travels with my Aunt,* 1969

Sometimes the same writer will even use both:

> ... the old steam-engines that used to chug around Edinburgh —David Daiches, *The Listener,* 13 Dec. 1973

> ... railway line that ran right round the city —David Daiches, *The Listener,* 13 Dec. 1973

And these are American examples of both *round* and *around* in the same expression:

> So I worked on him a bit, you know, telling him how he owes me and he starts to come around and then he says "... I'll see what I can do." —Philadelphia bar patron, quoted in Michael J. Bell, *The World from Brown's Lounge,* 1983

> A great obstacle to nuptials would seem to be O'Neal's ... children ... but apparently they have now come round —Kristin McMurran, *People,* 11 May 1981

Clearly you can use whichever word you feel is most natural for you, whether you are British or American.

arrant   See ERRANT, ARRANT.

array   The verb *array* is used with many prepositions. When used in the sense of "dress," it usually takes *in:*

> ... the subsequent arraying of their persons in the poppy-colored jerseys that she considered suitable to the gloom of the day —Elizabeth Goudge, *Pilgrim's Inn,* 1948

> ... arrayed in gaudy attire —Walter Pater, *Marius the Epicurean,* 1885

> ... had arrayed herself in lipstick, rouge, perfume — Herman Wouk, *Marjorie Morningstar,* 1955

If the sense is close to "equip," *in* or *with* may be used:

> ... almost every county of England arrayed in arms against the throne —T. B. Macaulay, *The History of England,* vol. I, 1849

> ... arrayed with the most advanced equipment — *General Electric Investor,* Summer 1972

Many prepositions are used when the meaning is "to get or place in order":

> ... had his students arrayed on the stage —Gilbert Rogin, *New Yorker,* 5 June 1971

> They arrayed themselves before us —Leon Uris, *Battle Cry,* 1953

... chairs were rounded up and arrayed in front of the Muller platform —John Brooks, *New Yorker*, 27 Apr. 1957

... chairs arrayed before a platform —Clifton Daniel, *N.Y. Times Mag.,* 12 Dec. 1954

Food was his material; his life's art was to array it upon mahogany and damask —*British Books of the Month*, March 1953

... scarcely had time to array his men at the townward wall —A. C. Whitehead, *The Standard Bearer*, 1915

... four brass buttons arrayed in a hollow square — Lois Long, *New Yorker*, 30 Oct. 1954

When there is a notion of drawing up forces, *against* is usual:

... arraying formidable resources against persons who gather and disseminate news —*Playboy*, April 1973

... the French encyclopedists, who were arrayed against the church —Harry S. Ashmore, *Center Occasional Papers*, February 1971

... each group is arrayed against one or more other groups —Margaret Mead, in *Personality in Nature, Society, and Culture*, ed. Clyde Kluckhohn & Henry A. Murray, 1948

arrive **1.** The question of what prepositions to use with *arrive* has been a matter of comment since 1770. Baker 1770 prescribes *at*, rather than *to*, for literal senses; either *at* or *to* for figurative senses. The figurative senses do not seem to occur to later commentators: Raub 1897 says "*at* a place, *in* a vehicle, *from* a place," and Bernstein 1965 says only *at* or *in* without explanation. We will take up literal and figurative senses separately, the literal first.

When the place of arrival is the object, we find *in* and *at:*

... arrived in the United States —*Current Biography*, April 1968

... when we first arrived in Stonington —Dana Burnet, *New England Journeys*, 1953

Ninety per cent of the emigrants arrive in New York City —*Geographical Rev.*, January 1954

Safely arrived at the capital —*Christian Herald*, October 1967

... members arrived at the classroom with arms full of books —Marel Brown, *Christian Herald*, March 1954

Either may be used of birth:

When Harley Johnston came into the world, he arrived at a small manor house —Donn Byrne, *A Daughter of the Medici*, 1935

Late that autumn a boy baby arrived in their home —Irving Bacheller, *A Man for the Ages*, 1919

On or *upon* may be used in some instances:

... by early morning the uniformed youngsters began to arrive on the dock —Frank Oliver, *The Reporter*, 6 July 1954

American tenor Jess Thomas arrived on the roster of the New York Metropolitan Opera in 1962 —*Current Biography*, June 1964

Two policemen at length arrived upon the scene — OED

Into is also sometimes used:

Neighbors arrive into what is already a madhouse scene —Elizabeth Bowen, *New Republic*, 9 Mar. 1953

... with which persons may arrive into the world at birth —*Psychiatry*, May 1945

When things—material or immaterial—arrive, we find *in, at,* or *on:*

... a just appreciation of Baudelaire has been slow to arrive in England —T. S. Eliot, "Baudelaire," in *Selected Essays*, 1932

... was safe when Allen's lob to Johnson arrived at the bag too late —Joseph Durso, *N.Y. Times*, 7 Sept. 1969

Swift's words arrive on the page with the regular tap of a day's rain —V. S. Pritchett, *Books In General*, 1953

... the day that particular issue ... arrived on the New Hampshire newsstands —*The Reporter*, 17 Aug. 1954

If the object is the point of departure, *from* is the most common, with *out of* finding a little use:

... many of them recently arrived from the hill country —Cabell Phillips, *N.Y. Times Mag.*, 30 May 1954

... who arrived in 1849 from Munich —*American Guide Series: Tennessee*, 1939

When material aid arrived from the Soviet Union — *Current Biography*, June 1967

... a lost begrimed dark burnt army abruptly arrived out of some holocaust —Marshall Frady, *Harper's*, November 1970

... belches begin arriving out of your body —Richard Brautigan, *A Confederate General from Big Sur*, 1964

When the object is the means of arrival, we find *by, on,* and occasionally *in:*

... but, after arriving by boat, it was found to be too heavy to transport —*American Guide Series: Louisiana*, 1941

... the visitor who arrives, as I did, by air —George Lichtheim, *Commentary*, October 1957

Francis Cooke, who arrived on the *Mayflower* — *Current Biography*, February 1967

... other invisible persons arriving in close carriages —Herman Melville, *Pierre*, 1852

In figurative use, the object in mind is almost always the point of arrival and the preposition in modern use is overwhelmingly *at*. The OED recognizes the use of *to*, which it labels obsolete. *To* is perhaps not quite obsolete, but it was more common in the 18th century (when Baker took note of it) than it is in the 20th.

> I have arrived to vast courage and skill that way — Lady Mary Wortley Montagu, reprinted in *Encore,* November 1944

> . . . and those, who could not otherwise arrive to a Perfection, . . . made use of the same Experiment to acquire it —Jonathan Swift, "A Discourse Concerning the Mechanical Operation of the Spirit," 1710

> . . . power arrives to them accidentally and late in their careers —Hilaire Belloc, *Richelieu,* 1930

> . . . he had at least arrived at what he considered a reasonable point —Norman Mailer, *Harper's,* March 1971

> The investigator arrives at a list of units —W. F. Bolton, *A Short History of Literary English,* 1967

> . . . want to do considerable exploring in college before arriving at a career decision —Milton S. Eisenhower, *Johns Hopkins Mag.,* February 1966

> . . . when their eldest child was arriving at school age —Frederick Lewis Allen, *The Big Change,* 1952

> . . . each in his own way, suddenly arrived at inventing twentieth-century art —Janet Flanner, *New Yorker,* 6 Oct. 1956

> . . . to arrive at general conclusions —Robert A. Hall, Jr., *A Short History of Italian Literature,* 1951

> . . . the deepest secret of the universe at which we can arrive —John Cowper Powys, *The Meaning of Culture,* 1939

> It's restful to arrive at a decision —Robert Frost, *New Hampshire,* 1923

> . . . began to arrive at a certain importance —Osbert Sitwell, *Triple Fugue,* 1924

From may indicate a figurative as well as a literal source:

> . . . a century in which totalitarianism arrives as easily from the Right as from the Left —Barbara Ward, *N.Y. Times Mag.,* 20 June 1954

2. Harper 1975, 1985 notes with regret the transitive use of *arrive* and *depart* by airlines people—simply the usual verb without the preposition. The OED shows such use (not in airlines lingo, though) from the late 17th century; even Tennyson indulged in it once. Our files show no evidence of a spread from the airlines to general use.

3. How long does it take a new sense of a word to make itself at home? The sense of *arrive* meaning "to achieve success" is recorded in the OED Supplement as making its arrival in 1889; its first appearance is marked by inclusion in quotation marks. This sense took its time: here are two examples more than 60 years later with the word still enclosed in quotation marks:

> The new rich, financiers and industrialists, had "arrived." —*Times Literary Supp.,* 15 June 1951

> . . . the railroad had decidedly "arrived" —G. Ferris Cronkhite, *American Quarterly,* Summer 1954

Quotation marks are no longer used; the sense is fully established.

ary   *Ary,* from *e'er a,* from *ever a,* is a dialectal term meaning "any, a single; either." The Dictionary of American Regional English records its occurrence throughout the U.S., but it is most frequent in Southern and Midland speech.

> See, I was loading more coal than ary a man they had down there —Gobel Sloan of Haysi, Virginia, quoted in *Our Appalachia,* ed. Laurel Shackelford & Bill Weinberg, 1977

In the 19th century *ary* was considered a New Englandism; it was in use there, and was not entirely confined to the usage of the less educated:

> . . . which, though very clean, yet hasn't the vestige of a table-cloth on ary a table —Henry Adams, letter, 9 Feb. 1859

The spelling *ary* seems to be American, but the construction is old:

> Has the old man e'er a son, sir —Shakespeare, *The Winter's Tale,* 1611

> . . . and I'd foot it with e'er a Captain in the county —Richard Brinsley Sheridan, *The Rivals,* 1775

It turns up spelled *arrow* in Fielding's *Tom Jones:*

> "I don't believe there is arrow a servant in the house." (OED)

The OED also cites Smollett's *Humphrey Clinker;* Schele De Vere's *Americanisms* (1872) quotes another instance from *Tom Jones.*

The only use of *ary* in modern English writing is in the representation of speech, especially in fiction:

> "If I said ary thing, I don't remember it now" — Charley Robertson, *Shadow of a Cloud,* 1950

> ". . . a street so wide it has footpaths on ary side . . ." —Conrad Richter, *The Trees,* 1940

James Whitcomb Riley used it in verse:

> Nary bee in ary hive —*Farm-Rhymes,* 1883

as   There are a number of questions—both picky and more substantial—involving the little word *as*—"one of the most overworked words in the English language," according to Shaw 1970. Overwork is a fate shared by most small function words in English; Mr. Shaw himself works *as* as hard as anyone else. (*As* is the fourteenth most frequent word in the Brown University Corpus, according to Kučera & Francis 1967.)

We will treat at this entry several uses of *as* that tend to be lumped together in handbooks. When *as* forms part of a compound, correlative, or phrase whose use is questioned, the whole construction will be found at its own alphabetical place. A number of these follow the present article. See also LIKE, AS, AS IF.

1. *Causal "as."* Bryant 1962 reports that causal *as* appears in standard contexts but is quite a bit less frequent than *because* and *since.* Many other commentators object to the use; the most frequent objection is the possibility of ambiguity in the uncertainty, in certain made-up sentences, whether *as* signifies "because" or "while." Here, for example, is the ambiguous sentence from Copperud 1970:

> As the door was locked, he turned and walked away.

The weakness of an example like this is that it is presented with no supporting context. The context would disambiguate, as linguists say, the sentence. We might know that the locking of this particular door was a process sufficiently lengthy to permit our protagonist to turn and walk away, or that our protagonist was simply balked of his purpose. On the other hand, if you have difficulty imagining a context into which this sentence would fit comfortably, that fact is a sign that the example has little demonstrative value.

Actually, cases where causal *as* is clearly ambiguous are hard to find; the objection seems somewhat flimsy. The objection of Copperud 1970 and one or two others that causal *as* is unidiomatic will not bear scrutiny. Here are some genuine examples of causal *as;* you can judge whether they are ambiguous or unidiomatic:

> The class of '24's valedictorian did not make it from Southern California this year, for instance, as his wife had died —Tom Gavin, *Sunday Denver Post,* 7 Oct. 1984

> As you are but young in the trade, you will excuse me if I tell you, that some little inaccuracies have escaped your eye —Thomas Gray, letter, 10 Aug. 1757

> THESEUS. Oh! then as I'm a respectable man, and rather particular about the company I keep, I think I'll go —W. S. Gilbert, *Thespis,* 1871

> "... I shall prepare my most plaintive airs against his return, in compassion to his feelings, as I know his horse will lose." —Jane Austen, *Mansfield Park,* 1814

> Martin told Jimmy Miranda to take the 3-year-old colt to the lead, and the strategy seemed brilliant as no one challenged Ten Below through slow early fractions —Steven Crist, *N.Y. Times,* 26 Sept. 1982

> ... and as it is always well to prepare for contingencies, I will just notify you —Henry Adams, letter, 9 Apr. 1859

> ... in cases of doubt I often leave them out, but I am apt to put them in, as they help the reader —Oliver Wendell Holmes d. 1935, letter, 27 July 1931

> ... I accepted at once as I like to make trips by plane —Flannery O'Connor, letter, 11 Sept. 1955

> At the last possible minute, John carefully polishes all the brass, as it tarnishes so easily —Suzy Lucine, *Morgan Horse,* April 1983

> As this chapter had no observable merits it did not seem worth reprinting here —Robert Burchfield, Note on the Text, 1984 reprint of Cobbett 1823

Causal *as* is a standard and acceptable alternative to *because* and *since,* but it is less frequently used than either. Objection to it on grounds of ambiguity seems dubious at best, since ambiguous examples in published writing are hard to come by.

See also SINCE 1.

2. *Relative pronoun.* The use that is questioned here breaks down into two kinds of constructions, one perfectly standard and one chiefly dialectal. In the standard construction, the relative pronoun *as* is preceded by *such* or *same:*

> Therefore let Princes, or States, choose such Servants, as have not this marke —Francis Bacon, *Essays,* 1625

> Simpling our Author goes from Field to Field,
> And culls such Fools, as may Diversion yield
> —George Farquhar, Prologue,
> *The Beaux Strategem,* 1707

> Each house shall keep a journal of its proceedings, and from time to time publish the same, excepting such parts as may in their judgment require secrecy —*Constitution of the United States,* 1787

> ... appreciation of and interest in such fine, pleasant, and funny things as may still be around —James Thurber, letter, 20 Jan. 1938

> ... with such poor things as are our own —Leacock 1943

> Plato and Aristotle faced the same problems of man in society as confront the modern philosopher —*Report: Royal Commission on National Development in the Arts, Letters, & Sciences, 1949–1951* (Ottawa, Canada)

> ... faced by the same sort of problem as confronts many local housing committees —*Times Literary Supp.,* 1 Oct. 1954

> ... such innovations as they actually have made —James Sledd, in *Essays on Language and Usage,* 2d ed., ed. Leonard F. Dean & Kenneth G. Wilson, 1963

> The same people as objected to "Inkhorn terms" ... poured derision upon those who "peppered their talk with oversea language" —David C. Brazil, *The True Book about Our Language,* 1965

> ... a tarred timber barn, behind which such of the young as fancied and some as didn't used to box — Benedict Kiely, *New Yorker,* 20 Aug. 1973

> A banjo can set up such a racket as will work the fillings loose from your teeth —Michael O'Rourke, *Nation Rev.* (Melbourne), 24 Apr. 1975

In this construction *as* cannot be easily replaced by another relative pronoun like *that* or *which.*

The relative pronoun *as* without a preceding *such* or *same* is a more complex matter. The OED found it obsolete in standard English but current in various dialects; the Dictionary of American Regional English declares it formerly widespread in American English but now restricted to the Midland and Southern areas. We have three kinds of evidence in our files. First, we have transcriptions of actual speech:

> 'I writes notes and letters for some as buys paper of me....' —Henry Mayhew, *London Labour and the London Poor,* 1851

> She said to me: 'There's a lot of old maids in this village, sir, as wants men....' —*The Journals of Arnold Bennett,* ed. Frank Swinnerton, 1954

> "Not," he said, "what you would call bookshops. There's some as stocks novels; there's some as stocks religion...." —Harold J. Laski, letter, 26 Aug. 1925

Then there is other dialectal evidence (British and American):

> Agriculture was ordained by Him as made us, for our chief occupation —Thomas C. Haliburton, *The Clockmaker,* 1837

. . . we was goin to tell the Gospel to them as had ears —Robert Penn Warren, in *New Directions,* 1947

. . . a lot of things happened inside of you as never ought to —Richard Llewellyn, *None But the Lonely Heart,* 1943

"Never trust a bloke as says that," Bert said —Alan Sillitoe, *Saturday Night and Sunday Morning,* 1958

I had me a little spell and took some pills as cost 60¢ a throw —Flannery O'Connor, letter, 4 Aug. 1957

And, curiously, we have as a third group a few examples appearing in contexts intended to be standard. These examples may simply reflect the natural idiom of the writer.

He has only to shake his well-stocked sleeves to provide a shower of comic images as point to what he calls "his relish for the ridiculous." —*Times Literary Supp.,* 3 Mar. 1950

There has never before been a time as exists today when school committees needed to present a united front —Alton S. Cavicchi, *MASC Jour.* (Mass.), February 1968

. . . coffeehouse featuring many of the performers as have appeared on Robert Lurtsema's "Morning Pro Musica" —advt., *WFCR* (Amherst, Mass.) *Program Guide,* February 1978

In addition, there is a fixed phrase beginning "them as" followed by a third-person present singular verb. In the first of the examples below, the phrase is represented as the speech of an unlettered character. In the other two the fixed phrase is used—as are many fixed phrases with *ain't*—in such a way as to disinfect it of the suspicion of illiteracy and make it a leavening agent in the writing.

'Them as looks down their nose don't see far beyond it,' said Laffin —Robert Gibbings, *Lovely Is the Lee,* 1945

I'll stick to my casualty page; them as likes that kind of thing can have their newsworthy floozies —Alan Villiers, *Ships and the Sea,* January 1953

In literature, for example, it is often said that "the novel is dead", or that "the sentence is obsolete". All right for them as thinks so —Clancy Sigal, *Times Literary Supp.,* 6 Aug. 1964

The plain relative pronoun *as* without *such* or *same* is a survival of older use. It must have been fading in the middle of the 18th century, for Lowth 1763 remarks in a footnote that it is no longer common. Here are three of his examples, all from the 17th century:

An it had not been for a civil gentleman, as came by —William Congreve, *The Old Bachelor*

The Duke had not behaved with that loyalty, as he ought to have done —Edward Hyde, Earl of Clarendon (title not given)

In the order, as they lie in his preface —Thomas Middleton, *Works*

It looks to us as if the plain relative pronoun *as* would be a little tricky to use if it is not part of your natural idiom. You need not, of course, avoid its survival in this proverb:

Handsome is as handsome does.

3. *Conjunction.* The use of *as* as a conjunction where *that,* or sometimes *if* or *whether,* could be substituted has been attacked by various commentators at least since Ayres 1881 discovered "Not as I know." Subsequent commentators from Bierce 1909 to Janis 1984 and Guth 1985 have decried it as ungrammatical, incorrect, or nonstandard. None of these commentators gives us a reason for the condemnation; in fact, none of them has much to say about it beyond the criticism.

This use, like the one discussed in section 2 above, is a survival of an older one. The OED notes its existence from Caxton's time in the 15th century. Lowth 1763 lists it in a footnote of old-fashioned or out-of-date uses. It had high literary use in the 17th and early 18th centuries:

And certainly, it is the Nature of Extreme *Selfe-Lovers;* As they will set an House on Fire, and it were but to roast their Egges —Francis Bacon, *Essays,* 1625

> I gain'd a son;
And such a son, as all men hail'd me happy
—John Milton, *Samson Agonistes,* 1671 (in Lowth)

. . . disposed to conclude a peace upon such conditions, as it was not worth the life of a grenadier to refuse them —Jonathan Swift, *The Four Last Years of the Queen* (in Lowth)

We should sufficiently weigh the objects of our hope; whether they be such, as we may reasonably expect from them what they propose in their fruition — Joseph Addison, *The Spectator,* No. 535 (in Lowth)

These literary uses have dropped away. The OED notes survival in southern British dialects; the DARE in American. It remains almost entirely an oral use in American English. It can occasionally be found in positive constructions:

Billy Sessions asked me if I thought you all would read his play & I allowed as I thot you would —Flannery O'Connor, letter, 1 July 1959

But usually it is followed in negative constructions, usually after the verbs *know, see,* or *say:*

I don't know as you'll like the appearance of our place —Harriet Beecher Stowe, *Dred,* 1856 (in OED)

I don't know as it makes any difference in respect to danger —Walt Whitman, letter, 9 Feb. 1863

"Just as you say," returned the rejected. "I ain't sure as you'd be exactly the one. . . ." —Francis Lee Pratt, "Captain Ben's Choice," in *Mark Twain's Library of Humor,* 1888

I don't see as it's been any use —Edith Wharton, *Ethan Frome,* 1911 (in American Dialect Dictionary)

I didn't know as I'd go —Thornton Wilder, *Our Town,* 1938 (in ADD)

But the last five years anyway we've managed to market it all in retail containers. I don't know as I should say all, but the majority of it —Mac Joslyn, quoted in *New England Farmer,* October 1984

This *as* must have been a regular feature of the idiolect of the detective novelist Erle Stanley Gardner. He put it into the language of many of the characters in his stories—including characters whose speech is standard. One sample:

> Well, after reading that letter, I don't know as I blame Minerva —*The Case of the Negligent Nymph,* 1949

This use of the conjunction *as* is not ungrammatical, erroneous, or illiterate, but you must remember that it is now a speech form—whether dialectal or not—and is not found in ordinary expository prose.

See also AS HOW.

4. *Preposition.* Phythian 1979 believes that "correct grammar" does not accept *as* as a preposition, but that is not the case. *As* has a few prepositional uses no one quibbles about:

> When I sailed as a boy, yachting was confined to relatively few centers —Carleton Mitchell, *Boating,* January 1984

> . . . language is primarily learned as speech —William Stafford, *Writing the Australian Crawl,* 1978

> He acted as her manager —E. L. Doctorow, *Ragtime,* 1975

> It was as Julie Lamber in *Theatre* . . . that she first won almost unanimous praise from Broadway critics —*Current Biography,* December 1964

> . . . they respect every man as a man —J. Bronowski, *American Scholar,* Autumn 1969

> Here's a good Ph.D. thesis for somebody: Weber as a literary man —Harold C. Schonberg, *N.Y. Times,* 16 July 1967

There is another sense of the preposition *as* that means the same as *like:*

> . . . each of them, as their predecessors, neatly tailored to the pocket —*Times Literary Supp.,* 26 Jan. 1967

> Then I said, "Do you think that he is not as other men?" —Jim Henderson, *Open Country Muster,* 1974

> . . . that grimness is as nothing compared to what was to come —Robert Penn Warren, *Democracy and Poetry,* 1975

Because of the propensity of conjunctional *as* to be used with what are called truncated clauses, it is sometimes hard to tell whether the conjunction or preposition was intended:

> Comeau was thin and Adams was fat, but after years of association they moved as matched planets — John Updike, *Couples,* 1968

> It sounds and reads as a forced word —John O. Barbour, quoted in Harper 1985

Some writers choose *as* automatically out of fear of misusing *like;* such uses are often ambiguous because the *as* can be understood in its "like" sense or in its "in the character or capacity of" sense. In the E. L. Doctorow quotation above, "He acted as her manager," *as* reflects the latter sense; it is easy to see how "He acted like her manager" would mean something quite different. Copperud 1964, Freeman 1983, and others warn against

using *as* in its "like" sense when it can be taken for the other. Here is an example:

> . . . convicted of assaulting a security guard . . . and breaking up the hotel's furniture. Said the judge to the defendants upon sentencing them: "You acted as buffoons." —*TV Guide,* 4 Jan. 1985

If the judge had used *like,* his meaning would have been apparent at once.

5. Copperud 1970 and one or two others raise an objection to the preposition *as* used after what they term "designating verbs": *name, appoint, elect,* and the like. Verbs like *elect* and *appoint* are complex transitive verbs—they take a complement and a direct object:

> We elected Helene president.

> He was appointed vicar.

> They named her their trade representative.

The problem with a blanket objection to the insertion of *as* between the object and the complement is that some similar verbs, such as *install,* are not complex transitives:

> He was installed as vicar last week.

If the occasional insertion of an unnecessary but harmless *as* in

> He was appointed as vicar.

avoids the unidiomatic

> He was installed vicar.

it is a minor fault indeed.

6. *As, such as.* Sellers 1975 objects to *as* used for *such as,* calling it "a sloppy Americanism." His compatriot Phythian 1979 finds it entirely acceptable. These two examples show that it is not an Americanism, and is not necessarily sloppy.

> . . . some little inaccuracies have escaped your eye, as in the 9th page *Lab'rinth's & Echo's,* (which are Nominatives plural,) with Apostrophes after them, as tho' they were Genitives singular —Thomas Gray, letter, 10 Aug. 1757

> I was often astonished when my mother did me some deed of generosity, as when she bought me my first Sunday suit with long pants —Russell Baker, *Growing Up,* 1982

as . . . as   **1.** *As . . . as, so . . . as.* As a general rule, it is safe to observe that *as . . . as* is regularly used in positive statements, and either *as . . . as* or *so . . . as* in negative statements. This state of affairs was not always the case.

Lamberts 1972 says that up until about a century ago, *so . . . as* was the regular form in negative statements. It is a very old construction; the OED shows *so . . . as* from the 13th century on. Apparently *as . . . as* began to be used in negative statements sometime in the 18th century; Marckwardt & Walcott 1938 cite a study that found the construction in Swift, Johnson, Boswell, and others. Leonard 1929 notes that a grammarian named J. Mennye in 1785 was apparently the first to insist on *so* after *not.* Since 18th-century grammarians prescribed most of their rules in cases of divided usage, we can fairly assume that Mennye was aware of *as . . . as* being used after *not.* Lowth 1762 was probably not aware of divided usage: he describes the *so . . . as* construction, illustrated entirely with examples of negative statements, but states no rule and uses neither the word *negative* or *not.* Mennye's book was published in New York. Leonard says that he had a large number of followers in the authors of 19th-century grammars and handbooks. In a grammar by Joseph Hervey Hull published in Boston in 1829, for example, the sentence "This is not as good as that" appears in a list of "incorrect phrases" to be corrected by the pupil.

Bryant 1962 cites a study showing that in the middle of the 19th century only about 11 percent of the writers studied were using negative *as . . . as;* by the middle of the 20th century negative *as . . . as* was used by more than 52 percent of the writers studied. As early as 1927, G. P. Krapp asserted that negative *as . . . as* was usual in speech. Surveys—Leonard 1932, Mittins et al. 1970, Crisp 1971—all show it to be established.

Handbooks, however, followed their 19th-century counterparts and continued to insist on *so . . . as* in negative contexts well into the first half of the 20th century. The prescription may be most firmly established in the field of business writing; we have one such text (Himstreet & Baty) prescribing *so* in negative contexts as recently as 1977. Most current handbooks join Bernstein 1971 in counting it among Miss Thistlebottom's hobgoblins; they all recognize the legitimacy of both constructions, although a few (for instance Janis 1984, Freeman 1983) find the *so . . . as* construction more formal or more appropriate in formal contexts.

Assertions about relative formality, however, do not bear much scrutiny, at least with respect to writing. A study made at Merriam-Webster before the publication of Webster's Third and based on citations gathered from the late 1930s up to the early 1950s showed the negative *as . . . as* more common than *so . . . as,* but the great bulk of the citations for both constructions are from the same sources and in a few instances from the same authors. There is no particular difference in formality. Further, evidence from collections of letters (such as Jane Austen's or Henry Adams's) shows a tendency to follow the prevailing mode. Jane Austen, writing in the early 19th century, regularly uses *as . . . as* in positive contexts:

> . . . I was as civil to them as their bad breath would allow me —20 Nov. 1800

and *so . . . as* in negative ones:

> She is not so pretty as I expected —12 May 1801

Henry Adams, writing at the end of the 19th century, uses both *as . . . as* and *so . . . as* in negative contexts:

> The Church never was as rotten as the stock-exchange now is —17 Feb. 1896

> No history . . . contains contrasts so dramatic and so gorgeously tragic, as the contrast between the Cathedrals of the 13th and the Chateaux of the 15th centuries —25 Sept. 1895

Our recent evidence, too, shows little difference in elevation between the constructions:

> Serious first novels don't do nearly as well as they should —John Irving, *N.Y. Times Book Rev.,* 25 May 1980

> He would eat hot soup and drink whiskey and sweat—my Uncle Jake did not, decidedly, do anything so delicate as perspire —Aristides, *American Scholar,* Winter 1981–82

The mystery about *as . . . as* and *so . . . as* is why *so . . . as* has begun to decline in regularity of usage (although certainly it is far from defunct). There is probably no one reason, but three possible contributing factors can be identified. First, English does not in general have different grammatical structures for negative statements; in most cases they are simply positive statements negated. Second, as Bryant and others point out, many *as . . . as* comparisons are fixed in English as regular patterns (*as cool as a cucumber, as sly as a fox, as clean as a whistle, as dry as dust,* etc.) where negation would not normally produce an introductory *so.* And third, the grammarians themselves may have made a contribution. By the time *not as . . . as* began to draw even with *not so . . . as,* Mennye's prescription had been repeated for about a century. Some observers feel that the constant use of false syntax—the presentation of examples to be corrected—served to reinforce rather the patterns the grammarians deemed incorrect than those supposed to be correct.

We should not overlook the occurrence of *so . . . as* in positive contexts. While it does not appear to have been especially common at any time, neither does it appear to have been rare. The OED has examples from the 15th century to the 19th century. It survives especially in a few expressions concerned with time. Boswell used these:

> . . . a spinnet, which, though made so long ago as 1667, was still very well toned —*Journal of a Tour to the Hebrides,* 1785

He even more or less puts it into Dr. Johnson's speech:

> He told me that "so long ago as 1748 he had read 'The Grave, a Poem' but did not like it much." —*Life of Samuel Johnson,* 1791

H. L. Mencken used a similar expression:

> . . . so late as 1870 —*The American Language, Supplement II,* 1948

More often, however, we find positive *so . . . as* where *as . . . as* might have been used when the writer appears to want the additional emphasis of *so* that comes from its use as a degree word:

> Super-duper profs even go so far as to try to enter real politics —Anthony Lambeth, *Change,* Summer 1971

> Now it may strike us as somewhat incredible that a viewpoint ostensibly so liberating as that of Boas could lead to a defense of traditionalism —*New Republic,* 19 Apr. 1939

> . . . delighted musicians so different as Paul Whiteman and Duke Ellington —Gilbert McKean, *Saturday Rev.,* 27 Sept. 1947

Both *as . . . as* and *so . . . as* are used in negative constructions; you can choose the one that sounds better in any given instance. In positive constructions *as . . . as* is the prevalent form; positive *so . . . as* is not wrong but simply much less common.

2. Copperud 1970 notes a couple of commentators who object to *as . . . as* constructions with the first *as* omitted; he also notes that Evans 1957 considers it acceptable. The OED records it without stigma and lists citations from about 1200 on, including ones from such writers as Wyclif, Shakespeare, Spenser, Milton, and

Richardson. Here are a couple of more modern instances:

> It was jolly as could be —Henry Adams, letter, 22 Apr. 1859

> He's hooked bad as I am —Robert Strauss, quoted in *N.Y. Times Mag.,* 20 May 1984

3. If a pronoun follows an *as . . . as* comparison, is it to be in the nominative case or the objective case? Is it "She is as tall as I" or "She is as tall as me"? Commentators differ. Longman 1984 prefers the nominative; Heritage 1982 permits either but says that traditionalists prefer the nominative; Phythian 1979 thinks that the nominative is pretentious even though correct; Evans 1957 thinks the objective is preferred.

Our evidence is of little help in this instance, because the typical "Is Mary as tall as I (or me)" construction is very rare in the sort of discursive prose most of our evidence comes from. What is more, *as* is often omitted from concordances of prose works precisely because its great frequency of occurrence would add to the bulk of the work. And as it is not a dialectal construction, those dictionaries that concern themselves with speech forms are not much help either. Grammarians and commentators have their opinions, but hard evidence seems difficult to come by. The apparent trend among commentators toward approving the objective case seems to be related to the use of the objective case after linking verbs.

See also IT'S ME; THAN 1.

4. See AS GOOD OR BETTER THAN.

as bad or worse than   See AS GOOD OR BETTER THAN.

as best   James J. Kilpatrick, in a column printed in the *Portland Oregonian* of 2 Nov. 1985, worries about his use of "we must do as best we can"—several of his readers had written in to chide him about it. Kilpatrick believes "as best we can" to be a respectable idiom but concedes that it might be a Southern regionalism and wonders if anyone else uses it. The answer is yes, other people use it, and no, it is not a Southern regionalism. Bernstein 1977 specifically approves it:

> It is perfectly proper to say, "He did the job as best he could."

Although Janis 1984 stigmatizes it as nonstandard, the expression has attracted little notice. Our evidence shows that *as best* has been around at least since the early 19th century:

> . . . blow 'em up as best suits our convenience — Washington Irving, *Salmagundi,* 14 Aug. 1807

A somewhat later example comes from Jane Austen's niece:

> But . . . he then found himself a ruined Man, and bound to provide as best he could for his Mother and Aunt —Caroline Austen, *Reminiscences*

These later examples show widespread use:

> . . . tells him to worry through with his doubts and sins and troubles as best he can —H. Rider Haggard, diary, 23 May 1918

> . . . must fill the place of a national theatre as best it can —George Bernard Shaw, letter, 19 Oct. 1929

> But I do as best I can —Harry S. Truman, letter, 18 Aug. 1948

> The cops had to get the sick and injured to hospital as best they could —H. L. Mencken, *Happy Days,* 1940

> . . . to where, or where as best he could see in the dark, she had gone through her rites —John Cheever, *The Wapshot Chronicle,* 1957

> . . . to answer all questions that arise, as best I can — Robert Graves, *The Greek Myths,* Vol. I, 1955

> . . . labour as best he might in the old vineyard — Flann O'Brien, *The Dalkey Archive,* 1964

> He pictured himself as this hard, lonely man—sidestepping the Byron cliché as best he could, only to land splat in the Bogart —Wilfrid Sheed, *People Will Always Be Kind,* 1973

> . . . leaving the spectators to make out as best they could what was going on —Robertson Davies, *The Lyre of Orpheus,* 1989

It looks like a perfectly respectable idiom to us.

ascent, assent   One of the 8th-grade English texts in our collection warns students not to confuse *ascent* and *assent*—a quick check in your dictionary will show you that although they sound the same, they are not at all related. Whoever wrote this should have checked a dictionary, or an 8th-grade English text:

> He analyzes the course of Russia's assent to superpower status —Advance Book Information, Oxford University Press, July 1983

ascertain   As late as Nicholson 1957 we find objection to the use of *ascertain* used to mean simply "to find out"; Nicholson insists it must mean "to find out or learn for a certainty, by experiment, investigation, or examination." The problem with this insistence is that it depends upon the ways definers in various dictionaries have handled *ascertain* and neglects the far more important question of how good writers have actually used *ascertain.* Definers may have been influenced by the etymology of the word and a desire to semantically tie this one surviving sense to older defunct senses. It is certainly hard to tell, in a great many contexts, the difference between "finding out or learning" and "finding out or learning for certain."

The objection is of obscure origin, perhaps alluded to as early as 1889 by Walter Pater in his *Appreciations.* It seems to have been in its fullest flower in the 1920s: Whipple 1924 emphasizes "definitely," and in 1927 both Krapp and Emily Post object to its use as simply "find out." These three suggest that the use may have been a popular one at the time, and quite likely a conversational one. Krapp's example—"I will ascertain if Mr. Jones is free to see you"—is not typical of our examples of written use. But Jane Austen had already established the less strenuous use:

> Morland produced his watch, and ascertained the fact —*Northanger Abbey,* 1818

> . . . they had the advantage of ascertaining from an upper window that he wore a blue coat, and rode a black horse —*Pride and Prejudice,* 1813

It was thereafter available for other writers to use, and use it they certainly have:

> It was not difficult for one who knew the city well, to find his house without asking any question. Having ascertained its situation ... —Charles Dickens, *A Tale of Two Cities,* 1859

> The boy crept along under the bank to ascertain from the nature of the proceedings if it would be prudent to interrupt so splendid a creature as Miss Eustacia on his poor trivial account —Thomas Hardy, *The Return of the Native,* 1878

> ... even went the length of reading the play of "King John" in order to ascertain what it was all about — George Bernard Shaw, *Cashel Byron's Profession,* 1886

> ... his whole attention concentrated on ascertaining by ear what he had been accustomed to judge by sight —C. S. Forester, *The African Queen,* 1935

> ... to catch intermittent glimpses of the Germans and so ascertain that they were still alive —Jeremy Bernstein, *New Yorker,* 30 Oct. 1971

There is no problem with this use of *ascertain,* and probably there never was.

as far as, so far as   **1.** In the October 1962 issue of *American Speech,* Paul Faris commented on the prepositional use of *as far as.* Although he had recorded a great many instances of the construction in speech and in writing, he found that dictionaries and usage books in general seemed unaware of the construction. He found only Fowler 1926 dealing with the subject.

Fowler 1926 (Fowler 1907 contained a single example for correction) deals with two aspects of *as (so) far as.* We will call one literal, for it depends on the meaning of *far.* Fowler approves such expressions as "went as far as York" and "He knows algebra as far as quadratics" and "I have gone so far as to collect, *or* so far as to collecting, statistics."

> ... as far at least as the moon —Henry Adams, letter, 3 Sept. 1863

> ... our concern about our fellow man extends only as far as our pocketbook or our discomfort —Melvin J. Lerner, *Psychology Today,* June 1971

The second prepositional use—the one that Fowler condemns—can also be seen from a different angle as the conjunction *as far as* used to introduce an elliptical clause, one from which the verb (such as *goes* or *is concerned*) has been omitted. This is the construction Faris is discussing, and it is the one that American usage commentators, starting with Bernstein 1962, comment unfavorably upon. (Later commentators include Copperud 1970, Harper 1975, 1985, Ebbitt & Ebbitt 1982, Bernstein 1977, Einstein 1985, Freeman 1983.) Let us begin our review of the matter with a few examples from print:

> As far as getting the money he asked for, Mr. Churchill had little difficulty —in Fowler 1926

> The cabin ... was in perfect condition so far as frame and covering until 1868 —Henry Seidel Canby, *Thoreau,* 1939 (in Faris)

> As far as disturbing a writer at his work, this hotel bedroom might just as well have been filled with howling monkeys this past week, for all the work I've been able to get done —E. B. White, letter, 8 Feb. 1942

> The Bikini was originally called the "atome" by M. Heim, and the sky was the limit so far as advertising it —*N.Y. Times,* 20 Feb. 1959 (in Bernstein 1962)

> Pauls would be taken seriously, they felt, and as far as doing business with Germany this was the most important long-range consideration —James Feron, *N.Y. Times Mag.,* 31 Oct. 1965

> As far as being mentioned in the Ten Commandments, I think it is —Billy Graham, newspaper column, 1974

> As far as temperament, the Abyssinian cat is a most affectionate and loving companion —Ruth A. Zimmermann, *Cats Mag.,* December 1980

Although these examples are characteristic of the construction and some of them are among the oldest citations for it, they are not exactly typical of our evidence. Most of our citations are from speech, either as recorded off the air or as reproduced in newspapers and magazines. We will begin with examples reproduced in print. The expression seems to have been part of President Kennedy's vocabulary; he turns up in our first two examples.

> But as far as whether I could attend this sort of a function in your church ... then I could attend — John F. Kennedy, quoted in *U.S. News & World Report,* 1960 (in Faris)

> So far as the next program, it will be developed later —John F. Kennedy, quoted in *Saturday Rev.,* 14 Nov. 1964

> But as far as the drug culture that they used to talk about, it's not as heavy as it was back ten years ago —Kris Kristofferson, quoted in *Cosmopolitan,* December 1977

> "I still have most of my mother's values as far as manners," says Mackenzie, "but I guess I always wanted to be like my father...." —Mackenzie Phillips, quoted in *People,* 2 Mar. 1981

> ... lived a heck of a lot better than Larry or I ever did as far as standard of living —Billie Jean King, quoted in *People,* 25 May 1981

> Not only was she a great actress, she was the Carole Lombard of her time, as far as being able to do comedy —Jack Lemmon, quoted in *Playboy,* June 1981

> It was probably one of the worst, if not the worst, conditions I've played in as far as wind —John McEnroe, quoted in *Springfield* (Mass.) *Republican,* 8 May 1983

> As far as raising kids, he didn't have a clue —Gary Crosby, quoted in *People,* 21 Mar. 1983

> As far as my ability, I think I've proven I can play —Alan Wiggins, quoted in *Springfield* (Mass.) *Daily News,* 6 July 1985

> Regan may be the ultimate guy to work for as far as getting the whole story —Larry Speakes, quoted in *People,* 12 Aug. 1985

Citations taken directly from broadcasts do not differ from the printed reports:

> I wonder if he's got a physical problem as far as running —Earl Weaver, *ABC Game of the Week,* 15 Aug. 1983

> . . . as far as bringing this sort of thing to a halt —Ara Parseghian, CBS football telecast, 25 Dec. 1986

We even have a few instances of facetious use. The first two are comments on the construction, the third a parody of a press conference given by President Reagan:

> 19. As far as incomplete constructions, they are wrong —George W. Feinstein, "Letter from a Triple-Threat Grammarian," *College English,* April 1960

> Only those will accept this who are irresponsible as far as their grammar —Willard R. Espy, in Harper 1985

> As far as Jack Kemp, it's not my job to make trades for the Yankees, but they bought a pig in a poke there —Veronica Geng, *New Yorker,* 30 Aug. 1982

Our commentators, from Fowler 1926 to Harper 1985 and Einstein 1985, are nearly unanimous in condemning the construction; only Faris in *American Speech* thinks it deserves more consideration. And why do they condemn it? As is so often the case, many do not give a reason. Fowler did so perhaps partly because of novelty; but both he and others have probably been affected by their frustrated expectation of the formulaic verb *goes* or *is concerned.* Ecountering *as far as* and then having the verb withheld is a bit like not hearing the other shoe drop. But as for novelty, it is not clear how much of a novelty the construction is. Faris recorded some 60 examples from both speech and writing in a single year, proving that it can be found when someone looks for it—and our newest evidence bears this out. From Fowler's first example, reprinted in 1907, more than half a century passed with no one else taking notice. While the construction was certainly not common, it may have been around, undetected, for quite a long time; lexicographers are sometimes not as alert to phrases as they are to new words:

> Then the king don Peter answered the prince and said; 'Right dear cousin, as far as the gold, silver and treasure that I have brought hither, which is not the thirtieth part so much as I have left behind me, as long as that will endure, I shall give and part therewith to your people.' —Lord Berners, translation of Froissart's *Chronicles,* 1523

Despite the last example prepositional *as far as* must be considered essentially a 20th-century form on the basis of what we now know. While we have by no means exhausted the possibilities, we have not yet found a 19th-century example, even in that most reliable repository of the informal language, letters.

There can be no question, after more than three quarters of a century, that prepositional *as far as* is established in speech; it was clearly established in 1962 when Faris published his findings. Reference books have been slow to catch up in this instance. But speech and reports of speech aside, the expression has made little inroad into ordinary prose. Our most recent evidence shows it still primarily a speech form.

2. Vizetelly 1906 and a few later commentators endeavor to discriminate between *as far as* and *so far as.* Their discriminations are applicable only to those uses of the phrases that are dependent on the individual meanings of *as, so,* and *far;* they do not apply to the phrases when used as compound conjunctions or prepositions. In these latter uses they are simple variants; *as far as* is somewhat more common as a conjunction, and much more common as a preposition, than *so far as.*

3. Bolinger 1980 asserts that *as far as* (the preposition) is substituted for *in* in jargon. His comment fits the example he shows to illustrate it, but if you will try *in* for *as far as* in the quotations we give above, you will find that it does not fit very well very often. Since most of our citations are from speech, they are perhaps not especially representative of jargon.

Copperud 1970 and Nickles 1974 object to *as far as* in any use as wordy or long-winded. *As far as* may indeed be long-winded in some instances, but it cannot be easily replaced by a shorter formula in many others. The examples that follow are from letters, where conciseness of expression is usually not of prime importance. We suspect that in these examples at least, it would not be easy to replace *as far as* with something shorter and better:

> I endeavour as far as I can to supply your place & be useful —Jane Austen, letter, 14 Sept. 1804

> My Rochdale affairs are understood to be settled as far as the law can settle them —Lord Byron, letter, 9 Sept. 1811

> We are in a state of anarchy so far as the President goes —Henry Adams, letter, 22 Dec. 1860

> . . . but, so far as I can see, I shall be in town on or before the 20th —Lewis Carroll, letter, 10 June 1864

> Those two seem to me achievements as far as the writing goes —Flannery O'Connor, letter, 2 Aug. 1958

4. Because the verb in the clause following the conjunction *as far as* is often separated by a few words from its subject, there is occasionally the possibility of a mismatch of number between subject and verb. Pyles 1979 sets down three examples of this problem from the 1954 Army-McCarthy hearings:

> . . . as far as the infiltration of the armed services were concerned —Roy Cohn

> . . . as far as coddling Communists are concerned — Roy Cohn

> . . . as far as Mr. Adams and Mr. Cohn is concerned —Senator McCarthy

The problem seems to occur chiefly in speech. We have only a single instance in print:

> . . . at least as far as liberality in movie themes are concerned —Kathleen Karr, *Media & Methods,* January 1971

The mismatch in each of these is caused by the intervention of a noun of different number from the subject between subject and verb. See AGREEMENT, SUBJECT-VERB: THE PRINCIPLE OF PROXIMITY.

as follows   If you are really interested, *as follows* regularly has the singular form of the verb—*follows*—even if preceded by a plural.

> The principal parts of *lay* are as follows: —Macmillan 1982

All the experts agree—Copperud 1970, 1980, Harper 1975, 1985, Longman 1984, Freeman 1983, Phythian 1979, Bremner 1980, Johnson 1982, Heritage 1969, Bernstein 1977, and undoubtedly many others.

One of the more interesting aspects of this subject is its longevity—it was first discussed in Baker 1770. Baker argued that *as follows* was preferable to *as follow,* which he says some 18th-century writers, including Addison, used. (The OED does show at least one 18th-century *as follow,* but not from Addison.) Campbell 1776 concurred with Baker and pronounced what seems to have been the final word: "When a verb is used impersonally, it ought undoubtedly to be in the singular number, whether the neuter pronoun be expressed or understood. . . ." No one seems to have disagreed subsequently; Lindley Murray 1795 took Campbell over into a footnote, and no modern commentator even gives Campbell's reasoning a thought.

The only modern wrinkle on the subject comes from a couple of Harper usage panelists, who think *as follows* can often be omitted. In a construction such as the one from Macmillan 1982 above, it could indeed be omitted. It seldom is omitted, however, perhaps in part because style manuals usually recommend that a colon be used only after a complete clause. *As follows* (or *the following*) serve to complete the clause in contexts like the one from Macmillan.

as for   Bierce 1909 objected to *as for,* prescribing *as to;* Bernstein 1977 cannot figure out why he did so and neither can we. Maybe Bierce was sick of Patrick Henry:

> I know not what course others may take, but as for me, give me liberty, or give me death! —speech in the Virginia Convention, 23 Mar. 1775

There is no reason to avoid *as for.* It is still in common and completely respectable use; Copperud 1980 opines that it is probably more common than *as to*—perhaps a debatable observation.

as good as   This adverbial phrase is disparaged by MacCracken & Sandison 1917 as an "undesirable colloquialism" for *practically,* and Shaw 1975 finds it "wordy" for *practically.* You can safely ignore both criticisms. Consider, for instance, Shaw's objection. *As good as* has eight letters and two blank spaces and has three syllables. *Practically* has eleven letters, three syllables in the most common pronunciation and four syllables in another. *Practically* has more letters and as many or more syllables.

Here are several impeccably standard examples:

> Goethe is quite explicit about this to Eckermann; he as good as says that a masterpiece is a gift from on high —Lucien Price, *Dialogues of Alfred North Whitehead,* 1954

> The floating laborer of our society . . . is as good as unheard-of among them —A. L. Kroeber, *Anthropology,* rev. ed., 1948

> . . . the Defense Ministry as good as admitted that most of the R.A.F.'s fighters are too slow —*Time,* 28 Feb. 1955

as good or better than   Under this heading we will discuss a construction involving both the positive and comparative of several adjectives (*good* seems only to be the most common of them) that has been the subject of corrective efforts since the 18th century. (Bryant 1962

calls the construction *dual comparison* and Bernstein 1977 *incomplete alternative comparison.*) Correction begins with Campbell 1776, who exhibits this sentence:

> Will it be urged that the four Gospels are as old, or even older, than tradition? —Bolingbroke, *Philosophical Essays*

What exercises Campbell is that *than,* which goes with *older,* does not go with *old.* Insert *as* after *old,* says Campbell, and everything will be put right. Lindley Murray 1795 picked up the example and the solution (he did sanitize the example by replacing *four Gospels* with *book;* Murray brooked no questioning of Christianity) and passed both on to the 20th century, where we can find them in various guises in Copperud 1970, Shaw 1970, Johnson 1982, Janis 1984, Harper 1985, and more.

This issue arises from the 18th-century grammarians' concern with developing a perfectly logical language—logical from the point of view of Latin grammar—and eliminating as many untidy English idioms as possible. If Campbell had not noticed it, this locution might now be considered simply another idiomatic usage. It certainly is a venial fault, since no reader is confused by the construction.

Let us look at a few examples:

> In Philadelphia she lived on Chestnut Hill, which considers itself as good if not better than the Main Line —*Life,* 15 Apr. 1940 (in Bryant 1962)

> . . . other slums, as bad or worse than those marked for obliteration —*N.Y. Times,* 1 Apr. 1954

> You will observe that I admire my own work as much if not more than anybody else does —Flannery O'Connor, letter, 4 May 1955

> . . . a rate it said was as good or better than conventional trains —*N.Y. Times,* 9 Apr. 1970

> . . . but the mayors have as good if not a better point —Glenn A. Briere, *Springfield* (Mass.) *Sunday Republican,* 1 Dec. 1985

These are the simple, or unpunctuated, variety of the expression. You can see that they are readily understandable and do not require correction on that score; the *as* that would follow the positive adjective if it were used alone has been omitted and the *than* that would normally follow the comparative has been retained—the proximate adjective has determined the choice of conjunction.

The construction can be found occasionally in a more elaborate and punctuated form:

> It was as great, or perhaps greater than the glow that came when, as a cub, he read his first paragraph in the paper —Stanley Walker, *N.Y. Herald Tribune Book Rev.,* 19 Oct. 1941

This is a perplexing example. It can be reasonably argued that since the adjectives are being separated by a comma, the second *as* should not have been omitted. And there should have been a comma after *greater,* which perhaps the typesetter left out inadvertently. If your comparative is going to be elaborated enough to require that you interrupt the flow of the sentence with commas, you might do well to insert the balancing *as.*

With the insertion of punctuation, however, you can stumble into a different problem. In the following example, the *or more* seems to have been an afterthought.

The *as* of the positive has been retained, and no *than* supplied for the comparative:

> ... the first step towards making bookselling there as much, or more, of a profession as it is in other countries —*Publishers Weekly,* 10 Feb. 1951

We think that the *as good or better than* construction is probably simply a long-lived English idiom; it need not be routinely revised out of general writing that does not strive for elevation. If you disagree, and prefer your constructions always unelided, there are at least two things you can do. We will use an example from Bernstein 1977 for illustration:

> ... a giant rocket with lifting power as great or greater than the Saturn 5's.

The time-honored suggestion is to supply the missing *as;* supplying it will require two commas:

> ... a giant rocket with lifting power as great as, or greater than, the Saturn 5's.

Bernstein thinks this solution a bit "on the prissy side." He suggests as an alternative putting the *or greater* at the end; it will need to be set off with a comma.

> ... a giant rocket with lifting power as great as the Saturn 5's, or greater.

He finds this solution more graceful than the first. He also suggests that the following revision is a way out, if you don't like all the commas:

> ... a giant rocket with lifting power at least as great as the Saturn 5's.

as great or greater than   See AS GOOD OR BETTER THAN.

as how   *As how* is aspersed by Phythian 1979 as incorrect and by Copperud 1970 as substandard for *that.* It is neither, however. It is simply dialectal: the OED characterizes it as southern (English) dialect; the Dictionary of American Regional English calls it chiefly Southern and Midland. It has had some literary use by Tobias Smollett (*Roderick Random,* 1748; *Humphry Clinker,* 1771), Captain Marryat (*Peter Simple* 1834), Bret Harte (*The Luck of Roaring Camp,* 1870), and Edward Eggleston (*The Hoosier Schoolmaster,* 1871). We have little evidence of current literary use.

It is found in the combinations *being as how* and *seeing as how,* and is also fairly common after *allow:*

> She didn't know I had sent it to her ... but she allowed as how she liked the book —Flannery O'Connor, letter, 24 Jan. 1962

This expression has current use in journalism and especially political journalism perhaps, as Reader's Digest 1983 suggests, for its "mildly satirical effect." Or perhaps it aims simply to provide an air of studied informality:

> Nixon allowed as how the best way to knock Romney down in the polls was to remove his winner status by beating him in New Hampshire —William Safire, *Before The Fall* (cited in Reader's Digest 1983)

> Premier Chou expressed cordiality toward the United States but allowed as how neither he nor ... Chairman Mao ... are planning American visits —

John Hughes, *Christian Science Monitor,* 10 Oct. 1972

It is also used to ascribe a countrified air to someone indirectly quoted:

> The man came, measured the height and girth of the tree, and allowed as how this was one of the most firmly rooted junipers he'd ever seen —Gordon Kahn, *Atlantic,* December 1947

> Even the nurseryman was uncertain of its exact origin, although he did allow as how it was a local product —Michael Olmert, *Horticulture,* February 1983

Asian, Asiatic, Oriental   As we move toward the end of the 20th century, *Asian* is the preferred word, noun or adjective, especially for ethnic purposes; *Asiatic* is held to be at least mildly offensive. For evidence we have Fowler 1965, Foster 1968, Copperud 1970, 1980, Harper 1975, 1985, and several dictionaries, both British and American. How this state of affairs came about is curious.

Asian is the slightly older word (1599 to *Asiatic*'s 1602), but the younger and longer word gradually replaced the older and shorter word. Our files, for instance, show no examples of *Asian* from about World War I to the 1940s. In the 1940s, however, *Asian* began a comeback. The reason was that the use of *Asiatic* as a racial designation began to be considered offensive, especially as associated with British or American colonial policies; persons and groups interested in appealing to or at least in not offending the downtrodden began using *Asian* instead. The Communists, for instance, switched their slogan from "Asia for the Asiatics" to "Asia for the Asians" during the 1940s. Sir Ernest Gowers in Fowler 1965 notes that *Asiatic* had always had a "contemptuous nuance" clinging to it from a literary use to describe an ornate prose style (Gowers mentions Matthew Arnold as having used it) which was unfavorably contrasted with a plainer one styled *Attic.* But the disreputable literary odor probably had little to do with the modern switch to *Asian;* that seems to have had primarily a political motivation.

Although *Asian* began to reappear in our citations during the 1940s, the reasons behind the switch did not begin to surface here until about 1950, when citations turn up from India and Australia as well as the U.S. A *New Yorker* writer in October 1950 caught the *Daily Worker* criticizing Walter Lippmann for writing "Asiatic forces" and then using *Asiatic* themselves a few issues later.

Whatever appeal the longer form seems to have has kept *Asiatic* from falling into disuse; we find it, for instance, used by some British writers interchangeably with *Asian* as a geographical designator:

> But according to Herodotus Chalcedon on the Asiatic side of the Bosporus was founded seventeen years before Byzantium. ... If its founding fathers had had eyes, they would not have chosen the inferior site on the Asian side of the Bosporus —Howard 1980

A correspondent criticized Dear Abby for using *Asiatic* in 1979. And we still have some evidence that the word is used neutrally:

> Let me tell you one of the difficulties. An English writer can say, I went to Salisbury and began to live in a cottage, but it's very hard for me to do that in that bald way. An Asiatic from the Caribbean mov-

ing near Stonehenge—if you're writing about it, it needs to be explained —V. S. Naipaul, quoted in *N.Y. Times Book Rev.,* 16 Sept. 1984

But most writers choose *Asian.*

There is an interesting situation developing in African English. In white-controlled South Africa *Asiatic* is a standard racial designation; in many black-controlled countries the official term is *Asian.* But in both instances the people so designated are discriminated against politically. Will *Asian* too become an offensive term?

Safire 1986 mentions that *Oriental* as a noun designating a person is felt to be offensive. We have relatively little evidence of such use, but what we have does not seem to be diminishing yet. We believe Safire is the only usage commentator so far to have mentioned the matter, although it also drew attention in a *TV Guide* article (13 Jan. 1984). Writers should be aware that *Oriental* may be becoming a touchy term.

aside from   *Aside from* is a compound preposition found in American English; some writers hold it to be the American equivalent of *apart from* (which see), but both British and American writers use *apart from.*

> Aside from bending into a stance, which is good for most waistlines, there is considerable walking in our game —Willie Mosconi, *Winning Pocket Billiards,* 1965

> Aside from the members of the society, millions read the magazines involved in the debate —Georgie Anne Geyer, *Saturday Rev.,* 25 Dec. 1971

> . . . but aside from these two teachers there was no great offering of courses at the graduate level —Samuel Flagg Bemis, *The New-England Galaxy,* Fall 1969

> Aside from being six feet tall, my image seemed inappropriate —Robben W. Fleming, *Michigan Business Rev.,* July 1968

You will note that in the first two examples *aside from* mean "besides" and in the second two "except for." Lurie 1927 gives an example, perhaps manufactured, where the first was intended but the second could be readily understood:

> Miss Robinson will enter the speaking contest and will read her selection. Aside from this, a very interesting program will be given.

The example seems a bit contrived, but you can see that misunderstanding might be possible. Make your context clear.

as if, as though   1. At one time the propriety of *as though* used for *as if* was considered dubious. Bierce 1909 damns the locution with faint recognition, mentioning that *as though* does have its defenders. Bernstein wrestled with the problem in a 1957 *Winners & Sinners;* by Bernstein 1971 he has accepted it. Everyone else who even mentions the matter finds *as though* and *as if* interchangeable.

2. What Bierce did not notice was that his example of *as though*—"She wept as though her heart was broken."— follows *as though* with a verb in the indicative mood. Several commentators insist on the subjunctive. Fowler 1926 considered the indicative an illiteracy (he condemned the future after *as though* equally). Simon 1980 plumps for the subjunctive; Flesch 1964 says the subjunctive is extinct after *as if* and *as though.* A number of other commentators (such as Harper 1985, Janis 1984, Scott, Foresman 1981) allow either the indicative or the subjunctive, reserving the subjunctive for formal occasions (newspaper reporting counts as formal in Harper).

Evidence in our files shows both subjunctive and indicative in frequent respectable use. There seems to be little difference in formality. Some examples:

> . . . it seemed to me as if every other man was sensible —Irving Wallace, *The Writer,* November 1968

> It is as if there were some psychic healing tissue — Irving Wallace, *The Writer,* November 1968

> . . . as though the eyes and brain are undistorting windows —Richard Gregory, *Times Literary Supp.,* 23 June 1972

> . . . as though there were no distinction —Philip Roth, *Reading Myself and Others,* 1975

> . . . felt as if he was being observed —E. L. Doctorow, *Ragtime,* 1975

> . . . as though she were inviting us to watch her — Mollie Panter-Downes, *New Yorker,* 4 Nov. 1985

3. See also LIKE, AS, AS IF.

as is   Harper 1985 reminds us that *as is,* most frequently used of goods to be sold, is always singular, regardless of the number of items, since it is almost always used adverbially or adjectivally.

> . . . sold on an "as is" basis —Diana Shaman, *N.Y. Times,* 20 Apr. 1980

> . . . made up of odds and ends; sold as is —Henry M. Ellis, *Stamps for Fun and Profit,* 1953

ask   Evans 1957 notes that *ask* may be followed by an infinitive or a clause:

> . . . was asked to arrange and perform the music for the sound track —*Current Biography,* October 1966

> . . . sent my brother upstairs to ask that I switch to the news —Otto Friedrich, *Harper's,* May 1971

> . . . asks whether the appointment of chaplains to the two Houses of Congress is "consistent with the Constitution. . . ." —Joseph L. Blau, *Rev. of Religion,* No. 3, 1950

Raub 1897 prescribes as follows: "Ask *of* a person, *for* what is wanted, *after* one's health."

> . . . if you ask it of him, he returns a hasty negative —Henry Fairlie, *N.Y. Times Mag.,* 11 July 1965

> . . . the two or three people of whom I asked his whereabouts —F. Scott Fitzgerald, *The Great Gatsby,* 1925

Of may also be used with inanimate objects:

> Comfort, beauty, and spacesaving efficiency are the three big things we ask of our rooms —*Better Homes and Gardens,* June 1954

From may be similarly used:

> . . . an increasing number were asking many things from philosophy —Henry O. Taylor, *The Mediaeval Mind,* 4th ed., 1925

For does indeed take what is wanted as its object:

> ... getting a reasonable portion of what it was asking for —Philip D. Lang, quoted in *Change,* January–February, 1971

> Just yesterday a letter came in from a girl your age in South Carolina asking for biographical material —James Thurber, letter, 4 Jan. 1958

Ask for is often used idiomatically with *trouble* or *it* in a figurative sense:

> Dili had been asking for trouble ever since she left school —Richard Vaughan, *Moulded in Earth,* 1951

> "You certainly made an ass of me today, Eloise. But I kept reminding myself that I was the one who had asked for it. . . ." —Louis Auchincloss, *A Law for the Lion,* 1953

After is indeed for health:

> You ask after my health —Lord Byron, letter, 9 Sept. 1811

> Another time a friend asked after King George VI's health —H. Durant Osborne, *Springfield* (Mass.) *Union,* 24 Mar. 1955

When information is sought, *ask* is often used with the preposition *about:*

> The truck driver would have asked about me in the drugstore —Phil Stong, *New England Journeys,* No. 3, 1955

When *ask* means "invite" it may be used with the adverb *out* or the preposition *to:*

> ... the other young men in Sargentville asked Ann out —Charles Bracelen Flood, *Omnibook,* June 1954

> ... they were known collectively as the Grateful Hearts but seldom asked to the house —Osbert Lancaster, *All Done From Memory,* 1953

as long as, so long as   It is a little hard to understand the objection that some textbooks used to make to *as long as;* Evans 1957 says it is not used in formal prose with the meaning "since," but Bryant 1962 and dictionaries find it standard.

> As long as they were there, they might as well be teaching —J. Kirk Sale, *Change,* July–August 1969

As long as and *so long as* are simply variants. Evans foung *so long as* much less common, but Bryant and our files show them to be roughly equal in frequency. *So long as* does not seem to be much used in the sense "since." The two are used pretty much interchangeably in the sense "provided that" and in the more literal sense "for the period of time that."

> There was no reason why industry could not do the job as long as it realized the size of the job to be done —*Time,* 7 Jan. 1946

> But so long as allowance for this is made it forms an obvious starting point —*Times Literary Supp.,* 14 May 1970

> As long as there are sovereign nations possessing great power, war is inevitable —Albert Einstein, *Atlantic,* November 1945

> I put it off as long as I can —William Faulkner, 5 June 1957, in *Faulkner in the University,* 1959

> So long as the wind blows the air away in the morning you don't have a pollution problem —Dr. Ruth Patrick, quoted in *Smithsonian,* August 1970

> And they'll stick around so long as sales of subsidiary rights ... bring in more money —Charles Kaiser, *Saturday Rev.,* August 1981

as much or more than   See AS GOOD OR BETTER THAN.

as of   It is a bit surprising how often you scratch a disapproved locution and find an Americanism that some British commentator has castigated. *As of* appears to be such a one:

> Let me now turn to the strange American delusion that the words "as of" can always be used before a date as if they were a temporal preposition. . . . An additional illiteracy is introduced when the words "as of" precede not a date, but the adverb "now." "As of now" is a barbarism which only a love of illiteracy for its own sake can explain. What is generally meant is "at present." —Lord Conesford, *Saturday Evening Post,* 13 July 1957

American commentators soon appeared in support of Lord Conesford's view: Copperud 1964, Flesch 1964, Follett 1966, Nickles 1974, Barzun 1985, and newspaper columnist Sally Bright in September 1986.

The first thing we must point out about *as of* is that even Lord Conesford and Barzun recognize that it has a legitimate use—"restricted," Barzun calls it. It is used when something in a letter or other writing carries a different date than that of the document itself.

> Statistics as of June 30, 1943 —*Britannica Book of the Year 1944*

> The tractors, said he, were costing Ford more to make than Ferguson paid for them. So Breech ended the contract, as of June 30 —*Time,* 21 July 1947

> This article was written and published by the Center in 1957. In the present version I have revised the figures as of the end of 1967 —Adolf A. Berle, *Center Mag.,* January 1969

The function of *as of* in these examples was explained by a Merriam editor in 1939 as "indicating an arbitrary, often official, designation for record or convenience . . . ." Another aspect of the arbitrariness underlined by *as of* is that the date given may not be precisely accurate: a heading such as "Balance as of August 31" may mean no more than "Balance at the end of business in the month of August" since the 31st may fall on a Sunday or some other day when the business is closed.

This use of *as of* need never be avoided; it constitutes the bulk of our printed evidence for the phrase. You should be aware that most of our evidence comes from business sources—annual reports and such—and from reference sources—*Current Biography, Britannica Book of the Year,* etc.—with occasional evidence from the news media.

There is another use, chiefly oral, of *as of.* In this use *as of* occurs with words relating to time other than dates; these words include the adverb *now* mentioned by Lord Conesford. Some examples:

> ... an almost morbid resemblance to the Roosevelt–Landon figures as of about this time in 1936 —Elmo Roper, quoted in *Time,* 13 Sept. 1948

Santayana's *The Last Puritan,* of a wider range, ends as of a period two decades earlier than the other two —Lucian Price, *Dialogues of Alfred North Whitehead,* 1954

I am saying, as of now anyway, that Ross never knew of Fleischmann's offer of his job to you —James Thurber, letter, 7 Aug. 1958

Dr. Edward Teller announced that "the best scientists as of this moment are not in the United States but in Moscow." —*Current Biography,* November 1964

Notwithstanding Lord Conesford's easy generalization, Roper and Whitehead and Thurber and Teller are not showing a love of illiteracy for its own sake—they are simply using an ordinary idiom. The idiom seems to be American, but Whitehead was an Englishman— maybe he picked it up while he was at Harvard. Brief idioms like *as of,* made up usually of particles, regularly serve two purposes in the language: they serve as spacers between the context words, and they give the mouth something to do while the brain races to keep ahead. It is true that they often add little to written discourse. It is equally true that there is no reason to try to expunge all traces of speech patterns from your writing, unless special circumstances compel you to write very compactly.

as per *As per* is a compound preposition whose origins are somewhat obscure. It appears to have originated sometime during the 19th century, probably in that area of life where business and law intersect: contracts, bills of exchange, and the like. We have very little actual 19th-century evidence, no one seems to have paid any attention to the phrase until the 1920s, when it turns up in a few glossaries in such phrases as *as per advice* and *as per invoice.* About the same time it also pops up in Whipple 1924 and Krapp 1927 as a term to be avoided. Such later commentators as have troubled to notice *as per*—Partridge 1942, Janis 1984, Freeman 1983, Guth 1985—belong to the avoidance school, but many apparently are not sufficiently troubled by it to give it space.
 In the May 1926 issue of *American Speech,* Maurice H. Weseen reported that *as per* was on its way out of use in business correspondence. The business letter, said Weseen, was no longer considered a formal legal document, and legalistic jargon was falling out of use in it. His crystal ball seems to have been somewhat clouded, since we find *as per* being used more than a half century later in about the same ways it was in 1926. If Weseen seems to have thought business letters were becoming less formal, Freeman 1983 thinks the opposite: he thinks *as per* inappropriate in formal style. Whether *as per* is too formal or not formal enough, it has caused little trouble in the legal world. It is defined in various law citations as meaning "in accordance with" or "in accordance with the terms of." It is not listed in David Mellinkoff's *The Language of the Law* (1963) as a troublesome term.
 We find *as per* used in two ways. It is still in use in business correspondence and in straightforward but somewhat stiff prose similar to such correspondence:

The second flight singles out a rear element, as per training method —H. H. Arnold & Ira C. Eaker, *Army Flyer,* 5th ed., 1942

The computer justifies and hyphenates the copy as per typographical specifications —John Markus, *American Documentation,* April 1966

... perform a few moves with this as per the sleight of hand section in this book —Ian Adair, *Conjuring as a Craft,* 1970

Just pre-heat or pre-chill as per directions on the bottom —mail order catalog, Spring 1980

More curious, perhaps, is the use of *as per* in contexts quite unlike business letters or "how-to" prose. Some of these examples are using the business-letter style for fun.

Here we were arranged at table as per diagram — Henry Adams, letter, 17 May 1859

I note, as per your esteemed letter, that you cannot beg —George Bernard Shaw, letter, 2 Apr. 1913

When we say we do not like big girls, as per our letter of yesterday, we do not mean ... —H. L. Mencken, in *The Intimate Notebooks of George Jean Nathan,* 1932

The opening scene is fantastic. The Devil calling in his coach as per family arrangement for the Marquis —*Times Literary Supp.,* 8 Feb. 1936

When challenged by the Committee for Nuclear Responsibility for not having properly inserted the negative points in the A.E.C. statement—as per President Nixon's shiny new Environmental Policy Act —*New Yorker,* 20 Nov. 1971

As our class of Old Blues sang "For God, for Country and for Yale" and (as per tradition) waved our pocket handkerchiefs —Carll Tucker, *Saturday Rev.,* 22 July 1978

Your decision to use *as per* or not would seem to be a matter of personal choice and taste; the tonal needs of a particular passage may make it useful at times even if you avoid it ordinarily.
 See also PER.

aspiration *Aspiration,* says Bernstein 1965, takes *toward* or sometimes *after.* He is apparently talking about older literary, rather than modern, use. *Aspiration* is usually not used with a preposition now, except the expected *of* that shows whose aspirations are being talked about. When a preposition is used, it will most likely be *for:*

... the aspirations of Alexander for the Bosporus — *Times Literary Supp.,* 4 Jan. 1952

... those who have no power aspirations for themselves —Harry Levinson, *Think,* May–June 1967

The natural aspiration for justice —*The Autobiography of William Allen White,* 1946

... designs and aspirations for national or social betterment —John Galsworthy, *The Inn of Tranquility,* 1912

... the aspiration of decent Americans for a just and lasting peace —Bruce Bliven, *New Republic,* 22 Nov. 1954

Of is used, followed by a gerund:

... with logical aspirations of getting there —William H. Whyte, Jr., *Is Anybody Listening?,* 1952

... Oak Ridge's aspiration of becoming an ordinary place —Daniel Lang, *New Yorker,* 31 Oct. 1953

We had aspirations of winning the NCAA championship this year —Wayne Vandenburg, quoted in *Sports Illustrated,* 15 July 1968

To may be used followed by either a noun or an infinitive:

... wide-eyed aspirations to become a television star —Richard Corbin, *The Teaching of Writing in Our Schools,* 1966

... aspirations to objectivity —*Times Literary Supp.,* 19 Feb. 1971

... the aspiration to touch the superlative in one's work —Oliver Wendell Holmes d. 1935, letter, 12 July 1921

Aspiration may be followed by a clause:

... the aspiration that gainful activities should be socially serviceable —J. M. Clark, *Yale Rev.,* Autumn 1953

Toward is also found:

The aspiration of America is still upward, toward a better job —Bernard DeVoto, *The World of Fiction,* 1950

aspire Bernstein 1965 will allow us *to, after,* and *toward* as prepositions; Raub 1897, *to* and *after;* Evans 1957, the infinitive. All are in use except for *after,* of which we have no evidence in the Merriam-Webster files and which is unattested after 1794 in the OED. *At* is attested a bit later:

... others aspired at nothing beyond his remembering the catchword, and the first line of his speech — Jane Austen, *Mansfield Park,* 1814

To is the predominant preposition:

... the social class to which they aspire —James Sledd, in *The English Language Today,* ed. Sidney Greenbaum, 1985

... students who do not aspire to graduate school — Nicholas S. Thompson, *Change,* October 1971

... aspire to prestigious cultural properties —Pauline Kael, *Harper's,* February 1969

... the Russian aspires to hard, materialist, dialectically sound explanations —Arthur Miller, *Harper's,* September 1969

... a wife who aspires to the style of life affected by her sister —*Playboy,* April 1966

... Romans who aspired to philosophy —Benjamin Farrington, *Greek Science,* 1953

To followed by the infinitive is also common:

Aspiring to be the leader of a nation of third-rate men —H. L. Mencken, *Prejudices: Second Series,* 1920

... aspired to become a professional breeder of ferrets —Sherwood Anderson, *Winesburg, Ohio,* 1919

In a country that aspires to be democratic —Robert M. Hutchins, *Center Mag.,* March 1968

... those who merely aspire to clean up a mess — Aldous Huxley, *Brave New World Revisited,* 1958

Toward and *towards* are both found:

... it aspires toward a ritualization of conflict — Irving Howe, *Harper's,* April 1970

... the literary values towards which he aspired — *Times Literary Supp.,* 25 Jan. 1968

For is sometimes used:

The Administration still seems to aspire for what is vaguely called an honorable agreement —J. William Fulbright, *The Progressive,* June 1969

as regards See REGARD 1.

assay, essay Copperud 1970, 1980 tells us these verbs are sometimes confused; the Oxford American Dictionary warns us against confusing them; Shaw 1975 exhibits the differences. Fowler 1926 says that the two verbs tend to be differentiated, and we think his summing-up of the situation comes very close to the truth. *Assay* is usually used in the sense of "test, evaluate" and *essay* in the sense "try, attempt." The differentiation, to use Fowler's word, is not complete, however.

The two verbs are etymologically the same; one of the earliest senses of *assay* was "try, attempt":

And when Saul was come to Jerusalem, he assayed to join himself to the disciples —Acts 9:26 (AV), 1611

     ... assayed
To stanch the blood
—John Dryden, *Stanzas on Oliver Cromwell,* 1658

This older variant still occasionally is used in current English:

... the most versatile writer that has ever assayed to use the dialect —Henry Hess Reichard, in *The Pennsylvania Germans,* ed. Ralph Wood, 1942

... has assayed to penetrate a field that by its very nature requires consummate skill —John W. Chase, *N.Y. Times Book Rev.,* 25 July 1954

How they accomplished this was a mystery, for they would draw the canvas curtains about his bed before they assayed such a task —Bette Howland, *Commentary,* August 1972

But *essay* is the more usual spelling for the "try" sense. We would suggest that you use *essay* to avoid puzzling your readers. Here are a couple of the more usual uses of *assay* in its figurative application:

... she would walk to the full-length mirror and assay herself —Mary McCarthy, *New Yorker,* 23 Mar. 1957

... I try to assay the man's or woman's importance —Alden Whitman, *Saturday Rev.,* 11 Dec. 1971

assent When the verb *assent* takes a preposition, it is *to:*

They did not readily assent to the selection —Irving Louis Horowitz, *Change,* January–February 1970

It is difficult now to assent to Lamb's words —T. S. Eliot, "John Ford," in *Selected Essays,* 1932

... in assenting to dance she had made a mistake of some kind —Thomas Hardy, *The Mayor of Casterbridge,* 1886

assimilate Bernstein 1965 says that *assimilate* takes *to* and infrequently *with;* this is true as far as it goes. *To* is indeed the most frequent preposition:

... helping them assimilate to the conditions of urban American life —Louis Berkowitz, quoted in *N.Y. Times,* 22 May 1980

... expounding a science, or a body of truth which he seeks to assimilate to a science —*Selected Writings Of Benjamin N. Cardozo,* ed. Margaret E. Hall, 1947

... felt an aristocratic horror for anything that assimilated a man to a craftsman —Havelock Ellis, *The Dance of Life,* 1923

Our manufacturing class was assimilated in no time to the conservative classes —H. G. Wells, *Mr. Britling Sees It Through,* 1916

But Mr. Eliot was the one who assimilated the French achievement to English literature —H. Marshall McLuhan, *Sewanee Rev.,* Winter 1947

Into is the next most frequently used preposition:

Jews who had assimilated into German, Russian and other cultures —Elenore Lester, *N.Y. Times Mag.,* 2 Dec. 1979

The Italian brilliance of execution was soon assimilated into the Russian style —Ivor Guest, *The Dancer's Heritage,* 1960

In order to be assimilated into a collective medium a person has to be stripped of his individual distinctness —Eric Hoffer, *The True Believer,* 1951

... poetry which attempted to assimilate the catastrophic events of the World War into the individual and social consciousness —Fred B. Millett, *Contemporary British Literature,* 3d ed., rev., 1944

By, as you would expect, indicates the agent:

... I was educated in, and assimilated by, the very bosom of the Yankee motherland —James Fallows, *Harper's,* February 1976

... conquered and forcibly assimilated by the West —Arnold J. Toynbee, *Horizon,* August 1947

With, in, and *as* are quite infrequent:

As the matured area assimilated itself with the region just to the east —Ray Allen Billington, *Westward Expansion,* 1949

Some of the present hard-core unemployed can be assimilated in industry —Henry Ford II, *Michigan Business Rev.,* July 1968

Countless Chinese have truly been assimilated as Americans —Mary Ellen Leary, *Atlantic,* March 1970

assist 1. A Japanese correspondent wrote us a few years ago asking about the verb complements that go with the transitive verb *assist* and a direct object. He was puzzled because the reference works in which he had looked up these constructions differed as to the propriety of *assist* followed by the object and *to* and the infinitive, or the infinitive without *to.* Evans 1957, for instance, says that the infinitive forms are not standard; other sources our correspondent quoted found them standard, and one declared the construction formal.

On investigating the subject, we found that it has not been especially well documented. Here, therefore, are examples—several supplied by our correspondent—of the chief verb complements that occur with *assist.*

The most commonly met construction is *assist* + object + *in* + gerund:

The main effort, however, is to assist these young people in obtaining employment —James B. Conant, *Slums and Suburbs,* 1961

... call upon our allies ... to assist this country in formulating a program of land reform —Representative Morris K. Udall, in *A Center Occasional Paper,* June 1968

These same techniques assisted him in evaluating the molecular structure —*Current Biography 1949*

Children are assisted in making notes —*American Guide Series: Minnesota,* 1938

Standard but somewhat less common is *assist* + object + *to* + infinitive:

Mr. A. is assisting his wife to show a book of photographic portraits —*Punch* (in Poutsma 1904–26)

And a spanking will probably assist you to bear that in mind —Clarence Day, *Life With Mother,* 1937 (from correspondent)

... assisted slum schools ... to demonstrate that ... —M. A. Farber, *N.Y. Times,* 9 Jan. 1969

... it may assist some tourists to set out with a better appreciation —*N.Y. Times,* 9 May 1952

Still less frequent is *assist* + object + infinitive (without *to*):

... an information service to assist British publishers and audio-visual manufacturers make contact with appropriate Japanese bodies, both trade and professional —Catalog, Tokyo English Language Book Fair, 1980 (from correspondent)

... we have with the benefit of informed advice tried to assist the developing world gain a better understanding of its language problems —Melvin J. Fox & Betty P. Skolnick, *Ford Foundation Report,* 1975

Sometimes *assist* occurs without a noun or pronoun object but with *to* and an infinitive complement:

... it is also true that they assist to give the place its character —Alfred Buchanan (1907), in *Wanderers in Australia,* ed. Colin Roderick, 1949

"... I assisted to carry him there." —Dorothy L. Sayers, *Murder Must Advertise,* 1933

... which suggested that imagination had often assisted to improve memory —Antony Flew, *A New Approach to Psychical Research,* 1953

2. When *assist* means "to be present," it regularly takes *at:*

The lady is one of the most intelligent and best-bred persons I have known in any country. We assisted at her conversazione, which was numerous —Tobias Smollett, *Travels Through France and Italy,* 1766

The picture of a saint being slowly flayed alive . . . will not produce the same physical sensations of sickening disgust that a modern man would feel if he could assist at the actual event —Roger Fry, *Vision and Design,* 1920

She waited there, hesitant, not exactly on the watch, not exactly unwilling to assist at an interview between Amy and Amy's mistress —Arnold Bennett, *The Old Wives' Tale,* 1908

. . . compare the ugly, grinning peasant bystanders surrounding an Adoration or a Nativity in northern painting with the ideal figures assisting at Italian holy scenes —Mary McCarthy, *Occasional Prose,* 1985

It is not certain that every *assist at* means no more than "to be present at":

The Russian party moves through the streets at a clip that suggests they have been called to assist at a rather serious fire —Mollie Panter-Downes, *New Yorker,* 5 May 1956

. . . invited me to assist at the burning of a huge pile of manuscripts —Henry Miller, *The Air-Conditioned Nightmare,* 1945

My conscience stirs as if, in my impulse to do violence to my enemy, I had assisted at his crime — Katherine Anne Porter, *The Never-Ending Wrong,* 1977

When *assist* clearly means "help," however, *in* and *with* are usual. *In* can be used before a noun or a gerund:

The teacher, college students, and seventh-grade students all assist in the project —Rexine A. Langen, *The Instructor,* March 1968

. . . was assisted in the preparation of a manual — *Annual Report, National Bureau of Standards,* 1950

. . . have assisted in making plans —Robert M. Hutchins, *Center Mag.,* September 1969

. . . turned to stage design in 1948, when he assisted Salvador Dali with the extraordinary sets —*Current Biography,* December 1964

The Captain and the cook was playing a duet on the mouth harp while your correspondent assisted with the vocals —Richard Bissell, *Atlantic,* December 1954

A few other prepositions—*to, into, by* (+ gerund)—are found occasionally:

. . . the artist could assist all humanity to a similar flight —Thomas Munro, *The Arts and Their Interrelations,* 1949

. . . a fetish used to assist a childless woman to fertility —R. E. Kirk, *Introduction to Zuni Fetishism,* 1943

. . . 120 (24 per cent) were assisted into the world by instrumental and other operative methods —Ira S. Wile & Rose Davis, in *Personality in Nature, Society, and Culture,* ed. Clyde Kluckhohn & Henry A. Murray, 1948

. . . assisted the war effort by broadcasting messages —*Current Biography 1947*

Towards was formerly used:

He never . . . heard a circumstance, which might assist towards her moral instruction that he did not haste to tell it her —Mrs. Elizabeth Inchbald, *Nature and Art,* 1796

3. Most of the quibbles about the propriety of this or that sense of *assist* have receded into the past. The propriety of *assist at* meaning "be present at" was an exciting issue in the 1920s—Fowler 1926, Krapp 1927, Lurie 1927 all discussed it—but no one seems to care any more. In the 1940s it was fashionable to call *assist* overworked and recommend *help* instead. Since *help* in the Brown Corpus (Kučera & Francis 1967) appears more than 14 times as often as *assist,* that recommendation need give you no pause.

as such Copperud 1970 notes a couple of his sources find *as such* sometimes used meaninglessly; Evans 1957 makes the same observation. "The test of its utility," says Copperud, "is to leave the expression out and decide whether anything is lost." You must remember, though, that what is lost may not be meaning but a desired rhythm or emphasis. The real test of utility here is made by your ear—the question is not only whether the sentence will stand without *as such* but also whether it sounds better to you with the phrase in or out. Here are a few examples you may judge. In the first, *as such* is used for emphasis, and the speaker obviously thought it essential to his meaning:

The U.S. has no commitment and no purpose to defend the coastal islands as such. I repeat, as such —John Foster Dulles, quoted in *Time,* 28 Feb. 1955

The love of humanity as such is mitigated by violent dislike of the next-door neighbor —*The Wit and Wisdom of Alfred North Whitehead,* ed. A. H. Johnson, 1947

I suppose that the reason why a philosophical theory of the nature of error as such is rejected . . . —John E. Smith, *New Republic,* 29 Nov. 1954

The author's emphasis, then, is not on Moslem resurgence as such but on the prevailing unrest among the Moslems —E. A. Speiser, *Yale Rev.,* Autumn 1954

. . . the absence of a general perspective, an indication of the way in which legal controls as such operate —Ian Brownlie, *Times Literary Supp.,* 22 May 1981

assume, presume Many commentators are at pains to distinguish these two words; besides the ones listed in Copperud 1970 we have Freeman 1983, Bremner 1980, Janis 1984, Einstein 1985, Shaw 1975, Macmillan 1982, and Chambers 1985. Freeman tells us that the two are generally synonymous, which is not accurate. The two words are generally synonymous only in one sense of each. Any good dictionary will show you when they are and when they are not synonymous. The difference in shading and emphasis that distinguishes the two words in their shared sense should also be clear from the dictionary definitions. These are from *Webster's Ninth New Collegiate Dictionary:*

assume . . . **5** : to take as granted or true : SUPPOSE presume ... 2 : to expect or assume esp. with confidence

In other words, *presume* tends to be more positive in its supposition than *assume.* This is not true, however, in the famous legal catch phrase of "presumed innocent until proved guilty." That sense is separately defined in the Ninth Collegiate as

3 : to suppose to be true without proof

It is worth observing that *assume* has more meanings than *presume* and is a much more frequently used word.

Here are a few examples of *assume* and *presume* used in the shared sense.

He assumed that he could negotiate with Mitterrand, the way he would have negotiated with a sharp investment banker —Jane Kramer, *New Yorker,* 18 Jan. 1982

... the conversation implicitly assumes that Oxford is the centre of the universe —Harold J. Laski, letter, 1 May 1932

As long as people assumed that learning a language was the product of an advanced intelligence, scholars were reluctant to place the birth of language too far in the past —Edmund Blair Bolles, *Saturday Rev.,* 18 Mar. 1972

... had always assumed that the last volumes would be distinctive, simply because of their sources — *Times Literary Supp.,* 19 Feb. 1971

Because of her intransigent radicalism, many Catholic reformers assume she is on their side when they press for drastic changes inside the Church — Dwight Macdonald, *N.Y. Rev. of Books,* 28 Jan. 1971

Nobody in Baskul had known much about him except that he had arrived from Persia, where it was presumed he had something to do with oil —James Hilton, *Lost Horizon,* 1933

... the reading public, who might be presumed to know that dynamite and poison have a certain deadly quality —Sir Norman Birkett, *Books of the Month,* June–July 1953

Of course, Eloise would never presume that they could still be friends —Louis Auchincloss, *A Law for the Lion,* 1953

Granite shot was used for guns in Plymouth in the sixteenth century, and it may be presumed that these are of similar date —E. Estyn Evans, *Irish Digest,* June 1954

You can see that the two words would be interchangeable in some of the examples in this way: *assume* could have been used in every instance for *presume,* but something would have been lost in so doing. However, *presume* could not very easily be substituted in the examples of *assume.* Interchange would appear to be easier in one direction than the other—the less specific word can more readily replace the more specific the other way round.

assure 1. See ENSURE, INSURE, ASSURE.
2. A couple of commentators have different points to make about the syntax of *assure.* Copperud 1970 insists that it takes an object—and it does. Bernstein 1965 says *assure* takes *of,* and it also does that sometimes, as we shall see.

Assure can take an ordinary noun object:

... the most positive way available to assure ultimate success —Clinton F. Robinson, *Dun's,* January 1954

The direct object may also be a clause:

... mothers anxious to assure that their daughters get noticed socially —Vance Packard, *The Sexual Wilderness,* 1968

But most often *assure*—much like *promise*—takes two objects—a direct and an indirect. The indirect object can be a personal noun but is usually a pronoun. The direct object may be a noun:

... and thus assured it the entire vote of New York —*Dictionary of American Biography,* 1929

More often it will be a clause, with or without *that:*

... a car trader, who would assure us that our car could not possibly make the crossing —William Faulkner, *New England Journeys,* No. 2, 1954

Linda assured me this was a verbatim translation — Cobey Black, *Saturday Rev.,* 23 Oct. 1971

Sometimes the clause is replaced by a phrase with *of:*

... to assure them of academic due process —*AAUP Bulletin,* December 1967

as the crow flies Copperud 1970, 1980 reports two critics calling this expression a cliché and an archaism. This criticism is self-contradictory: if it is a cliché it is current, and if it is an archaism it is not current. Neither view seems justified with respect to writing; however, our evidence suggests this is a more common expression in speech than in writing.
Bernstein 1965 finds the phrase battered and asks why not say "in a straight line" or "by air." But the replacement will not always work well, as you will see if you try either of those substitutes in this fairly recent example:

The main access route, Forest Service Road 99, takes you to Windy Ridge, within 4 miles as the crow flies of the crater's edge, for a view into the smoking maw of the volcano —*Sunset,* June 1983

as though See AS IF, AS THOUGH.

as to 1. This homely little two-word preposition seems to trouble the writers of books on composition. McMahan & Day 1980, 1984 give a typical handbook injunction:

Many people feel that this phrase does nothing but clutter your sentence; they consider it a borrowing from the worst and wordiest of legalese. You can probably substitute the single word *about.*

Except for the reference to legalese, which is off base, essentially the same information is to be found in a dozen handbooks. It deserves examination. This wordy bit of clutter contains four letters, one blank space, two syllables. If we replace it with *about,* we have five letters, no space, two syllables. How much have we gained? Nothing—the example shown in Prentice-Hall 1978 shows that the substitution of *about* for *as to* makes the sentence set slightly longer. If we substitute *concerning* or *regarding,* recommended in James Gordon Bennett's

"Don't List" for the *New York Herald* (reprinted in Bernstein 1971), we have expended even more space and more syllables. Clearly, then, *wordy* can have reference to neither space nor syllable count.

The problem seems to be that *as to* is a compound preposition. Most of the criticism directed at it seems to have originated with H. W. Fowler. *The King's English* (1907) has a whole section devoted to the alarmingly increasing use of compound prepositions and conjunctions, and nearly a page is devoted to *as to*. Fowler 1926 treats it in even more detail—though in the later book he finds one use to be worthwhile. Most of Copperud 1970's summary comes from Fowler.

As to is found chiefly in four constructions: as an introducer (the use approved by Fowler and his followers) and to link a noun, an adjective, or a verb with following matter. These four examples of Dr. Johnson's conversation (from Boswell's *Life,* 1791) will illustrate them:

> He would begin thus: "Why, Sir, as to the good or evil of card playing—" "Now, (said Garrick,) he is thinking which side he shall take."

> Sir, there is no doubt as to peculiarities. . . .

> . . . the worst thing you can do to an author is to be silent as to his works.

> We are all agreed as to our own liberty. . . .

These constructions are all still current in standard English.

The OED gives Wycliffe (ca. 1375) as its earliest example of the preposition. It seems to have been kept in steady use by literary figures and others ever since. Here is a healthy sample from our files, covering the time from the late 17th century to the present:

> . . . with the proviso that he would not that night make any statement as to what the fleet would do —Dean Acheson, quoted in Merle Miller, *Plain Speaking,* 1973

> . . . she remembered the purport of her note, and was not less sanguine as to its effect than she had been the night before —Jane Austen, *Mansfield Park,* 1814

> But as to the letters, they were forced from him, and exposed —Aphra Behn, *The Fair Jilt,* 1688

> I doubted as to the last article of this eulogy —James Boswell, *Life of Samuel Johnson,* 1791

> . . . you don't agree with my view as to said photographer? —Lewis Carroll, letter, 1 Apr. 1887

> As to this new word with which he has dignified our language —Sir Winston Churchill, quoted by William Safire, *N.Y. Times Mag.,* 10 Oct. 1982

> As to the old one, I knew not what to do with him, he was so fierce —Daniel Defoe, *Robinson Crusoe,* 1719

> . . . a costly litigation . . . as to who should possess the Sirens cast up by the sea on the Grand Master's shores —Norman Douglas, *Siren Land,* 1911

> Look ye, madam, as to that slender particular of your virtue, we shan't quarrel about it —George Farquhar, *The Constant Couple,* 1699

The opinions of relatives as to a man's powers are very commonly of little value —Oliver Wendell Holmes d. 1894, *The Autocrat of the Breakfast-Table,* 1858

> . . . there were no special constitutional principles as to strong drink —Oliver Wendell Holmes d. 1935, letter, 20 May 1920

> . . . my relation with the reader, which was another affair altogether and as to which I felt no one to be trusted but myself —Henry James, *The Art of the Novel,* 1934

> . . . sounded me as to my willingness to be guardian to this William —Charles Lamb, letter, 1810

> . . . who were clear as to their goal and confident as to their victory —Lewis Mumford, *Technics and Civilization,* 1934

> Opportunistic as to means, he was tenaciously consistent as to ends —Allan Nevins & Henry Steele Commager, *The Pocket History of the U.S.,* 1942

> As to the money, which I care no more about than I do, say, my respiratory apparatus —John O'Hara, letter, Fall 1949

> I could not help speculating as to the possibility of my filling the vacancy —George Bernard Shaw, preface, *The Shaw–Terry letters,* 1931

> . . . counted up a phantom savings of $6 billion from rooting out fraud, waste and abuse without any serious recommendations as to how —David A. Stockman, *Newsweek,* 28 Apr. 1986

Even writers on usage use it:

> . . . needs to be deliberately considered and analyzed; first, as to the exact meaning, and then, as to the best method —Gould 1870

> . . . where are we to look for guidance as to correct English? —Leacock 1943

> . . . opinion as to the propriety of particular words —Lounsbury 1908

> Peremptory and unreasoned pronouncements as to what is bad English are not the least of the minor pests which vex our enlightened age —Fitzedward Hall, "English Rational and Irrational," 1880

We think that it should be self-evident that *as to* is not legalese, as those "some people" referred to by McMahan & Day think. Rather, it is a common compound preposition in wide use at every level of formality that apparently goes unnoticed by usage commentators, except in places where they are displeased by it.

All of the constructions used by Dr. Johnson are still current. You can use any of them when they sound right to you.

2. One of the chief complaints made about *as to* is its superfluity in many instances especially when used in front of such conjunctions as *how, why,* and *whether:*

> . . . the question as to how they should be referred to —H. L. Mencken, in *Essays on Language and Usage,* ed. Leonard F. Dean & Kenneth G. Wilson, 2d ed., 1963

> The issue raised by the word is as to how the understanding is done—what parts you have to be con-

scious of —William Empson, *The Structure of Complex Words,* 1951

. . . it should be clear as to why Joyce could find no inspiration in a cultural renaissance that found so much of theme and subject in a legendary Irish past —James T. Farrell, *The League of Frightened Philistines,* 1945

The most frequent of these constructions is with *whether:*

My uncertainty as to whether *I* can so manage as to go *personally* —Lord Byron, letter, 7 Apr. 1823

. . . there ensued a long conversation as they walked as to whether waiters made more in actual wages than in tips —F. Scott Fitzgerald, "May Day," in *The Portable F. Scott Fitzgerald,* 1945

In the argument over this issue the question arose as to whether a great power could not only veto the coercion of itself —Walter Lippmann, *Atlantic,* December 1944

In the event of a dispute as to whether the Court has jurisdiction —Charter of the United Nations, 1945

. . . a first inquiry as to whether we do not fail both in the types of our teaching and in the kind of intellectual material we attempt to handle —*Selected Writings of Louise Pound,* 1949

. . . there was some mild speculation among the crowds as to whether he would come along with his mother —Mollie Panter-Downes, *New Yorker,* 6 Oct. 1951

They got into a discussion as to whether the hills of Africa were in fact green, as Hemingway said —John Barkham, *Saturday Rev.,* 13 Feb. 1954

As to whether is a particular bugbear of the handbooks. Here is a typical injunction:

This formulation occurs frequently in the speech and writing of those who will never use a single word where three can be found. Example: "There is some question *as to whether* the bill will pass." The *as to* can simply be deleted. *Whether* says it all —Harper 1975, 1985

Sometime after Harper 1975 was published, an item in the *New Yorker* pointed out that the 1975 edition of Harper used *as to whether* at least three times, as here, under *excellent:*

A reader raises the question as to whether "very excellent" is acceptable . . .

The 1985 edition has emended the passage to:

A reader raises the question whether "very excellent" is acceptable . . .

All the 1985 emendation accomplishes is to gain Harper consistency between precept and practice and to demonstrate that *as to* can be omitted; it has not demonstrated that *as to* must be omitted. Its omission is mandatory only if you are writing a telegram. Otherwise omission or retention of *as to* is entirely a matter of your own ear, taste, or style.

astonished In Bernstein 1965 we find the information that *astonished at* suggests disapproval, and *aston-*

ished by approval. Lincoln Library 1924 takes a different approach. It says astonished "*at* a situation or a person's attitude, *by* an event." *Astonished* can be used with either *at* or *by;* the rest is simply editors' guesswork.

Astonished was formerly used with *with:*

. . . astonish'd with surprize —John Dryden, 1697 (OED)

. . . his wits astonished with sorrow —Sir Philip Sidney, 1580 (OED)

Our evidence for *astonished* followed by a preposition is not great enough to suggest statistical reliability, but we have considerably more evidence for *at:*

In central Chile I was astonished at the structure of a vast mound —Charles Darwin, *On the Origin Of Species by Means of Natural Selection,* 1859

. . . you shall be astonished at the gay dresses and painted cheeks —"Aguecheek," *My Unknown Chum,* 1912

. . . astonished at the ease with which she managed to make him drop into his seat again —Joseph Conrad, *Chance,* 1913

We hefted one and were astonished at how heavy it was —*New Yorker,* 25 Oct. 1952

. . . astonished at the havoc wrought —F. Kingdon-Ward, *Geographical Jour.,* June 1953

We have little evidence for *by* followed by a noun, but much more for *by* followed by a gerund. It may be the latter construction that prompted Lincoln Library to tie this combination to events.

One can never enter St. Peter's without being astonished by its vastness and its majesty —Arthur Milton, *Rome in Seven Days,* 1924

. . . Mrs. Pontifex astonished the whole village by showing unmistakable signs of a disposition to present her husband with an heir or heiress —Samuel Butler, *The Way of All Flesh,* 1903

. . . astonished his fellows by buying and smoking ten-cent cigars —Sherwood Anderson, *Poor White,* 1920

astronomical Copperud 1970, 1980 records three of his authorities as finding *astronomical* "overused and inappropriate to convey the idea of a large number." He further notes that all dictionaries recognize the use as standard. The OED Supplement shows the sense as early as 1899, but it seems not to have become established until the middle of the 1930s:

The odds against a poor person becoming a millionaire are of astronomical magnitude —George Bernard Shaw, preface to *Too True to Be Good,* 1934 (OED Supplement)

Figures like that are too astronomical —Sinclair Lewis, *It Can't Happen Here,* 1935

. . . an income reaching astronomical proportions —*Manchester Guardian Weekly,* 12 Mar. 1937

. . . continued astronomical expenditures for arms would mean eventual bankruptcy for all nations —*Time,* 6 Mar. 1939

The sense has become firmly established since then. Curiously, Follett 1966 approved *astronomical* for distances, but not other uses. We do have a few examples with *distance:*

> The distance between the library and the bedroom is astronomical —Arthur Koestler, *Partisan Rev.,* Summer 1944

While it is hard to see why this use is inappropriate, the view that *astronomical* is overused may have more merit. Here are just a few examples of other astronomical things:

> . . . glamorous resorts bearing astronomical pricetags —Abby Rand, *Harper's Bazaar,* November 1979

> . . . the price . . . will be astronomical, but about $1,000 less astronomical than it was last year —Carrie Donovan, *N.Y. Times Mag.,* 20 Apr. 1980

> . . . the federal debt would become so astronomical that the credit of the federal government would be shaken —Frederick Lewis Allen, *The Big Change,* 1952

> . . . the uncontrolled sale of astronomical amounts of ammunition —Farley Mowat, *People of the Deer,* 1952

> . . . an astronomical rise in the total number of paperbacks —*Reveille,* 20 Mar. 1968

> The rate of VD in the United States has reached astronomical proportions —David R. Reuben, M.D., *McCall's,* March 1971

> . . . inflation that has raised modern-art prices to astronomical heights —Janet Flanner, *New Yorker,* 16 Mar. 1957

> . . . to overcome the astronomical unemployment — Don Bohning, *Saturday Rev.,* 11 Dec. 1976

If you agree that *astronomical* is overused, a wide range of alternatives—*vast, huge, immense, enormous,* and their synonyms and near-synonyms—is available.

as well as   *As well as* is mentioned in usage books chiefly in regard to its effect on the number of the verb following two nouns or pronouns between which it appears. These discussions typically betray some uncertainty about whether *as well as* is a conjunction or a preposition, and not infrequently they depend on examples which have been made up and bear little resemblance to actual usage. We will try to make matters clearer with examples of actual use.

We first take note of literal use, in which the phrase is used as the simple sum of its three words. Irmscher 1976 finds this literal use likely to be ambiguous by being confusable with the conjunction. A made-up example is presented to prove the point. Our real examples, however, are not ambiguous:

> However, I endeavoured to calm my mind as well as I could —Henry Fielding, *A Journey from This World to the Next,* 1743

> If you will always remember to act as well as I act, you will never get in trouble —Flannery O'Connor, letter, 13 Jan. 1960

> Abercrombie-Smith's eyes went flinty. He knew when someone was taking the mickey as well as the next man —Desmond Bagley, *Windfall,* 1982

This use is far too common to be legislated out of existence in favor of some other use.

As well as is also used as a preposition. In this function it is usually followed by a gerund:

> . . . they tell stories that become the myths of the tribe, as well as presenting characters that can serve as tribal heroes and villains —Malcolm Cowley, *New Republic,* 4 Oct. 1954

> . . . makes use of a variety of papers as well as providing a better jacket —*Times Literary Supp.,* 14 May 1970

> But Stevenson as well as being a romancer was an aesthete —J. I. M. Stewart, *Eight Modern Writers,* 1963

An ordinary noun is sometimes the object of the preposition:

> As well as a new dress, Pam will be wearing another family present, a . . . necklace, when she receives her guests —Jill Gray, *The Age* (Melbourne), 2 May 1975

Prepositional use of *as well as* is not as common as conjunctive use; indeed, the most common use of the phrase is as a conjunction. It joins nouns and noun phrases:

> There were two filling stations at the intersection with Union Avenue, as well as an A & P, a fruit stand, a bakery, a barber shop, Zuccarelli's drugstore, and a diner —Russell Baker, *Growing Up,* 1982

> Words for him must become objects in themselves, as well as automatic signallers of meaning —Barzun 1985

> I have endorsed each of these measures, as well as the more difficult route of constitutional amendment —Ronald Reagan, *Abortion and the Conscience of the Nation,* 1984

It joins prepositional phrases:

> . . . as it may have appeared from Versailles, as well as from Paris —*Times Literary Supp.,* 27 Aug. 1971

> . . . caught fish for supper as well as for sport —Tom & Lucia Taylor, *Center Mag.,* July–August 1971

> . . . became king in name as well as in fact —*Current Biography,* May 1966

It joins verbs and verbal phrases:

> . . . who acted the role as well as sang it —Leighton Kerner, *Village Voice,* 28 Feb. 1968

> . . . was directed as well as written by Valdez — Thomas Thompson, *N.Y. Times Mag.,* 11 Mar. 1979

> . . . were responsible for building roads as well as running the courthouse —Margaret Truman, *Harry S. Truman,* 1972

> . . . has done much to cement our society together— as well as to make it more rigid —Edgar Z. Friedenberg, *Change,* May–June 1969

It joins adjectives:

> . . . legislators and rulers, civil as well as ecclesiastical —Thomas Jefferson, *The Statute of Virginia for Religious Freedom,* 1777

... the placing of the preposition before the relative, is more graceful, as well as more perspicuous — Lowth 1762

... looked quite good, as well as understandably happy —Elizabeth Drew, *New Yorker,* 3 Dec. 1984

... has become so firmly established, in written as well as spoken English —Howard 1984

It also joins pronouns. Several handbooks recommend that the pronoun following *as well as* be in the same case as the pronoun preceding. Our evidence is sparse, the modern English case system being what it is, but seems to indicate that the second pronoun does tend to match the case of the first.

You see I have a spirit, as well as yourself —Jane Austen, letter, 8 Feb. 1807

... and I want to see them again, as well as you — James Thurber, letter, 1 Aug. 1958

... headlines that hurt us as well as them —Len Morgan, *Flying,* March 1984

Sometimes *as well as* joins two words or phrases that are the subject of the same verb. While this is the function that gets most of the attention of the commentators, it is less frequent in our citations than the conjunctive functions just illustrated. In about two thirds of the instances in our files the first subject is plural, and the verb must likewise be plural. In the instances where the first subject is singular, usage is mixed.

Descriptive grammarians from Poutsma 1904–26 and Jespersen 1909–49 to Quirk et al. 1985 all say that the singular verb is more common, but that the plural is used. Evans 1957 concurs. Ebbitt & Ebbitt 1982 and Janis 1984 also recognize mixed usage. The rest of the handbooks that we have seen insist on the singular verb.

The root of this disagreement lies in the fact that *as well as* is what Quirk calls a quasi-coordinator: it is often felt to be adding something of a parenthetical nature. This characteristic is usually signaled by the use of commas—see the examples above. Ebbitt & Ebbitt observes that in general when a writer considers the *as well as* segment part of the subject (and hence uses a plural verb), he or she does not set it off with commas. This is a general, but not an iron-clad rule; Bernstein 1962 shows this example, complete with commas:

He, as well as the producer, Jack H. Silverman, are Broadway newcomers —*N.Y. Times*

But more typical are these examples with plural verbs and no commas:

But the vocalism as well as the identity of the signs impose caution upon us —Cyrus H. Gordon, *Antiquity,* September 1957

The enormous increase in college enrollments as well as the large amounts business now is investing in the continued education and training of all levels of employees attest to the pervasiveness of our race to gain new knowledge —Charles R. Bowen, in *Automation, Education and Human Values,* ed. W. W. Brickman & S. Lehrer, 1966

We find the singular verb with and without commas:

This theme, as well as the writer's art, makes the novel a work of art —John T. Metz, in *Classroom Practices in Teaching English,* 1968–1969

... and available evidence as well as past experience suggests that the Soviet will attempt to mobilize maximum diplomatic, political and military force — Gene Gregory, *Atlas,* October 1969

These examples will, we hope, dispel any notion that in the real world *as well as* is used in simple sentences like "John as well as Jane was late for dinner."

Our advice to you is that if you join singular subjects with *as well as,* you should follow your instinctive feeling for the singular or plural verb, but it will help your readers if you omit the commas with the plural verb and insert them with the singular verb. If your instinct does not lead you to prefer one approach over the other and you do not want to rewrite (as with *and*), choose commas and a singular verb. That will offend no one.

at   Handbook writers from Vizetelly 1906 to Harper 1985 have been concerned over the use of the preposition *at* somewhere in the vicinity of and especially after the adverb *where.* This combination is evidently chiefly an Americanism (attested by the OED Supplement and entered in the Dictionary of American Regional English), but not entirely unknown in British dialects. It is first attested as an American idiom in Bartlett's 1859 *Dictionary of Americanisms.* Mark Twain in *Life on the Mississippi* (1883) associated it with Southern speech; the DARE calls it chiefly Southern and Midland. It is, of course, entirely futile to attempt to eradicate a speech form by denouncing it in books on writing. And a more harmless idiom would be hard to imagine.

Our evidence shows the idiom to be nearly nonexistent in discursive prose, although it occurs in letters and transcriptions of speech:

'Fore you begins for to wipe your eyes 'bout Br' Rabbit, you wait and see where 'bouts Br' Rabbit gwine to fetch up at —Joel Chandler Harris, *Uncle Remus: His Songs and Sayings,* 1880, in *The Mirth of a Nation,* ed. Walter Blair & Raven I. McDavid, Jr., 1983

In half the stories I felt he didn't know himself where he was coming out at —Flannery O'Connor, letter, 2 Aug. 1958

In current speech, the *at* serves to provide a word at the end of the sentence that can be given stress. It tends to follow a noun or pronoun to which the verb has been elided, as in this utterance by an editor here at the dictionary factory:

Have any idea where Kathy's at?

You will note that *at* cannot simply be omitted; the *'s* must be expanded to *is* to produce an idiomatic sentence if the *at* is to be avoided.

For a particular mid-20th-century use of this idiom, see WHERE ... AT.

at about   This two-word, three-syllable phrase has been the subject of an unlikely amount of discussion at least since the middle 1930s (our earliest note is from Jensen 1935). The standard objection is that the phrase is redundant. Evans 1957, who is almost the only usage writer who stands out from the crowd (Copperud 1964, 1970, 1980, Follett 1966, Janis 1984, Bryson 1984, Shaw 1970, 1975, Guth 1985, Ebbitt & Ebbitt 1982), points out that redundancy is not a reasonable claim, since *at,* a preposition, is frequently followed by adverbs (such as *almost, approximately, nearly, exactly*) and *about,* an adverb in this construction, is frequently used with other prepositions (Evans instances *for about an hour, in about a week, by about Christmas*). Follett admits that in some situations—those involving prices and rates, for instance—*at about* is appropriate:

> ... holding the domestic price index for plastic products as a whole at about the 1969 level —*Annual Report, Union Carbide Corp.,* 1970

> ... offered to buy gold at a fixed pound price and to sell gold at about that same price —Paul A. Samuelson, *Economics,* 5th ed., 1961

The basis for the assertion that *at about* is redundant is that *about* can be a preposition as well as an adverb, and as a preposition has nearly the same meaning as *at about*. It is not reasonable, of course, to require a writer to use *about* as a preposition where it works (or only sounds) better as an adverb, but handbooks tend to overlook this point, for all their devotion to logic in other parts of the usage arena. "*At about* can be reduced to either *at* or *about*," says Ebbitt & Ebbitt. But consider this sentence:

> Another leading librarian wrote at about the same time that it was the considered judgment of ... —Eva Goldschmidt, *College & Research Libraries,* January 1969

If only *at* is used, the intended notion of approximate time is removed; if only *about* is used, ambiguity is introduced by the uncertainty whether *about* "approximately" or *about* "concerning" is intended. Obviously *at about* is the proper choice. Here are a couple of other examples in which neither *at* nor *about* can be omitted:

> ... With a Bare Bodkin ... is Mr. Hare at about his best —M. R. Ridley, *London Calling,* 6 Jan. 1955

> ... as contrasted to superimposing scientific and professional education upon a cut-off liberal experience at about the age of twenty-one —Milton S. Eisenhower, *Johns Hopkins Mag.,* February 1966

At about is another instance in which the usage writers appear not to know of literary use. Edward C. Fletcher, in *American Speech,* October 1947, defended *at about* as reputable and established. He presented more than fifty examples from literary sources. Among the authors he cited are George Borrow, Herman Melville, Henry James, Anthony Trollope, Charles Eliot Norton, E. M. Forster, Henry Adams, Edith Wharton, Katherine Mansfield, Virgina Woolf, John Dos Passos, Thomas Wolfe, Ezra Pound, Logan Pearsall Smith, D. H. Lawrence, Edmund Wilson, Carson McCullers, Wolcott Gibbs, J. Frank Dobie, I. A. Richards, Ludwig Bemelmans, George Santayana, Osbert Sitwell, Evelyn Waugh, Robert Graves, Morris L. Ernst, John Hersey, John O'Hara, and John P. Marquand. You can compare this list with the list of handbook writers who condemn *at about* and decide which list offers the better guides to the art of writing English.

Here are just a few more examples from our files:

> ... and at about half after twelve ... we separated —Henry Adams, letter, 17 May 1859

> But at about this time —Edmund Wilson, *Axel's Castle,* 1931

> A careful examination of Mr. Pound's work shows two very obvious changes at about this time —*Times Literary Supp.,* 13 Jan. 1950

> At about this time, she took me on as a kind of secretary —Louis Bromfield, "The Big Smash," 1952

At about is most frequently used with expressions of time, according to our evidence. In many of these cases, *about* can be used alone. But it need not be. When *at about* makes better sense or simply sounds better, use it without fear and with the encouragement of one contemporary commentator:

> June Guilford of Cleveland challenges a sentence in which I said "at about the same time...." She wanted to know what that "at" was doing in there. Darned if I know. I suppose that "about the same time" would have sufficed, but "at about" just sounds better to me —James J. Kilpatrick, *Portland Oregonian* (syndicated column), 2 Nov. 1985

at home   See HOME, *adverb*.

atop   Use of *atop* as a preposition is called "well established journalese" by Evans 1957; he has some doubts about its use in literary English. G. V. Carey, in *American Into English* (1953), says the preposition is frequent in American prose but rare in British prose. Copperud 1970 says other criticisms of the preposition are sometimes heard, but we have not seen them.

The organization of Murray's definition in the OED suggests that he thought *atop* was first an adverb, which came to be used with *of* for an object, and then became a preposition by omission of *of*. This explanation is plausible enough (it is similar to the development of *alongside*), but the earliest citation for the preposition is a year or two older than the earliest for the adverb. It seems equally possible that adverb and preposition developed concurrently.

Except for his use of the pejorative *journalese,* Evans seems to have been on the right track essentially. Our evidence shows that the preposition became established in American journalism during the first quarter of the 20th century. The preposition is now the prevalent use and is no longer confined to journalism. The adverb *atop* and the compound preposition *atop of,* which Evans suggested avoiding as too literary, are simply not often used any more.

We have nothing very recent for *atop of:*

> Atop of the great hill she stopped for breath —Maurice Hewlett, *Halfway House,* 1908

The adverb pops up once in a while:

> He [a horse] had a heart murmur, a deformed front foot, and his fifteen hands were almost all taken up by legs, with a reedy, angular body atop —R. C. Rodgers, *Northeast Horseman,* February 1980

The preposition prevails in American use, and it even turns up now and then in British:

> ... a small church with timbered bell cote and a high timbered porch sits atop a hill —Sheila Green, *Country Quest* (Wrexham, Wales), May 1975

> ... sits atop the nonfiction best-seller list —Christopher Lehmann-Haupt, *N.Y. Times,* 2 Aug. 1983

> ... commemorated in stone atop a monumental column in Mountain Grove Cemetery —E. L. Doctorow, *Ragtime,* 1975

> ... material of varying shapes and sizes piled atop one another —Philip Roth, *Reading Myself and Others,* 1975

at present, at the present time Copperud 1964 and Bernstein 1965 discourage the use of these phrases in place of *now*. It is difficult to see why. We have no evidence that either of these phrases is likely to preempt more than its share of the language, and what virtue there is in trying to limit the number of choices a writer has in expressing an idea is unclear to us. Bernstein suggests that if the verb is in the present tense (and it is with these phrases), an indication of time may be unnecessary. Bernstein's observation may account for why we are not inundated with examples of the phrases.

> This view finds favour at the present time because . . . —Kathleen Raine, *CEA Chap Book,* 1969

> At present, in addition to his day-to-day coverage, Smith writes a column —*Current Biography,* December 1964

> Few of the drawings he mentions are at present known —*Times Literary Supp.,* 6 June 1980

> The fact that these "pro-British" people are now skirmishing against the British Army, which is at present defending the "anti-British," is only superficially paradoxical —Conor Cruise O'Brien, *N.Y. Rev. of Books,* 6 Nov. 1969

These uses of the phrase seem harmless to us, at the very least. In the example from O'Brien *at present* forestalls an awkward repetition of *now* and is a virtue. Both phrases can also be useful in subtly emphasizing a contrast with time past or time future in a way that the less noticeable *now* cannot accomplish. You should feel free to use them when they sound right.

See also PRESENTLY.

attain 1. Bryson 1984 finds fault with a less than entirely felicitous sentence from *The Times* of London referring to "The uncomfortable debt level attained. . . ." *Attain,* says Bryson, "suggests the reaching of a desired goal." A good dictionary, however, will show you that *attain* is not so limited in meaning. The reaching of a desired goal is indeed one of the main aspects of the verb, but it is also frequently used to indicate the reaching of a limit or the end of some sort of progression. It was this sense the *Times* writer probably had in mind. Here are a few examples of the use:

> . . . an atomic bomb was to be detonated by attaining critical mass —Murray Leinster, *The Writer,* May 1968

> The maximum orbit attained by the capsule —*Current Biography,* November 1965

> The great mountain blacksnake, entirely harmless, attains a length of eleven feet —*American Guide Series: New Jersey,* 1939

> We see that the maximum value . . . is attained at the right endpoint —School Mathematics Study Group, *Calculus of Elementary Functions,* Part 1, 1969

2. The intransitive *attain* is usually used with *to:*

> . . . Gulliver's impulse to self-advantage is such that he can attain only to a fantasy of political power — Paul Fussell, *Samuel Johnson and the Life of Writing,* 1971

> Some writers of this sort of verse have even attained to something like celebrity —Leacock 1943

> A not dissimilar kind of childlike Latin could attain to a remarkable symmetry and balance —Henry O. Taylor, *The Mediaeval Mind,* 4th ed., 1925

attempt 1. The noun *attempt,* Bernstein 1965 tells us, takes *at.* It does, but it takes other prepositions too. Here we have *at:*

> . . . the first attempt at a broad outline —*Times Literary Supp.,* 9 Apr. 1970

> . . . inspired him to make his first attempts at writing —*Current Biography,* November 1967

> This figure swung a silver tray in an attempt at careless grace —Kingsley Amis, *Lucky Jim,* 1954

On is the usual preposition when *attempt* means "an attempt to kill"; it is also used in other contexts.

> . . . the Orsini attempt on the life of Napoleon III — *Times Literary Supp.,* 18 Apr. 1968

> . . . believe the state to be so constituted that attempts on its authority are not easily justified — Michael Walzer, *Dissent,* September–October 1969

> Before we could make an attempt on the summit — Sir John Hunt & Sir Edmund Hillary, *Geographical Jour.,* December 1953

Against and *upon* are also used:

> . . . assassination attempt against President Ford — radio newscast, 22 Sept. 1975

> . . . any attempt . . . against the integrity . . . of the territory —Vera Micheles Dean, *The Four Cornerstones of Peace,* 1946

> . . . the four attempts upon Mussolini's life —*Times Literary Supp.,* 3 Apr. 1969

A very common construction is *to* and the infinitive:

> . . . plunged into the water in an attempt to escape — *Current Biography,* July 1965

> . . . to record with special sympathy the attempts of others to deal with like situations —Alice P. Kenney, *New-England Galaxy,* Fall 1970

> . . . any attempt to offer evidence in the place of conjecture is welcome —*Times Literary Supp.,* 26 Mar. 1970

2. Zinsser 1976 lists *attempt*—apparently the verb—as a "long word that is no better than the short word"—in this case, *try.* Many good writers have found *attempt* adequate:

> . . . to attempt a broad reconciliation of the diverging views in the church —Tad Szulc, *N.Y. Times Mag.,* 27 May 1979

> It is best never to attempt to joke —Ernest Hemingway, "Miss Mary's Lion," 1956

> Why he attempted it at all is an insoluble puzzle — T. S. Eliot, "Hamlet and His Problems," in *Selected Essays,* 1932

> I attempt no chronicle —Hilaire Belloc, *Richelieu,* 1930

> Some man was talking to him in a low voice and attempting, from time to time, to lay a hand on his

shoulder —F. Scott Fitzgerald, *The Great Gatsby,* 1925

attend 1. Raub 1897 tells us that *to* follows this verb when it means "listen" and *upon* when it means "wait." There is a bit more to the matter than that. When *attend* suggests application of the mind, the attention, or care, the intransitive regularly takes *to:*

You must attend to words when you read, when you speak, when others speak —Barzun 1985

... Sarah Shepard had always attended to the buying of his clothes —Sherwood Anderson, *Poor White,* 1920

He walked along towards home without attending to paths —Thomas Hardy, *The Return of the Native,* 1878

How difficult it is to attend to the argument —F. R. Leavis, *Revaluation,* 1947

... has business to attend to outside —Martin Levin, *Saturday Rev.,* 8 Jan. 1972

When *attend* is used to mean "to be ready for service" or "to be present," *upon* is most common, while *on* and *at* are occasionally used.

The Nemesis that attends upon human pride —G. Lowes Dickinson, *The Greek View of Life,* 7th ed., 1925

... how he attended upon Wishart when the latter preached in Haddington —Kenneth Scott Latourette, *A History of Christianity,* 1953

Byron, George Eliot, Tolstoy—did the valet attend on them? —*Times Literary Supp.,* 22 Oct. 1971

After all, we constantly attend at music that is presented second-rate or worse —Stark Young, *New Republic,* 26 Jan. 1942

2. In the past participle, says Bernstein 1965, *attend* takes *with* for things and *by* for persons. The real world is not so tidy. While *with* is indeed used for things, it is not so frequent as it may have been in the past, and *by* is now being used for both persons and things.

The use of metals in this rude state was attended with two very considerable inconveniences —Adam Smith, *The Wealth of Nations,* 1776

... always attended with a certain degree of risk — George Fielding Eliot, *Harper's,* November 1939

... the qualification which enables him to do so may be attended with a disadvantage —F. R. Leavis, *The Common Pursuit,* 1952

He was attended by a half-dozen servants —Lloyd C. Douglas, *The Big Fisherman,* 1948

... battalions, attended by all their baggage and artillery —T. B. Macaulay, *The History of England,* vol. I, 1849

... fifty broad-wheeled waggons, attended by a hundred men —Adam Smith, *The Wealth of Nations,* 1776

Attended by heron, tern, cormorant, and gull, these adorable mammals ... —Doone Beal, *Gourmet,* August 1980

... any resolution of it is bound to be attended by risks —Charles Frankel, *Columbia Forum,* Summer 1970

I was much happier here ... attended by smokey Scotch —Larry L. King, *Harper's,* July 1969

... this may become inflamed and be attended by pain —W. A. D. Anderson, ed., *Pathology,* 1948

... his few efforts have been attended by instant failure —John Buchan, *Castle Gay,* 1930

at the present time See AT PRESENT, AT THE PRESENT TIME.

at this point in time See POINT IN TIME.

attitude *Attitude* is generally followed by the prepositions *toward, towards,* and *to.*
Toward is the most frequent in American English:

... corporate attitudes toward day care —Anita Shreve, *N.Y. Times Mag.,* 21 Nov. 1982

... a new attitude toward sex —Marcia Seligson, *McCall's,* March 1971

... his attitude toward almost all of his close collaborators —William L. Shirer, *The Rise and Fall of the Third Reich,* 1960

Thackeray's fruitfully ambivalent attitude toward his own class —Clifton Fadiman, *Holiday,* October 1954

Towards is found chiefly in British English:

... a mental attitude towards the quality —George Bernard Shaw, *Harper's,* October 1971

... this cavalier attitude towards the established practices of his profession —*The Observer,* 29 Sept. 1963 (in *Current Biography,* July 1965)

... his pugnacious attitude towards other geckos — Gerald Durrell, *My Family and Other Animals,* 1956

To is more common in British than in American English.

... similar attitudes to the Middle East crisis —*The Times* (London), 17 Nov. 1973

... the attitude of these boys to everyday honesty — *Times Literary Supp.,* 26 Mar. 1970

... St. Gregory's attitude to the slave trade —Angus Wilson, *Anglo-Saxon Attitudes,* 1956

His intensely ambivalent attitude to his father — Anne Fremantle, *Commonweal,* 6 Dec. 1946

About has some use, usually spoken, in American English:

Some of them have an attitude about it —Janiece Walters, quoted in *Fortune,* 11 Nov. 1985

I'll tell you his attitude about those dangers —Joe Garagiola, radio broadcast, 14 Feb. 1974

... for not having a sufficiently serious attitude about his work —*Current Biography,* June 1953

Compound prepositions are sometimes used in what we may call wordier contexts:

> ... compensate for the failure of the inventionistic approach to justify anticipation by taking up a conventionalist attitude as regards the universal truth of inductive conclusions —Georg Henrik Von Wright, *A Treatise on Induction and Probability*, 1951

> The fear of a specific object is an affect. The attitude with respect to this affect.... —Abram Kardiner, *The Individual and His Society*, 1939

attraction See AGREEMENT, SUBJECT-VERB: THE PRINCIPLE OF PROXIMITY.

attributive *Attributive* is an adjective that describes the position of a modifier directly in front of the word it modifies: *black* tie, *silly* remark, *big* toe, *kitchen* sink, *lobster* salad, *computer* terminal. That nouns can function like adjectives in this position is a feature of English noticed as long ago as Lindley Murray 1795. He mentions two-word compounds of which the first element is a noun, and notices that they are sometimes open (he cites *adjective pronoun, silver watch, stone cistern*), hyphened (he cites *coal-mine, corn-mill, fruit-tree*), and solid (he cites *honeycomb, gingerbread, inkhorn*).

John Simon, in Michaels & Ricks 1980, objects to the combination *language deterioration;* Simon says *deterioration of language* would be better (he does not, however, mention that *language change* is used in the same paragraph). A combination like *language deterioration* (or *language change*) is not quite the animal that Lindley Murray was talking about in 1795; Murray's combinations we would call compounds, some of them self-explanatory. Combinations like *language deterioration* represent simply the free modification of one noun by another. Otto Jespersen, in the second volume of his seven-volume grammar (1909–49), comments on this characteristic of the language; he attributes both compound-forming and free modification to "the want in English of an adequate manner of forming adjectives from substantives to denote the vague relations indicated by Latin *-alis, -anus,* etc."

The formation of compounds from one noun annexed to another goes back to Old English, where it was the standard way of forming compounds. The noun attributive as a free modifier of another noun appears to be somewhat more recent: Jespersen's examples mostly start with Shakespeare, but he has few examples between Shakespeare and the 19th century. The practice, then, may be a revival. At any rate it is flourishing now.

A single page of a journal (*EDF Letter*, May 1986, a newsletter for people interested in environmental issues) yields these examples: *beef industry, health aspects, beef consumption, beef production, bank and government funds, bank policies, rain forest work, board member, ecology subjects, Home Loan Bank, Reagan Administration, U.S.-Panama Commission, Santa Margarita River Foundation, San Diego investment counseling firm, brokerage and venture capital business.* And there are compounds too, of course: *rain forest, field guide.* And the ordinary reader will find these understandable and will probably not notice them as being in the least out of the ordinary. Quinn 1980 gives some long strings of attributive nouns from a single picture caption in a 1980 Philadelphia newspaper: "the Chapel of the Four Chaplains Annual Awards Banquet" at which "the Rabbi Louis Paris Hall of Heroes Gold Medallion" was awarded to "Former NATO commander Alexander M. Haig Jr."

Quinn's strings raise two minor questions concerning attributive nouns. The first is the use of the plural noun as an attributive: *Awards Banquet.* Both Foster 1968 and Safire 1982 have comments on the subject. It seems that the norm has been to have singular nouns used as attributives—*billiards,* for instance, even lost its *-s* to give us *billiard ball* and *billiard table.* What seems to be a fairly recent trend toward using plural attributives in contemporary English has attracted some attention and raised a few eyebrows. Of course there always had been a few plural attributives—*scissors grinder, physics laboratory, Civil Liberties Union, mathematics book*—but what about the apparently sudden influx of *weapons system, communications technology, operations program, systems analyst, earth-resources satellite, singles bar, enemies list?* The answer appears to be that such plural attributives are standard. Many of these combinations come from specialized fields of endeavor, and the plural form seems to be chosen to differentiate the meaning of the combination with the plural from whatever the singular attributive might connote. In more general cases, like that of *awards banquet,* perhaps the intent is simply to stress plurality: more than one award will be presented.

The second question is represented by "Former NATO commander Alexander M. Haig Jr." The attributive descriptor "former NATO commander" is a journalistic device probably intended to compress information into a minimum amount of space. It is common in picture captions (as in this case) and in news articles, where it appears to be a basic tenet of journalism that no reader will remember who a public figure is from one day to the next. There are various objections to the practice but the chief one—that such strings are hard to understand—is patently off-base. You will find a brief, more general discussion under FALSE TITLES.

audience It is not uncommon in the usage business for a specific usage to cause a broad general principle to be erected to correct it. When the movies became popular in the early years of the 20th century, the people who sat in front of the silent screen watching the action were designated by the name used for the people who sat in front of a stage watching the action: *audience.* Amateurs of Latin were appalled: an audience listens; spectators look. After all, *audience* is derived from the Latin verb for "to hear." Numerous handbooks lent their weight to the opinion: Utter 1916, MacCracken & Sandison 1917, Ball 1923, Powell 1925, Hyde 1926, Krapp 1927, *Morrow's Word Finder,* 1927, and more. The opinion was still being repeated by Bernstein 1965 (he reversed himself in 1971).

But the battle had been lost before it began; *audience* had over a century earlier been transferred to seeing in reference to books by Ben Franklin. By the time movies came along, it had been fairly common for several decades at least. This counter-etymological application had gone entirely unnoticed, except in dictionaries. Some examples:

> The stricken poet of Racanati had no country, for an Italy in his day did not exist; he had no audience, no celebrity —Matthew Arnold, *Essays in Criticism, Second Series,* 1888

> Every author writes for money, for money represents an audience —Henry Seidel Canby, *Thoreau,* 1939

... for the scholar-writer to lose the sense of addressing a broad audience —Malcolm Cowley, *New Republic,* 22 Nov. 1954

... the quick reader (who is nearly all your audience) —Norman Mailer, *Advertisements for Myself,* 1959

The sense applied to readers is still in use. It was recognized in Webster's 1909 and the Merriam-Webster editors added a sense especially for the silent movies in the 1922 Addenda section of that book.

The transfer of the meaning of *audience* in reference to books simply reflects a change in our culture. Before the development of printing, a poet's audience would have been primarily listeners, and only secondarily people who could read the poems in manuscript. After printing, they became primarily readers. And since both the hearers and the readers bore the same relationship to the poet, they inherited the same name, cutting the word off from its Latin root. The transfer to the silent-movie audience was a similar process—adaptation of the word to a new technology.

In current English *audience* is applied to those who see and hear concerts, operas, plays, movies, circuses, and radio and television.

... became known to network radio as well as television audiences as newscaster —*Current Biography,* February 1966

In the sense of the reading, viewing, or listening public, it is applied to books and records, as well as to those who view works of visual art. It has even been applied to international high fashion:

While the Dior business was directed towards the Establishment customers on both sides of the Atlantic, Saint Laurent appealed to a much more avant-garde audience —Stanley Marcus, *Minding the Store,* 1974

These uses are all standard.

auger, augur Reader's Digest 1983 notes that these similar-sounding and similarly spelled words are sometimes confused. *Auger* as a noun refers to various boring tools, and as a verb to boring holes. *Augur,* noun and verb, deals with foretelling future events from omens. The verb *augur* is often used in the phrase *augur well for.* With words as disparate as these in meaning, any confusion is purely a matter of spelling. If in doubt, check your dictionary. We have found the confusion in unexpected places:

In the event, these appetizers auger well for the rest of the menu —*Notes and Queries,* December 1984

aught Copperud 1970 cites three of his authorities—Evans, Flesch, and Fowler—who stigmatize *aught* as archaic. He has incompletely reported Fowler, who both in 1926 and 1965 (revised by Gowers) recognizes "for aught I know" as still in use; Evans 1957 says only that some uses of *aught* have "a decidedly archaic tone," and he, too, recognizes the currency of "for aught I know." Copperud adds on his own that its use is "perhaps, pretentious"—a view not concurred in by other authorities and unsupported by our evidence.

A glance at the entries in a dictionary such as Webster's Ninth New Collegiate Dictionary will show you that *aught* is archaic as an adverb and as a noun in the sense "nonentity, nothing"; it is still in use as a pronoun

meaning "anything, all" and as a noun meaning "zero." Here are a few examples of the pronoun:

... and would disdain as much as a lord to do or say aught to conciliate one —Ralph Waldo Emerson, "Self-Reliance," 1841

... appeal to aught that there may be of painter or poet in any one of us —Max Beerbohm, *And Even Now,* 1920

"... for all they say I couldn't see aught but Jack...." —Zane Grey, *The Mysterious Rider,* 1921

... no one ever read fiction for aught else —Bernard DeVoto, *The World of Fiction,* 1950

For aught he knew to the contrary, it might have been some quack —Gerald W. Johnson, *New Republic,* 20 June 1955

But it is a rare evening when the breeze carries the odor of aught but blossoms —Melvin R. Ellis, *National Geographic,* August 1955

... Cora still lay without a stone, and for aught he knew he would someday return to the cemetery and find her grave gone —Bernard Malamud, *The Magic Barrel,* 1958

... nor even in the Andes has this onlooker ever beheld aught to match it —Irvin S. Cobb, *Arizona Highways,* July 1971

Even the senses of *aught* that are still alive are not especially common. The *for aught* construction may have been kept alive by its frequent occurrence in Shakespeare. Here are three out of many examples:

Nor is he dead, for aught that I can tell —*Midsummer Night's Dream,* 1596

... for aught I see —*The Merchant of Venice,* 1597

It might be yours or hers for aught I know —*All's Well That Ends Well,* 1603

augment *Augment,* often in the form of its past participle *augmented,* is used frequently with the preposition *by* and less frequently with *with.*

... he augmented his scholarship from the American Legion by working six nights a week as saxophonist with a jazz band —*Current Biography,* February 1967

... or was he to throw up his job, retire on pension, and augment this income by selling other books? —James Leasor, *Irish Digest,* January 1953

... in subfreezing temperatures augmented by a 35-mph wind —David Brudnoy, *National Rev.,* 29 Dec. 1970

... villages ... augment their water-control farming by cultivating the nearby hillsides —Kent V. Flannery et al., *Science,* 27 Oct. 1967

... has twice augmented a couponing blitz by pledging to give a nickel to the Special Olympics for retarded children each time a coupon was redeemed —*Wall Street Jour.,* 25 Mar. 1982

Augmented at times of downpour by spillover from the great central lake, the water penetrated gradually into the peat beds —Fred Ward, *National Geographic,* January 1972

. . . skillfully augment the melodramatics of modern crime detection with these terrors inherent in our metropolises —Arthur Knight, *Saturday Rev.,* 6 Nov. 1971

. . . the pianist got hold of a vintage upright whose hammers had been augmented with thumbtacks in an effort to simulate the harpsichord —Wilder Hobson, *Saturday Rev.,* 28 Nov. 1953

To the north and east the forms descend from Anglian, as these have been altered, corrupted, and augmented with influence from Old Norse —Charlton Laird, *The Miracle of Language,* 1953

augur   **1.** See AUGER, AUGUR.
2. Finegan 1980 cites Newman 1974 as saying "Augur does not take for after it. It cannot take for after it." But in modern English *augur* very frequently takes *for,* and after the phrase *augur well* (or sometimes *ill*), *for* is usual:

. . . the book sets a standard that augurs well for the future —R. D. Martin, *Nature,* 29 Aug. 1984

. . . doesn't augur especially well for "6 O'Clock Follies." —John J. O'Connor, *N.Y. Times,* 24 Apr. 1980

. . . his very survival augurs well for his future mastery —Robert Coles, *Harper's,* November 1971

The record augurs well for the prospects of Britain's girls —*Illustrated London News,* 31 Aug. 1968

. . . felt that the hopefuls now in the field augur well for the party —*Time,* 7 Apr. 1952

Neither point of view augurs well for the arousing of American interest —*Selected Writings of Edward Sapir,* ed. David G. Mandelbaum, 1949

. . . this is the significant message of his song that augurs bright for the working class —*Indian Rev.,* January 1946

. . . greater facility in negotiating with each other, which augurs well for the peace of the world — Franklin D. Roosevelt, report to Congress, 1 Mar. 1945, *in Voices of History 1945–46,* ed. Nathan Ausubel, 1946

. . . her appearance augured ill for the interview — Fred Whishaw, *At the Court of Catherine the Great,* 1899

Of is less frequently used now than formerly, but it too is standard:

This seemed to augur ill of Christianity —Kenneth Scott Latourette, *A History of Christianity,* 1953

We might augur more hopefully of Spain's attempt —Irving Babbitt, *Spanish Character and Other Essays,* 1940

. . . an unloved brother, of whom worse things had been augured —George Eliot, *Silas Marner,* 1861

Fletcher, from the beginning had augured ill of the enterprise —T. B. Macaulay, *The History of England,* vol. I, 1849

To seems to be no longer in use:

One vote, which augurs ill to the rights of the people —Thomas Jefferson, *Writings,* 1788 (OED)

auspicious   Phythian 1979 and Bryson 1984 would like to limit *auspicious* to the sense "propitious, promising, of good omen." They both are suspicious of the public speaker's "on this auspicious occasion," in which they interpret *auspicious* to mean "special, memorable, distinguished." If they wished merely to call the phrase a cliché, it would be hard to disagree with them, but in their reading of the meaning of *auspicious,* they are in error. The sense that they misinterpret is dated back to the 17th century in the OED; it means "marked by good auspices, prosperous."

. . . documents an auspicious period in the history of the music —*Bluegrass Unlimited,* April 1982

. . . it seems perhaps an auspicious moment to quantify some of the feelings and reactions I have had in more than 20 years as director —S. Dillon Ripley, *Smithsonian,* September 1984

This sense is perfectly well established and standard.

author   You will have no trouble finding people who dislike *author* used as a verb: Copperud 1964, 1970, 1980, Follett 1966, Flesch 1964, Reader's Digest 1983, Nickles 1974, Kilpatrick 1984, Ebbitt & Ebbitt 1982, Harper 1975, 1985, Zinsser 1976, McMahan & Day 1980, Janis 1984, Watt 1967, the Oxford American Dictionary, Gowers 1948, Ivor Brown 1945. There are probably more for the dedicated researcher to unearth. Heritage 1969 stigmatized it, but Heritage 1982 dropped the note.

This verb has a very strange history marked by many inexplicable gaps in the record. Such gaps, however, are not uncommon in the backgrounds of little-used words, and until after World War II the verb *author* was a little-used word. It first appears in Chapman's translation of Homer in 1596:

The last foul thing Thou ever author'dst (OED)

Chapman's verb means "to be the author of," but his author is not a writer—a doer or perpetrator instead. The OED shows a few 17th-century examples like Chapman's, and then the evidence seems to dry up. The OED also records another 17th-century sense that did not survive to the 18th.

Our next evidence comes from the 18th century. Henry Fielding in *Joseph Andrews* (1742) pulls it out of his hat as an intransitive—actually as a gerund:

There are certain mysteries or secrets in all trades, from the highest to the lowest, from that of *prime-ministering* to this of *authoring,* which are seldom discovered, unless to members of the same calling.

Fielding's italics suggest that he knew he was using a nonce word. But it did not vanish entirely. About a century and a half later we find it without italics, used by a book reviewer:

What is a reviewer's duty to a book like this? Ignore it, and so implicitly encourage the author to go on authoring . . . ? —*N.Y. Times Book Rev.,* 7 July 1918

We have little evidence since for Fielding's intransitive verb, and you will not find it recorded in a dictionary.

An author authors, but never in the present tense. No one says, when asked what he or she is doing, "I'm authoring." —Roy Blount, Jr., *N.Y. Times Book Rev.,* 17 Oct. 1982

Our next bit of evidence is the surfacing of Chapman's verb again, applied to the game of ice hockey:

> ... when Buddy Maracle authored the goal which roused the ire of Coach Eddie Powers —J. Earl Chevalier, *Springfield* (Mass.) *Republican,* 22 Jan. 1931

The use of Chapman's verb in sports seems not to have died out, although our evidence is quite sporadic:

> ... no-hitters authored by Koufax, Haddix and Feller —Alan C. Hoffman, *Away,* Summer 1981

Chapman's verb has occasional use in areas other than sports, too:

> ... his acts ... are conditioned by his own character as a living creature and by the environment in which he lives, but he authors them out of these materials —Iredell Jenkins, *Rev. of Metaphysics,* December 1951

> ... seems to treat these urges as if they, too, were authored by some outside agency —James C. Moloney, *Psychoanalytic Rev.,* April 1948

Finally we come to the transitive verb that everyone loves to hate:

> The edition on painting is authored by a number of leading authorities on the subject —*Birmingham* (Mich.) *Eccentric,* 10 Sept. 1936

> He authored a saying, oft repeated among dairymen, "Treat the cow kindly, boys; remember she's a lady—and a mother." —*American Guide Series: Minnesota,* 1938

> Samuel Hopkins Adams authored the screen success called "It Happened One Night" —*N.Y. Herald Tribune Book Rev.,* 26 Feb. 1939

> ... Volume I of this series, published in 1937 and authored by Dorothy Garrod and Dorothea Bate —*Science,* 3 May 1940

> As the Princess Sapieha, she authored two best sellers of her own —Bennett Cerf, *Saturday Rev.,* 23 Aug. 1947

> ... Christopher Morley has authored, co-authored, and edited over fifty books of poetry, fiction, autobiography, essays, and drama —Whitney Balliett, *Saturday Rev.,* 26 Dec. 1953

> He has in fact authored more than 700 magazine pieces —Cleveland Amory, *Saturday Rev.,* 30 Oct. 1971

The last three examples suggest that *author* as a verb has appeared with some frequency in the pages of *Saturday Review.* H. L. Mencken ascribes it to *Variety,* but he gives no actual citations. In a footnote in his fourth edition of *The American Language,* he opines that the American use of the verb originated in the show-business journal, but says his earliest actual example comes from *Editor and Publisher,* 27 Aug. 1927. He does not print the example, though.

These examples reveal another interesting point: *author* is not limited to books, as most of the commentators suppose. Two of our three earliest citations are not about books: in one a saying is authored, in the other a screen success. Almost half the evidence in our files is for something other than a literary production.

The nonliterary writings that are most frequently authored are legislative bills, legal opinions, and such:

> ... authored a postal pay reclassification bill —*Current Biography,* February 1964

> One of the incipient "Stop Muskie" plans being discussed ... has been largely authored by Representative Bella Abzug —Richard Reeves, *New York,* 7 Feb. 1972

> ... authored one of several resolutions introduced in Congress —*Current Biography 1950*

> He authored last May's conservative-leaning opinion —*Time,* 20 Oct. 1958

> ... a compromise version, along the lines of the House bill, will be quickly substituted. Who authors this substitute will bear heavily on the final vote — *New Republic,* 15 May 1950

In addition, we have references to movies, the books of musicals, radio or television programs, songs, games, and so on. And, of course, software for the computer:

> ... uses a microcomputer game he authored to teach high-ranking managers how to make decisions — William W. Gunn, *InfoWorld,* 16 May 1983

You may have noticed that *author* is used of things like legislation, plans, and musical plays in which more than one hand is likely to have been involved. It is often used when joint effort is explicitly indicated:

> A description of Latin syntax, authored by two scholars —Ernst Pulgram, *Word,* April 1954

> Authored by N. E. Welch, D. S. Billingsley, and C. D. Holland of the Department of Chemical Engineering —*Texas Engineering Experiment Station News,* September 1961

> ... as stressed in the jointly authored document — Paul E. Fenlon, *AAUP Bulletin,* December 1967

The fuss over this verb has been somewhat overblown. We have seen that the oldest sense—the Chapman sense—continues in sporadic use; it has never been censured. The Fielding intransitive, still not recognized by dictionaries, may yet accrete enough evidence to get into future unabridged dictionaries, if only through facetious use. The 20th-century transitive—the Mencken *Variety* sense, if you will—is used chiefly in journalism and is not a literary word. It is easily avoided by those who dislike it. The most useful function of *author* would seem to be in connection with joint effort in production of a piece, and in connection with things like computer games that are not regularly associated with writing.

authoress Reader's Digest 1983 confidently informs us that "most women now regard the term *authoress* as demeaning." We do not presume to speak for most women; the evidence in our files suggests that the opinion of very few women has been sought for this word. Herbert Mitgang in the *New York Times Book Review* (19 Aug. 1979) calls the term "condescending." The use described by Mitgang—that of a South African censor banning a book by Nadine Gordimer—probably was intended to be condescending. Copperud 1970, 1980 opines that *authoress* has fallen into disuse—a premature observation, as examples below will demonstrate.

Authoress has been the subject of commentary in print at least since 1867, when Edward S. Gould took up the cudgels. Gould's discussion seems to be a continuation of one in Alford 1866 on the subject of feminine nouns, especially those ending in -*ess*. (See -ESS.) Alford was apparently set off by some clergyman's using *governess* in reference to Queen Victoria in a prayer, and he does not mention *authoress*. Gould ranges over several nouns ending in -*ess,* finding some useful and some not. *Authoress* he finds "superfluous" because *author* does not indicate sex. Ayres 1881 and Lurie 1927 simply abridge Gould's remarks. Richard Grant White 1870 finds *authoress* not especially objectionable, although he notes that it has been condemned by writers. Fowler 1926 also notes literary objections to the word, but he seems to find the superciliousness of the objectors more annoying than the word:

> **authoress** is a word regarded with dislike in literary circles, on the grounds, perhaps, that sex is irrelevant to art, & that the common unliterary public has no concern with its superiors' personality.

It is probably worth noting that all of these early commentators are men (and so are Bierce 1909, Utter 1916, and Krapp 1927, who also comment along the same lines). The sole exception is an unnamed literary woman cited in Lounsbury 1908 as being indignant at the designation *authoress;* whoever she was, she seems to have anticipated the comment of the Reader's Digest staff. Fowler, on the other hand, found *authoress* "a useful word."

Authoress has never been what you would call an overused or even a heavily used word. The OED, which dates it back to Caxton in 1478, notes that *author* is the usual term, and *authoress* is used chiefly when the sex is being purposely emphasized. In other words, *authoress* replaces some periphrastic designation like *woman writer* or *female author.* The choice of one word over two seems to be the reason for *authoress* in these examples:

> I dined with people that you never heard of, nor is it worth your while to know; an authoress and a printer —Jonathan Swift, *Journal to Stella,* 4 Jan. 1711

> ... & this work of which I am myself the Authoress —Jane Austen, letter, 5 Apr. 1809 (she signed this letter M.A.D.)

> ... the playwright, a distinguished authoress who shall also here be nameless —Cornelia Otis Skinner, *New Yorker,* 19 Mar. 1949

> ... the reputation that was to label her for all time to come: the first professional English authoress — Robert Phelps, introduction, *Selected Writings of the Ingenious Mrs. Aphra Behn,* 1950

But in a great many instances there seems to be no particular reason for picking the word, since the writer's sex is already apparent:

> It is not necessary for Miss M. to be an authoress, indeed I do not think publishing at all creditable to men or women —Lord Byron, letter, 1 May 1812

> ... Miss Katherine Mayo, authoress of *Mother India* —*Atlantic,* April 1928

> ... a very famous title of an unknown play by Helmina von Chézy, the authoress of the libretto to Weber's *Euryanthe* —Otto Erich Deutsch, *Modern Language Notes,* February 1948

> Miss Rebecca West, the authoress, has made a special study —*London Calling,* 15 July 1954

> Their mother, the famous authoress, seems to have had great charm —W. H. Auden, *New Yorker,* 1 Apr. 1972

> She also is a board member of a large department-store chain; a working authoress of cookbooks — Melvin Durslag, *TV Guide,* 14 Apr. 1973

> ... Margaret Zellers shares some of her favorite small and special places in a country that has become second home to this globe-trotting, trustworthy authoress —Linda Gwinn, *Town & Country,* July 1980

In some instances the word seems somewhat pejorative:

> Their heroines go through the motions of sexuality, usually wholesale, merely by way of retaliation for what their authoresses believe to be the habits of men —G. Legman, *Love and Death,* 1949

> ... my wife, and the women in her consciousness-raising group, and the authoresses in *Ms.* magazine ... have decided it's all my fault —John Updike, *Playboy,* January 1975

> Murdoch cares too much to play the authoress paring her fingernails —Linda Kuehl, *Saturday Rev.,* 8 Jan. 1977

> The result is an uneasy book in which one feels that the authoress has ventured into an unfamiliar territory —Quentin Bell, *Times Literary Supp.,* 21 Mar. 1980

Insofar as offense inheres in *authoress* itself and not simply in the whole class of gender-specific occupational names, it is probably uses like these that have given it a bad odor.

To summarize: *Authoress* is not a heavily used word, and it is one that you can easily avoid if the risk of giving offense seems great. Still, writers have found it useful on occasion down through the past 500 years. Jane Austen used it of herself without qualm:

> I may boast myself with all possible vanity to be the most unlearned and uninformed female who ever dared to be an authoress —letter, 1 Dec. 1815 (in Lounsbury 1908)

It can be used condescendingly but is more often simply neutral.

authority When *authority* refers to a person, it is most often followed by *on,* but several other prepositions are possible:

> I'm not an authority on civil rights —Johnny Mathis, quoted in *Globe and Mail* (Toronto), 18 May 1964

> ... Mr. H. R. Palmer, a high authority on the history of Northern Nigeria —Sir James G. Frazer, *Aftermath,* 1937

> ... who was an authority upon mushrooms —Eric Partridge, *From Sanskrit to Brazil,* 1952

> He has attained identification as an authority in a certain vein of knowledge —Paul Horgan, *Ladies' Home Jour.,* January 1971

Man is the final authority of what he wants —James B. Coulter, quoted in *Johns Hopkins Mag.,* Summer 1971

When *authority* refers to a cited source, *for* is usual:

... one never knows the exact authority for any one statement —*Times Literary Supp.,* 29 May 1969

When it refers to a power or convincing force, several prepositions may be used:

... the central government had no real authority over the states —Leon H. Canfield & Howard B. Wilder, *The Making of Modern America,* 1962

... local-government units are created by, or on authority of, the state in which they are situated —Frederic A. Ogg & P. Orman Ray, *Introduction to American Government,* 8th ed., 1945

... that formal authority under which ... he was able to record some part of life —John Malcolm Brinnin, *New Republic,* 17 Nov. 1952

... his similar constructions of the 1960's have the authority to mock the avant-garde as conservative —*Current Biography,* December 1965

... is close enough to college to have authority about campus life —Walter Havighurst, *Saturday Rev.,* 13 Feb. 1954

... a fantasist's pose of authority on such matters —Theodore Sturgeon, *E Pluribus Unicorn,* 1953

avenge, revenge Watt 1967 puts the distinction between these two words this way: "*Avenge* ... suggests an act of just retribution, often for wrongs done to others. *Revenge* ... suggests malice or resentment rather than justice and usually applies to an injury, real or fancied, against oneself." Copperud 1970 cites four commentators in agreement, and Shaw 1975, Bryson 1984, Chambers 1985, Lurie 1927, MacCracken & Sandison 1917, and Utter 1916 are likewise in agreement. It is a nice distinction, which we commend to your attention. Our evidence shows, however, that the distinction is only sometimes observed.

Here are a few examples of *avenge* that observe the distinction:

During his second term he was impeached and removed from office. His wife ... in 1924 entered the gubernatorial campaign to avenge her husband —*American Guide Series: Texas,* 1940

... it was a son who would some day avenge his father —Charles Dickens, *A Tale of Two Cities,* 1859

But here we find *revenge* used in the same way:

... has left little doubt that she is out to revenge her father's death —Geoffrey Godsell, *Christian Science Monitor,* 14 Sept. 1979

... bands of Maryland men set out to revenge the deaths of their comrades —Howard Fast, *The Unvanquished,* 1942

The special use of *revenge* is to indicate a getting even on one's own account:

Since then, the Administration has been revenging itself on the Post —Russell Watson, *Newsweek,* 15 Jan. 1973

... revenging himself in a most devilish manner upon his greatest enemies —Roald Dahl, *Someone Like You,* 1953

... the hope of revenging himself on me was a strong inducement —Jane Austen, *Pride and Prejudice,* 1813

The doctor, who was a person of nice honour, resolving to revenge the flagrant insult, immediately flew to the chimney-piece, and taking down a rusty blunderbuss, drew the trigger upon the defiler of his bed —Oliver Goldsmith, *The Citizen of the World,* 1762

But *avenge* is also used in the same fashion:

... its outraged victim finally avenged himself —John Hohenberg, *Saturday Rev.,* 13 Nov. 1971

He had an insult to avenge, a dishonor to be washed off his imaginary escutcheon —James T. Farrell, *What Time Collects,* 1964

... thought he always avenged an injury, he never bore malice for one —Charles Kingsley, *Hereward the Wake,* 1866

... boastful of what he would do to avenge himself on the rascal-people —Charles Dickens, *A Tale of Two Cities,* 1859

Although the distinction described above is a useful one which we would advise you to follow, it is actually ignored almost as often as it is observed.

aver Copperud 1970, 1980 calls *aver* objectionable when it means "say." Although he adds the opinions of Bernstein and Flesch to his own, the fact is that except in legal contexts *aver* hardly ever means anything else. Copperud's objection appears to be based on dictionary definitions—for instance "to declare positively." But one must remember that the degree of positiveness is often more apparent to the writer than it is to the reader. These are typical uses:

The Duchess of Rutland, who ventured nearest, was even heard to aver that she discerned a tear in Elizabeth's eye —Sir Walter Scott, *Kenilworth,* 1821

But where was Richard? Adrian positively averred he was not with his wife —George Meredith, *The Ordeal of Richard Feverel,* 1859

"No American as rich as Mrs. Ballintin," the architect solemnly averred, "need ever be entirely without heirlooms." —Mary Austin, *Starry Adventure,* 1931

The tragedy of the nineteenth century, Pope Leo XIII averred, was that the workers were lost to the Church —Anne Fremantle, *Saturday Rev.,* 6 Mar. 1954

Strato had proudly averred that he did not need the help of the gods to make a world —Benjamin Farrington, *Greek Science,* 1953

... truth, indeed, may not exist; science avers it to be only a relation —Henry Adams, *Mont-Saint-Michel and Chartres,* 1904

The money saved by improved surveying, Dee averred, would suffice to found a mathematical readership in each of the two universities —S. F. Mason, *Main Currents of Scientific Thought,* 1953

In 1899 most scientists would have unhesitatingly averred that nature was like this —Sir James Jeans, *The New Background of Science,* 1934

If, as some people aver, animals are not talking when they make noises, what is it they are doing? —Emily Hahn, *New Yorker,* 24 Apr. 1971

... the hypocrisy of the Poles, both I. S. and V. aver, exceeds even that of the Viennese —Robert Craft, *Stravinsky,* 1972

This, members of the inner circle of art aver, would be a "disaster." —Joanne Dann, *Saturday Rev.,* 8 Jan. 1977

average *Average,* says Jensen 1935, should not be used to mean "customary, ordinary, usual"; Evans 1957 concurs; Copperud 1970 notes that Bernstein 1965 and Follett 1966 do not agree. Even though an occasional writer puts this sense in quotation marks,

... an ideal crowd of "average" American men —Joyce Carol Oates, *Harper's,* April 1972

this is a dead issue. The use has been completely standard for many years.

The average reader of the newspaper —Charles W. Eliot, *Education for Efficiency,* 1909

Can we study in Dante and Milton the faith of the average man? —Albert Guérard, *Education of a Humanist,* 1949

The law in charging them with such a duty has shaped its rules in disregard of the common standards of conduct, the everyday beliefs and practices, of the average man and woman —*Selected Writings of Benjamin N. Cardozo,* ed. Margaret E. Hall, 1947

... makes them, perhaps, less able to understand the average man —Bertrand Russell, *Education and the Good Life,* 1926

If you pay too much by mistake, the average Briton will give you your proper change —Richard Joseph, *Your Trip to Britain,* 1954

The average graduate of the grammar school in 1870 could not read with ease, nor could he write an ordinary letter in good English in a legible hand —*Dictionary of American Biography,* 1928

The average family doctor today works about 60 hours a week —Dodi Schultz, *Ladies' Home Jour.,* August 1971

averse to, from Samuel Johnson, in his Dictionary of 1755, has this comment at sense 3 of *averse:* "It has most properly *from* before the object of aversion." He illustrates this with quotations from Hooker, Clarendon, and Pope. At sense 4 he adds, "Very frequently, but improperly, *to.*" This he illustrates with quotations from Clarendon and Swift. Lowth 1762 agrees with Johnson: "So the noun *aversion,* (that is, a turning away,) as likewise the adjective *averse,* seems to require the preposition *from* after it; and not so properly to admit of *to,* or *for,* which are often used with it."

Lowth's opinion, as you can see, is based on translating the Latin roots of the English word, and then selecting the preposition that translates Latin *a* as the appropriate complement. Johnson's statements are presum-

ably also based on the Latin. But not everyone agreed with Lowth and Johnson. Priestley in 1768 notes some writers using *averse from* and some *averse to;* the latter he finds "more truly English." Campbell 1776 favors *to* and rejects the etymological argument, and so does Lindley Murray in the edition cited in Baron 1982.

The preponderance of usage has been on the side of Priestley, Murray, and Campbell. Even Sam Johnson the conversationalist did not heed Johnson the lexicographer:

Why, Sir, you cannot call that pleasure to which all are averse —1769, in Boswell, *Life of Samuel Johnson,* 1791

Although Hodgson 1889 terms *averse to* a blunder, he acknowledges it to be "almost universal"; Vizetelly 1906 says that "present usage prefers *averse to.*" But *averse from* has not disappeared. Although some American handbooks (Raub 1897 corrects British examples of *averse from* to *averse to*) advise against using it and others (Reader's Digest 1983 for instance) find it pedantic, *averse from* is still in good, albeit predominantly British, usage.

... Democratic senators from the East were no less averse from free trade than their Republican colleagues —Samuel Eliot Morison, *Oxford History of the American People,* 1965

... was not at all averse from a spice of gossip —Bonamy Dobrée, *English Literature in the Early Eighteenth Century, 1700–1740,* 1959

He was by no means averse from constructing a theory first, making observations second —D. H. Pennington, *Seventeenth Century Europe,* 1970

... averse from killing, he just tells the ... bank staff that this is the greatest day in their lives —Dilys Powell, *The Sunday Times* (London), 2 June 1974

... tries to strike a middle course, averse both from exaggeration and from whitewashing —*Times Literary Supp.,* 10 Dec. 1954

I am inveterately averse from any sort of fuss —Max Beerbohm, *Seven Men,* 1920

Twentieth-century British commentators have differed over the question. The Fowler brothers (1907) favor *averse to,* and Fowler 1926 terms *averse from* a pedantry, as does Partridge 1942. Gowers 1948 favors *averse from,* but lets Fowler's opinion stand in his revision (Fowler 1965). Mittins et al. 1970 cites a number of other British commentators with varying opinions. Sellers 1975 finds *averse to* more common, as does Phythian 1979; neither condemns *averse from. Averse to* is, in fact, the more common phrase in both varieties of English:

Not that the Princetonian is always averse to putting on the glitz —Guy D. Garcia, *Time,* 28 Nov. 1983

They are not averse to sipping human blood on occasion —Donald Dale Jackson, *Smithsonian,* November 1982

... naturally he was not totally averse to the promotion he got from the defenders of the peculiar institution —*Times Literary Supp.,* 12 Feb. 1970

Although Campbell is not averse to polemics —Stephen Spender, *New Republic,* 2 Feb. 1953

No wonder he was averse to the novels of Stendhal —W. H. Auden, *New Yorker,* 2 May 1953

... a horror of cruelty which made me very averse to war —Bertrand Russell, *London Calling,* 24 Mar. 1955

Gaunt had never been averse to an audience at these moments —Ngaio Marsh, *Colour Scheme,* 1943

See also ADVERSE, AVERSE.

aversion   There has been less controversy over the years about the prepositions that go with *aversion* than about the ones that go with *averse.* Reader's Digest 1983 will admit *to* or *for,* Phythian 1979 *to, from,* and *for,* with *to* more common than *from* and *for.* Our files bear out Phythian's observation.

There are a few prepositions of which we have in our files but a single example. Phythian singles out for censure a British public speaker's *aversion of;* we have no other examples with *of.* We do have a single *against:*

> ... some particular word or expression against which he cherishes a special aversion —Lounsbury 1908

Lounsbury elsewhere uses *to.* And Boswell seems to have used *at* at least once:

> He said that mankind had a great aversion at intellectual employment —James Boswell, *London Journal, 1762–1763,* ed. Frederick A. Pottle, 1950

When Boswell reconstructed Johnson's words for the *Life,* however, they came out this way:

> Mankind have a great aversion to intellectual labour —*Life of Samuel Johnson,* 1791

To is, as Phythian observed, the most common preposition:

> But I have no aversion to the issues being discussed —Jimmy Carter, quoted in *N.Y. Times,* 14 Feb. 1980

> ... had an aversion to makeup —Garson Kanin, *Cosmopolitan,* March 1972

> And all aversions to ordinary humanity have this general character —G. K. Chesterton, in *A Century of the Essay,* ed. David Daiches, 1951

> Bill was consistent in his aversion to noise —Joseph Mitchell, *McSorley's Wonderful Saloon,* 1938

> ... their aversion to the split infinitive springs not from instinctive good taste, but from tame acceptance of the misinterpreted opinion of others —H. W. Fowler, *S.P.E. Tract 15,* 1923

> Nonetheless, I believe that my aversion to Studio 54 has deeper wellsprings —Carll Tucker, *Saturday Rev.,* 28 Apr. 1979

From has the next greatest amount of use:

> He felt an aversion from expressing his views — Angus Wilson, *The Middle Age of Mrs. Eliot,* 1958

> My aversion from the word "teach" —F. R. Leavis, *Times Literary Supp.,* 29 May 1969

> ... she had an instinctive aversion from the past — Elizabeth Bowen, *A World of Love,* 1955

> ... a Puritan aversion from sex —Leslie A. Fiedler, *Encounter,* April 1954

> ... his aversion from pipes and increasing affection for after-dinner cigars —Howard Nemerov, *Federigo, or, The Power of Love,* 1954

The use of *for* goes back quite a ways, but seems to be less common now than either *to* or *from:*

> But, of all the names in the universe, he had the most unconquerable aversion for Tristram —Laurence Sterne, *Tristram Shandy,* 1762

> For society indeed of all sorts ... he had an unconquerable aversion —Samuel Butler, *The Way of All Flesh,* 1903

> The aversion for boiled milk may be older than certain beliefs —Morris R. Cohen, *The Faith of a Liberal,* 1946

> ... it had a marked aversion for the notes of the new age, enthusiasm, mysticism, rapture —Van Wyck Brooks, *The Flowering of New England, 1815–1865,* rev. ed., 1946

Besides these, the OED shows that Bacon used *towards* in the 17th century (we have no modern examples with *towards*) and also has an example from Addison with *against* (like the use by Lounsbury quoted above). But in the 20th century, *to, from,* and to a lesser extent *for* hold sway.

avid   *"Avid,"* says Barzun 1985, "means hungry, greedy, moved by physical appetite." With this definition as his point of reference, he goes on to criticize several uses of the word that do not fit his conception of the word's meaning. Kingsley Amis, in Michaels & Ricks 1980, seems to concur. Barzun's definition, however, cannot be found in the OED or Webster's Second or Webster's Third, and for good reason—it does not represent what the word usually means. Barzun perhaps based his notion on the meaning of the French word from which *avid* is derived, but his emphasis on "physical appetite" is mistaken. In English the use of the word to denote physical appetite is rare. The OED has an 1866 example of a "dragon avid for his prey." We have these:

> ... on arms exposed to avid *Aedes aegypti* —C. N. Smith, *Pesticide Progress,* July 1968

> ... has been an avid smoker ever since —*Time,* 19 Mar. 1951

> ... giving her accumulated richness over to that tiny blind mouth so avid to suck —John Updike, *Couples,* 1968

The notion of physical appetite underlies this use too:

> So I really must get rid of that original rat nightmare, and the idea of that closing-in circle of thousands of avid glittering eyes —Elizabeth Bowen, letter, reprinted in *Partisan Rev.,* 1948

But those are all our examples. From the beginning (1769) the usual use has been to denote desire or eagerness rather than physical appetite.

The basic meaning of *avid* is "eager." But *avid* is generally a more intense word than *eager.* It adds to *eager,* in use that tends to be literary, the notion of great desire or greed, or, in use that runs more to journalism and standard reference works, the notion of great enthusiasm. The first of these two somewhat divergent uses is the longer established.

Avid is often applied to people; in such use it may stress either desire and greed or enthusiasm:

> To all of these avid participants, the bargainers made representations —*American Guide Series: Minnesota,* 1938

> . . . the duty of all musical organizations to play for this avid and absorptive public —Virgil Thomson, *The Musical Scene,* 1947

> . . . every month hundreds of millions of dollars in new securities were snapped up by avid investors — Allan Nevins & Henry Steele Commager, *The Pocket History of the U.S.,* 1942

> . . . an avid collector of matchboxes —*Time,* 7 Jan. 1946

> . . . you are almost snatched inside the shops by avid proprietors —Claudia Cassidy, *Europe—On the Aisle,* 1954

> . . . an avid student of Sandburg —Gerald W. Johnson, *New Republic,* 15 Dec. 1952

> . . . taken over by an avid fisherman —Horace Sutton, *Saturday Rev.,* 12 June 1954

> . . . a talented musician, an avid bowler, and a student of existentialist literature —*Johns Hopkins Mag.,* October 1965

> . . . an avid reader, an opera buff, and is very much up on politics —William Nolen, M.D., *McCall's,* October 1971

> . . . was an avid botanist, as this superb estate of 11 hectares bears witness —Geri Trotta, *Gourmet,* December 1982

It is also applied to personified abstractions and to parts of people:

> . . . business has never been an especially avid supporter of these programs —Andrew Hacker, *N.Y. Times Book Rev.,* 2 Sept. 1979

> Beautifully made books can be shared with an interested grownup as avid little fingers are guided in careful handling —Alice Rusk, *Library Jour.,* 15 Mar. 1967

> . . . the usual group of ghouls who materialize from nowhere to feast their avid eyes on tragedy —Van Siller, *Cosmopolitan,* March 1972

> . . . had given his obviously avid mind an opportunity to pick up matters far beyond the ken of most —John McNulty, *New Yorker,* 13 June 1953

And to ordinary abstractions:

> . . . still takes an avid interest in Tanzanian politics —William Edgett Smith, *New Yorker,* 30 Oct. 1971

> . . . frown on what they consider his avid fondness for the limelight —*Time,* 3 June 1946

> His avid thirst for knowledge —*Times Literary Supp.,* 21 Jan. 1955

> . . . my dominant emotion was one of avid curiosity —S. S. Van Dine, *The Greene Murder Case,* 1927

The foregoing examples have shown *avid* in an attributive position. It is also used as a predicate adjective, and in that position tends to be followed by *for* or *of* or by *to* and an infinitive:

> He was convivial, bawdy, robustly avid for pleasure —F. Scott Fitzgerald, "The Rich Boy," 1926

> He was not avid for responsibility —C. S. Forester, *The African Queen,* 1935

> She watched him eagerly, avid for any gleam of surprise or disapproval —Margery Allingham, *More Work for the Undertaker,* 1949

> He was writing for a public avid for gruesome details —*New Yorker,* 20 June 1953

> The press, always avid for personality clashes —*I. F. Stone's Bi-Weekly,* 22 Mar. 1971

> A powerful will grown to manhood, avid of glory — H. A. Overstreet, *About Ourselves,* 1927

> Sinclair Lewis is close akin to his own Babbitt; avid of quick effects and immediate rewards —Ben Ray Redman, *Saturday Rev.,* 15 Feb. 1947

> The two cultures are equally avid of message — Edmund White, *Saturday Rev.,* 6 Jan. 1973

> The island markets were filled with all sorts of delectable sea food, and Sallie was always avid to learn new dishes —*The Autobiography of William Allen White,* 1946

> . . . avid to spend such spare time as they possessed reading better things —Anthony Powell, *Punch,* 30 Dec. 1953

> . . . employs 1,450 people and is avid to demonstrate that it deserves its current $53.5-million budget — Herman Nickel, *Fortune,* 2 June 1980

> . . . people were avid to be consumers —Andrew Hacker, *N.Y. Times Book Rev.,* 24 June 1984

Avid is a relatively recent word and was not widely used until the 20th century. The foregoing examples illustrate typical 20th-century usage and are a reliable guide for your use of the word.

awake, awaken *Awake* is a verb that has not yet settled down from its long and tangled history. It, like *wake* (see WAKE, WAKEN), is a blend of two older verbs, one transitive (or causative) and the other intransitive. These two verbs had different principal parts—one set being irregular and the other regular. The OED says that one of these inflected forms in Old English became used as a separate verb with regular inflections added; this verb became our modern *awaken. Awaken* is still regular, with *awakened* as its past and past participle.

Awake, on the other hand, still has its mixture of regular *(awaked)* and irregular *(awoke, awoken)* principal parts. The frequency with which these are employed has varied over the years. The OED points out that Shakespeare used only *awaked.* Fowler 1926 found *awoke* commoner than *awaked* in the past and *awaked* commoner than *awoke* in the past participle. Fowler does not mention *awoken,* which was labeled obsolete in Webster 1909. Gowers in Fowler 1965 keeps the original note on the past *(awoke* rarely *awaked)* but changes the note on the past participle to "*awaked* sometimes *awoken* and rarely *awoke.*"

Awoken presents a special problem. The OED notes that the past participle of the Old English equivalent of *awake* was (in modern spelling) *awaken,* but by the 13th century the *-n* had been lost, leaving a past participle *awake,* which survives now only as an adjective. As *awake* fell into adjectival use, a new past participle *awoken* was formed from the irregular past *awoke.* *Awoken* was so little attested that Webster 1909 listed both it and the original *awaken* as obsolete. Webster's Second continued the obsolete designation, apparently through someone's carelessness—there was 20th-century evidence for *awoken* in the Merriam-Webster files when the book was edited.

British commentators are in some disarray. Partridge 1942 discovered *awoken* in a mystery by Agatha Christie. He called it wrong. Bryson 1984 simply repeats Partridge. Phythian 1979 thinks that *awoken* does not exist. Gowers in Fowler 1965 recognizes it, but the OED Supplement takes no notice. Longman 1984 gives *awoken* as the only past participle.

Awoken has staged a strong comeback in the 20th century. The evidence in our files begins during World War I and comes primarily from British sources:

> . . . I was awoken by a very persistent lark —Robert Graves, letter, 22 May 1915

> . . . with eyes like sparks and his blood awoken —John Masefield, *Reynard the Fox,* 1919

> . . . his sense of insecurity was awoken —E. M. Forster, *A Passage to India,* 1924

> The boy had awoken to this sound —*Horizon,* October 1941

> . . . where a dozing visitor is awoken by a padding maid with an afternoon tea —Nigel Dennis, *Partisan Rev.,* July–August 1943

> . . . the householder spirit had awoken in me —P. G. Wodehouse, *Joy in the Morning,* 1946

> He had awoken in this rare mood —Evelyn Waugh, *Scott-King's Modern Europe,* 1947

> Donald had awoken at six —Angus Wilson, "Mother's Sense of Fun," 1947

> . . . should not have awoken to the truth —Arnold J. Toynbee, *Saturday Rev.,* 16 Aug. 1947

> . . . the town was awoken by a wild yelling —Alan Moorehead, *The White Nile,* 1960

> Among the lads thus rudely awoken —Ivor Herbert, *Winter's Tale,* 1974

> This reference has awoken some expensive memories —*Private Eye,* 7 Mar. 1975

It is probable that *awoken* is the prevailing past participle in British English today, and we know it also exists, at least orally, in American English. Our written evidence for American English use is weak, possibly because the verb itself is less common in American English than British English. So at the present time American English has both *awaked* and *awoken* as past participle; *awoken* predominates in British English; *awoke* is considerably less common in both British and American English.

The original past participle *awaken* appears still to exist in Jamaican English:

> Mr. L. C. . . . told the Gleaner that he was awaken by noise and heat —*Jamaica Weekly Gleaner,* 13 Feb. 1974

awaken See AWAKE, AWAKEN.

awesome The use of *awesome* as a generalized term of approval is relatively recent and has not received much comment in usage books. Harper 1985 tested their usage panel on the subject with the expression. The panel may have been bemused by the example sentence, which referred to the New York Yankees' relief pitcher Goose Gossage. Several panel members were sufficiently impressed with Gossage's fastball to feel the description apt.

Awesome has been part of the standard hyperbole of sports broadcasting and writing for several years. It may have been popularized by professional football broadcasts; when *great* came to be applied freely to plays and players of average to good quality, *awesome* was rushed in to supply the idea of better than average. The use of the word in sportswriting is not quite so recent as you might imagine, although our earliest citation appears to be sarcastic:

> After this awesome exhibition the Yanks settled down and played baseball —*N.Y. Times,* 21 June 1925

A couple of more recent examples:

> . . . finished his season in awesome fashion, winning eight of his last nine decisions and posting a 1.07 earned-run average for that span —Roger Angell, *New Yorker,* 3 Dec. 1984

> The depth of quality on the Steeler squad is awesome—there is no apparent weakness anywhere —Anson Mount, *Playboy,* August 1979

Such use is, however, far from limited to the world of sports. Howard 1984 says that preppies favor the word. Our files are perhaps not finely attuned enough to the usage of preppies to confirm this transatlantic observation, but we do have evidence of its use in the speech and writing of young people:

> The article on Henry Thomas of E.T. was totally awesome —letter to editor, *People,* 13 Sept. 1982

> Wildlife Camp was good to me too. My Quest was called Lakes and Streams. It was awesome —letter to editor, *Ranger Rick,* March 1985

> "It's totally awesome," said 9-year-old Robin Meisner of Newton —Bella English & Patricia Currier, *Boston Globe,* 1 Jan. 1986

This use, which appears to be chiefly oral, often attracts the intensifier *totally.* It is strictly a generalized term of approval.

Marge Piercy, one of the Harper panelists, wrote "We lost 'awful' so then we needed 'awesome'. . . ." It is quite possible that her summary of the situation helps account for the growth in the use of *awesome.* The OED marks *awesome* "Chiefly Scotch." Its introduction into present-day English seems to have come from Sir Walter Scott early in the 19th century, at approximately the same time that the weakened sense, "disagreeable, objectionable," of *awful* was developing. This sense, and the simple intensive sense that developed later may well have influenced some writers to choose *awesome* for "inspiring awe." Here are a few representative older examples:

> To harness its power in peaceful and productive service was even then our hope and our goal, but its awesome destructiveness overshadowed its potential for good —Dwight D. Eisenhower, message on atomic energy, 17 Feb. 1954

> Your nomination, awesome as I find it, has not enlarged my capacities —Adlai E. Stevenson, *Speeches,* ed. Richard Harrity, 1952

> ... the physician's awesome responsibility for life and death —Gerald Wendt, *N.Y. Herald Tribune Book Rev.,* 9 Oct. 1949

> ... in the past three years have come awesome but not inspiring improvements upon the original forms of atomic death —Norman Cousins, *Saturday Rev.,* 7 Aug. 1948

> One night this week, the flood reached its awesome crest —*Time,* 7 July 1947

> It was an awesome sight to watch the great seas piling in —Charles Nordhoff & James Norman Hall, *Pitcairn's Island,* 1934

Compare these with these more recent examples:

> ... there is something manic, even awesome, about the sergeant's pious belief in the infallibility of his polygraph —William Styron, *This Quiet Dust and Other Writings,* 1982

> ... embryonic development in every species poses some of the most awesome mysteries —Gary Blonston, *Science 84,* March 1984

> The number of orchestral and operatic works based on his poems is awesome —D. J. R. Bruckner, *N.Y. Times Book Rev.,* 16 Oct. 1983

> ... for several years they were considered too costly to import, even by stores that offer other luxury goods. Now, thanks to the strengthening dollar, the prices no longer seem awesome —Abby Rand, *Town & Country,* December 1982

> The U.S. economy looks awesome, especially to outsiders —*Wall Street Jour.,* 8 Oct. 1984

> ... some of the more awesome vintages of Bordeaux and Burgundy —Jay Jacobs, *Gourmet,* March 1980

Awesome has not lost its primary meanings, but even if we set the sports and spoken use as a generalized term of approval aside, it seems to be becoming less intense. It may well be following a pattern of development similar to that followed by *awful* a century earlier.

awful, awfully

> The word *awful* should however be used with caution, and a due sense of its importance; I have heard even well-bred ladies now and then attribute that term too lightly in their common conversation, connecting it with substances beneath its dignity —Hester Lynch Piozzi, *British Synonymy,* 1794

Mrs. Piozzi appears to have been the first person to remark in print on the weakened sense of *awful* that was developing in spoken English toward the end of the 18th century. She did not give us any examples of the use, and it is more than a decade before written examples are found. This may be one of the earlier ones; it sounds like the weakened sense, but the context is a bit short to be certain:

> This is an awful thing to say to oil painters —William Blake, *A Descriptive Catalogue of Pictures ...,* 1809

These next two are more certain:

> It is an awful while since you have heard from me —John Keats, letter, 27 Apr. 1818 (OED Supplement)

> ... there was an awful crowd —Sir Walter Scott, letter, 20 Feb. 1827 (in George Loane, *A Thousand and One Notes on A New English Dictionary,* 1920)

The OED shows Charles Lamb before 1834 as its earliest example. The sense became well established during the 19th century:

> ... the awful chandeliers and dreary blank mirrors —W. M. Thackeray, *Vanity Fair,* 1848

> What an awful blunder that Preston Brooks business was! —Jefferson Davis, quoted by Mary Chesnut, diary, 27 June 1861

> It is awful to be in the hands of the wholesale professional dealers in misfortune —Oliver Wendell Holmes d. 1894, *The Autocrat of the Breakfast-Table,* 1857

Although Joseph Hervey Hull's *English Grammar* of 1829 put "the weather is awful" in a list of "incorrect phrases," there seem not to have been a great many decriers of the use before the 20th century. Richard Grant White 1870 objected to the use of *awfully* as an intensive, calling it a Briticism, and Bardeen 1883 mentioned two other 19th-century commentators as critics. But in the first quarter of the 20th century or so the use was roundly thumped by numerous commentators, including Vizetelly 1906, Utter 1916, MacCracken & Sandison 1917, Whipple 1924, Lincoln Library 1924, and Lurie 1927, among others. "*Awful* does not mean *ugly* or *disagreeable,*" wrote Utter, belatedly objecting to a sense that had been in use for more than a century. It has continued to flourish in the 20th century, in two distinct senses, "extremely disagreeable or objectionable" and "exceedingly great":

> ... what an awful lot shoe-laces can tell you —Logan Pearsall Smith, *All Trivia,* 1934

> He had rented a pretty awful house —Edmund Wilson, *Memoirs of Hecate County,* 1946

> On this last we all had an awful time with Hull —Sir Winston Churchill, *Closing the Ring,* 1951

> I do an awful lot of talking and singing —Cornelia Otis Skinner, quoted in *Los Angeles Examiner,* 20 Apr. 1952

> The weather has been awful —Janet Flanner, *New Yorker,* 27 June 1953

> Much of it is about what you might expect, pretty awful —W. G. Constable, quoted in Lucien Price, *Dialogues of Alfred North Whitehead,* 1954

... but when it gets off its toes and settles down to trying to unsnarl its plot, it is pretty awful —John McCarten, *New Yorker,* 7 Jan. 1956

The color was awful, like in bad MGM musicals —Pauline Kael, *Harper's,* February 1969

... his bronchial troubles are extravagantly awful —V. S. Pritchett, *N.Y. Times Book Rev.,* 10 June 1979

discreet, discrete This is awful —Einstein 1985

Vulgar and awful, but useful —James MacGregor Burns, in Harper 1985

After all, an awful lot of people learn American English —Janet Whitcut, in Greenbaum 1985

Awful is also used as an intensive adverb, like *awfully,* but in our evidence is not as common in writing as *awfully* is:

It's a sad state of affairs and awful tough on art —H. L. Mencken, *Prejudices: Second Series,* 1920

... and an awful little is too much —Joseph Wood Krutch, *Saturday Rev.,* 24 July 1954

While the weakened senses were developing, the original senses continued in use:

She had not been used to feel alarm from wind, but now every blast seemed fraught with awful intelligence —Jane Austen, *Northanger Abbey,* 1818

... the awful striking of the church clock so terrified Young Jerry, that he made off —Charles Dickens, *A Tale of Two Cities,* 1859

... had applied to the War Department for an extension of ten days, and was awaiting an answer from that awful headquarters —John William DeForest, *Miss Ravenel's Conversion from Secession to Loyalty,* 1867

... I am in fear—in awful fear—and there is no escape for me —Bram Stoker, *Dracula,* 1897

The awful arithmetic of the atomic bomb —Dwight D. Eisenhower, address to U.N., 8 Dec. 1953

... in the half-light it had an awful majesty, so vast, so high, and so silent —Edward Weeks, *Atlantic,* July 1956

... something unknown and awful was going to happen —James T. Farrell, *What Time Collects,* 1964

It was an awful war, one of the worst —William Styron, *This Quiet Dust and Other Writings,* 1982

A few commentators feel that *awful* can no longer be used in its original senses, but it obviously can when the context is clear. An ambiguous context will, of course, leave the reader uncertain. Ambiguity can even be created as between the two weakened senses:

General Hood is an awful flatterer; I mean an awkward flatterer —Mary Chesnut, diary, 1 Jan. 1864

The intensive adverb *awfully* was attacked as a Briticism by Richard Grant White in 1870. The Oxford American Dictionary as recently as 1980 continues the depreciation of the intensive with the remarkable claim that "careful writers" avoid it. Perhaps so, but good writers have certainly not avoided it since it became established in the mid-19th century. Some of our exam-

ples are from fiction and drama, but others are from ordinary discursive prose:

"... Would you think it awfully rude of me if I asked you to go away?" —Oscar Wilde, *The Picture of Dorian Gray,* 1891

... and they like it awfully —Rudyard Kipling, *The Day's Work,* 1898

... the awfully rich young American —Henry James, *The Wings of the Dove,* 1902

... who seemed so awfully afraid of anything that wasn't usual —John Galsworthy, *The Dark Flower,* 1913

I used to learn quotations; they are awfully genteel —Lord Dunsany, *The Glittering Gate,* 1909 in *Five Plays,* 1914

... one of those awfully nice, well-brought-up, uneducated young creatures —Aldous Huxley, *Those Barren Leaves,* 1925

... staring at them with those awfully brilliant eyes of his —Dorothy Canfield, *The Brimming Cup,* 1921

It's most awfully nice of you to think of it —Willa Cather, *The Professor's House,* 1925

... was something more than an awfully nice girl —*The Autobiography of William Allen White,* 1946

"I'm awfully sorry," I said —W. Somerset Maugham, "The Alien Corn," 1931

... suddenly all the frocks in size fourteen seem awfully girlish —Phyllis McGinley, *Saturday Rev.,* 21 Feb. 1953

... a masterpiece of its kind, and if the kind is not awfully profound ... —*Times Literary Supp.,* 30 June 1966

... seemed awfully cold and self-possessed —Edith Oliver, *New Yorker,* 22 Oct. 1966

That word "I" makes you seem awfully responsible, doesn't it? —Bailey 1984

Awfully has other uses than just that of intensifier; however, these are not so frequently met:

I should have been asleep instantly, but he of the red nightcap now commenced snoring awfully —George Borrow, *The Bible in Spain,* 1843

There is no time at which what the Italians call *la figlia della Morte* lays her cold hand upon a man more awfully than during the first half hour that he is alone with a woman whom he has married but never genuinely loved —Samuel Butler, *The Way of All Flesh,* 1903

They sat, awfully gazing into the distance —Ford Madox Ford, *It Was the Nightingale,* 1933

... paused, to direct his eyeglass awfully upon a small boy sitting just beneath the lectern —Dorothy L. Sayers, *Busman's Honeymoon,* 1937

According to Mary Hiatt, in *The Way Women Write* (1977), there is a notion abroad that *awfully* is a typically feminine intensifier. As the preceding examples show, it is not particularly marked for sex.

The history of *awful* and *awfully* is not unique; *dread-*

ful, dreadfully, frightful, frightfully, horrid, horridly, terrible, and *terribly,* for instance, had all undergone similar weakening to become used in intensive function earlier than *awful* and *awfully.* The process seems to be a normal one in English. Some writers have turned to *awesome* to avoid having their *awfuls* misunderstood, but even *awesome* now seems to be undergoing a similar change. A few other writers—mostly British—are trying to revive the old spelling *aweful* for the earlier senses:

> . . . the aweful art of biography —Jill Tweedie, *The Guardian,* 8 Nov. 1973

> . . . a grotesque figure with a huge and aweful wooden mask —Richard Southern, *The Seven Ages of the Theatre,* 1964

> . . . striking originality and awe-ful grandeur — *Times Literary Supp.,* 12 Feb. 1970

awhile, a while For a word that has been in use in English since before the 12th century, *awhile* has taken a long time to achieve a final form, and there is good evidence that the process is not yet complete. The underlying problem is etymology: *awhile* is compounded from the article *a* and the noun *while* and has been written as one word in adverbial function since the 14th century.

Now the usual prescription, propounded at least as early as Krapp 1927, is that when *awhile* is an adverb, it should be written as one word and when it functions as a noun phrase, it should be written as two words. Here are two examples that fit the theory:

> . . . it gives him a chance to chat awhile —Edward Hoagland, *Harper's,* February 1971

> ". . . and I'll stay outside for a while . . ." —James Stephens, *The Crock of Gold,* 1912

The prescription is neat and it seems sensible enough, but there are two problems with it. First, *awhile* is often written or printed as one word after a preposition, such as *for, in,* or *after,* where theory holds it should be two words, and second, *a while* is often written or printed as two words after a verb where theory holds it should be one word. Our evidence indicates that neither of these floutings of the prescription has shown the least tendency to abate. Let us look at them in turn.

It is the use of the one-word *awhile* after a preposition that attracts the most attention, for it is the easier of the two problems to be dogmatic about. The number of commentators who touch on it is very large: Krapp 1927, Bernstein 1958, 1965, 1977, Fennell 1980, Irmscher 1976, Little, Brown 1980, McMahan & Day 1980, Harper 1975, 1985, Shaw 1970, Johnson 1982, Nickles 1974, Bryson 1984, Phythian 1979, Janis 1984, Freeman 1983, Heritage 1982, Longman 1984, Copperud 1970, 1980, Corder 1981, and many more. Harper opines that copy editors frequently "correct" *a while* to *awhile* in phrases like "a while ago," and that this "correction" accounts for many instances of the one-word *awhile* found in print where two words might have been expected. Harper's is a plausible theory, but it unfortunately cannot be proved, and it is vitiated slightly by the OED's showing the first *awhile ago* to have been printed by Caxton in 1489. And the plain fact of the matter is that, in spite of the universal opposition of the above-listed commentators (and more), *awhile* is often spelled as one word in phrases like *awhile ago* or *after awhile.* Look at these examples:

> . . . try to get its members to show up for work once in awhile —*Wall Street Jour.,* 10 July 1980

> We forgot, for awhile, the terrible troubles —Barbara Cressman, letter to the editor, *Harper's,* February 1971

> After awhile, the policemen arrested the three men —H. L. Stevenson, *UPI Reporter,* 1 July 1982

> . . . a time-delay switch that keeps it shining for awhile —*Consumer Reports,* November 1978

> The price of gold has been at $500 for awhile —Barbara Ettorre, *N.Y. Times,* 29 May 1980

> . . . even went to college for awhile —*N.Y. Times,* 13 Aug. 1976

> That got old after awhile —Richard Chamberlain et al., *Quarter Horse Jour.,* July 1983

> He had to suspend publication of the Weekly for awhile —Thomas Powers, *Rolling Stone,* 17 Feb. 1972

> . . . if prices turned up for awhile —Roy W. Jastram, *Wall Street Jour.,* 11 Nov. 1980

> . . . I got better for awhile —Randall Jarrell, letter, March 1965

> All she needs is a little guiding once in awhile — Katie Whitmore, quoted in *Christian Herald,* June 1967

> After awhile, even the professors. . . . —Paul Potter, *Johns Hopkins Mag.,* October 1965

> I lived with him and his wife for awhile —Sally Kempton, *Village Voice,* 28 Feb. 1968

And these examples are from just the last two decades; we have many others from the preceding five. The OED has 19th-century examples from Ouida in 1882 and Keats in 1872 as well.

Now let's look briefly at the opposite side of the coin: the two-word *a while* where *awhile* might be expected. Freeman 1983, for instance, believes in a strict dichotomy of style: two words after a preposition, one word after a verb. Heritage 1982, however, would allow either one or two words after a verb while calling for two words after a preposition. Consider, for instance, these variant stylings:

> . . . the commitments you mentioned awhile back — Cynthia Lofsness, quoted in William Stafford, *Writing the Australian Crawl,* 1978

> . . . used a while back to dispose of cooking grease — *New Yorker,* 3 Dec. 1984

> . . . and it will take a while —Flannery O'Connor, letter, 9 Nov. 1962

> "And that's going to take awhile." —Martin Karpiscak, quoted in *Christian Science Monitor,* 21 Oct. 1980

> . . . it has taken me awhile to read it —Jerome Beatty, Jr., *Saturday Rev.,* 11 Feb. 1967

The difficulty of deciding that a single form is correct for adverbial use is illustrated by the example given in Corder 1981:

Can you stay awhile?

The difficulty can be seen if we recall that a number of noun phrases—all functioning adverbially—can be used in the same slot *awhile* occupies:

Can you stay a week?

Can you stay a few minutes longer?

Can you stay a little while longer?

In short, many noun phrases beginning with *a* and a space function as adverbs in English, and there is no compelling reason to prefer *awhile* to *a while* in such contexts.

What conclusion can we reach? It is obvious that both *awhile* and *a while* are in wide use in places where some commentators believe the opposite form belongs. It is also obvious that your using *awhile* or *a while* makes no great difference to the reader. And both forms are etymologically and semantically identical, the only difference being the presence or absence of a space after *a*. The problem is a compounding problem. And except for the fact that almost every handbook in existence worries about it, it is not important at all.

There are, therefore, two things you can do. You can follow your own feel for the expression and write it as one word when that seems right and as two words when that seems right. If you don't trust your own feeling for language that far, you can use a rule of thumb based on the consensus of the handbooks: use *a while* after a preposition and before *ago*, and use either *awhile* or *a while* in other places. You can substitute the phrase "for a while" for the one-word form in your context to help you decide.

We close with some more examples. The first three fit our rule of thumb. But how about the last three? Would you write *a while* or *awhile?*

So let us escape from all this for a while —Simon 1980

A while later I followed the workers —E. L. Doctorow, *Loon Lake,* 1979

She would only stay awhile —E. L. Doctorow, *Ragtime,* 1975

And the flapdoodle has lasted quite awhile longer —Thomas J. Bray, *Wall Street Jour.,* 14 Jan. 1981

. . . till I had been to college a while —Marge Piercy, in Harper 1985

. . . he would dictate a while, then lapse into a coma —Flannery O'Connor, letter, 20 Apr. 1957

B

back   For use with *return, refer,* etc., see REDUNDANCY.

back-formations   *Back-formation* is a term used by linguists, lexicographers, and etymologists to describe a word formed by removing an affix—real or supposed—from an already existing word. Back-formation is an active process of word-formation: the front matter of *12,000 Words* mentions such relatively recent examples as *gangle* from *gangling, lase* from *laser, free-associate* from *free association,* and *one-up* from *one-upmanship.* It has been an active process for quite a long time and has given us *burgle* (1870) from *burglar, peddle* (1532) from *peddler, grovel* (1593) from *groveling, enthuse* (1827) from *enthusiasm, diagnose* (ca. 1860) from *diagnosis, donate* (1785) from *donation, televise* (1927) from *television,* and *typewrite* (1887) from *typewriter.* Verbs are not the only kinds of words produced by back-formation. Another fairly numerous group consists of singular nouns formed from real or supposed plurals. Among these are *statistic* (1898) from *statistics, pea* (1666) from *pease,* and *kudo* (1926) from *kudos.*

Back-formations are mentioned here because a number of them have irritated commentators on usage from time to time. Some—for instance *burgle, donate,* and *enthuse*—have been carried from book to book for years, while others, such as *kudo,* are of more recent vintage. You will find several of these treated at their own alphabetical places.

background   Copperud 1970 lists Flesch 1964 and Gowers in Fowler 1965 as objecting to *background* as a fad or vogue word. In his 1980 edition Copperud adds this remark: "The popularity and usefulness of *background,* however, is such that few are likely to be influenced by such criticism." True. The criticism had, in fact, simply gone out of date; apparently very few paid any attention. Here are some examples of the criticized uses; they are perfectly standard.

. . . courses designed to prepare kids with poor backgrounds for college work —Steven V. Roberts, *Commonweal,* 30 Jan. 1970

. . . the differences in the two boys' backgrounds are annihilated by their age —Pauline Clark, *Times Literary Supp.,* 2 Apr. 1971

. . . an ambivalent figure, suspect on the right for friendship with Nelson A. Rockefeller, a Harvard background, entree in Georgetown, and flexibility on Russia —Barbara W. Tuchman, *N.Y. Times Book Rev.,* 11 Nov. 1979

The word has developed a specialized use, usually attributive, in the reporting of American politics:

. . . "deep background" information not for any attribution for which the reporters must assume responsibility if they use it and "background" information —*UPI Reporter,* 6 June 1974

. . . could not recall whether the four censored passages were background or deep background —*N.Y. Times,* 30 May 1976

. . . prefers to speak on a background basis himself, i.e., no direct quotations —Aaron Latham, *New York,* 29 Mar. 1976

back of, in back of   In 1909 Ambrose Bierce included *back of* in his book of words and expressions to be banned. He did not mention *in back of.* In 1917 MacCracken & Sandison found *back of* "colloquial" and added a note for *in back of:* "undesirable." Fowler 1926 mentions *back of* as an Americanism (as had Fitzedward Hall in 1880) without aspersing it. From these slender beginnings arose a tradition of condemning these inoffensive phrases for one reason or another that has lasted some 70 years. Here are a few of the mixed reviews:

> *Back of* is colloquial only. *In back of* is a vulgarism —J. C. French, *Writing,* 1924

> *Behind* is Literary English; *back of,* colloquial; *in back of,* childish —J. C. Tressler, *English in Action, Course 1,* 1935

> *back of* for *behind* is a colloquialism; *in back of* for *behind* is an illiteracy. *In front of* is good English — Partridge 1942

This sort of inconsistent criticism persists at least to Guth 1985. A few commentators—Shaw 1975 and Prentice Hall 1978, for instance—are sure there must be something wrong (it wouldn't be in those other books if there weren't something wrong), but they are not sure quite what; they settle for "wordy." Other commentators have found nothing wrong: Lurie 1927, Evans 1957, Copperud 1970 (retracting his earlier faultfinding), Reader's Digest 1983. Bernstein 1965, 1971 finds both standard but still has a preference for *behind.*

So what was wrong with these phrases? Nothing really. They are Americanisms, as far as we know now; perhaps the native nervousness of American usageasters toward Americanisms is to blame.

Back of is traced by the OED Supplement to 1694. Here are a few examples:

> "I hunted one season back of the Kaatskills" — James Fenimore Cooper, *The Pioneers,* 1823

> If he misstated, he asked his friends from Georgia, back of him, to correct him —John C. Calhoun, *Works,* 1840 (in Thornton, 1939)

> Back of the bluffs extends a fine agricultural region —William Cullen Bryant, *Letters of A Traveller,* 1850

> To be vested with enormous authority is a fine thing.... There was nothing back of me that could approach it —Mark Twain, *A Connecticut Yankee in King Arthur's Court,* 1889 (*A Mark Twain Lexicon,* 1938)

> Back of the purely objective system of sounds ... there is a more restricted "inner" or "ideal" system —Edward Sapir, *Language,* 1921

> Bill placed it on the wall back of the bar —Joseph Mitchell, *McSorley's Wonderful Saloon,* 1938

> ... back of every exquisite dinner stands a temperamental chef —*Time,* 16 June 1952

> Franklin stood back of me in everything I wanted to do —Eleanor Roosevelt, quoted by Catherine Drinker Bowen, *Atlantic,* March 1970

> Back of the glittering facade of new office buildings is, perhaps, the most angry and unpleasant ghetto in all the country —John Kenneth Galbraith, *New York,* 15 Nov. 1971

> ... back of my activity there will be the coherence of my self —William Stafford, *Writing the Australian Crawl,* 1978

In back of is more recent and is not as well attested in our files. Curiously, Webster's Second labeled *back of* "*Colloq., U.S.*" but left *in back of* unstigmatized. Nobody knows why. This quirk of labeling has been noticed in several usage books and may have influenced the usage panel of Heritage 1969 in finding *in back of* slightly less objectionable than *back of.* A few examples:

> The picture represents a burning martyr. He is in back of the smoke —Mark Twain, "How to Make History Dates Stick," 1899 (*A Mark Twain Lexicon,* 1938)

> ... the expectations that lie in back of this charge — Abram Kardiner, *The Individual and His Society,* 1939

> One day, I was sitting in the tiny parlor in back of the store —John McNulty, *New Yorker,* 23 July 1949

> ... the Navy has always been strongly in back of the venture —Thomas Wood, *N.Y. Herald Tribune,* 21 June 1953

Both *back of* and *in back of* are standard in American English.

bacteria   *Bacteria* is regularly a plural in scientific and pedagogical use. In speech and in journalism it is also used as a singular to mean "a variety or strain of bacteria":

> ... the first authorized outdoor release of a genetically-altered bacteria —Neil Strassman, *The News-Dispatch* (Michigan City, Ind.), 11 Mar. 1987

In this use a plural *bacterias* is sometimes found:

> ... more resistant to chlorine and elevated water temperatures than other bacterias —Allan Bruckheim, M.D., *Chicago Tribune,* 8 Feb. 1990

These are acceptable uses in journalism, and were first accurately described in Evans 1957.

For other foreign plurals, see LATIN PLURALS.

bad, badly   **1.** The adverb *bad* is not as old as the adverb *badly.* The OED notes a couple of instances of the former from the 17th century; the OED Supplement picks it up from the early 19th century, calling it "chiefly U.S." But it must have existed in 18th-century British English, because Baker 1770 complains about it:

> Some writers employ the word *bad* as an Adverb, and would not scruple to say *That was done very bad:* which is not English.... *bad* is only an Adjective. The Adverb is *badly.*

In modern use the adverb *bad* falls into two general areas of use, one of which is standard, and the other of which sounds more like a mistake and is usually considered less than standard.

The standard use of the adverb *bad* is equivalent in meaning to *badly.* It often occurs with *off:*

> The Americans didn't know how bad off they were until daylight —E. J. Kahn, Jr., *New Yorker,* 13 June 1953

> Are living composers really that bad off? —Ned Rorem, *N.Y. Times,* 20 Apr. 1975

After *do* and a few other verbs, *bad* is interchangeable with *badly:*

> . . . so I didn't do too bad —Denny McLain, quoted in *Sports Illustrated,* 29 July 1968

> The revenge Watson sought was not against any person, of course, but against Winged Foot itself, where the rule is: Hit it bad and it'll eat your lunch —J. O. Tate, *National Rev.,* 24 Aug. 1984

> A bad moving sow will soon go off her legs, and then you must look out for trouble —E. Walford Lloyd, *Pigs and Their Management,* 1950

Bad is also interchangeable with *badly* after *want* or *need:*

> . . . the war which he says will surely come, though Prussia wants bad to dodge it —Henry Adams, letter, 9 Apr. 1859

> . . . while we continually shout for peace and security, we don't seem to want it bad enough to prepare adequately —Brig. Gen. Robert C. Dean, quoted in *Springfield* (Mass.) *Union,* 15 May 1953

> . . . needed dough, and he needed it bad —James Atlas, *N.Y. Times Mag.,* 9 Sept. 1979

> I wanted to get a mandolin real bad —Bill Holt, quoted in *Bluegrass Unlimited,* 11 May 1982

You should note that most of these examples are from speech.

When *bad* functions in an intensive sense, more or less equivalent to *severely,* it sounds wrong to more people and is less likely to be considered standard, though Evans 1957 believes that this use will eventually become standard. Here are a number of examples. You will find that some of them are less jarring than others:

> . . . letting himself sink back down into the luxurious willess [sic] irresponsibility that is the nicest thing about being bad sick —James Jones, *From Here to Eternity,* 1951

> . . . was only a Trotskyist, and hated Communists bad —G. Legman, *The Fake Revolt,* 1967

> He has had frozen feet pretty bad —Walt Whitman, *Brooklyn Eagle,* 19 Mar. 1863

> ". . .And the Russians use twenty-five per cent of their population in food production and screw it up so bad they have to buy from the United States. . . ." —Len Deighton, *Spy Story,* 1974

> If the ratings fall a point or two, how bad can you hurt? —Jerry Solomon, quoted in *Forbes,* 14 Feb. 1983

2. Vizetelly 1906 and MacCracken & Sandison 1917 (and many others of that era) warned against using *badly* after *want* in the sense of "very much." By 1958 Bernstein was correcting *bad* after *want* to *badly,* indicating that *badly* was fully acceptable in this use.

> I want to live here badly —Jodie Foster, quoted in *TV Guide,* 11 Mar. 1983

As we have seen, *bad* is frequent in this use, but most of our evidence is from speech.

Similar use of *badly* in the expressions "badly in need of" and "need badly," although criticized by commentators in the past, was found acceptable by the majority

of the usage panels of Heritage 1969 and Harper 1975, 1985. It is standard.

> I told all my people to go home and get some sleep, which they needed very badly, having missed one night entirely —Dean Acheson, quoted in Merle Miller, *Plain Speaking,* 1973

3. The use of *badly* after a copula (or linking verb) is widely discussed, with many handbooks warning of divided usage or warning against the use of *badly. Badly* comes most frequently after the verb *feel,* and for the subtleties of that usage, you should see FEEL BAD, FEEL BADLY.

Our evidence shows *badly* less common after other linking verbs. The examples that follow all come from standard usage; *badly* is considered an adjective in this construction:

> Henry looked badly —Francis Hackett, *Henry the Eighth,* 1929

> If a body of water is muddy, or otherwise discolored, or smells badly . . . we can regard it as polluted —George S. Hunt, *Bioscience,* March 1965

> The stuff tasted badly —Stephen Nemo, *Avant-Garde,* March 1968

Even though dictionaries recognize this standard use of *badly* as an adjective, our relatively spare evidence suggests that most writers use *bad* instead.

4. Evans 1957 notes that the comparative and superlative of *bad* and *badly* are *worse* and *worst.* At one time *badder* and *baddest* were used, but they dropped out of the standard language in the 18th century, surviving only in dialectal use. In recent time *badder* and *baddest* have been revived, but only in relation to the slang sense of *bad* meaning "good, great."

5. See also FLAT ADVERBS.

bail, bale A person looking these words up in Webster's Ninth New Collegiate Dictionary would find seven homographs of *bail* and three of *bale,* most of which fortunately never get entangled. A verb *bail,* derived ultimately from Middle English *baille* "bucket," however, is often spelled *bale* in British English. Gowers in Fowler 1965 and Chambers 1985 both comment on the fact, and the OED Supplement shows corroborating evidence. When *bail out* means "to dip and throw water" or "jump from an airplane with a parachute," Americans use the *bail* spelling and many Britons use *bale.*

> . . . had no sooner bailed out than he was hit on the head by a piece of falling engine —Edwards Park, *Smithsonian,* June 1982

> The British airman who baled out —*London Calling,* 23 Feb. 1956

Our evidence shows that the *bale* spelling was used in the U.S. as recently as 1939, and the OED Supplement shows that the *bail* spelling is sometimes used in British English. There seems to be general agreement about the other homographs of *bail* and *bale.* If you are in doubt, check your dictionary.

baited, bated Heritage 1982 and Bryson 1984 point out that in the phrase "with bated breath" the *bated* is sometimes misspelled *baited:*

> . . . we wait and wait with baited breath —*N.Y. Times,* 15 June 1980

Bryson has an example from a British newspaper.

The verb *bate* is related to *abate*. Here are a couple of proper examples:

> . . . find yourself waiting with bated breath for the next issue —Randall Collins, *Change,* Winter 1972–73

> And you are less than human if the exorcism sequence and its build-up don't bate your breath —Judith Crist, *New York,* 21 Jan. 1974

balance The extension of the meaning of this word to the remainder or rest of something other than money is an Americanism. It seems to have been first noticed in John Pickering's *Vocabulary* of 1816; the excerpt from this work quoted in the Dictionary of American English shows that Pickering considered it to be a Southernism. The earliest citation in the DAE, however, is from Pennsylvania, dated 1788. Noah Webster in a letter to Pickering in 1817 found the usage forced and unwarranted; he left it out of his 1828 dictionary. Joseph Hervey Hull's *English Grammar, by Lectures* of 1829 mentioned it in a list of incorrect phrases.

Subsequently, the expression was damned in a number of 19th-century books, including Bache 1869, Richard Grant White 1870, and Ayres 1881. Grant White denies that the expression is an Americanism, citing an example from a publication called "Once a Week," which must have been British. Citations in the OED show that this sense of *balance* began to appear in British English in the latter half of the 19th century. The chorus of objection continued unabated into the 20th century: Vizetelly 1906, Bierce 1909, MacCracken & Sandison 1917, Jensen 1935, and many others right up to Copperud 1980 and Janis 1984. Heritage 1969 dislikes it, too, downplaying the fact that 53 precent of their usage panel has found it acceptable.

But Heritage 1982 drops the usage note. Harper 1975, 1985 finds the usage entirely acceptable in informal contexts, and Reader's Digest 1983 finds it acceptable.

The sense has now been in use for two centuries, and has been carped at—to no avail—for more than a century and a half. No solid reason for avoiding the sense has been brought forward in all that time, although a few commentators have tried to construct something based on the original meaning—"scales"—of *balance.* The whole controversy has been nothing more than a repetition from one usage book to another. Uses like the following are entirely standard:

> About the balance of the book . . . one can only say that it is so bad . . . —William F. Buckley, Jr., *N.Y. Times Book Rev.* 6 June 1976

> The balance of the party was turned around and sent home —E. L. Doctorow, *Ragtime,* 1975

balding The adjective *balding* seems to have originated in *Time* magazine in 1938. It was the particular bugbear of Theodore Bernstein, who denounced it repeatedly as nonexistent and needless. Few other commentators seem to have been offended by it, and even two well-known usage panels have found it acceptable. The word seems to have filled a need, for it has become rapidly established in American English. Foster 1968 mentions a British critic who questioned its need in British English, but it seems to have established some sort of foothold there as well. The OED Supplement has a British citation that antedates the critic by five years. The following examples demonstrate how rapidly the

word went from *Time*-style journalism to other publishing:

> . . . he crams a golf cap on his balding grey head — *Time,* 5 Dec. 1938

> A gaunt, balding, tight-lipped man —John Fischer, *Harper's,* May 1945

> . . . two middle-aged balding fat men —*The Autobiography of William Allen White,* 1946

> . . . a big balding six-footer —Truman Capote, *Other Voices, Other Rooms,* 1948

> A little, reddish-haired, balding fellow —William Carlos Williams, *The Build-Up,* 1952

> . . . pulled over his lap the balding buffalo robe — Wallace Stegner, "The Traveler" in *Perspectives USA,* Summer 1953

> He was a round balding man —E. L. Doctorow, *Ragtime,* 1975

> . . . a balding, thirtyish, would have been eroticist — Philip Roth, *Reading Myself and Others,* 1975

> . . . is bespectacled and balding —William Styron, *This Quiet Dust and Other Writings,* 1982

> The owner appears to be the balding man —Jay McInerney, *Bright Lights, Big City,* 1984

Besides being applied to buffalo robes, the adjective has begun to spread to other figurative uses:

> . . . as far as a balding hill near Kallista —Ray Davie, *The Age* (Melbourne), 26 Apr. 1975

> . . . the "pictures," unexpectedly, winning out today over the balding prose —*Vogue,* December 1982

bale See BAIL, BALE.

baleful, baneful These two words are somewhat similar in meaning as well as appearance and are sometimes used in quite similar contexts, but in the main they differ in emphasis. *Baleful,* the older and more frequently used word, typically describes what threatens or portends evil:

> . . . despite the baleful economic outlook —DeWitt C. Morrill, *Wall Street Jour.,* 23 Mar. 1954

> "Pest!" he said sharply and gave Waldo a baleful look —Jean Stafford, *Children Are Bored on Sunday,* 1953

> Men! Her gaze rested upon her husband with baleful intensity —Katherine Anne Porter, *Accent,* Summer 1946

> Complete with "uranium reactor," powerful atom smashers, a "hot lab" and other baleful equipment —*Time,* 18 Nov. 1946

But *baleful* is also used of what has an evil or pernicious influence or effect:

> . . . the baleful arts of sorcerers —Sir James G. Frazer, *The Golden Bough,* 1935

> . . . she had been launched under some baleful star; and so, was a luckless ship —Herman Melville, *Omoo,* 1847

... the baleful power of fanaticisms and superstitions —Edmund Wilson, *New Yorker,* 14 May 1955

Baneful applies typically to what causes evil or destruction:

He felt that some baneful secret in his life might be exposed —John Cheever, *The Wapshot Chronicle,* 1957

... the ugly, baneful and largely avoidable excretions of their employers' plants —Donald Gould, *Smithsonian,* May 1972

... were responsible for baneful policies still in force —Elmer Davis, *But We Were Born Free,* 1954

... her love for him is a possessive and baneful love —J. D. Scott, *Saturday Rev.,* 7 May 1955

Both words are used to modify terms like *influence, effect, result;* in such use there is little to choose between them:

From this dismal malady he never afterwards was perfectly relieved; and all his labours, and all his enjoyments, were but temporary interruptions of its baleful influence —James Boswell, *Life of Samuel Johnson,* 1791

The baneful influence of this narrow construction on all the operations of the government —John Marshall, *McCulloch* v. *Maryland,* 1819

balmy, barmy   *Balmy* is an old word, going back to the 15th century. It was used in contexts like these:

... sallied forth to enjoy the balmy breeze of morning —Thomas Love Peacock, *Headlong Hall,* 1816

The balmy summer air, the restful quiet —Mark Twain, *Tom Sawyer,* 1876

Around the middle of the 19th century it developed a new sense suggesting weakness or unbalance of mind. This sense is used in contexts like these:

"... I think I'd have gone balmy if it weren't for Walt Whitman.... —Christopher Morley, *The Haunted Bookshop,* 1919

"Two breakfasts? Wanting to let the child bathe? The man's balmy." —Evelyn Waugh, *A Handful of Dust,* 1934

Gowers in Fowler 1965 considers this later sense of *balmy* a misspelling of *barmy,* which has the same meaning:

... He knew He had to get out of it or go barmy — Richard Llewellyn, *None But the Lonely Heart,* 1943

Gower's objection to *balmy* was raised earlier by someone writing in the *Westminster Gazette* of 30 May 1896, as a citation in the OED Supplement shows. The Supplement editors stand firmly against both Gowers and *Gazette: barmy* in this sense is an alteration of the earlier—by some forty years—*balmy.* You need not worry about using the spelling *balmy.*

Both *barmy* and *balmy* are originally British. Our files show *balmy* to be more common in American English than *barmy.*

baneful   See BALEFUL, BANEFUL.

banquet   Copperud 1970 reports *banquet* as highflown when it is used for present-day public dinners; his 1980 book finds it both quaint and pretentious. He brings in Evans 1957 and Bernstein 1965 to buttress his assertion. However, Evans and Bernstein in his 1971 book devote most of their remarks to noting how the quality and quantity of food offered at a banquet has declined from times past. That sad fact had been noted earlier:

... a routine banquet menu (grapefruit, chicken, peas, ice cream) —*Time,* 15 Nov. 1948

How different things were in the old days!

... Leckerbiss Pasha of Roumelia, then Chief Galeongee of the Porte, gave a diplomatic banquet at his summer palace at Bujukdere.... He was an enormous eater. Amongst the dishes a very large one was placed before him of a lamb dressed in its wool, stuffed with prunes, garlic, assafœtida, capsicums, and other condiments, the most abominable mixture that ever mortal smelt or tasted —W. M. Thackeray, *The Book of Snobs,* 1846

State banquets like that given by the Galeongee of Roumelia—less revolting, no doubt—are still given from time to time:

... a recent banquet in Hong Kong, which featured simple preparations like rolled fillet of fish stuffed with mustard greens and Yunan ham, and more complex dishes like baby oysters stir-fried with scrambled eggs —George Lang & Jenifer Harvey Lang, *N.Y. Times Mag.,* 25 Jan. 1987

There can be no criticizing this use of the word. But perhaps a more typical use of *banquet* is to be found in reports like these:

Girl Scout Troop 103 held its second annual banquet and court of awards Saturday night in St. Mary's Church Hall —*Springfield* (Mass.) *Daily News,* 16 June 1953

... was honored as the '86 Horse of the Year at Saratoga Raceway at the recent USHWA Award Banquet held at the track —*Hoof Beats,* January 1987

At this sort of gathering the speeches and the presentations are the important thing, not the food. A later paragraph in the first report, for instance, tells us that the Girl Scouts were fed baked ham. The entry in the OED suggests that banquets were heading in this direction as far back as the end of the 19th century.

So why the fuss? It is true that in her new and revised edition of *Etiquette* in 1927 Mrs. Emily Post listed *banquet* among several expressions she held to be pretentious and not used by "Best Society." But Mrs. Post was unlikely to have been concerned with the Girl Scouts or the horse of the year. A more likely answer is the fact that *banquet* was laid under interdiction by William Cullen Bryant in his *Index Expurgatorius,* compiled when he was editor of the *N.Y. Evening Post* and published in 1877. Bierce 1909 repeated the rejection. Old newspaper prejudices never die—and some don't even fade away.

Bantu   *Winners & Sinners*—house organ of the *N.Y. Times*—warned in November 1983 that *Bantu,* a word used in scholarly writing for a group of African languages and a family of African peoples, is considered offensive because of its use by the South African government.

> ... the official term "Bantu," which, like "non-white," most black Africans find offensive —Charles Mohr, *N.Y. Times,* 17 Nov. 1974

> ... a new phrase to replace "bantu" ... , a word despised by blacks —*Christian Science Monitor,* 17 Feb. 1978

Typical uses of the word that may give offense are these:

> ... today 60% of GM's South African employees are Bantus or Coloreds —*Annual Report, General Motors Corp.,* 1971

> Permanent employment offered to respectable and honest man, Bantu or Coloured. ... Bring reference book, NI card, UI card and testimonials —advt., *Cape Times* (South Africa), 1 Feb. 1975

barbarian, barbaric, barbarous Although these words are well treated in books that discriminate synonyms from one another (such as Webster's New Dictionary of Synonyms), a few usage books also venture to comment on them. Reader's Digest 1983 gives a number of examples of how the words are used, while Chambers 1985 and Bryson 1984 try to emphasize what they think the distinctions should be.

Barbarian is primarily used as a noun. When used as an adjective, it usually means "of or relating to barbarians":

> ... survives as a tribute to our barbarian ancestors —*Times Literary Supp.,* 28 May 1971

> ... border troops were increasingly recruited in the later Empire from barbarian tribes —Weston La Barre, *The Human Animal,* 1954

> ... some thirty years after the barbarian penetration of Britain had been checked —F. M. Stenton, *Anglo-Saxon England,* 2d ed., 1947

It is also used to suggest lack of refinement or culture:

> ... attacked the romance for its confusion and lack of unity, considering it a barbarian invention unworthy of literature of classical stamp —Robert A. Hall, Jr., *A Short History of Italian Literature,* 1951

> ... had laid Newport open to the barbarian invasions of the new millionaires —Marcia Davenport, *My Brother's Keeper,* 1954

Barbaric is also used to mean "of or relating to barbarians":

> ... specimens of graphic art found among extant barbaric folk —Edward Clodd, *The Story of the Alphabet,* 1900

> ... the advance of barbaric horsemen —Vivian J. Scheinmann, *N.Y. Times Book Rev.,* 24 Oct. 1976

In anthropology it signifies a state between savagery and civilization:

> Men may be considered to have risen into the next or *barbaric* state when they take to agriculture —Sir Edward B. Tylor, *Anthropology,* 1930

Barbaric is also used in a sense of "wild, primitive, uncultivated" that is not pejorative:

> I sound my barbaric yawp over the roofs of the world —Walt Whitman, "Song of Myself," 1855

> When Emerson does allude to artificial life, it is to find buried there the startling, strange, barbaric life of nature —Richard Poirier, *A World Elsewhere,* 1966

> ... produced the tangled, loose, barbaric magnificence of the Elizabethan drama —Marchette Chute, *Ben Jonson of Westminster,* quoted in *Think,* November 1953

> ... a barbaric quality that fits into the current mood of jewelry design —advt., *N.Y. Times,* 8 June 1981

But the wild and uncivilized has its negative side too:

> ... installed himself in a pad at the Dorchester of such barbaric tastelessness that it must have been shipped piecemeal from Las Vegas —S. J. Perelman, *New Yorker,* 1 Jan. 1972

> He felt embattled, a guardian of high culture during the barbaric Eisenhower years —James Atlas, *Atlantic,* April 1982

Barbaric is also used to denote or suggest the cruelty and inhumanity that civilized people associate with barbarians:

> ... intended to demonstrate that the human race is even more barbaric now than it was in 1431 —Wolcott Gibbs, *New Yorker,* 13 Oct. 1951

> ... yet I knew the barbaric devil that lurked in his breast and belied all the softness and tenderness —Jack London, *The Sea-Wolf,* 1904

> ... the first and second planetary wars have helped to make of this half century the most barbaric interval of the Christian era —Adlai E. Stevenson, *Call to Greatness,* 1954

> ... the barbaric treatment of Soviet prisoners of war —William L. Shirer, *The Rise and Fall of the Third Reich,* 1960

Barbarous is sometimes used to mean "of or relating to barbarians":

> Further, we find, that the Roman Legions here, were at length all recalled to help their Country against the Goths, and other barbarous Invaders —Jonathan Swift, "A Proposal for Correcting ... the English Tongue," 1712

> Caesar's short sketch of the Germans gives the impression of barbarous peoples. ... They had not reached the agricultural stage, but were devoted to war and hunting —Henry O. Taylor, *The Mediaeval Mind,* 4th ed., 1925

It often means simply "uncivilized":

> Italic culture would have been quite barbarous had it remained untouched by Greek or Etruscan influences —C. A. Robinson, Jr., *Saturday Rev.,* 1 May 1954

> ... Troy, which the narrow-minded Greeks called a barbarous city, though Helen found it, I dare say, far pleasanter than Sparta —George Santayana, *Atlantic,* April 1948

Both were frontier states, less cultivated and hardier than the others, and regarded as barbarous and only half Chinese —A. L. Kroeber, *Anthropology,* rev. ed., 1948

It is also used to mean "harsh, cruel":

You have been wantonly attacked by a ruthless and barbarous aggressor —Sir Winston Churchill, *The Unrelenting Struggle,* 1942

... the barbarous conflicts between nations that call themselves Christian —Edmund Wilson, *A Piece of My Mind,* 1956

Barbarous is frequently used to suggest lack of culture and refinement:

... the civilizing of the barbarous talk show —Karl E. Meyer, *Saturday Rev.,* 15 Apr. 1978

... what a barbarous gut-rotting drink your German beer is —Robert Graves, *I, Claudius,* 1934

... the author may have a good deal of difficulty in persuading his publisher to give him a large enough advance to permit him to escape perhaps from this barbarous country to lodgings in Paris or Rome — Harrison Smith, *Saturday Rev.,* 14 Nov. 1953

Barbarous has a special tendency to be applied to language. When it is not merely being used to express general disapproval, it means "full of barbarisms"—barbarisms being a diffuse class of words and expressions that offend in some way. For a discussion of these, see BARBARISM.

We breed barbarous Centaur-words such as *quadraphonics* from Latin sires out of Greek dams —Howard 1980

... the usual scholarly biography, written in barbarous academese —Dwight Macdonald, *New Yorker,* 12 Mar. 1955

... when the language had been so refined, that Elizabethan poetry was commonly thought crude and barbarous —Charles C. Bell, *PMLA,* September 1947

... when he is at his worst Faulkner's style is barbarous—barbarous in its abundant solecisms, barbarous in its intolerable purple passages —Edward Wagenknecht, *New Republic,* 23 June 1952

... offensively elitist in its barbarous jargon —Terry Eagleton, *N.Y. Times Book Rev.,* 9 Dec. 1984

To summarize the evidence: *barbaric* and *barbarous* share most of their uses. They are even used in a weakened sense as generalized terms of disapproval:

... the barbaric heat of late August —*Time,* 1 Dec. 1947

... the barbarous Midwestern climate —Mary McCarthy, *New Yorker,* 23 Mar. 1957

They differ chiefly in two uses: *barbaric* is often used in its nonpejorative "wild, primitive" sense in which *barbarous* is rare; and *barbarous* is used of language, while *barbaric* rarely is. *Barbarian* is still available as an adjective but is used less than either *barbaric* or *barbarous.*

barbarism In the simpler times of Campbell 1776 the rhetorical world had a symmetry and balance we can only admire now. Purity of expression, he said, implies three things, and accordingly it may be injured in three ways: by barbarisms, solecisms, and improprieties. Continuing the tripartite organization, Campbell found three kinds of barbarisms: the use of obsolete words, the use of new words, and the use of words "new-modelled"—cobbled up out of existing words or word elements. This classification of barbarisms was thereafter solemnly repeated from book to book and could be found as late as A. S. Hill 1895.

By the time Fowler 1926 was writing, the first two of Campbell's barbarisms were no longer a subject of debate, even though they might be listed in rhetoric texts. The barbarisms that Fowler wrote about were compounds that violated the principles of classical word formation, usually by being compounded from Greek and Latin elements, or English in combination with Greek or Latin. Among the words that Fowler lists as disputed on this ground are *bureaucrat, cablegram, electrocute,* and *Pleistocene;* more recent examples are *speedometer* and *television.*

Fowler, as a man educated in the classics, does not approve the coming of barbarisms, but he considers complaining about them a waste of time. Most people do not know *television* or *bureaucrat* to be malformed words; they just use them when they need to and go about their business. Fowler recognizes this, too, and the realization underlies his refusal to get overly exercised by the subject. And in actual fact, the fuss is over nothing: there is no requirement handed down from Dionysius Thrax or Priscian that forces English to form its words according to the principles obtaining for Greek or Latin. English follows its own processes of word formation.

We have no particular evidence to show that even writers on usage and grammar have applied the term *barbarism* with anything approaching precision; in fact they no longer even define it with precision:

A **barbarism** is an obviously incorrect use of words, usually illiterate or eccentric rather than vulgar — Lee T. Lemon, *A Glossary for the Study of English,* 1971

A barbarism is an expression in the mouth of an educated speaker which is so at variance with good sense and good usage that it startles the hearer —Follett 1966

Here we see that not only Campbell's notion of the word has been lost, but also Fowler's more restricted sense. The term has simply become an epithet of disparagement, a handy club for the usagist or reviewer to use in belaboring some poor expression or author. Here are a few examples, from Fowler's sense down to the modern:

But "antibody" has no such respectable derivation. It is, in fact, a barbarism, and a mongrel at that — Quiller-Couch 1916

... even preachers sometimes are guilty of barbarisms in pronunciation —Andrew Thomas Weaver, *Speech—Forms and Principles,* 1942

... never slips into the jargon or barbarisms that have disfigured some recent social history —R. K. Webb, *N.Y. Times Book Rev.,* 1 Apr. 1984

Surely we can agree, at least, that 'different than' is a solecism and a barbarism? —Howard 1984

barbiturate The prevailing pronunciation today stresses the second syllable, \bär-ˈbich-ə-rət\ and minor variants. A version stressing the third syllable, as \ˌbär-bə-ˈtyủr-ət\, may still be heard, especially among doctors. Increasingly common among ordinary educated speakers, and going against the spelling, is a version that does not reflect the second *r* in the spelling: \bär-ˈbich-ə-wət\. In accordance with this pronunciation, one sometimes finds the misspelling *barbituate* in print.

barely A couple of handbooks mention constructions with *barely* that they feel should be avoided. One comments on this sort of construction:

> He had barely begun his judicial experience, however, when the United States was drawn into World War I —*Current Biography 1951*

The handbook warns against the use of *than* in place of *when.* All our examples of this construction from edited prose use *when,* but it is not an especially frequent construction.

The other, a schoolbook, warns against using a negative verb with *barely* in this sort of construction:

> And you could barely see the black lines of the trees —R. H. Newman, *Far from Home,* 1941

> . . . he was trying to talk last time he was up here and he barely could talk above a whisper —Birch Monroe, quoted in *Bluegrass Unlimited,* September 1982

In these you are supposed to avoid *couldn't,* on the grounds that *couldn't barely* constitutes a double negative. The *couldn't barely* construction may exist in speech and student writing, but it is unattested in our files of edited prose.

The likelihood is that these books have made entries for *barely* on the basis of constructions that are much more likely with *hardly.* See HARDLY.

Here are some examples of the most common uses of *barely:*

> . . . so slight a movement it was barely noticeable —Roald Dahl, *Someone Like You,* 1953

> . . . the danger from which we barely escaped —Morris R. Cohen, *The Faith of a Liberal,* 1946

> . . . although I am barely in my dotage —Clifton Daniel, *N.Y. Times Mag.,* 3 June 1984

bargain The verb *bargain,* says Raub 1897, takes *with* a person, *for* a thing. Since 1897 a few prepositions have joined this pair, as the following examples show.
With a person or group of persons:

> The employer must not bargain with any group other than the one which has gained the majority vote —Horace Kidger & William E. Dunwiddie, *Problems Facing America and You,* 1959

> Judges bargain about reality with defendants —*Trans-Action,* March 1970

With may also be used with something considered as a helpful tool:

> I didn't have much to bargain with when they presented me with my 1965 figures at contract time —baseball player quoted in *Sporting News,* 26 Mar. 1966

For something:

> We had to bargain for everything, live on a shoestring —Lenora Slaughter, quoted in *Ladies' Home Jour.,* September 1971

> All you bargained for was a little music —Howard Taubman, *N.Y. Times Mag.,* 14 Mar. 1954

> The Wise Youth had not bargained for personal servitude —George Meredith, *The Ordeal of Richard Feverel,* 1859

About or *on* something or some subject:

> . . . right to organize into unions and to bargain about wages —Marshall Smelser & Harry W. Kirwin, *Conceived in Liberty,* 1955

> It ruled unanimously that management must bargain on pensions —*Time,* 4 Oct. 1948

To can also be used, when *bargain* is transitive:

> . . . the right to bargain his services to the highest bidder —*Springfield* (Mass.) *Daily News,* 26 May 1953

Bargain may also be used with a number of handy little adverbs. A sample:

> We bargained out our differences —*Wall Street Jour.,* 19 May 1955

> . . . unwilling to bargain away the twelve West German divisions —*Time,* 8 May 1954

> . . . you can sometimes bargain the price down —Izak Haber, *Rolling Stone,* 8 June 1972

barmy See BALMY, BARMY.

bar sinister In 1903 the prolific writer Richard Harding Davis published a novel titled *The Bar Sinister.* Its publication created a bit of controversy in the press over the correctness of the term *bar sinister.* The press clippings in our file concerning this affair are lengthy explanations of heraldic terminology. Bierce 1909 put it much more succinctly: "There is no such thing in heraldry as a bar sinister."

Maybe there is not one in heraldry, but there is one in English literature. *Bar sinister* seems to have been introduced by Sir Walter Scott in *Quentin Durward,* 1823, as a heraldic charge that was a mark of bastardy. A couple of sources opine that Scott might have picked up the term from French, in which language *barre* means "bend sinister," which is a band running from the lower left to the upper right on a coat of arms.

Bierce assumed that the *bar* in *bar sinister* was a misuse for *bend*—a bar is a horizontal line in heraldry and a bend a diagonal one. That may be true; however, *bend sinister* has nothing to do with bastardy. The *sinister* terms that do have to do with bastardy are *baton sinister* and *bendlet sinister.* If you are interested in distinguishing these terms, you need not seek out a book on heraldry; Reader's Digest 1983 covers this matter pretty thoroughly.

But it was Scott's *bar sinister* that caught the imagination of the public and the novel writer, and it has stayed in use since. As early as 1926 Fowler dismissed its controversial aspects, calling its correction "pedantry" except in technical contexts (and it is not found in technical contexts). Copperud 1980 calls Fowler's advice sensible. So do we. Here are a few examples:

... how he had started with the initial handicap of the bar sinister, the illegitimate son of a small Ayrshire farmer and a peasant woman —George D. Brown, *The House with the Green Shutters,* 1911

... supported the attempt to erase the bar sinister with which the United Nations had labeled Spain —Harold L. Ickes, *New Republic,* 6 Feb. 1950

... two who claimed a royal bar sinister —*Time,* 1 Aug. 1955

... the destinies of an estate and a fortune are decided by the intervention of a stranger whose connexion with the family is by a bar sinister —*Times Literary Supp.,* 27 Nov. 1969

In later years [T.E.] Lawrence treated his bastard status lightly, remarking that "bars sinister are rather jolly ornaments." In fact, the bar sinister was a tall hurdle to overcome —James C. Simmons, *Passionate Pilgrims,* 1987

baseball The idioms of baseball are strictly beyond the purview of this book. They present, however, a ready trap for the unwary who are casually tempted to mix baseball with usage. Three brief instances will suffice to make the point.

Mr. Vin Scully, a television sportscaster of considerable experience, stumbled over the expression "wait on the pitch" while announcing a World Series game in 1984. Apparently recalling some ancient or recent admonition to eschew *wait on* in favor of *wait for,* he made a remark about the ungrammaticality of the phrase. He had forgotten the game in his concern for "correct English." There is little reason to say a baseball batter is "waiting for" a pitch; if there were, the batter would in fact be waiting for the pitcher to do something. But when a batter "waits on" a pitch, the pitch is on its way and the batter is exercising self-discipline in order not to swing too soon. There is no matter of correctness here; the two phrases mean different things.

The other two instances concern the expression *between each.* Freeman 1983 states that you cannot say "the pitcher rests between each inning." This is true; the baseball idiom is usually "between innings," and the statement itself is absurd. Between innings the teams exchange places, the fans visit the concession stands or the toilet, and the radio and television stations play beer commercials.

Nicholson 1957 is essentially Fowler 1926 with some surface Americanization. Fowler's discussion of *between each* includes a lengthy illustrative example drawn from cricket. It was rather uncritically translated to baseball, with these somewhat ludicrous results:

NOT *A pitcher who tried to gain time by blowing his nose* between *every ball;* this must be corrected to *after every ball, between the balls,* or *between every ball & the next.*

It may be cricket, but it sure ain't baseball.

based When used to mean "established, founded" and when followed by a preposition, *based* is most often used with *on:*

As the university tradition came to America, it was based on four ultimate sources of strength —James B. Conant, *Atlantic,* May 1946

Less often, *based* is used with *upon:*

... perhaps only in the end based upon a complication in economics and machinery —T. S. Eliot, "Tradition and the Individual Talent," 1917

And least often, it is used with *in:*

... the non-denominational religion based in the hope of progress —Reinhold Niebuhr, *New Republic,* 23 Oct. 1953

Based, when used to mean "stationed or located at a base," is most often followed by the prepositions *at* or *in:* "a fleet based at the island," "She was based in California."

From 1781 to 1788 he was based in Leeds, touring in other north country towns —George Metcalfe, *Country Quest* (Wrexham, Wales), June 1974

... a couple of young Australian lawyers who were based at the hotel —David Butwin, *Saturday Rev.,* 13 Nov. 1971

Use of this sense with the preposition *on* is chiefly British:

... the roving correspondent of a leading Dutch newspaper, who has been based on London for the past twenty years —*London Calling,* 17 June 1954

Only occasionally is *on* found in American usage:

General Benjamin Lincoln, after failing to recapture Savannah, was now based on Charleston —Samuel Eliot Morison, *Oxford History of the American People,* 1965

Over may also be seen occasionally in special contexts:

... the fact that so many of the firms controlling this wealth are based over the border is one which Canadians often mention with anxiety —Andrew Walker, *Modern Times,* 1975

based on, based upon When *based on* begins a sentence, language commentators get worried. The problem is that in such a position, the phrase tends to be a dangling modifier:

Based on futures prices today for October delivery, Cuba will pay around $1.5 million —*N.Y. Times,* 25 Apr. 1964

Based on a systems planning approach, Battelle will come up with a number of procedures —*American School Board Jour.,* Septebmer 1968

Based upon is occasionally used in the same way:

Based upon these prior inquiries, we believe that appropriate club quarters can be provided —form letter quoted in Edmund Wilson, *The Bit Between My Teeth,* 1965

The sin here is a venial one. Some of the commentators on the use of *based on* (for instance, Barzun 1985, Freeman 1983, Bernstein 1965) readily admit that there are other fixed participial phrases used similarly—*owing to, strictly speaking, given, speaking of, according to,* for example—and never questioned. These writers feel that *based on* simply has not yet become established in the function of an absolute participle. Grammatically it works in the same way as the others, however, and the sentences given above as examples are perfectly understandable at first reading. Our evidence for the construction, however, is quite scanty; perhaps the construction is not common enough to have become solidly established. Note that when a *based on* phrase clearly modifies an element later in the sentence, it is not dangling and is fully acceptable:

> Based on the evidence to date, the best answer is that both are probably involved —Jeanne Chall, *The Instructor,* March 1968

basic Both *basic* and *basal* are relatively recent words formed in the 19th century. Fowler 1926 comments on them; his notion is that both adjectives were formed for use in scientific texts where *fundamental* might have been misleading. But Fowler notes *basic* being used in general contexts in place of *fundamental,* and of this he disapproves. Fowler's disapproval has been echoed by later British commentators such as Phythian 1979 and Longman 1984.

Howard 1978, however, notes that *basic* has won its place and that one would be pedantic to grumble about it. Probably few modern users of *basic* are aware of the word's origin in scientific writing. Although Fowler laid increasing use of the word to the desire of people to sound "up-to-date & scientific," its shortness has probably had as much to do as anything with its rapid establishment. Phythian is especially unhappy with the expressions *basic idea* and *basic reason.* The dearth of evidence in our recent files for these combinations suggests that they are probably speech forms and are not much used in edited prose. It would be pointless, if not pedantic, for us to censure speech forms in a book for writers.

Related to these speech forms is a use of *basic* after *your* that is apparently intended to be humorous:

> Madison, New Jersey . . . is your basic polyester suburbia —Alan Rich, *New York,* 6 Oct. 1975

> In both versions, Allegra Clayton, your basic blonde heroine, is cool, . . . accomplished —Eden Ross Lipson, *N.Y. Times Book Rev.,* 23 Dec. 1984

basically 1. Copperud 1970 notes that what he calls the "correct form" of the adverb—*basicly*—although sometimes seen in print, is unrecognized by dictionaries. Our evidence for the spelling is very slight: a 1916 issue of *Scientific American,* a book on criminology published in 1942, and a book in linguistics from 1953. Correspondents wrote in to us in 1921 and 1927 suggesting the word be entered in our dictionaries. For some reason the spelling simply has not caught on, even though it is etymologically impeccable. Since dictionaries do not enter what is not used, *basicly* seems doomed to continue unrecognized.
2. Several British commentators—Bryson 1984, Phythian 1979, Longman 1984, and Howard 1978—object to what they consider to be the unnecessary use of *basically.* From the scanty evidence they supply, it would appear that they chiefly object to the use of *basically* as a sentence adverb. A couple of American commentators, Nickles 1974 and Macmillan 1982, join the British.

The construction in question seems to be primarily a spoken one:

> Basically, the sun excites the crystalline structure of the cell —Ray Morgan, quoted in *Smithsonian,* February 1981

> Shock basically means that your legs and arms are getting no circulating blood anymore —Dr. Thomas E. Root, quoted in *N.Y. Times Mag.,* 19 Sept. 1982

This construction also appears in edited prose, however:

> Basically, it is an index of names and topics; it is not a concordance —*Times Literary Supp.,* 14 Nov. 1968

> Basically, we try to test and report on cars that are most widely sold —*Consumer Reports,* April 1977

> Basically, he's a God-fearing, red-blooded all-American boy who feels strongly about a lot of things —Ahmad Rashad, *Sports Illustrated,* 25 Oct. 1982

> . . . the doctors told me I would need an operation. . . . I basically had no choice —Edward J. Rollins, *People,* 22 Aug. 1983

> Basically, the cursor shows you where you are —*National Shorthand Reporter,* July 1985

"Nineteen sentences out of twenty in which *basically* appears would be sharpened by its deletion," says Howard. Well, maybe so. But the rigorous pursuit of excising *basically* does not look like an important path to better prose. *Basically,* as it is used in the examples here, is one of those little space-makers carried over from speech to speech-like prose; it does not seem to be so heinous a fault in the kind of prose in which it appears. You will notice that none of the examples above is of the high style—no deep discussions of political philosophy, religion, or literature here. In breezy journalistic writing an occasional *basically* will not hurt, but it should not be overdone.

basis 1. *Basis* figures in two somewhat long-winded phrases that are just the sort of thing to make usage writers foam at the mouth. The first of these phrases is *on the basis of* (or sometimes *on a basis of*), which is often made a candidate for replacement. However, when your geometry book says

> . . . this cannot be proved on the basis of the postulates that we have stated so far —School Mathematics Study Group, *Geometry, Part 1,* 1965

you cannot improve the sentence by substituting *on, by, after,* or *because of,* as suggested by Copperud 1970. The periphrastic preposition is right for the geometrical statement, and no simple substitution will improve it. But this is not to say that it can never be replaced without improvement or reduction in long-windedness. In this sentence, for instance,

> Hence, we find that a primary characteristic of propaganda is the effort to gain the acceptance of a view not on the basis of the merits of that view but, instead, by appealing to other motives. —Herbert Blumer, in *Principles of Sociology,* rev. ed., 1951

you could well replace "on the basis of the merits of that view" with "on its own merits," but that involves more than a simple replacement of *on the basis of* with *on.* Let us draw a hasty conclusion: when you meet your *on the basis of* in revising, consider how it fits the whole context of your piece and how it fits the rhythm and sense of the sentence. A mechanical replacement will not necessarily make your text more readable. (For practice you might try playing around with the sentence quoted just above. It can be tightened up considerably; still, in some revisions you might find retention of *on the basis of* helpful.)

The more challenging phrase is *on a ____ basis.* This phrase functions as an adverb and is guaranteed to make a usage commentator see red. It is a phrase which looks and sounds awkward and which is found quite often in less-than-elegant writing. Its awkwardness seems to be its chief virtue, for it allows a writer to write what might otherwise not be easily expressible:

> Baseball as at present conducted is a gigantic monopoly intolerant of opposition and run on a grab-all-that-there-is-in-sight basis —Cap Anson, 1897, quoted in *The Ultimate Baseball Book,* ed. Daniel Okrent & Harris Lewine, 1984

> Routine and remedial maintenance are available via resident engineers, single or multi-shift maintenance contracts, or on a per call basis —computer advt., May 1969

> . . . one lithographer announced commercial availability of continuous tone lithography on a production basis —Wallace B. Sadauskas, *Book Production Industry,* June 1967

In each of these examples the writer used the *basis* phrase to say something that would have been difficult to express in a less cumbersome way. You will note that the last two are of a technical nature; the phrase is not uncommon in technical contexts.

In these next examples the phrase is used in somewhat simpler contexts but in each case is not readily replaced by a plain adverb:

> . . . they're on a first-name basis with the agents — Joe Eszterhas, *Rolling Stone,* 17 Feb. 1972

> . . . transfer them to authorities which could handle them on a permanent peacetime basis —C. E. Black & E. C. Helmreich, *Twentieth Century Europe,* 1950

> . . . operates on a contract basis —*Current Biography 1948*

> . . . an appropriation of $7.5 million a year for a five-year period, allotted to the states on a matching basis —*Saturday Rev.,* 26 June 1954

> . . . will be run on a non-profit-making basis —Hardiman Scott, *London Calling,* 13 Jan. 1955

In the next example, *on a daily basis* means something different than *daily:*

> The accountants work on a daily basis in management's offices, plants and board rooms —*Forbes,* 15 May 1967

Now do not jump to the conclusion that we are recommending *on a ___ basis* as an all-purpose tool. It is awkward, and it can often be revised to advantage. Here, for example, is a sentence where "on a linage basis" could have been turned into "by the line" and been not only simpler but more easily understandable:

> Whether from their training as pedagogues or whether they were accustomed to being paid on a linage basis, their literary style was circumloquacious in the extreme —Gordon Clark, *The Reporter,* 6 Apr. 1967

The matter of revision is not always simple, though. Safire 1984 reprints a sentence of his own using the phrase

> . . . my cap is reverently doffed to Executive Editor A. M. Rosenthal, whose idea it was to thrust me into the language dodge on a weekly basis.

A correspondent of Safire's—perhaps frightened by a usage writer while young—objects to the *basis* phrase and asks why *weekly* or *every week* wouldn't do. The question answers itself. Not only do "thrust me into the language dodge weekly" and "thrust me into the language dodge every week" spoil the rhythm of the sentence, but they do not mean the same thing as what was written. The knee-jerk substitution simply does not work. In order to avoid *on a weekly basis* Safire would have to rewrite, perhaps coming up with the starchier "whose idea it was to have me write a weekly column on language." Safire did better the first time.

The conclusion to be reached here is that *on a ___ basis,* while generally awkward, can sometimes be useful. It is not a phrase found in very formal writing. But care and judgment are required in revising it out of your text; it may be better left alone than hastily revised.

2. When used with a preposition, *basis* usually takes *of* or *for:*

> The basis of optimism is sheer terror —Oscar Wilde, *The Picture of Dorian Gray,* 1891

> . . . the frustrating task of putting international affairs on a permanent basis of law and order —Adlai E. Stevenson, *Speeches,* ed. Richard Harrity, 1952

> . . . Indian trails . . . were the basis for many of their roads —*American Guide Series: North Carolina,* 1939

> . . . his theory of synthetic cubism involves abstraction as a basis for painting —Herbert Read, *The Philosophy of Modern Art,* 1952

When *basis* is used with *in,* the phrase *basis in fact* is usual:

> . . . the common . . . rationalization . . . has no real basis in fact —William Styron, *This Quiet Dust and Other Writings,* 1982

Basis may also be followed by an infinitive:

> . . . three-man committee which was studying a basis to arrange a cease-fire plan —*Current Biography 1951*

bated See BAITED, BATED.

B.C. See A.D., B.C.

be **1.** The history of this verb is long and complex, as anyone who looks at its entry in the OED will see plainly. Our present verb is made up of bits and pieces of three older verbs. In the 16th century, Strang 1970 tells us, *be* was regularly used for the second person singular and plural and the first and third persons plural in the present tense: we be, you be, they be. About this same time, *are,* a form surviving in northern dialects of English, began to stage a comeback. Eventually *are* ousted *be* from all its present indicative uses in standard English, and *be* was reduced in standard English to its subjunctive function. It has kept its older indicative uses in various dialects and in a few fossilized expressions such as "the powers that be."

The OED notes that *are* has even begun to drive *be* out of its subjunctive uses. This process may still be going on, but so far, we note, *be* has continued in its subjunctive uses:

> Whether you be black or white, if you're poor, you're poor —B. B. King, quoted in *Rolling Stone,* 21 Feb. 1980

If that be good fortune, it has recently become better —Vermont Royster, *Wall Street Jour.*, 21 July 1982

But love when practiced that way, be it surrounded by however many hearts and flowers, is really just a mask for men's aggressions —Merle Shain, *Some Men Are More Perfect Than Others,* 1973

The father's reconciliation with his son, figurative though it be, pays tribute to the myth of the eleventh-hour reconciliation —Molly Haskell, *Vogue,* March 1982

The subjunctive *be* is especially strong in a few fixed phrases:

Be that as it may, this work is as important —Martin Bookspan, *Consumer Reports,* September 1980

If I'm accused of male chauvinism, so be it! —William C. Vergara, quoted in Harper 1985

2. A good deal has been written about the use of *be* in Black English to indicate habitual or continued action, as it does in these examples:

Just before the post bar closed, the black custodian stepped out into the street. . . . "No telling how long any American Legion post can keep going, the way the members be getting older and older," he remarks —Jon Nordheimer, *N.Y. Times,* 27 Oct. 1974

. . . even though he only sings in church now, Little Richard still knows how to work a crowd. "People be leapin' outta their seats," he says —Vicki Jo Radovsky, *US,* 19 Nov. 1984

Monroe K. Spears in Michaels & Ricks 1980 points out that use of *be* is known in other dialects of English as well as in Black English. Here are a couple of Irish examples:

"Let me sit here for a while and play with the little dog, sir," said she, "sure the roads do be lonesome —" —James Stephens, *The Crock of Gold,* 1912

The Government does be callin the brother in for consultations —Myles na gCopaleen (Flann O'Brien), *The Best of Myles,* 1968

The ability of a verb form or auxiliary to indicate continuation or duration of an action is called by grammarians and linguists *aspect.* Since English is somewhat deficient in aspect, compared to some other languages, these dialectal forms do constitute an enrichment of the language. But they are not yet available to the writer of ordinary standard English, and no one knows if they ever will be.

There is a great deal more on the dialectal uses of *be* to be found in the Dictionary of American Regional English.

beat, beaten "The use of *beat* where *beaten* is called for . . . is illiterate," says Harper 1985. Don't you believe it. The statement betrays ignorance: no verb form used by Steele, Dr. Arbuthnot, and Dr. Johnson is illiterate:

He had beat the Romans in a pitched battle —Sir Richard Steele, *The Spectator,* No. 180, 1711 (OED)

They were beat . . . and turned out of doors —Dr. Arbuthnot, *The History of John Bull,* 1712

I have beat many a fellow, but the rest have had the wit to hold their tongues —Samuel Johnson, letter to Mrs. Thrale, in John Wain, *Samuel Johnson,* 1974

Sir, a game of jokes is composed partly of skill, partly of chance; a man may be beat at times by one who has not a tenth part of his wit —Samuel Johnson, in James Boswell, *Life of Samuel Johnson,* 1791

Reader's Digest 1983 calls *beat* "the old variant participle" and notes that it remains in "good, though slightly informal, use, especially in the sense 'defeated.'" This is much closer to the mark than Harper's casual damnation. Here are some examples:

He is persuaded that Montgomery could have beat the Russians to Berlin —Geoffrey Bruun, *Saturday Rev.,* 24 Feb. 1951

Some Very Peculiar Types have beat a path to my door these last few years —Flannery O'Connor, letter, 8 May 1955

But this one really had me beat —Roald Dahl, *Avant-Garde,* March 1968

What was unforeseeable is now known: Johnson can be beat —*New Republic,* 23 Mar. 1968

He ran for the Senate and was beat —Harry S. Truman, quoted in Merle Miller, *Plain Speaking,* 1973

Narrowly but decisively John Lennon had beat those odds —*People,* 5 Mar. 1984

There are two constructions in which *beat* rather than *beaten* seems to turn up with regularity. One occurs when the verb *get* replaces the usual auxiliary *have;* it is fairly common in sports contexts.

So if they get beat a step on a pass, they're still tall enough to go up and spike the ball —Tom Brookshier, quoted in *Sports Illustrated,* 21 Oct. 1963

Navratilova got beat —Curry Kirkpatrick, *Sports Illustrated,* 20 Sept. 1982

At least I'm not getting the hell beat out of me like in those TV series —James Garner, quoted in *TV Guide,* 5 Oct. 1984

The second is the phrase "can't be beat." *Beaten* does not seem to be used in this phrase.

. . . for tabloid readability John Gunther can't be beat —*Time,* 3 Nov. 1941

The weather couldn't be beat —Audax Minor, *New Yorker,* 31 Oct. 1953

. . . the dry temperate summers can't be beat — Andrea Chambers, *People,* 16 Aug. 1982

Our conclusion is that *beaten* is by far the more common form of the past participle. *Beat* is found in older writing, but is still used in respectable circles. It is common after *get* and usual in *can't be beat.*

beau Harper 1975 tells us that *beau* is obsolescent, if not obsolete, and that the plural *beaux* is obsolete in the U.S. Harper is wrong on both counts. Although not as common as *boyfriend, beau* is still in frequent use, even in the gossipy personality magazines. The plural spelling *beaux* is usual in American English. Some examples:

Her old beaux have forgiven her —Jill Pearlman, *US,* 31 Dec. 1984

. . . whose beaux have included . . . Russian film director Andrei Mikhalkov-Konchalovsky —Fred Bernstein, *People,* 10 Jan. 1983

... the unemployed Prince Gottfried von Hohen-lohe-Langenburg, one of Big Gloria's beaux — Edmund Morris, *N.Y. Times Book Rev.,* 22 June 1980

She should probably have married one of her local beaux —Mark Schorer, *Atlantic,* August 1970

... taking messages when her daughter's many beaux call —Angela Taylor, *N.Y. Times,* 1 July 1976

... her beaux would leave her a single petal of the magnolia with a message pricked upon it with a pin —Nancy Milford, *Harper's,* January 1969

Suggestion: if you want to know what is obsolete and what is not, check a good dictionary.

beauteous   You wouldn't think that this little-used synonym of *beautiful* would excite comment by usage writers, but it does. Fowler 1926 considers it a poeticism; Krapp 1927 says it is "archaic and poetical"; Flesch 1964 calls it "an ugly, barbaric word"; Copperud 1970, 1980 thinks it may have a derogatory tinge and may be intended to dilute a tribute; Harper 1985 says it is used chiefly by people trying for a bit of elegance.

If you suspect that our most recent commentators are shooting in the dark, you are probably right. *Beauteous* is a word that has greatly decreased in literary use during the last couple of centuries. The OED shows that *beauteous* is an older word than *beautiful,* by nearly a century. A check into the concordances of several poets shows that in the 16th, 17th, and 18th centuries, *beauteous* was more frequently used than *beautiful.* While Spenser used *beautiful* slightly more often than *beauteous,* Shakespeare and Marlowe both heavily favored *beauteous;* Jonson, Donne, Herrick, George Herbert, Milton, and Marvell all favored *beauteous* (a few didn't use *beautiful* at all); Thomas Traherne used both equally. In the 18th century Swift used *beautiful* slightly more than *beauteous,* but Pope and Johnson used *beauteous* much more often.

With the onset of Romanticism the preference shifted. Blake used *beautiful* 97 times to 7 for *beauteous;* Byron, Shelley, Keats, and Wordsworth all preferred *beautiful,* using *beauteous* only occasionally. The Romantics seem to have set the tone: later 19th century poets such as Arnold, Browning, and Tennyson all used *beautiful* more often. By the 20th century the switch was complete: Milton and Donne did not use *beautiful;* Dylan Thomas did not use *beauteous.*

The evidence of the concordances shows that sometime around the beginning of the 19th century *beautiful* surpassed *beauteous* as the literary word of choice, and the use of the older word has dwindled since. Thus the uncertainty of recent commentators: they do not meet the word very often and are puzzled what to make of it when they do. Our recent evidence is too scanty to base many generalizations on, so we can neither confirm nor refute the suspicions of Copperud and Harper. The only intended effect we have noticed is its use in a couple of *New York Times* reviews (both quoted below) to suggest earlier times. Here are some examples—first a few of the older literary uses, and then some more recent ones.

Bags of fiery opals, sapphires, amethysts,
Jacinths, hard topaz, grass-green emeralds,
Beauteous rubies, sparkling diamonds
            —Christopher Marlowe, *The Jew of Malta,* ca. 1590

How beauteous mankind is! O brave new world — Shakespeare, *The Tempest,* 1612

The one as famous for a scolding tongue
As is the other for beauteous modesty
            —Shakespeare, *The Taming of the Shrew,* 1594

Now beauteous Daphnis cloath'd with heav'nly light —Samuel Johnson, "The Hymns to Daphnis from the Fifth Pastoral of Virgil," 1726

Was high-born, wealthy by her father's will,
And beauteous, even where beauties most abound
            —Lord Byron, *Don Juan,* Canto xiii, 1823

As light and beauteous as a squirrel —William Wordsworth, "Peter Bell—A Tale," 1819

... the orchestral playing was of the beauteous kind that only Boston gives us regularly any more —Virgil Thomson, *The Musical Scene,* 1947

There is music and dance and beauteous liberation in that shop —Thomas J. Cottle, *Saturday Rev.,* 19 June 1971

This time, we're in early 19th-century Styria. Carmilla, the beauteous, last descendant of the undead Karnstein nobility ... —A. H. Weiler, *N.Y. Times,* 4 Feb. 1971

And the Incredible Merlin the Magician is preparing for his joust with Feste, the fire-eating fool, by making beauteous damsels levitate and disappear —Nan Robertson, *N.Y. Times,* 4 May 1979

... out on Rhode Island Sound 10 beauteous 12-meter yachts raced —Sarah Pileggi, *Sports Illustrated,* 8 Aug. 1983

We can see no sneaky pejorative intent or overblown elegance in these recent citations. *Beauteous* is a word that is no longer much used, though it is not archaic. Perhaps you could use it for an old-fashioned effect, but *beautiful* will always be safe.

because   **1.** *Is because.* Someone—we do not know precisely who—decided that *because* could only be used to introduce an adverbial clause; it could not introduce a noun clause. This rule was devised, presumably, for the purpose of denouncing the expression *the reason is because* (see REASON IS BECAUSE). However, *because* had all along been used to introduce noun clauses, even in sentences where the word *reason* did not appear:

Because may certainly introduce a noun clause that is joined to *it, this,* or *that* by some form of the verb *to be.* ... This has been standard English for centuries —Evans 1957

In the February 1933 issue of *American Speech,* Fannye N. Cherry of the University of Texas discussed the issue, citing the opinions of college textbooks of the late 1920s and early 1930s as well as Fowler 1926—a relatively recent book then. She concluded her discussion with a large number of examples extending from Francis Bacon in the 17th century to many contemporary authors of the 1920s and 1930s. Her earliest examples all had the word *reason,* but most of her later examples did not. Here is a selection of examples; those marked with her name are taken from the *American Speech* article.

For to know much of other Mens Matters, cannot be, because all that Adoe may concern his owne Estate —Francis Bacon, *Essays*, 1625

Is it because liberty in the abstract may be classed amongst the blessings of mankind . . . ? —Edmund Burke, *Reflections on the Revolution in France*, 1790 (Cherry)

"Coward! it was because you dared not run the risk of the wrong." —W. M. Thackeray, *The Newcomes*, 1853 (Cherry)

It is true, that he is entitled, at times, Antiochus Epimanes—Antiochus the madman—but that is because all people have not the capacity to appreciate his merits —Edgar Allan Poe, "Four Beasts in One," 1833 (Cherry)

Perhaps this staunchness was because Knight ever treated him as a mere disciple —Thomas Hardy, *A Pair of Blue Eyes,* 1873 (Cherry)

There is indeed no mystery about why people go wrong; it is because, if the thing had to be said without the use of the verb *like, would* & not *should* is the form to use —Fowler 1926 (Cherry)

But that would be because we did not know the tots —Robert Benchley, *Of All Things*, 1921 (Cherry)

It would seem that his fondness for the village of Clee St. Margaret is because . . . it is "doubly secluded." —*Times Literary Supp.*, 28 Feb. 1948

This is largely because they take care of each other —Herbert Hoover, *Memoirs*, 1951

. . . the absence of Philip Wakem from the river trip which compromises Maggie and Stephen is because he is ill —Geoffrey Tillotson, *Sewanee Rev.*, Spring 1953

No doubt . . . this is because the market apparatus of our consumer society has devoted a deal of wit to cultivating the age-consciousness of old and young alike —Theodore Roszak, *The Making of a Counter Culture*, 1969

. . . this is because, unlike them, he has been continuously engaged in university teaching —*Times Literary Supp.*, 19 Feb. 1970

When *is because* is used without *reason,* it is so ordinary as to quite escape notice; you see that Fowler, who condemned *reason is because,* used *it is because* himself without thinking. The construction is common, and it is entirely standard.
2. Related to the *is because* construction is one in which a clause beginning with *because* is the subject of a sentence. This construction alarms Follett 1966, because he thinks *because* and not the whole clause is the subject.

But merely because this distinction is not significant to the physicist does not mean that it is not meaningful in other sectors of science —Leslie A. White, *The Science of Culture*, 1949

Otto Jespersen in his *Modern English Grammar* (volume 3) discusses this sort of construction, which he terms a "modern colloquialism." He gives these examples, among others:

Just because I'm here now doesn't mean I didn't go, does it? —Booth Tarkington, *The Flirt*, 1913

Just because a fellow calls on a girl is no sign that she likes him —George Ade, *Artie,* 1897

Because I say Republicans are stupid, does not make me a Socialist —Jack London, *Martin Eden,* 1909

Our evidence for this construction shows it to be more typical of speech than of highly serious discursive writing. It is not wrong, but you probably will not want to use it in anything of a formal nature.
3. Muriel Harris of Purdue University in an article in the May 1979 *College Composition and Communication* reported surveying several hundred incoming freshmen to find out what they had been taught about writing before they came to college. Seventy-five percent of them said they had been told never to begin a sentence with *because*. This rule is a myth. *Because* is frequently used to begin sentences, particularly in magazine and newspaper writing.

Because they place a high value on education, they had built some years ago a two-year community college —John Fischer, *Harper's,* February 1971

Because she is the emblem of spending ability and the chief spender, she is also the most effective seller —Germaine Greer, *McCall's,* March 1971

We do note that most of our sentences beginning with *because* are of the sort illustrated here, where the *because* clause could have followed the main clause but has been placed first in the sentence for greater emphasis.
4. A number of handbooks along with Heritage 1982 and Longman 1984 point out that there can be ambiguity when *because* follows a negative verb in a sentence. A typical illustrative sentence might be

He didn't leave because he was afraid.

The question is, did he leave or did he stay? The usual advice is to solve the ambiguity with a comma:

He didn't leave, because he was afraid.

In this case he stayed; he was afraid to leave. If the comma is omitted

He didn't leave because he was afraid.

the sentence presumably means he left, but not because he was afraid. What should be obvious to you by now is that sentences like the example are better rewritten than merely given or left without a comma. Our evidence shows that sentences of this type are very rare in edited prose. Professional writers seem to revise them and you should too.
5. See AS 1; SINCE 1.

begin *Begin* belongs to a class of irregular verbs that in Old English had different singular and plural forms in the past tense. In the case of *begin,* the singular past was *began,* the plural *begun;* the past participle was *begun* (these are modernized versions). At some point the distinction between the singular and plural forms began to break down, but it was observed at least sporadically into the 18th century. Thus when Addison wrote in the *Spectator* "the men begun" and Pope in his *Essay on Criticism* wrote "the Goths begun," they were making the correct distinction. But in the 1660s Samuel Pepys was writing in his diary:

But Sir. W. Pen most basely told me that the Comptroller is to do it, and so begun to employ Mr. Turner about it.

And Pope elsewhere had written "the bard begun."

Johnson in his 1755 Dictionary listed both *began* and *begun* for the past tense. But grammarians tended to be less tolerant. Both Priestley in 1761 and Lowth in 1762 preferred only *began* for the past—Lowth, in fact, listed the Pope and Addison snippets above in a footnote as errors. It is likely that neither Priestley nor Lowth understood the origin of the dual forms; certainly Richard Grant White 1870 did not when he reran Lowth's footnote and examples in somewhat expanded form.

Webster 1909 and Webster's Second (1934) listed the past tense *begun* in the pearl section at the foot of the page with other rare words and forms; Webster's Second added the label *archaic.* Webster's Third (1961) put it back at the main entry for *begin* but labeled it *dialectal.*

Begun as the past tense has survived chiefly in dialectal and vernacular use. It can be found with considerable frequency in the 19th-century American humorists and local colorists:

> There was a place on my ankle that got to itching, but I dasn't scratch it; and then my ear begun to itch —Mark Twain, *Huckleberry Finn,* 1884

The Dictionary of American Regional English notes that the usual past tense is *began; begun* is still in use but is found chiefly among speakers who have little formal education. There is also a chiefly Southern and South Midland past *begin.*

Lowth noted variation creeping into the past participle too; he lists a *have began* by Dryden and a *had began* by the Earl of Clarendon in his 1763 footnote full of errors. These forms too have survived into the 20th century. The DARE notes that while *begun* is usual, *began* is found among speakers with little formal education. *Begin*—still Southern and South Midland—apparently has less use as a past participle than as a past.

beg the question   Suppose you are a member of a debating team faced with the task of upholding the positive side of a stirring proposition such as "Resolved, that the seventeen-year locust is a harmful creature." Now after listening to an opponent talk about the charm and rarity of the critters, you electrify your audience with a series of proposals for counteracting the damage done by the locusts. The audience cheers, but the judges give you a bad mark. What you have done is assume that the locust is a harmful creature and go on from there instead of proving that it is a harmful creature. You have used a fallacious argument known as *petitio principii*—a Latin term borrowed into English.

Petitio principii has been translated into English as *begging the question,* a translation that, as Bernstein 1971 notes, offers no clue to the logical fault it is supposed to represent.

To return to our hypothetical case. What people will have noticed about your presentation is the result of your argument—you sidestepped the whole problem of proving the locust harmful and went on to further concerns. They may not recognize the logical fallacy by which you accomplished this, but they will note the practical result.

It is not surprising, then, that many people, untrained in the finer points of logical argument, apply the phrase *beg the question* to the obvious result—dodging the issue—without worrying about the manner in which the dodging was accomplished. And the result of these people's use of the phrase is a new meaning of *beg* that the lexicographers must account for: "to evade, sidestep." As the examples that follow show, this sense of *beg* is used not only with *question* but also with plural *questions* and other words as well. It is fully established as standard.

> However I hope we shall do better as we go on and as long as there's no dodging or begging the question on our side, I'm not afraid —Henry Adams, letter, 6 May 1860

> On the contrary, the conditions of profit, of control, demand that the real question be side-stepped. The formula of entertainment is the means of begging the question —James T. Farrell, *Literature and Morality,* 1947

> I may well be accused of begging the question of dictatorship by saying that the American system simply would not permit it —Clinton Rossiter, *The American Presidency,* 1956

> Maynard begs the difficulties set by the *Utopia* for a medievalist by designating its principles as "simply Christian" —Charles T. Harrison, *Sewanee Rev.,* 1949

> To shake a fist at a swollen federal bureaucracy may be satisfying, but it begs the point —Elizabeth Drew, *Atlantic,* April 1971

> Pentagon and State Department officials beg the point when they suggest that sturdier barriers might have forced the terrorists to resort to aerial bombardment —*Time,* 8 Oct. 1984

behalf   Numerous commentators, from Utter 1916 and Krapp 1927 to Bremner 1980, Janis 1984, and Harper 1985, insist on a distinction between *in behalf of* and *on behalf of. In behalf of,* they say, means "for the benefit or advantage of," while *on behalf of* means "as the agent, representative, or spokesman for." Reader's Digest 1983, Einstein 1985, and Copperud 1970, 1980 believe that the phrases are interchangeable; Johnson 1982 also notes that the distinction is no longer observed.

There are further complications. James A. H. Murray in the OED (1887) at *behalf* noted that *on* was being used where he thought *in* should be; he opined that a useful distinction was being lost. Murray may indeed have noticed a trend developing; a recent British dictionary, Longman 1984, says that only *on* is used in current British English, and Quirk et al. 1985 labels *in behalf of* American English. Bryson 1984, on the other hand, finds a distinction (different from everyone else's) between *in* and *on.* In short we have a muddle of opinion here.

Murray seems to have been the first to notice a distinction between *in behalf of* and *on behalf of.* He also seems to have been misled by his evidence. He gives "in the name of" as the first sense of *in behalf of* (*behalf,* 2a) and marks it obsolete with a cross-reference to *on behalf of,* suggesting that the *on* phrase had replaced the *in* phrase in that function. At the second sense (2b) Murray cites Shakespeare as the earliest user:

> Let me have thy voice in my behalf —*The Merry Wives of Windsor* (spelling modernized)

Bartlett's *Concordance to Shakespeare,* although begun in 1876, was not published until 1894, seven years later than the part of the OED that includes *behalf.* The first citation for *behalf* in the concordance is the same one given by Murray. A little farther down the list we find this:

I come to whet your thoughts On his behalf — *Twelfth Night*

And toward the end of the list this:

... good Cassio, I will do All my abilities in thy behalf —*Othello,* act 3, scene 3

Tell him I have mov'd my lord on his behalf and hope all will be well —*Othello,* act 3, scene 4

It seems likely that if Murray had had the concordance, he would have realized that there never was such a distinction in the first place.

Murray's earliest citation for *on behalf of* "for the benefit of" is from William Cowper in 1791. But it was in use between Shakespeare and Cowper:

As for the Warres, which were anciently made, on the behalfe, of a kinde of Partie, or tacite Conformitie of Estate —Francis Bacon, *Essays,* 1625

Bacon's language is a bit obscure now, but references later in this lengthy sentence make it quite clear he is thinking about one entity waging war for the supposed benefit of another.

ZARA. And after did solicite you, on his behalf — William Congreve, *The Mourning Bride,* 1697

In Congreve's tragedy, Zara—a captive queen—is accusing the king's daughter of intervening in favor of another prisoner.

Modern American usage simply continues the interchanging of the *in* and *on* phrases that obtained in Shakespeare's time:

... I am certainly much obliged to you and Mavis for all your effort in my behalf —Flannery O'Connor, letter, 26 Oct. 1949

... let me thank you again ... for everything you have tried to do on my behalf —Archibald Mac-Leish, letter, 15 Dec. 1944

... to sign the legal papers in his son's behalf —Gay Talese, *Harper's,* January 1969

"On behalf of every workingman who has gone down under the club or been shot in the back, I consign you to that place...." —E. L. Doctorow, *Loon Lake,* 1979

... the all-Brahms recital ... on behalf of that institution's Student Fund —Irving Kolodin, *Saturday Rev.,* 13 Nov. 1971

Our 20th-century British evidence is all for *on behalf of:*

... the ultimate triumph of Archibald Douglas—to which Boswell's vigorous pamphleteering on his behalf contributed —*Times Literary Supp.,* 17 Apr. 1953

... reseach on behalf of the authors by an Arab scholar —*Times Literary Supp.,* 2 Oct. 1969

Our evidence would thus appear to support the Longman 1984 contention that modern British writers use only *on.* But our British evidence is somewhat sparse, and it is true that one British commentator—Bryson—thinks *in* still used.

Conclusion: the OED shows that the "agent" sense is older; the "benefit" sense—presumably because your agent should be working for your benefit—developed from it in Shakespeare's time. But Shakespeare himself used both *in* and *on* in this sense, and since *in* had earlier been used in the "agent" sense, there never was a distinction in meaning based on the choice of preposition. Modern British usage appears to favor *on* in all instances, but both *in* and *on* are used interchangeably in American English.

behest Reader's Digest 1983 calls this an old word now used as a fancy synonym for *command* and for *urging* or *strong suggestion.* Flesch 1964 thinks it old-fashioned; he recommends using *request* instead. *Behest* is indeed an old word, but it is still in current use. It suggests a stronger urging than *request* does. You can decide for yourself how fancy these contexts are:

... charges that he shaved points at the behest of gamblers —Jerry Kirshenbaum, *Sports Illustrated,* 15 Feb. 1982

... largely at the behest of well-heeled corporate lobbyists —Robert E. Litan, *N.Y. Times Book Rev.,* 16 Oct. 1983

... a candy bar that will be attached to the inside of his helmet at the behest of dietitians —Henry S. F. Cooper, Jr., *New Yorker,* 17 July 1971

... were not accustomed to gathering, at the behest of a mere governor —John Fischer, *Harper's,* November 1970

... the Toleration Act, which the assembly at his behest passed on 21 April 1649 —Samuel Eliot Morison, *Oxford History of the American People,* 1965

... to tell his story at the behest of the Athens government —*Time,* 4 Oct. 1954

behoove, behove Those commentators who bring up the subject—Evans 1957, Bryson 1984—agree with the OED Supplement that *behoove* is the usual spelling in the U.S. and *behove* is the usual spelling in the U.K. Our evidence confirms the observation, our last British *behoove* and our last American *behove* both dating from the 1940s.

Behoove and *behove* are usually found in impersonal constructions beginning with *it:*

... it behooves us to conform to it out of deference to public opinion —Geoffrey Nunberg, *Atlantic,* December 1983

... it may behoove us at this time to re-examine the grounds —Charles G. Tierney, *Saturday Rev.,* 18 Dec. 1971

... had informed me ... that it would behoove me not to swing violently at the ball —John Lowenstein, quoted in *Sports Illustrated,* 16 Aug. 1982

Any commentator who says *beho(o)ve* can take only *it* for a subject, however, is wrong—for instance, Phythian 1979, Sir Bruce Fraser in Gowers 1973, Bryson 1984, and Reader's Digest 1983. *It* is the usual subject, not the only possible one. Sometimes we find an example with a personal subject:

... as good scientists we are behooved to discard this model with its fortuitously correct results —J. J. Zuckerman, *Jour. of Chemical Education,* April 1966

... one sees It so seldom one is behooved to be impressed —Liz Smith, *Cosmopolitan,* February 1972

Such uses are fairly uncommon, but are not wrong.

Before criticizing other uses of *beho(o)ve,* critics should have looked in unabridged dictionaries. Bryson 1984 has taken from Fraser in Gowers 1973 an example of a sentence containing the construction "it ill behoves." Bryson and Fraser assume this must mean "become," but it need not, since one sense of *beho(o)ve* is "to be proper." The construction with *ill* is rare, however. Bryson and Fraser could come up with but a single example; our files likewise have just one, and that from a radio show. *Ill behoove,* we assume, must be chiefly in oral use.

A few other comments have been made on the subject of this verb that we mention only for you to beware of. A 1927 survey of 227 judges reported in *The English Journal* called *behoove* illiterate, which it most certainly is not. A few of the British commentators think it old-fashioned or even archaic, but we continue to collect evidence of its use. Krapp 1927 called it "slightly archaic and literary." But it is not. *TV Guide* and *Sports Illustrated,* from which we have recent citations, are hardly literary in content. *Behoove* may not be the most common word in English, but it is still alive and kicking.

being, being as, being as how, being that   If your regional dialect or personal vocabulary does not include the conjunction *being* or its compound forms, you might very well wonder at the wide coverage these terms receive in handbooks. But covered they are: Reader's Digest 1983, Macmillan 1982, Nickles 1974, Janis 1984, Bremner 1980, Irmscher 1976, Bell and Cohn 1981, Corder 1981, Prentice Hall 1978, Shaw 1970, 1975, Guth 1980, 1985, Copperud 1970, McMahan & Day 1980, Little, Brown 1980. And these are only the fairly recent ones. Even a British dictionary, Longman 1984, comments on them. The epithets usually applied to the terms are "nonstandard," "substandard," "barbarian," and "illiterate." One essayist (Paul Fussell, "Notes on Class," in *The Contemporary Essay,* 1984) finds *being that* "pseudo-genteel." He is alone. Only the first two listed books, Reader's Digest and Macmillan, correctly identify these as dialectal.

The conjunctions *being, being as,* and *being that* had at least some literary use in the 16th and 17th centuries:

Sir John, you loiter here too long, being you are to take soldiers up in counties as you go —Shakespeare, *2 Henry IV,* 1598

Being that I flow in grief,
The smallest twine may lead me
—Shakespeare, *Much Ado About Nothing,* 1599

And being you have
Declined his means, you have increased his malice
—Beaumont and Fletcher (Webster 1909)

The OED has citations from Sir Thomas More, a prose work of Milton's, and some other 17th-century prose writers. The conjunctive *being* and its compound forms seem to have been used mostly in prose—notes in our files show them used by John Bunyan and Jeremy Taylor, for instance—but we have almost no evidence of their being used in poetry.

The OED shows no examples from the 18th century—presumably the forms faded into dialect during that time. British evidence from the 19th century is

mostly dialectal—the English Dialect Dictionary has abundant evidence—with occasional other use. The EDD cites Charles Kingsley's *Westward Ho* (1855) for *being that;* the same form turns up in Jane Austen's correspondence:

Southey's Life of Nelson;—I am tired of Lives of Nelson, being that I never read any. I will read this, however, if Frank is mentioned in it —letter, 11 Oct. 1813

The Dictionary of American English and Dictionary of American Regional English both record 17th-century citations from Rhode Island; obviously these forms came here with early settlers. But after one early 18th-century citation, the rest of the evidence is 19th-century or later, and mainly dialectal. The DARE notes that currently these forms are chiefly Southern, South Midland, and New England.

Our current evidence shows that these forms turn up from time to time in print, chiefly in the indicated dialect areas. The media in which they appear are essentially informal—letters, transcribed speech, newspaper articles. Here are a few samples:

Being she isn't about to mingle with other domestics in the servants' mess, Bobo's meals are brought to her suite —Fred Sparks, *Springfield* (Mass.) *Union,* 30 Mar. 1971

Being as the exploitation began at the same time [in] almost every watershed there was simply not enough people —Warren Wright, quoted in *Our Appalachia,* 1977

While I was in NC I heard somebody recite a barroom ballad. I don't remember anything but the end but beinst you all are poets I will give it to you —Flannery O'Connor, letter, 1 Apr. 1955

That is when the kids get up early—naturally they get up early on Saturday mornings, being as how that is one of the two days in the week they do not have to get up early —George V. Higgins, *Boston Globe Mag.,* 21 Oct. 1979

I was appreciative that any woman would come onstage in that state, being that it was the state of California —Martin Mull, quoted in *Rolling Stone,* 17 July 1975

The people quoted are two New Englanders, a Kentuckian, a Georgian, and the anomalous Martin Mull, who was born in Chicago. Flannery O'Connor's *beinst* is a variant spelling based on pronunciation (she spelled it *beingst* once, too).

It is clear that the conjunction *being* survives dialectally in current English. If it—or its compounds—is part of your dialect, there is no reason you should avoid it. You should be aware, however, that when you use it in writing it is likely to be noticed by those who do not have it in their dialects.

belabor, labor   Barzun 1975, 1985, Einstein 1985, and Bremner 1980 (quoting Barzun) object to the use of *belabor* instead of *labor* in such expressions as "belabor a point." Copperud 1980 notes that dictionaries agree the two words are interchangeable. The evidence is on the side of Copperud and the dictionaries.

If you are looking for a reason to choose between *labor* and *belabor* there are these facts: *labor* is older and shorter. *Belabor* carries the connotation of its primary sense—beating. Both verbs seem to be American in this use; we have no British evidence for either. Take your choice. Here are a few examples of each:

> ... and for that reason I needn't belabor here the question —Brendan Gill, *New Yorker*, 1 Jan. 1972

> ... the playwright often tends to labor a point —Edith Oliver, *New Yorker*, 20 Nov. 1971

> ... it does not ... belabor an argument —Edward Weeks, *Atlantic*, August 1954

> ... has a tendency to labor his points —John Kenneth Galbraith, *Atlantic*, November 1982

> It would be only belaboring the obvious to say that "A Solo In Tom-Toms" is "uneven" —Stanley Walker, *N.Y. Herald Tribune Book Rev.*, 21 Apr. 1946

> ... which made champions of English respectability so anxious to labor the obvious differences between them —Joseph Wood Krutch, *Samuel Johnson*, 1944

> I do not wish to belabor this ancestor theme —Alben W. Barkley, *Saturday Evening Post*, 17 Apr. 1954

> I have labored a slight example —Allen Tate, *New Republic*, 2 Mar. 1953

belie Follett 1966 worries that "this useful word" is "being distorted" into its opposite meaning—being used in the general sense of "to give evidence of." He produces only one example of distortion, however, and that from someone identified only as a delegate to the United Nations. We do not even know if we are dealing with a native speaker of English. A correspondent of William Safire, in Safire 1982, produced two more examples, one from an automobile advertisement, and another from a newspaper story which read "Slight twitches in his eyes and hands belied his nervousness." This writer apparently wrote *belie* while thinking *betray*.

Our files contain no evidence of this reported use and we thus assume that it is not very widespread. This is a more typical use of *belie:*

> ... he remained the master of a great feudal estate whose amenities and luxuries, though modest, belied his primitivist credo —Edwin M. Yoder, Jr., *Harper's*, March 1971

believe, think "In casual speech and writing," says Kilpatrick 1984, "the two words are interchangeable. The precise usage scarcely justifies prolonged fussing. ..." Bremner 1980 believes in fussing. His rule of thumb: you believe from the heart; you think with the intellect. Sounds simple, but it's not. Evans 1961 points out that *believe* covers a wide range of credulity, and at the less intense end of the range has long been interchangeable with *think*. Kilpatrick is right in suggesting the matter is scarcely worth fussing over.

Here are some examples of *believe,* from the 18th century to the 20th. See which ones you can confidently assign to the heart or the mind.

> But I, who smell a rat at a considerable distance, do believe in private that Mrs Howard and his Lordship have a friendship that borders upon the tender —Lady Mary Wortley Montagu, letter, August 1725

> ... how much happier that man is who believes his native town to be the world —Mary Shelley, *Frankenstein*, 1818

> Good day—I believe you are a Sorcerer —W. S. Gilbert, *The Sorcerer*, 1877

> Consequently, we must believe that "emotion recollected in tranquillity" is an inexact formula —T. S. Eliot, "Tradition and the Individual Talent," 1917

> ... the Czar of Russia was a man of uncertain temper who believed he had great interests in the Mediterranean —C. S. Forester, *The Barbary Pirates*, 1953

> ... I believe they picked her up without stopping —Eudora Welty, *The Ponder Heart*, 1954

> These axioms, though they believed them to be unnecessary, were always introduced in their mathematical works —Bertrand Russell, *Foundations of Geometry*, 1897

> ... he believed he was better with a knife than any man in all of New York —Norman Mailer, *Advertisements for Myself*, 1959

See also FEEL.

belly The committee for the defense of *belly* as applied to people seems to have been formed by Fowler 1926, and Copperud 1970, 1980 lists nearly every commentator he checked as a member of it. We can add Partridge 1942 and Bremner 1980 to the list. Although none of our 19th-century sources mention the word, there seems to have been a notion around that it was not polite. Krapp 1927 notes that *belly* was not then used in polite conversation or writing with reference to human beings. This newspaper article refers to the question:

> ... a good time to scrap the Victorian version of belly and explain that since the gay nineties it has not been necessary to confuse belly with stomach or abdomen in order to show your good breeding —*Bronx* (N.Y.) *Home News*, 12 May 1937

It hardly seems necessary to prove by illustration that such a staunchly defended fine old English word is in current use. There is a fairly long discussion of *belly* and some of the terms substituted for it in Evans 1957.

bemuse The OED cites a 1705 letter by Alexander Pope:

> When those incorrigible things, Poets, are once irrecoverably Be-mus'd. ....

Murray defines this use as "*humorously,* To devote entirely to the Muses." He defines the main sense as "To make utterly confused or muddled, as with intoxicating liquor ... to stupefy." The earliest citation is also from Pope, dated 1735. It is shown thus:

> A parson much be-mus'd in beer.

Dr. Johnson in his 1755 dictionary entered the word as an adjective *bemused.* He defined it "Overcome with musing; dreaming: a word of contempt." Johnson quotes Pope, too, but more fully:

> Is there a parson much bemus'd in beer,
> A maudlin poetess, a rhiming peer?

Noah Webster in 1828 picked up Johnson word for word but omitted the quotation.

There is no question that Pope's 1735 usage is the springboard from which our modern use starts. Webster 1864, Webster 1890, and Webster 1909 all used the Pope quotation, truncated as it is in the OED. But it seems likely that the interpretation that has given us our modern meaning comes from taking Pope's line out of context. Here are the first 22 lines of *An Epistle to Dr. Arbuthnot,* from which it comes:

> Shut, shut the door, good John! fatigu'd, I said,
> Tie up the knocker, say I'm sick, I'm dead.
> The Dog-star rages! nay 'tis past a doubt,
> All Bedlam, or Parnassus, is let out:
> Fire in each eye, and papers in each hand,
> They rave, recite, and madden round the land.
> 　　What walls can guard me, or what shades can hide?
> They pierce my thickets, thro' my Grot they glide;
> By land, by water, they renew the charge;
> They stop the chariot, and they board the barge.
> No place is sacred, not the Church is free;
> Ev'n Sunday shines no Sabbath-day to me;
> Then from the Mint walks forth the Man of rhyme,
> Happy to catch me just at Dinner-time.
> 　　Is there a Parson, much bemus'd in beer,
> A maudlin Poetess, a rhyming Peer,
> A Clerk, foredoom'd his father's soul to cross,
> Who pens a Stanza, when he should *engross?*
> Is there, who, lock'd from ink and paper, scrawls
> With desp'rate charcoal round his darken'd walls?
> All fly to Twit'nam, and in humble strain
> Apply to me, to keep them mad or vain.

In this context, where Pope is besieged by would-be poets who want him to read their verses, it seems quite likely that Pope is suggesting that the parson found his muse in beer—in other words, he is using *bemused* in much the same way he had in 1705. A parson who is simply muddled by beer would not make much sense in the larger context of the poem.

Harper 1985 says that centuries ago *amuse* and *bemuse* were synonyms, but that they are no longer. This is not quite accurate. The OED shows that the usual senses of *amuse* in the 17th and 18th centuries were approximately "distract, mislead, deceive." These senses have fallen into disuse and during the 19th century seem to have been transferred to a certain extent to *bemuse.*

Bemuse, then, is a somewhat slippery word. Harper 1975, 1985, Freeman 1983, and Bernstein 1977 warn against using *bemuse* as a synonym for *amuse.* We have no evidence that *bemuse* is actually equated with *amuse.* But, perhaps because of the word's uncertain origins, we have quite a few citations of uncertain meaning, uses that fall between the cracks of dictionary definitions. We will first show you a few mainstream citations, where the meaning is clear:

> We know that the commission salesman will, if we let him into our homes, dazzle and bemuse us with the beauty, durability, unexcelled value of his product —Jessica Mitford, *Atlantic,* July 1970

> Ella stood with her sandals sinking into the beach, bemused and peaceful in her rapt look of mystery, tears streaming down her wrinkled face —William Styron, *Lie Down in Darkness,* 1951

> But it may be that he drinketh strong waters which do bemuse a man, and make him even as the wild beasts of the desert! —W. S. Gilbert, *Ruddigore,* 1887

> . . . he, bemused in his Neoplatonism and rapt . . . in the "egotistical sublime" —Robert Penn Warren, *Democracy and Poetry,* 1975

> . . . more serious claim is that the Soviet Union is marching irresistibly across a bemused and flabby world —Arthur M. Schlesinger, Jr., *Saturday Rev.,* June 1980

Then we have ambiguous or uncertain uses. The first two are letters to the editor. The first of these could be interpreted as *amused;* however, our context is too short to be certain. The second starts out as though *amused* or even *pleased* is meant, but then a complaint follows.

> I was initially bemused by your Aug. 14 front page story on the Dull Men's Club —letter to the editor, *Wall Street Jour.,* 28 Aug. 1980

> It bemused me greatly to read. . . . In an otherwise representative piece, she neglected to give any mention to Canada's highly acclaimed classical musicians —letter to the editor, *Vogue,* October 1982

The rest of the examples were written by professionals but are equally ambiguous:

> . . . the band whose piledriver precision so bemused Composer Igor Stravinsky that he wrote his *Ebony Concerto* for it —*Time,* 31 May 1954

> . . . we have a giddy child out to "blow his mind" and bemused to see all the pretty balloons go up —Theodore Roszak, *The Making of a Counter Culture,* 1969

> There is probably no one in the world more bemused by the eccentric aspects of crime than the urbane, rubicund Alfred Hitchcock —Arthur Knight, *Saturday Rev.,* 24 June 1972

> Some political analysts here [in Zimbabwe] are bemused at the naively gleeful reaction of many whites to the recent arrest —Tony Hawkins, *Christian Science Monitor,* 15 Aug. 1980

> Gable plays his he-man part with the bemused ease to be expected of a man who has done the same thing many times before —*Time,* 12 Oct. 1953

> He also began to develop an attitude toward whites, a kind of bemused disdain for their foolishness —Richard M. Levine, *Harper's,* March 1969

Part of the problem with *bemuse* may be that lexicographers have not analyzed its use as well as they should have. At least some of the above examples would fit into one of the obsolete senses of *amuse* that *bemuse* has presumably taken over: "to occupy the attention of, absorb." But while there seem to be several lexicographical loose ends to *bemuse,* we do not have convincing evidence that it often infringes on current senses of *amuse.* We merely advise you to note that it is a bit slippery to handle.

benedict　 This term for a newly married man who has long been a bachelor is derived from Benedick, a character in Shakespeare's *Much Ado About Nothing.* Benedick professes to be a confirmed bachelor but at the end of the play marries Beatrice, with whom he has exchanged barbed remarks throughout. Somehow the spelling got changed to *benedict;* it is spelled with a *-ct* by Sir Walter Scott in 1821. A few commentators—Fowler 1926, Krapp 1927—point out that the *-ct* spelling is unetymological, but it has become the established one. The spelling may perhaps have been influenced by a use of *benedict* meaning "a bachelor." We have very scant evidence that such a use was known; one source derives it from St. Benedict, whom it calls "patron saint of celibates." The "bachelor" sense, in any case, appears not to have been widespread. Copperud 1970 calls *benedict* "society-page lingo," but none of our evidence is from society pages. Here are a few examples:

> Some are bachelors, others benedicts —*Esquire,* July 1970

> . . . when, one evening, the Canadian benedict began extolling Jacqueline Susann's "The Love Machine" —S. J. Perelman, *New Yorker,* 12 Feb. 1972

> He had married our great-aunt Margaret shortly before the death of our parents and so became our guardian while still a benedict —Mary McCarthy, *New Yorker,* 15 Dec. 1951

The spelling *benedick* has occasionally been used:

> . . . tho' less likely than ever to become a Benedick —Lord Byron, letter, 29 Nov. 1813

We have no actual 20th-century citations for Shakespeare's spelling. You can consider *benedict* the established form. The word does not seem to be used very frequently any more.

bereaved, bereft The variant past participles of *bereave*—*bereaved* and *bereft*—have developed somewhat separate adjectival uses. *Bereaved* is the word most frequently chosen to mean "suffering the death of a loved one":

> . . . he spoke . . . as an unsuccessful and unhappy man might relate the biography of a successful and happy brother lately dead, for Kipling . . . had very much the air of a man bereaved —Maurice Cranston, *London Calling,* 19 Aug. 1954

When *bereaved* is followed by a preposition, it is *of:*

> . . . orphans, spinsters and bachelors bereaved of their other relatives —Alice P. Kenney, *New-England Galaxy,* Fall 1970

Bereft usually denotes the loss, lack or deprivation of something and is almost always used with the preposition *of:*

> Both players are instantly bereft of their poise —Albert E. Wier, *The Piano,* 1940

> . . . the book is . . . completely bereft of an index —*Times Literary Supp.,* 27 June 1968

> Bereft of their independence . . . —C. Vann Woodward, *N.Y. Rev. of Books,* 12 Aug. 1971

> These are hollow men, bereft of purpose —Clive Barnes, *N.Y. Times,* 4 May 1972

Bereft is also used, although less frequently than *bereaved,* in the sense "suffering the death of a loved one":

> . . . thinking of herself as a bereft daughter mourning here —Ben Ames Williams, *Leave Her to Heaven,* 1944

> . . . the weeping widow, the bereft children —John Cogley, *Center Mag.,* September 1968

If a preposition is used, again it is *of:*

> . . . why a young man so full of promise was cut off in his youth, why a woman was widowed . . . why a country was bereft of one who might have served it greatly —Alan Paton, *Cry, the Beloved Country,* 1948

beseech *Beseech* and *seek* are related words. At one time both *seech* and *seek* were in use; *seek* prevailed in the simple verb, but *seech* prevailed in the compound. The past and past tense, then, should be *sought* in both cases. But *beseeched* has been around since the 16th century. Shakespeare used *beseeched* but not *besought;* on the other hand Wyatt, Spenser, Sidney, Milton, and Pope used *besought* but not *beseeched.* In the 19th century *beseeched* was considered incorrect, according to the OED (1885), and Richard Grant White in 1870 opined that no good writer at that time used *beseeched* for *besought.* But *beseeched* did not vanish from use, and it has been staging a comeback in the 20th century.

Copperud 1970 records some difference of opinion among his authorities: Flesch 1964 plumps for *beseeched,* while the rest favor *besought.* Lamberts 1972 feels that *beseeched* is usual and that *besought* is found only in special contexts. Copperud 1970, however, finds that observable usage is "all but invariably" *besought.*

Our evidence doesn't favor either side. While we have more citations for *besought,* they cover a span of about 140 years; our smaller number of *beseeched* citations cover a span of about 60 years. We have a few more citations for *beseeched* than for *besought* from the past 25 years. A few typical examples of each follow:

> . . . his hostess beseeched him to sing —Christopher Sykes, *Evelyn Waugh: a Biography,* 1975

> . . . as for years they had beseeched us to understand —William F. Buckley, Jr., speech, 29 Sept. 1968

> . . . Nixon was beseeched by Republican leaders everywhere to urge . . . —Richard H. Rovere, *New Yorker,* 13 Oct. 1956

> . . . unpretentious, altogether delightful, and frenziedly besought Italian restaurant —Jay Jacobs, *Gourmet,* May 1980

> He besought us to lie doggo, collect the weekly stipend, and thank our lucky stars —S. J. Perelman, *Holiday,* October 1957

> President Truman has been besought by many reputable newspapers . . . to veto . . . —Harold L. Ickes, *New Republic,* 24 Oct. 1949

Both forms are still in completely respectable use. You can use *beseeched,* like Shakespeare, or *besought,* like Spenser, Milton, and Pope.

beside, besides As a number of commentators remark and all conscientious dictionaries show, there is a certain amount of overlap between these two words. The OED shows that historically there was even more than there is now.

It was Edward S. Gould who, in 1856 as he himself tells us, first undertook to distinguish between the two for a benighted and confused world, since the dictionaries of his day did not. His distinction was to restrict *beside* to use as a preposition; *besides* was both adverb and preposition, and when a preposition meant "in addition to." He declared *beside* when meaning "in addition to" to be an error. Gould's distinction has been repeated and repeated (we have it more than thirty times in our files) right down to Einstein 1985. Moreover, in general Gould's distinction is reflective of the trend of modern usage, although it is not exact in all particulars.

Modern commentators, while repeating Gould, have tended to further simplify his pronouncements; some try to reduce *beside* to a single sense and *besides* to one sense for the preposition and one for the adverb. Consultation of a dictionary will disabuse anyone misled by such oversimplification.

Besides is the easier word to deal with. It has the adverbial action all to itself; *beside,* the older adverb, is archaic.

> ... lost her social position, job, and husband, and was broke besides —Sally Quinn, *Cosmopolitan,* November 1972

As a preposition, *besides* usually means "except, other than, together with":

> There were other irritations, besides the voice — Martha Gellhorn, *Atlantic,* March 1953

> ... often we know a good deal about them besides the name —W. F. Bolton, *A Short History of Literary English,* 1967

> You wish you could remember something about Spinoza, besides the fact that he was excommunicated —Jay McInerney, *Bright Lights, Big City,* 1984

Beside is always approved in prepositional uses like these:

> ... a sputtering old Model T ... coughed and died right beside the schoolyard —Russell Baker, *Growing Up,* 1982

> In the ditch beside the road —F. Scott Fitzgerald, *The Great Gatsby,* 1925

> But the conception is really nothing, you know, beside the delivery —Philip Roth, *Reading Myself and Others,* 1975

The only question arises when *beside* is used in the preposition sense of *besides.* Gould disliked this use, and most commentators since his time simply avoid it by not mentioning it at all. Although it is not nearly as frequent as *besides,* it is well attested. It has been in use since the 14th century and appears in the King James version of the Bible in several places. Our modern evidence for this sense of *beside* is modestly literary:

> A hundred incidents beside those here chosen would have served as well —Carl Van Doren, *The American Novel,* 1940

> Beside the resident members, other members dropped in and out during the day —*The Autobiography of William Butler Yeats,* 1953

> Beside being taken into a world of escapist literature a thoughtful reader can go somewhat further —John P. Marquand, *Book-of-the-Month-Club News,* April 1946

> ... his other mythical theme beside the South —Leslie A. Fiedler, *New Republic,* 23 Aug. 1954

While this use of *beside* is not wrong, nor rare, nor nonstandard, *besides* is the word most people use.

best foot forward Evans 1961 and Bernstein 1971 remind everyone that this ancient idiom is perfectly all right in spite of applying the superlative degree to only two. See also SUPERLATIVE OF TWO.

bestow Back in the 18th century the grammarian Lowth corrected a Swiftian *bestow to* to *bestow upon;* Lindley Murray corrected a *bestow of* to *bestow upon.* Lowth and Murray seem to have had an accurate feel for what idiomatic usage would be: in modern use *upon* and *on* are the usual prepositions.

> Dolly bestowed upon him her highest compliment —Clarence Budington Kelland, *Saturday Evening Post,* 25 Dec. 1954

> ... the Queen is the fountain of honours and when she bestows a peerage upon a subject ... —Nancy Mitford, *Noblesse Oblige,* 1956

> ... bestowing half-abstracted nods of greeting from time to time on passing acquaintances —Thomas Wolfe, *You Can't Go Home Again,* 1940

> ... the instant hero status that the press bestowed on these first seven astronauts —C. D. B. Bryan, *N.Y. Times Book Rev.,* 23 Sept. 1979

This example with *at* is probably influenced by *glance:*

> But if you are to understand the new Oxford you must bestow a glance at the old —S. P. B. Mais, *The English Scene To-day,* 2d ed., 1949

When *bestow* means "to put in a place, stow," however, it often takes *in:*

> Instead of bestowing the envelope safely in his pocket —Dorothy L. Sayers, *Murder Must Advertise,* 1933

> ... parcels which she bestowed in the corners of the vehicle —Arnold Bennett, *The Old Wives' Tale,* 1908

be sure and See TRY AND.

bet The verb *bet* has two forms of the past and past participle: *bet* and *betted.* Bierce 1909 and Follett 1966 believed firmly that only *betted* was proper. No one else agrees. In this country, *bet* is usual:

> ... he hasn't bet on a single race —Anthony J. Aliberti, *Hub Rail,* January/February 1987

> ... has been helped by the fact that she bet on a writer who was becoming a new cult figure —*N.Y. Times Book Rev.,* 26 Sept. 1976

> He bet basketball, baseball, football and ... hockey games —Pat Jordan, *Sports Illustrated,* 9 Feb. 1987

Betted is rather unusual in American English; Reader's Digest 1983 believes it is becoming rare, and it might very well be.

Betted is not nearly as uncommon in British English as it is in American English. Our most recent British sources, however, Quirk et al. 1985 and Longman 1984, say that *bet* is usual in British English too, and *betted* less frequent. Longman repeats an observation also given in Evans 1957: *bet* is the past form used for a definite transaction:

> ... she bet me £5 I couldn't do it —Longman 1984

while *betted* is used more indefinitely:

> Dixon betted himself it would be there before them —Kingsley Amis, *Lucky Jim,* 1954

Our evidence also shows *betted* used in reference books where the author is perhaps more consciously formal:

> ... if there is a tremendous amount of money betted on it then they will make that horse 'odds on' —John Welcome, *A Light-hearted Guide to British Racing,* 1973

betake oneself Nickles 1974 lists *betake oneself* as a "raconteur's cliché." You, however, need not avoid the expression, for it is the only remaining live use of the verb.

> Perkin Warbeck betook himself to the Netherlands —James A. Williamson, *The Tudor Age,* 1964

> ... betook himself to the trackless wasteland of the Sinai Peninsula —Raymond A. Sokolov, *N.Y. Times Book Rev.,* 20 Apr. 1980

> ... the firm ... betook itself to the far shore of the Hudson, where rents are more merciful —G. Bruce Boyers, *Town & Country,* February 1983

bête noire, bête noir Copperud 1980 notes that three commentators label *bête noir* a misspelling, but Webster's Third recognizes it as a variant spelling. Most of the commentators, for example Partridge 1942, wonder why people do not use good old English *bugbear* instead.

One trouble with fussing over the presence or absence of a final *-e* in a phrase pinched from French is that any number of other freedoms taken with the conventions of French spelling and compounding are overlooked. In English context a circumflex may disappear or a superfluous hyphen may be added, and the term is sometimes printed in roman and sometimes in italic. A French phrase in English is likely to undergo a few changes; it is idle to pick on just one of them to label a mistake.

Bête noire has been in English since 1844, according to the OED; the *e*-less spelling dates from 1860. Here are a few examples of its use from our files:

> ... the old bête noir of labor —*Atlantic,* October 1922

> ... and *bête noir* of Disraeli —Bennett Cerf, *Saturday Rev.,* 11 Dec. 1954

> ... which has always made him a *bête noir* in Quebec —Donald C. Masters, *A Short History of Canada,* 1958

> ... the real *bête noir* in the Vietnam situation —William O. Douglas, *Center Mag.,* March 1969

> ... in his view the *bête noir* of behavioral psychology —*N.Y. Times Book Rev.,* 16 Sept. 1973

Flesch 1964 thinks the *e*-less spelling is used nine times out of ten, but it is not. Our evidence shows *bête noire* to be four or five times more common.

better   **1.** See ABSOLUTE COMPARATIVE.
2. The use of *better* for *had better,* (see also HAD BETTER, HAD BEST) is rejected by a couple of critics, but Copperud 1970 says that the consensus is that it is not open to serious criticism. Longman 1984 notes that it is also used

in informal British English. Our examples here suggest that while it is an acceptable idiom, it is not found in very formal surroundings.

> ... an internist, which is what you ought to see. You better listen to me —Flannery O'Connor, letter, 9 Oct. 1962

> ... a stubblehead German with an accent you better not laugh at —E. L. Doctorow, *Loon Lake,* 1979

> You better buy it too —Pete Carey, *Popular Computing,* January 1985

> ... they're going to be awfully mad at me, and we better figure that in, too — John F. Kennedy, quoted in *Harper's,* February 1971

3. The idiom *better than* used to mean "more than" is disliked by the usage panel of Heritage 1969, 1982 and by the Oxford American Dictionary; Harper 1985 and Lurie 1927 find it unacceptable in careful writing or literary English but passable in speech. Reader's Digest 1983 has fewer reservations about it, calling it "slightly informal" but "widespread and perfectly legitimate." Not one of these sources brings forth a better reason for questioning the expression than that more is not necessarily better, a truism irrelevant to a matter of idiomatic English. Lurie does say, though, that some dictionaries label it *colloquial. Better than* is primarily a spoken idiom (it is attested in some varieties of Irish English and in some English dialects), and like many spoken idioms it is not generally found in the more formal kinds of writing.

> ... it would take better than a fifty-degree incline to flip the moon car —Henry S. F. Cooper, Jr., *New Yorker,* 17 July 1971

> ... who has hit better than .300 for the last 14 seasons —Bill Lyon, *Hartford* (Conn.) *Courant,* 12 July 1983

> We were whistling along at slightly better than Mach 2 —Horace Sutton, *Saturday Rev.,* 23 June 1979

> ... added up to better than 16 percent of consumer expenditures for health care —*American Labor,* July–August 1969

4. The idiom *the better part of* in the sense of "most" or "more than half of" is disliked by Bremner 1980, for no apparent reason. "Why *better?*" he asks. But why not? That's how the idiom goes. It is used with expressions of time.

> We stayed in Seoul the better part of two days — Norman Cousins, *Saturday Rev.,* 4 Mar. 1978

> ... including the better part of a year spent living with the Blood Indians —Frank Getlein, *Smithsonian,* May 1972

> For the better part of two decades the forces of expansion were in the saddle —Eli Ginzberg, *Columbia Forum,* Fall 1970

> ... and Buenos Aires, with the better part of two days at the last —David D. Tennant, *Illustrated London News,* 31 Aug. 1968

between   **1.** *Between, among.* James A. H. Murray in the OED says it as clearly and succinctly as anyone: "It [*between*] is still the only word available to express the relation of a thing to many surrounding things severally and individually, *among* expressing a relation to them collectively and vaguely." Still, the unfounded notion that *between* can be used of only two items persists, most perniciously, perhaps, in schoolbooks. The notion has its origin in the etymology of *between*—the *-tween* derives from an Old English form related to the Old English word for "two"; Samuel Johnson in his Dictionary (1755) took note of it. "*Between* is properly used of two, and *among* of more," he wrote, but being aware of actual use he added "but perhaps this accuracy is not always preserved." He himself did not always preserve this accuracy:

> ... and sincerely hope, that between public business, improving studies, and domestic pleasures, neither melancholy nor caprice will find any place for entrance —Samuel Johnson, letter to James Boswell, 20 June 1771

Noah Webster in 1828 included in his definition of *between:* "We observe that *between* is not restricted to *two*." The originators of the restriction to two, then, ignored the evidence of the two most famous dictionaries of that time. Our earliest evidence for the prescribed restriction to two comes from Goold Brown's *Grammar of English Grammars* (1851). Goold Brown, who was not shy about admitting his superior intellectual powers, skewered an earlier grammarian (T. O. Churchill, 1823) for writing "between more than two": "This is a misapplication of the word *between,* which cannot have reference to more than two. . . ." Another early proponent of the restriction is William B. Hodgson (1881), a Scot who was very fond of finding the correct meaning of English words in their roots—his usual favorites being Greek and Latin. Hodgson is aware of Johnson and Webster, both of whom he relegates to a footnote. As early as 1917 (MacCracken & Sandison), however, we find *between* being admitted as usable for more than two; the great majority of usage commentators since have followed the lines pointed out in the OED definition. But there are a few holdouts for Goold Brown's position: the Harper 1975 usage panel, Simon 1980, Einstein 1985, Sellers 1975, Safire 1982, Bander 1978, and an occasional schoolbook (*Building English Skills,* orange level, 1982) among them.

    What of actual use? The OED shows citations for *between* used of more than two from 971 to 1885; we ourselves have citations from 1303 to 1985. The usage is better than a thousand years old; the attempt to restrict to two, if we take Goold Brown as the originator, less than a century and a half.

    Actually, the enormous amount of ink spilled in the explication of the subtleties of *between* and *among* has been largely a waste; it is difficult for a native speaker of English who is not distracted by irrelevant considerations to misuse the two words. One of the major distractions is, in fact, excessive concern for number. For instance, Einstein 1985 applauds a "correct use of *among*" in a sentence commenting on the ability of certain pianists to play together without interference "to a degree that must have been unique among pianists." In this instance the writer could hardly have been wrong: no native speaker of English would use *between* in such a construction.

    Here is a generous handful of examples of *between* used idiomatically of three or more or used with a plural noun, often of indeterminate number. Some are old (we have already met Dr. Johnson) and some are more recent. For the use of *between* with a singular noun, see the next section.

Phœbus was Judge betweene *Jove, Mars,* and *Love* —Sir Philip Sidney, *Astrophel and Stella,* 1591

This, of course, is between our three discreet selves —Jane Austen, letter, 11 Oct. 1813

Of course that's between you and me and Jack Mum —Myles na gCopaleen (Flann O'Brien), *The Best of Myles,* 1968

... loosely, it applies to a choice between *two or more* —MacCracken & Sandison 1917

... a choice between more than two things or decisions —Partridge 1942

There were three different conclusions to be drawn from his silence, between which her mind was in fluctuation —Jane Austen, *Mansfield Park,* 1814

All the difference in the world, Dinny, between the 'buck,' the 'dandy,' the 'swell,' the 'masher,' the 'blood,' the 'nut,' and what's the last variety called —John Galsworthy, *Flowering Wilderness,* 1932

... those who have not time to choose between *possession, gain, advantage, resource,* & other synonyms —Fowler 1926 (s.v. *asset*)

Undoubtedly there is something in common between the three (Dante, Chaucer, Villon) —T. S. Eliot, "Dante," in *Selected Essays,* 1932

... the relation between grammar, Latin, and social power —Robert Pattison, *On Literacy,* 1982

... under the shadowing trees between whose tops looked down from afar the bold brow of some wooded bluff —Francis Parkman, *La Salle and the Discovery of the Great West,* 1869

The real basis for distinguishing between levels of usage —Barnard 1979

Between doing all these things I read an advertisement that amused me —Randall Jarrell, letter, May 1952

Between the mountains that cradled the yard there seemed to be thousands of freight cars —Russell Baker, *Growing Up,* 1982

Here a few examples of *among:*

Also, could the children be *let alone* while I talk to them, and *not* have (. . .) people going about among them, stirring up the inattentive ones —Lewis Carroll, letter, 2 Sept. 1897

My mother came home with that [joke] the other day. She circulates among all and sundry —Flannery O'Connor, letter, 1 Dec. 1957

... the tribes of north-west Germany were continuously on the move; such movements probably contributed to the diminution of racial distinctions among them —D. J. V. Fisher, *The Anglo-Saxon Age,* 1973

... it is no mere happenstance that Dilsey, alone among the four central figures . . . is seen from the outside —William Styron, *This Quiet Dust and Other Writings,* 1982

Between is not a possibility in any of these except perhaps the Fisher example, where *among* nonetheless does not seem at all forced. In the following example, note how *between* emphasizes differences between one person and each of a number of others, or the whole of them collectively, while *among* shows an indefinite relationship within the group:

> ... it is doubtful whether the differences between Burchfield and the Americans are greater than the differences among the Americans themselves — Robert F. Ilson, in Greenbaum 1985

The following examples of *among* show signs of its having been chosen strictly on the basis of referring to more than two. The first was criticized by Theodore Bernstein in *Winners & Sinners:*

> The psychiatrist said under cross-examination ... that he would include simultaneous intercourse among two men and a woman—a scene shown in the film—in the category of normal —*N.Y. Times,* 30 Dec. 1972

> There is an interesting discussion of language ... among Professor Ross, Richard Buckle (...), and Philip Howard —Simon 1980

> ... is a worthy book that nevertheless falls among many stools —John Simon, *N.Y. Times Book Rev.,* 14 Oct. 1979

> ... the author alternates among mod slang, clichés and quotes from literary giants —Albert H. Johnston, *Publishers Weekly,* 24 July 1978

We suggest that in choosing between *among* and *between* you are going to be better off following your own instincts than trying to follow someone else's theory of what is correct. Our final exhibit shows one prescriber of usage laying down the law and then following his own instincts.

> **among, between:** *Among* may apply to any number; *between* applies to two only —Vizetelly 1906, p. 14

> **bring, carry, fetch:** Discriminate carefully between these words —Vizetelly 1906, p. 40

> **contemptible, contemptibly, contemptuous, contemptuously:** Discriminate carefully between these words —Vizetelly 1906, p. 55

2. *Between each, between every: between* with a singular noun.
Fowler 1926 says "B[*etween*] ... must not be followed by a single expression in which a distributive such as *each* or *every* is supposed to represent a plural." One might well ask why not? Fowler does not tell us. Evans 1961 is more expansive:

> But, actually, *each* is what is called a "distributive." That is, it refers to an individual but only in its quality as a member of a group. There is always a plural in mind when we say *each....* When we say "between each," as in "He rested between each stroke," we are saying by elision, "He rested between each stroke and the next one." And the language permits elision.

Evans goes on to point out that the expression has been used from Shakespeare to John Mason Brown and "must be accepted as idiomatic English."
The question of this construction goes back long before Fowler to the 18th century; Leonard 1929 mentions Robert Baker's comment on it in 1779. And it con-

tinues into the 19th: Hodgson 1889 lists examples of *between each* and *between every* from the 1860s among his examples of errors, including this one from the novelist Elizabeth Gaskell:

> Where, between every stitch, she could look up and see what was going on in the street —*Mr. Harrison's Confessions,* 1866

The construction does go back as far as Shakespeare:

> Between each kiss her oaths of true love swearing — *The Passionate Pilgrim,* 1599

Hall 1917 lists—besides Shakespeare—Jeremy Taylor, Pope, Fielding, Goldsmith, Coleridge, Scott, the historian Motley, Dickens, and George Eliot as authors in whose works he found the construction. He quotes two instances from *Adam Bede:*

> ... pausing between every sentence to rap the floor ...

> ... said Mr. Poyser, turning his head on one side in a dubitative manner, and giving a precautionary puff to his pipe between each sentence.

Volume 2 of Jespersen's *Modern English Grammar* quotes Dickens in addition:

> ... with a shake of her head between every rapid sentence —*A Tale of Two Cities*

Jane Austen, in one of her letters, provides the following breathless example:

> ... & after them succeeded Mrs. White, Mrs. Hughes & her two children, Mr. Moore, Harriot & Louisa, & John Bridges, with such short intervals between any, as to make it a matter of wonder to me, that Mrs. K. & I ever should have ten minutes alone —letter, 26 June 1808

We judge that even though Fowler dislikes it, Nickles 1974 thinks it an illiteracy, and Freeman 1983 and others think it illogical, *between each (every)* is, as Evans 1961 asserts, an acceptable idiom. Too many literary lights have used it to allow any other conclusion.
3. Copperud 1970, Corder 1981, Freeman 1983, Fowler 1926, and others point out that when two (or more) items are enumerated after *between,* the connective used should be *and,* not *or* or *to. And* is, in fact, the connective usually chosen.

between you and I   "What is this *between you and I* ... and where does it come from?" asks Simon 1980. The question is rhetorical; while Simon makes clear his disapproval, he does not dig deeply into the origin of this construction. He seems to think it the fault of sloppy modern education. He also thinks *between you and I* is reinforced by the conscious avoidance of *me* in *it's me.* Barzun 1985 goes further, finding the origin of the expression there:

> This blunder has been the result of a well-meant but foolish conspiracy to root out the use of *it's me.* The wrongheaded war against that quite idiomatic, informal locution created a bugbear in the minds of the ignorant or timid, which drives them to saying *I* whenever they have a chance. The upshot is the illiterate *between you and I....*

The technical term for avoiding one grammatical trap only to fall in another is *hypercorrection.* Hypercorrection is mentioned as a cause or reinforcement of *between you and I* by several other commentators, among them Copperud 1980, Roberts 1962, and Mencken 1963 (abridged). Barnard 1979 will not accept hypercorrection as the cause, however:

> But in the Stratford Grammar School where Shakespeare was a pupil, it had not occurred to anybody that English grammar needed to be taught—only Latin. Yet the Bard has one of his heroes, Antonio in *The Merchant of Venice,* tell his friend Bassanio: "all debts are cleared between you and I." And this is not in light conversation, but in a letter written in the face of death.

The most sophisticated expression of the hypercorrection theory is one of the earliest. In his *New English Grammar* (1892), Henry Sweet takes cognizance of the existence of *between you and I* in early modern English and credits the campaign against *it is me* only for reviving the older construction.

Sweet suggests that the early modern English *between you and I* resulted from *you and I* being so frequently joined together as subject of a sentence that the words formed a sort of group compound with an invariable last element. There may be something to this since binary units like *you and I, man and wife,* are known to have syntactic peculiarities in some other languages—Arabic and German, for instance. But Sweet's incompletely worked-out notion does not explain the coexistence of *between you and me* in early modern English. The question clearly needs more study.

Freeman 1983 mentions a completely different theory: that *I* is substituted for *me* because it sounds softer, less emphatic, and less egotistical than *me.* This is a sort of reversal of the theory that explains *it's me* on the analogy of the French "c'est moi," in which *moi* is called a disjunctive nominative—a form used wherever the word is stressed. Some commentators have called the *me* of *it's me* a disjunctive nominative too. We should remember, however, that the French system does not work in reverse. (See also IT'S ME.)

So for all that has been written about *between you and I,* little is really known about it. If Sweet's hypothesis is correct and modern use is a revival of the early modern English use, we ought not to find much in the way of evidence for the phrase from, say, the end of the 17th century until some time in the middle of the 19th century, when schoolmastering of *it's me* would have had time to take effect. (We find *between you and I* censured in Bache 1869, and Shirley Brice Heath in Shopen & Williams 1980 reports a speaker to graduates of a female Academy in 1846 advising against it.) As it happens, we do have evidence from the late 16th century, the 17th century, and the early years of the 18th century—then nothing for about 150 years. Wyld 1920 mentions examples from the middle of the 17th century but does not quote the texts.

> ... it is an argument too deepe to be discussed between you and I —Thomas Deloney, *Jacke of Newberie,* 1597

> LADY FROTH. ... For between you and I, I had Whymsies and Vapours —William Congreve, *The Double-Dealer,* 1694

> BELINDA. Between you and I, it must all light upon Heartfree and I —Sir John Vanbrugh, *The Provok'd Wife,* 1697 (cited in OED, Wyld, and in *Literary Digest,* 27 June 1925)

> CLINCHER. ... for, hark ye, captain, between you and I, there's a fine Lady in the wind —George Farquhar, *Sir Harry Wildair,* 1701

You might be interested to note that the examples from the Restoration playwrights here are all of what we might call the "confidential" *between you and I.* Curiously enough, the earliest example of this use in the OED is from 1588 and is *between you and me.* All of our 18th century examples have *me:*

> Between you and me, I am often apt to imagine it has had some whimsical Effect upon my Brain —Sir Richard Steele, *The Spectator,* No. 118, 1711 (OED)

> And, between you and me, I believe Lord North is no friend to me —Samuel Johnson, in James Boswell, *Life of Samuel Johnson* 1791

> Between you and me, the *Lyrical Ballads* are but drowsy performances —Charles Lamb, letter, February 1801

But then, in the mid-19th century, we find this:

> Between you and I, I believe that the secret of Ma's willingness to allow me to go to South America lies in the fact that she is afraid I am going to get married —Samuel Clemens, letter, 5 Aug. 1856

H. L. Mencken remarks that Twain regularly used *between you and I* until William Dean Howells took him in hand. The return of the expression to the other side of the Atlantic is attested by a reviewer in the *Times Literary Supplement* (21 Sept. 1967) who cites it as occurring in an 1896 letter of Lady Randolph Churchill, an American by birth. It is probably the "confidential" use that accounts for most modern instances of *between you and I.* We must believe that the use is chiefly spoken, for we have precious little evidence in print.

You have perhaps noticed that Shakespeare's and Deloney's *between you and I* was not of the "confidential" type; it simply indicated some sort of transaction between two people. Farquhar gives us a later example:

> YOUNG MIRABEL. ... I tell thee, child, there is not the least occasion for morals in any business between you and I —*The Inconstant,* 1702

Curiously, Congreve, who used *I* in the "confidential" phrase, uses *me* in the transactional:

> MRS. FORESIGHT. ... Now as to this Affair between you and me —*Love for Love,* 1695

There is only one "confidential" use in Congreve's plays and several of the other. It is possible, of course, that Congreve is suggesting a trait of character with Lady Froth's *between you and I,* but it is hard to see such subtlety in Farquhar's use.

So far we have dealt exclusively with *between you and I,* which is only the most commonly commented-upon variety of a general phrase *between x and y* in which *x* or *y* or both are pronouns. Shakespeare, in such constructions, almost invariably used the objective case of the pronoun, although he has one of the merry wives of Windsor say "There is such a league between my good man and he!" When the *x* is a proper name we sometimes find *I* in the second spot:

> ... and many high words between Mr. Povy and I —Samuel Pepys, diary, 31 Mar. 1664

There was nothing between Mr. Robert and I — Daniel Defoe, *Moll Flanders,* 1722

But evidence for such constructions is sparse, and it is hard to figure out why they occur. Curiously, *he* appears in the *x* slot in these recent examples:

The principal difference between he and I is stamina —Tennessee Williams, quoted in *Esquire,* 5 June 1979 (in Simon 1980)

Rhonda's assessment of Darrin's casual attitude . . . seemed to be borne out by an "interview" with him. This consisted of interrupting a game of catch between he and Brian in Opryland's parking lot — Brett F. Devan, *Bluegrass Unlimited,* September 1983

. . . relations between he and the two bosses are acrimonious as usual —Greg Gumbel, television broadcast, ESPN, 21 Oct. 1985

Can any conclusions be drawn from this welter of opinion and actual use? Everybody criticizes *between you and I,* but it keeps occurring, although examples in print, especially recent ones, are hard to find. When a third item is added to *between you and I* as in the Irish "between you and me and John Mum" or the English and American "between you and me and the gate-post (or lamppost)," *me* is the usual form of the pronoun. Although Mark Twain in 1856 wrote "between you and I and the fence," examples in the Dictionary of American Regional English are predominantly of *me.*

The linguist Noam Chomsky, in his *Barriers,* 1986, has suggested that compound phrases like *you and I* are barriers to the assignment of grammatical case. This means that *between* can assign the objective case only to the whole compound, which cannot be declined, and the individual words in the phrase are free to be nominative or objective or even be reflexives. This is the closest thing to an explanation anyone has offered yet.

Conclusion: you are probably safe in retaining *between you and I* in your casual speech, if it exists there naturally, and you would be true to life in placing it in the mouths of fictional characters. But you had better avoid it in essays and other works of a discursive nature. It seems to have no place in modern edited prose. For more instances of the anomalous use of pronouns, see MYSELF; PRONOUNS; WHO, WHOM 1.

betwixt   James A.H. Murray in the OED considered *betwixt* to be archaic, and *between* to be the living word. The OED citations for *betwixt* are fairly numerous, beginning in the 900s but falling off considerably in number toward the end of the 17th century; there are only a handful from the 18th and 19th centuries. *Betwixt* is used essentially like *between,* even of more than two (see BETWEEN 1).

The word has not yet fallen into disuse. Evidence in the Merriam-Webster files and in the Dictionary of American Regional English show its survival in American dialectal use, especially in the Southern and South Midland areas:

Did you see him betwixt us & the light? —Jesse Stuart, "Uncle Joe's Boys," 1936 (American Dialect Dictionary)

Well, betwixt us two, I do not identify myself with St. Catherine —Flannery O'Connor, letter, 16 Dec. 1955

It also appears, of course, in older literature:

Where the red bird stops to stick its
Ruddy beak betwixt the pickets
Of the truant's rustic trap
    —James Whitcomb Riley, *Farm-Rhymes,* 1883

So he set down on the ground betwixt me and Tom —Mark Twain, *Huckleberry Finn,* 1884

and in a few specialized contexts:

. . . the sun in his glory betwixt nine stars three two three and one arg. —*Burke's Peerage,* 1949

And it is also established in the fixed phrase *betwixt and between,* used occasionally as a compound preposition:

. . . writers already named, who move betwixt and between these criminal branches —Julian Symons, *N.Y. Times Book Rev.,* 30 Sept. 1979

Most often, however, the phrase is used as an adverb or adjective meaning "in an intermediate position" or "neither one thing nor the other":

"Sweet Thursday" makes one feel betwixt and between —Harvey Curtis Webster, *Saturday Rev.,* 12 June 1954

Sometimes such an expression belongs to the vernacular; sometimes to some technical vocabulary; sometimes it is betwixt and between —Gilbert Ryle, in *Ordinary Language,* ed. V. C. Chappell, 1964

A few commentators (such as Nickles 1974, Watt 1967) consider *betwixt and between* a cliché; it is, however, relatively infrequent in print and probably does not really deserve the label.

Except in dialect and the fixed phrase *betwixt and between, betwixt* is uncommon enough nowadays to call attention to itself. It is sometimes used for that very purpose:

. . . but she's not pitching percale here but rather the animal splendor short-sheeted betwixt —*People,* 3 Jan. 1977

bi-   Dictionary editors receive a lot of letters about time words formed with the prefix *bi-,* especially *bimonthly* and *biweekly.* The typical letter writer is outraged or distressed that *bimonthly,* for example, may mean either "every two months" or "twice a month." Many of our correspondents accuse us of abdicating our responsibility by not setting things straight. The trouble is that it is much too late to set things straight. People have been using these words in two different meanings for quite some time, and now we all simply have to live with that fact.

Perhaps the most irritating thing of all is that the writers who use these words almost always assume you know exactly what they mean. In the publishing world, for instance, everyone assumes you know *bimonthly* means "every two months." Only once in a while are you given a clue:

. . . there will now be 6 issues a year. Each bimonthly issue will have 48 pages —*Scouting,* January–February 1970

On the other hand, we have evidence that in the world of education *bimonthly* usually means "twice a month";

a correspondent reports being confused by the publishing use when he was familiar only with "bimonthly examinations." And then we have this passage from a novel with an academic setting:

> "Please listen," O'Connor said. "None of us has time to meet twice a week. The casebooks have grown like tapeworms. We simply have to get organized. I propose we shift to bi-monthly meetings." —John Jay Osborne, Jr., *The Paper Chase,* 1971

We find the same situation with *biweekly.* Writers assume that their meaning is your meaning:

> ... turns in a bi-weekly column —Jerome J. Shestack, *N.Y. Times,* 26 June 1973

What's your guess? Twice a week? Every other week? The writer does not tell us.
Here again the context helps us:

> They are repaid by weekly, biweekly, or monthly payments —McKee Fisk & James C. Snapp, *Applied Business Law.,* 8th ed., 1960

> ... is living in the house herself and giving bi-weekly square dances.... Many guests were told at the beginning of the season that they would be expected every Thursday and Sunday —Millie Considine, *The Diplomat,* April 1965

In a few cases there are contrasting words. For instance, we have *biannual* for "twice a year" and *biennial* for "every two years." But unfortunately *biannual* has sometimes been used to mean *biennial.* Here a solution is easy: skip *biannual* altogether and use in its place the common *semiannual.*
Semiannual reminds us of one possible general solution: use a *semi-* compound for "twice a" and a *bi-* compound for "every two." Apparently many writers do so, for a majority of our citations for *bimonthly, biweekly,* etc. seem to be for "every two." The trouble is that there are just enough of the other uses to leave the reader uncertain. Another solution is to avoid the *bi-* compounds altogether and come right out with it: "twice a week" or "every other month."
These words present a problem that you will have to decide how to deal with case by case. One very important consideration is that if you find yourself in a situation where only a *bi-* word will do, you should give your reader a contextual clue as to your intended meaning.

biannual, biennial See BI-.

bid 1. *Noun.* Copperud 1970 reports that the sense of *bid* meaning "an attempt or effort to win," often seen in newspaper headlines, has been much criticized. This is a dead issue. The OED Supplement shows that this use has been around since the 1880s; it is recognized as standard by dictionaries, and even the Heritage 1969 usage panel found it unobjectionable.

> In his bid for support in the South —John Kenneth Galbraith, *New York,* 15 Nov. 1971

> ... subject only to the market, bankruptcy, a takeover bid —John Fischer, *Harper's,* March 1971

2. *Verb.* Bid has irregular inflected forms. When it means "to make a bid" it usually has the unchanged *bid* as both past and past participle:

> ... was pleased when Betty Franklin, one of his black material handlers, bid for the job —Stephen Sahlein, *The Affirmative Action Handbook,* 1978

> She was bid on by a man from a French agency — Audax Minor, *New Yorker,* 26 Feb. 1972

Bidded can be found but is not usual:

> ... specified other particular suppliers on other bidded contracts —Jonathan Kwitny, *Wall Street Jour.,* 21 Jan. 1975

In other senses the most common past is *bade:*

> ... bade his marshals make the scene as lavish as possible —S. J. Perelman, *New Yorker,* 1 Jan. 1972

> ... the pianist bade us follow him —Horace Sutton, *Saturday Rev.,* 19 June 1971

Bid is sometimes also found:

> The outgoing Truman bid a similar farewell eight years ago —*Trends,* 24 Nov. 1960

In the phrase *bid fair to, bid* is more frequent as past, though *bade* is also used:

> ... first appeared in 1953 and together bid fair to become an institution —Martin James, *Saturday Rev.,* 10 July 1954

> The summer of 1885 bid fair to be one of more than ordinary interest —*Dictionary of American Biography,* 1928

> ... what with the sweat and Indeharu's exertions it bade fair to disintegrate —C. S. Forester, *The Sky and the Forest,* 1948

As past participle, *bid* and *bidden* are the most usual:

> ... those manuscripts that he had once bid Max Brod to dispose of —Philip Roth, *Reading Myself and Others,* 1975

> ... we have bid adieu to most historical problems — John Wilkinson, *Center Mag.,* May 1968

> ... she was bidden to dine at Windsor —Georgina Battiscombe, *Queen Alexandra,* 1969

> ... was bidden to listen to brief prayers —Lady Bird Johnson, *McCall's,* November 1970

Bade is a less frequent past participle:

> ... friends were bade farewell —*Dartmouth Alumni Mag.,* May 1954

billion Copperud 1970, Reader's Digest 1983, and others comment on the fact that in American English *billion* means "a thousand million" and in British English "a million million." Our latest British source, Longman 1984, says that the American sense of *billion* is increasingly being used in British English because it is standard both in American English and international scientific English. Longman does warn of the possibility of confusion in British English.

bimonthly See BI-.

bit 1. Vizetelly 1906 called the use of *bit* for liquids— "there's not a bit of water on the farm"—an error; Longman 1984 mentions that some people in the U.K. still think it is wrong. No one objects to *bit* used of abstractions:

> The Neapolitan Court was always prime for a bit of scandal —Mollie Hardwick, *Emma, Lady Hamilton,* 1969

. . . fill up any spaces in the oven with a bit of baking —Mary Dene, *Woman's Realm,* 21 Sept. 1974

Since neither the abstraction nor the liquid is particulate, it seems a bit nit-picking to object to one but not the other.

2. Everybody has heard of a bit part in a theatrical production. There is another theatrical use of *bit* that refers to a routine or to some business onstage:

Yes, yes, yes, I see what you mean about the "headless man" bit —Ellen Terry, letter, 24 Sept. 1896

This theatrical use spread into more general use gradually and was especially prominent in hip use of the 1960s and 1970s. Predictably, the usage panels hated it, although the Harper 1975 group expressed a willingness to put up with it in speech. This use is by now well established, but from the examples below (the first is apparently from speech) you can see that it is most at home in a breezy style.

I did the starving writer routine, the full La Boheme bit —Les Dawson, quoted in *Annabel,* July 1974

So what's with this "lady" bit, that seems to have come into fashion over the last two or three years? —Margaret Sydney, *Australian Women's Weekly,* 16 Apr. 1975

No, I didn't get my impression of the Civil War from home. I got it from the air around me (with the ambiguous Lincoln bit probably from a schoolroom) —Robert Penn Warren, *Jefferson Davis Gets His Citizenship Back,* 1980

bite *Bite* has two past participles, *bitten* and *bit. Bitten* is by far the more common—it is the usual form of the past participle. *Bit,* the less common form, was thought archaic when the OED was edited. The Dictionary of American Regional English reports several dialect surveys on the subject; *bit* is used especially by respondents that are male and less educated. The highest reported use of *bit* was by 33 percent of respondents in California and Nevada in 1971.

At any rate the dialect geographers have established that *bit* as past participle is alive and well in speech. How does it fare in print? Our evidence shows that it still occurs, and in standard English contexts, but not nearly as often as *bitten.*

Harper 1975, 1985 has an interesting observation. *Bitten,* they say, can be used as past participle in both active and passive constructions, but *bit* can be used only in active ones. Our recent evidence agrees in general, but not in every particular. In the examples below you will see that in print the past participle *bit* occurs more often in several fixed phrases than in more general and literal senses of *bite.* While the passive construction is not usual, it is not impossible (it seems to be not uncommon in speech).

They'd bit their own hook —*The Collected Verse of A. B. Paterson,* 1946

I have bit my tongue and held back —William Howells, *The Heathens,* 1948

. . . few leases have bit the dust —William F. Longgood, *Saturday Evening Post,* 4 Dec. 1954

I have bit off more than I can chew —Flannery O'Conner, letter, 9 Nov. 1962

. . . hoping not to get bit by mosquitoes —Robert Coover, *Harper's,* January 1972

He's bit the bullet and we haven't —Senator Mike Mansfield, quoted in *The Economist,* 31 May 1975

In the past year or so, most of the large independents have bit the dust —Stephen J. Sansweet, *Wall Street Jour.,* 23 June 1982

. . . ceiling molding—fittings that might have bit the bin a short decade ago —Donald Vining, *Metropolitan Home,* October 1982

Conclusion: these citations, spanning about 40 years, are not evidence that *bit* is beginning to rival *bitten* in frequency, but only that *bit* continues to be used now and then, especially in various fixed phrases of *bite.* It almost always occurs in an active construction. *Bitten* is the usual past participle.

biweekly See BI-.

black Quite a few commentators mention the use of *black* in the sense of *Negro,* a revival of an old use that seems to have begun with the civil rights movement in the 1960s. The OED reports instances of *black* in the sense from the 17th century; evidently it began as a translation of the Spanish *Negro,* which had earlier been used in English. The term seems to have been neutral in the 18th century:

The negro case is not yet decided. . . . Maclaurin is made happy by your approbation of his memorial for the black —James Boswell, letter to Samuel Johnson, 14 Feb. 1777

Reader's Digest 1983 says that *black, Negro,* and *colored* were all in neutral use during the time of slavery; after the Civil War *colored* was the preferred term, with *Negro* replacing it in favor around the turn of the century. Changes in the preference for one term over another are always gradual. Copperud 1970, 1980 reports a *Newsweek* poll taken in 1969 that showed *Negro* ahead of *colored* just slightly ahead of *black.* By the end of the 1970s *black* was clearly preferred. It is sometimes capitalized.

. . . when the idea of enlisting blacks for Confederate armies (with the implied promise of freedom) was successfully brought forward —Robert Penn Warren, *Jefferson Davis Gets His Citizenship Back,* 1980

. . . two black men in overalls lifting off a plank — Russell Baker, *Growing Up,* 1982

. . . and there are Blacks in the exclusive clubs of Harvard, Yale, and Princeton —Geoffrey Nunberg, in *Standards and Dialects in English,* 1980

More recently, *Afro-American* (a 19th-century word) and *African-American* (1984) have become terms of choice. The former is used mostly as an adjective, while the latter is about equally noun and adjective. *African-American* is perhaps on its way to becoming the preferred term, but *black* is still just about as frequent. See also COLORED.

Black English *Black English* is a term going back only to 1969. It is used almost exclusively as the name for a dialect of American English spoken by many black Americans.

During the 1970s a great deal was written about Black English. It has two competing theories of origin: one theory holds that the characteristic features of Black English have their origin in a creole at least partly derived from African languages; the other holds that Black English shares most of its features with the Southern dialect spoken by whites. The proponents of the two theories do not, it appears, speak to one another. Black English has also been embroiled in several disputes relating to educational theory in recent time and a law suit decided in some Federal District Court.

All of this controversy has perhaps generated more heat than light on the purely linguistic side of the subject; it will likely be many years (maybe even generations) before the various political and educational disputes are set aside and Black English can be studied disinterestedly and dispassionately. The interconnections and influences of the various dialects of British and American English appear to be complex and subtle and well worth study; it seems a shame that so much of the effort in connection with Black English is spent on polemics.

Bolinger 1980 lists three features of Black English on which almost everyone is agreed (the examples here are Bolinger's):

> Omission of the copula *is:* [modern linguists often call this "copula deletion"]: *You out the game.*

> Dropping of the present-tense inflection *-s* [others generalize this to "not marking the verb for person"]: *He fast in everything he do.*

> Use of *be* to mean "repeated occurrence" . . . : *Some of them be big.* [See BE for other examples.]

Many other features are also mentioned by one commentator or another, among them multiple negation, the use of double subjects, and the use of nominative pronouns in place of genitive forms. This last was noticed briefly by H. L. Mencken in *The American Language* (4th edition, 1936). Mencken in turn had found it mentioned by the grammarian George O. Curme (*Parts of Speech and Accidence*, 1935). The example Mencken cites—"He roll he eyeballs"—was found by Curme in one of Joel Chandler Harris's Uncle Remus stories.

Those who are interested in the subject can find several books published on it as well as articles in such periodicals as *American Speech, The English Journal,* and *The Journal of English Linguistics,* among others. Reader's Digest 1983 has a substantial article with attached word lists, and there are also discussions in Barnard 1979, Bolinger 1980, and Quinn 1980. Some specific features of Black English are treated in a general way in this book—see, for instance, BE; DOUBLE NEGATIVE 1; DOUBLE SUBJECTS.

blame, *noun.* The noun *blame* may be followed by the prepositions *for, with,* or *on:*

> I take all the blame for not seeing further than my nose —C. P. Snow, *The Conscience of the Rich,* 1958

> She could not bear any implied blame of him —Angus Wilson, *The Middle Age of Mrs. Eliot,* 1958

> . . . and just as vaguely puts the blame on downtown businessmen —Jack Olsen, *Sports Illustrated,* 15 July 1968

blame on, blame for The real difference between "blame someone for" and "blame something on" is the direct object; in the first the direct object is the cause—usually a person—of the problem, and in the second the direct object is the problem. The first construction is older; the second is not attested in the OED until 1835.

In 1881 the pseudonymous Alfred Ayres in *The Verbalist* took note of the newer construction. *Blame on,* said Ayres, "is a gross vulgarism which we sometimes hear from persons of considerable culture." Ayres does not stop to explain why it is a vulgarism or how such cultured persons are capable of using such a vulgarism—or even to prescribe *blame for.* It is a simple ex cathedra pronouncement, and from Ayres it spread rapidly into other American usage books, textbooks, and dictionaries and eventually even into British publications. Vizetelly 1906 called it "indefensible slang," and he blackened the expression in his dictionary, Funk & Wagnalls 1913, and in his later books. Censure of one kind or another turns up in Utter 1916, MacCracken & Sandison 1917, Lincoln Library 1924, Whipple 1924, Lurie 1927, Krapp 1927, Jensen 1935 and so on down to more recent publications such as Bernstein 1958, 1965, Shaw 1970, 1975, Gowers in Fowler 1965 (Fowler 1926 ignored it), Phythian 1979, Bremner 1980, Oxford American Dictionary 1980, Freeman 1983. Others along the way had found the construction standard—Evans 1957, Copperud 1964, 1970, 1980, Flesch 1964, Bryant 1962, Harper 1975, 1985, Heritage 1969—as indeed it had been all the time.

Our files show *blame on* and *blame for* to be about equally frequent.

> The firm blame the closures on "heavy losses and a world-wide fall in demand" —Keith Mason & Ian Hepburn, *The Sun* (London), 31 Oct. 1974

> . . . begins by blaming everything on the parents —Pauline Kael, *Harper's,* February 1969

> . . . maneuvering to blame any breakdown in the talks on the other side —*I. F. Stone's Bi-Weekly,* 5 Apr. 1971

> . . . have only themselves to blame for the fact that alimony is necessary —Germaine Greer, *McCall's,* March 1971

> . . . parents blame the urban school system for their children's failures —Fred M. Hechinger, *N.Y. Times,* 9 Jan. 1969

> . . . blames this culture for conceiving of art as having to do with personal privilege and pleasure —Lionel Trilling, *N.Y. Times Book Rev.,* 7 Mar. 1954

A few other prepositions are used with *blame,* but less often:

> . . . not to blame onto Latin the results of sloppy teaching —Marion Friedmann, in *Verbatim,* December 1974

> . . . tended to blame the evasion of such subject-matter . . . to the persistence of the romantic tradition —*Times Literary Supp.,* 21 July 1966

> . . . she blamed us with killing the canary birds, too —*New Yorker,* 25 Sept. 1926

blasé When *blasé* is followed by a preposition, it is usually *about:*

> Twelve years ago it was still considered a tremendous journalistic coup to discover . . . a single dissenter. Now our correspondents have grown somewhat blasé about the breed —Adam B. Ulam, *Saturday Rev.,* 7 Feb. 1976

. . . has been less blasé about the activities of the Sandinist National Liberation Front —Alan Riding, *Saturday Rev.,* 12 Nov. 1977

There is also evidence for *with* and *at:*

. . . but in time, we became jaded and blase with ordinary heiresses with American fortunes —Eve Babitz, *Rolling Stone,* 3 Feb. 1972

. . . to act a bit blasé at the prospect of yet another famous . . . customer holding forth —Allan Ripp, *Avenue,* March 1984

blatant, flagrant Several commentators note that these words "are confused," which, being interpreted, means "have senses that overlap in meaning." This is a relatively new subject—one first noticed, apparently, in Partridge 1942, which records Anthony Eden saying "a blatant breach of good faith" in a 1936 speech. Evans 1957 worked out a distinction between *blatant* and *flagrant* and so did Bernstein 1965, along somewhat different lines. Most subsequent commentators echo one of these two.

Blatant is usually the point of the comment. One matter that draws notice is the extension of *blatant* from its earliest "noisy" senses to a sense "glaringly conspicuous or obtrusive"—a shift from the ear to the eye, so to speak. The OED Supplement dates this development from the end of the 19th century. The sense was given in Webster 1909 but was deleted by a short-sighted editor working on Webster's Second (1934). It has become the predominant sense in modern use.

The conspicuousness denoted by both *blatant* and *flagrant* is almost always of an undesirable kind. Several commentators from Evans and Bernstein on note that *flagrant* stresses scandalous or wicked behavior. This is its most common use, and it commonly modifies such nouns as *violation* and *abuse.*

. . . in flagrant violation of the Hague and Geneva conventions —William L. Shirer, *The Rise and Fall of the Third Reich,* 1960

. . . uncovered flagrant discrimination —Francis X. Gannon, *Change,* September 1971

. . . I, who even in the most flagrant crimes had denied the justice and righteousness of capital punishment —Jack London, *The Sea-Wolf,* 1904

Blatant is sometimes used similarly:

. . . more graft, more mismanagement and more blatant knavery —Harold L. Ickes, *New Republic,* 16 May 1949

. . . the most blatant and public forms of sex discrimination —Lillian Foster, *McCall's,* March 1971

. . . this blatant violation of human dignity and international law —Edward Weisband & Thomas M. Franck, *Trans-Action,* October 1971

Blatant, in general, carries less moral freight than *flagrant:*

Interpolated essays or apostrophes by the novelist are of course a blatant violation of the principle —Bernard DeVoto, *The World of Fiction,* 1950

Still, *flagrant* is not limited to expressions of moral outrage, as one or two commentators suggest it is. It can mean merely "conspicuous." In such use it is more or less interchangeable with *blatant:*

. . . his son is a flagrant homosexual —*Saturday Rev.,* 8 Jan. 1955

. . . let's say a blatant homosexual —Merle Miller, *Saturday Rev.,* 2 Jan. 1971

There is no more flagrant example of poetic diction —Irving Babbitt, *The New Laokoon,* 1910

. . . the poeticism was real poetry, and it was far from shamefaced, in fact it was blatant —Dwight Macdonald, in *The Film,* 1968

In summary, while *blatant* and *flagrant* may both mean merely "conspicuous," *blatant* is usually used of someone, some action, or something that attracts disapproving attention:

The most blatant instance is provided by the recent colloquial use of *like* whenever the speaker halts for an idea —Barzun 1985

Flagrant is used in the same way but usually carries a heavier weight of violated morality:

. . . this was a very flagrant instance of filial disobedience and rebellion —Thomas Love Peacock, *Nightmare Abbey,* 1818

We recently heard the announcer of a hockey game refer to "a blatant hook"—hooking is a common infraction in ice hockey—that the referee failed to call. A generation earlier he would probably have used *flagrant.* The fact is that the use of *blatant* is now growing faster than that of *flagrant.* In another generation, perhaps, the two words will be more frequently interchangeable than they are today.

bleeding See BLOODY.

blend Bernstein 1965 and Partridge 1942 say that blend is followed by *with:*

. . . blending the cadences of the liturgy with those of perplexed brooding thought —Edmund Wilson, *Axel's Castle,* 1931

. . . whose life had been so strangely blended with hers —Winston Churchill, *The Crisis,* 1901

. . . elation which comes when man feels himself blended with nature —Walter Prescott Webb, *The Great Frontier,* 1952

Partridge disapproves *blend* with *into,* but it is quite common and standard:

The painting would blend into nature —Harold Rosenberg, *New Yorker,* 20 Nov. 1971

. . . ordering their cadres to blend themselves into the government landscape —Robert Shaplen, *New Yorker,* 24 Apr. 1971

Sometimes we find *blend in* followed by *with:*

. . . how well he blends in with the background —Andrew Sarris, in *The Film,* 1968

. . . more imaginative sets, which are unfortunately blended in with others that are pretty poor —Henry Hewes, *Saturday Rev.,* 28 Feb. 1953

And in cookery, *blend* is followed by *in:*

> Blend in four tablespoons flour —Jane Nickerson, *N.Y. Times Mag.*, 10 Oct. 1954

blind agreement See AGREEMENT, SUBJECT-VERB: THE PRINCIPLE OF PROXIMITY.

blink, blink at The verb *blink* has a transitive sense "to refuse to recognize, to close one's eyes to, ignore." This has often been used in the phrase *blink the fact:*

> ... another escape hatch to allow us to blink facts — Stanley Kauffmann, *Atlantic*, March 1973

> ... there is no blinking the fact that ... —Albert H. Marckwardt, in *The College Teaching of English*, ed. John C. Gerber, 1965

> The fact cannot be blinked —*Times Literary Supp.*, 24 Sept. 1964

But it is also used with many other direct objects:

> But it would be foolish to blink the pitfalls —Vermont Royster, *Wall Street Jour.*, 15 Apr. 1981

> But without blinking that frightening connection — William Stafford, *Writing the Australian Crawl*, 1978

> He does not blink the weaknesses of the West — James Reston, *N.Y. Times*, 24 June 1979

> ... it seems necessary ... not to blink realities — Dell Hymes, in *Language as a Human Problem*, ed. Morton Bloomfield & Einar Haugen 1974

> There is evil in it, no blinking that —Wilfrid Sheed, *N.Y. Times Book Rev.*, 21 Nov. 1976

This sense is turned into an intransitive with *at* once in a while:

> ... modern popular philosophy blinks at these facts —Morris R. Cohen, *The Faith of a Liberal*, 1946

> ... poem, which neither blinks at the brutality nor plays down ... —Babette Deutsch, *Yale Rev.*, December 1953

> Carter had to blink at these differences in order to bring off a peace treaty —Sidney Zion & Uri Dan, *N.Y. Times Mag.*, 8 Apr. 1979

The OED first noted the *at* construction in an 1857 citation, which it considered improper. Copperud 1970, 1980 echoes the OED disapproval, with the implication that *blink at* is not idiomatic. It is idiomatic, however; it is simply rare.

Blink at is used in a related sense which means "to view with surprise or dismay":

> When an eminent critic called them "stark as the Welsh mountains" I blinked at the implication — Waldo Williams, *Dock Leaves*, Winter 1953

> ... no one's even blinking at the $450 tag —*Vogue*, September 1976

> ... American propaganda (there is no use in blinking at the word) —Harrison Smith, *Saturday Rev.*, 24 Feb. 1951

bloc, block The spelling *bloc* is usual for the sense of a political combination. The OED Supplement shows no use of *block* in this sense more recent than 1957.

> ... Iran's two main power blocs —James Dorsey, *Christian Science Monitor*, 8 Dec. 1980

> ... to please every voter bloc and interest group — Louis Winnick, *N.Y. Times Book Rev.*, 13 Jan. 1985

> ... the power of the women's bloc vote —Nancy J. Walker, *N.Y. Times Book Rev.*, 11 Mar. 1984

blond, blonde Do you use *blond* or *blonde?* Both? Do you reserve *blonde* for female applications and *blond* for male ones? Do you make no distinction? The *e* meant feminine in the Middle French word which was brought into English, but its force is somewhat weaker in English. We have studied fourteen handbooks offering occasionally conflicting advice to help you choose between *blond* and *blonde;* rather than try to untangle their various formulas, we will simply describe what our most recent evidence shows.

Blonde, when used as a noun of a human, is currently used only of females:

> Promise Land, a blonde who lives up to her blissful name —Alan Bold, *Times Literary Supp.*, 27 Nov. 1981

> ... her lightest, funniest performance, rivalled only by her dippy blonde in "Beat the Devil" —Elizabeth Tallent, *New Yorker*, 10 Jan. 1983

Blond, when used as a noun of a human, is currently used of either males or females:

> ... got off the plane with an incredible looking blond in tow—Seleina Marlow —Jeremy Bernstein, *American Scholar*, Winter 1981/1982

> ... the lanky blond lies across the bed, his wrists tied to the bedpost —John Stark, *People*, 13 Aug. 1984

The *blond* spelling is applied slightly more often to males than to females.

As an adjective applied to humans, *blonde* is used of both males and females, but more often of females:

> ... her streaked blonde hair swept up in a hive — James Atlas, *Atlantic*, April 1982

> He shakes his blonde, layered locks —Rochelle Chadakoff, *US*, 8 June 1982

> A handsome blonde lady —William Weber Johnson, *Smithsonian*, March 1983

> He was a Northern Frenchman, very blonde —Richard Cobb, *The Listener*, 18 July 1974

> Out fell six nude photographs of a blonde girl — *Cape Times* (South Africa), 1 Feb. 1975

As an adjective applied to humans, *blond* is used of both males and females:

> ... the tall, blue-eyed blond Dutch actor Rutger Hauer —Pauline Kael, *New Yorker*, 12 July 1982

> The girl—she looked about twenty—was slim and blond and beautiful —Berton Roueché, *New Yorker*, 28 Dec. 1981

> ... the blond boys —*People*, 13 Feb. 1984

> ... the blond actress who plays one of her two daughters —David Gritten, *People*, 4 Oct. 1982

> ... the "British Blondes," a popular troupe of women entertainers. Thanks to them, blond hair for

the first time became a mark of feminine beauty —
Carl N. Degler, *N.Y. Times Book Rev.,* 17 Apr. 1983

. . . a lovely blond Englishwoman —G. Y. Dryansky,
Town & Country, April 1984

The adjective *blond,* like *blonde,* is more often applied
to females than males.

When the word is applied to a nonhuman object, you
can use either spelling. Here are two things to which it
is applied—wood and beer:

. . . blond wooden tables —Katharine Andres, *New
Yorker,* 9 Jan. 1984

Blonde wood handles —*Crate & Barrel Catalogue,*
Spring and Summer 1981

In a blond beer —Norman S. Roby, *Cuisine,* August
1983

. . . blonde barley beer —Peter Dragadze, *Town &
Country,* April 1983

In sum, the adjective is applied more often to females
than males in both spellings. The noun *blonde* is used of
females; the noun *blond,* of both sexes. You can use
either spelling for nonhuman objects.

See also BRUNET, BRUNETTE.

bloody   The use of *bloody* as an intensive adverb and
intensive adjective is more of a usage problem in British
English than it is in American English. Harper 1975,
1985 has a short sketch on *bloody,* ending with a warning to Americans to have a care for English sensibilities.

The most curious thing about *bloody* to Americans is
the revulsion with which the word has been regarded in
British English; it carries no particularly vulgar tinge in
American English, even when used as an all-purpose
intensive as it is in British English. And nobody really
knows how *bloody* acquired its bad odor. The OED
shows that the intensive use was current in the second
half of the 17th century. Its first known occurrence in
print is in Sir George Etherege's play *The Man of Mode*
in 1676. The passage is of uncertain meaning. It occurs
when one of two rakish gentlemen who have been ral-
lying a shoemaker about his home life and his drinking
directs his servant to pay the shoemaker half a crown.
The other gentleman says:

Not without he will promise to be bloody drunk.

This may be a simple intensive use, or it may not be. A
single occurrence is hard to interpret.

James A. H. Murray in the OED says that *bloody* was
in "general colloquial use" from the Restoration to the
middle of the 18th century. During that time it seems to
have had no particular offensive taint:

It was bloody hot walking to-day —Jonathan Swift,
Journal to Stella, 8 May 1711

What happened after about 1750 no one seems to
know. But *bloody* went out of use by the fashionable and
polite and became confined to the speech of the lower
orders of society. It seems likely that Samuel Johnson's
Dictionary had some effect. In the second edition
(1755), he entered the adverb, defined it "very; as *bloody*
sick, *bloody* drunk" and added the note "this is very vulgar." The entry seems to have been considered vulgar
by Johnson's successors; the entry is omitted from the
8th edition, which appeared in 1798 and 1799, and is
also missing from Todd's edition (1818). But Noah

Webster picked it up in his 1828 dictionary, keeping
Johnson's original entry intact.

Still the word could be found occasionally in print.
Byron put the word into the mouth of an English highwayman shot by his hero Don Juan:

'Oh Jack! I'm floor'd by that 'ere bloody Frenchman!' —*Don Juan,* Canto xi, 1823

But as the 19th century went along, the word seemed to
mysteriously acquire even more loathsome connotations. The OED notes Ruskin in 1880 writing:

The use of the word 'bloody' in modern low English
is a deeper corruption, not altering the form of the
word, but defiling the thought of it.

If *bloody* were as tainted by "deeper corruption" as
Ruskin says, it is little wonder that George Bernard
Shaw could create a sensation in 1914 by putting it in
the mouth of Eliza Doolittle in *Pygmalion* and having
it spoken in public on the stage. The *New York Times*
correspondent wrote that the utterance of the forbidden
word was the chief interest in the play, and that the
audience heard it shudderingly. Mrs. Patrick Campbell
remembered it somewhat differently; in her autobiography she wrote that

The 'bloody' almost ruined the play; people laughed
too much.

After World War I the word began to creep into
respectable literature again, appearing in works by such
writers as W. Somerset Maugham, John Masefield, and
Aldous Huxley. Still, Webster's Second (1934) could
add "regarded in England as a gross vulgarism."
Between the wars there was some interest in speculating
on the origin of *bloody*'s stigma. H. L. Mencken in *The
American Language* (4th ed., 1936) notes: "Various
amateur etymologists have sought to account for its
present evil fame by giving it loathsome derivations,
sometimes theological and sometimes catamenial, but
the professional etymologists all agree that these derivations are invalid, though when it comes to providing
a better one they unhappily disagree."

Foster 1968 notes the appearance of *bloody* in public
speeches as part of the general casting off of linguistic
restraints after World War II. He quotes Lord Boothby
in a 1963 speech saying "I was bloody nearly mental till
I was nineteen. . . ." This use is not very different from
that of Fielding's Old Mutable:

STEDFAST. . . . If you change your mind again before
they are married, they shall never be married at all,
that I am resolved.
OLD MUTABLE. [Aside.] This is a bloody positive old
fellow.
                               —*The Wedding-Day,* 1743

Earlier *bloody* had such a bad reputation that several
euphemisms were used in its place: *ruddy, bleeding, sanguinary,* and *blooming,* among others. *Ruddy* gained
enough taint of its own to be considered a bit of a swear-
word itself, and Gilbert and Sullivan created such an
outcry when they introduced the operetta *Ruddygore* in
1887 that they changed the spelling to *Ruddigore* after
the fourth performance. Even that spelling seems to
have raised eyebrows. Foster 1968 notes that the Duke
of Edinburgh uttered the phrase "ruddy well" in a 1956
newsreel, and that has taken some of the sting out of the
word.

Foster also points out that the use of *ruddy* and
blooming as euphemisms in British English has some-

what tainted their use in other senses, so that references to "a ruddy color" may bring snickers. Longman 1984 makes the same point about bloody itself, warning that the slang sense might interfere with a use of an older sense. The senses conflict in such a context as this:

> . . . and saw my foot slung up to a gantry, swathed in bloody great bandages —R. F. Delderfield, *To Serve Them All My Days,* 1972

But some Americans worry about the opposite reaction:

> Unfortunately titled (for those turned off by implications of violence and justifiably unaware of the veddy British use of "bloody" as an intensive), John Schlesinger's *Sunday Bloody Sunday* . . . —Judith Crist, *New York,* 27 Sept. 1971

But the intensive use is known in American English, even though it is not as common as it is in British English. Leacock 1943 is amused by a passage from James Fenimore Cooper, in which mild expletives are represented by dashes, but *bloody* is untouched:

> . . ."D———e," said the bosun, "what the d———l, does the bloody fellow mean?"

And Eliza Doolittle's "not bloody likely" cannot even raise an American eyebrow:

> . . . wishes he would "try a more laid-back look and Hawaiian shirts." Not bloody likely —*People,* 29 Sept. 1980

In British use *bloody* has slowly been finding its way into print. The OED back in 1887 commented on the practice of the British popular press of representing it, when they had to, as *b———y.* In 1946 *Newsweek* had some fun with the British press when a Lady Elisabeth White said in court, "yes, I stole the bloody things." *Newsweek* reported that "from the *Daily Worker* on up" the London papers printed the word as ——— or *b———.* The press has gotten braver since:

> . . . said last night that the Glasgow firemen would be "bloody fools" if they did not accept the new agreement —Rosemary Collins & Peter Cole, *The Guardian,* 3 Nov. 1973

> What a bloody shame that when something went wrong, it had to happen this way —Norman Thompson, quoted in *The Sunday Times* (London), 7 Apr. 1974

> I'm bloody browned off —Joe Gormley, quoted in *Daily Mirror* (London), 31 Oct. 1974

Now it turns up in print not only in the U.K. but also in Canada, South Africa, New Zealand, and Australia.

Australia is of particular interest. Howard 1980 and 1984 comments on the wide use of *bloody* in Australia, as do several earlier commentators. It appears that the word there long ago lost some of the stigma it had in England. A poem published in 1904 made fun of its frequency of occurrence in Australian English (this version was printed in *Time,* 24 Apr. 1944):

> The sunburnt bloody stockman stood
> And, in a dismal bloody mood,
> Apostrophised his bloody cuddy;
> The bloody nag's no bloody good,
> He couldn't earn his bloody food!
> A regular bloody brumby. Bloody!

This same poem is given in a footnote in *American Speech,* October, 1960, and is identified as being from W. T. Goodge, *Hits, Skits and Jingles,* Sydney, 1904. It is interesting that the original apparently printed dashes in place of *Time's bloody.*

Our most recent evidence of British English suggests that intensive *bloody* is now what older dictionaries would have described as "colloquial." It is generally found only in reported speech and in fictitious speech in literature. It probably still offends more delicate sensibilities.

blooming   See BLOODY.

blow   *Blow* belongs to a class of verbs some of whose members have regular inflected forms and some irregular. The usual inflected forms of *blow* are irregular: *blew* and *blown.* The regular variant of these, *blowed,* says Phythian 1979, is allowed only in the expression "I'll be blowed." The OED also shows *blowed* only in that sense. Lamberts 1972 notes, however, that the regular forms are common in nonstandard English. The Dictionary of American Regional English narrows this observation, finding *blowed* to be chiefly Southern and South Midland with some scattered use in Northern areas. The DARE additionally notes that *blowed* occurs especially frequently among less educated male speakers.

Blowed does not seem to have had much literary use. Shakespeare puts it into the mouth of his Irish captain Macmorris in *Henry V:*

> I would have blowed up the town. . . .

Defoe gave it to Robinson Crusoe:

> May 16.   It had blowed hard in the night. . . .

Blowed was apparently in the dialect of William Cobbett. In his 1819 *Grammar* he has this passage:

> . . . as, *the tree, which stood close beside the barn, is blowed down.* In this last instance, we are not only informed that a tree is blowed down, but the sentence also informs us what particular tree it is.

Our American citations of recent vintage are all from speech and fall within the dialect areas described by the DARE.

boast   Copperud 1970 cites himself as questioning the transitive sense "to possess and call attention to" but notes that dictionaries recognize the meaning; so do the two famous usage panels. The OED shows that the sense has been in use since the late 17th century. It has always been standard.

> . . . whether she boasts any offspring besides a grand pianoforte did not appear —Jane Austen, letter, 7 Jan. 1807

> Philadelphia, which boasts history galore —Lewis Mumford, *New Yorker,* 13 Apr. 1957

> . . . the Southwest's financial capital . . . boasting the establishment of more new insurance companies last year than any other city in the country —Theodore H. White, *The Reporter,* 8 June 1954

> One of these carvings in particular . . . boasts a refinement not seen again until the Christian Middle Ages —Hilton Kramer, *N.Y. Times,* 16 Nov. 1976

When *boast* is used as an intransitive with a preposition, *of* and *about* are usual:

... this world of Capitalism, with its astonishing spread of ignorance and helplessness, boasting ... of its spread of education and enlightenment —George Bernard Shaw, *The Intelligent Woman's Guide to Socialism and Capitalism,* 1928

... the magazine could boast of a critic ... whose interest in the theatre was exceeded only by his interest in the living human drama —*Saturday Rev.,* 23 Apr. 1955

... he allows environmental pollution ... at the same time that he boasts about playground facilities and law and order —Henry Hewes, *Saturday Rev.,* 3 June 1972

boat   Almost everyone knows a ship is bigger than a boat, and a number of usage writers—Kilpatrick 1984, Harper 1985, Shaw 1975, for instance—allow themselves a display of their nautical lore by elaborating on the theme. This is all part of the folklore of newspapering, and goes back at least as far as James Gordon Bennett's "Don't List" of the *New York Herald,* in which everyone is directed not to use *boat* "(except in describing a small craft propelled by oars)." Copperud calls the attempt to restrict *boat* to this sense "a naval fetish." The literate general public, no doubt mostly landlubbers, pays no attention to the restriction and uses *boat* for a floating contrivance of whatever size it wishes. Such use is entirely standard, of course, except in nautical circles:

When he reached Alexandria he came up to his boat, a paddle steamer built of steel —E. L. Doctorow, *Ragtime,* 1975

bodacious   Although this word is entered in Reader's Digest 1983, Bremner 1980, and Nickles 1974, there is no usage problem attached to it. It's an American dialect term; the Dictionary of American Regional English labels it chiefly Southern and South Midland. Nickles calls it a "crackerbarrel term." Many people have met the word through the comic strip "Snuffy Smith," produced by Fred Lasswell. A typical use (we omit the cartoonist's balloon):

Elviney!! I got some bodacious gossip for ye ...

The term has occasionally been adopted by the city slickers:

The bodacious business of buying and selling network television time —Geoffrey Colvin, *Fortune,* 20 Oct. 1980

The most bodacious example in the U.S. of the plushy Victorian architecture —*Time,* 4 Sept. 1944

The word's origin is somewhat conjectural. It is probably related to *audacious* and to a British dialect term *boldacious,* believed to be a blend of *bold* and *audacious,* which is attested somewhat later than the American word. The adverb *bodaciously* is attested even earlier than *bodacious,* which makes it possible that *bodacious* is a back-formation. If we had more early evidence, we would need less guesswork.

boggle   When a usage writer is determined to find something wrong with an expression, he will disapprove

no matter how difficult constructing a rationale for the disapproval turns out to be. Both Barzun 1985 and Bremner 1980 dislike the expression "(something) boggles the mind." Bremner says it is an example of the error of making a transitive out of an intransitive. Presumably this means that if "the water boils" is earlier in standard use, then "boil the water" must be an error. Of course it isn't, as anyone willing to take a short tour through the verbs in a dictionary will see. Barzun thinks that making a transitive out of *boggle* is contrary to usage. If it were truly contrary to usage, however, he would not have had to write about it. Barzun also says *boggle* describes what a horse does when it is startled and refuses to budge, and that's why "the mind boggles" makes sense. (Horse sense, perhaps.) But a verb's original physical sense—and that of *boggle* was used of people about as early as it was of horses, by the way—cannot be taken as controlling the legitimate direction of the verb's later semantic development. If it could, we might have to disapprove many well-established verb uses, such as "the situation cries out for action" because the earliest uses of *cry* involved loud noise. Such objections as the ones just discussed have a decidedly ad hoc cast to them.

What really irks these writers is that the transitive use of *boggle* in this sense is quite recent. Our evidence for it began to appear in the mid-1950s, and in our early examples it is not the mind but the imagination that is boggled:

Efforts to capture the atmosphere of a European musical center come off on the whole far better than might be expected, but not without several moments that boggle the imagination —Arthur Knight, *Saturday Rev.,* 20 Mar. 1954

The amount of litigation that would be set off ... boggles the imagination —*The Reporter,* 6 Apr. 1967

It was also used with a personal direct object:

Lack of a clear-cut mission is only one of several problems which can boggle even the brightest, best-paid, and most dedicated commissioner —Sanford Brown & Robert Vermillion, *Newsweek,* 2 Jan. 1961

What boggled her, though, was why her uptight husband ... was suddenly a sex symbol —Cyra McFadden, *The Serial,* 1977

Our files do not hold any evidence for "boggle the mind" before 1970, although it was undoubtedly in use earlier:

... even good small claims courts tend to impose procedural requirements that boggle the mind of most laymen —Philip C. Schrag, *Columbia Forum,* Summer 1970

The impressions of the vast land that is Russia boggle the mind —Richard Dunlop, *Chicago,* September/October 1972

It is the forum in which all this ends up which boggles the mind —Douglas Kiker, *The Washingtonian,* October 1973

There is another transitive sense of boggle: "to mess up, botch":

... a ne'er-do-well New Yorker who held minor government posts and had a talent for boggling nearly every job he put his hand to —H. Allen Smith, *People Named Smith,* 1950

The master of ceremonies ... seemed to boggle everything that seemingly could be boggled —Rust Hills, *Esquire,* September 1974

The intransitive uses have not been pushed aside by the transitive. The intransitive equivalent of "boggle the mind" is not only older but more frequent:

> ... so much for a movie sale, so much for a major book club selection, and so on until even the statistical mind boggles —Robert Stein, *New York,* 30 Aug. 1971

> When Bette abruptly dropped out for more than a year, show business minds boggled —Patricia Burstein, *People,* 30 June 1975

> ... has more dresses and skirts than your average boutique. On the other side of the hallway is another walk-in closet that—well, the mind boggles —Lisa See, *TV Guide,* 30 Dec. 1984

And the old standard *boggle at* construction is still in use:

> ... not inclined to boggle at the way much of it was achieved —Wallace Stegner, *Saturday Rev.,* 14 Jan. 1967

> ... who dishonestly pretends to be an old Etonian but honestly boggles at the peculations he finds his sister involved in —John Simon, *Esquire,* February 1974

> ... who, however, might boggle at the chef's inclusion of butter —Jay Jacobs, *Gourmet,* June 1982

In summary, you can either have your mind boggle at something or have something boggle your mind—both are standard and frequent in American English. Our evidence shows that the intransitive predominates in British English, but the adjectival compound *mind-boggling,* which implies a transitive verb, is used in British English as well as American:

> ... sets the seal to her mind-boggling trajectory — Clive James, *Observer Mag.,* 4 Nov. 1973

bona fides Funny things have been known to happen to Latin words once they become incorporated into the English language. We have Latin plurals that look like singulars and so have become singular in English (see LATIN PLURALS for several examples), and here we have a singular that looks like a plural and seems to be in the process of becoming one.

Bona fides came out of law Latin in the 19th century. There is not much 19th-century evidence about it; presumably the term stayed close enough to the law to avoid adventuresome treatment. But it began to widen its use in the 20th century. Fowler 1926 seems to have been the first to spot an irregularity. He mentions an instance in which someone had pruned off the final -*s* to make a noun *bona fide.* The next irregularity was spotted by Partridge 1942—a use of *bona fides* with a plural verb:

> As though Kingdom's *bona fides* were not accepted —R. Philmore, *No Mourning in the Family,* 1937

The OED Supplement has a similar example from someone who submitted it to the scholarly journal *Notes and Queries* in 1944:

> If Mina's *bona fides* are once questioned. . . .

These examples are too brief to give us a very certain idea of what the writer had in mind. But in 1954 a Merriam–Webster editor wondered if a new sense of the word was developing. He said he thought he had met it in contexts where it meant something like "evidences or proofs of genuineness or trustworthiness"—a sense roughly equivalent to *credentials.* Such a sense was, in fact, beginning to be used:

> If bona fides to the union were necessary—and they probably were—the employer offered them in most substantial form —Clark Kerr & Lloyd Fisher, *Atlantic,* September 1949

In this example *bona fides* clearly means "evidences of good faith." But the intuition of one editor and a single confirming citation were not enough to establish the currency of the meaning, and it was omitted from Webster's Third.

In the meantime several commentators followed in Partridge's footsteps and declared that *bona fides* was not a plural. None of them seems to have suspected a new sense developing, not even Reader's Digest 1983, which produces this example as an error:

> [Question by CIA:] "How were Oswald's *bona fides* established?"

The source of the question—the CIA—is very interesting, for a correspondent of William Safire, reprinted in Safire 1982, comments on the terminology used in the intelligence and counterintelligence business and notes among other things that there are people who volunteer information to intelligence services "whose 'bona fides' must be ascertained in order to establish their credibility." Is this, then, an established usage in the cloak-and-dagger business? Evidently so:

> My bona fides in this extraordinary case are known to the Turks, to the British and to security officers of JAMMAT (Joint Allied Military Mission to Aid Turkey) —Ray Brock, letter to editor of *Time,* 31 Mar. 1952

> He [John A. McCone] added that "the bona fides of the man," which "were not known at the time of the testimony," had subsequently been established by the Central Intelligence Agency —quoted in *N.Y. Times,* 10 Oct. 1975

> When the war ended German intelligence archives were captured . . . and Fritz Kolbe's bona fides were unambiguously established —Edward Jay Epstein, *N.Y. Times Book Rev.,* 16 Jan. 1983

It would thus seem that the plural use is an established one in the intelligence world. But it is not limited to that milieu:

> Once, Max was told, a Braxton Bragg had presented as his *bona fides* the photoinset ID wallet of an F.B.I. agent —Allen Lang, *Ellery Queen's Mystery Mag.,* January 1962

> Yes, he said, the supply truck would be able to take me as soon as he had my *bona fides* —Emily Hahn, *New Yorker,* 15 Apr. 1967

> Spending on strategic forces is a kind of bona fides for Schlesinger of American intentions to keep up world responsibilities —Leslie H. Gelb, *N.Y. Times Mag.,* 4 Aug. 1974

He makes something of a try at the authentic, but he keeps letting his literary bona fides leak in —Stanley Kauffmann, *Before My Eyes,* 1980

And, you will have noted, this meaning is not always plural. Between the original sense and the one just discussed there is a transitional use which persists:

That should be sufficient to establish his bona fides as a Southerner —Emile Capouya, *Saturday Rev.,* 25 July 1964

... there was no question about his bona fides as a college student; he was president of the Student Council —Robert Rice, *New Yorker,* 5 Mar. 1955

... I was anxious to establish his *bona fides* as a serious practitioner of the arts —Lawrence Durrell, *Horizon,* July 1949

In these examples *bona fides* means not "good faith" but "the fact of being what one claims to be." It is not a long stretch from "the fact of being" to "proof of the fact of being."

In conclusion, we can say that *bona fides* is a word in transition. It is too late to drag in Latin to prove that the English word is supposed to be singular; it is an established plural in the intelligence-gathering community, and is treated as a plural or as if it were a plural by others. Actual usage is more complex than the simple examples in the handbooks would suggest. There seems to have been a sense development from "good faith" to "the fact of being genuine" to "evidence(s) or proof(s) of being genuine." The last sense is often but not invariably used with a plural verb. The first two are seldom used with plural verbs. It is not unreasonable to object to use of a plural verb with the first two meanings. But even that use may someday become established. We must remember that *bona fides* is also English now, not just Latin.

Incidentally, we have not yet collected an example like Fowler's of a singular *bona fide* meaning "an item of proof."

boost For some mysterious reason American commentators tend to be uncomfortable in the presence of full-blown Americanisms. *Boost,* both noun and verb, is such a one. Vizetelly 1906 thought it a vulgarism and Copperud 1964 and Bernstein 1965 dislike the noun in the sense of "increase, raise, rise." Copperud 1970 admits that dictionaries find these senses standard.

The noun is popular in business reporting:

A boost in the banking industry's prime rate —Edward P. Foldessy, *Wall Street Jour.,* 18 Jan. 1982

... sold fairly well initially, but then two boosts made sales skyrocket —Miriam Berkley, *Publishers Weekly,* 28 Sept. 1984

It also has technical uses:

In order to use a gravity boost at Saturn to propel Voyager 2 on toward ... Uranus —*Science,* 29 Jan. 1982

When the boost is in, however, the Toyota twin-cam is anything but stock —Jean Lindamood, *Car and Driver,* August 1983

No one since Vizetelly has grumbled at the verb. The OED Supplement notes that it is now used even in British English:

The injections contain this hormone to boost your natural supplies —Dr. Jane Vosper, *Woman's Realm,* 26 Oct. 1974

border When *border* is used to mean "to approach the nature of a specific thing" and is followed by a preposition, *on* is usually the choice:

... even talking to one's friends in these days you came to racial issues that bordered on a party line —John P. Marquand, *So Little Time,* 1943

... a passionate dedication that borders on fanaticism —Michael Novak, *Center Mag.,* September 1969

... a waste of intellect bordering on the absurd —Joseph Conrad, *Chance,* 1913

... she did nothing but walk up and down ... in a state bordering on stupefaction —Thomas Hardy, *The Return of the Native,* 1878

When the literal sense of *border* is used in the passive, the preposition most often used is *by; with* is less frequent:

... rice paddies bordered by earthen dikes —E. J. Kahn, Jr., *New Yorker,* 12 May 1951

... the river bordered with wild flags and mottled plane trees —Louis Bromfield, *The Man Who Had Everything,* 1935

born, borne When George Farquhar wrote in 1707

But I must tell you, Sir, that this is not to be born —*The Beaux Stratagem*

the conventions of English spelling were not as firmly established as they are today. Today we have a dozen or more handbooks and commentators to tell us that *bear* has two past participles, *born* and *borne*. As a verb *born* is used only in the passive of the literal or figurative act of birth; it is also used as an adjective:

I was born in his second-floor bedroom —Russell Baker, *Growing Up,* 1982

Some are born whole; others must seek this blessed state —Bernard Malamud, *N.Y. Times Book Rev.,* 28 Aug. 1983

Transplanted Southwesterners, born losers, they live arid lives —Stanley Ellin, *N.Y. Times Book Rev.,* 31 July 1983

The active past participle for giving birth is *borne:*

... a younger woman who had borne an illegitimate child —Russell Baker, *Growing Up,* 1982

Borne is used for all other senses:

Critics ... charge that the Americans were borne to Paris on ideological wings —Walter Goodman, *N.Y. Times Book Rev.,* 17 Apr. 1983

... luxury almost too rich to be borne —Russell Baker, *Growing Up,* 1982

A modest revelation indeed, and not one fully borne out by the text —Noel Perrin, *N.Y. Times Book Rev.,* 6 Sept. 1981

The principal problem, and one which should be borne in mind by facility planners —E. M. Hargreaves, *Area Development,* August 1970

Our collection of errors shows that *born* is used in place of *borne* about twice as often as *borne* for *born.* The errors are both British and American.

borrow 1. The usual preposition linking *borrow* to the person or source is *from:*

... consents to borrow money from a usurer — Moody E. Prior, *American Scholar,* Autumn 1981

... borrowed a scene from another play —*Current Biography,* September 1965

... items of erudition borrowed directly from ancient sources —Robert A. Hall, Jr., *A Short History of Italian Literature,* 1951

"I like him because I have not read the books from which he has borrowed his opinions...." —George Bernard Shaw, *Cashel Byron's Profession,* 1886

Of is used, but seems old-fashioned:

... my desire to borrow them of their parents — Henry Miller, *The Air-Conditioned Nightmare,* 1945

... what? not one single book? Oh, but ... you can borrow of the parson —Jonathan Swift, *Journal to Stella,* 15 July 1711

On may also be used:

... borrowing heavily on the ideas of their European colleagues —*Dictionary of American History,* 1940

The prepositions *off* and *off of* appear to be limited to speech. Occasionally they may turn up in fiction:

... she even used to borrow books off me sometimes —Margaret Drabble, *The Needle's Eye,* 1972

Of is also used sometimes to link *borrow* with the object borrowed:

A few decades ago, songwriters borrowed freely of these words —*Phoenix Flame,* 1954

Mr. Jim had a lantern to peer out the ruts of the road.... Effie Turpin walked behind him to borrow of his light —Elizabeth Madox Roberts, *The Time of Man,* 1926

A preposition may likewise be used with *borrow* to indicate the collateral put up for a loan. *On* seems to have been used first and is still current:

" ... One time I borrowed on my saddle from the fella that was promotin' the show...." —Richard Wormser, *The Lonesome Quarter,* 1951

... lived on what he could borrow on his expectations —John Fulton, quoted in *Sports Illustrated,* 29 July 1968

The present favorite in financial circles is *against:*

... policyholders who can borrow against the cash value of their life insurance policies —*Changing Times,* May 1981

2. The use of *borrow* to mean "lend" is dialectal. The Dictionary of American Regional English finds it most prevalent in the Northern area west of the Great Lakes.

bosom Copperud is especially interested in this word, treating it briefly in 1970 but in extenso in 1964 and 1980. From his entries in 1970 and 1980—*bosom(s)*—it is not certain whether he is pinning the labels *euphemism* and *nice-Nellyism* on the singular *bosom* or the plural *bosoms* when it refers to a woman's breasts, or both. But what seems to have drawn his attention is this example:

... reaching a memorable peak of something or other at the end of the first act, when he causes his heroine to tear the false bosoms from a rival's dress and fling them triumphantly across the stage —Wolcott Gibbs, *New Yorker,* 3 Nov. 1956

Whether Gibbs considered *falsies* too slangy for his review we'll never know, but prudishness does not seem to be the intent here.

The use of *bosom,* usually but not always in the plural, may have started as a euphemism. It sounds Victorian, but we have no evidence of its use before 1924 and no very frequent evidence until the 1950s. It is apparently of American origin.

... without concealing her withered naked bosoms —Raymond Paton, *The Autobiography of a Blackguard,* 1924

After slipping a quilted housecoat over her broad, erect shoulders, pinning it across her ample bosoms —Viola Goode Liddell, *Georgia Rev.,* Fall 1950

... the 1917 "Bathers by a River," in which the women's bosoms seem to have been drawn with a compass —Janet Flanner, *New Yorker,* 22 Dec. 1951

... leaped like a damp naiad from behind the shower curtain, into my arms. Her dewy bosoms, none too firm, crushed into my shirt front —John Barth, *The Floating Opera,* 1956

... the future Congresswoman with bosoms which spoke of butter, milk, carnal abundance —Norman Mailer, *Harper's,* March 1971

... likes to perform clad only in shorts with electrical tape and shaving cream on her bosoms —*People,* 9 Feb. 1981

Our only British evidence comes from an interview with a British actress of considerable residence in the U.S.:

And I thought, 'Oh my God, my bosoms are being seen....' —Jacqueline Bisset, quoted in *Cosmopolitan* (London), October 1974

This no longer appears to be a real euphemism anyway. It sometimes seems to be chosen because it sounds faintly prudish and is seemingly intended to have a lightening effect. It does not seem to be used in prose that is intended to be either stately or erotic.

both *Both* is used in a number of idiomatic constructions that have come under attack by usage experts from the 18th century to the 20th. Most of these criticisms occur between 1870 and the 1920s, but a surprising number of them have been repeated right into the 1980s. Here is a representative selection.
1. Redundant (or, in the old days, pleonastic) uses: the censure of uses of *both*—primarily in mild emphasis— that are held to be pleonastic is a favorite game of usage writers going back to Baker 1770, who finds that this line

from an unidentified work of Swift's "seems to make Nonsense":

> They both met upon a Trial of Skill.

In 1889 William B. Hodgson finds fault with this as pleonastic:

> You and I both agree —Matthew Arnold, *Literature and Dogma,* 1873

He then proceeds to correct some other examples. He takes from a Mary Ann Kelty this sentence:

> "I'm sure I would if I could," agreed both of the literary ladies.

To correct the pleonasm of *both,* he revises to "the two literary ladies." What makes *two* acceptable and *both* wrong is not explained.

The majority of Hodgson's examples combine *both* with *agree.* This combination echoes down the ages. Here we have Copperud 1980: "Since *both* indicates duality, it is redundant with such words as *equal, alike, agree, together:* ... 'Both agreed.' *They agreed.*" But who has limited *agree* to an implication of duality that makes *both* redundant? Not users of English, certainly.

Copperud mentions the combinations *both alike* and *both together.* These are great favorites; they have been given particular notice by Bernstein 1962, 1977, Freeman 1983, MacCracken & Sandison 1917, Ayres 1881, Vizetelly 1906, Lurie 1927, Jensen 1935, Partridge 1942, Heritage 1982, Richard Grant White 1870, and others. Why this is such an important issue is uncertain. We know that a writer named Shakespeare used these combinations:

> That very hour, and in the selfsame inn,
> A meaner woman was delivered
> Of such a burthen, male twins, both alike
> —*The Comedy of Errors,* 1593

A look into a Shakespeare concordance will show that he used *both alike* six times in the plays and *both together* three times. William Blake used *both alike.* Probably other poets did too, though it is hard to prove; concordances tend to suppress *both.* But Hodgson had no examples in his prose collection, and they are rare in our files. We have no citations at all for the constructions the usage books tell you to avoid. Are they then trying to correct some oral use? If so, why?

In the end, after two centuries and more of comment, this molehill is still a molehill. It is a trivial matter and not worth worrying about.

2. *Both ... as well as.* Copperud 1970, 1980 tells us that "*Both* is also redundant with *as well as,*" whatever that may mean. He then compounds the confusion by recommending that *as well as* be changed to *and.* How does that cure redundancy? Bernstein 1977 and Johnson 1982 say the same thing. Chambers 1985 and Partridge 1942 say that *as well as* is incorrect after *both;* of course they can't and don't tell us why. *As well as* is used as a correlative in a manner somewhat like *and* (see AS WELL AS), but how that fact is relevant to either of the foregoing comments is obscure at best. In our files the use of *both ... as well as* is uncommon, but it does occur:

> ... for fear such an impression might produce ill will both in the United States as well as in Formosa and Seoul —*N.Y. Times,* 9 Aug. 1955

> At later stages in my life, I had opportunity to eat both the presumably very best food in the world, as

well as the very worst —Herbert Hoover, *Memoirs,* 1951

The worst that can be said of these is that they are not very elegant. Since the construction is fairly rare, it doesn't seem worth fussing about.

3. *Both ... and.* Bernstein 1977, Phythian 1979, Bryson 1984, and Chambers 1985 all stress the necessity of placing the same construction after *both* and after *and* for the most pleasingly well-balanced results. This seems sensible enough. Bernstein pulls an example from the *N.Y. Times:*

> The Senator said that both from the viewpoint of economics and morality the nation must practice self-denial.

He points out that *From the viewpoint of economics* follows *both* but only *morality* follows *and.* He shows two ways to correct the problem and adds "Logical tidiness is always an asset in the use of language." The point to note here is that the quotation begins with "The Senator said." Presumably the reporter is transcribing very nearly what was said. What is said is spoken English, not written English, a distinction that in this case Bernstein does not take into account.

Dean Alford in 1866 had heard all of this before; he traces it back to Lindley Murray's *English Grammar* of 1795 (there's not much new in the usage game). Alford believes that a statement of the same form as the Senator's is "plain colloquial English"; he finds a revised and entirely parallel construction "harsh and cramped." He quotes a snippet from Shakespeare's *The Tempest:*

> Having both the key
> Of officer and office, set all hearts i' th' state
> To what tune pleased his ear.

The sensible conclusion would seem to be this: when transcribing speech, even indirectly, leave the rhythms and constructions of speech undisturbed. In writing discursive prose, you might do well to seek out parallel constructions.

4. *Both of.* Evans 1962 writes: "Many correspondents have timidly asked if it is permissible to say *both of them* and many more have roundly asserted that it is not permissible. ..." This issue seems to have been current before the turn of the century; Hall 1917 notes that a rhetorician named Quackenbos objected to it in an 1896 textbook. Utter 1916 found it acceptable: "No one, not even the most careful speaker, need avoid this phrase." But we have later books denouncing it as well as Dean Alford's muddled 1866 defense. The objection appears to have been centered in obscure and specious reasoning, to judge from Hall's epitome of Quackenbos, and the exact reasons were early discarded in favor of simple imperatives:

> Say, "I saw *them both,*" not "I saw *both of them.*" — Frederic J. Haskin, *The Word Book,* no date (before 1934)

Both of is just like *all of* (which see). The *of* after *both* can be omitted before a plural noun (although it need not be), but it must be kept before a pronoun in the objective case. Evans points out that the construction is as old as Shakespeare; it occurs 11 times in his plays, and in works of Christopher Marlowe and George Herbert as well. Evans also instances the King James Bible. This appears to have been a perfectly standard idiomatic construction all along that was fixed on by someone during the 19th century as a solecism. It is entirely blameless.

> *That* was a new experience for both of us —Lewis Carroll, letter, 26 Jan. 1883

> Therefore she was equally concerned about both of them —James Stephens, *The Crock of Gold,* 1912

> It is only false if both of its terms are false —Robert W. Marks, *The New Mathematics Dictionary and Handbook,* 1964

> . . . both of whom insisted —David A. Stockman, *Newsweek,* 28 Apr. 1986

> . . . both of whom now dance the ballet more often —Arlene Croce, *New Yorker,* 4 Aug. 1986

5. *The both.* Correspondents more recent than Evans's have written to ask about the propriety of such expressions as *the both of you* which, they aver, are in constant use on television. *The both* has been occasionally sniped at in a few of the more obscure handbooks, such as *Morrow's Word Finder* (1927) and Whitford & Foster's *American Standards of Writing* (1937), but most commentators and handbooks do not notice it. Theodore Bernstein found an example for treatment in a 1969 *Winners & Sinners:*

> Mr. Epstein has two choice offerings to himself, 'Mack the Knife' and 'September Song,' lovely the both of them, in the writing and the doing —*N.Y. Times,* 17 June 1969

As this seems a little more elegant than the usual review, Bernstein found fault with it, calling *the both* "catachrestic"—an unusual and none too clear application of that sesquipedalianism, which is ordinarily applied to a word wrong for its context or to a forced figure of speech.

Perrin & Ebbitt 1972, on the other hand, note that *the both* is a fairly common spoken idiom, usually avoided in writing. This observation may be reasonably accurate: we have no great deal of evidence for it in print.

> He found it impossible to earn a living, and Alice's private income could not support the both of them —Andrew Raeburn, *Boston Symphony Orchestra Program,* 21 Oct. 1972

E. L. Doctorow puts it into the mouth of Emma Goldman in one of his novels:

> You would sit across the dinner table from each other in bondage, in terrible bondage to what you thought was love. The both of you —*Ragtime,* 1975

All of our other evidence is from speech. The expression appears to be an Americanism, at least as far as we can tell from the evidence we now have. There is no reason you should avoid it if it is your normal idiom.
6. *Possessive.* A couple of dictionaries, Longman 1984 and Heritage 1982, mention the formation of the possessive with *both.* Evans 1957 notes that the *'s* genitive can be used but that the *of* genitive is more common: "the fault of both of us" being more common than either "both our faults" or "both's faults."
7. *Both* of more than two. Chaucer in *The Knight's Tale* has these lines:

> O chaste goddesse of the wodes grene,
> To whom bothe hevene and erthe and see is sene.

The lines were reprinted in more modern spelling in one of the editions of Richard Grant White's *Words and Their Uses* (apparently not the 1870 edition), and they appear to have upset him, because he says "it is impossible that the same word can mean two and three." Fitzedward Hall in *Modern English* (1873) solved the problem. White, he said, had befuddled himself by confounding the conjunction *both* with the pronoun *both.* Hall goes on to point out that the pronoun is not used of three, but the conjunction, which is used in much the same way as *either, neither,* and *whether* are, can be used of two or more. The OED shows examples from Chaucer's in 1386 to 1839. Vizetelly 1906 comments that the usage has been challenged but has abundant literary authority and antedates Chaucer. Here are three examples; all are in the OED, a couple in briefer form:

> . . . they answered that they would take better advice and so return again, both prelates, bishops, abbots, barons and knights —Lord Berners, translation of Froissart's *Chronicles,* 1523

> My dwelling is but melancholy. Both Williams and Desmoulins and myself, are very sickly —Samuel Johnson, letter, 2 Mar. 1782

> He prayeth well, who loveth well
> Both man and bird and beast
> —Samuel Taylor Coleridge, "The Rime of the Ancient Mariner," 1798

Our recent evidence for this construction is sparse. You might have thought Hall and Vizetelly had laid this question to rest, but no, Partridge 1942 complains about this line:

> . . . whilst still permitting her to give full run to minor eccentricities, both in speech, deed and dress —R. B. Cunninghame Graham, "Aunt Eleanor," 1914

Bernstein 1977 also insists on reference to two only. Neither Partridge nor Bernstein seems to have noticed the difference between conjunction and pronoun.

The construction has reached at least to the middle of the 20th century:

> . . . is both a musician, an archaeologist, and an anti-Fascist —Cyril Connolly, *Horizon,* March 1946

bottleneck Bottleneck is a metaphorical term still in use that seems to have reached a peak of popularity during World War II, when, as Watt 1967 observes, it became fashionable to refer to any place, person, or thing that retards progress as a bottleneck. In the flood tide of popular use it was inevitable that the word would sometimes find its way into contexts in which it looked ludicrous—if one stopped to think of the origin of the metaphor. Comment on *bottleneck* in eight or nine usage books—mostly British—can be traced to one man, Henry Strauss, Lord Conesford. He compiled a list of some of the sillier combinations, such as bottlenecks that needed to be ironed out, and sent them to *The Times,* where they were published. From *The Times* the list went into Gowers 1948, and his later editions, then into the pseudonymous Vigilans's *Chamber of Horrors* (1952), Evans 1957, Watt 1967, and so forth. Lord Conesford ran the whole list in the *Saturday Evening Post* (13 July 1957). In somewhat diluted form it seems to account for the entries in Phythian 1979, Bryson 1984, and Longman 1984. Sir Bruce Fraser dropped the list and shortened the entry for the 1973 edition of *The Complete Plain Words.*

The problem seems to have been essentially a British one all along. Our file of usages from the World War II era is fairly large and notably devoid of humorous combinations. We have only one instance of "big bottleneck," which is often pointed at:

Lack of home-finding social workers is another big bottleneck here —*PM*, 10 July 1941

The verb of choice with *bottleneck* was not *iron out* but *break:*

... to increase scarce materials and facilities, break bottlenecks, channel production to meet essential needs —Harry S. Truman, message to Congress, 6 Sept. 1945

We do have a recent *ease,* which seems not unreasonable:

... could be undertaken to ease certain civilian bottlenecks —Abraham S. Becker, *Wall Street Jour.,* 21 June 1982

With the passing of the surge of usage following the World War II era, the point of the commentary has become lost. The word is still in use and is still applied to any person, place, or thing that impedes progress. But the funny combinations are gone.

bottom line   *Bottom line* is a term of recent popularity which draws notice in Harper 1975, 1985, Bremner 1980, and Janis 1984. The first calls it slang and associates it with the Watergate hearings, the second says it is business jargon, the third says that as a term for the culmination or definitive part of anything it is much overworked.

Bottom line was in the flood tide of its popularity from the mid-1970s to the mid-1980s; it remains to be seen how long its popularity will last. Most of its uses are metaphorical. The basis for these metaphorical uses is the line at the bottom of a balance sheet where profit or loss is shown:

... estimates that only $350,000 was brought down to the bottom line. That works out to a before-tax profit margin of 14 percent —Gwen Kinkead, *Fortune,* 3 Dec. 1979

This use was easily extended to the notion of profit and profitability:

... is better known for its growth, its bottom line, and its product —Susan Brenner, *Inc. Mag.,* March 1981

Their constant concerns were the bottom line and projections of future profit-and-loss —Ray Walters, *N.Y. Times Book Rev.,* 17 July 1983

And this use in turn, was easily extended beyond business:

The bottom line at Oklahoma showed 14 conference championships in 17 years —Bruce Newman, *Sports Illustrated,* 31 July 1978

Since profitability is obviously a primary concern in business, the term was spread to other instances of primary considerations or salient points. This is a very common use:

I have a tendency to say, "Get to the point, get to the bottom line." —Barbara Walters, quoted in *TV Guide,* 30 Dec. 1972

"The bottom line is, if she was pregnant, like I heard, then it was me. ... " —Patrick Anderson, *The President's Mistress,* 1976

... what really mattered, in the final analysis, was that Carol had got clear. Getting clear was the bottom line —Cyra McFadden, *The Serial,* 1977

The bottom line is this: You write in order to change the world, knowing perfectly well that you probably can't, but also knowing that literature is indispensable to the world —James Baldwin, quoted in *N.Y. Times Book Rev.,* 23 Sept. 1979

The bottom line on whether or not to do a limited edition is the appraisal of the market —William Goldstein, *Publishers Weekly,* 9 July 1982

Sometimes the main point is a summary or conclusion:

Its bottom line is that Turkey's crisis is "the most immediate threat to US interests" —John K. Cooley, *Christian Science Monitor,* 11 Mar. 1980

The bottom line here is that in Lotusland the good guys and the bad guys get all mixed up in the scum —Mason Buck, *N.Y. Times Book Rev.,* 29 Apr. 1984

The bottom line is that software is an uncharted wilderness —Stephen T. McClellan, *Datamation,* 1 May 1984

These are the chief uses of the noun at present. It shows no particular sign of being confined to just these uses. In political contexts there is a use—perhaps growing—in which *bottom line* means something like "about as far as you can go":

But what is the territorial bottom line? How far can an Israeli government withdraw —Terence Smith, *N.Y. Times,* 13 July 1975

But the Soviets' often-stated insistence that the Polish Communists must retain a "leading role" in the country is seen as nonnegotiable. "This," said one Western analyst, "seems the bottom line." —*Christian Science Monitor,* 14 Apr. 1981

There is also a hyphenated adjective. You will find it entered in responsible dictionaries.

boughten   *Boughten* is an adjective formed from *bought* and *-en.* It apparently has some dialectal use as an actual past participle, but such usage as there may be is poorly attested, since most interest is centered in the adjective.

Evans 1962 says that *boughten* was once widely used in the U.S. but that by the middle of the 19th century it was becoming rustic. It is hard to verify this. Evidence in the Dictionary of American English and OED Supplement is not overwhelming, and it is not clear that the writers cited constitute "wide" use. The 20th-century evidence in the Dictionary of American Regional English is chiefly Northern and North Midland; the DARE map shows dots speckled right across the northern half of the country, with a few sneaking south in California. It is also hard to pinpoint the time when the term began to be considered rustic or uneducated. Critics in our files date from the 1920s—Lincoln Library 1924, Lurie 1927, Krapp 1927, and a couple of notices in the *Literary Digest* of that era—and we have a few more recent writers—Shaw 1970 and Harper 1985—who beat the same drum.

The OED shows literary use at the end of the 18th century—Coleridge 1793—and at the beginning of the 19th—Southey in 1805. The earliest attested American use is dated 1801. American use tends to differ from the British original, as we shall see. The early British uses meant "purchased," as distinguished from what should have been freely given or volunteered. This sense is not dead but turns up from time to time, even in American use:

> Better to go down dignified
> With boughten friendship at your side
>   —Robert Frost, *Complete Poems,* 1949

> ... the good will of boughten allies —Garet Garrett, *Rise of Empire,* 1952

> ... hatred of plastic posh, boughten elegance, empty sophistication —Benjamin DeMott, *Saturday Rev.,* 11 Dec. 1971

The usual American use, however, contrasts *boughten* with *homemade:*

> More boughten goods, to eat, to wear, to use —Josephine Young Case, *At Midnight on the 31st of March,* 1938

> ... the ordeal of his first boughten haircut —*Time,* 12 Sept. 1949

> ... a very passable imitation of boughten ice-cream —H. L. Mencken, *Happy Days,* 1940

> ... my red sled, and my boughten wagon —*The Autobiography of William Allen White,* 1946

> ... for this reason homemade and frozen pies often do not come up to the quality of boughten ones — Dennis E. Baron, *American Speech,* Summer 1981

This use is known in English dialect, as evidence in the English Dialect Dictionary shows, and it is also used in Canada:

> "You shouldn't drink so much of that stuff," Jess said. "It's not like boughten liquor. . . ." —Margaret Laurence, *The Stone Angel,* 1964

> The "boughten" posts he's had experience with have held up 18 to 20 years —*The Citizen* (Prince George, B.C.), 12 May 1975

brand   Copperud 1970 notes sharp criticism by Bernstein 1965 of the earlier extended sense that means "a class of goods identified by name"

> ... sixty minutes of the Army's brand of football — James Jones, *From Here to Eternity,* 1951

He also finds Evans 1957 equivocal about it and says that Webster is the only dictionary that recognizes the sense. His 1980 edition has the same information with the names omitted.

What Bernstein says is that "there is no need for this kind of extension." Evans notes that Partridge 1942 objects to the use, instancing a 1937 book about Margaret of Navarre, apparently written by an American. Evans assumes that this use of *brand* is of American origin.

We cannot even be sure that this is originally American, much as it sounds American. The earliest citation in our files is British:

> ... its picture pages were the best of their kind; every brand of notable, at high fees, enlivened its pages — John Buchan, *Castle Gay,* 1930

And we have other British examples:

> Sussex plays a brand of cricket which is notably her own —S. P. B. Mais, *The English Scene To-day,* 2d ed., 1949

> He would, I believe, have a sense of humour, rather different from the English brand —Cyril Cusack, *Irish Digest,* January 1953

> ... a pleasant, easy brand of irony —*Times Literary Supp.,* 22 Oct. 1971

The Webster mentioned by Copperud is Webster's Third. We take wry satisfaction in our having recognized the sense; a usage that has been around since at least 1930 and that has been disapproved in two usage books ought to have been noticed by someone. As far as we know, Longman 1984 has the first British recognition of the sense. It is far from rare in American use:

> And I think that Berlin and Rome and Tokyo ... would now gladly use all they could get of that same brand of madness —Franklin D. Roosevelt, State of the Union Message, 7 Jan. 1943, in *Franklin D. Roosevelt's Own Story*, ed. Donald Day, 1951

> ... we might also look for six brands of nominalism, to go with each of our six philosophies —Kenneth Burke, in *Twentieth Century English,* ed. William S. Knickerbocker, 1946

> Yet we do not make the mistake of believing that the answer to communist materialism is a different brand of materialism —Adlai E. Stevenson, *Speeches,* ed. Richard Harrity, 1952

> ... a more polished brand of American English — Albert H. Marckwardt, *Word Study,* May 1952

> ... the American brand of the English language — Harry R. Warfel, *Who Killed Grammar?,* 1952

> ... simply because they do not like their brand of government —Clifton Daniel, *N.Y. Times,* 22 Mar. 1953

> And it does take a special brand of courage to present a television program live —Goodman Ace, *Saturday Rev.,* 6 Mar. 1954

> ... her own peculiarly feminine brand of common sense —C. Vann Woodward, *N.Y. Herald Tribune Book Rev.,* 31 Jan. 1954

> ... the pestilential proposition that the world needs to be saved in a hurry by their own brand of righteousness —Charles J. Rolo, *Atlantic,* October 1954

We could add many additional citations of more recent vintage, but we think these should make it clear that in 1961, when Webster's Third was published, this use of *brand* was well established as standard. It still is.

breach, breech   Copperud 1970, 1980 and Bryson 1984 say that these two words are frequently confused. Our files contain no evidence of such confusion. Simon 1980 cites an instance of "breech the gap" from *Time* in which the *breech* is apparently a typo for *breach* used mistakenly for *bridge.* Bryson builds his case on this same citation, but one blooper is not evidence of a serious problem. If you have any doubts about which word to choose, a dictionary will put you straight.

break 1. Copperud 1970, 1980 says that newspaper stylists used to object to "Mrs. Jones broke her arm" unless it was meant that she broke the arm on purpose. Copperud suggests that the stylists are wrong and that the idiom is standard. We do not know what stylists objected to, but the usage itself is entirely standard.

> . . . she had broken her left foot in a fall —*Current Biography,* November 1965

2. The usual principal parts of *break* are *broke* for the past and *broken* for the past participle. The variant past participle *broke,* the OED tells us, was formed from *broken* in the 14th century and was in widespread use in the 17th and 18th centuries. By the 19th century its use was receding, but the OED notes that it was still used in poetry—by Tennyson, for instance—for metrical purposes. McKnight 1928 points out that Jane Austen in *Mansfield Park* (1814) put *broke* in the mouths of her upper-class Bertrams and their friends like Miss Crawford:

> If your Miss Bertrams do not like to have their hearts broke. . . .

But the middle-class Mrs. Norris uses *broken:*

> . . . a poor, helpless, forlorn widow, unfit for anything, my spirits quite broken down. . . .

This presumably illustrates the fact that older forms, forms going out of fashion in the use of the middle classes, often persist longer in the upper and lower classes. Jane Austen herself used *broke:*

> . . . the Maypole bearing the weathercock was broke in two —letter, 8 Nov. 1800

The Dictionary of American Regional English reports that the past participle *broke* is found chiefly in the speech of less educated Americans. It may also be found in the informal use of others:

> . . . turnip green potliquor with cornbread broke up in it —Flannery O'Connor, letter, fall 1952

It is also the current past participle among those who train horses:

> If you do a good job of driving a colt, you can have him broke well enough so that. . . . —Oscar Crigler, quoted in *Western Horseman,* May 1980

> . . . where he had been broke as a yearling —Mary Fleming, *Western Horseman,* October 1981

> Both colts were broke to drive singly —*Morgan Horse,* April 1983

This usage has been standard in the horse-training business for many years (citations in the Dictionary of American English go back to 1833). A correspondent in 1937 made this point: "A *broken* horse, they say, is infirm, weak, aged; a *broke* horse, tamed and disciplined." In view of this distinction, it is easy to understand the preference for *broke.*

breakdown The fuss over the use of *breakdown* in the sense of "division into categories" or "something analyzed by categories" was started, says Copperud 1970, 1980, by the same Lord Conesford who gave us the question at *bottleneck.* If Lord Conesford started it, it was picked up by Sir Ernest Gowers in his 1954 *Complete Plain Words,* where it still can be found in the 1973

edition. It has also found its way into a few American books, including Watt 1967, Bernstein 1965, and Shaw 1975.

The gist of the problem seems to be first, that *breakdown* is too frequently used in this sense—it had a brief run as a hot political term in the early 1950s—and second, that it can result in ludicrous combinations when applied to nouns that stand for things which can be physically broken down.

Our evidence shows that while *breakdown* was fashionable and even faddish for a while, that period has passed. Further, the possibility of ludicrous combinations is low. You need not fret at all about the word.

> . . . ratings services issue the individual breakdowns for 203 cities —Les Brown, *N.Y. Times,* 1 Dec. 1979

> So it is not surprising that Professor Emery should be more interested in Thomas's language than his thought; and the most valuable part of the introduction is a breakdown of the words Thomas used most often —*Times Literary Supp.,* 30 July 1971

> It includes a breakdown of who sang what on every Drifters' single —Jon Landau, *Rolling Stone,* 20 Jan. 1972

> In a breakdown of these statistics, M. Henry disclosed that in an average year about seventy-five percent of the accidents occur in good weather —Jeremy Bernstein, *New Yorker,* 30 Oct. 1971

breakthrough The chief criticism of *breakthrough* as overused dates back to the mid-1960s; the other criticism that it is sometimes indifferently printed as hyphened or open is too trivial to worry about. Many compound words are so treated.

Breakthrough denotes an advance through a barrier. The advance need not be a deeply significant or a startling one:

> . . . accomplished her breakthrough into musical comedy —*Current Biography,* December 1967

> . . . a technological breakthrough in rainwear —*Orvis catalog,* 1980

> One of the illustrations for this book actually shows a *girl* holding a snake. Another breakthrough! —Barbara Brenner, *N.Y. Times Book Rev.,* 4 May 1975

To stress importance, adjectives are often added:

> This is a major breakthrough —Robert Lewis Shayon, *Saturday Rev.,* 4 Mar. 1972

> The big breakthrough came in 1960 —Norman Cousins, *Saturday Rev.,* 13 Nov. 1976

> . . . one of the most significant trade breakthroughs of the century —*St. Louis Post-Dispatch,* 27 Dec. 1971

> . . . where you can be wiped out by a dramatic breakthrough overnight —George W. Blackwood, quoted in *Annual Report, W. R. Grace & Co.,* 1970

break up The most recent sense of *break up*—"to laugh or cause to laugh uncontrollably"—is reported by Copperud 1970 as stigmatized as *slang.* The expression seems originally to have been show-business lingo and to have gradually worked its way into more general circulation. The meaning was not in general use early enough to have been included in Webster's Third. We do have some citations taken from interviews with entertainers, but none of our evidence seems particularly slangy.

> It broke me up. I laughed so hard that I was punished ... for disrupting the class —Art Garfunkel, quoted in *N.Y. Times Mag.*, 13 Oct. 1968

> Between pants, he giggles a little, then a lot. Then he breaks up completely, laughing himself into a coughing fit —Gene Williams, *New Yorker*, 30 Oct. 1965

> ... on this particular night one of the chickens nosedived into the pit, landed on the timpani, then raced around among the orchestra. The musicians broke up, they couldn't play for giggling —Robert Daley, *Cosmopolitan*, July 1972

> He can write piercingly acute descriptive passages and comic scenes that break you up —L. E. Sissman, *New Yorker*, 11 Sept. 1971

breech   See BREACH, BREECH.

bridegroom   See GROOM.

bright   Safire 1986 says that *bright*, applied to an adult, "as used today" is a term of mild derogation or very faint praise. He finds it unfailingly complimentary when applied to children, but warns that it may not be so understood when applied to an adult. This nuance, he notes, is unrecorded in dictionaries.

Safire reprints three letters he received in response to his original column: one, a New Yorker, disagrees; another New Yorker agrees but says the quasi-pejorative *bright* is usually applied to women by men; the third, from Illinois, has not heard of the quasi-pejorative use.

Dictionaries don't recognize the use for want of citational evidence. Safire's discussion and his one confirming correspondent suggest that the usage is probably an oral one and perhaps geographically or socially limited. If it spreads into general use, new dictionaries will let you know.

bring   1. *Bring, take.* Although one would imagine that most native speakers of English have mastered the directional complexities of *bring* and *take* by the time they are old enough to read, a surprisingly large number of usage commentators have felt it incumbent upon themselves to explain this subtlety to adults. The basic point they make is this: *bring* implies movement toward the speaker, and *take* implies movement away. It is a point well made, and it holds for all cases to which it applies. It does not, alas, apply to all cases of actual use of these verbs, and hence the commentators' despair: Harper 1975, 1985 says, "The distinction between *bring* and *take* is one that today is honored in the breach almost as often as in the observance." The problem, however, is not one of usage; it is one of oversimplification on the part of the prescribers.

Longman 1984 makes an important point most commentators overlook: "Either verb can be used where the point of view is irrelevant." This irrelevance to the reader (or hearer) can be illustrated by several examples. The first is hypothetical.

Let us suppose that the editor and his wife are about to go to an outdoor concert at the park. They have folding chairs and perhaps picnic things to take. The editor's wife sees some cumulus clouds in the western sky.

"Don't forget to bring the umbrella," she tells the editor, as they prepare to leave. The use of *bring* here instead of *take* suggests that the editor's wife is already thinking of being at the concert and possibly needing the umbrella. The notion of direction exists entirely in her head; it does not refer to her immediate external surroundings. The direction implicit in *bring* (or *take*) in this instance is irrelevant to both the editor and to any third party who may overhear. The message is to make sure the umbrella is at the park in case of rain.

Shakespeare provides a similar example. In *Much Ado About Nothing* (act 3, scene 5), the constable Dogberry has gone before a magistrate with news of the capture of a couple of suspicious characters whom he would like the magistrate to examine; the magistrate is in haste to be elsewhere and tells Dogberry to examine the men himself. As the magistrate leaves, Dogberry says to his partner Verges:

> Go, good partner, go get you to Francis Seacoal; bid him bring his pen and inkhorn to the jail.

Like the editor's wife above, Dogberry is thinking ahead.

Shakespeare provides us with another example in *The Comedy of Errors*. In this exchange each of the men thinks that the other has the gold chain they are talking about:

> ANTIPHOLUS (OF EPHESUS). And with you take the chain, and bid my wife
> Disburse the sum on the receipt thereof.
> Perchance I will be there as soon as you.
> ANGELO. Then you will bring the chain to her yourself?

Again the notion of direction is irrelevant to the audience.

More recent examples are not hard to find:

> In 1934 the rise of Hitler brought to Michael Ustinov uncomfortable memories of the repression he had once experienced in Russia, and he brought his family back to Stockholm —*Current Biography*, November 1965

> Copies will be given to pupils to bring home to their parents —*N.Y. Times*, 5 Mar. 1970

> John Thompson talks about the youngster who was doing poorly in school, whose father couldn't read or write, whose mother was concerned about her son's potential. She brought him to a professional educator, a doctor.... —Bruce Lowitt & Ira Rosenfeld (AP), *Morning Union* (Springfield, Mass.), 17 Mar. 1985

The notion of direction is irrelevant to the reader in each of these cases. Yet Theodore Bernstein criticized the second in his *Winners & Sinners*, and a correspondent sent the third in to us, believing it to be an error. Neither one is an error. It is pointless to try to impose one's own point of view on something that has been written from a different point of view. And in the two newspaper examples, the reporters may well have been paraphrasing an original statement, distancing the reader even further from the point of view of the original user of *bring*. Harper 1975, 1985 considers this use of *bring* "a debasement of our language." If it is such, the process of debasement has been going on for nearly 400 years, if not longer.

There is a related use of *bring*, in which the subject

and object are both persons. It means approximately "to cause to come or go along with; to escort, accompany." It too is common in Shakespeare's plays:

> ... in the morn
> I'll bring you to your ship
> —*The Tempest,* 1612

> I will bring thee where Mistress Anne Page is —*The Merry Wives of Windsor,* 1601

> Will you go to them? I will bring you thither —*Romeo and Juliet,* 1595

The OED marks this sense *Obs. exc. dial.* It has survived in the U.S.:

> I had a sudden desire to see Sheela myself ... and when Florrie offered to bring me along with her that evening I took her up at once —Mary Deasy, *Saturday Evening Post,* 16 May 1964

U.S. survival seems to be chiefly dialectal; the Dictionary of American Regional English lists examples from several geographical areas, chiefly in relation to going or returning from a social event such as a dance. The use is not directional: someone can be brought to the dance and brought home afterward. It is perhaps permanently fixed in the country expression (slightly altered here):

> I've got to dance with the ones what brung me —Representative Philip Gramm, quoted in *People,* 24 Jan. 1983

The American dialectal survival is probably another one of those older English usages that came over to this continent with early settlers and stayed in use here after falling into general disuse in Great Britain. For another such survival, see LOAN, LEND.

Conclusion: a native speaker of English will hardly ever misuse *bring* or *take;* the problem exists in the minds of the usage commentators, who have formulated incomplete rules for the use of *bring.* The non-native speaker can easily follow the commentators' simple rules. But *bring* and *take* are used in a great many idiomatic phrases—*bring to bear, take to task, bring to mind*—in which the verbs are never interchanged. The non-native speaker will find no guidance to these in our usage writers; he or she must have recourse to a good dictionary.

2. The Dictionary of American Regional English notes a widespread occurrence of the secondary variant past and past participle *brung.* It is used, as noted above, in the fixed phrase "dance with the one what brung me." While the DARE information suggests no educational level for users of *brung,* it is widely perceived as a form used by less educated persons:

> "... guess what? I brung along me new boyfriend...." —David French, *Leaving Home,* 1972

It is used for humorous effect too:

> "Well, Mr. Ambassador," drawled South Carolina Democratic Sen. Ernest (Fritz) Hollings ... , "we brung you a half." —Albert R. Hunt, *Wall Street Jour.,* 8 Aug. 1983

bring up See RAISE, REAR.

Brit *Brit* is a relatively modern word, unattested before 1901, that is a shortening of *Briton, Britisher,* or *British.* It is used to designate a native of England, and

its use has been accelerating rapidly since the 1970s. It has several virtues that undoubtedly have helped foster its use: it is short, it can be made plural (as *British* cannot), it is not easily confused in speech (as *Briton* and *Britain* can be), and it is unmarked for gender (as *Englishman, Englishwoman* are not). Its usage is, however, a bit tricky. Reader's Digest 1983 says *Brit* is used by Australians and Americans, but is not liked by the British. Safire 1986 uses it but says it is a term not used by the British although it is not especially derogatory. It appears in the OED Supplement with no usage label.

Some British sources in our files confirm Reader's Digest's suggestion of British touchiness. The first quotation is from an article on the Australian press:

> For generations, the British have been the *Poms,*—the word not without overtones of affection. Now, they are the *Brits,* and this apparently milder appellation always carries an edge of dislike and contempt —*Times Literary Supp.,* 10 May 1974

> ... the Brits—as we are elegantly known in Dublin —John Vaizey, *The Listener,* 11 Oct. 1973

These quotations suggest that the term has been used with a certain edge of derogation in some of the English-speaking nations, and our evidence suggests that—at least in the mid-1970s—*Brit* had at least some coloration of disdain in Australia, New Zealand, Ireland, Scotland, and Canada. A couple of examples should suffice:

> ... three, including an unarmed internee, have been killed by the Brits —*Rosc Catha* (Ireland), November/December 1974

> The amount of space the "left" wing Brits devoted to the farce of a trial —letter to editor, *Glasgow News,* 19 Nov. 1974

> Isn't that typical of the crafty Brits? They don't even grow the stuff, yet they make a fortune getting it off someone else, then flogging it —*The Sun* (Melbourne), 2 May 1975

Recent American use, which is on the increase, does not, as Safire observes, seem especially derogatory:

> ... if the forces of Providence were behind all this, having whimsically decided to kick around the Mexicans and the Brits —*Wall Street Jour.,* 3 Nov. 1976

> ... has hired three Brits to write copy that will move the hearts and minds —Peter W. Bernstein et al., *Fortune,* 2 May 1983

> The events attract all the young Brits, but don't expect it to be tweedy —*Town & Country,* April 1981

> Cleese narrowly wins our Funny Brit award over Peter Cook —*People,* 11 June 1984

The Brits themselves use the term. Longman 1984 labels this use *informal:*

> No doubt young Brits, influenced by television, films, and magazines, will pick up the slang —Howard 1980

> ... has learned something about dialogue.... His Hong Kong Chinese sound like the real thing, as do his Americans—the Cousins, as the Brits call them —Anthony Burgess, *N.Y. Times Book Rev.,* 25 Sept. 1977

The inscrutable Americans, or Brits, or French, or Germans —William Davis, *Punch,* 16 Mar. 1976

The True Brit is the man who thinks God made us great and glorious —Bernard Crick, *The Observer,* 19 May 1974

The trend of American and British usage seems to suggest that *Brit* is on its way to becoming a relatively neutral, informal term used in place of the longer *Briton, Britisher,* or *Englishman.* It seems likely to continue to hold its edge of dislike and contempt in some other places, however. Its increasing rate of growth may be in part ascribable to the controversies that have clung to *Briton* and *Britisher* for the past century or more. See BRITON, BRITISHER.

Briton, Britisher   While the recently popular term *Brit* is making some inroads into the use of these two words in informal contexts, both *Briton* and *Britisher* are in reputable use for "a native of England, Great Britain, or the United Kingdom"—and they are sometimes taken to include people from the Commonwealth nations—often in contrast to *American.*
   Briton, the OED tells us, was extremely popular in the 18th century; its use seems to have receded somewhat in the late 19th and early 20th centuries but to have come back a bit since then. It is more used in the U.K. than in the U.S.:

   ... we Britons by our situation —James Harris, *Hermes,* 1751

   ... I had the inalienable right of a freeborn Briton to make a morning call —Lewis Carroll, letter, 11 May 1859

   It was deep in Alabama that a fellow Briton persuaded me to change my ways —Vincent Mulchrone, *Punch,* 2 June 1976

   A MORI poll taken in Britain in February found that, although two-thirds of Britons said they liked Americans, over half did not trust Mr. Reagan's judgment —*The Economist,* 26 Apr. 1986

   ... difference between the speech of Americans and Britons —Baron 1982

Britisher is more common in American than in British English:

   ... I had become used to being the only Britisher permanently established in the region —R. C. H. Sweeney, *Grappling With a Griffon,* 1969

   ... it is naturally favored by Britishers on holiday — *Town & Country,* January 1983

   ... no more intriguing ... than any number of other pleasant Britishers might have been —Ethan Mordden, *N.Y. Times Book Rev.,* 23 Dec. 1984

   "I am a Britisher," May cheerfully tells everyone in the accent of her native Yorkshire —Giovanna Breu, *People,* 2 July 1984

While both of these terms appear to be in current good use, both have been and perhaps still are involved in some controversy:

   ... are we Britons or Britishers? I don't like either very much —Hardcastle, *Punch,* 20 May 1975

Nobody likes to be called a *Briton,* though it saves space in journalism. ... *Britisher* is an Americanism —Longman 1984

   ... we beg him to avoid in future the odious and meaningless word "Britisher" —Anthony Powell, *Punch,* 8 July 1953

   The OED says that *Britisher* is apparently of American origin (as does the Dictionary of American English)—a point disputed by Richard Grant White. White in turn was disputed by Fitzedward Hall. Brander Matthews in *Americanisms and Briticisms* (1892) pointed out that none of the authors cited under *Britisher* in the OED were American. Nevertheless, Americans did use the term:

   ... to excuse the curiosity of a Britisher —William Dean Howells, *The Lady of the Aroostook,* 1879

White's contention, apparently supported by Matthews, seems to embody a view shared by contemporary dictionary editors; Fowler 1926 notes that many of them attach pejorative or other warning labels to the term. Fowler, however, doubted (correctly it appears) the accuracy of the labels in American dictionaries, and commented that if *Britisher* was used by Americans in reference to the English, the English had no right to object. The controversy seems to have subsided somewhat since then, except for a few flare-ups like those quoted above.
   Briton seems to have hit its low point shortly after World War I. The OED says that in the late 19th century it was used chiefly in poetical and rhetorical contexts, and Henry Bradley in The Society For Pure English's *S.P.E. Tract XIV* (1923) says that it suffered from its use in the 18th-century patriotic song "Rule Britannia." From this bottom it appears to have rebounded.
   It seems possible that the lingering memories of these old controversies may partly explain the recent popularity of the more informal and sometimes derogatory *Brit.* See BRIT.

broke   **1.** There is some disagreement over the status of the participial adjective *broke* meaning "without funds, penniless." Harper 1985 calls it "informal," Phythian 1979 "slang," Bell & Cohn 1980 and Macmillan 1982 "colloquial," Vizetelly 1906 "misused," and Bryant 1962 "standard formal English." Our evidence shows that Bryant is closest to the mark.

   Duncan's company, which had patented the name, went broke in 1965 —Ray Walters, *N.Y. Times Book Rev.,* 28 May 1978

   ... there were times when he was downright irrational, as when he claimed in unbecoming panic to be going broke —Brendan Gill, *New Yorker,* 18 Sept. 1971

   We didn't have bank examiners and federal deposit insurance until banks started to go broke —J. Irwin Miller, *Center Mag.,* September 1969

   Companies have crashed, leaving shareholders broke —Terry George, *Weekend* (London), 29 Oct. 1968

   Economically, Indonesia is broke and the quick answer to the problem is a massive injection of foreign aid —John Hughes, *New Republic,* 30 Apr. 1966

. . . bought a controlling interest in the old German mining firms, which had gone broke during the war —Emily Hahn, *New Yorker,* 29 Sept. 1956

Thus far no toll road has gone broke —*Fortune,* July 1954

Sometimes he was broke, and we would force ourselves to think of ways in which he might earn money —Stephen Spender, *Partisan Rev.,* December 1948

. . . which will build us a more lasting prosperity. I have said that we cannot attain that in a nation half boom and half broke —Franklin D. Roosevelt, radio appeal for the NRA, 24 July 1933, in *Nothing to Fear,* ed. B. D. Zevin, 1946

This use derives from the verb *break,* which was used both transitively and intransitively, beginning in the 16th and 17th centuries, in the sense "to run out or cause to run out of money, go bankrupt." At the time, both *broke* and *broken* were in use as past participles, and both were used adjectivally in this sense—*broken* as early as Shakespeare, and *broke* as early as Samuel Pepys:

. . . I had a letter from his poor father at Cambridge, who is broke, it seems, and desires me to get him . . . a place of employment —Samuel Pepys, diary, 4 Nov. 1663

Swift used the word too; he wrote of a shopkeeper recently turned army officer:

. . . I fancy he was broke, and has got a commission —Jonathan Swift, *Journal to Stella,* 25 Dec. 1710

Our evidence supports Bryant's view that the sense is standard English, at least in America. Perhaps it is time for usage writers to stop worrying about a usage some three centuries old.
2. For the use of *broke* in reference to horses, see BREAK 2.

brunch Why is *brunch* in a usage book? It comes in for mention in Evans 1957, Harper 1975, 1985, and Reader's Digest 1983. Evans and Reader's Digest note the existence of opinion disparaging the word.

. . . you might wind up for breakfast-luncheon (we're still allergic to that word *brunch*) —*Mademoiselle,* October 1948

Reader's Digest quotes a disparaging remark by Heywood Broun, and Mimi Sheraton, a writer on food, does too:

. . . of which the late Heywood Broun said, "There may be some perfectly nice people who use the word 'brunch,' but I prefer not to know about them." — *N.Y. Times,* 18 Mar. 1977

The word was once often printed in quotation marks, too, suggesting some uncertainty as to its status. Harper notes that "Sunday brunch" was commonly advertised in the 1930s; it still is today.
The word is a coinage blended from *breakfast* and *lunch,* going back only to 1896. The 1896 citation in the OED Supplement is from *Punch,* and *Punch* claimed the coinage for "Mr. Guy Beringer, in the now defunct *Hunter's Weekly*" in 1895. Apparently no actual example of Mr. Beringer's use has surfaced.

Here are a few early examples and a few of more recent vintage. You can see the change of status.

Brunch, as we suppose everybody knows, is, or better was, that halfway meal between breakfast and lunch, which indolence or impecuniosity long ago invented —*The Nation,* 23 Mar. 1921

. . . not a luncheon, you see, nor even that meal of profligates, "brunch" —*Manchester Guardian Weekly,* 31 July 1925

Brunch, as far as Miss Bankhead is concerned, is a much more satisfactory way of entertaining than the formal eight-o'clock dinner —*Cincinnati Enquirer,* 14 Aug. 1932

Brunch is an urban phenomenon, and the term covers virtually any meal eaten on Sunday between 11 a.m. and 4 p.m. It is a sort of culinary status symbol —Dave Salyers, *Chicago,* September/October 1972

. . . on weekends it's fun to entertain at breakfast or brunch —Ann Valentine, *Houston Post,* 5 Sept. 1984

At brunch (our holiday routine) my father said grace as usual —Ronald Hugh Morrieson, *Landfall 112,* December 1974

Brunch is always lovely foods—never ordinary weekly fare —Victoria Van Antwerp, *Western Massachusetts Mag.,* March/April 1984

brunet, brunette It would be nice to be able to say that these words are used in a way exactly parallel to *blond* and *blonde* (which see). Such, however, is not the case. These words are much less frequently used than *blond* and *blonde,* and our evidence shows that both spellings are almost exclusively applied to females. The only apparent difference between the spellings is that *brunet* is used somewhat more frequently as an adjective than as a noun, and *brunette* somewhat more frequently as a noun.

. . . tucked her blond locks under a series of brunet wigs —Guy D. Garcia, *Time,* 18 Mar. 1985

The voluptuous brunette in a satin robe is being chased around her boudoir —John Stark, *People,* 5 Nov. 1984

bug Various senses of *bug,* as a noun and as a verb, have been commented upon by usage writers. A selection:
1. Electronic eavesdropping. Copperud 1970 reports both the noun and verb considered standard in some dictionaries; Ebbitt 1982 says they are established in general usage. The Harper 1975, 1985 panel seems to have some doubts about using them in "a formal report to Congress." The Ebbitt evaluation fits our evidence rather well. *Bug* appears a bit more common as a verb or gerund than as a noun.

. . . who ordered the bugging of the Democratic headquarters —Brian Beedham, *The Listener,* 18 July 1974

. . . making them live in one of the official ghettos for foreigners, bugging their apartments —Phillip Knightley, *N.Y. Times Book Rev.,* 25 Jan. 1976

. . . paid spies and informers, phone tappings, bugs and seeing eyes —Harriet Bolton, *Sunday Times* (South Africa), 10 Nov. 1974

France's most juicy scandal at the moment is the affair of the bugging of *Canard Enchaîné* satirical magazine by the internal secret police —*Punch,* 8 July 1975

. . . setting each other up, taping and bugging reciprocally —Garry Wills, *Saturday Rev.,* 11 Dec. 1976

2. The use of the verb *bug* in the sense of "annoy, bother" troubles the Harper 1975, 1985 usage panel in print but not in casual speech. Our evidence shows it used in the same sort of general publications the electronic bug is found in:

Of course, academics and television have been bugging Mr. Nixon for most of his career —Telford Taylor, *N.Y. Times Book Rev.,* 31 Oct. 1982

He still bugs Andrea about her tennis —Barry McDermott, *Sports Illustrated,* 9 Apr. 1984

3. Finally we present three more *bug*s as lagniappe. Other usage books have not yet discovered these. They are all established in the same kind of general publications as the preceding uses. First the "unexpected flaw or defect":

. . . freedom from program bugs and errors —*Datamation,* December 1980

. . . "support" their systems by visiting users when bugs in the software show up —*Christian Science Monitor,* 22 Apr. 1982

Then the "unspecified sickness":

. . . getting up after a tummy bug to keep the date because children were concerned —Doreen Taylor, *Scottish Field,* July 1975

. . . who has allergies and is always fighting some kind of bug —Newgate Callendar, *N.Y. Times Book Rev.,* 27 Feb. 1983

And last, "sudden enthusiasm":

. . . got the gliding bug two months ago —*Evening Gazette* (Middlesbrough, England), 27 May 1974

But he still had the baseball bug, and in 1956 the Phillies signed him —Jim Kaplan, *Sports Illustrated,* 22 Aug. 1983

But the building bug has spread to projects that could saddle Glaswegians with two large white elephants —*Time,* 5 Mar. 1984

bugger Copperud 1970, 1980 and Evans 1957 warn against the unsavory associations of this word. Their comments appear to be dated, in view of the greater frankness in print that has characterized the past quarter century or so.
1. *Noun.* The sexual sense, which goes back to the 16th century, is used in both American and British English, though it is probably more frequent in British use. Our evidence suggests that the word was once popular in certain British intellectual circles because of its salty or vulgar edge. Such citations as we have suggest that *bugger* is currently only slightly more vulgar than the clinical *sodomist* or *sodomite.*
  The semi-vulgarity of extended uses of the noun depends upon the user's or hearer's knowledge of the

original sense. It is used of persons as a generalized term of abuse:

The technically accomplished buggers are two a penny in any period —John Fowles, *The Collector,* 1963

The sly old bugger, Mal thought —Max Braithwaite, *A Privilege and a Pleasure,* 1973

Tidmarsh said, "I knew some bugger on a terminal had been tying up more free time this year. I should have goddamn known it would be your terminal." —Micheal Z. Lewin, *Hard Line,* 1982

But more frequently—and especially in American English—it is used in a much milder sense. This milder sense is often signaled by a down-toning adjective like *poor:*

I think Harry might still be trying, poor bugger —John Lennon, quoted in *Playboy,* January 1981

My father was a bull, a tough bugger, y'know —James Caan, quoted in *Cleo,* April 1975

They've gotten a lot of praise for their well-crafted albums—and the shrewd buggers make great singles, too —Michael Musto, *US,* 26 Mar. 1984

In British English bugger is mildly pejorative when combined with *silly:*

. . . disdain for silly buggers who get trapped into marriage —Martin Amis, *The Listener,* 11 Apr. 1974

When *silly bugger* is combined with *play,* it means "to behave or act foolishly":

He's encouraging Michael Foot and Wedgie Benn to play silly buggers, as he puts it, so that when unemployment passes the 3,000,000 mark in 18 months' time they will be blamed for it —Auberon Waugh, *Private Eye,* 2 May 1975

When used in British or American English of some nonhuman subject, *bugger* is not particularly vulgar. Its pejorativeness is usually indicated by the context:

. . . never felt squeamish until she was asked to pick up a spider. She hates the little buggers —Michael Small, *People,* 12 Nov. 1984

. . . I had *plans* for this car. I was looking forward to flashing around Las Vegas in the bugger —Hunter S. Thompson, *Fear and Loathing in Las Vegas,* 1972

Competition? "It's going to be a tough bugger. . . ." —Bill Rodgers, quoted by Bob Wischnia, *Runners World,* June 1981

If you think I'm going to bowl into a wind like this bugger after the season's work I've done you can bloody think again because I shan't —Fred Trueman, quoted in John Arlott, *Fred: Portrait of a Fast Bowler,* 1971

Zapping . . . is what we in the shadowy world of VCR owners do to commercials. We push the fast-forward button right through the buggers —Ellen Goodman, quoted by William Safire, *N.Y. Times Mag.,* 12 Feb. 1984

In British English it is used to mean "damn":

> Frankly, I don't care a bugger how it works —Robert Chartham, quoted in *N.Y. Times Mag.,* 2 Dec. 1973

> As it turns out, Dan couldn't give a bugger whether I'm there or not —Glenda Jackson, quoted in *Cosmopolitan,* April 1976

And in British English *bugger-all* means "nothing":

> . . . who have houses in the south of France and in the West Indies and sit around doing bugger all — Lord Carrington, quoted in *N.Y. Times,* 22 May 1979

> . . . some people he could mention ought to watch themselves when they knew bugger-all whereof they spoke —Alan Coren, *Punch,* 6 Nov. 1974

2. *Verb.* In its sexual sense, *bugger* is more common in British than in American English. A British writer—Gavin Ewart—in Michaels & Ricks 1980 twits American pretentiousness in using *sodomize* instead of *bugger.* In British English the verb is extended into use as a generalized denunciation:

> . . . I said to my seventeen-year-old mate, 'Bugger him. We'll go off and join the army.' —a farmworker, quoted in Ronald Blythe, *Akenfield,* 1969

> 'Bugger philosophy!' Jerry said angrily —André P. Brink, *Looking on Darkness,* 1974

> 'Bugger her. She walked out on me, didn't she?' — Jean Watson, *Stand in the Rain,* 1965

> "I'm buggered if I'll apologize to that Yankee bastard. . . ." —John Rowe, *Count Your Dead,* 1968

The participial adjective—also British—means "tired out." It does not seem to be notably vulgar.

> When I reached the trenches I was pretty well buggered —Raymond Gardner, *The Australian,* 26 Apr. 1975

Bugger about and *bugger around* are also British, and not greatly offensive, apparently. In the intransitive they mean "to potter around, do things ineffectually, waste time":

> '. . . What these chaps get paid for beats me: buggering about all the time like blue-arsed flies in a bakery and never doing a stroke of honest work.' —Bruce Marshall, *Vespers in Vienna,* 1947

> ". . . What the hell do you mean by buggering about like this? . ." —Kingsley Amis, *Lucky Jim,* 1954

> . . . buggering about unnecessarily in implementing the legislation —Alan Ramsey, *Nation Rev.* (Melbourne), 29 May 1975

> . . . generally buggering around with the positions of a lot of lower ranks —C. M. Evans, *Nation Rev.* (Melbourne), 17 Apr. 1975

Bugger about is sometimes used transitively:

> ". . . you get used to being buggered about a bit by head office." —Colin Watson, *Kissing Covens,* 1972

Bugger off—likewise British—is a bit more of a problem. Some American references call it extremely vulgar, but others call it colloquial, or slang. It means "to leave" but is usually used as an imperative, equivalent to "scram, beat it":

> To people who come up and criticize me in public, I have a simple answer. . . . Bugger off —Kingsley Amis, quoted in *Publishers Weekly,* 28 Oct. 1974

> When I recovered, I said, 'Okay, bugger off then,' and I am afraid she did just that —Richard Burton, quoted in *People,* 15 Mar. 1982

> . . . when she'd finally buggered off I gave way a bit and had a good cry —Noel Coward, *Pretty Polly and Other Stories,* 1965

> "Do you want me to stay with you, Daddy, till the doctor comes?"
> "I want you to bugger off."
> —Iris Murdoch, *A Fairly Honourable Defeat,* 1970

Finally we have *bugger up* meaning "to botch, bungle" (many American equivalents will quickly come to mind):

> The Common Market has done wonders for fishing and buggered up everything else —Tim Goddard, quoted in *Punch,* 27 Mar. 1974

There seems to be, or has been, a taint of vulgarity clinging to *bugger up,* as this next example suggests. Note, however, that it was published quite a few years earlier than the example from *Punch:*

> '. . . I hope your private investigations haven't buggered up the situation prematurely.'
> The copperess looked at the varnished ceiling. 'Oh, pardon,' the Detective-sergeant said. 'It's still hard, after all these years, to remember we have ladies in the Force.' —Colin MacInnes, *Mr Love and Justice,* 1960, in *The London Novels of Colin MacInness,* 1969

All of the extended uses of *bugger,* noun and verb, are marked *coarse slang* in the OED Supplement. Longman 1984 marks most of them *slang* but not *vulgar.* Other references give varying readings; there is even a suggestion that the degree of vulgarity varies from the South to the North of England. It is difficult to judge such things from this side of the Atlantic. The examples quoted above, which are typical, seem to suggest that the terms may not be as vulgar in actual usage as the reference books say they are. The only sense—the "little bugger"—that is very common in the U.S. is not vulgar here.

bulk Bryson 1984 notes that "a few authorities"—among them Copperud 1970, Longman 1984, Phythian 1979, Janis 1984, Shaw 1975—object to the use of *the bulk of* when it means "the greater part of, the majority of" and would restrict it to contexts involving volume and mass. He discounts this criticism noting that Gowers in Fowler 1965 says the usage is more than 200 years old (the OED cites it from Addison in 1711) and that Bernstein 1965 thinks no other word conveys quite the same idea of generalized and unquantified assessment. "So use it as you will," he recommends.

Such criticism as there is tends to be somewhat diffuse: it is not clear whether the objection is to the use of *bulk* with things that are abstract and have no physical quantity, or to its use with count nouns. Our most recent evidence shows these facts:

The bulk of is used with plural count nouns that may be thought of as a mass:

> But in the bulk of Connolly's writings such thoughtful, sharp-eyed perceptions are the exception —Hilton Kramer, *N.Y. Times Book Rev.,* 19 Feb. 1984

> A word isn't given legitimate status by a vote . . . but by a subtle consensus—by its being used by the bulk of literate people —Thomas H. Middleton, *Saturday Rev.,* 8 Feb. 1975

> . . . even behind the Iron Curtain, where the bulk of the citizens dread war as much as we do —Donald R. Morris, *Houston Post,* 14 Sept. 1984

The bulk of is equally often used with mass nouns, to many of which no physical dimensions can be assigned:

> . . . units which were doing the bulk of the fighting —*Times Literary Supp.,* 22 Oct. 1971

> According to the vast bulk of evidence —Thomas H. Middleton, *Saturday Rev.,* August 1978

> . . . does the bulk of the work himself —Newgate Callendar, *N.Y. Times Book Rev.,* 24 Apr. 1983

> . . . the bulk of the precinct is wretchedly ugly —Dan Greenburg, *Playboy,* June 1980

All of these uses are perfectly standard. "So use it as you will"—to quote Bryson once more.

bunch   Whatever it is that seems to be wrong with *bunch* appears to be a singularly American problem, and one commented upon chiefly by writers of college handbooks. Our evidence shows what seems to be a sharp increase in the use of *bunch* both as a generalized collective and as a word for a group of people just after the turn of this century. Typical early examples are these:

> I'd rather be William S. Devery than a whole bunch of kings —*Hudson* (N.Y.) *Register,* 4 Nov. 1902

> . . . the trust is a bunch of beef companies put together —*Star of Hope,* 3 Oct. 1903

> The whole bunch should be at Dixmont, which would be the proper place for them to stop —*Automobile Rev.,* 1 Nov. 1903

> Somehow he did not take with the bunch and one of the crowd walked up to him —*N.Y. Sun,* 20 Dec. 1903

> Then he finishes his hogs with corn he raises himself, ships the hogs to Sioux City and has another bunch of clean cash —*The Farmer and Breeder,* 1 Apr. 1903

Uses like these—the word must have been common in speech—ruffled some writers on usage. The earliest we have found is Utter 1916, who objects to the collective use: "it is not heard on the lips of the fastidious." MacCracken & Sandison 1917 objected to the use for a group of people (they condemned *crowd* at the same time): "unaccepted colloquialisms or slang for *group* or *set.*" Most of the other early critics take the MacCracken & Sandison tack: Vizetelly in *Slips of Speech* (1922), F. K. Ball's *Constructive English* (1923), Lurie 1927, Jensen 1935. Krapp 1927 hits both usages. After World War II the emphasis of the handbooks shifts to the general collective, with the "group of people" sense taking a back seat. Repeating more or less the same strictures are

Watt 1967, Evans 1957, Shaw 1970, 1975, Bell & Cohn 1980, Little, Brown 1980, Macmillan 1982, and Janis 1984. Evans 1957 introduced a new strain, calling the use of *bunch* meaning "lot" (as in, "that's a bunch of baloney") "definitely wrong." Janis 1984 calls it nonstandard.

Let's examine some actual examples of the three disputed usages. First, the group of people:

> ". . . there isn't a private school in the state that's got as swell a bunch as we got in Gamma Digamma this year. . . ." —Sinclair Lewis, *Babbitt,* 1922

> ". . . And think of what my bunch will say if I go back home and tell 'em we went to a night club and I couldn't have a cocktail. . . ." —*American Mercury,* January 1928

The "my bunch, the bunch" use is no longer current. But the word has continued in a less personal use:

> . . . that high hat bunch which seems to be reading the Saturday Review —*Saturday Rev.,* 11 Apr. 1925

> . . . along with some of the radical students they were looked upon as a queer bunch —*American Mercury,* April 1928

> By that hour, we were usually an overheated, irritable bunch —J. D. Salinger, *Nine Stories,* 1953

> The new management trims out all the excess expenses . . . blaming the low earnings that result on the old bunch —*Forbes,* 15 May 1967

> They were a tough-looking bunch —Daphne du Maurier, *Ladies' Home Jour.,* September 1971

> . . . my colleagues are, for the most part, an eminently lovable bunch —Alan Rich, *New York,* 10 Jan. 1972

This sense appears to be established as standard, at least in what Perrin & Ebbitt 1972 call general use.

The general collective use, which dates back to the 17th century, would seem to be well established:

> A bunch of the boys were whooping it up in the Malemute saloon —Robert W. Service, "The Shooting of Dan McGrew," 1907

> They raise houses in skyscraping piles of a hundred dwellings one on top of another . . . so that in place of one horizontal street you have bunches of perpendicular ones —George Bernard Shaw, *The Intelligent Woman's Guide to Socialism and Capitalism,* 1928

> ". . . He's a group-manager. Looks after a bunch of clients. . . ." —Dorothy Sayers, *Murder Must Advertise,* 1933

> The first bunch of twenty-one characters, by Overbury and others, was added to the second impression of his poem —Douglas Bush, *English Literature in the Earlier Seventeenth Century, 1600–1660,* 1945

> . . . he did correspondence courses in philosophy at a bunch of universities —Saul Bellow, *The Adventures of Augie March,* 1953

> . . . a little bunch of us drifted away and into an open doorway —E. B. White, *New Yorker,* 7 Apr. 1956

> . . . and of course the familiar bunch of hippies from my own country —Daphne du Maurier, *Don't Look Now,* 1966

... the best-looking bunch of guarantees they had ever been offered —Mollie Panter-Downes, *New Yorker,* 26 Aug. 1972

... a whole bunch of activities that had nothing to do with the intricate business of collecting and distributing accurate secret intelligence —John le Carré, *N.Y. Times Book Rev.,* 14 Oct. 1979

Finally, the use of *bunch* with a mass noun. As Evans' illustration—"that's a bunch of baloney"—suggests, this sense is well established in speech. It goes all the way back to Dr. Johnson:

I am glad the Ministry is removed. Such a bunch of imbecility never disgraced a country —in Boswell's *Life,* 1791 (OED)

However, it does not appear in print very often. Nonetheless rarity does not make it wrong, or even nonstandard.

Did you ever hear such a bunch of nonsense in your life? —*Everybody's,* October 1914

... he would have a bunch of money —Upton Sinclair, *The Goslings,* 1924

In spite of the prickly bunch of dissent disconcertingly handed to Mr. Wilson —Mollie Panter-Downes, *New Yorker,* 11 Feb. 1967

... and listen to a bunch of sentimental drivel —Paul Kresh, *Stereo Rev.,* July 1971

On the basis of this and much similar evidence, we think that the continued objection to these uses of *bunch* is nothing more than a tradition in usage commentary dating back to before the 1920s. The hair-splitting reasoning that finds "a bunch of roses" and "a bunch of keys" formal but "a bunch of individualists" and "a bunch of numbers" and "a bunch of nonsense" informal or colloquial or slang is purely factitious. You can observe it if you wish, but there is no reason to do so beyond your own preference.

bunk into   Harper 1975, 1985 and Safire 1982 note that *bunk into* is used for *bump into* in New York City. The Dictionary of American Regional English confirms their observation, labeling it "N[ew] Y[ork] C[ity], esp[ecially] Brooklyn."

burgeon, burgeoning   It appears that no one was concerned about the figurative uses of *burgeon* until the 1960s, when Theodore Bernstein (in *Winners & Sinners* at least as early as 1964), Flesch 1964, and Follett 1966 discovered it. The recommendation of Flesch is short and to the point: "*burgeon* is a fancy word that can easily be replaced." And in fact it is a fancy word—you have to learn it, and if you learn it from an older dictionary, as Bernstein and Follett did, you learn that it means "to send forth buds or shoots"—Webster's Second defines it simply as "to bud, sprout."

There is a perfectly sound reason for this brief 1934 dictionary treatment. At the time the book was edited, there was but little evidence of figurative use. The OED lists some, from the 14th century to the 19th, but the editors of Webster's Second had no recent evidence and omitted a definition to cover figurative use (notes in the file show that the need for a figurative sense occurred to at least one editor).

As a result, Bernstein and Follett, knowing from the Second that *burgeon* meant "to bud, sprout," were shocked to discover that it was being used in a much broader way in the public prints. And a usage problem was born.

The evidence in our files suggests that the use of *burgeon* and especially the participial adjective *burgeoning* in a broader sense connoting rapid and flourishing growth began to increase in frequency in the late 1930s. Here it is, for instance, used in a book review:

With 1933 the focus takes in the Reichstag fire and burgeoning Hitlerism —*N.Y. Times,* 29 Jan. 1937

Widespread popular use began around the end of World War II. Copperud 1970 credits much of this popularization to *Time* magazine. Indeed, it did appear in the pages of *Time* with some frequency:

Sometimes new settlements, unmarked on the maps, had burgeoned into large communities in only two or three years —*Time,* 7 Aug. 1944

Quebec's burgeoning industries —*Time,* 16 Sept. 1946

... channeled the city's burgeoning population into neatly curving rows of comfortable frame houses —*Time,* 12 Dec. 1949

The use was not limited to *Time,* however:

... who learns that the little stitch in the side is cancer and that he is carrying around inside himself that mysterious, apocalyptic, burgeoning thing which is part of himself but is, at the same time, not part of himself but the enemy —Robert Penn Warren, *All the King's Men,* 1946

The American Legion and the Veterans of Foreign Wars must accept responsibility for the drum majorette. They cannot escape it. It has been at their conventions that she has burgeoned —Frank Sullivan, *A Rock in Every Snowball,* 1946

... one could go on at length listing the burgeoning varieties of periodicals —Frederick Lewis Allen, *Atlantic,* November 1947

By the 1950s the extended senses were firmly established:

... what may well be the most difficult period of the burgeoning Western alliance —Richard H. Rovere, *New Yorker,* 10 Nov. 1951

... there is in Japan a hospitality toward ... the American way of life which is sincere, clear-eyed, burgeoning with affection —Perry Miller, *Atlantic,* August 1953

Suburban towns with burgeoning populations need more police and fire protection —*N.Y. Times,* 28 Feb. 1954

... not one of those feminizing Faulknerians, who via Katherine Anne Porter and Eudora Welty have burgeoned into the fullblown epicene school —Leslie A. Fiedler, *New Republic,* 26 Sept. 1955

... the high walls of the Kremlin were burgeoning with new mysteries —Harrison E. Salisbury, *N.Y. Times Mag.,* 21 Aug. 1955

The evidence makes the point. The extended uses of *burgeon* had been appearing in the august pages of the *New York Times* for more than a quarter century before

Theodore Bernstein looked up a dated entry in Webster's Second and made an issue out of it. It is probably impossible anyway to pen in the meaning of a word once it begins to be frequently used figuratively. Uses with the connotation of rapid or flourishing growth are the predominant ones today. The budding connotation has not been lost, as the following two examples show, but it is now a less frequent use:

I weighed this. It sounded promising. Hope began to burgeon —P. G. Wodehouse, *Joy in the Morning,* 1946

... the so-called 'little renaissance" in poetry then burgeoning —Robert E. Spiller, *CEA Critic,* January 1971

"Ah," you may object, "couldn't Spiller's use mean 'flourishing'?" Yes, it could be so interpreted; you have discovered the difficulty of pinning down a figurative use to a single interpretation.

Unless you are a lover of causes that were lost before they were begun, do not trouble yourself to limit *burgeon* to "to bud, sprout." There is no essential difference between the usage of the 1970s and 1980s and that of the 1940s and 1950s with this word.

burglarize, burgle Apparently somebody about 1870 felt that a verb was needed to express the meaning "to commit burglary." We don't know why—*rob* had always served the purpose—but *burgle* (1870) and *burglarize* (1871) were coined at about the same time to supply the felt need. Perhaps some pedantic newspaper editor objected to *rob:* "rob means to commit robbery; it can't mean to commit burglary. There's a distinction between robbery and burglary, you know." (See BURGLARY, ROBBERY). We'll probably never know. But in 1870 this line appeared:

The Waverly National Bank burgled —*Philadelphia Press,* 15 Mar. 1870 (Dictionary of American English)

Our first citation for *burglarize* comes from an April 1871 magazine article quoted by M. Schele de Vere in his 1872 book of Americanisms. The citation was written about the use of the word in an English magazine; it was clearly used earlier, but no one has so far found the actual citations. Both *burgle* and *burglarize* seem to be Americanisms, but they must either have crossed the Atlantic quickly or have been independently coined in England at about the same time: we have Schele de Vere's citation for *burglarize* and an 1872 citation in the OED for *burgle.* The OED, incidentally, indicates that a verb of this specific meaning had existed in English law-Latin from the 14th century—*burgulāre,* which, had it been brought into English, might have produced something on the order of *burgulate.*

Both *burgle* and *burglarize* were quickly under a cloud. Bardeen 1883 puts both in his "indefensible" category on the basis of remarks by Schele de Vere and Richard Grant White. The 1885 volume of the OED lists *burglarize* as *U.S.* and *burgle* as *facetious*—a judgment perhaps colored by W. S. Gilbert's use in *The Pirates of Penzance* (1879):

When the enterprising burglar's not a-burgling. . . .

American commentators have generally tended to disparage *burgle,* partly, at least, because it is a back-formation. Lounsbury 1908 had his doubts about it; Lurie 1927 despised it; Krapp 1927 considered it facetious;

later commentators, such as Bernstein 1971 and Kilpatrick 1984, find it funny. British usage differs. In 1926 the magisterial H. W. Fowler looked at both words and said "it is to be hoped that *burgle* may outgrow its present facetiousness & become generally current." Fowler's wish has come true in British English—indeed such use had started earlier:

... which led him to imagine that the residence of M. Dagnan-Bouveret, the well-known artist, was to be burgled —*Auckland* (New Zealand) *Weekly News,* 1 Oct. 1903

There was a story that he had once been caught burgling a house —H. G. Wells, *Joan and Peter,* 1918

In 1617 his house was burgled by Henry Baldwin and others —E. K. Chambers, *The Elizabethan Stage,* 1923

And while Mr Ede sits and waits, how many holiday makers will find their empty houses burgled this Easter? —*The Economist,* 27 Mar. 1948

... in spite of having his cabin burgled by an enterprising gentleman —*Times Literary Supp.,* 19 Feb. 1971

The last anti-*burgle* shot in British English seems to have been fired by Partridge 1942, standing by the OED label *facetious* and opting for *rob.* And in spite of the doubts of the American commentators, *burgle* has begun to turn up in serious contexts here:

The O.S.S. did not burgle the Japanese Embassy in Portugal —Cornelius Ryan, *N.Y. Times Book Rev.,* 17 Sept. 1972

They burgle supermarkets, pharmaceutical houses and other cash repositories —John Crosby, *N.Y. Times Book Rev.,* 31 Oct. 1976

... the government will burgle us if we don't watch out —John Leonard, *Vogue,* November 1976

Burglarize, in the meantime, has won grudging acceptance in American use. There is still British resistance to it:

What I cannot abide is to read in one of our own papers that a house has been *burglarised* rather than burgled —Honor Tracy, *Encounter,* January 1975

It was criticized as journalese by Evans 1957 and as "colloquial" by Bernstein 1962 (he recanted in 1971), but most current commentators find it acceptable. The following are typical instances:

... he and his partner burglarize the Academy's clerical office —Mary Perot Nichols, *N.Y. Times Book Rev.,* 27 May 1973

A car had been burglarized —G. Christian Hill, *Wall Street Jour.,* 18 Mar. 1974

No sooner was the first batch of paintings returned ... than the museum was burglarized again —Katharine Kuh, *Saturday Rev.,* 26 July 1975

Conclusion: if you go on the assumption that a verb distinct from *rob* is needed, there has never really been anything wrong with either *burgle* or *burglarize.* The whole fuss has really depended on the fact that *burgle* is a back-formation and *burglarize* an *-ize* verb (see -IZE 2).

Both are in respectable use in the U.S.; there seems to be a preference for *burgle* in British English.

burglary, robbery The distinction between these words is spelled out in Kilpatrick 1984, Harper 1975, 1985, and Copperud 1970, 1980, and no doubt in countless law texts. If you really feel uncertainty on the point, check any conscientious dictionary, where you will find everything made clear. *Robbery* (13th century) is older and more general than *burglary* (16th century).

burgle See BURGLARIZE, BURGLE.

burn *Burn* has variants in both past and past participle—*burned* and *burnt*. Longman 1984 tells us that *burned* is commoner than *burnt* for intransitive uses and *burnt* commoner than *burned* for transitive uses. Our evidence bears out this observation for British English:

> ... the days burned into weeks and months —Samuel Selvon, *A Brighter Sun,* 1952

> Burnt my fingers defending an Old Boy —R. F. Delderfield, *To Serve Them All My Days,* 1972

> ... in danger of being burnt as witches —Phyllis Grosskurth, *Times Literary Supp.,* 6 June 1980

In American English *burned* is the more common in both intransitive and transitive uses:

> Yet he burned for retribution —Kenny Moore, *Sports Illustrated,* 29 Aug. 1983

> He also showed that carbohydrates are burned faster when consumed in the morning —Jane E. Brody, *N.Y. Times,* 11 Aug. 1981

Transitive *burned* and intransitive *burnt* are not unknown in British English, and transitive *burnt* is not rare in American English. We have no recent American examples of intransitive *burnt*.
Burnt is the usual form in British English when the participle is used as an adjective:

> ... ground magnesian limestone and its burnt equivalent —*Fream's Elements of Agriculture,* 15th ed., 1975

In American English both *burnt* and *burned* are used as adjectives:

> ... blue sky showed through the charred skeleton of the burnt church —John Updike, *Couples,* 1968

> ... a large, sun-scorched, burned section —Nathaniel Nitkin, *New-England Galaxy,* Fall 1967

> I generally get burnt almond or chocolate chip — Edward Koch, quoted in *Harper's Bazaar,* February 1981

> ... I stopped off at various burned almond booths —Lillian Langseth-Christensen, *Gourmet,* December 1980

Our most recent evidence shows a few more examples of *burnt* than *burned* in straight adjectival use; the evidence gets more complicated when compounds like *burned-out, burnt-out, burned up, burnt umber, burnt cream* are considered. You may have to consult a reference book if you are unsure of some of these compounds.

burst The usual past and past participle is *burst:*

> Tuesday about 400 persons burst into a Santa Barbara city council meeting —*Berkeley Barb,* 17 Apr. 1969

> ... and then to her shame she burst into tears — Daphne du Maurier, *Ladies' Home Jour.,* September 1971

The past and past participle *bursted* is not wrong, as some handbooks suggest, but it is old-fashioned in writing and dialectal in speech.

> ... something of the sundering energy of a bursted shell comes vividly before my senses —Rhys Carpenter, *The Esthetic Basis of Greek Art,* 1921

We have no recent evidence for *bursted* in print; the Dictionary of American Regional English records recent evidence in speech.
See also BUST.

bus A few years ago there was a minor fuss over the verb *bus*—it was rejected by a narrow margin by the Heritage 1969 usage panel. The rejection may have been as much political as linguistic, since there was considerable controversy at the time about transporting children to school by bus to achieve racial balance. The panel of Heritage 1982 recanted; the verb was all right all along, of course. Note that both *-s-* and *-ss-* are in use in spelling the inflected forms:

> ... the guests, who were bused in —*Women's Wear Daily,* 21 July 1975

> ... and visitors and hostesses alike were bussed to the day-camp site —Judy Van Vliet Cook, *Girl Scout Leader,* March 1968

> ... the painless crusade against busing —*Harper's,* January 1973

> ... necessitating bussing of approximately 50 percent of the students —Ron Hollander, *Town & Country,* October 1979

Many people prefer the double *-s* spellings because they better indicate the pronunciation. The same concern for pronunciation makes some prefer the plural *busses* over *buses* for the noun in spite of the fact some handbooks prescribe the simple *-s* form. Both spellings are, in fact, in reputable use.

> ... on double-decker buses —Ray Walters, *N.Y. Times Book Rev.,* 9 Sept. 1979

> ... people walked into the busses —Alfred Kazin, *Prose,* Spring 1973

business As an example of the silly stuff usage writers sometimes get into, we give you this stricture:

> *Business* is used colloquially for "right" or "obligation," but it has no grammatical sanction: "You have no business spending as much as you do" is better expressed as: "You have no right to spend as much as you do." —Powell 1925

The same sentiments are found in Vizetelly, *Slips of Speech,* 1922, and Jensen 1935; Krapp 1927 goes only as far as calling the construction colloquial.
This use of *business,* defined as "Right of action," can

be found in Samuel Johnson's Dictionary of 1755, with a late 17th century citation:

> What *business* has a tortoise among the clouds? —L'Estrange

The expression "no business" was current in the early 19th century:

> ... my politics being as perverse as my rhymes, I had, in fact, "no business there" —Lord Byron, letter, 6 July 1812

That usage writers from the first third of the 20th century should find something amiss about this use can be explained only by their ignorance of its history.

bust, *verb.* *Bust* is a verb that originated in an \r\-less pronunciation of *burst* apparently common in many dialect areas in the 19th century and earlier. Evans 1962 comments that the pronunciation is more old-fashioned than vulgar. *Bust,* however, in the 19th century moved from being a variant or dialectal pronunciation to become a separate verb, its separateness emphasized by the fact that its past and past participle is regularly *busted* (less often *bust*) while that of *burst* is *burst* (and rarely now *bursted*). The past and past participle *bust* appears to be more common at present in British English than it is in American.

Bust is now established as a separate verb, with many senses in which *burst* (or *break*) cannot be substituted. So the first thing you have to do is to disregard the oversimplification prevalent in school grammars (such as Warriner 1982) and college handbooks (such as Bell & Cohn 1980, McMahan & Day 1980) claiming *bust* to be wrong for *burst* or *break,* or *busted* wrong for *broke.* These books are expressing opinion that is well over a half century old and that has no relevance to current 20th-century usage—indeed, it was scarcely relevant to current usage 50 years ago.

Back in 1942 John R. Bethel, then in charge of Merriam editorial work, put a note in our files pointing out that *bust* was changing its status "under our noses" from Slang, Dial., and Inelegant (the labels of Webster's Second) to Colloq. and in some contexts Standard. The note enjoined future editors to collect as much evidence as possible so as to be up-to-date on the status of the word. This we have done—we have many citations. Examination of them would show you that most of what you read in the usage books is pure and simple malarkey. Look at the following examples and make up your own mind:

> ... this extraordinary piston-engined pusher was primarily for busting tanks with its 75 mm gun —Bill Gunston, *Attack Aircraft of the West,* 1974

> In winter they blame him when hungry elk and deer are busting their fences and devouring their haystacks —Robert C. Wurmstedt, *Time,* 5 Nov. 1984

> Even a man couldn't have bust it down —John Fowles, *The Collector,* 1963

> ... police officers searching for a gasoline bomb factory busted their way with sledgehammers into 11 houses —*N.Y. Times,* 19 July 1981

> Courts enjoined them, police busted their heads —E. L. Doctorow, *Ragtime,* 1975

> James boxes—or did, until his jaw was busted —*New Yorker,* 17 Oct. 1983

Naturally, all hell busted loose again. The GSA quickly tore down the huts —Jim Fain, *Atlanta Jour.-Constitution,* 23 Sept. 1984

> ... Grant, a convinced Union partisan, joined the 21st Illinois Regiment to replace a colonel busted for overdrinking —Alden Whitman, *Atlanta Jour.-Constitution,* 16 Sept. 1984

> ... misfields it and busts his silly old ankle again —Alan Coren, *The Times* (London), 9 Jan. 1974

> ... had thrown away career and respectability to bust her client out of prison and vanish with him into the hills of eastern Tennessee —Joyce Wadler, *People,* 23 Apr. 1984

The foregoing examples are all for senses that *bust* shares with either *break* or *burst;* they come from recent fiction, nonfiction, newspapers, and magazines. They show *bust* established as standard in what some handbooks call General English. We have no evidence that *bust* has reached the highest levels of formality—no examples from disquisitions upon ethics, linguistics, genetics, philosophy, or theology, for instance, and no examples from the prose of the bureaucrat.

You may wonder if the establishment of *bust* in this sort of publication is recent. The answer is no. Although there may be a wider spectrum of use now, the same usages can be found from a quarter century or so earlier:

> We approach the scullery window. He busts in. I raise the alarm —P. G. Wodehouse, *Joy in the Morning,* 1946

> ... unable to bust the tradition —*Newsweek,* 5 July 1948

> We have busted out in an epidemic of industrialization —James Street, *Holiday,* October 1954

> ... were busting out all over with their own ideas —*Investor's Reader,* 9 Feb. 1955

> ... but suddenly the Nazis bust loose and the captain's cowardice is revealed —John McCarten, *New Yorker,* 29 Sept. 1956

> ... feeling that an orchestra would suddenly appear and bust loose with Cole Porter —*Theatre Arts,* April 1957

In addition, there are other uses in which *bust* is the verb of choice:

> Federal labor law would have been declared, once again, superior to harsh union-busting state laws —T. R. B., *New Republic,* 17 Aug. 1953

> The best headline is no good if it busts —Leslie Sellers, *The Simple Subs Book,* 1968

> The Northern Securities trust was busted, and Morgan could do nothing but writhe —*Business Week,* 20 Apr. 1981

> ... full of all kinds of budget-busting measures —David A. Stockman, quoted in *Atlantic,* December 1981

The use of *bust* to mean "arrest, raid" is still slangy but has begun moving in more respectable circles of late. It seems to have originated in the jargon of police and those the police arrest.

Jerry and I had just busted (arrested) two guys inside for pushing heroin —a police officer named Spinosa, quoted in *Headquarters Detective,* 12 Sept. 1956

. . . first tipping off the Drug Squad with an anonymous call. They busted him just as he was setting off —Alexander Frater, *Punch,* 29 May 1974

. . . my house in Culloden Rd, Eastwood, was busted —Mark Butler, in *Coast to Coast: Australian Stories 1973*

There is simply no legal basis for busting a bailed rape suspect who had fooled a judge —Alan M. Dershowitz, *TV Guide,* 31 May 1985

Bust is also the usual verb in a large number of phrases beginning *bust my* (or *your* or *our,* etc.) _____, some of which are rather vulgar and others not. Here are examples of some of the latter variety:

Every time I hear of a critic who is hardly getting enough to eat I laugh until I bust my galluses — Theodore Dreiser, quoted in *The Intimate Notebooks of George Jean Nathan,* 1932

We are busting our guts to get this war settled — Major General Henry I. Hodes, quoted in *Newsweek,* 12 Nov. 1951

Don't bust a gut to wash out the teapot every time you use it —Jonathan Sale, *Punch,* 19 Aug. 1975

We made every customer happy. But we had to bust our tails to do it —Gary P. Spoleta, quoted in *N.Y. Times,* 8 June 1984

These phrases have a distinctly informal flavor.

There is no point in basing your use of *bust* on backward-looking opinions. *Bust* has been gaining in respectability for a half century and in some contexts is absolutely the right word to use.

See also BURST.

bust *adjective,* **busted** Among the usagists' complaints about the verb *bust* are mixed some shots at adjective use of the past participle:

Don't write busted if you mean *broke* —McMahan & Day 1980, 1984

This seems a curiously antediluvian attitude when you compare it with this over 80 year old observation:

busted: A slang term for financially broken, but used by persons accustomed to a refined diction —Vizetelly 1906

The sentence "The stock market collapse left me busted" was included in Leonard's 1931 usage survey; the respondents found it "disputable." Crisp's 1971 replication of the survey yielded essentially the same result. The reason for the unchanged status across 40 years— during which the *bust* group has gained considerable status in print—may be that the adjective uses of *bust* and *busted* have become differentiated.

Webster's Third has an entry for *bust* or *busted* defined as "broke, bankrupt." There was good evidence for *busted* in the late 1950s:

. . . eventually went completely *busted* as a publisher —William Manchester, *Disturber of the Peace,* 1951

The town was a busted mining camp, than which there is nothing sadder to see —Bennett Cerf, *Saturday Rev.,* 31 July 1948

FDR . . . was dealing with a busted nation —Gerald W. Johnson, *New Republic,* 29 Nov. 1954

. . . to play roulette side by side with a busted but still imperious grand duke —David Dodge, *Holiday,* February 1955

But the tendency since 1961 has been to use *bust*— usually as a predicate adjective and quite often in the phrase *go bust*—for the sense of "bankrupt, broke":

One is rich, one is poor. One is booming, one perennially half bust —James Morris, *The Road to Huddersfield,* 1963

And when the Penn Central went bust —Robert Townsend, *Center Mag.,* January/February 1972

At one time a man who went bust was treated almost as a leper —William Davis, *Punch,* 17 Apr. 1974

. . . dropping out or selling out or going bust —Betsy Morris, *Wall Street Jour.,* 23 Dec. 1981

. . . the profits generated by one hit show pay for the 20 to 25 other projects that go bust —Brandon Tartikoff, *TV Guide,* 13 Sept. 1985

Busted, on the other hand, is used as both an attributive and a predicate adjective chiefly in the sense "broken":

. . . broken homes and busted marriages —Peter Carlson, *People,* 17 Feb. 1986

. . . a trial run at the last minute revealed that the damn thing was busted —Alan Lightman, *Science,* September 1984

. . . writing fiery memos to his staff about every yawning pothole, busted street light or littered playground he sees —David M. Alpern, *Newsweek,* 26 July 1982

She had a busted ankle and was on crutches at the time —John Hepworth, *Nation Rev.* (Melbourne), 17 Apr. 1975

Bust is sometimes used to mean "broken":

Ours are starting to crumble to bits now, the kettle and iron going bust —Simon Williams, quoted in *Annabel,* March 1975

My fantasies were dashed, my new friendship gone bust —Mark Harris, *N.Y. Times Book Rev.,* 4 Nov. 1984

Busted "bankrupt, broke" still seems to be of low status because usage has shifted to *bust* in this sense; *busted* "broken" seems to be gaining in status and appears with some frequency in well-edited and widely distributed publications. *Bust* "bankrupt" seems to be standard, especially in the phrase *go bust.*

but **1.** Part of the folklore of usage is the belief that there is something wrong in beginning a sentence with *but:*

Many of us were taught that no sentence should begin with "but." If that's what you learned, unlearn it—there is no stronger word at the start. It announces total contrast with what has gone before, and the reader is primed for the change —Zinsser 1976

Everybody who mentions this question agrees with Zinsser. The only generally expressed warning is not to follow the *but* with a comma, as in this example:

> But, hasty, ill-considered and emotional prohibitions can seriously threaten individual industries — *Annual Report, Owens-Illinois,* 1970

The argument is that the force of the *but* is weakened by the unneeded comma. Such commas are rare in the materials in our files. This example is more typical:

> . . . performing-arts organizations in this country are in desperate straits. But that is not for lack of public support —Harold C. Schonberg, *Harper's,* February 1971

A comma after *but* is, of course, all right if it is one of a pair setting off a parenthetical clause:

> But, as one industry analyst says, . . . —*Forbes,* 1 Dec. 1970

2. One of the more vexatious questions the usage folks have to deal with is the question of whether *but* is a preposition or a conjunction in usages like this:

> The boy stood on the burning deck,
> Whence all but he had fled;. . . .

These lines, you may remember, are from a poem named "Casabianca" (1829) by the English poet Felicia D. Hemans (1794–1835). It appears that Mrs. Hemans originally wrote "but him," but someone seems to have persuaded her to change it—or perhaps some editor changed it without asking. *Bartlett's Familiar Quotations* now carries the version with *he,* and that is the form of the line most people remember.

How is it possible to be able to write both "but he" and "but him": is one correct and the other wrong? Are they both all right? Is *but* a preposition? Is *but* a conjunction? The answer to all these questions is "yes"— just ask an expert.

Goold Brown devotes almost two full pages of tiny type to the question in his *Grammar of English Grammars* (10th edition, 1880). Goold Brown, buttressing his position with numerous examples from the King James Bible, Dryden, Pope, and other literary and theological notables, is a conjunction man. He pillories nearly two dozen other 19th-century grammarians who believe *but* to be a preposition, and he is especially scornful of a couple who would have it both ways. Bierce 1909 is with Goold Brown. Baker 1927 takes the opposite view: *but* is a preposition, "but he" is an error. Hall 1917 finds differing views in his survey: one grammarian for the preposition, two for the conjunction, two for both or either. MacCracken & Sandison 1917 admit mixed usage, but they prefer the preposition; the argument for the conjunction they think is a weak one. Williams 1897 reprints an exchange he had with Fitzedward Hall in the pages of *The Dial* in 1893: both admit unsettled usage, but Hall thinks the preposition is normal in modern usage. Follett 1966 is a preposition man. He spends most of his two or three pages on the subject denigrating the treatment given *but* in dictionaries, including Webster's Second and the OED. Follett thinks that *but he* is idiomatically correct at times, though not grammatically correct. Bernstein in several of his books is unsure,

but he suggests a rule of thumb: if the *but* and pronoun come early in the sentence, use the nominative form of the pronoun; if late in the sentence, use the objective case. Bremner 1980 has no use for Bernstein's compromise. He is for the preposition. Cook 1985 summarizes several views; she leans toward calling *but* a preposition and would opt for one part of Bernstein's solution— always putting *but* and the objective pronoun toward the end of the sentence, if she hit a sentence in which *but him* sounded awkward farther forward in the sentence, rather than changing *him* to *he.*

We could add many more opinions and suggestions, but they would serve no purpose. All of this confusion and contradiction comes from trying to cram an English function word with varying functions into a single mold.

The information in the OED that irritated Follett shows that *but* functioned as a preposition (taking a dative) in Old English. It also functioned as a conjunction after which the case of a noun or pronoun was determined by the construction it was in. Nowadays, of course, only pronouns show case in these constructions. Both uses have come down to present-day English, to the bafflement of grammarians and would-be grammarians.

The proponents of the conjunction have collected examples more assiduously than the proponents of the preposition have and have shown that the use of the nominative after *but* has a long history in literature:

> There is none but he,
> Whose being I doe feare
> —Shakespeare, *Macbeth* (in Williams 1897)

> No man but I has right to do her justice —Aphra Behn, *The Dutch Lover,* 1673

> There was nobody but he and I —Jonathan Swift, *Journal to Stella,* 8 Sept. 1711

> . . . since none puts by
> The curtain I have drawn for you, but I
> —Robert Browning, "My Last Duchess" (in Williams 1897)

> . . . any men but they would have had a strong leaning towards what is called "Conservatism" —John Henry Newman, *Historical Sketches,* 1885 (in Williams 1897)

The use of the nominative in like constructions is still found:

> . . . none but he can have seen them all —*Times Literary Supp.,* 16 June 1966

> . . . since no one but I myself had yet printed any of my work —Paul Bowles, *Without Stopping,* 1972

> . . . it carried him farther than anyone but he dared dream —R. W. Apple, Jr., *N.Y. Times Mag.,* 3 Dec. 1978

But can also be interpreted as a conjunction followed by the objective case when the pronoun stands in a position normally calling for the objective:

> Abuse everybody but me —Jane Austen, letter, 7 Jan. 1807

> . . . I didn't even know of anyone else but him —Bill Holt, quoted in *Bluegrass Unlimited,* May 1982

Of course, one can equally well argue that *but* in each of these examples is a preposition. In the next two examples, *but* is clearly a preposition. Note that the style is more nearly conversational than it was in the examples with the nominative pronouns. The first is fictional speech.

> ... it was his misfortune to save her from a passel of raiding enemy in a situation that everybody but her is trying to forget —"My Grandmother Millard," in *The Collected Stories of William Faulkner,* 1950

> Everybody but me among us old codgers proudly insists that he and his wife were married just like the kids of today —James Thurber, letter, 22 Dec. 1952

Our conclusion is that the absolutists who insist that *but* is only a conjunction or only a preposition are wrong. *But* has functioned in both capacities since Old English and still does. You are correct in choosing to use it either way. Bear in mind, however, that conjunctive *but* followed by a nominative pronoun seems rather more literary than the preposition.

3. *Except for* functions as a compound preposition. Although it is found less often, *but* works with *for* in exactly the same way:

> But for the name of its author ... it would not have had a hope of publication —*Times Literary Supp.,* 22 Oct. 1971

> He liked to think of himself as Fitzgerald's mentor but for whom Scott's talents might never have fully matured —Norman Cousins, *Saturday Rev.,* April 1981

4. Otto Jespersen, in *Negation in English and Other Languages* (1917), wrote: "By a curious transition *but* has come to mean the same thing as 'only'; at first it required a preceding negative: *I will not say but one word,* i.e., 'not except (save) one word'. . . ." He points out that eventually the negative came to be dropped, creating one of those curious expressions we have in English in which a negative construction and a positive one mean the same thing (see also COULD CARE LESS, COULDN'T CARE LESS). The positive form came to be considered normal:

> ... with an urgency which differed from his but in being more gentle —Jane Austen, *Mansfield Park,* 1814

> ... which in all probability, had he but picked it up and carried it openly away, nobody would have remarked or cared —"Centaur in Brass," in *The Collected Stories of William Faulkner,* 1950

> He contributes but four words to the Epilogue — Robert Craft, *Stravinsky,* 1972

> No wonder Purdey's produces but seventy a year — C. P. Reynolds, *Gourmet,* March 1985

The original form with the negative, however, did not disappear. It kept right on being used, chiefly in speech (see NOT . . . BUT). This has led several commentators (among them Bernstein 1977, Prentice Hall 1978, Little, Brown 1980, Johnson 1982) to label it a double negative—in ignorance of the origin of the use. Here are a few samples of the older construction:

> ... they didn't go but a little ways before they come to another branch —William Tappan Thompson, "A Coon Hunt in a Fency Country," 1847, in *The Mirth of a Nation,* ed. Walter Blair & Raven I. McDavid, Jr., 1983

A long time ago, my husband and I were talking about what makes a good prose style. . . . "I never knew but one man who was *born* with a fine prose style," he said —Rosemary C. Benét, *Book-of-the-Month Club News,* February 1948

> I never heard of but one skipper who did not arrive at the quarter deck by way of the hawsepipe —Captain Harry Allen Chippendale, *Sails and Whales,* 1951

> ... the other tenant who, bless his heart, isn't but two months behind in his rent —Flannery O'Connor, letter, 25 Apr. 1959

> I'd be right there with him—I didn't lack but three lengths of the hoe —Gloria Naylor, *People,* 11 Mar. 1985

When *but* means "only," the later positive form of the construction is the one used in standard prose; the older negative form is found chiefly in speech.

5. *But that, but what.* The use of these expressions is governed by idiom, so it is no surprise that grammarians and usage commentators have, in general, found them worrisome. French idioms generally do not trouble the teacher of French, but English idioms seldom fail to perplex English teachers—or so it seems at times. As a result, the advice tendered is usually not very helpful—often muddled and occasionally self-contradictory. The concern over these phrases is old, going back at least to Lindley Murray 1795. Murray may also have established the tradition of self-contradiction; he condemns *but that* after a negative accompanied by *doubt* but uses it himself with a different negative:

> ... yet it is not done so generally, but that good writers, even in prose, use it when speaking of things.

But that. Jespersen notes in *Negation in English and Other Languages,* 1917 that *but that* is used to introduce a conditional clause in which it means "if . . . not"; the form of the sentence is not necessarily negative:

> I waited upon him accordingly, and should have taken Collins with me, but that he was not sober — Benjamin Franklin, *Autobiography,* 1771

Jespersen has many more examples of such constructions, down to the time when he was writing. Our files contain mostly negative sentences, a situation which would seem to indicate that *but that* is usually found in negative constructions nowadays.

One of the problems that usage commentators find with *but that* comes from the fact that in some contexts *but* alone can be used:

> I don't see but that sheet has become as frankly partisan as any party paper —Oliver Wendell Holmes d. 1935, letter, 11 Oct. 1928

> ... the words of E. B. White, who once wrote: "I'm sure there isn't a humorist alive but can recall the day when. . . ." —Kathleen Fury, *TV Guide,* 30 Dec. 1984

And sometimes *that* alone can be used:

> ... there is no doubt that Jewison's use of his camera and his fluid editing make for superior entertainment —Hollis Alpert, *Saturday Rev.,* 13 Nov. 1971

As a result, some commentators find *but that* wordy. The two-word idiom, however, has impressive literary credentials extending (in Jespersen's examples) back to Caxton in the 15th century. Here are a handful of examples, old and modern:

> I don't say but that very entertaining and useful characters, and proper for comedy, may be drawn from Affectations —William Congreve, "Concerning Humour in Comedy," 1695

> For half a minute I was not sure, but that it was You transported into England by some strange Chance —Thomas Gray, letter, 24 May 1742

> I cannot be persuaded but that marriage is one of the means of happiness —Samuel Johnson, *Rambler,* 1752 (in Jespersen 1917)

> . . . I never see such a performance but that I later go out of the theatre and . . . become just such another —Sherwood Anderson (1923), cited in *New Yorker,* 12 Nov. 1984

> There can be no question but that the play gives Mr. Muni a rare opportunity —Wolcott Gibbs, *New Yorker,* 26 Feb. 1949

> Nothing is so absurd but that some philosopher has said it, Cicero told them —David Brudnoy, *National Rev.,* 19 Nov. 1971

The common use of *but that* with *doubt* has been questioned since Murray 1795, but without much reason.

> I do not doubt but that I shall set many a reader's teeth on edge —John Ruskin, *Time and Tide by Weare and Tyne,* 1867 (in Jespersen 1917)

> There can be no doubt but that economic disorders are fundamental —*Times Literary Supp.,* 5 Oct. 1940

> There is no doubt but that Congress was impressed —*New Republic,* 7 Feb. 1944

> . . . there is little doubt but that modern air freight received its real impetus from the second world war —*Newsweek,* 19 Jan. 1953

> There is no doubt but that Communists will associate themselves with it —Stanley K. Sheinbaum, in *Johns Hopkins Mag.,* December 1965

These usages are all standard, as even some handbooks (Perrin & Ebbitt 1972, Macmillan 1982) recognize.

But what. This is a more recent combination; it is attested as early as the 17th century, but most of the evidence for it comes from the 19th and 20th. The OED has little and mostly subliterary evidence for the construction; still, evidence in Jespersen and later dictionaries shows it to have been in good literary use:

> I had no agreeable diversion but what had something or other of this in it —Daniel Defoe, *Robinson Crusoe,* 1719 (in Jespersen 1917)

> . . . scarce a farmer's daughter within ten miles round but what had found him successful —Oliver Goldsmith, *The Vicar of Wakefield,* 1766 (in Jespersen 1917)

> . . . not that I think Mr. M. would ever marry anybody but what had had some education —Jane Austen, *Emma,* 1816 (in Jespersen 1917)

> I don't know but what it would —Charles Dickens, *Nicholas Nickleby,* 1838 (in Jespersen 1917)

> Her needle is not so absolutely perfect . . . but what my superintendence is advisable —Sir Walter Scott (Webster 1909)

> I don't see but what he'll have to be impeached —Henry Adams, letter, 29 Dec. 1860

> I did not know but what he was altogether 'conscientious' in that matter —Abraham Lincoln, debate with Douglas, 27 Aug. 1858

And use continues, as these 20th-century examples testify:

> There is no question but what all general vocational subjects . . . can be taught better in an organized class —G. A. McGarvey & H. H. Sherman, *Granite Cutting,* 1938

> I don't doubt but what she could do it —Flannery O'Connor, letter, 1952

> There were, to be sure, a few motorcars, but not so many but what I could pretend not to see them —James Norman Hall, *Atlantic,* December 1952

> There is no question but what all linguists . . . agree in principle with Stewart's point of view —Lawrence M. Davis, in *Black-White Speech Relationships,* 1971

> . . . hardly a year goes by but what we need a bull or a billy goat or a ram —Richard M. Ketchum, *Blair & Ketchum's Country Jour.,* November 1982

But what was declared standard by Whitford & Foster, *American Standards of Writing* (1931) and Bryant 1962; Perrin & Ebbitt 1972 offers the same view but the authors find it less common than *but that* in print. Denigration of the phrase began with Murray 1795 and is still repeated by some modern commentators. Our more recent evidence suggests that *but what* is a standard idiom, but one more likely to be found in speech, fictional and reported, and in the less formal kinds of writing than in elevated prose.

6. *But however.* A few handbooks warn against using *but* in combination with *however* or *yet.* Our files show almost no evidence of such use in edited prose.

but which, but who　　See AND WHICH, AND WHO.

buy　**1.** *Noun.* Copperud 1970 notes that some commentators quibble over the sense of *buy* that means "bargain"; in addition to this group, Harper 1985 also views it askance. Copperud opines that the use must be well on the way to acceptance. It should be, since it has been in use since 1879. Here are some examples:

> It's not only the OTCs that are buys —Robert S. Kane, *Saturday Rev.,* 20 Mar. 1976

> . . . dollar for dollar, penny for penny, the very best buy on the market today —Sam Aaron & Clifton Fadiman, *Saturday Rev.,* December 1978

> . . . to convince investors that Denny's success . . . makes its stock a good buy —Earl C. Gottschalk, Jr., *Wall Street Jour.,* 5 Jan. 1981

> Among the great buys . . . is the so-called kitchen Ming —Geri Trotta, *Gourmet,* December 1982

2. *Verb.* The sense of the verb meaning "accept, believe" is called slang by Copperud 1970 and Harper 1985. That label is out of date; the sense is now standard:

> Professor Handlin is too knowledgeable a historian of the political and social currents in the nation to buy that line of reasoning —Herbert Mitgang, *N.Y. Times Book Rev.,* 26 Oct. 1980

> The Oxford English Dictionary doesn't buy the Scandinavian connection, though —Thomas H. Middleton, *Saturday Rev.,* March 1981

> One sympathizes with the effort, even if one doesn't buy his overall thesis —James R. Mellow, *N.Y. Times Book Rev.,* 7 Nov. 1982

> . . . a group of young House activists who don't buy the old ways of doing business —Elizabeth Drew, *New Yorker,* 10 Sept. 1984

> But the President soon made it clear that he didn't buy the notion that delaying the tax cut had become unavoidable —David A. Stockman, *Newsweek,* 28 Apr. 1986

by means of   Copperud 1970 quotes himself and Bernstein 1965 as finding *by means of* "redundant" for *by* or "some other preposition." This assertion is illustrated by an example sentence of great simplicity in which *in* or *with* is suggested as a substitute.

But of course *by means of* did not come into use to vex editors pressed for space. *By means of* is, in fact, seldom used in very simple sentences and is often used precisely to avoid a simpler preposition when the simpler one might be ambiguous—*by,* for instance, has ten or a dozen meanings shown in Webster's Ninth New Collegiate Dictionary. Consider these examples:

> . . . the exploration of Palestine's rich past by means of material remains left behind by the Jews of Biblical times —*Current Biography,* February 1966

> . . . on the . . . mosaic two scenes are telescoped into one by means of an awkwardly posed single figure doing double duty —*Times Literary Supp.,* 18 Dec. 1969

> All I hope is that I will not gloss over my puzzlement by means of an overheated "literary" rhetoric —Irving Howe, *Harper's,* March 1969

It may be generally true that shorter is better, but longer can be clearer, especially if the shorter preposition is capable of several interpretations and the longer of only one.

by the same token   See TOKEN.

C

cache   See HYPERFOREIGNISMS.

caesarean   See CESAREAN, CAESAREAN.

calculate   There is more fuss about this word than is warranted in recent handbooks, which hasten to point out that when *calculate* is used to mean "to judge to be true or probable, suppose, think" and sometimes "to intend," it is dialectal, colloquial, or informal. The use is an Americanism and has been the subject of censure at least since Hull's grammar of 1829. Some commentators on Americanisms believe that in the early days of the Republic the Yankee's *calculate* contrasted with the Southerner's *reckon* or *allow.* The Dictionary of American Regional English identifies *calculate* as originally a New Englandism that spread. Evans 1957 thinks its use dying out; in partial confirmation the DARE says it is somewhat old-fashioned. A few examples of "judge to be true or probable, think":

> It is probable that the hospital poison has affected my system, and I find it worse than I calculated —Walt Whitman, letter, 14 June 1864

> . . . demonstrates that I am not calculated to be soft on such a subject —Arthur H. Vandenberg, quoted in *Time,* 14 Apr. 1947

> An old fellow with a carpet bag calculated it was good exercise to walk to Quincey —Mark Twain, *The Adventures of T. J. Snodgrass,* 1856 (*A Mark Twain Lexicon,* 1938)

> We had reason to calculate, that they had good guides —Zebulon M. Pike, *An Account of Expeditions to the Sources of the Mississippi,* 1810

And a couple of "intend":

> We calculate to go up to the city to-morrow —Cyrus Hurd, Jr., letter or journal entry, 9 Mar. 1849, in *Yale Rev.,* Summer 1947

> He ketched a frog one day, and took him home, and said he cal'lated to educate him —Mark Twain, "The Notorious Jumping Frog of Calaveras County," 1865, in *Mark Twain's Library of Humor,* 1888

calculated   On etymological grounds Richard Grant White 1870 belabored the use of *calculated* in the sense of "apt, likely" as an error. He brought forth a quotation from Oliver Goldsmith as an example of the error. His objection, however, was entirely factitious; the participial adjective had been used in that sense for a century and a half before he decided it must be wrong. Still, White had a number of followers, and his objections were repeated at least as late as Jensen 1935. The sense is standard. A few examples:

> . . . with all the modest feeling which the idea of representing Edmund was so strongly calculated to inspire —Jane Austen, *Mansfield Park,* 1814

> DESPARD. Hush. This is not well. This is calculated to provoke remark —W. S. Gilbert, *Ruddigore,* 1887

> . . . the way in which this Debate came about was calculated to give one the feeling of a challenge —Sir Winston Churchill, *The Unrelenting Struggle,* 1942

> . . . some news of late that sounds to me better calculated to provoke distaste for us than respect —Adlai E. Stevenson, *New Republic,* 23 Feb. 1953

What they found was not calculated to encourage an optimistic report —*Time,* 7 June 1954

Note that *calculated* can also be used in a sense "intended" which must be related to the dialectal sense of *calculate* meaning "intend." The participial adjective in this sense is not dialectal:

> ... forms of evasion calculated precisely to prevent me from getting information —Walker Gibson, in *The Hues of Modern English,* 1969

calligraphy Writers have been accused of misusing this word by commentators from Hodgson 1881 to Partridge 1942, Bernstein 1965, and Bryson 1984. Their objections are based on their belief that calligraphy means "beautiful handwriting." This is the etymological fallacy—the confounding of an English word with its etymology: *calligraphy* is formed from Greek elements meaning "beautiful writing."

In writings dealing with art, inscriptions, typographic design, and the like, *calligraphy* is most often applied to artistic or decorative lettering—often in alphabets other than our familiar Roman—or to the art of producing such lettering.

> Arabic inscriptions are now usually more closely integrated into the design-scheme, and cursive calligraphy has supplanted the strong uprights and right-angles of the earlier alphabets —Phyllis Ackerman, *Ciba Rev.,* June 1953

> His father was a sign painter and lettering artist, and ... the only one of the 'revolutionary' artists of the twenties and thirties ... to have been trained in lettering and calligraphy —*Printing World,* 26 Dec. 1975

> One point of contention is whether the use of raised gold distinguishes illumination from calligraphy — Annalyn Swan, *Wall Street Jour.,* 9 Aug. 1972

> The artist's debts are to Matisse ... and to Chinese caligraphy and landscape scrolls —Emily Genauer, *N.Y. Herald Tribune Book Rev.,* 28 Nov. 1954

It is also used in an extended sense in reference to the use of line by an artist:

> Calligraphy, or expressive draftsmanship for its own sake, is the virtue of Charles Seliger's delicate oils — Stuart Preston, *N.Y. Times,* 20 Feb. 1955

> ... others hailed him as a gifted exponent of sculptural calligraphy—or "drawing in space" —Robert F. Moss, *Saturday Rev.,* 15 Nov. 1975

This extended use is occasionally stretched further as a metaphor:

> His face ... registers only furrows and a knitted brow—the calligraphy of doubt —Alexandra Johnson, *Christian Science Monitor,* 18 Nov. 1976

In general literary use, without reference to art, *calligraphy* is used for ordinary handwriting—a sense faulted by our critics on the basis of etymology.

> ... written in a clear, and rather bold round hand, the caligraphy particularly, for so old a man, being exceptionally good —*Curiosities of Street Literature,* 1871

> My father's letter (his calligraphy, I had noted, had neither become less neat nor more mature) —Jean Stafford, *Partisan Rev.,* Fall 1944

Calligraphy is sometimes extended to the lettering of signs, whether decorative or not:

> We lunched at one of those Chinese restaurants on Mott Street, whose name hung above the sidewalk in neon-tube calligraphy —Bernard Taper, *New Yorker,* 2 June 1956

> ... it is a sad sign, a pale reflection of the original's exuberant calligraphy —Colin Eisler, *Harper's,* August 1983

These are the ways in which *calligraphy* is currently used. The spelling *caligraphy,* which occurs in a couple of our examples, is old-fashioned and no longer in use. Do not confuse the meaning of the word's Greek roots with the word's meaning in English.

callous, callus The main point on which usage writers agree about these words is that *callus* is a noun and *callous* is an adjective. Beyond that point they start to differ. Rather than describe the ins and outs of their opinions, we will concentrate here on how these words are really used.

Taken together, *callous* and *callus* have use in three parts of speech and with two general categories of meaning, which we may label "physical" and "emotional." Both words come to us from the same Latin word *callus,* though *callous* took a slightly circuitous route through Middle French to arrive. It is not too surprising, then, that these two words, which sound alike, look very similar, and have the same source, should be the cause of some confusion. Let's examine them according to their function as parts of speech.

As a noun, *callus* is the predominant spelling, and physical meanings are the predominant ones:

> ... connecting cambium in the callus —H. J. Fuller & O. Tippo, *College Botany,* 1950

> ... bunions, corns and calluses —*Harper's Bazaar,* November 1979

> Callus is an unorganized meshwork of woven bone —Heather Smith Thomas, *Chronicle of the Horse,* 2 Nov. 1984

The spelling *callous* is an infrequent one (at least in edited prose) for the physical sense of the noun:

> ... the thumb of my left hand, where the callous had formed —Charles Spielberger, *Partisan Rev.,* Summer 1946

> ... a callous formed there large as a bowl —Pearl Buck, *The Good Earth,* 1931

Extended uses of the noun occur with either spelling but are quite rare.

> ... these moral callouses which she simply could not understand —Gilbert Knox, *The Land of Afternoon,* 1924

> ... a protective callus of cynicism —Martin Levin, *N.Y. Times Book Rev.,* 17 Aug. 1975

Now for the adjective: *callous* is the spelling used, almost exclusively with emotional meaning.

> ... a callous disregard for human rights —William O. Douglas, *Being an American,* 1948

> ... her elegant and callous mother —John Cheever, *The Wapshot Chronicle,* 1957

... the callous murder of one good man —Martin Booth, *British Book News,* October 1984

... the presence of callous ulcers —*JAMA,* 18 Aug. 1962

Callus is not used as an adjective, but both *calloused* and *callused* are. *Calloused* usually has emotional connotations, and *callused* always has physical ones.

... had become so stupid and calloused about the birds —Ernest Hemingway, "Miss Mary's Lion," 1956

... thought it calloused to prolong the war —Irving Howe, *N.Y. Times Mag.,* 19 Sept. 1982

The tree wound was heavily calloused —Sandra L. Anagnostakis, *Science,* 29 Jan. 1982

His hands were rough, callused, competent —Russell Baker, *Growing Up,* 1982

Lastly, the verb: *callous* and *callus* in purely verbal uses (which are uncommon) parallel the uses of the adjectives in *-ed; callous* is usually emotional and *callus* is physical.

... long association with the police had utterly calloused him to human misery —Erle Stanley Gardner, *The Case of the Crooked Candle,* 1944

... these men don't ... actually sweat and callous their hands —Alan Paton, *Cry, The Beloved Country,* 1948

... let ends [of a broken tuber] callus over before you plant —*Sunset,* May 1982

In summary, emotional meanings are almost entirely confined to *callous,* regardless of part of speech. Physical meanings are usually spelled *callus,* sometimes spelled *callous.*

calvary, cavalry The word *cavalry* refers to a component of the army traditionally mounted on horseback, while *Calvary* is the hill near Jerusalem where Jesus was crucified and *calvary* (lowercase) refers either to an open-air representation of the Crucifixion or to an experience of intense mental suffering. Don't confuse the spellings of these two words, as is occasionally done.

can, may 1. *Can* and *may* are most frequently interchangeable in senses denoting possibility. The definition of *can* in Webster 1909 gave *may* as a synonym in a definition dealing with possibility and illustrated with this example:

Here can I sit alone, unseen of any —Shakespeare, *The Two Gentlemen of Verona,* 1595

The *can* in the quotation denotes neither power nor permission but possibility. So does this one:

Can we, with manners, ask what was the difference —Shakespeare, *Cymbeline,* 1610

It's not much of a stretch of meaning from the use in *Cymbeline* to

"Can I come in, Frank?" —Anthony Trollope, *Dr. Thorne,* 1858

Can in its original form meant "to know of, to know how," and when it came to be used as an auxiliary verb it carried the notion of knowing how to do something—

mental ability rather than physical ability. This mental connotation is still common:

I can visualize the helpful comment on my paper —Jessica Mitford, *Atlantic,* July 1970

... one of the advantages of written speech is that it says the same thing to everyone who can read it —John Holt, *Atlantic,* May 1971

From mental ability *can* was extended to physical ability:

... the snow ... gets so deep he can walk right onto the roof —Edward Hoagland, *Atlantic,* July 1971

Anyone who can handle a fly rod —Forrest N. Yockey, *Ford Times,* November 1967

From these two uses, *can* came to take on the connotation of possibility; if our files are reasonably accurate reflections of present-day use, the "possibility" sense of *can* is the one most frequently used in edited prose:

Naturally, we are always asking: Can I marry the girl I love? Can I sell my house? —W. H. Auden, *Columbia Forum,* Winter 1970

Maybe then, with some honest grub sticking to my ribs, I can become a passable writer —Jean Stafford, *Vogue,* 1 Jan. 1972

... an infinite number of lines ... can be drawn through a point —Robert W. Marks, *The New Mathematics Dictionary and Handbook,* 1964

One can but admire his restrained use of the material —Suzanne Slesin, *N.Y. Times Mag.,* 14 Apr. 1985

The transition from "possibility" to "permission" is subtler than the handbooks think. Noah Webster's 1828 dictionary contained this as part of his definition 5:

... to be free from any restraint of moral, civil or political obligation, or from any positive prohibition.

This sense involves nothing more than permission given by not prohibiting. It constitutes the most common "permission" sense we find written:

... took off from her [the bride's] head the myrtle wreath, which only maidens can wear —Henry Adams, letter, 17 May 1859

If the President wants the nomination, he can have it —Elizabeth Drew, *Atlantic,* May 1971

Greece is the only country in the Eastern Mediterranean where the Sixth Fleet may count on landing. Theoretically it can land in Turkey, but ... —Elizabeth Drew, *Atlantic,* November 1971

The new prayers are not compulsory, and vicars can use the old forms if they like —*N.Y. Times,* 11 Nov. 1979

New members are required to wait forty-eight hours after signing up before they can play —James K. Glassman, *Atlantic,* September 1971

You cannot enter, but you can walk round part of the thick white walls —Nadine Gordimer, *Atlantic,* November 1971

The *cannot* in the last example distinctly implies a denial of permission. Lamberts 1972 points out that for negative uses in which permission is denied, *cannot* and *can't* have largely replaced *may not* and *mayn't*.

The use of *can* in a direct question to request permission is basically an oral use. Note that all of our examples come from recorded speech or fictional speech:

Can I proceed without interruption? —Senator Stuart Symington, at the 1953 Army–McCarthy hearings (Pyles 1979)

"Can I speak to Detective-Sergeant Sparrow?" I asked —Graham Greene, *Travels with My Aunt,* 1969

She licked the cream off her fingers, slowly, one at a time, with an appreciative popping sound. "Beaut. Can I have another piece?" —Anne Mulcock, *Landscape with Figures,* 1971

Can I turn to the subject on which you are being most attacked at the moment . . . ? —Nicholas Woolley (BBC interviewer), *The Listener,* 8 Aug. 1974

If this is almost exclusively an oral use, why should we find it so often mentioned in books on writing? Yet we do find in, for instance, Cook 1985—a handbook published by The Modern Language Association of America presumably for college or graduate-school students—this sort of statement:

In formal contexts, the rule goes, *may* refers to permission, *can* to ability: *May I leave now? Can she bake a cherry pie?*

What sort of formal context is being referred to here? Need anyone write "May I go now?" or "Can she bake a cherry pie?" in a journal essay? In a report to the President? In an address to a learned society? It would seem unlikely. But what other formal context could be referred to in a book with the subtitle *How to Improve Your Own Writing*?

The answer was probably discovered by Compton 1898, who found the quotation from Trollope's *Dr. Thorne* that we quoted earlier. Compton excuses Trollope's use of *can* in the question by noting that Trollope put the word in the mouth of a young speaker; Compton opines that the misuse of *can* for *may* is an error that belongs mostly to one's childhood years. When you add this opinion to the fact that a great many of the books that insist on the distinction were written for schoolchildren, it becomes clear that we are dealing with a pedagogical tradition. The *can/may* distinction is a traditional part of the American school curriculum. The fact that the distinction is largely ignored by people once out of school is also a tradition.

Conclusion: The uses of *can* which request permission are seldom found in edited prose. In general, this use of *can* belongs to speech, reported or fictional. In negative statements, *cannot* and *can't* are much more frequently used than *may not* and *mayn't*; use in negative contexts is seldom noticed or criticized. *May* is still used, of course:

And I said, 'Mr. President, I want to talk to you. If I may, I'll come right up there and see you.' —Harry S. Truman, quoted in Merle Miller, *Plain Speaking,* 1973

2. An important aspect of the business of distinguishing the proper uses of *can* and *may* is the erection of a strict line of demarcation between the two. As far as we know, Samuel Johnson was one of the first to do this:

3. It is distinguished from *may,* as *power* from *permission;* I *can* do it, it is in my power; I *may* do it, it is allowed me: but in poetry they are confounded.

We can find much the same statement made more recently:

In formal English a distinction is drawn between *can* and *may. Can* is used when indicating physical ability to do something: "I *can* jump more than five feet." *May* is used when indicating permission to do something: "You *may* stay home from school tomorrow." However, it is only fair to say that the distinction is often ignored . . . —Harper 1985

Johnson's 1755 definition of *can* shows that he was ignorant of the origin of the word; he did not know that its earliest senses implied mental ability, and he did not recognize the uses implying possibility, although such uses may have been the "confounded" ones he found in poetry. If Boswell reports correctly, Johnson himself was one of the confounders:

He was particularly indignant against the almost universal use of the word *idea,* in the sense of *notion* or *opinion,* when it is clear that *idea* can only signify something of which an image can be formed in the mind —*Life of Samuel Johnson,* 1791

The sense of the first *can* in Boswell's paraphrase concerns neither power nor permission but possibility, and particularly that part of the realm of possibility dealing with what ought to be rather than what can be or what is. There is no admixture of the notion of power or of physical ability here. This use is standard and very common in the English of those who write on usage:

That *d[ifferent]* can only be followed by *from* & not by *to* is a SUPERSTITION —Fowler 1926

. . . *amorous* can only be used of persons —Follett 1966

Responsibility can be put only on people, not on things —Sellers 1975

. . . *despondent,* which can apply only to people —Simon 1980

Here is Bryson 1984 discussing the subject:

can, may. You have probably heard it a thousand times before, but it bears repeating that *can* applies to what is possible and *may* to what is permissible. You can drive your car the wrong way down a one-way street, but you may not (or must not or should not). In spite of the simplicity of the rule, errors abound. Here is William Safire writing in *The New York Times* on the pronunciation of *junta:* 'The worst mistake is to mix languages: You cannot say "joonta" and you cannot say "hunta".' But you can—and quite easily. What Safire meant was 'should not' or 'may not' or 'ought not'.

Bryson is clearly unaware that Safire's usage is standard in the trade. He is also unaware that he uses it himself:

substitute can only be followed by 'for' —Bryson 1984 (p. 137)

See also CANNOT 2.

can but See CANNOT BUT, CANNOT HELP, CANNOT HELP BUT.

cancel out Freeman 1983 tells us that a meeting that is discontinued is canceled, not canceled out. To this we can say that he is correct insofar as our evidence is reliable. *Cancel out* is not used in the transitive sense of *cancel* meaning "to call off." *Cancel out* is, however, in idiomatic use with other senses of *cancel*. Harper 1985 says *cancel out* is often heard from bureaucrats. This we cannot confirm, as we do not have a single citation from a bureaucrat; *cancel out* is apparently not even used by the Postal Service, where many bureaucrats are employed.

Harper also calls *cancel out* redundant, which is their way of telling you that some people use *out* idiomatically with *cancel* and others do not. Here are some completely acceptable examples of the senses in which *cancel out* is used.

As an intransitive, *cancel out* is used chiefly in the sense "to neutralize each other's effect":

> . . . these colors cancel out and make the room poorer than it would have been if a more limited palette had been used —Lewis Mumford, *New Yorker,* 15 Oct. 1955

> . . . the various pressure groups to a large degree canceled out —James B. Conant, *Atlantic,* May 1946

It also occurs in mathematics:

> The units "cancel out," and the ratio remains 4:5 — William L. Schaaf, *Mathematics For Everyday Use,* 1942

And it is used in the intransitive equivalent of "to call off an event":

> . . . a little rain wouldn't make people cancel out — Jeff Brown, *Holiday,* June 1966

> . . . we've more than once landed our rebuilt army warplanes on Chicago's Maywood field when other lines canceled out —Charles A. Lindbergh, *The Spirit of St. Louis,* 1953

The most frequent use, however, is the transitive sense that means "to match in force or effect, offset":

> . . . a state whose two Senators representing 100,000 permanent residents, can cancel out the votes cast by the Senators representing the fourteen million residents . . . —D. W. Brogan, in *Aspects of American Government,* ed. Sydney D. Bailey, 1950

> . . . just as his irritability cancelled out his natural kindness —Osbert Sitwell, *Horizon,* July 1947

> . . . every definite piece of advice he gives is cancelled out by another, equally definite, contrary piece of advice —*Times Literary Supp.,* 29 Apr. 1955

> Ironies breed before our eyes, cancel each other out —Irving Kristol, *Encounter,* December 1954

> When smoking cigarettes, I should drink green tea to cancel out the poison —Shirley Glaser, *New York,* 27 Sept. 1971

> Pratt's conversation often seems to cancel itself out, as do some of his lyrics: "Who am I talking to I know but I don't know. . . ." —Ken Emerson, *New Times,* 20 Aug. 1976

candelabra Originally the plural of *candelabrum,* *candelabra* has been used as a singular with the plural *candelabras* since at least 1815:

> Four silver candelabras, holding great waxen torches —Sir Walter Scott, *Ivanhoe,* 1819 (OED)

> Surrounded by gauzy nymphs and staglike men with candelabras, Zorina appeared barefoot —Arlene Croce, *New Yorker,* 12 July 1982

Even though Fowler 1926 disliked the usage, it is so well established (unlike, for instance, the singular use of *criteria*) that it goes almost entirely unnoticed. *Candelabra* is also still used as a plural of *candelabrum:*

> There were white peacocks (stuffed) on the lawn, a tent hung with chandeliers and decorated with candelabra —Jody Jacobs, *Los Angeles Times,* 23 Sept. 1984

For other foreign plurals, see LATIN PLURALS.

canine Copperud 1980 asserts that *canine* used as a noun meaning "dog" is journalese and is discouraged by three authorities (one of which is himself). The second claim we may take as true, but the first is, to be more or less polite, questionable. The objection is an old one, going back to Vizetelly 1906, who simply said that *canine* should not be used for *dog.* Jensen 1935 came up with a reason: "*Canine* is an adjective and should not be used as a noun." Actually, the noun *canine* is older than the corresponding adjective, though the oldest sense is that of a tooth.

Our evidence shows that *canine* is usually given a broad, not a specific, application:

> . . . canines reproduce young in 62 days —Hope Ryden, *N.Y. Times,* 15 Dec. 1974

> A world expert on the canines, he keeps two rare breeds —Paulette Pratt, *Observer Mag.,* 16 Dec. 1973

> The family Canidae consists of two main subgroups, the vulpines (foxes) and the canines (wolves, coyotes, jackals, and dogs) —Michael W. Fox, *The Soul of the Wolf,* 1980

We have only one "journalistic" citation in our files:

> A sozzled Australian, accompanied by a dog, got on to a tram and was quickly . . . told by the N.A. conductor that he and his canine couldn't travel together —*The Bulletin* (Sydney, Australia), 20 Jan. 1954

See also EQUINE; FELINE.

cannot 1. *Cannot, can not.* Both spellings are acceptable, but *cannot* is more frequent in current use. Chambers 1985 insists that *cannot* must be used in British English unless the *not* is to receive particular emphasis. A couple of American sources (Oxford American Dictionary 1980, Trimble 1975) mention that the two-word form can be used to indicate special emphasis, although Irmscher 1976 warns that publishing-house style may prevail over your emphasis. Emphasis on *not* appears to be intended in this passage:

> You said a while ago, says your man, that you were a better man than any man here. Can you jump?
> I can not, says the sergeant, but I'm no worse than the next man —Flann O'Brien, *At Swim-Two-Birds,* 1939

In general, however, the one-word form is used:

> Dr Bourne cannot yet call her out of danger —Jane Austen, letter, 10 Jan. 1809
>
> ... a simple fact that ... the C.C.C.C.'er cannot admit —Simon 1980

2. *Cannot* is in regular use by writers on usage in the sense "should not, ought not." This usage conflicts with their commonly repeated oversimplification of the relation of *can* and *may*, as William Safire, in the *New York Times Magazine* (17 Feb. 1980) noted, when he reprinted a sentence of his:

> You can flout convention and you can flout authority, but you cannot use flaunt for flout.

A correspondent, he reported, suggested that *may not* should have been used in place of *cannot*. But this use is so clear and firmly established in writing on usage that it should not be quibbled at. Look at these examples:

> ... being quite superfluous, cannot be defended by an appeal to the secondary meaning of *aggravare* —Hodgson 1889
>
> But a person cannot be aggravated —Bierce 1909
>
> 'Purport' cannot be used in the passive —Bernstein 1962
>
> ... *as* cannot be used as a preposition —Phythian 1979
>
> ... a thing cannot be more or less or rather or somewhat or very unique —Kilpatrick 1984
>
> *Plus* cannot be used as a substitute for *also* —Harper 1985

cannot but, cannot help, cannot help but A lot has been written about these phrases. To put as charitable a light on the matter as possible, most of what you may read is out of date. We have hundreds of citations for these phrases, and we can tell you two things for certain: these phrases all mean the same thing—"to be unable to do otherwise than"—and they are all standard. To the usual three we can add *can but* and *cannot choose but,* which also have the same meaning but are less frequently met with. We will take up each of the five in turn. Our evidence is much heavier for *cannot but* and *cannot help but* than it is for the other three, and accordingly more examples of them will appear.

Can but is characterized as "pompous" by Bernstein 1971, but it seems natural enough in these examples:

> No scholar facing a subject such as this can be but overwhelmed —Robert F. Byrnes, *ACLS Newsletter,* November 1968
>
> Howard Hawks devotees and admirers can but sigh at his self-borrowings in Rio Lobo —Judith Crist, *New York,* 15 Feb. 1971

Cannot choose but is attested in the OED from 1557. Apparently 1798 was a big year for this phrase:

> The eye—it cannot choose but see;
> We cannot bid the ear be still
> —William Wordsworth, "Expostulation and
> Reply," 1798

> The Wedding-Guest sat on a stone:
> He cannot choose but hear
> —Samuel Taylor Coleridge, "The Rime of the
> Ancient Mariner," 1798

Modern uses are likely to be echoes of 1798:

> But James, as always, wins in the end and we cannot choose but hear —Katherine Hoskins, *Hudson Rev.,* Spring 1948
>
> I clutched my stem glass ... and listened as the wedding guest listened. I could not choose but hear —S. P. B. Mais, *The English Scene To-day,* 2d ed., 1949

Cannot help is grammatically the odd one of the five. It is followed by a present participle, whereas the others are followed by the bare infinitive. As you can see, it has been in use quite a long time:

> ... yet I cannot help thinking, that ... our Conversation hath very much degenerated —Jonathan Swift, "A Proposal for Correcting, Improving and Ascertaining the English Tongue," 1712
>
> ... I can hardly help imagining that we shall go again —Samuel Johnson, letter, 22 July 1777
>
> ... but I cannot help thinking that Nature will struggle again & produce a revival —Jane Austen, letter, 8 Apr. 1805
>
> Efforts against unemployment made in the same educational and helpful terms ... cannot help producing results —Franklin D. Roosevelt, 29 Mar. 1930, in *Franklin D. Roosevelt's Own Story,* ed. Donald Day, 1951
>
> ... you cannot help sensing how maleducated we are —John Mason Brown, *Saturday Rev.,* 8 Aug. 1942
>
> ... and everybody else at Town Hall can't help knowing how their bosses feel —John Fischer, *Harper's,* January 1969
>
> In my grimmest imaginings I could not help thinking that he might have raped my daughter instead — William Styron, *This Quiet Dust and Other Writings,* 1982

Cannot but is an old established idiom. It has even been a favorite of some of our old warhorses of usage— Henry Alford, Richard Grant White, Fitzedward Hall— but instead of citing them we give you a goodly sample of others from across nearly three centuries:

> ... I can't but laugh to think how they'll spunge the sheet before the errata be blotted out —George Farquhar, *Love and a Bottle,* 1698
>
> I cannot but confess the failures of my correspondence —Samuel Johnson, letter, 1750
>
> I cannot but applaud your zeal —Benjamin Franklin, letter, 26 Dec. 1789
>
> I cannot but think of dear Sir Thomas's delight — Jane Austen, *Mansfield Park,* 1814
>
> ... and I cannot but regret that the part of Ordonio was disposed of —Lord Byron, letter, 31 Mar. 1815
>
> ... the poetry or vision that one cannot but look for in fiction of this contemporary stamp —*Times Literary Supp.,* 13 Feb. 1943
>
> ... in which both Stendhal and Byron, with the prodigious example of Napoleon before them, could not but believe —John Peale Bishop, *New Republic,* 22 Nov. 1954

The outsider cannot but be struck by the frequent reluctance of the learned world —Edmund Wilson, *New Yorker,* 14 May 1955

You cannot but be entertained —Newgate Callendar, *N.Y. Times Book Rev.,* 1 Sept. 1974

One cannot but wonder if the image . . . flashed before the mind of Davis —Robert Penn Warren, *Jefferson Davis Gets His Citizenship Back,* 1980

. . . which cannot but help him as he assumes his difficult task —Daniel Southerland, *Christian Science Monitor,* 16 Jan. 1981

Cannot help but, which may have been formed as a syntactic blend of *cannot but* and *cannot help,* is the most recent of the phrases. It appears to have arisen just before the turn of the 20th century. Three sources—the OED, Curme 1931, and Poutsma 1904–26—all give the English novelist Hall Caine as the earliest source. Two of his novels, *The Manxman* (1894) and *The Christian* (1897) are cited. We began to acquire citations in the 1920s, and a great many from 1940 on. Here is a sample:

Since I cannot help but write to you —Vachel Lindsay, in *Yale Rev.,* Autumn 1943

. . . we cannot help but feel that many of them . . . —Clifton Fadiman, *Saturday Rev.,* 5 Aug. 1944

. . . I could not help but reflect that if I hadn't been so noble . . . —Robert Penn Warren, *All the King's Men,* 1946

. . . you just cannot help but accept the invitation —S. P. B. Mais, *The English Scene To-day,* 2d ed., 1949

. . . she couldn't help but feel proud of Dandy —John Dos Passos, *Chosen Country,* 1951

I couldn't help but feel that it was in some way a recognition —Robert M. Coates, *New Yorker,* 18 Oct. 1952

". . . if fellows like you go about sneering he cannot help but find out," I said —Oliver St. John Gogarty, *It Isn't This Time of Year At All!,* 1954

. . . could not help but be a little impressed by what Dottie disclosed —Mary McCarthy, *The Group,* 1963

. . . one cannot help but admire the freshness of his approach —*Times Literary Supp.,* 17 Oct. 1968

Reformers cannot help but think that there are far more effective ways —Robert A. Nisbet, *Change,* January–February 1971

. . . they cannot help but provide us with important clues —Katharine Kuh, *Saturday Rev.,* 22 Jan. 1977

One cannot help but rejoice for those who escaped —Margaret Drabble, *N.Y. Times Book Rev.,* 14 Nov. 1982

But I can't help but wonder what would happen —Emily Grotta, *Houston Post,* 14 Sept. 1984

Only *cannot but* and *cannot help but* have been the subject of much criticism. Vizetelly 1906 warned readers to distinguish between *can but* and *cannot but*—as if they meant something different; Bierce 1909 condemned *cannot help but;* Utter 1916—the only one with

foresight—recommended simply accepting *can but, cannot but,* and *cannot help but* as idioms. A great many other commentators have had their say, many of them finding fault with one or the other by resorting to logic—their own brand—but of course logic cannot measure idioms. Degree of formality appears to be determined not by the phrase but by the choice of *cannot* or *can't* in the phrase. You can use whichever one seems most natural to you; all are standard.

cannot choose but   See CANNOT BUT, CANNOT HELP, CANNOT HELP BUT.

cannot help, cannot help but   See CANNOT BUT, CANNOT HELP, CANNOT HELP BUT.

can't but   See CANNOT BUT, CANNOT HELP, CANNOT HELP BUT.

can't hardly   See HARDLY.

can't help, can't help but   See CANNOT BUT, CANNOT HELP, CANNOT HELP BUT.

can't seem

I must be nervous this afternoon. I can't seem to settle down to anything —Kathleen Norris, *The Passing Show,* 6 Dec. 1933 (in Partridge 1942)

The expression *can't seem* is an idiom that came under critical scrutiny during the last quarter of the 19th century. It was apparently first noticed by Schele De Vere in his 1872 book of Americanisms. He characterizes it as an odd use Yankees make of *seem,* apparently quoting or paraphrasing a comment made somewhere by James Russell Lowell. Bardeen 1883 interprets this to mean that *seem* is used redundantly. There were others who found redundancy in this use—Utter 1916 mentions it as a criticism of the phrase—and Shaw 1975 is still working that vein of criticism.

Another criticism is that the expression is illogical or involves, as Partridge 1942 puts it, "misplacement of words." Partridge has correctly identified the process, but it is not an error. Bolinger 1980 calls it "raising"— a name linguists use for the process by which a negative (or sometimes another element) gets moved from a subordinate clause to the main clause. Another well-known example of raising is "I don't think it'll rain today" for "I think it won't rain today." Negatives often tend to be raised in conjunction with *seem.* Look at these examples:

My problem is that I cannot seem to remember this —Kilpatrick 1984

It never seems to have occurred to him that . . . —*Dictionary of American Biography,* 1928

. . . they do not seem to be seriously engaged in anything other than being oppressed —John Corry, *Harper's,* November 1970

Senate members don't seem to recall any such understanding —*Time,* 23 Mar. 1953

. . . we did not seem to breed that type in Australia —*Auckland* (New Zealand) *Weekly News,* 19 Nov. 1925

Partridge would correct "I can't seem to settle down" to "I seem unable to settle down" which his American editor, W. Cabell Greet, characterizes as awkward though logical. The unraised negative with *seem* is also in use, but not so frequently as the *can't seem, don't seem* constructions. A couple of examples:

> ... he seems not to have been deflected from his political views —*Dictionary of American Biography,* 1928

> It is surprising how many otherwise quite rational people seem not to know this —Rexford G. Tugwell, *Center Mag.,* July/August 1970

Conclusion: while *can't seem* itself appears to be mostly used in speech, its cousins *cannot seem, don't seem, did not seem,* etc., are not uncommon in print, are all formed by negative-raising, and are all standard idioms. The more logical construction, with the negative in the subordinate part of the sentence, can be used, but it is less frequent. See RAISING.

canvas, canvass Usage books tell you that the noun *canvas* refers to cloth, and the verb and noun *canvass* usually refer to the soliciting of votes or opinions. You will certainly not go wrong in making this division a rule of thumb. Actual usage, however, is not quite so clear-cut. These two words are closely related etymologically (the oldest sense, now obsolete, of the verb *canvass* was "to toss in a canvas sheet in sport or punishment"), and from their earliest occurrences both words, to varying degrees, have been spelled both ways. Here is a summary of modern usage:

The noun which the usage books say is only *canvas* is occasionally spelled *canvass.*

> ... for the painter to transfer his imaginative conception to canvass —John Dewey, *Art as Experience,* 1934

> ... canvasses by Mondrian —Kermit Lansner, *New Republic,* 26 Jan. 1953

The verb meaning "to cover, line, or furnish with canvas" is spelled *canvas* but may be inflected with either a single or double *s.*

> An over-canvassed craft would be a liability —Bill Wallace, *Sailing,* rev. ed., 1966

> ... the one hundred-foot-long Gallery, canvased from floor to ceiling with dozens of masterpieces by Reubens, Sir Joshua Reynolds ... —*Town & Country,* April 1984

The much more common verb discussed in usage books has several senses (including "to examine in detail" and "to solicit support or determine opinions") and is usually spelled *canvass* but occasionally *canvas.*

> ... the tendency of some of the members of the Advisory Council to canvas their government's interests not only at the Council table —Ann Dearden, *Middle East Jour.,* October 1950

The noun derived from this verb is also usually *canvass* but occasionally *canvas.*

> Funds for the bridge were raised by a house-to-house canvas —*American Guide Series: Maryland,* 1940

Except for the verb inflections of *canvas,* the secondary spellings are currently much less common than the primary spellings.

capability *Capability* is commonly followed by *of* or *for* when it is used with a preposition:

> They were viewing the country with the eyes of persons accustomed to drawing; and decided on its capability of being formed into pictures —Jane Austen, *Northanger Abbey,* 1818

> With childish faith in the capabilities of science —I. I. Rabi, *Atlantic,* October 1945

> Their ignorance of Man's capabilities for mischief — J. Stevenson-Hamilton, *Wild Life in South Africa,* 1947

> Today's student constituency has shown a thirst and capability for serious responsibility —Jean-Louis D'Heilly, *Change,* December 1970

It is also commonly followed by *to* and an infinitive:

> The capability of a great state to expand its influence —*New Republic,* 27 Jan. 1968

> ... has revealed several areas of weakness in world capability to accelerate agricultural output —*Rockefeller Foundation President's Five-Year Review & Annual Report,* 1968

> ... our capability to stop these bombers —Stuart Symington, *New Republic,* 13 July 1953

> ... research activities aimed at developing man's capability to work in the sea —*Annual Report, Union Carbide Corp.,* 1970

capable When followed by a preposition, *capable* nearly always appears with *of:*

> ... when those muscles and joints were rendered capable of motion —Mary Shelley, *Frankenstein,* 1818

> ... individually so capable of charm —Edmund Wilson, *A Piece of My Mind,* 1956

> ... although he is not capable of using you ill —Jonathan Swift, "Letter to a Very Young Lady on Her Marriage," reprinted in *Encore,* June 1945

> ... I became myself capable of bestowing animation upon lifeless matter —Mary Shelley, *Frankenstein,* 1818

> ... people who valued machines more than men were capable under these conditions of governing men —Lewis Mumford, *Technics and Civilization,* 1934

The last three illustrations above show *capable of* used with a gerund in the active voice. While occurring less frequently, *capable of* may be found used with a verb in the passive voice; although some language arbiters decry this construction, it has been used by careful writers for quite some time:

> An ideal so expansive is no longer capable of being compressed —*Selected Writings of Benjamin N. Cardozo,* ed. Margaret E. Hall, 1947

> ... a formal doctrine, capable of being expressed in a few catchwords —Lewis Mumford, *Technics and Civilization,* 1934

> ... your language wardrobe is capable of being enlarged many times over —Jerome Martin & Dor-

othy Carnahan Olson, *Patterns of Language,* Level G (textbook), 1977

capacity *Capacity,* when it refers to ability, potential, facility, or power, may be followed by *to* and the infinitive:

. . . has the capacity . . . to experiment with a variety of novelistic techniques —John W. Aldridge, *Saturday Rev.,* 6 Sept. 1975

. . . the capacity to live and learn, as it were —Maxwell Geismar, *American Moderns,* 1958

It may also be followed by the preposition *for* and a noun:

. . . astounding him with their fearless capacity for denouement —Robert Coover, *Harper's,* January 1972

. . . she developed a fine capacity for mischief — George Eliot, *Silas Marner,* 1861

A gerund phrase may follow the preposition when *capacity* is used with *for:*

. . . demonstrate a capacity for solving the critical problems in our own society —James M. Gavin, "On Post Cold War Strategy," *Center Report,* June 1972

. . . his capacity for feeling snubbed by those whose superiority he recognized —Van Wyck Brooks, *The Flowering of New England, 1815–1865,* rev. ed., 1946

Capacity in this sense may even be found with *of* and a noun, although this combination is less frequent:

. . . bold adventurous people without nerves, minds, or the capacity of observation —Archibald MacLeish, *Yale Rev.,* Autumn 1941

If my career were of that better kind that there was any opportunity or capacity of sacrifice in it — Charles Dickens, *A Tale of Two Cities,* 1859

Of may also be followed by a gerund phrase, but this use is infrequent:

. . . when they wanted the capacity of interesting those who wished to dedicate themselves —Lawrence J. Shehan, *Bulletin of the National Catholic Education Association,* August 1949

David Lloyd George in England also had the capacity of glamorizing himself —Victor L. Albjerg, *Current History,* September 1952

When *capacity* is used to designate volume, the preposition *of* follows it:

One modern cement elevator has a storage capacity of 114,000 barrels —*American Guide Series: Minnesota,* 1938

When denoting a position or role, *capacity* is used a little more often in the construction *in his* (*her, our,* etc.) *capacity as,* than in the construction *in the* (*his, her,* etc.) *capacity of:*

. . . in their capacity as historians they have pointed out the effect of specific economic factors —John Dewey, *Freedom and Culture,* 1939

In the capacity of vice-president of the federation — *Current Biography 1950*

capital, capitol There are a number of things the spelling *capital* is used for—letters, money, cities—but *capitol* always refers to a building, even when used figuratively:

Not going to my grandmother's side of the road was an impossibility . . . for Ida Rebecca's house was the capitol of Morrisonville —Russell Baker, *Growing Up,* 1982

caption Copperud 1970, 1980 notes that Fowler 1926 did not like *caption* used for a title or heading. He was echoing an old complaint that probably started with Richard Grant White 1870. White objected to the use on the grounds of etymology; he cited its Latin source and claimed that *caption* therefore had to mean "seizure"; he also said that those who used it for "heading" must think the word is derived from the Latin word for "head." Ayres 1881 repeats the same argument, and from time to time (Evans 1957, Bryson 1984) this supposed Latin-based reason for not using *caption* "heading" is mentioned. We have not, however, been able to find a single source out of the several that insist on *caption* "heading"—generally in contrast with *legend* for the matter under a picture—that also makes any mention of Latin. Partridge 1942, for instance, merely says that *caption* is being misused for "a legend underneath (instead of above, as it should be). . . ." The meaning "heading" perhaps simply stems from legal use, where *caption* signifies a particular kind of heading.

All the former criticism notwithstanding, *caption* is established in American use both for a heading and for the legend under a picture or cartoon.

. . . an editorial which appeared in your issue of December 9th under the caption "The Woollcott Menace" —Alexander Woollcott, letter, 19 Dec. 1935

He soon became a regular contributor to various comic periodicals and turned out quips, cartoon captions, and sketches —Marc Slonim, *Saturday Rev.,* 12 June 1954

carat, karat, caret *Carat* is a unit of weight for precious stones; *karat* (also spelled *carat* sometimes) is a unit of fineness for gold; *caret* is a wedge-shaped mark used by copy editors and proofreaders to mark a place in text where something is to be inserted. It is really unlikely that you will confuse these, let alone fuddle them with Bugs Bunny's old favorite *carrot,* as Shaw 1975 worries. If in doubt, check a good dictionary. We do have an instance of *carat* wrongly spelled with two *r*'s in a direct-mail advertisement for precious gems available "directly from those fabled mines in India"— an offer probably as dubious as the spelling.

care 1. Chambers 1985 and Raub 1987 remind us that the verb *care* is often followed by *for* and *about;* Chambers also mentions *to* and the infinitive.

. . . have always cared for patients beyond customary norms —Leonard Gross, *McCall's,* March 1971

. . . he and his brother were cared for by a guardian —*Current Biography,* October 1967

. . . to prove that the rest of the country really cares about their problems —Henry Ford II, *Michigan Business Rev.,* July 1968

... thought the United States would not care too much about a few missiles in Cuba —A. M. Rosenthal, *N.Y. Times Book Rev.,* 3 June 1973

... spent more time in church on Sundays than I care to remember —Mrs. Medgar Evers, *Ladies' Home Jour.,* September 1971

Was there anything he cared to say? —Paul Horgan, *Ladies' Home Jour.,* January 1971

2. The noun *care* is commonly followed by *for* or *of*.

... to provide medical care for the aged —*Current Biography,* October 1965

... discreetly, and with every care for her ... dignity —Doris Lessing, *Ms.,* April 1973

... the care of the aged and care of the insane —Paul Goodman, quoted in *Psychology Today,* November 1971

... leaving her patient in the care of his daughter —Daphne du Maurier, *Ladies' Home Jour.,* August 1971

careen, career The verbs *careen* and *career* look a lot alike, sound a lot alike, and to many people mean much the same thing. Disapproving usage writers hark back to the older (though still living) sense of *careen* which refers to leaning a boat over on its side to expose the keel for cleaning or repair. From this and from the intransitive nautical sense of *careen* that means "to heel over," Follett 1966, Bremner 1980, and Bryson 1984 conclude that any extended use of *careen* should involve sideways motion such as swaying, tilting, or rocking. And it is true that *careen* is used this way.

Cars rocketed out of the six tunnels ... and careened in wild zigzags —Mark Murphy, *New Yorker,* 18 June 1949

We were careening from side to side and going like nobody's business —Thomas B. Bluff, *N.Y. Times Mag.,* 6 June 1954

... the car careened around abrupt corners —E. L. Doctorow, *Loon Lake,* 1979

But it is also true that *careen,* influenced no doubt by *career* and also by the associated idea of speed that is apparent even in the examples of sideways motion above, often refers to rapid headlong movement.

... the taxi careened west on Forty-seventh Street ... (he had three minutes in which to make the train) —Philip Hamburger, *New Yorker,* 29 Mar. 1952

... and wind careened down the streets and past the corners —Lacey Fosburgh, *Cosmopolitan,* June 1976

Part of the problem in trying to pin down objectively the movement described by *careen* or *career* is that since the movement is headlong, reckless, or uncontrolled, some kind of sideways movement may be involved, actually or potentially. So it is often not clear exactly what a careening or careering object is doing. This indeterminacy may distress usage critics but seems not to bother most writers.

... the birds careen wildly —Claudia Cassidy, *Europe—On the Aisle,* 1954

A bus careened out of control over a precipice — *N.Y. Times,* 10 Apr. 1955

... everyone careens around on roller skates —Jane Howard, *N.Y. Times Book Rev.,* 11 May 1980

... oil-rich sheikhs careening over sand dunes in their ... four-wheel drives —Dora Jane Hamblin, *Smithsonian,* September 1983

... sending the craft careening out of control —J. Eberhart et al., *Science News,* 10 May 1986

... send him careering through the salons on a bicycle —*Time,* 8 Apr. 1946

... intoxicated cats careering through our houses — Frank Swinnerton, *Tokefield Papers,* 1949

... and birds career through its open space —Ward Just, *Atlantic,* June 1975

... causing high-performance military aircraft to career out of control —*Flight International,* 11 Sept. 1976

Figurative uses of *careen,* of which there are many, are equally imprecise.

... his mind veered away, careened back giddily to the rock on which he was sitting —Norman Mailer, *The Naked and the Dead,* 1948

The action careens across the ancient world, breathless in its pace —John Mason Brown, *Saturday Rev.,* 20 Dec. 1947

... suicidal Vietnam veteran who is careening through his last days on earth by staying high —Sara Blackburn, *N.Y. Times Book Rev.,* 9 Sept. 1973

... the book careens off into political interpretations —James Fallows, *Harper's,* February 1976

... we careened on toward Christmas —John Irving, *The Hotel New Hampshire,* 1981

Not all usage writers lament over the broadened meaning of *careen.* Harper's 1985 usage panel gives the "use of *careen* in the sense of to move fast with a lurching or swerving motion" an 87 percent vote of confidence. Reader's Digest 1983 approves of several extended senses (including a figurative use), adding sensibly: "Trying to discourage the use of perfectly legitimate extensions like this one is what earns 'usage experts' a bad name. Whatever its parentage, *careen* is a vivid and entirely satisfying word...."

The disapproving Follett, along with Colter 1981 and Kilpatrick 1984, says that the extended use of *careen* has elbowed out *career.* We have healthy evidence for recent use of *career,* however, so the takeover by *careen* is far from complete and may very well stay that way.

Another point expressed or implied by Follett, Gowers in Fowler 1965, and Evans 1962 is that the use of *careen* as a synonym for *career* is an Americanism. The OED Supplement calls it "Chiefly *U.S.,*" and as far as we can tell (since most of our citation-collecting is from American sources anyway), this is the case. So if you simply cannot accept the fact that the broadened uses of *careen* are here to stay, you might have to pack your bags and head for the more congenial clime of British English.

careful, careless 1. *Careful,* when used with a complement, is most often followed by the preposition *of* and a noun or a pronoun, or by an infinitive:

> At first she had been careful ... of him —Hugh MacLennan, *Two Solitudes,* 1945

> ... in most cases the savages were careful to leave Quaker families unmolested —W. R. Inge, *The Church in the World,* 1928

When *careful* is used to mean "exercising prudence," however, it may be followed by *about* or *with:*

> It is true that they generally are careful about money —John Fischer, *Harper's,* January 1969

> The thrifty Scot, ordinarily so careful with a dollar —W. A. Swanberg, *True,* June 1954

2. *Careless,* according to our evidence, is most often used with *of* when it takes a complement:

> Careless of all his advice, she swung at it ... and poled it far over the fence —E. L. Doctorow, *Loon Lake,* 1979

> ... he was careless of facts, misty in principles —J. J. Plumb, *N.Y. Times Mag.,* 11 Feb. 1973

3. Both *careful* and *careless* are also used with *in* followed by a noun or gerund. This use is less frequent than use with the other prepositions or with an infinitive dealt with above:

> ... was short in stature, deep-chested, careful in dress —*Dictionary of American Biography,* 1929

> Congreve's plays were deplorably careless in construction —Peter Forster, *London Calling,* 7 Apr. 1955

> ... who was as careless in handling his own money —*Dictionary of American Biography,* 1936

careful writer The careful writer is a fiction often invoked by usage commentators. Conveniently, the careful writer follows whatever precept the commentator is laying down at the moment. The example below is the only one we have in which the epithet is applied to an actual person:

> In a famous dictum by Nero Wolfe, that careful writer Rex Stout disallowed *contact* as an all-purpose verb —Barzun 1985

When you meet the careful writer in usage books, you should be careful to distinguish him from the good writer.

careless See CAREFUL, CARELESS.

care less See COULD CARE LESS, COULDN'T CARE LESS.

caret See CARAT, KARET, CARET.

case Sir Arthur Quiller-Couch in his book *On the Art of Writing* (1916)—a collection of lectures delivered at Cambridge in 1914 and 1915—includes a lecture in which he has a little fun with the jargon of bureaucrats, some of whom were evidently employed at Cambridge. The word that is the chief butt of the lecture is *case* in a few of its typical phrases. Although Copperud 1970 says that the use of *case* is "unforgettably ridiculed," the actual humor of the lecture depends first on the audacity

of tweaking the noses of the university examiners and second on the deliberate misconstrual of some harmlessly stodgy formula used by the poor clerk of a local board. If you are looking for unforgettable ridicule, you would do better to read Mark Twain on Fenimore Cooper.

In any case—to use one of the aspersed phrases—Quiller-Couch, once committed to print, became the source of a copious flow of imitation, from MacCracken & Sandison 1917 on. The usual criticism picks out one or two phrases and appends some comment like "wordy and usually unnecessary."

Copperud notes with some surprise that "these expressions seem immune to attack"—which simply means that writers regularly use the offending phrases without paying attention to the critics. So here—perhaps for the first time anywhere—you may see how real writers use some of the offending expressions.

In any case:

> ... others say, universities in any case are good for very litte —George W. Bonham, *Change,* October 1971

> In any case, it would take a genealogist some days clambering around a man's family tree to determine whether he was entitled to the suffix of esquire —Howard 1980

> ... under threat of a scandal which, in any case, would drive him out of public life —Samuel Hopkins Adams, *Success,* 1921

> He is physically so extraordinary, in any case, that nothing less than a life-size statue ... could convey his uniqueness —Robert Craft, *Harper's,* December 1968

In case:

> ... a literary party where one is expected to know all the guests but the host keeps murmuring their names in one's ear just in case —Humphrey Carpenter, *N.Y. Times Book Rev.,* 24 Apr. 1983

> ... and taking into consideration the vagaries of the English climate, I like to take some woollens just in case —Graham Greene, *Travels with My Aunt,* 1969

> And in case the President still thinks law and order and Vietnam are what count —Anne Chamberlin, *McCall's,* March 1971

> ... pledged mutual assistance in case either country engaged in hostilities —*Collier's Year Book,* 1949

In case of:

> ... presiding over the Senate, where he casts a vote in case of a tie —*Current Biography,* April 1966

> The roof must be completed in case of rain —Thomas J. Smith, *Yankee,* July 1968

> An underground passage gave safe access to a spring in case of need —*American Guide Series: Virginia,* 1941

In that case:

> He told me that he was not at the Writers' Workshop and in fact had no connection at all with the university. When I asked why in that case he was here, he looked at me with perplexity —Laurence Lafore, *Harper's,* October 1971

In that case, I'd change my money first and pay in British currency —Richard Joseph, *Your Trip to Britain,* 1954

He asked if, in that case, America would "maintain the adequate military, naval, and air forces" —Stephen E. Ambrose, *Johns Hopkins Mag.,* April 1966

The foregoing phrases are not easily removed, although sometimes they may be replaced by another phrase. *In the case of,* however, is a phrase that several handbooks believe can readily be done without or, as Copperud suggests, replaced by *concerning.* You will see in these next examples that you cannot always make the suggested expedients work. You may well be able to think of different, more workable revisions, though.

In the case of cancer or heart disease the only person who literally gets hurt is the one who failed to get to his doctor in time —Glenn V. Carmichael, *Ford Times,* September 1966

. . . asked if he would, in the case of an emergency, be willing to lend me some money —Jane Harriman, *Atlantic,* March 1970

. . . averring that leniency would be a mistake in the case of the confirmed young criminal —*Current Biography* 1947

In the case of the Hollywood writers, some of the accused took their case to the courts —*Collier's Year Book,* 1949

Posterity, if she doesn't ignore him altogether, is far more likely to confirm and even to emphasize the vulgar judgment of his contemporaries, as she has done in the case of Doyle and Holmes —*New Yorker,* 12 Feb. 1949

In these last few examples, the expression containing *case* can probably be revised for the better. If you try, remember that you are looking for an improvement, not just a substitution.

There are quite a number of so-called "magnetic hills" . . . located wherever the configuration of the landscape presents the illusion of nonexistent grades. It is usually a case of a slope of moderate steepness occurring between two steeper slopes —Donald A. Whiting, *Ford Times,* February 1968

If it is a truism that the quality of every college depends chiefly upon its faculty, it was even more the case at the Wyandanch College Center —Jerome M. Ziegler, *Change,* June 1972

. . . she wouldn't expect any payment. Which proved to be the case —Gail Cameron, *Ladies' Home Jour.,* August 1971

Each environmental problem requires a specific solution, even in cases where the products made are similar in nature —*Annual Report, National Lead Co.,* 1970

Conclusion: sometimes phrases with *case* are superfluous, sometimes they are long-winded, and sometimes they are neither. You have to decide each case on its merits.

casket, coffin It is perhaps a bit surprising to see comment on the use of the all-American euphemism *casket* still being published in the 1980s. But it is there in Harper 1985 (as also in the 1975 edition) and Bremner 1980.

The earliest citation in print is Nathaniel Hawthorne's disapproving notice of 1863: "a vile modern phrase" (OED Supplement). The usages that incurred Hawthorne's disapproval have so far escaped lexicographers. The OED Supplement reproduces an earlier citation (1849) from a letter written by a woman in North Carolina. Her use, however, is clearly metaphorical (the bracketed gloss was supplied by Norman Eliason, the editor of the book, *Tarheel Talk,* 1956, where the letter is cited):

. . . casket, which held this jewel [her dead friend], was worthy of it.

Eliason notes that aside from this single *casket,* the term used was *coffin* (p. 189); it is unlikely this single metaphor is the origin of the use to which Hawthorne objected. That must have come in around the time of the Civil War; Mencken 1936 notes that *case* competed with *casket* at this time, ultimately losing out. An 1869 commentator (Bache, *Vulgarisms*) thought the use of *casket* to be "trifling with a serious thing." The term was put on William Cullen Bryant's *Index Expurgatorius* (published in 1877 but compiled earlier) as a euphemism and carried from there into the style rules of various newspapers. It was still being disapproved at the *New York Times* by Theodore Bernstein in 1958 *(Watch Your Language).*

From around the turn of the century, the adoption of *casket* in preference to *coffin* was being urged by the undertaking trade, along with various other changes in terminology. Although usage commentators disparaged the term, and although the suspicion that a casket was more expensive than a coffin received public expression, the term nevertheless seems to have reached acceptance. There is no evidence that it raises an eyebrow anymore. Several sources—a trade source cited by Mencken, and Jessica Mitford, cited by the OED Supplement—point out that in the U.S. a casket is of rectangular design, while a coffin has the traditional tapered shape. *Coffin* is the standard term in British English.

casualty Partridge 1942, citing A. P. Herbert, strongly disapproves of the sense of *casualty* that means "a person killed or injured"; he would restrict it to its original meaning of "a serious or fatal accident." Copperud 1970 reports that all of his authorities consider the extended sense standard, and the OED Supplement dates it back to 1844. The objection would seem to be a dead issue. The extended sense has even sprung further extensions:

. . . those whose minds and livers fell casualty to the two-martini lunch —Michael Korda, *N.Y. Times,* 2 Nov. 1977

The TV season claimed its first casualty yesterday when ABC announced it was yanking its rapidly failing new comedy —*Baltimore Sun,* 12 Nov. 1981

. . . strongly suggests the need for new and better ways of handling the casualties of divorce —Daniel Goldstine, *N.Y. Times Book Rev.,* 24 July 1983

catachresis *Catachresis* is a term from classical rhetoric for "the use of a wrong word for the context." We present first a couple of examples of the thing:

There was quite an ecliptic collection of whale artifacts —*Antiques and the Arts Weekly,* 29 Oct. 1982

The Royals made three errors in the first five innings, but the Orioles failed to materialize on the mistakes —*Morning Union* (Springfield, Mass.) (AP), 17 Mar. 1987

The catachreses are the use of *ecliptic* for *eclectic* and *materialize* for *capitalize*.

Catachresis has become part of the jargon of 20th-century usage writers. It can be found in Fowler, and Partridge uses it with some frequency. It is a favorite word of John Simon's, and we have recent examples from him and from Philip Howard. Occasionally, other writers will flourish it as well.

Usage writers tend to apply the term loosely, using it as a sesquipedalian term of disparagement for whatever usage they choose not to approve. Fowler 1926, for instance, applies the term to the use of *mutual* where he would prefer *common*, as in "our mutual friend"—a long-established usage even in his day. Simon 1980 hangs it on the phrase "reasonably entranced," even though *reasonable* has a sense "moderate," which makes it difficult to tease out something objectionable from this use of the adverb. It has been pointed out at least once that usage writers themselves are not immune to the fault:

> *Catachresis* for instance is grammarians' jargon for using a word in a wrong sense. When grammarians call writing jargon merely because it is verbose, circumlocutory and flabby, they themselves commit the sin of catachresis —Gowers 1948

The derivative adjective is *catachrestic.*

catalyst   *Catalyst* is a term borrowed from chemistry and popularized, Reader's Digest 1983 believes, by its familiarity from high-school science classes. The word is commonly used metaphorically, usually meaning "an agent that provokes or speeds change." Two British commentators, Sir Bruce Fraser (in Gowers 1973) and Phythian 1979, worry that the metaphor may be misapplied. Fraser cites a British politician who spoke of an agreement that "would automatically act as a catalyst for bridging the gap." Similar examples exist in our files:

> I agree that government is the developmental catalyst necessary to bring the private sector to water — letter to editor, *Area Development,* May 1970

> . . . they've become either catalysts or pawns in schemes of those who stand to profit —Thomas Moran, *Woman's Wear Daily,* 15 Nov. 1976

What these somewhat blundering uses prove is that the metaphorical sense has become so well established that it is separated from its chemical beginnings, at least in the minds of some of its users. The examples that follow are more typical:

> . . . at most a catalyst accelerating a reaction which had begun in the embryonic hours of Christianity — Norman Mailer, *Harper's,* March 1971

> Some Westerners even envisage trade as a catalyst for liberalization in the USSR —Hedrick Smith, *Atlantic,* December 1974

> . . . taking lovers often is a catalyst for divorce — Albert H. Johnston, *Publishers Weekly,* 21 Apr. 1975

> The regimen provides some guests the catalyst they need for changing their life-styles —Jerry Kirshenbaum et al., *Sports Illustrated,* 7 Feb. 1983

Catalyst is commonly applied to a person who gets things going:

> The main thing is for me to be the catalyst and to let the viewers decide —David Frost, quoted in *People,* 1 Sept. 1975

> You've got to have somebody who's going to be a catalyst, to bring out the excitement in the other guy —a source at ESPN (television network), quoted in *TV Guide,* 15 July 1983

> . . . left-fielder and team catalyst Gary Matthews — Craig Neff, *Sports Illustrated,* 13 May 1985

> She acts as a catalyst to overcome this lack —*Times Literary Supp.,* 22 Oct. 1971

catastrophe, catastrophes   Copperud 1970, 1980 notes that these are sometimes misspelled *catastrophy* and *catastrophies.* Our files contain one example of the first and four of the second. A sly Merriam-Webster editor some thirty years ago discovered that six members of the editorial staff at that time would have used the plural *-phies.* Don't you do it.

catch   *Catch* is a verb with a muddled history. It originally came to us from French, with regular principal parts—equivalent to *catched*—and with a meaning of "hunt, chase." Somehow it got muddled with an English verb that was the ancestor of *latch* (onto), from which it acquired its primary surviving meanings and an analogical past and past participle *caught.* The original meaning was taken up by a slightly later French import, the ancestor of *chase,* and *catch* was left with the meaning of *latch* and the competing verb forms *catched* and *caught* (while *latch,* in the meantime, had become regular, as it is today).

The fickleness of literary usage with regard to *catched* and *caught* is curious. Lamberts 1972 notes *caught* in Shakespeare and the King James Bible; *catched* in Bunyan, Steele, Defoe, and Isaac Watts. Shakespeare did use *caught,* but used *catched* once in a while; so did Spenser. Ben Jonson used both, but Marlowe in his plays and Sidney in his poems used *caught* only. Milton used both (but mostly *caught* in poetry), Donne used both, and Pope used both. Samuel Johnson seems to have used *caught* in his poems and *catched* in conversation. Dryden and Swift, at least in their poetry, used only *caught.* After Johnson and Boswell it is hard to find literary *catched.* Wordsworth, Coleridge, Byron, Shelley, and Keats all use *caught.*

Richard Grant White 1870 wrote that "no good writer now uses" *catched* for *caught.* He seems to be right, even now. *Catched* seriously contested *caught* in the 17th and 18th centuries but has now receded pretty much to dialectal use. The information in the Dictionary of American Regional English shows *catched* widespread but infrequent; *caught* is the prevalent form, even in speech, and the only form used seriously in writing.

catchup   See CATSUP, KETCHUP, CATCHUP.

category   Copperud 1970 disparages the use of *category* in connections other than the scientific and philosophical and buttresses his opinion with that of three other writers, one of whom is reported to concede grudgingly that *category* in the sense of "class" is standard in the U.S. Shaw 1975 also concedes that the "class" use exists, but insists that *category* is really proper only in science or philosophy.

Now had these experts looked in the OED, they would have found that *category* has been used in the sense of "class" since 1660, and further that such use was stigmatized as "bad English" by a Lord Granville as far back as 1883. If you doubt that this horse, still being flogged by some usage writers, is truly dead, here are more than enough examples to demonstrate that the use is standard:

The impromptu writing must have . . . declined faster and faster into the questionable category — Thomas Carlyle, review of Lockhart's *Life of Sir Walter Scott,* in *London and Westminster Rev.,* 1838

. . . a rundown on the average proportions of our after-tax spending dollars Americans are now laying out in each major spending category —Sylvia Porter, *Ladies' Home Jour.,* August 1971

Dr. Harper's generosity in money matters, personal and official, was embarrassing in both categories — Robert Morss Lovett, *All Our Years,* 1948

It isn't so broad a category as postwar fiction —Malcolm Cowley, *Harper's,* April 1953

. . . none of the writings of the fathers of the English Church belongs to the category of speculative philosophy —T. S. Eliot, "Lancelot Andrewes" (1926), in *Selected Essays,* 1932

. . . in the realm (or category . . .) of women's literature —Joyce Carol Oates, *N.Y. Times Book Rev.,* 5 June 1977

In speech, *category* is frequently used with *fall in* or *into:*

I don't think those things fall in the same category —Senator Lowell Weicker, radio interview, 28 Nov. 1975

Some fall into that category; some do not —Representative Christopher Dodd, radio interview, 10 Sept. 1981

cater In current American usage, the predominant preposition after *cater* is *to:*

. . . stores that cater more to lower- and middle-income customers —Isadore Barmash, *N.Y. Times,* 12 Mar. 1980

So, our government, always on the alert to cater to the peace of mind of its citizens . . . —Goodman Ace, *Saturday Rev.,* 6 Mar. 1971

Both were in any case catering to a great appetite for self-expression —Marya Mannes, *The Reporter,* 28 Apr. 1953

In British usage the predominant preposition is *for:*

. . . in this book he caters for professionals and amateurs —Russell Meiggs, *Times Literary Supp.,* 19 Nov. 1982

The pulps catered for a large audience, literate but not literary —Julian Symons, *Bloody Murder,* 1985

Australia's large public hospitals are operating to capacity catering for road accident victims —James E. Breheny, *The Age* (Melbourne), 14 Apr. 1975

To is also found in British English, perhaps a bit more often than *for* is found in American:

. . . when most British companies had not even thought seriously about catering to French tastes — *The Economist,* 16 Mar. 1974

Showmen is devoid of politics. They hain't got any principles! They know how to cater for the public — Artemus Ward, "Interview with President Lincoln," 1861, in *The Mirth of a Nation,* ed. Walter Blair & Raven I. McDavid, Jr., 1983

. . . the plutocratic St. Moritzers for whom our popular dramatists cater —T. S. Eliot, "A Dialogue on Dramatic Poetry" (1928), in *Selected Essays,* 1932

How this largely divergent practice came about is uncertain. We do know from the OED that *for* came first; it was used by Shakespeare:

. . . providently caters for the sparrow —*As You Like It,* 1600

To is first attested in 1840 in the writing of Thackeray:

Catering to the national taste and vanity —*The Paris Sketch Book*

Since the *to* originally turned up in the figurative use of *cater,* Murray suggests it may have been influenced by the use of *to* with the figurative sense of *pander.* Whatever the cause, most writers of British English follow Shakespeare, and most Americans follow Thackeray.

Catholic, catholic A number of commentators note that the capitalized *Catholic* is used by Christian institutions other than the Roman Catholic Church, but in American use it is usually taken to mean "Roman Catholic" unless otherwise modified.

Books in the tradition of what we sometimes call "the Catholic novel" —Doris Grumbach, *Saturday Rev.,* 4 Mar. 1978

. . . memories of growing up Catholic on the South Side of Chicago —Martin Levin, *N.Y. Times Book Rev.,* 22 Apr. 1973

The lowercase *catholic* does not refer to religion but to broadness of tastes or interests:

. . . they demonstrated a catholic taste in what they selected for the different rooms of this house —Rita Reif, *N.Y. Times,* 10 May 1979

. . . a model of how to be Left without being gauche. A man of catholic attainments and no side —Alex Hamilton, *The Guardian,* 3 Nov. 1973

. . . one of the most catholic of physicians in his willingness to try unorthodox methods —Gilbert Cant, *N.Y. Times Mag.,* 3 Feb. 1974

catsup, ketchup, catchup The spellings *catsup* and *ketchup* are used with about equal frequency; *catchup* is not as common as the other two, but it is used; all three spellings are standard. You can accept this statement as given or, if you feel contentious, you can advocate one of these spellings over the others. Your choice might be based on the brand you eat (Del Monte calls it *catsup,* Heinz and Hunts call it *ketchup*), the writers you read

(J. D. Salinger and John Dos Passos used the spelling *catsup,* Eudora Welty and Norman Mailer used *ketchup,* William Faulkner used both, and Ernest Hemingway used *catchup*), or just personal preference.

causal *as*   See AS 1.

cause   **1.** Copperud 1970 says that the expression "the cause . . . is due to" is redundant. Perhaps it is, but we have no reason to believe that anyone uses it, at least in print. We have examined our entire file of the citations collected for *cause* during the past half century without finding a single example. H. W. Fowler seems to have found it once in a British newspaper sometime before 1926. Perhaps it is time to forget the matter.
2. The noun *cause* may be followed by the prepositions *of* and *for:*

> . . . used his fame to champion the cause of the hand-icapped —*Current Biography,* January 1966

> . . . New Englanders realize that the cause for land preservation is not yet hopeless —Eleanor Sterling, *Yankee,* July 1968

> . . . admitted that recent bank failures were a cause of concern —*Current Biography,* July 1965

> . . . there would be little cause for apprehension at the present time —Robert A. Nisbet, *Psychology Today,* March 1971

caution   When the verb *caution* is used with a preposition, it is generally followed by *against:*

> . . . I intend directly to introduce myself, caution you against certain possible interpretations of my name —John Barth, *The Floating Opera,* 1956

Less often, *caution* is used with *about:*

> . . . Mother had cautioned them more than once about saying things like that —Mary Austin, *Starry Adventure,* 1931

Infrequently, *caution* is found with *of:*

> . . . Professor Hay cautioned of a great debate on how far we should look on the spread of Renaissance values —*Times Literary Supp.,* 21 Mar. 1968

Caution is also used with *to* in both positive and negative constructions:

> . . . encouraged her in this plan but cautioned her to involve Dr. Taylor in any reassignments —*AAUP Bulletin,* December 1967

> She cautioned Miss Pollitzer not to show them to anyone else —*Current Biography,* February 1964

cavalry   See CALVARY, CAVALRY.

ceiling, floor   The abuse of underlying metaphors when *ceiling* means "a prescribed upper limit" and, to a lesser extent, when *floor* means "a prescribed lower limit" is primarily a British concern. We find Gowers 1954, Sir Bruce Fraser in Gowers 1973, Gowers in Fowler 1965, Howard 1980, Bryson 1984, and Longman 1984 all working the issue over. With commendable economy of effort both Fowler 1965 and Howard 1980 use the sentence "The effect of this announcement is that the total figure of £410 million can be regarded as a floor as well as a ceiling," and Bryson 1984 credits

them both while rerunning it yet again. The mixed metaphors in this example, as well as talk about raising, lowering, and removing floors and ceilings, simply show that the meaning has become so well established its metaphorical origin has been forgotten. You can find some amusing examples in the books mentioned above, if you are interested. Copperud 1980 opines: "Regardless, usefulness has solidly established both terms." We can only agree. Most of our recent examples do not contain a problem. Here is a sample:

> . . . the establishment by Congress of a ceiling on outlays and a floor on revenues —Edwin L. Dale, Jr., *N.Y. Times Mag.,* 22 Aug. 1976

> . . . our subsidy programs must be expanded by raising the ceilings on both income and price —Abraham Ribicoff, *Saturday Rev.,* 22 Apr. 1972

> . . . faintly better dressed than the older generation, with a faintly higher ceiling on his ambitions — Penelope Gilliatt, *New Yorker,* 11 Sept. 1971

> Many banks . . . have threatened to move their credit card operations to other states unless New York raises or abandons the ceiling on consumer credit charges —Karen W. Arenson, *N.Y. Times,* 16 Nov. 1980

celebrant, celebrator   *Celebrant* is a 19th-century word that was originally applied to one who celebrates a Mass or some other religious rite. *Celebrater* is a 17th-century word for a person who celebrates anything; the spelling *celebrator* superseded *celebrater* in the 19th century. Sometime in the 1930s, apparently, *celebrant* began to be used in the more general sense. Our earliest citation is from 1937:

> Half a million celebrants tramped the streets from dawn to dusk today when New Orleans cast aside everyday cares to observe the century-old Mardi Gras —*N.Y. Times* (AP), 10 Feb. 1937

This use had perhaps been prefigured by Yeats' extension of the religious sense:

> . . . Velasquez seemed the first bored celebrant of boredom —William Butler Yeats, *The Trembling of the Veil,* 1922

Yeats' book, however, was privately printed and probably had but a small circulation; it seems to have had no effect on British use of *celebrant.* The broader sense has been missed by the OED Supplement and is almost entirely American.
The use established itself quickly enough:

> Railroads run special excursion trains, on which celebrants eat and sleep while the Round-Up is in progress —*American Guide Series: Oregon,* 1940

> Some of the celebrants had been flown in by a former R.C.A.F. flying instructor —*Time,* 11 Feb. 1946

> The beer is magnificent; 10¢ for the biggest glass in Europe (and for celebrants, the biggest hangover, too) —Temple Fielding, *Fielding's New Travel Guide to Europe,* rev. ed., 1949

> Printing took Walt from a Long Island farm to Brooklyn and to New York, whose celebrant he became —Henry Seidel Canby, *Turn West, Turn East,* 1951

The streets reek with wine, garlic, and smoking olive oil, while the torches flare down on a sea of yelling, reeling celebrants —Carl de Suze, *Atlantic,* September 1953

If anyone objects to a subjective appraisal . . . it should not be his enthusiastic celebrants —Richard McLaughlin, *American Mercury,* February 1953

Whitman was also a celebrant of the West as natural innocence —*Times Literary Supp.,* 17 Sept. 1954

The highlight for all, however, is the monthly party for members whose birthdays occur that month. After a program and just before the cake, each celebrant speaks briefly —Howard A. Rusk, M.D., *N.Y. Times,* 19 Dec. 1954

All of these examples (and others in our files) have one thing in common—they were printed before Theodore Bernstein discovered that this use was an error (*Winners & Sinners,* 19 Jan. 1955). Evans 1957 also noted the usage, calling it "at the best ambiguous." It is not, however, ambiguous in context. Compare the examples above with these typical examples of the religious celebrant:

... the people themselves, the celebrants officiating in liturgical rites and feasts —Thomas Merton, *Center Mag.,* March 1968

The Conference opened with a celebration of Holy Communion in the Cathedral at which the Rt. Rev. Walter H. Gray, Bishop of Connecticut, was celebrant —*Hartford Times,* 2 Jan. 1954

To make the Eucharist depend for its validity on the episcopal ordination of the celebrant —*Times Literary Supp.,* 10 June 1955

Celebrator, the word recommended as a replacement for the broadened *celebrant,* is still in use but is not quite as frequent as *celebrant:*

... one of the celebrators is 50 years old —*My Weekly Reader,* 18 Jan. 1952

... still others consider him the celebrator of a Third Sex —Leslie A. Fiedler, *Encounter,* January 1955

... as facile celebrators of Vatican II thought their church could do —Garry Wills, *New York,* 2 Aug. 1971

No difference in the level of formality between *celebrant* and *celebrator* is detectable from our citations. Both are in reputable use, with *celebrant* slightly more frequent.

... or a better celebrant of its variety —Philip Larkin, *Required Writing,* 1983

... celebrators feast on corn bread, fried potatoes — Susan Carey, *Wall Street Jour.,* 26 Apr. 1983

... women have been America's chief celebrants of the art —Nancy Goldner, *Dance News,* May 1982

... gaily garbed celebrators parading through the streets —James Kelly, *Time,* 13 May 1985

Celtic As part of the name of a sports team, such as the Boston Celtics, this is pronounced \\'sel-tik\\. You will also hear this pronunciation in other contexts, and at times from very well-educated speakers. But the closer you get to circles substantively concerned with Celtic lore and languages, the more likely you are to hear \\'kel-tik\\.

cement, concrete Some time around the year 1300, according to the OED, a writer described a certain kind of clay as being strong as iron, stone, or cement. This writer was not sent a corrective letter pointing out that he must have meant concrete, since cement is only one ingredient of concrete—because the word *concrete* had not yet entered the language. Modern writers are not so lucky. Let a writer in the *Wall Street Journal* mention dragging a carton "across the cement floor," and someone will send a letter to the editor, giving the information above and (odds are) adding a recipe for concrete into the bargain.

The first thing to realize here is that if confusion exists, it lies solely in the realm of words, not things. The contractor who laid the floor had no difficulty in distinguishing the material cement from the material concrete. And once the floor is laid, what you call it is of little consequence. You can call it "cement," as our ancestors did, or "concrete," as the letter writer does; the floor remains unaffected.

As a term for a mixture of ingredients that sets hard when combined with water, *cement* is a term some 500 years older than *concrete. Concrete* began as an adjective, and was not used as a noun of the building material until the 19th century. *Concrete* is a more frequently used word than *cement.* In general, as distinguished from technical, writing, both are most common in figurative uses:

... the social cement that held the Fore hamlets together —E. Richard Sorenson, *Smithsonian,* May 1977

There were boys and young men all over the halls, lounging, smoking, spitting, talking loudly in the concrete accents of the New York streets —Irwin Shaw, *The Young Lions,* 1948

On this symbolic issue, he declared, his feet were set in cement —Richard J. Whalen, *N.Y. Times Mag.,* 22 Feb. 1976

... a mythology is being slowly, steadily, set in concrete —Eric Sevareid, *Saturday Rev.,* 2 Oct. 1976

Property having been the cement of their marriage —Sonya O'Sullivan, *Cosmopolitan,* April 1976

... they limit our vision and persuade us that we can exercise choice over that which is set in the concrete of the present —*Harper's,* December 1971

In reference to the building material, we find *concrete* currently more frequent than *cement,* quite possibly because of the increased use of concrete as a building material. Both words are still used of some familiar things:

The cement floors and sheetrock walls ring with industry and joy —Judson Jerome, *Change,* September 1971

... ochre-stained concrete floors —*Southern Living,* November 1971

Tap . . . tap . . . tap.
Heels on the cement walk
—John Rechy, *Evergreen,* December 1967

. . . garden apartments situated on a hilly mound, with a pond and concrete paths —John Coyne & Thomas Herbert, *Change,* Winter 1971–1972

But in some combinations only *concrete* is found:

The white beams crossing white beams, all of pre-stressed concrete —Horace Sutton, *Saturday Rev.,* December 1978

Conclusion: the use of *cement* to refer to various building materials now mostly known as *concrete* has been around for some 600 years. Objection to its use, in other than technical contexts, in such combinations as "cement floors" or "cement walks" is pedantic. However, more people are using *concrete* than *cement* to describe such things these days, and there is certainly nothing wrong either with maintaining the technical distinction in general writing.

censor, censure, censer   We have in our collection as many as 15 handbooks, from 1917 to 1984, warning against confusing *censor* with *censure.* A few toss in *censer* for good measure. A couple say the confusion is common but not where it is common. We have not a single example of such confusion in our files. Maybe students muddle them by poor spelling. If adults confuse them, however, they seem to be smart enough to look in a dictionary before committing to print. You should do the same if you have doubts.

center   The intransitive verb *center* is idiomatically used with the prepositions *on, upon, around, round, about, in,* and *at:*

I wanted the Heisman, but my whole life wasn't centered on it —Jim Plunkett, quoted in *Sports Illustrated,* 23 Jan. 1984

. . . the town was a close-built brick huddle centered on a black river —John Updike, *Bech is Back,* 1982

By May her thoughts were centered on him —Garrison Keillor, *Lake Wobegon Days,* 1985

. . . the play centers upon the death of an eight-year-old flute-playing shepherd boy —*Current Biography,* March 1967

The attack, slanderous and vile, centered around her prison story —Iris Noble, "First Woman Reporter," in *Dreams and Decisions,* ed. Carl B. Smith et al., 1983

The novel itself is centered around a Norwegian village hostelry —Maxwell Geismar, *N.Y. Herald Tribune Book Rev.,* 7 Apr. 1940

One group of apparent ironies, we noted, centred round the deflation of emotional considerations by practical ones —Ian Watt, *The Rise of the Novel,* 1957

His delusions centered about money —John Updike, *Couples,* 1968

. . . the automobile that the accident seemed to center about was a 1932 Ford V-8 operated by one James Thurberg —James Thurber, letter, August 1935

. . . every literary movement centers about a political program —George Orwell, *New Republic,* 14 July 1941

. . . over 70 per cent of our expanding population continuing to center in the nation's major metropolitan areas —Sylvia Porter, *Springfield* (Mass.) *Daily News,* 13 Aug. 1969

. . . the love interest centers in Henry's chronic courtship of Beatrix —John E. Tilford, Jr., *PMLA,* September 1952

. . . for any interval $[-a,a]$ centered at the origin — School Mathematics Study Group, *Calculus, Part II,* 1965

Then I is simply an interval in S centered at 0 — Casper Goffman, *Mathematics Mag.,* January 1974

The OED evidence, from the 17th century to the 19th century, shows primarily *center in* but includes some citations with *upon, on,* and *around.* Current American usage favors *on* and *around. About* has strong literary backing but is not as frequent as *around. Upon* is occasional; *round* is British. *In* seems to be less used than it was in the past. *At* is primarily mathematical.

Beginning sometime in the 1920s, *center around* and (by implication) *center round* and *center about* were attacked as illogical. Most of the critics merely assert the illogic of *center around* without explanation or demonstration, and some (mostly contemporary college handbooks) do not even assert; they simply tell us that "many" or "some people" or people "generally" consider it illogical. One who does elaborate a bit is Theodore Bernstein, for whom *center around* was a favorite subject (he dealt with it in *Winners & Sinners* from 1956 until at least 1969 and devoted an article to it in his 1965 book). But to make his argument he has to claim that intransitive *center* possesses only a single narrow meaning, "to be collected or gathered at a point," and that, because of the idea of *point,* such a meaning requires *in* or *on* or *at.* Neither Evans 1962 nor Barnard 1979 mentions Bernstein, but both discussions show how inadequate his definition is: many centers are not points in the mathematical or any other sense, nor does the meaning of the verb always involve gathering or collecting. Probably no definition much less broad than "to have a center" (picking up the varied meanings of *center* the noun) is really adequate to the actual intransitive use of the verb. And this definition will easily allow any of the prepositions illustrated above.

Bremner 1980 rejects *center around* because "it is physically impossible to *center around.*" His observation must be true, since citations for *center around* tend not to refer to anything physical. But it does not follow that one should therefore always use *center on,* as Bremner claims.

As you can see, the logic of those who call *center around* illogical is itself open to some question. But questionable or sound, logic is simply not the point. *Center around* is a standard idiom, as commentators increasingly concede (for example, Harper 1975, 1985, Chambers 1985, Ebbitt & Ebbitt 1982), even when they prefer another combination. You can use it freely, if you want to. *Center on,* however, is more common in current American use and is also standard. In addition, *revolve* and similar verbs will combine satisfactorily with *around* in many contexts where *center* and a particle typically appear. There is no lack of alternatives here.

centimeter   See HYPERFOREIGNISMS; KILOMETER.

ceremonial, ceremonious   *Ceremonious* is a word brought in from the French in the 16th century. It was first used as a synonym for *ceremonial,* which had been brought in from the French in the 14th century. George Campbell, in his 1776 *Philosophy of Rhetoric,* seems to have been the first person to try to distinguish the two; he disparaged the use of *ceremonious* as a synonym for *ceremonial* and said that *ceremonious* properly related to a form of civility and *ceremonial* to a religious rite. No one in the 19th century seems to have followed up on Campbell.

Fowler 1926 revived the question, but was apparently unaware of Campbell's distinction, which he could have elaborated slightly to the advantage of his own article, had he known it. Fowler begins with a distinction that initially seems clear enough, relating *ceremonial* to the countable use of *ceremony* ("a piece of ritual") and *ceremonious* to the use that is not countable ("attention to forms"), but the following discussion and example are not entirely transparent.

Later commentators, including Copperud 1970, 1980, Heritage 1969, 1982, Longman 1984, Harper 1985, Shaw 1975, and Reader's Digest 1983, have concentrated primarily on trying to make Fowler's treatment clear. Sometimes they have oversimplified, as Shaw 1975 does by saying *ceremonial* applies to things and *ceremonious* to people and things. As we shall see, both adjectives are applied to persons and to things.

Without trying to discuss and exemplify all the distinctions of meaning that dictionaries show, let us indicate the general tendencies of the two words. We will do this by revising Campbell's distinction somewhat. *Ceremonious* tends to be used in a way that suggests behavior while *ceremonial* tends to be used so as to suggest compliance or involvement with a ritual, which may be civil or personal as well as religious. This distinction is perhaps easiest to see in the application of the words to people:

> A large percent of the poultry products in the large cities must be ceremonially butchered. It is a matter of record that many of these ceremonial butchers . . . —Thurman W. Arnold, *The Bottlenecks of Business,* 1940

> He was not a very ceremonious beau; he never sent her flowers or whispered silly things in her ear — Louis Auchincloss, *Atlantic,* December 1949

The same distinction can be seen when the words are applied to a person's speech:

> He read in a synthetic ceremonial tone of voice that sounded preposterous as well as insincere, but he was conducting the marriage ceremony precisely as he had conducted countless previous ones —James T. Farrell, *What Time Collects,* 1964

> . . . his ceremonious diction wore the aspect of pomposity —Sir Winston Churchill, *Maxims and Reflections,* 1949

As generally applied, *ceremonial* tends to be the everyday adjective relating to any kind of ceremony, religious or otherwise:

> True ceremonial centers sprang up all over central and north-central Peru —Edward P. Lanning, *Peru Before the Incas,* 1967

> . . . the ceremonial role of flowers at weddings and funerals —Genevieve Stuttaford, *Publishers Weekly,* 6 Sept. 1976

> . . . an Administration which seems to conceive its role as a ceremonial one —Haynes Johnson, *The Progressive,* December 1969

> On ceremonial occasions, such as my grandfather's birthday or Christmas —Osbert Lancaster, *All Done from Memory,* 1953

Ceremonious tends to emphasize actions and behavior:

> . . . just as a priest kneels before an altar piled with oranges and bread and performs some ceremonious hand flourishes —Robert Craft, *Stravinsky,* 1972

> . . . the cold and ceremonious politeness of her curtsey and address to his friend —Jane Austen, *Pride and Prejudice,* 1813

> . . . the ceremonious extinguishing of the candles — Logan Pearsall Smith, *All Trivia,* 1934

> . . . love's perfection is what in more ceremonious days was called rapture or bliss —George P. Elliott, *Harper's,* September 1970

> . . . wrapped in a ceremonious and almost awkward reserve —Norman Douglas, *Siren Land,* 1911

> He left her on her doorstep with a ceremonious little bow —Louis Auchincloss, *A Law for the Lion,* 1953

Ceremonious is sometimes used to emphasize the meaninglessness of the ritual performed:

> The cold bath that he took each morning was ceremonious—it was sometimes nothing else since he almost never used soap —John Cheever, *The Wapshot Chronicle,* 1957

> "Most standardized tests are by and large ceremonious," charged Edys Quellmalz of the Center for the Study of Evaluation —*Council-Grams,* September 1982

In broad terms, then, *ceremonious* tends to stress a way of acting, doing, or behaving while *ceremonial* serves as the simple adjective for *ceremony.* This example shows typical uses in successive sentences:

> The Zuñi are a ceremonious people, a people who value sobriety and inoffensiveness above all other virtues. Their interest is centred upon their rich and complex ceremonial life —Ruth Benedict, *Patterns of Culture,* 1934

The broad generalizations are attended, however, with a couple of complications. First we have instances in which perhaps either word might have been chosen, and some people would no doubt have chosen the one that the author did not:

> . . . Owner Fleitz marched off with the three-foot silver trophy, after a ceremonious ducking in the refuse-filled Almendares River —*Time,* 9 Dec. 1946

> Napoleon rarely appeared in public. . . . When he did emerge, it was in a ceremonial manner, with an escort of six dogs —George Orwell, *Animal Farm,* 1945

The second complication is frequency of use. Our files show *ceremonial* to be used more often than *ceremonious.* The Brown Corpus statistics in Kučera & Francis 1967 tend to confirm our own numbers. *Ceremonial* seems to have reclaimed the territory where Campbell saw conflicting usage in the 18th century. It may possibly be spreading into areas where *ceremonious* would ordinarily have been used until recently. Only time will tell. You, in the meantime, will be perfectly safe if your usage is in general accord with the broad outlines of use described and illustrated here.

certain 1. A large majority of the Heritage 1969 usage panel found nothing wrong with the construction "nothing is more certain. . . ." This question is the echo of an old objection to the use of adverbs with *certain* on the gounds that *certain* is an absolute adjective. A couple of older books say this:

> There are no degrees of certainty —G. M. Hyde, *Handbook for Newspaper Workers,* 1926

> That which is *certain* is sure, and therefore does not admit of comparison —Vizetelly 1922

The fact that the usage panel was unimpressed shows that the issue is dead. We have plenty of evidence of standard use:

> The summer traveler is almost certain to see a mirage —*American Guide Series: Texas,* 1940

> . . . was reasonably certain that his invention was original —M. M. Musselman, *Atlantic,* October 1945

> . . . finds his magnetic compass a less certain guide —Lawrence Lafore, *Harper's,* October 1971

> . . . if one were more certain that education and ability were identical —Ivar Berg, *Change,* September 1971

2. Cook 1985 notes that *certain* can be used ambiguously. All the same, the "uncertain" use of *certain* is one of its chief uses:

> . . . "average" American men, fairly good-looking, of a certain height —Joyce Carol Oates, *Harper's,* April 1972

> . . . as a result of the acceptance of certain miracles —*Times Literary Supp.,* 2 Apr. 1971

> New York's nightpeople of a certain age and condition indulged themselves —Judith Crist, *New York,* 15 Nov. 1971

The OED Supplement traces "of a certain age" back to the middle of the 18th century and notes that this use of *certain* was popular in euphemistic phrases, such as "in a certain condition" for *pregnant* and "a certain disease" for *venereal disease.* Euphemistic use has declined. The "specific but unspecified" notion, however, continues in vigorous use, and it is very popular in such places as annual reports:

> . . . problems that had been creating strains in certain areas of manufacturing —*Annual Report, American Can Co.,* 1970

> . . . remains in effect at certain locations —*Annual Report, Owens-Illinois,* 1970

> In addition, certain other companies were acquired —*Annual Report, Borden Co.,* 1970

certainly Three editions of Strunk & White (1959, 1972, 1979) contain an objection to the indiscriminate use of *certainly* as an intensive. The admonition carries no specific examples and is vaguely worded; it is not very clear what the usage to be avoided is. However, as this is an issue surviving from the 1920s and 1930s, we can get a more definite idea from older sources. Jensen 1935 objects to "we *certainly* had a good time" and Whipple 1924 to "it is *certainly* true" and "we will *certainly* do so." We also have a couple of newspaper clippings from the 1930s that say about the same thing. If you look at the expressions objected to, you can easily understand why this is a dead issue. The expressions are perfectly standard in speech and are common enough in writing:

> This is certainly true in the case of medicine —T. R. McConnell, *AAUP Bulletin,* September 1969

> I would certainly like to work in journalism for a while —James Brady, quoted in *Book Digest,* February 1978

> . . . not many persons in the Roman world could have afforded them since they were certainly extremely costly —*Times Literary Supp.,* 18 Dec. 1969

> . . . it is certainly true that the set of integers is a subset of itself —Mary P. Dolciani et al., *Modern Algebra and Trigonometry,* 1973

certificated A correspondent whose letter is printed in Safire 1984 expresses dismay at the participial adjective *certificated* applied to a person who has been given a certificate. This correspondent is a bit late coming to the discovery of the term:

> . . . they enter the normal school where they remain two years as with us, and then become certificated teachers —*Jour. of Education,* vol. 18, 1883

Certificated does not appear to compete much with *certified;* its use is largely limited to education (in both British and American English) and air transportation. A few examples of use:

> . . . a certificated parachute technician —Charles A. Zweng, *Parachute Technician,* 1944

> . . . the certificated airlines have carried more cargo —*Air Transportation,* December 1948

> Certificated teachers used the tawse to enforce discipline —Mary Paterson, *Scots Mag.,* February 1956

> . . . the steel-nosed Captain Morgan (pirate and certificated teacher) —*Times Literary Supp.,* 30 Nov. 1967

> . . . moved to England, where she studied ballet for 11 years, actually becoming a certificated teacher — Vincent Canby, *N.Y. Times,* 11 Mar. 1973

Since *certificated* has been in use for at least a century (the verb *certificate* itself is attested as early as 1818 in British English), there is little point in complaining about it. It is the correct term in a small number of applications and can otherwise be ignored.

cesarean, caesarean The first spelling, *cesarean,* is the one now most frequently used in medical writing; *caesarean* is also acceptable. The spellings with an *-ian* termination are considerably less frequent but not wrong. The *c* is not usually capitalized.

chaff, chafe Copperud 1970, 1980 and Bryson 1984 warn against confusing *chaff* with *chafe*. Since, in the senses cited, *chaff* means "to tease good-naturedly" and *chafe* "to irritate, vex," you might well wonder how the words could be confused. Copperud gives us an example: "The mayor was chaffing at his confinement...." The example makes things clearer—this is an intransitive sense we are dealing with, not the transitive ones cited. And, in fact, this problem does not involve the 19th-century verb *chaff* that means "tease, banter" at all.

It appears from evidence in the OED that back in the bad old days before printers—and schoolmasters in their wake—had normalized English spelling, the verb we now know as *chafe* was also spelled *chaff*, among many other ways. We can find this double *-f* spelling in Caxton, Sterne, and others. The OED says the spelling was fairly common from the 16th to the 19th century, and Webster's Third lists it as an archaic variant.

The sense of *chafe* in which the *chaff* spelling seems to turn up occasionally is the one that means "to feel or show irritation or discontent." Here are a couple of examples of it in the usual spelling:

> There are scientists, however, who chafe at such restrictions —Otto Friedrich, *Time,* 10 Sept. 1984

> ... who for years has chafed under the burden of a WASP culture —Alfred Kazin, *Atlantic,* January 1983

Here are three examples with the double *-f* spelling:

> At that time the German army was chaffing under conservative policies of the old-line generals —*Commonweal,* 16 Feb. 1940

> With much of Europe chaffing under the growing U.S. economic domination —Charles A. Wells, *Between the Lines,* 1 Jan. 1967

> ... and he is chaffing today because of the 26 per cent service charge on his hotel bill —Robert Craft, *Stravinsky,* 1972

These occasional occurrences—we have only three to dozens and dozens of *chafe*—suggest that the old spelling is still used once in a great while, that it is not so much archaic as just quite rare. You can use it, if it looks and sounds right to you, but do so with the knowledge that it is rare and is likely to be thought a misspelling or a confusion.

chain reaction Your dictionary can tell you that *chain reaction,* in general (not technical) terms, means "a series of events so related to each other that each one initiates the next." This notion underlies the use of the word in physics and such figurative uses as this one:

> ... ploughed into the car ahead, starting a 10-car chain reaction that left eight people seriously injured —Eric Timm, *New Zealand Woman's Weekly,* 6 Jan. 1975

Copperud 1964, 1970, 1980 complains, however, that *chain reaction* is often misused in being applied to instances in which events do not follow one from another. He cites as an example (based on one given in Bernstein 1965) a report of a single event that set off a chain reaction of telephone calls—in other words, a rapid succession of events, all following a single cause but not following one from the other. We find a similar use in this report on race riots in 1967:

> The worst came during a 2-week period in July, first in Newark and then in Detroit. Each set off a chain reaction in neighboring communities —*Report of the National Advisory Commission on Civil Disorders,* 1968

We need to notice two things here. First, Copperud is measuring uses like these by dictionary definitions and no dictionary seems to recognize such use. Second, this is a figurative use, not a literal use. A figurative use can be inspired by any of several aspects of a literal term and not every writer will think of the same one. The Kerner Commission report quoted above used *chain reaction* metaphorically for a series of similar events that were triggered by a primary event and that happened in rapid succession, even though they were not dependent one upon the next. Another aspect of a chain reaction is its cumulative effect:

> West Berlin's political crisis could start a chain reaction undermining the Social Democratic-Liberal coalition —*Christian Science Monitor,* 19 Jan. 1981

> ... were alert to a possible "panic" (a domino chain reaction of firms unable to meet debts on margin) — Richard L. Strout, *Christian Science Monitor,* 3 Apr. 1980

The notion that a chain reaction may become self-sustaining can underlie other uses:

> ... the movie is expected to trigger a self-sustaining chain reaction of U.F.O. sightings —Boyce Rensberger, *N.Y. Times,* 9 Dec. 1977

We see no real problem in these uses. It is unrealistic to expect that every writer will seize on the same aspect of something as evocative as a nuclear chain reaction when using the term figuratively. Dictionaries will eventually catch up with what has happened with this term.

chair 1. *Verb.* *Chair* is a verb formed by functional shift from the noun. On this basis Bernstein 1958, 1965 denounces the use of the verb *chair* in the meaning "to preside as chairman of"; Copperud 1970, 1980 calls it journalese. *Chair* had been made a verb—in different meanings—as long ago as the 16th century, so that Bernstein's scorn of the term on the grounds of neologism was misplaced. The sense to which he objected, however, has been in use only since the 1920s; the OED Supplement has a citation from 1921. Both Copperud and Bryson 1984 note that dictionaries accept the term without comment. It is standard.

> ... he willingly chaired committees and gave his energies selflessly —John Kenneth Galbraith, *The Scotch,* 1964

> ... a public meeting chaired by Governor Hindmarsh —*Australian Dictionary of Biography,* 1967

> ... chaired a contributors conference in April — *Times Literary Supp.,* 19 Feb. 1971

> ... opposition in the committee hearings, chaired by Senator Sam Ervin —*N.Y. Times,* 1 Feb. 1972

Copperud finds *chairman* in the same sense "even more disagreeable." *Chairman* has been used as a verb since 1888. *Chair* would seem to be simpler.

2. *Noun.* It has been fashionable for a few years for persons unacquainted with the forms of parliamentary procedure to disparage the use of *chair* in the sense "chairman, chairwoman" as an ugly creation of the Women's Liberation movement. There is, of course, no law that requires people to know anything about the history of what they disparage, but we can tell those who are curious that *chair* has been used in this sense since the middle of the 17th century. Its earliest citation in the OED is dated 1658–9; it is only four years more recent than *chairman*. It is, moreover, a standard term of parliamentary procedure:

> Sometimes the chair "appoints," in which case he names the members of the committee —*Robert's Rules of Order,* 2nd ed., 1893

> I second the motion. (The seconder need not stand up, address the chair, or be recognized.) —J. C. Tressler & Henry I. Christ, *English in Action,* 7th ed., 1960

> In the event of a change or an addition, the member addresses the Chair, waits for recognition, and states his point —John V. Irwin & Marjorie Rosenberger, *Modern Speech,* 1961

Our evidence suggests that this sense of *chair* may perhaps be more often encountered in programs, directions for the submission of papers, and the like, than it is in running context. It is not, however, unusual in running context.

> The Conservative chairwoman . . . was far more liberal than the Labour chair had been in calling speakers who opposed the motion —Mollie Panter-Downes, *New Yorker,* 30 Oct. 1971

Harper 1985 and Reader's Digest 1983 recommend the use of *chair* in place of *chairperson.* See also CHAIRMAN, CHAIRWOMAN, CHAIRPERSON, CHAIRLADY.

chairman, chairwoman, chairperson, chairlady

A fair amount of ink has been spilled in the discussion of the propriety and appropriateness of these terms. Usage writers who venture an opinion on the subject tend to dislike *chairperson* and recommend *chairman, chairman* or *chairwoman,* or *chair* (see CHAIR).

Chairman is the oldest of these words (1654) and the most widely used. It has been and still is used of women:

> As chairman of Scholarship, Mrs. George Hervert of El Cerrito will announce the scholarship amount —*Berkeley* (Cal.) *Daily Gazette,* 31 Oct. 1973

> . . . Sophie Meldrim Shonnard, honorary chairman of the benefit committee —*Town & Country,* March 1980

> . . . the commission's chairman, Rachel Evans —Joan Cook & Judith Cummings, *N.Y. Times,* 21 Mar. 1980

Because *chairman* is used of both men and women, some commentators claim that its *-man* element is not masculine, buttressing their arguments with reference to the Anglo-Saxon. However, the 17th-century origin of the term vitiates the Anglo-Saxon argument, and the fact that *chairwoman* appeared as early as 1699 suggests that *chairman* was not entirely gender-neutral even in the 17th century. But there is ample precedent for using *chairman* of both men and women.

Chairwoman is an entirely respectable word dating from 1699, but it seems not to have been used as often

as it might, probably because it has long competed with *chairman* in application to women and has recently had competition from *chairperson.*

Chairperson is a recent coinage (1971) as a gender-neutral term to be used in place of *chairman* and *chairwoman,* one of several such gender-neutral coinages containing *-person* (see PERSON 2). It was greeted with much resistance by usage writers and others resistant to neologism, but seems to have quickly gained acceptance in a wide variety of publications. A number of commentators have noted that although *chairperson* was intended to be gender-neutral, it is chiefly used of vacant posts (in advertisements) and of women; apparently when men fill such vacancies, they style themselves *chairmen.* Our evidence shows this to be generally true even now, although our most recent evidence shows a greater percentage of men designated *chairperson* than our earlier evidence did. Thus *chairperson* tends to be truly neutral when the position is vacant or when no name is associated with the office. But when a name is mentioned, *chairperson* is still more likely to stand for a woman than for a man.

In spite of the attacks of usage writers and others, *chairperson* has won fairly wide acceptance. A sample of citations from the early 1980s shows it to be used in *Business Week, Science, People, College English, TV Guide, US, Inc., Publishers Weekly,* and *Saturday Review,* as well as in a wide variety of more specialized publications. In recent use it appears to be almost as frequent as *chairman.* Harper 1985 and Reader's Digest 1983 suggest using *chair* in place of *chairperson.* Our evidence, however, shows *chair* is not nearly as commonly used as *chairperson.*

Clearly all three of these words (or four, if you count *chair*) are in standard use, and you can use whichever you like best.

A curious term that is not really a contender for favor here is *chairlady.* This is an infrequent alternative to *chairwoman* that we have found once or twice in British use, but mostly in American. Leo Rosten in *The Joys of Yiddish* (1968) associates the term with American Jewish culture, and we have a little evidence supporting his observation. But our evidence also suggests that at one time *chairlady* might have been best established in labor-union usage:

> This is when we had the union. I was the chairlady —Evelyn Finn, quoted in Studs Terkel, *Hard Times,* 1970

> . . . she's union chairlady in her section —Richard Bissell, *7½ Cents,* 1953

We have no current evidence of such use. It has perhaps been supplanted by *chairperson:*

> Teresa works in a textile factory and, as her union's chairperson . . . —Judith Crist, *Saturday Rev.,* August 1980

We have scattered evidence for *chairlady* through the 1970s, but none since. It is not a serious contender with *chairman, chairwoman,* and *chairperson.*

chaise lounge, chaise longue

Chaise-longue is a French word that was brought into English around 1800. It designated a kind of elongated chair, and the word probably followed the piece of furniture to England. *Chaise lounge* is formed from the French word by a process known as folk etymology. In folk etymology, words or word elements are transformed in such a way as to make them closer to more familiar or better understood words or word elements. In the case of *chaise longue, longue* is not an English word, but *lounge,* spelled with the same letters, is. In addition, there was in 19th-century American use a noun *lounge* that designated a similar piece of furniture (this *lounge* appears in *Uncle Tom's Cabin,* for instance). It would seem, then, that the French *chaise longue* became combined with the American *lounge* to produce *chaise lounge.*

Of course things are not quite that simple. *Chaise-longue* (it seems to have been regularly hyphenated during the 19th century) seems not to have been entered in an English dictionary until it appeared in a section of the OED in 1889. It did not appear in one of our dictionaries until Webster 1909. In both the OED and Webster 1909 it was marked with double bars, indicating that the editors considered it a foreign word. (Editors of Webster's Second 1934 removed the bars.)

The OED mentions that Ogilvie's dictionary enters the word in the form *chaise-lounge,* a spelling not recognized in the OED, all of whose citations were for the French spelling. The Ogilvie's dictionary referred to turns out to be the 1855 Supplement to *The Imperial Dictionary,* edited by John Ogilvie and published in Edinburgh and London. *Chaise-lounge* is so marked that we know Ogilvie intended the second part to be pronounced like English *lounge.* That he entered the term suggests that it was probably current in Edinburgh at the time he was editing the supplement. Unfortunately he gives us no citation of its use in print.

The American *chaise lounge* began to appear in print in the 1920s; undoubtedly it had been used in speech for some time earlier. As a printed term it seems to have become established first in the trade; many of our early citations are from manufacturers' catalogs and newspaper advertisements. When the spelling began to appear in both the Montgomery Ward and the Sears and Roebuck catalogs, it could no longer be ignored—millions of people would be familiar with it. *Chaise lounge* did have some general and literary use too, but the bulk of such use belonged to the French spelling. The current situation is not much different. *Chaise lounge* is still most common in commercial use. It also continues in general and literary use to some extent, but there *chaise longue* predominates. The latter is usual in British use of all kinds.

In current American use *chaise lounge* is most often used for poolside, patio, or deck furniture, while *chaise longue* and the shortened *chaise* are somewhat more often used for indoor furniture.

> In California we would lie on a chaise lounge . . . on the patio —Donald Charles, *Sky and Telescope,* December 1983

> . . . chairs, chaise longues and ottomans slipcovered in Thai cotton —Anthony Haden-Guest, *Architectural Digest,* November 1985

> A custom-made leather chaise opposite the television —Susannah Masten, *Southern Accents,* July/August 1984

chance   1. *Noun.* The preposition used most commonly after *chance* is *of:*

> . . . would have only a small chance of hitting us — Thomas C. Butler, *Johns Hopkins Mag.,* Summer 1971

> We must take him on if there was any chance of success —Ernest Hemingway, "Miss Mary's Lion," 1956

Chance is also used, in varying senses, with *at, for,* and *on:*

> . . . his team has the chance at a question —*NEA Jour.,* January 1965

> . . . historians, who will get their chance at it . . . in the future —Jonathan Daniels, *N.Y. Times Book Rev.,* 9 May 1954

> . . . Italy's best chance for progress —*N.Y. Times,* 10 Dec. 1963

> . . . the best chance for future society —E. M. Forster, reprinted in *Encore,* November 1944

> . . . took advantage of a free chance on a set of 10 storm windows —*Springfield* (Mass.) *Union,* 21 Sept. 1955

And it is used with *to* and the infinitive:

> Even if we have the happy chance to fall in love — Graham Greene, *Travels with My Aunt,* 1969

> . . . to give the swagman a chance to incriminate himself —William Power, *Yale Rev.,* Summer 1954

2. *Verb.* The verb *chance* may be followed by the prepositions *on* or *upon:*

> . . . unless one chances on him while he is already laughing —Hiram Haydn, *American Scholar,* Summer 1964

> We chanced upon a pocket air-pollution indicator — *McCall's,* October 1971

It is also frequently followed by *to* and the infinitive:

> Chancing to pick up a copy —L. N. Wright, *CEA Critic,* May 1971

> Arnvid chances to rescue a young woman — Edmund Fuller, *Saturday Rev.,* 16 Oct. 1954

Other prepositions are occasionally used:

> . . . 24 Bewick . . . swans chanced into Slimbridge from their breeding grounds 2,600 miles away — Sophy Burnham, *N.Y. Times Mag.,* 27 Apr. 1980

> . . . I chanced by a bookstall —Deedee Moore, *Cosmopolitan,* January 1972

character   Copperud 1970, 1980, Strunk & White 1959, 1972, 1979, Watt 1967, and Prentice-Hall 1978 all point out that *character* is often used for unneeded padding. How often, we cannot judge; we know it happens at least now and then:

> . . . that were partly economic and partly political in character —*Collier's Year Book,* 1949

> The measured dipole moment is about one-sixth of this value, suggesting that HCl is about 16% ionic in character —Ralph H. Petrucci, *General Chemistry,* 1972

But in the bulk of our citations the vagueness of the word seems to be useful, and it cannot easily be replaced:

> . . . wanted the furnishings to be mostly a traditional counterpoint to the open contemporary character of the house —Gary E. McCalla, *Southern Living,* November 1971

Despite the increasingly political character of the movement —Jon Margolis, *Esquire,* March 1970

But the character of these changes differed from one age to the next —W. F. Bolton, *A Short History of Literary English,* 1967

If *character* is sometimes used unnecessarily, it would seem to be a small matter and certainly no reason to forego use of the word entirely.

characteristic In general, when the adjective *characteristic* is followed by a preposition, the preposition is *of:*

> It's particularly characteristic of the Western industrialized society —Margaret Mead, *Barnard Alumnae,* Winter 1971

> . . . are related in different ways from those which are characteristic of the comprehensive high school — James B. Conant, *Slums and Suburbs,* 1961

Less frequently, *characteristic* may be used with *in* or *for:*

> The cough is so characteristic in whooping cough — Morris Fishbein, *The Popular Medical Encyclopedia,* 1946

> . . . which seem to be characteristic for the different organic groups —S. S. Tomkins, ed., *Contemporary Psychopathology,* 1943

charisma *Charisma* is an originally theological term that was first appropriated for secular use by the German sociologist Max Weber. The work of Weber's in which he uses the term was not translated into English until 1947, but it was known to people who were familiar with his thought:

> Charisma is, then, a quality of things and persons by virtue of which they are specifically set apart from the ordinary, the everyday, the routine —Talcott Parsons, *The Structure of Social Action,* 1937

Thus, the earliest uses of the word in English are elucidations of Weber's theories or applications to Germany:

> . . . the strange German conception of the leader's "charisma," a combination of manliness, recklessness, and intellectualism —Louis L. Snyder, *Annals of the American Academy of Political and Social Science,* July 1947

> The superficial adulation paid to Mussolini never approached the aura—the *charisma,* as some Germans name it—surrounding the Führer —R. M. MacIver, *The Web of Government,* 1947

It was not long before *charisma* turned up in literary criticism:

> . . . for Paul radiates what the sociologists, borrowing the name from theology, call *charisma,* the charm of power, the gift of leadership —Lionel Trilling, *The Liberal Imagination,* 1950

> What the junior editor means is that the author of the manuscript, although lacking in sales appeal, has a high value on the literary stock exchange. He has . . . what political sociologists would call charisma — Malcolm Cowley, *The Literary Situation,* 1954

So the word was current in some intellectual circles when John F. Kennedy was elected president in 1960.

The frequent application of *charisma* to Kennedy seems to have been in large measure responsible for the popularity of the word in the press. By the end of the 1960s, *charisma* was busting out all over:

> Beauty, wealth, birth—where could you find a better summary of what gives the Kennedys . . . their charisma? —Max Lerner, *N.Y. Post,* 28 June 1968

> . . . Jesse Jackson, who has been described as being closer than anyone else to Dr. King in charisma — Charlayne A. Hunter, *Trans-Action,* October 1968

> . . . those gifted with the charisma to lead us out of the wilderness —W. Warren Wagar, *Center Mag.,* September 1968

> . . . has at least as much to do with United States blindness as with Fidel Castro's well-established charisma —Irving Louis Horowitz —*Trans-Action,* April 1969

The boom has continued through the 1970s:

> She had more than charisma; it was almost an inner radiance —Ralph G. Martin, *McCall's,* November 1971

> Of all the world's capitals, this city seems to be the *most* gifted with charisma —Patrick McGivern, *Cosmopolitan,* March 1972

> The charisma of the aerospace and defense industries —Gary DeWard Brown, *Datamation,* March 1972

> Autumn is Libra's special season, and through Thanksgiving, the private you is blessed with extra sparkle and charisma —Lila Spencer, *Cosmopolitan,* October 1976

> What she lacked was charisma, the magic that leaped out from the screen —Sidney Sheldon, *Cosmopolitan,* September 1976

> . . . whose acting in *Sunday Too Far Away* and *Caddie* leaves no doubt of his intelligence and charisma —S. S. Prawer, *Times Literary Supp.,* 18 July 1980

You can perhaps detect here—as several commentators have—a certain devaluation or trivialization of the word from its early application to national leaders like Hitler, Kennedy, or Castro to its extension to movie actors, the aerospace industry, and even to the ordinary Libra (at least through Thanksgiving). We could give further examples, but the point has been made. Commentators such as Howard 1977, Phythian 1979, Bremner 1980, and Harper 1985 object mildly to the trend. The word may have descended in application from the definition Weber gave it—quoted in translation in Howard 1977 and in the OED Supplement—but Parsons had already deflated it somewhat in 1937, and its spread to literary criticism also sowed the seeds for most current use. If the coin is somewhat devalued, it is nonetheless in wide circulation.

chary *Chary* is often followed by *of* and somewhat less often by *about:*

> My business experience has taught me to be chary of committing anything of a confidential nature to any more concrete medium than speech —William Faulkner, *The Sound and the Fury,* 1929

I wanted my father's good opinion because he was chary of his compliments —*The Autobiography of William Allen White,* 1946

. . . should make us chary of allowing new meanings to obscure one of the fundamental properties of space —Bertrand Russell, *Foundations of Geometry,* 1897

For the most part, Beard is chary about expressing his own opinion very directly —John M. Mathews, *American Political Science Rev.,* December 1946

. . . he himself was chary about the psychoanalytical technique in serious mental illness —Alfred Kazin, *N.Y. Times Mag.,* 6 May 1956

Occasionally, *chary* may be found with *as to, in,* or *with:*

. . . the cautious and taciturn Yankees were sometimes very chary as to their answers —F. Eliot, *Atlantic,* July 1953

Such persons are usually expected to be chary in the exercise of their real power —Ralph Linton, *The Cultural Background of Personality,* 1945

I am always very chary with percentages . . . I like short words and vulgar fractions —Sir Winston Churchill, quoted in *Time,* 19 Oct. 1953

chastened   By and large, when *chastened* is used with a preposition, it is *by:*

. . . were chastened but not defeated by the New Left experience —Michael Harrington, *N.Y. Times Book Rev.,* 11 Mar. 1973

. . . the process by which what is private is chastened and socialized by being made to enter public life — Charles Frankel, *Antioch Rev.,* Fall 1955

However, when *chastened* is used with a preposition, the choice of the preposition is dictated not by the meaning of the word, but rather by the meaning of the prepositional phrase. Thus, *by* denotes the agent doing the chastening and, among other prepositions that are used, *for* indicates the reason for the chastening and *to,* the state into which something is chastened or the extent of the chastening, while *in* may signify the circumstances that do the chastening:

. . . the proud have been chastened for their manifest sins —Albert Guérard, *Education of a Humanist,* 1949

. . . his character chastened to a Christ-like degree — James D. Hart, *The Popular Book: A History of America's Literary Taste,* 1950

. . . had been chastened in two marriages —*Time,* 29 Aug. 1955

chastise   Copperud 1970, 1980 and Fowler 1926 warn against spelling this word *chastize.* The OED shows the spelling with *z* in use—along with a variety of other spellings—from the 16th to the 19th centuries. Webster 1909 marks *chastize* as a "reformed spelling"—apparently one of the aims of the reform movement was to have verbs in *-ise* spelled in the same way as verbs in *-ize.* We have very little 20th century evidence of the *-ize* spelling. We suggest that you go with the overwhelming majority and spell it *chastise.*

chauvinism, chauvinist   It has become fashionable to take note—usually with disapproval—of the use of *chauvinism* and *chauvinist* to mean "male chauvinism" and "male chauvinist." Reader's Digest 1983 and Ebbitt 1982 point out that such use can be confusing, since the words do have other meanings. Consider, for instance, this letter to the editor:

Judge Greenfield's chauvinism was glaringly exposed when he leaned over backwards to acquit Martin Evans of rape charges —*Harper's Weekly,* 4 July 1975

If the hint contained in the reference to rape charges does not clear up the meaning of *chauvinism* instantly, then this use could be called unclear. But the sentence is quoted in isolation, and it is quite likely that a larger context would make the meaning clear. In fact, most of our unmodified examples of *chauvinism* and *chauvinist* that imply *male* are made perfectly clear by their contexts:

. . . think V. Woolf could have written even better if she'd had a happier sex life. What a chauvinist remark! Yet it is also a deeply feminist remark — Margaret Drabble, *The Listener,* 27 Sept. 1973

She becomes a Fem Man-Hate heroine and is inevitably shot by a chauvinist redneck —Anthony Burgess, *Saturday Rev.,* 3 Feb. 1979

The Canadian hierarchy this year gave serious attention to women who advocated the ordination of female priests—a cause that gets only chauvinist chuckles from U.S. bishops —Robert G. Hoyt, *Harper's,* October 1971

Even most instances of *chauvinism* and *chauvinist* in the original meaning, "excessive patriotism or nationalism," which is the sense most often encountered bereft of limiting modifiers, are clarified by context. It is sound advice, though, to be sure that either your context or your modifiers make your meaning plain; these words have spread quite a bit from their originally narrow nationalistic meanings.

Of more interest, perhaps, are the commentators who disapprove the truncated use. The Harper 1975, 1985 panel disapproves by a wide margin (no breakdown of the vote by sex is given). Simon 1980 calls it a "trendy misuse." The assumption underlying this criticism seems to be that *chauvinism* has only recently been perverted from its original sense by feminists. Such, however, is not the case. *Chauvinism* has been used in English only since 1870 and by early in the 20th century it was having its boundaries stretched:

The literary chauvinism of the famous lecture on "The American Scholar" is perhaps more apparent than real —George Saintsbury, *A History of Criticism and Literary Taste in Europe,* 1904

He warned the New Yorker against the besetting sin of "Chauvinism, that intolerant attitude of mind which brooks no regard for anything outside his own circle and his own school" —H. W. Cushing, *The Life of Sir William Osler,* 1925

Political nationalism expresses itself in economic Chauvinism —*Contemporary Rev.,* March 1927

By the 1940s and 1950s this sort of use was common:

. . . the rise of a Negro business spirit and Negro business chauvinism —*Psychological Abstracts,* March 1948

A genial exercise in state chauvinism by one of this state's most assiduous, and readable, drum-beaters —*New Yorker,* 26 Nov. 1950

. . . if the inevitable professional chauvinisms can be abandoned —Wilbur Zelinsky, *Geographical Rev.,* January 1951

Mr. Hersey's chauvinism for Yale '36 —letter to the editor, *Time,* 29 Sept. 1952

If we adjust these accounts for the understandable chauvinism of their authors, many of whom were Chippewa —Bernard J. James, *American Anthropologist,* April 1954

A pivotal role in the change from the notion of "great or undue partiality or attachment to one's own group or place" to that of "an attitude of superiority," which we find in *male chauvinism* and *female chauvinism,* was apparently played by the usage of Marxists. We have abundant evidence that *chauvinism* and *chauvinist* were used as generalized terms of abuse by and of Communists of various factions; such epithets as *petty bourgeois chauvinism, Great Russian chauvinism, social chauvinism, race chauvinism,* and *white chauvinism* were used with some frequency to attack individuals or groups within the Marxist movement. So common was *chauvinism* as a derogatory term, that a pamphlet issued by the U.S. Army during the heyday of McCarthyism on "How to Spot a Communist" used the word as one of its "clues." Here is another example from that period:

> White chauvinism: The private Communist expression for racial prejudice against the Negroes. The Communists have other uses, or misuses, of the word chauvinism; a man who tends to relegate women to a secondary role is a "male chauvinist" — Herbert A. Philbrick, *I Led 3 Lives,* 1952

One of the favorite games of *Time* in those days was twitting the *Daily Worker* about some of their sillier exercises in self-abasement in the face of some change or other in the party line. On 16 May 1949 and 9 January 1950 *Time* quoted the *Daily Worker's* sports editor apologizing for errors he had made with respect to "white chauvinism" and again on 26 June 1950 quoted a headline apologizing for "white chauvinist errors." But the terminology had its uses:

> . . . drew a deep breath and let fly with a hot blast of pure male chauvinism —*Time,* 27 Mar. 1950

Male chauvinism was escaping from the jargon of Marxist abusing Marxist into general use.

We close with a little bouquet of *chauvinism* and *chauvinist* to give you some indication of the range of the words' application in current use. (We assure you that *male chauvinism* and *female chauvinism* are in frequent use, though we do not show them here.)

> . . . English is the world's great pickpocket of language. It borrows pretty or useful words from every other tongue. . . . It would be daft not to make use of our great wealth because of linguistic chauvinism — Howard 1980

> If there should be life on the moon, we must begin by fearing it. . . . It says something about our century, our attitude toward life . . . our human chauvinism —Lewis Thomas, *The Lives of a Cell,* 1974

> . . . this is a matter of social politics (and, he might well have added, of heterosexual chauvinism) — John Fowles, *Saturday Rev.,* July 1980

They may not have been nearly as slow and stupid as we, in our mammalian chauvinism, always assumed —Georgess McHargue, *N.Y. Times Book Rev.,* 13 Nov. 1983

. . . this book is the perfect tool for combating the prejudices of Western art chauvinists —Ralph Novak, *People,* 25 Mar. 1985

. . . a beleaguered, defiant community of New York chauvinists —Richard Corliss, *Time,* 20 Feb. 1984

Who are the "health chauvinists" you rail against? —James Gorman, *People,* 21 Mar. 1983

. . . might please even the most adamant . . . culinary chauvinists —Jay Jacobs, *Gourmet,* December 1982

cheap   1. Copperud 1980 warns of the derogatory connotations of *cheap* meaning "inexpensive," and Reader's Digest 1983 worries that the pejorative uses are driving the "inexpensive" sense out of use. The neutral sense, however, is not being driven out of use:

> If there is a cheaper hobby in the world than the collection of homonyms, I have yet to find it —James J. Kilpatrick, *Smithsonian,* April 1984

> . . . was discovering how simple and cheap the sport can be —David Butwin, *Saturday Rev.,* 29 Jan. 1972

> The initial purposes of the public development of the St. Lawrence . . . had been to supply home consumers . . . with cheap power —*Current Biography,* May 1967

> . . . a new segment of the population that wouldn't travel at all without cheap group rates —Barbara Johnson, *Saturday Rev.,* 4 Mar. 1972

> . . . at a time when every federal penny is to be watched and pinched, good basic science comes relatively cheap —Lewis Thomas, *Late Night Thoughts on Listening to Mahler's Ninth Symphony,* 1983

Pejorative senses can easily be told from the context, in most cases:

> I won't tell you the brand name, but I bought it cheap, because it doesn't get used very much. And you know what I got? A cheap stove —Betty Furness, quoted in *Money,* December 1980

> . . . motivated by insatiable vanity and a desire for cheap thrills —Barbara Tritel, *N.Y. Times Book Rev.,* 23 Feb. 1986

> Clara was wearing a gown of sequined silver. She looked cheap —E. L. Doctorow, *Loon Lake,* 1979

> . . . a cheap array of tawdry glitter —*Current Biography,* May 1965

You probably need not worry about the neutral sense being taken as pejorative except when *cheap* is used attributively—directly ahead of the noun it modifies. In the next example *cheap* connotes shoddiness as well as low price:

> . . . a desk, good but battered . . . , a bed serving also as a sofa, a cheap carpet —Janice Elliott, *Angels Falling,* 1969

The likelihood of the pejorative connotation creeping in is greatest when the noun denotes a physical object—no one is confused about *cheap electric power* or *cheap travel rates*. If you mean to say that an object is not expensive by using *cheap*, you had better take care to make your meaning unmistakable in context.

2. Bernstein 1971 reminds us that *cheap* is an adverb as well as *cheaply*. The adverb *cheap* is most frequently found in contexts of buying and selling, and it regularly follows the word it modifies:

> . . . if there is an abandoned shed in your neighborhood that you can buy cheap —Daniel B. Weems, *Raising Goats*, 1983

> . . . the multinationals got the licences cheap —Neal Ascherson, *Observer Rev.*, 3 Mar. 1974

> You could then launch these little spacecraft wonderfully cheap —Freeman Dyson, *Science 85*, November 1985

Cheaply is used in a wider range of meanings and may either precede or follow the word it modifies:

> . . . which diminish his capacity to produce efficiently and cheaply —Ivar Berg, *Change*, September 1971

> . . . sell their cheaply made goods to America — Goodman Ace, *Saturday Rev.*, 25 Mar. 1972

> . . . probably the worst historical novel ever penned, and certainly the most cheaply melodramatic — Albert Guérard, *Education of a Humanist*, 1949

> . . . real estate speculators blockbusted their West Side neighborhoods, snapping up homes cheaply — John Saar, *People*, 11 Apr. 1983

There are people who believe that all adverbs end in *-ly* and who avoid flat adverbs like *cheap* (see FLAT ADVERBS). It is therefore pretty common to see *cheaply* in a context where *cheap* would also have been perfectly idiomatic:

> For this reason, the Lutzes get the house cheaply — Stephen King, *Playboy*, January 1981

The adverb *cheaply* sometimes replaces the adjective *cheap* after a copulative verb. This is a phenomenon of fairly long standing; the OED has examples of the phrase *to hold cheap* "to think little of"—which dates from Shakespeare's time—written as *to hold cheaply* in the 19th century. This sort of substitution is one kind of hypercorrection. Here are a couple of more recent examples, first the adjective and then the hypercorrect adverb:

> . . . he needed money to acquire Old Masters, which never come cheap —Robert Wernick, *Smithsonian*, September 1979

> Quality, as one might expect, does not exactly come cheaply —G. Bruce Boyer, *Town & Country*, February 1983

check The common English particles—*up, on, over, into*, for instance—are a frequent irritation to the usage commentator, who tends to suspect that they are often superfluous. But they are idiomatic and cannot simply be wished away. *Check* as a verb is used with a number of these.

Copperud 1970, 1980 comments especially on the use of *check into*, which seems to have been a particular bugbear of Theodore Bernstein. Bernstein, in *Winners & Sinners* (23 June 1954) disapproved of these two examples:

> . . . is kept busy checking into developments —*N.Y. Times*, 11 June 1954

> He said he also had asked Mr. Carr to check into such rumors —*N.Y. Times*, 12 June 1954 (proof)

Copperud points out that the *into* in each of these examples serves the purpose of disambiguation; without it *check* could be understood in the sense of "to slow or bring to a stop." This seems to be a reasonable point, and it is likely that the use of such idiomatic and "superfluous" particles often has the singling out of one sense of a multisense word as a main function.

Let us, then, not worry about alleged superfluity or redundancy in these idiomatic combinations of *check*, but look at those that are in current use and see by example what sorts of contexts they are found in.

Out seems to be the particle in most frequent use at the present time. You will note in these examples that *check* with *out* is not reserved to a single meaning:

> . . . try something on a small scale and check out the result —Richard M. Brett, *Blair & Ketchum's Country Jour.*, February 1980

> . . . her answer that evening, and I have checked this out with others, was, "What should I say? . . ." — Alan Rich, *New York*, 3 Apr. 1972

> . . . they stop visitors and question them, and check out parked cars —B. J. Phillips, *Ms.*, March 1973

> Check it out with Gladys —*Jamaica Weekly Gleaner*, 13 Feb. 1974

> Instead, he began to check out Donohue's story — Anatole Broyard, *N.Y. Times*, 23 Feb. 1972

> . . . there was no time to check stories out —Thomas Parker, *Harper's*, August 1969

> Be sure to check out the prettily embroidered place mats —Merrie A. Leeds, *Town & Country*, May 1980

> . . . so we might as well go check out that crowd to see who we're going to be hanging out with —Carolyn Becknell Mann, *Harper's Weekly*, 16 May 1975

On is also common:

> . . . going to I Corps near Da Nang and checking on the Marines' progress there —David Halberstam, *Harper's*, February 1971

> Through the monitoring center, physicians can check on a patient from anywhere inside or outside the hospital —*Psychology Today*, March 1971

> Wilbur G. Kurtz, an artist and historian of the South, was retained to check on every matter of detail —Gavin Lambert, *Atlantic*, March 1973

Check up and *check up on* can also be found. *Check up* followed by a clause appears to be British; *check up on* is predominantly American:

> Check up that the child has the means of obtaining any materials or books she may need —Ailsa Brambleby et al., *A Handbook for Guiders*, 1968

> . . . I had got up to look out of the window to check up if there was going to be a frost —Ian Cross, *The God Boy*, 1957

. . . she planted herself in the front row of the House visitors' gallery to check up on the vote —James Egan, *McCall's,* March 1971

One may work his head off or just think and loaf. No one checks up on you —Albert Halper, *American Scholar,* Winter 1981–1982

. . . told two flat falsehoods about what had happened in secret session where no reporters were present to check up on him —Elmer Davis, *But We Were Born Free,* 1954

And there are also *over* and *around:*

They asked for volunteers to check over the registration lists —*Boy's Life,* August 1952

. . . mothers who brought their babies in to be checked over by a city doctor —*The Lamp,* September 1953

. . . staying there just long enough to be checked over by Al Getman —Alexander Woollcott, letter, 2 Sept. 1940

The White House people had quietly checked around and found . . . —David Halberstam, *Harper's,* February 1971

Chicano The remarks on this term in Copperud 1980, Bremner 1980, and Harper 1985 suggest that there is some misapprehension about this word. It is a word, as Copperud notes, applied by some Mexican-Americans to themselves. It seems to have been introduced into American English in the late 1940s or early 1950s. It was first used by politically active groups and hence is a term considered offensive by those Mexican-Americans of different or opposed political views. Our evidence for objection to *Chicano* suggests that the objection is primarily political; we have no evidence from printed sources that *Chicano* has been used as a pejorative term by either Mexican-Americans or other Americans.

Chicano has been frequently used in the Anglo press since 1968 or 1969 and is still in frequent use. The term is no longer limited to certain militant groups of Mexican-Americans; with wider application it has become a less politicized term, and expressed objection to it has largely subsided, although there are undoubtedly still some Mexican-Americans who find it offensive. We have had a correspondent object to it as recently as 1982.

Contrary to the opinion of Copperud, *Chicano* is more frequently capitalized now than it used to be.

chide When used with a preposition, *chide* is usually used with *for* to designate what has provoked the chiding:

. . . his wife . . . was forever chiding him for his grammatical lapses —William Styron, *Lie Down in Darkness,* 1951

Always the schoolmarm when it came to words, my mother chided him for ignorance —Russell Baker, *Growing Up,* 1982

There is evidence, though, for the use of *chide* with several other prepositions—*with, on, as,* and *about:*

. . . is chided with the fact that he, while declaring himself inimical to everything the Festival represents, still uses it —Irwin Shaw, *Harper's,* September 1970

. . . chided the administration on farm . . . policies — *Wall Street Jour.,* 2 Sept. 1954

. . . chided advertisers and their agencies as being "the arch-conservatives of the contemporary world" —Tom Donlon, *Advertising Age,* 6 Apr. 1970

The last fellow who chided me about Southern ancestry was a Westerner —James Street, *Holiday,* October 1954

The past tense and past participle of *chide* have yet to settle in form. Although, as you can see from the last three illustrations, *chided* is usual in active constructions in American English, our evidence indicates that *chid* is more often used in British English:

I chid her for this unnecessary demonstration — Augustus John, *Chiaroscuro,* 1952

. . . chid them for drinking —Elizabeth Taylor, *A Game of Hide-and-Seek,* 1951

When the passive voice is used, the choice of past participle is not so clear-cut: *chidden* is found in both American and British writing, while *chided* seems to occur mainly in American English:

. . . [she] is chidden for continuing to write novels in her original mode —Frances Taliaferro, *Harper's,* February 1983

. . . like children who have been chidden —William Faulkner, *Spotted Horses,* 1940

. . . the disturbers glanced round . . . as though chidden by an intruder in their own home —Vita Sackville-West, *The Edwardians,* 1930

. . . the Cardinal was chided for his words —Gay Talese, *Harper's,* January 1969

Less frequent is the form *chid:*

"Ah, no!" she sighs, and is chid —George Meredith, *The Ordeal of Richard Feverel,* 1859

chief justice Copperud 1970, 1980 says the proper title is *chief justice of the United States* not *chief justice of the Supreme Court;* Harper 1985 says there is a distinction between the terms even though the same judge holds both positions. This has all the appearance of a legal technicality having little or no bearing on the usage of the ordinary person. We find both terms in good use:

. . . the nomination of Abe Fortas as Chief Justice of the United States —John Corry, *Harper's,* December 1968

The Chief Justice of the Supreme Court presides over the Senate during the impeachment trial — Stanley E. Dimond & Elmer F. Pflieger, *Our American Government,* 1961

As a compromise you can roll the two together:

. . . to the position of Chief Justice of the Supreme Court of the United States —Lewis Paul Todd et al., *Rise of the American Nation,* 1961

childish, childlike The conventional wisdom holds that *childlike* has positive or neutral connotations while *childish* has negative connotations. As a general guideline (though not, we shall see, as a strict rule), this is true. *Childlike* usually connotes some good quality such as innocence, trustfulness, or ingenuousness; it is also used in neutral description. *Childish* usually implies a quality such as immaturity or lack of complexity; occasionally it refers to the mental deterioration of old age.

> ... the simple, direct, childlike quality which all observers note in the Chinese themselves —Havelock Ellis, *The Dance of Life,* 1923

> He was a devout man, with a childlike trust in God —Charles Nordhoff & James Norman Hall, *Men Against the Sea,* 1934

> Her brow and eyes and hair are beautiful and childlike —Mabel F. Hale, *New-England Galaxy,* Winter 1965

> ... an adult should be an adult, occasionally childlike perhaps, but never childish —John R. Silber, *Center Mag.,* September/October 1971

> Every problem becomes very childish when once it is explained to you —Sir Arthur Conan Doyle, *The Return of Sherlock Holmes,* 1904

> Nodding, for it would have been childish to cut him, I walked on quickly —W. Somerset Maugham, *The Moon and Sixpence,* 1919

> ... she was living a childish fantasy —Herman Wouk, *Marjorie Morningstar,* 1955

> ... shaking their fists and calling childish phrases — Katherine Anne Porter, *The Never-Ending Wrong,* 1977

> ... his parents.... they were both getting childish and needed care —Pearl Buck, *The Long Love,* 1949

Fowler 1926 says that *childlike* should always be used of adults or their qualities, and the evidence agrees. *Childish,* not *childlike,* is used as a neutral adjective to refer to children. In this way writers avoid saying that something is *like* a child's when it *is* a child's.

> ... a light, airy, childish laugh, in which ... he recognized the tones of little Pearl —Nathaniel Hawthorne, *The Scarlet Letter,* 1850

> ... the clear, childish accents of the little children — Charles Nordhoff & James Norman Hall, *Pitcairn's Island,* 1934

When something other than children is being referred to, *childish* is sometimes used in a neutral or positive context, whereas *childlike* is only rarely used in a negative context. These are the uses for which you may find yourself criticized.

> ... the simple and childish virtues of veracity and honesty —Ralph Waldo Emerson, "Illusions," 1860, in *A Century of the Essay,* ed. David Daiches, 1951

> ... those memories had indeed made this day poignantly perfect, childish in its brazen delight —William Styron, *Lie Down in Darkness,* 1951

> She is a woman of beauty, very small, with childish wrists and ankles —Joyce Carol Oates, *Harper's,* August 1971

> ... assumptions that workers are basically lazy, conniving and childlike —John R. Coleman, *N.Y. Times Book Rev.,* 5 Oct. 1975

Chinaman   Most dictionaries and usage commentators note that *Chinaman* meaning "a Chinese" is considered offensive. The term is originally an Americanism and dates from the middle of the 19th century when Chinese immigrants encountered the Gold Rush boom on the West Coast. From American English the term found its way into British English, where, according to our most recent sources, it is also considered offensive.

Current usage is a bit hard to describe. Our American evidence shows some examples of the old naive use—as if the user had no notion anyone found the term offensive—but more of knowing use that is intended satirically or is intended to hark back to those days when the expression was common. We have also seen it applied to porcelain figures—whether punningly we cannot be certain. Recent British use is somewhat puzzling: the term is used in literary contexts of fictional figures and in humorous contexts in *Punch,* but it is hard for an American to understand the intent—if there is any—of such use. *Chinaman* has one entirely inoffensive use in British English—it is the name of a cricket bowling delivery whose rough equivalent in baseball would be a slow breaking pitch. It is often lowercase in this use:

> "Not many of these blokes," I told myself, "can read my chinaman and googly." —Gary Sobers, *The People,* 18 June 1967

choice, *noun*   The origin of some notions about usage is as mysterious as the origin of many folk beliefs. A correspondent in Safire 1984 says that he often sees, "He has two choices, either A or B." "Of course," the correspondent goes on, "there is only one choice." This correspondent's belief, which seems to rest on the notion that *choice* has but a single meaning, is of very obscure origin, unless the correspondent himself thought it up. We have been unable to find such a concern expressed in our collection of usage books, perhaps because many of them offer *choice* as a word to be used in place of *alternative:*

> To the purist one should never speak of three *alternatives,* rather of three "choices" —Harper 1985

Choice, however, has several senses, and the one being objected to by Safire's correspondent is the same sense used in the compound adjective *multiple-choice,* which is used of tests. While it is not the most common sense of *choice,* it is by no means rare:

> A single light in a computer can only be in one of two states, on or off; it thus expresses a two-choice situation —Robert W. Marks, *The New Mathematics Dictionary and Handbook,* 1964

You can use this sense if you need to. It is standard.

choice, *adjective*   This adjective is used by a few grammarians—George O. Curme and Paul Roberts, for instance—to describe the most careful and conservative kind of English. It is probably a better descriptor of that kind of English than is *formal,* which is the term used by most commentators but which is confusingly applied to different ranges of written material by different commentators. See also FORMAL.

chord, cord   Everyone agrees that *chord* is used for a group of musical tones, and *cord* for a string. Beyond this there is some disagreement and some misinformation. Copperud 1970, 1980 says that *cord* and *chord* come from the same ancestor, which is only partly true. The musical *chord* is derived ultimately from *accord*, and is not related to the string *cord*. There is, however, another noun *chord* which is related to *cord;* it was originally spelled *cord,* but its spelling was altered in the 16th century to conform to Latin *chorda* or perhaps the Latin's Greek original. This *chord* has a few regular uses: technical (truss chord, the chord of an airplane wing), mathematical (the chord of a circle), and emotional:

> John's work has always awakened responsive chords in a large and loyal body of admirers —David Piper, *Times Literary Supp.,* 1 Feb. 1980

> During his interview he struck exactly the right chord —E. M. Swift, *Sports Illustrated,* 7 Mar. 1983

The emotional uses frequently suggest some musical influence.

Then we have anatomical use, in which both spellings can be found:

> Chordates are defined by the presence of three features. One is the nerve chord in the spinal cord — Chet Raymo, *Boston Globe,* 21 July 1986

> . . . *foramen magnum* (hole at the base of the skull where the spinal chord enters) —C. Loring Brace, *The Stages of Human Evolution,* 1967

American commentators (Copperud 1970, 1980, Bernstein 1958, 1965, 1977, Bremner 1980, Kilpatrick 1984) insist on the *cord* spelling in such combinations as *vocal cords, spinal cord,* and reject the *chord* spelling as an error. British commentators (Fowler 1926, 1965, Treble & Vallins 1937, Longman 1984, Chambers 1985) are more perceptive; they recognize both spellings. OED evidence shows that *chord* was perhaps somewhat more common than *cord* in the 19th century; Fowler thought *chord* was predominant in the first quarter of the 20th. Longman recognizes both spellings; so does Chambers, but Chambers says that *cord* has become more common. *Cord* seems to predominate in American use.

The *chord* spelling can still be found in American sources in combination with *spinal* and more frequently with *vocal,* where the unrelated musical *chord* may affect people's spelling:

> . . . whose spinal chord was severed in a mugging incident —Barry Schatz, *Springfield* (Mass.) *Union,* 13 May 1985

> . . . making my living by my pen and on occasion by agitating my vocal chords —Clifton Fadiman, *Holiday,* April 1957

> . . . paralysis in one vocal chord —*Current Biography,* February 1968

> A girl's pipes are her vocal chords —Sherman Louis Sergel, ed., *The Language of Show Biz,* 1973

The compound *dischord* (for *discord*), found in a nationally syndicated comic strip in the late 1970s, is undoubtedly influenced by the musical *chord,* but it is a misspelling.

Conclusion: even though the *chord* spelling with adjectives like *vocal* and *spinal* is historically justified and considered acceptable by a number of British authorities, it is widely understood to be a misspelling in American usage. While it is not really a misspelling, we recommend that you use the commoner *cord* spelling.

chronic   Copperud 1970, 1980 warns against misuse of *chronic* to mean "severe." This is a puzzling adjuration on the surface; we can find no evidence in our files of such use in edited prose. Two British sources, Phythian 1979 and Chambers 1985, mention a sense "bad, very bad, deplorable, intense, severe" that they describe as slangy or informal. This sense, it appears, is primarily British oral usage. Webster's Third describes it as British slang and the OED Supplement as "used colloq[uially] as a vague expression of disapproval."

The evidence in the OED Supplement suggests that even this use is not especially common in written sources; its most common use seems to be in the generally adverbial combination *something chronic:*

> It's made my eyes water something chronic —H. G. Wells, *Mr. Polly,* 1910 (OED Supplement)

> So she started howling, and carrying on there something chronic —Richard Llewellyn, *None But the Lonely Heart,* 1943

> But that blasted curvilinear geometry of theirs, it stirred you up something chronic —Donald Jack, *That's Me in the Middle,* 1973

The only American use in our files remotely approaching this is the following one from O. Henry:

> "Bill," says I, "there isn't any heart disease in your family, is there?"
> "No," says Bill, "nothing chronic except malaria and accidents. Why?"
> —"The Ransom of Red Chief," 1907

And even O. Henry is not markedly astray from the usual senses of the word. If there really is a usage problem here, it appears to be British.

circle   There are some language commentators who decry the use of the verb *circle* with *around* or *round* as redundant. The OED evidence shows that these words, along with *about,* have been used with *circle* for a long time:

> So cerclith it the welle aboute —[Geoffrey Chaucer,] *The Romaunt of the Rose,* ca. 1400 (OED)

> The Sea which circles us around —Abraham Cowley, *Works,* ca. 1667 (OED)

> The busy whisper circling round Convey'd the dismal tidings when he frown'd —Oliver Goldsmith, *The Deserted Village,* 1770 (OED)

> That proud ring Of peers who circled round the King —Sir Walter Scott, *The Lady of the Lake,* 1810 (OED)

Although it is true that *circle* in this sense is now most frequently used by itself, there is contemporary evidence for its still taking *around, round,* or *about* in a complement:

> . . . hired a sound truck that circled around the home —Theodore H. White, *The Reporter,* 8 June 1954

> . . . he circled mentally round and round the core of the matter —Marcia Davenport, *My Brother's Keeper,* 1954

> . . . female circles about youngster —Robert M. McClung, *Massachusetts Audubon,* June 1968

Note that in the example from Marcia Davenport *round* suggests cautious avoidance of or a failing to come to grips with something. *Around* is similarly used:

... after circling around the problem for years, finally took the plunge and committed itself —George W. Bonham, *Change,* Winter 1971–1972

... they circle warily around the resulting void at the centre of popular humanistic thought —Joan Fox, in *The Film,* 1968

Or it may add a note of confusion:

Adding to the congestion are befuddled drivers circling around the cargo center searching for the passenger terminals —Frank E. Emerson, *New York,* 22 Nov. 1971

There seems to be no compelling reason to avoid *around, round,* or *about.*

These are not the only particles in use with *circle.* Here are the adverbs *back, up,* and *in,* usually in conjunction with a preposition:

... to allow the mind free play, to circle back on one's own arguments —James R. Kincaid, *N.Y. Times Book Rev.,* 24 Jan. 1982

... thinks of his life as being a sort of long, boring, nonstop flight from Cuba that will eventually circle back there —Vincent Canby, *N.Y. Times,* 29 Apr. 1979

I can circle up behind him, she thought —Bill Pronzini, *The Stalker,* 1971

As they begin, first slowly, then with increasing cold certainty, to circle in on each other —Barbara A. Bannon, *Publishers Weekly,* 4 Aug. 1975

circumstances There has been a fairly long-lived dispute as to the propriety of the use of the preposition *under* as opposed to the preposition *in* with *circumstances.* The list of commentators from Fowler 1926 on who specifically approve *under* is quite impressive, and you can be assured that both constructions are in good odor and in standard use. Before we trace the history of the controversy, let's look at a few examples of use:

... men have written good verses under the inspiration of passion, who cannot write well under any other circumstances —Ralph Waldo Emerson, "Love," 1841

There, then, is a rough-and-ready description of the development of feudalism, as a practical necessity under the circumstances of that time —G. G. Coulton, *Medieval Panorama,* 1938

... they frequently hand out business cards under social circumstances, which is, of course, not correct —Amy Vanderbilt, *Ladies' Home Jour.,* September 1971

... died in 1944 under circumstances that indicated "his departure from this earth may have been somewhat accelerated." —Norman Cousins, *Saturday Rev.,* 30 Oct. 1971

With as benign a smile as I could under the circumstances manage I suggested that the general ask the President that question —Dean Acheson, quoted in Merle Miller, *Plain Speaking,* 1973

... and others who are Snobs only in certain circumstances and relations of life —W. M. Thackeray, *The Book of Snobs,* 1846

In the best circumstances, waiting for action was hard —T. E. Lawrence, *Seven Pillars of Wisdom,* 1935

... some you see in bright canvas deck chairs on green lawns in country circumstances —E. B. White, in *Perspectives USA,* Summer 1953

A German irredentist movement is something very natural in the present circumstances —Arnold J. Toynbee, *London Calling,* 18 Mar. 1954

In no circumstances will the Chinese leadership allow the country to become dependent on one major trading partner —Alastair Buchan, *The Listener,* 6 Dec. 1973

In seems to be more common than *under* in British usage, while both are in frequent use in the U.S. When *circumstances* means "financial situation," *in* is the preposition of choice; *under* is rare:

... living useful lives in reduced circumstances —Norman Stone, *N.Y. Times Book Rev.,* 28 Oct. 1984

While growing up in comfortable circumstances in Pasadena —*Current Biography,* February 1967

She lived at Nice in very modest circumstances —*Dictionary of American Biography,* 1936

You should not think, however, that *under* and *in* are the only prepositions to go with *circumstances;* others are used when the situation dictates. Here are just two others, but the selection is hardly exhaustive:

... it may be the right one for the circumstances of that nation —Donald McLachlan, *London Calling,* 24 June 1954

Life may be good or bad according to circumstances —Bertrand Russell, *Education and the Good Life,* 1926

The controversy over *in* and *under* seems to have had its origin in one of Walter Savage Landor's *Imaginary Conversations* (1824) in which Horne Tooke talks with, or perhaps at, Dr. Johnson. Landor's reason for reprehending *under* is etymological: *circum* means "round or around" in Latin and therefore *in* is appropriate and *under* is not. Many of you will recognize this sort of reasoning as your old friend, the etymological fallacy. Others will grow familiar with it through repeated encounters in these pages. Fowler demolished Landor's logic, but a century too late for that gentleman's edification.

Nearly a century passed after Landor's original pronouncement before the question of *under* or *in the circumstances* began to appear in works on usage. It is a question notably absent from our standard 19th century sources: Alford 1864, White 1870, Gould 1870, Ayres 1881, Hodgson 1881. We don't know who first reintroduced the question, but comments in John O'London's *Is It Good English?* (1925) and Partridge 1942 suggest that it may have been a British newspaper editor. At any rate the earliest comments from Americans (MacCracken & Sandison 1917, *Literary Digest* in 1917, 1918, and 1923, Lincoln Library 1924) in our files approve both prepositions; the *Literary Digest* follows the same distinction between the prepositions that is set down in the OED (1893): "Mere situation is expressed by '*in* the circumstances', action affected is performed '*under* the circumstances.'" Perhaps not all Americans were in accord with these commentators: Evans 1962 says that Woodrow Wilson insisted on *in*.

When Fowler dismissed the argument for the insistence on *in* as "puerile," he also mentioned the OED distinction and mentioned in passing that *under* seemed natural when pressure is suggested. Both of these points continue to pop up here and there: Phythian 1979, for instance, likes *in* but will accept *under* when pressure is suggested.

The OED distinction is dismissed by Treble & Vallins 1937; they find it "cryptic" and "difficult to follow," as indeed it is. Nevertheless Partridge 1942 presents it as a rule to follow, and so do Follett 1966, Bernstein 1965, 1971, and Cook 1985. At any rate subsequent usage has failed to confirm the OED distinction with any degree of certainty, and most recent commentators merely find both phrases acceptable—as of course, they have been all along. *Under* is attested as long ago as 1665, nearly two centuries earlier than the OED's first example with *in* (our example from Thackeray is older than the OED's earliest *in*, however, and the construction is doubtless older than that).

The etymological fallacy dies hard, however. Evans 1962 notes that Harold Ickes refused to sign letters containing *under the circumstances.* Gowers 1948 rejected *under* on logical grounds, but he recanted in his 1954 book and left the choice to the reader's own taste, while continuing to express his preference for *in.* And as recently as 1984 a correspondent has written to this company to inveigh against *under* on etymological grounds. You, we know, will not be taken in by the etymological fallacy.

cite, site, sight A number of handbooks, primarily those aimed at college and high-school students, point out that these three homophones (or any pair of them) should not be confused. That the meanings are entirely distinct you can tell at a glance at your dictionary; substitution of *site* or *sight* for one of the others (we have no examples of *cite* wrongly applied) is made on the basis of sound alone—and presumably little or no forethought. You would think this never happens except in the writing of careless students, but it does.

> I have sighted only two examples —letter from an irate correspondent to Merriam-Webster, February 1980

> Set your sites on the future —advt., *Morgan Horse,* April 1983

> . . . a policeman who claims to have sited UFOs — *TV Guide,* 2 Sept. 1981

All together now: the first should have been *cited,* the second *sights,* the third *sighted.* Pay attention when you write, seems to be the appropriate motto here.

civilian Copperud 1970, 1980 complains that Merriam-Webster dictionaries are the only ones that recognize a use of *civilian* in which the word distinguishes the civilian from a member of a uniformed force such as a police force or fire department, as well as from a member of the military. Copperud does not like the extension beyond the military, and while Bernstein 1965 will accept extension to police and firefighting forces, he draws the line there.

A check of some recent desk-sized dictionaries shows that at least one recognizes the extension to police and

fire-fighting units (making it as up-to-date as Webster's Third, published in 1961) and another recognizes extension to police forces. Small wonder. The use has been around since the late 1940s or early 1950s, and here are a couple of examples:

> Until the fall of 1954 New York was the only city with a population of more than 1,000,000 that shunned the use of civilians as school-crossing guards —Joseph C. Ingraham, *Modern Traffic Control,* 1954

> Police forces of the stature of the Royal Canadian Mounted Police must have a proper concern for the traditions that make membership in the force something different from holding down a nine-to-five civilian job —*Globe and Mail* (Toronto), 30 Apr. 1975

The extension of *civilian* to distinguish ordinary people from members of any group, regardless of whether the group is uniformed or not, is what Bernstein objects to. This use is not especially new; our files show that the meaning was listed as new in the 1948 *Britannica Book of the Year.* It has become well established and is more frequent in our files at the present time than the sense that contrasts civilians with police or fire fighters. Here are some representative examples:

> . . . pension fund managers are presumed to be dealing with sophisticated corporate minds, not the gullible civilian kind —Everett Mattlin, *New York,* 1 Nov. 1971

> While a civilian girl will often try a new haircut at whim, for a model a haircut is serious business — Richard Natale, *Cosmopolitan,* April 1974

> We could only conclude that either belly dancers have vastly bigger navels than civilians or that inflation has had some queer effects —Betsy Wade, *N.Y. Times Book Rev.,* 2 Mar. 1975

> A pretty strong case could be made that the last person genuinely qualified to report on travel is a professional travel writer. After all, we seldom endure any of the common catastrophes that afflict civilian travelers —Stephen Birnbaum, *Esquire,* June 1977

> "As a man of medicine, I don't understand you civilians at all. . . ." —quoted by Goodman Ace, *Saturday Rev.,* 14 Oct. 1978

> . . . Ellen Schwamm's second novel. . . . In civilian life, Schwamm is married to the fiction writer Harold Brodkey —James Wolcott, *Harper's,* August 1983

It appears that you can safely ignore the strictures of Bernstein and Copperud, who are looking backward. These extended uses of *civilian* are common, well established, and standard. More dictionaries will doubtless be recording them as time goes on.

clad This participial adjective, from the irregular past participle of *clothe,* is denigrated as bookish, archaic, or affected by a number of commentators—Flesch 1964, for instance, says that *clad* is obsolete and the modern word is *dressed.* Flesch rather vitiates his argument by producing four examples of *clad,* apparently from contemporary newspapers, which would seem to demonstrate nonobsolescence rather conclusively.

Just what the point of such objections is is hard to fathom. It is certainly easy enough to find bookish or old-fashioned examples:

In the vast forest here,
Clad in my warlike gear
—Henry Wadsworth Longfellow,
"The Skeleton in Armor," 1842

They were pitiably clad; like many farm-children, indeed, they could hardly be said to be clad at all —Hamlin Garland, *Prairie Folks,* rev. ed., 1899

They are pretty; they are clad in very costly robes of silk —Lafcadio Hearn, *Glimpses of Unfamiliar Japan,* 1894

. . . people going about poorly clad, or even without shoes and stockings —Samuel Butler, *The Way of All Flesh,* 1903

Her thin hands, clad in knitted woolen gloves —Louis Bromfield, *The Green Bay Tree,* 1924

But note that the use continues right through mid-century:

. . . was meticulously clad in morning clothes with a red geranium as a boutonniere —*The Autobiography of William Allen White,* 1946

. . . elegant objects in themselves, though usually clad against the cold in thick rugs —Osbert Sitwell, *Noble Essences,* 1950

The children, clad in bright snow suits —Grace Metalious, *Peyton Place,* 1956

Clad even appears at that time in publications for children:

. . . went about in all weathers clad in a torn undershirt —*Story Parade,* September 1951

Clad in furry hoods —*My Weekly Reader,* 3 Mar. 1952

. . . rather poorly clad —*American Girl,* March 1953

And regular use continues:

. . . the new chancellor, who was clad in a ceremonial robe of midnight-blue silk —*Current Biography,* January 1966

. . . solemn strippers undulate scantily clad bodies well into the morning hours —*The Changing Middle South,* No. 3, 1970

Virtually no one tells his guests how to be clad anymore —Raymond A. Sokolov, *Saturday Rev.,* 16 Dec. 1972

. . . I appeared in that annual class picture clad as a cowboy —Dan Greenburg, *N.Y. Times Book Rev.,* 2 Jan. 1977

A common use of *clad* involves attaching it to a preceding noun to make a compound modifier:

The little cocker spaniel hurries to and fro about the vine-clad porch —Donn Byrne, *A Daughter of the Medici,* 1935

. . . upland plains filled with wild life, and snow-clad mountains —Tom Marvel, *The New Congo,* 1948

This pretty grey stone ivy-clad world of Princeton —Randall Jarrell, letter, September 1951

. . . with her feet thickly wool-clad —Marcia Davenport, *My Brother's Keeper,* 1954

. . . row after row of magnificent ice-clad peaks —Sir Edmund Hillary, *National Geographic,* November 1955

. . . a mysterious jean-clad fraternity man —Susan Walters, *Women's Wear Daily,* 19 May 1975

. . . or a hillside of hard maple and birch, or one oak-clad ridge —*N.Y. Times,* 3 Oct. 1976

By now you should be persuaded that *clad* has been in regular use all along and that its use does not make contemporary writing sound bookish, archaic, or affected.

claim The disapproval of the verb *claim* used in a meaning close to "assert, contend, maintain" is a hoary American newspaper tradition stretching from William Cullen Bryant's *Index Expurgatorius* and James Gordon Bennett's *Don't List,* both dating from before the turn of the century, and Bierce 1909 to Bernstein 1958, 1965, Copperud 1964, 1970, 1980, Bremner 1980, and Kilpatrick 1984. Bryant's *Index* was probably compiled around 1870, so the tradition has continued for more than a century. There have been defectors: Utter 1916 reports that the *New York Evening Post,* the paper for which Bryant compiled his *Index,* approved the use of *claim* as an alternative to *assert.*

Bryant's *Index* was reprinted in Ayres 1881 and probably found its way into American usage books early in the 20th century. The subject seems to have become a favorite from Vizetelly 1906 to Strunk & White 1959, 1972, 1979; there were numerous commentators in the 1920s. But comment in usage books outside the newspaper field was more varied and not uniformly disapproving, though most did express disapproval.

The subject reached British readers through the attention of the Fowler brothers, who discovered it in their 1907 *The King's English.* H. W. Fowler revised and expanded his treatment in 1926, and most subsequent British commentators have been mindful of his remarks. Fowler found the use first, a vulgarism, and second, a violation of English idiom. He recognized *claim* followed by *to* and an infinitive as legitimate when *claim* was active and the subject of *claim* and the infinitive was the same; the passive and all other uses with an infinitive he rejected as false idiom, illustrating his objections with examples that seem perfectly idiomatic today. He also rejected sentences with *claim* followed by a dependent clause except when *claim* meant "demand." Again, his rejected examples seem perfectly ordinary today.

The unmentioned secret behind the Fowlers' detection of a violation of English idiom in this use is that the use is of American origin. The OED included the sense, without illustrations, on the authority of Fitzedward Hall, an American philologist and controversialist living in England, who contributed to the dictionary. (Hall in an 1880 magazine article twitted William Cullen Bryant for using *claim* in the proscribed sense in a book of his own travels.) The Supplement to the OED supplies the examples, and they come from mid-19th-century America. The Dictionary of American English quotes Mark Twain:

. . . it is claimed that they were accepted gospel twelve or fifteen centuries ago —*Innocents Abroad,* 1869 (DAE)

The Fowler brothers found it in Richard Grant White:

> Usage, therefore, is not, as it is often claimed to be, the absolute law of language — *Words and Their Uses,* 1870 (Fowler 1907)

Just how the usage reached Great Britain from the U.S. is uncertain. Perhaps transatlantic passage was not necessary, for the uses cited with distaste in Fowler 1907 are not very far removed from the more recent of the citations given in the OED under one of its unstigmatized senses. Here are a pair of examples from the Fowlers and one from the OED:

> The gun which made its first public appearance on Saturday is claimed to be the most serviceable weapon of its kind — *Times* (Fowler 1907)

> The constant failure to live up to what we claim to be our most serious convictions — *Daily Telegraph* (Fowler 1907)

> It is claimed, then, on behalf of Christianity, that there is a Holy Ghost — Joseph Parker, *The Paraclete,* 1874 (OED)

As you will see from the following examples, the Fowlers' examples are not what would now be considered violations of English idiom. Our examples are from both British and American sources.

> . . . if he really loved her better than himself, as he claimed, he would not stand in her way — *Smart Set,* March 1907

> Some, like Jacobi, have claimed that faith is its own evidence — W. R. Inge, *The Church in the World,* 1928

> He had always claimed that he was working for the glory of British Art — Aldous Huxley, *The Olive Tree,* 1937

> He will claim that he has not only kept the country out of war . . . — *New Republic,* 1 June 1938

> . . . has a world-wide membership of 2,500 and is claimed to be the Nation's only nonessential organization — *American Guide Series: Michigan,* 1941

> The CW20 airplane is claimed to have other new safety features — Harry G. Armstrong, *Principles and Practice of Aviation Medicine,* 1939

> . . . Henry James, an old friend, who claimed perhaps a little too often that he was an artist and nothing else — W. Somerset Maugham, *Saturday Rev.,* 11 Apr. 1953

> Their efforts were not so unsuccessful as is often claimed — Noam Chomsky, *Columbia Forum,* Winter 1969

> He accuses Britain and the West of consistently siding with the forces of White repression in southern Africa in defence of what they claim to be the "free world" — *Times Literary Supp.,* 27 Aug. 1971

> . . . bothering him right on mike about a threatening phone call she had received, claiming him to have been the nasty, horrible caller — R. Meltzer, *Rolling Stone,* 22 June 1972

> This volume's dust jacket claims that the mighty Argentine fantasist "has come into English in haphazard fashion. . . ." — John Updike, *New Yorker,* 24 May 1982

In reading your way through all the examples, you will have probably noticed the advantage *claim* can have over any of the words—*contend, assert, maintain,* etc.—proposed as superior. It regularly introduces a connotation of doubt or skepticism—the notion that what is claimed may well be disputed. Thus *claim* is seldom—perhaps never—used where *assert, maintain,* or *say* would work better. *Claim* does its job so well that it seems to have been in standard use almost from the beginning, and it continues in standard use in spite of the opposition of the newspaper stylists and many other commentators.

It is, therefore, useful to remember that *claim* followed by an infinitive phrase or a clause regularly introduces an element of doubt. In its other meanings, *claim* regularly takes a noun phrase as object.

clandestine   In a newspaper column in 1985 James J. Kilpatrick questioned the use of *clandestine* in a wire-service dispatch reporting the marriage of a rock star "in a clandestine ceremony." Kilpatrick says that *clandestine* is the wrong word here because it "implies something illicit." The problem with Kilpatrick's criticism is that it takes a narrower view of the application of *clandestine* than actual usage warrants.

Clandestine is indeed used of things kept secret because they are unlawful:

> . . . to establish a control which would make the clandestine possession of bombs impossible — Sir George Thomson, *New Republic,* 14 Mar. 1955

> The actual number of clandestine abortions — Julienne Travers, *Ms.,* April 1973

> . . . the clandestine marketing of heroin in New York — Richard Grenier, *Cosmopolitan,* March 1972

Of course, sometimes the writer does not approve of those who make the activity unlawful, and then the term does not carry a connotation of evil:

> Portugal's clandestine anti-Fascist Committee — *Time,* 4 Nov. 1946

> The editor of the Czecho-Slovak *clandestine* newspaper . . . was executed — *New Republic,* 10 Aug. 1942

> The organized resistance, through the vital clandestine radio transmitters . . . informs the people about what is really happening — Constantine C. Menges, *Trans-Action,* December 1968

> . . . the determination and persistence of Tyndale's friends in their clandestine importing of his New Testaments into England — Ira M. Price, *The Ancestry of Our English Bible,* 1949

It is often used of covert government operations such as spying:

> . . . the co-operation of the British clandestine services — Arthur M. Schlesinger, Jr., *N.Y. Herald Tribune Book Rev.,* 24 Feb. 1946

> . . . the scandalous clandestine involvement of the CIA in the affairs of the National Student Association — Edgar Z. Friedenberg, *Change,* Winter 1971–1972

> The Forty Committee under Kissinger approved another clandestine subsidy for Angola — Roger Morris, *N.Y. Times Mag.,* 30 May 1976

Quite often the rule a clandestine action transgresses is vague or informal—sometimes it amounts to no more than the usual way society expects people to behave, or what is expected by peers, supervisors, or spouses:

> . . . they managed frequent clandestine meetings and kept up a constant exchange of letters —Nancy Wilson Ross, *Saturday Rev.,* 15 Apr. 1972

> A girl who is excited by clandestine sex in a man's apartment —David R. Reuben, M.D., *McCall's,* March 1971

> A physician, for instance, may engage in clandestine fee splitting —*Fortune,* February 1954

> . . . that clandestine interest in the macabre and morbid that is to be found throughout the course of nineteenth century literature —Bernard Smith, *Place, Taste and Tradition,* 1945

> . . . in the spirit of a dipsomaniac hiding bottles for his clandestine use —Wilmarth Sheldon Lewis, *Atlantic,* February 1947

> She proposed a clandestine marriage, but he swore that when afterwards detected, it would cause his dismissal —Anthony Trollope, *The Macdermots of Ballycloran,* 1847

The common thread running through most of these uses, besides the denotation of secrecy, is the connotation of fear of discovery. In Trollope's use of *clandestine* about a marriage, the man fears for his job if the marriage is discovered: this is a mainstream use of *clandestine.* In the wire-service story at the beginning of this article, fear is not involved: the rock star may be shunning the news media, but he certainly does not fear them. And this is why the wire-service use strikes us, as well as James J. Kilpatrick, as a bit odd.

classic, classical These two adjectives began life as variants in the early 17th century, and it is not surprising that they share several senses. But over the course of three centuries some differentiation has occurred, so that *classic* is the usual choice in some situations and *classical* in others. Usage writers have often noted this differentiation, but many of them tend to believe differentiation complete where it is not and others bog themselves down in trying to define the terms—for definitions we suggest you look in a good desk dictionary.

Classic is used in preference to *classical* in two rather recently established applications that usage writers tend to disparage rather than to recognize—sports and fashion:

> The five classic races are . . . —*The Oxford Companion to Sports and Games,* ed. John Arlott, 1975

> . . . has learned to box in classic, upright form — Michael Shapiro, *Sport,* July 1983

> . . . the classic pure jump-shooting guard —Bruce Newman, *Sports Illustrated,* 20 Nov. 1985

> . . . these classic khaki trousers are the best — *Banana Republic Catalog,* Summer 1984

> . . . clothes rendered in extremely classic ways — Carrie Donovan, *N.Y. Times Mag.,* 29 Aug. 1982

Classical is the scientific choice:

> According to classical electrodynamics, the electrons should radiate energy continually —Dietrick E. Thomsen, *Science News,* 11 Jan. 1986

> . . . Pavlovian conditioning—also known as classical conditioning —Gerald Jonas, *New Yorker,* 26 Aug. 1972

> . . . the classical canonical forms of matrices —John Duncan, *British Book News,* October 1971

Classical is also usual in music:

> His training was mainly in classical music, and for a time he was a member of an amateur operatic group —*Current Biography,* July 1965

> . . . have recorded everything baroque from Albinoni to Zelenka but have rarely invaded the classical period —Stephen Wadsworth, *Saturday Rev.,* November 1980

> The records were mostly classical, Mozart, Haydn, Bach, stacks of them —Daphne du Maurier, *Ladies' Home Jour.,* September 1971

In reference to the language, art, and civilization of the ancient Greeks and Romans, *classical* is usual but *classic* is not unknown:

> Where English designers . . . had interpreted Classical decorative elements . . . Napoleon wanted to follow, as closely as possible, true Greek and Roman forms —William C. Ketchum, Jr., *Antique Monthly,* October 1981

> . . . won a classical scholarship to Trinity College, Cambridge —*Current Biography,* December 1965

> . . . the transition from the stiffer archaic style to the freer classical period —James A. Blachowicz, *N.Y. Times,* 27 Feb. 1983

> But no one will ever again present a "criticism of life" in classic Greek —Barnard 1979

> . . . from back in the old classic times. It might have fauns and satyrs and the gods and—from Greece, from Olympus in it somewhere —William Faulkner, 30 May 1957, in *Faulkner in the University,* 1959

In the senses of "serving as a standard of excellence," "memorable," and "typical," *classic* is more commonly used and is the form prescribed by most usage writers, but in fact *classical* is also used quite frequently:

> Far from being the classic period of explosion and tempestuous growth, my adolescence was more or less a period of suspended animation —Philip Roth, *Reading Myself and Others,* 1975

> . . . I knew that long before his father's time the buffalo had found their classic habitat on the Great Plains —Robert Penn Warren, *Jefferson Davis Gets His Citizenship Back,* 1980

> The manually operated elevators were frequently out of action; when not, the call buttons had the classic Bellevue notice affixed: "Ring Up for Down." — Gerald Weissman, *The Woods Hole Cantata,* 1975

> It was just a classic error, that's all, not getting residuals —Charles Adams, quoted in *Washington Post,* 17 Nov. 1982

> He was a classic sales go-getter —William Oscar Johnson, *Sports Illustrated,* 20 Sept. 1982

> The Orioles won the thing in the eighth, in equally classical style —Roger Angell, *New Yorker,* 7 May 1984

It was a kind of classical exhibition of Georgia politics —Flannery O'Connor, letter, 21 July 1962

... would be one response to such a classical Oedipal situation —Norman MacKenzie, *The Listener,* 25 April 1974

classifying genitive See GENITIVE 1.

clean, cleanse According to the OED, *cleanse,* the older of these two words, was originally the common word for both the literal and figurative senses of "to make clean." *Clean* was formed by functional shift from the adjective in the 15th century and gradually took on most of the everyday dirt, with *cleanse* becoming the more elevated word. Consequently *cleanse* became more frequent in figurative use.

Although *clean* remains the more common verb, *cleanse* has never lost its literal meaning. It tends to be used most often of the human body:

... if your skin feels "tight" cleanse it with a liquid cleansing lotion or a soft cream —*American Girl,* December 1952

... their carefully cleansed skins glowed —Rebecca West, *The Thinking Reed,* 1936

Transplant candidates require dialysis to cleanse their blood —Neil A. Martin, *Dun's,* October 1971

Sometimes its use carries a whiff of ritual:

... he plunged the knife into the earth and so cleansed it —John Steinbeck, *The Pearl,* 1947

It is occasionally called in to do duty for the environment:

The rivers and the air need to be cleansed —Fred M. Hechinger, *Saturday Rev.,* 7 Aug. 1976

It also serves for the taste buds:

Throw in a crisp lemon sorbet after a rich dish to cleanse the palate —Shirley Lowe, *Sunday Mirror* (London), 30 June 1968

But mostly *cleanse* is used figuratively:

... Bowdler scoured Shakespeare word by word to cleanse him of every last smudge of impropriety — Richard Hanser, *Saturday Rev.,* 23 Apr. 1955

The whole world must be cleansed of the evil from which half the world has been freed —Harry S. Truman, broadcast, 8 May 1945

A group of sinners reveal their wickedness and are cleansed —A. M. Sullivan, *Saturday Rev.,* 22 Oct. 1949

For at least 10 days I was possessed by fury, at everyone. One morning I awoke and felt for the first time cleansed and filled with hope —Nan Robertson, *N.Y. Times Mag.,* 19 Sept. 1982

clear, clearly Both *clear* and *clearly* are adverbs, but in recent use they do not overlap. *Clear* is most often used in the sense "all the way":

... my ticket from San Francisco clear to New York City —Jack Kerouac, *Esquire,* March 1970

... a model son who had just gone clear out of his mind —Renata Adler, *New Yorker,* 24 Apr. 1971

... there is a good chance that the bay will freeze clear across —E. B. White, letter, 18 Jan. 1940

... with his shirt soaked clear through —Robert Greenfield, *Rolling Stone,* 20 July 1972

Clearly is used in the sense "in a clear manner":

... writes clearly and helpfully —*Times Literary Supp.,* 16 Apr. 1970

His skull shone clearly in the gaslight —Flann O'Brien, *At Swim-Two-Birds,* 1939

... looked clearly at their country and set it down freshly —*Smithsonian,* November 1982

It is also used to mean "without doubt or question":

He clearly knows his way about the complex and abstruse issues —*Times Literary Supp.,* 2 Oct. 1970

... except when national security is clearly involved —John Fischer, *Harper's,* October 1970

... walked toward them calmly and sanely, clearly not armed with bottles or stones —James Jones, *Harper's,* February 1971

In this second sense *clearly* appears also as a sentence adverb, a use that is criticized by Howard 1980 and Safire 1980 as a vogue use. Both commentators seem a bit tardy in discovering this use, which has been around quite a few years and is established:

Clearly, we must look further and find a rational test —Zechariah Chafee, Jr., *Free Speech in the United States,* 1941

Clearly it is a good thing to have material conveniences —Sir Richard Livingstone, *Atlantic,* March 1953

Clearly we are in a transitional stage —Vera Micheles Dean, *The Four Cornerstones of Peace,* 1946

Clearly some literalist recourses to law are offensive to the sense of justice —Alexander Comfort, *Center Mag.,* May 1970

Clearly our aqueous environment is being subjected to an accelerating stress —Barry Commoner, *Columbia Forum,* Spring 1968

clew, clue In the detective sense and its derivative uses, the usual spelling is *clue.*

After I wrote down all the clues, I knew it had to be you —Marjorie Seddon Johnson et al., *Hopes* (Second-grade text), 1977

The discovery of the crime, by the clues left behind —H. A. L. Craig, *London Calling,* 17 Mar. 1955

... tried to look for clues as to why some patients with malaria would suddenly become worse and die —Thomas C. Butler, *Johns Hopkins Mag.,* Summer 1971

God knows how the Medawars came to select the topics they did. ... There is no clue in the introduction —Jeremy Bernstein, *N.Y. Times Book Rev.,* 2 Oct. 1983

... the Russians don't have a clue about making shock absorbers, so their cars hop and bobble down the road —P. J. O'Rourke, *Car and Driver,* August 1983

The original spelling was *clew*. An early meaning of *clew* was "ball of thread, yarn, or string." Because of the use of a ball of thread to effect an escape from a labyrinth in various mythological stories—that of Theseus in the labyrinth of Crete, most notably—*clew* came to be used of anything that could guide you through a difficult place and, eventually, to be used of bits and pieces of evidence. The variant spelling *clue*, says the OED, began to be used in the 15th century, became frequent in the 17th, and in the late 19th became predominant in the "evidence" sense.

> . . . I'll follow up the clue (Clew? my stylograph won't spell) —Ellen Terry, letter, 4 July 1892

Partridge 1942 calls *clew* an American spelling. We do have fairly frequent evidence of it in the 1940s and early 1950s, but it has largely dropped out of use since then. The nautical use is always *clew*.

cliché   *Cliché* is in origin a French word for a stereotyped printing surface. The *C* volume of the OED (1893) recognized it only as a foreign word with this meaning. Its use to mean "a trite phrase or expression" is only attested in the OED Supplement from 1892. It seems to have caught on very quickly; by the 1920s it was already being disparaged as "worn":

> The word *'cliche'* itself, we have seen, is a cliche, a worn counter of a word —Havelock Ellis, *The Dance of Life,* 1923

Most usage books and handbooks devote themselves to talking about what a cliché is. We will try to do that and also pay some attention to the word itself.
1. *The word.* Reader's Digest 1983 notes that *cliché* is regularly used as a term of disparagement, which should surprise no one. From the following examples you can see that it has been extended semantically from words to ideas to visual images to things of various kinds:

> The dialog is largely cliches decked out in current jargon —Howard Kissel, *Women's Wear Daily,* 27 Dec. 1976

> . . . his mischief with the clichés in our language —John Irving, *N.Y. Times Book Rev.,* 10 June 1979

> . . . "investing in human capital" is the cliche for this —Leonard Silk, *Saturday Rev.,* 22 Jan. 1972

> . . . a dubious cliché about the upper-class Englishman's habit of understatement —Arthur Mizener, *The Saddest Story,* 1971

> . . . an absolutely hilarious parody of every possible cliché ever invented about the American male —Arthur Knight, *Saturday Rev.,* 13 May 1972

> A recurring media cliché is the "human interest" story about the grandmother graduating from college —Fred M. Hechinger, *Saturday Rev.,* 20 Sept. 1975

> Some of the illustrations for this volume are so familiar they have become cliches —Michael Kammen, *N.Y. Times Book Rev.,* 4 July 1976

> . . . the visual clichés with which the televising of music is cursed —Irving Kolodin, *Saturday Rev.,* 1 Nov. 1975

> . . . tired and disconnected routines that drew on little more than the clichés of modern dance —Alan Rich, *New York,* 24 Apr. 1972

> . . . malls have, in the past 10 years, become almost a cliché of so-called urban renewal —William Marlin, *Saturday Rev.,* 7 Feb. 1976

> The Georgetown cocktail party, by now, is as much of a political cliché as the rubber-chicken dinner —Linda Charlton, *N.Y. Times,* 19 Apr. 1976

> . . . an anthology of threadbare clichés of *haute* and bistro cuisine —Jay Jacobs, *Gourmet,* December 1980

Copperud 1970, 1980 notes that *cliché* is used redundantly with *old* and *usual.* Such qualifiers seem to go naturally with *cliché* much as *old* seems to go with *adage* and *maxim.* Our evidence suggests that such combinations are not preponderant, but also not uncommon. See OLD CLICHÉ, OLD MAXIM; OLD ADAGE.

You may also have noted that the unaccented *cliche* is sometimes used but the accented *cliché* is much more common.
2. *The thing.* Although many commentators and handbooks discuss clichés, there is not a great deal to be learned from reading their discussions. You will be advised in most instances simply to avoid clichés. You will not have the reasons for your avoiding them very well explained; you will be told only that they weaken your writing or are an insult to the intelligence of your readers. Perhaps there is a hidden suggestion that you will sound like a journalist:

> After two years studying what rewrite men did with the facts I phoned them, I knew that journalism was essentially a task of stringing together seamlessly an endless series of clichés —Russell Baker, *Growing Up,* 1982

You will also not learn much about what is and what is not a cliché. Oh, everybody agrees on a definition—the one given at the beginning of this article is typical—but there is little agreement about what fits the description. For instance, can a single word be a cliché? Or must a cliché be a phrase or longer expression? Earlier we saw that Havelock Ellis called the word *cliché* a cliché way back in 1923. Christopher Ricks in Michaels & Ricks 1980 calls single words clichés, and apparently so have many others between those two dates: a letter to the editor of the *Saturday Review* in 1965 complained specifically about *cliché* being applied to single words in the pages of that magazine. The editors of Reader's Digest 1983 raise several questions (similar ones can also be found in Copperud 1970, 1980 and Harper's 1975, 1985) about what distinguishes a cliché from any number of other frequently used stock phrases and expressions such as *how do you do* or *thank you.* The questions have a serious point, but no one seems to know the answer.

We will offer only two suggestions. The first is that in all the use of *trite, overused, stale, outworn, threadbare* and such descriptors there is probably a connecting thread of meaninglessness. You might, then, want to base your notion of the cliché not on the expression itself but on its use: if it seems to be used without much reference to a definite meaning, it is then perhaps a cliché. But even this line of attack fails to separate cliché from the common forms of polite social intercourse. A second and more workable approach would be simply to call a cliché whatever word or expression you have heard or seen often enough to find annoying.

Many writers, in fact, do seem to use some such

rough-and-ready definition. Here, for instance, is a book reviewer:

> He doles out his ghoulish clichés to the exorcists with equal largesse: the priest's panic "was marinated in a tide of sullenness"; "Slivers of agony jabbed and pierced through his buttocks and groins." —Francine Du Plessix Gray, *N.Y. Times Book Rev.,* 14 Mar. 1976

Now those expressions may be clichés to the reviewer of exorcism novels, but there are plenty of nonreaders of the genre who have never seen them before. Indeed, you are likely to find, when you read anyone's list of clichés, at least a few that you have never seen or heard before.

Christopher Ricks in Michaels & Ricks 1980 observes that writers against clichés invariably use clichés to make their point. This observation suggests that there is an inconsistency in the dogged pursuit and cornering of clichés that is akin to the suggestion that opponents of gun control be shot. If clichés can only be shot down with other clichés, there would seem to be little point in trying too hard.

Moreover, many of our commentators conclude that the utter avoidance of clichés is impossible for one reason or another. Therefore, they advise, if you come to a situation where a cliché is the best way to express an idea, go ahead and use it. "The most overworked cliché is better than an extravagant phrase that does not come off," says Howard 1984. Several other commentators concur. The advice seems sound to us.

For those who are interested in collecting expressions others have thought to be clichés, Copperud mentions headings under which they may be found in Follett and Fowler. The longest list we have seen is in Partridge 1942, where he includes most of his *Dictionary of Clichés* (1940); the list runs for more than 20 pages.

3. If you suspect that *one-way ticket to oblivion* in "This is one of the many hoary newspaper clichés that have long since earned one-way tickets to oblivion" (Harper 1985) is a bit of a cliché, you may then realize that writers on usage and compilers of handbooks are not immune to the attraction of clichés in their own writing. Such frequently invoked terms as *the careful writer, strictly speaking, a more precise term, formal speech and writing, casual speech, anything goes, permissive linguist,* and the like, and such descriptive terms as *colloquial, overworked, wordy, awkward, illiterate, overused,* are certainly reflexive enough and devoid enough of content in much of their use to qualify as clichés. A number of these that present particular problems will receive separate treatment in this book.

client A few commentators—Copperud 1970, 1980, Shaw 1975, Chambers 1985, Janis 1984—comment on *client* and *customer.* The gist of their comments is that a customer buys goods while a client buys services from a professional and especially a lawyer. As a general rule this observation is true, even if some stores catering to high-class trade prefer to think of their customers as clients, as Janis observes. If you remember to construe *professional* broadly, most of the following examples are not out of line:

> . . . frequently represented clients in the federal courts —*Current Biography,* October 1967

> It is not so bad for a client and architect to serve a common public purpose —Roger G. Kennedy, *Smithsonian,* November 1982

> Other commission agents act as buyers for their clients —Nelda W. Roueche, *Business Mathematics,* 1969

> Catholic schools are expected by their clients to maintain standards —John Cogley, *Saturday Rev.,* 15 Oct. 1966

> Hoteliers are reluctant to disclose the extent to which their light-fingered guests help themselves, not wanting to brand their clients as pilferers —Michael S. Lasky, *N.Y. Times,* 27 Jan. 1974

> . . . like a client in a brothel maintaining his dignity during a police raid —Robert J. Clements, *Saturday Rev.,* 17 July 1971

> . . . pawnshop owner . . . , his relationships with his clients —*Current Biography,* June 1965

> . . . reportedly got into a fist fight with a nightclub client —*Current Biography,* July 1965

> . . . a fine meal tastes infinitely better to a cold client than to a hot one —Richard Eder, *Saturday Rev.,* 8 Jan. 1977

> With the growing importance of institutional clients stockbrokers have invested heavily in research departments —Jack Revell, *The British Financial System,* 1973

The distinction between goods and services, may, however, be blurred occasionally, as you can see.

Janis 1984 remarks on the euphemistic use of *client* for the recipient of social services; this use dates back to the 1920s and seems to be a true euphemism—the agencies did not think people wanted to be referred to as *cases.* Over the years the social-service use has been extended in various directions to other government agencies—police, tax collectors, urban renewal specialists. Much of this seems to have occurred in British usage, but we do have American evidence from former federal budget chief David Stockman, who uses the term apparently for those groups that do or do not get federal subsidies:

> For now, Stockman would concede this much: that "weak clients" suffered for their weakness —William Greider, *Atlantic,* December 1981

This sort of use brings *client* full circle and back to its early meaning "dependent."

climactic, climatic When nine or ten handbooks make haste to tell you that *climactic* relates to *climax* and *climatic* to *climate* and you should not confuse the two, you might suppose that there is some insidious tendency for the words to be muddled in somewhat similar contexts. Not so. This is a simple matter of spelling, and from what we can find in our files the error is more often mentioned in handbooks than it occurs in edited prose. *Climactic* is the rather more frequent word; it is useful to book and movie reviewers, among others. *Climatic* is used mostly in technical contexts, but occasionally creeps into ordinary public view in articles on ice ages and such. Our scanty evidence suggests that when the spelling or the typesetting goes wrong, it is *climatic* that turns up in the place of *climactic.*

Here are two examples of each word used correctly and one of *climatic* for *climactic.*

> . . . this average citizen who is projected into the climactic American dream of parking his toothbrush at

the White House —Maxwell Geismar, *The Last of the Provincials,* 1947

... they send a squad of gunmen to wipe him out, and in the climactic gun battle they succeed —Arthur Knight, *Saturday Rev.,* 24 July 1971

... a sudden violent climatic change, as ... in the ice age —W. H. Auden, *Columbia Forum,* Winter 1970

... he got a bit dotty: he extrapolated his climatic theories into a theory that superior races, evolved under just the right climatic conditions, were able to carry on this superiority as they moved into new climes —*Times Literary Supp.,* 28 May 1971

Not long ago, the car chase was just the climatic ingredient in movies —Peter Davalle, *Annabel,* March 1975

The likelihood of a typo or misspelling extends to the compound *anti-climactic* too. The first example is an error, the second is written as it should be.

When you reach the first-act finale ... you do not have the feeling that it is anti-climatic —*Current Biography,* June 1965

This example happens to occur in quoted material, so that we cannot be sure whether the error was made in the original source or in the reprinter. In this final example, in any case, all is copacetic:

The debate, however, proved anti-climactic —Norman Mailer, *Harper's,* November 1968

climax Theodore Bernstein knew the etymology of *climax*—it comes from a Greek word meaning "ladder"—and from his knowledge of the Greek he reached the conclusion that the English word could not properly mean "highest point, culmination, acme, apex," which is, of course, precisely what it means to most people.

The issue seems to have been first discovered by Hodgson 1889; it is repeated in Allbutt, *Notes on the Composition of Scientific Papers* (1923), F. K. Ball, *Constructive English* (1923), and G. M. Hyde, *Handbook for Newspaper Workers* (1926). Perhaps Bernstein picked up the topic from Hyde.

Allbutt calls the use "a modern abuse unknown to Samuel Johnson." Unknown to Johnson it certainly was; the earliest OED citation for the "acme" sense is dated 1789. The date, however, suggests that the use was not especially modern even in 1923. Copperud 1970, 1980 and Bryson 1984 tend to think Bernstein a little far-out; they go along with the recognition of the meaning in Evans 1957, Fowler 1965, and all dictionaries. You need not give *climax* a second thought. The etymologically pure meaning exists only as a technical term in rhetoric.

Bryson 1984 adds a curious note of his own, saying that "the authorities" agree that *climax* should not be used as a verb and that it should not be used to indicate a lowest point. "The authorities" for the second objection seem to be Bryson himself and Bernstein 1962, 1965. Bernstein used the same example from the *New York Times* in both books. We have not been able to locate any other unmistakable examples, although one of Hodgson's cited authors (from 1826) could be so interpreted. A use of *climax* meaning "nadir" we conclude not to be a matter for serious concern; at least, evidence for it is hard to come by.

And the only authority we have been able to discover

who objects to *climax* as a verb is Bryson himself. OED evidence for the verb begins in the 1830s and 1840s. Our citations suggest it might have been a popular journalistic use earlier in this century:

Mrs. Hansel's appearance climaxed a day of sensational charges against the aged cult leader —*Springfield* (Mass.) *Union,* 27 May 1927

The vote climaxed three hours of furious debate —*Vancouver Star,* 9 Feb. 1926

But even popular journalistic use seems to have drawn no comment until Bryson. In any case, use of the verb is also perfectly standard.

climb 1. *Climb* was originally an irregular verb of the same class as *sing* and *begin.* It began to be used with regular inflections around the 16th century. Webster's Third shows three surviving forms of the old strong inflections for both past and past participle: *clim, clomb, clum.* All are marked as dialectal. The Dictionary of American Regional English shows *clum* (also spelled *clumb*) to be fairly widespread; *clim* is found in the Atlantic states and New England; *clomb* is chiefly Midland. It also reports *clam* as a Southern form used chiefly by blacks. A recent survey of Canadian English (Scargill 1974) found *clumb* still in occasional use there.

Johnson's 1755 dictionary showed *clomb* as the first variant for both past and past participle; *clomb* was used as a rhyme word by both Coleridge and Wordsworth; it turns up in the journals of Lewis and Clark at about the same period (1805). But in the latter part of the 20th century, it has dwindled to dialectal use, along with *clim* and *clum(b).*

... in the night sometime he got powerful thirsty and clumb out on to the porch-roof —Mark Twain, *Huckleberry Finn,* 1884

2. *Climb down, climb up.* Several 20th-century commentators, including Vizetelly 1906, Bierce 1909, and Einstein 1985, have decided that the use of *down* with *climb* (which has been going on since about 1300) must be wrong since *climb* means "to go up." These same writers, along with Bryson 1984, Partridge 1942, and Bernstein 1965, also censure *climb up* (which has been around since 1123) as redundant.

"How can you climb down?" asks Einstein rhetorically—a question that no doubt has occurred to several who have found themselves up trees. Certainly you need not take Vizetelly's advice: he prescribes *crawl down,* which (if we are determined to be literal-minded) might work for caterpillars or snakes, but not so well for the rest of us. Actually, as some of the following examples show, *climb down* is not always used literally.

... she began to smile, and MacIver climbed down off the stool —Robert Murphy, *Saturday Evening Post,* 4 Dec. 1954

... the embarrassment ... to the United States of climbing down from the perch from which we denounced all deals —Michael Straight, *New Republic,* 11 July 1955

He climbs amiably down mine shafts —Pierre Berton, *Maclean's Canada,* 15 June 1953

... they've had to confess their mistake ... and soon they'll have to climb down about the interview —John Buchan, *Castle Gay,* 1930

Typical of the critics' remarks about *climb up* is this from Bryson 1984:

> But in a sentence such as 'He climbed up the ladder', the *up* does nothing but take up space.

The *up* after *climb* is really no different than Bryson's *up* after *take:* it is an idiomatic accompaniment adding a little emphasis that helps prevent a one-syllable verb from being overlooked. Even usage writers cannot avoid those idiomatic particles, and there is not the least reason that you should worry about yours. Also note that many uses of *climb up* are not especially literal:

> ... the hills that climb dizzily up from Bernkastel's narrow cobblestone streets —Frank J. Prial, *N.Y. Times,* 3 Nov. 1976

> Your road, pleasant with shade-trees, climbs up and down steep little hills —Thomas Wood, *Cobbers,* 1938

> A major who climbed up to take a look —Burtt Evans, in *The Best from Yank,* 1945

> It takes what seems a long time ... for anti-aircraft fire to climb up from muzzle to target —Ira Wolfert, *Torpedo 8,* 1943

The fact is that *climb* is very frequently used with adverbs, prepositions, and combinations of both, like *down from* and *up from.* Here is a selection of other adverbs and prepositions that the usage experts do not bother to mention:

> West of Iron River US 2 climbs steadily upward — *American Guide Series: Michigan,* 1941

> They exchanged glares and he climbed reluctantly out of the car —Mary Jane Rolfs, *No Vacancy,* 1951

> His profession was, in fact, the main avenue by which individuals might climb out of the class of manual workers —Benjamin Farrington, *Greek Science,* 1953

> ... let me climb out on a limb and tell you what the general sales outlook seems to be —Richard C. Bond, *Toys and Novelties,* March 1954

> ... Uncle Daniel and I climbed in my trusty Ford — Eudora Welty, *The Ponder Heart,* 1954

> ... has no hesitation about climbing in & out of her filmy clothes —*Time,* 22 June 1953

> ... knocked Sihanouk off his perch and let the Khmer Rouge climb into his place —Ross Terrill, *N.Y. Times Book Rev.,* 15 June 1975

> ... temperatures will climb into the upper 70s — *Atlanta Constitution,* 19 Sept. 1984

> ... ivy climbs over the thick white porch columns —*American Guide Series: Louisiana,* 1941

> ... the clear young flame climbed lithely through the shavings —Charles G. D. Roberts, *Hoof and Claw,* 1914

> But after considering, the bear climbed back up — Edward Hoagland, *Harper's,* February 1971

> ... the Dow Jones industrials had climbed back into the 780–790 range —John W. Schulz, *Forbes,* 1 Dec. 1970

> ... the world population might climb to the 10,000 million mark —Lord Boyd Orr, *Books of the Month,* April 1953

> ... climb on a plane in New York —Horace Sutton, *Saturday Rev.,* 2 Jan. 1954

> ... has been unable to climb above third place — Joel Colton, *Yale Rev.,* March 1954

Those selections should give you a good idea of the adverbs and prepositions that regularly go with *climb.* It is not, however, an exhaustive list. Our advice is to use any of the ones that seem appropriate in a given context.

cling   *Cling* is an irregular verb of the same class that *climb* formerly belonged to. It had principal parts analogous to those of *ring: clang, clung. Clang* was the singular form of the past tense; it has dropped out of standard use, although the OED notes it continuing in northern dialect through the 19th century. Presumably people from the northern areas of Great Britain brought it to this country. The Dictionary of American Regional English calls it *archaic,* but it is still around, although it is rare:

> I clang to it —University of Massachusetts undergraduate, in conversation, 19 Nov. 1979

The OED notes some use of the regular inflection *clinged* in the 17th and 18th centuries; by the 19th the OED considered the form dialectal. It, too, is rare but not obsolete:

> Bryant, once up 7–3, clinged ... to a 7–6 margin — Dick Baker, *Springfield* (Mass.) *Daily News,* 24 Apr. 1980

The majority of us use *clung:*

> He clung to the railing —E. L. Doctorow, *Ragtime,* 1975

> They clung to what gave their status meaning in a desperate embrace of the past —Barbara W. Tuchman, in *The Contemporary Essay,* ed. Donald Hall, 1984

> ... early morning mist clung to the river —John Rowe, *Count Your Dead,* 1968

clipped forms   See ABBREVIATIONS.

clique   The only dispute over *clique* seems to be the appropriateness of the anglicized pronunciation \ˈklik\ for this word imported from French in the 18th century. By now the anglicized pronunciation must be judged acceptable, even if it is less frequent than \ˈklēk\.

clone   *Clone* is such a recent and useful addition to the general vocabulary from the realm of science that even though it receives brief mention in Reader's Digest 1983 and Harper 1985, no one seems to disparage it even as the "popularized technicality" it is.

Until the 1970s *clone* was found mostly in scientific contexts. It may have reached the general public through science fiction:

> The clone is the most terrifying monster to come to life in science fiction for a long time —*Publishers Weekly,* 1 Nov. 1965

At any rate, by the mid-1970s the term was catching on:

> In Boston, while the President is making a speech, a body is found—the exact double of the President, even to fingerprints. This has happened once before. Who is in the White House? The real thing? A clone? —Newgate Callendar, *N.Y. Times Book Rev.,* 29 Aug. 1976

Applied to people, *clone* can be neutral, but it is normally at least faintly derogatory. Sometimes it is decidedly pejorative:

> There's a whole new legion of Brooke Shields clones coming along —John Peden, quoted in *N.Y. Times,* 26 May 1980

> . . . Peter Lorre and Sidney Greenstreet clones out to commit dastardly acts —Pat Sellers, *US,* 28 Sept. 1982

> The picknicking K.C.s, until he got up close, resembled clones —Noel Perrin, *N.Y. Times Book Rev.,* 6 Sept. 1981

> What I like about Christine is that she's not a clone. She isn't one of those airheads you usually see on the tube —King Harris, quoted in *People,* 15 Nov. 1982

The word tends to be pejorative when applied to such things as movies, television shows, and such:

> . . . an increase in "me too" publishing, the issuance of volumes that are clones of books that have been selling well —Ray Walters, *N.Y. Times Book Rev.,* 27 Dec. 1981

> Clones of his broad-shouldered, man-tailored casual look have been appearing in almost every collection since the fall —Bernadine Morris, *N.Y. Times,* 15 Mar. 1984

Clone is used as a verb, too.

> . . . tend to look as though they were cloned rather than recruited —Berkeley Rice, *N.Y. Times Mag.,* 30 May 1976

> . . . someone has cloned Farrah Fawcett-Majors and Donny Osmond and sent them to newsrooms all over America —Ron Nessen, *TV Guide,* 8 Dec. 1978

> . . . no less than three of his Japanese classics have been cloned in the West —Dianna Waggoner, *People,* 27 Oct. 1980

> . . . set out in 1959 to clone a nationwide chain of Burger Kings from their five stores in Florida —Lee Smith, *Fortune,* 16 June 1980

Clone's popularity shows no sign of abating at present. Perhaps all we need to do is to remind you that it often carries a pejorative overtone.

close proximity This phrase is called redundant by a number of recent commentators such as Harper 1985, Heritage 1982, Bryson 1984, and Macmillan 1982. The difficulty is not really a recent discovery: it can be found as far back as Krapp 1927 and Vizetelly 1920. What is interesting is that both the older books recognize that there are degrees of nearness, an idea that recent commentators neglect to mention. Of course there are

degrees of proximity, and *close proximity* simply emphasizes the closeness. Here are a few examples:

> But then the prospect of a lot
> Of dull M.P.'s in close proximity,
> All thinking for themselves, is what
> No man can face with equanimity
> —W. S. Gilbert, *Iolanthe,* 1882

> However, she admits that the herb [tansy] works only on plants in very close proximity —Ken Druse, *N.Y. Times Mag.,* 22 June 1980

> Mr. Beard and Miss Compton disagreed on the distance of meat from heat, probably because Mr. Beard had in mind a smaller fire-bed to which the steak could be in closer proximity —Jane Nickerson, *N.Y. Times Mag.,* 27 June 1954

> Swallow means porch-bird, and for centuries and centuries their nests have been placed in the closest proximity to man —Richard Jefferies, *The Open Air,* 1885

> . . . move the two magnets into close proximity —Bell Telephone Laboratories, *The Formation of Ferromagnetic Domains,* 1959

clothed See CLAD.

cloture Bernstein 1965 disparages *cloture* as an unnecessary word imported from French; he prefers the more general term *closure.* Bremner 1980 disagrees: "The word is not a fancy word for *closure. Cloture* is a parliamentary term for ending debate and voting on a measure." Usage and dictionaries agree with Bremner.

clue See CLEW, CLUE.

coalesce When *coalesce* is used with a preposition, *into* is the one used most often, whatever the sense of the verb:

> Eventually they will coalesce into a single metropolitan area —John Fischer, *Harper's,* April 1972

Less frequently, *coalesce* may be followed by *with* or *in:*

> It was in this way that it coalesced so readily with the anti-rationalistic bias of the historical revolt —Alfred North Whitehead, *Science and the Modern World,* 1925

> . . . hardly soluble problems have coalesced in one problem which solves itself —George Bernard Shaw, *Back to Methuselah,* 1921

When *coalesce* is used to mean "to unite for a common end," it may be also used with *around* or, occasionally, *on:*

> . . . causing a sizable number of party faithful to coalesce around Kennedy —Godfrey Sperling, Jr., *Christian Science Monitor,* 11 Feb. 1980

> . . . the Republican, Democratic, and Liberal Parties coalesced on a candidate —Gus Tyler, *New Republic,* 23 Aug. 1954

coarse, course Chambers 1985 and a couple of schoolbooks discriminate between these two words. Since *coarse* is an adjective and *course* a noun and a verb, there is no serious chance of confusing them in use. This is merely a matter of spelling or careless handwriting that makes *a* and *u* indistinguishable.

coed Bremner 1980 notes that this word was formerly an acceptable word for a female student at a coeducational institution, but is now in disfavor. Our evidence suggests he may be right; at least we have gathered fewer and fewer citations for its use in recent years. This example tends to corroborate Bremner's view:

> At that time it was customary to locate a suitable female spectator (then known as a "coed") —Philip G. Howlett, *Sports Illustrated,* 31 Aug. 1981

The adjective *coed* continues to be used, most often in the sense "open to or used by both men and women."

coequal Bryson 1984 disparages this word as "a fatuous addition to the language." But *coequal* was actually added to the language in the 14th century and has been found useful now for about 600 years.

> A confederacy of coequal, sovereign states had been tried and found wanting —Samuel Eliot Morison & Henry Steele Commager, *The Growth of the American Republic,* 3d ed., 1942

> At one time botany and zoology were roughly coequal in biology at universities —Philip H. Abelson, *Science,* 18 June 1971

> All the coequal ingredients—choreography, music, book, design—of ballet —Walter Terry, *Saturday Rev.,* 24 July 1976

> . . . personal and political disputes among its six coequal members —Paul Kemezis, *N.Y. Times,* 22 Aug. 1976

It's used as a noun, too:

> By 1970 he had eclipsed Prime Minister Aleksei N. Kosygin, his coequal at the beginning —Craig R. Whitney, *N.Y. Times Mag.,* 10 June 1979

You can use the word without fear. As the examples suggest, *coequal* tends to be used in contexts where the equality is established on some formal basis, and it is frequent in political contexts.

coffin See CASKET, COFFIN.

cohort About 1950 people began to notice a new sense of *cohort,* one meaning "companion, colleague, follower." There was brief mention of it in *Word Study* in 1950 and by John W. Clark in *British and American English Since 1900* (1951); it received longer treatment in *American Speech* in 1953. Jacques Barzun listed it with other usages he disliked in an article in 1957, and Bernstein 1958 included it. From there it spread into a great number of other usage books, many of which assert that *cohort* does not mean "companion, colleague, follower" but means rather some subdivision of a Roman legion or "band, company."

How the new sense developed is a bit mysterious. Everybody agrees that it happened in America. Here is one idea of how the development may have occurred. First the word referred to a Roman military force—one tenth of a Roman legion:

> When the cohort superseded the maniple, the signum of the first maniple in each cohort was used as the standard of the cohort —*The Oxford Classical Dictionary,* 1949

There even were German cohorts in some of the Roman legions —W. Nelson Francis, *The English Language,* 1965

Then it developed a sense meaning any body of troops:

> The Assyrian came down like the wolf on the fold,
> And his cohorts were gleaming in purple and gold
> —Lord Byron, "The Destruction
> of Sennacherib," 1815

Then the word was extended to any group or band:

> . . . to the dining room, where a cohort of brown-habited monks were already engaged in an orgy of swallowing ices —Osbert Sitwell, *Noble Essences,* 1950

> When the day came for Rabbi Silver to be inducted, Harry, with a loyal cohort of adherents, forcibly barred his entrance —S. N. Behrman, *New Yorker,* 1 May 1954

This "band, group" sense was also used in the plural:

> If the Wood cohorts captured the Ohio delegation for their man, it would follow that Wood's adherents in the state would take over the party machinery — Samuel Hopkins Adams, *Incredible Era,* 1939

The problem with plural use is that it could be understood either as "groups"—as presumably the writer intended—or as "followers, colleagues"—understood as referring to a number of individuals forming one group rather than to a number of groups. Consider this example:

> Twenty-one months ago Dr. Mossadegh and his cohorts nationalized the British-owned oil concession in southern Iran —*N.Y. Times,* 25 Jan. 1953

The *cohorts* there could refer to followers or to groups, but there seems to be a tendency—particularly on the part of those not versed in the traditions of the Roman military—to interpret such a *cohorts* as referring to individuals. The earliest example of uncertain interpretation in our files dates from 1929:

> Meanwhile Mart Strong had taken advantage of the momentary respite to close and lock his doors, and as Carry Nation and her cohorts swarmed forward and pounded the panels with fists and stones he could be heard frantically dragging furniture across the room and piling it into a barricade —Herbert Asbury, *Carry Nation,* 1929

The author uses the word here in a context describing a mob scene involving five hundred or more persons, not all of whom were supporters of Carry Nation—some were in opposition to her, and many were simply curious onlookers. Some pages later he uses the word again:

> When Carry Nation led her embattled cohorts against the drug store O. L. Day had already applied for a permit to sell liquor for medicinal purposes. . . .

Here the "embattled cohorts" demonstrates the appeal of the military metaphor, but the body of troops actually referred to were the members of the Medicine Lodge, Kansas, chapter of W.C.T.U. in 1899. Clearly Asbury was envisioning this troop of women as a Roman army marching into battle, but there is no comparison from the standpoint of numbers—probably no more than two or three dozen women were involved. The use of *cohorts* here is undoubtedly based on the similarity of the crusading women to soldiers marching into battle, and the matter of numbers probably never entered the author's mind. Still it is very easy for the reader to interpret the word as "friends, collaborators," or something similar. And it is probably from a number of similar figurative uses similarly interpreted that the new sense developed.

The Byron quotation for the "group of soldiers" sense was chosen on purpose. At least two commentators, Gilbert Highet (quoted in Harper 1985) and Howard 1983, speculate that the popularity of the Byron poem fixed the word in the American consciousness, perhaps through the medium of 19th-century American schoolbooks, and thus led to the new sense. The theory is interesting but unprovable.

At any rate the sense was establishing itself by the 1940s. It is too firmly established in American English to be eradicated by commentators demonstrating their knowledge of Roman military organization. Here is a selection of examples from the 1940s to the present:

This convention ... formulated a second constitution which virtually restricted the suffrage to the freedmen and their white cohorts —*Dictionary of American History,* 1940

With Dickinson and his cohorts perusing it in the meanwhile with critical eyes, it is not difficult to imagine the suffering of the too sensitive author — Claude G. Bowers, *The Young Jefferson 1743–1789,* 1945

He also enlisted in the café cohorts of Pablo Picasso —*Time,* 4 Apr. 1949

It was on the night of Jan. 16, 1938, that Benny Goodman and his now-illustrious cohorts took over Carnegie Hall —*Newsweek,* 18 Dec. 1950

... the rarer acknowledgment that the performers have also achieved what they were working for can be made about Miss Thompson and her cohorts — *New Yorker,* 20 Oct. 1951

He was on the phone, talking to Henry Cabot Lodge or Tex McCrary or some such cohort —*New Yorker,* 5 Apr. 1952

... such cohorts as Trumpeter Buck Clayton, Vibraphonist Red Norvo —*Time,* 28 Apr. 1952

The old poet had left, accompanied by two of his cohorts —Mary McCarthy, *The Groves of Academe,* 1952

... brought in such cohorts as Senator Ferguson ... and Senator Knowland —Richard H. Rovere, *New Yorker,* 31 Jan. 1953

... and my special, only technically unassigned cohort grinned up at me —J. D. Salinger, *New Yorker,* 19 Nov. 1955

... Bishop Lowth and his cohorts introduced a smug this-is-correct attitude into the study of English — John Nist, *A Structural History of English,* 1966

It is also the time to ask yourself how he cuts it in the A.M.—as a man, beyond being a sexual cohort — Jacqueline Brandwynne, *Cosmopolitan,* July 1975

Nixon and his cohorts remain targets, not subjects —Max Lerner, *Saturday Rev.,* 29 May 1976

... considering the appreciable evolutionary gap between us and our simian cohorts —John Pfeiffer, *Smithsonian,* June 1980

After the death of Mao Zedong and the downfall of his widow and her cohorts —John Hersey, *New Yorker,* 10 May 1982

... centralizing the power in the hands of Stalin and his cohorts —Richard Lowenthal, *N.Y. Times Book Rev.,* 3 Feb. 1985

It would appear that the *New Yorker* may have been influential in establishing this sense in sophisticated writing. The use seems to have spread even to British English (the OED Supplement has another example more recent than this):

It is more the pity then that he should use the new American vulgarism of "cohort" meaning "partner" —*Times Literary Supp.,* 25 Nov. 1965

The "new American vulgarism" has firmly established itself in standard use in the past thirty or so years. Is it all Byron's doing? We'll probably never know.

coiffeur, coiffure Both of these words were imported into English from French, *coiffure* in 1631 and *coiffeur* in 1847. They are not new; people should be used to them by now. *Coiffure* is the hairdo; *coiffeur* the hairdresser. All the same, they are sometimes muddled, and we get the hairdresser for the hairdo:

... to model a most un-Beatle-like coiffeur —*People,* 11 June 1984

The spelling *coiffeure,* which we have seen on at least one hairdressing establishment, is neither French nor English.

cold slaw, coleslaw Evans 1962 and Reader's Digest 1983 comment on the form *cold slaw* used for *coleslaw.* *Cold slaw* is an American folk etymology based on the Dutch *koolsla.* It dates back to 1794 and is about a half century older than the presently much more common and etymologically more accurate *coleslaw.*

Evans says that most of the populace gets cold slaw, but our files show relatively little recent evidence of the term's use in print. It undoubtedly still appears on menus, however, and the Dictionary of American Regional English has collected evidence on its questionnaires as recently as 1970.

collaborate Einstein 1985 calls *collaborate together* redundant (see REDUNDANCY). It represents an intensive use of the adverb, or would if actually so used. We have no evidence of its use in print. What we do find is that *collaborate* is frequently used with *in, on,* and *with:*

... unless the best minds of its time have collaborated in its construction —T. S. Eliot, "Lancelot Andrewes," *Selected Essays,* 1932

The nation's press generally collaborated in information distortion —Robert Lewis Shayon, *Saturday Rev.,* 4 Mar. 1972

... American and Soviet scientists have already collaborated on studies of pollution —Anthony Wolff, *Saturday Rev.,* 17 Apr. 1976

She is currently collaborating on a book about birth defects —*Current Biography,* February 1968

So it's our particular senses that collaborate with whatever's going on outside to make an event — Allen Ginsberg, *American Poetry Rev.,* vol. 3, no. 3, 1974

... the mere suspicion that they are collaborating with their clients in activities of a criminal gang nature —John Dornberg, *Saturday Rev.*, 10 June 1978

... enlisted three experienced psychoanalysts to collaborate with him —Peter Loewenberg, *Los Angeles Times Book Rev.*, 24 Sept. 1972

With is often used with either *in* or *on* in the pattern "collaborate with someone in (or on) something":

... to collaborate with his old friend Howard Hawks on a screenplay —Bennett Cerf, *Saturday Rev.*, 26 Dec. 1953

... was to collaborate with her husband in many of his writings —*Current Biography 1948*

At is also possible:

... repudiated Nixon's suggestion that they were collaborating at the job in the last months of 1968 — Garry Wills, *Harper's,* January 1972

collectable, collectible   Janis 1984 reports a tendency toward differentiation between these spellings. He says that *collectable* is being used more as an adjective in relation to bills, while *collectible* is being used as a noun for things like glassware, furniture, political campaign buttons, and posters that are collected. Our evidence does not corroborate his observation. We find that both *collectible* and *collectable* are used as nouns for items to be collected, with *collectible* the more frequent spelling. We find both spellings used for the adjective, again with *collectible* somewhat more frequent. You can use whichever spelling you prefer.

collective   Copperud 1964, 1970, 1980 cocks an individual snook at the use of the adjective *collective* in such uses as "industry has its collective eye on Washington" and "experts cocked their collective eyebrow at the prediction." This use of *collective* in the sense "shared by all members of a group" is owing to the writer's intention of extending a figure of speech normally associated with an individual to a group. It is in frequent and unnoticed use with many nonanatomical nouns:

... the most fantastic outburst of collective insanity —Noam Chomsky, *Columbia Forum,* Winter 1969

... the Republican Party's collective memory — Emmet John Hughes, *Saturday Rev.*, 13 Dec. 1975

... a collective shudder swept across the city —Robert Bloch, *Cosmopolitan,* November 1972

... we can almost hear the bobby-soxers in the listening audience offer a collective swoon —Mel Gussow, *N.Y. Times,* 30 Nov. 1979

... the only ethnic example of collective culinary genius —Peter S. Feibleman, *Saturday Rev.*, 4 Sept. 1976

... citizens can continue to rely on their own collective judgment —Barry Commoner, *Columbia Forum,* Spring 1968

... good for our collective health —Albert Rosenfeld, *Saturday Rev.*, 14 Oct. 1978

When the figure of speech involves an anatomical noun, Copperud takes disapproving notice, but the usage is not really different.

It [language] takes its locus in their collective larynx and ear —Paul Ziff, *Semantic Analysis,* 1960

The effulgent reality is in the collective brain — Anthony Burgess, *Saturday Rev.*, 2 Sept. 1978

... washing and scouring the great collective brain —Norman Mailer, *Harper's,* March 1971

... or even to scratch their collective head —Stringfellow Barr, *Center Mag.*, May 1968

If you feel the urge to use this sort of figurative expression, we advise you to keep the noun modified by *collective* in the singular. Notice that the plural noun in the following two examples makes *collective* unnecessary:

... if we hide our collective heads in the sand — James V. McConnell, *Psychology Today,* April 1970

... the promises ... that flowed so trippingly off their collective tongues —*Women's Wear Daily,* 26 Mar. 1973

collective nouns   1. *Subject-verb agreement.* Collective nouns—singular nouns that stand for a number of persons or things considered as a group—have had the characteristic of being used with both singular and plural verbs since Middle English. The principle involved—referred to elsewhere in this book as notional agreement—is simple: when the group is considered as a unit, the singular verb is used; when it is thought of as a collection of individuals, the plural verb is used. All grammarians and usage commentators agree on the basic principle.

Chambers 1985 points out that one class of collective nouns—those like *baggage, cutlery, dinnerware* that stand for a collection of inanimate objects—can be omitted from consideration; they are regularly singular:

Your luggage has been sent to Kansas City by mistake.

Those commentators who mention British–American differences agree in general that singular verbs are more common in American English and plural verbs more common in British English. Beyond this generality it can be unsafe to venture; where notional agreement operates, there are no absolutes. For instance, Bryant 1962 states that British usage employs the plural verb with *government:*

In effect the Government are facing three distinct crises —David Basnett, *The Times* (London), 17 Dec. 1973

But though the plural verb with *government* is usual, it is not universal:

... the Government delegates to the BBC responsibility for ... —*BBC Year Book 1952*

... the Government has already made it clear —*The Economist,* 15 Feb. 1975

The difference in British and American usage may be illustrated by the word *family.* While Mittins et al. 1970 report a surprising amount of resistance in their survey to "his family are in Bournemouth," our evidence suggests that the plural verb is quite a bit more common in British English:

I hope all the family are in a convalescent State — Lord Byron, letter, 12 Nov. 1805

The family were not consumptive —Jane Austen, *Mansfield Park,* 1814

. . . an economist whose family are prominent —*Manchester Guardian Weekly,* 28 Aug. 1936

. . . the Royal Family take the train —Carol Wright, *In Britain,* June 1974

. . . but his family were respectable upper-crust —Gabriele Annan, *Times Literary Supp.,* 14 Mar. 1980

My family are nearly all gone —Sir John Gielgud, in *People,* 19 Oct. 1981

But there is also singular use:

. . . to determine where, for legal purposes, a family ends —Edward Jenks, *The Book of English Law,* 5th ed., 1953

The modern family is increasingly to be viewed as the family of procreation —Peter G. Hollowell, *The Lorry Driver,* 1968

Quirk et al. 1985 say that in British English the plural verb is more frequently used with collective nouns in speaking than in writing. In American English, the singular verb is more common:

The family was miserably poor —John Gunther, *Inside Europe,* rev. ed., 1937

The family includes a poodle —*TV Guide,* 23 Apr. 1954

The family was a closely-knit one —*Current Biography,* September 1964

A last family is leaving —Alice Mattison, *New Yorker,* 10 June 1985

But the plural verb is not at all rare:

His family were enormously wealthy —F. Scott Fitzgerald, *The Great Gatsby,* 1925

. . . when her family come to grief —*Time,* 26 Feb. 1951

. . . checked with her family, who prefer the latter spelling —Erich Segal, *N.Y. Times Book Rev.,* 3 June 1984

Two areas often singled out to illustrate British–American differences are politics and sports: Quirk and Harper 1985, for instance, mention both. In British English terms like *Parliament, public, government, committee* are frequently used with plural verbs; the same (and similar) terms in American English are more likely to be used with singular verbs. The contrast in sports comes when the name of a city (or country) is used as the name of a team. A British headline might read

Liverpool triumph over Swansea

while its American counterpart might read

Oakland defeats Baltimore

2. *Pronoun agreement.* Collective nouns are often referred to by plural pronouns, though singular in form. This characteristic, too, is ascribable to the operation of notional agreement. A handful of examples:

The congregation rose and settled again on its benches —James Joyce, *Dubliners,* 1914

. . . the crowd surged to its feet —*Time,* 21 June 1948

. . . a majority of the Committee expressed its preference —G. H. C. Bodenhausen, *UNESCO Copyright Bulletin,* No. 3, 1951

. . . Laurel's government moved to northern Luzon and in March they were flown to Tokyo —*Current Biography,* June 1953

. . . the party, who at his suggestion, now seated themselves —Jane Austen, *Mansfield Park,* 1814

The main difficulty with the South is that they are living eighty years behind the times —Harry S. Truman, letter, 18 Aug. 1948

. . . challenge which now confronts the faculty. They have undertaken —James B. Conant, *President's Report, Harvard University,* 1945

Copperud 1970 lists a half dozen commentators who agree that writers should take care to match their pronouns and verbs, singular with singular, plural with plural. Evidence shows that writers have sometimes adhered to this policy and sometimes ignored it. Here are some examples of the approved practice.

Plural verb, plural pronoun:

The Norton family have featured some of the greatest entertainers of all time at their park —Thomas J. Smith, *Yankee,* July 1968

. . . why a democratic people need to know something more about their legislative proceedings —J. R. Wiggins, *Nieman Reports,* July 1952

One thing the God-fearing Scandinavian and German stock of Wisconsin obviously like about their senior senator —Peter Ross Range, *Cosmopolitan,* December 1978

Singular verb, singular pronoun:

. . . the majority does not necessarily trust in the correctness of its own language —Finegan 1980

. . . an enemy which is as pitiful as it is vicious —*N.Y. Herald Tribune Book Rev.,* 28 Sept. 1952

An appeal lies to a Personnel Security Review Board. . . . It in turn makes recommendations —Ralph S. Brown, Jr., *Annals of the American Academy of Political and Social Science,* November 1953

When verb and pronouns do not match, it is usually that a plural pronoun is being used after a singular verb; the reverse mismatch is highly unlikely. A collective noun with singular verb and plural pronoun exhibits the same pattern as many indefinite pronouns (see AGREEMENT, INDEFINITE PRONOUNS):

. . . no example of a nation that has preserved their words and phrases from mutability —Samuel Johnson, preface to the Dictionary, 1755

The entire diplomatic class has, in my forty years of acquaintance with them —Henry Adams, letter, 1 Feb. 1900

. . . a cross-section of the public is interviewed each day about their listening —*BBC Year Book 1952*

What industry now fears is that the government will move into their plants —*Newsweek,* 18 Aug. 1952

3. A collective noun followed by *of* and a plural noun (Curme 1931 calls this a "partitive group") follows the same notional agreement as collective nouns in general. Thus we find James J. Kilpatrick (*Pittsburgh Press Sunday Mag.,* 11 Aug. 1985) expressing approval of the use of a plural verb in a sentence beginning "A rash of stories"—the notion is clearly plural. Here are a few other examples:

> Whether the higher order of seraphim illuminati ever *sneer?* —Charles Lamb, letter, 28 July 1798

> . . . the only lodge of Christians who never try to get us barred off the newsstands —H. L. Mencken, letter, in *The Intimate Notebooks of George Jean Nathan,* 1932

> The great majority of marriages that go on the rocks are those contracted in earlier years —George Jean Nathan, *Testament of a Critic,* 1931

When the idea of oneness or wholeness is stressed, the verb is singular:

> The bulk of the stories by new writers is fairly dull —Valentine Cunningham, *Times Literary Supp.,* 13 Aug. 1976

4. See also AGREEMENT: ORGANIZATIONS CONSIDERED AS COLLECTIVE NOUNS; AGREEMENT, SUBJECT-VERB: A BUNCH OF THE BOYS; NOTIONAL AGREEMENT, NOTIONAL CONCORD.

collide It is a tradition for newspaper editors—or at least those who write usage books—to believe that *collide* can only be used when both objects in the encounter are moving. The notion can be found in Bryson 1984, who probably got it from Bernstein 1958, 1965, or 1977, or from various *Winners & Sinners* going back at least to 1955, and Bernstein may well have gotten it from G. M. Hyde's *Handbook for Newspaper Workers* (1926). Hyde may have picked it up from William Cullen Bryant; *collided* appears without explanation in his *Index Expurgatorius,* compiled during his years as a newspaper editor in New York and first published in 1877.

The OED notes that when *collide* came to be used of train and ship accidents the usage was widely disparaged as an Americanism. Schele de Vere, *Americanisms* (1872), is aware of this criticism, but says *collide* is a good English word. (He also says the British prefer *to collision,* a verb not attested in the OED.) Schele de Vere includes the notion of two bodies in motion in his definition of the word. Where he got the notion is uncertain; it is not implicit in the etymology of the word, and most 19th-century dictionaries contented themselves with minor variations on Samuel Johnson's 1755 definition (intended originally as a transitive), which did not include it. There seems to be little historical basis for the insistence; the OED shows a citation from 1746 in which blood collides with the aorta wall.

Our citations for the literal sense of *collide* that come from sources other than newspaper accounts of plane, train, ship, or automobile accidents show that it is usually celestial objects, particles, vehicles, and people that tend to collide. In some instances—as with celestial objects and particles—it is clear that all bodies are in motion. In some instances it is not clear, and in others one object appears to be stationary. Here are two examples of the last type:

> . . . short time it took Mr. Phelps to dodge inside the library, skid into the librarian, upset a stack of

books, wreck a fernery and collide with The Mudhen at a table —*Boy's Life,* March 1953

> The hawk turned and stooped, only to collide with some bushes under which the duck had managed to find shelter —Edward A. Armstrong, *Bird Display and Behaviour,* 2d ed., 1947

By far the greatest number of our citations for *collide* are figurative, in which ideologies, politicians, nations, searing glances, and the like collide. In these uses relative motion is not a consideration. We thus suspect that you will seldom have to worry about this matter. If you do, you may be assured that *collide* is standard, even when only one body is in motion.

colloquial *Colloquial* is an adjective evidently introduced into English by Samuel Johnson, even though he did not enter the word in his 1755 dictionary. Its first meaning is "conversational":

> . . . I found him highly satisfied with his colloquial prowess the preceding evening. "Well," said he, "we had a good talk." BOSWELL. "Yes, sir; you tossed and gored several persons." —James Boswell, *Life of Samuel Johnson,* 1791

According to OED evidence, Johnson introduced this sense in a paper in *The Rambler* in 1751; in 1752 he used the now more familiar sense "characteristic of familiar conversation" in another number of *The Rambler.* Boswell again echoes Johnson's use:

> But Johnson was at all times jealous of infractions upon the genuine English language, and prompt to repress colloquial barbarisms —*Life of Samuel Johnson,* 1791

It is this sense that has come to be used as a label by writers on language and by dictionaries.

One early combination involving *colloquial* that is found in the writings of grammarians is the phrase *colloquial speech.* The phrase designated ordinary conversational speech—the sort of talk you would engage in as part of any gathering—at a party, on the street corner, at the country store, or at the dinner table. It was contrasted with what was sometimes called *platform speech.* Platform speech was an artificially articulated version of English intended to make a speaker understood at a distance; it was the customary form of English for politicians and preachers addressing large audiences. The development of electronic public-address systems and radio and television has essentially eliminated the need for platform speech. We hear our preachers and politicians today speaking in a more ordinary—colloquial—way.

Colloquial, however, was probably a poor choice of term for describing ordinary everyday speech. It is a learned term and, especially in its abbreviated form *colloq.,* removed from everyday connotations. It is not surprising, really, that it was misunderstood as a pejorative label, in spite of the fact that dictionaries using the label were at pains to explain that it was not pejorative. The misunderstanding became so widespread that many dictionaries and handbooks abandoned the label altogether. The editors of Webster's Third decided not to try to distinguish the standard written from the standard spoken language. Other dictionaries and handbooks replaced *colloquial* with other labels, of which *informal* is the most common.

That *colloquial* is widely assumed to be pejorative is amply attested:

> In particular teachers have treated spoken English as simply an inferior form of written English, instead of a properly different form, and assumed that "colloquial" means corrupt —Herbert J. Muller, *The Uses of English,* 1967

> ... the use of *like* as a conjunction. It *was* colloquial; it is now correct —Clifton Fadiman, *Holiday,* March 1957

> The tone is informal but not colloquial or condescending —Delores McColm, *Library Jour.,* 15 May 1966

> Its writing is often wordy and sometimes rather jarringly colloquial —Colin Thubron, *Times Literary Supp.,* 3 Nov. 1978

> I'm glad we took into full membership all sorts of robust words that previous dictionaries had derided as "colloquial" —Zinsser 1976

It would have been bad enough that the general public and schoolteachers misinterpreted *colloquial,* but there is abundant evidence that it was likewise misinterpreted by writers on usage—sometimes in spite of their explanations to the contrary. Here is one example:

> COLLOQUIAL Commonly used in speech but inappropriate in all but the most informal writing —Prentice Hall 1978

> **anyplace** Colloquial for *any place* —Prentice Hall 1978

Since the blank space between *any* and *place* has no sound, it cannot be detected in speech, and therefore it is meaningless to say that *anyplace* is "commonly used in speech"; *anyplace* and *any place* simply sound the same in the same environment. As applied to *anyplace,* therefore, *colloquial* is being used as some sort of stigmatizing label, and the intention is that the reader of the book avoid *anyplace* and use *any place.*

The use of *colloquial* with pejorative overtones is fairly common with usage writers:

> ... but it is easy to avoid it, and with it the faultfinding of the censorious, who condemn it as colloquial —Utter 1916

> ... derived from a colloquial and childish synonym —Howard 1980

> ... must be considered at best colloquial —Bryson 1984

as. (1) Highly colloquial when used in place of *that* or *whether* —Macmillan 1982

Whether "plenty" is being used here as an adjective or an adverb, it is colloquial —Bernstein 1958

Out loud is thought to be both unidiomatic and colloquial —Shaw 1970

Another word often used carelessly is *alibi.* In colloquial speech it frequently replaces the noun "excuse" —Freeman 1983

At its mildest, hypallage contributes a colloquial taint to technical writing —John Dirckx, *The Language of Medicine,* 2d ed., 1983

prepositions often criticized.... *Back of* for *behind* ..., *inside of* for *within* ..., and *over with* for *over* ... are colloquial —Guth 1985

Aggravate should not be used in its colloquial meaning of "irritate" or "exasperate" —Little, Brown 1986

So for *True....* "Is that so?" Colloquial and worse —Bierce 1909

All colloquial expressions are little foxes that spoil the grapes of perfect diction —Emily Post, *Etiquette,* 1927

Perhaps some of the taint of Dr. Johnson's "colloquial barbarisms" has rubbed off on *colloquial.* If you see the term used regularly in a handbook or other book on usage, you can be reasonably sure it is thought of as disparaging by the author, no matter what explanation is attached to it when (and if) the term is explained.

collusion From the time of Samuel Johnson's 1755 dictionary and even before, *collusion* has been defined to show that it involves practices that are underhanded, deceptive, dishonest, or illegal. Typical uses look like these:

> He knew that every bill for gasoline, oil, tires, and overhauling was padded, that the chauffeur was in collusion with the garage owner for this purpose —Thomas Wolfe, *You Can't Go Home Again,* 1940

> They suspected with some justification ... collusion between the French and British and the internal enemies of Bolshevism —George F. Kennan, *Soviet Foreign Policy, 1917–1941,* 1960

> ... the wretched police collusion, false and perjured evidence —William Styron, *This Quiet Dust and Other Writings,* 1982

From Fowler 1926 to Bryson 1984 usage commentators have warned against the use of *collusion* in a weakened sense where *cooperation, concert,* or *collaboration* might do. Such use is typically labeled "confusion," but from our evidence it is clear that there is usually no confusion. *Collusion* seems to have been chosen for its effect:

> By collusion of nature and riotous living he was an extremely ugly man —Florette Henri, *Kings Mountain,* 1950

> ... this escapade, achieved with the unwitting collusion of their grandmother —*Current Biography* 1948

> ... Bay was the official and I the unofficial representative of the Board of Trade—another happy collusion —Francis Meynell, *My Lives,* 1971

> Probably it is blowing the whistle to reveal collusion between these competitors, but they did achieve a happy arrangement —Red Smith, *N.Y. Times,* 17 Mar. 1978

> ... one of those authors who seem to write almost in collusion with their audience —Anatole Broyard, *N.Y. Times Book Rev.,* 9 Mar. 1986

In these examples, where nothing really underhanded or dishonest is going on, *collusion* has been chosen for an effect, such as irony or humor. But examples like

... if merged, the two would form the biggest cigarette combine anywhere —Gwen Kinkead, *Fortune,* 29 June 1981

... the United Scouting Combine, which pools information on college players —Allan Zullo, *Popular Computing,* November 1982

... a great mining and metallurgical combine in Siberia —Edward Crankshaw, *N.Y. Times Mag.,* 30 Nov. 1975

So in recent use if the derogatory overtones are desired, they must be clearly signaled by context:

... a would-be courier for the Mediterranean heroin combine —Don DeLillo, *Esquire,* December 1971

... the hefty Hibernian hustlers of the Manhattan combine known as Tammany —Walter Wager, *Telefon,* 1975

... a university-industrial combine which is even more pervasive and which has been far more powerful in determining the shape of the university —T. R. McConnell, *AAUP Bulletin,* September 1969

come and See TRY AND.

comic, comical A number of commentators hasten to distinguish between these words, generally on the grounds that *comic* applies to what is intentionally funny and *comical* to what is unintentionally funny. Most of these commentators also note some interchangeability of the two; Chambers 1985, for instance, notes some usurping of *comical*'s territory by *comic.* Copperud 1970 notes that dictionaries do not make the same distinction.

The dictionaries are closer to reality than the commentators, whose analysis fails in two points. First, *comic* is a much more common word than *comical.* Being more familiar, *comic* tends to be used in places where *comical* might have been chosen. And second, the distinction the commentators draw is somewhat off base. Such distinction as there is rests on the fact that while *comic* can be used of anything that is funny, *comical* tends to be used of what is funny by reason of being unexpected or startling. *Comic* is the all-purpose adjective for comedy; *comical* is not used in that way. *Comic* may stress thoughtful amusement; *comical* spontaneous, unrestrained hilarity. Here are examples of each:

... with but the smallest twist, Gladstone's words and actions can be transformed from Victorian gold into comic lead —Sheldon Rothblatt, *N.Y. Times Book Rev.,* 5 Aug. 1984

... a constant sad and funny picture too. It is the knight that goes out to defend somebody who don't want to be defended. ... It is comical and a little sad —William Faulkner, 13 May 1957, in *Faulkner in the University,* 1959

These aren't cheerful tales, though they're often sharp and grotesquely comic —*Times Literary Supp.,* 23 Apr. 1970

... he looked so comical that some of the natives laughed —*Boy's Life,* June 1953

The police appear as comic figures who have no intention of arresting anybody —Lewis H. Lapham, *Harper's,* November 1971

I doubt if the Bugner combine will accept the bid — Desmond Hackett, *Daily Express,* 8 Oct. 1970

... France's largest perfume and cosmetics combine —Michael Braham, *The Observer,* 14 Apr. 1974

Thus the overtone of something shady is American. The term seems to have been first applied to an unsavory political alliance in New York around 1886, and many early citations, whether referring to combinations of persons or corporations, have a derogatory overtone. But the term has ameliorated over the years, and much of our recent American evidence is similar in tone to our British evidence:

... frightened France and Russia into their own protective combine 15 years later —Paul Kennedy, *N.Y. Times Book Rev.,* 21 Oct. 1984

... arrayed in clothes so shapeless and ill fitting that they gave his figure a comical air of having been loosely and inaccurately strung together from a selection of stuffed bags of cloth —Leslie Charteris, *The Happy Highwayman,* 1935

We are dealing with a comic perspective —Norman Mailer, *Harper's,* March 1971

comma A great deal of space is devoted in many handbooks to the various standard uses of the comma. Since this information is so widely available—in Webster's Ninth New Collegiate Dictionary and *Webster's Standard American Style Manual,* among other sound guides—we will not repeat it here. There is also a good deal of comment on the use or nonuse of a comma before the coordinating conjunction in a series of three or more. In spite of all the discussion, practice boils down to the writer's personal preference, or sometimes a house or organizational style. Additional comment is not needed. There are, however, a few other issues involving the comma.
1. See COMMA FAULT.
2. Comma between subject and predicate. It is no longer cricket to separate the subject and predicate with punctuation. "How," asks Simon 1980 rhetorically, "can one possibly separate the subject . . . from the predicate . . . by a comma?" The comma between subject and predicate is an old convention that has fallen into disuse and disfavor. It was common in the 18th century:

What Methods they will take, is not for me to prescribe —Jonathan Swift, "A Proposal for Correcting, Improving and Ascertaining the English Tongue," 1712

The words *for all that,* seem too low —Murray 1795

The first thing to be studied here, is grammatical propriety —Murray 1795

This comma is now universally frowned on and tends to be found only as a vice of comic-strip writers, advertisers, and others who are not on their guard. You should avoid the practice.

comma blunder, comma error See COMMA FAULT.

comma fault Comma fault is one of the names (others are *comma splice, comma blunder, comma error*) that composition teachers give to the joining of two independent clauses by a comma alone. It is one species of run-on sentence and has been denounced as an error at least since MacCracken & Sandison 1917. The modern comma fault seems to be a survivor from an older, looser form of punctuation:

As to the old one, I knew not what to do with him, he was so fierce I durst not go into the pit to him —Daniel Defoe, *Robinson Crusoe,* 1719

Why, sure *Betty,* thou art bewitcht, this cream is burnt too —Jonathan Swift, *Polite Conversation,* 1738

The New Jersey job was obtained, I contrived a copperplate press for it —Benjamin Franklin, *Autobiography,* 1771

These examples were not considered faulty when they were written, as 18th century punctuation did not follow the conventions that we practice today. But even as the standards of punctuation were evolving during the 19th century to those we are familiar with, the older, looser punctuation continued to be employed in personal letters:

I have found your white mittens, they were folded up within my clean nightcap —Jane Austen, letter, 24 Aug. 1805

It is not necessary for Miss M. to be an authoress, indeed I do not think publishing at all creditable either to men or women —Lord Byron, letter, 1 May 1812

Well, I won't talk about myself, it is not a healthy topic —Lewis Carroll, letter, 29(?) July 1885

The epistolary comma fault has continued into the 20th century:

This is a big picture as it has a million dollar budget and I think it is going to be a good one, it will be some time before it is finished —Ronald Reagan, letter, 2 Aug. 1938

Tell Johnny to read Santayana for a little while, it will improve his sentence structure —E. B. White, letter, 11 Mar. 1963

It seems most probable that the origin of the comma splice is the use of the comma to represent a relatively brief pause in speech (18th-century prose is closer to actual speech than it often appears now, and letters are often a close approximation of speech). Further evidence for this hypothesis can be found in modern transcriptions of speech. In the next example, the speech is fictitious:

The Ambassador . . . responded with a blast of enthusiasm. "Those weren't tough questions, those were kid-glove questions. . . ." —John Updike, *Bech Is Back,* 1982

The two independent clauses beginning with *those* would have been spoken so rapidly that any punctuation other than a comma would hardly have been possible. The comma similarly used turns up in transcriptions of actual speech:

. . . and I think that the first books, *God's Little Acre* and the short stories, that's enough for any man, he should be content with that, but knowing writers, I know he's not —William Faulkner, 13 May 1957, in *Faulkner in the University,* 1959

The Encyclopaedia Britannica lives off installment buying, this is our whole business —William Benton, quoted in Studs Terkel, *Hard Times,* 1970

And I thought, 'Oh my God, my bosoms are being seen for God's sake, I can't stand it!' —Jacqueline Bisset, quoted in *Cosmopolitan* (London), October 1974

Composition teachers, however, are rather more concerned with inadvertent comma faults that creep into student papers in ordinary expository prose. It is probably a tribute to these teachers that uncorrected examples are so hard to find in print. The example we show you below comes from a specialized journal more concerned with the dissemination of information than with literary values. It also, the sharp-eyed will note, contains a misspelling.

An unusual and beautiful coiffeur is not all that embellishes Daisy, she also has very long thick eye lashes and thin, flat, elongated nostrils —*Chronicle of the Horse,* 16 Mar. 1984

The comma fault in discursive prose is sometimes purposely used by writers for stylistic effect. As a device it can be found in the fiction of William Faulkner, Edna Ferber, E. L. Doctorow, and many others. You probably should not try the device unless you are very sure of what you want it to accomplish. Here are three examples:

> Orvie was being very helpful, he organized dances and games, he had passed plates of chicken and ice cream, he danced with some of the more awful wives —Edna Ferber, *Come and Get It,* 1935

> If I came in early I distracted them, if I came in late I enraged them, it was my life they resented, the juicy fullness of being they couldn't abide —E. L. Doctorow, *Loon Lake,* 1979

> Her face is intelligent. The hair is somewhere between strawberry and gold, you can't tell in this light —Jay McInerney, *Bright Lights, Big City,* 1984

comma splice See COMMA FAULT.

commence   *Commence* has come in for various kinds of criticism since the middle of the 19th century. There were originally three objections, of which only one survives.

The first was raised by George Perkins Marsh, in his 1859 *Lectures on the English Language.* Marsh comments in a footnote that good writers do not follow *commence* with *to* and an infinitive, but with a noun or gerund. Marsh also notes that there is no grammatical objection to such use. The OED notes that Fitzedward Hall and Miss Charlotte Yonge also commented negatively on the use. But the objection seems then to have died. The construction did not:

> . . . when the man climbed over the wall the ass commenced to crop the grass —James Stephens, *The Crock of Gold,* 1912

> "In fact," Ambrose says, "I am commencing to wonder if the cat has got its tongue. It is the most noncommittal parrot I ever see in all my life." —Damon Runyon, *Runyon à la Carte,* 1944

> After discussing the day's prospects . . . then commence to see the customers —Harry S. Truman, diary entry, 1 June 1945

The second objection was raised by Richard Grant White 1870 to a British idiom in which *commence* means "to begin to be":

> If Wit so much from Ign'rance undergo,
> Ah let not Learning too commence its foe!
>   —Alexander Pope, "Essay on Criticism," 1711

> Blake commenced pupil—Swinburne (in White 1870)

Ayres 1881 notices this use but also says that Fitzedward Hall had defended it. After Ayres there seems to be no comment. Perhaps Hall had overpowered all opposition; the OED marks the sense *archaic,* which may also account for the silence of later critics.

The third, and longest-lived, objection was started by Alford 1866. He objects to the frequent use in the newspapers of *commence* where *begin* might have served. He was also plagued by printers changing his *begin*s in

church announcements to *commence*s. Apparently *commence* was popular with journalists and printers at the time, and the Dean preferred *begin.* Ayres 1881 also opted for *begin,* as did Bierce 1909 and many subsequent commentators down to Janis 1984 and Einstein 1985. A few—Vizetelly 1906, MacCracken & Sandison 1917, Bremner 1980, and some others—distinguish *commence* and *begin* and often *start.* The consensus of those who compare is that *commence* is more formal. Other commentators supply other labels: Janis 1984 calls it "pretentious," Bryson 1984 "an unnecessary genteelism," Copperud 1970, 1980 "old-fashioned and inappropriate," Longman 1984 "bookish or pedantic."

There is a grain of truth in all these comments, but they should not be too insistently urged. The word has, after all, been in regular use in English since the 14th century, and it is not surprising that it has been used by writers of every stripe, from the artless to the humorous to the pedantic.

The word is simply too valuable to take a narrowly dim view of. It has been used to make fun of stuffed shirts:

> MOCKMODE.   . . . our friendship commenced in the college-cellar, and we loved one another like two brothers, till we unluckily fell out afterwards at a game at tables —George Farquhar, *Love and a Bottle,* 1698

> . . . things never began with Mr. Borthrop Trumbull; they always commenced —George Eliot (in Longman 1984)

> How to begin—or, as we professionals would say, "how to commence" —Ring Lardner, preface, *How to Write Short Stories,* 1924

It was part of the arsenal of 19th-century American humorists:

> Directly I spy the heathens they commence takin' on, and the spirit it begin to move 'em, they gin to kinda groan and whine —William C. Hall, "How Sally Hooter Got Snakebit," 1850, in *The Mirth of a Nation,* ed. Walter Blair & Raven I. McDavid, Jr., 1983

> . . . after she commenced her miserable gift of the gab —Frances Lee Pratt, "Captain Ben's Choice," in *Mark Twain's Library of Humor,* 1888

It is also used by writers in a serious vein:

> The Period wherein the English Tongue received most Improvement, I take to commence with the beginning of Queen Elizabeth's Reign —Jonathan Swift, "A Proposal for Correcting, Improving and Ascertaining the English Tongue," 1712

> His friendship with Arbuthnot was just now commencing —Sir Walter Scott, footnote in Swift's *Journal to Stella,* 1824

> Before Webster commenced his tinkering, the spelling of those two hundred words, however irregular to his apprehension, was more uniform than probably it will ever be again —Gould 1870

> You probably remember that when Wolcott Balestier commenced publishing in London . . . , he asked Edmund Gosse to find him a willing and inexpensive office boy —Alexander Woollcott, letter, 29 Sept. 1942

The Report was an aid to my stopping a two-pack-a-day habit which commenced in early infancy —William Styron, *This Quiet Dust and Other Writings,* 1982

And in ordinary fiction:

The ruggedness vanishes as quickly as it commenced in the east —Ernest K. Gann, *Fate Is the Hunter,* 1961

At eleven-thirty he would dash through the city room to commence drinking his lunch —Gregory McDonald, *Fletch,* 1974

The Buckeye State Used Cars enterprise looked grim and satisfactorily seedy, I turned in there and commenced a negotiation —E. L. Doctorow, *Loon Lake,* 1979

Commence, then, is a word capable of being used in several ways. You need not routinely change it to *begin* or *start.*

commend   When *commend* means "praise," it is usually used in the pattern "commend someone for" or "commend someone on":

... his wife seriously commended Mr Collins for having spoken so sensibly —Jane Austen, *Pride and Prejudice,* 1813

... commended her for her beautiful grasp and projection of the role —*Current Biography,* April 1966

... commended the membership on carrying on a half-million dollar operation with a quarter-million dollar budget —George W. Corrigan, *Connecticut Teacher,* April 1963

When it means "entrust" or "recommend," the pattern is usually "commend someone or something to":

Richard had commended her to the care of Lord Mountfalcon —George Meredith, *The Ordeal of Richard Feverel,* 1859

To thy fraternal care
   Thy sister I commend
—W. S. Gilbert, *The Yeomen of the Guard,* 1888

... a university don ... who had ventured to commend "Leaves of Grass" to the young gentlemen of his seminary —H. L. Mencken, *Prejudices: Second Series,* 1920

These two counts alone are sufficient to commend the authors to the wise and wary —Oscar Cargill, *CEA Critic,* March 1971

... the limits beyond which the Church cannot go in commending itself to Free Churchmen —T. S. Eliot, "Thoughts After Lambeth," in *Selected Essays,* 1932

commensurate   *Commensurate,* when followed by a preposition, usually takes *with:*

They say only gracious things, commensurate with the gratitude and exaltation they feel —John Updike, *Harper's,* July 1972

... to project their voices at a volume commensurate with the music —Molly Haskell, *Saturday Rev.,* 30 Oct. 1971

It is sometimes also used with *to:*

... face to face for the last time in history with something commensurate to his capacity for wonder —Richard Poirier, *A World Elsewhere,* 1966

commentate   *Commentate* is a back-formation from *commentator;* it was first used as a transitive verb in the late 18th century and then as an intransitive verb in the early 19th. A number of American writers on usage in the latter half of the 20th century have taken umbrage at its use. We have the usage panel of Heritage 1969, Shaw 1970, Bremner 1980, Janis 1984, and Harper 1985, all registering their disapproval. (Heritage 1982 rejects only the transitive use.) The amount of attention devoted to a word so little used is a little puzzling. We know of no British denigration of the word, however.

Commentate is often not used in quite the same way as *comment,* which is often recommended in its place; it tends to refer to the making of an extended, even systematic commentary or to the presentation of commentary on a regular basis rather than to scattered comments. Some examples:

Commentate upon it, and return it enriched —Charles Lamb (in Webster 1909)

... remarked to a Mr. Broun that Lardner was the country's only sports writer who had ever had any business commentating on politics —*Commonweal,* 31 Mar. 1939

Raymond Moley, after seven months of professorial commentating, decided to call it quits —*Time,* 1 Oct. 1945

... Weekend's Helen Gougeon commentated at yesterday's Fur Fashion Award Show —Harriet Hill, *The Gazette* (Montreal), 15 Apr. 1953

... Stanley Marcus ... will commentate the winning citations —Arnold Gingrich, *Esquire,* January 1974

... the fashion show commentated by Saks fashion director Patricia Fox —Kim Blair, *Los Angeles Times,* 20 Nov. 1979

There is a very true blue and pukka British centaur called Dorian Williams who always commentates on horsefests —Philip Howard, *Verbatim,* Autumn 1980

commiserate   At one time language commentators warned against using a preposition with *commiserate.* While the transitive use of *commiserate* is still in evidence, the intransitive use followed by *with* is now somewhat more common:

... conjoin to commiserate as well as to promote the teaching assistant's cause —Ann M. Heiss, *AAUP Bulletin,* December 1969

... before my trip New Yorkers commiserated with me —David Butwin, *Saturday Rev.,* 3 Apr. 1971

... I commiserated with her once about the great lost fortune —Russell Baker, *Growing Up,* 1982

Commiserate is also used with *over:*

... white liberals, who commiserate today over being excluded from the "Movement" —Harvey Wheeler, *Saturday Rev.,* 11 May 1968

commitment Phythian 1979, Bremner 1980, and Chambers 1985 remind everyone that there is only one *t* in the middle of *commitment,* which contrasts with the spelling of *committed, committing, committal,* and *committee.*

committee *Committee* is one of those collective nouns that are much more often used with a plural verb in British English than in American English. See COLLECTIVE NOUNS.

common See MUTUAL, COMMON.

commonality Howard 1978 seems to be the only commentator to take exception to the modern and predominantly American use of *commonality;* he belabors it with a handy quotation from the *Harvard Business Review.* The use or uses to which he objects seem to have become established since World War II; the origin may have been technical or military. Here are a few typical examples; you can judge for yourself whether you need to use the word, which is clearly established in standard use.

... sweating and sleeping fitfully in the overheated coach, they seemed, to Badger, to share a great commonality of intimacy and weariness —John Cheever, *The Wapshot Chronicle,* 1957

On many tractors and vehicles there is considerable commonality of parts between different makes — *Farmer's Weekly* (South Africa), 23 May 1962

Mankind's left brain, the speech region, must also have evolved; here lies the structural basis for the deep commonality of all human grammars —Philip Morrison, *Scientific American,* August 1973

... his sensitive feeling for black people and for the South, the commonality of his and their hard, church-centered, rural life —William V. Shannon, *N.Y. Times Book Rev.,* 6 June 1976

... three distinct agents whose only basic commonality of action is to effect an increase in cellular Na$^+$ —Clarence D. Cone, Jr. & Charlotte M. Cone, *Science,* 9 Apr. 1976

The commonality of the American people is politics —John Leonard, *N.Y. Times,* 17 May 1977

There are, therefore, big differences between runners, just as there are differences between all people. Yet there are commonalities —*Runners World,* December 1980

commune The verb *commune,* in its modern usage, is almost always intransitive and followed by *with:*

His very capacity to commune with peasant villagers —John K. Fairbank, *N.Y. Times Book Rev.,* 28 Aug. 1977

... they commune briefly with their only child — Winthrop Sargeant, *New Yorker,* 1 Apr. 1972

An older combination may be seen in the following:

They had much earnest conversation, freely communing on the highest matters —Thomas Carlyle, *The Life of John Sterling,* 1851

communicate, communication 1. Terms of considerable popularity, especially when they are much used

in educational institutions, tend to come under the disapproving scrutiny of usage commentators. The disapprobation expressed of *communicate* and *communication* is a bit on the nebulous side; the words are said to be overused or pretentious or unnecessary. An occasional commentator expresses a general uneasiness about the use of the terms; Copperud 1980 is disturbed by their invasion of schools of journalism, and Edmund Wilson, in *The Bit Between My Teeth* (1965), expresses nearly the same concern in a wider perspective. All the while the usage panel of Heritage 1982 finds the intransitive use of *communicate* acceptable. There does not appear to be a burning issue here.

The intransitive *communicate* is more than a hundred years old but has blossomed in the 20th century:

Because the objects of art are expressive, they communicate —John Dewey, *Art as Experience,* 1934

... genuine poetry can communicate before it is understood —T. S. Eliot, "Dante," in *Selected Essays,* 1932

If I had been a little older than eight, and Mr. Yarnall a little younger than eighty, we might have communicated more largely —Christopher Morley, *Saturday Rev.,* 28 Aug. 1954

... that love of practical jokes that is often the desperate attempt of the solitary and the shy to communicate —May Sarton, *New Yorker,* 9 Jan. 1954

That was not the same understanding that the French had. We did not communicate adequately — Jimmy Carter, quoted in *N.Y. Times,* 14 Feb. 1980

This sort of use is too well established to quibble about. **2.** Janis 1984 objects to *communication* when it does not imply reciprocity, and Follett 1966 objects when it refers to concrete carriers of information. Both would disapprove this example, but it is nonetheless a completely standard use:

Great books are original communications. Their authors are communicating what they themselves have discovered —Mortimer J. Adler, *Playboy,* January 1966

3. One of our older handbooks, Raub 1897, says that *communicate* should be followed by *to* for a singular noun and by *with* for a plural. Our evidence shows *with* in most cases, singular or plural, but *to* is still in idiomatic use.

... how could Moses communicate to him that the thread of a woman's life might depend on his consideration? —John Cheever, *The Wapshot Chronicle,* 1957

... Cynthia forced Cabot to communicate with her entirely through the keyhole —James Purdy, *Cabot Wright Begins,* 1964

Now if you wish to communicate with someone — Huntington Hartford, *American Mercury,* March 1955

Suppose ... that there are actually human beings existing in our midst who are able to communicate with each other in this spin-off of the mother tongue —Thomas H. Middleton, *Saturday Rev.,* 16 Oct. 1976 comparable   See INCOMPARABLE.

comparative   See ABSOLUTE COMPARATIVE; DOUBLE COMPARISON; IMPLICIT COMPARATIVE; SUPERLATIVE OF TWO.

comparatively   1. The point made about this adverb by commentators is that it should not be used when no comparison is stated or implied. It should not be used for "somewhat" or "fairly," say the critics. The crux here is the interpretation of *implied.* James A. H. Murray in the OED seems to have placed a loose construction on the notion. His definition reads, in part, "As compared with something else implied or thought of; not positively or absolutely; somewhat, rather."

The realization that a problem exists does not seem to have come until Gowers 1948. He includes *comparatively* and *relatively* in a list of "adverbial dressing-gowns" that are presumably of frequent use in British official prose to cover up "the nakedness of an unqualified statement." Gowers offers no example of *comparatively* so used but does give an example of *relatively* from "a circular." He added much the same discussion to Fowler 1965, again without any real example of *comparatively* used objectionably. From this modest start, *comparatively* has appeared in a succession of British usage books and dictionaries—Sellers 1975, Phythian 1979, Bryson 1984, and even Longman 1984. It has been treated in a few American sources too—Evans 1957, Bernstein 1965, Shaw 1975. Of the Americans, Bernstein and Shaw are primarily interested in *relatively,* and none of them produces a genuine example of *comparatively* used in the way they say it should not be. Only Bryson 1984 produces a real citation, and he limits it to a single sentence so that we have no way of judging for ourselves if a comparison is "clearly implied" to use his standard.

If all the discussion has been erected upon a supposed misuse buttressed by a single citation produced after the fact, you might suspect that the alleged misuse is so rare as to be beneath notice. But quite the contrary: it is common enough to be entirely established, as the OED definition confirmed from the beginning. The OED shows an example dated 1840 that is not materially different from the construction in Bryson. And here is an 18th-century example that is older than the OED's first citation:

> ... the necessity that everything should be raised and enlarged beyond its natural state, that the full effect, which otherwise would be lost in the comparatively extensive space of the theater, may come home to the spectator —Sir Joshua Reynolds, "Why Naturalism Is Not High Art" (1790 or before), reprinted in *Encore,* July 1947

And some later British examples show that the use has not faded:

> Casual people are useless in modern industry; and ... those who want to work longer and harder than the rest, find that they cannot do it except in comparatively solitary occupations —George Bernard Shaw, *The Intelligent Woman's Guide to Socialism and Capitalism,* 1928

> Indeed with so much money wagered by the public, it was an uphill struggle for noble patrons to keep either the turf or the ring even comparatively honest —G. M. Trevelyan, *English Social History,* 1942

> ... created by a comparatively small body of soldiers, sailors, administrators, missionaries and busi-

ness men —D. W. Brogan, *N.Y. Times Mag.,* 15 Aug. 1954

The point of giving these examples is not to suggest that *comparatively* is used predominantly without reference to a stated or implied comparison, for such is not the case. But uses where the comparison is not obvious have existed all along beside those in which the comparison is explicitly stated or "clearly implied."

> Nicanor Parra, a generation younger than Neruda, has, on the other hand, led a comparatively obscure and quiet life —*Times Literary Supp.,* 14 Nov. 1968

> ... died ... at the comparatively early age of fifty-two —*Times Literary Supp.,* 16 Apr. 1970

> The realistic theatre is itself a comparatively recent development—hardly much more than a hundred years old —Harold Clurman, *Harper's,* February 1971

In our judgment, there is nothing one need be concerned about here. The OED had the matter right, and it is unreasonable to expect that usage would suddenly march to the critics' tune after it had been marching to another for a century and a half. See also RELATIVELY, which has drawn the same criticism and most of the same critics.

2. Fowler 1926 devoted a considerable amount of space to attacking (at *few*) the expression "a comparatively few," and as a result the phrase is noticed as improper in Copperud 1970 and Phythian 1979 too. It is hard for us to tell you that there is a real problem, because we have no examples of its occurrence in our files. Perhaps the expression was a transient phenomenon of British journalistic writing.

compare to, compare with   Our files contain slips from about 50 commentators who are all eager to explain the difference between *compare to* and *compare with.* Their basic rule is easy to state: when you mean "to liken," use *compare to;* when you mean "to examine so as to discover the resemblances and differences," use *compare with.* Raub 1897 put it more succinctly: "Compare *with* in quality, *to* for illustration." The real world of discourse, however, is not as tidy as the rule. Part of the problem can be seen in the initial summing up: how different is "liken" from "examine to discover resemblances"? Not very, and in practice *compare* is frequently used in such a way as to make the distinction between senses uncertain, a fact commented upon as long ago as Fowler 1926.

Back in 1947 a Mr. Bernstein wrote a letter to the editor of *Word Study,* published by Merriam-Webster, objecting to a *compare to* that he thought should, on the basis of Fowler and Webster's Second, be *compare with.* The editor undertook an examination of the evidence then in the files and discovered considerable variance from the prescribed rule. He found no more than 55% observing the rule for the "liken" sense and an even split between *with* and *to* in the "examine" sense. (He also discovered that the basic distinction was first set down in the 1847 Webster unabridged.)

How do things stand some 40 years later? Without attempting statistics, we think we can give you a clear notion by examining the citations a little differently than the *Word Study* editor did in 1947.

First we will look at the active verb. For the "liken" sense, the basic rule prescribes *compare to.* Shakespeare's Sonnet XVIII is frequently set forth as an example:

Shall I compare thee to a summer's day? —1609

Modern speakers and writers have not abandoned the rule:

I know Patrick doesn't care about being compared to anybody. He's his own self —Moses Malone, quoted in *Springfield* (Mass.) *Sunday Republican,* 1 Dec. 1985

Mr. Ridley is surely not just to compare what Henry did to convicted felons in 38 years of rule to what Hitler did to innocent civilians —Maureen Quilligan, *N.Y. Times Book Rev.,* 11 Aug. 1985

The deeds of modern heroes are constantly compared to those of Greek and Roman epic and legend —Gilbert Highet, *The Classical Tradition,* 1949

They were blue, but a blue so deep that I can only compare it to the color of the night sky —Robert Penn Warren, *Partisan Rev.,* Fall 1944

... to be compared to Homer passed the time pleasantly —William Butler Yeats, *The Trembling of the Veil,* 1922

Some writers—they are a minority—use *with:*

Though Irwin is often compared with both Chaplin and Keaton as a silent clown, he is actually closer in attitude to Harold Lloyd —Mel Gussow, *New Yorker,* 11 Nov. 1985

... the first poem in which images seen are compared with sounds heard —Stephen Spender, *New Republic,* 2 Feb. 1953

So when *compare* is an active verb used in the "liken" sense, the basic rule is more often observed than not.

When *compare* is an active verb and used in the sense "examine so as to discover resemblances and differences," there is more variation in practice. Our citations show that more writers use *with* (as the basic rule prescribes) than use *to,* but the numerical difference between the majority and the minority is not as great as for the "liken" sense. Here are some examples from both groups:

That compares with a 6% year-to-year decline in the 1981 fourth quarter — *Wall Street Jour.,* 6 May 1982

This compares to an effective tax rate of 52.5 percent —*Annual Report, Colgate-Palmolive Company,* 1981

Comparing himself physically with Keaton, he said, "My body is this sort of long spaghetti noodle and his was like a whippet." —Mel Gussow, *New Yorker,* 11 Nov. 1985

... of the other three only Susana could be compared to her ancestors in vital fiber —George Santayana, *Persons and Places,* 1944

... what is now called Humanism, of which I must here say something, if only to contrast it and compare it with the Aestheticism of Pater —T. S. Eliot, "Arnold and Pater," in *Selected Essays,* 1932

... she is often asked to compare the old theatre with the new —*Current Biography,* January 1968

We can conclude, then, that when *compare* is used as an active verb in the "examine" sense, the basic rule calling for *with* is more often observed than not, but quite a few writers use *to.* One other point should be mentioned: the possibility of uncertainty as to which sense of *compare* a writer has intended. Look at the Santayana quotation above—couldn't the sense be "liken" just as easily? Or look at this example:

Mr. Eliot compares them in their possible wide effectiveness with the present body of segregated intellectuals who now write only for each other —Lionel Trilling, *Partisan Rev.,* September–October 1940

If *compare* can be used as an active verb in such a way that we cannot be sure which sense is intended, when *compared* is used as a detached past participle, sometimes introduced by *as,* it is much harder to try to distinguish between the prescribed *to* and *with* senses. Fowler 1926 was the first to take note of this fact. He puts it this way:

Compared with, or *to, him I am a bungler* (this is a common type in which either sense is applicable).

More recently we find James J. Kilpatrick observing:

I will never in my life comprehend the distinction between *compared to* and *compared with.* My ear hears nothing amiss in "This year's corn crop, compared *to* last year's," or in "This year's corn crop, compared *with* last year's." —Kilpatrick 1984

Our files show that *with* and *to* are used about equally after the past participle. In spite of Fowler's comment about either sense being applicable, most of the following examples, we think, you will find to be of the "examine for resemblances and differences" sense.

... a million people will go abroad for a holiday this year, compared with 750,000 in 1952 —Vincent Mulchrone, quoting an unknown speaker in *Punch,* 8 July 1975

Only 9 percent of American doctors are women, compared to 24 percent in Great Britain —Leonard Gross, *McCall's,* March 1971

American text treatments are conservative, compared with ours —Allen Hutt, *Newspaper Design,* 2d ed., 1971

So much of the action of hockey was freewheeling, imaginative, instinctive, as compared to football with its precise routes and exact assignments — George Plimpton, *Sports Illustrated,* 30 Jan. 1978

... political thinking in the United States is skewed sharply to the right as compared with the other Western democracies —Noam Chomsky, *Columbia Forum,* Winter 1969

... the house is luxurious compared to some of the cabins up the hollow —Robert Coles, *Harper's,* November 1971

Sixty-two million people are now gainfully employed, compared with fifty-one million 7 years ago —Harry S. Truman, State of the Union Message, 7 Jan. 1953

But that's just a minor difference compared to the major agreements on which we base present and future policy —Jimmy Carter, quoted in *N.Y. Times,* 14 Feb. 1980

... our flag officers and senior captains are old compared with those of other navies —Hanson W. Baldwin, *Harper's,* April 1941

... will have four armored, or tank, divisions, as compared to the single brigade ... available a year ago —Hanson W. Baldwin, *Foreign Affairs,* October 1940

Compared with the earls and the actresses, the Knapweed-Knapweeds are numerous —Aldous Huxley, *The Olive Tree,* 1937

... will not challenge a stag in possession of a harem if his rival's antlers are too big compared to his own —Julian Huxley, *Yale Rev.,* Autumn 1943

... this is the third novelty in his work as compared with that of the past decade —Malcolm Cowley, *New Republic,* 7 Apr. 1941

Compared to the language of Michelet ... , Renan's prose is pale —Edmund Wilson, *To the Finland Station,* 1940

... Europe's economy is doing quite nicely, thank you, compared with the years after the second world war —*The Economist,* 26 Apr. 1986

Unemployment is low compared to that of other tribes —David Edmunds, *Wilson Quarterly,* New Year's 1986

Compared with the fables, my own work is insignificant —Marianne Moore, quoted in *Time,* 24 May 1954

... you always seemed so firm to me compared to myself —E. B. White, letter, 13 Feb. 1972

We can conclude, then, that in 20th-century practice, the general rule of the handbooks is followed more often than not when *compare* is used as an active verb, but both *with* and *to* are used equally with the past participle. The rule can be looked upon as a guide that you may choose to observe if you wish to. Many writers obviously do not.

There is one more point of interest. Fowler says that with the intransitive verb, only *with* is possible. The construction he gives as an example is a negative one. In modern practice, both *with* and *to* are used:

And while Mr. Wilson doesn't compare with Miss Murdoch, the metaphysical playfulness in his book reminds us of her —Anatole Broyard, *N.Y. Times Book Rev.,* 9 Mar. 1986

... ham and bamboo shoots did not compare to those made at Ying's —Mimi Sheraton, *N.Y. Times,* 16 Dec. 1977

For all-around dependability ... nothing else compares with a Cleveland —advt., *Bookbinding and Book Production,* June 1953

Nothing compares to the actual handling of a multitude of concrete cases —Thomas F. McNally, *Bulletin of the National Catholic Education Association,* August 1949

Not even the collapse of the Roman Empire compared with a calamity so serious —Henry Adams, *Mont-Saint-Michel and Chartres,* 1904

No other auto race in the U.S. quite compares to the Sebring grind —*Time,* 14 Mar. 1955

comparison 1. See ABSOLUTE ADJECTIVES; ABSOLUTE COMPARATIVE; DOUBLE COMPARISON; IMPLICIT COMPARATIVE; SUPERLATIVE OF TWO.

2. Illogical comparison. Copperud 1970, 1980 notes that some people object to constructions like "the finback has the tallest spout of any whale" (R. C. Murphy, *Logbook for Grace,* 1947, cited in Bryant 1962) on the grounds that *any* includes the thing being compared in the group it is being compared with. This is rather subtle reasoning for everyday use, and it is little wonder that it is often ignored or unthought of. Bryant notes that such constructions have been used since Chaucer's time and can be found in informal and sometimes in formal prose. The one statistical study she mentions found the superlative with *any* about 30 percent of the time and the superlative with *all*—which is held to be more logical—about 70 percent of the time.

... 13 years in that high office—the longest of any President —*Boy's Life,* May 1968

... the tallest of all the girls —Patricia Browning Griffith, *Harper's,* March 1969

Bryant also notes the occasional use of the comparative in this construction—"a more intolerable wrong of nature than any which man has devised" (*Reader's Digest,* November 1957, cited in Bryant)—but finds it much less common than the same construction with *any other* in place of *any.* Most commentators who mention the problem recommend the use of *any other.*

Your father would probably remember Franklin Delano Roosevelt, the 32nd President, better than any other —*Boy's Life,* May 1968

3. Phythian 1979 says that the word *comparison* should be followed by *with* and not by *to. Comparison* is indeed followed by *with:*

... minor projects in comparison with the work he was doing —*Current Biography,* December 1967

... the English language was not fit to bear comparison with the learned languages of Europe —W. F. Bolton, *A Short History of Literary English,* 1967

Poor in comparison with rich relatives on either side —*Times Literary Supp.,* 22 Oct. 1971

... he considered himself a saint in comparison with Florabelle's mother —Erskine Caldwell, *Tragic Ground,* 1944

It is also, but somewhat less frequently, followed by *to:*

... waspish by comparison to the cars he was accustomed to —Terry Southern, *Flash and Filigree,* 1958

... sales so pale and unpromising in comparison to those of the thirties —John Brooks, *New Yorker,* 27 Apr. 1957

... our own language is nothing special in comparison to other languages —Robert A. Hall, Jr., *Leave Your Language Alone,* 1950

Formerly *of* was used:

They who think everything, in comparison of that honor, to be dust and ashes —Edmund Burke, speech, 1780

... would be frail and light in comparison of ourselves —Thomas De Quincey, "The Vision of Sudden Death," 1849

Between is also used in constructions where both items being compared appear after *comparison:*

> ... draws an interesting comparison between Marcion's rejection of the Old Testament and Bultmann's existential approach —*Times Literary Supp.,* 18 Jan. 1968

> ... there is little comparison between Michelangelo's *Sonnets* and his sculpture and paintings —René Wellek & Austin Warren, *Theory of Literature,* 1949

compatible   When *compatible* is used with a preposition, it is usually *with:*

> ... how to make full employment compatible with reasonable price stability —Charles L. Schultze, *Saturday Rev.,* 22 Jan. 1972

> ... forms of adventure and danger ... which are compatible with the civilized way of life —Bertrand Russell, *Authority and the Individual,* 1949

If *compatible* is applied to devices, again the choice is usually *with.* However, there is evidence that *to* is sometimes used:

> The system also will be compatible with cable television, and can provide 20 channels —*Wall Street Jour.* 31 Mar. 1982

> It seems like a tragic waste, if quad records are compatible to ordinary stereo systems, that more records aren't being made —Alan Rich, *New York,* 16 Aug. 1976

compendious   In 1806 Noah Webster published *A Compendious Dictionary of the English Language.* Its vocabulary runs to 355 pages, and, when back matter and front matter are added in, the book amounts to more than 400 pages. It is not a slim volume. What is most noticeable about the book is that most of its 37,000 words are defined in a single line each. The *Compendious Dictionary* is tightly packed and its definitions are concise; it illustrates the definition of *compendious* that is found in Webster's Ninth New Collegiate Dictionary: "marked by brief expression of a comprehensive matter."

Compendious has another salient characteristic: it sounds big. Many people, when they first read or hear the word, get the notion that it means "big and comprehensive" or simply "comprehensive." Probably most of them have to learn that it is also supposed to connote conciseness, compactness, brevity. Some never do learn this, and thus usage writers gain another topic for discussion.

And here is where the trouble begins. Evans 1957 says that the word "means concise, or containing the substance of a subject in brief form. ..." His definition adequately covers Noah Webster's title and uses like this:

> For readers too anemic to face up to the 868 double-column pages ... Twitchell gives a compendious summary in an appendix —S. Schoenbaum, *N.Y. Rev. of Books,* 30 Jan. 1986

But Evans goes on to say "A *compendious* work may be large or small, but its compendiousness has nothing to do with its size." Now let us assume he is right. Let us further suppose that a reader to whom the word is unfamiliar sees this passage:

> Goold Brown ... in his compendious, and bulky, *Grammar of English Grammars* —Julia P. Stanley, *College English,* March 1978

If Evans is right, this book can be both compendious in its treatment and bulky in size. But how can the reader know that Goold Brown has treated his matter concisely? There is no way, unless he or she is already familiar with the book. The natural inclination of the reader seeing *compendious* linked with *bulky* is to think of comprehensiveness.

And to judge from our evidence, comprehensiveness is the usual connotation that readers pick up and, apparently, is also what writers intend. Our evidence runs from 1798 to 1986. In our earliest example, Jane Austen is commenting on a one-sentence description:

> A short and compendious history of Miss Debarry! —letter, 25 Nov. 1798

The combining of *short* with *compendious* suggests that comprehensiveness was in Miss Austen's mind. She is not the only writer to use the combination:

> Such looseness cannot be afforded in a short and compendious book —*Times Literary Supp.,* 7 Dec. 1951

In this second example, the writer may have been following Evans's definition, but the reader has no way of knowing it for certain. And the same may be said for a few of the following examples. But we believe that not only is comprehensiveness the connotation the reader will take from these examples, it is in most cases clearly what the writer had in mind too:

> Scott's "Specialized Catalogue of United States Stamps" for 1975, the 53d edition of this work, has now become available, a little bit later than in other years, but not a bit less compendious or useful to the collector —Samuel A. Tower, *N.Y. Times,* 23 Feb. 1975

> ... offered a most diversified and compendious program at the APA meetings —*The Americana Annual* 1953

> ... Miss Mainwaring's achievement is, so far as my fairly compendious memory stretches, unmatched —Anthony Boucher, *N.Y. Times Book Rev.,* 15 Aug. 1954

> In times of violent action and rapid change, compendious treatises of political philosophy can scarcely be expected —W. L. Renwick, *English Literature 1789–1815,* 1963

> As for the writing of our more extreme, compendious, sociological novelists —Glenway Wescott, *Images of Truth,* 1962

> ... his costumes, which are the fruit of a compendious knowledge —a reviewer, quoted in *Current Biography,* October 1964

> ... which stocks what must be one of the most compendious collections of jackknives in the known universe —Jay Jacobs, *Gourmet,* December 1982

> ... most of the texts I selected can also be found in either the Arndt or the Fennell, for their books are compendious, and there is bound to be some agreement on what is the best —D. M. Thomas, *N.Y. Times Book Rev.,* 24 Oct. 1982

> It is doubtful that even the most compendious traditional or teaching grammar notes such simple facts —Noam Chomsky, *Knowledge of Language,* 1986

It appears to us that *compendious* tends to be generally understood as and frequently used for the "comprehensive" half of its older "concise and comprehensive" meaning. This understanding probably results from learning the word by reading it in contexts where, if Evans's analysis is correct, the "conciseness" half of its meaning can be ascertained only by acquaintance with the thing being described. Consequently, most of us are aware only of the "comprehensive" idea. Dictionaries have been slow to recognize this development, but they will inevitably have to do so.

compendium   Bernstein 1962, 1965 and Copperud 1964, 1970, 1980 assert that a compendium must be an abridgment or something brief—something little, not big. Bryson 1984 says size has nothing to do with it—the point is the concise treatment. All three have unfortunately fixed on one use of a multipurpose word and assumed that their use is the only correct use. *Compendium* is not a narrowly or precisely applied word. It has been used of items as diverse as books, people, packages of stationery, periodicals, buildings, and collections of several kinds. The doubtful should look at the examples given in the OED, the OED Supplement, or Webster's Third. Or read the fairly recent examples shown below. The plurals *compendia* and *compendiums,* by the way, are both acceptable.

Polio victims are a compendium of all the virtues —Wilfrid Sheed, *People Will Always Be Kind,* 1973

Important is naturally the most overused word in these compendia, which are now easily available in museum bookshops —Marina Vaizey, in Michaels & Ricks 1980

Changing Climate, a compendium of reviews, original contributions, and synthesis —John S. Perry, *Nature,* 24 Oct. 1984

His compendia of shibboleths run for scores of pages —Harvey A. Daniels, *Famous Last Words,* 1983

... stationery in a wide choice of colors, ready-packaged in compendiums whose boxes are a stately form of gift wrap in themselves —*New Yorker,* 21 Nov. 1983

... compendia, ranging from extensive but unoriginal compilations all the way to mere reproductions of lecture-notes —Robert A. Hall, Jr., *External History of the Romance Languages,* 1974

She suddenly became a compendium of knowledge about Maoris and kiwi birds and sheep dipping —Cynthia Heimel, *Playboy,* November 1983

Hyannis is a concrete compendium of shopping malls, fast-food drive-ins and tourist stands —Milton Moore, *N.Y. Times,* 17 July 1983

... her role ... is a compendium of her previous roles —Pauline Kael, *New Yorker,* 30 Jan. 1971

The buildings themselves are a compendium of clichés of modern architecture —Paul Goldberger, *N.Y. Times,* 2 July 1976

From the administration's point of view, the direct subsidy to the Russians is a drop in the bucket compared with the full compendium of direct and indirect subsidies —*Wall Street Jour.,* 13 Aug. 1986

competence, competency   Copperud 1970, 1980 finds the two forms interchangeable in American usage, with *competence* the predominant form. Fowler 1926 also says the forms are interchangeable, a statement repeated by Gowers in Fowler 1965, with the additional observation that *competency* is preferred (in British usage) for the sense "a sufficiency of means for life" and *competence* for the rest. Gowers may be right, but his observation is not substantiated by our evidence nor by the treatment given the words in Longman 1984, a contemporary British dictionary. The "sufficiency of means" sense, which is not especially common, is perhaps more evenly divided between the two variants than other senses:

... their pockets were well lined, for without a considerable competence, a man could not be a Senator at all —*Times Literary Supp.,* 22 Oct. 1971

Having acquired a competency there, he returned to England —*Australian Dictionary of Biography,* 1967

... and retired with an ample competence in 1868 —*Dictionary of American Biography,* 1929

He remained in business with his three brothers ... only until he had acquired a competency —*Dictionary of American Biography,* 1929

Longman 1984 calls this sense *formal,* and the sources quoted suggest that it is not especially likely to be met with in everyday conversation.

The variants are not quite as interchangeable as the usage writers would suggest, and dictionaries seldom have the space to spell out preferences in much detail. We can tell you that *competence* is much more frequently used in general than *competency; competence* seems to be the only form used in the linguistic sense (where it contrasts with *performance*); and *competency* seems to be most frequently used in the fields of education and law. Mitchell 1979 has noticed the educational use: "Thus the school people have changed 'competence' to 'competency,' gaining thereby some small increase in self-esteem and a twenty-five percent increase in syllables...." Mr. Mitchell's years of teaching presumably make him competent to speak to educators' self-esteem, but his apparent suggestion that *competency* is a neologism is as faulty as his arithmetic. *Competency* is not the creation of school people; it has been around since the end of the 16th century, and though its use in general is dwindling, it can still be met in literary works—generally older ones—as well as in journals and columns devoted to specialized and technical subjects:

... with a decent competency of onion sauce —Washington Irving, "The Legend of Sleepy Hollow," 1820

... had the thrift to remove a modest competency of the gold —Ambrose Bierce, *In The Midst of Life,* 1891

Powell could not defend himself from some sympathy for that thick, bald man ... who was so tactfully ready to take his competency for granted —Joseph Conrad, *Chance,* 1913

Educational use in our files tends to be plural—"skills, knowledge, and competencies"—or attributive, as in "minimum competency requirements" or "competency testing." Since many of the attributive uses refer to state laws or requirements, one suspects an overlay of legal usage upon the educational.

complacent, complaisant **1.** A number of commentators (Kilpatrick 1984, Bryson 1984, and Copperud 1970, 1980 among them) warn against the confusion of these words. If the words were used only in the senses assigned by these gentlemen, they would never be confused, of course. Conveniently overlooked in their defining is the fact that *complacent* has been and is used to mean "marked by an inclination to please or oblige"—the first sense of *complaisant* in Webster's Ninth New Collegiate Dictionary. This is, in fact, the only meaning Johnson's 1755 dictionary gives *complacent*. Johnson's biographer Boswell also used this sense:

> Though for several years her temper had not been complacent, she had valuable qualities —James Boswell, *Life of Samuel Johnson,* 1791

Perhaps part of the problem was precipitated by the publication of the OED, which enters this sense of *complacent* but also wonders if it is obsolete. Despite the speculation, the OED cites three sources: Burke from 1790, Scott from 1821, and Charlotte Brontë from 1849. This evidence notwithstanding, language critics at the turn of the century began labeling this use of *complacent* as an error. That the sense is still in occasional use the Merriam-Webster files attest:

> ... the man of feeling, the man of action and the man of thought. The one is tolerant, complacent, easy going, convivial, loving —*Horizon,* December 1946

> The University of Colorado courteously released me from my contract, but the Garrett Biblical Institute was less complacent —Robert Morss Lovett, *All Our Years,* 1948

On the whole, however, modern writers regularly spell this meaning *complaisant*. *Complacent* in its modern senses is used more commonly than *complaisant*. If you are doubtful about the meaning of either word, a good dictionary will solve your problem.
2. When *complacent* is used with a preposition, it is most likely to be *about:*

> She's not very complacent about having done that — Robert Penn Warren, *All the King's Men,* 1946

Less frequently used are *with, of,* or *to:*

> ... with my office building paid for, is it any wonder that I grew complacent with the status quo —*The Autobiography of William Allen White,* 1946

> For several years, the U.S., complacent of its ability to stay ahead of Russia in all things technological — *Time,* 10 Jan. 1955

> But then, as she quickly reminded herself, she had been no more complacent to him ... than she had been to half-a-dozen others. Men were so stupid! — *The Strand,* December 1913

Unlike *complacent, complaisant* hardly ever is used with a preposition:

> ... who is known in history largely as the complaisant husband of his wife —Claude G. Bowers, *The Young Jefferson, 1743–1789,* 1945

compleat Labeled an obsolete spelling of *complete* in the OED, *compleat* is entered in the OED Supplement with the notation "Revived in imitation of its 17th-cent. use. ..." The spelling seems to have made its comeback by means of book titles such as *The Compleat Bachelor, The Compleat Pediatrician, The Compleat Strategyst.* These titles were, of course, modeled on Izaak Walton's *The Compleat Angler.* Around the middle of the 20th century, *compleat* began to creep back into running text as well:

> A compleat decoration and consulting service — advt., *Antiques,* October 1952

> As a help in breaking down the Prime Minister's compleat personality —John Haverstick, *Saturday Rev.,* 4 Dec. 1954

> The compleat idler is a recurrent American dream —*Time,* 24 June 1957

> ... one of the most decorated officers in the Army and a compleat professional —Ward Just, *Atlantic,* October 1970

> Again Mr. Thomas showed himself to be the compleat maestro —Winthrop Sargeant, *New Yorker,* 20 Nov. 1971

> ... one gazed on the compleat politician, accepted him as such, and did not much consider the man — Henry Fairlie, *Harper's,* January 1973

> ... playing Dracula as the compleat ladykiller — Janet Maslin, *N.Y. Times,* 13 July 1979

> ... clarion calls for the compleat physician —*JAMA,* 29 Aug. 1980

complected Not an error, nor a dialectal term, nor an illiteracy, nor nonstandard—all of which it has been labeled—*complected* is simply an Americanism, and apparently a 19th-century Americanism. It seems to be nonexistent in British English. It is attested as early as 1806 in the *Journals of Lewis & Clark,* used by Meriwether Lewis. Until the early 20th century it excited no notice except from compilers of Americanisms and regional terms. (Those who subscribe to the opinion that it is regional dialect—such as Harper 1985—should know that the Dictionary of American Regional English reports it "widespread.") Beginning with Vizetelly 1906, however, it began to raise hackles, and it has been variously aspersed in nearly every American handbook and usage book published from that time to the present. No British book mentions it.

There seems to be no very substantial objection to the term, other than the considerable diffidence American usage writers feel about Americanisms. It is irregularly formed, to be sure, but so are many other words. It has been used by some of our better-known authors:

> You look lots like yer mother: Purty much same in size;
> And about the same complected
> —James Whitcomb Riley, *Love-Lyrics,* 1883

> Here is the dark-complected hand with a potato on its fork ... there the light-complected head's got it —Mark Twain, *Those Extraordinary Twins,* 1894 (*A Mark Twain Lexicon,* 1938)

> A heavy-sot man, sandy complected —O. Henry, *The Trimmed Lamp,* 1916 (OED Supplement)

... the man they meant wasn't dark complected — William Faulkner, *Light in August,* 1932 (OED Supplement)

... a blue-eyed, fair-complected man —A. B. Guthrie, Jr., *The Way West,* 1949

... a tall, thin man, fairly dark complected —E. J. Kahn, Jr., *The Peculiar War,* 1952

... his face, though lined a little, was fresh and well complected —Robert Penn Warren, *Band of Angels,* 1955

... a stocky man with a red-complected shining brown face —E. L. Doctorow, *Ragtime,* 1975

Complexioned, universally recommended as a substitute for *complected,* has less use than *complected:*

... all look too coarse complexioned and dowdy — Henry Adams, letter, 17 May 1859

... a red-complexioned man of medium height — Santha Rama Rau, *The Reporter,* 16 Mar. 1954

... the pale-complexioned women —Alan Moorehead, *New Yorker,* 1 May 1954

A heavy-set, swarthy-complexioned man —Vern E. Smith, *The Jones Men,* 1974

Our recent evidence shows that neither of these words is in very frequent use in print. Here are two examples:

Mussels in a tangy ravigote dressing have been right on the mark on several tries: corpulent, clear-complected specimens —Jay Jacobs, *Gourmet,* May 1982

He is pink-complexioned with lemon-colored hair —W. P. Kinsella, *Sports Illustrated,* 14 Apr. 1986

While both are still in use, many writers apparently avoid using either one. Literary use slightly favors *complected.*

complement, compliment A very large number of usage books and handbooks, from the grade-school level up, warn against confusing *complement* and *compliment.* This is really a spelling problem, as your dictionary will demonstrate, since the two words share no meanings whatsoever, as either noun or verb. The evidence we have of the misspelling tends to be the use of the commoner *compliment* in place of *complement:*

The assignments and exercises were challenging and complimented points the instructor was making — quoted in *New Yorker,* 1 Nov. 1982

To compliment the butter campaign, American Dairy Association has created new butter point-of-purchase materials —*Eastern Milk Producer,* April 1985

... a knowledge of the possibilities of their branching pattern, complimented by nerve dissection with fine instruments —*Biological Abstracts,* July 1954

A quick check of your dictionary should clear up any doubts about which spelling you need. The same caution applies to the adjectives *complementary* and *complimentary.*

complete, completely *Complete* is one of those words some people think are absolute adjectives—

adjectives that cannot be logically modified by *more, most,* or *less.* It is, for instance, on the huge list of such adjectives compiled in Partridge 1942. For a discussion of these, see ABSOLUTE ADJECTIVES.

Complete itself does not upset many commentators when modified; the usage panel of Heritage 1969, 1982 finds it acceptable, as do Harper 1985 and Bryson 1984. The pointlessness of worrying about the modification of *complete* can perhaps be illustrated by these quite ordinary examples:

Today the separation is even more complete —John Fischer, *Harper's,* March 1971

Yet even after the most complete victory in history —Denis Brogan, *Esquire,* March 1970

His technical ignorance had proved even more complete than he thought —Norman Mailer, *Harper's,* March 1971

The composer with whom he was in closest and most complete sympathy —*Times Literary Supp.,* 16 Apr. 1970

... taking special pains to give an impression of completest normalcy —Saul Bellow, *Herzog,* 1964

The adverb *completely* is similarly modified, despite occasional objection (as by Sellers 1975):

But if Swift was ... let in to all their secrets (more completely than has usually been thought) —Bonamy Dobrée, *English Literature in the Early Eighteenth Century, 1700–1740,* 1959

complex Copperud 1970, 1980 reports that some commentators object to the use of *complex* in nontechnical prose in a figurative sense derived from psychological use (as in *Oedipus complex*). The books that contain these criticisms (Bernstein 1965, Evans 1957, Fowler 1965) are now more than a quarter century old. The OED Supplement shows that this figurative use began as far back as 1927, and Copperud notes that most dictionaries consider it standard. If the use was a bit of a fad 30 or 40 years ago, it no longer is; other senses of the noun are currently in much more frequent use. But the figurative sense is still occasionally encountered. As these examples suggest, it is not used very often in highly serious writing:

My childhood passed rather uneventfully, getting only pimples and a complex to remember it by — Pat Rutter, quoted in *Rolling Stone,* 22 June 1972

... Jemima, the Blackface ewe with the Houdini complex. No respecter of confining fences —*Scottish Field,* June 1974

... the British do not share our superstar complex —Karl E. Meyer, *Saturday Rev.,* 25 Nov. 1978

... there is a distinct feeling that if the Royals lose the first game, they will be overcome by their Yankee complex —Murray Chass, *N.Y. Times,* 6 Oct. 1980

I think in the arts and in all matters that relate to the intellectual, we still have a colonial complex —Tom Wolfe, quoted in *Saturday Rev.,* April 1981

complexioned See COMPLECTED.

compliance Murray 1795 corrected two 18th-century examples of "in compliance to" to "in compliance with." Murray seems to have had a good sense of the way the idiom was changing in this case. The standard pattern in current English is *compliance with* (something) and *compliance of* (someone).

> . . . to compel state compliance with acts of Congress —Eugene J. McCarthy, *Dictionary of American Politics,* 1968

> . . . they can no longer count on the automatic compliance of the countries of Eastern Europe —Arthur M. Schlesinger, Jr., *Harper's,* March 1969

compliment, complimentary See COMPLEMENT, COMPLIMENT.

comply A couple of handbooks insist on *comply with* and reject *comply to,* but they fail to make an important distinction. When the agent is human, the preposition is *with.* When it is mechanical, however, either *with* or *to* may be used.

> . . . should you think ill of that person for complying with the desire —Jane Austen, *Pride and Prejudice,* 1813

> . . . if you do not comply with my wishes —Thomas Love Peacock, *Nightmare Abbey,* 1818

> Rather than comply with various rulings of the Supreme Court, he . . . —E. J. Kahn, Jr., *New Yorker,* 10 Apr. 1971

> In 1969, 10 percent of the automobile parts tested . . . failed to comply with federal safety standards — Philip G. Schrag, *Columbia Forum,* Summer 1970

> . . . has softer front rubber insulators, and allows front wheels to comply to road shocks —*Motor Trend,* November 1967

compose See COMPRISE.

compound subjects See AGREEMENT, SUBJECT-VERB: COMPOUND SUBJECTS.

comprise Between thirty and forty commentators are represented in our files as subscribing to this dictum (from Copperud 1970): "The whole *comprises* the parts; thus *is comprised of* is wrong." The subject was a particular favorite of Theodore Bernstein; he put it in his 1958, 1965, and 1977 books and treated it many times in *Winners & Sinners.* Our commentators are both British and American, and as far as we can discover, all are citizens of the 20th century. We have not yet discovered any 19th-century comment. The earliest we have found is in an American printers' trade journal, the *Inland Printer,* March 1903. Our earliest British source is Fowler 1907.
  Copperud's brief summary is a bit too succinct. There are actually two constructions involved in the disputed usage: the passive one Copperud mentions and an active one that is most easily spotted when a plural noun is the subject of *comprise:*

> The words they found comprise, if not the language of enormity, a language for enormity —David Reid, in Michaels & Ricks 1980

The *Inland Printer* writer found two similar uses: "the companies that comprise the regiment" and "the houses that comprise the row," which, he avers, "are actual quotations from print." The active construction is the

older of the two. The OED records it in the late 18th century, but the editors did not have much evidence and labeled the use *rare.* The OED Supplement has collected many later examples. The most noteworthy characteristic of the construction is that from the beginning into the early 20th century, it seems to have been rather more frequent in technical and scientific writing than in belles lettres. It seems to have gained increasing use, and especially nontechnical use, in the 20th century:

> It was these last words that proved to Joseph that the ringlets and bracelets did not comprise the whole of this young man's soul —George Moore, *The Brook Kerith,* 1916

> . . . each number . . . carries our names up in the corner as comprising the editorial staff —Alexander Woollcott, letter, Spring 1918

> . . . the ceremonies which comprise the abdication — Sir James G. Frazer, *Aftermath,* 1937

> . . . they comprise the only repertory that is unique to it —Virgil Thomson, *The Musical Scene,* 1947

> The basic assumptions and techniques which comprise the scientific way of interpreting reality —Leslie A. White, *The Science of Culture,* 1949

> Adjacent rock formations determine the sand and pebbles comprising a beach —Joyce Allan, *Australian Shells,* 1950

> The receipts . . . comprised the fifth-largest gate in boxing history —John Lardner, *New Yorker,* 17 Mar. 1951

> . . . individuals who comprised the planting aristocracy —Oscar Handlin, *The American People in the Twentieth Century,* 1954

> The buildings that comprise the Nunnery quadrangle —Katharine Kuh, *Saturday Rev.,* 28 June 1969

> . . . the $750 billion of tax cuts through 1986 that comprise the heart of the Reagan program —Kenneth H. Bacon, *Wall Street Jour.,* 31 Aug. 1981

> . . . the sixty or so scowling citizens who comprised the forward section of the line —T. Coraghessan Boyle, *Atlantic,* January 1982

> . . . the moralistic qualities that comprised Carter's systematic weakness in foreign policy —Joseph Kraft, *Los Angeles Times,* 26 Sept. 1984

> Seven boys comprised the choir —Garrison Keillor, *Lake Wobegon Days,* 1985

This sense—"compose, constitute"—can be found from time to time with a singular subject:

> Miss Sally Fagg has a pretty figure, & that comprises all the good looks of the family —Jane Austen, letter, 14 Oct. 1813

> For too long there has existed a misconception as to what comprises a literary generation —William Styron, *N.Y. Times Book Rev.,* 6 May 1973

> Weaver, whose .597 percentage over the last 14 years comprises baseball's third-best all-time —Ron Powers, *Inside Sports,* August 1982

The active construction, we can see, is flourishing and can be found in quite a wide range of writing.

The passive construction is the one that caught the eye of the Fowler brothers in 1907. They reproduced this example:

A few companies, comprised mainly of militiamen —*Times*

The passive construction is not as old as the active; the OED Supplement dates it from 1874. H. W. Fowler intended to give it extended treatment in his 1926 book, but the paragraph was accidentally omitted, and he had to content himself with publishing it five years later in *S.P.E.* (Society for Pure English) *Tract 36.* The passive construction too appears to be in a flourishing condition today, as does the detached past participle:

... it was universally believed that mankind was comprised of a single species —Ashley Montagu, *Man's Most Dangerous Myth: The Fallacy of Race,* 2d ed., 1945

... his vision of environment as comprised of chemic, economic, and natural force —Richard Poirier, *A World Elsewhere,* 1966

Like any other system comprised of complex feedback cycles —Barry Commoner, *Columbia Forum,* Spring 1968

... a great many of the present-day centers are comprised of militant groups —Irving Louis Horowitz, *Center Mag.,* May 1969

Social situations ... are comprised of complex interrelated variables —V. L. Allen, *Social Analysis,* 1975

Comprised of a Chinese managing director, British manager, French concierge, German food and beverage director ... this talented multi-lingual team ... —Linda Gwinn, *Town & Country,* June 1980

The audience, comprised mainly of undergraduates in sneakers and denim —William Kucewicz, *Wall Street Jour.,* 19 Jan 1981

... a series of 30 gates comprised of red and green poles —Patrick Strickler, *Sports Illustrated,* 10 Dec. 1984

But do not think that the vigorous condition of the disputed constructions has tended to crowd the older senses out of use. Not at all. *Comprise* seems to have increased in overall use enough so that all the senses current within the last 200 years are still in good health. Here is a small sample of the two most common older senses. You should notice that they come from many of the same sources as the disputed constructions:

Three months comprised thirteen weeks —Jane Austen, *Mansfield Park,* 1814

... civilization as Lenin used the term would then certainly have comprised the changes that are now associated in our minds with "developed" rather than "developing" states —*Times Literary Supp.,* 5 Mar. 1970

... a series ... that eventually comprised more than 200 titles —Judith Appelbaum, *N.Y. Times Book Rev.,* 2 Jan. 1983

Originally the Hogs comprised only the Skins' offensive linemen —Jack McCallum, *Sports Illustrated,* 6 June 1983

... a Senate comprising free-lance egos —*Wall Street Jour.,* 8 Nov. 1984

The course of studies comprised Classics, Theology, and Commercial —Garrison Keillor, *Lake Wobegon Days,* 1985

Conclusion: the aspersed active construction of *comprise* has been in use for nearly two centuries; the passive construction for more than a century. It is a little hard to understand why these constructions that are so obviously established are still the source of so much discontent. (They have been defined in Merriam-Webster dictionaries since 1934.) Perhaps the critics are worried about the older senses:

Unlike all but a few modern writers, Mrs. Spark uses the verb "comprise" correctly —John Updike, *New Yorker,* 23 July 1984

But our evidence shows no diminution of vitality in the older senses—"include" and "be made up of." Even sportswriters use them. If the criticism has had any noticeable effect, it may be that it causes some writers to avoid the passive construction, which is slightly less well attested in our files than we might have expected. The active construction is the harder one to detect and so has not received as much antagonistic notice. Our advice to you is to realize that the disputed sense is established and standard, but nevertheless liable to criticism. If such criticism concerns you, you can probably avoid *comprise* by using *compose, constitute,* or *make up,* whichever fits your sentence best.

concensus   See CONSENSUS 3.

concept   Bryson 1984, Janis 1984, Ebbitt 1982, Macmillan 1982, and Copperud 1970, 1980 are among those who complain of a fad use of *concept* in a sense approximating *idea* (or any of a number of other words trotted out to suit the need). College handbooks may be trying to eliminate this from the writing of students in Freshman English, but the real problem here is that the commentators are all criticizing business and advertising use without saying so. Our files are full of examples of *concept* from the annual reports of U.S. corporations. And we have this sort of thing:

... they perceive their roles as selling merchandise when they should be marketing a concept —Joel B. Portugal, *N.Y. Times,* 7 Dec. 1980

And this:

... weaknesses come to the fore on this concept album about the songwriting team's scuffling days — Jon Landau, *Rolling Stone,* 17 July 1975

The language of business and showbiz is not especially amenable to correction by those who write college English handbooks.

Still more important is the fact that these commentators start from the wrong basic premise: they assume that *concept* is originally and basically a word from philosophy meaning "an abstract or generic idea generalized from specific instances." The OED shows that *concept* is a Latinized form of *conceit* introduced in the 16th century; its earliest meaning was, in fact, "idea, notion." The philosophers then came along in the 17th century and made a narrower application of the earlier general term. The general sense "idea, notion" has been used all along.

Our evidence suggests that *concept* is currently not in extensive use for literary purposes. We have, however, winnowed out some examples in which "notion, idea" is the prevalent meaning yet which are not specialized uses. You can judge for yourself how faddish these examples are.

... the elevators in loft buildings, castles, hospitals and warehouses—that, infirm and dolorous to hear, seem to touch on our concepts of damnation —John Cheever, *The Wapshot Chronicle,* 1957

... "honor"—a word ... of which they had such a curious concept —William L. Shirer, *The Rise and Fall of the Third Reich,* 1960

... we must expand the concept of conservation to meet the imperious problems of the new age —John F. Kennedy, Introduction to Stewart L. Udall, *The Quiet Crisis,* 1963

... my inherited concept of New Englanders —John Fischer, *Harper's,* January 1969

Were there two human minds functioning separately from each other in the same brain? The concept was shattering —Irving Stone, *McCall's,* March 1971

... the Falstaff who simply and fully enjoyed life and wasn't about to sacrifice it to some idiot concept of battlefield honor —Martin Gottfried, *Saturday Rev.,* 23 June 1979

concern When *concern* means "an uneasy state of blended interest, uncertainty, and apprehension," it is used especially with the prepositions *over, for,* and *about:*

... concern over the influence of the screen on the minds of young people —*Current Biography,* May 1965

... their concern over issues of racism, poverty, war and ecology —Israel Kugler, *Change,* October 1971

... to show courtesy and concern for the safety of other vehicles on the road —Julie Candler, *Ford Truck Times,* Summer 1970

Their militant concern for the environment —Donald Gould, *Smithsonian,* May 1972

We are now beginning to see more concern about the prison system —Willard Gaylin, *Harper's,* November 1971

... growing concerns about the environment —Fred J. Borch, *General Electric Investor,* Winter 1970

With is also used with this sense:

... expression of a concern with the quality of American life —James R. Dickenson, *National Observer,* 3 Feb. 1973

... concern with fallout and nuclear war —Barry Commoner, *Columbia Forum,* Spring 1968

When *concern* denotes interest or involvement, the usual preposition is *with* or *in:*

... his concern with bringing new rhythms into English poetry —Alan Holder, *Berkshire Rev.,* Winter 1966

... concern with the nature and transmutability of matter —*Times Literary Supp.,* 17 July 1969

... public concern with building a society of university trained and educated youth —Jerome Evans, *Change,* September 1971

Much of the concern of ... Doxiadis in the problems of human settlements —*Current Biography,* September 1964

concerned When *concerned* suggests worry or anxiety, it can be followed by any of several prepositions. The most frequent are *about* and *for:*

... were concerned about both their children — Eileen Hughes, *Ladies' Home Jour.,* September 1971

... especially concerned about the effects of extended use —T. George Harris, *Psychology Today,* May 1971

... she was deeply concerned about them —Gail Cameron, *Ladies' Home Jour.,* August 1971

"... I'm rather concerned for the poor devil...." — Michael Arlen, *These Charming People,* 1924

... young people of today are concerned for others —Elisabeth Elliot, *Christian Herald,* June 1967

Over, at, and *by* are also used:

... educators have been greatly concerned over the reading program in the elementary grades —Catherine Zimmer & Marjorie Pratt, *Quarterly Jour. of Speech,* April 1941

... was concerned at the mounting indignation of the people against Americans —Robert Payne, *Saturday Rev.,* 27 June 1953

The Kremlin was getting increasingly concerned by the stubborn survival of ... Christianity, inside the Soviet Union —*Time,* 23 Aug. 1954

When *concerned* conveys the notion of interested engagement, *with* is the most common preposition:

... concerned with obtaining Congressional approval —Eli Ginzberg, *Columbia Forum,* Fall 1970

This book is more concerned with the earlier peoples than with the Incas —Edward P. Lanning, *Peru Before the Incas,* 1967

They are concerned with the way individual human situations snowball into political situations —Erica Jong, *Barnard Alumnae,* Winter 1971

In is also used. It tends to suggest involvement:

The British have been deeply concerned in foreign relations for a thousand years —Joyce Cary, *Holiday,* November 1954

... none of the states which we wanted invited to the peace conference could be said to be not directly concerned in the peace —James F. Byrnes, broadcast speech, 5 Oct. 1945

In is used especially when something criminal is suggested:

Was Mary Thoday ... really after all concerned in the theft? —Dorothy L. Sayers, *The Nine Tailors,* 1934

. . . a charge of being concerned in registering bets on horses —*Springfield* (Mass.) *Daily News,* 23 June 1953

. . . accused of being concerned in murdering Thomas Smithson —*The Times* (London), 24 Jan. 1974

Concerned in the following three examples rather blends the notions of worry and interest:

. . . not particularly interested in perspective, but he was much concerned about techniques of painting —*Current Biography,* May 1967

. . . he has always been concerned for the relevance of philosophy —*Times Literary Supp.,* 19 Feb. 1970

. . . is as concerned with status and prestige as the businessman is —Stephanie Dudek, *Psychology Today,* May 1971

When *concerned* suggests interest or care, it can also be followed by *to* and an infinitive. Our evidence shows this practice currently more common in British English than in American:

. . . is concerned only to present one side of the case —*Times Literary Supp.,* 26 June 1969

. . . some of the subjects were concerned not to make fools of themselves —Bert R. Brown, *Psychology Today,* May 1971

. . . is concerned to depict the tangled politics of Renaissance Italy —*British Book News,* April 1953

. . . a single department concerned to carry out a single policy —E. H. Carr, *Foreign Affairs,* October 1946

conciseness, concision *Conciseness* is a 17th-century word still in use. *Concision* is an even older word, but its original senses are now archaic or obsolete; it began to be used as a synonym of *conciseness* in the 18th century. *Concision* was used in some piece written by Henry James and noticed by the Fowler brothers (Fowler 1907) who thought it a bit exotic for *conciseness.* Fowler 1926 took up the subject again, this time recommending *conciseness* and calling *concision* a "literary critics' word"; Sir Ernest Gowers left the remarks in his revision, Fowler 1965. In spite of Fowler's preference for *conciseness, concision* seems to be the word of choice in reviews. *Concision* appears in our files with a bit more frequency than *conciseness.* Some examples of each follow:

Conciseness is generally a strength of this book — *Physics Today,* September 1984

. . . argues with elegant conciseness —Dennis H. Wrong, *Change,* April 1972

The first six volumes set a high standard for conciseness —*Times Literary Supp.,* 31 Oct. 1968

. . . the magnificent conciseness, the neatness —Bonamy Dobrée, *English Literature in the Early Eighteenth Century, 1700–1740,* 1959

Though Seneca is long-winded, he is not diffuse; he is capable of great concision —T. S. Eliot, "Seneca in Elizabethan Translation," in *Selected Essays,* 1932

. . . the concision and compactness of the metaphor —John Livingston Lowes, *Convention and Revolt in Poetry,* 1919

. . . forced upon me a concision that my practice as a dramatist had made grateful to me —W. Somerset Maugham, *The Summing Up,* 1938

. . . the writing of the "Memoirs" is perfect in concision and clearness —Edmund Wilson, *New Yorker,* 4 Apr. 1953

. . . the introduction and commentary are exemplary in their concision and lucidity —*Times Literary Supp.,* 9 Feb. 1967

Stendhal is a master of concision —John Russell, *N.Y. Times Book Rev.,* 26 July 1981

Concision is occasionally used of visual images:

The flowers are drawn with delicate concision and utter botanical veracity —*New Yorker,* 3 Dec. 1966

. . . "open," airy, three-dimensional images of extraordinary delicacy and concision —Hilton Kramer, *N.Y. Times,* 11 Apr. 1976

Even television can be the subject:

The eye of the television camera craves concision—anecdotes, jokes, statements, rather than musings —Carll Tucker, *Saturday Rev.,* 2 Sept. 1978

conclave It occasionally happens that a journalistic practice popular at a particular time will be unfavorably noticed by a usage commentator in a book and from that time will continue to be mentioned in usage books, even after the popularity of the practice has waned. This appears to be the case with *conclave.* During the 1940s and 1950s many journalists were using *conclave* for any gathering of a group or association; there were references to conclaves of doctors, Boy Scouts, American Legionnaires, United Nations delegates, and on and on. This use is a figurative extension of the word as applied to the meeting of the College of Cardinals to elect a Pope. Such figurative use is not, of course, abnormal; one sense or another of *conclave* has been used figuratively from the 17th century on.

Theodore Bernstein denounced the journalistic use in 1965, basing his objection on the Latin etymology of the word (it is based on Latin *clavis* "key") and the fact that the word first designated a room. Except in specific reference to the room in which the College of Cardinals elects the Pope, this sense is obsolete. The entire development of *conclave* in English has occurred through the adding of extended meanings unrelated to the etymology, so the Latin origin has no bearing on current use. From the place, the word was extended to the meeting held there and to the people at the meeting. The first meetings called conclaves were meetings of ecclesiastics; later it referred to meetings of lay people, and, from about the middle of the 20th century, to meetings of lay people not necessarily held behind closed doors.

We present some 20th-century examples. All are living uses of the word in English, and all are perfectly standard.

. . . after a short conclave of a few hours, the cardinals unanimously elected pope the youngest among them —Philip Hughes, *Popular History of the Catholic Church,* 1954

We look upon the Moscow festival as a conclave of cinema artists —George Stevens, Jr., quoted in *Current Biography,* December 1965

... the opening session of the First Annual A. J. Liebling Counter-Convention, a two-day conclave of newspaper and magazine writers —Thomas Meehan, *Saturday Rev.,* 3 June 1972

The clergy met in unofficial but well-attended conclave to deliberate —Norman Douglas, *South Wind,* 1917

... to make her views known ... at high-level conclaves in the Pentagon —Marshall Smith, *Cosmopolitan,* July 1976

... bandying heterodoxies in a conclave of poets outside some little café on the Rive Gauche —Max Beerbohm, *Atlantic,* December 1950

The ball was a vast conclave of seeming strangers whom, it turned out, one mostly knew —John Kenneth Galbraith, *Ambassador's Journal,* 1969

The piece at the Broadhurst ... deals with a United States delegate to a conclave of the United Nations —Wolcott Gibbs, *New Yorker,* 26 Dec. 1953

conclude *Conclude* has been subject to the separate criticism of two of its meanings for quite a while now, and since both of them still surface in usage books from time to time, we will give each brief mention.
1. The use of *conclude* in its sense meaning "decide" appears to have been first attacked by Fitzedward Hall in his 1872 *Recent Exemplifications of False Philology.* Hall's attack is listed in Bardeen 1883 with Bardeen's conclusion that the use was legitimate though carped at. MacCracken & Sandison 1917 also noted that the use was legitimate though opposed. But it is labeled a misuse in G. M. Hyde's *Handbook for Newspaper Workers* (1926) and in Jensen 1935 and Partridge 1942. Evans 1957 calls the sense standard. Copperud 1980 omits mention of the sense but does note the construction in which *conclude* is followed by *to* and an infinitive (the most common construction for the "decide" sense) "unidiomatic."
    The "decide" sense of *conclude* goes back to the 15th century with Lydgate and Caxton. Shakespeare used it:

They did conclude to bear dead Lucrece thence,
To show her bleeding body thorough Rome,
    And so to publish Tarquin's foul offence —*The Rape of Lucrece,* 1594

Here are a few other examples:

This being a good Situation ... we Concluded to delay at this place a few days —William Clark, 22 July 1804, in *The Journals of Lewis and Clark,* ed. Bernard DeVoto, 1953

... if she concludes to make arrangements —Francis Lee Pratt, "Captain Ben's Choice," in *Mark Twain's Library of Humor,* 1888

So we concluded to walk —Mark Twain, *Report from Paradise,* 1909

... and Stone concluded to go to bed —Carolyn Wells, *The Clue of the Eyelash,* 1933 (in Partridge 1942)

Although Evans says that this sense is also followed by a clause, we have more evidence for the construction with *to* and the infinitive. When *conclude* is followed by a clause and especially one introduced by *that,* it is most often being used in the sense "to reach as a conclusion; infer":

... he concluded that she was less simple than she seemed —Edith Wharton, *The Age of Innocence,* 1920

We suspect from our citations that the "decide" sense of *conclude* is no longer as common as it was in the past, although its appearance in Copperud's recent book suggests that it has not entirely passed out of use.
2. A slightly less frequently treated subject has been the sense "to bring or come to an end; close." Vizetelly 1906 seems to have decided something was wrong with the use; he held that *conclude* is a mental process while *close* is a physical process. He did not further elaborate this dictum, so its basis is unclear. A 1923 book titled *Editing the Day's News,* George C. Bastian et al., which reached its fourth edition in 1956, simply repeated Vizetelly. In Bremner 1980 the Vizetelly dictum has become a suggestion to avoid the meaning "end" in newspaper stories of interviews and speeches, lest, presumably, it be mistaken for the meaning "draw a conclusion." Confusion is actually unlikely because the "draw a conclusion" sense is typically followed by a clause, and the "end" sense, when transitive, by a noun. Since it is uncertain whether Vizetelly was worried about transitive or intransitive use, we include both in our examples:

The Period wherein the English Tongue received most Improvement, I take to commence with the beginning of Queen Elizabeth's Reign, and to conclude with the Great Rebellion in Forty Two —Jonathan Swift, *A Proposal for Correcting, Improving and Ascertaining the English Tongue,* 1712

The sexton concluded his speech with an approving smile at his own sagacity —Thomas Love Peacock, *Headlong Hall,* 1816

For little men may plan out their successes and more or less conclude the programme to their own satisfaction during their little lives —Hilaire Belloc, *Richelieu,* 1930

But there were, to repeat and to conclude, three saving accidents at work in the body of Emily Dickinson's work —R. P. Blackmur, "Emily Dickinson: Notes on Prejudice and Fact," in *American Harvest,* ed. Allen Tate & John Peale Bishop, 1942

They had exactly fifteen minutes to conclude their business —Helen MacInnes, *The Venetian Affair,* 1963

He concludes by reporting, with approval, the greeting of a German prisoner —*Times Literary Supp.,* 19 June 1969

... they were eager for me to conclude my fifteen minutes of distilled wisdom —Jerome S. Bruner, *Saturday Rev.,* 15 Jan. 1972

concord See the articles beginning with AGREEMENT.

concord, notional See NOTIONAL AGREEMENT, NOTIONAL CONCORD.

concrete   See CEMENT, CONCRETE.

concretize   Harper 1985 expresses horror at this term, complaining that dictionaries do not even recognize it as slang (and displaying at the same time an unusual notion of what slang is). *Concretize* is, they say, "a favorite of business administrators, bureaucrats, and other semi-literates," though the evidence suggests this view is more wish than fact:

> . . . are either poorly chosen or insufficiently concretized vehicles for the psychic content —John Simon, *New York,* 5 Apr. 1976

Copperud 1970, 1980, on the other hand, thinks the word is standard but concedes that it is subject to the sort of opprobrium that Harper has heaped upon it. The kinds of users that Harper believes are fond of *concretize* do not figure significantly in our citations for it. We find it most frequent in literary criticism and political commentary and in works on religion, philosophy, anthropology, and the like, where the terminology runs to sesquipedalian technicalities and the general tone is decidedly intellectual. We have extracted some examples from our files to show you how the word is used, just in case you are not familiar with it. These are, incidentally, among our most readable examples:

> . . . many of us will end his book still held more by the Idea of Huey P. Newton than by this particular effort to concretize himself —Murray Kempton, *N.Y. Times Book Rev.,* 20 May 1973

> Throughout there are references to individual cases which concretize their message —Albert H. Johnston, *Publishers Weekly,* 3 Feb. 1975

> . . . a relatively simple policy statement is introduced for discussion. This is kicked around a bit, as the saying goes, . . . until finally the original statement has been at once pointed up, toned down, . . . concretized, amended, and resolved —*Fortune,* November 1950

> His fourth stanza will concretize, or "materialize," the act, by dwelling upon its appropriate ground —Kenneth Burke, *A Grammar of Motives,* 1945

> In Orlick is concretized all the undefined evil of the Dickens world —Dorothy Van Ghent, *Sewanee Rev.,* Summer 1950

> . . . a reality that derives from the history of Ireland's defeats and that is focused, concretized, in the very quality of the men of Dublin —James T. Farrell, *The League of Frightened Philistines,* 1945

> . . . when H. L. Mencken said of this country and Poe, "They let him die like a cat up an alley," he was merely concretizing the hatred that literary artists have always felt in this society towards a citizenry that has found them ornamental rather than basic — Seymour Krim, *Evergreen,* August 1967

Concretize has been in use since the 1880s. You can use it in its proper sphere without concern. Most writers most of the time will not find it especially useful, however.

concur   *Concur* may be used with various prepositions, chief among them being *with, in,* and *to:*

> . . . I asked him whether he concurs with the opinion of most psychiatrists that the creative impulse is a

kind of neurosis —Jim Gaines, *Saturday Rev.,* 29 Apr. 1972

> This recommendation, concurred in by all members of the Department —*AAUP Bulletin,* September 1971

> Physical and moral causes had concurred to prevent civilisation from spreading to that region —T. B. Macaulay, *The History of England,* vol. I, 1849

Less frequently *concur* may be found with *on:*

> We all concurred on the argument that when you have news, you have to print it —Katharine Graham, quoted in *McCall's,* September 1971

condemn, contemn   Two or three commentators warn us not to confuse *condemn* and *contemn.* Likely no one has any trouble with *condemn;* the problem is *contemn,* which is a rather bookish word and is not much used. Your dictionary defines *contemn* as "to view or treat with contempt; scorn." Keep the definition in mind as you read the examples.

The real difficulty seems to be that a writer who chooses *contemn* instead of *scorn, sneer at,* or *despise* runs a certain risk of being thought to have spelled *condemn* wrong or to have otherwise been mistaken, when the context does not rule out the sense of *condemn.* We have no examples of confusion in our files, but we do have examples in which a reader unfamiliar with this relatively rare word could easily read *condemn* for *contemn.* Look at these examples:

> Scandal besmirched the officeholders; the ballot box, corrupted, no longer recorded the voice of the people; and the law, contemned, exercised no restraint over criminals —Oscar Handlin, *The American People in the Twentieth Century,* 1954

> Historically, the word vulgar was used in fairly neutral description up to the last quarter of the seventeenth century to mean and describe the common people. Vulgar was common but not yet contemned —Aristides, *American Scholar,* Winter 1981–1982

> The priestly function transcended the individual, and an unworthy priest was contemned, not for performing service when unfit to do so, but for neglecting to do it at all —James A. Williamson, *The Tudor Age,* 1964

> . . . his own early drawings of moss-roses and picturesque castles—things that he now mercilessly contemned —Arnold Bennett, *The Old Wives' Tale,* 1908

> So long as the aspirations of surrealism are granted any validity—and even those who have contemned its visual art have not hesitated to admit the worth of its literary products —David Sylvester, *Encounter,* September 1954

> Much of the out-of-state press, with which Wallace had carried on a running feud for years, contemned Mrs. Wallace's candidacy —*Current Biography,* September 1967

In how many of these examples might the unwary reader read *condemn?* It is not very likely in the first two but not impossible or even improbable in the rest. So the real problem, we think, is not that writers confuse the two words, but that some readers may mistake *contemn* as *condemn.*

condition Copperud 1970 states that his earlier (1964) characterization of *condition* used in *heart condition* as a "faceless euphemism for *ailment, disease*" is a common criticism in newspaper circles. The criticism may be widespread, but this use of *condition* is not usually a euphemism.

Condition has been used euphemistically in such time-honored combinations as *in an interesting* (or *delicate* or *certain*) *condition* to avoid *pregnant* (Nickles 1974 lists these and so does the OED Supplement). It can also refer to pregnancy without euphemism:

> Unwilling to face the stigma attached to unwed mothers in her own country or to reveal her condition to her elderly parents, Olga Scarpetta left Colombia and came to New York ... to have her child in secrecy —Eileen Hughes, *Ladies' Home Jour.*, September 1971

Condition in the sense Copperud objects to is, as Harper 1985 remarks, "hardly a precise term." Its very imprecision is its chief virtue, for it is often used when the precise ailment is unknown or not understood. As a generalized term, its usefulness can be seen in these examples:

> One of the major factors in his reversal of fortune was a series of physical ailments, the worst of which was a painful chest condition that beset him in 1962. The condition, apparently caused by a muscle spasm or pinched nerve, evaded specific medical diagnosis —*Current Biography*, April 1966

> ... in treating Paget's disease, which is a condition characterized by excessive bone formation —*Annual Report, Pfizer*, 1970

> My husband is impotent. What can be done about it? A. That depends on what the problem really is ... there *are* a few specific physical conditions that can cause this difficulty —Dodi Shultz, *Ladies' Home Jour.*, August 1971

If newspaper editors want to fret over this use of *condition*, let them. You needn't worry about it at all.

conducive It is hard to understand why language commentators persist in reminding us that *conducive* is used with *to* and not *of*. The evidence in the Merriam-Webster citation files is unmistakable: *conducive* is almost always used with *to:*

> Thus a feeling of apprehensiveness, conducive to attention, is aroused in the reader —T. S. Eliot, "Charles Whibley," in *Selected Essays*, 1932

The language critics insist that *of* should never be used with *conducive* and the fact is that it is not so used— not, at least, in contemporary English. We have no citations for this combination. The OED mentions it but labels it obsolete and shows just one citation, that from 1793. The OED also labels as obsolete the construction *conducive for*. We do have a single example of this use taken from the letter of a correspondent in 1975. The evidence, though, is overwhelming for *conducive to*.

conferencing Harper 1975, under the heading *educationese*, reports receiving a letter asking about the propriety of the word *conferencing*, used in the phrase "from much conferencing experience" by a junior high school principal in a letter to a parent. The Harper editors conclude by recommending the use of *conferring*,

which would sound very strange indeed in the construction the principal used.

Thomas H. Middleton encountered the word in 1978:

> One of my prime candidates for quick death is *conferencing* —*Saturday Rev.*, 7 Jan. 1978

He too found it in an educational context, but the reference—"Clearly, conferencing is a booming business"—is not to parent-teacher conferences, but to large-scale meetings. In both cases, however, the meaning is "the holding of conferences."

Our files have citations from educational sources from about the same period that use *conferencing* as a word for a technique for teaching writing, one apparently employing discussions between the writer and the teacher and sometimes involving the whole class too. These citations and the ones that came to the attention of Harper and Middleton suggest that *conferencing* exists as a somewhat technical term in educational jargon. It has not yet sufficiently emerged from its technical domain to warrant entry in a general dictionary.

"*Conferencing* may be getting entrenched, though," says Middleton in conclusion. He may be right, but for reasons he did not suspect. A somewhat later use of *conferencing* has developed—probably independently—in the world of computers. Our first inkling was from a publication of the New Jersey Institute of Technology:

> Computerized conferencing systems under development at NJIT advanced dramatically during the year —Paul H. Newell, Jr., *Nexus*, October 1976

It has appeared at least once to our knowledge in a publication intended for the general public:

> ... the latest in "computer conferencing" ... which eventually will substitute communication by computer terminal for old-fashioned speeches and panel discussions —Ada Louise Huxtable, *N.Y. Times*, 12 Oct. 1980

But so far it has appeared mostly in trade and technical sources:

> Communications actually got under way last July, but were suspended briefly in October while the DOC decided whether computer conferencing—the exchange of electronic messages—comes within the purview of export regulations —Clifford Barney, *Electronics*, 11 Nov. 1985

This *conferencing* may burst into general use before the educational one does. We have but one citation for the word in a context that is neither of teaching nor of electronics:

> It took over two years and many hours of conferencing to reach agreement on the selection of works to be included —Mortimer J. Adler, *Know*, Fall 1972/ Winter 1973

confess For reasons that are hard to guess, Copperud 1970 finds the intransitive *confess* followed by the preposition *to* "clumsy" and unidiomatic. He even invokes Evans 1957 as support, but he has misread Evans, who rejects *confess to* only when it is followed by a perfect infinitive *("I confess to have heard ...").* Evans and Shaw 1987 both note that *confess to* is often followed by a gerund:

> ... I must confess to having done some flagrant cheating —Cornelia Otis Skinner, *N.Y. Times Mag.*, 23 Jan. 1955

... will confess to having had at least one spontaneous apparently telepathic or clairvoyant experience —Antony Flew, *A New Approach to Psychical
Research,* 1953

... no one had ever confessed to having locked it —
William de Morgan, *It Never Can Happen Again,*
1909

We must confess to being somewhat conservative —
ita bulletin, Spring 1965

George Bernard Shaw even used *of* with the gerund:

> ... no Irishman ever again confessed of being Irish
> —*Back to Methuselah,* 1921

We may tell you that *confess to* is also often followed
by a noun:

> ... and then confessed to the crime under the urgent
> moral persuasion of the company's chairman —C.
> R. Hewitt & Jenifer Wayne, *London Calling,* 19 Aug.
> 1954

> ... I confess to a certain reluctance —Herbert Read,
> *The Philosophy of Modern Art,* 1952

> Rhee confesses to 78 years and is probably older —
> Gerald W. Johnson, *New Republic,* 15 June 1953

> Let me begin by confessing to prejudice —Dudley
> Fitts, *N.Y. Times Book Rev.,* 4 July 1954

> ... I confess to a firm belief in the tonic properties
> of crags —John Livingston Lowes, *Convention and
> Revolt in Poetry,* 1919

In short, there seems to be no real problem here. All of
the examples are idiomatic and only GBS's is unusual.

confidant   1. *Confidant, confidante.* The usage books
seem to present only a partial picture of the usage of
these words: Fowler 1926 calls *confidant* masculine and
confidante feminine; Copperud 1970, citing other commentators for support, agrees on *confidante* but says
confidant is bisexual. In actual usage, *confidant* usually
refers to a male:

> ... had him as a confidant and friend —Gay Talese,
> *Harper's,* January 1969

> ... the same detective and his friend and confidant,
> Dr. Watson —A. C. Ward, *British Book News,* May
> 1954

It is also used of females:

> ... shows her caliber in permitting Miss Alice Mar-
> riott to be her confidant —Elizabeth S. Sergeant, *Sat-
> urday Rev.,* 24 July 1948

> She had specialized as the confidant and friend —
> Osbert Sitwell, *Horizon,* July 1947

Confidante is usually applied to females:

> ... Emma moved from kitchen maid to royal confi-
> dante —Charles Lee, *Saturday Rev.,* 12 Mar. 1955

> ... if he would be thoughtful, considerate, and treat
> her as a partner and confidante —Joseph P. Lash,
> *McCall's,* October 1971

But it is also used of males:

> ... the minister, assumed to be a confidante of
> Eisenhower, reported his findings to the President —
> *Current Biography,* November 1967

The informer, Douglass Durham, was the chief aide
and confidante —John Kifner, *N.Y. Times,* 13 Mar.
1975

2. Some handbooks warn us not to confuse *confidant*
and *confident.* They undoubtedly mean the adjective
when they specify *confident,* and surely no one able to
read this book would mistake the noun *confidant* for the
adjective *confident.*

But there is a curious historical sidelight involved.
The noun *confidant* came to English in the 17th century
from the French, in which it was spelled *confident.* The
17th-century English spelling of the word was the same
as the French: *confident.*

> WORTHY. ... engage her in an intrigue of her own,
> making yourself her confident —Sir John Vanbrugh,
> *The Relapse,* 1696

The OED notes that the spelling with *a* did not come
into use until the 18th century. *Confidant* and *confidante* gradually replaced the older spelling—the OED
does find a few *-ent* spellings still in use in the 19th century and we have an example from a distinguished British serial in 1947—and the *-a-* spellings are the only
ones in current use. Another curiosity: *confidante* is an
entirely English word formed on analogy with French.

confide   In its intransitive senses *confide* is often used
with *in:*

> "... I have been so nearly caught once or twice
> already, that I cannot confide any longer in my own
> ingenuity" —Thomas Love Peacock, *Nightmare
> Abbey,* 1818

> ... patients too awed by the doctor to confide in him
> —Leonard Gross, *McCall's,* March 1971

The use of *in* with *confide* was mentioned as long ago as
1795 in Murray's *Grammar,* where he corrects *on* to *in:*

> "Intrusted to persons on whom the parliament could
> confide;" "*in* whom."

Confide may also be followed by a dependent clause:

> One husband confided that his wife buys an extra
> supply of cards —Goodman Ace, *Saturday Rev.,* 13
> Nov. 1971

In its transitive senses, *confide* may be followed by *to*
and the indirect object, which may be found before or
after the direct object:

> ... began confiding to her all the daily twists and
> turns in her affair with a waiter —Herman Wouk,
> *Marjorie Morningstar,* 1955

> ... do not confide your children to strangers —
> Mavis Gallant, *New Yorker,* 1 Feb. 1964

confident   When this adjective is followed by a preposition, *in* and *of* are the ones most likely to be used—
they occur with equal frequency:

> Why should he not walk confident in his own high
> purpose —Vernon Louis Parrington, *Main Currents
> in American Thought,* 1930

> ... people were confident of a golden future —
> Thomas Wolfe, *You Can't Go Home Again,* 1940

Less frequently, *about* or *at* may be found:

> ... make him more confident about speaking at length —Bernard H. & Charles D. McKenna, *American School Board Jour.*, June 1968

> ... but few would be at all confident at assigning him a particular place in the history of English writing —*Times Literary Supp.*, 17 Apr. 1969

And still less frequently, but nevertheless idiomatically, *confident* is used with *as to* or *on:*

> ... who were clear as to their goal and confident as to their victory —Lewis Mumford, *Technics and Civilization,* 1934

> ... the Democrats were confident on the point and the Republicans fearful —*Wall Street Jour.*, 4 Nov. 1954

Very often, of course, *confident* is followed not by a prepositional phrase but by a dependent clause:

> We are confident that the budget ... will permit both major segments of higher education to meet California's education needs ... —Ronald Reagan, quoted in *Change,* September 1971

conform   When *conform* is followed by a preposition, it is most likely to be either *to* or *with.* According to our evidence, the use of *to* is more frequent by a considerable margin:

> ... unwilling to conform to American ways —Oscar Handlin, *The American People in the Twentieth Century,* 1954

> ... in *1984,* the members of the Party are compelled to conform to a sexual ethic of more than Puritan severity —Aldous Huxley, *Brave New World Revisited,* 1958

> ... have modified my views of conduct to conform with what seem to me the implications of my beliefs —T. S. Eliot, "Thoughts After Lambeth," in *Selected Essays,* 1932

Another adverbial prepositional phrase may sometimes intervene between *conform* and the phrase with *to* or *with:*

> ... provided they conform in dimensions to those publicly owned —Charlton Ogburn, *Harper's,* October 1971

conformity   When followed by a preposition, *conformity* usually takes *to* or *with.* *With* is perhaps slightly more common, but the difference is small, if there is any:

> Conformity to the discipline of a small society had become almost his second nature —Edith Wharton, *The Age of Innocence,* 1920

> Ideas are tested not in give and take, but in their conformity to doctrine —Ward Just, *Atlantic,* October 1970

> In conformity with his father's wishes —*Current Biography,* April 1967

> ... in conformity with international law —*Foreign Affairs,* July 1940

A common phrase in the annual reports of many businesses is typified by this example:

> ... in conformity with generally accepted accounting principles —*Annual Report, Owens-Illinois,* 1970

Several special constructions should also be noted. When the things between which the relationship exists are both named after *conformity,* the preposition may be *between* or *of:*

> ... this is conformity between the old and the new —T. S. Eliot, "Tradition and the Individual Talent," 1917, in *Selected Essays,* 1932

> ... the close conformity of many of the tortuous veins with relic structures —*Jour. of Geology,* September 1948

When the prepositional phrase specifies, instead, the area of thought or experience where the conformity exists, *of* or *in* may be found:

> ... such grants encourage a conformity of approach to scientific problems —Henry T. Yost, Jr., *AAUP Bulletin,* September 1969

> Conformity in habit of growth should be maintained even more than conformity in texture —M. E. Bottomley, *New Designs of Small Properties,* rev. ed., 1948

confusion   Almost all handbooks have warnings about various pairs of words that are "often confused." Many of these pairs are homophones, such as *hail* and *hale,* that are substituted for each other because they sound alike. Many others are pairs that don't necessarily sound alike but are close in spelling, such as *confidant* and *confident,* so that one may be written inadvertently in place of the other. Many of these pairs receive separate treatment in this book.

In addition we sometimes encounter substitutions of one word for another that shares perhaps some elements of pronunciation with it. These are not easily explained; they are not commonplace occurrences—if they were they would perhaps be worth individual treatment. Some of them no doubt result from garbled or inattentive transcription of tape recordings. They are not strictly malapropisms, which are usually the result of reaching for an unfamiliar word in speech (or sometimes in writing). The names of the perpetrators of these examples, when known, have been suppressed. See also MALAPROPISM.

> ... but "after 'Canadian Sunset' all the guys went into their record binge and got out my old material and it kept us living." —*N.Y. Times,* 4 July 1980

> ... but neither did they try to spur me on. They simply clapped gentiley —*World Tennis,* December 1969

> ... consisting of plutonium oxide and geranium oxide —*Predicasts Technology Update,* 6 Oct. 1984

> ... do not look backwards, but forage blindly and bravely ahead —*Vogue,* August 1983

> Whenever McCredie would hit an apparent winner, Cashman would answer with a point-ending repartee —*Hartford* (Conn.) *Courant,* 7 June 1982

> So enhanced was I with the Chinese repousse that I devoted a good deal of time to developing a special

fiber for working it —*Springfield* (Mass.) *Daily News*, 1 Dec. 1975

It is also strongly suggested that you require . . . an FeLV-negative test, and, if plausible, an FIP test —*Cats Mag.*, February 1980

. . . a *salade de chasse:* slices of hot chicken and ruffled grouse —*Town & Country*, April 1984

congenial   By and large, when *congenial* is used with a preposition, the preposition is *to:*

. . . such things are common here, and congenial to the Persian character —Elinor Wylie, *Jennifer Lorn*, 1923

. . . our earth is becoming less congenial to life with each passing year —Norman Cousins, *Saturday Rev.*, 27 Nov. 1976

Congenial used with *with* may also be found, but far less frequently:

By temperament Decter is congenial with static law —Muriel Haynes, *Saturday Rev.*, 13 Nov. 1971

When the word modified by *congenial* is inanimate, there is a possibility that *for* may be used:

. . . when the climate was much more congenial for such enterprise —Henry Ladd Smith, *New Republic*, 22 Nov. 1954

congruence   See INFLUENCE 2.

conjunctive adverb   See ALSO.

connect   *Connect* is regularly used with the prepositions *with* and *to*. Some commentators have tried to limit the use of *with* to figurative senses and of *to* to concrete senses; this restriction is generally but not always followed in practice. There is a tendency for *with* to go with figurative senses and *to* to go with literal senses, but fully idiomatic exceptions are not hard to find. Some examples of *with:*

His policy was identical with Lincoln's, but he was unable to connect with Northern sentiment —Samuel Eliot Morison, *Oxford History of the American People*, 1965

The alleged message . . . simply does not connect with the plot of the film —Arthur M. Schlesinger, Jr., *Saturday Rev.*, 15 Apr. 1978

Military leaders, particularly those connected with the Air Force, vehemently disagreed —Jon M. Van Dyke, *Center Mag.*, July/August 1970

. . . realized that if he was going to connect with his generation he had better start finding out about America —Anthony Wolff, *Saturday Rev.*, 26 Aug. 1972

I don't connect her with Christmas, but maybe I connect her with joy —Robert Henderson, *New Yorker*, 24 Dec. 1967

. . . the power of language to connect us with the world —Harry Levin, *N.Y. Times Book Rev.*, 5 Aug. 1979

. . . the trading centers which connect Finland with the outside world —Samuel Van Valkenburg & Ellsworth Huntington, *Europe*, 1935

. . . built roads connecting the Fezzan with Tunisia —*Collier's Year Book*, 1949

We have plotted a few points and connected them with a smooth curve —School Mathematics Study Group, *Calculus of Elementary Functions, Part I*, 1969

He must nose a heavy ferryboat into a . . . slip and connect the bow with a bridge —Leonard A. Stevens, *Saturday Evening Post*, 30 June 1956

Here are a few examples of *to:*

. . . to measure people's responsiveness by connecting them to wires and laboratory devices —Marcia Seligson, *McCall's*, March 1971

. . . long staircases that connect to the road —*Ford Truck Times*, Summer 1970

None of Thaw's impressive series of five Goyas overtly connects to death —Thomas B. Hess, *New York*, 26 Jan. 1976

The draft is what connects Kansas Wesleyan to the war —Calvin Trillin, *New Yorker*, 22 Apr. 1967

Two things may also be connected *by* still another thing:

. . . we connect the points by a smooth curve —School Mathematics Study Group, *Elementary Functions*, 1965

The world of sports has its own set of prepositions:

. . . connected for his first home run since Aug. 19 —Jim Fox, *Springfield* (Mass.) *Union*, 25 Sept. 1967

Finding Morris Bradshaw free, he connected with him on a 50-yard scoring pass —Ron Reid, *Sports Illustrated*, 6 Aug. 1979

. . . Sipe connected on a 45-yard bomb to Reggie Rucker —Gerald Eskenazi, *N.Y. Times*, 8 Dec. 1980

connection   See IN CONNECTION WITH.

consensus   1. The consensus of opinion among writers on usage since the 1940s is that the phrase *consensus of opinion* is redundant. We have added "of opinion" advisedly; this is indeed a matter of opinion and not of fact, as will appear in what follows.

Consensus, it appears from OED evidence, rather suddenly developed at least three different new uses around the middle of the 19th century. The OED suggests the word itself first insinuated its way into the language through a physiological meaning introduced in a 16th-century book on physiology apparently written in Latin. In 1854 we have a "consensus of forces," in 1858 a "consensus of . . . evidence," in 1861 a "consensus of the Protestant missionaries," and in 1874 a "consensus of opinion." The connection between the physiologist's and the modern uses is perhaps illustrated by this citation from John Stuart Mill's *A System of Logic*. Unfortunately our nearly hundred-year-old slip does not tell us whether the passage was taken from the third edition of 1851 or the eighth of 1872; if it was the 1851, this would be an early citation indeed:

There is, in short, what physiologists term a *consensus*, similar to that existing among the various organs and functions of the physical frame of man and the more perfect animals, and constituting one of the many analogies which have rendered universal such expressions as the "body politic" —John Stuart Mill, *A System of Logic*

The early citations suggest that *consensus* was not then limited to opinion, and indeed it has not been since. The Merriam-Webster files have instances of "consensus of views," "consensus of preference," "consensus of support," "consensus of political comments," "consensus of advanced thinking," "consensus of experts," "consensus of agreement," "consensus of behavior," "consensus of values," "consensus of belief," "consensus of readings," "consensus of dissent," "consensus of conscience," "consensus of scholarship," and "consensus of usage." Thus, the cautious writer might well be tempted to write *consensus of opinion,* being aware that *consensus* can be used of other things. This is the point made in the following passage, probably written by Frank H. Vizetelly:

> The accepted meaning of *consensus* is "general agreement." It is commonly defined as "a collective unanimous opinion of a number of persons," and on this account the phrase "consensus of opinion" appears to be tautological. But as there may be consensus of thought, of functions, of forces, etc., it is not tautological to speak of a "consensus of opinion." Besides, the phrase is an English idiom —*Literary Digest,* 1 May 1926

The opinion that *consensus of opinion* is redundant appears to have begun with James Gordon Bennett the younger, who ran the New York *Herald* from 1867 until 1918. A list of his Don'ts for use by editors of the paper is reprinted in an appendix in Bernstein 1971. The list is not dated, but *consensus of opinion* was probably added to the list toward the end of Bennett's tenure; none of our late-19th-century or early-20th-century usage books mention it. Even Fowler 1926 notes *consensus* only because he found it confused with *census.* Although the question must have been in the air in 1926, as the excerpt from the *Literary Digest* above indicates, we find little discussion of it in books until the 1940s. Since that time nearly every writer on usage has clambered onto the bandwagon.

Of all our recent writers on usage, only Freeman 1983 seems to be aware of the issues discussed in the *Literary Digest.* He has also read Webster's Second, which has this note: "The expression *consensus of opinion,* although objected to by some, is now generally accepted as in good use."

> Such is the consensus of opinion of the leading authorities on international law —Thomas F. Bayard (U.S. Secretary of State), dispatch, 1 Nov. 1887

> The following comments are indicative of the present consensus of opinion —MacCracken & Sandison 1917

> It was the consensus of opinion of all their speeches that there was a lot of drinking going on —Will Rogers, *The Illiterate Digest,* 1924

> We made a systematic attempt to ascertain the consensus of usage throughout the English-speaking world —Frank H. Vizetelly, *N.Y. Times,* 2 Jan. 1927

> . . . the consensus of scholarship . . . assigns the two plays to Tourneur —T. S. Eliot, "Cyril Tourneur," in *Selected Essays,* 1932

> Tennyson's reaction to the consensus of critical opinion —*PMLA,* September 1951

> This language, according to a consensus of scholarly opinion —W. K. Matthews, *Languages of the U.S.S.R.,* 1951

> It is a consensus of opinion which derives additional significance from the fact that . . . —*Times Literary Supp.,* 13 Feb. 1943

> In the end, without a vote, but because it seemed to be the consensus of opinion —*The Autobiography of William Allen White,* 1946

> In place of authority in science, we have and we need to have only the consensus of informed opinion — J. Robert Oppenheimer, *New Republic,* 26 Apr. 1954

> The consensus of their opinion, based on reports that had drifted back from the border —John Hersey, *New Yorker,* 2 Mar. 1957

> . . . in a manner that maintains a consensus of public opinion—avoiding disruptive attack from Right and Left —Gaddis Smith, *N.Y. Times Book Rev.,* 3 June 1973

The decision for you is whether you want to use *consensus of opinion,* and make your meaning perfectly clear while running the risk of being wrongly censured for redundancy, or use *consensus* alone and risk less than full clarity, perhaps. Technically, *consensus of opinion* is not a redundancy, but many nonetheless believe it is. You are safe using *consensus* alone when it is clear that you mean consensus of opinion, and most writers in fact do so.

2. *General consensus.* Some of the writers who condemn *consensus of opinion* as a redundancy do the same for *general consensus.* Their argument in this case is on a better footing, for generality is indeed part of the meaning of *consensus.* The added *general* is probably felt by the writers who use it to have an intensive effect:

> There is a general consensus that some social plan of production for the needs of the community, rather than for individual profit, is necessary if the routine of civilized life is to continue —Morris R. Cohen, *The Faith of a Liberal,* 1946

General is sometimes added to *consensus of opinion,* though perhaps more often formerly than nowadays.

> . . . the general consensus of opinion in the City — *The Spectator,* 3 Jan. 1925

3. *Concensus.* Freeman 1983, Reader's Digest 1983, Howard 1977, and Copperud 1970 all note *concensus* as a frequent misspelling of *consensus.* We have a fair amount of evidence of its turning up in publications where it should have been detected. Perhaps the most amusing example is reported in Daniels 1983: he found it in an invitation issued by a large university for him to participate in a project to study problems of student illiteracy. The OED notes the spelling as an obsolete variant of *consensus.* It is no longer acceptable.

consequent When *consequent* is used with a preposition, the preposition is usually *on* or *upon:*

> The stillness consequent on the cessation of the rumbling and labouring of the coach —Charles Dickens, *A Tale of Two Cities,* 1859

The false perceptions of Mussolini . . . were consequent upon Pound's wanting his epic to be actively engaged in the process of history —A. D. Moody, *Times Literary Supp.,* 15 Aug. 1980

Consequent may also be followed by *to,* but that preposition appears far less frequently:

> . . . the subsequent disorders consequent to the diverse demands of internal factions —*Current History,* March 1937

consequential Here we have a most curious case. The sense of *consequential* meaning "important" was rejected by some two thirds of the Heritage 1969 usage panel, for reasons that are not given. (Heritage 1982 has no comment on this subject.) Harper 1975, 1985 notes that the sense is disputed, but finds it logical and predicts eventual acceptance. Earlier American objection we have not found, and therefore we assume the Heritage question was based on H. W. Fowler's 1926 comment that "*c.* does not mean of consequence." "Of consequence" is part of the definition in the OED at *consequential* 5; but Fowler selected as an example of what "would not now be English" an OED citation at sense 6a "having social consequence." Of course both of these senses mean the same thing; the OED separated uses of the adjective applied to nonhuman things from uses of the adjective applied to humans. The OED marks the earlier, nonhuman sense obsolete, but not the human sense. So it is not clear what Fowler had in mind—was he in effect saying that the human sense was also no longer in use?

Our files show almost no use of the human sense he gave as an example. (We do have evidence of the "self-important" sense—OED 6b—that Fowler said was still alive.) But if the example given by Copperud 1970, 1980 in reporting Heritage 1969 is accurate, the Heritage panel was objecting to the nonhuman sense (OED 5). This sense has a curious history too.

The OED shows it to start with Henry Fielding in 1728. In a comedy called *Love in Several Masques,* Fielding put the word into the mouth of Lord Formal, an updated Restoration fop with a taste for fancy language. Lord Formal takes the adjective, based till then on other senses of *consequence,* and bases it on the sense meaning "importance." These are his words as he takes leave of another character:

> For the sweetness of your conversation has perfumed my senses to the forgetfulness of an affair, which being of consequential essence, obliges me to assure you that I am your humble servant.

If this sense started out as part of the fancy talk of Fielding's fop, it was also in serious use; the OED shows later and straight-faced citations from the mid-18th century to the early 19th. But its last quotation is dated 1821, and the editor thought the sense obsolete.

Nevertheless, the use reappeared in the middle of the 20th century. We do not know whether the sense had continued all along, and the OED simply lacked citations, or whether it was re-formed from the same elements Fielding had used. In either case there is none of Fielding's playing with words in these examples:

> Impressionism has proved itself the most consequential of the efforts of the nineteenth-century painters to reorganize the data of vision —Wylie Sypher, *Partisan Rev.,* March–April 1947

The social effects were more consequential —Oscar Handlin, *N.Y. Times Book Rev.,* 11 Apr. 1954

. . . the single consequential work of fiction so far this year by any of the French intellectuals —Janet Flanner, *New Yorker,* 14 July 1956

. . . so severely indifferent to the events the rest of us think consequential in our politics —Murray Kempton, *N.Y. Rev. of Books,* 23 Oct. 1969

Separately, none of these responsibilities seems very consequential —Albert R. Hunt, *Wall Street Jour.,* 24 July 1972

. . . provocative, constantly interesting, and in some regards profoundly consequential —Rodney Needham, *Times Literary Supp.,* 25 Jan. 1980

Such views that have to do with that nonissue can sever the very consequential friendly relationship that is now being built up —Malcolm S. Forbes, *Forbes,* 3 Jan. 1983

These examples, as you can see, are perfectly standard. The "self-important" sense applied to humans has been in use all along, as Fowler observed:

> As for the Housekeeper, she was more consequential than ever, having been intrusted with a secret —William Black, *A Daughter of Heth,* 1871

> He was a very short, fat little man, with immensely long grey side-whiskers, and a most consequential manner —Lord Frederic Hamilton, *Vanished Pomps of Yesterday,* 1934

> . . . we might reflect that a weighty, consequential, humourless manner can still draw the plaudits of the intellectuals —Kingsley Amis, *Encounter,* April 1955

It can even be extended to the inanimate:

> . . . kept a couple of Rollses in the garage. . . . One was an old Phantom, I think, and stood gleaming in the half-light, immensely long, terrifically black and enormously consequential —Jan Morris, *N.Y. Times Mag.,* 2 Feb. 1975

conservative Bierce 1909 and Fowler 1926 objected to what was in their time a new use of *conservative* meaning "marked by moderation or caution" and applied especially to estimates. Gowers in Fowler 1965 noted that it had become established in the U.K. Howard 1977 also notes the use in British English and says it sounds odd to some British ears because of the connection of *conservative* with one of the major British political parties. The sense is an early 20th-century Americanism that has spread to British English. It is standard in American English, and now that it is entered without stigma in the OED Supplement and other recent British dictionaries (as Longman 1984), it is presumably standard in British English too.

> Assuming that only 30 per cent of the men and 10 per cent of the women want and need jobs—a conservative estimate —Abraham Ribicoff, *Saturday Rev.,* 22 Apr. 1972

> By the most conservative estimates, half a million children of survivors are alive today —Joan Barthel, *N.Y. Times Book Rev.,* 29 Apr. 1979

With in-depth counselling, neither of these boys would have been operated on. This is the reason we are so conservative and insist on long periods of observation —Dr. Jon Meyer, quoted in *Johns Hopkins Mag.,* Summer 1971

consider 1. *Consider* ran into trouble with usage writers in 1870. In that year Richard Grant White, by misconstruing its etymology, decided that it should not be used as a synonym for *suppose, think, regard*—a use that has existed since the 16th century. Ayres 1881 quoted White. Hall 1917 cited a writer named Genung as condemning the use in 1893 and recanting in 1900. Utter 1916 referred to White's condemned use as a "weaker" sense and said that it was established in the usage of good writers. MacCracken & Sandison 1917 followed White's lead and added a wrinkle of their own: when used in a sense close to "regard," *consider* should not be followed by *as* (this construction dates back to the 17th century). Hall 1917 established by counting examples of what Utter had observed: the "weaker" sense of *consider* was well established in literature.

In more recent commentators we find a similar variety of opinion. Partridge 1942 and Bemner 1980 tend to agree with Utter and Hall; Evans 1957 is lukewarm toward the use; Copperud 1964, 1970, 1980 goes with Richard Grant White. The *as* construction criticized as illogical by MacCracken & Sandison is called unidiomatic by Copperud and by Gowers in Fowler 1965, and Strunk & White 1959, 1972, 1979 also disapprove *as* when *consider* means "believe to be." Evans and Copperud raise a third issue: Evans says that *consider* can be followed by an infinitive but that a *that* clause is generally preferred, while Copperud declares the following clause to be unidiomatic.

Let us examine these three issues in the light of the evidence. The first is easily disposed of. Richard Grant White has fallen into the etymological fallacy—a favorite pitfall of his—and besides, half of his etymologizing is wrong. The OED dates the use from before 1533. Here are a couple of examples (and the examples for the constructions below also illustrate this long established sense):

I considered this one of the most unhandsome speeches ever made —Robert Louis Stevenson (in Hall 1917)

Who is the man most to be admired? Sometimes the man who is so considered officially by his class — Sinclair Lewis, *Yale Literary Mag.,* June 1906

The question of the construction with *as* is more interesting. *Consider,* in the sense under consideration here, can be used with several kinds of complements. It may be followed by a noun:

... does not class himself with performers he considers great popular singers —*Current Biography,* February 1968

... the daily threat of death was considered part of the business —*Science News,* 14 June 1969

It may be followed by an adjective:

... honeymoons in Europe were not considered necessary —Charles Bracelen Flood, *Omnibook,* June 1954

It may be followed by an adjectival prepositional phrase:

Pine was the only timber then considered of commercial value —*American Guide Series: Michigan,* 1941

It may be followed by two nouns (or pronoun and noun), one the direct object and the other its complement:

... many close friends now had to consider each other enemies —Martha F. Child, *New-England Galaxy,* Fall 1970

... many well-placed doctors consider nurses the most important component —Leonard Gross, *McCall's,* March 1971

His fellow clerks ... had come to consider him a very prickly sort of fellow —Thomas B. Costain, *The Black Rose,* 1945

It may be followed by a noun (or pronoun) and an adjective:

... considered her so totally unamiable —Jane Austen, *Sense and Sensibility,* 1811

... to consider war inevitable and prepare for it — *Wall Street Jour.,* 26 Mar. 1954

It may also be followed by a noun and a phrase introduced by an infinitive:

... we consider the results to be satisfactory — *Annual Report, National Distillers and Chemical Corp.,* 1969

Consider is also used in many of the same constructions with *as.* For instance, with a single noun:

... the "bastard-wing" in birds may be safely considered as a digit in a rudimentary state —Charles Darwin, *On the Origin of Species by Means of Natural Selection,* 1859

... all the problems which can be considered as that problem in disguise —W. W. Sawyer, *Prelude to Mathematics,* 1955

... that metal, which was peculiarly considered as the standard or measure of value —Adam Smith, *The Wealth of Nations,* 1776

... what has been considered as possibly Gallegos' finest novel —*Current Biography 1948*

With an adjective:

... could not but consider it as absolutely unnecessary —Jane Austen, *Mansfield Park,* 1814

... they consider Marx as outdated —Edmond Taylor, *The Reporter,* 17 Aug. 1954

With two nouns or a pronoun and a noun:

... we have considered science as a steadily advancing army of ascertained facts —W. R. Inge, *The Church in the World,* 1928

... are reported to consider polished stone axes, and in general all polished pebbles, as thunderstone —Sir James G. Frazer, *Aftermath,* 1937

We must consider government as our servant — Rexford G. Tugwell, quoted in *Center Mag.,* March 1968

. . . I considered him and deferred to him as an older man —T. S. Matthews, *Saturday Rev.,* 17 May 1975

It can also be followed by a participle:

Throughout this section all figures will be considered as lying in a fixed plane —School Mathematics Study Group, *Geometry, Part II,* 1965

You will have noted some older writers cited above. Our evidence suggests that the *as* constructions are perfectly idiomatic but are not as common in recent use as they have been in the past. Nonetheless, they are still in use and are standard.

Our last question is about complementizing with a clause. Evans notes that *consider* may be followed by an infinitive phrase:

. . . is considered to excel in the interpretation of modern works —*Current Biography 1948*

But he says that a *that* clause is likely to be preferred. Copperud, on the other hand, says that a clause is unidiomatic. Our evidence shows Copperud's notion to be unfounded:

I do not consider that the replaying of all that classical truck shows a raising of the Goldman Band's cultural standard —Virgil Thomson, *The Musical Scene,* 1947

. . . they considered that . . . a state of war now existed —Sir Winston Churchill, *The Unrelenting Struggle,* 1942

We can understand Tacitus considering that a man who lives outside *la ville* must be a lunatic —Norman Douglas, *Siren Land,* 1911

Then there are those friends . . . who consider that the diaries make him out an extremely unpleasant person —Auberon Waugh, *N.Y. Times Mag.,* 7 Oct. 1973

We must conclude that all the illustrated uses of *consider* are proper and standard; they are well-established in literature and in general writing. There never has been anything wrong with them. We do note, however, some apparent reduction in recent use of the *as* constructions, even though they are by no means archaic.

2. *Consider* can also be used with *for:*

. . . considered for an official position —*Dictionary of American Biography,* 1929

. . . was being considered for a new and rather difficult assignment —*Current Biography,* July 1965

3. The construction *consider of* is called by the OED "somewhat archaic." It does seem a bit old-fashioned:

She took three days to consider of his proposals —Jane Austen, *Mansfield Park,* 1814

"I will consider of her punishment." —Mark Twain, *The Prince and The Pauper,* 1881 (*A Mark Twain Lexicon,* 1938)

. . . they were to consider of their verdict —*Selected Writings of Benjamin N. Cardozo,* ed. Margaret E. Hall, 1947

considerable *Considerable* is involved in issues as an adjective, adverb, and noun. We will take them up separately.

1. *Adjective.* It is first necessary to eliminate from this discussion the most common construction in which the adjective occurs. This is one in which *considerable* is usually preceded by a word like *a, the, his, one, any, no:* the play was a considerable success, her considerable fortune, no considerable effort was made. These uses are standard and universal, and no one questions them except Phythian 1979, who thinks *considerable* is used too much. But when *considerable* modifies a mass noun, with no determiner like *an* or *our,* Fowler 1926, 1965 notes a difference between British and American usage. Fowler says that in British usage *considerable* is used only with nouns for immaterial things, while in American usage it is used of nouns for material things. Evans 1957 also makes much the same statement without mentioning any use as specifically British. In fact Fowler's British use is both British and American:

. . . scenes of considerable crime —Robert Shaplen, *New Yorker,* 6 Sept. 1982

. . . a time of corruption, hatreds, sadism and considerable hysteria —Ernest Hemingway, "Miss Mary's Lion," 1956

. . . did considerable harm to the prestige of his country —Elmer Davis, *But We Were Born Free,* 1954

He did it with considerable energy —Joseph Conrad, *Chance,* 1913

. . . good wages, with considerable social prestige — Aldous Huxley, *The Olive Tree,* 1937

He was a man of wide reading and considerable culture —*The Autobiography of William Allen White,* 1946

This use is standard and universal. The use with mass nouns of material does seem to be American. It is considerably less frequent than use with immaterial mass nouns. It occurs in standard English, but in works of a general and not a literary nature.

. . . thereby liberating considerable dust —Louis Shnidman, ed., *Gaseous Fuels,* 1948

. . . has room for considerable luggage —Burgess H. Scott, *Ford Times,* September 1966

The product contains considerable salt —Raymond E. Kirk & Donald F. Othmer, eds., *Encyclopedia of Chemical Technology,* 1950

The Japanese . . . were equipped with considerable radio equipment —Herbert L. Merillat, *The Island,* 1944

Fore Shank—Rich in flavor, considerable bone — *Meat and Meat Cookery,* 1942

2. *Adverb.* The most ink has been spilled in the attempt to stamp out the old flat adverb *considerable* used to mean "to a considerable extent or degree; quite a bit." This use is not an Americanism in origin, but it seems to have survived chiefly in this country. Like most flat adverbs it seems to be primarily a speech form and like most flat adverbs, more common formerly than now. (See FLAT ADVERBS.) We have good evidence of its currency in 19th-century American English, especially from the humorists.

. . . the charge half a dollar to each person; which being about the price of half a fat sheep, I thought "pretty considerable much," if I may be permitted to use an expressive phrase of the country —Frances Trollope, *Domestic Manners of the Americans,* 1832

"What air you here for?" I continued, warmin up considerable. "Can't you give Abe a minute's peace?" —Artemus Ward, "Interview with President Lincoln," 1861, in *The Mirth of a Nation,* ed. Walter Blair & Raven I. McDavid, Jr., 1983

. . . considerable many warts —Mark Twain, *Tom Sawyer,* 1876

. . . loafs around considerable —Mark Twain, *Tom Sawyer,* 1876

In 20th-century use the adverb is found chiefly in speech, fictional and genuine, and in letters and similar speechlike prose.

. . . I thought we had very frankly made a mistake and prayed considerable during about three days that the Communists would reject it —Walter George, U.S. Senator from Georgia, quoted in *Time,* 18 June 1951

My two new swans . . . have high voices and use them considerable —Flannery O'Connor, letter, 15 Feb. 1964

. . . I bought my first professional mixer, one with a dough hook that kneaded the dough for me. That speeded things up considerable —Everett Burton, quoted in *American Way,* July 1984

Although two of the three users we have quoted happen to be Georgians, the Dictionary of American Regional English gives no regional limitation to the adverb, nor do our other citations suggest one. Only occasionally does the adverb appear in edited prose:

. . . Theodore Roosevelt received considerable more help —Victor L. Albjerg, *Current History,* September 1952

. . . the children of the upper and middle classes received the best schooling available with considerable greater frequency —Charles Frankel, *Columbia Forum,* Summer 1970

The flat adverb *considerable,* then, is still alive in speech. It is seldom used in edited prose other than fiction.
3. *Noun.* The noun use of *considerable* is evidently American. There is some disagreement among dictionaries as to which constructions are the adjective used absolutely and which are the noun. There is a construction "a considerable of (a)" which everyone calls a noun. It is, however, somewhat old-fashioned and may be going out of use. This is the most recent example we have found of it:

It was a kind of mixed hound, with a little bird dog & some collie & maybe a considerable of almost anything else —William Faulkner, "Shingles," 1943 (American Dialect Dictionary)

This Faulkner quotation also appears in the OED Supplement and the Dictionary of American Regional English.
The following examples are felt to be adjectives by some dictionary editors and nouns by others. In either case they are standard usages, but they are perhaps passing out of use in edited prose.

. . . the older McMath was inclined to spend considerable on liquor —Roy Bosson, quoted in *Current Biography 1949*

. . . considerable is known concerning the literature of the Babylonians —*The Encyclopedia Americana,* 1943

. . . it explains considerable but has to be strained beyond belief to explain all it is supposed to —Herbert J. Muller, *Science and Criticism,* 1943

. . . Arnold Shaw, who reputedly knows considerable about the business —*Saturday Rev.,* 21 Feb. 1953

. . . *The McGill News* apparently caused considerable of a furore by printing a "top secret" picture of the famous fence —*McGill News,* Spring 1954

. . . and that is considerable of an understatement —Rolfe Humphries, ed., *New Poems by American Poets,* 1953

. . . Robert Hunter, who at that time was considerable of a Socialist —*The Autobiography of William Allen White,* 1946

consistent When *consistent* is used with a preposition, *with* is by far the most common:

Father John did not think it to be consistent with his dignity to answer this sally —Anthony Trollope, *The Macdermots of Ballycloran,* 1847

Other prepositions, although found less often, also appear in idiomatic English with *consistent,* the choice determined by the intended meaning:

. . . the influence of America should be consistent in seeking for humanity a final peace —Franklin D. Roosevelt, fireside chat, 3 Sept. 1939, in *Nothing to Fear,* ed. B. D. Zevin, 1946

The employed labor force in 1948 worked a weekly average of hours that was fairly consistent within the industry group —*Collier's Year Book,* 1949

The anti-German element in French defence thinking is consistent throughout this period —*Times Literary Supp.,* 27 Aug. 1971

Hume, it will be remembered, was the most consistent of the empiricists —John H. Randall, Jr., *The Making of the Modern Mind,* 1926

Opportunistic as to means, he was tenaciously consistent as to ends —Allan Nevins & Henry Steele Commager, *The Pocket History of the U.S.,* 1942

consist in, consist of The world of usage writers tends to be tidier than the real world, and in drawing the customary distinction between *consist in* "lie, reside (in)" and *consist of* "to be composed or made up (of)" they take advantage of that artificial tidiness. The distinction is, in fact, usual—most writers observe it and so should you—but the OED shows that historical practice has not been consistent, and our evidence shows that current practice, while more consistent than in the past, is still not perfectly so. Here is one example each of mainstream use:

The skill . . . consists in making them talk like little fishes —Oliver Goldsmith, quoted in Boswell's *Life of Samuel Johnson,* 1791

The committee . . . consists of a baker's dozen of academics —Simon 1980

It is easy to see that when the subject is singular and the noun following is plural, *of* is the right preposition:

The remaining two-thirds consists of extracts of speeches —*Times Literary Supp.,* 5 Mar. 1970

But when *consist* appears with a singular noun on each side, there can be uncertainty. Sometimes the context is not sufficient to make it clear which meaning is intended:

. . . a new look at what Shaw's "reality" consisted in —*Times Literary Supp.,* 18 June 1971

Bernstein 1962 cites an example of *consist of* that he maintains should have been *consist in,* but most of the ambiguous or uncertain examples in our files are uses of *consist in* where *consist of* might have made more sense:

Hypallage may consist in simple jumbling of the words in a sentence —John Dirckx, *The Language of Medicine,* 2d ed., 1983

Poe's reply consisted in a series of five articles — Nelson F. Adkins, *Papers of the Bibliographical Society of America,* 3d quarter, 1948

. . . for travelling, he said, was travelling in one part of the world as well as another: it consisted in being such a time from home, and in traversing so many leagues —Henry Fielding, *Jonathan Wild,* 1743

. . . a religious course that does not consist in memory work alone —Paul F. Klenke, *Bulletin of the National Catholic Education Association,* August 1949

Chambers 1985 says that *consist in* is more formal than *consist of;* this may account for some writers' being uncertain in handling it since it is likely to be less familiar. At any rate our evidence indicates that writers are more likely to stray from the usual and recommended idiom with *consist in* than with *consist of.* If you are uncertain, these two final mainstream examples may serve as points of reference:

The mistake that is made on television consists in believing that anyone can speak interestingly — Edwin Newman, PBS television program, 8 Mar. 1979

. . . the city seemed to me to consist of three areas — Stephen Spender, *N.Y. Times Mag.,* 30 Oct. 1977

consonant When used with a preposition in contemporary English idiom, the adjective *consonant* is almost always followed by *with:*

. . . he regarded his photography as an entirely wholesome pastime, consonant with his religious principles —Richard Ellmann, *N.Y. Times Book Rev.,* 17 June 1979

In earlier English (as far back as the 15th century, the OED attests), *consonant* was also used with *to.* This usage seems to have disappeared during the early part of the 20th century: our last citation is this:

This, being consonant to tradition, need have done no harm —G. K. Chesterton, reprinted in *The Pocket Book of Father Brown,* 1946

constitute See COMPRISE.

consul See COUNCIL, COUNSEL, CONSUL.

consummate Bryson 1984 complains that *consummate* is used too much as an adjective, and Copperud 1970, 1980 complains that it is used too loosely by music critics. Copperud, however, is able to reach his conclusion because he arbitrarily restricts *consummate* to the single narrow sense "perfect." This is the sort of use he objects to:

Victoria de los Angeles' consummate artistry is again evinced . . . —*Cambridge Rev.,* 22 Apr. 1950

Consummate here means "of the highest degree," a different sense from Copperud's and one recognized by most dictionaries. This sense is not always used flatteringly:

. . . the only reason that anyone would buy things of such consummate ugliness —John Corry, *Harper's,* November 1970

Applied to a person, it suggests great skill and proficiency:

. . . a reputation as a consummate professional — Don Heckman, *Stereo Rev.,* September 1971

Onstage she is brash . . . the consummate hussy — Richard Grenier, *Cosmopolitan,* May 1973

These uses are not recent developments, as evidence in the OED shows. They are established beyond cavil.

contact The noun *contact* was turned into a verb about 1834. Its use was primarily technical, and it was noted by the OED in 1891. Sometime in the 1920s a nontechnical use of *contact* as a transitive verb began in the United States. The earliest citation in the OED Supplement is also, so far as we know, the earliest complaint about the use. It is from a 1927 review in *The Spectator,* a British periodical, of Theodore Dreiser's *An American Tragedy.* Dreiser's use, if someone should find it, would then be the earliest on record, as the novel was published in 1925.

It is unlikely that Dreiser invented the use. In all probability he simply used something that was in the air. Our earliest citation does not suggest that this *contact* was suspected to be anything unusual:

Men are divided in thought and feeling. They are no longer satisfied to be either churchmen or atheists, but are beginning to contact God vaguely, uncertainly, in many ways —*Springfield* (Mass.) *Union,* 14 Jan. 1926

Our next example does place the word in quotation marks as if it were new or special; one of our editors thought it might be intended to mean "to subject to the attentions of a contact man":

The Bureau also began to "contact" national advertisers, to divulge the secret that newspapers were as good as magazines for national campaigning —*Tide,* April 1928

Our third citation shows a use that helps explain why *contact* has remained alive; the substitutes usually recommended as "more precise" will not work very well here. Try *consult, talk with, telephone, write to* (the list from Little, Brown 1986) in this context:

Bourne said he had been unable to contact Santo Domingo since the last weather report was received here at 2:12 p.m. —*Springfield* (Mass.) *Republican,* 14 Sept. 1930

Although the earliest objection to the use was published in England, our files show no direct British influence on the earliest American objectors. Reader's Digest 1983 opines that "the anglophile literary establishment" was a prime force in the controversy, but our evidence suggests that it started in the newspapers. Two events in the early 1930s seem to have fueled the controversy. On 1 Dec. 1931 several newspapers (we have clippings from the *New York Times* and the *Boston Post*) carried a story about one F. W. Lienau, a high official of Western Union, who denounced the verb *contact* and tried to get other officials of the company to forbid its use. The ensuing publicity lasted into 1932. Then in March 1932 the Lindbergh baby was kidnapped. There was intense publicity about the case, and *contact* cropped up often in the reporting of it, as in this news summary from an edition of the *Los Angeles Times:* "Lindbergh twice contacts kidnappers."

A 1935 clipping duly notes the presence of the literary establishment. A columnist in the *Brooklyn Times-Union* quotes Yale English professor William Lyon Phelps, who had a column in *Scribner's,* as denouncing the word. In 1938 the *New Republic* decided to campaign against the word. Opdyke 1939 is the first of the commentators in our library to express disapproval. From the 1940s on there is quite a lot of negative comment, and subsequently *contact* has become part of the standard furniture of usage books and college handbooks.

The assault on *contact* seems to have been based on two factors: the verb was formed from the noun by functional shift, and the use is supposed to have originated in business jargon. The first objection has been made for many other words of similar origin; yet, no objection has been raised to an even larger number of words formed in the same way. Functional shift has been an increasingly common method of word-formation in our language since Middle English. And the original functional shift of *contact* had taken place nearly a century earlier than the emergence of the disputed usage. It does not appear to be a strong basis for objection.

Of the ascribed origin in business jargon we cannot be certain. Early evidence is too sparse to support a judgment, even though there is plenty of later evidence of business use. Further doubt is cast by the speculations of a 1935 Brooklyn newspaper columnist, who claims a telegrapher told him that telegraphers had been using it for years. The same columnist also mentions army use in World War I. No evidence has yet appeared to confirm these speculations. Our present knowledge of the origin of the use, then, is still incomplete.

The objection in Great Britain to *contact* as an Americanism is on sounder ground, but it has proved so useful there, according to Longman 1984, that it is commonly used in all but the most formal contexts. The OED Supplement gives no warning label.

The real reason for the American objection is most likely popularity, as Safire 1982 observes. Sudden popularity underlies many a usage problem—see, for instance, HOPEFULLY and SPLIT INFINITIVE. Safire goes on to comment that *contact* "has fought its way into standard usage."

One of the interesting features of the dispute over *contact* is the growing number of commentators who have thrown in the towel. One of the earliest must have been the British critic Ivor Brown, who is quoted in Mencken 1963 as denouncing the word in 1940 and by Gowers

1948 as allowing that it might be justified (his reluctant change of heart was published in Brown 1945). Copperud 1970 lists several commentators who find it acceptable, and Bernstein 1971, Kilpatrick 1984, and Reader's Digest 1983 can be added to his list. Geoffrey Nunberg, writing in *The Atlantic* (December 1983), wonders why anyone bothered to object; he represents the younger generation of the split between generations that Follett 1966 forecast. While Copperud claims the consensus of commentators to approve the usage, it has curiously become a fixture in the lists of disapproved usages reproduced in college handbooks. Thus we find that the newspaper writers who first raised the hue and cry have come to terms with usage, but the college English teachers, who came late into the game, are still fighting it.

All the fuss seems to have had no effect on actual use. The verb's usefulness seems to lie in the two characteristics mentioned by Bernstein when he came to accept it. It is short, usually replacing a longer phrase like "get in touch with." It is also not specific (*vague* is the term its disparagers prefer) and for that reason is especially useful in such expressions—common in advertising—as "contact your local dealer." Such contact could be made by telephone, by mail, or simply by walking in. The writer does not need to speculate on how it might happen.

> . . . more people are using a computer at home to contact information services —Erik Sandberg-Diment, *N.Y. Times,* 15 Feb. 1983

> . . . editors could do so by contacting Moses' man, who would contact Moses —Gay Talese, *Harper's,* January 1969

> Alumnae interested in attending should contact the Public Relations Office —Erica Jong, *Barnard Alumnae,* Winter 1971

> What do you believe would be the effect on humanity if the earth were contacted by a race of such ungodlike but technologically superior beings? —*Playboy,* September 1968

Our evidence indicates that the verb *contact* is standard. It is not much used in literary contexts nor in the most elevated style. It is all right virtually anywhere else, however, with the probable exception of freshman English papers, where the instructors are likely to be observing the continuing opposition of the handbooks.

contact clauses   *Contact clause* is one of several terms grammarians use for a dependent clause attached to its antecedent without benefit of a relative pronoun. Some dictionaries and usage commentators discuss contact clauses under the heading *that, omission of;* in practice, however, any relative pronoun (as *who, whom,* or *which*) may be felt to be missing in a given instance.

Here are a few samples of contact clauses, all taken from the third volume of Jespersen 1909–49:

> Where is the thousand markes ∧ I gaue thee, villaine? —Shakespeare

> Here she set up the same trade ∧ she had followed in Ireland —Daniel Defoe

> The seed ∧ ye sow, another reaps —Shelley

> This wind ∧ you talke of —Shakespeare

> Those nice people ∧ I stayed in Manchester with — Mrs. Humphrey Ward

> I am not the man ∧ I was —Dickens

In each of these examples a relative pronoun could be inserted at the caret but is clearly not needed. Constructions such as these are appropriate in any variety of writing.

Historically the contact clause is the result of a paratactic construction of two independent clauses, not a relative clause with the relative pronoun omitted. Jespersen conjectures that contact clauses have been common in everyday speech for some six or seven hundred years; they seem to have come into literature as the forms of everyday speech came into it. In the 18th century, when the first influential grammars of English were written, English was analyzed by analogy with Latin. In Latin, relative clauses require the relative pronoun; English grammarians analyzing English in terms of Latin grammar decided that contact clauses must be relative clauses with the relative pronoun omitted. Their analysis has come down to the present day and may even be found in grammars not following Latin outlines:

> In this transform the relative pronoun *which* replaces the noun phrase *the street.* If we wish, we may delete the relative pronoun and have a contact clause.... The transform is "The street we live on is quiet." —Harold B. Allen et al., *New Dimensions in English,* 1968

Since contact clauses did not exist in Latin, the 18th-century grammarians looked at them askance. Lindley Murray 1795 termed the construction "omitting the relative" and stated that "in all writings of a serious and dignified kind, it ought to be avoided." Jespersen quotes Samuel Johnson as calling the omission of the relative "a colloquial barbarism" (and also notes that examples can be found in Johnson's letters).

It may be of interest that the contact clause was used in early modern English in constructions not found in present-day English. In present-day English the presumed pronoun of a contact clause would be the object of a verb or preposition: "The key you lost," "Here is the boy you sent for." In early modern English, however, the contact clause was also commonly used in subject relationship, where the "missing" pronoun would have been nominative, as in Shakespeare's "My father had a daughter loved a man" (*Twelfth Night,* 1602). That such constructions could easily lead to ambiguity is shown by Shakespeare's "I see a man here needs not live by shifts" (*The Comedy of Errors,* 1593) and "She loved me well deliver'd it to me" (*The Two Gentlemen of Verona,* 1595). Strang 1970 points out that ambiguity probably contributed to the decline of such use; in present-day English, contact clauses in subject relationship are seldom found except in constructions introduced by *it is* or *there is (are):*

> ... it was haste killed the yellow snake —Rudyard Kipling (in Jespersen)

> ... there are lots of vulgar people live in Grosvenor Square —Oscar Wilde (in Jespersen)

> ... but the business of beauty—there is no person at all knows what that is —James Stephens, *The Crock of Gold,* 1912

Grammarians seem not to include within the domain of the contact clause a noun clause lacking the conjunction *that:*

> Would you believe some reprocessing firms do not even remove the labels from old stock —Henry Hunt, *Houston Post,* 9 Sept. 1984

This is a closely related phenomenon, however, and it is often included in treatments headed *that, omission of.* It is as long and well established in English as the contact clause and is appropriate in any variety of writing. It is probably relatively more common in casual and general prose and relatively less common in prose that aims to fly high; it is probably more common after some verbs (as *believe, hope, say, think*) than others (as *assert, calculate, hold, intend*). All the same, it is at home in virtually any modern context.

contagious, infectious Several usage books, including Bryson 1984, Phythian 1979, Bremner 1980, Copperud 1970, 1980, and Shaw 1975, inform us that contagious diseases are spread by contact and infectious diseases by infectious agents. All contagious diseases are also infectious, but not all infectious diseases are contagious. Not many writers are likely to need to worry about the medical distinction between *contagious* and *infectious;* if they do, they can always consult a good dictionary, where the distinction will be made clear.

Shaw, however, goes beyond the technical to the figurative uses. *Contagious,* he says, emphasizes speed while *infectious* emphasizes irresistible force. Bremner likes this distinction; on the other hand, Bryson sees no difference between the two when used figuratively. Our evidence from the past 15 or 20 years suggests that Bryson is closer to the mark. If there is a distinction in recent use, it is this: *contagious* can be used of pleasant and unpleasant things, but *infectious* is almost always used of pleasant things.

> ... European leaders felt terrorism could become contagious —Edward Girardet, *Christian Science Monitor,* 3 Apr. 1980

> ... put an end to contagious ideological heresy —John Darnton, *N.Y. Times Mag.,* 13 Apr. 1980

> ... disturbed behavior is highly contagious —Constance Holden, *Science,* 17 Aug. 1973

> ... the tremendous excitement he generated, an excitement that was contagious —Thelma Nason, *Johns Hopkins Mag.,* February 1970

> ... the women's enthusiasm so contagious, that I for one could not keep my heart from beating faster —Germaine Greer, *Harper's,* October 1972

> ... radiating energy and vitality, a magnetic, irresistible current of warmth and contagious good humor —Tad Szulc, *N.Y. Times Mag.,* 27 May 1979

> ... a languid lyricism and elegance which proved highly infectious —*Times Literary Supp.,* 18 June 1971

> ... a freckled, impish face whose infectious grin reveals widely spaced teeth —Patrick O'Higgins, *Cosmopolitan,* July 1972

> ... with an enthusiasm that can be infectious —Tony Schwartz, *N.Y. Times Book Rev.,* 9 Dec. 1979

> His temperament was as fiery as his red hair, and his vitality was infectious —John Walker, *Atlantic,* February 1972

contemn See CONDEMN, CONTEMN.

contemporaneous See CONTEMPORARY.

contemporary Back in the 1960s Theodore Bernstein was denouncing in *Winners & Sinners* uses of *contem-*

porary in the sense "present-day, modern" that he had observed in the *New York Times.* He may, in part, have condemned the sense because he could not find it in his Webster's Second. Gowers in Fowler 1965 has a similar problem: he cannot find the meaning in the OED.

Webster's Second might well have served Mr. Bernstein better. Evidence in the OED Supplement and our own files shows that our editors simply missed the meaning. The oldest Supplement citation is the title of *The Contemporary Review,* which goes back to 1866. That title was known to the editors of Webster's Second, as was *Contemporary American Literature,* the title of a book from which citations for the dictionary were taken. And the use existed in other books marked for citations. For instance, here is George Bernard Shaw using the word in a way that illustrates the transition from "existing at the same time" to "present-day":

> In the preface to my Plays for Puritans I explained the predicament of our contemporary English drama —preface, *Man and Superman,* 1903

A little later in the same preface Shaw uses the word in the new sense:

> . . . what we call education and culture is for the most part nothing but the substitution of reading for experience, of literature for life, of the obsolete fictitious for the contemporary real . . .

These passages had been marked by our editors for other words than *contemporary,* as had this one:

> . . . very high in the waist, very full and long in the skirt; a frock that was at once old-fashioned and tremendously contemporary —Aldous Huxley, *Those Barren Leaves,* 1925

So our editors missed the sense and thereby contributed to the creation of a usage issue.

The new sense had become fully established by the late 1940s:

> . . . and put them into a novel that is clamorously contemporary —John William Rogers, *Saturday Rev.,* 17 July 1948

> Their aim was to bring poetry closer to its real self and to make it more vivid, more intense and more contemporary —Maurice Bowra, *New Republic,* 25 Nov. 1946

> The first of these, characteristic of the 1920's, was known to its adepts as Contemporary Music —Virgil Thomson, *The Musical Scene,* 1947

> . . . whose work is quite as contemporary as that of Austin Clarke even if he is no longer among the living —Babette Deutsch, *New Republic,* 21 Mar. 1949

Since this meaning is to be found in all recent American dictionaries as well as the OED Supplement, and is even part of the title of Evans 1957 and Harper 1975, 1985, you can assume that it is entirely standard.

The establishment of the "present-day" sense has led to two other issues mentioned in some usage books. The first is a warning—in Cook 1985 and a couple of others—about the likelihood of ambiguity in sentences like this:

> . . . but no one would consider Byron's poetry licentious by contemporary standards —*N.Y. Times,* 7 May 1968

The argument is that *contemporary* might refer either to Byron's time or to the present. While the possibility of ambiguity does exist, it seems remote unless the context has been deliberately removed. Even in the *New York Times* excerpt (cited in an issue of *Winners & Sinners*), the intent is made quite plain by "would consider"; if the writer had meant to refer to Byron's time the verb probably would have been "considered" or "would have considered." It is not very likely that a reader will be misled with the complete context to read.

Einstein 1985 recommends the use of *contemporaneous* for "existing at the same time" if the use of *contemporary* might cause confusion. *Contemporary* and *contemporaneous* have been synonymous since the 17th century. For many years the synonymy discriminations in Merriam-Webster dictionaries noted that *contemporary* was likely to be applied to people and *contemporaneous* to events. This distinction was only broadly true; *contemporaneous* was less frequently applied to people than *contemporary* and more often to things or events. But the development of the newer sense of *contemporary* has altered the relationship between the two words. Since the late 1940s the "modern, present-day" meaning of *contemporary* has become its predominant use. *Contemporaneous,* in spite of two or three false starts in the direction of *contemporary,* has essentially retained its original sense. What we are beginning to see is what H. W. Fowler called "differentiation": *contemporary* is being used chiefly in its most recent sense, and *contemporaneous* is being used for "existing at the same time"—more or less replacing *contemporary* in that sense. While this differentiation is not complete, it does permit writers to contrast the two words in a single sentence:

> But now that we have not merely contemporary but almost contemporaneous history, putting events in their place almost as they roll off the production line —*Times Literary Supp.,* 9 Jan. 1964

> The world of the Jews in Germany, France, England, Holland, Italy, Austria, was vastly different from the world of *shtetl* Jews in eastern Europe. The world of the first was contemporary; the world of the second only contemporaneous —Leo Rosten, *The Joys of Yiddish,* 1968

So the "present-day, modern" sense of *contemporary* has become fully established, and *contemporaneous* appears to be replacing *contemporary* in its older sense. You will be able to observe whether this differentiation develops so completely that the sense Bernstein and Follett and Gowers thought to be the only correct one actually becomes old-fashioned. Do not expect the result to be too tidy, however; a countervailing force exists in the noun *contemporary,* for which the older meaning remains in vigorous use.

contemptible See CONTEMPTUOUS 1.

contemptuous 1. *Contemptible, contemptuous.* In the 16th, 17th, and 18th centuries these two words were used interchangeably, as the citations in the OED show. Shakespeare, in particular, provides a good example of the practice of those times: the four Shakespearean citations listed in the OED at *contemptible* and *contemptuous* are the only ones listed in Bartlett's *Concordance to Shakespeare* (1894), and these four citations constitute one use of each word with each meaning.

By 1770, however, at least one person was voicing dissatisfaction over the ambiguity of the adverb forms of these words:

> If I hear it said that one Man treats another contemptibly, I hardly know whether the Meaning is that he treats him with Contempt, or that his own Behaviour is contemptible —Baker 1770

The ambiguity is of the kind that can become a springboard for wit. Bache 1869 relates an anecdote about "Dr. Parr" (possibly Dr. Samuel Parr 1747–1825, an English pedagogue known as a vastly learned but dogmatic conversationalist):

> A man once said to Dr. Parr:—"Sir, I have a contemptible opinion of you." "Sir," replied the Doctor, "that does not surprise me: all your opinions are contemptible."

This riposte caught the fancy of Ayres 1881, who took the anecdote for his own book, and Lurie 1927, who did likewise.

Baker's complaint and Parr's retort were probably reflections of the attitudes and usage developing around them. The date of the last citation in the OED for *contemptuous* meaning "worthy of contempt" is 1796, for *contemptible* meaning "full of contempt" is 1816, and for *contemptibly* meaning "with contempt" is 1827. The evidence we have for later uses of these meanings is scanty: Fowler 1926 quotes a citation for *contemptibly*, and Patrick Cosgrave (in the February 1975 issue of *Encounter*) alludes to a speech by the British political leader Edward Heath. Besides that we have one citation in our files:

> ... it looks so contemptuous to see a grown man or woman chewing in public —Monica Sheridan, *Irish Digest*, March 1955

Though we have little direct evidence for the continued use of these meanings, there is plenty of indirect evidence in the form of injunctions against such uses. We know of more than twenty sources from the past century or so which advise readers not to confuse *contemptible* and *contemptuous*. No doubt some of these commentators include this topic simply because a predecessor did. However, the subject has been revived so often that it may be true that some people are inclined to use *contemptible* to mean "showing contempt" and *contemptuous* to mean "worthy of contempt" in speech and casual writing, even though such uses rarely find their way into print. We are therefore joining the ranks of the cautious in advising you to keep *contemptible* and *contemptuous* distinct.

2. When *contemptuous* is used in the predicate and followed by a prepositional-phrase complement, the preposition is always *of:*

> ... I have been indifferent to, if not indeed contemptuous of, blame —Havelock Ellis, *My Life,* 1939

> ... they seem to grow more sullen, sloppy, and contemptuous of the public they are supposed to serve —John Fischer, *Harper's,* November 1971

contend The word *contend* is very commonly found followed by a clause:

> ... contending that he will be editing the one journal no one could damage —John Kenneth Galbraith, *New York,* 15 Nov. 1971

Contend is also used with prepositions, and *with* is the one most often found:

> We must constantly—in an infinite variety of ways—be contending with one another —Edmund Wilson, *A Piece of My Mind,* 1956

> ... they had contended first with wind and sandstorms, and now with cold —Willa Cather, *Death Comes for the Archbishop,* 1927

Less frequently, *contend* is used with *against* in this same relation:

> ... some of the difficulties against which the French business man had to contend —Paul Johnson, *New Statesman & Nation,* 19 Sept. 1953

When the object of the preposition is the source of contention, *for* is the choice:

> ... a gray stone castle, for whose keep Bruces and Comyns and Macdowalls contended seven centuries ago —John Buchan, *Castle Gay,* 1930

Earlier in this century, some usage books, among them Ball 1923, Weseen 1928, and Lincoln Library 1924 mention that *contend* may also be used with *about.* Interestingly enough, our citation files have no evidence for this use in running text, but quite a lot for *for.* The OED does mention *about* at the entry for *contend,* but only one quotation for *contend about* is shown, and that is from the 17th century.

continual, continuous As far as we can tell, the first person to draw a distinction between *continual* and *continuous* was Elizabeth Jane Whately, in her book *A Collection of English Synonyms,* published under her father's name in 1851.

> A 'continuous' action is one which is uninterrupted, and goes on unceasingly *as long as it lasts,* though that time may be longer or shorter. 'Continual' is that which is constantly renewed and recurring, though it may be interrupted as frequently as it is renewed.

Miss Whately's distinction has been repeated with some frequency since; our files hold examples from about 50 handbooks and usage guides published between the turn of the century and 1986. The restatements have generally been briefer; here, for instance, is Prentice Hall 1978:

> *Continual* means "frequently repeated".... *Continuous* means "without interruption"....

You may well wonder why this distinction needs such frequent repeating. Margaret M. Bryant, writing in *Word Study* (May 1956) seems to have found the reason:

> As explicit as all handbooks for writing are, they have not succeeded in establishing a definite difference in *continual* and *continuous* in the minds of many.

The reasons for this failure are, as we shall see, historical. *Continual* is the older word, dating from the 14th century. The definition given first in the OED encompasses both the sense Miss Whately prescribes for *continuous* and the one she prescribes for *continual;* the latter is marked "less strictly" in the OED. *Continuous* came along in the 17th century and was first applied to continuity in space. The earliest distinction between the two words may be the one made by Dr. Johnson in his 1755 dictionary: "*Continual* is used of time, and *continuous* of place." The meaning of *continuous* prescribed by Miss Whately did not become established until her own time—from the 1830s on.

It is quite possible that Miss Whately was basing her discrimination on what she believed to be the cultivated practice of her time, although she gives us no actual examples nor does she cite any author who makes the distinction. She seems to have been entirely unaware of the earlier use of either word and of the fact that the original sense of *continual* had not died. When the first example below was written, *continuous* hardly existed in English:

> ... the plot being busy (though I think not intricate) and so requiring a continual attention —Aphra Behn, epistle to the reader, *The Dutch Lover*, 1673

> What dreadful hot weather we have! It keeps one in a continual state of Inelegance —Jane Austen, letter, 18 Sept. 1796

> ... a continual supply of the most amiable and innocent enjoyments —Jane Austen, *Mansfield Park*, 1814

> ... the waves, which poured in one continual torrent from the forecastle down upon the decks below — Captain Frederick Marryat, *Peter Simple*, 1834

> ... I was in a state of continual boozyness from the repeated seidels ... of bier which I had to drink — Henry Adams, letter, 7 June 1859

> The cold evening breeze ... sprinkled the floor with a continual rain of fine sand —Robert Louis Stevenson, *Treasure Island*, 1883

So this sense of *continual* persisted in use, while at the same time *continuous* was developing a new sense to compete with it. And in spite of the inroads of *continuous*, this sense of *continual* is still used now:

> ... the continual dread of falling into poverty — George Bernard Shaw, *The Intelligent Woman's Guide to Socialism and Capitalism*, 1928

> We live in a country where His Majesty's Cabinet governs subject to the continual superintendence, correction and authority of Parliament —Sir Winston Churchill, *The Unrelenting Struggle*, 1942

> Actually, there has been a kind of continual biological progression over the years —Adolf A. Berle, *Center Mag.*, January 1969

> Or will the continual presence of abstraction in man's thought dry up ... the old springs of poetry? —Robert Penn Warren, *Democracy and Poetry*, 1975

Ironically, Miss Whately missed one genuine distinction, the one noted by Dr. Johnson. *Continuous* and not *continual* is used of continuity in space (even though *continual* was first in this use too, *continuous* had replaced it by Johnson's time):

> Small windows, too, are pierced through the whole line of ancient wall, so that it seems a row of dwellings with one continuous front —Nathaniel Hawthorne, *The Marble Faun*, 1860

> Continuous quantity resists and even defies description in terms of disjunct ultimate units —Josiah Royce, *The Spirit of Modern Philosophy*, 1892

> ... the horses and chariots alone ... extended in a continuous line for more than six English miles — Sir James G. Frazer, *The Golden Bough*, 1935

> ... had transformed the woods and swamps of northern Europe into a continuous vista of wood and field —Lewis Mumford, *Technics and Civilization*, 1934

> Paper tape is a continuous medium —Susan Artandi, *An Introduction to Computers in Information Science*, 1968

But something must be conceded to Miss Whately's observation: *continual* is more likely than *continuous* to be used for repetition of something that may be interrupted.

> His face had a beery, bruised appearance of a continual drinker's —Robert Louis Stevenson, *New Arabian Nights*, 1882

> There were continual quarrels —William Butler Yeats, *Dramatis Personae*, 1936

> What happens is a continual surrender of himself — T. S. Eliot, "Tradition and the Individual Talent," 1917

> I found it a continual agreeable surprise to realize that she was not "common" —Edmund Wilson, *Memoirs of Hecate County*, 1946

> You will also have to get used to continual visits from all the unbalanced people on the island, who love to plague editors —James Thurber, letter, 21 May 1954

And only *continuous* is used in a construction with *with* that emphasizes unbroken connection:

> He believed that the former was continuous with the Middle Ages and the world of antiquity —J. M. Cameron, *N.Y. Rev. of Books*, 6 Nov. 1969

> Some claim that the animals acquired the essentials of human language and, in so doing, revealed capacities continuous with human cognition —Colin Beer, *Natural History*, May 1986

But we have many instances where both words are used in similar contexts:

> ... though it was a mild night on the sea, there was a continual chorus of the creaking timbers and bulkheads —Jack London, *The Sea-Wolf*, 1904

> ... the continuous thunder of the surf —Robert Louis Stevenson, *Treasure Island*, 1883

> ... the air was full of a continual din of horns — Leslie C. Stevens, *Atlantic*, August 1953

> There was a continuous rumble and grumble of bombardment —Siegfried Sassoon, *Memoirs of a Fox-Hunting Man*, 1928

> ... waspish, continual chatter about boys on the campus whom he suspected of perversion —William Styron, *Lie Down in Darkness*, 1951

> Thus, all the continuous talk of a "new Nixon" — George Stricker, *Saturday Rev.*, 29 Apr. 1972

... a time of almost continual war —John Richard Green, *The History of the English People,* 1880

... a state of almost continuous warfare —Ted Morgan, *Saturday Rev.,* 1 Nov. 1975

... as if some deep continual laughter was repressed —Hallam Tennyson, *Encounter,* December 1954

... the irrepressible and continuous crying which her happiness caused here —E. L. Doctorow, *Ragtime,* 1975

Part of the seeming indifference on the part of writers to a distinction so often repeated is to be explained by the writer's point of view—whether the writer perceives the subject as uninterrupted or not over time. This is obvious in the next two examples: clearly the wars and the trials had some actual breaks between them, but the writer views them as an ongoing and uninterrupted sequence.

... the subcontinent will be rent by innumerable and continuous local wars —Hyman P. Minsky, *Trans-Action,* February 1970

From 1948 on, purges and trials have been continuous —Wayne S. Vucinich, *Current History,* February 1952

To summarize the discussion thus far: many factors enter into the choice between *continual* and *continuous.* As we have seen, *continuous* is the usual word when the application is to physical continuation, continuation in space; nobody uses *continual* in this way. And it is true (though we have not tried to illustrate) that *continuous* is the only choice in a large number of technical applications, in mathematics, construction, manufacturing, biology, and more; *continual* has almost no technical applications. And because it has a much broader spectrum of application, *continuous* is the more common word. Yet, *continual* has been used since the 14th century in its primary sense of "continuing indefinitely in time without interruption" and is still used in that sense. *Continuous* is more recent in this application, having become established in it only in the 1830s, but it is very frequently so used in current English. *Continual* is the word most often chosen when the meaning is "recurring." It is possible for you to follow Miss Whately's distinction or one of its modern versions, and many good writers do so. Others equally good do not, however.

If you are a person who likes careful distinctions, H. W. Fowler's may lie closer to the actual use of *continual* and *continuous* in the areas in which they actually compete. Fowler 1926 says that that which is *continual* "either is always going on or recurs at short intervals & never comes (or is regarded as never coming) to an end." That which is *continuous* is that "in which no break occurs between the beginning & the (not necessarily or even presumably long-deferred) end." Here are two examples illustrating Fowler's distinction, and you may also wish to test it against the examples given above:

The promised visit from "her friend" ... was a formidable threat to Fanny, and she lived in continual terror of it —Jane Austen, *Mansfield Park,* 1814

... that, for 100 days or more, during the primary season, his life could be in continuous jeopardy —James MacGregor Burns, *N.Y. Times,* 14 Sept. 1979

continually, continuously The first thing that needs to be said about these adverbs is that they are used in similar contexts so much of the time that it is very difficult to discern a marked difference between them. For the record, *continually* had a 350-year head start on *continuously,* which in its early uses was found principally in technical contexts. *Continuously* is currently used about as frequently as *continually* and for the most part in essentially the same contexts. However, two specific kinds of uses (which constitute only a small minority of all the uses in our files) are handled by *continuously* alone. It is the adverb used when something continues in space rather than time:

The hand binding will show a sewing thread running continuously from the first needle hole to the last —Edith Diehl, *Bookbinding,* 1946

... the frieze decorated continuously with mythical battle scenes —*Antiques and the Arts Weekly,* 3 Dec. 1982

And *continuously* does all the technical work:

Let *f* and *g* map *B* continuously into itself —Simeon Reich, *American Mathematical Monthly,* January 1974

... compare the amount ... when interest is compounded continuously —School Mathematics Study Group, *Calculus of Elementary Functions,* 1969

A few commentators from Bierce 1909 to Bremner 1980 have tried to extend to these adverbs the distinction between the adjectives *continual* and *continuous* that was first made by Miss Whately in her book of synonyms published in 1851 (see CONTINUAL, CONTINUOUS). Unfortunately, that distinction has even less to do with the way the adverbs are used in standard English than it does with the adjectives. The distinction between the adjectives made by Fowler 1926 (also mentioned at CONTINUAL, CONTINUOUS) describes the use of *continually* pretty well, but fails for *continuously.*

If *continuously* and *continually* are to be distinguished, they must be distinguished by criteria other than those advanced for the adjectives. We can do this best by pointing out the typical uses of each. *Continuously* has the two unshared uses mentioned above. It is also used to contrast with adverbs other than *continually* for the purpose of stressing that something happens steadily and imperceptibly without discrete stages or episodes:

Rocker arms are now pressure lubricated continuously rather than intermittently —*Car Life,* December 1954

Its proponents think that species evolve episodically, not continuously —*N.Y. Times Book Rev.,* 5 Dec. 1982

... the seatback angle can be adjusted continuously, rather than in steps —*Consumer Reports,* May 1979

Continuously is also used where stress is laid on an unbroken succession of discrete time periods:

The mayor ... , elected continuously since 1945 —*Current Biography,* September 1965

After holding the international chess title continuously for nine years —*Current Biography,* June 1965

... has been appearing each week ever since, the oldest continuously published newspaper in the United

States —*American Guide Series: New Hampshire,* 1938

For 137 years services were held continuously in Long Street Church —*American Guide Series: North Carolina,* 1939

Continually is used especially when something continues to exist or happen, with or without interruptions, for an indefinite period of time (this is what Fowler observed):

> It may therefore, perhaps, be necessary, in order to preserve both men and angels in a state of rectitude, that they should have continually before them the punishment of those who have deviated from it — Samuel Johnson, quoted in James Boswell, *Life of Samuel Johnson,* 1791

> The solar cells continually face the sun —Newlan MacDonnell Ulsch, *Boston Globe Mag.,* 21 June 1981

> ... the expression ... of a beautiful secret continually tasted, was still on his face —John Updike, *Couples,* 1968

> ... tells of the loneliness that has been continually present in his life since he became blind and deaf — *Current Biography,* December 1966

> Nothing is ever dry: land and air are continually saturated —C. Daryll Forde, *Habitat, Economy and Society,* 8th ed., 1950

> "I'll find the right place and the right people and then I'll begin," he continually said to himself —Sherwood Anderson, *Poor White,* 1920

> His hands were small and prehensile, ... and they were continually flickering in front of him in violent and expressive pantomime —Robert Louis Stevenson, *New Arabian Nights,* 1882

> The wines are the continually underrated local ones —John Vinocur, *N.Y. Times Mag.,* 9 Oct. 1983

Continually is also the adverb of choice when repetition is emphasized:

> The youngsters continually deserted their meal in order to put their arms about the cow's neck — James Stephens, *The Crock of Gold,* 1912

> ... and indeed I was deeply and continually honored wherever I went —Garrison Keillor, *Lake Wobegon Days,* 1985

> My job is to edit copy continually —E. B. White, letter, September 1921

> ... there are two works I do reread continually — Muriel Spark, quoted in *N.Y. Times Book Rev.,* 12 June 1983

These examples show uses of *continually* and *continuously* in which a fastidious writer can make a rational choice. But these do not represent all usage. Many times the words are used as if they were interchangeable. The majority of the interchangeable uses are uses of *continuously* in contexts where *continually* would have worked as well and might have been expected; the use of *continually* in a context that is typical of *continuously* is relatively infrequent. The intrusion of *continuously* into the territory of *continually* is probably the result of

the increase in the use of both *continuous* and *continuously* that has been going on for three centuries, rather than the result of confusion, indifference, or a failure of standards.

You can observe the distinctions described and illustrated above (or even the traditionally prescribed distinction), if you want to; quite a few writers, however, seem to make virtually no distinction at all.

continue on   A half dozen or more commentators from Ayres 1881 to Chambers 1985 have dismissed *continue on* as a redundancy, with the *on* considered (usually) superfluous. Ayres himself found the *on* to be "euphonious" in some expressions, but superfluous in others. Later commentators seem to have missed the euphony. One, however, Safire 1984, defends the expression when applied to travel.

Our evidence does not suggest that *continue on* is a favorite phrase in English; its use does not even make up a significant percentage of our evidence for *continue.* The citations we have are about evenly divided between use involving travel or movement and other use. Some of the travel examples:

> They continued on for a quarter of a mile, squatting under the foliage and bellying over the ledges —Norman Mailer, *The Naked and the Dead,* 1948

> ... some to continue on to ports around the world —*From Natchez to Greenville,* No. 3, 1970

> Mr. Kovarnik bowed slightly, picked up his briefcase, and continued on down the hall —Frederick L. Keefe, *New Yorker,* 15 Sept. 1951

And a few of the others:

> ... decides to make no investment at all and continues on with the old equipment —Ralph E. Cross, *Dun's,* January 1954

> Old forms linger in the chronology of the earth, discarded shapes continue on in a new age —Emma Hawkridge, *The Wisdom Tree,* 1945

> ... it continued on for many years in crippled form —Rondo E. Cameron, *Jour. of Political Economy,* December 1953

This is clearly a matter of no special importance. It hardly seems that anyone need worry about the space wasted by a two-letter word, especially one which may help the rhythm (or euphony) of a sentence or even (as in several of our examples) serve usefully to underline continuation where cessation might have been expected. If you are one of the few who use *continue on,* you may keep right on using it. And if you do not use it, of course, there is no reason to begin.

See also REDUNDANCY.

continuous   See CONTINUAL, CONTINUOUS.

continuously   See CONTINUALLY, CONTINUOUSLY.

contractions   Contractions became unfashionable in the 18th century and continued so until the early 20th century at least; in 1901 a correspondent of *The Ladies' Home Journal* was still wondering if *can't, couldn't,* and *won't* were permissible. Today many handbooks for writers recommend contractions to avoid sounding stilted. See AIN'T; AN'T, A'N'T; DON'T; EN'T; HAIN'T; HAN'T; WON'T. See also ABBREVIATIONS.

contrast   **1.** As a noun, *contrast* is used with the prepositions *between, with,* and *to:*

What a contrast . . . between this gray apathy and the way the Germans had gone to war in 1914 —William L. Shirer, *The Rise and Fall of the Third Reich,* 1960

The contrast between the wealthy citizenry of Potosí and the Indian miners —*Times Literary Supp.,* 23 Feb. 1967

. . . identified through comparison or contrast with the history of other societies —Peter J. Parish, *N.Y. Times Book Rev.,* 3 Feb. 1985

. . . a congenial contrast with his more bourgeois background —Gay Talese, *Harper's,* January 1969

The starting five was black, . . . and they made a startling contrast to Adolph Rupp's lily-white aggregation —Jack Olsen, *Sports Illustrated,* 15 July 1968

When preceded by *in, contrast* may be followed by either *to* or *with; to* seems somewhat more common in American English.

His gaily striped tie was in odd contrast to his haggard face —Van Siller, *Cosmopolitan,* March 1972

The enforced simplicity in this diary of half-living is in contrast to the intensity of his former life —*Times Literary Supp.,* 21 Mar. 1968

. . . dispassionate style and clear organization of this article are in sharp contrast to his sentimental meandering . . . in other essays —George Victor, *Change,* November 1971

In contrast with Mr Chou, Mr Nguyen Huu Tho was strongly critical —David Bonavia, *The Times* (London), 19 Nov. 1973

Morrissey himself, in contrast with his present surroundings, is all New York —Melton S. Davis, *N.Y. Times,* 15 July 1973

2. The commentators are of several minds on the question of the verb *contrast* used with *with* or *to.* Alford 1866 allows both but prefers *to;* Bernstein 1965 and Safire 1984 allow both but think *to* implies a stronger contrast than *with;* Longman 1984 and Simon 1980 think *with* the only choice in modern use. The OED finds *with* more common than *to,* and *with* predominates in our most recent evidence.
Some examples of *with:*

The Activity of his Character is now to be contrasted with the Gravity of Nestor's —Alexander Pope, footnote, *The Iliad,* 1715

. . . the luxury of the soft beaten sand as contrasted with the paved centre —Thomas De Quincey, "The Vision of Sudden Death," 1849

. . . contrasting her with other women and thinking how deliciously ingenuous she was —Vita Sackville-West, *The Edwardians,* 1930

. . . to contrast the optimism of Teilhard de Chardin with the pessimism of Pascal —Thomas Merton, *Commonweal,* 27 Oct. 1967

It does not contrast the woman riveter with the chic mannequin —Arthur Miller, *Harper's,* September 1969

. . . a mountain whose majestic calm contrasts with the extraordinary scenes of human cruelty —Diane Johnson, *N.Y. Times Book Rev.,* 27 Mar. 1983

Some examples of *to:*

. . . the fixity and establishment-mindedness of all law ethics as contrasted to love ethics —Joseph Fletcher, *Situation Ethics,* 1966

It is interesting to contrast the policies of the two German states to the use of German and English — Richard E. Wood, *English Around the World,* November 1976

. . . and what more comfortingly square profession could there be to contrast to the danger and self-righteousness of his parents' endeavors? —Mopsy Strange Kennedy, *N.Y. Times Book Rev.,* 25 Nov. 1984

We find little evidence of a difference of intensity between *with* and *to. With* is simply more often used.

convenient   As a predicate adjective *convenient* can be followed by *to* and the infinitive:

. . . it is convenient to divide it into three parts — Norman Fisher, *London Calling,* 13 May 1954

. . . they find it more convenient to conform —John Foster Dulles, quoted in *New Republic,* 30 May 1955

It can also be followed by prepositional phrases introduced by *for* or *to. For* is used mostly for persons or their convenience:

. . . whichever is more convenient for you —Gwen Ford, *Young Miss,* November 1967

. . . everything necessary and convenient for the skipper's use —Captain Harry Allen Chippendale, *Sails and Whales,* 1951

. . . convenient for carrying packages to the pantry shelf —*Phoenix Flame,* 1953

To is used for persons but also for places:

. . . hours convenient to the workingman —radio advt., 6 May 1975

In a few constituencies it is convenient to the party managers if a good Jewish or Catholic candidate wins —D. W. Brogan, *The English People,* 1943

. . . not located convenient to large cities —*Dictionary of American History,* 1940

. . . a point convenient to a group of plantations — *American Guide Series: Virginia,* 1941

conversant   *Conversant* usually takes the preposition *with:*

. . . obviously conversant with all of Wodehouse's characters —*New Yorker,* 30 Oct. 1971

. . . woe to the liberal politician who was not quickly conversant with them —Norman Mailer, *Harper's,* March 1971

. . . two authors conversant with a large number of widely differing languages —Margaret Masterman, *Times Literary Supp.,* 19 Mar. 1970

British officers recruiting Gurkhas must be conversant with the ways of a dozen or more castes and tribes —Christopher Rand, *New Yorker,* 6 Nov. 1954

It also takes *in,* but less frequently:

... may prefer to speak Spanish but are often conversant in English as well —John M. Crewdson, *N.Y. Times,* 8 Aug. 1979

This produced officers conversant in many matters, but proficient in very few —Col. David H. Hackworth, *Harper's,* July 1972

convict When the verb *convict* is followed by a preposition, often the preposition is *of:*

... was convicted of perjury and sentenced to prison —Stanley E. Dimond & Elmer F. Pflieger, *Our American Government,* 1961

Big words are hopelessly out of place when they convict an author of insincerity —Eugene S. McCartney, *Recurrent Maladies in Scholarly Writing,* 1953

Less frequently, *convict* is used with *on:*

... pronounced sentence on the defendents convicted on the indictment —International Military Trials—Nurnburg, *Nazi Conspiracy and Aggression,* 1947

... was convicted ... on the less serious charge — *Current Biography 1947*

Some language commentators deplore the use of *for* with *convict,* but it does not appear to be in widespread use. The Merriam-Webster files contain only one citation for it:

If we cannot convict some of them for their disloyal activities perhaps we can convict some of them for perjury —Joseph McCarthy, quoted in *New Republic,* 14 Feb. 1955

convince, persuade The use of *convince* in a construction in which it is followed by *to* and an infinitive phrase has been controversial since about 1958. Edwin Newman is often mentioned in discussions of this issue, but he came late (1974) upon the scene; Bernstein, Copperud, Follett, and Shaw all had preceded him. Most recent comment centers on criticism of the construction with *to* and the infinitive, but accepts as legitimate complement phrases beginning with *of* and clauses usually beginning with *that.* Some commentators try to distinguish *convince* and *persuade* on the basis of various subtle differences in meaning that they descry; these commentators are a link to the past, as we shall see. A few—Bremner 1980, Barnard 1979—see no point in the controversy.

Barnard 1979 says that a half century ago, when he was a freshman in college, he was taught that *convince* meant "mental acceptance," and *persuade* mental acceptance followed by action. Barnard's summary connects that era with ours, because the ascribed meanings are currently put to use to make a point about syntax whereas earlier they were used simply to distinguish the two words without explicit reference to syntax. The typical constructions—*convince* with *that* or *of* and *persuade* with *to* and the infinitive—were then used only in illustrating what was supposed to be a distinction in meaning. Both Vizetelly 1906 and Whipple 1924, for

instance, employ the constructions as illustrations but make no explicit mention of them.

The current use of *convince* with *to* and an infinitive can be seen as the final development in a long historical process in which these two verbs have moved into each other's sphere of influence. Richard Grant White 1870 is the earliest commentator we have found on this subject. His complaint is with *persuaded.* He finds *persuaded* used where *convinced* should have been used, and laments that the use is too well entrenched—he cites the King James Bible twice and Shakespeare once—to be eradicated. A "tender and delicate sense" has been lost.

It is clear from White's examples that the use of *persuaded* he does not like involves its use where, to use Barnard's paraphrase, only mental acceptance is involved; no action is implied. This use of *persuade* is still current:

"There's no such thing as ghosts. People just make them up and think they see them." I still wasn't persuaded. I had been there and seen the ghost's dreadful effect on my grandmother —Russell Baker, *Growing Up,* 1982

It is probable that the handbooks of the early 20th century were attempting to tidy up usage in the way that White would have liked to see; they must have been concerned with fencing *persuade* off from *convince,* because we have no evidence of *convince* being used to suggest mental acceptance followed by action until the middle of the 20th century.

In 1969 P. B. Gove, Merriam's editor in chief, answered a letter from a linguist about the construction in which *convince* is followed by the infinitive. He said that it was not in his idiolect and went on to explain why the construction was not illustrated in Webster's Third: the definer had only three examples of it as opposed to 61 of a clause following the verb. The definer no doubt thought it too infrequent a construction to be worth quoting. The definer has proved a poor prognosticator, however. Of the citations gathered between the editing of the Third and 1969, nearly 60 percent showed the infinitive construction. Flesch 1964 said that *convince to* was "a new idiom springing up under our noses," and he was right.

Our earliest evidence for the new idiom comes from 1952:

A new political party, the Constitutional Party, is formed to try to convince the Electoral College to vote for Gen. MacArthur and Sen. Byrd —*Current History,* November 1952

It had undoubtedly already existed in speech for some time, and it gradually increased in use in print:

... a method by which Congress in 1913 convinced Woodrow Wilson to modify his stand on currency reform —*New Republic,* 2 Aug. 1954

He convinced the Russians to let him exhibit anyway —*N.Y. Times,* 13 Sept. 1958

Widows and girls may be hired for the purpose of delivering love messages, patching quarrels, or convincing a girl to become someone's *novia* —Oscar Lewis, *Tepoztlán: Village in Mexico,* 1960

This convinced me to fight —Darryl F. Zanuck, quoted in *Newsweek,* 6 Aug. 1962

. . . something I could never convince him to read —
John Lahr, *N.Y. Times Book Rev.,* 3 Dec. 1967

. . . asking me to convince McCarthy to do it —
David Halberstam, *Harper's,* December 1968

. . . convinced the group to seek their pleasures elsewhere —*Massachusetts Wildlife,* September–October 1969

. . . to convince his compatriots to leave the country
—Theodore Draper, *N.Y. Rev. of Books,* 12 Mar.
1970

The construction is fully established now:

She said to hell with it, she would skip Italy. . . . You
convinced her to go —Jay McInerney, *Bright Lights,
Big City,* 1984

. . . how his publisher had once tried to convince him
to change a word in one of his manuscripts —Leslie
Aldridge Westoff, *N.Y. Times Mag.,* 10 May 1987

When Theodore Bernstein first noticed the construction in 1958, one of the corrections he suggested was the
substitution of a *that*-clause for the infinitive phrase:
"He convinced the Russians that they should let
him. . . ." Such a use of the clause complement when
action is involved is apparently rare, however. We do
have a few examples:

. . . was convinced by his teachers that he should take
a senior high school biology course —C. Robert
Haywood, *NEA Jour.,* January 1965

When is a spoofy movie not quite convinced it
should act like one? —Liz Smith, *Cosmopolitan,*
December 1976

A review of the evidence in our files shows that almost
always when *convince* is followed by a clause, mental
acceptance only is connoted:

. . . I doubt not your rising from the perusal convinced that our nation . . . has enjoyed a continuous
blessing —Quiller-Couch 1916

. . . which is to convince itself that there are too
many lines in a sonnet —James Thurber, letter, 23
June 1952

. . . after he convinced himself that she was all right
—"Centaur in Brass," in *The Collected Stories of
William Faulkner,* 1950

He had tried for weeks to forget her, he said, convinced that she was too young for him —Herman
Wouk, *Marjorie Morningstar,* 1955

The agency lawyers were convinced the decision was
a fluke —Eileen Hughes, *Ladies' Home Jour.,* September 1971

And do not believe that *persuade* has disappeared from
the use involving action:

. . . Freud was persuaded to make an expedition to
the great natural wonder of Niagara Falls —E. L.
Doctorow, *Ragtime,* 1975

Could language somehow be persuaded to come
closer to experience? —Howard Nemerov, *Prose,*
Fall 1971

Follett 1966 observes of the verb *contact* that most of
those remaining who object to it probably remember it

as a neologism. This seems to be the case with *convince
to* as well. We suspect that people born in the 1930s or
1940s or later do not even notice the construction, while
those born earlier do. And in another generation people
may wonder what all the fuss was about.

To sum up: long ago *persuade* became established in
a use connoting mental acceptance without following
action—a sense Richard Grant White thought should be
reserved for *convince. Persuade* still has this use, often
with the same *of* and *that* constructions regularly found
with *convince.* Sometime around the middle of this century, *convince* began to be used to connote mental
acceptance followed by action, usually in a construction
in which an infinitive phrase follows the verb. This construction is now a fully established idiom. The earlier
usage writers who tried to fence off *persuade* from *convince* and the later ones who tried to fence off *convince*
from *persuade* have failed alike. And in another generation perhaps no one will care.

cop   A few commentators worry about the status of
cop for "police officer." Bremner 1980 says it is gaining
respectability. It has gained respectability, and is used
regularly in the general English of newspapers and magazines in the United States and in Great Britain and
other countries using British English. It is, of course,
used in novels and occasionally turns up in collections
of essays and such, although it does not appear often in
the most elevated kinds of writing.

. . . we were surprised to learn that he makes his living as a traffic cop in midtown Manhattan —*New
Yorker,* 28 June 1982

Equally fine is Kinderman, the cop —Keith S. Felton, *Los Angeles Times,* 23 May 1971

I grew up in Ohio when the cop on the corner was a
girl's best friend —Eleanor Perry, *Ms.,* September
1972

Don McKillop continues as the local cop —Paul
Foster, *Scottish Field,* May 1974

. . . cops were allowed to behave like real people —
Joan Bakewell, *The Listener,* 13 June 1974

cope   *Cope* in the sense "to deal with and try to overcome problems and difficulties" has been used since
Milton's time with the preposition *with:*

. . . was beginning to feel a way towards a plan for
coping with that old incubus —Stella Gibbons, *Cold
Comfort Farm,* 1932

. . . it was this sudden change of mood that he felt he
could never cope with —William Styron, *Lie Down
in Darkness,* 1951

. . . had simply not been able to cope with the revolutionary new tactics —William L. Shirer, *The Rise
and Fall of the Third Reich,* 1960

Until the 1930s this appears to have been the only construction. *Cope* then came to be used absolutely, with no
object added in a phrase introduced by *with.* This use is
much like the absolute use of the verb *manage.* The
Shorter OED dates it from 1932, the OED Supplement
from 1934. It first appeared in British English and
apparently became established there during World War
II and its aftermath. A writer in the *Yale Review* in 1947
noted the appearance of the word in descriptions of
making do under difficult circumstances in postwar

Great Britain. In fiction it seems to have been primarily used in speech:

> Heaven knows, I wish Roderick were free enough and old enough to cope! —Elizabeth Bowen, *The Heat of the Day,* 1949

> "My cousin Pamela Lyson is coping. . . ." —Elizabeth Goudge, *Pilgrim's Inn,* 1948

> "She's not the sort to cope." —Joyce Cary, *A Fearful Joy,* 1949

> "We can cope," she said —H. E. Bates, *The Scarlet Sword,* 1951

But not all use was in fictional speech. Foster 1968 found it in a British soldier's account of his wartime experiences at Anzio in 1944. And it was used in general running text:

> Imperceptibly it became easier. You were beginning to cope —Fred Majdalany, *Patrol,* 1953

> . . . only 9 per cent were unable to cope at all — *Times Literary Supp.,* 10 Sept. 1954

> After all, since the flying boats stopped, the old aerodrome, opened in the 1920s, has been coping — Robert Finigan, *London Calling,* 3 Mar. 1955

In the 1950s the new construction began to appear in American English:

> . . . and on that occasion reliable old Schrafft will be on hand to help you cope —*New Yorker,* 8 Dec. 1951

> Nevertheless, said he, the conference would have to cope —*Time,* 12 Dec. 1955

> Four divisions of Russian occupation forces couldn't cope —*Newsweek,* 5 Nov. 1956

In the 1960s the usage came to the attention of American commentators. Copperud 1964 may have been the first; he thought it correct but so unusual that people were likely to think it a mistake. The Heritage 1969 panel did not like it in formal writing, and Bremner 1980 does not like it at all, while the Harper 1975, 1985 panels accept it only in speech. E. B. White in his second and third editions of Strunk & White (1972, 1979) characterizes it as "jocular"; he seems to have been unfamiliar with contemporaneous use of the construction in the *New Yorker.* None of these American commentators reveals knowledge that the construction is fully established in British use; no British commentator that we have seen so much as mentions it. The OED Supplement, perhaps, is chary of it, labeling it *colloq.* But they seem to have less evidence than we've shown you so far; they reproduce only Elizabeth Bowen from 1934 and two comments on the construction from the 1950s. It has however continued steadily in British use:

> I was too green to know that all cynicism masks a failure to cope—an impotence, in short —John Fowles, *The Magus,* 1966

> Never mind, she could cope —Daphne du Maurier, *Ladies' Home Jour.,* Sept. 1971

> . . . the French authorities would either have to confess their inability to cope or would have to find new methods —*Times Literary Supp.,* 28 Apr. 1972

> The casualty department at the hospital, which dealt with 100 cases, coped very satisfactorily —Robin Morgan, *Yorkshire Post,* 7 June 1974

> . . . the struggles of a young middle-class married couple who could not really cope —Margaret Crosland, *British Book News,* May 1982

And furthermore it appears to be well established in general American use too:

> . . . Marshal Pétain, "due to age," a little less able to cope —Ward Just, *Atlantic,* October 1970

> . . . their wraith-like mother, unable to cope since the recent death of the father —Dorothy B. Hughes, *Los Angeles Times,* 23 May 1971

> . . . wresting their living from a precipitous land that seems to defy the very idea of giving man back any return for his sweat and labor. But the Sikkimese cope —Harrison E. Salisbury, *Vogue,* 15 Oct. 1971

> . . . the astronauts would have been increasingly unable to cope —Henry S. F. Cooper, Jr., *New Yorker,* 18 Nov. 1972

> . . . candid interviews with families struggling to cope —Ellen Chesler, *N.Y. Times Book Rev.,* 28 Aug. 1983

The absolute use of *cope* is well established; it has had no effect whatsoever on the *cope with* construction.

cord   See CHORD, CORD.

coronate   Back in 1967 one Darcy Curwen wrote this:

> A short while ago I heard one of the better radio announcers say, "When Pope Pius was coronated. . . ." There is no such word; the fellow meant crowned —*Bulletin of Emma Willard School,* June 1967

Nickles 1974 doesn't like *coronate* either, listing it among a bunch of "bastard" words, as he terms back-formations. William Safire in the *New York Times Magazine* for 16 March 1980 called it "wrong."

A look into Webster's Third or the OED will give you a different slant on the word. *Coronate* has been around since the 17th century. It is derived from Latin *coronatus,* past participle of *coronare* "to crown"; it is not a back-formation from *coronation.*

Coronate is a relatively rare verb. It last got fairly frequent play back at the accession of Queen Elizabeth II:

> Queen Elizabeth II will probably be coronated sometime between August and the spring of 1953 —*Wall Street Jour.,* 9 Feb. 1952

It has been used only occasionally since.

> The police asked today all drivers to keep off the streets Thursday when the Shah and Empress Farah will be coronated —*N.Y. Times* (AP), 23 Oct. 1967

Perhaps some writers are too young to remember 1953, and the Shah is long gone, having been replaced by the Ayatollah Khomeini, who was not coronated (or crowned). Most people use *crown.* But *coronate* is available if you need it, and it is a perfectly legitimate word.

correct   *Correct* is on some lists of absolute adjectives (see ABSOLUTE ADJECTIVES). It has, of course, been frequently used in the comparative and superlative.

> . . . has wrote a more correct account of Italy than any before him —Joseph Addison, preface to *Remarks on Italy,* 1705 (cited in OED under *any*)

... recommends them to his readers as most correct —Baron 1982

As far as we can judge, from rhymes and other clues, the American accent and stress of English is more 'correct', i.e. older, than the British accent —Howard 1984

correspond   *Correspond,* in the senses meaning "to be in conformity or agreement" or "to compare closely, match," may be followed by either *to* or *with;* according to our evidence, *to* is used more often:

... the man whose consciousness does not correspond to that of the majority is a madman —George Bernard Shaw, *Man and Superman,* 1903

Their political position corresponds further to their military strength —*New Republic,* 3 May 1954

... all quotations should *correspond* exactly with the originals in wording —*MLA Style Sheet,* 2d ed., 1970

When meaning "to write to someone," *correspond* is used with *with* exclusively:

In 1943 he began to correspond with a young Welsh poet, Lynette Roberts —Michael Glover, *British Book News,* July 1985

cosmetic, cosmeticize, cosmetize   Harper 1975, 1985 in disparaging the verb *cosmetize* (one of those *-ize* verbs) seemingly bewails the fact that there is no verb derived from *cosmetic* to be found in unabridged dictionaries. Howard 1977 found one in the 1976 Addenda Section of Webster's Third: *cosmeticize.* Cosmeticize was coined in the 19th century and can also be found in the OED. It was apparently first used literally in the sense of "to apply a cosmetic to" (although the earliest—1824—cited use may be figurative), but in its modern use it is usually figurative:

Euphemism would enter in only if language ... tried to prettify or cosmeticize the effect —Robert M. Adams, in *Fair of Speech,* ed. D. J. Enright, 1985

Hollywood used to cosmeticize lives —Stanley Kauffman, *Before My Eyes,* 1980

... with a brashness that has been cosmeticized into proto-polish —Simon 1980

The verb *cosmetize*—still waiting for entrée to the unabridged—has been used more often literally than figuratively:

... artistically cosmetized corpses —Richard Brissell, *A Stretch on the River,* 1950

The body is embalmed and cosmetized —*Newsweek,* 9 Sept. 1963

... the old dead were cosmetized into an overdrawn image of younger times —Harry J. Boyle, *The Great Canadian Novel,* 1972

Another possibility for making a verb from *cosmetic* is to go the route of the plain functional shift:

... they display themselves—corseted and cosmeticked—in the streets —G. Legman, *Rationale of the Dirty Joke,* 2d series, 1975

Its ugliness mocks every beauty real and cosmeticked —Milton Mayer, in *The Great Ideas Today,* eds. Robert M. Hutchins & Mortimer J. Adler, 1965

Cosmetize will perhaps eventually make its way into an unabridged dictionary; its chances will be even better if it continues to be used in a way distinct from *cosmeticize. Cosmetic* looks like a long shot at the present time. If you need a verb formed from *cosmetic, cosmeticize* is available and is in dictionaries. Though they are less well established, you can use the others, too, if you like; some writers already have or we wouldn't have collected the examples here. You should be aware, however, that both *cosmeticize* and *cosmetize* are likely to draw some of the unfavorable attention that comes to most modern verbs ending in *-ize.*

could care less, couldn't care less   Everyone knows that *couldn't care less* is the older form of the expression. Eric Partridge in *A Dictionary of Catch Phrases* (2d ed., 1985) says that the phrase arose around 1940 and was probably prompted by an earlier catch phrase, "I couldn't agree with you more." If we assume Partridge's date of origin refers to speech, it is hard to quibble. We do have a 1945 citation from a BBC war correspondent covering a British commando operation:

You would have thought that they were embarking on a Union picnic; they just couldn't care less — Stewart Macpherson, 24 Mar. 1945, in *The Oxford Book of English Talk,* ed. James Sunderland, 1953

The OED Supplement and the editor of the second edition of Partridge's book cite the phrase as the title of a book published in 1946. William Carigan, writing in the *CEA Forum* (October 1972), opines that the phrase was brought to the U.S. by GI's returning from World War II. The hypothesis is plausible even though we lack, at the present time, examples of immediate postwar use in the U.S. It was clearly established by the late 1950s and early 1960s:

To me the elaborate framework, and symbolism, was too much for such petty characters. I couldn't have cared less what happened to any of them —Flannery O'Connor, letter, 17 Jan. 1958

'Listen, Cuckoo, are you sure about Duddy and Yvette? I couldn't care less, but....' —Mordecai Richler, *The Apprenticeship of Duddy Kravitz,* 1959

"... Some place with air conditioning. And without a TV set. I couldn't care less about baseball." — James Baldwin, *Another Country,* 1962

This time, the monkey could not have cared less; the snake held no terrors for it —Dean E. Wooldridge, *The Machinery of the Brain,* 1963

The origin of *could care less* is also obscure. All we know about it for sure is that it came later. Harper 1975, 1985 reports getting letters asking about the expression starting in 1960. That would suggest its existence in speech around that time. No printed examples have so far turned up that antedate the 1966 examples collected by James B. McMillan and cited in his article in *American Speech* (Fall 1978). Our earliest citation is from what appears to be a wire-service picture caption:

This roarless wonder at Chicago's Brookfield Zoo could care less about the old saying dealing with the advent of March —*Springfield* (Mass.) *Republican,* 2 Mar. 1968

The reason why the negative particle was lost without changing the meaning of the phrase has been the subject of much speculation, most of it not very convincing. No one seems to have advanced the simple idea that the rhythm of the phrase may be better for purposes of emphatic sarcasm with *could care less,* which would have its main stress on *care,* than with *couldn't care less,* where the stress would be more nearly equal on *could* and *care.* You, however, may not find this argument very convincing either.

Another consideration not previously mentioned, we believe, is the existence of an intermediate form in which the negative element is divorced from *could* and comes earlier in the sentence:

> ... none of these writers could care less about the "tradition of the novel" —Alfred Kazin, *Saturday Rev.,* 3 July 1971

> But in Bloomingdale's nobody could care less, while here, everyone cares —Donald S. Warner, *Punch,* 12 Mar. 1975

These examples are, of course, too late to prove anything. If they had come before 1960, however, a line of development might have been postulated.

The attitude of the commentators toward *could care less* has in general been negative, with Harper perhaps making the point most vehemently by calling it "an ignorant debasement of the language." Safire 1980 saw usage of *could care less* as having peaked in 1973; he dismissed it as defunct in 1980. But it has not disappeared:

> Funny, ... it comes at a time when I really could care less —Robert Preston, quoted in *People,* 28 June 1982

Bernstein 1971 thought it not quite established then; if it becomes established, he says, it will be another example of "reverse English." Pairs of words or phrases that look like opposites but mean the same thing are not unknown in English: *ravel/unravel, can but/cannot but,* for instance. (For another case in which a negative construction and a positive construction mean the same thing, see BUT 4.)

This is what our present evidence suggests: while *could care less* may be superior in speech for purposes of sarcasm, it is hard to be obviously sarcastic in print. This may explain why most writers, faced with putting the words on paper, choose the clearer *couldn't care less.*

could of   This is a transcription of *could've,* the contracted form of *could have.* Sometimes it is used intentionally—for instance, by Ring Lardner in his fiction. Most of you will want *could have* or *could've.* See OF 2.

council, counsel, consul   A sizable number of handbooks and schoolbooks going back at least as far as Utter 1916 warn against the confusion of *council* and *counsel;* a few even add *consul* to the broth. According to the OED, *council* and *counsel* were hopelessly muddled in medieval times; and our present division of meanings, which apparently matches neither the Latin nor the French from which both are derived, began to establish itself in the 16th century. In current English, *council* generally stands for some sort of deliberative or administrative body, while *counsel* is used for advice or for a lawyer and as a verb meaning "to advise" or "to consult." *Consul* in modern use refers to a diplomatic official.

Our evidence shows that the chief confusion likely to be encountered is the substitution of *council*—the more common word—for one of the three main uses of *counsel.* In the following three examples, *counsel* should have been the spelling chosen:

> ... who can council students —*Linguistic Reporter,* March 1979

> ... his council is sought by leaders of city and nation —*Current Biography,* September 1966

> ... they're still self-conscious about their council being a woman —*American Labor,* July–August 1969

Our advice to you is first, don't try to use *council, counsel* and *consul* in a single sentence as some of the handbooks do—you'll only muddle people. And second, if you have some doubt about which form you want, a look in your dictionary will clear things up.

councillor, councilor, counselor, counsellor   These derivative nouns follow the spellings of their root words. See COUNCIL, COUNSEL, CONSUL.

counterproductive, self-defeating   Phythian 1979 and Harper 1975, 1985 are not pleased with the adjective *counterproductive,* a fairly recent (about 1962) addition to the English vocabulary. Phythian complains that it is too often used as "a loose alternative to *unprofitable, detrimental,* etc." Harper calls it a vogue word which "says nothing that *self-defeating* doesn't say quite as well."

Both these comments miss the point. *Counterproductive* seems to have found a little gap in the language in which to establish itself: no other word has quite the same meaning. Try, for instance, any of the three suggested substitutes in this recent example:

> ... where everybody in the room is pretty sharp, competition in the counterproductive sense goes down, reciprocal respect goes up —John Barth, *N.Y. Times Book Rev.,* 16 June 1985

In the unprofitable sense? In the detrimental sense? In the self-defeating sense? None is a very likely replacement.

When applied to actions, *self-defeating* carries a strong suggestion of failure:

> ... may have convinced millions of Americans ... that violence is a self-defeating and futile way to relieve frustration —Frank K. Kelly, *Center Mag.,* May 1968

> ... tried to rebut the reports, but his praise ... was so fulsome as to be self-defeating —*Current Biography,* January 1968

Counterproductive stresses the producing of results contrary to those intended but tends to suggest a hindering rather than a failure of attainment:

> But some Protestant clergymen now tend to think that professional fund raising is counterproductive —*Time,* 4 Sept. 1964

> ... retailers must be sure that its impact will not be advantageous in one season of the year only to be counterproductive in another —Michael LaBaire, *Publishers Weekly,* 28 Mar. 1980

Our evidence suggests that *counterproductive* has found a place in the language. Its vogue has lasted for more than a quarter of a century and shows no sign of abating. It is beginning to move from the prose of sociologists, bureaucrats, and political scientists—many of whom also use *self-defeating*—into more general and, occasionally, even literary contexts. You can use it if you need it.

couple, *noun* **1.** *Agreement. Couple* is a singular noun but it often takes a plural verb. Several commentators recommend the plural verb when the sentence also has a pronoun referring to *couple* since the pronoun will almost always be *they, their,* or *them.*

> The couple remain friends and share custody of their four children —*People,* 10 May 1982

The governing principle here is notional agreement; if the writer is thinking of two people, the verb is plural:

> The couple were married on April 21 —*Current Biography,* March 1966

> Our young couple from Catonsville were driving by —Alexander Woollcott, *Long,Long Ago,* 1943

> ... the couple have featured in sixteen plays — *Times Literary Supp.,* 8 Feb. 1974

> Before long the young couple have vanished —Patricia T. O'Conner, *N.Y. Times Book Rev.,* 16 Feb. 1986

When the writer thinks of the couple as a unit, the verb is singular:

> The couple has three children —*Current Biography,* February 1967

> The couple has an apartment in Dallas —*N.Y. Times,* 1 Dec. 1970

> The couple dislikes fussy food —Francesca Stanfill, *N.Y. Times Mag.,* 21 Dec. 1980

You will note that the verb seems naturally to be plural when the writing concerns a wedding, as two people are wed, and singular when it concerns children, as joint action is often involved. Consequently when children are mentioned and a pronoun reference follows, editors are likely to be upset:

> The couple has four children of their own —*N.Y. Times,* 24 Mar. 1966 (in *Winners & Sinners,* 31 Mar. 1966)

But *they, their,* and *them* are the standard pronouns of reference for *couple,* especially when people are referred to, regardless of the number of the verb. (See THEY, THEIR, THEM.) In the example just quoted, *his* or *her* are impossible and *its* would sound silly. The substitution of the plural verb might tend to suggest that the couple had children by previous marriages. Although *they, their,* and *them* have been used to refer to nouns and pronouns that take singular verbs for centuries, many newspaper editors seem not to realize it. If a sentence like the one above makes your editor see red, you'll have some complicated rewriting to do. In other instances you could simply use the plural verb:

> A Dayton couple was slain in their home today — *N.Y. Times,* 30 July 1961 (in *Winners & Sinners,* 17 Aug. 1961)

In this example, the plural verb would work fine.

2. *A couple of.* The use of *couple* meaning "two" came under attack in the 19th century. Richard Grant White 1870 seems to have been in the vanguard (Hall 1917 gives 1867 as the first publication of the objection). The basis for the objection seems to be the etymological fallacy—*couple* is derived from Latin *copula* "bond." White's objection is raised with varying degrees of vehemence in several other American usage books—among them Bache 1869, Ayres 1881, and William Cullen Bryant's *Index Expurgatorius* (1877)—until sometime after the turn of the century. Vizetelly 1906 is typical:

> *couple:* Does not mean merely two, but two united, as it were by links.

This usage had been around since the 14th century. Webster 1909, for instance, illustrated it with quotations from Sir Philip Sidney, the King James Bible, Addison, Dickens, and Carlyle. It is not surprising then, that White's objection rather fizzled out early in this century. Here are some other examples of the use:

> A couple of senseless rascals —George Villiers, *The Rehearsal,* 1672

> We finished a couple of bottles of port —James Boswell, *Life of Samuel Johnson,* 1791

> Edward & Fly went out yesterday very early in a couple of Shooting Jackets and came home like a couple of Bad Shots, for they killed nothing at all —Jane Austen, letter, 15 Sept. 1796

> The tribe lost a couple of their best hunters —Rudyard Kipling, *The Second Jungle Book,* 1895

> ... during a couple of years that I spent abroad — Henry James, *The Ivory Tower,* 1917

The objection shifted from White's etymological one to the more general charge of colloquialism or to an objection to the use of the phrase in the sense of "a small but indefinite number." Vizetelly 1906 seems to be the earliest to object to the indefinite use; many later commentators follow. Bierce 1909 takes the opposite point of view, stating that *couple* should only be used when the idea of number is unimportant. The tendency of *couple* to be indefinite is shown in these examples:

> For a couple of years the company succeeded in keeping clear of further disaster —E. K. Chambers, *The Elizabethan Stage,* 1923

> ... a cotton mill run by a hard-bitten North country working man who had borrowed a couple of hundred pounds to start the business —G. M. Trevelyan, *A Shortened History of England,* 1942

> It apparently made relatively slow progress at the start, but after a couple of years it was in wide and indeed almost general use —H. L. Mencken, *The American Language, Supplement 1,* 1945

> A couple of times I gave up —E. B. White, letter, 2 Jan. 1957

Some handbooks still stigmatize *a couple of* as colloquial or informal, but we think you need not worry too much about the propriety of a phrase that has been in use for 500 years. To those who might urge that it is to be questioned only when it means "a few," we point out that the works of E. K. Chambers, G. M. Trevelyan, and H. L. Mencken cited above are not noted for their breezy style.

For a more recent concern of the commentators, see COUPLE, *adjective.*

couple, *adjective* While the commentators were worrying whether the noun *couple* could be used to mean simply "two" and whether it could mean "a few" (see COUPLE, *noun*), the word itself was following the path of development that *dozen* had taken centuries earlier—dropping its following *of* and being used like an adjective. We are not sure when this process began in speech, but we begin to find written evidence in the 1920s. Sinclair Lewis heard it in the dictation of George W. Babbitt:

> ... all my experience indicates he is all right, means to do business, looked into his financial record which is fine—that sentence seems to be a little balled up, Miss McGoun; make a couple sentences out of it if you have to —Sinclair Lewis, *Babbitt,* 1922

Lewis was not the only one to use it:

> ... where the land rises to a couple or three or four feet —W. H. Hudson, *Far Away and Long Ago,* 1924

> ... in the phrases *a couple peaches, a couple of peaches,* only two should be meant —Krapp 1927

G. P. Krapp is the first commentator to mention the construction, but he evidently saw nothing wrong with it. A decade later, however, it was thought to be wrong:

> **couple.** Not an adj.; must be followed by "of" and preceded by article —Muriel B. Carr & John W. Clark, *An A B C of Idiom and Diction,* 1937

Of all the subsequent commentators who have disapproved the omission of *of,* Evans 1957 has the most interesting observation. While insisting that standard English requires *of* between *couple* and a following noun, he points out that the *of* is omitted before a degree word such as *more* or *less.* And indeed this construction is found in standard English:

> ... to emphasize his sincerity he swore a couple more oaths —C. S. Forester, *Hornblower and the Atropos,* 1953

> We can end this chapter by looking at a couple more examples of Middle English writing —Charles Barber, *The Flux of Language,* 1965

> ... middle-aged men expecting a couple more promotions —Peter Preston, *Punch,* 28 Nov. 1973

These examples are all British; the construction is explicitly recognized by a recent British dictionary, Longman 1984. The construction occurs in American English too:

> ... till they had taken a couple more first-class lickings —Elmer Davis, *But We Were Born Free,* 1954

But American English usage seems to have been influenced by the number of commentators stressing the necessity of *of.* The result is the occasional "a couple of more":

> ... a couple of more wins from Jim Palmer —Jim Kaplan, *Sports Illustrated,* 10 Apr. 1978

Nickles 1974 refers to this construction as a "garble" and opines that it results from confusion of *a couple of* with some such construction as *a few more;* he fails to

recognize the standard *a couple more.* Theodore Bernstein seems to have encountered the construction, too; in a June 1967 *Winners & Sinners* he quotes Evans with a measure of approval, but questions whether all degree words fit the pattern. He comes a cropper by confusing Evans's "degree words" with ordinary adjectives. Of course he is right that *a couple of* is used before an adjective and noun:

> ... to develop a couple of new techniques —J. S. Anderson, *General Electric Investor,* Summer 1971

> ... philosophical criticism by a couple of other professors —Robert Penn Warren, *N.Y. Times Book Rev.,* 20 May 1984

Bernstein was unable to find any specific comment in usage books on "a couple of more" and concludes therefore that it is not wrong, though "ungraceful." If you find it ungraceful also and do not care to omit the *of* before *more,* you can put the *more* after the noun instead; the example above would become "a couple of wins more from Jim Palmer." Bernstein also notes that when *more* is promoted to pronoun by omission of the following noun, *of* is not used, as in ". . . I think I'll have a couple more."

But we have strayed from the red-blooded, 100-percent-American adjective before a plural noun that Sinclair Lewis heard in the speech of the middle-class Middle West. The usage is apparently not found in British English, although we do have one example from Jamaica. Here are a few American ones:

> He got off the bus a couple blocks up and sauntered down past the alleyway —James Jones, *From Here to Eternity,* 1951

> ... plumped up a chintz-covered cushion with a couple slaps of his hand —Maritta Wolff, *Back of Town,* 1952

> The first couple chapters are pretty good —E. B. White, letter, 26 Oct. 1959

> ... I haven't heard their last couple albums —Leonard Feather, *Down Beat,* 25 Nov. 1971

> So let's start with a couple samples —Quinn 1980

> Afterward, I met Mark Mullaney upstairs for a couple beers —Ahmad Rashad, *Sports Illustrated,* 25 Oct. 1982

> ... though Mr. Shaw himself still operated a couple wagons for hire —Garrison Keillor, *Lake Wobegon Days,* 1985

This construction seems well established in American English. Everyone who comments knows it to be common in speech. It is now quite common in general prose, but we have seldom found it in prose that aspires to formality and elegance. Its two most frequent uses are with periods of time and with number words like *dozen, hundred,* and *thousand*:

> ... about the eighth century A.D., although Vaillant (1941) would make it a couple centuries sooner — Raymond W. Murray, *Man's Unknown Ancestors,* 1943

> ... have surfaced dramatically in the last couple weeks —James P. Gannon, *Wall Street Jour.,* 16 Oct. 1970

... waiting a couple years before he'd be ready to compete —Kurt Markus, *Western Horseman,* May 1980

There must have been a couple million people in the heart of London yesterday —an American businessman quoted by Bob Considine, *Springfield* (Mass.) *Union,* 9 June 1953

A couple thousand cases of liquor —*Wall Street Jour.,* 14 July 1969

... contains a couple hundred poems —William Cole, *Saturday Rev.,* 18 Sept. 1976

... one of the couple dozen or so really *hip* people —Dean Latimer, *East Village Other,* 30 Mar. 1971

To recapitulate: *a couple* without *of* seems to have begun being used like *a few* and *a dozen* in the 1920s. Our earliest evidence is from that careful listener to American speech, Sinclair Lewis. It is interesting to note that another careful listener, Ring Lardner, had his busher say *a couple of* only a few years earlier:

I could of beat them easy with any kind of support. I walked a couple of guys in the forth and Chase drops a throw —Ring Lardner, *You Know Me Al,* 1916

A couple without *of* is firmly established in American speech and in general writing (though not the more elevated varieties) when it is used directly before a plural noun or a number word. Before *more, a couple* is used without *of* in both British and American English and in this context is often preferred even by American commentators.

course **1.** See COARSE, COURSE.
2. Copperud 1970, 1980 finds *course* as used in such phrases as *in the course of* or *during the course of* redundant for *during, at,* etc. Phrases like these are often used for rhythm or space in a sentence—to keep the content words spaced out so they don't interfere with one another; content words can be too tightly packed to be immediately understood. In addition, these phrases add emphasis to the notion of duration. Let us look at a few examples to see when these phrases are unnecessary and when they are useful:

When in the Course of human events, it becomes necessary for one people to dissolve the political bands which have connected them with another — *Declaration of Independence,* 1776

This example is perhaps unfamiliar to writers on usage. The phrase here helps build a stately and formal opening. The idea can be more briefly expressed: "when one people has to split from another ... ," but more than patriotic sentiment prevents us from seeing that as an improvement.

... the Italian star Silvana Mangano, whom De Laurentiis married in the course of making the picture —*Current Biography,* May 1965

If the phrase is reduced to *in* here, only puzzlement would result. "During the making of the picture" is no improvement either. *While* would be idiomatic here but might import a ludicrous hint that they were married on the set.

... was doing an article on Kim Novak and, in the course of it, met Miss Novak's personal PR girl — Cleveland Amory, *Saturday Rev.,* 30 Oct. 1971

Is the phrase redundant here? If not, it is hard to think of a more concise equivalent.

During the course of the Early Horizon, region after region seems to have broken free from the Chavin influence —Edward P. Lanning, *Peru Before the Incas,* 1967

Here "the course of" would seem omissible; it does no more than emphasize somewhat the length of the period and suggest a happening gradually. But if not at all essential, the phrase is at least harmless, and little is gained by its omission.

For, in the course of an exactly and beautifully written childhood narrative, Iduarte unobtrusively and unargumentatively writes of philosophical or moral uncertainties that afflict many people in many societies —Naomi Bliven, *New Yorker,* 17 July 1971

This seems to be a leisurely review. Avoidance of unnecessary words is no object here. You could undoubtedly put the matter more briefly, but the author didn't have to and clearly didn't want to.

Almost 500 million transactions were handled by our business offices in the course of the year — *Annual Report, American Telephone & Telegraph Co.,* 1970

... were settled during the course of 1970 on a basis which the Company considers favorable —*Annual Report, International Business Machines Corp.,* 1970

... both of which were merged into National Bank of North America in the course of the year —*Annual Report, CIT Financial Corp.,* 1971

All of these seem to be abridgeable.

During the course of this meeting, she told him about her overload —*AAUP Bulletin,* December 1967

Academics are not notably terser than businessmen in their prose.

We conclude that phrases like *in the course of* and *during the course of* can be useful as well as flatulent. You need not avoid them on principle, but you would do well to weigh their use.

craft **1.** The editors of Harper 1985 asked their usage panel about *craft* used as a verb by President Reagan in "the wisdom to craft a system of government...." Sixty-nine percent of the panel turned thumbs down on the use, but panelist James J. Kilpatrick saw nothing wrong with it. Bernstein 1965 seems to have been the first to notice the verb; he identifies the use of the past participle in advertising.

The OED has a single 15th-century example of *craft* used as a transitive verb, so the 20th-century use is a sort of revival. It does seem to have started in advertising, chiefly as a past participle, shortly after World War II:

Which means they're *more* than wonderfully smart and exquisitely crafted —advt., *Life,* 16 Sept. 1946

Crafted with the great beauty and care that make every ... shoe a masterpiece in footwear —advt., *Harper's Bazaar,* October 1947

Crafted in fine mahoganies and choice, hand-rubbed mahogany veneers —advt., *N.Y. Herald Tribune,* 15 July 1951

The intention is to suggest the workmanship and skill of master craftsmen. The revival was not long in reaching more general contexts:

Even the beautifully crafted mosaics on the walls were dingy —Lloyd C. Douglas, *The Big Fisherman,* 1948

... meticulous 1/8-scale models he has crafted — *Newsweek,* 9 Feb 1953

There are ten stories in the collection, most of them superbly crafted —Ann F. Wolfe, *Saturday Rev.,* 3 Sept. 1955

Recent use has followed the same general lines. *Craft* and *crafted* are used literally:

... showing aborigines crafting boomerangs with Stone-Age techniques —*Smithsonian,* August 1970

Indian artisans crafted the idol before Columbus discovered the New World —*National Geographic School Bulletin,* 18 Jan. 1971

... one of the most sophisticated and highly evolved machines that man has yet crafted —David F. Salisbury, *Christian Science Monitor,* 9 Oct. 1979

More frequently, though, they are found in figurative use, very often referring to writing:

The beautifully crafted intricacy of plot forbids brief summary —Edmund Fuller, *Chicago Tribune Mag. of Books,* 26 May 1963

... ballets give the observer the illusion of spontaneous and self-created emotional events rather than crafted choreography —*Current Biography,* October 1971

... it's a carefully crafted poem —Robert Weaver, *Books in Canada,* January 1972

... fifty guidelines for crafting a sales pitch —Walter McQuade, *Fortune,* 21 Apr. 1980

The novel deal was crafted to avoid restrictions in federal law —*Business Week,* 2 Mar. 1981

... offering bribes to venal literary editors, crafting ecstatic reviews of each other's books —Martin Amis, *N.Y. Times Book Rev.,* 5 Apr. 1981

There are those in the current White House who spend all their time crafting the President's image — Alexander M. Haig, Jr., *TV Guide,* 15 Mar. 1985

The President, or his speech writer, is miles ahead of most of the Harper usage panel. *Craft,* both as verb and participial adjective, is well established in current American use. It has also been used in British English.

2. A few commentators remind us that when the noun *craft* means boat, aircraft, or spacecraft, the plural is usually the uninflected plural *craft,* although *crafts* is sometimes also used. This information is in your dictionary.

3. *Craft, kraft.* A few people unfamiliar with the word think that *kraft,* the kind of paper your brown supermarket bag is made of, is spelled *craft.* It is not; use *k* for this paper.

crass *Crass* is an adjective that writers have no difficulty in using but dictionaries seem unable to define. And if dictionaries are muddled, you can imagine the condition of the few usage writers who venture to say that it is often misused. Bernstein 1965 seems to have begun the discussion. He was under the impression that the basic meaning of *crass* is "stupid," a view which is not sustained by the evidence. Little wonder, then, that he found fault with two uses where the word pretty clearly did not mean "stupid." Copperud 1970 interprets Bernstein's examples to be using the word to mean "cheap, mercenary, greedy"; Copperud's interpretation is possible in some contexts, and undoubtedly some people do use the word in this way. His interpretation seems to fit one of Bernstein's examples, which refers to "the bit of insurance a crass employer paid," but other interpretations of that phrase are also possible. It seems likely that Copperud brought this meaning to the example rather than deriving the meaning from the example. Bryson 1984 is somewhat more cautious, saying that *crass* does not mean "merely coarse or tasteless." Of these commentators only Bernstein provides real examples; none has a very certain idea of what *crass* means.

But let's not be too hard on our commentators. Once they were launched upon this issue, they had to depend on dictionaries for guidance, and the dictionaries failed them. The problem for the lexicographer is this: *crass* is a word of wide application and little specific content. It is always unflattering and usually pejorative. It is a handy word for condemnation. But its meaning tends to be colored by the associations of the word it modifies.

Perhaps the easiest place to begin an examination of *crass* is at the beginning. It was dragged into English from Latin; the Latin original meant "thick, gross." Its earliest use in English was to describe physical entities. This use is now virtually archaic. The word was used to distinguish what was thick, coarse, heavy from what was thin, delicate, light. Such use may still turn up on rare occasions:

Crass vultures and hawks fly with delicate finches, hummingbirds and doves —Nancy Lyon, *N.Y. Times,* 4 Mar. 1973

But *crass* is now used almost entirely in figurative applications. In such use it is overwhelmingly negative; it regularly emphasizes the lack of some desirable characteristic. Quite often the missing characteristic is delicacy of feeling, sensitivity, or consideration:

To a crass world it does appear extraordinary that two beings who need each other desperately, and who do not know how soon they may be wrenched apart, should treasure every golden moment —Mary Webb, *The Golden Arrow,* 1916

... whereas we ourselves live in an Age of Anxiety, our progenitors were often distinguished by their crass complacency —Peter Quennell, *N.Y. Times Book Rev.,* 11 July 1954

Nobody on Wall Street would be so crass as to use the word "enormous"; the preferred expression is "a reasonable profit commensurate with the risk." — Lewis H. Lapham, *Harper's,* May 1971

... despite the same crass reliance on methods of intimidation —Anthony Bailey, *N.Y. Times Book Rev.,* 6 May 1973

The crass, expedient handling of the French underground —Hanson W. Baldwin, *Saturday Rev.,* 6 Mar. 1976

It may suggest a lack of subtlety or discrimination, or an inability to discriminate or to appreciate subtlety:

> ... in deep disgust at the farrier's crass incompetence to apprehend the conditions of ghostly phenomena —George Eliot, *Silas Marner,* 1861

> ... misconceived literature in the crassest possible way —Alfred Kazin, *Saturday Rev.,* 3 May 1975

> ... a phrase far too grand to designate the crass traditional views of nature which prevailed —Henry O. Taylor, *The Mediaeval Mind,* 4th ed., 1925

> Among yachtsmen, the distinction between big and little boats is a matter of clubby politesse.... For insurance purposes, the distinction is much crasser but just as blurred —Eugene Sullivan, *Money,* July 1973

Sometimes *crass* suggests that what it is applied to should be beneath one:

> ... a culture daintily remote from the crass concerns of everyday life —Frederick Lewis Allen, *The Big Change,* 1952

> ... returning from the Holy Land to find his friends taken up with the small and crass details of a commerce that he had never learned —Louis Auchincloss, *A Law for the Lion,* 1953

> Her anxieties for her children's future, which were considered crass and reactionary by Tolstoy's followers —Katha Pollitt, *Saturday Rev.,* 13 May 1978

One common use of *crass* is as an intensifier with pejorative overtones. In this use it is difficult to discern much in the way of a precise denotation:

> Why did this crass flattery matter to Stalin ... ? — *Time,* 22 Mar. 1948

> The crass partisanship of Chairman Vinson cannot be condoned —Harold L. Ickes, *New Republic,* 7 Nov. 1949

> ... you should not enshrine a crass oversimplification of it —John Simon, *New York,* 30 Aug. 1971

It can also be used as a rather general term of disapproval. In such uses the writer may have a more precise denotation in mind, but it does not necessarily come through to the reader:

> Virginia is perhaps the best of the south to-day, and Georgia is perhaps the worst. The one is simply senile; the other is crass, gross, vulgar and obnoxious —H. L. Mencken, *Prejudices: Second Series,* 1920

> ... literate, frequently funny, brash, and on occasion crass concept of what television programming will be like —Judith Crist, *Saturday Rev.,* 21 Aug. 1976

> The strength of "The Bush Soldiers" resides not in the writing, which is often crass, but in its story of endurance —Craig McGregor, *N.Y. Times Book Rev.,* 9 Dec. 1984

The interpretation "cheap, mercenary, greedy" is possible when the surrounding context points the way. You can find such a meaning in these next three examples, although the writers probably did not have it in mind:

> ... the new business buildings in the City of London represent British philistinism in its most crass and shortsighted form —Lewis Mumford, *New Yorker,* 26 Sept. 1953

> He resented him as a crass and stupid person who had fallen through luck into flowing prosperity —Bernard Malamud, *The Assistant,* 1957

> He had removed her from that crass monied Middle Atlantic society —John Updike, *Couples,* 1968

The authors probably meant something closer to "insensitive," but you can easily see how Copperud's interpretation could be applied instead.

We think the examples here illustrate most of the chief dimensions of the use of *crass* in modern English. You will perhaps understand the difficulties lexicographers and commentators have had in getting a firm grip on its quicksilver usage.

credence, credibility Phythian 1979 says that *credence* "is sometimes confused with *credibility*." A letter to the editor of *Nature* (6 Dec. 1984) makes the same point, calling the confusion "a new verbal abuse." It isn't very new; Fowler 1926 shows an example of the usage they are talking about in his discussion of the overlap in sense between *credence* and *credit.*

The crucial constructions here are *give credence to* and *lend credence to.* When the subject of the phrase is a person, the meaning of *credence* is the familiar one of "belief":

> ... the directors of information in the Kremlin gave as little credence to their own agents as they did to Churchill —*Times Literary Supp.,* 4 July 1968

> ... though I can't give much credence to that suggestion —Stanley Kubrick, quoted in *Playboy,* September 1968

> It is a pity if the Premier (Mr. Hamer) as he was reported yesterday is now lending credence to the conspiracy theory.... Such sentiments are more in line perhaps with the States-rights troglodytes —*The Age* (Melbourne), 30 Apr. 1975

The familiar sense is being used even when the construction is made passive:

> Should baseball statistics since World War II be given the same credence as those from the years ... ? —William Claire, *Smithsonian,* April 1984

> ... and all that had made charming and delightful earlier American literature can no longer be given simple credence —Irving Howe, *N.Y. Times Book Rev.,* 4 July 1976

It is when the subject of these phrases is inanimate that we get a use closer in meaning to *credibility:*

> Two results stand out ... ; neither of these gives any credence to the assertions of Lord Ridley —in Fowler 1926

> The nautical rope molding in the cornices and door trim gives credence to the theory that ... —*American Guide Series: North Carolina,* 1939

> The evidence lends some credence to the view that American electoral politics is undergoing a long-term transition —Walter Dean Burnham, *Trans-Action,* December 1969

> His theory on the origin of human cancer has lent credence to the idea that cancer can be conquered by

a massive infusion of funds —Lucy Eisenberg, *Harper's,* November 1971

The problem here is not really a question of confused usage. It is a problem created by the limits of lexicography. *Credence* in these typical constructions is a quality. When it inheres in humans, the lexicographer defines it by the name of a similar quality known to inhere in humans: *belief.* But when the quality of *credence* inheres in something inanimate—a theory, an action, evidence—the lexicographer has to resort to a different word—*believability*—to define the quality because *belief* is most readily understood as applying to humans. The difficulty for the lexicographer here is with *belief* and *believability,* not *credence,* for *credence* is applied to both persons and things in exactly the same constructions.

We do not mean to suggest that *credence,* whether applied to persons or things, is limited to the two constructions so far discussed. It is not, although they are the most frequent. Here are two examples differently constructed:

He placed complete credence in everything that anyone said to him —Rebecca West, *The Thinking Reed,* 1936

... the charge has a certain credence —Karl V. Teeter, in *Language as a Human Problem,* ed. Morton Bloomfield & Einar Haugen, 1974

The criticized use seems to be of 20th-century origin, although the OED has one 19th-century citation referring to the credence of a person's senses. In its usual constructions it is certainly of the 20th century. Our evidence suggests that the application to things is increasing, especially in the construction *lend credence to.* There is nothing in the sources in which this construction is found to suggest that it is anything less than standard. It is used in both British and American English.

The OED notes that *credence* and *credit* have historically shared senses—*credence,* for instance, once had a financial sense that *credit* has taken over completely. One sense of *credit* that the OED marks obsolete means "credibility" or "believability."(The obsolete status is doubtful because Fowler's discussion of *credence* and *credit* includes two citations of what is apparently this sense.) Perhaps—by way of speculation—the dominance of the financial senses of *credit* has led to *credence*'s taking over this sense from *credit.* Compare these two examples:

Many things which are false are transmitted from book to book, and gain credit in the world —Samuel Johnson, in James Boswell, *Life of Samuel Johnson,* 1791

The legend gained new credence when dredging operations of recent years brought up several rotting wagon hubs —*American Guide Series: Tennessee,* 1939

And we note, finally, that *credence* is used with *lend* quite a bit more often than *credibility* is. Here, however, are two examples of *lend credibility to.*

... cast him as a Parisian dress designer, a character to which he nevertheless managed to lend some credibility —*Current Biography,* January 1967

... the blacks' report charged that blacks had been invited to the conference only to lend it credibility —Don Mitchell, *Harper's,* August 1971

In the first example, with its human subject, *credence* simply would not have been chosen. In the second we have an inanimate subject—an action. But the political overtones militate in favor of *credibility.* It may be that the recent politicization of *credibility* has also contributed to the increasing use of *credence* in other contexts.

credibility See CREDENCE, CREDIBILITY; CREDULITY, CREDIBILITY.

credible, creditable, credulous Commentators from at least as far back as Hodgson 1889 have been commenting upon or warning against confusion of these words. Hodgson gets off on the wrong foot, holding up the novelist Tobias Smollett for criticism for his use of *creditable* in this passage:

Two creditable witnesses ... affirmed the appearance of the same man —*The Expedition of Humphry Clinker,* 1771

Hodgson thought Smollett should have used *credible,* but Smollett was right: the first sense of *creditable* was "believable," and it was certainly current at the time Smollett was writing. This sense has mostly dropped out of use now; *credible* has taken over the field, and if this sense of *creditable* is not archaic, it is certainly rare. We have but one example of its use since the 19th century, and the meaning of the word here is not absolutely certain:

Few of his fellow Americans listened—just as they had not listened when similar messages had come from more creditable sources —Fred M. Hechinger, *Saturday Rev.,* 21 Sept. 1974

The use here may have been intended to mean "estimable" or "praiseworthy," but "credible" would also fit. The sense meaning "credible" is entered in some law dictionaries, too. Most writers use *credible* for this meaning, however; *creditable* is most frequently used as a rather tepid word of praise:

The restaurant's salads and vegetables are generally creditable, if not altogether imaginative —Jay Jacobs, *Gourmet,* September 1980

Credulous, which when applied to people, contrasts with *skeptical,* does not appear to be misused very often. We have but a single instance in which it is used to mean "credible":

If it strikes you as credulous that the eminently successful producer of popular television games shows ... doubled as a hit man for the CIA ..., then you can credit this book —*Publishers Weekly,* 9 Mar. 1984

This leaves us with the substitution of *credible* for *creditable* or *credulous.* This has certainly happened, but our evidence for it indicates it is not common. We have one oldish example—

He has done credible work —*Anthology of Magazine Verse 1926*

—in which *creditable* seems to have been intended. And we have a more recent one—

So long as our popular science writers depict science as an esoteric and inexact pursuit, the credible public will never dare judge the policy consequences or moral implications —*Trans-Action*, January/February 1967

—in which *credulous* is apparently intended.

Apart from the question of whether the "credible" sense of *creditable* is still a live use, there appears to be very little to worry about here. Most writers know the differences of meaning that separate the three words, or they trust their dictionaries.

See also INCREDULOUS, INCREDIBLE.

credit 1. See CREDENCE, CREDIBILITY.
2. Bernstein 1965 and Evans 1957 believe that the verb *credit* should not be used to attribute something unfavorable or discreditable. Their view overgeneralizes what is usually done into what must be always done. Actual usage is more various and offers the opportunity to use *credit* in several ways. It is a good idea to remember that in many instances there will be two points of view about the desirability of the thing credited—as witness the frequent claiming of credit for bombings, killings, and kidnappings by terrorist groups. The possibility of two points of view may actually be emphasized by yoking *credit* with *blame:*

Historically, the quality of children's lives has been blamed on or credited to their parents —Carll Tucker, *Saturday Rev.*, 15 Oct. 1977

... in his own era, Samuel Adams was often credited with or blamed for creating the Revolution all by himself —Carol Berkin, *N.Y. Times Book Rev.*, 12 Sept. 1976

Moreover, *credit* can be and frequently has been used entirely neutrally:

... a persistent but unsubstantiated legend credits a trader, La Ronde or Laland, with the operation of a sloop as early as 1731 —*American Guide Series: Minnesota*, 1938

The ambiguity ... that few may credit to *Tess* — Robert B. Heilman, *Southern Rev.*, April 1970

Any differences were automatically credited to aging —*Johns Hopkins Mag.*, Spring 1968

This use can easily apply to what is or can be interpreted as less than desirable:

"Our company was credited with hundreds of kills," Reid told a reporter —Seymour M. Hersh, *Harper's*, May 1970

The great heart of the Atlantic has been credited with powers which make of it almost a sentient monster —William Beebe, *The Arcturus Adventure*, 1926

... was credited by the London *Daily Express* with scathing remarks on English prisons —*Current Biography 1950*

... some New York critics refused to credit Rauschenberg and Cunningham with much more than a bad practical joke —*Current Biography*, May 1966

... the Republican National Committee in the canvass of 1880, was widely credited with having carried the State of Indiana by the use of money —*Dictionary of American Biography*, 1929

... overpopulation must be credited as a major factor in the vicious border war between El Salvador and Honduras —F. Herbert Bormann, *Massachusetts Audubon*, June 1971

In summary, then, *credit* is usually used to assign what is laudable, but not always. You may want to be credited with something I find reprehensible. And *credit* is also used for things that fall between the entirely laudable and the entirely blameworthy.
3. Simon 1980 seems to feel that *with* is the only preposition the verb *credit* is to be used with; he specifically objects to *for*. *With* is the most common preposition, but it is by no means the only one. The illustrations above show not only *with* but also (in different constructions) *to* and *as*. *For* is also in reputable use:

These procedures proved successful ... , and coupled with changes in agricultural practices, were credited for the success of control programs in a number of other tropical areas —Lloyd E. Rozeboom, *Johns Hopkins Mag.*, Spring 1971

Credit Mobil, its final sponsor, for not being nervous about sex after 40 —Judith Crist, *New York*, 10 Feb. 1975

creditable See CREDIBLE, CREDITABLE, CREDULOUS.

credulity, credibility *Credulity* and *credibility* come close in meaning only when used with such verbs as *strain, tax,* or *stretch*. Even here use is quite straightforward in most instances. *Credulity* is used of the receiver:

It is hard, without an inordinate strain upon the credulity, to believe any such thing —H. L. Mencken, *Prejudices: Second Series*, 1920

... this bird—whose fabulous numbers, estimated from two to five billion, had taxed the credulity of spectators —Thomas Foster, *N.Y. Times Book Rev.*, 27 Feb. 1955

He stretched credulity beyond the limits of all but the inner circle of the faithful —George E. Reedy, *N.Y. Times Book Rev.*, 18 Oct. 1981

Credibility is used of the sender:

... she has occasionally stretched credibility far in reaching the solution of a problem —A. C. Ward, *British Book News*, May 1954

Howard's sudden transformation ... puts a strain on the novel's credibility —Harry T. Moore, *Saturday Rev.*, 12 Feb. 1972

... because the author places too much weight on these characters' shoulders, their credibility is strained —Susan Isaacs, *N.Y. Times Book Rev.*, 26 Sept. 1982

But *credulity* carries overtones of gullibility, an aspect often stressed in dictionary definitions. As a result, some writers have used *credibility* of the receiver in an apparent attempt to avoid the negative overtones of the alternative:

... the contrast between the respectable exterior and the turbulent interior of this family strains her reader's credibility —*Times Literary Supp.*, 4 May 1951

... wants us to believe that the narrator wrote this manuscript in a few hours on that Sunday afternoon, which somewhat taxes credibility —Ivan Gold, *N.Y. Times Book Rev.*, 12 Aug. 1979

Most writers, however, are content to use *credulity* of the receiver; the neutral use of *credulity* is not rare, even though somewhat underemphasized in the dictionaries.

credulous   See CREDIBLE, CREDITABLE, CREDULOUS.

creep   *Creep* is one of an interesting class of English verbs having a long vowel in the infinitive and a short one in the past and past participle. In Middle English *creep* was a strong verb—one that is inflected by internal vowel change—that came over into the weak class in the 15th century, developing the now prevalent *crept* as past and past participle (the dental stop \t\ is the hallmark of past and past participle of weak verbs and also the clue to the regularity of this form). The dialectal *crep* and *crope* are survivors from Middle English.

Like other members of this class—*leap, kneel, dream*—*creep* has developed an even more regular past and past participle with the same vowel as the infinitive: *creeped*. The OED has examples of *creeped* from a 17th-century playwright, an 18th-century historian, and a 19th-century anthropologist. It is still used in the 20th century. Most of our recent evidence for *creeped* comes from speech; we have seen little of it in print yet, where *crept* is usual. Here are some recent examples:

Bumbry may have creeped up —Tony Kubek, NBC baseball telecast, 5 Oct. 1983

The shade which has now creeped across the court —Al Trautwig, USA network telecast, 18 Feb. 1984

The interest rate has creeped up a little bit —Michael Ashe, Springfield (Mass.) news telecast, 11 July 1984

You might be interested in keeping your eyes and ears open for *creeped*. This verb has not yet settled down from the changes that began five centuries ago.

crescendo   A couple of American newspapermen-commentators, Bernstein 1958, 1965 and Bremner 1980, and a couple of British ones, Howard 1978 and Bryson 1984, object to the use of *crescendo* to mean "a peak of intensity." The proper use, they say, is to mean "a gradual increase in intensity." Since the increase has to reach some sort of climax, the extension of the word to the climax from the increase hardly seems surprising. The extended use may be American in origin:

In July he was ordered abroad, and their tenderness and desire reached a crescendo —F. Scott Fitzgerald, "The Rich Boy," 1926

The infrequent lamps mounted to crescendo beneath the arcade of a filling-station at the corner —William Faulkner, *Sanctuary,* 1931

. . . until it reaches a crescendo of romantic opulence in the emotional climaxes —Mark Schorer, in *Forms of Modern Fiction,* ed. William Van O'Connor, 1948

. . . the bombardment rose to a deafening crescendo —*N.Y. Times,* 12 July 1953

Last week the sound and fury of his performance reached a new crescendo —*Time,* 2 July 1956

The sense is not limited to the United States, however:

. . . the crescendo where for an instant all the trumpets blare —Stuart Cloete, *Against These Three,* 1945

. . . it was built to order for the flies, and these rose to a crescendo of hungry activity —Farley Mowat, *People of the Deer,* 1952

. . . gales were well-nigh continuous. One reached its crescendo at one o'clock in the morning with a gust that had everyone wondering what would go —*The Countryman,* Autumn 1950

And it is still with us:

While no one yet imagines the protests reaching a Vietnam-like crescendo —Roger M. Williams, *Saturday Rev.,* 30 Sept. 1978

. . . its episodes too neatly arranged to build to the quiet crescendo of the boy protagonist's weaning from his family —Tom Dowling, *San Francisco Examiner,* 19 Nov. 1985

The "peak, climax" sense of *crescendo* is still a minority use, and it shows no sign of driving the earlier senses from use. You can avoid it if you wish to, but it is clearly a fully established meaning.

cripple   As a noun for a person with a physical disability *cripple* seems to have been largely replaced by such euphemisms as *handicapped, disadvantaged,* and *disabled*—a replacement noted by Malcolm Muggeridge (in *Esquire,* April 1974) and Robert A. Nisbet (in *Fair of Speech,* 1985). It is found only occasionally now:

They don't want weakness in the Presidency. If they do pick a cripple, it'll be out of superstition—they think he's stronger than other people, inner strength and all that —Wilfrid Sheed, *People Will Always Be Kind,* 1973

But modified by some limiting adjective which takes it out of the realm where it is felt to be objectionable, *cripple* continues to flourish:

. . . whom he portrays here as a moral cripple lusting for power —Robert Manning, *N.Y. Times Book Rev.,* 23 Sept. 1984

. . . many may be regarded as dental cripples —A. Bryan Wade, *Basic Periodontology,* 2d ed., 1965

Not more than twenty years ago homosexuals were told by physicians that they were mental cripples —O. B. Hardison, Jr., *Entering the Maze,* 1981

. . . a sentimental, manipulating emotional cripple, who attempted to destroy her children —Anne Roiphe, *N.Y. Times Book Rev.,* 8 July 1984

. . . failure to have these talents would have set a man apart as a social cripple —Robert Pattison, *On Literacy,* 1982

criterion, criteria, criterions   *Criterion* is a learned word taken from the Greek in the 17th century; in those more learned times, the OED informs us, it was not uncommon for writers to spell the word in Greek letters. Things are different in these less learned times, as we shall see.

Criterion has two plural forms, the classical *criteria* and the analogical English form *criterions*. The English *criterions* seems to have more approvers in usage books than actual users, if our citation file represents the matter fairly. It had a spate of popularity in the late 1940s and early 1950s, but is quite rare since then. It is still in occasional use, however:

> . . . insisted in his lecture that language levels should be distinguished by social criterions —Harold B. Allen, *The Linguistic Institute in the Days of Bloomfield,* 1983

But the usual plural is *criteria,* by an overwhelming margin. *Criteria* is in fact so common that it is met more often than the singular *criterion.* And it is undoubtedly this frequency of *criteria* that has led to its perception by many as a singular. We cannot be sure when use of *criteria* as a singular first began. It probably occurred in speech before writing and in casual writing before print, but we have no direct evidence. Our first singular example appeared—perhaps fittingly, some would say—in a pamphlet on education published by an agency of the U.S. government:

> In some cities the area to be covered, or number of schools rather than number of children, is the criteria considered in visiting teacher assignments — Katherine M. Cook, *The Place of Visiting Teacher Services in the School Program,* 1945

Our next example is from a publisher's advertising. It appears in a rather fancily printed flyer—with ligatured *ct*s and *st*s:

> Dr. Harbage is writing about a criteria for great literature of all times —advt. flyer, Macmillan Co., October 1947

Then we found it in philosophy:

> . . . Hsuntze proposes another criteria by which "we will not suffer from the misfortune of being misunderstood. . . ." —Jack Kaminsky, *Philosophy & Phenomenological Research,* September 1951

It is nearly 20 years from our earliest example of the singular *criteria* to the first mention of the singular in a usage book, Copperud 1964. Bernstein 1965, Follett 1966, and Watt 1967 followed closely. The lapse of time is not surprising, however, as our evidence for the singular is fairly rare until the mid 1960s. Since the remarks of the first commentators, there has been a crescendo of warnings against using *criteria* as a singular. We now have about 20 in our files. The increase in comment is not to be mistaken for a revival of classical letters—one commentator firmly (through three editions) believes *criteria* to be Latin.

The singular *criteria* seems pretty well established in speech. The following examples were all taken from radio or television broadcasts:

> . . . to act independently and with complete liberty with only one criteria, the greatest good for the greatest number —Lyndon B. Johnson (in Harper 1985)

Let me now return to the third criteria —Richard M. Nixon, 20 Apr. 1970

> . . . that really is the criteria because . . . —Bert Lance, former Director of the Office of Management and Budget, 15 or 16 Sept. 1977

> . . . predisposition is not the criteria —William Webster, former Director of the FBI, 4 Mar. 1980

The criteria was . . . —Caspar Weinberger, former U.S. Secretary of Defense, 14 Apr. 1986

If this sort of spoken testimony were all we had, it would be easy to dismiss the singular *criteria* as one of those inadvertences to which the spoken language is always liable. But there is this sort of evidence in cold print:

> I find it difficult, for instance, to believe that Daniel Aaron wrote, "His own esthetic criteria emerges . . . ," and yet that is what I find in his introduction —Granville Hicks, *Saturday Rev.,* 7 May 1966

Professor Kira then examines the modern American bathroom from the standpoint of ergonomics or human engineering, whose criteria is that form follows function —*N.Y. Times,* 9 May 1966

> . . . the criteria for motivating a constituent is not well established —Bruce Fraser, "Some Remarks on the Verb-Particle Construction in English," in *Monograph Series on Languages & Linguistics,* ed. F. P. Dinneen, 1966

The historically dominant criteria for adopting particular technological innovations was . . . —Raymond Bauer, *Center Mag.,* January/February 1972

No criteria, however, exists for gauging the longevity of a "new word" —Donald B. Sands, *College English,* March 1976

There is as yet no widely accepted test criteria for mopeds —*Consumer Reports,* June 1978

Into this he includes a criteria which assures proper and decent working conditions —advt. flyer, Oxford University Press, April 1981

The number of examples above could easily be extended by examples from sources with more modest pretensions to an elevated style and from printed reported speech.

Two commentators stand apart from the rest. Howard 1978 is more interested in how such singulars as *criteria* develop than in complaining about them: ". . . English grammar evolves with majestic disregard for the susceptibilities of classical scholars." Barnard 1979 believes that *criterion* is rare in ordinary usage and that *criteria* is the regular singular as well as plural. Our evidence, however, shows that *criterion* still has plenty of use as a singular. We have, incidentally, heard *criterias* used as the plural of *criteria,* but we have yet to see it in print.

Some foreign plurals are so well established as singulars that no one notices them: *stamina, agenda, candelabra,* for instance. *Criteria* is certainly not in that class. Others have become established as singulars but are still disputed. *Data,* for instance, is a mass noun with either a singular or plural verb. But *data* is rarely, if ever, a count noun, and *criteria* is regularly a count noun, whether singular or plural. *Media* and *strata* are used as singular count nouns in certain specialized fields, but *criteria* seems to have no specialized haven.

Criteria is at this point: it definitely exists as a singular count noun, and it is definitely criticized. Only time will tell whether it will reach the unquestioned acceptability of *agenda.* In the meantime you should be aware that the singular *criteria* is still a minority use and that its legitimacy is disputed.

For other foreign plurals, see LATIN PLURALS.

criticize   Bierce 1909 disparaged the common use of *criticize* to mean "censure." Jensen 1935 notes that the "censure" sense is the one most students associate with the verb and tries to rehabilitate it. He also notes that *censure* itself originally meant "evaluate, judge" and gradually became entirely negative—a point also commented upon by Brander Matthews 1921. Bernstein 1971 also takes note of the common understanding of *criticize* as "censure," and Copperud 1980 believes there is no use arguing (as Jensen tries to do) that it should be used only in its neutral sense. Bernstein and Copperud both point out that context usually makes the meaning clear but that there is no escaping the usual connotations of disfavor. It is probably the disparaging overtones of *criticize* that helped the revival of *critique* as a verb. See CRITIQUE 2.

critique   1. *Noun.* It is hard to understand why there has been any controversy about this noun. Fowler 1926 disliked it (he gives us no reason for his dislike) and thought it might die out. It didn't. Flesch 1964 called it a "fad word" and Evans 1957 thought it "highfalutin." Why this 20th-century antagonism to a word that had been in continuous use for more than two centuries? Copperud 1980 characterizes these criticisms as "dated and pedantic."

We don't know why the word was used in the first place, but the desire may have been to have a word free from the original, usually censorious sense of *criticism*. The word was first spelled *critic* or *critick* and gradually—during a period stretching from Dryden to the early 19th century—was made over on the French pattern. Addison and Pope may have been influential, both using *critique,* but Johnson spelled it *critick* in his dictionary. Todd revised Johnson's spelling to *critique* in his early-19th-century edition.

The word seems never to have dropped out of use.

. . . I was more anxious to hear your critique, however severe, than the praises of the million —Lord Byron, letter, 6 Mar. 1807

I wonder if you could cut out, and send me, *The Times* critique on *Sowing the Wind?* —Lewis Carroll, letter, 5 Oct. 1893

. . . and their critiques were very commonly either mere summaries or scrappy "puffs" —George Saintsbury, *A History of Nineteenth Century Literature,* 1896

. . . did his best to persuade Thoreau to write brief critiques of his eminent Concord friends —Henry Seidel Canby, *Thoreau,* 1939

. . . the unfavorable critiques of the last thirty years —Janet Flanner, *New Yorker,* 29 Dec. 1951

In their critique of criticism these writers give a salutary warning —*Times Literary Supp.,* 6 Feb. 1953

. . . reading a book for my *Inquiry* (somebody's critique of Adam Smith's economics, I do believe) —John Barth, *The Floating Opera,* 1956

. . . the ideal critique is itself a work of art as well as an explication of and meditation on the work of art it examines —John Simon, *Movies Into Film,* 1971

. . . "reviews," which assumes the reader has not seen the work, and "critiques," which assume he or she has seen (or read) it —Robert L. Boyce, *Library Jour.,* 1 June 1976

The word is useful and will undoubtedly continue to be used.

2. *Verb.* More recent criticism (Cook 1985, Harper 1985, Heritage 1982, Janis 1984, *Winners & Sinners,* 20 Jan. 1986) has been directed toward *critique* used as a verb. The assumption of most critics appears to be that *critique* is a neologism, but it has been in use since 1751, albeit not as regularly as the noun.

Our evidence suggests that the current use of the verb is more of a revival than a real continuation, starting apparently in the 1950s. *Critique* is at the first step of a line of historical development that began with *censure,* which originally meant "estimate, judge" but gradually came to be used only for fault-finding. *Criticize* has followed the same path, and even though its neutral sense is still in use, the usual negative overtones it carries for most people have probably prompted the choice of *critique.* The majority of our citations come from the world of education and are quite clearly the result of a desire to avoid the negative implications of *criticize.*

In 1981 or 1982 the cover of a *New York Times Magazine* carried the headline "Betty Friedan Critiques the Women's Movement." You can see the reason for using *critique* here. *Criticize* would be interpreted as "censure," and *review* would have suggested more of a historical overview than a critical examination. Here are a couple of other examples from outside the educational world:

. . . the insights of experts from many other countries invited to critique the plans —Hazel Henderson, *Saturday Rev.,* 18 Dec. 1973

. . . Theodore M. Bernstein, who critiqued *The New York Times* —Copperud 1980

You can use this verb or avoid it. It is sometimes particularly useful, and it does—so far—avoid the overtones of disparagement commonly carried by *criticize.* But there is resistance to its use of which you should be aware.

crochet, crotchet, crotchety   Copperud 1964, 1970, 1980 and Evans 1957 note a spelling problem here. To our surprise we found more examples of *crochet* for *crotchet* and *crochety* for *crotchety* than we expected.

Evans points out that *crotchet* and *crotchet* were originally the same word, but they have become considerably differentiated, with *crochet* limited to needlework and *crotchet* to several other senses, "idiosyncracy, quirk" being the one we find most often misspelled.

Ethel Strainchamps in *College English,* January 1966, found *crochet* for *crotchet* in the *New York Times,* the *Saturday Review,* and the *New Statesman;* our files also have the *New York Times Book Review* and *Harper's.* We have *crochety* for *crotchety* in a publication of The National Council of Teachers of English, in *Boy's Life,* and in *Current Biography.* We have even see *crocheted* (the past of the verb *crochet*) rendered as *croched* in a mail-order catalog. These are all careless errors.

culminate   1. When culminate is used with a preposition, the choice is usually *in:*

. . . must face the prospect of a steady physiological decline that culminates in senility and death — Albert Rosenfeld, *Saturday Rev.,* 2 Oct. 1976

If they were allowed their own way, every comedy would have a tragic ending, and every tragedy would culminate in a farce —Oscar Wilde, *The Picture of Dorian Gray,* 1891

Culminate is also used with *with* occasionally:

> This rite . . . culminates with the sacrifice of a llama —W. Stanley Rycroft, ed., *Indians of the High Andes,* 1946

Other prepositions—*as, at, into,* and *over*—have also appeared, but not so often:

> . . . the forces . . . culminate as a tendency to force the liquid toward the periphery and not to rotate it —Harry G. Armstrong, *Principles and Practice of Aviation Medicine,* 1939

> . . . the mountain-building forces were active at irregular intervals culminating at the close of the Carboniferous —*American Guide Series: New Hampshire,* 1938

> The pseudoplasmodium . . . migrates for a considerable distance before it culminates into a sporocarp —Constantine John Alexopoulos, *Introductory Mycology,* 2nd ed., 1962

> It culminates over the question of which of the two will complete the mission —Alan Brody, *Hartford Studies in Literature,* vol. 1, no. 1, 1969

2. Bernstein 1965 objects to *culminate* used transitively because it "is generally considered exceptional." The OED had labeled the sense *rare,* but the Supplement contains the note, "Delete *rare* and add later examples." The examples here are later than those in the Supplement:

> The disagreement over Indo-China culminates a series of incidents —Denis Healey, *New Republic,* 17 May 1954

> . . . as a marriage ceremony used to culminate a romance —Frederick Andrews, *Wall Street Jour.,* 6 Mar. 1975

> . . . the two Great Pyramids of Giza that culminated this period —Walter Sullivan, *N.Y. Times,* 29 Jan. 1975

3. Bernstein 1965 and Bryson 1984 both insist that *culminate* must mean "to rise to the highest point." Both are newspapermen, and as such are likely to ignore literary usage and perhaps to cast an excessively cold eye on journalistic usage when it takes a direction which they are unfamiliar with. In short, their objection is a quibble, apparently based on etymology. In 20th-century writing *culminate* is used overwhelmingly in a figurative sense, and the "highest point" is very often simply the end point of some sequence:

> . . . a state of nervousness that culminated as Lydia entered —George Bernard Shaw, *Cashel Byron's Profession,* 1886

> . . . the process of disintegration which for our generation culminates in that treaty —T. S. Eliot, "Dante," in *Selected Essays,* 1932

> Self-mortification tended to assume more and more violent forms, till it culminated in the strange aberrations of Egyptian eremitism —W. R. Inge, *The Church in the World,* 1928

> . . . abstract moral speculations, culminating in rigid maxims, are necessarily sterile and vain —Havelock Ellis, *The Dance of Life,* 1923

> . . . his growing pallor, in the end to culminate in a touch of green —Osbert Sitwell, *Noble Essences,* 1950

> . . . such a paroxysm of indignation as could culminate only in giving one's immediate notice —Vita Sackville-West, *The Edwardians,* 1930

> . . . exile and savage persecution culminating in the most fantastic outburst of collective insanity in human history —Noam Chomsky, *Columbia Forum,* Winter 1969

> . . . the somewhat lax proof-reading throughout, which culminates in the extraordinary vision of a "sadistic madam" (read "madman") perched on the throne of the Caesars —*Times Literary Supp.,* 19 Mar. 1971

Such uses as these are entirely proper even when they occur in journalistic rather than literary prose.

cultivated, cultured The commentators who discuss these words seem to be going in several different directions, apart from agreeing that both adjectives mean "having or showing education and refinement." *Cultured* seems to have been condemned by some American commentators around the turn of the century; it is defended by Hall 1917, who nevertheless uses *cultivated* himself. Gowers in Fowler 1965 would prefer *cultured* to *cultivated,* but fears it has been tainted by *kultur,* with its racist-imperialist associations. Copperud 1970, 1980 thinks *cultured* may also suffer from being linked with the institutionalized, ideological culture of the Communist world. And if you need further adverse influence, Mrs. Emily Post in 1927 opined that *culture* was a word "rarely used by those who truly possess it." While Copperud says that *cultured* has acquired an unfavorable connotation, Shaw 1975, 1987 thinks *cultured* is "the more elegant and refined word." And Daniel J. Kevles (*The Physicists,* 1971) thought that *cultivated* was going out of fashion "in part because it had acquired a connotation of preciousness."

Both words can be used with unpleasant connotations:

> The cultivated lady in Bryn Mawr raises her sherry glass and stares speculatively at me over its rim — Laurence Lafore, *Harper's,* October 1971

> Actually, the reason he is often asked to read a book is so that some day he can say that he read it, which will make him cultured —Jerry Richard, *Change,* October 1971

And both can be used without such overtones:

> . . . the indifference to modern drama which so many otherwise cultivated people feel —Thomas R. Edwards, *N.Y. Times Book Rev.,* 8 Sept. 1974

> That Smith himself was very widely read, immensely cultured, . . . these lectures leave no doubt —Patrick Cruttwell, *Washington Post Book World,* 26 Sept. 1971

When Copperud thinks more careful writers use *cultivated* because it is free from ideological and other taint, he may be right. Our evidence shows more use for *cultivated* recently than for *cultured.* The usage of those who write about language has clearly shifted to *cultivated:*

> And how much harder it has become, after forty-odd years, to pass judgment on usage, for if there has been a gain in what might be called educated speech and writing, there has been a loss in what might be called cultivated —Louis Kronenberger, *Atlantic,* September 1970

> . . . the informal conversation of cultivated speakers —William Card et al., *Jour. of English Linguistics,* 1984

> It is in cultivated homes that the babies without euphemism shit in their pants —Janet Whitcut, in Greenbaum 1985

cum *Cum* is a Latin preposition that was taken over into English in the second half of the 19th century. Because it is Latin, it is considered snobbish by Flesch 1964 and as pretentious and intellectually ostentatious by Copperud 1964, 1970, 1980. In his 1980 edition Copperud worries further about its puzzling those who do not know Latin. The examples below indicate that journalists and other writers need have no concern about the word's being widely understood. The matter of intellectual ostentation is for individual judgment, of course.

  Cum is used in two ways in English: as an ordinary preposition and as a sort of combining word attached to the preceding and following nouns or adjectives by hyphens. Even now it is fairly often italicized, a practice indicating that not all writers feel it is fully English. Since our commentators concentrated on the hyphenated form, we will illustrate that first:

> . . . whoops it up with them in the saloon-cum-cathouse —John Simon, *New York,* 31 May 1976

> . . . gives the role a tough-*cum*-innocent quality — Arnold Hano, *TV Guide,* 21 Apr. 1979

> . . . an engineer-cum-producer who gained his reputation partly through the Hendrix albums —Chris Hodenfield, *Rolling Stone,* 2 Mar. 1972

> . . . doing a 1929 gangster-movie-cum-musical spoof —Judith Crist, *Saturday Rev.,* 2 Oct. 1976

> . . . to grill our hamburger-cum-hotdog supper —Al Statman, *N.Y. Times,* 15 Dec. 1974

> . . . executives on a business-cum-pleasure jaunt — John Godwin, *Cosmopolitan,* July 1973

> It is true that the notion of Homer as a kind of Moses-cum-Jeeves is not dead —Colin MacLeod, *Times Literary Supp.,* 18 July 1980

As a plain preposition it looks like this:

> . . . the President threatened the economy with a new oil import fee cum gasoline tax —*Wall Street Jour.,* 15 May 1980

> . . . a fashionable restaurant cum boutique on the East Side —John Corry, *N.Y. Times,* 20 Apr. 1977

> Her full-throttle delivery of nostalgia cum schlock — Patricia Burstein, *People,* 30 June 1975

> . . . parents' traditional educational *cum* recreational functions —Richard Schickel, *Harper's,* April 1971

> . . . also visited the Maharajah, *cum* Governor, in his palace —John Kenneth Galbraith, *Ambassador's Journal,* 1969

Cum looks standard to us in a considerable variety of contexts.

cupful The Oxford American Dictionary 1980 and Harper 1985 believe *cupfuls* is the only correct plural. They are wrong. It is, however, the more common plural. See -FUL.

cured *Cured* is usually used with the preposition *of* in the sense and construction typified in the following quotations:

> A patient can be said to be cured of his infection — William A. Sodeman, ed., *Pathologic Physiology,* 1950

> . . . the students have been cured of their ignorance —William D. Schaefer, *Profession 78,* 1978

Evidence in our files seems to indicate that *cure* followed by *from* was once in use in the U.S. and still may be, as a regionalism:

> . . . thanks were thus rendered to the good carpenter for curing one of its [family] members from cancer —*Southern Folklore Quarterly,* September 1940

Some doubt is cast upon the matter, however, by the fact that this combination is not recorded in the Dictionary of American Regional English.

curriculum *Curriculum* has two plurals: *curricula* and *curriculums.* *Curricula* is quite a bit more frequent, but both are standard. We have no very recent evidence of *curricula* being mistaken for a singular. For other foreign plurals, see LATIN PLURALS.

customer See CLIENT.

cute *Cute* came about as an 18th-century shortening of *acute.* Used in this sense, it has often been printed or written with a preceding apostrophe:

> Mr. Snow struggles gamely to be objective, but can be held to have succeeded only on the assumption that every Chinese who follows Lenin is 'cute, hilarious and indomitable —*Times Literary Supp.,* 23 Oct. 1937

Mrs. Piozzi wrinkled her nose at the expression in her synonym book of 1794, ascribing it to "coarse people" and "low Londoners." Early-20th-century commentators—Vizetelly 1906, for instance—more or less repeated Mrs. Piozzi's disapproval.

  In the meantime, 19th-century America had added a new meaning—"attractive or pretty especially in a dainty or delicate way." It is presumably this meaning that inspired the following remark:

> The reviewer will also ever pray in the interest of the English language . . . that the word "cute" be banished from the pages of serious literature —*The Nation,* 22 Apr. 1909

Of course it was not:

> Cute four-room California bungalow —Sinclair Lewis, *Babbitt,* 1922

Individual, cute, blue paper-baskets stuffed with salted almonds were beside each plate —Carl Van Vechten, *The Tattooed Countess,* 1924

After a while she brought the pants, and they were cute little things —*New Yorker,* 28 Aug. 1926

Emily Post in 1927 laid the use under a mild ban—she termed it "provincial," which was her label for some of the more venial linguistic sins. Some handbooks (Prentice Hall 1978, Macmillan 1982, for instance) are still repeating the opinions of *The Nation*'s reviewer and Emily Post.

In the 20th century, *cute* further developed a disparaging sense:

It is a disconcerting experience to revisit a play that once appeared wonderfully brilliant and original and to discover . . . that considerable sections of it now seem alarmingly cute —Wolcott Gibbs, *New Yorker,* 27 Aug. 1955

. . . a ranch-style home with Early American maple, nautical brasswork and muslin curtains; just too cute

for words —Christopher Isherwood, *The World in the Evening,* 1952

When it is not embarrassingly cute, it is blatantly idiotic —Arthur M. Schlesinger, Jr., *Saturday Rev.,* August 1979

No one has condemned this use. We don't think you have to worry much about any of these uses. The second sense—"attractive, pretty"—is still used mostly in speech, real or fictional, and in informal writing:

. . . there was my Liebfraumilch (well-named) and the cute bottle of beer, too —Randall Jarrell, letter, 6 May 1952

". . . Oh, don't worry; you know Chauncy wouldn't fix you up with a dog or anything—he's probably very acceptably cute." —Shylah Boyd, *American Made,* 1975

cut in half   See HALF 3.

D

dais   This odd-looking word for a raised platform has suffered a lot of phonological knocking about in the course of its descent from Latin *discus* (it is also related to our word *dish*), and the pronunciation has reflected some uncertainty. For a time the recommended pronunciation was \\'dās\\, rhyming with *lace,* but this is largely restricted to British English. The most usual pronunciation now is \\'dā-əs\\, rhyming with *pay us,* and while this version was once denounced as "pedantic," it now is generally recommended. The second most common pronunciation is \\'dī-əs\\, as though the word were spelled (as it is, in fact, sometimes misspelled) *dias.*

See also PODIUM.

danglers   See DANGLING MODIFIERS.

dangling adverb   See SENTENCE ADVERB.

dangling constructions, dangling gerunds, dangling infinitives   See DANGLING MODIFIERS.

dangling modifiers   English has a common construction called the *participial phrase:*

Happening to meet Sir Adam Ferguson, I presented him to Dr. Johnson —James Boswell, *Life of Samuel Johnson,* 1791

In Boswell's sentence, the subject of the main clause—I—is the same as that of the phrase, and it is accordingly omitted from the phrase, leaving the phrase to modify the subject of the main clause. But frequently the subject of the phrase is omitted when it would have been different from that of the main clause; the resultant participial phrase is often called a *dangling participle*—the most commonly mentioned kind of dangling modifier:

Drake continued his course for Porto Rico; and riding within the road, a shot from the Castle entered

the steerage of the ship —Thomas Fuller, *The Holy State and the Profane State,* 1642 (in Hall 1917)

Speaking as an old friend, there has been a disturbing tendency in statements emanating from Peking to question the good faith of President Reagan —Richard M. Nixon (cited by William Safire, *N.Y. Times Mag.,* 19 June 1983)

Now when the same construction can be found in the writings of Thomas Fuller in the 17th century and a speech of Richard Nixon in 1983, you might suspect that it is a very common one indeed. It is, and a venerable one: Hall 1917 cites studies that have found it as far back as Chaucer; he himself found it in the writings of 68 authors from Shakespeare to Robert Louis Stevenson. Yet just about every rhetoric, grammar, and handbook written since the latter part of the 19th century warns the student against such constructions. Why the fuss?

Bryant 1962 states the reason succinctly: "in some sentences the reader is misled into attaching the modifier to a subject which it does not meaningfully modify." When such misleading actually occurs, the result can be a howler. Here are a few examples (the sources given are the books wherein they are cited):

Turning the corner, a handsome school building appeared —Bryant 1962

Flying low, a herd of cattle could be seen —Paul Roberts, *Understanding Grammar,* 1954

Walking over the hill on the left, the clubhouse can be clearly seen —Freeman 1983

Quickly summoning an ambulance, the corpse was carried to the mortuary —Barzun 1985

The point that must be made here is that these funny examples have apparently been invented for the purpose of illustration. Actual dangling participles are more often of such nature as to excite little mirth; indeed, they may hardly be noticeable except to the practicing rhetorician or usage expert. We have already seen two genuine examples; here are a few more:

> Returning to a consideration of the extracurricular activities of the undergraduate, the continued significance of the intramural program of athletics should be stressed —James B. Conant, *President's Report, Harvard University,* 1950–1951

> Unless appreciated when young an effort is required to "get into them" —Leacock 1943

> ... wanting to be alone with his family, the presence of a stranger superior to Mr. Yates must have been irksome —Jane Austen, *Mansfield Park,* 1814

> Born and raised in city apartments, it was always a marvel to me —Arthur Miller (in Simon 1980)

When a genuinely funny dangler actually occurs, it is sure to be repeated in a collection of humorous mistakes, as this one was:

> After years of being lost under a pile of dust, Walter P. Stanley, III, left, found all the old records of the Bangor Lions Club —*Bangor Daily News,* 20 Jan. 1978 (reprinted in *SQUAD HELPS DOG BITE VICTIM and Other Flubs,* 1980)

Dangling participles are not the only dangling modifier that students are warned against—clauses, prepositional phrases, infinitives, and appositives can all be misrelated in such a way as to be characterized as dangling:

> It is a fact often observed, that men have written good verses under the inspiration of passion, who cannot write well under any other circumstances — Ralph Waldo Emerson (in Hall 1917)

> The patience of all the founders of the Society was at last exhausted, except me and Roebuck —John Stuart Mill (in Barzun 1985)

> Distinguished public servant, exemplar for the United States Foreign Service, tireless seeker of peace, your work in arduous posts around the globe has repeatedly demonstrated —in Harper 1985

Like the dangling participle, these other dangling constructions are both common and of considerable historical and literary background. Hall 1917 found more than 800 examples in more than 100 authors from Bishop Latimer in the 16th century to his own time. The usual reason given for avoiding such constructions is clarity, but in most cases the meaning can be readily discovered, even if the sentence is not expressed in the most elegant manner. The important thing to avoid is a juxtaposition that produces an unintended humorous effect. Unintentional humor seems most likely to be created when writing of an unusually compact nature is intended—a caption under a picture, a newspaper account, a dictionary definition. Here is a single example from each; the perpetrators have not been named, but we must confess that the dictionary definition formerly appeared in a Merriam-Webster dictionary:

> After being crushed to predetermined particle size Babcock's fluidized bed combustor can be fired with any solid, liquid, or gas fuel —caption

> Jerry Remy then hit an RBI single off Haas' leg, which rolled into right field —newspaper account

> [a plant] native to Europe but introduced elsewhere with silky hairs over the entire plant —dictionary definition

The last two of these illustrate a problem that many writers working under deadline have faced: given two different kinds of modifiers following a noun, which order do you put them in? In some circumstances there may be no entirely satisfactory answer, and under a deadline there may not be much time for rewriting.

Conclusion: dangling modifiers are common, old, and well-established in English literature. When the meaning is not ambiguous, Bryant 1962 allows them to be "informal standard usage." The evidence in Hall 1917 and other sources shows they are not infrequent in literature of a more elevated sort. Who has censured the dangling modifier in these lines from Pope?

> Vice is a creature of such frightful mien
> As, to be hated, needs but to be seen.
> But seen too oft, familiar with her face,
> We first endure, then pity, then embrace.
> —in Barnard 1979

The one pitfall that must be avoided is unconscious humor, which is perhaps most likely when a writer has two different modifiers—say, a prepositional phrase and a clause—that attach to the same noun. The dangling modifier is a venial sin at most, but if you commit an unintentional howler, you are liable to be ridiculed.

See also SENTENCE ADVERB.

dangling participles   See DANGLING MODIFIERS.

dare   1. Although almost everything you need to know about *dare* can be found in a dictionary, several usage books also comment on its peculiarities. These peculiarities arise from the fact that *dare* is both an ordinary verb and an auxiliary verb. As an auxiliary verb *dare* has in its present tense the uninflected third person singular *dare,* which caught the eye of the first commentator to mention it, Robert Baker in 1770. He didn't like it. Neither did Campbell 1776. But they did not realize that they were dealing with what is now called a modal auxiliary, rather than with a misuse of the ordinary verb, since the auxiliary cannot really be told from the ordinary verb except by such grammatical clues as the uninflected third person singular.

The modal auxiliary is regularly followed by an infinitive phrase without *to:*

> ... they being so absolutely his masters that he dare not write a letter to a newspaper ... without their approval —George Bernard Shaw, in *Harper's,* October 1971

> ... the victory policy Nixon dare not too openly avow —I. F. Stone's *Bi-Weekly,* 17 May 1971

> We dare not deal with even the most remote and orderly revolutions as isolated events —Clinton Rossiter, *Center Mag.,* May/June 1971

> ... claims that he daren't specialize —Gareth Lloyd Evans, *The Guardian,* 27 Sept. 1971

As a regular verb, *dare* has *dares* in the present third singular. It can be followed by an infinitive phrase with *to:*

> And yet Erica Mann Jong dares to call her book of poems "Fruits & Vegetables" —Erica Jong, *Barnard Alumnae,* Winter 1971

> . . . so one might dare to enter them —Norman Mailer, *Harper's,* March 1971

> . . . or they would dare to criticize Castro —Paul Goodman, quoted in *Psychology Today,* November 1971

In other examples may be seen a blend of the modal and the ordinary uses; here *dare* is followed by the infinitive without *to,* yet is preceded by other auxiliaries (as *might, would,* and *do*):

> . . . not even there did I dare say the words —George P. Elliott, *Harper's,* September 1970

> . . . the hardiest germ would hardly dare approach her —Edith-Jane Bahr, *Ladies' Home Jour.,* October 1971

> Do we dare assume that . . . —Lloyd E. Rozeboom, *Johns Hopkins Mag.,* Spring 1971

The regular verb can also take a noun object:

> . . . the willingness with which she dares personal exposure —Richard Schickel, *Harper's,* March 1971

> At the least one dares profound humiliation —Norman Mailer, *Harper's,* March 1971

2. The past tense *durst* has been superseded in modern use by *dared.* It is now archaic or dialectal.

daresay, dare say   This compound verb is used in the first person singular of the present tense. It has hardly ever been used otherwise; the OED shows a single example of "he durst say" from Sterne in the 18th century, and Sylvia Townsend Warner ventured a "Philip . . . daresayed" in a story in the *New Yorker* in 1954. You can write it as one word or two. Old handbooks—around the turn of the century—prescribed two words, and Chambers 1985 believes two words to be usual. But our evidence shows the one-word styling slightly more common.

Heritage 1982 says *daresay* is more common in British than American English. It may be, but it is not the least bit unusual in American English.

In its transitive use *daresay* is followed by a clause. Formerly the clause would never have been introduced by *that,* but in recent use *that* is used. Some examples without and with *that:*

> Well, I daresay my boiling point is lower than Baby Doll's —Harry Kurnitz, *Holiday,* February 1957

> I daresay it's silly to look for the winner beyond Canonero II —Audax Minor, *New Yorker,* 5 June 1971

> I dare say the case is no different for the trade literature of morticians —Robert Lekachman, *Change,* September 1972

> I daresay that the chief reason that the invitation to supply this historical sketch came to *me* is . . . —Louise Pound, *PADS,* April 1952

> . . . and I dare say that my children . . . have a livelier time of it —Alec Waugh, *National Rev.,* 23 Feb. 1971

> . . . and I daresay that if it had been stuck into one of Mr. Buckley's novels . . . —Nora Ephron, *N.Y. Times Book Rev.,* 7 Aug. 1983

dassent, dassn't   Safire 1984 quotes a correspondent who uses the spelling *dassent* and another who wonders if it shouldn't have been *dassn't.* This contraction—from *dares not,* apparently—was common in the 19th century and the early 20th (the American Dialect Dictionary shows many spellings) and was used for *dares not, dare not* and *dared not.* The spelling variations are presumably intended to approximate speech. *Dassent* as a spelling was neither the most frequent nor the rarest:

> . . . and he said he would like to go, but he dassent —Marietta Holley, "A Pleasure Exertion," in *Mark Twain's Library of Humor,* 1888

> ". . . I whipped Ed Walker twice, Saturday. I don't like girls. You dassent catch toads unless with a string. . . ." —O. Henry, "The Ransom of Red Chief," 1907

Dassn't (now the commonest form) and its variations are basically dialectal but, as the use by a correspondent of Safire's suggests, are among those countrified terms trotted out for effect—usually emphasis—in otherwise straightforward writing.

> You will not look, because you dassn't,
> At what is hidden in his bag
>   —"Letter to V——," in *Collected Poems of Elinor Wylie,* 1932

> Like those beetles on the waterpond, you can bend the surface tension film but you dassn't break through —Christopher Morley, *The Man Who Made Friends With Himself,* 1949

> . . . chortling openly at the things a bigot thinks but dassn't utter —Jack O'Brien, *Springfield* (Mass.) *Union,* 1 Dec. 1973

dastard   *Dastard* is a fairly rare word. It first meant a dullard, and then a coward. By the time Fowler 1926 was complaining about its being misused, the sense of "coward" was slipping into the past and the word, when used, generally meant some sort of underhanded or treacherous villain:

> . . . a girl who took the wrong turning when some dastard, responsible for her condition, had worked his own sweet will on her —James Joyce, *Ulysses,* 1922

> Sherlock Holmes would have dismissed Mike Hammer as a dastard and a cad —Hal Boyle, *Springfield* (Mass.) *Union,* 29 June 1954

> Bounty hunters are usually dastards in Westerns — *Current Biography,* October 1966

dastardly   In 1926 H. W. Fowler, with his eye fixed firmly on the 19th century, pronounced the opinion that *dastardly* must mean "cowardly" and that to apply it to acts that involved or persons who took any risk was to misuse it. This opinion was repeated by Evans 1957 and carried unchanged by Gowers into Fowler 1965; Heritage 1982 offers a slightly modified version. Now, you can in fact find such use if you look back far enough:

> She now determined that a virtuous woman
> Should rather face and overcome temptation,
> That flight was base and dastardly
>   —Lord Byron, *Don Juan,* Canto i, 1819

Choosing the safe side, however, appeared to me to be playing a rather dastardly part —George Borrow, *The Romany Rye,* 1857

But it is hard to find this sense applied to persons. In the following examples there is an element of cowardice, but it would not appear to be the dominant notion:

Sir, you are no brutal dastardly idiot like your brother I frightened to death: let us understand one another —Robert Browning, *Pippa Passes,* 1841

. . . he would have fought him to the death; but he had no such opportunity; the dastardly brute had trampled on him when he could not turn against him —Anthony Trollope, *The Macdermots of Bally-cloran,* 1847

. . . expected to see the sturdy yeomanry of the village armed with scythes and pitchforks beating the countryside for the dastardly kidnapers —O. Henry, "The Ransom of Red Chief," 1907

Dastardly seems to emphasize something done behind another's back, underhandedly, sneakily, or treacherously—or a person who would do such things—rather than mere cowardice. Even Fowler noted this aspect of meaning—"acts . . . so carried out as not to give the victim a sporting chance"—in deprecating the use.

But Flesch 1964 puts his finger on another characteristic that keeps *dastardly*—a fairly uncommon word in literary use—alive: "*dastardly* is a piece of oldfashioned rhetoric." And indeed it is. It is quite regularly used in the public denunciation of some reprehensible deed:

The horrible tragedy . . . has been summarily avenged, and the last of the perpetrators and participants have made atonement with their lives for the dastardly crime —*Tombstone Republican,* 28 Mar. 1884, in Douglas D. Martin, *Tombstone's Epitaph,* 1951

I ask that the Congress declare that since the unprovoked and dastardly attack by Japan on Sunday, December 7th, a state of war has existed —Franklin D. Roosevelt, war message to Congress, 8 Dec. 1941, in *Nothing to Fear,* ed. B. D. Zevin, 1946

But during late years oil money from outside has gone into the Fourth Texas District in a dastardly effort to defeat a man who had represented not only his district, but his state, with distinction —Harold L. Ickes, *New Republic,* 15 May 1950

It would appear to be the faint odor of the black-caped villains of 19th-century popular melodrama, twirling their mustaches and gloating evilly over their misdeeds, that clings to *dastardly* and keeps it in contemporary use:

. . . when Dallas' dastardly J. R. Ewing reweds Sue Ellen on CBS this week —Sue Reilly, *People,* 6 Dec. 1982

. . . the worst the dastardly villain . . . could think of in the torture line was briskly pummeling his victim with a truncheon —Robert Lekachman, *N.Y. Times Book Rev.,* 19 Feb. 1984

. . . to help uncover the dastardly scheme hatched by Madame Bardoff —Caroline Seebohm, *N.Y. Times Book Rev.,* 5 June 1977

. . . Peter Lorre and Sidney Greenstreet clones out to commit dastardly acts of espionage and other malevolent mischief —Pat Sellers, *US,* 28 Sept. 1982

The rhetorical use has even spawned another use of *dastardly* that simply expresses disapproval:

. . . when the stool-mouse Patrick discovers the dastardly truth and bravely reveals all —*Times Literary Supp.,* 16 Apr. 1970

What is this dastardly threat to pleasure at sundown . . . ? —Donald J. Gonzales, "Crisis at the Cocktail Hour," *Saturday Rev.,* 15 Nov. 1975

But history had a dastardly trick in store for those helpful birds —Neil Dana Glukin, *Early American Life,* June 1977

In effect, the "cowardly" sense of *dastardly* has been fading out of use for a century or more and seems destined to join the original sense of "dull, stupid" in the obscurity of the historical dictionaries. During a period from around 1850 to around 1950, *dastardly* often connoted underhandedness and treachery. Since about 1950 the word has been kept in use by its overtones of rhetorical denunciation and the stage villain of melodrama, and it is now even weakening into use as a generalized term of disapproval. There is no point in looking backwards.

data, datum   1. The word *data* is a queer fish. It is an English word formed from a Latin plural; however, it leads a life of its own quite independent of its Latin ancestor and equally independent of the English word *datum,* of which it is supposed to be the plural. Ordinary plurals—that is, the plurals of count nouns, like *toes, women,* or *criteria*—can be modified by cardinal numbers; that is, we can say *five toes,* or *five women,* or *five criteria.* But *data* is not used with a cardinal number; no one, it seems, can tell you how many *data. Datum,* incidentally, is a count noun; in one of its senses it has a plural *datums,* which is used with a cardinal number:

. . . in place of a single reference system today we have about 80 more or less independently derived reference systems or datums —Homer E. Newell & Leonard Jaffe, *Science,* 7 July 1967

In its current use, *data* occurs in two constructions: as a plural noun (like *earnings*) taking a plural verb and certain plural modifiers (such as *these, many, a few of*) but not cardinal numbers, and serving as a referent for plural pronouns (such as *they, them*); and as an abstract mass noun (like *information*), taking a singular verb and singular modifiers (such as *this, much, little*), and being referred to by a singular pronoun (*it*). Both of these constructions are standard. The plural construction is much the more common, since evidence (which we shall see) suggests that the plural construction is mandated as house style by several publishers. Evans 1957 points out that usage differs in different sciences, although the passage of time has undoubtedly invalidated some of his specific observations.

Data was not a common word until the 20th century. There are only scattered examples from the 17th and 18th centuries; in the mid-19th century it and *datum* began to appear with some frequency in philosophical works. Not until the end of the 19th century did its usual modern sense—facts and figures—become established. The earliest attestation for mass noun use with a singular verb is dated 1902; it is American. The singular construction must have soon become fairly common, for it is recognized and corrected in Utter 1916 and Mac-Cracken & Sandison 1917. Merriam-Webster editors apparently did not begin to gather evidence until the 1920s; what they collected showed both the singular and plural constructions to be in vigorous use. The struggle of the Latinists against the singular mass noun use was equally vigorous; we have numerous citations from handbooks of the 1920s reprehending the use. One indeed has to struggle for correctness:

> Although it sounds awkward to use the plural verb with *data,* yet it is correct to do so —Whipple 1924

The differentiation of *data* and *datum* was noticed at a fairly early date:

> ... in ordinary use, "data" is not the mere plural of "datum." The two words possess quite different connotations. "Datum" appears to be almost exclusively used for a primary level in surveying while "data" connotes information or facts. Hence "data" as the plural of "datum" is a syntactical plural while "data" in the sense of facts is a collective which is preferably treated as a singular —*Science,* 1 July 1927

But insights such as those of the *Science* editor only slowly reached the citadels of usage pronouncement. And by about the middle of the 20th century, when usage writers began to recognize the mass singular use as established and standard (it was recognized without stigma in Webster's Second), more editors appear to have become convinced that only the plural construction was correct. So it happens that at present we have the anomaly of a majority of usage writers recognizing or approving the mass noun singular construction while a majority of the citations collected here are in the plural. That the preference for the plural is editorially inspired is indicated by such examples as these:

> ... much of the data are still tentative —James Q. Wilson, *N.Y. Times,* 6 Oct. 1974 (the singular modifier *much* with plural verb shows that some copy editor routinely corrected the verb without thinking)

> There is no great amount of special data that begin to move upward many months before the economy as a whole —Leonard H. Lempert, *Christian Science Monitor,* 18 Sept. 1980 (the verb after *data* has been made plural even though the actual subject is *amount*)

> ... investing in their own computer systems to interpret the raw digital data that are transmitted by the satellite. By massaging the data themselves, rather than buying it from the government —*Business Week,* 23 Aug. 1982 (the editor failed to notice *it* in the second sentence)

In none of the above examples is it likely that the author used anything but the mass noun singular construction; a later editorial hand is clearly evident. In addition, the singular construction is sometimes decorated with a supercilious [sic]:

> ... "there is [*sic*] no scientific data which conclusively demonstrates [*sic*] —Chief Justice Warren Burger, quoted by John Leonard, *N.Y. Times Book Rev.,* 8 July 1973

To summarize, *data* has never been the plural of a count noun in English. It is used in two constructions—plural, with plural apparatus, and singular, as a mass noun, with singular apparatus. Both constructions are fully standard at any level of formality. The plural construction is more common. If you are an editor for a publisher whose house style insists on the plural construction only, take care to be consistent (such care is advised by Evans 1957, Bernstein 1971, 1977, Macmillan 1982, and Einstein 1985, among others).

2. *Datum.* There is a common misapprehension among usage writers that *datum* is rarely used. While it is not nearly so frequently used as *data,* it is far from being a rare word. It is well attested both as a surveying term (as mentioned above in the 1927 *Science* quotation) and as a term in other disciplines—philosophy, mathematics, and the social sciences, among others—and in criticism. All citations up until about the middle 1960s occur in decidedly learned media. There have been more occurrences of *datum* in popular sources since then. Perhaps the insistence of many editors that *data* is a plural has accelerated the tendency for *datum* to be used as a singular of *data:*

> Very soon I expect to be 52, a datum I do not expect will rouse the statisticians —William F. Buckley, Jr., *Pueblo Star-Jour.,* 5 Oct. 1977

> Gun metal chills fingers far faster than does a wooden pencil—the first datum of the day —Ronald Jager, *Blair & Ketchum's Country Jour.,* November 1980

In fact, it looks like *datum* is beginning to be simply a fancy substitute for *fact:*

> I'd estimate the median age of Manhattan Market's clientele to be well on the sunny side of thirty-five. Armed with this demographic datum, one may suspect ... —Jay Jacobs, *Gourmet,* September 1981

For other foreign plurals, see LATIN PLURALS.

date 1. College handbooks used to carry warnings against the use of *date* in the sense of a social engagement usually with a person of the opposite sex, or in the sense of a person with whom one has such an engagement. Jensen 1935, for instance, warned against it, and Macmillan 1982 suggests that it wouldn't be appropriate for an appointment with the dean. Most recent books seem to have dropped the subject; Bryant 1962 called it standard. Janis 1984 thinks it a bit informal and warns that it is not used of a person with whom one has a business appointment.

> Then I went on to my dinner date with friends — Ruth Mooney, *Harper's,* April 1972

> She cares little for dates or school social affairs — *Current Biography,* October 1966

> Stradlater was in the back, with his date —J. D. Salinger, *Catcher in the Rye,* 1951 (OED Supplement)

The appointment sense goes back to the 1880s and the person sense to the 1920s. This is a dead issue.

2. Leonard's 1932 survey of usage found that the verb *date,* meaning roughly "to show signs of age, become outmoded" was considered in dispute. Crisp's 1971 survey showed that there was still residual resistance. What notion this resistance is based on, we do not know, for the usage is entirely standard. It is fairly common in general and literary contexts, and dates back before the turn of the century.

> The well-tailored suit that does not date —Phyllis Feldkamp, *Christian Science Monitor,* 17 Sept. 1979

Comedy—except for the greatest—dates much more quickly than any other genre —John Simon, *New York,* 30 Aug. 1971

. . . this book has dated since its original publication ten years ago —*Times Literary Supp.,* 18 Dec. 1970

3. When the verb *date* is used to point to a date of origin, it may be used with *from, back to,* or *to.*

. . . a variety of ravishing screens dating from the late sixteenth to the mid-nineteenth centuries —John Gruen, *New York,* 8 Feb. 1971

. . . the Cronkite film, though dating back to 1962, was the most popular —Martin Mayer, *Harper's,* December 1971

Much of what would come about in 1968 . . . would date to this testimony in August of 1967 —David Halberstam, *Harper's,* February 1971

datum   See DATA, DATUM.

daylight savings time   See SAVING, SAVINGS.

days   See ADVERBIAL GENITIVE.

dead   Sometimes considered to be an absolute adjective. See ABSOLUTE ADJECTIVES.

deadwood   *Deadwood* is what handbook writers call words that they feel should be pruned out to produce a desirably brief freshman English paper. While one may sympathize with the task of the freshman English instructor, many of the phrases and words so labeled have a useful function in the real world. The question will come up at various entries in this book. See also REDUNDANCY; WORDINESS.

deal   1. *Deal* belongs to a class of weak or regular verbs including *feel, creep, kneel,* and *mean* in which the past and past participle have a short vowel contrasting with the long vowel of the infinitive. Some of these (see KNEEL; CREEP) have variants. *Deal* seems always to have *dealt:*

He dealt with them out of his constant sorrow —E. L. Doctorow, *Ragtime,* 1975

It seemed everybody I knew either did drugs or dealt drugs —J. Poet, *Rolling Stone,* 17 July 1975

We have a citation postulating *dealed* in uneducated black speech from a novel about drug dealing. We do not know if the form is actually used.

2. Whipple 1924 thought *deal* was a bit vulgar; he advised using *arrangement, transaction,* or *agreement* instead. A half century later Himstreet & Baty 1977 were still warning against *deal,* although they did not use the word *vulgar.* A number of college handbooks, too, from Jensen 1935 to Prentice Hall 1978 and Macmillan 1982, express reservations about various uses of the word. Almost every use objected to is an original Americanism, mostly from the 19th century. Whether relating to business or to politics, these uses are all now standard in general use. Here are some examples:

And the company could lose perhaps as much as $2 million on a deal with Jimmy Ling —*Forbes,* 1 Dec. 1970

. . . travelled to California, where the big drug deal was arranged —*Publishers Weekly,* 2 Feb. 1976

. . . is offering to buy your stock in it at a price that may or may not be a good deal for you —Sylvia Porter, *Ladies' Home Jour.,* October 1971

Prime Minister Margaret Thatcher faces almost certain defeat in her belligerent campaign to win a better deal for Britain from the European Economic Community —R. W. Apple, Jr., *N.Y. Times,* 29 Nov. 1979

Surely the government must be entering into secret deals with Israel or the Arab states —Lewis H. Lapham, *Harper's,* January 1972

3. When the intransitive verb *deal* means "concern oneself" or "take action," its usual preposition is *with:*

To deal with that new movement, quite obviously it will be necessary to develop a really new criticism —Leslie A. Fiedler, *Los Angeles Times Book Rev.,* 23 May 1971

It deals with the illusions of youth —Paul D. Zimmerman, *Newsweek,* 4 Dec. 1972

This was a state of mind, or point of view, which many of the anxious friends from another class of society found very hard to deal with —Katherine Anne Porter, *The Never-Ending Wrong,* 1977

When *deal* is used in relation to selling—literally or figuratively—the usual preposition is *in:*

Specializing in ancient coins is like handling old masters: you have to be educated to deal in them —Bruce McNall, quoted in *Money,* January 1981

. . . never known to have actually dealt in the drug —Dan Rosen, *N.Y. Times Mag.,* 15 June 1975

. . . the liberal arts deal in symbols and universal ideas —Scott Buchanan, "So Reason Can Rule," 1967

dear, dearly   The adverbs *dear* and *dearly* are interchangeable only in contexts dealing with cost:

The present version has cost Britain dear —*The Economist,* 1 Feb. 1985

. . . negligence on the part of the British government (for which it later paid dear) —Samuel Eliot Morison, *Oxford History of the American People,* 1965

Their high wages are dearly bought with monotonous labour —*Times Literary Supp.,* 5 Mar. 1970

. . . has cost the United States dearly in men and money —Richard H. Rovere, *New Yorker,* 5 June 1971

Dearly is used in other contexts:

The social word still matters dearly to her —Gail Cameron, *Ladies' Home Jour.,* August 1971

. . . in that he dearly loved a fight —*Times Literary Supp.,* 19 Feb. 1971

. . . he wished so dearly to live that he let his life be taken from him rather than take it himself —Katherine Anne Porter, *The Never-Ending Wrong,* 1977

debacle   This word was borrowed from French and is normally stressed in accordance with its pronunciation in that language: \di-ˈbäk-əl\ or, less often, \di-ˈbakəl\, along with minor variants of these. Those who say \'deb-i-kəl\ have been the target of frowns, but one could argue that they have a point. The word as normally written has already lost both its original diacritics (the French form is *débâcle*); why should it not, after almost two centuries as part of English, fall in with the stress pattern of such other French-derived words as *miracle, manacle,* and *spectacle?*

debar   When it is used with a preposition, *debar* most often appears with *from:*

> . . . nothing can more surely debar the Germans from establishing and shaping the new Europe —Sir Winston Churchill, *The Unrelenting Struggle,* 1942

> It seems to me axiomatic that a verse translator . . . shall not be debarred from a strictly liberal translation —D. M. Thomas, *N.Y. Times Book Rev.,* 24 Oct. 1982

At one time, *debar* was also used with some frequency with the preposition *of;* however, in contemporary usage this combination occurs infrequently:

> . . . but the absence of some is not to debar the others of amusement —Jane Austen, *Mansfield Park,* 1814

> . . . they would debar the citizen of his right to resort to the courts of justice —Justice Peter V. Daniel, quoted in *Harvard Law Rev.,* June 1953

debut   The verb *debut* is disapproved of by many usage writers (as Bernstein 1977, Bremner 1980, and the usage panels of both editions of Harper and Heritage). Intransitive uses have been around since 1830 but transitive uses, which are even more strongly disliked and are less common, only since the 1950s. This verb comes in handy in newspaper and magazine articles, where it is most often found, since newsy writing often discusses first appearances of people, products, and the like. In general prose of this sort it is standard but it seems to have almost no use in literature and other more elevated varieties of writing. It is worth noting, too, that the transitive uses have a more jargonish flavor than the intransitive.

> A series called *Trio* debuted —Joseph Finnigan, *TV Guide,* 19 Feb. 1966

> The new monthly with a 50-cent cover price will debut this week —Philip H. Dougherty, *N.Y. Times,* 18 Nov. 1975

> The Panama Canal Treaty will debut on the Senate Floor Wednesday —Senator Robert Byrd, U.S. Senate debate, 8 Feb. 1978

> Willie Nelson returns occasionally, after debuting on one of the first shows —Jorjanna Price, *Houston Post,* 30 Aug. 1984

> Key Biscayne is debuting an all-condo shopping center —*Metropolitan Home,* January 1982

> CompuServe jointly debuted electronic shopping service with LM Berry —*Predicasts Technology Update,* 18 Feb. 1985

decide   Intransitive *decide* is used with several prepositions, of which *on, upon, for,* and *against* are the most common.

> . . . had also received an offer to play with a Canadian team for more money, but he decided on the Packers —*Current Biography,* January 1968

> . . . impetuously decided on another of his spectacular displays —Woodrow Wyatt, *The Reporter,* 8 June 1954

> . . . led him to decide upon law as his career —*Current Biography,* December 1967

> . . . the issue had been regarded as the gravest the nation had to decide upon in this century —Walter Laqueur, *Commentary,* January 1972

> They decided against both the tea and the talk — Flannery O'Connor, letter, 5 May 1956

> . . . decided against attending any of the public night schools of Pittsburgh —*Current Biography 1949*

> In any case, events have decided against Mondrian —Harold Rosenberg, *New Yorker,* 20 Nov. 1971

> The trinity thought it over and gloomily decided for bacon and eggs —Honor Tracy, *Irish Digest,* January 1954

> . . . he had decided for the cloth —*Newsweek,* 24 May 1954

Sometimes a periphrastic preposition may replace *for:*

> They decided in favor of a bridge —*The Americana Annual 1953*

Between and *about* are also used:

> . . . helps you decide between . . . vegetable crops or flowers —radio commentator, 16 Apr. 1975

> . . . I have already decided about the value of my work —William Faulkner, 13 Mar. 1958, in *Faulkner in the University,* 1959

decimate   The Roman army took discipline seriously. They had a practice of keeping mutinous units in line by selecting one tenth of the men by lot and executing them. We are not certain how much the practice improved performance, but its memorable ferocity helped carry the word from Latin into English as *decimate.*

From Richard Grant White in 1870 down to the present day, numerous commentators have ridiculed or disapproved the way the word has been used in English. White ridiculed its use by war correspondents of the Civil War; another critic chastised war correspondents of the Crimean War. In 1941 the *Plain Dealer* (Cleveland, Ohio) criticized its use by war correspondents in World War II (and in 1944 took a slap at radio broadcasters too). War correspondents were not alone in taking their lumps; a poor farmer of 1859 was belabored in Hodgson 1889 for using the term to describe the destruction wrought on his turnip field by frost. And more recently, we read a troubled writer to the editor of the *Saturday Review* in 1971:

> I also grieve over what has happened to "decimate," though no less an authority than *The New York Times* has assured me I am wrong in thinking it can only mean "to destroy every tenth man."

All of these critics have learned the etymology of *decimate,* but none of them have bothered to examine its history and use in English. Such an examination would have relieved the grieving letter writer above; *decimate* has seldom meant "to destroy every tenth man" in English, and then only in historical references.

Aside from a few technical uses, *decimate* has had three main applications in English. The first, attested since 1600, refers to the Roman disciplinary procedure. The earliest citations note that the practice was revived by the Earl of Essex in Ireland; all later citations refer to the Romans.

The second application, attested from 1659, refers to a ten percent tax and specifically to a ten percent tax levied by Oliver Cromwell in 1655 on the defeated Royalists. This sense is of some literary interest—Dryden, for instance, refers to someone as being "poor as a decimated Cavalier"—but it has no current use.

The third, first attested in 1663, is the use that is criticized on etymological grounds. Labeled "*rhetorically or loosely*" in the OED, it is the only sense of the word that has continued to thrive in English. It is an emphatic word, and probably owes its continued use in English to the arbitrary ferocity of the Roman practice rather than to its arithmetic. It is most frequently used to denote great loss of life or serious or drastic reduction in number:

> . . . the male population of the United States will be decimated by cancer of the lung in another fifty years if cigarette smoking increases as it has in the past — Dr. Alton Ochsner, quoted in *Current Biography,* October 1966

> . . . hoping that Nazi brutality would serve to decimate the German Social-Democratic leadership — George F. Kennan, *Soviet Foreign Policy, 1917–1941,* 1960

> . . . had survived an American ambush that decimated a group of stragglers he'd been travelling with —E. J. Kahn, Jr., *New Yorker,* 24 Mar. 1962

> The Voice of America has almost been decimated, its feature staffs and desks virtually eliminated — Daniel Bell, *New Republic,* 17 Aug. 1953

> . . . high populations of gypsy moth larvae are usually decimated by the wilt disease virus —*Massachusetts Audubon News,* May–June 1971

> Though the buffalo herds have been decimated, . . . this is still the frontier —John Updike, *New Yorker,* 30 Mar. 1987

Sometimes it denotes a reduction in amount:

> When a brokerage firm is sued and fined for decimating a widow's net worth through excessive buying and selling—that makes the headlines —Paul A. Samuelson, *Newsweek,* 23 Sept. 1968

Often the word denotes great damage or destruction:

> . . . a severe frost set in . . . and my field of turnips was absolutely decimated; *scarce a root was left untouched —Scotsman,* 1859 (in Hodgson 1889)

> . . . how parking lots decimated the downtowns they were intended to serve —Ada Louise Huxtable, *N.Y. Times,* 30 Aug. 1979

> . . . mercantile districts of cities are likely to be decimated by direct hits of explosive bombs or incendiary bombs —Horatio Bond, ed., *Fire Defense,* 1941

When used of localities, *decimate* may connote a considerable reduction of population:

> . . . the cholera epidemic which decimated Ohio in 1833 —*Dictionary of American Biography,* 1929

It is even used occasionally for humorous overstatement:

> The mercury's caprice decimated the scheduled dawn services, but brought out unprecedented throngs for the traditional fashion parade —*N.Y. Times,* 10 Apr. 1939

> One of them is murdered backstage. Then another. Somebody is out to decimate the country-and-western population —Newgate Callendar, *N.Y. Times Book Rev.,* 11 Oct. 1987

Sir James Murray inserted a definition in the OED, "To kill, destroy, or remove one in every ten of" before the extended sense just discussed. He presumably did this to provide a semantic bridge from the earlier senses (and especially the Roman sense) to the extended sense, but he produced no citations to indicate its actual use. Apparently *decimate* has never been so used in English. Although a few commentators still cling to the Latin—"To reduce by one tenth, not to destroy entirely" (Macmillan 1982)—most recent usage books recognize that the Latin etymology does not rule the English word. Many of them warn against "illogical" uses, such as putting *decimate* with percentage. Our evidence shows this to be an infrequent problem.

deduce, deduct *Deduce* and *deduct* formerly had a greater number of meanings than they do now. Some of the meanings, including the most common of today's senses, were shared by both words. *Deduce* once meant "subtract, deduct," and *deduct* meant "infer, deduce," but according to the OED both of these senses are now obsolete. It seems odd, then, that several modern usage books advise you not to get the two words confused.

What we have found is that, despite the OED, *deduct* is still occasionally used to mean "infer, deduce." To our way of thinking, such use shows that this sense is not obsolete after all, though it may, of course, be less common than formerly:

> ". . . leave the deducting to the cops. . . ." —Gypsy Rose Lee, *The G-String Murders,* 1941

> . . . its earlier use is deducted from the writings of later commentators —Richard Southern, *The Seven Ages of the Theatre,* 1964

> . . . some anthropologists deduct that the ability to make tools . . . did not depend upon an enlargement of the brain —*Science News Letter,* 17 Apr. 1965

Why has the "infer" sense remained with *deduct* when it is now much more commonly associated with *deduce?* Probably because of the familiar noun *deduction,* which can refer to the action or result of either verb but is closer in spelling to *deduct.* When someone, by inferring something, is making a deduction, it doesn't sound illogical to say that he is deducting, since such a verb does exist. Without the benefit of similar reinforcement, the "subtract" sense of *deduce* has not survived.

While the context will usually make your intention clear if you use *deduct* to refer to an operation of the mind, you might reasonably choose to avoid even the appearance of confusion and use *deduce* for that meaning.

deem A few commentators—Flesch 1964, Fowler 1926, 1965, and Evans 1957—express variously some reservations about the old verb *deem*. At issue seems to be a use by politicians—including many U.S. presidents—that these people deem pretentious. The word is in wide literary and journalistic use, and has been for generations:

> My parents deemed it necessary that I should adopt some profession —George Borrow, *Lavengro,* 1851

> ... to inspect all the sites that were deemed eligible —Emily Hahn, *New Yorker,* 24 Apr. 1971

> ... pleasure and my own personal happiness ... are all I deem worth a hoot —George Jean Nathan, *Testament of a Critic,* 1931

> ... a general fling at the sex we may deem pardonable —George Meredith, *Diana of the Crossways,* 1885

> In one of their exchanges Holmes and Pollock name those they deem to be literature's great letter writers —Aristides, *American Scholar,* Autumn 1979

> The Congress, whenever two thirds of both houses shall deem it necessary —*Constitution of the United States,* 1787

> Should the new films be deemed too licentious —Harold Clurman, *Harper's,* May 1971

> ... his hope, which he had deemed dead, blossomed with miraculous suddenness —Arnold Bennett, *The Old Wives' Tale,* 1908

> The average layman—or Congressman—is deemed unable to comprehend the mystic intricacies and intrigues of foreign affairs —John F. Kennedy, *N.Y. Times Mag.,* 8 Aug. 1954

> ... the porcupine is deemed to be a very propitious animal for crops —Sir James G. Frazer, *Aftermath,* 1937

It is hard to see that there can be any problem with this word.

defect Bernstein 1965 claims that *defect* is followed by "*in* (an artifact); *of* (a person)" but the Merriam-Webster files do not support this distinction. Rather there is evidence that the two prepositions are used interchangeably in both American and British English:

> Language is alive only by a metaphor drawn from the life of its users. Hence every defect in the language is a defect in somebody —Jacques Barzun, *Atlantic,* December 1953

> ... defect in a work [of art] is always traceable ultimately to an excess on one side or the other —John Dewey, *Art as Experience,* 1934

> All such fanaticisms have in a greater or less degree the defect which I found in the Moscow Marxists —Bertrand Russell, *London Calling,* 24 Mar. 1955

> ... a permanent aristocracy, possessing the merits and defects of the Spartans —*Selected Papers of Bertrand Russell,* 1927

> ... because I have a speech defect, kind of a lisp, and I'm conscious of defects in others —Willis Crenshaw, quoted in *Sports Illustrated,* 29 July 1968

> In the coaster-brake business A. J.'s worst headache was the basic defect of all friction brakes: they wear out —M. M. Musselman, *Atlantic,* October 1945

> To give one example of Mrs. Dickson's defect of method, she quotes liberally —*Times Literary Supp.,* 1 Mar. 1974

> ... due to defects both of legislation and of administration —Lillian L. Shapiro, *Library Jour.,* 1 Jan. 1976

defective, deficient Some recent British commentators (Phythian 1979, Bryson 1984, Chambers 1985) are at pains to distinguish these words. Their consensus seems to be that *defective* emphasizes a flaw, while *deficient* emphasizes a lack—or, put another way, that *defective* is more qualitative and *deficient* more quantitative. Fair enough, if you remember that these are tendencies and not absolute distinctions. Contexts will occur in which either one might be used. Here are a few typical examples:

> ... problems of children with defective eyesight —*Current Biography,* March 1966

> ... knew that the door was defective and would likely blow out —Robert Sherrill, *N.Y. Times Book Rev.,* 10 Oct. 1976

> ... it must have seemed a defective and in some respects tendentious piece of work —*Times Literary Supp.,* 19 Feb. 1971

> ... her dedication as an artist was as total as her humanity was defective —Peter Davison, *Atlantic,* February 1972

> Its answers were inadequate, ... its vision deficient —Andrew M. Greeley, *Change,* April 1972

> ... because of deficient rains in Ethiopia —Robert Claiborne, *Saturday Rev.,* 13 Nov. 1976

> ... which makes sprightly reading but is seriously deficient in American historical perspective —Walter Arnold, *N.Y. Times Book Rev.,* 11 Mar. 1973

> ... are deficient in hiring and promoting women —Susanna McBee, *McCall's,* September 1971

Both can be used as nouns:

> ... as something resembling a mental defective —*N.Y. Times,* 1969

> ... doesn't treat the reader like a mental deficient —Ted Morgan, *Saturday Rev.,* 29 Sept. 1979

See also DEFICIENT.

defend *Defend* may be followed by *against* or *from;* the distinction made in Raub 1897—"Defend others *from,* ourselves *against*"—is not necessarily observed in contemporary use:

> ... a part of Schleswig Holstein where strong dikes defend the land against the furor of winter storms —Samuel Van Valkenburg & Ellsworth Huntington, *Europe,* 1935

> The antitrust laws must constantly defend the ideal of industrial democracy against all sorts of pressures —Thurman W. Arnold, *The Bottlenecks of Business,* 1940

... watching him defend his high and rigid standards against the endless assault our times mount against them —Richard Schickel, *Harper's,* March 1971

Powell could not defend himself from some sympathy for that thick, bald man —Joseph Conrad, *Chance,* 1913

... a floor of double boards to defend the old woman's bones from the dampness —Ellen Glasgow, *Vein of Iron,* 1935

The playwright defended *Come Back, Little Sheba* from the criticism that it was depressing —*Current Biography,* June 1953

defenestrate Defenestration has been a mode of political expression for centuries, and a member of the Harper 1975, 1985 usage panel wondered if there shouldn't be a verb *defenestrate* to go along with it. Almost two thirds of the panel thought there ought to be. Well, there is. It is a recent verb for which our earliest citation is figurative. In subsequent use it has been both literal and figurative.

Now he had to have somebody to contrast him with unfavorably—an Articulate Englishman. Such a person is a contradiction in popular-fiction terms, like a scrutable Oriental. To produce one, Green had to defenestrate all the traits by which a whodunit reader identifies an Englishman —A. J. Liebling, *New Yorker,* 7 Apr. 1956

In a California college, I saw books thrown through a window.... Shouting and burning, defenestrating the memory of mankind, they feel at least they are doing *something,* not just sitting on their butts — Anthony Burgess, *American Scholar,* Autumn 1969

If you get your dates wrong and defenestrate yourself before the waiting period has expired, the most your beneficiaries will receive is a refund of the premiums you've paid —John Erno Russell, *Moneysworth,* 21 July 1975

Perhaps the chief distinction of the picture is the number of things getting defenestrated in it: an overnight bag, a book, some manuscript pages, an attaché case —John Simon, *New York,* 8 Dec. 1975

He says that this used to make his colleagues rather cross, but that they have got used to it over the years. I am amazed that they have not defenestrated him —Howard 1980

Our evidence indicates that usage of this back-formation is on the increase, but it is still not an especially common word. It has been in use for more than thirty years, and you can feel safe in using it if you need it.

deficient When *deficient* is used with a preposition, the preposition is almost always *in:*

The report that Diggory had brought of the wedding ... was deficient in one significant particular — Thomas Hardy, *The Return of the Native,* 1878

But this view is held to be deficient in intelligence, liberalism, and democracy —Lionel Trilling, in *Forms of Modern Fiction,* ed. William Van O'Connor, 1948

In our files there is just a single instance of *deficient* used with *of:*

... with scant need for imagination, of which she was very deficient —*The Encyclopedia Americana,* 1943

See also DEFECTIVE, DEFICIENT.

defile When used with a prepositional phrase expressing means or agent, *defile* is followed by *by* or *with; by* occurs a little more frequently than *with:*

... the academic institution ... suddenly defiled by the crude political demands of people unfit to pass through its gates —Jerome Karabel, *Change,* May 1972

Now he saw why he had sanctified his body and refused to defile it with a woman —Sholem Asch, *The Apostle,* 1943

definite 1. Phythian 1979 and Copperud 1980 warn against the misspelling *definate.* It, *definately,* and *defination* are all attested in our files. Watch out for that second *i.*

2. *Definite, definitely.* Copperud 1970, 1980 lists three objections to the use or overuse of these words as intensives. To his list can be added Phythian 1979, Bell & Cohn 1981, Janis 1984, Watt 1967, Prentice Hall 1978, and Perrin & Ebbitt 1972.

Beyond the supposed overuse, the objectors call any use of the words in this way "meaningless," "imprecise," "vague." Since they are so consistently called "overworked" by the commentators, one might suspect that they were the objects of a passing vogue, but in fact that seems not to be the case. The OED Supplement ignores this use but covers the similar use of *definitely* as an emphatic *yes,* which it dates to 1931. The evidence of our citations for the use under consideration here goes back to about the same time—1932 for the adjective and 1938 for the adverb. In 1938 the adverb was already being condemned as a fad use that would debase the word. But a fifty-year-long fad is a paradoxical beast, and the use has continued to the present. (Nor has it driven out older uses of the words.) The following examples evidence its establishment in general prose; it seems to have little use in literature and virtually none in any sort of elevated discourse, however:

He had gone into newspaper work because he had definite writing abilities. But he soon hated his work —William J. Reilly, *Life Planning for College Students,* 1954

... began to look out through the room with the small, sour eyes of a definite maniac —Johanna Kaplan, *Harper's,* March 1971

Now "Ragtime" has brought an undisclosed amount of money and a definite, if indeterminate, quantity of hope to the block —Richard F. Shepard, *N.Y. Times,* 28 July 1980

He is a pupil of the late Edgar Wallace and has definitely made good in literature —*N.Y. Herald Tribune,* 24 July 1938

What was definitely overlooked was the fact that the troposphere is not continuous —Lord Ritchie-Calder, *Center Mag.,* May 1969

We had always hoped there would come a time when there would be dancing in the aisles of the U.N. But this was definitely not it —Goodman Ace, *Saturday Rev.,* 20 Nov. 1971

3. *Definite, definitive.* Warnings against the confusion of these words can be found in quite a large number of usage books and handbooks: Harper 1975, 1985, Sellers 1975, Copperud 1970, Bernstein 1965, Evans 1957, Fowler 1926, 1965, Phythian 1979, Chambers 1985, Shaw 1975, 1987, Prentice Hall 1978. Almost all of them tell you what the words mean—information readily available in dictionaries. Harper and Fowler assert that the error consists in using *definitive* in place of *definite.* We have collected no evidence of such substitution during the last quarter century, and the usage books give no quoted examples.

The operative word here is "clear-cut," however, as it is not always easy to tell in a given case whether *definitive* has been used in place of *definite* or has been used innocently in one of its own well-established senses but in a context where error may be perceived by one so inclined:

> They all want definitive answers, not carefully hedged responses stated in terms of probabilities full of "ifs" and "buts" and other uncertainties —Seymour Martin Lipset, *N.Y. Times Mag.,* 30 Aug. 1964

Definite would fit smoothly into this sentence, but that is not to say that the author did not mean *definitive* in its sense "serving to supply a final answer," as Webster's Third puts it. Nearly all our examples of the possible misuse of *definitive* are of this variety, as are several of Fowler's examples. Examples like the following are not numerous and not recent:

> No one denies that the cease-fire brings a definitive strengthening of the Communist position in Asia — Denis Healey, *New Republic,* 9 Aug. 1954

Most of the time, writers seem to have little trouble keeping these words distinct; if, however, you are confronted by a situation in which your correctly used *definitive* might be taken for a confused use in place of *definite,* the better part of valor might be to avoid both words and use one like *conclusive, categorical,* or *final* instead.

Misuses of *definite* for *definitive* are easy to spot but rarely find their way into print. They do not constitute a serious problem. Our most recent example is this:

> The publication as Christmas gifts of a definite edition of the poems of Rudyard Kipling —*Times Literary Supp.,* 7 Dec. 1940

definitive See DEFINITE 3.

degree Various phrases based on *to a degree* receive some mention in a few usage books. Bernstein 1965 begins by observing that *to a degree* once had the meaning "to the last degree" or "to a remarkable extent" but that it now means "in moderate measure" or "in a small way." Fowler 1926 remarked on the first of these uses, calling it illogical but established and tracing it back to 18th-century literary sources. This older use seems fairly unlikely to appear in current American English, but its occurrences in older, more literary, and usually British English are not difficult to recognize, most of the time:

> She was indeed extraordinarily clever . . . ; but in some things she must have been stupid to a degree —Ira Victor Morris, *Covering Two Years,* 1933

The newer sense, the common one now in American English, was condemned by Follett 1966, but is recognized by Bernstein and dictionaries (as Webster's Ninth New Collegiate). It emphasizes limitation. It can usually be told from the older use:

> To a degree this attitude is held by many in the Peace Now movement —David K. Shipler, *N.Y. Times Mag.,* 6 Apr. 1980

Sometimes, though, the context is such that you cannot be sure which meaning was intended. This example is probably of the newer meaning, but the older could be understood in its place:

> . . . the Princeton attitude toward passes thrown by other teams is still innocent to a degree —*New Yorker,* 6 Oct. 1951

In these quantified times, many American writers express the older sense with a different phrase, *to the nth degree:*

> The four players are adjusted to the nth degree, . . . and not a wisp of sound is out of place —Theodore Strongin, *N.Y. Times,* 19 Nov. 1967

> . . . they were honest to the nth degree —John K. Fairbank, *Harvard Today,* Autumn 1968

Bernstein objects to phrases of the form *to an x degree,* in which *x* represents some adjective, as wasteful of space. In his very simple examples, he is of course right, but such clear-cut stuff is not typical of real use. In actual use these phrases serve as periphrastic adverbs and seem to be employed chiefly where a seemingly equivalent single word might be ambiguous or misleading. Here are a few typical examples:

> . . . they will be dealing to a large degree with government bodies —*Forbes,* 1 May 1967

> To a startling degree, the reverse seems to be true — Michael Lerner, *Change,* September 1971

> . . . authoritarian systems have the advantage of being able to force saving, to a considerable degree, while democratic systems must rely on voluntary self-denial —John Fischer, *Harper's,* March 1971

> Speakers pointed out that universities are now dependent to an extraordinary degree . . . upon Defense Department funds for "basic" research — Doris Grumbach, *Commonweal,* 30 Jan. 1970

> The staff, however, soon became bogged down in bureaucratic red tape and, to a certain degree, in its own idealism —Peter Linkow, *Change,* January–February 1971

degreed This adjective is termed "a linguistic horror" by Harper 1975, 1985 and is laid to the jargon of the employment placement industry. James J. Kilpatrick, however, thinks "If a dog can be pedigreed, I see no reason why a professor couldn't be degreed" (*Mayville* [Ky.] *Ledger-Independent,* 25 Aug. 1984). The formation of *degreed* from a noun by addition of *-ed* is no different from that of *pedigreed* or *footed* or the famous "fruited plains" of "America the Beautiful." The OED shows that *degreed* has been in existence since 1560, so no modern-day personnel supervisor should be blamed for coining the word. Employers do get a lot of mileage out of it, though; more than half of our citations come from help-wanted ads. Here are a few examples of use:

> Degreed Blacks are finding that as bad as the economy is, if they have the right degree they can get a job —*Black Collegian,* March/April 1975

> Its staff includes three degreed librarians, paraprofessionals, and graduate assistants —Lisa Harbatkin, *Bluegrass Unlimited,* October 1981

> ... hospital undergoing major expansion seeks degreed Accountant —advt., *N.Y. Times,* 9 May 1982

> Dressage instructor, degreed and trained in Germany is seeking position —advt., *Chronicle of the Horse,* 3 Aug. 1984

> We are seeking degreed engineers in all disciplines — advt., *Engineering Opportunities,* August 1967

déjà vu *Nostalgia* was once a medical term (notes Harper 1985) that has been taken over by popular usage in an entirely different sense. Using a *New York Times* headline that had been castigated in *Winners & Sinners* in 1981, the Harper editors put the question of the similarly popularized use of *déjà vu* to their panel. A bit more than a third approved. Bremner 1980 seems to have noticed the popular use, too, although he does not mention it specifically; he explains its technical meaning instead.

Déjà vu is a psychological term brought into English from French just after the turn of the century. It was used for an illusory feeling of having previously experienced something that was, in fact, happening for the first time. For about a half century, the term led an uneventful existence in psychological journals and texts, with only an occasional glossed appearance in popular works. Then it began to appear on its own, unglossed, in nontechnical writing.

The point of divergence of popular use from technical use lies in the differing viewpoints of the technical writer and reader and the popular writer and reader. The psychologist and his reader are interested in the illusory experience. The popular author and his reader are interested in the fact that it all seems so familiar:

> For a while this bloated, exasperating, corny, interminable tear-jerker is apt to give the reader a maddening sensation of *déjà vu* —John Brooks, *N.Y. Times Book Rev.,* 16 Apr. 1950

The OED Supplement has a similar use from a British book review:

> Although better than her last novel, *Aimez-vous Brahms* ... has a depressing air of *déjà vu* —*The Times* (London), 18 Feb. 1960

Both of these reviewers are pointing out that the authors have done again what has been done before, but they are not suggesting that they have actually read the same material before. Here the material is new, the books are being read for the first time, but the situations, the characters, the sentiments, have been similarly treated before—the feeling that it is all familiar is no illusion.

We get a similar use in this report on the Tet offensive from Saigon:

> ... the early morning sunlight seemed to etch every detail of the scene in my mind—the gray paving stones of the street, the pale terra cotta bricks on the basilica wall. The feeling of *déjà vu* was strong. I had seen all this a hundred times before in every movie about the fighting during World War II in the streets of Paris. But now, the soldiers crouching along the wall were real soldiers —John Donnelly, *Newsweek,* 12 Feb. 1968

Similar uses—stressing the familiar and especially the too familiar—abound:

> ... there is small fear of posthumous libel but the stale, sickly aroma of *déjà vu* pervades these pages —*Times Literary Supp.,* 13 Apr. 1967

> ... and to most liberals who had hoped for a fresh wind the appointment seems like a case of déjà vu —Edward B. Fiske, *N.Y. Times,* 10 Mar. 1968

> There was a general feeling of déjà vu in this beachfront community this week as the countdown for Apollo 12 was being conducted —Sandra Blakeslee, *N.Y. Times,* 14 Nov. 1969

> To the American, on the other hand, who views them with a growing sense of *déjà vu,* they are likely to seem part of a syndrome he knows only too well —Hillel Halkin, *Commentary,* May 1972

> Two can lunch on dreary déjà vu for $47 in our town's temples of serious French cooking —Gael Greene, *New York,* 3 Mar. 1975

> Yet as one reads "Castles Burning," it is almost with a feeling of déjà vu, so closely does it follow the patterns established by the private eye writers of the 1930's —Newgate Callendar, *N.Y. Times Book Rev.,* 3 Feb. 1980

The popular use was established before it was discovered: it had been used in the *New York Times* for thirty years before the language guardians there took notice of it. And so far as we know, no commentator has yet noticed the offspring of the popular use—an adjective:

> Once the human body is accepted, dressed or not, all the permissiveness in movies and plays will be deja vu —Jane Fonda, quoted in *N.Y. Times,* 5 Dec. 1969

> ... much of what was blasted as revolutionary in 1931 has long since become déjà vu —Lamberts 1972

> ... these ... looked to me less *déjà-vu* than usual — John Canaday, *N.Y. Times,* 2 Sept. 1973

> ... it's that *nouvelle-vague* décor, with bed-mattress on floor, records and player at hand, the Scotch and pernod being poured from the end table endlessly, the photos tacked to the walls—all too too *déjà vu* —Judith Crist, *New York,* 25 Mar. 1974

> While short skirts seem déjà vu, short pants have a lively, contemporary air —Bernadine Morris, *N.Y. Times,* 18 Nov. 1980

> There's something familiar about such straightforwardness, something faintly déjà vu —Bob Ottum, *Sports Illustrated,* 9 Nov. 1981

Both of these popular uses are established in standard sources written by professional writers. You can use them if you need them.

Sharper-eyed readers may have noticed a few vagaries of accent, hyphenation, and italicization in the examples. The most common form has both accents and no hyphen: *déjà vu.* The word is still italicized about half the time.

delectable   Fowler 1926, using part of a note in the OED, pronounced *delectable* as being chiefly in ironic use; Gowers in Fowler 1965 left the remarks intact except to edit out a reference to an apparently defunct sweet, Delectable Lozenges. Evans 1957 denies ironic use in the U.S.; in America, he says, it is "a club woman gush word." Flesch 1964 says it is "arch" and should not be used. Reader's Digest 1983 merely notes that *delectable* is frequently synonymous with *delightful* and *delicious* but "has a flavor all its own."

Our evidence shows that *delectable* is pretty frequently used by British writers to describe places and scenery. This use is perhaps a residual effect of Bunyan's "delectable Mountains." You will note that some of our examples might have influenced H. W. Fowler's views, had he come across them, and that all of them appeared before Gowers did his revision.

> ... the Isle of Wight: a very delectable place for a month's residence —George Meredith, *The Ordeal of Richard Feverel,* 1859

> ... have already by private gift or public subscription enclosed delectable woodlands to be an eternal delight and precept to their children —Norman Douglas, *Siren Land,* 1911

> ... a bicycle or walking tour round some specially delectable section of our coastline —S. P. B. Mais, *The English Scene To-day,* 2d ed., 1949

> ... surprising but delectable views of Snowdonia — W. A. Poucher, *Country Life,* 16 Nov. 1951

> ... a leisurely exploration of this delectable region —*British Book News,* February 1953

> ... it was only a little piece of a vast and delectable countryside —John Buchan, *Castle Gay,* 1930

There seems to be nothing noticeably peculiar to either British or American English in these other applications, but neither do they seem especially ironic, gushy, or arch:

> The gossip moreover was always of the most delectable kind —Vita Sackville-West, *The Edwardians,* 1930

> ... the custom of performing this delectable score with string ensembles of various sizes —Martin Bookspan, *Stereo Rev.,* October 1971

> ... some delectable full-page illustrations —E. S. Turner, *Times Literary Supp.,* 4 Dec. 1981

> ... Hirschfeld's delectable inky squiggles in the *Times* —Brendan Gill, *Horizon,* August 1979

> Not since October 13, 1939, had I been cheered by such delectable tidings —Sir Winston Churchill, *The Unrelenting Struggle,* 1942

> ... a delectable as well as an intelligent woman — Arthur M. Schlesinger, Jr., *Saturday Rev.,* 1 Apr. 1978

> ... the quality of Rousseau's own delectable style — Malcolm Muggeridge, *Punch,* 22 July 1953

> ... imparts a flavor some old-timers profess to think delectable —John Fischer, *Harper's,* April 1971

> ... It was spicy sherry; and we drank out of the halves of fresh citron melons. Delectable goblets! — Herman Melville, *Omoo,* 1847

> ... Double Gloucester cheese with chives, and delectable old ports —James Villas, *Town & Country,* April 1980

> ... the made-on-the-premises pâté, which is as delectable as ... the best of French pâté —Elin Schoen, *New York,* 26 April 1971

We do have one genuinely ironic example, though:

> ... Irishmen intent on the destruction of the British Empire by conspiracy, murder, slander, and all the other delectable schemes that come to life so readily in the Gaelic brain —Liam O'Flaherty, *The Informer,* 1925

You needn't give a passing thought to all the criticism. If the word fits, use it.

delusion, illusion   Although warnings not to confuse these two words have been issued since the late 1800s, *delusion* and *illusion* are often used in ways that apparently overlap in meaning. This is probably so because *delusion* refers to a misleading of the mind and *illusion* to a misleading of the mind as well as to a misleading of the senses. When *illusion* refers only to the senses, there is a neat differentiation, and many of the usage books—mostly the older ones—make haste to point it out. But real usage is (predictably) not so neat, as we shall see.

Let's begin by setting aside technical use. Psychologists and other scientists interested in phenomena of the mind and senses we will assume to be consistent and unconfused. We will concern ourselves with nontechnical popular use, where the two words appear to have overlapping areas of operation in referring to a misleading of the mind. H. W. Fowler was the first to recognize and come to grips with this situation. His treatment (in both the 1926 and 1965 editions) is the longest and most detailed that has been done. But in spite of its length, it is more suggestive than explicit. We will work with two points implicit in his discussion. First, *delusion* is the stronger word; it denotes a longer lasting, more tenacious, and sometimes more harmful or dangerous notion. Second, even when the two words are denotatively quite similar, they tend to be used in constructions where they are not actually interchangeable. Sometimes the verb will dictate the selection of one word rather than the other, and sometimes another word or phrase in the context will do so. Some specifics follow the examples.

In the first of the examples below, the writer uses both words; *delusion* appears to be the stronger one. In the rest of the examples, we show both words in various contexts. We think that you will seldom find the words interchangeable in these.

> The illusion of continental self-sufficiency persists in an era when technology has utterly demolished it. That self-sufficiency may have been an approximation of the truth fifty years ago. But today it is a delusion endangering our very existence —Marquis Childs, *Yale Rev.,* Spring 1947

> Hess, always a muddled man ... , flew on his own to Britain under the delusion that he could arrange a peace settlement —William L. Shirer, *The Rise and Fall of the Third Reich,* 1960

... seems to be labouring under the delusion that the majority of fore-edge paintings now to be found ... are contemporary with the books they decorate — *Times Literary Supp.,* 29 June 1967

... I am under no illusion that such a school can always overcome the strong divisive community attitudes —James B. Conant, *Slums and Suburbs,* 1961

... lived most of our lives with the comfortable illusion of our own enlightenment —Dan Wakefield, *Los Angeles Times Book Rev.,* 25 Apr. 1971

... the easygoing world of higher education that I remember—no doubt, with a bit of good-old-days delusion —Tom Wicker, *Change,* September 1971

I indulged, on this last trip, the illusion of visiting again the Paris and London of my youth —Edmund Wilson, *A Piece of My Mind,* 1956

... the National Park Service, which in recent years has suffered the delusion that it is a federation of highway departments —Jon Margolis, *Esquire,* March 1970

I had the beautiful feeling and illusion that I was young and vital and renewed —E. V. Cunningham, *Cosmopolitan,* February 1973

The fighting in Laos is destroying the Buck Rogers delusion behind the Nixon Doctrine —*I. F. Stone's Bi-Weekly,* 8 Mar. 1971

... the shattering of an illusion about a boy with whom she had a long affair —Caroline Seebohm, *N.Y. Times Book Rev.,* 29 July 1979

... our short-run delusions about international economics may prove just as damaging —Frank Gibney, *Harper's,* January 1972

All the governments of France since 1791 lived in the illusion that they had made themselves popular —*Times Literary Supp.,* 19 Feb. 1971

But it is sham or delusion or both to label either "urban growth policy" —Donald Canty, *City,* March–April 1972

Du Bois was, indeed, nursing an illusion when he thought there could have been a joint Freedmen and Poor White revolution —*Times Literary Supp.,* 4 Nov. 1965

It is a snare and a delusion, says Herbert Hill — *Trans-Action,* October 1971

... a megalomaniac with unlimited ambitions, few scruples, and the wildest illusions about the capabilities of air power —John Fischer, *Harper's,* December 1971

... when sober he became depressed, and when well-oiled he had delusions of grandeur —James P. O'Donnell, *Saturday Evening Post,* 15 Jan. 1955

The fact that Miss Hale comes of a family of painters and has published a number of novels must be said to have given her delusions of competence —John Russell, *N.Y. Times Book Rev.,* 31 Aug. 1975

... had no illusions about the kind of people he was dealing with —Andrew M. Greeley, *Change,* April 1972

The reporter who regularly goes to dinner with an Undersecretary of Defense ... comes to think of himself as a minister without portfolio. This is an illusion, but it is a seductive one —Lewis H. Lapham, *Harper's,* January 1972

Delusion and *illusion* can sometimes be interchanged (the quotations above from Wicker, *Times Literary Supp.,* 4 Nov. 1965, and Fischer are perhaps examples), but in most cases they cannot. The reasons for this are that *illusion* is the more common word, that *delusion* tends more often than *illusion* to be used technically, and that each tends typically to be used in its own surroundings. This last characteristic is more marked with *delusion,* which tends to be coupled with *snare* and *sham* and to occur in such fixed phrases as *labor under a delusion* and *delusions of grandeur. Delusion* also tends more often to be used with verbs of negative import, like *suffer,* while *illusion* can be used with such verbs as *indulge.* An illusion can be *comfortable* or *seductive* or *beautiful,* and when it is gone, the illusion has been *shattered;* such words are seldom found with *delusion.* And we believe that when you have a context in which either word fits comfortably, you will probably choose *illusion*—more writers do.

demand   The noun *demand* is idiomatically used with the prepositions *for, on* or *upon,* and *of:*

> ... demands for measures to safeguard the income of the small farmer —*Current Biography,* February 1966

> ... the overwhelming demand for doctors during World War II —*Current Biography,* October 1967

> ... so many demands on our time —Jamienne Studley, *Barnard Alumnae,* Winter 1971

> ... reducing demands on the root system —*Better Homes and Gardens,* April 1973

> ... the demands upon the infant must be limited — Ernest R. Hilgard & Richard C. Atkinson, *Introduction to Psychology,* 4th ed., 1967

> ... because of the increasing demands of her career she discontinued her studies —*Current Biography,* October 1967

> ... this is the demand of major art —Jonathan Aaron, *Harper's,* February 1971

demanding   According to Bernstein 1965, *demanding* is idiomatically followed by *of.* However, we find *demanding* very seldom used with a complement introduced by a preposition, and we have no examples with *of.* While *demanding of* certainly sounds idiomatic, the only preposition we have recorded is *in:*

> ... because the State Board of Education was always a bit more demanding in the requirements that high school teachers had to meet —Phil Tracy, *Commonweal,* 27 Feb. 1970

demean   *Demean* is two verbs. The first, related to *demeanor,* dates from the 14th century. The second, formed from the prefix *de-* and the adjective *mean,* apparently on the model of *debase,* dates from the 17th century. Some 18th-century pundits—Baker 1770 and Campbell 1776—disapproved of the second verb on the grounds that it was a misuse of the first. Baker for instance says it "is used by all the lower People, as well as by great Numbers of their Betters, to signify *Debase* or *Lessen.* It is also found in the same Sense in bad Writers." Among the bad writers Baker numbers Richardson, whose novel *Pamela* he calls "emetic." He supposes that occurrence of the second *demean* in Swift and Bolingbroke was due to "oversight."

The mistaken opinions of 18th-century commentators often have long lives. This one continued through the 19th century: we find it in Gould 1870 and Ayres 1881, and it seems to have been discussed at length by Fitzedward Hall in an 1891 magazine article (Hall produced many examples but didn't like the usage). The topic persisted into the 20th century with Vizetelly 1906, Bierce 1909, MacCracken & Sandison 1917, John O'London's 1925 *Is It Good English?,* and a great many other commentators of the 1920s. Fowler 1926 recognized that there were two verbs, but he disapproved of the second one. Still later we find Partridge 1942 and Follett 1966 registering disapproval.

Defenders of the second *demean* came late into the field. Hall 1917 added citations from Dickens, Thackeray, and Emerson to the authors Fitzedward Hall and others had mentioned; Bernstein 1965, 1971 and Evans 1957 called it standard.

In the meantime it had appeared in dictionaries. Samuel Johnson seems to have been the first lexicographer to recognize it (it is not in Nathan Bailey's earlier dictionary); he included it as a second sense under the first *demean.* If Richardson and Goldsmith had used the meaning, Johnson was probably familiar with it. But he illustrated it with a passage from Shakespeare in which the first *demean* was probably intended but the context permitted either interpretation:

> Now, out of doubt, Antipholus is mad;
> Else he would never so demean himself
> —*The Comedy of Errors,* 1593

Webster picked it up from Johnson, and Worcester from Webster, and the OED notes it without censure, giving a 1601 citation as the earliest.

Partridge found the second *demean* to be growing obsolescent in the 1940's, but quite the opposite is the case today: the second *demean* is almost the only one in current use; the first *demean* has become rare. Here are some examples of the first *demean:*

> . . . it shall be my earnest endeavour to demean myself with grateful respect towards her Ladyship —Jane Austen, *Pride and Prejudice,* 1813

> . . . he might have been observed to demean himself as a person with nothing to do —Henry James, *The Wings of the Dove,* 1902

> Might not your paper demean itself with more attention to the niceties of diction? —letter to the editor, *Washington Post & Times Herald,* 21 Oct. 1954

And a few of the second:

> . . . expected the same services from me as he would from another, while I thought he demeaned me too much in some he required of me, who from a brother expected more indulgence —Benjamin Franklin, *Autobiography,* 1771

> A narrow life in Budmouth might have completely demeaned her —Thomas Hardy, *The Return of the Native,* 1878

> No statistical description can either explain or demean a poem —R. P. Blackmur, in *American Lit-*

erary Criticism 1900–1950, by Charles I. Glicksberg, 1951

> . . . I don't think it demeans her elegant classical style in the least —Arlene Croce, *Harper's,* April 1971

The first *demean* is used reflexively, usually with a phrase specifying how one demeans oneself; the second *demean* may be used reflexively or not. The first *demean* is now a rather bookish word, and since the equally bookish *comport* is available as a replacement (not to mention the plainer *conduct* and *behave*), its continuing in vigorous use appears somewhat unlikely. The second *demean* has the field practically to itself. The most recent usage books in our collection fail even to mention the issue.

demise Three commentators feel *demise* is pretentious for *death* in ordinary contexts (whatever those may be), and Bryson 1984 considers the use "an unnecessary euphemism." Bryson's real objection, however, is to the use of *demise* in a sense close to *decline.* None of this criticism is borne out by recent evidence. In current nonlegal use *demise* means "death" or "a cessation of existence or activity" or "a loss of position or status." Here are some typical examples:

> . . . turns out to be a gratifyingly loutish, brutish fellow. It is quite clear that everyone who knows him would welcome his conveniently accidental demise —Richard Schickel, *Life,* 14 Aug. 1970

> Shortly after the Emperor's demise his son Antoninus not only had his brother, Geta, stabbed to death but ordered the slaughter of some 20,000 of his brother's followers —Robert Payne, *Saturday Rev.,* 18 Mar. 1972

> . . . contained extracts from English magazines and contributions by local writers, whose dilatoriness in delivering copy, according to Tegg, caused its demise —*Australian Dictionary of Biography,* 1969

> . . . the impending demise of freedom in Thailand —H. L. Stevenson, *UPI Reporter,* 6 Jan. 1977

> . . . the New Hampshire primary has played a key role in the demise of two sitting presidents —Charles Kenney, *Boston Globe Mag.,* 3 Feb. 1980

> The memoirs that spring forth after an Administration's demise —Walter Goodman, *N.Y. Times Book Rev.,* 29 May 1983

> While several trade magazines are predicting the demise of pants, many manufacturers . . . are selling more pants —Margaret Pacey, *Barron's,* 24 July 1972

> . . . a couple of extra years of inept handling . . . may greatly hasten the wine's demise —Frank J. Prial, *N.Y. Times,* 5 May 1976

These uses are all standard.

Democrat, Democratic Harper 1975, 1985, Copperud 1970, 1980, and Heritage 1982 all comment on the use of *Democrat* as an adjective by some Republican politicians. Heritage notes the usage does not have much acceptance off the campaign stump, and Copperud notes that it is not recognized in dictionaries. It is, however, unlikely to require notice in dictionaries because it is simply an attributive use of the noun.

The longest and most interesting treatments of the subject are in Copperud 1980 and *Safire's Political Dictionary* (1978). Safire traces the use back to Leonard Hall in 1955 and, apparently, earlier to Thomas E. Dewey.

The usage is primarily a spoken one. In print, *Democratic* with a capital *D* serves to distinguish the political designation from the broader lowercase use.

depart 1. Quite a number of prepositions are used with *depart;* the choice is determined by the meaning and purpose of the prepositional phrase. *On* or *in* for the time, *on* for the nature of the activity, *for* for the destination, and *from* for the point of departure, whether physical or nonphysical, are probably the most common, but others appear from time to time:

> Alvarado departed on the adventure late in 1523 — Chester Lloyd Jones, *Guatemala Past and Present,* 1940

> ... and thus departed for Bucharest that December with his Queen —*Current Biography 1947*

> ... persons who thus departed from the house — Herman Melville, *Pierre,* 1852

> ... a measure of the amount by which a curve departs from a straight line —Bertrand Russell, *Foundations of Geometry,* 1897

> ... monetary policy departed from acute restraint — John W. Schulz, *Forbes,* 1 Dec. 1970

> ... he had a "formula" ... and was not encouraged to depart from it —Seymour Krim, *Evergreen,* August 1967

2. From the evidence produced by a correspondent reprinted in Safire 1984, some wire service stylebooks (and perhaps some newspaper stylebooks too) insist on *from* after *depart,* disapproving the transitive use of the verb. The OED (the volume covering *D* was published in 1897) marked the transitive use *rare* except in *depart this life.* If the transitive was rare at the end of the 19th century, it no longer is. Copperud 1980 calls the use "unexceptionable"; it certainly seems common enough:

> So on August 2, 1943, Wahoo departed Pearl Harbor for the Japan Sea —Edward L. Beach, *Submarine,* 1946

> When Four-two-zero first departed Honolulu — Ernest K. Gann, *The High and the Mighty,* 1953

> ... when they are departing scientific fact for scientific speculation and when they are departing science altogether —Meg Greenfield, *The Reporter,* 26 Sept. 1963

> ... one boiling morning in July, we departed my father's house —Larry L. King, *Harper's,* April 1971

> The Washington Senators baseball team has departed the ball park in the nation's capital — Goodman Ace, *Saturday Rev.,* 6 Nov. 1971

> The presidents of Columbia and Harvard have departed office —John Kenneth Galbraith, *New York,* 15 Nov. 1971

> ... a harsh contrast to ... the Hawaii they had so recently departed —Robert Craft, *Stravinsky,* 1972

> ... having seen the Greeks at last depart their shores after 10 years of siege —John Keegan, *N.Y. Times Book Rev.,* 11 Mar. 1984

Even *depart this life,* mistakenly marked *archaic* in Webster's Second, is still with us:

> ... and when her gentle spirit departs this life the world will be much poorer —John Lane, *In a Tuscan Garden,* 1902

> Thelma J. Ivory departed this life Friday, September 7, 1984 —*Houston Post,* 14 Sept. 1984

depend In most senses *depend* is followed by *on* or *upon:*

> This is the way it goes with the writers: they resent you to the degree that they depend on you —Jay McInerney, *Bright Lights, Big City,* 1984

> If I whimpered about having to get up early in the morning, I could depend on her to say, "The early bird gets the worm." —Russell Baker, *Growing Up,* 1982

> ... it was, rather, that no one could depend upon them —George F. Kennan, *New Yorker,* 1 May 1971

> ... steam from 5 to 10 minutes, depending upon the type and age of the beans —James Beard, *American Cookery,* 1972

> ... "the sick man of Europe" was, or (depending on one's outlook) is, Turkey —Simon 1980

When *depend* means "hang down"—a live but not very common use—it often is followed by *from:*

> ... a watch chain depended from his pocket —Paul Theroux, *N.Y. Times Book Rev.,* 22 July 1979

> ... in the painting of the half melted watches depending limply from a tree —Lewis Mumford, *New Republic,* 5 Apr. 1954

This sense is occasionally figurative:

> ... the painting of the "Redeemer in Glory" ... depends at second hand from Raphael's "Vision of Ezechial" —*Times Literary Supp.,* 30 Mar. 1967

Depend is also used absolutely, though chiefly in conversation:

> In the timehonored phrase, it depends —Irving Kolodin, *Saturday Rev.,* 11 Dec. 1954

> "Oh well ... I'm not sure. It rather depends." — Daphne du Maurier, *Ladies' Home Jour.,* August 1971

Many commentators point out that in speech this construction can be followed by a clause with no *on* or *upon* intervening, as in "It depends how many times you've seen it" or "It all depends whether it rains." We have no evidence of these conversational patterns in ordinary discursive prose.

dependant See DEPENDENT.

dependent 1. *Adjective.* Like the verb *depend,* the adjective *dependent* is frequently used with *on* or *upon:*

> Parents have little escape and are dependent on each other for too many different roles —John Platt in

Information Please Almanac 1971, ed. Dan Golenpaul

. . . forsaken and dependent upon music for any interest whatsoever in their lives —Eve Babitz, *Rolling Stone,* 3 Feb. 1972

The spelling *dependant* is no longer current for the adjective.
2. *Noun.* The noun is usually spelled *dependant* in British English and *dependent* in American English.

depositary, depository The idea that a *depositary* is a person or an institution, while a *depository* is a place, was expressed most often in the early part of this century, though it may occasionally be found today. It is often tempered by a comment to the effect that such a distinction would be nice to make but isn't always made. The last observation is correct: in actual usage, *depositary* usually refers to a person or institution and *depository,* a much commoner word, often refers to a place, but the distinction is by no means strictly followed. Historically, both words have referred to persons and institutions since the 17th century and to places since the 18th century. And in many contexts either interpretation is possible. A bank, for example, is both an institution and a place. Here is a sampling of citations:

. . . in exercising his functions as a depositary —William W. Bishop, Jr., *American Jour. of International Law,* July 1951

. . . the immense experience of which we are the depositaries and the inheritors —Max Ascoli, *The Reporter,* 1 Dec. 1955

. . . the stock had to be at Fluor's depositary that same day —Richard L. Hudson, *Wall Street Jour.,* 26 Nov. 1982

. . . family confidences; of which he is known to be the silent depository —Charles Dickens, *Bleak House,* 1853

. . . to cope with any large-scale attack on the bullion depository —Alan Hynd, *Saturday Evening Post,* 29 May 1954

. . . Congress officially became the depository of Burma's gift —Cecil Hobbs in *Understanding Other Cultures,* ed. William A. Parker, 1954

. . . the ocean deeps . . . cannot be considered a safe depository for radioactive wastes —*Current Biography,* December 1965

deprecate, depreciate Contrary to the views of thirty or forty guardians of the language, *deprecate* and *depreciate* are seldom confused. Most of such confusion as exists has been introduced by those who have sought to illuminate, but have only befogged. Among the befoggers must be counted lexicographers, for our attempts to define and discriminate have not been notably successful.
Depreciate is the easier of the two words to deal with. Its oldest use is what for convenience we shall refer to as the disparaging sense. This sense manifests itself in two ways in modern English. First, it is used in its own right:

True politeness in China demands that you should depreciate everything of your own and exalt every-

thing belonging to your correspondent —Lord Frederic Hamilton, *Vanished Pomps of Yesterday,* 1934

. . . Household is at pains to depreciate and disclaim such pure thrillers as "A Rough Shoot," which he regards as rather dishonorable potboilers —L. E. Sissman, *New Yorker,* 1 May 1971

Knowledge is a great thing. Nobody should depreciate it —Robert M. Hutchins, *Center Mag.,* March 1968

There is a tendency to depreciate the present knowledge of adsorption on solid metals —Morris Cohen, *Science,* 7 June 1968

This use appears to be receding, as *depreciate* comes more and more to be perceived as a technical term relating to monetary matters. But the figurative use of its monetary sense provides *depreciate* with a second way of denoting disparagement:

The body-count by which the Vietnam war is officially and journalistically reported is as good an illustration as any of how we have depreciated the value of human life —Ramsey Clark, *Center Mag.,* July/August 1970

Such overuse depreciates the value of useful words —Howard 1977

We should note in passing that this latter use—with *value* as the direct object—is not replaced by *deprecate* in ordinary serious writing.
If *depreciate* is a relatively simple word to deal with, *deprecate* is not. Its early uses are strongly influenced by the religious associations of *deprecation,* its older relative, which was used as the name of a particular kind of prayer—a prayer for the removal or averting of something evil or disastrous. We can see this notion of praying or hoping to ward off or avert something in Samuel Johnson's use:

. . . to call upon the sun for peace and gaiety, to deprecate the clouds lest sorrow should overwhelm us, is the cowardice of idleness, and idolatry of folly —*The Idler,* 24 June 1758

The notion of seeking or hoping to turn aside or avert something undesirable, with or without the intercession of some higher power, can be seen in these examples:

It was the road . . . by which the ambassadors of so many kingdoms and states approached the seat of empire, to deprecate the wrath . . . or sue for the protection of the Roman people —Tobias Smollett, *Travels Through France and Italy,* 1766

. . . smilingly placed himself opposite him, with the look of one who deprecates an expected reproof —John Cowper Powys, *Ducdame,* 1925

. . . it would bring about the war we all dread and deprecate —Albert Guérard, *Education of a Humanist,* 1949

We might say that the thing deprecated in the foregoing examples is viewed with a certain amount of dread. One may also wish to ward off or avert something of which one does not approve. And in these next examples we can see the notion of disapproval mixed with that of seeking to avert or avoid:

The evil principle deprecated in that religion, is the orderly sequence by which the seed brings forth a crop after its kind —George Eliot, *Silas Marner,* 1861

His eye, which was growing quick to read Naomi's face, saw at once . . . that she deprecated even the slightest reference to her weakness —Sir Arthur Quiller-Couch, *The Delectable Duchy,* 1893

"No, seriously," he said, in his quality of an amateur of dogs; "she is very fine." Even then he could not help adding: "What you can see of her!"
Whereupon Sophia shook her head, deprecating such wit —Arnold Bennett, *The Old Wives' Tale,* 1908

As a Protector of the People Tiberius was held in great awe by the Rhodians. . . . But he insisted that he was merely a private citizen and deprecated any public honours paid to him. He usually dispensed with his official escort of yeomen —Robert Graves, *I, Claudius,* 1934

We may even find both dread and disapproval mixed with the seeking to ward off:

Terrible as are the potentialities of the atomic bomb, we must not waste time in deprecating its use. Instead, we must be more determined than ever to prevent the recurrence of war —Vera Micheles Dean, *The Four Cornerstones of Peace,* 1946

The notion of disapproval often takes over so thoroughly that the notion of seeking to ward off or avert is greatly diminished or even completely lost.

Master Cruncher . . . turning to his mother, strongly deprecated any praying away of his personal board —Charles Dickens, *A Tale of Two Cities,* 1859

A man who advocates aesthetic effort and deprecates social effort —Thomas Hardy, *The Return of the Native,* 1878

Always a moderate, he deprecated extremists of both sections —*Dictionary of American Biography,* 1936

Another group . . . deprecated all dogmas, and pled for a purely ethical religion —Will Durant, *The Age of Faith,* 1950

. . . it is because his championship was successful that we can now afford to deprecate his tactics — Harry Levin, *Yale Rev.,* Summer 1954

The flaunting lascivious attitudes toward sex so deprecated by groups wishing to restrict sexual communication to narrow channels —Lester A. Kirkendall, *ETC,* June 1968

Novels, though not forbidden, were deprecated by their parents —K. M. Elisabeth Murray, *Caught in the Web of Words,* 1977

The use of dashes for commas is deprecated —Howard 1984

All needless repetition is to be deprecated —Barzun 1985

The editors of *Webster's New Dictionary of Synonyms* found a tinge of regret in *deprecate,* which would seem to move it in the direction of *deplore.* The notion of regret is stronger in some of the next group of examples than in others, but the interpretation is possible in all of them (some are also cited in our synonym book):

There is nothing I more deprecate than the use of the Fourteenth Amendment beyond the absolute compulsion of its words to prevent the making of social experiments —Oliver Wendell Holmes d. 1935, *Truax v. Corrigan,* 1921

. . . in which Wallace earnestly deprecates the modern tendency to disparage reason —W. R. Inge, *The Church in the World,* 1928

I very much deprecate the House falling unduly into the debating of details and routine, and losing sight of its larger duty —Sir Winston Churchill, *The Unrelenting Struggle,* 1942

I not only deprecate, I deplore, monkeyshines in Congress —Harold L. Ickes, *New Republic,* 2 Aug. 1943

. . . is hardly his fault, and I will content myself with deprecating the conspicuous waste of a distinguished talent —Wolcott Gibbs, *New Yorker,* 16 Apr. 1955

I deprecate public debate about what the Cabinet should be doing, by members of the Cabinet —Harold Wilson, quoted in *The Listener,* 8 Aug. 1974

We should pause now to observe that we have entered the realm of controversy. The first use of *deprecate* to be criticized is its "disapprove" sense, by Ayres 1881, who believes it to be used as a synonym of *disapprove, censure, condemn.* Even though Ayres is not very sure what *deprecate* does mean—he gives several different definitions—his remarks are repeated in MacCracken & Sandison 1917 and Powell 1925, but then disappear in the growing controversy involving *deprecate.*

We do not really know how this most controversial use—or, really, two uses—of *deprecate* arose. Readers Digest 1983 has the most ingenious suggestion. They found it used by Thackeray in *Vanity Fair* (1848). He places the phrase "deprecate the value of" in the mouth of a fast-talking but ill-educated auctioneer, and in the view of Reader's Digest Thackeray has used a common malapropism of the day to mark his character. But since we have no genuine evidence of *deprecate* with *value* as object and no evidence of *deprecate* used for the monetary sense of *depreciate,* we are rather doubtful. And our earliest evidence for a changed sense is not for the "disparage" sense either; it is for what we could call the "modest" sense:

He said much of their kindness to him, and his wish that he could ever have the chance to do anything for them; while they politely deprecated anything that they had done —Margaret Deland, *Old Chester Tales,* 1898

This use might be defined as "to make little of, play down, belittle modestly." It is clearly related to similar uses of the adjectives *deprecating, deprecatory,* and their apparently later compounds with *self-.* It is a separate use of the verb that has continued:

I remember that he deprecated the very general belief in his success or his efficiency, and I think with sincerity —William Butler Yeats, *The Trembling of the Veil,* 1922

To his many admirers his most engaging characteristic was the way in which he deprecated his achievements —A. J. Cronin, *Keys of the Kingdom,* 1941

He speaks five languages . . . , but deprecates this facility —*Time,* 1 Dec. 1952

. . . the man who knows he too has been successful but can't help deprecating his position as an artist — Taliaferro Boatwright, *N.Y. Herald Tribune Book Rev.,* 31 Oct. 1954

. . . was quite right to be confident, however much he might deprecate his own achievements —Goronwy Rees, *The Listener,* 30 Jan. 1975

He amusingly deprecates his melodic gifts by saying that canon is good for him as he only has to write one melody —*Record Roundup,* November–December 1984

You have noted that in this last use of *deprecate,* the belittling is always directed by the subject toward himself or what he has done. When it is directed toward a second person or toward a thing, *deprecate* comes closer in meaning to *disparage* or *belittle.*

"I am not deprecating your individual talent, Joseph," the Bishop continued, "but, when one thinks of it, a soup like this is not the work of one man. . . ." —Willa Cather, *Death Comes for the Archbishop,* 1927

The general tone of most of the clubs was . . . all but abjectly respectful of the mother-country, and members spoke of "His Majesty's ship" in the harbour, while they deprecated American fruits and productions —Van Wyck Brooks, *The World of Washington Irving,* 1944

It is customary to deprecate the literary achievement of the past decade —James Laughlin, *Spearhead,* 1947

Among Chicagoans of more than grade-school education, there is a disposition to deprecate the Colonel. . . . Some of the scoffers . . . —A. J. Liebling, *New Yorker,* 19 Jan. 1952

. . . perhaps the most reluctantly admired and least easily deprecated of twentieth-century American novelists —*New Yorker,* 17 Dec. 1955

And golfers by nature almost invariably deprecate any golf course they cannot break par on —Charles Price, *Esquire,* August 1965

. . . Western society places a premium on masculinity while often deprecating femininity —Marvin Reznikoff & Tannah Hirsch, *Psychology Today,* May 1970

It is instructive, we think, to try substituting *depreciate* for *deprecate* in these examples. In most of them *depreciate* simply does not sound quite right. We believe that it has become too strongly associated with the world of finance to sound totally suitable in literary or even psychological contexts. *Belittle* or *disparage* or even *denigrate* or *put down* will work better. It would appear that *depreciate* has been vacating this semantic area and that *deprecate* has been moving in.

Now a brief look at the commentators. The issue of *depreciation* was introduced by the brothers Fowler in *The King's English* (1907). They simultaneously introduced the first obfuscation of the issue. Their objection is raised not by a use of *deprecate* but by a use of *self-deprecatory.* It can be a dangerous (because misleading) practice to base a criticism of a root verb on a use of a compound of a related adjective because to do so is to

ignore the often pertinent consideration of separate semantic development. The Fowlers further obscured the issue by defining *deprecate* as to "pray against." The numerous commentators who followed the Fowlers' lead have not provided much additional light. A different approach was taken by Flesch 1964, who suggested avoiding the problem by replacing *deprecate* or *depreciate* with some other word or phrase. His approach suggests the complexity of *deprecate:* he substitutes a different word or phrase for it in each of his several examples.

If you have read all the examples here, you already know a good deal about how *deprecate* is used. To recapitulate, we see these historical trends: *depreciate* has for some time been retreating into specialization as a financial term; it is less and less used as a term of disparagement. *Deprecate* has taken over much of *depreciate's* old territory, although its "modest" use is one *depreciate* was seldom used for. You can use *deprecate* in any of the ways here illustrated—the sources are impeccably standard. Or you can try Flesch's approach and substitute some other word or phrase in order to avoid some of *deprecate's* ambiguities.

See also DEPRECATING, DEPRECATORY, DEPRECIATORY; SELF-DEPRECATING, SELF-DEPRECATORY.

deprecating, deprecatory, depreciatory These three adjectives have been introduced into the discussion of *deprecate* and *depreciate* by some commentators. Such introduction tends to be irrelevant to an understanding of the verbs, for only *deprecating* is derived from the verb and the adjectives have led their own separate existence.

The oldest of the set is *deprecatory.* The OED shows that it was originally used of prayer—this is the connection to *deprecation* that *deprecatory* shares with *deprecate.* Swift in 1704 took the adjective into the secular world, where it has been used in the sense "seeking to avert disapproval, apologetic" ever since.

"Why did you not wait for me, sir, to escort me downstairs?" she said, giving a little toss of her head and a most sarcastic curtsey.
"I couldn't stand up in the passage," he answered with a comical deprecatory look —W. M. Thackeray, *Vanity Fair,* 1848

Why, we ourselves, the official advocates of study, generally feel constrained to express our admiration of it in deprecatory terms —C. H. Grandgent, *Old and New,* 1920

. . . made a politely deprecatory little speech. "We may not be as good as you remember us," she said —*Time,* 18 Sept. 1950

Krapp 1927 understood this sense, but not Bernstein 1958, who, misled by H. W. Fowler's discussion of the verb, confused it with *depreciatory.*

Deprecatory later—probably under the influence of the verb—developed its second sense of "disapproving":

. . . quotation marks are not normally employed with words of common usage, *except* in a deprecatory or ironic sense —Rosemary Neiswender, *Library Jour.,* 15 Mar. 1966

In some examples of this sense, disparagement is clearly mixed with or is perhaps more important than disapproval:

If it were true that [Henry] Adams's deprecatory estimate of what education did for him was applicable to everybody, we should be obliged to be more than a little appalled —Mark Sullivan, *Our Times,* vol. 2, 1927

... some deprecatory title such as "the moron course" —*Educational Research Bulletin,* 19 Jan. 1949

... the modernized disciplines have become academic again in the old, deprecatory sense of the term —Steven Marcus, *Times Literary Supp.,* 27 Aug. 1976

In such use the word is hard to distinguish from *depreciatory.*

Depreciatory is a 19th-century word that regularly means "disparaging":

... a depreciatory term conveying the notion of a shallow critic or trifling virtuoso —*Everyday Phrases Explained,* 1913

... as *little* is not often used with depreciatory adjectives —Jespersen 1917

... nonart (the word is not to be taken as depreciatory) —Wayne Shumaker, *Elements of Critical Theory,* 1952

We have but a single example of *depreciatory* used by mistake for the first sense of *deprecatory.* Perhaps, to borrow a notion from Flesch 1964, the writer was scared into it by some usage commentator:

Santayana laughed his gentle, depreciatory laugh — George Biddle, *The Reporter,* 28 Apr. 1953

Deprecating, from the present participle of the verb, is another 19th-century word. It is used like *deprecatory,* but it is hard to be quite certain whether its sense development is exactly parallel to that of *deprecatory* or not, as the OED Supplement does not discriminate meanings. The citations in our files suggest that the net semantic result has been about the same, in any case:

"He wants to take to ballooning. It seems he's been up once."
Constance made a deprecating noise with her lips —Arnold Bennett, *The Old Wives' Tale,* 1908

Matthew Arnold had been wandering among us with many deprecating gestures of those superangelic hands of his —Van Wyck Brooks, *The Ordeal of Mark Twain,* 1920

Mrs. Shane became falsely deprecating of Lily's charms. "She is a good girl," she said. "But hardly as charming as all that...." —Louis Bromfield, *The Green Bay Tree,* 1924

They will turn off with a deprecating laugh any too portentous remark —Bertrand Russell, *The Scientific Outlook,* 1931

... the sort of physical possession ruled out by his deprecating comments on age and a gal's fancy — Richard Poirier, *A World Elsewhere,* 1966

Allagash tells you, with a deprecating roll of his eyes, that Vicky is studying Philosophy at Princeton —Jay McInerney, *Bright Lights, Big City,* 1984

For me the word has a slightly humorous, slightly deprecating quality. I would use it only in joking — Peter S. Prescott, in Harper 1985

Do not be misled by the occasional failure of a critic to understand the older of the two modern senses of *deprecatory.* Our present evidence shows that the use of *deprecating* is increasing slightly while that of *deprecatory* and *depreciatory* is not.

See also DEPRECATE, DEPRECIATE; SELF-DEPRECATING, SELF-DEPRECATORY.

deprecative, depreciative These are relatively rare alternatives to *deprecatory* and *depreciatory.* See the article at DEPRECATING, DEPRECATORY, DEPRECIATORY.

deprecatory See DEPRECATING, DEPRECATORY, DEPRECIATORY.

depreciate See DEPRECATE, DEPRECIATE.

depreciative See DEPRECATIVE, DEPRECIATIVE.

depreciatory See DEPRECATING, DEPRECATORY, DEPRECIATORY.

deprive *Deprive* is usually used in the construction "deprive (someone or something) of (something)":

It will not do merely to deprive the Court of its power to legislate —Rexford G. Tugwell, *Center Mag.,* January 1968

... their acquiescence is a "singing" lyricism which deprived Yiddish poetry of intellectual bite —Irving Howe, *Commentary,* January 1972

If another world war deprives man of civilization and all that it entails —Mortimer J. Adler, *Playboy,* January 1966

Deprive is also used with *from* but, judging by its representation in the Merriam-Webster files, not very often:

How can we improve a situation if we are deprived by terminology from knowing what the situation really is? —James B. Conant, *Slums and Suburbs,* 1961

They contrived it often with an elaborate will, Willfulness even, recognizing the freedom of death From which no tyrannies deprived them
—Philip Murray, in *New Poems by American Poets,* ed. Rolfe Humphries, 1953

de rigueur Bremner 1980 and Bryson 1984 warn users of this adjective to be careful of its spelling. There is a *u* both before and after the *e.* Bryson has seen *de rigeur* and we have seen *de riguer.* This word requires some attention.

derisive, derisory *Derisive* and *derisory* both came into the language during the 17th century, the former in 1662 and the latter in 1618, as recorded in the OED. Both words then meant about the same thing, "causing or expressing derision." After a long period of time, in the late 19th and early 20th centuries, each word developed a second sense, "worthy of ridicule"; thus, the synonymy of the two words was extended. Despite the opinions of critics Chambers 1985, Bryson 1984, and Phythian 1979, *derisive* and *derisory* are to some extent still used synonymously in contemporary writing:

... there was heard derisive laughter from the boorish revelers —Goodman Ace, *Saturday Rev.,* 25 Dec. 1971

... pointing a derisory finger at me he roared, "Look at him! The Yellow Press lapdog!" —R. F. Delderfield, *For My Own Amusement,* 1968

The put-on artist draws out that derisive moment — Jacob Brackman, *New Yorker,* 24 June 1967

What a moment for "Pheeleep"—the derisory name by which that strange ... baronet was known — *Times Literary Supp.,* 22 Oct. 1971

According to the Merriam-Webster files, though, there does seem to be a distinction growing between the two words. The evidence shows that over the last 40 years or so, writers have been more often choosing *derisive* for its original sense "causing or expressing derision," while opting for *derisory* when they mean "worthy of ridicule":

... he stopped just outside the door, waiting; and of course it came: the burst of derisive laughter —Morley Callaghan, *The Loved and the Lost,* 1951

Instead, Mailer became his own most derisive critic ... always finally being put down hardest by himself —John W. Aldridge, *Saturday Rev.,* 13 Nov. 1971

... even our President recently permitted himself some derisive remarks about intellectuals —Adlai E. Stevenson, *New Republic,* 22 Nov. 1954

The old stallion rolled one white, derisive eye —Nelson Algren, *The Man with the Golden Arm,* 1949

The small-town editor pays derisory fees—$5 or less—for these syndicated columns —E. S. Turner, *Times Literary Supp.,* 17 Aug. 1984

He makes his rounds in a derisory excuse for an automobile, which is always in danger of breaking down —A. J. Liebling, *New Yorker,* 3 Nov. 1956

... it was selling them for derisory prices by our standards —Joseph Alsop, *N.Y. Times Mag.,* 18 Mar. 1973

The wages paid to the seasonal labourers are derisory —V. S. Pritchett, *The Spanish Temper,* 1954

A note of interest suggested by our files is that *derisory* (usually in its second sense) recently seems to have been occurring with much more frequency than has *derisive* (in either of its senses).

derive   *Derive* is usually used with a prepositional-phrase complement, which nearly always begins with *from:*

Mr. Vidal's Lincoln, however, derives from the mainstream of modern scholarship —Joyce Carol Oates, *N.Y. Times Book Rev.,* 3 June 1984

... the social stratum from which he derived —Carl Van Doren, *The American Novel,* 1940

In an analogous way, *derive* is also found, though less frequently, with the adverb *therefrom* and the conjunction *whence,* both of which are equivalent to a phrase introduced by *from:*

Her characters do not move in an ordered, stable world and derive therefrom a personal sense of order —William Van O'Connor, in *Forms of Modern Fiction,* and its ed., 1948

... the sound-signs whence are derived the alphabets of the civilised world —Edward Clodd, *The Story of the Alphabet,* 1900

In our files there are a few instances for the use of *derive* with *in, of, out,* and *through:*

... the two electoral triumphs by Woodrow Wilson derived essentially in the inability of the Republicans to compromise —Cortez A. M. Ewing, in *Aspects of American Government,* ed. Sydney D. Bailey, 1950

... derived of the poorest African stock —Melville J. Herskovits, *Saturday Rev.,* 10 Jan. 1942

Modern international law, deriving out of the summary by Hugo Grotius —Frederic L. Paxson, *Pre-War Years 1913-1917,* 1936

... the cherub of our grave-stone cutters is derived through the Hebrews —Edward Clodd, *The Story of the Alphabet,* 1900

At one time *derive* was also used with *to;* this usage, along with the sense conveyed, is now archaic:

... inconvenience that will be derived to them from stopping all imports —Thomas Jefferson, *Writings,* ca. 1826 (OED)

derogate   In its intransitive senses, *derogate* is used with *from:*

... increase the authority of each Dominion and not derogate from it —Robert Gordon Menzies, *Foreign Affairs,* January 1949

... special agreements which do not derogate from the rights of prisoners —Dean Acheson, *Harper's,* January 1953

... and should I, at leaving it, procure the society of one so lovely ... who should say that I derogated from the rank which I am virtually renouncing? — Sir Walter Scott, *The Fortunes of Nigel,* 1822

derogation   *Derogation* when followed by a complement usually takes *of* or *from,* with *of* occurring more frequently:

... our ... peevish derogation of the immense spectrum of cultures in what is referred to as the third world —Edward Hoagland, *N.Y. Times Book Rev.,* 22 Jan. 1984

While the use of *from* with *derogation* may still be found sporadically in contemporary writing, it is more often found in writing dating from the 1950s and before:

It is no necessary derogation from his book that the humor is about the humor of alumni magazines — Howard Mumford Jones, *Saturday Rev.,* 12 Apr. 1941

descriptive genitive   See GENITIVE 1.

desert, deserts, dessert   This is really just a matter of paying attention to spelling. There are two nouns spelled *desert.* The first of these is the barren *desert,* and by reason of pronunciation if no other, it seems seldom to be mistaken for the others. The second *desert* is related to *deserve* and is pronounced like *dessert.* It is frequently used as a plural, especially in the phrase *just deserts* (which one gets). Here we have the real spelling problem. We find *desert* in place of *dessert* from 1833 to 1984 (and we suspect we have not seen the last of it). And the opposite error—*just desserts,* as if chocolate cake or cherries jubilee were being substituted for what one deserves—has been detected by Bernstein 1962 in the *New York Times,* by Simon 1980 in *Time,* and by one of our editors in a 1986 "Bloom County" comic strip. Care is all that is needed here. Take your time, think, trust your dictionary, and reform your ways (if need be).

And don't you just know that somewhere there is an ice-cream emporium called Just Desserts?

desideratum   The plural of this borrowing from Latin is *desiderata.* Evans 1957 says *desideratums* may also be used, but we have no record of its use in our files.

The use of *desiderata* as a singular is quite rare—we have no unequivocal example since 1927. Its development as a singular has probably been stunted by the flourishing condition of the singular *desideratum.* See the list at LATIN PLURALS for other borrowings whose plurals may or may not present problems.

> . . . in a civilization where intellect is a minor desideratum —Norman Sheresky & Marya Mannes, *Cosmopolitan,* November 1972

> The other desideratum is a pitcher with good control —Roger Angell, *New Yorker,* 12 Mar. 1984

> Sense and intelligence are desiderata of drama — George Jean Nathan, *The Theatre Book of the Year, 1946–1947*

> Such knowledge and attitudes may not be just desiderata—they may be *imperatives* —Edwin O. Reischauer, *Saturday Rev.,* 29 May 1976

design, intend   Einstein 1985 says that "common usage now freely substitutes *design* for *intend.*" He doesn't like it, however. Copperud 1970, 1980, opines that *design* is overused in journalism. Here are what seem to be some typical journalistic uses:

> President Reagan, in an appearance at Jefferson Junior High School in Washington, D.C., that was designed to show his interest in educational issues — *Publishers Weekly,* 14 Sept. 1984

> . . . a move designed to bolster confidence in the pound sterling —*Current Biography,* February 1968

> . . . a list of questions designed to find out just what our readers thought —*McCall's,* March 1971

The writer in each of these examples might have used *intend,* but it is hard to see what improvement would come from a substitution. The use of *design* in senses close to *intend* dates back at least to the 17th century. Here is an example from a literary source:

> The conference was neither so short nor so conclusive as the lady had designed —Jane Austen, *Mansfield Park,* 1814

This is not to suggest that *design* and *intend* are freely interchangeable. Einstein's advice to stop and think when you go to write *design* is sound; sometimes *intend* will indeed be the better choice. And sometimes not. In this last example, the use of *intend* would have muddled the intended meaning:

> Then she went out in search of a new lifestyle, one better designed to elude threats to her well-being — Don Gold, *Cosmopolitan,* June 1976

desirous   *Desirous* has been used with both *of* and *to* for a long time:

> . . . desirous at once of having her time to herself — Jane Austen, *Mansfield Park,* 1814

> I returned to London, very desirous to see Dr. Johnson —James Boswell, *Life of Samuel Johnson,* 1791

> . . . King William the Third was desirous to ascertain the comparative strength of the religious sects —T. B. Macaulay, *The History of England,* vol. I, 1849

> Desirous of living on the cozy footing of a father-in-law —Herman Melville, *Omoo,* 1847

In contemporary writing, while *desirous to* is used now and then, *desirous of* is the more common construction:

> They seem very desirous of getting back —Flannery O'Connor, letter, 1958

> . . . poetry designed to appeal to ears desirous of rhetoric —Eric Partridge, *British and American English Since 1900,* 1951

desist   When *desist* takes a prepositional-phrase complement, the preposition is usually *from;* less frequently, *desist* is followed by *in:*

> . . . to desist from attempts at suppression —Elmer Rice, *New Republic,* 13 Apr. 1953

> . . . had desisted in his effort to press love upon her —Sherwood Anderson, *Poor White,* 1920

despair   The verb *despair,* when used with a preposition, is usually used with *of:*

> Unless one despairs of mankind altogether —John Cogley, *Center Mag.,* July/August 1970

> Poetry has its roots in incantation . . . but it may well despair of competing with the incantation of Big Business, Bigger Navies, Brighter Churches —C. Day Lewis, *A Hope for Poetry,* 3d ed., 1936

Despair has also been used with *at,* but this use is much less frequent:

> . . . our parents sometimes despaired at our inability to understand —Paul Potter, *Johns Hopkins Mag.,* October 1965

despoil   When *despoil* is used with a preposition, it is *of:*

> . . . individual monasteries were occasionally despoiled of their land and revenues —Owen & Eleanor Lattimore, *The Making of Modern China,* 1944

> . . . the Dons sought unsuccessfully in New Mexico the kind of wealth of which they had despoiled the Aztecs —*American Speech,* Spring/Summer 1975

despondent Simon 1980 makes the claim that *despondent* "can apply only to people." Wrong. It is usually applied to people, true, but there are a few instances in which it is not:

The house ... needed paint badly, and looked gloomy and despondent among its smart Queen Anne neighbors —Willa Cather, *The Song of the Lark,* 1915

... Mark Twain was filled with a despondent desire ... to stop writing altogether —Van Wyck Brooks, *The Ordeal of Mark Twain,* 1920

The sonata is a wonderful instance of Bartók's inspired enlargement of the gamut of sonorous effects. Its slow movement ... is more active than his characteristically despondent ones —Arthur Berger, *Saturday Rev.,* 27 May 1950

Over against the ecstatic apocalypse, in every prophetic tradition, there stands the despondent psalm —Frederick A. Pottle, *PMLA,* September 1952

In the more despondent literatures of Europe — *Times Literary Supp.,* 14 Nov. 1968

dessert See DESERT, DESERTS, DESSERT.

destined *Destined* is almost always used with a preposition, either *to* or *for. Destined to* is most common when it is followed by an infinitive:

The affair seemed destined to end unfortunately — Zane Grey, *Desert Gold,* 1913

... were destined to battle with each other for the control of the road —Harrison Smith, *Saturday Rev.,* 5 June 1954

Frazer's *Golden Bough* suggested that the mere primitiveness of religious belief proves it is destined to be left behind on the march to civilization —Mary Douglas, *Commonweal,* 9 Oct. 1970

Destined to may also be followed by an object, although this is less frequent than the infinitive:

... he was destined to a bright and leading role in the world —H. G. Wells, *Joan and Peter,* 1918

After finishing high school he returned to California to study engineering at Stanford University in order to escape the legal profession to which he seemed to have been destined by family ties —*Current Biography,* June 1964

When *destined* is used with *for,* it is followed by a noun or noun phrase:

... it seemed that her graph of accomplishment was destined for a downward dip —*Saturday Rev.,* 26 Mar. 1955

A committee won't sit if its drivelings are not destined for print —Jacques Barzun, *Atlantic,* December 1953

... he's the kind of actor who seems destined for an Oscar —Stephen Schaefer, *US,* 11 Feb. 1985

destroy Harper 1975, 1985, Copperud 1980, and Bryson 1984 take up the problem of whether the phrases *completely destroyed* and *partially* (or *partly*) *destroyed* are acceptable. The Harper panel split down the middle

on *completely destroyed* and approved *partially destroyed.* Why is the question raised at all? It seems to be the residue of an old concern of newspaper editors. We have a citation taken from a book called *Editing the Day's News,* published in 1923, objecting to *partially destroy.* The issue is dead today, however, and need not concern you.

destruct, self-destruct Ever since the 1950s people have been writing to ask if there is such a word as *destruct.* The *Chicago Tribune* in March 1962 reprinted a denunciation of the word that seems to have originated in the *Cedar Rapids Gazette.* Barzun 1985, prompted by an instance of *self-destruct* printed on the bottom of a grocery bag, claims there is no verb *destruct.*

The verb *destruct* has been entered in our unabridged New International Dictionary since 1909. It was originally formed in the 17th century from the past participle of the same Latin verb that gave us *destroy.* It was simply a rare alternative to *destroy* that had only the advantage of contrasting prettily with *construct.* When it was revived as part of aerospace jargon in the 1950s, its coiners and users probably had no notion that the verb already existed. They probably created it by back-formation from *destruction.*

The revived *destruct* is not used in quite the same way as *destroy.* For one thing, it is usually used with *self-,* and *destroy* is not (except as a participial adjective in *self-destroying*). What is more, *destruct* carries the connotation of destroying for some positive purpose, such as safety.

... a $50 million weather satellite which was deliberately destructed on launch —*Springfield* (Mass.) *Sunday Republican,* 19 May 1968

A noun *destruct* was formed at the same time as the revived verb. It is often used attributively:

... an attaché case with instant destruct equipment —Walter Wager, *Telefon,* 1975

Both the noun and verb *destruct* are seldom found outside the areas of aerospace, the military, and cloak-and-dagger stories. Such is not the case, however, with *self-destruct. Self-destruct* was popularized by its use in the television series "Mission Impossible." The opening of each show included a tape of recorded instructions that burned itself up after the words, "This tape will self-destruct in five seconds."

We have evidence from technical sources for *self-destruct* used as an adjective (*self-destruct mechanism,* for instance), but not for the verb. The verb seems to have sprung full-grown from the heads of the "Mission Impossible" writers. The notion of self-destruction seemed to fill a need, for the verb rapidly became popular, established itself, and has continued to be widely used in general contexts. Here is a selection of typical uses:

... we've designed a leaf bag ... which will self-destruct when it is left in the rain —Norman Seltzer, quoted in *Springfield* (Mass.) *Union,* 19 Aug. 1970

A second homing device went into operation there this afternoon. Both devices will self destruct at 2:00 A.M. —Hugh C. McDonald, *The Hour of the Blue Fox,* 1975

... the hypothesis that all authority can and should "self-destruct" after it has served its purpose — David V. J. Bell, *Power, Influence, and Authority,* 1975

Do you psychologically self-destruct every time you double-fault in tennis? —Janice Harayda, *Money,* June 1976

There are also other ways, of course, for a film director to self-destruct —John Simon, *New York,* 10 Jan. 1977

But no amount of guidance can guarantee that your carefully constructed portfolio won't self-destruct — William G. McDonald, *Fortune,* 15 Dec. 1980

Even in a high-vacuum system, the compounds can self-destruct —*McGraw-Hill Yearbook of Science and Technology,* 1981

. . . an inventive time-travel story that unexpectedly self-destructs at the end —Gerald Jonas, *N.Y. Times Book Rev.,* 31 July 1983

destructive When it is used with a preposition, *destructive* is most often used with *of* or *to,* with *of* occurring more frequently:

. . . whenever any form of government becomes destructive of these ends, the people have the right to alter it —Linus Pauling, *Center Mag.,* September 1968

. . . a very violent . . . motion which is extremely destructive to the ligaments of the right shoulder — Ernest Hemingway, "African Journal," 1956

Much less often, *destructive* is used with *toward:*

. . . persons . . . are apt to be *destructive* toward themselves or others —Kenneth Goodall, *Psychology Today,* May 1971

detract, distract Some language commentators warn against confusing the use of *detract* and *distract.* While it is true that *detract* is used most commonly to mean "to take away something," it is also used to mean "to divert." The OED records this sense as dating from the 16th century, and the citation it quotes from the early 19th century shows the verb with the word *attention* as its direct object. This sense of *detract* has been entered in Merriam-Webster dictionaries since Webster's Second (1934), and Merriam-Webster editors have collected some half dozen instances of its use during the 20th century:

The anxious drama of the political and economic crises . . . has tended to detract attention from many of the more prosaic yet profound changes —Arthur Sweetser, *Foreign Affairs,* October 1940

These exaggerated reports tend to detract attention from the real issue —John Scott, *Time,* 3 Mar. 1947

The fact of the matter is that while "distract (the) attention" is by far the more commonly used phrase, "detract (the) attention" is also attested in irreproachably standard contexts.

When *detract* is used with a preposition, it is used with *from:*

. . . the little room was furnished as a chapel, though very simply, so as not to detract from the glory of the frescoes —Elizabeth Goudge, *Pilgrim's Inn,* 1948

An individual's image enhances or detracts from his power to persuade —Carll Tucker, *Saturday Rev.,* 25 Nov. 1978

deviate When *deviate* is used with a preposition, it is now most often used with *from:*

The building deviates considerably from the classic tradition —*American Guide Series: N.Y. City,* 1939

. . . sticking as close as possible to . . . the printed score, deviating as little as possible from strict tempo —Winthrop Sargeant, *New Yorker,* 10 Mar. 1955

. . . exercise censorship over any one of the Big Six Negro leaders who tried to deviate from the script — Malcolm X, *Evergreen,* December 1967

Deviate used with the preposition *into* is more commonly found in literature of the past:

. . . Shadwell never deviates into sense —John Dryden, *Mac Flecknoe,* 1682 (OED)

Our travellers deviated into a much less frequented track —Henry Fielding, *Tom Jones,* 1749 (OED)

But it continues to be found sporadically in modern writing, sometimes with allusion to Dryden's use in *Mac Flecknoe:*

For an additional 10¢ the driver will deviate into side streets —*American Guide Series: New Jersey,* 1939

. . . has been known to deviate into sense, but this is not one of those times —*New York,* 17 Nov. 1975

device, devise Several books call attention to the possibility of a spelling problem here. We have seen *devise* used for *device. Device* is a noun, *devise* primarily a verb and secondarily a noun used only in legal contexts. Checking your dictionary for the relevant meaning will keep you on the right path.

devolve When used with a preposition, *devolve* usually appears with *on* or *upon:*

In Case of the Removal of the President from Office, or of his Death, Resignation, or Inability to discharge the Powers and Duties of the said Office, the Same shall devolve on the Vice President —*Constitution of the United States,* 1787

. . . as they see the final power over curricular design slip from them and devolve on students —Lewis B. Mayhew, *Change,* January–February 1971

. . . the basic coverage of political conventions may devolve upon cable television —Neil Hickey, *TV Guide,* 1 Aug. 1980

Upon Leonard Woolf the editorship of the diary has devolved —Elizabeth Bowen, *N.Y. Times Book Rev.,* 21 Feb. 1954

Less frequently *devolve* is used with *to* or *into:*

. . . if the newspaper organization dissolves, no part of the assets should devolve to members —H. L. Ewbank, *AAUP Bulletin,* December 1969

The reason is that the economy had devolved into five separate economies that no longer act as one — *Business Week,* 1 June 1981

Curiously enough, while *devolve* followed by *from* had at one time faded from use, it now is appearing again, at least sporadically. *Evolve,* which commonly combines with *from,* may be an influence here:

> His allegedly subversive campaigns . . . all devolve from his belief in basic American rights —Frank Deford, *Sports Illustrated,* 8 Aug. 1983

> . . . the Code of Conduct for prisoners of war, which devolved from the Korean War —Ivor Peterson, *N.Y. Times,* 14 May 1979

diagnose Lurie 1927 disapproves of using the verb *diagnose* with a person as its object, even though there is often no other way of avoiding a stilted sentence. Several other more recent complaints have been lodged against this use, but not all of the commentary has been negative. Evans 1962 gives his approval: "there is bitter wisdom in the popular usage, for a man and his sickness are one. . . . It is a soothing fiction that the man "has" the malady; too often the malady has him."

Because this use sounds very familiar in spite of the fact that we have only a relatively small amount of evidence for it in our files, we believe that it is more frequently found in speech than in writing. However, the usefulness of this sense of *diagnose* is manifest, and its use in writing may well increase.

> . . . the women . . . have diagnosed themselves accurately —Joseph P. Donnelly, M.D., *Redbook,* March 1964

> . . . Yang was diagnosed mentally ill —Alan M. Dershowitz, *Psychology Today,* February 1969

> Cindy was first diagnosed over a year ago . . . as having a tumor —Janice Eidus, *Johns Hopkins Mag.,* May 1977

> Dr. Root, the first to diagnose me correctly —Nan Robertson, *N.Y. Times Mag.,* 19 Sept. 1982

dialogue 1. The spelling *dialogue* is much more commonly used than *dialog.*
2. There is a variety of comment on the noun *dialogue.* Kilpatrick 1984 says, "At some point in recent semantic history, a curious notion took root that *dialogue* should be restricted to describe a conversation between two persons only." This is apparently a delicate allusion to, among others, Edwin Newman, whose discussion of Gerald Ford's use of *dialogue* (in *Esquire,* December 1975) is based on that notion, and Shaw 1975, 1987, where *dialogue* is said to be from the Greek for "two words." Not only is Shaw in thrall to the etymological fallacy, but the Greek etymon does not contain the notion "two" at all. Anyone who reads the etymology of the word in a good dictionary will see that Greek *dia* means "through, across, apart" and several other things, but never "two." Restriction to two is also mentioned at the entry in the OED, where it is called a tendency.

More commentators seem concerned about the sense of *dialogue* that means "an exchange of ideas and opinions." This sense is called a "fad word" by Flesch 1964, and is mentioned or discussed also in Bremner 1980, Reader's Digest 1983, and Shaw 1975, 1987, and is the subject of Newman's remarks about President Ford's use. Here are some examples of the use:

> Rhetoric and anger partially yielded to dialogue — Robert Liebert, *Change,* October 1971

> However, the beginnings of a dialogue between church and complex have been established —Cynthia Proulx, *Saturday Rev.,* May 1973

> . . . encouraging unions and management to develop a day-to-day dialogue in which long-term problems can be discussed —*Current Biography,* January 1967

> . . . shows how the dialogue about British economic growth has developed —*Times Literary Supp.,* 5 Mar. 1970

There is no doubt that this sense has enjoyed a considerable vogue which is still going on. It is standard in general prose. The sense seems to have been prefigured by Thomas Hobbes:

> To enter into Dispute, and Dialogue with him — *Leviathan,* 1651 (OED)

3. Reader's Digest 1983 opines that the verb *dialogue* developed from the noun in the "exchange of ideas" sense discussed above, and the editors don't much care for it. That the verb is formed from the noun there is no question. And if the OED evidence is conclusive, Shakespeare was the first to use it—both transitively and intransitively. Among other users of the verb cited by the OED are Richardson, Coleridge, and Carlyle. What seems to have happened is that this verb has fallen out of serious literary use but has persisted or been revived in speech and speech-like writing. Here are some examples of typical recent use:

> What I especially appreciate is your willingness to dialogue about issues —Louis Shores, *RQ,* Spring 1973

> . . . to dialogue with Jesus Christ —radio talk show, 22 June 1975

This sort of use has been held up for our amusement by a contemporary satirical novelist:

> Nor could he get her to dialogue with him beyond an inflectionless "Far out." —Cyra McFadden, *The Serial,* 1977

diamond, diaper See VEHICLE.

dice See DIE *noun,* DICE.

dichotomy After reading and rereading our stack of citations for the use of *dichotomy,* we have come to the conclusion that many people who use this word (and probably even more people who read or hear it) have only a general idea of what it means. This haziness on the part of purveyors of English has resulted in a word whose meaning, aside from technical uses, is likewise hazy. For someone evaluating good and bad usage or even merely trying to describe usage accurately, *dichotomy* presents a ticklish problem. You begin with a word whose boundaries of meaning are so fuzzy that definitions by dictionaries (or usage commentators, for that matter) really fail to do it justice. Then, if you decide to approve only those uses covered by a given group of definitions, you will probably condemn more uses than you intended to, because even some of the relatively straightforward senses are hard to define thoroughly and precisely.

Several usage commentators have responded to the uneasiness that *dichotomy* engenders by simply saying that it should not be used in general contexts to mean "division" or "split." Frankly, we welcome such uses because they, at least, can be pinned down to a single, clear definition.

... the sharp dichotomy between undergraduate education and graduate professional study —*Current Biography,* June 1964

... the dichotomy between mind and body —Rollo May, *Psychology Today,* August 1969

Howard 1978 disapproves of using *dichotomy* "to mean anything divided into two or resulting from such a division; and thence to mean something paradoxical or ambivalent." Howard has paraphrased these definitions from the OED Supplement, which lumps them under one sense and illustrates them with four citations. Three of these citations are meant to be covered by the first definition (which is quite close in wording to a definition already given in the OED—one example of just how hard this word is to define). In the remaining citation *dichotomy* means "paradox":

By a dichotomy familiar to us all, a woman requires her own baby to be perfectly normal, and at the same time superior to all other babies —John Wyndham, *The Midwich Cuckoos,* 1957 (OED Supplement)

We, too, have citations in which *dichotomy* means "paradox" or has some other extended meaning which may not be readily decipherable from the context:

Herbert Hoover, a Quaker, fed milk to Belgian babies; Herbert Hoover as President of the United States had the war veterans of the Bonus Army bombed out of Washington by tear gas. What is this profound dichotomy? —Alfred North Whitehead, *Atlantic,* March 1939

... this same false dichotomy, "take us, or you will get Communism," ... was until recently, the strongest shield of the big dictators —Garrett Mattingly, *Saturday Rev.,* 17 July 1948

It is a well-known paradox that the lover of the sea craves for dry land—the sailor's love-hate extension of our old dichotomy to want to be where we are not —William Sansom, *N.Y. Times Mag.,* 10 May 1964

... the Eskimo today lives in a dichotomy, in a kind of cultural and economic never-never world —D. M. Whitworth, *Westways,* September 1965

... the dichotomy or contradictions within the American mind —Richard Beale Davis, *Key Reporter,* Spring 1968

... invoking a traditional ... dichotomy, how can we understand an indefinable term except through acquaintance with what the term denotes? —Arthur Danto, *Columbia Forum,* Fall 1969

... the false dichotomy between attitudes and institutions —Todd Gitlin, *Psychology Today,* January 1970

... the traitor-patriot dichotomy has been resolved decisively in favour of the latter interpretation — Michael S. Cross, *Books in Canada,* June–July 1974

... spinning lovely dichotomies (all fairy stories have female heroines: all science comes from the ego, not the self) —*Times Literary Supp.,* 7 July 1978

In many cases of such dichotomizing, the message that gets across to the reader is chiefly that the writer is using a fancy, academic-sounding word. If this is the impression you want to convey, *dichotomy* will surely serve you. If you are mainly interested in having your sentence understood, however, you might be better off finding another way to word it.

diction Harper 1975, 1985, Copperud 1980, and Bernstein 1971 all agree that *diction* in the sense of "enunciation" is established and acceptable in spite of earlier criticism:

But he is generally recognized to be a good orator, with crystal-clear diction —*Current Biography,* April 1966

The concern over the propriety of this sense appears to have started at the beginning of this century. It continued long enough for Follett 1966 to object to the use. At least part of the blame for spurring the debate on can be laid to the editor who failed to include the sense in Webster 1909, even though it was entered in the OED with citations from Dr. Johnson, Macaulay, and Ruskin.

Our earliest evidence for discussion of the issue dates from 1901. A reviewer of Alfred Ayres's *Some Ill-Used Words* in *The Critic,* May 1901, dismissed Ayres's contention that the sense "delivery" or "utterance" should be accompanied by an explanatory footnote as "pure pedantry." From Ayres's book the dispute moved into American newspapers, evidently fueled by frequent use of the sense in reviews of plays and operas. A 1913 newspaper objects to a critic's use of *diction* in reference to an opera singer. We also have a 1928 newspaper clipping questioning the application of *diction* to both a speaker and a singer, as well as a 1931 clipping belaboring the drama critic of the *New York Herald Tribune* on this issue. All three of these mention the nonexistence of the sense in large American dictionaries. The editors of Webster's Second (1934) included senses for both speaking and singing, and the controversy subsequently began to wane. Still, some remembered it:

Yet a certain indistinctness of what is miscalled diction interfered with no part so much as his —Eric Bentley, *New Republic,* 18 Oct. 1954

A reviewer of Harper 1975 in the *Saturday Review* speaks of the matter as a lost battle. From the start it was a typical purist's battle, begun after the disputed use had been current for a century and a half in the works of several standard authors.

dictum While the plurals *dicta* and *dictums* are both in standard use, our evidence shows that *dicta* is quite a bit more commonly used.

Partridge 1942 contains an example of *dicta* used as a singular. Our files have no examples that are clearly singular; this does not appear to be a serious problem.

For other foreign plurals, some of which present usage problems, see LATIN PLURALS.

didn't ought See HAD OUGHT, HADN'T OUGHT; OUGHT 1, 3.

die, *verb* From as far back as Ayres 1881 there have been varying pronouncements as to which prepositions may be used with which objects after the verb *die.* Sometimes disapproval is expressed of one preposition or another; Vizetelly 1906 and Copperud 1964, 1970, 1980 do not like *from,* and Ayres 1881 and Jensen 1935 do not like *with.* Since as many specifically approve these two prepositions as object to them, there cannot be much of a question of propriety here. But there is still the question of idiom. Here we have some sample contexts in which prepositions are used with *die* in various senses. *Of* seems to be the most commonly used:

> ... dying of kidney disease —Dr. C. L. Mengis, *National Observer*, 10 Mar. 1973

> Otherwise, like many another self-congratulatory society, they would have died of too much love —Robert K. Merton, *Columbia Forum*, Spring 1968

> ... I die of horror at what we're doing —Marya Mannes, quoted in *Harper's Weekly*, 11 Apr. 1975

> For years his mind had been dying of inanition —Van Wyck Brooks, *The Flowering of New England, 1815–1865*, rev. ed., 1946

> Diddloff is a dandy who would die of a rose in aromatic pain —W. M. Thackeray, *The Book of Snobs*, 1846

> ... nearly died of starvation —*Current Biography 1947*

From:

> ... Alexander died from an infection —*Current Biography 1947*

> Plans for community projects died from lack of enthusiasm —Jack Hamilton, *Town Jour.*, January 1954

> ... suspicions ... which had withered and died since from too much doubt —Louis Bromfield, *The Green Bay Tree*, 1924

For:

> It died for lack of support —James O. Goldsborough, *N.Y. Times Mag.*, 27 Apr. 1980

> Men die from time to time, ... but not for love —Lewis H. Lapham, *Harper's*, November 1971

> They had not come to the colonies to die for a creed —Edith Wharton, *The Old Maid*, 1924

> ... I was dying, yes, dying for someone really to care for me —Mary Deasy, *The Hour of Spring*, 1948

> He may be dying for a cigarette, but he has been taught to wait —Emily Hahn et al., *Meet the British*, 1953

> ... to do and die for the company —Clyde Haberman, *N.Y. Times*, 16 Jan. 1984

With:

> Odalie and Bizette had died with pneumonia —Lyle Saxon, *Children of Strangers*, 1937

> ... she, the children, and her father all died with the cholera —Raymond W. Thorp, *Bowie Knife*, 1948

In some religious contexts, *to* is used:

> ... that we might die to sin —1 Peter 2:24 (RSV)

> ... to be lost to all created things, to die to them and to the knowledge of them —Thomas Merton, *The Seven Storey Mountain*, 1948

And a few others appear less frequently:

> ... where the penal laws were dying through nonenforcement —*Dictionary of American Biography*, 1929

> ... at roll-top desks that were to die over —Cyra McFadden, *The Serial*, 1977

Many other prepositions are possible when the phrases are adverbial ones of location. Since these are not a matter of idiom with *die*, we have not included any here. In addition many varying older combinations can be found in the OED.

die *noun,* **dice**   The use of *dice* as a singular for one of the small cubes thrown in various games has been the object of some discussion. Krapp 1927 and Evans 1957 both mention its use, with Evans saying that *dice* is the usual singular. A letter to *Word Study* in 1947 made the claim that *dice* was the usual singular used by those who gambled with dice, and the Merriam editor who replied to the letter agreed, even though the use was not recognized in Webster's Second. Copperud 1970, 1980, finding the singular *dice* entered only in Webster's New World Dictionary (he missed the coverage in Webster's Third and the Collegiate dictionaries edited from it), disapproves the use.

The OED shows that the singular *dice* has been in use since the 14th century. It is apparently primarily a spoken use, for it is fairly rare in print. If dice players scorn *die* as a singular in speech, they (or their editors) seem to prefer it in print.

differ   The basic advice of the usage books is this: when *differ* means "to be unlike," it is followed by the preposition *from;* when *differ* means "to disagree," it is followed by the preposition *with* or *from*. This advice is more or less a consensus of upwards of twenty commentators from Ayres 1881 to the present. Writers have apparently had no difficulty using these words, and the only controversy has been the disagreement of the usage writers among themselves about the propriety or desirability of *with* or *from* in the "disagree" sense.

Most of the commentary consists of a few observations and a made-up example or two. Here are some actual examples. They include some other prepositions usually not mentioned, as well as those that stir contention. The sense "to be unlike" does, in fact, select *from:*

> ... the mind of the mature poet differs from that of the immature one —T. S. Eliot, "Tradition and the Individual Talent," 1917

> ... in these features lunar materials differ from most terrestrial and meteoric rocks —Caryl P. Haskins, *President's Report, Carnegie Institution of Washington, D.C., 1969–1970*

> ... here Mercian, spoken between the Thames and the Humber, differed from Northumbrian, spoken north of the Humber —W. F. Bolton, *A Short History of Literary English*, 1967

> Society folk in Philadelphia certainly differ from the Boston breed —Bennett Cerf, *Saturday Rev.*, 23 Apr. 1955

> They differ considerably from other tapeworms in structure —Libbie Henrietta Hyman, *The Invertebrates*, 1951

In its "disagree" sense, *differ* in current use takes *with* most frequently; but it is not a recent construction:

> ... said that only one player had differed with the majority —Murray Chass, *N.Y. Times*, 30 Mar. 1980

... he arrives at interpretations that often differ with those of other critics —Richard Ellmann, *N.Y. Times Book Rev.,* 4 Apr. 1976

... if they differ at all with American policy ... they are accused of being against us —Lester Markel, *N.Y. Times Mag.,* 10 Jan. 1965

The founders of Massachusetts, though they had come to America to seek religious freedom for themselves, would not allow it to others who differed with them —*Dictionary of American History,* 1940

... into conflict with his imperious uncle ... with whom he was hereafter to differ on almost every subject —*Dictionary of American Biography,* 1929

... the secretary, who told me how he had differed with his friends in parliament —Jonathan Swift, *Journal to Stella,* 29 Apr. 1711

Differ from in the "disagree" sense is a bit older than *differ with,* but it is not so frequent nowadays:

... I saw him almost daily, listened to him, sometimes differed from him, at any rate listened to him —Sir John Squire, *Britain To-Day,* October 1953

In this respect he differed profoundly from Burke —*Times Literary Supp.,* 16 May 1935

I read the *Cicero,* not because I differ a whit from you as to the author, but because it offered me some information I wanted —Oliver Wendell Holmes d. 1935, letter, 8 Jan. 1917

I differed from him, because we are surer of the odiousness of one, than the errour of the other —James Boswell, *Life of Samuel Johnson,* 1791

Among is also found with this sense:

Primitive rules of moral action, greatly as they differ among themselves, are all more or less advantageous —Havelock Ellis, *The Dance of Life,* 1923

Sometimes *differ from* can be interpreted in either sense:

... the economic man has become dominant almost to the point of excluding values and interests that differ from his —Kenneth S. Davis, *N.Y. Times Mag.,* 27 June 1954

When *with* is used with *differ* in its "be unlike" sense, as happens occasionally, it does not quite parallel the use of *from* with this sense of the verb. Here *with* means something like "in the case of":

... details of the car-hire arrangement differ with each company —Richard Joseph, *Your Trip to Britain,* 1954

Man probably gets ... , his "world view," from the language he learns, and it differs with every language —Stuart Chase, *Power of Words,* 1954

Several prepositions are used to indicate the subject of the difference. Here are a few typical examples:

... frequently differed on policy matters —*Current Biography 1949*

Opinions differ as to who were the first white visitors to Arizona —*Dictionary of American History,* 1940

... if they differ about the end itself —Brand Blanshard, *Saturday Rev.,* 29 Jan. 1955

... there was little persecution of those who differed in religious matters —*American Guide Series: New Hampshire,* 1938

different At least three different commentators—Cook 1985, Copperud 1970, 1980, and Bryson 1984—say that *different* as just used in this sentence is unnecessary. Unnecessary it may be, but including it is no great sin. The use of *different* after a number is simply an emphatic use. There is no law against emphasis. You can certainly leave the *different* out if you wish, but unless you are writing a telegram or are pressed for space, there is no need to. Let your ear be your guide. Note that the following writers found no need to excise the emphatic *different:*

Purity, it was said, implies three things. Accordingly, in three different ways it may be injured —Campbell 1776

I'll make it up to you twenty different ways —Samuel Johnson, in Boswell's *Life,* 1791

There were three different conclusions to be drawn from his silence —Jane Austen, *Mansfield Park,* 1814

... published at least five different books on grammar —Simon 1980 (in Bryson 1984)

Concur has three different meanings —Harper 1985

different from, than, to We have about 80 commentators in our files who discourse on the propriety of *different than* or *different to.* The amount of comment—thousands and thousands of words—might lead you to believe that there is a very complicated or subtle problem here, but there is not. These three phrases can be very simply explained: *different from* is the most common and is standard in both British and American usage; *different than* is standard in American and British usage, especially when a clause follows *than,* but is more frequent in American; *different to* is standard in British usage but rare in American usage. Here are a few examples of each construction:

My wish has been to try at something different from my former efforts —Lord Byron, letter, 20 Feb. 1816

... English would be a very different tongue from what it is —Brander Matthews, *Essays on English,* 1921

... not being afraid to be different from the rest of them —Flannery O'Connor, letter, 23 Dec. 1959

And the place where he was safe from that was in that penitentiary, which wasn't so different from the life he would have led if he'd been home —William Faulkner, 20 May 1957, in *Faulkner in the University,* 1959

Auden is gentleness itself ... and the evening is smooth, quiet, affectionate. How different he is from his new public persona —Robert Craft, *Stravinsky,* 1972

I agree, although my definition of ignorance and stupidity is quite different from his —Daniels 1983

She, too, had one day hoped for a different lot than to be wedded to a little gentleman who rapped his teeth —W. M. Thackeray, *Pendennis,* 1848

... the children grow older too and turn against them or prove to be far different than early parenthood had dreamed —Bernard De Voto, *The World of Fiction,* 1950

... and when Helen handed it to me, I said, "I thought these things were different than they used to be." —James Thurber, letter, 31 July 1952

Our emotions in the 20th century are affected by different conditions than in the 13th —Flannery O'Connor, letter, 19 Apr. 1958

Life in cadet school for Major Major was no different than life had been for him all along —Joseph Heller, *Catch-22,* 1961 (in Guth 1985)

... because the college campus of 1985 is markedly different than its namesake of 1955 —John R. Thelin, *Wall Street Jour.,* 11 Dec. 1985

But man was then a very different animal to what he now is —Thomas Love Peacock, *Headlong Hall,* 1816

"... Perhaps gentlemen are different to what they were when I was young...." —E. M. Forster, *A Room with a View,* 1908

Sometimes a speech, because it has been prepared in the expectation of the House being in a different mood to the one it assumes in the event, may misfire —Woodrow Wyatt, *Encounter,* April 1954

... it soon became apparent that I would find an architectural style there quite different to anything else —Neil Ray, *Geographical Mag.,* December 1983

... gives a sense different to the one intended — Howard 1984

The history of the controversy about *different than* and *different to* has two strands. The first is the history of the usage itself. The evidence shows *to* and *unto* as the first prepositions used, as early as the 1520s. *From* is first attested in Shakespeare:

This week he hath been heavy, sour, sad,
And much much different from the man he was
—*The Comedy of Errors,* 1593

The OED cites a 1603 comedy coauthored by Thomas Dekker for the use *different to* and a 1644 work by Sir Kenelm Digby for *different than.* From the 18th century the OED lists Addison with *different from,* Fielding with *different to,* and Goldsmith with *different than.*

The OED entry notes that *different from* was then (1897) usual, and that *different to* was well-attested and common in speech, but disapproved by some as incorrect. No mention is made of disapproval of *different than,* but a long list of standard British authors who had used it is appended. The OED opines (as does the grammarian H. Poutsma) that *different than* is patterned after *other than.* Jespersen 1909–49 (vol. 7), on the other hand, observes that *different* is often felt to be a kind of comparative. He mentions as confirming evidence not only the construction with *than* but also the tendency for *different* to be modified by such adverbs as *much, not much, no,* and *any,* which are frequently used with comparatives. He gives as his earliest instance the "much different" of Shakespeare's cited above. Here are some examples from our files of *different* with such adverbs:

The Libyan horse was far different in formation than any of the wild horses —Frank G. Menke, *The New Encyclopedia of Sports,* 1947

I'm no different than you —Frank Shorter, quoted in *Springfield* (Mass.) *Daily News,* 3 June 1986

... would probably require a much different philosophic idiom —Kenneth Burke, *A Grammar of Motives,* 1945

... not greatly different than in the U. S. —*Time,* 11 Aug. 1947

And the construction after *different* in this next example also has the feeling of a comparative:

... which is different than any other piece we've done lately —*Harper's,* March 1949

The OED list of standard authors using *different than* had been compiled by Fitzedward Hall in his *Modern English* of 1872. The original objection to *different than* appears in Baker 1770. He found this sentence in William Melmoth's translation of Cicero's letters, published in 1753:

I found your Affairs had been managed in a different Manner than what I had advised.

Commented Baker: "*A different Manner than* is not English. We say *different to* and *different from;* to the last of which Expressions I have in another Place given the Preference, as seeming to make the best Sense." Leonard 1929 found the subject in no other 18th-century grammars, but Sundby et al. 1991 shows that Baker's opinion was carried down to the 19th century by a few less well-known grammarians, James Wood, John Knowles, and Alexander Bicknell. Hall may have picked it up from one of them. Goold Brown's mid-19th-century *Grammar of English Grammars* does not seem to mention it (at least it is not in the index of the 1880 edition), although he does object to *different to* and specify *different from* as correct. Hall's discussion was chiefly concerned with *different to,* which had been the subject of continuing discussion from Baker's time; mention of *different than,* of which Hall disapproved, was relegated to a footnote.

At any rate, Hodgson 1889 and Raub 1897 object to *different than,* and it has become a favorite topic of 20th-century comment. In the first half of the century *different than* was regularly condemned. In the second half some still condemn it, but a majority find it acceptable to introduce a clause, because insisting on *from* in such instances often produces clumsy or wordy formulations. But there is still quite a bit of residual hostility to *than,* especially when it is followed by a noun or pronoun. This may have more to do with the question of whether *than* can be a preposition (see THAN 1) than with *different* itself.

Different to has been the subject of more nearly continuous dispute. Disapproval began with Priestley in 1768. Baker 1770 preferred *from* to *to* and he raised the often repeated point that the verb *differ* takes *from* and not *to.* The argument from the verb was repeated by Lewis Carroll in an 1886 letter, by Compton 1898, Vizetelly 1906, and many others. Fowler 1926 dismissed it as mere pedantry; notwithstanding his scorn, the argument can be found as recently as Strunk & White 1979 and Phythian 1979.

Baker's objection turns up in Murray 1795, where *different to* is corrected to *different from* in two places. It probably went from Murray into other grammar books. It pops up in Alford 1866, where Alford presents the problem as sent him by a correspondent who introduces a new argument, based on the meaning of the prefix *dis-* in Latin: "apart." This argument is repeated as recently as Cook 1985.

Fowler 1926 stoutly defends *different to,* and his defense has probably done much to lessen British objection to the expression, although objection still lingers in many letters to *The Times,* as Howard 1980 reports.

In summary we can say that there need have been no problem here at all, since all three expressions have been in standard use since the 16th and 17th centuries and all three continue to be in standard use. Mencken 1963 (abridged) comments on a flurry in the newspapers over *different than* that took place in 1922. Mencken cites with approval this comment from the New York *Sun:*

> The excellent tribe of grammarians, the precisians and all others who strive to be correct and correctors, have as much power to prohibit a single word or phrase as a gray squirrel has to put out Orion with a flicker of its tail.

differentiate When *differentiate* is used with a preposition, it is most often *from:*

> At his best he could differentiate one poem from another —Randall Jarrell, *N.Y. Times Book Rev.,* 15 Aug. 1954

> ... it was the end of a continuous spectrum, differentiated from other states only by degree —J. Anthony Lukas, *N.Y. Times Mag.,* 14 Jan. 1973

Less frequently, differentiate is used with *between:*

> ... without ever being able to differentiate between their relative significances —Lois Armstrong, *People,* 5 July 1976

Differentiate is also used with *among,* but very infrequently, perhaps because it tends to lead to somewhat muddled sentences like this example:

> Then he will try to differentiate among those who might assume larger responsibilities from those who cannot —Harry Levinson, *Think,* May–June 1967

dilapidated **1.** The argument, raised by Bierce 1909 and referred to by Copperud 1980, that *dilapidated* can only be used of a stone structure because it is derived from Latin *lapis* "stone," has not attracted the fancy of modern commentators. Their indifference reflects their good sense, because the argument fails as to both etymology and actual usage. *Dilapidate* comes from Latin *dilapidatus,* the past participle of *dilapidare* "to squander, destroy." *Dilapidare* was formed from the prefix *dis-* plus the verb *lapidare* "to throw stones," which in turn came from *lapis* "stone." So even Latin *dilapidatus* was at several semantic removes from *lapis* and was in no way tied to a meaning that involved stone. Neither the English verb *dilapidate* nor the adjective *dilapidated* has ever been restricted to referring only to things of stone. People, vehicles, buildings (many of them made of brick or other materials), and a host of other things have been and can be described as dilapidated.
2. The spelling *delapidate(d)* has very occasionally been used since the 17th century, but it is considered a misspelling.

dilemma Contrary to the beliefs expressed by members of what Kilpatrick 1984 calls the "Society for the Protection of *Dilemma,*" the word has several meanings.

The earliest use of *dilemma* in English was in the 16th century as a term in rhetoric for an argument presenting usually two alternatives to an opponent, both of which were conclusive against him. By the end of the 16th century, the word had spread from argument to situations involving action. The earliest citation for such use shown in the OED comes from the dramatist and poet Robert Greene:

> Every motion was entangled with a dilemma: ... the love of Francesco ... the feare of her Fathers displeasure —*Never Too Late,* 1590

In Greene's play the heroine is faced with a hard choice between alternatives—Francesco's love and her father's good will—that appear to be unattainable at the same time, perhaps mutually exclusive.

Shakespeare extended the word to the state of mind of a person faced with such a choice:

> Here, Master Doctor, in perplexity and doubtful dilemma —*The Merry Wives of Windsor,* 1601

By the middle of the 17th century, a third use had arisen: the application of the word to a situation in which a person is faced with alternatives each of which is likely or sure to be unsatisfactory. This use is closest to the original use in rhetoric.

> ... this doleful Dilemma; either voluntarily, by resigning, to depose himself; or violently ... to be deposed by others —Thomas Fuller, *The Church-History of Britain,* 1655 (OED)

The dilemma described by Fuller, we note in passing, is not without parallels in modern history.

All three of these extended senses—Greene's, Shakespeare's, and Fuller's—have continued in use down to the present. Here, for instance, we find Greene's sense of a choice between alternatives that appear to be mutually exclusive, although perhaps they should not be:

> ... presents the dilemma of whether one wants to be correct or endure —Heywood Hale Broun, in Harper 1985

> Those who hold both the beauty of the countryside and the prosperity of agriculture equally dear have dreaded the time when our present methods of "progressive" husbandry might lead the nation to a cruel dilemma—the choice between agriculture and a satisfying landscape —Robert Waller, *New Scientist,* 24 Apr. 1969

> For the Greeks, the Roman Empire was a necessity of life and at the same time an intolerable affront to their pride. This was, for them, a formidable psychological dilemma —Arnold J. Toynbee, *Horizon,* August 1947

Here we have Shakespeare's extension to the decider's state of mind:

> ... lived in a constant dilemma between disapproval of Lucy's frivolity, and rapturous fascination —Vita Sackville-West, *The Edwardians,* 1930

In *Man and Superman* (1903) George Bernard Shaw managed to use both Greene's sense and Shakespeare's sense in a single brief passage of dialogue:

> RAMSDEN. If I am to be your guardian, I positively forbid you to read that book, Annie.
> ANN. Of course not if you don't wish it.
> TANNER. If one guardian is to forbid you to read the other guardian's book, how are we to settle it? Suppose I order you to read it! What about your duty to me?
> ANN. I am sure you would never purposely force me into a painful dilemma, Jack.
> RAMSDEN. Yes, Yes, Annie: this is all very well, and, as I said, quite natural and becoming. But you must make a choice one way or the other. We are as much in a dilemma as you.

Here are some examples of Fuller's use, with unsatisfactory or undesirable options:

> In either Case, an equal Chance is run:
> For, keep, or turn him out, my Lord's undone. . . .
> A strong Dilemma in a desp'rate Case!
> To act with Infamy, or quit the Place
> —Jonathan Swift, "To Mr. Gay," 1735

> . . . the unpleasant dilemma of being obliged either to kill the father or give up the daughter —Jedidiah Morse, *The American Universal Geography,* 1796 (OED)

> . . . here is the dilemma. If German industry is not allowed to develop, most of Europe will be without its customary supplies; if Germany is allowed to become a great industrial nation, she will be able to wage another war —Frank Abbott Magruder, *National Governments and International Relations,* 1950

> . . . Goldschmidt was faced with a real dilemma: to grant the permit and further anger those upset by the first demonstration, or to refuse the permit and deny the constitutional right to demonstrate peaceably — Manson Kennedy, *City,* Summer 1972

Now if you stop to reflect, you will realize that the Greene sense and the Fuller sense are in essence the same; the difference between them is entirely a matter of how the author presents the dilemma. Fuller, for instance, might have presented his instance as a choice between resigning and staying alive or being deposed by force and perhaps not staying alive: the choice between life and possible death is not one between two equally undesirable options. Often what is most unsatisfactory, even positively painful, is the necessity of making the choice:

> Either everything in man can be traced as a development from below, or something must come from above. There is no avoiding that dilemma: you must be either a naturalist or a supernaturalist —T. S. Eliot, "Second Thoughts on Humanism," in *Selected Essays,* 1932

> . . . mothers tend to put themselves in a cruel dilemma. They know they want a life beyond their children, but they also want to be everything to their children —Bruno Bettelheim, *Ladies' Home Jour.,* September 1971

> . . . like most of the other professionals of the era, he could not escape the tragic dilemma of the Western liberal world, confronted by two brutal and regressive dictatorships neither one of which it could overcome without the help of the other —Walter Mills, *Center Mag.,* March 1968

The word has come gradually to be used in contexts in which just what the choice is or just what the alternatives are is not made explicit, leaving the reader to infer part of what is intended:

> . . . the dilemma between art and life in our own times —*Times Literary Supp.,* 28 Dec. 1951

> The dilemma which faces all moralists is that the repression of instincts is apt to breed a worse disease than their free expression —Herbert Read, *The Philosophy of Modern Art,* 1952

> But they were in a real dilemma. It seems to be a law of the imagination that bad characters are more fun to write and read about than good ones —W. H. Auden, *New Yorker,* 1 Apr. 1972

And if no alternatives are mentioned at all, the word becomes very close in meaning to *problem, difficulty, predicament:*

> . . . man's relation to nature and man's dilemma in society —E. B. White, *Yale Rev.,* Autumn 1954

> Capt. Moore with about forty dragoons . . . led the pursuit and became separated from the others. . . . Discovering their dilemma, more than 150 Mexicans turned upon them and did terrible execution —*The Dictionary of American History,* 1940

> . . . with Kennedy's withdrawal, the Democrats' dilemma becomes glaringly apparent —Kilpatrick 1984

> The personal dilemma of the poet with his fortune to make —Henry O. Taylor, *The Mediaeval Mind,* 4th ed., 1925

> . . . to take man's dilemma, the old familiar things in which there's nothing new . . . and . . . to make something which was a little different —William Faulkner, 1 May 1958, in *Faulkner in the University,* 1959

This use of *dilemma* without specific alternatives was noted by Krapp 1927: "now in general colloquial use as a synonym for *predicament, uncomfortable position, a fix.*" It is by far the most common use in the second half of the 20th century. H. W. Fowler noted it, with disapproval, around the turn of the century. After a false start in *The King's English* of 1907, he laid down the law for the fraternity of usage prescribers in 1926:

> The use of *d*[ilemma] as a mere finer word for *difficulty* when the question of alternatives does not definitely arise is a SLIPSHOD EXTENSION; it should be used only when there is a pair, or at least a definite number, of lines that might be taken in argument or action, & each is unsatisfactory.

We can see that Fowler has two points here: first, he objects to the relatively new extension of *dilemma* to uses involving no question of alternatives—an objection which has proved to be futile—and second, he recommends confining the word within limits it had already outgrown in 1590. Fowler's followers have done little more than pursue their own reasoning into regions more and more remote from actual usage. Bernstein 1958, 1965 chooses to revise Fowler's *unsatisfactory* (the adjective used in Webster's Second and subsequent

Merriam-Webster dictionaries) to *distasteful;* Copperud 1964 chooses the even stronger *evil.* Copperud goes on to explain to us that "a choice between the love of two beautiful women is not a true dilemma"; but unless the ladies in question are entirely indifferent, it is the same dilemma presented, for instance, by Shaw: to please one is to displease the other. Freeman 1983 may be on sounder theoretical ground when he states that "it is not a dilemma to have to choose between apple pie and chocolate custard"; however, in all our examples of the use of *dilemma* in edited prose, we have none of the word's being applied to so trivial a choice.

Conclusion: *dilemma,* in the senses extended from the original application to argument, has never been as restricted in meaning as Fowler and his successors have wished it to become. Its further extension to instances in which no alternatives are expressed or implied has become the prevailing use in the 20th century, even though disapproved by Fowler and two leading usage panels. Your use of the word in the sense of *problem* or *predicament* should not be a concern—even E. B. White used it that way.

diminution For pronunciation problems with this word, see NUCLEAR.

diphtheria, diphthong See PHTH.

direct, directly These adverbs are sometimes interchangeable:

> . . . will take you and your car direct from Dover to Stirling —Andrew S. Stoke, *In Britain,* February 1972

> . . . took her directly from the closing night at the theater to the hospital —Anne Edward, *Book Digest,* January 1978

> . . . suggesting I write to her direct —John Willett, *Times Literary Supp.,* 26 Mar. 1970

> . . . letters . . . sent directly to me —John C. Messenger, *Psychology Today,* May 1971

> . . . flown direct to Hong Kong —Geri Trotta, *Town & Country,* March 1980

> . . . flew directly to Boston —Gail Cameron, *Ladies' Home Jour.,* August 1971

> . . . Shakespeare's *Hamlet* speaks direct to our condition —R. J. Kaufmann, *American Scholar,* Summer 1967

> The books . . . speak directly to children —*Times Literary Supp.,* 22 Oct. 1971

> . . . put the question direct —Harold C. Schonberg, *Harper's,* February 1971

> We asked the ministers directly —Rodney Stark et al., *Psychology Today,* April 1970

> . . . went into the hotel business direct —*American Labor,* December 1969

> Most graduates go directly into industry —James B. Conant, *Slums and Suburbs,* 1961

> ". . . the luggage is to be loaded direct on to the aircraft. . . ." —Graham Greene, *Travels with My Aunt,* 1969

> . . . it could be loaded directly onto barges —John Fischer, *Harper's,* January 1969

Directly is always used in preference to *direct* as a contrasting adverb paired with *indirectly:*

> . . . problems related directly or indirectly to the Vietnam War —Mary & Kenneth Gergen, *Change,* January–February 1971

Overall, *directly* is used quite a bit more often than *direct.* It has uses and meanings that it does not share with *direct.* An important exclusive use of *directly* is before the word or phrase it modifies; *direct* is not used in that way as an adverb.

> There are more directly relevant pictures —*Times Literary Supp.,* 22 Oct. 1971

> Directly in front of us, two men . . . began attacking the pavement with a crowbar —James Jones, *Harper's,* February 1971

> Nobody left, unless he was directly told to —Jane O'Reilly, *New York,* 15 Feb. 1971

> . . . supported by directly assisting a professor — Robert T. Blackburn, *AAUP Bulletin,* December 1967

> . . . hand-stitch them to the pocket pieces directly underneath —Mary Johnson, *Woman's Day,* October 1971

> . . . another handicap directly related to the predilection for violence —Richard J. Barnet, *Harper's,* November 1971

In addition, *direct* will not fit into the following uses, in which the adverb technically modifies the preceding verb form but is also tightly bound to the prepositional phrase that follows:

> . . . will vary directly with these selected variables — Matthew Besdine, *Psychology Today,* March 1971

> . . . a fuel gauge viewed through a plate glass window set directly on the gas tank —*Ford Truck Times,* Summer 1970

> . . . landing directly against the microphone —Robert Thompson, *Harper's,* October 1971

> . . . the mountain that rose directly above our camp —Jane Goodall, *Ladies' Home Jour.,* October 1971

Direct is likewise not used in the sometimes criticized senses relating to time that are discussed below at DIRECTLY.

directly 1. A sense that *directly* does not share with the adverb *direct* is "immediately." Vizetelly 1906 notes the existence of some objectors to this use in America (we can count Bierce 1909 among these), but he says the use is popular in England. It has been in British use since Shakespeare's time.

> With undoubting decision she directly began her adieus —Jane Austen, *Mansfield Park,* 1814

> . . . reading it directly after Rowe's most tense contribution to the form —Bonamy Dobrée, *English Literature in the Early Eighteenth Century, 1700–1740,* 1959

It is also in American use:

> . . . he may start off with an idea, but almost directly he is back to type —Otis Ferguson, *New Republic,* 22 Nov. 1954

... in the 50 or 75 years directly before he began to write —Irving Howe, *New Republic,* 4 July 1955

Directly after his graduation —*Current Biography,* January 1965

Some commentators (Jensen 1935, Longman 1984) worry that this sense of *directly* might be confused with other senses. Ambiguous examples do occur, but they would seem not to bother the reader much because the senses invoked seem to reinforce each other rather than conflict. Here are a few:

... the most proper thing to be done was for him to walk down to the parsonage directly, and call on Mr. Crawford —Jane Austen, *Mansfield Park,* 1814

Let me say directly that the definition of the naturalistic school will vary somewhat in the case of each literary historian —Maxwell Geismar, *College English,* January 1954

When Joe Kennedy finished saying a few terse words to his family, he went directly to his room —Gail Cameron, *Ladies' Home Jour.,* August 1971

2. There is also a weakened sense that means "after awhile, shortly"; it is chiefly, but not exclusively, American.

Pretty soon it darkened up, and ... directly it begun to rain —Mark Twain, *Huckleberry Finn,* 1884 (*A Mark Twain Lexicon,* 1938)

I expect Rachel in directly, as she said she should not stay a moment after Tregenna and Bella were gone —*The Letters of Rachel Henning Written between 1853 and 1882,* published in Sydney, Australia, 1952

We are uncertain to what extent this use may be limited geographically in current use. Our most recent citations are South Midland or Southern. The Dictionary of American Regional English should have the final word when the volume containing *D* appears.

3. The conjunction *directly* meaning "as soon as" has drawn fire from American critics in the past (for instance Ayres 1881, MacCracken & Sandison 1917, and Jensen 1935) but is in standard British use.

See how silly H. I. is directly I turn my back —Ellen Terry, letter, 26 Dec. 1896

... and directly we enter it we breast some new wave of emotion —Virginia Woolf, in *A Century of the Essay,* ed. David Daiches, 1951

Directly you slip it on, this shoe feels like an old friend —advt., *Punch,* 24 Jan. 1951

... I decided that directly I had £500 I would escape —Alan Moorehead, *A Late Education,* 1970

... it gets very cold at sea directly the sun sets —Robin Brandon, *The Good Crewman,* 1972

See also IMMEDIATELY.

disagree Phythian 1979 says *disagree* takes *with,* not *from.* The OED shows that *from* is obsolete — there are no citations after the 17th century, except one 19th-century legal use. *To* seems still to be found in legal contexts, especially in *disagreed to,* which may be paired with the more modern-sounding *agreed to.*

In ordinary use, *with* is common but other prepositions can be found, especially when the object refers to

the general subject of discussion rather than the rejected viewpoint:

One can disagree with his views, but one can't refute them —Henry Miller, *The Air-Conditioned Nightmare,* 1945

It is possible to disagree with the U.S. proposal —Norman Cousins, *Saturday Rev.,* 30 Oct. 1971

... the authorities disagree about the procedure to be followed —F. S. C. Northrop, *The Logic of the Sciences and the Humanities,* 1947

Mr. Beard and Miss Compton disagreed on the distance of meat from heat —Jane Nickerson, *N.Y. Times Mag.,* 27 June 1954

disappointed When *disappointed* is used with a preposition in contemporary writing, it may take any one of several prepositions: *about, at, by, in, over,* or *with.* It may also be followed by *to* used with an infinitive. At one time, *disappointed of* was common, but during the 20th century, *disappointed in* has become the most prevalent usage:

... to be contradicted by events, to be disappointed in his hopes —Sir Winston Churchill, quoted in William L. Shirer, *The Rise and Fall of the Third Reich,* 1960

By 1843, when he came home disappointed in journalism but eager to write books —Henry Seidel Canby, *Thoreau,* 1939

During the 19th and early 20th centuries, some writers, T. B. Macaulay and W. H. Hudson to name two, used *disappointed* with the word *agreeably.* The juxtaposition was deliberate, and, while some usage commentators cautioned against the use, others conceded that under the right circumstances it served a legitimate purpose: to convey a certain whimsical paradox. The use is not attested in contemporary writing:

On approaching the house I was agreeably disappointed at having no pack of loud-mouthed, ferocious dogs rushing forth —W. H. Hudson, *The Purple Land,* 1885

disapprove When used with a preposition, *disapprove* is generally used with *of:*

... the familiar agreement that a reporter need not sign an article of which he disapproves and may withhold permission to management for the use of his name —John Hohenberg, *Saturday Rev.,* 13 Nov. 1971

... was to have a "house-wedding," though Episcopalian society was beginning to disapprove of such ceremonies —Edith Wharton, *The Old Maid,* 1924

When the object of the preposition is the one disapproving, however, *by* appears:

The Faribault alliance was disapproved by the annual Faribault school meeting in 1892 —*American Guide Series: Minnesota,* 1938

disassemble **1.** *Disassemble, dissemble.* *Dissemble* means "to hide under a false appearance" or "to put on a false appearance":

... had been trained to dissemble and conceal his real thoughts —M. S. Handler, introduction to *The Autobiography of Malcolm X,* 1966

When Banquo returns as a ghost, however, Macbeth can dissemble no longer —Julius Novick, *N.Y. Times,* 15 July 1973

Disassemble means "to take apart":

Then we disassembled the mixers and examined them for signs of wear —*Consumer Reports,* July 1980

Several commentators caution their readers not to confuse these words. Our files contain no evidence of such confusion, but Gowers in Fowler1965 cites an instance in which *dissemble* is used when *disassemble* is meant. **2.** *Disassemble* is a relatively recent coinage in its current sense. The OED has a citation from 1611 for *disassemble* used to mean "disperse," but "take apart" as a sense of the word was not recorded until 1903. Its common use by mechanics in the early 20th century caused a little consternation among the nonmechanical. Its strongest critic seems to have been A. P. Herbert, the English writer and politician:

What a wicked word! Dis-assemble! The engineers of our glorious Navy say 'strip an engine'—swift and metaphorical and true. That should be good enough for any motor-monger ashore —A. P. Herbert, *What a Word!,* 1935

"Motor-mongers" continued to say "disassemble" anyway, despite its wickedness, and the word quickly established itself in standard English. The only recent critic to find fault with it is Follett 1966, who regards it as a needless word.

disassociate   See DISSOCIATE, DISASSOCIATE.

disburse   The Oxford American Dictionary warns against confusion of *disburse,* which usually means "to pay out (money)" or "to distribute (property)," with *disperse.* Such confusion probably accounts for this:

Cottontail rabbit management study indicates . . . that stocked or marked rabbits disburse widely —*Biological Abstracts,* June 1954

James J. Kilpatrick in his newspaper column (29 Sept. 1985) has also mentioned having found an instance in which demonstrators were "asked to disburse."

The OED has a figurative sense of *disburse* defined as "To . . . give out or away." It is marked obsolete with only 16th and 17th century citations. The next example may represent a revival of that sense, even though it could be seen as an error for the current *dispense:*

Of course, the advice disbursed . . . is semiliterate trash —Simon 1980

discomfit   Several usage commentators have, in the past, tried to convince their readers that *discomfit* means "to rout, completely defeat" and not "to discomfort, embarrass, disconcert, make uneasy." However, most of the recent commentary agrees with the evidence we have: the sense "to discomfort, disconcert" has become thoroughly established and is the most prevalent meaning:

. . . his habit of discomfiting an opponent with a sudden profession of ignorance —T. S. Eliot, "Francis Herbert Bradley," in *Selected Essays,* 1932

Discomfited by Labor heckling . . . , Eden lost his usual urbanity —*Time,* 19 Mar. 1956

. . . parents get inarticulate and discomfited when it comes to discussing love —Linda Wolfe, *N.Y. Times Book Rev.,* 15 Feb. 1976

. . . people like to see the pompous scientific establishment discomfited —James S. Trefil, *Saturday Rev.,* 29 Apr. 1978

. . . he saw that his boss was discomfited and at a loss —David A. Stockman, *Newsweek,* 28 Apr. 1986

The use of *discomfit* to refer to defeat in battle is now rare, and extended uses meaning "to frustrate the plans of, thwart" are uncommon.

Although, as Harper 1985 says, "*discomfit* has now come to be practically synonymous with 'discomfort,'" there is a difference between the two words. *Discomfit* is used almost exclusively as a verb (*discomfiture* is the related noun), while *discomfort* is much more commonly used as a noun than a verb.

discontent   The noun *discontent* may be followed by *with:*

. . . a widely voiced discontent with the Vietnam war —John J. Corson, *Saturday Rev.,* 10 Jan. 1970

. . . this majority comes about through the accident of discontent with an incumbent administration —Wilfred E. Binkley, *New Republic,* 16 Nov. 1953

. . . their growing discontent with British rule —Margaret Stimmann Branson, ed., *America's Heritage,* 1982

. . . from discontent with student wages to dissatisfaction with the number of pianos available —John W. Moscow, *N.Y. Times,* 9 Jan. 1969

Less frequently, *discontent* is used with *over:*

Some discontent over ROTC lingers —D. Park Teter, *Change,* September 1971

. . . when popular discontent over a massive new tax program . . . erupted in strikes —*Current Biography,* April 1967

discourage   When *discourage* is used with a preposition, it is usually *from,* which in turn is often followed by a gerund phrase as its object:

. . . some employers discourage them from taking that much time —David Butwin, *Saturday Rev.,* 23 Oct. 1971

Occasionally *discourage from* is followed by a noun phrase:

. . . directors who . . . are being discouraged from the normal play of their talents —Gilbert Seldes, *Perspectives USA,* Summer 1953

Discourage has also been used occasionally with *into* and *with* as the following examples show:

. . . a generally negative attitude toward the environment had almost discouraged me into discounting my own high estimation of that exceptional project —John Lear, *Saturday Rev.,* 6 Nov. 1971

. . . certain books which . . . tend to discourage us rather with Renanian irony and pity —Edmund Wilson, *Axel's Castle,* 1931

discover, invent The original meaning of *invent* in English is "to come upon, find, discover," a meaning quite close to the meaning of the Latin word from which it was taken. Toward the end of the 18th century this original sense was decreasing in use, while two newer senses—still in use today—were flourishing. The OED has a citation from the Scots rhetorician Hugh Blair in 1783 that is probably the first discrimination between *invent* and *discover*, whose current sense was taking the place of *invent's* original sense:

> We invent things that are new; we discover what was before hidden. Galileo invented the telescope; Harvey discovered the circulation of the blood —*Lectures on Rhetoric and Belles Lettres*, 1783

What Blair was doing, in effect, was distinguishing a current sense of *invent* from a current sense of *discover* which was in competition with a dying sense of *invent* (it is now archaic).

Blair's book was widely used in schools. Perhaps Noah Webster was familiar with it from its use as a textbook. At any rate he included Blair's discrimination in his 1828 dictionary:

> *Discover* differs from *invent*. We *discover* what before existed, though to us unknown; we *invent* what did not before exist.

Noah changed Blair's "what was before hidden" to "what before existed, though to us unknown" in the explanation of *discover*. He may have thought this a sharper point of discrimination than Blair's wording. It has since become the only point of dispute.

Webster's discrimination has become a regular part of school textbooks and handbooks. Here is a modern example:

> *Discover* means "to find something existing that was not known before." *Invent* means "to create" or "to originate." —Battles et al. 1982

And here is an older one:

> A person *discovers* a thing already existing but hitherto unknown; he *invents* something entirely new —MacCracken & Sandison 1917

Now, if we look at typical examples given to show the distinction, we find:

> Marie Curie *discovered* radium.
> Edison *invented* the phonograph.

But does anyone write "Marie Curie invented radium" or "Edison discovered the phonograph"? Probably not, unless the writer is trying for humor from incongruity. The plain fact is that no one with a school child's command of the language confuses these two words used in such an obvious way. But look at this:

> Newton invented the differential and the integral calculus and discovered the laws of motion. I might perhaps have said that he discovered the calculus and invented the laws of motion, for the distinction between "discovery" and "invention," which used to be so carefully drilled into us at school, is not so sharp in the upper strata of mathematics and physics —K. K. Darrow, *Renaissance of Physics*, 1936

What Professor Darrow was questioning is the appropriateness of Noah Webster's "what before existed" to the conditions of abstract physics and mathematics. We don't need to dally in the upper strata of mathematics

and physics to discover that if Noah's comment was apropos in 1828 it no longer is in the 20th century.

> We shall never know who first discovered how to pound up metal-bearing rock and heat it in the fire —Tom Wintringham, *The Story of Weapons and Tactics*, 1943

> ... two brothers named Roberts discovered that it was possible to apply a coating of dissolved rubber to silk fabric and thereby secure an airtight covering —*The Encyclopedia Americana*, 1943

> Long before vaccination was discovered, attempts had been made to lessen the ravages of smallpox —Victor Heiser, *An American Doctor's Odyssey*, 1936

> It was discovered how to hollow out logs to provide a vessel of some stability and lightness for water transport. The canoe was invented —E. Adamson Hoebel, *Man in the Primitive World*, 1949

None of the processes above can really be said to have existed before. Yet *invent* cannot be used in place of *discover* in any of the sentences. The reason is syntactical: *discover* can take a noun, clause, or *how to* phrase as its object, but *invent* takes only a noun. Thus in many cases the distinction between the two words will be entirely grammatical, without Noah's semantic considerations entering the question at all.

And when a noun is the direct object? Here we find some disputed usages:

> The material was discovered in 1954 by Goodrich-Gulf scientists —*N.Y. Times*, 16 Oct. 1956

> A number of drug companies that hope to discover new medicines are synthesizing variants of the THC molecule —Solomon H. Snyder, *Psychology Today*, May 1971

The first of these examples refers to a synthetic rubber, and was criticized in *Winners & Sinners* on the basis of Noah Webster's then 128-year-old "what before existed." But it is a good idea to remember that even Noah did not make this criterion part of his definition—it was simply part of a word discrimination. His definition of this sense of *discover* reads:

> To find out; to obtain the first knowledge of; to come to the knowledge of something sought or before unknown.

Nothing in the definition suggests *discover* is inapplicable to synthetic rubber—a substance undreamt of in 1828.

The second example contains an important clue. We have learned a lot more about inventing than was known when Blair and Webster were alive. We now know, for instance, that inventions may have unexpected consequences. Many an inventor who has set out to invent a specific thing has wound up with something that has an entirely different application. A man who hoped to invent an artificial substitute for quinine actually produced the first artificial dye. In other words, he invented a substance and discovered that it had an entirely different use. The same result can occur when scientists synthesize or invent new compounds in hopes of discovering new medicines. *Discover* can suggest serendipity or surprise:

> After trying hundreds of hydrocarbons on several mosquito species, they discovered a hyrdocarbon

approximately thirty-five times more active —Lawrence Locke, *The Lamp,* Summer 1971

To summarize, Noah Webster's "what before existed" applies well enough to *discover* in uses that do not compete at all with *invent.* In some constructions *discover* can be used where *invent* cannot. And in sentences with noun objects where the two words can compete, *discover* is more likely than *invent* to suggest an accidental, unexpected, or merely hoped-for result.

discreet, discrete A number of usage books define *discreet* as "prudent," "judicious," "tactful," or "circumspect" and *discrete* as "separate" or "distinct," with the implication that these are two completely different words which should not be confused. However, the history and spelling of *discreet* and *discrete* are more closely intertwined than is commonly realized. *Discreet* came into Middle English from Middle Latin *discretus* (the past participle of Latin *discernere,* "to separate, distinguish between") via Middle French *discret.* According to the OED, our English word *discrete* came into Middle English as a translation of this same Latin *discretus* in 1398 "but app[arently] was not in general use till late in 16th c[entury]." In its early life *discrete* was sometimes spelled *discreet,* but only rarely. *Discreet,* on the other hand, used to have the spelling *discrete* as a common variant:

... *discrete* was the prevalent spelling in all senses until late in the 16th c., when on the analogy of native or early-adopted words in *ee* from ME. close *ē* (as *feet, sweet, beet),* the spelling *discreet* (occasional from 1400) became established in the popular sense, leaving *discrete* for the scholastic and technical sense in which the kinship to L. *discrētus* is more obvious —OED

Since the first half of the 17th century, the two spellings have been perceived as separate words with separate meanings. In that time, confused spellings have undoubtedly occurred (hence the interest shown by usage book writers). The words are, after all, homophones and can be confused by simply transposing two adjacent letters.

In spite of misspellings the separate identities of the two words have been firmly established. But are they irrevocably established? Although there is no way to tell whether a particular misspelling is merely a typographical error or whether it originated with the author, the "misspelled" forms of *discreet* and *discrete* seem to be appearing more frequently in reputable publications lately. We wonder if a reversion to the days of dual spellings for both words is in the offing. Here are some recent citations:

He is conservatively dressed. . . . so discrete is he that there is almost nothing to mark him physically —*N.Y. Times Mag.,* 27 Apr. 1980

... discretely silent —*Christian Science Monitor,* 26 June 1980

He looks smooth and discrete, like a mortician —*Boston Globe Mag.,* 23 Nov. 1980

... allowing more than a discrete amount of sentiment to filter into my work —*Southwest Art,* September 1984

... tries to count the uncountable (i.e., cultures, which . . . are not discreet units) —*American Anthropologist,* September 1976

... breaking up the desired educational task into discreet parts —*College English,* September 1977

... it is now freed from the limitations of space and polemical purpose which accompanied the original publication. In this extended setting, Professor Raphael is able to provide a discreet analysis of Hobbes on causation —*Times Literary Supp.,* 3 Nov. 1978

The upper notes are distinct and discreet —*Science 80,* May/June 1980

But behind the tangle of Taylors are five discreet performers with a wealth of idiosyncracies —*People,* 22 July 1985

Examples like these, while surprisingly numerous, are by no means usual. The separate identities of the two words remain standard for now.

disinformation There has been some comment about the relatively recent (1939) word *disinformation.* It is not an error for *misinformation,* as has been alleged, nor is it a euphemism for *propaganda.* It means "false information deliberately and often covertly spread." It seems to be used chiefly in the spy business, or, as the current phrase goes, the intelligence-gathering services. Its use has spread to other fields upon occasion. Robert Kirk Mueller (*Buzzwords,* 1974) mentions its occasional use in the business world; our most recent evidence from this sector indicates that it turns up in the mysterious surrounds of hostile corporate takeovers. We have also found it in reference to an ordinary criminal case and to domestic politics:

Much of what Brill told Spear was what the police wanted Spear to hear. Indeed, some of it was untrue—"disinformation." —Timothy Dwyer et al., *Boston Globe Mag.,* 13 Apr. 1980

The press, looking at government, sees a colossus, rich in resources for evasion, disinformation, even intimidation —Hedley Donovan, *Fortune,* 29 Dec. 1980

One of the more interesting facts about this word is that several of its earliest appearances are as translations of the titles of functioning groups within foreign governments:

... Gen. Krivitsky's account of the German "Disinformation Service," engaged in manufacturing fake military plans for the express purpose of having them stolen by foreign governments —*N.Y. Herald Tribune Book Rev.,* 19 Nov. 1939

... Soviet experts, whose special bureau for the purpose bears the stunning, Orwellian title, "Disinformation Office." —Ben H. Bagdikian, *N.Y. Times Mag.,* 14 June 1964

But in 1959 the Kremlin put such operations on a formal basis by establishing within its espionage branch of the KGB, a special Department of Disinformation —Everett G. Martin, *Wall Street Jour.,* 23 Sept. 1971

disinterest, disinterestedness, uninterest Robert F. Ilson, in an article in Greenbaum 1985, states that "the spread of *disinterested* at the expense of *uninterested* is bound to be helped by the existence of the noun *disinterest* and the non-existence of a noun *uninterest.*"

Not only has *disinterest* strengthened the position of the adjective, it has also fueled the controversy surrounding the adjective. For instance, a letter to the editor of the *American Scholar* asks:

> Is the ugly word "disinterest," used to mean "lack of interest," going to have to be accepted? . . . And the noble word "disinterested" is thus being lost —Ruth Shepard Phelps Morand, *American Scholar,* Winter 1949–50

and a writer to the *Times Literary Supplement* finds fault with a sentence containing the words "utter disinterest in other people's opinions," going on to remark:

> The confusion of the word "disinterested" or the use of this new word "disinterest" with the idea of disregard or indifference is becoming common —J. R. Pole, *Times Literary Supp.,* 6 Feb. 1964

And Gowers' paragraph on *disinterested,* added in his 1965 edition of Fowler, contains four citations, two of them for the noun *disinterest.* What of this word *disinterest*?

The OED editor, James A. H. Murray, seems to have had little evidence for the noun. He finds three senses. The first, "something . . . disadvantageous," is labeled "Now *rare*"; the second, "disinterestedness, impartiality," is labeled *"Obs.";* the third, "absence of interest," is labeled *"rare."* The Supplement of 1933 drops the second and third labels, adding citations from the early 20th century. The 1972 Supplement adds nothing to the second sense, but several citations to the third; the "absence of interest" sense appears to be flourishing.

Evidence in the Merriam-Webster files shows that both OED senses 2 and 3 continue in use. Phythian 1979 insists *disinterest* must mean only "impartiality," but he is wrong. Its primary use is to mean "absence of interest":

> This self-contained economy creates in the hillman a comparative disinterest in the world's affairs — *American Guide Series: Arkansas,* 1941

> As a result of general disinterest, the poets of the United States find themselves writing for an audience which grows increasingly smaller —Louis Untermeyer, *Américas,* September 1954

> . . . seemed always to display a disinterest in current affairs —Osbert Lancaster, *With an Eye to the Future,* 1967

> She greeted Moses with marked disinterest —John Cheever, *The Wapshot Chronicle,* 1957

> The officers heard this with disinterest —E. L. Doctorow, *Ragtime,* 1975

> . . . its total disinterest in normal sex —G. Legman, *The Fake Revolt,* 1967

The OED's second sense also is in use:

> . . . Arnold was temperamentally incapable of disinterest where his sense of propriety was outraged — *Times Literary Supp.,* 27 Mar. 1969

> . . . flourish best only as they achieve a degree of disinterest and detachment —Nathan M. Pusey, *President's Report, Harvard University,* 1966–1967

> . . . reexamine these contentious issues . . . with admirable disinterest and dispassion —Bernard Wasserstein, *N.Y. Times Book Rev.,* 24 May 1987

> All these books Irwin feigned to approach with scientific disinterest, but Duddy was not fooled —Mordecai Richler, *The Apprenticeship of Duddy Kravitz,* 1959

This sense might be in more frequent use if it were not in competition with the synonymous *disinterestedness,* which is almost never used except in the sense of "freedom from selfish motive or interest":

> I believe it is generally admitted that one of the ingredients of justice is disinterestedness —Thomas Love Peacock, *Headlong Hall,* 1816

> I had a feeling of noble disinterestedness in my anger —Malcolm Cowley, *Exile's Return,* 1934

> . . . his assumptions of scholarly disinterestedness and moral superiority —Angus Wilson, *Death Dance,* 1957

> . . . no longer enlightened self-interest, but enlightened disinterestedness —Donald Milner, *The Listener,* 30 May 1974

The evidence indicates that *disinterestedness* is quite a bit more frequent than *disinterest* in the same sense. Thus there appears to be a tendency to use *disinterest* for "lack of interest" and *disinterestedness* for "freedom from selfish interest."

The last term of our trio, *uninterest,* does in fact exist. The OED lists a single 1890 example; Merriam-Webster files contain a few others. It means "lack of interest" but is not a commonly used word.

> . . . his blank uninterest in poor and black citizens — Julian Symons, *Times Literary Supp.,* 9 Jan. 1981

> . . . the author expresses marked uninterest in writing about academe —Richard R. Lingeman, *N.Y. Times Book Rev.,* 18 June 1978

Since most of our evidence for this word is fairly recent and comes from sources in which the *disinterested/uninterested* controversy is frequently mentioned, we have some suspicion that *uninterest* may have been used chiefly to avoid the accusation of linguistic wrongdoing that *disinterest* might bring.

disinterested, uninterested Copperud 1970 says the following (among other things) about these words: "The umpire, ideally, would be *disinterested;* one who did not care about the game would be *uninterested.* A useful distinction is being blurred. Flesch concludes the battle is already lost, and Fowler wistfully wonders whether rescue is still possible. . . . Despite the critics, the battle does seem lost. . . ." Dozens of other commentators on the subject echo the same sentiments.

So far from being lost or blurred, however, the ethical sense of *disinterested* makes up more than 70 percent of the citations for the word gathered by Merriam-Webster from about 1934 to the 1970s. It constitutes even more than 70 percent of the citations gathered in the 1980s. The "beautiful older sense of the word" (to quote John Wain, *N.Y. Times Book Rev.,* 20 July 1980) is alive and well, as it has been throughout the 20th century; reports of its demise are greatly exaggerated.

The discovery that *disinterested* and *uninterested* were differentiated in meaning seems to have been an American one, and it was made at nearly the same time as the discovery that *disinterested* was being used to mean "uninterested." Our earliest evidence is from The Century Dictionary of 1889, where in a synonymy the editors note, "*Disinterested* and *uninterested* are sometimes confounded in speech, though rarely in writing." They then distinguish between the two. The first edition (1907) of Woolley 1920 also warns against the confusion. Utter 1916 thinks the "uninterested" sense of *disinterested* is obsolete, but he is alone. MacCracken & Sandison 1917 follow Woolley. (MacCracken & Sandison, incidentally, appear to be the first to use the illustrative phrase "a disinterested judge," which is reused with considerable frequency by usage writers right into the 1980s, notwithstanding that, as far as we can tell, it is almost never used by writers employing *disinterested* in ordinary discourse. We have no citations for it used as an attributive adjective before *judge*.

Several commentators distinguish *disinterested* and *uninterested* in the 20s, 30s, and 40s; lament for the lost distinction does not appear to have begun until about 1950:

> . . . the noble word "disinterested" is thus being lost, because so few writers (and virtually no journalists) will write the word "uninterested" any longer — Ruth Shepard Phelps Morand, letter to the editor, *American Scholar,* Winter 1949–50

> We are always a little sad when we see a word losing a pristine meaning that is still useful. We feel that way about "disinterested," for example — *The Pleasures of Publishing,* July 1953

> More people seem to be saying *disinterested* when they mean *uninterested.* . . . If the Linguistic Scientist found the whole world writing and speaking so, that would only mean that a noble distinction, hard to replace, had been lost — I. A. Richards, *Confluence,* March 1954

The sense of loss continues unabated today:

> . . . she must be—to use a good old word that is rapidly losing its usefulness—disinterested —Wayne C. Booth, in *Introduction to Scholarship in Modern Languages and Literatures,* ed. Joseph Gibaldi, 1981

The notion that the ethical sense is older (as expressed by John Wain, above, and numerous others) is erroneous. The OED shows that the earlier sense of *disinterested* is the simple negative of *interested;* it is dated before 1612; the earliest attestation of the ethical sense is 1659. Curiously, the earliest uses of *uninterested* are for ethical senses (both 17th century); the modern use is not attested until 1771. The OED editor, James A. H. Murray, was uncertain of the status in his time of the simple negative sense of *disinterested,* marking it "? *Obs*[olete]." The 1933 Supplement removed the label and presented, without comment, three modern citations, all British, all dated 1928. This evidence refutes the assertion of Anthony Burgess, quoted in Harper 1985, that this use of *disinterested* is "one of the worst of all American solecisms." On the contrary, it is the discovery of the usage problem that is American. The, issue was unknown to Fowler 1926 (the Fowler mentioned by Copperud 1970 is, in fact, Sir Ernest Gowers in his 1965 revision of Fowler), and it is unremarked in the 1933 OED Supplement. Treble & Vallins 1937 make the distinction; Partridge 1942 calls the use of *disinterested* for *uninterested* a mistake; the 1972 OED Supplement notes that it is "Often regarded as a loose use." The vehemence of opinion directed against the earliest sense of *disinterested* appears to have increased over the years with American leadership. Harper 1985, for example, shows 100 percent rejection of the use; in 1975 it had only been 91 percent.

We have mentioned the OED evidence. What of other dictionaries? Samuel Johnson in 1755 recognizes both the ethical and the simple negative senses of *disinterested;* he lists the ethical sense first—it was his own use:

> Sir, you have a right to that kind of respect, and are arguing for yourself. I am supporting the principle, and am disinterested in doing it, as I have no such right —quoted in James Boswell, *Life of Samuel Johnson,* 1791

Noah Webster in 1828 also recognizes both senses, and he adds this comment: "This word is more generally used than *uninterested.*" Webster's observation still holds true, and it is likely that the relative infrequency of *uninterested* has contributed to the continued use of *disinterested* in its place.

What of actual usage, historical and modern? As with many issues of English usage, when much heat of opinion is generated, the subtleties of genuine use by purposeful writers are frequently overlooked (compare, for instance, ENORMITY, ENORMOUSNESS). The evidence shows a marked distinction between the way in which the ethical sense is used and that in which the simple negative sense is used. The ethical sense is applied more than half of the time to abstract nouns:

> Disinterested intellectual curiosity is the life-blood of real civilization —G. M. Trevelyan, *English Social History,* 1942

> . . . because a disinterested love of learning is here first implanted in its students —Nathan M. Pusey, "A Program for Harvard College," 8 Oct. 1956

> . . . the old man was tripped up by a gaily-colored hoop sent rolling at him, with a kind of disinterested deliberation, by a grim little girl —James Thurber, *Fables for Our Time, and Famous Poems Illustrated,* 1940

Jane Austen uses the term with a suggestion of being free from selfish sexual motive:

> He was now the Mr. Crawford who was addressing herself with ardent, disinterested love; whose feelings were apparently become all that was honourable and upright —*Mansfield Park,* 1814

This use finds an occasional modern echo:

> Usually it was just the three of us, but we would often end the evening with a friend of his. These junkets were in all ways delightful and disinterested. Lewis had a serious interest in a classmate of Elaine; and at that time neither Elaine nor I had any serious interests whatever —Katherine Hoskins, "Notes on a Navy Childhood," *Prose,* 1974

You will perceive that these two uses are not far from the simple negative sense, except that the underlying *interested* is in these cases more heavily charged with meaning than it usually is at present. The word *interested,* indeed, was a more intense word in the past than now:

> No day has passed . . . without my most interested wishes for your health —Samuel Pepys, letter, 4 Sept. 1665 (OED)

Here *interested* is close in meaning to modern uses of *concerned.* It is the greater intensity of *interested* that makes earlier simple negative uses of *disinterested* hard for us moderns to distinguish from uses of the ethical sense. Here is Jane Austen again; the interest must be chiefly monetary:

> His choice is disinterested, at least, for he must know my father can give her nothing —*Pride and Prejudice,* 1813

The ethical sense is also applied to people:

> ... in which we see the best side of the people and their most disinterested selves —Roger N. Baldwin, *Civil Liberties,* March 1955

> ... to insure that all work is well evaluated ... by knowledgeable yet disinterested referees —Eugene Wall, *American Documentation,* April 1967

> Don't you think that priests make more disinterested rulers than lay politicians? —Wilfrid Sheed, *People Will Always Be Kind,* 1973

It is when the ethical sense is applied to people that its meaning can be understood as the simple negative sense, especially if the construction and context are not unmistakable:

> A clergyman cannot be disinterested about theology, nor a soldier about war —Bertrand Russell, *Education and The Good Life,* 1926

The construction in which *disinterested* is followed by a preposition can create some ambiguity and raise the possibility of misinterpretation, especially when the moral sense is the one intended. The modern simple negative sense is followed by a preposition just about half the time, but it is almost always *in:*

> Unsocial, but not antisocial. ... Contemptuous of other people. Disinterested in women —Dr. James A. Brussel, profile of a so-called "Mad Bomber," reprinted in *Rolling Stone,* 15 Nov. 1979

The simple negative sense, in its earlier uses, carries the stronger senses of *interested,* which are now largely out of use. Here is an example of it in a context where lack of financial interest is the underlying meaning:

> But they are far from being disinterested, and if they are the most trustworthy ... , they in general demand for the transport of articles, a sum at least double to what others of the trade would esteem a reasonable recompense —George Borrow, *The Bible in Spain,* 1843

By the early 20th century, our weakened sense of *interested* is detectable in the use of *disinterested:*

> The only discordant note now is the services conducted perfunctorily by ignorant or disinterested priests —William Roscoe Thayer, letter, 26 Oct. 1906

> ... an editor who in a disinterested voice sat issuing assignments for the day —Ben Hecht, *Erik Dorn,* 1921

> The inquiry was answered in a vague and disinterested manner —*The Spectator,* 1 May 1926

In most recent citations, the weakening is patent:

> Although Sister Bear is anxious to learn baseball, Papa Bear forces lessons on her disinterested brother —*TV Guide,* 2 May 1985

Lamberts 1972 makes the point that in English many pairs beginning with *dis-* and *un-* are differentiated:

unarmed, disarmed; unengaged, disengaged; unproved, disproved; unable, disable; unaffected, disaffected; unconnected, disconnected. He notes the *dis-* in each case means "was once but is no longer," "From here," he says, "it is only a short jump to *uninterested, disinterested.*" This meaning of *dis-* does, in fact, color many uses of *disinterested,* beginning early in the 20th century:

> When I grow tired or disinterested in anything, I experience a disgust —Jack London, letter, 24 Feb. 1914

> What often happens in such cases is that husband and wife become disinterested in each other —Theodore Isaac Rubin, *Ladies' Home Jour.,* September 1971

> Those spotted are usually taught so slowly they grow disinterested and quit —*N.Y. Times,* 25 June 1967

> ... I can recall that I was becoming increasingly disinterested in physical exertion and exercise —Mort Diamond, *Scouting,* April 1966

The simple negative sense of *disinterested,* then, has lost, with the weakening of *interested,* the more highly charged meaning that it had in the 17th to 19th centuries, but it has gained a subsense with the meaning "having lost interest."

Uninterested is, of course, in use, although with not so great a frequency as *disinterested* in the same sense. Here are a few examples:

> ... but the greater part of the young gentlemen having no particular parents to speak of, were wholly uninterested in the thing —Charles Dickens, *Nicholas Nickleby,* 1839

> ... seems totally uninterested in Manhattan, its bright lights, glamour, style —Curry Kirkpatrick, *Sports Illustrated,* 26 Nov. 1984

> My fear of deep water left the Navy simply uninterested —Russell Baker, *Growing Up,* 1982

Conclusion: The alleged confusion between *disinterested* and *uninterested* does not exist. Nor has the ethical sense of *disinterested* been lost—Merriam-Webster files show it used more than twice as often as the other senses. *Disinterested* carries the bulk of use for all meanings; *uninterested* is much less frequently used. In current use, *disinterested* has three meanings: an ethical one, "free from selfish motive or bias"; a simple negative one, "not interested"; and a slightly more emphatic one, "having lost interest." Of these the simple negative is the oldest, the ethical one next, and "having lost interest" the most recent.

The ethical sense of *disinterested* is applied both to human and abstract subjects, but more often to the latter; the simple negative sense is usually applied to human subjects. About half the time it is used in the construction *disinterested in*—this construction is not used for the ethical sense.

Uninterested originally had ethical senses (its earliest), which appear to be dead, although a Harper 1975 usage panelist noted getting a letter from a lawyer referring to "uninterested witnesses." A single citation, however, is not sufficient evidence to attest to a survival of the older meaning.

For another contributor to the *disinterested/uninterested* problem, see DISINTEREST, DISINTERESTEDNESS, UNINTEREST.

disinterestedness See DISINTEREST, DISINTERESTED-NESS, UNINTEREST.

disjuncts See IRONICALLY.

dislike 1. *Noun.* Partridge 1942 says *dislike to* is incorrect and should be *dislike of*. We disagree. *Dislike* can take the prepositions *of, for,* and *to; to* is the least common. A few examples:

> . . . his dislike of Robbe-Grillet is bizarre —*Times Literary Supp.,* 19 June 1969

> . . . a wholesome dislike of sophistry and rhetoric — W. R. Inge, *The Church in the World,* 1928

> Dislike of America ran much deeper —*Time,* 13 Jan. 1947

> . . . contempt and dislike for human beings —Angus Wilson, *The Middle Age of Mrs. Eliot,* 1958

> The coyote, which has an atavistic dislike for water —*National Geographic,* October 1939

> Burger's dislike for television cameras —Cynthia Mills, *UPI Reporter,* 21 June 1979

> My dislike for the tidies of the world is particularly strong this week —*And More by Andy Rooney,* 1982

> I have always had a dislike to managers losing money over me —W. Somerset Maugham, *The Summing Up,* 1938

> . . . a man who takes an unreasonable dislike to another —*Time,* 26 May 1952

> The flour took a cordial dislike to the eggs and humped itself up —*Boy's Life,* May 1952

It would appear that *take a dislike* tends to select *to* as its preposition.

2. *Verb.* Besides a noun object, the verb *dislike* can take a participial phrase or an infinitive phrase, according to Evans 1959. Longman 1984 says that the infinitive complement is not possible in British English; our evidence is not extensive enough to confirm but certainly does not refute. It is possible in American English, though not common and especially rare in edited prose. The *-ing* construction is more common. An example of each:

> . . . reports that Miss West disliked working with Fields —*Current Biography,* November 1967

> I dislike to bother you with "trivia" —letter received at Merriam-Webster from Forest Park, Illinois, 26 Jan. 1983

dismayed Colter 1981 recommends *with* after *dismayed,* which is a little surprising, as *by* is the usual preposition. *With* and *at* may also be used:

> Dismayed by the plans —*Current Biography,* July 1965

> . . . dismayed by the fall of Premier Mendes-France —Mollie Panter-Downes, *New Yorker,* 19 Feb. 1955

> Dickens . . . was dismayed by the little he received for the huge success of his *Christmas Carol* — George Bernard Shaw, *American Mercury,* January 1946

> I am dismayed by the frequent assumption of our modern critics that only nervous degenerates can really write —Harold J. Laski, letter, 19 Feb. 1917

> . . . became dismayed with the timidity and nationalist bickering displayed there —*Current Biography,* September 1953

> . . . was dismayed at the "yawning listlessness" of many —*Dictionary of American Biography,* 1928

disparate Reader's Digest 1983 notes *disparate* as a useful word meaning "strongly different, differing in real character." Safire 1984 disputes this use, feeling that *disparate* means "unequal" rather than "markedly dissimilar." It does seem to mean "unequal" in some legal contexts, notably in the phrase *disparate treatment,* which crops up in employment-discrimination cases. And inequality can easily be seen in uses such as these:

> . . . election of local government officials from districts of disparate size —*American School Board Jour.,* June 1968

> . . . economically disparate groups do not make congenial neighbors —Urban Land Institute finding, in *Center Mag.,* September 1968

> . . . enjoying disparate levels of development — Claude A. Buss, *Wilson Library Bulletin,* November 1968

> The book consists of two rather disparate parts —A. H. Stride, *Nature,* 15 Feb. 1969

Still, "markedly dissimilar" is the most frequent sense. It is hard to find the notion of inequality in these examples:

> . . . few areas of study offer as much scope for tantalizing speculation as the disparate fields of astronomy and molecular biology —*Britannica Yearbook of Science and the Future,* 1969

> Pianists as disparate as Vladimir Horowitz and Fats Waller get equal consideration —Hans Fantel, *N.Y. Times Book Rev.,* 22 July 1979

> . . . romantic encounters with four disparate women —*Boston Spectator,* October 1966

> . . . the disparate interests of heterogeneous faculties —Lewis B. Mayhew, *Change,* March 1972

> The welding together of such disparate creeds into a coherent work of art is in itself no mean achievement —*Envoy,* May 1968

Disparate is also used of what is made up of diverse or incongruous elements:

> This disparate and uneasy coalition —Maurice R. Berube, *Commonweal,* 11 Apr. 1969

> At first the cast Visconti has chosen seems quite disparate —Frederic Morton, *Harper's,* April 1970

> . . . a disparate gathering of art that hasn't focused on any one period or style —David L. Shirey, *N.Y. Times,* 14 July 1971

Disparate is occasionally accompanied by intensifiers (*totally* and *wildly* are favorites). Since *disparate* is already a stronger word than *different,* some would no doubt find the intensifiers unnecessary. We add here a few examples; you can decide for yourself whether you would use them.

> . . . a doomed attempt to bind together two totally disparate sections of Asia —James A. Michener, *N.Y. Times Mag.,* 9 Jan. 1972

They have wildly disparate personalities —Barbara Walters, *McCall's,* November 1970

. . . students of widely disparate experience and ability —Barbara Bock, *Media & Methods,* March 1969

. . . look at divorce from totally disparate points of view —Arthur Knight, *Saturday Rev.,* 13 May 1972

dispassionate, impassionate Although The Right Handbook 1986 warns against confusing these words, we think you have little reason to worry. The basis for the warning seems to be that there are two adjectives *impassionate,* one of which means "impassioned" and the other "dispassionate." That situation does sound like a potential source of confusion. But neither of these adjectives seems to have been used since the middle of the 19th century, and both were rare to begin with. We doubt you will need either of them, with *impassioned* and *dispassionate* currently available.

dispense When *dispense* is used with a preposition, *with* is the usual choice, since *dispense with* is a fixed expression with its own meanings, "to suspend the operation of" and "to do without":

. . . why the government is so vigorously asserting its right to dispense with warrants in national-security cases —Alan M. Dershowitz, *Commentary,* January 1972

Miss de Momerie seemed ready to dispense with convention —Dorothy L. Sayers, *Murder Must Advertise,* 1933

When the verb is used in any of its senses involving portioning out or administering and the phrase denotes the receiver, *dispense* is naturally used with *to:*

We were in Yeats' debt because he dispensed some of his worthwhile sketches to his humble listeners — Fred R. Jones, *N.Y. Times Book Rev.,* 16 May 1954

When it is used in the less frequent meaning "to exempt," *dispense* may be found with *from:*

. . . claiming to dispense the clergy from obeying the very laws which as bishops they are pledged to enforce —W. R. Inge, *The Church in the World,* 1928

disposal, disposition The comments about *disposal* and *disposition* made by Fowler 1926 and revived by a few latter-day usage writers are correct for the most part. The two words overlap in some areas of usage, but each tends to specialize in certain jobs.
Disposal refers to the getting rid of or destruction of something. It also gets used in the phrases *at one's disposal* and *at the disposal of.* Instances in which *disposition* replaces *disposal* in these uses are quite uncommon:

. . . the disposal of 300 tons of solid waste —*Annual Report, Eastman Kodak Co.,* 1970

. . . can use any means at their disposal —James F. Reed III, *Center Mag.,* May 1969

. . . to place the facilities of both institutions at the disposal of graduate students —*Current Biography,* December 1964

Disposition is the usual choice when talking about things that are administered, arranged, settled, or taken care of; *disposal* is only infrequently used in such cases.

And *disposal* does not, of course, refer to temperament or inclination, as *disposition* does.

. . . had informed Octavian of the general plan . . . and he made his dispositions accordingly —John Buchan, *Augustus,* 1937

. . . disposition of the 800,000 wretched Arab refugees —Adlai E. Stevenson, *Look,* 22 Sept. 1953

. . . the board's disposition of his case —*AAUP Bulletin,* December 1967

. . . the future disposition of the Panama Canal — Stanley Karnow, *Saturday Rev.,* 24 July 1976

. . . showed no disposition to be bored —Vita Sackville-West, *The Edwardians,* 1930

dispossess *Dispossess* is sometimes used with a preposition. When it is, *of* is the one generally used, although the use of *from* is also attested:

. . . dispossessing the nobles of their wealth —C. B. A. Behrens, *N.Y. Rev. of Books,* 3 June 1971

. . . dispossessing the French from the southern shores of the Mediterranean —Percy Winner, *New Republic,* 9 June 1952

disqualify When used with a preposition, *disqualify* is used with either *from* or *for:*

. . . Teachers of English or even of writing are not thereby disqualified from writing stories —William Saroyan, *N.Y. Times Book Rev.,* 8 June 1980

. . . failure to pass [examinations] would presumably disqualify them for parenthood —Vance Packard, *Saturday Rev.,* 20 Aug. 1977

disregard The noun *disregard* may be followed by *for* or *of.* At one time use of *of* predominated; now the two appear with about equal frequency:

. . . the slave-owners' total disregard for the humanity of their workers —*Times Literary Supp.,* 27 Aug. 1971

. . . his flip disregard for the consequences of his actions —Arthur Knight, *Saturday Rev.,* 26 June 1954

The disregard for Japanese interests shown in the way the President moved toward Peking —Leslie H. Gelb & Morton H. Halperin, *Harper's,* November 1971

. . . the disregard of the true shape of things themselves —Laurence Binyon, *The Flight of the Dragon,* 1911

. . . a disregard of the judicial system —Julian Towster, *Saturday Rev.,* 19 Dec. 1953

. . . the Administration's disregard of the realities of power —Richard J. Whalen, *Harper's,* August 1971

The phrases *with disregard for, with disregard of* are both quite common; however, when *disregard* is preceded by *in,* it is followed by *of:*

. . . with contemptuous disregard of the rights — Robert Ellis Standen, *Atlantic,* October 1940

... with complete disregard of danger —*Current Biography,* February 1953

... with ruthless disregard for the exhaustibility of the resources they exploited —Joseph Kinsey Howard, *Yale Rev.,* Spring 1947

... rears her orphaned nephew with a disregard for convention —*Current Biography,* September 1967

... he was like a flame burning on in miraculous disregard of the fact that there was no more fuel —Aldous Huxley, *The Olive Tree,* 1937

... can no longer pursue their destinies in disregard of others.... —Wyndham White, quoted in *Time,* 26 May 1967

Disregard has been used with *to,* but very infrequently:

... a total disregard to the ordinary decencies —Charles G. Norris, *Brass,* 1921

disremember On the whole, criticism of *disremember* has softened over time. Bache 1869 labels it both "obsolete" and "a low vulgarism." Ayres 1881 says it is "vulgarly used in the sense of *forget.*" Vizetelly 1906 commands: "Avoid this term as provincial and archaic, and use *forget* instead." Krapp 1927 says it is "dialectal and humorous." Shaw gives an old-fashionedly harsh opinion in 1970 ("An illiteracy. Never use this word in standard English.") but has mellowed somewhat by 1975 ("This word is dialectal rather than illiterate, but good speakers prefer *forget* or *fail to remember*"). Reader's Digest 1983 calls *disremember* "a dialectal word" which "is sometimes used by standard speakers for folksy effect; this is an informal use."

So much for opinion; now for the actual evidence. *Disremember* can be found in dialect studies of the U.S. (especially the South) and Great Britain. It has been used in narrative and dialogue by fictional characters from various parts of the U.S., often with humorous effect or to suggest the rustic and uneducated. And it is very occasionally found in nonfiction.

... there didn't happen to be no candle burnin if I don't disremember —Frances Miriam Whitcher, "Hezekiah Bedott," 1855, in *The Mirth of a Nation,* ed. Walter Blair & Raven I. McDavid, Jr., 1983

"... one of those Massachusetts fellers—I disremember his name...." —Kenneth Roberts, *Oliver Wiswell,* 1940

"It was the British who did it," I said quickly. "I disremember the place and time" —E. L. Doctorow, *Loon Lake,* 1979

... when the composer, well on toward the patriarchal age of eighty-one ..., disremembered so much —Irving Kolodin, *Saturday Rev.,* 29 May 1954

We are not sure how common *disremember* is in standard spoken English, though it does not appear in the million-word corpus analyzed by Hartvig Dahl in *Word Frequencies of Spoken American English* (1979). Nonetheless, we suspect that it is basically a spoken word that only occasionally finds its way into print, and then usually for a particular effect.

dissatisfied, unsatisfied Though *dissatisfied* and *unsatisfied* appear to be synonyms, there are distinctions evident in the usage examples in the Merriam-Webster files. These examples show that *unsatisfied* is more frequently used to modify nonhuman terms (such as *ambition, debts, curiosity, demands, claims*) than human ones and that in all instances the meaning is generally of something or someone being "unfulfilled" or "unappeased":

... although every one was curious the curiosity was unsatisfied —Sherwood Anderson, *Poor White,* 1920

... the deep creative instinct within her ... is teased, suppressed, tantalized, unsatisfied —John Cowper Powys, *The Meaning of Culture,* 1939

... a large unsatisfied demand for education at university level —*Times Literary Supp.,* 5 Feb. 1970

Dissatisfied, in contrast, is used primarily with respect to persons or groups in the sense of "not pleased or gratified":

Dissatisfied landowners stopped action —*American Guide Series: Minnesota,* 1938

... the young adult is dissatisfied more often with the job than the older worker —Dale B. Harris, in *Automation, Education and Human Values,* ed. W. W. Brickman & S. Lehrer, 1966

While both *dissatisfied* and *unsatisfied,* when used with a preposition, are usually followed by *with,* both words, according to our evidence, may be followed by *by:*

... became dissatisfied with most of what was then known ... as psychological research —David Loye, *Psychology Today,* 12 May 1971

They were unsatisfied with the composition of the appointed embassy —William Mitford, *History of Greece,* 1808 (OED)

... he was dissatisfied by the picture she represented —Eric Linklater, *Private Angelo,* 1946

... unsatisfied by what he characterized as "nothing but double talk" —*Library Jour.,* 1 Dec. 1966

dissemble See DISASSEMBLE 1.

dissent Language commentators have for some time discussed the use of *dissent* followed by the preposition *with.* From the evidence in the Merriam-Webster files, it appears *dissent with* is not found in 20th-century writing. The OED records it, but labels the use of *with* obsolete and shows only a 1710 quotation from Addison. The OED and our files agree that *dissent from* is the usual combination:

All who dissent from its orthodox doctrines are scoundrels —H. L. Mencken, *Prejudices: Second Series,* 1923

... he must dissent from the central doctrine of that encyclical —Neil H. Jacoby, "The Progress of Peoples," 1969

The use of *dissent to* has also raised some hackles in the past. While it is not a very common usage, it may still be found, along with *dissent against:*

... dissenting to the most outrageous invasion of private right ever set forth as a decison of the court —Julian P. Boyd, *American Scholar,* Winter 1952–1953

It is summarized, dissented against and reviewed at ever-higher levels —David Binder, *N.Y. Times,* 26 Dec. 1976

The noun *dissent,* when used with a preposition, is usually followed by *from:*

> ... was writing in dissent from a majority position —Willard Gaylin, *Harper's,* November 1971

Rarely it may also be found with *to:*

> ... Maryland had confirmed its 88-year-old dissent to the 14th Amendment —*Time,* 18 Apr. 1955

dissimilar Some language commentators insist that *dissimilar* should be followed by *to* when it needs the complement or a prepositional phrase, but in actual usage, *dissimilar* is just as likely to be followed by *from:*

> These pumps ... were not dissimilar to those once familiar to everyone on a farm —James B. Conant, *On Understanding Science,* 1947

> ... but the military requirements are not dissimilar from those for defense —Fletcher Pratt, *New Republic,* 24 Feb. 1941

dissociate, disassociate *Dissociate* and *disassociate* share the sense "to separate from association or union with another," and either word may be used in that sense. *Dissociate* is recommended by a number of commentators on the ground that it is shorter, which it is by a grand total of two letters—not the firmest ground for decision. One commentator (Colter 1981) thinks *dissociate* is older, but he has not looked in the OED: *disassociate* dates from 1603, *dissociate* from 1623. Both words are in current good use, but *dissociate* is used more often. That may be grounds for your decision.

When used with a preposition, both *dissociate* and *disassociate* are usually used with *from:*

> ... some flight attendants dissociate themselves from the job —Gail Sheehy, *N.Y. Times Book Rev.,* 23 Oct. 1983

> ... she tries to disassociate herself from the film's apocalyptic ending —Stephen J. Sansweet, *Wall Street Jour.,* 10 Dec. 1981

Both words, however, are used with other prepositions from time to time:

> ... the restaurant, which he became disassociated with in June 1983 —Julie Gilbert, *Houston Post,* 3 Sept. 1984

> ... Albertine is ... dissociated into so many different images —Edmund Wilson, *Axel's Castle,* 1931

> ... there is a rule in English which dissociates consonants out of the onsets of unstressed syllables — program of annual meeting, Linguistic Society of America, 27–30 Dec. 1983

Dissociate has a chemical sense which *disassociate* lacks and which can take the preposition *into:*

> ... hydrochloric acid dissociates into hydrogen ions and chloride ions —William D. McElroy, *Cellular Physiology and Biochemistry,* 1961

distaff Although disparaged by Copperud 1964, 1970, 1980 as "journalese" and by Flesh 1964 as pretentious, and viewed cautiously by Reader's Digest 1983 as liable to annoy women, the adjective use of *distaff* shows no sign of waning usage. Its primary use is as an alternative to *female.* Here are some current examples:

> ... felt that most tournaments did not allot a big enough share of the prize money to the distaff side of the proceedings —Herbert Warren Wind, *New Yorker,* 2 Oct. 1971

> ... a serious and thoughtful study of the distaff Ivy League colleges —Marylin Bender, *N.Y. Times Book Rev.,* 17 Oct. 1976

> ... the distaff tradition in English fiction —Albert H. Johnston, *Publishers Weekly,* 10 Jan. 1977

> ... even other women in the audience sometimes seem embarrassed at the outrageous things they hear from a distaff comic —Karen Stabiner, *Mother Jones,* July 1979

> ... spun off a distaff line after women began snapping up her small size men's jackets —Martha K. Babcock, *People,* 2 Mar. 1981

> ... the first distaff jockey to win a race in Mexico — *Horse Illustrated,* July 1980

It is also applied to horses with some frequency:

> Another with notable distaff relations is Mr. D. Simpson's Joshua colt from the Sandwich Stakes heroine Mayfell —Alan Yuill Walker, *British Racehorse,* October 1979

> Delta Marron is the top weight in the distaff field and probably will be the post time choice in the race off her impressive record —Ed Fricke, *Times-Picayune* (New Orleans), 22 Sept. 1979

> ... the distaff side was asserting its earning power in the minds of buyers, owners and breeders —Wendy Insinger, *Town & Country,* July 1981

> Two distaff champions, Landaluce and Princess Rooney, both completed their 2-year-old campaigns undefeated —Janet Carlson, *Town & Country,* July 1983

Our evidence at the present time shows little objection to the adjective *distaff* by women writers. It seems possible that its etymological connection is remote enough even to be unknown to many who use it, and it seems not to have been used with a disparaging intent. It would thus appear to be an acceptable alternative to *female,* if you need one.

distaste When used with a preposition, *distaste* overwhelmingly takes *for:*

> ... made no effort to conceal his distaste for the drink —Terry Southern, *Flash and Filigree,* 1958

> ... had an obvious distaste for the corruption of modern politics —Irving Howe, *Harper's,* January 1969

Less often, *distaste* may also be used with *at, of, toward,* or *towards:*

> ... the girls in Women's Lib who talk about their distaste at being thought of as sex objects —John Corry, *Harper's,* November 1970

> ... well known for his distaste of books too forthrightly sexual —Norman Mailer, *Advertisements for Myself,* 1959

. . . the attitude of fear and distaste toward mathematics — Bruce Dearing, in *Automation, Education and Human Values,* ed. W. W. Brickman & S. Lehrer, 1966

. . . the personal distaste Churchill and deGaulle nursed towards each other —*Atlantic,* October 1945

distill, distil *Distill* and *distil* are variant spellings, and although the spelling *distil* is used in contemporary writing, *distill* is found far more often. The word may be used with any one of various prepositions, but it occurs most frequently with either *from* or *into:*

. . . in 600 pages of conference documentation, distilled from many thousands of pages —Barry Commoner, *Harper's,* June 1972

. . . has distilled into these two volumes a lifetime of research and thought —Allan Nevins, "Book-of-the-Month-Club News," December 1945

Other prepositions used with *distill* are *out of, through,* and *to:*

. . . the preciousness of existence may be distilled out of its very precariousness —Frederick Morton, *Saturday Rev.,* 22 May 1954

Most filmmakers distill life through the conventions of fiction —Susan Rice, *Media & Methods,* March 1969

Distilled to its essence, the Marshall Plan is simply this —Clarence B. Randall, *Atlantic,* October 1950

Of is a much less common alternative to *from* and *out of:*

. . . the place had an overmastering silence, a quiet distilled of the blue heavens —John Buchan, *Castle Gay,* 1930

distinctive, distinct, distinguished Several fairly recent British publications (as Sellers 1975, Chambers 1985) warn against confusing *distinctive* with *distinct* and a few, mostly American, ones (as Copperud 1970, 1980) warn against confusing *distinctive* with *distinguished.* We are frankly puzzled by all these warnings, for we have no recent evidence that suggests any confusion at all. The words are adequately defined in standard dictionaries and require no further clarification here. We offer a few typical examples of each:

. . . the platypus has a distinct reptilian walk —Janet L. Hopson, *Smithsonian,* January 1981

The functions of banking as distinct from the procedures —Martin Mayer, *The Bankers,* 1974

The reprinting of old guide books, then, is a distinct service to scholars —*Times Literary Supp.,* 19 Feb. 1971

. . . science fiction is as distinct a genre as satire or comedy —Murray Leinster, *The Writer,* May 1968

. . . what its distinctive contribution is to society — Robert A. Nisbet, *Psychology Today,* March 1971

To be sexy to a woman, a man must be distinctive —David R. Reuben, M.D., *Woman's Day,* October 1971

The distinctive feature of this compilation was its emphasis on science —*Times Literary Supp.,* 19 Feb. 1971

. . . acted in 1527 before Henry VIII and a distinguished audience —F. P. Wilson, *The English Drama 1485–1585,* 1968

. . . a distinguished writer in the field of nature and the wilderness —David McCord, *Saturday Rev.,* 25 Mar. 1972

. . . even the layman was able to make distinguished contributions —Nicolas H. Charney, *Saturday Rev.,* 19 Feb. 1972

distinguish When *distinguish* is used with a preposition, the preposition is most likely to be either *between* or *from.* They are used with about equal frequency:

. . . a child under four will hardly distinguish between yesterday and a week ago —Bertrand Russell, *Education and the Good Life,* 1926

. . . a transistorized instrument accurate enough to distinguish between sandy, hard, or rocky bottom — Jan Adkins, *Harper's,* October 1971

It had its stone wall . . . to protect it, distinguishing it from an open village —G. M. Trevelyan, *English Social History,* 1942

. . . permits us to distinguish the styles of the North American Indians . . . from those of the better-known African, Mesoamerican and South Pacific primitive cultures —Barbara Rose, *New York,* 10 Jan. 1972

Less often, *distinguish* is used with *among.* From the few examples which we have of *among,* it seems that the writers may have been influenced by the notion that *between* can be used only of two items and that *among* must be used for more than two:

. . . impossible to distinguish among the fat vases, fancy lampshades, and ladies' hats —David Denby, *Atlantic,* September 1971

See BETWEEN 1.

Very infrequently, *distinguish* may be used with *into:*

The following is a summary of the various suggestions . . . distinguished into the following categories —Felix M. Keesing, *Social Anthropology in Polynesia,* 1953

And we have one citation for *distinguish* with *above:*

. . . what distinguishes his memoir above others —S. L. A. Marshall, *Saturday Rev.,* 17 Apr. 1954

distinguished See DISTINCTIVE, DISTINCT, DISTINGUISHED.

distract See DETRACT, DISTRACT.

distrait Longman 1984 objects to the use of *distrait* in the sense "anxious," a gloss which the writer of the usage note extracted from the definition "inattentive or mildly distraught because of anxiety or apprehension"; the abridgment seems rather to misrepresent the problem. Bryson 1984 distinguishes *distrait* from *distraught.* Fowler 1907, 1926, 1965 objects generally to use of the term as a pretentious Gallicism.

Distrait is a fairly rare literary word. The fact that it is mentioned as a usage problem only in British books and dictionaries would suggest it is more commonly used in British English than in American English, but we do have American evidence. It has an unusual history. The OED shows that it was used in the 14th and 15th centuries in a sense approximating "distraught." It appears to have been reborrowed from French in a milder sense during the 18th century (no direct connection can be established from the 15th century to the 18th). The word *absentminded* has been used to define the reborrowed use since Webster 1864. This definition was probably brought over from French dictionaries by translation, and it is unfortunate, because in English *absentminded* suggests a habitual condition and *distrait* does not.

Another peculiarity of the word is that it tends to be treated in English as if it were still a French word: it is frequently italicized, it has a feminine variant *distraite* like a French adjective, and it is pronounced as if French. It thus tends to advertise the self-consciousness with which it is used.

The word, partly because of its low frequency, is difficult for lexicographers to define. It fits into a group of words including *abstracted, absent, absentminded, distracted, distraught,* and *preoccupied,* but its placement in the group is not perfectly clear. Sometimes it suggests agitation and is fairly close to, but apparently not as strong as, *distraught:*

> She sat on thorns, and was so distrait she could hardly answer the simplest question —Charles Reade, *Put Yourself in His Place,* 1870

> The hall porter, seeing her a little *distraite,* went up to her and asked if he could assist madame in any way —M. Barnard Eldershaw, *The Glasshouse,* 1937

> ... she habitually seated herself on any paper or papers she had collected; at the post, to be forced off her papers by any duty made her as *distraite* as a mother bird —Elizabeth Bowen, *The Heat of the Day,* 1949

More often it seems to indicate such a preoccupation of mind as makes the subject unaware of his or her immediate surroundings; it suggests mental agitation but no specific cause. In the first of these examples, the subject is in love; in the second he has seen a ghostly friar; the third subject has just murdered her husband.

> Scythrop grew every day more reserved, mysterious, and *distrait;* and gradually lengthened the duration of his diurnal seclusions in his tower —Thomas Love Peacock, *Nightmare Abbey,* 1818

> And Juan took his place, he knew not where,
> Confused, in the confusion, and distrait,
> And sitting as if nail'd upon his chair:
> Though knives and forks clank'd round as in a fray,
> He seem'd unconscious of all passing there
> —Lord Byron, *Don Juan,* Canto xvi, 1824

> She was just a touch distraite throughout the evening, and her friends rallied her jocosely because she could not bear to spend even a few hours at the theater without her Ernest —Katherine Anne Porter, *Ladies' Home Jour.,* August 1971

> ... the signs of boredom under the perfection of the royal manner. Not that the King could be called distrait; no, but he had begun to fiddle with the silver bracelet round his wrist —Vita Sackville-West, *The Edwardians,* 1930

distrustful *Of* is the preposition used with *distrustful:*

> ... the Russians were at once distrustful of their new comrades —William L. Shirer, *The Rise and Fall of the Third Reich,* 1960

dive, dived See DOVE.

divest When followed by a prepositional phrase, *divest* appears with *of:*

> It will divest itself of its local phone companies —Laura Landro, *Wall Street Jour.,* 18 Mar. 1982

> ... divesting themselves of all claim to moral and intellectual leadership —George F. Kennan, *New Republic,* 24 Aug. 1953

> ... as if his woolen small-clothes had been disarranged in the divesting of his street-coat —Flann O'Brien, *At Swim-Two-Birds,* 1939

It is interesting to note that until recently, *divest* in its business sense was usually a reflexive verb, as shown in the first example above. Although that usage is still predominant, another has recently cropped up alongside it in which *divest* takes as a direct object the thing that is given up:

> GAF Corp. is in the process of divesting eight businesses—about half of its revenue base —*Business Week,* 1 June 1981

Barzun 1985 considers that, with this use, "an important verb has lost its bearings." This use might be seen as a contemporary revival of a sense "to lay aside, abandon" labeled "now rare" in the OED and "archaic" in Webster's Third, though earlier instances of this sense show no orientation to business. But whether the recent use is a new sense or a revival, we must wait to see how well it establishes itself.

divide 1. The verb *divide* is used with a large number of prepositions, some of which are used rarely, others of which are used frequently. In the Merriam-Webster citation files there are occasional instances of *divide* being used with *as to, to, against,* and *towards,* but there is extensive evidence for its use, depending upon the sense, with a variety of other prepositions. The one used most often is *into:*

> People who respond to international politics divide temperamentally into two schools —Arthur M. Schlesinger, Jr., *Harper's,* August 1971

> Those concerned with this matter divide into several groups —Lewis Mumford, *New Yorker,* 9 Feb. 1957

> ... a plane that divides a geometric figure into parts equal in measure —Robert W. Marks, *The New Mathematics Dictionary and Handbook,* 1964

Divide is also used with *between* and *among,* with *between* occurring far more often. The choice seems often to be dictated by the old distinction that insists on *between* for two and *among* for more than two. However, some citations show that writers may ignore that distinction:

> ... divide their time between Paris and Athens —*Current Biography,* July 1965

> ... the initiative, instead of being concentrated, is divided between many laboratories —A. W. Haslett, *London Calling,* 18 Mar. 1954

... the remainder is to be divided equally among his four sons —Mary P. Dolciani et al., *Modern Algebra and Trigonometry,* 1973

... political prestige is divided among Socialists and Nazis —*Current History,* August 1936

The use of *divide* with *from* is also common especially when both divisions are mentioned and one is the direct object:

... the piece of knowledge that more than anything else divides women from girls —Herman Wouk, *Marjorie Morningstar,* 1955

In addition to the common mathematical use of *divide* with *by, divide by* is used in other contexts:

... that town was roughly divided in half by the high and rugged Gardner Mountain Range —*American Guide Series: New Hampshire,* 1938

... more alike ... in feeling than any other two writers divided by three centuries —G. M. Trevelyan, *English Social History,* 1942

Divide may be used with *on, upon* or *over* when the matter that causes the division is the object of the preposition. *On* occurs most frequently, *upon* and *over* less often:

The doubtful civil liberties cases are those on which the court divides —John P. Frank, *N.Y. Times,* 3 Oct. 1954

Experts divide over whether Mr. Reagan represents the vanguard of a tidal swing in the 1980s —Richard J. Cattani, *Christian Science Monitor,* 15 July 1980

Agricultural workers are divided upon the question —F. D. Smith & Barbara Wilcox, *The Country Companion,* 1950

Divide with occurs, but not very often:

... the *American Weekly Mercury* divided the honor with the *Boston Gazette* —*American Guide Series: Pennsylvania,* 1940

2. Many language commentators deplore what they consider the unnecessary use of the adverb *up* with certain verbs, *divide* among them. *Divide up* has been around for quite some time and continues to be used by writers of good repute:

... to enable women to divide up domestic tasks —Sir Winston Churchill, *The Unrelenting Struggle,* 1942

We divide up nouns into "masculine," "feminine" and "neuter" —Mario Pei, *The Story of Language,* 1949

... he might divide up a supply of jelly beans —John Holt, *Atlantic,* May 1971

divorce The verb *divorce* is almost always used with *from* when followed by a prepositional phrase:

... some of them [artists] quite divorced from any earthly, temporal dimension at all —Joyce Carol Oates, *Saturday Rev.,* 6 Jan. 1973

The isolationism of the 1920's had not divorced America from the world's perplexing problems —Oscar Handlin, *The American People in the Twentieth Century,* 1954

There is one example with *of* in our files:

It was divorced of any significance for America —Sy Kahn, *Jour. of Modern Literature,* 1st issue, 1970

divulge Three commentators criticize *divulge* used as a casual variant for *say, tell,* or *announce.* Since the most recent of these books was published in 1964, it may come as no surprise that we have no recent examples of such use in our files, although it may still occur. We have a few older examples like this one:

... it seemed to me an occasion to divulge my real ideas and hopes for the Commonwealth —Logan Pearsall Smith, *All Trivia,* 1934

More typical of the current use of *divulge* are these examples:

As a special mark of favor to Elena, whom she had invited to tea, she confided a family recipe, which was not to be divulged even to me —Edmund Wilson, *New Yorker,* 5 June 1971

Another folder ... divulges Nixon's early fixation on discrediting his left-wing detractors —Paul Grabowicz, *Mother Jones,* May 1979

The Navy, whatever its reasons, was reluctant to divulge the details —Hal Dareff, *Saturday Rev.,* 5 Feb. 1972

... does not divulge prices to journalists —Janet Malcolm, *New Yorker,* 10 Apr. 1971

do Quirk et al. 1985 has a section on the use of *do* as a pro-form—that is, as a substitute for the predicate of an earlier part of the sentence. The uses discussed, in which *do* follows a modal auxiliary like *may* and *must* or perfective *have* (usually with a modal auxiliary), are idioms principally found in British English. These are not recent idioms; they have been under attack and examination at least since Cobbett 1823. Let's put down some examples here to relieve the abstractness of this grammatical talk. First, *do* after a modal (or after *used to,* here functioning somewhat like a modal):

... but my money has not held out so well as it used to do —Samuel Johnson, letter, 22 July 1777

... Mrs. Stent gives us quite as much of her company as we wish for, & rather more than she used to do —Jane Austen, letter, 30 Nov. 1800

... but if your mention of "a less expensive paper" implies (as I presume it must do) that you propose to lower the price of the book —Lewis Carroll, letter, 24 Aug. 1866

"But you must do. I thought all men had to know ..." —John Fowles, *The Collector,* 1963

'Recognize it?' the man said, whipping the thing out again.
    'I might do.'
        — Colin MacInnes, *Mr Love and Justice,* 1960

... and she said, Does money grow on trees Bill? It might do, I said ...
        —*The Stories of Frank Sargeson,* 1974

And here are some examples of *do* after perfective *have.* The first of these is a quotation that Cobbett worried to death for nearly half a page before concluding that it made no sense. Our evidence suggests that this is the more common form of the idiom at present.

> It is somewhat unfortunate, that this Number of the Spectator did not end, as it might very well have done, with the former beautiful period —Hugh Blair, *Lectures on Rhetoric and Belles Lettres,* 1783

> "In the month of June last, do you remember a parcel arriving for Mr. Lawrence Cavendish . . . ?"
> "I don't remember, sir. It may have done, but Mr. Lawrence was away. . . ." —Agatha Christie, *The Mysterious Affair at Styles,* 1920

> 'She must have transferred her affections to some foul blister she met out there.'
> 'No, no.'
> 'Don't keep saying "No, no." She must have done.'
>   —P. G. Wodehouse, *Right Ho, Jeeves,* 1934

> "Did you leave the front door open, Roddy?"
> "No."
> "There's an awful draught swirling round my ankles. I think you must have done."
>   —Elizabeth Taylor, *At Mrs Lippincote's,* 1945

> . . . you are inclined to say, "Yes, but I've seen this before. St. Vincent looked just like this."
> It may have done, but there'll be differences — Alec Waugh, *Love and the Caribbean,* 1958

> The question that most concerns the British reader is: "Can it happen here?" The short answer is: "It has done" —*Times Literary Supp.,* 25 Apr. 1968

> . . . no longer looks as safe as it would have done before —*Times Literary Supp.,* 12 June 1969

> "We felt this man did not have the same service he would have done had he been white," said Mr. Hunte —*Evening Mail* (Birmingham, England), 13 June 1974

As you will have noted, most of these examples come from quoted or fictional conversation or from letters. It would thus appear that British writers tend to avoid the construction in more dignified prose. Our few recent American examples show no such limitation, probably because the idiom is not a common conversational one in American English.

> The energy crisis has not yet overwhelmed us, but it will do if we do not act quickly —Jimmy Carter, radio talk, quoted by J. R. Pole in Michaels & Ricks 1980

> . . . the OCF didn't begin as well as it could have done —Stanley Kauffmann, *Before My Eyes,* 1980

> Assuming that the first galaxies formed in the densest regions—as they almost certainly would have done —M. Mitchell Waldrop, *Science,* 26 Sept. 1986

dŏck   The distinction between *dock* and *pier* or *wharf* seems to have been first made by Richard Grant White in 1870. His dictum—"to say that he fell off a dock is no better than to say that he fell off a hole"—was memorable enough to be repeated by Ayres 1881 (without attribution) and Vizetelly 1906 (with attribution). The use of *dock* "pier" was on the Don't List of the *New York Herald* (before 1918), and the prohibition became

part of the lore of the newspaper trade. Bernstein 1962, 1965 cleaves to the newspaper tradition, along with Follett 1966, but Copperud 1964 dissents, calling it "nautical cant." Harper 1975, 1985, Ebbitt and Ebbitt 1982, and Evans 1957 accept the "wharf, pier" sense.

It appears to be chiefly an American usage. The Dictionary of Americanisms gives citations from as early as 1817, but the OED does not recognize it at all. Longman 1984 labels it North American. In American English it is standard.

> . . . staring about me, until we came alongside the dock —Charles Dickens, *American Notes,* 1842

> Jean was on the dock when the ship came in —Mark Twain, *Harper's Monthly Mag.,* January 1911

> . . . and now they are rotting on the dock at Liverpool —H. L. Mencken, letter, 9 Oct. 1919

> . . . I thought of Gatsby's wonder when he first picked out the green light at the end of Daisy's dock —F. Scott Fitzgerald, *The Great Gatsby,* 1925

> Then she walked across the dock and up the steep sandy road —*Short Stories of Ernest Hemingway,* (1926) 1938

> . . . and on a cold, blue, and unusually calm afternoon in February I found myself stepping onto the Cuttyhunk dock —Richard Todd, *New England Monthly,* December 1987

> . . . was on the dock waving a bill —Samuel Eliot Morison, *John Paul Jones: A Sailor's Biography,* 1959

doesn't   See DON'T.

dominate, domineer   *Dominate* is used far more often than *domineer.* If either word is used intransitively with a complement, the preposition used is *over:*

> . . . he dominated over his party —Claude G. Bowers, *Jefferson in Power,* 1936

> . . . a power . . . which soon began to domineer over all orders and all parties —T. B. Macaulay, *The History of England,* vol. I, 1849

When *dominate* is used in the passive voice, the agent is named in a phrase beginning with *by:*

> Farrell of course resented the fact that his reputation was dominated by "Studs" —Alfred Kazin, *N.Y. Times Book Rev.,* 16 Sept. 1979

Domineer occurs most frequently now as its present participle, *domineering,* which has taken on adjectival status:

> Servile and fawning as he had been before, he was now as domineering and bellicose —Jack London, *The Sea-Wolf,* 1904

donate   *Donate* is one of those pesky back-formations that have frequently come under the gun of critics. Richard Grant White was probably first. He is mentioned in the fourth edition of Gould 1870 as having attacked the word in a magazine article. "Webster, of course, records the word," sneers Gould, who was a partisan of Worcester in the 19th-century American dictionary war. *Donate* had been first entered in Webster 1864, and Gould attacked—correctly, from the standpoint of modern etymology—the Latin origin postulated for it there.

Richard Grant White included his attack in his 1870 book and *donate* became part of William Cullen Bryant's *Index Expurgatorius,* compiled when he was editor of the *N.Y. Evening Post* and published in 1877. Bardeen 1883 lists five works discussing it (and he missed Gould); Ayres 1881 cites Gould. By the turn of the century, and for quite a few years thereafter, it was roundly condemned on all sides, although dissenting voices were here and there heard. With Utter 1916 the popular epithet becomes "vulgar"; it is used by Whipple 1924, too, and in 1925 Merriam-Webster editors yielded to the contemporary view and added the label by plate-change to the dictionary. But Vizetelly, following his own dictionary, Funk & Wagnalls 1913, was measured in his comments, allowing *donate* certain legitimate uses (as Utter did too, though grudgingly). Lounsbury 1908 considered it needlessly abused, and Hall 1917 opined that if the millionaire philanthropists and their clients needed a new word, they might as well have it.

Donate is an original Americanism, first attested in 1785. It has some British use, too, as H. L. Mencken noted in *The American Language.* Fowler 1926 does not condemn it, but calls it "chiefly U.S." and notes it as a back-formation; Gowers in Fowler 1965 observes that it has become a formal word for *give* in British English. In American use it seems to be the word of choice when the giving, usually to a cause or charity, is public or is intended to be publicized. It is no longer controversial.

> Magazines donated space. Artists and writers donated their services. Peace was what people were groping for, and when Americans grope for something they turn naturally to display advertising —E. B. White, *The Wild Flag,* 1946

> . . . the receipts of the gala premier performance of the film would be donated to the League —Tom Buckley, *Harper's,* August 1971

done   **1.** *Done* in the sense of "finished" has been subject to a certain amount of criticism over the years for reasons that are not readily apparent. The use of *done* as an adjective in this sense dates back to the 14th and 15th centuries, but the construction usually objected to—*be done*—is of more recent origin, attested by examples in the OED from the second half of the 18th century. Otto Jespersen, in his seven-volume grammar (1909–1949), has examples of the construction from several well-known 19th-century writers beginning with Dickens. In earlier English the usual auxiliary with *done* had been *have.* From Jespersen's examples it would appear that during the 19th century the use of *have* with *done* became more and more limited to the fixed expression *have done with,* which is still in use; if his examples are indeed representative, this tendency may well have strengthened the position of *be done.*

The earliest objection to *be done* in our files is from MacCracken & Sandison 1917. They do not say what is wrong with it but prescribe *have finished* in its place. (The fact that the OED and Curme 1931 note it as chiefly Irish, Scots, and U.S. may show how the objection originated.) This must have been a regular part of many schools' grammar lessons, for 47 percent of the usage panel of Heritage 1969 remembered them well enough to disapprove the construction. Theodore Bernstein objected to *done* for *finished* in 1958 but by 1971 and 1977 was on the way to accepting it. The construction is standard. *Finished,* too, has been used with *be*

since the later 18th century. (See FINISHED and THROUGH.)

How old the construction really is may depend on how old the first example below is, and of course no one knows that. Perhaps the proverb in this form dates only from the later 18th century.

> Man's work lasts till set of sun,
> Woman's work is never done —proverb

> A terrible sound arose when the reading of this document was done —Charles Dickens, *A Tale of Two Cities,* 1859

> I am done with official life for the present —Mark Twain, *Sketches, New and Old,* 1872 (Dictionary of American English)

> . . . the character I don't forget, and when the book is finished, that character is not done —William Faulkner, 13 Apr. 1957, in *Faulkner in the University,* 1959

> . . . as soon as she is done shooting this movie — Richard Boeth, *Cosmopolitan,* June 1976

2. The use of *done* as the past tense rather than past participle of *do* is not recorded in the OED. Evidence in the English Dialect Dictionary and the Dictionary of American English suggests that it may be more recent than one might expect, dating only from the 19th century. It may be of dialectal origin, and it is quite possible that there will never be a sufficient early record to date the use with any certainty. It is likely that the form was corrected by schoolteachers almost as soon as it was noticed; it is still in school grammars for correction (we note it in Warriner 1986, for instance). Our oldest comment on the use is from Richard Grant White 1870, who says it is common among completely illiterate people. Reader's Digest 1983 calls the usage nonstandard; Bryant 1962 says it is colloquial but is a receding usage. It is very occasionally used in standard contexts, but only in such specialized ways as this:

> To outline the highly intricate plot . . . is impossible in a short review, and in any case would be comparable to revealing who done it in a review of a who-dunnit —Peter Lewis, *Times Literary Supp.,* 21 May 1982

3. We do not yet know the definitive word on *done* used as a completive or perfective auxiliary. Raven I. McDavid, in his 1963 abridgment of H. L. Mencken's *The American Language,* observes that the usage occurs chiefly but not exclusively in Southern and South Midland dialects; it is also mentioned in works on Black English and Appalachian English. Examples in the American Dialect Dictionary substantially accord with McDavid's observations; many of them are indicated to have been used by black speakers. We are not certain of the social status of this usage; McDavid suggests that in most places that constituted the Confederacy it probably has a somewhat higher status than grammarians and school teachers would concede. We hope that in time the Dictionary of American Regional English will provide further light on the subject.

All we can do is warn you that the use is evidently regionally restricted and that it is probably subject to some social restrictions as well. Some examples:

> "When Brother James he see that, he thought she'd done got good. . . ." —William C. Hall, "How Sally Hooter Got Snakebit," 1850, in *The Mirth of a*

Nation, ed. Walter Blair & Raven I. McDavid, Jr., 1983

Old Eagle had done already took off —William Faulkner, *Saturday Evening Post,* 5 Mar. 1955

. . . her voice, which had all the sad languor of the upper Pamunkey River. "The Japanese," she said, "they done bombed Pearl Harbor." —William Styron, *This Quiet Dust and Other Writings,* 1982

. . . and you play the same thing, then it ain't great no more. It's done been played —Carlton Haney, quoted in *Bluegrass Unlimited,* September 1983

4. See DO.

don't   In the 17th century several contracted negative verb forms came into use—among them *don't, won't, shan't, an't* (an ancestor of *ain't*), *han't, wa'n't*—that are noticeable because their pronunciation differs rather markedly from that of the positive elements from which they were formed. This somewhat obscured phonological relationship allowed several of these to be multipurpose forms: *an't* was used for *am not* and *are not; don't* for *do not* and *does not; han't* for *has not* and *have not.* The 17th century got by with fewer of these contractions than we use today.

No one is sure how *don't* came by its pronunciation; it matches neither *do* nor *does.* The most likely explanation, accepted by Strang 1970 and tentatively accepted by Jespersen 1909–49, is that the pronunciation comes by way of analogy with *won't.* The spelling obviously comes from *do* and *not,* but how this spelling came to be used for the third person singular is not so obvious, though (since *don't* was a spoken form long before it was written down) it seems likely that one or more phonological processes were involved. A contributing factor may well have been the unsettled condition of the third person singular of *do,* in the 17th century. The northern form *does* had long been competing with the southern *doth* (both variously spelled) for several centuries. In addition to these two there was in the 16th and 17th century an uninflected form *do.* This form was regularly used by Samuel Pepys in his diary:

. . . the Duke of York do give himself up to business, and is like to prove a noble prince; and so indeed I do from my heart think he will. . . . but I should be more glad that the King himself would look after business, which it seems he do not —21 Jan. 1664

It is possible that this uninflected form had some influence on the written *don't.*

From the 17th century through the 19th century, *don't* seems to have had unimpeachable status. Our examples here begin with works of the Restoration playwrights, who have supplied many of our earliest examples in print of these contracted forms.

OLD BELLAIR. No matter for that; go, bid her dance no more. It don't become her, it don't become her — George Etherege, *The Man of Mode,* 1676

LANDLADY.   . . . you know it, sir.
GAYMAN. Ah, but your husband don't —Aphra Behn, *The Lucky Chance,* 1686

LOVELESS. So, thus far all's well. . . . my wife don't expect me home till four o'clock —Sir John Vanbrugh, *The Relapse,* 1696

It don't appear that he knew any thing of your book —Thomas Gray, letter, 14 Feb. 1768

Putting as much contempt as I could into my look and tone, I said, "Dr. Johnson don't!—humph!" — Horace Walpole, letter, 26 May 1791

. . . and if Wordsworth don't send me an order for one upon Longman, I will buy it —Charles Lamb, letter, 7 June 1809

But never mind;—'God save the king!' and kings!
   For if *he* don't, I doubt if *men* will longer
      —Lord Byron, *Don Juan,* Canto viii, 1823

. . . and the sun dont shine, . . . and the wind dont blow, . . . and the birds dont sing —Emily Dickinson, letter, 5 Apr. 1852

However, it don't matter if you've read the play — George Bernard Shaw, letter, 24 Dec. 1897

Indicative of the social status of third singular *don't* in the mid-19th century is this example:

There is one other phrase which will soon come to be decisive of a man's social *status,* if it is not already: "That tells the whole story." It is an expression which vulgar and conceited people particularly affect, and which well-meaning ones, who know better, catch from them. It is intended to stop all debate, like the previous question in the General Court. Only it don't —Oliver Wendell Holmes d. 1894, *The Autocrat of the Breakfast-Table,* 1858

The attack on third singular *don't* seems to have begun in the second half of the 19th century and in the U.S. Longman 1984 says that it was "common in educated informal speech" in British English "well into the 20th century," and gives an Aldous Huxley letter as an example. Partridge 1942 says it "is now a solecism." It seems to have lost status earlier in the United States. The earliest attack on its use that we have seen comes from George Perkins Marsh in 1859. He represents the two directions of attack on *don't.* The older one is a general attack on contracted forms that had been carried on since the time of Swift and Addison; in the United States it seems to have been particularly directed against *don't, won't,* and *ain't,* all of whose origins were unknown to or considered erroneous by the attackers. Marsh wrinkles his nose at *don't* meaning "do not" and opines that only careless speakers use it for "does not." Schele de Vere 1872 considers the third singular use "objectionable slang"; Ayres 1881 does not like it; Bardeen 1883 lists five sources who object. It must have rapidly gotten into school books and handbooks; almost all of our early 20th-century sources condemn the use. The usage survey reported in Crisp 1971 shows that third singular *don't* then had lower status than it had had in the survey of Leonard in 1932.

Earlier in this century it could still be found in both British and American poetry:

To-night he's in the pink; but soon he'll die.
And still the war goes on; he don't know why
      —Siegfried Sassoon, in
      Georgian Poetry 1916–1917, 1919

"He don't consider it a case for God" —Robert Frost, *Mountain Interval,* 1921

And in American fiction of that period, third singular *don't* was being put into the mouths of ordinary middle-class and working-class characters, whose conversations tended to depart considerably from the norms taught in grammar school:

> "Old wind-bag," he sputtered. "Why does he want to be bragging? Why don't he shut up?" —Sherwood Anderson, *Winesburg, Ohio,* 1919

> ". . . It makes elegant reading, but it don't say nothing . . ." —Sinclair Lewis, *Babbitt,* 1922

> "I says 'Lay it down,'" says Cap. "If that don't mean 'bunt,' what does it mean?" —Ring Lardner, *How to Write Short Stories,* 1924

It still is used in speech, mostly but not exclusively by the less educated, and in casual writing:

> . . . the carpenter don't build a house just to drive nails —William Faulkner, 11 Mar. 1957, in *Faulkner in the University,* 1959

> . . . I judge Fr. C. belongs to the tribe that knows what's bad but don't know what's good —Flannery O'Connor, letter, 19 Apr. 1958

> And them bass fiddles that's electrified, they're so loud, and the average man that plays 'em don't know how to turn 'em down —Birch Monroe, quoted in *Bluegrass Unlimited,* September 1982

Doesn't is a more recent formation than *don't.* No one seems to have turned up an example earlier than one from 1818 reported by Karl W. Dykema (*English Journal,* September 1947). Byron seems not to have known it; at least he used only *don't* for all persons throughout *Don Juan,* although he uses both *does* and *doth* in positive constructions. Nor will *doesn't* be found in the fiction of Jane Austen. Although third person singular *don't* appears in her dialogue, *does not* is the preferred form. *Don't* is, of course, still standard in all uses except the third person singular, but in that use it has lost all the status it once enjoyed. It is instructive to note that the reduction of status of third singular *don't* was in large part accomplished by those who were zealous to improve and correct the language but who were utterly ignorant of the origin and earlier literary use of *don't.* As Flesch 1964 notes, *don't* is not an illiteracy. But neither is it standard any longer in edited prose.

See also AIN'T.

don't seem See CAN'T SEEM.

don't think The placement of the negative in such sentences as "I don't think it will rain tonight" and "I don't think they have a chance" is a characteristic English idiom that is sometimes objected to on the grounds of logic. Such sentences are briefly discussed at RAISING.

dote When *dote* is used with a preposition—and it almost always is—*on* is the overwhelming choice, although our files show instances of *dote upon* and *dote over:*

> . . . the spectators dote on his quips and his banter —Herbert Warren Wind, *New Yorker,* 17 July 1971

> How he doted on this terrible lodger of theirs — Glenway Wescott, *Apartment in Athens,* 1945

> . . . it is precisely the sort upon which the dilettante etymologist dotes —Thomas Pyles, *Words and Ways of American English,* 1952

> He has been assembling the stamps since boyhood and still dotes over them —*N.Y. Times,* 7 Oct. 1951

double comparative See DOUBLE COMPARISON.

double comparison Double comparison consists chiefly of the use of *more* or *most* with an adjective already inflected for the comparative or superlative degree. Lamberts 1972 observes that besides marking the comparative and superlative, *more* and *most* were used as intensives long before Shakespeare's time. This use is still with us: when we say to our host or hostess, "That was a most enjoyable meal," we are using *most* as an intensive, in much the same way as we might use *very.* Back in the 14th century *more* and *most* came to be used in intensive function with adjectives already inflected for comparative and superlative. OED evidence suggests that the practice continued from the 14th through the 17th centuries. It was common in Lord Berners' translation of Froissart and fairly frequent in Shakespeare's plays; it also occurred in the King James version of the Bible. Some examples:

> . . . he took new councillors of the most noblest and sagest persons of his realm —Lord Berners, translation of Froissart's *Chronicles,* 1523

> More fairer than fair, beautiful than beauteous — Shakespeare, *Love's Labour's Lost,* 1595

> How much more elder art thou than thy looks! — Shakespeare, *The Merchant of Venice,* 1597

> This was the most unkindest cut of all —Shakespeare, *Julius Caesar,* 1600

> But that I love thee best, O most best, believe it — Shakespeare, *Hamlet,* 1601

> . . . that after the most straitest sect of our religion I lived a Pharisee —Acts 25:5 (AV), 1611

The OED evidence for this use of *more* and *most* suggests a marked decline after the 17th century. Part of the decline can be attributed to the attack mounted against the construction by several 18th-century grammarians, including Lowth in 1763. "Double comparatives and superlatives are improper," says he, and sets out Shakespeare and the translators of the book of Acts, cited above, for correction. The bishop, however, was willing to indulge poets in occasional improprieties, and he could not bring himself to condemn "most highest" applied to God in an old translation of the Psalms. Priestley, who was not a bishop, was not diffident about criticizing this construction in his revised edition of 1798 nor was Lindley Murray 1795. And by the middle of the 19th century, Goold Brown felt no compunction about telling Shakespeare and King James's translators what they should have written.

Lindley Murray based his grammar on that of Lowth, Priestley, and others. It was widely used as a school grammar, and widely imitated by other writers of school grammars. So the strictures on the double comparative and double superlative became part of every schoolchild's lessons—and they still are. The result has been that double comparison has pretty much vanished from standard writing. The OED found a "more lovelier" in Tennyson, and Hall 1917 a "most dimmest" in Swinburne, but such examples are hard to find and, when found, often prove to be allusions to older literary use. Double comparison does, however, linger in speech and in such familiar writing as letters—wherever it may serve some specified purpose. The television weatherman who in March 1980 spoke of the "least snowiest winter" perhaps did so inadvertently. But Lewis Carroll could write on purpose in a letter to a child

> . . . and of all that race none is more ungratefuller, more worser —13 Mar. 1869

The actress Ellen Terry used double superlatives with some frequency in her letters:

> . . . I must yet ask you to take my very bestest thanks —29 June 1892

The last two examples show double comparison by inflection. Americans have been conscious of this possibility at least since Nathan Bedford Forrest was reputed to have said, "Git thar fustest with the mostest." Formations such as *firstest, mostest,* and *bestest* are perhaps most typical of the speech of young children before they are influenced by school and the language of their peers. The best-attested of all the inflectional double comparatives and superlatives seems to be *worser.* The evidence in the OED shows it to have been very common in the 16th and 17th centuries; Shakespeare used it many times, for instance. Use dropped off in the 18th and 19th centuries; here again we are probably seeing some of the effect of the 18th-century grammarians and their successors. Some examples of *worser* from its heyday:

> Were my state far worser than it is, I would not wed her —Shakespeare, *The Taming of the Shrew,* 1594

> I cannot hate thee worser than I do —Shakespeare, *Antony and Cleopatra,* 1607

> But to divert myself in doing this,
> From worser thoughts, which make me do amiss
> —John Bunyan, "Author's Apology,"
> *The Pilgrim's Progress,* 1678

By the middle of the 19th century, novelists such as Dickens and Thackeray were putting *worser* into the mouths of their least-educated characters. But it could still be found in the speech and familiar writing of the educated:

> To begin with, perhaps, if I were a better man, I might feel inclined to become a clergyman. But as I'm very much a worser man, we'll count that out — Henry Adams, letter, 9 Feb. 1859

Worser has become archaic from the standpoint of literature, but it still persists in speech, especially among the less educated. The hostility of the grammarians since the 18th century has essentially eliminated double comparison as a method of emphasis in standard written English. See also LESSER, considered by some to be a double comparative.

double genitive Almost every native speaker of English has read or heard expressions like these:

> . . . that place of Dorothy Thompson's is only sixty miles away —Alexander Woollcott, letter, 18 Mar. 1940

> . . . two very nice girls who were friends of yours — Flannery O'Connor, letter, 9 Apr. 1960

The most noticeable thing about "place of Dorothy Thompson's" and "friends of yours" is that the possessive relationship is marked both by the preposition *of* and the genitive inflection. This construction is known as the *double genitive* or *double possessive.* It is an idiomatic construction of long standing in English—going back before Chaucer's time—and should be of little interest except to learners of the language, because, as far as we know, it gives native speakers no trouble whatsoever.

But the double genitive was discovered by the 18th-century grammarians and has consequently been the subject of considerable speculation, explanation, and other (sometimes disapproving) comment. Before we examine the history of comment on the construction, let us take a look at the construction itself.

The genitive in English has more functions than the simple indication of possession (see the article at GENITIVE). The double genitive construction is a characteristic that separates the possessive genitive from all other functions of the genitive. Here is how the matter is typically explained: "Jane's picture," out of context, can be considered ambiguous. If *Jane's* is an objective genitive, we can clear up the possible confusion by using the *of* construction: "a picture of Jane." If the picture belongs to Jane, and *Jane's* is a possessive genitive, using the *of* construction, we get "a picture of Jane's." In other words, when *of* is used with a possessive genitive, the noun or pronoun regularly retains its genitive inflection. No native speaker of English would write our first example as "that place of Dorothy Thompson."

The double genitive is a perfectly acceptable, perfectly normal form in modern English. But those 18th-century grammarians weren't so sure. Lowth 1762 may have been the first to notice it. In his discussion of the possessive, he runs afoul of "a soldier of the king's." He seems to have mulled it over awhile; he begins by conceding that sometimes both the *'s* and *of* may be used, but then adds—apparently as the idea strikes him—that "here are really two possessives; for it means 'one *of* the soldiers *of* the king.'" The treatment of Priestley in his 1768 edition is fuller than Lowth's, and he is the first to use the picture example, pointing out the difference between "this picture of my friend" and "this picture of my friend's."

Lindley Murray 1795 bases his treatment on Lowth and Priestley. He is not very happy with the construction. He seems somewhat relieved to be able to repeat Priestley's statement that where the double genitive is not necessary to distinguish the sense (as in the picture example), it is generally avoided, "especially in a grave style" of writing. Murray in his later editions also adds that some grammarians advise avoiding the construction altogether. One of them was James Buchanan, who in *A Regular English Syntax* (1767) wrote, "*Of* being the sign of the Genitive Case, we cannot put it before a Noun with (*'s*) for this is making two Genitives" (cited in Leonard 1929). The 18th-century grammarians simply had a horror of anything double, because such constructions did not occur in Latin.

Lowth's explanation is of interest only because it survived into the 20th century. His "one of the soldiers" construction is what later grammarians called a *partitive genitive.* The partitive explanation was adopted because it avoided the idea of the possessive duplicated. In the third volume of his *Grammar* (1909–1949) and in *S.P.E. Tract No. XXV* (1926), Otto Jespersen seems to have finally disposed of the partitive explanation. It could have been exploded by anyone who happened to try it out on Priestley's example with a pronoun. His example comes from the first volume of *Tristram Shandy* (1759): "This exactness of his." Try it for yourself.

Jespersen cites another historical grammarian, L. Kellner, in his edition of *Caxton's Blanchardyn* (1890), as having proposed that the development of the construction occurred in three stages: first, possession with possessive pronoun; second, with possessive case of the noun; and third, with an extended sense of possession (as in "that beard of thine") that we still use today. We close with a few examples of the extended use:

... a good friend of my father's —Heywood Hale Broun (spoken), 18 Dec. 1985

... many a guest of ours inside the house at Seaforth —James Thurber, letter, 23 June 1955

They grump now, with some justification, that Serbia's political leaders are the most mediocre of any of the republics' —David Binner, *N.Y. Times Mag.,* 25 Dec. 1983

... a favorite phrase of your delighted mother's — Emily Dickinson, letter, 1 Oct. 1851

double modal *Double modal* is a term used by linguists to describe such expressions as *might can, might could,* and *might should.* Several of these have received comment in usage books. Those that survive in present-day American English tend to be used in speech rather than writing, and are generally old-fashioned or dialectal. *Might could* (which see) seems to be a still flourishing speech form in the Southern U.S. There are other combinations at OUGHT.

double negative Otto Jespersen, in *Negation in English and Other Languages* (1917), has an interesting observation. He notes that negation in a sentence is very important logically but that it is often formally unimportant in the structure of the sentence—in many instances in English it is marked by no more than an unstressed particle like *ne* or modern *-n't.* Hence, there has long been a tendency to strengthen the negative idea by adding more negative elements to the sentence. This tendency is perhaps properly called *multiple negation,* but it is usually referred to in modern handbooks and commentaries as the *double negative.*

The double negative functions in two ways in present-day English: as an emphatic negative, and as an unemphatic positive. We will examine each of these separately.

1. *Emphatic negative.* The multiple negative for emphasis or reinforcement of the negative idea of a sentence is very old, going back much farther than Chaucer, whose description of his knight is often given as an example:

He nevere yet no vileynye ne sayde
In al his lyf unto no maner wight
    —General Prologue, *The Canterbury Tales,* ca. 1387

The construction was common at least through Shakespeare's time:

... they could not find no more forage—Lord Berners, translation of Froissart's *Chronicles,* 1523

And that no woman has; nor never none
Shall mistress be of it
        —Shakespeare, *Twelfth Night,* 1602 (in Strang 1970)

        She cannot love,
Nor take no shape nor project of affection
        —Shakespeare, *Much Ado About Nothing,* 1599 (in Lowth 1762)

The more effusive multiple negatives seem to have gone out of literary favor some time after Shakespeare, but the double negative—like Lord Berners'—kept in use:

QUACK. ... your process is so new that we do not know but it may succeed.
HORNER. Not so new neither; *probatum est,* doctor.
    —William Wycherly, *The Country Wife,* 1675

I cannot by no means allow him, that this argument must prove.... —Richard Bentley, *Dissertation on Epistles of Phalaris,* 1699 (in Lowth 1775)

... lost no time, nor abated no Diligence —Daniel Defoe, *Robinson Crusoe,* 1719 (in McKnight 1928)

It was during the 18th century that the double negative began to attract the unfavorable notice of grammarians. Leonard 1929 cites such early 18th-century grammarians as James Greenwood (*An Essay Towards a Practical English Grammar,* 1711), but it seems to have been Lowth 1763 who gave the classic form to the statement:

Two negatives in English destroy one another, or are equivalent to an affirmative. ...

Lowth's statement was repeated word for word by Murray 1795 and in various forms by many other grammarians; it has become part of the warp and woof of pedagogy.

Lowth's statement is not original with him—it is simply a rule of Latin grammar. And it was a well-known rule; as early as 1591 Sir Philip Sidney in *Astrophel and Stella* had written a joking sonnet based on the principle that two negatives make an affirmative (quoted in Baron 1982). Lowth was aware of earlier use of multiple negation for emphasis; in a footnote he too cites Chaucer and Shakespeare. But he thought the old practice was obsolete.

It was later and lesser grammarians (Leonard cites J. Mennye's *An English Grammar* in 1785 and John Clarke's *Rational Spelling Book* in 1796) that made absolute the dictum about two negatives making a positive. From the absolute position seems to have arisen the often urged argument that the statement is based on logic. As Lamberts 1972 has pointed out, it all depends on what logic you choose. Two negatives may make a positive in the logic of Latin grammar, but not in the logic of algebra: $-a + -a = -2a$. Algebraic logic yields approximately the same result as the old multiple negative—simply a stronger negative.

The old multiple negative and the common or garden double negative were passing out of literature in Lowth's time. What was happening was that their sphere of use was contracting; they were still available but were restricted to familiar use—conversation and letters. And, since old forms persist the longest among the least educated, the double negative became associated with the speech of the unlettered. In modern use, the double negative is widely perceived as a rustic or uneducated form, and is indeed common in the speech of less educated people:

... I never had nary bit of desire to drink no strong drinks since I felt the Lord forgive me —Sam Johnson, quoted in *Our Appalachia,* ed. Laurel Shackelford & Bill Weinberg, 1977

... my daddy was all gray and didn't have no bank account and no Blue Cross. He didn't have nothin', and he worked himself to death —Louis Banks, quoted in Studs Terkel, *Hard Times,* 1970

I went and saw the Allen Brothers in a free concert . . . and I didn't know nothing about bluegrass — Rick Stacy, quoted in *Bluegrass Unlimited,* July 1982

We ain't had no breakfast, we're going hungry, so what do you mean we can't get no relief? —Nannie Washburn, quoted in *Harper's Weekly,* 16 May 1975

"It just wouldn't do no good," John Francis Michalski said from his corner stool in Uncle John's Bar —James T. Wooten, *N.Y. Times,* 1 Sept. 1974

And of course, the double negative is put into the speech of similar characters in fiction:

". . . and then there warn't no raft in sight. . . ." — Mark Twain, *Huckleberry Finn,* 1884

". . . the refreshin' rain-drops will begin to fall without none of your help. . . ." —Marietta Holley, "A Pleasure Exertion," in *Mark Twain's Library of Humor,* 1888

". . . pretty near everybody uses that once in a wile without no bad after effects." —Ring Lardner, *The Big Town,* 1921

'Mr. Rosen, my husband didn't have no friends.' — Bernard Malamud, *The Magic Barrel,* 1958

I won't have nothing to do with those people, Houdini told his manager —E. L. Doctorow, *Ragtime,* 1975

It still occurs in the casual speech and writing of more sophisticated and better educated people:

I never believe nothing until I got the money —Flannery O'Connor, letter, April 1952

There's one more volume which I hope will be the last but I haven't no assurance that it will be —William Faulkner, 5 June 1957, in *Faulkner in the University,* 1959

Anyway, as you know, Ez hasn't changed none — Archibald MacLeish, letter, 30 Sept. 1958

You can't do nothing with nobody that doesn't want to win —Robert Frost, letter, 20 Sept. 1962

The double negative may even be trotted out in discursive prose for effect:

The sailplane sure ain't no 747! —Susan Ochshorn, *Saturday Rev.,* 14 Apr. 1979

The range of use of the double negative has shrunk considerably in the past 400 years—partly through the hostility of the 18th-century grammarians and their followers—but it has not disappeared. If it's part of your normal speech, you certainly don't need to eradicate it when talking to your family and friends. But it is not a prestige form; you are not likely to impress the boss, the teacher, or the job interviewer by using double negatives. But, as the examples above show, it does have its uses. You just have to pick your occasions.

2. Weak affirmative. Lowth, when he lays down the rule about two negatives making an affirmative, quotes Milton. The double negative as a weak positive was in use as early as 1537; it was a rhetorical device (the usual name for it is *litotes* or *meiosis;* see LITOTES) that would

have been included in 16th-century books on rhetoric. The intention of this double negative is just the opposite of the traditional one: instead of emphasizing, it is meant as understatement. Here are a few examples:

Fanny looked on and listened, not unamused to observe the selfishness which, more or less disguised, seemed to govern them all —Jane Austen, *Mansfield Park,* 1814

". . . I have (I flatter myself) made no inconsiderable progress in her affections. . . ." —Jane Austen, *Mansfield Park,* 1814

Indeed, I am not sure you have not a far clearer view of things —Alexander Woollcott, letter, 4 Dec. 1917

He turned his blue eyes on Mother. And keeping the home fires burning ain't so easy either, he said. He was not without charm —E. L. Doctorow, *Ragtime,* 1975

. . . had what *Opera News* not unfairly called "the kind of performance that gives the composer a bad reputation." —Andrew Porter, *New Yorker,* 29 July 1985

When this device is overused, reviewers and commentators on style can get annoyed:

. . . an annoying penchant for the double negative ("should not pass unnoticed" appears three times, "not dissimilar" twice) —Graham Forst, *Books in Canada,* February 1976

One can cure oneself of the *not un-* formation by memorizing this sentence: *A not unblack dog was chasing a not unsmall rabbit across a not ungreen field* —George Orwell, footnote to "Politics and the English Language," 1946

double passive The construction known as the *double passive* looks like this:

The mystery was assiduously, though vainly, endeavoured to be discovered —in Fowler 1926, 1965

It is, you can see, awkward. The subject is examined in some detail in Bernstein 1965 and Fowler 1926, 1965; it gets shorter treatment in Copperud 1970, 1980 and Janis 1984. We cannot tell how much of a problem the double passive presents in current use; Gowers appears to have added nothing in 1965 to Fowler's original treatment. Janis 1984 does show how it might occur in business writing and how it might create a problem:

The seminars were asked to be given by top management itself.

(Is the meaning that top management asked for the seminars to be given or that top management was asked to give the seminars?)

The double passive construction is the sort of thing that is easily passed over when dictionary editors collect examples of individual words, and so we have no examples to quote for you. If you would like to see more examples, you can find them in Fowler and in Bernstein; no sources are given, however.

See also PASSIVE VOICE.

double possessive See DOUBLE GENITIVE.

double subjects In 1672 John Dryden wrote an essay called "Defence of the Epilogue," in which he asserts that the English used by writers of his day is more proper, more correct, than the English used by writers in the age of Shakespeare, Fletcher, and Jonson. To illustrate his point, Dryden introduces several passages from Jonson's play *Catiline,* in which he finds various improprieties of diction. One of the lines criticized reads "Such Men they do not succour more the cause. . . ." Dryden observes: "*They* redundant."

Ben Jonson's *they* after *men* is what grammarians refer to as a *double subject.* The appositive pronoun after the subject of the sentence is an old technique for emphasizing the subject. It goes back to Old English and Middle English; it still survives to a certain extent in poetry (mostly older poetry, now) and in some dialects (it is sometimes mentioned, for example, as a characteristic of Black English), and, to judge from its stigmatized appearance in schoolbooks, it occurs in the speech of children and other unschooled persons.

Hall 1917 has an imposing list of poets who have used the double subject. One familiar example will do here:

The eye—it cannot choose but see;
We cannot bid the ear be still
—William Wordsworth, "Expostulation and
Reply," 1798

The old-fashioned mode of expression is obviously helpful in getting lines of poetry to scan.

The double subject is rare in modern prose. Older writers—including Dryden himself—occasionally fall into the old pattern, but it is seldom used today. It can, however, still be heard in casual speech:

But a first-rate scoundrel, like a first-rate artist, he's an individualist —William Faulkner, 7 Mar. 1957, in *Faulkner in the University,* 1959

Anyone who sees any illegal dumping on state land, they should get the plate number and we can take it from there —Carroll Holmes, quoted in *Sunday Republican* (Springfield, Mass.), 6 Dec. 1987

It is noticeable that in both of these examples, the repeated subject comes after an intervening phrase or clause; this contrasts somewhat with the pattern of Black English, in which the repeated subject may follow the subject directly, as well as follow an intervening phrase. From the punctuation of examples in such books as Geneva Smitherman's *Talkin and Testifyin* (1977), it would appear that a pause is normal before the repeated subject. Pauses are similarly indicated in the examples we have of Faulkner's double subjects, too.

The double subject seems not to have been treated very exhaustively in the sources available to us—we have depended a good deal on Hall 1917 for historical information. However, the rarity of the construction in prose—and we suppose it is pretty rare in modern poetry, too—would seem to relegate the subject to well-earned obscurity.

double superlative   See DOUBLE COMPARISON.

doubt, *verb*   The transitive verb *doubt* may take a clause as its object. The clause may be a sort of contact clause (which see) without a conjunction or a clause introduced by *that, whether,* or *if:*

Some cancer researchers doubt hyperthermia will ever emerge as a primary therapy —Walter L. Updegrave, *N.Y. Times Mag.,* 23 Mar. 1980

There is nothing for it but to doubt such diseases exist —H. G. Wells (in Fowler 1907)

. . . but I doubt that this represents a judgment of relative merit —Malcolm Cowley, *New Republic,* 22 Sept. 1941

. . . I doubt that this kind of disagreement produces many divorces —Elizabeth Janeway, *Atlantic,* March 1970

. . . I seriously doubt whether the stuff I give them makes anyone else feel good —*And More by Andy Rooney,* 1982

I doubt if he had read a play of Shakespeare's even at the end of his life —*The Autobiography of William Butler Yeats,* 1953

. . . I doubt if one writer ever has a satisfactory conversation with another writer —William Faulkner, 16 May 1957, in *Faulkner in the University,* 1959

The clause that follows *doubt* could also in the past be introduced by *but* or *but that,* especially when the main clause is negative or interrogative; these constructions now seem to be rare with the verb, although we do have examples of *but that* with the noun.

. . . I don't doubt but she may endure —Sir John Vanbrugh, *The Relapse,* 1696

. . . nor do we doubt but our reader . . . will concur with us —Henry Fielding, *Jonathan Wild,* 1743

So far, things are reasonably simple. Now enter the usage writers, headed by Vizetelly 1906, who rejects *doubt but that* and prescribes *doubt that.* His comment may be the first evidence that the constructions with *but* are beginning to sound old-fashioned.

Then come the brothers Fowler in 1907. They erect a set of three rules for the proper use of the verb that depend on the writer's considering the doubt reasonable, the writer's disapproving the doubt, or the writer's using the "vivid" *whether.* These rules have more than a whiff of excogitation about them, an observation borne out by two facts: Meredith, Trollope, Thackeray, and H. G. Wells are cited as bad examples (there are no good examples), and H. W. Fowler threw the whole treatment out in 1926 and did it over.

Fowler's 1926 version begins by finding the use of *that* after *doubt* in a positive statement "contrary to idiom," a finding contradicted by the dozen or so examples he produces, all using *that.* He allows *that* when the main clause is negative or interrogative, but his real purpose seems to be to restore *whether,* the older of the two usages, in every possible instance. If the OED evidence is representative, the use of *that* and *if,* the latter of which Fowler does not mention, began in the 19th century. It is perhaps a bit surprising that he does not endorse negative and interrogative *but* and *but that,* both of which are older constructions than the *that* construction he does allow.

The *doubt if* construction ignored by Fowler was certainly established in everyday speech both in British and American English in the 19th century:

But never mind;—'God save the king!' and kings!
For if *he* don't, I doubt if *men* will longer . . .
—Lord Byron, *Don Juan,*Canto viii, 1823

I doubt if I should trouble them if they did come —Henry Adams, letter, 7 June 1859

. . . and I doubt if she can be heard at all beyond that distance —Lewis Carroll, letter, 15 Jan. 1884

By the time Fowler gave his 1926 theories to the general public, there was already a separate American set of rules, as expressed in F. K. Ball's *Constructive English* (1923), for example. These were based on the following nuances: *that* (or *if*) could be used after *doubt* when there was no doubt; *whether* (or *if*) when there was a doubt. Over the course of time, the American rules and Fowler's rules became conflated. The ministrations of a couple of dozen commentators since Fowler have resulted in this contemporary consensus:

1. Use *that* for questions and negative sentences.
2. Use *whether* or *if* to express uncertainty.
3. Use *that,* even in positive statements, to express disbelief rather than uncertainty.

You can follow these rules to guide your own practice if you want to. But can you judge the practice of others by them? No. The reason is simple: to know whether uncertainty or disbelief is intended, you must have either a clearly indicative context or an almost clairvoyant knowledge of an author's intentions. For instance, the usage panel of Heritage 1969 was given no more than "I doubt that he will come" for comment. In order to elicit an opinion, it was necessary to gloss the sentence to indicate that it was supposed to express genuine doubt. One cannot tell the intention from the sentence itself. And such is the case with the great majority of our citations. But the point to remember is this: you need not pay any attention to the rules to understand these writers:

I doubted at first whether I should attempt the creation of a being like myself, or one of simpler organization —Mary Shelley, *Frankenstein,* 1818

Ben is here seeking a family, but I doubt if he gets what he wants —Henry Adams, letter, 22 Apr. 1859

Pessimists doubt that the United Nations will be able to resolve the problems that face them —Vera Micheles Dean, *The Four Cornerstones of Peace,* 1946

... I doubt very much if they will last the season through —Stella Harrison, in *Canadian Forum,* June 1952

I doubt myself whether this would have made much difference —Quintin Hogg, *Times Literary Supp.,* 22 Jan. 1970

It was quite wonderful that she should ... never have doubted that it would occur —Louis Auchincloss, *A Law for the Lion,* 1953

... Jordanian and Israeli army officers doubt that the systems they live within do provide means for peaceful change —*Commonweal,* 9 Oct. 1970

The house is furnished but they ask me to buy dishes and carpets, or bring these with me which I doubt if I can do —Robert Frost, letter, 16 July 1921

Nor did mediaeval logic doubt that its processes could elucidate and express the veritable natures of things —Henry O. Taylor, *The Mediaeval Mind,* 4th ed., 1925

In his thirty-eight years as a critic I doubt if he ever wrote a single paragraph that was not carefully planned —Deems Taylor, *Music to My Ears,* 1949

We would conclude that *that* is used when the main clause is negative; *that* also seems to be picked for use with a third-person subject more often than *whether* and *if.* But most of our examples have a first-person subject, and in those sentences the writers seem to pick *if, that,* or *whether* according to personal preference.

See also IF 1.

doubt, *noun* **1.** A few commentators drag the noun *doubt* into the morass of rules propounded for the verb. This is a mistake. The noun, when followed by a clause, may take a clause introduced by any of the conjunctions used for the verb:

... there is little doubt that strategic nuclear weapons would be used —*I. F. Stone's Bi-Weekly,* 8 Mar. 1971

... there was no doubt that the King would return —*Current Biography 1950*

... some doubt whether the view ... through a Russian prism may not sometimes have a distorting effect —*Times Literary Supp.,* 1 Dec. 1966

... the expression of some doubt if very many citizens will ever read all of these 949 pages —Elmer Davis, *Saturday Rev.,* 20 May 1939

... no fair-minded person can be left in any doubt but that the murder was planned —Leonard Schapiro, *London Calling,* 15 July 1954

There can be no doubt but many men have been named and painted great who were vastly smaller than he —Thomas Carlyle, *London and Westminster Rev.,* 1838

2. *Doubt,* whether as a singular or a plural, is followed idiomatically by a number of prepositions:

... if there was any doubt about his condition — Daphne du Maurier, *Ladies' Home Jour.,* August 1971

... had some doubts about sending this boy on a man's job —Ellen Lewis Buell, *N.Y. Times Book Rev.,* 16 May 1954

... in Bolshevik theory the slightest doubt of the regime is interpreted as bitter enmity —*New Republic,* 17 Mar. 1952

... so that all who could vote might be under no doubt of the road to reward —J. H. Plumb, *England in the Eighteenth Century,* 1950

... Byron's ... may have been intended for some other woman, but there is no doubt over Shelley's — *Times Literary Supp.,* 3 July 1969

There is no doubt as to the accuracy of his portrayal —Klaus Lambrecht, *New Republic,* 2 June 1941

doubtful Fowler 1926 includes *doubtful* in his disquisition upon the verb *doubt,* and numerous later commentators have followed suit. See the article at DOUBT, *verb,* for the main theoretical lines. In practice, *doubtful* is usually not followed by a clause, but when it is the clause can begin with *that, whether,* or *if.* We also find the conjunction omitted occasionally.

... it seems doubtful that the university can expect a substantial reduction of conflict —Jerome H. Skolnick, *AAUP Bulletin,* September 1969

... it is doubtful whether the Czechs resented it — *Times Literary Supp.,* 9 Apr. 1970

. . . it is doubtful if any brief biography can recapture the essence of Benjamin Franklin —Carl Bridenbaugh, *N.Y. Herald Tribune Book Rev.,* 4 July 1954

It is doubtful France would be willing to forswear testing —Gerard Smith, *Interplay,* February 1969

See also DUBIOUS, DOUBTFUL.

doubtless, no doubt, undoubtedly   The basic premise of the usage writers (Fowler 1926, Evans 1957, Follett 1966, Bremner 1980, and Bryson 1984) who discuss the relative strength of these words is correct: *doubtless* and *no doubt* (and also *doubtlessly,* which see) are often used to mean "probably"; *undoubtedly* tends to carry more conviction, but it too is often used with less than literal force.

> . . . the poor woman . . . fearfully listening and doubtless misinterpreting it all —Glenway Wescott, *Apartment in Athens,* 1945

> The labor unions spent an estimated thirty million nationally, and industry doubtless matched it —Henry S. Ashmore, *Center Mag.,* January 1969

> In due time, "The Other" will doubtless become one of the classics of horror tales —Dorothy B. Hughes, *Los Angeles Times,* 23 May 1971

> To-day, in search, no doubt, of new subscribers, the exploiters of snobbery go forth —Aldous Huxley, *The Olive Tree,* 1937

> . . . his example will no doubt help others to further explorations —Harold Clurman, *Harper's,* February 1971

> . . . had built a reputation as an academic innovator, no doubt leaving behind some miffed feelings —George W. Bonham, *Change,* October 1971

> . . . Moscow also is undoubtedly willing to pay a high price for Chinese support —Harry Schwartz, *N.Y. Times Mag.,* 11 July 1954

> . . . she will undoubtedly be more careful next time —Lenore Hershey, *Ladies' Home Jour.,* January 1971

Ways of expressing greater certainty include the sometimes maligned *indubitably* (which see); either of Fowler's suggestions, "without (a) doubt" and "beyond a doubt"; and even longer phrases such as "there can be no doubt" or "there is no doubt at all," which by their very cumbersomeness are likely to come across as heartfelt. Part of the reason why *doubtless, no doubt,* and *undoubtedly* lack full strength is that they fit into sentences so smoothly that writers tend to use them as stylistic tools to adjust the rhythm of their prose. Also, *doubtless, no doubt,* and *undoubtedly* all imply that the writer is speculating on or assuming something or is expressing a strong conviction rather than asserting something that has been proven to be true. So these words may carry more conviction for the one who writes them than for the one who reads them.

doubtlessly   Because *doubtless* functions as an adverb, *doubtlessly* has remained an uncommon word during its half-millennium sojourn in the English language. Some people find it superfluous and would like to get rid of it altogether, but after such a long time it seems unlikely to disappear.

Doubtlessly owes its existence to the fact that *-ly* is used so regularly to form adverbs from adjectives in English that adverbs without the *-ly* tend to sound a little incomplete. Even William Safire, in an article defending the use of sentence modifiers, is lured into using *doubtlessly:*

> Doubtlessly, my deliberate decision to adopt "hopefully" in its sentence-coloring sense . . . will be attacked —Safire 1980

When *doubtlessly* modifies an adjective, the inclusion of the *-ly* can help the sentence to read smoothly and be readily understood:

> . . . reduces everybody and everything to stereotypes, overlaid with doubtlessly unintentional vestiges of white colonialist mentalities —John J. O'Connor, *N.Y. Times,* 7 June 1979

See also DOUBTLESS, NO DOUBT, UNDOUBTEDLY.

dove   *Dive* is a weak verb with the past tense *dived.* In the 19th century it developed a past tense *dove*—probably by analogy with *drive, drove*—in some British dialects and in North America. As far as we know, Longfellow was the first person to put it into print:

> Dove as if he were a beaver —*The Song of Hiawatha,* 1855

Hall 1917 notes that Longfellow changed this to *dived* in later editions, probably at the suggestion of critics. The OED Supplement shows an 1857 comment on the prevalence of *dove* in Canada.

Although some older books (such as Jensen 1935) have called *dove* incorrect, most, and especially the more recent ones, accept both *dived* and *dove* as correct. The usage of *dove* is really governed by geography rather than by social class or notions of correctness. Linguistic geographers have found it to be the prevalent past tense in the northern U.S. and some parts of Canada. A 1971 survey found it the prevalent past tense in California and Nevada. Some note that it is spreading southward in the U.S., having become common in some parts of Pennsylvania and eastern South Carolina and Georgia. Undoubtedly the Dictionary of American Regional English will give a more complete picture of its distribution in time.

One notable enclave of *dived* in the northeastern U.S. is the editorial offices of the *New York Times;* their *Winners & Sinners* has been objecting to *dove* since the editorship of Theodore Bernstein. His successors have complained about *dove* at least as recently as March 1987.

Here are a few examples of both forms:

> When I dived in, several others climbed out —John Kenneth Galbraith, *Ambassador's Journal,* 1969

> One of the women dove in smartly and rose up past the tank window —E. L. Doctorow, *World's Fair,* 1985

> The plane dived and smartly landed —John Updike, *Bech is Back,* 1982

> Black dove the airplane, from a dizzy height that permitted him to see simultaneously London and Cherbourg —William F. Buckley, Jr., *Cosmopolitan,* October 1976

> Evans, a 16-year veteran, dived for the ball —Ron Fimrite, *Sports Illustrated,* 15 Oct. 1984

And when I dove, the ball appeared to be 5 yards over my head —Joe Bellino, quoted in *Boston Sunday Globe,* 2 Dec. 1984

... he swam out and dived down to the bottom —Mordecai Richler, *The Apprenticeship of Duddy Kravitz,* 1959

Little boys dove in to grab the brass shell casings —Garrison Keillor, *Lake Wobegon Days,* 1985

Although *dived* is somewhat more common in writing in the U.S. and is usual in British English, *dove* is an acceptable variant. We suggest that you use whichever is more natural to you.

downplay Copperud 1980 terms this verb "journalese," and William Safire publicly apologized in his *New York Times* column of 24 July 1983 for using it. New York journalists seem a bit diffident about using compound words of which adverbs form the first part (see, for instance, UPCOMING).

Downplay is a relatively new verb, evidently going back no farther than 1954. Its main use does seem to be in journalism: almost all of our evidence comes from newspapers and magazines. Thirty years in the business seems to have established it for general use. Here is a cross-section of our evidence:

Actor Stewart happily downplays his boyish charm —*Time,* 2 Aug. 1954

... he will downplay the need for economic and social reform —*Newsweek,* 30 Mar. 1964

White doggedly downplays this kind of talk —Wilfrid Sheed, *N.Y. Times Book Rev.,* 21 Nov. 1976

... the UN downplayed the problem —*Wall Street Jour.,* 10 July 1973

... a two-week field training exercise which will downplay his role as the Prince of Wales —*The Canadian* (Charlottetown, P.E.I.), 8 May 1975

... downplays any territorial competitiveness —David McQuay, *Sunday Denver Post,* 23 Sept. 1984

He downplays others' labor without substituting a convincing personal struggle or achievement of his own —Garry Wills, *Harper's,* January 1972

As president of the show, McDevitt modestly downplays his role —Suzanne Wilding, *Town & Country,* May 1980

dozen *Dozen* has two plurals, a zero form *dozen* (just like the singular) and an inflected *dozens.* When a number is put before the noun, the zero form plural is used:

He that kills me some six or seven dozen of Scots —Shakespeare, *I Henry IV,* 1598

... stript away ten dozen Yards of Fringe —Jonathan Swift, *A Tale of a Tub,* 1710

... several million dozen pairs —B. Eldred Ellis, *Gloves and the Glove Trade,* 1921

... consuming ... twelve dozen oysters, eight quarts of orange juice —Frank Sullivan, *The Night the Old Nostalgia Burned Down,* 1953

When the number is not specified, *dozens* is used:

... worked in dozens of minor roles in television plays —*Current Biography,* June 1965

Evans 1957 notes that *of* used to be common after *dozen:*

I bought you a dozen of shirts —Shakespeare, *I Henry IV,* 1598

... a dozen or so of people were sitting about —Archibald Marshall, *Anthony Dare,* 1923

This construction is now felt to be old-fashioned and is no longer used much. We do, of course, retain *of* after *dozens:*

Dozens of times since ... I have been asked ... —Joseph Wood Krutch, *American Scholar,* Spring 1955

draft, draught Longman 1984 and Chambers 1985 remind us that in current British English *draft* is used for a preliminary sketch and for the corresponding verb, and also for an order for payment (a bank draft). But *draught* is used for beer, horses, and a current of air, and *draughts* is used as the name for the game of checkers. American English uses *draft* in all cases, except, of course, that it calls checkers *checkers.*

drank See DRINK.

drapes, draperies A food and restaurant critic for the *New York Times* and the cartoonist of the strip "Garfield" are taken to task by Kilpatrick 1984 for using the noun *drapes.* "Drape isn't a noun," says Kilpatrick. "It's a verb." Simon 1980 also wrinkles his nose at the word, but his criticism has a social rather than a grammatical basis.

These are brave men, however, apparently the first males ever to venture into this subject, hitherto an exclusively female domain. The only earlier comment that we have found in a usage book is in Margaret Nicholson 1957. The subject seems to have originated with Emily Post, about 1927. Post's approach is straightforward: Never say *drapes;* say *"curtains,* or, if necessary, *draperies."*

The OED Supplement sheds interesting light on this issue. The earliest citations for *drapes,* which is labeled North American, are from the catalogs of Montgomery Ward and Sears and Roebuck. Now, we may safely assume that Emily Post's window hangings were not ordered from a catalog, and—if the word's being a crass Americanism rather than a cultured Briticism weren't enough to put her off it—she would certainly not use a catalog's word for them. No, that's for Miss Noback-ground: "Say, Murree, the new drapes in my home are dandy" (1945 edition).

Post's substitutes, *curtains* and *draperies,* deserve brief comment. *Curtains* has long been in use on both sides of the Atlantic. Her qualifying words, "or, if necessary," may represent tacit recognition of the fact that in America *curtains* and *drapes* or *draperies* often designate somewhat different hangings. *Draperies,* interestingly enough, is also identified as North American in the OED Supplement. Its first citation is from an 1895 Montgomery Ward catalog.

Nicholson appears to have originated the dictum, repeated by Kilpatrick, that *drape* is properly a verb and that the noun is *drapery.* We have already noted that the plural use of both *drape* and *drapery* is North American and dates from around the turn of the century. *Drape* as a verb goes back to the 15th century in obsolete senses; it goes back only to 1847 in reference to cloth. *Drapery* in reference to cloth dates from 1686. *Drape* as a noun relating to cloth or drapery dates back to 1611, and is thus the oldest of the three. The objection to it is (excuse the pun) made from whole cloth.

Beginning with Post, disapproval of *drapes* has occasionally been recorded in the press and in other printed sources, and women have from time to time written to this company to protest the word's appearance in the dictionary. One of the earlier complaints appeared in the *Saturday Review* in April 1928. The writer found the use of *drapes* "ghastly"; however, the word was being used in reference to the theater, in which it is a technical term. *Drapes* is also a technical term in the operating room, where the patient to be operated on is covered with sterile drapes.

The identification of *drapes* as North American seems accurate, although there are signs it is beginning to be used in Britain. Sellers 1975 complains that the Americanism is creeping into British use, and the OED Supplement has a 1970 British citation. All of our evidence is U.S. and Canadian. Here are a few examples:

> Some of the windows were masked by long cretonne drapes —Raymond Chandler, *The Simple Art of Murder,* 1950

> ... on the West Coast families drew the drapes across their bedroom windows —Pierre Salinger, *On Instructions of My Government,* 1971

> ... the new gimmicks: the green printed drapes, pink-and-green waiter and waitress outfits —Linda Wolfe, *New York,* 10 Jan. 1972

> ...a shabby brownstone with dark-green shades and sleazy drapes at the windows —Betty Ferm, *Cosmopolitan,* May 1974

We must conclude that there is no linguistic reason for choosing between *drapes* and *draperies.* Both are of the same plebeian North American origin and the same age, and are equally well established. If you have always used one instead of the other, by all means you should continue to do so. If you have no fixed preference, *draperies* is the safer choice.

draught   See DRAFT, DRAUGHT.

dream   **1.** The verb *dream* has the past and past participle forms *dreamt* and *dreamed.* Evidence in the OED suggests *dreamt* is somewhat older than *dreamed;* Lamberts 1972 suggests that *dreamed* is the earlier form, and the evidence in the Middle English Dictionary allows that possibility. Both forms are nearly 700 years old in any case. Phythian 1979 says that *dreamt* is the more common form in England; our evidence confirms his observation. Watt 1967, Shaw 1987, and Lamberts find *dreamed* more common in the U.S.; the Brown Corpus (Kučera & Francis 1967) strongly backs their contention, while our evidence finds both forms flourishing in American use.
2. We have been surprised to find that the usage writers, most of them inveterate critics of redundancy, seem not to object to the tautologous "dreamed a dream." The expression is, of course, entirely standard:

> I had almost forgotten to tell you of a dream which I dreamed —Emily Dickinson, letter, 21 Oct. 1847

> ... a dream he had dreamt while awake —Joyce Carol Oates, *Harper's,* August 1971

3. Shaw 1987 mentions *dream* taking *of* before a gerund; *of* can also be used with a noun object, and so can *about:*

> ... men who might never have dreamed of advocating massacres —*New Yorker,* 10 Apr. 1971

> ... she often dreamt of the assassination of Kennedy —Joyce Carol Oates, *McCall's,* July 1971

> I dreamt about the boy who Rock and big Stoop had thrown off that roof —Claude Brown, *Manchild in the Promised Land,* 1965

> He dreamt again about somebody else's bulldozers clearing his land —Mordecai Richler, *The Apprenticeship of Duddy Kravitz,* 1959

drench   *Drench* is often used with a complement introduced by *in* or *with:*

> She was drenched in furs and diamonds —Richard Brautigan, *A Confederate General from Big Sur,* 1964

> ... desserts drenched in brandy or Cointreau —Dwight Macdonald, *New Yorker,* 18 July 1953

> "... after detonation the ground-zero circle is drenched with fallout" —Don DeLillo, *End Zone,* 1972

> The sun went up in triumph and drenched the parkland with gold —Elizabeth Taylor, *New Yorker,* 14 Apr. 1956

When *drench* is used in the passive voice, *by* may begin the phrase:

> She was drenched ... by compassion for the immense disaster of her sister's life —Arnold Bennett, *The Old Wives' Tale,* 1908

The locution *drench to the skin,* or *drench one to the skin* is occasionally attested in our files:

> ... a thunderstorm which would have drenched them to the skin —Marcia Davenport, *My Brother's Keeper,* 1954

Particular contexts also allow *drench* to be used with *on* or *from:*

> ... snow and sleet, which drenched cruelly down on little townships —Mollie Panter-Downes, *New Yorker,* 21 Feb. 1953

> Sometimes they ... make awful confidences, or drench us from sentimental slop-pails —Logan Pearsall Smith, *All Trivia,* 1934

drink   The usual 20th-century past tense of this verb is *drank* and the past participle, *drunk.* Usage is not entirely uniform yet, although it is closer to uniform than it has been in the past. The OED notes that the past tense *drunk* was in good use from the 16th through the 19th centuries; Johnson's 1755 Dictionary gives it as a standard variant. Its status has receded since, and it now seems to be relegated to dialect and to what H. L. Mencken called the vulgate:

> "He said he drunk very little," she reminded me —Ring Lardner, *The Big Town,* 1921

The past participle *drank* is a more complex problem. The OED says that it came in during the 17th century.

It seems to have been used commonly from the 17th century at least until Jane Austen's time:

> NURSE. That, miss, is for fear you should be drank before you are ripe —Sir John Vanbrugh, *The Relapse,* 1696

> ... having read somewhere that cold water drank plentifully was good for a fever —Benjamin Franklin, *Autobiography,* 1771

> Monboddo dined with me lately, and having drank tea, we were a good while by ourselves —James Boswell, letter, 14 Feb. 1777

> It is evening; we have drank tea —Jane Austen, letter, 2 Mar. 1814

Johnson's Dictionary did not give *drank* as a past participle—only *drunk* and *drunken*—but to illustrate one sense of *drink* Johnson quotes Dr. Arbuthnot using *had drank,* and the OED shows that Johnson himself used the form. Hall 1917 cites authors as recent as Robert Louis Stevenson for the form and further informs us that it had in his own time considerable vogue in polite spoken English.

On the other hand, Cobbett 1823 disapproved *drank* as a past participle. So did Richard Grant White 1870. White's remarks were objections to the use of irregular verbs by Sterne, Pope, and Swift; he was caught out for this by Fitzedward Hall in *Recent Exemplifications of False Philology* (1872). Hall must have made a convincing case for *drank,* for Bardeen 1883 put it among the words he styled legitimate, though carped at by some critics.

Still, most early 20th-century comment ran against the form. Handbooks such as Utter 1916, Krapp 1927, and Lurie 1927 did not approve it; the editors of Webster's Second (1934) moved it from the main entry of *drink,* where it had been in Webster 1909, and stuck it in the pearl section at the bottom of the page, labeled erroneous.

Linguistic geographers around the middle of the century discovered, however, that the handbooks and Webster's Second were treating *drank* with less respect than it deserved. It was still in polite spoken use in some parts of the U.S. and Canada, and indeed was the majority use in a few areas. It is primarily a spoken form, but it does pop up from time to time in prose written by someone whose dialect still contains the form:

> Two inmates at the Berkshire County House of Correction were taken to Hillcrest Hospital Tuesday evening after they had reportedly drank Lysol —*Springfield* (Mass.) *Morning Union,* 21 Nov. 1984

In writing, you will want to use the past *drank* and the past participle *drunk.* The past *drunk* is essentially dialectal. The past participle *drank* is still in standard spoken use in some parts of the U.S. and Canada, but it is seldom used in print.

See also DRUNK, DRUNKEN.

drought, drouth These variant spellings for the dry spell receive more diverse comment than you would suspect: Shaw 1987, Harper 1985, and Watt 1967 say that both are correct but that *drought* is more common than *drouth.* Our evidence confirms this. Copperud 1980 finds *drouth* in greater favor, a comment that is not supported by our evidence. Longman 1984 says that *drouth* is poetic except in Irish, Scottish, and North American English; our evidence cannot dispute this.

Evans 1957 calls *drouth* dialectal in England, but standard and interchangeable with *drought* in the U.S.; our evidence shows that *drouth* was more common in 1957 than it is now. The Oxford American Dictionary says that careful writers and speakers do not use *drouth.* This remark is simply not true:

> But weather seemed loath to bedevil the hardy island further, except with drouth —Christopher Morley, in *A Century of the Essay,* ed. David Daiches, 1951

> 'Tis not enough on roots and in the mouth,
> But give me water heavy on the head
> In all the passion of a broken drouth
>   —Robert Frost, *A Witness Tree,* 1942

> ... the desolation, the aesthetic and spiritual drouth, of Anglo-Saxon middle-class society —Edmund Wilson, *Axel's Castle,* 1931

> I know it was a year of drouth —*The Autobiography of William Allen White,* 1946

> A drouth or a plague of insects may cause crop failure along the river —Charles F. Hockett, *Man's Place in Nature,* 1973

At the present time, *drouth* is less frequent than *drought* in American English, but both forms are standard.

droves *Drove* is an old collective noun for a herd of animals. It has been used figuratively for upwards of nine centuries. By Defoe's time, it was being used in the plural as a collective, like *throngs* and *crowds,* to indicate a great number. This use is still current:

> Now tourists arrive in such droves that the best you can do is get into step with the stampede —David Butwin, *Saturday Rev.,* 5 Feb. 1972

> ... produced droves of famously beautiful women —William Styron, *This Quiet Dust and Other Writings,* 1982

> Everyone who can afford it wants to live downtown.... They're coming in droves —Jeanne Wayling, quoted in *Audubon Mag.,* November 1982

> Today, fan letters ... come to her in droves — Lucinda Franks, *Saturday Rev.,* January 1981

Since the word was in common use to describe large numbers of people flocking to attend an event, some facetious writer decided that it might be cleverly used to express the opposite notion. We don't know whose idea this was, but it has certainly caught on:

> ... not only stifled the members' interest, but which ... sent them away in droves —Ralph Ellison, *Invisible Man,* 1952

> ... militant anti-Communists stay away in droves —Frank Gorrell, *New Republic,* 14 June 1954

> ... foolish moviegoers stayed away from the Music Hall in droves —Judith Crist, *New York,* 24 July 1972

> ... consumers stayed away from dealers' showrooms in droves —*Wall Street Jour.,* 3 Feb. 1976

> ... the networks spent more lavishly than ever to televise it. Nonetheless, television viewers stayed away in droves —Neil Hickey, *TV Guide,* 1 Aug. 1980

Copperud 1980 thinks that "stayed away in droves" is about the only use of *droves,* but it is not; according to our citations it is not even the most common use. He also thinks that it is a cliché, an opinion from which it is hard to dissent.

drown 1. *Drowned, drownded.* Sometime between the age of Chaucer and that of Shakespeare, several English verbs ending with a nasal vowel acquired an unetymological *-d* at the end. The added *-d* became permanent in some of these: *astound, lend, sound.* In others it did not:

> ... wou'd be ready To swound at the sight of a new face —Thomas Shadwell, *The Sullen Lovers,* 1668

Where Shadwell has *swound,* we would now write *swoon.*

Drown was one of the verbs that acquired an intrusive *d.* The variant *drownd,* says the *OED,* flourished in the 16th and 17th centuries. By the 18th century it seems to have been felt to be dialectal: Swift puts it into the mouth of Tom Neverout in *Polite Conversation* (1738):

> ... don't throw Water on a drownded Rat.

But other characters in this piece say *drown'd;* for instance, Colonel Atwit:

> ... he that is born to be hang'd, will never be drown'd.

Drownd was apparently first attacked by John Witherspoon in *The Druid,* 16 May 1781, who called it "a vulgarism in England and America" (cited in Mencken 1963, abridged). It has been used in rural humor:

> And sing like a medder-lark all day long,
> And drownd her cares in the joys o' song
> —James Whitcomb Riley, *Farm-Rhymes,* 1883

> "Mebby I shall be drounded on dry land, Josiah Allen, but I don't believe it." —Marietta Holley, "A Pleasure Exertion," in *Mark Twain's Library of Humor,* 1888

It is still put into the mouths of fictional characters of rural background or of little education. It is no longer part of standard written or spoken English.

2. *Drowned, was drowned.* It is a convention of newspaper writers and editors that *drowned* should be used for an accidental drowning, and *was drowned* for an intentional drowning. Thus, "she drowned in the lake" should imply an accident, and "she was drowned in the lake" should bring *An American Tragedy* to mind.

The convention may be usefully observed in journalistic reports of drownings, but it is not much observed in other kinds of writing, especially when there is no implication of foul play:

> ... Cessair, a fictitious granddaughter of Noah, comes to Ireland forty days early to escape the Flood ... only to be drowned ... with her brother and fifty maidens —George Brandon Saul, *The Shadow of the Three Queens,* 1953

In some figurative uses the matter of intention may be moot:

> ... a Caesar salad that is fine when not drowned in dressing —Mimi Sheraton, *N.Y. Times,* 18 Jan. 1980

Unless you are reporting an actual drowning, you probably need not worry about using the passive.

drunk, drunken The usual observation is that *drunk* is regularly used as a predicate adjective and that *drunken* is usual in the attributive position, before the modified noun. This observation is, in general, still true.

Drunk is used both literally and figuratively as a predicate adjective:

> By nine he was incoherently drunk —Gregory McDonald, *Fletch,* 1974

> ... watching the cream of Bluegrass Society getting drunker and drunker —Hunter S. Thompson, *Rolling Stone,* 5 July 1973

> ... he was drunk with the shape and sound of words —Morris Dickstein, *N.Y. Times Book Rev.* 3 July 1983

Overall it has only occasional attributive use in speech:

> It occurred to me then that no general can win a war with a drunk army —Jesse Jackson, quoted by Robert Friedman, *Esquire,* December 1979

But it is regularly used attributively before the words *driver* and *driving.* It has been so used for some time, judging from the frequency with which Theodore Bernstein censured its appearance in the *New York Times,* and, especially since the 1980s, is preferred in that use:

> ... the Europeans are particularly tough on drunk driving —Paul Hoffman, *Saturday Rev.,* 10 Feb. 1973

> ... about three Americans are killed and 80 are injured by drunk drivers every hour of every day — *Newsweek,* 13 Sept. 1982

> Law enforcement is only one part of the nationwide campaign against drunk drivers —editorial, *Springfield* (Mass.) *Daily News,* 16 Dec. 1985

When *drunk* is a past participle modifying a noun, it may also precede the noun:

> ... and a half drunk cup of black coffee ... on the bedside table —Tim Cahill, *Rolling Stone,* 2 Mar. 1972

Drunken is the usual choice in attributive uses with words other than *driver* or *driving:*

> Might not the presence of the police chief's small son, if physically unimposing, yet have stayed the drunken hand that plunged the knife? —James Park Sloan, *The Case History of Comrade V.,* 1972

> The drunken slaughter over the past decade is a staggering one-quarter of a million Americans —*Newsweek,* 13 Sept. 1982

Drunken, rather than *drunk,* is used to indicate habitual drinking as distinguished from a state of intoxication. In this use it may even be found as a predicate adjective:

> A brother drinks and the family is dubbed drunken —Carll Tucker, *Saturday Rev.,* 23 June 1979

dual A thousand years ago and more, Old English had a grammatical number system consisting of singular (for one), dual (for two), and plural (for more than two). The plural long ago supplanted the dual, and all we have as reminders of its former existence are such words as *either, neither, between, both, other,* and *whether,* whose ancestors were connected with it. These words and the

comparative inflection -er can still serve to remind us of
things in twos, but the notion is greatly weakened now
and in some instances nearly forgotten. It is, however,
salutary to remember how long the formal dual number
has been defunct when a commentator invokes it to justify a supposed limitation on usage.

dual comparison See AS GOOD OR BETTER THAN.

dubious, doubtful Is it permissible to say that you
are dubious about something? Follett 1966 states that
"when the word is used with discrimination, the doubt
is elsewhere than in the person or thing described as
dubious. This person or thing is the object of doubt by
another or others, not the author or abode of doubt."
Macmillan 1982 is of the same opinion: "The result of
an action or the truth of a statement may be *dubious,*
while the person who questions either is *doubtful.*" We
are dubious about this distinction. *Dubious* has been
used—even by writers of discrimination—to mean
"doubting, unsettled in opinion, suspicious."

> Mr. Cruncher was soothed, but shook his head in a
> dubious and moral way —Charles Dickens, *A Tale
> of Two Cities,* 1859

> Mamma had shaken a dubious head —Rose Macau-
> lay, *Told by an Idiot,* 1923

> He had never heard of me and was a little dubious
> about signing his name —Henry Miller, *The Air-
> Conditioned Nightmare,* 1945

> When I was hired, old George was dubious, and with
> reason, because as a salesman I was tongue-tied —
> Bill Gerry, *Yale Rev.,* Winter 1948

> ... one project about which their top management
> was very dubious —Peter F. Drucker, *Harper's,* Jan-
> uary 1972

Follett's objection may possibly stem from the fact
that the "doubting" sense of *dubious* is not as common
as the senses that taken together mean "giving rise to
uncertainty." But the "doubting" sense is also only one
segment of the meaning of *doubtful.* Both *dubious* and
doubtful are frequently used to refer to the object of
doubt. *Doubtful* may imply a simple lack of conviction
or certainty, while *dubious* usually implies suspicion,
mistrust, or hesitation; however, in many contexts
either word can be used.

due to Concern over the propriety of *due to* is one of
those long-lived controversies in which the grounds for
objection have entirely changed over time. The present-
day objection is to *due to* used as a preposition in the
sense of "owing to" or "because of," but the controversy
began in the 18th century with *owing.* There were some,
apparently, who objected to the use of *owing,* an "active
participle," in the sense "owed, due," which was held to
be proper only for the "passive participle" *owed* (or
due). Johnson's Dictionary notes this controversy
(under *owe*) and comments that Lord Bolingbroke had
been aware of it, and avoided *owing* by using *due* in the
sense "attributable": "*Bolinbroke* [sic] says, the effect is
due to the cause." Johnson did not agree; he thought
most writers used *due* only of debt. Johnson did not
enter Bolingbroke's use of *due* in his first (1755) edition.
He inserted it in a later edition, however, with a quotation from Robert Boyle and the annotation, "proper,
but not usual."

Somehow Johnson's comments on *due* at his entry for
owe (or perhaps just his attitude) were transmitted to
American handbooks of the second half of the 19th century: Bache 1869, Ayres 1881, Compton 1898. The gist
of their argument is objection to the use of *due* where
there is no notion of debt. Johnson's comment was not,
however, repeated by Webster 1828.

In the 20th century the grounds of objection change.
A few writers—Vizetelly 1906, Josephine Turck Baker
1927—repeat the 19th-century objection. But with Utter
1916, MacCracken & Sandison 1917, Fowler 1926,
Krapp 1927, the sense "attributable" is acceptable as
long as *due* is clearly an adjective; when *due to* is used
as a preposition introducing a phrase that modifies anything but a particular noun, it is objectionable. A new
issue has been born, and subsequent commentators
have generally followed the newer line of attack.

Owing to and *due to* developed along precisely parallel lines, according to a detailed study by John S. Kenyon published in *American Speech,* October 1930. The
difference is that *owing to* crept imperceptibly into use
as a preposition while the focus of criticism was on the
active-passive issue. *Due to* did not begin life as a preposition until nearly the 20th century (the OED Supplement has an 1897 citation). Once the critics noticed the
new use, they laid aside old objections and belabored
due to for its new function.

The basic argument is this: *due to* is all right when it
clearly has a noun or pronoun to modify or when it follows a linking verb:

> ... a Jonah's gourd,
> Up in one night, and due to sudden sun
> —Alfred, Lord Tennyson,
> *The Princess,* 1847 (OED)

> ... the failure to nail currant jelly to a wall is not due
> to the nail —Theodore Roosevelt, 1915, quoted by
> William Safire, *N.Y. Times,* 6 Apr. 1986

> It must be due to my lack of polish —Robert Frost,
> letter, 25 Apr. 1915

> ... its gradual supersession by the less efficient hand-
> gun of Tudor times appears to have been due to the
> village neglect of archery —G. M. Trevelyan, *A
> Shortened History of England,* 1942

But when there is no linking verb, the construction is
suspect:

> Largely due to the literary activities of Alfred the
> Great and the political supremacy reached by his
> kingdom of Wessex ... , the language of Wessex
> became accepted as the standard form of the lan-
> guage in literary composition —George H.
> McKnight, *English Words and Their Background,*
> 1923

> Although I myself, due doubtless to defective skill,
> have to work pretty hard —George Jean Nathan,
> *Testament of a Critic,* 1931

> ... Ross is famous for his old conviction that
> women do not belong in offices. This has mellowed
> somewhat, partly due to his discovery during the war
> that several of them could be as competent as men
> —James Thurber, letter, 6 Sept. 1947

> ... the slips were not introduced until the first of
> May (due to complications in securing them) —Nor-
> man V. McCullough, *College English,* April 1960

... there is an outside chance at least that Ben Reid—due to those considerations of environment and mentality ...—may have his sentence commuted —William Styron, *This Quiet Dust and Other Writings,* 1982

Webster's Second originally described *due* as being "often erroneously used in the phrase *due to* ... in the manner of a compound preposition," but at the end of the 1940s Merriam editors revised the entry to read: "Prepositional *due to, ...* though objected to by some, is in common and reputable use." Since that time some commentators have agreed that the use is valid, while others have stood by the opinions of 1916 and 1917. All allow that *due to* is unobjectionable after the verb *to be.* But many of those who admit that prepositional *due to* is established are quick to put in a disclaimer, such as that many people object to it or that it is informal. *Due to* has entered the folklore of usage.

Perhaps it is time for the critics to find a new basis for disparaging *due to.* A sure sign of the reflexiveness of the present objections is beginning to appear in careless restatements of them. Two college handbooks of the 1980s call *due to* an adjective rather than a preposition, for example. A general handbook of the same time says that *due to* is a wordy way of saying *because. Because,* however, is a conjunction and *due to* is a preposition; *due to* competes with *because of.* (And what can *wordy* mean in this case? *Because* has the same number of syllables and two more letters than *due to.*)

In our judgment, *due to* is as impeccable grammatically as *owing to,* which is frequently recommended as a substitute for it. There never has been a grammatical ground for objection, although the objection formulated in the early part of this century persists in the minds of some usage commentators. The preposition is used by reputable writers and is even officially part of the Queen's English—the OED Supplement gives a quotation from Queen Elizabeth II. There is no solid reason to avoid using *due to.*

due to the fact that Most of the commentators who mention this phrase condemn it as "wordy for *because.*" There are a couple of things you should keep in mind when presented with such advice. First, remember that, being human, we tend to see wordiness as a characteristic of someone else's writing; we ourselves always use just the right number of words.

Most importantly, remember that *due to the fact that* is a wordy way of saying the short and simple word *since* —Shaw 1970

Second, it is a good idea to test the advice in a real context. Here are a few examples:

The success of the Channel 13 report was due mainly to the fact that it let both sides ... speak for themselves —Stephanie Harrington, *Village Voice,* 28 Feb. 1968

Would you improve this passage by changing it to "was mainly because it ..." or "was mainly since it ..."?

[The ship] was taxed to her capacity, due to the fact that, instead of proceeding direct to Melbourne from Bluff, she was advertised to go first to Adelaide —S. T. Colver, *Paul Travers' Adventures,* 1897 (in Dictionary of American English and OED Supplement)

Here *because,* or even *since,* would work very nicely; but this was written before the phrase had been labeled wordy. It is also the earliest attestation for the preposition *due to.*

This is due to the fact that the cost of prescription drugs borders on the exorbitant —Henry Gewirtz & Saxon Graham, *Trans-Action,* February 1970

"This is because" is usable here (*since* is not). You should be aware, though, that there is a considerable amount of opinion to the effect that *because* should not be used to introduce a clause functioning as a noun, though *because* is indeed often so used. So our handbook writers, in effect, recommend a usage here that they warn you against elsewhere in the book.

But enough. You can usually work your way around *due to the fact that,* if you want to. But you obviously cannot simply replace it with *because* or *since* in every context. Adding *the fact that* to *due to* allows the preposition to function as a conjunction; it may even come in handy sometime.

dumb Commentators as far apart as Utter 1916 and Harper 1985 have decried the use of *dumb* to mean stupid. In spite of the opposition of these commentators, the usage has become well established, even in writing:

He assured me that musical people, though singularly dumb, were so sexually depraved that we could acquire platoons of budding sopranos for the price of a Coke and a hamburger —Russell Baker, *Growing Up,* 1982

The result of this sense's becoming established is that the "mute" sense of *dumb* has come to be considered offensive to those persons who cannot speak. The substitute usually recommended is *mute.*

dummy subject See THERE; THERE IS, THERE ARE.

dwell 1. Although there are two spellings, *dwelt* and *dwelled,* for the past tense of *dwell,* the original form *dwelled* has steadily lost ground over the centuries. *Dwelled* is still used, but *dwelt* is found far more often:

... the great-hearted ... sufferer who dwelt behind the hulking and lugubrious facade —William Styron, *This Quiet Dust and Other Writings,* 1982

... it was on Roelf that her eyes dwelt and rested — Edna Ferber, *So Big,* 1924

He dwelled on his own sensations and liked to talk about them —E. L. Doctorow, *Ragtime,* 1975

2. Some language commentators warn against using *dwell* when (to them) the more everyday word *live* is meant. The commentators were contending as far back as the early part of this century that *dwell* had given way in use to *live.* While *live* may be the more common usage, *dwell* has by no means disappeared:

... now dwells within a half-mile of a subway — *American Guide Series: N.Y. City,* 1939

... less [people] than had dwelled in his own town —C. S. Forester, *The Sky and the Forest,* 1948

... I learned that she dwelt at 16 Charlotte Street — Samuel Flagg Bemis, *New-England Galaxy,* Fall 1969

3. *Dwell* may take any of any number of prepositions. In addition to *behind, on, within, in,* and *at* (shown in

the quotations above), *dwell* is used with *among, beneath, outside, over, under, upon,* and *with:*

... God ... taking flesh and coming down and dwelling among us as a man —Samuel Butler, *The Way of All Flesh,* 1903

... "by my twin soul which dwells beneath the banana plant, will I do it!" —Charles Beadle, *Witch-Doctors,* 1922

... elements of the society which support but dwell outside the campus —Anthony Lambeth, *Change,* Summer 1971

It is useless to dwell over the sufferings of these heroic men —John Buchan, *The Last Secrets,* 1923

He could not hinder himself from dwelling upon it —Stephen Crane, *The Red Badge of Courage,* 1895

... divert attention from the sorrow and prevent the sufferer from dwelling upon it —Edith Sitwell, *I Live Under a Black Sun,* 1937

Yet Goldsmith has a peculiar reticence which forbids us to dwell with him in complete intimacy — Virginia Woolf, *The Captain's Death Bed and Other Essays,* 1950 ed.

To judge by the evidence found in the Merriam-Webster citation files, *dwell* is used most often with *on,* followed by *in* and *upon.* The other prepositions are used less frequently.

dying, dyeing Several commentators warn, sensibly enough, against the careless use of *dying,* the present participle of *die,* when *dyeing,* the present participle of *dye,* is intended.

E

each There are a number of niggling problems about *each* and its agreement with either verb or pronoun. These problems mostly were discovered in the 18th century, when the conflict of grammatical agreement and notional agreement first began to trouble grammarians. We will take up a few of these separately. See also AGREEMENT: INDEFINITE PRONOUNS.
1. *Each,* pronoun, as simple subject. The rule of thumb from the 18th century on has been that *each* takes a singular verb. This is the usual case in modern practice:

... each is believed capable of producing 10,000 barrels —*Annual Report, Phillips Petroleum Co.,* 1970

... for each who achieves it —*Times Literary Supp.,* 28 Mar. 1968

Each was alert to snatch any advantage —*Dictionary of American Biography,* 1928

Each derives its authority directly from the Constitution —*N.Y. Times Mag.,* 27 Feb. 1955

Notional agreement interferes with the singularity of *each* only when *each* has a plural antecedent. The notional plurality may then bring a plural verb into use:

... in Naples a number of families will join in a carriage, and each have their own emblazoned doors — *The Journals of Arnold Bennett,* ed. Frank Swinnerton, 1954

... the quarrel scene between the two leaders was superbly conducted and each die in the grand manner —T. C. Worsley, *Britain To-Day,* June 1953

... Antony in *Antony and Cleopatra* and Aecius in *Valentinian....* Each command a subordinate — Murray Abend, *Notes and Queries,* 16 Aug. 1952

Both KB Moulding and Driwood Moulding offer.... Each are assembled of at least three mouldings —Lawrence Grow, *The Old House Catalogue,* 1976

Sticklers for grammatical agreement will insist on a singular verb. The singular is more usual and will not attract attention.
2. *Each,* adjective, modifying a singular noun subject. The singular verb is regularly used:

Each Division brings to bear ... its special expertise —*Annual Report, CPC International,* 1970

... each sex is distinguished from the other — Stephanie Dudek, *Psychology Today,* May 1971

... a general belief that each person possesses four souls —Sir James G. Frazer, *Aftermath,* 1937

3. *Each,* pronoun, followed by a phrase introduced by *of.* Since the *of* phrase always contains a plural noun or pronoun, notional plurality is strong in these constructions. Those who always insist on grammatical agreement insist on the singular verb, but Copperud 1970, ·1980 notes that the commentators he summarizes are evenly split on the propriety of the plural verb. Copperud also says that instances of *each (of)* with a plural verb are increasing in carefully edited prose—in other words, notional agreement appears to be gaining ground over grammatical agreement. Evidence in the Merriam-Webster files shows actual usage to be about as evenly split as Copperud's commentators. First a few examples with singular verbs:

Each of them is a decisive way —Ronald Reagan, *Abortion and the Conscience of the Nation,* 1984

Each of the articles ... relates to one central theme —T. George Harris, *Psychology Today,* May 1971

... but each of the other high roads has much to make its traverse exciting —Alicita and Warren Hamilton, *Ford Times,* July 1954

But each of us harbors our own special interests — Tom Lewis, *Harper's Weekly,* 26 July 1976

And each of them was busy in arranging their particular concerns —Jane Austen, *Sense and Sensibility,* 1811 (in Hodgson 1889)

Note the contrast in possessive pronouns in the last three citations; there is more on pronoun agreement in section 5 below. Now some plural examples:

> We still record our observations in "bits of data", each of which do possess the character of simple location —Allen Aardsma, *Undergraduate Jour. of Philosophy,* May 1969

> He usually has about eight pupils, each of whom pay about $200 a month —*Time,* 3 June 1946

> Each of his ideas are stated —*Down Beat,* 20 Oct. 1950

> Each of these texts have been further validated —*Training Manual for Auxiliary Firemen,* 1942

> Each of Mr. Fugard's plays . . . are themselves acts of contrition —Mel Gussow, *N.Y. Times,* cited in Simon 1980

It seems likely that notional agreement is the decisive force in most of these examples, singular and plural. If you are thinking of *each* as individualizing, you will use the singular verb; if you think of it as collecting, you will use the plural. Many writers use the idiomatically common pattern of a singular verb and a succeeding plural pronoun.

4. *Each,* adjective, following a plural noun subject. The usage panel of Heritage 1969 rejected "they each have large followings" by a whopping 95 percent. They were marching alone, apparently; Copperud 1970, 1980 cites his commentators (except the panel) as accepting the plural verb, while Heritage 1982, Chambers 1985, Johnson 1982, Freeman 1983, and Bernstein 1958 all allow it. Heritage 1982 also approves the plural pronoun in such instances. The examples of this construction in our files are plural:

> . . . they each have too many possible meanings —Linda Costigan Lederman, *New Dimensions,* 1977

> Our containerboard mills each conduct five-year programs —*Annual Report, Owens-Illinois,* 1970

> If we and our Atlantic community partners each take our respective share —Dean Acheson, *U.S. Dept. of State Bulletin,* 12 June 1950

> . . . these and millions of other organized groups each possess their own individuality —Pitirim A. Sorokin, *Society, Culture, and Personality: Their Structure and Dynamics,* 1947

> Gates and Mifflin each publicly avowed their entire confidence in Washington —Horace E. Scudder, *George Washington,* 1885

5. Pronoun reference. It is abundantly clear that *each* shares with many indefinite pronouns the tendency to take a plural pronoun in reference, and equally clear that notional agreement rules in most instances, singular or plural. Nonetheless, use of a plural pronoun in reference to *each* has often been censured, for example by Lurie 1927, Follett 1966, Phythian 1979, and Heritage 1982. Let us begin with one of the earliest examples to be censured; Addison wrote it and Campbell 1776 rejected it:

> Each of the sexes should keep within its particular bounds, and content themselves to exult within their respective districts —*The Spectator,* No. 505

Here we can see Addison's mind shifting from considering the two groups separately to considering them collectively. Campbell insists on grammatical agreement; a more reasonable objection would be to the shift from singular to plural in the same sentence. Addison's contemporaries probably never noticed. Modern instances can be found where such a shift takes place in adjacent sentences:

> These nations are in every way equal to each other. Each is responsible for its own home and foreign policy. But they are also parts of a greater whole —Lord Salisbury, quoted in *British Information Services,* 14 Apr. 1952

Usually, however, a writer or speaker tends to maintain either the singular or the plural notion without sudden shifts. Frequently the notion is singular:

> Each house shall keep a journal of its proceedings —*Constitution of the United States,* 1787

> . . . each having its own council and academic board and controlling its own teaching —Sir James Mountford, *British Universities,* 1966

> The romanticist and the realist try to capture them, each in his own way —Leacock 1943

> . . . each of them should feel ashamed for the rest of his natural life for his part in this —William H. Lundquist, letter to the editor, *Newsweek,* 14 July 1952

> . . . to each according to his weakness and his heart's desire —Glenway Wescott, *Prose,* Fall 1971

We even find George Bernard Shaw thinking of individual actors of both sexes:

> Each claimed as of right the part which came nearest to his or her speciality; and each played all his or her parts in exactly the same way —Preface, *The Shaw-Terry Letters,* 1931

More often, however, the notion seems to be plural:

> Thirteen of these unfortunate rivals entered the lists; and each of them in their turn paid the Forfeiture of their lives —William Melmoth, translation of Cicero's Letters, 1753 (in Baker 1770)

> I found myself that same morning with three or four of the groundkeepers, each of us with a pick or shovel on our shoulders —E. L. Doctorow, *Loon Lake,* 1979

> . . . but in lowliness of mind let each esteem other better than themselves —Philippians 2:3 (AV), 1611

> Each in their own way, the Indians, Indo-Chinese and Indonesians, were asking —*Time,* 3 Dec. 1945

> . . . the independence of the tribes was marked by their peculiar dialects; but each, after their own, allowed a just preference —Edward Gibbon, *The Decline and Fall of the Roman Empire,* 1788

> Each of these people undoubtedly modified Latin in accordance with their own speech habits —Albert C. Baugh, *A History of the English Language,* 2d ed., 1951

> Each in their way broke fresh ground —*Times Literary Supp.,* 5 Nov. 1971

> . . . each candidate had to overcome special barriers thrown in their way by local bigots —*New Republic,* 25 May 1953

Note that *each,* like other indefinite pronouns, partakes of that idiomatic construction in which the pronoun takes a singular verb but a plural pronoun:

> And each of them was busy in arranging their particular concerns, and endeavoring, by placing around them their books and other possessions —Jane Austen, *Sense and Sensibility,* 1811 (in Hodgson 1889)

> Each woman enrolled in the WAAC has postponed the induction of a man since they are counted as a man in computing ... manpower requirements —George C. Marshall, *The United States at War,* 8 Sept. 1943

> Each, first of all, has to provide their home listeners with the best possible service —Robert McCall, *BBC Year Book 1952*

In pronoun reference to *each,* trust notional agreement.
6. *Each,* pronoun, referring to a plural subject, but following the verb. Copperud 1970 reports the agreement of Fowler 1965 and Bernstein 1965 that when *each* follows the verb, the reference to the subject should be singular; Copperud gives this example:

> We are each responsible for his own family.

Not only does the example seem awkward, but the Merriam-Webster files have not a single example of the prescribed form with the singular. Actual usage seems to prefer the plural:

> ... strong unsubsidized lines can each carry their share of money-losing routes —*Time,* 17 May 1954

Bernstein and Fowler appear to be agreeing on theory only; the examples they present, of course, have plural pronouns. Our files have very few examples of this particular construction, which suggests this problem may be encountered less often than some of the others discussed in this article.
7. Evans 1957 states, "The pronoun *each* itself does not have a genitive form. We cannot say *each's.*" He is wrong; the form is rare but does exist.

> Incentives for faculty come from rewards in each's discipline —Robert T. Blackburn, *AAUP Bulletin,* December 1967

8. In the 19th century there was some debate about whether *each*—pronoun or adjective—could properly refer to more than two. The issue was apparently started by Walter Savage Landor, who prescribes *every* when the reference was to more than two. Landor's prescription was mentioned with approbation by Fitzedward Hall in one of his polemical articles on language. Williams 1897 devotes a whole chapter, with numerous examples, to rebutting Hall. It is no longer an issue; *each* frequently refers to more than two.

each and every, each and all *Each and every* is an emphatic form, damned on all sides (Copperud 1970, 1980, Watt 1967, Shaw 1975, Bryson 1984, Janis 1984, and more) as pompous, redundant, wordy, officialese, trite, and a cliché—a wide-ranging selection from the language critic's stock of disapproving descriptors. (Watt does, however, point out that it is not strictly tautological.) Strunk & White 1972, 1979 calls it "pitchman's jargon," to be avoided except in dialogue. It is, in fact, used in fictional speech. In this example, the author

has purposely created a context that seems to justify the critics' adjectives:

> "My friends, the time has come when each and every one of us must face the fact that pornography, no matter what disguise it wears, still remains outright obscenity and a threat to our families, to our future, and to the health of this great nation. . . ." —Irving Wallace, *The Seven Minutes,* 1969

But mostly *each and every* is simply used as an emphatic modifier:

> ... if a man is lucky to avoid such intimate confrontation with the failure of his deepest projects each and every month —Norman Mailer, *Harper's,* March 1971

> I decided to do what most of the correspondents have no patience or need to do, and that is cover each and every one of the press briefings —Irving Wallace, *The Plot,* 1967

> Not only has the Report apparently found criteria ... but also a way to apply them to each and every one of 1,187 faculties —Samuel McCracken, *Change,* June 1972

> By now, every woman knows it's all right not to get an orgasm each and every time she goes to bed with a man —Jane DeLynn, *Cosmopolitan,* December 1976

There is a less common variant *each and all,* similarly used:

> ... a wild assortment of vital and trivial statistics about each and all of us —Malcolm S. Forbes, *Forbes,* 1 Feb. 1974

> ... what we are looking for is a special chemistry for each and all of our publications —Rupert Murdoch, quoted in *UPI Reporter,* 28 Apr. 1977

The evidence suggests that writers fail to take the strictures of the commentators very seriously and that they use *each and every* simply as an emphatic form of *each* or *every* or they use it, as Irving Wallace did in his fictional political speech, to help achieve a particular effect. It is available for you to use, if it seems useful, or to avoid, if it strikes you as it does the commentators.

each other   **1.** *Each other, one another.* Bardeen 1883 indicates that the use of *each other* for *one another* is legitimate, though carped at by some critics; Bardeen had found his carping critic in Ayres 1881. Actually the prescriptive rule that *each other* is to be restricted to two and *one another* to more than two goes back even farther than Ayres. Goold Brown 1851 cites the rule with approbation, and quotes it from an even earlier grammarian, one T. O. Churchill (*A New Grammar of the English Language,* London, 1823). Churchill did not invent the rule; although Brown mentions no earlier instance, Sundby et al. 1991 have found it in a 1785 grammar by a George N. Ussher. But Goold Brown also notes that "misapplications of the foregoing reciprocal terms are very frequent in books" and goes on to cite Samuel Johnson and Noah Webster in error. He further notes that "it is strange that phrases so very common should not be rightly understood." It is perhaps easier now than it was in 1851 to see why: evidence in the

OED shows that the restriction has never existed in practice; the interchangeability of *each other* and *one another* had been established centuries before Ussher or somebody even earlier thought up the rule.

Fowler 1926 notes that some writers follow the rule but goes on to state that "the differentiation is neither of present utility nor based on historical usage; the old distributive of two as opposed to several was not *e*[*ach*], but *either*; & *either other*, which formerly existed beside *e*[*ach*] *o*[*ther*] & *one another* would doubtless have survived if its special meaning had been required." Even Fowler's high reputation among usage commentators has not convinced those to whom the rule is dear; many still prescribe it. A few examples may illustrate the rule's baselessness:

Sixteen ministers who meet weekly at each other's houses —Samuel Johnson, *Life of Swift* (in Brown 1851)

Most of whom live remote from each other —Noah Webster, *Essays* (in *Literary Digest,* 5 July 1924)

The spouse aspires to an union with Christ, their mutual love for one another —chapter gloss, *Canticle of Canticles* (Douay Version), 1609

Two negatives in English destroy one another — Lowth 1763

It is a bad thing that men should hate each other; but it is far worse that they should contract the habit of cutting one another's throats without hatred —T. B. Macaulay (in Webster 1909)

. . . and the charity of every one of you all toward each other aboundeth —2 Thessalonians 1:3 (AV), 1611

. . . he and Bikki were extremely jealous of one another —Stella Gibbons, *Cold Comfort Farm,* 1932

. . . and there is a chain of witnesses who confirm each other —G. K. Chesterton, "The Oracle of the Dog," 1923

. . . Janet and Marcia would, by way of greeting, neigh at one another —John Updike, *Couples,* 1968

They had been marrying one another for so many centuries that they had bred into themselves just the qualities, ignorance and idiocy, they could least afford. At the funeral of Edward VII in London they had pushed and shoved and elbowed each other like children for places in the cortege —E. L. Doctorow, *Ragtime,* 1975

A few commentators believe the rule to be followed in "formal discourse." This belief will not bear examination: Samuel Johnson's discourse is perhaps the most consistently formal that exists in English literature, and he has been cited in violation of the rule.

We conclude that the rule restricting *each other* to two and *one another* to more than two was cut out of the whole cloth. There is no sin in its violation. It is, however, easy and painless to observe if you so wish.

2. *Each other's, one another's.* Goold Brown 1851 cites some unidentified writer as using *each others'*, which he finds wrong in that instance. In Johnson's use, cited above, however, he thinks *each others'* more logical. The evidence in Merriam-Webster files indicates that the possessive is regularly *each other's, one another's*. We have no evidence that Goold Brown's reasoning has been followed.

Johnson 1982 notes that the following noun can be either singular or plural; our evidence agrees:

. . . all entities or factors in the universe are essentially relevant to each other's existence —Alfred North Whitehead, *Essays in Science and Philosophy,* 1947

. . . its members still frequently exchange visits to each other's homes —*Current Biography,* January 1968

3. Henry Bradley, in the *E* volume of the OED, observes that the use of *each other* as the subject of a clause is "a vulgarism occasionally heard"; he does not, however, present either substantiation or quoted example. Fowler 1926 and Partridge 1942 agree; so does Heritage 1982, which cautiously bans it only from "formal writing," however. Evidence in the Merriam-Webster files indicates that such use is nearly nonexistent in edited prose. If *each other* is by now a fully established pronoun, there is no grammatical reason it could not be the subject of a clause, but it is simply not so used. Perhaps uncertainty about the number of the verb is a deterrent.

eager When *eager* is used with a preposition, the preposition is usually *to* and it is followed by an infinitive:

He himself was eager to have the Cathedral begun — Willa Cather, *Death Comes for the Archbishop,* 1927

. . . members of the public eager to understand those principles —Quintin Hogg, *Times Literary Supp.,* 22 Jan. 1970

Although in the past *eager* was used with a variety of prepositions besides *to*—among them *about, after, for, in, of,* and *upon*—the Merriam-Webster files attest to the continuing use of only *for* and *in* during the last 100 years. And while *eager for* is frequent in contemporary writing, *eager in* is much less often used:

. . . all were eager for more trips —Ruth Saberski Goldenheim, *Barnard Alumnae,* Winter 1971

. . . as eager for human companionship as a spaniel pup —Phil Stong, in *The Aspirin Age 1919–1941,* ed. Isabel Leighton, 1949

. . . he was less learned than swift and eager in his reading —Horace Gregory, *The Shield of Achilles,* 1944

early on This adverb is sometimes objected to in American writing as an obtrusive Briticism. It is a relative newcomer to the language, having arisen in British English around 1928.

'It might have been *given* him earlier.' . . . 'Well— not too early on, Peter. Suppose he had died a lot too soon.' —Dorothy L. Sayers, *The Unpleasantness at the Bellona Club,* 1928 (OED Supplement)

Early on came into frequent use in American English in the late 1960s and is now well established on both sides of the Atlantic.

Another objection by commentators is that the *on* is superfluous; *early* will do. Looking at our evidence for the way that *early on* is used, we find that *early* could be substituted in some, but certainly not all, cases. When a sentence modifier is required, for example, the *on* is needed.

Early on, the project reached a climax of sorts —Jack Fincher, *Smithsonian,* July 1982

Early on, Gould did such a good job as bulldozer operator, that Steiner hired him fulltime as ranch manager —Doug Perkins, *The Cattleman,* December 1983

Early on is a more specific adverb than *early* and refers to an early point or stage in a process or course of events. James McCawley is credited in William Safire's "On Language" column (12 Apr. 1981) with pointing out that *early on* "is never used when referring only to clock times: One does not say, 'Alice usually gets up early on.'" Our evidence bears out this observation.

On the subject of this adverb's proper sphere of usage, Harper 1985 says, "there is nothing wrong with the formulation and it is rather charming, especially in casual speech," which may be a case of damning with faint praise. *Early on* is equally at home in speech and writing.

Early on, I was a conservative, snobby, Buckley type —Gore Vidal, quoted in *Look,* 29 July 1969

. . . my mother told me early on you don't sell diamonds at the five and dime —Robert Mitchum, quoted in *Cosmopolitan,* November 1976

. . . he had that particular cast of features which comes to maturity comparatively early on in life —Paul Scott, *A Male Child,* 1956

Despite his unsuccess early on, one has the impression of a considerable manipulator of his own fortunes —Stephen Spender, *N.Y. Times Book Rev.,* 26 May 1957

. . . very early on, Samuel Johnson learnt to fear the hours of stagnant idleness —John Wain, *Samuel Johnson,* 1974

. . . a former film student spotted early on by . . . the president of Universal Studios —Hollis Alpert, *Saturday Rev.,* 12 July 1975

He was a liar who early on saw the incendiary power of his lies —Robert Leiter, *American Scholar,* Winter 1981/82

earth The names of planets other than our own are invariably capitalized, but *earth* is more often than not lowercased. Capitalization is most likely when the earth is being referred to in astronomical terms:

. . . the effects which the cosmos has on the planet Earth —David W. Hughes, *Nature,* 14 June 1969

When the other planets are also referred to, there is some tendency both to capitalize *Earth* and to omit the definite article *the* which normally precedes it:

. . . for the moon, Mercury, Venus, Mars, and Earth —Brian T. O'Leary et al., *Science,* 15 Aug. 1969

Some writers, however, choose to lowercase *earth* and to include *the* even when referring to the other planets:

The earth is uniquely favored among the planets. . . . The large planets (Jupiter, Saturn, Uranus and Neptune) have only a small solid core —Sir Edward Bullard, *Scientific American,* September 1969

Both treatments are perfectly acceptable. The sensible thing to do is to choose whichever styling seems most natural to you in a particular context, and to use that styling consistently in similar contexts.

easy, easily As an adverb, *easy* has a long history of reputable use. It was first recorded in 1400 and can be found in the works of such authors as Spenser, Shakespeare, and Byron. In current English it has many uses, most of which have a somewhat informal quality:

. . . Bauer knows when to go easy on players —*Current Biography,* February 1967

In the daytime I'm working in the studios, $10 an hour. Making $300, $400 a week easy —Jimmy McPartland, quoted in Studs Terkel, *Hard Times,* 1970

. . . was just a matter of rest and quiet, and taking things easy —Daphne du Maurier, *Ladies' Home Jour.,* August 1971

. . . lets no one off easy —Richard Howard, *N.Y. Times Book Rev.,* 24 Nov. 1974

Laughs come easy nowadays —Jeffrey Klein, *N.Y. Times Book Rev.,* 24 Oct. 1976

All those out there who may have wondered what Atlantic City would be without Bert Parks can rest easy —Judith Cummings, *N.Y. Times,* 14 Apr. 1980

Go easy on the salad dressing —Martha Smilgis, *People,* 21 July 1980

Take it easy when you first start a new exercise program —Martha Davis Dunn et al., *Living, Learning, and Caring,* 1981

These uses of *easy* are, in general, distinct from the uses of *easily. Easily* is a more common adverb than *easy,* and it has a wider range of applications. It can and often does come before the verb it modifies, in which position *easy* is not possible:

. . . a distrust that easily erodes the thin crust of knowledge —Theodore Schwartz, *Psychology Today,* March 1971

. . . need not be so easily fooled —Stephen Steinberg, *Commentary,* January 1972

Easily usually cannot be replaced idiomatically by *easy,* even when it follows the verb:

. . . seem to be able to suppress the drug's effects easily —Solomon H. Snyder, *Psychology Today,* May 1971

. . . a gentleman who moves easily in exalted circles —John Thompson, *Harper's,* October 1971

In contexts where both adverbs are possible (such as "Laughs come easy" or "Laughs come easily"), you should choose whichever seems most natural and most appropriate to the tone of your writing.

echelon *Echelon* is originally a French word meaning literally "a rung on a ladder." It was borrowed into English in the late 18th century in a figurative sense denoting a step-like military formation, and it remained primarily a military word for about 150 years thereafter, developing several additional senses during that time.

One military sense it had developed by the end of World War II was "a level in a chain of command":

> It is a principle that a higher echelon maintain communications to the next lower echelon —*Coast Artillery Jour.,* November–December 1944

In this sense, *echelon* began to appear commonly in general publications:

> Both were highly placed staff officers at top-echelon headquarters —Edward Weeks, *Atlantic,* June 1946

And it quickly came to be applied to civilian as well as military organizations:

> . . . twelve men who formed the party's top echelon —*Newsweek,* 2 Aug. 1948

> Primary attention is given to the highest echelons of the public service —John W. Gardner, *Yale Rev.,* Summer 1949

This is now the most common use of *echelon.*

Several commentators have objected to the popular extended sense of *echelon,* essentially because they regard it as overused. Sir Ernest Gowers (in Fowler 1965) describes it as a "slipshod extension" of the "step-like formation" sense, but it should be noted that the new sense is perfectly consistent with the original meaning, "a rung on a ladder." In any case, as Copperud 1980 notes, the new sense "is now so popular that uprooting it would be a fearsome task." It would, in fact, be impossible.

ecology *Ecology* is a scientific word that in recent years has come into widespread use among nonscientists. In its oldest sense, it means "a branch of science concerned with the interrelation of organisms and their environments." It can also refer in scientific use to the interrelationship itself, rather than to the study of it:

> . . . must be sought among the complex interactions of living organisms and their environments, in other words, in their ecologies —George L. Rotramel, *Systematic Zoology,* September 1973

This use of *ecology* is well established and above reproach. Such difficulties as arise with *ecology* have to do with its use by general (nonscientific) writers to mean "the environment" or "the natural world." Several recent commentators have noted and criticized this use of the word. Our files contain a few clear-cut examples of it, including the following:

> To implement this policy in all corporate activities relating to the ecology —*Annual Report, Owens-Illinois,* 1970

> As to the furor over the ecology, it seems to me that its proponents are jousting windmills —letter to the editor, *Johns Hopkins Mag.,* Spring 1971

> And it not only saves money; it's good for the ecology, too —television commentator, 30 Aug. 1977

Most of our evidence for *ecology* in this sense is from the early 1970s, when the environmental movement was first coming into its own and its terminology was still relatively new and unfamiliar to many people. No doubt *ecology* is still sometimes used to mean "environment," but our evidence suggests that such usage, which was never very common, is becoming increasingly rare. A current writer or speaker is far more likely to use *envi-*

ronment than *ecology* in such contexts as those quoted above.

economic, economical *Economic,* which usually refers to economics or an economy, has a wider range of application than *economical,* which usually refers to the quality of economy and means "thrifty" or "not wasteful." The discussion of these words in usage books generally consists of a description of the separate meanings of *economic* and *economical* and an injunction not to confuse the two.

However, many *-ic* and *-ical* adjectives (such as *geologic* and *geological* or *symmetrical* and *symmetric*) are variant forms of the same word and are partially or wholly synonymous with each other, so it is not surprising to find that occasionally there is some crossover of meaning between *economic* and *economical.*

> . . . he introduces them in his slow, careful, reticent, economic way —John Cowper Powys, *The Meaning of Culture,* 1939

> . . . he plays remarkably pure, fundamental, indeed economic basketball —David Halberstam, *Inside Sports,* 30 Apr. 1980

> . . . the political, economical and cultural history of Europe —Geoffrey Bruun, *N.Y. Herald Tribune Book Rev.,* 21 June 1953

> Each country was considered carefully for its economical and weather status —Joan Casanova, *Multihulls,* November–December 1980

ecstacy Copperud 1980 says that *ecstacy* is "likely to be regarded as a misspelling; only Webster gives it as a variant." The Webster he's referring to is Webster's Third, which lists it as a relatively uncommon variant of *ecstasy.* These citations from our files show why we included *ecstacy* in Webster's Third:

> I get carried away in an ecstacy of mendacity — George Bernard Shaw, *Man and Superman,* 1903

> . . . his meditations approached ecstacy —Thornton Wilder, *The Cabala,* 1926

> . . . occasions of ecstacy at the sights he saw —W. L. Schurz, *N.Y. Times Book Rev.,* 9 Dec. 1956

> . . . religious ecstacy —*Harper's,* June 1969

Although *ecstacy* is definitely an infrequent variant, it has been in use since the late 17th century. It persists because *-acy* words (as *celibacy, delicacy, democracy, diplomacy, fallacy, intestacy, privacy*) are much more numerous in English than *-asy* words (as *apostasy, fantasy*).

ect. See ETC.

edifice This word has been cited as a pompous synonym for *building* by commentators dating back as far as Fowler 1926, but our evidence suggests that pomposity is not so much a characteristic of the word itself as of the buildings it describes. *Edifice* almost always refers to a large, massive, and imposing structure, in which use it is not pompous but descriptively appropriate:

> . . . various imposing San Antonio edifices, including the old Opera House —Green Peyton, *San Antonio: City in the Sun,* 1946

The lastest Hilton edifice is scheduled to open for business in July in Beverly Hills. It is a $15,000,000 450-room hideaway on an eight-acre tract —Gladwin Hill, *N.Y. Times,* 10 Apr. 1955

... an immense, cupolaed edifice of red brick on the hill —Richard Wolkomir, *Vermont Life,* Winter 1969

editorial The propriety of *editorial* was a subject of minor controversy in the late 19th and early 20th centuries. This noun was criticized in 1870 by Richard Grant White, who described it as an "unpleasant Americanism" to be shunned in favor of the British *leader* or *leading article.* White felt that *editorial* could only be correctly used as an adjective. Not enough people agreed with him, however, to give *editorial* any lasting notoriety, at least in the U.S., and no American commentator since Krapp 1927 (who defended the noun use) has addressed the subject. The British, on the other hand, still seem to have mixed feelings about it:

Editorial... is now a strong rival of 'leading article' and 'leader,' and it is probable that it will oust them in due course, being much more self-explanatory — Foster 1968

Editorial: ... *Not* the leading article. To use it that way is *really* unprofessional —Sellers 1975

editorial *we* See WE 1.

educationist In British English, *educationist* is an ordinary word synonymous with *educator:*

The author is a well-known educationist who for twenty years has taught at St. Luke's College — *Times Literary Supp.,* 2 Apr. 1970

But in American English, *educationist* rarely describes an actual, specific person. It most often serves instead as a term of disparagement for a stereotypically muddleheaded educational theorist, whose dubious ideas have contributed greatly—in the writer's view—to the downfall of American education:

... the educationist is someone who can take an easy subject and make it difficult —Dr. Laurence T. Peter, *The Peter Prescription,* 1972

... English grammar has been denigrated by large numbers of influential educationists —Thomas H. Middleton, *Saturday Rev.,* 1 Mar. 1980

Its disparaging connotations are also apparent in adjective use:

Intellectually *The Greening of America* resembles nothing so much as your typical educationist tractate: a stock of truism ... spiced with trivia —Samuel McCracken, *Change,* January–February 1971

educator A few commentators have cited *educator* as a pompous synonym for *teacher.* Evans 1957 notes that it is more often used of administrators in education than of actual teachers, and our evidence confirms this. *Educator* is also used to denote a scholar or theorist in the field of education. Its application to an actual teacher is relatively rare and usually carries implications of responsibility or achievement outside the classroom. Here are some typical examples of its use:

A faculty member seeking leave should recognize that he has a primary obligation ... to his growth as

an educator and scholar —*AAUP Bulletin,* September 1969

Margaret Mead, sociologist, anthropologist, educator, philosopher —Donald Robinson, *Ladies' Home Jour.,* January 1971

... an educator who comes to the Montana town ... to become principal of the community's first high school —William S. Murphy, *Los Angeles Times Book Rev.,* 15 Apr. 1971

-ee One of the two suffixes *-ee* in English—the one in *trainee,* not the one in *bootee*—comes via Middle English from Middle French. It has proved surprisingly productive in English and is used in many words where various syntactic and formal considerations would have prohibited its use in French. These extensions of the suffix, Jespersen 1905 tells us, first took place in legal language and later reached the general language. The most common use of the suffix is to form what Jespersen calls "passive nouns"—that is, nouns designating the receiver of the action of a verb, words like *appointee, draftee, grantee.*

A number of observers—Bernstein 1977, Follett 1966, Safire 1982, and Gowers in Fowler 1965—are not especially pleased with the productiveness of the suffix; they discourage the coining of such words. But *-ee* is often used for nonce coinages, often for humorous effect. There seems to be a long-standing tradition of easy witticism based on contrasting *-er* (or *-or*) and *-ee* forms. It can be found as far back as Sterne (who, interestingly enough, felt the suffix still to be French):

The *Mortgager* and *Mortgagée* differ the one from the other, not more in length of purse, than the *Jester* and *Jestée* do, in that of memory, —*Tristram Shandy,* 1760

And so it has gone, down to our own time. It is probably this sort of joking that lends the humorous or whimsical quality to many coinages:

I have ... a luncheon engagement for Friday which I am now trying to break. The lunchee is out of town —Archibald MacLeish, letter, 24 Nov. 1931

In times past I was the giver; now things are reversed, and I'm the givee —Harry S. Truman, diary, 14 Feb. 1948

But not all coinages with *-ee* are whimsical or facetious; your dictionary will show you quite a few that have stuck around as useful. And William Safire in his column has noticed such coinages as *asylee* for one seeking asylum and *mentee* for one who learns from a mentor, both of which were apparently intended seriously. Only time will tell if they establish themselves in the language (so far they have not).

Some of these same commentators may not like the receiver-of-an-action *-ee* but have been propelled into embracing it by the appearance of another sense of the suffix that can be viewed as nearly synonymous with *-er,* that designates more of a doer than a receiver. Gowers in Fowler 1965, for instance, abominates *escapee* (which see), recommending the older but less used *escaper* in its place. Gowers is about a century too late to prevent the establishment of *escapee* (and so are Follett 1966 and Nickles 1974). Since *absentee* (1605) is about the earliest of the productions of this sense of *-ee,* you can see how untimely and futile are the complaints. Another commonly mentioned example is *standee,* which has been with us since around 1880. They may be illogical if the receiver sense is taken as the logical norm, but it's just too late for logicians to turn back the clock. All we can do is accept the fact that a number of these formations exist, as Safire 1982 advises. You do not have to use them yourself, of course.

And even logic despairs in some cases.

> Mr. Wingate, a periodic contributor, is a Wilmington, Del. retiree —*Wall Street Jour.,* 11 Dec. 1985

What about *retiree?* Is it "one who has retired" (and thus attackable) or "one who has been retired" (and thus acceptable)? You could argue either side persuasively. But to what end? The word is established in usage.

effect   See AFFECT, EFFECT.

effectuate   *Effectuate* is not a new verb (it was first recorded in 1580), but it has something of the quality of an awkward neologism, and its use has been subject to occasional criticism since the 19th century. It is not a word that occurs naturally in casual conversation; you aren't likely to hear anyone say "That was the hardest thing I ever effectuated" or "We finally effectuated a settlement of our argument." Most often it occurs in prose having a formal or legalistic quality, and it describes actions taken on an official or governmental level:

> . . . it would help effectuate the purposes of the law —*American Labor,* July 1968

> . . . choose new social values and effectuate the changes conducive to progress —Neil H. Jacoby, "The Progress of Peoples," 1969

> . . . the principle that the majority . . . ought to be able to effectuate its desires —Thurgood Marshall, *Center Mag.,* September 1969

> . . . emphasizing the importance of institutions in effectuating good works —Aaron Wildavsky, *N.Y. Times Book Rev.,* 9 Dec 1984

effete   *Effete* is derived from the Latin *effetus,* meaning "no longer fruitful." It had some early use in English in its literal sense, chiefly describing domestic animals no longer capable of producing offspring, but its principal English uses have always been figurative. Until the 20th century, its usual figurative sense was "exhausted, worn out":

> They find the old governments effete, worn out — Edmund Burke, *Reflections on the Revolution in France,* 1790 (OED)

But the uses in which the word is now familiar to most people are not suggestive of exhaustion so much as of overrefinement, weakness of character, snobbery, and effeminacy. *Effete* first showed signs of acquiring these shades of meaning in the 1920s:

> "You're much too effete—that's your great shortcomin'. You don't feel—you are no child of nature. . . ." —S. S. Van Dine, *The Bishop Murder Case,* 1929

But it wasn't until the 1940s that the new *effete* clearly established itself in reputable writing:

> . . . there are a few critics (principally effete members of English Departments) who attack me in order to belabor the entire tradition of realism —James T. Farrell, *New Republic,* 28 Oct. 1940

> . . . the fear of being snobbish or effete leads thinkers to make a virtue of the very limitations of the common man —Herbert J. Muller, *Science and Criticism,* 1943

> It is a part of American folklore as respects Englishmen to suppose that they are "effete" —J. Frank Dobie, *A Texan in England,* 1945

> . . . now and then some effete customer would order a stinger or an anisette —John Steinbeck, *Cannery Row,* 1945

> . . . nothing so effete as the art-for-art's-sake of Oxford's esthetic Walter Pater —*Time,* 20 Aug. 1945

> She cannot manage masculine men. Her males are either overtly effete . . . or possessed by a feline power-mania —Edward Sackville West, *Horizon,* June 1946

These new uses of *effete* have made it a much more common word than it ever was in its "exhausted" sense, which is now almost never seen.

The new *effete* has received occasional criticism from such commentators as Evans 1957, Bernstein 1965, and Bryson 1984, but resistance to it has not been widespread. Although it is true that the senses in which *effete* is now used have no strong connection with its original literal sense, it is also true that these senses have gained a firmly established place in the language of educated speakers and writers. Current dictionaries routinely recognize them as standard.

e.g.   See I.E., E.G.

egregious   We agree with some earlier usage writers that this word's former positive sense "distinguished, outstanding" has been replaced by a usually pejorative meaning, but just what that meaning is is harder to pin down than you might think. A single definition, such as is commonly given by usage commentators and desk-sized dictionaries, does not cover all of the citations we have, yet the three separate definitions in Webster's Third—sense 2 ("conspicuous for bad quality or taste, notorious"), sense 3a ("extraordinary, extreme"), and sense 3b ("flagrant")—end up being a case of overkill, since more than one of these definitions can apply to a single use. It is probably this nebulous quality that prompted Flesch 1964 to say of *egregious,* "Many people don't know its exact meaning, and so it's better to avoid it." However, it can be useful to have available a word that encompasses a range of meanings not easily expressed in any other way. The following citations show how *egregious* (as well as its derivative adverb *egregiously*) varies from a word with a distinct meaning to a word with several possible nuances.

> During this quarrel, the egregious Ma called in newspaper reporters —Carey McWilliams, in *The Aspirin Age 1919–1941,* ed. Isabel Leighton, 1949

> . . . the egregious Rorschach test, which turns students . . . into helpless victims of modern diviners — William F. Albright, *N.Y. Herald Tribune Book Rev.,* 20 June 1954

> . . . the most egregious idiot —John P. Roche, *New Republic,* 24 Jan. 1955

> . . . an egregiously tedious newsboy —Thomas Meehan, *N.Y. Times Mag.,* 28 June 1964

. . . so many egregious errors —*Times Literary Supp.,* 2 May 1968

. . . to cover up teaching inadequacies or egregious political activities by teachers —George W. Bonham, *Change,* Winter 1971–72

. . . the egregiously optimistic belief that people will believe anything —John Kenneth Galbraith, *N.Y. Times Book Rev.,* 15 Sept. 1974

The famous style . . . strikes me as egregiously ersatz —Hilton Kramer, *N.Y. Times,* 30 Mar. 1975

. . . a rather egregious box of imitation ostrich leather complete with two plastic tiger-teeth clasps —*N.Y. Times Book Rev.,* 5 Dec. 1976

. . . lines of such egregious insipidity —Arthur M. Schlesinger, Jr., *Saturday Rev.,* 13 May 1978

either 1. One of the older strictures on the use of *either* is the objection to its use in the sense of "each." The examples that seem to have started the controversy are biblical:

And the king of Israel and Jehoshaphat king of Judah sat either of them on his throne —2 Chronicles 18:9 (AV), 1611

. . . and on either side of the river, was there the tree of life —Revelation 22:2 (AV), 1611

The discoverer of these "improper" uses was Bishop Lowth in 1763 (he added more examples in later editions). From Lowth the subject was picked up by many other grammarians, including Lindley Murray 1795. Bache 1869 disapproves, as do many commentators in this century (the most recent being Bremner 1980 and an Associated Press publication cited in Harper 1985).

But the sense had been recognized in Johnson's 1755 Dictionary, and it had a few defenders (Utter 1916) as well as a few who would tolerate it (Ayres 1881), though preferring *each.* The OED shows the use as an adjective to go back to King Alfred and as a pronoun to about the year 1000. It is the oldest sense of *either.* And the opposition of the grammarians appears to have had little effect on writers: Hall 1917 lists forty or so writers from the 19th and early 20th century using this sense of *either.*

Fowler 1926, who had obviously never seen or heard of Hall 1917, decided that the sense was archaic. He was perhaps trying to accommodate both the grammarians' disapproval and the OED evidence, and the OED had much less 19th-century evidence than Hall had found. But Fowler was wrong:

The two men walked one on either side of the cart —James Stephens, *The Crock of Gold,* 1912

. . . she had a spot of colour in either cheek —Henry James, *The American,* 1877

Gowers in Fowler 1965 revised the entry to express a preference for *each,* but he finds *either* idiomatic. Bernstein 1971 and Harper 1985 find the use acceptable. But what the commentators have not done explicitly is to distinguish the adjective use from the pronoun use. If you look back at the two biblical examples, you will see that *either* is a pronoun in the first and an adjective in the second. If the first sounds a little strange to you, don't be surprised. The pronoun in this sense has pretty much dropped out of use; Webster's Third marks it *archaic.* The adjective, however—and it was the adjec-

tive that Fowler 1926 called archaic—is still in common use, though it is probably not as common as *each.* Some examples:

. . . a wide boulevard with shade trees along either side —Nancy Milford, *Harper's,* January 1969

Poor in comparison with rich relatives on either side —*Times Literary Supp.,* 22 Oct. 1971

Mary Fitzpatrick, a spokesman, said the debris apparently came down "safely" on either side of the Equator —*N.Y. Times,* 4 Nov. 1979

An antique torchère and an ornate Ch'ing Dynasty lacquered screen anchor either end of the room —Anthony Haden-Guest, *Architectural Digest,* November 1985

. . . a majestic sweep of flesh on either side of a small blunt nose —William Faulkner, *Sanctuary,* 1931

. . . fragilely bound into the house by French windows at either end —F. Scott Fitzgerald, *The Great Gatsby,* 1925

2. *Either* of more than two. Now here we have an odd situation. This topic, into which *neither* is often introduced, is a fairly old one, but the older commentators in our collection—Richard Grant White 1870, Ayres 1881—treat it rather liberally. They find *either* in relation to more than two to be in use, and both White and Ayres find it a convenient usage that they think will prevail. It is commentators from around the turn of the century on who insist on the limitation to two. Hall 1917 cites writers named Quackenbos (1896) and Genung (1900) as insisting, and he catches Genung himself using it of three. Our files show Vizetelly 1906, Hyde 1926, and Jensen 1935 in the absolutist camp; there are many more recent writers who insist on two, right down to Chambers 1985, Bell & Cohn 1981, Fennell 1980, Cook 1985, and Trimmer & McCrimmon 1988, among others.

Bernstein 1971 in his discussion of the problem distinguishes between the use of *either* as a conjunction, and as a pronoun and adjective. (It is one of the striking characteristics of the absolutists that they fail to make such distinctions.) Bernstein observes that when *either* is a conjunction, use of more than two is not at all uncommon. Our files confirm his observation:

. . . the scantiest serious attention from either biographers, scholars, or critics —Edmund Wilson, *The Wound and the Bow,* 1941

. . . *Bleak House* is topped either by *Pickwick, David Copperfield,* or *Great Expectations* —Alexander Woollcott, letter, 21 Feb. 1941

. . . for in such case the population will either (a) die, (b) migrate, or (c) plunge into economic chaos —*Memoirs of Herbert Hoover, 1874–1920,* 1951

Animals are raised and children are either reared or raised or drug up —Bremner 1980

The majority of his paintings feature either children, fishermen or old people —*This England,* Autumn 1983

Use of the pronoun for more than two, on the other hand, is fairly uncommon:

Allowing passage in either of four directions —Webster 1909, definition of *four-way,* adjective

. . . beside him was a telephone through which he could communicate with anyone, on either of the three trains —Hector Bolitho, *A Century of British Monarchy,* 1951

You can see that we have no really recent examples of the pronoun used of three or more, and we have almost none at all of the adjective. You can therefore conclude that *either* is rarely used of more than two when a pronoun or adjective; but the conjunction is commonly so used.

3. A minor question raised in a few recent handbooks has to do with parallelism in *either . . . or* constructions. Some commentators refer to it as misplacement of *either.* Here's a case in point:

. . . there is no record of his having taken a Doctor's degree either at Oxford, Cambridge, or Dublin — William Barclay Squire, in *Grove's Dictionary of Music and Musicians,* 3d ed., 1927

The commentators would prefer that *either* followed *at,* or that *at* be repeated before *Cambridge* and *Dublin.* Now there is no question that such a correction would be an improvement in elegance, but the sentence poses no problem of understanding as it is. (The quotation from Alexander Woollcott at section 2 above is a similar example.) We think you should try for the improved parallelism, but it is fair to say that this is not a life-and-death matter.

4. The question of the number of the verb governed by the pronoun *either* or by nouns or pronouns joined by *either . . . or* has been treated by various commentators from Baker 1770 to the present. The result has been an abundance of rules, conditions, and invented examples. But evidence of actual use of *either* as a subject seems almost to be less common than rules prescribing that usage. The paucity of evidence comes from the fact that *either* is less frequently used as a pronoun than as a conjunction, adverb, or adjective and that even as a pronoun it appears more often as an object than a subject. (*Neither* is more generously attested; see the article there.)

Bremner 1980 has a compendious summary of the rules that are usually given:

When *either* is the subject of a clause, it takes a singular verb and singular referents. . . .
When *either* and *or* join singular subjects, the verb is singular. . . . When *either* and *or* join a singular subject and a plural subject, put the plural subject second and make the verb plural. . . .
When *either* and *or* join subjects of different person, make the verb agree with the nearer subject. . . .

These rules are commonsensical enough, and you will not go wrong if you follow them. But the little evidence we have suggests that there is some deviation from them—mostly on account of notional agreement. Several commentators, such as Longman 1984, Heritage 1982, Copperud 1964, 1970, 1980, Janis 1984, Perrin & Ebbitt 1972, and Evans 1957, recognize this.

When the pronoun *either* is the subject of the verb, we do find singular agreement:

. . . Welsh and Irish are closer to each other than either is to English —William W. Heist, *Speculum,* April 1968 (in Perrin & Ebbitt 1972)

And although almost everyone agrees that singular is usual, plural agreement is also attested. Curiously, the OED has 16th and 17th century examples with plural

agreement, but apparently none with singular agreement. Plural agreement seems most likely when *either* is followed by *of* and a plural noun or pronoun:

. . . either of them are enough to drive any man to distraction —Henry Fielding, *Tom Jones,* 1749 (in Jespersen 1909–49)

. . . it was not a subject on which either of them were fond of dwelling —Jane Austen, *Sense and Sensibility,* 1811 (in Jespersen)

Are either of you dining with Stewart to-night? — Edward F. Benson, *The Babe,* 1911 (in Jespersen)

I personally do not find that either of these critics make my flesh creep —John Wain, *New Republic,* 28 Jan. 1960 (in Perrin & Ebbitt)

It seems likely that plural agreement is more common in spoken than in written English in such constructions; even the example in Baker 1770 seems to come from speech.

Perrin & Ebbitt 1972 have even found usage that varies from the general *either . . . or* rule that the verb should agree with the nearer subject. But, all things considered, we recommend that you follow the general rule; it is always safe.

See NOTIONAL AGREEMENT, NOTIONAL CONCORD and AGREEMENT: INDEFINITE PRONOUNS; see also NEITHER.

either . . . or See EITHER 3, 4.

eke (out) Evans 1957, Bernstein 1977, Bryson 1984, and Barzun 1985 all say that a supply can be eked out, or made to last, "either by adding to it or by consuming it frugally" (Bryson). Fowler 1926 and Phythian 1979 are more restrictive, saying that *eke out* means only "to make something, by adding to it, go further or last longer or do more than it would without such addition" (Fowler). The commentators' approval, such as it is, of the use of *eke out* is derived from the verb *eke*'s archaic meaning "to increase or lengthen" and from the noun *eke*'s meaning "an addition or extension."

What these commentators are unanimous in objecting to is the use of *eke out* in "they managed to eke out a living." This sense, "to get with great difficulty," which is sometimes expressed simply by *eke* without the *out,* has been the predominant sense since the 1950s. For the thirty years before that it was a fairly close runner-up to the older sense in frequency of use. Continuing back through time, we find this sense attested in the first half of the 18th century. It has continued in use since then with increasing frequency:

Some runaway slaves . . . contrived to eke out a subsistence —Charles Darwin, *The Voyage of the Beagle,* 1845 (OED)

. . . eked out a subsistence upon the modest sum his pen procured him —George Meredith, *Diana of the Crossways,* 1885

. . . eked out a livelihood as village schoolmaster — *Dictionary of American Biography,* 1929

. . . to eke a living from eroded or starved land — *American Guide Series: Virginia,* 1941

. . . using obsolete equipment and backbreaking labor to eke out small hauls from old veins [of coal] —*Time,* 20 Aug. 1956

... eking out a torpid but endurable existence — Richard Freedman, *Washington Post,* 26 Sept. 1971

... to witness the Celtics eke out a thrilling overtime victory —Jonathan Evan Maslow, *Saturday Rev.,* 21 Jan. 1978

... eked out just 18% of the vote —Deborah A. Randolph, *Wall Street Jour.,* 27 Aug. 1980

So although someone may criticize you for saying that you're eking out a living, you should be well protected by the knowledge that it falls well within standard English usage.

elder, eldest There is no real controversy concerning these words, but certain observations regarding them have been included in many books on usage, dating back as far as Vizetelly 1906. The primary point stressed by the commentators is that *elder* and *eldest* are used only of persons ("her elder brother"), while *older* and *oldest* are used of both persons and things ("her older brother," "an older house"). This observation is generally true, but it should not be thought of as a hard and fast rule. In addition to serving as a comparative of *old,* *elder* is also sometimes used to mean "former," in which sense its use in describing things is entirely correct:

He remembered a thousand hard actualities of those elder circumstances —Carl Van Doren, *The American Novel,* 1940

... Henry James's personal preference for the finer forms of the elder arrogance —Willard L. Sperry, *Religion in America,* 1946

... a more vivid statement of the doctrine of an elder day —*Selected Writings of Benjamin N. Cardozo,* ed. Margaret E. Hall, 1947

His poems are of the elder New England tradition — Horace Gregory, *Saturday Rev.,* 14 Mar. 1953

Other uses of *elder* and *eldest* in describing things are rare, and they therefore tend to have something of an unidiomatic ring to them:

The elder service flag was a magnet of cobwebby bunting which drew him down the room —MacKinlay Kantor, *God and My Country,* 1954

Montauk, the eldest of the five, was preceded by 17 earlier lighthouses —Mary Zimmer, *Ford Times,* February 1968

Another point made by some commentators is that *elder* and *eldest* are used chiefly in describing seniority within a family. This is undoubtedly true:

... hatred of the mother and elder sister —Joan Aiken, *The Writer,* May 1968

... the relationship between elder and younger brother —*Times Literary Supp.,* 2 Apr. 1971

... the second eldest of the family —James Traub, *Saturday Rev.,* 27 May 1978

Eldest is almost never used except in describing a family member, but *elder* is more versatile. It occurs in the common phrase *elder statesman* and in similar phrases

in which it has connotations (sometimes ironic) of experience and wisdom:

... invited by an elder thinker to concur in his calm exposure of human folly —*Times Literary Supp.,* 14 May 1970

... as indifferent to genuine novelty as some of those elder sages —Harry Levin, *N.Y. Times Book Rev.,* 5 Aug. 1979

As we elder journalists like to say —Vermont Royster, *Wall Street Jour.,* 2 May 1984

Some commentators also note—and our evidence confirms—that *elder* is not used to make comparisons with *than* (as in "she was elder than her sister"). It is, however (as Evans 1957 points out), used to make comparisons with *of:*

... the elder of the two daughters —Herbert Warren Wind, *New Yorker,* 13 Oct. 1986

elegant British travelers in America during the 19th century frequently commented unfavorably on the American use of *elegant* as a synonym of *fine* or *excellent,* as in "it's an elegant morning." H. L. Mencken, in *The American Language, Supplement I* (1945), notes that various commentators have recorded the use of *elegant* with such nouns as *potatoes, mill, lighthouse, hogs, bacon, corn,* and *whiskey,* to name a few. Such usage seems to have been confined almost entirely to speech. Here's an example of it from the dialogue of a novel set in Virginia around 1870:

"I'll take her right to the hospital and give her to the doctor in charge.... She has an elegant chance of pulling through, there...." —Joseph Hergesheimer, *Mountain Blood,* 1915

Chances are you've never seen or heard *elegant* used in this way. We don't know for certain how widespread such usage was in the past, but we feel safe in saying that it is now extremely rare, if it continues to occur at all.

A somewhat similar use of *elegant* is in such sentences as "we had an elegant time" and "we were served an elegant meal":

... until dinnertime, when an elegant roast was served —Andrew W. Turnbull, *New Yorker,* 7 Apr. 1956

Criticism of such usage was common in the early 20th century, and it can still be heard on occasion. The critics regard *elegant* in such sentences as nothing more than a generalized term of approval equivalent to *pleasing* or *agreeable,* but that view strikes us as an oversimplification. To describe a time or a meal as elegant is to imply not simply that it was pleasing, but that it was pleasing to persons of refinement and cultivation. Such implications may seem pretentious or affected in many cases, but they are not inconsistent with the normal connotations of *elegant.*

In any case, the criticized uses of *elegant* are less common than they once were, and the strong objections they once invited seem to have been largely forgotten.

elegant variation *Elegant variation* is a term invented by Fowler 1926 for the inelegant use of a synonym merely to avoid using the same word two or more times in a sentence, or in a short space of text. It also receives mention in Janis 1984, Johnson 1982, and Copperud 1970, 1980. The sensible advice generally given is to avoid elegant variation. Fowler 1926, 1965 has the most extended treatment.

elegy, eulogy Strictly speaking, an elegy (from the Greek *elegos,* "song of mourning") is a sorrowful or melancholy song or poem, and a eulogy (from the Greek *eulogia,* "praise") is a formal statement or oration expressing praise. A funeral oration is called a eulogy because it typically praises the accomplishments and character of the person who has died. It also, of course, expresses sorrow, and many people no doubt associate the word *eulogy* more strongly with sorrow than with praise. Such associations might be expected to cause some tendency to confuse *elegy* and *eulogy,* but our evidence gives little indication that such confusion has occurred. *Eulogy* is never used to mean "a sorrowful song or poem." Nor is *elegy* used to mean "a speech of praise." *Elegy* is, however, sometimes used in figurative contexts to mean in essence "a funeral oration":

> He concludes his elegy for the literature of the past by remarking that those writers "had class in both senses of the word...." —Michele Murray, *National Observer,* 16 June 1973

> They write like undertakers: an elegy on every page —David Rains Wallace, *N.Y. Times Book Rev.,* 22 July 1984

If you use *elegy* in this way, you may find yourself being corrected.

elicit, illicit Warnings against confusion of the verb *elicit,* "to draw forth," and the adjective *illicit,* "unlawful," can be found in a few usage handbooks. It may seem that such confusion is unlikely in the real world because the words are of different parts of speech. But pronunciation tends to bring them together, and our files provide some evidence that confusion does exist:

> The court majority said, and I quote: "We hold only that when the process . . . focuses on the accused and its purpose is to illicit a confession...." —*Police,* September–October 1967

A good desk dictionary will sort the matter out for you, should you be confused for a moment.

eligible *Eligible* may be used with a complementary prepositional phrase, and *for* or *to* are the prepositions used most often. When the construction is *eligible for,* a noun phrase almost always follows it:

> ... were eligible for the university —William L. Shirer, *The Rise and Fall of the Third Reich,* 1960

> ... there's some standard [insurance] policy she's eligible for —James Gould Cozzens, *Guard of Honor,* 1948

When *eligible* is used with *to,* an infinitive usually follows, although occasionally a noun may follow instead:

> He's eligible to start receiving benefits after the second week —Bill Moyers, *Harper's,* December 1970

> ... membership in State and county organizations made one eligible to membership in A.M.A. —*Current Biography 1950*

elope, elopement People who elope don't necessarily get married, as Bernstein 1965 points out. In its original sense, still sometimes seen, *elope* describes the actions of a married woman who runs away from her husband with her lover:

> ... his unfaithful wife had eloped with her latest lover —Harrison Smith, *Saturday Rev.,* 20 Mar. 1954

It can also be used to mean simply "run away," with no implications of love or marriage:

> ... she finally eloped to London, to try her luck in the theatre —Peter Quennell, *The Marble Foot: An Autobiography,* 1976

In general use, however, *elope* calls to mind strong images of young lovers stealing away to be married in the dead of night (often by way of an unsteady ladder leaning against the sill of an upstairs window). The associations that *elope* and *elopement* have with marriage are so strong that it is usually unnecessary to state specifically that two people who have eloped have, in fact, gotten married:

> Defying her family, they eloped, built a crude cabin here, and lived happily the rest of their lives — *American Guide Series: Connecticut,* 1938

> When Hollywood's one genuine movie star eloped with soft drink king Al Steele last spring —Aline Mosby, *Springfield* (Mass.) *Daily News,* 8 Sept. 1955

When the marriage does not come off, on the other hand, it is a good idea to say so:

> Sixteen-year-old Christine ... ended a two-week elopement without benefit of marriage with tears in her eyes —*Springfield* (Mass.) *Union* (UPI), 3 July 1957

else In present-day English, compound pronouns with *else—anybody else, somebody else, who else,* for instance—take the *-'s* of the possessive on the *else:*

> It's fun reading somebody else's poems —Randall Jarrell, letter, May 1953

> At least this is an individual book. I can't think of anybody else's that it might remind you of —Flannery O'Connor, letter, 14 Nov. 1959

> I could picture Blount's people getting cautiously off the floor, and God knows who else's people —Wilfrid Sheed, *People Will Always Be Kind,* 1973

> ... they were ideas not unlike anybody else's — Philip Roth, *Reading Myself and Others,* 1975

> They just didn't seem to give a damn about life— theirs or anyone else's —*And More by Andy Rooney,* 1982

It seems strange, perhaps, to readers at the tail end of the 20th century that this subject needs to be mentioned at all. But a century ago it was a red-hot issue in usage. The reason for the dispute was a shift in general practice: before about 1840 the *-'s* went with the pronoun, and forms like *somebody's else* were considered standard. Gould 1870 and Ayres 1881 were still calling for these forms in the face of changing usage, but not long after the turn of the century the modern forms began to gain increasing acceptance among the commentators.

But change comes hard for some people; there is evidence that some English instructors were still trying to inculcate *somebody's else* as late as the 1950s. The old forms may still be heard or seen, but the form with *else's* is now the overwhelming choice.

elude See ALLUDE 2.

elusive, illusive Admonitions not to confuse *elusive* ("hard to perceive or comprehend") and *illusive* ("based on illusion; illusory") can be found in a few books on usage. Such confusion is rare. The mistake that can occur—usually, we would think, because of simple inattention—is the use of the relatively uncommon *illusive* in place of *elusive:*

> . . . probably the appendix acting up. It was very illusive and not detected until the day of the operation —letter received at Merriam-Webster, 2 Sept. 1954

emanate *Emanate* is usually used with the preposition *from:*

> . . . the radio broadcasts and editorials emanating from Hanoi —Robert Shaplen, *New Yorker,* 11 Sept. 1971

> . . . one of the queerest bits of logic emanating from this group —Howard Mumford Jones, *The Theory of American Literature,* 1948

Very rarely you might encounter *in:*

> All works will have emanated in either Spanish, Portuguese, or French . . . whether or not they have been translated —*Library Jour.* 1 May 1967

embark *Embark* may be used with a number of different prepositions, but by a large margin the usual choice is *on* or *upon,* the former being more common:

> . . . its avowed intention to embark on unconstitutional action —J. H. Plumb, *England in the Eighteenth Century,* 1950

> . . . they embarked upon a thoroughgoing rediscovery of their Englishness —Oscar Handlin, *The American People in the Twentieth Century,* 1954

Embark is used with *for* when the object denotes destination:

> Clark embarked most of the party . . . for the Three Forks —Bernard DeVoto, *The Course of Empire,* 1952

And we have a few citations for *embark from* to indicate the point of departure:

> . . . four companions, embarking from Floyd Bennett Field, circled the globe —*American Guide Series: N.Y. City,* 1939

At one time, *embark in* was a fairly common construction; however, it seems to have been dropping out of use during the last 40 years or so, as travel by ship has decreased.

embellish *Embellish* is most often used with *with* when it takes a complement:

> The book is embellished with some excellent photographs —*Times Literary Supp.,* 12 Feb. 1970

The influence of that usage accounts for our one example of *embellish* with *wherewith:*

> Religion is tending to degenerate into a decent formula wherewith to embellish a comfortable life — Alfred North Whitehead, *Science and the Modern World,* 1925

Embellish is also used with *by:*

> His text is embellished by a large number of extremely well-produced illustrations —*Times Literary Supp.,* 24 June 1955

emend See AMEND, EMEND.

emerge When *emerge* is used with a preposition, the choice is most often *from:*

> She began it officially by emerging from the back room clad in a dragon-embroidered kimono — Thomas Pynchon, *V.,* 1963

> One further finding of interest emerged from Cowdry's study —Kenneth Keniston, *Change,* November-December, 1969

It is also very frequently used with *as:*

> . . . outside of the framework of what soon emerged as the new "common sense" —Noam Chomsky, *Columbia Forum,* Spring 1968

> . . . America, emerging as the greatest power after the Second World War . . . —Hannah Arendt, *N.Y. Rev. of Books,* 18 Nov. 1971

Sometimes it appears with both:

> . . . emerged from the war as a creditor nation —*The Encyclopedia Americana,* 1943

Other prepositions commonly used with *emerge* include *at, in, into, on, onto, out of, through, upon,* and *with:*

> . . . the character of dominant individuals who happen to emerge at a formative period —*Selected Papers of Bertrand Russell,* 1927

> . . . only then did his pure and completely characteristic style emerge in all its integrity and originality — Herbert Read, *The Philosophy of Modern Art,* 1952

> . . . a great many points of interest . . . , some of which will emerge into importance in succeeding lectures —Alfred North Whitehead, *Science and the Modern World,* 1925

> . . . the first post-depression, post-war generation to emerge into the world —Paul Potter, *Johns Hopkins Mag.,* October 1965

> . . . allowing the patient to work through it and emerge on the other side —Richard Schickel, *Harper's,* April 1971

> . . . emerged onto the Pennypacker Mills Pike . . . — F. Van Wyck Mason, *The Winter at Valley Forge,* 1953

> . . . it is important that the announcement should emerge out of the present Conference —Sir Winston Churchill, *Closing the Ring,* 1951

> . . . their plots emerge through a juxtaposition of different elements —Joan Aiken, *The Writer,* May 1968

... soon emerged upon wild bleak downs —George Borrow, *The Bible in Spain,* 1843

If we emerge with a new tariff . . . —Alan Valentine, *Yale Rev.,* Autumn 1954

Emerge is also sometimes followed by *that* and a clause:

It emerges that her husband is somehow involved with the dead girl —Anthony Quinton, *Encounter,* December 1954

emigrate, immigrate *Emigrate* and *immigrate* make a case in which English has two words where it could easily have made do with only one. The two words have the same essential meaning—"to leave one country to live in another"—and differ only in emphasis or point of view: *emigrate* stressing leaving, and *immigrate* stressing entering. A large number of handbooks, from MacCracken & Sandison 1917 to Janis 1984, warn us not to confuse the two. Our evidence shows that almost no one does, at least in edited prose. A handy clue to identity is provided by the prepositions each takes. *Emigrate* tends to go with *from:*

... Ezekiel Wapshot, who emigrated from England aboard the *Arbella* in 1630 —John Cheever, *The Wapshot Chronicle,* 1957

Bernstein 1965 recommends only *from.* However, when the writer is thinking in terms of the new country, *to* is also used:

... this difficult writer, who was recently permitted to emigrate to the West —Patricia Blake, *N.Y. Times Book Rev.,* 29 Feb. 1976

He was a Dane, a big, yellow-haired, outgoing man in his late forties, and a widower. He had emigrated to the United States after his wife's death —Russell Baker, *Growing Up,* 1982

Immigrate, with its stress on entering, usually is used with *to* and *into:*

... left the family farm there . . . to immigrate to the United States —*Current Biography,* May 1965

... the foreign scientists and engineers who immigrate into the United States —Robert M. Hutchins, *Center Mag.,* March 1968

Immigrate is sometimes used with *from.* Just as *emigrate to* can be understood as "to leave there and come to", *immigrate from* can be understood as "to come here from":

Pettigrew comes from Richmond, Virginia, but his father immigrated from Scotland —Godfrey Hodgson, *Atlantic,* March 1973

Distinguishing these words may be less of a problem than is often suggested, as your meaning is essentially the same no matter which you use. To emphasize the notion of leaving, use *emigrate* with *from;* to emphasize the notion of arriving, use *immigrate* with *to* or *into.*

eminent, imminent Almost all books on usage include a warning about confusion of *eminent* and *imminent* (occasionally the much less used word *immanent* is included for good measure). The meanings are actually quite distinct: *eminent* means "prominent" (as in "an eminent author"); *imminent* means "soon to occur, impending" (as in "imminent danger"). Use of

one word in place of the other is now extremely rare in edited prose, but it does seem to occur from time to time in writing that has not been so closely scrutinized (as in a quiz given several years ago to aspiring emergency medical technicians, which included a question about the proper course of action with a pregnant woman when "the birth is eminent"). Such confusion appears to have been somewhat more common in the past:

The eminent Danger I had been in —Daniel Defoe, *A Journal of the Plague Year,* 1722 (OED)

See also IMMINENT 1.

emote The verb *emote* was coined as a back-formation of the noun *emotion* in the early 20th century. From the first, its use has tended to be something less than entirely serious:

And you let me sit there and emote all over the place —Megrue & Hackett, *It Pays to Advertise,* 1917 (OED Supplement)

The basic meaning of *emote* is "to express emotion." Its most familiar use is undoubtedly in humorously or deprecatingly describing the work of actors:

A Method actor can sit on a stage, feeling deeply and emoting strangely, but it's no good if the audience hasn't the faintest idea of what is going on —Carol Tavris, *Harper's,* January 1983

It is also used in a similar way to describe theatrical behavior by nonactors:

Remember, this is politics; it doesn't have to make sense so long as you emote instead of asking questions —Russell Baker, *N.Y. Times,* 8 May 1976

Uses of *emote* without humorous or deprecating connotations are relatively uncommon, but we do encounter them from time to time:

... there was still room for a talented performer to emote with class and style —Horace Sutton, *Saturday Rev.,* 29 Jan. 1972

Crying, especially on-camera, is considerably more difficult for the actress, but Bob Fosse . . . helped her learn to emote —Peter Greenberg, *Cosmopolitan,* October 1976

Like many another back-formation, *emote* has met with some disapproval among usage commentators, but because its normal uses are facetious rather than serious, it does not invite strong criticism. Recent commentators (such as Bernstein 1965) have limited their censure to cases in which *emote* is used without humorous intent. Such usage cannot be called nonstandard, but it is inconsistent with the usual connotations of the word, and you may well want to avoid it for that reason.

emotional, emotive The use of these adjectives in British English has undergone an interesting development in recent decades. H. W. Fowler described *emotive* as a "superfluous word" in 1926, feeling that it served no purpose not better served by *emotional.* In his 1965 revision of Fowler's *Modern English Usage,* however, Sir Ernest Gowers noted that *emotive* had come to be used in a distinct way and had become the preferred choice in the sense "appealing to the emotions; evoking an emotional response," as in "an emotive speech" or "an emotive political issue." Gowers' observation is confirmed by our recent evidence from British sources:

> The decision had been taken because executions were an emotive issue —*The Age* (Melbourne), 23 Apr. 1975

> ... an emotive and currently much discussed topic —Ann Oakley, *British Book News,* June 1979

> ... it was reflected in the calm treatment of an emotive issue: euthanasia —*The Economist,* 30 Aug. 1985

Emotive is now so well established in this use among the British that one recent commentator, Phythian 1979, warns against confusion of *emotional* and *emotive,* by which he apparently means the use of *emotional* to mean "appealing to or evoking emotions." Such usage is in fact perfectly reputable, as H. W. Fowler could have told him. It is especially so in American English:

> ... he is already ... identified with a strong emotional issue —Joseph P. Albright, *N.Y. Times Mag.,* 1 Sept. 1974

> The nuclear-power controversy has become so emotional —Wadsworth Likely, *Saturday Rev.,* 22 Jan. 1977

employ   *Employ* is occasionally cited as a pretentious substitute for *use.* The two verbs are in fact often interchangeable, but *employ* is most appropriately used (or employed) when the conscious application of something for a particular end is being stressed:

> Some there are ... who employ incomprehensible wording to confuse, impress, or dazzle the unsophisticated —Mary C. Bromage, *Michigan Business Rev.,* July 1968

> ... his best poems employ ironically the conventions he rejects —Kenneth Fields, *Southern Rev.,* April 1970

> ... will refrain from employing their military strength in new political power plays —Anatole Shub, *Harper's,* January 1972

employe, employee   The French word *employé* (rhymes with *say*) was first used in English in the early 19th century. Its form is that of the past participle of the verb *employer,* "to use, employ," and its meaning is basically "employed one." The feminine form is *employée,* "a female employe." The feminine form never had much success in English, but *employé* continued in occasional use well into the 20th century:

> The depositors were wage-earners; railroad employé's, mechanics, and day labourers —Willa Cather, *A Lost Lady,* 1923

Eventually, of course, both *employé* and *employée* were superseded by the English *employee,* formed by combination of *employ* and the familiar suffix *-ee.* The earliest known occurrence of *employee* is in Thoreau's *Walden,* published in 1854. The OED indicated in 1897 that *employee* was rare in the U.S., but by 1926 it was well enough established for H. W. Fowler to promote its use by describing it as "a good plain word with no questions of spelling & pronunciation & accents & italics & genders about it. . . ." Fowler had no use for the French *employé,* and he would be glad to know that *employee*

appears now to be the invariable choice in British English.

In the U.S., however, the ghost of *employé* lives on. Although *employee* is undoubtedly the usual spelling in American English, there are some publications and writers that show a preference for the variant *employe,* apparently out of deference to *employé.* The implication is that *employee* is in some way a corruption of the French term, but, in fact, as Fowler pointed out, it is a perfectly good English word, logically and formally consistent with other words of its kind. *Employe,* on the other hand, is a strange hybrid—spelled like the French word (minus the acute accent) but pronounced like the English one (rhyming with *see* rather than *say*) and used like the English word to refer to a woman as well as to a man. *Employe* aims to be a more logical and precise spelling than *employee,* but it fails on both counts. Its use is not incorrect, however. It occurs regularly in highly reputable publications, and it has clearly established itself as a respectable spelling variant in American English:

> ... stemming from poor employe training —*Wall Street Jour.,* 3 June 1980

> The employe ... maintained in the suit that he was threatened with dismissal —*Washington Post,* 5 May 1982

> ... 45 percent of the workers were office employes —Michael H. Brown, *Audubon Mag.,* November 1982

> Employes have no legal standing to challenge settlements —*U.S. News & World Report,* 29 Aug. 1983

> ... is studying "cafeteria-style" benefits for state employes —*USA Today,* 23 Apr. 1984

emporium   The literal meaning of *emporium* in Latin is "a place of trade; marketplace." As used in English, it now typically denotes a store or restaurant that is notably large, notably busy, or notably pretentious. It has two plurals, *emporiums* and *emporia,* both of which are in good use:

> ... turn them into fast-food burger and chicken emporiums —Glenn Collins, *N.Y. Times,* 4 Feb. 1973

> ... the huge emporia that do their brisk trade in shopping centers —William Safire, *N.Y. Times,* 6 May 1974

> ... established their imposing emporiums along Broadway —Dorothy Seiberling, *New York,* 20 May 1974

> ... found ... prices to be higher than those of the fancy gourmet emporia —Lee Aitken, *New England Monthly,* April 1984

Emporiums is the more common of the two.

enable   "To make possible, practical, or easy" is a sense of *enable* that appeared for a time in the 17th century then fell into disuse before resurfacing again at the end of the 19th century. In recent years this sense has had regular use, though it remains much less common than the sense "to make able". A few critics dislike it, but most usage writers favor it with a healthy neglect.

> ... to enable admission of the best candidates —*N.Y. Times,* 22 June 1952

... it enabled passage of the anti-poll-tax law — Henry F. & Katharine Pringle, *Saturday Evening Post,* 19 June 1954

... a congenial literary form that would enable coherence and control —Robert Coles, *New Republic,* 15 Apr. 1967

... a new design was produced that enables the resolution of volume strain into areal ... and vertical strains —Caryl P. Haskins, *President's Report, Carnegie Institution of Washington, D.C.,* 1969–1970

enamor   In current English, *enamor* is used most often in the passive and when used with a preposition usually appears with *of:*

... Querelle ... becomes enamored of the policeman and betrays Gil to the law —Edmund Wilson, *New Yorker,* 5 June 1971

... an alarming number of our college graduates were enamored of a future security tucked into a job with a pension —Bennett Cerf, *Saturday Rev.,* 21 June 1952

Less frequently, *enamor* is used with *with:*

... a peculiar mélange ... that will, alas, disappoint those enamored with the Yugoslavian filmmaker — Judith Crist, *New York,* 1 Nov. 1971

Although some language commentators frown on the practice, *enamor* is used with *by,* but not very often:

... she wouldn't have been quite so enamoured by the list of ingredients —June Bibb, *Christian Science Monitor,* 17 Feb. 1965

enclose, inclose   These variant spellings are equally old (both date from around 1400) and equally respectable, but *enclose* has now become so much the more common of the two that *inclose* is almost never seen. The same distribution holds true for *enclosure* and *inclosure.* The *in-* forms seem now most likely to be found in legal writing:

Rights of common may be ... wholly extinguished by inclosure —E. H. Burn, *Cheshire's Modern Law of Real Property,* 11th ed., 1972

encounter   Kilpatrick 1984 notes that he was once criticized by a correspondent for using *encounter* to mean "meet with" or "come across," as in "books I have encountered." He agrees with his critic that such usage is incorrect and that *encounter* properly means "to meet as an adversary or enemy; to engage in conflict with; to run into a complication." Certainly *encounter* has those meanings, but we wonder why Kilpatrick is so ready to abandon its "meet with" sense, which the OED shows to have been in use since the 14th century. J. Leslie Hall investigated the pedigree of this sense in 1917 and found that it had been used by such writers as Samuel Johnson, Sir Walter Scott, Edgar Allan Poe, Nathaniel Hawthorne, George Eliot, and Robert Louis Stevenson. Hall considered it a somewhat "old-fashioned" sense, but our evidence shows that its occurrence in current English is common and perfectly idiomatic:

... they experienced under simulated conditions the sensations they would encounter in space —*Current Biography,* November 1965

... she stole on tiptoe downstairs ... praying devoutly that she would encounter no one —Katherine Anne Porter, *Ladies' Home Jour.,* August 1971

... will be happy to encounter once again the author's balanced prose —William V. Shannon, *Saturday Rev.,* 7 Aug. 1976

encroach   When used with a preposition, *encroach* is usually used with *on* or *upon:*

Today, the enemy is vague, the work seems done, ... the expert encroaches on the artist —Norman Mailer, *Advertisements for Myself,* 1959

... groups of houses encroaching suddenly upon the desolation of the marshland —William Styron, *Lie Down in Darkness,* 1951

Occasionally *encroach* is used with *into, onto,* and *to:*

... the building originally encroached into Nassau County —Michael Kramer, *New York,* 2 Sept. 1974

... burnt-out cars had been dragged to the gutters, sometimes encroaching up onto the sidewalk — James Jones, *Harper's,* February 1971

... fishermen encroached closer and closer to the Alaskan waters —Frank Abbott Magruder, *National Governments and International Relations,* 1950

end   When *end* is used intransitively with a preposition, it may be used with *by:*

Van Dusen ended by setting up the entire itinerary and going along —*Time,* 19 Apr. 1954

Somewhat less frequently (but still commonly), *end* is used with *as, at,* and *on:*

... he ended as an Air Service supply officer — James Gould Cozzens, *Guard of Honor,* 1948

The bridge ended at the island —*American Guide Series: Minnesota,* 1938

The interview ends on a note of close harmony — Stuart Chase, *Power of Words,* 1953

Infrequently, *end* has been used with *along:*

This typical mediterranean vegetation ends abruptly along the Río Bío-Bío —Preston E. James, *Latin America,* rev. ed., 1950

See also END UP.

endeavor   As a synonym for *attempt* or *try,* the verb *endeavor* has several distinguishing characteristics, the most obvious of which is its relative formality. It also carries connotations of a continuing and earnest effort, as in attempting to enact a long-range policy or to achieve a lasting result:

The American Jewish Committee ... endeavors to foster cultural expression of American Jewry —*Collier's Year Book,* 1949

And, I might add, I would endeavor to have these schools offer a far broader array of practical courses —James B. Conant, *Slums and Suburbs,* 1961

It should be noted that the committee endeavored to cover both the needs and interests of the students — Ben F. Wheless, *Junior College Jour.,* October 1970

ended, ending These words have caused some minor disagreements among usage commentators. The point at issue is whether *ending* can properly be used in describing a period that is in the past, as in "We were there for the week ending July 22." A few critics, dating back to Weseen 1928, have contended that *ended* is required in such a context (". . . for the week ended July 22"), and that *ending* is only appropriate when speaking of the future ("We'll be there for the week ending April 4"). Other commentators, such as Partridge 1942, have argued that the use of *ending* to speak of the past is common and respectable. The most telling point has been made by Sir Ernest Gowers, who has noted (in Fowler 1965) that we always use *beginning* rather than *begun* when referring to a past period in terms of its start ("We were there for the week beginning July 15"). This use of *beginning* has been criticized by no one. Gowers calls the criticism of *ending* "pedantic," and we agree. Both *ended* and *ending* are idiomatic when speaking of the past. Use the one that seems more natural to you:

> . . . in the year ended last Sept. 30 —*Newsweek,* 19 Apr. 1948

> . . . in the year ending last March 31 —*Newsweek,* 29 Nov. 1948

endemic, epidemic We have no evidence showing that these words have ever been confused, but the similarities of their spelling, pronunciation, and application are such that they look confusable, and books on usage have been explaining the distinction between them for many years. One more time can't hurt: medically speaking, *endemic* describes a disease that is constantly present to a greater or lesser extent in a particular place; *epidemic* describes a severe outbreak of a disease affecting many people within a community or region at one time. To the basic distinction we may also add that *endemic* can be followed by either *in* or *to:*

> . . . the gravely debilitating . . . parasitic disease that is endemic in lower Egypt —William Styron, *This Quiet Dust and Other Writings,* 1982

> . . . to study diseases endemic to the developing areas of the world —*Johns Hopkins Mag.,* Summer 1967

Epidemic is more commonly used as a noun than as an adjective:

> . . . a typhus epidemic that killed more than 65,000 people in the British Isles in 1816 —Timothy Ferris, *N.Y. Times Book Rev.,* 31 July 1983

Its most familiar adjectival use is in the phrase *epidemic proportions:*

> . . . AIDS was proclaimed as reaching *epidemic* proportions —Edwin Diamond, *TV Guide,* 28 Oct. 1983

Both words, of course, are also commonly used in nonmedical contexts:

> The problems endemic to translating poetry — Genevieve Stuttaford, *Publishers Weekly,* 22 Oct. 1982

> Early in this century there was an epidemic of picture postcards —*People,* 14 Dec. 1981

Another point of some concern to usage commentators is the use of *epidemic* to describe outbreaks of disease affecting animals rather than people. Bernstein 1965 considers this a "loose usage," since *epidemic* is derived from the Greek *epi-,* "on, at," and *demos,* "people." He argues that the correct word for an outbreak among animals is *epizootic.* The distinction he promotes is in fact sometimes observed, particularly in scientific writing:

> An epidemic of plague in human beings is usually preceded by a rat epizootic —*Merck Manual,* 8th ed., 1950

But the etymological connection between *epidemic* and "people" is now entirely lost in general usage, and the use of *epidemic* to describe nonhuman outbreaks of disease is established as standard:

> . . . epidemics of the disease during winter and spring months —H. E. Biester & L. H. Schwarte, ed., *Diseases of Poultry,* 2d ed., 1948

> As administrator he advanced game conservation . . . and fought a severe epidemic of rinderpest — *Current Biography,* December 1965

Commentators who have defended such usage include Gowers in Fowler 1965 and Copperud 1980.

ending See ENDED, ENDING.

endless Some objections have been made to the common use of *endless* as a synonym of *innumerable.* The original criticism, as expressed by Weseen 1928, seems to have been based on logic: "endless instances" should be revised to "an endless list of instances," apparently because the instances themselves cannot logically be said to have no end, but the "list" or number of them can (hyperbolically speaking). Later critics, such as Partridge 1942 and Evans 1957, have taken an entirely different approach, focusing their relatively mild disapproval on the exaggerated quality of the "innumerable" *endless* rather than its lack of logic. Of course, that same exaggerated quality is apparent in Weseen's suggested correction, "an endless list," and, for that matter, in *innumerable.* This seems to be a case in which the original reason for disliking the sense has been forgotten or disregarded, but because the sense has gained a certain notoriety a new reason for disliking it has been devised, and a (minor) controversy persists.

Even so, we do not think you have to worry about this sense of *endless.* Most critics pay it no attention, and its use in reputable writing continues to be common and unremarkable:

> . . . greedy demand for endless encores —John Browning, *N.Y. Times,* 4 Apr. 1971

> . . . dreary chronicle of her endless public appearances —*Times Literary Supp.,* 27 Aug. 1971

> Endless books on Ireland —Daphne du Maurier, *Ladies' Home Jour.,* September 1971

> . . . the endless, wittily devious ways of women's organizations —Katherine Anne Porter, *The Never-Ending Wrong,* 1977

> . . . on endless fact-finding missions —*Sports Illustrated,* 21 June 1982

endorse 1. *Endorse on the back.* *Endorse* is derived from the Old French verb *endosser,* "to put on the back." This etymology has led some critics, dating back at least to Vizetelly 1906, to contend that the phrase *endorse on the back* is redundant. A good argument against that contention is made by Krapp 1927, who points out that the "on the back" connotations of *endorse* are "no longer strongly felt," and that the main idea in endorsing a check is to prepare it for cashing by signing it—that the signing is done on the back is almost incidental. If someone were to hand you a legal document and tell you to endorse it, you might reasonably ask, "Where?" *Endorse* still retains some associations with the idea of "back" in certain of its uses, but those associations are secondary to the principal idea of signing one's name. The redundancy of *endorse on the back* is more imaginary than real.

2. *Endorse* meaning "approve." The use of *endorse* to mean "approve, sanction" originated in the 19th century:

> This book . . . the world has endorsed, by translating it into all tongues —Ralph Waldo Emerson, *Representative Men,* 1847 (OED)

Criticism of it followed soon afterward from such commentators as Richard Grant White 1870 and Ayres 1881. Its foremost critic in the 20th century has been Fowler 1926, who described it as a "solecism." Fowler objected in particular to its use in advertisements, such as (Fowler's example) "Paderewski endorses the pianola," in which its full sense is "to express support for or approval of publicly." Some resistance to this use of *endorse* has persisted among British commentators, but its place in American English has long been established, and no American critic that we know of has faulted it since the early part of the 20th century. Its most common occurrences continue to be in advertising and politics:

> . . . [players] of the Baltimore Colts football team also endorse UNIROYAL's All-Sports shoes —*Annual Report, UNIROYAL Incorporated,* 1970

> . . . he alienated Democratic leaders by endorsing Richard Nixon for President —*Current Biography,* January 1967

But it occurs commonly in other contexts as well:

> . . . the American Medical Association endorsed community vaccination programs —*Current Biography,* March 1968

> He fully endorses the modern appreciation of Erasmus as a deeply religious writer —*Times Literary Supp.,* 30 July 1971

3. *Endorse, indorse.* These spellings are equally reputable, but *endorse* is now far and away the more common of the two. Most of the scanty recent evidence we have for the *in-* spelling is from legal contexts:

> An indorsement must be written on the instrument by or on behalf of the holder —Lowell B. Howard, *Business Law,* 1965

> . . . a specially indorsed writ —*Palmer's Company Law,* 22d ed., 1976

endow   *Endow* is very often used with a preposition, and usually the preposition is *with:*

> Endow such men with religious zeal —Vernon Louis Parrington, *Main Currents in American Thought,* 1930

> I was endowed with rights to a White House car — John Kenneth Galbraith, *Ambassador's Journal,* 1969

There is also, of course, the common construction of *endow* used with *by* when the verb is used in the passive and the object names the agent:

> The library, which was endowed by Andrew Carnegie, has approximately 36,000 volumes —*American Guide Series: Louisiana,* 1941

Our files show *endow* with other prepositions, but these are fairly rare:

> A chair of agriculture, endowed in the sum of $125,000, has been provided —*Science,* 21 Dec. 1928

> . . . people who have been overgenerously endowed in the way of height —Hamilton Basso, *The View From Pompey's Head,* 1954

> . . . the mellow wisdom which once he had dreamed that the slow advance of years would endow upon him —James T. Farrell, *What Time Collects,* 1964

end result, end product   Those people to whom redundancy is anathema do not take kindly to *end product* and *end result.* Of the two terms, *end result* is closer to a simple redundancy; it basically means "result" but may emphasize the finality of the result.

> We may look at schizophrenic utterances as the end result of a combination of two factors —Brendan Maher, *Psychology Today,* November 1968

> It is obviously too soon to predict the nature of the end-result —Aaron Copland, quoted in *N.Y. Times,* 13 May 1951

> . . . the end result was the same, no matter how it was reached —Shelby Foote, *Love in a Dry Season,* 1951

> . . . only the end results of changes over many thousands of centuries can be seen —Dr. Alex B. Novikoff, *Science,* 2 Mar. 1945

End product, on the other hand, has two uses. Especially in science and manufacturing, an end product is the final product of a series of processes or activities and is often distinguished from a by-product. In most general contexts it simply means "result" or "product."

> . . . the digestible materials have been acted on by enzymes and their end-products —Edwin B. Steen & Ashley Montagu, *Anatomy and Physiology,* 1959

> In areas where little residual fuel oil is used, road oil and coke may be the end-products —John W. Frey, in *World Geography of Petroleum,* eds. Wallace E. Pratt & Dorothy Good, 1950

> These schemes give not the faintest thought to the immediate results . . . or the end product —Lewis Mumford, *New Yorker,* 19 Mar. 1955

> He is the end-product of poll taxes and machine politics —J. Lacey Reynolds, *New Republic,* 27 Mar. 1944

> . . . this is the end product of a lot of work —Jeremy Bernstein, *N.Y. Times Book Rev.,* 28 Feb. 1982

In *end result* and the looser, noncontrastive uses of *end product,* the question of whether *end* is superfluous or whether it serves as an intensifier depends occasionally on the context but usually on your opinion of redundancy (which see).

end up   1. *End up* is an "unacceptable colloquialism for *end* or *conclude*" proclaims Macmillan 1982. (According to the introduction to their guide to usage, a colloquialism is ipso facto unacceptable in formal writing.) Setting aside for now the matter of whether *end up* is a colloquialism, let's take a look at the difference between *end* and *end up*. The first point to notice is that *end up* is not substituted for all senses of the verb *end* but almost always is used to mean "to reach a specified ultimate rank or situation."

> ... the dinner-glasses disappeared one by one ... , the last one ending up, scarred and maimed, as a tooth-brush holder —F. Scott Fitzgerald, "The Cut-Glass Bowl," 1920, in *The Portable F. Scott Fitzgerald,* 1945

> "... He might even end up by wanting me to pull drill with the Company. ..." —James Jones, *From Here to Eternity,* 1951

> ... the party ended up with a minority in Congress —Gus Tyler, *New Republic,* 21 June 1954

> Hollywood parties, those celebrated institutions which so frequently ... end up in romance or in tragedy —Peter Ustinov, *London Calling,* 5 Aug. 1954

> ... we still end up with a total of 25,137 possible morpheme shapes —William G. Moulton, *NEA Jour.,* January 1965

> They ended up fighting it out among themselves —Tom Wolfe, *New York,* 27 Sept. 1971

> ... he ended up at a ferry pier and had to dive into the water to escape —Fox Butterfield, *N.Y. Times,* 16 June 1979

Although *end* also gets used in contexts like these, such use is far outnumbered both by the use of *end up* and by the use of *end* in other senses. We suspect, moreover, that *end* used with this meaning often reveals the hand of a copy editor who followed the advice of a handbook like Macmillan. *End* alone does not sound as natural as *end up* in many contexts:

> ... an able engineer who ended as a general —Waldemar Kaempffert, *N.Y. Times Book Rev.,* 13 June 1954

> ... he was warned his body would end in a ditch if he did not stop complaining —A. H. Raskin, *N.Y. Times Mag.,* 7 Nov. 1976

Because *end up* so commonly expresses the meaning "to wind up," its use emphasizes the notion of everything that led up to a certain result, while *end* emphasizes the notion of finality and more or less ignores what came before. As a result, *end* can be not only an awkward synonym for *end up,* but sometimes no synonym at all. This is especially true when *end up* is followed by a subject complement. *End* cannot be substituted in the following sentences without changing or losing the meaning.

> ... he's probably going straight ahead from here and will end up Governor of Mississippi —Eudora Welty, *The Ponder Heart,* 1954

> ... like everyone else I don't want to end up a festering heap —John Lennon, quoted in *Current Biography,* December 1965

> ... the October "election" in South Vietnam will end up an utterly meaningless exercise —Richard H. Rovere, *New Yorker,* 18 Sept. 1971

In the course of this discussion you have seen a sampling of the kinds of contexts in which *end up* normally appears. It should be obvious that "colloquialism" is not an appropriate label for *end up.* What's more, there is really no difference between the formality of the contexts that *end up* appears in and those that *end* appears in. The only difference between the two verbs is one of meaning.

2. When *end up* is followed by a preposition, the preposition is usually (in rough order of frequency) *with, in, as, by,* or *at.* Examples are cited in section 1 above.

enervate   To *enervate* is "to lessen the vitality or strength of" or "to reduce the mental or moral vigor of." Some people use this word without really knowing what it means, a fact testified to by a few cryptic uses preserved in our files and by the usage books which admonish their readers not to use *enervate* to mean "stimulate," "invigorate," or "energize." Don't be misled by the superficial resemblance of *enervate* to these other words. It comes from Latin *enervare,* which was itself formed from the prefix *e-* ("out, out of") and *-nervare* (from *nervus,* "sinew, nerve"). The etymological meaning still lingers in *enervate.*

> ... compelled the sluggish arms of an enervated system to begin to flail —Donald Kirk, *Saturday Rev.,* 8 Jan. 1977

engage   *Engage* may be used with any number of prepositions, but by far it is most often used with *in,* which in turn is most often followed by a gerund or a noun:

> ... but was busily engaged, on the farther side of the piano, in examining a picture —Edith Wharton, *New Year's Day,* 1924

> The police are engaged in the rounding up of suspects —Anthony Burgess, *MF,* 1971

> ... where students and scholars engage together in the imaginative exploration of the past —Henry Steele Commager, *N.Y. Times Book Rev.,* 4 Apr. 1954

> ... the reader (whom Miss Piercy does engage in argument, however feverish) —John Updike, *New Yorker,* 10 Apr. 1971

Less frequently and about equally, *engage* is used with *with* or *on* (*upon* being a less common variant of *on*); our files indicate that *engage on* is chiefly a British usage:

> ... he might engage on topics that his brother might like to regard as private —Ford Madox Ford, *The Last Post,* 1928

> The class under whose work he was engaged on this particular evening —Robertson Davies, *Tempest-tost,* 1951

> We hurry about in inadequate clothing and are too engaged with fighting to feel the cold —Marjorie Kinnan Rawlings, *Cross Creek,* 1942

. . . he was no longer as actively engaged with his old publishing house —Bennett Cerf, *Saturday Rev.,* 19 Dec. 1953

I allowed as how I didn't have anything being engaged upon the production of a novel —Flannery O'Connor, letter, 5 Oct. 1957

Engage may be used with *to,* especially in the familiar "engaged to be married" and "the man she was engaged to" phrases. We also find such other uses with the infinitive as these:

I was engaged to lunch with him in New York — Edmund Fuller, *Wall Street Jour.,* 10 July 1980

. . . the author engages himself to reassess literary reputations —Riley Hughes, *New Scholasticism,* July 1951

"Engage somebody to stay with him, or—or send him away?" —Ellen Glasgow, *Barren Ground,* 1925

". . . I hope to engage you to be serious likewise." — Jane Austen, *Pride and Prejudice,* 1813

Engage may be used with *for:*

. . . she engaged for the London cast of David Belasco's production —*Current Biography 1949*

Mr. Lorry readily engaged for that, and the conference was ended —Charles Dickens, *A Tale of Two Cities,* 1859

Engage is also used with *by:*

. . . students trying to force their way . . . were engaged by police wielding canes —*N.Y. Times,* 8 Nov. 1953

. . . students aren't terribly engaged by the majority of courses —Robert S. Powell, Jr., *Saturday Rev.,* 10 Jan. 1970

. . . I was engaged by a newspaper to be its first dance critic —Walter Terry, *Saturday Rev.,* 27 Nov. 1976

and with *as:*

. . . she had engaged herself as a servant —Kenneth Roberts, *Oliver Wiswell,* 1940

enhance The use of *enhance* with a personal object was called obsolete by Fowler 1926 and is cited as an error in one recent dictionary (Longman 1984). Evidence in the OED shows that *enhance* with a personal object was once common, but that it fell into disuse during the 17th century. Its occurrence in current English is rare but not obsolete:

I think clothes should enhance the woman, not the designer —Margaret Gunster, quoted in *Women's Wear Daily,* 6 Dec. 1976

A successful run enhances a runner in his own eyes —Dr. Brent Waters, *Runners World,* June 1981

Enhance now almost always has a thing—often an abstract quality—as its object:

. . . the general effect, enhanced by a ceiling of pale-blue metal plates —*New Yorker,* 10 Apr. 1971

The fresh flavour of the vegetables is . . . enhanced by the other ingredients —Marguerite Patten, *Health Food Cookery,* 1972

We have done little to enhance the productivity of programmers —John R. Ehrman, *Datamation,* 4 Mar. 1980

Enhance normally describes the improvement or heightening of something desirable, but its use with a negative object is not incorrect:

. . . the very circumstance which at present enhances your loss, must gradually reconcile you to it better —Jane Austen, letter, 8 Apr. 1798

Bernstein 1965 finds that such usage occurs "not uncommonly." Our evidence shows, however, that it is now about as rare as the use of *enhance* with a personal object. The "make better" associations of *enhance* are now so well established that its use to mean "make worse" puts some strain on idiom:

. . . such evils as distracting youngsters from more nutritious foodstuffs, enhancing obesity, ruining teeth and causing diabetes —Jane E. Brody, *N.Y. Times,* 25 May 1977

enigmatic Copperud 1970, 1980 finds that *enigmatic* is often incorrectly used to mean "dubious, questionable," and he quotes one example of such misuse. Our files contain no further evidence of it, however. In edited writing, at least, *enigmatic* seems to be holding firmly to its established sense, "mysterious, puzzling":

. . . she remained enigmatic about her own life — John Thompson, *Harper's,* March 1971

The enigmatic Cedeno has been a mystery mainly to pitchers so far —E. M. Swift, *Sports Illustrated,* 7 May 1979

. . . Baudelaire remains an enigmatic figure —Victor Brombert, *N.Y. Times Book Rev.,* 21 Nov. 1982

enjoin 1. Fowler 1926 dislikes the use of *enjoin* with a personal object followed by an infinitive, as in "They enjoined him to be careful." He finds some support for such a construction in the OED, but he argues that "ordinary modern use" requires an impersonal object followed by *upon,* as in "They enjoined caution upon him." Sir Ernest Gowers keeps this argument essentially unchanged in his 1965 revision of Fowler, but our evidence suggests that whatever validity it may have had in 1926 is now entirely lost. As Evans 1957 notes, when *enjoin* is used to mean "to direct or admonish" it now usually takes the infinitive:

. . . and enjoined him to bequeath them to his heirs —*Times Literary Supp.,* 28 May 1971

. . . my temperament enjoins me to believe —Arthur M. Schlesinger, Jr., *Harper's,* August 1971

. . . takes personal command, and enjoins the men to move forward —Col. David H. Hackworth, *Harper's,* July 1972

The construction favored by Fowler (with *upon* or *on*) is now relatively uncommon. Note that the sense of *enjoin* differs somewhat in this construction, being not so much "to direct" as "to impose" or "to urge as a duty or necessity":

We must at last practice what we enjoin on others — H. H. Lippincott, *Time,* 21 Feb. 1955

. . . displayed the charity enjoined on Christians — Naomi Bliven, *New Yorker,* 17 July 1971

2. A point of interest raised by several commentators is that *enjoin* has two main senses which are almost directly opposite to each other: "to direct or urge" and "to forbid or prohibit." Both senses are centuries old, and there is no question about the respectability of either. The "forbid or prohibit" sense is most familiar in—but not limited to—legal contexts:

... claims the right ... to enjoin newspapers from telling their readers what the government is up to — Archibald MacLeish, *Saturday Rev.,* 13 Nov. 1971

... girls enjoined from getting soiled; boys forbidden to play with dolls —Letty Cottin Pogrebin, *New York,* 27 Dec. 1971

... a judge permanently enjoined him from shipping excess oranges —Guerney Breckenfeld, *Saturday Rev.,* 10 July 1976

enjoy Two uses of this verb have drawn occasional criticism since the 19th century. One of them, in the phrase *enjoy oneself,* can now safely be classed as a dead issue. This old idiom (first recorded in 1656) was faulted by Hodgson 1889, and apprehensions about its propriety persisted in the minds of some people well into the 20th century. Its supposed offense was that it illogically (and, perhaps, indecently) implied taking pleasure in oneself, inasmuch as the "correct" meaning of *enjoy* is "to take pleasure or satisfaction in." Even Hodgson admitted, however, that this supposedly incorrect phrase was used "by the best writers." The case against it was in fact so weak that no other commentator we know of took up the cause, but it was promoted by enough English teachers to give it some currency among certain members of the general public. Indications are, however, that the currency is now past. There may be a few diehards out there who continue to look askance at this common phrase, but let there be no doubt in your mind about it—*enjoy oneself* is nothing less than perfectly respectable:

... and she settled down to enjoy herself alone, working, thinking, living —D. H. Lawrence, *Sons and Lovers,* 1913

There they all were. Enjoying themselves —Stella Gibbons, *Cold Comfort Farm,* 1932

... as if he doesn't quite approve of enjoying himself too much —Elizabeth Drew, *New Yorker,* 14 Dec. 1987

The other criticized use appears in such a sentence as "He enjoys poor health," in which *enjoy* is being used as if it were simply a neutral synonym of *experience.* This use of *enjoy* is an outgrowth of its common sense, "to have the benefit of; have for one's use or lot":

... has enjoyed a long and varied career in the United States —*Current Biography,* September 1967

... natural gas will continue to enjoy its historic price advantage —*Annual Report, Pacific Lighting Corporation,* 1970

This sense of *enjoy* dates back to the 15th century. The criticized use is also quite old, having been recorded as early as 1577. Such commentators as Richard Grant White 1870 and Ayres 1881 took unfavorable notice of it in the late 1800s, and objections to it can still be found in some usage handbooks. It is not now—and never has

been—common in writing, but it does persist in making written appearances from time to time:

... Mendes appears to have enjoyed poor health — Stephen Birmingham, *The Grandees,* 1971

... could relegate OE to even more profound organizational insignificance than it presently enjoys — Samuel Halperin, *Change,* January–February 1971

The OED notes that this use of *enjoy* occurs chiefly "where the [object of the verb] has properly a favourable sense, qualified adversely by the adj[ective]." In essence, then, "to enjoy poor health" serves as another way of saying "to fail to enjoy good health." The problem, of course, is that *enjoy* so strongly suggests "take pleasure in" that its use with a negative object sounds peculiar. That is why such usage is criticized and why it continues to be uncommon.

enormity, enormousness The usage experts insist that *enormity* is improperly used to denote large size and is properly used only to denote wickedness, outrage, or crime. *Enormousness* is the word recommended for large size. This recommendation from Strunk & White 1979 for *enormity* is typical: "Use only in the sense 'monstrous wickedness.'" The recommendation is not just simple, it is an oversimplification, as the first definition of *enormity* in Webster's Second shows:

1. State or quality of exceeding a measure or rule, or of being immoderate, monstrous, or outrageous; as, the *enormity* of an offense.

This suggests a much wider range of application than just "monstrous wickedness." Let's have a look at some of these applications.

First, we find that *enormity* can carry overtones of moral transgression:

Sin, remember, is a twofold enormity —James Joyce, *A Portrait of the Artist as a Young Man,* 1916

... the always ugly inequality in the distribution of this world's goods, in ceasing to be a practical necessity, has become a moral enormity —Arnold J. Toynbee, *Civilization on Trial,* 1948

Twenty years after the war we stand shocked and amazed at the enormity of the German crimes — *Times Literary Supp.,* 30 Dec. 1965

It may also denote an outrage against one's sense of decency or one's sense of what is right:

One should pause to absorb this in its full innovative enormity—a United States Senator tapped and trailed on his legislative rounds by *American* Army agents? —Andrew St. George, *Harper's,* November 1973

The vulgarity of his age has suddenly been revealed to him in all its enormity —Albert Dasnoy, *Encounter,* February 1955

At other times it may stress the gravity of a situation, the seriousness of what may happen because of some act or event. The emphasis here is on the dire consequences, rather than the moral obloquy:

I confess the crime, and own the enormity of its consequences, and the danger of its example —Samuel Johnson, letter written for Dr. Dodd, June 1777

She was violently ill, and she was afraid that she was dying. She was too frightened to let Tom-Tom go for help, and while he dosed her as he could, she confessed to him about herself and Turl. As soon as she told it she became easier and went off to sleep, either before she had time to realize the enormity of what she had done, or while she was still too occupied in being alive to care —"Centaur in Brass," in *The Collected Stories of William Faulkner,* 1950

Now the enormity of his running away rode heavily on him —*Read and Young America Mag.,* 15 Nov. 1952

She perceived as no one in the family could the enormity of the misfortune —E. L. Doctorow, *Ragtime,* 1975

The grave situation described may carry distinct overtones of being a considerable departure from what is normal:

They awakened; they sat up; and then the enormity of their situation burst upon them.
"How did the fire start?" asked Pablo plaintively, and no one knew —John Steinbeck, *Tortilla Flat,* 1935

But in spite of what the critics say, *enormity* is often used simply to denote great size or extent. It is applied to things that are literally or figuratively great in size:

... explains to a certain extent the enormity of its craters and the loftiness of its mountain peaks —*The Strand,* May 1905

The enormity of the explosion gives us several things to think about —*Manchester Guardian Weekly,* 30 Sept. 1921

... demonstrating ... the enormity and joyous function of his genital member —Robert Coover, *Evergreen,* June 1967

What has given the battle its special flavor and intensity, however, is not just the size of the combatants and the enormity of the prize —Richard Austin Smith, *Fortune,* January 1966

Husband doubts friend appreciates enormity of his good fortune —John Barth, *The Floating Opera,* 1956

Quite often *enormity* will be used to suggest a size that is beyond normal bounds, a size that is unexpectedly great. Here the notion of monstrousness may creep in, but without the notion of wickedness. This use can be either literal or figurative. For instance, the first quotation below describes the dirigible *Hindenberg* as seen by a child on the streets of New York:

The enormity of her was out of scale with everything, out of scale with the houses and the cars on the street and the people now shouting and pointing and looking up; she was like a scoop of sky come down to earth, or a floating building —E. L. Doctorow, *World's Fair,* 1985

... it was as though one had flown near enough to the sun to realize its monstrous enormity, and had then returned to earth again appalled by its distance from us —Sacheverell Sitwell, *All Summer in a Day,* 1926

Now the singer can be heard on her first recital album and while the positive impression of her singing is sustained, the real enormity of the voice can be inferred.
Listeners at Carnegie Hall were driven back into their seats by the volume of the Jones super-voice —Howard Klein, *N.Y. Times,* 18 Dec. 1966

In many instances the notion of great size is colored by aspects of the first sense of *enormity* as defined in Webster's Second. One common figurative use blends together the notions of immoderateness, excess, and monstrousness to suggest a size that is daunting or overwhelming:

... the enormity of the task of teachers in slum schools —James B. Conant, *Slums and Suburbs,* 1961

In view of the enormity of population pressures in India, the condom machine is like a black joke —Michael T. Kaufman, *N.Y. Times,* 11 Nov. 1979

... helpful, self-effacing individuals, whose own creative powers may well be devoured by the enormity of the task before them —Joyce Carol Oates, *American Poetry Rev.,* vol. 3, no. 5, 1974

Interestingly, it is this use that most often catches the eye of the commentators:

"Impressed by the enormity of the job and the far-reaching scope of the military, Mr. Lovett knows ..." "The enormity of the collection long ago discouraged the academy with its limited staff." Authorities on usage are virtually unanimous in reserving "enormity" for the idea of wickedness —Bernstein 1958

On the challenge of the Presidency, Mr. Reagan said: "I have always been well aware of the enormity of it, the difficulties. . . ." —William Safire, *N.Y. Times,* 8 Mar. 1981

Writers since the last half of the 19th century have used the interplay of the notions of enormous size and of wickedness or outrageousness to give their uses of the word a richness of meaning that they have directed in various ways. Here, for instance, we have a writer combining size with moral outrage:

The enormity of existing stockpiles of atomic weapons —*New Republic,* 21 Dec. 1953

Here we have a writer combining the two notions in order to get in a sly dig at an opponent:

My other correspondent has a somewhat juster notion of the magnitude of his proposition, or, as I should rather say, of its enormity —Richard Grant White 1870

Another writer uses it for humorous effect:

That is one of the lessons that buses remind you of ... the enormity of the female behind —Beverly Nichols, *Punch,* 12 Dec. 1973

Sometimes even the "enormous wickedness" sense has been employed tongue-in-cheek:

Lecture her two boys on the enormity of telling a fib —William Black, *The Strange Adventures of a Phaeton,* 1872 (OED)

... that solemn warning against the enormity of the split infinitive —Havelock Ellis, *The Dance of Life,* 1923

In their rush to correct misuses the commentators tend to leave the impression that *enormity* is a mass noun meaning "monstrous wickedness." This impression overlooks long and frequent use of the word as a count noun. The count use has been recognized by dictionaries since Samuel Johnson's of 1755. Its application ranges from atrocious, sinful, or vicious acts to lesser sins and peccadilloes. It is seldom applied to things that are merely big.

We shall speak of the particular abuses and enormities of the government —Edmund Spenser, quoted in Johnson 1755

Hastily excusing herself to Lady Mendip, with whom she had been discussing the latest enormities of the Government —Dorothy L. Sayers, *Murder Must Advertise,* 1933

... have as little success in achieving integration as they are having in preventing U.S. enormities and escalation in Indo-China —W. H. Ferry, *Center Mag.,* March 1968

Actually, Johnson adored London and was exhilarated no end by its racy surface, enormities included —Paul Fussell, *Samuel Johnson and the Life of Writing,* 1971

There are many little enormities in the world, which our preachers would be very glad to see removed — Joseph Addison, quoted in Johnson 1755

... Miss Loos saw that, far more amusing than a brash, frank narrative ... would be for Lorelei to practise her enormities with the most complete and wide-eyed naïveté —Peter Forster, *London Calling,* 22 Apr. 1954

But what about *enormousness?* It has simply never been a very popular word. It developed in the 17th century, later than *enormity,* and its original sense, too, was associated with wickedness:

Such is the infinitenesse and enormousnesse of our rebellious Sin —John Donne, sermon, ca. 1631 (OED)

This sense appears to have dropped out of use.
It developed the meaning of "enormous size" about the same time that *enormity* did; the earliest OED example for this sense is dated 1802 and the earliest two for the same sense of *enormity* are 1792 and 1802. It is, indeed, sometimes used in this sense, as the critics recommend that it be:

The plane, the hangar, the assembly equipment, the very workers themselves conveyed an impression of almost antiseptic cleanliness, and this, along with the enormousness of everything, gave the scene a feeling of unreality —John Brooks, *New Yorker,* 26 Apr. 1969

... in contrast to the general shapeless enormousness of the vegetation —Richard Hughes, *A High Wind in Jamaica,* 1929

It is also used on occasion as what appears to be a mechanical replacement for *enormity*—in contexts where standard, well-attested uses of *enormity* (like those we have already examined) would have been at least as appropriate:

... Bengali civil servants ... are dispirited, unhopeful, buried in mindless routine, and crushed by the enormousness of their daily challenges —C. Stephen Baldwin, *Saturday Rev.,* 6 Nov. 1971

As I see it, there is still another telling Kafkaesque dimension to Watergate now that President Ford has written his version of The End. It is the enormousness of the frustration ..., the sense of waste, futility, and hopelessness —Philip Roth, *Reading Myself and Others,* 1975

But in spite of the adjurations of the critics, *enormousness* does not find a great many users.
The reasons for stigmatizing the size sense of *enormity* are not known. It was simply characterized without explanation by Henry Bradley, editor of the *E* volume of the OED (1893), in these words: "this use is now regarded as incorrect." The sense was labeled obsolete or rare in Webster 1909, but the labels were removed in Webster's Second, leaving the sense unstigmatized. Both editions have synonymy notes that distinguish between *enormity* and *enormousness* by stressing the sense of wickedness for *enormity.* It seems possible that the critics derived their opinion from the synonymy notes, since they clearly have not heeded the definitions. The earliest usage book statement we have, from MacCracken & Sandison 1917, appears to have been taken directly from the Webster 1909 synonymy: "*Enormity* refers to abnormal wickedness, *enormousness* to excessive size." This summary has been repeated with minor variations by numerous subsequent critics, but there is some recent evidence that a different view is beginning to find expression:

... I think the time has come to abandon the ramparts on "enormity's" connotation of wickedness — William Safire, *N.Y. Times,* 8 Mar. 1981

Conservatives hold that *enormity* means only 'extreme badness,' never 'enormous size.' We feel that this rule is obsolete and that it is acceptable to use the word in either sense, or in both at once — Reader's Digest 1983

We agree with these two commentators. We have seen that there is no clear basis for the "rule" at all. We suggest that you follow the writers rather than the critics: writers use *enormity* with a richness and subtlety that the critics have failed to take account of. The stigmatized sense is entirely standard and has been for more than a century and a half.

enquire See INQUIRE, ENQUIRE.

enquirer See INQUIRER, ENQUIRER.

enquiry See INQUIRY, ENQUIRY.

en route This French phrase was first used in English in the 19th century. Its assimilation into our language was completed long ago, and there is no longer any need to underline or italicize it as a foreign term. It is used as both an adverb and an adjective, and it is written both as one word and two. Copperud 1980 prefers the two-word form, and our evidence shows that it continues to be the more common choice:

> ... essential that the civil en route services be provided —R. W. Faulks, *Principles of Transport,* 1973

> The Apollo can be calibrated en route —Richard L. Collins, *Flying,* March 1984

> ... their first-night stopover enroute to Florida — Robert Towers, *N.Y. Times Book Rev.,* 13 June 1976

Because the *en* of *en route* sounds just like *on* in one of its pronunciations, the potential for an embarrassing error exists:

> They are "intermediate" systems in that they mark stages on route to mastery ... of written, academic discourse —*College Composition and Communication,* October 1980

> ... in spite of the fact that, on route to the show, the van brakes failed —*Chronicle of the Horse,* 3 Aug. 1984

Authors and proofreaders beware.

ensure, insure, assure Quite a few commentators insist on distinctions between these words, but Bernstein 1977 says there are none, flatly contradicting Einstein 1985 who says that each means something different. Usage agrees better with Bernstein. Here is what the synonymy paragraph in Webster's Ninth New Collegiate Dictionary says:

> *Ensure, insure,* and *assure* are interchangeable in many contexts where they indicate the making certain or inevitable of an outcome, but *insure* sometimes stresses the taking of necessary measures beforehand, and *assure* distinctively implies the removal of doubt and suspense from a person's mind.

And here are three typical examples:

> ... but the state has blocked the sale until Witco assures that any pollution on the property will be cleaned up —Barry Meier, *Wall Street Jour.,* 7 Aug. 1985

> ... claims that his system will ensure uniformity in pronunciation —Baron 1982

> ... held that school officials had the right to insure that a high-school assembly proceed in an orderly manner —William Safire, *N.Y. Times,* 24 Aug. 1986

A few commentators, such as Trimble 1975 and Sellers 1975, suggest *assure* for people, *ensure* for things, and *insure* for money and guarantees (insurance). These are nice distinctions, and you can follow them if you want to. *Assure* is almost always used of people, in fact:

> But I am writing to assure you no jury would convict if you wanted to join me in murdering Eddy Duchin —Alexander Woollcott, letter, 22 Feb. 1933

The rest of the recommendation rests on using *ensure* for general senses and reserving *insure* for financial senses. This distinction has been urged at least since Fowler 1926, especially by British commentators. It is in general true that *insure* is used for the financial uses (it must vex the British commentators to find *assure* still occasionally used in this sense by British technical writ-

ers). However, both *insure* and *ensure* are used in general senses:

> A solicitor is a man whose profession ensures that whenever you telephone him, he is in court —Alan Brien, *Punch,* 11 Sept. 1974

> ... so simple a thing as ensure that all third-grade teachers will be expert in spelling —Mitchell 1979

> ... would insure against any awkward second marriage —Mollie Hardwick, *Emma, Lady Hamilton,* 1969

> ... his sudden fame probably insured a backlash — Calvin Tomkins, *New Yorker,* 6 Dec. 1982

Our most recent evidence shows that the distinction between *ensure* and *insure* is made more often in British written English than in American written English, and a few commentators hold that *insure* is more common than *ensure* in American English.

en't *En't* is a contraction that is equivalent to *is not* and is probably one of the old forms that helped *ain't* acquire the sense of "is not" in addition to "am not" and "are not." It is most abundantly attested in Swift:

> It en't my fault, 'tis Patrick's fault —*Journal to Stella,* 29 Mar. 1711

See AIN'T.

enter *Enter* is a verb which may be used with many prepositions, but most often it is used with *into* or with *upon* or *on;* of these, *into* occurs most frequently:

> Mr. Sloane didn't enter into the conversation —F. Scott Fitzgerald, *The Great Gatsby,* 1925

> Nor shall I enter into details concerning the ensuing half-dozen nights —Katherine Anne Porter, *Ladies' Home Jour.,* August 1971

> ... wondered whether ... this marriage had been entered upon late —Jean Stafford, *Children Are Bored on Sunday,* 1953

> ... the house has now entered on a distinctly new phase —Edmund Wilson, *New Yorker,* 5 June 1971

Less often, *enter* is used with *in:*

> Where doubt enters in, there enters the judicial function —*Selected Writings of Benjamin N. Cardozo,* ed. Margaret E. Hall, 1947

Enter is also used with complements introduced by *for, as, at, by,* and *with.* Of this group *for* and *as* appear more often than the others:

> Six ... were entered for the English Derby —George Whiting, *Irish Digest,* June 1954

> ... the United States Army, which he entered as a captain —*Current Biography,* December 1964

> ... he had come to America, probably entering at the port of Charleston, S.C. —*Dictionary of American Biography,* 1928

> ... even though such language entered by way of the ruling classes —W. F. Bolton, *A Short History of Literary English,* 1967

. . . a United States Naval Reserve chaplain, entering with the rank of lieutenant (j.g.) —*Current Biography,* January 1964

A final example shows vividly the wide range of prepositions that can be used with *enter:*

Christianity entered the region of upstate New York from two directions, under two flags, and in two forms —*American Guide Series: New York,* 1940

enthrall   Usually, when *enthrall* is used with a preposition, it is used with *by:*

. . . I am most enthralled by the past world that Borges offers up —John Riley, *Los Angeles Times Book Rev.,* 23 Jan. 1972

As a less frequent alternative, *enthrall* may be used with *with:*

. . . Nelly, with whom he is enthralled —Tom Bishop, *Saturday Rev.,* 5 Feb. 1972

enthuse   The road to respectability has been a long one for *enthuse,* and there are some who feel that it still has not arrived. It originated as a back-formation of the noun *enthusiasm* in the early 19th-century. The earliest record of its use is in a letter written in 1827 by a young Scotsman who was traveling in the Pacific Northwest:

My humble exertions will I trust convey and enthuse, and draw attention to the beautifully varied verdure of N.W. America —in *American Speech,* 1947 and OED Supplement

Enthuse has been the object of critical attention at least since Richard Grant White 1870 called it "ridiculous." White described it as being "in vogue in the southern part of the United States," but no other evidence establishes that its popularity was limited to the South. Ayres 1881 was somewhat more moderate in his judgment than White, saying only that *enthuse* had not yet won acceptance and that "for the present . . . it is studiously shunned by those who are at all careful in the selection of their language." Unlike White, Ayres recognized the possibility that *enthuse* might one day cease to be "shunned." Its written use during Ayres's time seems to have been chiefly confined to newspapers (as it is now), but journalists were not the only writers to employ it:

. . . I have been very much interested in the memorial; and I have been enthused over what I conceive to be Lanier's theories of art —Robert Frost, letter, 10 June 1894

The attitude of usage commentators toward *enthuse* has been fairly consistent throughout the 20th century. In general, their criticism has been expressed more in the relatively moderate tones of Ayres than in the strident tones of Richard Grant White. The origins of *enthuse* as a back-formation are not now usually regarded as an unpardonable sin, but doubts persist about its suitability in formal writing. The typical advice now given is to avoid written use of *enthuse* because its reputation remains suspect. Only a few commentators (notably Kilpatrick 1984) continue to claim that the word is intrinsically flawed.

Like opinion about it, actual usage of *enthuse* seems to have changed little through the years, except that it occurs much more commonly in writing than it once did. One of its most familiar uses is in the form of the

past participle *enthused,* which functions as an adjective more or less equivalent to *enthusiastic:*

But experts . . . are not unanimously enthused —John Lear, *Saturday Rev.,* 28 June 1969

. . . because I'm enthused and excited about it —John Bremer, *Media & Methods,* January 1970

So enthused was the lanky Perkins —Callan, *Punch,* 3 Apr. 1974

. . . when he spoke of being an actor, he sounded enthused —Dave Anderson, *N.Y. Times,* 2 June 1974

. . . technocrats are now enthused about wind power —Christopher Flavin quoted in *Christian Science Monitor,* 10 Aug. 1981

The President was enthused —H. R. Haldeman, *Forbes,* 15 Mar. 1982

Its other common uses are as a transitive verb meaning "to say with enthusiasm":

. . . he enthuses, "She looks so seductive. . . ." — *Harper's Bazaar,* November 1972

"It will be the dream ticket," one Humphrey strategist enthused —Robert Sam Anson, *New Times,* 28 May 1976

"Tremendously useful" he enthused —Hardcastle, *Punch,* 27 May 1975

"I think it's great," a woman from Omaha enthused —Marquis Childs, *Smithsonian,* June 1985

and as an intransitive verb meaning "to express enthusiasm":

I cannot enthuse over the things as Leslie does — Wilfred Owen, letter, 22 Sept. 1912 (OED Supplement)

I must enthuse a little, too, over some old favourites —Harold J. Laski, letter, 1921

. . . to hear the youngsters of today enthusing about the croissants —Frank Sullivan, *The Night the Old Nostalgia Burned Down,* 1953

. . . it does not enthuse, presuppose values, or have many lyrical moments —*Times Literary Supp.,* 25 Nov. 1965

. . . and I was enthusing over it —Julian Huxley, *Memories,* 1970

. . . he never enthused too loudly about his son's accomplishments —Craig Waters, *The Washingtonian,* May 1974

. . . enthuses over the joys and beauties of . . . homestead crafts —John D. Tierney, *Wall Street Jour.,* 18 Aug. 1981

Our evidence does not show that *enthuse* is a remarkably informal word, but it does confirm that it is not used in highly formal writing. (This restriction may be partly explained by the fact that the behavior it names is not, itself, highly formal.) The common applications of the word make it most useful—and most often used—in journalistic prose. The stigma attached to it is not a strong one, but it is persistent; we would not bet against its lingering for some years yet. There are clear signs, however, that the stigma has at least begun to wane. The usage panel of Heritage 1969 rejected *enthuse* in "serious writing" by a margin of 3 to 1, but the panel of Heritage 1982 took no vote at all on this issue, and William Safire has recently (11 Mar. 1984) indicated in his language column his acceptance of the word. In another hundred years or so, who knows?—maybe everyone will have forgotten why there was ever any fuss over *enthuse.*

entitle   *Entitle* has two common meanings: "to give a title to, title" and "to give a right to." Sources as diverse as Emily Post 1927 and Bremner 1980 have expressed disapproval of using *entitled* to mean "titled." However, this well-established usage has been common for over 500 years and is the older of the two senses.

> . . . a sermon entitled "Popular Government by Divine Right" —Stuart W. Chapman, *Yale Rev.,* Summer 1954

> . . . describes himself as an "elephant tramp" for the purpose of entitling his autobiography —Robert Lewis Taylor, *N.Y. Times Book Rev.,* 27 Feb. 1955

> . . . shows entitled "Sesame Street" —*Annual Report, Carnegie Corp.,* 1969

> . . . a chapter entitled *Eugene Onegin* —*Times Literary Supp.,* 30 July 1971

> I was impelled to entitle a recent political column about the Saudi oil minister, Sheik Ahmed Yamani, "Yamani or Ya Life" —Safire 1984

The sense "to give a right to" has inspired commentary rather than criticism. Evans 1957 notes that it "is not followed by the *-ing* form of a verb, as in *this entitles you to going,*" and Fowler 1926 says that "it does not mean bound (*to* do) or liable (*to* a penalty)." We agree with both of these statements because none of the citations we have fits either of the patterns described. *Entitle* is almost always used with *to* plus an infinitive or a noun phrase, and in all cases the thing that is entitled to be had or done is something that is desired or desirable.

> . . . felt entitled to advise her in such matters —Louis Auchincloss, *A Law for the Lion,* 1953

> We were entitled to believe . . . that there was a general acceptance of the principles —John Foster Dulles, *U.S. News & World Report,* 16 July 1954

> When children are cheated of these happy times to which they are entitled —Frances R. Horwich, *NEA Jour.,* February 1965

> . . . we're entitled to our half of the country —Ian Douglas Smith, quoted in *Time,* 26 Nov. 1965

> This rank entitles us to full membership —Naomi F. Levin, *Barnard Alumnae,* Winter 1971

enure   See INURE, ENURE.

envelop   See ENVELOPE 2.

envelope   1. The two pronunciations of the noun, \ˈen-və-ˌlōp\ and \ˈän-və-ˌlōp\, are used with about equal frequency and are both fully acceptable, but the \ˈän-\ version is sometimes stridently decried. Evans 1962 calls it "a strange, ignorant mispronunciation," and approvingly cites Kenyon and Knott's dismissal of

it as "pseudo-French" in A Pronouncing Dictionary of American English (1944).

It is really not pseudo-French, nor ignorant, and as used by most speakers today it appears naturally, with no affectation or striving for style. If you were to try to anglicize the French word *enveloppe,* \ˈän-və-ˌlōp\ is exactly what you would come up with—a pronunciation like that of *encore, ennui,* and many others. A fairly reasonable objection one might make to it is that *envelope* has been in our language since the early 18th century, so that it deserves to be spoken like such other old borrowings from French as *envy* and *environ* rather than to vary between two versions, as do *enclave* and *en route,* which were borrowed more recently.

Such a calmly philological consideration cannot well be the source of the peculiar venom directed against \ˈän-\, however. For this we must look to more revealing animadversions, such as one in the February 1926 issue of *American Speech,* which refers to someone who "is tempted to invest in a very high silk hat such as the doorkeeper uses at the British Museum, take to using *onvelopes,* write only *cheques* at the bank. . . ." Or this from Vladimir Nabokov's *Lolita* (1958):

> Oh, she was very genteel: she said "excuse me" whenever a slight burp interrupted her flowing speech, called an envelope an ahnvelope. . . .

Thus, \ˈän-və-ˌlōp\ is (or was) considered not so much wrong as non-U: a dreadful indication of the middle classes getting above themselves.
2. *Envelop, envelope.* The use of *envelope* as a variant spelling for the verb and of *envelop* as a variant spelling for the noun is now so uncommon as to look downright peculiar:

> She looked as though she might somehow envelope me —Gerald Warner Brace, *Bell's Landing,* 1955

> . . . nor did he mention his promotions, though they were revealed on his envelops —Gerald Sykes, *The Center of the Stage,* 1952

envious, enviable   At one time, *envious* and *enviable* shared a sense, "highly desirable," but this sense has just about faded from general usage. That is to say, *envious* has lost the sense while *enviable* has retained it. Some language commentators warn not to mix up the two words, but our files show that such confusion is unlikely, because *envious* is not now used in the shared sense except in such contexts as poetry:

> Theirs was an envious gift, but lightly held — Thomas Cole, *Interim,* vol. 4, 1954

Envious, when used with a preposition, is usually used with *of:*

> . . . were envious of the easier way of life of their Kikuyu neighbours —L. S. B. Leakey, *Mau Mau and the Kikuyu,* 1952

envisage, envision   *Envisage* got started in English in the early 19th century with the sense, now archaic, of "to meet squarely," "confront," "face."

> Must I recognize the bitter truth? . . . I have envisaged it —George Meredith, *The Egoist,* 1879 (OED)

By 1837 a second sense was developing which the OED defines as "To obtain a mental view of, set before the mind's eye; to contemplate; *chiefly,* to view or regard under a particular aspect." Webster's Third divides this sense into two subsenses, using a total of five rephrasings and two synonyms to thoroughly cover the different shades of meaning.

In 1926 Fowler took exception to *envisage*, calling it "a 19th-century word only, & a surely undesirable GALLICISM. *Face, confront, contemplate, recognize, realize, view & regard* seem equal between them to all requirements." How can a word that is so obviously useful, carrying such a wide range of meaning, be "surely undesirable"? We do not understand Fowler's judgment, but Nicholson 1957 and Gowers in Fowler 1965 agreed with it enough to put versions of his article in their respective revisions of his book.

Nicholson and Gowers perceive two uses for *envisage*. The first is the one for which we are advised to use a word from the multisynonym list (to which Gowers adds *imagine, intend,* and *visualize*); they follow Fowler's lead in berating this sense. The second is what Nicholson defines as "the current meaning, 'obtain a mental view,' 'set before the mind's eye'" and what Gowers defines as "forming a mental picture of something that may exist in the future"; this sense they perceive as allowable. Now, according to the definitions in Webster's Third and the OED, the second sense approved by Nicholson and Gowers is actually the same sense as the one which belongs to most of the verbs in those lists of synonyms. They do not like the sense when it is defined by synonym, but they are willing to give it limited approval when they have redefined it themselves. This is what comes of trying to adjust reality and received opinion to each other instead of taking a fresh view of reality.

Since the distinction that Nicholson and Gowers make is an artificial one, it comes as no surprise that people actually using *envisage* do not make it. *Envisage* can express a broad range of nuances and is a very useful word—so useful that it has a look-alike twin, *envision.*

Envision appeared on the scene by 1919—late enough, apparently, to escape Fowler's censorious eye and, as a result, to be ignored by Nicholson and Gowers. Evans 1957 accepts both words but claims that *envision* is the more poetic of the two and "is properly confined to those ecstatic or alarming foreshadowings that visions are made on." Bryson 1984 has a milder version of the same opinion: "*Envision* is slightly the loftier of the two." In actual practice this distinction does not hold true, as the examples below will show you.

Bryson also says, "If there is no mental image involved, neither word is correct. A rough rule is that if you find yourself following either word with 'that' you are using it incorrectly." We disagree. *Envisage* and *envision* are almost never followed by *that,* yet in spite of this fact they can both be used in sentences that conjure up no mental picture. Sometimes the thing envisaged or envisioned is a concept more abstract than a mental image. When a specific picture is in mind, however, writers tend to use *envision* more than *envisage.* None of the critics mention this.

Here are some citations which show how *envisage* and *envision* are used and how the distinctions that usage writers have made are not always reflected in actual usage.

> . . . I could envisage without difficulty a typical . . . day —P. G. Wodehouse, *Joy in the Morning,* 1946

> . . . because she thought of the path *as* running, she envisaged all else as standing still —Elizabeth Bowen, *The Heat of the Day,* 1949

> . . . a social salvation . . . which he envisages as the possible and necessary experience of millions of individuals —Lionel Trilling, *New Yorker,* 24 Nov. 1951

> . . . all utopias . . . envisage a different kind of men and women from any that we know —*Times Literary Supp.,* 23 Apr. 1971

> . . . we envisage booming demand for political scientists —Alan Abelson, *Barron's,* 8 May 1972

> . . . he envisages sex as a sort of universal spiritual energy —Iris Murdoch, *The Fire and The Sun,* 1977

> . . . by envisioning the religious pattern within our lives —Stephen Spender, *New Republic,* 3 Aug. 1953

> The dingy office, pathetic with an out-moded elegance of brass rail and threadbare carpet, was exactly what Mr. Campion had envisioned —Margery Allingham, *More Work for the Undertaker,* 1949

> We envision this new sytem being in production in about two years —J. S. Anderson, quoted in *General Electric Investor,* Summer 1971

> . . . he had come to envision himself as a symptomatic consciousness —John W. Aldridge, *Saturday Rev.,* 13 Nov. 1971

> . . . had envisioned only the possibility of humiliation —Stanley Marcus, *Minding the Store,* 1974

> . . . we may envision the appalled face of Emerson —Robert Penn Warren, *Democracy and Poetry,* 1975

These examples show that, in many respects, *envisage* and *envision* are interchangeable. Reader's Digest 1983 concedes as much and so does Shaw 1975, though he spoils the effect by saying that "both words are so ponderous that neither should be used in ordinary circumstances." Once again, we beg to differ. *Envisage* and *envision* may not pop up in the day-to-day conversation of most people or in very informal kinds of writing, but they have established a firm place for themselves in all other varieties of standard English.

epic   Various popular uses of this literary word have been criticized from time to time. In its primary sense, *epic* denotes a long narrative poem such as the *Iliad* or the *Odyssey,* in which the deeds of historic or legendary figures are recounted. It also has several extended senses in which it applies to such modern phenomena as big-budget historical movies and double-overtime basketball games. These extended senses are sometimes used in hyperbolic ways and that makes them easy targets for anyone who scorns hyperbole, but they persist in widespread and largely uncontroversial use:

> . . . the faculty at Oxford . . . put on an epic demonstration of power —Gus Tyler, *Change,* Winter 1971–72

> . . . this most durable of film epics is still going strong —Robert Manning, *Atlantic,* February 1973

> The most spirited and satisfying new Western epic in several years —*New Yorker,* 31 Oct. 1983

> . . . an upset, lacrosse followers say, of nearly epic proportions —Bob Kravitz, *Sports Illustrated,* 4 Aug. 1986

epicene pronouns A problem of long standing in English is finding a gender-neutral singular pronoun to use in reference to indefinite pronouns like *anyone, everyone,* and *someone*. The spoken language has long used *they, their,* and *them,* but this folk solution has not sufficed for the academically trained and grammatically oriented, for whom number sometimes seems to be more important than common sense. The most usual grammarian's solution (buttressed at least once by the British parliament) has been to recommend the masculine *he, his, him*. Some grammarians and theorists, beginning in the 19th century, have chosen the road of neologism. This has led to such proposed forms as *ne, nis, nim, hiser, thon, en, unus, talis, ir, iro, im, ons, he'er, shis, heris, co, cos, tey, ter, tem, s/he,* and so on and on. The latest we have heard of are *che, chim, chis, chimself,* proposed by someone from Texas in December 1985. There may never be an end to these ingenious proposals. The best, most informative, and most entertaining summary of this whole matter is an article by Dennis E. Baron in *American Speech,* vol. 56, no. 2, Summer 1981. The same discussion is presented in a somewhat revised form as the tenth chapter of his book *Grammar and Gender* (1986).

Under this heading Nickles 1974 disapproves of *they, their,* and *them* used in reference to indefinite pronouns. We discuss the matter at THEY, THEIR, THEM 1.

epidemic See ENDEMIC, EPIDEMIC.

epithet Gould 1870 complained that *epithet* was misunderstood by "many men who are well educated, and many who are not so." Gould believed that the only proper meaning of *epithet* was "an adjective denoting any quality, good or bad." He objected in part to its use in denoting a descriptive noun rather than an adjective (such usage was, in fact, called erroneous by both Samuel Johnson and Noah Webster), but his main objection was to the widespread notion that *epithet* referred only to such negative terms as *vile* and *cowardly* and not to such terms of praise as *good* and *honest*.

The argument that *epithet* should be applied only to adjectives is no longer heard, but resistance to its use in a specifically negative sense has not entirely died out. In its oldest uses, *epithet* is a neutral word, derived from the Greek *epitheton,* "adjective; characterizing term." It has had this sense in English since the 16th century. The point at which it began to develop its more limited negative sense is impossible to determine, but there is reason to believe that it may have been as early as the 1700s. (In 1755, Johnson specifically indicated in his dictionary that it could refer to both good and bad qualities, and his feeling the need to make that point suggests that the word was already being understood—or misunderstood, in Johnson's view—as referring only to the bad.) In any case, the disputed sense was obviously well developed by Gould's time. Its common occurrence in writing, however, is a fairly recent phenomenon:

No one should be afraid to have epithets hurled against him by the enemy — *Yale Rev.,* July 1919

... was what we now call a lowbrow; but that epithet had not then been invented —George Bernard Shaw, *American Mercury,* January 1946

But this time G.M. and the U.A.W. were not exchanging four-letter epithets —*Time,* 7 June 1948

... forbade the union ... from using epithets or offensive language against the company's employes —*Wall Street Jour.,* 5 Aug. 1948

... his name has come to be almost as much of an epithet as that of the late Quisling —Bob Considine, *Springfield* (Mass.) *Union,* 26 Nov. 1954

This sense of *epithet* is now quite common, but it has not displaced the older, comprehensive sense, which also continues in regular use:

... as worthless as the epithets, "great," "wonderful," or "marvellous" —J. C. Trewin, *John O'London's Weekly,* 24 June 1949

... earned him the affectionate epithet of "peanut ambassador" —*Current Biography,* April 1966

... their search for the just adjective, the refined epithet —Kathleen Raine, *CEA Chap Book,* 1969

Recent usage commentators have in general either been willing to acknowledge that the negative sense of *epithet* is now established as standard (Reader's Digest 1983) or omitted it as something less than a real problem (Phythian 1979, Bryson 1984, Shaw 1985). A notable exception is Sir Ernest Gowers, who in Fowler 1965 describes this sense as a "corruption." No doubt there are some people who continue to regard it in that way, but they are becoming more and more of a minority. Dictionaries now routinely enter "derogatory term" or the like as a sense of *epithet*. If you feel any unease about its use, the thing to do is to modify it with an appropriate adjective such as *insulting* or *disparaging*. Such usage will offend no one.

... I do not employ the word "bureaucracy" as a disparaging epithet —Robert K. Merton, *Columbia Forum,* Spring 1968

Shrilly repeated negative epithets abound —Benjamin DeMott, *Saturday Rev.,* 13 May 1978

epitome The best-known sense of *epitome* is "a typical or ideal example," "embodiment." A few usage writers mention that *epitome* can be used of something bad as well as something good; this is true.

He was the epitome of the ruthless business titan — S. N. Behrman, *New Yorker,* 27 Oct. 1951

... can be the epitome of evil —*Southern Living,* April 1972

Even when used with the intended meaning "embodiment," *epitome* can sometimes be interpreted as meaning "acme," "high point."

To me it [a country store] seemed the epitome of plenty and luxury —Della Lutes, *The Country Kitchen,* 1936

Such rides are my earliest recollection. They remain in memory as the epitome of happiness —Frank Swinnerton, *Tokefield Papers,* 1949

... those jobs at IBM and Chase Manhattan many ... view as the epitome of success —Stephen V. Roberts, *Commonweal,* 30 Jan. 1970

Harper 1985 and others advise against using *epitome* to mean "acme." The problem with sentences such as these last three examples is that there is no certain way to tell from the context whether the intended meaning is "embodiment" or "acme." In fact, we currently lack any clear-cut evidence that *epitome* is intentionally used to mean "acme" (for instance, in a sentence such as "that hit play was the epitome of her career"), and so we have not recognized this aspect of meaning as a distinct sense in our dictionaries. Such a sense, however, may be developing.

epoch Bernstein 1965 considers the proper meaning of *epoch* to be "the beginning of a new period, a turning point." That is, in fact, one of the oldest senses of the word, but it is now rarely seen:

> The adherence of the United States to such a convention would mark an epoch in the international copyright relations of this country —Arthur Fisher, *Annual Report of the Librarian of Congress,* 1952

Far more common is the use of *epoch* to mean "an extended and distinct period of time." Bernstein contends that only *era* properly has this sense, but he acknowledges that "probably the distortion of *epoch* has gone too far to be reversible." A look in the OED sheds some interesting light on this subject. *Epoch* has actually been used in the sense disliked by Bernstein since the 17th century, while *era* has had this sense only since the 18th. *Era* originally, like *epoch,* referred to a point marking the beginning of a period rather than the period itself. In other words *era* has undergone exactly the same "distortion" that *epoch* has undergone, but more recently. The "period of time" sense of *epoch* is entirely proper:

> ... the leading international lawyer of his epoch — *Times Literary Supp.,* 25 Jan. 1974

> In the Cartesian epoch ... man conceived of the universe as a watch —Robert Penn Warren, *Democracy and Poetry,* 1975

equable, equitable Warnings against confusion of these adjectives are sometimes heard. *Equable* has the basic meaning, "steady and moderate." Its most familiar uses are in characterizing a moderate climate and an even temperament:

> The outstanding features of Hawaii's climate include mild and equable temperatures the year round — *Atlas of Hawaii,* ed. R. Warwick Armstrong, 1973

> By nature he is an equable dog —*Dog World,* June 1982

Equitable is a synonym of *fair:*

> ... help us come to honest and equitable terms with one another —Susan Edmiston, *New York,* 27 Dec. 1971

> ... the claim of the public to an equitable share in the seashore —Anthony Wolff, *Saturday Rev.,* 22 July 1978

Appearances of one of these words where the other is usual are uncommon, at least in edited prose; but they do turn up from time to time. *Equitable* is a bit more likely to be applied to climate and temperament than is *equable* to be applied to, say, an evenhanded discussion of conflicting views.

equal 1. When *equal* is used with a preposition, it is used most often with *to:*

> ... whether the idea of maximum personal liberty is equal to the idea of maximum personal discipline — Adlai E. Stevenson, *Speeches,* ed. Richard Harrity, 1952

> He was equal to extended walks by this time — Thomas B. Costain, *The Black Rose,* 1945

Equal to may also be used with a verbal, in which case the gerund is the most likely form, although there is sporadic evidence for the use of the infinitive:

> ... become equal to solving the problems of every conceivable environment —William J. Reilly, *Life Planning for College Students,* 1954

> She was very equal, therefore, to address Mr. Bingley on the subject of the ball —Jane Austen, *Pride and Prejudice,* 1813

Although the use of *equal* with *with* occurs more often in older writings, it is still in occasional use in contemporary English:

> ... maintain social services in his country on a level equal with those in the rest of the United Kingdom —*Current Biography,* September 1968

Phythian 1979 cautions against using the preposition *for* with *equal.* We have little evidence in our files that the use occurs in edited prose.

2. *Equal* is one of those adjectives that some commentators (such as Partridge 1942, Bernstein 1965, Shaw 1970, 1987) insist are absolute and incapable of comparison. They therefore disapprove of the combination *more equal.* As do many other statements about the absolute quality of adjectives (see ABSOLUTE ADJECTIVES), this opinion suffers from two weaknesses. It ignores history—*equal* has been compared since at least the 17th century—and it fails to recognize the common use of *more* and *most* to mean "more nearly," "most nearly." Here are some ordinary uses of *more equal* in the sense of "more nearly equal":

> ... but if we keep edging toward it, American society will become more just, more equal, and more evenhanded in the distribution of power —John Fischer, *Harper's,* March 1971

> ... that the American woman is not the same as other women: that she is freer in her manners and that she is freer because she is more equal —Henry Fairlie, *American Scholar,* Winter 1976/1977

> So even though income distribution among unmarried individuals grew more equal over the decade, among families it grew less equal —David Osborne, *Harper's,* January 1983

More equal cannot be allowed to depart without a notice of George Orwell's use of the phrase in *Animal Farm.* There he used *equal* in a way not normally compared and put *more* with it to show the duplicitous ways in which totalitarian regimes use the language for their own advantage. All animals, say the ruling pigs, are equal, but some are more equal than others. Orwell's *more equal than* has frequently been echoed by later writers:

> ... those who are less equal than others must find the power —Tom Hayden, *American Scholar,* Autumn 1967

> ... in a professional situation where some must by definition be more equal than others —Harold Perkin, *Times Literary Supp.,* 19 Mar. 1970

> ... a rule of all great egalitarian bureaucracies, as George Orwell pointed out, is that some people are

more equal than others —John Hersey, *New Yorker,* 31 May 1982

equally as This phrase has been denigrated in books on English usage for more than a hundred years. Nineteenth-century commentators such as William Blackley (in *Word Gossip,* 1869) and Ayres 1881 concerned themselves in particular with the phrase *equally as well,* which Ayres described as "a redundant form of expression." Commentators throughout the 20th century have expressed much the same opinion. The definitive seal of disapproval was given by Fowler 1926, who called *equally as* "an illiterate tautology."

The reason *equally as* is considered redundant is that either *equally* or *as* can stand alone in most of the contexts in which the phrase is used. "The old show was awful, and the new show is equally as bad" can be revised to " . . . the new show is equally bad" or " . . . the new show is as bad" with no change of meaning. What will change, of course, is emphasis, especially if *equally* is deleted in favor of *as.* As Bernstein 1965 notes, *as* by itself is far less emphatic than either *equally as* or *equally.* The point of the *equally* in *equally as* is to make it clear that the comparison being made is unqualified. Other adverbs and adverbial phrases are also used with *as* for the same purpose; for example, "the new show is just as bad" or " . . . every bit as bad." The difference is that only *equally* can also be used to replace *as* altogether (except in such constructions as "One is equally as bad as the other," in which *as* cannot be deleted).

Equally as is certainly not "illiterate," and its redundancy is more apparent than real. We would describe it as an idiomatic phrase that is equivalent to *just as* and that is widely regarded as redundant. It no doubt occurs commonly in speech, but its reputation is bad enough to make it relatively rare in edited prose:

There are others equally as dedicated —*Forbes,* 15 Sept. 1970

. . . retaliated with two thorough slaughters of the Redmen. . . . Their two get-back whippings of Syracuse were equally as brutal —Curry Kirkpatrick, *Sports Illustrated,* 25 Mar. 1985

This innocuous phrase has drawn more vehement criticism than is warranted, but you may well want to prefer *just as* in your writing or to use *equally* by itself for emphasis where your construction permits it.

equine *Equine* is chiefly an adjective meaning "of, relating to, or resembling a horse or the horse family":

. . . the recent outbreak of an equine venereal disease on two breeding farms —*N.Y. Times,* 17 Mar. 1978

It also occasionally occurs as a noun, usually synonymous with *horse:*

Flannery's horseflesh is several stables away from the stiffly noble equines of the classic English and American horse-painter schools —*Time,* 29 Oct. 1951

Both the adjective and the noun occur most naturally in scientific contexts. Their use in general contexts in which the writer is being playfully fancy or is trying to avoid repeating the word *horse* is discouraged by Flesch 1964 and Copperud 1980.

See also CANINE; FELINE.

equitable See EQUABLE, EQUITABLE.

equivalent 1. When the adjective *equivalent* is used with a preposition, the choice is usually *to:*

It is also misleading to talk as if a mere liking . . . for the ritual . . . of one of the Christian churches were equivalent to a religion —Edmund Wilson, *A Piece of My Mind,* 1956

Much less often it is used with *with:*

A third additional trial would be equivalent with the first one made originally —J. M. Wolfe, *First Course in Cryptanalysis,* vol. II, rev. ed., 1943

2. When the noun *equivalent* is used with a preposition, it is usually used with *of:*

In economics, the equivalent of a beautifully composed work of art is the smoothly running factory — Aldous Huxley, *Brave New World Revisited,* 1958

Less frequently it may be used with *to,* and still less frequently with *for:*

. . . the intellectual equivalent to a certain surgical operation —*The Autobiography of William Butler Yeats,* 1953

. . . France is almost without an equivalent for the old "newspapers of information" —*Manchester Guardian Weekly,* 10 Nov. 1944

equivocal, ambiguous, ambivalent Following the lead of dictionaries of synonyms (such as *Webster's New Dictionary of Synonyms)* Copperud 1970 and a few other commentators note that *ambiguous* and *equivocal* are essentially synonymous but that *equivocal* may suggest intent to deceive or evade. The word to be stressed here is *may.* Here are some examples that connote deceit or evasiveness:

. . . the dubiety engendered by the equivocal proceedings of James Macpherson —W. L. Renwick, *English Literature 1789–1815,* 1963

. . . had made powerful enemies within the party by his support for the Munich pact and his equivocal attitude on Suez —*Current Biography,* September 1964

. . . there was nothing equivocal about him. One was struck at once by his straightforwardness —Jack London, *The Sea-Wolf,* 1904

. . . no pollsters have ever stopped me on the street to tap the fount of my colossal knowledge. They would never get an equivocal answer if they ever asked me —Goodman Ace, *Saturday Rev.,* 22 Jan. 1972

But often *equivocal* suggests no more than *ambiguous:*

She is far from a knee-jerk Catholic in her literary responses, equivocal about Greene and Waugh and bored by Bernanos —Mary Gordon, *Saturday Rev.,* 14 Apr. 1979

. . . science in all its aspects is now perceived as irremediably equivocal in its bearing upon human happiness—capable of producing good but also evil — Donald Fleming, *Atlantic,* September 1970

For his will is ambiguous, good as well as bad —Paul Tillich, *Center Mag.,* September 1969

In both studies, results for Negro children were ambiguous —*Annual Report, Educational Testing Service,* 1966–1967

... as murky and ambiguous as the results of the aborted landslide of 1968 —Walter Dean Burnham, *Trans-Action,* December 1968

... such equivocal terms as Socialism and Communism are frequently used with different meanings. These ambiguities.... —Francis Conklin, *New Scholasticism,* October 1953

... the more responsible among us assert that these words are ambiguous —Nehemiah Jordan, *Themes in Speculative Psychology,* 1968

... it may be pointed out that the terms general and common are equivocal —John Dewey, *Art as Experience,* 1934

In reality, as has been already observed, an æquivocal or ambiguous word is not one name, but two names —John Stuart Mill, *A System of Logic,* 1843

Ambivalent may also be used in a sense close to *equivocal* or *ambiguous:*

My attitude toward the plan ... will be called by some of my friends ambiguous, or perhaps—since the word is now in fashion—"ambivalent" —Albert Guérard, *Education of a Humanist,* 1949

More examples are given at AMBIVALENT, AMBIGUOUS.

erotica *Erotica* has the form of a Greek plural, but it is now usually understood as a mass noun meaning "erotic material," and, as Bernstein 1971 observes, it is now more often than not construed as singular:

... the erotica is explicit —Thomas Lask, *N.Y. Times,* 15 Oct. 1966

... erotica was often associated with left-wing politics —*Times Literary Supp.,* 22 Oct. 1971

Is all erotica male fantasy then ... ? —Shana Alexander, *Newsweek,* 5 Feb. 1973

Treatment of *erotica* as a plural still occurs, however, and is not incorrect:

There is also a top row of erotica and I asked the man if he sold many of these —Bill Moyers, *Harper's,* December 1970

For other foreign plurals, see LATIN PLURALS.

err The dust of controversy swirls thickly about the pronunciation of this word. The traditional pronunciation can be illustrated from the works of Alexander Pope, who also gave us the phrase "to err is human" and is thus partly responsible for the continued familiarity of this humble stump of a word:

In doubt his Mind or Body to prefer;
Born but to die, and reas'ning but to err
   —"Essay on Man," 1734

Similarly Swift:

Observe the case: I state it thus:
You may compare your Trull to us;
But think how damnably you err
When you compare us Clouds to her
  —"An Answer to a Late Scandalous Poem," 1733

Nor, if *err* and *air* were homophones, would Wordsworth have written:

(Surely I do not err) that pensive air
  —"Lines Suggested by a Portrait from the
    Pencil of F. Stone," 1835

But in our own century we find this witness, from a less celebrated pen, to the existence of an untraditional pronunciation:

Those who err and call it *air*
Can be met with everywhere.
Educated men and women
Fondly quote: "To air is human."
  —Katherine Buxbaum, in a publication of the
   Iowa State Teachers College, no date

Those who condemn \'er\ for *err* typically advance no reason other than the implicit one of tradition. Since *err* is both a semantic and etymological relative of *error,* \'er\ has what commentators usually call "logic" on its side; and the tradition has, precisely, partly dissolved in current usage, where \'er\ preponderates. Further, some speakers who are quite aware that they are "supposed" to say \'ər\ nevertheless eschew that version for its indistinct vowel. We may, then, endorse the further sentiments of Katherine Buxbaum:

Blame the speakers? Let's be fairer:
Blame the language for the error.
Error is a proper word,
"Ur-ur" would be quite absurd.
Is it natural to infer
That making errors is to err?
Wherefore, purists, don't despair,
Thoughts of punishment forbear,
Just give the erring ones the air.

A similar moral could even be drawn from Pope, whom we give the last word:

The Vulgar thus through Imitation err;
As oft the Learn'd by being singular
   —"Essay on Criticism," 1711

For a related but distinct question of pronunciation, see ERRANT, ARRANT 2.

errant, arrant **1.** *Errant* and *arrant* were once synonymous words, but they long ago came to be distinguished from each other in their principal senses. The fundamental meaning of *errant* is "wandering" (as in "an errant knight"), while *arrant,* which also once meant "wandering," now has the sense "utterly bad" (as in "arrant nonsense"). The OED shows that *arrant* originated as a variant of *errant,* and that its current sense developed from its use in such phrases as "an arrant thief," which originally meant a wandering, vagrant thief but came eventually to be understood as an utterly bad thief. "Utterly bad" has been the principal sense of *arrant* since at least Shakespeare's time:

We are arrant knaves all; believe none of us —Shakespeare, *Hamlet,* 1601

Errant has also been used in this sense:

They are errant cowards —Daniel Defoe, *Robinson Crusoe,* 1719 (OED)

But this sense of *errant* seems never to have been very common and is now usually considered obsolete.

As a topic for discussion by usage commentators, the

distinction between *errant* and *arrant* has a long but otherwise unimpressive history. The first to broach the subject was Robert Baker 1770, who complained that the words were frequently confused, and that *errant* in particular was often mistakenly used in place of *arrant,* even by good writers (such as Daniel Defoe). No other critic took up the matter for almost 200 years—until 1957, to be precise, when Bergen and Cornelia Evans suggested that it might be a good idea to avoid both words, on the grounds that *errant* had become "archaic and literary" and that *arrant* was rarely used except in clichés. Copperud 1964 simply warned against confusing one word for the other. What our evidence shows is that both words continue in fairly common use. The distinction in meaning prescribed by Baker and Copperud definitely is generally observed in modern usage, but *errant* still turns up on rare occasions in place of *arrant:*

> ... it is errant stupidity to look for simplicity in so-called simple cultures —Farley Mowat, *People of the Deer,* 1952

> ... find it insulting, if not errant nonsense —David L. Shores, in *Papers in Language Variation,* ed. David L. Shores & Carole P. Hines, 1977

Such usage can be defended on historical grounds, but you would probably do better to choose *arrant* when you mean "utterly bad."

2. In accordance with the difference in spelling between *errant* and *arrant,* there has arisen a distinction in pronunciation, \'er-ənt\ versus \'ar-ənt\; but for a great many speakers who do not distinguish \e\ and \a\ before \r\ the distinction is impossible to maintain. Both pronunciations must therefore be considered acceptable for either word.

For a related but distinct question of pronunciation, see ERR.

errata This little-used word leads a double life. Its primary existence is as the plural of *erratum,* a fancy synonym for "error" that is used principally to mean "an error in a printed work discovered after printing and shown with its correction on a separate sheet." But *errata* is also used in the publishing world in a distinct sense denoting either a list of such errors or the page on which such a list is printed. Usage commentators such as Shaw 1975, Harper 1975, 1985, and the panelists of Heritage 1969 and Heritage 1982 take a peculiar attitude toward this sense of *errata.* They accept the sense itself but advise that *errata* should always be construed as a plural, even when its meaning is "a list" or "a page." It appears to us that this advice is impossible to follow:

> The Errata, if included, is a list of errors —C. A. Hurst & F. R. Lawrence, *Letterpress Composition and Machine-Work,* 1963

One could not say "The Errata are a list ..." When *errata* is clearly being used in its singular sense, it cannot logically be used with a plural verb—such usage would be equivalent to saying, "The list are ..." or "The page are ..." In cases where a plural verb can be substituted without resulting in an ungrammatical sentence, the effect of the substitution is to change the meaning of *errata.* For example, if "The errata is in the appendix" is revised to "The errata are in the appendix," *errata* no longer means "list" in the revised sentence, but is serving instead as the plural of *erratum.*

Confusing, isn't it? The point is that when the commentators say *errata* should always be treated as a plu-

ral, they are saying in effect that the use of *errata* to mean "a list" or "a page" is incorrect. What our evidence says is that the singular use of *errata* is limited to—and is correct in—the world of publishing:

> ... this reissue ... differs from the original only in the additions of an explanatory preface and an end errata —Glenn O. Carey, *CEA Critic,* January 1972

For other foreign plurals, see LATIN PLURALS.

erstwhile, quondam, whilom These three strange-looking words are all adjectives that mean "former." *Erstwhile* is also an uncommon, and *whilom* an archaic, adverb meaning "formerly."

The adverb *erstwhile* dates from the 15th century and is still in occasional use today, especially modifying adjectives:

> The requirements of modern war have outrun the erstwhile satisfactory formal organization —Vannevar Bush, *Infantry Jour.,* October 1945

> ... Berryman's erstwhile uncollected essays and reviews and stories —Donald David, *N.Y. Times Book Rev.,* 25 Apr. 1976

The adjective *erstwhile* has a somewhat mysterious and confused history. It is not mentioned in the OED, and the earliest citation we know of appears in the OED Supplement and is dated 1901; yet, Webster 1909 and Webster's Second (1934) mistakenly label it archaic. Whatever its past, *erstwhile* now is widely used as an adjective:

> ... one of its erstwhile allies —Arnold Wolfers, *Yale Rev.,* Summer 1954

> ... his erstwhile colleague's [paper] ... on industrial policies and growth —*Times Literary Supp.,* 27 Aug. 1971

> ... George Harrison of the erstwhile Beatles —Faubion Bowers, *Atlantic,* February 1972

> ... all those erstwhile budget-stretchers such as fish, liver, heart, and stew meat —Jennie Douglas, *Christian Science Monitor,* 17 July 1980

> ... started an erstwhile wide receiver ... at quarterback —Paul Zimmerman, *Sports Illustrated,* 10 Jan. 1983

Though less common than *erstwhile, quondam* appears in a wide variety of contexts:

> ... Randy Turpin, the quondam middleweight champion —*The Ring,* October 1952

> ... antagonized his quondam collaborator —W. L. Renwick, *English Literature 1789–1815,* 1963

> ... the vineyards of Corton-Charlemagne—named after their quondam owner, the Emperor Charlemagne —*Consumer Reports,* November 1971

> A quondam grocery store now displays early prints and maps —Alan L. Otten, *Wall Street Jour.,* 10 June 1981

Whilom gets used occasionally:

> ... a handsome whilom golf pro —Tex Maule, *Sports Illustrated,* 11 Oct. 1965

... the whilom seaport that once rivaled Philadelphia —William Least Heat Moon, *Blue Highways,* 1982

Harper 1985 says that "*erstwhile* is seldom used except in formal writing and even then it is often misunderstood." While we cannot agree that this is true of *erstwhile,* we do think it is true of *quondam* and *whilom.* If you decide to use one of these last two for reasons of style, you run the risk of confusing or mystifying your readers. *Quondam* and *whilom* are not archaic, but they do have an archaic quality that may interfere with their being readily understood or make you look like a striver for clever effects. They do not look like other English adjectives, and they are used so infrequently that they will probably be unfamiliar to many of your readers. If they were used as often as *erstwhile,* no doubt they would lose their standoffish quality.

escalate   *Escalate* is a back-formation from the noun *escalator.* It was first used in the early 20th century with the literal sense, "to ride up on an escalator":

> I dreamt I saw a Proctor 'escalating', Rushing up a quickly moving stair —*The Granta,* 10 Nov. 1922 (OED Supplement)

But the figurative *escalate* that we now use appears to have developed from figurative uses of *escalation* and *escalator* that originated in the 1930s. *Escalation* was first used in reference to a provision in naval treaties allowing a country the right—the "right of escalation"—to increase the size and number of its warships in order to keep up with any increase made by the other country. *Escalator* was used in describing a provision in labor contracts—an "escalator clause"—allowing for increases in wages and prices to reflect increases in costs. When *escalate* began to be used figuratively, it was also in reference to military and financial matters:

> ... a contractor performing on a lump sum, unit price, or escalated job —*Jour. of Accountancy,* May 1950

> The possibility of local wars 'escalating into all-out atomic wars' —*Manchester Guardian,* 12 Nov. 1959 (OED Supplement)

Escalate became a common word in the 1960s, when it was used constantly in speaking of the increasing U.S. involvement in the war in Vietnam. As its range of applications expanded, it was inevitably criticized as a vogue word, but it fared better than many other back-formations; the usage panel of Heritage 1969, for example, found it acceptable by a large majority. Much of the criticism that has been directed at it has come from British sources. Several British commentators, including Howard 1978, have contended that it can be appropriately used only in describing increases that occur in successive stages, but our evidence suggests that these critics have misread the word's connotations. *Escalate* typically implies a continuing and usually undesirable increase or expansion, often with the added implication that each stage of the increase provokes even further increases:

> ... the violence escalated to include gunfire and gang warfare —*Newsweek,* 6 Mar. 1967

> ... the problem escalates so rapidly that it gets out of hand before significant improvement is achieved —D. J. Rowe, *Reviews of Modern Physics,* January 1968

> The costs are already too high, and they escalate higher each year —Lewis Thomas, in *The Contemporary Essay,* ed. Donald Hall, 1984

> ... that the K.G.B. and the C.I.A. have escalated their secret operations ... in an action-counteraction process that has overpopulated the world with secret agents —Harry Howe Ransom, *N.Y. Times Book Rev.,* 4 Mar. 1984

Less often, *escalate* serves simply as a synonym of *increase* or *grow:*

> His interest escalated as his knowledge and skill deepened —Margaret Carter, *Living,* July 1974

> The grin escalates into a chuckle, the chuckle to a chortle —Robert Palm, *TV Guide,* 21 Mar. 1986

escalator   For pronunciation problems with this word, see NUCLEAR.

escape   Does a prisoner escape jail or escape *from* jail? *Escape from* is the usual idiom, but *escape* is also occasionally used as a transitive verb in such a context, without *from:*

> ... after escaping a Russian prison camp in his youth —Stanley Ellin, *N.Y. Times Book Rev.,* 20 July 1975

This sense of the verb is "to get free of." Its use, like that of the intransitive *escape (from),* is naturally not limited to descriptions of jailbreaks:

> ... machine-gunned those who tried to escape the burning ruins —William L. Shirer, *The Rise and Fall of the Third Reich,* 1960

> ... and escaped the jungle to carry forward the struggle —James Atlas, *N.Y. Times Book Rev.,* 19 Sept. 1976

A distinctive modern use of transitive *escape* is in contexts relating to space travel:

> ... to escape the earth's gravitational pull —Edwina Deans et al., *Unifying Mathematics,* 2d ed., 1968

> ... the second spacecraft to escape the Solar System —S. W. H. Cowley, *Nature,* 27 Mar. 1980

Evidence in the OED shows that this transitive *escape* is extremely old, being first attested in the 14th century. By the end of the 1600s, however, it had fallen into disuse, and until quite recently it was either omitted altogether from dictionaries or was labeled obsolete, as it is in the OED and in *Webster's Third.* Its recent revival—more accurately, its recent recoinage—dates only from the late 1950s, according to our evidence. Relatively few usage commentators have taken note of it, but those that have (Bernstein 1962, 1965; Harper 1975, 1985; and the usage panel of Heritage 1969) regard it as an error, arguing that as a transitive verb *escape* properly means "to avoid" (as in "escape possible punishment"). On the other hand, most current dictionaries (including Heritage 1982) now treat *escape* in the sense "get free of" as standard. Our evidence shows that it is far less common than *escape from,* but the contexts in which it occurs are standard, and we can see no compelling reason to shun it. After three decades of reputable use, it seems clear that this old sense of *escape* has come back to stay.

escapee *Escapee* has occasionally been criticized as a mistake for *escaper,* on the assumption that the suffix *-ee* can properly form only words that refer to the object of an action. It is, however, a standard word and is recognized as such by all current dictionaries. It was first used in the second half of the 19th century, when it occurred in both the U.S. (the earliest citation for it is from Walt Whitman's *Specimen Days* in 1865) and Australia. It made its way back to Britain at about the turn of the century. *Escaper* is an older word, first recorded in 1611. It is now rarely seen, having been all but eclipsed by *escapee:*

> ... she ran off the dunes like an escapee —Gail Sheehy, *New York,* 10 Jan. 1972

> Escapees tended to be much younger —Peter Watson, *The Sunday Times* (London), 17 Mar. 1974

> ... nursery escapees with the toughness to survive —Wallace Stegner, *Blair & Ketchum's Country Jour.,* December 1979

> ... an elegant escapee from the boredom of suburbia —Robert Sherrill, *N.Y. Times Book Rev.,* 14 Sept. 1980

Our scanty recent evidence for *escaper* is all from British sources:

> ... they are not the only zoo escapers to have prospered —*In Britain,* November 1975

> One of her escapers was Freud's "Wolf Man" — Rosemary Dinnage, *Times Literary Supp.,* 19 Aug. 1983

See also -EE.

especial, especially See SPECIAL, SPECIALLY, ESPECIAL, ESPECIALLY.

espresso, expresso The strong coffee made by forcing steam under pressure through finely ground coffee beans is known in Italian as *caffè espresso,* or just *espresso* for short. Contrary to a popular belief of English-speakers, the *espresso* means not "fast" but "pressed out"—it refers to the process by which the coffee is made, not the speed of the process. The idea that *caffè espresso* means "fast coffee" may have contributed somewhat to the occurrence in English of the variant *expresso,* or the variant may have originated simply because it more closely resembles a familiar English word than does *espresso.* In any case, *expresso* is in widespread use, both on menus and in edited prose:

> Jérôme sidled to the expresso bar —Jerome Charyn, *Antaeus,* Winter 1976

> ... thick expresso with a shot of Calvados —Patricia Wells, *N.Y. Times,* 6 June 1982

Several current dictionaries, including Webster's Ninth New Collegiate Dictionary and the OED Supplement, recognize *expresso* as an established variant, but there are others that omit it altogether or treat it as a mistake. *Espresso* is undoubtedly the more common form, at least in writing, and is undoubtedly favored by the cognoscenti.

Esquire *Esquire* means literally "shield-bearer." In the days of chivalry, it denoted a young candidate for knighthood who, as the OED puts it, "attended upon a knight, carried his shield, and rendered him other services." It later acquired the meaning "a member of the English gentry ranking immediately below a knight," in which sense it was appended to such a man's name as a title of respect in formal address. Eventually it came to be used more broadly in British English as a respectful title used in addressing correspondence to any man who could otherwise be referred to as "Mr."—in other words, just about any man at all. The British continue to use it that way in the abbreviated form *Esq.* (or sometimes *Esqr.* or *Esqre.*). Its use in American English is far less common, persisting mainly among attorneys, who use it when referring to or addressing each other in writing.

There has recently been some controversy in American legal circles about using *Esq.* after the name of a woman lawyer. Some lawyers are all in favor of such usage, it seems, while some others are strongly opposed to it. Indications are that the pros are gradually winning out over the antis, but arguments for both sides can still be heard. Lawyers being lawyers, it seems likely that this issue will stay alive for some years yet.

Note that when *Esq.* is used as a title following a name, no other title or term of address is used before the name. You can write *Mr. John Smith* or *John Smith, Esq.,* but if you are concerned with observing proper form (as you presumably are when you use *Esq.* in an address) you should not write *Mr. John Smith, Esq.*

-ess In 1855 Archbishop Richard Chevenix Trench, in *English Past and Present,* devoted a chapter to English words that were disappearing from use. One class of words he found greatly diminished in 19th-century English was feminine nouns—most of them designating occupations—ending in *-ess.* From the literature of the 14th, 15th, 16th, and 17th centuries he brought forth such interesting specimens as *teacheress, sinneress, neighbouress, herdess, constabless, ministress, flatteress, saintess, soldieress, impostress,* and *builderess.* According to H. L. Mencken (*The American Language, Supplement I,* 1945), a copy of Trench's book found its way into the hands of Mrs. Sarah Josepha Hale, editress (her term) of *Godey's Lady's Book,* in 1865. In the period around the Civil War, American women had begun their movement for civil rights, for the vote, and for a more active role in public life generally. Mrs. Hale made a stirring plea for the revival and establishment of many of these terms; it was her belief, apparently, that the regular use of these terms would add dignity to the women whose professions or occupations they described. She set forth one list of twenty-five occupational or professional titles and another of thirty-three more general titles which had, or for which she proposed, *-ess* equivalents (the lists are in Mencken).

Many of the words on these lists had been in general use all along—*empress, duchess, princess, lioness, abbess, goddess, waitress, prioress,* and so forth—and had never been the subject of much discussion—indeed, most of these are impeccable today. But others of them, including such established words as *authoress* and *poetess,* ran afoul of the male establishment. They were derogated by the intellectually elite as ugly, pedantic, and unnecessary. At the other end of the spectrum, 19th-century American humorists like Artemus Ward and Petroleum V. Nasby used such terms as *beastess, championess,* and *prestidigitateuress* to satirize the serious use by women and of women of some of the terms the *Godey's* writer had recommended. Mamie Meredith has an interesting survey of such use in *American Speech* (August 1930).

By the time we get to the 20th century, we find women turning against many of these terms too; the words are held to be demeaning in that they inject the consideration of sex where it is unnecessary. This argument had already been one of many put forth by 19th-century male critics of *poetess* and *authoress.* Most recent feminist opinion also opposes such forms. Wilson 1987 notes with wry amusement that it is almost always the masculine term *(actor, priest, shepherd)* that feminists want to have as the standard generic noun (but the same is not true for pronouns—see EPICENE PRONOUNS).

These feminine forms have not lacked defenders. A couple of the more surprising ones are Richard Grant White 1870 and Fowler 1926. White noted that many critics condemned such words as *poetess* and *authoress,* but he had run across words of that kind in some of the old authors that Archbishop Trench was writing about, and he thought the words deserved a place in the language. Fowler thought that *-ess* words (and other feminine forms) were useful, and he thought there should be more of them. Interestingly, some of the less successful *-ess* words that Fowler champions can be found on the 1865 list in *Godey's Lady's Book.*

So far we have seen that *-ess* forms have been urged by women and condemned by women, and condemned by men and defended by men. A mixed bag of opinions, at least through the period of Fowler. Is modern opinion clearer? Yes and no. Though *-ess* forms would find few proponents among feminists today, the commentators—mostly men, of course—present less than a clear picture. For instance, Shaw 1975, 1987 says that *Negress* and *Jewess* were considered offensive long before the Women's Liberation movement; Simon 1980 says that these words are not pejorative. Kilpatrick 1984 advises a man married to a sculptor not to call her a sculptress; Simon thinks *sculptress* is not a pejorative term.

In this book the four *-ess* words most frequently mentioned by usage commentators—*authoress, poetess, Jewess, Negress*—are accorded individual treatment. We cannot give you any easy advice about *-ess* words in general. Not enough research has yet been done to tell us if the forms Trench thought were dying out were actually in everyday use, to tell us if there was a revival of *-ess* forms during the 19th century in England as well as in the United States, or to tell us what attitudes such a revival in England might reveal. And modern use, though much written about, has perhaps not been dispassionately recorded.

We can offer only a few indications. There seem to have been at least a few people in 19th century England who found some *-ess* forms polite:

> Mr. Lewis Carroll has much pleasure in giving to the editresses of the proposed magazine permission to use . . . —Lewis Carroll, letter, 6 Feb. 1888

And some found them rather humorous:

> How do you like the Mandarinesses? Are you on some little footing with any of them? —Charles Lamb, letter, 29 Mar. 1809

> Now enough of political economy, which I inflict on you only to educate you as a manageress —George Bernard Shaw, letter, 3 Oct. 1899

And at least a few modern writers have found the virtue noted by Fowler of packing two kinds of information in a single word useful:

> As Bech talked, and his translatress feverishly scribbled notes upon his complicated gist —John Updike, *Bech Is Back,* 1982

> . . . immediately my young love becomes a young giantess looking down at me —E. L. Doctorow, *Loon Lake,* 1979

> . . . where he had learned to do the high-life (his instructress's waist like a live, slow snake in his hands) —John Updike, *Bech Is Back,* 1982

One would probably do well to approach these words in a somewhat gingerly manner. Some are unmistakably out of favor now. Others, however, such as the traditional titles of female nobility, go their merry way. Even those of humbler station often continue in frequent use. *Waitress* shows no real sign, at this point, of being permanently displaced by the genderless neologisms *waitperson* and *waitron;* indeed, *waitress* has even become more common in print as an informal verb over the last 20 years or so. And the word *manageress,* which Shaw seems to have used humorously, continues in frequent and serious use in British English, our evidence suggests. Clearly this portion of our vocabulary is still evolving.

essay See ASSAY, ESSAY.

essential, *adjective* **1.** *Essential* is used most often with the preposition *to* when the construction requires a preposition:

> . . . you are essential to her perfect happiness —Charles Dickens, *A Tale of Two Cities,* 1859

Less frequently but still quite commonly, *essential* may be used with *for:*

> . . . a good liberal education during the undergraduate years is essential for every librarian —*Current Biography,* June 1964

Sometimes it is used with *in:*

> . . . he possesses the charismatic warmth, color, and conviction essential in a national leader —*Current Biography,* September 1964

Still less often *essential* is used with *as:*

> . . . socioeconomic status classifications are essential as a means of giving some meaning to the huge amounts of data —*Annual Report, Educational Testing Service,* 1966–1967

2. A few commentators claim *essential* is an absolute adjective and object to its use with adverbial qualifiers (see ABSOLUTE ADJECTIVES). Follett 1966 says it does not admit of *more* or *less* or even *so.* Partridge 1942 and Jacques Barzun, in *American Scholar,* Summer 1957, seem to be making the same objection. Harper 1975, 1985, while objecting to *more,* finds *most essential* acceptable because it is an idiom used for emphasis rather than comparison.

Most essential is indeed used for emphasis:

> The animal nature, indeed, is a most essential part of the Faun's composition —Nathaniel Hawthorne, *The Marble Faun,* 1860

> This reasonableness was a quality which events were to prove most essential in meeting the unexpected difficulties —*Dictionary of American Biography,* 1928

And also *absolutely essential:*

> . . . it is now fairly clear that they are absolutely essential to him as a man and as a writer —Richard Poirier, *Saturday Rev.,* 22 Apr. 1972

So essential seems likewise to be chiefly emphatic:

> In any highly civilised society disguise plays so large a part, politeness is so essential, that to throw off the ceremonies . . . is as much a necessity as a breath of air in a hot room —Virginia Woolf, *The Second Common Reader,* 1932

> So essential was the service rendered by the Abbott mills that the employees were exempted from the draft —*Dictionary of American Biography,* 1928

> . . . the savage bulls so essential to . . . bullfighting — William D. Patterson, *Saturday Rev.,* 26 Dec. 1953

Most, absolutely, and *so* are the chief intensifiers with *essential.* We have a few examples with *very,* but they seem curiously flat:

> The sound financing of the building is very essential —Loretta Quinlan, *Massachusetts Teacher,* May 1965

> For many of us who travel to Germany, that is a very essential thing to remember —Richard Atcheson, *Saturday Rev.,* 25 Mar. 1972

But writers do also use *more* and *most* with *essential* for comparison and the use must be considered standard:

> The most essential characteristic of mind is memory —Bertrand Russell, in *Encore,* July 1946

> Glubb asked that the Legion be allowed to serve also in Italy, but this the British refused, feeling that the protection of the oil pipelines in the Arab countries was more essential —*Current Biography 1951*

> The most enduring and most essential qualities of mind and personality are founded in the early years of life —Robert Havighurst, quoted in *Girl Scout Leader,* November 1967

> . . . the determination of what we had and what we needed being more essential than the qualities of the old-style professional production man —David Halberstam, *Harper's,* February 1971

> Once the ranks are filled with career soldiers, a "civilian-oriented leadership" will be more essential than ever —D. Park Teter, *Change,* September 1971

essential, *noun* When the noun *essential* is used with a preposition, it is used most often with *of:*

> . . . these mountain people, albeit unlettered, have acquired so many of the essentials of culture —F. R. Leavis, *The Common Pursuit,* 1952

Less frequently, *essential* appears with *in, for,* or *to:*

> . . . felt that religion was decent and right, an essential in an honest man's life —Pearl Buck, *The Long Love,* 1949

> . . . has plenty of at least one essential for success as an Albany lobbyist —Dwight Macdonald, *New Yorker,* 22 Aug. 1953

> . . . a change of underclothes and of socks are almost an essential to me —Graham Greene, *Travels with My Aunt,* 1969

estimate **1.** When the verb *estimate* is used with a preposition, it is usually *at:*

> . . . German populations estimated at between 10 and 15 million —Vera Micheles Dean, *The Four Cornerstones of Peace,* 1946

See also ABOUT 3.

There is also evidence in our files for the use of *as, by, for,* and *from:*

> . . . half a dozen ears of dried corn which Chuck estimated as being over seven hundred years old — *Boy's Life,* February 1953

> The child is sexless, the adult estimates his virility by his sexual activities —Ruth Benedict, in *Personality in Nature, Society, and Culture,* ed. Clyde Kluckhohn & Henry A. Murray, 1948

> . . . the almost three billion pounds of candy estimated for 1948 —*Collier's Year Book,* 1949

> Their attainments in their studies will be estimated from their school records —*1952 Catalogue of Phillips Academy,* Autumn 1951

2. The noun *estimate* is often used with *of:*

> . . . it involved making an estimate of a man's character —C. S. Forester, *The African Queen,* 1935

estimation Fowler 1926 expresses a curious dislike for the use of this word to mean "opinion, judgment," and he especially considers its use in such phrases as *in my estimation* to be nothing less than "illiterate." Presumably he was unaware that this sense of *estimation* dates back to the 14th century, when Chaucer used it in his translation of Boethius's *De Consolatione Philosophiae* (as the OED shows), and that it has been recognized as standard in dictionaries going all the way back to Samuel Johnson's (1755), in which it is illustrated with a quotation from Francis Bacon. It is, beyond doubt, an entirely reputable sense, and Fowler's disapproval of it (which has been echoed by some later commentators) can only be regarded as a personal idiosyncrasy.

> . . . rose therefore in the estimation of the regiment —Rudyard Kipling, *Wee Willie Winkie, and Other Child Stories,* 1888

> To divert interest from the poet to the poetry is a laudable aim: for it would conduce to a juster estimation of actual poetry, good and bad —T.S. Eliot, "Tradition and the Individual Talent," 1917, in *Selected Essays,* 1932

> Dictatorial propaganda aims first of all at the legitimizing in popular estimation of the dictator's government —Aldous Huxley, *The Olive Tree,* 1937

> . . . apart from his own estimation of certain modern composers —Warwick Braithwaite, *The Conductor's Art,* 1952

> In the estimation of Picasso's friends, it acts like a memorandum for him —Janet Flanner, *New Yorker,* 9 Mar. 1957

estrange When used with a preposition in contemporary English, *estrange* is used with *from:*

> ... such critical approaches ... can only estrange him from the audience he deserves —Irving Howe, *New Rupublic,* 28 Mar. 1955

Moreover, *estrange* is now found used most often in the passive:

> ... she telephoned her husband, who was estranged from her and living in Boston —John Updike, *Playboy,* January 1982

> ... so completely estranged from the life of her own time —Maxwell Geismar, *The Last of the Provincials,* 1947

et al. This Latin abbreviation means "and others" or "and the others." Some commentators have contended that it should only be used of people, regarding it strictly as an abbreviation of the masculine *et alii* and the feminine *et aliae,* but in fact it also serves as an abbreviation of the neuter *et alia,* and its use of things is not incorrect. It is, however, uncommon. The most frequent use of *et al.* is in citing (as in a footnote or bibliography) a publication that has several or many authors. To save space, one or two of the authors' names are given, followed by *et al.:*

> Ruth I. Anderson et al., *The Administrative Secretary: Resource* (New York: McGraw-Hill, 1970), p. 357.

Commentators generally discourage the use of *et al.* and similar abbreviations in expository writing, but our evidence shows that such use is common. There is considerable variation in the way *et al.* is styled. It sometimes is printed in italics, and the period following *al* is sometimes omitted; but the favored choice is to retain the period and to print *et al.* in regular roman type:

> ... to put maximum pressure on Nixon et al. abruptly to pull out of Asia —William F. Buckley, Jr., *National Rev.,* 30 June 1970

> ... memories of the big numbers from *The Green Pastures,* et al. —Alan Rich, *New York,* 10 Jan. 1972

> The solicitude of Simon, Newman, et al. for correct usage —Robert Pattison, *On Literacy,* 1982

> Apparently John Updike, Saul Bellow et al. were going to welcome me —Susan Brownmiller, *N.Y. Times Book Rev.,* 12 Jan. 1986

etc. This abbreviation of the Latin *et cetera* means literally "and others of the same kind." Most commentators have one or two things to say about its proper use.
The most frequently repeated point is that *etc.* should not be preceded by *and,* since *et* means "and" in Latin. Our evidence suggests that this is not a serious problem in edited prose, inasmuch as we have no examples of *and etc.* in our files. A few commentators also warn that *etc.* should not be used at the end of a list introduced by *for example* or *such as* (as in "... such photographic materials as lenses, filters, etc."). The redundancy of *etc.* in such contexts is not strongly felt, however, and the usage considered erroneous by the commentators does occur in standard writing:

> ... had such Indian names applied to them as *coon, moose, possum, skunk,* etc. —Mathews 1931

... by such function words as *can, must, should, have,* etc. —C. C. Fries, *The Structure of English,* 1952

There is disagreement about the contexts in which *etc.* can be appropriately used. Some critics favor restricting it to such special contexts as footnotes and technical writing, but others find its use in ordinary prose unobjectionable, recommending only that it be avoided in formal usage. What our evidence shows is that *etc.* now occurs commonly in ordinary expository writing:

> ... the full texts of pastoral letters, ... private communications, speeches, etc. —Doris Grumbach, *N.Y. Times Book Rev.,* 8 July 1979

> ... street language, dialects, admixtures of foreign tongues, etc. —Simon 1980

If you dislike the sound of *etc.* in such contexts, alternatives are *and so on, and so forth,* and *and the like.*
The use of *etc.* in reference to persons rather than to things is defended by Fowler 1926, but other commentators have been less tolerant of it (Partridge 1942 considers it "insulting"). Its occurrence is rare enough that the question of its acceptability is largely moot. Here is one of our few examples:

> ... the novels of Proust, James, Hardy, Twain, Forster, Huxley, etc. —*N.Y. Times,* 20 Oct. 1967

A far more likely choice in such a context would be *et al.*
Et cetera is often mispronounced \ek-ˈset-ər-ə\. The analogous mispronunciation, substituting \ek-\ for \et-\, also occurs in French, and the reason is doubtless the same in both languages: assimilation of an unusual initial sound-sequence (no other familiar word in either language begins with \ets-\) to a common one. Words like *exceptional, ecstatic,* and *eccentric* abound in English. Whether influenced by this pronunciation or by purely orthographical considerations (*ct* being a more common sequence of letters than *tc*), *etc.* itself is often misspelled *ect.* This was, for instance, the form regularly used by F. Scott Fitzgerald in his letters. Remembering that the phrase begins with Latin *et* "and" should prevent you from committing either the mispronunciation or the misspelling.

ethnic designations: pronunciation The word *Italian* is not infrequently pronounced with initial long *i,* \ī-ˈtal-yən\, in some regions of the United States, especially among older or less well-educated speakers. Less common is *Arab* with a long initial vowel and secondary stress on the last syllable: \ˈā-ˌrab\. Both of these local and, in intent, socially neutral pronunciations are sometimes mimicked by others with humorous intent:

> ... the seeming rebelliousness of a nice Jewish girl from Central Park West marrying an A-Rab —Erica Jong, *Fear of Flying,* 1973

But such variant pronunciations can give strong offense even if innocently meant. We suggest you use the short vowels, and pronounce these words as \ˈar-əb\ and \ə-ˈtal-yən\ or \i-ˈtal-yən\.

etymological fallacy *Etymological fallacy* is a term used by philologists and linguists to describe the insistence that a word in present-day English derived from a foreign (and especially Greek or Latin) word must have the same meaning as the foreign word or must have its meaning limited in some way. Such insistence has long been popular with many usage writers, from Richard Grant White 1870 and earlier right down to the present. The appeal to etymology is a very seductive one, especially to those who know a little Latin or Greek. You will find the etymological fallacy mentioned in quite a few of the articles in this book.

One thing to remember when you read or hear someone insisting that an English word must have a certain meaning because of its Latin or Greek roots is that these insisters apply their etymologies very selectively. You will find few of them who object to *December* being used for the twelfth month, when its Latin root means "ten," or to *manure* being used as a noun meaning "dung" when it originally was a verb meaning "to work (land) by hand." So when you read, for example, that *caption* must refer to matter above a picture because it comes from Latin *caput* "head," keep *manure* in mind.

eulogy   See ELEGY, EULOGY.

euphemisms   **1.** A euphemism is an inoffensive expression substituted for another that may offend or suggest something unpleasant. Euphemisms have been around much longer than the word itself, which dates only from the 17th century. Euphemisms are—how shall we say it?—culturally and socially mediated; they are perhaps less a subject for the student of grammar and usage than for the student of the social sciences more generally.

Euphemism is used as a pejorative label by quite a few writers on usage. It probably has little point as a label, most of the time, since one salient fact about euphemisms is that almost everyone knows what they are being used in place of; only the newest and most abstruse euphemisms are likely to puzzle the reader. But usage writers tend to fancy themselves blunt, forthright, and plainspoken people, and poking a little fun at the po-faced and the mealy-mouthed is one of their favorite sports. Of course, even the plainspoken can miss a euphemism now and then: witness Copperud 1980 who gets in a jab at *bathroom* and *restroom* being euphemisms for "the more exact toilet," but does not mention that this use of *toilet* was itself originally a euphemism (as, indeed, once was *privy*).

The use of euphemisms for political purposes—when *taxes* become *revenue enhancements, invasions* become *incursions,* and *murder* becomes *liquidation*—has been viewed with alarm by various writers, among them George Orwell. Bolinger 1980 also discusses the subject, especially in reference to the deceptive use of euphemisms.

You probably need not be very concerned about euphemisms in your writing. It is not practical to worry about any except those you recognize as euphemisms; those that you recognize, you will use or avoid according to what you are writing and the audience you are writing for.

2. *Euphemism, euphuism.* Fowler 1907, 1926, 1965 has a warning about confusing these words. It is doubtful that these words are often confused, as Fowler asserts. In 1907 there are two 19th century examples and in 1926 (and 1965) an unidentified newspaper example, but we have little in our files. *Euphuism* is a literary word that seldom reaches the nonliterary public. Inadvertency would probably account for *euphuism* used as a gloss on the misspelling *uphemism* in Peter & Craig Norback, *The Misspeller's Dictionary,* 1974.

evacuate   The use of *evacuate* to mean "to remove (people) especially from a military zone or dangerous area" was once controversial. It is not new by any means (its roots go back to the 17th century), but its widespread occurrence is a fairly recent development, dating back only to the first World War:

> . . . the English system of evacuating the wounded — *Yale Rev.,* April 1916

Early critics of *evacuate* in this sense believed that only the place from which the people were removed could properly serve as the object of the verb: "the city was evacuated" but not "the people were evacuated from the city." The argument was based on etymology—*evacuate* is derived from the Latin *evacuare,* "to make empty." To speak of evacuating people, in the view of the critics, was to speak of making them empty, which was a pretty peculiar thing to speak of.

This issue was taken up by a few commentators up to and through the period of World War II, but the "remove" sense of *evacuate* had by then proved to be so useful and popular that any criticism of it had the hollow ring of pure pedantry, and the controversy quickly died out. The respectability of this sense is no longer subject to question:

> . . . sent planes to evacuate the British residents of Kashmir —Robert Sherrod, *Saturday Evening Post,* 19 June 1954

> . . . the Rostropovich family was evacuated to the city of Orenburg —*Current Biography,* May 1966

> . . . was also counted on to evacuate ARVN troops if a retreat proved necessary —*I. F. Stone's Bi-Weekly,* 8 Mar. 1971

even   *Even* is an adverb whose placement can affect its meaning, according to the relatively few commentators who bother to mention it. In speech the location of *even* in the sentence is not especially important, since its intention is clearly signaled by stress. In this respect it is like *only,* which almost every commentator has discussed at length.

Longman 1984 observes that a natural place for *even* to fall in the sentence is just before the verb: "John even works on Sundays." The meaning of this example would be perfectly clear in speech and, in fact, would be hard to misconstrue in writing. But the example is very simple. Safire 1984 produces a more complex example from the headline of a book advertisement:

> Only NAL Could Publish a Book That Even Scared Stephen King

Here we find *even* placed in the familiar speech pattern given in Longman, but the context is sufficiently complex to raise at least some doubt as to the meaning of the sentence. It pleased a correspondent of Mr. Safire's to ring several possible interpretive changes upon the sentence, which can be easily disambiguated in print by placing *even* directly in front of *Stephen King,* though at the cost of a possibly humorous *even Stephen.*

This, then, is our general advice: if your sentence is complex enough to cause possible confusion when it is read silently, without the assistance of the voice, put the *even* directly in front of the word or phrase it qualifies, as has been done in this example:

> Colloquialisms are necessarily used even in the formal writing of dialogue —Shaw 1980

If your sentence is as simple as the Longman example, normal speech placement of *even* is unlikely to cause confusion.

See also ONLY 1.

event The phrase *in the event that* serves as a somewhat formal substitute for *if:*

> ... next in line for the Presidency in the event that there is no Vice-President —*Current Biography 1947*

The *that* is often omitted:

> In the event a vehicle is disabled by shelling —Carl Mann, *He's In The Signal Corps Now,* 1943

Both versions invite predictable criticism for wordiness and pomposity, and there are certainly many contexts in which neither would be appropriate ("In the event that I had a hammer, I'd hammer in the mornin'"). But their distinctive tone and rhythm make them useful in other contexts. In writing that has an elevated quality, for instance, they are entirely at home:

> ... which currency would, moreover, be available for immediate use in the event our negotiations with the Russians should utterly collapse and separate action in the West should be required —Jack Bennett, *Annals of the American Academy of Political and Social Science,* January 1950

eventuate *Eventuate,* which means "to result, come to pass, come about," started life as an Americanism in the late 18th century and was stigmatized for that reason in the 19th century. Alford 1866, a British commentator, called it "another horrible word, which is fast getting into our language through the provincial press." Richard Grant White 1870 and Ayres 1881, both Americans, lifted their cudgels in turn but berated *eventuate* with a different meaning of *provincial* in mind. According to Ayres, *eventuate* (in addition to *effectuate* and *ratiocinate*) was "said to be a great favorite with the rural members of the Arkansas legislature." Next came a couple of moderating opinions which noted the past criticism of *eventuate* but claimed that "it has been employed by good writers in England" (OED) and therefore "may be considered good English" (Vizetelly 1906). Fowler 1926 and Krapp 1927 then tried a new tack by blaming journalists for using *eventuate.* Modern-day critics have for the most part contented themselves with deriding the word itself (but not the people who use it) as pompous, ponderous, and unnecessary.

In our time *eventuate* has been used on both sides of the Atlantic primarily in scholarly and scientific writing and in the rather dry prose of textbooks and reference works. It has also had some use in popular magazines and newspapers, but it is not the best choice when you are aiming for simplicity, informality, or forcefulness in your style.

> ... this usually eventuated in some kind of legislation —Frederic A. Ogg & Harold Zink, *Modern Foreign Governments,* 1949

> ... some disease that could not be cured and which would eventuate in death —Tennessee Williams, *The Roman Spring of Mrs. Stone,* 1950

> How shall the teacher mediate music to the pupil so that the desirable changes I have been enumerating shall actually eventuate? —Karl Wilson Gehrkens, *Educational Music Mag.,* September–October 1954

> ... rarely does some good fail to eventuate —Ernest K. Lindley, *Newsweek,* 11 Feb. 1957

> ... the Nazi-Fascist millenium [sic] which mercifully never eventuated —*Times Literary Supp.,* 15 Aug. 1980

> ... a possible cognitive-social mechanism by which deafness may eventuate in paranoia —Philip G. Zimbardo, *Science,* 26 June 1981

every **1.** *Subject-verb agreement.* Since *every* regularly modifies a singular noun, it is not too surprising that a singular verb usually follows. The pronoun *every* is archaic, so *every* is not bedeviled by quite the same number of conflicts between grammatical agreement and notional agreement that *each* and the other indefinite pronouns are.

> ... every snob thinks that the common people must be kept in their present place —George Bernard Shaw, *The Intelligent Woman's Guide to Socialism and Capitalism,* 1928

> ... given to every Sioux girl who was the first-born child —*American Guide Series: Minnesota,* 1938

> By now, every woman knows it's all right —Jane DeLynn, *Cosmopolitan,* December 1976

When *every* modifies two or more nouns joined by *and,* there is mixed usage, at least in part because of the rule that compound subjects joined by *and* are both grammatically and notionally plural. *Every,* however, tends to emphasize each noun separately, and the singular verb is common. The possibility of nouns joined by *and* being considered individually and thus taking a singular verb had been recognized as early as Lowth 1762; Fernald 1916 makes a specific exception to the rule of a plural verb for nouns modified by *each, every,* and *no.* Our evidence shows that the singular verb is more common:

> Every legislator, every doctor, and every citizen needs to recognize ... —Ronald Reagan, *Abortion and the Conscience of the Nation,* 1984

> Every kitchen, office and shop in Sun Valley was on his beat —Peter J. Ognibene, *Smithsonian,* December 1984

> This every beginning college teacher and graduate student knows —The Hazon Foundation, *The Importance of Teaching,* 1968

But the plural verb is not rare:

> ... every phrase, every line and every stanza are indissolubly welded —Marjorie Gullan, *The Speech Choir,* 1937

> Every single word and meaning of great ancient writers like Geoffrey Chaucer were recorded in the OED —Robert Burchfield, *U.S. News & World Report,* 11 Aug. 1986

2. *Pronoun reference.* Longman 1984, in a usage note at *every,* opines that since *every* modifies a singular noun, it would seem logical that it would be followed by singular pronouns. But it often is not; the effect of notional agreement and considerations of sex often work to bring in plural pronouns. Evans 1957 has a rather succinct set of rules (we omit the examples) to sum up the situation:

> It [*every*] is also followed by a singular pronoun when there is no question whether it is males or

females that are being talked about. . . . But when the reference is to both men and women, or the sex is unknown, a plural pronoun is generally preferred, . . . although some grammarians insist on the generic *his.* The plural pronoun is required in speaking of something owned in common . . .

The difference in Evans's approach and that of "some grammarians" is illustrated by this excerpt from Harper 1985:

> "I want *every* supervisor and employee to continually ask themselves these questions" is an example of a common error in choice of personal pronoun.

Evans would prefer *themselves,* since the sex is unkown, but Harper—in 1985 liberated enough not to require the generic *his*—calls for *himself or herself.* But notional agreement suggests the plural here too.

Actual usage is not quite as tidy as Evans's rules are. For instance, when there is no problem about males or females, the singular pronoun is usually used:

> . . . every woman knows it's all right not to get an orgasm each and every time she goes to bed with a man —Jane DeLynn, *Cosmopolitan,* December 1976

> Every bumptious idiot thinks himself a born ruler of men —George Bernard Shaw, *The Intelligent Woman's Guide to Socialism and Capitalism,* 1928

> . . . she lived in every moment entire as it came — Pearl Buck, *The Long Love,* 1949

Sometimes notional agreement will by itself attract a plural pronoun, even when there is no question of gender:

> I said, 'Now you wait and see. Every man in this United States that's got a daughter will be on my side,' and it turned out they were —Harry S. Truman, in Merle Miller, *Plain Speaking,* 1973

The pull of notional agreement is especially strong when inanimate objects are involved:

> Every kitchen, office and shop in Sun Valley was on his beat, and he visited them all —Peter J. Ognibene, *Smithsonian,* December 1984

> . . . every country that could produce the required goods was inundated with orders far beyond their capacity to supply —John A. Todd, *The Mechanism of Exchange,* 6th ed., 1949

> Every species of atoms or ultimate particles of bodies will be found to have their peculiar powers of attraction for heat —Leonard K. Nash, *Atomic-Molecular Theory,* 1950

> EVERY proper name in the Bible, with reference to passages where they occur —advt., quoted in Follett 1966

When the reference is to men and women or when the sex is unknown, the plural pronoun is almost always used:

> If we can succeed in persuading every man and woman, every nation to do their utmost —Herbert Hoover, quoted in *Time,* 27 May 1946

> I wish it were possible for every man and woman in this country to see for themselves what World War II has done —Basil O'Connor, *Key Reporter,* Summer 1946

> . . . the right of every nation, of every people, of every individual to develop in their own way — Dean Acheson, *New Republic,* 23 Jan. 1950

> . . . having a clerk telephone every U.S. correspondent in the capital, urging them to come to the embassy —*Time,* 11 Aug. 1952

> I saw every student before they went away —example from the Survey of English Usage (spoken), quoted in Longman 1984

Evans's observations are very close to the mark.

3. Copperud 1970, 1980 mentions some disagreement among grammarians and other observers over whether *every* is an adjective only, or is also an adverb. Dictionaries generally enter it as an adjective (*every* the pronoun is archaic). Bryant 1962 points out that it is an adverb in such phrases as *every now and then* or *every so often.* Merriam-Webster dictionaries treat these phrases as fixed idioms. The issue seems to have little practical importance.

everybody, everyone   Most of the discussions written about the indefinite pronouns *everybody* and *everyone* in usage books overlook important considerations. Here is a typical example:

> *Pronoun after "everyone."* The pronoun to be used after the word "everyone" apparently troubles even our most careful writers, as witness: "Give everyone credit for having the courage of their convictions." This might get by in colloquial speech but it is not sanctioned in good writing —Bernstein 1958

The problem is, of course, the same one we find with almost all the indefinite pronouns (see AGREEMENT: INDEFINITE PRONOUNS)—*everyone* and *everybody* are grammatically singular but notionally plural. Their natural tendency is to take singular verbs and plural pronouns. Some four years later Bernstein is concerned about *everybody:*

> "And so everybody took their guitars and songs, their poetry and perambulators, their high-bouncers and dogs, and went peacefully home." Here is an instance in which the proper pronouns—"his" or "his or her" won't work —Bernstein 1962

Indeed, the "proper pronouns" would make silly stuff out of the sentence. Bernstein's solution, of course, is to write the sentence over, to "face frankly this inadequacy of the language." But there is really nothing wrong with the pronouns in the sentence as it stands.

Bernstein is one of numerous modern descendants of the 18th-century grammarians Lowth and Lindley Murray, who first decided such pronouns should be singular. Bernstein has company: Bremner 1980, Shaw 1975, Nickles 1974, Colter 1981, Kilpatrick 1984, Simon 1980 all agree with his views. On the other side of the question, Copperud 1970 cites Evans 1957 and Flesch 1964. Longman 1984, Heritage 1982, and Reader's Digest 1983 find the plural pronouns acceptable. Jacques Barzun puts it more strongly:

> . . . it seems to me clear that good sense requires us to say "Everybody took their hats and filed out." — *Atlantic,* January 1946

One of the points made about notional plurality in several sources is that a pronoun in a coordinate clause or in a following sentence referring back to *everyone* or *everybody* is always plural—must be plural in normal English. To demonstrate this point we will call on dancer Sally Rand, as recorded by Studs Terkel:

> Flashlights went off and the music played, and everybody was happy. They said: do it again —*Hard Times,* 1970

Try substituting *he* or *he or she* in that second sentence, and see how absurd it is.

In our first citation from Bernstein above, there is an assertion that reference to *everyone* (or *everybody*) by *they, their, them* is not sanctioned in good writing. The assertion is false. Such reference may be found in important literature and other reputable writing from the 16th century to the present. Here is an extensive selection of examples (many of these are taken from Jespersen 1909–49, Hodgson 1889, and McKnight 1926).

> . . . every one prepared themselves —George Pettie, *A Petite Pallace of Pettie his Pleasure,* 1576 (in McKnight)

> . . . but God send every one their heart's desire —Shakespeare, *Much Ado About Nothing,* 1599

> . . . when every body else is upon their knees —*The Spectator,* No. 171 (in Jespersen)

> . . . frighted every body else out of their senses —Thomas Gray, letter, 15 July 1736

> . . . everybody had their due importance —Jane Austen, *Mansfield Park,* 1814

> . . . entreating everybody to drown themselves —P. B. Shelley, *Essays and Letters,* ca. 1822 (in Jespersen)

> . . . every body has played the fool in their turn —Sir Walter Scott, *The Antiquary,* 1815 (in Jespersen)

> Let us give everybody their due —Charles Dickens, *Nicholas Nickleby,* 1839 (in Jespersen)

> . . . everybody might have been born idiots, instead of having their right senses —George Eliot, *The Lifted Veil,* 1859 (in Jespersen)

> . . . everybody conjectured that I perished last night; and they were wondering how they must set about the search for my remains —Emily Brontë, *Wuthering Heights,* 1847

> It is true that when perspective was first discovered, everybody amused themselves with it —John Ruskin, *The Elements of Drawing,* 1857 (in Hodgson)

> . . . everybody can select which they please —Lewis Carroll, letter, 14 Nov. 1883

> Experience is the name everyone gives to their mistakes —Oscar Wilde, *Lady Windermere's Fan,* 1893

> . . . everybody has to take their chance in this world —James Stephens, *The Crock of Gold,* 1912

> Everybody ought to do what they can —Willa Cather, *O Pioneers!,* 1913

> . . . a definite plan for everybody in my department to help maintain their physical condition —Franklin

D. Roosevelt, letter, 2 June 1917, in *Franklin D. Roosevelt's Own Story,* ed. Donald Day, 1951

> . . . can time any little irregularity of your own so that everybody else is so blind that they don't see or care —F. Scott Fitzgerald, *The Great Gatsby,* 1925

> I mean we want every one to have all the *good, clean fun* they can —*New Yorker,* 28 Aug. 1926

> Everybody joined in several hymns, their firm warm voices carrying all through the ship —Katherine Anne Porter, *Accent,* Summer 1946

> . . . I want everyone here in this country and in the world to feel their personal concern in the success of the United Nations —Clement Attlee, speech, 22 Nov. 1945

> Everybody has a right to describe their own party machine as they choose —Sir Winston Churchill, in *Encounter,* April 1954

> Everyone was on their best behaviour —Elizabeth Taylor, *The Soul of Kindness,* 1964

> ". . . everyone would rise to their feet." —Malcolm Muggeridge, *The Green Stick,* 1972

> Everybody involved . . . disclosed their illiteracy —Charlene & Arn Tibbetts, *What's Happening to American English,* 1978

> Everyone knew where they stood —E. L. Doctorow, *Loon Lake,* 1979

> Almost everyone in the car is watching and pretending they're not —Jay McInerney, *Bright Lights, Big City,* 1984

They, their, them have been used in reference to *everybody* and *everyone* for more than 400 years in literature. You should not be dismayed by the fact that *everyone* and *everybody* regularly take a singular verb but a plural pronoun referent. That's just the way the indefinite pronouns behave in idiomatic English. Reader's Digest 1983 says "If you prefer *everyone . . . they* as being more natural, don't apologize." We agree. But do not feel that you have to use *they, their,* or *them,* if they do not seem natural to you. The choice is yours. Sometimes even first-person pronouns are used quite naturally:

> She's the doctor from Australia who goes around telling everybody we're all gonna die —Arlo Guthrie, quoted in *Yankee,* August 1986

It is worth mentioning that evidence in the Merriam-Webster files—drawn almost entirely from written prose—shows that both *everyone* and *everybody* have been more frequently used with plural pronouns than singular ones in the 20th century. *Everyone* is more than twice as likely as *everybody* to be used with a singular pronoun, perhaps from the underlying pressure toward singularity created by *-one.*

See also NOTIONAL AGREEMENT, NOTIONAL CONCORD; THEY, THEIR, THEM.

everyday, every day The single word *everyday* is an adjective ("an everyday occurrence," "part of everyday life"); the two-word phrase combining *every* and *day* functions either as a noun ("Every day is new") or as an adverb ("I see her every day"). The adverbial phrase is being written as a single word with increasing frequency:

Everyday I see or read about other women in similar roles —K. L. Gorby, *Vogue,* November 1980

Everyday it seems as though I am treated to matching scandals —Meg Greenfield, *Newsweek,* 16 Nov. 1987

This form may well get into the dictionaries someday, but for now the two-word styling for the adverbial phrase is still more common.

everyone See EVERYBODY, EVERYONE.

everyplace The history of *everyplace* parallels that of *anyplace.* It is a word of apparently American origin that has only recently begun to appear in print with any regularity. The objections that have been made to *anyplace* have also been made to *everyplace* (and also to *no place* and *someplace*). Its status in current English is as a somewhat informal synonym of *everywhere:*

"... and everyplace we stopped on the way up, people smiled at us ..." —*Rolling Stone,* 1 Mar. 1973

Although, like everyplace else, the White Elephant had engaged a corps of college students —Horace Sutton, *Saturday Rev.,* 16 Oct. 1976

See also ANYPLACE; NOPLACE; SOMEPLACE.

everytime, every time *Every* and *time* form a common adverbial phrase that is normally written as two words ("They'll do it every time"; "Every time it rains ..."). There is, however, a persistent tendency to treat this two-word phrase as a single-word adverb, especially when it occurs at the beginning of a clause and is essentially synonymous with *whenever:*

Everytime I read an Irish story —*Irish Statesman,* 13 Sept. 1924

... and everytime the business failed, we children inherited a new legacy —Charles Jones, quoted in *Psychology Today,* April 1968

Everytime a field was cleared of timber —Julian Fish, *Early American Life,* April 1976

Such usage seems to be growing slowly more common, but the two-word styling is still more widely preferred. As Copperud 1980 notes, no dictionary has yet entered the single word *everytime.*

every which way This expressive Americanism, attested as early as 1824, has made a few commentators nervous: Vizetelly 1906 calls it "a pleonastic colloquialism"; MacCracken & Sandison 1917, Shaw 1962, 1970, and Prentice Hall 1978 all call it colloquial. Baker 1927 labels it incorrect and appends the following instruction:

Instead of saying, "He ran *every which way,*" one should say, "He ran in all directions."

It is a mystery why American commentators tend to be so timorous about Americanisms. Evidence in the OED Supplement shows that the expression has even caught on to some extent in Great Britain now. Here are a few unvarnished samples, all American:

... dozens of cameras perched all over the city ... always relentlessly prying and probing every which way —Philip Hamburger, *New Yorker,* 19 July 1952

... he attempted to perfect a relaxing chair—an overstuffed piece of furniture that started to pulsate gently every which way as soon as it was occupied — *New Yorker,* 29 May 1954

... in 1912 when the Democratic Party was split every which way —Harry S. Truman, in Merle Miller, *Plain Speaking,* 1973

... to send the company on a wild-goose chase shipping its damn machines every which way —E. L. Doctorow, *Loon Lake,* 1979

evidence *Evidence* has been used as a transitive verb for many centuries, but it has retained something of a formal quality that has invited occasional hostility from usage commentators. Fowler 1926 approved its use when its meaning was clearly "to serve as evidence of; prove the existence, occurrence, or truth of" (as in "The book evidences the author's careful scholarship"), but he considered it incorrect when used simply as a synonym of *show* or *exhibit* (as in "The author evidences careful scholarship"). Later commentators have not concerned themselves with any such distinction, being content to describe *evidence* as "ugly" (Partridge 1942), "pretentious" (Copperud 1964), and "not as good a word as *show*" (Flesch 1964).

The distinction promoted by Fowler is one that will undoubtedly seem obscure to many people, and it is not widely observed:

... spruce trees ... evidencing similar but less spectacular golden traits —George E. Toles, *Trees,* Winter 1975

Mr. Pais evidences Einstein's cast of mind —Timothy Ferris, *N.Y. Times Book Rev.,* 28 Nov. 1982

... a mistaken adverbial punctiliousness that is often evidenced even at Harvard —Lynn M. Salerno, letter, in Safire 1984

... the ensemble evidences a puzzling equivocation —Peter Plagens, *Art in America,* July 1986

Each of these passages would be criticized by Fowler, but the contexts are obviously standard, and the use is no longer seriously regarded as erroneous (except, perhaps, by a few of Fowler's more devoted disciples). The formality of *evidence* is the characteristic that best distinguishes it from *show* and even from *exhibit.* This formality is apparent in all its uses:

The intellectual climate of our time evidences a rebirth of interest in philosophical first principles — Frederick Sontag, *Jour. of Religion,* July 1954

... is evidenced most clearly in what we may refer to as "the creative aspect of language use" —Noam Chomsky, *Columbia Forum,* Spring 1968

... it evidenced an appallingly petty malevolence on their part —Marshall Frady, *N.Y. Rev. of Books,* 6 Apr. 1972

Such formality can sometimes be inappropriate (or pretentious, as Copperud puts it), but it is not invariably so. The question to ask yourself when considering the use of *evidence* is whether the audience, tone, and subject of your writing make formality suitable. If they do, then *evidence* is as good a verb as any other.

evidently See APPARENTLY, EVIDENTLY.

evoke, invoke Warnings against confusion of these verbs are sometimes given. The basic distinction between them is simple enough. *Evoke* is derived from the Latin *evocare,* "to call forth." Its usual senses in current English are "to elicit," "to bring to mind," and "to recreate imaginatively":

> . . . never fails to evoke a tumultuous response from its audiences —*Current Biography,* March 1968

> . . . her twin hulls evoke images of the South Seas —Earl Arnett, *Maryland Mag.,* Winter 1970

> Some movies have the mysterious power to evoke an era —Liz Smith, *Cosmopolitan,* December 1973

Invoke is derived from the Latin *invocare* "to call upon, appeal to." Among its many English senses are "to solicit," "to appeal to or cite as an authority," and "to implement":

> . . . is entitled to invoke the assistance of the court —James W. Coull & Eric W. Merry, *Principles and Practice of Scots Law,* 1971

> . . . I foolishly invoked the name of Julia Child —Gael Greene, *New York,* 13 Sept. 1971

> . . . as a way of invoking the death penalty —George Freeman Solomon, *People,* 17 Jan. 1977

Our evidence indicates that these verbs are almost always used in distinct ways, except that *evoke* sometimes occurs as a synonym of *invoke* in its sense "to appeal to or cite as an authority":

> The name of Socrates is not one that would ordinarily be evoked by a defender of artists —*Times Literary Supp.,* 6 Feb. 1943

> The names of Ascoli, Bréal, Gaston Paris, Pio Rajna are evoked —M. Sandmann, *Modern Language Notes,* December 1955

> . . . in that essay I evoked the name of Flaubert and the example of Emma Bovary —Philip Roth, *Reading Myself and Others,* 1975

The contexts in which such usage occurs are standard, but the usage itself is still liable to criticism. Most writers would choose *invoke* in such contexts, and we recommend that you do so as well.

evolute The verb *evolute* is a back-formation of *evolution* that originated as an Americanism in the late 19th century. It is synonymous with *evolve* in both its intransitive and transitive senses:

> If those miserable vagrants could only evolute into respectable people —*Cambridge* (Mass.) *Tribune,* 15 Aug. 1884 (OED Supplement)

> . . . has been standardizing and slowly evoluting new patterns —*Emporia* (Kans.) *Gazette,* 9 Sept. 1927

Evolute is too rarely used to have provoked a major controversy among usage commentators, but the few critics who have taken note of it have, of course, disliked it. Weseen 1928 called it an "inadmissable coinage"; Jensen 1935 asserted that "there is no such word"; and Evans 1957 called it "an ignorant blunder." More recently, William Safire (*N.Y. Times Mag.,* 14 Aug. 1983) has called *evolute* a mistake, although he acknowledges the possibility that it could one day gain accep-

tance. The word itself, meanwhile, has continued in uncommon use:

> Cows have not evoluted to the stage where they can be born and into production within eight months, yet! —*Burlington* (Vt.) *Free Press,* 22 Apr. 1982

> Shoulders, though still emphasized, are evoluting —Patricia McColl, *N.Y. Times Mag.,* 6 Oct. 1985

If you use *evolute,* you can be sure that most of your readers will find it peculiar, if not actually incorrect. Remember that *evolve* is fully synonymous with *evolute* and is available as a less problematic substitute.

ex- 1. The use of *ex-,* a hyphenated prefix meaning "former," to modify a noun phrase ignited the wrath of Fowler 1926, who deplored "such patent yet prevalent absurdities as *ex-Lord Mayor*" and *"ex-Chief Whip."* A few present-day critics keep the flame burning: "Does 'ex French general' mean that the man is no longer French?" ponders Bremner 1980.

In 1956 the editors of *Winners & Sinners,* the editorial watchdog bulletin of the *New York Times,* considered advocating the use of *ex* without a hyphen to modify noun phrases. Their aim was to find a way of making *ex-* compounds unambiguous and silencing followers of Fowler, thereby preventing overzealous copy editors from devising such concoctions as "tax ex-official." After some consideration they decided to shelve the issue and continue the hyphenated styling as in "ex-tax official." This is, in fact, what usually occurs in edited prose generally. While this styling of *ex-* compounds may not be a perfect solution, their meaning is transparent enough except to those who take extra pains to misunderstand them. Bremner's "ex-French general" is a case where *ex-* modifies not the adjective "French" but the substantive phrase "French general." Although *ex-* can modify only the attributive part of a noun phrase (as in the first citation below), it usually modifies the whole phrase.

> . . . an Italian ex-Catholic father and an ex-Mormon mother —Alfred Kazin, *Saturday Rev.,* 3 May 1975

> . . . two bishops and two ex-college presidents —Robert M. Hutchins, *Center Mag.,* March 1968

> . . . a burly twenty-nine-year-old ex-surf bum —Burr Snider, *Esquire,* June 1973

> . . . a teenage ex-porno queen —Richard P. Brickner, *N.Y. Times Book Rev.,* 5 Sept. 1976

Occasionally *ex-* is used in such a way that it could be interpreted as modifying either the attributive or the whole substantive, but we doubt that such uses cause problems for the reader.

> . . . his position as an Englishman in an ex-colonial country —*Current Biography,* June 1967

Ex- is widely used in general contexts but is largely avoided in those that are very elevated or literary.
2. Reader's Digest 1983 proposes a distinction between *ex-* and *former* in a limited set of cases. The suggestion is that *ex-* attached to a title or a word expressing relationship should mean the immediate past incumbent; all earlier ones should be designated *former.* Thus, there can be only one ex-President of the U.S. at a time, though any number of former presidents, and no matter how many spouses you may have had, only the one most recently divorced is your ex-husband or ex-wife.

The distinction is easily enough followed, if you care to do so, in those relatively infrequent circumstances when it becomes relevant. We have, however, no citations clearly showing a writer observing the distinction and a few older ones showing it being ignored. In the nature of things, proof positive of a distinction so limited in its scope is difficult to come by, but we must doubt that the distinction is well established in practice.

exact same   This common phrase is sometimes criticized, chiefly on the assumption that *exact* is being misused in it as an adverb. It is, of course, possible to interpret *exact* as an adverb in *exact same* (much like *very* in *very same*), but we feel that it is better regarded as an adjective being used with another adjective for emphasis. One reason for such an interpretation is that *exact* has no other adverbial use in modern English. Perhaps a better reason (at least, a more convincing one) is that the two words of the phrase are sometimes transposed ("the same exact thing"), and such interchangeability strongly suggests that both of them are functioning as adjectives. Other adjectives are also occasionally used to give added emphasis to *same:*

> . . . the pure snap-shot illustrates the same identical method of leading —Bob Nichols, *Skeet and How to Shoot It,* 1947

In any case, the part of speech of *exact* in *exact same* is of secondary importance. The primary question is whether the phrase is used by educated speakers and writers, and the answer to that question is yes:

> . . . all their authors give the exact same interview — Wilfrid Sheed, *N.Y. Times Book Rev.,* 7 Oct. 1973

> . . . have been used in the exact same sense —W. P. McCafferty et al., *Systematic Zoology,* March 1974

> . . . all made of the exact same sweet white bread dough —Mimi Sheraton, *N.Y. Times,* 1 June 1976

> The exact same photograph —Wright Morris, *American Scholar,* Autumn 1979

> The exact same ninety-word quotation from Chesterton —John Updike, *New Yorker,* 24 May 1982

Its use is especially common in speech.
Exact same has also been criticized as redundant, like many another emphatic phrase. For a discussion of the validity of such criticism, see REDUNDANCY.

exceedingly, excessively   The distinction between these adverbs is noted in many books on usage. *Exceedingly* is used only as a synonym of *extremely:*

> . . . is in an exceedingly precarious position —Robert A. Nisbet, *Psychology Today,* March 1971

> . . . did exceedingly well in the advertising business —William Stadiem, *Town & Country,* September 1980

Excessively normally functions as a synonym of *overly:*

> . . . an attempt to escape an excessively literal world —*Current Biography,* July 1966

> Without being excessively indulgent —Robert K. Merton, *Columbia Forum,* Spring 1968

This distinction became a topic for usage commentators in the late 19th century, when Ayres 1881 among others

disparaged the use of *excessively* in contexts which required, in their view, *exceedingly* or *extremely.* Such usage actually has a highly respectable history:

> Elizabeth was excessively disappointed; she had set her heart on seeing the Lakes, and still thought there might have been time enough —Jane Austen, *Pride and Prejudice,* 1813

> There came forth from it nothing but smoke . . . at which he wondered excessively —Edward W. Lane, *A Thousand and One Nights,* 1841 (OED)

But it seems never to have been very common; at any rate, it certainly is not common now. The "overly" sense of *excessively* is now so strongly established that any use to mean "extremely" stands out as peculiar. Here is a sampling of the scanty evidence we have gathered for it in the 20th century:

> . . . only an excessively small amount of glass is taken off —*Scientific American Supp.,* 13 Oct. 1916

> . . . a set of pamphlets . . . which are excessively interesting —Harold J. Laski, letter, 22 Apr. 1928

> . . . a volume of poems that has become, as they say in the book collectors' catalogues, excessively rare — Anthony West, *New Yorker,* 10 Nov. 1951

except   See ACCEPT, EXCEPT.

exception   *Exception* has been used over the years with many different prepositions, some of which are still current, others of which have faded from use. Among the latter are *at, against,* and *from:*

> And yet she takes exceptions at your person — Shakespeare, *The Two Gentlemen of Verona,* 1595

> Thou hast taken against me a most just exception — Shakespeare, *Othello,* 1605

> Only a little exception from the amiable tenor of their conduct —Albany Fonblanque, *England Under Seven Administrations,* 1829 (OED)

Now *exception* usually takes either *of* or *to:*

> . . . he made an exception of his rigid nonhandshaking policy —Charles W. Ferguson, *Fifty Million Brothers,* 1937

> . . . What makes Minneapolis businesses an exception to the general rule —Roland Gelatt, *Saturday Rev.,* 29 Oct. 1977

In addition, when *of* or *to* is used, each is found most often in a particular idiom, *with the exception of* or *take exception to:*

> . . . taught at the university for four years, with the exception of the academic year 1952–53 —*Current Biography,* January 1966

> The Aga Khan took strong exception to the remark and fought back —Robert Payne, *N.Y. Times Book Rev.,* 26 Sept. 1954

See also WITH THE EXCEPTION OF.

exceptionable, exceptional   The foremost distinction to be made between these two words is that one is extremely rare and the other is extremely common. *Exceptionable* is a word most likely to occur in discussions by usage commentators who are concerned that it should not be confused with *exceptional.* They should put their minds at rest. Although *exceptionable* was in fact occasionally used with the same meaning as *exceptional* in the 19th century, we have no evidence of such usage in the 20th. On the rare occasions when *exceptionable* is now used in running text, it means "objectionable":

> At its least exceptionable, ecology is a housekeeping movement —Richard Neuhaus, *Harper's,* October 1971

Exceptional, of course, is a common word of which the basic meaning is "forming an exception":

> ... very much in keeping with the exceptional moral nature of America —Milton Viorst, *Interplay,* February 1969

It often describes someone or something that is significantly better than average:

> His talent was too exceptional to allow for casual predictions —Norman Mailer, *Advertisements for Myself,* 1959

Exceptional also has a special use among teachers, sociologists, and psychologists to describe children who in some significant way differ from normal children. It refers especially to mentally retarded, physically handicapped, emotionally disturbed, or learning disabled children, although it can also refer to children who are unusually intelligent or otherwise gifted:

> He must think more particularly of the exceptional child who is deficient (not so much of the one who is gifted) —*The Exceptional Child,* 20 Mar. 1951

> ... has embraced the cause of the exceptional child. It requires that every school system must provide for special education of retarded children —Sarah Bassinor, *Massachusetts Teacher,* March 1965

This use of *exceptional* is well-established: our first record of it is from 1911. It has been criticized as a euphemism for *retarded* or *feeble-minded* by a few writers who apparently pride themselves on their refusal to spare anyone's feelings. Harper 1985, on the other hand, regards it with approval.
    See also UNEXCEPTIONABLE, UNEXCEPTIONAL.

excess   See ACCESS 1; IN EXCESS OF.

excessively   See EXCEEDINGLY, EXCESSIVELY.

exclude   When *exclude* is used with a preposition, it is usually *from:*

> The humane judgement of the experienced literary man is excluded from consideration —Iris Murdoch, *The Fire and the Sun,* 1977

> He was shut up in a room from which all light was excluded —Thomas Hardy, *The Return of the Native,* 1878

exclusive   When *exclusive* is used with a preposition and the object names what is excluded, the preposition is *of:*

> Few tourists come to Guadalcanal; the number last year was 1,809 ... exclusive of one-day callers from occasional cruise ships —Robert Trumbull, *Saturday Rev.,* 23 Oct. 1971

When the object names what is actually included and excludes others, the preposition is *to:*

> The belief in "peaceful coexistence" is not exclusive to Socialists in Britain —*Time,* 20 Sept. 1954

excuse   When the verb *excuse* is used with a preposition, it ordinarily is used with *from,* less often with *for.* Moreover, when the word is used in this way, it usually, although not always, appears in the passive:

> ... the compulsory education law permitted children to be excused from public schools —*American Guide Series: Minnesota,* 1938

> ... enabled an even greater number of officers to excuse themselves from any personal responsibility —William L. Shirer, *The Rise and Fall of the Third Reich,* 1960

> ... one may be excused for supposing that he, too, would have been in the Canadian League long ago —Jack Olsen, *Sports Illustrated,* 29 July 1968

The Merriam-Webster files also attest the use of *excuse* with *of* instead of *from,* but this use is infrequent:

> Has any other General been excused of the necessity of giving an accounting —*New Republic,* 29 Aug. 1949

These observations pertain chiefly to American usage because it seems that, although at one time British English also used *excuse* with *from* or *for,* the word now appears more often with no preposition:

> ... these students are excused the normal degree course entry qualifications of two A levels —Peter Wilby, *The Observer,* 19 May 1974

execute   **1.** As early as 1824 Walter Savage Landor, in his *Imaginary Conversations,* objected to using *execute* to mean "to put to death." However, the most widely read and strident manifesto on this subject was that of Richard Grant White 1870, who scathingly referred to the "vicious use of this word" which "produces sheer nonsense" because, he claimed, it is only a law or a sentence that gets executed, not a person. White called for "a vigorous and persistent effort on the part of the best speakers and writers and professional teachers" to fight this use even though—as he himself said—*execute* had meant "to put to death" for quite a long time to quite a number of people. He was apparently spurred on rather than deterred by the fact that his convictions ran totally counter to actual usage.
    The response to his remarks must have been a disappointment to him. Ayres 1881 did reprise White's argument, ascribing it to "some of our careful speakers," but only after noting that "the dictionaries and almost universal usage say that [*execute*] also means to put to death in conformity with a judicial sentence." Ayres refrained from stating an opinion of his own about *execute;* he only reported the opinions of others. This was as close as White got to support for his views among contemporary usage writers. Fitzedward Hall in *Recent Exemplifications of False Philology* (1872) argued that the sense was valid because otherwise "*Executioner,* which we use only in one sense, would pass clear out of our language, under Mr. White's purification of it." Since White's time other writers have referred to his opinion, but most have made it clear that the weight of usage is overwhelmingly against it. The sense of *execute*

meaning "to put to death" has been around since at least 1483, was used by Shakespeare, Gibbon, and Macaulay, and is firmly established in standard English.

> ... four days after their trial, Rochford and the four other condemned men were executed —Edith Sitwell, *Fanfare for Elizabeth,* 1946

2. Recent usage books have included only a smattering of comment about *execute.* Flesch 1964 and Janis 1984 disapprove of using it to mean "sign" when referring to a document. We lack evidence for this use in general contexts and suspect it may be common only in the legal and business worlds.

Harper 1985 says that *execute* is not a synonym for *kill* or *murder* and that it means "to kill [a person] in compliance with a military order or judicial decision." Terrorists and others who seek to justify their actions are probably the most likely to use *execute* to mean "kill." Such semantic tinkering is objectionable on moral rather than linguistic grounds.

exemplary   *Exemplary* is etymologically related to *example,* and its fundamental meaning is "serving as an example or pattern." More often than not, it describes something praiseworthy and has the sense "deserving imitation:"

> ... with exemplary tact and discretion —George F. Kennan, *New Yorker,* 1 May 1971

> ... every exemplary act of bravery —Marge Piercy, *N.Y. Times Book Rev.,* 23 May 1976

But it can also be used in neutral contexts:

> ... presents exemplary details and sums up over large areas —John Hollander, *Harper's,* March 1971

And even, on occasion, in negative ones:

> ... faithfully mirroring the work's exemplary mediocrity —John Simon, *New York,* 7 Feb. 1972

The meaning here seems to be something like "quintessential."

Commentators have sometimes warned against using *exemplary* as if it were simply a synonym of *excellent,* but clear-cut instances of such usage are hard to come by. When *exemplary* describes something excellent, as it often does, it seems always to carry the further suggestion that the thing described, because of its excellence, is worthy of imitation. The usage disliked by the commentators is presumably in such contexts as the following:

> An otherwise exemplary twelve-ounce prime sirloin steak —Jay Jacobs, *Gourmet,* December 1982

> ... they serve exemplary pastries —George V. Higgins, *N.Y. Times Mag.,* 9 Oct. 1983

Such usage is atypical, but it is not actually incorrect. *Exemplary* is a stronger word (if not a better-chosen word) than *excellent,* even when it only describes a pastry.

exhaustive, exhausting   *Exhaustive* ordinarily means "testing all possibilities or considering all elements; thorough." Only very rarely is it used with the same meaning as *exhausting,* and then it runs the risk of being misunderstood. Though something that is

exhaustive may prove to be exhausting as well, the meanings of the two words are distinct.

> ... it re-creates in exhaustive (and sometimes exhausting) detail the roller-coaster feel of the campaign —Ken Auletta, *N.Y. Times Book Rev.,* 28 July 1985

exhibit, exhibition   Bernstein 1965 and Shaw 1975 want to enforce a distinction between *exhibit* and *exhibition,* the gist of which is that *exhibit* should refer only to an item or group of items on display in an exhibition and not to the exhibition itself. The use of *exhibit* which these writers consider an error is in such a sentence as "Ten thousand people have so far attended the art exhibit." This use of *exhibit* is criticized by no other commentator, however, and is consistent with the general sense of the word, "something exhibited." It is also common:

> ... on the final day of the August exhibit —*Retailing Daily,* 16 Aug. 1954

> ... taking their best work to the gallery for the art exhibit —Kay Haugaard, in *Networks,* ed. Marjorie Seddon Johnson et al., 1977

exhilarate, exhilaration   Spell these words with caution, noting well that they contain not just one *a,* but two. The first *a* can easily turn into an *i* or an *e:*

> ... we feel so comfortable and so exhilerated —*Massachusetts Audubon Newsletter,* December 1970

It may help to remember the etymological connection of these words with *hilarious.*

exhorbitant   See EXORBITANT.

exhuberance, exhuberant   See EXUBERANCE, EXUBERANT.

existence, existent   The spelling *existance* for *existence* has been reported by Irmscher 1976 and Copperud 1980 and has caught our eye several times over the years. We also have some evidence for an -*ant* spelling of *existent* which probably involves some element of confusion with the word *extant.* Both *existance* and *existant* are still considered misspellings and should be avoided.

exonerate   *Exonerate,* when used with a preposition, is usually used with *from* or *of. From* is more common:

> ... a society in which an understanding of human frailty means to exonerate ourselves from all moral judgment —Harold Clurman, *Harper's,* May 1971

> ... exonerated him of complicity in the Iquitos uprising —*Current Biography,* April 1967

Two other prepositions are found in our files:

> ... he cannot be exonerated for his negligence — O. S. Nock, *The Railways of Britain,* 1947

> ... the contents of which tended very strongly to exonerate defendant as to the charge in the indictment —*State* v. *Pietranton,* 72 S.E. 2d 617, 13 Nov. 1952

exorbitant   Note that there is no *h* following the *x* of *exorbitant.* This is a spelling error that's easily made, although its occurrence in published writing is relatively rare.

> ... with tickets being sold at exhorbitant prices — *Variety,* 3 Oct. 1979

expatriate The spelling *expatriot,* created by the influence of *patriot,* is occasionally used for the noun *expatriate.*

> ... potentially dangerous expatriots such as Lee Harvey Oswald —*N.Y. Times,* 24 May 1965

> ... the German expatriot poet Heine —*N.Y. University Bulletin,* Spring 1967

Expatriot is perceived as a misspelling and is not entered in current dictionaries. However, its use is frequent enough to allow the possibility of its becoming an acceptable variant spelling in the future. Until that happens, expect criticism if you use it.

expatriot See EXPATRIATE.

expect 1. We have collected over 40 comments and admonitions about *expect* from the past century or so, and all of them discuss the same issue: using *expect* to mean "suppose" or "think" in sentences such as "I expect you were sorry to hear that." Criticism of this usage has more often than not been based on such reasoning as that used by Richard Grant White in 1870: "*Expect* refers only to that which is to come, and which, therefore, is looked for.... We cannot expect backward." Many commentators echoed White's opinion during the late 19th and, in particular, early 20th centuries.

The OED shows that the "suppose" sense of *expect* is actually quite old, dating back to the 16th century. But the OED's editors, writing in 1894, were evidently no more fond of this sense than was Richard Grant White; they described it in the following terms:

> Now *rare* in literary use. The misuse of the word as a synonym of *suppose,* without any notion of 'anticipating' or 'looking for', is often cited as an Americanism, but is very common in dialectal, vulgar or carelessly colloquial speech in England.

Questions about whether the Americans or the British were to blame for this sense persisted for some years, but that part of the controversy has now died out entirely. Our evidence shows that the "suppose" sense of *expect* is now common on both sides of the Atlantic.

Many recent handbooks have followed the OED's lead in calling the "suppose" sense colloquial (White's point about "expecting backward" is now rarely heard). Our evidence gives some support to that characterization, but only if *colloquial* is understood as meaning "characteristic of informal conversation" rather than as a term of disparagement. When *expect* means "suppose," it is almost invariably used in the first person, and it therefore appears most often in speech and in the kinds of writing which make use of the first person—correspondence, dialogue, and informal prose:

> I shall be able, I expect, to dispatch the waggon — Thomas Jefferson, letter, 27 Feb. 1809

> ... it was loose or something, I expect —Francis Lee Pratt, "Captain Ben's Choice," in *Mark Twain's Library of Humor,* 1888

> I expect that Shakespeare devised Iago with a gusto —W. Somerset Maugham, *The Moon and Sixpence,* 1919

> "He won't go quite as high as I do, I expect ... " — D. H. Lawrence, "The Rocking-horse Winner," 1933

> "George knows, I expect," said Virginia —Agatha Christie, *The Secret of Chimneys,* 1925

> ... do look at the book on him by Grégoire Leroy, I expect in the Library of Congress —Harold J. Laski, letter, 18 Jan. 1930

> I expect you're familiar with them —Heathcote Williams, *Evergreen,* December 1967

> To be fair, I expect that the same situation obtains in the editorial page —Lawrence Dietz, *Los Angeles Times Book Rev.,* 27 Feb. 1972

The use of this sense with a subject other than *I* is rare and is most likely to occur in an indirect quotation:

> ... she would announce ... that she expected that Osbert would like a little walk —Osbert Lancaster, *All Done From Memory,* 1953

The "suppose" sense of *expect* is now far less controversial than it once was, although it still has its detractors. It has also had some staunch defenders in its time, including Fowler 1926, who declared, "This extension of meaning is, however, so natural that it seems needless PURISM to resist it.... there is no sound objection to it." We agree. Whenever *I* is appropriate in a written context, the "suppose" sense of *expect* is likely to be appropriate also.

2. *Expect* is very often followed by *to* and the infinitive:

> ... the anthropologists expect to find some degree of fit between religious beliefs and the institutions they sustain —Mary Douglas, *Commonweal,* 9 Oct. 1970

> For the system to work, the individual must not only expect to pay that price, he must consider it proper to do so —Ramsey Clark, in *Center Mag.,* July/August 1970

> "Jacques d'Amboise ... is now about as elegant a danseur noble as one can expect to see." —Winthrop Sargeant, in *Current Biography,* September 1964

> ... Bainbridge's men could expect to be starved and cold —C. S. Forester, *The Barbary Pirates,* 1953

Less often, but still very commonly, *expect* is used with *from* or *of:*

> As was to be expected from such a large number of writers —Morris R. Cohen, *The Faith of a Liberal,* 1946

> ... a new student gets some idea from these records of what to expect from himself —Howard Warshaw, *Center Mag.,* July/August 1970

> ... he was not interested in poetry and there could be small hope of expecting poetry from him —John Ciardi, *Saturday Rev.,* 11 Mar. 1972

> What he expected of me was to extricate him from a difficult situation —Joseph Conrad, *Chance,* 1913

> ... magazines offer printed information on what one can expect of fabrics —Mary S. Switzer, in *The Wonderful World of Books,* ed. Alfred Stefferud, 1952

A fine ear for the music of words is expected of a poet —Michael Williams, in *Little Reviews Anthology 1949,* ed. Denys Val Baker

expectorate   Back in the days when chewing tobacco was a common habit, *expectorate* enjoyed some popularity among the genteel as a euphemism for *spit*. Like most euphemisms, it provoked a certain amount of criticism. Our files include a clipping from the *Springfield* (Mass.) *Republican* of 10 Apr. 1903, in which "elegant people" are reported to have been writing letters to New York's board of health complaining about the use of *spit* in public signs, and suggesting the substitution of *expectorate*. The story goes on—

> But the president, Dr Lederle, produced a letter written by Theodore Roosevelt when he was police commissioner, asking: "Can't you have our form of notice changed so as to read 'spit' instead of 'expectorate?' Expectorate is a vile word, and the health board ought to use good English." Mr. Roosevelt was right, and the health board did well to take his advice.

The clipping ends with the assertion that, other than in medical use, *expectorate* "is of no value except in the punning observation: 'A man who expectorates on the floor cannot expect to rate as a gentleman.'"
   Expectorate is still sometimes used to mean "spit," but the user is now more likely to be trying for humor than politeness. The noun *expectoration* has the same quality:

> ... became something of a folk figure partly because of the enormous chaw that bulged out his cheek, and his thoughtful, brooding expectorations were relentlessly depicted by the television cameras —Robert W. Creamer, *Sports Illustrated,* 24 Jan. 1983

Such usage no longer provokes letters, pro or con. *Expectorate* and *expectoration* now occur chiefly in medical writing, in which they usually describe the expulsion of material from the lungs.

expediate   *Expediate* is a rare version of *expedite* that has been turning up at intervals since the 17th century. The OED lists it as a "spurious word," because, as far as the editors knew, it was created by error and thenceforth appeared only in dictionaries. It is originally attested in a 1605 book, in which it was changed to *expedite* by 1629. It was picked up in Henry Cockeram's 1623 dictionary of hard words (Cockeram includes *expedite,* too, but only as an adjective). From Cockeram it somehow found its way into Todd's edition (1818) of Johnson's Dictionary. But it has also been in editions of the Merriam-Webster unabridged since 1909 because it has continued in sporadic use over the last hundred years or so.
   We have no idea why *expediate* continues to pop up. One of our etymologists has theorized that it may be a spontaneous coinage in each instance, the product of the common verb ending *-ate* operating on *expedient* or *expedite.* It is unlikely to be a mere misspelling or typographical error, and our most recent example is reported from speech. *Expedited* would not be mistaken as *expediated* when spoken.

> Clay said the board is seeking "expediated bargaining" in this year's teacher negotiations—by limiting talks to four or five issues —Jeri Kornegay, *Jackson* (Mich.) *Citizen Patriot,* 20 Jan. 1985

It is also possible that *expediate* is a spoken form that seldom finds its way into print and thereby eludes the notice of lexicographers, who would be glad to hear of documented occurrences, we are sure.
   For now it must be said that wary writers use *expedite* but very few use *expediate.*

expedite   See EXPEDIATE.

expel   1. When *expel* is used with a preposition, the choice is almost always *from:*

> ... had been expelled from his seat in the Senate for plotting with the British —Richard B. Morris, *N.Y. Times Book Rev.,* 25 July 1954

> ... if powerful blowers could be set up to expel the fumes away from the area —Bertrand de Jouvenel, *Center Mag.,* September 1969

An interesting twist on this use of *expel* may be seen in the following example, which is, however, not typical:

> ... the Chilean government expelled an American expatriate named Michael Townley into United States custody —Thomas Hauser, *N.Y. Times Book Rev.,* 27 July 1980

2. Although some language commentators warn their readers not to misspell *expel* as *expell,* the warning seems unnecessary: judging from the Merriam-Webster files, *expell* hardly ever occurs, at least in edited prose.

experience   1. Perhaps influenced by Alford 1866, who condemns the use of the word *experience* as a verb, American language commentators, among them Richard Grant White 1870, Ayres 1881, and Bierce 1909, continued into the beginning of the 20th century to caution against its use. The criticism persisted despite the fact that the verb *experience* had been in use as far back as the 16th century (as the OED shows) and had remained in continuous use since that time. *Experience* never did fade from use, and the language critics eventually accepted its legitimacy, so that contemporary usage books seldom even touch on the earlier controversy.
2. When the verb *experience* is used with a preposition, the form of the verb is usually the past participle, and the preposition most frequently is *in:*

> Also experienced in expressing his ideas in writing —*Current Biography 1953*

> ... highly experienced in industrial management and financial policy —*Times Literary Supp.,* 9 Mar. 1967

Less frequently, *experience* is used with *as:*

> ... with the help of a staff of twenty-three people experienced as parents —*Current Biography,* May 1965

expert   1. *Adjective.* When the adjective *expert* is used with a preposition, it is usually *in:*

> ... he is an artist expert in shaping his material into one comprehensive design —Samuel C. Chew, *N.Y. Herald Tribune Book Rev.,* 15 Apr. 1951

It may be used with *at:*

> Lanny had become expert at learning scientific formulas —Upton Sinclair, *Presidential Mission,* 1947

2. *Noun.* The noun *expert,* when used with a preposition, is most often used with *on:*

> ... half a dozen specialists—experts on various regions of the world —Ernest O. Hauser, *Saturday Evening Post,* 29 May 1954

Somewhat less frequently, *expert* is used with *in,* and still less frequently, with *at:*

> ... a highly qualified lawyer, an expert in education —Jack Witkowsky, *Saturday Rev.,* 20 Nov. 1971

> ... the town's expert at repairing cane-seated chairs —Elizabeth Van Steenwyk, *Ford Times,* November 1967

expertise   This French borrowing was first used in English more than a century ago, but its establishment as a full-fledged English word has occurred only in recent decades. Its older sense, "expert opinion or commentary," is now relatively rare:

> But there is no evidence in the fairly numerous records of such expertises as have survived of any attempts at similarly precise analyses —Rowland Mainstone, *Developments in Structural Form,* 1975

But its newer sense, "expert knowledge or skill," is extremely common:

> ... with what sort of expertise does he judge a poet to be great? —Iris Murdoch, *The Fire and the Sun,* 1977

> ... showed his expertise at civil service —Joseph Wambaugh, *The Black Marble,* 1978

> ... the very model of musical comedy expertise — Martin Gottfried, *Saturday Rev.,* 15 Apr. 1978

> ... despite the bluegrass expertise McCoy has gained —Larry Rhodes, *Bluegrass Unlimited,* January 1981

> ... the professionalism and increasing expertise of nurses today —Laurie Repchull, *Health Care,* 14 June 1982

Because it is both highly popular and fairly new, *expertise* is susceptible to criticism as a vogue word, and a number of commentators have called it one. Harper 1985 suggests that it "may well fall into disuse," but our growing collection of evidence for it suggests the process has not begun yet. It is equally possible that the voices of criticism will themselves eventually die out, as it becomes increasingly obvious that *expertise* is here to stay.

exposé   *Exposé* has been used in English since the early 19th century. Of its various applications in current English, the most common is in describing a journalistic work in which something disreputable is revealed:

> ... an angry, often emotional exposé —Joyce Milton, *Saturday Rev.,* June 1980

> ... a hard-hitting, arresting exposé of the horrific conditions of America's penal institutions —Mel Watkins, *N.Y. Times Book Rev.,* 11 Dec. 1983

> ... the thousandth exposé of life under Communism —William F. Buckley, Jr., *N.Y. Times Book Rev.,* 8 July 1984

As Copperud 1980 notes, *exposé* has occasionally been criticized as a needless synonym for *exposition* or *expo-*

sure, but its connotations and uses are in general distinct from those of the longer words. You should feel no hesitation about using it.

Exposé can be written either with or without an acute accent:

> ... an exposé of female oppression —Daniel Seligman, *Fortune,* 29 Dec. 1980

> ... this particular expose is a bit of a revelation — Walter McVitty, *Nation Rev.* (Melbourne), 15 May 1975

Both forms are widely used. The accented form is the more common of the two, perhaps because it clearly indicates how the word is pronounced, \ˌek-spō-ˈzā\.

expressive   When it takes a prepositional-phrase complement, *expressive* is used with *of:*

> ... her stiff back and neck eloquently expressive of outraged innocence —Thomas Wolfe, *You Can't Go Home Again,* 1940

expresso   See ESPRESSO, EXPRESSO.

exquisite   In a 1926 issue of *American Speech,* we read the following admonition:

> Another word by which social reputations rise and fall is *exquisite.* Here the ante-penultimate accent is the hall-mark of linguistic propriety; the penultimate accent gives the signal for the ejection to an outer social limbo. On his own head, therefore, be the fate of him who ventures to say that anything is *exquis'-ite* —John L. Haney, *American Speech,* April 1926

Similar advice, in less awesome tones, is offered by later usage writers.

Half a century later, educated speakers of English remain unimpressed: second-syllable stress in *exquisite* is as widespread as initial stress. It is not clear what the basis of the objection to \ek-ˈskwiz-ət\ is; for what it may be worth, the word comes from Latin *exquīsītus,* with both *i*'s long.

extemporaneous, impromptu   If you have ever taken a class in public speaking, you have probably been taught to distinguish between these adjectives. Teachers of speech will tell you that an extemporaneous speech is one that has been thoroughly prepared and planned but not memorized, so that the exact words used by the speaker are chosen as the speech is actually being made. An impromptu speech is distinguished as a speech for which the speaker has made no preparations—a genuinely spur-of-the-moment, off-the-cuff speech. This distinction undoubtedly has value in discussing different types of speeches, but it is not strictly observed in general usage. *Extemporaneous* in its oldest sense is simply synonymous with *impromptu,* and its use in describing off-the-cuff remarks is common and correct:

> ... the ready wit of a detective who has had to resort to extemporaneous prevarications on numerous occasions —Erle Stanley Gardner, *The Case of the Stuttering Bishop,* 1936

> ... asked him to reminisce.... He responded eagerly and delivered a four-minute extemporaneous recollection —*New Republic,* 11 July 1955

But the distinction does have some existence outside the speech classroom. *Extemporaneous* is also used to describe a prepared speech given without notes or text, while *impromptu* is almost always used in describing speech that is truly unprepared:

> He spoke without a note, and he is a superb extemporaneous speaker —*New Republic,* 16 June 1952

> It might be misleading to say that these Churchill talks were "impromptu"—for it is doubtful that he was ever unprepared for a speech —Robert Sherwood, *Roosevelt and Hopkins,* 1948

extended Used as an adjective, *extended* often has the sense, "notably long; prolonged, lengthy":

> . . . went on an extended vacation —*Current Biography,* October 1965

> . . . even after extended exposure to mirrors —Gordon G. Gallup, Jr., *Psychology Today,* March 1971

> . . . had been to Europe on an extended trip —Gail Cameron, *Ladies' Home Jour.,* August 1971

This sense is both old and respectable, but two recent commentators (Flesch 1964 and Copperud 1970, 1980) have expressed disapproval of it, regarding it as, at best, a poor substitute for *long.* We see little basis for such an opinion, and the usage is, in any case, clearly standard in the examples above and many others in our files.

extension The spelling *extention* was once a respectable variant of *extension,* but it fell into disuse several centuries ago. It occurs now only as an occasional error:

> . . . the line of extention of the range —*Science and Culture,* May 1941

> . . . the southern extention of the new road —*Country Quest* (Wrexham, Wales), July 1975

extract When the verb *extract* is used with a preposition, the choice is almost always *from:*

> He seemed to extract a vicious enjoyment from her reaction —Harry Hervey, *Barracoon,* 1950

Extract has also been used with *out of* for several hundred years, but in our century this use has been sporadic:

> May it be possible, that foreign hire Could out of thee extract one spark of evil? —Shakespeare, *Henry V,* 1599

> . . . its captain resolved to extract the uttermost fare out of every refugee he took to London —H. G. Wells, *Mr. Britling Sees It Through,* 1916

exuberance, exuberant The same spelling error that occurs with *exorbitant* also occurs with *exuberance* and *exuberant*—an *h* slips in unobtrusively following the *x:*

> He has an exhuberance, and abounding interest in good living —*The Californian,* Fall 1952

> . . . the exhuberant clapping and backslapping —*Automation, Education and Human Values,* 1966

Watch out for that *h.*

exude *Exude,* when used with a preposition, is usually used with *from:*

> . . . oil exudes from discrete openings that are typically 0.5 cm in diameter —Alan A. Allen et al., *Science,* 27 Nov. 1970

> . . . Mr. Stryver, exuding patronage of the most offensive quality from every pore —Charles Dickens, *A Tale of Two Cities,* 1859

F

fabulous A number of commentators disparage the weakened sense of *fabulous,* in which it becomes a sort of generalized word of approval. Given the taste of English speakers and writers for hyperbole, such a development seems inevitable. With a little care you can still use the word in a heightened sense, pregnant with the notion of being worthy of fable or legend. But the word carries the germ of its own weakening, as you may notice in these examples:

> His manner was very much that of a man who has sailed strange seas and seen . . . the fabulous buried cache of forgotten pirates' plundering —Thomas Wolfe, *You Can't Go Home Again,* 1940

> The fabulous Jerry O'Shaugnessy, thinks Sam. In the old days, in the Party, they had made a legend of him —Norman Mailer, *Advertisements for Myself,* 1959

> . . . a man fabulous, rather than famous, in many of the diplomatic and social salons of the Europe of his day —George F. Kennan, *New Yorker,* 1 May 1971

> . . . tons upon tons of good winter wheat and other supplies were sent in fabulous quantities —Katherine Anne Porter, *The Never-Ending Wrong,* 1977

> . . . recall how thirty-six years ago Hitler dominated the Olympic Games and turned them into such a fabulous propaganda success —William L. Shirer, *Saturday Rev.,* 25 Mar. 1972

> . . . the voice of a man divulging fabulous professional secrets —Roald Dahl, *Someone Like You,* 1953

> . . . her final fabulous success as a real estate magnate —James Purdy, *Cabot Wright Begins,* 1964

faced When *faced* is used adjectivally with a preposition, it is usually *with:*

> . . . a federal system faced with the challenges of a militant civil-rights movement —James Q. Wilson, *Commentary,* January 1972

In the sense specific to having covered the front or surface of something, *faced* is used equally with *with* or *in:*

> . . . an enormous foyer faced with marble —Eleanor Munro, *Saturday Rev.,* 24 July 1976

> . . . insisting that the house be faced entirely in the native Virginia beige fieldstone —Robert A. Caro, *Atlantic,* November 1982

face up to *Face up,* which is almost always followed by *to,* is considered to be an Americanism and has been soundly belabored by British critics going back to Partridge 1942 and Ivor Brown 1945; Copperud 1970, 1980 also mentions Lord Conesford, who found many things to dislike in American English shortly after World War II. The apparent spur to comment was the growing use of the expression in British English:

> . . . he could face up to the fact that Ernest was not everybody's cup of tea —Nevil Shute, *Most Secret,* 1945

> . . . we should bury the past in its entirety, and face up exclusively to the present —*Horizon,* November 1945

> Judaism today must face up to such problems — Raphael Lowe, *London Calling,* 25 Mar. 1954

> . . . not facing up to life —Angus Macleod, *New Statesman & Nation,* 26 Dec. 1953

The general thrust of British criticism is that the *up to* is superfluous, since *face* says it all. This charge is rebutted by Bernstein 1965, Copperud, and Harper 1975, 1985. In general, then, American commentators defend the phrase and British commentators denigrate it.

The claim that the phrase is an Americanism is made on doubtful grounds. The earliest attestation of it is from an Oxford professor, Sir Walter Raleigh, who used it in a letter dated 4 September 1920. The citation is given in the OED Supplement and in Foster 1968. Foster says that Raleigh had been in the United States before 1920, and assumes he picked up the phrase here. The assumption may well be true, but printed American evidence for *face up to* does not appear in our files until 1924, 1926, and 1927, and the OED Supplement has British examples from 1925 and 1935 too. The phrase was apparently making progress on both sides of the Atlantic at the same time.

Face up to is common in American English:

> . . . how a British family faced up to the dark realities of the war —Allan Nevins, *Saturday Rev.,* 20 Sept. 1941

> It faces up frankly to Russia's known opposition — Adlai E. Stevenson, *Saturday Rev.,* 28 Feb. 1953

> I wanted to get her to face up to what would happen —Claude Brown, *Manchild in the Promised Land,* 1965

> Custine finally faced up to this situation —George F. Kennan, *New Yorker,* 1 May 1971

> Movies and songs about growing up and facing up —Richard Corliss, *Apartment Life,* July 1980

British use seems to have continued unabated in spite of the critics. It is interesting to compare these examples two decades apart:

> . . . though it could be wished that the author had not been so "genuinely bilingual" as to adopt with enthusiasm the phrase "facing up to" —*Times Literary Supp.,* 16 Dec. 1949

> The British educational establishment did not on the whole face up to the Hegelian-Marxist challenge — *Times Literary Supp.,* 5 Mar. 1970

facilitate Fowler 1926 said that only things could be facilitated and that an example he had in which police officers were facilitated was "a slipshod extension." Fowler is wrong on style but right in substance. *Facilitate* with a personal direct object is attested in the OED from the 17th to the 19th centuries; Fowler found it in the 20th. It is, however, a rare use; it is almost always a thing that is facilitated.

Flesch 1964 and Zinsser 1976 disparage *facilitate* where *ease* would do (Flesch would also allow *help*). The shorter word, though, is not always the automatic choice. Neither *ease* nor *help* would convey the full intended meaning in these examples:

> . . . a practice facilitated, once the war broke out, by the blackout —William L. Shirer, *The Rise and Fall of the Third Reich,* 1960

> . . . smallpox, which decimated tribes in what was to be New England at the start of the 17th century and facilitated the first European settlements there — William S. McFeely, *N.Y. Times Book Rev.,* 14 Aug. 1983

> Mr. Archer facilitates his own task of destruction, and avoids offending popular opinion, by making an exception of Shakespeare —T. S. Eliot, "Four Elizabethan Dramatists," in *Selected Essays,* 1932

> . . . the World Bank concentrated on facilitating loans and investment —*Current Biography,* July 1965

Simple solutions are not always good solutions, and monosyllabic words are not always the best words.

fact 1. Quite a few phrases built around *fact—the fact that, in point of fact,* and *the fact is,* for example—are attacked in various handbooks as wordy deadwood. They undoubtedly are in many cases. What few commentators seem to notice, however, is that such phrases serve just as often to help the writer get a sentence organized or make an awkward transition. Try deleting or replacing the *fact* phrase in these examples and see if you have improved things or not:

> We might as well get used to the fact that no head of state down there can stay in office without a policy of nationalizing foreign holdings —James M. Garvin, *Center Report,* June 1972

> The fact is not that officials do uniquely badly but that they are uniquely vulnerable —Gowers 1948

> And the fact seems to be that it needed just one more book to clinch my business —Robert Frost, letter, 17 Sept. 1914

> The plain fact is that the President is not really a very good politician —Stewart Alsop, *Atlantic,* February 1972

> Although Al Capone was easily the best-known gangster of his own or any other time, he was in point of fact rather a parochial figure —Joseph Epstein, *Commentary,* January 1972

> Our newfound fascination with China should not blind us to the fact that American relations with Japan are much more important to U.S. security — Leslie H. Gelb & Morton H. Halperin, *Harper's,* November 1971

I can see no reason why the fact that Mr. Kallman and I have been close friends for over thirty years should debar me from reviewing him —W. H. Auden, *Harper's,* March 1972

We're not constantly made aware of the fact that the writer understands what he's talking about — Kingsley Amis, quoted in *The Writer's Place,* ed. Peter Firchow, 1974

Apart, however, from the fact that he was a younger son . . . —P. G. Wodehouse, *Something Fresh,* 1915

We are not recommending that you plug these phrases into every other paragraph; like any verbal tic they can grow annoying. But you should be aware that they can secure a needed emphasis, effect a smooth transition, or otherwise make themselves useful stylistically. They are not always superfluous.

2. See TRUE FACTS.

fact that   See FACT 1.

factor   Most of the criticism that *factor* is imprecise or vague suffers from exactly the same fault—it is imprecise and vague. Prentice Hall 1978 even calls it "wordy"—how does a six-letter, two-syllable word get to be "wordy"? We are also told that the word is overworked, and this criticism has greater validity. A few commentators will allow *factor* to be used for "a cause contributing to a result"—one of about eight senses in Webster's Ninth New Collegiate Dictionary. Some of the "more precise" words that *factor* displaces are *consideration, circumstance, characteristic, constituent, component, ingredient*—all of them obviously longer and windier.

Let's test these criticisms on an example:

But such factors as Reid's youth at the time of his crime, his slum background, his marginal mentality, had caused Wright . . . to feel that execution would be an injustice —William Styron, *This Quiet Dust and Other Writings,* 1982

Now, what are these factors? *Contributing causes* to the crime? *Mitigating circumstances?* Simply *considerations* that the judge is taking into account? Or perhaps all of these at once? If we substitute any of these more precise terms, do we then improve the sentence, or do we simply add syllables and lose part of the meaning carried by *factors?*

Contributing factor is criticized in a few books as a redundancy. As *factor* is a word of several senses, the addition of *contributing* may serve to narrow the word's focus or to set off less significant from more significant factors; the question of redundancy in such contexts is irrelevant. The main consideration may often be whether the sentence sounds better with or without *contributing.*

It looks like the criticism of *factor* started as a reaction to a noticeable increase in its use, perhaps around the time of World War II, and most of what we see now are the original criticisms rehashed. Trimble 1975 seems dated in its remark, "Doesn't it have a lovely scientific ring to it?" No more. *Factor* is old hat. *Parameter* is a much flashier word.

We think it is perfectly all right to use *factor* in favor of any of those longer, "more precise" substitutes. But remember that *factor* is a well-worked word; you should not beat it to death.

faculty   *Faculty* has several senses that relate to the world of academics. The British use it chiefly to denote a particular branch of learning in an educational institution, as in "the Faculty of Philosophy," which in the U.S. would be "the Department of Philosophy." *Faculty* in American English most often serves as a collective noun meaning "the teaching and administrative staff in an educational institution":

Most of the faculty . . . does not favor or see as possible any such ambitious role for the university — Nathan Glazer, *American Scholar,* Spring 1967

But *faculty* is also used in the U.S. as a plural having the sense "faculty members." This use of *faculty* was first recorded in 1843:

That was all I could ever get from him on the subject—'that the Faculty were funny fellows . . .' — *Yale Literary Mag.* (OED Supplement)

Evidence of its common occurrence in writing was a long time coming, however. We at Merriam-Webster came across it only in 1953:

. . . her feeling that the faculty of her school are persecuting her —Wolcott Gibbs, *New Yorker,* 3 Jan. 1953

The military faculty desire to teach their subjects well —Harold W. Dodds, *Atlantic,* March 1953

And we did not encounter it frequently until the 1960s:

Faculty from many colleges and disciplines are participating —*AAUP Bulletin,* September 1965

. . . its appeal is strong enough to attract many faculty —Paul Potter, *Johns Hopkins Mag.,* October 1965

. . . not all faculty even yet concur in this resolve — Nathan M. Pusey, *President's Report, Harvard University,* 1968–1969

This plural use of *faculty* has drawn the disapproval of several commentators. Follett 1966, for one, considers it tantamount to saying "three army" instead of "three army men." It continues to be common, however, and has clearly established a secure place for itself in the language of academics. If you dislike it, use "faculty members" or "teachers" instead.

fail   **1.** As late as Jensen 1935 some commentators were still proscribing the transitive uses "to be unsuccessful in passing" and "to grade (as a student) as not passing." These uses appeared in the early 20th century and became widespread in the 1940s and 1950s. Although they have not supplanted the corresponding intransitive senses of fail, the transitive uses are now firmly established and occur more often:

'Got through all right, sir?' For all answer I dropped a half-crown into his soft broad palm. 'Well,' says he . . . , 'I never knew him keep any of you gentlemen so long. He failed two second mates this morning before your turn came. . . .' —Joseph Conrad, *Chance,* 1913

An applicant upon failing any prescribed theoretical examination may reapply —Charles A. Zweng, *Parachute Technician,* 1944

... students who ... might have failed it altogether if I had graded them in rhetoric —Alfred Whitney Griswold, *Essays on Education,* 1954

... European schools ... fail a large percentage of their students —James B. Conant, *Slums and Suburbs,* 1961

... it was disclosed that the race horse ... had failed his fertility test —Richard Haitch, *N.Y. Times,* 10 Oct. 1976

2. Some commentators, among them Copperud 1964, 1970, 1980 and Flesch 1964, say that the verb *fail* should be used only when an attempt of some sort is involved. Bernstein 1965, 1971 and Bremner 1980 are somewhat less restrictive, allowing *fail* to be used when an obligation or expectation is not met. But all disapprove the use of *fail* as a sort of general-purpose negative. They are fighting for a lost cause, nonetheless, for the use is established:

One might question the wisdom of a man who made two trips to Spain and failed to visit the Escorial — *Times Literary Supp.,* 19 Feb. 1971

Into that intimate and loose little society of the garrison Stella and Robert both gravitated, and having done so could hardly fail to meet —Elizabeth Bowen, *The Heat of the Day,* 1949

... those who failed to see that pain is as necessary morally as it undoubtedly is biologically —Havelock Ellis, *The Dance of Life,* 1923

... neither of the great powers can conceivably fail to fear such a conflict —Noam Chomsky, *Columbia Forum,* Winter 1969

For a few weeks, he trailed around after his unit, buttoned into an uncomfortable uniform ... but he obviously failed to enjoy it, and soon gave it up — George F. Kennan, *New Yorker,* 1 May 1971

3. When *fail* is used with a preposition, the construction often involves *to* and the infinitive:

Amy ... had criminally failed to latch the streetdoor of the parlour —Arnold Bennett, *The Old Wives' Tale,* 1908

If Glasgow as a city should fail to interest the visitor —L. Dudley Stamp, *The Face of Britain,* rev. ed., 1944

He had a genius for explosive statements that rarely failed to startle his hearers —Dwight D. Eisenhower, *Crusade in Europe,* 1948

... that one-horse teachers' college whose recruiter failed to sway me thirty years ago —Tom Wicker, *Change,* September 1971

Fail is also used with *of,* but this use was more frequent up through the 1950s than it has been since:

... all these things Gale turned over and over in his mind, only to fail of any definite conclusion —Zane Grey, *Desert Gold,* 1913

... voters by the million could not fail of having some effect upon public affairs —Gerald W. Johnson, *Our English Heritage,* 1949

... since no love affair's wild heart lets itself be netted in words, this chronicle of a passion may fail of effect —Clifton Fadiman, *Holiday,* July 1957

A lottery bill, for which King voted, failed of passage —*Current Biography,* May 1964

Fail is also sometimes used with *in* or *at:*

He had originally intended to become a mathematician, but after failing in calculus, he decided ... to turn to history —*Current Biography 1951*

Many men are almost as afraid of abandonment, of failing in marriage —Germaine Greer, *McCall's,* March 1971

He sold the farm to become an architect, at which he failed —Donald Hogan, *Harper's,* January 1972

... an incoherent tale of a brilliant scapegrace who had deliberately failed at school —Herman Wouk, *Marjorie Morningstar,* 1955

Occasionally, *fail* is found with *as, by, for, from, on,* or *with:*

The one piece in the collection which fails as a short story —Robert Kiely, *N.Y. Times Book Rev.,* 3 June 1973

... speculation about the lives of Ross Lockridge Jr. and Thomas Heggen, two writers failed by success — *N.Y. Times Book Rev.,* 25 Aug. 1974

How could he fail the centuries behind him for what might not live more than a few years? —Sheila Kaye-Smith, *The End of the House of Alard,* 1923

... this enterprise failed from lack of capital —*Dictionary of American Biography,* 1928

... he falls for the Hollywood fleshpots, drinks too much, fails on his deadlines —Anthony Burgess, *Saturday Rev.,* July 1981

He turns then to Delphine, and with her he does not fail —E. K. Brown, *Rhythm in the Novel,* 1950

fallacy Gowers in Fowler 1965, set off by an example of "a fallacious report," explains at some length what a fallacy in logic is; Bernstein 1965 likewise describes a logical fallacy; Macmillan 1982 would also restrict the word to logic. Copperud 1970, 1980 says that dictionary definitions bear out these restrictive views.

But dictionaries do not, in fact, bear out the restrictions; the OED shows that *fallacy* has never been restricted to reasoning and logic—the logicians' use is but one of several senses of the word. Explanation of what a fallacy is in logic may be of interest in itself but is simply irrelevant to the question of English usage. Here are some examples that dictionary definitions are based on:

... warn biographical critics against the fallacy of supposing that Browning's reserve was weakness — *Times Literary Supp.,* 19 Feb. 1971

The arguments of the Federalist are intended to prove the fallacy of these apprehensions —John Marshall, *McCulloch v. Maryland,* 1819

That is a statement which, I believe, physicists accept almost as a truism, and philosophers generally condemn as a hoary fallacy —Sir Arthur Eddington, *New Pathways in Science,* 1935

It is a common fallacy that a writer, if he is talented enough, can achieve this poignant quality by improving upon his subject-matter —Willa Cather, *Not Under Forty,* 1936

One of the fallacies most widely believed about the academic world is that practically everything has been done in the way of elucidation of the past — Wilmarth Sheldon Lewis, *Yale Rev.,* Spring 1947

Such a picture of him is not, I believe, a true description of Stalin's sense of identity, although I cannot claim the fallacy to have been demonstrated —Robert C. Tucker, *Saturday Rev.,* 8 Jan. 1972

Parents also console themselves by the American fallacy that one can only be young once —Elizabeth Bowen, *Punch,* 19 Aug. 1953

Fallacy is neither originally nor primarily a term in logic.

false comparison *False comparison* is a name used by a few commentators (such as Johnson 1982, Copperud 1970, 1980) for a writer's careless omission of a word or two that would make a comparison perfectly clear and logical—"carrying ellipsis too far," Copperud calls it. Handbooks sometimes treat it as a variety of *illogical comparison* or *incomplete comparison.* This is a rather insignificant mistake in terms of its hindrance of communication, because readers tend to go right past such false comparisons without even noticing them. Here are a couple of examples of the fault from a writer of impeccable credentials, with the probable missing words supplied in brackets:

> ... in many counties Negroes outnumber whites in a ratio resembling [that in] parts of Alabama and Mississippi —William Styron, *This Quiet Dust and Other Writings,* 1982

> ... that fine and funny book, in which horror and laughter are commingled like [in] the beginning of a scream —William Styron, *This Quiet Dust and Other Writings,* 1982

From these and the examples in Johnson and Copperud it appears that *in* is often the word or one of the words omitted in false comparison. There are, however, others (see ANY 3, AS GOOD OR BETTER THAN). We think that you can see from the examples how easily the construction slips by. But even if readers are not likely to be often puzzled by false comparisons, we think it is a good idea for you to try to avoid them.

false titles This is Copperud's term for what Bernstein calls "coined titles" and Safire calls "bogus titling"—the journalistic practice of placing descriptive terms in front of a person's name in a news story: "globe-trotting diplomat Henry Kissinger" or "consumer advocate Ralph Nader." Copperud and Bernstein associate the practice with *Time* magazine, which probably popularized the practice if it did not invent it. Copperud 1964, 1970, 1980 and Bernstein 1958, 1965 find the practice distasteful—apparently many newspaper stylebooks object to it. Safire 1980 notes how these descriptors tend to be regularly attached to particular names. Newman 1974 amuses himself to some length by pretending that they are first names. The practice also exists in British journalism; it is noted by Sellers 1975 as "*Time*-style adjectives" and in a review of a book on the tabloid press in the *Times Literary Supplement* (22 May 1981) as "the attributive queue."

The practice seems to show no sign of waning (Cop-

perud gives twice as much space to it in 1980 as he did in 1970) and at any rate presents no problem of understanding to the reader. The practice probably derives its appeal from the compact way in which it identifies people for the reader.

If you're not a journalist, you need never worry about it in your writing. Examples such as this are highly unlikely outside of journalism:

> ... candidate for a Ph.D. under famed New Left philosopher Herbert Marcuse —Marcia Gillespie & Ronald Van Downing, *Essence,* November 1970

famed *Famed* has been aspersed by some commentators (Bernstein 1965, Flesch 1964, Copperud 1964, Fennell 1980, Watt 1967, Ebbitt & Ebbitt 1982) as journalese; Zinsser 1976 associates it with *Time* magazine. But the OED tells a different story: the first journalist listed there is Shakespeare. The OED also has examples from Sir Richard Steele, George Washington, Lord Byron, and Nathaniel Hawthorne. Webster's Second has a quotation from Milton. With these important literary sources, it is no wonder that dictionaries recognize *famed* as standard. *Famous* may be more often used, but that does not mean everyone must use *famous.*

> And when you find him evenly deriv'd
> From his most fam'd of famous ancestors,
> Edward the Third ...
>   —Shakespeare, *Henry V,* 1600

> Like those Hesperian gardens, famed of old —John Milton, *Paradise Lost,* 1667

In present-day use *famed* is both a predicate adjective, often with *for,* and an attributive adjective.

> Denver, once famed for its clear mountain air, is now subject to smog —Barry Commoner, *Columbia Forum,* Spring 1968

> ... Harold's famed Reno gambling casino —Bennett Cerf, *Saturday Rev.,* 22 May 1954

Famed is perfectly standard, even if it has been used by *Time:*

> ... Ruskin's famed friend, Painter Sir John Millais —*Time,* 29 Dec. 1947

familiar The usual prepositions used with *familiar* when it is a predicate adjective are *with* and *to;* someone is *familiar with* something, and someone or something is *familiar to* someone.

> His older black colleagues, more familiar with administrative procedures —David M. Rafky, *Change,* October 1971

> It is in this way that we become familiar with a language —Gerald Durrell, *My Family and Other Animals,* 1956

> ... this breeze, so familiar to her because of its nearly predictable comings and goings —William Styron, *Lie Down in Darkness,* 1951

> ... the Poles are familiar to him as a people involved for centuries in Russian affairs —*Times Literary Supp.,* 9 Apr. 1970

Once in a while *from* identifies a source of familiarity:

> ... traditional commercial patterns familiar from the American past —Harvey Wheeler, *Center Report,* June 1972

farther, further About every usage commentator in the 20th century—from Vizetelly 1906 to Trimmer & McCrimmon 1988—has had something to say about *farther* and *further* (and sometimes *farthest* and *furthest*) as to how they should be used or how they seem to be used. Only a few venture beyond Vizetelly's original pronouncement:

> *Farther* should be used to designate longitudinal distance; *further* to signify quantity or degree.

Vizetelly's dictum did not account for the educated usage of his own time or for that of the past, and it has only partially predicted usage since his time.

Farther and *further* are historically the same word, so it is not surprising that the two have long been used more or less interchangeably. *Further* is the older of the two; it appears to have originated as the comparative form of a Germanic ancestor of English *forth*. *Farther* originated in Middle English as a variant of *further* that was influenced by the comparative (spelled *ferre*) of *far* (then spelled *fer*) which it (and *further*) eventually replaced. So neither word was originally connected with *far*, but gradually they have both become so.

Henry Bradley, editor of the *F* volume of the OED (published in 1897), summed up what he considered standard English practice at the time. He said that *farther* is usually preferred as the comparative of *far*, that *further* was used where the notion of *far* was absent, and that there was a large intermediate class of uses in which the choice between the two was arbitrary. Fowler 1926 disagreed, seeing Bradley's description as more theoretical than actual. Fowler believed that most people did not use both terms, as they would have to do if they followed Bradley's scheme; most people made do with one or the other and the one Fowler saw as usual was *further*. He therefore opined that *further* would eventually replace *farther* altogether. So far it has not.

What Fowler probably saw was that *farther*'s range of application was shrinking. This development seems to be part of a process of differentiation—a process Fowler thought would end in the demise of *farther*. The differentiation is most noticeable—most nearly complete—when *farther* and *further* are used as adjectives.

As adjectives, both words could at one time be used in the sense "additional":

> . . . I have now no farther thought of danger —Thomas Gray, letter, 12 Sept. 1756

> You will e'er long I suppose receive further intelligence of him —Jane Austen, letter, 11 Feb. 1801

> . . . in that delightful state when farther beauty is known to be at hand —Jane Austen, *Mansfield Park,* 1814

> He became aware that Mr. Jackson was clearing his throat preparatory to farther revelations —Edith Wharton, *The Age of Innocence,* 1920

But in present-day English *further* has taken over this function entirely:

> "Well," he began, without any further greeting —Katherine Anne Porter, *Ladies' Home Jour.,* August 1971

> . . . a further volume of uncollected essays —Peter Stansky, *N.Y. Times Book Rev.,* 1 June 1975

> . . . no further deliveries of military equipment —Chester Bowles, *Saturday Rev.,* 6 Nov. 1971

> . . . hums like a tuning fork between all these fainter and further thoughts —William H. Gass, *Harper's,* February 1984

Farther has been relegated as an adjective to instances where either literal or figurative distance is involved:

> The farther floe was pulling away in the grip of the tide —Berton Roueché, *New Yorker,* 22 Oct. 1966

> . . . at the farthest remove imaginable from regional writing —Ivan Gold, *N.Y. Times Book Rev.,* 24 Apr. 1983

And even in this function *further* is presenting formidable competition:

> The Viking settlements had cut greater Northumbria in two, and the further part had fallen under the influence of the Celtic Highland powers —Frank Barlow, *The Feudal Kingdom of England 1042–1216,* 3d ed., 1972

> . . . it was the furthest thing from everyone's mind —E. L. Doctorow, *Loon Lake,* 1979

> . . . the furthest point west that Columbus reached —Graham Greene, *Getting to Know the General,* 1984

So for the adjective we can see that *further* has squeezed *farther* out of the "additional" sense and is giving it considerable pressure in the "more distant" sense. Fowler would probably see this situation as confirming his prediction that *further* would eventually win out.

As adverbs, *farther* and *further* are less well differentiated. Differentiation is most nearly complete in the "degree" sense, where there is no notion of distance. This is the use that OED editor Bradley said *further* was preferred for. We can find *farther* in this sense, but our examples are getting a bit old:

> . . . without consulting farther with any soul living —Laurence Sterne, *Tristram Shandy,* 1759

> Please see to it that I do not have to act any farther in the matter —Bernard DeVoto, letter, 7 June 1943

Further is now the usual choice, as Bradley predicted:

> DeGaulle's violent remarks . . . further strained relations —Stephen E. Ambrose, *Johns Hopkins Mag.,* April 1966

> Before she could protest further they had seized her arms and were marching her down to the boat —Daphne du Maurier, *Ladies' Home Jour.,* August 1971

> . . . I recommend that you have nothing further to do with this person nor with these arms transfers —Robert C. McFarlane, quoted in *The Tower Commission Report,* 1987

Further is also used as a sentence adverb; *farther* is not.

> Further, I am monolingual and have no way of knowing whether a translation is faithful to the original —E. B. White, letter, 13 May 1957

> I am certain, further, that she has known it could come about in just such a form —Peter Taylor, *The Old Forest and Other Stories,* 1985

But when spatial, temporal, or metaphorical distance is involved, *farther* is still thriving, *pace* Fowler's prediction:

> ... too tired, too unhappy to go farther —Bernard Malamud, *The Magic Barrel,* 1958

> ... irrigate a million acres of dry land farther downstream —John Lear, *Saturday Rev.,* 6 Nov. 1971

> I asked how much farther it was to Dublin —Renata Adler, *Pitch Dark,* 1983

> Farther along, the obese gypsy Madame Katrinka beckons you to enter her storefront parlor —Jay McInerney, *Bright Lights, Big City,* 1984

> Statecraft was his business, and he knew more and saw farther than they did —James A. Williamson, *The Tudor Age,* 1964

> ... has taken the effect one step farther —Susan Kenney, *N.Y. Times Book Rev.,* 26 Jan. 1986

> Cod, he pointed out, is farther down in the food chain —Garrison Keillor, *Lake Wobegon Days,* 1985

> Nothing could be farther from the truth —Godfrey Hodgson, *N.Y. Times Book Rev.,* 30 Jan. 1983

But *further* is giving *farther* plenty of competition for the same uses:

> He could not only walk further but he walked faster —Mordecai Richler, *The Apprenticeship of Duddy Kravitz,* 1959

> ... he moved on to spread despondency further — Graham Greene, *Travels with My Aunt,* 1969

> ... 300 miles further down the river —Noel Perrin, *N.Y. Times Book Rev.,* 6 Sept. 1981

> I park my car in a better spot, further from the curve —Renata Adler, *Pitch Dark,* 1983

> ... but he got no further than Portland —Gerald Weales, *Smithsonian,* December 1985

> ... ranged still further back to Saxon and British times —John Butt, *English Literature in the Mid-Eighteenth Century,* edited & completed by Geoffrey Carnall, 1979

> But Messrs. Lindblom and Cohen go further. They suggest that ... —Andrew Hacker, *N.Y. Times Book Rev.,* 29 July 1979

> ... put us one step further on the road to a police state —*I. F. Stone's Bi-Weekly,* 9 Feb. 1970

So in adverbial use *further* dominates when there is no sense of distance and as a sentence adverb, but both *farther* and *further* are in flourishing use whenever spatial, temporal, or metaphorical distance is involved.

Fowler would be pleased to discover that *further* is more commonly attested than *farther* in our recent files and in the Brown University corpus (Kučera & Francis, 1967). Fowler's prediction of the demise of *farther* has come true only in certain uses, however. *Further* has all but eclipsed *farther* in adjective use, with *farther* competing only for a portion of the "more distant" use. *Further* has pretty well eliminated the adverbial *farther* from non-distance uses, and it has the sentence adverb function all to itself. But both forms are in vigorous

competition in the adverbial distance uses. Fowler's prediction may be more accurate for British usage than it is for American; the British evidence in our files shows *further* more common than *farther* in all senses.

farthest See FARTHER, FURTHER.

fascinated Some language commentators, Bernstein 1965 and Phythian 1979 among them, have noted that when *fascinated* is used with a preposition, *by* is limited to a human fascinator, while *with* signals a nonhuman fascinator. Our evidence shows that the situation is not so simple. First off, *fascinated* is more often used with *by* than with any other preposition, and *by* can take as its object either a human or nonhuman fascinator:

> Alice began to be fascinated by her, and to wonder what she was thinking about —George Bernard Shaw, *Cashel Byron's Profession,* 1886

> ... I continued to be fascinated by the Senator and especially his two assistants —Ernest Hemingway, "African Journal," 1956

> She was at once fascinated and repelled by the disclosures —Herman Wouk, *Marjorie Morningstar,* 1955

> The truth is that in common with most of us, he is fascinated by pornography —Norman Mailer, *Advertisements for Myself,* 1959

Used less frequently, *fascinated with* does seem to occur only when something nonhuman is indicated:

> ... a more general German tendency to be fascinated with power —Talcott Parsons, *Psychiatry,* February 1945

> The male, of course, has long been fascinated with combat —Vance Packard, *The Sexual Wilderness,* 1968

Nonhuman objects are also the rule in the scattered examples we have of the use of *fascinated* with *at, in, over,* or *to* and the infinitive:

> He was fascinated at the thought of what the day meant to Grant —Sherwood Anderson, *Poor White,* 1920

> ... he became fascinated in the detailed lineaments of what he claimed to find oppressive —Richard Poirier, *A World Elsewhere,* 1966

> He can become more fascinated over the fact that a stream is named "Donner and Blitzen River" — Richard L. Neuberger, *N.Y. Times,* 27 July 1952

> I was fascinated to hear Mr. Harrington equate power with the status quo —Henry Steele Commager, *Center Mag.,* July/August 1971

fascination 1. As near as can be determined, the sense of *fascination* meaning "the state of being fascinated" was first entered in dictionaries in the closing years of the 19th century: first the Century Dictionary (1889), then Webster 1890, then the OED (1897). Not long after, language critics took to admonishing against this use of *fascination.* MacCracken & Sandison 1917 had this to offer:

> To say "I've always *had a fascination for* Becky Sharp" means "I have always fascinated Becky

Sharp." A bewitching person *exercises a fascination on* or *over* (more colloquially, *has a fascination for*) the person who is charmed.

Despite the disapprobation of some critics, this sense of the word remained in use, and a definition of it was carried through into Webster's Second 1934. At about this same time use of the sense in print began to increase, and it became widespread particularly during the 1950s. Hence, by the time Webster's Third was published in 1961, this sense of *fascination* was in very common use:

> ... an extreme example of James's fascination by brutality and violence —John Farrelly, *New Republic,* 5 July 1948

> ... his lifelong fascination for clowns and their art —*Current Biography,* June 1953

> ... his fascination with politics goes beyond his work —*Current Biography,* May 1966

Although the sense of the word is now fully established, some critics persist in warning against its use: Phythian 1979 and Barzun 1985 repeat MacCracken & Sandison's criticisms from 1917. What triggered the outcry against this use of *fascination* can only be guessed at. It is true that sometimes one cannot be quite sure what the intent of the writer is:

> I find a fascination, like the fascination for the moth of a star, in those who hold aloof and disdain me —Logan Pearsall Smith, *All Trivia,* 1934

By suggesting that we revise this use of *fascination* out of our sentences, language commentators are probably hoping to avoid the sort of puzzlement offered by Smith. The fact of the matter is, however, that most contexts in which *fascination* is used in this sense are quite straightforward. Current evidence offers no reason to avoid it, if the writer will exercise care in its application.
2. When used with a preposition, *fascination* is most often used with *for, of,* or *with:*

> ... there is a pride and fascination for them in a new love adventure —H. G. Wells, *Joan and Peter,* 1918

> He felt the strange fascination of shadowy religious places —D. H. Lawrence, *Sons and Lovers,* 1913

> ... Hunt's fascination with the mechanics and engineering of public opinion —Theodore H. White, *The Reporter,* 8 June 1954

Less often, it appears with *about, before, by,* or *in:*

> There is, however, a terrible human fascination about the miniature —Loren C. Eiseley, *Harper's,* March 1953

> ... lived in a constant dilemma between disapproval of Lucy's frivolity, and rapturous fascination before her femininity —Vita Sackville-West, *The Edwardians,* 1930

> ... an intensely strong attraction toward beauty and an equally intense fascination by the ugliness which is contrasted with it —T. S. Eliot, "Tradition and the Indvidual Talent," 1917

> There is today, among some labor bosses, the same childlike fascination in finance, in deals, in handling big chunks of money —Eric Sevareid, *The Reporter,* 18 Sept. 1958

fatal, fateful Quite a few writers on usage are at pains to distinguish between *fatal* and *fateful.* It all began when H. W. Fowler found a passage in a newspaper using *fateful* where he felt *fatal* would have been better. Fowler's OED would have told him that the sense used in the newspaper was first attested in 1764 and the sense he thought *fateful* was created for was not attested until 1800. *Fateful* seems actually to have been invented by Alexander Pope earlier in the 18th century for a meaning close to "oracular" or "prophetic." Both Pope's sense and the newspaper's "deadly" sense are uncommon in present-day English.

Fowler also made the pronouncement that *fateful* could indicate a good outcome as well as an unpleasant one. Almost all subsequent commentators repeat this part of Fowler's treatment. To it, many recent ones add a limitation on *fatal.* Perhaps the most compendious summary is that of Copperud 1980:

> *Fatal* means death-dealing, *fateful* productive of great consequences, for either good or evil.

As a description of actual usage, this is something of an oversimplification, and it especially oversimplifies the range of use of *fatal.*

Fatal is the original adjective for *fate.* It carries the usual simple relational sense: the Fates are "the fatal sisters." It also has (and has had since Chaucer's time) the sense of "involving momentous consequences, portentous" that the critics prefer to assign to *fateful.* The usual direction of this portent is toward evil, as Fowler observed:

> ... if I had been superstitiously inclined to observe days as fatal or fortunate —Daniel Defoe, *Robinson Crusoe,* 1719

> ... the constable had orders to take him into custody and lodge him in prison.... The news of *this* effectually frightened him, and he delivered up the 14 negatives ... before the fatal day arrived —Lewis Carroll, letter, 11 Nov. 1886

> Then came the fatal letter, the desolating letter — Arnold Bennett, *The Old Wives' Tale,* 1908

> ... ever since she had got back to the Vassar club that fatal morning —Mary McCarthy, *The Group,* 1963

> ... at Pearl Harbor on the fatal day —David McCullough, *Saturday Rev.,* 27 Nov. 1971

Fateful is used in about the same way:

> ... the Fuehrer actually made his fateful decision to declare war on the United States on December 9 — William L. Shirer, *The Rise and Fall of the Third Reich,* 1960

> ... the Gulf of Tonkin resolution, the fateful declaration adopted by Congress —*The Progressive,* January 1970

> Edwardian England dug the grave into which British colonialism fell in 1945, and the story of that fateful shoveling is told by Mr. Martin —Alden Whitman, *Saturday Rev.,* 6 Nov. 1971

> The fateful decision to cover up what we knew to be the true budget numbers —David A. Stockman, *Newsweek,* 28 Apr. 1986

Fateful does sometimes have at least a neutral, if not quite positive, connotation:

> ... the day when the fateful letter from the college admission office is due —James B. Conant, *Slums and Suburbs,* 1961

> It is sixty years since Mann undertook that fateful holiday in Venice ... which gave him the basic material for the novella —*Times Literary Supp.,* 30 July 1971

Fatal developed its sense "causing death, destruction, or ruin" in the 16th century. When the meaning is strictly "causing death," it is a sense not shared by *fateful:*

> Although an individual can live with just one kidney, the failure of both is fatal —Neil A. Martin, *Dun's,* October 1971

> ... demonstration had been set off by the fatal shooting of ... a prisoner —Paul Jacobs, *Center Mag.,* May 1969

> The infection of the fallopian tubes could be fatal — *Human Reproduction* (9th grade textbook), 1981

Fatal also indicates destruction or ruin, often with the notion of death commingled:

> Queen's favours might be fatal gifts, but they were much more fatal to reject than to accept —Henry Adams, *Mont-Saint-Michel and Chartres,* 1904

> He discerns a fatal flaw in the theory —Ronald Gross, *N.Y. Times Book Rev.,* 25 Mar. 1973

> ... a point of view fatal to any moral force —Katherine Anne Porter, *The Never-Ending Wrong,* 1977

> ... an error fatal to his entire scientific methodology —Patrick Gardiner, *N.Y. Rev. of Books,* 20 May 1971

Fateful has been used sporadically in this sense. It is never constructed with *to,* however, as *fatal* can be.

> He hath loosed the fateful lightning of His terrible, swift sword —Julia Ward Howe, "Battle Hymn of the Republic," 1862

And *fatal* has a weakened sense that has developed from the "causing death or destruction" sense. The OED suggests that this sense may have come from the human tendency to overstate things, to be hyperbolical.

> *Being that* is a fatal way to begin any sentence — Barzun 1985

> Natural logarithms struck the fatal blow. The day the professor broached that subject, my brain sent up a warning signal —Susan McDonald, *Hampshire Life,* 7 Feb. 1986

> Tediousness is the most fatal of all faults —Samuel Johnson, *Life of Prior,* ca. 1781

> For what he wanted as a captain seems to have been ... authority. He should have known that of all wants this is the most fatal —T. B. Macaulay, *The History of England,* vol. I, 1849

Fateful is not used in this sense. Nor is it used in the sense of *fatal* that applies to a powerful and dangerous attraction:

> ... I look forward to becoming a middle-aged sex object of fatal charms —Joan Rivers, *McCall's,* October 1971

> ... has a fatal attraction for the stalest figures of speech in the language —Joseph Lelyveld, *Saturday Rev.,* July 1980

> ... his pursuit of her fatal daughter —Robert M. Adams, *N.Y. Times Book Rev.,* 31 Mar. 1985

Fatal has the wider range of application, and is the more common of the two adjectives.

father   Use of *father* as an intransitive verb meaning "to act as a father in rearing a child" is a fairly recent development that has not been universally welcomed. Heritage 1982 reports that a majority of its usage panel disapproves *father* in this sense, perhaps because they feel that it has a jargonistic quality, or perhaps because they simply dislike its newness. It does not seem otherwise objectionable in our examples. In any case, our evidence indicates that this intransitive *father* is not especially common. When it is used, it is most likely to be in the form of the gerund, *fathering,* often in conjunction with the analogous term *mothering:*

> ... whether mothering and fathering can really be learned outside an intimate family environment — Kenneth L. Woodward, *Newsweek,* 10 June 1974

> ... provides a frank discussion of fathering in its many forms —catalog, *Harvard University Press,* 1981

fault   There have been complaints by Follett 1966, Copperud 1964, and the usage panel of Harper 1975, 1985 about the transitive use of the verb *fault* in the sense "to find fault with." A slight majority of the panel of Heritage 1969, 1982 finds it acceptable. Gowers in Fowler 1965 and Bernstein 1971 wonder what the fuss is about—the use has been around since the middle of the 16th century. It appears to have become common only in the middle of the 20th century, however, which is probably why its critics have thought it a fad. It is no fad; it is standard usage.

> ... I certainly can't fault someone who is overpowered by a collection of ... taboos —Thomas H. Middleton, *Saturday Rev.,* 11 Dec. 1976

> No one can fault the peformers in this comedy — *New Yorker,* 19 Oct. 1963

> ... and no one is to be faulted for allowing them to enter his life —Irving Howe, *Harper's,* February 1971

> It is difficult to fault this book —*Times Literary Supp.,* 29 Dec. 1972

faulty parallelism   *Faulty parallelism* is a term used by composition teachers for the placement of different structures in coordination with each other. Very often such faulty parallelism occurs with the conjunctions *and* and *or* with such other coordinators as *either* and *neither.* Here are a couple of made-up examples for illustrative purposes:

> The old car was a relic and rusty.

> To drink heavily and taking too many drugs are bad for your health.

These examples—one from the teacher's guide to an English text and the other from a text reported in a technical journal—show the vice in a plain and simple form. In the first a noun and an adjective are coordinated; in the second, an infinitive phrase and a participial phrase. Those who teach composition in high school or in college are necessarily very fierce on such constructions.

But when we get away from the writing of the tyro and into the world of the professional and presumably polished writer, we have a different problem. Faulty parallelisms still occur, but they tend to be almost invisible. This new invisibility would suggest that in edited prose faulty parallelism may generally be accounted a venial sin—if the writer doesn't notice it and the editor doesn't notice it and the reader doesn't notice it, how serious can it be?

Moreover, what if the usage writer doesn't notice it? In Strunk & White 1959 we find this rule (printed in boldface italics in the book):

15. Express co-ordinate ideas in similar form.

This is followed by numerous examples of faulty parallelism, complete with corrected versions. We assume that E. B. White, who presumably polished this up from Strunk's original, believed in the rule. E. B. White the grammarian, at least. What about E. B. White the essayist? Joseph M. Williams, in "The Phenomenology of Error," (*College Composition and Communications,* May 1981) quotes this passage:

I have written this account in penitence and in grief, as a man who failed to raise his pig, and to explain my deviation from the classic course of so many raised pigs. The grave in the woods is unmarked, but Fred can direct the mourner to it unerringly and with immense good will . . . —"Death of a Pig," *Essays of E. B. White,* 1977

Did you notice any faulty parallelisms there? (Williams says there are two.) But White presumably didn't notice any, and neither have most of his readers.

Here are a few more examples:

The award, which carries a $1,000 cash prize with it, goes to a trade-book editor under 40 who has shown special talent in discovering and/or getting the best work out of his authors —Victor S. Navasky, *N.Y. Times Book Rev.,* 15 Apr. 1973

. . . the stripes are either plainer or appear more commonly in the young —Charles Darwin, *On the Origin of Species by Means of Natural Selection,* 1859

In the Warrington family, and to distinguish them from other personages of that respectable race, these effigies have always gone by the name of 'The Virginians.' —W. M. Thackeray, *The Virginians,* 1857 (in A. S. Hill 1895)

. . . a lady very learned in stones, ferns, plants, and vermin, and who had written a book about petals — Anthony Trollope, *Barchester Towers,* 1857 (in Hill)

. . . before I was capable, either of Understanding my Case, or how to Amend it —Daniel Defoe, *Moll Flanders,* 1722

You could probably find such examples by the dozen, if you were to sharpen your eye so as to be able to detect them readily. These are, as we said, venial sins; they are not ornaments or nice turns of phrase to be imitated. We think you should try to avoid them in your writing. But if you slip, no one may notice.

favorable When *favorable* is followed by a preposition, the preposition is usually either *to* or *for.* When the

meaning of *favorable* is "feeling or expressing support or approval," *to* is used:

. . . stengthened the hand of those favorable to the council —Paul Sigmund, *Change,* March 1973

. . . because all men are favorable to that process — Walter Prescott Webb, *The Great Frontier,* 1952

Several . . . generals were mentioned as favorable to the scheme —*American Guide Series: Texas,* 1940

For is the usual choice when *favorable* means "suitable":

. . . the university structure is more favorable for accurate evaluation of societal problems —Halton Arp, *AAUP Bulletin,* September 1969

. . . to select those most favorable for hybridization —*Current Biography,* January 1964

Both *to* and *for* are used when *favorable* means "advantageous." *To* is more common:

. . . constructive acts favorable to the status of the Negro —James B. Conant, *Slums and Suburbs,* 1961

Existing credit law, sometimes archaic and traditionally favorable to the lender —Lucia Mouat, *The Consumer Fights Back,* 1970

. . . the reform was favorable for wage earners but the opposite for pensioners —*Current Biography 1950*

An alternative preposition after *favorable* is *toward,* which is used from time to time in the same way as *to:*

. . . reviewers were not too favorable toward the production —*Current Biography 1953*

faze, phase, feaze, feeze 1. *Faze* is a 19th-century American variant of a much older verb *feeze* (spelled in about a dozen different ways) with a meaning not attested for the older word: "disconcert, daunt." It has existed in American use in four chief spellings, *faze, phase, feaze,* and *feeze,* as noted by Bernstein 1971. A writer in the Buffalo, N.Y., *Express,* 17 Sept. 1894, who was quite pleased with the word, noted the spellings *faze, phase,* and *feaze.* A letter to the editor of a New York paper in June 1915 noted *feaze* in one magazine, *phase* in a second, and *faze* in a third. This writer had found so many variant spellings in the dictionaries he consulted that he said, "At present it holds the unique position of being the only English word that cannot be misspelled, however one tries." He favored *faze,* as do Bernstein and numerous other commentators, most of whom believe *phase* to be an error. Only Webster's Third and Bernstein recognize *phase* as a legitimate variant. Of the four variants, *faze* is by far the most usual. We find *phase* the next most frequent:

A woman arriving alone in sunglasses and Nike jogging shoes did not phase the solitary waiter —*Town & Country,* May 1983

Rainstorms do not phase them —*Christian Science Monitor,* 11 Nov. 1977

. . . not even the sight of the evening's star in purple-pink underwear . . . seemed to phase anyone —*Rolling Stone,* 16 Mar. 1972

Feaze and *feeze* are becoming quite rare. Our last *feeze* is from 1947:

> That didn't feeze the gaunt Kaltenbrunner —Victor H. Burnstein, *Final Judgment,* 1947

Feaze is seen a bit more often:

> It didn't feaze her any —James M. Cain, *Double Indemnity,* 1936

> It takes a lot to feaze a Texan —Robert M. Denhardt, *The Horse of the Americas,* rev. ed., 1975

The unrelated *phase* is usually a noun, but it is also a verb and it seems to be getting more play as a verb in recent years, especially in such combinations as *phase out, phase in,* and *phase into.* We have at least one instance of the verb *phase* (with *out*) spelled *faze.* So in the interests of lessening confusion in the world, we recommend that you use *faze* to mean "daunt" and let *phase* have its own distinctive use. However, the *phase* spelling of *faze* is almost a century old now, and we are not especially hopeful that it will be phased out.

2. *Faze,* being an Americanism, was naturally suspect by the usage and dictionary community. Vizetelly 1906 seems to be the earliest commentator to recommend avoiding it as slang. Its entry in older dictionaries was variously labeled colloquial, dialectal, slang, or informal, and a few usage commentators still carry similiar warnings. But Merriam-Webster dictionaries, Reader's Digest 1983, and Bernstein 1971 know that it is standard. Bernstein makes this point: *faze* has a connotation that such synonyms as *daunt* and *disconcert* simply cannot supply. He thinks *daunt* might be closest, but finds it too high-flown for a context that is typical of *faze.* He gives an example like this one:

> It hit Marciano flush on the right side of the jaw, but it didn't seem to faze him a bit —A. J. Liebling, *New Yorker,* 17 Nov. 1951

It might have been appropriate to use *daunt* in such a context when John L. Sullivan was fighting, but not when Rocky Marciano was fighting, and not now.

Quite a few commentators note that *faze* is most commonly found in negative contexts: While this is true, it is incidental to the meaning of *faze*—not being fazed is more worthy of remark than being fazed. Here are a few more examples:

> He had ice water in his veins. Nothing fazed him, not insult or anger or violence —Robert Penn Warren, *All the King's Men,* 1946

> "... It never fazed her for a moment and we can't let it faze us." —John Dos Passos, *The Grand Design,* 1949

> Leopardi got a threat letter yesterday.... It didn't faze him, though. He tore it up —Raymond Chandler, *The Simple Art of Murder,* 1950

> ... I was too well schooled in the Christian ethic— all worthwhile things are difficult, you must stand up to life's challenges—to let that faze me —Jane Harriman, *Atlantic,* March 1970

> ... the wines, which do not faze him, fuddle me — Robert Craft, *Stravinsky,* 1972

> Dry snow didn't faze the Dynamark, but a normal mouthful of wet snow clogged it —*Consumer Reports,* January 1983

feasible   *Feasible* has three senses in the OED. As defined briefly in Webster's Ninth New Collegiate Dictionary, they are, in historical order, "capable of being done or carried out," "capable of being used or dealt with successfully," and "reasonable, likely." In 1926 H. W. Fowler announced that he did not like the third sense, which he had noticed coming into common use. It was his opinion that the third sense of *feasible* was simply a fancy substitution for *possible* or *probable,* and he attacked it by insisting that *feasible* be limited to its first sense (he ignores the second) and by bringing in the first half of an OED note on the third sense to the effect that the sense was not justified etymologically (*feasible* goes back to the Latin verb for *do*) and was recognized in no other dictionary. He omitted the rest of the note: "though supported by considerable literary authority." Indeed, the sense goes back to Thomas Hobbes in the 17th century and had been in use about 250 years when Fowler was offended by it.

To clinch his point about the proper uses of *possible* and *feasible,* Fowler tells us that a thunderstorm is possible but not feasible (an example repeated, with minor changes, in Bremner 1980, Longman 1984, Shaw 1987, and Copperud 1970, 1980). The example, however, is beside the point: writers do not use *feasible* of storms.

The three definitions are not really discrete, in spite of the etymological disclaimer in the OED. In order to frame a definition of reasonable length, the lexicographer often has to sort examples of an adjective according to the kinds of nouns it modifies. The second and third senses in the OED account for the application of *feasible* to things that are not doable, even though the underlying notion of *feasible* is not much changed.

> Sand is used as a filter medium in preference to other feasible materials —Herbert R. Mauersberger, *American Handbook of Synthetic Textiles,* 1952

> ... the cove off which the ship lay at anchor offered the only feasible landing place —Charles Nordhoff & James Norman Hall, *Pitcairn's Island,* 1934

> ... where a qualified judgment respecting his fitness is clearly feasible —William Van Alstyne, *AAUP Bulletin,* September 1971

> ... to keep as cool as feasible, and to wait —Ned Temko, *Christian Science Monitor,* 12 Dec. 1979

> I am not here concerned with the question whether such a "humanistic" civilization ... is or is not *desirable;* only with the question whether it is *feasible* —T. S. Eliot, "The Humanism of Irving Babbitt," in *Selected Essays,* 1932

> The most feasible interpretation is that dust and breccia probably were formed at an early stage in the history of the moon —Mitsunobu Tatsumoto & John N. Rosholt, *Science,* 30 Jan. 1970

> ... by crossing the one and only feasible pass — Douglas Carruthers, *Beyond the Caspian,* 1949

None of the things described as *feasible* in these examples can be done; in each case the word suggests that whatever is in question is within the realm of practical possibility or reasonable likelihood. *Possible* cannot be substituted for *feasible* in some of these contexts and still make sense; in those where it can be substituted it often changes the meaning.

There is one construction—"it is feasible that"—in which *possible* can substitute very nicely. Some of Fowler's examples are of this construction. All of our examples of it are British:

> As the Chapel pre-dated any knowledge of printing, it is feasible that the founder planned to give the people religious instruction by the pictorial medium — Martin Thornbill, *Explorer's Scotland,* 1952

> It is quite feasible that the line is corrupt —Norman Blake, *The English Language in Medieval Literature,* 1977

Whatever is feasible is more reasonable or more likely than what is merely possible. To point a finger at a use of *feasible* and say that *possible* was meant is to try to read the writer's mind. These are cases where we would do better to give the writer credit for having chosen the right word to convey the intended meaning.

feature 1. Back in the 1920s there was much negative comment in usage circles and in various handbooks on the propriety of *feature* as a verb in advertising and journalism. Bernstein 1971 thinks the fact that it is a verb formed by functional shift from a noun may have triggered the hostile reaction. Noticeable popularity at the time was probably at least as important a cause: "overused and hackneyed" is the verdict of Hyde 1926. Fowler 1926 saw it as a repulsive Americanism that he feared would make its way into popular British use. (It did.) Because it was mentioned in handbooks then, it is still in handbooks, though now chiefly to explain that it is in standard use (as it had been since about 1888). Here are a few typical examples:

> The exhibition will feature first editions and related manuscripts —Erica Jong, *Barnard Alumnae,* Winter 1971

> When my husband and I dine in a restaurant that features a buffet —Amy Vanderbilt, *Ladies' Home Jour.,* August 1971

> The film . . . evolved into a series, featuring Mickey Rooney as Andy Hardy —*Current Biography,* September 1965

2. Strunk & White 1959 (and subsequent editions) also considers *feature* hackneyed, but it differs from most in disliking the older noun use as well as the verb. The example of disapproved use (which goes back to the original Strunk circa 1920) is interesting:

> A feature of the entertainment especially worthy of mention was the singing of Miss A.

The advice given is this: "Better use the same number of words to tell what Miss A. sang and how she sang it." This advice seems a bit naive; it is distinctly possible that the example is a minor masterpiece of tact. If Miss A. happens to have more friends than talent, it may be better not to tell what she sang and how she sang it. We may have the same politic avoidance of judgment in this example:

> A feature of the program was a panel discussion in which visitors from other institutions shared the benefits of their own, related experience —Calvin H. Plimpton, *Amherst College Bulletin,* November 1967

3. Shaw 1975, 1987 and Trimmer & McCrimmon 1988 worry about a verb sense of *feature* meaning "imagine, fancy." Shaw thinks it informal and dialectal, Trimmer & McCrimmon slang.

> "A necktie!" he exclaimed indignantly. "Can you feature wearing a necktie out here?" —Kenneth M. Dodson, *Away All Boats,* 1954

> "And these are my two little country bumpkins. They already want to go home. Can you feature it?" —Jean Stafford, *The Mountain Lion,* 1947

> "So you can feature what she said about Wurssun," Jonas said. "*Less* than nothing. . . ." —Anne Tyler, *Southern Rev.,* April 1965

This seems to be chiefly an oral use, going back at least to the era of World War II and perhaps less common now than formerly. These examples do not sound especially slangy, though all record imagined speech.

feaze See FAZE, PHASE, FEAZE, FEEZE.

February A succession of \r\'s in different syllables of the same word presents an articulatory hurdle to many speakers, not only in English but in other languages. One solution is for one of the \r\'s to dissimilate, either becoming a different sound, or dropping out altogether. Several words that come to us from Romance show the first process, with \l\ substituted for \r\: compare *pilgrim* with the etymologically related *peregrine*. Within English, in a number of words with unstressed \ər\ before a consonant, the \r\ drops from this position in favor of another \r\ more prominently placed. Thus *caterpillar* is often pronounced \'kat-ə-ˌpil-ər\, and the first \r\ of *elderberry, governor, offertory, surprise, thermometer,* and *vernacular* and the second \r\ of *paraphernalia* are often dropped without exciting any notice or comment. *February,* by contrast, is a shibboleth. The most widespread pronunciation of this word among educated speakers is \'feb-yə-ˌwer-ē\, and while the consensus of usage writers is tolerant of this version, most of us can recall having been admonished to say \'feb-rù-ˌwer-ē\ at some point in our school days.

The status of other words in which \r\ is sometimes dropped from the end of a consonant cluster (as in *February*) varies. *Library* is perhaps pronounced \'lī-ˌber-ē\ more often by children than by adults, and that pronunciation draws general disapproval. But *synchrotron* and *temperature* often come out \'siŋ-kə-ˌträn\ and \'tem-pə-chər\ without causing eyebrows to be raised.

feed *Feed,* when used with a preposition, is most often used with *on:*

> Tom seeks to escape from regularity by romanticism. He feeds on detective and adventure stories — James T. Farrell, *The League of Frightened Philistines,* 1945

> When writing turns to mush, thought, which feeds on writing, suffers from malnutrition —Thomas H. Middleton, *Saturday Rev.,* 24 Nov. 1979

Feed has also been used with *upon* or *off.* Although still less frequent than *on,* recent evidence suggests that the use of *upon* and *off* has been growing:

> . . . to think again; to feed upon memory —Walter De la Mare, *Encounter,* December 1954

> . . . shifted his stance toward his art and the experience that his art fed upon —Donald Davie, *N.Y. Times Book Rev.,* 25 Apr. 1976

The dread of the new place mounts up in her and feeds off the complaints in his letters —Oscar Handlin, *The Uprooted,* 1951

... have the sort of hardcover sale that ... the softcover could feed off the celebrity —N. R. Kleinfield, *N.Y. Times Book Rev.,* 16 Sept. 1979

Feed may even occur with *from,* but this seems to be a far from usual combination:

... in a position to reward those who ... are content to feed from officially provided sources —Thomas B. Littlewood, *Saturday Rev.,* 15 Apr. 1972

feel   Copperud 1964 quotes one Alice Hamilton, M.D., from an article in the *Atlantic* (September 1954), as being amused by "the increasing rejection of *believe* and *think* in favor of *feel.*" This is our earliest attested objection to the use, although Copperud seems to know of earlier objections based on the assertion that nothing can be felt that is not apprehended by the sense of touch. Shaw 1987 (at *sense*) says that apprehension by touch was a restriction on *feel* that held at an earlier time, but the evidence in the OED shows the presumed restriction has never existed.

The earliest commentator we have seen is Evans 1957. Gowers added the topic to Fowler 1965, commenting on this use of *feel* in British government circles. A number of college handbooks, such as Macmillan 1982 and Ebbitt & Ebbitt 1982, object to the use, and Bernstein comments on it somewhat cautiously in his 1962 and 1971 books.

Copperud defends the use, noting that it has been around for a long time (the modern construction goes back to Shakespeare) and that a number of respected authors—Trollope, Hardy, Lincoln—have used it. He also mentions that Webster's Third quotes an Alice Hamilton for the "think, believe" sense. Could it be the same Alice Hamilton? Yes, indeed, and from the same article:

I am a reader, so I feel I have a right to criticize authors —Alice Hamilton, M.D., *Atlantic,* September 1954

In the examples below you will see that this sense of *feel* tends to be colored by the notion of emotion or intuition; it doesn't seem to mean "think" in the sense of using powers of reasoning.

But I feel that I have not yet made my peace with God —Emily Dickinson, letter, 8 Sept. 1846

... there still remained my relation with the reader, which was another affair altogether and as to which I felt no one to be trusted but myself —Henry James, *The Art of the Novel,* 1934

A person can admire New York and so on, and all that, but I feel it is absolutely impossible to love the place —James Thurber, letter, 20 Jan. 1938

But our panel evidently felt that the Manhattan commuter's daily trek is no less arduous —Zinsser 1976

Gibbon evidently felt that this first memoir had betrayed him into garrulity —John Butt, *English Literature in the Mid-Eighteenth Century,* edited & completed by Geoffrey Carnall, 1979

Some people feel that if we arm ourselves with a lot of nuclear weapons, the Russians will never dare attack us —*And More by Andy Rooney,* 1982

... some of us felt that this wasn't an appropriate time to celebrate —Tip O'Neill with William Novak, *Man of the House,* 1987

This use is entirely standard.

feel bad, feel badly   It is a standard joke of usage writers to remark that someone who says "I feel badly" must be complaining about a defective sense of touch, or thick gloves, or numb fingers. The Joe Miller who invented this hoary witticism may have been Frank Vizetelly, whose 1906 *A Desk-Book of Errors in English* has this: "However, *feel badly* is correct when the intention is to say that one's power of touch is defective...." Subsequently joining the merry band of misunderstanders we find Bierce 1909, Evans 1962, Harper 1975, 1985, Freeman 1983, Kilpatrick 1984, and others. Of course, they know and we know that people who say "I feel badly" simply mean they feel bad.

How do we explain the persistence of *feel badly?* One of the more frequently mentioned causes involves hypercorrection, often labeled with such words as *gentility, overrefinement,* or *elegance*—that is, the use of an incorrect form in one place in reaction to being corrected upon using the replaced form in some other construction. If hypercorrection is one of the influences on *feel badly,* its historical roots would go back to the campaign against flat adverbs—that is adverbs like *bad, right, slow, sure* that have the same form as adjectives—that was begun in the second half of the 18th century. (See FLAT ADVERBS.) The explanation would be, then, that correction of *bad* in *hurt bad,* or *need it bad* would result in *badly* after *feel* too. Bernstein 1965, however, thinks this explanation will not bear close inspection. He points out that other adjectives after *feel* are seldom if ever corrected to adverbs: no one seems to use "I feel sadly" or "I feel angrily," for instance.

If hypercorrection is not a persuasive explanation, we must look elsewhere. We can find several other influences, but probably no single comprehensive explanation.

First, *feel* plus an adverb is not a nonstandard construction; *feel* is often followed by adverbs when they qualify the degree or way of feeling. Thus one may feel strongly about an issue, or feel differently about it now. Bernstein 1965, 1977 points out that it is possible for *badly* to be used in such a construction; he posits "I feel badly the need for more discussion of this issue."

Second, the *feel bad, feel badly* choice is related to the *feel good, feel well* choice, where many people choose one or the other depending on whether they are talking about a physical or mental state (see GOOD 1). Those who differentiate use *feel well* for health and *feel good* for emotion; many make the same distinction with *bad* and *badly,* choosing *feel bad* for health and *feel badly* for emotion. Here, for instance, is Harper panelist David Schoenbrun:

"I use 'I feel bad' to express a physical condition, but 'I feel badly' to express an emotional response."

The following examples are other evidence for *badly* used of emotion:

... I know you must have felt very badly when you cleaned out Mamma's closet —Harry S. Truman, letter, 21 Oct. 1947

We feel very badly about your only having one turkey, worth a paltry half grand —James Thurber, letter, Fall 1938

. . . I was laughing, but trying not to for some reason, feeling badly that I laughed, feeling ashamed —E. L. Doctorow, *Loon Lake*, 1979

The other waiters began to feel badly. 'Aw, lay off,' Bernie Altman said —Mordecai Richler, *The Apprenticeship of Duddy Kravitz*, 1959

Don't feel badly if you didn't do too well on this little test —advertising letter, March 1980

Bryant 1962 cites Ernest Hemingway and Walter Lippmann as also using *badly* for the emotional state. The choice of an adverb for the emotional state instead of the related adjective is also attested with other adverbs:

. . . it [a letter] had effect enough over me to make me feel unpleasantly for two days —Henry Adams, letter, 9 Feb. 1859

But Bryant and others point out that the evidence of surveys shows that many people do not differentiate, and use *badly* for health as well as *bad* for the emotional state:

I do not feel so badly this forenoon—but I have bad nights —Walt Whitman, letter, 17 June 1864

At once he felt bad, for he usually charged two twenty-five for this kind of job —Bernard Malamud, *The Magic Barrel*, 1958

Still, I feel bad about not having written you —E. B. White, letter, 23 June 1946

In fact Bryant sums up several surveys by saying they show usage to be almost evenly divided between *feel bad* and *feel badly*, regardless of whether health or emotional state is the topic. Our printed evidence, however, shows *feel badly* being used most often for the emotional state.

Third, Evans 1962 notes that some people may choose *badly* because they think *"bad* could only mean wicked." This is not an idle supposition. An American handbook, *Vulgarisms and Other Errors of Speech,* published in 1869, explicitly prescribes the usage now decried as erroneous:

"He feels very *bad,"* is sometimes said as descriptive of one's feeling very sick. *To feel bad* is to feel conscious of depravity; to feel *badly* is to feel sick.

It is not unlikely that the association of *bad* with moral turpitude has survived in many American families and has given further strength to the use of *badly*.

Fourth, we cannot entirely dismiss the influence of *well,* preached as an adverb in innumerable schoolbooks yet entirely acceptable after *feel*—so much so that it has been recognized as an adjective in this function by most dictionaries. As long ago as 1927, Josephine Turck Baker *(The Correct Word: How to Use It)* mentioned that some authorities (but not a majority) proposed recognition of *badly* as an adjective. It has been so recognized in some unabridged dictionaries—in Webster's Second and Webster's Third, for instance.

The attitudes of the usage books to *feel badly* is interesting. Almost all of the school handbooks, from grade-school to college level, prescribe *feel bad;* it is clearly the pedagogical standard. But Copperud 1980 sums up his survey of dictionaries and the more general usage books with this observation: "The consensus is that *feel bad*

and *feel badly* are standard and interchangeable with respect to both emotional state and physical condition."

Conclusion: the controversy over *feel bad* and *feel badly* has been going on for more than a century, and since its beginnings lie in two opposing prescriptive standards—that of the 1869 handbook prescribing *feel badly* and that of the 20th-century schoolbooks prescribing *feel bad*— it is unlikely to die out very soon. People will go on about as they do now—some differentiating *bad* and *badly,* some not, some avoiding *badly,* some not. You can see that the question is not as simple as it is often claimed to be, and, with those considerations in mind, make your own choice. Whatever it is, you will have some worthy comrades and some worthy opponents.

feel good, feel well   See GOOD 1.

feet   See FOOT.

feeze   See FAZE, PHASE, FEAZE, FEEZE.

feisty   Nickles 1974 disparages those who use *feisty* without knowing its origin. Bremner 1980 repeats much of Nickles verbatim but places more emphasis on the etymology itself: *feisty* comes from *feist* (spelled *fice* by William Faulkner in his writings), a small dog, from obsolete *fisting hound,* from obsolete *fist* "to break wind." Flesch 1983 approves the word, in spite of its "unappetizing origins."

Nickles's slighting comments were probably provoked by the fairly recent popularity of *feisty,* which is what brought it to Flesch's attention. *Feisty* is of dialectal origin, and it seems to have had mainly pejorative overtones in dialect:

". . . I don't aim to take no snot offen him, and if he gets feisty with me, I'll take and learn him a little respeck." —Emmett Gowen, *The Dark Noon of March,* 1933

Savage was lean, needlessly dirty, with a feisty unshaven face —Luke Short, *Vengeance Valley,* 1950

But as the term moved into general use, it lost the pejorative overtones and has come to be used of someone or something that is admirably, if a bit uncomfortably, full of fighting spirit:

. . . if you're for him, he's feisty; if you're not, he's arrogant —George V. Higgins, quoted in *People,* 1 Dec. 1975

His concession speech is feisty as ever—the truth, he says, will rise again —David Halberstam, *Harper's,* January 1971

. . . this tiny, feisty, dark-haired woman of seemingly limitless energy and a propensity for throwing caution to the wind —Hays Gorey, *N.Y. Times Mag.,* 22 Jan. 1978

. . . rejecting crabs that are technically alive but half ossified by ice in favor of those fresh and feisty enough to snap their claws —Caroline Bates, *Gourmet,* March 1977

Of course, I was committing an elitist sin even to mention Mozart's name, but then I get to feeling feisty at times and dare to do the unthinkable — Martha Banta, *College English,* October 1980

A few reference works call *feisty* slang or colloquial, but it is in standard use.

feline The noun is discouraged by Copperud 1970, 1980 and Flesch 1964 as a journalese variant of *cat*. Flesch produces as example only a headline, Copperud nothing. Our files hold very little evidence of noun use. Just this sort of thing, for the consumption of young people:

> ... the blood-curdling screech of the strange feline, known to be found around Scout camps on odd evenings —*Boy's Life*, March 1953

And this sort of literarily pejorative use:

> The possibility of this happening as a general social fact has brought out the feline in her and her class —Christopher Hitchens, *N.Y. Times Mag.*, 1 June 1975

The much more usual use of *feline* is as an adjective, which can be admiring or disparaging:

> What Cassidy had on his side all this time was a youthful feline quality —*The Story of Pop*, 1973

> ... a lanky, feline Brazilian beauty —Roland Gelatt, *Saturday Rev.*, 21 June 1969

> ... the feline party intriguer and critic —David Thomson, *Europe Since Napoleon*, 2d ed., rev., 1962

> He said as much in his column, in that feline way of his —Grundy, *Punch*, 23 Dec. 1975

See also CANINE; EQUINE.

fell swoop The phrase *at one fell swoop* is uttered by Macduff in Shakespeare's *Macbeth* when he learns that Macbeth has murdered his wife and children, as several commentators remind us. The metaphor is that of a hawk swooping down on defenseless prey, and *fell* here means "cruel, savage, ruthless." Evans 1957 points out that the phrase conveys both Macduff's sense of the suddenness of the murderous attack and also the helplessness of his wife and children in the face of a murderous tyrant. Bremner 1980 calls the phrase a cliché in modern use, and Evans says "the phrase is now worn smooth of meaning and feeling."

Actually, what has happened is this. *Fell* has become a rarely used literary, rhetorical, poetic term, rather removed from common experience. It is not obsolete and you can still find it, but not often, and not in ordinary places. So the present-day reader of the Shakespearean phrase tends to understand Macduff's sense of the suddenness of the attack and to skip over the meaning of *fell*; the *fell* has worn smooth of meaning, but the notion of suddenness still adheres to the phrase.

And the phrase has become an idiom, really; it has lost its literal meaning and has come to mean "all at once." It is neutral in application, not necessarily introducing a disastrous event. And Shakespeare's *at* often becomes *in* or *with*.

> These controls should be ended at one fell swoop —Milton Friedman, reprinted column, 1969

> What cosmic process created the stars and planets? Are new ones still being formed? Or were all that now exist made in one fell swoop? —Fred L. Whipple, *Scientific American Reader*, 1953

> EMP could incapacitate everything in one fell swoop —Thomas W. Buckman, quoted in *Wall Street Jour.*, 29 May 1981

> With one fell swoop, I seized the door and pulled it wide open —Cleveland Amory, *Saturday Rev.*, 6 Sept. 1975

The phrase does get quite a lot of work, and one is not entirely unreasonable to consider it a bit of a cliché; but it has a fine pedigree. If you use it, with *at* or *in* or *with*, you should pay Shakespeare the respect of getting the rest right (though a typo may thwart your intent):

> It would not mean Utopia at one fell stroke —Douglas MacArthur, quoted in *Springfield* (Mass.) *Union*, 27 Jan. 1955

> They offered a cutesy-wootsy amendment to abolish 44 programs in one full swoop —James J. Kilpatrick, *Springfield* (Mass.) *Morning Union*, 1 May 1986

female The status of *female* as a noun equivalent in meaning to *woman* has gone through some remarkable changes over the centuries. The fullest account of its early history is in Lounsbury 1908; Hall 1917 also has a fairly generous treatment. The word came into Middle English from the French *femelle* originally as a noun. The modern spelling comes from the influence of the word *male*, to which it is not related; the OED notes that it was spelled *female* to rhyme with *male* in a poem as early as 1375. It was applied to humans and lower animals alike, perhaps earliest to women.

Lounsbury traces its slow progress in literature. Wycliffe used it at least once, and so did Chaucer; it turns up in a few other early writers. Shakespeare used it only 11 times, compared to some 400 instances of *woman*. Lounsbury remarks that a couple of Shakespeare's uses suggest that *female* was considered somewhat of a fancy word at the time—one of what Ben Jonson called "perfumed phrases." The word also had occasional use by such dramatists as Massinger and Fletcher, but it was not until the 18th century that it became fully established in literary use. Lounsbury notes it was used with some, but not great, frequency by such writers as Addison and Steele; by the middle of the century it appeared frequently in literary use, being common in Richardson, Fielding, and Smollett. Although Goldsmith used it in his poem "The Deserted Village"—Lounsbury quotes the line "where the poor houseless shivering female lies" and Hall the line "As some fair female, unadorned and plain" from the poem—the word seems to have been used chiefly in prose. Its use in literary works continued unabated through the end of the 18th century and into the first half of the 19th; it is found in such writers as Fanny Burney, Jane Austen, Sir Walter Scott, James Fenimore Cooper, Poe, Dickens, Thackeray, Charles Reade, Elizabeth Barrett Browning, Bulwer-Lytton, Charles Lamb, Washington Irving, and Hawthorne. Hall lists a great many others.

In the middle of the 19th century, however, a change took place—numerous commentators began to condemn the use as vulgar, a misuse, poor taste, or a perversion of language. Alford 1866 asks, "Why should a *woman* be degraded from her position as a rational being, and be expressed by a word which might belong to any animal tribe ... ?" Richard Grant White 1870 protests that "this is one of those perversions which are justified by no example, however eminent.... when a woman calls herself a female, she merely shares her sex with all her fellow-females throughout the brute creation." An early objection along the same lines—a letter to the editor of the *Manchester Examiner and Times* in March 1858—is quoted by Hodgson 1889: "Why should women be confounded with lower animals of the feminine gender?" The same sentiment is expressed by a number of other critics of the mid to late 19th century. The editor of *F* for the OED, Henry Bradley, adds his comment: "Now commonly avoided by good writers, exc[ept] with contemptuous implication." (Lounsbury censures the OED treatment as misleading since its entry cites no well-known literary figure after Steele in 1713; he assumes—perhaps unfairly—the OED editor must have been aware of the literary usage.)

There are a few interesting observations to be made about all this late Victorian furor. First, the most vociferous objectors are men. We know that Sarah Josepha Hale, editor of *Godey's Lady's Book,* agreed with Alford, but we really do not know if women found the usage offensive or not. Clearly they had not earlier; Fanny Burney had used *female* of the Princess Royal, and Jane Austen not only of the characters in her novels but of herself:

> I think I may boast myself with all possible vanity to be the most unlearned and uninformed female who ever dared to be an authoress —letter, 1 Dec. 1815 (in Lounsbury)

Perhaps women found the usage unobjectionable even later:

> We read only the other day a report of a lecture on the poet Crabbe, in which she who was afterward Mrs. Crabbe was spoken of as "a female to whom he had formed an attachment." To us, indeed, it seems that a man's wife should be spoken of in some way which is not equally applicable to a ewe lamb or a favorite mare. But it was a "female" who delivered the lecture, and we suppose the females know best about their own affairs —William Matthews, *Words; their Use and their Abuse,* 1880 (cited in Bardeen 1883)

Second, the objection is ostensibly based on the word's leveling of women with lower animals, but the gallantry of this argument may well be largely factitious. The real basis for objection to this use of *female* is much more likely to have been its regular appearance in the newspapers of the day. Lounsbury elsewhere remarks that during the 19th century, newspapers were widely blamed for the degeneracy of the language. The correspondent to the *Manchester Examiner and Times* in 1858 states it baldly: "Newspapers, I grieve to say it, are the great corruptors of our language, if not of every other." Richard Grant White too draws most of his objectionable uses from newspapers. The transparency of the stated basis for objection is clear from our earliest evidence, the Manchester letter writer. The passage to which he objects read "a female had been found dead at a road-side." He purports to be anxious to discover whether it had been a "a cow, or a mare, or a she ass." Had it been a cow, mare, or she ass, of course, it wouldn't have made the newspapers, even in 1858. On such a flimsy pretext more than one linguistic prejudice is based.

Third, we are not given much evidence of how *female* was actually used. Of the objectors, only Hodgson gives quotations, and both Lounsbury and Hall list far more authors than they quote. So our knowledge of genuine usage is somewhat sketchy. Still, we can trace a few distinct uses.

Female as a term correlative to *male* seems not to have been objected to, except by a few commentators such as Bache 1869 and Ayres 1881 who disliked both *male* and *female.* A typical example of this use Hall quotes from Macaulay:

> Though in families the number of males and females differs widely, yet in great collections of human beings the disparity almost disappears.

This sort of use is specifically approved by some commentators as scientific or statistical.

The use as a simple synonym of *woman* we have seen from Goldsmith and Jane Austen earlier. A couple of examples more:

> . . . attention paid by the females of quality, who so regularly visited David Ramsay's shop —Sir Walter Scott, *The Fortunes of Nigel,* 1822

> The alarmed female shrieked as she recovered her feet —James Fenimore Cooper, *The Pilot,* 1823

Mark Twain, writing after the mid-Victorian assault, made fun of Cooper's penchant for using it.

The "woman" use seems to have led in two directions. First, and perhaps most handily, *female* was used in the singular when the age of the person referred to was unknown or uncertain, and in the plural to indicate a group of mixed or undetermined ages:

> . . . the females of the family —Jane Austen, *Pride and Prejudice,* 1813

> . . . the small party of females were pretty well composed —Jane Austen, *Mansfield Park,* 1814

> In short, there was not a female within ten miles of them that was in possession of a gold watch, a pearl necklace, or a piece of Mechlin lace, but they examined her title to it —Joseph Addison, *The Guardian* (cited by Hall)

> . . . all naked pictures, which may be a reason they don't show it [a picture gallery] to females —Charles Lamb, letter, 9 Aug. 1810

> It opened into the house, where the females were already astir —Emily Brontë, *Wuthering Heights,* 1847

Second, a humorous or facetious use:

> . . . I sometimes add my vocal powers to her execution of
> "Thou, thou reign'st in this bosom," —
> not, however, unless her mother or some other other discreet female is present, to prevent misinterpretation —Oliver Wendell Holmes d. 1894, *The Autocrat of the Breakfast-Table,* 1858

The frequent statements of the 19th century on the opprobrium attached to the use of *female* is overstated. The most opprobrious citation produced to back up the assertion is from an 1889 daily newspaper by an anonymous author who says it is a term of opprobrium. There is, however, a faintly or mildly pejorative use. Hodgson says the "contemptuous sense is justified by ample precedents" and produces this example:

> He did not bid him go and sell himself to the first female he could find possessed of wealth —Anthony Trollope, *Doctor Thorne,* 1858

Trollope's contempt here does not seem especially strong. Holmes uses the word another time in making a distinction of social class:

> When a young female wears a flat circular side-curl, gummed on each temple,—when she walks with a male, not arm in arm, but his arm against the back of hers,—and she says "Yes?" with a note of interrogation, you are generally safe in asking her what wages she gets, and who the "feller" was —*The Autocrat of the Breakfast-Table,* 1858

All of this brings us up to the turn of the 20th century, just after which Hall and Lounsbury were writing. How has the noun *female* fared in this century?

The mid-19th century strictures seem to have driven the neutral use of Austen, Scott, Cooper, et al. pretty much out of currency. It is but rarely attested:

> She was above average height, with a Roman nose, firm chin, dark eyes, heavy brows—a commanding female, in brief —*Dictionary of American Biography,* 1936

> I'm strictly a female female —Oscar Hammerstein II, "I Enjoy Being a Girl" (song), 1958

The application to lower animals continues to flourish, although writers on zoological subjects tend often to prefer more specialized terms, such as *mare, cow, bitch, queen,* and *hen.*

> The leopards will stay at rest until the light fades and evening shadows deepen. Then the female will hide her young in a safe place —*National Geographic World,* June 1986

The scientific or statistical use is still common:

> Of the membership, females are in the majority in the ratio of three to one —Macum Phelan, *Handbook of All Denominations,* 3d ed., 1924

> The distribution represented about 42.7 million males and about 17.3 females —*Collier's Year Book,* 1949

> The claim that males can be transformed, by means of hormones and surgery, into females, and vice versa, is, of course, a lie —Thomas S. Szasz, *N.Y. Times Book Rev.,* 10 June 1979

The humorous use has also continued, though examples are not many in our files:

> I will read her a wholesome lecture, for her soul's good, on the proper treatment a self-respecting female should apply to the modern young man —William J. Locke, *Simon the Jester,* 1910

> Such prominent females as Helen Wills, Gertrude Ederle, Amelia Earhart, and Babe Didrikson left him cold. In his opinion, there hadn't been an athletic gal worth looking at since Annette Kellerman —James Thurber, *New Yorker,* 5 Jan. 1952

The more-or-less mildly pejorative use likewise persists:

> He's just about on a par with this bone-pounding chiropractor female, Mrs. Mattie Gooch —Sinclair Lewis, *Main Street,* 1920

> Henry Adams said that the magazine-made female has not a feature that would have been recognized by Adam —Agnes Repplier, *Under Dispute,* 1924

> What a poisonous female she was! Bob could have her —Russell Thacher, *The Tender Age,* 1952

> Once at a party he met a name-dropping female who kept asking him "Do you know So-and-so?" —T. S. Matthews, *The Selected Letters of Charles Lamb,* 1956

Bolinger 1980 maintains that *female* in ordinary conversation is always derogatory. We can neither prove nor disprove the assertion.

Convenient in this function, *female* has continued to be used in reference to a group of women and girls or to those whose age is not readily apparent or is irrelevant—in short, in rather indefinite instances. This use can still be found, even in literature. Our earliest citation reads almost as if it had come from Jane Austen:

> Refinement is a characteristic of the females of our family, Dorothea —Margaret Deland, *Old Chester Tales,* 1898

> If you do that, then the fellow, or female, you are trying to tell the truth to thinks you are feeling sorry for yourself —Robert Penn Warren, *All the King's Men,* 1946

> And from that hour to this, the Gazette has referred to all females as women except that police-court characters were always to be designated as "ladies" —*The Autobiography of William Allen White,* 1946

> . . . the tombstone shop opposite . . . in which the Christian emblems and the white marble specters of weeping females —Osbert Sitwell, *Noble Essences,* 1950

> When she was a few days old, she became, upon the death of her mother, whose entire dowry she inherited, the richest female in France —William Maxwell, *New Yorker,* 7 Jan. 1956

> . . . just as small children call all females mother, so sailors . . . should call all barmaids Beatrice — Thomas Pynchon, *V.,* 1963

> Terms like "pioneer," "farmer," and "settler" should clearly include females as well as males — Harper 1985

> The female who had laughed behind the lights, he saw, was the producer, a leggy girl pale as untinted oleo —John Updike, *Bech Is Back,* 1982

To sum up: the noun *female* had slow growth in literary use from the 14th to the 18th centuries; from the mid-18th to the mid-19th century it was commonly used in literature. In the middle of the 19th century it began to be disparaged, most likely because it was a popular word in newspapers, and not chiefly for the reason usually given—that it demeaned women by equating them with cows, sows, and mares. The censure continued well into the 20th century and has undoubtedly curtailed the word's use in written English, especially in the simple neutral use by which Jane Austen could refer to herself as a female or Fanny Burney could refer to the Princess Royal as "the second female in the kingdom." The facetious use is apparently still alive, as is the mildly pejorative use—this latter especially in ordinary conversation, according to Dwight Bolinger. The indefinite or indeterminate use—where age is unknown or irrelevant or where groups consist of mixed ages—appears to be the most common current use in writing, and it still is in good standing in literature.

feminine forms, female-gender word forms, feminine designations Long, learned, and speculative discussions of nouns whose terminations in English mark them as intended for women can be found under these and related headings in Fowler 1926, 1965, Reader's Digest 1983, Copperud 1970, 1980, and other sources. The largest group of these words, those ending in -*ess,* we have treated separately under that heading in this book.

Writers who express opinions about feminine forms in general can be divided into three groups: those (mostly men) who believe them falling into disuse; those (some 19th-century women and Fowler 1926) who find them desirable; and those (chiefly women) who find them offensive for one reason or another. We do not yet know if 20th-century feminism will have much effect on the use of these words; our evidence does show, however, that many of those confidently pronounced by commentators years ago to have gone out of use as long ago as the 18th century are in fact still used.

Fowler 1926 rather stands alone. He did not disparage feminine forms but found them useful, and actually hoped that more would come into use. He urged the adoption of such words as *doctoress, teacheress, singeress,* and *danceress* (he didn't care for *cantatrice* and *danseuse*). Fowler here was being generally consistent with his approval of the multiplication of distinctions in the language. He thought feminine terms packed two kinds of information in a single word, and he liked that. That characteristic probably accounts for the survival of many that are still in use.

See -ESS; see also PERSON 2.

ferment, foment The Oxford American Dictionary 1980 says "Do not confuse *ferment* with *foment*." Bremner 1980 says "In their figurative senses, . . . *ferment* and *foment* are almost interchangeable"; Shaw 1975 agrees. Here is what our evidence tells us:

The literal senses are clearly distinct and cause no problem. *Ferment* refers to the chemical process of fermentation, and *foment* refers to treating the body with applications of moist heat.

The figurative senses are more tangled, but looking at them according to parts of speech helps to sort them out. As nouns, *ferment* and *foment* differ greatly. *Foment* is practically never used with a figurative meaning, but *ferment* has two common figurative senses, "a state of unrest" or "agitation" and "a process of active, often disorderly development."

> The decline in coffee prices is causing economic ferment —*Newsweek,* 28 Feb. 1955

> Since he visited only troubled schools, his impression was one of a system in ferment —Peter Binzen, *Saturday Rev.,* 5 Feb. 1972

> . . . one of the greatest eras of intellectual ferment and creativity in history —Robert E. Herzstein, *N.Y. University Bulletin,* Spring 1967

> . . . there is a more healthy ferment in cognitive psychology . . . than there has been for many years — Noam Chomsky, *Columbia Forum,* Spring 1968

Now for the figurative verb senses. *Ferment* has the intransitive sense "to be in a state of agitation or intense activity":

> . . . these truths have been fermenting in the minds of a great many people —C. E. Ayres, *Saturday Rev.,* 14 Oct. 1950

> . . . whenever a new plot begins to ferment —Joan Aiken, *The Writer,* May 1968

It also has a transitive sense "to work up (as into a state of agitation)." *Foment* also has a figurative transitive sense "to promote the growth and development of"; and it is in these senses, in some contexts, that the words can be virtually synonymous.

There is, however, some difference in usage between the two words. Things that are fermented can be good or bad; things that are fomented are usually bad. And transitive uses of *foment,* which are virtually its only figurative uses, are much more common than transitive uses of *ferment,* which are just a small part of that word's orbit.

> . . . intelligence, which, fermented by much thought and travel in many lands, made him the raciest of wits —Vernon Louis Parrington, *Main Currents in American Thought,* 1930

> . . . the present outbreak of lawlessness—fermented by the Mau Mau —L. S. B. Leakey, *Mau Mau and the Kikuyu,* 1952

> . . . the notion that wars are fomented by munitions makers —Frederick Lewis Allen, *The Big Change,* 1952

> . . . seeking to foment revolution everywhere —Fred W. Neal, *Center Mag.,* May/June 1972

fewer See LESS, FEWER.

field It is a bit of a convention in the field of college handbooks to disparage the phrase *in the field of* as deadwood, which it certainly is in such examples as "He is majoring in the field of physics." The complaint is probably more of a warning to freshman English students and other college writers than a generalization on usage at large.

In our files we have a handful of citations from which the phrase could have been harmlessly omitted. But our citations seldom have it attached to well-known areas of intellectual endeavor such as psychology, history, or medicine. More often it is used to flag some other noun as standing for a field of study or endeavor when that meaning might not otherwise be the first to come to mind:

> Until Lévi-Strauss entered the field of mythology — John Bamberger, *N.Y. Times Book Rev.,* 3 June 1973

> . . . a writer of the utmost distinction in the crime field —Julian Symons, *N.Y. Times Book Rev.,* 30 Sept. 1979

> . . . the company applied its expertise and credit resources to the field of finance leasing —*Annual Report, General American Transportation Corp.,* 1970

> . . . casting my memory back over the field of musicals —Hollis Alpert, *Saturday Rev.,* 13 Nov. 1971

> . . . to dominate the radio news field —*Current Biography,* October 1966

The phrase *the field of* is probably generally omissible before the name of a well-known field such as chemistry or mathematics or philosophy, but it may be useful in preventing misunderstanding if the field is passenger cars or mystery novels.

fight with Chambers 1985 and Copperud 1970, 1980 point out that *fight with* can be ambiguous. This can be true if you phrase the sentence just right (or perhaps we should say, just wrong) and remove it entirely from context. But real sentences are far less likely to be troublesome. These are typical:

They had to be together, share with each other, fight with each other, quarrel with each other —Virginia Woolf, *Mrs. Dalloway,* 1925

. . . I fight and grapple with them —Charles Lamb, *The Essays of Elia,* 1823

When *fight* is figurative, ambiguity is nearly impossible:

. . . the losing battle that the plot fights with the characters —E. M. Forster, *American Scholar,* Autumn 1953

. . . the child should not have to fight with the book's pages —Bernice McLaren & Lawrence Dennis, *Children's House,* vol. 3, no. 5, 1969

figure *Figure* meaning "conclude, decide, think" is another apparent Americanism that has a few usage commentators worried. It was termed a provincialism by Emily Post back in 1927, and maybe that judgment persists in some. It is standard, in fact, but as the examples show, not especially formal:

. . . he doubtless figures it will make the Americans happy —Robert Shaplen, *New Yorker,* 11 Sept. 1971

He figures he and the Lord are lucky in any particular year to come out even —John Kenneth Galbraith, *Ambassador's Journal,* 1969

If you don't have the money, they figure you're not going anywhere —Fred R. Harris, *Harper's,* May 1972

figurehead Copperud 1970, 1980 says that *figurehead* is "often misapplied to people" which is a statement not easy to understand in itself, since the word's chief use when not designating a figure on a ship's bow is its application to people. What Copperud offers by way of clarification is a couple of examples in which the term is not applied in its usual pejorative sense of "a head or chief in name only." But the application of *figurehead* to people is a metaphorical extension; Copperud seems to have found two uses in which the writers had a different notion of the metaphor from the accepted one. We have a similar example:

The child who does not honor his father and mother will seldom honor teacher, business senior or the figureheads of state and government —H. H. Arnold & Ira C. Eaker, *Army Flyer,* 5th ed., 1942

And here is another one, somewhat different, but still not pejorative:

For surely Amory Blaine . . . is an odd figurehead for the Jazz Age —Maxwell Geismar, *The Last of the Provincials,* 1947

We frankly cannot say that these are mistakes. They are metaphorical extensions of the original sense, but it is not easy to define them. What we may have in them is a different sense that is of such infrequent occurrence in print that dictionary editors have had no need to try to figure out its meaning yet. It may even be passé already; the dates on the examples are not especially recent. It is possible that such a use could cause confusion on the part of the reader, to whom the pejorative sense may be the most familiar. But our evidence shows that pejorative use tends to be signaled by the context: *only, mere, merely* are often used, or the context otherwise makes the meaning plain. Even the familiar use, "a head or chief in name only," can be without much in the way of pejorative overtones:

The Crown Prince moved in a circle of silly young officers, who talked in bellicose and boastful terms; and he was sometimes tempted to put himself forward as figurehead for the most aggressive German militarists —*Times Literary Supp.,* 3 Sept. 1954

fillers *Filler* is a term used for words, phrases, and sounds (often spelled *er, uh, um*) that are used to fill gaps or pauses in discourse by speakers, as Burchfield 1981 diplomatically puts it, "who temporarily lose their fluency." A number of these—*actually, like, you know, for instance*—have been denigrated by usage writers, many of whom seem unaware of their function.

One astute observer of the language describes the function of fillers this way:

For the speaker, they give time for formulating the coming material, and for both speaker and hearer, they signal that the speaker will continue; the hearer's turn to reply has not come —Archibald A. Hill, in *Studies in English Linguistics,* ed. Sidney Greenbaum et al., 1979

Some fillers—*well, oh*—introduce an utterance, and others—*actually, you know, isn't it?*—are used as tags at the end of an utterance. Robert F. Ilson, in *The English Language Today* (1985), notes that British English has a wider variety of these than American English. It also appears that some of the British fillers are considered indicative of social class.

Fillers have been studied to some extent by linguists, but there is undoubtedly a great deal that we do not know about their functions and the constraints under which they are used. Just remember, when you read this or that writer discoursing on the subject, that fillers are characteristic of speech, not of written prose.

final Phythian 1979, Partridge 1942, Einstein 1985, Ayres 1881, and Copperud 1970, 1980 all carry brief warnings that *final* used in combination with *completion* (the first four), *ending, upshot* (Phythian and Partridge), and *culmination* (Copperud) is redundant. That our files—which are fairly wide-ranging—contain no examples of these combinations suggests that the problem does not arise often. When *final* is used with such words, or with *end, consumer, destination, outcome,* it is merely intended to reinforce the notion of finality. See REDUNDANCY.

final analysis See ANALYSIS.

finalize It has been fashionable to scorn *finalize* for more than four decades now. Its magic year seems to have been 1942: Perrin & Ebbitt 1972 says that Maury Maverick put *finalize* on his original list of gobbledygook in that year, and Partridge 1942 got in the first blows for the British. The British were quicker to follow up their initial attack than the Americans. A. P. Herbert went after it in *Punch* in 1945, Ivor Brown in *A Word in Your Ear* in 1945, and Sir Ernest Gowers in *Plain Words* in 1948. Gowers quoted Herbert, who, apparently facetiously, used *finalize* to mean "terminate."

Except for a 1944 review of Maverick's gobbledygook list in *Time,* American comment seems to have waited until the 1950s, especially when President Eisenhower used the word in a speech in 1958. After that everybody seems to have got on the bandwagon.

There was quite a bit of confusion about the origin of the word at first. Gowers was sure it was an Americanism, and so were a few 1950s reference works. Even as late as 1980, commentators were writing that President Eisenhower had introduced the word, if not actually coined it. And all the while it had been sitting quietly at the foot of page 948 in Webster's Second 1934—in the pearl section that holds the lower-frequency words.

It got into Webster's Second from Australia, chiefly. The earliest evidence we had then was from a business letter sent here from Melbourne in 1922. In 1923 our agent in Melbourne wrote to report losing the sale of a dictionary because *finalize* was not in it. The word was apparently quite common in Australia and New Zealand in the 1920s, especially in business circles:

> Negotiations are in progress between the New Zealand Co-operative Dairy Company and Mr. H. H. Sterling . . . with a view to his taking a position with the company. The matter has not been finalised — *Auckland* (New Zealand) *Weekly News,* 12 Nov. 1925

By 1927 the word had reached the U.S., apparently through the medium of the U.S. Navy; it turns up in the U.S. Naval Institute *Proceedings* in May of that year. The OED Supplement has British examples from 1930. It seems never to have been considered anything but standard in Australia and New Zealand. It is probably the widespread adoption of the word by various bureaucracies around the time of World War II that brought it to unfavorable notice.

Evidence in our files and in the OED Supplement shows that *finalize* is used in all of the major English-speaking areas of the world. (In British English both *-ise* and *-ize* spellings are used, with *-ise* the more common.) It is still a favorite in business and official English, and thus tends to be found in relatively formal contexts. It is occasionally found in breezy or tongue-in-cheek writing:

> In this decent if oppressive garb, she receives from Orloff a ring plighting their troth, and amid protracted twittering the couple finalize plans to marry at once —S. J. Perelman, *New Yorker,* 27 June 1953

> As I'm Prime Minister today, I thought you'd like to know what's going to be in the forty-one Queen's Speeches, now we've got them all gummed together into one. Of course, it's not exactly finalised yet — Alan Coren, *Punch,* 24 July 1974

> A total of 32 gigs has so far been finalised —*New Musical Express,* 31 Jan. 1976

> . . . she and Harvey hadn't finalized the parameters of their own interface —Cyra McFadden, *The Serial,* 1977

But more often it is used in contexts like these:

> No advertising budget has been finalised —*Evening Press* (Dublin, Ireland), 5 June 1974

> The scientist points out, though, that more tests must be conducted before these results are finalized —Barbara Ford, *National Wildlife,* June–July 1982

Private placement is legal in all but four states . . . , and like agency adoption, it is finalized through the court —Lynne McTaggart, *Saturday Rev.,* 10 Nov. 1979

> . . . has finalized a deal with a Canadian music distributor to handle these sales —Valerie Thompson, *Quill & Quire,* August 1976

> Final regulations were proposed last April, and an I.R.S. official testified today that they may be finalized in about 2 1/2 weeks —Frances Cerra, *N.Y. Times,* 22 Sept. 1976

> . . . in 1824 he journeyed to London to finalize his colonial accounts —*Australian Dictionary of Biography,* 1967

You do not have to use *finalize* at all, of course, but it is by now well established as standard. You would have little occasion for it in belles-lettres, but in contexts such as those illustrated here, writers seem to find it useful.

fine 1. If you had to plow through the abundant evidence for the adjective *fine* in our files, you might tend to agree with those handbooks that call it, when used to denote superior quality, an overused counterword. But what is equally obvious is that writers don't seem to feel it the least bit empty of content. It is used especially, though not at all exclusively, by reviewers, for whom it apparently suggests a measured or discriminating appreciation of something good. It seems to be able to denote superior quality without the suggestion of overstatement. It is frequently used in the superlative. Here are some samples of use:

> It is a very fine army—the best in South America — Graham Greene, *Harper's,* March 1972

> . . . where a translator, however fine a scholar, is not a writer . . . —Leo Rosten, *Harper's,* July 1972

> On balance, however, 1970 should prove a fine year, and a benison to the wine lover —Robert J. Misch, *McCall's,* March 1971

> A fine detective story, admirably bolstered with trade expertise —*Times Literary Supp.,* 22 Oct. 1971

> . . . there are few indications that its culture was more than superficial; fine clothes rather than fine feelings —James Sutherland, *English Literature of the Late Seventeenth Century,* 1969

> Yet his writing over the past two decades has included some of his finest poems —*Times Literary Supp.,* 16 Apr. 1970

> . . . the scripts . . . are in the finest traditions of the BBC —Gene Shalit, *Ladies' Home Jour.,* August 1971

As a predicate adjective it tends to be a more generalized (and less emphatic) term of approval:

> The job was fine—for a while —Vivian Cadden, *McCall's,* October 1971

> Unsaturated olive and corn and peanut oils are fine for cooking and salads —Dodi Schultz, *Ladies' Home Jour.,* August 1971

> This is no "value-free" book, which is fine with me —Peter Steinfels, *Commonweal,* 9 Oct. 1970

2. The adverb *fine* is called colloquial by a number of commentators, but *colloquial,* which is often used to disparage rather than merely to refer to standard spoken English, is a misleading label. In present-day use adverbial *fine* has two chief meanings. The less frequent one, "with a very narrow margin of time or space," usually goes with the verbs *cut* or *run:*

He had only forty minutes left, and would be cutting it too fine if he tried to find Hood —Pierre Salinger, *On Instructions of My Government,* 1971

The more frequent sense means "very well, excellently":

I liked your Maine poems fine —Archibald MacLeish, letter, 25 Jan. 1929

The dress . . . is beautiful and fits fine —Flannery O'Connor, letter, 1 Jan. 1959

Miss Lillian withstood the operation extremely fine —Dr. John R. Robinson 3d, quoted in *N.Y. Times,* 3 Oct. 1980

The adverb *fine* can be found in discursive prose as well as in speech and friendly correspondence:

This bloodless September stuff suits me fine — Edward Hoagland, *Harper's,* February 1971

A set of miniature chisels from Korea . . . held up fine —Claude D. Crowley, *Early American Life,* February 1977

They could walk fine in real life, but in front of the fashion photographers' cameras they were forced to become physical incompetents —*New Yorker,* 5 Oct. 1981

In these two uses the adverbial *fine* is not idiomatically interchangeable with *finely.*

finished In 1985 an American woman living in Germany wrote to us about two sentences containing *finished* that had been marked wrong by a German instructor on an English examination taken by her son (who had attended elementary school in the United States). The sentences were "I'm not finished yet" and "you aren't finished yet." The instructor was looking for *haven't* in each case. The woman had written to a British publisher on the same question and had been told that *am not* and *are not* with *finished* were not standard British usage, although they were "popular" in the U.S. and might occur in "informal" British speech. The question, then, was one of British English as taught from a textbook and British and American usage as it actually is.

That the school text is based on an artificial standard is fairly obvious from Strang 1970, who says that the construction *be finished with* arose in the 19th century, and from Otto Jespersen 1909–49 (volume 4) who found the construction in English literature as far back as Oliver Goldsmith's *Vicar of Wakefield* (1766). Jespersen also found examples from Jane Austen, Hall Caine, Arnold Bennett, George Bernard Shaw, Hugh Walpole, Frank Swinnerton, and W. Somerset Maugham. To this list we can add James Joyce:

Are you not finished with him yet . . . ? —*Ulysses,* 1922

Since a good many of the examples appear to have been spoken by characters in these books, it seems reasonable to suppose that the construction is chiefly found in ordinary speech. We cannot be sure whether the construction is better established in American speech than in British speech since most of our evidence is from discursive prose.

It seems apparent that *finished* began to become common in this construction during the 19th century, at the same time that the participial adjective (which had also arisen earlier) was becoming established. It also seems clear that the dispute over the propriety of the construction centers upon its use with a personal subject. With an inanimate subject, the construction can be understood as passive (rather than intransitive). We have several examples of this usage, which has not been a matter of dispute:

. . . the strife was finished; the vision was closed — Thomas DeQuincey, "The Vision of Sudden Death," 1849

At three o'clock his business was finished —Sherwood Anderson, *Poor White,* 1920

If the finished sketch was really finished —Dorothy L. Sayers, *Murder Must Advertise,* 1933

. . . the character I don't forget, and when the book is finished, that character is not done —William Faulkner, 13 Apr. 1957, in *Faulkner in the University,* 1959

. . . a complete clean-up by the contractor's crew when work is finished —Sylvia Porter, *Ladies' Home Jour.,* August 1971

The somewhat later use of *finished* to mean "done for" seems not to have been disputed either, even though it takes a personal subject.

. . . it may mean I am finished—an old fogey no longer able to keep the pace —Oliver Wendell Holmes d. 1935, letter, 1 Aug. 1925

See also DONE 1; THROUGH.

fire off Two commentators—Zinsser 1976 and Copperud 1980—disparage *fire off* as journalistic when it is used of something written. Zinsser pins his accusation on *Time,* and Copperud on *Newsweek.* Our examples are more wide-ranging:

What Woody did was compose and immediately fire off a TWX message to the Chief of Air Staff —James Gould Cozzens, *Guard of Honor,* 1948

. . . fired off a telegram to FDA Commissioner Charles Edwards —Nicholas Wade, *Science,* 19 Nov. 1971

. . . fired off a letter to Bunny Sandler's boss —John Mathews, *Change,* Summer 1971

The President's mood was reflected in a memorandum he fired off almost immediately —Chester Bowles, *Promises to Keep,* 1971

. . . contented themselves with firing off peremptory messages —Robert M. Bleiberg, *Barron's,* 8 May 1972

Some years ago a newspaper publisher fired off a memo to his staff saying, "If I see the word 'upcoming' once more, I'm going to be downcoming and the person responsible will be outgoing." —Edwin McDowell, *N.Y. Times,* 29 June 1983

The term seems generally to connote a sending in haste and sometimes in anger. It seems appropriate in such circumstances.

firm 1. *Noun.* Bernstein 1965 and Copperud 1970, 1980 object to the nontechnical use of *firm* as a synonym for any sort of business: Bernstein objects in particular to its use for a corporation, a different sort of legal entity; Copperud claims no dictionary recognizes the "corporation" use except Merriam-Webster dictionaries. The technical sense is "a partnership of two or more persons not recognized as a legal person distinct from the members composing it."

There are two matters to set straight here. First, no Merriam-Webster dictionary equates *firm* with *corporation;* our dictionaries do recognize a current extended sense, however, "a business unit or enterprise." This sense is well attested:

> ... the engineering firm that built the Chesapeake Bay bridge —*Dun's,* October 1971

> The new firm started operations in early 1971 as a major supplier of die cast parts —*Annual Report, National Lead Co.,* 1970

> ... established his own firm as a manufacturer of lamps —*Current Biography,* April 1966

> Sally does mechanical drawing for an engineering firm —Edwina Deans et al., *Basic Mathematics,* Book G, 1977

The second point is that the reader of these examples and similar reports has no need to know and probably does not care to know what legal basis the firm is established on. The consideration is irrelevant to the reader, and so is the objection.

Firm is a collective noun that is treated as singular in American English. In British English, however, it may take a plural verb:

> One sympathetic firm have sent Mr. Lawrence a pair of "indestructible" socks —*The People,* 25 Feb. 1968

2. *Adverb.* The adverb *firm* is usually found in just a few fixed phrases, such as *hold firm* and *stand firm:*

> On legalization of the Communist Party the Government is also standing firm —David Holden, *N.Y. Times Mag.,* 3 Oct. 1976

Firmly serves for other adverbial uses:

> ... held my hand firmly —Jane Goodall, *Ladies' Home Jour.,* October 1971

> ... the more she brooded, the more firmly she decided that it could not be done —Katherine Anne Porter, *Ladies' Home Jour.,* August 1971

> ... keeps buzzing until the door is firmly closed — Hubbard H. Cobb, *Woman's Day,* October 1971

> He firmly believes that shipbuilding will turn up with economy —Gerald R. Rosen, *Dun's,* October 1971

first Evans 1962 reports an exasperated husband who is annoyed by his wife's saying "When we were first married" meaning "soon after we were married." The husband evidently feels that *first* only means "for the first time." A similar understanding must underlie Lurie 1927's remarks on the curiosity of the same phrase.

Lurie quotes a man from Cincinnati who thought the expression a Germanism. But it apparently is not, to judge from the remarks and examples given by Jespersen 1909–49 (volume 4) under the heading "inchoative *first.*" Jespersen notes that the OED missed this use of *first* (as has Webster's Third) which he describes as denoting or emphasizing the beginning of a state, action, or change of state. A few examples of the same use in different contexts:

> "The name was gilded there when first I got the guitar...." —Herman Melville, *Pierre,* 1852

> I saw he was drunk when he first came into the room —Charles Dickens, *The Pickwick Papers,* 1837 (in Jespersen)

> When I first arrived in the country and spoke Dutch still —William Petersen, *Encounter,* December 1954

For another use of *first* disputed on the grounds of its having only one meaning, see FIRST TWO, TWO FIRST. See also FIRSTLY.

first and foremost This alliterative phrase is called redundant, trite, and meaningless by Evans 1957, political bombast by Copperud 1964, and a cliché by Macmillan 1982. No doubt there is some justice in all these criticisms, and you may want to keep them in mind the next time you are called upon to make a campaign speech ("First and foremost, let me thank the good people of this fair city ... "). *First and foremost* has other uses than as an introduction to windy oratory, however. Its alliteration and rhythm give it an emphatic quality which may make it attractive to good writers as an occasional alternative to *primarily* or *primary:*

> Its first and foremost component is the conscious cultivation of man's intellectual and expressive powers —Thomas F. O'Dea, *Center Mag.,* May 1969

> ... what they needed first and foremost was a giant statistical brain —David Halberstam, *Harper's,* February 1971

> ... the danger of Russia's strength was always, first and foremost, a function of Europe's own weakness —George F. Kennan, *New Yorker,* 1 May 1971

firstly Two objections have been lodged against this word. The first is a 19th-century prejudice against *firstly* on the grounds of propriety. Thomas De Quincey, for instance, said in 1847 that he detested the pedantic neologism *firstly.* Ayres 1881 seems to agree, although he does mention the approbation of Moon 1864; both Ayres and Gould 1870 note that Webster 1864 called it improper (and it was rare for Gould to agree with Webster). Later commentators who are lined up against *firstly* include Vizetelly 1906 and Bierce 1909.

All this criticism involved a certain amount of misunderstanding, however. De Quincey thought *firstly* a neologism, but it had been in use for more than 300 years when he wrote. Moon seems to have approved *firstly* because he thought *first* wasn't an adverb; but it is. Fowler 1926 pooh-poohed the whole fuss as "one of the harmless pedantries." Fowler thought that only pedants would insist on beginning a list with *first,* for no one did it naturally. But here Fowler was off base, for enumerations beginning *first* and going on with *secondly,* etc., can be found in the writings of such literary men as Thomas Gray (in 1758) and William Hazlitt (in 1808) well before there was a controversy.

Fowler's dismissal of the objections to *firstly* rather took the wind out of the sails of the controversy, though, and it gradually drifted to a stop, although Bernstein 1971 (agreeing with Fowler and Evans 1957, 1962) found one mid-20th-century American commentator still leery of it (as are Harper 1985 and Montgomery & Stratton 1981 more recently). Evans, in support of Fowler, lists such well-known 19th-century writers as Dickens, Scott, Gladstone, Byron, Thackeray, and Kingsley as users of *firstly*. This list makes it probable that the cause of the *firstly* fuss was the simple objection to what is perceived as new and popular—the cause of many another usage issue chronicled in this book.

Since Fowler took the original objection away from the commentators, they have come up with a second one. Almost universally they admit that *firstly* is all right, but they still prefer that you not use it. They want you to use *first* instead because it is shorter. Whether or not the commentators' advice has had any effect, *first* is a much more common and much more generally useful word than *firstly*, which is almost never used except to begin an enumeration. Our evidence also suggests that *firstly* is more frequent in British English than in American English.

All of this brings us to a final point. A good many recent handbooks feel you should be consistent in your enumerations. They prefer *first, second, third,* etc., but will allow you *firstly, secondly, thirdly,* etc. if you really favor those. Now there is nothing wrong with consistency—it is desirable—but it is only fair to note that writers and speakers have often played fast and loose with these enumerators. President Carter, for instance, used *first of all, secondly, third.* But that was in speech, you object. True. But Thomas Gray in 1758 used *first, 2dly, 3dly,* up to *6thly.* And William Hazlitt in 1808 used *first, secondly,* etc., up to *eighthly,* then *lastly.* And Fitzedward Hall 1873 used *first of all, secondly, in the third place.* And the English novelist Colin MacInnes in about 1957 used *firstly, next, thirdly.* So while we do not suggest you be purposely inconsistent, it does appear that consistency in this specific usage has not always had a particularly high priority with good writers.

first two, two first When *first* and a cardinal number are used together, there are two ways of ordering them: either "the three first Gospels" (an example from Alford 1866) or "the first three Gospels." The OED shows that the first of these constructions is the older, dating back to at least the 14th century. The latter construction is attested from the late 16th century. The OED editor suggests that the latter construction is the result of the common people's perception of *first* as an ordinal.

The OED explanation works very well for *first,* but Jespersen 1909–49 (volume 2) notes that the same competition in word order occurs with *last* and *next* as well as *first.* The development of the two competing constructions, then, is not likely to be explained by simple logic; let us just accept it as historical fact.

The older construction—"the two first"—became the subject of commentary and controversy in the second half of the 18th century. Lounsbury 1908, who devotes nearly 10 pages to a discussion of the controversy, mentions several separate occasions in which the older use was criticized, including a dispute the poet Thomas Moore had with a critic and with his printer in 1833. The first of the usage writers in our collection to mention the issue is Alford 1866, who defends his use of "the three first Gospels" against critics. Since that time, the subject has been reviewed in a large number of usage books, most of them coming between Alford and the

1930s, although it does appear in some books as recent as Freeman 1983 and Harper 1985.

There is no shortage of literary evidence for the older construction:

> I cast my eyes but by chance on *Catiline;* and in the three or four first pages, found enough to conclude that *Johnson* writ not correctly —John Dryden, "Defence of the Epilogue," 1672

> ... and procure a transcript of the ten or twenty first lines of each —Samuel Johnson, letter, 7 Aug. 1755

> Why, the two last volumes are worse than the four first —Thomas Gray, letter, 8 Mar. 1758

> ... the seven first years of his pacific reign —Daniel Defoe, *The True Born Englishman,* 1701 (in Lounsbury)

> ... the three next pictures —*The Spectator,* No. 167 (in Jespersen)

> The Examiner has been down this month, and was very silly the five or six last papers —Jonathan Swift, *Journal to Stella,* 24 Aug. 1711

> ... the preface to the five first imperfect editions — Alexander Pope, appendix to *The Dunciad,* 1743 edition (in Lounsbury)

> ... the average price of the sixty-four first years of the present century —Edward Gibbon, *The Decline and Fall of the Roman Empire,* 1788 (in Lounsbury)

> ... during the two or three last years of his life, he was more fond of company than ever —Oliver Goldsmith, quoted in a footnote to Swift's *Journal to Stella,* 1824 edition

> The two last days were very pleasant —Jane Austen, letter, 8 Sept. 1816

The basis for the objection to the older construction is logic, supposedly; the argument urged is that there can be one first and one last. Jespersen comments on this argument:

> Pedants have objected to combinations like *the three first lines* on the absurd plea that there is only one first line (as if it were not possible to speak of the first years of one's life!)

Alford attacks the logic of the usage from a somewhat different angle. He objects to "the first three Gospels"— the correction urged upon him by his critics—on the grounds that "the first three" to him implied the existence of a second three—and there are only four Gospels. Lounsbury also makes use of this argument.

The appeal to logic against the older construction depends on the assumption that *first* has but one meaning—the first in a denumerable series—the falsity of which Jespersen demonstrated. The fact that this argument is fallacious has not prevented its often being repeated—as recently as Freeman 1983. The argument of Alford and Lounsbury is not especially strong either: the meaning they ascribe to the newer construction does sometimes occur, but in speech, at least, Alford's meaning for "the first three Gospels" is likely to be differentiated from his critics' meaning for the same expression by stress and intonation. More simple-minded commentators have merely called the older construction wrong, but, of course, it is not.

What is true, however, is that the older construction

is falling out of use. Longman 1984 describes it as old-fashioned. The survey of the usage panel in Harper 1975, 1985 shows 19 percent of the panelists using the older construction and 81 percent the newer construction. Our files have very few examples of the older construction, although it does turn up from time to time:

> ... published the year before the two first volumes of Tristram Shandy —John Butt, *English Literature in the Mid-Eighteenth Century,* edited & completed by Geoffrey Carnall, 1979

But the newer construction is the one you will usually find:

> Between his last two comedies he went on some diplomatic mission to Constantinople —Bonamy Dobrée, *Restoration Comedy,* 1924

> The first couple chapters are pretty good —E. B. White, letter, 26 Oct. 1959

> The first six volumes set a high standard —*Times Literary Supp.,* 31 Oct. 1968

> This play ... drags rather badly for the first two acts —James Sutherland, *English Literature of the Late Seventeenth Century,* 1969

We think that the newer construction is right now the more common one idiomatically, and if you have been born since the 1920s, it is the one you will use automatically. But remember that anyone who happens to still use the older order is not wrong.

fit, fitted **1.** There seems to be a bit of confusion about the alternative past and past participle forms of the verb *fit.* Both *fitted* and *fit* are used in the United States; only *fitted* appears to be used in British English. The Linguistic Atlas information given in Bryant 1962 shows that there are American regional considerations involved too, and the Dictionary of American Regional English shows that *fit* predominates in all parts of the U.S. except New England. There should perhaps be a tiny isogloss in New York City in the area of the *New York Times* offices: Theodore Bernstein 1962, 1965, 1971, 1977 insists on *fitted* (in 1971 he allowed *fit* fit for speech, but not for print), and so does his successor, as recently as in *Winners & Sinners,* 20 Mar. 1987.

Evans 1957, Bryant 1962, Lamberts 1972, and Heritage 1982 present opinion or evidence showing some preference for *fitted* when the verb is used in a causative sense:

> During the off-season he was fitted with glasses — Rick Telander, *Sports Illustrated,* 2 Aug. 1982

Our evidence for this sense does not confirm the dominance of *fitted,* even though it seems right intuitively. It does not seem especially unlikely that dialectal preference for *fit* might sometimes counter this general trend of using *fitted* for the causative sense. For instance, we have this example:

> A fine shirtmaker will tell you that ... you are perfectly capable of being fit —G. Bruce Boyer, *Town & Country,* February 1983

One problem here is that we don't really know that much about the development of *fit* as an irregular past and past participle. No one to this point seems to have put together a great deal of information about it.

For now you need only remember that in American

English both *fitted* and *fit* are correct; your preference in a particular instance will probably be conditioned by where you were born. British English uses *fitted.* The Dictionary of American Regional English shows *fit* more common than *fitted* in most of the U.S. Our files show *fitted* somewhat more common than *fit* in print.
2. There is also an adjective *fit* which in its earliest and still current sense, "adapted to an end or design," goes back to the 14th century. It is actually a couple of hundred years older than the verb. This adjective is frequently used as a predicate adjective followed by *for* or *to* and an infinitive:

> It was a hearse fit for a royal corpse —Russell Baker, *Growing Up,* 1982

> ... I write a great deal that is not fit to read —Flannery O'Connor, letter, 4 May 1955

In British English especially, the participial adjective *fitted* is often used in place of *fit:*

> I have attained to all the wisdom which I am fitted to bear —James Stephens, *The Crock of Gold,* 1912

> Dryden was a natural laureate, fitted for the post by outlook, ambition and poetic temper —John Gross, *N.Y. Times Book Rev.,* 15 July 1984

It seems likely that confusion with the verb—the senses of verb and adjective overlap to a certain degree—accounts for some instances in which *fitted* is used. When *fit* is used in its newest sense, "in sound physical condition," it is never replaced by *fitted.*

fix **1.** Back in 1839 Captain Frederick Marryat, the nautical novelist, paid a visit to America. Among the things he noticed was the American use of the verb *fix.* "The verb 'to fix' is universal. It means to do anything," he wrote in his diary. The editors of the Dictionary of American English used Marryat's comment to preface their treatment of the verb, for which they were able to descry some thirty senses and subsenses of American provenience. While a good many of these originated later than 1839, some go back to the 17th and 18th centuries.

Captain Marryat is not noted for his effect on American usage writers. But Schele de Vere 1872 expanded quite a bit on Marryat's comment, and it was perhaps from this source that the subject was picked up by turn-of-the-century commentators. Vizetelly 1906 finds *fix* "repair" to be "inelegant and indefinite." Bierce 1909 disapproves it in the senses "repair" and "prepare." MacCracken & Sandison 1917 find it an "inaccurate colloquialism" in the same senses.

From these older sources *fix* has found its way into quite a large number of handbooks. Many of these complain that the word is overused or has too many meanings and recommend that some more exact word be substituted for it. On examination you can see that the reason given for the recommendation is inexact. Is "repair my watch" more specific than "fix my watch"? Or is "prepare some supper" more precise than "fix some supper"? Clearly not. Shaw 1987 goes beyond the mere suggestion of using a more precise substitute; he says that it doesn't make much sense to use the same word for such widely diverse meanings. But *fix* is no more semantically diffuse than many common verbs in English. For instance, you can "take a swim," "take a drink," "take your time," "take it on the chin," or "take a size six." Who is confused by such everyday phrases?

And *fix* has many fewer senses than such verbs as *set, break, turn, do,* or *run.*

This seems to be a case—one out of many—of the well-attested but inexplicable nervousness of American usage commentators when faced with Americanisms. There is no reason Americans need be diffident about their own language. Here are a few fairly recent examples of several senses that are mentioned in the usage books:

> ... the Windham Garage, where cars and farm machines get fixed —Vance Bourjaily, *Atlantic,* February 1973

> ... a searching criticism of the whole legal system, which they said was too seriously flawed for a legal services program to fix —David Riley, *The Washingtonian,* November 1970

> "Do you want me to fix you a piece of jelly bread?" she asked —Russell Baker, *Growing Up,* 1982

> Her hair looked as if it had just been professionally done, although she fixes it herself —Lally Weymouth, *N.Y. Times Mag.,* 26 Oct. 1980

> Did you go and try to fix this case behind my back? —F. Lee Bailey, quoted in *N.Y. Times,* 6 Mar. 1976

> ... fixing traffic tickets for wayward drivers —William Nack, *Sports Illustrated,* 22 Sept. 1980

> ... don't bother either to have their cats fixed or to feed them —Anthony Bailey, *New Yorker,* 20 Nov. 1971

> ... to make some money and get her Latino nose fixed to American standards —Richard Boeth, *Cosmopolitan,* June 1976

These uses are all standard though not, perhaps, characteristic of the most elevated prose.

Safire 1984 prints a letter in which a correspondent takes him to task for writing "a chance to fix their mistakes." The correspondent pretends this must mean "a chance to make their mistakes permanent." This is the game of willful misinterpretation of plain American English that is pleasureful to those who dislike some meaning or other of a word for some reason or other or for no reason. We recommend that you not play it. These uses of *fix* are perfectly all right in American English.

2. The intransitive sense of *fix* meaning "to get set, be on the verge" is showing signs of breaking out of its regional shell. It seems to be most often used in the southern United States, but now and then pops up in a national publication. It is almost always found in the form *fixing to* now. The evidence in the Dictionary of American English shows *fixing for* in the 18th century. There is a long article on the subtleties of *fixing to* by Marvin K. L. Ching in *American Speech,* Winter 1987.

> I am fixing to paint this afternoon —Flannery O'Connor, letter, 28 Feb. 1960

> ... Muhammad Ali and Joe Frazier are fixing to come out of retirement —*Sports Illustrated,* 31 Aug. 1981

This construction is not found in very formal contexts.
3. The noun *fix* has less frequently been aspersed, but it receives occasional mention. Bernstein 1971 says most senses of the noun are useful and acceptable, but he questions the sense "a shot of a narcotic." The examples here will show you how that sense has developed since 1971:

> ... the urgent frisking for notes and small change of boys desperate for a fix —Anthony Burgess, *MF,* 1971

> ... leaves the Radio 3–saturated listener wondering where to go for his evening fix —Christopher Driver, *The Listener,* 27 June 1974

> ... Dopey Americans will pay anything for their coffee fix —William Safire, *N.Y. Times,* 13 Jan. 1977

> Beauty contest addicts can get another giant fix tomorrow —John J. O'Connor, *N.Y. Times,* 9 Sept. 1977

> To the baseball addict, box scores ... are his daily fix —Ronnie Virgets, *New Orleans Times-Picayune,* 12 Oct. 1979

Here are two other common and even more recent uses of the noun:

> There is no quick fix to the interest-rate dilemma —Christopher Byron et al., *Time,* 12 Oct. 1981

> These are technological fixes once undreamed of —Horace Freeland Judson, *Science 84,* November 1984

flack   See FLAK, FLACK.

flagrant   See BLATANT, FLAGRANT.

flair   1. *Flair* is a fairly recent import from French, first attested in English in its current manifestation in 1881. Our evidence from the early 20th century regularly puts the word in quotation marks or italics: writers (or editors) seemed to feel the word was foreign. Fowler 1926 with his nose for etymology insisted that the primary meaning of the word must be "keen scent, capacity for getting on the scent of something desired, a good nose *for* something"—the word means "sense of smell" in French. Obviously it was not so used in English—Fowler picks for censure a completely normal-looking example in which a woman is described as having a flair for cooking and a flair for writing. But once Fowler had started a hare, there were others willing to follow:

> Indeed, I am thinking of doing a broadcast about it, calling upon the people to rise and kill off all those who use *flair* under the impression that it means knack or talent or aptitude —Alexander Woollcott, letter, 23 Jan. 1937

But this was how the word was (and is) being used:

> ... the same insight into average men and women, the same *flair* for differences of character —*Harper's,* September 1915

> ... Barnum's amazing flair for publicity —*The Nation,* 11 Apr. 1923

> ... men with less fire but more flair for constructive effort —*American Mercury,* May 1926

> ... a graduate of Jones Commercial High School with a flair for the *mot juste* —S. I. Hayakawa, *Chicago Sun Book Week,* 8 Sept. 1946

> ... an unexpected flair for light comedy —*Current Biography,* February 1968

... a flair for getting the most out of each tidbit — Nicholas Lemann, *N.Y. Times Book Rev.,* 26 June 1983

Flair is also used to mean "inclination, tendency, penchant":

The Greeks, who had a flair for renaming everything they came in contact with —Lowell Thomas, *Beyond the Khyber Pass,* 1925

... their flair for dramatic public announcements — Leslie H. Gelb & Morton H. Halperin, *Harper's,* November 1971

And there's a sense for an attractive quality—"style, verve, panache":

... no politician ... who has rushed into print can compare with Mr. Churchill in historical *flair,* literary skill —*Political Science Quarterly,* December 1923

When carried off with real flair, the general flow of the music makes one willing to overlook any momentary reminiscences —Aaron Copland, *Our New Music,* 1941

... and his neckties, well, they had flair —Robert Henderson, *New Yorker,* 22 Apr. 1967

Not only did the Reds lose, but they lost with flair —Herm Weiskopf, *Sports Illustrated,* 19 July 1982

These uses have been standard all along. The issue appears to be dead now.

2. *Flair, flare.* A number of handbooks warn against confusing these homophones. Part of the trouble is that *flair* is an occasional variant of *flare* in the sense of "a spreading outward." When pants with flared legs were fashionable, they were sometimes spelled *flairs* and sometimes *flares.* Aside from this, we have little recent evidence for *flair* in this sense. In other senses we find occasional uncertainty about spelling. In the first of these examples *flare* would be more usual; in the second it should be *flair:*

A bloop hit is a flair —Phil Pepe, in *Baseball Digest,* November 1974

... Gift Selections with an Early American Flare — advt., *Early American Life,* December 1979

flak, flack   *Flak* was originally antiaircraft fire, and more recently hostile or at least unfriendly criticism. *Flack* was originally a press agent. Copperud 1980 is worried that the difference between the two is threatened. As far as spelling is concerned, the difference has already eroded to a certain extent: *flack* is established as a variant spelling of *flak,* and *flak* is used occasionally for *flack.* However, neither variant is as common as the original spelling, so spelling will clue you to meaning most of the time. In other cases, you will have to pay attention to the context. The words are never confused, even if their spellings are sometimes interchanged. You will not mistake the meanings in these examples:

A flak man for Senator Dymally —Paul Wieck, *New Republic,* 27 Jan. 1968

... they would not hire a flak to keep their names in the press —E. V. Cunningham, *Cosmopolitan,* February 1973

Flack is much more usual:

... the same nervous agents, press flacks, and hangers-on —Larry L. King, *Harper's,* July 1968

... the rhetoric of a White House flack —Gaddis Smith, *N.Y. Times Book Rev.,* 3 June 1973

Flak is often run into, caught, or taken:

... the administration has run into flak —Andy Pasztor, *Wall Street Jour.,* 18 Feb. 1983

The Budget Director also caught flak for statements that ... —Rich Jaroslovsky, *Wall Street Jour.,* 12 Nov. 1981

Now we're taking the flak from all the rest —David A. Stockman, quoted in *Atlantic,* December 1981

This sometimes comes spelled *flack* (the original sense was also sometimes spelled this way):

This modest proposal ran into flack —Charles MacDonald, *Library Jour.,* August 1967

There was a lot of flack when you took your stand —R. Allen Leider, *Celebrity,* October 1976

We recommend that you go with the original and still dominant spellings for each word.

flammable, inflammable   These two words are synonymous. *Flammable* is a much newer word, apparently coined in 1813 to serve in a translation from Latin. In the 1920s it was adopted by the National Fire Protection Association in place of *inflammable.* Underwriters and others interested in fire safety followed suit. The reason given for its adoption was the possibility that the *in-* of *inflammable* might be misunderstood as a negative prefix. We do not know whether such a misunderstanding has ever actually occurred. We have a 1949 citation in which a scientist working on a fireproof airplane engine is quoted as saying that in the proposed system the fuel would be "virtually inflammable." The clipping, however, is so shot through with typographical errors that we cannot be positive what was actually said. It does, however, suggest that there may be some basis for the concern about misunderstanding.

The publicity campaign undertaken to urge wider adoption of *flammable* put the word in the public eye on numerous occasions over the years. Eventually the ivory tower—where nothing burns, apparently—began to be heard bemoaning the loss of a fine literary word *(inflammable)* which was being shunted aside by a "corrupt" form. The combination of publicity and occasional outbreaks of lamentation have probably helped in landing the subject in so many usage books.

Our files show that both forms continue to be used. *Flammable* seems to be less common in British English than it is in American English and *inflammable* correspondingly more common. *Flammable* is used literally; figurative use belongs to *inflammable:*

The vision of a single young woman is said to have overcome the inflammable Monk —George Meredith, *The Ordeal of Richard Feverel,* 1859

But the inflammable and inflammatory materials were there to be ignited by critics of the scientific-military Establishment —Donald Fleming, *Atlantic,* September 1970

Nonflammable is the usual negative compound of *flammable.*

flare   See FLAIR 2.

flat adverbs   A flat adverb is an adverb that has the same form as its related adjective: *fast* in "drive fast," *slow* in "go slow," *sure* in "you sure fooled me," *bright* in "the moon is shining bright," *flat* in "she turned me down flat," *hard* and *right* in "he hit the ball hard but right at the shortstop." Flat adverbs have been a problem for grammarians and schoolmasters for a couple of centuries now, and more recently usage writers have continued to wrestle with them.

Flat adverbs were more abundant and used in greater variety formerly than they are now. They were used then as ordinary adverbs and as intensifiers:

> . . . commanding him incontinent to avoid out of his realm and to make no war —Lord Berners, translation of Froissart's *Chronicles,* 1523

> . . . I was horrid angry, and would not go —Samuel Pepys, diary, 29 May 1667

> . . . the weather was so violent hot —Daniel Defoe, *Robinson Crusoe,* 1719

> . . . the five ladies were monstrous fine —Jonathan Swift, *Journal to Stella,* 6 Feb. 1712

> . . . I will not be extreme bitter —William Wycherly, *The Country Wife,* 1675

You would be hard pressed to find modern examples of these particular uses.

Originally such adverbs had not been identical with adjectives; they had been marked by case endings—usually a dative -*e*—but over the course of Middle English the ending disappeared. The 18th-century grammarians, such as Lowth 1762, Priestley 1798, and Murray 1795, could not explain how these words were adverbs. They saw them as adjectives, and they considered it a grammatical mistake to use an adjective for an adverb. Their preference was for the suffixal adverb ending in -*ly*.

Two centuries of chipping away by schoolmasters and grammarians has reduced the number of flat adverbs in common use and has lowered the status of quite a few others. Many of them continue in standard use, but most of them compete with an -*ly* form. Bernstein 1971, for instance, lists such pairs as *bad, badly; bright, brightly; close, closely; fair, fairly; hard, hardly; loud, loudly; right, rightly; sharp, sharply; tight, tightly.* Many of these pairs have become differentiated, and now the flat adverb fits in some expressions while the -*ly* adverb goes in others. And a few flat adverbs—*fast* and *soon,* for instance—have managed to survive as the only choice (though in the latter case the adjective has all but disappeared).

The controversy or uncertainty over the status of this or that flat adverb is a legacy of our not having had an adequate grammar. The Latin grammar that was all the 18th-century grammarians knew could not explain how the same word could be both an adjective and an adverb. Thus common usages such as the intensive *exceeding* were vexing to the grammarians:

> . . . was so exceeding harmless —John Dryden, "Defence of the Epilogue," 1672

> . . . having an exceeding good memory —Benjamin Franklin, *Autobiography,* 1784

> . . . an exceeding good ball last night —Jane Austen, letter, 9 Jan. 1796

English has many words that can function both as adverb and adjective. If the early grammarians had realized that English was not the same as Latin, a whole lot of agonizing and rationalizing could have been avoided. And we might also have avoided those supernumerary adverbs like *muchly* and *thusly*—often criticized as hypercorrect—formed in accordance with the grammarians' predilection for -*ly* forms.

Several articles in this book deal with the question of flat adverbs; see BAD, BADLY; CHEAP 2; CONSIDERABLE 2; NEAR, NEARLY; QUICK, QUICKLY; SCARCELY 1; SLOW, SLOWLY; TIGHT, TIGHTLY.

flaunt, flout   A letter to the editor of the *San Francisco Chronicle* in 1932 noted "the curious new error" of confusing *flaunt* with *flout:*

> This new error, which I am informed is sweeping the country, is one more indication that we Americans are growing less and less language minded. Is this growth due to the machine age? —letter, *San Francisco Chronicle,* 25 June 1932

This is the first record we have of anyone objecting to this "curious new error." Our earliest evidence of the error itself is from 1918:

> They flaunt his every title to affection or respect — *Yale Rev.,* October 1918

Further evidence turned up sporadically in the 1920s and 1930s, but we began to see this use of *flaunt* frequently only in the late 1940s.

This is one issue about which there is no dissent among usage commentators. All of them regard the use of *flaunt* to mean "flout" as nothing less than an ignorant mistake. Many of them also note with dismay or astonishment that this ignorant mistake is extremely common, and that it occurs even among the well-educated (Partridge 1942 even candidly admits to having made it himself). Nowhere is there the least suggestion, however, that its common occurrence among the highly educated makes it at all defensible. Even those commentators who are relatively liberal in other matters take a hard line when it comes to *flaunt* and *flout.*

Flaunt in its approved senses can mean "to display oneself to public notice," "to wave showily," and especially "to display ostentatiously":

> . . . some books that flaunt a brand name are doing little more than beckoning to a market —Hugh Kenner, *Harper's,* March 1984

> . . . to allow a minority to openly flaunt its differences with the rest of society —*Houston Post,* 16 Sept. 1984

Flout means "to treat with contemptuous disregard":

> . . . is crushed by the conventions she flouts —Robert Pattison, *On Literacy,* 1982

> . . . many of them flout the rules on amateurism — Bob Ottum, *Sports Illustrated,* 6 Feb. 1984

Both words are used to describe open, unashamed behavior, and both typically suggest disapproval of such behavior. They are, in fact, used in such similar ways that they go together easily in a single sentence:

> They are secure enough in their womanhood to neither flaunt it (like a starlet) nor flout it (like some feminists) —*People,* 3 Jan. 1983

... a young woman notoriously wild, flaunting her sexual power, flouting the decorum deemed fitting a maiden queen —Maureen Quilligan, *N.Y. Times Book Rev.,* 3 Apr. 1983

Add to this similarity of use the obvious similarity of the words themselves, and you have a situation ripe for confusion.

It is an oversimplification, however, to say that the use of *flaunt* to mean "to treat with contemptuous disregard" is merely the result of confusion. Certainly this sense originated from confusion of *flaunt* with *flout,* but those who now use it do so not because they are confused—they do so because they have heard and seen it so often that its use seems natural and idiomatic. They use it, in other words, because they are familiar with it as an established sense of *flaunt:*

They observed with horror the flaunting of their authority —Marchette Chute, *Shakespeare of London,* 1949

... she flaunted the rules, was continually reprimanded —Louis Untermeyer, *Saturday Rev.,* 7 June 1969

... burning-out with drugs, daring authority, flaunting tradition —Edwin S. Shneidman, *Psychology Today,* June 1971

... whose code of respectability he flaunts or violates —Philip Roth, *Reading Myself and Others,* 1975

... the impulse ... to flaunt the taboos of the tribe —O. B. Hardison, Jr., *Entering the Maze,* 1981

No one can deny that this sense of *flaunt* is now alive and well, despite its lowly origins.

Nevertheless, the notoriety of *flaunt* used for *flout* is so great, and the belief that it is simply an error is so deep-seated and persistent, that we think you well-advised to avoid it, at least when writing for publication. Its occurrence in a published work is almost certain to draw criticism (assuming that it gets past the eye of the copy editor). If you use it in casual speech, open criticism is less likely—if only because most people are not that rude—but you do run the risk of giving some of your listeners the mistaken impression that they are smarter than you are.

Nor do we recommend that you use *flout* to mean "to display ostentatiously; flaunt." Such usage does turn up in print on occasion:

"I think the flouting of indecent and offensive displays ... should be curtailed" —Patrick Cormack, quoted in *Express & Star* (Wolverhampton, Eng.), 8 June 1974

The Ku Klux Klan ... is openly flouting its racial hatred —Julian Bond, letter, 1981

But it is extremely uncommon and can only be regarded as a genuine error.

See also MITIGATE.

flautist, flutist   A musician who plays the flute can be called either a flautist or a flutist. *Flutist* is the older word, first recorded in 1603, and is the one preferred by usage commentators. *Flautist* is of Italian derivation. The earliest record of its occurrence in English is from 1860, when Hawthorne used it in *The Marble Faun.* Fowler 1926 was the first to express disapproval of it, essentially because he found it pretentious. Despite his

objections, however, *flautist* has become the preferred term in British English. In American English, both words are used but *flutist* is by far the more common choice.

fleshly, fleshy   A few critics, starting with Fowler 1926, distinguish between *fleshly* and *fleshy* and warn against confusing them. The two words, the OED shows, have been occasionally synonymous for many years—at least since Chaucer used them both in the sense of "plump." To show the main directions of development while not getting bogged down in unnecessarily specific details, we can say that each word has two main divisions of meaning. The first relates to the flesh as substance, the second to flesh as opposed to the spirit or to what is immaterial.

The senses relating to flesh as a substance and its physical attributes have come to predominate with *fleshy:*

A charming, fleshy, latter-day Jay Gatsby —Aljean Harmetz, *N.Y. Times Mag.,* 5 Oct. 1980

... right angles are softened by curves and fleshy pillows —Michael Walker, *Metropolitan Home,* April 1983

The senses contrasting with *spiritual* are those that have come to predominate with *fleshly:*

Paul has to bring these fleshly pagans over to a more ascetic faith —Anthony Burgess, *TV Guide,* 5 Apr. 1985

... this vision of life without tears in a fleshly paradise —Malcolm Muggeridge, in Ronald Reagan, *Abortion and the Conscience of the Nation,* 1984

There are quite a few instances in which both words can be used similarly, or even synonymously. These uses are well justified historically and are not wrong, but they tend to be counter to what the reader would normally expect.

floating adverb   See SENTENCE ADVERB.

floor   See CEILING, FLOOR.

flounder, founder   A person flounders by struggling to move or obtain footing, while a ship founders by filling with water and sinking. Usage writers say that these two words are often confused, and we have found that *flounder* and *founder,* whether used literally or figuratively, sometimes do borrow each other's meaning.

... Cabeza de Vaca's boat had floundered in 1528 — Bernard DeVoto, *The Course of Empire,* 1952

... our political parties must never flounder on the rocks of moral equivocation —Adlai E. Stevenson, *Speeches,* ed. Richard Harrity, 1952

Their discourse floundered.... They sat staring numbly at each other —Margaret Cousins, *Ladies' Home Jour.,* October 1971

... bloodhounds ... raced confidently through the campus right to the highway ... and there they foundered —Edward Corsetti, *True Police Cases,* October 1959

Flounder for *founder* is a substitution much likelier to be encountered than the reverse. And the uses of *founder* for *flounder* tend to read as though some third verb might be what the writer really wanted. Crossover uses of *flounder* are more straightforwardly cases of confusion with *founder.* We do not have enough evidence to say that a new sense has become established in either case.

Critics such as Bernstein 1958 and Freeman 1983 also disapprove of *founder* paired with *sink* as redundant:

> The ship carrying Manoel's rhinoceros foundered off the coast of Genoa and sank with all hands —Calvin Tomkins, *New Yorker,* 20 Nov. 1971

The redundancy is undeniable, but the offense seems minor. *Founder and sink* is not much different from other redundant pairs long sanctioned by idiom: *dead and gone, fear and trembling, huff and puff.*

Occasionally a sentence will allow either *flounder* or *founder* to be used.

> ... the thick yellow hawser visible beyond my porthole was ... what a life preserver was to the floundering man —John Hawkes, "The Ship," in *Fiction,* vol. 1, no. 4, 1973

Except for such contexts, however, it is probably better to keep the meanings of these two words distinct.

flout   See FLAUNT, FLOUT.

flunk   A number of college handbooks (including Little, Brown 1980, 1986, Prentice Hall 1978, Macmillan 1982) and at least one high-school handbook (Guth 1980) stigmatize *flunk* as "colloquial"—whatever that may mean to their respective editors. Flesch 1983, in contrast, approves the term, which he finds more forceful than *fail.* It is probably this forcefulness that is moving *flunk* from the schoolroom and the campus into wider general use. Here are a few examples:

> ... why Professor Schlesinger flunks Nixon as a President —Garry Wills, *N.Y. Times Book Rev.,* 18 Nov. 1973

> ... publicizing the names of violators who had flunked two inspections in a row —Richard Haitch, *N.Y. Times,* 4 July 1976

> ... millions would flunk the examinations —Vance Packard, *The People Shapers,* 1977

> ... I had, I recall, flunked trigonometry four times in a row —William Styron, *This Quiet Dust and Other Writings,* 1982

It is Flesch's contention that *flunk* connotes failure by a generous margin. His contention is supported by this example:

> My latest accomplishment is that I flunked the driver's test. ... I drove the patrolman around the block. He sat crouched in the corner, picking his teeth nervously while I went up a hill in the wrong gear, came down on the other side with the car out of control and stopped abruptly on somebody's lawn —Flannery O'Connor, letter, 2 July 1958

fluorine, fluorescent   Bremner 1980 and Copperud 1970, 1980 note that words derived from and related to *fluorine* are often misspelled by transposing the vowels to *flour-.* We have plenty of evidence for such mistakes, so they are worth watching out for.

flutist   See FLAUTIST, FLUTIST.

foist, fob off   Fowler 1926 discovered a sentence in a British newspaper beginning, "The general public is much too easily foisted off with the old cry...." This construction, said Fowler, was wrong; *fob off* could be used in "the public can be fobbed off with something" or in "something can be fobbed off on the public," but *foist* could only be used in the second construction. Evans 1957 repeats the gist of Fowler's comments about the construction, but illustrates *foist* with *foisted on.* Copperud 1970, 1980 omits the original construction problem altogether, although citing Fowler and Evans. He insists on *fob off on* and *foist on* and says *foist off* is wrong. Longman 1984 takes Fowler's position.

We have two separate issues mingled here. The original—Fowler's—concerns the construction in which the public or an individual is *foisted off with.* Except for the single example he produced, we have no evidence of that construction. Fowler correctly identified the normal idiomatic construction.

Copperud's notion of which prepositions may be used with *foist,* however, conflicts with the evidence we have. *Foist*—in the construction Fowler considered idiomatic—is used with *on, upon, into,* and *off on. On* and *upon* are by far the most common:

> ... a sort of military remittance man foisted on the Europeans —Richard C. Longworth, *Saturday Rev.,* 12 June 1976

> The cause of their sorrow was a unique coffin foisted upon them by their chief supplier of funeral goods —Russell Baker, *Growing Up,* 1982

Into is much less common; all of our evidence for it is British.

> ... if one may foist a pun into *Lycidas* —*Notes and Queries,* 10 June 1950

Foist off on, which may be in origin a syntactic blend of *foist on* and *fob off on,* is a construction that seems to be slightly on the increase. Our evidence for it goes back to 1937:

> ... accusing him of gross dishonesty in foisting off on the public a palpable fiction in the guise of an authentic travel book —Charles Roberts Anderson, *American Literature,* March 1937

> It is indeed remarkable what nonsense about words can be foisted off on scholars having international reputations —Mitford M. Mathews, *American Speech,* October 1954

> ... those who think that Emma foisted off someone else's child on Nelson —Mollie Hardwick, *Emma, Lady Hamilton,* 1969

> ... to foist off the cost of inflation on somebody else —David Osborne, *Harper's,* January 1983

We also find *foist off* without *on:*

> ... authors who try to foist off the ancient Greek philosopher as some sort of modern biologist —Jeremy Bernstein, *N.Y. Times Book Rev.,* 2 Oct. 1983

To recapitulate: the construction with *foist off* that Fowler criticized in 1926 is uncommon or unidiomatic enough that it does not appear in our files. The objection to *foist off* that Copperud built from Fowler is without basis, as the combination is completely standard.

folk, folks Both *folk* and *folks* have been subjected to criticism for quite a while. There are two streams of comment. The British one begins with Fowler 1926; he thought *folk* a lingering Saxonism on its way out of ordinary use. Gowers heavily revised the opinion in 1965 but still endorsed the notion that *people* was replacing *folk*. It is true that *people* is much more common than *folk*, but *folk* has not vanished by any means, even in British English. Gowers also thought *folk* and *folks* were more common in American English than in British, which may well be true. *Folks*, at least, is almost entirely American. Gowers, it may be noted, did not disparage *folks*.

But Vizetelly 1906 and MacCracken & Sandison 1917 had disparaged it, and Emily Post in 1927 called it "provincial" (a venial fault in Mrs. Post's system of labeling). From these and other sources, the question of the propriety of *folks* has come down to recent times. Our most recent evidence suggests that the comments in most of the handbooks are backward-looking.

Let's begin with a cursory glance at British English. Gowers noted that *folks* was often used in direct address by American entertainers and was similarly used by British entertainers in imitation of that practice. Our only two fairly recent examples of British *folks*—and these both from Commonwealth sources—are of this construction:

But seriously, folks, the story is beyond belief —Caroline Egerton, *Nation Rev.* (Melbourne), 29 May 1975

So, come folks, let's not wait —Jill, *Advocate-News* (Barbados), 15 Feb. 1975

Much of our British evidence for *folk* is not especially different from American use, although *folk* seems always to be used even in situations where Americans would tend to use *folks:*

She hadn't wanted to discuss her broken marriage with the folk at home —Sybil Josty, *Annabel,* February 1974

Canadians are shrewd folk —H. S. Ferns, *Times Literary Supp.,* 15 Feb. 1980

... those pompous round-robins from literary folk —Auberon Waugh, *N.Y. Times Book Rev.,* 17 June 1979

The Highland Pony ... is rather suspicious of strange folk —Colonel Sir Richard Glyn Bart, *The World's Finest Horses and Ponies,* 1971

In American English we find that *folks* is still used for people generally and for one's family:

... the time of year when folks travel —Susan Hallsten McGarry, *Southwest Art,* July 1984

... a standard resource for kids whose folks are divorced —Randy Shipp, *Christian Science Monitor,* 14 Dec. 1979

... up to their old hijinks, robbing, getting folks killed —Genevieve Stuttaford, *Publishers Weekly,* 2 Aug. 1976

... would not be some folks' cup of tea —Carll Tucker, *Saturday Rev.,* 17 Feb. 1979

It is also used, although not as often as *folk,* for people of a particular class or kind.

My momma could never understand how white folks could twist the words of the Bible around to justify racial segregation —Dick Gregory, in *The Bedford Reader,* ed. X. J. Kennedy & Dorothy M. Kennedy, 2d ed., 1985

... the good parts of his book are about the folks at the top —Jeff Greenfield, *N.Y. Times Book Rev.,* 6 July 1980

In 1784, when folks in what is now Tennessee began talking of creating a new state —John G. Mitchell, *Smithsonian,* November 1982

Cubs fans ... were ready to ram the TV folks through the ivy-covered walls —Richard Rothschild, *Houston Post,* 31 Aug. 1984

Folk seems to be somewhat more frequent in this sense:

Houdini entertained the circus folk —E. L. Doctorow, *Ragtime,* 1975

... the rich and famous and infamous folk —Simon 1980

... we literary folk can make a brave display —John Updike, *Publishers Weekly,* 14 May 1982

The mountain folk around the Gap —Frank DeFord, *Sports Illustrated,* 19 Nov. 1984

... have closer ties with ... urban elites than with rural folk —S. Frederick Starr, *N.Y. Times Book Rev.,* 15 July 1984

Folk and *folks* have come a long way since Emily Post disdained them. These uses are standard, although *folks* still seems to be a tad breezier or more informal than *folk.* Either can be used as an alternative to *people* in an appropriate context.

follow, follows See AS FOLLOWS.

following The fourth definition of the preposition *after* in Webster's Second 1934 contains this defining phrase: "following the expiration of." The word *following* in that phrase is used as a preposition. It must have seemed natural to the editor who wrote it, and it passed unnoticed by other editors working on the dictionary, but they did not enter *following* as a preposition in Webster's Second (1934) (it was added to the Addenda Section in 1955). The phrase does not occur in the definition of *after* in Webster 1909, so apparently the prepositional use became established in the period between the editing of the two dictionaries. Our earliest notice of it is in Hyde 1926 where it is called a misuse for *after.* It was presumably appearing in newspapers at that time, but we do not have an actual example. The Addenda and Corrigenda to the Shorter Oxford English Dictionary entered *following* as a preposition in 1955 with citations dated 1851 and 1914. These citations are not included in the OED Supplement; perhaps the Oxford editors were doubtful of their authenticity.

The prepositional use went virtually unnoticed until Gowers 1948 complained about it. Even then he thought it was too late to block its use, and in his 1965 revision of Fowler he grudgingly accepted it when "it implies something more than a merely temporal connexion between two events, something more than *after* but less than *in consequence of.*" Bernstein 1971 observes that this is a fine distinction to make and predicts that writers are not likely to make it. Several

English commentators (Sellers 1975, Phythian 1979, Bryson 1980, Longman 1984, Burchfield 1981) have followed Gowers in finding fault with the preposition. Our reading indicates that it is more of an issue in Britain than in America.

A good deal of our evidence of use comes from brief biographical sketches:

> Following a journey to Russia, in 1882, he imported into the Northwest from that country hardier varieties of fruit trees —*Dictionary of American Biography,* 1929

> Following the armistice Minton remained with the Army of Occupation —*Current Biography 1949*

This suggests that one appeal of *following* is as an alternative to *after.* It may also suggest itself to a writer as a counterpart to another participial preposition, *during:*

> During World War II, we helped train and equip twenty Nationalist divisions to oppose the Japanese and following the war helped train and equip forty more to oppose Mao Tse-tung —Chester Bowles, *Saturday Rev.,* 6 Nov. 1971

The chief argument of the British critics is that *following* can be used to ludicrous effect. They illustrate this by making up ludicrous examples or by reproducing real examples which must be misread to prove the point. Our files contain no particularly silly examples. We do find examples from time to time, however, in which *following* has been used in a context where its meaning is less than clear:

> In March 1863, following the manifest intention of the British ministry to enforce the Foreign Enlistment Act more strictly, he went to Paris —*Dictionary of American Biography,* 1929

There is nothing grammatically objectionable in the use of *following* as a preposition. We do suggest, however, that if you use it you make sure it cannot be misread as a simple participle.

foment   See FERMENT, FOMENT.

fond   *Fond,* when it is used with a preposition and has a sense involving affection, is most often used with *of* followed by a noun phrase or a gerund:

> ... I do own that she's as devilish fond of me as she can be —W. M. Thackeray, *Vanity Fair,* 1848

> ... a round, amiable, commanding man of whom he was very fond —Donald Barthelme, *New Yorker,* 3 May 1982

> ... critics are fond of comparing the American public high school with ... the British Grammar Schools —James B. Conant, *Slums and Suburbs,* 1961

> He is also fond of swimming, reading, and going to the theater —*Current Biography,* October 1966

In the past, *fond* in this sense was used with *on,* most notably by Shakespeare:

> That he may prove More fond on her than she upon her love —Shakespeare, *Midsummer Night's Dream,* 1596

> And I, poor monster, fond as much on him —Shakespeare, *Twelfth Night,* 1602

In its sense "foolish," *fond* was formerly used with *to* and an infinitive, but this construction no longer occurs in contemporary writing:

> I wonder he is so fond To trust the mockery of unquiet slumbers —Shakespeare, *Richard III,* 1593

> Should such a man, too fond to rule alone —Alexander Pope, *An Epistle to Dr. Arbuthnot,* 1735

> ... I am not fond enough to hope that anything said here ... will unsettle any fixed habit of speech —Richard Grant White 1870

fondness   *Fondness* is usually used with the preposition *for,* followed by a noun or a gerund:

> They have no particular fondness for organizations —Norman Cousins, *Saturday Rev.,* 20 Nov. 1971

> His fondness for rigid alternatives goes to such lengths —Irving Kristol, *Encounter,* December 1954

> ... a strange fondness for keeping a brief diary on beech trees —John Mason Brown, *Daniel Boone,* 1952

foot   *Foot* has three plurals. The regular one is *feet.* The second is *foots,* which is used in only a couple of specialized senses (for instance, when *foots* means "footlights"):

> He wanted to jump over the foots after the guy —Gail Garber, quoted in John Lahr, *Notes on a Cowardly Lion,* 1969

The third is the zero form *foot.* This plural also has limited use. It is used in the chiefly British sense of "foot soldiers, infantry":

> ... the majority of the foot, as of old, were pikemen and billmen —James A. Williamson, *The Tudor Age,* 1964

The more common use of the plural *foot* is in the sense of the nonmetric unit of measure, and even here it is restricted. It regularly occurs (and *feet* does not) between a number and a noun. In this position it is usually joined to the number with a hyphen.

> ... cleared a seven-foot fence to get away —*Sports Illustrated,* 24 Apr. 1967

> ... the 15-foot high statue —Ronald Leir, *Jersey Jour. and Jersey Observer,* 23 Apr. 1985

> ... a 340-by-120-foot auditorium —Norris Willatt, *Barron's,* 9 Feb. 1970

> ... the twenty-eight foot thirteen-ton cutter *Gipsy Moth III* —*Current Biography,* December 1967

The plurals *feet* and *foot* both occur between a number and an adjective:

> ... is five feet six inches tall —*Current Biography,* October 1965

> ... neither the Russians nor the Chinese were ten foot tall —Michael Howard, *Times Literary Supp.,* 21 Dec. 1979

> ... six foot wide and four foot deep —Daniel Defoe, *Robinson Crusoe,* 1719

In present-day American printed use, *feet* is more common than *foot,* and is prescribed by many handbooks.

Foot seems to be more frequent in print in British English. In speech, *foot* is common in both varieties:

> He was a short man, only about five foot six —Harry S. Truman, quoted in Merle Miller, *Plain Speaking,* 1973

> ... ten to eleven thousand foot deep —Margaret Thatcher, speech to National Press Club, 19 Sept. 1975

Evans 1957 points out that formerly *foot* could always be used as a plural after a number, even if it is not immediately followed by a noun or adjective. This practice is less common now. We see it sometimes in British English:

> ... wingless ants have been captured at heights up to 5,000 foot —V. B. Wigglesworth, *Nature,* 16 Nov. 1973

In American English we find it chiefly in speech:

> It was about 12-foot plus —surfer quoted by Robert Sherrill, *N.Y. Times Mag.,* 16 July 1967

> ... which is 15 foot in diameter —Leon Lederman, speech at meeting of American Association for the Advancement of Science, 1977

Many of the handbooks take the erroneous position that *foot* is only a singular and that *feet* is the only correct plural. The plural *foot* is limited to the uses shown here, but in them it is not an error. Belief that *foot* is wrong leads to this sort of unthinking hypercorrection:

> ... which grows to a height of one feet —*N.Y. Times,* 6 July 1980

forbid 1. The past tense of *forbid* for a long time was written either *forbade* or *forbad,* with about equal occurrence. During the last 50 years or so, however, the spelling has gone heavily in favor of *forbade,* despite the fact that the more usual pronunciation of the word is analogous to that of *bad.*
2. When *forbid* is used with a preposition, *to* is the commonest choice, and while usually the construction is *to* and the infinitive, occasionally it may be *to* and an object:

> ... given only bread and water, and forbidden to speak to his sisters —Bertrand Russell, *Education and the Good Life,* 1926

> ... they did not outright forbid me to see the Babcocks —George P. Elliott, *Harper's,* September 1970

> ... her inability to come to terms with herself forbade it to be otherwise —George F. Kennan, *New Yorker,* 1 May 1971

> ... had died in some awful combination of exile and expatriation, since their health forbade England to them —Mary McCarthy, *N.Y. Rev. of Books,* 9 Mar. 1972

Forbid is also used, although less often, with *from.* Critics deny that this usage is idiomatic, but it has been around for a long time. The OED enters it, and although it labels the sense rare and restricts the verb in this sense to use "with the personal object only," it provides evidence of usage from 1526. Our more recent evidence

shows that while it is still used with the personal object, it is also applied to other kinds:

> The Vatican issued an order forbidding all Catholic clergy from participating in Illich's Center —"Radical Cleric," *A Center Occasional Paper,* February 1971

> The new rules would ... forbid them [American companies] from giving the Soviet Union technology and expertise —Richard Burt, *N.Y. Times,* 19 Mar. 1980

> ... the electric utilities are forbidden from burning the plentiful high sulphur Eastern coal —Lorana Sullivan & Robert Samuelson, *Sunday Times* (London), 17 Mar. 1974

Forbid is also used with a gerund:

> Foxy wasn't sure if the rules forbad using associations others had used —John Updike, *Couples,* 1968

> ... a promise to her family forbids her writing another book for a year —*Publishers Weekly,* 24 Jan. 1966

Language critics find this construction acceptable, but most say that *forbid* with *to* is more common. The evidence bears them out. An interesting thing to note, though, is that when *forbid* is used with *from* it is followed by a gerund, as the examples given earlier show.

forceful, forcible, forced There probably never would have been a problem about these words had not H. W. Fowler taken offense at a vogue for *forceful* in the British press in the 1920s. Fowler 1926 sprang to the defense of *forcible,* calling it "the ordinary word" and saying that *forceful* was reserved for poetic and other special contexts. He claimed more force for *forceful* than for *forcible,* and enigmatically illustrated this difference with a figurative example of *forceful* and a literal one of *forcible.* He then turned to his examples of *forceful* in order to damn them. Later commentators—Evans 1957, Copperud 1964, 1970, 1980, Shaw 1975, 1985, Bryson 1984, Janis 1984, Heritage 1982, Longman 1984—have come forward to try to clarify what Fowler muddied. Here is our summary of the situation in actual usage.
Forceful is generally used figuratively in present-day American English:

> ... has been a forceful advocate of the Army's viewpoint —*Current Biography,* November 1965

> ... a clearer and more forceful statement —Michael Kitzmiller & Kenneth Tollett, *Center Mag.,* November 1969

It is less often used literally; when it is it means "characterized by force":

> ... an explosion perhaps 500 times as forceful as the atomic bomb —Richard L. Williams, *Smithsonian,* January 1981

> ... obvious, forceful contractions —Russell L. Cecil & Robert F. Loeb, *Textbook of Medicine,* 8th ed., 1951

Forcible is most commonly—almost always in America—used literally. It suggests something done by force:

> In those 10 decades China suffered forcible entry from Western imperial powers —Horace Sutton, *Saturday Rev.,* 17 Mar. 1979

... believed to favor forcible seizure of power — *Current Biography,* February 1966

Forcible also has an older figurative use, practically identical with modern *forceful:*

... many compliments too numerous and forcible to repeat —Charles Dickens, *A Tale of Two Cities,* 1859

A copious and forcible language —T. B. Macaulay, *The History of England,* vol. I, 1849

This was probably the use Fowler wished to defend. It is still found in British English, but not in American:

To his contemporaries he seemed clear-cut and forcible —*Times Literary Supp.,* 19 Mar. 1964

Forced is added to the group by a couple of commentators. It shares with *forcible* the notion of being produced or done by force. But it tends not to be physical force but rather legal force or force of circumstances:

... a discussion of forced busing —Judith Crist, *Saturday Rev.,* 16 Oct. 1976

Protection against forced labor —Carol L. Thompson, *Current History,* November 1952

... assignment to forced residence, which is really a form of imprisonment —Mary McCarthy, *N.Y. Rev. of Books,* 9 Mar. 1972

Forcible is not normally used in this way. In the following example, *forced* is the word one expects:

... John Adams was hurt by his forcible retirement from the Presidency —Garry Wills, *N.Y. Times Book Rev.,* 20 Feb. 1983

Forced is also used of something produced by willpower or effort:

... in this vein of forced lightness —Katherine Anne Porter, *Ladies' Home Jour.,* August 1971

forego, forgo If you look in your Webster's Ninth New Collegiate Dictionary (or other good contemporary dictionary), you will find a verb *forego* that means "to go before" and a verb *forgo* that means "to abstain from, do without." You will also find that the verb *forgo* is sometimes spelled *forego,* but the verb *forego* is spelled only *forego.*
Some commentators (for example, Evans 1957, Shaw 1962, 1975, 1987, and Bremner 1980) record this variation accurately, but several (for example, Simon 1980 and Bryson 1984) try to deny it.

foreign plurals For a list of those that are most frequently the subject of usage writers, see LATIN PLURALS.

foreseeable future This phrase is denigrated by Shaw 1975 as "trite" and "lacking in good sense" and by Nickles 1974 as "haphazard writing." These two writers base their objection on the assertion that it is not possible to see into the future. But this phrase has to do with forecasting, not with prophecy. Webster's Third defines this sense of *foreseeable* as "lying within the range for which forecasts are possible." Forecasting may be an imperfect science, but it is carried on with some regularity.
The phrase is not attested before 1932, but it caught on rapidly, and *future* is now the noun of choice with

foreseeable, outnumbering in our files all other nouns by more than two to one. The phrase is used mostly by politicians, sociologists, educators, and planners; it does not appear to have much in the way of literary use. The use of the phrase does not appear to be diminishing. Here are a few examples:

Second, to form world-wide international organizations, and to arrange to use the armed force of the sovereign nations of the world to make another war impossible within the foreseeable future —Franklin D. Roosevelt, radio address, 20 July 1944, in *Nothing to Fear,* ed. B. D. Zevin, 1946

Secretary of State John Foster Dulles was reported to have told the Senate Foreign Relations Committee today he is optimistic that plans can be worked out for new disarmament talks with Russia "in the foreseeable future." —*Springfield* (Mass.) *Union,* 10 Jan. 1958

We live in a world of words, and no computers, mechanization, or new discoveries are going to change that ... not in the foreseeable future anyway —Alfred Fleishman, *Sense and Nonsense,* 1971

... available sources of power are ample to meet needs for the foreseeable future —John Lear, *Saturday Rev.,* 1 Jan. 1972

... agriculture seems likely to be the mainstay of the nation in the foreseeable future —Horace Sutton, *Saturday Rev.,* 17 Mar. 1979

foreword, forward Venolia 1982, Shaw 1970, 1975, 1987, Bremner 1980, and others warn against confusing the spellings of these two words. No one confuses the words themselves, and, as far as we know, no one has gone to print using the misspelling *foreward* for the directional *forward.* But the prefatory *foreword* does occasionally have the directional word put in its place:

... will contain a forward by Jamie Lee —*US,* 27 Aug. 1984

In the forward to his book —*Newsweek,* 18 Aug. 1986

It is sometimes muddled as *foreward* too.
Baron 1982 notes that *foreword* is one of a handful of Saxonisms—words of native stock proposed by Victorian philologist William Barnes and his followers to be used in place of words of French or Latin provenience—that have stuck successfully in the current language. *Foreword* was coined as a substitute for *preface* in 1842. Fowler 1926 condemned it as a vogue word and thought from 1924 evidence that it was on its way out. He "allowed himself a paragraph of exultation," as Evans 1957 puts it. But *foreword* is established. The paragraph of exultation was dropped by Gowers from the 1965 edition.

for free *For free,* as far as we know, was first aspersed in the *Saturday Evening Post,* 20 Feb. 1943; the citation is in the American Dialect Dictionary. What is interesting is that the earliest citation shown in the ADD is an anonymous quotation printed in an article in the same magazine, 12 Dec. 1942—just about two months earlier. The phrase must have had quite a bit of popular use at the time. Since 1943 it has become rather fashionable for writers of usage books to disparage the phrase. Shaw 1975, 1987 calls it "wordy slang ... used by careless speakers." Harper 1985 calls it slang and says it is "used only facetiously by careful writers." Bernstein 1965 calls it "semihumorous slang, perhaps originally used by semiliterates." Bernstein's successor at *Winners & Sinners* (29 Nov. 1985) calls it "comic-book Brooklynese."

A couple of commentators dissent. James J. Kilpatrick in a newspaper column (11 Aug. 1985) calls the Harper entry "sniffy" and wonders if the phrase is becoming respectable. He says that the phrase is "shorter than the stiff and formal" phrase *without charge.* Flesch 1983 defends *for free* as an idiom.

When an idiom that seems to be as recently formed as *for free* begins to compete with *free, gratis,* and *without charge,* speakers and writers probably feel some real need for it. Kilpatrick has given us one hint as to why. You can discover another hint by trying *free* where these writers wrote *for free:*

> The drivers will pay their transportation . . . , but will have the run of the inn for free —*N.Y. Times,* 25 Dec. 1963

> . . . it seemed best to find a way to live for free then —Jane Harriman, *Atlantic,* March 1970

> The hat they throw in extra for free —James Jones, *From Here to Eternity,* 1951

You can see here that the *for* obviates the ambiguous combinations *inn free, live free, extra free.* In the next example, the removal of *for* would require its replacement with *away* in order to preserve normally idiomatic English:

> . . . to avoid accusations it was giving billable services for free —*Datamation,* 15 Aug. 1970

And many writers clearly think it lends the right informal note:

> . . . sunset, the only thing they get for free —Christopher Morley, *The Man Who Made Friends With Himself,* 1949

> . . . the French Parliament, still wrangling in its three-month-old deadlock on whether French children shall receive a Catholic-school education for free —Janet Flanner, *New Yorker,* 15 Sept. 1951

> . . . baby bottles will be warmed for free —B. A. Young, *Punch,* 1 July 1953

> Here, lessons in how to toss a stole or cape around in ways never thought possible are for free —Lois Lang, *New Yorker,* 20 Oct. 1951

> Then offer it—for free—to the British Museum — Bennett Cerf, *Saturday Rev.,* 31 Jan. 1948

This idiom is well established in general prose, and you can safely disregard the objections. It is not used in writings of high solemnity, however.

forget The past tense of *forget* is *forgot;* the past participle is *forgot* or *forgotten.* Both past participles are used in American English (*forgotten* is more common):

> . . . I've forgot, don't remember, the name of the other —Harry S. Truman, quoted in Merle Miller, *Plain Speaking,* 1973

> . . . one of the shabbier pretensions gets almost forgotten —Robert Penn Warren, *Democracy and Poetry,* 1975

Longman 1984 and Evans 1957 remind us that *forgotten* is standard in present-day British use; *forgot* is considered archaic.

> . . . an acknowledgment that he had quite forgot her —Jane Austen, *Mansfield Park,* 1814

forgo See FOREGO, FORGO.

formal *Formal* is a term used in a great many usage books to distinguish that kind of writing and speech that is most mannered and remote from ordinary conversational English. In spite of its wide use, it presents problems as a label, because there is a good deal of uncertainty about just what *formal* is meant to cover. Two responsible commentators can use the term differently. Bryant 1962, for instance, includes among formal sources many of the same sources Perrin & Ebbitt 1972 considers general.

When *formal* is used in this book, it is used only as a vague indicator of general tendency and not as the marker of a class of writings with uniform characteristics. We would suggest that you take prescriptions of "not used in formal English" or "unacceptable in formal English" with a considerable grain of salt. Perhaps Bishop Lowth's "elevated style" would have been a more generally useful label.

See also CHOICE, *adjective;* INFORMAL; LEVELS OF USAGE.

formal agreement See NOTIONAL AGREEMENT, NOTIONAL CONCORD.

former **1.** *Former, latter.* Just about any usage book will tell you that *former* is used to refer to the first of two and *latter* to the second of two and that *former* and *latter* should not be used when three or more persons or things are being discussed.

Let's take a look at the evidence: *former* and *latter* are certainly used when two persons or things are being discussed:

> This book is addressed . . . both to "new" and to "experienced" collectors. The former will be misled and the latter irritated by the text —*Times Literary Supp.,* 5 Feb. 1970

> . . . was the Truman administration's internal security program a deliberate attempt to build support for foreign aid, or was it essentially an incompletely examined response to domestic political pressures? Freeland stresses the importance of the former. . . . A more plausible analysis might place greater emphasis on the latter explanation —Robert Griffith, *Saturday Rev.,* 22 Apr. 1972

> However, the triumphant welfare state principle means a fundamental trade-off between capitalist prosperity and economic security. As a nation we have chosen to have less of the former in order to have more of the latter —David A. Stockman, *Newsweek,* 28 Apr. 1986

But more often only one word or the other is used:

> . . . the decision to base the civil rights bill on both the commerce clause and the 14th Amendment, with the heavier emphasis on the former —*Current Biography,* February 1965

> . . . the home of Dr. and Mrs. Perley Marsh, the latter a descendant of Colonel Hinsdale —*American Guide Series: New Hampshire,* 1938

... he will try to differentiate among those who might assume larger responsibilities from those who cannot. He will not persist in trying to remake the latter —Harry Levinson, *Think,* May–June 1967

Would Neill say that Jimmy was not self-directed ... ? Or would he see a child learning new satisfactions ... ? I would hope the latter —Emmanuel Bernstein, *Psychology Today,* October 1968

... citing the films *Stiletto* and *The Wild Bunch.* The latter film had been well received —Mark Phillips, *Media & Methods,* September 1969

And *former* and *latter* are not restricted to just two possible referents; they are often used with three or more—often enough that such use really can be considered acceptable, at least in most varieties of general prose.

... there were three sorts of recruits: ... The former of these probably joined with a view to an eventual captaincy —*Times Literary Supp.,* 30 Dec. 1949

Pronunciation may be indicated by diacritical marks, by Trager-Smith phoneme symbols, or by the International Phonetic Alphabet. The most easily understood system ... is the former —*Booklist,* 1 July 1979

Does 'well' refer to aesthetic or emotional or moral values? Or to all three? Surely not the latter —C. Day Lewis, *A Hope for Poetry,* 3d ed., 1936

... though her bibliography includes Hecht, Snyder, and Daiches, she omits the latter's first name —DeLancey Ferguson, *Modern Language Notes,* February 1957

These materials are resistant to corrosion, abrasion, and extremes of temperature, the latter stemming from a coefficient of thermal expansion near zero —*Annual Report, Owens-Illinois,* 1970

Their three primary gathering places are the Grand Ole Opry backstage, the Station Inn, and the Bluegrass Inn, the latter being Nashville's oldest bluegrass club —Brett F. Devan, *Bluegrass Unlimited,* October 1982

Even less restricted uses of *latter* occur. Sometimes it refers to a group of things:

Among these latter were the great German poet, Friedrich Schiller, and New England's Henry Wadsworth Longfellow —*American Guide Series: Minnesota,* 1938

He is a fellow of the three latter societies —*Current Biography,* November 1966

Follow the roads past the three lakes. The upland forests adjacent to the latter two present a magnificent sight —Eileene Coffield, *Ford Times,* November 1967

The artist, the teacher, and the soldier are probably as old in their service to society as the minister, the physician, and the lawyer. Unlike the latter, however, they operate outside the personal thoughts of the individual —Ralph Crawshaw, *Center Mag.,* May 1969

And sometimes *latter* simply refers to the last person or thing named previously, especially at the end of a clause or phrase:

... they generally go to the nearest water to drink, afterwards returning to sleep near what may be left of the meat; or, should the latter be finished, not going very far —J. Stevenson-Hamilton, *Wild Life in South Africa,* 1947

The skipper, or if the latter is the navigator, the bos'n, will be having a final look around —Peter Heaton, *Cruising,* 1952

He appears to be an out-and-out Martin Johnson kind of man. The latter devoted his films and writings to explode the shoot-and-shiver myths of too articulate Brethren of the Safari —Hans Christian Adamson, *Saturday Rev.,* 10 July 1954

Obviously, the usagists' simple dictum that *former* and *latter* can only refer to the first and second of two is unrealistically restrictive. However, when discussing more than three items, you can, of course, use the alternatives (such as *last* or *last-named* instead of *latter*) that the usage books recommend, and many writers do so:

The last of these died at a comparatively early age, but the other four all achieved considerable eminence as teachers and writers —*Dictionary of American Biography,* 1928

The last mentioned, as well as the others, almost inevitably causes strains —Robert T. Blackburn, *AAUP Bulletin,* December 1967

It was followed by *The Girl in the News* (1940), *Kipps* (1940 ...), and *The Young Mr. Pitt* (1941). The last-named presented the life of the famous English prime minister —*Current Biography 1950*

Some usage books will also tell you that it is a good idea to avoid *former* and *latter* altogether, because these words interfere with smooth reading and rapid comprehension by forcing the reader to look back and reread in order to see what is being referred to. But since some writers are using *former* and *latter* left and right, how can we tell whether other writers avoid them? Well, for one thing, *latter* (as you may have noticed in the citations shown above) gets a lot more use than *former,* and the reason is probably that writers avoid using *former* because it involves too much of an interruption. The referent of *former* is usually some distance away, which means (1) that it is rarely remembered without a rereading and (2) that the reader may have quite a hunt to find it. The referent of *latter* is usually close at hand and is often remembered without a look back. In fact, uses of *latter* with three or more choices indicate that the reader is merely expected to retain the last of the series and associate it with the word *latter,* without going back to find out what kind or how many came before.

So, should you use *former* and *latter* in your writing? They make it easy to refer to earlier phrases or clauses that are not easily distilled down to a word or two (the passage by Robert Griffith near the beginning of this article is a good example). They let the writer start a new sentence without having to repeat a word or phrase. *Latter,* especially, can often be used without interrupting the reader's train of thought, and both words are appropriate in formal contexts where the reader expects to progress slowly. Just keep in mind that *former* and *latter* are basically conveniences for the writer. They are potential nuisances for the reader unless handled with care, and you have no right to demand more from your reader than your subject is worth. Repetition of the word or phrase that *former* or *latter* might replace is in many cases a good alternative.

2. See EX- 2.

formula Both plural forms, *formulas* and *formulae,* are common and correct. Although the choice of which one to use may vary from person to person and publication to publication, our evidence reveals no general patterns that show that one form or the other is preferred in a particular field.

formulate Several usage writers have felt that this word would be better replaced by a shorter synonym, such as *form* or *make,* in phrases like "formulate an opinion" and "formulate a plan." As with many other common but criticized usages, *formulate* can be seen to have some advantages over its suggested replacements. Its greater length, which makes it sound "pretentious" to Evans 1957 and "grandiose" to Bremner 1980, helps it to imply greater complexity or more deliberate intent than *form* or *make.* This is borne out in our citations, where plans and policies are formulated much more often than opinions.

We are sure that *formulate* can sound pretentious if used pretentiously, but in everyday, businesslike prose (where it is frequently found) it draws no more attention to itself than is seemly.

... in the excitement of recent events he had not formulated a plan —Theodore Dreiser, *Sister Carrie,* 1900

The principles of economics formulated two generations ago can no longer be relied on today —Morris R. Cohen, *The Faith of a Liberal,* 1946

... a means ... of formulating student opinion on various issues —*AAUP Bulletin,* December 1967

... formulate measures to streamline certain administrative procedures —*Current Biography,* November 1967

... long-range plans are being formulated —*Annual Report, National Lead Co.,* 1970

... the new educational policies now being formulated in Washington —Henry S. Resnik, *Saturday Rev.,* 4 Mar. 1972

forte This word in the sense of "one's strong point" is derived from the French. In this sense, usage writers recommend that the word be pronounced like *fort.* It is also very often pronounced like the musical term *forte,* which represents the same Latin root meaning "strong" but which in this case is derived immediately from the Italian. The musical term is pronounced, with usage experts concurring, \\'fòr-ˌtā\\, or sometimes \\'fòrt-ē\\ (the last like *forty*). All three versions may be heard from well-educated speakers in reference to a strong point, but the last two have incurred vociferous disapproval.

Those who object to the pronunciations in question point out that the word comes from the French, and \\'fòr-ˌtā\\ is not at all the way the French pronounce it. Against this objection several points may be made:

First, it is now an English word, which we may pronounce as we see fit. A comparable case is that of *apostrophe* in the sense of a punctuation mark. This comes probably from the French and would be pronounced by them without the long *e,* roughly \\ˌá-pòs-'tròf\\, yet we pronounce it \\ə-'päs-trə-fē\\, just like the rhetorical term (meaning "addressing of an absent person") that comes to us via Latin from the ancient Greek. With both *forte* and *apostrophe* we have to do with a very old word that has reached us twice by different routes.

Second, the spelling isn't French either—in French the word is *le fort*—so any quest for Gallic purism is doomed from the start.

Third, the recommended pronunciation, rhyming with *fort,* also is not the French one, which rhymes rather with *for.*

A more ticklish objection is that the pronunciation \\'fòr-ˌtā\\ isn't exactly English either, but pseudo-foreign: we are here pronouncing the word as if it were Italian, or French with an acute-accented *e,* when in fact it is French with an unaccented *e.* In this view, the pronunciation is ridiculous because it represents a failed attempt at foreignness (see HYPERFOREIGNISMS).

Now, normally we would counsel against hyperforeignisms, since for these you have no one in your corner. The lofty look down on them, and the humble are annoyed. But in the present case even those who have heard the objections often persist in the pronunciation \\'fòr-ˌtā\\ as being more familiar to them or as being less likely to be mistaken for the much commoner word *fort.* Since there is, in fact, no etymologically respectable pronunciation available for this word, we might as well select one that feels natural and that aids communication. All three discussed here are standard.

forthcoming Janis 1984 and Copperud 1980 are worried about a sense of *forthcoming* that they believe is displacing *forthright.* The use is not new; the OED dates it back to 1835. It is, however, not very felicitously defined in dictionaries, and that is probably part of the problem.

The use, which seems to be originally British, is almost always a predicate adjective and only rarely an attributive adjective. It is often used in negative constructions. It is applied to people and, less often, to what they say or write. In its earliest attestations it describes a social characteristic that suggests openness and willingness to talk. In these applications it is perhaps closer in meaning to *outgoing* than to *forthright.* It is still used in this way:

But though she was friendly she was not very forthcoming. She replied courteously and sweetly when spoken to, but she never told anybody anything —Elizabeth Goudge, *Pilgrim's Inn,* 1948

"... She's extraordinarily forthcoming, isn't she, bubbling over, uncontrollably effervescent?" —L. P. Hartley, *The Hireling,* 1957

From Bertram Shaw, who was candid and forthcoming, he obtained what he required without appreciable trouble —Edgar Lustgarten, *Defender's Triumph,* 1951

... Viennese girls ... are attractive, amusing, forthcoming, and fairly chic —Ian Fleming, *Thrilling Cities,* 1963

Even people ... who would have been, in India or other formerly colonial lands, at once servile and distant, were open and forthcoming in Nepal —Merry I. White, *Atlantic,* August 1970

When people are in a position where they are, for reasons of policy, expected to be closemouthed or evasive, *forthcoming* comes fairly close to *frank* or *candid* or *forthright:*

> . . . made what a member of the EEC gold lobby has characterised as a "rather forthcoming speech" — *The Economist,* 13 Apr. 1974

> . . . but Joe tended to be a little too forthcoming and perhaps easily led into saying things that were *ex officio* —Milton Helpern, MD, with Bernard Knight, MD, *Autopsy: The Memoirs of Milton Helpern,* 1977

> The doctor was forthcoming and impregnable in the best tradition of American technicians. His understanding of events was too coherent to permit him to be tricked into inconsistency —Suzanne Garment, *Wall Street Jour.,* 3 Apr. 1981

> . . . the publisher, a pale, languid man of 30, was even more forthcoming. "I'm in it for the money", he said —*The Times* (London), 1 Nov. 1973

> . . . the personal contact between the editor and local officials is friendly, if not always forthcoming — Keith Williams, *In Britain,* April 1975

It may suggest generosity or readiness to give out information:

> His parents were very strict, German, authoritarian, and not forthcoming with explanations —Tony Kornheiser, *Inside Sports,* October 1979

> . . . the dust-jacket gives no information about him, except that he lived in West Cornwall for several years. The publishers should be a little more forthcoming —D. M. Thomas, *Times Literary Supp.,* 1 Aug. 1980

> The woman on the other end is clearly new, else she would not be so forthcoming with the information —Jay McInerney, *Bright Lights, Big City,* 1984

These are the chief ways in which the disputed sense is used. *Forthright* is in no danger of being usurped.

fortuitous   Our evidence at the present time is not conclusive, but it appears that sometime after World War I—certainly by the 1920s—*fortuitous* began to be used in a sense meaning "fortunate, lucky." Fowler 1926 seems to have been the first to notice the use. He laid the development to the sound of *fortunate* and the meaning of *lucky.* It is impossible to know for certain, but *felicitous* may also have had some influence. After all, *fortuitous* sounds like a blend of *fortunate* and *felicitous,* and its new meaning resembles a blend of its original meaning and the meaning of *felicitous.*

Fowler was apparently alone in noticing the new sense (he considered it an error) until well after World War II. The next commentator in our collection who mentions the use is Bernstein 1958. After Bernstein there are many commentators (we have about twenty) who disapprove the use. We do have one (Shaw 1975, 1987) who merely notices the use and two (Harper 1975, 1985 and Copperud 1970, 1980) who notice that the sense is already recorded in American dictionaries.

The oldest meaning of *fortuitous*—which has been the predominant sense all along—is "occurring by chance":

> . . . a certain Fortuitous Concourse of all Mens Opinions —Jonathan Swift, *A Tale of a Tub,* 1710

His presence in Berlin was quite fortuitous. He had come to deliver a memorial address —William L. Shirer, *The Rise and Fall of the Third Reich,* 1960

Samuel Johnson even used it to mean "controlled by chance" in one of the memoranda he wrote to himself for purposes of self-correction:

> Of this vacillation and vagrancy of mind I impute a great part to a fortuitous and unsettled life, and therefore purpose to spend my time with more method —day after Easter, 1778, quoted in Paul Fussell, *Samuel Johnson and the Life of Writing,* 1971

There is, as Reader's Digest 1983 observes, a use intermediate between "by chance" and "fortunate." It is applied to something that is a chance occurrence, but has a favorable result. The seeds for this use were planted long ago. In the following 18th-century example, the writer is using the primary sense. But notice how easy it is to find overtones of good fortune:

> Acquisitions of knowledge, like blazes of genius, are often fortuitous. Those who had proposed to themselves a methodical course of reading, light by accident on a new book, which seizes their thoughts and kindles their curiosity, and opens an unexpected prospect —Bennett Langton, *The Idler,* 28 July 1759

This sort of context probably prefigured our intermediate sense, which has occurred, until very recently, about as often as the "fortunate" sense does in our files. Some examples:

> Our expansion as a world power was helped by acquisition of the Panama Canal project which had bankrupted a French company. This piece of business was aided and abetted by a fortuitous revolution in Panama that had a suspicious smell, though the President denied he had any part in promoting it —John Kieran ed., *Information Please Almanac* 1948

> I think I reported not long ago in *The New Yorker* . . . how I was saved in college one night by the fortuitous appearance in the night skies of the most brilliant aurora borealis seen in Ohio since the Civil War —James Thurber, letter, 21 May 1954

> It was on the second night, July 27–28, that Bomber Command came nearest to its objective of total destruction, through a number of circumstances, largely fortuitous. The weather was fine. Clear skies, as well as luck and judgment, meant exceptionally accurate marking —Geoffrey Wheatcroft, *Times Literary Supp.,* 26 Dec. 1980

> She panted into the underground, snatched a ticket from the machine, belted down the stairs, and there was a fortuitous train —Doris Lessing, *The Good Terrorist,* 1985

> It hit because of a fortuitous combination of historical forces —Louise Bernikow, *Playboy,* August 1986

It is tempting to speculate, then, that the sense development of *fortuitous* went from "chance" to "chance with a good outcome" to "fortunate." Such development is plausible, but cannot be supported by evidence in our files, unless one wants to interpret Bennett Langton as using the intermediate sense—and we do not think he was. The earliest evidence we have for a changed sense, both in our own files and in Fowler's examples, is for the "fortunate" sense:

> Take, for example, the peculiarly fortuitous circumstances under which he entered the Scribner publishing house —Edward Bok, *The Americanization of Edward Bok,* 1920

We did not collect any more examples until after World War II.

> . . . a fortuitous escape from the seemingly inevitable death sentence —Franklin L. Ford, *Saturday Rev.,* 10 May 1947

> It has been pointed out that it was fortuitous for Dunning that he had versed himself so well in radio fundamentals —*Current Biography 1948*

> We have a great and fortuitous advantage, for if there is nothing the Kremlin wants more than to rule the world, there is nothing the United States wants less than to rule the world —Adlai E. Stevenson, *Call to Greatness,* 1954

> This circumstance was a fortuitous one for Abraham Lockwood —John O'Hara, *The Lockwood Concern,* 1965

> . . . one of the most fortuitous events in the recent history of pop music —Jon Landau, *Rolling Stone,* 13 May 1971

> But from a cost standpoint, the company's timing is fortuitous —*Business Week,* 13 Dec. 1982

> The opening of his firm had come at an extremely fortuitous time —Connie Bruck, *Atlantic,* December 1984

In present-day English we have three senses of *fortuitous* forming a gradation: "happening by chance," "happening by a lucky chance," and "lucky, fortunate." The third of these has been in use for almost seventy years and is recognized in several dictionaries. There is no question that it is established, especially in newspaper and magazine use, and even though it has lately received a great deal of unfavorable notice, it is showing no signs of going away. You can use the sense, but you must be prepared to catch a little flak if you do.

It is harder to advise you about the intermediate use. It seems likely to continue in use, and because the element of chance is present in its meaning, it is unlikely to cause much stir. Only one commentator has noticed it so far, but it has also not yet been recognized in dictionaries. Our guess is that if you use *fortuitous* to mean "happening by a lucky chance," you have nothing to worry about.

fortuitously The adverb *fortuitously* has been subject to the same strictures as *fortuitous,* but not as often, possibly because the adverb is a good deal less frequent than the adjective. It gets quite a bit of attention in Safire 1984. Safire in a newspaper column (22 Nov. 1981) found fault with a sentence in a *Time* article about airplanes that had been ordered by the Shah of Iran shortly before his fall. The offending sentence ended ". . . planes that fortuitously were never delivered." Safire interpreted the adverb to mean "fortunately" because it seemed obvious to him that it was fortunate that the Ayatollah didn't get his hands on the planes. The *Time* writer defended his choice of the word. He said he had picked it deliberately because the planes had been not delivered by happenstance, or, as he put it, "sheer dumb luck."

We have here perhaps the first recorded dispute that can be ascribed to the failure of dictionaries to recognize the intermediate sense of *fortuitous* (see FORTUITOUS and its citations from James Thurber, Doris Lessing, and others for this sense). The *Time* use of the adverb falls midway between "by chance" and "luckily." The blending of the notions of chance and luck seems to be present in the following examples, too:

> Here I do not wish to suggest that there was something so fortuitously creative about that afternoon as to lead us to discover right then, once and for all, what we wished the magazine to "be" —William Styron, *This Quiet Dust and Other Writings,* 1982

> The needs of the gross anatomy laboratory have been fortuitously met by the big refrigerators of the former dining hall —John Walsh, *Science,* 6 Oct. 1972

> We followed him out the door, into the elevator, and into a taxi that had fortuitously stopped in front of the hotel —*New Yorker,* 1 Dec. 1951

The other two meanings of *fortuitous* also exist in the adverb:

> It's fashionable these days to shuck off whatever's happening out there in the American ghetto, the barrio or slum. As the not-so-subliminal message of these Reagan years suggests: "Who cares? Out of sight, out of mind."
> Fortuitously, some smart people disagree —Neal R. Peirce, *Boston Globe,* 14 July 1986

> Fortuitously, wells drilled here have yielded carbon dioxide; so lucky farmers find cheaply at hand plenty of dry ice in which to pack their crops for shipment —*National Geographic,* June 1941

> . . . reliance has to be placed on the memories of aging trade unionists and on their fortuitously preserved collections of papers —*Times Literary Supp.,* 19 Feb. 1970

> An edition can be uniform with an impression only fortuitously when it is confined to a single impression —Fredson Bowers, *Principles of Bibliographical Description,* 1949

forward See FOREWORD, FORWARD.

founded *Founded,* when used with a preposition in general applications, is used most often with *on:*

> . . . tales of real life, high and low, and founded on fact! —Henry David Thoreau, *Walden,* 1854

> . . . his instinctive dislike of the middle class was founded on its intellectual sterility —Vernon Louis Parrington, *Main Currents in American Thought,* 1927

Founded is used in just the same way with *upon* but our evidence suggests that this use has become somewhat less frequent over the last 25 years:

> . . . her value as a human being was founded upon a durable, if an intangible, basis —Ellen Glasgow, *Barren Ground,* 1925

> . . . early poems founded upon old French models — *The Autobiography of William Butler Yeats,* 1953

Founded is also used quite frequently with *in.* Although this use may have a general application, like that of *founded on* (as in the first of the following examples), more frequently *in* signifies a date or place:

> ... this criticism is founded in misconception of the true significance of literature —*Selected Writings of Benjamin N. Cardozo,* ed. Margaret E. Hall, 1947

> The first big-city tutorials were founded in 1962 — Jack J. Levine, *Columbia Forum,* Spring 1968

> ... Shawn and his wife founded the first of the Denishawn schools, in Los Angeles —*Current Biography 1949*

founder See FLOUNDER, FOUNDER.

Frankenstein For sheer triviality, few subjects can top the question of whether it is all right to use *Frankenstein* to refer to the creation, the monster, and not just to its creator. The palm for unearthing this issue seems to go to F. H. Collins, who put it in his *Author and Printer*—a book for the guidance of printers and proofreaders—published in 1905. Fowler 1926 took up the cudgels against the usage, although he seemed rather to feel that it was too well established to beat down.

On this side of the Atlantic the editors of Webster 1909 followed Collins's advice, but in 1934 those of Webster's Second threw out the admonition and entered the sense as a second definition. The editors of the Second had seen these examples:

> But this machine is a Frankenstein that will turn on its own creators and work their destruction together with its own —*Atlantic,* October 1917

> Before that measure, a bureau was a kind of Frankenstein created by Act of Congress —*Yale Rev.,* October 1918

> The gigantic post-War industrial Frankenstein erected by Herr Stinnes is conceivable among no other people —*Time,* 30 Aug. 1926

But even recognition in Webster's Second would not satisfy all the sticklers; still fighting the good fight we find Bernstein 1958, 1965, Harper 1975, 1985, Bremner 1980 and Shaw 1975, 1987, who are still disposed to view the use as an error. On the other hand, we have Evans 1957, Copperud 1964, 1970, 1980, Watt 1967, Follett 1966, and Barzun 1985 accepting the extended sense. Here is Barzun:

> Pedantry is a misplaced attention to trifles which then prides itself on its poor judgment. The editors who would have everyone write *a Frankenstein's monster* instead of *a Frankenstein* are pedants. ...

freedom *Freedom* is used with a number of prepositions, but use with *of* occurs far more often than with any other:

> There is a great deal of fuss nowadays about freedom of speech —T. S. Eliot, "Charles Whibley," *Selected Essays,* 1932

Among other prepositional combinations, those occurring most often are *for, from, in,* and *to.* The collocation *freedom to* is usually followed by an infinitive:

> His political philosophy revolves around the concept of freedom for the individual —*Current Biography,* February 1966

> ... a reasonably stable government ... and at least a modicum of efficiency and freedom from graft — Elspeth Huxley, *N.Y. Times Mag.,* 18 July 1954

> ... freedom in thought, the liberty to try and err — H. L. Mencken, *Prejudices: Second Series,* 1920

> ... follow the Kremlin's political line as a price for their limited freedom to preach and teach —Tom Whitney, *Wall Street Jour.,* 25 Mar. 1954

free gift *Free gift* is cited as a redundancy by many commentators. It appears most commonly nowadays in advertising copy. Since most of us do not have to write advertising copy, the criticism seems rather trivial. The phrase has been in use since at least the 18th century, and in older use serves to distinguish what is given voluntarily from what is cajoled or required. (Edward Gibbon, in his *Decline and Fall of the Roman Empire,* 1788, tells us that Roman emperors exacted gifts from the people on certain state occasions.) Benjamin Franklin used it in suggesting a line to take in dealing with Parliament:

> *Redress our Grievances.* ... If you would have our free Gifts, desist from your Compulsive Methods — letter to the Massachusetts House of Representatives, 7 July 1773

The notion of "freely given" can still be found:

> It's true that grace is the free gift of God —Flannery O'Connor, letter, 21 June 1959

> ... something new and amiable, a free gift from science and high technology —Lewis Thomas, *Late Night Thoughts on Listening to Mahler's Ninth Symphony,* 1983

The commentators uniformly assume *free* means "without charge" in *free gift.* The assumption may not always be warranted.

friend The preposition used with *friend* is most often *of:*

> ... known in Boston, ... as the inexhaustible friend of all good causes —Van Wyck Brooks, *The Flowering of New England, 1815–1865,* rev. ed., 1946

> ... was an official and congressional friend of the same company —C. Vann Woodward, *Reunion and Reaction,* 2d ed. rev., 1956

Less often, *friend* is used with *to:*

> ... the young, the oversensitive ones, and the displaced ones, do not need it, and it is no friend to them —Edna O'Brien, *Cosmopolitan,* February 1973

Friend may also be used with *with;* this usually occurs in the idiomatic phrases *be friends with* or *make friends with:*

> Whitman could be friends with anyone who was genuine, not a snob, not a prig —Henry Seidel Canby, *Walt Whitman,* 1943

> Yet many a man is making friends with death
> Even as I speak, for lack of love alone
> —Edna St. Vincent Millay, in *Time,* 17 Nov. 1952

Be friends to has been used in the past, but there is no 20th-century evidence in the Merriam-Webster files:

> ... the widow's been good friends to me sometimes —Mark Twain, *Tom Sawyer,* 1876

friendly, *adjective* When *friendly* is used with a preposition, it is used most often with *to:*

> Not all general officers were insensible to the advantages of a press friendly to them personally —James Gould Cozzens, *Guard of Honor,* 1948

> . . . she had always been extremely friendly to me and to my work —Eric F. Goldman, *Harper's,* January 1969

Less frequently, *friendly* is followed by *with:*

> "His Grace is never very friendly with anyone. . . ." —Sir Arthur Conan Doyle, *The Return of Sherlock Holmes,* 1904

> ". . . we must keep smiling faces and be friendly with him no matter how repulsive it may be" —Jack London, *The Sea-Wolf,* 1904

One might expect to find *friendly toward* or *towards* paralleling the use of *friendly to;* however, there is only a little evidence in our files for either preposition:

> Congress is friendly also toward giving the board responsibility only to decide cases —*Nation's Business,* June 1953

> This would have been unfair of me because towards myself Thursby was always unusually friendly — *Horizon,* December 1946

Friendly is used with *for* infrequently:

> Grateful for this relief, Dost Mohammad . . . kept Afghanistan friendly for Britain —G. M. Trevelyan, *British History in the Nineteenth Century,* 1922

friendly *adverb,* **friendlily** Both *friendly* and *friendlily* have been in use as adverbs for quite some time. According to the OED, the first written example of *friendly* dates from around the 12th century, and the adverb has had continuous use through the ensuing centuries. According to our evidence, it is still in use in the 20th century:

> Fayre had the thought, maybe Waits was laughing at him, but more than likely he meant it friendly — Maristan Chapman, *The Happy Mountain,* 1928

> . . . thought that all large trees were the abode of spirits, which were friendly disposed unless a person interfered with the tree —Sir James G. Frazer, *Aftermath,* 1937

> He was . . . friendly disposed towards the British — W. Gordon Harmon, *Royal Central Asian Jour.,* January 1951

The use of *friendlily,* according to the OED, dates from 1680. The OED's evidence for it since then appears to be less than its evidence for *friendly;* however, the Merriam-Webster files indicate that in the 20th century, the use of *friendlily* is preferred to the use of *friendly,* at least in edited prose, although Krapp 1927 called it "too awkward for general use."

> The invitation was made friendlily and genuinely enough —Alec Waugh, *My Place in the Bazaar,* 1961

> The horses of the general and Fittleworth . . . minced friendlily along the road —Ford Madox Ford, *The Last Post,* 1928

> The German sat down in the seat opposite and smiled friendlily at the Austrian woman —Erskine Caldwell, *New Republic,* 8 Mar. 1939

> Lorene said goodby to the Fort DeRussey surfboard rider friendlily out in the hall —James Jones, *From Here to Eternity,* 1951

> Came out into the reception area to greet them friendlily —Lawrence Sanders, *The Second Deadly Sin,* 1977

> 'But you can do a bit of labouring, can't you?' said the clerk, quite friendlily —Colin MacInnes, *Mr Love and Justice,* 1960

> He answered my letter at last, as he did yours, and very friendlily —J. R. Ackerley, *The Listener,* 9 May 1974

It seems likely that some writers avoid the choice by means of paraphrase: "in a friendly way," or something similar.

frightened The prepositions used after *frightened* are *of, by, at,* and *about. Frightened of* has a history of being criticized which apparently started in the middle of the last century. The OED quotes an 1858 issue of *Saturday Review* as saying, "It is not usual for educated people to perpetrate such sentences as . . . 'I was frightened *of* her.'" The OED's own comment is that "in recent colloquial use *frightened of* (cf. 'afraid of') is common."

More than a century after the *Saturday Review's* criticism, the stigma attached to *frightened of* lingers in the minds of some usage writers. *Winners & Sinners* (9 Aug. 1962) calls it a "substandard *colloquialism.*" Bernstein 1965 labels it a "casualism," and Freeman 1983 says, "Rather than *of, by* should follow *frighten.*" While some critics suggest *by* and *at* as replacements for *of,* others take the opposite tack and recommend *afraid of* instead of *frightened of.*

Even if *frightened of* did deserve at one time to be called a colloquialism, it deserves it no longer. Our evidence indicates that when a preposition follows *frightened, of* is probably more common than *by* and certainly more common than *at.* All three can be considered standard.

> We are frightened of any urge that would lift us out of the muck —Henry Miller, *The Air-Conditioned Nightmare,* 1945

> We are not frightened of being outsmarted —Hugh Gaitskell, *N.Y. Times Mag.,* 27 June 1954

> I was really rather frightened of being with her — Adrian Henri, *Times Literary Supp.,* 10 Apr. 1969

> . . . frightened of allegations contained in the manuscript —Michael Gordon, *The Age* (Melbourne), 24 Mar. 1975

> . . . frightened out of their wits by the fierce impact —Thomas B. Costain, *The Black Rose,* 1945

> . . . people who like classical music but are frightened by its scope —Ann M. Lingg, *Think,* September 1954

> They were all frightened at the collapse of their lives —D. H. Lawrence, "The Horse Dealer's Daughter," in *England, My England,* 1922

Chambers 1985 accepts *of, by,* and *at* after *frightened* and says that *about* can also be the choice in colloquia'

English when *frightened* "is used of a short-lived state of fear at a particular time in the present or future: *There's nothing to be frightened about—the doctor won't hurt you.*" Even in more general circumstances than these and in written English, we think *frightened about* sounds idiomatic.

> ... the owning and managerial classes were then frightened, not only of Labour, but also about their own economic survival —G. D. H. Cole, *New Statesman & Nation,* 21 Nov. 1953

from whence, from thence, from hence Present-day usage writers take the position that *from* is redundant with *whence, thence,* and *hence.* The basis for this assertion is that the notion of *from* is already present in the words. The objection boils down to a conflict you will encounter again and again in this book: English idiom against logic based on Latin.

The questioning of these phrases is not recent. Samuel Johnson in his Dictionary of 1755 termed *from whence* "A vitious mode of speech." (*Vicious* was not so strong a word in 1755 as it is now.) And after the comment, Johnson quotes Spenser and Shakespeare. It was not a mode of speech unfamiliar to him:

> There is nothing served about there; neither tea, nor coffee, nor lemonade, nor anything whatever; and depend upon it, Sir, a man does not love to go to a place from whence he comes exactly as he went in —Samuel Johnson, quoted in Boswell's *Life,* 1791

Among the 18th-century grammarians who discussed the subject, Priestley 1798 noted that the sense of the preposition was present in the words and thought that the preposition seemed superfluous. But he knew the practice was common (16th-, 17th-, and 18th-century literature is full of the phrases), and he felt that the omission of the preposition in many cases might seem "stiff and disagreeable." Priestley here had reached the heart of the problem: writers used the preposition when it sounded right and left it out when it sounded right.

Priestley was aware of literary usage—he quotes Dryden and Swift. Hodgson 1889 is also aware of literary usage, quoting Smollett and Kingsley. American usage writers of the late 19th century (Bache 1869 and Ayres 1881) are more severe towards the phrases and less interested in literary practice. More recent usage commentators are for the most part dogmatic, for two reasons: the phrases are much less common than they were two centuries earlier, and the commentators may be unacquainted with the older literary sources.

Here are a few instances from the past, to give you a feel for how the phrases have been used:

> From hence the long continuance of the club, which I shall have frequent occasion to speak further of —Benjamin Franklin, *Autobiography,* 1771

> I shall be able, I expect, to dispatch the waggon with the servants from hence, about the 9th. of March —Thomas Jefferson, letter, 27 Feb. 1809

> ... I suppose he will write to us from thence —Jonathan Swift, *Journal to Stella,* 10 Apr. 1711

> How many unsolicitous hours should I bask away, warmed in bed by the sun's glorious beams, could I, like them, tumble from thence in a moment —Samuel Johnson, *The Idler,* 10 June 1758

> I from thence considered industry, as a means of obtaining wealth and distinction —Benjamin Franklin, *Autobiography,* 2d part, 1784

> Let them be whipp'd through every market town till they come to Berwick, from whence they came —Shakespeare, *2 Henry VI,* 1592

> Love still has something of the sea
> From whence his mother rose
> —Sir Charles Sedley, "Song," before 1702

> ... he went soon after to Carolina, from whence he sent me next year two long letters —Benjamin Franklin, *Autobiography,* 1771

> She is at present in a mad house, from whence I fear she must be moved to an hospital —Charles Lamb, letter, 27 Sept. 1796

Even though Benjamin Franklin knew and used all these phrases, there is little likelihood that you will. *From hence* has hardly penetrated the 20th century. A reason contributing to its dropping from the active lexicon is that *hence* is little used today in reference to a physical location. It is more often used of time—"five years hence"—and in other senses. *From hence* is to all intents and purposes an archaism.

From thence does have 20th-century use, but it can hardly be called frequent—it is, in fact, quite rare.

> ... he timed the run from Watford to Mark Lane, and the farther walk from thence to the entrance to the docks —Freeman Wills Crofts, *The Loss of the 'Jane Vosper',* 1936

Thence, however, is used of place, and therefore the possibility of *from thence* is greater. Most of our 20th-century examples of *from thence* come from British publications; it may be less common in American English.

From whence is still alive in both British and American English. Its frequency has made it the chief focus of critical comment, from Samuel Johnson's time to the present. We have plenty of 20th-century evidence of its use, although it is not nearly as common as *whence* alone. *From whence* is a very old phrase, going back at least to 1388. It may have been kept fresher in the public consciousness by its occurrence in the King James Bible, especially in the 121st Psalm: "I will lift up mine eyes unto the hills, from whence cometh my help." This passage may also help account for the frequent occurrence of *from whence* with the verb *come.*

> Mr. Praeger, as orderly and meticulous as Vienna, (from whence he came) —*N.Y. Times,* 11 Aug. 1957

> ... dumps them on flat, sanded earth in the sun, from whence in a few days he takes them to the kiln —*The Autobiography of William Allen White,* 1946

> ... shot through the hedge and down a thirty-foot drop into a midden, from whence he emerged with no bones broken, but covered with smelly mud —K. M. Elisabeth Murray, *Caught in the Web of Words,* 1977

> The fourth lesson was to remember, always, from whence I came —Tip O'Neill with William Novak, *Man of the House,* 1987

From whence is the only one of the three phrases that shows signs of continuing vitality, even though it is undoubtedly less common then it was a century or two ago. We see no great fault in using it where it sounds right—and great writers have used it where it sounded right all along.

frown Of all the prepositions used with *frown, upon* and *on* are the most frequent, with *upon* a shade more frequent than *on:*

> In a day of slipping labels ... such language is frowned upon —Jessamyn West, *N.Y. Herald Tribune Book Rev.,* 30 May 1954

> Lotteries, a form of fund-raising now frowned upon in many quarters —*N.Y. Times,* 17 Jan. 1954

> ... the fact that he is frowned upon by some people —Roy Blount, Jr., *Sports Illustrated,* 23 Aug. 1982

> ... we tend to encourage rigid ideological unity ... and to frown on insurgent individualism —John F. Kennedy, *N.Y. Times Mag.,* 18 Dec. 1955

> Music was not desired by Quakers, it was frowned on —Catherine Drinker Bowen, *Atlantic,* March 1970

Less often, *frown* is used with *at:*

> ... turning his head to frown grotesquely at the man in the back —Terry Southern, *Flash and Filigree,* 1958

> ... she sat in bed frowning nervously at herself in the mirror across the room —Louis Auchincloss, *A Law for the Lion,* 1953

Occasionally, *frown* may be used with *from* or *over:*

> ... the tacit admonition frowned from every corner that these treasures are displayed for study —Clive Bell, *Art,* 1914

> Bulky Georgian mansions frowned over iron fences —*American Guide Series: Michigan,* 1941

fruitful When *fruitful* is used with a preposition, it is most often followed by *of,* less often by *in,* and occasionally by *for* or *to:*

> ... its mathematical aspect ... is less complicated and less fruitful of controversy —Bertrand Russell, *Foundations of Geometry,* 1897

> History is fruitful of recurrences and therefore of analogies —Reinhold Niebuhr, *Atlantic,* July 1954

> ... the same environment appears to be fruitful in one instance and sterile in another —Arnold J. Toynbee, *A Study of History,* vol. 1, 1934

> ... deliberation at this point may be fruitful in that respect —Terry Southern, *Flash and Filigree,* 1958

> The year 1892 was fruitful for Chekhov —*Times Literary Supp.,* 22 Oct. 1971

> ... the fund of available analogies that prove fruitful to diverse minds —Morris R. Cohen, *The Faith of a Liberal,* 1946

fruition The original sense of *fruition* is "enjoyment." The sense is found in the King James Bible and the Book of Common Prayer, and it is common in older literature:

> ... I must observe it once more, that the hours we pass with happy prospects in view are more pleasing

than those crowned with fruition —Oliver Goldsmith, *The Vicar of Wakefield,* 1766

Sometime in the 19th century the word began to be used in the sense of "a bearing of fruit" or, in its more usual figurative application, "realization, accomplishment." The OED was one of the first dictionaries to record this use; the editor of *F,* Henry Bradley, thought it must be a blunder based on an erroneous association with the word *fruit.* He found the sense in use in both England and America but noted it was not countenanced by British dictionaries or by Webster or Worcester in America. His examples are all American: one from context, and two from other American dictionaries—both probably more recent than the Webster and Worcester he had checked.

The new sense seems not to have excited much comment at first. There was a little flurry of newspaper interest and some letters of inquiry to Merriam-Webster editors in the 1920s, mostly because Webster 1909 had omitted the sense. But Webster's Second entered it in 1934, and after that the inquiries stopped. Then in the middle 1960s, several commentators discovered the original sense practically all at once. Flesch 1964, Bernstein 1965, and Gowers in Fowler 1965 all disparaged the new sense. Copperud 1970, 1980 observes that the old sense was practically unknown by then and dismisses their objections as pedantry. Howard 1977 and Bryson 1984 also accept the figurative use.

The original sense, because of its liturgical use, is not yet archaic, though liturgies are changing and older versions of the English Bible are being replaced. All the same, it is pretty unusual in everyday contexts. The original extension to the ripening of fruit or crops is also seldom met. The ordinary use is the entirely figurative one:

> It is no accident for the soul to be embodied: her very essence is to express and bring to fruition the functions and resources of the body —George Santayana, in *A Century of the Essay,* ed. David Daiches, 1951

> ... we then think of him as still mindful of the old ideals and sure to bring them elsewhere to fruition —William James, *Pragmatism,* 1907

> The remarkable human relationship that dominated Cubism between 1909, when it came into full fruition, and 1914 —Janet Flanner, *New Yorker,* 13 Oct. 1956

> ... harbors large ambitions that require a helpmate rather than a playfellow to bring them to fruition —Joseph P. Lash, *McCall's,* October 1971

fugitive 1. When the noun *fugitive* is followed by a preposition, the preposition is usually *from:*

> ... the character seems like a fugitive from a Molière comedy —*Time,* 20 Aug. 1951

> I stand before you today as a fugitive from a sweat shop —Adlai E. Stevenson, *Speeches,* ed. Richard Harrity, 1952

2. In its specialized sense "likely to evaporate, deteriorate, or change," the adjective *fugitive* may be followed by *to:*

> ... good money value pigments are generally very fugitive to light —William von Fischer, ed., *Paint and Varnish Technology,* 1948

In other senses, *fugitive* is occasionally used with *from* or *in:*

> . . . poor Indians . . . whose clothes were sometimes fugitive from better wardrobes —John Steinbeck, *Tortilla Flat,* 1935

> . . . colors were fixed in space and sounds were fugitive in time —Irving Babbitt, *The New Laokoön,* 1910

-ful   Nouns ending in *-ful,* such as *cupful, spoonful, bagful,* and so forth, regularly form the plural by adding *-s* at the end: *cupfuls, spoonfuls, bagfuls.*

> . . . he brought home two large bagfuls of stuff —Bernard Malamud, *The Magic Barrel,* 1958

The plural of these words has long been a puzzle to the public. The earliest commentary we have encountered is Dean Alford's 1866 response to a query about the plural of *spoonful.* The Dean prescribed *spoonfuls,* if it was to be written as one word; *spoons full* if it was to be written as two words. The same advice has been often repeated to seekers after the same information.

There seem to be two factors contributing to the public's continuing perplexity. Most of these words began as two-word compounds of noun and adjective, and the noun took the plural—all will remember the nursery rhyme and its "three bags full." And somewhere, sometime, there seem to have been teachers who were convinced that internal pluralization was more proper or more elegant. We have had many letters from people who remember their teachers telling them that the proper plural is *cupsful* or *handsful.* We have not discovered what schoolbooks prompted these teachers; all of our usage books disagree. But the notion is surely alive, and the questions continue to come in.

The result of the continuing uncertainty is the existence of less frequent variants such as *cupsful* or *teaspoonsful.* These variants are called wrong by some recent handbooks. They are not wrong, but most people use *cupfuls* and *teaspoonfuls.*

full   *Full* is very often followed by *of:*

> The groundwork of this narrative is . . . more full of details which Hawthorne had personally observed —Carl Van Doren, *The American Novel,* 1940

> All his motions were full of tender concern —Morley Callaghan, *The Loved and the Lost,* 1951

> Then one night, Ring came round, fuller of bounce than ever —Frank O'Connor, *Harper's,* April 1971

The phrase *to have one's hands full,* however, is followed by *with* when it takes a preposition:

> Why a man who already had his hands full with two such posts should then begin to cultivate so great a passion for a university presidency —Harold Taylor, *Saturday Rev.,* 14 Apr. 1973

fulsome   When words formerly common come to be used rarely, the lexicographer may have some difficulty in interpreting them. *Fulsome* is such a word. It appears to have had some frequency in Middle English; the Middle English Dictionary lists three main senses. These appear to have subdivided and proliferated in the 16th and 17th centuries particularly, to judge from the evidence in the OED, which lists seven main senses with six subsenses. By the time the *F* section of the OED was

edited—it was published in 1897—the floodtide of usage had receded considerably; the evidence for most of the senses runs out in either the 17th or the 18th century. The OED editor duly marked all but two senses obsolete, and one of the remaining two probably obsolete. Samuel Johnson, in his Dictionary of 1755, was closer to the point of receding usage, but in his limited citational resources he saw only four senses, each attested by 16th or 17th century works. He missed the first two senses listed in the OED as well as the only sense the OED considered live: *fulsome* praise, flattery, cant. Noah Webster in 1828 noticed something peculiar about Johnson's definitions. He printed them verbatim but added this note: "These are the English definitions of *fulsome,* but I have never witnessed such applications of the word in the United States." He included, under the spelling *fullsome,* a definition of the sense he found current:

> Gross; disgusting by plainness, grossness or excess; as *fullsome* flattery or praise.

This is, of course, the same sense the OED editor considered to be live.

The considerable comment about the frequent use or misuse of *fulsome* is an American phenomenon of only recent occurrence, starting in the late 1940s or early 1950s in response to the word's beginning to appear with some frequency in newspapers and magazines. The following filler from the June 30, 1951, issue of the *New Yorker* is typical:

> Nick Schenk, head of Loew's Inc., is at work now drafting the letter of acceptance of L. B. Mayer's resignation—to make it so fulsome that even Mr. Mayer will like it. —*Leonard Lyons in the Post.*
>
> You mean so coarse, gross, foul, satiating, nauseating, sickening? Or you mean so repulsive, disgusting, and offensive to moral sensibility?

All of the synonymous terms supplied by the *New Yorker* editor are taken from Webster's Second, published in 1934. They illustrate the contribution of this dictionary and its predecessor to the problem. The editor of *fulsome* for Webster 1909 had available ·in the OED the full history of the word, but little evidence of current use. He clearly used the OED information in revising the definition of the 1890 unabridged. But he did two things that would have future repercussions: he included in the definition hints from two definitions the OED editor considered obsolete, or probably obsolete; and he added at the end, apparently out of his own head, the words "insincerity or baseness of motive." Both of these characteristics of the 1909 definition were carried over into the 1934 book.

The history of *fulsome* is quite complex, as the OED treatment shows. But when 19th- and 20th-century citations are compared with those of the 16th, 17th, and 18th centuries, it is pretty clear that the word had stronger negative implications in older use than it has in modern use. Thus the retention of terms used to define the older uses has resulted in a definition too strongly worded to describe 20th-century use very accurately.

The addition of "insincerity or baseness of motive" was also unfortunate. It appears to have been the 1909 editor's notion of why fulsome praise might be offered, but it has never been a meaning of the adjective itself. In other words, fulsome praise, fulsome tributes, and so forth, may connote insincerity or baseness of motive, but the adjective *fulsome* does not denote such a thing, as the OED definition and citations demonstrate.

So one major contributor to the controversy has been an overembellished dictionary definition written sometime before 1909, reprinted in the 1934 unabridged (and, with variations, in numerous smaller dictionaries and handbooks on usage) and then repeated, with varying degrees of accuracy of recall, by members of usage panels. A measure of misreading has sometimes added to the problem: the first string of adjectives listed by the *New Yorker* editor are from a definition labeled obsolete in both the 1909 and 1934 Webster. The citation reprehended in the *New Yorker,* incidentally, seems to fit reasonably well within the OED definition: "Of language, style, behaviour, etc.: Offensive to good taste; *esp.* offending from excess or want of measure or from being 'over-done'. Now chiefly used in reference to gross or excessive flattery, over-demonstrative affection, or the like." Leonard Lyons does not appear to be ascribing good taste to L. B. Mayer, although perhaps *effusive* might have served the writer's purpose less controversially.

Then how is *fulsome* actually used in the 20th century? The largest part of our citations deal with praise, but a number of the earlier senses listed in the OED still persist, if attested only occasionally. The etymologically purest sense (OED 1)—"characterized by abundance; copious, full"—is still in use. This is the sense that draws the most frequent criticism:

> ... illustrating with fulsome quotations both the underlying philosophy and the nature of its expression in poetry —*Times Literary Supp.,* 16 June 1966

> The Ecclesiological Society, which the author describes in fulsome detail, seems to have been a redoubtable and influential institution —George N. Shuster, *Key Reporter,* Spring 1963

> The quick passing of the hours will make them more cherished, and lend more fulsome importance and value to their use —Kenneth L. Patton, *The Humanist,* Summer 1947

> Their promises, while fulsome, were clothed in substance —*Consumer Reports,* April 1969

> The chief resentment against the President is the belief that he has made no fulsome effort to clean up the mess —editorial, *Springfield* (Mass.) *Union,* 18 Mar. 1951

The sense applied to the roundness or fullness of the figure (OED 2) turns up now and then:

> Crisp sheer shantung dresses over crinolines give fulsome billowy figure flattery —*Women's Wear Daily,* 2 Apr. 1952

> ... *Life* (May 19, 1958, p. 2) referred to Miss Margaret O'Brien as "a fulsome 20-year-old" with "sinuous curves" —Evans 1962

The sense applied to the flavor or taste of food (OED 3b) was alive as late as 1927, although much weakened in force:

> ... an exquisite wine, Sainte Croix du Mont, which called itself a Sauternes. I could not make out why it lacked the rather fulsome sweetness of ordinary Sauternes ... —Stephen Gwynn, *In Praise of France,* 1927

The sense of "offensive to normal tastes or sensibilities" (OED 6) also finds occasional use:

> Color photography ... has already reflected, in its uses, the true fresh beauties (as well as the fulsome

inanities) of the age —Walker Evans, *Fortune,* July 1954

There is one additional use. It pertains to music, is of recent development, and is related to the earliest sense of the word:

> Angel's soloists may be a shade more fulsome, but Argo's choral forces and organist collaborate to create a uniquely chaste atmosphere of sunny Easter-morning devotion —Peter G. Davis, *High Fidelity,* August 1970

> The fulsome sonority of Wagner filled the giant shed at Tanglewood last night and a soprano new to Tanglewood audiences stole their hearts —R. C. Hammerich, *Springfield* (Mass.) *Republican,* 13 Aug. 1972

> ... and she was in generally fulsome, limpid voice, a few rough moments aside —Thor Eckert, Jr., *Christian Science Monitor,* 13 Feb. 1980

But most of our citations deal with complimentary language or those who produce such language. In most cases the use is pejorative and causes the critics no concern. It emphasizes the notion of excess or effusiveness:

> "... A cast of your skull, sir, ... would be an ornament to any anthropological museum. It is not my intention to be fulsome, but I confess that I covet your skull." —Sir Arthur Conan Doyle, *The Hound of the Baskervilles,* 1902

> ... has written in your praise in the Harvard Law Review warmly but without being fulsome —Sir Frederick Pollock, letter, 26 Jan. 1928

> ... addressing the spirit as Princess Splendid in terms of fulsome flattery —Sir James G. Frazer, *Aftermath,* 1937

> The opposition dug up Harding's old encomium of the boss in all its fulsome gush of 'deference and devotion.' —Samuel Hopkins Adams, *Incredible Era,* 1939

> I gazed at her with an admiration whose extent I did not express, lest I be thought fulsome —A. J. Liebling, *New Yorker,* 15 Oct. 1955

> ... scorn is heaped ... in measure to equal the fulsome tribute paid every Democratic achievement since the bank holiday —Tom Wicker, *N.Y. Times,* 17 Oct. 1968

> ... the *Sydney Gazette* and the *Australian* both carried fulsome tributes, elegiac verses were penned — *Australian Dictionary of Biography,* 1967

> Rarely have I found the praise tendered me to be fulsome —Aristides, *American Scholar,* Autumn 1979

It is sometimes applied tongue-in-cheek:

> ... *Guardian* paid him a fulsome compliment: "one of the best-known Canadians in England" —*Time,* 25 Dec. 1944

> Mr. Lovell recklessly allowed himself to become even more fulsome. "I'll say this for you—when you carve a ham, you don't *squinch!*" he said. —James Reid Parker, *New Yorker,* 21 Oct. 1950

But there is a real problem with the use of *fulsome* when it is applied to praise, to an introduction, or to similar ceremonial devices. *Fulsome* is unusual enough that its attachment to *praise* or *introduction* does not immediately connote disparagement to the mind of the hearer, reader, or user encountering it for the first time. There is plenty of evidence that *fulsome* is taken to be either neutral, meaning approximately "full and detailed," or even complimentary, meaning approximately "generous." The latter use can be illustrated with a remark made by Arkansas Congressman Brooks Hays after a rather long and detailed introduction:

> You do me great honor, Betsy, and I'm grateful for this very friendly and very fulsome introduction . . . —speech, 4 Oct. 1968

A writer also took the term to be complimentary in a pamphlet on American railroads:

> There has been fulsome praise of the gigantic task that the railroads performed during the war —R. Fletcher, "The Way to Better Rail Transporation," March 1947

President Reagan has used it as a neutral term:

> I got a very fulsome apology from the President of Iraq —quoted on NBC News, 19 May 1987

Such interpretations of the word are fostered by its application in contexts where the writer's or speaker's intent is not clear and the sense is ambiguous:

> Name of Stassen Also to Fore in Light of Fulsome Praise of Both by Dewey —subhead, *N.Y. Times,* 18 Oct. 1948

> In both the House of Commons and the House of Lords, the adoption of the traditional "humble address" of congratulation provided the setting for fulsome tributes to the royal family —*Washington Post,* 17 Nov. 1948

> Cotton Mather became unduly fulsome in his comment on her [Anne Bradstreet's] life —*Dictionary of American Biography,* 1929

> Back came some of the most fulsome praise for a vegetable that Thomas ever received —*Christian Science Monitor,* cited by James J. Kilpatrick, syndicated column, 3 July 1985

In the first two of these, "high praise" is probably intended; a pejorative sense would have been a sly dig out of place in a straight news context—nevertheless, such an implication could be inferred by the reader. The second two are ambiguous because the average reader is unlikely to know how effusive Cotton Mather ordinarily was (or what "duly fulsome" might mean) and to what degree new vegetables are normally praised.

The watchword obviously must be care. If you are tempted to use *fulsome,* remember that it is quite likely to be misunderstood by both the innocent reader and the gimlet-eyed purist unless your context makes your intended meaning abundantly clear. It is not a word familiar enough to carry an ambiguous context to a clear conclusion.

Let's try to sum this all up. *Fulsome* is probably more commonly used in the second half of the 20th century than it has been at any time since the end of the 17th, and curiously enough, our modern mildly pejorative uses are quite similar to those used by the Restoration dramatists—*fulsome* seems to have been an all-purpose term of abuse in the speech of the stylish people of that time (and it was often bracketed with *nauseous*). We offer three examples here for their flavor:

> SMITH. Now the devil take thee for a silly, confident, unnatural, fulsome rogue! —George Villiers, *The Rehearsal,* 1672

> HEARTWELL. I confess I have not been sneering fulsome Lies and nauseous Flattery —William Congreve, *The Old Bachelor,* 1693

> BOY. Sir, there are two men below desire to have the honour of kissing your hand.
> LYRIC. They must be knaves or fools, by their fulsome compliment
> —George Farquhar, *Love and a Bottle,* 1698

In present-day use *fulsome* is no more strongly negative than it is in these old uses. Its most common use is in mildly depreciatory contexts, but keep in mind that several nonpejorative meanings, one limited to music, are still current.

Most usage commentators and handbooks are still measuring current usage with the rather overblown definition of 1909, and as a result they tend to censure any use they feel is insufficiently pejorative. Modern lexicography will eventually catch up with present-day use, and the commentators, one hopes, will soften their remarks. One commentator has in fact changed his position. Rudolf Flesch in his 1964 book censured the usual modern examples of the word. But in his 1983 book, he said:

> If you want to use *fulsome* in the sense of copious and abundant, go right ahead.

We would urge a bit more caution. If you do use the nonpejorative senses, make sure your context is unambiguous.

fun   A few commentators and handbooks deplore the use of *fun* as an adjective, several others term it informal, and a couple who dislike it themselves still note how nouns have a way of turning into adjectives in English. Quite a few members of all groups believe the usage is new—Flesch 1983, for instance, thinks it only about twenty years old; Copperud 1980 concurs; Harper 1985 finds it a vogue usage of the early 1970s; Macmillan 1982 thinks it transitory.

The OED Supplement, however, shows that it is a bit older. The Supplement calls it an attributive use of the noun passing into an adjective and cites examples from the middle of the 19th century on, including this title from 1853, which does have a modern ring:

> Fun jottings; or, Laughs I have taken pen to.

The recent flurry of use that has caught the attention of the commentators seems to have started after World War II:

> This language problem has its fun side, too —*Time,* 2 Sept. 1946

> ". . . We may not be the best motel on the Highway but The Bluebird is certainly the cutest. A fun place. . . ." —Mary Jane Rolfs, *No Vacancy,* 1951

> New fun ideas are the poncho and the all-in-one shirt and shorts "walking suit" —Virginia Pope, *N.Y. Times Mag.,* 13 June 1954

The usage had really caught on by the middle 1960s, helped, probably, by advertising for fun cars and fun furs. It has turned up in some unexpected places:

> . . . there were countless small boats for racing, fishing, or just fun sailing —Samuel Eliot Morison, *Oxford History of the American People*, 1965

And more predictable ones:

> "A Few Selected Exits" is a fun book to read —Clive Barnes, *N.Y. Times*, 15 Apr. 1969

> . . . doing the boogaloo on the beaches at Fort Lauderdale and other fun spots —*Newsweek*, 3 Apr. 1967

And it can be found outside the usual publishing centers:

> . . . two of the more fun nights he had had all summer —Kim Vought, *The Beachcomber* (Ocean City, Md.), 14 Aug. 1970

> . . . a fun evening with a worship service and lots of food —Ellen Houx, *Mineral Independent* (Superior, Mont.), 4 Jan. 1973

It is used in the 1980s in just the way it was used in 1946:

> Vocabulary is, indeed, the fun part of dialectology — Robert Claiborne, *Our Marvelous Native Tongue*, 1983

All of the examples shown so far are for attributive uses. No commentator has attempted to tackle the question of whether *fun* is a predicate adjective as well, and probably with good reason, for there is no sure way to prove that *fun* in "That was fun" is either an adjective or a noun. But notice that it is often linked with another adjective:

> "The money's in the cave!"
> "Tom—honest injun, now—is it fun or earnest?"
> "Earnest, Huck. . . ."
> —Mark Twain, *Tom Sawyer*, 1876

It is challenging and fun for children —Frances R. Horwich, *NEA Jour.*, February 1965

> They think it is fun and good for young people — Rosemary Brown, *Ladies' Home Jour.*, September 1971

These uses suggest that some writers may well feel it to be a predicate as well as an attributive adjective. So does at least one speaker:

> Things have changed. It hasn't been all that fun lately —Lawrence K. Grossman, quoted in *Springfield* (Mass.) *Union-News*, 1 Aug. 1988

We also have spoken evidence for *so fun, funner,* and *funnest,* which attest to adjective status in speech.
  As an attributive adjective, *fun* is not often found in elevated contexts; as a quasi-predicate adjective, it is found in all contexts.

funny It is a bit funny that the sense of *funny* that means "strange, odd, peculiar" is still being treated as something less than standard. Here is a recent comment:

> Often used in conversation as a utility word that has no precise meaning but may be clear enough in its

context. It is generally too vague for college writing —Trimmer & McCrimmon 1988

This is little more than an elaboration of MacCracken & Sandison 1917:

> . . . inaccurate colloquialism for *strange, odd.*

The OED traces this sense back to 1806. It labels the sense colloquial, and its examples seem to be from letters or transcribed conversation. It does appear to be a spoken use in origin.

> She supposes my silence may have proceeded from resentment of her not having written. . . . &c. She is a funny one —Jane Austen, letter, 7 Jan. 1807

It was moving into more general use even before the turn of the century, and it is still common in standard, although perhaps not stodgily formal, sources.

> "I am in Lady Agatha's black books at present," answered Dorian, with a funny look of penitence — Oscar Wilde, *The Picture of Dorian Gray*, 1891

> Once more Hastings got that funny impression of something put on and artificial in her tone —John Cowper Powys, *Ducdame*, 1925

> It is a funny place, this world of Capitalism — George Bernard Shaw, *The Intelligent Woman's Guide to Socialism and Capitalism*, 1928

> . . . where everybody would expect you to stay and think it funny when you wouldn't —William Faulkner, *Sanctuary*, 1931

> For some funny reason we have never been accepted as Vermonters —Robert Frost, letter, May 1931

> . . . being funny that way, she had had an intuition that something was really going to happen this time —Elizabeth Bowen, *The Heat of the Day*, 1949

> She was funny that way—that was the only explanation —Mary McCarthy, *New Yorker*, 23 Mar. 1957

> They make charming little beginning-of-the-world music on funny little instruments —Elizabeth Hardwick, *N.Y. Rev. of Books*, 6 Nov. 1969

> It's a very funny kind of sin—because you do it with the approval of the Dean of Women, your Minister, and both sets of parents —Margaret Mead, *Barnard Alumnae*, Winter 1971

> But chickens or tomatoes or detergent soap earmarked for the cooperatives have a funny way of falling into the busy hands of black marketeers — Ned Temko & Michael Winston, *Christian Science Monitor*, 19 May 1980

> Funny, nothing in Whitman ever seemed to me unwholesome —Robert Boyers, *Times Literary Supp.*, 30 May 1980

> Considering how hard a man works to get himself into the White House, it's funny that once he gets there he can't wait to leave —*And More by Andy Rooney*, 1982

Unless your prose is of a truly elevated sort, there seems to be no real reason to avoid this use of *funny.*

further, furthest See FARTHER, FURTHER.

fused participle See POSSESSIVE WITH GERUND.

G

gage See GAUGE.

gainsay This synonym for *deny* has a vaguely Shakespearean quality. Fowler 1926 classes it as a literary word, and he notes that it now usually occurs in negative contexts. Our evidence confirms his observation:

> This is not to gainsay the boldness of his concepts — Henry Kamen, *Times Literary Supp.,* 15 Oct. 1982

> . . . he could not gainsay Krushchev's testimony — Robert C. Tucker, *N.Y. Times Book Rev.,* 2 Jan. 1983

> There is no gainsaying such certainty of misinformation —John Algeo, in Greenbaum 1985

galore *Galore* is derived from the Irish Gaelic *go leor,* "enough." Some usage commentators have written about it as if it still had a strongly Irish quality, but in fact it has been used in English since the 17th century and has long since been thoroughly assimilated into the mainstream of our language. Its most strident critics have been Fowler 1926, who considered it "no part of the Englishman's natural vocabulary," and Bernstein 1965, who found it appropriate only for "jocular or breezy or slangy effect." Our evidence shows that it is a common, standard word most likely to occur in writing that has an informal tone, as most writing now does. It occasionally appears in more formal contexts, but it would be out of place—and therefore is not used—when a somber or highly serious tone is called for. You will not find it, for example, in such a sentence as "The battlefield was strewn with bodies galore." Here are some examples of typical use from our files:

> Legends galore . . . have clustered round his name — Norman Douglas, *South Wind,* 1917

> . . . tables (several of them, covered with Oriental carpeting), chairs galore, plush settees —Truman Capote, *New Yorker,* 27 Oct. 1956

> And what is left? Technical achievements, technical achievements galore —Peter Ustinov, *Center Mag.,* January 1969

> . . . with loyalty galore to invest if only he could earn it back with interest —John le Carré, *N.Y. Times Book Rev.,* 14 Oct. 1979

> There is sleuthing galore ahead of the reader —William F. Buckley, Jr., *N.Y. Times Book Rev.,* 13 Mar. 1983

gambit A *gambit* is a chess opening in which a player risks one or more minor pieces to gain an advantage in position. Some usage writers would like to rein extended uses in as close as possible to the original meaning. Bernstein 1958, Follett 1966, and Bryson 1984 all think that a gambit should involve some sort of concession or sacrifice. When this happens in actual practice, the writer is usually deliberately employing the metaphor of a chess game, and such uses are rare.

> Yet it may be that the figure of twelve million was never more than a gambit, advanced in order to win a force that is still too high —*New Republic,* 2 Nov. 1942

> . . . it is clear that the U.S.S.R. was playing a gambit: among the captured Russian material exhibited in Helsinki at the close of the campaign was none of the first-class equipment that the Germans subsequently came up against on the Russian front —Eric Dancy, *Foreign Affairs,* April 1946

In the evidence we have accumulated, *gambit* is freely used to mean merely "a calculated move" or "stratagem." Other common meanings are "a remark intended to start a conversation or make a telling point" and "a topic."

> Ibsen as we know had a meagre power of invention. . . . It is not a gross exaggeration to say that his only gambit is the sudden arrival of a stranger who comes into a stuffy room and opens the windows — W. Somerset Maugham, *The Summing Up,* 1938

> . . . the Russian gambit which has rarely been beaten. . . . The man in the government bureau you want to see is not there, is sick, is in hospital, or is away on his vacation —John Steinbeck, *A Russian Journal,* 1948

> . . . the problem of the child confronting the adult world must recall to us how useful this gambit was to Henry James —Elizabeth Janeway, *N.Y. Times Book Rev.,* 25 July 1954

> . . . to avoid the multitude of taxes and assessments, the standard gambit of the peasant was to "dress poor" and "talk poor" —Stanley J. Idzerda, *Background of the French Revolution,* 1959

> . . . uses a foxier gambit to achieve his ends. He employs the infantile, or blubber-mouth approach —S. J. Perelman, *New Yorker,* 9 July 1949

> . . . a favorite gambit of reporters who are pressing the President for information is: "There has been a report that you are going to . . ." —*Newsweek,* 26 Sept. 1949

> In desperation one seeks an artificial gambit. I remember one from an English girl: "Oh, I say, are you frightfully keen on cats and dogs?" —George C. McGhee, *Saturday Rev.,* 28 June 1975

> . . . always carried turtle eggs in his pockets and bounced them on bars as a conversational gambit — Bergen Evans, *Saturday Rev.,* 26 June 1954

Bryson objects to the phrase *opening gambit* as a redundancy, but with extended meanings so far removed from the original, the question of redundancy loses whatever importance it might have in more literal contexts:

> "How nice of you to come and see an old woman, dear," said Lucilla. This was her usual opening gambit with the young —Elizabeth Goudge, *Pilgrim's Inn,* 1948

> . . . if a stranger just ahead drops a rosary, don't take any notice. That's the opening gambit of the oldest trick in the world —Francis Aldor, *The Good Time Guide to London,* 1951

If you happen to be criticized for using *gambit* in a general way, we do not think you should take the criticism too seriously.

gamut   *Gamut* in its literal sense, which is now almost never used, means "the whole series of recognized musical notes." Most people are familiar with *gamut* as a figurative word meaning "an entire range or series." It occurs especially in the phrase *run the gamut*, which usually has the sense "to range all the way; vary":

> . . . ran the gamut from mildly piquant and creamy to firmer, well-ripened specimens —Mimi Sheraton, *N.Y. Times,* 2 May 1979

> . . . the outdoor furniture runs the gamut from prim poolside pieces to the frankly zany —*N.Y. Times,* 10 Apr. 1980

Possible confusion of *run the gamut* with *run the gauntlet* is noted by several commentators. Reader's Digest 1983 and Harper 1985 cite a few examples of such confusion, but it does not appear to be a widespread problem. Our own files contain not a single instance. See, however, GAUNTLET 2.

gantlet   See GAUNTLET 1.

gap   The use of *gap* in such phrases as *generation gap* and *credibility gap* is discouraged as hackneyed by several commentators. Its popularity continues unabated, however, and there seems to be no end to the variety of its applications:

> There is also a "frustration gap" between new students and those who campaigned in support of the school —Cheryl Bentsen, *Change,* October 1971

> . . . was no television then, and we filled the trash gap with glorious, pulpy . . . fiction —Arthur Prager, *Cosmopolitan,* May 1972

> . . . consumer advocates fear a "protection gap" while new rules are written —John Curley, *Wall Street Jour.,* 20 Apr. 1982

> . . . distrust plus loss of self-confidence equals the confidence gap —Theodore J. Lowi, *N.Y. Times Book Rev.,* 10 Apr. 1983

garb   Some criticism has been directed at *garb,* essentially because it is seen as a needless synonym for more straightforward words, such as *clothes* and *clothing. Garb* continues in reputable use, however, both as a noun and as a verb, and its use should give you little concern. The noun in its literal sense most often denotes a highly distinctive outfit, and it is likely chosen over a more ordinary word because the clothes it describes are themselves out of the ordinary:

> . . . the baroque, beaded beauty of ceremonial garb —S. K. Oberbeck, *Newsweek,* 15 Jan. 1973

> . . . a man in priestly garb was selling medallions — Lawrence Van Gelder, *N.Y. Times,* 3 Oct. 1979

> . . . got hold of some traditional Hasidic garb —John Gross, *N.Y. Times Book Rev.,* 1 Apr. 1984

The noun also has a common figurative use, in which it typically describes a deliberately deceptive outward appearance:

> . . . cloak ordinary observations in a garb of specious profundity —Walter Kendrick, *N.Y. Times Book Rev.,* 4 Sept. 1983

The verb *garb* occurs most often as a past participle. Like the noun, it has both literal and figurative uses:

> . . . garbed impeccably but anachronistically in Forties evening dress —Bruce Cook, *Saturday Rev.,* 1 Nov. 1975

> . . . do not relish magnificent dishonesty garbed as gospel —Fred Rodell, *Saturday Rev.,* 14 Mar. 1953

gauge   Note well the spelling of *gauge.* A common error puts the *u* before the *a:*

> . . . when you guage present progress with past aspirations —*Rolling Stone,* 13 May 1971

The old and respectable variant spelling *gage* avoids the problem altogether, but it is now rarely used for the verb. Its most common use is in reference to scientific instruments used to make measurements:

> . . . gages for measuring extremely high pressures — Benjamin Petkof, *Mineral Facts and Problems,* 1965

gauntlet   **1.** *Gauntlet, gantlet.* Some confusion exists about the status of these spelling variants. The argument is sometimes heard that they represent etymologically distinct words, and that *gantlet* is the only correct choice—or at least is the preferable one—in the common phrase *run the ga(u)ntlet.* This argument is mistaken. There is, in fact, more than one *gauntlet* in the English language, but *gauntlet* and *gantlet* are not themselves etymologically distinct—they are spelling variants, pure and simple.

The older *gauntlet* was borrowed from French in the 15th century. Its literal meaning in French is "little glove," and it originally described a protective glove worn with medieval armor. The phrases *throw down the gauntlet* and *pick up the gauntlet* arose from the medieval custom of throwing down a glove to issue a challenge. These phrases (with many variations) persist in figurative use, and *gauntlet* also now describes several varieties of glove, both protective and fashionable:

> . . . not picking up the gauntlet so callously thrown to them by Nixon —Ralph J. Gleason, *Rolling Stone,* 8 June 1972

> In the first paragraph he throws down the gauntlet — *Time,* 12 Dec. 1983

> . . . wears his engineer's cap, coveralls and work gauntlets —*Saturday Evening Post,* 16 Nov. 1956

> Wool-knit gauntlets in navy, cobalt, or black —*New Yorker,* 21 Nov. 1983

The *gauntlet* of *run the gauntlet* has a more complex history. The reference in *run the gauntlet* is to a form of military punishment in which a prisoner was made to pass between two rows of men armed with clubs or other weapons. The original name for such a punishment in English was *gantlope,* a derivative of the Swedish *gatlopp,* from *gata,* "road," and *lop,* "course."

Gauntlet came to be used in place of *gantlope* through the process of folk etymology—that is, the substitution of a familiar word for an unfamiliar one. The earliest citations for *gauntlet* meaning "gantlope" are from the 17th century:

> To print, is to run the gantlet —Joseph Glanvill, *The Vanity of Dogmatizing,* 1661 (OED)

> They stripped them naked, and caused them to run the Gauntlet —Increase Mather, *The History of King Philip's War,* 1862 (originally published in 1676) (OED)

Gantlet was simply one of several spelling variants. It was also used for the "glove" sense of *gauntlet:*

> Yee that fling out the gantlet to him that calls you Coward —Nathaniel Ward, *The Simple Cobler of Aggawam,* 1647 (OED)

We do not know exactly how *gantlet* came to be regarded as the "preferred" spelling in *run the ga(u)ntlet.* The distinction *gantlet* (punishment)/*gauntlet* (glove) seems to have arisen in the U.S. during the 19th century. Our own dictionaries recognized it—for reasons which are not at all clear—and probably played a significant role in promoting it up until the publication of Webster's Third in 1961. British dictionaries have never recognized the distinction, and *gantlet* has long since dropped out of use as a spelling variant in British English. In American English, mistaken notions about its correctness (for which we have to take our share of blame) have assured its continued use as a variant of *gauntlet* in its "gantlope" sense:

> ... send it through the FDA gantlet —Paul H. Blachly, *Psychology Today,* May 1971

> The gantlet of congressional committees ... remains to be run —William G. McDonald, *Fortune,* 15 Dec. 1980

The more common spelling, however, is *gauntlet:*

> ... could run the Republican primary gauntlet — Kaye Northcott, *Mother Jones,* January 1980

> ... found himself running a gauntlet of 1,200 women —Linda Marx, *People,* 4 Oct. 1982

> ... running a gauntlet of hostile bulls —Fred Bruemmer, *National Wildlife,* June/July 1985

2. Many commentators warn against confusion of *run the gauntlet* for *run the gamut.* Such confusion does not appear to be widespread, but we do have some evidence of it:

> Customers run the gauntlet from state and local governments to public libraries and big corporations — *Datamation,* May 1977

When the sense of the phrase is "range," the correct choice is *gamut.*
See also GAMUT.

gay   By now everyone knows that homosexuals have made *gay* the word of choice for "homosexual." Copperud 1980 notes that *gay* shares with *black* and *Chicano* the distinction of being both self-applied by the segment of society it describes and adopted generally. The general acceptance of the term in its new sense has brought it to the attention of usage writers, many of whom are sure that the homosexual use of *gay* has destroyed the word for its older uses. Our evidence shows, however, that the older senses of *gay* are still with us.

It would take a certain willful perverseness to read "homosexual" into the use of *gay* applied to inanimate nouns in contexts like these:

> ... crossed the street under the clear starry sky toward the gay lights of the municipal tree —Garrison Keillor, *Lake Wobegon Days,* 1985

> ... stepping nimbly between the piles of garbage to the gay marimba rhythms in your head —Jay McInerney, *Bright Lights, Big City,* 1984

> ... gay and witty clothes —*Vogue,* August 1983

> ... Miss Pym's gay, confident gift invests everything it handles with an individual—comedy, is it? — Philip Larkin, *Required Writing,* 1983

Applied to humans, it can be more easily ambiguous:

> We walked along Beauchamp Place encountering a gay fellow dressed as King Charles —Robert Morley, *Punch,* 10 Feb. 1976

But note how the placement of *gay* in the next two examples makes the meaning clear:

> Where would a gay student feel most comfortable? —*People,* 17 Sept. 1984

> ... the leader of a gay band of Sorbonne students — Mary McCarthy, *Occasional Prose,* 1985

The bemoaning of the loss of the traditional senses of *gay* is premature, to put it mildly. The traditional senses are still in regular use. Attention to the context will almost always ensure that your intended meaning comes through clearly. Nonetheless, the new sense creates enough potential for unintended humor or serious miscommunication to exact some thoughtful care from you in your use of the word.

gendarme   Objections are sometimes made to the use in English of *gendarme* as a general term for a French policeman, because *gendarme* in French refers specifically to the equivalent of the American state policeman. Against those objections it should be noted that the English word *gendarme* has its own independent existence, like any other foreign word borrowed into our language, and that, in any case, the French themselves appear not to be such sticklers about how they use *gendarme. Harrap's New Standard French and English Dictionary* shows that the French *gendarme* has the "approx[imate]" sense "police constable," and that plural *gendarmes* occurs in several French idioms in which its meaning is simply "police." In short, the objections strike us as somewhat pedantic. In English *gendarme* is a not very precise term used especially for an armed policeman in a French-speaking country. It also occurs as a playful synonym of *policeman* without reference to French-speaking countries, although such usage seems now to be fairly uncommon:

> ... got a first hand view of local gendarmes performing routine duties and was given rides in a swivel chair —*Springfield* (Mass.) *Union,* 22 Aug. 1953

gender The use of *gender* to mean "sex" has been cited with disapproval in books on usage for many years. Fowler 1926 seems to have been the first to raise the issue, and his remarks are typical:

> **gender**... is a grammatical term only. To talk of *persons* or *creatures of the masculine* or *feminine g.,* meaning *of the male* or *female sex,* is either a jocularity (permissible or not according to context) or a blunder.

The grammatical *gender* denotes a subclass of words that is usually partly based on sex and that determines agreement with other words or grammatical forms. For example, a French noun of the feminine gender, such as *femme,* "woman," takes the definite article *la,* while a noun of the masculine gender, such as *fils,* "son," takes *le.* As many commentators point out, sex does not always enter into it: the French word for "pen," *plume,* belongs to the feminine gender and takes *la;* the word for "pencil," *crayon,* is masculine and takes *le.* So much for grammar. The "sex" sense of *gender* is actually centuries old. The OED records it as early as the 1300s, and it was included as a standard sense in the dictionaries of both Samuel Johnson (1755) and Noah Webster (1828). Its use during much of the 19th century seems to have been, if not common, at least unremarkable:

> ... black divinities of the feminine gender —Charles Dickens, *A Tale of Two Cities,* 1859

But by the turn of the century dictionaries had begun to give it restrictive labels. The OED described it as "now only *jocular*" in 1898, and Merriam-Webster dictionaries at the same time were calling it "obsolete or colloquial."

Whether obsolete, colloquial, or jocular, the "sex" sense of gender continued in occasional use. By the publication of Webster's Third in 1961, we had accumulated enough evidence of its straightforward use in written contexts to see that the restrictive labels of the past no longer applied. But the real boom in its popularity was still to come. In the past two decades, the "sex" sense of *gender* has become increasingly common in standard writing:

> Both genders usually use the same basic bag —*Consumer Reports,* March 1971

> ... have nothing to do with the author's gender —Erica Jong, *N.Y. Times Book Rev.,* 12 Sept. 1976

> ... of a different gender... from their characters —Arthur M. Schlesinger, Jr., *Saturday Rev.,* 2 Sept. 1978

> ... routinely screen for gonorrhea irrespective of gender —John J. Potterat et al., *JAMA,* 13 Feb. 1981

> ... excluded persons of their gender —Daniel Seligman, *Fortune,* 5 Apr. 1982

Its use as an attributive adjective where *sexual* would otherwise appear is especially widespread:

> ... shifts in gender identity —Robert T. Rubin et al., *Science,* 20 Mar. 1981

> ... gender expectations —Frederika Randall, *N.Y. Times Book Rev.,* 12 Dec. 1982

> ... the gender gap—the pattern of women voting differently from men —Nancy J. Walker, *N.Y. Times Book Rev.,* 11 Mar. 1984

> ... what we call gender harassment —*People,* 15 Oct. 1984

> ... gender roles within the family are broader —Elizabeth Janeway, quoted in Harper 1985

And it has given rise to the derivative term, *genderless:*

> ... belonged to a different, genderless world —Colette Dowling, *N.Y. Times Mag.,* 28 Nov. 1976

> In these genderless times —James J. Kilpatrick, quoted in Harper 1985

The revival of *gender* in its "sex" sense may be partly attributable to the increased public attention now being given to issues involving men and women, as well as to the increased use of the word *sex* in senses relating to physical intercourse. (A column that appeared in the *Boston Globe* in 1983 plausibly suggests that *gender* is being used as a "reverse euphemism," inasmuch as *sex* "has become so much identified with TV violence and steamy soap operas.") In any case, there is no denying that the "sex" sense of *gender* is now more common than it has ever been. Most current dictionaries recognize it as standard, but there are still some books on usage (such as Harper 1985 and Shaw 1987) that discourage its use.

genealogy *Genealogy* is formed ultimately from the Greek roots *genea* "race, family" and *-logia,* a combining form derived from *logos* "word, reason" and denoting expression or study. The exact English correspondent of *-logia* is *-logy,* as in *eulogy* (where it is appended to the Greek combining form *eu-* meaning "good"). However, *-logy* frequently follows combining forms ending in a thematic vowel *-o-,* which in these combinations (rather perversely from a semantic standpoint) receives the stress (as in *psychology*). As a result, many speakers think of *-ology* as being the suffix, and it is in this form that the suffix has been made a noun *(isms and ologies).* Yielding to the tug of this neologistic suffix, most speakers pronounce *genealogy* \ˌjē-nē-ˈäl-ə-jē\, as though it were spelled *geneology.* Sometimes the inattentive even spell it that way. Those who understand the formation of the word or whose pronunciation is simply more influenced by spelling will tend to say \ˌjē-nē-ˈal-ə-jē\ (rhyming with *analogy*) or, even more meticulously, \ˌjen-ē-ˈal-ə-jē\ (with the first *e* short—no doubt in reminiscence of the epsilon of the Greek).

In a similar condition are *mineralogy* and *mammalogy,* both rather irregularly formed. For the first, \ˌmin-ə-ˈral-ə-jē\ appears to predominate, at least among people in the field, but you will also hear \ˌmin-ə-ˈräl-ə-jē\ from the educated. The misspelling *minerology* is seen occasionally. For *mammalogy* our pronunciation evidence is too slender to indicate a preferred version, but it is clear that both \-ˈmäl-\ and \-ˈmal-\ are in respectable use.

general consensus See CONSENSUS 2.

genitive **1.** There are informative discussions of the genitive case in Fries 1940, Evans 1957, and Roberts 1954, and undoubtedly in many other sources. Our brief overview will be based chiefly on these three, with many examples taken from one or another of them.

The genitive case comes in two forms for nouns: an inflected form marked by an apostrophe and an *s* (*'s*) or sometimes just an apostrophe at the end of the noun, and a periphrastic form with the preposition *of.* The personal pronouns have a set of forms *(my, our, your, his, her, their)* that are the equivalent of the genitive of nouns (some analysts consider them adjectives). Bishop Lowth in 1762 used the word *possessive* in place of the older term *genitive;* so then did other 18th-century grammarians, and many grammarians since have used it. This change in terminology has led to a few minor usage problems based on the erroneous supposition that the only function of the genitive is to show possession (see section 2 below). The only statistical investigation of the genitive that we are aware of can be found in Fries 1940. Fries found that the possessive genitive was the most common, but that it accounted for only 40 percent of all genitives. The other 60 percent was split up among various functions. We summarize a number of these here. The categories are not universally agreed upon—a characteristic that you may have noticed is one of the banes of grammatical study—and a single category may be given different names by different analysts.

Subjective genitive and *genitive of origin.* Fries lumps these together, but Roberts separates them. Together they make up 29 percent of Fries's examples:

> his mother's request
> Leroy's dancing
> the general's letter
> Shakespeare's plays

Objective genitive or *object genitive.* These make up 17 percent of Fries's count. Roberts notes that object genitives tend to modify nouns denoting some sort of action:

> contributed toward the family's support
> my son's discharge
> Caesar's murderers

Descriptive genitive or *classifying genitive.* Fries adds the *genitive of measure* to this:

> the room's furnishings
> the airplane's speed
> the building's foundation
> one day's leave
> a dollar's worth
> a year's wages
> the Eighty Years' War

Evans singles out some descriptive genitives which he labels the *genitive of purpose:*

> men's shirts
> a girls' school

Evans points out that the periphrastic form of these genitives of purpose is made with the preposition *for,* rather than *of:*

> shirts for men
> a school for girls

There are other genitives that receive occasional recognition. One of these is the idiomatic form known as the *group genitive,* which is characterized by the placement of the *'s* at the end of a descriptive phrase:

> the King of England's army
> the Department of Science's Antarctic division

According to Baron 1982, although Bishop Lowth found such constructions acceptable, Noah Webster in 1784 did not. There seems to be no recent controversy involving the construction.

Roberts also mentions an *appositive genitive,* which is always periphrastic in form:

> the city of San Francisco
> the state of Wyoming
> the fine art of flattery
> the title of treasurer

This outline of the functions of the genitive, brief and incomplete though it is, shows how misleading it is to think of the genitive in English as showing only possession.
2. *Genitive with inanimate nouns.* Look at this list of phrases:

> the nation's capital
> a week's pay
> a dollar's worth
> a stone's throw
> the Hundred Years' War
> land's end
> on a winter's night

In each of the phrases the noun in the possessive case stands for something inanimate. One of the curious things about these constructions is that a considerable number of 19th-century grammarians reasoned themselves into believing that they did not exist or were wrong. Some 20th-century commentators—Follett 1966, for instance—still think they are wrong. And why? Because you are not supposed to be able to attribute possession to something inanimate.

The argument is a case of fooling oneself with one's own terminology. After the 18th-century grammarians began to refer to the genitive case as the possessive case, grammarians and other commentators got it into their heads that the only use of the case was to show possession. But not one of the examples in the list is a possessive genitive; they are subjective or objective or descriptive genitives, as described in section 1 above. And they are all perfectly standard.

Simply changing the name of the genitive does not change or eliminate any of its multiple functions. The choice between the *'s* form and the phrasal form with *of* should be determined by the sound of the sentence.

> . . . at half an hour's notice —Henry James, *The American,* 1877

> All the movie's Texans . . . keep their word —*Time,* 21 Jan. 1952

> . . . trailer parks right up to the water's edge —James Jones, *Holiday,* July 1952

> . . . the whales, as though to divide the sea's food resources among them —Rachel Carson, *The Sea Around Us,* 1951

> One of the veranda's functions —Frank Sullivan, *The Night the Old Nostalgia Burned Down,* 1953

> . . . the importance of science's carefully tested finding —Arthur Holly Compton, *Key Reporter,* February 1952

> Around the chimney's base the roof looked eroded —Doris Lessing, *The Good Terrorist,* 1985

> . . . the best known of central Kentucky's Bluegrass farms —Boyd Keenan, *Key Reporter,* August 1952

> . . . one of Napa Valley's most respected producers —advt., *Town & Country,* November 1987

3. There is mixed usage with regard to indicating the genitive case of a singular noun ending in an \s\ or \z\ sound with an apostrophe plus *s* or an apostrophe alone. Our evidence shows that for common nouns more writers use *'s* than the apostrophe alone: *the boss's desk, the princess's wedding* are more common than *the boss' desk, the princess' wedding.* But when a polysyllabic *s* or *z* noun is followed by a word beginning with an *s* or *z* sound, the apostrophe alone is more frequent: *for convenience' sake.*

This same basic observation can be made of proper nouns: *Jones's house, Dickens's novels* are more common than *Jones' house, Dickens' novels.* There are more exceptions with proper names, however: *Jesus' time, Moses' law.* Multisyllabic names and particularly those of biblical and classical origin usually take only the apostrophe: *Odysseus' journey, Aristophanes' plays.* Single-syllable names, however, even the classical ones, more often have *'s: Zeus's anger.*

4. See also APOSTROPHE 2, 4; DOUBLE GENITIVE; POSSESSIVE WITH GERUND.

gent This shortened form of *gentleman* was once vilified by the cultivated and would-be cultivated, but no one seems to care much about it any more. The OED notes that "Early in the [19th] century the word was colloquial and slightly jocular; about 1840 its use came to be regarded as a mark of low breeding." American commentators in particular seem to have regarded *gent* with loathing; for example, Ayres 1881 described it as "perhaps, the most offensive" of vulgarisms, and Emily Post 1927 dismissed it as "unspeakable." Many other late 19th- and early 20th-century critics, both American and British, took unfavorable notice of the word, but among current commentators its use has become a non-issue (the one exception is Gowers in Fowler 1965, who revises somewhat the comments made by Fowler 1926). Many dictionaries, on the other hand, continue to give this word a restrictive label, such as *slang, informal,* or *colloquial.*

What our evidence indicates is that *gent* still turns up commonly in published writing, but the writers who use it, by and large, do not take it very seriously. It has something of a British quality to American ears, and much of our recent evidence for it is from British sources:

> . . . they struck poses, later to be copied by gents who invaded the bathroom —Philip Hope-Wallace, *The Guardian,* 14 Nov. 1973

> . . . implicit separation of the gents from the chaps —William Feaver, *The Listener,* 18 July 1974

> . . . a back view of a muscular gent on page ten — Marje Proops, *Daily Mirror* (London), 25 Feb. 1975

American writers use it in much the same ironic or mildly mocking way:

> . . . an antiquated . . . gent who wouldn't stop yelling and pounding his cane —John Schulian, *Inside Sports,* 31 Aug. 1981

> . . . his voice is majestically bland. (If he weren't such an impressive gent, he could be Salieri to Pavarotti's Mozart.) —Pauline Kael, *New Yorker,* 29 Oct. 1984

And it is also the word of choice when describing a dapper Englishman:

> . . . an English gent dropped in the other day and ordered twenty-eight shirts —John de St. Jorre, *Town & Country,* November 1982

Until recently in London, you could tell a true city gent by his bowler and brolly —Leslie Maudel-Viney, *N.Y. Times,* 24 Aug. 1986

In addition, *gent* is sometimes used in place of *gentleman* when the longer word seems inappropriately formal:

> That meant one 95-year-old gent took the lead. The poor fellow looked absolutely ancient —David R. Papke, *Commonweal,* 3 Oct. 1969

> He is a slender, soft-spoken gent with wide-spaced pale-blue eyes —Roger Angell, *New Yorker,* 12 Mar. 1984

genuine The usual pronunciation of this word among educated speakers has a short final vowel, \'jen-yə-wən\ or \'jen-yə-win\. A variant with long final vowel, \'jen-yə-ˌwīn\, is found in most regions of the United States, and in some places is even the predominant form in less educated speech. This variant has a friendly, folksy ring to it and is often used in jest by educated speakers. But these observations are generalizations; our pronunciation files show occasional use of \'jen-yə-ˌwīn\ in a nonfacetious context by educated speakers, for instance by the Irish author Sean O'Faolain, and by a former headmaster of a prestigious New England preparatory school.

gerund See POSSESSIVE WITH GERUND.

gesticulation, gesture Fowler 1926 notes that the principal meaning of *gesticulation* is abstract, "the use of gestures" and the principal meaning of *gesture* is particular, "an act of gesticulation; an expressive bodily movement." But he also observes that either word can serve in place of the other when its connotations (or lack of connotations) make it an appropriate choice—that is, *gesticulation* can be used to denote a particularly theatrical or emotional gesture, and *gesture* can be used to mean "the use of gestures" when the writer wants to avoid the overtly theatrical connotations of *gesticulation.* That description of the ways in which these words are used was accurate in 1926 and is still accurate today:

> . . . show the same interest in dramatic gesticulation and facial expression —E. H. Gombrich, *N.Y. Rev. of Books,* 12 Mar. 1970

> . . . with a great gesticulation of my whole body I motioned him to stay —Samuel Beckett, *Evergreen,* June 1967

> . . . dismiss legislation with the impatient gesture of an old man's hand —Lewis H. Lapham, *Harper's,* January 1972

> . . . the resources of . . . gesture from which a characterization is composed —Irving Kolodin, *Saturday Rev.,* 3 Apr. 1971

get **1.** One of the more important verbs in English, *get* is handled with considerable diffidence in the handbooks. Part of the problem, as the handbooks see it, is the large number of vigorously expressive idioms *get* enters into; the "Choice English"—to use the term of Roberts 1954—that college freshmen are expected to cultivate much prefers colorlessness to vigor. Vigorous expressions are often suspected by usage critics of being "colloquial"—that is, slightly improper in some way or other not easily specified. If you are writing with the idea of getting your point across, however, you will not avoid the rich fund of idiomatic phrases with *get.*

One very important use of *get* is to form a sort of passive with the past participle. Bryant 1962 says that this construction emphasizes the idea of process. A couple of other commentators call it emphatic and unambiguous. Roberts 1954 says it is felt to be somewhat colloquial and thus avoided in Choice English. Evans 1957 says that the construction was condemned by grammarians in the 19th century, who prescribed *become* or *be* as substitutes. Both Evans and Flesch 1964 think that such substitution results in a weaker, less emphatic statement. Here are examples of the passive with *get:*

There are times when the French get aggravated and displeased by us —Jimmy Carter, quoted in *N.Y. Times,* 14 Feb. 1980

... propaganda in the form of news items which I doubt ever got printed —Katherine Anne Porter, *The Never-Ending Wrong,* 1977

... Neither partner will be, ultimately, the person who got married in the beginning —Germaine Greer, *McCall's,* March 1971

Perhaps the letter had got lost in the post and never arrived at all —Hugh Fleetwood, *Cosmopolitan,* June 1973

2. There has been some mild controversy over *get* in the sense of *obtain.* Bernstein 1965 prefers *obtain,* which he thinks stronger than *get,* but Copperud 1970, 1980 considers the substitution of *obtain* for *get* an affectation when *get* is more natural. You can use whichever sounds better to you without concern. Here are some samples of *get:*

... sign the inventory. Get a copy —Anna Fisher Rush, *McCall's,* March 1971

... has missed out on the help that can be gotten from the academic community —Barry Commoner, quoted in *N.Y. Times,* 17 Mar. 1980

... administrators can easily get agreement from almost every unit —Ivar Berg, *Change,* September 1971

3. The past tense of *get* is *got;* the past participle is *got* or *gotten.* See GOT, GOTTEN; HAVE GOT.

4. The pronunciation \(ˈ)git\ has been noted as a feature of some British and American dialects since the 16th century. In the phonetic spelling of his own speech Benjamin Franklin records *git.* However, since at least the 17th century some grammarians and teachers have deprecated this pronunciation. It nonetheless remains in widespead and unpredictable use in many dialects, often, but not exclusively, in weakly stressed positions followed by a strong stress, as in "get up!"

get ahold of   See AHOLD.

gibe   See JIBE, GIBE.

gift   The use of *gift* as a verb has drawn scorn and even expressions of despair from some commentators on language. Their criticism is directed specifically at its use in contexts where it serves essentially as a synonym of *present,* as in "He gifted her with a new coat," although a number of the critics acknowledge that such usage dates back to the 17th century. Even older is the use of

gift to mean "to endow with some power or attribute," which was first recorded in the 1500s. The OED includes many citations for both the "endow" and "present" senses of *gift:*

... the inspiration with which we writers are gifted —Henry Fielding, *Tom Jones,* 1749 (OED)

The Regent Murray gifted all the church Property to Lord Sempill —J. C. Lees, *Abbey of Paisley,* 1878 (OED)

Gift did not become a controversial verb until it began to appear with some regularity in American newspapers and magazines. Its adoption by Hollywood gossip columnists probably did nothing to help its reputation:

Glen Ford gifted Eleanor Powell with a brand new kitchen —*Movieland,* March 1951

He gifted her with a large heart-shaped diamond —Louella O. Parsons, syndicated column in *Springfield* (Mass.) *Daily News,* 28 July 1958

Most of the criticism of this verb has been from American sources. Usage panelists in particular cannot abide it—the major panels have consistently rejected it by better than a nine to one margin. The British seem to regard it with somewhat greater tolerance, perhaps because of its long history of reputable use in Scotland (the OED labels the "present" sense "chiefly Scottish," and much of our own evidence for it is from Scottish sources). Dictionaries, both British and American, treat it as standard. Its detractors say the usual things about the impropriety of using a noun as a verb, but that argument obviously does not stand up either against more than 400 years of historical evidence or against the many noun–verb pairs that draw absolutely no critical attention whatever. There is nothing fundamentally wrong with the verb *gift.* It is, however, an uncommon word, and an unpopular one as well. Unless you happen to be either Scottish or a gossip columnist, you probably won't have much occasion to use it.

See also FREE GIFT.

gild the lily   This idiomatic phrase is cited as a misquotation by many commentators, who point out that the passage in Shakespeare's *King John* (1597) from which it is derived actually reads:

To gild refined gold, to paint the lily,
To throw a perfume on the violet,
. . . .
Is wasteful and ridiculous excess.

Of course, those who use *gild the lily* are not actually quoting Shakespeare or anyone else—they are simply using an established idiom in a familiar way:

To gild the lily, the food and service are virtually as good as the setting —Malcolm S. Forbes, *Forbes,* 1 June 1967

An appeals court, gilding the lily of nonsense, agreed —George F. Will, *Newsweek,* 21 July 1986

Gild the lily has probably had more success as an idiom than *paint the lily* because the repeated *-il-* of *gild* and *lily* gives it a more memorable sound. You can, of course, use *paint the lily* if you like, but we doubt that Shakespeare would insist on it.

Gipsy   See GYPSY, GIPSY.

gladiolus One gladiolus may make for a sparse bouquet, but at least it spares you from having to figure out what to call more than one of them. Do you say *gladioli* (or is that too stuffy?), *gladiolus* (too incomplete?), or *gladioluses* (too awkward?)? Each of these plurals is used and each has its detractors. Happy are those for whom the word is *gladiola* and the plural *gladiolas* (though some will say that's a case of ignorance being bliss).

Gladioli is the commonest plural of *gladiolus* and is found in both technical and nontechnical sources.

> Plant out more gladioli —*New Zealand Jour. of Agriculture,* September 1948

> . . . sweet corn, gladioli, butter and potatoes —John Cheever, *The Wapshot Chronicle,* 1957

> . . . our misshapen gladioli bulbs —Alexander Frater, *Punch,* 16 Sept. 1975

> Gladioli, with their rich, varied colors —catalog, Springhill Nurseries, Spring 1987

The plural *gladiolus,* though not quite as common, also appears in a wide range of sources.

> . . . begin spraying all Gladiolus when leaves are up four to six inches —*The Gladiolus—Supplement,* April 1943

> . . . the beckoning display of roses in bud, full-blown chrysanthemums, and stately gladiolus —Caron Howe Platt, *Gourmet,* November 1981

> Hardy Gladiolus have long been a favorite —catalog, Park Seed Co., Spring 1987

Gladioluses is less common and appears in general periodicals and books but not in technical sources.

> . . . orange-pink gladioluses —Edmund Wilson, *Memoirs of Hecate County,* 1946

> . . . lilies, gladioluses, dahlias —*N.Y. Times,* 31 Jan. 1982

The spelling *gladiola* originated through back-formation when people heard the word *gladiolus* and thought it was a plural form. *Gladiola* and *gladiolas* are relatively uncommon in print but are frequent enough not to be considered misspellings. They appear in general publications only.

> . . . he had planted what I took to be a gladiola — Nevil Shute, *In the Wet,* 1953

> . . . lush gladiolas, display dahlias —John Updike, *Couples,* 1968

> . . . an arrangement of gladiolas —Patricia Browning Griffith, *Harper's,* March 1969

One further option in nontechnical contexts is to bypass the whole issue and call the flowers *glads.*

> . . . varieties of annuals, dahlias, glads, peonies — *Better Homes and Gardens,* August 1946

> . . . appear at a paramour's door with a bunch of glads and a box of marzipan —Alan Coren, *Punch,* 10 Apr. 1974

glamour 1. *Glamour* has an interesting history. It originated as a Scottish derivative of *grammar* that meant "a magic spell"—a sense attributable to the for-mer popular association of scholarly knowledge with occult practices. The OED indicates that it was "introduced into the literary language" by Sir Walter Scott in the early 19th century. By the middle of the 1800s, it had acquired the meaning "a magical or illusory beauty or charm," from which sense developed its now common use to describe the kind of dazzling appeal associated with movie stars and fashion models. Its former connotations of magic have now been largely replaced by connotations of glitter:

> . . . shuns the glitz and glamour of the world he creates —Rebecca Bricker, *People,* 22 Nov. 1982

> . . . intoxicated by the glamour of show business — Molly Haskell, *N.Y. Times Book Rev.,* 30 Oct. 1983

> . . . retains her model's figure and glamour —William E. Geist, *N.Y. Times Mag.,* 8 Apr. 1984

> To the outsider the city has more glamour than ever —William E. Blundell, *Wall Street Jour.,* 9 May 1986

A few commentators (such as Bernstein 1965) have regretted seeing *glamour* lose its magic, but the new uses of the word are far too well established to be seriously controversial.

2. The spelling variant *glamor* originated in the U.S. on analogy with such other American spellings as *honor* and *odor.* Some commentators have been reluctant to accept it as a respectable variant, but our evidence shows that it occurs widely in American periodicals:

> . . . have built-in glamor —*New York,* 30 Aug. 1971

> . . . glamor and performance —*Harper's,* May 1972

> . . . the glamor of the stage —*Wall Street Jour.,* 19 Nov. 1980

> Has the glamor faded . . . ? —*Science,* 16 Jan. 1981

> White House evenings—glamor, glamor, glamor — *Women's Wear Daily,* 9 Mar. 1981

Glamour is, however, appreciably more common than *glamor* in the U.S. and is the only spelling used in Great Britain.

glance See GLIMPSE, GLANCE.

glean On the subject of *glean,* Bryson 1984 says this: "Enough of its original meaning lingers that it should still convey the idea of gathering thoroughly and arduously." The original meaning referred to is "to gather grain or other produce left by reapers." Bernstein 1965 notes that "by metaphorical extension it means to collect bits with great effort"; his objection of the word's usage covers Bryson's objection as well: "By improper extension it [*glean*] is misused to mean merely to gather."

The extended sense of *glean* that both these authors are discussing developed, as indicated in the OED, during the 13th century; when it first came into use, it was indeed a simple extension of the original literal use of *glean* and implied the drudgery involved in that process. Over the years, though, and especially in the 20th century, *glean* has also come to be used frequently to mean merely "to find out, learn, ascertain." Both the original extended sense and the newer one are perfectly valid uses of *glean:*

> "Of your inner life, my dear, we know nothing beyond such scraps as we can glean in spite of you,

from little things which escape you almost before you know that you have said them." —Samuel Butler, *The Way of All Flesh,* 1903

Mrs. Truax, in her last letter, intimates that she can tell pretty exactly where I am, but she never gleaned it, I imagine, from any letter of mine —Alexander Woollcott, letter, 14 Feb. 1918

. . . taking down one book after another until she had gleaned all the information the library contained about the late Dr. Adam Savage —Robertson Davies, *Tempest-tost,* 1951

The picture could be pieced together from hints and information gleaned at the President's press conference —*N.Y. Times,* 22 Feb. 1953

. . . much of what is believed about the United States Government can conveniently be gleaned from the memoirs of President Calvin Coolidge —John Kenneth Galbraith, *New York,* 15 Nov. 1971

But I also fail to glean any insight from the man concerning the other oddities of his artistic eidos —Robert Craft, *Stravinsky,* 1972

. . . brought back a tale from which we were able to glean a new clarity about ourselves —*Harper's,* March 1971

. . . an eager British newsman, in a last and possibly desperate attempt to glean anything from the congress which would be even remotely intelligible — John Horgan, *Commonweal,* 9 Oct. 1970

The latest gossip is eagerly gleaned —Timothy Green, *Smithsonian,* November 1982

glimpse, glance Discussion of this pair of words goes back to Fowler 1926, who points out that "you *take* or *give* a glance at something, but *get* a glimpse of it." On the basis of the citations he gives as examples of what not to do, it would seem that his specific complaint was about the use of "a glimpse at" to replace "a glance at." We think that this must be a relatively unusual combination, because we do not have a single example for it in our files. All we have are one or two citations in which *glimpse* might, with some effort, be construed as meaning "glance." And we have only one citation in which *glance* means "glimpse." Clearly, these two nouns are, in the main, successfully distinguished by writers of English.

Since Fowler's time a few usage books have included this topic, but most of these have not gone beyond merely restating the appropriate roles of the nouns *glance* and *glimpse.* Shaw 1975 adds, however, that "to glimpse is to obtain a brief view of something," and Harper 1985 is more expansive on the topic of verb uses. Harper's most pointed remarks concern whether *glimpse* is used as an intransitive verb to mean "to take a brief look." The editors believe that "it will probably be a surprise to most people to learn that dictionaries also give *glimpse* in the same sense and the same function [as *glance*]. Despite this, it is rare to hear or read statements such as 'She *glimpsed* at the stranger as he passed her.'" Harper is correct. Although *glimpse* is entered as an intransitive verb in some dictionaries (including ours), such use is very uncommon:

The purposes of life are beyond us, though glimpsed at by all revelation in the arts and religions of mankind —*Times Literary Supp.,* 6 May 1955

. . . this helps them, I think, glimpse around the next corner of history —Jack Newfield, *Evergreen,* June 1967

Glance as a transitive verb synonymous with *glimpse* is not mentioned in the usage books, but, for the record, this use is archaic.

glow When the verb *glow* is used with a preposition, use of *with* occurs most frequently:

. . . the fire that burned within him, that glowed with so strange and marvellous a radiance —Aldous Huxley, *The Olive Tree,* 1937

. . . she was a positive creature, self-assured, beautiful and glowing with an interior smile —Jean Stafford, *The Mountain Lion,* 1947

. . . the whole tiered and layered place glowed with new paint —Bernard Malamud, *The Assistant,* 1957

Glow is less frequently used with *about, at, from, in, into, of, over,* and *to* in various relations and senses:

. . . regard it as perfectly proper to study and glow about the marvels of Roman aqueducts —Sidney Hook, *Education for Modern Man,* 1946

. . . sitting alertly in the drawing-room, glowing at friends —Elizabeth Bowen, *The Hotel,* 1927

. . . her gentle, eager personality glowing from her fine features —Rex Ingamells, *Of Us Now Living,* 1952

. . . the leaves of the maple trees glowed red and yellow in the sunlight —John P. Marquand, *So Little Time,* 1943

Opposing opinions glow into acrimony —Morris Longstreth, *Book-of-the-Month Club News,* March 1951

. . . the Gilbert apartment, never brightly lit, glowed of itself —Lloyd Alexander, *Discovery,* March 1954

. . . he glowed over the marvels of modern gadgetry that could reduce hard work —James Aldredge, *Irish Digest,* February 1955

They kindled him and made him glow to his work —D. H. Lawrence, *Sons and Lovers,* 1913

go 1. The past tense of *go* is *went;* the past participle is *gone.* Those of you who are interested in etymology might try looking up the history of *went,* which was borrowed by *go* from another Middle English verb. In the speech of the less educated—H. L. Mencken's vulgate—the two forms are often interchanged.

The people on our place always say, "we gone to see it," or "we gone and done it," when the action is past—never "went" when "went" would be correct —Flannery O'Connor, letter, 4 May 1955

Miss O'Connor herself used *went* as a past participle facetiously:

. . . I can forget about going to Europe, having went —letter, 17 May 1958

Others use it unconsciously:

. . . would have went home —radio sports announcer, 1 June 1984

These uses are not standard.

2. The newest sense of *go* as a transitive verb means "say." This sense has been noticed in Safire 1984 and by various correspondents to this company and to newspapers. The use, which seems to have first attracted attention in the mid 1970s, has been noted as common in the speech of children and young adults. It is a speech form, seldom seen in print. Here is one of our few examples:

> I'm the last person to admit I've achieved anything. . . . But now my friends say it to me, and I go, "You're right, I can't deny it any more. We've made it." —Steve Martin, quoted in *Newsweek,* 3 Apr. 1978

One of Safire's correspondents points out that in speech *go* can differentiate between direct and indirect quotation. In speech there is little or no difference between "She says you're cute" and "She says, 'You're cute.'" But "She goes, 'You're cute'" is always direct quotation. This is a clever explanation, but there are ways to disambiguate "She says you're cute" through intonation, stress, and juncture without using *go* for *say.*

The usage appears to exist in British English too. Our pronunciation editor noted this pun on it in a British radio comedy called "I'm Sorry, I'll Read That Again" in June 1976:

> ANNOUNCER. . . . the Lone Stranger's horse went lame.
> HORSE. Neigh. Lame, lame, lame.

Just remember that this sense of *go* is a spoken use.
3. See GO AND.

go and   *Go and* is often used to emphasize a following verb:

> . . . but now she has gone and . . . married that monsieur de Wolmar —Thomas Gray, letter, December 1760

> . . . a subject too well painted by others for me to go and daub —Charles Reade, quoted in *PMLA,* March 1945

> It went a long way toward making him touchy about what Uncle Daniel had gone and done —Eudora Welty, *The Ponder Heart,* 1954

> "What's he want to go and do that for?" —Helen Eustis, *The Fool Killer,* 1954

This emphatic use does not imply any actual motion. It can be used without *and*—"Go jump in the lake"— as well. It has the punch and directness of speech and is seldom used in ordinary discursive prose.

See also TAKE AND; TRY AND; UP, *verb* 2.

gobbledygook   This word for turgid and generally unintelligible prose has been in use only since the 1940s, but the phenomenon it describes is much older. Many usage books from Cobbett 1823 to Bailey 1984 have entertaining and horrifying examples. Entries under *gobbledygook* can be found in Janis 1984, Watt 1967, Copperud 1970, 1980, Perrin & Ebbitt 1972, Evans 1957, and Shaw 1970. If you want to look at some samples for amusement or instruction, we recommend these books to you. In other books examples will appear under the heading *jargon.*

See also JARGON.

goes without saying   It is surprising to learn that this common idiomatic phrase is hardly more than a hundred years old. A translation of the French *cela va sans dire,* it was first recorded in 1878, and it was still enough of a novelty some 16 years later for Lewis Carroll to feel a bit self-conscious about using it:

> To say I am well "goes without saying" with me — Lewis Carroll, letter, 21 Aug. 1894

By 1926, however, it was well enough established for H. W. Fowler to regard it with a somewhat grudging acceptance, despite its Gallic origins.

Fowler's approval of *goes without saying* might have marked the beginning and end of its career as a usage topic, except that a few recent critics have seen fit to fault it on logical grounds, pointing out that if something truly goes without saying there is, of course, no need to say it. Such literal-minded criticism of an idiomatic phrase is itself illogical, however, and it has not caught on widely among current commentators. *Goes without saying* continues in common and reputable use:

> They have, it goes without saying, an excellent case against the Left —Wilfrid Sheed, *The Good Word and Other Words,* 1978

> It goes without saying that the language-exposure of an Anglo-Saxon villager was not like this —Strang 1970

See also NEEDLESS TO SAY.

good   **1.** *Feel good, feel well.* Some surprising assertions have been made about this rather ordinary pair of expressions. The Oxford American Dictionary, published in 1980, assures us that "it is also incorrect to say *I feel good* when speaking for one's health." This view is not without some support in usage books, although we had to hunt back over a goodly span of years to find the next most recent assertion of it: it is in MacCracken & Sandison 1917. Before them we find Vizetelly 1906. We do not know where Vizetelly got the idea. Mac-Cracken & Sandison further inform us that "'He feels (looks) *good*' really means 'He feels (looks) *virtuous.*'" The correlative of this notion can be found in the comments on *bad* made by Bache 1869 (see BAD, BADLY). Opposed to the OAD is Harper 1985, wherein *feel good* is prescribed to refer to health.

Today virtually everybody agrees that both *good* and *well* after *feel* and *look* are predicate adjectives. The years of disagreement over which was correct seem to have contributed to some differentiation. *Look well* and *feel well* tend to express good health. *Feel good* can express good health or it can suggest good spirits in addition to good health. *Look good* does not generally refer to health, it relates to some aspect of appearance. This need not be personal appearance:

> Somebody in the company decided it would look good if they bought cheaper paper towels —*And More by Andy Rooney,* 1982

See also FEEL BAD, FEEL BADLY.
2. *Good* as an adverb. Although the adverbial use of *good* dates back to the 13th century, the patterns it appears in in present-day English seem to have established themselves in the 19th century. And in the 19th century also we find the beginning of the tradition of reprehending those uses—our earliest commentator is Bache 1869. We can fairly confidently assume a spoken

origin here; Bache antedates the earliest 19th-century example in the OED by about twenty years.

All of the schoolbooks and many of the college handbooks and other usage books that we have consulted insist that *good* is an adjective only. The more enlightened commentators recognize the adverb's existence. They correctly associate it primarily with speech. The schoolmasterly insistence on *well* for the adverb may have contributed to the thriving condition of adverbial *good:*

> Insistence on *well* rather than *good* . . . has created a semantic split related to the adjective-adverb distinction but extending beyond it: *good* has become emotionally charged, *well* is colorless. *He treats me good* expresses more appreciation than *He treats me well,* and *She scolded him, but good* can hardly be expressed with *well* at all —Bolinger 1980

The justice of Bolinger's observation is nowhere better illustrated than in the world of American professional sports, where *good* is the emotionally charged adverb of choice:

> It was a sinker low and inside. I've been in a little slump the last two weeks. Today, I was swinging the bat good —Tony Armas, quoted in *Springfield* (Mass.) *Union,* 4 Sept. 1984

> Guidry hung a slider. I just exploded all over it. I mean, it was *kissed.* I hadn't hit the ball good in a month —Reggie Jackson with Mike Lupica, *Playboy,* June 1984

> "The boys did good," Manager Bamberger said, smiling —Roger Angell, *New Yorker,* 10 May 1982

> . . . I haggled pretty good and got almost as much as the top guys —Billie Jean King, quoted in *Ms.,* July 1973

The adverbial *good* is not, however, limited to sports:

> It pays good and keeps the boys in school —Archibald MacLeish, letter, 14 Oct. 1936

> . . . the press which implies only a kind of competitive point-scoring with the Communists. They goose us; we goose them back good —John Kenneth Galbraith, *Ambassador's Journal,* 1969

> This works pretty good. Roxanne pats his hand and tells him not to get upset —Garrison Keillor, *Lake Wobegon Days,* 1985

> I like "Noon Wine" pretty good but the others tend to be coy —Flannery O'Connor, letter, 26 July 1962

> Test pilots are at home writing technical flight reports, but we don't do so good when it comes to rich, lyrical prose —Virgil "Gus" Grissom, *Gemini: A Personal Account of Man's Venture into Space,* 1968

> . . . Doc Moore's car had a tree fall on it and smash it up real good —Bill Paul, *Wall Street Jour.,* 27 May 1975

Our evidence shows that adverbial *good* is common in the speech of the less educated, but is also known and used by the better educated. It is almost de rigueur in professional sports. Bernstein 1977 reports that the adverb as used in sports grates on Edwin Newman (1974). But it does not grate on Reggie Jackson or Tony Armas or Billie Jean King, the ones who know the lingo.

And one should not assume that *well* is avoided out of ignorance—a professional basketball coach interviewed on television after a game began by saying that the team played good but in mentioning the contributing factors said that they shot well and they rebounded well. The nuances here are plain to sports fans but are overlooked by usage writers.

As the quotations above suggest, adverbial *good* is still primarily a speech form. Our evidence is mostly from reported or fictional speech, letters, and similar breezy and familiar contexts. It is not likely to be needed in a book review or a doctoral dissertation.

See also BAD, BADLY.

3. Most commentators fail to mention the intensive use of adverbial *good.* It often modifies *many* or a number and is preceded by *a:*

> . . . something Hilaire Belloc noted a good 50 years ago —John Simon, *N.Y. Times Book Rev.,* 14 Oct. 1979

> But a good many other Americans at that time could take a college education or leave it alone —Tom Wicker, *Change,* September 1971

This is an entirely standard use. It was listed as an "incorrect phrase" in Joseph Hervey Hull's *Grammar* of 1829, however.

4. See AS GOOD AS.

good and *Good and* functions as an intensive adverb. A few other adjectives—*nice* is the most familiar one—can also be joined by *and* to another adjective to function as an intensive. *Nice and* is generally restricted to approving phrases (like *nice and warm*), but *good and* is a straight intensive:

> Why you *have* been good and busy! —Ellen Terry, letter, 1 Dec. 1896

> His Irish was good and up —Wilfrid Sheed, *People Will Always Be Kind,* 1973

> . . . she'll be good and ready to come home by then —Flannery O'Connor, letter, 16 May 1963

> I'll be good and damned if I give Hussey a bottle of vermouth to change the padré into a Presbyterian — George Jean Nathan, letter, in *The Intimate Notebooks of George Jean Nathan,* 1932

As these examples suggest, *good and* is not often found in very lofty surroundings. Evans 1961 thinks it is used chiefly in spoken American English; several handbooks also suggest it is informal or colloquial. In spite of Ellen Terry, the usage seems to be primarily American.

goodwill, good will *Goodwill* can be spelled either as one word or as two. Our evidence shows that *goodwill* is the prevalent form, but *good will* is also very common, especially when the sense is "benevolent interest or concern":

> . . . he left with nothing but good will —Eugene DiMaria, *Metropolitan Home,* November 1982

> . . . carting good will around as part of her luggage — Edwin Newman, *N.Y. Times Book Rev.,* 3 June 1984

When the sense relates to the value of a business, the single word *goodwill* is almost invariably used:

> . . . is carried on the acquiring company's books as nontaxable goodwill —*Business Week,* 12 Apr. 1982

And when the term is being used adjectively ("a good-will tour") it is written either as a single word or, less often, as a hyphenated compound:

> ... has served as goodwill ambassador —*Current Biography,* September 1966

> ... most hotels run their lost-and-found departments as a good-will operation —Robert J. Dunphy, *N.Y. Times,* 13 Nov. 1977

got, gotten The past participle of *get* is either *got* or *gotten.* Strang 1970 says that both forms were in free variation in 17th-century English. In British English *got* has come to predominate, while in North America *gotten* predominates in some constructions and *got* in others. Marckwardt 1958 points out that in North American English *have gotten* means that something has been obtained, while *have got* denotes simple possession:

> ... they could have gotten $50,000 for their old house —*And More by Andy Rooney,* 1982

> *Wise Blood* finally came out in England and has gotten good reviews —Flannery O'Connor, letter, 21 Oct. 1955

> I haven't got a son —Mordecai Richler, *The Apprenticeship of Duddy Kravitz,* 1959

> ... as long as I have got a chance to win —Dwight D. Eisenhower, quoted in *U.S. News & World Report,* 16 July 1954

This practice is not absolutely uniform, however:

> If you haven't got your license yet —James Thurber, letter, 1937

Gotten has been under attack in American handbooks as somehow improper. Lindley Murray 1795 apparently started the controversy by calling *gotten* nearly obsolete. It was indeed passing out of use in British English at that time, though it was still usable in the 1820s:

> As the Greeks have gotten their loan, they may as well repay mine —Lord Byron, letter, 9 Apr. 1824

Murray's books were widely used in American schools, too, and his opinion was adopted by American usage books like Bache 1869 and Ayres 1881; MacCracken & Sandison 1917 called *gotten* "less acceptable in general" and Jensen 1935 repeated Murray's judgment that it was obsolete. One version of this notion, even though it is wrong, persists as recently as Einstein 1985, who insists on *got* only. The schoolmastering has perhaps kept *got* more current than it might have been had natural selection been allowed free play. Thus we find both *got* and *gotten* in use as past participle. Freeman 1983 says that *gotten* is preferred to *got* when there is a notion of progression involved. This is frequently true:

> Squirrels had gotten into the mattress —John Cheever, *The Wapshot Chronicle,* 1957

> ... it was recommended that the President not inform Congress until we had gotten the hostages back —Edwin Meese 3d, quoted in *The Tower Commission Report,* 1987

> He had not really gotten used to the food —E. L. Doctorow, *Ragtime,* 1975

But it is also used where there is no idea of progression:

> I had gotten up to go to the men's room —William Styron, *This Quiet Dust and Other Writings,* 1982

> Cars had stopped in the street and drivers had gotten out —E. L. Doctorow, *World's Fair,* 1985

And *got* is used both when the notion of progression is present and when it is not:

> ... in composing my list of guests I haven't got beyond him and Anne Parrish —Alexander Woollcott, letter, 19 Nov. 1936

> Since he has got grown, it's the races, of course, he likes —Peter Taylor, *The Old Forest and Other Stories,* 1985

> They had then got to the approaches of French Canada —John Cheever, *The Wapshot Chronicle,* 1957

> ... until a small group of friends could be got to sit still for a few minutes —Russell Lynes, *Harper's,* April 1970

> ... had got word that Tom Bird wanted to meet with him again —Calvin Trillin, *New Yorker,* 6 Jan. 1986

English speakers in North America seem to use both *got* and *gotten* in a way that is almost freely variable. The observation of Marckwardt is largely true; that of Freeman less so. The learner of English might find it useful to follow their distinctions, but the native speaker will pick whichever form seems more natural at the time.

For other questions involving this verb, see GET; HAVE GOT.

gourmand, gourmet These similar words have dissimilar histories. *Gourmand* was a synonym for *glutton* when it was borrowed from French in the 15th century. *Gourmet,* which once meant "a wine merchant's assistant" and, later, "a connoisseur of wine" in French, did not appear in English until the 19th century, by which time it had developed the sense "a connoisseur of food and drink." *Gourmand* had by that time developed a similar "connoisseur" sense of its own, but it still retained suggestions of a hearty appetite. The distinction between the two words became a topic for discussion as soon as *gourmet* entered the language:

> The *gourmand* unites theory with practice.... The *gourmet* is merely theoretical —A. D. MacQuin, footnote, *Tabella Cibaria,* 1820 (OED)

In the 20th century, the distinction has been expressed somewhat differently, usually along the following lines: a gourmet is a knowledgeable and fastidious epicure; a gourmand is a person who likes good food in large quantities—a gourmet who eats too much. *Gourmand* is often described as having contemptuous overtones that *gourmet* lacks.

What our evidence shows, primarily, is that *gourmet* is a far more common word than *gourmand. Gourmand* seems to be little used except by those who consciously distinguish it from *gourmet.* The contemptuous overtones of *gourmand,* however, are no longer strong, and are often entirely absent:

> ... thousands of gourmets and gourmands of all ages were busily indulging in the specialties —Leslie Maitland, *N.Y. Times,* 17 May 1976

In this capital of dedicated gourmands, the classic banquet takes on staggering proportions —Bruce David Colen, *Town & Country,* May 1980

... a delightful haven for gourmet, gourmand, and epicure —Michael T. Kaufman, *N.Y. Times,* 23 Jan. 1983

Gourmand sometimes occurs in contexts where it seems to be serving as little more than a synonym of *gourmet:*

Deaths due to tetrodotoxin continue because several species of poisonous puffers ... are highly prized by Oriental gourmands —Joseph S. Levine, *Smithsonian,* September 1981

But such usage seems unlikely to become common, if only because *gourmet* itself has become so well established as the word for "connoisseur." The meaning of *gourmand* is now certainly closer to *gourmet* than it is to *glutton,* but our evidence shows clearly that *gourmand* and *gourmet* are still words with distinct meanings in the bulk of their use, and are likely to remain so.

government Both *government* and *environment* are often pronounced with varying degrees of compression, reaching as far as \ˈgəm-int\ and \in-ˈvīr-mint\. But even educated speakers speaking slowly are likely to omit the *n* before the *m,* and this pronunciation must be considered standard. Our files bristle with professors and senators saying \ˈgəv-ər-mənt\ and \en-ˈvī-rə-mənt\. One accordingly runs across the misspellings *goverment* and *enviroment* from time to time; *goverment* is even listed in the OED as an "obsolete form" of *government.* Recalling the connection with *govern* and *environs* will immunize you against such spelling errors.

graduate The verb *graduate* first became controversial in the 19th century, when its use as an intransitive in a construction such as "He graduated from college" was censured by several American commentators, including Gould 1880 and Ayres 1881. The critics argued that since the college conferred the degree on the student, *graduate* should only be used transitively with the student as its object or in the passive construction "He was graduated from college." How such an idea originated is not clear. The OED shows that the intransitive *graduate* occurred in writing as early as 1807 (the transitive *graduate* is older, dating from the 15th century):

Four years are then to be passed at college before the student can graduate —Robert Southey, *Letters from England,* 1807 (OED)

By 1828 it was well enough established for Noah Webster to include it in his dictionary. The objections of the critics some 50 years later no doubt caused a few people to shun it, but its widespread use by the well-educated seems not to have been seriously affected.

I graduated from the Lawrence High School as many as five years ago —Robert Frost, letter, 11 Sept. 1897

The continued common use of the intransitive *graduate* has long since persuaded most commentators to admit its acceptability, but notions about its impropriety have not died out entirely among the general public. There are still people who make a point of saying "he was graduated" rather than "he graduated," although some commentators (such as Bernstein 1971

and Freeman 1983) now actually criticize such usage as old-fashioned. Those who indulge in it are, at the very least, in the minority; the intransitive *graduate* is now more common by far.

The use of *graduate* most likely to be criticized these days is a new transitive sense meaning "to graduate from":

... won't graduate high school in New York —advt., *N.Y. Times,* 19 June 1979

This use of *graduate* without *from* has been cited as an error by usage commentators dating back to Evans 1957. It occurs frequently in speech, but its appearance in edited prose is still relatively uncommon. Here are a few more examples of it from our files:

I was a lawyer, I had graduated law school —Arthur Frommer, quoted in *Harper's,* July 1972

... as Toby ... graduates Cambridge —Erica Abeel, *N.Y. Times Book Rev.,* 28 Sept. 1975

"I graduated college in 1974," says Schwartz —Robert Lipsyte, *N.Y. Post,* 2 May 1977

"... I knew her as a probation officer before she graduated law school...." —Scott Turow, *Presumed Innocent,* 1987

graffiti, graffito Before the 1960's, *graffiti* and its singular *graffito* most often referred to writings or drawings on ancient walls or artifacts. Art historians, language historians, archaeologists, and the like were the main users of this term (which came into English from Italian), and they discriminated between the singular and plural forms.

... a graffito in hieroglyphic Hittite —Maurice Vieyra, *Hittite Art 2300–750 B.C.,* 1955

Among the many *graffiti* left on the pedestal —M. R. Dobie, translation of Alexandre Moret, *The Nile and Egyptian Civilization,* 1927

In the 1960s the creation of graffiti evolved from an incidental to an obtrusive cultural phenomenon, and as the phenomenon overspread public places, the word *graffiti* invaded the household. Many people came to know the word only as *graffiti,* not realizing that *graffito* was available when a singular was needed. As a result, *graffiti* is sometimes used as a mass noun with a singular verb:

... the graffiti is being covered with fresh paint — *Springfield* (Mass.) *Union,* 8 Jan. 1970

Graffiti comes in various styles —S. K. Oberbeck, *Newsweek,* 1 Oct. 1973

... urban surfaces where graffiti is typically found — Mark Mendel, *Visible Language,* Summer 1975

This use is not yet as well established as the mass-noun use of *data,* but it does fill a gap left by *graffito,* which is virtually always a count noun, not a mass noun.

... a crudely drawn graffito —Herbert Mitgang, *N.Y. Times,* 13 Mar. 1983

... a lovely graffito I saw recently —David Halberstam, *Playboy,* July 1973

Use of *graffiti* as a singular count noun is rare in print, but together with the rare use of *graffito* as a plural, it reveals how confusing some people find this word—even (or maybe especially) when they are trying their hardest to get it right:

> . . . a graffiti on the wall —*Times Literary Supp.,* 30 Apr. 1971

> . . . one of the most sophisticated graffito I have ever encountered —Clive Barnes, *Punch,* 23 Mar. 1976

> Graffiti . . . is evidently growing by leaps and occasionally out of bounds. . . .
> . . . told us he has collected more than 2,000 individual graffito—yes, that's the singular —Cleveland Amory, *Saturday Rev.,* 7 Jan. 1967

The evidence we have for this word used as an attributive shows that either form can be used. To our ear, at least, unless the sense is clearly one of a single inscription or slogan, *graffiti* sounds better as an attributive than *graffito,* probably because of *graffiti*'s dual role as a plural and as a singular mass noun.

> . . . recorded in graffiti inscriptions —Louis H. Gray, *Foundations of Language,* 1939

> . . . the names of other graffito-writers —Bill Wingell, *National Observer,* 2 Aug. 1971

> Picasso's graffito manner fits in well with the anonymous political daubs on the walls nearby —Anthony Burgess, *N.Y. Times Mag.,* 4 Dec. 1977

> . . . ubiquitous icons of graffiti art —Cathleen McGuigan, *N.Y. Times Mag.,* 10 Feb. 1985

Mass-noun use of *graffiti* continues to grow apace and may establish itself fully in time. For now, however, we feel that traditional count use is safer:

> The graffiti announce that we have left the Catholic area and are moving in Protestant streets —Brian Moore, *Atlantic,* September 1970

For other foreign plurals, see LATIN PLURALS.

grammatical agreement See NOTIONAL AGREEMENT, NOTIONAL CONCORD.

grammatical error It must have been a humorist who in the 19th century attacked the phrase *grammatical error* in exactly the same way the guardians of the language had attacked many an idiom: "How can an error be grammatical?" This slyboots elicited a lengthy defense of the phrase from Bache 1869, which was reprinted in Ayres 1881. It must have been a later wit who drew a similar defense from Follett 1966.

It should be pointed out, however, that the phrase is used as a generalized term of abuse in usage commentary. Phythian 1979, for instance, calls the use of *uninterested* that he disapproves a grammatical error, even though no grammar is involved in the problem.

grapple *Grapple* is usually used as an intransitive verb, and as such it is almost always used with *with:*

> . . . the architect has grappled with more problems than one need hope to see solved in any single church —Henry Adams, *Mont-Saint-Michel and Chartres,* 1904

> . . . the Administration will soon realize that it is grappling with fact, not theory —John Kenneth Galbraith, *The Reporter,* 14 Apr. 1953

> . . . the crisis of the American spirit grappling with its destiny —Robert Penn Warren, *Democracy and Poetry,* 1975

Very occasionally it is used with *for, on,* or *over:*

> . . . in her incessant grappling for affection —Frederic Morton, *N.Y. Herald Tribune Book Rev.,* 31 Aug. 1952

> I'll not be overanxious to venture my life
> In meddling with Death. What Death grapples on
> Is better abandoned
> —Donagh MacDonagh, "Gravedigger," in *New World Writing,* 1954

> . . . men sweating and grappling over state problems —Emily Taft Douglas, *New Republic,* 4 Oct. 1954

Modern transitive uses of *grapple* with *to* are echoes of one of Shakespeare's famous lines:

> Those friends thou hast, and their adoption tried,
> Grapple them unto thy soul with hoops of steel
> —*Hamlet,* 1601

> . . . Amy still jeered, being of those who obtain one idea at a time and grapple it to their souls with hoops of steel —Rose Macaulay, *Told by an Idiot,* 1923

> The once detested Mr. Carlyle was grappled to our souls with hoops of steel —Samuel Hopkins Adams, *Grandfather Stories,* 1955

> . . . that America would grapple democracy to its citizens with hooks [sic] of steel —*Times Literary Supp.,* 13 Nov. 1948

grateful *Grateful* in its sense meaning "appreciative" may be used with the prepositions *for* or *to.* In general, *grateful for* is used with benefits received, *grateful to* with people:

> Separated from his dream, he was sickened at its ugliness and grateful for the lights and sounds of day —John Cheever, *The Wapshot Chronicle,* 1957

> The world was grateful for this moment of fresh air —Thomas Merton, *Center Mag.,* September 1969

> I am uncommonly grateful to you for drawing my attention to it —Dorothy L. Sayers, *The Nine Tailors,* 1934

> She was touched by the offer of the rings, and grateful to George —Herman Wouk, *Marjorie Morningstar,* 1955

When *grateful* means "pleasing" and is used with a preposition, the preposition is usually *to.*

> . . . the sight of Clara was grateful to his senses as a glass of iced wine —Elinor Wylie, *Mr. Hodge and Mr. Hazard,* 1928

> . . . gave me ample room to develop my theme, but forced upon me a concision that my practice as a dramatist had made grateful to me —W. Somerset Maugham, *The Summing Up,* 1938

> . . . expertly composed in full romantic vein, lavish with melody, grateful to the voices —Herbert Weinstock, *Saturday Rev.,* 23 Mar. 1968

gray, grey Both spellings are correct and common. In American English, the preference is for *gray,* but *grey* is also widely used. The British have a very definite preference for *grey*.

Grecian, Greek The distinction between these adjectives has been variously described by commentators dating back to Fowler 1926. What our evidence shows is that the distinction is not observed as consistently as some of the commentators would like. Both adjectives are used in referring to both ancient and modern Greece, although *Greek* is certainly the more common and more widely applied of the two. Some commentators have wanted to restrict *Grecian* to the architecture and art of ancient Greece and to human features suggestive of that art ("a Grecian nose"), but the evidence simply does not support such a narrow restriction:

> . . . essential for full Grecian participation in the war —*Atlantic,* June 1944

> A Grecian pruning saw . . . is perfect for this —Millicent Taylor, *Christian Science Monitor,* 26 Dec. 1975

> . . . German tourists are beginning to people Grecian beaches —Frank Riley, *Saturday Rev.,* 30 Oct. 1976

Such usage may now deserve to be called atypical, but it is not actually incorrect. *Grecian* and *Greek* are basically synonymous words. We recommend that you rely on your own sense of idiom to choose between them in a given context.

grey See GRAY, GREY.

grieve When *grieve* is used with a preposition, it is used most often with *for:*

> Last Winter she died also, and my days
> Are passed in work, lest I should grieve for her
>   —Amy Lowell, *Sword Blades and Poppy Seed,* 1914

> . . . the people, threatened by hostile Indians, grieved for their old homes —*American Guide Series: Texas,* 1940

Somewhat less frequently *grieve* is used with *at* or *over:*

> . . . somewhat grieved at the smallness of this customer's appetite —Osbert Sitwell, *Noble Essences,* 1950

> . . . the President . . . grieved over the people's disappointment which he was helpless to prevent — Samuel Hopkins Adams, *Incredible Era,* 1939

Grieve is also used with *to* and the infinitive:

> . . . he grieved, like an honest lad, to see his comrade left to face calamity alone —George Meredith, *The Ordeal of Richard Feverel,* 1859

grievous, grievously In contravention of its spelling, *grievous* is sometimes pronounced \\'grē-vē-əs\\, so that it rhymes with *previous.* We have evidence for this pronunciation from some educated speakers of the language, including several prominent politicians, but it is not common by any means and is widely regarded with scorn. The standard pronunciation of *grievous* is \\'grē-vəs\\.

Usage commentators warn against the \\'grē-vē-əs\\ pronunciation, and some of them also warn against the spelling *grievious.* If this misspelling does occur, it is extremely rare in print, at least according to our evidence. The only example in our files is a citation for the adverb *grieviously,* in which the misspelling is being deliberately used in a fictional representation of nonstandard speech:

> . . . havin' in mind more pertic'larly the unobstructed fact that . . . the pastoral subscriptions has fallen off so grieviously —Francis T. Hoover, *Not in His Steps,* 1911

See also MISCHIEVOUS.

grill, grille The word for a cooking surface that resembles a grating is spelled *grill;* the word for a grating that forms a barrier or screen, such as on the front end of an automobile, is spelled either *grille* or *grill.* Copperud 1980 feels that *grille* is "somewhat pretentious," but our evidence suggests that its use is not at all uncommon:

> A properly designed air dam under the grille —*Playboy,* April 1982

> . . . semis that park their grilles right in your rearview mirror like giant menacing grins —Lesley Jane Nonkin, *Vogue,* November 1985

The Oxford American Dictionary warns against confusion of *grille* with *grill,* by which it apparently means the use of *grille* when referring to the cooking surface. We have no evidence of such usage in print, though one will doubtless see it from time to time in the name of a restaurant or some similar place.

grisly, grizzly The adjective that means "inspiring horror or disgust" is usually spelled *grisly:*

> . . . that grisly and still mysterious disease —Nan Robertson, *N.Y. Times Mag.,* 19 Sept. 1982

> . . . one of the grisliest bloodbaths in all history — *Wall Street Jour.,* 26 Jan. 1982

The adjective that means "somewhat gray" is spelled *grizzly:*

> . . . the grizzly old Field Marshal —William L. Shirer, *The Rise and Fall of the Third Reich,* 1960

> . . . the man, a grizzly old country preacher —Richard M. Levine, *Harper's,* April 1971

The grizzly bear is so named because its fur has a grayish appearance. When most people think of grizzly bears, however, the images that come to mind (rightly or wrongly) are of a fierce and terrifying animal, the color of whose fur is of no special importance. The association of grizzly bears with fierceness may be part of the reason why the "inspiring horror or disgust" adjective is often spelled *grizzly.* Another part of the reason is that this spelling reflects the word's pronunciation, \\'griz-lē\\, more accurately than *grisly* does.

> Why otherwise torture their victims . . . ? . . . It is not for themselves or for us these grizzly dramas are played out —Archibald MacLeish, *Atlantic,* June 1950

> . . . the grizzly tale of Lizzie Borden —Suzanne K. Steinmetz & Murray A. Straus, *Society,* September–October 1973

> . . . reduced the abstract issue of capital punishment to grizzly reality —C. Robert Zelnick, *Christian Science Monitor,* 2 Dec. 1976

... three dozen or so grizzly murders —*People,* 20 Sept. 1982

We have substantial evidence for this spelling, and like the OED we treat it as a legitimate variant in our dictionaries. It is far less common than the *grisly* spelling, however, and there are many people who regard it simply as an error.

groom A strange prejudice against the use of *groom* to mean "bridegroom" lingers in a few usage handbooks. The apparent reason for this prejudice is that *groom* is thought to have associations with the stable, owing to the use of its older homograph in the sense "a person who takes care of horses." The same reasoning might be expected to find fault with the word *bridegroom* itself, on the grounds that it implies that the bride resembles a horse. *Bridegroom* has, in fact, been criticized in the past by no less a personage than Noah Webster, who felt that the word should be *bridegoom,* and who went so far as to enter and define *bridegoom* in his Dictionary in 1828. Webster's preference for *bridegoom* had an etymological basis: the Middle English word was *bridegome,* from the Old English *brȳdguma,* a compound of *brȳd,* "bride," and *guma,* "man." As far as Webster was concerned, *bridegroom* (which acquired the intrusive *r* by folk etymology) was a "gross corruption" that ought not be tolerated.

In attempting to revive the dead word *bridegoom,* Webster was fighting a battle that had been lost centuries before. The OED shows that *bridegome* had fallen into disuse by the end of the 1300s. *Bridegroom* (originally spelled *brydegrome*) first appeared in writing some time later, in 1526. The only forms in use thereafter were *bridegroom* and *groom,* which was first recorded in Shakespeare's *Othello* (1604). Both *bridegroom* and *groom* were treated as standard in Samuel Johnson's Dictionary in 1755. Webster's attempt to promote *bridegoom* seems to have had no success at all, but his opinions may perhaps have had some influence in encouraging a prejudice against *groom.* For whatever reason, that prejudice has now hung on, although barely, for more than 150 years. We recommend that you not take it seriously. The "bridegroom" sense of *groom* is recognized as standard by all dictionaries, and there is no sensible reason to avoid its use.

grope *Grope* is used most often with *for:*

... it found the connection for which subconsciously it must have been groping —Hamilton Basso, *The View from Pompey's Head,* 1954

Groping for sleep, all he found was a welter of thoughts —Hugh MacLennan, *Two Solitudes,* 1945

... his eyes groping painfully for a sight of whoever stood on the landing —Kay Boyle, *A Frenchman Must Die,* 1946

We must all grope for richer roles, however we can —Francine Du Plessix Gray, *N.Y. Times Book Rev.,* 10 Oct. 1976

Much less frequently, *grope* in this sense is used with *after:*

It was as though she groped after something which was vanishing —Vita Sackville-West, *The Edwardians,* 1930

Even the costumes ... seemed to grope ineptly after some notion of eroticism —Mimi Kramer, *New Yorker,* 26 Oct. 1987

In other relations, *grope* may be used with any number of prepositions, among them *into, through, to, toward,* and *towards:*

Let me grope into a series of formulations, not intended to be sequential-cumulative —William Stafford, *Writing the Australian Crawl,* 1978

But tens of thousands of people groped through it [fog] and crowded the city —Robert D. McFadden, *N.Y. Times,* 24 Nov. 1979

Government mediators ... groped closer to a solution to the dispute —*Newsweek,* 18 Apr. 1955

Like other state governments, California's is ... often thwarted as it gropes toward a future of awesome complexity —Trevor Armbrister, *Saturday Evening Post,* 12 Feb. 1966

... they grope towards an understanding of their loss —*Times Literary Supp.,* 19 Feb. 1971

ground zero The term *ground zero* is a product of the nuclear age; it designates the point on the earth's surface above which, below which, or at which an atomic explosion occurs. Its figurative use in describing the central point of something, such as an area undergoing rapid change, is uncontroversial:

Mahal is located at ground zero of a district "that in five years will be completely Indianized" —Jay Jacobs, *Gourmet,* July 1981

But recent years have also seen *ground zero* being used on occasion as a synonym of *square one,* meaning "the very beginning":

... then we can start from ground zero again — Rabbi Isaac Swift, quoted in *Time,* 8 Dec. 1975

... you will not have to start from ground zero — Shirley M. Hufstedler, *N.Y. Times Mag.,* 11 Jan. 1981

... you can spend years of effort just trying to return to ground zero —*Wall Street Jour.,* 3 Feb. 1981

It is not hard to see how this extension of meaning has occurred; after all, *zero* more strongly suggests a starting point than it does a central point, and to those unfamiliar with its origins, *ground zero* is probably more suggestive of rocket launches than of nuclear explosions. But, of course, those who *are* familiar with its origins tend to regard its use to mean "the very beginning" as an error. The usage panel of Harper 1985 turned thumbs down on this sense by a margin of better than nine to one. The contexts in which it occurs are certainly standard, but our evidence does not show that it is common enough yet to be regarded as well established. In light of that situation, we recommend avoiding it.

group genitive See GENITIVE 1.

grow One of the many senses of *grow* is "to become," a sense that has been in common use for many centuries:

... black beard will turn white, a curl'd pate will grow bald —Shakespeare, *Henry V,* 1599

Fortunately for Shakespeare, he did not have Richard Grant White as a copy editor:

> Now, *grow* means increase, the enlargement of a present quality or condition, not a change in character of that quality or condition. A rough sea may grow rougher, a dark sky grow black, but a smooth sea becomes rough, a clear sky becomes black, ... and the moon, or anything else that lessens, does not grow [smaller], but becomes smaller —Richard Grant White 1870

White would have told Shakespeare that a curled pate does not grow bald, but becomes bald. What Shakespeare would have told White we can only guess.

White's opinions were influential enough in the late 19th century to persuade many people that there was something wrong with the "become" sense of *grow,* especially in the phrase *grow smaller.* A few writers on usage were still raising the issue in the 1920s, but the groundlessness of White's objection was by that time widely recognized: such commentators as Vizetelly 1906, Utter 1916, and Hall 1926 pointed out that the "become" sense had a long history of highly respectable use. Later commentators such as Partridge 1942, Evans 1957, and Bernstein 1971 have also defended the "become" sense, but the issue appears not to be entirely dead. Longman 1984 includes the note, "Some people dislike the combination *grow smaller* as illogical."

Be that as it may, we cannot recommend that you devote much effort to avoiding *grow smaller. Grow* in its "become" sense usually implies a gradual, continuous process of change, and its use with those implications is entirely appropriate whether the change involves an increase or a decrease—in size or in any other quality:

> ... the lighting grows gradually dimmer —*American Guide Series: Minnesota,* 1938

> As technical arguments grew more complex —Homer Page, *Not Man Apart,* July 1971

> ... as the world itself grows smaller, its institutions perforce grow bigger —Osborn Elliott, *One Nation Divisible* (published speech), November 1969

guarantee, guaranty As a look in any good dictionary will show, these two words are interchangeable in almost all of their uses. The principal distinction to be made between them is the one made by Copperud 1970, 1980: "... *guarantee* is by far the more commonly used." Some writers formerly preferred *guaranty* for the noun and *guarantee* for the verb, but *guarantee* is now the usual choice for both. The advice given by Fowler 1926 is still sound: "Those who wish to avoid mistakes have in fact only to use *-ee* always."

guerrilla, guerilla The literal meaning of *guerrilla* in Spanish is "little war." It was once used in English, as in Spanish, to denote irregular warfare carried on by independent bands of fighters, but the word in that sense was replaced more than a hundred years ago by such phrases as *guerrilla war* and *guerrilla warfare.* The principal use of *guerrilla* in English has long been to denote a fighter engaged in such warfare:

> ... would train our new guerrillas for all kinds of conditions —Garry Wills, *Atlantic,* February 1982

The Spanish word for such a fighter is *guerrillero,* and it has sometimes been suggested that *guerrillero* should also be the preferred word in English. *Guerrillero* has almost never been used in English, however, except to refer specifically to Spanish guerrillas.

The spellings *guerrilla* and *guerilla* are established as reputable variants in English (the Spanish spelling is *guerrilla*). Most of the evidence in the OED is for the *guerilla* spelling, but our modern evidence shows clearly that *guerrilla* is now the more common form. Usage commentators accept both.

guess Look at the use of *guess* in these two examples.

> "Well, I don't *expect* to marry. I don't know as I do, at my time of life," responded the spinster. "I rather guess my day for chances is gone by." —Francis Lee Pratt, "Captain Ben's Choice," in *Mark Twain's Library of Humor,* 1888

> "I guess I'll use lemon instead of vinegar," she said —*And More by Andy Rooney,* 1982

Such uses of *I guess* were long accounted Americanisms and have long been looked down on by some of our British cousins (Phythian 1979 still thinks the expression "worth resisting"). American defenders from James Russell Lowell (*Introduction to the Bigelow Papers,* 2d series, 1867) to H. L. Mencken (*The American Language,* 3d edition, 1923) to Harper 1975, 1985 have shown that the expression is an old one in English that came over to this country straight from the language of Shakespeare's time. Howard 1977 agrees: "*I guess,* in the sense I am pretty sure, was good English before it became good American." Howard finds it coming back into British use from American.

Some American commentators—Lurie 1927, Jensen 1935, Guth 1985, Macmillan 1982, for instance—have been diffident about it. American uncertainty goes back at least to Joseph Hervey Hull's *Grammar* of 1829, but American English is nothing to be ashamed of.

We are not advising you to use *I guess* in your starchiest formal discourse, and we doubt that you would be inclined to. In contexts like those shown above, however, it is perfectly acceptable.

guts The sense of *guts* meaning "courage" has been around for quite some time now: the OED Supplement gives the first use as occurring in 1893. We have little evidence for its use until after 1915.

> We've got to work up our end ... and fall to and bring the English out. It's the one race in this world that's got the guts —Walter H. Page, letter, 22 June 1916

Although Walter H. Page seems to have felt nothing was particularly coarse about the word, *guts* could and did provoke some strong reactions:

> Since the publication of my dialogue on Modern Disillusion a little while ago I have received a number of protests—some unfortunately anonymous—against my use of the word "guts" to signify mental courage. One correspondent has sent me a clipping from a Western magazine called *All's Well* in which the writer says: "When I came upon it [guts] in a high-class magazine I was not only nauseated but astonished that the editor would allow it." —Lewis Mumford, letter to the editor, *The Nation,* 11 Feb. 1925

Its use makes the commentators a little nervous even today. Evans 1957 found it "coarse but effective"; Copperud 1970, 1980 thinks the word is always used with the deliberate intent to shock or to sound rough-hewn; Flesch 1983 quotes a use by William Safire and seems a little surprised that his editors let him get away with it; both Flesch and Shaw 1975, 1987 feel that it is slang. As you read through the following examples, you will see that critical opinion has not caught up to actual use yet. However, the word is indeed plain and forthright, and if you are not prepared to be plain and forthright (or feel your audience is not prepared to have you so), you might want to choose an alternative such as *courage, mettle, pluck, spirit, resolution*—or even that old periphrastic warhorse, *intestinal fortitude.*

> ... I'm trying to prove to myself right now that I've got the guts to stick it out here —*Hearst's Mag.,* March 1917

> ". . . Just tell them straight from the shoulder . . . here we intend to stay until some one kicks us out. . . . Put all the guts into it that you can!" —O. E. Rölvaag, *Giants In the Earth,* 1927

> Finally, he has the guts to grab the job, if grabbing is necessary —John Gunther, *Inside Europe,* rev. ed., 1937

> The point is that my "social sympathies" should have made me a communist, and would have done so if I had only had the guts —*Yale Rev.,* Summer 1939

> But they should be songs with what has been called "the real intestines"—not to use the plain word *guts* —*Saturday Rev.,* 25 Apr. 1942

> ... what had taken place . . . apparently involved just guts, the revolt of a man against the pure footlessness which had held him in bondage —William Styron, *Lie Down In Darkness,* 1951

> These facts speak eloquently of the guts and stamina of these two men —Sir John Hunt & Sir Edmund Hillary, *Geographical Jour.,* December 1953

> There was no one in the house who had guts enough to say that *Some Came Running* was a washerwoman at 1,200 pages, and could be fair at 400 — Norman Mailer, *Advertisements for Myself,* 1959

> ... Charlotte shows some guts in telling the Matron how to run her hospital —*Times Literary Supp.,* 19 May 1966

> ... those who might have challenged him didn't have the guts to do it —Merle Miller, *N.Y. Times Book Rev.,* 23 Nov. 1975

> ... but people so much want a poet with guts that they cling to him like a port in a storm —Virginia Woolf, letter, 1930 (in *Times Literary Supp.,* 28 May 1982)

> Otherwise, the members would raise hell, and it would look as if the Democrats didn't have any guts —Tip O'Neill with William Novak, *Man of the House,* 1987

guttural   Bryson 1984 warns that this word is frequently misspelled *gutteral.* His observation is borne out by evidence in our files. Remember that there are two *u*'s.

guy   Stephen Leacock put it this way:

> The fact is we are always hard up for neutral words to mean "just a person"; each new one gets spoiled and has to be replaced. . . . Hence the need for "guy," which will gradually rise from ridicule to respectability —Leacock 1943

Flesch 1983 announces that *guy* has reached respectability. A few commentators, however, demur. Shaw 1975, 1987, Bell & Cohn 1981, and Macmillan 1982 are not sure it belongs in standard English. Harper 1985 is more neutral. But *guy* has filled the need described by Leacock and is in common use in standard journalism. This use of *guy* was once thought to be an Americanism (the only citation in the original OED is from a late 19th-century American source), but evidence in the OED Supplement shows that it had a British origin around the middle of the 19th century.

We will here follow the precedent of Flesch and give several examples of current use. You will note that it can also be used of women and corporations; it truly has become a term for "just any person." These examples show many of the currently popular expressions that *guy* is used in.

> As for Mr. Symons' readers, they can't tell the good guys from the bad —Mary Cantwell, *N.Y. Times Book Rev.,* 20 Mar. 1983

> Cunning is the refuge of the little guy —Stephen Jay Gould, "Were Dinosaurs Dumb?," 1980, in *The Contemporary Essay,* ed. Donald Hall, 1984

> In short, small banks can go down in flames. The big guys? Never. —Milton Moskowitz, *Houston Post,* 3 Sept. 1984

> ... a small cabal of very tough guys who really run that country —Alistair Cooke, quoted in *Women's Wear Daily,* 10 Mar. 1975

> ... eager to assure us that he is no ivory tower intellectual but a regular guy —Paul Robinson, *N.Y. Times Book Rev.,* 25 Sept. 1983

> He's sneaky-bright. . . . He doesn't flaunt it, because he wants to be one of the guys —Jay Daniel, quoted in *Newsweek,* 8 Sept. 1986

> Amy Irving likes it that Santa Fe isn't a swinging place. "The people are down-home—I'm just a normal guy here," she says —Andrea Chambers, *People,* 16 Aug. 1982

> ... the inability of people to put themselves in the other guy's shoes —Ishmael Reed, *N.Y. Times Book Rev.,* 4 Nov. 1984

> But he was a tenacious old guy who wrote some interesting poems —William Stafford, *Writing the Australian Crawl,* 1978

gynecology   The most widespread pronunciation of *gynecology* among both physicians and laypeople is \\,gī-nə-'käl-ə-jē\. A respectable runner-up among physicians is \\,jin-ə-'käl-ə-jē\; this version is less well known to the general public. Some medical sources even sanction \\,jī-nə-'käl-ə-jē\, though one physician has expressed the opinion that he had never heard the \\,jī\ version from anyone that he felt "ought to be using the word."

gyp For some time now there has been a tendency to call attention to oneself or one's group by taking public umbrage at some term or other as an ethnic slur. The verb *gyp,* reports Safire 1986, is one of those words. *Gyp,* which means "to cheat or swindle" is probably derived from a noun that is probably short for *Gypsy.* This is a fairly remote derivation to take offense at, and we have no evidence that *gyp* is ever used in an ethnically derogatory way. But since a few have taken offense, it is likely that others will follow. You should at least be aware that the issue has been raised and that sensitivities are now keener in this area than perhaps they were formerly. The verb, incidentally, is an Americanism of late 19th-century origin.

Gypsy, Gipsy These spelling variants have established themselves on opposite sides of the Atlantic: *Gypsy* is the almost invariable choice in American English; *Gipsy* is just about as dominant in British English. Fowler 1926 argued that *Gypsy* should be preferred because of its consistency with *Egyptian,* from which the word is derived, but his opinion appears to have had no effect on the British preference for *Gipsy.*

H

h

Hear them down in Soho Square,
dropping aitches ev'rywhere,
Speaking English any way they like.
—Alan Jay Lerner, "Why Can't the English?"
in *My Fair Lady,* 1956

The pattern that elicited this plaint from Professor Higgins was the familiar Cockney one, a pattern not found in the United States. The emotion with which the question was fraught sprang from the fact that, in England, *h*-dropping is the verbal class distinction par excellence. In America, on the other hand, although there is one pattern in which \h\ is normally dropped by some people and not by others, the variation does not correlate so starkly with social class.

The pattern in question is that of \h\ before the semivowels \w\ and \y\, as in *when* or *human.* Some educated people say \'hwen\ and \'hyü-mən\; others—probably the majority—say \'wen\ and \'yü-mən\. (Strictly speaking, what we transcribe as \hw\ and \hy\ are not literally \h\ followed by a semivowel, but a single sound that we may call a voiceless version of that semivowel. The distinction is unimportant for this discussion, however.) The \'wen\ style has long prevailed in southern England, home territory of standard British English, and cannot be regarded as incorrect, though it is under persistent pressure from the spelling. In America, \hw-\ gets an additional boost from the admixture of the northern strand of English speech where \hw-\ did not die out. Accordingly, in this country, when language is put under a lens, the \'wen\ style sometimes appears in an invidious light, as when Ring Lardner suggests the semi-educated vernacular of one of his characters by making him say

She was playing bridge w'ist with another gal and two dudes —*The Big Town,* 1921

All the same, it is entirely standard.

Another subclass of *h*-words may be defined not phonologically but etymologically: those borrowed from French, the *h* not being pronounced in the lender language. In many of these, \h\ has been added at the suggestion of the spelling: the \h\ we now pronounce in *hotel, habit, heritage,* etc., is an innovation. In others, the \h\-less pronunciation persists—*hour, honor, hon-*

est, heir, etc.—though here too there have been struggles, as Charles Lamb attests:

Martin Burney is as odd as ever. We had a dispute about the word 'heir' which I contended was pronounced like 'air'—he said that it might be in common parlance, or that we might so use it, speaking of the 'Heir at Law' a comedy, but that in the Law Courts it was necessary to give it a full aspiration, & to say *Hayer*—he thought it might even vitiate a cause, if a Counsel pronounced it otherwise. In conclusion he 'would consult Sergeant Wilde'—who gave it against him. Sometimes he falleth into the water, sometimes into the fire —letter, 24 May 1830

In the case of *herb* (from French *herbe* \erb\), the battle fell out differently in different ages and areas:

"When my Father was a boy every well-brought-up Canadian child learned that 'herb' was pronounced without the 'h'; you still hear it now and again, and modern Englishmen think it's ignorance...." —Robertson Davies, *The Rebel Angels,* 1981

The situation today is: Americans normally do not pronounce the \h\, Englishmen normally do, and Canadians are divided. Canadian phonology in general matches the American much more nearly than it does the British, but anglophone Canadians tend to follow Britian's lead on individual lexical shibboleths like *herb* and *schedule.*

Finally, *vehicle* (from French *véhicule*) is in anomalous position: the most widespread pronunciation and the one most often recommended is without \h\, but the \h\ variant, far from smacking of book-learning, strikes some as rustic, especially if the middle syllable is stressed, so that this version seems to them doubly a "hick" pronunciation. This \h\ variant is discussed at greater length at VEHICLE.

See also A, AN.

had better, had best These are standard English idioms.

... a word which had better be eschewed by all those who do not wish to talk high-flying nonsense —Richard Grant White 1870

... somewhat mysteriously hinted that I had better be at his house ... at seven o'clock in the evening —

The Intimate Notebooks of George Jean Nathan,
1932

. . . he had better think again —Barzun 1985

It had best be a good letter —Penelope Gilliatt, *New
Yorker,* 1 May 1971

A great many handbooks find it necessary to assure you
that *had better* and *had best* are standard, because these
expressions were attacked as illogical in the 19th century. Walter Savage Landor and William Cobbett seem
to have been key figures in the attack. The controversy
was a sort of spin-off of the older controversy about *had
rather,* which dates back to the 18th century (see HAD
RATHER). The form Landor prescribed was *would better,*
and according to the historical sketches in Lounsbury
1908 and McKnight 1928 Landor prevailed on Robert
Browning to revise a *had better* in *Pippa Passes* to *would
better.* Someone erected a theoretical basis for the controversy: *had better* was supposed to have been an erroneous expansion of *"'d better,* in which the *'d* was supposed to have been contracted from *would.* Bierce 1909
repeats it all. Cobbett 1823 criticizes the use of *had better* by the 18th-century rhetorician Hugh Blair as a
vulgarism.

Lounsbury devotes quite a bit of space to an account
of his researches into literature to try to discover when
had better came into common use; his findings suggest
that it was more commonly used in the 19th century
than earlier. The OED dates it all the way back to 971;
Shakespeare used it once (Lounsbury wonders if perhaps Fletcher wrote that particular line). It was certainly
known to the dramatist George Farquhar at the beginning of the 18th century:

You had best talk to him —*Love and a Bottle,* 1698

. . . but you had better walk about and cool by
Degrees —*The Beaux Stratagem,* 1707

The point to remember here is that there has been nothing wrong with these phrases all along.

A few of the critics who approve *had better* are less
certain about it when the *had* is omitted. See BETTER 2.

had have, had of   See PLUPLUPERFECT.

had ought, hadn't ought   Bache 1869 said that he
had it on good authority that the New Englandisms *had
ought* and *hadn't ought* were "making progress among
us"—Bache's anonymous book was published in Philadelphia—and he therefore gave the expressions some
room for disapproval. Since 1869 many schoolbooks
and handbooks have taken up the cudgels against them,
but apparently to little or no avail, for they are still the
speech forms that they seem to have been all along. You
will not find them in polished personal essays or in art
criticism or even in ordinary reporting.

There has been a notion from the beginning that *had
ought* and *hadn't ought* are regionalisms. Linguistic surveys show that Bache was not too much off base in 1869
in calling them New Englandisms. They seem to be predominantly Northern forms, although we have seen a
few anomalous examples. E. Bagby Atwood's *A Survey
of Verb Forms in the Eastern United States* (1953) shows
hadn't ought in New England, New York, northern
Pennsylvania, and New Jersey, as well as in small areas
of Ohio and northeastern North Carolina.

The fullest account seems to be in Visser 1969. He
suggests that the expressions are more common in normal coversation than the printed record would indicate,

and he has a generous half page of printed citations dating from 1836 to 1964. Here are a few examples not in
Visser:

"I hadn't ought to think anything."
"Say 'Shouldn't think,' Landry."
                    —Frank Norris, *The Pit,* 1903

. . . it's father Bedott's name, and he and mother
Bedott both used to think that names had ought to
go down from generation to generation —Frances
Miriam Whitcher, "Hezekiah Bedott," 1855, in *The
Mirth of a Nation,* ed. Walter Blair & Raven I.
McDavid, Jr., 1983

He come to hire it just before I made up my mind
that I hadn't ort to go —Marietta Holley, "A Pleasure Exertion," in *Mark Twain's Library of Humor,*
1888

If you don't like people, you hadn't ought to be in
politics at all —Harry S. Truman, quoted in Merle
Miller, *Plain Speaking,* 1973

Among the interesting anomalies are citations in Visser
from Robert Louis Stevenson's *Treasure Island* and
from a couple of novels by William Faulkner. These,
and the quotation from Harry Truman above, suggest
that the whole story of *hadn't ought* and *had ought* is
not yet known. Perhaps there will be fuller information
when the volume of the Dictionary of American
Regional English including *O* is published (it's not
entered under *H*). The earlier American Dialect Dictionary also has a mysterious citation from Georgia.

Regardless of what the schoolbooks and handbooks
might say, neither *had ought* nor *hadn't ought* is wrong;
they are simply regionalisms. But they are still confined
to speech and fictional speech.

Visser, incidentally, devotes about as much space to
didn't ought and *doesn't ought,* which are attested in
British English from Dickens to J. R. R. Tolkien,
Atwood found a few examples in New England. The
handbooks and schoolbooks seem not to know that
these forms exist.

See also OUGHT 1, 3.

had rather   *Had rather* is a perfectly respectable and
perfectly standard English idiom. It seems to have come
into use during the 15th century. It competed with the
older *had liefer* (sometimes spelled with a *v* as *lever* or
liever) and by Shakespeare's time had pretty well
replaced the older phrase. From the middle of the 18th
century until early in the 20th, it was the subject of considerable controversy. It appears in present-day handbooks chiefly in the form of notices that both *had rather*
and *would rather,* the alternative prescribed during the
controversy, are standard.

The controversy seems to have had its origin in Samuel Johnson's Dictionary of 1755. Under *rather* is this
notice:

6. *To have* RATHER. [this is, I think, a barbarous
expression of late intrusion into our language, for
which it is better to say *will rather.*]

Here Johnson made two blunders. He had failed to read
his Shakespeare attentively: *had rather* is used thirty-
eight times in Shakespeare's plays. And he seems not to
have considered whether he used it himself. Later evidence shows that it was part of his vocabulary:

. . . and every hour shows the careful observer those
who had rather live in ease than in plenty —*The
Idler,* 10 June 1758

The first experiment, however, was bold, and deserved applause and reward: but since it has been performed, and its event is known, I had rather now find a medicine that can ease an asthma —letter, 6 Oct. 1784

From Johnson's Dictionary the question spread to the 18th-century grammarians—Lowth, Campbell, Lindley Murray. In his later editions Lowth has a footnote on the subject in which he cites "two grammatical essays" of 1768 (Leonard 1923 identifies the author as William Salisbury) in which the origin of *had* is explained as a mistaken expansion of *'d*—as in *I'd rather*—which was asserted to be a contraction of *would*. Salisbury's explanation proved to be popular; it was repeated by many later commentators, including Campbell 1776, Webster 1828, Alford 1866, Ayres 1881, and Bierce 1909.

Another question about *had rather* troubled Lowth. He did not understand how the past *had* could be used to signify present time. What he missed was the fact that *had* was a subjunctive. McKnight 1928 explains how the historical development of these expressions involved the subjunctive all along, from the early impersonal *me were lever* (*me* is a dative there and the whole phrase means "it would be preferable to me") to the later personal form *I had lever,* in which *rather* replaced *lever* by Shakespeare's time.

Noah Webster was accounted an opponent of *had rather.* He undoubtedly picked the controversy up from Johnson's Dictionary, on which he based his 1828 edition. Noah seems to have been a bit skeptical; he repeats Salisbury's explanation but qualifies it with *supposed* and *may have been.* He unequivocally recommends *would rather,* however, as had all the 18th-century commentators. The editors of Webster 1864 stated the case in stronger language, calling *had* "a blundering interpretation" of the supposed *'d* in their version of Salisbury's explanation. This eventually brought them a strong rebuke from the *New England Journal of Education* (reprinted in Bardeen 1883) for not having made use of more recent philological information.

Would rather, universally recommended, and *should rather* were combinations that had actually been in use for some time before the controversy.

Your knowing of Mr. Dorimant, in my mind, should rather make you hate all mankind —George Etherege, *The Man of Mode,* 1676

... my loaves (cakes I should rather call them) of barley bread —Daniel Defoe, *Robinson Crusoe,* 1719

Hall 1917 thinks *would rather* may actually be older than *had rather;* he found an instance in Chaucer and another in Sir Thomas More. McKnight cites a European study claiming eight instances of *would rather* in the First Folio of Shakespeare, though they do not turn up in the Concordance to Shakespeare (there is one instance of *rather would*). Be that as it may, *would rather* was an existing form available to compete with *had rather,* and it has done so right down to the present day. Bryant 1962 reports two studies, one of which found *would rather* in the majority and the other of which found *had rather* in the majority.

So in present-day English you can use either *had rather* or *would rather.* No one objects to either form any more. In speech, of course, you'll find *'d rather,* which you are free to interpret as you please.

I wouldn't let them do it, though. I'd rather die in the poorhouse than do a thing like that —Harry S.

Truman, quoted in Merle Miller, *Plain Speaking,* 1973

There are long and detailed treatments of *had rather* in Lounsbury 1908 and Hall 1917. See also HAD BETTER, HAD BEST.

hail, hale Confusion about which of these spellings should be used in a particular context one would expect to be common, but we have relatively little evidence of it in our files. Perhaps proofreaders and copy editors have especially sharp eyes when it comes to *hail* and *hale.* Even so, it seems worthwhile to point out possible areas of confusion.

The spelling *hale* is the established choice for the verb meaning "to compel to go":

... he was haled before a summary court —Hugh Trevor-Roper, *American Scholar,* Winter 1981/82

Usage commentators find that this verb is often mistakenly spelled *hail.* We've collected only two examples of this error, the most recent of which is from 1949:

... Albania was challenging Great Britain's competence to hail it before the International Court of Justice —*Collier's Year Book,* 1949

Hale is also the spelling used for the adjective meaning "healthy":

... a tall, hale blond of thirty —Sara Davidson, *Harper's,* June 1972

In this case we have collected three errors within the last 15 years, so the problem may be greater:

... most young Israelis ... are tough, confident, hail-and-hearty —*The Economist,* 26 July 1985

The spelling *hail* is correctly used for the noun and verb relating to icy lumps of precipitation and for the verb meaning "greet" or "acclaim." It also occurs in the idiom "hail from":

They hail from any number of Western states — Gary Schmitz, *Denver Post,* 31 Aug. 1984

And in the term *hail-fellow-well-met:*

... a fun guy, a genuine hail-fellow-well-met —William Taaffe, *Sports Illustrated,* 10 Mar. 1986

hain't *Hain't* meaning "have not" or "has not" seems to be a spelling of one pronunciation of earlier *han't* (which see), itself more obviously a contraction of *have not* or *has not. Han't* can be found in the works of the Restoration dramatists of the late 17th century. *Hain't* seems to have been quite common in 19th-century American English, especially rural speech, if we can trust the evidence of the humorists of that era:

Huldy's well meanin', and she's good at her work, and good in the singers' seat, but Lordy massy! she hain't got no experience —Harriet Beecher Stowe, "The Minister's Housekeeper," 1871, in *The Mirth of a Nation,* ed. Walter Blair & Raven I. McDavid, Jr., 1983

Showmen is devoid of politics. They hain't got any principles! —Artemus Ward, "Interview with President Lincoln," 1861, in *The Mirth of a Nation,* ed. Walter Blair & Raven I. McDavid, Jr., 1983

Hain't is one of the dialect verb forms attested in the Linguistic Atlas surveys of the United States, but it seems to have been passing out of use gradually for decades. The later contractions *haven't* and *hasn't* are standard, and also far more frequent.

Hain't is also a variant pronunciation of *ain't*. And *ain't* is also used for "have not, has not." Those who are interested in the history of these contractions should see the entries at AIN'T and DON'T.

hairbrained Most often this word is spelled *harebrained,* and that is how usage writers tell you to spell it. Heritage 1982 sums up the prevailing attitude: "Though *hairbrained* has a long history, this spelling is not established usage." Their statement makes one wonder just what the "long history" of *hairbrained* may be. Going to the OED, we see that a third of the citations quoted at *harebrained* and related terms are for the *hair-*spelling and that both spellings are attested from the 16th century onward. *Hairbrained* has continued to the present day as an infrequent but regular variant.

> The hair brained escapades of the poet —*The Bookman,* April 1927

> . . . he'll pull some hair brained deal —James Jones, *From Here to Eternity,* 1951

> . . . their hairbrained folly —Christopher Lasch, *N.Y. Times Book Rev.,* 25 Jan. 1976

While the Heritage statement about the "long history" is certainly true, whether *hairbrained* is an established usage or not is a matter of opinion. Our opinion based on the evidence is that it is established.

hale See HAIL, HALE.

hale and hearty This is one of those alliterative duplications, says Evans 1957, which become clichés. The phrase denotes robust good health and is almost always used of older persons. It is so familiar that it can be misspelled by those who, as the saying goes, "spell by ear."

> . . . who at 91 years of age looked hale and hardy —*Johns Hopkins Mag.,* Spring 1983

If you use the phrase, mind the spelling. See also HAIL, HALE; HARDY, HEARTY.

half 1. A few commentators—among them Sellers 1975, Longman 1984, Chambers 1985, and Corder 1981—discuss *half* with respect to verb agreement. They all tell us that when *half,* either noun or adjective, is followed by a singular noun it takes a singular verb; when followed by a plural noun, a plural verb. This makes good sense, because it follows notional agreement and also allows for the principle of proximity. Those who use the wrong verb, as Sellers says some do, have perhaps been frightened by traditional grammar or the school exercise of diagramming sentences into believing that the formal subject, *half,* must govern the verb, when in fact the true subject is the following noun.

Such constructions are not very common in our files. Perhaps the problem only surfaces occasionally. Here are three examples:

> . . . half of whose population votes —Gustave Mersu, *American Mercury,* October 1952

> . . . a half of the children drop out —James B. Conant, *Slums and Suburbs,* 1961

> . . . half the citizens don't know or care —Robert Penn Warren, *Jefferson Davis Gets His Citizenship Back,* 1980

2. Handbooks going back as far as MacCracken & Sandison 1917 say that both *half a* (or *an*) and *a half* are all right, but *a half a* is redundant. A few of the more recent ones, like Scott Foresman 1981, notice that the *a half a* construction seems to be mostly a spoken usage. This is our opinion, too, for we have very little evidence of its use in print. It would seem most likely to occur with fixed phrases like *half an hour* or *half a dollar,* which are thought of as units and which are frequently found hyphenated in print. Here is an instance quoted from speech:

> . . . I learned . . . that almost no woman who has gone beyond the eighth grade ever calls a 50-cent piece a half-a-dollar —John O'Hara, foreword to *Assembly,* 1961

In edited prose *a half* and *half a* and *half an* are usual:

> . . . eating a half grapefruit —E. L. Doctorow, *Loon Lake,* 1979

> Given half a chance —Aristides, *American Scholar,* Autumn 1981

> . . . to make you listen with half an ear —Donal Henahan, *N.Y. Times,* 28 Nov. 1967

3. *Cut in half.* Bernstein 1971 and Copperud 1980 note that there was formerly a considerable to-do about the propriety of *in half* used after verbs like *cut, break, divide,* or *fold.* (The subject is mentioned in Vizetelly 1906.) The argument was that there are incontrovertibly two halves resulting from whatever verb action is applied and that the plural *halves* must therefore be used. The singular is not used with *thirds* or *quarters,* for instance. Bernstein and Copperud pooh-pooh the argument on the grounds of idiom; they also point out that *half* functions in several other cases differently from the other fractions. But Bernstein's and Copperud's "formerly" is not quite right, for Freeman 1983 is still favoring *in halves* in formal English. Our evidence shows that *in half* is the prevailing form, even in mathematics texts:

> Fold the bill in half and then in half again —Max A. Sabel et al., *Essentials of Mathematics,* Book 1, 1977

> Rotifers . . . whose nutritional intake was cut roughly in half increased their life span —*Johns Hopkins Mag.,* Spring 1968

In halves is sometimes used. This example may have been influenced by the plural *avocados,* however:

> Cut avocados in halves and prepare as described —Anne Mason, *Starters & Afters,* 1974

half-mast, half-staff Harper 1975, 1985 says that *half-mast* is the more common term for the position in which a flag is flown as a symbol of mourning, noting that the entries in dictionaries bear out the contention. Bremner 1980 and the *New York Times Style Book* (1962) insist that *half-mast* be reserved for naval flags and *half-staff* for all others. Copperud 1980 hints rather broadly that such insistence is pedantry. Both forms are correct: *half-mast* is used for any flag; *half-staff* is used for any flag other than a naval flag.

hamstring H. W. Fowler made the verb *hamstring* a minor usage issue in 1926 by arguing that its past tense and past participle should be *hamstringed* and not *hamstrung,* inasmuch as it is derived from the noun *hamstring* and has no relation to the verb *string.* Later commentators have had to balance their respect for Fowler's opinions against the evidence of actual usage, which shows clearly that *hamstrung* is the form now established in standard use. Many commentators compromise by saying that both *hamstringed* and *hamstrung* are acceptable, but our own evidence indicates that *hamstringed* has now fallen entirely out of use—we have no 20th-century example of it in our files. Most dictionaries now recognize only *hamstrung,* and we recommend that form to you. Notice how unidiomatic *hamstringed* would sound in any of the following passages:

> A few other U.S. attorneys hamstrung specialists by refusing to let them deal with state and local officials —Robert E. Taylor, *Wall Street Jour.,* 28 Sept. 1981

> . . . had been hamstrung by Roosevelt's reluctance — Robert A. Caro, *Atlantic,* November 1981

> . . . an arrogant brilliance that has the local cops hamstrung —Jack Kroll, *Newsweek,* 9 June 1986

handful *Handful* has two plurals, *handfuls* and *handsful.* The first is the more common, and the one recommended in several handbooks. See -FUL.

hands-on This now-common adjective is a recent coinage. Our earliest evidence of its use is from 1969:

> The high point of the classes is the great amount of hands-on time available to the students —Philip H. Braverman, *Datamation,* November 1969

It first became widespread in the phrase *hands-on experience,* denoting practical experience in the actual operation of something, such as a computer, or in the performance of a job. Much of our early evidence for it relates to education.

> . . . unusual teaching methods that emphasize active, hands-on experience —Larry A. Van Dyne, *Change,* February 1973

But by the early 1980s, *hands-on* was being more widely applied, describing everything from a museum featuring articles meant to be touched to a corporate executive taking an active role in running a business:

> ". . . didn't think Valente was hands-on enough." Mr. Valente, he [unidentified speaker] said, "didn't dig into the business enough. . . ." —Jeffrey A. Tannenbaum, *Wall Street Jour.,* 19 June 1980

Its adoption in the world of business has given *hands-on* a measure of notoriety that it never had in the world of education, and such commentators as Safire 1986 and the usage panel of Harper 1985 have in recent years considered it jargon. Whatever validity that description has (and it does have some, certainly), the use of *hands-on* in the business world is established, and it will probably gain in respectability in the non-business world as its occurrence becomes less of a novelty. Our only recommendation is that you avoid it in contexts where it may be more suggestive of physical groping than of practical involvement:

> ". . . we're all looking for ways to get a hands-on feel for the consumer" —Alexander MacGregor, quoted in *N.Y. Times Book Rev.,* 3 Apr. 1983

hang, hanged, hung One of the more widely known and frequently repeated observations on usage is that *hanged* is preferred as the past and past participle of *hang* when the verb has the sense "to hang by the neck until dead" and that *hung* is the correct choice for all other senses of the word. This distinction arose out of the complex history of *hang.* The OED shows that *hang* developed from two Old English verbs, one of which was a weak (or, in effect, regular) verb giving rise to the inflected form *hanged,* and the other of which was a strong (or, in effect, irregular) verb giving rise to *hung.* (These verbs, Lamberts 1972 tells us, were originally a transitive–intransitive pair, like *set–sit, lay–lie,* that eventually fell together as a single verb.) The two forms were more or less interchangeable for many centuries, but the weak form was eventually superseded by the strong form except in the "execute by hanging" sense, in which *hanged* probably persisted because it was the form favored by judges in pronouncing sentence. Even in the "execute" sense, however, the strong form made inroads:

> . . . for these rogues that burned this house to be hung in some conspicuous place in town —Samuel Pepys, diary, 4 July 1667

> . . . to-day I am laid by the heels, and to-morrow shall be hung by the neck —George Farquhar, *The Constant Couple,* 1699

> . . . should not escape unpunished. I hope he hung himself —Jane Austen, letter, 6 Dec. 1815

> These men were . . . at last brought to the scaffold and hung —Percy Bysshe Shelley, *Address,* 1817 (OED)

> I have not the least objection to a rogue being hung —W. M. Thackeray, *The Newcomes,* 1853 (cited by Otto Jespersen, *S.P.E. Tract 25,* 1926)

In 1898, the OED noted that writers and speakers in southern England often used *hung* in this sense.

The distinction between *hanged* and *hung* has been a topic for commentary since Joseph Priestley first broached the subject in 1769. The issue was raised by only a few writers in the 19th century, but 20th-century commentators have taken up the cause wholeheartedly, and almost all books on usage now include some mention of *hanged* and *hung.* The primary concern of the critics is that *hung* should not be used in the "execute" sense, or that such use should at least be avoided in formal writing. Many commentators recognize that *hung* for *hanged* is now common in standard English, but more than a few persist in describing it as an error, pure and simple.

Our evidence shows that *hung* for *hanged* is certainly not an error. Educated speakers and writers use it commonly and have for many years:

> . . . that if he was hung he would plant flowers on his grave —James Stephens, *The Crock of Gold,* 1912

> The negro murderer was to be hung on a Saturday without pomp —William Faulkner, *Sanctuary,* 1931

> . . . soldiers convicted of appalling crimes are being hung and shot —*Times Literary Supp.,* 29 Nov. 1941

> . . . a man in jail just about to be hung —William Faulkner, 13 May 1957, in *Faulkner in the University,* 1959

... insists that IRA terrorists can be hung by the law now —Noyes Thomas, *News of the World* (London), 24 Nov. 1974

... a 13-year-old evangelist, who hung himself because his mother spanked him for sassing her —Flannery O'Connor, letter, 23 Apr. 1960

Placed in solitary he hung himself —Horace Sutton, *Saturday Rev.,* 1 Mar. 1980

Hanged is, however, more common than *hung* in writing. It is especially prevalent when an official execution is being described, but it is used in referring to other types of hanging as well:

... that he might be put on his trial and hanged —James Stephens, *The Crock of Gold,* 1912

... I dreamed that we hanged The Informer —Ernest Hemingway, "Miss Mary's Lion," 1956

Nobody is hanged for stealing bread any more —William Faulkner, 15 Feb. 1957, in *Faulkner in the University,* 1959

After a long investigation and trial, Dr. John Webster ... was hanged for Parkman's murder —John Thompson, *Harper's,* October 1971

... were promptly hanged outside the Portcullis Gate —John Updike, *Bech Is Back,* 1982

... he had fled Europe ... to avoid being hanged —Russell Baker, *N.Y. Times Mag.,* 15 Feb. 1976

... was found hanged in his family's home —Lena Williams, *N.Y. Times,* 23 Feb. 1984

Hanged also occurs in several old-fashioned idiomatic expressions in which *hung* is not possible:

But equally I'm hanged if I want to be bullied by it —Sinclair Lewis, *Main Street,* 1920

I'll be hanged if I'll be mournful —Peter B. Kyne, *The Pride of Palomar,* 1921

But *hung* is more likely than *hanged* when the hanging described is in effigy:

George Washington, kidnapped, and hung (in effigy) —*Time,* 4 Mar. 1946

... by morning I'll be hung in effigy —Ronald Reagan, quoted by William Safire, *N.Y. Times Mag.,* 8 Mar. 1981

Local feelings ran so strong against the plan that Eddie and I were booed out of the town hall in Eastham and were hung in effigy in Truro —Tip O'Neill with William Novak, *Man of the House,* 1987

And E. Bagby Atwood's *A Survey of Verb Forms in the Eastern United States* (1953) found that in speech "*hung* ... predominates in all areas and among all types [of informants considered with respect to age and level of education]."

The distinction between *hanged* and *hung* is not an especially useful one (although a few commentators claim otherwise). It is, however, a simple one and certainly easy to remember. Therein lies its popularity. If you make a point of observing the distinction in your writing, you will not thereby become a better writer, but you will spare yourself the annoyance of being corrected for having done something that is not wrong.

hangar The name for a building in which aircraft are housed is *hangar,* not *hanger.* The spelling mistake is easily made:

... a variety of military buildings including jet hangers —*Johns Hopkins Mag.,* Summer 1971

But its occurrence in edited prose is, according to our evidence, rare.

hanker *Hanker,* when used with a preposition, is most frequently combined with *after:*

Mrs. Morel wanted to buy him a little sable brush that he hankered after. But this indulgence he refused —D. H. Lawrence, *Sons and Lovers,* 1913

... betrays himself when he hankers too yearningly after common human fulfilments —Aldous Huxley, *The Olive Tree,* 1937

... a moment when he hankered after other, strange delights —Robertson Davies, *Tempest-tost,* 1951

Nearly as often, *hanker* is used with *for* or with *to* and the infinitive:

At the bottom of my heart I hankered for Larry, but as long as I didn't see him it didn't really bother me —W. Somerset Maugham, *The Razor's Edge,* 1944

... one hankers for the character he played in "The Blackboard Jungle" instead of the point-making prigs he takes on now —Penelope Gilliatt, *New Yorker,* 17 June 1967

... making me thus kind of hanker, for dear "amusement's" sake, to decorate the thing —Henry James, "Notes for *The Ivory Tower,*" 1917

... any fourteen historical characters with whom you hanker to spend an evening —Clifton Fadiman, *Holiday,* June 1953

The evidence also includes an occasional use of *hanker* with *toward:*

... those who were soon to call themselves 'sophisticated' were hankering toward Dorian Gray's aesthetic life —James D. Hart, *The Popular Book: A History of America's Literary Taste,* 1950

han't *Han't,* sometimes spelled *ha'n't,* is one of those efficient negative contractions that came into fashionable use during the 17th century in England. It is the contraction for both *have not* and *has not.* It was common in the Restoration comedies of Wycherly, Congreve, Vanbrugh, and Farquhar, and was used by Jonathan Swift in his *Journal to Stella.* Some examples:

Han't I always been thy friend ... ? —William Wycherly, *The Country Wife,* 1675

Pray heaven that old rogue Coupler han't sent us to fetch milk out of the gunroom! —Sir John Vanbrugh, *The Relapse,* 1696

I han't seen Lord Pembroke yet —Jonathan Swift, *Journal to Stella,* 21 Oct. 1711

In 1815 an American named David Humphrey, one of the "Hartford Wits," published a play titled *The Yankey in England.* The play was apparently intended for an English audience, for at the back of the volume Humphrey included a glossary of Americanisms used by the Yankey, Doolittle, in the play. Among those listed was *han't,* listed alongside *havn't,* for *have not.* The inclusion of *han't* suggests that it did have some American use as well. Later in the 19th century the usual spelling was *hain't* (which see). It has been replaced by *haven't* and *hasn't.*

If you are interested in the history of these contracted forms, see AIN'T and DON'T.

happening   This is another issue that can be traced directly to Fowler 1926, who had this to say about the noun *happening* as a synonym for *event* or *occurrence:*

> It is a VOGUE-WORD, which has had a startlingly rapid success, & which many of us hope to see wither away as quickly as it has grown. There is nothing to be said against it on the score of correctness; but it is a child of art & not of nature; may it prove sickly, & die young!

Fowler regarded *happening* as a literary affectation, but the early death he hoped for (not so early, actually, since *happening* in its "event" sense was first recorded in 1581) has not occurred. The basic sense has, in fact, produced offspring. In the late 1950s and early 60s, *happening* was first used to denote bizarre artistic or theatrical events designed to provoke spontaneous reactions:

> The . . . Happening was a Peruvian painter playing jazz at the piano while Harold Stevenson, another painter, read selections from a biology book —Elaine Dundy, *Esquire,* October 1964

Sounds like fun, doesn't it? *Happening* later came to be used more broadly to describe just about any event of particular or unusual interest:

> The hearing is a happening, one of those unique events . . . which will be talked about for years —Douglas Kiker, *The Washingtonian,* October 1973

It has even been used to describe an interesting person:

> At home or in the ring, Ali is a . . . one-man happening —*Time,* 8 Mar. 1971

Fowler's criticism of *happening* can still be found in Gowers's 1965 revision, but no other commentator has taken up the cause. The basic "event" sense of *happening* continues in common use:

> . . . the list of happenings at the start of this survey —Craig McGregor, *N.Y. Times Book Rev.,* 19 May 1985

The "artistic event" sense of *happening* is now rare, as are such events themselves, but the "interestingly unusual event" sense still occurs with some regularity:

> . . . the engaging repartee that made Monday Night a happening even for non-football fans —William Taaffe, *Sports Illustrated,* 7 Oct. 1985

harangue, tirade   Several commentators, from Evans 1957 forward, have made the following distinctions between these words: *harangue* referes to a prolonged and vehement speech, not necessarily hostile, addressed to a group or at least to more than one person; *tirade* refers always to a hostile speech, one that may be addressed to any number of people, including just one. Our evidence does show that not all harangues are hos-

tile, but it gives no support to the notion that they require an audience of more than one:

> That lady was still haranguing the girl —Ford Madox Ford, *The Last Post,* 1928

> . . . said in chilling, ominous tones which . . ., indicating an endless harangue, made him want to get out of there: "There are things that I can never forgive you for." —William Styron, *Lie Down in Darkness,* 1951

As for *tirade,* it once could be used like *harangue* to describe vehement speech without necessary implications of hostility:

> She listened with a melancholy smile to her guide's tirade in praise of liberty —Sir Walter Scott, *Quentin Durward,* 1823 (OED)

But it does now seem always to imply a violently abusive tone:

> . . . erupts into an hysterical tirade that betrays all her past misery —Elaine Louise Lawrence, *LIT,* Spring 1966

> . . . bursts out in a tirade against all womankind —Harold McCurdy, *Psychology Today,* April 1968

harass   Copperud 1980 points out that *harass* is sometimes misspelled with two *r's.* Our evidence confirms this. Please pay attention.

hard, hardly   Of these two adverbs, *hard* is the older by a couple of centuries. *Hardly* was formed in the 13th century as an ordinary adverbial derivative of the adjective *hard.* Its oldest senses have passed out of use, but the senses "with force," "harshly," and "with difficulty" are still alive, although they are more common in British use than in American.

> . . . where the means of existence was wrung so hardly from the soil —Sir Winston Churchill, *The Unrelenting Struggle,* 1942

> . . . the belief that protection bore hardly on the farmers —*Dictionary of American Biography,* 1936

> Professor Bowers has been hardly treated by those he is anxious to help —*Times Literary Supp.,* 24 Mar. 1966

> . . . were told over and over again by their most idealistic advisers that Germany had been hardly used —A. J. P. Taylor, *Saturday Rev.,* 11 Dec. 1954

The problem that hangs over these senses is the likelihood of confusion with the "scarcely" sense of *hardly,* which is the dominant use in present-day English. This sense can even modify the same verbs as the early senses, and the reader must concentrate on the context in order not to be misled:

> Marquis' vocabulary and literary and historical references are pleasures to play with. Because they are different and hardly used, students delight . . . —Winfield Carlough, *Media & Methods,* November 1968

The recommendation of all the commentators is that you use *hard* in all uses where it fits. Our evidence suggests that most American writers seem to find other words—like the glosses given above—to use in place of *hardly* when it doesn't mean "scarcely."

hardly The hastier usage commentators and school-book compilers assure us that *hardly* is a negative. More cautious observers say that *hardly* has the force of a negative or that it has a negative meaning. *Hardly* is not a negative. There is an important difference between

> I hardly studied at all —Harvey Wheeler, in *A Center Occasional Paper,* April 1971

and the same sentence expressed negatively:

> I didn't study at all.

Try making a negative out of *hardly* in the following examples and you will see what we mean:

> They had hardly known each other then —Robert Canzoneri, *McCall's,* March 1971

> . . . mothers are often tired but hardly ever lazy —Bruno Bettelheim, *Ladies' Home Jour.,* January 1971

> Trembling in every limb, hardly able to set one foot before the other, she opened the door —Katherine Anne Porter, *Ladies' Home Jour.,* August 1971

> . . . provide the translators with the problem—which they hardly solve—of finding reasonable English equivalents for his florid indignation —*Times Literary Supp.,* 2 Oct. 1970

You can see that *hardly* approaches a negative but doesn't quite get there. Otto Jespersen (*Negation in English and Other Languages,* 1917) calls it an *approximate negative.*

Approximate negative or not, the schoolbooks and handbooks are nearly universal in calling *hardly* with a negative (*can't* is the one most frequently named) a *double negative.* This is a misnomer in two ways. First, a word not a negative plus a negative cannot logically be called two negatives; second, and more important, the effect of two genuine negatives is usually reinforcement of the negation (see DOUBLE NEGATIVE 1), while a negative with *hardly* is actually weakened (*softened* is Jespersen's word). To see the difference, let's compare constructions.

> I got up and tried to untie her, but I was so excited my hands shook so I couldn't hardly do anything with them —Mark Twain, *Huckleberry Finn,* 1884

Huck is saying in this passage that his hands were shaking so much that he had considerable trouble in untying her, but he did untie her. Now let's make a true double negative out of it:

> My hands shook so much I couldn't do nothing with them.

If Mark Twain had had Huck say that, the female in question would still be tied up.

So analysis of *can't hardly* as a double negative is wrong, and if it is to be stigmatized, that must be done on some other basis than association with *don't never* and the like.

Now let's see where these constructions with *hardly* and a negative occur. They are found in speech:

> . . . and you couldn't hardly get a job —Edward Santander, quoted in Studs Terkel, *Hard Times,* 1970

> There's not hardly an hour goes by that his face, or just the thought of him, doesn't flash through my mind —Terry Bradshaw, quoted in *Playboy,* March 1980

> Prenuptial agreements, [Mick] Jagger recently said, "don't stand up in court hardly." —*Time,* 12 Mar. 1984

> . . . and nobody hardly took notice of him —Jonathan Swift, *Journal to Stella,* ca. 1712 (in Jespersen)

It occurs in fictional speech and in fictional first-person narration:

> . . . it gave us not time hardly to say, O God! —Daniel Defoe, *Robinson Crusoe,* 1719 (in Jespersen)

> "I don't know," she says. "He acts kind of shy. He hasn't hardly said a word to me all evening." —Ring Lardner, *The Big Town,* 1921

> Now here's a funny thing about me: the first night on a sleeper, I can't hardly sleep at all —Sinclair Lewis, *The Man Who Knew Coolidge,* 1928

The combination *without hardly* seems to turn up in newspaper reporting from time to time:

> The rest are left to wander the flat lowlands of West Bengal without hardly a trace of food or shelter —*N.Y. Times,* 13 June 1971

> . . . a nice spacing of seven hits by Nelson to win without hardly breaking a sweat —Gerry Finn, *Springfield* (Mass.) *Morning Union,* 2 Aug. 1985

Summary: *hardly* with a negative produces a weaker, not a stronger, negative; it is not, therefore, a double negative. But it is a speech form not used in discursive prose. The difference between *hardly* with a negative and *hardly* without a negative is neatly illustrated in the examples from Katherine Anne Porter and Mark Twain. Katherine Anne Porter is writing as the omniscient narrator, and she uses *hardly* without a negative. Mark Twain uses Huck Finn as first-person narrator; Huck uses *hardly* with a negative—the construction that would have been natural to his speech. Keep this distinction in mind if you use *can't hardly* or other negative constructions with *hardly* in writing: use them only where they are natural to the narrator or speaker.

See also HARD, HARDLY; SCARCELY 2.

hardly . . . than The sequence *hardly . . . when* is considered correct and standard by all commentators.

> His studies had hardly begun when he was drafted into a cavalry unit of the *Wehrmacht* in 1943 —*Current Biography,* February 1967

This sequence means the same thing as *no sooner . . . than.* The perhaps more familiar *no sooner . . . than* sticks in the minds of some writers using *hardly,* and *hardly . . . than* results:

> Hardly have I organized the fancy in my mind than a raucous company of sightseers comes loudly down the quay —Jan Morris, *N.Y. Times Mag.,* 20 July 1975

Hardly . . . than is a syntactic blend (which see). It seems to be of rather recent origin; the OED has, at the third sense of *than,* a single instance from 1903 (and a *scarcely . . . than* from 1864).

Fowler 1926 was the first to make an issue of this construction. He called it "surprisingly common" and gave three instances, all probably taken from British newspapers. Jespersen 1909–49 (volume 7) has examples from two little-known authors (one of whom used the construction several times in the same book). Bryant 1962 has a 1958 example but cites a study which found the construction rare. Our file of citations shows only the one example given above. It may be that the construction is more prevalent in British English (Jan Morris is British) than in American, or it may simply be infrequent.

Most of the commentators in our collection who mention the construction consider it an error; several of them point out that both *barely* and *scarcely* can occur with *than* in the same syntactic blend. Our evidence suggests that neither the approved *hardly . . . when* or the disapproved *hardly . . . than* is a commonly met construction. Use of the syntactic blend is only a minor error.

See also SCARCELY. . .THAN.

hard put   Follett 1966 calls *hard put* an unidiomatic clipped form of *hard put to it;* Bernstein 1965 accepts either form. Copperud 1970, 1980 notes that dictionaries all recognize *hard put*. One reason for clipping the longer phrase is obvious from the following example— the awkward *to it to* is avoided.

> I am hard put to explain how they ever got a man in space —*And More by Andy Rooney,* 1982

hardy, hearty   These two words do not look alike, but they sound much alike in American English. They are vaguely similar in meaning in some of their senses, but they are not interchangeable. The substitution of one for the other, then, must be accounted a mistake. We have a "hearty crop" from *Newsweek* in 1976, and "a particularly hearty flower" from *Parade Magazine* in 1977, both of which should have been *hardy*. And in the *New York Times Magazine* we have a 1982 "hardy soups," which should have been *hearty*.

English is a very difficult language to spell by ear. We suggest you consult a dictionary whenever you are in any doubt—even if you are using a word processor.

harebrained   See HAIRBRAINED.

hark back, harken back, hearken back   To understand the problem here, we have to spend a moment on *hark, harken,* and *hearken*. These words are related, and all have the basic sense "to listen, listen carefully," *Harken* is just a spelling variant of *hearken;* the OED shows *harken* to have been used earlier, but *hearken* came to predominate. *Harken* was probably given some impetus in American use by its having been put forward as a reformed spelling—the *Chicago Tribune* adopted it in 1934—and most of our 20th-century evidence for it is American. Both *harken* and *hearken* are still used in their basic meaning.

Hark, however, is now rare in its sense of "listen." From its use as a cry in hunting, it had developed various uses for actions in hunting; in these it was usually accompanied by an adverb such as *away, on, forward,* or *back. Hark back* was a 19th-century formation which quickly acquired a figurative meaning "to turn back to an earlier topic or circumstance." This has become an established use and is the most frequent employment of *hark,* although it can still be found with *forward, after,* and *to.*

In the 20th century *hark back* began to influence *hearken* and *harken*. Our earliest evidence is from 1933:

> And so on, until a fairly complete image of the room has been constructed to which one's mind can at any moment hearken back —Ira Victor Morris, *Covering Two Years,* 1933

> . . . they hearken back to the good old days of a century ago —Bernard Berelson, *Saturday Rev.,* 12 May 1951

> This ancestral harkening back to Mark Twain — John Henry Raleigh, *New Republic,* 8 Feb. 1954

> There are purists, of course, who hearken back to pre-lift days —William Gilman, *N.Y. Times,* 16 Jan. 1955

> . . . the recipes hearken back to yesteryear —Horace Sutton, *Saturday Rev.,* 20 Mar. 1971

> . . . tales . . . harken back to an earlier time —George Carey, *Johns Hopkins Mag.,* January 1976

> The quadrangles of countless universities and museums hearken back to this monastic original — Michael Olmert, *Smithsonian,* June 1980

> Many illustrators . . . continue to harken back to the pseudomedievalism of Randolph Caldecott —John Seelye, *N.Y. Times Book Rev.,* 11 Nov. 1984

It appears from our most recent evidence that the spelling *harken* is beginning to prevail in this use in American English. In the 1980s it has begun to differentiate further from *hearken;* it has developed a sense meaning "hark back" without *back:*

> . . . an unflawed specimen that harkens to the days of Sherlock Holmes —Carleton Jones, *Maryland Mag.,* Spring 1982

> The biographies and legends harken to those his grandfather told him —Samuel G. Freedman, *N.Y. Times Mag.,* 23 Oct. 1983

> One very dusty bottle in the cellars . . . harkens to the days of Napoleon —Anne Marshall Zwack, *Gourmet,* September 1985

Three commentators—Theodore Bernstein in a *Winners & Sinners* from about 1970, Copperud 1980, and Reader's Digest 1983—have noticed the *h(e)arken back* construction. They think it must be a mistake. But it is already fairly well established in general writing and is continuing to gain ground. If the present trend continues, *harken,* with or without *back,* may come to be regularly used to mean "hark back" in American English. We have no evidence that *hearken back* is establishing itself in British use, though it has occasional use in the U.S. At the present time, however, neither *hearken back* nor *harken back* appears to be replacing *hark back,* which continues in frequent use, both British and American.

has got   See HAVE GOT.

hassel   See HASSLE 2.

hassle   **1.** *Hassle* is not a colloquial term, or perhaps we should say it is not just a colloquial term. A good portion of the evidence we have collected for *hassle* comes from quoted speech, but over half of our evidence is from running text in newspaper and magazine articles. The noun is more common than the verb and appears proportionately more often in ordinary prose. However, neither the noun nor the verb is used in elevated or literary prose. Here is a sampling of citations:

Car pooling is seen by most people as a hassle — Martin Nemirow, *The Washingtonian,* October 1973

. . . who are too blasé to hassle him —*People,* 5 Apr. 1976

. . . few Belgians think the political hassle will go so far —David R. Francis, *Christian Science Monitor,* 17 Apr. 1980

. . . drugs are as much a solace and joy for the police as they are for those they hassle —Gore Vidal, quoted in *Rolling Stone,* 15 May 1980

. . . frustrated by hassles over leaks to the press — Jerry Kirshenbaum, *Sports Illustrated,* 25 Oct. 1982

It's a place where a face can go and not be hassled — John Chancellor, quoted in *Town & Country,* January 1983

Mr. Watt describes his controversial tenure as an unequaled "success story" despite "tremendous hassle and abuse" —Andy Pasztor, *Wall Street Jour.,* 18 Feb. 1983

2. The spelling *hassel* is a variant of *hassle* but is quite rare these days. Its heyday was in the early 1950s, when the word usually referred to a heated argument or a fight, but even then *hassle* was more common.

have got 1. Marckwardt 1958 points out that to many—perhaps most—Americans *have got* denotes mere possession, while *have gotten* denotes obtaining:

I haven't got a dime myself —E. L. Doctorow, *Loon Lake,* 1979

However much money you have gotten from Thaw it is only as much as he wanted to give you —E. L. Doctorow, *Ragtime,* 1975

Have got is believed by several British commentators (including Longman 1984 and Strang 1970) to be more common in British English than in American English. Historically it goes back to the 16th century. Marckwardt says that it developed in reaction to a weakening in the ability of *have* to denote possession because of its increasing use as an auxiliary verb. Thomas L. Crowell in *American Speech,* December 1959, and Gowers in Fowler 1965 suggest that *got* may have been inserted in the construction because of the tendency for *have* to occur as *'ve* in unstressed positions in the sentence.
Have got came under fire in American English from Richard Grant White 1870. White considered the *get* superfluous in the construction, and he also objected because he felt the use was not the original meaning of *get.* (Evans 1962 explains, however, that it was a perfectly natural extension of meaning.) It was White's first objection that went into the handbooks and grammar books. Hall 1917 mentions three such from about the turn of the century. Bierce 1909 objects, and so do many others. But by the time of Evans 1962 and Bernstein 1971 a greater tolerance had developed. Bernstein quotes Gowers in Fowler 1965 on the side of acceptance. Curiously, later British commentators—Phythian

1979, Longman 1984, Chambers 1985—pick up criticizing where the Americans left off. This resumption of an old theme is even more curious with the conjoined names of Fowler and Gowers on the side of acceptance. Here are some examples, old and new, of the use:

. . . ask George if he has got a new song for me — Jane Austen, letter, 27 Oct. 1798

Is it a farm you have got? —Charles Lamb, letter, 10 Jan. 1797

. . . has not Hobhouse got a journal? —Lord Byron, letter, 3 May 1810

Haven't you got your little camera with you? — Lewis Carroll, letter, 10 Aug. 1897

The Chinese haven't got anybody who'll protect them —Gough Whitlam, quoted in *The Listener,* 3 Jan. 1974

. . . how we have achieved the spelling that we have got today —Howard 1984

. . . Mat's got the notion that you dont care much for home or old friends —Emily Dickinson, letter, 24 Mar. 1852

"But have you got the grit, the character, the never-say-quit spirit it takes . . . ?" —Russell Baker, *Growing Up,* 1982

She knows she hasn't got real talent —Linda Wolfe, *N.Y. Times Book Rev.,* 27 Apr. 1986

Have will do perfectly well in writing that avoids the natural rhythms of speech. But in speech, or prose that resembles speech, you will probably want *have got.*
2. *Have got to.* Here we have another curiosity. *I have got to go* is listed as an incorrect expression in Joseph Hervey Hull's *Grammar* of 1829. But our earliest printed examples come from the middle of the 19th century. The early examples are British and literary—Disraeli, Dickens, George Eliot, Trollope, Ruskin, Oscar Wilde, H. G. Wells, George Bernard Shaw—while Hull's grammar book was written for school use and published in Boston. Later negative comment on this construction comes from Vizetelly 1920, Jensen 1935, Shaw 1970, 1975, 1987, and Harper 1975, 1985. In addition to the literary names mentioned (they are from Jespersen 1909–49, volume 4), we have these examples:

South Carolina has got to eat dirt —Henry Adams, letter, 2 Jan. 1861

But I've got to face the situation —Harry S. Truman, letter, 14 Nov. 1947

We have got to come into court—the high court of public opinion—with clean hands —Dwight D. Eisenhower, quoted in *Newsweek,* 30 June 1952

But I, as President, have got to maintain the accurate image that we do have a crisis —Jimmy Carter, quoted in *N.Y. Times,* 14 Feb. 1980

"You've got to be kidding," I said —Tip O'Neill with William Novak, *Man of the House,* 1987

Every man has got to stand on his own feet —William Faulkner, 8 May 1957, in *Faulkner in the University,* 1959

Have got to, have to, and the frequently recommended *must* can all be used in the present tense, but only *had to* can be used in the past. *Got to,* with the *have* omitted, is also used in the present tense, but primarily in speech. It is not, as Harper says, illiterate.

> "You just got to grow up a little, honey," she said — John Irving, *The Hotel New Hampshire,* 1981

> You got to get away where you can see yourself and everybody else. I really believe you got to do that — James Thurber, letter, 20 Jan. 1938

havoc See WREAK, WRECK.

he, he or she Many handbooks, among them Scott, Foresman 1981, Little, Brown 1980, 1986, Corder 1981, Irmscher 1976, Ebbitt & Ebbitt 1982, Trimmer & McCrimmon 1988, and other usage books such as Reader's Digest 1983 and Copperud 1970, 1980 have articles of varying length dealing with the problem of what third person singular pronoun to use in referring to a singular noun antecedent that can apply to either sex.

Everybody says that the traditional solution has been to use *he, his, him, himself,* the masculine third person singular. One researcher (Julia Penelope in *The English Language Today,* 1985) found that the prescribing of *he* as the generic third person singular seems to go back no further than Lindley Murray 1795. The actual practice, however, is much older (and *his* did duty as a neuter before *its* became established), but it was not the only solution available.

The use of generic *he* as a common-gender and common-number pronoun has lately been attacked as offensive by feminists and others. Bolinger 1980 points out that the problem was not discovered by feminists, but is an old one in the language. The lack of a common-gender and common-number pronoun has been felt since at least as far back as Middle English. The common solution has been to substitute the plural *they* (or *them* or *their);* even Chaucer used this dodge. We have many examples of how writers have dealt with the difficulty at THEY, THEIR, THEM 1, at the articles dealing with pronouns at AGREEMENT, and at the separate entries for the indefinite pronouns.

The use of the double pronoun *he or she, him or her, his or her,* is not recent either. Bolinger notes that it dates back at least to the 18th century and cites a quotation found by Otto Jespersen in a work by Henry Fielding: "the reader's heart (if he or she have any)." The double pronoun works well at times, but its frequent use leaves the writer open to two kinds of error. The first is the failure to follow through. Reader's Digest 1983 has an example: "The true measure of a human being is how he or she treats his fellow man." The other likely fault is the use of the double pronoun when the antecedent is plural. Allan Metcalf, in *American Speech,* Fall 1984, has this example: ". . . would add little or nothing to the citizens' understanding of the situation and advance his or her accomplishments." Besides susceptibility to these inconsistencies, the double pronoun has the disadvantage of awkwardness, as numerous commentators point out, especially when a context calls for it repeatedly.

Many of the books mentioned above suggest and exemplify other ways of avoiding generic *he.* Among them are casting the sentence in the plural, addressing the reader directly in the second person, and revising to avoid the pronoun altogether.

We suggest that you solve the difficulty in the way that you think will work best in a given situation—it is not likely you will want to use the same strategy every time for every audience. Those who are committed to the generic *he* will undoubtedly keep on using it. Those who are not will search for other solutions. See SEXISM 2.

The lack of a common-gender third person singular pronoun has stimulated many ingenious folk over the years to invent such a form. See EPICENE PRONOUNS.

head over heels Part of the appeal of this adverbial phrase suggesting a somersault is its lack of logic; the head is, after all, normally over the heels. The original phrase was *heels over head,* which was recorded as early as the 14th century. The variant *head over heels* has been in use since the 1700s. The OED described it as "a corruption" of *heels over head* in 1898, and some critics, such as Bierce 1909, cited it as an error, but common use had by then already made any questions about its logic purely academic. *Head over heels* has now entirely superseded *heels over head,* both in its literal sense:

> . . . tumbling him head over heels into the foam rubber pit —Gwilym S. Brown, *Sports Illustrated,* 6 July 1964

and in its figurative sense, in which it serves essentially as a synonym for *deeply* or *completely:*

> . . . when she falls head over heels for Barbra Streisand —Robert Brustein, *N.Y. Times Book Rev.,* 4 Apr. 1976

> . . . to which the Russians had committed themselves head over heels after a Marxist revolutionary government took power —Craig R. Whitney, *N.Y. Times Mag.,* 20 Apr. 1980

headquarter The verb *headquarter* is a relatively recent word. It was first recorded in 1903 and, according to our evidence, did not become common until the 1950s. It has both a transitive sense, "to place in headquarters," and an intransitive sense, "to make one's headquarters." The transitive verb is usually seen in the form of the past participle *headquartered:*

> . . . is headquartered a few blocks from the White House —Julia Malone, *Christian Science Monitor,* 10 Feb. 1981

> . . . both headquartered in Texas —David Tuller, *TV Guide,* 11 June 1982

> . . . a Xerox subsidiary headquartered in Ann Arbor —*Publishers Weekly,* 7 Oct. 1983

The intransitive *headquarter* is relatively uncommon, although its use dates back to at least the 1920s:

> News that Henry J. Allen . . . will headquarter in Washington —*Emporia* (Kans.) *Gazette,* 26 Dec. 1928

> . . . oil companies seemed unsure where to headquarter —*Newsweek,* 5 July 1954

> . . . who now lives and headquarters in San Antonio —Cleveland Grammar, *Houston Post,* 10 Sept. 1984

Headquarter became the object of scrutiny when the usage panel of Heritage 1969 was asked to vote on its acceptability "on a formal level," and proceeded to give it a resounding rejection. The panel of Heritage 1982 has repeated that rejection, and Harper 1985 has warned that *headquarter* "can still cause careful users of the language to shudder." While we do not doubt the truth of that observation, we suspect that there are also many careful users of the language who wonder, as we do, what the shuddering is about. In its usual use as a past participle (". . . is headquartered in New York"), *headquarter* is a clear, concise verb that is guilty of no offense other than newness. Its occurrence in ordinary writing should dismay no reasonable person. If any shuddering is merited, it may be for the intransitive *headquarter* (". . . will headquarter in New York"), which, because of its relative rarity, may sound odd to some ears.

head up   Like many other verbs, *head* is often used with *up;* a person can either *head* a committee or *head up* a committee. Because the *up* appears to add nothing to the meaning of *head* (although it might be argued that *head up* in some way implies a more active and energetic leadership than does *head* by itself), language watchers regard it as superfluous and therefore, as Harper 1985 puts it, "unacceptable to careful speakers and writers." Evidence of actual usage shows, however, that *head up* is extremely common both in speech and in writing. Our earliest record of it is from the 1940s, and we have found it to be in widespread use since the 1950s:

> Energetic, imaginative, forceful Sir James Stevenson headed up a committee of experts —William Haynes & Ernst A. Hauser, *Rationed Rubber,* 1942

> . . . who unselfishly headed up the fund —Harvey Breit, *N.Y. Times Book Rev.,* 18 Apr. 1954

> . . . casting about for a man to head up his political-science department —Thomas Drake Durrance, *Saturday Evening Post,* 29 May 1954

> . . . a dynamic young businessman who was heading up a forty-million-dollar a year enterprise —Tom McCarthy, *The Writer,* November 1968

> . . . Saxophonist Cannonball Adderley . . . heads up his quintet —*New Yorker,* 20 Aug. 1973

> . . . a bearded outdoorsman who heads up a private consortium of environmental groups —Jane Eblen Keller, *Smithsonian,* February 1980

We see nothing wrong with such usage, but you should be aware that it stands some chance of being criticized.

healthy, healthful   In the *Saturday Review* of 17 Mar. 1979 Thomas H. Middleton wrote, "The sad truth is that *healthy* has so often been used to mean 'healthful' that any dictionary worth its flyleaf just has to list 'healthful' as one of *healthy*'s meanings." This and a notice in a column by James J. Kilpatrick (28 June 1985) attest to the flourishing condition of the old issue of the distinction between *healthful* and *healthy.* Here is the gist of the prescription: *healthful* means "conducive to health" (it does) and *healthy* means "enjoying or evincing health" (it does), and never the twain shall change places. The trouble is that *healthy* is used for the sense of *healthful* just given. How long has this sloppy confusion of distinct words been going on? Since the middle of the 16th century—in other words, for more than four hundred years.

The distinction itself was invented by Alfred Ayres only in 1881. It has certainly been repeated many times since, right up into the 1980s. But it should surprise no one that the distinction has often not been observed: there never was a distinction in the first place (unless you count the 150-year head start *healthful* had on *healthy*).

Healthy, since its introduction in the middle of the 16th century, has been used much more frequently than *healthful* in both senses. So if you observe the distinction between *healthful* and *healthy* you are absolutely correct, and in the minority. If you ignore the distinction you are absolutely correct, and in the majority.

Here are some examples of each word in its main acceptations:

> . . . they demand more food and beer than the natives consider either decent or healthful —Anthony Burgess, *Saturday Rev.,* 22 July 1978

> He felt incapable of looking into the girl's pretty, healthful face —Saul Bellow, *Herzog,* 1964

> . . . would almost certainly result in a healthy marine back to normal duty within a week —Thomas C. Butler, *Johns Hopkins Mag.,* Summer 1971

> . . . to achieve more genteel or healthier living habits —J. M. Richards, *Times Literary Supp.,* 27 Nov. 1981

> As food costs rise, so does the price of a healthy diet —Patricia Wells, *N.Y. Times,* 6 June 1979

Bernstein 1965, 1971 disapproves *healthy* meaning "considerable," thinking it slangy. You can see from these examples that it is not:

> Count Frontenac, who had a healthy respect for the Iroquois —Samuel Eliot Morison, *Oxford History of the American People,* 1965

> Signed manuscripts by living novelists generally drew the healthiest prices —Richard R. Lingeman, *N.Y. Times Book Rev.,* 21 May 1978

heap, heaps   *Heap* has been used to mean "a great deal" since the 16th century. This sense may have developed from the use of *heap* to mean "a multitude; a crowd," which dates back to the period of Old English. The "great deal" sense was not recorded by either Samuel Johnson or Noah Webster, and it seems not to have come into widespread written use until fairly recently. It was first entered in a Merriam-Webster dictionary in 1864, when it was described as "low or humorous." Usage commentators in the 20th century have generally regarded it as a colloquialism. Our written evidence for it is considerable, and not all of it is notably informal, but it does confirm that this sense of *heap* is most at home in writing that has a conversational tone:

> Then Sankey roped me in to do a heap of things for him —Harold J. Laski, letter, 6 Aug. 1931

> It took a heap of work to settle the wilderness — Meridel Le Sueur, *North Star Country,* 1945

> . . . means the National League West is in a heap of trouble —Henry Hecht, *Sports Illustrated,* 11 June 1984

The plural *heaps* in this sense has much the same quality:

> There are heaps of things in the world which I should like to see changed —T. S. Eliot, "A Dialogue on Dramatic Poetry," in *Selected Essays,* 1932

> . . . you can landscape with heaps of annuals while these other things get going —Millicent Taylor, *Christian Science Monitor,* 9 Apr. 1971

There is also the adverbial phrase *a heap,* which is used to mean "much" or "very much." Its occurrence in writing is limited primarily to representations of rustic speech:

> "Hit pleasures me a heap to see you," John said — Elizabeth Madox Roberts, *Jingling in the Wind,* 1928

> Every time we see her she screams something like, "There's a heap worse things than death let me tell you. . . ." —Flannery O'Connor, letter, 27 Apr. 1963

hearken back   See HARK BACK, HARKEN BACK, HEARKEN BACK.

heartrending   Two commentators (Shaw 1987 and Copperud 1980) recommend *heartrending*—to be found in almost every dictionary—over *heart-rendering*—not to be found in any dictionary that we know of. *Heart-rendering* does exist—we have a citation for it in our files—but it is of such low frequency that we do not think you will ever be much tempted to use it.

hearty   See HARDY, HEARTY.

heave   In standard English *heave* has two past tense and past participle forms, *heaved* and *hove.* In nautical contexts *hove* is used.

> . . . cable can be hove in or veered under power — Great Britain Admiralty, *Manual of Seamanship,* 1951

> . . . the vessel is hove ahead by the capstan or windlass —Carl D. Lane *The Boatman's Manual,* 1951

> We . . . hove up the anchor —Roland Barker, *Ships & the Sea,* July 1953

> Aspinwall backed the foresail a bit and hove to on the starboard . . . tack —Anthony Burgess, *MF,* 1971

> . . . a small skiff that had just hove in sight —Nelson Bryant, *N.Y. Times,* 2 Jan. 1983

Hove is also used when the nautical meaning "to move in an indicated way" is borrowed for general contexts, especially in fixed phrases.

> I hove to at the stripling's side —P. G. Wodehouse, *Joy in the Morning,* 1946

> Towards the summit my two pathmakers hove in sight —W. K. M. Wood, *Scots Mag.,* May 1958

> She first hove into view on a *Family* episode last season —*Time,* 25 Sept. 1972

> . . . long before Mr. Agee hove on the horizon with a 46-page critique —Frederick Taylor, *Wall Street Jour.,* 21 Aug. 1981

Other uses of *hove* are for the most part folksy or dialectal.

> And in ploughing deep . . . there was hove into the light of day a very large and dead-looking toad —Della Lutes, *The Country Kitchen,* 1936

> . . . whoever hove those things in here —Mark Twain, *Tom Sawyer,* 1876

When a past tense or past participle is needed for *heave* in a context not involving nautical lingo, *heaved* is usually used.

> . . . the brakemen heaved large chunks of coal over the fence —Sherwood Anderson, *Poor White,* 1920

> . . . boiling seas and burning mountains heaved and tossed —*Selected Papers of Bertrand Russell,* 1927

> The Sheriff heaved massively in the chair —Robert Penn Warren, *All the King's Men,* 1946

> His stomach heaved —Marcia Davenport, *My Brother's Keeper,* 1954

> . . . heaved a sigh of relief —Daphne du Maurier, *Don't Look Now,* 1966

> . . . the Earth's crust was heaved up —Paul F. Brandwein et al., *Concepts in Science,* 1975

hectic   This word is mentioned in several books of usage, including Bremner 1980, Copperud 1970, 1980, Bernstein 1965, and Evans 1957, and has been submitted to the usage panels of Heritage 1969 and Harper 1975, 1985—all because of its treatment in Fowler 1926. Fowler was upset with what is now the prevalent sense of the adjective: "filled with excitement or confusion." He based his objection on etymology, thus, as Copperud observes, failing to take note of his own observation that etymology does not always determine meaning, an observation which he had tucked under the heading *True & False Etymology.* (See ETYMOLOGICAL FALLACY.)

Hectic is derived from a Greek word meaning "habitual." In English it was applied to a persistent fever present in some diseases, and then it came to mean "having such a fever" and then "red, flushed" and eventually acquired (around 1904) its present usual sense, which is similar to the figurative use of *feverish.* Here are a few examples that relate to the several fever senses, in case you are unfamiliar with them:

> Amelia found him up very early the next morning, more eager, more hectic, and more shaky than ever —W. M. Thackeray, *Vanity Fair,* 1848

> Hectic spots of red burned on his cheeks —Oscar Wilde, *The Picture of Dorian Gray,* 1891

> . . . identify it with the hectic flush of a consumptive —Robert M. Adams, *N.Y. Rev. of Books,* 20 May 1971

These will probably seem more familiar:

> I had a pretty hectic time for a while —John Buchan, *Greenmantle,* 1916

> No single reporter could do justice to the hectic weekend at the Waldorf —Joseph P. Lash, *New Republic,* 18 Apr. 1949

> . . . which had survived the hectic activity —Norman Mailer, *Harper's,* March 1971

No one after Fowler finds fault with the extended sense.

height   There are two problems here. The first is spelling. This word was originally formed in Old English from the Old English version of *high* and the suffix *-th;* the formation is exactly analogous to *breadth, width,* and *length.* The spellings *heighth* and *highth* are, therefore, the purest from the standpoint of etymology. However, they have been replaced in prevalent standard use by *height.*

Height comes into use by way of northern English dialects. The OED tells us that the *th* after the sound our *gh* used to stand for was pronounced \t\ in the north and \th\ in the south. As a result, northern spelling had no final *h* while southern spelling did. Milton spelled the word *highth.* But the northern version has come to prevail in modern use. *Highth* seems to have dropped out of use altogether, but *heighth* persisted into the first half of the 20th century at least, and is still occasionally used to stand for the pronunciation \ˈhīth\. Even though *heighth* and *highth* are etymologically pure and are not errors, we recommend that you stick to the mainstream spelling *height.*

Pronunciation is a different matter. The modern \ˈhīth\ is a bit of a phonological curiosity in itself, being a sort of combination of the more usual \ˈhīt\ and an older and apparently mostly disused \ˈhīth\, which would have been used for *highth.* It may have been influenced by the usual pronunciation of *eighth.* It is, however, a pronunciation too widespread among the highly educated and the highly placed to be considered anything but a standard variant. If it is your natural pronunciation, stick with it.

heist Copperud 1980 pronounces *heist* only fit for casual use and says well-edited publications avoid it. Flesch 1983 flatly contradicts him, saying that it is frequent in well-edited publications. Flesch produces evidence that he is right. He notes that all dictionaries label it *slang,* and suggests that it is in widespread use because it lends color to writing.

> The whole affair was neatly reckoned as *"le fric-frac du siècle,"* the heist of the century —Peter Andrews, *N.Y. Times,* 29 July 1979
>
> . . . as suspenseful as any movie heist since *Rififi* —Arthur Knight, *Saturday Rev.,* 6 Nov. 1971
>
> Missing the big jewel heist . . . was the low point for me —William Safire, *N.Y. Times,* 23 Sept. 1974
>
> . . . a gang of international crooks who have heisted an American atomic scientist —*Playboy,* April 1966
>
> Enter Supercrook, determined to heist the heroin —Newgate Callendar, *N.Y. Times Book Rev.,* 3 June 1979

help See CANNOT BUT, CANNOT HELP, CANNOT HELP BUT.

helpmate, helpmeet Both these words are standard. *Helpmeet* is the older and is formed by a misunderstanding from a verse in the King James Bible:

> And the Lord God said, It is not good that man should be alone; I will make him an help meet for him —Genesis 2:18

In the passage, *meet* is an adjective meaning "suitable." However, the reference was to the impending creation of Eve, and gradually *help meet* came to be understood as one word meaning "wife." *Helpmate* was formed by folk etymology from *helpmeet,* and is today the commoner word.

hence See FROM WHENCE, FROM THENCE, FROM HENCE.

he or she See HE, HE OR SHE.

her See IT'S ME.

herb See H.

here is, here are See THERE IS, THERE ARE.

heroics Evans 1957 says that *heroics* is usually meant derisively, an opinion that accords with the OED treatment. The use Evans is talking about seems to have had its origin in the bombast and rhetoric of the heroic tragedies popular during the Restoration. The original use seems to have referred to the overwrought and high-flown language typical of the plays, but it has come also to be applied to the flamboyant posturing and action involved. Heroics are what the real hero does not indulge in:

> He showed no enthusiasm, however, and merely remarked, without heroics, that it was up to him — *N.Y. Tribune,* November 1917
>
> . . . representing in his outlook the majority of his contemporaries, who have no time for heroics but only for heroism —*Times Literary Supp.,* 2 Jan. 1943
>
> The French soldiers were in fact played by German policemen, and Kubrick ruefully recalls how difficult it was to persuade them to stop playing at heroics and act scared —Andrew Bailey, *Rolling Stone,* 20 Jan. 1972

But the word has not been uniformly slighting or pejorative. Some authors have felt it to mean simply "heroic behavior":

> . . . contact with the Phoenicians conferred upon the Greeks the art of perpetuating their heroics in visible, graphic form —William Mason, *A History of the Art of Writing,* 1920
>
> It is impossible to exaggerate his veneration for the heroes and heroics of the American Revolution — Henry Seidel Canby, *Walt Whitman,* 1943

And it has been used of actions and efforts not really involving heroism at all, but rather determined or valiant effort. It turns up in sports reporting:

> Willie's heroics were a notable part of the Giants' sweep of last week's crucial three-game series with Brooklyn —*Newsweek,* 19 July 1954

More recently it has been applied to the efforts of medical and rescue personnel. Copperud found a reference to rescue workers after an earthquake that puzzled him, because his dictionaries defined only the bombast and posturing. Dictionaries can sometimes miss new developments. Uses like Copperud's are simply the application of the sports use to situations in real life which demand performance under difficult circumstances:

> . . . enough damage had already been done that the most extraordinary medical heroics were still in vain —Robin Marantz Henig, *N.Y. Times Mag.,* 28 Feb. 1982

There is really no problem here. The context will make the intent of the writer clear in most cases, and dictionaries will eventually catch up with writers.

hers *Hers* is another one of those pronouns from the northern dialects of Britain that became ultimately successful, driving the southern form—*hern*—out of standard use. *Hern* still exists in nonstandard varieties of English.

Hers was frequently spelled with an apostrophe two or three hundred years ago:

> . . . I sent for a dozen bottles of her's —Samuel Pepys, diary, 17 June 1663

Bishop Lowth used the form with the apostrophe in his grammar book of 1762. But in present-day use, *her's* is accounted a mistake in spelling.

See also YOURS.

herself   See MYSELF.

hesitant   *Hesitant* may often be followed by *about* or by *to* and the infinitive:

> . . . was not at all hesitant about presenting his strong objections to the Bay of Pigs plan —Irving Janis, *Psychology Today,* November 1971

> . . . is hesitant to offend any of the fraternity by impertinence —Paul Potter, *Johns Hopkins Mag.,* October 1965

Less often, *hesitant* is used with *in:*

> . . . we would be even less hesitant in embarking on foreign adventures of the Vietnamese sort —Joseph Shoben, *Change,* November–December 1969

hiccup, hiccough   *Hiccup* is the older spelling, and the one preferred by usage commentators, but *hiccough* has also been in use for several centuries (from 1628). *Hiccough* undoubtedly originated through a misunderstanding of *hiccup,* and the OED suggested in 1898 that it "ought to be abandoned as a mere error." It hasn't been, however. *Hiccup* is the more common spelling, but *hiccough* also continues in widespread, reputable use:

> 1918 appears as no more than a hiccough in this book —*Times Literary Supp.,* 10 May 1974

> . . . treatment for such afflictions as . . . stroke, food poisoning, hiccoughs —Sally A. Lodge, *Publishers Weekly,* 1 Oct. 1982

> . . . with hardly a hiccough —*The Economist,* 12 July 1985

The word is pronounced so that it rhymes with *stickup,* regardless of its spelling.

high, highly   Both *high* and *highly* are adverbs, but they are seldom used in the same situations. *High* is used for both literal and figurative distance up: climbed *higher,* rose *high* in the corporation, aims *high,* prices have gone too *high.* It is also used for rich living: living too *high* on the hog. *Highly* can denote high position in a scale: *highly* placed officials, *highly* paid. Most often, *highly* is used before an adjective or a participle in an intensive function: *highly* successful, *highly* polished, *highly* interesting, *highly* amused. *Highly* is occasionally used after verbs, sometimes in intensive function:

> . . . some of whom he respected highly —Eric F. Goldman, *Harper's,* January 1969

It is also used in the sense of "with approval or favor":

> . . . corporations thought highly of university-sponsored executive-development programs —*Dun's,* October 1971

> . . . does not think highly of many of his films —*Current Biography 1947*

Copperud 1970 expresses a preference for *high-priced* over *highly priced.* When used with *priced, highly* seems more idiomatic before the participle than following it:

> . . . a short, highly priced book —Malcolm Muggeridge, *Esquire,* December 1971

> . . . are not priced highly —*Sky and Telescope,* December 1969

hike   The use of *hike* to mean "increase" is strongly censured by Bernstein 1965, but it is disparaged by no other commentator. Our evidence shows that this sense has been in use since at least the 1920s. Our earliest evidence for both the noun and the verb is from William Allen White's *Emporia Gazette:*

> . . . shared in the wage hike under the new contract —*Emporia* (Kans.) *Gazette,* 16 Nov. 1926

> . . . any attempt to hike the cost of building in Emporia —*Emporia* (Kans.) *Gazette,* 2 May 1927

Much of our early evidence is from headlines, in which the word's brevity gives it an obvious advantage. Its use outside of headlines has been common for decades, however. The contexts in which it occurs almost always have to do with money, and the increases it describes tend to be abrupt rather than gradual:

> . . . the Administration's planned budget . . . has been hiked to $103 million —David L. Martin, *General Electric Investor,* Summer 1971

> . . . these charges are just another way to hike your overall room rate —Sylvia Porter, *Ladies' Home Jour.,* October 1971

> . . . the first drastic hike in oil prices during the 1973 Mideast war —Donald Kirk, *Saturday Rev.,* 19 Mar. 1977

> She also insists that the . . . program will not necessitate a tax hike —Al Green, *Houston Post,* 9 Sept. 1984

These uses of *hike* occur chiefly in American English.

him   See IT'S ME.

him or her   See HE, HE OR SHE.

himself   See MYSELF.

hinder   When *hinder* is used with a preposition, the choice is usually *from:*

> He could not hinder himself from dwelling upon it —Stephen Crane, *The Red Badge of Courage,* 1895

> . . . did not hinder her from giving spirited interpretations in comedy —*Current Biography,* March 1953

Occasionally, *hinder* may be found with *in:*

> My various societies . . . boost or hinder me in my scholarly endeavors —Wayne C. Booth, in *Introduction to Scholarship in Modern Languages and Literatures,* ed. Joseph Gibaldi, 1981

In the passive voice, *hinder* is often used with *by* to express agency or means:

> . . . whose scientific work is hindered by extreme eccentricity —*Times Literary Supp.,* 22 Oct. 1971

hindrance   **1.** *Hindrance* is the common spelling for this word, but the variant *hinderance* is still occasionally found in 20th-century writing:

> The purpose of the stricter judgment of the Fed. [sic] Court is to prevent hinderance of industry by too

easily obtained patents —*Jour. of the Patent Office Society,* June 1943

The subsequent omission of this facility is not a great hinderance as it is located in an urban enclave —James L. Mulvihill, *Professional Geographer,* August 1979

2. When used with a preposition, *hindrance* is usually used with *to:*

... his very superiorities and advantages would be the surest hindrance to success —Edith Wharton, *The Age of Innocence,* 1920

... all these are great hindrances to the development of the world on a liberal scale —Arnold J. Toynbee, quoted in Arnold J. Toynbee et al., "Will Businessmen Unite the World?" April 1971

Less frequently but still commonly, *hindrance* is used with *of,* as in the Patent Office Society example above and in the following:

... he still felt his rebellion against odious fate, everyone's fate, death, war; his tremor of knee and hindrance of speech —Glenway Wescott, *Apartment in Athens,* 1945

hint When used with a preposition, *hint* is usually used with *at:*

... a slender selection of essays, which hint quietly at what may be expected —Edmund Wilson, *Axel's Castle,* 1931

He was drinking too much and his neck and the under chin hinted at a plumpness which was not altogether a good sign —Victor Canning, *The Chasm,* 1947

... a submerged feeling or memory, that the two of them can only hint at but cannot express —Joyce Carol Oates, *Harper's,* August 1971

Less frequently, *hint* is used with *of:*

The face of the old retainer hinted of things still untold —Thomas B. Costain, *The Black Rose,* 1945

The evidence shows that once in a while *hint* is also used with *about, against,* or *for:*

"Why do you even hint about shame to me? . . ." —E. Temple Thurston, *The Green Bough,* 1921

Her husband's tutor was found to hint very strongly against such a step —Thomas Hardy, *A Group of Noble Dames,* 1891 (OED Supplement)

... not answering letters hinting broadly for invitations to visit —Grace Metalious, *Peyton Place,* 1956

his It was at one time believed—and the story still crops up from time to time—that the origin of the possessive -*'s* was as an elision of *his.* Although the supposition is wrong, *his* was actually sometimes used to mark the possessive.

... my cozen Edward Pepys his lady —Samuel Pepys, diary, 17 June 1663

See APOSTROPHE 2, 4; GENITIVE.

his or her See HE, HE OR SHE.

hisself Anyone who stops to think about it will notice that our standard reflexive pronouns are not very consistently formed. Some are formed on the genitive case of the pronoun: *myself, ourselves, yourself, yourselves. Herself* might be considered as a genitive as might *itself* if we allowed for merging of the two *s*'s. But then we have *himself* and *themselves,* patently formed on the objective case, and we have to admit that the third person reflexives are just different. Bishop Lowth back in 1762 was aware of the anomaly and opposed *himself* and *themselves* as corruptions. He plumped for *his self* and *their selves* instead, citing the first from Sir Philip Sidney and the second from some statutes of Henry VI. He seems to have found *himself* and *themselves* particularly objectionable when used in apposition to the subject of a sentence: "He himself did it." Here the use of the objective case as a nominative troubled him, although Lindley Murray 1795 would later accept it. Lowth was not, incidentally, bothered by the genitive in "I myself," because 18th-century printers regularly printed the genitive forms of the reflexive pronouns as two words—*my self, your self,* and so forth.

But usage paid no attention to the Bishop's plea for a more rational and consistent set of pronouns. *Hisself* and *theirselves* still exist, but they are considered nonstandard. You will find them, and *theirself,* in dialectal speech, in fiction as part of the speech of rustic characters, and occasionally used for humorous effect.

They run off as though Satan hisself was a'ter them with a red-hot ten-pronged pitchfork —Artemus Ward, "Interview with President Lincoln," 1861, in *The Mirth of a Nation,* ed. Walter Blair & Raven I. McDavid, Jr., 1983

I wouldn't want nobody to have to strain hisself —Flannery O'Connor, letter, 28 Feb. 1960

See also THEIRSELVES.

historic, historical *Historic* and *historical* are simply variants. Over the course of two or three hundred years of use, they have tended to diverge somewhat. *Historical* is the usual choice for the broad and general uses relating to history:

... an historical survey of the United States Army in wartime —*Current Biography,* January 1968

... a historical survey of popular music —John J. O'Connor, *N.Y. Times,* 10 May 1981

... an historical interpretation of Bonhoeffer's theology —*Times Literary Supp.,* 30 July 1971

... a possible way out of a political and historical tangle —Norman Cousins, *Saturday Rev.,* 30 Oct. 1971

Historic is most commonly used for something famous or important in history:

What I think marks both those times is that people who were in either of them knew they were in a historic moment —Arlo Guthrie, quoted in *Yankee,* August 1986

Greetings from historic Milledgeville where the ladies and gents wash in separate tubs —Flannery O'Connor, letter, 19 May 1957

On May 10, 1973, in a historic decision, the House voted 219 to 188 to stop the Defense Department from spending any more money on the war in Vietnam —Tip O'Neill with William Novak, *Man of the House,* 1987

But this is not a complete differentiation. *Historic* still crops up in the general sense:

> . . . the literal satirist, who might be only of limited historic significance —Robert B. Heilman, *Southern Rev.,* April 1970

Historical also means "important in history," but this sense does not appear to be very widely used any more:

> . . . the Dean, speaking from that most historical pulpit —Hamlin Garland, *Back-Trailers from the Middle Border,* 1928

Most of the usage writers pretend that the differentiation is more absolute than it actually is. But we would suggest that you go along with the general trend; bucking it may be historically justified but is more likely to interfere with the smooth transfer of your ideas from paper to reader.

You will have noticed that both *a* and *an* are used before *historic* and *historical.* A number of commentators prescribe *a* here, but you should feel free to use *an* if it sounds more natural to you. We find that more writers use *a* than *an* but that both are common. For more on the use of *a* and *an,* see A, AN.

hither   1. *Hither, thither, whither.* These three analogous adverbs, which basically mean "to here," "to there," and "to where," have been described by various commentators as old-fashioned, archaic, obsolescent, formal, pompous, and literary. The adequacy of any of those descriptions may be questioned ("old-fashioned" is probably best), but it is clear, in any case, that these are not ordinary words in common, everyday use.

Of the three, *hither* is least likely to be used alone.

> Hither Beecher removed his household in 1810 — *Dictionary of American Biography,* 1929

It occurs most often in the company of *thither* or *yon:*

> . . . the flame . . . blew hither and thither on the wind —James Stephens, *The Crock of Gold,* 1912

> . . . have continued to do, hither and thither in the world —Glenway Wescott, *Prose,* Fall 1971

> . . . elegant wood carvings jutting out hither and yon —Russell Baker, *Growing Up,* 1982

> . . . her fevered eyes roamed hither and yon over the headlines —Katherine Anne Porter, *Ladies' Home Jour.,* August 1971

It also continues to be used in the adjective *come-hither:*

> . . . a pretty girl with a well turned ankle and a come-hither smile —*The Autobiography of William Allen White,* 1946

Thither occurs considerably more often as a solitary adverb than *hither.* When used straightforwardly, it usually relates to movement to a geographical location, especially when such movement is on a large scale or is a major undertaking:

> . . . who seem to have migrated thither from Sennar —Sir James G. Frazer, *Aftermath,* 1937

> . . . the merchants had flocked thither from the South and West with their households to taste of all the lus-

cious feasts —F. Scott Fitzgerald, "May Day," in *The Portable F. Scott Fitzgerald,* 1945

> . . . to support any British army that marched thither —Samuel Eliot Morison, *Oxford History of the American People,* 1965

> He had relatives in New York and thither he sailed —*Dictionary of American Biography,* 1944

Thither is also sometimes used to deliberately evoke the language of the past:

> . . . has assembled accessories from all over the store, and thither we advise you to hie —*New Yorker,* 10 Dec. 1949

It is also used with *hither,* of course, and less commonly, with *yon:*

> . . . random couples necking thither and yon —Bennett M. Berger, *Trans-Action,* May 1971

The most common—or least uncommon—of these adverbs in current English is *whither.* It occurs in the same kinds of contexts as *thither:*

> . . . had left Chicago, whither he had emigrated, for the Soviet Union —Horace Sutton, *Saturday Rev.,* 5 June 1971

> . . . born in Quebec, whither his parents had removed —*Dictionary of American Biography,* 1928

> . . . the voyage from New York whither they had flown from the West Indies —Peter D. Whitney, *N.Y. Times,* 2 May 1954

Whither is also used figuratively:

> The . . . self-serving leader must try to imagine whither this restlessness may lead in the next five years —Michael Novak, *Center Mag.,* March–April 1971

> . . . describe the general musical situation in America and whither we are heading —Thomas Lask, *N.Y. Times,* 12 Mar. 1971

> . . . to discover whither modern science is hurrying us —Howard Mumford Jones, *Saturday Rev.,* 12 June 1954

A related figurative use is in rhetorical questions, which typically consist simply of *whither* followed by a noun, with no accompanying verb:

> With the exodus of the beautiful people and a generation gap among present upperclassmen and underclassmen, whither Harvard? —Franklin Chu, *Change,* December 1970

> . . . many a symposium on whither the arts —John Leonard, *N.Y. Times Book Rev.,* 15 Feb. 1976

> Whither the phonograph record? —Paul Kresh, *Stereo Rev.,* September 1971

Hither, thither, and *whither* show no sign of passing into obsolescence in the near future. Their place in current English is not large, but it appears to be firmly established.

2. In addition to its adverbial uses, *hither* has been used as an adjective meaning "near" since the 14th century:

> . . . this was just the hither edge of the oil slick — Archibald MacLeish, *N.Y. Times,* 17 June 1973

. . . at the hither side of the great bell —William Dean Howells, *Venetian Life,* new ed., 1872

. . . in the steppes of eastern Europe or hither Asia — W. P. Lehmann, *Language,* January–March 1954

Although not in the vocabulary of most people, this adjective has obvious staying power. The only commentators to have taken note of it are Hall 1917 and Evans 1957, both of whom regarded it with approval.

hitherto There are two complaints about *hitherto.* Flesch 1964 and Janis 1984 suggest avoiding *hitherto* because it is old-fashioned. For Janis if it is not old-fashioned, it is overformal. But neither label is borne out by the evidence. *Hitherto* is in frequent current use; it is not old-fashioned. And Bremner 1980 produces an example from the sports pages, not noted for their overformality, to complain about.

Bremner 1980 says the word means "up to now" and not "up to then." This is the gist of the second complaint, which can also be found in Bernstein 1965, Copperud 1970, 1980, and Bryson 1984. We find the argument back in a 1956 *Winners & Sinners;* there Bernstein says that now is the time implied by *hitherto.* It is, but we must be careful not to restrict our notion of time so severely that *now* refers only to today and everything else is *then.* For look at this example, which is typical of a certain approach to writing about the past:

> Bogus naturalization of immigrants and repeating at elections were now carried to hitherto unknown lengths —*Dictionary of American Biography,* 1936

The *now* in that passage refers to 1869 or 1870 (the article is about Boss Tweed) and means "at the time we are talking about," and *hitherto* there means "up until the time we are talking about." This use of *hitherto* is not rare in the 20th century:

> Hitherto when in London I had stayed with my family in Bedford Park —William Butler Yeats, *The Trembling of the Veil,* 1922

> No, Owen was a poet—a War Poet only because the brief span of his maturity coincided with a war of hitherto unparalleled sweep, viciousness and stupidity —Osbert Sitwell, *Noble Essences,* 1950

> Locke, too, saw the necessity of examining the problem of knowledge more thoroughly than had hitherto been attempted —Frank Thilly, *A History of Philosophy,* rev. ed. by Ledger Wood, 1951

> Hitherto Scottish students had in the main gone to John Balliol's college in Oxford —Sir James Mountford, *British Universities,* 1966

> They claimed only the power to exclude it from federal territories, where it had never hitherto existed —Harry V. Jaffa, *National Rev.,* 29 Dec. 1970

Underlying the critics' objection, though not always mentioned, is the existence of a contrasting word for *hitherto* that decidedly means "up until then"—*thitherto.* Two commentators, Bryson and Bremner, are clearly aware of the word. It is a nice word but very rare. It is strange for newspapermen like these to recommend it, for we have no evidence of its being used in newspapers. Here are two examples:

> . . . the ruts in the lane—thitherto as deep as the Union trenches before Vicksburg—had mysteriously

filled up by themselves —S. J. Perelman, *New Yorker,* 6 June 1953

> . . . was interrupted when his younger daughter, thitherto immersed in her reading, asked . . . —John Simon, *New York,* 5 Jan. 1976

Now if you want to devote yourself to the preservation of *thitherto,* we commend it to your use—it is a fine word. If not, you can go right ahead and use *hitherto* in the sense of "up until the time we are talking about" like William Butler Yeats. Or you can try the journalists' other suggestions: *theretofore* (almost as rare and bookish as *thitherto*) and *previously* (acceptable to all).

hoard, horde These words are homophones, and Chambers 1985, Bryson 1984, Shaw 1987, and Copperud 1980 all warn against confusing them. But as your dictionary will show you, there is no reason to confuse them from the standpoint of meaning. This is a spelling problem. Our evidence suggests that *hoard*—maybe the spelling just seems more familiar—is used in place of *horde:* "hoards of local golfers," "hoards of warriors." One creative misspeller, in a journal designed for educational consumption, managed to combine the two words: "hoardes of seagulls." If you think you are apt to misspell either of these words, check your dictionary.

hoi polloi 1. *Use with "the." Hoi polloi* is a Greek term that literally means "the many." Its use in English stretches back to a time when a good education consisted largely of mastering Greek and Latin. *Hoi polloi* was adopted by the well-educated as a term for the unprivileged masses. It was originally written in Greek letters:

> If by the people you understand the multitude, the οἱ πολλοὶ —John Dryden, *Of Dramatick Poesie, An Essay,* 1668 (OED Supplement)

> . . . one or two others, with myself, put on masks, and went on the stage with the οἱ πολλοι —Lord Byron, *Detached Thoughts,* 1821

As its use became more widespread in the 19th century, the transliterated form *hoi polloi* (rarely *oi polloi*) came to be preferred:

> After which the *oi polloi* are enrolled as they can find interest —James Fenimore Cooper, *Gleanings from Europe,* 1837 (OED Supplement)

> The *hoi polloi,* as we say at Oxford, are mindless—all blank —*Read & Reflect,* 1855 (OED Supplement)

Proper usage of *hoi polloi* did not become a subject of controversy until the early 20th century, when the argument that this term should not be preceded by *the*—because *hoi* literally means "the"—first began to be heard. The issue was not taken up by usage commentators until 1926, when H. W. Fowler asserted that "These Greek words . . . are equally uncomfortable in English whether *the* (= *hoi*) is prefixed to them or not . . ." and recommended avoiding the term entirely. Similar advice has since been given by Evans 1957 and Bernstein 1977. Other recent critics, such as Shaw 1975, have said only that *hoi polloi* should not be used with *the.* It is interesting to note that when *hoi polloi* was used by writers who had actually been educated in Greek, it was invariably preceded by *the.* Perhaps writers such as Dryden and Byron understood that English and Greek are two different languages, and that, whatever its literal meaning in Greek, *hoi* does not mean "the" in English. There is, in fact, no such independent word as *hoi* in English—there is only the term *hoi polloi*, which functions not as two words but as one, the sense of which is basically "commoners" or "rabble." In idiomatic English, it is no more redundant to say "the hoi polloi" than it is to say "the rabble," and most writers who use the term continue to precede it with *the:*

> ... the local hoi polloi —Herbert R. Mayes, *Saturday Rev.,* 9 Oct. 1971

> ... the hoi polloi like us —*Daily Mirror* (London), 7 Nov. 1974

> ... trouble with the *hoi polloi* —John Taylor, *Punch,* 27 Nov. 1974

> ... the hoi polloi ... can actually walk in off the street —Mordecai Richler, *N.Y. Times Book Rev.,* 5 Jan. 1975

> ... letting in the hoi polloi —Judy Klemesrud, *N.Y. Times,* 19 Dec. 1975

> ... mingling with the Roman hoi polloi —Richard Grenier, *Cosmopolitan,* October 1976

> Let the hoi polloi stand around —Abby Rand, *Harper's Bazaar,* November 1980

> ... the hoi polloi finally began —Frank Deford, *Sports Illustrated,* 9 July 1984

Use of *hoi polloi* without *the* is considerably less common, although not rare:

> ... while it "brought the news" of the world to hoi polloi —Eliot Fremont-Smith, *New York,* 15 Oct. 1973

> ... nauseating the civilized filmgoer, while around him *hoi polloi* laugh their heads off —John Simon, *N.Y. Times,* 24 Nov. 1974

> The critic walls out *hoi polloi* —Richard A. Lanham, *Style: An Anti-Textbook,* 1974

> ... tales of hoi polloi successfully routed from our private oceans —Russell Baker, *N.Y. Times,* 13 June 1982

Hoi polloi without *the* is certainly standard, but it sometimes has an unidiomatic ring to it (Bernstein 1977 describes it as "clumsy"). The decision you have to make as an intelligent writer, therefore, is whether you care more for etymology than for idiom. We recommend that you favor idiom, but if etymology has won you over, keep in mind that simply omitting *the* is not always enough. The purist should find fault with both of the following quotations:

> ... the chic and the near chic, and plain hoi polloi —John Corry, *N.Y. Times,* 27 Mar. 1974

> ... an aloof ... intellectual who did not cater to hoi-polloi —Harry Markson, *N.Y. Times,* 5 June 1983

The first, in the purist's view, is like saying "plain the masses," and in the second there ought not to be a hyphen, as we do not join "the" and "masses" with a hyphen.
2. An issue about which there has been surprisingly little comment is the use of *hoi polloi* to mean "the snobby elite," a sense which is almost directly opposed to the term's original meaning. Only Bernstein 1977 and Bry-

son 1984 have mentioned (and censured) this sense. Perhaps other commentators have chosen to ignore it—or have simply been unaware of it—because it occurs so rarely in print. We have only two written examples of it in our files, well separated in time:

> I could fly over to Europe and join the rich hoi polloi at Monte Carlo —Westbrook Pegler, *Times News-Tribune* (Tacoma, Wash.), 25 Sept. 1955

> It was the beginning of his Christmas present to them—a day away from their desks ... dining and drinking elbow-to-elbow with the Palm Beach hoi polloi —James T. Wooten, *N.Y. Times,* 21 Dec. 1972

Indications are, however, that this sense of *hoi polloi* is extremely common in speech. We first heard of it in the early 1950s, when it was reported to be well established in spoken use in such diverse locales as central New Jersey, southern California, Cleveland, Ohio, and Las Vegas, Nevada. Several members of our editoral staff at that time also testified to its common occurrence, and similar testimony in the years since strongly suggests that this sense of *hoi polloi* may now be more widely known and frequently used in speech than the older, etymologically accurate sense. We do not know for certain how this new sense originated. Bernstein 1977 speculates that it may have come about because of association of *hoi* with *high.* Another possibility is that the new sense developed out of the inherent snobbery of *hoi polloi.* In its original sense, *hoi polloi* is a term used by snobs or—more often—in mocking imitation of snobs. Even its sound has a quality of haughtiness and condescension (much like that of *hoity-toity,* a term that has undergone a similar extension of meaning in the 20th century, from its former sense, "frivolous," to its current sense, "marked by an air of superiority"). It may be that people unfamiliar with the meaning of *hoi polloi,* but conscious of its strong associations with snobbery, have misunderstood it as an arrogant term for the haves rather than a contemptuous term for the have-nots.

hold, *verb* Kilpatrick 1984 mentions an Indiana newspaper editor who objects to *hold a meeting,* but Kilpatrick is tolerant of it. He has looked it up in the OED and found that meetings were held as long ago as 1735 and that there was a reference of 1450 having to do with friends who held a great council. Copperud 1970, 1980 says that *hold a meeting* is widely aspersed in journalism, but we are not sure by whom. We agree with Kilpatrick and Copperud that *hold a meeting* is entirely standard.

hold, *noun* See AHOLD.

holocaust Usage writers who claim that *holocaust* is not a synonym for *disaster* and who, because of the older sense of a completely burnt sacrificial offering, say that *holocaust* has the more specific meaning "fiery destruction entailing loss of life" (Bernstein 1965) or "wholesale destruction by fire" (Bremner 1980) are taking advantage of the critic's license to discuss only a small incident in the whole story. *Holocaust* has had a more complicated semantic development than this restriction suggests.

The "burnt sacrifice" sense appeared in English by the middle of the 13th century, and related figurative uses are attested in the OED from 1497 on, although they are rarely found today. Uses in which the notions of death and destruction are preeminent did not develop until a couple of centuries later, but once started, they flourished more vigorously than the uses related to sacrifice. As a result, *holocaust* commonly refers to large-scale destruction, loss of life, fire, or all three at once:

> In many cases the population of guano birds shows marked cyclical changes—usually a gradual build-up followed by holocaust —*Nature,* 1 Dec. 1951

> . . . no fewer than seventy revolutions or civil wars up to 1903. Then the fighting stopped, after a terrible holocaust —H. Mathews, *The Nation,* 8 Nov. 1952

> In the July 1967 holocaust . . . about 2700 stores were ransacked —Russell Dynes & E. L. Quarantells, *Trans-Action,* May 1968

> . . . our long repressed fear of nuclear holocaust —*Vogue,* October 1982

> . . . the building burns . . . in a luridly awful holocaust —Valentine Cunningham, *Times Literary Supp.,* 23 Sept. 1983

> . . . increase the threat of global holocaust —Natalie Angier, *Time,* 24 Dec. 1984

One specific application of the word is, of course, to the genocidal slaughter of European Jews by the Nazis during World War II. When used this way, *holocaust* is often capitalized and is usually preceded by *the* unless it is used as an attributive:

> . . . a survivor of the holocaust —Barbara A. Bannon, *Publishers Weekly,* 3 Jan. 1977

> . . . a country so obsessed by the Holocaust —*Atlantic,* April 1983

> . . . concentration camps where Holocaust victims were exterminated —William R. Doerner, *Time,* 13 May 1985

Figurative meanings branch out in several directions from the basic meanings discussed above. Some are synonymous with *disaster* or describe some natural disaster (these are what critics specifically disapprove of). Some allude to the Holocaust, and others have a more tenuous connection to one of the basic meanings.

> . . . the holocaust of bank failures —E. W. Kemmerer, *The ABC of the Federal Reserve System,* 1936

> . . . a spiritual holocaust —Maxwell Geismar, *The Last of the Provincials,* 1947

> The Edsel holocaust threw us into The Dark Age of Applied Science —Jim Siegelman, *Harper's Weekly,* 12 July 1976

> . . . awakens to the ethical holocaust around him —Judith Crist, *Saturday Rev.,* 2 Oct. 1976

> . . . turn an ordinary matrimonial war into an explosive do-or-die end-of-the-world holocaust —J. Alan Ornstein, *The Lion's Share: A Combat Manual for the Divorcing Male,* 1978

> . . . Jackson's policy of Indian removal—a particularly shocking episode in America's home-grown holocaust —Eric Foner, *N.Y. Times Book Rev.,* 2 Mar. 1980

> . . . after the tornado . . . in a township garage that had survived the holocaust —Civia Tamarkin, *People,* 9 July 1984

Holocaust is still in the process of acquiring new shades of meaning, and the current interest in the Holocaust seems likely to spur this development on. The criticized "disaster" meaning is a part of this natural evolutionary process, so we see no reason to single it out as being particularly worthy of censure.

home, *adverb* Longman 1984 has a note saying that the adverb *home* is used with verbs of motion, the implication being that such use is standard. And so it is, and has been since Old English. It can be even used with *be* when there is the notion of movement.

> . . . Tuesday I raced home from school —Russell Baker, *Growing Up,* 1982

> . . . was called home to help his father —*Current Biography,* April 1966

> They knew that they were home and dry within five minutes —June Goodfield, *Science 84,* March 1984

This use is common in sports and in figurative use:

> . . . Kirk Gibson doubled home two runs —Herm Weiskopf, *Sports Illustrated,* 12 July 1982

> Turner hit the last ball to square leg for the Pilgrims to scamper home —T. A. L. Huskinson, *Cricketer International,* August 1976

> . . . Bach's music always brings us home —Otto L. Bettmann, *American Scholar,* Winter 1985/86

But there seems to have been some question about its use when no movement is implied, when its sense is "at home." Such use is called questionable by MacCracken & Sandison 1917 and colloquial by Watt 1967 and Bryant 1962. Copperud 1970, 1980 cites two other commentators who say that the use is good American usage, but not British; Longman 1984 says *at home* is better than *home* alone in formal British English. Our evidence shows this *home* to be standard in American English, at least in the more ordinary sorts of prose:

> . . . were willing to stay home —Thomas C. Butler, *Johns Hopkins Mag.,* Summer 1971

> . . . I would come and sketch in the late afternoon when the children were home from school —Aaron Shikler, *McCall's,* March 1971

> . . . my first weeks home were a delight —William Pennell Rock, *Center Mag.,* November/December 1971

> I am sitting home —Russell Baker, *N.Y. Times Mag.,* 7 Aug. 1977

> . . . their constituents back home are crying for more federal aid —Woody Klein, *N.Y. University Bulletin,* Spring 1967

It is also figurative:

> . . . walked into an economics course . . . and knew that he was home —Leonard Silk, *N.Y. Times Mag.,* 10 Aug. 1975

Copperud's commentators seem to be right. Adverbial *home* is apparently no issue in American English, but we have almost no recent British evidence for its use instead of *at home.*

home *noun,* **house** The folks who disparage the use of *home* in the sense of "house" divide roughly into two groups. One group is often associated by usage writers with Edgar A. Guest and his famous line, "It takes a heap o' livin' in a house t' make a home." They write like this:

> We build a *home* with love and time, and build a *house* with a hammer and saw —A. M. Stires, Jr., letter to editor, *Fine Homebuilding,* February/March 1981

> How can you in English buy a home any more than love or Killarney? You can buy a house and hope to make your home there —Ian Robinson, *Encounter,* January 1975

The other group distinguishes the words on the basis of class: Simon 1980 identifies *home* as non-U, while Paul Fussell, in *Class* (1983), identifies it with the middle class. Both of these gentlemen were anticipated by Emily Post 1927, who based her opinion on exactly the same grounds.

Both groups like to place the blame for *home* meaning "house" on the advertising of real-estate agents. Bernstein 1965, 1971, 1977 at least partially exculpates them from the charge. And well he should. The usage is much older than modern real-estate agents.

In Webster's Ninth New Collegiate Dictionary you will find the first sense of *home* divided into two parts, "domicile" and "house." The distinction represents modern use. The OED does not separate these senses, probably because the distinction is hard to make in the oldest examples. The earliest citation comes from the *Lindisfarne Gospels,* which are dated around 950, and is a translation of a passage from the New Testament that in the King James Version is the familiar "In my father's house are many mansions" (John 14:2). In the *Lindisfarne Gospels* the word rendered as *mansions* by the King James translators is *hamas*—the Old English for *homes.* Modern use seems to have begun with Felicia D. Hemans around 1835, in a reference to "the stately homes of England." Even Mrs. Hemans is nearly a century earlier than Babbitt and his real-estate promoters.

If we forget the practice of real-estate agents and advertising writers and turn to ordinary prose writers, we find that Bernstein is right in his observation that *home* and *house* are often interchangeable. Writers sometimes contrast them and at other times do not.

> Their house, I assume, gives them a large measure of happiness. Yet why does my calling their home vulgar also give me such a measure of happiness? —Aristides, *American Scholar,* Winter 1981/82

> ... had come down to New York from her home in Bridgeport, a clapboard house —E. L. Doctorow, *Ragtime,* 1975

> I saw the home of General Walker in Dallas—a big two-story battleship-grey clapboard house —Flannery O'Connor, letter, 17 Nov. 1962

> Our house is our home. We live there —*And More by Andy Rooney,* 1982

> ... 107 acres of land with a home on it —Stephen Singular, *New York,* 8 Dec. 1975

> ... a loan they were trying to get at the bank to make their house smaller —*And More by Andy Rooney,* 1982

> ... half of Foxy's home rested on a few cedar posts and Lally columns footed on cinder block —John Updike, *Couples,* 1968

A number of commentators have remarked on the tendency to buy a home and sell a house:

> ... he bought a home in the Hollywood Hills formerly owned by Howard Hughes —*Current Biography,* July 1965

> They talked about buying a new, smaller home.... They figured they could get $75,000 for their old house —*And More by Andy Rooney,* 1982

There is nothing wrong with distinguishing *home* and *house* if you want to. But be aware that many writers other than those involved in real estate will sometimes use them interchangeably.

home in on See HONE IN ON.

homograph, homophone, homonym Our correspondence shows that people are occasionally muddled by these words. *Homograph* is used for words that are spelled alike but are different in meaning or derivation or pronunciation: the *bow* of a ship, a *bow* and arrow. *Homophone* is used for words that sound alike but are different in meaning or derivation or spelling: *to, too, two; magnate, magnet; rack, wrack. Homonym* is used for homographs or homophones; sometimes it is used more specifically to designate words that are both homographs and homophones, like the verb *quail* and the noun *quail.*

John Algeo, in *The English Language Today* (1985), reports that confusion of homophones is a major subject of writers on usage in the popular press. Homophones certainly present spelling problems, and you will find plenty of them in this book. Homophones are also a primary source of puns.

Hon. See HONORABLE.

hone in on An issue looming on the usage horizon is the propriety of the phrase *hone in on.* George Bush's use of this phrase in the 1980 presidential campaign (he talked of "honing in on the issues") caught the critical eye of political columnist Mary McGrory, and her comments on it were noted, approved, and expanded by William Safire. Safire observed that *hone in on* is a confused variant of *home in on,* and there seems to be little doubt that he was right. *Home in on* is a fairly new phrase itself, one whose origins can be traced to the verb *home* as it relates to homing pigeons. The OED shows that *home* was first used in the sense "to fly back home after being released at a distant point" in the late 19th century. The extended use of this verb from which *home in on* is directly derived was first recorded in 1920 in a magazine called *Wireless World:* "The pilot can detect instantly from the signals, especially if 'homing' towards a beacon" (OED Supplement). Our evidence indicates that this use of *home* was confined chiefly to the military until the 1950s. It often occurred with *on,* as in "The missile homed on the target." Our first example of *home in on* is from 1951, in a context having to do with aviation. Our earliest record of its figurative use in a general context is from 1956. We did not encounter *hone in on* until George Bush used it in 1980, but we did record two instances of *hone in* in the '60s:

> ... looking back for the ball honing in to intercept his line of flight —George Plimpton, *Paper Lion,* 1965

> Wallace has been able to "hone in some basic issues ...," Bush said —*Houston Post,* 14 July 1968

George Bush again? Probably so. He was a congressman from Houston in 1968.

Recent evidence suggests that *hone in on* is becoming increasingly common. We have found it twice in the past few years on the pages of a popular magazine:

> . . . boys tend to hone in on a few concentrated fields of interest —Ruth Duskin Feldman, quoted in *People,* 20 Dec. 1982

> . . . Springsteen hones in on the plights and victories of the common man —Lisa Russell, *People,* 10 Sept. 1984

We have also noted its use in speech, and we received a phone call not long ago from an articulate and obviously well-educated woman who had read *home in on* in the newspaper and wanted to know if it was an error for *hone in on.* It may be that eventually *hone in on* will become so common that dictionaries will begin to enter it as a standard phrase; and usage commentators will then routinely rail against it as an ignorant corruption of the language. That is a development we can all look forward to, but its time is not yet. In the meantime, we recommend that you use *home in on* instead.

honeymoon   A curiosity noted with bemusement by Copperud 1970, 1980 is that some newspapers have regarded *honeymoon* as a word to be shunned in favor of *wedding trip.* We have evidence of this peculiar prejudice in our own files:

> Betty White's Honeymoon Center . . . was almost the subject for a Herald-Tribune resort-section article. The idea was given up when they couldn't dope a way to avoid using the word "honeymoon." That gazette has a rule against using the word in its editorial columns —Walter Winchell, syndicated column, 19 Apr. 1950

Bernstein 1971 also notes that some "conservative newspaper society pages" dislike *honeymoon,* and he traces the issue back to Bierce 1909, who asserted that such usage as "a week's honeymoon" was incorrect because the *-moon* in *honeymoon* means "month." There is good reason to believe, however, that the origins of the newspapers' objections to *honeymoon* may have nothing to do with Bierce's devotion to the etymological fallacy. Walter Winchell, in the column quoted above, also reported that the Herald-Tribune banned the word *body.* The implication is that *honeymoon* and *body* were felt to have risqué connotations offensive to the sensibilities of genteel readers.

Fortunately, readers are not now quite as genteel as they once were, and we seriously doubt that there are any so prudish as to take offense at *honeymoon.* We also doubt that any current newspapers continue to ban this innocuous word, but even if a few still do, there is no reason why you should.

honor   **1.** When used with a preposition, the verb *honor* may select *by* or *with,* the former occurring a little more frequently than the latter:

> . . . would honor its obligation to provide equal treatment to the would-be Negro attorney by establishing a law school —Harry S. Ashmore, *Center Mag.,* May 1968

> . . . the only American of Norwegian birth honored by a statue in Oslo —*American Guide Series: Minnesota,* 1938

In 1945 the Museum of Modern Art honored Strand with a widely praised one-man show —*Current Biography,* July 1965

> . . . the only Englishman in all history that the world honors with the surname of Great —Kemp Malone, *Emory University Quarterly,* October 1949

Honor is used less frequently with *for, at,* or *in:*

> . . . was honored for excellence in teaching —*Emory & Henry Alumnus,* Summer–Fall 1970

> . . . has been honored at half a dozen public luncheons —Joe Alex Morris, *Saturday Evening Post,* 10 July 1954

> . . . this principle has been honored in the original allocation of powers —Scott Buchanan, *Center Mag.,* September 1969

Very occasionally, *honor* may be found with *through:*

> The creators were honored through association of their names with their achievements —Lawson M. McKenzie, *Science,* 25 Dec. 1953

2. *Honor in the breach.* This phrase has continued in use since Shakespeare:

> It is a custom More honour'd in the breach than the observance —*Hamlet,* 1601

> Perhaps these provisions are most honored in the breach —*Yale Rev.,* Winter 1944

> . . . even this requirement is often honored in the breach —James B. Conant, *Slums and Suburbs,* 1961

> . . . titles are more honored in the breach than the observance —Charles Trueheart, *Publishers Weekly,* 24 Sept. 1982

Honorable   *Honorable* is a title of respect in American use but one with no official standing, and—perhaps not surprisingly—it is the subject of a number of conflicting commentaries. We set aside the vexed question of who is entitled to an *Honorable* and who is not as essentially a matter for books on etiquette, and concentrate here on the more linguistic aspects of the issue.

We can tell you this: the word is capitalized when used as an honorific. It is generally preceded by *the* (a terrible row over the omission of *the* seems to have gone on in the 1870s). It is generally followed by the given name, initials, or some other title (as *Mr.*). It is abbreviated to *Hon.* when appropriate (though the abbreviation was on William Cullen Bryant's *Index Expurgatorius* of the 1870s).

Copperud 1980 points out that H. L. Mencken was using the term derisively fifty years ago, and there is evidence that others do not always use the term with solemnity either:

> My former Secretary of Agriculture, the Hon. Charlie Brannan —Harry S. Truman, diary, 24 June 1955

It looks like this in more straightforward surroundings:

> . . . the court of the Honorable Harmon T. Langley —Frank De Felitta, *Cosmopolitan,* August 1976

Outright disapproval lasted into the 1930s:

> No American is "Honorable." "The Hon. Franklin D. Roosevelt" is as incorrect as "The Hon. Bath

House John Coughlin." It is strictly a British handle —Stanley Walker, *City Editor*, 1934

Copperud opines that the term seems "to be going out of use in our blunter age," but that sort of prediction does not always come true.
See also REVEREND.

hoof   Both the plurals *hoofs* and *hooves* are in standard use. Phythian 1979 and Copperud 1970, 1980—citing older commentators—say that *hoofs* is more common. But in contemporary print, *hooves* is more common, and especially so in the trade journals of those concerned with horses, cattle, goats, and mules:

... trampled the grass with their hooves —Daniel B. Weems, *Raising Goats,* 1983

A farrier visits every four to five weeks to trim hooves and reset shoes —Marcia Werts, *Morgan Horse,* July 1984

And it is also more common in general sources:

The hooves furnished glue —William Least Heat Moon, *Blue Highways,* 1982

... a horse with golden trappings and gilded hooves —E. J. Kahn, Jr., *New Yorker,* 9 July 1984

... take nails out of tires as well as horses' hooves —Hardcastle, *Punch,* 25 Sept. 1974

Llamas are good climbers, and their padded feet are less damaging to wilderness paths than the hard hooves of horses —*Ranger Rick,* April 1985

But *hoofs* is not rare:

... its tiny hoofs —Charles C. Mann, *Natural History,* June 1986

... pull the yuletide king through the air on winged hoofs —*Dallas Morning News,* 10 Dec. 1984

The Secret of Healthy Hoofs —advt., *Quarter Horse Track,* February 1984

hope   1. *Hope,* when used with a preposition, is usually followed by *of* or, a little less frequently, by *for:*

... America was the hope of liberty —Van Wyck Brooks, *The Flowering of New England, 1815–1865,* 1936

... the next year low water defeated hopes of grandscale river navigation —*American Guide Series: Minnesota,* 1938

... the ability of the present Soviet leaders to fulfil their hopes of efficiency —*Times Literary Supp.,* 9 Apr. 1970

... continuation of the War threw a dark cloud over his hope for professional employment —Harry R. Warfel, *Noah Webster: Schoolmaster to America,* 1936

... it was sufficiently promising to arouse hopes for his future —*Times Literary Supp.,* 15 Sept. 1966

... he took his manuscript back from a large New York firm that had low hopes for it —Judith Appelbaum, *N.Y. Times Book Rev.,* 11 May 1983

Very occasionally *hope* is used with *in, on, over* or *to* plus the infinitive:

He had previously put his hopes in Gambetta —*Times Literary Supp.,* 12 June 1969

... she does not place her hopes on books ... smuggled out of Russia —*Times Literary Supp.,* 18 May 1967

... a faint stirring of hope over the possibilities of a Korean truce —*Current History,* July 1952

... was their only hope to keep North Carolina from voting so heavily for Wallace —Robert Sherrill, *Saturday Rev.,* 17 June 1972

Hope may also be followed by a clause introduced by *that:*

... expressed his hope that the young artist would not abandon photography —*Current Biography,* December 1964

... expressed his hopes that such programs could reverse "the worst tendency in ... education ..." —*Current Biography,* January 1966

2. *Hope* is used idiomatically in all the following phrases: *in the hope(s) of, in hope(s) of, in the hope(s) that,* and *in hope(s) that.*

In the hope of bringing about a peaceful settlement —Senator Mike Mansfield, in *A Center Occasional Paper,* June 1968

They put to sea ... in the hopes of drifting across the Pacific —Geoffrey Murray, *Christian Science Monitor,* 4 June 1980

... do not invert the normal order of words in hopes of sounding more genteel —Barzun 1985

... doping out basketball scores in hope of one day winning a pool —Evan Hunter, *N.Y. Times Book Rev.,* 13 Nov. 1983

... in the hope that the issue could be resolved —Bernard Gwertzman, *N.Y. Times Mag.,* 4 May 1980

We're lumping them all together here in the hopes that somewhere in the pile you will come across just what you need —*New Yorker,* 17 Dec. 1950

In hopes that something good might be brought out of the ruins, he began to pick up —John Fischer, *Harper's,* December 1969

At one time an infinitive may have followed *in hopes,* but this construction seems not to occur in contemporary writing:

... to see the End of it, and in Hopes to make something of it at last —Daniel Defoe, *Moll Flanders,* 1722

Also occurring in idiomatic use are the phrases *with the hope(s) of* and *with the hope that.* The former occurs with either the singular or plural of *hope,* although the singular occurs more often. The latter is attested in our evidence only in the singular:

... with the hope of establishing a government that was both anti-Communist and anti-Fascist —*Current Biography,* June 1964

. . . and with the hopes of having it repaid them with interest, whenever they have occasion to return the visit —Thomas Gray, letter, 9 Oct. 1740

. . . to ascertain student views with the hope that they might understand —Donald McDonald, *Center Mag.*, July–August 1970

With the hope of has some slight variations, such as *with little hope of, with any hope of,* and *with its hope of.*

hopefully No one knows why a word or phrase or construction suddenly becomes popular—it just happens. And when it does, it is sure to attract the displeased attention of some guardian of the language. The split infinitive, for instance, seems to have become suddenly popular during the 19th century, and there are still people who worry about it. The sentence-modifying use of the adverb *hopefully* is a like case, and it is recent enough that its history can be traced reasonably clearly.

The adverb has been in use since the 17th century; Samuel Johnson in his 1755 dictionary lists two senses; Noah Webster in 1828 lists three. Neither seems to have encountered the word as a sentence modifier, but Johnson's third quotation may point to a source from which such a use could develop:

> From your promising and generous endeavors we may hopefully expect a considerable enlargement of the history of nature. *Glanville.*

But *hopefully* does not appear to have been very widely used; it was available if writers needed it, but few writers did. No clear-cut example of the sentence-modifying use has been found earlier than the 1932 example given in the OED Supplement. Even as late as the middle 1950s, examples are scarce. Our files have just a couple that are unmistakable:

> The benefits to me and hopefully to our bank have been many —Richard A. Booth, *U.S. Investor*, 29 May 1954

> This gift was, of course, intended to help each of these institutions, but also at the same time to call attention dramatically to the inadequacy of salaries in the whole college-teaching profession, and hopefully, to encourage others to assist in improving what is clearly a very serious deficiency —Nathan M. Pusey, *President's Report, Harvard University,* 1955–1956

We have, besides these, several somewhat ambiguous examples.

> The doctor had said hopefully two weeks in hospital, two weeks more in town, and then we could leave. Things didn't turn out as planned —Helen Thurber, letter, 14 July 1941

(If the doctor used the word, we have an example of the new use, but if it merely characterizes his manner and attitude as he spoke, the use is traditional. The context will not let us be sure which is the case.)

> They are popular only in the sense of being, most of them, hopefully designed for the people —John W. Clark, in *British and American English Since 1900*, 1951

> If they . . . confuse the advisability of pregnancy with that of having another highball, the hopefully unexpectant mother should demand a change of venue — James Thurber, letter, 6 Dec. 1954

Copperud 1970, 1980 gives the date of the rapid expansion of use of *hopefully* as a sentence modifier as "about 1960." Bernstein 1962 exhibits a clear-cut example, presumably from the *New York Times,* and calls it solecistic. A 1963 edition of Funk & Wagnalls *Standard College Dictionary* recognizes the use. Copperud 1964 and Flesch 1964 both produce examples from unidentified newspapers and disapprove the use. The evidence in our files shows a considerable increase beginning in 1964.

The onslaught against *hopefully* in the popular press began in 1965, with denunciations in the *Saturday Review* (January), the *New Yorker* (March) and the *New York Times* (December). The ranks of *hopefully* haters grew steadily, reaching a peak around 1975, which is the year the issue seems to have crossed the Atlantic (the OED Supplement has British examples of use dating from 1970). Viewers with alarm there would repeat all the things American viewers with alarm had said, and add the charge of "Americanism" to them.

The *locus classicus* of most of the charges leveled against sentence-modifying *hopefully* is Follett 1966. Follett died in January 1963 (Jacques Barzun later editing the manuscript for posthumous publication), and it is likely that his analysis was one of the earliest to be written down. He seems to have been the originator of the theory that this use of *hopefully* was un-English and that it came from "hack translators" of German who used it to translate the German *hoffentlich.* But he does not produce any hack translations to back up his assertion; all his examples seem to be from American newspapers. Follett also tosses off in passing two of the other points that M. Stanley Whitley, in *American Speech,* Summer 1983, identifies as the chief objections to *hopefully:* a grammatical one concerned with the function of the adverb ("strains the sense of *-ly* to the breaking point"), and a social one objecting to people who use vogue words. He also complains that this *hopefully* lacks point of view (another much repeated charge), which seems reasonably close to the charges of ambiguity made by E. B. White in the *New Yorker,* 27 Mar. 1965, and in Strunk & White 1972, as well as by Barzun 1985 and others. His discussion lacks only a complaint about the loss of the original sense of the word.

There is a good deal of entertainment to be had in examining many of the statements made about *hopefully,* but we haven't enough space here for so much detail; you will have to look into such books as Nickles 1974, Cook 1985, Harper 1975, 1985, Copperud 1964, 1970, 1980, Phythian 1979, Bremner 1980, Colter 1981, Johnson 1982, Freeman 1983, Einstein 1985, Newman 1974, and Michaels & Ricks 1980 for some of the more entertaining comments.

We will, however, look a bit further at the supposed un-English origin of this use. Follett suggested that *hopefully* came from the translation of German *hoffentlich* as we have noted; Bernstein 1965 seems to be the first to have put that theory into print. German *hoffentlich* receives quite a bit of notice by the critics. Also mentioned by both American and British commentators is German *hoffnungsvoll,* which can be translated by *hopefully* in its uncontroversial sense. In addition we have a Southern California academic who, in a 1972 letter to the *Times Literary Supplement* mentions Yiddish; Simeon Potter, who is British, in the 1972 *Compton Yearbook* says he thinks it came through American Yiddish or Pennsylvania Dutch; and Einstein 1985 quotes a correspondent—also British—who would not have us overlook a Dutch word. All this is very ingenious but is not supported by a single shred of evidence. The earliest citation is from the *New York Times Book Review,* and all of the other early citations are American, so those British observers who complain about it as an Americanism, at least, are on solid ground. But we find no overt association with any foreign language in the early examples, nor are they from the sort of lofty academic prose in which one might detect a German influence. With such models as *surely* and *certainly* already long established, a foreign origin need not be sought.

We should point out that opinion has not been unanimously opposed to this usage. Thomas H. Middleton expressed his acceptance of it in the *Saturday Review* in 1974, 1975, and 1976 at the height of the outcry against it. Many college handbooks took a measured approach, noting both widespread acceptance and opposition. Some opponents predicted that it would be accepted, and others gave up:

> I regard the word "hopefully" as beyond recall. I'm afraid it's here to stay, like pollution and sex and death and taxes —E. B. White, letter, 16 Feb. 1970

Still other commentators changed their minds:

> . . . I sweat with embarrassment to read the article that I wrote about 'hopefully' in 1975 —Howard 1983

> To be quite honest, a decade ago I was on the side of the objectors, but in recent years additional thought about the matter has changed my mind —Bernstein 1977

William Safire came around to acceptance, his defection sourly noted by Kilpatrick 1984, still holding out. And Rudolf Flesch, who in 1964 was one of the earliest objectors, was by 1983 plugging the word:

> After a quarter century of furious struggle, the purists have been roundly defeated. . . . It's an established, accepted, often needed English word. Don't shy away from it. —Flesch 1983

In general, much of the furor in the press has abated since the high tide of the mid-1970s. True, Edwin Newman has not changed his mind:

> In addition, the "hopefully" disease is far advanced —*San Francisco Examiner,* 7 Oct. 1987

And all usage books and handbooks now have to take some notice of the question. But the storm appears to be moderating. And on 10 November 1985 the Prince of Wales used the word during a televised press conference at the Smithsonian Institution in Washington. What more prestigious cachet can be put on it? Academics and literary people also use it, at least occasionally:

> Hopefully some examples, especially those of Chapter IX, have already given rise to reflections —Strang 1970

> If you begin to elaborate it, you may gain something, but you'll lose the heart of it. That is, what the poem hopefully has —William Stafford, *Writing the Australian Crawl,* 1978

The sentence-modifying *hopefully* has by no means driven the older senses from use:

> . . . tempers the gloom, adding hopefully, "and there may be a lesson in that." —Baron 1982

> . . . many who have set out hopefully upon it have turned back, frustrated and disheartened —Barnard 1979

To sum up: *hopefully* had been in sporadic American use as a sentence modifier for some thirty years before it suddenly caught fire in the early 1960s. What is newly popular will often be disparaged, and criticism followed rapidly, starting in 1962 and reaching a high point around 1975. There has been a considerable abatement in the fuss since and many commentators now accept the usage, but it seems safe to predict that there will be some who continue to revile it well into the next century. You can use it if you need it, or avoid it if you do not like it. There never was anything really wrong with it; it was censured, as Bolinger 1980 notes, because it was new, and it is not very new any more.

Two substitutions, incidentally, have been proposed for sentence-modifying *hopefully.* One is *hopingly,* which is in Johnson 1755 and Webster 1828; it has not, however, been attested in use since 1883. The other is *hopably* or *hopeably.* Bremner 1980 asserts that it has been used, and he uses it himself, but Bernstein 1965, 1971, Safire 1980, and Cook 1985 call it nonexistent. We have no evidence of its use apart from Bremner.

See also SENTENCE ADVERB.

horde See HOARD, HORDE.

host The credit for first raising the question of the propriety of *host* as a verb seems to belong to Roy Copperud; he has dealt with it in his 1960, 1964, 1970, and 1980 books. Copperud blames the usage on society columnists. Flesch 1964 calls it journalistic. Two usage panels, those of Heritage 1969 and Harper 1975, have also condemned it.

The thrust of the criticism assumes that *host* is a modern invention, whether of society writers or other journalists or of radio and television. These assumptions are, as Quinn 1980 points out, incorrect. The OED dates the verb back to the 15th century; it was used by Spenser (and by Shakespeare, though in a different sense). Evidence of its use apparently stops early in the 17th century and then reappears at the end of the 19th. It seems to have survived dialectally in the U.S.; the American Dialect Dictionary has an early 20th-century regional American example. The OED Supplement records a 1939 example, and then many from the 1950s on. The verb is widely used, in the press and elsewhere, and is entirely standard in spite of the critics' reservations.

> . . . read at the celebration dinner hosted (invariably) by Anson himself —Isaac Asimov, *Whiff of Death,* 1958 (OED Supplement)

> Moscow had backed out of its promise to host the World's Fair —Frank Deford, *Sports Illustrated,* 28 Sept. 1970

> . . . on television in Pittsburgh, where he briefly hosted an afternoon variety show —*Current Biography,* February 1967

> . . . I hosted a luncheon —William L. Shirer, *Saturday Rev.,* 25 Mar. 1972

> . . . where he hosted a dinner last night —*Jamaica Weekly Gleaner,* 13 Feb. 1974

> Though the scores of friends he generously hosted at the Savile were given no reason to suspect it, he remained a man of acutely slender means —Randolph Quirk, *Style and Communication in the English Language,* 1982

house See HOME *noun,* HOUSE.

hove   See HEAVE.

how   *How* as a conjunction in the sense of *that* is
aspersed by Ayres 1881, Vizetelly 1906, Bernstein 1965,
and Phythian 1979—which makes nearly a century of
aspersing. The usage itself is a bit older, however; the
OED tracks it back to Aelfric, the Anglo-Saxon grammarian and writer of religious prose, around 1000. It is
a little unfair to equate the usage flatly with *that,*
although the OED does so and our dictionaries do too.
It is, in fact, a usage in which the underlying notion of
"the way or manner in which" is weakened to varying
extents, and in many cases appears—at least to the
modern reader—to be entirely absent. Here are a few
older examples of the use:

> And anon the tidings came to king Philip of France
> how the King of England was at Boulogne —Lord
> Berners, translation of Froissart's *Chronicles,* 1523

> When therefore the Lord knew how the Pharisees
> had heard that Jesus made and baptized more dis-
> ciples than John —John 1:4 (AV), 1611

> And it is pretty to hear how the King had some
> notice of this challenge a week or two ago, and did
> give it to my Lord General to confine the Duke —
> Samuel Pepys, diary, 17 Jan. 1668

> I have heard how some critics have been pacified
> with claret and a supper, and others laid asleep with
> soft notes of flattery —Samuel Johnson (in Ayres
> 1881)

> Bob Cratchit told them how he had a situation in his
> eye for Master Peter —Charles Dickens, *A Christ-
> mas Carol,* 1844 (in OED)

If there is a problem with this use of *how*—and Evans
1957 declares it standard—it may be that it is falling out
of literary and written use and being more and more
confined to speech. We do have 20th-century evidence,
but not a great deal since mid-century, except in speech:

> It was odd how writers never seemed to have any-
> thing to do except write or live —Martha Gellhorn,
> *Atlantic,* March 1953

> I won't waste your time this afternoon in telling you,
> in the political tradition, all about how I am myself
> a farmer —Adlai E. Stevenson, *Speeches,* ed. Rich-
> ard Harrity, 1952

The OED notes that this sense of *how* has appeared as
part of the compounds *how that* (found in Chaucer and
the King James Bible) and *as how* (attested as early as
Smollett's *Roderick Random* in 1748); *how that* is
apparently no longer used, but *as how* continues in
modern use. See AS HOW.

how come   *How come* is a familiar phrase of obscure
origin that first came to attention as an Americanism in
the middle of the 19th century. We say "of obscure origin" because for a time there was considerable speculation about its origin. It was considered dialectal and was
supposed to be a shortening of such phrases as "How are
you coming on?" "How are things coming toward you?"
"How comes it that . . . ?" "How came it . . . ?" and
"How do you come on?" Some of these expressions
were used in the East, according to Vizetelly 1922, and
one or two were held to be common in northern Ireland.
A later commentator, in *Proceedings of the American
Dialect Society* 14 (November 1950), associates the

phrase with Gullah *hukkuh.* Interest in its origin seems
to have waned since.
   Vizetelly finds the phrase to be "of ambiguous meaning," as well he might, given the strange phrases he lists
as its possible origin. But the only obscure example we
have seen is in the OED Supplement and is taken from
T. S. Eliot's *Sweeney Agonistes.* All the others seem to
mean "why," and, if we do need a longer phrase to
derive it from, "how comes it . . ." would seem adequate
from the standpoint of meaning (Krapp 1927 phrases it
as "how does it come," which seems a bit stilted.)
   Krapp labels it colloquial and slang; Evans 1957,
Bernstein 1965, and Harper 1975, 1985 (deriving it from
"How does it come about that . . . ?") find *how come*
unsuitable in writing. Reader's Digest 1983 dismisses it
as "informal only." Flesch 1964 finds it an acceptable
and useful idiom, however, and Safire 1982 defends it
spiritedly against Bernstein, Evans, and Harper, as well
as a couple of correspondents. One of Safire's correspondents mentions being corrected in fourth grade, so the
disapproval of *how come* may be part of the school-
teacher tradition too.
   How come is a little bit like the verb *bust:* its use in
writing is on a higher level than its use in speech seems
to be—it is a social climber in print. Its rise in respectability probably started after World War II. We have
many journalistic examples:

> If a marine's "everyday routine" is so simple, how
> come the Army couldn't hold the Naktong River
> *twice* without them? —*Time,* 23 Apr. 1951

> And yet for all this self-indulgence, he has managed
> somehow to achieve what Max Beerbohm called in
> his own case "a very pleasant little reputation." How
> come? —Joseph Wood Krutch, *Saturday Rev.,* 30
> Jan. 1954

> One thing they're studying now is how come the por-
> poise can swim so fast with so little power —Richard
> Joseph, *Esquire,* August 1965

> How come the ensemble can dance precisely in 5/4
> time, but when 16 swans bow to the prince they bend
> over haphazardly at 16 different angles? —Nancy
> Goldner, *N.Y. Times Mag.,* 30 May 1976

> And, for that matter, how come they never have
> donuts in Peking . . . ? —*And More by Andy Rooney,*
> 1982

> Construction was obviously not stone, but iron.
> How come? —Edwards Park, *Smithsonian,* Febru-
> ary 1985

> Most of the "eak" verbs are regular—leaked, peaked,
> squeaked, streaked. Then you get speak-spoke. How
> come? I don't know —James J. Kilpatrick, *Pitts-
> burgh Press Sunday Mag.,* 29 Sept. 1985

   Writers simply seem to find *how come* a sassier—
Safire says "nastier"—and more emphatic *why.* We
have not yet found it in surroundings more elevated
than those we have quoted.

however   The main problem raised by the commentators about *however* is its placement in the sentence.
When used to mean "on the other hand, nevertheless,
but" some commentators—Strunk & White 1959, 1972,
1979 and Zinsser 1976 among them—hold that *however*
should not begin a sentence. This opinion is older than
Strunk & White, but we are not certain where it began.
Harper 1975, 1985, Bremner 1980, Bernstein 1971, and

Heritage 1982 disagree with the prohibition; Bremner calls it a myth. Copperud 1970, 1980, Bremner, Bernstein, and Janis 1984 make the point that the *however* should be placed where it most effectively emphasizes the words the writer wants to emphasize. Here are a few examples of how other writers have chosen to place *however:*

> ... made the 17th century Holland's Golden Era. In the 18th century, however, Holland suffered a gradual decline —William Petersen, *Encounter,* December 1954

> Critics were in general agreement in praising his sensitivity and fluent technique.... Some, however, found fault —*Current Biography,* July 1967

> Clearly the Guevara diaries were documents of the greatest political and historical interest and importance. However, neither the Bolivians nor the Americans ... were at first prepared to authorize their publication —*Times Literary Supp.,* 14 Nov. 1968

> ... seeing sights on a flaming July day is tough. However, I found it very pleasant —Henry Adams, letter, 3 July 1859

> Black revolutionaries also face ethical dilemmas, however —Denis Goulet, *Center Mag.,* May 1969

> It would have to come when I was in no state to answer your letter with words of cheer. However, better late than never —James Thurber, letter, 19 Mar. 1940

The only point that needs to be made is that there is no absolute rule for the placement of *however;* each writer must decide each instance on its own merits, and place the word where it best accomplishes its purpose.

The treatment of the subject in Strunk & White suggests that placing *however* first in the sentence makes it mean "to whatever extent" or "in whatever way." In fact, the context determines this sense of *however* no matter where it occurs in the sentence:

> Such are the harsh facts, and no new formulas, however ingenious, ... can make them disappear —Walter Laqueur, *Commentary,* January 1972

There are also some objections to the combination of *but however* as redundant. Longman 1984, with an example in which the *but* and *however* are separated, rebuts the objections, saying that the combination is widely and respectably used. The objection seems to be grounded chiefly in Fowler 1926 and 1965; the examples in Fowler 1965 seem to be of the very kind recognized by Longman. This issue, then, is apparently primarily a British concern.

See also WHATEVER 1.

human At the noun entry for *human* in the OED, Murray, the editor, observes that it was formerly much used and starts off with an example from Lord Berners in the 16th century. But, he continues, it is "now chiefly *humorous* or *affected.*" It is hard to find much that seems either humorous or affected in the 19th-century examples he offers, however. Bierce 1909 is the first American objector. He succinctly states the usefulness of the term:

> We have no single word having the general yet limited meaning that this is sometimes used to express—a meaning corresponding to that of the

word *animals,* as the word *men* would if it included women and children.

But he rejects it.

From such slender beginnings arose a minor industry of disparaging the noun use—an industry almost entirely based on not looking at the OED examples, as Jensen 1935 attests. Writing more than 400 years after Lord Berners, he says that *human* "has not yet acquired good standing as a noun."

The curious thing about this issue is its persistence in what has been called the folklore of usage—that is, persistence in believing something is wrong with this noun in spite of its having been declared standard by such commentators as Bernstein 1965, 1971, Evans 1957, and Flesch 1964. The persistence of both views is reflected in contemporary handbooks: Guth 1985 says it is not generally accepted while Irmscher 1978 says it is acceptable. Copperud 1970, 1980 says there is still substantial objection to it. And the evidence seems to show that writers tend to avoid it even now; our recent citations include a great many more examples of *human being* than of *human.* Those who use the noun use it just the way Bierce described:

> ... he can give scientific reasons for thinking that humans (or some humans) might have been expected to have tails —Howard 1983

> ... that microbes ... caused diseases and that insects carried them to humans —*Johns Hopkins Mag.,* Summer 1967

> While lower animals can deceive and mislead through camouflage and similar devices, as far as we know only humans can consciously and deliberately lie —Carol Z. Malatesta, *N.Y. Times Book Rev.,* 31 Mar. 1985

Our conclusion is that even though this noun has been standard for some 450 years, many people still believe that it is somehow tainted and avoid it.

hung See HANG, HANGED, HUNG.

hypallage See RAISING.

hypercorrection Sir Isaac Newton set down three laws of motion, the third of which is often stated thus: "For every action there is an equal and opposite reaction." If we were to translate this—albeit roughly—to apply to usage and grammar, we might get something like "For every correction there is an equal and opposite hypercorrection." *Hypercorrection* is a term used by linguists and grammarians for "equal and opposite" errors made in the course of avoiding other errors which are frequently subjected to correction.

The most frequently discussed hypercorrections involve pronouns, especially the use of a nominative pronoun in a slot calling for an objective pronoun. Examples:

> ... the most irritating thing to we military people — four-star general on television, 6 Nov. 1983

> ... designed for you and I —radio commercial, 3 Mar. 1980

Such pronoun mistakes are particularly frequent in compound objects such as *you and I, my wife and I.* How many of these are really the result of hypercorrection is a matter that can be disputed, since such usages can be found dating back farther than the inception of traditional grammar. *Between you and I* is frequently mentioned as a hypercorrection; yet it can be found as long ago as the diary of Samuel Pepys, who wrote "between my wife and I" on 5 July 1663. And we hear it put in the mouths of characters in Restoration comedies:

> ... Impertinent people, which, between you and I *Jack,* are so numerous —Thomas Shadwell, *The Sullen Lovers,* 1668

You will find more on this subject at BETWEEN YOU AND I and at PRONOUNS.

Another hypercorrect pronoun usage is the substitution of *whom* for *who* in sentences like "Whom shall I say is calling?" You will find more on this at WHO, WHOM 1.

Another common hypercorrection involves the use of an *-ly* adverb where an adjective or flat adverb is called for:

> ... there's an awfully lot of methane and ammonia in the universe —exobiologist quoted in *Science News,* 16 Aug. 1969

> ... the seldomly used player —network television baseball announcer, Fall 1986

> ... because he tested positively for steroids —network television sports announcer, 25 Dec. 1986

> ... unless my eyes have gone badly —cable television sports announcer, 3 Nov. 1985

> ... go home and think deeply, longly, and ... —Boston city councilman, 4 Aug. 1983

> I once had a dentist who never failed to say "open widely" —John Ciardi, in Harper 1985

Lamberts 1972 lists the disputed adverbs *muchly, thusly,* and *soonly* as forms created by hypercorrection. Similarly we will sometimes find *well* for *good:*

> ... make your dog look as well as possible —dog handler at Westminster dog show, 11 Feb. 1985

> A correct use, cited just to show how well it sounds —Copperud 1964

Some instances of what look like hypercorrect adverbs after linking verbs may be lingering traces of an older style of using adverbs instead of adjectives after such verbs. You will find one common example of this practice discussed at LOOK 1.

Another substitution occasionally mentioned as a hypercorrection is the use of *as* in place of *like:*

> All three lamps are pure brass, and not brass plated, as some similar looking products —advt., *New Yorker,* 1 Feb. 1988

This is another practice with long-standing antecedents. See LIKE, AS, AS IF 2.

Perrin & Ebbitt 1972 also mentions as hypercorrections the substitution of some verb forms for others, such as using *lie* for *lay,* and certain pronunciations. Robert F. Ilson, in *The English Language Today* (1985), mentions the involuted sentences typically produced in trying to avoid a terminal preposition. And Allan Metcalf, in *American Speech,* Fall 1984, mentions a new one: the insistence by some on using *his or her* as a nonsexist substitute for generic *his* or disapproved *their* is

leading to the use of the singular form even when the antecedent is plural. See HE, HE OR SHE.

Hypercorrections are also called *hyperurbanisms.* You may find them discussed under this heading in Johnson 1982, for instance.

See also SUBJUNCTIVE.

hyperforeignisms   By analogy with the terms *hypercorrection* (which see) and *hyperurbanism* ("aiming for a prestige form and overshooting the mark"), we suggest the term *hyperforeignism* to denote an unsuccessful attempt to give an authentic foreign pronunciation to a foreign-derived word being used in English context. Such flubs open the speaker up to ridicule much more than garden-variety, down-home mispronunciations such as \ˈrev-ə-lənt\ for *relevant,* since the spectacle of people seemingly trying to get above themselves and then coming a cropper attracts the hoots of both democrats and aristocrats. A veteran columnist writes:

> One of our most famous TV anchorpersons ... pronounces coup de grâce "coo dee grah." How refeened —Herb Caen, *San Francisco Chronicle,* 16 Oct. 1987

The hapless anchorperson may have misguidedly dropped the final \s\ with *Mardi Gras* (pronounced \ˈmärd-ē-ˌgrä\) in mind. More than one ambitious diner has likewise overgeneralized and committed the faux pas (\fō-ˈpä\) of ordering vichyssoise as \ˌvē-shē-ˈswä\. (As a rule of thumb, French leaves *s* silent only when it is the last letter of a word.)

Another Gallic trap lies in the pronunciation of *e,* especially at the end of a word, where most of the problems arise. When surmounted by an acute accent (as in *café* or *attaché*) or followed by silent *r* or *t* (as in *beret* or *pourparler*), the pronunciation is \ā\; but when not so accompanied (as in *cache* \ˈkash\ or *vichyssoise* or *à la carte*) the final *e* is silent. Yet we have occasionally recorded educated speakers rendering *cache* as \ka-ˈshā\, perhaps misled by *cachet,* which is indeed pronounced that way. A different problem arises in the cases of words like *chancre,* where a truly French pronunciation would violate phonological constraints of English. The usual solution, especially with older loanwords of this type *(massacre, mediocre, reconnoitre/reconnoiter, theatre/theater),* is to end the word with a fully anglicized \-ər\. *Raison d'être,* a more recent loan and still quite foreign-looking, gets either an authentic French pronunciation with voiceless final \r\ or the nearest more-or-less-English equivalent, with \-rə\. *Cadre* is a special case, the most common pronunciations being \ˈkad-rē\ and \ˈkäd-rä\—the latter rhyming with, and possibly modeled on, the Spanish loan *padre.* For more on final *e,* see FORTE.

Our passing reference above to "silent *r*" skirts another area of difficulty. Again a rule of thumb: French *r* is silent only at the end of a word after *e,* and not always then. The rather widespread pronunciation of *reservoir* as \ˈrez-ə(r)-ˌvwä\ is pseudo-French.

In a curious position are a couple of words long naturalized in English which sometimes get partly French pronunciations even from people who have no idea that the words were borrowed from French. The case of *envelope,* of which the \ˈän-\ version has attracted some withering comment, is discussed at ENVELOPE 1. The pronunciation \ˈsänt-ə-ˌmēt-er\ for *centimeter* may have conceivably been influenced by *centime,* though it is specially prevalent not among money people but among nurses and doctors. These pronunciations are not incorrect—they are French as far as they go—but by now one would expect to hear consistently the fully anglicized \en\ in these words.

Queen of the hyperforeignisms is *lingerie.* Of the multitudinous pronunciation variants for this word, the most common seems to be \ˌlän-jə-ˈrā\, the product of some extremely tenuous analogies with words like *entrée.* An approximation to the French would be \ˌlanᵖ-zhə-ˈrē\, but, while that pronunciation is certainly established, so many others are also established that it is unlikely to sweep the field.

In another category of hyperforeignism, a form is created not by the overly enthusiastic application of sound–spelling correspondence rules from the lender language, but by the application of more familiar rules from a *different* language. Thus, Americans are aware, from examples like *chancre* and *cachet* and a dozen others, that the French pronounce *ch* as \sh\. Having mastered this much, they proceed to rechristen Chile's president Augusto Pinochet (\ˌpē-nō-ˈchet\) Gallically as \ˌpēnō-ˈshä\, though Spanish *ch* is pronounced \ch\ as in English. Among generic words, Italian-derived *adagio* \ä-ˈdä-jō\ gets Frenchified as \ä-ˈdäzh-ō\, but gets its revenge when we pronounce the Latin-derived *viva voce* (\ˌvī-və-ˈvō-sē\) as if it were from Italian, \ˌvē-və-ˈvō-chä\. Both of these pronunciations are well established.

hyphen, hyphenate Phythian 1979 objects to *hyphenate* as unnecessarily long since *hyphen* is already a verb. *Hyphenate,* however, is the more common of the two:

. . . although long-lived is hyphenated —Simon 1980

Photocomposition is particularly stupid at breaking words and hyphenating them in the wrong places — Howard 1984

Hyphenate is probably reinforced in its preferred position by the noun *hyphenation,* the noun *hyphenate,* and the adjective *hyphenated.* There is also a verb *hyphenize,* which is very seldom used.

hypothecate, hypothesize Einstein 1985 admits that in his head *hypothecate* and *hypothesize* mean essentially the same thing and that his ear prefers *hypothecate.* He then bemoans the fact that they mean different things—as you will be told they do if you listen to Shaw 1987 or Bernstein 1962 or Fowler 1926, or if you look in an old dictionary. But if you look in Webster's Third you will find two verbs spelled *hypothecate* with different derivations. The newer one (dating from 1906) does mean "hypothesize." The newer one can also be found in the OED Supplement, which, however, does not accord it a separate entry.

Neither verb *hypothecate* is often used, and the two appear not only in different contexts but in different sources. The older *hypothecate,* which has to do with pledging something for security, appears in business and legal contexts. The newer *hypothecate,* meaning "hypothesize," seems to be found most often in scientific writing and in linguistics, and only occasionally elsewhere—the OED Supplement has a letter of Ezra Pound's and we have an example from a high-school text on art history.

So, Mr. Einstein and others can feel free to use the word their ear prefers. Many more writers use *hypothesize;* in our files it is more than twice as common as both verbs *hypothecate* put together.

I

I The entries at *I* in many usage books—Cook 1985, Nickles 1974, Copperud 1970, 1980, Venolia 1982, and Bryson 1984, among others—deal primarily with issues discussed to some extent elsewhere in the same book or in someone else's book. The leading topic of commentary is the use of *I* in some object position where *me* would be expected, and especially as the second part of a compound of the "someone and I" type.

I have been planning a piece on personal pronouns and the death of the accusative. Nobody says "I gave it to they," but "me" is almost dead, and I have heard its dying screams from Bermuda to Columbus: "He gave it to Janey and I." . . . Love to you and she from Helen and I —James Thurber, letter, 25 June 1956

You will find more on this and related subjects in the articles at BETWEEN YOU AND I; HYPERCORRECTION; IT'S ME; MYSELF; PRONOUNS.

Other aspects of the first person singular pronoun and its use or avoidance can be found at WE 1 and PRESENT WRITER.

-ic, -ical English contains a considerable number of adjective pairs ending in *-ic* and *-ical:* for instance, *biologic, biological; electric, electrical; ironic, ironical; mythic, mythical.* Some of these pairs are essentially

interchangeable while others are differentiated in use. Sometimes the *-ical* variant will have a wider or more transferred semantic range than its counterpart in *-ic*—and sometimes not. A number of these pairs have been treated in usage books, and you'll find some of them here: see CLASSIC, CLASSICAL; ECONOMIC, ECONOMICAL; HISTORIC, HISTORICAL.

If you are uncertain which of a given pair of these adjectives to use, you had better rely on a good dictionary, such as Webster's Ninth New Collegiate Dictionary. A good dictionary will show you which senses belong to which variants if they are indeed differentiated in use. Sometimes there is less differentiation than usage writers would like there to be.

ice cream, ice water It is sometimes instructive to take a look at the usage issues of the past, so that we may be chastened and not so easily carried away by those of the present. It may be hard to believe that the innocuous terms *ice cream* and *ice water* were once a subject of intense scrutiny and cerebration. (They were hyphenated then.)

By mere carelessness in enunciation these compound words have come to be used for *iced-water* and *iced-cream*—most incorrectly and with a real confusion of language, if not of thought. For what is called ice-water is not made from ice, but is simply water iced, that is, made cold by ice; and ice-water might be warm, as snow-water often is. Ice-cream is unknown —Richard Grant White 1870

As for ice-cream, there is no such thing, as ice-cream would be the product of frozen cream, i.e., cream made from ice by melting. What is called ice-cream is cream *iced;* hence, properly, *iced* cream and not *ice*-cream. The product of melted ice is *ice*-water, whether it be cold or warm; but water made cold with ice is *iced* water, and not *ice-water* —Ayres 1881

These paragraphs are the product of intellectual reasoning upon idiom by two important commentators of another age, many of whose other opinions are still kept alive in usage books today. Think about that over your next bowl of ice cream or glass of ice water.

idea From Jensen 1935 to Trimmer & McCrimmon 1988 we find a modest tradition in handbooks—mostly those intended for college freshmen—fostering the view that *idea* means "mental conception, notion" and that its use in other significations is vague, imprecise, or indiscriminate. This restriction will not withstand examination of even a modest selection of typical modern uses of *idea.* To begin with, it is worth observing that the sense the handbooks insist upon as being the precise meaning is the very one decried as "modern cant" by Dr. Johnson (reported by James Boswell in *Life of Samuel Johnson,* 1791). Richard Chenevix Trench quotes Boswell and adds his own thoughts on the subject (in the 13th edition of *English Past & Present,* 1886):

What now is 'idea' for us? How infinite the fall of this word from the time when Milton sang of the Creator contemplating his newly-created world,
    'how it showed,
      Answering his great *idea,*'
to the present use, when this person 'has an *idea* that the train has started,' and the other 'had no *idea* that the dinner would be so bad.' Matters have not mended since the times of Dr. Johnson; who, as Boswell tells us, 'was particularly indignant against the almost universal use of the word *idea* in the sense of *notion* or *opinion,* when it is clear that *idea* can only signify something of which an image can be formed in the mind.' There is perhaps no word in the whole compass of the language so ill treated, so rarely employed with any tolerable correctness; in none is the distance so immense between what properly it means, and the slovenly uses which popularly it is made to serve.

Before looking at those modern uses, let us remind ourselves that *idea* is a polysemous word—that is, a word of many meanings—and compared to such workhorses as *break, run, set,* and *take,* it is a word of little semantic spread indeed. The following uses are all standard:

The idea rather is to terrorize liberal Senators with the thought of a runaway convention —Arlen J. Large, *Wall Street Jour.,* 2 June 1969

. . . but they die comforted, in cleanliness and in dignity. That was the idea of the place —Michael T. Kaufman, *N.Y. Times Mag.,* 9 Dec. 1979

. . . a booster dose . . . every three or four years is a good idea —Dodi Schultz, *Ladies' Home Jour.,* August 1971

They begin with an ideological premise rather than with an idea for a story —Lewis H. Lapham, *Harper's,* November 1971

. . . it greatly strengthened his romantic attachment to the idea of the English gentleman —Arthur Mizener, *The Saddest Story,* 1971

The natty look of navy and white is having a strong revival this spring with classical nautical shapes as well as Oriental ideas —*Women's Wear Daily,* 25 Oct. 1980

. . . had little idea of what they wanted to do —Larry A. Van Dyne, *Change,* September 1971

We have very very little idea about Indian population here —Everett H. Emerson, radio interview, 3 July 1975

. . . our compensation was a room in the Allerton Hotel. The idea being: if we showed enough initiative, we'd rent the room and thus have compensation for our singing —Win Stracke, quoted in Studs Terkel, *Hard Times,* 1970

The plot of his opera is an original idea about life after death —Rosemary Brown, *Ladies' Home Jour.,* September 1971

ideal *Ideal* is sometimes considered to be an absolute adjective. See ABSOLUTE ADJECTIVES.

identical *Identical,* says Bernstein 1965, takes the preposition *with* or *to.* But in *Winners & Sinners,* 15 Oct. 1964, he had taken a different view. Criticizing this sentence,

He said that Presidents Dwight D. Eisenhower and John F. Kennedy, faced with similar legislation, had taken positions identical to his —*N.Y. Times,* 9 Oct. 1964

Bernstein said "the favored preposition is 'with,' not 'to.'" Where he derived this idea is uncertain, unless he saw Follett 1966 in manuscript (Follett prescribes *with* but shows only examples with *to*) or Treble & Vallins 1937 (who prescribe *with,* not mentioning *to*).
    Opinion on the matter is divided between Treble & Vallins 1937, Sellers 1975, Phythian 1979 (all British), Colter 1981 (Canadian), Himstreet & Baty 1977 (U.S.), and Follett 1966 (U.S.), who prescribe *identical with* and Bernstein 1965, Copperud 1970, 1980, Harper 1975, 1985, Heritage 1982 and Longman 1984, who accept both *with* and *to.*
    Evidence shows *identical with* to be the older form, attested in the OED as far back as the 17th century. Follett claims that *identical to* is an Americanism, but the evidence is too sketchy to be certain of that. Our earliest citation for *identical to* is American:

Such a situation is identical to that which would exist if . . . —*Scientific American,* June 1922

But its use is not exclusively American; Longman 1984 recognizes British use, and we have a few examples:

. . . and yet the decoration of the Cheyenne tepee and 'chief sticks', and their version of the Sun Dance, were not identical to those of their neighbours —H. W. M. Hodges, *Antiquity,* September 1957

This situation is identical to the survival in North America of earlier English terms that have long since passed out of use in the mother country —John Geipel, *The Viking Legacy,* 1971

In 1950 our evidence showed *identical with* to be about twice as frequent as *identical to;* since then new accessions for each form have been about equal. Neither preposition appears to be eclipsing the other, and both are fully acceptable. We note only one trace of preference in our evidence: all of our mathematical citations use *with.* Here are a handful of examples of both constructions:

> The boat was small, identical to the one in which they landed —Norman Mailer, *The Naked and the Dead,* 1948

> . . . a preliminary injunction almost identical to his original restraining order —*Newsweek,* 16 Dec. 1946

> . . . when 0 is added to any given number, the sum is identical with the given number —Mary P. Dolciani et al., *Modern Algebra and Trigonometry,* 1973

> . . . advantages almost identical with those that we ourselves obtain —John Wyndham, *The Kraken Wakes,* 1953

> . . . some of their implements were identical with those displayed in museums at New Bedford —Henry Bettle Hough, *N.Y. Times Book Rev.,* 25 Apr. 1954

identify   When *identify* is used with a preposition, it is usually *with:*

> . . . his audiences identify themselves closely with his predicaments and revel in his triumphs —*Current Biography,* June 1953

> He identified vigorously with J. Edgar Hoover, the great sleuth —A. J. Liebling, *New Yorker,* 9 Oct. 1954

> . . . my father in some way identified himself with the Great Commoner, and this seemed to me purely a pose —Edmund Wilson, *A Piece of My Mind,* 1956

> . . . the reader watches an imagined consciousness unfold and identifies with it —Howard Mumford Jones, *Saturday Rev.,* 23 Apr. 1955

> . . . Henry Adams had personal reasons to identify himself with Washington; he was the grandson and great grandson of Presidents —Alfred Kazin, *Harper's,* December 1968

> . . . Whitman found himself as man and artist by identifying with New York —Alfred Kazin, *Harper's,* December 1968

This sense of *identify* apparently was borrowed from the field of psychology in which it began to be used in the early 20th century. The OED Supplement shows the earliest use to be from A. A. Brill's translation of Freud's *Interpretation of Dreams,* 1913. There is no disagreement among language commentators with the fact that the use is firmly established and is acceptable. Rather, disagreement arises about the use or nonuse of the reflexive pronoun. Follett 1966, Macmillan 1982, Harper 1985 and Simon 1980 all maintain that omission of the pronoun is an error arising from the jargon of psychology. Up until the 1940s, our evidence shows that the pronoun was used more often than not; however, over the last 35 or 40 years, use of the pronoun has become optional, as you can see from the examples

above. The usage panel of Heritage 1982 finds either use or nonuse of the pronoun equally acceptable.

idiom   *Idiom* is a word you will find with some frequency in this book, as in most usage books. It is not an especially precise word—Roberts 1954 calls it "loose and unscientific"—and it is generally used by usage writers for some construction or expression that they approve of but cannot analyze.

Roberts observes that for some reason *idiom* often refers in English to combinations involving prepositions and adverbs—you will find plenty of those throughout this book. The word is also frequently applied to those expressions or constructions that either are not transparent from the usual current meanings of the individual words that make them up or that appear to violate some grammatical precept. Vizetelly 1906, for example, defended *ice cream* and *ice water* as idioms, because they had been attacked as illogical (see ICE CREAM, ICE WATER).

The tension between idiomatic usage and logical analysis is one of the chief sources of usage comment, and has been since at least the middle of the 18th century. For a typical 18th-century treatment of an idiom, see HAD RATHER.

idiosyncrasy, idiosyncracy   A number of critics since Fowler 1926 (Watt 1967, Copperud 1964, 1970, 1980, Bryson 1984) warn against the *-cy* spelling, calling it a misspelling. Fowler also claimed that the *-cy* spelling spoiled the sense, but he had trapped himself in his etymological musings—there is no evidence that any one using the *-cy* spelling meant anything except *idiosyncrasy.*

The evidence in the OED shows that the *-cy* spelling goes back as far as Sir Thomas Browne's *Pseudodoxia Epidemica* in 1650; there are also some 19th-century examples. An article in *Word Study,* May 1957, listed 19 citations for the *-cy* spelling from 1892 to 1953 found in such sources as *Notes and Queries, PMLA, English Studies, American Speech,* the *New Republic, Saturday Review, Time,* and several books, including Jespersen 1909–49. The most amusing example was from a 1931 book written by J. Middleton Murry, who six years later wrote an article in the *Times Literary Supplement* (3 Apr. 1937) decrying the *-cy* spelling. The editor of the word for Webster's Third was impressed by the documentation and entered *idiosyncracy* as a secondary variant.

Since *idiosyncracy* has been in use for nearly 350 years, it is probably time to stop thinking of it as a misspelling; it is a misspelling only from the standpoint of etymology, not of educated usage. But we remind you that it is a secondary variant—*idiosyncrasy* is much more common—and you will probably be better off sticking to the more common spelling.

idiot savant   See SAVANT.

idle   *Idle* has been used as a transitive verb meaning "to make idle" since the 18th century, but such usage has become common only in the past several decades. Its current popularity is chiefly journalistic. It occurs in reports about workers who are not working, usually because of a strike, and in reports about athletes who are not playing, usually because of injuries or illness:

> . . . its men were idled amid the walkout by two locals —Peter Schuck & Harrison Wellford, *Harper's,* May 1972

... idled for part of two seasons with a knee injury —Ed Gillooly, *Boston Sunday Advertiser,* 10 Oct. 1971

This use of *idle* has fared well among usage commentators. Harper 1975, 1985 considers its acceptability beyond question, and the usage panel of Heritage 1982 approves it "on all levels of speech and writing."

i.e., e.g.   Usage books note that these two abbreviations tend to be confused with each other. Our evidence shows that the usual error is the use of *i.e.* in place of *e.g.* The error is relatively rare in edited material, but it does seem to occur widely in speech and casual writing. To avoid it, remember that *i.e.* is an abbreviation for the Latin *id est* and means "that is"; *e.g.* is an abbreviation of *exempli gratia* and means "for example." *I.e.,* like *that is,* typically introduces a rewording or clarification of a statement that has just been made or of a word that has just been used:

> Most of the new books are sold through 3,500 Christian (i.e., Protestant) bookstores —*N.Y. Times Book Rev.,* 31 Oct. 1976

> It is money that wasn't absorbed by government, i.e. the administration tax cuts, that is spurring current growth —Joe Sneed & John Tatlock, *Houston Post,* 31 Aug. 1984

E.g. introduces one or more examples that illustrate something stated directly or shortly before it:

> Poets whose lack of these isn't made up by an inescapable intensity of personal presence (e.g. Sylvia Plath) simply aren't represented —Hugh Kenner, *N.Y. Times Book Rev.,* 17 Oct. 1976

> ... rent them to responsible tenants, e.g., retired naval officers —David Schoenbaum, *N.Y. Times,* 3 July 1977

If you feel uncertain about which abbreviation is called for in a particular context, try substituting *that is* or *for example,* or else revise the sentence so that neither is required.

if   1. *If, whether.* Evans 1957 says that the notion that *if* may not introduce a noun clause, as *whether* may, is a recent one. Actually, it is not quite as recent as Evans thought. Leonard 1929 traces the notion back to an obscure 18th-century dictionary editor, J. Johnson. This Johnson—not to be confused with Samuel Johnson—prefixed a 20-page grammar to his New Royal and Universal English Dictionary of 1762 and in it he attacked a number of Scotticisms that he had extracted from the writings of David Hume. Among these he listed *question if* for *question whether;* apparently Hume had used *if* to introduce a noun clause as object of the verb *question.*

The *if* that J. Johnson disparaged as a Scotticism is almost always used to introduce a noun clause that is the object of a verb such as *doubt, see, ask, wonder, decide,* and *know.* If Johnson had read his Bible more attentively, he would have learned that it was not a Scotticism:

> Also he sent forth a dove from him, to see if the waters were abated from off the face of the ground —Genesis 8:8 (AV), 1611

And if he had looked in the greater Johnson's dictionary, he would have found the sense listed, with quotations from Dryden and Prior.

We know of no other comments on *if* "whether" after J. Johnson until the issue turns up a century later in Alford 1866. Alford clearly had the question raised by a correspondent who thought that *if* should not be so used. Alford says, "I cannot see that there is anything to complain of in it" and duly notes its use in the Book of Genesis and in Dryden and Prior. But Ayres 1881 condemns it, and so do Vizetelly 1906, Krapp 1927, Jensen 1935, Partridge 1942, and a great many other commentators of the 1920s and 1930s.

More recent American commentators, however, tend to take Alford's attitude. Evans, Copperud 1964, 1970, 1980, Bernstein 1965, 1971, Perrin & Ebbitt 1972, Watt 1967, Irmscher 1976, Bryant 1962, and others find the usage standard. A number of these as well as Janis 1984 and Shaw 1987 also add that *whether* is the word more often used in formal contexts. Our evidence supports this observation fairly well. Holdouts for Ayres's position include Harper 1975, 1985 and Edwin Newman as one of their panelists, as well as a few British sources—Sellers 1975, Phythian 1979, and Chambers 1985.

The OED and Jespersen 1909–49 (vol. 3) trace the construction back to Old English. Jespersen finds it in Shakespeare:

> How shall I know if I do choose the right? —*The Merchant of Venice,* 1597

As Evans points out, this use of *if* has never actually been restricted; the whole question of its propriety is factitious. Yet the notion that *whether* and not *if* should be used to introduce such a clause is still at large; Mary Vaiana Taylor in *College English,* April 1974, found 20 percent of the teaching assistants she polled marking *if* wrong in such sentences. It may be the persistence of this notion that makes *whether* predominate in formal contexts. Here are some other examples of this use of *if:*

> ... I asked her if she was engaged to Sam Fiske —Emily Dickinson, letter, 19 Mar. 1854

> I don't know if that Etiquette thing is spelled right, or not —Will Rogers, *The Illiterate Digest,* 1924

> Dr. Crowther fingered his tie to feel if it were straight —Aldous Huxley, *Point Counter Point,* 1928

> We've been having days I doubt if you could beat in Colorado —Robert Frost, letter, 1 Nov. 1927

> I cannot cross the gap yet. I do not know if I ever shall —Agnes Newton Keith, *Atlantic,* February 1946

> ... I doubt if one writer ever has a satisfactory conversation with another writer —William Faulkner, 16 May 1957, in *Faulkner in the University,* 1959

> Someone inquired if that wasn't a pretty expensive way to educate a single student —Harry S. Ashmore, *Center Mag.,* May 1968

> And keep an eye on the temperature gauge to see if the engine runs too hot —*Consumer Reports,* April 1980

> If there's a swindler in the bookkeeping department at the bank, I doubt if he's going to pick my account to steal from —*And More by Andy Rooney,* 1982

We can use the example by Andy Rooney to illustrate a point made by Otto Jespersen: the "whether" sense of *if* is not used at the beginning of a sentence. Initial *if* (the first word in the example) is understood as the ordinary conditional use. The "whether" sense is rarely found except after a verb, although it is sometimes used after adjectives:

> It is extremely doubtful if it could be used with any success —Raymond W. Bliss, *Atlantic,* November 1952

We should also point out that other fine points are brought into the argument by a few commentators to buttress the original objection. The most common of these is the insistence on *whether* when an alternative is specified, as in the example above from Will Rogers. Copperud dismisses this view as "a superstition." It appears to have no more basis in fact than J. Johnson's finding the construction to be a Scotticism.

2. Copperud 1970, 1980 cites Flesch 1964 and Fowler 1965 as being opposed to *if* in the sense of "though"; Harper 1985 and Heritage 1982 also object. These seem to be examples of the construction questioned:

> ... sets out to make a fairly routine, if exhaustive, search of the caves —John S. Bowman, *Saturday Rev.,* 23 Oct. 1971

> ... a man possessed of such satanic, if controlled, fury on a football field —George Plimpton, *Harper's,* May 1971

> ... the excellence of its traditional, if routine, services —Nicholas Pileggi, *New York,* 24 July 1972

> ... but they are unwilling, if not unable, to make close personal contacts —Stephanie Dudek, *Psychology Today,* May 1971

And they seem unlikely to cause confusion. We conclude that the construction is standard—and it is quite common.

3. From Fowler 1907 to Bryson 1984, there are a few commentators who express concern over the use or nonuse of the subjunctive after *if.* The Fowler brothers were expecting the imminent demise of the subjunctive—in a generation, they thought—and they were mainly concerned with the avoidance of sentences in which the subjunctive might be used. However, the subjunctive has not died, and Bernstein 1971 and Bryson 1984 try to distinguish between uses of *if* where the subjunctive is called for and uses where it is to be avoided. Both allow the subjunctive after *if* when the clause contains a condition that is hypothetical or contrary to fact, but neither gives a satisfactory rule of thumb for identifying such clauses. The problem is that the dividing line between what is or could well be true and what is hypothetical or not true is not consistently clear—in fact it can often be an entirely subjective judgment made by the writer.

The indicative is called for in the first example below; the subjunctive is proper in the second; the third and fourth seem to be in that gray area of subjective judgment.

> But if the CIA was not responsible . . . , who was? —Norman Cousins, *Saturday Rev.,* 28 Apr. 1979

> If there were a single word . . . , it might be "modest" —Carolyn Balducci, *N.Y. Times Book Rev.,* 3 June 1973

> If Japan was threatened, the situation could well be different —Keyes Beech, *Saturday Rev.,* 23 Aug. 1975

> ... the inevitable graduate student preparing for another long night in the lab might hear . . . if he weren't too absorbed to notice —*Johns Hopkins Mag.,* Fall 1971

See SUBJUNCTIVE.

if and when   This rather innocuous-looking phrase (which is sometimes reversed to *when and if*) has been the subject of attack from Fowler 1907 on—look at this list: Fowler 1907, 1926, 1965, Partridge 1942, Copperud 1964, 1970, 1980, Flesch 1964, Follett 1966, Bernstein 1965, Shaw 1975, 1987, Phythian 1979, Morris 1975, 1985, Freeman 1983, and Kenneth Darling in *American Speech,* February 1941. Only Janis 1984 will allow the phrase to have any use, and even he cautions against using it carelessly (to be completely accurate, Fowler 1907 does excuse one use by the British statesman Gladstone).

If and when seems to have some small standing in legal parlance, and it is such use that Janis finds justified. (Similar considerations seem to lie behind the Fowlers' excusing of Gladstone.)

The amount of critical fire (and especially the diatribe in Fowler 1926) seems disproportionate to the problem. Fowler 1907 and Fowler 1926 have abundant examples of the phrase, drawn primarily from British newspapers. Almost no one since has produced a live instance, so it is hard to tell whether *if and when* is really a common phrase. The Fowlers collected more examples than the readers for the Merriam-Webster files have collected since then. Is the phrase perhaps less frequent today than in 1907 and 1926? Or is it now primarily an oral expression that does not find its way into print? We cannot be sure. Here are a few of our examples; they do not seem especially dreadful:

> If and when you do come to America, I hope to have due notice —Alexander Woollcott, letter, 1 Aug. 1935

> The state is eager to get at the 30-year-old osteopath if and when he takes the witness stand to defend himself —*Springfield* (Mass.) *Union,* 25 Oct. 1954

> ... wondering if and when her life would ever get underway —Philip Roth, *The Professor of Desire,* 1977

Our files do have examples of two constructions not to be found in Fowler. The first of these is use of the phrase at the end of a statement:

> "I think the Old Man has it in mind to give Bus the Tactical Air Force for the invasion of the Japanese home islands; if and when. . . ." —James Gould Cozzens, *Guard of Honor,* 1948

> ... he could not be trusted to save Israel if and when —Ralph J. Gleason, *Rolling Stone,* 7 Dec. 1972

In the second, *if and when* (or *when and if*) is followed by *to* and an infinitive. This construction shows that the writers (and Gould especially) considered the phrase as a fixed unit, because *if* in the sense used here is not normally followed by *to* and the infinitive. It would seem reasonable that this construction could be attacked on the grounds of faulty parallelism.

> The disagreement over *if* and *when* to teach quantum chemistry —Peter O'D. Offenhartz, *Jour. of Chemical Education,* December 1967

. . . new attitudes are developing about marriage and when and if to have children —Jane Schwartz Gould, *Barnard Alumnae,* Winter 1971

We suspect you will seldom have a real need for *if and when,* but if it slips out, it is a trivial offense. We do not recommend the construction with *to* and the infinitive, however, since it seems liable to more substantive objection. If you feel the need to use this construction, you might consider replacing the *if* with *whether;* this would restore the parallelism and defuse that aspect of the criticism.

if worst comes to worst   See WORST COMES TO WORST.

ignoramus   Fowler 1926 and Evans 1957 insist that the only plural for *ignoramus* is *ignoramuses,* not *ignorami.* Fowler justifies his assertion on the grounds that it is derived from a Latin verb and not from a noun. Well, in legal language it is. But the common use comes from a character in a play (*Ignoramus,* 1615, by George Ruggle) whose name came from the legal term. And one suspects that Fowler and Evans would not have protested *ignorami* if it had not been used. It has, but it has not made the dictionary yet.

Ignorami began to turn up in our files in the 1920s. It was perhaps a facetious formation, but one can hardly tell from examples like these:

. . . free of the cheap and hokum stagework of those coxcombish ignorami who call themselves actors —*Plain Talk,* March 1928

. . . the gawks and ignorami who circulated around the schoolhouse back in Hickory Creek —*Literary Digest,* 5 May 1923

We have about half a dozen examples from the 1920s, but nothing after that until the mid 1960s:

And you can't think how it annoys me to see the New Ignorami of criticism refer to him merely as *Twain,* as if that were his real name —Katherine Anne Porter, *N.Y. Herald Tribune Book Week,* 26 Dec. 1965

Such missteps, while often howlingly funny to ignorami like us, are deadly serious concerns to psychologists and linguists —Roger Rosenblatt, in *The Bedford Reader,* ed. X. J. Kennedy & Dorothy M. Kennedy, 1985

These ignorami should never have been invited to the party —Michael I. Miller, *American Speech,* Summer 1984

The revival is continuing, and *ignorami* is beginning to be recorded in dictionaries as a secondary variant. *Ignoramuses* is still the usual plural, however.

I guess   See GUESS.

ilk   The story of *ilk* is a familiar one to readers of usage books. The word in Old English was a pronoun synonymous with *same.* It persisted in that sense only among the Scots, who used it in the phrase *of that ilk,* meaning, as the OED explains, "of the same place, territorial designation, or name: chiefly in names of landed families, as *Guthrie of that Ilk, Wemyss of that ilk* = Guthrie of Guthrie, Wemyss of Wemyss." It was apparently a misunderstanding of the Scottish use that gave rise to the "kind or sort" sense of *ilk* which became

established in the 19th century and which is the only sense of the word now used outside of Scotland.

The extended meaning of *ilk* has been censured by usage commentators for more than a hundred years:

Ilk is a much abused word, being constantly substituted for stamp, class, or society. "Men of that *ilk* are seldom good for anything." "We want to have nothing to do with Governor Swann, and men of that *ilk.*" (Washington *Chronicle,* January 27, 1869.) — Schele de Vere 1872

The long list of 20th-century commentators who have repeated such criticism includes such prominent names as Fowler 1926, Partridge 1942, and Bernstein 1965. But recent decades have seen increasing recognition that the "kind or sort" sense of *ilk* is now standard English. Evans 1957 calls it standard, and Copperud 1970, 1980 agrees, noting the acceptance of this sense by current dictionaries. Simon 1980, having been criticized by a correspondent for using the sense himself, finds that this is one extension of meaning he is inclined to accept.

Our evidence shows clearly that, whatever its origins, the "kind or sort" sense of *ilk* has long since made a place for itself in the vocabulary of standard English. Probably its most distinctive characteristic is its suggestion of contempt, which is apparent in the two sentences cited by Schele de Vere in 1872, and which is still apparent in much current use:

The titillating mush of Cartland and her ilk —Germaine Greer, *The Female Eunuch,* 1970

. . . pilgrims of that Beautiful People ilk park their limos on West 10th Street —Gael Greene, *New York,* 3 Mar. 1975

But *ilk* is also commonly used with no disparaging connotations:

. . . Twain, Conrad and others of the lofty ilk — Leonard Michaels, *N.Y. Times Book Rev.,* 16 May 1976

. . . others of their compact but luxurious ilk —*Consumer Reports,* February 1980

. . . the success of Michael Arlen, P. G. Wodehouse and their ilk —Margaret Crosland, *British Book News,* May 1982

Such usage certainly still has its enemies, but their spirited defense of the old and little-used Scottish sense of *ilk* is far more passionate than reasonable. The facts are these: *ilk* once meant "same"; it now means "sort." Such is the way of language.

ill   Raub 1897 advocated using *ill of* when a preposition was called for. Some years later, *Literary Digest* was saying that the preferred modern use was *ill with* (1929). More than 50 years later, it does appear that *ill with* is the more commonly found construction; however, the evidence in our files shows that *ill of* is still in use:

Actually I only once went ill with thirst —T. E. Lawrence, *Seven Pillars of Wisdom,* 1935

. . . incurably ill with cancer —*Time,* 14 Mar. 1949

. . . he was ill with tuberculosis —*Current Biography,* July 1966

. . . she was ill of a fever —Harrison Smith, *Saturday Rev.,* 28 Feb. 1953

He was put in bed ill of the fever —Joseph Whitehill, *American Scholar,* Winter 1967–68

illegible, unreadable The distinction to be made between these words is that *illegible* means "impossible to read; indecipherable" and *unreadable* chiefly means "lacking interest or attraction as reading; extremely dull or badly written":

> ... the handwriting, though expressive, is almost illegible —*Times Literary Supp.,* 12 Feb. 1970

> Protect prescription labels with transparent tape, so they won't become smudged and illegible —Dodi Schultz, *Ladies' Home Jour.,* August 1971

> ... prose that was graceless, inflated, and very nearly unreadable —David Littlejohn, *Commonweal,* 30 Jan. 1970

> ... issued their second highly technical, distinctly unreadable text —Marcia Seligson, *McCall's,* March 1971

This distinction has been noted by many commentators, dating back as far as Utter 1916. Several commentators, including Utter, Evans 1957, and Shaw 1975, have also noted that *unreadable* can sometimes mean "indecipherable," Fowler 1926, Krapp 1927, Partridge 1942, and Phythian 1979 will not allow this sense of *unreadable,* but it is treated as standard in dictionaries. It was first recorded in 1830. According to our written evidence, its use in current English is extremely rare. In fact, the closest thing we have to recent evidence of its use is a single citation from the magazine *Infoworld,* in which its meaning is not so much "impossible to decipher" as it is "impossible to see clearly enough for reading":

> ... permitting them to function in reduced light conditions where LCDs [liquid crystal displays] are unreadable —Nancy Groth, *Infoworld,* 27 Jan. 1986

illicit See ELICIT, ILLICIT.

illogical comparison See ANY 3; FALSE COMPARISON.

illusion See DELUSION, ILLUSION.

illusive See ELUSIVE, ILLUSIVE.

illustrate When *illustrate* is used with a preposition, it may be used with *by, in,* or *with:*

> ... a large number of new behaviors to meet new situations are abundantly illustrated by the plight of the current group of European refugees —Ralph Linton, *The Cultural Background of Personality,* 1945

> How is this illustrated by the books in hand? —Thomas Caldecotte Chubb, *Saturday Rev.,* 13 June 1953

> The rich diversity of his life is abundantly illustrated in the correspondence which flowed across the Channel —Dumas Malone, *N.Y. Times Book Rev.,* 1 Aug. 1954

> The same competitive spirit was illustrated in Smith's coverage of President Kennedy's assassination —*Current Biography,* December 1964

> His portly hard middle hung over with a shirt illustrated with pineapples —Saul Bellow, *The Adventures of Augie March,* 1953

> Mr. Tracey illustrates, with recordings, how drums are used for different purposes —*London Calling,* 18 Feb. 1954

Illustrate may occasionally be used with *from* to suggest a different relation:

> ... then proceeded to discuss and illustrate these apophthegms from his own knowledge of books —Gilbert Highet, *The Classical Tradition,* 1949

The use of *illustrate* with these prepositions will most often call for the verb to be a past participle; however, as the Highet and *London Calling* examples above show, there are instances using other verb forms.

illy This little-used adverb was once the object of impassioned criticism:

> The Illy Haters Union is not so strong in numbers as the Anti-Infinitive Splitters Guild, but its members are of more desperate and determined character. They are embattled minute men, sworn that only over their dead bodies shall the adverb illy be admitted to literary respectability —*N.Y. Sun,* 10 Nov. 1931

Illy is actually quite an old word, recorded in writing as early as 1549. Its written use has never been truly common, however. Samuel Johnson did not include it in his dictionary of 1755, and British travelers, hearing it spoken in the U.S., mistook it for an Americanism in the early 1800s (as is noted in Mencken 1936). *Illy* did not originate in America, but it does seem to have had far more use in the U.S. than in Great Britain. Its career as a usage issue has also been chiefly American. It was routinely vilified by American commentators throughout the late 19th and early 20th centuries.

The argument against *illy* ran as follows: since *ill* is established as both an adverb and adjective, *illy* is superfluous, and its use is equivalent to using *welly* in place of *well.* What this argument ignores is that there are many similar adverbial pairs in English—for example, *full* and *fully, right* and *rightly.* There is, in fact, nothing intrinsically wrong with *illy.* The reason for its existence may be that adverbs ending in *-ly* are normally preferred when the adverb precedes the verb or participle it modifies ("It was rightly done" or "It was done right" but not "It was right done"). Most of the evidence for *illy* shows it occuring before a verb or participle:

> Beauty is jealous, and illy bears the presence of a rival —Thomas Jefferson, *Writings,* 1785 (OED)

> Never were two beings more illy assorted —Washington Irving, *Oliver Goldsmith,* 1849 (OED)

> I fear it has been illy and inadequately done —*The Private Papers of Senator Vandenberg,* ed. Arthur H. Vandenberg, Jr., 1952

> ... no graceful memoir of a life well or illy spent —*Saturday Rev.,* 5 June 1965 (OED Supplement)

Of course, *ill* is also used before verbs and participles, and is far more common than *illy.* (More common than either are such synonymous adverbs as *poorly* and *badly.*)

Illy is no longer a hot issue among usage commentators—partly, we suppose, because it is such an uncommon word, and partly because the most influential usage book of the 20th century, Fowler 1926, makes no mention of it. *Illy* seems now to have fallen entirely out of use in British English. In American English, it is standard but rare. There are probably still some people who cringe at the sight or sound of it, but we feel almost certain that the Illy Haters Union has long since been disbanded.

image   *Image* in its relatively recent sense of "popular or perceived conception, public impression" is called a fad word by Flesch 1964, Bernstein 1965, Fowler 1965, and Watt 1967, although Flesch thinks it seems to fill a need. The usage panel of Harper 1975, 1985 disapproves it. Phythian 1979 and Ebbitt & Ebbitt 1982 say it is established, and by implication so does Janis 1984, who merely explains it. Bernstein thought the fad would probably fade out, but that has not happened. It is well established, as these examples attest:

> ... how his media consultants formed, marketed and sold an image —Ronald Steel, *N.Y. Times Book Rev.,* 5 Aug. 1984

> He's devoted a large part of his creative life to demolishing the image of the ballerina as nun — Arlene Croce, *Harper's,* April 1971

> For others, clothes become a way to express themselves—although whether they are expressing their true personality or trying to create an image is often far from clear —John de St. Jorre, *Town & Country,* November 1982

> ... has been quite frank in discussing the image he hopes Germany will present to the world at Munich —William L. Shirer, *Saturday Rev.,* 25 Mar. 1972

It can be used attributively, too:

> We were concerned about the perception that some corporations were paying no tax, and that just wasn't right, says John E. Chapoton, Assistant Treasury Secretary for tax policy. "We're dealing with an image problem." —Gene Koretz, *Business Week,* 1 Mar. 1982

> ... the decisive battle for the Reagan Revolution got reduced to an image contest between the Speaker and the President —David A. Stockman, *Newsweek,* 28 Apr. 1986

imaginary, imaginative   Shaw 1975, 1987, Phythian 1979, and Copperud 1970, 1980 all differentiate between *imaginary* and *imaginative,* agreeing roughly that the first means "existing in the imagination, not real" and the second "characterized by or showing use of the imagination." They do so on obvious grounds. It is hard to imagine the words interchanged in examples like these:

> Many of the ailments were imaginary —Joyce Carol Oates, *Harper's,* August 1971

> ... threatening her with some very imaginative mutilations —Katherine Anne Porter, *The Never-Ending Wrong,* 1977

> He had liked each tree—one for climbing, another to play beneath with tiny, imaginary people —Robert Canzoneri, *McCall's,* March 1971

> ... an imaginative and unassuming ... architectural genius —P. W. Stone, *Catholic Digest,* December 1968

But the words can be much closer in meaning:

> His canvases, chiefly imaginary, somber landscapes —*Current Biography,* June 1965

> ... romantic in the sense that they deal with an imaginative realm to which men and women like to resort to escape the drabness of their daily routine — Morris R. Cohen, *The Faith of a Liberal,* 1946

> ... works that create through language an essentially imaginative environment for the hero —Richard Poirier, *A World Elsewhere,* 1946

In such use, relating to art and literature, *imaginative* is more common, and it stresses what is produced by the imagination as distinct from what merely exists in the imagination, for which *imaginary* is the usual word.

> The Alderman's son is Shakespeare, and the book is an imaginative reconstruction of his early life —M. R. Ridley, *London Calling,* 29 Apr. 1954

> ... works of imaginative literature —Walter Arnold, *Saturday Rev.,* 7 July 1979

imbecile, imbecilic   Simon 1980 says in passing that *imbecilic* is "a substandard adjective derived by faulty analogy." We do not know on what basis this assertion is made, but the formation from the noun *imbecile* and the adjective ending *-ic,* as shown in the OED Supplement, is entirely regular.

The word *imbecilic* appears to be a 20th-century coinage. The earliest citation in the OED Supplement is dated 1918. We first heard of it in 1909 through a letter from a physician in Markey, Michigan, who was perhaps suggesting that his wife had coined the word:

> Whenever this word was used by my wife in the presence of educated people it occasioned remark and favorable comment.

It was written down as early as 1917:

> ... two statements by Professor Harry Elmer Barnes, of Smith College. The first was written in June, 1917: "... the extreme Pan-Germanic junker party—allied itself to the semi-imbecilic Crown Prince." —*American Mercury,* August 1927

It should not be considered substandard English:

> ... a remark more imbecilic than the first —Jean Stafford, *Children Are Bored on Sunday,* 1953

> ... the imbecilic but eternally triumphant Inspector Clouseau —Arthur M. Schlesinger, Jr., *Saturday Rev.,* 28 Oct. 1978

> ... Arnheiter's imbecilic game of hide-and-seek with the Chinese submarine —William Styron, *This Quiet Dust and Other Writings,* 1982

There is even a derivative adverb:

> ... simper imbecilically under the floodlights on some demicelebrity's arm —John Fowles, *Holiday,* June 1966

immanent   See EMINENT, IMMINENT; IMMINENT 2.

immediately   *Immediately* has been used as a conjunction equivalent to *as soon as* for well over a hundred years, but it has never really succeeded in establishing itself in American English. Many American commentators have cited it as an error, and our evidence shows that its use by American writers has been rare. In British English, however, it is common and standard:

> Immediately he had finished tea he rose —D. H. Lawrence, *Sons and Lovers,* 1913

> . . . they should always be summoned immediately an accident happens —Alan Blackshaw, *Mountaineering,* 1965

> I started writing *Jill* immediately I left Oxford —Philip Larkin, *Required Writing,* 1983

See also DIRECTLY 3.

immigrate See EMIGRATE, IMMIGRATE.

imminent 1. *Imminent* in the past has been spelled *eminent* (see EMINENT, IMMINENT), but the spelling is now avoided as an error. It was denounced as long ago as Baker 1770. He blamed it on the French. The opposite mistake may possibly have been made in the following example, but it seems more likely that a pun involving *imminent arrival* and *eminent* was intended:

> Miami Beach's tensely anxious Sans Souci Hotel readied the full treatment for its imminent guests, the touring Shah of Iran and his luscious Queen —*Time,* 24 Jan. 1955

2. *Imminent, immanent.* Sellers 1975 and others warn against confusing these words, which would appear hard to do from the disparity in their meanings; *immanent* is more likely to be found in philosophy than in ordinary discourse. But the spellings are close, and sure enough *imminent* has been used in the sense of "immanent" since 1605. The OED has three 17th-century examples, and one from the 19th. Here are a couple of ours from the 20th:

> . . . suddenly the young woman she is to be is imminent in her manners and her looks —Irwin Edman, *American Scholar,* Winter 1950–1951

> It is possible to act to change the world because we are not totally imminent in it —Richard Lichtman, *Center Mag.,* September 1969

Now it is entirely possible that these are simply typographical errors and not deliberate revivals of the 17th-century spelling. We firmly recommend that you keep the two words distinct in spelling so that you do not confuse your readers.

immune In general, when *immune* is used with a preposition, *from* and *to* appear about equally:

> . . . his [Donne's] contemporaries, who often seem . . . to exist immune from our perplexities and swept by passions which we admire but cannot feel —Virginia Woolf, *The Second Common Reader,* 1932

> . . . had some source of strength that made him immune from being imposed on by a woman of character like herself —Frank O'Connor, *New Yorker,* 2 Aug. 1952

> . . . it could hardly have been immune from scrutiny by curious and critical official eyes —George F. Kennan, *New Yorker,* 1 May 1971

> To the extent that people develop personal and esthetic interests, they are immune to trivial changes

in style —Lewis Mumford, *Technics and Civilization,* 1934

> And what pilot is immune to errors? —Charles A. Lindbergh, *The Spirit of St. Louis,* 1953

> . . . these were not problems wholly immune to those immutable laws of change that eventually affect all societies —George F. Kennan, *Saturday Rev.,* 6 Mar. 1976

Much less frequently, *immune* is used with *against:*

> His name is now immune against partisan rancor —Richard M. Weaver, *The Ethics of Rhetoric,* 1953

> . . . rendered communistic peoples more or less immune against fear —Raymond W. Bliss, *Atlantic,* November 1952

In its biological/medical sense, although *immune* has been used with *against, from,* and *to,* current evidence shows a preference for use of *to:*

> . . . furnish satisfactory evidence . . . to the effect that he was immune against smallpox —Victor Heiser, *An American Doctor's Odyssey,* 1936

> . . . immune from nervous and organic disorders —Alexis Carrel, *Man, the Unknown,* 1935

> An individual is immune to a virus as long as the corresponding antibodies are present in his circulatory system —J. D. Watson, *Molecular Biology of the Gene,* 1965

Some language commentators have said that *immune* may be used with *of;* if it has been or is now so used, the occurrence is not common. Our files have no evidence for this usage.

immunity When *immunity* is used with a preposition in its general sense, it is most commonly found with *from* when the object names the threat:

> In return he had been promised immunity from criminal prosecution —*Time,* 27 May 1946

Of is common to mark other relations:

> . . . prohibiting the abridgement of the privileges or immunities of citizens —Kenneth S. Tollett, *Center Mag.,* November/December 1971

Less frequently, *immunity* is used in its general sense with *against* or *to* when the object names the threat, and with *in* or *for* in other relations:

> . . . give the youngsters some kind of immunity against the slums and social injustices —Gertrude Samuels, *N.Y. Times Mag.,* 13 June 1954

> . . . a feeling of security . . . of absolute immunity to onslaught from above —H. L. Mencken, *Prejudices: Second Series,* 1920

> . . . gangsters in those days . . . enjoyed a curious immunity in society —Katherine Anne Porter, *The Never-Ending Wrong,* 1977

> . . . offering him immunity for past offenses —*American Guide Series: Louisiana,* 1941

In its biological/medical sense, *immunity* is used most often with *to,* and less frequently with *against* or *from:*

> No instance of natural immunity to cowpox has been conclusively demonstrated —Kenneth F.

Maxcy, *Preventive Medicine and Hygiene,* 7th ed., 1951

. . . a mild disease, cowpox, confers immunity against . . . smallpox —Gordon Alexander, *Biology,* 8th ed., 1962

Since there was complete immunity from symptoms due to bubbles —Harry G. Armstrong, *Principles and Practice of Aviation Medicine,* 1939

Occasionally, this sense is found with *in* or *of* marking other relations:

. . . may produce fairly satisfactory immunity in man which lasts for several months —Henry Pinkerton, in *Pathology,* ed. W. A. D. Anderson, 1948

. . . the passive immunity of the newborn provided by nature is a highly efficient mechanism —T. F. McNair Scott, in a seminar given by the Medical Division of Sharp and Dohme, Summer 1953

immure When used with a preposition, *immure* is most often found with *in. Immure* is most commonly found in the form of the past participle, although occasionally other forms are found:

. . . one cannot immure himself in an ivory tower — Gerald W. Johnson, *New Republic,* 14 Mar. 1955

. . . immured in the deep, dark, stony bowels of a pyramid —Walter de la Mare, *Encounter,* December 1954

. . . to be immured from birth in an unbreakable circle of private experience —*Times Literary Supp.,* 8 Oct. 1954

In the same relation *immure* is used less frequently with *behind* or *within:*

. . . accretion of objects . . . behind which he seems to immure himself in order to feel at ease —Janet Flanner, *New Yorker,* 9 Mar. 1957

He immured himself so closely within the walls of the old theocratic temple —Vernon Louis Parrington, *Main Currents in American Thought,* 1927

In other relations, *immure* has been used occasionally with *at, against,* and *with:*

. . . she was taken off and immured at La Roche — Sir Basil Thomson, *The Mystery of the French Milliner,* 1937

She is as wary of good fortune as she is immured against the bad —Walker Percy, *The Moviegoer,* 1961

. . . in the dingy office on lower Sixth Avenue where I daily immured myself with an intractable typewriter —S. J. Perelman, *New Yorker,* 1 Jan. 1972

impact This word comes in for adverse criticism both as a noun and as a verb in figurative use. The criticism is relatively recent, beginning evidently in the 1960s with Bernstein 1965, Fowler 1965, and Follett 1966. These three (and also Bremner 1980) are concerned with the noun; later writers take up the cudgels against the verb. The gist of most of the criticism is fairly well summed up in this portion of the discussion in Cook 1985:

impact A word fit to describe the crash of a wrecker's ball against its target, *impact* has become a substitute

for *bearing, influence, significance,* and *effect.* It's so overworked in officialese and journalese that the more appropriate terms are falling into disuse. Both Follett and Bernstein have harsh words for this "faddish" abasement of the noun. How much more horrified they might have been had they lived to see the current vogue of the verb *impact* in the sense of "to have an impact" or "to have an impact on" *(Loose usage adversely impacts the language).*

Let us examine the noun use first. Cook's assertion that *impact* is so overworked that its synonyms are falling into disuse has no real basis; all of the listed synonyms continue to flourish. As to the overuse in officialese and journalese, we cannot be so positive. *Impact* may well be overworked in those areas, but as we shall see, it did not become established there first, nor is it limited to those areas.

The historical background of the figurative use goes back to Samuel Taylor Coleridge in 1817, according to evidence in the OED. But it gives few 19th-century quotations, which leads us to believe that the use did not really become common until the 20th century. In spite of the suggestion about official language and journalism, the bulk of our early evidence comes from sources that must be generally described as literary:

It seems to me that intensity is the only thing. A day's impact is better than a month of dead pull — Oliver Wendell Holmes d. 1935, letter, 4 Apr. 1909

. . . the various impacts of science upon thought — Alfred North Whitehead, *Science and the Modern World,* 1925

. . . expose the mind bare to the poem, and transcribe in all its haste and imperfection whatever may be the result of the impact —Virginia Woolf, *The Second Common Reader,* 1932

. . . the impact of industrialism on a country only beginning to create an art and literature —Granville Hicks, *The Great Tradition,* 1933

. . . one feels as one reads the sheer impact of immediate experience —John Livingston Lowes, *Essays in Appreciation,* 1936

The first impact of this policy on Octavius's mind — John Buchan, *Augustus,* 1937

Events are sensational in the degree in which they make a strong impact in isolation —John Dewey, *Freedom and Culture,* 1939

Everything which happened to me to-day was curiously without impact —Christopher Isherwood, *The Berlin Stories,* 1946

Here is the impact of the South on the sun-starved North —Eudora Welty, *Saturday Rev.,* 23 Sept. 1950

But in the immediate impact of this scene we are unconscious of the medium of its expression —T. S. Eliot, *Atlantic,* February 1951

By the early 1950s, the figurative sense seems to have become immensely popular—at least we have abundant evidence of its use. It was probably the spread of the sense to the nonliterary material read by usage commentators that led to the initial adverse criticism. The earliest negative comment in our files is from an issue of *Saturday Review* in late 1944. The writer, whose name we failed to record, objected to the term in a sociological book.

Copperud 1970, 1980 notes that dictionaries all consider the figurative use of the noun standard; from the sample of relatively early use given above, you can see why they do. The use was established as standard nearly a half century before Bremner discovered it to be faddish.

With the verb we have a somewhat more complicated situation. Not only is the figurative extension of the verb much more recent (the OED Supplement's earliest citation is from 1935) but so is the adverse criticism (apparently the earliest is that of the Heritage usage panel in 1982). But since part of the criticism seems to be based on the erroneous notion that the verb is derived from the noun by functional shift, we must first pursue a little etymology.

Here are a few noun-used-as-verb comments:

Americans also use . . . nouns as verbs (e.g., 'impact,' 'vacation') —Andrew Knight, *N.Y. Times,* 7 May 1978

. . . "caveat" and "impact" became verbs [in the speech of Secretary of State Alexander Haig] —James H. Boren, *Washington Post Mag.,* 23 Jan. 1983

It may be that my children will use *gift* and *impact* as verbs without the slightest compunction —Geoffrey Nunberg, *Atlantic,* December 1983

". . . *impact* as a verb." The former noun has been used so often in its verb form in bored rooms that *impact on* has lost its punch —Safire 1986

But *impact* was a verb in English before it was a noun; it is first attested in 1601 and was brought in straight from the past participle of the Latin verb that also gave us *impinge.* The relatively recent figurative uses of the verb are parallel to, though no doubt influenced by, the figurative sense of the noun; this is not a case of a verb derived from an earlier noun.

Our earliest evidence for figurative use of the verb is, like the figurative use of the noun, primarily literary:

The world did not impact upon me until I got to the Post Office and picked up my mail —Christopher Morley, *The Man Who Made Friends with Himself,* 1949

. . . the images impacting the human retina —Thomas Hart Benton, *University of Kansas City Rev.,* Autumn 1950

How will total war impact on such a poet? —*Times Literary Supp.,* 4 May 1951

It hardly impacted even on the guests' subconscious —Enid Bagnold, *Atlantic,* October 1952

The verb, however, did not establish itself as steadily and rapidly as the noun did. Instead we find only a trickle of use in the 1950s and 1960s; not until about 1970 is there a noticeable increase in use, and even through the 1970s the increase is modest. The biggest jump in use in our files occurs around 1980, and it is this advance that attracted the criticism to be found in Heritage 1982, Harper 1985, Kilpatrick 1984, and Cook 1985.

There is now a difference in where the word is found, too. The newer citations come from quotations from politicians, from business and financial sources, and from other reportage. Some examples:

Requirements of the war have impacted very heavily on the services' pilot inventory —Senator John Stennis, quoted by Bergen Evans in *Famous Writers Mag.,* Spring 1968

More governmentese—Environmental Protection Administrator Ruckelshaus talks of ways to "advantageously impact" the auto pollution problem —*Wall Street Jour.,* 2 Mar. 1973

. . . a variety of efforts to impact energy —Senator Edward M. Kennedy, quoted in *N.Y. Times Mag.,* 24 June 1979

Imports of stainless steel products continued to impact the Division's profits during 1970 —*Annual Report, Armco Steel Corp.,* 1970

This need to hold stock for 12 months will impact mutual funds —Robert Lenzer, *Barron's,* 20 Dec. 1976

. . . lets us spend more on R&D without impacting the bottom line —Jessie I. Aweida, quoted in *Business Week,* 26 Jan. 1981

. . . says he's not worried about IBM impacting Apple sales in the West —*Financial Post* (Toronto), 23 Jan. 1982

. . . has grown considerably since transplanted here in 1972, impacting the city with full brontosaurian force a year later, when 54 concerts were stuffed into ten days —Gary Giddins, *New York,* 30 June 1975

. . . these differences impact on and often adversely affect the communications process —Geneva Smitherman, *English Jour.,* February 1976

The production and use of energy stands out by far as the single most critical item impacting on the environment —Leon Lindsay, *Christian Science Monitor,* 30 Jan. 1980

. . . attributes much of that problem to inflation as it impacts upon the tax system —Soma Golden, *N.Y. Times Mag.,* 23 Mar. 1980

. . . more Americans are traveling to the United Kingdom, which may impact art and antiques sales there —*Antique Monthly,* October 1981

At the technology session that impacted on the development of electronic publishing —*Publishers Weekly,* 1 Jan. 1982

No one knows how the proposed changes will impact Europe's air —*Civil Engineering,* August 1982

. . . said the proposal . . . could impact all women seeking abortions —*Denver Post,* 5 Sept. 1984

. . . two issues which at first blush may seem noneducational in nature, but which in reality impact heavily on the choices which Smith students make —Barbara B. Reinhold, *Smith Alumnae Quarterly,* Winter 1984

The variety of sources quoted here (and we have even more in our files) suggests that the figurative senses of the verb *impact* are standard and reasonably well established. The financial uses tend to occur in surroundings that include more jargon than do the rest, and we have a couple of citations that show the verb in the context of military jargon. Many of our citations are of quoted speech. Curiously, this verb is no longer prominent in the literary sources from which it sprang; it seems not to have established its use in literary writing, as the noun did. We find no difference in degree of formality or typical context between transitive and intransitive uses.

You need not use this verb if you find it unappealing; a periphrastic substitute (often including the noun) will suggest itself for nearly any context in which the verb might be used, and sometimes another verb such as *affect, influence, impinge,* or *hit* may serve. But it is too late now for complaint to prevent the establishment of this use.

impassionate   See DISPASSIONATE, IMPASSIONATE.

impatient   When used with a preposition, *impatient* is most often followed by *of:*

His sisters . . . were quite as impatient of his advice, quite as unyielding to his representation —Jane Austen, *Mansfield Park,* 1814

He was always impatient of delay —Edmund Wilson, *A Piece of My Mind,* 1956

Less frequently, *impatient* is used with *for, to,* or *with,* and occasionally with *at:*

. . . a Cadillac cowboy impatient for his father's death —*Current Biography,* September 1964

Winterbourne was impatient to see her again —Henry James, *Daisy Miller,* 1879

. . . had always been impatient with doctrines and systems —William H. Whyte, Jr., *The Organization Man,* 1956

. . . impatient at Benson's presence —George Meredith, *The Ordeal of Richard Feverel,* 1859

impeach   1. When used with a preposition, *impeach* is usually used with *for:*

. . . (who, by the way, was later impeached for corruption!) —Julian Huxley, *Memories,* 1970

. . . why should he be impeaching the Reverend George Barnard for exceptional futility? —Compton Mackenzie, *The Parson's Progress,* 1923

Once in a while, *impeach* is used with *on:*

. . . attempted to impeach Culligan on a variety of counts of misfeasance —Richard R. Lingeman, *N.Y. Times,* 14 Feb. 1970

At one time *impeach* was used with *of,* but in modern prose that combination seldom occurs:

. . . in the name of all the commons of England, impeached Thomas earl of Strafford . . . of high treason —Earl of Clarendon, *The History of the Rebellion and Civil Wars in England,* 1647 (OED)

2. Look again at the citation from Julian Huxley in section 1 above saying that somebody "was later impeached for corruption." Was this person removed from office or simply charged with misconduct? This question is related to the central usage problem involving *impeach.*

Theodore Bernstein in 1970 conducted a small poll in connection with a number of news reports about the threat of impeachment proceedings against Justice William O. Douglas of the Supreme Court. He polled thirteen people, all of whom worked for the *New York Times,* and found that ten of them thought *impeach* meant "to remove from office." This is not a new under-

standing of the word. We have evidence of it going back to before World War I. But it is rarely found in print (our earliest printed evidence is from an editorial in the *New York Sun* in 1913). You could call the people's "remove from office" a folk usage—it exists in people's minds, in their conversation (two of our earliest citations involve arguments about whether President Andrew Johnson was impeached or not), and on signs ("Impeach Earl Warren" signs used to be fairly common). Once in a while it pops up in print:

When the supreme court found several of Peron's early decrees illegal, he had his rubber-stamp congress impeach it, then filled the vacancies with his followers —Michael Scully, *Reader's Digest,* January 1956

If a great many people believe *impeach* means "to remove from office," then it does mean that. The interpretation is scarcely devoid of reason since removal from office is the whole point of impeachment. The meaning can be found in Webster's Third, but it is too rarely used in print to be entered in desk dictionaries. Still, a writer must reckon with its existence. If you need to use *impeach* in your writing and wish not to be misunderstood, you had better phrase your context carefully.

impecunious   Evans 1957 calls *impecunious* "formal" and Flesch 1964 tags it as "an unnecessarily long word for *poor."* Although the word is not encountered all that often, when *impecunious* is used our evidence shows that it can carry connotations of its own. As Webster's New Dictionary of Synonyms says, *impecunious* "may imply the deprivation of money but it more often suggests a habitual being without money and, sometimes, connotes also the habit of borrowing or of living upon one's friends":

. . . this eager impecunious young man who had fared so richly in his poverty —Edith Wharton, *The Age of Innocence,* 1920

. . . the impecunious artists and writers of New York gathered for cheap meals and free talk —Jerome Mellquist, *Perspectives USA,* Summer 1953

My greatest treat as a small and impecunious Scots boy, was to visit friends of my mother who were "big people" in the then prosperous Belfast linen industry —Aylmer Vallance, *Irish Digest,* July 1954

In her present guise of impecunious daughter of impecunious lately dead peer, earning her living as . . . part-time cook —*Times Literary Supp.,* 19 Mar. 1970

The real fright, for this reviewer, lay in the book's depiction of impecunious academics living in Manhattan —Arthur Krystal, *N.Y. Times Book Rev.,* 29 July 1984

Impecunious can upon occasion be a useful word.

impenetrable   *Impenetrable* is now usually used with *to* when a complementary prepositional phrase is needed:

Five volleys plunged the files in banked smoke impenetrable to the eye —Rudyard Kipling, *Wee Willie Winkie and Other Child Stories,* 1888

This gentleman was impenetrable to ideas —Padraic Colum, Introduction to James Joyce's *Dubliners,* 1926

. . . why should black novels, paintings, or symphonies be impenetrable to whites? —Robert F. Moss, *Saturday Rev.*, 15 Nov. 1975

At one time, *impenetrable* also occurred with *by*, but this use is extremely infrequent in contemporary prose:

> Aristocracies are, as such, naturally impenetrable by ideas —Matthew Arnold, *Essays in Criticism*, 1865 (OED)

imperfect passive   See PROGRESSIVE PASSIVE.

impervious   When *impervious* is used with a preposition, the choice is almost always *to:*

> . . . so hard a bark, as to be almost impervious to a bullet —Herman Melville, *Omoo*, 1847

> But he had long since grown impervious to these alarms —Arnold Bennett, *The Old Wives' Tale*, 1908

> He looked at her, impervious to her tears —Jean Stafford, *Children Are Bored on Sunday*, 1953

> . . . Berlin struck me, above all, as impervious to any political reactions whatever —Stephen Spender, *N.Y. Times Mag.*, 30 Oct. 1977

implement   The OED shows that the verb *implement*, meaning "to carry into effect," originated in the language of Scottish law at the beginning of the 19th century. Its more widespread use began to occur about a hundred years later:

> . . . council has been prepared to implement that agreement —*Westminster Gazette*, 30 Aug. 1909 (OED Supplement)

Implement proved to be such a useful verb that before long it became common, thereby attracting the attention of usage commentators. Its early popularity was among the British, and its early critics were also British. They seem to have regarded it as too fancy and obscure a word for general use. Fowler 1926 considered its use in newspapers to be "pedantry," and Partridge 1942 classed it as a "literarism," by which he meant an unusual word "used only by the literary or the learned." Later critics, such as Follett 1966, found instead that *implement* had the quality of bureaucratic jargon. More recent commentators, however, tend to agree that there is nothing actually wrong with *implement* except that it is overused.

Overuse tends to be in the eye of the beholder, but we do concede that *implement* is a very common word. It typically describes the taking of concrete measures to carry out an official policy or program:

> . . . once plans for a volunteer army are implemented —D. Park Teter, *Change*, September 1971

> Even should the amendment pass, however, it will take years of action in the courts to implement it —Susan Edmiston, *New York*, 27 Dec. 1971

> . . . to implement New Orleans's court-ordered desegregation —Kenneth L. Woodward, *Cosmopolitan*, February 1973

In such contexts, *implement* is an entirely appropriate word. You should feel no uneasiness about using it.

implicit   *Implicit* is often used with a preposition, and that prepositon is usually *in:*

> He was immensely relieved by Shiloh's permission to remain, implicit in a quick gesture of the hand — Elinor Wylie, *The Orphan Angel*, 1926

> The movies borrowed from other arts on the way to finding methods implicit in their medium —Bernard DeVoto, *The World of Fiction*, 1950

> This assumption, implicit in innumerable statements by President Reagan —Henry Steele Commager, *Atlantic*, March 1982

In other relations and other senses *implicit* may also be found, less frequently, with *from, with,* or *within:*

> . . . in the best stories the end is implicit from the beginning —Joan Aiken, *The Writer*, May 1968

> The black dead ocean looked like a mirror of the night; it was cold, implicit with dread and death — Norman Mailer, *The Naked and the Dead*, 1948

> The goodness and strength implicit within Pen unfold but slowly —John DeBruyn, *LIT*, Spring 1966

implicit comparative   We are indebted to Quirk et al. 1985 for the name of this topic. Implicit comparatives make up a small group of words which were comparative adjectives in Latin and have come to be used in English in some of the ways that true English comparatives are. According to Quirk, "they are not true comparatives in English, since they cannot be used in comparative constructions with *than* as explicit basis of comparison."

The implicit comparatives are comparative not so much through syntax as through meaning. In some cases, though, the comparative meaning affects the syntax. *Minor, major, inferior,* and *superior,* for example, are apparently perceived as having more absolutely comparative connotations than *junior* and *senior:* of these six adjectives, only *junior* and *senior* are regularly used with *more* and *most:*

> When a more junior man leaves, does it make any difference? —Elizabeth Drew, *Atlantic*, August 1970

> The more senior the officer, the more time he has — George S. Patton, *War as I Knew It*, 1947

> . . . power and prestige for even the most junior Congressmen —Gerald R. Rosen, *Dun's*, October 1971

> Tribute should be paid here to certain of our most senior colleagues —*Professional Geographer*, March 1949

Usage commentators generally cover this difference not by discussing implicit comparison but by proclaiming that *more* should not be used with *major, inferior,* or *superior* while ignoring *junior* and *senior.*

A further indication of the idiosyncratic nature of implied comparatives shows up in the following two citations for *senior:*

> Durbrow, the Minister-Counselor, is next senior to Ambassador Smith —Leslie C. Stevens, *Atlantic*, August 1953

> Diana Cartier, a somewhat more senior performer than the others —Walter Terry, *Saturday Rev.*, 6 Nov. 1971

In the passage by Stevens, *senior* follows *next* (a position normally occupied by a superlative but sometimes by a comparative) and is followed, as Quirk describes, by *to*. In the one by Terry, *senior* follows *more* (a construction that normally calls for a positive adjective) and, with its comparative connotation thus negated, is followed by *than*. Both sentences sound idiomatic; the hybrid nature of this implicit comparative makes it versatile enough to adapt to the demands of its context.

Other constructions are normally reserved for positive adjectives but are not as strong markers of comparison as *more* is. With these, the various implicit comparatives occur more indiscriminately.

... too much concentration on the anatomy and physical functions of very inferior bodies and too little on ... the novel itself —Oscar Cargill, in *The Range of English,* 1968

Pop music may be a very minor art form —Paul Hofmann, *N.Y. Times,* 22 Apr. 1973

He thought a cave a very superior kind of house —Willa Cather, *O Pioneers!,* 1913

... I had served under him as a very junior officer —Sumner Welles, *Seven Decisions That Shaped History,* 1950

Should Venturi and Rauch have been asked to design so major an effort? —Thomas B. Hess, *New York,* 5 Apr. 1976

... he is young for so senior a post —William Ridsdale, *London Calling,* 14 Apr. 1955

... so inferior that they are afraid of criticism —Sinclair Lewis, Nobel Prize acceptance speech, revised, 1931

"We were trying to be too superior...." —Ellen Glasgow, *They Stooped to Folly,* 1929

... as minor as a program formulated by a single foreman —Harold Koontz & Cyril O'Donnell, *Principles of Management,* 1955

... there is such a major drive to get the Chinese Communists into the U.N. —*U.S. News & World Report,* 16 July 1954

See also INFERIOR, SUPERIOR; MAJOR.

imply See INFER, IMPLY.

important 1. *Important, importantly, more* (or *most*) *important, more* (or *most*) *importantly.* Copperud 1970 reports that the usage panel of Heritage 1969 was evenly divided on the question of the acceptability of *more importantly* but notes that the subject is (at that time) mentioned in no dictionary of usage. The phrase *more importantly* had come to our attention only a short time before:

"More importantly, Shafer will be trying to take the first of the uncommitted power blocs into the Rockefeller camp ..." (June 13). The adverbial phrase "more importantly" modifies nothing in the sentence. What is wanted in constructions of this kind is "more important," an ellipsis of the phrase "what is more important." —*Winners & Sinners,* 11 July 1968

There was no great rush to judgment following the split decision by Heritage, but Strunk & White 1972

gave the subject brief mention, advising readers to avoid the adverb by rephrasing. Then Newman 1974 gave the controversy a boost:

Why, after centuries, has more importantly, misused, begun to replace more important?

The Harper 1975 panel rejected *more importantly* by three to one. But Bernstein 1977, after a fairly long discussion, changed his 1968 opinion and concluded that neither *important* nor *importantly* was wrong (an opinion concurred in by Safire 1984).

Most of the published opinion has come in the 1980s: Simon 1980, Bremner 1980, Copperud 1980, Burchfield 1981, Johnson 1982, Macmillan 1982, Janis 1984, Bryson 1984, Longman 1984, and Safire 1984. The best summary of the whole matter is in Safire.

American commentators tend to object to the adverb and to recommend the adjective. Objections are made primarily on grammatical grounds. Many repeat Bernstein's original statement that *more importantly* modifies nothing in the sentence. But from the same point of view, neither does *more important.* So a longer phrase, *what is more important,* is postulated and ellipsis adduced to explain the inconvenient absence of *what is.* (In support of this explanation, it is worth noting that our evidence for the phrase—beginning with either *what* or *which*—is older than that for *more/most important.* Darwin uses the phrase fairly often in *Origin of Species,* 1859.) Quirk et al. 1985 describes the grammar of the adjective as a "supplementive adjective clause"; no longer expression needs to be postulated to explain it. Quirk adds that a corresponding adverb can replace the adjective with little or no change in meaning. The OED Supplement simplifies the grammar by calling *more important* "a kind of sentence adjective" and *more importantly* "a kind of sentence adverb." Both forms can be explained grammatically, so there is no real ground for objection in grammar. Only one grammatical limitation needs to be kept in mind: the adjective is used in this way only with *more* or *most;* the adverb can stand alone, but usually has *more* or *most.*

Proponents of the adjective also assert—as Newman 1974 does—that the adjective construction is much older. This assertion cannot be proved with the information now available. The OED Supplement shows *more important* from 1964 and *more importantly* from 1938. Our evidence tells us that both are older than that, but we know this only by chance. The phrases were of little interest just a few years ago and were easily passed over by citation gatherers. Our oldest examples of each phrase are found on citations marked originally for some other term. There are undoubtedly earlier examples to be found, if someone interested were to look for them. So far, the adverb is still older:

No one could overestimate the cost of that struggle to the English, not only in men and money, but also and more importantly in the things of the spirit —H. L. Mencken, *Prejudices: First Series,* 1919

In this country a frontier is no more than something which affects the hours during which licensed premises may be open ... or, more importantly, where the system of government of the Established Church changes —*Times Literary Supp.,* 3 Apr. 1937

More important, the passion of Giovanni and Annabella is not shown as an affinity of temperament —T. S. Eliot, "John Ford," in *Selected Essays,* 1932

But at the end, on every point, unanimous agreement was reached. And more important even than the agreement of words, I may say we achieved a unity of thought and a way of getting along together —Franklin D. Roosevelt, address, 1 Mar. 1945, in *Nothing to Fear,* ed. B. D. Zevin, 1946

You can, then, use either the adjective or the adverb; both are defensible grammatically and both are in respectable use. As Bryson says, "the choice of which to use must be entirely a matter of preference." Usage writers use both:

More important, there is no verb *destruct* —Barzun 1985

More important, do not confuse *masterful* with *masterly* —Safire 1984

. . . but, more importantly, I thought it would help users and readers of English —Bernstein 1977

Importantly, the editor of Webster's New World Dictionary, David Guralnik, agrees —Safire 1980

Most importantly, remember that *due to the fact that* is a wordy way of saying the short and simple word *since* —Shaw 1970

2. *Important* may be complemented by prepositional phrases beginning with *for, in,* or *to:*

Impressions and experiences which are important for the man —T. S. Eliot, "Tradition and the Individual Talent," 1917, in *American Harvest,* ed. Allen Tate & John Peale Bishop, 1942

What kinds of involvement with language are most important for students? —Dwight L. Burton, in *The Range of English,* 1968

. . . tea is very important in British life —Michael Davie, *London Calling,* 19 May 1955

. . . was important in the development of the cotton oil business —*Current Biography 1950*

. . . the matter imitated is important at least to the sale of the goods —Oliver Wendell Holmes d. 1935, in *The Dissenting Opinions of Mr. Justice Holmes,* ed. Alfred Lief, 1929

. . . an end she thinks more important than extra health to her family —Herbert Spencer, reprinted in *Encore,* November 1944

To is sometimes followed by an infinitive phrase:

It is no doubt important to resist pain, but it is also important that it should be there to resist —Havelock Ellis, *The Dance of Life,* 1923

After the superlative, *most important,* one may often find a prepositional phrase beginning with *of:*

The most important of these opportunities came in May 1965 —*Current Biography,* December 1965

impose When used with a preposition, transitive *impose* is used most often with *on;* while *impose* is also used with *upon, on* occurs almost twice as often:

They [churches] impose their views on the public schools —Walter Lippmann, *A Preface to Morals,* 1929

He had greatly disliked the outlandish style imposed on him —Arthur Mizener, *The Saddest Story,* 1971

To impose the baler on those big, hay-grown fields, mastering all their produce —Edmund Wilson, *New Yorker,* 5 June 1971

. . . it must impose ever greater restrictions upon the activities of its subjects —Aldous Huxley, *Brave New World Revisited,* 1958

By making forms he understands the world, grasps the world, imposes himself upon the world —Robert Penn Warren, *Democracy and Poetry,* 1975

Much less frequently, *impose* occurs with *as* or *from:*

A great writer—yes; that account still imposes itself as fitting —F. R. Leavis, *The Common Pursuit,* 1952

Order is something evolved from within, not something imposed from without —E. M. Forster, in *Encore,* November 1944

Occasionally, *impose* is used with *against, around, between, in, into,* or *over:*

If there were any risk that I might be simply imposing one interpretation against another —Frederick J. Hoffman, *Southern Rev.,* April 1965

. . . the United Kingdom's Defense Ministry imposed a new 200-mile war zone around the Falklands —*Wall Street Jour.,* 29 Apr. 1982

He imposed the huge, native stone building between his rambling lodge and his old stable —*Ford Times,* February 1968

They imposed respect if not affection in Europe — D. W. Brogan, *The English People,* 1943

. . . the imposing of reason and moderation into the bosoms of some fifteen gentlemen of birth —Stella Gibbons, *Cold Comfort Farm,* 1932

. . . the Romans imposed a uniform organisation over the whole of Lowland Britain —L. Dudley Stamp, *The Face of Britain,* rev. ed., 1944

impossible This word is sometimes considered to be an absolute adjective. See ABSOLUTE ADJECTIVES.

impractical, impracticable *Impracticable* applies to what is not feasible:

". . . a delicious idea, but so impracticable it doesn't really bear thinking about at all." —Roald Dahl, *Someone Like You,* 1953

. . . numerous uncertainties made a single chronological order impracticable —*Times Literary Supp.,* 16 Apr. 1970

Impractical is a 19th-century word that was quite rare when the OED was originally edited. It has since outstripped the older (17th-century) *impracticable* in use. It is sometimes just an antonym of *practical:*

For Clyde's parents had proved impractical in the matter of the future of their children —Theodore Dreiser, *An American Tragedy,* 1925 (OED Supplement)

It may be applied to what has no practical value:

. . . in fact, "book learning" beyond the Three R's was historically considered somewhat impractical — Tom Wicker, *Change,* September 1971

... living austerely and owning little, but rich in impractical and priceless honor —William Laurence Sullivan, *Epigrams and Criticisms in Miniature,* 1936

It is also used for what is not feasible:

Even the largest of cargo planes can carry but a fraction of the tonnage of a cargo ship and many cargoes are of such a nature as to make air transportation entirely impractical —*California Maritime Academy General Catalog,* 1969–1970

Visits ... were impractical for a considerable number of students living in isolated areas —Peter J. Smith, *Saturday Rev.,* 29 Apr. 1972

Impractical is easier to pronounce and spell than *impracticable;* that fact may in the future make it even more dominant than it already is.

impresario Copperud 1970, 1980 notes this is often misspelled *impressario;* we can confirm his observation. It has nothing to do, etymologically or semantically, with *impress,* and you should not let this more common word influence your spelling of a less common one. Only one *s,* please.

impress *Impress* is used with any one of numerous prepositions; among them *by* or *with* occur most frequently:

... this group ... is impressed by actual gains that have come about —John Dewey, *Freedom and Culture,* 1939

... her first novel ... impresses by its assurance and finish —*British Book News,* August 1967

... he sure had been impressed by the fellow with the Stacomb in his hair —David Halberstam, *Harper's,* July 1969

He had impressed the village with his urbanity and his sharp clothes —John Cheever, *The Wapshot Chronicle,* 1957

... although people consciously deny being impressed by testimonials there is a strong suspicion that unconsciously they are impressed with them —Vance Packard, *The Hidden Persuaders,* 1957

... I am impressed with the way it [a book] hangs together thematically —Erica Jong, *Barnard Alumnae,* Winter 1971

Impress is also found quite often with *on* or *upon:*

... it was the general custom for boys to be whipped on certain days to impress things on their memories —Thomas B. Costain, *The Black Rose,* 1945

His view of art ... impressed itself upon a number of writers —T. S. Eliot, "Arnold and Pater," in *Selected Essays,* 1932

... impressing his will upon others by sheer force of character —Vernon Louis Parrington, *Main Currents in American Thought,* 1927

Somewhat less frequently, *impress* is used with *as* or *into:*

... the criminals released from jail and the foreigners impressed into service —Upton Sinclair, *Presidential Mission,* 1947

Her full lower lip was impressed into a suggestion of voluptuousness —E. L. Doctorow, *Loon Lake,* 1979

... [Khrushchev] impressed us as a very rugged, forceful individual —Don Dallas, *London Calling,* 21 Apr. 1955

Very occasionally, *impress* is used with *at, for,* or *in:*

... neither awed nor visibly impressed at being the center of attention —Joseph N. Bell, *Saturday Evening Post,* 25 Dec. 1954

All able-bodied survivors were impressed for the task —*American Guide Series: Texas,* 1940

The poem does not contain a series of ... fine phrases. It only impresses in its totality —A. T. Tolley, *Southern Rev.,* April 1970

impromptu See EXTEMPORANEOUS, IMPROMPTU.

improve When *improve* is used with a preposition, it is usually *on* or *upon:*

... remembered all the backwoods stories his customers told him—and doubtlessly improved on them a little —George Sessions Perry, *Saturday Evening Post,* 3 July 1954

The book is hard to improve on —Daniel Melcher, *Children's House,* Holiday issue, 1969

It is a common fallacy that a writer ... can achieve this poignant quality by improving upon his subectmatter —Willa Cather, *Not Under Forty,* 1936

... a mass of people as a whole seems to improve upon the better nature of the parts —Edward Hoagland, *Harper's,* October 1970

Very occasionally, *improve* is used with *over:*

... although he improves over Johnson by entering more respellings —*Language,* January–March 1946

improvement The chief prepositions used with *improvement* are *on, in, of,* and *to.*

... some of whom offered improvements on Patterson's original proposal —*Current Biography 1947*

... where life would be such an improvement on dull dingy Paris —Vladimir Nabokov, *Lolita,* 1958

... studies for possible improvements in State and Federal social security legislation —*Current Biography 1947*

... spent every dollar he earned on the comfort of his family and the improvement of their station in life —Herman Wouk, *Marjorie Morningstar,* 1955

... the patents taken out by Watt for improvements to the steam engine —*Times Literary Supp.,* 5 Mar. 1970

in, into You will not find many subjects in this book over which more ink has been spilled to as little purpose as this one—the distinguishing of the prepositions *in* and *into.* The real distinction is simply stated: *into* is used with verbs of motion; *in* is used with verbs that show location and also with some verbs of motion. The OED gives the history: in Old English *in* originally had all the work; with verbs of location it took a noun in the dative case, and with verbs of motion a noun in the accusative case. Eventually the two cases became indistinguishable, and *to* was dragged in to help with the accusative instances. By modern times, *into* had carved out a pretty sizable piece of the original territory of *in.*

The grammarians, though, want usage to be even simpler. There must be one function for *in,* one function for *into,* and no sharing. They have been insisting on this simplification of English since at least Joseph Hervey Hull's *Grammar* of 1829 (and he very likely was not the first), and they are still beating the same drum as recently as Shaw 1987, Belanoff et al. 1986, and Little, Brown 1986. It is a hoary tradition.

But *in* has remained in use with verbs of motion all along. There seem to be various reasons for its survival. The OED lists several verbs with which *in* is regularly and idiomatically associated—one or two of them appear in the examples that follow. There are other idiomatic expressions that require *in* rather than *into* (the poker game, for instance, is *spit in the ocean*). And there is the constant influential presence of the adverb *in,* which combines idiomatically with many verbs. Goold Brown (10th edition, 1880) also notes the influence of speech patterns; he finds a grammarian's "split into two" less satisfactory than "split in two" because, he says, the shorter word is better in the unemphatic position (*split* also happens to be on the OED list).

Here are a few examples of *in* with verbs expressing motion, spread over about 300 years:

> FLORIO. My Rosaura!   *They embrace.*
> *Enter* Podesta *and* Bricklayer.
> ROSAURA. My husband! Faint, faint in my arms!
> —John Crowne, *City Politiques,* 1683

> Your plants were taken in one very cold blustering day & placed in the Dining room —Jane Austen, letter, 1 Oct. 1808

> . . . will turn round halfway in his chair and spit in the fire! —Mary Chesnut, diary, 1 Jan. 1864

> You never know when something you may say might make them go jump in the lake —Flannery O'Connor, letter, 20 May 1960

> You can't get a waiter to wait ten seconds. You go in a restaurant, he hands you a menu . . . , and in three seconds he starts tapping his pencil —*And More by Andy Rooney,* 1982

The last example above makes another point: *into* would have given more prominence to the fact of entering the restaurant than the writer wanted.

The points to remember are these. Sometimes you need *into* to distinguish motion from location, as in this example:

> . . . their sturdy little ship, the Roosevelt, backed out of her berth into the East River —E. L. Doctorow, *Ragtime,* 1975

Some verbs and some expressions idiomatically call for *in*—we've seen "go jump in the lake" and "split in two," for instance. Cook 1985 says that *place* requires *in;* nobody had to explain that to Jane Austen. And when you have a choice, remember that *into* gives more prominence to the idea of entrance; if you want to deemphasize that, as Andy Rooney did, you use *in.* Both *in* and *into* are standard with verbs of motion no matter how some commentators might wish things to be. But you must, as always, use your ear.

inaccessible   *Inaccessible,* when used with a preposition, is almost always used with *to:*

> Mary was not . . . so inaccessible to all influence of hers —Jane Austen, *Persuasion,* 1818

> . . . there were things in us fundamentally inaccessible to one another —George Santayana, *Persons and Places,* 1944

> . . . our classical authors remained uncollected, with much of their work inaccessible to the reading public —Malcolm Cowley, *N.Y. Times Book Rev.,* 25 Apr. 1982

Very occasionally, *inaccessible* may be used with *for:*

> . . . its deliberately national and middle-class image make it inaccessible or unattractive for most of the children —Wallace Roberts, *Change,* November–December 1969

In its physical sense *inaccessible* may be used with *by:*

> Places inaccessible by any road may be quickly reached by plane —George Gaylord Simpson, *Attending Marvels,* 1934

> . . . areas near the capital were inaccessible by rivers —Chester Lloyd Jones, *Guatemala Past and Present,* 1940

in addition to   A couple of commentators disparage *in addition to* as a wordy alternative to *besides.* It is, rather, a longer alternative to *besides* that may be chosen for variety or for sentence rhythm. It can also be paired with another longer phrase where *besides* would work poorly:

> . . . research and publication and community service should be carried on in addition to, rather than as a substitute for, class and seminar instruction —Bruce Dearing, *CEA Forum,* April 1971

> All this in addition to, and even in defiance of, whatever real or pretended sex education . . . may be offered —G. Legman, *Rationale of the Dirty Joke,* 1st series, 1968

When the phrase is most nearly literal, *besides* will not substitute well for it:

> . . . a core of educational experiences, in addition to the basic core for the technician aide, could be directed toward preparing students —Arden L. Pratt, *Junior College Jour.,* December 1970–January 1971

> . . . was appointed the Stratford company's general manager, in addition to his other duties —*Current Biography,* September 1965

In addition to is most easily interchangeable with *besides* when it begins a sentence, and if our evidence is typical, this is its most common position:

> In addition to everything else, Hemming proved to have an odd sense of mischief —Jeremy Bernstein, *New Yorker,* 30 Oct. 1971

> In addition to these regular reminders Dr. Adams recently put out . . . an excellent guidebook —*Times Literary Supp.,* 5 Feb. 1970

We are also warned that *in addition to,* unlike *and,* does not add one subject of a sentence to another and thus does not affect the number of the verb. We cannot show you an example of this construction, because we have none in our files. We suspect it to be rare in edited prose.

in advance of   Copperud 1980 disparages *in advance of* as wordy for *before;* Janis 1984, with greater insight, notes that *before* is simpler but does not always carry the same force. The phrase is more specific than *before* in that it has fewer meanings, and it may be occasionally preferred to *before* for that reason.

> However, Washington never really ceased to give substantial military assistance to Chiang Kai-shek in advance of democratic performances —Lawrence K. Rosinger, *New Republic,* 5 Aug. 1946

And other senses of *advance* may occur in the phrase:

> . . . the laws were in advance of English common law —*Dictionary of American Biography,* 1936

in any case   See CASE.

inasmuch as   This phrase is disparaged by several commentators (such as Follett 1966, Evans 1957, Copperud 1960, 1964, 1970, 1980, Flesch 1964) in terms only slightly varied from those of Fowler 1926. Fowler calls it "pompous," and later critics apply such labels as "formal" and "stilted." As Janis 1984 and Evans 1957 point out, *since, as,* and *because* are simpler. But if you want a longer expression, there is nothing wrong with *inasmuch as;* the objections are trifling.

> . . . though sometimes I have been not a little inclined to quarrel with it, inasmuch as it effectually deprives one of the assistance of the men —Fanny Kemble, *Journal of a Residence on a Georgian Plantation in 1838–1839,* 1863

> Dickens was a smash hit at the age of 24. This was not quite an accident, except inasmuch as genius is always a divine accident —John Wain, *N.Y. Times Book Rev.,* 24 June 1979

> . . . which is just as well, inasmuch as it is by no means clear that he'd have understood it —William F. Buckley, Jr., *National Rev.,* 25 Aug. 1970

inaugurate   Copperud 1960, 1964, 1970, 1980 is following a long journalistic tradition when he disparages *inaugurate* for *open, begin,* or *start* as journalese; it goes back to Bierce 1909 and before him to William Cullen Bryant's *Index Expurgatorius,* compiled when he was editor of the *New York Evening Post* and published in 1877. *Inaugurate* was also disparaged by Richard Grant White 1870 and Ayres 1881, and (according to Vizetelly 1906) by Yale professor William Lyons Phelps, inaugurating (if we may) an extra-journalistic tradition followed by Partridge 1942, Evans 1957, and Flesch 1964. Vizetelly notes that lexicographers ignore these strictures, and indeed they have—the sense "to begin" was recognized in Samuel Johnson's Dictionary (1755).
   To be frank, were it not for the strength of the tradition, this would have been a dead issue long ago. Here are a few examples of what is clearly a standard, and not especially journalistic, usage:

> . . . the era of galvanized sesquipedalism and sonorous cadences, inaugurated by Johnson —Fitzedward Hall 1873

> Who inaugurated the custom of working by day? —Brooks Atkinson, *Saturday Rev.,* 21 Aug. 1954

> . . . turning from the hero to the common man, we inaugurated the era of realism —Joseph Wood Krutch, *The Modern Temper,* 1929

> . . . thereby inaugurating a terror which would become dreadfully familiar to hundreds of millions — William L. Shirer, *The Rise and Fall of the Third Reich,* 1960

> . . . inaugurated the train of disasters —Robert B. Heilman, *Southern Rev.,* April 1970

> Yet it would be unreasonable to demand that a writer both inaugurate a new era of scholarship and solve all the problems he has raised —Richard Sennett, *N.Y. Times Book Rev.,* 19 Oct. 1980

in back of   See BACK OF, IN BACK OF.

in behalf of   See BEHALF. ’

in case   See CASE.

in case of   See CASE.

incentive   When *incentive* is used with a preposition, it is usually *to:*

> And these lucky chances had been no incentive to further effort —H. G. Wells, *Mr. Britling Sees It Through,* 1916

> . . . add that terrible but effective incentive to greater effort: fear of losing a job —*New Republic,* 19 Sept. 1949

> This of course provides an incentive to make the next release particularly interesting —Chris Albertson, *Saturday Rev.,* 27 Nov. 1971

Less often but still quite commonly, *incentive* is used with *for:*

> That eliminated the incentive for judicial tests of legality —Irving Brant, *New Republic,* 20 Dec. 1954

> . . . reducing the incentives for South Africans, Israelis and Pakistanis to use nuclear weapons —James Fallows, *N.Y. Times Book Rev.,* 26 June 1983

Incentive also occasionally is used with *toward:*

> . . . rivermen provided the first incentive toward establishing a settlement here —*American Guide Series: Pennsylvania,* 1940

When the prepositional phrase specifies the incentive, the preposition is, naturally enough, *of:*

> . . . the Nipmucks and Valley Tribes only needed the incentive of Philip's arrival to take up the tomahawk —Ray Allen Billington, *Westward Expansion,* 1949

> . . . the old incentive of competition —S. P. B. Mais, *The English Scene To-day,* 2d ed., 1949

incentivize   This is perhaps the most recent of the infamous verbs that end in *-ize.* Its meaning is "to give incentives to," as in "ways for companies to incentivize their employees." We first heard of it in 1970 from a correspondent who told us that it was in common use by people in the advertising business. In published writing, however, it was anything *but* common, and we didn't encounter it again until an instance of its use in the *Wall Street Journal* was cited in Harper 1985. The Harper panelists rejected it almost unanimously with varying degrees of disgust and horror. Our continued lack of evidence for it suggests that those who despise it have little to fear. For the time being, anyway, *incentivize* shows no sign of working its way into the mainstream of English.

inchoate A number of British commentators, beginning with Ivor Brown 1945 and running through Gowers in Fowler 1965, Howard 1977, and Bryson 1984, complain about the extension of meaning of *inchoate* from "incipient, immature, or just beginning" (Howard's definitions) to "amorphous, incoherent, or disorganized" (Howard again). A couple of American commentators, Flesch 1964 and Shaw 1987, agree. But the extended use is natural and probably inevitable: what is just begun is also unfinished, incomplete, and often also disorganized or incoherent. There is no need to bring forward a putative confusion with *chaotic* to explain the development. And unfortunately for the complainers, the extension of meaning was already three decades old or more when Brown noticed it.

> ... all the world of men outside seemed inchoate, purposeless, like the swarming, slimy, minute life in stagnant water —Mary Webb, *The Golden Arrow,* 1916

> ... had to seek the help of their conquered subjects, or of more vigorous foreigners, to administer their ill-knit and inchoate empires —T. E. Lawrence, *The Seven Pillars of Wisdom,* 1935

> Sometimes her sweltering and inchoate fury was so great that she threw him on the floor and stamped on him —Thomas Wolfe, *Look Homeward, Angel,* 1929

> The heart of the crowd is undoubtedly a thing of vague, inchoate yearnings to be touched —John Livingston Lowes, *Convention and Revolt in Poetry,* 1919

It is now one of the words regularly used by reviewers:

> ... it threatens to dominate their narratives, as something inchoate, unchannelled, mysterious — John Updike, *New Yorker,* 10 Apr. 1971

> ... the pieces seem almost inchoate: ideas struggling to be realized, works waiting to be born —Lisa Hammel, *N.Y. Times,* 9 Mar. 1976

> ... about 132 pages of inchoate material in this new collection —Joyce Carol Oates, *N.Y. Times Book Rev.,* 1 Apr. 1979

It also has considerable use in other kinds of writing:

> In the colleges ... it [composition] falls characteristically into the least experienced hands, where it is pawed and plied into a thousand inchoate shapes — Walker Gibson, in *The Hues of English,* 1969

> ... his unique set of blocks, inhibitions, and inchoate anxieties —Norman Mailer, *Harper's,* March 1971

> ... can help us to examine the often inchoate assumptions underlying our relationships —Susan Edmiston, *New York,* 27 Dec. 1971

American dictionaries and at least one British one have already acknowledged this spread of meaning.

incident Harper 1975, 1985 and Copperud 1970, 1980 are disturbed by the use of *incident* as an all-purpose word for some unpleasant or potentially dangerous occurrence—Copperud and Gowers in Fowler 1965 call it a euphemism. The basis of their concern is found in the assertion that *incident* means only "a minor or unimportant occurrence." But the assertion is without foundation and suggests that dictionaries have not been "perused with attention" (to use a line from Dr. Johnson). Here are three examples of actual use:

> There were frequent border incidents leading to armed clashes —*Current Biography,* November 1967

> The students were earlier declared ineligible following a weekend incident involving alcoholic beverages —*Ouray County* (Colo.) *Plaindealer,* 8 Mar. 1973

> Whenever an incident occurred in the neighborhood, he was one of the first to be suspected —C. Knight Aldrich, *Psychology Today,* March 1971

The sense displayed in these examples has been established since before World War I in reference to discrete occurrences of serious diplomatic import, and in the period since World War I has spread to other areas. The OED Supplement has numerous examples from 1913 on. When Gowers says that it is often used as a euphemism for *affray,* its value becomes apparent—it suggests an unfortunate occurrence while avoiding the need to specify its character, which may not always be immediately certain. The sense is impeccably standard. Its potential for being used euphemistically should not be overlooked, however. Here, for instance, is Thomas H. Middleton reporting on the jargon of the nuclear power people:

> A nuclear accident isn't called an accident; it's an "abnormal occurrence" or an "incident." —*Saturday Rev.,* 1 May 1976

incidental When used with a preposition, *incidental* is usually combined with *to:*

> ... labor problems incidental to rapidly expanding factories —*American Guide Series: Massachusetts,* 1937

> There is, in hockey, no idiotic propaganda that violence is only incidental to the game —Jeff Greenfield, *Harper's,* January 1972

> These projects were always incidental to our games, which dominated our days —Jim Strain, *Sports Illustrated,* 22 June 1981

> ... Gibraltar is a Crown Colony and *habeas corpus* is incidental thereto —Harold J. Laski, letter, 11 Feb. 1923

Very occasionally, *incidental* occurs with *on:*

> One oligarchic critic emphasises the casual profits incidental on Athens' position as an imperial city — A. H. M. Jones, *Past and Present,* February 1952

incidentally 1. The spelling *incidently* is a rare variant of *incidentally* that is noted in a number of large dictionaries, including the OED and Webster's Third; it goes back to Sir Thomas More. It has never been entirely out of use:

> Incidently, no self-respecting scientist would make the same mistake —Horace Gregory, *N.Y. Times Book Rev.,* 11 Mar. 1962

Some commentators consider it an error, but it is not. It is not a spelling that we recommend your using, however.

Incidently would also be the spelling of an adverb derived from the adjective *incident,* should one be needed.

2. Fowler 1926 and Gowers at greater length in Fowler 1965 disparage the use of *incidentally* as a sentence adverb. When used this way—as it commonly is in speech, letters, and lighter prose—*incidentally* introduces an aside or digression; there is nothing wrong with such use.

> Incidentally, I had lunch with T. S. Eliot the other day —James Thurber, letter, 12 Dec. 1950

> ... Cervantes's masterpiece . . . —incidentally, now available in a new and accomplished translation —Malcolm Muggeridge, *Punch,* 8 Apr. 1953

> Incidentally, I am only coming to Princeton to research, not to teach —Albert Einstein, letter, quoted in *Change,* January–February 1971

> ... was fortunate in having a good teacher, Mrs. Lottie Ross—still living, incidentally —John Fischer, *Harper's,* October 1970

incidently See INCIDENTALLY 1.

inclose, inclosure See ENCLOSE, INCLOSE.

include There are quite a few commentators—Bryson 1984, Barzun 1985, Flesch 1964, Copperud 1960, 1964, 1970, 1980, and Bernstein 1965 among them—who maintain that *include* should not be used when a complete list of items follows the verb.

> The prison includes 22 enclosed acres and a farm of 1,000 acres west and south of the walls —*American Guide Series: Minnesota,* 1938

> His clubs include the Athenaeum, the Carlton, the Farmers', the Beefsteak, and Grillion's —*Current Biography,* September 1964

There is nothing wrong with either of these examples. They fit the requirements of Fowler 1926, 1965 perfectly:

> With *include,* there is no presumption (though it is often the fact) that all or even most of the components are mentioned. . . .

The critics above, however, have somehow reasoned themselves into the notion that with *include* all of the components must not be mentioned, which has never been the case. Fowler's comments accurately describe how *include* is used.

incomparable A number of derivatives ending in *-ble* are accented on a syllable other than the one corresponding to the stressed syllable of the underlying verb. Thus *incomparable, irrevocable, irrefutable,* and *irreparable* are normally stressed on the second syllable. The disparity of stress often corresponds to a certain disparity of meaning. *Incomparable,* for example, typically

does not mean literally "not subject to comparison" but "matchless, beyond compare."

A few words of this type have not definitely settled on a single pronunciation style: *lamentable* varies widely between the specially stressed \ˈlam-ən-tə-bəl\ and \lə-ˈment-ə-bəl\, stressed by analogy with the verb *lament.* And a minority of educated speakers use verb-like pronunciations even for words like *irrevocable,* although such pronunciations are scorned by some. But we are not dealing here with mere error. Every so often we receive a letter from a correspondent consciously defending \kəm-ˈpar-ə-bəl\ for *comparable* when the sense is not "roughly equal" but "suitable for comparison," a meaning more closely tied to the underlying verb. Thus, five cents and a billion dollars would be (in this view) \kəm-ˈpar-ə-bəl\, whereas one hour and one acre would not be.

There are similar cases of different pronunciations for different senses of a word. *Ablative* gets stress on its first syllable when it is used in the grammatical sense but is pronounced \a-ˈblāt-iv\ when it means "tending to ablate." *Protractor* may be pronounced \ˈprō-ˌtrak-tər\ when it designates the geometrical instrument and no longer, in the speaker's mind, has connection with any verb, but \prō-ˈtrak-tər\ when it refers to "something that protracts."

incomparables See ABSOLUTE ADJECTIVES.

incomplete comparison See ABSOLUTE COMPARATIVE; AS GOOD OR BETTER THAN; FALSE COMPARISON.

incongruous *Incongruous* may be used with the preposition *to* or *with:*

> ... it would be ... incongruous to meet her at the end of a chapter —Herman Wouk, *Aurora Dawn,* 1947

> ... an efflorescence of hope that must have seemed highly incongruous to those who knew his situation —James Atlas, *N.Y. Times Book Rev.,* 8 July 1979

> He ate enormously, with a zest which seemed incongruous with his spare frame —Willa Cather, *The Song of the Lark,* 1915

> It is astonishingly incongruous with what we feel we know —T. S. Eliot, "Cyril Tourneur," in *Selected Essays,* 1932

Less frequently, *incongruous* occurs with *about, in,* or *on:*

> There is something incongruous about Oslo —Hugh C. McDonald, *The Hour of the Blue Fox,* 1975

> ... settlements incongruous in material and often startling in their ugliness —S. P. B. Mais, *The English Scene To-day,* 2d ed., 1949

> He was smoking a cigar which looked incongruous on his thin face —Norman Mailer, *The Naked and the Dead,* 1948

in connection with *In connection with* and one or two other phrases containing *connection* are disparaged as wordy in such books at Phythian 1979, Janis 1984, Copperud 1960, 1964, 1970, 1980, and Shaw 1975, 1987. The usual argument is that some simple preposition—*about* is the one most often mentioned—is preferable. The guess here is that the commentators have paid little attention to the way their corrections would read in a range of actual contexts.

> Our financial practices put the Company in a very favorable position in connection with the currency disturbances in Europe —Paul E. Wallendorf, quoted in *General Electric Investor,* Summer 1971

"A favorable position about the currency disturbances"? Not likely.

> The World Bank . . . was founded in connection with the United Nations at the end of World War II — *Current Biography,* July 1965

About? By? From? At? Of? Concerning? Several of these substitutes are clearly impossible; others will produce a meaningful sentence but not a sentence with the same meaning as this sentence.

> These options, granted in connection with the acquisition of various corporations —*Annual Report, Phillips Petroleum Co.,* 1970

Our files contain many examples like those above where it is not easy to replace the phrase with one of the suggested single-word prepositions.

True, the phrase does also occur in simpler contexts where a shorter preposition is a viable option:

> . . . offered the following in connection with this aspect of the situation —*AAUP Bulletin,* December 1967

> One thing I want to point out . . . in connection with these prices —Richard Joseph, *Your Trip to Britain,* 1954

In connection with, then, can sometimes be replaced by a shorter preposition and sometimes not. You as a writer are going to have to make that decision. The automatic substitution of *about* or *concerning* can result in gibberish.

incorporate When *incorporate* is used with a preposition, it is used usually, with about equal frequency, with *in* or *into:*

> . . . the Germans had just simply dropped on Mr. Schatzweiler in their pleasant way, incorporated him in their forces and had sent him to the front —Ford Madox Ford, *The Last Post,* 1928

> . . . so our allies can incorporate the bomb in their military plans —Omar N. Bradley, *Saturday Evening Post,* 10 Apr. 1951

> . . . to incorporate into the community of scholars a community of students —James B. Conant, *Atlantic,* May 1946

> . . . to accept new findings of fact . . . and incorporate them into our teaching —W. Nelson Francis, *College English,* March 1953

Incorporate is sometimes used with *with:*

> . . . where music has been for a hundred and fifty years integrated and incorporated with the whole intellectual tradition —Virgil Thomson, *The Musical Scene,* 1947

Incorporate is used only infrequently with *on:*

> . . . innovations in engine and body design which may be incorporated on coming car models —*The Americana Annual 1953*

incredulous, incredible Many books on usage explain the distinction between these words, which is that *incredible* means "impossible to believe" or "hard to believe" ("an incredible story") and *incredulous* means "unwilling to believe; disbelieving" ("an incredulous audience"). What the commentators are chiefly concerned about is the use of *incredulous* where *incredible* is usual:

> . . . so began the incredulous success story we all know —*Disco 45 Annual 1976*

Such usage was once in good repute. The OED gives "not to be believed" as an obsolete sense of *incredulous* and shows it occurring in the works of such writers as Sir Thomas Browne and William Shakespeare:

> No obstacle, no incredulous or unsafe circumstance —Shakespeare, *Twelfth Night,* 1602

But this sense of *incredulous* had fallen into disuse by the end of the 18th century. Its reappearance in recent years has been sporadic, although there are signs that the usage may be growing more widespread:

> I think it's rather incredulous to say that you can't defend this country without a 10 percent increase — Senator Pete Domenici, quoted in *Springfield* (Mass.) *Morning Union,* 8 Apr. 1983

> . . . their tales of woe seemed almost incredulous — William L. Shirer, *The Nightmare Years,* 1984

> . . . her incredulous performance. . . . It does strain credibility —*People,* 3 June 1985

Even so, *incredible* is still the usual and standard word in such contexts. Most writers continue to restrict *incredulous* to its "disbelieving" sense, and we recommend that you do so as well:

> He was greeted with incredulous laughter —Robert M. Hutchins, *Center Mag.,* September 1968

> The author was incredulous and investigated. "It was true," he discovered. —Mel Gussow, *N.Y. Times Mag.,* 1 Jan. 1984

See also CREDIBLE, CREDITABLE, CREDULOUS.

inculcate When *inculcate* is used with a preposition, and the direct object denotes what is inculcated, the preposition is usually *in* or *into:*

> Hatred of America is systematically inculcated in Russians —*Time,* 27 Sept. 1948

> His task, rather, is to inculcate in the government and the people basic ecological attitudes —William Murdoch & Joseph Connell, *Center Mag.,* January–February 1970

> The blatant irrationalism and blind violence inculcated into the dupes of the totalitarian despots — *Times Literary Supp.,* 18 Jan. 1941

> By the time I was four years old "Take a Pair of Sparkling Eyes" . . . had been fairly inculcated into my bloodstream —Noel Coward, *Punch,* 8 July 1953

Infrequently, *inculcate* is also used with *on* or *upon:*

> . . . thorough instruction in all phases of weather . . . designed to inculcate judgment on what to do in emergency —Phil Gustafson, *Saturday Evening Post,* 12 June 1954

... the figure primarily responsible for inculcating upon vast numbers of young and needy minds ... the primer-simple notion that LSD has "something" to do with religion —Theodore Roszak, *The Making of a Counter Culture,* 1969

More controversial is the use of *inculcate* with *with* and a personal direct object. Although this practice rouses the opposition of some language commentators (Evans 1957, Phythian 1979, Bryson 1984, for example), most seem not to notice that when the use occurs, the sense of the verb is a little different from the sense implied when *inculcate* is used with the other prepositions mentioned above: "to cause to be impressed" rather than "to impress". Copperud 1970, 1980 is an exception in this regard, and he is also one commentator who seems not to be disturbed by passages like these:

... the disinterested teachers who fail to inculcate them with American ideals —James J. Joliff, letter to the editor, *Newsweek,* 22 July 1957

The children ... were early inculcated with their parents' moral code —*Current Biography,* July 1965

This construction, though standard, is much less common than the uncontroversial one discussed first.

incumbent **1.** When the adjective *incumbent* is used with a preposition, it is usually used with *upon* or *on:* use of *upon* occurs a little more frequently. Use of *on* or *upon* usually means that the object of the preposition is followed by *to* with an infinitive:

After taking off his coat, he felt it incumbent upon him to make some little report of his day —Theodore Dreiser, *Sister Carrie,* 1900

It is incumbent upon the press to act not in its own best interests, but in society's best interests —Carll Tucker, *Saturday Rev.,* 23 June 1979

... Mr. Lorry felt it incumbent on him to speak a word or two of reassurance —Charles Dickens, *A Tale of Two Cities,* 1859

It is not the Russian people as a whole on whom it is incumbent to respond to the challenge —George F. Kennan, *New Yorker,* 1 May 1971

Occasionally, the preposition is simply followed by a noun:

Expression of that emotional experience has been incumbent upon modern fiction —Warren Beck in *Forms of Modern Fiction,* ed. William Van O'Connor, 1948

... the various types of obligation incumbent on the members of the profession —R. M. MacIver, *Annals of the American Academy of Political and Social Science,* January 1955

Far less frequently, *incumbent* is used with *for:*

... is it therefore incumbent for us to abandon our search ... ? —Ernest Nagel, *New Republic,* 28 June 1954

2. See PRESENT INCUMBENT.

indefinite pronouns Many indefinite pronouns, such as *anyone, somebody, none, each, either,* and *one,* are involved in usage questions of one kind or another. You will find most of these treated separately. They are also part of the discussions in the articles at AGREEMENT: INDEFINITE PRONOUNS; NOTIONAL AGREEMENT, NOTIONAL CONCORD; THEY, THEIR, THEM.

indefinite *you* See YOU 2.

independence When used with a preposition, *independence* is used with either *from* or *of:*

... and he would say, with enough diffidence to mark his respect for his elders, yet a complete independence of their views —Edith Wharton, *The Spark,* 1924

Countries that have been sluggish in their social and economic adaptations have not attained independence of foreign aid —Neil H. Jacoby, "The Progress of Peoples," 1969

... to work toward Korea's independence from Peking —David J. Dallin, *The Rise of Russia in Asia,* 1949

... the logical independence of the axiom of parallels from the rest, is the guiding motive of the work —Bertrand Russell, *Foundations of Geometry,* 1897

independent *Independent,* when used with a preposition, is usually used with *of:*

... detached from and independent of the dark stretches below —Thomas Hardy, *The Return of the Native,* 1878

... our anxiety to make judges independent of the popular will —Morris R. Cohen, *The Faith of a Liberal,* 1946

... they would ... unanimously bring up to me, independent of any questions I'd ask them, the claim that the morale in the field was ... high —William Ruckelshaus, quoted in *N.Y. Times Mag.,* 19 Aug. 1973

Perhaps by analogy with *independence, independent* is occasionally used with *from:*

... all ... apparently on a par and independent from each other —*Newsweek,* 1 May 1972

Indian See NATIVE AMERICAN.

indifferent The preposition used with *indifferent* is almost always *to:*

... aspects of language that the earlier grammarians were indifferent to —Geoffrey Nunberg, *Atlantic,* December 1983

... singularly indifferent to landscape —*Times Literary Supp.,* 21 May 1971

... grow indifferent to and even contemptuous of such democratic impedimenta —Irving Howe, *Harper's,* July 1969

Rarely we find a compound preposition—*as to* or *with respect to*—instead:

For it is commonly said and commonly believed that science is completely neutral and indifferent as to the ends and values which move men to act —John Dewey, *Freedom and Culture,* 1939

individual The contention of most commentators in the controversy over *individual* as a noun meaning "a human being" is this: it is acceptable when the individual is contrasted with a larger unit, such as society or the family, and it is acceptable when it stresses some special quality. These two examples illustrate:

> The individual rebelled against restraint; society wanted to do what it pleased; all disliked the laws which Church and State were trying to fasten on them —Henry Adams, *Mont-Saint-Michel and Chartres,* 1904

> But Donne would have been an individual at any time and place —T. S. Eliot, "Andrew Marvell," in *Selected Essays,* 1932

But there is something wrong with it when it points to no obvious contrast or no obvious special trait and simply means "person":

> Now I hold it is not proper for a scientific gent
> To say another is an ass, at least to all intent;
> Nor should the individual who happens to be meant
> Reply by heaving rocks at him, to any great extent
> —Bret Harte, "The Society upon the Stanislaus"
> (in Utter 1916)

> There were many individuals of dashing appearance, whom I easily understood as belonging to the race of swell pick-pockets —Edgar Allan Poe, "The Man of the Crowd," reprinted in *Encore,* September 1945

The above distinction is essentially that given in Fowler 1926. But the controversy is older than Fowler, dating back at least to Bache 1869, who objects for no specific reason. Ayres 1881 objects more clearly. His objection is based on etymology: since *individual* suggests one that cannot be divided, it has to be used in opposition to an aggregate that is divisible. Bierce 1909 repeats the etymological objection. Our evidence shows that from sometime around the period of Ayres and Bache until the 1920s, it was fashionable to disparage *individual* used in the manner illustrated by Poe and Harte above.

The OED marks a sort of midpoint in the early history of the controversy. The *I* sections were published in 1900; at this sense of *individual,* James A. H. Murray put a note: "Now chiefly as a colloquial vulgarism, or as a term of disparagement." The citations shown in the OED do not bear out this judgment, although the latest one (1888) does contain the phrase "unpleasant individual."

Hall 1917 expresses puzzlement over the attack on the sense. He lists 38 authors in whose works he has seen it. Most of the authors are 18th- and 19th-century grammarians and philologists. Hall opines that literary use is on the decline, which may have been what Murray was getting at indirectly in the OED note.

The earliest OED citation is from Samuel Johnson in 1742. Hall claims to have found it in Sir Thomas Browne a century earlier (he does not reproduce the citation, however), and Samuel Johnson had found it in Bacon and Pope (but the citations are curiously under the adjective in his Dictionary).

> Neither is it enough to consult concerning *Persons,* ... what the Kinde and Character of the *Person* should be; For the greatest Errours are committed, and the most Iudgement is shewne, in the choice of *Individuals* —Francis Bacon, *Essays,* 1625

> Know, all the good that individuals find,
> Or God and Nature meant to mere Mankind,
> Reason's whole pleasure, all the joys of Sense,
> Lie in three words, Health, Peace, and Competence
> —Alexander Pope, "Essay on Man," 1734

Johnson had abridged both of these. It seems likely, from these and the long list in Hall, that the OED readers did not pay much attention to the use. (The same can be said for Merriam-Webster editors, too. We have a citation that complains of George Borrow's using the term seven times in three pages of *The Romany Rye,* and even though that book was quite heavily marked for citations here, no one found *individual.*)

The OED treatment had a curious effect. Murray's note presumably reflected use at the end of the 1890s, but it began to be repeated in American sources only about 20 years later—Utter 1916 has a version of it and so does Lincoln Library 1924. Webster 1909 carried the sense unlabeled, but the editors—apparently on the basis of a number of published opinions condemning the use—added a note similar to the OED's in 1925 (the note was kept in softened form in Webster's Second 1934; Webster's Third 1961 went back to the original stance of Webster 1909).

It was clearly not the usage of Bacon or Pope or Johnson that brought on the controversy. The source of the complaints seems to have come from two quarters. Fowler notes that the "person" sense of *individual* was a jocular commonplace among 19th-century novelists, and Hall's evidence bears him out—Hall's most frequent users include Cooper, Hawthorne, Poe, and Dickens (Coleridge used it a lot, too). And it seems to have been a regular ornament of mid-19th-century journalism: Alford 1866 mentions it in passing on his way to an attack on the similar use of *party.* Mencken 1963 (abridged) quotes Alford and remarks that he could have been talking about American newspapers as well as British. Quite possibly journalistic overuse was behind the complaints of Bache, Ayres, and Bierce.

We don't know which writers soured Fowler on the word, but we suspect that what might be termed high-toned use of the disputed sense of *individual* was never questioned:

> Every decent and well-spoken individual affects and sways me more than is right —Ralph Waldo Emerson, "Self-Reliance," 1841

> Alas and alas! you may take it how you will, but the services of no single individual are indispensable — Robert Louis Stevenson, *Virginibus Puerisque and Other Papers,* 1881

> Faith, in the agonized hands of the individual, becomes an imaginative experiment —R. P. Blackmur, "Emily Dickinson," in *American Harvest,* ed. Allen Tate & John Peale Bishop, 1942

The journalistic mannerisms of late Victorian times are gone now. The disparaging use mentioned by Murray seems to have passed as well.

If we are correct in our guess that late Victorian journalistic practice was the probable cause of the outcry, the whole issue should have died with the cause. But it has not. We find it mentioned (after Fowler) in Krapp 1927, Jensen 1935, Evans 1957, Copperud 1960, 1964, 1970, 1980, Bernstein 1965, Watt 1967, Heritage 1969, Shaw 1975, 1987, Zinsser 1976, Prentice Hall 1978, Little, Brown 1980, 1986, Bremner 1980, Reader's Digest 1983, Longman 1984, Bryson 1984, Trimmer & McCrimmon 1988, and undoubtedly many others. What do these people say about a subject that has been empty of content for, say, half a century? Mostly they repeat Fowler 1926 in one way or another. A few find new reasons for disapproval. Zinsser does not like *indi-*

vidual because it is a longer word than *person;* Trimmer & McCrimmon says it is disapproved because it is overdone in college writing. It is interesting that not one commentator since Hall 1914 has commented on the literary background of the use.

Our evidence from the last fifty years or so shows that *individual* as a noun is most often used in contrast to some larger group—just as Fowler said it should be. When the contrast is not evident, the word almost always seems to carry the notion of one person considered separately. We have no recent evidence of the older facetious use nor of the disparaging use. The following examples are typical:

> His profession was, in fact, the main avenue by which individuals might climb out of the class of manual workers —Benjamin Farrington, *Greek Science,* 1953

> We must first be born as free individuals if we are to move beyond our individual limitations —Wayne C. Booth, *Now Don't Try to Reason with Me,* 1970

> Every individual is capable of injuring or killing himself —Thomas S. Szasz, *Harper's,* April 1972

> ... though he works with individuals, he thinks socially —Norman Mailer, *Advertisements for Myself,* 1959

> The accounts are rendered by individuals from the rank and file who took part —Ellen Cantarow, *Change,* May 1972

> Colleges and universities, like the majority of individuals, have usually been too passive —Calvin H. Plimpton, *Amherst College Bulletin,* November 1967

We see no need for continuing concern over *individual.* Almost all the examples we have from edited prose fit well within the guidelines suggested by Fowler and his followers. It seems probable that the usages that provoked the original criticism have simply gone out of fashion.

For some other controversies that have been at least partly fueled by 19th-century journalistic fashion, see FEMALE; PARTY; TRANSPIRE.

indorse, indorsement See ENDORSE 3.

indubitably *Indubitably* is criticized as pretentious or stuffy by Evans 1957, Bremner 1980, and Bryson 1984. However, the description in Shaw 1975 is not as uncompromising and is closer to actual usage; Shaw says it "is less often used" than *undoubtedly* "because it sounds somewhat more formal and pretentious."

Indubitably is not the kind of word that gets used in everyday conversation, except perhaps for humorous effect. In formal prose, where it usually appears, it can come across as pretentious, but generally only when the writer is adopting a lofty tone. Often, *indubitably* merely acts as an emphatic equivalent of *undoubtedly.*

> None of these disclaimers can obviate the fact that *Sacre* was indubitably composed to support a choreographic story line —James Lyons, *Boston Symphony Orchestra program,* 8 Jan. 1972

> ... believes itself to be impregnably in the right and its opponents indubitably in the wrong —A. C. Benson, *From A College Window,* 1906

> ... this intense and serious and indubitably great poetry —T. S. Eliot, "Marlowe," in *Selected Essays,* 1932

> ... the incongruity of having equal numerical representation in the General Assembly for countries indubitably unequal in many respects —Vera Micheles Dean, *The Four Cornerstones of Peace,* 1946

> Indubitably, execution deters its victim from repeating his crime —George Stevens, *Saturday Rev.,* 25 Sept. 1971

See also DOUBTLESS, NO DOUBT, UNDOUBTEDLY.

indulge When *indulge* is used intransitively and with a preposition, the preposition is usually *in:*

> A wedding is nothing but an excuse for indulging in indecency under respectable guise —Vita Sackville-West, *The Edwardians,* 1930

> People who know the facts can never be quite so free to indulge in fantasy as those who don't —Aldous Huxley, *The Olive Tree,* 1936

> ... the ordinary man's occasional fear of indulging involuntarily in overstrong language —Osbert Sitwell, *Noble Essences,* 1950

When *indulge* is used transitively and with a preposition, the preposition is usually *in* or *with; in* occurs a little more frequently:

> I thank the House for having indulged me in this manner —Sir Winston Churchill, *The Unrelenting Struggle,* 1942

> ... indulged themselves in factitious pity —William Styron, *Lie Down in Darkness,* 1951

> ... and it was only on occasion of a present like this, that Silas indulged himself with roast-meat — George Eliot, *Silas Marner,* 1861

> ... continues to indulge his whimsy with brocade and doeskin neckties —*Current Biography,* March 1965

Transitive *indulge* is occasionally used with *by;* when it is, the object of *by* is generally a gerund:

> ... a post-war Italy that brims with talent yet indulges its recent shame by condescending toward its greatest novelist —*New Republic,* 4 Aug. 1952

indulgent When *indulgent* is used with a preposition, it may be *in, of, to* or *with:*

> It is true, again, that "wealth" has become far more indulgent in its treatment of intellectuals —Irving Howe, *Partisan Rev.,* January–February 1954

> ... is so indulgent in its enumerations of irrelevant detail —*N.Y. Times Book Rev.,* 24 Dec. 1978

> ... more appreciative of his success, more indulgent of his short-comings —Nathaniel Hawthorne, *The Marble Faun,* 1860

> Is his library board indulgent of his absences? — Nancy R. McAdams, *Library Jour.,* 1 Dec. 1966

> ... would perhaps be more indulgent to my vivacity —Matthew Arnold, Preface to *Essays in Criticism,* First Series, 1865

... are indulgent to the cruelties of Russia —Raymond Aron, *Encounter,* January 1955

He is, therefore, often cynical or gently indulgent with the wonder and admiration of the common man for scientific predictions —Stephen C. Pepper, *World Hypotheses,* 1942

The fans could afford to be indulgent with the antics of Moose —*Boy's Life,* February 1953

inedible, uneatable One commentator observes that *inedible* describes that which by its nature cannot be used as food, as in "an inedible plant," and that *uneatable* describes food which is in no condition to be eaten, as in "a rotten, uneatable egg." Another commentator makes exactly the opposite distinction. And yet another commentator notes instead that a tough piece of meat is uneatable while a spoiled or poisonous piece of meat is inedible.

What our evidence indicates is that the words are used more or less interchangeably except in strictly scientific contexts, where *inedible* is preferred. *Inedible* is a considerably more common word overall than *uneatable:*

... those portions of the crops which were inedible to man —Norman C. Wright, *Farmer's Weekly* (South Africa), 25 Nov. 1953

... inedible fats of both plant and animal origin —Harold L. Wilcke, *Duquesne Science Counselor,* December 1966

Prison riots are always caused by unbearable conditions—inedible food, brutality of the guards ... —Donn Pearce, *Esquire,* March 1970

... a real truffle, the kind people like to eat, or an uneatable one —J. Henri Fabre, *Insect Adventures,* retold by Louise S. Hasbrouck, 1917

... they were so undercooked as to be uneatable —Sylvia Townsend Warner, *New Yorker,* 20 Nov. 1954

in excess of This phrase has drawn some criticism as a pompous substitute for *more than* or *over.* It seems to be most at home in writing that has to do with large quantities of material or large sums of money:

... a fifteen-year project costing in excess of $6,000,000 —*Current Biography,* February 1967

... a capacity in excess of 450,000 tons a year —*Annual Report, The Mead Corp.,* 1970

Total expenditure will be in excess of $5.5 million —*Area Development,* July 1970

inexecrable Usage books by two commentators—Shaw 1975, 1987 and Einstein 1985—talk about this mysterious hard word as if they had actually seen or heard it in recent times. We do have a note on it that appeared in the British scholarly publication *Notes and Queries* in 1967. But we have little hard information on the word and no modern examples of use (as distinct from discussion) at all.

It appears to be an obsolete Englishing of Medieval Latin *inexecrabilis* "unappeasable." Its best-known occurrence is in Shakespeare's *The Merchant of Venice* (1597):

O, be thou damn'd, inexecrable dog!

Shakespeare's use has been emended to *inexorable* in modern editions of the play. Since the epithet is flung at Shylock in the scene in which he will not be dissuaded from collecting the pound of flesh, the change is reasonable; the senses of the two words are very close. But it is worth noting that when the line is removed from context, *inexecrable* can easily be interpreted as an intensive form of *execrable* "detestable."

The OED has one other example, from 1594, and the word was also used by Thomas Kyd in *The Spanish Tragedy* (1592).

If in modern use (of which we have only the inferential evidence mentioned above) the word means "inexorable," it could be viewed as a mistake—which is how Shaw views it—or as a revival of the obsolete meaning. We suspect, however, that *inexecrable* is more likely to be used as a strong synonym of *execrable.*

infatuated *Infatuated* takes *with* when it uses a preposition:

Stock investors are infatuated with growth —Heinz G. Biel, *Forbes,* 15 Aug. 1972

Kubrick seems infatuated with the hypnotic possibilities of static setups —Pauline Kael, *New Yorker,* 1 Jan. 1972

... he is infatuated—via newspaper pictures—with Evelyn Nesbit Thaw —Stanley Kauffmann, *Saturday Rev.,* 26 July 1975

infectious See CONTAGIOUS, INFECTIOUS.

infer, imply We have in our collection more than fifty writers on usage, from 1917 to 1988, who insist that a certain distinction between *infer* and *imply* be observed and preserved. Rather than explain, let us illustrate:

Given some utterance, a person may infer from it all sorts of things which neither the utterance nor the utterer implied —I. A. Richards, *Confluence,* March 1954

Richards' usages are exactly those approved and recommended by our more than fifty commentators. They are not, however, the only usages of these words. And there's the rub. Real life is not as simple as commentators would like it to be. A glance at any good dictionary would suggest the same to you: Webster's Ninth New Collegiate, for instance, lists four transitive senses of *imply* (one is obsolete) and five of *infer.* We will not confuse you by discussing all of these, but there are three distinct uses of *infer* we must deal with, and a couple of *imply.* We will start with *imply,* which is simpler and less controversial.

For simplicity we lump together the two chief uses of *imply,* noting only that the first involves no human agent and that the second may or may not. Examples of each, in order:

Amnesty, like pardon, implied crime, and he admitted none —Robert Penn Warren, *Jefferson Davis Gets His Citizenship Back,* 1980

And further, an utterer may imply things which his hearers cannot reasonably infer from what he says —I. A. Richards, *Confluence,* March 1954

There once was minor controversy about a sense of *imply* meaning "hint" used with a personal subject. A note in the Merriam-Webster files written in 1935 said:

> Of course "imply" in the sense of "hint" is careless or vulgar English.

A similar opinion had also appeared in print:

> *Imply* carries with it a tinge of offensiveness when we say, "What do you mean to *imply?*" —*Literary Digest*, 4 Apr. 1931

We seldom find this use in edited prose except in fictional speech:

> "Don't imply you inherit your flibbertigibbet ways from me. . . ." —*American Girl*, December 1951

But keep this *imply* in mind. It is used in exactly the same way as a disputed sense of *infer*, though not so often.

Now, for *infer*, which is the real bone of contention. We are going to identify only three main uses of *infer*, and for the sake of convenience we label them historically. The first is the use of *infer* that everybody approves. We will call it "More 1528," because Sir Thomas More introduced it to English in that year:

> Wherupon is inferred . . . that the messenger wold have fled fro by force —*A Dyaloge . . . of the Veneration and Worshyp of Ymagys*, 1528 (OED, sense 3)

The second use we will call "More 1533," for Sir Thomas gave it to English in that year (in fact he had introduced the usual use of *imply*, too, in 1528). It means the same as *imply:*

> The fyrste parte is not the proofe of the second, but rather contrary wyse, the seconde inferreth well ye fyrst —*Answer to Frith*, 1533 (OED, sense 4)

A distinguishing characteristic of More 1533 is that it does not occur with a human subject.

Now More 1528 and More 1533 coexisted in literary writing for 400 years or so, and no one was confused, so far as the record shows. Here are some examples of More 1528:

> . . . and Sir J. Minnes would needs infer the temper of the people from their joy at the doing of this —Samuel Pepys, diary, 14 Dec. 1663

> I found that he inferred from thence . . . that I either had the more money, or the more judgment —Daniel Defoe, *Moll Flanders*, 1722

> . . . he . . . would hardly answer me the most common question without asking first: What do you intend to infer from that? —Benjamin Franklin, *Autobiography*, 1771

> . . . nor can any thing be more fairly inferred from the Preface, than that Johnson . . . was pleased —James Boswell, *Life of Samuel Johnson*, 1791

> She seldom saw him—never alone; he probably avoided being alone with her. What was to be inferred? —Jane Austen, *Mansfield Park*, 1814

> Mr. Anderson did not say this, but I infer it —Henry Adams, letter, 17 Jan. 1861

> . . . I infer that Swinburne found an adequate outlet for the creative impulse in his poetry —T. S. Eliot, *The Sacred Wood*, 1920

More 1533, the OED shows, was used continuously up to the time the book was edited; Milton and James Mill are among those quoted. Here are some examples not in the OED:

> He used Metcalf as an agent in all proceedings which did concern that foundation; which will infer him to be both a wise and an honest man —Thomas Fuller, *The Holy State and the Profane State*, 1642

> For the principles we lay down, if narrowly looked into, do not infer that —Jonathan Edwards, "Notes on the Mind," 1716–1720

> However, as I have often heard Dr. Johnson observe as to the Universities, bad practice does not infer that the *constitution* is bad —James Boswell, *Life of Samuel Johnson*, 1791

> Lucy . . . reseated herself with an alacrity and cheerfulness which seemed to infer that she could taste no greater delight —Jane Austen, *Sense and Sensibility*, 1811

This use still occurs in the 20th century:

> . . . but the levels of restricted syntactic relationships infer an individual complication of language — Joshua Whatmough, in *New World Writing*, 1954

> . . . to be a literary man infers a certain amount of— well, even formal education —William Faulkner, 25 Feb. 1957, in *Faulkner in the University*, 1959

More 1533 is not itself really the subject of much controversy, but it is recognized in dictionaries, and that recognition leads the commentators not to trust the dictionaries.

We may call the real disputed sense "personal *infer*" because—in distinct contrast with More 1533—it usually has a personal subject. And contrary to all those fifty or more commentators, it does not really equal *imply* in the latter's full range of meanings—it means "hint, suggest," in other words, *imply* only in the sense considered a bit less than acceptable in the 1930s. The personal *infer* is relatively recent. We have found no examples earlier than this one:

> I should think you *did* miss my letters. I know it! but . . . you missed them in another way than you infer, you little minx! —Ellen Terry, letter, 3 Oct. 1896

Our earliest American example comes from a list of Kansas words submitted to *Dialect Notes* in 1914 by Judge J. C. Ruppenthal of Russell, Kansas. His example of the use reads this way:

> He *infers* by his remarks that things are not going right.

This sense is clearly an oral use at the beginning—we have no examples of it in print, except in usage books, until the middle of this century. But it is obscure in origin—was it a theater usage? Or possibly an Americanism Ellen Terry picked up on one of her American tours?

The development of *infer-imply* as a usage issue is curious, too. The earliest mention of the subject is in MacCracken & Sandison 1917, an English handbook apparently originally intended for use at Vassar College. Here is what it says:

> A speaker or his statement *implies* (suggests, expresses, though not explicitly) something which a hearer *infers* (draws or deduces) from the statement. *Infer* is constantly used where *imply* is intended. CORRECT: Do you mean to *imply* [not *infer*] that I am deceiving you?

You will note that the example shown has a personal subject and that the authors say "*infer* is constantly used." Since we know of no printed evidence existing in 1917, we infer the usage to be spoken.

Our next evidence is from the *Lincoln Library,* a sort of one-volume encyclopedia for young people published in 1924. It has a section on good usage, in which it was noted that *imply* and *infer* were frequently confused. MacCracken, who was president of Vassar, was a grammatical consultant to the *Lincoln Library,* and he is probably responsible for the notice there. The comment about confusion has been repeated often in the 60 years following.

Infer and *imply* also turned up in Whipple 1924, a handbook on business-letter writing published by the Westinghouse Technical Night School Press. There is no apparent connection between Whipple and MacCracken & Sandison other than the treatment of business letters in the 1917 book. But MacCracken & Sandison is listed as one of the sources of Lurie 1927, the next book to take up the subject. Lurie seems to be the first to have noticed that dictionaries did not support the distinction.

And indeed they did not. The OED defined More 1533 without comment, as did Webster 1909 and undoubtedly other dictionaries. But in 1932 a member of the philosophy department at Boston University wrote to the Merriam editorial department questioning the definition of More 1533 in Webster 1909. In his opinion the sense was no longer in current good use. After some preliminaries about logic, he got to the point:

> ... no cultured person has in my hearing ever confused the two words. It is, however, the constant practice of the uneducated and the half-educated, to use *infer* for *imply.*

The logician is, of course, talking not about More 1533 but personal *infer.*

The editors gave serious consideration to the complaint—and by that time they also had collected our first four commentators and a couple of clippings from the *Literary Digest* that rather preferred *infer* in this use to *imply,* because *imply* seemed a bit offensive (see the quotation in the discussion of *imply* above). One editor suggested adding a note to the definition of More 1533, but he was overruled by another who observed—as we have here—that the sense in question was not quite the same as More 1533. Instead they added a new definition, "5. Loosely and erroneously, to imply," which appeared in Webster's Second (1934). Thus the dispute was established, although most of the usage-book comment came after World War II.

What can we conclude from all this? The first obvious point is that all the commentators from the very beginning missed the fact that it was an oral use they were objecting to—no one distinguished book use from spoken use. And the dictionaries did not support the distinction the commentators were trying to make because the dictionaries recorded only book use. The second point is that the words are not and never have been confused. We have seen that the same writer could use both More 1528 and More 1533 without mental distress. And personal *infer* has never been muddled with anything else, although it may have replaced the similar use of *imply* that was mildly disparaged in the 1930s. Third, logic is irrelevant to the dispute. *Infer* and *imply* are not interchanged by logicians. The personal *infer* is never used in logic. The objection is social—the personal *infer* has been associated with uncultured persons. Fourth, no distinctions are being lost. The distinctions between the

main uses of *infer*—More 1528, More 1533, personal *infer*—and *imply* have remained the same all along. They are not the same distinction the commentators are talking about, but the commentators' distinction—roughly, that *imply* always means transmission and *infer* reception—is wishful and has not existed in usage since 1533. Fifth, it seems likely that the repeated injunction not to use *infer* for *imply* has diminished the literary use of More 1533, and if anything is in real danger of being lost, it is that long-standard use.

We have no evidence of personal *infer* in print before the 1950s—setting aside Ellen Terry's letter quoted above, which was published in 1932. Here is a sampling of what we have collected:

> I have heard Italians complain of the American accent, inferring that American culture is unworthy of notice —W. Cabell Greet, *Word Study,* October 1952

> The actor ... may, by using a certain inflection or adopting a certain attitude, give a quite contrary impression, infer a meaning or eliminate one —Cyril Cusack, *Irish Digest,* January 1953

> ... "fit to be President," the New York *Post* was digging up evidence to infer that he is not —*New Republic,* 9 Mar. 1953

> Jake liked to think of himself as a high-rolling broncbuster, and if somebody inferred that he couldn't ride a particular horse, that was the horse Jake was bound to try —Fred Gipson, *Cowhand: The Story of a Working Cowboy,* 1953

> May I remark here that although I seem to infer that private communication is an unholy mess of grammatical barbarism, ... such is not my intent —V. Louise Higgins, "Approaching Usage in the Classroom," *English Jour.,* March 1960

One probable effect of the controversy should be noted here. Although our collection of usage books is by no means exhaustive, the ones we have show that the *imply–infer* issue did not become intensely treated until the very end of the 1950s. The writers just quoted—excepting Gipson, who was consciously using a colloquial expression (probably a direct descendant of our 1914 Kansas use)—probably did not even know there was a usage question. Later, it became virtually impossible not to know, and our evidence shows a marked decline of occurrence of personal *infer* in edited prose. It pops up here and there, as in letters to the editor, but it is scarce in edited material. As far as we know, spoken use has not been affected.

When you are weighing the importance of the controversy in your mind, consider this example:

> Leavis infers that Eliot's whole achievement is compromised by the inadequacies which his criticism reveals —*Times Literary Supp.,* 30 Nov. 1967

If a writer says that a third person infers something, it is not possible without the preceding context (missing from our clipping) to know for certain whether the third person is hinting or suggesting or is deducing or concluding. But even though you cannot be sure about the meaning of *infer* in the sentence, do you have any trouble understanding what is being said about Eliot?

If you have had the fortitude to stick with us this far, you know that the commentators' intense concern over preserving the all-important distinction between *infer* and *imply* goes back to a spoken use prevalent among certain less cultured undergraduates at Vassar before 1917. It has been the chiefly oral use of *infer* with a personal subject that has been under attack all along, and that seems not to pose much of a problem for writers. The dwindling use of the More 1533 sense of *infer*, however, may well suggest that writers are increasingly following the commentators' preferred distinction between *infer* and *imply*. That distinction is easy enough to observe, certainly.

inferior, superior   *Inferior* and *superior,* as a result of the somewhat tricky role they have as implicit comparatives in English, are favorite subjects of usage commentators. The most commonly raised issue is that idiomatically they should be followed by *to* rather than *than* (a telling point that shows they are not true comparatives, according to Quirk et al. 1985). All the commentators are agreed on this. And, unlike Partridge 1942 and Shaw 1975, we find that writers almost always do follow *inferior* and *superior* with *to:*

> ... regarded as inferior to the earlier work —*Current Biography,* June 1966

> No longer do workers and peasants feel inferior to the university-trained —Rhea Menzel Whitehead, *Saturday Rev.,* 4 Mar. 1972

> ... nor is the tuition greatly superior to that of the tax-supported schools —B. K. Sandwell, *The Canadian Peoples,* 1941

> On the whole, they were infinitely superior to the situation —Andrew Sarris, *Village Voice,* 28 Feb. 1968

The only evidence we have for *than* is second-hand: Fowler 1926 gives two citations without attribution for *superior than;* Partridge 1942 harks back to an 1898 issue of the *Fortnightly Review* for an example of *inferior than;* and Bernstein 1977 cites a radio commercial for *superior than.*
See also IMPLICIT COMPARATIVE.

infest   When *infest* is used with a preposition, the choice is most often *with:*

> ... a little hotel ... infested with congressmen, judges, and statesmen —*The Autobiography of William Allen White,* 1946

> ... a brisk, gorsy, suburban place infested with fox terriers and healthy children —Anthony West, *New Yorker,* 10 Nov. 1951

> ... a division's command post ... in an apple orchard infested with snipers —A. J. Liebling, *New Yorker,* 10 Dec. 1955

Less frequently, *infest* is used with *by:*

> ... the dockworkers union that was kicked out of the American Federation of Labor on charges that it was infested by racketeers —*Wall Street Jour.,* 22 Sept. 1954

> ... her tenement was infested by rats and overpriced —*New Yorker,* 10 Dec. 1966

As may be seen in the examples given above, when *infest* is used with a preposition, the verb form is usually the past participle; exceptions, however, do occur:

> ... I curse computers for infesting the language with terms like *input, readout,* and *interface* —Thomas H. Middleton, *Saturday Rev.,* 1 Apr. 1978

infiltrate   When *infiltrate* is used with a preposition, *into* is by far the one used most often:

> ... political agents are known to be infiltrating into Chilean army and conservative circles —*Atlantic,* February 1944

> ... the discovery by man that only ... in self-consciously infiltrating himself into the harmony of the universe—is the peace which he seeks to be accomplished —*Saturday Rev.,* 1 Mar. 1952

> ... many Hebrew idioms have infiltrated, in translated forms, into the various Jewish dialects —William Chomsky, *Hebrew: The Eternal Language,* 1957

> ... police undercover agents cannot infiltrate into the inbred, closely-knit Mafia —*Times Literary Supp.,* 14 May 1970

> ... how much of a force they had in reserve as opposed to the force they had infiltrated into the South —David Halberstam, *Harper's,* February 1971

Occasionally, *infiltrate* may be found with *to:*

> They tend rather to infiltrate to supply lines and rear installations —*Cavalry Jour.,* November–December 1942

> Another complete failure followed—this time in a step-ladder factory to which his father had infiltrated him —*English Digest,* May 1953

When the object names the one doing the infiltrating, *infiltrate* is also used with *with* or *by:*

> ... there will be efforts to infiltrate the bandits with police operatives —*Christian Science Monitor,* 23 Apr. 1952

> ... one radical organization decided to infiltrate his class with a *kung fu* fighter —Tom Wolfe, *New York,* 27 Sept. 1971

> ... a language that has become infiltrated by patterns and loan words from English —R. Somerville Graham, *Word,* December 1956

Less frequently and in various relations, *infiltrate* is used with *through, among,* or *from:*

> ... it will be next to impossible to keep the Reds from infiltrating through any dividing line —*Newsweek,* 17 May 1954

> They learn how to keep out of the street itself (it's a deathtrap) and how to infiltrate instead from house to house —*Newsweek,* 22 Mar. 1943

> ... the salt water trickles down on the rocks; steam rises. The salt steam infiltrates among the clams — Hugh Cave, *New England Journeys,* 1953

In technical use the choice of prepositions used with *infiltrate* is even wider: the military does not restrict itself to *into, to* or *through;* use of *toward* or *within* also occurs:

> ... a momentary glimpse of Guillermo's section to our left, infiltrating rapidly toward the rise —Alvah Bessie, *Men in Battle,* 1939

> ... one or two lone infantrymen ... could infiltrate within rifle range and quickly kill the gun crew — *Coast Artillery Jour.,* September–October 1942

infiltration When *infiltration* is used with a preposition, *of* is often chosen:

> Not long before the coming of the white man, the irresistible infiltration of the Iroquois had begun —*American Guide Series: New York,* 1940

> The charges of heavy communist infiltration of the book trade —*Publishers Weekly,* 3 Mar. 1951

> ... articles expounding at length on the Soviet infiltration of the international disarmament movement —Elizabeth Grossman, *N.Y. Times Book Rev.,* 30 Jan. 1983

Somewhat less frequently, *infiltration* is used with *into:*

> There is no evidence of Communist infiltration into the union movement —*N.Y. Times,* 28 June 1953

> ... the danger of infiltration of professional gamblers into college athletics —*Current Biography 1951*

> ... the progressive infiltration into their staffs of persons bringing with them the professional ... standards —*AAUP Bulletin,* May 1965

Infiltration has also been used with *among,* although infrequently:

> ... to keep an eye on Guatemalan infiltration among its neighbors —*Time,* 21 June 1954

Occasionally, *in* is used:

> ... investigations into charges of Communist infiltration in the State Department —*Current Biography 1953*

infinitive The infinitive is the simple form of a verb. It can be used as a noun or as a modifier and it can control a word group used as a noun or modifier. The preposition *to* frequently but not always occurs with the infinitive. Since the 18th century there has been an assumption that the *to* is part of the infinitive, though that is not so. This belief has given us two usage controversies, which you will find at SPLIT INFINTIVE and TRY AND.

inflammable See FLAMMABLE, INFLAMMABLE.

inflict, afflict Are *inflict* and *afflict* in conflict? Quite a few commentators think so, and they warn us not to confuse the two. As is often true in these cases, the confusion is imaginary. What is perceived as confusion is in fact persistence of the oldest sense of *inflict,* which means the same as *afflict.*

Inflict typically occurs in constructions in which something is inflicted on, or upon, somebody:

> ... once in a great while I inflict it upon people —Thomas H. Middleton, *Saturday Rev.,* August 1981

> ... I am resolved not to inflict boredom on even the most deserving —Oliver St. John Gogarty, *It Isn't This Time of Year At All!,* 1954

> ... a model knight on whom God suddenly inflicts leprosy —*Times Literary Supp.,* 1 Dec. 1966

Afflict typically occurs in constructions in which someone is afflicted with or by something:

> I found myself afflicted with a sense of the staleness and glibness of my verse —Donald Hall, *Goatfoot Milktongue Twinbird,* 1978

> Evelina is afflicted by a sense of responsibility for actions which she opposed —John Butt, *English Literature in the Mid-Eighteenth Century,* edited & completed by Geoffrey Carnall, 1979

> ... how a composer's work is both aided and afflicted by the power of record companies —Langdon Winner, *N.Y. Times Book Rev.,* 17 April 1983

These are not the only constructions in use, but they are typical. And they match the guidelines set up by the commentators. The thing to note is that the typical direct object of *inflict* is some unpleasant circumstance and the typical direct object of *afflict* is a person. The older sense of *inflict* works just like *afflict:*

> The miners are still out, and industry, as a result, is inflicted with a kind of creeping paralysis —Harold J. Laski, letter, 30 May 1926

> ... a sick man inflicted with an incurable ailment —*Manchester Guardian Weekly,* 20 Nov. 1936

> ... inflicting us with a meddlesome cub —Warwick Deeping, *Sincerity,* 1934

The dates of the examples, our most recent, are worth noticing. Maybe this older use is passing away, but we cannot be sure. At any rate it has never been very common, and we do not recommend that you try to resurrect it.

influence **1.** When the noun *influence* is used with a preposition, *of* predominates and usually introduces the influence itself:

> ... we find primitive men thinking that almost everything is significant and can exert influence of some sort —William James, *Pragmatism,* 1907

> The influence of Seneca is much more apparent in the Elizabethan drama —T. S. Eliot, "Shakespeare and the Stoicism of Seneca," in *Selected Essays,* 1932

> All confessions are carefully scrutinized for the influence of fear and coercion —William O. Douglas, in *Omnibook,* October 1953

In the opposite relation, introducing the one influenced, it is often used with *on* or *in;* use of *on* occurs a little more frequently:

> We are not concerned with details, but with ultimate influences on thought —Alfred North Whitehead, *Science and the Modern World,* 1925

> I had read *The Sound and the Fury* a month or two earlier and it had a long influence on me —Norman Mailer, *Advertisements for Myself,* 1959

> ... the need to conform has a powerful influence on the thinking and behavior of Americans —Ralph White, *Psychology Today,* November 1971

> ... Greek morals, in their finest essence, have been a vivifying influence in our modern world —Havelock Ellis, *The Dance of Life,* 1923

> ... his enormous influence in the party organization —*New Republic,* 8 Mar. 1954

> ... her dresses have become an important influence in the fashion industry —*Current Biography,* May 1953

In the same relation but less often, *influence* is used with *over* or *upon:*

> As provost of the Swedish clergymen he exercised a quickening influence over all the Swedish congregations —*Dictionary of American Biography,* 1928

> For this reason, he gained unbounded influence over Alexis's mother, the Tsarina —*Times Literary Supp.,* 1 Feb. 1968

> ... its paralysing influence upon the production and enjoyment of wealth —J. A. Hobson, *Poverty in Plenty,* 1931

> ... heredity ... exercised a greater influence upon him than did living people —Osbert Sitwell, *Noble Essences,* 1950

Influence has occasionally also been used with *among, for, from,* or *with:*

> It thus became a major goal of American foreign policy to weaken Communist influences among unions —*Collier's Year Book,* 1949

> She didn't approve of Mack in the least. Thought he was a bad influence for Duveaux —Olive Higgins Prouty, *Now, Voyager,* 1941

> ... the younger man was subjected to a deep and lasting influence from the older writer —Emile DeLaveny, *Times Literary Supp.,* 17 Apr. 1969

> ... the Russians took steps to gain influence with the governments of Eastern Europe —C. E. Black & E. C. Helmreich, *Twentieth Century Europe,* 1950

2. Simon 1980 is not gentle with people who stress this word on the second syllable:

> What makes *inflúence* so ghastly is not necessarily its sound (though I think it is ugly) but its demonstration of the existence of people so uneducated, so deaf to what others are saying, so unable to learn the obvious that they are bound to be a major source of verbal pollution, linguistic corruption, cultural erosion.

We cite this passage to illustrate what passions a fairly minor linguistic variation can arouse. The pronunciation \in-ˈflü-əns\ is chiefly Southern—we have recorded it spoken by former President Jimmy Carter, journalist Tom Wicker, and various Southern senators and governors. The point to notice is that, in some communities, \in-ˈflü-əns\ *is* what others are saying. It is thus largely a mark, not of the nescient, but of those who happen to have been born and raised in the South.

The same variation is found in *congruence,* some stressing the first syllable and some the second. In this case, however, so far as we know, the variation correlates neither with schooling nor with region.

informal Informal is often used—even overused—by usage writers, handbook writers, and dictionaries as a replacement for the much misunderstood label *colloquial.* It is of vague application; beyond the fact that it represents a different part of the usage spectrum from *formal,* its meaning is rather elusive. Here are two attempts to pin it down:

> Informal style is marked by relatively short loose sentences, the use of simile rather than metaphor, casual rhythms and stresses —Barnard 1979

> Informal English is the spoken language of cultured people and the language used in writing when casual or familiar expression is desired —Janis 1984

When we have used it in this book, we have used it much as others have—simply in contrast to *formal* (which see).

See also LEVELS OF USAGE.

informant, informer An *informer* may simply be someone who informs but is usually someone who informs against someone else underhandedly, as a spy or a police informer who gets paid for information. An *informant* may be the same thing as an *informer,* but most often *informant* denotes someone who informs in a general way or provides cultural or linguistic information to a researcher.

> ... a rich storehouse of information ... the informers are (among others) Herodotus, Frank Stockton, Marco Polo —Jean Stafford, *New Yorker,* 3 Dec. 1973

> ... he began using informers to convict rich men of real or imaginary crimes —Robert Graves, *I, Claudius,* 1934

> Still another cause for disciplinary action is the charge of being an informer —J. Edgar Hoover, *Masters of Deceit,* 1958

> The intrigue in Mrs. Gutierrez's life has been created by her career. She is a professional informant.... Between 1968 and the present, Mrs. Gutierrez has been a paid informer —Nicholas M. Horrock, *N.Y. Times,* 2 Apr. 1975

> If the Government thinks the need to deport a given individual is great enough, it may decide to name its informants —*Harvard Law Rev.,* February 1953

> ... we had lately received a very alarming account from Paragon. Miss Arnold was the informant then, and she spoke of ... —Jane Austen, letter, 10 Jan. 1809

> ... choosing informants for the preparation of a dialect atlas —G. L. Brook, *English Dialects,* 1963

> ... some of Mayer's other findings were more surprising. One informant after another revealed that American films stirred a deep discontent —David Robinson, *Saturday Rev.,* 13 Dec. 1975

infrastructure This word is first attested in English in 1927 used in reference to the Maginot Line. Sir Winston Churchill characterized it as jargon in 1950, and it got wide publicity in 1951 and 1952 from its occurrence in NATO documents issuing from General Eisenhower's headquarters. From these beginnings its use has grown considerably. To the military, *infrastructure* refers to the permanent installations that a military force requires, but elsewhere it is of vague application, usually referring to things that underlie and support an enterprise. Here are some typical examples of its use in general contexts:

> In the West, industrialization goes forward in swift momentum. In the new states, it is impeded by a lack of basic technical skills, of power, of transport, and of the economic and social infrastructure necessary for fruitful investment —Abba Eban, *Center Mag.,* September 1969

... the Koch administration's inability to spend enough money to rebuild streets, sewers, bridges and other parts of the city's deteriorating infrastructure —Ronald Smothers, *N.Y. Times,* 11 Nov. 1979

... because the Orinoco belt has not been developed, an entire infrastucture, including roads and refineries, must be built —Linda Grant, *Los Angeles Times,* 27 Nov. 1979

Despite the "Phoenix" program to "neutralize" (kill or jail) members of the VC infrastructure, it seems to be pretty much intact —*I. F. Stone's Bi-Weekly,* 23 Feb. 1970

... that redoubtable intellectual infrastructure which has grown up around business—the faculties of the leading graduate business schools and the management consultants —Robert Lubar, *Fortune,* 13 July 1981

It has been called a "buzz word" by Janis 1984 and "gobbledygook" by Shaw 1987, but it drew the support of a surprisingly large minority of the Harper 1985 usage panel (43 percent).

infringe A few people may still believe that there is something wrong with using *infringe* as an intransitive verb followed by *on* or *upon,* as in "to infringe on the rights of others." Whatever doubts persist are directly attributable to Fowler 1926, who discussed the subject at some length and ended with a recommendation to use *infringe* only as a transitive verb ("infringe the rights of others") and "to abstain altogether from i[*nfringe*] *upon* as an erroneous phrase." Fowler was aware that the OED treated the intransitive *infringe* as standard and included evidence for it dating back to 1762, but he mistakenly regarded its common use as a recent development, and he found several reasons for disparaging it.

Fowler's criticism has not, in this case, been widely taken up by other usage commentators. The intransitive *infringe* is both common and respectable, as it was during Fowler's time, and as it was long before Fowler's time. The very first dictionary ever published by this company (Webster 1847) included at the entry for *infringe* this note: "This word is very frequently followed by *on* or *upon;* as, to *infringe upon* one's rights." That observation still holds true today:

... did not ... infringe upon the interests of other groups —Frances Fox Piven, *Columbia Forum,* Summer 1970

... tried to infringe on their power —Pete Axthelm, *New York,* 1 Nov. 1971

... might infringe on that talismanic privacy — Francine Du Plessix Gray, *N.Y. Times Book Rev.,* 15 July 1979

The transitive *infringe* is also alive and well. It occurs most often in writing relating to the law:

... many modern statutes have infringed it —David M. Walker, *The Scottish Legal System,* 3d ed., 1969

... is not free to infringe the patent —John D. Upham, *Chemical & Engineering News,* 9 Feb. 1987

infuse When *infuse* is used with a preposition, it is usually *with:*

... we know that broad social feelings should be infused with warmth —Lionel Trilling, in *Forms of Modern Fiction,* ed. William Van O'Connor, 1948

... infused only with her passion for her child — Ethel Wilson, *Lilly's Story,* 1952

His facile, free use of pen and brush infuses the massive subjects with a joyful vitality —Ada Louise Huxtable, *N.Y. Times,* 27 Apr. 1980

Less frequently, *infuse* is used with *by:*

Subsequent chapters ... are infused by a remarkable grasp of the facts —Hal Lehrman, *N.Y. Times Book Rev.,* 7 Aug. 1955

In another often encountered sense—"introduce, insinuate"—*infuse* is used with *into:*

... infusing life into an inanimate body —Mary Shelley, *Frankenstein,* 1818

... was of too cold a temperament to infuse a powerful current of life into the old tradition —Laurence Binyon, *The Flight of the Dragon,* 1911

... a tendency to infuse more and more of myself into the apprehension of the world —George Santayana, *Saturday Rev.,* 15 May 1954

Infuse also has been used with *in* or *to:*

These words, these looks, infuse new life in me — Shakespeare, *Titus Andronicus,* 1594

... with the arrival of Sir Gerald Templer early in 1952 a new spirit was infused both to civilians and security forces —*The Americana Annual 1953*

Shakespeare, in addition to using *infuse* with *in, into,* and *with,* also used it with *on;* this last use is not found in contemporary prose:

With those clear rays which she infused on me That beauty am I bless'd with which you see —*Henry VI,* 1592

There have been some critics, Evans 1957 and Phythian 1979 among them, who object to "infusing a person with something." The fact of the matter is that it is a long-established use dating back to the 16th century. It may be that the OED, in labeling the use obsolete, influenced language commentators against it. The OED, it turns out, was premature in calling the sense obsolete. In the first OED Supplement (1933) this sense of *infuse* receives further treatment, including a directive to remove the obsolete label, and the sense is illustrated with two quotations, dated 1900 and 1928. Our own files indicate continuing widespread use:

... the self-respect with which men had been infused —Dixon Wecter, *When Johnny Comes Marching Home,* 1944

... infusing both older cadres and younger masses with devotion —Robert C. North, *New Republic,* 4 July 1955

... his ability to infuse others with his own enthusiasm —*Current Biography,* November 1967

ingenious, ingenuous, ingenuity Confusion of *ingenious* and *ingenuous* is not now much of a problem, but the distinction between these words was not so widely observed several centuries ago. *Ingenious* is the older word, having been borrowed from French in the 1400s. It is derived from the Latin *ingeniosus,* which means "talented, clever." *Ingenuous* was first used in English in the late 1500s. The Latin source from which it arose is *ingenuus,* "native, free born." Both words have developed several senses since their first use in English, but the fundamental meaning of *ingenious* has always been "clever":

> ... the plot is ingenious and the going is good-humored —*New Yorker,* 1 May 1971

> ... an ingenious method of checking errors —W. David Gardner, *Datamation,* June 1982

Ingenuous had some early use in the sense "noble or honorable," but its primary use in English has been to describe a person or personality characterized by frankness and openness, owing either to good character or—now more often—innocence:

> ... the jolly, disarming, ingenuous friendliness of this farm boy —*Johns Hopkins Mag.,* Summer 1967

> ... his frankness of expression, his ingenuous American informality —William F. Buckley, Jr., *Cosmopolitan,* October 1976

The OED shows that, in addition to their customary and distinct uses, *ingenious* and *ingenuous* were used fairly regularly as synonyms for many years:

> Our Lord having heard this ingenious confession —William Beveridge, *Sermons,* ca. 1680 (OED)

> If their Sonnes be ingenuous, they shall want no instruction —Shakespeare, *Love's Labour's Lost,* 1595 (OED)

It may be that the publication in 1755 of Samuel Johnson's Dictionary, in which these synonymous uses are not recognized, had something to do with establishing *ingenious* and *ingenuous* as distinct words. For whatever reason, they appear to have ceased being used as synonyms by about 1800. Many 20th-century usage commentators warn that these words are often confused, but we have only two clear examples of such confusion in our files:

> "But are they fair?" she asked ingeniously —Rose Macaulay, *Potterism,* 1920

> ... by developing ingenuous new devices and methods, which greatly increased efficiency —Sidney L. Pressey, in *Addresses on Current Issues in Higher Education,* 1951

And even these may simply be typographical errors rather than the product of authorial confusion.

A related subject is the history of the noun *ingenuity. Ingenuity* is derived from *ingenuous,* but its meaning is "the quality or state of being ingenious":

> ... substituting technical ingenuity for a lack of good musical material —Peter Hellman, *Cosmopolitan,* January 1973

> ... the tenacity and ingenuity of Vermont hill farmers —*N.Y. Times,* 21 Aug. 1983

Ingenuity acquired this sense in the 17th century, when *ingenuous* and *ingenious* were being used as synonyms. It was sufficiently well-established in the 18th century for Johnson to include it in his Dictionary, and for Baker 1770 to disapprove of it: "It is a considerable Blemish in our Language, that the Word *Ingenuity* has two Senses; for hereby it often becomes unintelligible." Baker wanted *ingenuity* to be used only in its older "ingenuous" sense, and he suggested that *ingeniety* be

adopted as the noun of *ingenious.* He was fighting a battle already lost, however. The older sense of *ingenuity* had already been largely superseded by *ingenuousness* in Baker's time. It is now obsolete.

in hope(s) of See HOPE 2.

in hope(s) that See HOPE 2.

inhuman See UNHUMAN, INHUMAN.

inimical, inimicable When *inimical* or its less often encountered synonym, *inimicable,* is used with a preposition, the preposition is *to:*

> Both heat and cold are inimical to man, and he exists precariously balanced between them —Upton Sinclair, *Presidential Mission,* 1947

> ... local control is only a form of control, and it may be inimical to liberty —George F. Will, *National Rev.,* 30 June 1970

> Pleasure is by nature immoderate and indefinite and inimical to right proportion —Iris Murdoch, *The Fire and the Sun,* 1977

> ... those deficits seem to me directly inimicable to the progress we want to see on inflation —Paul Volcker, quoted in *Wall Street Jour.,* 10 Mar. 1982

initialisms See ACRONYMS.

initials We had a bit of a challenge from a correspondent some time ago. He wondered how names like *O'Hara* and *McCarthy* are abbreviated—with just the *O.* and the *M.* or with *O'H.* and *McC.?* We hunted through our collection of usage books and stylebooks without learning much. According to the books, prefixed names retain the prefix when abbreviated: *de Belleville* should be abbreviated *de B.* We found this to be done in practice when we encountered *V. de S. Pinto, George de F. Lord,* and Madame *de B.* And the Irish writer Myles na gCopaleen abbreviated his name to *M. na gC.*

But we found no advice for *O'Hara* and *McCarthy.* So we began looking for evidence instead of guidance. It appears that the same prefixing principle applies: John O'Hara became *J. O'H.* and Georgia O'Keeffe became *G. O'K.* For the *Mc*'s we found *Robert McC. Adams* and *George McT. Kahin.*

We conclude, then, that standard practice is to keep the capitalized initial elements when abbreviating.

ink Bremner 1980 and Copperud 1980 both look down on the verb *ink* as sportswriterese or sports headlinese, but this transitive verb has long since leaked from the sports pages into wider use:

> The contract safely inked, I was interviewed —Jessica Mitford, *Atlantic,* October 1974

> No sooner is his contract inked than mighty lumberjacks start to make their axes ring —Peter Andrews, *N.Y. Times Book Rev.,* 18 May 1975

> If the Alliance can complete negotiations and ink a new pact before Jan. 1 —George B. Merry, *Christian Science Monitor,* 23 Nov. 1979

> ... the comedian inked a 30-year contract with NBC —*People,* 6 Dec. 1982

. . . she has been inked to do the part of a judge in an HBO special —Marge Crumbaker, *Houston Post,* 12 Sept. 1984

Before you ink the next big deal —Phyllis Berman, *Forbes,* 3 Dec. 1984

You should not expect to find it or use it in the more solemn kinds of discourse, however.

in line   See ON LINE.

innate   When *innate* is used with a preposition, it is usually *in:*

The faculty for myth is innate in the human race — W. Somerset Maugham, *The Moon and Sixpence,* 1919

. . . the delays innate in both serial and book publication —Walter Rundell, *AAUP Bulletin,* September 1971

Very occasionally, *innate* is used with *to:*

. . . the materials for conflict are innate to social life —Richard Sennett, *Psychology Today,* November 1970

innocent   Back in 1926, H. W. Fowler decided that *innocent of* in the sense "lacking in" was worn-out humor. Gowers continued the notice in Fowler 1965. Other commentators have largely ignored this usage. It seems harmless enough in these typical examples.

So I . . . proceeded to take ideas they didn't know they had out of them as a prestidigitator takes rabbits and pigeons you have declared yourself innocent of out of your pockets —Robert Frost, letter, 12 Aug. 1924

. . . finds the story is "meaningless," apparently because it is innocent of satire or moral —James Thurber, letter, 13 Dec. 1950

. . . an equally unfiery *kung-pao* chicken was innocent of the peanuts that give it character —Caroline Bates, *Gourmet,* April 1977

He took some samples, which eventually proved to be innocent of silver —John McPhee, *Basin and Range,* 1980

See also PLEAD 2.

inoculate   Bremner 1980 and Copperud 1970, 1980 note that this word is misspelled with two *n*'s. The mistake does turn up in print from time to time, and so *inoculate* appears to be a bit of a problem word for copy editors and proofreaders as well as writers. Distinguish *inoculate* from *innocuous,* which does have two *n*'s.

in order that   There is a strictly British issue concerning this phrasal conjunction that began with Fowler 1926 and is still to be found in Phythian 1979 and Longman 1984. Fowler likes *may* or *might* after the phrase and will tolerate *should* and sometimes *shall,* but he calls use of *can, could, will,* and *would* "unidiomatic." American writers and commentators both seem indifferent to the matter.

in order to   Commentators concerned with saving words (including Bremner 1980, Flesch 1964, Bernstein 1965, and Copperud 1960, 1964, 1970, 1980) would

have you regularly delete *in order* from this useful phrase. Follett 1966, on the other hand, says that objections to the phrase are pedantic.

One thing the phrase accomplishes is to eliminate the possibility of ambiguity. It is often used in contexts where reduction to *to* would be ambiguous.

I had to borrow $2,500 from Elliott Nugent, and damn near left *The New Yorker* for Paramount Pictures in order to live —James Thurber, letter, 2 June 1958

It may therefore, perhaps, be necessary, in order to preserve both men and angels in a state of rectitude —Samuel Johnson, quoted in James Boswell, *Life of Samuel Johnson,* 1791

Of course, there are many contexts where ambiguity is not a problem. It may prove useful to look over these examples—they span some two and a half centuries— from the point of determining how many would be improved by deleting *in order:*

. . . till better Care be taken in the Education of our young Nobility, that they may set out into the World with some Foundation of Literature, in order to qualify them for Patterns of Politeness —Jonathan Swift, *A Proposal for Correcting, Improving and Ascertaining the English Tongue,* 1712

As whisk and swabbers was the game then in the chief vogue, they were obliged to look for a fourth person, in order to make up their parties —Henry Fielding, *Jonathan Wild,* 1743

. . . even went the length of reading the play of "King John" in order to ascertain what it was all about — George Bernard Shaw, *Cashel Byron's Profession,* 1886

I dreamed last night that I had to pass a written examination in order to pass the inspection there — Robert Frost, letter, 22 Mar. 1915

With which understanding one may with all propriety open a discourse on poetry in order to show that poetry is older than prose —Leacock 1943

. . . it is always strange to what involved and complex methods a man will resort in order to steal something —William Faulkner, "Centaur in Brass," in *Collected Stories,* 1950

The critic betrays an unconscious admiration . . . in the sublime images he is driven to in order to express the depths of his exasperation —John Butt, *English Literature in the Mid-Eighteenth Century,* edited & completed by Geoffrey Carnall, 1979

First let me say that it is with great reluctance that I am raising my own allowance. In order to do that, I am increasing the self-imposed debt limit —*And More by Andy Rooney,* 1982

We suspect you will not find many improvements made simply by dropping *in order.* In several cases (perhaps especially those of Frost and Butt/Carnall) *in order* avoids real awkwardness. In others considerations of rhythm and emphasis may be judged to apply. The thoughtful writer strives not for mere conciseness, but also for ease of communication. Many of the little phrases that brevity buffs think unnecessary are the lubrication that helps to smooth the way for your message to get across.

input This fashionable word, which has spread into general use from the world of computers, is disparaged as jargon and bureaucratese by Heritage 1982, Shaw 1987, Bremner 1980, Bryson 1984, Janis 1984, Mitchell 1979, and Zinsser 1976. Most of the objections are directed at the noun. And the sense which seems to provoke the most irritation is a broad one: "advice, opinion, comment."

Let us concede *input* to be jargonish and faddish; yet, it must be in some way useful if it continues to be chosen so frequently by such a variety of writers as the ones quoted below. We'll let you decide how useful it can be in this sampling of the citations in our files.

> Some lakes can withstand inputs of acids for many years because they sit in or near beds of limestone —Robert Alvo, *Natural History,* September 1986

> Vegetable producers and home gardeners alike depend upon seed companies for one of their most essential inputs —Ann Ingerson, *New England Farmer,* November 1983

> ... getting the process started would require an input equivalent to that spent on the Apollo program —Isaac Asimov, *Saturday Rev.,* 28 June 1975

> ... the best way for farmers to protect their profits is to cut input costs —*Wall Street Jour.,* 18 Dec. 1985

> ... a home-cooked dinner on a weeknight often requires more input than the committed career woman can summon at the day's end —Ruth Spear, *New York,* 25 Oct. 1976

> Her one rule as a writer is succinct: never show anything to anybody while in the process. There can be nothing worse than input from well-meaning family or friends —Sybil Steinberg, *Publishers Weekly,* 24 Aug. 1984

> ... the raw sensory material, actually, the input right into his own ear from the streets —Allen Ginsberg, *American Poetry Rev.,* Vol. 3, No. 3, 1974

> Where, as in Vietnam and Laos, the frustration has been nearly total, the bureaucratic input has been all but infinite —John Kenneth Galbraith, *ADA World Mag.,* March 1971

> ... the musical design was rounded rather than rugged, the level of expressivity restrained by Kim's much too restricted scale of personal input —Irving Kolodin, *Saturday Rev.,* 3 Apr. 1976

> The Soviet economy may be viewed as confronting a growth dilemma arising from the simultaneous slowing in the growth of inputs of labor and capital and in the productive use of those inputs —Abraham S. Becker, *Wall Street Jour.,* 21 June 1982

These examples may give you some idea of the semantic spread of *input* as used outside bureaucracy and the worlds of science and technology. Whether you use it is obviously your choice. One aspect of the matter worth your considering is how many words are needed to replace it effectively in each of these examples. You will not always find a one-for-one exchange possible. This use of *input* may yet be a novelty and may carry with it unwanted connotations of technology, but it is concise.

inquire, enquire 1. Both *inquire* and *enquire* are used in American and British English. *Enquire* appears more frequently in British English than in American English.

When *enquire* does appear in American English, it is usually in bookish or formal contexts. Overall, in American English *inquire* occurs more often than *enquire;* in British English *inquire* occurs about as often as does *enquire.*

2. When *inquire* and *enquire* are used with a preposition, it is most often *about* or *into:*

> ... their host inquired about the horses —*American Guide Series: Louisiana,* 1941

> ... but he did inquire about it. ... —*Times Literary Supp.,* 17 July 1969

> ... before we enquire into the affirmative aspects of this hope —McGeorge Bundy, ed., *The Pattern of Responsibility,* 1951

> ... he enquired into dynamical problems involving the measures of time and velocity —S. F. Mason, *Main Currents of Scientific Thought,* 1953

Inquire and *enquire* are used less frequently with *after* or *for:*

> The parents of the boys he played with always inquired after his father and mother —F. Scott Fitzgerald, "The Rich Boy," 1926

> ... as if she enquired after a favorite child —Katherine Anne Porter, "The Source," in *Mid Country,* ed. Lowry C. Wimberly, 1945

> It was soon evident that this was the reddleman who had inquired for her —Thomas Hardy, *The Return of the Native,* 1878

> ... enquiring for news of the war —*Yale Rev.,* October 1919

There is also some evidence of use with *as to* and *concerning:*

> ... when he told a man who enquired as to the progress of his comedy that he had finished it —Matthew Arnold, reprinted in *Encore,* November 1944

> ... a man who was carrying a load of pottery to market stopped his horse against my field and inquired concerning Wyman the younger —Henry David Thoreau, *Walden,* 1854

Inquire and *enquire* are usually used with *of* when the object is the person asked; less frequently *from* is used in this relation:

> Let spendthrifts' heirs enquire of yours—who's wiser —Lord Byron, *Don Juan,* Canto XII, 1823

> ... he had long inquired of himself what great principle or idea it was that had created the Union —Archibald MacLeish, *Saturday Rev.,* 13 Nov. 1971

> ... when he inquired from his friend, David Garnett, whether the rest of the party really liked him —*Times Literary Supp.,* 19 May 1971

inquirer, enquirer Of the variants *inquirer* and *enquirer,* the former appears more frequently. When *enquirer* is used, it is likely to be found in British prose; however, it has not gone entirely out of use in the U.S.— witness the newspaper title the *National Enquirer.*

inquiry, enquiry 1. The evidence for *inquiry* and *enquiry* points to a pattern of usage much like that of *inquire* and *enquire,* but with one difference: *enquiry* appears in current American usage more often than does the spelling *enquire.* Still, both *inquiry* and *enquiry* are used in American and British English, with the *i* spelling occurring more often. There has been some discussion that British English, unlike American English, may be showing a preference for the *e* spelling when the word denotes an investigation. According to our evidence, there may be a movement in this direction, but the pattern does not seem settled yet; moreover, the evidence we do have points to any shift occurring only in the English of England—other British English usage continues to make the two spellings interchangeable:

> . . . the rest of the play being occupied by a primitive but effective police inquiry —T. S. Eliot, "Seneca in Elizabethan Translation," in *Selected Essays,* 1932

> . . . the full account of the B.M.A.'s field survey and postal inquiry among general practitioners —*New Statesman & Nation,* 3 Oct. 1953

> . . . she said nothing to him beyond the traditional words of welcome and the traditional enquiry after his family —Padraic Fallon, in *44 Irish Short Stories,* ed. Devin A. Garrity, 1955

> . . . Mrs. Musto in spite of her enquiry, was preoccupied —Patrick White, *The Solid Mandala,* 1966

> . . . he was accustomed to travel throughout England, making enquiry into the decisions of local officials and chastening the negligent —D. J. V. Fisher, *The Anglo-Saxon Age,* 1973

> . . . heading an enquiry into the effects of reports on pornography —*Punch,* 11 Sept. 1974

> Due to considerable customer interest, enquiries from builders . . . are invited —Australian advt., in *Multihulls,* September–October 1981

2. When *inquiry* and *enquiry* are used with a preposition, *into* is found most often:

> . . . distinguish between legitimate legislative inquiry into the acts of a man . . . and illegitimate inquiry into opinions —Norman Thomas, in *New Republic,* 28 Feb. 1955

> This book is an enquiry into the causes of the English blindness to Racine —John Loftis, *Modern Language Notes,* November 1958

Less frequently, the two words are used with *about, as to, in, of, on,* or *with* in various relations and senses:

> The next day I made such exhaustive enquiries about women with golden hair, that some people thought me mad —John Berry, *Antioch Rev.,* December 1956

> . . . his head was tilted at the precise angle of inquiry as to where he should put Muhlenberg's drink — Theodore Sturgeon, *E Pluribus Unicorn,* 1953

> . . . Research Council fosters scientific inquiry in the social fields —*Current Biography 1950*

> . . . made inquiries of other libraries when a particular book was needed —*Current Biography,* June 1967

> During the Parliamentary enquiry on the Liverpool and Manchester Railway Bill —O. S. Nock, *The Railways of Britain,* 1947

> . . . his casual inquiry with other publishers who thought they had not had the same experience — Curtis G. Benjamin, letter to the editor, *Times Literary Supp.,* 19 June 1969

in regard to, in regards to   See REGARD 1.

in respect of, in respect to, with respect to   These phrases have been the subject of considerable dispute for over a century. *In respect of* was attacked as an error or affectation by Marsh 1859. Marsh condemned the phrase in spite of its use by Sir Francis Bacon; he also noted it to be frequent in Coleridge, but he thought Coleridge's influence could not account for its currency. Alford 1866 defended the phrase (he used it himself), citing Bacon, among others. Fitzedward Hall 1873 cudgeled both the earlier commentators; he tended to dislike *in respect of* (he did credit Coleridge for its revival), but he was contemptuous of Marsh's reasons. Ayres 1881 was content to repeat Marsh; Bardeen 1883 quoted Hall. All of this argumentation boiled down to no more than whether *of* or *to* should be the preposition following *respect.*

As inconsequential as this issue may seem, it did not die off with the dawn of the 20th century. Fowler 1926 helped keep it alive by simply suggesting that the phrases are better avoided than used, which advice is somewhat embellished by Gowers in the 1965 edition. Copperud 1970, 1980 contrives to find something ambiguous about *in respect to,* and joins with Gowers in recommending *about* instead of any of the phrases—an oversimple recommendation that, if applied consistently, would make nonsense out of many sentences in which the phrases are used. Phythian 1979 goes his own way, prescribing *in respect of* and not *to.* With Phythian we have come 120 years and 180 degrees from Marsh.

None of the foregoing opinion has a solid, practical connection to actual usage. Our evidence tells us that all three of these phrases are in current good use. You will notice that our examples tend to come from academic writing rather than the popular press. *In respect of* has much more British than American use.

> Hull remains completely obdurate about not using the word "recognition" in respect of the French Committee —Sir Winston Churchill, *Closing the Ring,* 1951

> . . . a map of the world in which all principal features should be correctly placed in respect of mathematically determined parallels of latitude —Benjamin Farrington, *Greek Science,* 1953

> This is particularly so in respect of his concept of lateral thinking —*Times Literary Supp.,* 12 Feb. 1970

In respect to is the least common of the three. It is much more frequent in American English than British English:

> The most intriguing in the group of paintings is the one which, in respect to its replicas, has figured simply as the *Weavers* in the modern literature —W. R. Rearick, *Johns Hopkins Mag.,* Spring 1967

> . . . perhaps prejudices my judgment in respect to the perfection of her model —George Santayana, *Persons and Places,* 1944

With respect to is currently the most common of the three in American English, and it has British use as well:

. . . four points I made in my first report with respect to vocational education —James B. Conant, *Slums and Suburbs,* 1961

. . . creates its share of problems with respect to language —Albert H. Marckwardt, *Linguistics and the Teaching of English,* 1966

. . . a more advantageous position with respect to the larger more comprehensive problem —Nehemiah Jordan, *Themes in Speculative Psychology,* 1968

. . . our conception of the physical world can be exhibited as a theory with respect to our experiences —A. J. Ayer, quoted in *Times Literary Supp.,* 19 Feb. 1970

inroad   *Inroad,* according to our evidence, is often used in the plural, but the significant number of citations for its use in the singular precludes our labeling *inroad* as usually used in the plural. When *inroad* is used with a preposition, it is used with one of any number. Occurring frequently are *into* and *on:*

. . . he had drunk three times as much brandy as was his custom and had made a great inroad into the package of Egyptian Prettiests which he never smoked after supper —Jean Stafford, *Children Are Bored on Sunday,* 1953

. . . the development of synthetic materials made deep inroads into the use of leather —John F. W. Anderson, in *The New International Year Book,* 1951

. . . the appearance, if not the reality, of Republican inroads into a Democratic stronghold —Iver Peterson, *N.Y. Times,* 7 Nov. 1979

. . . so harassed by Sutter's threats and commands that they made little inroad on the valley supply of pelts —Julian Dana, *The Sacramento,* 1939

. . . another sharp inroad on the principle of free speech —*Civil Liberties,* February 1954

. . . the continuing inroads on moviegoing . . . via the Public Broadcasting Service, cable, and Home Box Office —Judith Crist, *Saturday Rev.,* 8 Jan. 1977

Inroad is also used, somewhat less frequently, with *in* or *upon:*

. . . the idea of making inroads in the Democratic camp to split off the Southerners —C. Vann Woodward, *Reunion and Reaction,* 2d ed. rev., 1956

. . . Maharishi and meditation have made remarkable inroads in colleges and high schools —Malcolm Scully, *Saturday Rev.,* 14 Apr. 1973

Sometimes the inroads upon justice are subtle and insidious —*Selected Writings of Benjamin N. Cardozo,* ed. Margaret E. Hall, 1947

. . . this inroad upon my rural peace is in the highest degree distasteful —John Buchan, *Castle Gay,* 1930

Very occasionally, *inroad* is used with *against, among,* or *with:*

. . . their power to make dramatic inroads against an injustice of long standing —Milton S. Eisenhower, *Johns Hopkins Mag.,* February 1966

. . . trade unionism made some inroads among the skilled construction crafts —Murray Ross, *Annals of the American Academy of Political and Social Science,* November 1947

A rapidly growing Mexican sulphur industry . . . is now making inroads with domestic customers —*Newsweek,* 2 July 1956

insanitary   See UNSANITARY, INSANITARY.

insensible   When *insensible* is used with a preposition, it is usually *to:*

. . . Archer had never been insensible to such advantages —Edith Wharton, *The Age of Innocence,* 1920

. . . the strange thing is that a boy so sentient of his surroundings should have been so insensible to the real world about him —*The Autobiography of William Allen White,* 1946

I never knew a member of the Vietnam press corps who was insensible to what happened when the words "war" and "correspondent" got joined — Michael Herr, *Esquire,* April 1970

At one time, *insensible* was also used with *of,* although not so often as with *to.* Over the last 30 years, however, *insensible of* has seldom turned up in our reading:

If there was one man in the world she hated because he was insensible of her attraction it was Mark — Ford Madox Ford, *The Last Post,* 1928

. . . the primitive . . . mind . . . is untrammelled by logic, and insensible of the law of contradiction — Sir James G. Frazer, *Aftermath,* 1937

insensitive   When *insensitive* is used with a preposition, it is used with *to:*

He was insensitive to all kinds of discourtesy — James Joyce, *Dubliners,* 1914

. . . we will only impede progress if we rely on threats or are insensitive to many difficulties and basic fears —Adlai E. Stevenson, *New Republic,* 28 Sept. 1953

One would have to be astonishingly insensitive to these pleas —Fred M. Hechinger, *Saturday Rev.,* 29 May 1976

inseparable   When used with a preposition, *inseparable* is followed by *from:*

. . . the strengthening of discipline, the summoning of moral resources are by no means inseparable from the formulas of religion —Edmund Wilson, *A Piece of My Mind,* 1956

. . . employment policy is inseparable from demographic policy —Anthony Wolff, *RF Illustrated,* August 1975

inside of   Bierce 1909 seems to have been the first to insist on the omission of *of* from the compound preposition *inside of.* He has been followed by a considerable number of handbooks right up to the present. There are two types of dissent that counter the tradition established by Bierce.
Bryant 1962 cites two studies that show *inside of* occurs in standard contexts as a variant of *inside;* she thus concludes that *inside of* is standard, as it is. (Our

evidence shows that *inside* is more common than *inside of,* however.)

The second form of dissent starts as early as Mac-Cracken & Sandison 1917 and continues as recently as Trimmer & McCrimmon 1988; it finds *inside of* less reprehensible when used with expressions of time. Strunk & White 1959, 1972, 1979 and Reader's Digest 1983 join Bryant in finding this use acceptable also.

It seems likely that *inside of* originated as a speech form in which *of* served to create a bit of space between *inside* and the next content word. It would, therefore, be fair to characterize it as colloquial in the nonpejorative sense of the word. You use it or omit it according to the rhythmic requirements of your sentence. Here are a few examples:

> . . . had such a roaring time of it that she killed herself inside of two years —George Bernard Shaw, letter, 31 Dec. 1897

> ". . . inside of a week I got a package from Croirier's with a new evening gown in it." —F. Scott Fitzgerald, *The Great Gatsby,* 1925

> Isn't it disheartening to see a magnificent sunburn . . . disappear entirely inside of a fortnight? —Bennett Cerf, *Saturday Rev.,* 11 Apr. 1953

> . . . turned a sprawling village of 2,412 in 1825 into a city of 10,000 inside of seven years —*Newsweek,* 15 Aug. 1955

> But usually . . . the lift started up again inside of a minute —Polly Frost, quoted in *New Yorker,* 27 Jan. 1986

> . . . how to live with and inside of paradox — R. D. Rosen, *Psychobabble,* 1977

> The yokel had simply stepped inside of his opponent's sense of time —Ralph Ellison, *Invisible Man,* 1952

As these suggest, the use with expressions of time is the more frequent. See also OUTSIDE OF.

insight When *insight* is used with a preposition, the choice is usually *into:*

> . . . uncover useful insights into the social history of Victorian England —Carlos Baker, *Saturday Rev.,* 1 May 1954

> . . . the sudden insight into the nature of things — Edmund Wilson, *A Piece of My Mind,* 1956

> . . . realizing this gave me no insight into how to correct it —Bartley McSwine, *Change,* May–June 1971

Occasionally, *insight* is also used with *about, as to, in, on, regarding,* or *to;* of this group *on* occurs a little more frequently than the others:

> . . . I had a big insight and a little insight about the book —Rust Hills, *Esquire,* April 1973

> . . . might well offer fresh insights as to the character and extent of the social adaptation involved — George C. Barker, *ETC,* Summer 1945

> I had the highest respect for Harris Wofford's insight in realizing the critical importance of having students honestly involved —Jacqueline Grennan, *Change,* March–April 1969

> There is no doubt that certain unusually able ex-Communists . . . can offer brilliant insights on our present difficulties —*New Republic,* 22 Oct. 1951

> . . . shows a keen insight regarding the genetic relationships of American Indian languages —*Dictionary of American Biography,* 1929

> . . . gave us new insights to their concerns and objectives —Chester Bowles, *Promises to Keep,* 1971

insightful This relatively new adjective (first recorded in 1907) has lately become something of a minor irritant to a few usage commentators, who have described it variously as "journalese" (Zinsser 1976), "a suspicious overstatement for 'perceptive'" (Strunk & White 1979), and "jargon" (Janis 1984). Dictionaries, on the other hand, routinely treat it as an ordinary, inoffensive word. Its use is common and has been for several decades. Here is a representative sampling of the ways in which it is used:

> . . . Royko is as insightful as he is humorous —Dan Walker, *Saturday Rev.,* 24 Apr. 1971

> . . . as readable as it is insightful —William Manchester, *N.Y. Times Book Rev.,* 12 Sept. 1976

> As a diarist, Coward could be insightful about himself —Mel Gussow, *N.Y. Times Book Rev.,* 28 Nov. 1976

> . . . this insightful reinterpretation of recent American abstraction —Barbara Rose, *Vogue,* October 1976

> . . . is also very insightful about Burton's acting — *Wall Street Jour.,* 18 Dec. 1981

insignia *Insignia* has the form of a Latin plural, the singular of which is *insigne.* But as an English word, *insignia* is used both as a plural and as a singular:

> . . . the magazine's insignia has been a rabbit dressed in evening clothes —*Current Biography,* September 1968

> . . . all the insignia and stigmata of Old World nationalism —Henry Steele Commager, *Saturday Rev.,* 13 Dec. 1975

When *insignia* is understood as a singular, it often has *insignias* as its plural:

> Precise or elegant usage is seen as one of the insignias of class —Anatole Broyard, *N.Y. Times Book Rev.,* 22 Mar. 1981

The singular *insignia* is recorded in the OED as early as 1774, but its use seems not to have become common until the 20th century. Usage commentators have in general regarded it with tolerance, although it has had its critics (such as Follett 1966). The alternative singular *insigne* is preferred by some writers:

> . . . a red beret with the Amtrak arrow insigne — David Butwin, *Saturday Rev.,* 22 Jan. 1972

However, *insignia* is a far more common choice in such contexts, and *insigne* is itself sometimes criticized as pretentious. *Insignia* appears still to be used primarily as a plural in British English, but in American English, the singular *insignia* and the plural *insignias* (as well as the plural *insignia*) are now unquestionably standard. You need not hesitate to use them.

insist When *insist* is used with a preposition, it is used with *on* or (less often) *upon:*

> ... he liked to insist more strongly than ever on the altruistic, the self-sacrificingly patriotic character of his whole career —Aldous Huxley, *The Olive Tree,* 1937

> ... he certainly insists on the superiority of man to nonhuman nature —Eric Bentley, in *Forms of Modern Fiction,* ed. William Van O'Connor, 1948

> ... she insisted on reading them pleasant stories about nice boys and girls —Louis Auchincloss, *A Law for the Lion,* 1953

> ... but he himself, though capable of firm opinions, never insisted upon them —Robert Penn Warren, *Commonweal,* 15 Aug. 1947

> ... she has added ... the sense of raw pity which is all the more remarkable because she never insists upon it —Robert Payne, *N.Y. Times Book Rev.,* 9 May 1954

In its transitive use, *insist* is used with a clause as object:

> ... if a powerful writer insists for long enough that you are half-dead, why, then, you begin to ... believe it —C. Day Lewis, *A Hope for Poetry,* 3d ed., 1936

> ... in some suburban schools where parents insist their children take certain academic subjects — James B. Conant, *Slums and Suburbs,* 1961

inspire When *inspire* is used with a preposition, it generally is used with *by* and the verb form is usually the past participle:

> He refused to admit to himself that he was inspired by passion. He despised passion —Liam O'Flaherty, *The Informer,* 1925

> ... inspired by the most genuine passion for the rights and liberties of mankind —Virginia Woolf, *The Second Common Reader,* 1932

> ... inspired by a subconscious desire to compensate for these humiliations —George F. Kennan, *New Yorker,* 1 May 1971

Inspire is also used quite frequently with *in, to,* or *with; to* and *with* occur more often than *in.* The verb may take any of its forms.

> The disgust he had inspired in me before, when gloating over anticipated tortures —W. H. Hudson, *Green Mansions,* 1904

> The bribe had inspired nothing but fright in the old man —Irving Wallace, *The Plot,* 1967

> The crammed, violent life of Catfish Row inspired George Gershwin to something beyond show music —*Time,* 23 Mar. 1953

> ... inspiring Americans to visit Europe —Horace Sutton, *Saturday Rev.,* 1 Jan. 1972

> The old rooms in the candlelight inspired him with a tenderness —Vita Sackville-West, *The Edwardians,* 1930

> ... observation of warlike crowds inspired me with thoughts having much affinity with those of psychoanalysts —Bertrand Russell, *London Calling,* 24 Mar. 1955

Occasionally, *inspire* may also be used with the prepositions *among, from, into, through,* or *toward:*

> ... the political mobsters in the play appeared to inspire more fascination than hate among Moscow playgoers —Tom Whitney, *Wall Street Jour.,* 25 Mar. 1954

> Great artists know or believe that they are inspired from something outside themselves —S. Alexander, *Beauty and Other Forms of Value,* 1933

> ... Dante's earnestness of purpose ... inspires life into the dry bones of his formal scholasticism — Charles Eliot Norton, in *World's Best Literature,* 1896

> ... a Boston architect who had studied in France, inspired a large following through his brilliant creations —*American Guide Series: Michigan,* 1941

> The famed Armory Show of 1913 inspired her toward abstract painting —*The Americana Annual* 1953

in spite of the fact that This phrase is disparaged by a few commentators as wordy or excessive. The basic issue is discussed at FACT 1.

instance Two commentators, Phythian 1979 and Copperud 1970, 1980, say that *instance* is frequently used in wordy phrases. They both single out *in the instance of:*

> In the instance of *Where's Charley?,* he adapted the original play *(Charley's Aunt)* to the book of the musical —*Current Biography,* October 1965

We find relatively few examples of this phrase, which makes us wonder how real the overuse of the phrase is. Both commentators object to *instance* on the same grounds as they object to *case.* See the article at CASE for a discussion of phrases that have been criticized as wordy.

instil, instill 1. Both *instil* and *instill* are used, but the double *l* spelling occurs more frequently. The single *l* spelling seems to be favored by the British, but it occurs also in American English use. The matter of determining spelling preference is made more difficult by the fact that when inflecting the verb, British English automatically doubles the *l,* giving *instilled, instilling.*
2. When *instil* or *instill* is used with a preposition, it is most often *in:*

> His desire to share this understanding with his countrymen and to instil in them a persistent impulse toward inquiry —Roger Burlingame, *Backgrounds of Power,* 1949

> School teachers, anxious to instil a love of the outdoors in young folk —*Scots Mag.,* July 1958

> ... inevitability of violence could be instilled in the minds of his contemporaries —Richard Hofstadter, *Harper's,* April 1970

Less frequently, but still quite often, the preposition *into* is used:

> My plan is one for instilling high knowledge into empty minds —Thomas Hardy, *The Return of the Native,* 1878

... the conventional English education instils into us a prejudice against that kind of disquisition —Max Beerbohm, *Atlantic,* December 1950

Some language critics are adamant against the use of *instil, instill* with the preposition *with,* as in "to instill something or someone with" (a similar point may be found at INFUSE). This use has been around for a long time; the OED enters it, but labels it *rare* and shows a quotation from Milton, 1644. *Instill with* has survived into contemporary writing, but occurs only occasionally:

... instilling everybody who meets him with renewed confidence and equanimity —Bennett Cerf, *Saturday Rev.,* 26 May 1951

... it was the Chinese who instilled them with principles of national communism —*Times Literary Supp.,* 13 May 1965

Instil and *instill* have also been used, although infrequently, with *among, through,* or *within:*

The police also back the Church in her endeavors to instil modesty of dress among women —*Living Church,* 27 Mar. 1926

He planned to instil lofty ideals through his painting —*Times Literary Supp.,* 30 Oct. 1981

The aim was to instill within bright children a desire to continue their education —James B. Conant, *Slums and Suburbs,* 1961

instruct When *instruct* is used with a preposition, the one that occurs most frequently is *to* followed by an infinitive:

... they told them so because they had been instructed to tell them so —H. R. Trevor-Roper, *New Statesman & Nation,* 5 Dec. 1953

... an urgent call from the White House instructing him to draw up a legal brief —*Current Biography,* July 1965

Almost as frequently *instruct* is used with *in:*

... present need should instruct America in drawing the plans of a new system of government —Vernon Louis Parrington, *Main Currents in American Thought,* 1930

... a teacher was secured in Philadelphia to instruct in English grammar —*American Guide Series: Delaware,* 1938

Occasionally, *instruct* is used with *as to* or *for:*

... instruct them as to which candidate to vote for —Dayton D. McKean, *Party and Pressure Politics,* 1949

Of the 382 delegates thus chosen, 278 were instructed for Roosevelt, 68 for Taft —David Saville Muzzey, *Our Country's History,* new ed., 1961

insure See ENSURE, INSURE, ASSURE.

integral See METATHESIS.

intend Here are the chief constructions (besides the simple direct object) that are used with *intend:*
It may be followed by an infinitive:

They never intended to strike Jacksontown —E. L. Doctorow, *Loon Lake,* 1979

It may be followed by a direct object and an infinitive phrase.

... seems to have intended the happy ending to show the purification of our corrupt society —John Butt, *English Literature in the Mid-Eighteenth Century,* edited & completed by Geoffrey Carnall, 1979

It may be followed by a gerund:

... I saw that the child had reached the fence and intended climbing it —Peter Taylor, *The Old Forest and Other Stories,* 1985

It may be followed by a clause, with or without *that.* The verb in the clause will be a subjunctive or the equivalent of a subjunctive. This construction seems less common than the foregoing:

... in everything Richelieu undertook things happened as Richelieu had intended they should happen —Hilaire Belloc, *Richelieu,* 1930

Intend may take a prepositional phrase introduced by *for:*

At first intended for the church, he was educated at ... —*Australian Dictionary of Biography,* 1967

In speech and speechlike writing, it is sometimes followed by *on* and a gerund:

... I intend on protecting myself and my loved ones —letter to the editor, *Saturday Evening Post,* October 1981

Longman 1984 warns against *intend* followed by *for,* a noun or pronoun object, and an infinitive with *to,* as in "I didn't intend for her to hear." We have no examples of this construction in edited prose, and assume that it is a verbal use like *intend on.*
See also DESIGN, INTEND.

intense See INTENSIVE, INTENSE.

intensifiers A recent correspondent of ours was curious to know what an intensifier is—a new part of speech? she asked. Not really a new part of speech. An intensifier—or intensive, as it is also called—is a linguistic element used to give emphasis or additional strength to another word or a statement. Intensifiers come from several parts of speech and other grammatical categories. Our correspondent sent us a couple of nouns:

Where *the dickens* have you been?
What *the hell* are you doing?

Adverbs are the largest class:

a *very* hot day
it was *so* sweet of you
a *mighty* fine time
You know that *full* well.
a *really* big show
awfully bad weather
wet *clear* through

Adjectives are used too:

you *bloody* idiot
It's a *complete* lie.
utter nonsense

And participles:

stark raving mad
a *blooming* fool

And pronouns:

> She *herself* did it.
> Borrowing is *itself* a bad habit.

Prepositional phrases can serve as intensifiers:

> Where *in heaven's name* have you been?
> What *in the world* does he think he's doing?

Good and and *nice and* are also used:

> when I'm *good and* ready
> It's *nice and* warm here.

Intensifiers are a frequent bone of contention in usage books. Since they very often indicate a conversational style, many handbooks discourage their use. And there are long-standing disputes about the propriety of adjectives and flat adverbs in intensive function.

Historical observers like Lamberts 1972 and Strang 1970 note that the words used as intensifiers have tended to change over the years. Such intensifiers as *sore, wondrous, plaguey, powerful, devilish, prodigious,* which were formerly quite common, are little used nowadays. Those that survive from older use are often objects of dispute.

intensive, intense   The controversy over these two words was started by Fowler 1926. His complaint was that *intensive* was replacing *intense* in a sense meaning approximately "highly concentrated." He laid the blame for this change on two phrases that apparently began to appear frequently around the time of World War I— *intensive farming* (this sense of *intensive* now has become more specialized and has a separate definition) and *intensive bombardment.* He thus charged other use of this *intensive* with being a popularized technicality and plumped for *intense* instead.

The vehemence of Fowler's remarks has impressed later usage writers, and we have a number of subsequent treatments of the two words as a result. Nickles 1974 and Bryson 1982 more or less repeat Fowler. Evans 1957 discusses Fowler's treatment at greater length and in an enlightened fashion. Most commentators—Shaw 1975, 1987, Chambers 1985, Heritage 1982—simply differentiate the two words, using examples of each in which the words would not be interchanged. Flesch 1964 adds the view that *intensive* is overused.

What Fowler seems to have noticed was a change in usage in progress. The OED shows that the two earliest senses of *intensive* are synonymous with two senses of *intense*: "very strong or acute" and "highly concentrated." The OED marked both these senses of *intensive* obsolete because their evidence ended with the 17th century. The first of these is indeed obsolete: Robert Burton wrote *intensive pleasure* but nowadays only *intense* is used in such a context. The second sense, if indeed it was obsolete, has been revived in the 20th century, and in the second half of the 20th century it has all but replaced *intense* in the "highly concentrated" sense.

In the 20th century the words have tended to differentiate along different lines from those Fowler was defending. *Intense* has tended to become limited to describing some inherent characteristic:

> . . . in the intense sunlight —Nancy Milford, *Harper's*, January 1969

> But tonight . . . the excitement was more intense —James Jones, *Harper's*, February 1971

> . . . there was intense concern for his health —Norman Cousins, *Saturday Rev.*, 30 Oct. 1971

> . . . requiring intense concentration —Stanley Marcus, *Minding the Store*, 1974

> . . . the intense dislike she arouses —Alfred Kazin, *Harper's*, August 1971

Intensive would never be used in those contexts. *Intensive* tends to connote something that is applied from outside:

> . . . gave them six years of intensive training for leadership —William L. Shirer, *The Rise and Fall of the Third Reich*, 1960

> . . . Grissom and Glenn underwent intensive preparation for the next space flight —*Current Biography*, June 1965

> . . . nine days of intensive screenings, panel sessions, and lectures —Arthur Knight, *Saturday Rev.*, 12 Feb. 1972

> . . . the trees, once started, would need no intensive attention —Rexford G. Tugwell, *Center Mag.*, September 1968

> The foreign children in Cologne are taught intensive German for two years —Deborah Churchman, *Christian Science Monitor*, 7 July 1980

It would appear that the "highly concentrated" sense is generally viewed as externally applied rather than an inherent characteristic and is thus displacing *intense* in this use. *Intense* is not dead in this use, but it is dwindling:

> . . . an intense barrage of anti-personnel gunfire —*Current Biography*, April 1966

> But some of them, in spite of care and intense treatment, can never fly well enough to defend themselves or hunt —Margery Facklam, "Kay McKeever and a Parliament of Owls," in *Chains of Light* (8th-grade textbook), ed. Theodore Clymer, 1982

intensives   See INTENSIFIERS.

intent, *noun*   See INTENTION 1.

intent, *adjective*   When the adjective *intent* is used with a preposition, it is usually *on:*

> . . . he would walk right past purple cows, so intent was he on his quest —James Thurber, *Fables for Our Time, and Famous Poems Illustrated*, 1940

> . . . the author is so intent on being clever that he usually forgets to be anything more —Babette Deutsch, *Yale Rev.*, December 1953

Less frequently, *intent* is used with *upon:*

> . . . comes Fred MacMurray, so intent upon making his way in the corporation —Lee Rogow, *Saturday Rev.*, 23 Oct. 1954

Intent has also been used, but not very often, with *in* or *to* plus the infinitive:

> . . . several lanes of traffic . . . intent in tracing the most direct route between two given points —Emily Hahn et al., *Meet the British*, 1953

> The Federalists were intent to create a strong government —Claude G. Bowers, *Atlantic*, January 1953

intention   **1.** *Intention, intent. Intention* and *intent* are used very nearly interchangeably in many cases:

> Dos Passos' trilogy, *U.S.A.,* is thoroughly political in intention —Philip Rahv, *Image and Idea,* 1949

> . . . she didn't have any wish, intention, desire . . . to become any kind of a female bum —James T. Farrell, *What Time Collects,* 1964

> When a person offers us a piece of his mind, we suspect him of hostile intent —Samuel McChord Crothers, *The Cheerful Giver,* 1923

> The title is the simple evidence of Maugham's intent —Edmund Fuller, *American Scholar,* Winter 1946–47

However, there are a few instances in which *intention* and *intent* do not substitute easily for each other in an idiomatic way; a preference for one or the other is evident according to the context:

> . . . he had returned to lay claim to one of Texas's most curvesome blonds . . . and, with no intentions toward marriage, to carry her away to Chicago —Gay Talese, *Esquire,* December 1979

> His day began with an heroic offering of its every moment of thought or action for the intentions of the sovereign pontiff —James Joyce, *A Portrait of the Artist as a Young Man,* 1916

> . . . have a general intention to pray for the intentions of the Pope or the Church —Aloysius McDonough, C.P., *The Sign,* July 1959

> She is vitally concerned therefore with human motivation, what trial lawyers call *intent* —Catherine Drinker Bowen, *Atlantic,* March 1970

> . . . the clear intent of the Taft-Hartley law's provision on secondary boycotts —*Wall Street Jour.,* 26 Mar. 1954

2. When *intention* is used with a preposition, it is used most often with *of,* which is followed by a gerund or a noun:

> ". . . may we very humbly entreat you to sign this gentleman's manifesto with some intention of putting your promise into practice?" —Virginia Woolf, *Three Guineas,* 1939

> The great novelists knew that manners indicate the largest intentions of men's souls —Lionel Trilling, in *Forms of Modern Fiction,* ed. William Van O'Connor, 1948

> The main intention of the poem has been to make dramatically visible the conflict —Allen Tate, *On the Limits of Poetry,* 1948

Almost as frequently, *intention* is used with *to,* which is followed by an infinitive:

> . . . a young child's statements are often objectively untrue, but without the slightest intention to deceive —Bertrand Russell, *Education and the Good Life,* 1926

> . . . the government's intention to implement the Industrial Training Act —*Current Biography,* July 1967

Intention has also been used with *against, behind, toward,* or *towards:*

> "He said the U.S. harbors no military intentions against Saudi Arabian oil fields" —NBC radio newscast, 19 Mar. 1975

> . . . in her wise innocence she had divined the intention behind her mother's tolerance —James Joyce, *Dubliners,* 1914

> . . . their keen perception of Soviet actions and intentions toward Yugoslavia —Alex Dragnich, *Current History,* July 1952

> Recently, Young informed the ICC of his intentions towards the Central —*Time,* 1 Feb. 1954

intercede   *Intercede* is used with a variety of prepositions; those found most often are *for, in,* or *with:*

> . . . to intercede for her afore she commits the sin that cannot be forgiven —Sir Arthur Quiller-Couch, *The Delectable Duchy,* 1893

> . . . and she it was now . . . who interceded for the old woman with her uncle —Hilaire Belloc, *Richelieu,* 1930

> It was not the task of the government to intercede in this process —Herbert I. London, *Arts and Sciences,* Spring 1967

> . . . successfully interceded in a conflict between Hindus and Moslems —*Current Biography,* December 1964

> . . . will intercede with the deity on their behalf —*National Geographic,* October 1947

> Jack then stupidly asked another Cosa Nostra member to intercede with the collector —Donald R. Cressey, *Harper's,* February 1969

Once in a while, *intercede* is used with *against* or *between:*

> Only the law, it seems, can effectively intercede against the threat of irreversible depredations —Hilton Kramer, *N.Y. Times,* 22 Apr. 1979

> "Resists making judgments that intercede between teenagers and the codes and beliefs of their parents" —publisher's catalog, August 1981

interesting, interestingly   *Interesting* has drawn occasional criticism from usage commentators dating back to Partridge 1942, primarily on the grounds that it is an overused and imprecise adjective. It is, of course, an extremely common word.

> What was most interesting about Daniel's speech . . . —Gay Talese, *Harper's,* January 1969

> . . . for more interesting part-time jobs —Jane Schwartz Gould, *Barnard Alumnae,* Winter 1971

> . . . these letters are interesting but not fascinating —Robert F. Byrnes, *Saturday Rev.,* 5 Apr. 1975

Its imprecision is part of what makes it useful, and we see no need to make a policy of avoiding it. No doubt there are times, however, when a more precise adjective does make a good substitute for *interesting.*

More interestingly, the adverb *interestingly* is often

now used as a sentence modifier, as we have used it in this sentence. Such usage has been common since the 1960s:

... and, interestingly, no public funds at any level could have been used —James B. Conant, *Slums and Suburbs,* 1961

Interestingly, Young thinks the Atlanta experience is essentially national —Richard Reeves, *New York,* 12 July 1976

Interestingly, Weinberger once served as a young captain —Hedrick Smith, *N.Y. Times Mag.,* 1 Nov. 1981

It occurs commonly with *enough:*

Interestingly enough . . . , the students who have the most trouble . . . —John Coyne, *Change,* March 1973

Interestingly enough, these handbooks . . . are bound in the manner of real books —Erik Sandberg-Diment, *N.Y. Times,* 20 Mar. 1984

The sentence-modifying *interestingly* is somewhat similar to the sentence-modifying *hopefully* (which see), but no usage commentator that we know of has so far criticized it.

interface *Interface,* like *input,* is a word given wide currency by the computer revolution, and as both noun and verb it is viewed with alarm and distaste by the usage panel of Harper 1985, as well as by Bremner 1980, Bryson 1984, Phythian 1979, Longman 1984, Cook 1985, Howard 1977, Mitchell 1979, and Janis 1984. It is treated a bit more cautiously by Sir Bruce Fraser in Gowers 1973, and a correspondent quoted in Safire 1984 assures everyone that it is passé in business management. The word has also been roundly cudgeled in the press.

Our evidence, however, suggests there is not much reason for alarm. Unlike *input, interface* has not made much headway in general edited prose. Many of our examples from newspapers and magazines comment on the word rather than use it. A great many other examples are direct quotations from people using it in speech:

... the question of how the C.I.A. interfaced with the Presidency —Senator Howard H. Baker, Jr., quoted in *N.Y. Times,* 28 Feb. 1975

In this technological century, we need an interface between science and the public —Carl Sagan, quoted in *People,* 22 Nov. 1976

In a recent speech he gushed with an adman's grandiloquence . . . : ". . . to establish, at a single moment in time, eyeball-to-eyeball interface with the man in the street on a global scale. . . ." —Jeremy Bullmore, quoted in *Wall Street Jour.,* 22 Mar. 1982

We also find it in the help-wanted ads:

... the ability to interface at various management levels —advt., *New Orleans Times-Picayune,* 26 Sept. 1979

This indiv will interface with the patient, staff & physician —advt., *N.Y. Times,* 25 Jan. 1987

And we find it used tongue in cheek at times:

... had calluses on his pen hand and his chair interface —*C Biologics,* 15 July 1977

It occurs in edited prose in serious contexts, too, but not with great frequency:

... represented in medieval times a physical, economic and cultural interface between the Indian Ocean and western Pacific —A. D. Couper, *The Geography of Sea Transport,* 1972

... will find its greatest use at the school-university interface —C. A. Stace, *Nature,* 19 Dec. 1984

... cutting out much of the interface problem between management and computer personnel — Michael Stewart & Graham Bond, in *Handbook for Managers,* vol. 3, ed. Malcolm E. Levene et al., 1975

Today, it's the computer wizards who are interfacing with the lexicon —Patrick Bedard, *Car and Driver,* October 1983

It is perhaps significant that three out of four of these examples are British. Our evidence shows that in American English *interface* is found in technical contexts almost all of the time; it does not appear to be catching on in ordinary prose.

in terms of *In terms of* is a compound preposition that seems to have taken hold only after World War II. It apparently struck a responsive chord, for we have many examples of its use from the early 1950s. It also appears to be habit-forming; we have many cases of multiple examples having been drawn from the same writer in the same book or article. It did not take long to draw unfriendly attention: the editor of the *Journal of Communication* disapproved in 1954. The usage books have followed suit: Bernstein 1962, 1965, Copperud 1964, 1970, 1980, Follett 1966, Strunk & White 1979, Macmillan 1982, Montgomery & Stratton 1981, Janis 1984, Guth 1985, and Trimmer & McCrimmon 1988 all dislike the phrase. The usual advice is to omit it or to substitute a simple preposition for it. You are warned, however, that you cannot make such a change—at least in the sentences we have collected—without additional revision or without altering the meaning of the passage somewhat.

Guth's characterization of *in terms of* as "a vague all-purpose connective" is fairly accurate. It seems to be one of those terms whose imprecision is its greatest virtue—writers don't always want to be precise. It may have had its origin in mathematical uses like this one:

To add or subtract unlike fractions it is necessary first to express the given fractions in terms of a common denominator —Robert W. Marks, *The New Mathematics Dictionary and Handbook,* 1964

It is certainly common enough in mathematics—where it is not imprecise—and probably has been for quite some time. This is speculation, however; our earliest citations for it are not mathematical.

We give you here a selection of actual uses of the phrase. We find no single easy way to replace *in terms of* in them.

Of course Clark, Charlie and all the rest of my good friends are thinking in terms of 1948—and I'm not —Harry S. Truman, letter, 20 Sept. 1946

... the method is delightfully remote from academicism, and the theme comes to life in terms of people and wagons, horses and dogs —*Times Literary Supp.,* 28 Dec. 1951

And so McCarthy in the hearings saw all issues and conditions in terms of himself —Michael Straight, *New Republic,* 28 June 1954

... a scheme for an orderly arrangement of the elementary particles. The particles were described in terms of eight quantum numbers —*Current Biography,* February 1966

... he has no thought of overdoing the simple life; he is thinking in terms of £500 a year, with a few good servants and horses —James Sutherland, *English Literature of the Late Seventeenth Century,* 1969

Pointlessly exploring your pockets, you come up with a small glass vial, Tad's gift. In terms of improving your mood, this might be just what the doctor ordered —Jay McInerney, *Bright Lights, Big City,* 1984

Darman meant that the President did not think in terms of more than one year at a time —David A. Stockman, *Newsweek,* 28 Apr. 1986

internecine *Internecine* is a useful word today because of a mistake that wasn't caught. The word began its history in English in Samuel Butler's satirical poem *Hudibras* (1663). According to the OED, Butler apparently used the phrase *internecine war* as a translation of Latin *internecīnum bellum,* which was a term for a war of extermination. Samuel Johnson's Dictionary (1755) was the first dictionary to enter the adjective, and Johnson, apparently misled by Latin *inter-* (which does not have in this word its usual "mutual" or "reciprocal" sense), defined it as "endeavouring mutual destruction." Johnson's definition was of course carried into later dictionaries—lexicographers are frequently respectful enough of their predecessors to copy them. Before too long, Johnson's sense was the dominant meaning of the word. And a good thing, said Fowler 1926, for without Johnson's misunderstanding, the word would have had no particular use in the language, since its Latin sense has plenty of substitutes in English, including *destructive, slaughterous, murderous, bloody,* and *sanguinary.*
So Johnson's mistake has given English a useful, if somewhat learned, word. It is really more of an interesting story than a usage issue; even the major usage panels find the mistaken use acceptable. The last complaint we know of is in Bernstein 1958; he objected to its use for internal conflict without the notion of slaughter. It is true that other words are available for this use, but *intramural* sounds too much like fun and games and *intertribal* too anthropological. In the second half of the 20th century, if our evidence is representative, the bloodless sense has become predominant. Here are a few examples:

The rivalry between the various cities of Texas is an interesting phenomenon.... The Easterner, or tenderfoot, will not comprehend this keen, internecine rivalry —Frank Sullivan, *The Night the Old Nostalgia Burned Down,* 1953

Thereafter the consolidation of Pictish power ... and the increasing strength of the kingdom of the Mercians combined with internecine troubles to force Northumbria on to the defensive —D. J. V. Fisher, *The Anglo-Saxon Age,* 1973

Did you then remember that, for all their internecine squabbling, trade unionists always call one another "brother"? —Grundy, *Punch,* 20 July 1976

... public broadcasting ... survived the internecine rivalry between its two governing bodies —Peter Caranicas, *Saturday Rev.,* January 1981

In any society, Hegel contends, an élite of masters, potentially in internecine conflict, will dominate —George Steiner, *New Yorker,* 12 July 1982

interpose When used with a preposition, *interpose* most commonly appears with *between* in modern writing:

She actually interposed her body between him and the street door —Edna Ferber, *Cimarron,* 1929

... the tendency to interpose objects of worship between God and man —W. R. Inge, *The Church in the World,* 1928

... the tops of the trees behind him interposed between him and the sun —C. S. Forester, *The Sky and the Forest,* 1948

... interpose himself between the police and the body of one demonstrator —Norman Mailer, *Harper's,* November 1968

Much less often, *interpose* is used with *in:*

... the Senate has shown restraint in interposing vetoes in the case of major appointments —Lindsay Rogers, in *Aspects of American Government,* ed. Sydney D. Bailey, 1950

And, once in a while, *interpose* is followed by *against, on, upon,* or *with* in various senses and relations:

... 1966, when Robert Kennedy interposed his formidable presence against what appeared to be the certain election of Arthur Klein —Richard Cohen, *New York,* 13 Sept. 1971

For a while I listened ... and at length interposed once more on the old man's side —W. H. Hudson, *Green Mansions,* 1904

Mountain systems are significant ... because of the barriers that they interpose upon the movements of people —Vernor C. Finch & Glenn T. Trewartha, *Elements of Geography,* 2d ed., 1942

... the McCarthy fight against Harvard and Dr. James Conant was interposed with the statement that Conant had so little understanding of Communism —*The Reporter,* 16 Feb. 1954

interpretative, interpretive These words are synonyms. *Interpretative* is older by a century or so. The OED labeled *interpretive* "rare," having only one 17th-century and one 19th-century citation, but the OED Supplement contains plenty of 20th-century evidence, as do our files. Fowler 1926 and Gowers in Fowler 1965 prescribe *interpretative* on the basis of the underlying Latin form and call *interpretive* wrong. Evans 1957 and Bernstein 1965 give the nod to the older and longer form: Bernstein notes that some writers appear to use *interpretive* on the analogy of *preventive* (Fowler condemns the longer form *preventative*). Watt 1967 and Shaw 1975, 1987 are neutral. Copperud 1960, 1964 prefers *interpretive;* in his consensus books (1970, 1980) he notes ruefully that the consensus seems to run against him and concedes that dictionaries favor *interpretative*.

The definitions in Webster's Third are at *interpretative,* and *interpretive* is defined only by a cross-reference to *interpretative*. This arrangement probably reflects nothing more than alphabetical chance—the definitions had to go at one or the other, and *interpretative* comes first. The editors of the Third had about equal evidence for both words.

Evidence gathered since the publication of the Third, however, runs heavily in favor of the shorter *interpretive*. So both forms are well established.

intervene   *Intervene* is used with a variety of prepositions, but it occurs most often with *in:*

> . . . he will intervene directly in his novel to comment on the characters and action —Carlos Lynes, Jr., in *Forms of Modern Fiction,* ed. William Van O'Connor, 1948

> . . . the new board was shorn by Congress of any power to intervene in industrial disputes —Mary K. Hammond, *Current History,* November 1952

> There were, at that time, only two places where the Allies could intervene in Russia —George F. Kennan, *Soviet Foreign Policy, 1917–1941,* 1960

Less frequently, *intervene* is used with *between* or *with; between* occurs a little more often:

> There still intervenes a narrow space between the last house of London and the ancient Forest Hall —Richard Jefferies, *The Open Air,* 1885

> . . . the trained self-consciousness . . . intervenes between the poet's moods and his poetry —C. Day Lewis, *A Hope for Poetry,* 3d ed., 1936

> She intervened with Monsignor Seipel to keep an eye on her boy —John Gunther, *Inside Europe,* rev. ed., 1937

> . . . had called for the government to intervene with Federal troops —Malcolm X, *Evergreen,* December 1967

Intervene has also been used with *after, against,* and *into:*

> The reign of the great Napoleon intervened after the fall of the first republic —De Forest Stull & Roy W. Hatch, *Our World Today: Europe and Europe Overseas* (textbook), 1948

> . . . appealed to Pope Paul VI to intervene against possible obstructive tactics —*Current Biography,* December 1964

> . . . Mr. Dubos says that man must continue to intervene into nature, but we must do it with a sense of responsibility —William Kucewicz, *Wall Street Jour.,* 13 June 1980

in that case, in the case of   See CASE.

in the circumstances   See CIRCUMSTANCES.

in the course of   See COURSE 2.

in the event that   See EVENT.

in the final analysis   See ANALYSIS.

in the hope(s) of, in the hope(s) that   See HOPE 2.

in the worst way   See WORST WAY.

into   **1.** See IN, INTO.
2. *Into, in to.* Quite a few handbooks, beginning at least as far back as Fowler 1926, point out that the adverb *in* followed by the preposition *to* is not to be confused with the preposition *into*. The matter is probably not one of real mental confusion but of inadvertence or carelessness; it seems most likely to occur where *in* idiomatically belongs to the preceding verb and *to* goes with a human object. *Turn* is a verb often chosen for illustration, because *turn something in* carries the notion of handing over and contrasts strikingly with the "transform, change" sense of *turn* which is idiomatically used with *into*. Thus, we find in the handbooks more than one illustrative instance of "suspects turned themselves into police." Our own bad example is not quite as striking, but you may still say "abracadabra" at the end of it:

> . . . turn this form into your department head —internal memo, Merriam-Webster Inc., 1986

It should be *in to.*

intrigue   The most common sense of the verb *intrigue* is "to arouse the interest and curiosity of," as in "the story intrigued them." This sense is now so well established and widely used that anyone unfamiliar with its history will probably be surprised to learn that it did not exist until about a hundred years ago. The earliest evidence of its use (in the OED Supplement) is from 1894. Once it had been introduced, however, it caught on quickly, and within a few decades it had become both extremely common and, among certain people, extremely unpopular.

The new and common sense of *intrigue* was widely disliked in the early 20th century for two basic reasons: it was new and it was common. Its frequent appearance in newspapers sent some readers to their dictionaries, where they found only such definitions for the verb *intrigue* as "to cheat or trick," and "to plot or scheme." Where had the new sense come from? It appears to have been borrowed directly from French, where it had developed from a sense essentially synonymous with *puzzle* (which had itself developed from the "cheat or trick" sense). Its French origin enabled Fowler 1926 to attack it as a "Gallicism" having "no merit whatever except that of unfamiliarity to the English reader, & at the same time the great demerit of being identical with & therefore confusing the sense of a good English word." Fowler condemned *intrigue* as a worthless and pretentious substitute for such verbs as *puzzle, fascinate,* and *interest.*

The new sense of *intrigue* was already firmly established in English by the time Fowler censured it. It has been included as a standard sense in Merriam-Webster dictionaries since 1919, when it was added to the New Words section of Webster 1909. Its widespread use has continued unabated throughout the 20th century. Critical attacks against it have also continued, but since the 1940s they have been relatively rare and relatively mild. New reasons have been devised for disliking it; Partridge 1942 and Bernstein 1965, for example, claim that it is incorrectly derived from the French verb, which, they say, means "to puzzle." In fact, the French verb means both "to puzzle" and "to arouse the curiosity of." By far the most popular criticism in recent decades has been that *intrigue* is "overworked," a description that has the advantage of being both insubstantial and impossible to refute. Almost all commentators now acknowledge that the disputed sense of *intrigue* is standard. The one recent exception is Simon 1980, who echoes Fowler when he describes it as "a flagrant Gallicism."

We include all this information solely as a matter of interest—not to suggest that you should feel the least hesitation about using *intrigue*. This useful verb may have been a gallicism in the 1890s, but it is certainly not a gallicism now. As several commentators have pointed out, it has connotations that distinguish it from *fascinate, interest,* and other such verbs; something that intrigues us not only fascinates us, it fascinates us by making us curious, by making us want to find out more. Sir Ernest Gowers rightly suggests in Fowler 1965 that the popularity of *intrigue* is largely explained by the fact that no other verb has quite the same meaning.

> "I must confess," he said, "the New Woman and the New Girl intrigue me profoundly...." —H. G. Wells, *Ann Veronica,* 1909

> ... were naturally intrigued by hearing Judith refer to herself ... as a Used Gourd —Stella Gibbons, *Cold Comfort Farm,* 1932

> "I read about your party ... and I was intrigued by a woman who preferred Kreisler to a jewel." — George Bernard Shaw, quoted in *Woman's Home Companion,* April 1954

> My seatmate's business, incidentally, intrigued me —Bennett Cerf, *Saturday Rev.,* 29 May 1954

> ... a problem that intrigued the seventeenth-century mind as fully as it does our own —Noam Chomsky, *Columbia Forum,* Spring 1968

> ... friends would be intrigued by the difference in Bundy —David Halberstam, *Harper's,* July 1969

introduce   When *introduce* is used with a preposition, it is usually used with *to* or *into;* use of *to* occurs just a little more frequently:

> "... I dressed, had some dinner at that little Italian restaurant in Rupert Street you introduced me to...." —Oscar Wilde, *The Picture of Dorian Gray,* 1891

> "I could introduce him to oils and help him start landscapes...." —Agnes Sligh Turnbull, *The Gown of Glory,* 1952

> Craft introduced her to the noted composer Igor Stravinsky —*Current Biography,* July 1967

> ... my idea of introducing him that evening to the broad cultural connection between Siberian Slavic dancers and Czechs —Jane O'Reilly, *New York,* 15 Feb. 1971

> ... the first Merino sheep ever imported into this country ... and introduced into Claremont by his kinsman —*American Guide Series: New Hampshire,* 1938

> The artist evenings at the Museum ... seem to have introduced a new spirit into Virginia art —*Southern Literary Messenger,* September 1940

> ... a bit of finely filiated platinum is introduced into a chamber containing oxygen —T. S. Eliot, "Tradi-

tion and the Individual Talent," 1917, in *American Harvest,* ed. Allen Tate & John Peale Bishop, 1942

> ... the suspense of someone who introduces one part of life into another, feeling insecurely that they may clash —John Cheever, *The Wapshot Chronicle,* 1957

Once in a while, when one would expect to find *into, in* occurs instead:

> General David Humphreys, ... and the first man to introduce merino sheep in America —*American Guide Series: Connecticut,* 1938

> The air or oxygen was introduced in the helmet at the side of the window —Harry G. Armstrong, *Principles and Practice of Aviation Medicine,* 1939

Introduce has also occurred with *among, at, between, for, round,* and *within:*

> ... a Russian campaign to divide Germany from the Atlantic Community and to introduce friction among the European powers —*Current History,* May 1952

> In 1819, the use of the power loom was introduced at the Amoskeag Mills —*American Guide Series: New Hampshire,* 1938

> ... the inhabitants saw Penn's claim to revenue from soil and trade as a wedge introduced between them and the Crown —*American Guide Series: Delaware,* 1938

> During the second year of his ministry he introduced a gradual change for this evening service —Virginia Douglas Dawson & Betty Douglas Wilson, *The Shape of Sunday,* 1952

> ... small figures in relief, called 'weepers', were introduced round the base of the tomb —O. Elfrida Saunders, *A History of English Art in the Middle Ages,* 1932

> When directed change is, however, introduced within segments of a culture, latent dissatisfactions are brought to the surface —Lewis S. Feuer, *Jour. of Philosophy,* 11 Nov. 1954

intrude   When *intrude* is used with a preposition, the choice most often is *into:*

> No industry intrudes into the peaceful village — *American Guide Series: Connecticut,* 1938

> ... the old-established aristocratic society into which they intruded with their outlandish ways —G. M. Trevelyan, *English Social History,* 1942

> Thereafter Nazi influences intruded ever more forcefully into the organized life of German-Americans — Oscar Handlin, *The American People in the Twentieth Century,* 1954

Just a little less frequently, *intrude* is used with *on* or *upon:*

> ... not wishing to intrude himself too much on the attention of men who stood for substance —Thomas Wolfe, *You Can't Go Home Again,* 1940

> ... he was someone intruding too quickly on that moment of understanding shared with Peggy in the hall —Morley Callaghan, *The Loved and the Lost,* 1951

... he was not sure that he should intrude upon his uncle's sorrow —Jean Stafford, *The Mountain Lion,* 1947

... most of these parents love their children but admit that they have intruded upon the marital relationship —Morton Hunt, *N.Y. Times Book Rev.,* 5 June 1977

Intrude is occasionally also used with *between* or *in:*

... we are kept at a distance because Mailer's personality intrudes between us and the experience —Tom Seligson, *N.Y. Times Book Rev.,* 15 July 1973

We will not allow any other people to intrude in our way of life —*Current Biography 1947*

inundate When *inundate* is used with a preposition, *with* is usual:

Her face was inundated with an angry colour —James Joyce, *Dubliners,* 1914

We were soon inundated with letters —William H. Whyte, Jr., *The Organization Man,* 1956

... I have never felt lonelier in my life, more inundated with frustration —John Mason Brown, *Saturday Rev.,* 18 April 1953

Less often *inundate* is used with *by:*

CBS was inundated by calls, telegrams, and letters —Marya Mannes, *The Reporter,* 27 Apr. 1954

The ballet public is inundated—truly it is—by *Swan Lake*s galore —Walter Terry, *Saturday Rev.,* 20 Sept. 1975

Infrequently *inundate* has been used with *in:*

... this gluts the market and inundates the viewer in a morass of mediocrity or worse —Amos Vogel, *Evergreen,* June 1967

inure, enure The spelling *inure* is found much more often than is the variant *enure.*
Inure, when used with a preposition, almost always takes *to,* whatever its meaning:

Inured to television and radio, that audience is accustomed to being distracted —Aldous Huxley, *Brave New World Revisited,* 1958

Americans have become inured to red meat, well tabascoed —Anthony Burgess, *Saturday Rev.,* 3 Feb. 1979

... the treatment therein of corporate income taxes is bound to inure to the benefit of the profession —*Jour. of Accountancy,* February 1945

... such an identity of interest between the taxpayers that a refund to one will inure to the benefit of the other —William T. Plumb, Jr., *Harvard Law Rev.,* December 1952

Inure, however, has also at times been followed by *against* or *with:*

... we have learned, too, that museums can inure us against the reality of function —Leonard Kriegel, *Change,* March–April 1969

... those people still inured with gentler passions —George W. Bonham, *Change,* October 1971

Enure when used with a preposition in its meaning "habituate" is usually used with *to,* in much the same way as *inure* is used. The variant *enure* in this sense is found more often in British than in American use:

... the jungle odour renders it difficult for anyone, not enured to it, to complete the tour —Osbert Sitwell, *Escape with Me!,* 1939

... a people that is by now enured to crises —*The Economist,* 9 Aug. 1947

Enure, in its sense "accrue," has a more complicated pattern of usage than does *inure.* As shown above, *inure* in both senses is used with *to. Enure,* when meaning "accrue," is used with *to* or *for* in British English and usually with *to* in American English:

... like all fair bargains, it should enure to the benefit of both sides —*The Economist,* 28 June 1947

... even though they enure not for the company's benefit but for that of the secretary himself —*Palmer's Company Law,* 22d ed., 1976

The grant does not convey power ... which can enure solely to the benefit of the grantee —John Marshall, *Gibbons v. Ogden,* 1824

invent See DISCOVER, INVENT.

invest There are two different verbs *invest,* the first preceding the second by some 80 years (1533; 1613). The earlier *invest,* which comes directly from the Latin *investire,* is usually used with *with:*

During a few years the book was invested with a significance ... which its ... merits could not justify —Aldous Huxley, *The Olive Tree,* 1937

... Meredith showed an extraordinary power for investing brainwork with imagery —C. Day Lewis, *The Poetic Image,* 1947

... invest a prelate with the symbols of his office —Herbert Agar, *Declaration of Faith,* 1952

... which permitted the Victorians to invest medieval art and architecture with Victorian values —Janet Malcolm, *New Yorker,* 18 Sept. 1971

When this *invest* is used with *by,* the verb is usually in the form of the past participle:

He was one of 30 officials, courtiers and dignitaries invested by the queen —*Springfield* (Mass.) *Union,* 23 June 1953

Dukes were originally invested by girding them with a sword, as earls had long been invested —*Chambers's Encyclopaedia,* new ed., 1950

The western base of Big Round Top was invested by the Confederates —*American Guide Series: Pennsylvania,* 1940

When the second verb *invest,* which comes through the Italian *investire,* is used with a preposition, it is usually *in:*

Pension plans are less heavily invested in stocks than generally believed —George Anders, *Wall Street Jour.,* 18 Dec. 1981

The refugees themselves are willing to invest their suffering as well as their time in the cause —John Cogley, *Commonweal,* 25 Dec. 1953

One might say one invests one's identity *in* one's memory —Elizabeth Bowen, *Saturday Rev.,* 27 May 1950

. . . the superficial adoption of this tradition by one who was unwilling to invest in its authentic vitality —George Steiner, *Times Literary Supp.,* 27 June 1980

in view of the fact that   This is one of the longer phrases involving *fact;* all of them are questioned by one or another critic. Like the others this one has its uses, but you probably do not need it at the beginning of a sentence. See FACT 1.

invite   The noun *invite* was formed by the same process—functional shift—that gave us the nouns *command* and *request.* It has been in use for more than 300 years—since 1659—and its users include Fanny Burney (in her diary) and Thackeray (in a letter), among others. It was first disparaged by Gould 1867, who mentions it in passing. Since then Bardeen 1883, Vizetelly 1906, Fowler 1926, 1965, Partridge 1942, Bryant 1962, Watt 1967, Copperud 1964, 1970, 1980, Irmscher 1976, Perrin & Ebbitt 1972, Phythian 1979, Janis 1984, and Barzun 1985 have all had at it; only Evans 1957 seems tolerant. It has been labeled (some of the following epithets have been reduced to adjectives from more elaborate invective) ignorant, vulgar, humorous, informal, slang, dialectal, barbarous, colloquial, unrespectable, incorrect, and ill-bred. Such a variety of opinion is uninformative about the nature of the problem, but it does suggest that the critics consider *invite* just a bit below the salt.

You can make up your own mind about *invite* on the basis of these examples, which represent fairly the range of its usage. It does seem certain that some writers have used it in the speech of their less educated characters and that others have used it when being deliberately light or humorous.

Lyddy sot a good deal by her. She never had a quilting or a sewing-bee but what nothing would do but she must give Rachel Doolittle an invite —Francis Lee Pratt, "Captain Ben's Choice," in *Mark Twain's Library of Humor,* 1888

"You sound like you didn't get no invite to the dance" —Richard Bissell, *A Stretch on the River,* 1950

"What are you dressing up for, Nobby?" asked someone. "Didn't your invite say evening dress optional?" —C. S. Forester, *Saturday Evening Post,* 15 Nov. 1958

Thanks for the invite —Flannery O'Connor, letter, 17 May 1961

. . . an invitation, mailed on May 12, to a reception at Maple Leaf Gardens to be held on May 14. Since I didn't get the invite until the 16th, I don't see how I can make it —Susan Ford, *Sunday Sun* (Toronto), 18 May 1975

Charlie MacArthur said an invite of Woollcott's was like a call to the jury panel —Ruth Gordon, *Myself Among Others,* 1971

. . . a classy invite to an art gallery —Sally Vincent, *Punch,* 28 Nov. 1973

I acted smug, Republican and nonchalant and waved my blackmarket ticket and invite —Joe Eszterhas, *Rolling Stone,* 1 Mar. 1973

. . . one Nobel Peace Prize nominator wants to call him with an invite to Oslo —Jonathan Cooper, *People,* 5 Aug. 1985

Authorities gently (but oh so firmly) returned word that Mrs. Marcos just didn't rate an invite —*People,* 3 Aug. 1981

invoke   See EVOKE, INVOKE.

involve   **1.** Some language critics, among them Phythian 1979, Follet 1966, and Evans 1957, deplore the use of this word as imprecise when there is no suggestion of complication or entanglement, as in sentences like "Representatives of several groups were involved in the discussions." However, the choice of *involve* in these cases may have been deliberate on the part of a writer who was looking for a less specific but no less meaningful word than *entail, necessitate,* or *affect* (all of which Phythian suggests as substitutes). At any rate, *involve* has over the centuries acquired various shades of meaning. It is standardly used in any number of senses without apparently generating misunderstandings on the part of the reading public, and also without any serious loss of use of those other putatively more precise words, which continue to be called upon when writers need them.

2. When *involve* is used with a preposition, it occurs with many, but the one chosen most often is *in:*

Involved in these imaginings she knew nothing of time —Thomas Hardy, *The Return of the Native,* 1878

Involved in its meaning is the idea of power conceived in a particular way —Lionel Trilling, in *Forms of Modern Fiction,* ed. William Van O'Connor, 1948

. . . approve the costs that were involved in building new roads —Edwin O. Reischauer, *N.Y. Times Book Rev.,* 23 May 1954

It seems inconceivable that such a man could be involved in questionable deals —Trevor Armbrister, *Saturday Evening Post,* 12 Feb. 1966

Involve is also used often with *with:*

. . . become emotionally involved with their jobs, and take pleasure in accomplishment —Herbert Gold, *Yale Rev.,* Autumn 1954

The less parochial among British radical students . . . are rightly involved with the problem of world hunger —*Times Literary Supp.,* 9 Apr. 1970

When Jo is away, he finds himself simultaneously involved with Anna, a Brooklyn waitress . . . and Imogen, the romantically beautiful wife —Alfred Kazin, *Partisan Rev.,* Summer 1946

The second floor of a three-story frame building is fully involved with fire —Dennis Smith, *Report from Engine Co. 82,* 1972

Infrequently, *involve* has been used with *against, around, for,* or *into:*

At present about 400,000 soldiers, some 95,000 of them European, are involved against Ho's forces — Frank Gorrell, *New Republic,* 3 Aug. 1953

... the true business of the literary artist is to plait or weave his meaning, involving it around itself — Samuel C. Brownstein & Mitchel Weiner, *How to Prepare for College Entrance Examinations,* ed. Stanley H. Kaplan, 1954

"He says it'd be lovely and so on. But I don't think he sees what's involved for me." —Nigel Balchin, *A Way Through the Wood,* 1951

"That'll be quite enough." He involved a thousand-volt charge into his primness and succeeded in looking like the Angel of the Lord —Margery Allingham, *More Work for the Undertaker,* 1949

invulnerable This word is sometimes considered to be an absolute adjective. See ABSOLUTE ADJECTIVES.

in whole and in part See WHOLE.

iridescent Reader's Digest 1983 and Gowers in Fowler 1965 remind us that this is sometimes misspelled *irridescent.* The word should have only one *r.*

ironically Bremner 1980 advises us to let the reader decide whether something we write is ironic or not, and not to preface the remark with *ironically*—and especially not with *ironically enough.* Bremner is objecting to *ironically* as a sentence adverb, but he has missed an important point. *Ironically* as a sentence adverb is what some grammarians call a disjunct; disjuncts tell you what the writer or speaker thinks about a statement, not what the reader or hearer is supposed to think.

Bremner is the only American usage writer we have found who mentions this primarily British issue. The British commentators—Howard 1978, Burchfield 1981, Longman 1984, and Robert F. Ilson in *The English Language Today* (1985)—base their objections on semantic grounds. Howard may speak for the group:

Ironically is a powerful and explicit word. It is being weakened by use as an all-purpose introductory word to draw attention to every trivial oddity, and often to no oddity at all.

Howard's summary fits the objections of the other British commentators reasonably well. A couple of American academics have taken up the same line: Wayne C. Booth—who is not disinterested, having written a book on irony—in *Harper's* (May 1984), and Hugh Kenner in the *Times Literary Supplement* (17 Oct. 1986). Part of the fun of this line of criticism is trying to think up plausible substitutes for *ironically. Oddly, embarrassingly, incongruously, paradoxically, strangely,* even *sadly* and *tragically* have been suggested.

The usage itself has been a long time coming to light. It is about as old as sentence-adverbial *hopefully* (half a century or so), but is only now being discovered. Here are some examples from over the years:

Ironically enough, it was Boston and Cambridge that grew to seem provincial —Van Wyck Brooks, *The Flowering of New England, 1815-1865,* rev. ed., 1946

Scott, Dickens, Thackeray, Hawthorne, Cooper, Bulwer-Lytton, and George Eliot were most in demand, and with the passing of instruction in Greek and Latin literature, these novelists were, ironically, called 'classics.' —James D. Hart, *The Popular Book: A History of America's Literary Taste,* 1950

Ironically, the President found himself agreeing with the same companies his administration had just indicted ... as a wicked oil cartel —*Time,* 8 Sept. 1952

... laid the foundations of his fortune with a novel called, ironically enough, *The Light that Failed* — Maurice Cranston, *London Calling,* 19 Aug. 1954

Ironically, one's first impression of Melville Cane, unless one chances on him while he is already laughing, is that of melancholy —Hiram Haydn, *American Scholar,* Summer 1964

Ironically the bombing of London was a blessing to the youthful generations that followed —Iona & Peter Opie, *Children's Games in Street and Playground,* 1969

... decline from their former economic strength (which has, ironically, been accompanied by an upsurge in appreciation in the intellectual community) —Richard Schickel, *Harper's,* October 1970

The good weather, ironically, was in part responsible for this perhaps record toll —Jeremy Bernstein, *New Yorker,* 30 Oct. 1971

Ironically, the most likely source of hidden value lies in the company's older properties —Frederick Rose, quoted in *Wall Street Jour.,* 23 May 1980

These should be enough to give you a good idea of the standardness of their usage. It has been waiting to be discovered for some time, and no doubt commentators in this country will eventually recognize the potential it offers as a target for criticism. The older use of *ironically,* incidentally, seems to be moving right along unaffected by the newer use.

irrefutable See INCOMPARABLE.

irregardless This adverb, apparently a blend of *irrespective* and *regardless,* originated in dialectal American speech in the early 20th century (according to the American Dialect Dictionary, it was first recorded in western Indiana in 1912). Its use in nonstandard speech had become widespread enough by the 1920s to make it a natural in a story by Ring Lardner:

I told them that irregardless of what you read in books, they's some members of the theatrical profession that occasionally visits the place where they sleep —Ring Lardner, *The Big Town,* 1921

Its widespread use also made it a natural in books by usage commentators, and it has appeared in such books regularly at least since Krapp 1927. The most frequently repeated comment about it is that "there is no such word."

Word or not, *irregardless* has continued in fairly common spoken use, although its bad reputation has not improved with the years. It does occur in the casual speech and writing of educated people, and it even finds its way into edited prose on rare occasion:

... allow the supplier to deliver his product, irregardless of whether or not his problem is solved — John Cosgrove, *Datamation,* 1 Dec. 1971

... irrespective of whether the source is identified and irregardless of whether all that news is disseminated to the general public —Robert Hanley, *N.Y. Times,* 25 Oct. 1977

The spherical agglomerates occur in these powders, irregardless of starting composition —*Predicasts Technology Update,* 25 Aug. 1984

But *irregardless* is still a long way from winning general acceptance as a standard English word. Use *regardless* instead.

irrelevant   Fowler 1926 notes that the OED contains a warning against the misspelling *irrevelant;* the same problem is mentioned by Copperud 1970, 1980, Bremner 1980, and Janis 1984. We have examples of the misspelling in our files, so care is warranted.

Fowler also says that *irrevelant* is probably spoken a hundred times for every time it appears in print. The process that produces *irrevelant* from *irrelevant* in speech is called metathesis (which see). Metathesis has had a hand in producing some of our common words, like *burn.* Transposing the *l* and the *v* in speech could lead to the same transposition in writing. A similar metathesis is discussed at CALVARY, CAVALRY.

irreparable   See INCOMPARABLE.

irrevocable   See INCOMPARABLE.

is because   See BECAUSE 1; REASON IS BECAUSE.

is being   See PROGRESSIVE PASSIVE.

isolate   When *isolate* is used with a preposition, the choice is usually *from:*

Daphne looked at him brightly, her eyes isolated from them all —Hugh MacLennan, *Two Solitudes,* 1945

... peoples were so isolated from one another, so impeded by their different languages —Edmund Wilson, *A Piece of My Mind,* 1956

Occasionally, *isolate* is used with *in:*

... isolated in the conventional productivity statistics —Robert M. Solow, *Think,* May–June 1967

And, once in a while, *isolate* is found with *by* or *with:*

The unit was isolated by standard isolation pads located between it and the steel beams —*Trane Weather Magic,* April 1955

The tooth was isolated with cotton rolls, the caries removed and the cavity dried —*1952 Year Book of Dentistry*

issue   In British English, the transitive verb *issue* is often followed by *with:*

... schoolchildren are not issued with school-books, but with vouchers for buying them —Margaret Lane, *Times Literary Supp.,* 9 Mar. 1967

... at lunch yesterday I was issued with a roll whose "crust" must literally have been painted on — Kingsley Amis, *Times Literary Supp.,* 15 July 1983

Such usage first occurred in the early 20th century. Its common occurrence has led to its acceptance by British commentators (such as Partridge 1942 and Gowers in Fowler 1965). Speakers of American English would say "provided with" or "supplied with" instead.

is when, is where   See WHEN, WHERE.

it   For *it* in reference to preceding ideas, topics, sentences, or paragraphs, see THIS 1.

Italian   See ETHNIC DESIGNATIONS: PRONUNCIATION.

iterate   See REITERATE.

it is I who, it is they who   Constructions in which *it is* is followed by a first or second person pronoun or by a plural were troubling to 18th-century commentators, beginning at least as early as Samuel Johnson's Dictionary (1755). Campbell 1776 and Lindley Murray 1795 also discuss these problems. What troubles them the most seems to be the occurrence of the constructions in writers like Shakespeare, Dryden, Pope, and Prior.

Let us sort things out a bit. With plurals the problem was never specified. Johnson and Campbell are simply made uneasy by the presence of a plural after *it is,* though they concede good precedent. Modern usage consistently goes right along with Shakespeare and Pope, and no modern critic sees a problem here:

'Tis these that early taint the female soul —Alexander Pope (in Johnson and in Campbell)

It is they who argue for military intervention — Arthur M. Schlesinger, Jr., *Harper's,* March 1969

It takes *is,* and the later verb agrees with the plural referent of its subject. Gowers in Fowler 1965 cites a similar construction.

Strang 1970 and Copperud 1970, 1980 note that there is conflicting usage with the first person pronoun: "It is I who (is? am?)." Strang points out that in earlier stages of the language such a sentence would have been unmistakably governed by the first person pronoun and would have begun "It am I. . . ." But over the years the position of *it* caused it to be felt to be the true subject, and the third person verb *is* replaced *am* and sometimes governed throughout the sentence. Copperud opines that, strictly speaking, *am* should follow *I,* but says that "there is a strong tendency to use *is,* since *am* sounds artificial." Copperud's remarks confirm Strang's comment that this conflict is not yet resolved. The construction does not turn up often, and it may be that writers sometimes avoid it in favor of a more concise and less problematic wording. Such evidence as we have, however—both old and modern—suggests that Copperud's strict construction predominates in print:

... but *'tis I* that am not able to come up to her Terms —Daniel Defoe, *Moll Flanders,* 1722

It is I who possess these attributes —Walter Prescott Webb, *The Great Frontier,* 1952

See also IT'S ME.

its, it's   It is easy to state the standard rule (after all, we have seen it in about forty usage books, handbooks, and schoolbooks): *it's* is the contraction of *it is* and *it has; its* is the third person neuter possessive pronoun. But these two forms have been frequently interchanged and entangled throughout their history, and you can be sure that they still are—or forty books would not have to carry reminders.

Both forms seem to have come into use around the beginning of the 17th century. Let's begin with the pronoun. It is first attested in 1598 as *its* in an Italian-English dictionary written by John Florio. Strang 1970 terms Florio a foreigner; he was the son of an Italian Protestant refugee, but he was probably born in London.

Before this the usual possessive (in writing, at least) was *his*. Richard Mulcaster, for instance, in his *Elementarie* of 1582 has this:

> ... euerie word almost either wanting letters, for his necessarie sound, or having ...

Another popular solution to the neuter possessive problem was to use the uninflected *it*, as Shakespeare did:

> ... it had it head bit off by it young —*King Lear*, 1606 (in Strang, OED)

Shakespeare seems not to have used *its*, although the OED says he might have written the *it's* used as an absolute adjective in *Henry VIII* (acted in 1613). Editors began putting *its* in Shakespeare's plays later (McKnight 1928 gives an example of *it* changed to *its* in the Third Folio, 1664). Wyld 1920 notes that *its* is not used in the 1611 Bible. And it does not appear as one of the possessive pronouns in Ben Jonson's grammar (published posthumously in 1640). Nevertheless it established itself during the 17th century, and Strang says that after mid-century the alternative *his* signifies an element of personification.

The troublesome fact for us moderns is that the predominant form in printing was *it's*. The apostrophized form was used by the above-mentioned Florio as early as 1603. It may have been given this form because it was felt not to be a separate possessive pronoun like *his, her,* or *their* but simply *it* with the *'s* of the genitive attached to it. This possibility is borne out to a certain extent by Priestley 1761; he lists *it's* as the genitive of *it* and does not include it in the list of possessive pronouns at all.

It's was apparently the more common form of the pronoun throughout the 17th and 18th centuries. In the 18th century we find such uses as these:

> ... our language has made it's way singly by it's own weight and merit —Lord Chesterfield, letter to *The World,* 28 Nov. 1754

> ... of it's real import —Adam Smith (in Leonard 1929)

> ... when it is omitted and it's Place supplied with an Apostrophe —Baker 1770

Late 18th-century users carried it into the early 19th century:

> ... estimate it's merit —Thomas Jefferson, letter, 21 May 1787

> ... will work it's effect —Thomas Jefferson, letter, 21 Aug. 1818

> ... the assurance of it's being ... —Jane Austen, letter, 8 Nov. 1800

The unapostrophized *its* was in competition with *it's* from the beginning and began its rise to dominance in the mid 18th century. Lowth 1762 gave *its* as the possessive form of *it* (even though he seems to have favored *her's*, etc.). Baker gave *it's* in 1770, as we saw above, but switched to *its* in his 1779 edition. Lindley Murray 1795 used the unapostrophized form even to the point of muddlement: Campbell 1776 had complained about the genitive *it's* being misused for *'tis*, the contraction of *it is*. Murray elaborated on this topic but used *its* even in his example of misuse: "Its my book."

The modern assumption that *its* came to predominate for the pronoun in order to distinguish it from *it's* "it is" is supported by Campbell's complaint. Campbell

also makes the point that *'tis* was the usual contraction of *it is*. But even if *'tis* predominated, *it's* was in at least occasional use:

> ... and it's come to pass ...
> This tractable obedience is a slave
> To each incensed will
> —Shakespeare, *Henry VIII,* 1613

> Why, sir, it's your own fault —Sir John Vanbrugh, *The Relapse,* 1696

Since we all know that *it's* predominates over *'tis* today, we may reasonably suppose that *its* came to be preferred as a contrasting pronoun form.

Another more recent assumption is that this distinction, which presumably developed during the 19th and early 20th centuries, is being lost. The reappearance of prenominal *it's* (which may never have completely disappeared) is certainly well documented. It is frequently noticed in signs and posters, as by Simon 1980, for instance. We have also found it in letters, advertisements, flyers, mail-order catalogs, and animal-husbandry journals. But—and if you are an alarmist, you may view this with alarm—we have also found it in edited, more widely circulated publications: *Vogue* (1985), *New York Times Magazine* (1984), *Southern Living* (1983), *Springfield* (Mass.) *Morning Union* (1983), *This England* (1983), *People* (1982), and *Gourmet* (1981). These cannot all be typos, can they?

And the distinction is under milder pressure from the other side—from the George Bernard Shaws who eschew the apostrophe in general and use only *its* for all purposes.

We tend to agree with Reader's Digest 1983 that the insistence on *its* for the pronoun as necessary to distinguish the pronoun from the contraction does not make much sense, since the *'s* does everything for the noun. *Jean's* can be possessive in "Jean's coat" and it can be a contraction in "Jean's here" and "Jean's already read it." Use of one form in three functions with the noun does not seem to trouble anyone.

Still, we do not recommend that you rush to espouse the apostrophized pronoun. The possessive pronouns were a complete muddle in the 18th century. The grammarians were divided between apostrophized and unapostrophized forms, and frequently their own usage contradicted whatever conclusions they had reached. Over time the confusion has sorted itself out, and we now have a modestly consistent set of unapostrophized pronouns. So even though the apostrophe is on the rise (see the article at APOSTROPHE), we see no particular reason to go back to 18th-century usage. We recommend that you stick with *its* for the pronoun and *it's* for the contraction.

it's me   The venerable argument over the nominative versus the objective case after the verb *to be* is a memorable part of our linguistic heritage. Nearly everyone has heard it in one form or another. You should be aware that, while the discussion is still going on, its grounds have been shifted:

> The choice between "It is I" and "It's me" is a choice not between standard and nonstandard usage but between formal and colloquial styles —Trimmer & McCrimmon 1988

So instead of the old choice between right and wrong we are now choosing a style; it is a choice that is much closer to the reality of usage than the old one was.

Copperud 1970, 1980 cites Follett 1966 as prescribing the nominative in constructions where a personal pronoun follows *to be,* and we do find instances when the nominative is used, but probably for the reason alluded to above by Trimmer & McCrimmon: these constructions tend to be rather formal.

> Let me urge you not to forget that it was I ... whom you burdened with the job —*The Intimate Notebooks of George Jean Nathan,* 1932

> It was she who ... paid no longer any attention to religion —William Styron, *This Quiet Dust and Other Writings,* 1982

In older English we find the nominative even in speech written for the stage:

> Is't he that speaks nothing but Greek or Latine, or English Fustian? —Thomas Shadwell, *The Humorists,* 1671

> Alas, this is not he whom I expected —Aphra Behn, *The Dutch Lover,* 1673

But the more relaxed colloquial style could also be found in earlier writing:

> It is not me you are in love with —Sir Richard Steele, *The Spectator,* No. 290, 1 Feb. 1712

Leonard 1929 remarks that Campbell 1776 argued Steele's *me* was correct because it was governed by the preposition *with* but that Lowth 1762 had analyzed the construction and concluded that the preposition really governed the omitted relative pronoun—and the sequence *he who͞m* in the Aphra Behn example suggests Lowth was on the right track.

The main argument, however, is on much broader grounds. From the beginning in the 18th century, there were two camps. The earlier, apparently, is represented by Priestley 1761, who favors accepting *it is me* on grounds of custom. Priestley mentions that grammarians opposed his position, but he doesn't say who they were. Lowth 1762 heads the partisans of *it is I,* who clearly had Priestley outnumbered: Baker 1770, Campbell 1776, and Lindley Murray 1795 were on the side of the nominative. And these were the commentators whose preachments were accepted as gospel by the schoolmasters. Priestley's opinion had to wait until Alford 1864 to find a sympathizer.

If the great tide of expressed opinion favored *it is I,* how is it that *it is me* survived to reach its at least semi-respectable status today? The strongest force operating in favor of *it is me* is probably that of word position: the pronoun after *is* is in the usual position for a direct object, and the objective case feels right in that position. It is probably just as simple as that—we find the strength of word order at work on initial *whom* also, turning it frequently into *who,* even when it is an object in its clause—but early grammarians knew nothing of the power of word order in English, and they had to find other explanations.

One of the more interesting explanations was the "French analogy." This was apparently first set forth by Priestley. In his discussion of the uses of the oblique (Priestley preferred Johnson's *oblique* to Lowth's *objective*) cases of the pronoun in place of the nominative, he notices that French has similar constructions, notably *c'est moi.* Campbell rejected the French analogy out of hand; French, he said, had no influence on English. Now we know that French had indeed had a rather forcible impact on English beginning in 1066 (and even earlier),

but as the Middle English that resulted from that collision does not seem to have the modern *it is me* (it is first attested in the 16th century), we cannot really find its source there.

Priestley also asserts that the reason the grammarians won't accept *it is me* is that it does not match the pattern of Latin (which is why he brought up French). It is probably true that Latin is the theoretical reason for the insistence on the nominative. But besides theory, there was actual usage. Unless all the Restoration playwrights had tin ears or were for some unfathomable reason following an artificial convention, the people of quality they portrayed on the stage did use the nominative:

> MARCEL. By Heavens, 'tis she: Vile Strumpet! —Aphra Behn, *The Dutch Lover,* 1673

> MRS. LOVEIT. Oh, that's he, that's he! —George Etherege, *The Man of Mode,* 1676

> LADY TOUCHWOOD. ... but when you found out 'twas I, you turned away —William Congreve, *The Double Dealer,* 1693

> LYRIC. ... If ever the muses had a horse, I am he —George Farquhar, *Love and a Bottle,* 1698

A number of recent commentators maintain that *me* is more common than *us, them, him,* or *her* after *be.* This at least sounds likely, but we do not know how it can be proved. We do know that all of the objective pronouns can be found in the construction:

> "It's me," I said.
> "How are you?" she replied
> —Russell Baker, *Growing Up,* 1982

From the way the president moved his head, I realized that his real audience wasn't us at all —Tip O'Neill with William Novak, *Man of the House,* 1987

... if I were them, I would —George Schultz, Secretary of State, television interview, 6 Dec. 1985

... can sometimes act like it's him against the world —Penelope Wang, *Newsweek,* 29 Dec. 1986

... but it's her, the same girl, returned to my life — E. L. Doctorow, *Loon Lake,* 1979

Here are some more third-person examples:

> ... thinking verily it had been her —Samuel Pepys, diary, 1 Oct. 1666 (in OED)

> And if anybody had to feel of the hot water and get burned it was always her —Will Rogers, *The Illiterate Digest,* 1924

> I went out in a hurry hoping it might be her —Mickey Spillane, *The Big Kill,* 1951

> If I were him I would put in everything now —Ernest Hemingway, *Life,* 1 Sept. 1952

> ... always looking around ... to see if any of the girls playing in the street was her —Bernard Malamud, *The Magic Barrel,* 1958

We also have a couple of later examples in the pattern of Richard Steele above:

> Ah, it is her you love —Charles Reade, *Hard Cash,* 1863 (in Hall 1873)

For it was not her one hated but the idea of her —
Virginia Woolf, *Mrs. Dalloway,* 1925

Clearly, both the *it is I* and *it's me* patterns are in
reputable use and have been for a considerable time. *It
is I* tends to be used in more formal or more stuffy situations; *it's me* predominates in real and fictional
speech and in a more relaxed writing style. *Him, her,
us,* and *them* may be less common after the verb *to be*
than *me* is, but they are far from rare and are equally
good.

For more on the vagaries of pronouns, see BETWEEN
YOU AND I; PRONOUNS; THAN 1; THEY, THEIR, THEM; WHO,
WHOM 1.

-ize   1. *-ize, -ise.* The American form of this suffix is
-ize; the British typically use *-ise,* although some of the
more etymology-conscious publishing houses may insist
on the *-ize* termination for some words, following OED
practice. Longman 1984 has a list of verbs (such as
advertise, chastise, circumcise, despise, and *surmise*)
that must be spelled *-ise* in both language varieties, but
these words are not formed from the suffix *-ize.*
2. According to the OED, the suffix *-ize* itself was first
mentioned by Thomas Nashe in 1591. He was none too
politely tweaking the noses of his "reprehenders,"
whom he was apparently pleased to have nettled with
his verb coinages ending in *-ize.* Ever since, it has been
possible to raise hackles with newly coined verbs that
end in this suffix.

Such verbs have aroused much comment in the 19th
and 20th centuries. Critics were upset by Noah Webster's inclusion of *demoralize, Americanize,* and *deputize* in his 1828 dictionary. Bache 1869 hated *jeopardize*
(which was almost as big an object of scorn in the 19th
century as *finalize* is in this) and *signalize.* Schele de
Vere 1872 was offended by *barberize* (which is what bar-
bers were supposed to do). Richard Grant White 1870
denounced *resurrectionize;* his denunciation led Fitzedward Hall 1873 to rain down dozens of other similarly
formed *-ize* verbs on him. Not content with pelting
White, Hall produced a few dozen additional examples
in another part of the book. He himself unloaded *neo-
terize* in the course of this latter disquisition and then

allowed his "philological patience" to be severely tested
by T. A. Huxley's *depauperize.* Compton 1898 wanted
to ban *deputize* and *jeopardize.*

With this admirable head of steam built up, the issue
roared into the 20th century, where *finalize* replaced
jeopardize as the object of the most heat and least ratio-
nality. But plenty of other *-ize* words have come under
the gun: *accessorize, burglarize,* and *prioritize* are some
you will find discussed in this book. The anathematizing
(we couldn't resist) of *-ize* verbs shows no sign of letting
up: a recent handbook, Trimmer & McCrimmon 1988,
counsels students to "avoid such pretentious and unnecessary jargon as *finalize, prioritize,* and *theorize.*" The
pretentious and unnecessary *theorize* has been with us
since 1638 and has been used by Coleridge, Howells,
Joyce, Dreiser, and Forster, among others.

If you are one of those persons of tender sensibilities
whose nerves are grated by *-ize* verbs, you would be better off learning to live with the problem, as everybody
knows that the jargoneers of the government, the military, and the various hard and soft sciences have a sweet
tooth for these words. And they are not the only ones.
Samuel Pepys, for instance, came up with *divertising* in
1667. Truman Capote used *artificialize,* Mary
McCarthy *sloganized* and *sonorized,* Coleridge *melan-
cholize,* Charlotte Brontë *colloquize,* and Robert
Southey *physiognomize.*

But you can take some comfort in the thought that
many of these coinages do not last. A check through
Hall's 1873 list turns up such confections as *excursion-
ize, pulpitize, sororize, sultanize, sensize, dissocialize,
soberize*—have you ever encountered them? One suspects that more recent coinages such as *laymanize,
impossibilize, disasterize, explitize, incentize,* and *prom-
inentized* will be similarly forgotten.

So *-ize* is a very productive suffix in English; for 400
years or more it has been freely attached to nouns,
adjectives, proper names, and sometimes other roots to
produce verbs for immediate use. These are often nonce
words (we have a *Colorado-ize* used by someone getting
ready to go backpacking in the mountains), but many
others have stuck. Who today blinks at *popularize, for-
malize, economize, legalize, politicize, terrorize,* or *capitalize?*

J

Jap, Japanese   The word *Jap* is a clipped form of
Japanese that has been around since the end of the 19th
century. It is also found as a slang term for a professional gambler in New Orleans around 1886, but the
etymology of this particular use is obscure.

Clipped terms are often felt to be somewhat less than
respectful—even such inoffensive terms as *prof* and *doc*
have been criticized—and clipped ethnic terms are doubly suspect. In the United States, this term has a considerable history of pejorative use: according to evidence
in our files it was used with derogatory intent by newspapers on the West Coast from the first decade of this
century. Such use did not take long to appear in fiction:

I've got that boundary line to patrol—to keep out
Chinks and Japs —Zane Grey, *Desert Gold,* 1913

Americans were not unaware that the term was offensive. The first commentator to note this in print seems

to have been Hyde 1926, who did not specifically term
it offensive but did not approve its use in newspapers.
H. L. Mencken in *The American Language* (the 1963
abridgment) says that Japanese-Americans on the West
Coast had long objected to the use, but to little avail.
And then World War II gave a great boost to the usage.
Not only did *Jap* have brevity to recommend it, but it
probably served a psychological purpose:

The epithets "Kraut," "Jap," "Gook"—all are shorthand ways of excluding the enemy from the ranks of
human beings —Anne Roiphe, *Cosmopolitan,* April
1975

World War II is more than forty years behind us, and
attitudes have changed. Spiro T. Agnew noted changing
attitudes in 1968:

People are getting too edgy, the Republican Vice-
Presidential candidate believes, when they take

umbrage at being called "Polacks" or "Japs" in a spirit of fun —Homer Bigart, *N.Y. Times,* 25 Sept. 1968

That sort of fun has seldom been shared in by the ethnic groups so designated.

Jap is generally either used disparagingly or taken to be offensive, even in innocent use. Unless your intent is to recreate the atmosphere of World War II for some purpose, use *Japanese.*

jargon Chaucer used *jargon* to mean the twittering of birds; the word has declined in status since then. The OED shows that it embarked upon its career as a pejorative term in the 17th century. According to Perrin & Ebbitt 1972, Sir Arthur Quiller-Couch, in his *On the Art of Writing* (1916), popularized the word as an all-purpose bludgeon for various kinds of verbal fuzziness. Sir Arthur's treatment would hardly pass muster nowadays for an investigation of jargon; he wanders too easily from the subject. Much more to the point is the chapter in Bolinger 1980.

In modern use *jargon* is a pejorative term meaning more or less "obscure and often pretentious language." This meaning is very closely related to another: "the technical terminology or characteristic idiom of a special activity or group." The pejorative meaning represents the outsider's opinion of the specialist's or insider's technical terminology. The technical usages have their defenders:

Specialized wording selectively employed between colleagues and co-workers is no blight. It is, in fact, preferable for quick, accurate messages. Jargon is not prone to double meanings —Mary C. Bromage, *Michigan Business Rev.,* July 1968

Scientists use jargon because they are obsessed with the desire to show that their work really does belong within a reputable context; they feel that it must conform to the conventions of the particular audience to which it is directed, and that they must use the appropriate technical language of the subject, however clumsy and contrived this may seem to the outsider —J. M. Ziman, *Nature,* 25 Oct. 1969

Let the outsider beware, then. If you are going to pry into material written for the specialist, you are going to have to learn the specialist's language. Of course many outsiders resent having to learn the language—and not without some reason. The defenders of jargon may point out that it eliminates ambiguities and is the quickest way for one professional to talk to another, but there is good reason to suspect that part of the function of jargon is to keep outsiders in the dark.

The beginnings of this function can be found in the Renaissance. As new knowledge accumulated, those who possessed it felt some proprietary right in it. Their protective jargon was Latin:

However, when professional secrets might be revealed by the use of a tongue comprehensible to any "man in the street," it was a different matter. Priests, lawyers, and doctors all had specialised knowledge, which many of them did not wish to have made generally accessible. They had a common language, Latin, which served them very well for professional cryptolalia. To expound trade-secrets in the vernacular was to betray one's cause and one's fellow-practitioners. Consequently, during the sixteenth century, various ordinances were passed against the writing of medical or legal treatises in any language except Latin. The great sixteenth-century French surgeon, Ambroise Paré (ca. 1510–1590) was strongly criticised for publishing his works in French, and was brought to court by his fellow-doctors for doing so —Robert A. Hall, Jr., *The External History of the Romance Languages,* 1974

Latin is gone now as the language of learning, but in the vernacular languages, jargon can serve a similar purpose:

One enemy of communication is jargon, which can be used contemptuously or even sadistically, to reinforce the majesty of the scientific message and the layman's sense of exclusion from a privileged body of knowledge —*Times Literary Supp.,* 27 June 1968

The jargon that is most likely to distress the ordinary person is that used by governments; few citizens these days can avoid directly confronting bureaucratic jargon in such places as tax returns and other official forms that must be dealt with. Consequently, bureaucratic jargon has probably drawn more hostile criticism than any other jargon. It has even been attacked by politicians from Sir Winston Churchill to Secretary of Commerce Malcolm Baldrige. It made a career for Sir Ernest Gowers, who was hired to help English bureaucrats simplify their jargon. His original *Plain Words* (1948) has passed through at least two subsequent enlargements and will undoubtedly see more. And British official prose, like its American counterpart, will march on in majestic disregard of all suggestions for improvement. Bureaucratic jargon is the official language bureaucrats write for bureaucrats to read. If you need the official approval of a bureaucrat, you will probably have to learn how to cope with the idiom. It is not going away.

We do not intend to apologize for jargon, but to be fair you have to recognize that many of its critics simply refuse to understand it. For one small example, Barzun 1980 disparages the word *containerize* as unnecessary jargon. Not needed, he says, since we already have the verb *to box.* He then goes on to explain that *box* wouldn't do because, as he mockingly suggests, "it wouldn't have sounded like the heroic, scientific conquest of mind over matter." He omits to notice that *box* (or for that matter *crate* or *package* or *wrap* or *carton*) was not used because it does not mean the same thing to people in the business as *containerize* does. As Harper 1985 says, "Containerize is among the least objectionable of the 'ize' coinages of recent years because it was a result of the development of a new method of shipping cargo and thus serves a real need." Willful misunderstanding is no corrective to jargon.

jealous 1. Some language commentators warn against confusing the words *jealous* and *zealous.* At one time, as the OED indicates, the two words were considered synonyms and were used as such, most particularly in the Bible and in related religious writings:

And he said, I have been very jealous for the Lord God of hosts —1 Kings 19:10 (AV), 1611

To spoyle the zelous God of his honour —*Homilies II,* 1563 (OED)

According to our evidence, *jealous* and *zealous* are not otherwise used interchangeably. Their closest approach in meaning now occurs when *jealous* is used to mean "vigilant in guarding a possession":

All the authors I have met are diligent in their work, sober, earnest, jealous of their craft, eager to perfect their art —Allan McMahan, in *The Wonderful World of Books,* ed. Alfred Stefferud, 1952

... toward a more passionate assertion of the demands of individual freedom, or a more jealous insistence upon the precedence of the community — Archibald MacLeish, *American Scholar,* Autumn 1953

2. When *Jealous* is used with a preposition, it is usually used with *of:*

Up the stairs ... came the model, at whom Beppo looked askance, jealous of an encroacher on his rightful domain —Nathaniel Hawthorne, *The Marble Faun,* 1860

I know that religion, science, and art are all jealous of each other —W. R. Inge, *The Church in the World,* 1928

... the 1944 campaign cost the French many lives and untold property, of which the Normands are so traditionally jealous —David Butwin, *Saturday Rev.,* 21 June 1969

Once in a while, *jealous* is used with *for:*

They were like sons to him, he was jealous for their welfare, and was always available for advice and help —*Dictionary of American Biography,* 1929

Infrequently, *jealous* has been used with *to* and an infinitive or with *over:*

The old legal constitution of the country gave him the whole judicial power, and William was jealous to retain and heighten this —John Richard Green, *The History of the English People,* 1880

Ape-women, mannish Russian scientists, stewardesses wearing impossible caps, ... they are all there, and who would get jealous over *them?* —Robert Plank, *Hartford Studies in Literature,* vol. 1, no. 1, 1969

jeer When *jeer* is used with a preposition, it is usually followed by *at:*

Isabelle knew she would be jeered at as yet another American heiress who had forced her way — Rebecca West, *The Thinking Reed,* 1936

You had to be as old as a cadet to know a girl without being jeered at —Hugh MacLennan, *Two Solitudes,* 1945

... the exiles of an earlier period, who ... had jeered at the United States —Edmund Wilson, *Memoirs of Hecate County,* 1946

Jeer has also been infrequently used with *to:*

... The women jeered to one another, "What can be done with a new world like this?" —Josephine Young Case, *Atlantic,* May 1946

jejune Todd & Hancock 1986 call attention to a curious fact about *jejune;* derived from a Latin word originally meaning "fasting, hungry," it is usually used figuratively for what is devoid of substance or nutriment for the mind—uninteresting, insipid, or trite stuff. But it has also become associated with an unoriginality that bespeaks immaturity, and so it is used in senses approximating "puerile, juvenile, naive." Todd & Hancock

suggest that this semantic "slide," as they put it, may be due to contamination from French *jeune* "young." Ben Ray Redman had made the same suggestion in the *Saturday Review,* 2 Mar. 1957.

The great difficulty with this word is the ambiguity of many of its uses. Look at this one:

... unburdens himself of his somewhat naïve reflections on the evils of unemployment, and engages in jejune conversations with Foxhall Edwards, his editor, which sound suspiciously like the bull sessions of a college sophomore —Leo Gurko, *The Angry Decade,* 1947

This example seems to suggest immaturity, but may or may not have been so intended. The mainstream of current use runs in this channel:

It was a gasbag of a speech, soft, loose, jejune, thin gruel for a man who has been at the center of events for more than two decades.... Is this all he has to say? —Ward Just, *New England Monthly,* October 1984

But on the outer edges the word has eddies and bywaters that are hard to chart. Take this sample:

We pass in the world for sects and schools, for erudition and piety, and we are all the time jejune babes —Ralph Waldo Emerson, "Spiritual Laws," 1841

If I were Harvard University, or the General Motors Corporation, I would buy and remove The Anchor ... to somewhere in the States; to show the young and jejune what a pub should look like —Christopher Morley, in *A Century of the Essay,* ed. David Daiches, 1951

... he had reached his majority before it ever occurred to him that a white woman might make quite as agreeable a mistress as the octaroons of his jejune fancy —H. L. Mencken, *Prejudices: Second Series,* 1920

... there is so little other decent fiction around to tickle a jejune man's fantasies —George Stade, *N.Y. Times Book Rev.,* 12 Aug. 1984

It was just twenty years ago that the Museum of Modern Art held its first jejune exhibition of modern architecture —Lewis Mumford, *New Yorker,* 11 Oct. 1952

Edmund Wilson, in *The Bit Between My Teeth* (1965), comments without etymologizing on the use of *jejune* in the sense "callow." Wilson was familiar with this use, for in 1922 he received this in a letter:

I changed the meaning of *jejune* eight or ten years ago. That is to say, I added a new special meaning, to wit, that of youthful feebleness —H. L. Mencken, letter, 17 May 1922

If you look back at the Emerson quotation, you may feel that Mencken was perhaps taking a bit more credit for invention than he deserved. Nevertheless, *jejune* seems to be capable of breaking out in any of several directions. It will be interesting to watch it and see where it goes.

jeopardize Richard Grant White called *jeopardize* "a foolish and intolerable word" in 1870, and he was not the only one who thought so. A popular view among American critics in the 19th century was that the proper verb was *jeopard,* an older word which, according to the OED, had fallen into disuse by the end of the 1600s. The first record of *jeopardize* is from 1646, but there is no further evidence of its use until it turns up in Noah Webster's American Dictionary in 1828 with the note, "This is a modern word used by respectable writers in America, but synonymous with *jeopard,* and therefore useless." Useless or not, *jeopardize* became increasingly common, both in America and in Great Britain, as attempts to resurrect *jeopard* met with predictable failure. The voices of protest against *jeopardize,* all of which had been American, began to die down by about 1900, and it was not long before this minor controversy was entirely forgotten. It has now been many decades since anyone found anything wrong with *jeopardize.*

See -IZE 2.

Jew, jew down *Jew* used as an adjective and the phrasal verb *jew down* are usually considered offensive. The former should be replaced by *Jewish,* and the latter avoided altogether.

jewelry This word is sometimes pronounced \'jü-lə-rē\, a switched-around form of \'jü-əl-rē\ that is an example of *metathesis* (which see). A similar case is *Realtor,* often pronounced \'rē-lət-ər\. Neither pronunciation is very well established as standard.

Jewess *Jewess* is a word of relatively low frequency and of uncertain status. Copperud 1964, 1970, 1980 and Evans 1957 say it is often considered derogatory; evidence in H. L. Mencken (*The American Language, Supplement I,* 1945) confirms that opinion, but it is evidence from the middle 1930s. *Jewess* is often bracketed with *Negress,* with commentators finding them both derogatory (Evans) or not (Simon 1980).

An important factor in the status of such words is who uses them. We have evidence, for instance, that Jewish women may use *Jewess* of themselves:

> I sat and thought to myself, here is the head of the church, sitting face to face with the Jewess from Israel, and he's listening to what I'm saying —Golda Meir, quoted in *N.Y. Times,* 20 Jan. 1973

Most of our literary evidence seems to be neutral, although it is not always easy to detect covert social commentary that may underlie a usage. Here are a few American examples:

> His wife had been a German Jewess, above him socially, so she thought —Saul Bellow, *Mr. Sammler's Planet,* 1969

> The sexual yearning is for the Other. The dream of the shiksa—counterpart to the Gentile dream of the Jewess, often adjectively described as "melon-breasted." —Philip Roth, *Reading Myself and Others,* 1975

> ... they had been refugees in Portugal during World War II, and when it was over, only Australia would let them in. An Australian Jewess, Bech thought — John Updike, *Bech Is Back,* 1982

Jewess seems to be a word that can be used by those who are deft enough to illuminate social attitudes in a subtle way; perhaps most of us are not clever enough to use it. Our British evidence is enigmatic; the little we have suggests from the way it is used that it could give offense, but British sensibilities may be different on this point.

See also -ESS; NEGRESS.

jibe, gibe The distinction between *jibe* and *gibe* is not as clear-cut as some commentators would like it to be. *Jibe* is the more common spelling. It is used both for the verb meaning "to be in accord; agree" ("jibe with") and for the verb and noun of nautical parlance ("jibe the mainsail," "a risky jibe in heavy seas"). It is also used as a variant of *gibe* for the verb meaning "to utter taunting words; to deride or tease" and for the noun meaning "a taunting remark; jeer." *Gibe* is more common in these uses and is preferred by the critics, but *jibe* is also in widespread use, and the evidence shows clearly that it is a respectable spelling variant:

> Alas poore Yorick ... Where be your Jibes now? — Shakespeare, *Hamlet,* 1602 (OED)

> ... my jibe at the Socialists of the eighteen-eighties —George Bernard Shaw, *The Intelligent Woman's Guide to Socialism and Capitalism,* 1928

> ... with some new jibe at Mr. Dillon or Mr. Redmond —*The Autobiography of William Butler Yeats,* 1953

> ... a blasphemous boy jibes at them —Robert Craft, *Stravinsky,* 1972

> ... rankled by jibes in the national media —Eugene Kennedy, *N.Y. Times Mag.,* 9 Mar. 1980

Jibe has been recognized as a standard variant of *gibe* since the publication of the fourth volume of the OED in 1900. The critics worry that its use may cause confusion, but the context in which it occurs always makes its meaning clear. The distinction promoted by the critics appears to have no practical value, but if you like to observe such distinctions you may well want to observe this one.

There is some evidence for *gibe* used as a variant of *jibe* in both the "agree" sense and the nautical uses, and it is recognized as such in both Webster's Second and Webster's Third. However, this use is very rare and in most contexts would probably be considered an error by readers.

job action This term denotes any of various tactics—usually short of a strike—by which disgruntled workers express their disgruntlement. Most commonly it applies to forms of protest undertaken by workers who are legally barred from striking:

> Spokesmen for police and firemen's benevolent organizations said yesterday a loss of jobs ... could cause massive sick calls, mass rallies, demonstrations and other job actions —*Boston Sunday Advertiser,* 6 Feb. 1972

Our earliest record of its use is from 1968. Most dictionaries now recognize it as a standard term, but not everyone likes *job action*—most notably, the usage panel of Harper 1975, 1985 rejects it by almost a 2 to 1 margin. Some of its detractors cite it as a euphemism, but much of the criticism may derive more from disapproval of the actions themselves than from disapproval of the term that denotes them.

jobless *Jobless* is a fairly new word, first attested in 1919:

> ... soldiers who have jobs awaiting them are being held while those who are jobless, in many instances, are being released —*Leslie's Weekly,* 22 Feb. 1919

A less objectionable coinage is hard to imagine, but Copperud 1980 reports that *jobless* was formerly criticized "as an unnecessary invention," and Phythian 1979 shows that it still occasionally is: "A word invented by journalists because *unemployed* takes up too much headline space. This is not sufficient reason for admitting it into the language." Copperud also credits journalists (specifically, headline writers) with having invented *jobless,* but he finds nothing wrong with that fact or with the word itself. No other critic broaches this subject.

We do not know for certain how, why, or by whom *jobless* was invented, but we do know that it is now common and entirely standard:

> . . . that jobless scientists and engineers could be put back at work —John Lear, *Saturday Rev.,* 1 Jan. 1972

> . . . to right those wrongs and put the jobless back to work —*The Economist,* 3 Nov. 1984

join 1. *Join* is used with any of several prepositions; those occurring most often are *in, to,* or *with.* When *in* is used, it is followed by a noun or by a gerund:

> . . . Snowy felt ashamed to have joined in the laugh —Richard Llewellyn, *A Few Flowers for Shiner,* 1950

> If others went ahead and engaged in name calling, at least he could refuse to join in it —William Lee Miller, *The Reporter,* 8 June 1954

> . . . urged the United States to join in the acceptance of Communist China by the United Nations —*Current Biography,* January 1966

> . . . he at once joined in organizing Tualatin Academy —*Dictionary of American Biography,* 1928

> Scientific management thus joined trade-union pressure . . . in shortening the work week —Stuart Chase, *N.Y. Times Mag.,* 30 May 1954

When *join* is used with *to* or *with,* at least one early commentator (Raub 1897) thought that with the choice of preposition a distinction is made as to the type of object: "Join *to* something greater, *with* something equal". Our files do not indicate that usage is so clear-cut. *To* and *with* are used about equally, and both occur in many situations:

> . . . the agitation of his mind, joined to the pain of his wound, kept him awake all night —Francis Parkman, in *The Practical Cogitator,* ed. Charles P. Curtis, Jr. & Ferris Greenslet, 1945

> All my life I have looked for . . . a writer with spiritual health and goodness joined to literary genius — Francis Hackett, *Saturday Rev.,* 16 Feb. 1946

> . . . it describes its author's struggle to assert her sexuality, to join it to creativity —Leonard Kriegel, *N.Y. Times Book Rev.,* 11 May 1980

> . . . I joined with a group of persons to go in a taxi to the prison —Katherine Anne Porter, *The Never-Ending Wrong,* 1977

> . . . Pennsylvanians under Wayne . . . joined their units with men from New Hampshire —F. Van Wyck Mason, *The Winter at Valley Forge,* 1953

> . . . detailed research joined with a splendid narrative style —*American Scholar,* Spring 1953

It seems that if *join* is being used of persons, *with* is the more likely preposition to occur, as in the Porter and Van Wyck Mason examples above; however, *join to* may also be found:

> He was then joined to Gen. Scott's command and was actively engaged at the seige —*Dictionary of American Biography,* 1929

Occasionally, *join* is used with *into:*

> . . . when the thirteen colonies joined into a Federal Union —Vera Micheles Dean, *The Four Cornerstones of Peace,* 1946

2. There are many language commentators who disapprove using *together* with *join;* they call it redundant. *Join together* is primarily a spoken idiom in which the purpose of *together* is to add emphasis. Probably the best known example of these words is in the Bible:

> What therefore God hath joined together, let not man put asunder —Matthew 19:6 (AV), 1611

Contemporary examples can also be found:

> . . . loose alliances of local factions that join together every four years for purposes of contesting Presidential elections —Robert K. Carr, *N.Y. Herald Tribune Book Rev.,* 13 Apr. 1952

> ". . . two people joined together . . . by hatred—a deep, abiding, mutual hatred." —Hamilton Basso, *The View From Pompey's Head,* 1954

> . . . the art which joins all men together at their deepest and simplest level of response —Leslie A. Fiedler, *Los Angeles Times Book Rev.,* 23 May 1971

There is no need to avoid familiar idioms like *join together* simply because the second word iterates and emphasizes part of the meaning of the first.

See REDUNDANCY; WORDINESS.

judgment, judgement Both ways to spell this word have been in use for centuries. *Judgment* was once the only spelling shown in dictionaries, but that changed with the publication of the OED, in which *judgment* and *judgement* are treated as equal variants. Most dictionaries now show both spellings. Usage commentators generally allow that both are acceptable, but the Americans among them tend to prefer *judgment* while the British preference is for *judgement.* Our own most recent evidence shows *judgment* leading *judgement* in American sources by a ratio of about 2 to 1. Our British evidence has *judgement* out in front by about 3 to 2. This evidence does not constitute a perfect, scientific sampling of current usage, but it does show clearly that both spellings are in reputable use on both sides of the Atlantic. It also supports the general observation that *judgment* is more common in the U.S. and *judgement* more common in Britain.

judicial, judicious These two adjectives are close etymological relatives whose meanings have shown a tendency to overlap ever since *judicious* entered the language in the late 16th century (*judicial* is an older word, first recorded in a work written before 1382). The distinction between their principal senses remains clear, however: *judicial* has to do primarily with judges and the law (as in "the judicial branch of the government"), while *judicious* relates to sound judgment of a general kind (as in "a fair and judicious critic"). *Judicious* was also once used in a sense synonymous with *judicial,* but that use was last attested in 1632 and is now obsolete. Use of *judicial* as a synonym of *judicious,* which first occurred in 1581, has also been labeled obsolete, but a review of recent evidence shows that label to be mistaken:

> ... is not only urbane, but judicial; not only noble, but edifying —Sir James Bryce, *Studies in History and Jurisprudence,* 1901

> ... made an evident effort to be judicial and fair minded —John C. McCloskey, *Philological Quarterly,* January 1946

> One likes one's academicians objective, critical and judicial —*Times Literary Supp.,* 14 Nov. 1968

> ... requires the judicial appraisal of other people's management —Franklin D. Roosevelt, 12 Mar. 1935, in Donald Day, *Franklin D. Roosevelt's Own Story,* 1951

This sense of *judicial* is considered erroneous by usage commentators. As the above quotations show, it occurs in standard, even academic, contexts, but it is not common. Most writers will choose *judicious* in its place.

juncture *Juncture* has several meanings, the most common of which is "a point in time." It is used especially to denote an important or critical point brought about by a concurrence of circumstances or events:

> ... the juncture where relations between father- and son-in-law began to break down —Marcus A. McCorison, *New-England Galaxy,* Winter 1965

> At this critical juncture in history only the fullest resources ... can do the job —*City,* March–April 1972

> ... stave off the danger of a schism that has seemed looming at some junctures in the last few years —Paul Hofmann, *N.Y. Times,* 14 Jan. 1980

Use without implications of particular importance or crisis is not uncommon, however:

> At this juncture, the future looks bright in the extreme for Barbra Streisand —Burt Korall, *Saturday Rev.,* 11 Jan. 1969

> ... is about the only obvious depressant hanging over the stock market at this juncture —Sydney Rutberg, *Women's Wear Daily,* 27 Oct. 1975

> ... their difficulties at a later juncture in their schooling —Charles Lawrence III, *Saturday Rev.,* 15 Oct. 1977

Dictionaries treat these uses of *juncture* as standard, as they are, but Evans 1957 and Gowers in Fowler 1965 dislike *juncture* when *point* or *time* would serve as well—that is, when there is no underlying sense of events converging or coming to a head. The only other critic to remark on *juncture* is Flesch 1964, who regards *at this juncture* as a pompous way to say "now."

junior See IMPLICIT COMPARATIVE.

junta Though this Spanish-derived word has been in English since the early 17th century, the pronunciations we most frequently record are the still Spanish-sounding \ˈhün-tə\ and \ˈhu̇n-tə\. (English retains the Spanish

\h\ pronunciation of *j* in *jai alai, jalapeño,* and *jicama* as well.) Also well attested is the frankly anglicized \ˈjən-tə\. Less frequent but still standard are the hybrids \ˈjün-tə\ and \ˈhən-tə\, the latter heard from Presidents Kennedy and Reagan. Very occasionally we hear someone overshooting Spanish and landing in pseudo-French: \ˈzhən-tə\ (see HYPERFOREIGNISMS).

jurist The use of *jurist* as a synonym for *judge* is deprecated by several commentators, who point out that *jurist* has the general sense "one who is versed in the law" and is therefore not strictly limited in application to judges. It should be noted, however, that *jurist* is now relatively rare in American English except in referring to a judge (the British use it differently, to denote a legal scholar or writer). It does not, as a rule, stand alone in place of *judge* as a pure synonym; a judge asked what he or she does for a living would be unlikely to reply, "I'm a jurist." It typically serves instead as a respectful term for a person whose status as a judge is already known:

> Mr. Murphy went to Judge Kaufman in chambers and threw the problem in the jurist's lap —A. J. Liebling, *New Yorker,* 23 July 1949

Such usage is not incompatible with the general sense of *jurist.*

just As an adverb, *just* has many uses, almost all of which have a somewhat informal quality. It can mean "exactly" ("just right"), "very recently" ("someone just called"), "barely" ("just in time"), "immediately" ("just west of here"), "only" ("just a reminder"), "very" ("just wonderful"), and "possibly" ("it just might work"). Handbooks on writing occasionally cite one or more of these senses as a colloquialism (the "very" sense, in particular, has often been singled out), but all of them occur commonly in writing that is not unusually lofty in subject matter or tone.

The phrase *just exactly* has been frequently criticized as a redundancy since Fowler 1926 described it as a "bad tautology." Our evidence indicates that its occurrence in edited prose is extremely rare.

justify When *justify* is used with a preposition, it often occurs with *by* or *in.* When *by* is used, it is followed more often by a noun, less often by a gerund; when *in* is used, it is followed more often by a gerund, less often by a noun:

> ... their immediate jubilant reaction has been abundantly justified by the sales —Peter Forster, *London Calling,* 20 May 1954

> ... he did not so much apologize as justify both by argument and instance the life he had led —Irwin Edman, *Atlantic,* February 1953

> ... he tried to justify his enthusiasm by pretending that it was in truth an intellectual interest —Douglas Hubble, *Horizon,* August 1946

> His business was so nearly concluded as to justify him in proposing to take his passage —Jane Austen, *Mansfield Park,* 1814

> When is a physician justified in not being completely candid with the patient? —Norman Cousins, *Saturday Rev.,* 1 Oct. 1977

... their own lives are to be justified ... only in the accomplishment of their children —Romeyn Berry, *N.Y. Times Mag.,* 16 May 1954

Less frequently, *justify* is used with *as* or *to:*

... the playhouse was forced to justify itself as a serious cultural endeavor —*American Guide Series: Pennsylvania,* 1940

... Ruark himself justifies it as a journalistic device —Bruce Bliven, Jr., *Saturday Rev.,* 23 Apr. 1955

She loved him so much that she justified to herself his every fault —Ruth Park, *The Harp in the South,* 1948

... the physician is duty bound and morally justified to relieve suffering —Louis Lasagna, *Johns Hopkins Mag.,* Spring 1968

Justify has occurred infrequently with *for* or *of:*

The decision to keep the original arrangement of the poems ... is entirely justifed for its critical value — *Times Literary Supp.,* 19 Feb. 1971

It is not necessarily and uniquely poetic, though it justifies itself of his poetic experience —Cyril Connolly, *Horizon,* April 1946

Justify, with some frequency, is also followed by the idiom(s) *on (*or *upon) the ground(s):*

... Batista justified his seizure of power on the grounds of an alleged conspiracy —*The Americana Annual 1953*

Locke justified the right of revolution not upon the ground of hostile acts of the people —*Dictionary of American History,* 1940

The plan is justified on the ground that the farm cannot be divided —Walter Prescott Webb, *The Great Frontier,* 1952

K

karat See CARAT, KARAT, CARET.

ketchup See CATSUP, KETCHUP, CATCHUP.

kibosh *Kibosh* is one of those words whose origins have never been definitely determined. It has been suggested that Yiddish or Irish Gaelic could have been the source, but these ideas remain no more than suggestions. The word, in a variant spelling, is first attested in 1836:

("Hooroar," ejaculates a pot-boy in parenthesis, "put the kye-bosk [sic] on her, Mary!") —Charles Dickens, *Sketches by Boz*

Dickens preferred the *y* spelling and it is still used, although less frequently than the *i* spelling. Additionally, almost all the evidence in the Merriam-Webster files for the spelling *kybosh* is British:

Robbing Peter to pay Paul. Gob, that puts the bloody kybosh on it if old sloppy eyes is mucking up the show —James Joyce, *Ulysses,* 1914

"He has properly put the kybosh on the trysting place of Uncle Percy and his nautical pal." —P. G. Wodehouse, *Joy in the Morning,* 1946

In New York, though, it's the soot puts the kybosh on horticulture —Caterine Milinaire, *Punch,* 5 May 1976

Kibosh appears to be mainly an American spelling:

"... one of the best ways it can put the kibosh on cranks is to apply this social boycott business to folks...." —Sinclair Lewis, *Babbitt,* 1922

... finally shows up with a woman whom he had decided to bring home with him. Ma Stroup puts the kibosh on that —Erskine Caldwell, *N.Y. Herald Tribune Book Rev.,* 25 Apr. 1943

She was all for turning them in to the authorities and you put the kibosh on that —Mickey Spillane, *The Big Kill,* 1951

... the directive puts the kibosh on one of the few potentially valuable efforts that the United States has been making —Richard H. Rovere, *New Yorker,* 7 Mar. 1953

As in the foregoing examples, the noun *kibosh* is usually used in the phrase *put the kibosh on.* The construction is usually in the active voice but may at times be passive:

... Pop's picture broke down the press and the kibosh has been put upon further pictorial presentation —*Star of Hope,* 25 July 1903

The kibosh was put on the plan by one of the many former friends and present enemies of John L. Lewis —*Life,* 2 Feb. 1942

kick off Copperud 1970, 1980 indulges in some critical alliteration when he describes this verb as "a frayed figure from the football field." Evans 1957, on the other hand, considers it slang that is "on the way to becoming accepted spoken English." We find that it now occurs commonly in written English as well, and while its tone is not of the highest seriousness, it is no longer slang. Its most characteristic use is in describing the beginning— often ceremonial—of large-scale public events or activities:

... will kick off a painting and sculpture show of works pertaining to George Washington —Grace Glueck, *N.Y. Times,* 30 Jan. 1966

In August the premier amateur racing series on the planet kicked off its season —*Outside,* December 1985

Last year's convention kicked off a day early —Austin Murphy, *Sports Illustrated,* 28 Apr. 1986

kid Admonitions not to use *kid* to mean "child" seem to have come more from English teachers than from usage commentators, although they do appear in many books written in the early 20th century (such as Vizetelly 1906 and Krapp 1927). As is now generally recognized, the "child" sense of *kid* is actually quite old, having been recorded as early as 1599. The OED indicates that it was originally "low slang," but it became established in more general use during the 19th century:

Passed a few days happily with my wife and kids — Lord Shaftesbury, diary, 16 Aug. 1841 (OED)

. . . and I work too for other people. My kids, and Henry, and my friends —Ellen Terry, letter, 23 Sept. 1896

The "child" sense of *kid* first became common among the British, but its career as a usage issue has been strictly American. No British commentator that we know of has criticized it. The early resistance to it by Americans has also now largely subsided in the face of many years of widespread use, although it does still have some detractors (Harper 1975, 1985 finds that it is "viewed with distaste by many"). Several recent commentators have defended it staunchly. Flesch 1983, for example, considers it "more personal, more affectionate, more intimate" than *child*. It has, undoubtedly, an informal quality, but that need not be seen as a disadvantage. As Copperud 1970, 1980 puts it, "The consensus is that it is informal, which means well suited to most contexts."

They were clean enough—the school sees to that. But some of them were pitiful little kids —Robert Frost, letter, 7 Jan. 1913

. . . during their sad little walks with the kids —Bernard Malamud, *The Magic Barrel,* 1958

When I was a kid, there were no such things as holidays for me —Frank O'Connor, *New Yorker,* 28 July 1956

. . . looking like a somber little man among the American kids —Mary McCarthy, *Occasional Prose,* 1985

They would thus start kids out on the right path — Simon 1980

This can drive some kids to even greater rebellion, which often lands them in jail —*The Economist,* 11 Apr. 1986

kilometer In North America, *kilometer* is most often pronounced with the principal stress on the second syllable: \kə-ˈläm-ət-ər\. This pronunciation has drawn heated objections from some quarters. Since *centimeter, millimeter,* etc., are pronounced with principal stress on the first syllable, it stands to reason that *kilometer* should be too. For just one word of the series to receive second-syllable stress seems to violate the very spirit of uniformity which the metric system represents.

The proposal to use only first-syllable stress in these words is not a lost cause. First, \ˈkil-ə-ˌmēt-ər\ is a fairly close runner-up already, especially among scientists. Second, those who have been saying \kə-ˈläm-ət-ər\ and are made aware of the issues are sometimes contrite. The great American chemist Harold C. Urey wrote the following letter to the journal *Science* in 1972:

Some years ago, I noticed that a European friend pronounced the word for a thousand meters, kiˈlo··

me´ter, whereas I was pronouncing it ki·lom´e·ter´. I consulted my dictionary, *Webster's New International Dictionary of the English Language* (Merriam-Webster, Springfield, Mass., ed. 2, 1950). It said that this word should be pronounced kil´o·me´ter, but sometimes pronounced ki·lom´e·ter´ "by false analogy with" ba·rom´e·ter. Following this, I tried to correct my pronunciation of the word and succeeded in doing so.

Because many scientists are still using the second (erroneous) pronunciation, I again consulted a dictionary. *Webster's Third New International Dictionary* (1961) gives both pronunciations as acceptable. This is because we scientists have used the wrong pronunciation for many years, and, of course, the dictionary tries to keep up with us, or perhaps better to keep down with us. Should we then use the following pronunciations—mil·lim´e·ter´, cen·tim´e·ter´, ki·log´ram, ki·lov´olt, and so forth?

May I appeal to all my friends (if I have any friends after complaining about such details) to use the same pronunciations that are used in European countries.

Unfortunately the matter is not quite so simple.

Interestingly enough, second-syllable stress was, in fact, the only option shown for *millimeter* and *centimeter* in Noah Webster's original 1828 dictionary: in that book, *kilometer* rhymed with *barometer,* and *centimeter* rhymed with *perimeter.* The analogy between these sets of words is false in the sense that the semantic relations between prefix and suffix are different in the two cases, but in both cases the same Greek word meaning "measure" is at the root of *-meter.* Nor will European example help us much. The \kə-ˈläm-ət-ər\ variant is quite widespread in the British Isles as well—we have heard it for instance from an editor of *Nature* (English counterpart of the American periodical *Science*), along with such characteristically British pronunciations as \kən-ˈträv-ər-sē\ for *controversy* and \kə-ˈräl-ə-rē\ for *corollary.* The stress pattern in non-English-speaking European countries is not especially relevant to questions of English pronunciation, but for what it may be worth, the local equivalent of *kilometer* is pronounced with second-syllable stress in Spanish and Italian, and with third-syllable stress in German, French, and Russian.

It might seem desirable to many to have a standard pronunciation for *kilometer,* but in the present case there is an inherent dilemma which cannot be dismissed out of hand. Normally a pronunciation wins out over its rivals not by reason of etymology or logical niceties but because of the bandwagon effect. In the case of *kilometer,* however, there is at present no bandwagon. The currently most widespread American pronunciation, \kə-ˈläm-ət-ər\, faces a plausible challenge from \ˈkil-ə-ˌmēt-ər\, and it is anyone's bet what the outcome will be. It is entirely conceivable that there will be no outcome, in the sense that one variant will drive out the other.

We may be wise to remember that it is really not all that unusual for words that might well be pronounced analogously to differ, even in the vocabulary of science. For instance, two closely related areas of mathematics are *homology* theory and *homotopy* theory, often pronounced in the same breath. But the former is pronounced \hō-ˈmäl-ə-jē\, the latter \ˈhō-mə-ˌtäp-ē\. And there is another odd-man-out among the *-meter* words of the metric system: *centimeter* is often given a quasi-French pronunciation \ˈsänt-ə-ˌmēt-ər\, especially by doctors and nurses (see also HYPERFOREIGNISMS).

kilt In Scotland, the traditional knee-length skirt worn by men is called a kilt. Outside of Scotland, the established singular form is also *kilt,* but analogy with such familiar words as *pants* and *trousers* occasionally leads to the addition of an *-s:*

> The Indian wearing kilts was supposed to represent the "Mohawks" who had staged the Tea Party — Leslie Thomas, *Long May It Wave,* 1941

This use of *kilts,* which our evidence shows to be rare, has been cited as an error by several commentators. You can be sure that the Scottish dislike it as well.

kin The usual sense of *kin* is collective—"relatives":

> ... the pressures close kin ... can exert on the would-be childbearer —Shirley Lindenbaum, *N.Y. Times Book Rev.,* 29 Apr. 1984

But it also has occasional use as a countable singular—"kinsman":

> ... below it, Old Heidelberg, a close kin to Liederkranz —*Esquire,* February 1974

The singular *kin* is not new; the earliest record of its use is from the 13th century. It is, however, uncommon enough to call attention to itself. Evans 1957 considers it archaic, repeating the judgment made by the OED in 1901. Bernstein 1965 and Harper 1985 go a step further, citing it as an error. What our evidence shows is simply that it is rare. It should not be confused with the adjective *kin,* which is uncontroversial:

> ... going for another stay with some of that Tolliver family she was kin to —Peter Taylor, *The Old Forest and Other Stories,* 1985

See also KITH AND KIN.

kind 1. *These* (or *those*) *kind* (or *sort*) *of.* We will tell you first what most of the handbooks and usage books say: use *this* or *that* with singular *kind* or *sort* and follow *of* with a singular noun; use *these* or *those* with plural *kinds* or *sorts* and follow *of* with a plural noun. But we will warn you second that this advice applies only to American English, and that it presents an unrealistically narrow set of options. Real usage—even in American English—is much more varied and much more complex.

The history of these expressions as a usage issue goes back to the 18th century. According to Leonard 1929, Robert Baker in his 1779 book disapproved *these* or *those* before singular *sort* and thus established the party line for American commentators of the 19th and 20th centuries. Leonard also notes that Lowth 1762 (in one of his later editions) and Lindley Murray 1795 touched on the construction; Murray cited "these kind of sufferings" for correction.

Leonard says the issue was considered a more serious problem in the 19th century. In this country Noah Webster (*Grammatical Institute,* 1804), Goold Brown (*Grammar of English Grammars,* 1851 and later), Richard Grant White 1870, and Ayres 1881 disapprove; presumably there were many others. And if White and Ayres are typical, most American commentators were entirely ignorant of any literary precedent for the expressions (Goold Brown does mention Shakespeare but still calls his use an impropriety). You may be likewise unaware of the literary backing, so we will put in some examples here:

> Those kind of objections —Sir Philip Sidney, *The Defence of Poesie,* 1595 (in McKnight 1928)

> These kind of knaves I know —Shakespeare, *King Lear,* 1608

> ... these kind of Testimonies —John Milton, *Of Prelatical Episcopacy,* 1641

> ... these kind of thoughts —John Dryden, *Of Dramatick Poesie, An Essay,* 1668 (in McKnight)

> ... these kind of structures —Jonathan Swift, *A Tale of a Tub,* 1710

> ... these sort of authors are poor —Alexander Pope (in Alford 1866)

> These Sort of people ask Opinions —Sir Richard Steele, *The Tatler,* No. 25, 7 June 1709

> You don't know those Sort of People Child —Daniel Defoe, *Moll Flanders,* 1722

> The Apprehension of these kind of Fleers —Colley Cibber, *An Apology for the Life of Mr Colley Cibber, Comedian,* 1740

> ... engaged in these sort of hopes —Jane Austen, *Mansfield Park,* 1814

> These sort of people —Charles Dickens, *Nicholas Nickleby,* 1839 (in Jespersen 1909–49)

> ... these sort of impertinences —Sydney Smith, letter, 6 Jan. 1843 (in Hodgson 1889)

These constructions do not stop in the middle of the 19th century, but the examples should give you a general idea of what could have been found by 19th-century commentators had they chosen to look. And undoubtedly there are more to be found. (Commentators are many, but collectors of evidence are few.)

The reaction to the expressions has been more mixed in Great Britain. You might expect more tolerance from British commentators, since the examples above are all from British literature. Alford 1866 is a defender of the construction, but Hodgson 1889 is a critic. Fowler 1926 is somewhat tolerant, while Gowers in Fowler 1965 promotes it to the status of "sturdy indefensible." Chambers 1985 finds it acceptable in informal language. But Phythian 1979, Howard 1980, and Bryson 1984 take the American point of view (or perhaps they have come full circle to Baker and Lindley Murray again).

The phrases did not develop uniformly. *Manner,* which most commentators simply ignore, seems to have been the first so used (as in Shakespeare's "all manner of men"), followed shortly by *kind.* It is important to note that the constructions with *kind* have many premodifiers other than *these* and *those*—in fact *these* apparently occurs only twice in Shakespeare. He uses *such* ("such kind of men"—*Much Ado About Nothing*), *some* ("some kind of men"—*Twelfth Night*), *all* ("all kind of natures"—*Timon of Athens*), and other modifiers ("the newest kind of ways"—*2 Henry IV*) as well as a singular before with a plural after ("a kind of men"—*Othello*). Milton, writing about forty years later, also uses this last pattern. He has in his English prose works "what kind of Bishops," "such kind of deceavers," "which kind of Monsters," "such kind of incursions," and "a kind of Chariots" in addition to his uses with *these.*

Sort, which comes along later, probably gives us a clue to how the idioms developed. Shakespeare regularly uses it with *a* before and the plural after ("a sort of men"—*Merchant of Venice,* "a sort of vagabonds"—*Richard III*). When Shakespeare uses a plural premodifier, he uses *sorts* ("all sorts of deer"—*Merry Wives of Windsor,* "several sorts of reasons"—*Hamlet*). A concordance of Milton's English prose works shows that Milton follows the same pattern. The singular premodifier and *sort* is commonly followed by a plural noun; we find "this sort of men," "the younger sort of servants," "the better sort of them." He also uses the plural premodifier and *sorts:* "all sorts of men," "two sorts of persons," but his singular followed by a plural is about seven times more common. He apparently did not find much use for the all-plural form. We might conjecture then, from this little information about *sort,* that the idioms first form with the singular felt to be a mass noun, frequently with a plural complement, and gradually the *kind of, sort of* comes to be felt to be more or less of an adjective (this is the supposition of the OED, Jespersen, and Jensen 1935)—with no particular effect on the preceding modifier or the following noun. *Sort* falls into the same patterns as *kind*—with plural modifiers and plural nouns—in the 18th century.

To complete the picture, we find both Shakespeare and Milton using plural *kinds* followed by a singular, too—the singular being a mass noun. Shakespeare gives us "Some kinds of baseness"; Milton, "various kinds of style," "other kinds of licensing." Shakespeare (but not Milton, apparently) also has *kinds* with a plural: "All kinds of sores and shames."

To sum up: when Jespersen says that with *kind* and *sort* "we often find seeming irregularities of number," he has not overstated the case. We can find both *kind* and *sort* in the singular preceded by a singular and followed by a singular; in the singular preceded by a singular and followed by a plural; and in the singular preceded by a plural and followed by a plural. And *kinds* and *sorts* are followed both by singulars and plurals. All these permutations have been in use since the 18th century or earlier, and they are still in use. Witness these examples:

... the kind of fear here treated —Charles Lamb, *The Essays of Elia,* 1823

"What kind of angel is this?" —Bernard Malamud, *The Magic Barrel,* 1958

I hate to write this kind of thing —Flannery O'Connor, letter, 26 Oct. 1958

... started as a kind of narrative —John Houseman, quoted in *Publishers Weekly,* 19 Aug. 1983

... a sort of Modern Authors —Jonathan Swift, *The Mechanical Operation of the Spirit,* 1710

I love this sort of poems —Charles Lamb, letter, 20 Mar. 1799

This sort of verbs is purely Saxon —Noah Webster, *Grammatical Institute,* 1804 (in Leonard 1929)

... stockbrokers, sugar-bakers—that sort of people —W. M. Thackeray, *Punch,* 27 Sept. 1845

... the kind of questions that must be asked —Herbert J. Muller, *The Uses of English,* 1967

... this kind of records —Dan Gibson, quoted in *New Yorker,* 16 July 1984

... to see what sort of books occupied the lowest ... bookshelves —Lewis Carroll, letter, 11 May 1859

If there are any other kind of farmers —Leacock 1943

... what kind of jobs they'll find —Robert Boyd, *Miami Herald,* 26 Sept. 1968

... what kind of adjustments he must make —Gideon Ariel, quoted in *Popular Computing,* November 1982

... those kind of guys —Ring Lardner, *The Big Town,* 1921

... these kind of sensational statements —Sir Winston Churchill, *The Unrelenting Struggle,* 1942

... many years of participating in these kind of forays —Robert Morley, *Punch,* 28 Sept. 1976

Those were the kind of big plays —William N. Wallace, *N.Y. Times,* 6 Jan. 1980

These are the kind of worries I can handle —*And More by Andy Rooney,* 1982

Those kind of letters —Art Buchwald, *Springfield* (Mass.) *Republican,* 2 Oct. 1983

Those are the kind of thoughtful comments —Jeff Greenfield, *Springfield* (Mass.) *Morning Union,* 2 May 1986

... a trend toward different kinds of living —Margaret Mead, *Barnard Alumnae,* Winter 1971

There are all kinds of chic on Long Island —Walter Wager, *Telefon,* 1975

... a writer of several kinds of distinction —R. W. B. Lewis, *N.Y. Times Book Rev.,* 2 Jan. 1983

... those kinds of excess —Jeff Greenfield, *Springfield* (Mass.) *Morning Union,* 2 May 1986

... does all sorts of outrageous things —Henry Adams, letter, 29 Dec. 1860

... what kinds of people they happen to despise —Daniels 1983

These are the kinds of books a grandmother should give —*People,* 14 Feb. 1983

And although it is seldom mentioned by the handbooks, *type* has fallen into the same sort of pattern:

And in America we don't do those type of things —Carl Ekern, quoted in *Newsweek,* 21 July 1986

Conclusion: *kind* and *sort,* in the singular, preceded by *these* or *those* and followed by a plural noun is an idiom well established in British usage—from the 16th century to the present. It is a bugbear of American handbooks, and such use as it has had in American English has until quite recently (as the dates on the examples show) been confined chiefly to speech. It seems now to be establishing itself in written American English. The grammar books and handbooks may nonetheless continue to repeat themselves and to follow Robert Baker and Lindley Murray. Many of them will be so concerned with *these* and *those* that they will entirely miss the fact that "that kind of sailboats" (from a recent 7th-grade English text) is just as anomalous from the point of view of narrow grammatical logic as "those kind of sailboats." But you are aware by now that a much greater variety of constructions is in respectable use than the handbooks realize.

If *kind of* and *sort of* are adjectives in these constructions, as the OED, Jespersen, and Jensen believe they are, the agreement of *these* or *this* with *kind* or *kinds* is, of course, irrelevant. But the variety of constructions suggests that writers and speakers have not intuitively felt them to be true adjectives, for determiners like *this* and *these* agree with the following noun and are unaffected by an intervening adjective. Thus, if *kind of* were a true adjective, we would find only "these kind of sailboats," but in fact we find *this, that, a,* and so forth as well as the plural forms.

2. See KIND OF, SORT OF; KIND OF A, SORT OF A.

kindly *Kindly* is used both as an adjective ("a kindly smile") and as an adverb ("he smiled kindly"). In one of its many adverbial uses it serves as a synonym of *please:*

> The old woman did not know it but she spoke in a hoity-toity voice.... "Kindly order me a conveyance" —Rumer Godden, *Ladies' Home Jour.,* December 1970

> "And now you'll kindly do me the favor to pack a suitcase full of clothes and send it on to me. I'll give you just one week for it, too." —Katherine Anne Porter, *Ladies' Home Jour.,* August 1971

These passages illustrate two ways in which *kindly* differs from *please:* it tends to have a highly formal sound, and it often has an imperious quality, so that the request being made comes across as a command. If someone you disliked were to clap a hand on your shoulder in a hearty gesture of insincere friendship, you might find yourself saying, "Kindly take your grubby paw off me." *Please* just wouldn't be appropriate at such a moment.

The "please" sense of *kindly* is standard, but a few commentators regard it with varying degrees of disapproval. Flesch 1964 states flatly that it "shouldn't be used." Evans 1957 finds that it "has a touch of unctuousness about it that may defeat its intention of being elegant or ingratiating" when used in such a phrase as *kindly remit.* Our evidence suggests, however, that its use in such a phrase is not meant to be ingratiating, but forceful. As Bremner 1980 puts it, "*kindly* is stronger and more formal than *please* and tends to connote the idea of 'Do this—or else.'"

A related use of *kindly* cited by Fowler 1926 is in such a sentence as "You are kindly requested to return the enclosed form within 30 days." This is a fairly common way of making a formal request, but Fowler dislikes it because it seems to imply that the requester is giving himself credit for being kind.

kind of, sort of These phrases slid imperceptibly into adverbial function from their various uses sometime around the end of the 18th century. They began to draw unfavorable notice from the commentators a little more than a century later. Vizetelly 1906 and Bierce 1909 opened fire on *kind of;* MacCracken & Sandison 1917 added *sort of.* They received mention by all of the 1920s commentators in our collection. Jensen 1935 sums up the majority opinion: "These are adjectival phrases and should never be used adverbially."

And why is that? Vizetelly gave his reasons for *kind of.* He said it was an American provincialism that had no literary authorization. The OED has examples from English, Irish, and Scots sources (Dickens among them). The Dictionary of American English has earlier evidence, and it is American, but clearly this is not an American provincialism.

Vizetelly may have been on sounder grounds in denying *kind of* any status in literature. The earliest example is from a broadside of some sort and may be below literary notice. In 1804 it was used in a poem by Thomas G. Fessenden, who is noted here and there in H. L. Mencken's *The American Language* and its second supplement as a person not averse to publishing comments on the correctness or incorrectness of American provincialisms. Perhaps Vizetelly was being a literary critic in this instance. But he might have spotted *kind of* in these two American authors, if he had looked:

> ... kind of stood by me —Mark Twain, *Tom Sawyer,* 1876

> And so on—fourteen verses. It was kind of poor —Mark Twain, *Life on the Mississippi,* 1883

> ... didn't have the family brains, and he was kind of soft-hearted —Winston Churchill, *The Crisis,* 1901

Kind of and *sort of* (for which the earliest evidence is British) are simply speech forms—idioms commonly used in ordinary speech. Krapp 1927 called them "colloquial," which was his way of saying the same thing. Krapp's word is the one most frequently repeated in recent handbooks, but one tends to suspect that recent commentators are unfamiliar with Krapp's sense of the word. McMahan & Day 1980, for instance, use the label *colloquial* but follow it up with this remark: "The phrases can be used in standard English, but not as adverbs." But *colloquial* and *nonstandard* are not synonymous; *kind of* and *sort of* are regularly used in standard English all the time. The thing you must remember is that they are primarily spoken idioms, and thus are most at home in speech, fictional speech, and prose written in a light or familiar style. Here is a generous sample of typical instances:

> ... it made me feel kind of shaky for a while —Archibald MacLeish, letter, 12 Aug. 1910

> I kind of thought it was —Booth Tarkington, *Penrod,* 1914

> "... I could stand it if we didn't go back to the lovin' wives, ... but just kind of stayed in Monarch...." —Sinclair Lewis, *Babbitt,* 1922

> And I kind of want to make *her* Moyra —Henry James, "Notes for *The Ivory Tower,*" 1917

> "... You see, they're tennis shoes, and I'm sort of helpless without them...." —F. Scott Fitzgerald, *The Great Gatsby,* 1925

> We've been having practice raids here, and I dash around the roads at night blowing a horn and feeling kind of silly —E. B. White, letter, 21 May 1942

> Funny as hell, isn't it? Kind of like a tenderfoot Boy Scout trying to clean up the Paris red-light district —Bill Mauldin, *N.Y. Herald Tribune Book Rev.,* 7 July 1946

> He wasn't even a politician, and it's kind of hard to explain why he stayed in politics —James Thurber, *New Yorker,* 9 June 1951

> ... and it's kind of true —Randall Jarrell, letter, 24 Sept. 1951

> ... they all sort of work together —Lord Snowden, quoted in *Australian Women's Weekly,* 30 Apr. 1975

The book kind of dribbles to a close —Tim Bowden, *Nation Rev.* (Melbourne), 8 May 1975

... I kind of liked him too —*And More by Andy Rooney*, 1982

... then coming up with insights, sort of, to match the latter —Joan Barthel, *N.Y. Times Book Rev.*, 27 May 1984

Jim believed that God sort of generally watched over the world —Garrison Keillor, *Lake Wobegon Days*, 1985

... they were to be transferred in amounts sort of as drawn —Caspar Weinberger, Secretary of Defense, quoted in *The Tower Commission Report*, 1987

kind of a, sort of a   Here we have another English idiom that has come under the disapproving scrutiny of the critics. Leonard 1929 identifies Robert Baker, in his 1779 book, as the first to notice the construction. "Would not the *a* or *an* be better omitted? and is not 'a strange sort of man'.... a more correct, as well as a more elegant, way of speaking?" he asks. Apparently no one was listening; at least none of our 19th-century sources mentions the construction. Vizetelly 1906 rediscovered it. Bierce 1909 mentions it too, but he adds a fillip of his own; he lays logic on the problem: "Say that kind of man. Man here is generic, and a genus comprises many kinds. But there cannot be more than one kind of thing." We find the same logic solemnly repeated by Bernstein 1958, Shaw 1970, Bremner 1980, and Cook 1985. Most of the rest of the commentators simply advise omitting the *a* or *an* (as Baker did) and differ over whether the construction is informal or colloquial or wholly inadmissible.

Curme 1931 finds the construction—with *manner* rather than *kind* or *sort*—as far back as the 14th-century travel book associated with the name of Sir John Mandeville. He described the crocodile as "a manner of a long serpent." These later examples use *kind* and *sort*:

... and yet I have the wit to think my master is a kind of a knave —Shakespeare, *The Two Gentlemen of Verona*, 1595

... made a kind of a Jest —Daniel Defoe, *Moll Flanders*, 1722

... a very good sort of a fellow —Henry Fielding, *Tom Jones*, 1749 (in Curme and Jespersen 1909–49)

... he left off the study of projectiles in a kind of a huff —Laurence Sterne, *Tristram Shandy*, 1759

... the men looked hard at him, anxious to see what sort of a looking "cove" he was —Herman Melville, *Omoo*, 1847

You know what sort of a man King is —Henry Adams, letter, 17 Jan. 1861

... a couple card rooms and a kind of a summer parlor —Ring Lardner, *The Big Town*, 1921

... an answer to the question: "What sort of a man was Robert Burns?" —*Saturday Rev.*, 1 Apr. 1939

Lord Allenby, who was no kind of a mystic —*Times Literary Supp.*, 2 Jan. 1943

"... It is probably," the Doc concluded, "some sort of a millennium." —Thomas Heggen, *Mister Roberts*, 1946

... what kind of an ambassador he was —William Harlan Hale, *The Reporter*, 12 Jan. 1956

It is apparently that kind of a show —Clive Barnes, *N.Y. Times*, 19 Nov. 1968

Type, incidentally, can also be found in this construction:

... that type of a threat —Joseph McCarthy, 1954, quoted in Pyles 1979

Our files show that *kind of* or *sort of* without the following *a* or *an* is a much more common construction than the one with the article. No doubt many writers use both—Defoe writes both "a kind of a Jest" and "a kind of Jest" in *Moll Flanders*. But you are more likely to use the form without the article in most writing. Still, there never has been a sound reason for aspersing the less common idiom. If it is your idiom, there's no need to avoid it, especially in speech or in familiar writing.

kith and kin   This alliterative phrase has been cited as a cliché by several commentators, beginning with Evans 1957. As clichés go, it is not an especially popular one; we have collected only a few examples of its use during the past several decades. The commentators like to point out that *kith* means—or formerly meant—"fellow countrymen," so that *kith and kin* should not, in their view, be taken as referring only to kinsfolk, but to countrymen or acquaintances and kinsfolk. (Similar reasoning could be used to argue that *kith* should not be understood as meaning "countrymen," since in an even older sense it meant "country," and the OED shows that the original meaning of *kith and kin* was actually "country and kinsfolk.") What our evidence shows is that *kith and kin* is variously used and is variously understood in current English. More often than not, it does seem to imply nothing more than "kinsfolk" and is thus open to a charge of redundancy, but its exact meaning is often hard to pin down. Clearly some writers do apply it to friends as well as to relatives:

... began to interview Sedgwick kith and kin. She talked with friends from Edie's years in Cambridge —Geoffrey Wolff, *N.Y. Times Book Rev.*, 4 July 1982

... a great network of kith and kin spread around the globe, among them artists as well as anthropologists, poets as well as psychoanalysts —Marshall Sahlins, *N.Y. Times Book Rev.*, 26 Aug. 1984

kneel   *Kneel* belongs to a group of verbs which offer a choice of variants for the past and past participle. For *kneel*, either *kneeled* or *knelt* is considered standard. *Knelt* occurs just a little more frequently than does *kneeled* in contemporary usage:

The boy knelt and held out his arms —E. L. Doctorow, *Ragtime*, 1975

Warren walked in bowed, kneeled on the straw mat —E. L. Doctorow, *Loon Lake*, 1979

The OED tells us that *kneeled* was the regular spelling until the latter part of the 19th century, when *knelt* began appearing. Shakespeare, for instance, never used *knelt*.

knit, knitted   As many commentators observe, the past tense and past participle of *knit* can be either *knit* or *knitted*. A few critics in the early 20th century regarded *knitted* as an error, but that issue was apparently laid to rest when Fowler 1926 accepted both forms, while noting some distinctions in their use. Our evidence shows that the two forms are interchangeable in most contexts ("a knit/knitted shirt"; "he knit/knitted his brows in concentration"). *Knit* is definitely preferred, however, with such adverbs as *closely* and *tightly* in figurative use:

> They rejected the closely knit but stifling family interaction —A. I. Rabin, *Psychology Today,* September 1969

> . . . a loosely knit state which allows for great variety —John W. Holmes, *The Lamp,* Fall 1971

> Always alone among strangers, the family grew tightly knit —Ross Milloy, *N.Y. Times Mag.,* 6 Apr. 1980

knot   Nautically speaking and strictly speaking, a knot is a unit of speed equal to one nautical mile per hour, and a vessel is described as traveling at (or "making") a certain number of knots. Also occasionally heard is such usage as "The ship was under way at 20 knots an hour," in which *knot* has the meaning "nautical mile." This sense of *knot* is widely derided by those in the know as a landlubber's mistake, and you would probably be prudent not to indulge in its use, at least within earshot of sailors or usage commentators. If you do happen to use it, however, and if some seafaring or word-watching type accuses you of gross ignorance, you might just point out that it was first entered in a dictionary in 1864 and was first recorded a century before that in the written works of two famous English sailors:

> The ship went ten knots an hour —Admiral George Anson, *Anson's Voyage Round the World,* 1748 (OED)

> The strong tide, though even here it ran five knots an hour —Captain James Cook, *Voyages,* published in 1790 (OED)

know   *Know* belongs to a class of verbs most of which (like *blow, fly, show*) have at least some irregular forms in the past and past participle but a few of which (like *flow*) have only regular ones. In standard English *know* has only *knew* and *known. Knowed,* although old—the OED dates it back to the 14th century—is now found only in dialectal and uneducated speech. *Knowed* has been frequently used by fiction writers for their special purposes:

> "I knowed it!" sighed Mrs. Davids —Francis Lee Pratt, "Captain Ben's Choice," in *Mark Twain's Library of Humor,* 1888

> Old Eagle had done already took off because he knowed where that old son of a gun would be laying as good as we did —William Faulkner, *Saturday Evening Post,* 5 Mar. 1955

know-how   Good old American *know-how:* the word, if not the quality it names, was first in evidence in 1838, but it began to appear commonly in print only about a hundred years later. Its great popularity in the decades since attests to its usefulness. It denotes a kind of practical knowledge and skill—an ability to solve problems and get things done—which no other word quite gets at (*expertise* perhaps comes closest, though its connotations are quite different). More often than not, the con-

texts in which it occurs have to do with business or technology:

> . . . failed in commercial ventures because they lacked marketing knowhow —*Forbes,* 1 May 1967

> We can develop the know-how, and we can train the people needed to get the job done —Robert C. Weaver, *Michigan Business Rev.,* July 1968

> . . . a nation with technical know-how but few energy resources —Janet L. Hopson, *Smithsonian,* November 1982

> . . . the knowhow of mature electronic engineers — Paul Preuss, *Science,* July/August 1985

Usage commentators in general have found little fault with *know-how.* Evans 1957 briefly notes that it is standard in American English, and Gowers in Fowler 1965 observes that it has come to be accepted in British English as well, despite its American origins. Bernstein 1965, Watt 1967, and Shaw 1987 consider it overused. Bremner 1980 says it is a handy word.

kraft   See CRAFT 3.

kudos, kudo   *Kudos* is a Greek word that was dragged into English as British university slang in the 19th century. The OED so notices, calling it in addition (and curiously) a colloquialism. Early users, conscious of its origin, sometimes printed it in Greek letters:

> "No money?"
> "Not much—perhaps a ten'ner," answered Drysdale, "but no end of κῦδος, I suppose."
> —Thomas Hughes, *Tom Brown at Oxford,* 1861

In this earliest use, the word referred to the prestige or renown one gained by having accomplished something noteworthy. The word became more popular than one might have expected for a bit of university slang. By the 1920s it had developed a second sense, "praise given for some accomplishment"—a reasonable extension of the original use. *Time* magazine is frequently credited with the popularizing of this second sense, but it probably did not originate with *Time* editors. In this example, for instance, it seems to suggest praise or acclaim rather than prestige:

> "If the secret were really kept, you'd be waiving all the kudos too," she added —Leonard Merrick, *The Man Who Understood Women, and Other Stories,* 1919

In construction *kudos* is originally a noncount noun, a mass noun, like *glory, acclaim, renown,* or *prestige:*

> . . . they had acquired much kudos among the pilgrims —John Buchan, *The Last Secrets,* 1923

> . . . Oliphant, who gained a little kudos —Leonard Merrick, *The Actor-Manager,* 4th ed., 1919

> . . . she was proud of sharing in Bresnahan's kudos —Sinclair Lewis, *Main Street,* 1920

During the 1920s the "praise" sense of *kudos* came to be understood as a plural count noun. *Time* magazine does seem to have been influential in this process. It was a policy of the editors to announce honorary degrees and like awards under an opening like this (from 28 June 1926):

> Another week of Commencements . . . and distinguished citizens from all walks of life were called to

many rostra to be honored. . . . Kudos conferred during the week:

And a list would follow. The notion of plurality also became associated with the word when it was linked with a plural noun:

> They were the recipients of honorary degrees—*kudos* conferred because of their wealth, position or service to humanity —*Time,* 27 June 1927

But while these examples suggest a plural count noun, they do not prove that *kudos* has been taken to be a plural. Our earliest unmistakably plural citation is a bit earlier and from a different source:

> Colonial mechanics have very few kudos thrown in their path —letter to editor, *Rand Daily Mail* (Johannesburg), 23 Dec. 1925

Demonstrably plural citations have not been as frequent as you might expect from the amount of attention *kudos* has received. Here are a few more of our earlier ones:

> There is no other weekly newspaper which in one short year has achieved so many kudos —*Time,* 9 June 1941

> All kudos, he says, are the due of Cranston Williams —*Advertising & Selling,* April 1948

> Its kudos for brilliance are few —Saul Carson, *New Republic,* 26 Jan. 1948

Far more of our citations are of uses in which *kudos* could be taken to be either a mass noun or a plural.

Once *kudos* was perceived as plural, though, it was inevitable that someone would prune the *s* from the end and create a singular. The earliest pruner in our files is Fred Allen. He did it in a letter written to Groucho Marx in which with a little pungent exaggeration he describes favorable reaction to a television show. He sets the scene in a delicatessen:

> . . . eating was suspended. chicken fat was shaken from fingers to point them. novy was shredded from snags of teeth to make way for encomiums. . . . a fat man put down a . . . celery tonic bottle and emitted an effervescent burp while he paid his tribute to the hour. a man sitting on a toilet bowl swung open the men's room door and added his kudo to the acclaim —October 1950

What Fred Allen could do in a letter, someone else was bound to do in print:

> To all three should go some kind of special kudo for refusing to succumb —Al Hine, *Holiday,* June 1953

Harper 1975, 1985 and Shaw 1975, 1987 tell us that there is no such thing as a kudo. But they are wrong. If there is no such thing as a kudo, there is no such thing as a cherry, a pea, an asset, a caterpillar, or a one-hoss shay. All of these terms were formed by back-formation from a supposed plural. Jespersen 1909–49, in his second volume, has many other examples. Mencken (1963 edition) also lists a number of similarly formed singulars that exist in the American vernacular.

Like it or not, *kudo* is here as a singular count noun and *kudos* as a plural count noun. A few more examples:

> All these kudos spread around the country —Goodman Ace, *Saturday Rev.,* 6 Nov. 1971

> . . . the real kudos obviously belong to good old Will Shakespeare —*Playboy,* January 1974

> Frazier delivered a kudo seldom uttered in high finance: "He's underpaid." —Joe Flaherty, *New York,* 23 Sept. 1974

> She added a kudo for HUD's Patricia Harris —Susan Watters, *Women's Wear Daily,* 26 June 1978

> . . . the rewards are the kudos that come from everywhere —Horace Sutton, *Saturday Rev.,* 2 Sept. 1978

> . . . a handsome number of kudos —Allen Drury, letter in *Publisher's Weekly,* 17 Feb. 1984

We think that *kudo* and *kudos* as count nouns are by now well established, although you will note that they have not yet penetrated the highest range of scholarly writing or literature. If you do choose to use the word, keep in mind that there are three separate uses: *kudo* as a singular count noun, *kudos* as a plural count noun, and *kudos* as a singular noncount noun. Do not fall into the error of thinking that criticism of *kudo* means that there is a singular count noun *kudos;* there is not. If you are thinking of a single instance of praise, you must either use *a kudo* or choose some other word.

Kudos is usually pronounced \ˈk(y)ü-ˌdäs\ or \ˈk(y)ü-ˌdōs\ by those who treat it as singular, \ˈk(y)ü-ˌdōz\ by those who make it plural.

L

labor See BELABOR, LABOR.

lack *In* and *for* are the prepositions used with the verb *lack. Lack in* has not been criticized, but the usage panel of Heritage 1969, 1982 prefers *lack* to *lack for* when no difference of meaning would result. We find, however, that the use with *for* turns up in negative constructions (the sample sentence offered by Heritage also has one) in standard writing.

> He will not lack for strategists willing to explain the war —David Halberstam, *Harper's,* January 1969

> The middle-class suburbanite does not lack for doctors —Walter Goodman, *Commentary,* January 1972

> She never lacked for self-knowledge in the matter of vanity —Wright Morris, *Plains Song,* 1980

> Steve Lasker hasn't lacked for news experience since his teens —Frederick C. Klein, *Wall Street Jour.,* 22 June 1983

We also have examples for *lack* used this way in folksy writing. Such an association may be the source of the Heritage criticism.

Here's hoping he'll never lack for friends —Mark Twain, *The American Claimant,* 1892 (OED Supplement)

Leon didn't lack for visitors the last few years —Garrison Keillor, *Lake Wobegon Days,* 1985

One of our citations has a negative construction without *for,* but the direct object in this case is modified by "a few," whereas the objects in the examples above are unmodified.

... certainly the river did not lack a few travelers —William Styron, *This Quiet Dust and Other Writings,* 1982

laden When *laden* is used with a preposition, the choice is almost always *with:*

... he ceased to speak to her as though she were a child and he a person laden with wisdom —Sinclair Lewis, *Arrowsmith,* 1925

... a dull serious novel, laden with coincidence one would not tolerate in fact, let alone fiction —Anthony Boucher, *N.Y. Times Book Rev.,* 14 Mar. 1954

... enigmatic space and Edward Hopper American houses that seem laden with disquiet —Irving Howe, *N.Y. Times Book Rev.,* 11 Sept. 1983

lady *Lady* is one of the fine old words of English. After perhaps 1100 years of use it began to be the subject of considerable discussion in usage books during the 19th century. As often happens, they did not agree with one another to any great extent. The use of *lady* in the sense of "wife" was considered a dreadful vulgarism by Gould 1867 and forbidden in the *New York Evening Post* by William Cullen Bryant at about the same time. Fitzedward Hall 1873 thought the usage archaic and cited two 18th-century authors, Oliver Goldsmith and Fanny Burney. Richard Grant White 1870 was not fazed by this usage at all; he said that he did not see what all the fuss was about and that if a man registering at a hotel wanted to designate his wife a lady, it was all right with him.

There was generally more agreement on the broader issues. Almost everyone—even Ayres 1881 and George Perkins Marsh 1859—agreed that *woman* was a better general designation for the sex than *lady,* but almost all of them allowed *lady* to be an acceptable word for a woman of superior breeding or social refinement. The occasion of all this discussion seems to have been an American journalistic convention of the time that mandated referring to women in news reports as *ladies.* Perhaps those "hack journalists," as Marsh termed them, thought *lady* somehow more polite than *woman;* they probably never realized the storm of controversy they had unleashed. Ayres pays special attention to the case of working women. If the better class of women—in short, ladies—are required "from any cause soever to work in a store," Ayres holds that they are content to be called *saleswomen.* But "your young woman" for whom a job in a store is a degree of social advancement—"She, Heaven bless her! boils with indignation if she is not denominated a sales *lady.*"

The commentators of the earlier part of the 20th century contented themselves with reviewing the same 19th-century topics in pretty much the 19th-century way. After World War II, however, commentators began to be a little more sophisticated in their approach—even wary in a few cases—because American women had become more emancipated in their attitudes. Reader's Digest 1983 seems to grasp particularly well not only the diversity of attitudes towards *lady* but also the complexity of actual usage when they call *lady* "a word so full of social overtones and built-in gender assumptions that no one can prescribe rules of its usage for others." The subject matter, however, has not changed; it is almost entirely the same question of which is better, *lady* or *woman,* to use as a general indicator of sex (*woman* is now the all but universal choice), and which is better to use in light of what is known about a person's social position or refinement. Even the recognition found in Copperud 1970 and others that *Ladies* is regularly used as a form of address to an audience of women can be traced back as far as Gould 1867. A good dictionary can tell you nearly all of this. All the uses commented upon are listed as separate senses of the noun *lady.* You can even find a few additional uses of *lady* if you are interested, and the dictionary offers these without the social moralizing.

If the subject matter of the commentators has remained essentially constant for more than a century now, what about usage? Is it any different? We can reply with some assurance that the 19th-century journalistic habit of referring to all women as *ladies* has nearly passed from the scene. Then too, *lady* has picked up at least one use since the old days: it is now used, especially in the gossip sheets and personality magazines, as a word for the young woman who is the usual but unmarried companion of a man who happens to be a television actor, a rock star, or some similar focus of fascinated attention. This is the old denigrated "wife" sense revived with a new, late-20th-century twist.

With lady Josephine and daughter Leah, 4, along for the ride ... —*People,* 9 May 1983

The examples that follow will tell you more about how *lady* is used in print; some simply use the word while others offer comment. One of the things you will probably notice is that no simple rule about when to use or not use *lady* will stand up against actual usage. People will choose between *lady* and *woman* in ways that seem most natural to them, although—as you will see—they sometimes do so to the displeasure of those to whom or about whom they are speaking. One of the considerations that affects one's attitude toward the word is who says or writes it and who hears or reads it. It will be of interest also to know when something was written. These examples cover a considerable span of years, though of course you will find more recent examples than old ones.

Talking of the ladies, methinks something should be observed of the Humour of the fair sex —William Congreve, "Concerning Humour in Comedy," 1695

Mrs. Reynolds is the name of the Lady to whom I will remember you to-morrow —Charles Lamb, letter, 1810

... a lady very learned in stones, ferns, plants, and vermin —Anthony Trollope, *Barchester Towers,* 1857 (in A. S. Hill 1895)

The woman who kissed him, and pinched his poke, was the lady that's known as Lou —Robert W. Service, "The Shooting of Dan McGrew," 1907

... the trunk had been lost but was now found that contained what some lady was going to wear —Robert Frost, letter, 10 Nov. 1920

A lady is—or in Ellen Terry's generation was—a person trained to the utmost attainable degree in the art and habit of concealing her feelings and maintaining an imperturbable composure under the most trying circumstances —George Bernard Shaw, preface, *The Shaw–Terry Letters,* 1931

It was years ago, I remember, one Christmas Eve when I was dining with friends: a lady beside me made in the course of talk one of those allusions — Henry James, *The Art of the Novel,* 1934

A lady who had paid a fine for streetwalking came in to protest not the publication of the news of her fine, but the fact that we called her a woman, and she assured us that she was as much of a lady as any of the other girls in this town. And from that hour to this, the Gazette has referred to all females as women except that police-court characters were always to be designated as "ladies" —*The Autobiography of William Allen White,* 1946

. . . it . . . no more enhances the quality of a lady's output than does the assumption of . . . cute and booksy *noms de plume* —James Thurber, *Thurber Country,* 1953

. . . [my mother]'s usually the only lady present at these things and gets treated in highstyle by the auctioneer —Flannery O'Connor, letter, 6 Oct. 1956

Whatever the fops and bullies may have thought of it, tragedy had a special appeal to the ladies —James Sutherland, *English Literature of the Late Seventeenth Century,* 1969

At the end of the lecture Miss Stein rose; we all got up; and amid the babble of goodnights the ladies came forward from their compound —Allen Tate, *Prose,* Fall 1971

. . . [Boswell] thought it overstepping the limit when a lady suggested to him that perhaps the sexes would be equal in the next world —John Wain, *Samuel Johnson,* 1974

She never has more than eight and serves sumptuous Haitian delicacies cooked by her Haitian lady — Andre Leon Talley, *Women's Wear Daily,* 17 Apr. 1978

A story I wrote . . . tells of a sixty-year-old man who has an adulterous affair with the lady across the street —Philip Roth, *Reading Myself and Others,* 1975

She was a very elegant, honest-looking lady —E. L. Doctorow, *Loon Lake,* 1979

. . . another female stereotype—the elderly lady who seems to be everybody's white-haired grandmother but actually is a sharp, observant old dame who knows much more than she pretends to —Newgate Callendar, *N.Y. Times Book Rev.,* 28 Aug. 1983

The auctioneer . . . looked out on an audience containing Betty Friedan, Nora Ephron and other enlightened friends. "There are no ladies here—just women," he said sternly —Michael Small, *People,* 19 Sept. 1983

Despite the efforts of feminists, working-class women across America, young and old, still resolutely refer to themselves as ladies —Michael Brody, *Fortune,* 11 Nov. 1985

His mother had been a scrubwoman, and he wasn't going to let these ladies suffer the way she had —Tip O'Neill with William Novak, *Man of the House,* 1987

For at least some speakers, the more demeaning the job, the more the person holding it . . . is likely to be described as a lady. Thus, cleaning lady is at least as common as cleaning woman, saleslady as saleswoman. But one says, normally, woman doctor. To say lady doctor is to be very condescending —Robin Lakoff, *Language and Woman's Place,* 1975

. . . explains how a lady artist (it was George Eliot) was able to deduce . . . —O. B. Hardison, Jr., *Entering the Maze,* 1981

One of my few unpublished stories . . . was written on the advice of the lady agent just mentioned — Donald Hamilton, in *Colloquium on Crime,* ed. Robin W. Winks, 1986

lady . . . avoid using this in place of "woman" unless you intend shadings of meaning that describe someone who is elegant, "refined," and conscious of propriety and correct behavior. In most contexts this word is perceived as (and often is) condescending — Rosalie Maggio, *The Nonsexist Word Finder,* 1987

lag When *lag* is used with a preposition, it is usually *behind:*

Two horsemen were within a hundred yards. . . . One, lagging behind the other, was Oldring's Masked Rider —Zane Grey, *Riders of the Purple Sage,* 1912

Behind him lagged the girl —Harriet La Barre, *Discovery,* March 1954

. . . the organized workers thus saw their pay lag behind the corporate returns —Michael Harrington, *Center Mag.,* September 1969

lament The verb *lament,* when used with a preposition, is used with *about, for,* or *over:*

. . . we need not gloat or lament about the limitations of finite minds —Antony Flew, *A New Approach to Psychical Research,* 1953

And Jeremiah lamented for Josiah —2 Chronicles, 35:25 (AV), 1611

. . . instigating some journalist friends of his at the same time to lament over the decay of the grand school of acting —George Bernard Shaw, *Cashel Byron's Profession,* 1886

lamentable See INCOMPARABLE.

large, largely The adverb *largely* is described as unidiomatic following the verbs *bulk* and *loom* by several commentators, dating back to Fowler 1926. Our evidence confirms that *large* is the usual choice:

These inner planets . . . do not bulk very large in the solar system as a whole —Carl Sagan, *Scientific American,* September 1975

. . . and America loomed large in their imagination —Garrison Keillor, *Lake Wobegon Days,* 1985

We do have substantial evidence for *bulk largely* in our files, but none more recent than 1949. Our only example of *loom largely* is from speech.

last Some usage writers make the distinction that *last* means "final" and *latest* means "most recent." Other writers admit that both words can mean "most recent" but insist that only *latest* conveys this meaning unambiguously. This difference of opinion has existed for quite some time, as we can see from a comparison of two comments published in 1927:

> "Last" means the end of a series, "latest" indicates the most recent. For example, we say: "This is the latest issue of this magazine," when we mean that the issue is the most recent one. But if we say, "This is the last issue of this magazine," we mean that the publishers have discontinued the issue of the magazine, and no more numbers are to come —Lurie

> *Last* in one of its senses means *latest;* in consequence, one may say, "The *last* issue of the magazine," meaning the *latest* issue. Some speakers, however, prefer to use *latest* instead of *last,* as more closely expressing the meaning to be conveyed — Baker

Topics such as a last/latest issue of a magazine or a writer's last/latest book are the typical illustrations chosen by commentators, presumably because such contexts might be ambiguous if the wrong word is chosen. However, we agree with Bryson 1984 that "the chances of ambiguity . . . are probably not as great as some authorities would have us believe." Our citations bear this out:

> . . . anyone who has read Professor Haines's study in our last issue —*The Nation,* 21 May 1924

> . . . which was reproduced in facsimile in the last issue of this news letter —Ruth Wedgwood Kennedy, *Renaissance News,* Autumn 1951

> . . . some hostile review in the *New Republic* of my last book —Harold J. Laski, letter, 28 Nov. 1920

> I scrounged around in my trash system trying to find if I had a carbon of my last to you —Flannery O'Connor, letter, 8 Oct. 1957

> This is another scrappy note written as a stop-gap between my last long letter to you and the next — Alexander Woollcott, letter, 26 Jan. 1918

> . . . indicates that respondents tend to remember best the last words they hear —Stanley L. Payne, *The Art of Asking Questions,* 1951

We believe that the general context or the subject under discussion, if not the immediate context, will usually provide enough information to make such uses of *last* unambiguous. A dead writer's last book, for example, is obviously not merely his latest one. And in cases where the meaning of *last* is ambiguous the ambiguity may be immaterial. Whether a living writer's last novel is his final one or merely his most recent is a question that usually can't be decided until he either writes another or dies; in the meantime *last* will serve the purpose well enough.

Of course, there may be times when, with no help from the larger context, you must make it clear that something is the final one of a series and not just the most recent. In such a case you can simply use *final,* or you can expand the immediate context and say, for example, "the last book she wrote before she died." Einstein 1985 says, "A prudent way to avoid such confusion is to use only *latest* for recency and only *last* for finality," but since other people use *last* with both meanings, you may not be able to avoid ambiguity just by restricting your own use. However careful you are to discriminate between *last* and *latest,* you cannot be sure that your reader or listener will realize that you have done so.

When nouns denoting time (such as *night, week, May, Tuesday*) are being modified, idiom calls for *last* or *past,* but not *latest,* even though the meaning is clearly "most recent" and not "final."

> . . . the last three or four years —William R. Eshelman, *Wilson Library Bulletin,* November 1968

> For eight of the past nine years —*Bowdoin Alumnus,* January 1971

See also FIRST TWO, TWO FIRST.

last analysis See ANALYSIS.

late Much thought has been given to the use of *the late* before the name of a dead person. The most frequently considered aspect of such use is just how long a person referred to as "the late" can have been dead. Here are a few opinions:

> . . . the statute of limitations might run for half a century —Bernstein 1971

> As a general rule, late is used in reference to persons whose death has occurred within the twenty or thirty years just past —Harper 1975

> . . . "the late" is used for about ten to fifteen years after death —Safire 1984

What everyone does agree on is that there is no hard and fast rule to be followed. Our evidence shows that *the late* can be applied to people whose lives were recent enough to exist at any point within the living memory of the writer or speaker. You should use your own judgment to decide whether it is appropriate in a particular instance.

Use of *the late* in referring to a person who has just died is also considered by Bernstein 1971, who finds it "ridiculous." Bernstein cites an example of such use in a newspaper caption, but we have no further evidence of it. *The late* normally serves as a respectful way of referring to a dead person when that person's death is no longer shocking news.

Still another consideration is the use of *the late* in referring to a famous person whose death is common knowledge. Bernstein 1971 and Safire 1984 discourage such use, regarding *the late* as superfluous. Safire acknowledges, however, that "some people use the phrase . . . to pay respects to the subject." Most people, in fact, use the phrase that way. *The late* is primarily a term of respect for a person who has recently died, and its use in referring to a famous person is both common and appropriate:

> The late Henry Ford —*N. Y. Times,* 27 Sept. 1950

> The late President John F. Kennedy —*Current Biography,* June 1967

> . . . the late, beloved Langston Hughes —Alfred Duckett, *Essence,* November 1970

> . . . the late Vince Lombardi and his legendary Packers —John Fischer, *Harper's,* February 1971

> . . . the late H. L. Mencken —Paul Fussell, *Los Angeles Times Book Rev.,* 25 Apr. 1971

Another aspect of the use of *the late* has also drawn comment. Kilpatrick 1984 warns against such a sentence as "The bill was signed by the late President Johnson" which, he says, "creates a startling and indeed a macabre image," implying that President Johnson was already "late" when he signed the bill. That seems to be an excellent point until you realize that *the late* can almost always be read in a macabre way by anyone determined to do so:

He heard an address in Boston by the late Charles Evans Hughes —*Current Biography 1951*

. . . chairman was the late Democratic Senator Estes Kefauver —*Current Biography,* January 1968

In a talk to Harvard's Nieman Fellows twenty years ago, the late A. J. Liebling declared that . . . —Joseph P. Lyford, *Center Mag.,* September 1969

As the late Joseph Levinson pointed out —Martin Bernal, *N.Y. Rev. of Books,* 23 Oct. 1969

The late Prof. Louise Pound collected them in a study of 1936 —Allen Walker Read, "The Geolinguistics of Verbal Taboo," 10 Jan. 1970

On Lowenstein's first day in the House, the late L. Mendel Rivers accosted him —John Corry, *Harper's,* April 1971

The late can legitimately be used in this way because it does not simply mean "the dead," it means "the now dead." It is actually no more macabre to say "the bill was signed by the late President Johnson" than to say "the bill was signed by the now dead President Johnson."

See also WIDOW, WIDOWER.

later on   The *on* of *later on* was much criticized as superfluous in the first half of the 20th century, but it no longer provokes controversy. It occurs commonly in both speech and writing:

. . . if you don't report him, he'll probably get into worse trouble later on —J. Edgar Hoover, *NEA Jour.,* January 1965

Later on their diagnoses got more specific —Conrad Rooks, quoted in *Evergreen,* December 1967

. . . his ability to resist, later on, the temptation to steal a television set —C. Knight Aldrich, *Psychology Today,* March 1971

For a parallel, but more recent, case see EARLY ON.

Latin plurals   One of the favorite subjects of usage writers over the years is the misuse of the plurals of foreign words—mostly but not all Latin—as singulars. For discussions of individual foreign plurals that are used as singulars, see AGENDA; BACTERIA; BONA FIDES; CANDELABRA; CRITERION, CRITERIA, CRITERIONS; CURRICULUM; DATA, DATUM; DESIDERATUM; DICTUM; EROTICA; ERRATA; GRAFFITI, GRAFFITO; MAGI; MEDIA; MEMORANDUM; MINUTIA; PAPARAZZO, PAPARAZZI; PARAPHERNALIA; PHENOMENON; PROLEGOMENON, PROLEGOMENA; STADIUM; STRATA, STRATUM; TRIVIA.

latter   See FORMER 1.

laudable, laudatory   Usage commentators are concerned about maintaining the distinction between these words, which is that *laudable* means "deserving praise; praiseworthy" ("laudable attempts to help the poor") and *laudatory* means "giving praise; praiseful" ("a laudatory book review"). This distinction is a real one. Aside from a 15th-century citation in the OED, the only evidence we have seen of *laudable* used in place of *laudatory* is a single passage cited by Fowler 1926. Use of *laudatory* in place of *laudable* is somewhat more common, according to our evidence:

Librarians are alert to . . . the need to re-allocate certain routine chores to others less qualified; this is laudatory —Mary Lee Bundy & Paul Wasserman, *College & Research Libraries,* January 1968

. . . both take pay cuts in order to do what really makes them happy. This laudatory stance fails to save either man from banality —Philippe Van Rjndt, *N.Y. Times Book Rev.,* 3 July 1983

But this use is still quite rare, and it cannot be regarded as standard.

laugh   The verb *laugh,* when used intransitively with a preposition whose object is what caused the laughter, is usually used with *at:*

. . . the ridiculous, *le rire,* the comic is what we laugh at —John Dewey, *Art as Experience,* 1934

. . . a butt, a clod, laughed at by looking-glasses — Virginia Woolf, *Between the Acts,* 1941

. . . a professor on this side of the Atlantic would be laughed at in the English weeklies —E. K. Brown, *Rhythm in the Novel,* 1950

It seems clear that *laugh* is still used idiomatically with *over;* most of our evidence for it, however, is old:

. . . let us every one go home
And laugh this sport o'er by a country fire
—Shakespeare, *The Merry Wives of Windsor,* 1601

Have you forgotten about . . . that capital story you told of the large loaf. A hundred times since, I have laughed over it —Herman Melville, *The Confidence-Man,* 1857

lawman   Sheriffs in the old West were not actually called lawmen, but that is what we call them now. The word *lawman* appears to have been first adopted by the writers of Westerns in the 1940s:

. . . Mariposa took Rio for a lawman. . . . A thrill-packed Western yarn —*Huntting's Monthly List,* February 1944

The burly lawman took the youth by the arm —Burt Arthur, *The Buckaroo,* 1947

By the 1950s, *lawman* had gained enough currency from its use in popular books and movies that journalists began applying it more widely as a general term for a law-enforcement officer:

. . . shot and killed three police officers . . . and stood off some 30 other lawmen in a 1½-hour gunbattle — *Springfield* (Mass.) *Sunday Republican,* 29 May 1955

The use of *lawmen* in the *N.Y. Times* in 1958 caught the critical eye of Theodore Bernstein, who evidently was no fan of Westerns:

What on earth are "lawmen" and what is the need for such a coinage? —*Winners & Sinners,* 5 Feb. 1958

Bernstein 1965 repeated this criticism, and it apparently has had some influence among other journalists; Harper 1975, 1985 notes that the Associated Press stylebook treats *lawman* as a word to be shunned. Copperud 1970, 1980, however, accepts it as a standard word, as do the several dictionaries that now enter it (including Webster's Third and Random House 1987). Its association with the old West remains strong enough to make it most appropriate for describing a law-enforcement officer who has—or is seen as having—some of the qualities of a gun-toting sheriff:

> That May day in 1936 I made Hoover's reputation as a fearless lawman —Alvin Karpis, quoted in *Los Angeles Times Book Rev.,* 23 May 1971

lay, lie   These verbs are one of the most popular subjects in the canons of usage. They first attracted attention in the second half of the 18th century, when educated usage seems to have been rather indifferent to the distinctions between them. Lounsbury 1908 says that when Laurence Sterne's *A Sentimental Journey* was published in 1768, a critic attacked the line "But Maria laid in my bosom," maintaining that readers might "conclude that Maria was the name of a favorite pullet." (It is highly improbable that anyone actually reading Sterne would be liable to such a misapprehension.)

The earliest commentator in our collection to mention *lay* and *lie* is Baker 1770. Early in his book he sets down the principal parts of the two verbs and gives examples of how they should be used. Later on he observes that *lie* is very seldom used for *lay* (this is still a true observation) but that he has found *lain* (the past participle of *lie*) used for *laid.* He cites a writer named Bluet who wrote this: "after they have lain aside all Pretences to it." *Lain* is a very literary-sounding substitution to 20th-century ears. However, Emily Dickinson had made the same substitution:

> Thank you for "the Sonnet"—I have lain it at her loved feet —letter, Spring 1886

The opposite change is much more common. Campbell 1776 criticized this passage:

> ... my studies having laid very much in churchyards —*The Spectator*, 24 Oct. 1712

Once the grammarians had picked up *lay* and *lie* as a subject, it was soon entrenched both in the schools and in the handbooks and usage books. Our collection includes about sixty commentators upon the subject. To them you could add the standard dictionaries, all of which mark the intransitive *lay* for *lie* as nonstandard in one way or another (Flesch 1983 cocks a snook at the dictionaries for being so prissy). Almost all of these commentators tell you what the principal parts of each verb are and note that even though many people have confused them, you should not; the details are in your dictionary.

Let's look first at the history of the usage. The OED shows that *lay* has been used intransitively in the sense of "lie" since around the year 1300. From then until the latter part of the 18th century, the usage was unmarked: Sir Francis Bacon, for instance, used it in the final and most polished edition of his essays in 1625. Lounsbury notes its occurrence in such 17th- and 18th-century writers as Pepys, Fielding, Horace Walpole, and Mrs. Montagu.

But from the 19th century on, there are fewer and fewer literary examples. Byron has a rather famous, or

infamous, "there let him lay" in *Childe Harold's Pilgrimage,* 1818; it is cited in the OED and many other places, but it does not really count. Byron was driven to it: he needed a rhyme for *spray* and *bay.* Jane Austen used it in an interesting way in *Mansfield Park,* 1814. She has her uncultured Mr. Price ask, "Whereabouts does the *Thrush* lay at Spithead? Near the *Canopus?*" According to McKnight 1928, Miss Austen does this to show the social class of Price, but it is just as likely that she used it to show Mr. Price's familiarity with nautical lingo. The OED notes that *lay* "lie" was established in nautical parlance in various expressions; Mr. Price in the novel had a son in the navy, and Jane Austen had two brothers in the navy. Whatever subtlety she intended, you may not even see the usage unless you read a carefully edited edition. In an inexpensive reprint we have seen, Miss Austen's *lay* has been silently corrected to *lie* by some unthinking editor.

If the grammarians and the schoolmasters and the schoolmarms and the usage writers have succeeded in largely establishing the transitive-intransitive distinction between *lay* and *lie* in standard discursive prose, they have not done so well in speech. The persistence of *lay* "lie" in speech in spite of the marshalled opposition of the schoolteachers is reinforced by several factors. First, there is the failure of what Bolinger 1980 calls contrast. The two verbs overlap in some ways: they share an identical form, *lay;* in the past tense the common use with *down* sounds about the same whether spelled *lay down* or *laid down.* Evans 1957 and the OED note in addition that *lay* once had a use with a reflexive pronoun that meant the same as *lie down:* "Now I lay me down to sleep."

> ... I laid me down flat on my belly —Daniel Defoe, *Robinson Crusoe,* 1719

Evans says that the pronoun dropped out but was understood, giving intransitive *lay.* Lamberts 1972 thinks that the irregular principal parts of *lie* sound a bit bookish in speech and that this feeling tends to promote the use of *laid* in place of *lay* and *lain.* This feeling is probably illustrated here:

> I got the knife away from the kid and made him lie down again. But, from that moment, Bill's spirit was broken. He laid down on his side of the bed, but he never closed an eye —O. Henry, "The Ransom of Red Chief," 1907

Then we have some idioms in which *lay* functions intransitively:

> ... I see that you, too, plan to lay off for Holy Week —Alexander Woollcott, letter, 21 Feb. 1941

> He begins by saying he can't get hold of enough books to find out whether we have any literature or not and then he proceeds to say we have none. I am sure he will lay for me somewhere —Robert Frost, letter, 22 Feb. 1914

And, finally, there is the simple longevity of intransitive *lay,* almost 700 years of continuous use.

The conflict between oral use and school instruction has resulted in the distinction between *lay* and *lie* becoming a social shibboleth—a marker of class and education. Thus, writers can use it to identify characters, as Jane Austen may have done as early as 1814, or to build up a dialectal integrity.

> He was troubled with a wonderful pain in his chest and amazin weakness in the spine of his back,

besides the pleurisy in the side, and having the aguer a considerable part of the time, and being broke of his rest of nights, cause he was so put to't for breath when he laid down —Frances Miriam Whitcher, "Hezekiah Bedott," 1855, in *The Mirth of a Nation,* ed. Walter Blair & Raven I. McDavid, Jr., 1983

Old Eagle had done already took off because he knowed where that old son of a gun would be laying —William Faulkner, *Saturday Evening Post,* 5 Mar. 1955

"I mean, I don't change sheets in the morning, after I wait on the breakfast eaters ... without having no place to lay down. . . ." —John Irving, *The Hotel New Hampshire,* 1981

A linguistic shibboleth is only a reliable social marker when an individual either uses or avoids it on all occasions. Persons whose education or status would lead them to avoid such use in formal situations may use the stigmatized word in informal, friendly circumstances:

She thinks every story must be built according to the pattern of the Roman arch . . . , but I'm letting it lay —Flannery O'Connor, letter, 25 July 1964

. . . I didn't want anybody, the workers or the contractors or anybody, to lay down on the job —Harry S. Truman, quoted in Merle Miller, *Plain Speaking,* 1973

And there is another curious influence on the use of transitive *lay* in speech: a folk distinction between *lay* and *lie* seems to be in operation that cuts across the distinction of the school books. Evans 1957 says, "There is a tendency in present-day English to prefer the verb *lay* in speaking of inanimate objects, and the verb *lie* in speaking of living creatures." A baseball announcer on television has put it in the pithier folk form: "*Lay* is for things, *lie* is for people." We even have some printed evidence of this "*lay* is for things" use:

. . . the book really lays flat when opened —Mabel C. Simmons, *New Orleans Times-Picayune,* 23 May 1976

. . . we block and size most every carpet we sell to be sure they lay flat —advertising brochure, 1981

The System Unit Board, laying flat at the bottom of the box, includes a 5 Mhz 8088 microprocessor —Sergio Mello-Grand, *InfoWorld,* 19 Dec. 1983

Notwithstanding the belief of some that social judgments can be solidly based on language use, the *lay-lie* shibboleth seems to be changing its status. For instance, several commentators, such as Evans 1957, Follett 1966, and Flesch 1983, are perfectly willing to give the distinction up; Bolinger 1980 thinks it is already a lost cause not worth defending; Copperud 1970, 1980 judges the consensus of his experts to be that at least some uses of *lay* for *lie* are verging on standard. Flesch even goes so far as to recommend using *lay* for *lie* if it comes naturally to you. We have some evidence that reporters have so used it; an angry letter to the editor of *Fortune* in 1982 complains about it, and the *Winners & Sinners* of 24 March 1988 points a finger at two recent examples from the *New York Times.* And we have this writer, too, drawing attention to an earlier usage of his own:

"The dead hand of the present should not lay on the future," I wrote in a recent harangue —William Safire, *N.Y. Times Mag.,* 11 Oct. 1987

Additional evidence of a change comes from the usage surveys. When Leonard made his survey in 1932, the intransitive *lay* examples were deemed "illiterate." When Crisp replicated the survey in 1971, the ranking of the usage had risen to "disputable" (one perhaps war-weary group of college English teachers felt it was established).

If *lay* "lie" is on the rise socially, however, it is likely to be a slow rise, as indignant letters to the editor attest. Bolinger observes sensibly that if you have invested some effort in learning the distinction, you will not want to admit that you have wasted your time. And by far the largest part of our printed evidence follows the school-book rules. On the other hand, evidence also shows no retreat of intransitive *lay* in oral use. So what should you do? The best advice seems to be Bolinger's:

Many people use *lay* for *lie,* but certain others will judge you uncultured if you do. Decide for yourself what is best for you.

lead, led   The past tense and past participle of the verb *lead* is spelled *led:*

. . . he led negotiations in a strike —*Current Biography,* February 1967

The strong tendency to spell it *lead* is presumably attributable in large part to analogy with the verb *read,* as well as to the influence of the noun *lead.*

. . . has lead a life of action —*American Poetry Rev.,* vol. 3, no. 5, 1974

. . . has lead the field —*Southwest Art,* May 1984

This is a common mistake in casual writing. Watch out for it.

See also MISLEAD, MISLED.

leading question   In a court of law, the term *leading question* denotes a question that is put in such a way as to guide the person being questioned towards a desired response, for example, "The defendant seemed unusually nervous that afternoon, didn't he?" Usage commentators dating all the way back to the Fowler brothers in 1907 have complained that *leading question* is often misused outside of legal circles to mean "a difficult, tricky, unfairly worded question," such as "When did you stop beating your wife?" We do not doubt that such usage does occur, but, surprisingly, we have no evidence in our files of its occurrence in print. Apparently it is limited primarily to speech, where it may, in fact, be quite common. As Howard 1983 suggests, a person being interviewed may object to a tricky question as "leading," implying that it was intended to lead to a too revealing or self-incriminating answer. Such usage does not strike us as illogical. The only objection that can be made to it is the one that has been repeatedly made by the critics: it is not strictly consistent with the narrow, legal sense of *leading question.*

lean   1. While both *leant* and *leaned* can be found in the past tense and past participle in British English, *leant* is preferred. In American English, *leaned* is used almost exclusively.

The train started. Snopes leaned into the aisle, looking back —William Faulkner, *Sanctuary,* 1931

Jake leaned against the counter. 'Say what kind of a place is this town?' —Carson McCullers, *The Heart Is a Lonely Hunter,* 1940

... the air-speed indicator leaned right until it rested on one hundred and twenty —James Gould Cozzens, *Guard of Honor,* 1948

She leant out of the porthole —Ngaio Marsh, *Death of a Peer,* 1940

Mr. Pondoroso leant his scooter against the Wayne Mews wall —Colin MacInnes, *Absolute Beginners,* 1959

... entered her child's room and leant over his sleeping form —Ray Smuts, *Sunday Times* (South Africa), 10 Nov. 1974

His anger vanished. His whole soul leaned out eagerly towards Gallagher, craving support —Liam O'Flaherty, *The Informer,* 1925

The IRS has leaned on him for money accrued from the movie —Joe Flaherty, *Inside Sports,* 31 Jan. 1981

2. *Lean* is used with a great number of prepositions, but by far the one most frequently found is *on:*

They leant on the counter, laughing and talking —John Fountain, *The Bulletin* (Sydney, Australia), 24 Feb. 1954

Both items lean heavily on nostalgia —Bennett Cerf, *Saturday Rev.,* 22 May 1954

This is a straight deal or the senora wouldn't be in it. You have no reason to lean on me —Pierre Salinger, *On Instructions of My Government,* 1971

... a factor ... never pointedly leant on by the playwright to underpin his case —John Bayley, *Times Literary Supp.,* 20 June 1980

Lean with *to, toward,* or *towards* is also quite common:

... many times have I, leaning to yonder Palm, admired the blessedness of it —Virginia Woolf, *The Second Common Reader,* 1932

... Mr. Horgan leans too heavily to the side of the friars and paints them whiter than the evidence justifies —Oliver La Farge, *American Scholar,* Spring 1955

... nearly everybody leans toward a timid conservatism with regard to unfamiliar music —Virgil Thomson, *The Musical Scene,* 1947

The woman leaned her hard eyes toward them: "The broken glass, monsieur, that'll cost you one franc extra." —Waldo Frank, *Island in the Atlantic,* 1946

... his aesthetic appreciation ... leaned towards the old rather than to the modern —A. L. Rowse, *West-Country Stories,* 1947

Without looking up at him she leant towards him —Ngaio Marsh, *Death of a Peer,* 1940

Lean is also found with other prepositions. Following are examples of *upon, in,* and *against:*

Shakespeare leaned, as it were, even as craftsman, upon the general fate of men and nations —*The Autobiography of William Butler Yeats,* 1954

I wasn't being lonely and sitting home and crying. I was leaning over in the opposite direction —Ethel Merman, quoted in *Saturday Evening Post,* 5 Mar. 1955

The old man leaned the mast with its wrapped sail against the wall —Ernest Hemingway, *Life,* 1 Sept. 1952

Earlier in this article are examples of *lean* with *into, out of,* and *over.*

leap *Leaped* and *leapt* are interchangeable both as the past tense ("He leaped/leapt over the ditch") and past participle ("The song has leaped/leapt to the top of the charts") of *leap. Leapt* is the more common choice in British English. In American English, *leaped* and *leapt* seem to be used with about equal frequency:

... remarks leaped to his tongue —Norman Mailer, *Harper's,* 1971

... fairly leapt at life in a hundred directions —James Dickey, *N.Y. Times Book Rev.,* 3 Oct. 1976

... Upshaw leapt in the air. ... (Currently, Upshaw denies this version, claiming that he leaped in the air on mere whim ...) —Melvin Durslag, *TV Guide,* 15 June 1973

learn 1. The use of *learn* to mean "teach" was once perfectly respectable:

Sweet prince, you learn me noble thankfulness —Shakespeare, *Much Ado About Nothing,* 1599

... having learned him English so well that he could answer me —Daniel Defoe, *Robinson Crusoe,* 1719

I have too much pride to stand indebted to Great Britain for books to learn our children the letters of the alphabet —Noah Webster, letter, *Weekly Monitor,* 15 Feb. 1785

The OED includes many citations for the "teach" sense of *learn,* dating back to the beginning of the 13th century. Samuel Johnson treated it as a standard sense in the first edition of his dictionary, published in 1755. But the 1785 edition included the note "This sense is now obsolete." By the last decades of the 18th century it had lost prestige. Noah Webster noted in his American Dictionary (1828) that "this use of learn is found in respectable writers, but is now deemed inelegant as well as improper." The OED labeled it "vulgar" in 1902.

The "teach" sense of *learn* has persisted in dialectal and uneducated speech, but its only use in writing is now in the representation or deliberate imitation of such speech:

... there is certainly no lack of correspondence schools that learns you the art of short-story writing —Ring Lardner, *How to Write Short Stories,* 1924

... if he'd only learned himself to speak good grammar he would probly be a Major today —James Jones, *From Here to Eternity,* 1951

I'll learn him to touch my gun! —Agnes Sligh Turnbull, *The Gown of Glory,* 1951

My daddy learned it to me —Leonard Eversole, quoted in *Our Appalachia,* ed. Laurel Shackelford & Bill Weinberg, 1977

2. Even though Lindley Murray disapproved *learnt* in 1795, the British use both *learnt* and *learned* as the past tense and past participle of *learn.*

... learned to live off man's left-overs —Gordon Hard & Frank Manolson, *Observer Mag.,* 25 Nov. 1973

When I went to my prep school, I learned the piano —Charles, Prince of Wales, quoted in *Observer Rev.,* 9 June 1974

... Magistrate Riley's colleagues have learnt their lesson —*Private Eye,* 5 Apr. 1974

... he first learnt, really learnt, the pleasure of reading —*British Book News,* July 1983

Learnt is no longer very common in American English. Simon 1980 criticizes an American book for using it; he calls it obsolescent and slightly fuddy-duddy. It turns up occasionally:

... according to the system learnt in their course —Ring Lardner, *How to Write Short Stories,* 1924

But the usual form in American English is *learned:*

... a slightly reticent girl who had learned to carry her beauty well —Frank Conroy, *Harper's,* November 1970

... was horrified when she learned what had happened —Jay McInerney, *Bright Lights, Big City,* 1984

learned See ALLEGED 2.

leary See LEERY, LEARY.

leastways, leastwise These two synonymous adverbs are both more at home in speech than in writing, although both have some sort of literary pedigree:

". . . or, leastwise, people'll think you've been defiled . . ." —Joseph Conrad & Ford Madox Ford, *The Inheritors,* 1900

He was own brother to a brimstone magpie—leastways Mrs. Smallweed —Charles Dickens, *Bleak House,* 1852 (OED)

Both words originated from phrases: *at the least way,* which dates back to the 14th century, and *at the least wise,* which was first recorded in 1534. The equivalent phrase now established in general use, of course, is simply *at least.* The single word *leastways* was labeled "*dial.* and *vulgar*" by the OED in 1902, and its use has continued to be chiefly dialectal:

"It might a-done the bashing, though," said Kirk, "leastways, the underneath part, or this here rounded end. . . ." —Dorothy L. Sayers, *Busman's Honeymoon,* 1937

"Reckon so," Dade admitted. "Leastways I'm the only one workin' there regular." —Harold Sinclair, *Music Out of Dixie,* 1952

The OED labeled *leastwise* "somewhat *rare,*" and somewhat rare it has remained. It does have some use in straightforward, albeit informal, writing:

... leastwise ever since Bill Crews, years ago, took his team out to play some little town across the hills —Newlin B. Wildes, *Yankee,* May 1967

But to other writers it clearly has much the same dialectal quality as *leastways:*

There ain't no sech massage. Leastwise, I haven't met it —*Chicago Daily Tribune,* 6 Nov. 1926

leave, let 1. The OED traces *leave* "let" in the combination *leave alone* back to about 1400. This *leave*

alone, however, does not seem to have been a very conspicuous part of the literary mainstream. Shakespeare, Congreve, and Defoe, for instance, use *leave alone* only in its literal sense of "leave in solitude"; they use *let alone* for "to refrain from bothering or using." Shakespeare, for example, has this:

So please you, let me now be left alone —*Romeo and Juliet,* 1595

It seems likely that *leave alone* "let alone" did not begin to appear in print often until the later 19th century (the OED has a 1798 example from Madame D'Arblay's diary, but it was not published until nearly 100 years later). This use was familiar in one special context early in the 19th century:

Little Bo-Peep has lost her sheep,
And can't tell where to find them;
Leave them alone, and they'll come home,
And bring their tails behind them.

The Oxford Dictionary of Nursery Rhymes (1952) dates this back to an 1805 manuscript. It appeared in print in editions published in 1810, 1842, 1853, and 1877 and undoubtedly did much to make the phrase familiar. We have another early 19th-century instance, but it too would not have been published until much later than it was written:

... and heartily pray that they would leave me alone —Charles Lamb, letter, 29 June 1829

Leave alone and other phrases using *leave* in the sense of "let" (the OED lists *leave go (of)* and *leave hold (of)* among others) must have begun to appear with some frequency by the last quarter of the 19th century, for that is when they first drew unfavorable notice, from Ayres 1881. He condemns such expressions as "leave me be" and "leave it alone" as vulgarisms. Compton 1898 and Vizetelly 1906 agree and so does Bierce 1909. Bierce is apparently the first to mention the "solitary" versus the "untouched" sense of *leave alone.*

Leave alone was not singled out for special treatment by commentators until sometime after World War II. Commentators in the 1920s and 1930s continued to lump it with other *leave* expressions when they mentioned it at all. Occasionally, as in the *Literary Digest* of 24 January 1925, it was contrasted with *let alone* along the "solitary"-"untouched" lines of Bierce. Since World War II, opinion has been divided between the insisters on the Biercian distinction (Copperud 1960, 1964, 1970, 1980 and Bernstein 1958, 1965, 1977) and just about everyone else (including Evans 1957, Bryant 1962, Watt 1967, Shaw 1975, 1987, Harper 1975, 1985, and Trimmer & McCrimmon 1988), who find *let alone* and *leave alone* acceptably interchangeable. Watt makes the point that the distinction between *leave alone* and *let alone* can be very slight, and it is hard to get exercised over the possibility of ambiguity—as Bernstein and Copperud do—in an example like that from Charles Lamb, which could be interpreted as "leave me by myself" or "don't bother me." Lamb's drift is unmistakable no matter which interpretation you choose.

F. Scott Fitzgerald had noticed the phrases being used interchangeably:

"Then you ought to leave it alone," countered Doctor Civet —*The Great Gatsby,* 1925

"Why not let her alone, old sport?" remarked Gatsby —*The Great Gatsby,* 1925

Some other examples of *leave alone:*

> ... your imagination. I say, leave it alone, let it do its own work —Hal Underhill, *The Writer,* May 1968

> But a good many other Americans at that time could take a college education or leave it alone —Tom Wicker, *Change,* September 1971

> My mother hated whisky and admired men who could leave it alone —Russell Baker, *Growing Up,* 1982

You should note that the "solitary" sense can still be used unmistakably when it is wanted:

> ... she was afraid that she would be left alone. Once you have lived with another, it is a great torture to have to live alone —Carson McCullers, *The Ballad of the Sad Café,* 1951

Leave alone is standard in both uses.

2. Many of the American commentators on *leave* and *let*—particularly those who write schoolbooks and college handbooks—make no mention of *leave* (or *let*) *alone* but concentrate on other uses of *leave* meaning "let." The construction usually condemned is *leave* followed by a pronoun and an infinitive without *to. Leave* in this use is often a mild imperative:

> Leave us only add that ... —Jonathan Evan Maslow, *Saturday Rev.,* 12 Apr. 1980

This construction is primarily oral. It has been so long and so often reprehended in the schools that one of its chief uses in print is to be facetious:

> Leave us not enquire how I happened to be running —Alan Coren, *Punch,* 7 Oct. 1975

When it is used seriously in print, the use has been taken from speech:

> If you put them in drums, and this is the easiest way to handle them, and you leave them stand, some free-liquid will surface over time —John Hernandez, quoted in *Civil Engineering,* December 1982

> As for the gap left by Sweet, "We will probably leave it be," says NBC casting chief Joel Thurm —*TV Guide,* 31 May 1985

One curious thing about these constructions is that they are held to be more reprehensible in American English than in British English. They have received almost no attention by British commentators, as far as we can tell, until quite recently, when Phythian 1979 and Longman 1984 take notice. Perhaps British indifference accounts for occasional serious (but not literary) use in British publications:

> Leave it steep for at least 4 hours —Elizabeth David, *Italian Food,* 1969

This example points out how minor the problem really is. In American English, "Let it steep" or "Leave it to steep" would both be acceptable. But no matter how you choose to define *let* and *leave* here, the same message has been given.

There are other idioms in which *leave* and *let* are involved, notably the OED's *leave go (of)* and *leave hold (of).* About these American commentators are in disarray, and the only British commentator to mention them, Phythian 1979, disapproves *leave go (of).* The OED simply identifies them with spoken—colloquial—idiom.

What conclusions can we draw? In American use, *let* plus the infinitive without *to* and *leave* plus *to* plus the infinitive are standard and acceptable to all parties. *Leave* without *to* but with the infinitive is monolithically opposed by American educational usage writers, still devoted to the opinion of Ayres 1881. It is, consequently, a construction limited to speech and to facetious use in print. British attitudes seem more latitudinarian, or perhaps just indifferent.

3. The last curiosity about *leave* and *let* to be mentioned here is the substitution of *let* for *leave,* which is discussed in Bryant 1962. Bryant's examples are dialectal, and were recorded in areas of Pennsylvania Dutch settlement. An example is "Don't close the door; let it open." A German verb *lassen,* which overlaps both *leave* and *let* in meaning, is supposed to be the influence behind the usage. H. L. Mencken in *The American Language,* with some confirmation by Raven McDavid, editor of the 1963 abridged edition, also mentions German as an influence in the confusion of *leave* and *let.* Here is a fictional example of the dialectal confusion:

> "Please, will you leave me let my books in school? ..." —Helen Reimensnyder Martin, *Tillie—A Mennonite Maid,* 1904

We might mention that hypercorrection seems to have reared its less than charming head in this matter. A well-known New York baseball announcer, who is distinctly not of German background, has been recorded on at least two occasions as saying "He's gonna let him in" when a baseball manager, after a visit to the mound, has decided to stick with the pitcher currently in the game. Most of us would say "leave him in." The *let* is presumably the result of frequent teacherly correction of *leave* constructions.

4. See also LET; LET ALONE.

lectern See PODIUM

led See LEAD, LED.

leery, leary 1. *Leery* and its less common variant *leary* have been in use for quite a while: Webster's Ninth New Collegiate Dictionary dates the spelling *leery* from about 1718. Perhaps because the word appeared first in thieves' cant, it formerly carried with it a slang label, a label which some language commentators still approve: Bernstein 1965, for one, suggests avoiding its use and substituting instead *chary* or *wary,* among others. The OED labels its entry slang, and while it is true that this sense of *leery* is seldom encountered in British English, it has become quite common in standard American English. The slang label of Webster's Second (1934) was dropped from Webster's Third (1961).

2. When *leery* or *leary* is used with a preposition, it is most likely to be followed by *of:*

> ... the presidency of the world would be an office of comparatively little power—nothing to be leery of —E. B. White, *Harper's,* July 1942

> ... is leery of wise New York politicians and reporters —Richard Reeves, *New York,* 27 Dec. 1971

> ... with nervous Republicans still leery of the supply-side theology —William Greider, *Atlantic,* December 1981

Leery or *leary* is also used less frequently with *about* and very occasionally with *as to:*

> ". . . I'm kind of leery about churches, and I'm kind of leery about preachers too." —Claude Brown, *Manchild in the Promised Land,* 1965

> ". . . This was something new and, frankly, some of us were a wee bit leery as to the outcome." —Edward N. Saveth & Ralph Bass, *Think,* July 1953

leeway As a nautical term, *leeway* denotes the drift or off-course lateral movement of a vessel caused by wind or currents. Most nonsailors are familiar with the word only in its figurative sense, "an allowable margin of freedom or variation." This sense seems to have originated in the early 20th century. The first of our dictionaries to enter it was Webster 1909, in which it was labeled "colloquial" and was explained by the following note: "This use of the word, now very common, arises from a confused idea of *leeway* as meaning room to leeward."

The "confused" sense of *leeway* took some time to become established in written use. Weseen 1928 cited it as a colloquialism, and it was still labeled as one in Webster's Second (1934). It wasn't until the 1940s that we began to find it commonly in writing.

> . . . give the hostess a much greater leeway in her menu planning —*June Platt's Plain and Fancy Cookbook,* 1941

> . . . the Union government allows them a considerable amount of leeway —Frederic A. Ogg & Harold Zink, *Modern Foreign Governments,* 1949

> You've got to make up your mind now, darling, there's no leeway any more —Arthur Miller, *Death of a Salesman,* 1949

Its written use in the decades since has become increasingly widespread. It is now the most common sense of the word.

> . . . they do not allow much leeway —Walter Goodman, *Harper's,* August 1971

> . . . perhaps with greater leeway —Randall Collins, *Change,* Winter 1972–73

> . . . with plenty of leeway for defensible shortfalls — *N.Y. Times,* 1 Oct. 1977

> . . . gives himself plenty of leeway —Paul Zweig, *N.Y. Times Book Rev.,* 25 July 1982

> . . . give too much leeway to children in the choice of books —Edwin McDowell, *N.Y. Times Book Rev.,* 15 Apr. 1984

The extended sense of *leeway* originated in American English, where its use has never been seriously controversial (no American commentator since Weseen 1928 has even mentioned it). Its relatively recent adoption by the British has, however, drawn criticism from two British commentators, Howard 1977 and Phythian 1979, both of whom fault it as illogical. But they are fighting a lost battle. The extended sense of *leeway* is now unquestionably standard, and it is recognized as such by current dictionaries, both British and American.

legitimate, legitimatize, legitimize Fowler noted in 1926 with some asperity that *legitimatize* and *legitimize* were edging out the usage of the older verb *legitimate*. *Legitimate* dates from 1586, *legitimatize* from 1791,

and *legitimize* from 1848. Phythian in 1979 echoed Fowler's complaint but had perhaps neglected to check current usage. While growth in the usage of *legitimatize* and especially of *legitimize* did occur in the first half of the 20th century, that growth has not had the effect of producing "the virtual exclusion of *legitimate*" that Phythian claims. In fact, according to our evidence, while *legitimize* was used more often than *legitimate* for a while, since the late 1960s and the early 1970s the two words have been occurring with about the same frequency:

> The "objectivity" which earlier scientists sought at their own life peril to legitimate in the era of church dogmatism —Carl Oglesby, *Center Mag.,* March/April 1971

> But what of their criminality? What role does it play for us? Paradoxically it serves, I believe, to legitimate them in our eyes as objects of interest —Norman Podhoretz, *Commentary,* January 1972

> . . . the ways in which schools and colleges legitimate and maintain inequality —Christopher Jencks, *N.Y. Times Book Rev.,* 15 Feb. 1976

> Poland has ceased being a nation with even a pretense of Communist rule, a rule that is legitimated by Marxist ideology —Irving Kristol, *Wall Street Jour.,* 11 Jan. 1982

> . . . they battle for their political positions, for educational reforms and for a goal of legitimizing their life-styles —Thomas J. Cottle, *Change,* January–February 1971

> . . . José Martí, who legitimized poetry as a revolutionary vocation —Peter Winn, *N.Y. Times Book Rev.,* 10 June 1979

> Ethnicity began to be legitimized as part of the fabric of American life —Arthur M. Schlesinger, Jr., *Saturday Rev.,* 12 Nov. 1977

> . . . that format went from English first into Fortran . . . and then back into English, which sort of legitimizes its descent —Howard 1983

Legitimatize, while found with regularity, is used less often than are the other two words:

> The only reasons for placing this story in 1916 were to legitimatize the fact that every idea in it is shopworn, and to build sets —Pauline Kael, *New Yorker,* 21 Nov. 1970

> . . . a series of controversial court decisions in several states has already had the effect of legitimatizing trespass on beaches in certain common situations — Anthony Wolff, *Saturday Rev.,* 22 July 1978

> . . . perception and more broadly subjective experience had become legitimatized in mainstream American psychology —Howard E. Gruber, *N.Y. Times Book Rev.,* 8 Jan. 1984

lend 1. See LOAN, LEND.
2. Some of the commentators who want to discourage the use of *loan* as a verb go on to comment that only *loan* is a noun, not *lend.* Well, almost right but not quite. *Lend* is a noun, though not in ordinary American English. It has been in the language since the end of the 16th century, but was at first spelled *len* or *lenne,* acquiring its terminal *d* only in the 18th century (the *d* on the

verb *lend* is also unetymological). It seems to have been used chiefly on the outskirts of mainstream British English, in northern dialects, in Scotland, in Australia and New Zealand; one of our American citations is from an Irish-American milieu, so it may have been used in Irish English too.

> "Run out to Mrs. Mullins in the Front Room and ask her for the lend of her brass fender," she cried — Mary Lavin, *Atlantic,* June 1956

> "... Why don't you get the lend of a truck one night. ..." —Ross Franklyn, in *Coast to Coast: Australian Stories 1946*

lengthy   *Lengthy* started its career as a usage issue in the late 1700s, when British critics began to attack it as an Americanism. The first record of its use is from about a hundred years earlier. Among the 18th-century American writers who used it were Thomas Jefferson, John Adams, Alexander Hamilton, George Washington, and Benjamin Franklin:

> An unwillingness to read any thing about them if it appears a little lengthy —Benjamin Franklin, letter, 1773 (OED)

The British first regarded *lengthy* as an unneeded synonym for *long,* but they soon began to use it themselves:

> One most lengthy and perplext proposition —Jeremy Bentham, *Chrestomathia,* 1816 (OED)

> This address ... was unusually lengthy for him — Charles Dickens, *Pickwick Papers,* 1837 (OED)

The history of the early dispute was recounted in detail by Albert Mathews in an article published in *The Dial* in 1898. Mathews reported, among other things, that a British nobleman named Lord Harrowby defended *lengthy* as early as 1818, finding that it "imported what was tedious as well as long, an idea that no other English word seemed to convey as well." *Lengthy* became so firmly established in British usage during the 19th century that Mathews felt safe in concluding that "the controversy may be said long ago to have ended."

As it turns out, Mathews's conclusion was a bit premature. *Lengthy* has continued to appear sporadically in books on usage (most of them American) throughout the 20th century. Bierce 1909 thought that it was "no better than breadthy, or thicknessy," but later commentators have been more tolerant. A typical opinion can be found in Evans 1957: "*Lengthy* is largely restricted to speeches and writings and carries the reproachful suggestion that they are longer than they need be." The use of *lengthy* without connotations of tediousness is discouraged by several commentators, although Harper 1975, 1985 finds that it "does not necessarily imply tediousness." Bernstein 1965 also questions the strength of its "tedious" connotations; he asserts that "the meaning of *lengthy* is not at all sharp" and recommends avoiding it altogether.

Our evidence shows that *lengthy* does retain its "overlong, tedious" connotations in much modern use:

> ... the disadvantages of the lengthy and histrionic discussions such television may invite —*N.Y. Times Mag.,* 12 Sept. 1954

> They were given lengthy lectures on the importance of neatness and lettering —David Wellman, *Trans-Action,* April 1968

> Completion of a lengthy form ... is often followed by equally lengthy delays —Robin Prestage, *Saturday Rev.,* 1 Jan. 1972

But note that if *long* were substituted for *lengthy* in the above passages, the implications of tediousness would hardly be less. Harper and Bernstein are right in observing that *lengthy* does not always carry such implications. It can simply be a synonym of *long.* Most typically, it describes something that is long in a noteworthy way, whether because of tediousness or, very often, because of comprehensiveness:

> A lengthy discussion between him and Professor Richard ... promoted liturgical interest and knowledge throughout the Church —*Dictionary of American Biography,* 1936

> ... embarked upon lengthy studies of all aspects of therapeutic application of X-rays —*Current Biography 1949*

> Commission members launched a lengthy probe — Trevor Armbrister, *Saturday Evening Post,* 12 Feb. 1966

> ... to undergo lengthy training in programming — Herbert A. Simon, *Think,* May–June 1967

Our evidence also shows that its use in describing things other than speech and writing is common:

> ... on a short trip, much less a lengthy one —Georgene Pitman, *Ford Times,* November 1967

> ... would certainly involve lengthy delays —Richard Eells, "Pacem in Maribus," *A Center Occasional Paper,* June 1970

> Wars were neither organized nor lengthy —William Glasser, *Saturday Rev.,* 19 Feb. 1972

> ... its lengthy Christmas holidays —Donna Martin, *Change,* Winter 1972–73

Its use in describing physical objects, however, is relatively rare:

> He twirled his lengthy key chain —Don Davis, in *The Best from Yank,* 1945

The upshot of this lengthy discussion (which you may find either tedious or comprehensive) is that *lengthy* is a venerable synonym of *long* which has been used by excellent writers for about three centuries. You need not hesitate to use it yourself.

less, fewer   Here is the rule as it is usually encountered: *fewer* refers to number among things that are counted, and *less* refers to quantity or amount among things that are measured. This rule is simple enough and easy enough to follow. It has only one fault—it is not accurate for all usage. If we were to write the rule from the observation of actual usage, it would be the same for *fewer*: *fewer* does refer to number among things that are counted. However, it would be different for *less*: *less* refers to quantity or amount among things that are measured and to number among things that are counted. Our amended rule describes the actual usage of the past thousand years or so.

As far as we have been able to discover, the received rule originated in 1770 as a comment on *less*:

> This Word is most commonly used in speaking of a Number; where I should think *Fewer* would do bet-

ter. *No Fewer than a Hundred* appears to me not only more elegant than *No less than a Hundred,* but more strictly proper —Baker 1770

Baker's remarks about *fewer* express clearly and modestly—"I should think," "appears to me"—his own taste and preference. It is instructive to compare Baker with one of the most recent college handbooks in our collection:

> *Fewer* refers to quantities that can be counted individually.... *Less* is used for collective quantities that are not counted individually . . . and for abstract characteristics —Trimmer & McCrimmon 1988

Notice how Baker's preference has here been generalized and elevated to an absolute status, and his notice of contrary usage has been omitted. This approach is quite common in handbooks and schoolbooks; many pedagogues seem reluctant to share the often complicated facts about English with their students.

How Baker's opinion came to be an inviolable rule, we do not know. But we do know that many people believe it is such. Simon 1980, for instance, calls the "less than 50,000 words" he found in a book about Joseph Conrad a "whopping" error. And usage writers are not the only ones:

> In Dunedin, Fla., Margaret Rice objects to the use of "less" when "fewer" is meant —James J. Kilpatrick, *Hackensack* (N.J.) *Record,* 28 June 1985

The OED shows that *less* has been used of countables since the time of King Alfred the Great—he used it that way in one of his own translations from Latin—more than a thousand years ago (in about 888). So essentially *less* has been used of countables in English for just about as long as there has been a written English language. After about 900 years Robert Baker opined that *fewer* might be more elegant and proper. Almost every usage writer since Baker has followed Baker's lead, and generations of English teachers have swelled the chorus. The result seems to be a fairly large number of people who now believe *less* used of countables to be wrong, though its standardness is easily demonstrated.

In present-day written usage, *less* is as likely as or more likely than *fewer* to appear in a few common constructions. One of the most frequent is the *less than* construction where *less* is a pronoun. The countables in this construction are often distances, sums of money, units of time, and statistical enumerations, which are often thought of as amounts rather than numbers. Some examples:

> The odometer showed less than ten thousand miles —E. L. Doctorow, *Loon Lake,* 1979

> . . . he had somewhat less than a million to his name when he went to Washington —David Halberstam, *Harper's,* February 1971

> I was never in Europe for less than fourteen months at a time —James Thurber, letter, 18 July 1952

> . . . the present enrollment of less than three thousand students —John Fischer, *Harper's,* February 1971

> Her agency, less than 5 years old, is a smashing success —Donald Robinson, *Ladies' Home Jour.,* January 1971

> Begun with a capital of less than twenty pounds, it brought . . . financial security —*Current Biography,* December 1965

> . . . an allied people, today less than 50,000 in number —W. B. Lockwood, *A Panorama of Indo-European Languages,* 1972

> ". . . I've known you less than twenty-four hours. . . ." —Agatha Christie, *Why Didn't They Ask Evans?,* 1934

Fewer can be used in the same constructions, but it appears less often than *less.* It is sometimes used in such a way as to make one suspect that an editor rather than a writer is responsible for the *fewer.*

> . . . Dudek's car has fewer than 600 miles on the odometer —Rick Reilly, *Sports Illustrated,* 2 Dec. 1985

> . . . has never gained fewer than 1,222 yards in a season —Rick Telander, *Sports Illustrated,* 5 Sept. 1984

> From fewer than 15,000 in 1960, they reached 60,000 by 1970 —Norman Myers, *International Wildlife,* January/February 1982

Some contemporary usage writers (as Bernstein 1977, Chambers 1985, Cook 1987) concede that this use of *less* is acceptable.

The *no less than* construction noticed by Baker tends—over 200 years later—still to have *less* more often than *fewer:*

> . . . about 26,000 acres worked by no less than 1,800 slaves —*Times Literary Supp.,* 27 Aug. 1971

> The class of 1974 . . . included no less than 71 new Democrats —Tip O'Neill with William Novak, *Man of the House,* 1987

> I can remember no less than five occasions when.... —Noël Gilroy Annan, *ACLS Newsletter,* January–February 1969

> It is spoken by no less than 100 millions in Bengal and bordering areas —W. B. Lockwood, *A Panorama of Indo-European Languages,* 1972

Many of you have seen signs on the express lanes at supermarkets saying, "Twelve items or less"; and others, perhaps, may recall the contests in which a sentence was to be completed "in twenty-five words or less." *Less* is the choice in this construction:

> . . . readers are encouraged to keep their comments to 500 words or less —*Change,* January–February 1971

> . . . of all the millions of families in the country, two out of three consist of only three persons or less — Mark Abrams, *London Calling,* 9 Oct. 1952

> . . . and now know enough to create little fictions that in 30 seconds or less get right to the heart of desire itself —Mark Crispin Miller, *Johns Hopkins Mag.,* Winter 1984

Kilpatrick 1984 defends this *less* and the one just above. *Less* is again the choice in mathematical usage:

> 8 times 2 is less than 6 times 3 —Max A. Sabel et al., *Mathematics,* Book 1, 1977

> In the geometries of Bolyai and Lobachevski . . . the sum of the angles of a triangle is always less than 180° —Robert W. Marks, *The New Mathematics Dictionary and Handbook,* 1964

Less is also frequent when it follows a number:

> ... almost $10 million less than for 1969 —*Annual Report, Borg-Warner Corp.,* 1970

> Many bulls fought in Madrid weigh 100 kilos less —Tex Maule, *Sports Illustrated,* 29 July 1968

> ... at thirty-three on my part, and few years less on yours —Lord Byron, letter, 17 Nov. 1821

And of course it follows *one:*

> ... one less scholarship —Les A. Schneider, letter to the editor, *Change,* September 1971

> One less reporter —Don Cook, *Saturday Rev.,* 24 June 1978

Less is also frequently used to modify ordinary plural count nouns. You will notice from the following examples that in present-day English this usage appears to be more common in speech (and reported speech) than it is in discursive writing. It must also be conceded that some of the plural nouns in the examples were probably thought of as uncountable amounts rather than numbers.

> We have more and more wonderful means of saying things, and less and less wonderful things to say —Leslie Lieber, quoted in Einstein 1985

> ... Goldsmith took less pains than Pope ... to create images of luxury in the reader's mind —John Butt, *English Literature in the Mid-Eighteenth Century,* edited & completed by Geoffrey Carnall, 1979

> ... Americans pay less taxes than most of the inhabitants of developed countries —Robert Lekachman, quoted in *Center Mag.,* January–February 1970

> ... has considered advertising the fact that he has less commercials —Robert Lewis Shayon, *Saturday Rev.,* 20 Aug. 1966

> The less sodium you consume, the less drugs you're likely to need —Jane E. Brody, *N.Y. Times,* 11 July 1979

> Less gallons means that they sometimes have to up their rates —Jack Cooper, quoted in *N.Y. Times,* 29 Oct. 1979

> You have to make less mistakes —Victor Temkin, quoted in *N.Y. Times,* 4 May 1980

> There are fewer industries and less job openings —*Illustrated London News,* 31 Aug. 1968

> ... lower rates ... lazy days, and less crowds —L. Dana Gatilin, *Christian Science Monitor,* 23 Oct. 1979

> Less people exercise their right to vote —William Scranton, quoted in *Celebrity,* October 1976

> When there are several distinct but equivalent mathematical proofs, that proof which has less steps and/or utilizes less theorems is considered to be the more elegant —Nehemiah Jordan, *Themes in Speculative Psychology,* 1968

The examples above show native speakers and writers of English using *less* of count nouns in various constructions. *Fewer* could have been used in many of them—at times it might have been more elegant, as Robert Baker thought—but in others no native speaker would use anything but *less.* If you are a native speaker, your use of *less* and *fewer* can reliably be guided by your ear. If you are not a native speaker, you will find that the simple rule with which we started is a safe guide, except for the constructions for which we have shown *less* to be preferred.

lesser 1. Samuel Johnson in his 1755 dictionary aspersed the formation of *lesser* as a "barbarous corruption" because he considered it a double comparative (see DOUBLE COMPARISON). *Less* does serve as a comparative of *little,* and it did so in Middle English when *lesser* was formed. Whoever coined *lesser* seems to have considered *less* not a comparative of *little,* but an independent adjective meaning "unimportant." At any rate Johnson recognized that the irregularity of its formation had had no effect on its literary use; he presents citations from Spenser, Shakespeare, Bishop Burnet, John Locke, and Pope. The tenth edition (1880) of Goold Brown 1851 demonstrates at considerable length that some 19th-century American grammarians pruned Johnson's remarks down to the "barbarous corruption" part, omitting his mitigating comments—"adopted by poets, and then by writers of prose, till it has all the authority which a mode originally erroneous can derive from custom" (these words are partly from the 1755 edition and partly from a later one)—and then lumped *lesser* with *badder, gooder,* and *worser.* This sort of thing created a usage problem that sputtered through the 19th century and died out. Alford 1866 found *lesser* acceptable though irregular, and even Ayres 1881 gave it the nod of approval.

Though its propriety was a 19th-century issue, *lesser* still appears in some handbooks, usually paired with *less.* The handbooks tend to hold that *lesser* is used to indicate a difference in value or importance. The observation is broadly correct:

> ... would have turned any lesser man to madness or suicide —Robert Graves, *New Republic,* 21 Mar. 1955

> ... a virtuous woman, though she might be of lesser birth —Edith Sitwell, *Fanfare for Elizabeth,* 1946

> ... lesser conductors analyze music better than they used to —Virgil Thomson, *The Musical Scene,* 1947

> The discussion has been confined so far to the lesser ode, but most poets attempted the greater ode as well —John Butt, *English Literature in the Mid-Eighteenth Century,* edited & completed by Geoffrey Carnall, 1979

It is also used of numerical quantities in contexts where *smaller* or *lower* is more usual:

> So $1 million a day would be taken out for each day they bargain. They would be bargaining for a lesser amount each day —Peter Ueberroth, quoted in *Springfield* (Mass.) *Morning Union,* 2 Aug. 1985

It is also used of size. Such use was more common in the past than it is now; most present-day use for size is confined to names of plants and animals like *lesser celandine* or *lesser yellowlegs.*

> ... offered to share the booty, and having divided the money into two unequal heaps, and added a golden snuff-box to the lesser heap, he desired Mr. Wild to take his choice —Henry Fielding, *Jonathan Wild,* 1749

Perhaps degree rather than size is what is involved in an example like this one:

> ... those for whom the gravity of the *Rambler* has a lesser appeal —John Butt, *English Literature in the Mid-Eighteenth Century,* edited & completed by Geoffrey Carnall, 1979

2. The adverb *lesser* raises an occasional question too. Shakespeare used it several times in his plays. In present-day use it is limited to modifying past participles—especially *known*—to which it may or may not be joined by a hyphen.

> The lesser known is the epitaph on Ben Franklin's tombstone —Harper 1985

> ... the lesser-known places within America's National Park System —Horace Sutton, *Saturday Rev.,* 14 Apr. 1979

> ... the lesser privileged group of Argentina's population —*Current Biography 1949*

lest This conjunction is almost always followed by a verb in the subjunctive mood:

> It is an idea that cannot safely be compromised with, lest it be utterly destroyed —E. B. White, letter, 29 Nov. 1947

> Lest there be any doubt —Alan M. Dershowitz, *N.Y. Times Book Rev.,* 26 June 1983

> ... to be very wary lest one become an accomplice —Robert Stone, quoted in *Publishers Weekly,* 21 Mar. 1986

It can also be followed by a *should* clause, a construction that seems to have been more common in the past than it is now:

> ... lest it should betray her into any observations seemingly unhandsome —Jane Austen, *Mansfield Park,* 1814

> ... the anxiety of the socialists lest they should lose —*Times Literary Supp.,* 19 Mar. 1970

The use of a verb in the indicative mood following *lest* has occasionally been cited as an error. Our evidence shows that such usage does occur in standard writing, but it is atypical:

> ... lest the United States finds itself a virtual dictatorship —Adolph A. Berle, "The Power of the President," October 1970

> ... lest its drift is lost on us —Roger Owen, *Times Literary Supp.,* 14 May 1982

let 1. See LEAVE, LET.
2. *Let, let's.* There is a modicum of published opinion about *let* and *let's* used as imperatives that is concerned with the case—nominative or objective—of a following pronoun. Besides case, the problem is seen by some as also involving redundancy. Though the commentators have been at the subject since the 1920s—even Fowler 1926 made his contribution—they have not reached any consistent conclusions. We must turn, then, to a few serious grammarians—mostly to Jespersen 1909–49 but also to Quirk et al. 1985—for an insight or two.

Back in Middle English the first-person imperative with *let*—"let us go," to use Jespersen's example—began to compete with the older form, "go we." (The

two can be found side by side in Chaucer—there's an example at *let* in the OED—and in Shakespeare). As the *us* shows, the objective case of the pronoun followed *let.* Sometime around the middle of the 16th century the nominative pronoun begins to appear. Jespersen has an example from the play *Ralph Roister Doister* (ca. 1553):

> Let all these matters passe, and we three sing a song.

The OED has a 17th-century version of Malory with a "let we . . . ," and our files include a modern instance from Trinidad:

> ". . . a restaurant in Queen Street way we cud get good *dhal pourri* and chicken curry, let we go." —Samuel Selvon, *A Brighter Sun,* 1952

But the nominative is much more common when there are two members joined by *and:*

> ... let thee and I go on —John Bunyan, *Pilgrim's Progress,* 1678 (in Jespersen)

> ... let my dear and I talk the matter over —George Farquhar, *The Beaux Stratagem,* 1707 (in Jespersen)

The two members are often in apposition to *us* but are still nominative:

> ... let us make a covenant, I and thou —Genesis 31:44 (AV), 1611

> Let us go then, you and I —T. S. Eliot, "The Love Song of J. Alfred Prufrock," 1917

There are a couple of related constructions not involving *us:*

> Let fortune go to hell for it, not I —Shakespeare, *The Merchant of Venice,* 1597

> Let He who made thee answer that —Lord Byron, *Cain,* 1821 (in Jespersen)

Jespersen calls this last an instance of "relative attraction" because of the influence of *who,* and says that later editors changed *He* to *Him.* The pattern persists in modern English; here, for instance, is a comic-strip paraphrase of a famous passage (John 8:7) of the King James Bible:

> Let he who is without sin cast the first stone —Joe Martin, "Mister Boffo," 25 Oct. 1986

The reason for the appearance of nominative pronouns in place of the objective in all these constructions, says Jespersen, is that the pronoun has come to be perceived as the subject of the following infinitive rather than the object of *let.* He calls it a notional or virtual subject. The construction is not peculiar to English; Jespersen finds it with both nominative and objective pronouns in Danish, Norwegian, and Dutch—languages cognate with English.

And then we have *let's.* This contraction of *let us* is found only with the imperative use of *let.* It dates back at least to Shakespeare's time:

> If you deny to dance, let's hold more chat —*Love's Labour's Lost,* 1598

By the 20th century *let's* is frequently treated as a unit, rather than as a contraction, and then it takes a following pronoun. When the pronoun is *us,* the construction is criticized as redundant, especially by the earlier commentators. Quirk et al. 1985 characterizes *let's us* as "familiar American English."

Let's can also be followed by a pair of pronouns in either the nominative or the objective case; the constructions occur in both American and British English.

> Let's you and I take 'em on for a set —William Faulkner, *Sartoris,* 1929 (in OED Supplement)

> . . . let's you and I go together —Arthur Wing Pinero, *The Benefit of the Doubt,* 1895 (in Jespersen)

> Let's you and me duck out of here —John D. MacDonald, *The Brass Cupcake,* 1950 (in OED Supplement)

> . . . the resulting photograph was really amusing. The caption under it read, or so Liz quipped: "Lady Bird, after this is over, let's you and me go out and have a drink." —Lady Bird Johnson, *A White House Diary,* 1970

The commentators on this construction concern themselves solely with the propriety of the nominative-case pronouns; Evans 1957 points out that not one of them observes that either *you and me* or *you and I* after *let's* is just as redundant as *us.*

Now, what are we to make of all this? The main point is, as the evidence from *Ralph Roister Doister* to the present shows, that these are idiomatic constructions—no matter what the case of the pronoun—found almost exclusively in spoken English. You can use whichever of them sounds right to you wherever you would use speech forms in writing. You will probably not need any of them in anything you write that is at all removed from speech.

3. The negative of *let's* is formed in three ways: *let's not,* which is widely used; *don't let's,* which is chiefly found in British English; and *let's don't,* which is an Americanism. Nickles 1974 terms this last an outright illiteracy. This form is typical of speech and casual writing, of course, but Nickles's characterization of it will not do, as this example from one of the most resolutely literary men of his time shows:

> In all events, let's don't celebrate it until it has done something —Alexander Woollcott, letter, 26 Jan. 1918

let alone   The phrase *let alone* is used as a conjunction to introduce a contrasting example for purposes of emphasis. In sentences with a negative construction or negative overtones, its sense is close to "much less":

> ". . . Great to read but bloody to speak, let alone sing. . . ." —Robertson Davies, *The Lyre of Orpheus,* 1989

> . . . it does so much worse for a million others that I don't feel justified in worrying let alone complaining —Robert Frost, letter, November 1914

> This is no mean feat for any author, let alone one who is also a Harvard professor —Rosemary Herbert, *Publishers Weekly,* 23 Jan. 1987

> He discovered that it is difficult to find good farm hands at any price, let alone for the wages he could afford to pay —Jack Cook, *Blair & Ketchum's Country Jour.,* March 1983

It is less often used in positive contexts, where its meaning is close to "not to mention" or "as well as":

> . . . his interest in music led him to comb Flanders, let alone Italy, for . . . singers —J. H. Plumb, *The Italian Renaissance,* 1961

Vizetelly 1922 and Lincoln Library 1924 disapproved of this usage. No subsequent commentator—Krapp 1927, Opdyke 1939, Evans 1957, Bryant 1962, Bremner 1980, Einstein 1985—has agreed, so the issue can be called dead.

Evans, Bryant, and Bremner do agree, however, that *leave alone* is not standard in the same use. This opinion seems to be related to American sensitivity to *leave-let* substitutions that British commentators seem to ignore. Our evidence for *leave alone* in this function is quite sparse, and almost all of it is British. Here are a couple of examples:

> This argument . . . does not serve the author as a starting-point for prophecy, leave alone for any planning for Utopia —*Times Literary Supp.,* 6 Mar. 1943

> . . . Mr. McKenzie deplored the fact that, when his shop had been recently broken into, the thieves would not even burgle, leave alone buy, his books — Michael Barratt, *The Bookseller,* 1 June 1974

Our only example from an American source is from a television play reprinted in a seventh-grade textbook. But the author is an Englishman living in Canada, the flight of the title is between two Canadian cities, and the doctor who has this line is presumably Canadian, too:

> Can't buy one truck, leave alone forty —Arthur Hailey, "Flight into Danger" in *Introduction to Literature,* ed. Betty Yvonne Welch et al., 1981

We suspect that Americans simply do not use *leave alone* in this way. It seems to be only a rather rare variant in British English, but it does not appear to be substandard there.

let's   See LET 2.

level   **1.** *Noun.* Flesch 1964, Gowers in Fowler 1965, Follett 1966, Prentice Hall 1978, Bremner 1980, Howard 1980, and Bryson 1984 are all censorious of the use of *level* in the sense "position in a scale or rank." Several object at considerable length to this relatively innocuous term that writers and especially journalists find very handy. If you are inclined to be influenced by such epithets as *automatic, vague, clutter,* and *avoidable,* you may want to avoid this use of *level;* however, consider the following examples, and ask yourself if they would be substantially improved by revising to eliminate the word *level:*

> In fact, recent legislation passed at the federal, state, and local levels requires some participation by recipient groups in planning and monitoring health care —*Carnegie Quarterly,* Summer 1970

> Really funny writers are so rare that when they appear in quantity . . . the general level of wit goes up around them —Calvin Tomkins, *N.Y. Times Book Rev.,* 14 Dec. 1975

> Mr. Gardner writes at a fine level of sophistication, neither oversimplifying nor talking down —*New Yorker,* 3 Feb. 1973

> Their story of a young Baltimore lawyer harried to distraction by the demented unfairness of courts and judges is out of control. The decibel level is too high —Arthur M. Schlesinger, Jr., *Saturday Rev.,* December 1979

But if the macho style can be killing on a local, domestic level, it becomes almost suicidal on an international scale —Pete Hamill, *Cosmopolitan,* April 1976

At the White House level the Office of Budget Management has been working for two years on a new government publication —John Lear, *Saturday Rev.,* 15 Apr. 1972

Like to have, in the sense of almost or nearly, is common on the level of folk or Dialect speech —Harper 1975

Given a more lucid style, this hodgepodge . . . of precariously connected subjects could work on a kind of Vienna-guidebook-cum-People-magazine level — Caroline Seebohm, *N.Y. Times Book Rev.,* 1 July 1979

The complete avoidance of *level* in this sense seems hardly worth aiming for.

2. *Verb.* The transitive verb takes *at* when it suggests aiming:

The conduct of Harris so infuriated the men that some of them leveled their muskets at him —George V. Rogers, *New-England Galaxy,* Fall 1970

. . . echo the charges . . . leveled at Surrealism — Annette Michelson, *Evergreen,* August 1967

The intransitive sense "to deal frankly or openly" takes *with:*

. . . the girls in the office who leveled with him about what it means to work for a company riddled with brilliant men — *Women's Wear Daily,* 8 June 1972

levels of usage   Back in the 18th century the grammarians recognized only two kinds of English, right and wrong. A usage was right or wrong according to the criteria of the one judging, who sometimes took into account the opinions of his predecessors or contemporaries. Judgments were independent of such considerations as the status of the writer or the variety or purpose of the writing. But a more sophisticated approach was hinted at as early as Lowth 1762; he mentions, just in passing, the solemn and elevated style and the familiar style.

What Lowth's casual observations amounted to was the application of stylistic categories from classical English rhetoric to grammar. McKnight 1928 quotes from Sir Thomas Wilson's *Arte of Rhetorique* (1553): "There are three maners of stiles of enditinges, the great or mightie kinde, when we vse great wordes, or vehement figures. The small kinde, when wee moderate our heate by meaner wordes. . . . The lowe kinde, when we . . . goe plainly to worke and speake altogether in common wordes." Sir Thomas's *great, small,* and *low* contrast quaintly with the traditional levels of usage, *formal, informal,* and *substandard,* listed by Bailey 1984.

Bailey's are the levels of usage that most concerned usage commentators and English teachers in approximately the first half of the 20th century. The terms could vary—Roberts 1954 used *choice, general, vulgate,* for instance—but the categories remained essentially the same. Bailey's objection to the system is its tendency, being arranged in a sequence of *best, good, bad,* to cause people to choose the hardest or longest word as the best word and hence to produce gobbledygook. McKnight notes the same tendency in 16th century writers: the low

or plain style with its lack of rhetorical figures was considered vulgar.

The usual set of usage categories was attacked by John S. Kenyon in *College English* (October 1948). Kenyon's thesis was that the usual levels of usage confused cultural levels—standard and nonstandard—with functional varieties of English, such as formal or familiar. Kenyon found the confusion common in his own earlier writings and in that of many of the best-known writers on usage.

Later commentators have found Kenyon's analysis somewhat oversimplified, but it seems to have had an effect—the few recent handbooks that we find mentioning levels of usage (McMahan & Day 1984, for instance) tend to stick to functional varieties. A more elaborate attempt to deal with these questions can be found in Martin Joos, *The Five Clocks* (1952).

See also FORMAL; INFORMAL.

liable   **1.** When *liable* means "responsible" and is followed by a prepositional phrase, the preposition is *for:*

. . . each alleged conspirator can be held liable for the statements and actions of the other conspirators — Herbert L. Packer, *N.Y. Rev. of Books,* 6 Nov. 1969

. . . a general partner liable for any excess of liabilities over the paid-in capital —*Dun's,* October 1971

When it means "in a position to incur," *to* is used:

Outside of eating with a sharp knife, there is no rule in the Book that lays you liable to as much criticism —Will Rogers, *The Illiterate Digest,* 1924

. . . will render a man liable to certain diseases of the personality —John Butt, *English Literature in the Mid-Eighteenth Century,* edited & completed by Geoffrey Carnall, 1979

2. *Liable, apt, likely.* These three words are often used in the same construction—with *to* and an infinitive following—and in meanings that are very nearly synonymous. Usage commentators began to insist on discriminating between them as far back as Richard Grant White 1870. White's chief object of concern was *apt,* but he threw in a shot at *liable* in passing. Ayres 1881 mentioned them both, and so did Vizetelly 1906 and Bierce 1909. White insisted that *apt* and *liable* be restricted to inherent characteristics of persons while *likely* was appropriate for what Vizetelly called "contingent events." The following citations from Oliver Wendell Holmes illustrate usages that Richard Grant White would have found acceptable. *Apt* is applied to a person and suggests an inherent quality. *Liable* too is applied to a person and carries the notion of being subject to something not especially desirable.

Little localized powers, and little narrow streaks of specialized knowledge, are things men are very apt to be conceited about —*The Autocrat of the Breakfast-Table,* 1857

. . . the man who thinks his wife, his baby, his house, his horse, his dog, and himself severally unequalled, is almost sure to be a good-humored person, though liable to be tedious at times —*The Autocrat of the Breakfast-Table,* 1857

Bierce went his own way. His rejection of *apt* was based on senses of *apt* not relevant to the construction he disliked, and his rejection of *liable* was based on its supposedly requiring *to* and a noun, not *to* and an infinitive. Much present-day criticism tends to be rather an amalgam of Bierce and his predecessors; irrelevant senses of both *apt* and *liable* are brought in for discussion, and Richard Grant White's analysis is still used. The majority of recent opinion accepts *apt* as broadly synonymous with *likely*. A few still bother with *apt,* and when they do you can see the ghost of Richard Grant White:

> *Apt* is more specific in meaning than *likely* and should be used only to indicate that its subject has a natural tendency to err or do something undesirable —Heritage 1982

Most commentators, however, expend the greater part of their critical efforts on *liable*. The emphasis is on the undesirable aspect of whatever it is that follows *liable,* although this aspect tends to be somewhat exaggerated by examples in which boilers are liable to explode. The disastrous is not required; Oliver Wendell Holmes gave us only tediousness. You might also note that the exploding boiler standard overlooks Richard Grant White's insistence that *liable* be used of a person; this aspect of his analysis is generally overlooked by recent commentators.

Let's begin with a few examples of *likely* which no one criticizes and everybody recommends. They can perhaps serve us as a sort of benchmark by which to judge examples of *apt* and *liable*. We think they present contexts in which different writers might have used *apt* or *liable.*

> . . . that man is always susceptible to phony religions, and that he is likely to further an epidemic by mistaking it for a religious activity —Robert B. Heilman, in *The Range of English,* 1968

> . . . strange subjective experiences, and because they are strange they are also likely to be upsetting —*Trans-Action,* March 1968

> If the student with limited ability fails to gain admission to a prestige college, the parents are likely to blame the public school —James B. Conant, *Slums and Suburbs,* 1961

> She is a down-to-earth woman who is likely to shake her head at being celebrated as "a living legend" —*Current Biography,* February 1968

> . . . my interests being what they are I am not likely to make even a good start —Charlton Laird, in *The Range of English,* 1968

Now we come to *apt.* The OED shows that the criticized construction with *apt* goes back to the 16th century, as does that with *liable*. It would appear that these constructions have an unbroken history of use. It also seems likely that they have been more common in speech and casual writing than in the more serious kinds of writing. We think the older examples here are not much different from the more recent ones:

> Not till the fiddles are in tune, pray, sir. Your lady's strings are apt to fly, I can tell you that, if they are wound up too hastily —Sir John Vanbrugh, *The Relapse,* 1696

> I am too apt to be negligent —Samuel Johnson, letter, 16 July 1754

> I wish, however, that the instrument might be less apt to decay, and that signs might be permanent —Samuel Johnson, Preface to the Dictionary, 1755

> Solitary reading is apt to give the headache —Charles Lamb, letter, 26 Feb. 1808

> . . . the danger is that we are apt to be huddled forward into all sorts of new expressions of no particular value —Leacock 1943

> . . . discovering the Church is apt to be a slow procedure —Flannery O'Connor, letter, 16 July 1957

If we remember that what is undesirable or unwanted is not necessarily a disaster of large proportions, we will find that *liable* is rather more often used of the undesirable than not:

> We have no reason to be sure that we shall then be no longer liable to offend against God —Samuel Johnson, 1777, in James Boswell, *Life of Samuel Johnson,* 1791

> . . . it seems to me that their cause is, I do not say, desperate, but liable to be overturned at what would seem to be a small thing —Henry Adams, letter, 23 Apr. 1863

> . . . I am so liable to say what I do not mean —Lewis Carroll, letter, 9 June 1879

> The simpler the word, the more liable I am to come up with a rare spelling —Flannery O'Connor, letter, 3 Mar. 1954

> . . . the pastor must set an example, he must illustrate his morality in public; and this is liable to result in hypocrisy —Edmund Wilson, *A Piece of My Mind,* 1956

> . . . images and association which would be suggestive to Japanese readers are liable to be meaningless to English readers —*Times Literary Supp.,* 22 Oct. 1971

> She is not as prone to fight with other dogs, and is less liable to stray —*The Complete Dog Book,* 1980

We do have good evidence of *liable* as simply synonymous with *likely:*

> "It's all kudu country," Pop said. "You're liable to jump one anywhere." —Ernest Hemingway, *Green Hills of Africa,* 1935

> . . . the parrot does not act as if it is liable to say anything important in the next hour —Damon Runyon, *Runyon à la Carte,* 1944

> . . . between these two dates, when most of the summer visitors are liable to be handy —Eleanor Sterling, *Yankee,* July 1968

> I am not liable to reach the city again though I consider myself very good on crutches —Flannery O'Connor, letter, 24 Nov. 1956

> Even while observing Arab etiquette . . . he is liable to drape an arm across royal shoulders and boom, "Well, your Excellency, how's the doubles game? . . ." —J. D. Reed, *Sports Illustrated,* 17 Nov. 1980

Our conclusion is that, except in the handbooks, which seem simply to repeat their predecessors, this is essentially a dead issue. Both *apt* and *liable* are still synonyms of *likely,* as they have been for some 400 years now. *Liable* is still more frequently used of things that are undesirable.

One curious note: to make a negative compound, you need *likely:*

> . . . any action . . . is liable, and not at all unlikely, to be blamed by *somebody* —Lewis Carroll, letter 21 Sept. 1893

liaise This back-formation from *liaison* is not as new a word as might be supposed; the OED Supplement includes a citation for it from 1928. It was originally a military word, but by the 1940s it appears to have become fairly well established in more general use among the British:

> 'To liaise' . . . was at first frowned on by the pundits: its usefulness . . . soon came to outweigh its objectionableness —*New Statesman,* 1 Aug. 1942 (OED Supplement)

The meaning of *liaise* can be either "to act as a liaison officer" or "to establish liaison." Its occurrence in British English is now common and unremarkable:

> . . . a school-based social worker to liaise with the social services department —*Times Educational Supp.,* 23 Nov. 1973

> . . . while liaising between management and men —Jeremy Kingston, *Punch,* 20 Mar. 1974

> Part of his job was to liaise between the unions and political leaders —*Daily Mirror* (London), 13 Nov. 1974

> . . . employed ombudsmen to liaise between journalists and their offended public —*The Economist,* 26 Apr. 1985

But in American English *liaise* is a very uncommon verb, and its occasional use still draws ridicule:

> Mr. Reagan has not yet committed the sin of verbifying his "layizon." Some bureaucrats talk of arranging for their agencies to "liaise with" others. . . . In Reaganese, that would be pronounced "laze with" —Safire 1984

liaison With its French origin and unusual sequence of vowels, *liaison* is inevitably going to present a puzzle to some people when it comes time to pronounce it. And, in fact, a bewildering array of pronunciations of this word can be found in our files. The two most common pronunciations in American English are \\ˈlē-ə-ˌzän\\ and \\lē-ˈā-ˌzän\\, both of which are established in standard speech. The variant \\ˈlā-ə-ˌzän\\ is well entrenched in the military, but in other circles it is widely regarded as an error. Its use by Ronald Reagan, for example, is criticized by Safire 1984.

The spelling of *liaison* also gives many people trouble. The tendency is to drop the second *i:*

> . . . permanent liason officer to the International Control Commission —*Village Voice,* 28 Feb. 1968

This error is rare in edited prose, but it is easily made in casual writing.

library See FEBRUARY.

lie See LAY, LIE.

lighted, lit A puzzled editor recently wrote to ask about the acceptability of *lighted* versus *lit* as past and past participle of *light,* both in general and in reference to stage lighting in particular. His letter was prompted by one of his authors—a university professor—who claimed that only *lighted* was proper; *lit* should be reserved for drunks.

The professor is right about drunks, but wrong otherwise. Both *lit* and *lighted* are acceptable and standard, and have been all along. The evidence in the Merriam-Webster files shows both forms to be used about equally. A few of the handbooks opine that *lighted* may be more frequent in adjectival use ("a clean, well-lighted place"), but even here our evidence shows about equal use of both forms. We have reputable citations for "a lit cigar" and "a lighted cigar" and "a lit window" and "a lighted window." The matter, then, is simply one of the author's preference—choose whichever sounds better in a given context.

Lit seems to have been originally called into question by a grammarian—perhaps William Ward—who in 1765 opined that it was "rather low." His opinion must have been repeated with some frequency; in an anonymous American handbook of 1869 entitled *Vulgarisms and Other Errors of Speech* we find "'The gas is *lit*,' is often said, instead of, 'The gas is *lighted.*' The word *lit* may be used as a colloquialism, but it should not be written, unless in representing conversation." In spite of the fact that modern handbooks and dictionaries recognize both *lit* and *lighted* as standard, someone must be repeating the old condemnation, with the confusion of others as a result:

> On the technical level, *Joe* is poorly shot, sloppily edited and miserably lit (lighted?) —Susan Rice, *Media & Methods,* October 1970

light-year In scientific usage, a light-year is a unit of distance equal to about 5,878,000,000,000 miles, the distance light travels in one year in the vacuum of space. But nonscientists sometimes have trouble thinking of a "year" as anything other than a unit of time:

> When I saw this interaction, I realized we are 50 light-years behind —Marya Mannes, quoted in *Harper's Weekly,* 11 Apr. 1975

> . . . ended six years, and several political light-years, ago —Michael Harrington, *N.Y. Times Book Rev.,* 26 Sept. 1976

> . . . has been taken for granted in the United States for light years —Margaret de Miraval, *Christian Science Monitor,* 16 Mar. 1981

> It seems light years ago that Scott Fitzgerald rhapsodized the lissome girls in grown-up gowns —*People,* 11 Oct. 1982

Such usage is not common in standard writing (although it may be growing more so), and it naturally attracts disapproval from the astronomically educated. It should not be confused with the widespread and established figurative use of *light-year* to mean "a very great distance," with the "distance" referred to typically being more cultural than physical:

> . . . it is light-years away from anything ever tried before —John Fischer, *Harper's,* February 1971

> They are two minutes and yet light-years away from the crowded village —Suzanne Patterson, *Gourmet,* June 1979

> . . . the world of music and the world of books were light-years apart —Ray Walters, *N.Y. Times Book Rev.,* 13 Sept. 1981

like, as, as if   1. *Conjunction.* Those who are old enough may still remember an American cigarette commercial back in the 1950s and early 1960s that contained the line "Winston tastes good, like a cigarette should." This line provoked a considerable controversy in the popular press, which is probably what the advertising agency hoped to achieve. The controversy lasted quite a long while, passing from the newspapers to magazines to usage books. Even the editors of the *New Yorker* took note of it:

> We hope Sir Winston Churchill, impeccable, old-school grammarian that he is, hasn't chanced to hear American radio or television commercials recently. It would pain him dreadfully, we're sure, to listen to the obnoxious and ubiquitous couplet "Winston tastes good, like a cigarette should." That pesky "like" is a problem for us Americans to solve, we guess, and anyway Sir Winston has his own problems —*New Yorker,* 26 May 1956

That pesky *like* seems not to have bothered the impeccable, old-school grammarian as he dealt with his other problems:

> We are overrun by them, like the Australians were by rabbits —Sir Winston Churchill (in Longman 1984)

So what is the problem with this pesky *like?* Is it a solecism typical of the uneducated? Some commentators think so:

> *Like* has long been widely misused by the illiterate; lately it has been taken up by the knowing and the well-informed, who find it catchy, or liberating, and who use it as though they were slumming —Strunk & White 1959, 1972, 1979

Let's take a look at the history of conjunctive *like* and see if Strunk & White's opinion is right.

Conjunctive *like* was for some time thought to have originated in the 16th century, or perhaps earlier, as a shortening of an older compound conjunction *like as.* But newer information published in the Middle English Dictionary shows that *like* by itself was used as a conjunction as long ago as *like as* was—from the late 14th century. It first turned up around 1380 in an anonymous work named *Cleanness* where it is used to mean approximately "as if." Chaucer used it in about 1385 to introduce a full clause in *The Complaint of Mars.* Both "as" and "as if" uses are attested in the 15th century—by James I of Scotland, Malory, Lydgate—and in the 16th—by Sir Thomas North, Lord Berners, Sir Thomas Elyot. In 1608 or 1609 Shakespeare (or his collaborator) used it to introduce a full clause near the end of the first scene of *Pericles:*

> ANTIOCHUS.   As thou
> Wilt live, fly after; and, like an arrow shot
> From a well-experienc'd archer hits the mark
> His eye doth level at, so thou ne'er return
> Unless thou say Prince Pericles is dead.

Shakespeare also used conjunctive *like* followed by a nominative pronoun:

> And yet no man like he doth grieve my heart —
> *Romeo and Juliet,* 1595

So we can say this much about conjunctive *like:* in the 14th, 15th, and 16th centuries it was used in serious literature, but not often. Shakespeare's use may be typical:

he uses *like* as verb, noun, adjective, adverb, and preposition with considerable frequency, but conjunctive *like* seldom.

Evidence from the 17th and 18th centuries is not plentiful either. And in these centuries it comes mostly from nonliterary works, including less formal sources such as letters and journals. This suggests that conjunctive *like* may be primarily a speech form only occasionally used in print. It might also suggest that the evidence has simply not been dug out yet. Otto Jespersen refers to examples produced by that indefatigable digger Fitzedward Hall in an 1892 article in *The Nation;* these include additional 16th-century evidence and citations from Dryden and others.

In the 19th and 20th centuries conjunctive *like* becomes much more common; Jespersen 1909–49 (vol. 5) tells us that "examples abound" and lists them from Keats, Emily Brontë, Thackeray, George Eliot, Dickens, Kipling, Bennett, Gissing, Wells, Shaw, Maugham, and others. So we must conclude that Strunk & White's relegation of conjunctive *like* to misuse by the illiterate is uninformed.

Where did the idea that *like* as a conjunction is an illiteracy come from? We are not sure. We do know that *like* became a subject of dispute in England during the 19th century. Jespersen cites an account by the English philologist Frederick Furnivall in his memoirs of an argument Furnivall had with Tennyson on the subject. Tennyson had corrected Prince Albert for using conjunctive *like;* he thought the use was recent, and incorrect. Furnivall pointed out that it was to be found in Shakespeare. Alford 1866 was an early commentator who also found conjunctive *like* "quite indefensible."

In America the earliest mention of the subject comes from Noah Webster's *Rudiments of English Grammar,* 1790. Webster included the sentence "He thinks like you do" in an 8-page list of "improper and vulgar expressions." A Philadelphia schoolmaster, Joseph Hutchins, followed in 1791. Joseph Hervey Hull, in an 1828 grammar, included the sentence "It feels like it has been burned" in a list like Webster's. Hull added a new construction to the controversy, but we don't know if he realized it. And we are not even sure that Webster originated the dispute. Apparently few other 19th-century grammarians noticed this use. Some 19th-century American commentators who opposed *like* for *as* are Bache 1869, Richard Grant White 1870, and Long 1888.

Although 19th-century commentators were in substantial agreement on this matter, the dictionaries were not quick to take it up. The conjunctive use of *like* was not controversial in the 18th century, and Samuel Johnson's *Dictionary* of 1755 had *like as* under the adverb entry; there was no preposition or conjunction. Webster 1828 and Worcester's Dictionary simply followed Johnson. The conjunction was unrecognized until the Century Dictionary entered it in 1889, with quotations from Shakespeare and Darwin and commentary from James Russell Lowell, who ascribed its use to Henry VIII and Charles I of England. Webster 1890 had no entry for a conjunction, but noted that one sense of the adverb was regarded by some grammarians as a preposition. Funk & Wagnalls 1890 entered the conjunctive use as sense 2 of the adverb, labeled it *Colloq.,* and added a quotation from Colonel John S. Mosby of Civil War fame. Webster 1909 recognized the conjunctive use in a synonymy note, calling it a provincialism and contrary to good usage.

The objection to conjunctive *like,* then, appears to be a 19th-century reaction to increased conjunctive use at that time, and the objectors were chiefly commentators on usage rather than grammarians or lexicographers. After World War I all three of these groups got in step to present a united front on the issue: it was incorrect to use *like* for *as* or *as if; like* was a preposition, not a conjunction. Webster's Second 1934 includes a thorough condemnation (Strunk & White's "illiterate" may have come from this source), which appears to be a digest of a number of heated opinions. It was inserted, we are embarrassed to say, in spite of copious evidence of standard use then in our files.

It might be useful here to give some examples of conjunctive *like* in typical contexts. Most of these are 20th-century examples, with a few earlier ones thrown in as a reminder of the historical dimension of this usage. They typify the chief constructions in which we find conjunctive *like*—and some of them seem to have eluded the commentators.

Since the "as if" sense seems to be the earliest attested, we will start with it. It is mostly used to introduce a full clause:

> ... the bustle and confusion of a railroad, where people are whirled along slam bang to eternal smash, like they were so many bales and boxes of dry-goods —William Tappan Thompson, "The Hoosier and the Salt Pile," 1848, in *The Mirth of a Nation,* ed. Walter Blair & Raven I. McDavid, Jr.,1983

> Seemed like I'd die if I couldn't scratch —Mark Twain, *Huckleberry Finn,* 1884

> But we soon felt like we knew each other —Will Rogers, *The Illiterate Digest,* 1924

> When they worked she looked like she had moles burrowing under her hide —Jessamyn West, *Atlantic,* July 1944

> ... it sounded like something came for the dog through the brush —Conrad Richter, *Atlantic,* January 1946

> ... and it looked like we were a pretty good combination —Harry S. Truman, quoted in Merle Miller, *Plain Speaking,* 1973

> ... looking like it aimed to run right through the shed —William Faulkner, *The Town,* 1957

> His face looked like it had been slicked down the middle and not put together right —Flannery O'Connor, letter, 20 Mar. 1961

> ... middle-aged men who looked like they might be out for their one night of the year —Norman Mailer, *Harper's,* November 1968

> She felt like I was talking to her —William L. Shirer, *The Nightmare Years,* 1984

> ... the back wheels spinning, stones flying like they were shot from guns —Garrison Keillor, *Lake Wobegon Days,* 1985

> ... you wake like someone hit you on the head —T. S. Eliot, "Sweeney Agonistes," 1932 (in OED Supplement)

> Her voice sounds like it could have levelled buildings and parted the waters —Robert Palmer, *Rolling Stone,* 12 Oct. 1972

> I remember that scene like it was yesterday —Tip O'Neill with William Novak, *Man of the House,* 1987

This sense of *like* seems especially common after verbs like *feel, look,* and *sound. Like* "as if" is also used in a few common short idiomatic phrases where it is followed by an adjective, especially *mad* or *crazy,* and the phrase is used adverbially:

> Thence by coach; with a mad coachman, that drove like mad —Samuel Pepys, diary, 13 June 1663

> And other writers were in the library studying like mad —William Stafford, *Writing the Australian Crawl,* 1978

> ... Brooks and friends are horsing around like crazy —Stanley Kauffmann, *Before My Eyes,* 1980

Like in the sense "as" occurs in four constructions, three of which are closely related. The first—this is the single most heavily criticized use of *like*—is to introduce a full clause:

> I expect we shall shortly carry our knives and forks, like the Chinese do their chop sticks, in our pockets —Washington Irving, *Morning Chronicle* (New York), 22 Jan. 1803

> Nobody will miss her like I shall —Charles Dickens, letter, 7 Jan. 1841 (in Jespersen)

> We go into litigation instinctively, like a young duck goes into the water —Mark Twain, *Morning Call* (San Francisco), 15 Sept. 1864

> Do you still recite, like you used to? —Arnold Bennett, *Hilda Lessways,* 1911

> Just like you used to be —Willa Cather, *O Pioneers!,* 1913

> ... I can go hungry again like I have gone hungry before —Carl Sandburg, *Smoke and Steel,* 1920

> ... instead of being embarrassed by the waiter, like he used to be —Sinclair Lewis, *Babbitt,* 1922

> ... second-rate people like we are hang about afraid of the plain conclusions of our own brains —H. G. Wells, *Mr. Blettsworthy on Rampole Island,* 1928

> Sir Oswald played bridge, like he did everything else, extremely well —Agatha Christie, *The Seven Dials Mystery,* 1929

> ... "you little know how surprised you ought to be to see me here" as Robert Bridges said (just like Bernard Haggin does) —Randall Jarrell, letter, November 1947

> I expected him to look a little haunted, like Humphrey sometimes used to —Angus Wilson, *Death Dance,* 1957

> ... just scratches him off like the old dog does fleas —William Faulkner, 15 Feb. 1957, in *Faulkner in the University,* 1959

> ... he's only just now hitting twenty, like we all are —Colin MacInnes, *Absolute Beginners,* 1959

> He has dark black-Irish good looks like a poet should —Herbert Gold, *Los Angeles Times Book Rev.,* 23 May 1971

> Well, as I told you, I did that just like I did everything else —Harry S. Truman, in Merle Miller, *Plain Speaking,* 1973

... she might not be an early riser, like he is —Jay McInerney, *Bright Lights, Big City,* 1984

As parents you may be wondering, like I do on frequent occasions —Charles, Prince of Wales, quoted in *N.Y. Times Mag.,* 28 Sept. 1986

The second construction is the sneakiest one. It is the one in which *like* introduces a clause from which the verb—and sometimes even more—has been omitted. The verb is usually to be understood from the preceding clause. This *like* is often taken to be a preposition because there is no following verb. The classic example of this construction is "He takes to it like a duck to water." Here are some more:

... as if it followed like the night the day, that "language is a living thing. ..." —Simon 1980

It is intended to stop all debate, like the previous question in the General Court —Oliver Wendell Holmes d. 1894, *The Autocrat of the Breakfast-Table,* 1857

Here I am, Madam, gazing whole hours at the Maison quarrée, like a lover at his mistress —Thomas Jefferson, letter, 20 Mar. 1787

I've had my share of criticism, but for the most part it has rolled off me like water off a duck —Tip O'Neill with William Novak, *Man of the House,* 1987

... so I stared at it, like Kant at his church steeple, for half an hour —F. Scott Fitzgerald, *The Great Gatsby,* 1925

... are related to those of Africa, like those of the Galapagos to America —Charles Darwin, *On the Origin of Species by Means of Natural Selection,* 1859

... until it sat like a walnut in icing —E. L. Doctorow, *Ragtime,* 1975

Such wits as he are, to a company of reasonable men, like rooks to the gamesters —William Wycherly, *The Country Wife,* 1675

... the fog began to rise and seemed to be lifted up from the water like the curtain at a playhouse —Benjamin Franklin, *Autobiography,* 1788

In the third construction, all of the following clause is omitted except its subject. If the subject is a noun, it is hard to tell whether *like* is a conjunction or only a preposition. In these three examples you might argue either way:

Philip d'Arteveld then kept a great stable of good horses like a great prince —Lord Berners, translation of Froissart's *Chronicles,* 1523

... she fries better than she did, but not like Jenny —Jane Austen, letter, 7 Jan. 1807

Like tuna, halibut are large fish —John E. Warriner, *English Grammar and Composition* (Second Course), 1982

But when the subject is a pronoun, the nominative case may tip off the use of the conjunction:

... there are still a few who, like thou and I, drink nothing but water —Tobias Smollett, translation of *Gil Blas,* 1749

... the poet, like you and I, dear reader —W. H. Auden, quoted in *Time,* 2 Feb. 1948

... she, like they, was one of the last of that Anglo-American cultural aristocracy —John Henry Raleigh, *New Republic,* 5 Apr. 1954

... [the Russians] like we, have a common interest in avoiding war —Prime Minister Harold Macmillan, quoted in *Springfield* (Mass.) *Union* (UPI), 20 Mar. 1959

... even if they, like we, have a few problems with electronic processing equipment —*Los Angeles Times,* 28 Sept. 1983

The fourth use of conjunctive *like* is another one that is often overlooked by the critics; it is the construction in which *like* is followed by a prepositional phrase:

The color was awful, like in bad MGM musicals — Pauline Kael, *Harper's,* February 1969

Like on most boats, there was a multitude of concealed storage places —Jimmy Sangster, *Blackball,* 1987

"... It's a backdrop of L.A., like on the Johnny Carson show." —*New Yorker,* 14 Nov. 1983

... just like under the present scheme —*The Age* (Melbourne), 25 Apr. 1975

... like in a Charlton Heston movie —George Vecsey, *N.Y. Times,* 1 May 1983

... just like in the movies —Michael Walker, *Metropolitan Home,* March 1984

These examples should suffice to show that conjunctive *like* is widely used in standard English prose, and that it is used in some constructions where it goes unnoticed—as it is in the citation from Simon 1980; Simon in the same book takes another writer to task for using conjunctive *like.* They also show that although it occurs in many literary sources, it is almost always used where a construction that is primarily a speech form may be used appropriately. If you keep that in mind, you are not likely to go wrong.

To summarize the controversy: *like* has been in use as a conjunction for more than 600 years. Its beginnings are literary, but the available evidence shows that it was fairly rare until the 19th century. A noticeable increase in use during the 19th century provoked the censure we are so familiar with. Still, the usage has never been less than standard, even if primarily spoken.

The belief that *like* is a preposition but not a conjunction has entered the folklore of usage. Handbooks, schoolbooks, newspaper pundits, and well-meaning friends for generations to come will tell you all about it. Be prepared.

Never mind those purists who can't stand the way America talks —Flesch 1983, at *like*

It is an amusing reflection on the repugnance that conjunctive *like* can evoke that almost from the beginning of the controversy, some commentators have theorized that the usage was characteristic of a particular region—almost always a region other than their own. As long ago as 1836 the Boston *Pearl* (a newspaper presumably) ascribed "like you do" to Southerners. In 1867 James Russell Lowell in the Introduction to the *Biglow Papers,* second series, commented, "*Like* for *as* is never used in New England but is universal in the South and West." A respondent to the survey of Crisp 1971 said the conjunction *like* was standard in the South but not in the North. Brander Matthews 1901 described conjunctive *like* as a Briticism, "very prevalent" among both the educated and the uneducated. W. Nelson Francis, in *The English Language* (1963), called it standard in England and the American South. British observers have disagreed. Mittins 1970 reported a British commentator, G. H. Vallins, calling the usage an Americanism. A British writer in the *New York Times* (7 May 1978) thought that *like* and *as* were hopelessly muddled in the minds of most Americans. Sellers 1975 says "It may be acceptable as colloquial American, but it is still not accepted as English." Swan 1980 describes it as "Informal American." Our evidence shows that the usage is not unusual in British English but is more common in American English.

2. *Preposition.* The frequent adjuration against conjunctional *like* is believed to have frightened some people into using *as* for all purposes, even for a preposition. This sort of overreaction is called hypercorrection, and it has given the commentators an additional usage to condemn when they have finished with conjunctive *like*. Here are a couple of samples drawn from handbooks:

> He was built as a swordfish —Ernest Hemingway (in Fennell 1980)

> ... the Basenji is the size of a fox-terrier and cleans itself as a cat —Natalie Winslow, *Providence Sunday Journal*, 17 Jan. 1971 (in Perrin & Ebbitt 1972)

Like is what the handbooks prescribe for these. Here are a few from our files:

> Delicate problems as this are pivotal factors in establishing enduring leadership —Joseph A. Jones, *Exporters' Digest and International Trade Rev.*, October 1951

> New York, as most major cities, has found that the general public is very apathetic —*N.Y. Times*, 12 Oct. 1970

> ... beaches do not naturally smell as rotten eggs — *Massachusetts Audubon News Letter*, April 1971

You could argue plausibly that each of these is a hypercorrection, but what could you say about the following?

> Golden lads and girls all must,
> As chimney sweepers, come to dust ...
> —Shakespeare, *Cymbeline,* 1610

> O God, I thanke thee, that I am not as other men — Luke 18:11 (Geneva Bible), 1560

Prepositional *as,* then is not a modern phenomenon, born in holy terror of using *like. As* has been used prepositionally, in one way or another, since the 13th century. But it probably is used hypercorrectly some of the time. In all of the examples from our files, we would recommend *like*—and especially for the passage about the beaches that smell "as rotten eggs." *Like* would eliminate speculation about the olfactory apparatus of rotten eggs.

like, such as The few commentators who mention *like* and *such as* express rather diverse opinions. Little, Brown 1980, 1986 and Sellers 1975 make a distinction between the two, reserving *such as* for examples and *like* for resemblances. Little, Brown prefers that *such as* not

be divided by the noun for which examples are to be supplied: "such saxophonists as Ben Webster and Coleman Hawkins" does not meet their approval. Kilpatrick 1984 does not care if *such as* is divided or not, but he does not want *like* used in its place. *Winners & Sinners,* 27 Apr. 1987, on the other hand, does not want *such as* used before a single example; *like* is to be used there. Bernstein 1971 and Follett 1966 think that the example-resemblance distinction is too fine to worry about; Bernstein describes those who do worry about it as nit-pickers. Kilpatrick says Follett and Bernstein are wrong.

The fact that opinions vary so greatly on this matter is enough to suggest that standard usage itself varies a good deal. We think that Bernstein and Follett are right here and that the issue of ambiguity, which evidently underlies the thinking of those who urge the distinction, is probably much overblown. In the examples that follow, the quotation from Emily Post is clearly an example of *like* used for resemblance; that from Guth is an example of *like* used for examples. In the passages from Copperud and Flannery O'Connor, you cannot be sure whether examples or resemblances are intended, but the meaning of each sentence works out to be the same under either interpretation. And in none of the examples that follow can you detect any ambiguity of meaning, either as they are written with *like* or as they would read if you substituted *such as:*

> "Attended" instead of "went to" is taboo with people like Mrs. Worldly —Emily Post, *Etiquette,* 1927

> ... and you get more benefit reading someone like Hemingway, where there is apparently a hunger for a Catholic completeness in life —Flannery O'Connor, letter, 16 Jan. 1956

> Phrases like *three military personnel* are irreproachable and convenient —Copperud 1964

> It has been used in advertising copy like the following —Harper 1975, 1985

> Avoid clipped forms like *bike, prof, doc* —Guth 1985

> ... a mere box-office success like *Kiss and Tell* — George Jean Nathan, *The Theatre Book of the Year, 1949–1950*

> A writer like Auden for instance, or like Rex Warner, might do a fruitful parody —G. S. Fraser, in *Little Reviews Anthology 1949,* ed. Denys Val Baker

> ... some very outré works, things like Swift's poem "A Beautiful Young Nymph Going to Bed." —Paul Fussell, *Samuel Johnson and the Life of Writing,* 1971

liked to See LIKE TO, LIKED TO.

like for *Like for* is a particular instance of the case where a verb takes an infinitive clause as its object and the clause is introduced by *for.* Jespersen 1909–49 (vol. 5) presents examples of many verbs so complementized, but only a single example of *like for,* from a novel by George Eliot. George Eliot put it in the mouth of a Warwickshire character, and we presume the *like for* was intended to be dialectal. Here is an example typical of American use:

> I'd like for you to go ahead —Jesse Stuart, *Beyond Dark Hills,* 1938 (in American Dialect Dictionary)

American commentators seem to have picked out the combination *like for* because it is fairly common in spoken American English. From the evidence we have—mostly from the ADD—it is primarily a Southern and Midland expression. (Jesse Stuart lived in and wrote about Kentucky.) Evidence from California (a letter in our files and a citation from Richard Nixon in Reader's Digest 1983) suggests that the locution moved where its speakers moved, and we would guess that when the Dictionary of American Regional English reaches this phrase, we will find that it has spread considerably beyond its original boundaries. Bryant 1962 says it is used by cultivated speakers throughout the country.

Those who object to the locution—Bremner 1980, Shaw 1975, 1987, Lurie 1927, Oxford American Dictionary, Heritage 1969, *Winners & Sinners* 17 Aug. 1961—apparently favor the Northern dialects in which *like for* does not occur naturally. The fact remains, however, that *like for* is hard to find in edited prose and seemingly always has been, even though Bryant traces it back to 1474. Our evidence suggests that the request, as in the quotation from Jesse Stuart above, is its most frequent use, though it does occur in other constructions. Here is one:

> . . . women are unanimous on one point: They don't like for their breasts to be handled roughly —"M", *The Sensuous Man,* 1971

likely   The use of *likely* as an adverb has drawn some negative comment in the 20th century. Bierce 1909 appears to have been the first to object. Although he finds *likely* perhaps a better choice than *probably* in "He will likely be elected," he revises the sentence to make *likely* an adjective: "He is likely to be elected." Sometime in the 1920s Bierce's reservations about the adverb were modified by others. The American Dialect Dictionary cites a stricture that the adverb *likely* must be accompanied by a qualifying adverb such as *very, most,* or *quite,* dating it simply "1920s cent. N.Y." Krapp 1927 also mentions such an opinion, although not subscribing to it. Fowler 1926 asserts the stricture absolutely, but he is referring to British usage; he allows that American usage may be different.

Theodore Bernstein, however, censured the unmodified *likely* in three books (1962, 1965, 1977) and in numerous issues of *Winners & Sinners,* though we may suspect that he was finding it in the *New York Times* so often because it was in fact an established usage. The usage panels of Harper 1985 and Heritage 1969, 1982 side with Bernstein, and so do a few other commentators, such as Bremner 1980 and Janis 1984. Others—Copperud 1964, Flesch 1964, Reader's Digest 1983—demur. No proponent of the qualifier explains what it adds to the sentence. Only Bernstein goes beyond simple assertion to say that idiom requires it.

What about the evidence? The OED shows the unmodified *likely* from 1380 to 1895, but the two late 19th-century citations are from Scotland and the north of England. Editor Henry Bradley marks the unqualified adverb as rare except in Scotland and in dialect. Gowers in Fowler 1965 notes spoken use in Scotland and Ireland. We have examples from Scotland, Ireland, and New Zealand in our files. The OED Supplement says the unqualified adverb is frequent in North America.

If the OED citations are representative, it would appear that the unqualified adverb began to drop out of use in mainstream British English in the 19th century while it continued to be used in areas remote from

the influence of London—Scotland, Ireland, North America (both the U.S. and Canada), and later New Zealand.

Our evidence shows the unmodified *likely* used chiefly in what some handbooks call "general English"—the everyday language of the press and of most periodicals. We have little literary evidence other than use in fictitious speech, and no evidence of use in the most elevated style. Here are some typical examples:

> A six-room apartment is not a house, and if you cook onions in one end of it, you'll likely smell them in the other —*New Yorker,* 29 Mar. 1952

> Canada likely will emphasize in the next few days that . . . —*The Gazette* (Montreal), 15 Apr. 1953

> The independents' future likely depends on just one thing—wresting away more of the market —*Wall Street Jour.,* 19 May 1955

> Currants for Christmas puddings will likely be dearer this year —*Sunday Post* (Glasgow), 15 Aug. 1954

> The music, likely English, is first known in a manuscript of 1746 —William L. Purcell, *American Record Guide,* December 1962

> . . . an expense which few card promoters would likely bear —*Newsweek,* 13 Nov. 1967

> Mr. Lowenstein, whose district likely never will win recognition for its wheat farms —*N.Y. Times,* 31 Jan. 1969

> . . . a novel means of spacecraft propulsion based upon the extraction of energy from the electromagnetic field of the solar wind. He claims that it is conceptually possible to sail upwind by coupling the energy extracted to an appropriate engine, likely an ion engine —Charles P. Sonett, *Science,* 8 Dec. 1972

> . . . and that money in turn will likely buy less — *Carnegie Quarterly,* Winter 1975

> . . . the Soviets likely would decide to purchase grain in the future from non-US sources —Jonathan Harsch, *Christian Science Monitor,* 7 May 1980

> The painting was likely finished in the winter of 1795 —Michael Olmert, *Smithsonian,* February 1982

> . . . it is not a scientific exercise professionals will likely cite —Peter G. Veit, *Natural History,* August 1983

> . . . has been the most contentious issue between the U.S. and China for 35 years, and will likely remain so —Kurt Andersen, *Time,* 7 May 1984

> But Ruthton women likely hadn't gone to college — Andrew H. Malcolm, *N.Y. Times Mag.,* 23 Mar. 1986

To sum up, the use of *likely* as an adverb without a qualifier such as *more, most, very,* or *quite* is well established in standard general use in North America. It is an old use, dating back to the 14th century. The strictures on it seem to have developed because it dropped out of mainstream literary use in England during the 19th century.

See also LIABLE 2.

liken The verb *liken* regularly takes the preposition *to:*

> ... one colonist likened it to sending a cow in pursuit of a hare —John Mason Brown, *Daniel Boone,* 1952

> ... economist Gary Becker would liken the institution of marriage to Adam Smith's pin factory — Peter Passell, *N.Y. Times Book Rev.,* 1 May 1983

likes of The phrase *the likes of* has been variously criticized in recent decades. Evans 1957 calls it "not literary English"; Bernstein 1965 dismisses it as "a casualism that has no place in serious writing"; and Shaw 1975 describes it as "nonstandard." We find little support for these assessments in our files, and certainly none for the last. *The likes of* is a common phrase, first recorded more than 200 years ago, which in current speech and writing has two principal uses, both of which are standard. In one of its uses, it has a single object, often a pronoun, and it typically carries overtones of disparagement:

> "Why should the likes of you come here?" she demanded —Fulton Oursler, *Reader's Digest,* October 1946

> ... who castigates his favorite grandson for ... marrying the likes of Anna —Julian Moynahan, *N.Y. Times Book Rev.,* 24 June 1979

> Don't want to be connected with the likes of him — A. G. Mojtabai, *Autumn,* 1982

In its other common use, *the likes of* has a multiple object in the form of a list of names, and its meaning is "such people as" or "such things as." It often implies that the list which follows is regarded as being in some way impressive or surprising. Disparaging connotations are rare:

> ... it's too bad that the likes of Paul Douglas, Ginger Rogers, and William Holden got caught up in it — John McCarten, *New Yorker,* 23 Jan. 1954

> Turning their backs on the likes of (get this) John Cheever, Philip Roth, Joan Didion, ... and John McPhee —Richard Locke, *N.Y. Times Book Rev.,* 23 Apr. 1978

> ... goblets and bowls coveted by the likes of The Smithsonian and The Metropolitan Museum of Art —advt., *N.Y. Times,* 9 Apr. 1980

> ... is now joined by the likes of Mr. Ludlum, Frederick Forsyth and ... John le Carré —Wilfrid Sheed, *N.Y. Times Book Rev.,* 6 July 1980

The likes of is appropriate and inoffensive in such contexts. The variant phrase *the like of* can also be used in some cases, and it is probably a better choice when the reference is to a single object and no disparagement is intended:

> ... colored by issues the like of which no political culture has yet encountered —Theodore Roszak, *The Making of a Counter Culture,* 1969

like to, liked to The *like* and *liked* in these expressions has been variously identified as adjective, verb, and auxiliary verb (the last is our present dictionary rubric). If the grammar is a bit perplexing, the meaning is not: "came near (to), almost." As idioms go, it is mod-

estly old, dating back to the 15th century. Around 1600 Shakespeare used both forms:

> We had lik'd to have had our two noses snapp'd off —*Much Ado About Nothing,* 1599

> ... I have had four quarrels, and like to have fought one —*As You Like It,* 1600

The idiom—if we call both variants one idiom—was quite common in literary sources during the 17th and 18th centuries:

> Stumbling from thought to thought, falls headlong down
> Into doubt's boundless sea, where, like to drown
> Books bear him up awhile....
> —John Wilmot, Earl of Rochester, *Satire Against Mankind,* 1675

> ... I had like to have lost my Comparison for want of Breath —William Congreve, *The Way of the World,* 1700

> Mr Prior was like to be insulted in the street for being supposed the author of it —Jonathan Swift, *Journal to Stella,* 9 Feb. 1711

> While he uttered this eloquent harangue, I had like to have laughed in his face —Tobias Smollett, translation of *Gil Blas,* 1749

> And such bellows too! Lord Mansfield with his cheeks like to burst —James Boswell, *Life of Samuel Johnson,* 1791

The evidence in the OED and OED Supplement shows that at least in the form *like to* the idiom continued in English literary use through the 19th century. But its translation to American English seems not to have been so literary. Consequently, Americans are likely to equate the terms with countrified or uneducated or old-fashioned speech. With the idiom's dropping out of literary use generally in the 20th century, most of our city-bred commentators think it uncouth. We will all know more about its distribution when the appropriate volume of the Dictionary of American Regional English appears, but our present information suggests that it is too widespread to be considered regional. It is a speech form that you will not need in discursive prose.

> ... Grover went to chewing on it and it liked to burn him up —Henry P. Scalf, quoted in *Our Appalachia,* ed. Laurel Shackelford & Bill Weinberg, 1977

> ... and he like to have never got away —Flannery O'Connor, letter, 11 Jan. 1958

limited This innocuous word first became controversial when Hodgson 1889 asserted that it was "often faultily employed" for such adjectives as *small, slight,* and *scant.* He quoted examples of what he considered to be misuse—"limited price" for "low or reduced price" and "limited acquaintance" for "slight acquaintance." Vizetelly 1906 repeated Hodgson's opinions almost exactly and cited the same examples in slightly reworded versions. Both Hodgson and Vizetelly did allow, however, that although they did not approve of using *limited* to describe "pecuniary circumstances," the use might be defended insofar as it was meant to contrast with *unlimited* in "unlimited wealth."

Similar criticism has been passed along from one usage book to another throughout the 20th century. Among the more recent commentators who have considered *limited* to be misused for *small* or *slight* are Partridge 1942, Evans 1957, Bernstein 1965, and Gowers in Fowler 1965. Despite their protests, however, such usage has continued to be common in standard speech and writing:

> Delia's experience was too limited for her to picture exactly what might happen —Edith Wharton, *The Old Maid,* 1924

> . . . a narrow mind, capable at most of the limited range of Marston —T. S. Eliot, "Cyril Tourneur," in *Selected Essays,* 1932

> . . . by young women of limited means —Morris R. Cohen, *The Faith of a Liberal,* 1946

> . . . my experience is probably a limited experience —William Faulkner, 25 Feb. 1957, in *Faulkner in the University,* 1959

> . . . our use of certain very limited natural resources —Dr. Ruth Patrick, quoted in *Smithsonian,* August 1970

> . . . so short that it is of very limited use to those interested in Sheraton —*Times Literary Supp.,* 19 Feb. 1971

> . . . employees with limited reading ability —William Serrin, *Saturday Rev.,* 2 Feb. 1980

Objections to these uses of *limited* appear to us to have no sound basis. The one real oddity cited originally by Hodgson was *limited price* for "low or reduced price." We do not know how widespread such usage was in Hodgson's time, but we have no current evidence for it.

lingerie   See HYPERFOREIGNISMS.

linking verbs   See LOOK 1.

lion's share   A clutch of commentators, including Kilpatrick 1984, Bernstein 1965, and William Safire (*N.Y. Times Mag.,* 16 Mar. 1986) complain that *lion's share* is frequently misused. Bernstein's criticism is typical:

> The *lion's share,* as conceived by Aesop, is all or almost all, not merely a majority or the larger part.

The dependency of these commentators on the fable of Aesop may in part be the fault—as much as we hate to admit it—of Merriam-Webster dictionaries.

Lion's share was entered in Webster 1864 with the definition "the larger part" and an explanatory note identifying Aesop's fable as the source of the phrase. The 1890 editor had apparently read Aesop too, and he interpreted Aesop as Bernstein would later. He put a new definition "all, or nearly all" in front of the 1864 definition, now elaborated into "the best or largest part." Editors of Webster 1909 and Webster's Second left the 1890 version untouched.

The trouble with the 1890 treatment was that the second part described English usage all right, but the first part, the part that Bernstein and the rest fixed on, represented only Aesop. And Aesop spoke no English, of course. The OED was not fooled by Aesop; the definition there reads "the largest or principal portion." The examples given, starting with Edmund Burke in 1790, illustrate the stated definition, not "all, or nearly all." Nor, in fact, do any of the citations that were in our files

before 1934 unmistakably illustrate "all, or nearly all" as a separate sense. Our citations show that it is often practically impossible to tell whether "most" or "nearly all" is intended but that when it is possible, the meaning is always the one criticized by the commentators, but recorded by modern dictionaries. Here are a few examples, beginning with some of our earliest:

> . . . partly from my own fault in assigning perhaps rather a lion's share to myself —Oliver Wendell Holmes d. 1935, letter, 1 Dec. 1899

> To old Esayoo I am glad to give the lion's share of the credit —Walter Elmer Ekblaw, *Four Years in the White North,* 1918

> . . . President Wilson's visit and the daily conferences of leading European statesmen have attracted the lion's share of public interest —*N.Y. Times,* 27 Dec. 1918

> Did she know the terror and the remorse that followed on the heels of it when one slyly sneaked the lion's share of buttered toast at tea? —Jean Stafford, *Children Are Bored on Sunday,* 1953

> The central Government collects and spends the lion's share of the citizens' tax dollar —Cabell Phillips, *N.Y. Times,* 1 Dec. 1957

> . . . a company that captured the lion's share of the deodorant and antiperspirant market —*Forbes,* 15 July 1971

> It was his life, rather than his art, that commanded the lion's share of attention —Hilton Kramer, *N.Y. Times Book Rev.,* 10 Aug. 1975

> . . . an elite that enjoys the lion's share of power and prosperity —Luther Spoehr, *Saturday Rev.,* 2 Feb. 1980

The moral of this tale is that usage commentators and lexicographers have to look at English usage to understand how English speakers use a term, no matter what source it comes from.

lit   See LIGHTED, LIT.

litany   1. *Litany* refers literally to a type of prayer in which a series of invocations and supplications are recited by the leader of a congregation, with alternate responses being made by the congregation as a whole. Recent decades have seen the development of two figurative senses, the first of which, "a repetitive recital," relates to the chantlike quality of a litany:

> . . . a litany of cheering phrases. "One of us is going to make it. . . . There's always room at the top. . . ." —Herman Wouk, *Marjorie Morningstar,* 1955

> "B-u-u-t . . ." and the Middlesex County Democrats picked up the now-familiar litany that the Democrats' vice-presidential candidate has been sounding up and down the land this autumn: ". . . not Senator Goldwater!" —Pete Hamill, *Saturday Evening Post,* 10 Oct. 1964

> . . . recited with her . . . a good-night prayer, a little litany of blessings into which Piet never knew whether or not to insert the names of his parents — John Updike, *Couples,* 1968

The second figurative sense is "a lengthy recitation or enumeration." It often carries implications of dreary familiarity:

> ... whenever she did so she had to listen to a litany of the unrecoverable debts he was owed —Michael McLaverty, *The Three Brothers,* 1948

But its meaning is sometimes hardly more than "list":

> ... published a breathless litany of Mara's virtues —Pete Axthelm, *New York,* 1 Nov. 1971

> ... its rather obvious litany of major American cities with large black populations —John Rockwell, *N.Y. Times,* 13 July 1980

These figurative uses of *litany* have so far met with little criticism. Among the best-known commentators, only Bernstein 1965 recommends restricting *litany* to its literal sense.

2. *Litany, liturgy.* Many commentators are at pains to distinguish between *litany* and *liturgy,* which means "a rite or body of rites prescribed for public worship." The literal senses of these words do not appear to be subject to confusion, but we have a few citations from recent years in which *liturgy* is being used figuratively where *litany* seems to be called for:

> ... the final words of the liturgy rang through the blockhouse public address system: "Ignition ... Mainstage ... Lift-off!" —Carmault B. Jackson, Jr., M.D., *National Geographic,* September 1961

> ... such slogans as "Not An Inch," "No Surrender," and "No Pope Here" are part of their political liturgy —Arthur Roth, *Harper's,* April 1972

literally

We have come to such a pass with this emphasizer that where the truth would require us to acknowledge our exaggeration with, "not literally, of course, but in a manner of speaking", we do not hesitate to insert the very word that we ought to be at pains to repudiate; such false coin makes honest traffic in words impossible —H. W. Fowler, *S.P.E. Tract 11,* 1922

The *L* volume of the OED, published in 1903, contained a citation for *literally* that had occasioned the editor of the volume, Henry Bradley, to append the note "Now often improperly used to indicate that some conventional metaphorical or hyperbolical phrase is to be taken in the strongest admissible sense." The citation in question was written by the English actress Fanny Kemble and published in 1863: "For the last four years . . . I literally coined money." Fanny Kemble did not originate the use; Charles Dickens had employed it years earlier in *Nicholas Nickleby* (1839):

> 'Lift him out,' said Squeers, after he had literally feasted his eyes in silence upon the culprit.

The use must have gained popularity by the time Bradley was doing his editing, and it continued to be popular enough to warrant notice in Webster 1909, where it was accorded the laconic usage note "often used hyperbolically." By 1922 H. W. Fowler sounded the call, and there has followed a steady stream of protesters and viewers-with-alarm ever since. Copperud 1980 writes, "Seldom is the word employed in its exact sense, which is *to the letter, precisely as stated.* Some examples: 'The

actor was literally floating on applause.' The word wanted was *figuratively,* unless levitation occurred. . . ."

How did things come to such a pass? The course of development is clear from the entry in the OED. There are four living uses of *literally.* The first (OED sense 2) means "in a literal manner; word for word"; the passage was translated literally. The second (OED sense 3) means "in a literal way"; some people interpret the Bible literally. The third (OED sense 3b) could be defined "actually" or "really" and is used to add emphasis. It seems to be of literary origin. Dryden in 1687 complained that his "daily bread is litt'rally implor'd"; Pope in 1708 commented "Euery day with me is literally another yesterday for it is exactly the same." In 1769 the political writer Junius asked rhetorically, "What punishment has he suffered? Literally none."

The purpose of the adverb in the foregoing instances is to add emphasis to the following word or phrase, which is intended in a literal sense. The hyperbolic use comes from placing the same intensifier in front of some figurative word or phrase which cannot be taken literally. Pope, with his "literally another yesterday," had already in 1708 prepared the way.

Has the hyperbolic use all but eclipsed the earlier uses of *literally,* as Copperud asserts? No. Merriam-Webster files show the three living earlier senses to be still in regular use; furthermore, these uses as monitored by our readers outnumber the hyperbolic use by a substantial margin.

Now a word about the critics. The chief assertions they make are that the hyperbolic use of *literally* is a misuse of the word or a mistake for *figuratively.* As we have seen, it is neither; it is an extension of intensive use from words and phrases of literal meaning to metaphorical ones. It is a not altogether surprising development from Alexander Pope's not quite literal "literally another yesterday."

If the hyperbolic use of *literally* is neither a misuse nor a mistake for some other word, should you use it? The point to be made here is that it is hyperbolic, and hyperbole requires care in handling. Is it necessary, or even useful, to add an intensifier like *literally* to a well-established metaphorical use of a word or phrase? Will the use add the desired emphasis without calling undue attention to itself, or will the older senses of *literally* intrude upon the reader's awareness and render the figure ludicrous, as was the case when a football play-by-play man we heard some years ago said the defensive linemen had "literally hammered the quarterback into the ground"? Here are a few examples to judge for yourself.

> ... make the whole scene literally glow with the fires of his imagination —Alfred Kazin, *Harper's,* December 1968

> They will literally turn the world upside down to combat cruelty or injustice —Norman Cousins, *Saturday Rev.,* 20 Nov. 1971

> Even Muff did not miss our periods of companionship, because about that time she grew up and started having literally millions of kittens —Jean Stafford, "Bad Characters," 1954

> This error and defeat in diplomacy literally broke Castiglione's heart —Robert A. Hall, Jr., *A Short History of Italian Literature,* 1951

> He literally glowed; without a word or a gesture of exultation a new well-being radiated from him and

filled the little room —F. Scott Fitzgerald, *The Great Gatsby,* 1925 (Reader's Digest 1983)

And with his eyes he literally scoured the corners of the cell —Vladimir Nabokov, *Invitation to a Beheading,* 1960 (OED Supplement)

Your very kind letter has left me as literally speechless as I remember —Archibald MacLeish, letter, 17 Feb. 1914

Lily, the caretaker's daughter, was literally run off her feet. Hardly had she brought one gentleman into the little pantry ... than the wheezy hall-door bell clanged again and she had to scamper along the bare hallway to let in another guest —James Joyce, *Dubliners,* 1914

... yet the wretch, absorbed in his victuals, and naturally of an unutterable dullness, did not make a single remark during dinner, whereas I literally blazed with wit —W. M. Thackeray, *Punch,* 30 Oct. 1847

litotes *Litotes* is a classical rhetorical device with a classical name—it is a form of understatement in which you assert a positive by using the negative of the contrary. The common expression "not bad" is an example. Litotes often takes the form *not un-* (as in "not unlikely") and in this form constitutes an acceptable kind of double negative; however, litotes does not require two negatives.

Not a few commentators have entries at *litotes.* Most of them are content to explain the term; a few have reservations about it. Safire 1980 does not care much for it; his objection is primarily to the *not un-* version. Howard 1978 quotes George Orwell in disapproval; again the *not un-* form is the one criticized. Kilpatrick 1984, however, notes that litotes can be used to convey subtleties not easily expressed otherwise. Everybody is against overusing the device, which is a sound enough principle. Reader's Digest 1983 warns that it can be ambiguous, and ambiguity may underlie Safire's objection, since his example is one garbled in speech by a secretary of defense.

The idea of litotes, the textbooks say, is to get emphasis by means of understatement. Bernstein 1958 suggests that humor and sarcasm are possible, too:

i spoke to goody this a.m., and dropped several hints that you would not be averse to getting a few laughs on the tallulah show come sunday —Fred Allen, letter, 30 Apr. 1951

He was not unaware that in his dress and as the owner of a car he was a provocation to many white people —E. L. Doctorow, *Ragtime,* 1975

Litotes can also be found in a number of fixed expressions:

... enclosing a check ... , and telling me in No Uncertain Terms, what I could do with it —Frank Sullivan, letter, 25 Oct. 1965

See the entry at NOT TOO for one of these fixed expressions that some commentators dislike. You will also find *litotes* mentioned at DOUBLE NEGATIVE 2.

liturgy See LITANY 2.

livid *Livid* is ultimately derived from the Latin verb *livere,* which means "to be blue." Its original use in English was as a synonym, more or less, of *black and*

blue, describing flesh that was discolored by or as if by a bruise:

There followed no carbuncle, no purple or livide spots —Francis Bacon, *The Historie of the Raigne of King Henry the Seventh,* 1622 (OED)

Its first extension of meaning gave it the sense "ashen or pallid," with the idea of blueness now secondary, if not entirely lost:

The light glared on the livid face of the corpse —Ann Radcliffe, *The Italian,* 1797 (OED)

... the shuddering native, whose brown face was now livid with cold —W. M. Thackeray, *Vanity Fair,* 1848

Mugridge's face was livid with fear at what he had done —Jack London, *The Sea-Wolf,* 1904

In this sense *livid* came to be used especially to characterize the appearance of a person pale with rage:

He was livid with fury —Compton Mackenzie, *The Early Life and Adventures of Sylvia Scarlett,* 1918 (OED Supplement)

This use gave rise in turn to a pair of new senses. Because the faces of angry people are reddened at least as often as they are ashen, and because *livid* is easily associated with such words as *lurid* and *vivid,* the images called to mind by such a phrase as *livid with fury* were for many people colorful rather than pallid, and the color they were full of—or at least tinged with—was red:

... she saw the girl's head, livid against the bed-linen, the brick-rose circles again visible under darkly shadowed lids —Edith Wharton, *The Old Maid,* 1924

... the plate window where a fan of gladiolas blushed livid —Truman Capote, *Other Voices, Other Rooms,* 1948

Livid also began to be understood as describing the angry state itself rather than the appearance produced by it:

Betsy is *livid.* She says now she will fight to the last ditch —Margaret Kennedy, *Together and Apart,* 1936 (OED Supplement)

The owners of large estates were ... livid at the prospect of his breaking up the bankrupt estates in the East —William L. Shirer, *The Rise and Fall of the Third Reich,* 1960

"Oh, Vernon, isn't it scrumptious?" some woman was exulting. "Those faculty wives will be livid! ..." —S. J. Perelman, *New Yorker,* 26 Nov. 1966

Such is the mottled history of *livid.* The history of critical comment about it is briefer and somewhat less varied. Most of the criticism has been directed at the "reddish" sense, dating back at least to a book titled *Handbook For Newspaper Workers,* published in 1926. The *Handbook* regarded "black and blue" as the correct meaning. Krapp 1927 described *livid* as "a somewhat literary word for *a bluish leaden color,* especially in the phrase *a livid bruise....*" Krapp did not single out the "reddish" sense, but he noted that *livid* "is often used ... with little realization of its definite meaning." A citation in our files from an unidentified newspaper in the

1950s takes the familiar line that "black and blue" is the proper meaning, but it also takes a somewhat unusual line in that the error it criticizes is the "ashen or pale" sense of the word. Bernstein 1958, 1965, 1977 sets the tone for more recent criticism by accepting both the "black and blue" and "ashen" senses while regarding the "reddish or red-faced" sense as an error. He does not mention the "furious" sense. The opinion of Freeman 1983 is like that of Bernstein. Bremner 1980 and Bryson 1984 also reject the "reddish" sense, but they both take note of—and accept—the "furious" sense. Kilpatrick 1984 is alone in regarding the "reddish" sense as established: "Only physicians and fuddy-duddies cling to the original meaning. When we learn that the president is *livid* at his budget director, we now infer that the president has a face like a Bloody Mary. So it goes." Note that the sense of *livid* in Kilpatrick's example is actually "furious."

Our own evidence shows that the usual meaning of *livid* in current English is "furious." This sense is so well established that a phrase like *livid with anger* now sounds almost redundant. The other senses, whether judged "correct" or "incorrect" by the critics, are now somewhat rare. Use of *livid* to mean "black and blue" is, in fact, so uncommon that many readers will no doubt find it bewildering:

> The grip of the dog's teeth, though kindly meant, was firm enough to give pain and to leave livid marks — John Updike, *Bech Is Back,* 1982

The "ashen" and "reddish" senses are hardly more common. It is often hard to tell which is meant:

> Suddenly Jerry seemed to petrify, features livid. . . . For a second, Barrett wondered whether Jerry might strike her or attempt to strangle her —Irving Wallace, *The Seven Minutes,* 1969

The truth is that *livid* seems no longer to have strong associations with any color. Whether red-faced or pale, a person who is filled with rage is now aptly described as *livid.*

loan, lend Copperud 1970, 1980 states flatly that the idea that *loan* is not good form as a verb is a superstition, but a surprisingly large number of commentators nonetheless express reservations about it. Among them are these, all Americans: Einstein 1985, Kilpatrick 1984, Bell & Cohn 1981, Bernstein 1965, 1971, 1977, Strunk & White 1959, 1972, 1979, Nickles 1974. In addition other commentators note a preference for *lend* in formal discourse—for instance Perrin & Ebbitt 1972 and Shaw 1970. Here is a recent comment:

> We do not accept, for example, that the noun *loan* can be used as a verb when *lend* is already there for that purpose, even though the banking community not only accepts it but is its most frequent user (or abuser) —Einstein 1985

The banking community aside, Mr. Einstein is essentially repeating a century-old opinion that can be traced back at least as far as Richard Grant White 1870.

But before we go into the history of the usage dispute, we should examine the history of the word. The verb *loan* was among the words brought to America by early English-speaking settlers who, in the words of James Russell Lowell, "unhappily could bring over no English better than Shakespeare's." The OED shows that verbal *loan* fell into disuse in England after the 17th century

but continued in use in America, which was essentially cut off from the literary and intellectual life of England. In 1796 an English traveler in America named Thomas Twining noticed *to loan* used by "the least cultivated ranks of society" (quotation in Dictionary of American English).

By the middle of the 19th century British letters were not as unfamiliar in the United States as they had been in earlier centuries, and American men of letters show some awareness of a certain provincial tone in the use of *loan* as a verb. James Russell Lowell put it in a fictitious press notice he wrote to fill up a blank page in the first series of *The Biglow Papers* (1848):

> . . . a pastoral by him, the manuscript of which was loaned us by a friend.

Lowell probably thought the word just right for a small-town editor. He commented on it in the introduction to the second series of *The Biglow Papers* (1867):

> *Loan* for *lend,* with which we have hitherto been blackened, I must retort upon the mother island, for it appears so long ago as in 'Albion's England.' (in Dictionary of American English)

Oliver Wendell Holmes's *Elsie Venner* (1861) also contains a comment:

> Loaned, as the inland folks say, when they mean 'lent.' (quoted in Lounsbury 1908)

Boston literary lights such as Holmes and Lowell may have felt the verb *loan* to be provincial, but what about the rest of the country? From the middle part of the 19th century the OED cites James C. Calhoun of South Carolina. To the west we find

> . . . officers of the Bank have loaned money at usurious rates —Abraham Lincoln, speech in the Illinois legislature, 11 Jan. 1837

Former president Martin Van Buren, a New Yorker, in his autobiography, begun in 1854, wrote

> . . . he pressed me to enter one of the prominent law offices in the city of New York, and offered to loan me the necessary funds. . . .

Benjamin Lundy, a New Jersey-born abolitionist editor and lecturer, noted in his journal in December 1834

> He also loaned me files of the Vermont Chronicle. . . .

Perhaps only the Brahmins felt diffident about verbal *loan.*

Still Richard Grant White 1870 went beyond a charge of provincialism and declared it wrong: "Loan is not a verb, but a noun." White based his objection on his derivation of the noun from the past participle of the Anglo-Saxon verb *laenan;* Lounsbury 1908 demonstrated that White was unable to tell a verb from a noun in Old English. (For lovers of etymology: *loan,* the noun, is of Scandinavian origin; it had replaced the related Old English word of the same meaning by early Middle English; its earliest use as a verb is by functional shift.) Nevertheless, the pronouncement stuck; from White it spread to William Cullen Bryant's *Index Expurgatorius* for the *New York Evening Post* (first published in 1877), Compton 1898, Vizetelly 1906, Bierce 1909, Mac-Cracken & Sandison 1917, and so on down to 1985.

British commentators appear satisfied in the main to label *loan* an Americanism and to assert the correctness of *lend* in British English. Fowler 1926 notes *loan*'s survival in the U.S. and "locally in U.K." Gowers 1948, however, notes with distaste the use of *to loan* in British government writing; in his revision of Fowler 1965 he changed "locally in U.K." to "and has now returned to provide us with a NEEDLESS VARIANT."

How is the verb *loan* actually used? The most striking thing is that it is used literally: you can loan money, books, art works, clothing, equipment, people or their services. *Lend* is also used for these purposes, but only *lend* is used for figurative purposes, such as lending a hand, lending an ear, or lending enchantment. It is a great joke of some usage writers (for instance, Bernstein, Einstein, Kilpatrick) to deride the use of *loan* by plugging it into Shakespeare: Loan me your ears. However, no one except facetious usage commentators appears ever to have used *loan* in such a way.

Here are some samples of how *loan* has been used:

> . . . a little matter of nine dollars and sixty-two cents . . . which he had loaned him about eighteen months ago, afore he had knowed him well —Petroleum V. Nasby, "The Reward of Virtue," 1866, in *The Mirth of a Nation,* ed. Walter Blair & Raven I. McDavid, Jr., 1983

> I wonder if Frederic Melcher of The Publishers Weekly wouldnt loan you his copy —Robert Frost, letter, 26 Mar. 1936

> . . . she offered to loan me the money —Archibald MacLeish, letter, 4 Feb. 1929

> Colonel Sartoris invented an involved tale to the effect that Miss Emily's father had loaned money to the town —William Faulkner, "A Rose for Emily," in *The Collected Stories of William Faulkner,* 1950

> . . . to the National Gallery he loans a picture —Eric Partridge, in *British and American English Since 1900,* 1951

> . . . an island cottage that Mittler owned and loaned them —John Cheever, *The Wapshot Chronicle,* 1957

> . . . telling him he wasn't going to loan him the eighty dollars —*And More by Andy Rooney,* 1982

> . . . the Magna Carta, which was being loaned to the United States for the Bicentennial —Tip O'Neill with William Novak, *Man of the House,* 1987

Loan as a verb is entirely standard, having been in use since the 16th century, at least; carried over to this continent in the language of early settlers, it has continued in use ever since. Its use is predominantly American and includes literature but not the more elevated kinds of discourse. If you use *loan* remember that its regular use is literal; for figurative expressions, you must use *lend.*

There is a curious disagreement about the past tenses of *loan* and *lend* in a few sources. Copperud 1970, 1980 notes that *loaned* seems to be used in place of *lent;* Perrin & Ebbitt 1972 makes the same observation; Kilpatrick 1984 admits the practice. But Einstein 1985 asserts the opposite—that *lent* is used for the past of both *lend* and *loan.* Our citational evidence is unable to confirm either observation.

loath, loathe, loth   Copperud 1970, 1980 points out that *loath* is an adjective, *loathe* a verb; so do several others. Bernstein 1977 begins, "A reputable newspaper contained this sentence: 'But, curiously, in an institu-

tion *loathe* to make decisions, they are ready to judge a President.' That is a gaffe that is not uncommon." Reader's Digest 1983 terms the spelling *loathe* for the adjective an error. Few dictionaries record the spelling: the OED notes *loathe* as a 17th century variant; Webster's Third allows it as a secondary *(also)* variant, as do its derivative dictionaries (Webster's Ninth New Collegiate Dictionary, for instance) and Longman 1984, which advises sticking to *loath* for the adjective, *loathe* for the verb.

If people would follow this advice, the language would no doubt be tidier; unfortunately they do not. The reason seems to be pronunciation: many people rhyme the adjective with the verb, voicing the *th,* and some of them use the spelling *loathe* which represents their pronunciation. There appears to be no confusion; all of our citations using the *loathe* spelling for the adjective, from 1924 to 1984, are unambiguous (as is Bernstein's example)—no one is likely to be misled. A recent example:

> . . . eager specialists who impressed me not only because they seemed to know what they were about but because they were articulate and not loathe . . . to let me learn —Laurence Urdang, *Datamation,* March 1984

The spelling *loth* is more common in British usage than American; American usage of *loth* was more common in the past than it is at present.

Things will be neater if you use *loath* (or *loth*) for the adjective, *loathe* for the verb. But if *loathe* represents your pronunciation of the adjective, you need not be afraid to use it. It is a legitimate variant.

locate   *Locate* seems to have come into use as an Americanism, and as an Americanism it has been subject to disparagement on three separate counts beginning as long ago as 1870.

1. *Locate* "settle." This intransitive use is the earliest recorded for the verb and dates back to the middle of the 17th century. Richard Grant White 1870 seems to have been the first to disparage it. He acknowledged it as an Americanism, and he apparently associated it with settlers in the Midwest, a group and a region with which he cared to have as little to do as possible. Although White's objection is social, he lists *locate* among the incorrect words; and it is so picked up by Ayres 1881.

Diffidence about Americanisms has long been a characteristic of American usage commentators; it is plain in Jensen 1935, who says *locate* is "sanctioned only as an Americanism" but is disguised behind the characterizations "colloquial" of MacCracken & Sandison 1917 and Watt 1967, "not regarded as standard" of Bernstein 1965, and "less refined and more dialectal" of Shaw 1987. It is possible that we are seeing some of the social aversion of 1870 still repeated in these comments; however, now that our rumbustious and uncouth ancestors have passed on to their rewards, there can be no objection to intransitive *locate* beyond its American origin. As these examples suggest, intransitive *locate* is not an overly literary term. It is, however, standard.

> Contra Costa County, Calif., Development Assn. would like to tell you why numerous chemical companies have located in the county —*Area Development,* May 1970

> Prefer to locate near a university granting Ph.D. or D.S.W. —advt., *AAUP Bulletin,* December 1969

In 1865 he located at Scranton, Pa. —*Dictionary of American Biography*, 1929

2. *Located* "situated." William Cullen Bryant put *located* on his *Index Expurgatorius* (published in 1877 but compiled earlier) without a gloss, so we do not really know what it was about the word that offended him. We do know that Bernstein 1962 found it objectionable in the sense of "situated" (he first went after it in a 1958 *Winners & Sinners*). Maybe he was the inheritor of the Bryant tradition. He considerably moderated his views in his 1965 book; apparently no one else agreed. The use is entirely standard.

> Located in a bad slum area now undergoing redevelopment, this school . . . —James B. Conant, *Slums and Suburbs*, 1961

> She lived in Brooklyn . . . and was an avid fan of the Dodgers baseball team when it was located in that borough —*Current Biography*, April 1968

> Settlements were typically located on or near the shore —Edward P. Lanning, *Peru Before the Incas*, 1967

Located is also disparaged as unnecessary or as deadwood in several books, such as Bernstein 1965, Flesch 1964, Perrin & Ebbitt 1972. If we take the Lanning quotation for an example, we can see that the sentence can still be understood when *located* is omitted. But its omission does not make a better sentence, just a shorter one. You should not hesitate to use *located*, even though it may be omissible for sense, when it gives a sentence better rhythmic structure.
3. *Locate* "find." MacCracken & Sandison 1917 seem to have been the first to raise an objection to *locate* in the sense of "find." This curious objection, too, has been repeated by more recent commentators. Evans 1957 would restrict *locate* for finding something by hunting for it; no one else makes this distinction. Flesch 1964 objects to *locate* as being a "stilted synonym" of *find*. Gowers in Fowler 1965 sets up a factitious distinction that Watt 1967 accepts: you *locate* the place where something or someone is, but you *find* the something or someone there. This is rather a subtle distinction, and it is not observed by the writers represented in our files. In the following examples, the first three are British, in the broad sense that comprehends the Commonwealth nations: one locates a place, one a thing, and the third might be interpreted either way. The rest of the examples are American.

> The young policeman was . . . trying to locate with his eyes the place in the garden where . . . —Doris Lessing, *The Good Terrorist*, 1985

> . . . one or more dogs that will locate the lion —J. Stevenson-Hamilton, *Wild Life in South Africa*, 1947

> . . . sent out to reconnoitre and to locate the kraal of the Kaffirs —Stuart Cloete, *The Turning Wheels*, 1937

> The next task is to locate a native speaker with no inhibitions —Stuart Chase, *Power of Words*, 1954

> . . . he soon located about two dozen other concerned students —*Johns Hopkins Mag.*, October 1965

> . . . instructed to locate two others with whom you would like to be in a group —Clyde Reid, *Christian Herald*, June 1969

> . . . this excerpt is very difficult to locate —George Jellinek, *Saturday Rev.*, 12 June 1954

> CIA officials sought to locate the source of the funding —*The Tower Commission Report*, 1987

You will note that not one of these violates Evans's distinction, but all except the first violate Gowers's distinction. Evans seems to have a clearer view of this matter. All of these examples are standard.

While we cannot say with Janis 1984 that "the quibbling about this word has ceased," there is not one of these three usages that need worry you. They are all thoroughly established in respectable usage.

look   1. Perrin & Ebbitt 1972 and Longman 1984 note that when *look* is used as an intransitive verb in the sense of "use one's eyes" it may be qualified by an adverb of manner: "look carefully," "look longingly." But when it functions as a linking verb, approximately equivalent to *appear* or *seem*, it takes an adjective: "You look beautiful," "You look tired." This is the modern analysis, and it dates from about the time of Alford 1866. But the OED shows that *look* in the latter meaning was formerly felt to be an intransitive and not a linking verb, and was usually qualified by an adverb of manner. Shirley Brice Heath in Shopen & Williams 1980 mentions an 1829 grammar that lists *look beautiful* as a "blunder." Old examples with the adverb are not especially hard to find:

> . . . my Lord Sandwich, who is in his gold-buttoned suit, as the mode is, and looks nobly —Samuel Pepys, diary, 17 June 1663

> . . . why you look more comically than an old-fashion'd Fellow —Thomas Shadwell, *The Sullen Lovers*, 1668

> The beauty remarks how frightfully she looks —Samuel Johnson, *The Rambler*, No. 193 (in Hall 1873)

> . . . holds a great deal commodiously without looking awkwardly —Jane Austen, letter, 8 Nov. 1800

> She has got her new teeth in, and I think they look very nicely —Emily Dickinson, letter, 20 June 1852

Here we have an instance where the general perception of how the verb functions has changed over the years. And what is true of *look* in this respect is also true of other verbs, such as *taste, feel, act, smell*, now treated as linking verbs. These verbs are not yet fully settled into their linking-verb roles, as occasional citations with adverbs of manner attest. Here are a couple:

> . . . everything was ashes. Even her cigarette tasted bitterly —Charles G. Norris, *Zelda Marsh*, 1927

> Abdullah wrinkled the edge of his flat nose and shook his head. They really smelled abominably —Ernest Hemingway, *Green Hills of Africa*, 1935

The OED notes that because the grammarians have insisted on the use of the adjective and condemned the adverb, the adverb of manner is rarely seen, unless it is *well, ill,* or *badly*. The first two are acceptable, of course, because they are adjectives as well as adverbs.

> "My house looks well, doesn't it?" he demanded —F. Scott Fitzgerald, *The Great Gatsby*, 1925

But you had better stick to adjectives. The occasional adverb of manner is beginning to look like some sort of hypercorrection, as indeed the passage just quoted from Fitzgerald does.

2. We have had a couple of inquiries in recent years about the propriety of *looking to* followed by an infinitive, and James J. Kilpatrick in a 1985 syndicated column recorded a correspondent's complaint about the same construction. Here is a typical example:

> I'm not looking to set a longevity record in this job —Dean Rusk, quoted in *Christian Science Monitor,* 17 Jan. 1968

There are actually three different uses in which *look* is followed by *to* and an infinitive. Two of the three go back several centuries, and two of the three are still of frequent occurrence. Let's take a look at them.

The first is a sense of *look* expressing anticipation or expectation. The OED shows that it began to be followed by an infinitive construction in the 17th century:

> Bruce, good morrow. What great author art thou chewing the cud upon? I look'd to have found you with your headache and morning qualms —Thomas Shadwell, *The Virtuoso,* 1676

This construction can still be found in the 20th century but is now less common than the others:

> In any reasonable world, the noted writer in question, and the young lady interviewers, could look to have their mouths washed out with soap —Emile Capouya, *Saturday Rev.,* 25 July 1964

In the 19th century this construction begins to turn up with *look* in the form of the present participle. The OED has Robert Southey in a letter written in 1830:

> I too had been looking to hear from you.

And a citation from A. E. Housman's *A Shropshire Lad* (1896):

> Two lovers looking to be wed.

Examples with *looking* are very common in recent use.

From the vantage point of the 1980s it is easy to look back at Southey and find hope as well as expectation and at Housman and find intention as well as anticipation. It is the notions of hope and intention that predominate in our most popular current use of *look* followed by *to* and the infinitive. Future dictionaries will probably have to give it a separate sense because the meaning has shifted away from expectation. It is most commonly found with *looking* but other forms of the verb are used as well.

> Long as I'm playin', I'm not lookin' to be on no high pedestal —Louis Armstrong, quoted in *N.Y. Times,* 20 Jan. 1960

> . . . Kierkegaard, whose work . . . looked to demonstrate that we cannot know the moral role we enact —Norman Mailer, *N.Y. Times Mag.,* 26 Sept. 1976

> "We weren't looking to trade Sam," said Giant Coach Allie Sherman —*Sports Illustrated,* 20 Apr. 1964

> . . . two men have been around looking to kill him —Lewis H. Lapham, *Harper's,* November 1971

> . . . Gremlins will arrive, looking to scare you silly — Richard Corliss, *Time,* 4 June 1984

> Today I'm a Commie-pinko-Antichrist looking to scalp Ron Reagan —Sam Donaldson, quoted in *People,* 14 June 1982

> . . . everyone is tired and looking to go home —Larry Cole, *TV Guide,* 12 Nov. 1982

The newer use is differentiated from the older chiefly by the notions of trying or hoping or intending to do something, the greater frequency of the present-participle construction, and the greater ease of using it in the negative.

There is a third use in which *look* is followed by *to* and the infinitive. This is the linking verb use of *look* in which it comes close in meaning to *seem* or *appear*. It has been used with an infinitive complement—almost always *to be*—since the later 18th century. It is almost always used with some form of *look* other than the present participle and is still common in current use:

> It looked to be hard, mean work —John G. Mitchell, *Smithsonian,* May 1981

> . . . looks to be a slow and laborious and rather uninteresting business —Howard Nemerov, *American Scholar,* Summer 1967

> If a fish looks to be in the contender class, the guide must keep it wet and alive —Horace Sutton, *Saturday Rev.,* 4 Feb. 1978

> And this is the only film that Spielberg has ever made where the editing looks to be from desperation —Pauline Kael, *New Yorker,* 30 Dec. 1985

> Although the SAT score decline actually looks, on further examination, to provide only trivial information —Daniels 1983

3. The *look to be* construction that we just examined leads us to two British idioms of similar meaning but different makeup. We will do no more than describe and illustrate these briefly, as they have (so far) drawn no criticism. The first is *look like* followed by a present participle:

> . . . *The Plain Dealer* looked like being a failure at its first performance —James Sutherland, *English Literature of the Late Seventeenth Century,* 1969

> . . . the timber industry looks like embarking on a period of rationalization —Edward Townsend, *The Times* (London), 21 Feb. 1974

The second idiom has *look* followed immediately by an object where an American would probably use *look like* or *look to be:*

> It looks a lucrative investment —Adrian McGregor, *National Times* (Sydney), 5 Apr. 1975

> This is why 1986 . . . looks a better prospect for an Arab-Israeli agreement —*The Economist,* 3 Jan. 1986

> . . . done up to the nines, and in the event, looking an ass compared with the rest of the soberly dressed audience —Edward Mace, *Observer Rev.,* 3 Mar. 1974

loose, lose Many handbooks include warnings about confusion of these two common words. The real problem, of course, is simply spelling. The verb *lose* rhymes with *choose,* and the urge to spell it with an extra *o* sometimes proves irresistible:

> . . . they loose her to a worthless motorcycle punk named Falbuck —*Media & Methods,* March 1969

This error is rare in edited material but fairly common in casual writing. A quick look in any dictionary is all that is needed to avoid it.

lost　Sometimes considered to be an absolute adjective.
　See ABSOLUTE ADJECTIVES.

loth　See LOATH, LOATHE, LOTH.

lots, a lot　Sir Ernest Gowers in Fowler 1965 notes that the Concise Oxford Dictionary labels *a lot* colloquial but that modern writers do not hesitate to use it in serious prose. He cites Sir Winston Churchill as one of his examples. *Colloquial* is the favorite handbook label for *a lot* and *lots:* about three quarters of those in our collection use it. And many of them think *colloquial* is something bad, as this comment demonstrates:

> *Lots of, a lot of, a whole lot.* These terms are colloquial for "many," "much," "a great deal." The chief objection is that each is a vague, general expression —Shaw 1970

This line of attack seems to descend directly from Jensen 1935 and Bierce 1909.
　Other people have noticed what Gowers noticed. Crisp's 1971 survey of attitudes toward usage problems listed all the surveyed groups as finding *lots, a lot* established. Perrin & Ebbitt 1972 says that all these expressions are established in general, though not formal, usage. Our evidence confirms Perrin & Ebbitt's observation and Gowers's too. These expressions have been used in serious but not overformal writing for a long time, and they still are. Here are some examples:

There were lots of people in Oxford like that —John Galsworthy, *The Dark Flower,* 1913

There is a lot of good in it —John Galsworthy, *Another Sheaf,* 1919

Freezing was not so bad as people thought. There were lots worse ways to die —Jack London, "To Build a Fire," in *Chains of Light* (8th grade textbook), ed. Theodore Clymer, 1982

There is a lot of good literature in the world —Barrett J. Mandel, *AAUP Bulletin,* September 1971

As to favorable comments I can stand a good lot —Oliver Wendell Holmes d. 1935, letter, 1 Nov. 1916

. . . give a lot of facts or details about the bird —John Burroughs, *Wake-Robin,* 1871

. . . there are lots of young men with their girls —Virgil Thomson, *The Musical Scene,* 1947

It was used a lot by the dons —Oliver St. John Gogarty, *It Isn't This Time of Year At All!,* 1954

The Seurat pictures want a lot of seeing to appreciate —*The Journals of Arnold Bennett,* ed. Frank Swinnerton, 1954

. . . will have to sacrifice a lot of academic sacred cows —John Fischer, *Harper's,* February 1971

Lots of Swiss are worried —Mollie Panter-Downes, *New Yorker,* 26 Nov. 1950

. . . we must have lots of consumers' representatives —Christopher Hollis, *Punch,* 9 Dec. 1953

. . . the fact that lots of these amateur officers had . . . —James Gould Cozzens, *Guard of Honor,* 1948

I had spent a lot of time —James Jones, *Harper's,* February 1971

See also ALOT, A LOT.

loud, loudly　*Loud* is most familiar as an adjective, but it is also an established adverb, as many commentators have noted. Its adverbial uses are more limited than those of *loudly;* it always follows the verb that it modifies, and it occurs chiefly with only a few simple and familiar verbs:

. . . if he talks loud and is rude to the waiters —Frank Swinnerton, *Tokefield Papers,* 1949

. . . and who screams loudest —A. C. Spectorsky, *The Exurbanites,* 1955

. . . those who shout loudest against the draft —Malcolm S. Forbes, *Forbes,* 1 Dec. 1970

. . . cheering as loud as their lungs would allow —R. W. Apple, Jr., *N.Y. Times,* 30 July 1981

Loudly could be substituted in any of the above passages ("most loudly" for "loudest") and is the adverb of choice with most other verbs and in most other contexts:

. . . many loudly proclaimed their conviction —George V. Rogers, *New England Galaxy,* Fall 1970

A clock on the wall ticked loudly —Daphne du Maurier, *Ladies' Home Jour.,* August 1971

. . . his loudly amplified guitar —Pete Welding, *Rolling Stone,* 11 May 1972

. . . a raucous company of sightseers comes loudly down the quay —Jan Morris, *N.Y. Times Mag.,* 20 July 1975

. . . are loudly proud of their gift for understatement —Herb Caen, *Architectural Digest,* June 1986

love　Many of us remember being taught when we were young that it was not proper to use the verb *love* in the sense "like." This is an old controversy, limited to the United States. Bache 1869 thought no one could properly love food (how wrong he was!); Richard Grant White 1870 wanted *love* reserved for a deeper emotion—his thoughts echoed as late as Evans 1957; Ayres 1881 thought women misused *love;* Jensen 1935 termed the use a vulgarism (using food as one of his examples). The OED tried to draw a distinction, listing without stigma the sense "to have a strong liking for; to be fond of; to be devoted or addicted to" but stigmatizing the use that is simply synonymous with *like* as a frequent vulgarism in the U.S. However, their examples of unstigmatized use include people loving sleep, a fat goose, grapes, and bread and butter with their tea, so it is a little difficult to see just how strong one's fondness must be before the use escapes the charge of vulgarism.
　Happily, all this nonsense has blown over. You can still achieve varying degrees of intensity any time you want ("I like spinach but I love pizza"), even with food as an object. You can use *love* for trivial occasions ("I'd love to go bowling but I have to do my income tax") or important ones ("I love my wife") without confusing or revolting anyone. Let's be glad that this issue seems to have died.

luck out According to Harper 1985, *luck out* was commonly used during World War II in some such sense as "to meet with bad luck; run out of luck," as in describing a soldier who was a casualty of battle ("He lucked out") or a poker player who lost his chips. The Harper panelists are asked if they think that the newer sense of *luck out,* "to succeed because of good luck," has now superseded the older sense. Most of them vote yes, but 26 percent vote no.

We find those "no" votes a bit peculiar, because we have collected almost no evidence of the older sense cited by Harper. An entry for it can be found in Wentworth & Flexner's *Dictionary of American Slang* (1960), indicating that it had *"some W.W. II use; some general use,"* but we have to wonder how common its use ever became. Several World War II veterans on the Harper panel have never heard of it, and our files include only a single citation:

> Elementary school children get a day off Feb. 17. . . . Junior and Senior High Schools are lucked out. . . . Both will be in session —*Springfield* (Mass.) *Union,* 31 Jan. 1958

The little evidence we have showing *luck* used as a verb during World War II is suggestive of good luck, not bad:

> "Landing was the real job, in that fog. I was pretty sure about my navigation . . . and decided to luck it and set her down. . . ." —pilot quoted by William L. White, *New Republic,* 20 Apr. 1942

> Just now I wouldn't give a nickel for the chances, but we may luck it through —Commander Frederick J. Bell, *Condition Red,* 1943

Such usage is consistent with the occasional use of *luck* as a verb dating back to the 16th century. Likewise, *luck out* in its now common sense "succeed by luck" is consistent with older uses of the verb. We first recorded this *luck out* in 1951:

> . . . had been arrested by a plainclothesman, who, as they say in Harlem, had lucked out on him; that is, the officer had picked him up merely on suspicion, searched him in a hallway, and found his dope outfit —Eugene Kinkead, *New Yorker,* 10 Nov. 1951

A brief article by James E. Miller, Jr. in the December, 1954 issue of *American Speech* testified to the common use of *luck out* in this sense by college freshmen. By the 1960s it had become established in more general use. It now occurs commonly in both speech and general writing:

> . . . I've lucked out on a couple of occasions —Jay Jacobs, *Gourmet,* July 1979

> He lucked out in other ways, too —Barbara Rowes, *People,* 22 Nov. 1982

> . . . would have been a complete disaster if I had not lucked out —Andrew Sarris, *Village Voice,* 12 Apr. 1983

Luck is also now commonly combined as a verb with prepositions, especially *into:*

> . . . fortunate enough to have lucked into the bawdy, rollicking Paris of Henry Miller —James Atlas, *N.Y. Times Book Rev.,* 5 June 1983

> You might just luck into tomorrow's action —John Barth, *N.Y. Times Book Rev.,* 16 June 1985

The sense of *luck out* cited by Harper, however, appears no longer to be used.

lunch, luncheon It seems hard to believe now, but people once looked down their noses at *lunch:*

> This word . . . may at the best be accounted an inelegant abbreviation of *luncheon* —Ayres 1881

The relative merits of *lunch* and *luncheon* provoked at least a few arguments in the late 19th and early 20th centuries. Our files include a clipping from an unidentified newspaper of the 1920s that tells the story of one such argument—between the American writer William Dean Howells, who liked *lunch,* and his wife, who preferred *luncheon.* To settle the dispute, they looked in the Century Dictionary:

> "Lunch is preferred!" cried Mr. Howells. "And who do you think," he slyly added, "is given as an authority?"
> "Who?"
> "William Dean Howells," answered that gentleman.
> "Oh, he's no authority!" smartly retorted his wife.

The OED observed in 1903 that *lunch* was "Now the usual word exc. in specially formal use, though many persons still object to it as vulgar."

Lunch is still the usual word, of course, and its propriety is no longer called into question. *Luncheon* now usually refers to a formal midday meal for a group of people, often as part of a meeting or as a way of entertaining a guest:

> He has been honored at half a dozen public luncheons and banquets —Joe Alex Morris, *Saturday Evening Post,* 10 July 1954

> Attorney General Robert Kennedy, during a luncheon conference with several newspaper editors — Malcolm X, *Evergreen,* December 1967

Luncheon also has occasional use as a somewhat formal synonym of *lunch:*

> Luncheon is $12.50 and includes, for example cream of mushroom soup, supreme of chicken with mustard sauce and a selection from the dessert table — Wallace Turner, *N.Y. Times,* 15 Jan. 1984

But *lunch* itself is not a notably informal word. It is, simply, an ordinary, everyday word, like *breakfast,* that is in constant use as both a noun and as a verb:

> . . . Blass lunches at the best restaurants —*Current Biography,* September 1966

> As the lunch crowd drifted away —Gail Sheehy, *New York,* 24 Apr. 1972

> . . . small tobacco tins containing money for lunch — Anthony Bailey, *New Yorker,* 29 Oct. 1973

> . . . for the benefit of 40 lunching tourists —Pat Orvis, *N.Y. Times,* 11 Apr. 1976

William Dean Howells would be pleased.

luxuriant, luxurious Readers of other usage books are warned not to confuse these words, but uses of *luxuriant* to mean "of, relating to, or marked by luxury" or "of the finest or richest kind" have appeared periodically since 1671 and uses of *luxurious* to mean "fertile," "lush," or "prolific" have been around since 1644.

> ... a luxuriant apartment —Susan E. Ferrier, *The Inheritance,* 1824 (OED)

> ... in luxuriant restaurants —Theodore Dreiser, *Sister Carrie,* 1900

> ... a dozen records with luxuriant gold and red seals —Walter Van Tilburg Clark, "The Portable Phonograph," 1941

> ... luxuriant suede, slate floors, crystal chandeliers —Margaret E. Morse, *Southern Accents,* September–October 1984

> ... a luxurious branch —Henry Vaughan, sermon, 1644 (OED)

> ... some luxurious misty timber jutted into the prairie —Henry David Thoreau, *A Week on the Concord and Merrimack Rivers,* 1849

> ... his luxurious whiskers —George Meredith, *The Ordeal of Richard Feverel,* 1859

> A luxurious growth of plants —*Industrial & Engineering Chemistry,* 3 Mar. 1953

> ... a luxurious growth of wet moss and lichen —Nathaniel Nitkin, *New-England Galaxy,* Fall 1967

These uses appear to be standard and several examples are literary, but admittedly they are not nearly as common as the so-called "correct" ones. Whether they fall outside the pale is a matter of opinion. Merriam-Webster puts them inside: *luxuriant* as a synonym of *luxurious* is recorded without stigma in Webster's Ninth New Collegiate Dictionary, and *luxurious* as a synonym of *luxuriant* in Webster's Third. The OED straddles the fence: six citations are given at the cross-over sense of *luxurious,* which is labeled "Now rare"; three citations are given at the cross-over sense of *luxuriant,* with the comment that it is misused for *luxurious.* If the OED editors had had a few more citations for *luxuriant,* they might very well have arrived at a more liberal judgment. We doubt, however, that usage commentators would soften their strictures, even if the cross-over meanings became fairly common. The setup—two similar-sounding words horning in on each other's territory—is an ideal opportunity for a prescriptivist to take a stand and dig in his heels.

M

machismo, macho Reader's Digest 1983 objects to the overlap of usage between these two words and recommends avoiding the use of *macho* as an abstract noun meaning "machismo" and the use of *machismo* as an attributive. The attributive use of *machismo* can be defended on the grounds that almost all nouns have the capacity to be used attributively; this is an inherent feature of the English language. We have no evidence for *machismo* used as a predicate adjective, but the attributive use does show up occasionally.

> ... flexing their muscles, Indian wrestling and performing other such machismo feats —Betty Friedan, *N.Y. Times,* 31 Jan. 1971

The abstract-noun use of *macho* is defensible by virtue of its regular appearance in well-edited publications.

> ... saluted the President for putting his macho on the table —William Greider, *Esquire,* September 1975

> ... repository of the old speakeasy tradition and bastion of boardroom macho —Frank J. Prial, *N.Y. Times,* 11 Nov. 1976

> Was Vietnam a case of macho raised to a world dimension? —Norman Cousins, *Saturday Rev.,* 28 Apr. 1979

> Adolescent macho is one of the most oppressive forms of macho —Bruce C. Appleby, letter in *English Jour.,* February 1981

Since neither of these uses seems likely to cause confusion or misunderstanding, there is no compelling reason not to include them in your repertoire, if you are so inclined. Equally, you may keep them distinct (*macho,* adjective, and *machismo,* noun) as they are in Spanish, if you are inclined that way.

mad 1. The use of *mad* to mean "angry" was criticized in 1781 by the Reverend John Witherspoon (reprinted in Mathews 1931), who said "In this instance mad is only a metaphor for angry.... It is not found in any accurate writer, nor used by any good speaker" except for rhetorical effect. He was uncertain of its geographical province, discussing it under the heading of Americanisms but saying it was "perhaps an English vulgarism." The issue resurfaced a century later when an Englishman named Richard A. Proctor blamed the usage on Americans, who had "manifestly impaired the language." In rebuttal, Ayres 1881 quoted from Shakespeare and the Bible to show that the "angry" meaning had a proper English pedigree; however, the notion that it is an Americanism recurs from time to time in later commentators. Several of Ayres's contemporaries found the usage unexceptionable, and though the 1881 edition of Worcester called it "colloquial," the rest of his comment was neutral rather than hostile.

Such leniency was dispelled in the early 1900s as Vizetelly 1906, Bierce 1909, MacCracken & Sandison 1917, Baker 1927, and Jensen 1935, among others, raised their pens in unanimous protest. A common complaint labeled the usage a "careless colloquialism"; the proper, formal meaning was held to be "insane" or "crazy." One or two commentators claimed that although the "angry" use had formerly been proper, it had become unacceptable.

More recent commentators hold a wider variety of opinions. Nicholson 1957 calls the usage "slang"; Guth 1985 calls it "informal"; some, such as Macmillan 1982 and Bell & Cohn 1981, reiterate the colloquial *angry*/formal *insane* distinction; and Flesch 1964, Bernstein 1971, and Reader's Digest 1983 all find the use of *mad* to mean "angry" perfectly acceptable. Copperud 1980 goes so far as to say that the objection "is now a nearly forgotten pedantry." Some people obviously have longer memories than others.

As Ayres and even some of the detractors have pointed out, the "angry" sense can be found in earlier British usage, including Shakespeare and the Bible. Evidence dating from the resurgence of the criticism to the present shows the "angry" sense of *mad* being used on several levels. There is evidence for a certain amount—though not a great deal—of literary use. More common use is found in general nonfiction, in fictional narrative and dialogue, in informal writing such as correspondence, and of course in speech:

> I am sometimes so mad with myself when I think over it all —Anthony Trollope, *The Last Chronicle of Barset,* 1867 (OED)

> Being mad that he did not answer, and more at his laughing so —William Butler Yeats, *The Green Helmet,* 1910

> The veterans formulated their own rules such as (1) to discuss their most intimate problems, (2) never to get mad and (3) to confine the discussions to the meeting-period —Nathan Blackman, *Psychiatric Quarterly,* January 1948

> Both the Moroccans and the Spanish are mad at France —*Time,* 1 Feb. 1954

> They do not much mind if Papandreou makes those important people mad —Jane Kramer, *New Yorker,* 24 May 1982

> "Marjorie," he pleaded, "what's the matter? Are you mad? . . ." —Booth Tarkington, *Penrod,* 1914

> I was so mad the way father was talking that I thought I could shoot the man —Liam O'Flaherty, *The Informer,* 1925

> "I've got a mean disposition. Attempted assassinations make me mad." —Dashiell Hammett, *Red Harvest,* 1929

> "I was mad," he said. "I have a pretty bad temper. . . ." —John Steinbeck, *The Moon Is Down,* 1942

> "Your dying-Jesus grin," Jane called it, when she was mad at me —Christopher Isherwood, in *New World Writing,* 1952

> . . . they get mad and stay that way about six hours and then everything is dandy again —Flannery O'Connor, letter, 5 Oct. 1957

> I *want* the North to be mad. —William H. Seward, quoted by Henry Adams, letter, 29 Dec. 1860

> He used to call me "boy." That made me mad — Senator Burton K. Wheeler, quoted in Studs Terkel, *Hard Times,* 1970

2. *Mad* can be followed by the prepositions *about, at, for, on, with,* and occasionally *over.* People who are angry are *mad at* or less often *mad with* people or things; they are also sometimes *mad about* things. People who are carried away by enthusiasm are *mad about, mad for,* or, if they are British, *mad on* something or someone. People who are frantic or wild are *mad with* something.

> . . . the farmers' union, mad at the administration because of low agricultural prices —Tad Szulc, *Saturday Rev.,* 29 Apr. 1978

> This boy is not calling me up to find out if I am mad with him —Flannery O'Connor, letter, 1 Aug. 1957

> Mad about the prices, mad about the sloppy workmanship and mad at myself for being so dumb about cars —Vivian Gerber, quoted in *Progressive Woman,* October 1972

> Patently, she's mad about him —Archibald MacLeish, *Botteghe Oscure,* Quaderno XI, 1953

> My family are nearly all gone, and I'm not mad about the few that are left —Sir John Gielgud, quoted in *People,* 19 Oct. 1981

> My friend, Mrs. Fraser, is mad for such a house — Jane Austen, *Mansfield Park,* 1814

> Jim, mad for the sea after his first taste of salt water, acquired a small schooner yacht —John Dos Passos, *Chosen Country,* 1951

> . . . middle-class Robbie and working-class Kevin, who are both mad on cars —*Times Literary Supp.,* 3 Dec. 1971

> . . . a stupid *cocotte* who has begun by driving him mad with jealousy —Edmund Wilson, *Axel's Castle,* 1931

> . . . he made his first appearance in Paris, which promptly went mad over him —Deems Taylor, *Music to My Ears,* 1949

3. *Like mad,* stigmatized as slang by Shaw 1975 and Freeman 1983, appears with some frequency in general publications as well as in speech:

> Big city department stores are decentralizing like mad, and supermarkets spring up overnight in the wilderness, their cash registers tinkling an obbligato to the bullfrog chorus from the surrounding swamps —Weare Holbrook, *Atlantic,* December 1954

> Anyway, the executive strode through the rain with his head erect and his brain executiving like mad — Ralph Knight, *Saturday Evening Post,* 25 Dec. 1954

> . . . people rush around like mad —Herman Wouk, *Marjorie Morningstar,* 1955

> . . . "the kids' program," advises Bob Kingsbury, "is expanding like mad." —*Dun's,* October 1971

> Made by his wife Rose, they were covered in plush stuffed with excelsior, and sold like mad —Catherine Calvert, *Town & Country,* December 1982

madding crowd Evans 1957, Reader's Digest 1983, and Harper 1985 claim that the phrase *madding crowd,* which comes down to us from Thomas Gray's "Elegy in a Country Churchyard" (1750) via the title of Thomas Hardy's novel, *Far from the Madding Crowd* (1874), is commonly miscorrected to *maddening crowd.* Both Reader's Digest and Harper advise against using the term; Reader's Digest calls it a cliché. Evans takes a laissez-faire attitude about the spelling and is noncommittal about the use.

The evidence in the Merriam-Webster citation files, on the other hand, shows that the phrase is in fact rarely changed to *maddening crowd* in print. To the extent that the problem is real, it must be a problem of speech.

> You will never catch us in the surging, madding crowds —Goodman Ace, *Saturday Rev.,* 11 Dec. 1971

> . . . the President was kept as far as possible from the potentially madding crowd —*The Economist,* 23 Nov. 1974

And while it is easier to call something a cliché than to prove that it is not one, this phrase appears with no more than reasonable frequency and might be more aptly and flatteringly described as an allusion. The phrase, after all, serves a purpose, and there is no good reason not to use it.

magi Those who know this word only in the context of the Three Wise Men may possibly be caught in the same mistake that others have made before them:

> She is a kind of Magi —work of literary criticism, 1966

> . . . a power-seeker, a Magi if you will —*Publishers Weekly,* 16 Feb. 1976

Magi is the plural of *magus* and is likely to remain so. Plural spellings used as singulars are often strongly—but not always successfully—resisted. For examples, see the list at LATIN PLURALS.

magic, magical According to Fowler 1926 the distinguishing features of *magic* and *magical* are that (1) *magic* is almost always used attributively and (2) *magic* is used literally and in fixed phrases while *magical* is used with extended meaning. Shaw 1975 objects to figurative uses of *magic* and *magical* because he believes they are overused; he also advises using *magical* when *magic* cannot be used attributively. Chambers 1985 assigns literal uses to *magic* and figurative uses to *magical.* We agree to some extent with Fowler and Shaw, but not with Chambers. Here is what we have found in the evidence we have collected.

The adjective *magic* is almost exclusively an attributive adjective, partly because the word *magic* after a linking verb can be construed either as a noun or an adjective. *Magical* can be either an attributive or a predicate adjective, but attributive uses are about three times as common as the others. So nonattributive uses of either word are relatively uncommon. Attributive uses that are part of fixed phrases (as *magic carpet, magic square,* and *magic number*) call for *magic,* not *magical.*

Both words are used with literal force to refer to the supernatural.

> . . . bulls and stags represented a greater magic potency —Katharine Kuh, *Saturday Rev.,* 20 Nov. 1971

> The practice of using human fat as a powerful magical ingredient —A. W. Howitt, in *A Reader in General Anthropology,* ed. Carleton S. Coon, 1948

And both are commonly used with extended meanings, though their connotations may differ. *Magic* often implies some kind of instant effect, while *magical* often involves a feeling such as enchantment. These are only tendencies, however, because the figurative uses of the two words overlap quite a bit.

> . . . the magic solution to the defense problem in Europe —J. F. Golay, *New Republic,* 19 Apr. 1954

> . . . a man who really had the magic touch —Leonard Bernstein, *Atlantic,* April 1955

> . . . the magic plainness of La Fontaine's language — Richard Wilbur, *N.Y. Times Book Rev.,* 14 Oct. 1979

> . . . looked more and more magical and silvery as it danced away —G. K. Chesterton, *The Innocence of Father Brown,* 1911

> . . . its magical mornings and its incomparable sunsets —Paul Bowles, *Holiday,* March 1957

> . . . the magical ease with which they are summoned forth —Daniel Menaker, *Harper's,* October 1972

Whether or not the figurative meanings are, as Shaw and Nickles 1974 say, overused to the point of weakening the strength of the words, is a matter of opinion and a matter beyond anyone's control. One problem here is that, having become sensitive to a word or turn of phrase, one tends to think of it as more frequently used than a careful statistical count would warrant. From a practical point of view, since many writers of quality find that *magic* and *magical* serve them well in figurative uses, there is no good reason for you to feel they are forbidden to you. As with any other word, however, avoid overusing *magic* or *magical* within the context of your own writing.

Magna Carta, Magna Charta There is some debate over whether or not this term should be spelled with *h.* You may want to use the *Carta* spelling because (1) it agrees with the pronunciation \\ˌmag-nə-ˈkärt-ə\\ that is used for either spelling, (2) it agrees with the vote by the House of Lords discussed by Gowers in Fowler 1965 (and therefore may be construed as the officially sanctioned spelling), and (3) it agrees with the larger portion of the citational evidence for this term in the Merriam-Webster files.

> Later generations undoubtedly read into the Magna Carta a great many guarantees —Henry W. Littlefield, *History of Europe 1500–1848,* 1959

> The first great step on the constitutional road was Magna Carta —G. M. Trevelyan, *A Shortened History of England,* 1942

> Magna Carta is a code of some sixty clauses —Frank Barlow, *The Feudal Kingdom of England 1042–1216,* 3d ed., 1972

> Runnymede (of Magna Carta fame) —P. F. Brooks, *Travel Holiday,* November 1977

> . . . the Wagner Act of 1935, labor's Magna Carta — Richard Margolis, *N.Y. Times Book Rev.,* 1 July 1984

On the other hand, if you already use and prefer the *Charta* spelling, you can defend your usage on the grounds that it has been around for over three and a half centuries and has been used by numerous reputable writers on both sides of the Atlantic. (By the way, the claim of Partridge 1942, echoed by Copperud, that *Charta* isn't Latin, is not true.)

> Considered to represent the penn'orth appointed by Magna Charta —Charles Dickens, *Our Mutual Friend,* 1865 (OED)

> The county law . . . has been called the *Magna Charta* of Prussian local government —Woodrow Wilson, *The State,* rev. ed., 1898

> . . . if such a Magna Charta existed —Robert Morss Lovett, *All Our Years,* 1948

One further point is worth mentioning: when the original document and not a latter-day counterpart is being referred to, *Magna C(h)arta* is usually not preceded by *the* (see the Trevelyan, Barlow, and Dickens citations above). Although literal American use with the definite article is occasionally found in print (see the Littlefield citation above), in British usage the article is omitted. We suspect, however, that many Americans who are familiar with the term only from their school days use the definite article.

magnate, magnet These two words are occasionally confused.

His manager was William Butler, textile magnet and baron of Massachusetts politics —*Boston Sunday Globe,* 24 Feb. 1985

Better check your dictionary if you are in doubt about them.

See also HOMOGRAPH, HOMOPHONE, HOMONYM.

magnitude 1. Flesch 1964 claims that the phrase *of the first magnitude* is a "silly cliché." Evans 1957 says

The use of the word *star* to designate a prominent actor or singer led to the adoption of the astronomical term to distinguish the highest degree of preëminence, but it is now worn out.

It is true that the phrase is used to refer to show-business personalities and to products that are being reviewed or promoted:

... a new supper club star of the first magnitude — Eugene Boe, *Cue,* 4 Jan. 1964

... a writer of first magnitude whose performance he has respected and admired for years —Richard Plant, *N.Y. Times Book Rev.,* 6 June 1954

It is also used, however, in other contexts and has been for quite some time:

Whatever be your Birth, you're sure to be A Peer of the First Magnitude to me —George Stepney, *Poems,* ca. 1707 (OED)

It is a question of the first magnitude —Oliver Wendell Holmes d. 1935, *Missouri* v. *Illinois and Sanitary District of Chicago,* 1905

... he made contributions of the first magnitude — J. H. Plumb, *England in the Eighteenth Century,* 1950

Judging from the citations in our files, we doubt that *of the first magnitude* is overused in general contexts. If you are not writing a high-powered, overblown promotional release, you can use *of the first magnitude* without worrying about producing cliché-ridden prose. And if you are writing a high-powered, overblown promotional release, you are probably not much concerned whether your writing is cliché-ridden or not.

2. Flesch 1964 also claims that *magnitude* is "a long word meaning size," with the implication that the shorter word is a better choice. His statement is an oversimplification which neglects the nonphysical uses of *magnitude* as well as the overtones of immensity it often carries when it is used to mean "size." There are many instances in which the substitution of *size* for *magnitude* would yield an awkward or even meaningless sentence. Even when *size* could adequately substitute in meaning, *magnitude* is an acceptable alternative. Here is a sampling of nontechnical uses from our files:

Nor could I consider the magnitude and complexity of my plan as any argument of its impracticability — Mary Shelley, *Frankenstein,* 1818

This Court can be insensible neither to the magnitude nor delicacy of this question —John Marshall, *Dartmouth College* v. *Woodward,* 1819

... a European catastrophe of a magnitude so appalling, and a scope so unpredictable —George Bernard Shaw, Preface to *Back to Methuselah,* 1921

... the magnitude of the task which confronted me —Stella Gibbons, *Cold Comfort Farm,* 1932

... sociological and political changes of considerable magnitude were in progress —James A. Michener, *Report of the County Chairman,* 1961

The magnitude of this increase becomes more apparent when you consider that 9¼ million tons of fuel were burned in 1970 —*Annual Report, Virginia Electric & Power Co.,* 1970

We should not underestimate the probable magnitude of psychological damage —Dr. Peter Wood, *Runners World,* September 1980

It was an egregious error, one of such magnitude that Herron might spend the rest of the summer, if not the next several years, reliving that goal —Parton Keese, *N.Y. Times,* 28 Apr. 1980

magus See MAGI.

major The two main points made about the adjective *major* by usage writers are that it is overused and that when it is used, it should be as a comparative and not a positive adjective.

It is true that *major* does tend to get a lot of use and that in contexts where it invariably appears its meaning gets diluted. The announcement of a "major motion picture," for example, means nothing more than that a movie is being released. But you should not be dissuaded from using a word simply because other people use it too much. Just don't overuse it yourself. And while *major* may not be a particularly precise or dazzling adjective, many of the words suggested as possible replacements are not exactly eye-openers either. Gowers in Fowler 1965 recommends "*chief, main, principal,* etc."; Phythian 1979 lists "*large, important, big, momentous, main, prominent, chief, principal,* etc."; and Bremner 1980 suggests "*big, great, important, serious, chief, main, principal.*" It is hard to see what advantage some of these hold over *major.*

Phythian and Bremner join Evans 1957, Follett 1966, and Nickles 1974 in claiming that *major* is a comparative in the same way that *greater* is and so should not be used as a positive adjective. They base their argument on the word's origin as the comparative of Latin *magnus,* conveniently ignoring the fact that Latin and English are two different languages. Evans says, "A major campaign speech may be more precisely an important campaign speech, though, of course, it may be *major* in the sense of being more important than other speeches"; Copperud 1980 sums up the objections of various commentators by saying, "Thus a major work would be one that stands out by comparison with others, not a great one in absolute terms." This discrimination of meaning seems somewhat forced. Would a speech that was relatively important compared to other speeches but not absolutely important taken by itself be called a major speech? We doubt it. By describing the "correct" use as a comparative and not a positive, the critics are being too extreme in two extremes. First of all, *major* does not function in English in the same way that *greater* does. Phythian says "the primary meaning of *major* is *greater,*" but it is hard to find a context in which *greater* can be idiomatically substituted for *major,* precisely because *greater* is a true English comparative and *major* is not. Secondly, we have such examples as these:

> ... an inquiry on the major needs of Jewish education in the communities —*The Americana Annual 1953*

> Only with increasing difficulty can France continue her claim to being a major nation with world-wide commitments and world-wide power —Edgar S. Furniss, Jr., *Yale Rev.,* Autumn 1954

> She also plans a new major novel with a Louisiana background —*Publishers Weekly,* 5 June 1954

> All satellite armies ... depend on Russia for their major arms —*Time,* 13 Dec. 1954

> ... the present political attitudes of most major nations —*Wall Street Jour.,* 9 June 1969

> ... for five years we have been in a major bear market —Charles J. Rolo, *N.Y. Times Mag.,* 9 June 1974

> ... an $88 million plan for a major tourist development—it would have to be major at that outlay—is under way —Horace Sutton, *Saturday Rev.,* 20 Mar. 1976

They typify the criticized use, but they are not as purely positive as some of the recommended alternatives such as *big, important,* and *principal;* that is, although *major* functions like a positive adjective it also carries the connotation of comparison. Follett complains that "the standard of comparison is in each case [when *major* is supposedly misused] assumed to be known to all." He is right, but his statement actually explains the advantage of using *major* rather than showing why it should be avoided. The implied comparison which lies behind *major* gives it an extra flavor that *big, important,* and *principal* lack. On the other hand, this implied comparison does lend force to Phythian's and Nickles's objections to *more major.* And, in fact, we have practically no evidence for such use.

See also IMPLICIT COMPARATIVE.

majority   **1.** *Majority* is a singular noun in frequent use as one of those collectives that take either a singular or plural verb depending, in this case, on the writer's notion of the majority as a unit or as a collection of individuals. Our evidence of recent use shows a couple of trends. When *majority* stands alone as the subject, it tends to be used with a singular verb:

> ... the majority has decided to go with front-wheel drive —*Blair & Ketchum's Country Jour.,* May 1980

> The silent majority ... has dwindled —*I. F. Stone's Bi-Weekly,* 17 May 1971

> The majority was persuaded that ... —Paul Lerman, *Trans-Action,* July/August 1971

Less often it takes the plural verb:

> ... hope that the silent majority are more or less happy with the Daily Service —Rev. Hubert Hoskins, *Home & Family,* September 1974

When *majority* is followed by *of* and a plural noun (a common construction), a plural verb is usual:

> The majority of its members were girls —Oliver St. John Gogarty, *Mourning Became Mrs. Spendlove,* 1948

> The majority of the residents of Crown Heights are black —Lis Harris, *New Yorker,* 16 Sept. 1985

> ... the majority of the letters are to Russell —*Times Literary Supp.,* 23 Mar. 1967

Occasionally we find a singular verb:

> The immense majority of the students is apathetic —Thomas Molnar, *Yale Literary Mag.,* December 1981

2. The use of *majority* is rather discouraged by most of the commentators, both British and American, when it is applied to something regarded as not countable, like *cake* or *weather* or *day.* This attitude appears to be the present residuum of an older aversion to the use of *majority* for anything that does not vote. The use is recognized in dictionaries, but our more recent evidence suggests it may occur chiefly in speech, because we do not have a great deal of evidence for it in edited prose. These examples are typical of what we find:

> Not only is the vast majority of strip mined land unreclaimable, but .... —Peter Harnik, *Environmental Action,* 15 May 1971

> ... the majority of the book is devoted to the Asian part of the trip —Lola Dudley, *Library Jour.,* 15 Mar. 1967

Perrin & Ebbitt 1972 says the use is sometimes found "in Informal and General usage"; our evidence confirms their observation. The use is certainly a reasonable extension of the countable use, and we cannot see why it should bulk large in anyone's list of worries. Even more insubstantial is objection to uses like these:

> On the majority of walks —Timothy Gelatt, *Saturday Rev.,* 4 Mar. 1972

> If Garlits were a cat with nine lives he would have used up the majority of them —Sam Moses, *Sports Illustrated,* 29 Sept. 1986

You can, of course, use *most* in these instances, and feel assured that you are beyond the reach of any criticism.

3. A few usage writers discuss modifiers of *majority.* Fowler 1926, 1965 objects to the use of *greater* and *greatest* (except in cases where two majorities are being compared) because they suggest falsely that *majority* means no more than "part" or "number." Heritage 1982 and Bremner 1980 favor the same restrictions. *Great* is approved by all. Our citations for *great,* inflected or not, as a modifier with *majority* are not very numerous, so this may be a problem that a writer does not face very often.

Bremner 1980 and Bryson 1984 think that *vast* as a modifier of *majority* is a bit of a cliché. Our files show *vast* to be the most common modifier, but it is unlikely to run *great, overwhelming, large,* and several others out of business. Bryson notes that *vast majority* has been used by Partridge, Fowler, and Bernstein, so you will not find a united front on the subject. We see no reason for you not to join with Partridge, Fowler, and Bernstein and use *vast* if it sounds right to you.

4. *Majority, plurality.* More of our handbooks undertake to rehearse the familiar distinction between these words in their electoral use than to comment on any other aspect of *majority*'s usage. Any decent dictionary will tell you that this use of *majority* refers to more than half the total votes while *plurality* refers to a number of votes that is less than half the total yet is greater than the number for any other candidate.

make

> He [Samuel Johnson] found fault with me for using the phrase to *make* money. "Don't you see," said he, "the impropriety of it? To *make* money is to *coin* it; you should say *get* money." The phrase, however, is, I think, pretty current —James Boswell, *Life of Samuel Johnson,* 1791

Boswell was right. The OED shows, in fact, that the "gain, earn" sense of *make* has been "pretty current" since the 14th century. Johnson's objection to it is hard to understand, especially since he included it without stigma in his Dictionary (sense 17, "to raise as profit from anything"). His opinion may have played some part in persuading such critics as Vizetelly 1906 and Bierce 1909 that the "earn" sense of *make* was an error. For whatever reason, this sense has had some slight notoriety until fairly recently. Evans 1957 notes that it "has been stoutly opposed by the purists but it is now so common that it must be accepted as standard." It really has been common and standard all along.

> Make all the money thou canst —Shakespeare, *Othello,* 1605

> "... how to make money—how to turn a good income into a better...." —Jane Austen, *Mansfield Park,* 1814

> But making money, slowly first, then quicker —Lord Byron, *Don Juan,* Canto xii, 1823

> "... the rest you can retail out at a premium, and so cure your cough, and make money by it...." —Herman Melville, *The Confidence-Man,* 1857

> Dixie makes his money on two-bit gin —Langston Hughes, *Shakespeare in Harlem,* 1942

malapropism   No writer likes to waste good material. Usage writers are no different, and we suspect that the heading *malapropism* in several books attests to this natural frugality. Entries can be found in Todd & Hancock 1986, Harper 1975, 1985, Reader's Digest 1983, Bremner 1980, Phythian 1979, Perrin & Ebbitt 1972, and Watt 1967, among others. We are joining the group.

Malapropism is much older as a phenomenon than it is as a word. The word, coined from Mrs. Malaprop, a character in Richard Brinsley Sheridan's *The Rivals* (1775), only came into use in the 19th century. But the botching of big words goes back at least to the 16th century, when writers of scholarly intent introduced many words from Latin into the language. McKnight 1928 notes that considerable fun was derived by writers from the difficulty uneducated or partially educated people had with hard words. Sir Thomas Wilson, in his *Arte of Rhetorique* of 1553—not a place you would ordinarily look for laughs—has several such passages purporting to be from genuine speech. McKnight observes that Shakespeare used the same sort of speech for some of his comic characters, notably the police officers Elbow and Dogberry, as well as Mrs. Quickly and various clowns

and country folk. Jespersen, in *Growth and Structure of the English Language* (1905), makes the point that English literature is richer in this sort of humor than that of any other language.

Jespersen and Bolinger 1980 discuss the causes of malapropism. Bolinger identifies it as a failure of contrast—the words are close enough in sound or appearance to be used one for the other. Jespersen notes that hard words are usually cut off from ordinary words; they share neither etymological roots nor associations of ideas with the common stock of the vocabulary. They must therefore be learned in isolation, and this isolation makes it easier for them to be exchanged for a similarly isolated hard word. Bolinger says that malapropism is a regular adornment of jargon, jargon being language that is full of specialized terms unconnected to ordinary discourse. He gives as an example from jargon a linguist's substitution of *tenant* for *tenet;* we have a like example in our own files:

> ... posits counter-arguments for some of Chomsky's basic tenants —*Linguistic Reporter,* September 1974

So we have two kinds of malapropism—the deliberate confusion of hard words for humorous effect that has been used by writers from Shakespeare's time and before, and inadvertent malapropisms committed by people not trying to be funny. Unconscious malapropisms are undoubtedly more common in speech than in writing. Here are three from local radio stations:

> Bob Lemon will be delegated to the front office —19 June 1979

> ... driving without a license or resignation —5 Jan. 1980

> ... arraigned ... on a charge of statuary rape —9 May 1983

They can also be found in reported speech:

> ... the ability to zero in on the essence of a problem and synthesize it for the Governor —in *N.Y. Times Mag.,* 29 June 1980

> ... what it's gonna affect is our truth and velocity with the citizens — in *Playboy,* November 1983

> Admiral Rickover worked deciduously during his 54 years of naval service —in James J. Kilpatrick's column, *Medford* (Oreg.) *Mail Tribune,* 8 Jan. 1985

And they turn up in writing too:

> There was some worry in the clubhouse, though, and it emulated from Lynn —reporter, *Springfield* (Mass.) *Republican,* 22 Apr. 1979

> ... one of those ersatz plaster-and-lathe motel complexes —reporter, *Rolling Stone,* 17 Feb. 1972

> The vision of Safirius Arbiter is an awesome one, since Safire is neither an entomologist nor an expert on usage —reviewer, *Saturday Rev.,* November 1980

> ... the most famous diet-conscious Red Sox because of his chicken regiment —reporter, *Springfield* (Mass.) *Morning Union,* 4 Sept. 1985

> ... you'll use these porcelains to dramatize a table or as limelights on an important armoire shelf —advt., *N.Y. Times,* 26 Apr. 1981

... recommended the merger as a money-saving mechanism that would eliminate the duplicity of services —reporter, *Springfield* (Mass.) *Morning Union,* 2 Nov. 1983

Malapropisms are venial sins. They are sometimes funny, and many writers on usage collect them, sometimes to prick pretension, sometimes to illustrate a threnody for the state of American education, or sometimes just for laughs. Humor writers will probably never stop using them. But they represent only a failure of the memory to retain the distinctive features of two different words. If you are trying to expand your vocabulary, you will probably drop a clanger now and then. We all do. An occasional linguistic pratfall seems not to be too high a price to pay for a richer vocabulary.

A related phenomenon is the mixed metaphor, likewise prominently displayed for fun in many usage books. And, yes, see also MIXED METAPHOR in this book.

male Although there has been a long-continued controversy over the use of *female* (which see), the parallel term *male* has been virtually ignored. Flesch 1964, however, does not like *male* used as a noun of humans. His objection is similar to that made to *female.* But unless our evidence is missing something, this is not much of a problem. *Male* is almost exclusively used as an adjective. As a noun it is used, as you would expect, biologically and in other contexts where it is paired with *female.*

> Terms like "pioneer," "farmer," and "settler" should clearly include females as well as males — Harper 1985

> ... followed by a singular pronoun when there is no question whether it is males or females that are being talked about —Evans 1957

It would seem to be a useful term when the age associations of *man* and *boy* need to be avoided, but we do not have evidence that it is much used this way. These are probably examples of such use:

> She is a trained observer of hotels, domestic service and the predatory habits of the Italian male —*British Book News,* September 1954

> She is twenty, unmarried and pregnant . . . ; it is not clear what obscure male is responsible —Mary McCarthy, *Occasional Prose,* 1985

Once in a while it turns up where *man* might be expected:

> ... in an age when the male doesn't even take off his hat or the woman her overcoat —James Thurber, letter, October 1936

You may not feel called upon to use the noun *male* very frequently except to pair it with *female,* but it is available for other uses if you want it.

man *Man* in its generic sense "a human being" has come under considerable attack in recent years by people who feel that because it is so widely understood in its somewhat more recent sense of "a male person," its generic sense slights women. This is not an unreasonable objection; however, the replacement of this generic *man* has been slowed by some mild resistance to replacing it with the four-syllable *human being* and greater, if less comprehensible, resistance to the two-syllable *human.* (For more on the *human–human being* controversy, see HUMAN.) *Human* and *human being* are making some progress as replacements on the schoolbook level; however, when we see them being used in place of *Man* by the intellectual elite of religion, science, and philosophy—those who deal with problems of cosmic dimension and treat everything in the large—we will know we have seen a successful revolution.

You, in the meantime, can use *human* or *human being* or even *person* if you dislike the generic *man.* Or you can keep on using *man.* One way or the other, you will probably please someone and displease another. You will find longer discussions in McMahan & Day 1980, 1984, Reader's Digest 1983, Irmscher 1976, and other handbooks, as well as in books that deal extensively with the questions of gender and sexism in English, such as Dennis Baron's *Grammar and Gender* (1986), Rosalie Maggio's *The Nonsexist Word Finder* (1987), and Casey Miller and Kate Swift's *Words and Women* (1976). Some of these also take up the matter of compounds with -*man* (*policeman, fireman,* etc.), which in this book are covered at SEXISM 1.

manifold, manyfold The adjective having such senses as "various" and "many" is spelled *manifold:*

> ... all are part of Roderick's manifold adventures — John Butt, *English Literature in the Mid-Eighteenth Century,* edited & completed by Geoffrey Carnall, 1979

The adverb meaning "by many times" is now almost always spelled *manyfold:*

> This investment, too, will be returned to us manyfold —Abraham Ribicoff, *Saturday Rev.,* 22 Apr. 1972

Manifold does have some adverbial use:

> ... the total extent of scientific knowledge gathered throughout history will be exceeded manifold within a few decades —John G. Meitner, ed., in Preface to *Astronautics for Science Teachers,* 1965

But such usage, although impressively old (dating back to before the 12th century), is extremely rare in modern English, and it stands a good chance of being cited as an error.

mankind *Mankind* has been open to some of the same objections as the generic use of *man* (which see). If our usage books are right, this is a subject less fervently pursued than *man,* probably because *mankind* in modern use is used almost exclusively to mean "the human race." It does, however, have a sense "men":

> PERT. Your knowing of Mr. Dorimant, in my mind, should rather make you hate all mankind.
> MRS. LOVEIT. So it does, besides himself.
> —George Etherege, *The Man of Mode,* 1676

This sense seems to be quite rare in the 20th century. Most modern use is of this type:

> It was to be more than a compilation of national histories; it was to tell the story of mankind —*Times Literary Supp.,* 19 Feb. 1971

If *mankind* is offensive to you, you have available *humankind, human beings, humans,* and *people,* at the very least, for replacements. *Humankind,* like *mankind,* is a mass noun that will force you to make up your mind about agreement; some people make such nouns plural, some singular. The other alternatives are all comfortably plural.

manner In *Hamlet* there is the phrase *to the manner born* which is used to mean "accustomed to a practice from birth." It seems to have caught the fancy of the literary set and has subsequently been stretched in one way or another to fit various somewhat similar contexts. This one is not too far from Shakespeare's meaning:

> She looks very pretty, breakfasting in bed as to the manner born —Vita Sackville-West, *The Edwardians,* 1980

For at least sixty years various commentators have warned against the spelling *manor* in place of *manner.* Among the more recent of these are Shaw 1987, Bremner 1980, and Copperud 1980. Some of these recognize that the spelling *manor* gives the phrase a different twist, but still disapprove. Reader's Digest 1983, however, simply treats *to the manor born* as a phrase meaning "of upper-class birth and education"—a sort of equivalent to *born with a silver spoon in one's mouth.* They provide a couple of examples, including this one:

> ... Kay, according to her, should have got married quietly in City Hall, instead of making Harald, who was not to the manor born, try to carry off a wedding in J. P. Morgan's church —Mary McCarthy, *The Group,* 1963

We think Reader's Digest has taken the more reasonable approach. If someone intends a meaning that is not Shakespeare's, why use Shakespeare's spelling? But you should note that both of these phrases are conspicuously literary, and you should not throw them around carelessly.

mantel, mantle These two words are now usually regarded as distinct from each other, with *mantel* used for a shelf above a fireplace, and *mantle* used for a cloak or a cover. However, they were originally nothing more than spelling variants (both derived from the Old French *mantel,* "cloak"), and *mantle* still occurs on occasion as a variant of *mantel:*

> An autographed picture of John Dewey dominates the mantle —William D. Lewis, *AAUP Bulletin,* December 1967

> Hand hewn beams, original mantle, plank floors throughout —advt., *N.Y. Times Mag.,* 25 May 1980

This use of *mantle* seems now to be largely confined to American English (American dictionaries treat it as standard, but British dictionaries do not recognize it). The few commentators who take note of it are all American, and all of them prefer *mantel* in such contexts. Our evidence shows that most writers prefer *mantel* as well:

> ... a bottle of J & B on the mantel —Donald Barthelme, *New Yorker,* 17 July 1971

> ... in a fishbowl on his mantel —Joseph Wambaugh, *The Black Marble,* 1978

> ... he pauses by the fireplace mantel —John Updike, *Playboy,* September 1981

many a The phrase *many a* is followed by a singular noun, and when that noun is the subject of a verb, a singular verb:

> ... many a student graduates without forming a firm conviction —Carl R. Woodward, *Phi Gamma Delta,* December 1968

> ... many a man before him has become confused —Ashley Montagu, *Psychology Today,* April 1968

But pronoun reference, when it occurs, is governed by notional agreement and may thus be plural or singular:

> ... and misled many a good body that put their trust in me —Thomas Gray, letter, 6 Sept. 1758

> Many a prophet who had predicted that business would slip ... changed his mind —*Time,* 30 Mar. 1953

manyfold See MANIFOLD, MANYFOLD.

mar When the verb *mar* is modified by a prepositional phrase, the preposition is usually *by:*

> ... all these gifts and qualities, ... were marred by prodigious faults —Virginia Woolf, *The Second Common Reader,* 1932

> ... his intellect, which was amazingly spotty, marred by great gaps —Norman Mailer, *The Naked and the Dead,* 1948

> ... little booklet is unfortunately marred by a multiplicity of minor errors —Randolph S. Churchill, *Books of the Month,* June–July 1953

Less frequently, *mar* is followed by *with:*

> ... a painstaking compilation, but ... marred with unscholarly remarks —*Dictionary of American History,* 1940

marathon Newman 1974 lampoons newspaper use of the phrase *marathon talks,* placing it within a tradition of "the hack phrase, the labored point, and the stereotyped treatment" that runs through American journalism. The term certainly is well established, as the following examples will show. Whether it qualifies as a hack phrase, labored point, or stereotyped treatment is a question of individual judgment. Comparing the dates in the first example, one may justifiably see its use in that case, at least, as no exaggeration:

> ... marathon talks, begun in 1955, are continuing —*Newsweek,* 23 June 1958

> ... his voice hoarse from marathon speechmaking —*Time,* 24 Mar. 1952

> ... both Houses of Congress, neglecting all other business, held a marathon debate ... on the admission of Kansas into the Union —Morton Hunt, *New Yorker,* 3 Nov. 1956

This attributive use perhaps derives from the marathon dances of the 1920s or earlier; at least we have plenty of evidence for the attributive from that time:

> Marathon bowling has generally fallen to the lot of the more ambitious male members of the bowling fraternity —*Springfield* (Mass.) *Union,* 8 June 1918

> ... what seems to have been a "Marathon talking test" in Hyde Park —*Manchester Guardian Weekly,* 19 June 1925

> ... Professor Camillo Baucia, "champion marathon pianist of Europe" —*Time,* 7 Dec. 1925

> The Wolf is still-hunter or marathon chaser —Ernest Thompson Seton, *Lives of Game Animals,* 1925

The attributive is fully established and perfectly standard.

Howard 1977 is distressed by the misuse of the noun for an endurance contest of any kind. The original idea, he says, was to cover the ground as quickly as possible, and, to be sure, that is exactly what the best marathoners still try to do. However, Mr. Howard himself observed in another connection that "English grammar evolves with majestic disregard for the susceptibilities of classical scholars" (*Weasel Words,* 1978), and the observation is as true of vocabulary as of grammar. It is the notion of endurance—an obvious factor in so long a race—that has attached itself so prominently to the word in English, even in reference books:

> . . . the marathon, the prize endurance event of the Olympics —*Collier's Year Book,* 1949

marginal Bernstein 1965, Gowers in Fowler 1965, Phythian 1979, and Bryson 1984 are all concerned in one way or other about figurative uses of *marginal.* The commentators have differing ideas of the proper scope of this adjective, and, in any event, they have reached the dike a little too late to stop the leak. The frequency of figurative use of this word does appear to have accelerated. It may be that the pressure of economics on the consciousness of the public is behind this development, although many of the figurative uses look fairly remote from technical economic uses. Most of what we find seems to stem from a figurative use dated back to 1887 in the OED; the general notion behind it is "barely acceptable" or "barely exceeding some minimum requirement." Here is a sample of recent use:

> . . . found themselves in marginal jobs stereotyped as feminine —Frederika Randall, *N.Y. Times Book Rev.,* 12 Dec. 1982

> . . . a man dulled by a marginal life —V. S. Naipaul, *Among the Believers,* 1981

> The "waiver" system, designed to facilitate the moving of marginal players —Robert W. Creamer, *Sports Illustrated,* 18 Sept. 1982

> . . . total, functional or marginal nonreaders —Jonathan Kozol, *N.Y. Times Book Rev.,* 3 Mar. 1985

Some of the economic citations seem very close to this general use, no matter how technically they might be defined:

> . . . marginal banks engage in frenzied borrowing and lending to look more liquid than they are —John W. Dizard, *Fortune,* 29 Nov. 1982

> . . . U.S. economic interests in the region are currently marginal—less than 2 percent of U.S. investments abroad are in Central America and less than 2 percent of our trade is with the region —Robert A. Pastor, *Atlantic,* July 1982

Sometimes the minimum requirement is that of perception or probability:

> . . . the bulk of the program's efforts—and expense— would be focused on threats that were marginal if not imaginary —Gregg Easterbrook, *Atlantic,* October 1982

> . . . coverage by the U.S. intelligence system is either marginal or nonexistent —report of U.S. Senate Intelligence Committee, quoted in *Wall Street Jour.,* 5 Mar. 1982

Some of the figurative uses derive from the original margin; they suggest the outside edges or the fringes:

> Connolly could also write well about certain individual writers, especially figures who are minor or marginal —Hilton Kramer, *N.Y. Times Book Rev.,* 19 Feb. 1984

> . . . you probably can't put together a majority coalition unless you are willing to deal with those marginal interests that will give you the votes needed to win —David A. Stockman, quoted in *Atlantic,* December 1981

> Miss Woodby, however, is only a marginal figure . . . , just one of the characters observed by a heroine —John Butt, *English Literature in the Mid-Eighteenth Century,* edited & completed by Geoffrey Carnall, 1979

There may be senses developing here that are not fully covered in current dictionaries, and it could turn out that lexicographers have some catching up to do.

marital, martial The issue here is not usage but typography. A slip on the keyboard easily transposes the *i* and the *t,* changing *marital* to *martial* or vice versa. We do not know how often this typo makes it into print, but it is common enough to have caught a few critical eyes. The Oxford American Dictionary, in fact, goes so far as to explicitly warn against confusion of these two words. We doubt very much that such confusion has ever occurred.

marshal, marshall The usual spelling of both the noun and verb is *marshal,* but a look in the OED shows that *marshall* has seen occasional use as a variant for centuries. We have a fair amount of recent evidence of its occurrence in edited prose:

> . . . reminds me of the two frontier town marshalls —Frederick Fox, letter, *N.Y. Times Book Rev.,* 21 Nov. 1965

> The fire marshall conducting the investigation — *New York,* 30 Aug. 1971

> . . . she attempted to marshall and refine her feelings —Albert H. Johnston, *Publishers Weekly,* 4 Aug. 1975

> . . . plants can marshall a complex array of chemical countermeasures —J. A. Miller, *Science News,* 25 May 1985

Nevertheless, *marshall* is regarded as a spelling error by several commentators. It seems to be a bit more likely in British English, where *marshalled* and *marshalling* are common for the inflected forms of the verb. In American English, especially, *marshal* is the better choice.

martial See MARITAL, MARTIAL.

martyr 1. *Noun.* When *martyr* is used with a preposition, it is usually followed by *to:*

> He'd been a martyr to asthma all his life —A. J. Cronin, *The Citadel,* 1937

> . . . Chaucer, as an amorous poet, made Aeneas fickle instead of a martyr to duty —Gilbert Highet, *The Classical Tradition,* 1949

Occasionally *martyr* is followed by *for* or *of:*

> ... she died as martyr for the new morality against the old —John Ardagh, *Washington Post Book World,* 26 Sept. 1971

> ... the common picture of her (Cleopatra) as a martyr of love, a mortal Aphrodite —John Buchan, *Augustus,* 1937

Raub 1897 suggests using "martyr *for* or *to* a cause, *to* a disease." According to our evidence, the distinction still exists. Of those citations in the Merriam-Webster files that show *martyr* used in connection with a physical condition, all follow it with *to,* as in the Cronin example above.

2. *Verb.* When the verb *martyr* is used with a preposition whose object is the reason, it is usually *for:*

> ... he is determined to martyr himself, if need be, for the anti-Nazi cause —*Time,* 14 Apr. 1941

> ... martyred by Diocletian for refusing to abjure the Christian faith —E. R. Leach, *London Calling,* 24 June 1954

massive The use of the word *massive* in its various extended senses has been drawing critical fire for some twenty-five years. Edmund Wilson was one of the first writers to pronounce against it:

> I have also written before of this stupid and oppressive word which seems to have become since then even more common as a ready cliché that acts as a blackout on thinking. One now meets it in every department: literary, political, scientific —*The Bit Between My Teeth,* 1965

Several other writers, among them Gowers in Fowler 1965, Watt 1967, Newman 1974, Howard 1977, Simon 1980, have also noted what they call the overuse of *massive.* While it is true that use of *massive* has become widespread, especially over the last forty years or so, the word has been in extended use for quite a long time. The OED dates the introduction of such a use from 1561. Our citation files testify to the frequency with which extended use of *massive* has occurred from the late 19th century through the mid 20th:

> Eustacia's manner was as a rule of a slumberous sort, her passions being of the massive rather than the vivacious kind —Thomas Hardy, *The Return of the Native,* 1878

> ... the far-reaching plans which his august and massive intellect might conceive —A. C. Whitehead, *The Standard Bearer,* 1915

> ... who gave to the service of their master a sober and massive obedience —Francis Hackett, *Henry the Eighth,* 1929

> ... she watched Grandmother move with a massive dignity —Ellen Glasgow, *Vein of Iron,* 1935

> If ever there was a massive chic she had personified it —Djuna Barnes, *Nightwood,* 1936

> ... when Ned had surpassed himself in massive playfulness —A. J. Cronin, *The Keys of the Kingdom,* 1941

> ... the U.S. people, still thunderstruck by the massive fact of Franklin Roosevelt's death —*Time,* 23 Apr. 1945

> ... his upper lip lifted under that nose to form a smile of somewhat massive irony —Robert Penn Warren, *All the King's Men,* 1946

> At a time when massive changes are occurring with lightning speed throughout the world —Harry S. Truman, Message to Congress, 14 Jan. 1946

> ... Ben, that funeral will be massive! They'll come from Maine, Massachusetts, Vermont, New Hampshire! —Arthur Miller, *Death of a Salesman,* 1949

Wilson suggests, as do others, that John Foster Dulles's use of "massive retaliation" in a speech given in 1954 might have been a spur to the widespread use of *massive.* However, Wilson goes on to say that broad use of *massive* had picked up its pace before that speech. *Massive* was in common use in reporting during World War II:

> For really effective massive night bombing, the radius is still between 450 and 500 miles —*Fortune,* January 1943

> ... he [MacArthur] was striking his massive blow, far behind the enemy's main positions —*Time,* 30 Oct. 1944

> A massive assault by the United States Army Air Forces —*Newsweek,* 25 Dec. 1944

> ... holding the reserves back and then launching a massive stroke at a chosen moment —H. Liddell Hart, *Harper's,* January 1946

> ... the Remagen bridgehead and the massive Russian breakthrough in March —Dixon Wecter, *Saturday Rev.,* 22 June 1946

The popularity this use of *massive* found in the 1940s seems to have increased in the postwar years and persisted to the present:

> A policy of massive dollar loans would do no more than postpone the problem —*The Economist,* 9 Aug. 1947

> The massive support given by the working class to Labour was natural enough —Roy Lewis & Angus Maude, *The English Middle Classes,* 1950

> ... the revolt against domination is so massive — Alan Paton, *Saturday Rev.,* 24 Nov. 1951

> ... her actual description of the relations between the sexes, as it unfolds in massive detail —Dwight Macdonald, *The Reporter,* 14 Apr. 1953

> There has been a massive, almost glacial, shift away from the passion for individual freedom —Archibald MacLeish, *American Scholar,* Autumn 1953

> ... theories and hypotheses solidly established on a massive foundation of experimental evidence — Aldous Huxley, *Brave New World Revisited,* 1958

> ... another massive publishing event, on which work was started in 1882 and was completed twenty years later —Katharine S. White, *New Yorker,* 10 Dec. 1966

> The massive intake of French vocabulary in Middle English was so great —W. F. Bolton, *A Short History of Literary English,* 1967

> ... the feeling of frustration, of being ineffectual, is massive —David Halberstam, *Harper's,* December 1968

The treatment of Constantine's most massive achievement —*Times Literary Supp.*, 16 Apr. 1970

... a massive march on City Hall —Selwyn Raab, *N.Y. Times,* 8 June 1975

... U.S. oil companies still have a massive stake in Libya —Bill Paul, *Wall Street Jour.*, 20 Aug. 1981

This first Chakkri king ... had the same massive common sense and instinct for leadership that Washington had —Roger Warner, *Smithsonian,* June 1982

... massive use of computer time —Paul Preuss, *Science 85*, July/August 1985

masterful, masterly The usage books, including Safire 1984, Bremner 1980, Shaw 1970, 1975, 1987, Simon 1980, Copperud 1960, 1964, 1970, 1980, Bernstein 1958, 1965, 1977, Phythian 1979, Sellers 1975, Harper 1975, 1985, Chambers 1985, Einstein 1985, just about uniformly insist that *masterful* must mean "domineering" and *masterly* "skillful, expert" and that it is a misuse of *masterful* to use it in the sense given for *masterly*. The two adjectives are thus distinct, and each—especially *masterful*—is to be kept in its proper place.

This distinction, however neat and convenient, is entirely factitious, the invention of H. W. Fowler in 1926. Fowler knew, as anyone who looks at the OED can, and said that the two words were for a long time interchangeable. Each of them had a "domineering" sense and a "skillful, expert" sense. The "domineering" sense of *masterly* dropped into disuse around the end of the 18th century. Fowler seems to have thought the world of English usage would be a tidier place if *masterful* too were limited to one sense. He therefore declared the differentiation between the two words to be complete, and followed with a number of examples that effectively showed it was not, but that he declared to be misuses. From then until now, usage writers have followed Fowler, condemning as misuse all the evidence that proved Fowler's opinion was only wishful thinking in the first place.

Here are some examples that show that the "obsolescent" (Partridge 1942) sense of *masterful* is as alive and well as it was in Fowler's day:

Lafe is a masterful letter writer, a practised hand, as it were —Henry Miller, *The Air-Conditioned Nightmare,* 1945

... the tradition of masterful treatment of medical problems in books for the general reader —Edgar Z. Friedenberg, *N.Y. Rev. of Books,* 30 Dec. 1971

... director Herbert Ross has done a masterful job of making his people act like humans —Arthur Knight, *Saturday Rev.*, 6 Nov. 1971

... sole ballottine blessed with a frame of masterful brioche —Gael Greene, *New York,* 3 Mar. 1975

It was once again a masterful performance —Dean Acheson, quoted in Merle Miller, *Plain Speaking,* 1973

A masterful place hitter and bunter, Keeler ... bridged the gap between ancient and modern baseball —David Nemec, in *The Ultimate Baseball Book,* ed. Daniel Okrent & Harris Lewine, 1984

... all were tied together in masterful television addresses —Douglas Hallett, *Wall Street Jour.*, 19 Aug. 1980

... Chaucer's masterful uses of the Song of Solomon —Edward Craney Jacobs, *Chaucer Rev.*, Fall 1980

... won the AFC Central title with a masterful game plan that shut down Cincinnati —*Springfield* (Mass.) *Morning Union* (AP), 19 Dec. 1986

... his dance criticism was masterful —Lois Draegin, *Harper's,* February 1984

Some writers use both *masterful* and *masterly* together:

He had a masterly sense of English and was a masterful copy-editor—the best, I am told by friends, they ever knew —Mary McCarthy, *Occasional Prose,* 1985

So the "skillful, expert" sense of *masterful* flourishes in standard prose. Its use has not diminished, as far as we can tell from our evidence, either the use of *masterly* or the use of the "domineering" sense of *masterful:*

... artists in their own right—several of them masterly ones —William Styron, *This Quiet Dust and Other Writings,* 1982

This is a masterly poem —Flannery O'Connor, letter, 30 Nov. 1957

They were masterly statesmen, not masterful supermen —David Thomson, *Europe Since Napoleon,* 2d ed., rev., 1962

"But then you don't seem powerless to me, either. Quite masterful, the way you run your TV crew." —John Updike, *Bech Is Back,* 1982

There are a few dissenters from the Fowler tradition, notably Bryson 1984 and Flesch 1983. Their dissent is based chiefly on the problem of adverbial use, which is also considered a bit of a problem by some of the commentators who follow Fowler. For an adverb counterpart, *masterful* has the readily available *masterfully,* but the choice is not so simple for *masterly. Masterly* is itself used as an adverb, but using the same form for both adjective and adverb may be a bit uncomfortable—at least for some—as is suggested by this circumlocution:

As Sir William Temple says of a great general, it is necessary not only that his designs be formed in a masterly manner, but ... —Samuel Johnson, in James Boswell, *Life of Samuel Johnson,* 1791

The alternative form *masterlily* is mentioned by a few writers, but no one seems to have actually used it. Dissatisfaction with *masterly* as an adverb and with the apparently unused *masterlily* leaves the Fowler-followers no solution to the adverb problem other than the Johnsonian circumlocution or rewriting in some other way. Bryson and Flesch recommend using *masterfully.* And at least one user of *masterly* as an adjective has done so:

... it so masterfully crystallized ... the sinister issues —William Styron, *This Quiet Dust and Other Writings,* 1982

There is some degree of differentiation between *masterful* and *masterly* used in the "skillful" sense. Our backing suggests that *masterly* is stronger in literary use; *masterful* in general use—in reviews, in sportswriting, in speech, and in other areas where high formality is not the order of the day. Both words are entirely standard and in quite respectable use. The recommended distinction is easy to observe, and you may prefer to do so, but you are in good company if you choose to ignore it.

mastery Both Lincoln Library 1924 and Bernstein 1965 note a distinction in preposition usage with the word *mastery:* it is *mastery of* a subject but *over* a person. Actual usage shows that things are not so clearcut. Generally, *mastery of* is, in fact, found when something impersonal is involved:

> ... had still far to go before he obtained absolute mastery of the government —J. H. Plumb, *England in the Eighteenth Century,* 1950

> Mastery of one's own discipline can be a lifework —Irving Kolodin, *Saturday Rev.,* 29 Jan. 1972

> ... mastery of managerial techniques —William H. Whyte, Jr., *The Organization Man,* 1956

However, use of *mastery of* may occasionally involve persons:

> ... leading on towards mastery of ourselves and our environment —Bertrand Russell, *Education and the Good Life,* 1926

Mastery over is found less often, but it too involves something impersonal more frequently than it involves persons:

> ... the mastery of the Alexandrians over the difficult art of the textbook —Benjamin Farrington, *Greek Science,* 1953

> The sun resumed its blessed mastery over the land —Oscar Handlin, *The Uprooted,* 1951

> It's amazing ... the complete mastery he's held over them —Ned Martin, radio baseball broadcast, 30 Apr. 1975

materialize Several common uses of this verb have been the object of critical commentary throughout much of the 20th century. In its oldest sense, *materialize* is a transitive verb meaning " to give material form to," as in "materialize an idea by writing it down." That sense dates back to 1710. The 19th century saw the development of several additional senses, including "to make materialistic," "to cause (a spirit) to appear in bodily form," and "to assume bodily form," as in "The ghost materialized." None of these senses have been disputed. But two other senses from the 19th century have not fared as well—"to make an appearance; appear suddenly":

> Some fifteen or twenty hounds that suddenly materialized among the bee-hives —Miss Murfree, *The Prophet of the Great Smoky Mountain,* 1885 (OED)

and "to come into existence; develop into something tangible":

> Year after year passed and these promises failed to materialise —*Blackwell's Mag.,* May 1891 (OED)

These uses have been treated as standard in dictionaries since 1905, when the OED entry for *materialize* was first published. They have been treated as standard in Merriam-Webster dictionaries since the publication of Webster 1909. They have been criticized by usage commentators at least since MacCracken & Sandison 1917.

The commentators have tended to regard *materialize* as an unnecessary, pretentious, or (at best) overused substitute for such plain verbs as *appear* and *happen.* A few would allow it in such a context as "The promised money never materialized," inasmuch as money does

have actual, material existence; but its use of something lacking material substance, as in "No new accusations have materialized," is routinely disparaged. Evans 1957, for example, finds that it is "incorrect and often borders on the silly." Yet, *materialize* is a common verb in its disputed senses, and its use is by no means limited to careless or pretentious writers. In its "appear" sense, it is especially useful in describing an appearance that is made suddenly, as if by magic:

> An instant later, a silk hat materialized in the air beside me —J. D. Salinger, *New Yorker,* 19 Nov. 1955

> A man on a bicycle suddenly materialized in front of our car —*Saturday Rev.,* 19 Feb. 1966

> ... an LBJ staffer materialized to get Sam into his formal attire —Larry L. King, *Harper's,* April 1970

> ... I reached absently for one only to have Mrs. Foster materialize at my elbow —Jay Jacobs, *Gourmet,* August 1973

> The drinks ... materialized on glass tables —John Updike, *Bech Is Back,* 1982

> ... several Israeli Army jeeps quickly materialized a month ago when students demonstrated —Trudy Rubin, *Christian Science Monitor,* 16 Jan. 1980

The sense "come into existence" also has distinct qualities. It usually occurs in negative constructions ("failed to materialize"), describing something that was hoped for or anticipated but did not happen or appear:

> It is heart-warming also to know that you had plans for me at Fortune even if they never did materialize —Archibald MacLeish, letter, September 1938

> The rain didn't materialize—instead we had a beautiful day —E. B. White, letter, 27 Aug. 1940

> The expected rally in Emerson failed to materialize —Malcolm Cowley, *The Literary Situation,* 1954

> ... a research fellowship would have been possible.... The fact that none ever materialised was a source of lasting disappointment —K. M. Elisabeth Murray, *Caught in the Web of Words,* 1977

> ... outfielders signed to expensive contracts last winter in order to lead the Yankees into a heralded new era of speed and contact hitting, were hesitantly and awkwardly moved in and out of the lineup, but the speedball attack never materialized —Roger Angell, *New Yorker,* 29 Nov. 1982

> ... a large sum of money that had been promised by an Eastern benefactor did not materialize —Garrison Keillor, *Lake Wobegon Days,* 1985

The old prejudice against these uses of *materialize* lingers on, but their place in standard English is nonetheless established, and has been for many decades.

maunder, meander A sense connoting "rambling about" is shared by *maunder* and *meander.* Some critics would allow *maunder* to refer only to speech while *meander* may apply to both speech and literal walking or rambling about. But the OED shows *maunder* used of walking or rambling from about 1746, while *meander* comes later, appearing in 1831. Over the years, though, *meander* has become the more often used word. While *maun-*

der has not dropped out of use in this sense, it is not found frequently:

> . . . a maundering and very leisurely railway nosed its way up the valley —H. Warner Allen, in *Wines of the World,* 1967

> . . . the dark unlit streets with only an occasional car maundering by —Malcolm Muggeridge, *Esquire,* April 1970

> . . . I thought I would maunder along the river — David Sheridan, *Smithsonian,* February 1983

One is more likely to encounter *meander:*

> . . . the rows of bricks that meandered along walls — Joy DeWeese-Wehen, *Horizon,* August 1979

> Black Creek is a wide, meandering stream with broad sandbars —Russell M. Daley, *Southern Living,* November 1971

> . . . fill up your gas tank and meander north —Theodore Fischer, *Apartment Life,* September 1979

> . . . a mere trickle of an unfledged watercourse meandering through the Piedmont —William Styron, *This Quiet Dust and Other Writings,* 1982

> . . . it [a road] lost heart . . . and meandered off in a lackadaisical path toward the mountain —Russell Baker, *Growing Up,* 1982

maxim   See OLD CLICHÉ, OLD MAXIM.

maximize   Janis 1984 says that *maximize* should not be modified by such adverbs as *further* and *greatly,* since its meaning is "to increase to a maximum." Phythian 1979 makes much the same point in a slightly different way by saying that it "should not be used as a synonym for simply *increase.*" Presumably the criticized usage does have some currency, but its occurrence in published writing is, according to our evidence, extremely rare. Our files do not include a single example of *maximize* modified by an adverb of degree or otherwise used to mean simply "increase."

Maximize is sometimes disparaged as jargon, perhaps because it occurs so commonly in business writing. Here are some typical examples of its use:

> . . . used to maximize social benefits and minimize adverse impacts —Michael Michaelis, *Wall Street Transcript,* 6 Mar. 1972

> . . . can multiply and maximize profit —John Gregory Dunne, *N.Y. Times Book Rev.,* 1 Apr. 1979

> . . . to maximize the ticket sales of the new soccer team —Phil Berger, *N.Y. Times Mag.,* 30 Sept. 1979

> . . . athletes who are always trying to maximize performance —*Runners World,* April 1981

may   1. See CAN, MAY.
2. *May, might.* Quite a few commentators include this heading, but most of them are content to offer ordinary dictionary-like explanations of the words' basic uses. There is nothing mysterious or controversial about these uses; if you have any question about them, we think you will find all the explanation you need in any good dictionary.

On a more mysterious note, a few commentators— Longman 1984, Barzun 1985, Howard 1984, Copperud 1970, 1980, Barnard 1979, Robert F. Ilson in Greenbaum 1985, Follett 1966—do note the puzzling use of *may* where *might* would be expected. There seem to be two places where such substitution occurs: in describing hypothetical conditions, and in a context normally calling for the past tense. Perhaps some examples would make things clearer. The first describes a hypothetical situation; it is taken from speech, as the *'d have* for *had* also indicates. It was spoken by a color analyst on a professional football telecast:

> If he'd have released the ball a second earlier—when [the pass receiver] made his cut—he may have had a touchdown —Dan Dierdorf, CBS television, 20 Dec. 1986

Here "might have had a touchdown" would have been expected.

In the second example we have a context where the past is called for:

> Born in Buffalo, N.Y., he may have gone to Princeton . . . but he made his reputation as a railroader — *Forbes,* 15 Sept. 1970

This one is especially confusing since *may* in such surroundings suggests that the writer does not know whether he went to Princeton; *might* (which is the verb we would have expected) would suggest that he could have gone if he had wanted to.

No one has a satisfying explanation for why these substitutions occur, and we are as stumped as everyone else. Here is about all we can tell you: we have more British evidence for the substitution (and more notice is taken of it by British commentators) than we have American evidence. But we do have both. The substitution is more frequent in speech than in writing. British evidence and British comment suggest that in print it is most likely to be found in the newspapers. It can be a puzzler when it occurs; notice in this example how you are at first led to believe that the boy survived:

> At first it was believed that the boy may have survived in a pocket of air, but when divers reached him yesterday it became obvious that he drowned soon after the trawler went over —*The Guardian,* 30 Oct. 1973

It will probably be some years before we know much more about this use of *may* for *might.* It receives but a brief footnote in Quirk et al. 1985; there it is related to some speakers' not perceiving any difference between "you may be right" and "you might be right." (The American example from sports broadcasting, however, could also be related to an often observed preference of players and other sports figures for casting what would be, in more formal circumstances, a past conditional sentence in the present tense: "If the pitcher doesn't walk [*for* hadn't walked] in the run, the Yankees win [*for* would have won] the game.") Until more is known about this usage, we advise you to use *might* in all contexts where the past tense is appropriate or where a hypothetical or highly unlikely situation is being referred to.

may of   See OF 2.

me   Everyone expects *me* to turn up as the object of a preposition or a verb:

> ". . . He's not a damned show-off like me." —Ernest Hemingway, *Green Hills of Africa,* 1935

Now he was going to show me something —Ernest Hemingway, *Green Hills of Africa,* 1935

But *me* also turns up in a number of places where traditional grammarians and commentators prescribe *I.* Many of these disputed uses of *me* result from the historical pressure of word position; language historians tell us that since sometime around the 16th century *me* has been appearing in places where *I* had before been regular—such as after *as* and *than* and the verb *be*—because those places are much like similar positions—such as after prepositions and transitive verbs—where *me,* or any other objective form, is usual.

Thus we find *me* used after *as* and *than:*

> . . . a good deal older than me —W. Somerset Maugham, quoted in *N.Y. Herald Tribune Book Rev.,* 5 Apr. 1953

> I had met a young man, barely older than *me* — Marya Mannes, *Out of My Time,* 1971

> LoPresti, who was a few years older than me —Tip O'Neill with William Novak, *Man of the House,* 1987

> . . . proved that she was just as good as them at running —Steven R. Weisman, *N.Y. Times Mag.,* 20 Apr. 1986

It is also common after *be* (there is more on this aspect of the subject at IT'S ME):

> . . . and I will say, whether anyone calls it pride or not, that if he *does* get up and around again it's me that saved his life —Walt Whitman, letter, 30 June 1863

> In gratitude, Churchill rolled off a recorded message to the workers: "This is me, Winston Churchill, speaking himself to you, and I am so glad to be able to thank you in this remarkable way." —*Time,* 1 Apr. 1946

> I meant it was me that couldn't encompass but one bill of goods metaphysically —Flannery O'Connor, letter, 31 Oct. 1959

Me is also used absolutely and in emphatic positions in the sentence:

> "Who, me?" said the lion —James Thurber, *Fables for Our Time, and Famous Poems Illustrated,* 1940

> "Why me?" I was going to ask —Simon 1980

> You should see us! Three baths! . . . And me with a valet!!! —Archibald MacLeish, letter, 7 Oct. 1926

> Me, I'll take the old sentimental shows —George Jean Nathan, *The Theatre Book of the Year, 1946–1947*

> Me, I am in transition from one college to another —Robert Frost, letter, 15 July 1943

All of the constructions so far mentioned are generally accepted by commentators as historically justified. You will note, however, that they are most likely to be found in speech and in writing of a relaxed personal or conversational style. In more formal contexts you may want to use *I* after *be* and after *as* and *than* when the first term of a comparison is the subject of a verb.

More problematical is what one of our correspondents dubbed "The *Someone and I* Syndrome" (this subject appears in another guise at BETWEEN YOU AND I and PRONOUNS). While traditional opinion prescribes *someone and I* for subject use—*I and someone* seems a bit impolite—in actual practice we also find *me and someone* and *someone and me:*

> She just walked along while me and Luke argued — William Saroyan, "The Sunday Zeppelin," reprinted in *Literature Lives* (9th grade text), ed. Hanna Beate Haupt et al., 1975

> Me and Enoch are living in the woods in Connecticut —Flannery O'Connor, letter, 1950

> . . . you and me can shake the eye-teeth of both the Democratic and Republican national parties — George C. Wallace, quoted in *Springfield* (Mass.) *Sunday Republican,* 30 June 1968

Of these two constructions, *me and someone* does have the minor virtue of putting the *me* in the emphatic position, where it is slightly less noticeable. Both are speech forms, often associated with the speech of children, and are likely to be unfavorably noticed in the speech and writing of adults except when used facetiously (as in Flannery O'Connor's letter).

Another *me* is the one used occasionally, especially in this country, as an indirect object where *myself* is more common:

> But one day I bought me a canary bird —Oliver Wendell Holmes d. 1894, *The Autocrat of the Breakfast-Table,* 1857

> . . . I must get me a place just like it —Alexander Woollcott, letter, March 1938

> . . . I have bought me some peafowl —Flannery O'Connor, letter, 17 March 1953

The OED Supplement says this is common in American speech; it does not appear to be much used in serious formal prose.

Our final use is of *me* for *my.* Our evidence suggests that this use is chiefly associated with Irish dialect; it is used humorously by others as well:

> ". . . wasn't me whole world lost?" —Paul Vincent Carroll, in *44 Irish Stories,* ed. Devin A. Garrity, 1955

> . . . I'll surely sleep through the day and I'll lose me job —Robert Gibbings, *Lovely Is the Lee,* 1945

> They are paying me well and unfortunately I have to earn me bread —Flannery O'Connor, letter, 2 Feb. 1959

meander	See MAUNDER, MEANDER.

meaningful	The history of *meaningful* shows how extremely popularity can, perversely, have a bad effect on a word's reputation. For about a hundred years after its first recorded use in 1852, *meaningful* existed quietly as an uncommon, unremarkable adjective. Even after it had become a fairly common word in the 1950s, it continued to pass unnoticed by the critics. But in the 1960s *meaningful* ceased to be ordinary. Its common use in such phrases as *meaningful dialogue* and *meaningful relationship* made it suddenly notorious, and it began to be criticized. E. B. White called it "a bankrupt adjective" in Strunk & White 1972, 1979, and the usage panel of Harper 1975 rejected it both in speech and in writing by a large majority. It was found to have various faults, but its chief failing was a simple one: it was overused. Hearing or reading the same word over and over can be like eating the same food day after day—no matter what its attractions, you tend to get sick of it. In the 1960s and 1970s, many people got sick of *meaningful,* and some have not yet recovered.

In the meantime, *meaningful* has continued in common use. It serves essentially as an antonym of *meaningless,* for which purpose it is well suited:

"Mexico is under tremendous time pressure to get people meaningful jobs," says Clark Reynolds, a professor of economics at Stanford University —Lawrence Rout, *Wall Street Jour.,* 25 Sept. 1981

. . . meaningful salary negotiations could take place only if the NFL were to shed its severe restrictions on free agency —*Sports Illustrated,* 11 Oct. 1982

Its notoriety is no longer great and will most likely continue to diminish as the years go by. Its use with *relationship* or *dialogue,* however, can still be counted on to draw a few groans.

means 1. The question whether *means* in the sense "something useful to a desired end" should appear in the singular or the plural form has occupied language commentators since as far back as the 18th century, and when Samuel Johnson was editing his Dictionary, he noted that *mean* "is often used in the plural." Shakespeare had used both *mean* and *means:*

And make the Douglas' son your only mean For powers in Scotland —*1 Henry IV,* 1598

Our sacks shall be a mean to sack the city —*1 Henry VI,* 1592

By this means Your lady is forthcoming yet at London —*2 Henry VI,* 1592

And so I chide the means that keeps me from it —*3 Henry VI,* 1592

Johnson noted with mild disapproval not that *mean* was used in the plural, but that it was used "by some not very grammatically with an adjective singular," as in the example from *2 Henry VI* above. Lowth 1762 also found this use worth criticizing in a line from a sermon by Bishop Francis Atterbury ". . . and by *that means* securing the continuance of his goodness," saying, "Ought it not to be, by *these means,* by *those means?* or by *this mean,* by *that mean,* in the singular number?" By the time of Noah Webster, however, *means* was in such widespread use that he could say

If *this means* and *a means* are now, and have immemorially been, used by good authors and the nation in general, neither Johnson, Lowth, nor any other person, however learned, has a right to say that the phrases are not good English —*Dissertations on the English Language,* 1789

In contemporary use, *mean* has been pretty well abandoned in favor of *means,* which may be either singular or plural in construction:

Blake, by his own poetic means, which essentially disdains the virtues of prose —F. R. Leavis, *Revaluation,* 1947

. . . it is not clear that redistributing authority over the police is the proper means —James Q. Wilson, *Harvard Today,* Autumn 1968

. . . any means that accomplishes this removal may be, and has been, employed —Betty J. Meggers, *Saturday Rev.,* 19 Feb. 1972

Other means come to mind but most important of all is the clear call to faculty to initiate inquiry — Robert T. Blackburn, *AAUP Bulletin,* December 1967

. . . many New Left activists believe that the means *determine* the ends —Norman Thomas, quoted in *The Progressive,* November 1969

The OED labels the singular use of *mean* in this sense as archaic (the *M* volume was published in 1908), and our evidence confirms that it has occurred very rarely in the 20th century:

This is a much more powerful mean of augmenting the fund of national industry —Frank William Taussig, ed., *Selected Readings in International Trade and Tariff Problems,* 1921

2. In the sense "material resources affording a secure life", *means* rather than *mean* is the invariable form:

In pre-war days many mothers with very limited means had no idea of the relative values of different foods —Margaret Biddle, *The Women of England,* 1941

. . . a short woman . . . decked out with furs . . . — one of those middle-aged women of means, it seems, whose emptyheadedness smacks of tragedy —John Cheever, *The Wapshot Chronicle,* 1957

. . . it takes defeat in war to persuade a Superpower that it has been living beyond its means —Arthur M. Schlesinger, Jr., *Harper's,* March 1969

When this sense of *means* takes a verb, the construction is plural:

. . . he came under the care of his maternal grandparents, whose means were sufficiently ample to enable them to afford him unusual educational advantages —*Dictionary of American Biography,* 1928

. . . while their means were always modest there was no trace of dire poverty —J. T. Ellis, *Irish Digest,* January 1954

At one time, this sense was also used in the singular construction; the OED labels it obsolete, and its latest use dates from the 17th century.

3. When used with a preposition, *means* is most often followed by *of:*

. . . agreement about the best means of organizing the state —Aldous Huxley, *Ends and Means,* 1937

. . . she [Emily Dickinson] never undertook the great profession of controlling the means of objective expression —R. P. Blackmur, in *American Harvest,* ed. Allen Tate & John Peale Bishop, 1942

. . . having developed the means of survival in the Harlem ghetto —*Current Biography,* November 1967

. . . essential to find a means of conveying the lessons —*Times Literary Supp.,* 19 Feb. 1971

Less frequently, *means* is used with *to, toward* or *for:*

. . . its unique place within the community is that it is an instrument of social purpose and a means to raise public taste —Sir William Haley, quoted in Thomas Owen Beachcroft, *British Broadcasting,* rev. ed., 1948

Many of our wants are means to a higher set of goals —Charles L. Schultze, *Saturday Rev.,* 22 Jan. 1972

. . . they would have little incentive to query hospital costs, even if they had the means to do so —Robert Claiborne, *Saturday Rev.,* 7 Jan. 1978

The two most important means toward reaching this goal —*Current Biography 1951*

High wages and slum clearance were the means toward abolition of group hatred —Oscar Handlin, *The American People in the Twentieth Century,* 1954

. . . the introduction of these new means for reproducing music —Aaron Copland, *Our New Music,* 1941

. . . technology has not as yet developed a means for dependable underground transmission of high voltage power —*Annual Report, Union Electric Co.,* 1970

4. See also BY MEANS OF.

meantime, meanwhile   Many American commentators have noted differences in the use of these two words. The usual observation is that *meantime* normally functions as a noun ("In the meantime, . . .") and *meanwhile* as an adverb ("Meanwhile, . . ."). The use of *meantime* as an adverb and *meanwhile* as a noun is generally discouraged, although most commentators allow that such usage is not incorrect; one of them (Bernstein 1971) defends the adverb *meantime* at some length, noting its frequent use by Shakespeare.

The evidence shows that *meantime* and *meanwhile* have been used interchangeably as nouns since the 14th century and as adverbs since the 16th century. The general observation that *meantime* is now the more common noun and *meanwhile* the more common adverb is undoubtedly true, but the adverb *meantime* and the noun *meanwhile* have been in continuous use for hundreds of years, and their use in current English is not rare:

Meantime I've had a letter from Paulhan and have written him —Archibald MacLeish, letter, 8 July 1949

Meantime there was a core of older contributors — *Times Literary Supp.,* 19 Feb. 1971

Meantime, he is headed in the right direction —E. B. White, letter, 4 Feb. 1974

Meantime, . . . those now in American racing have successfully cultivated a reserved, dignified image — Clive Gammon, *Sports Illustrated,* 1 Dec. 1986

And in the meanwhile, mum's the word —Alexander Woollcott, letter, 19 Nov. 1934

. . . were being developed in the meanwhile by engineers —S. I. Hayakawa, *ETC,* Summer 1952

But in the meanwhile a lot of people learned to read —Bergen Evans, "The Language We Speak," speech, June 1968

. . . gained a lot of other things in the meanwhile — *People,* 27 Apr. 1981

There is no need to make a point of avoiding such usage.

meddle   When *meddle* is used with a preposition, it often is followed by *with:*

. . . meddling with matters which lay beyond the sphere of the Estates of the realm —T. B. Macaulay, *The History of England,* vol. I, 1849

. . . it is inexpedient to meddle with questions of State in a land where men are highly paid to work them out for you —Rudyard Kipling, *Plain Tales from the Hills,* 1888

. . . she did not like other people to meddle with her property —Edmund Wilson, *New Yorker,* 5 June 1971

Meddle is also used with *in* and *into:*

. . . not in a condition to meddle nationally in any war —Claude G. Bowers, *The Young Jefferson 1743–1789,* 1945

Congress . . . has meddled in affairs that are properly within the jurisdiction of the courts —*New Yorker,* 10 Apr. 1971

. . . to abstain from the temptation to meddle into the inner affairs of other departments —*ACLS Newsletter,* vol. 5, no. 2, 1954

We also note that *meddle in* and *meddle into* often have *affairs* as their object; it appears that *meddle with* does not.

media   Edmund Wilson, in one of the essays collected in *The Bit Between My Teeth* (1965), says that the "habit of thinking in a Latin vocabulary does seem to be disappearing." Wilson's observation is not especially new, but its truth is perhaps nowhere better illustrated than in the cavalier fashion with which the plurals of Latin (and other foreign) loanwords have been treated by English speakers. *Media* is one of those, and certainly among the ones that have attracted the most comment.

Barnard 1979 observes that the widespread use of *media* is "so recent that no particular pattern has yet become standardized." In fact, the word seems at present to be developing in two somewhat contrary directions. The older, which is the use of *media* as a singular count noun, is not very recent; it dates back to the 1920s certainly and perhaps even a bit earlier. Louise Pound in *American Speech,* October 1927, has two unattributed citations for *media* as a singular; one, in the form of a plural *medias,* is clearly from advertising. The OED Supplement has a 1923 citation from a book on advertising using *mass media* as a singular. It thus appears that *media* as a singular count noun originated in advertising jargon, and our evidence shows that it has stayed in use in that field ever since, even though representatives of advertising such as Einstein 1985 occasionally object to it.

. . . our publication does not appeal to vast numbers as an advertising media —Helen Hurtig, *Jour. of the International Netsuke Collectors Society,* Summer 1973

It should be noted that singular *media* and plural *media* are both used by advertising people.

That the habit of thinking in a Latin vocabulary is disappearing in fields other than advertising became noticeable in our files as early as 1939 when *media* turned up as a singular noun in a medical text for the stuff on which cultures are grown. This sense—not the other singular *media* used in anatomy and phonology, incidentally—is unconnected with the advertising use, and presumably uncontaminated by it. It is a use that has persisted, although it is obviously nowhere near as common as the "mass media" use. Here are a couple of fairly early examples:

> ... producing a suitable media for organic life —*Britannica Book of the Year 1946*

> ... various salts of penicillin in an aqueous media can not be administered orally —*Science,* 16 Feb. 1945

A third independent singular *media* turned up in the field of art in a local museum bulletin in 1937. We have relatively little subsequent evidence of this use, but it too appears from time to time:

> ... "Experiments in Design" with Mrs. Varty which will include tissue paper, ink, string, a different media every day —Gladys E. Guilbert, *Spokesman-Review* (Spokane, Wash.), 30 Jan. 1966

And we have other miscellaneous uses of singular *media,* some of which we show you here. Note that the two most recent are technical (they both relate to computers):

> ... partly as a cultural media —K. L. Little, *American Jour. of Sociology,* July 1948

> ... necessary to rely on the mails as the contact media —Henry M. Ellis, *Stamps for Fun and Profit,* 1953

> Films ... will inevitably become more a media of personal expression —*Saturday Rev.,* 28 Dec. 1963

> These expatriate stars have become too large for one company or even one media to handle —Iris M. Fanger, *Christian Science Monitor,* 14 Sept. 1979

> ... a new ultra-high-density recording media — *Annual Report, Eastman Kodak Co.,* 1983

> ... an optical disc media —*Predicasts Technology Update,* 5 Jan. 1987

The singular count noun *media,* then, is fairly well established in a number of different specialized areas as the equivalent of *medium.* The plural *medias* is much less common than the singular *media,* and both are much less common than the plural *media* at the present time.

Development as a singular count noun is thus one direction this plural borrowed from Latin is taking. The other direction is toward use as a collective noun. A collective noun can take either a plural or a singular verb, and when *media* takes a plural verb no one notices it because the agreement does not differ from that of the traditional plural. When it takes a singular verb, it is distinguishable from the singular count noun in that it takes *the* rather than *a* or *one* or *this* and does not have a plural *medias.* The range of application of this *media* is narrow: it almost always refers to the mass media—television, radio, and the press especially. (It is also now being used as a plural collective to refer to representatives or members of these organizations.) It is a use well established in speech:

> Adds Fordham's Father Culkin: "Now the media goes directly to the public. ..." —Paul D. Zimmerman, *Newsweek,* 13 Nov. 1967

> The media, ... it probably could do a better job, but just the time limits you, the way they cut up the news —Huey Newton, quoted in *Rolling Stone,* 3 Aug. 1972

> You know, the news media gets on to something, and there's a certain herd instinct among writers — Edwin Meese 3d, quoted in *N.Y. Times,* 25 Sept. 1981

> I understand the media ... and it apparently understands me —Jesse Jackson, quoted in *Esquire,* December 1979

> There have been many changes in the media since you first came into it, since I first came into it — Marquis Childs, address to National Press Club, 17 Oct. 1975

> The media consumes you when you approach a milestone —Reggie Jackson, quoted in *Sports Illustrated,* 12 Aug. 1985

> I could care less what the media thinks —Mark Hughes, quoted in *Forbes,* 25 Feb. 1985

And it occurs in writing too, especially of a journalistic kind:

> There are signs that the media is going after him — John Leo, *New Times,* 31 May 1974

> Media is also concerned —R. R. Walker, *The Age* (Melbourne), 30 Apr. 1975

> ... the media gives insufficient coverage to what they do and say —William Davis, *Punch,* 12 Oct. 1976

> Most of the media continues to dwell on that period in their history —Cherie Moore, *People,* 2 Nov. 1981

> The American news media has its way of directing our attention —John Gilman, *UMass Collegian,* 12 Oct. 1983

The commentators by and large reject both of these developments; most seem unaware that there is more to the matter than a single phenomenon—one they see as being a plural noun misused as a singular. Among the nay-sayers are Chambers 1985, Trimmer & McCrimmon 1988, Bernstein 1962, Simon 1980, Kilpatrick 1984, Shaw 1975, 1987, and Safire (in his *New York Times* column of 24 Nov. 1985). Freeman 1983 and Howard 1978, 1984 do not exactly welcome the newer *media,* but they do locate it within a tradition that has brought singulars like *agenda* and *stamina* to respectability and view it without great alarm. Perrin & Ebbitt 1972, while conceding that many find uses like those illustrated above objectionable, point out that they are common in "General" (though not in "Formal") writing. The usage panel of Harper 1975, 1985 reveals an interesting difference in attitude as between the collective singular and the count singular with its plural *medias:* nearly one-third of the panelists accept the former in writing, but almost none accept the latter.

Despite the considerable expressed opposition, the illustrated uses of *media* are not on the wane. The evidence suggests, rather, that use of *media* is going to remain unsettled for some time because of these somewhat opposing pulls. But you should remember that *media* and *medium* are English words, even if naturalized, and are no longer subject to the rules of Latin. The evidence is that the singular count noun has been with us for more than fifty years, and shows no sign of retreat in spite of the hostility of the pundits. The collective use is more recent and seems to be following the direction of development of *data*. It too may well survive, although it is not at present as well established as the older mass use of *data*. And this is also worth remembering: our evidence shows that *media* is still being construed as a plural more often than it is either as a singular count noun or as a collective noun with a singular verb.

For more of these interesting foreign plurals, see the list at LATIN PLURALS.

mediate   *Mediate* is most often used with *between* when it takes a preposition:

> . . . our theory must mediate between all previous truths and certain new experiences —William James, *Pragmatism,* 1907

> I want to mediate between the two of you now, because if this breach continues it will be the ruin of us all —Robert Graves, *I, Claudius,* 1934

> . . . he mediates between the pole of nature and that of civilization —Robert Penn Warren, *Democracy and Poetry,* 1975

Occasionally, *mediate* is used with *for:*

> The learned professions have evolved to mediate for the individual —Ralph Crawshaw, *Center Mag.,* May 1969

Although Bernstein 1965 notes the use of *mediate* with *among,* our evidence shows that this use is infrequent:

> . . . the process of mediating among conflicting purposes and the anticipated needs of more than one reader —C. H. Knoblauch, *College Composition and Communication,* May 1980

Mediate is also found quite frequently in its transitive uses with *to* or *through:*

> . . . émigrés, who not only mediated western ideas to Russia . . . —*Times Literary Supp.,* 11 Oct. 1947

> . . . the individuals who, in the various cultural settings, mediate the culture to the child —Margaret Mead, in *Personality in Nature, Society and Culture,* ed. Clyde Kluckhohn & Henry A. Murray, 1950

> . . . what were once conceptions become the inherent meanings of material mediated through sense — John Dewey, *Art as Experience,* 1934

> . . . whose ideas are never likely to reach the common reader, except as mediated through the prose of shallower . . . disciples —*Times Literary Supp.,* 3 Sept. 1954

mediocre   This word is sometimes considered to be an absolute adjective. See ABSOLUTE ADJECTIVES.

meditate   When *meditate* is used with a preposition, the choice is usually *on:*

> . . . our only condition is that he turn them into poetry, and not merely meditate on them poetically —T. S. Eliot, "The Metaphysical Poets," in *Selected Essays,* 1932

> . . . meditated with concentrated attention on the problem of flight —Havelock Ellis, *The Dance of Life,* 1923

> . . . meditate on the fact that they were commanded by a man who meant business —C. S. Forester, *The Barbary Pirates,* 1953

Less frequently it is used with *upon:*

> While they went out of doors together, she meditated upon the fact of his usefulness —Ellen Glasgow, *Barren Ground,* 1925

> . . . the young priest blotted himself out of his own consciousness and meditated upon the anguish of his Lord —Willa Cather, *Death Comes for the Archbishop,* 1927

medium   See MEDIA.

meld   As a verb meaning "to blend or merge," *meld* is a fairly new word, although not nearly as new as some people believe. We first encountered it in 1936:

> . . . apple, currant, and raisin all melded into one sweetly tart aroma —Della Lutes, *The Country Kitchen,* 1936

By 1939, the editors of Webster's Second had seen enough evidence of this blend of *melt* and *weld* to be satisfied that it was established in standard use, and they added an entry for it to the "New Words Section" of that dictionary. It has been included in our dictionaries ever since.

Because the new *meld* is now a common word, it has attracted some unfavorable attention. Complicating the picture is the existence of an older *meld,* used to mean "to declare or announce (a card or cards) for a score in a card game (as pinochle or gin rummy)." Those who regard the new *meld* as an unwelcome development tend to perceive it as a misuse of the cardplayers' word:

> This word is frequently heard at meetings of businessmen or government officials when a difficulty arises which calls for uniting two diverse plans or proposals. The obvious cause of the misuse is the urge to say *weld* while suggesting a quiet and mild operation that will escape public notice. The fact is that *meld,* from the German *melden,* means to announce. It is a technical term of pinochle. To make it anything else is a MALAPROP —Follett 1966

But the new *meld* is in no sense a misuse of the older word. It is, instead, an entirely new coinage, and its popularity probably has far less to do with sneaky businessmen and politicians than with the way its sound so nicely reflects its meaning. *Meld* suggests a smooth and thorough blending of two or more things into a single, homogeneous whole. Connotations of smoothness are its most distinctive characteristic, and its sound reinforces those connotations. Safire 1984 recognizes the distinctive qualities of *meld* when he describes it as "a nice coinage," despite having received many letters complaining about his use of it. No other recent commentator mentions the word at all, but those letters to Safire make it clear that there are still some people who regard *meld* with strong disapproval.

Even so, we do not think you should feel nervous about using *meld.* Dictionaries have long recognized it as a standard word, and its use in reputable writing has been common for years.

This concentrated melding of diverse viewpoints — John R. Silber, *Center Mag.,* September/October 1971

He melded the operation of five U.S. affiliates into a smoothly functioning division —*Time,* 18 Feb. 1974

. . . in which he melds the musical traditions of these countries —Hans Fantel, *N.Y. Times Book Rev.,* 22 July 1979

. . . where Indian philosophy and custom met and melded with their Chinese counterparts —Gerri Trotta, *Gourmet,* May 1981

The verb has also given rise, by functional shift, to a related noun:

. . . the choreographer's meld of classic and folk idiom —Anna Kisselgoff, *N.Y. Times,* 25 Feb. 1971

. . . this meld of the mundane and the poetic —Robert Kirsch, *Los Angeles Times Book Rev.,* 6 June 1976

memento   See MOMENTO.

memorandum   Quite a bit has been written about the plural forms of *memorandum,* starting back in the 1870s when Richard Grant White put forward a plea for the English plural *memorandums.* Ayres 1881 demurred, on grounds too obscure now to be worth pursuing. Hall 1917 noted that *memorandums* was well established, citing Boswell and Defoe, among others.

Modern concern is over *memoranda* used as a singular (though it has not gone out of style as a plural) and was apparently first expressed by Vizetelly 1906. Since then quite a few commentators take on the subject, right up to Harper 1985 and Shaw 1987. Almost everybody discourages *memoranda* as a singular and abominates *memorandas,* except Evans 1957, who is the latitudinarian in this instance.

Ordinarily when there is so much discussion of a Latin plural, we have a lot of evidence for the alleged misuse, but not in this case: *memoranda,* singular, and *memorandas* almost never appear in print. We do have a little evidence from speech, particularly from congressional hearings. Pyles 1979 has examples of singular *memoranda* from attorney Joseph Welch during the Army–McCarthy hearings of 1954, and we recorded Robert MacFarlane using it at the Iran–Contra hearings in 1987. But even most testifiers before congressional committees seem to have few problems, although once in a great while *memorandum* as a plural will slip out.

So apparently there is not much of a problem here, and no real writing problem at all. *Memoranda* and *memorandums* are about equally common and both have good literary precedent; you can take your pick.

For more foreign plurals that vex English speakers, see LATIN PLURALS.

mentality   This was an uncommon word until the early 20th century, when it first came to be widely used in the sense "way of thinking; outlook." Its newly common use was noted with disapproval by Fowler 1926, who considered it a "superfluous word" and hoped that it would be allowed to "lapse into its former obscurity." That hope has not been realized. The "outlook" sense of *mentality* has continued to be common, and it has attracted relatively little critical attention since Fowler's time (a few commentators have considered it overused).

As Gowers notes in his revision of Fowler 1965, it often carries overtones of disparagement:

. . . top officers tended to have banana-boat mentalities in a jet age —Albert H. Johnston, *Publishers Weekly,* 2 Aug. 1976

. . . a study of greed, of the small-town mentality, of alienated youth —Newgate Callendar, *N.Y. Times Book Rev.,* 21 Aug. 1983

The herd mentality that led the world banking community to follow Mr. Wriston's lead —Ann Crittenden, *N.Y. Times Book Rev.,* 8 July 1984

metathesis   The process whereby a sound hops out of its proper place, so to speak, and pops up elsewhere in the word, or switches places with another sound in the word, is called *metathesis* (\mə-'tath-ə-səs\). A good example of metathesis is one pronunciation of *integral,* in which the \r\ has moved from after the \g\ to after the \t\, thus yielding \'in-trə-gəl\, as though the word were spelled "intregal." We have recorded this pronunciation from numerous educated speakers over the years, including former President Gerald Ford, Governor Nelson Rockefeller, broadcaster Edward R. Murrow, and professors Lionel Trilling and Marvin Harris. The reason for this alteration in the sequence of sounds is probably attraction to the pattern exemplified by such words as *intricate, introvert,* and (in one pronunciation variant) *interesting,* and also, at one remove, by words like *gentrified* and *centrally.* It is not a matter of \intr-\ being simply "easier to say" than \int . . . r-\, since under different accentual conditions that cluster is sometimes broken up in relaxed pronunciation: thus *introduced* commonly becomes \ˌint-ər-'düst\, in which form the first \t\, no longer protected by an immediately following \r\, drops out, and the word is pronounced as though spelled "innerduced." Again, such variations come from the lips of quite well-educated speakers; we have recorded \ˌkänt-ər-'byü-shən\ from no less a figure than Mitford M. Mathews, author of A Dictionary of Americanisms.

In the above examples, a single consonant has hopped out of place. But consonants can also exchange places, as in the mispronunciation of *relevant* as \'rev-ə-lənt\. Once again we apparently have a case of attraction to pattern: compare *reveille, revel(ing),* and more distantly, *envelope, invalid* (noun), and *revelation.*

When we hear such shifts occurring sporadically around us, they may sound to some like gross and hopeless slipups that could never become standard in the language. But the products of metathesis have indeed been taken up over the course of history. One notorious variant of *ask,* \'aks\, in effect goes all the way back to Old English, where *axian* and *ascian* existed side by side, and it is only by comparison with cognate forms in other languages that we can deduce that *-sk-* is the historically earlier order. In the case of *wasp,* it is rather the metathesized form that has become standard, since while Old English has both *wæsp* and *wæps* and Latin has *vespa,* overall comparative evidence points to a prehistoric *-ps-* as original. Similar vicissitudes mark the history of *bird, hasp,* and *tamarisk.* In the latter case the metathesis took place within the development of Latin, *tamariscus* out of earlier *tamarix* (where *sc* = \sk\ and *x* = \ks\), and English simply took over the result. Both metathesized and unmetathesized forms are visible in English *scintilla,* taken direct from the classical Latin *scintilla* "spark," and *stencil,* borrowed (via French) from a Vulgar Latin form we reconstruct as *stincilla. Palaver* and *parabola* are likewise metathetic doublets, though further sound change has obscured the relationship between them.

See also CALVARY, CAVALRY; IRRELEVANT.

meticulous This adjective, which is derived ultimately from the Latin *metus,* "fear," was a rare word until about the turn of the 20th century, after which it became both common and, for a time, controversial. The OED shows that it had some use in the 16th and 17th centuries as a fancy synonym of *fearful* and *timid,* but by 1700 it had fallen into disuse. In the 19th century it acquired (apparently by way of the French *méticuleux*) a second sense, "overly careful about small details":

> The decadence of Italian prose composition into laboured mannerism and meticulous propriety — John Addington Symonds, *Renaissance in Italy,* 1877 (OED)

This sense in turn gave rise to what is now its almost invariable sense, "painstakingly careful." *Meticulous* has been widely used in this sense for many decades:

> . . . gave to the fashioning of the written word all the fastidious, meticulous austerity of devotion that she knew —Rose Macaulay, *Told by an Idiot,* 1923

> His meticulous integrity in business and his accuracy in money matters —Henry Seidel Canby, *Thoreau,* 1939

> . . . she had observed a meticulous neutrality. . . . nothing could have been more correct than the behavior of her Government —Sir Winston Churchill, *The Unrelenting Struggle,* 1942

> The meticulous care with which the operation in Sicily was planned has paid dividends —Franklin D. Roosevelt, fireside chat, 28 July 1943, in *Nothing to Fear,* ed. B. D. Zevin, 1946

> . . . that fulness and meticulous documentation which the scholar requires —Gay Wilson Allen, *Saturday Rev.,* 5 Feb. 1955

> . . . a meticulous eye for detail —Howard E. Gruber, *N.Y. Times Book Rev.,* 22 July 1979

> . . . some kind of fine and meticulous craftsman — Doris Lessing, *The Good Terrorist,* 1985

The newly common *meticulous* attracted predictably unfavorable attention in the first half of the century. Its early critics (such as Fowler 1906) had no use for it in any sense, regarding it as a foreign affectation. But by about the 1930s the standard critical view had come to be that it was correctly used in its older and less common sense, "overly careful," and incorrectly used in its newer and popular sense, "painstakingly careful." The older sense was considered correct because it retains, however slightly, connotations of timidity and fearfulness, while the newer sense has lost such connotations altogether. Dictionaries, including our own, were also slow to recognize the newer sense, and its failure to appear in standard references no doubt encouraged many people to regard it as an error. Theodore Bernstein, whose dictionary of choice was Webster's Second 1934 (in which the newer sense does not appear), was still insisting in 1965 that *meticulous* should only mean "timorously careful and overcareful." A newer dictionary would have told him differently, as would most of

his fellow commentators (such as Evans 1957, Follett 1966, and Copperud 1970, 1980). The use of *meticulous* to mean "overly careful" is now rare. Its use to mean "painstakingly careful," on the other hand, is extremely common, and there is absolutely no question about its propriety.

might See MAY 2.

might could *Might could* is a double modal found in regional American speech, chiefly in Southern and Midland areas according to our evidence (the Dictionary of American Regional English may modify this labeling when it presents its evidence). *Might could* is the most conspicuous of a number of double modals with *might;* the others are *might can, might should,* and *might would.* The American Dialect Dictionary has, in addition, an instance of *might ought.*

The *might* in these constructions seems to intensify the notion of possibility or speculation; to the outsider who does not use the forms, the *might* seems to be similar in force to *perhaps.*

These constructions are not found in print except as part of reported or fictional speech. Dialect surveys and fictional use associate them with less educated or uneducated speakers. Dialect surveys report that cultured informants tend to avoid the construction; we cannot tell whether this is a result of schooling or is a mark of social status or is simply a typical pattern for a familiar form not used in the presence of strangers. Here are a few examples:

> ". . . My boy Sammy might could pay it for me. . . ." —Erskine Caldwell, *A House in the Uplands,* 1946

> He might could help 'em —John Faulkner, *Men Working,* 1941 (in ADD)

> I might can do it. I don't know now —Aunt Arie, quoted in *The Foxfire Book,* ed. Eliot Wigginton, 1972

> He might should've called a timeout the play before —John Hannah, professional football telecast, 16 Nov. 1986

> ". . . Doc's afraid it'd kick him—might would, I guess. . . ." —Charley Tyler, quoted in *The Foxfire Book,* ed. Eliot Wigginton, 1972

might of See OF 2.

might should See MIGHT COULD.

might would See MIGHT COULD.

mighty The use of *mighty* as an adverbial intensifier has been looked at askance since at least 1829, when the sentence "That is a mighty big dog" was given in Joseph Hervey Hull's *Grammar* as an "incorrect phrase" to be corrected. The issue is largely an American one; it does not appear much in British usage sources. And its origin appears to be in the assertion of Bostonian cultural superiority: not only was Hull's *Grammar* published in Boston, but the Boston *Pearl* of 20 Feb. 1836 is recorded in Thornton 1912 as labeling *mighty* a southern corruption.

Similar labels have, of course, been repeated right down to the present day by writers of usage books and college handbooks. The labels applied are most often *colloquial* and *informal;* others include *old-fashioned* and *quaint,* and several handbooks discourage its use in "most writing."

Hall 1917 seems to have been the first to investigate the use of *mighty.* The intensive use is not recent—the OED records it from before 1300; Hall adds many instances of his own finding from literature right down to his own time. He is unable to discover when the word dropped out of the literary language.

We have noted that the stigmatizing of *mighty* appears to have started in Boston. From this one would assume that it was not current in everyday English in New England, but such is not the case. *Mighty* turns up in the writing of such proper Bostonians as Oliver Wendell Holmes, the elder:

> But he said a mighty good thing about mathematics —*The Autocrat of the Breakfast-Table,* 1858

And Henry Adams:

> ... man knows mighty little, and may some day learn enough of his own ignorance to fall down and pray —quoted in John Buchan, *Pilgrim's Way,* 1940

It is of common occurrence in the letters of the younger Oliver Wendell Holmes:

> ... it is mighty interesting to look even through a keyhole on such great men —letter, 29 Nov. 1925

> ... I am mighty sceptical of hours of labor and minimum wages regulation —letter, 8 Jan. 1917

> His Corsican chauffeur was mighty careful not to run down a hen —letter, 29 July 1923

It is probably safe to assume, then, that the commentators who started questioning the propriety of *mighty* were not even thoroughly acquainted with the vocabulary of Bostonians.

Hall 1917 opines that *mighty* was brought to the U.S. at a time when it was current in London English—a conclusion safe enough, since the word seems to have been in current use in London English from the 17th through (at least) the 19th centuries. Our first writer concerned solely with the proprieties of English used it:

> This Expression is found in many Authors, who seem to value themselves not a little upon it, and think it mighty smart —Robert Baker, *Reflections on the English Language,* 1770

Boswell records it frequently in his *Life of Samuel Johnson* (1791) as appearing in the speech of the great man:

> An ancient estate should always go to males. It is mighty foolish to let a stranger have it because he marries your daughter. . . .

> No, Sir, this affectation will not pass;—it is mighty idle.

(Oddly, Johnson characterized the adverb *mighty* thus in his 1755 Dictionary: "Not to be used but in very low language." His animadversion seems to have had little effect, even on his own speech.)

Although our evidence of the currency of *mighty* in British English is equivocal because scarce, there is no doubt it is firmly established in American English—especially in the Southern and Midland areas, but by no means limited to them. It is quite common in newspaper and magazine writing.

In current American English it usually conveys a folksy, down-home feeling or a rural atmosphere:

> "It's plain and simple fare," said Aunt Tennie Cloer, "but mighty filling and mighty satisfying. . . ." —quoted by John Parris, *Asheville* (N.C.) *Citizen-Times,* 18 Jan. 1976

> A man must be mighty serious about his squirrel hunting —Stuart Williams, *Field & Stream,* February 1972

It is also a feature of a relaxed and chatty style:

> ... fried chicken, country ham, baked cheese grits, candied apples, turnip greens, corn bread and biscuits. That sounds mighty good to me, and I am all for trotting out American regional cooking —Julia Child, *N.Y. Times Mag.,* 16 Jan. 1977

> I'm still not crazy about cats, but I'm sure mighty grateful to that one —*And More by Andy Rooney,* 1982

> It sounded mighty formidable, like someone not to be trifled with —Garrison Keillor, quoted in *Update* (Univ. of Minn.), Fall 1981

It is common in the letters of literary people:

> ... and a mighty fine fellow you'll say he is —Robert Frost, letter, 1 July 1914

> ... a curious voyage that has really been mighty enjoyable —Alexander Woollcott, letter 11 Sept. 1917

> All in all we have had a mighty good winter —E. B. White, letter, 18 Jan. 1940

> It was mighty thoughtful of you to send me that quote from dear old Sam Adams's letter —James Thurber, letter, 3 Dec. 1958

> Well you are mighty right about the low rate of pious exchange —Flannery O'Connor, letter, 11 Aug. 1956

It is even used from time to time in more formal or more sophisticated contexts, where it can be counted on to add emphasis by being unexpected:

> ... the chairman made sure that there were mighty few of them —Mollie Panter-Downes, *New Yorker,* 30 Oct. 1971

> ... when Senator McClellan twists around in his chair and hoists his left shoulder, we know that he's feeling mighty put out over something —*New Yorker,* 12 June 1954

Hall 1917 thought perhaps you would not want to use *mighty* in a sermon, but judged it useful in other contexts where you might find it handy. Reader's Digest 1983 says this: "If not quite suitable for the most ceremonial of formal contexts, the adverb *mighty* is Standard American English in all others." We agree with both; *mighty* does have a force and flavor all its own, and if it is natural to you, you should not be afraid to use it where you think it will serve a purpose.

militate   **1.** According to our evidence, *militate* is almost always used with a preposition, and that preposition almost always is *against:*

> ... the thickness of population ... is the thing that most militates against individual distinction —Sinclair Lewis, *Good Housekeeping,* May 1935

. . . what he hated about America . . . was everything that militated against such a free life —Mark Schorer, *New Republic,* 6 Apr. 1953

. . . this has happened rarely so far, and a factor militating against the possibility is the variety of outlets of the reprint houses —James T. Farrell, *Literature and Morality,* 1947

Occasionally *militate* is used with *in favor (of):*

This fact alone militates in favor of Tunisia's French connection —Ray Alan, *New Republic,* 20 Sept. 1954

. . . considerations which at the time militated in their favor —Walter Millis, *N.Y. Herald Tribune Book Rev.,* 9 Feb. 1947

Although Richard Grant White writing in 1870 cautioned against using *militate against* and Ambrose Bierce in 1909 declared "there is no such word," *militate* has been around since 1642 and continues in widespread use in contemporary English. Modern commentators do not object to it.
2. See MITIGATE.

millennium One of the curious and sometimes frustrating things about our language is its spelling. The way that it has evolved is chiefly haphazard, and it was printers rather than educators who first began to squeeze English into its present state of somewhat uniform spelling. But variant spellings still exist for many words. Some of these variants are deemed acceptable and others are not, and differences of opinion exist on the acceptability of some variants. There seems to be, however, no widely used criterion for judging the relative acceptability of a spelling variant. Certainly simple frequency of use is not always the deciding factor. One of the best attested spelling variants in our files is the single -*n*- spelling of *millennium* and its derivative terms. No dictionary or spelling book that we are aware of recognizes *millenium.* Presumably the force of etymology still obtains in this case. You had better spell it with as many *n*'s as *l*'s.

mine See MY, MINE.

mineralogy See GENEALOGY.

minimal Why is there a problem about *minimal?* There seem to be two reasons: increase in use of the word in recent years, and dictionary definitions that fail to explain that use any too clearly. As a result the commentators are concerned, because they do not know how to gauge the usage that they see. Gowers in Fowler 1965 thinks *minimal* is supposed to be limited in meaning to "least possible" and is vexed when he finds it used otherwise; Shaw 1975, 1987 seems to share Gowers's view. Janis 1984 and Bolinger 1980 are conscious of ambiguity in some uses of the word. Bolinger gives this example from a sociologist:

The channels are organized so that minimal accuracy is maintained.

Bolinger recognizes that the writer cannot have meant "least possible"; he suspects that "at least some" was the intended meaning. But both interpretations are possible. The real problem here, we think, is the sociologist's failure to signal clearly the meaning he intended. The sense deduced by Bolinger is in widespread use, but in most

cases, as we think you will see from the examples, the sense is clearly signaled.

Contributing to all this uncertainty is a tendency of dictionary definers to try to cram everything into one definition—the definitions in the OED, Webster's Second, and Webster's Third all suffer from this weakness. Such treatment is perhaps inevitable when evidence of the divergence of meaning is not plentiful, but in fact evidence has been quite plentiful for quite a long time. It would thus appear that we lexicographers could have been more diligent—and more helpful.

If we set aside technical uses—including *minimal art* and its various related terms in theater, decoration, design, and fashion—we find that the general uses of *minimal* fall into three broad groups. The first of these is the "least possible" sense the commentators mention. This appears to be the smallest of the three groups; it is identified most readily by the application of *minimal* to a noun denoting something undesirable:

Their object was to deal China a crushing blow with a minimal expenditure of men and materials — Nathaniel Peffer, *Harper's,* September 1938

. . . it is contoured to slice through the air with minimal fuel-wasting drag —advt., *Wall Street Jour.,* 28 May 1980

Following the principle of self-reliance, the Chinese are proud that shops are set up with minimal expense —Rhea Menzel Whitehead, *Saturday Rev.,* 4 Mar. 1972

The formula could work this year if injuries are minimal —Paul Zimmerman, *Sports Illustrated,* 1 Sept. 1982

A more frequently met sense is the one noticed by Bolinger. In this use the etymological minimum is viewed as the least that is acceptable rather than possible. We could define it roughly as "being a bare minimum; barely adequate; at least some."

. . . recognition of the Russians as human entities, with certain minimal human rights —*Harper's,* June 1935

. . . the minimal virtues of good poetry are those of good prose —Joseph Wood Krutch, *Samuel Johnson,* 1944

. . . for the maintenance of minimal German living standards —William Harlan Hale, *Harper's,* December 1945

. . . held back in agreeing to even the minimal inspection —Norman Cousins, *Saturday Rev.,* 30 Oct. 1971

. . . too poorly trained and motivated to hold even minimal jobs —Sylvia Nasar, *Fortune,* 17 Mar. 1986

. . . hoping for a minimal excuse to hail Woody Allen —Stanley Kauffmann, *Before My Eyes,* 1980

. . . are making more than a minimal living —Henry Hewes, *Saturday Rev.,* 1 Nov. 1975

The third use probably would have been tagged "loosely" by the definers of 50 years ago, if they had defined it. In this use *minimal* merely means "very small," often with a connotation of insignificance; what is minimal is often hardly worth mentioning or hardly worthy of notice.

The opportunity of beating the opposition on a story is minimal —Harry Reasoner, quoted in *TV Guide,* 6 Nov. 1965

... brought together everything, with minimal exceptions —Irving Kolodin, *Saturday Rev.,* 28 June 1975

... touches Africa at two or three points on its tour around the world, but the students' exposure to Africa is minimal —John Coyne, *Change,* March 1973

... had a minimal interest in the world outside —Joyce Carol Oates, *N.Y. Times Book Rev.,* 15 Apr. 1973

... public opinion soon wrote off the Atlantic Charter as of minimal importance —*Times Literary Supp.,* 9 Apr. 1970

The anal emphasis is necessary because Miss Birkin has minimal mammaries and a second-rate face —John Simon, *New York,* 8 Mar. 1976

minimize   The commentary on *minimize* in the usage books consists of, first, objecting to the sense meaning "to estimate in the least possible terms" (a sense recorded in most dictionaries) and, second, objecting to its use with certain modifiers such as *greatly* or *as far as possible.*

The first of these complaints seems to hinge either on a wrongheaded insistence on the word's having only one meaning or on excessive concern with the word *estimate,* which is used in the definition in several dictionaries, including ours and the OED, as if *minimize* were therefore some technical term and hence could not mean "play down." However, *play down* is simply an idiomatic equivalent of what the dictionary definitions are really saying. Here are some examples of the sense:

... sources which have steadily rigged statistics to minimize adverse trends —*American Mercury,* February 1953

There was no disposition to slight industrial contractors or minimize the immense contribution they could make —James Phinney Baxter 3d, *Scientists Against Time,* 1946

... stresses the fun and minimizes the scholarship —B. A. Botkin, *N.Y. Times Book Rev.,* 24 Apr. 1955

... did not try to hide or minimize the uglier aspects of the Resistance —*Times Literary Supp.,* 18 Dec. 1969

... urged the public not to minimise the bomb problem —Andrew Boyle, *The Listener,* 30 Aug. 1973

... dresses for the maid of honor—all selected to minimize her sister Margaret's stockiness —Shirley Ann Grau, *Cosmopolitan,* January 1972

This sense is a century old and entirely standard.

The second objection may be a bit of a straw man. Bernstein 1965 does produce an example of "minimize as far as possible" and points out the redundancy of the "as far as possible." However, such usages are extremely rare in our files. If the usage is at all common, it may be primarily spoken rather than written.

miniscule, minuscule   This word is derived from the Latin adjective *minusculus* and is etymologically related

to *minus.* If you aim to be consistent with its etymology, therefore, you should spell it *minuscule.* Many people do:

... was now being followed in minuscule detail —*Sports Illustrated,* 18 Mar. 1974

... measured a surprisingly minuscule amount of noble gases —*Science News,* 12 Oct. 1985

two minuscule white geese in the blue water —Elizabeth Bishop, "Poem," in *The Complete Poems, 1927–1979,* 1983

The spelling *miniscule* is also extremely common, however. This spelling was first recorded at the end of the 19th century (*minuscule* dates back to 1705), but it did not begin to appear frequently in edited prose until the 1940s. Its increasingly common use parallels the increased use of the word itself, especially as an adjective meaning "very small." (This sense of the word is fairly new, having been first attested in 1893. In its older senses, both as a noun and as an adjective, *minuscule* is descriptive of lowercase letters and of several medieval writing styles featuring letters that are simplified and small.) The spelling *miniscule* presumably owes something to association with the combining form *mini-* and with such familiar words as *minimal* and *minimum.* Our evidence indicates that it now occurs in standard contexts just as commonly as *minuscule:*

... a miniscule animal called a rotifer —*Johns Hopkins Mag.,* Spring 1968

Transistors ... can be miniscule —*Center Mag.,* March/April 1971

The miniscule size of the cut —*Wall Street Jour.,* 20 Feb. 1974

... only a *miniscule* proportion of these books —*Language Arts,* April 1980

... current profits are miniscule —*Science,* 26 Sept. 1980

The miniscule Jewish data —*Maledicta 1983*

It may be, in fact, that *miniscule* is now the more common form. An article by Michael Kenney in the *Boston Globe* on 12 May 1985 noted that *miniscule* outnumbered *minuscule* by three to one in that newspaper's data base.

Nevertheless, *miniscule* continues to be widely regarded as a spelling error. No usage commentator will tolerate it, and most dictionaries either omit it or label it erroneous. Our own view is that any spelling which occurs so commonly, year after year, in perfectly reputable and carefully edited books and periodicals must be regarded as a standard variant. You should be aware, however, that you stand some chance of being corrected if you use it.

minister   The verb *minister* is most often used with *to:*

He pictured her then with a glow on her face ... that ministered to him alone —Winston Churchill, *The Crisis,* 1901

... a leader whom we all respect, but who has been called upon to minister to a hopeless case of political schizophrenia —Adlai E. Stevenson, *Speeches,* ed. Richard Harrity, 1952

... something still eludes us in the career of Jonathan Edwards and in the community to which he ministered —Edmund S. Morgan, *N.Y. Times Book Rev.,* 13 July 1980

It has also occurred infrequently with *among:*

> While ministering diligently among his rural parishioners —*Dictionary of American Biography,* 1936

minor   See IMPLICIT COMPARATIVE.

minus   *Minus* does not compare with *plus* (which see) as a generator of controversy, but its use as a preposition more or less equivalent to *without* has attracted occasional disapproval for many decades. Such usage dates back to the 19th century:

> We [arrived] ... about six in the evening, *minus* one horse —J. B. Fraser, *Travels in Koordistan,* 1840 (OED)

This use of *minus* was labeled colloquial by the OED in 1907, and it was discouraged in several handbooks on writing in the early 20th century. More recently, a few critics have stressed what they regard as its facetious quality; Bernstein 1965, for example, describes it as "a jocular casualism." Our evidence shows that it does sometimes occur in writing that has a playful tone:

> ... a reissue of the bearded representative who refused to sponsor an antiwar resolution. ... We find him about the same but minus the chin spinach — Julian Moynahan, *N.Y. Times Book Rev.,* 17 Oct. 1982

But *minus* is also commonly used in serious, if not highly solemn, writing:

> ... a condition for dealing with the Saigon regime minus Thieu —I. F. Stone, *N.Y. Rev. of Books,* 9 Mar. 1972

> The property is now a state farm, the castle, minus most of its looted furnishings, a museum —Eleanor Perenyi, *Green Thoughts,* 1983

> ... much of the National Democrats' vicious and intolerant nationalism—minus, of course, their Catholicism—was integrated into the official ideology of the Polish People's Republic —Norman Davies, *N.Y. Times Book Rev.,* 2 Sept. 1984

The full sense of *minus* in such contexts is usually "deprived of" or "having lost" rather than simply "without." The word still retains something of an informal quality, but that does not make it inappropriate in most current writing.

minuscule   See MINISCULE, MINUSCULE.

minutia   The meaning of *minutia* is "a minute or minor detail." The word is almost always now used in its plural form:

> ... seldom are minutiae piled on —Bradley Miller, *American Scholar,* Winter 1981/82

> ... only after ... all minutiae of a complex protocol have been observed —Fred Bruemmer, *Natural History,* December 1984

Evans 1957 finds that the plural can be either *minutias* or *minutiae;* however, our evidence shows that the only

form now used is *minutiae.* Bernstein 1965 cites as an error a sentence in which *minutiae* is used as a singular. This does not appear to be a widespread problem; we have no further evidence of the error in our files. Janis 1984, on the other hand, warns against using *minutia* as a plural (as though a singular *minutium* existed), and for this we do have some evidence:

> She has described her early years in their minutia — Herbert Lottman, *Columbia Forum,* Fall 1970

> ... acquiring encyclopedic knowledge about minutia —Frederick Goldman & Linda R. Burnett, *Need Johnny Read?,* 1971

This use of *minutia* is not established as standard.
For other foreign plurals, see LATIN PLURALS.

mischievous   A pronunciation \mis-'chē-vē-əs\, and consequent spelling *mischievious,* is of long standing: evidence for this spelling goes back to the 16th century. Our pronunciation files contain modern attestations ranging from dialect speakers of the islands of the Chesapeake Bay to Herbert Hoover. The pronunciation and spelling must be considered nonstandard but are in a somewhat special category, as they may be used deliberately and humorously, not to make fun of someone else's speech, but because the folksy sound and the echo from *devious* often add an appropriate flavor to the semantics of the word. See also GRIEVOUS, GRIEVOUSLY.

mishap   1. A commercially prepared list of supposed solecisms gotten up a few years ago by a publisher for the purpose of promoting a line of supplementary educational materials contained the words "lucky mishap," which were apparently meant to imply that *mishap* is wrongly used by the unlettered in place of *accident.* Bernstein 1965 and Shaw 1975 are also at pains to distinguish *accident* and *mishap.* While chance is a primary attribute of both *accident* and *mishap, mishap* always implies an undesirable result, and *accident* need not. If indeed the two words are ever confused, such confusion has escaped our attention. We have no evidence that the two words are actually muddled and cannot persuade ourselves that this is a genuine problem.
2. Bernstein 1958, 1965, Harper 1975, 1985 (citing the *Boston Globe* style manual), Shaw 1975, and Bryson 1984 all maintain that *mishap* should be reserved for minor unwanted accidents. There are, however, several factors working against the success of such a restriction.

First, there is history. The association of triviality with *mishap* is recent; older literary citations carry no such connotation. In Shakespeare's *The Comedy of Errors,* for instance, the old Syracusan merchant Ægeon tells "sad stories of [his] own mishaps," which include a shipwreck in which his wife and one of his twin sons were lost. Although Ægeon knows they were rescued and not drowned, the level of triviality is still not on a par with, say, spilling a glass of milk.

Second, the word is of a convenient length for newspaper headline writers, who often use it in place of the longer *accident* no matter how serious the occurrence. Thus we see headlines like these:

> Practice Mishap Kills Driver —*Springfield* (Mass.) *Morning Union,* 8 Feb. 1984

> 30 die in mishap —*The Times* (London), cited in Bryson 1984

> J. J. ASTOR DROWNED IN LINER MISHAP — headline over the report of the sinking of the *Titanic,* cited in Howard 1984

The headline use can carry over into ordinary prose:

> ... no mention of his having been killed in an auto mishap —Gregory Corso, *Evergreen*, August 1967

> The consequences of mishap are real. Two thousand villagers in Palomares, Spain, were exposed to radioactive debris —*New Republic*, 19 Mar. 1966

But undeniably *mishap* is also used for trivial occurrences:

> ... directed the concert without any of the mishaps expected of a twenty-year-old's performance —*Current Biography 1951*

> All sorts of little mishaps can blight a Broadway production —Bowen Northrup, *Wall Street Jour.*, 24 July 1972

> ... provoked by some mishap in the kitchen —Russell Baker, *Growing Up*, 1982

And sometimes no one can know how serious or trivial the mishap may be:

> They spent many hours in a simulated capsule ... preparing themselves for the possibility of mishap during flight —*Current Biography*, November 1965

In actual use, then, *mishap* may be applied to either serious or inconsequential occurrences, always unfortunate for the person involved. The wish to restrict it to minor accidents is perhaps slightly off the mark. The particular effect of *mishap* in most modern use is to downplay the seriousness of what happened, rather than to describe it. We see it used deliberately for this purpose:

> A spokesman for Metropolitan Edison, owners of the plant, insisted for several hours that a "mechanical mishap" had occurred, not a nuclear accident —H. L. Stevenson, *UPI Reporter*, 5 Apr. 1979

Mishap, then, is likely to be the word of choice when the unfortunate accident is of a trivial nature, and also when it seems desirable to downplay its seriousness.

mislead, misled The spelling error that occurs with the verb *lead* also occurs, not surprisingly, with *mislead*. The past tense and past participle, *misled*, is sometimes spelled *mislead*:

> ... if a checklist format is used to project the findings, the user can be mislead —*Language Arts*, October 1976

Remember, when the verb is being used in the past tense or past participle, get the *-lead* out.
See also LEAD, LED.

misplaced modifiers, misrelated modifiers See DANGLING MODIFIERS.

missile Bremner 1980 and Copperud 1970, 1980 note that *missile* is often misspelled *missle*. *Missile* is tough for us Americans; the same pronunciation also suggests such alternatives as *missal* and *mistle(toe)*. If you think of the British pronunciation with \-ˌīl\ at the end, you will have no trouble.
Copperud also mentions occasional confusion of *missile* with *missive*. We have not found this error in print, but composition teachers report it, and people have written to us to ask about it. It appears to be a mental

blend of *missive* and *epistle*. The only other confirmation that this confusion exists is *missile* entered under *letter* in one crossword-puzzle dictionary that we have seen.

misspell Copperud 1970, 1980 notes that "with ultimate perversity" this word is often misspelled *mispell*. The error is rare in edited writing, but we do have some evidence of it:

> Catch boss's typos, mispellings, etc. —*The Affirmative Action Handbook*, 1978

This ranks high on the list of Most Embarrassing Spelling Errors.

mistrustful *Mistrustful* is usually used with *of* when it takes a preposition:

> ... mistrustful of having made a mistake in his late demonstrations —Charles Dickens, *A Tale of Two Cities*, 1859

> ... the Russians are so mistrustful of everybody that they never know what to believe —Upton Sinclair, *A World to Win*, 1946

> ... be mistrustful of the ways of Western journalists —Norman Stone, *N.Y. Times Book Rev.*, 28 Oct. 1984

Sometimes *toward* is used:

> ... has described three such motherless children as ... mistrustful toward older people —Matthew Josephson, *Southern Rev.*, Winter 1973

mitigate This verb has several senses, but it functions primarily in current English as a synonym of *alleviate*, with suggestions of *moderate:*

> ... to mitigate injustices in both communist and capitalist societies —John Wilkinson, *Center Mag.*, March 1969

> ... mitigate the shocking conditions under which black people live there —Roger M. Williams, *Saturday Rev.*, 30 Sept. 1978

> ... did little to mitigate their unhappiness —*The Tower Commission Report*, 1987

It is not a rare word, but neither is it an extremely common one, and many people no doubt feel less than sure about its meaning. This uncertainty has in recent decades led to its being used with *against* in place of the similar but unrelated verb *militate*, meaning "to have weight or effect":

> ... some intangible and invisible social force that mitigates against him —"Centaur in Brass," in *The Collected Stories of William Faulkner*, 1950

> The self-respect they engender mitigates against their repetition —Harvey Wheeler, *Saturday Rev.*, 11 May 1968

> ... his looks tend to mitigate against him intellectually —David Halberstam, *McCall's*, November 1971

> ... they mitigate against inaccurate overstatement —Jeffrey Hirshberg, *American Speech*, Fall 1982

Such usage is comparable in several ways to the use of *flaunt* to mean "flout": it has its origins in the confusion of two similar words, it occurs primarily among educated people (poorly educated people are unlikely to use *mitigate* or *militate* in any sense), and it is universally regarded as an error by usage commentators.

Flesch 1983 lays the blame for this confusion on a method of teaching reading that downplayed phonics and was quite popular in the U.S. for a time, but it would seem unlikely that this system of pedagogy had any effect on William Faulkner. Edmund Wilson, in *The Bit Between My Teeth*, 1965, assigns the blame to the disappearing habit of thinking in a Latin vocabulary. Perhaps both reasons contribute. Flesch thinks the confusion is very widespread, but our files show it not as common as *flaunt-flout*. Flesch also says that we should give up and accept it as an American idiom. *Mitigate against* may reach that status someday—it shows no sign of going away—but it has not done so yet, and your use of it will probably attract some critical attention. We suggest you limit your use of *mitigate* to its moderating sense and use *militate against*.

See also FLAUNT, FLOUT.

mix When *mix* takes a preposition, it is most often *with:*

> Perique is used principally for blending and mixing with other and milder varieties —*American Guide Series: Louisiana*, 1941

> It must be remembered that he had never mixed on easy terms with boys and girls of his own age —Robertson Davies, *Tempest-tost*, 1951

> . . . a peculiar ability to merge and mix with other social groups —Walter Lippmann, *Atlantic*, March 1955

> Beard laughed aside academic rules . . . and mixed politics with economics and wit with both —C. Vann Woodward, *N.Y. Times Book Rev.*, 5 Sept. 1954

> . . . Mr. Strauss mixed a college deferment with some later luck on the draft lottery —J. Anthony Lukas, *N.Y. Times Book Rev.*, 11 June 1978

Mix is less often used with *in* or *into:*

> He informs all office seekers that it is not in keeping with his position as judge to mix in politics —*American Guide Series: Nevada*, 1940

> The society in which she mixed was very varied —Edith Sitwell, *I Live Under a Black Sun*, 1937

> Unfortunately prestige gets mixed into education at every turn —James B. Conant, *Slums and Suburbs*, 1961

Once in a while *mix* takes *within:*

> Political shifts and clashes which . . . were cast to mix within the vast crucible of the interior —Russell Lord, *Behold Our Land*, 1938

mixed metaphor This is an entry in several usage books and handbooks for the same reason *malapropism* is: it seems a shame to waste good comic material. Mixed metaphors are essentially a matter of beginning with one figurative expression and ending with another. These are doubtless more frequent in speech than in writing, for writers at least have the opportunity to go back and revise. Of course, they sometimes fail to do so.

Here are a few samples without their authors' names:

> This field of research is so virginal that no human eye has ever set foot in it —Ph.D. dissertation cited in *Linguistic Reporter*, April 1981

> The vacuum in the presidency that hung over the university —*Change*, March/April 1971

> The political equation was thus saturated with kerosene —*Newsweek*, 28 Apr. 1986

> . . . seems rather tame during the first taste or two, but gradually builds up a head of steam that leaves one breathing fire —*Gourmet*, January 1979

> . . . American scientists stole a trump on the Soviet Union —*Springfield* (Mass.) *Morning Union*, 12 Sept. 1985

> . . . an almost universal crescendo of hysteria and violence is the path through the horns of the dilemma —*A Center Occasional Paper*, 1971

It should be noted that sometimes a mixed metaphor may result when the writer is so accustomed to the figurative sense of a word that he or she forgets its metaphorical origin. Thus some mixed metaphors can be useful evidence for the lexicographer that an extended sense is established. These last two examples are perhaps such evidence:

> The ecologists are hammering away at the population growth bottleneck in an effort to shave it to reasonable proportions —cited in Bernstein 1971

> Bond's knees, the Achilles' heel of all skiers, were beginning to ache —Ian Fleming, cited in Barzun 1985

All we can suggest is that you look back over what you have written for any figurative language that may draw an unintended laugh.

See also MALAPROPISM; SYNTACTIC BLEND.

mock As a verb, *mock* is usually transitive; however, when it is intransitive and is used with a preposition, it is most often used with *at:*

> She was a handsome, insolent hussy, who mocked at the youth —D. H. Lawrence, *Sons and Lovers*, 1913

> Peacock was not mocking at his friend, but at what the eighteenth century so much distrusted, "enthusiasm" —*Times Literary Supp.*, 17 Apr. 1953

> . . . voices screaming and mocking at me —Frank Reynolds, *Evergreen*, June 1967

modal See DOUBLE MODAL.

molten Several commentators point out, as does the OED, that the adjective *molten* in its "liquefied by heat" sense is now limited in application to substances such as metals and rocks that require great heat to be melted. Our evidence, in general, supports that observation:

> . . . a stream of molten metal —*Times Literary Supp.*, 30 July 1971

> . . . effects that molten glass can produce —Helen Harris, *Town & Country*, August 1979

> . . . a fresh batch of molten rock —Richard A. Kerr, *Science*, 1 May 1981

Molten does, however, have some persistent use in describing melted cheese:

> ... molten Parmesan cheese —C. S. Forester, *Holiday,* October 1957

> ... a heat source that keeps the cheese molten — *Consumer Reports,* March 1972

> ... sautéed onions, molten cheese —Jane & Michael Stern, *Cook's,* September/October 1986

Such usage is not wrong, but it is atypical.

momentarily A relatively new sense of this word has drawn a fair number of attacks in recent years from a small but determined group of critics. The disputed sense is "at any moment; in a moment," as in "We'll be leaving momentarily." Its detractors insist that *momentarily* is correct only in its original sense, "for a moment," which was first recorded in 1654. This sense, although impressively old, appears to have been rarely used until the 20th century (the first of our dictionaries to enter it was Webster 1909), but it is now extremely common:

> ... the Pacific breezes momentarily gave way to a brisker wind —*Times Literary Supp.,* 16 Apr. 1970

> ... it is a momentarily heart-stopping ... experience —Marvin Grosswirth, *Datamation,* January 1981

Two additional senses of *momentarily* were used, albeit rarely, during the 19th century. One of them was "instantly," which was first recorded in 1799:

> This was momentarily agreed to —Richard Sicklemore, *Agnes and Leonora,* 1799 (OED)

And the other was "at every moment; from moment to moment," which dates from 1800:

> I am interrupted momentarily by visitors, like fleas, infesting a new-comer! —Robert Southey, letter, 1 May 1800 (OED)

The "from moment to moment" sense was the only one entered in Webster 1828, and it continued to be the only sense in Merriam-Webster dictionaries throughout the 19th century. It was never common, however, and it appears now to have passed entirely out of use, along with the equally rare "instantly" sense.

The history of *momentarily* is complicated by its connection with *momently,* a little-used adverb that at one time or another had (as the OED shows) each of the senses that *momentarily* has had. Webster 1828 gave *momently* two senses, the first of which was "for a moment"—which, of course, is now the prescribed sense of *momentarily*—and the second of which was really two senses in one, "in a moment; every moment." Webster's reason for giving two definitions for the second sense is revealed by the sentence he used to illustrate it, "We momently expect the arrival of the mail," which can be understood as either "We expect the arrival of the mail in a moment" or "We are at every moment expecting the arrival of the mail." Such usage with the verb *expect* seems to represent a transition between the sense "at every moment; from moment to moment" and the sense "at any moment; in a moment." This transition occurred with *momentarily* as well as with *momently:*

> During the early part of the morning, I momentarily expected his coming; he was not in the frequent habit

of entering the schoolroom, but ... I had the impression that he was sure to visit it that day —Charlotte Brontë, *Jane Eyre,* 1847

We have no further evidence from the 1800s showing *momentarily* used in this way, but it was through such usage (with *expect*) that *momentarily* "at any moment" first became common in American English in the 20th century:

> Arrests were expected momentarily as police continued their investigation —*Sun* (Baltimore), 13 Aug. 1928 (OED Supplement)

Fowler 1926 distinguished between *momentarily* and *momently,* asserting that *momentarily* meant "for a moment" and that *momently* meant "from moment to moment." That distinction was not to be found in any dictionary. The evidence, scanty as it is, suggests that at the beginning of the 20th century *momentarily* and *momently* were uncommon words that were used more or less interchangeably in several senses. In the years since, *momently* has continued to be uncommon, while *momentarily* has come into frequent use, first in its sense "for a moment" and soon afterward in its sense "at any moment; in a moment." These two senses have coexisted in American English for many decades (in British English, "at any moment" is rare). Neither one is inherently superior to the other, and neither one detracts in any way from the other. The meaning of each is always made clear by the context in which it occurs:

> ... more than ever convinced that the small unfamiliar stateroom ... had momentarily been filled and then emptied of black sea water —John Hawkes, *Fiction,* vol. 1, no. 4, 1973

> The menu said that momentarily we should be sipping consomme from shallow silver cups —John Hawkes, *Fiction,* vol. 1, no. 4, 1973

The notion that "at any moment" is in some way an error is attributable to the fact that "for a moment" was the first sense to become common (as well as to the mistaken assumption that a word can have only one meaning). This notion has not been widely promoted by usage commentators, but it does enjoy some popularity among certain writers, readers, and editors, and those who believe it are generally pretty sure of themselves:

> There may be comity between those who think ... *momentarily* means in a moment (airline captain over loudspeaker: "We'll be taking off momentarily, folks") and those who know it means for a moment. Members of these two classes can sit in adjoining seats on the plane and get along fine ... , but once the plane has emptied, they will proceed toward different destinations —Paul Fussell, in *The Contemporary Essay,* 1984

Since we at Merriam-Webster will be traveling with the people who "think" that *momentarily* can mean "in a moment," we cannot be sure where those people who "know" that it can mean only "for a moment" are headed. We hope, though, that they will consider a trip to the nearest library, where any number of good dictionaries will tell them that the airline captain was speaking standard English.

momento *Momento* is a rather rare spelling variant of *memento.* It is unetymological, since it obscures the word's relation to *memory* and *remember,* and probably shows the influence of *moment.* Some call it a misspelling, but it appears often enough in edited prose to have been considered acceptable for entry in at least two dictionaries: Webster's Third and the OED Supplement.

> ... a nostalgic momento of an earlier century — Joseph Wechsberg, *New Yorker,* 28 Mar. 1953

> ... a satisfyingly real momento of my enjoyment — Margaret Forster, *The Writer,* October 1968

> ... lexical momentos of the pop culture —John Algeo, *American Speech,* Winter 1980

The spelling is attested as early as 1853 in a letter written by Chauncey A. Goodrich, professor at Yale, son-in-law of Noah Webster, and first editor in chief of Merriam-Webster dictionaries. The OED Supplement instances George Eliot from 1871 and Dylan Thomas from 1951.

moneys, monies In most of its uses, *money* has no plural, but when the reference is to discrete sums of money, usually obtained from various sources or distributed to various individuals or groups, the plural *moneys* or *monies* is often used:

> ... the greater part of the moneys will have to come from the Federal Government —Lester Markel, *N.Y. Times,* 5 June 1967

> ... the basis for distributing many federal grant monies —Sandra Lauffer, *Change,* September 1971

> ... to raise the monies it will need from the large municipal corporations —Ian Breach, *The Sunday Times* (London), 20 Jan. 1974

> ... the present allocation of tax moneys and resources —Marcus Raskin, *N.Y. Times Book Rev.,* 11 Apr. 1976

> ... union pension-fund moneys are being used to destroy union jobs —Jeremy Rifkin & Randy Barber, *Saturday Rev.,* 2 Sept. 1978

> ... ad hoc collections of public and private monies —Fred Ferretti, *N.Y. Times,* 13 July 1980

The plural *monies* has occasionally been criticized because it suggests a singular *mony* rather than *money.* It is, however, an old and perfectly respectable variant that is used about as commonly as *moneys,* and it is recognized as standard in all current dictionaries.

monopoly *Monopoly* is used with several prepositions. Shaw 1972 and Bernstein 1965 prescribe the use of *of,* while Evans 1957 says that the use of *of* is British and the use of *on* is American. According to our evidence, *of* has been the preposition most commonly used with *monopoly* on both sides of the Atlantic, and probably still was when Shaw and Bernstein were writing:

> ... our illusions ... that we have a monopoly of energy, know-how, culture and morality —Adlai E. Stevenson, *Look,* 22 Sept. 1953

> ... a monopoly of atomic weapons —Barry Goldwater, *The Conscience of a Conservative,* 1960

> ... the clergy had enjoyed a fairly close monopoly of trained intelligence —G. M. Trevelyan, *English Social History,* 1942

The richer countries' monopoly of science and technology —*Times Literary Supp.,* 27 Aug. 1971

However, Evans may well have been detecting a trend, as our evidence for the past 25 years indicates that the use of *monopoly on* has been increasing in American English and is now probably more common than *monopoly of,* although *monopoly of* is still quite common:

> No one has a monopoly on virtue or truth —Bill Moyers, quoted in *N.Y. Herald Tribune,* 4 Jan. 1964

> In the cities, however, cadre members can still be easily singled out by ... their monopoly on conversation —Jonathan Mirsky, *Saturday Rev.,* 1 July 1972

> ... the Soviet Union has a monopoly on the best sable —Angela Taylor, *N.Y. Times,* 29 May 1976

> ... possessing as it does a shared monopoly of national television journalism —*Detroit News,* 23 Sept. 1981

There still appears to be no use of *monopoly on* in British English.

Monopoly is also used, although less frequently, with *in* and *over:*

> ... exercising a complete and official monopoly in that field since January 1950 —*Current Biography 1953*

> ... we believe that monopoly in anything, including monopoly in religion, is a source of corruption — Reinhold Niebuhr, quoted in *Time,* 29 Sept. 1947

> ... entrenched institutional interests that had previously obtained a monopoly over beliefs in, say, astronomy —John Dewey, *Freedom and Culture,* 1939

> ... give English merchants an almost complete monopoly over the colonial import trade —Leon H. Canfield & Howard B. Wilder, *The Making of Modern America,* 1962

Although Shaw mentions use of *monopoly for,* our files show scant evidence for it:

> ... a few among them possessed a virtual monopoly for the underwriting of government loans —Rondo E. Cameron, *Jour. of Political Economy,* December 1953

moot The adjective *moot* has a sense that means "open to question; debatable" (and a related sense "disputed") which causes no real concern amongst prescribers of usage. The sense that means "deprived of practical significance; purely academic," however, makes a few of them uneasy. They know it originated in legal use, and they are reluctant to see the shift into general use as acceptable.

> It is mistakenly used to signify that something is beyond argument, that there is no point in arguing the question, except in the technical legal sense that something moot is something previously decided — Bremner 1980

> Sometimes misused in the sense *hypothetical* or *academic.* This is a technical sense and out of place except in legal contexts ..., as the examples in Webster show —Copperud 1980

By "Webster" Copperud means Webster's Third, which illustrates this sense of *moot* with two citations about legal matters. In the late 1950s, when Webster's Third was being edited, legal citations for this sense in our files outnumbered nonlegal ones by about four to one. Since then, this sense has become as firmly fixed in general English as it is in legal English.

> Whether this type of proliferation is good or bad is a moot question. The facts of life are that it exists —Representative Frank Thompson, quoted in *American School Board Jour.*, September 1968

> Even inflation cannot justify charging $20 for a moderately-sized book. In Nash's case this complaint is moot, for his book would be expensive at any price —Philip Rosenberg, *N.Y. Times Book Rev.*, 20 June 1976

> . . . whether the Iranian government *can* free the hostages from the militants. But we have made the question moot, for the government's best interest is served by keeping them —Walter Guzzardi, Jr., *Fortune*, 2 June 1980

moral, morale We have on hand a good number of handbooks and schoolbooks that try to distinguish these two words on the most simplistic of lines. However, if you look up these two nouns in a good dictionary, you will see that they are intimately intertwined. The chief problem seems to be the sense "esprit de corps." In present-day English *morale* is the usual spelling for this sense; *moral* is likely to be considered a misspelling. But it is not; the OED shows that *moral* was the original spelling for this sense. It was the spelling in French, and the sense was taken over from the French. And current dictionaries, such as Webster's Ninth New Collegiate Dictionary, still recognize this sense as one of the meanings of *moral.*

We recommend, however, that you use *morale* for the "esprit de corps" sense—most people do. Few, if any, use *morale* instead of *moral* for the lesson in a story.

more important, more importantly See IMPORTANT 1.

more than one To listen to the usage writers, you would think there was no problem whatsoever with this phrase: Longman 1984, Shaw 1975, 1987, Phythian 1979, Copperud 1970, 1980, Evans 1957, Flesch 1964, Fowler 1926, 1965, Bernstein 1962, 1965, and the OED all confidently assert that *more than one* is followed by a singular verb; this, they say, in spite of the fact that the meaning is clearly plural. The cagier Bryant 1962 says "usually singular"; Jespersen 1909–49 says that *more than one* "seems" always to take the singular.

The two last-named commentators have good reason for their caution. *More than one* is a complicated little rascal. To begin with, it is not especially frequent as the subject of a verb and consequently most of those who would talk about it have very little evidence of use. And if we agree that it is plural in sense, then it must govern its verb on the basis of proximity (Jespersen calls it "attraction")—the *one* being the key item. From our limited evidence it appears that *more than one* is most often used as a group modifier of a singular noun, with the noun taking the singular verb:

> More than one woman has been known to like her —Anthony Hope, *The Dolly Dialogues*, 1894 (in Jespersen)

> Mr. Hannah said that more than one charge of discrimination was involved —*N.Y. Times* (in Bernstein 1962)

> More than one New England family still cherishes the . . . tea set —*House and Garden,* March 1957 (in Bryant 1962)

So far so good. But things, as you might suspect, are not that neat and simple. Eugene S. McCartney, in an article in *Word Study,* February 1953, investigated the problem and found variation in practice. The fly in the ointment is notional agreement. When the notion of plurality predominates, the plural verb is used. Sometimes this results in an awkward-sounding sentence:

> . . . which ensures that more than one tooth are in contact at all times —George Hessler, in *Tool Engineers Handbook,* ed. Frank W. Wilson, 1949

But sometimes the plural is simply required by common sense in the context of the whole sentence:

> If there are more than one, they are alphabetized among themselves —Webster's Second 1934, Explanatory Notes, Prepositional Phrases (in McCartney)

The singular would make no sense here, since a single phrase would not need alphabetizing. Even H. W. Fowler himself was led by notional agreement to the very brink of violating his own principle:

> The *l*[atter] should not be used when more than a pair are in question —Fowler 1926, 1965, under *latter*

Only the use of *a* and not *one* saves the rule in this case.

In the special situation where *one* is followed by *of* and a plural noun, the combination of the plural sense and of the proximate plural noun is likely to produce a plural verb:

> In the positions defined above in which more than one of these morphs occur —Charles F. Hockett, *Language,* January–March 1950

The first thing to remember is that these constructions in which *more than one* is the subject of a verb or is associated with the subject of a verb do not seem to be very numerous. When the phrase precedes a singular noun, the singular verb is usual, and sounds better too. In more complex sentences, however, the notion of plurality may well prevail—indeed, the plural may sometimes be required by sense. If you write yourself into one of those corners and cannot decide between singular and plural, you may want to try something like the Government Printing Office dodge. McCartney found a 1933 manual with

> Where there is more than one consonant, the last is carried over. . . .

And a 1936 one with

> Where there are more than one consonant, the last is carried over. . . .

A correspondent told *Word Study* that a 1953 edition of the manual dodged the problem thus:

> In a group of two or more consonants, division is made. . . .

mortician This word is an Americanism that was coined as a synonym for *undertaker* in the 1890s. Mencken 1936 notes that it first occurred in a publication titled *Embalmers' Monthly* in 1895 (we first heard of it in 1897, in a letter from the publisher of the *West-*

ern Undertaker). Its euphemistic qualities have naturally attracted some derision over the years, but few people now are conscious of it as a euphemism, and its use in American English is common and unremarkable:

> ... asked by the hospital which mortician you wish to have called —*Harper's Weekly,* 9 Feb. 1976

> ... increased cancers among such occupationally exposed groups as beauticians and morticians —Ben A. Franklin, *N.Y. Times,* 20 Mar. 1984

Undertakers themselves, interestingly enough, apparently prefer the term *funeral director,* which is actually an even older euphemism, first recorded in 1886.

Moslem, Muslim   *Moslem* is the older spelling, but *Muslim* is perhaps more used today both because it is preferred by those of whom it is used and because it is a closer representation of the Arabic. Either is likely to be preferred to *Mohammedan* or *Muhammadan,* which some people find offensive.

most, almost   The adverb *most* that is a shortening of *almost* has been attested in the written language since the early 17th century. It seems to have appeared in Scottish English in the 16th century with the spelling *maist.* At some point it made its way to this country, where it has flourished since the later part of the 18th century. It is in current use in speech and in standard writing of a not overly formal character.

In standard English *most* "almost" and the other familiar adverb *most* are in complementary distribution; that is, their usages do not conflict. *Most* "almost" is quite limited in application. It modifies the adjectives *all, every,* and *any;* the pronouns *all, anybody, anyone, anything, everybody, everyone,* and *everything;* the adverbs *always, anywhere,* and *everywhere.* There are other uses of *most* "almost" but they are dialectal or, perhaps, old-fashioned. Here are some examples of standard written use:

> ... it showers most all the time —Emily Dickinson, letter, 12 May 1842

> ... like most all of us, learned his racial prejudice at home —Dan Wakefield, *Los Angeles Times Book Rev.,* 25 Apr. 1971

> ... with a technical equipment equal to most any demands —Irving Kolodin, *Saturday Rev.,* 30 Jan. 1954

> ... witness ... German propaganda most anywhere in Europe —*N.Y. Herald Tribune Book Rev.,* 24 Dec. 1939

> ... and most every conceivable type of four-wheeled vehicle —Malcolm S. Forbes, *Forbes,* 1 Dec. 1970

> So most everybody in the bar was merely leaning on the bar —John McNulty, *New Yorker,* 31 Oct. 1953

> ... most everybody in the world today believes in his heart that life is more worth living for the average man in North America than anywhere else —John Dos Passos, quoted in *New Republic,* 1 Sept. 1941

> ... like most everyone else on the beach —David Arnold, *Boston Globe Mag.,* 2 Dec. 1979

> ... the quote is familiar to most every student of literature —Harvard O'Neille, *Southern Accents,* September–October 1984

> Most everything about a car ... is more or less essential —Henry Miller, *The Air-Conditioned Nightmare,* 1945

> These symbols ... are most always used in pairs —Joseph Lasky, *Proofreading and Copy-Preparation,* 1949

> ... accompanies him most everywhere —Frank Deford, *Sports Illustrated,* 8 Aug. 1983

> With that kind of power you could do most anything with a ball club —Alvin Dark & John Underwood, *Sports Illustrated,* 20 May 1974

> Most all of the poultry you purchase is ready-to-cook —Eva Medved, *The World of Food,* 3d ed., 1981

> ... the Tassels of most all the corn —George Washington, diary, 25 Aug. 1770 (OED Supplement)

All of these uses are standard. Here are a few samples of dialectal or old-fashioned use:

> It was most eleven when Josiah and me got to bed agin —Marietta Holley, "A Pleasure Exertion," in *Mark Twain's Library of Humor,* 1888

> It most froze me to hear such talk —Mark Twain, *Huckleberry Finn,* 1884, in *The Practical Cogitator,* ed. Charles P. Curtis, Jr., & Ferris Greenslet, 1945

> "I don't worry about myself," the old woman replied, "... my time has 'most come...." —Ellen Glasgow, *Vein of Iron,* 1935

> "There's your moon, Midge," he said. ...
> "I was watching it. It's most at the full."
> —Hamilton Basso, *The View from Pompey's Head,* 1954

A lot has been written about this *most.* From Bache 1869 to Trimmer & McCrimmon 1988 commentators and pedagogues disparage the word, calling it "inexcusable," "colloquial," "schoolgirlish," "dialectal," "incorrect," "folksy," "illiterate." Yet no native speaker of American English has any trouble with it, and it does not interfere with superlative *most.* As Evans 1957 observes, there is no theoretical or grammatical reason to object to the use. Indeed, the 120 years of opposition to *most* defy rational analysis. It is not even a covert marker of social status. It is simply an established American idiom; it has been in reputable use in speech and, somewhat less often, in writing from George Washington's time to the present. As you have noticed, its range of application is limited; it cannot be used everywhere that *almost* can. But within its sphere it is entirely respectable.

mostly   A number of handbooks comment on *most* and *mostly,* which you are warned not to confuse. The warning may be a lingering memory of the past, when *mostly* was used occasionally like *most* to mean "to the greatest degree." The OED marks this use obsolete, with its latest citation dated 1768. Our latest evidence is from Jane Austen:

> ... the person whose society she mostly prized —*Northanger Abbey,* 1818

This use seems to be so archaic that it is not worth worrying about. It has probably dropped out of use because it would conflict directly—in the same positions—with the now prevalent meaning, "for the greatest part, mainly." Our current *mostly* tones down the meaning of a verb or adjective; the older use emphasized it. You can imagine what confusion there would be if both senses were still in use and you read these examples:

> ... a pretty good training film, which is what this movie mostly resembles —*People,* 10 Oct. 1983

> Although the President carried his three-inch-thick briefing book as he padded to the beach ... , he mostly ignored it —Kurt Andersen, *Time,* 7 May 1984

> ... an eccentric lot who have mostly dropped out from the troublesome real world —Frank Rich, *N.Y. Times,* 5 Apr. 1983

There is also some question about the propriety of *mostly* when it modifies a verb directly, as in the three examples just above. Although this use may be questioned on the basis of its elegance, there is no question that it is standard and common.

Mostly is often used at the beginning of a sentence like a sentence adverb:

> Mostly everyone had a jolly good time —Rick Telander, *Sports Illustrated,* 11 Aug. 1986

> ... mostly, I have spoken at colleges —William F. Buckley, Jr., *New Yorker,* 31 Jan. 1983

It can also be placed after the words it modifies:

> ... a pamphlet which is to instruct and inspire filling station helpers and manicurists mostly —E. B. White, letter, 4 Feb. 1942

motive   *Motive* is often followed by the preposition *for,* which is, in turn, often followed by a gerund:

> Copernicus had no motive for misleading his fellow-men —George Bernard Shaw, *Man and Superman,* 1903

> ... had every motive for continued loyalty to Rome —*Times Literary Supp.,* 30 July 1971

> ... motives for doing something are often *not* good reasons for doing it —Wayne C. Booth, *Modern Dogma and the Rhetoric of Assent,* 1974

Motive is also sometimes followed by *of* or *behind:*

> ... the habit so prevalent with us of always seeking the motive of everyone's speech or behavior —W. C. Brownell, *French Traits,* 1889

> The Czechs at first suspected the purity of the mission's professed motive of helping them —*Current Biography,* May 1965

> One of these pits contained twenty-seven skulls. ... The motive behind this peculiar burial is not clear —Raymond W. Murray, *Man's Unknown Ancestors,* 1943

And sometimes *motive* is followed by *to* and an infinitive:

> This was sufficient motive to endanger the peace of the frontier —Ray Allen Billington, *Westward Expansion,* 1949

Ms.   *Ms.* is a blend of *Miss* and *Mrs.* and seems to have been originally devised as a convenience for business use in addressing letters when the sender did not know if the woman addressed was married or not. The

utility of such a designation seems to have been recognized as long ago as the 18th century; the OED Supplement (under *certain*) has a 1754 citation in which the writer wishes such a term existed. It took a couple of centuries for one to be invented.

Once *Ms.* began to be used with some frequency, the feminist movement adopted it as a desirable honorific because, like *Mr.,* it was unmarked for marital status. The result of this adoption was a certain amount of controversy, most of it of the unenlightening variety. Bolinger 1980 quotes a woman who says that *Ms.* has come to be associated with divorcees, widows, businesswomen, feminists, and some others of questionable social status, and that this has reduced its usefulness. Our evidence does not support this judgment. On the contrary, we believe that use of *Ms.* has become so widespread that it is now the standard form to use, especially in business correspondence, when a woman's marital status is unknown or irrelevant to matters at hand. One notable piece of evidence for the general acceptance of *Ms.* is that the *New York Times,* after years of believing that *Ms.* was not part of common usage, adopted its use in 1986 for references to women whose marital status is unknown or whose preference for *Ms.* is known.

There are substantial treatments of the history and development of *Ms.* in Reader's Digest 1983 under *Miss* and in Copperud 1980 under *Ms.*

muchly   Rather surprisingly, *muchly* has existed in our language for a long time. The first citation for it in the OED is dated 1621 and illustrates a straightforward use in a serious poetic context. The second OED citation, though, shows that in its early days *muchly* was also seen as something of an oddity:

> Commonly 'tis larded with fine new words, as Savingable, Muchly, Christ-Jesusness —J. Birkenhead, *Assembly-Man,* 1647 (OED)

Unlike *thusly* (which see), *muchly* has never really gained a foothold in mainstream English. It is rarely found in print and is most commonly used these days in speech, especially in the phrase "thank you muchly." People tend to use it instead of *much* when they want to inject a little interest or humor into a conventional or formulaic speech pattern; even after three and a half centuries, *muchly* retains the character of a novelty word.

mucous, mucus   As has been pointed out by several commentators, the noun is spelled *mucus,* and the adjective is spelled *mucous.* This is not a troublesome matter for most writers, since neither word is likely to appear with great frequency except in strictly medical contexts; still, the occasional mistake may occur in general writing:

> The mucus membrane ... could then proceed —*Harper's,* March 1971

> ... a sticky mucous that acts like flypaper to trap ants and termites —*International Wildlife,* January/February 1983

multiple negation   See DOUBLE NEGATIVE 1. Geneva Smitherman, in *Talkin and Testifyin* (1977), has a discussion of the subtleties and nuances achievable in Black English with multiple negatives.

munch   Copperud 1970, 1980 does not like *munch* when it is used of eating something that does not crunch. Our evidence suggests that it is frequently used without reference to sound and has been for some time:

> ... he munched Wisconsin cheese —*Time,* 12 Apr. 1948

> ... herds of cattle ... munching the succulent grasses —*American Guide Series: Louisiana,* 1941

> ... munching sandwiches and hard-boiled eggs — Katharine Newlin Burt, *A Man's Own Country,* 1931

> ... critically munching a fragment of pie-crust — Arnold Bennett, *The Old Wives' Tale,* 1908

Current use does not differ much from that of the first half-century. If there is any fault here, it may be that lexicographers have been too much influenced by the onomatopoeic origin of the word and not enough by the way writers use the word.

muse   *Muse* is used about equally with *on, upon,* or *over:*

> ... he took a moment or two to muse on it —Gertrude Samuels, *N.Y. Times,* 3 Oct. 1954

> ... her silent mother mused on other things than topography —Thomas Hardy, *The Mayor of Casterbridge,* 1886

> They settled back into reposeful attitudes with airs of having accepted the matter. And they mused upon it —Stephen Crane, *The Red Badge of Courage,* 1895

> ... muse upon the continuity and the tragic finality of life —Irving Howe, *New Republic,* 28 Mar. 1955

> ... muse with kindly condescension over this token of bygone fashion —Virginia Woolf, *The Second Common Reader,* 1932

> ... Cabot mused over the fact that the old bastard considered himself ... one of the eminences of the great metropolis —James Purdy, *Cabot Wright Begins,* 1964

Muse also occurs, much less frequently, with *about:*

> Ever since man first mused about his own nature — Eric H. Lenneberg, *Biological Foundations of Language,* 1967

Muslim   See MOSLEM, MUSLIM.

must   Use of *must* as a noun meaning "something essential" seems to have originated among American journalists in the late 19th century. The Dictionary of American English cites an 1892 article in *Dialect Notes* describing the journalistic *must* as follows: "An article marked with the word *must* is spoken of as a *must,* or emphatically—if there is absolutely no way of keeping it out of the paper—as a *dead must.*" *Must* in this sense was slow to become established in general use, but by the 1940s it had begun to appear regularly in print, both as an ordinary noun and as an attributive:

> ... its "must" legislation complete and a new Congress about to convene in six weeks —*Time,* 25 Nov. 1940

> ... it belongs at the top of the "must" book list of every prospective traveler —*N.Y. Herald Tribune Book Rev.,* 21 Sept. 1942

> ... high-quality insulation is not a must in tube sockets —*Radio News,* March 1944

> ... among the few "musts" in any retrospective of film history —*Hollywood Quarterly,* January 1946

> ... make considerable psychiatric ability a "must" for all physicians —*Diseases of the Nervous System,* May 1947

These uses of *must* continue to be common.

Usage commentators generally confine themselves to considering whether *must* should be set off by quotation marks when used as a noun and adjective. Copperud 1964 and Flesch 1964 say that it should not; Gowers in Fowler 1965 gives, with apparent approval, citations showing that it still is. Our own most recent evidence indicates that the quotation marks are now omitted more often than not.

must of   See OF 2.

mutual, common   It has long been the practice of usage writers to condemn the use of *mutual* in the senses "shared in common" and "joint" because, they maintain, *mutual* must include the notion of reciprocity. The basis for this long-lived criticism goes back to two sources in the 18th century. The first of these is Samuel Johnson's 1755 Dictionary, which gave only one definition, "reciprocal." Fitzedward Hall 1873 points out that this is an error on Johnson's part; the first quotation under *mutual* is from Shakespeare's *Merchant of Venice* (1597) and is for the "common" sense. Johnson simply missed the meaning, and his omission is what we may call the passive 18th-century source.

The active 18th-century source is Baker 1770. Baker claimed never to have seen Johnson's Dictionary before writing his book, so he must have developed his opinion independently or gotten it from some unidentified source. Baker insists on the "reciprocal" sense and objects to expressions like "our mutual benefactor" and "our mutual friend"; although he gives no actual citations of such use, he says that many writers use such expressions. He prescribes *common* as correct in such expressions and quotes with approbation a letter of John Locke's using "our common friend."

Subsequent criticism of the "common" sense of *mutual* seems to derive directly from Baker. The subject got a considerable boost in popularity when Charles Dickens published *Our Mutual Friend* in 1864. After Alford 1866 (who does not mention Dickens, though) almost every 19th-century commentator known to us has something to say on the subject, and so do a great many 20th-century commentators. Among the most recent holdouts for Baker's position are Phythian 1979, Simon 1980, and, a little lukewarmly, Bryson 1984.

The OED's first example of *mutual friend* is dated 1658. The other examples of its use are from Lady Mary Wortley Montagu, Edmund Burke, Sir Walter Scott, and George Eliot. Here are a few from our files:

> ... by the hands of our mutual friend, Mr. Boswell —Sir Alexander Dick, letter (to Samuel Johnson), 17 Feb. 1777

> I had it from a dear mutual friend —W. M. Thackeray, *The Book of Snobs,* 1846

> ... after I had paid ten dollars in court for having punched a mutual friend —Robert Frost, letter, January 1923

... after the burial of a mutual friend —James Joyce, *Ulysses*, 1922

... our mutual friend, T. R. Smith —*The Intimate Notebooks of George Jean Nathan*, 1932

Our mutual friend Libba Thayer has given me your address —James Thurber, letter, 2 May 1960

... at the home of mutual friends —Larry L. King, *Harper's*, April 1970

That same day, a mutual friend invited Mullins and myself to join him for a round of golf at his club —Tip O'Neill with William Novak, *Man of the House*, 1987

We even have an example or two of the stigmatized sense used with other nouns. Dean Alford managed to convince himself that the *mutual* in the following example denoted reciprocity, but it clearly does not: it refers to the faith of both Paul and the Christians in Rome in Jesus Christ:

That is, that I may be comforted together with you by the mutual faith both of you and me —Romans 1:12 (AV), 1611

Here are a couple of other examples:

... La femme de quarante ans has a husband and *three* lovers; all of whom find out their mutual connection one starry night —W. M. Thackeray, *The Paris Sketch Book*, 1840

So they all nudged each other toward a mutual fate —Garry Wills, *Saturday Rev.*, 11 Dec. 1976

Objection to *mutual* "common" has no basis other than Baker's *ipse dixit* of 1770 and the regrettable support given it by Samuel Johnson's failure to recognize the meaning in his 1755 Dictionary. The usages themselves go back to Shakespeare; they have been in continuous use for almost 400 years, they are eminently standard, and it is about time the matter was laid to rest.

my, mine These, like *thy, thine* and *no, none*, were originally variants for phonological reasons: the \n\ versions were used before vowels and after the word modified. Strang 1970 tells us that because the final position was pronominal, a new distribution of the words developed, based on grammatical considerations. *My* took over the adjectival duties and *mine* the pronominal ones. The use of *mine* in attributive position before words beginning with a vowel is now archaic, and found only in a few special contexts.

Copperud 1970, 1980 mentions some contradictory opinions about *my* and *mine* in Evans 1957 and Fowler 1926, 1965. Evans says that *mine* is used in combination with another possessive pronoun when the combination precedes the noun it refers to, as in "mine and her child." Fowler takes just the opposite position, calling for *my* in this position, as in "my or your informant." Copperud says that logic and consistency favor Fowler's position; however, we suspect that this is a case in which sound and familiarity of idiom weigh more heavily than logic. You should choose the wording that sounds best to your ear. Both Evans and Fowler do agree that the best solution is to rephrase the sentence whenever possible, using the construction that gives "my child and hers" and "my informant and yours."

myself In the *New York Times Magazine* for 1 Feb. 1981, William Safire quotes outgoing President Jimmy Carter:

I will work hard to make sure that the transition from myself to the next President is a good one.

Safire opines that the use of *myself* is "an unstylish, though not incorrect, use." He then goes on to recommend *myself* be used as an intensive, "not as a cutesy turning away from the harsh 'me'." Not mentioned in this article is the substitution of *myself* for *I*, in which Reader's Digest 1983 detected Safire indulging himself:

No longer were Price, Buchanan, and myself part of the innermost circle —*Before the Fall*, 1974

"One cannot escape the impression that over the last couple of decades or so there has been a marked increase in the use of 'myself' for 'me'," says Foster 1968. He gives a few examples, including this one:

The *Daily Express* immediately asked myself, Hastings and Osborne to contribute to a series of articles called "Angry Young Men" —Colin Wilson, *Encounter*, November 1959

If we look at the three examples so far given, we can see that in the first *myself* replaced *me* as the object of a preposition, in the second it replaced *I* as the subject of a verb, and in the third it replaced *me* as the object of a verb. These three functions are the chief ones in which *myself* replaces *I* or *me*. We will subdivide them somewhat, and pick out a few particular items for notice.

The substitution of *myself* for *I* or *me* had not escaped the notice of commentators earlier than Foster and Safire. Indeed it has been the subject of considerable comment for at least a century, from as early as Ayres 1881 to Harper 1985 and Trimmer & McCrimmon 1988. Two general statements can be made about what these critics say concerning *myself*: first, they do not like it, and second, they do not know why. An index to their uncertainty can be found in this list of descriptors that they have variously attached to the practice: snobbish, unstylish, self-indulgent, self-conscious, old-fashioned, timorous, colloquial, informal, formal, nonstandard, incorrect, mistaken, literary, and unacceptable in formal written English. Goold Brown's remark seems apropos here: "Grammarians would perhaps differ less, if they read more."

The handful of commentators who have done real research have found the usage surprisingly widespread in literary sources. Hall 1917, for instance, found it in 37 authors from Malory to Robert Louis Stevenson. But Hall is longer on lists of names than on actual quotations. We will try to be long on examples. We have grouped the examples according to the three main types of usage we mentioned above. Please note, by the way, that other reflexive pronouns—*ourselves, thyself, himself, herself*—are used in the same way as *myself*; a few examples of these are included among the greater number for *myself*.

First, *myself* as the subject of a sentence. As sole subject, *myself* is not common except in poetry:

Myself hath often overheard them say —Shakespeare, *Titus Andronicus*, 1594

My selfe am so neare drowning? —Ben Jonson, *Ode ἐνθουσιαστική*, 1601

Myself when young did eagerly frequent —Edward FitzGerald, *The Rubáiyát of Omar Khayyám*, 1859

Somehow myself survived the night —Emily Dickinson, poem, 1871

But when the reflexive pronoun is part of a compound subject, prose examples abound:

> ... Williams, and Desmoulins, and myself are very sickly —Samuel Johnson, letter, 2 Mar. 1782

> From the moment Mrs. Washington and myself adopted the two youngest children —George Washington, letter (in Pooley 1974)

> ... both myself & my Wife must —William Blake, letter, 6 July 1803

> ... the Post & not yourself must have been unpunctual —Jane Austen, letter, 1 Nov. 1800

> I will presume that Mr. Murry and myself can agree that for our purpose these counters are adequate — T. S. Eliot, "The Function of Criticism," in *Selected Essays,* 1932

> The King, myself, Lord Halifax, a British Admiral, Adm. Leahy, Lascelles, the Secretary of State in that order around the table —Harry S. Truman, diary, 5 Aug. 1945

> In fact, Colonel Jimmy Gault, his British Aide, and myself got in quite a sweat —George S. Patton, Jr., *War as I Knew It,* 1947

> Harry and myself had the black oursin needles in our toes —William Sansom, *The Face of Innocence,* 1952

> The Dewas party and myself got out at a desolate station —E. M. Forster, *The Hill of Devi,* 1953

> When writing an aria or an ensemble Chester Kallman and myself always find it helpful —W. H. Auden, *Times Literary Supp.,* 2 Nov. 1967

> Although Rosenman, others and myself continued to press for this postwar domestic legislation —Chester Bowles, *Promises to Keep,* 1971

We also find it tacked on to the subject in an appositive:

> ... but I had got tickets for 3, so we braved it, two young ladies ... and self —Lewis Carroll, letter, 12 Apr. 1881

> ... the four of us, John, Wally, Tom, and myself, moved into the astronaut quarters —Virgil "Gus" Grissom, *Gemini: A Personal Account of Man's Venture into Space,* 1968

> ... in the course of which several other film critics, myself included, have to take their lumps —Simon 1980

> The four of us—Baker, Darman, Regan and myself—were an odd lot —David A. Stockman, *Newsweek,* 28 Apr. 1986

Next, *myself* as the object of a verb and as a predicate noun. Most of these examples involve groups of names.

> The company was, Miss Hannah More, ... Mrs. Boscawen, Mrs. Elizabeth Carter, Sir Joshua Reynolds, Dr. Burney, Dr. Johnson, and myself —James Boswell, *Life of Samuel Johnson,* 1791

> ... appointed Mr. Francis, then attorney-general and myself to draw up constitutions for the government

of the academy —Benjamin Franklin, *Autobiography,* 1788

> ... it will find him here, as it will myself —Thomas Jefferson, letter, 27 Feb. 1809

> Mrs. Ives wants Mary Preston and myself to translate a French play —Mary Chesnut, diary, 4 Jan. 1864

> ... T. R. Smith, then managing editor of the *Century Magazine,* telephoned Mencken and myself at our office —*The Intimate Notebooks of George Jean Nathan,* 1932

> ... which will reconcile Max Lerner with Felix Frankfurter and myself with God —E. B. White, letter, 4 Feb. 1942

> ... Brinsley said that he was prepared to give myself and Donaghy a pint of stout apiece —Flann O'Brien, *At Swim-Two-Birds,* 1939

> During the lunch hour the male clerks usually went out, leaving myself and the three girls behind — Frank O'Connor, *New Yorker,* 11 Jan. 1958

> He said with a smile, "You Unitarians"—meaning Ted Sorensen and myself—"keep writing Catholic speeches." —Arthur M. Schlesinger, Jr., in *Life,* 16 July 1965

Before we move on to use of *myself* as the object of a preposition, we will give you some examples where the reflexive pronoun seems particularly popular—after those words whose status as preposition or conjunction is a matter of some dispute, words like *as, than,* and *like:*

> ... when mortals no bigger—no, not so big as—ourselves are looked up to —Henry Adams, letter, 13 Feb. 1861

> Some very odd people turn up hereabouts, usually hoping to find me as unconventional as themselves —Flannery O'Connor, letter, 6 Nov. 1960

> We are not unwilling to believe that Man wiser than ourselves —Samuel Johnson, *The Rambler* No. 87, 15 Jan. 1751

> ... no one would feel more gratified by the chance of obtaining his observations on a work than myself —Lord Byron, letter, 23 Aug. 1811

> ... Mr. Rushworth could hardly be more impatient for the marriage than herself —Jane Austen, *Mansfield Park,* 1814

> I think few persons have a greater disgust for plagiarism than myself —Oliver Wendell Holmes d. 1894, *The Autocrat of the Breakfast-Table,* 1857

> ... he judged her to be a year or so younger than himself —James Joyce, *Dubliners,* 1914

> ... her first husband, who was much older than herself —George Bernard Shaw, Preface, *The Shaw-Terry Letters,* 1937

> Her view is that he is a rare soul, a finer being either than herself or her husband —E. L. Doctorow, *Loon Lake,* 1979

> ... an eager lover like myself —William Wycherly, *The Country Wife,* 1675

I have, like yourself, a wonderful pleasure in recollecting our travels in those islands —James Boswell, letter to Samuel Johnson, 9 Sept. 1777

To-morrow I bury her, and then I shall be quite alone, with nothing but a cat to remind me that the house has been full of living things like myself —Charles Lamb, letter, 12 May 1800

Like myself, she was vexed at his getting married —Samuel Butler, *The Way of All Flesh,* 1903

... to see a man, who ... in the dusk looked for all the world like myself —Robert Frost, letter, 10 Feb. 1912

You know by now what a word from you means to any of the rest of us—& particularly to one like myself —Archibald MacLeish, letter, 9 Sept. 1926

Only among older chaps like myself —Kingsley Amis, quoted in *The Writer's Place,* ed. Peter Firchow, 1974

... as to which I felt no one to be trusted but myself —Henry James, *The Art of the Novel,* 1934

Finally, *myself* as the object of some ordinary prepositions:

Ye have seen what I did unto the Egyptians, and *how* I bare you on eagles' wings, and brought you unto myself —Exodus 19:4 (AV), 1611

But, I warrant you, I have a Proviso in the Obligation in favour of my self —William Congreve, *Love for Love,* 1695

The pheasant I gave to Mr. Richardson, the bustard to Dr. Lawrence, and the pot I placed with Miss Williams, to be eaten by myself —Samuel Johnson, letter, 9 Jan. 1758

So much for my patient—now for myself —Jane Austen, letter, 17 Nov. 1798

... the Russians were playing a double game, between ourselves —W. M. Thackeray, *The Book of Snobs,* 1846

... it will require the combined efforts of Maggie, Providence, and myself —Emily Dickinson, letter, April 1873

... with Dorothy Thompson and myself among the speakers —Alexander Woollcott, letter, 11 Nov. 1940

There are also two captions for Hokinson, one by myself and one by my secretary —James Thurber, letter, 20 Aug. 1948

Indeed I hope that you will have time, amongst your numerous engagements, to have a meal with my wife and myself —T. S. Eliot, letter, 7 May 1957

... a monitoring exercise of BBC radio in mid-1979 undertaken by Professor Denis Donoghue, Mr Andrew Timothy and myself —Burchfield 1981 (Introduction)

... and the Druid cannot imagine the magazine without himself —Jay McInerney, *Bright Lights, Big City,* 1984

If you have read this whole article, you have seen examples spoken or written by some forty-odd people— poets, politicians, playwrights, novelists, essayists, diarists, statesmen, even lexicographers. The evidence should make it plain that the practice of substituting *myself* or other reflexive pronouns for ordinary personal pronouns is not new—these examples range over four centuries—and is not rare. It is true that many of the examples are from speech and personal letters, suggesting familiarity and informality. But the practice is by no means limited to informal contexts. Only the use of *myself* as sole subject of a sentence seems to be restricted; all our examples are from older poetry.

Two observations may be made here, both gleaned from Frank Parker et al., "Untriggered Reflexive Pronouns in English," *American Speech,* Spring 1990. First, Noam Chomsky suggests that compounds like *Harry and myself* block the assignment of case by a governing verb or preposition to the individual constituents of the phrase, so that if they are pronouns they may be nominative or objective or may even be reflexives. The second involves a linguistic study called discourse analysis. You will observe that almost all the instances of first and second person reflexive pronouns here occur in contexts where the speaker or writer is referring to himself or herself or the listener or reader as a subject of the discourse, rather than as a participant in it. According to discourse analysis this is the way that English ordinarily works. Discourse analysis doesn't explain third person reflexives very well, but, in spite of what the critics may think, this use of the first and second person reflexives is a common and standard, though not mandatory, feature of the language.

Some writers no doubt use the reflexive pronouns for some of the many invidious reasons suggested by the commentators' labels. As an example of what you will want to avoid, we present this bit from a letter of inquiry received here in 1985; in trying to elevate his style beyond his capacity, the writer has violated the tenets of discourse analysis:

Quite recently, while using your lexicon, a rather interesting enigma manifested itself; one which I hope you can elucidate for myself.

If you can resist this sort of temptation, reasonable use of *myself* ought not to give you much trouble.

See also YOURSELF, YOURSELVES.

N

nag Heritage 1982 reports that some American dialects use the intransitive verb *nag* with *on:* "He is always nagging on me." This use is evidently a spoken one, for we have no printed examples in our files. In written English, the usual preposition with *nag* is *at:*

> . . . his senses nagged at him like pampered babies — Stephen Crane, *The Red Badge of Courage,* 1895

> People have been nagging at me to "stand up straight" for as long as I can remember —*And More by Andy Rooney,* 1982

> The novel *On the Way Back* nagged at me night and day —Graham Greene, *Getting to Know the General,* 1984

naïf, naïve, naïveté, naivety Many commentators discuss the relative status of these words in current English. What our evidence shows is that *naïf* and *naïve,* which in French are the masculine and feminine forms of one word, are in English now usually differentiated according to part of speech rather than gender: *naïve* is a common adjective used for both men and women; *naïf* is rarely used except as a noun meaning "a naïve person." The diaeresis is now omitted at least as often as it is retained:

> . . . still naïve enough to think she would be doing real police work —Joseph Wambaugh, *The Black Marble,* 1978

> . . . a naive young man —Robert Gilmore, *People,* 29 Nov. 1982

> . . . the naïve statement of a sheltered man —Ken Auletta, *N.Y. Times Book Rev.,* 22 Dec. 1985

> . . . couldn't believe how naive she had been —Peter Goldman & Lucille Beachy, *Newsweek,* 21 July 1986

> I am . . . just a naïf at heart —Philip Roth, *Reading Myself and Others,* 1975

> . . . a naif's contempt for figures of authority — James Carroll, *N.Y. Times Book Rev.,* 18 May 1986

The noun *naïveté* is greatly preferred in American English to the Anglicized *naivety.* It is still usually written with a diaeresis and an acute accent, but two other stylings, *naiveté* and *naivete,* are not at all uncommon:

> . . . an example of Mr. Wilson's naiveté —George F. Kennan, *Atlantic,* November 1982

> . . . have lost any such naivete —*Wall Street Jour.,* 20 Dec. 1982

> . . . what seems like carelessness and naïveté —Vicki Hearne, *N.Y. Times Book Rev.,* 27 May 1984

The British use *naïveté* as well, but they now seem to prefer *naivety:*

> . . . a wide-eyed naivety —John Elsom, *The Listener,* 25 Apr. 1974

> . . . amusing because of their naivety —William Davis, *Punch,* 26 Mar. 1975

naked, nude Several commentators distinguish between *naked* and *nude.* Here are a couple of comments by writers on usage:

> *Naked* and *nude* mean the same thing, but *nude* has classier connotations. It's "nude" in art. It's "naked" in the shower —Ebbitt & Ebbitt 1982

> Perhaps the distinction is subjective, but *naked* seems to be, shall we say, the barer word —Bernstein 1971

Other commentators make similar distinctions, though they shade them variously:

> To be naked is to be deprived of our clothes, and the word implies some of the embarrassment most of us feel in that condition. The word 'nude,' on the other hand, carries, in educated usage, no uncomfortable overtone —Anatole Broyard, *Town & Country,* October 1983

> Professor McLuhan also had a linguistic point to make, noting that streakers are nude but never naked. "It's only when you don't want to be seen that you're naked," he said —Robert D. McFadden, *N.Y. Times,* 8 Mar. 1974

Naked may also connote vulnerability or loss of dignity:

> I once saw a Czech film about a concentration camp. There was a line of naked prisoners. Now, that aspect of the human animal, in a state of great vulnerability, has not been explored by our filmmakers —Glenda Jackson, quoted in *Saturday Rev.,* March 1981

> It's hard to take an angry political statement seriously from a naked woman —*And More by Andy Rooney,* 1982

Nude is, as the Ebbitts observe, usual when the reference is to art. Lewis Carroll, in his letters written in the 1870s and 1880s, uses *naked* in reference to photography and *nude* in reference to drawing or painting. The status of photography has risen since then:

> Take a Picasso sketch of a nude. To me, that's much nuder than any nude in a photograph —Ansel Adams, quoted in *Playboy,* May 1983

Nude also is used for places where unclothed people congregate and for occupations that people perform without their clothes:

> . . . you got a lot of beaches in San Diego . . . and some of them are nude —Pete Rose, quoted in *Houston Post,* 8 Sept. 1984

> A nude dancer . . . is found shot —Sybil Steinberg, *Publishers Weekly,* 16 Mar. 1984

Naked has a more vigorous figurative life than *nude,* although both have figurative extensions. You would not normally find *nude* in contexts like these:

> The walls of the Guggenheim, which was between exhibitions, were completely naked —Christopher Petkanas, *Women's Wear Daily,* 5 Oct. 1981

... an arena of more naked struggle for national prestige and power —David Thomson, *Europe Since Napoleon,* 2d ed., rev., 1962

... to put obstacles of amour propre and naked vanity in the way —Archibald MacLeish, letter, 7 Sept. 1974

The battalion commander's briefing tent was harshly lit by two naked bulbs —John Rowe, *Count Your Dead,* 1968

naphtha See PHTH.

nary *Nary* started out as a dialect word and, when not followed by *a* or *an,* it still is.

... nary whiskey under any circumstances —Walt Whitman, letter, 15 Apr. 1863

... they don't have nary constables now —Albert Potter (a deputy sheriff in Kentucky), quoted in *N.Y. Times,* 5 Dec. 1976

Nary a/an, on the other hand, is now also used in mainstream English.

Nary a mention of it in the current summary —Sol M. Linowitz, *Saturday Rev.,* 24 Mar. 1956

They are so phrase-oriented that nary a single one passes without gentle sculpting at their hands —Lester Trimble, *Stereo Rev.,* October 1971

... old-fashioned Christmas displays with nary a neon tree —Mary Ellen Slate, *Antiques World,* November 1981

... nary an officer could be seen —David Freed, *Los Angeles Times,* 8 Sept. 1984

Flesch 1964 calls this use "archaic English," but that it clearly is not. Bremner 1980 says it "sounds phony and studiedly quaint except on provincial lips." You can test that view against the examples just given. *Nary* is, in any case, a word that gets used deliberately for effect; we doubt that it is used unself-consciously except by those who acquired it as part of their native dialect.

native Two British sources, Longman 1984 and Sellers 1975, note that *native* for a nonwhite, non-European person indigenous to some place is no longer considered polite. The offensiveness of the word, or the diffidence about it, seems to be a reaction to colonialism and its attitudes:

Plomer's voyagings put him in touch with people— "natives" as they were then called —Stephen Spender, *N.Y. Times Book Rev.,* 27 June 1976

The evil of colonialism is not oppression but contempt. Eminent Victorians despised their own lower classes and certainly the Irish ... as much as they did any other people they called natives —Eugene Weber, *N.Y. Times Book Rev.,* 16 June 1985

And the word is certainly charged with racial overtones in its use with respect to South Africa.

In North America we find *native* used nonpejoratively, especially in Alaska and western Canada, in the sense "Native American." In this use it is frequently capitalized.

... education seminars on Native cultures —*Discover Alaska,* Winter 1986

Native American *Native American* is a relatively new term that is now being used frequently in competition with *American Indian* and *Indian.* It has not yet replaced the other terms. The *Native* is sometimes spelled with a lowercase *n.*

Native American means American Indian, Indian, Native Hawaiian, and Alaskan Native —*Federal Register Part IV,* 15 Dec. 1983

He tells of a daydreaming child who sees a native American pass by his classroom window, but when he relates this to his teacher, she insists there are no Indians in Connecticut —Linda Hirsh, *Hartford (Conn.) Courant,* 3 June 1986

Much of the same can be said to people who attempt to portray Native Americans. I am a Flathead.... I ... get a little disgusted with the enormous romanticism with which the Indian is treated in the art world —Joanne Bigcrane Sandoval, letter to editor, *Southwest Art,* January 1985

Like so many Native Americans, the Moxos gradually gave up their lands when settlers moved into their territory —Allyn Maclean Stearman, *Natural History,* March 1986

nature *Nature* is one of those words, like *case, character,* and *fact,* that you find in handbooks accompanied by the label "wordy" or "superfluous" or "redundant" along with the assertion that such a quality is one of the chief characteristics of its use in English. Anyone who had to wade through the citational evidence for *nature* in our files in search of these wordy phrases would soon develop a contrary opinion; most uses of the word do not embed it in phrases like *in the nature of* or *of such a nature as to.*

Janis 1984 observes that it is difficult to frame a concise sentence using such phrases as *in the nature of.* His observation is true enough, but underlying it seems to be the notion that concise sentences are what every writer wants (or should want) all the time, which is patently false. The concise sentence has its uses and its great merits, but even Hemingway managed a long one from time to time. We think it fairly certain that when a writer chooses to tangle with *of the nature of, of such a nature,* or *in the nature of,* a concise sentence is not what he or she has in mind, and often for very sound reasons involving shades of meaning, authorial tone, sentence rhythm, or other important considerations.

The assumption the critics make when they call an example wordy or roundabout is that the sentence in which the construction occurs could be readily improved by omitting or shortening the expression. You might challenge this assumption by seeing what you would do with each of our examples below. How many can you shorten easily? And how many are noticeably improved by your revision? Does revision alter the meaning? Does it alter the tone?

I have observed, that a Reader seldom peruses a Book with Pleasure, 'till he knows whether the Writer of it be a black or a fair Man, of a mild or cholerick Disposition, Married or a Batchelor, with other Particulars of the like nature, that conduce very much to the right understanding of an Author —Joseph Addison, *The Spectator,* No. 1, 1 Mar. 1711

Her political affiliations are of a very independent Republican nature —*Current Biography 1951*

Something in the nature of an ovation was their reward —Virgil Thomson, *The Musical Scene,* 1947

They profess to be very concerned about the nature of the Soviet threat and want all we can give them on that score —Oliver North, in *The Tower Commission Report,* 1987

. . . the chapter dealing with the philosophical developments was in the nature of an afterthought — *Times Literary Supp.,* 19 Oct. 1951

. . . use a thin bookmarker. . . . Don't use scissors or old letters or anything of that nature —Lionel McColvin, in *The Wonderful World of Books,* ed. Alfred Stefferud, 1952

We are in a time of stress of a nature such as this country has never before experienced —Vannevar Bush, *N.Y. Times Mag.,* 13 June 1954

Yet the losses we inflicted upon them in the month of May were, I think, in the nature of three-quarters of the losses they inflicted upon us —Sir Winston Churchill, *The Unrelenting Struggle,* 1942

They are mostly books of a religious nature, popular rather than scholarly, and of passing value —*Dictionary of American Biography,* 1929

He also began to suffer from the intense nature of tennis —Adrian McGregor, *National Times* (Sydney), 5 Apr. 1975

Many stocks close for the month with prices a little lower than at the opening, but there has been nothing of a startling nature in the mild decline —*The Bulletin* (Sydney), 31 Mar. 1954

naught   1. *Naught, nought.* Two British commentators, Gowers in Fowler 1965 and Chambers 1985, prefer the spelling *nought* for "zero" and *naught* for "nothing." This, indeed, seems to be prevailing British practice:

It is when a certain number of noughts begins to appear at the end of the figures . . . that our eyes begin to glaze over —Hardcastle, *Punch,* 10 Apr. 1974

This precaution becomes as naught when the squad is turned about —John Peel, *Punch,* 13 May 1975

In American English, the word is not commonly used in either spelling to mean "zero"; *naught* is somewhat more common than *nought* when the meaning is "nothing."
2. Flesch 1964 and Copperud 1964, 1970, 1980 asperse *naught* "nothing" as quaint and bookish. Sometimes it is so for deliberate effect:

Say not the struggle naught availeth —Simon 1980

In most cases, however, the use of this word is limited not by quaintness but by the rather narrow range of constructions it idiomatically fits into. It is used primarily with *avail* or in such phrases as *come* (or *bring*) *to naught:*

It availed him naught —*The Economist,* 22 Sept. 1984

It occurred to me that the great care I was using in completing my diary might come to naught —Eric Randall, *Newsweek,* 15 Sept. 1986

. . . brought to naught by what Isak Dinesen called the business of being women —Abigail McCarthy, *N.Y. Times Book Rev.,* 6 Feb. 1983

nauseous, nauseating, nauseated   Behind the intense, though relatively recent, controversy over these words is a persistent belief, dear to the hearts of many American commentators, that *nauseous* has but a single sense: "causing nausea." There is, however, no basis for this belief. The OED lists three senses of *nauseous* that have been in existence since the 17th century.

The focus of the controversy is a sense of *nauseous* meaning "affected by nausea, feeling sick to one's stomach" that seems to have arisen shortly after World War II, undoubtedly in speech first. (Harper 1975, 1985 suspects it arose in the Bronx or Brooklyn.) It first came to our attention in 1949 in a letter to the editor of a periodical:

> SIR: One of the minor crosses which any physician has to bear is the experience of hearing patient after patient say, "Doctor, I am nauseous." . . . If the distinction I am making is not clear to you, may I point out that "nauseous" implies the quality of inducing nausea and that the person or animal in whom this sensation is induced is nauseated —Deborah C. Leary, M.D., *Saturday Rev.,* 4 June 1949

Dr. Leary was objecting to a similar use in an earlier *Saturday Review* article; before her objection we have no record of anyone's having made such a distinction, nor had we noticed in print the usage to which she objected. But by 1954 Theodore Bernstein had noticed it (*Winners & Sinners,* 28 Apr. 1954), and he reprinted the notice in Bernstein 1958. From this modest beginning, *nauseous* has become a standard entry in American usage books. We have found the subject discussed in more than 20 of them. But we have found it in only one British book, Bryson 1984, and Bryson is himself an American by birth. He cites Bernstein.

Dr. Leary's prescription is to use *nauseated* for "experiencing nausea" and *nauseous* for "causing nausea," and her prescription is repeated by almost all the subsequent usage books. A further concern is added by Perrin & Ebbitt 1972 and Ebbitt & Ebbitt 1982—the possibility that the use of *nauseous* to mean "sick" might be ambiguous to someone who had grown up with the distinction. But ambiguity is not a real problem. When *nauseous* means "sick," it is used in a restricted set of sentence patterns; when it means "disgusting" or "causing nausea," it is used in different patterns. Writers for the mass media who pretend to misunderstand common uses of the "sick" meaning show that they have not observed the difference in the patterns.

When *nauseous* means "sick," it is regularly used as a predicate adjective following a linking verb such as *be, feel, become,* or *grow.* The subject of the verb is of necessity always personal. (Use of this sense is generally literal but may occasionally be figurative, as in the last of this group of examples.)

But the heavy bread, the tepid meat, made him begin to feel nauseous —James Baldwin, *Another Country,* 1962

Dr. Gordon I. Kaye, a Columbia scientist . . . said "two persons who tried the filter had allergic reactions and a third became nauseous." —*Wall Street Jour.,* 21 June 1968

. . . drugs of various kinds to keep their Cosmonauts from becoming disoriented or growing nauseous —*Engineering Opportunities,* January 1968

When a cat is nauseous, it will often drool —Robert K. Lynch, B.S., V.M.D., *Cats Mag.,* February 1973

... soaking wet, and nauseous from the tossing of the wind-whipped water —Herman Wouk, *Marjorie Morningstar,* 1955

... some people were getting nauseous —Ira Flatow, PBS broadcast of "All Things Considered," 19 Jan. 1983

Sexism pervades every song these guys have written, so much so that looking at that fresh, innocent young woman's face on the cover of ... *but the little girls understand* is enough to make you nauseous —Dave Marsh, *Rolling Stone,* 3 Apr. 1980

When *nauseous* means "causing nausea, nauseating" in a literal sense it is seldom used with a personal subject. It is also much more often used as an attributive adjective—in front of the noun it modifies—than as a predicate adjective:

... sucked in the sides of his mouth so he would not taste the nauseous alcohol —Donald Windham, *The Dog Star,* 1950

After the involuntary shrinking consequent on the first nauseous whiff —Bram Stoker, *Dracula,* 1897

... clouds of nauseous fumes —William Beebe, *Jungle Peace,* 1918

... dangling over the nauseous water on which bobbed craft —Elizabeth Bowen, *The Little Girls,* 1964

... the sickly sweet smell which makes the neighbourhood of the leper nauseous —W. Somerset Maugham, *The Moon and Sixpence,* 1919

But even more important to remember than the differing syntactic patterns is that when *nauseous* means "nauseating" it is most likely to be used figuratively and not literally. This figurative use has a curious origin. It began in the second half of the 17th century (the OED's first citation is dated 1663). Wyld 1920 noted that *nauseous* and *filthy* (and *fulsome* too) were favorite counterwords during the Restoration period, used as generalized expressions of abuse or disapproval. This use often does appear with personal subjects and after linking verbs. But you will note that confusion with *nauseous* "sick"—even from our modern perspective—is not possible.

... and modesty is a kind of a youthful dress which, as it makes a young woman more amiable, makes an old one more nauseous —William Wycherly, dedication, *The Plain Dealer,* 1676

I hate that nauseous fool, you know I do —George Etherege, *The Man of Mode,* 1676

Sure, whilst I was but a knight, I was a very nauseous fellow —Sir John Vanbrugh, *The Relapse,* 1696

You would be as nauseous to the ladies as one of the old patriarchs, if you used that obsolete expression —George Farquhar, *Love and a Bottle,* 1698

This use of the figurative *nauseous*—applied to persons—seems to have pretty much died out with the 17th century. But figurative use applied to other things was equally common then and has continued right into the 20th century.

I confess I have not been sneering fulsome Lies and nauseous Flattery —William Congreve, *The Old Bachelor,* 1693

Fanatick Preaching ... in such a dirty, nauseous Style, as to be well resembled to Pilgrims Salve —Jonathan Swift, *A Tale of a Tub,* 1710

Pray, Mr. Wild, none of this nauseous behaviour —Henry Fielding, *Jonathan Wild,* 1743

... which in itself is a very insignificant one, quite nauseous and contemptible —Baker 1770

... when it was requisite to administer a corrective dose to the nation, Robespierre was found; a most foul and nauseous dose indeed —W. M. Thackeray, *The Book of Snobs,* 1846

... either of studied antiquarianism or nauseous pedantry —Fitzedward Hall 1873

... most evident and nauseous in the worst play which Ford himself ever wrote —T. S. Eliot, "John Ford," in *Selected Essays,* 1932

... the Government is guilty of nauseous hypocrisy —*New Statesman & Nation,* 21 Nov. 1953

... rebuked Rochester for his ribald and nauseous songs —James Sutherland, *English Literature of the Late Seventeenth Century,* 1969

... an addict friend, who exposes the nauseous act of shooting up —Annie Gottlieb, *N.Y. Times Book Rev.,* 16 June 1974

In present-day use, however, the "nauseating" sense of *nauseous* is becoming harder to find. The literal use has dropped off markedly since about 1920 and even the figurative use is dwindling. The cause of the decline seems to be that *nauseating* itself is taking over both of these uses. Here is the literal sense:

... a scent, either natural or artificial, may fascinate certain individuals and may be nauseating to others —A. Hyatt Verrill, "Perfumes Past and Present," 1940, in *Antaeus,* Spring/Summer 1976

I especially hated the cod liver oil, a nauseating goo tasting of raw liquefied fish —Russell Baker, *Growing Up,* 1982

Nauseating is considerably more frequent in figurative use, however:

Anything more nauseating she could not conceive. Prayer at this hour with that woman —Virginia Woolf, *Mrs. Dalloway,* 1925

... there isn't a single thinker of the first eminence, and I seem to have ploughed through reams of nauseating adulation —Harold J. Laski, letter, 10 Nov. 1925

Of course I condemned the nauseating combination of brutality and deceit in Frederick II and Bismarck —Albert Guérard, *Education of a Humanist,* 1949

Chamberlain's obsequiousness, his exaggerated flattery, in these letters can be nauseating —William L. Shirer, *The Rise and Fall of the Third Reich,* 1960

... that most nauseating of modern vices, self-pity —Pauline Clark, *Times Literary Supp.,* 2 Apr. 1971

The pomposity and self-satisfied moral rectitude of those bent on prosecution is, however, quite nauseating —J. H. Plumb, *N.Y. Times Book Rev.,* 5 Sept. 1976

... in which he deplored political corruption, the high crime rate, and the luxury of contemporary London, which he affected to find nauseating —Paul Fussell, *Samuel Johnson and the Life of Writing,* 1971

The most telling evidence of the growing preference for *nauseating* may come from E. B. White. In Strunk & White 1979, the third edition, White entered for the first time a warning on *nauseous:*

> **Nauseous. Nauseated.** The first means "sickening to contemplate"; the second means "sick at the stomach."

But on page 72 of the same edition he wrote:

> Rich, ornate prose is hard to digest, generally unwholesome, and sometimes nauseating.

Nauseated, prescribed by many usage books in place of *nauseous,* is less frequently used than either *nauseous* or *nauseating.* It has some figurative use:

> ... that famous, if dangerous, charm of his, nauseated as we may be by the excesses into which it so often misled him —John Mason Brown, *Saturday Rev.,* 20 May 1950

> ... the propaganda lies about the Czech treatment of the Sudeten Germans ... made me even more nauseated —William L. Shirer, *The Nightmare Years,* 1984

But most of its use is literal:

> A baby who gets too much to eat may become nauseated —Morris Fishbein, *The Popular Medical Encyclopedia,* 1946

> Nauseated with pain, Armitage roused himself — Jean Stafford, *The Mountain Lion,* 1947

> One did mention a patient who saw the movie and became nauseated —Hollis Alpert, *Saturday Rev.,* 15 June 1974

> ... was dizzy and nauseated when he penciled in the river that bears his name —Garrison Keillor, *Lake Wobegon Days,* 1985

There is a little evidence that *nauseous* and *nauseated* may be heading toward differentiation in their literal uses. In the PBS broadcast cited above, Ira Flatow did not go on to say that any of the passengers who felt nauseous actually became sick. Many of the citations we have for *nauseous* similarly connote that queasy feeling, not actual sickness.

> ... he munched some treated corn. After some observation, the bereft farmer relaxed; Harriman felt slightly nauseous for two days —Jake Page, *Science 81,* April 1981

> Suddenly, one of the contestants stepped back and shouted, Holy ———, I broke his ——— arm! I got nauseous —Melvin Durslag, *TV Guide,* 20 Mar. 1981

But a number of citations for *nauseated* suggest actual sickness:

> During the first three months of pregnancy, she may be nauseated, vomit often —"M", *The Sensuous Man,* 1971

> He spent the next 10 days in a hospital, nauseated, literally wanting to die —Rick Telander, *Sports Illustrated,* 28 Feb. 1983

> Chemotherapy and radiation help her toward remission, but they bald her skull and blast her mind, leaving her nauseated and irritable —Brina Caplan, *N.Y. Times Book Rev.,* 28 Nov. 1982

The evidence so far is only suggestive. Whether differentiation will continue on these lines remains to be seen.

Conclusion: At present, *nauseous* is most often used as a predicate adjective meaning "nauseated" literally; it has some figurative use as well. Usage writers decry these developments of the last 40 years, but they are now standard in general prose. The older sense of *nauseous* meaning "nauseating," both literal and figurative, seems to be in decline, being replaced by *nauseating. Nauseated* is usually literal, but is less common than *nauseous.* Any handbook that tells you that *nauseous* cannot mean "nauseated" is out of touch with the contemporary language. In current use it seldom means anything else.

near, nearly A few books express disapproval of the use of *near* in the sense "almost, nearly." Jensen 1935 tells his readers not to use it; Shaw 1975, 1987 recommends using *nearly* instead; and the Harper 1975, 1985 usage panel dealt with it in the combination *near-perfect* and passed it only 52 percent to 48 percent.

The sense is an old one (the OED dates it back to about 1200) and has been used by some respected literary figures, especially in less than lofty contexts:

> My uncle *Toby's* wound was near well —Laurence Sterne, *Tristram Shandy,* 1759

> ... we are not near ready —Emily Dickinson, letter, 15 June 1851

> ... but a bloody sweep came along and he near drove his gear into my eye —James Joyce, *Ulysses,* 1922

> This is pretty near a record —James Thurber, letter, November 1939

> The piece is pretty near done —E. B. White, letter, 21 Feb. 1942

> ... in my case it's not anything near as neat as a filing case, it's more like a junk box —William Faulkner, 6 May 1957, in *Faulkner in the University,* 1959

> Children don't have near as good taste as the experts would like to think —Flannery O'Connor, letter, 14 June 1958

Whether you use *near* or *nearly* in constructions like these and like *near-perfect* is a matter of your own ear. *Near* is one of those flat adverbs (*right* and *mighty* are two others) that may sound just a little old-fashioned to the modern ear. Although this use of *near* is idiomatic, more writers today would probably choose *nearly* instead, especially in anything meant to be published.

See also FLAT ADVERBS.

near miss People who like their language logical sometimes complain about this phrase, arguing that it ought to be *near collision* or *near hit.* As originally used during World War II, *near miss* described a bomb that exploded in the water near enough to a ship to damage its hull:

> Against surface vessels, a near miss by a dive bomber is often as effective as a direct hit, for it has all the underwater blasting effect of a torpedo —Lt. Robert A. Winston, *Aircraft Carrier,* 1942

But after the war *near miss* (sometimes styled as a hyphenated compound: *near-miss*) took on different associations, commonly describing a narrowly avoided collison or other mishap:

> ... if the sun had not experienced a near-miss from a passing star —Wilson D. Wallis, *Southwestern Jour. of Anthropology,* Spring 1950

> ... near misses by badly driven vehicles —*New Yorker,* 19 June 1954

The Federal Aviation Administration ... defines a near miss as two planes coming within 500 feet of each other —Jeremy Main, *Fortune,* 14 Oct. 1985

It also has widespread figurative use in describing an attempt that falls just short of success:

> The next two seasons saw near-misses in several big races —Bill Curling, *British Racehorse,* October 1979

Criticism of *near miss* has come more from the segment of the general public that writes letters to the editor than from usage commentators. Harper 1975, 1985 defends it, noting that the adjective *near* has as one of its senses "close, narrow" (as in "a near escape"), and that, in any case, *near miss* "is by now solidly entrenched in the American vocabulary" (as it is). Some writers and editors, especially in the field of aviation, have been persuaded to prefer *near collision,* but *near miss* continues to be a very common term, and, despite its apparent lack of logic, it is not an error.

necessary When used with a preposition, *necessary* is most often used with *to:*

> ... made himself so necessary to the company that by 1849 he was general superintendent of the road —*Dictionary of American Biography,* 1936

> Tennyson is as much a part of the nineteenth century as steam and as necessary to its understanding as Ricardo —Thomas F. O'Dea, *Center Mag.,* May 1969

> ... use all the police presence necessary to stanch the crime rise —Fred P. Graham, *Harper's,* September 1970

Less often, necessary is used with *for:*

> ... the grand tour ... became necessary for Americans —D. W. Brogan, *Saturday Rev.,* 17 Apr. 1954

> ... re-inventing the institutions that are necessary for human happiness —John Cogley, *Center Mag.,* July/August 1970

Necessary occasionally is used with *in:*

> ... a recognition that non-economic considerations were necessary in the distribution of economic goods —Thomas F. O'Dea, *Center Mag.,* May 1969

necessity When *necessity* is used with a preposition, the preposition is usually either *of* or, less often, *for.*

> ... the necessity of civil, academic and scientific liberty —George Soule, *New Republic,* 20 Jan. 1941

> ... the necessity of taking sides —Arnold Wolfers, *Yale Rev.,* Winter 1945

> ... the necessity of adopting a program of action — Mary E. Murphy, *Annals of the American Academy of Political and Social Science,* May 1948

> ... the necessity for greater precision —T. S. Eliot, "'Rhetoric' and Poetic Drama," in *Selected Essays,* 1932

> ... teaching them the necessity for authority —Sim O. Wilde, Jr., *Center Mag.,* May 1969

Harper 1985 claims that "an infinitive is never used after *necessity,*" but we have occasionally found it in quite reputable sources:

> ... the necessity to seek commercial markets — Roger Benedict, *Wall Street Jour.,* 17 Dec. 1957

> ... the necessity to formulate plans —Noël Gilroy Annan, *Times Literary Supp.,* 30 Apr. 1970

née The literal meaning of this word in French is "born." Its usual function in English is to introduce a married woman's maiden name, as in "Mrs. John Jones, née Smith." Usage commentators dating back as far as Bierce 1909 have warned against following it with a woman's given name, "Mrs. John Jones, née Mary Smith," because, they argue, a person is born only with a last name—the given name comes later. What that argument ignores is that *née* is not normally understood as meaning "born" when used in English. Its sense in English is closer to "formerly or originally known as" than to "born" and its use before a woman's maiden name is clearly meant to indicate what the woman was known as before her marriage, not at the moment of her birth. The facts of actual usage are that *née* is more often than not used as the critics say it should be, but its use with a given name is not uncommon. Such use is especially likely when the woman is referred to by her husband's full name ("Mrs. John Jones" rather than "Mrs. Mary Jones"), but it also occurs on occasion when the given name has already been indicated:

> Mrs. Fanny Harwood, nee Fanny Pain —*The Times* (London), 3 Nov. 1973 (OED Supplement)

This citation also illustrates that *née* is sometimes written without an acute accent. Both the accented and accentless versions are common.

Née has other uses which the critics do not generally consider, but which they surely would not like if they did:

> Lord Byron, nee George Pappas —Joseph Auslander & Audrey Wurdemann, *The Islands,* 1951

> Voltaire (nee François Arouet) —Aram Bakshian, Jr., *National Rev.,* 30 June 1970

> ... the Brewers nee Pilots who are also in their third year —Fred Ciampa, *Boston Sunday Advertiser,* 13 June 1971

> John Davis, nee Helmut Otto Kase —*Private Eye,* 14 Dec. 1973

... in the Palace, née the Chalfonte-Haddon Hall — Joan Kron, *N.Y. Times,* 14 Apr. 1977

Such usage demonstrates the extent to which *née* has lost its literal, French meaning in English.

need, *noun* Chambers 1985 says that *need* takes *for* except in the phrases *have need of* and *in need of.* Bernstein 1962 thinks that choosing *for* rather than *of* avoids the possibility that the reader could misinterpret *of* as being the genitive *of* (which connects *need* with the person or thing whose need it is) instead of the idiomatic *of* (which, like *for,* connects *need* with the description of what is needed).

Looking at the evidence we have accumulated over just the past few decades, we find that, overall, *for* and *of* are used with about equal frequency after *need.* Of the uses with *of,* half are for the genitive *of* and half for the idiomatic *of.* Uses of the phrase *in need of* make up about a quarter of the uses of idiomatic *of.* Both *have need of* and *have need for* are used but are less common. So in actual usage, the preposition that follows *need* is usually *for,* but *of* is also a common choice:

> ... the need for devising ways —Harvey Wheeler, quoted in *Center Mag.,* November 1969

> ... the need for regular checkups —Glenn V. Carmichael, *Ford Times,* September 1966

> ... the need of efficiency —Scott Buchanan, "So Reason Can Rule," 1967

> ... a condition in need of amendment —Norman Mailer, *Harper's,* March 1971

Bernstein's point about the confusion of idiomatic *of* with genitive *of* is undercut somewhat by the fact that genitive *of* usually follows the plural *needs* rather than the singular *need:*

> ... adapting it to the needs of the welfare state — *Current Biography,* July 1965

Although the fact is not mentioned by the commentators, *need* is also commonly followed by *to* and an infinitive:

> ... the need to look into the ecology —*Times Literary Supp.,* 9 Apr. 1970

> ... had the need to confess —Joseph Wambaugh, *Lines and Shadows,* 1984

need, *verb* **1.** *Need* is both a finite verb and an auxiliary. In its function as an auxiliary it does not inflect and is followed by the bare infinitive without *to:*

> No pressure group need apply —Harry S. Truman, diary, 20 Sept. 1945

> ... so that Louis need never know —Mavis Gallant, *New Yorker,* 8 July 1985

> ... all that Johnson or Nguyen need do is enroll — Michael Holzman, *College English,* March 1984

The finite verb does inflect; when followed by an infinitive, it requires *to:*

> The church bells needed to ring three times —Virginia Black, *This England,* Summer 1983

It can also be followed by a gerund:

> The facts are too well known to need repeating here —Tip O'Neill with William Novak, *Man of the House,* 1987

2. A curious construction in which *need* is followed directly by a past participle—"my car needs washed"— is called "widely disliked" by Longman 1984. The editors of *The Dictionary of American Regional English* know this as an American idiom too, found chiefly in the Midland area. The usual phrasing would be "needs to be washed", "needs washing", or "needs a wash."

needless to say Those who are determined to take their idioms literally are apt to have the same trouble with *needless to say* that they have with *goes without saying* (which see). If something truly need not be said, they wonder, then why say it? And if it does need to be said, why claim that it doesn't? The simple and obvious answer to these questions is that *needless to say* is not a logical, literal expression but an idiomatic phrase. It is used parenthetically for two main purposes—to emphasize that the writer or speaker regards the statement being made as in some way self-evident, and to provide a graceful transition between sentences or paragraphs:

> ... could then be discussions with the National Liberation Front. Needless to say, such discussions can hardly take place if the Saigon government regards even words of compromise as treasonable —Senator Mike Mansfield, in *A Center Occasional Paper,* June 1968

> ... steps which finally resulted in the atomic bomb.... Needless to say, ... all these decisions were made with the utmost secrecy —*Times Literary Supp.,* 5 Feb. 1970

We agree with Copperud 1964: "Criticism of the expression, except for overwork, is quibbling."

negation See DOUBLE NEGATIVE; RAISING.

negative See AFFIRMATIVE, NEGATIVE; DOUBLE NEGATIVE.

negative-raising See RAISING.

neglectful *Neglectful* is used with *of:*

> ... are utterly neglectful of what we consider the first requirements of decency —Edward Westermarck, *The History of Human Marriage,* 5th ed., 1921

> ... improper and neglectful of the low-income and non-politically oriented student —Fred Hill, *Change,* June 1972

negligent **1.** Some language commentators, among them Phythian 1979 and Shaw 1975, feel the need to distinguish between *negligent* and *negligible,* thus implying that there is some confusion about the use of the two words. Judging from the evidence in our files, however, the words are not used one for the other: they retain their separate meanings.
2. When *negligent* is used with a preposition, the choice is usually *in* or *of:*

> ... was perhaps somewhat negligent in his relations with his mother —Arnold Bennett, *The Old Wives' Tale,* 1908

> The insurer is negligent in failing to settle —R. E. Keeton, *Harvard Law Rev.,* May 1954

> ... almost deliberately negligent of the possibility of a war with Germany —H. G. Wells, *Mr. Britling Sees It Through,* 1916

... he was a careless workman, negligent of detail — Edith Hamilton, *The Greek Way to Western Civilization,* 1930

Negligent has also been occasionally used with *about:*

... is equally negligent about fiction —Charles Thomas Samuels, *Berkshire Rev.,* Winter 1970

negligible   See NEGLIGENT 1.

negotiate   The use of this verb to mean "to successfully travel along or over," as in "negotiate a sharp turn," was once disparaged as a colloquialism or worse, but it is now recognized as standard. The OED traces it to the language of hunting in the 19th century:

The first fence I negotiated most successfully —G. J. Whyte Melville, *Inside the Bar,* 1862 (OED)

This sense of *negotiate* became common enough in the early 20th century to attract some unfavorable attention. The earliest criticism recorded in our files is from the *New York Sun* of 22 Oct. 1906, in which the new sense is cited as a "barbarism creeping into the language." Fowler 1907 dismissed it briefly as slang, but its heyday as a usage topic did not come until the 1920s, when it was censured by many critics—including Fowler 1926, who asserted that any writer who used it was "literarily a barbarian." Despite that ringing condemnation, the voices of criticism in the years since have been few and relatively mild. Among current commentators, only Harper 1975, 1985 continues to find fault with it, claiming that it is "considered inappropriate in formal speech and writing." Our evidence does not show, however, that there is anything particularly informal about its use. As Gowers suggests in Fowler 1965, the distinguishing characteristic of *negotiate* is that it usually "implies a special need for skill and care":

She negotiated expertly the nerve-racking curves — Edna Ferber, *So Big,* 1924

... enables one to negotiate narrow channels —H. A. Calahan, *Yachtsman's Omnibus,* 1935

... the hairpin turn just beyond that you in your car will negotiate gingerly —Maynard Leahey, *New England Journeys,* No. 3, 1955

... might then have somehow negotiated the two miles up Carnelian to Bella Vista —Joan Didion, in *The Contemporary Essay,* ed. Donald Hall, 1984

With a catamaran bottom, she is able to negotiate the shallows —William Styron, *This Quiet Dust and Other Writings,* 1982

Negress   *Negress* was first used near the end of the 18th century; it became controversial in this country at about the time that there was considerable clamor in the press over the acceptability and capitalization of *Negro.* Hyde 1926 may have been the first to warn about use of *Negress,* although he did so in a somewhat obscure way, by calling it a misuse. Mencken 1945 relates in some detail several controversies in the press over the use of *Negress* in the 1930s. Our files have clippings from a 1931 Kentucky newspaper and *Time* magazine in 1946 in which use of the word was protested as being offensive. Some of the early objections mention that *Negress* was felt to be associated with the lower animals because its formation was similar to that of *lioness* and *tigress.*

One of the curiosities of the controversy about *Negress* is the tendency of the word to be associated with *Jewess* in much of the comment. At least two of the people quoted by Mencken yoke the two; so does the person who wrote to *Time* in 1946, and so does Simon 1980. One of Mencken's sources says that if *Negro* is acceptable, *Negress* should be, too; Simon takes the same line. Both also take about the same stance with *Jewess.* But examination of the problem from a supposedly logical point of view is irrelevant: the terms are offensive, at least to some people, and that is what the writer needs to remember.

Complaints about *Negress* have greatly reduced its use in American newspapers and magazines, although it still turns up in literary writing. It seems not to have been considered offensive in British English until about the 1970s. When it is used—chiefly by white male writers—it seems to be used neutrally. It is, however, a word that you should not use without considering the fact that some people are offended by it.

See also -ESS; JEWESS.

Negro   See BLACK; COLORED.

neither   *Neither* is a word about which many theoretical rules have been excogitated, beginning back in the 18th century, without regard to actual practice. Practice that deviates from the rules is regularly censured as error, regardless of the stature of the offending writer. But irregular (not to say, unruly) practice has continued in blithe disregard of the censorious grammarians, as materials collected in the OED, volume 2 of Jespersen 1909–49, and an article by William M. Ryan (*American Speech,* Fall–Winter 1976) abundantly attest. The worm in the apple of theory here is usually notional agreement, which was unknown to the grammarians who devised the rules and is unknown to or ignored by the handbook compilers who repeat them. We will take a look at four instances where precept and practice diverge.

1. *Pronoun. Neither,* the rules assure us, is singular. However, actual practice requires us to temper the absolute form of the rule and say that *neither* is usually singular. The reason it is sometimes plural is easy to see when you think about it. *Neither* serves as the negative counterpart of *either,* which is usually singular. But it also serves in the same way for *both,* which is usually plural. Suppose, for instance, you have written "when both are dead." If you wanted to use *alive* instead of *dead,* you might come up with Shakespeare's solution:

Thersites' body is as good as Ajax'
When neither are alive
           —*Cymbeline,* 1610

Other writers have done the same:

Both writ with wonderful facility and clearness; neither were great inventors —John Dryden, Preface to *Fables, Ancient and Modern,* 1700 (in OED)

Neither belong to this Saxon's company —Sir Walter Scott, *Ivanhoe,* 1819 (in Jespersen)

Neither were as good or as popular as his *First* — *Time,* 20 July 1942

The major characters dissolve into a stream of anxieties and musings, the minor ones are ferociously eccentric; and neither matter —Irving Howe, *New Republic,* 16 Nov. 1953

He had two job offers, but neither were ones he felt he could accept —Diana Diamond, *N.Y. Times,* 20 Oct. 1974 (in Ryan)

Though we will not illustrate the fact extensively, it is worth noting that *neither* by itself is more frequently singular:

Neither has a theatre of its own —Ronald Hayman, *The Set-Up,* 1973

. . . neither was able to go —K. M. Elisabeth Murray, *Caught in the Web of Words,* 1977

The singular number of *neither* is most likely to be ignored when it is followed by *of* and a plural noun or pronoun, for then both notional agreement and the principle of proximity (or "attraction" as Jespersen calls it) pull in the direction of a plural verb. A few commentators, such as Evans 1957, Copperud 1964, 1970, 1980, and Perrin & Ebbitt 1972, recognize this construction. The pull of these two forces is obvious in the first example below, where *neither* without the *of* phrase is singular:

Neither cares about decent homes for the citizens. Neither of these dragons care about skyrocketing prices —*Congressional Record,* 18 July 1951

. . . neither of 'em understand Mathematicks — Thomas Shadwell, *The Sullen Lovers,* 1668

. . . neither of them are a bit better than they should be —Henry Fielding, *Tom Jones,* 1749 (in Jespersen)

. . . but neither of these are the causes of it —John Ruskin, *The Crown of Wild Olive,* 1866 (in Jespersen)

Do you mean to say neither of you know your own numbers? —H. G. Wells, *A Modern Utopia,* 1905 (in Jespersen)

Neither of these two last examples were so intended —William Empson, *The Structure of Complex Words,* 1951

. . . neither of which are available in this country — Peter Stockham, in *Times Literary Supp.,* 15 June 1967

. . . Marx and Trotsky, neither of whom were notably gentle or vegetarian —Dwight Macdonald, *Esquire,* October 1966 (in Perrin & Ebbitt)

. . . the two hot spots, neither of which have ever been especially praised for their food —Judy Klemesrud, quoted in Simon 1980

Neither of these indicators are particularly accurate —Pat Ingram, *Chronicle of the Horse,* 13 Jan. 1984

Even in this construction a singular verb is very common:

. . . with whiskey and a deck of cards, but most of the time neither of these was available —J. L. Dillard, *American Talk,* 1976

Neither of you speaks a word until you're in the cab —Jay McInerney, *Bright Lights, Big City,* 1984

. . . neither of us was rational enough to be convinced of the other's position —John Barth, *The Floating Opera,* 1956

The pronoun *neither,* then, is not invariably singular, though it is more often so. When formal agreement obtains, it takes a singular verb. When notional agreement obtains, it takes either a singular or plural verb. These constructions are neither nonstandard or erroneous. If you are writing something in a highly formal style, you will probably want to use formal agreement throughout. Otherwise, follow your own inclination in choosing singular or plural constructions after *neither.*

2. *Neither . . . nor, neither . . . or.* Opinion on this topic seems nearly unanimous:

Neither cannot grammatically be followed by *or* — Campbell 1776

Always after *neither* use *nor* —Bierce 1909

neither   It's followed by *nor,* not *or* —Trimble 1975

. . . *neither* . . . is followed by *nor,* not *or* —Reader's Digest 1983

But although *nor* is usual after *neither, or* has also been used quite often from the 16th century to the present. It was Jonathan Swift who got Campbell exercised:

A petty constable will neither act cheerfully or wisely —*Some Free Thoughts &c.,* 1714

The *neither . . . or* construction is not at all rare:

. . . he would neither go with me, or let me go without him —Daniel Defoe, *Moll Flanders,* 1722

. . . for I neither ride or shoot or move over my Garden walls —Lord Byron, letter, 9 Sept. 1811

". . . if a man is neither to take orders with a living or without. . . ." —Jane Austen, *Mansfield Park,* 1814

An ordinary country girl, neither pretty or plain — Joyce Cary, quoted in *Time,* 20 Sept. 1948

Neither McCarthy's bigoted intolerance or Truman's excessive toleration can be allowed to weaken the government —Michael Straight, *New Republic,* 26 Mar. 1951

But justice is neither old or new —Mark Van Doren, *American Scholar,* Autumn 1951

. . . an author who is neither an infant, a fool, or a swindler —Eric Bentley, *New Republic,* 16 Feb. 1953

Neither Cadwallader, Oliffe or Mitcham would claim . . . —Tom Mangold, *The Listener,* 7 Nov. 1974

. . . the satellites are in thermal balance, neither heating up or cooling off —Robert C. Cowen, *Christian Science Monitor,* 23 Dec. 1982

Now, we can see no particular reason why anyone would prefer *or* to *nor* in these examples (except perhaps in the one from Jane Austen, where parallelism becomes a consideration). But obviously *or* seemed idiomatic to these writers, and their sentences are perfectly comprehensible. We suspect that you, like most people, will pick *nor* after *neither.* But if you do happen to use *or* instead, you will have committed no dreadful solecism.

3. Must *neither* refer to two only? The answer, as you might suspect from having read a few of the examples in the preceding section, is no. A few commentators

(Follett 1966 and Fowler 1926, 1965, for instance) hold out for two, but more consider what Fowler called the loose use to be neither solecistic nor nonstandard. It dates back to the 17th century, according to the OED. The adjective, the pronoun, and the conjunction are all sometimes used of more than two; such use is quite common with the conjunction.

I could do neither one of those three things —Henry Adams, letter, March or April, 1894

The French are descended from Gauls, Romans, and Germans, and neither of these elements was a distinct race —Carl D. Buck, *Comparative Grammar of Greek and Latin,* 1933

. . . neither of these last three materials is found in Japan —G. B. Sansom, *Japan: A Short Cultural History,* rev. ed., 1943

. . . neither tea, nor coffee, nor lemonade, nor anything whatever —Samuel Johnson, in James Boswell, *Life of Samuel Johnson,* 1791

Neither *Hamlet,* nor *Macbeth,* nor *Othello,* nor *Douglas,* nor *The Gamester* presented anything that could satisfy even the tragedians —Jane Austen, *Mansfield Park,* 1814

Neither you nor I nor anyone we know —Archibald MacLeish, letter, 27 Mar. 1920

. . . people who were neither beautiful, exciting, nor amusing —William Butler Yeats, *Dramatis Personae,* 1936

. . . this optimism, shared by neither labor, agriculture, nor industry —Paul A. Samuelson, *New Republic,* 18 Sept. 1944

. . . the rigid enforcement of antique decorum will help neither language, literature, nor literati —James Sledd, *English Jour.,* May 1973

We could cite dozens more. You may have noticed that the adjectival and pronominal uses are a bit jarring—they catch the attention more than they should—but the conjunctional uses seem humdrum. This suggests that you will probably want to avoid the first two—*none* is a perfectly good substitute—but you can use the conjunction freely. Note that *nor* is sometimes repeated and sometimes omitted for the intermediate words.

4. *"Neither . . . nor" and verb agreement.* Fowler 1926 is a bit irritated that Samuel Johnson and John Ruskin, as cited in the OED, transgressed his rule, which requires that if both subjects are singular the verb be singular. Fowler, of course, did not or would not understand notional agreement, which is what Johnson and Ruskin were following. Here is Johnson:

Neither search nor labour are necessary —*The Idler,* No. 44, 1759 (OED)

Dr. Johnson used singular agreement too:

. . . neither reason nor revelation denies —letter, 25 Sept. 1750 (in Fitzedward Hall 1873)

Conjunctional *neither . . . nor,* like the pronoun *neither,* acts as a negative for *either . . . or* (construed as singular) and for *both . . . and* (construed as plural); agreement therefore may be either singular or plural—notional agreement, pure and simple. Here are several examples with two singular subjects and with either a singular or a plural verb:

Neither wood nor plastic conducts heat the way metal does —*And More by Andy Rooney,* 1982

. . . neither force nor acceleration is directly defined —David Berlinski, *Black Mischief,* 1986

Neither moon nor Mars are habitable —Ashley Montagu, *Vista,* January–February 1970

Neither Cox nor Kepshire has shown any ill effects —Craig Neff, *Sports Illustrated,* 22 July 1985

. . . neither my father nor I were by nature inclined to faith in the unintelligible —George Santayana, *Persons and Places,* 1944

. . . neither George—nor the audience—knows what dragons await him —David Ansen, *Newsweek,* 16 June 1986

. . . has lasted almost a century because neither light, heat, nor humidity affect it —Ellen Ruppel Shell, *Science 84,* September 1984

Neither the *Los Angeles Times Book Review* nor the *Washington Post Book World,* for instance, name reviewers for their notices of new paperbacks —*Publishers Weekly,* 2 Aug. 1985

Neither . . . nor with two (or more) singular subjects, then, is governed by notional agreement and may take either a singular or a plural verb, as if the writer were imagining it as the negative of "either this or that" or the negative of "both this and that." When the subjects are plural, or the last subject is plural, a plural verb is expected:

Neither *montaña* nor Mexican origins are at all likely —Edward P. Lanning, *Peru Before the Incas,* 1967

A few books—Fowler 1926, Evans 1957, Chambers 1985—give conflicting advice on sentences containing constructions like "neither she nor I." Our evidence for such constructions is slim, but it shows that in actual practice (see the Santayana example above) the plural verb is usual.

If you are a native speaker of English, you will probably follow notional agreement without thinking, just as Samuel Johnson did. If you need a rule to follow consistently, use formal agreement—singular verb with singular subject and the verb to agree with the nearest subject otherwise. Formal agreement is always the safe choice in cases where you are uncertain.

5. See also AGREEMENT, INDEFINITE PRONOUNS; EITHER.

never A couple of handbooks, Scott Foresman 1981 and Colter 1981, would restrict *never* to the meaning "not ever, at no time" and disapprove its other chief meaning, "not in any degree," which is used like an emphatic *not.* The objection can be found as far back as Gould 1867. But just what is wrong with the typically spoken usages they give as examples is not made explicit. The use in question is quite old:

Thou canst not say I did it. Never shake
Thy gory locks at me.
                    —Shakespeare, *Macbeth,* 1606

Many uses of *never* seem to hover between a simple negative meaning and "at no time":

> ... the fly ash ... is trapped and never enters the atmosphere —*Annual Report, Virginia Electric & Power Co.,* 1970

> You never go through that kind of experience ... and come out the same —Mary Vespa, *People,* 16 May 1983

> ... holding onto a bag—probably popcorn that Naomi never finished —Johanna Kaplan, *Harper's,* March 1971

Such uses are standard.

next See FIRST TWO, TWO FIRST.

nice The use of *nice* as a general-purpose term of approval seems first to have been censured by Archdeacon Hare (Julius Charles Hare, 1795–1855), who was a friend of Walter Savage Landor and had some eccentric ideas about spelling. Ayres 1881 quotes his attack at some length, and Bardeen 1883 mentions him too. Bardeen lists quite a few late 19th-century commentators on the subject, none of whom approve.

The opinions of the critics of the late 19th century have been carried down to the present day. Copperud 1970, 1980 opines that complaints about *nice* meaning "agreeable" are heard less often than they were a generation ago in this country and that it has become more of an issue in British English than American. It certainly is still alive as an issue in Britain: Phythian 1979, Longman 1984, and Chambers 1985 all mention it. But it also remains a live topic in this country: Reader's Digest 1983 joins Copperud in dismissing it as an issue, but Shaw 1975, 1987, Perrin & Ebbitt 1972, Simon 1980, Trimmer & McCrimmon 1988, Macmillan 1982, Strunk & White 1979, Prentice Hall 1978, Bander 1978, and Irmscher 1976 all join the old-timers and line up against it. The usual objection is that *nice* is overused and should be avoided in writing.

The usage apparently antedates the criticism by about a century. Curiously, the earliest evidence seems to come from Dr. Johnson's circle. Hodgson 1889 quotes a 19th-century philologist named Kington Oliphant, who says the earliest instance he had seen was in Mrs. Thrale's conversation as recorded in Fanny Burney's diary. The earliest citation in the OED is from a 1769 letter of Mrs. Elizabeth Carter, who was also an acquaintance of Dr. Johnson. The usage seems to have come down through the 19th century to the present chiefly as conversational English.

It is certainly familiar to American writers, who take no trouble to avoid it in their casual moments:

> I have written you this nice long letter —Robert Frost, letter, 9 Oct. 1915

> It was uncommonly nice of you to write —Archibald MacLeish, letter, 9 Sept. 1926

> It was nice to see a great writer in our time —Ernest Hemingway, *The Green Hills of Africa,* 1935

> It's terribly nice, my boy, with the rosemary in bloom and the fragrance of the mimosa trees —James Thurber, letter, 20 Jan. 1938

> Of course when they began to bring in a little money, that was nice —William Faulkner, 13 Mar. 1958, in *Faulkner in the University,* 1959

> It was certainly damn nice of you to write me that telegram —F. Scott Fitzgerald, letter, 29 Jan. 1934

> Cary has been so nice—Ask him what he would like and I will try to paint it for him —Zelda Fitzgerald, letter, April 1934

> It was damned nice of you to write in your book for me —Robert Benchley, letter, 29 Apr. 1934

> ... the club cleared a nice profit at the bar —Groucho Marx, letter, summer 1940

There is certainly nothing wrong with an effort to get college freshmen to use a wider variety of adjectives in their writing, but there is also nothing inherently wrong with *nice* in its generalized use.

nicely Objections have been made in the past to the use of this adverb in a sense synonymous with *well* or *satisfactorily,* as in "That will do nicely." Criticism of such usage dates back to the 19th century:

> The very quintessence of popinjay vulgarity is reached when *nicely* is made to do service for *well,* in this wise: "How do you do?" *"Nicely."* "How are you?" *"Nicely."* —Ayres 1881

Ayres was actually criticizing two different uses. In the first one (with *do*) *nicely* functions as an adverb, and in the second one (with *be*) it functions as an adjective. The adjectival use of *nicely* may have been the peculiarity that actually caught Ayres's attention:

> "How is thee, Ruth?" she said ... "Nicely", said Ruth —Harriet Beecher Stowe, *Uncle Tom's Cabin,* 1852 (OED)

This adjective has had little, if any, use outside of dialectal speech. The adverb *nicely* in its sense "satisfactorily, very well," on the other hand, has appeared in reputable writing since the early 1800s:

> Your flesh, properly cured, might hang up nicely against the forthcoming bean-season —Walter Savage Landor, *Imaginary Conversations of Literary Men and Statesmen,* 1829 (OED)

Criticism of this adverb, which was not unusual among American commentators in the first part of the 20th century, might never have amounted to much if it were not for the adverb's association with the dialectal adjective. In any case, such criticism seems now to have died out altogether. It apparently breathed its last when 68 percent of the usage panel of Heritage 1969 found the "satisfactorily" sense of *nicely* acceptable in written use. This sense continues to occur commonly in writing, and no one now questions its propriety.

> It seems to be catching on nicely at Green Bay —John Fischer, *Harper's,* February 1971

> The cord-grass habitat ... was doing nicely, but there were no seaside sparrows —Norman Boucher, *N.Y. Times Mag.,* 13 Apr. 1980

> Nine months later, her father ... is recovering nicely —Christopher Stone, *US,* 12 Oct. 1982

> His own restaurant ... could stand up nicely to many of these places —Colman Andrews, *Metropolitan Home,* March 1984

> Rivers recovered nicely and began practice —Ed Burns, *Sports Illustrated,* 19 Nov. 1986

nickel, nickle *Nickel* is the original spelling, the usual spelling, and, in the opinion of many people, the only correct spelling. *Nickle,* on the other hand, is undoubtedly common in casual writing and not at all rare in edited prose:

> . . . identified its most promising nickle mining prospect —*Australian News Weekly Round-Up,* 15 July 1970

> . . . asking for a nickle, a dime, a quarter —Bill Taylor, *Northern Echo* (Darlington, England), 3 July 1974

> . . . wouldn't give you a nickle —*Bluegrass Unlimited,* September 1982

> . . . the recent nickle-a-gallon federal gas tax —J. Tevere MacFadyen, *Smithsonian,* April 1984

Even so, you are well-advised in this case to join the majority and spell it *nickel.*

nite *Nite* is a bit of a curiosity. Some people have thought it was associated with the spelling reform movement of the late 19th and early 20th centuries, but it seems not to have been: in the few dictionaries of simplified spellings in our library, *nite* is conspicuously absent. It seems to have been poorly thought of even by the reformers, possibly because it had gained a bad reputation from its employment by the willfully misspelling 19th-century American humorists:

> But the fack can't be no longer disgised that a Krysis is onto us, & I feel it's my dooty to accept your invite for one consecutive nite only —*Artemus Ward: His Book,* 1862

Nite is also attested in the works of Petroleum V. Nasby and could probably be found in the works of other humorists of that era.

Although snubbed by the reformers, *nite* has made considerable headway in the 20th century. Mencken 1963 (abridged) associates *nite* with advertising writers. Our earliest 20th-century attestation is from a discussion of the spelling in the *New York Times Magazine* (26 Oct. 1930), in which the writer also associates *nite* with advertisers and makers of electric signs. It is clear from the evidence that much of the advertising using *nite* was for entertainment and show business: combinations such as *nite club, nite life,* and *nite spot* are common. A slightly later development finds *nite* as part of the name of an event:

> The Tilbury Rotary Club will present a Holiday Festival Nite on Tuesday —*Chatham* (Ontario) *Daily News,* 26 June 1980

> Have this wish on Auction nite —*Prime Time,* April 1981

So *nite* is apparently an arbitrary respelling used by American humorists in the 19th century and by American advertisers from at least 1930. The OED Supplement shows it appearing in British English in the 1960s. It is probably older and more widespread than our evidence shows, but it does not seem to have made any inroads into standard written usage.

> . . . for at least the last forty years high school students have been substituting "nite" for "night" without affecting usage one iota —Paul Bixler, *Antioch Rev.,* December 1956

Mr Bixler's comment still holds. *Nite* will continue to be used in advertising and in the names of events like "Las Vegas Nite," but it is not a spelling you will want to use in ordinary prose.

no 1. *No* is often used in conjunction with other negatives, especially in speech. See DOUBLE NEGATIVE.
2. Ayres 1881 insists that when *no* introduces some sort of compound expression, it should correlate with *nor:* "no this nor that." Heritage 1982 insists that *or,* not *nor,* is required in the same situation. From this divergence of opinion we can infer that *or* was sometimes used in Ayres's time and that it has become prevalent during the century since:

> Mr Edwards is no scholar or man of letters —*Times Literary Supp.,* 22 Oct. 1971

> Rose sent no congratulations or messages —Gail Cameron, *Ladies' Home Jour.,* August 1971

> There would be no backing down or hiding behind a convenient wall —Billie Whitelaw, quoted in *Annabel,* April 1974

But *nor* is still found on occasion:

> . . . no experienced editors, no office staff nor a distributor for the books —Kenneth C. Davis, *Publishers Weekly,* 2 Aug. 1985

Nor could be considered more emphatic than *or,* but in present-day use, emphasis is usually achieved by repeating the *no:*

> There was no chair, no table, no sofa, no pictures — Graham Greene, *Travels with My Aunt,* 1969

> No pollution, no crime, no politics —John Fischer, *Harper's,* July 1972

3. *"No" in the sense of "not."* A few commentators around the end of the 19th century (Bardeen 1883 mentions three, one of which is Ayres 1881) objected to *no* qualifying a verb and meaning "not"—a matter chiefly of objecting to the phrase *whether or no.* Vizetelly 1906 said the practice had literary sanction. We have usually found *or no* (with or without *whether*) used in place of *or not* in literary contexts or by literary figures:

> . . . depends on whether or no his personal ambition is combined with intellectual ability —W. H. Auden, *Antaeus,* Spring/Summer 1976

> . . . so vulnerable she registers it whether she will or no —Elinor Langer, *N.Y. Times Book Rev.,* 4 Mar. 1984

> Laryngitis or no, the play has started off with a bang —Alexander Woollcott, letter, 19 Feb. 1940

> But personality or no, I have been aware of how much a part of you she was —E. B. White, letter, 20 Apr. 1957

> . . . Sister Mary Teresa emerges as a real human, nun or no —Newgate Callender, *N.Y. Times Book Rev.,* 1 Apr. 1984

See also WHETHER OR NOT.

nobody, no one These indefinite pronouns for the most part follow the same pattern of notional agreement as the other indefinite pronouns: they regularly take a singular verb but may be referred to by either a singular or plural pronoun. The handbooks that take a traditional position—mostly older ones—insist on the singular pronoun; newer ones recognize plural reference, although some of them avoid actual approval by limiting *they, their,* and *them* to informal use. Formal agreement looks like this:

> Nobody attains reality for my mother until he eats —Flannery O'Connor, letter, 28 June 1956

You can see right away one of the problems that formal singular agreement brings up—the question of sexism, conscious or otherwise. So there is an added advantage to favoring the plural pronoun: you avoid having to decide whether to use *he* or *she, his* or *her,* or *him* or *her.* Sometimes the notion of the many is so strong that the context simply calls for a plural:

> No one believes (they are right) —Adolf A. Berle, *The Reporter,* 8 Sept. 1955

> . . . but nobody really wanted to hear him speak. They wanted to see him grin —Harry S. Truman, quoted in Merle Miller, *Plain Speaking,* 1973

And the plural pronoun is often used even when the singular would present no problem:

> Nobody here seems to look into an Author, ancient or modern, if they can avoid it —Lord Byron, letter, 12 Nov. 1805

Byron was writing from Cambridge, and his reference could only have been to males. But he used the plural *they* anyway.

The use of the plural pronoun in reference to *nobody* and *no one* is not only very common, it is well established—the OED dates it back as far as 1548. It is as old-fashioned as Jane Austen and as modern as Doris Lessing:

> Nobody was in their right place —Jane Austen, *Mansfield Park,* 1814

> . . . nobody minds having what is too good for them —Jane Austen, *Mansfield Park,* 1814

> "But nobody uses it, do they?" —Doris Lessing, *The Good Terrorist,* 1985

Our advice to you is to not be afraid of using *they, their,* or *them* to refer to *nobody* or *no one* when the idea is clearly plural (as it is in the Berle and Truman examples above) or when you simply want to avoid a choice between masculine and feminine singular pronouns. When the sense is not necessarily plural, you can use singular pronouns in accordance with formal agreement. But meaning should come first.

For more on agreement with indefinite pronouns, see AGREEMENT: INDEFINITE PRONOUNS; NOTIONAL AGREEMENT, NOTIONAL CONCORD; THEY, THEIR, THEM.

no doubt See DOUBTLESS, NO DOUBT, UNDOUBTEDLY.

nohow This adverb appears never to have been common in standard written English, but it has had some reputable use in the sense "in no way":

> This is a modification . . . which we can no-how bring ourselves to conceive —Sir John F. W. Herschel, essay, 1841 (OED)

It is now rarely seen except in representations or transcriptions of nonstandard or dialectal speech, in which it typically follows another negative:

> "Well," the guy from the patrol said, "I guess I didn't expect it was no hotel nohow." —Robert O. Bowen, *The Weight of the Cross,* 1951

> . . . I wasn't on Dan's back much of the time nohow, but mostly jest strung out from my holt on Mister Ernest's belt —William Faulkner, *Saturday Evening Post,* 5 Mar. 1955

Nohow also has some dialectcal use in a sense synonymous with *anyway:*

> ". . . It's ten mile, nohow. Wouldn't you be a sight by daylight!" —Elizabeth Madox Roberts, *The Time of Man,* 1926

noisome While almost all English usage books find a need to caution against confusing *noisome* with *noisy,* our citation files show that *noisome* is almost always used to mean "noxious" or "disgusting":

> It [wine] has now become a noisome sulphur-and-vinegar compound —Norman Douglas, *Siren Land,* 1911

> Sol Levy had come over an immigrant in the noisome bowels of some dreadful ship —Edna Ferber, *Cimarron,* 1929

> . . . is zoned against livestock, partly owing to the fact that noisome pig farms once existed there — Christopher Rand, *New Yorker,* 11 Apr. 1964

> This morning's coffee shop is this afternoon's noisome, grease-spewing alfresco sandwich stand — Alexander Cohen, *N.Y. Times,* 13 Aug. 1972

A few citations in our files show *noisome* with extended meaning:

> Miss Karmel's debut is not of the noisome type with which so many "promising" writers enter upon—and usually depart from—the literary scene —Martin Rice, *Saturday Rev.,* 9 May 1953

> The reception of Charles Osborne's life of W. H. Auden and Ted Morgan's Somerset Maugham was predictably noisome —Richard Holmes, *N.Y. Times Book Rev.,* 29 June 1980

On the other hand, we have some evidence for *noisesome,* meaning "noisy," but so far not enough to warrant entry of this sense in the dictionary.

> . . . the suggestion that modern mothers . . . quieten their noisesome offspring by filling them up with chlorodyne —*Times Literary Supp.,* 5 Jan. 1967

> . . . our own necessarily noisesome and laborious progress through the thick bamboo forest —A. B. Anderson, *African Wild Life,* December 1950

no less than See LESS, FEWER.

none A specter is haunting English usage—the specter of the singular *none.* No one knows who set abroad the notion that *none* could only be singular, but abroad it is. Howard 1980 says, "A considerable number of readers of *The Times* are convinced beyond reason that the pronoun *none* is singular only"; Burchfield 1981 notes that listeners to the BBC are similarly convinced. The notion is not restricted to Britain: Mary Vaiana Taylor, in an article titled "The Folklore of Usage" in *American Speech* (April 1974), says that 60 percent of the graduate teaching assistants she surveyed marked *none* with a plural verb wrong in students' papers. William Safire, in the *New York Times Magazine* (1 Apr. 1984), mentions several correspondents who have written in protest of his "Obviously, none of these previous noun usages offer a clue. . . ."

The origin of the notion is simple enough to discover—the etymology of the word. Lounsbury 1908 supposed that "some student of speech" thought it to be a contraction of *no one*. Actually, the etymology explanation is at least as old as Lindley Murray 1795. Murray, after recording that "*None* is used in both numbers" goes on to observe, "It seems originally to have signified, according to its derivation, *not one,* and therefore to have had no plural. . . ." Murray is, in fact, only half right here. The Old English *nan* "none" was in fact formed from *ne* "not" and *an* "one," but Old English *nan* was inflected for both singular and plural. Hence it never has existed in the singular only; King Alfred the Great used it as a plural as long ago as A.D. 888. And even Murray concludes his observation by saying, "but there is good authority for the use of it in the plural number," and he quotes the Bible, Milton, Bishop Lowth, and rhetorician Hugh Blair.

We will probably never know who transformed Lindley Murray's etymological explanation into a law of usage and spread it about widely. Lounsbury could not identify the culprit and neither can we. All the sources since Murray that we have read and all those we have seen cited recognize plural use to some degree, even though they may quibble over details.

And direct evidence is hard to find. Our earliest and most straightforward example comes from the *Corvallis* (Oregon) *Gazette-Times,* sometime in October 1917 (we are unsure of the exact date, as the piece is reprinted in *The Oregonian* for 26 Oct. 1917). In it the *Corvallis* editorialist takes *The Oregonian* to task for saying, apparently in reply to a letter, that *none* generally takes the plural verb, but that either singular or plural is right.

> . . . but how "none," even though it may be plural in "sense," can escape its strict grammatical meaning of "no one," can escape taking a singular verb, is beyond the ken of strict construction, which should certainly prevail in matters of grammar. If there is any word in the English language that should be singular it should be "one."

So we do have evidence that belief in the strictly singular nature of *none* was alive in one editorial office over seventy years ago. Unfortunately, this editorialist vitiated his remarks by writing earlier in his editorial:

> . . . there have been many questions of grammar asked The Oregonian, and none of them have been answered correctly.

Once again, precept has come a cropper in practice.

However difficult it may be to say how this notion got started, we can find a number of adherents to it. Bierce 1909 appears to have been very unhappy with the stubborn insistence of popular usage that *none* is a plural when it refers to numbers rather than quantity. Gowers 1948 asked, "If reason is to prevail, for instance, what could be more obvious than that *none,* which is even less than *one,* cannot possibly take a plural verb . . . ?" Fennell 1980 tells us that *none* usually takes a singular verb (and gives only a singular example) and Simon

1980 finds fault with Barbara Walters for writing or saying "none are snobs."

Occasionally a commentator will have second thoughts, however. Strunk & White 1959 says that *none* "Takes the singular verb." The second edition (1972) allows for the plural verb "when *none* suggests more than one thing or person." This is illustrated wryly: "None are as fallible as those who are sure they're right." The third edition (1979) continues the second edition's line.

Most commentators, however, admit both singular and plural use. A number of them look for a basis for case-by-case decision. Sellers 1975, for instance, advises the singular verb when *none* means "no quantity," "no one," or "not one," and the plural verb when it means "not any," "no people," or "no things." Others will tell you that the plural is more common or the singular is more common, and still others will count up instances and try to get a statistical grip on the problem, perhaps with an eye to discerning trends.

Evidence in the Merriam-Webster files, all gathered in the 20th century, shows no trends. The possible effect of editorial opinion can occasionally be found: we have a pretty long run of *Time* citations that are mostly singular, and about as long a run from the *New Yorker* that are mostly plural. It appears that writers generally make it singular or plural according to whatever their idea is when they write. This matching of verb (or referring pronoun) to a pronoun by sense, rather than formal grammatical number, is known as notional agreement (see NOTIONAL AGREEMENT, NOTIONAL CONCORD and the various articles at AGREEMENT).

For instance, when *none* is followed by an *of* phrase containing a plural noun or pronoun, you might expect the plural verb to be more natural, as in the Bible's

> But none of these things move me —Acts 20:24 (AV), 1611

Our evidence, however, shows both the singular and plural verbs:

> How comes it, I wonder, that none of our scholars has written a monograph on him —Norman Douglas, *Siren Land,* 1911

> None of these are love letters in the conventional sense —W. H. Auden, *New Yorker,* 19 Mar. 1955

> None of its inhabitants expects to become a millionaire —Bernard DeVoto, *Holiday,* July 1955

> None of the lines are strikingly brilliant —Wolcott Gibbs, *New Yorker,* 5 Mar. 1955

> None of them is happily married today —Judith Krantz, *Cosmopolitan,* October 1976

> . . . when none of us in the West . . . have a very clear idea of where we are going —Edward Crankshaw, *N.Y. Times Mag.,* 30 Nov. 1975

Or perhaps you might think that *none* is more likely to take a singular verb when it butts right up against its verb. But here, too, both singular and plural are used:

> While some were poor, none was rich —John Kenneth Galbraith, *The Scotch,* 1964

> . . . when every dog howls at the locked door, and none go to their homes till the waning of the moon —Sacheverell Sitwell, *The Dance of the Quick and the Dead,* 1936

None is thought to have a distinguished prose style —Jane Tompkins, *Sensational Designs,* 1985

None were deeper in that labyrinthine ambition — G. K. Chesterton, reprinted in *The Pocket Book of Father Brown,* 1946

And if, among this wealth of possibilities, none seems exactly right —Barnard 1979

. . . and none say they read poetry for fun —James Sledd, in Greenbaum 1985

Clearly, then, *none* takes a singular verb when the writer thinks of it as singular, and plural when the writer thinks of it as plural. Perhaps the best evidence for this observation is found in examples from writers who use *none* sometimes as a singular and sometimes as a plural:

None of them seems cast specifically in the role of "thinker" —Tom Wicker, *N.Y. Times Mag.,* 3 May 1964

None of those statements are particularly disputable —Tom Wicker, *N.Y. Times Mag.,* 3 May 1964

. . . none of these sites has produced evidence of plant gathering —Edward P. Lanning, *Peru Before the Incas,* 1967

None of the inland camps have yet been excavated —Edward P. Lanning, *Peru Before the Incas,* 1967

None of them were trying to learn how to write —A. J. Liebling, *New Yorker,* 26 May 1956

. . . some were big and commodious, but none was handsome —A. J. Liebling, *New Yorker,* 18 June 1955

. . . I'm sorry to say none of my sisters are coming to London this summer —Lewis Carroll, letter, 23 May 1864

. . . and of all that race none is more ungratefuller — Lewis Carroll, letter, 13 Mar. 1869

Clearly, *none* has been both singular and plural since Old English and still is. The notion that it is singular only is a myth of unknown origin that appears to have arisen late in the 19th century. If in context it seems like a singular to you, use a singular verb; if it seems like a plural, use a plural verb. Both are acceptable beyond serious criticism.

none too See NOT TOO.

nonrestrictive appositives See APPOSITIVES.

nonstandard *Nonstandard* is a label frequently used in dictionaries and handbooks. It generally designates forms and constructions that are not characteristic of educated native speakers; these are very often regionalisms. Some books, such as Webster's Third, differentiate between *nonstandard* and *substandard,* using *substandard* as an indicator of social status. But many other books simply use *nonstandard* as a blanket replacement for *substandard, illiterate,* and various other now dated pejoratives. When it is applied indiscriminately like this, the label *nonstandard* should be regarded with a certain amount of healthy skepticism.

See also STANDARD, STANDARD ENGLISH; SUBSTANDARD.

no one See NOBODY, NO ONE.

noplace *Noplace,* meaning "nowhere," is condemned along with *anyplace, everyplace,* and *someplace* by a number of commentators on the grounds that *place,* a noun, should not be used as an adverb to mean "where." The objection does not hold water, as Bernstein 1971 points out at *anyplace,* because *place* is often used in combinations where it has adverbial force.

The evidence in our files and in the OED Supplement shows that *noplace* is found in American English rather than British English and that it is used in print less frequently than *anyplace* or *someplace* and about as frequently as *everyplace.* It is apparently more a spoken than a written form. In print it looks like this:

The car as a living room will have arrived, and getting from one place to another will be just as exciting as getting absolutely noplace —*New Yorker,* 29 Jan. 1955

The adverbial *noplace,* which is sometimes spelled as two words, should be distinguished from the simple combination of *no* and *place:*

Daring . . . had no place in the old role —Elizabeth Janeway, *Ms.,* April 1973

See also ANYPLACE; EVERYPLACE; SOMEPLACE.

nor **1.** For *nor* after *no,* see NO 2; for *nor* after *neither,* see NEITHER 2, 4.
2. *Nor* frequently replaces *or* in negative statements:

I don't think the barricades is an answer, nor giving up appreciation of and interest in such fine, pleasant, and funny things as may still be around —James Thurber, letter, 20 Jan. 1938

You cannot describe a house brick by brick, nor a wood leaf by leaf —Leacock 1943

. . . I wasn't interested in literature nor literary people —William Faulkner, 13 Mar. 1958, in *Faulkner in the University,* 1959

. . . not seeking to discount the study of grammar nor the analysis and practice of good written expression —Finegan 1980

It is clearly felt to be more emphatically negative than *or* in some instances:

. . . I recommend that you have nothing further to do with this person nor with these arms transfers — Robert C. McFarlane, quoted in *The Tower Commission Report,* 1987

3. There is a dialectal *nor* that means "than." It was commonly used by 19th-century American dialectal humorists:

. . . yet in the state of Indiany, where I live, there's no man as gits a bigger congregation nor what I gits —William Penn Brannan, "The Harp of a Thousand Strings," 1855, in *The Mirth of a Nation,* ed. Walter Blair & Raven I. McDavid, Jr., 1983

. . . & sez it is wuss nor cleanin house —*Artemus Ward: His Book,* 1862

normalcy *Normalcy* became a notorious word during the 1920 Presidential election, when Warren G. Harding proclaimed that what the country needed was a return to the "normalcy" of the days before World War I. Those who opposed Harding often criticized him for his less than exemplary use of the language, and they loudly derided *normalcy* as a characteristically laughable malapropism. The noun formed from the adjective *normal,* they pointed out, was *normality;* nouns ending in *-cy* were formed from adjectives and nouns ending in *-t* or *-te* (*accuracy* from *accurate, aristocracy* from *aristocrat,* etc.).

Harding's supporters quickly came to his defense, however, even going so far as to look in the OED, where it was discovered that *normalcy* had been recorded as early as 1857 in a dictionary of mathematics. It had also appeared in Webster 1864 as a rare word with the definition, "state or fact of being normal," and it had been used in the *Nation* in 1893 and in a book titled *Social Evolution* in 1894. It was an unusual and uncommon word, certainly, but Warren G. Harding had not invented it.

What Harding *had* done, of course, was to popularize the word. Despite those who regarded it as a "spurious hybrid" (Fowler 1926, for one), *normalcy* established itself in widespread use during the 1920s. Its notoriety was such that many of those who used it did so self-consciously, often in direct—and usually critical—reference to Harding and his term of office, and there was a persistent tendency to enclose the word in quotation marks:

> . . . to fear that we may be slipping back to a state of "normalcy" in politics —*World's Work,* September 1926

But it was also used straightforwardly on occasion:

> . . . will be restored to a state of normalcy on being put back into ordinary sea-water —Edwin E. Slosson, *Chats on Science,* 1924

> The woman whom change of status has left free to work out her own salvation . . . is bringing feminism to normalcy —*North American Rev.,* June 1928

During the 1930s, *normalcy* seems to have become something of a rare word again, as the memory of Harding's presidency faded. The years of World War II saw an appreciable increase in its use, however, and it has continued to be common in the decades since. Its most characteristic use is still in such phrases as *a return to normalcy,* but its association with Harding is no longer as prominent in people's minds. It often occurs simply as a straightforward synonym of *normality:*

> . . . from relative normalcy through marked eccentricity —John Barth, *The Floating Opera,* 1956

> . . . taking special pains to give an impression of completest normalcy —Saul Bellow, *Herzog,* 1964

> For both Faust and Buddha there is no such thing as normalcy —William Irwin Thompson, *Harper's,* December 1971

> They became distressed about total normalcy in their infants —Virginia E. Pomeranz, M.D., quoted in *Harper's Bazaar,* March 1981

Normalcy is now a perfectly reputable word, recognized as standard by all major dictionaries. The controversy that once surrounded it is now almost entirely dead, and there is no need to avoid its use.

no sooner   Quite a number of commentators—Janis 1984, Phythian 1979, Longman 1984, Johnson 1982, Bernstein 1965, Copperud 1964, 1970, 1980, Jensen 1935—insist that *no sooner* must be followed by *than* and not *when.* It usually is followed by *than; when* is so

rare in print we thought it was only a straw man raised to object to—until we unearthed this example:

> The moderator had no sooner asked for comments from the audience when a little man arose — *National Observer,* 26 Sept. 1966

If *when* is common after *no sooner,* it must be so only in speech. In print, *than* is the regular choice:

> . . . he had no sooner completed training than he was called to Ottawa —*Current Biography,* June 1966

> . . . the Romans had no sooner landed in Britain than they realised the importance of a crossing-place of the Thames —L. Dudley Stamp, *The Face of Britain,* rev. ed., 1944

> No sooner does John Riggins reluctantly drop out of sight . . . than Joe T. limps up to the booth —E. M. Swift, *Sports Illustrated,* 1 Sept. 1986

not about to   The idiom *not about to* has all the earmarks of being a relatively recent Americanism. It may have originally been regional, perhaps Southern and South Midland: the American Dialect Dictionary records it in West Virginia around 1942, and an article by Charles H. Hogan in *American Speech* (April 1945) identifies it with Texas. It was a feature of the speech of two American presidents (one from the Midland speech area and the other from close to the Southern):

> Had I done so, I would have surrendered the civilian control of your government to the military, and I was not about to do that —Harry S. Truman (in Reader's Digest 1983)

> Peace is the mission of the American people and we are not about to be deterred —Lyndon B. Johnson (in Harper 1975, 1985)

It began to catch on popularly about 1960:

> . . . a lot of intelligent people weren't about to buy this argument —James A. Pike, *Think,* March 1960

> The thrifty Dutch are not about to spend their liquid gold recklessly —*Time,* 19 Oct. 1962

> . . . but Miss Frutti, not about to miss anything, employed an ear trumpet —Harper Lee, *To Kill a Mockingbird,* 1960

> . . . is not about to back brother Bob in anti-Johnson rebellion —Robert D. Novak & Rowland Evans, Jr., *Plain Dealer* (Cleveland, Ohio), 29 July 1964

> . . . was not about to allow the rally to be turned into a fountain of . . . venom —*N.Y. Times,* 26 June 1966

> . . . Cardinal McIntyre, who was not about to be named anyway —John Leo, *Commonweal,* 2 Dec. 1966

> . . . he is not about to throw away any assets —Stewart Alsop, *Newsweek,* 27 Jan. 1969

> But Daley was not about to let the convention leave his city —Norman Mailer, *Harper's,* November 1968

The idiom did not come to the attention of critics until 1968, when Theodore Bernstein noticed it in the *New York Times* and decided it must be "substandard" (*Winners & Sinners,* 8 Aug. 1968). He found it again a year later, upgrading it (if that is the word) to "colloquial" (*Winners & Sinners,* 15 May 1969). The basis for most objections seems to be the possibility of ambiguity, since the phrase might be interpreted as the simple negative of *about to,* i.e., as meaning "not on the verge of." There is in fact no basis for this concern, because it simply is not used for that purpose and the context discourages such a reading; it is always used to express intention or determination.

There is one difficulty with our story so far. Nothing about the words *not about to* bars them from having been used to express intention before the middle of the 20th century. The words are, in fact, so unspectacularly ordinary that they might have been used in that way sporadically for quite a long time without being noticed:

> By the by, I expect Hanson to remit regularly; for I am not about to stay in this province for ever —Lord Byron, letter, 12 Nov. 1809

Byron is pretty clearly expressing intention here, but perhaps not determination. His use suggests that the expression may have been lurking unnoticed in the background all along; if there is anything peculiarly American about the idiom it may be the note of determination that is frequent in American use, and the frequency with which the phrase is now used.

Reader's Digest 1983 says that it was "at first regarded as informal, suitable only for spoken use" but that it is "now acceptable in formal writing also." The expression has gained wide currency in American English and is no longer regionally restricted, if it ever was. It is used in speech and in edited prose, especially that of newspapers and magazines. It does not seem to have much in the way of literary use, but it is still in evidence in political circles:

> Phil Gramm of Texas, my House supply-side ally, and I were not about to see the Reagan Revolution defeated by accounting gimmickry —David A. Stockman, *Newsweek,* 28 Apr. 1986

not all, all . . . not   See ALL 3.

not all that   See ALL THAT.

not as, not so   See AS . . . AS 1.

not . . . but   Under this heading a number of commentators take up the issue of *but* following a negative. It is aspersed as a double negative by some, but it is not a double negative (see the explanation at BUT 4). Bryant 1962 says that *not . . . but* is always followed by a number, though this is not quite true either. The construction is most frequently followed by a number (which may be either cardinal or ordinal), but other words (such as *few*) are used too.

The *not . . . but* construction is the older of a pair of expressions (the other lacks the negative) that mean the same thing. It is most common in speech, but not entirely limited to it. Here are a few examples from speech and letters:

> The last duel I fought didn't take but five minutes —Emily Dickinson, letter, 11 Jan. 1850

> You haven't done it but once —Flannery O'Connor, letter, 20 Sept. 1958

> . . . we never lost but very few logs —Elbert Herald, quoted in *Our Appalachia,* ed. Laurel Shackelford & Bill Weinberg, 1977

> "You . . . can't wear but one suit of clothes at a time," Mantzel says philosophically —Nancy Schommer, *People,* 18 Mar. 1985

Here is one from fiction:

> . . . and Miss Betty didn't have to be told but once —Peter Taylor, *The Old Forest and Other Stories,* 1985

Bryant calls this construction standard in speech. The respondents to Crisp's 1971 usage survey ranked it "disputable." What it seems to be, really, is a bit old-fashioned, and like many old-fashioned expressions may be more common in rural speech than in urban speech, and hence suspect to the city-dweller. It has been in the process of being replaced by the positive construction— especially in print—for quite some time now:

> It makes but one mistake —Emily Dickinson, letter, early 1878

> . . . had won 25 away games and lost but 15 — Anthony Cotton, *Sports Illustrated,* 30 Mar. 1981

> . . . he had but 12 days to go —C. D. B. Bryan, *N.Y. Times Book Rev.,* 16 Oct. 1983

Note that the meaning of *not . . . but* is "only." When *but* means "except," it is also common with negatives:

> No respect was paid but to merit —John Butt, *English Literature in the Mid-Eighteenth Century,* edited & completed by Geoffrey Carnall, 1979

> . . . there's no place for the kids to play but in the street —*And More by Andy Rooney,* 1982

For a negative followed by *but* and *that* or *what,* see BUT 5.

not hardly   See HARDLY.

notional agreement, notional concord   As Quirk et al. 1985 explains it, *notional agreement* (called *notional concord* by Quirk and others) is agreement of a verb with its subject or of a pronoun with its antecedent in accordance with the notion of number rather than with the presence of an overt grammatical marker for that notion. Another way to look at the matter is that of Roberts 1954, who explains that notional agreement is agreement based on meaning rather than form. We want to emphasize that this meaning is the meaning the expression has to the writer or speaker.

Notional agreement contrasts with formal, or grammatical, agreement, in which overt markers—form— determine singular or plural agreement. Formal agreement could also be called school-grammar agreement, for it is what is taught in school. We do not know who first realized that notional agreement exists as a powerful force in English grammar, but it must be a fairly recent discovery. The 18th-century grammarians never tumbled to it, even though their examples for correction showed it being widely followed. Most school grammars are based on their 18th-century forebears and do not mention notional agreement. And many (perhaps most) usage commentators seem likewise unaware of it.

But notional agreement has often been granted silent assent by normative grammarians in specific instances: formally plural nouns like *news, means,* and *mathematics* have long been accorded the privilege of taking singular verbs. So when a plural noun takes a singular verb because it is thought of as a single entity, we have notional agreement at work, but no one objects:

> I don't think the barricades is an answer —James Thurber, letter, 20 Jan. 1938

> The Philippines likewise wasn't interested —Chris Pritchard, *Christian Science Monitor,* 23 June 1986

Likewise, when a noun ostensibly singular takes a plural verb or pronoun—as in the case of many collective and institutional nouns in British English—we have notional agreement at work once again:

> Barclays Bank do not believe in regular statements, although I asked them to keep me posted —John O'Hara, letter, 8 Mar. 1964

> And so every Southern household when they bought books they bought Scott —William Faulkner, 13 May 1957, in *Faulkner in the University,* 1959

> The Brandt Commission have estimated that . . . —Christopher Terrill, *Geographical Mag.,* May 1984

> When in the Course of human events, it becomes necessary for one people to dissolve the political bands which have connected them with another —*Declaration of Independence,* 1776

More troubling to the traditional grammarian are instances in which a singular noun is used as if it were a generic collective and is referred to by a plural pronoun or is matched with a plural verb:

> A particular lady of quality is meant here; but every lady of quality, or no quality, are welcome to apply the character to themselves —Henry Fielding, *A Journey from This World to the Next,* 1743

> . . . and no small blame to our vaunted society that the man in the street . . . was debarred from seeing more of the world they lived in —James Joyce, *Ulysses,* 1922

> . . . a game of donkey baseball sounds pretty dull, but people who have seen them tell me different —John O'Hara, letter, 11 Sept. 1934

> I can usually spot a liberal Democrat or a conservative Republican at one hundred feet, and I have no trouble at all when they come close enough so I can hear them talk —*And More by Andy Rooney,* 1982

In this sort of notional agreement the plural pronoun is much more common than the plural verb.

Indefinite pronouns are heavily influenced by notional agreement, and in a peculiar way: they tend to take singular verbs but plural pronouns:

> "But nobody uses it, do they?" —Doris Lessing, *The Good Terrorist,* 1985

> . . . none has distinguished themselves —Carol Leggett, quoted in *Publishers Weekly,* 26 June 1987

> And suddenly she is there, and everybody knows, and they crane their heads backward to see her —Alice Adams, *Listening to Billie,* 1977

Notional agreement will also at times produce a singular verb after compound subjects joined by *and* and a plural verb after compound singular subjects joined by *or.* This is just the opposite of what formal agreement says should be the case:

> . . . time and chance happeneth to them all —Ecclesiastes 9:11 (AV), 1611

My admiration and affection for you both is bounded only by the Seven Seas —Groucho Marx, undated letter, in *The Groucho Letters,* 1967

> . . . in periods when vellum, parchment, or even paper were prohibitively expensive —Lee T. Lemon, *A Glossary for the Study of English,* 1971

> ". . . a feather or a fiddle are their pursuits and their pleasures. . . ." —Henry Fielding, *Jonathan Wild,* 1743

Notional agreement is mentioned at many entries in this book, because the conflict between notional and formal agreement is behind many disputed usages. (See, in particular, ONE OF THOSE WHO; THEY, THEIR, THEM; and the various articles at AGREEMENT.) Sometimes the conflict will drive a writer to produce a sentence even more startling than those produced by purely formal or purely notional agreement:

> Granted only a small fraction of lawyers actually besmirches their profession —*San Francisco Chronicle,* 13 Aug. 1986

notional subject   See LET 2.

not only . . . but also   The *also* in this set of correlative conjunctions is optional and is frequently omitted. Freeman 1983 says that when *also* is omitted, the words following *but* receive greater stress. This may be so, at least sometimes, but it is hard to demonstrate.

> . . . it is necessary not only that his designs be formed in a masterly manner, but that they should be attended with success —Samuel Johnson, in James Boswell, *Life of Samuel Johnson,* 1791

Also is often omitted in shorter constructions, where the omission is often desirable as it makes for tighter and smoother expression:

> Human society is not only multifaceted but often contradictory —Finegan 1980

> . . . an oafish brute who not only beat her but insisted on being addressed as father —Alexander Woollcott, letter, 24 Apr. 1942

> I not only feel, but know as a fact, that . . . —James Thurber, letter, 20 Jan. 1938

It would not matter whether Johnson had used *also,* but the other three examples would have been more awkward with the *also.*

The chief concern of the many commentators who discuss the *not only . . . but (also)* construction is parallelism: they insist that for clarity identical constructions be placed after both the *not only* and the *but (also).* The concern for the parallel construction goes back to the 19th century; it is mentioned in Ayres 1881 (in connection with *not . . . but only),* and Hall 1917 says that it was common in school rhetorics.

Despite the opinions of the commentators, the nonparallel construction is common enough to pass almost unnoticed. The fact that it often does pass unnoticed is evidence that it creates no confusion or misunderstanding. Hall 1917 collected about 125 nonparallel constructions from more than 50 authors, almost all literary. It is clear that constructions which are not precisely parallel are as much a part of standard English as those which are precisely parallel.

Here we have a few examples in which parallelism is not observed:

> I was not only endowed with the faculty of speech, but likewise with some rudiments of reason —Jonathan Swift, *Gulliver's Travels,* 1726 (OED)

> They not only tell lies but bad lies —Benjamin Jowett, translation of *The Dialogues of Plato,* 1871 (OED)

> Most of the luxuries, and many of the so called comforts of life, are not only not indispensable, but positive hindrances to the elevation of mankind — Henry David Thoreau, *Walden,* 1854

> North Haverhill is not only the seat of the country estate of Frances Parkinson Keyes but provides the locale for a number of her novels —*American Guide Series: New Hampshire,* 1938

> I was really impressed by your analysis of the show not only because of its complimentary tone, but because it so accurately described so many of the evils of radio —Groucho Marx, letter, 28 Dec. 1949

> A journal, both of them insisted, would give the Institute not only professional standing, but could provide a wide appeal for membership —Julia Child, *Jour. of Gastronomy,* Summer 1984

And here are a few examples in which it is observed:

> . . . for not only are their own Eleven all at home, but the three little Bridges are also with them —Jane Austen, letter, 30 June 1808

> . . . I am sure he would not only get over that trouble, but be as well and strong as he ever was —Walt Whitman, letter, 15 Apr. 1863

> . . . it was not only a Greek but a contemporary tragedy —Gilbert Highet, *The Classical Tradition,* 1949

> Miss Didion is wonderful not only at hearing her characters but at naming them —Mary McCarthy, *Occasional Prose,* 1985

We doubt that you had any trouble understanding any of the examples, though you may have preferred some over others. The worst of the nonparallel constructions above is that from the *American Guide Series,* where the two parts are different enough to be plainly noticeable; but it is the yoking of *is* with *provides* in addition to the placing of *not only* that makes it conspicuous. In the example from Julia Child, the matching of *would give* with *could provide* makes the placement of *not only* a secondary consideration. And in the example from Groucho Marx, repetition of the word *because* tends to disguise the fact that *because of,* a preposition, is matched with *because,* a conjunction. So as long as you take care that the groups of words joined by the conjunctions are not so dissimilar as to call attention to themselves, you need not worry all the time about achieving precise parallelism. It is more important for your sentence to sound natural and to make sense.

For the related issue of the placement of *only* in a sentence, see ONLY 1.

notorious Usage writers from Ayres 1881 to Harper 1985 have warned all and sundry not to confuse *notorious* with *famous, notable,* or *noted.* They point out that *notorious* has a pejorative connotation: "widely and unfavorably known." Other usage writers, from Vize-

telly 1906 to Copperud 1970, 1980 reply that the word is not always used pejoratively.

Notorious is a word that has suffered from guilt by association. It came into use in the middle of the 16th century with the neutral meaning "well or widely known," but very early it came to be used with nouns of unsavory meaning—one of the earliest uses shown in the OED is the combination "notorious sinners." And frequent use with nouns of this kind has colored the subsequent use of the word.

Notorious has a fairly frequent employment. Part of its popularity is the tang that clings to all uses of the word from its frequent use to mean "widely and unfavorably known." Even in its neutral uses, as we shall see, its association with the unfavorable, disreputable, and unsavory gives it a piquancy, an emphatic quality, that a mere *noted, notable, famous,* or even *celebrated* lacks. Thus, it is often the word chosen by writers who are aware of its particular flavor; writers who are not aware of that flavor can get themselves into trouble, as did the advertising copywriter who wrote a radio commercial for a local boutique calling attention to the availability of a painter in residence who was "notorious for his portraits."

Our evidence shows that most writers who use *notorious* are well aware of its overtones. Here are the ways in which it is used.

It is always pejorative when linked with a noun for an undesirable person:

> . . . a notorious gunman for the Profaci family — Tom Buckley, *Harper's,* August 1971

> . . . a notorious muddle-head, as Lenin unkindly described him —*Times Literary Supp.,* 31 Dec. 1971

> ". . . when he was a notorious bank robber. . . ." — Morley Callaghan, *More Joy in Heaven,* 1937

> . . . to ridicule the follies of Dr. John Hill, a notorious quack and hack writer —John Butt, *English Literature in the Mid-Eighteenth Century,* edited & completed by Geoffrey Carnall, 1979

When *notorious* is applied as an attributive or predicate adjective to a person, you can assume that it is being used pejoratively:

> . . . biography of someone as notorious as Adolf Hitler —John Kenneth Galbraith, *N.Y. Times Book Rev.,* 22 Apr. 1973

> . . . its first chiefs, the notorious Bielaski brothers — I. F. Stone's Bi-Weekly, 19 Apr. 1971

> . . . when the notorious Captain Bligh sailed into port in 1793 —Caleb Pirtle III, *Southern Living,* November 1971

> . . . whose audience is notorious as one of the most unruly in show business —*Current Biography,* April 1968

Often there will be clues that indicate a milder or even humorous use:

> . . . Alben and I had our pictures taken, as is usual when notorious persons leave or arrive in cities — Harry S. Truman, diary, 20 Sept. 1945

> . . . is a notorious soft touch for friends and strangers alike —*Current Biography,* April 1966

> . . . a notorious first-ball hitter, did just that. Only he hit it on the ground to third —Ron Fimrite, *Sports Illustrated,* 4 Nov. 1985

... Lady Demeter being a notorious non-smoker —William J. Locke, *The Great Pandolfo*, 1924

A totally uncharacteristic work by the century's most notorious modernist —*Time*, 22 Aug. 1955

Neither union officials nor executive vice presidents are notorious students of abstract truth —Richard E. Danielson, *Atlantic*, February 1947

Note that in each of these nonpejorative examples the selection of *notorious* rather than *well-known, notable, famous,* etc., is undoubtedly due to the word's overtones.

Notorious is frequently applied as an attributive or predicate adjective to nouns that the linguist would describe as "not human." The word verges on the neutral in many such applications. Still, in the absence of clues to the contrary, you will find the intent to be pejorative:

Some weeds have become notorious in tropical forestry —Charles J. Taylor, *Tropical Forestry*, 1962

... the President's veto of the notorious McCarran thought-control bill —Harold L. Ickes, *New Republic*, 29 Nov. 1950

A notorious district known as 'Hard Dig' was burned in 1826 by a mob of zealous citizens —*American Guide Series: Massachusetts*, 1937

... commander of a notorious Confederate prison camp —*Current Biography*, June 1966

... patrician style and plutocratic swagger; famous names and notorious fortunes —Louis Kronenberger, *Atlantic*, December 1971

Their school was St. Cyprian's, later notorious as the subject of Orwell's recollections —Marvin Mudrick, *Harper's*, January 1983

But very often there are no moral overtones; *notorious* is simply used as a more emphatic *celebrated, famous,* or *well-known:*

... the notorious mass-energy relation, $E = mc^2$ —P. W. Bridgman, *Yale Rev.*, Summer 1947

... the notorious thoroughness with which Clay conducts inspections —E. J. Kahn, Jr., *New Yorker*, 13 Jan. 1951

... one of those notorious dance marathons of the twenties —Richard Watts, Jr., *New Republic*, 1 Sept. 1947

... it is the chimpanzee ... that is the notorious chatterer —Weston La Barre, *The Human Animal*, 1954

... used iron sheets for the fronts of buildings, despite the fact that iron is a notorious conductor of heat —Lewis Mumford, *Technics and Civilization*, 1934

... they fill a notorious gap in the literature on ancient Rome —M. I. Finley, *N.Y. Rev. of Books*, 3 June 1971

The success and influence of the *alumni* of the Scottish universities in many spheres of national life is notorious —Sir James Mountford, *British Universities*, 1966

He was involved in a notorious controversy with the poet Swinburne —K. M. Elisabeth Murray, *Caught in the Web of Words*, 1977

In the construction *notorious for,* the strength of *notorious* is usually dependent on the matter following *for:*

... fields notorious for high risk and heavy start-up costs —*Dun's*, October 1971

... a man notorious for his unscrupulous business methods —Jane Addams, *Twenty Years at Hull-House*, 1910

... quickly became notorious for her abominable cruelties —Robert Penn Warren, *All the King's Men*, 1946

... I am notorious for my habit of looking on the bright side —John O'Hara, letter, 3 Aug. 1962

Presidents are, in the eyes of bureaucrats, notorious for putting off decisions —Leslie H. Gelb & Morton H. Halperin, *Harper's*, June 1972

The flight of the Loon is very swift and direct; it is notorious for its ability to dive instantly —Ralph Hoffmann, *Birds of the Pacific States*, 1927

Novelists are notorious for their howlers —V. S. Pritchett, *N.Y. Times Book Rev.*, 28 Nov. 1954

... Galicia, a region notorious for the shrewdness of its sons —*New Republic*, 22 Nov. 1948

... the American was to be notorious for his passion for gadgets —Henry Steele Commager, *Atlantic*, December 1946

In the construction *it is notorious that, notorious* is nearly always neutral; any pejorative intent has to be supplied by the matter following *that,* which seldom happens:

... and concerning taste it is notorious that there can be no dispute —Ashley Montagu, *Man's Most Dangerous Myth: The Fallacy of Race*, 2d ed., 1945

We have commentators, but it is notorious that they are not allowed to comment —Jacques Barzun, *Atlantic*, February 1947

That his dedicated intention was to write something that should not die is notorious —*Times Literary Supp.*, 28 Nov. 1942

That he was not always pleased is notorious —D. J. R. Bruckner, *N.Y. Times Book Rev.*, 16 Oct. 1983

It is notorious that Kant made a place for ethics in his system —Walter Lowrie, *Sewanee Rev.*, Summer 1950

You can see from the examples that most writers have no problem handling *notorious*. All you have to remember is that it always seems to have a certain piquancy, a certain bite, from its frequent association with persons and things of undesirable character. Even when it is neutral in denotation, it has that characteristic flavor.

not too *Too* in the sense of "very," a sense in which it almost always occurs with *not* or some other negative, came to the attention of the American public shortly after World War II. Our earliest evidence is from a column in the Cleveland *Plain Dealer* in 1946; the columnist, Ted Robinson, noted that the idiom *not too hot* or *not too good* was being used in place of *not so hot* or *not so good.* He seems to have found the idiom less than acceptable. In 1948 Jacques Barzun initiated a series of letters discussing the construction in *Word Study.* Barzun termed it a "dreadful modern use" then and has implacably opposed it ever since: in Barzun 1985 it is called a "widespread illiteracy."

Fowler 1926 had encountered the construction before the Americans. In a short list of illogical uses of *too* that he classified as "sturdy indefensibles," he had this example: "We need not attach too much importance to the differences between Liberal & Labour." So the two lines of opinion about the *not too* construction were born independently, with the Barzun line hostile and the Fowler line relatively tolerant. Except for Fowler all commentary has been American; the construction is apparently unnoticed in British English today.

Barzun supposed the *not too* construction to have been a corruption of *none too,* which seems rather unlikely given that the example he originally objected to concerned a student who "didn't study too much." It would take a pretty determined corrupter to turn "studied none too much" into "didn't study too much." Copperud 1970, 1980 assumes *not too* to be a Briticism, since Fowler was tolerant of it. But the idea of British origin does not fit in with the earliest American complaint. The two words are simply too easy to put together for their combination to be ascribable to any particular origin. Many times *not too* is all but invisible:

> He was up here not too long ago, playing his guitar and singing —James Thurber, letter, 30 Jan. 1951

> . . . I find myself 21 years later, still the owner of one-half share. In case you are not too familiar with current Wall Street prices, an entire share can be purchased for $1.10 —Groucho Marx, letter, 18 Oct. 1951

> today, i was informed that midgets are scarce "all of the good midgets are working, etc." i am not going to be able to shake off too many of these crises — Fred Allen, letter, 13 Oct. 1950

> This first slope wasn't too bad although it was steep —Leslie A. Viereck, *Dartmouth Alumni Mag.,* October 1954

Not too is most often a form of mild understatement:

> . . . academic appointments which leave him leisure for research are not too difficult to secure —*Report: Royal Commission on National Development in the Arts, Letters & Sciences, 1949–1951* (Ottawa, Canada)

> In southern Victoria the drainage-quality of some soils isn't too good —*The Bulletin* (Sydney, Australia), 24 Feb. 1954

> . . . can be not too arbitrarily divided into three periods —Edgar S. Furniss, Jr., *Yale Rev.,* Autumn 1954

> At its best a legislative investigation is not too satisfactory a place to be concerned with individual rights —Erwin N. Griswold, *Harvard Law School Record,* 21 Oct. 1954

> The great wars had not wrought too many changes in them —Saul Bellow, *New Republic,* 23 May 1955

> . . . the Szechuanese dialect is not too far from pure Mandarin —John Hersey, *A Single Pebble,* 1956

> . . . though they may differ on theoretical grounds, their end results are not too divergent —Albert H. Marckwardt, in *The College Teaching of English,* ed. John C. Gerber, 1965

> My God! Is decent diction itself to be consigned to rubble even before the next nuclear bomb is dropped? (As a former Secretary of the Army, I am not too surprised about the Air Force general.) — Elvis Stahr, Jr., in Harper 1985

A few instances are intended more ironically:

> . . . the truth is that Postmaster General Summerfield is privately not too happy with his lot in the Administration —*Newsweek,* 29 Nov. 1954

> There was plenty of applause to go around for everybody that night, but Henry was not any too friendly —Harry S. Truman, quoted in Merle Miller, *Plain Speaking,* 1973

The "very" sense of *too* is found occasionally with other negatives, like *never:*

> It never was too easy to find a publisher for a scholarly book —R. D. Altick, *The Scholar Adventurers,* 1950

> The purpose for this change has never been too satisfactorily articulated —Calvin H. Plimpton, *Amherst College Bulletin,* November 1967

A repeated complaint of the commentators who do not like the construction is that *not too* "not very" can be confused with *not too* "not excessively." But although the latter combination is used, it is quite easy to distinguish from the "not very" construction:

> Such a reaction should not too quickly be dismissed —Richard Poirier, *A World Elsewhere,* 1966

The commentators who, like Barzun, disapprove of *not too* include Cook 1985, Copperud 1970, 1980, the usage panels of Heritage 1969, 1982, Nickles 1974, Zinsser 1976, Follett 1966, and Bernstein 1958, 1965. Those who approve or are at least as tolerant as Fowler include the usage panels of Harper 1975, 1985, Evans 1962, and Thomas H. Middleton (*Saturday Rev.,* 19 Oct. 1974). Shaw 1975, 1987 is ambivalent.

So what is to be made of all this? If you look back at the examples, you will see no traces of illiteracy or of sloppy writing. *Not too* is simply one of the negative-construction forms of understatement (*not all that* is another; see ALL THAT) that have become popular since World War II and have drawn fire for just that reason. The examples are impeccably standard; so is the construction.

not to worry Sixty-two percent of the Harper 1985 usage panel disapproved the harmless British import *not to worry* in speech and 87 percent disapproved it in writing. Panelist Willard R. Espy dissented, finding *not to worry* diverting. In this he agrees with Flesch 1983.

The peculiarity of the expression lies in the imperative force of *not to*—equivalent to *don't.* The construction appears to be quite recent. The OED Supplement has a precursor of *not to worry* in "please not to mention that again" from George Eliot's *Middlemarch* (1872), but the earliest citation they show for *not to worry* is from 1958. Language historian Barbara M. H. Strang in a 1965 book review refers to it as a new construction.

The phrase began to appear in American English in the 1970s and is still to be found now and then:

> "I don't suppose you remembered that bagel," Megan says. "Not to worry, I'm not really hungry anyway...." —Jay McInerney, *Bright Lights, Big City,* 1984

> Our hero had just gone through a divorce, of which, mercifully, his journal says little directly; but, not to worry, there is sufficient dolorosity to go round — Aristides, *American Scholar,* Winter 1985/86

The construction turns up once in a while with other verbs:

> "We're gonna go outside for a while, okay?" she said. "Not to panic or anything. But I have this freaky feeling." —Cyra McFadden, *The Serial,* 1977

not un-   See DOUBLE NEGATIVE 2.

nought   See NAUGHT 1.

nouns as adjectives   See ATTRIBUTIVE.

nouns as verbs   It occasionally comes as a surprise to the linguistically unsophisticated that nouns can be put to work as verbs. This, like the use of nouns as adjectives, is a practice with a long history. Dean Alford 1866 commented on the subject; among the verbified nouns he mentions are *progress, head,* and *experience.* The Dean was not upset by the practice, but several recent commentators—Freeman 1983, Harper 1975, 1985, and Strunk & White 1972, 1979 among them—have criticized specific instances of the practice. The verbified nouns (or denominal verbs, to use a term many linguists use) that are objected to include *chair, host, gift,* and *debut,* all of which are treated separately in this book.

The opposite practice, that of turning verbs into nouns, also occurs. There is commentary on the subject in Safire 1980 and 1984.

nouns joined by *and, or*   See AGREEMENT, PRONOUN: NOUNS JOINED BY AND, OR.

now   Use of *now* as an adjective dates back to the 14th century. Its oldest sense, "present, existing," has impressive historical backing and has excited no animosity:

> ... into focus with the then or the now reality —Ezra Pound, *Polite Essays,* 1937

> ... the now Bishop Asbury had become well acquainted with the role —Dr. Asbury Smith, *Maryland Mag.,* Autumn 1971

But in the 1960s the adjective *now* suddenly became popular—and somewhat notorious—in two new uses: describing the mores and manners of the younger generation, and characterizing the generation itself:

> One agency music director in search of the "now sound" —*Newsweek,* 27 Nov. 1967

> ... fairly typical of the Now Generation —Henry S. Resnik, *Saturday Rev.,* 26 Oct. 1968

> ... has one advantage over most of the "now" tunes —Murray Chass, *N.Y. Times,* 24 Aug. 1969

These uses of *now* enjoyed a vogue of several years, but by the mid-1970s they had aged somewhat, as had the generation they applied to. In current English they have

a distinctly dated quality and are most likely to occur when the era of their popularity is being deliberately evoked. We have one citation, in fact, in which *Now* is being used to mean specifically "of or relating to the Now Generation of the late 1960s and early 1970s":

> Unlike many of the Now movies that were hastily produced right after the sumptuous success of "Easy Rider" —Nora Sayre, *N.Y. Times Book Rev.,* 1 Apr. 1984

See also THEN 1.

no way   From the evidence at hand it appears that *no way* as an emphatic negative is an Americanism that cropped up in the late 1960s. Our earliest printed evidence is from 1968:

> ... I can't forget those first seventeen years, no way! —Arthur Ashe, quoted in *N.Y. Amsterdam News,* 7 Sept. 1968

Did this use originate in the speech of black Americans? Is it college slang? Or is it simply part of the argot of the 1960s youth movement, as Howard 1978 suggests? It is hard, given that the related adverb *noway* has been around since the 13th century, not to suspect that it is a good deal older. Christopher Ricks, in Michaels & Ricks 1980, says it has been around a very long time, but he gives us no evidence.

Howard 1978 and Harper 1975, 1985 are sure the expression is on the way out; Reader's Digest 1983 and Flesch 1983 are sure it is here to stay. Shaw 1975, 1987 merely thinks it is hackneyed. Our current evidence does not suggest that the phrase is losing popularity.

As Reader's Digest notes, *no way* occurs in several constructions. The first of these, the interjectional use, is the earliest and the most common:

> So I ask myself ... do I want to go out on location in some godforsaken corner of McKeesport, Pennsylvania, and live in a motel for two months? No way —Robert Mitchum, quoted in *N.Y. Times,* 19 Sept. 1971

> The answer is—no way —Ada Louise Huxtable, *N.Y. Times,* 23 June 1974

> Liza was telling everybody there were no pictures in the nude, no way —David Taylor, *Punch,* 14 Aug. 1974

> ... when a friend asked him if he would do it again, Mr. [Jimmy] Carter looked back on his long quest and shook his head. "No, no way!" he said —James T. Wooten, *N.Y. Times,* 31 Oct. 1976

> You remember the Bolivian Marching Powder and realize you're not down yet. No way, José —Jay McInerney, *Bright Lights, Big City,* 1984

No way also frequently occurs after *there is* (or *was*). This construction is very close to being a simple combination of *no* and *way.* When followed by *for,* the phrase seems entirely transparent:

> ... said there was no way for Truman to win —Victor Emanuel, Sr., *Houston Post,* 15 Sept. 1984

But the *there is* construction without the *for* is more common:

> But after Nixon I say the hell with it, there's no way these kids should be punished and he gets away clean —John Sieler, quoted in *N.Y. Times,* 27 Oct. 1974

There's no way I could skate constantly for 20 minutes —Scott Hamilton, quoted in *Houston Post,* 4 Sept. 1984

There is no way you will be able to get everything in this article verified —Jay McInerney, *Bright Lights, Big City,* 1984

He was a turncoat, and there was no way we would support him —Tip O'Neill with William Novak, *Man of the House,* 1987

The *there is* can simply be omitted too:

No way you can put a ball over that scoreboard —John Candelaria, quoted in *Sports Illustrated,* 16 July 1979

No way the hottest name in Hollywood is supposed to act this uncool —Charles Leerhsen with Carl Robinson, *Newsweek,* 8 Dec. 1986

And, finally, the order of the verb and subject can be inverted after *no way:*

. . . and no way could Harvey explain a rack of lamb for two . . . when he was supposed to be working late —Cyra McFadden, *The Serial,* 1977

No way did I want to meet Mrs. Gregg again —Claire Miller, *Ranger Rick,* September 1985

No way were we going to do all the housework —Anne Taylor Fleming, *N.Y. Times Mag.,* 26 Oct. 1986

So far, *no way* seems to be limited to speech and prose of a personal or casual nature.

nowhere near Usage handbooks typically describe *nowhere near* as a colloquial or informal substitute for *not nearly.* The *Century Collegiate Handbook* back in 1924 went so far as to call it "vulgar," but most recent commentators have regarded it with more tolerance, limiting themselves to the advice that it should be avoided in formal speech and writing. The OED shows that it is an extremely old phrase, attested in writing (in the form *nowhere nigh*) as far back as 1413. Its common use in writing, however, seems not to have occurred until recently. The bulk of our written evidence for it is from the past several decades.

What that evidence shows is that the written contexts in which *nowhere near* occurs do, in fact, tend toward informality, but they need not be extremely informal. *Nowhere near* has a somewhat more emphatic quality than *not nearly,* and that can make it an appropriate choice in a variety of contexts:

. . . he wrote, "Western Europe has nowhere near the shocking degree of juvenile crime. . . ." —Dorothy Barclay, *N.Y. Times Mag.,* 9 Jan. 1955

Although a large majority of the respondents can justify extramarital sex, nowhere near as many are actually engaging in it —Robert Athanasiou et al., *Psychology Today,* July 1970

. . . household bulbs last nowhere near that long —*Forbes,* 1 Dec. 1970

. . . as a writer . . . Jackie Collins is nowhere near ready for the big time —Genevieve Stuttaford, *Publishers Weekly,* 14 Apr. 1975

. . . illustration after World War I was nowhere near as good as it had been before that —Newgate Callendar, *N.Y. Times Book Rev.,* 26 July 1981

It is certainly true, however, that *nowhere near* continues to be more common in speech than in writing.

A distinct use of *nowhere near* is in the sense "not at all close to":

Teddy bears, thank goodness, are nowhere near extinction —Carolyn Meyer, *McCall's,* March 1971

. . . our present health insurance policy comes nowhere near providing that —Sylvia Porter, *Ladies' Home Jour.,* August 1971

This sense has the same emphatic quality as the "not nearly" sense, and it also is most likely to occur in speech.

nowheres As several commentators point out, the adverb *nowheres* is not in standard use as a variant of *nowhere.* It occurs primarily in dialectal and nonstandard speech and in written representations of such speech:

I hain't been nowheres —Mark Twain, *Huckleberry Finn,* 1884 (OED Supplement)

I don't want to go nowheres and I'll take a job if it's the right kind —Ring Lardner, *The Big Town,* 1921

Nowheres, like *anywheres* and *somewheres* (which see), is an Americanism.

nth Fowler 1926 argues that since *n* means "an unspecified number" rather than "an infinite number" in mathematics, the derivative use of *nth* by nonmathematicians to mean "utmost," as in "to the nth degree," is wrong. His opinion has not been heeded in this case. No other commentator objects to the "utmost" sense of *nth* (Evans 1957 and Copperud 1970, 1980 consider it established in reputable use), and dictionaries have recognized it as standard throughout the 20th century. Here are a few examples of its use from our files:

. . . in the characters . . . developed to the nth degree —Judith Crist, *New York,* 27 Dec. 1971

. . . raised to the *n*th power of elegance —Audax Minor, *New Yorker,* 17 July 1971

. . . has raised to the *n*th degree our national failings of lethargy and wishful thinking —David Wheeler, *The Listener,* 15 May 1975

nubile *Nubile,* much more often used of young women than of young men, originally meant "of marriageable age or condition." This sense is still in use:

. . . a marriageable young lady. . . . she had . . . the most lithe and graspable of waists, in an age that greatly admired such a thing in a nubile female —Robert Penn Warren, *Jefferson Davis Gets His Citizenship Back,* 1980

It is easy to see how this use was extended to mean "sexually attractive." The extended sense has apparently been in American use since about the 1950s and in British use since the 1960s:

. . . the nubile chorus line at the Folies-Bergere —*N.Y. Herald Tribune,* 18 Mar. 1951

Birds of Britain is not a new Audubon but a fleshly paradise of nubile young women —*Times Literary Supp.,* 14 Dec. 1967

The few usage writers who mention this development (Bernstein 1971, Copperud 1970, 1980) do not find it at all troublesome.

nuclear In many recent usage books the reader is admonished to say \\'nü-klē-ər\\, not \\'nü-kyə-lər\\, and never mind what President Eisenhower used to say.

We wish first to confront a more interesting question. Why, when the pronunciation problems of *nuclear* are so well known that they are a continuing source of national wrath and mirth, do so many educated people—and especially members of Congress—persist in the condemned pronunciation? Why did \\'nü-kyə-lər\\ arise in the first place?

Since \\'nü-kyə-lər\\ is not a spelling pronunciation, it must have originated phonologically as a deviation from the target of \\'nü-klē-ər\\. The transformation is reminiscent of but cannot strictly be described as *metathesis* (which see); in any event *metathesis* is a label for a phenomenon, not an explanation. That the target pronunciation presents some articulatory difficulties is suggested by two other variants that may more clearly be seen as simplifications: the occasional \\'nü-kyir\\ and the fairly common \\'nü-klir\\ (which we have attested respectively from former President Jimmy Carter and from his mother, among others).

But besides any inherent difficulty involved in saying \\'nü-klē-ər\\, the pronunciation \\'nü-kyə-ler\\ was probably engendered by a process that functions in folk etymology as well: the replacement of a relatively less familiar sequence of sounds with one relatively more familiar. Now, there is *no* other common word in English that ends in \\-klē-ər\\, and just one uncommon one *(cochlear)*. But there are several that end in \\-kyə-lər\\ or \\-kyü-lər\\: *particular, spectacular, molecular, secular, oracular, vernacular.* So we believe that *nuclear* became \\'nü-kyə-lər\\ for the same reason that *et cetera* became \\ek-'set-ə-rə\\ (see ETC.): speakers have succumbed to the gravitational tug of a far more prevalent pattern.

This explanation is further bolstered by the case of *similar, percolator,* and *escalator,* which the less educated often pronounce respectively \\'sim-yə-lər\\, \\'pər-kyə-ˌlāt-ər\\, and \\'es-kyə-ˌlāt-ər\\. Here the vague explanation that the folk version is "simpler" will not hold water, because the folk version arises by *adding* a sound, \\y\\. What actually happens is that when saying *similar, percolator,* and *escalator,* some speakers conform to the more familiar pattern (stop consonant plus \\yəl\\ plus vowel) that shows up in such words as *fabulous, cellular, ridiculous, angular, populated,* and *masculine.*

A number of other pronunciation variants that go against the spelling of a word—the common \\'nəp-shə-wel\\ for *nuptial* (compare words like *conceptual* and *voluptuous*) and the less common \\ˌdim-yə-'nish-ən\\ for *diminution,* for example—can be explained along similar lines.

Returning to the status of \\'nü-kyə-lər\\, we must make several points. First, it is a minority pronunciation; \\'nü-klē-ər\\ is still much more common among educated speakers. Second, it is nonetheless a common pronunciation among the educated. Most of our evidence for it is from prominent political figures and journalists, but we have also recorded it from the mouths of college professors in a variety of academic disciplines. Third, if it is your natural pronunciation and you choose to continue with it, you will have a lot of distin-

guished company, but you are also likely to draw some unfriendly attention from those who consider it an error.

nude See NAKED, NUDE.

number 1. All commentators agree that the plural verb in the first example that follows is correct, and so is the singular verb in the second:

> Current statistics already show that, of the unemployed, a large number are illiterate —Adolf A. Berle, in *The Great Ideas Today,* ed. Robert M. Hutchins & Mortimer J. Adler, 1965

> The number of foreign-language and second-language users together adds up to 300 to 400 million —Braj B. Kachru, in Greenbaum 1985

The rule of thumb for this construction is stated succinctly by Bernstein 1977:

> In general, *a number* takes a plural verb and *the number* a singular.

Evidence in the Merriam-Webster files shows that the rule of thumb is generally observed. Even when the sentence begins with *there, a number of* commands the plural verb:

> "There are a number of telephone messages for you. . . ." —John P. Marquand, *So Little Time,* 1943

> There are a number of things to be said about the V.I.P. list —Arnold Gingrich, *Esquire,* April 1970

An adjective like *increasing* or *growing* tends to emphasize the word *number* in its singularity, and results in rather more mixed usage:

> . . . an increasing number of these students are earning —William Hamilton Jones, *Johns Hopkins Mag.,* October 1965

> An ever growing number of films is available —Arni T. Dunathan, *Vocatio,* April 1968

But even in these constructions, the plural verb is the more common.
2. See AMOUNT 1.
3. See the articles at AGREEMENT.

numerous. Normally an adjective ("Numerous species were sighted"), *numerous* gives occasional indications of taking on the function of a pronoun:

> . . . blunted the awareness of numerous of its inhabitants to the historical significance of many of its buildings —Norman Harrington, *N.Y. Times,* 7 Apr. 1968

Numerous is equivalent to *a number* or to the pronoun *many* in such a construction. Its use is similar to the use of *various* as a pronoun (as in "various of them"), except that it occurs far more rarely. It has been cited as an error by usage commentators dating back to Fowler 1926. Our relative lack of evidence for it suggests strongly that it is not yet established as standard.

See also VARIOUS.

nuptial See NUCLEAR.

O, oh Usage writers from Ayres 1881 to Shaw 1987 have been explaining the fine distinctions between these two variants of the same interjection. To us the matter looks much simpler. If you meet a capital *O* all by itself in current American prose, the odds are that you are looking at an abbreviation or a symbol or some other arbitrary designation. If you see it used interjectionally, you may be sure that you are reading a highly rhetorical writer fond of apostrophe:

> O for the times when one tended to go by the second edition of Webster's —Simon 1980

> O, the gallant self-effacement of the mountaineering fraternity —John G. Mitchell, *Wilderness,* Summer 1985

If you want to be an apostrophizer, you should be aware that veteran apostrophizers follow the ancient custom of putting no punctuation after the *O.*

Most plain people use *oh* nowadays. It is customary to separate *oh* from following matter with a comma or exclamation point. *Oh* is generally capitalized only when beginning a sentence. *O* is a rare spelling in ordinary interjectional use. When you see it, you are permitted to suspect that someone is after a particular effect, such as mockery:

> O, lackaday, the organization had betrayed me —Wayne C. Booth, *Now Don't Try to Reason with Me,* 1970

obedient When *obedient* is used with a preposition, it is *to:*

> Van Helsing stepped out, and, obedient to his gesture, we all advanced too —Bram Stoker, *Dracula,* 1897

> Faces of others seem like stars
> Obedient to symmetrical laws.
> I stare at them as though into a glass
> —Stephen Spender, "The Human Situation,"
> *Ruins and Visions,* 1942

> They [stories] are obedient not only to a genre . . . but also to the ideas they wish to see prevail — Thomas Sutcliffe, *Times Literary Supp.,* 2 Sept. 1983

object When *object* is used with a preposition, it usually takes *to.* What follows *to* may be a noun, pronoun, gerund, or infinitive:

> She had the desire to do something which she objected to doing —Arnold Bennett, *The Old Wives' Tale,* 1908

> Mademoiselle Lucy corrected her uncle's French, but objected to do more —George Meredith, *The Ordeal of Richard Feverel,* 1859

> ". . . But our silly husbands have a way of objecting to that sort of thing." —Roald Dahl, *Someone Like You,* 1953

> . . . but what good does objecting to Uncle Daniel do? You just get fired —Eudora Welty, *The Ponder Heart,* 1954

> . . . he at least strenuously objected to many of the German demands —William L. Shirer, *The Rise and Fall of the Third Reich,* 1960

Fowler 1926 says "the infinitive is deprecated & the gerund recommended. . . ." In actual usage, the infinitive is not frequent, but the quotation from Meredith above is an instance of it. The gerund, as in the quotation from Bennett, is found more often. *Object to* followed by a noun phrase is the most common construction.

Bernstein 1965 notes that *object* can also be followed by *against.* Examples in the OED show that *object against* was at one time in common use; in the 20th century, however, it is rare, and we have little evidence for it:

> It would be objected against these men that they would still be themselves and wreck illusion —*New Republic,* 15 Feb. 1939

objective Copperud 1970, 1980 cites a few commentators who object to *objective* as a noun where *object* or *aim* could be used; Shaw 1975, 1987 states roughly the same view. The usage disapproved dates back, according to the OED, to the 1880s. It apparently arose as a shortening of the 19th-century phrase *objective point.* Our evidence shows that *objective* tends to be found in serious discursive prose more frequently than in lighter writing.

If you choose to reduce your *objective* to *object,* you will pick up one syllable or three letters—not much of a gain, whether you are speaking or writing. We think it is your choice entirely. Here are three genuine examples for you to evaluate:

> In October, 1945 the Atomic Energy Commission laid down six objectives for the development of nuclear research —*Times Literary Supp.,* 27 Aug. 1971

> . . . their primary objective is not the enrollment of new voters but changing the party affiliation of old voters —Lawrence King, *Commonweal,* 9 Oct. 1970

> First objective is to collect old newspapers —James Egan, *McCall's,* March 1971

objective genitive, object genitive See GENITIVE 1.

objet d'art Copperud 1970, 1980 notes that this term is often mistakenly spelled *object d'art.* We have about half a dozen examples of this misspelling in our files, including the following:

> . . . fine paintings, sculptures and objects d'art both antique and contemporary —advt., *Town & Country,* July 1980

> . . . supplies sculptural objects d'art for store display —*Metropolitan Home,* June 1982

A moment's reflection or a quick look in the dictionary is all that is needed to prevent this mistake. Or you can use instead the completely English equivalent, *art object.*

obligated, obliged Usage comment about the verbs *obligate* and *oblige* seems to concern itself mostly with uses of the past participles. The first of these uses involves a sense of *obligated* meaning "indebted for a service or favor." The OED has 17th-, 18th-, and 19th-century evidence for the sense, but marks it "not now in good use." The OED Supplement shows that the sense went out of use except in northern England, Scotland, and the United States. The Dictionary of American English shows 18th- and 19th-century American examples; the OED Supplement has one from 1919. Mac-Cracken & Sandison 1917 and Copperud 1970, 1980 warn against the use of this sense; Janis 1984 suggests it has been replaced by *obliged*. Our evidence supports Janis; in writing, at least, we have no evidence for *obligated* in this sense. *Obliged* does indeed seem to have replaced it:

> I would be much obliged if you would send me six copies —Flannery O'Connor, letter, 19 July 1952

Part of the diffidence toward *obligated* that is to be found in usage books may come from its having dropped out of use in British English while remaining in Scottish and American use. British commentators and commentators born in areas of British speech are hostile to *obligated;* typical is Phythian 1979 who would relegate *obligate* to legal use. Bremner 1980 quotes with obvious satisfaction the fun George Bernard Shaw made of Woodrow Wilson's use of the word. Wilson was not, however, the first American president to use it:

> They were obligated, according to Promise, to give the Present —George Washington, *Writings,* 1753 (in DAE)

In the sense of being bound or constrained legally or morally, *obligated* and *obliged* are essentially interchangeable:

> ... Helen MacInnes feels obligated to make the background of her books as factual and authentic as possible —*Current Biography,* November 1967

> ... O'Connor from time to time felt obliged to answer those critics —Terry Pettit, *Averett Jour.,* Autumn 1970

> ... the false jauntiness that most of the high-circulation magazines still felt obligated to assume — Bruce Bliven, *New Republic,* 22 Nov. 1954

> ... to secure permissions which in many cases they have not been legally obliged to seek —*Times Literary Supp.,* 12 Feb. 1970

> Since I am challenged, however, I feel obligated to offer the evidence and documentation called for — Jessie Bernard, *American Sociological Rev.,* June 1950

> In return for C.E.P.A.'s help, the complainant is obliged to join the organization —Philip G. Schrag, *Columbia Forum,* Summer 1970

When the constraint is applied by physical force or by circumstances, however, *obliged* and not *obligated* is used:

> Subway riders are frequently obliged to step around a limousine idling softly while madam shops —Elizabeth Dailley Heaman, *Ford Times,* February 1968

> ... he speculated unprofitably, and in 1815 was obliged to resume his practice —*Australian Dictionary of Biography,* 1967

> ... not one of those children has been obliged to suffer the experience of a home-cooked meal —Gordon Lish, *Saturday Rev.,* 22 July 1978

oblivious Usage writers and other concerned language watchers in the early 20th century insisted that the correct meaning of *oblivious* was "forgetful; no longer mindful" and that it should only be followed by the preposition *of.* The basis of that opinion was etymological and historical. *Oblivious* is derived ultimately from the Latin verb *oblivisci,* "to forget," and its oldest senses in English, dating back to the 15th century, all have to do with forgetfulness. The sense of *oblivious* to which the critics objected was "not conscious or aware," which was first recorded in the middle 1800s. The OED labeled this sense erroneous in 1902, and it was censured by such critics as Ball 1923, Fowler 1926, and Krapp 1927. Much criticism was directed specifically at the phrase *oblivious to,* meaning "unaware of."

The "unaware" sense of *oblivious* has continued in extremely common use, however, and criticism of it is now largely a thing of the past. Our evidence shows that in current English it is far and away the most common meaning of the word. It typically describes a lack of awareness that is remarkable, especially because of its completeness, or that is in some way blameworthy; and in this sense the word is usually followed by the preposition *to:*

> ... writers are often oblivious to their readers — Mary C. Bromage, *Michigan Business Rev.,* July 1968

> Sigmund emerged oblivious to the shell-pink dusk —Irving Stone, *McCall's,* March 1971

> ... completely oblivious to the traffic of the street — Herb Goro, *New York,* 10 Jan. 1972

> ... oblivious to matters that don't have an immediate impact on his personal situation —Everett Groseclose, *Wall Street Jour.,* 16 Oct. 1972

> Father was oblivious to the man's speculative notice of his wife —E. L. Doctorow, *Ragtime,* 1974

> ... go-go girls oblivious to the rout outside —William Styron, *This Quiet Dust and Other Writings,* 1982

The "forgetful" sense of *oblivious* is still used, but it is now rare. It always takes the preposition *of:*

> Oblivious of any previous decisions not to stand together ..., the three stood in a tight group —Doris Lessing, *The Good Terrorist,* 1985

Some writers and editors prefer *of* to follow *oblivious* in its "unaware" sense as well. Such usage is not uncommon in current writing:

> ... play chess all afternoon oblivious of the business that might be transpiring in the courts and government buildings —Herbert Lottman, *Columbia Forum,* Summer 1970

> Johnson was not entirely oblivious of these beauties —John Butt, *English Literature in the Mid-Eighteenth Century,* edited & completed by Geoffrey Carnall, 1979

obnoxious *Obnoxious* in its oldest sense means "exposed to something unpleasant or harmful":

> O dangerous state of so sovereign pow'r!
> Obnoxious to the change of every hour.
> —George Villiers, *The Rehearsal*, 1672

> ". . . may render you only obnoxious to danger and disgrace. . . ." —Henry Fielding, *Jonathan Wild*, 1743

This sense is etmologically accurate: *obnoxious* is derived ultimately from the Latin *ob-*, "exposed to" and *noxa,* "harm." This sense has, however, been entirely superseded by a sense "extremely offensive," which apparently (as the OED suggests) owes something to association with *noxious.* This sense is by no means new, having been first recorded more than 300 years ago:

> A very obnoxious person; an ill neighbour —Anthony Wood, *Life,* 1675 (OED)

> Mr. Arthur Lee could not but be very obnoxious to Johnson, for he was not only a *patriot* but an *American* —James Boswell, *Life of Samuel Johnson*, 1791

Some commentators in the late 19th and early 20th centuries, led by Richard Grant White 1870, were unhappy about the "offensive" sense of *obnoxious,* but most seem to have realized that it was far too well established to be seriously opposed. No one now questions the correctness of this sense.

observance, observation The distinction between these words has been explained and recommended in books on usage for more than a century. It is a simple one: *observance* is to be used in the sense "an act or instance of following a custom, rule, or law," as in "observance of the Sabbath" and "observance of the speed limit"; *observation* is to be used in the sense "an act or instance of watching," as in "observation of a lunar eclipse." This distinction is, in fact, usually followed in actual usage:

> Her only hope lay in strict observance of court procedure —*American Girl,* March 1953

> His observation of the readiness of churchgoers to accept Hitler —*Current Biography,* September 1984

But *observance* and *observation* are also sometimes used as synonyms. Many commentators acknowledge that such usage was once respectable (it occurs in the works of such writers as Shakespeare, Coleridge, and Macaulay), but most of them now want it to be regarded as an error. A more reasonable view is to regard it simply as rare. The use of *observation* to mean "an act of following a custom or law" is especially uncommon:

> The South has never been solemn in the observation of this sacred day —*American Guide Series: North Carolina,* 1939

The use of *observance* to mean "an act of watching" occurs somewhat more often, although it is certainly far less common than the use of *observation* in this sense:

> . . . evidence of Inge's faithful observance of life —*Current Biography,* June 1953

> . . . made paranoiac by his observance of my rage —Sally Kempton, *Esquire,* July 1970

Dictionaries treat such usage as standard.

You may very well want to keep *observance* and *observation* distinct in your own writing (you probably do so already without thinking about it), but there is certainly no rule that says you have to.

observant *Observant,* when used with a preposition, takes *of:*

> . . . his eyes were often upon her, intensely observant of her gaiety —Maurice Hewlett, *Halfway House,* 1908

> . . . be meekly observant of religious custom on Sunday —*Selected Writings of Edward Sapir,* ed. David G. Mandelbaum, 1949

> . . . acutely observant of traffic laws —*Current Biography,* June 1965

observation See OBSERVANCE, OBSERVATION.

obsess When *obsess* is used with a preposition, it appears as a past participle, often as part of a passive construction. It is used with *with* about twice as often as with *by:*

> . . . those who . . . are obsessed with stupid, male vanity —Sherwood Anderson, *Poor White,* 1920

> . . . they had grown so obsessed with the idea that they could not willingly contemplate any action —C. S. Forester, *The African Queen,* 1935

> . . . become obsessed with the suspicion that most of the talk they cannot hear consists in plottings —James Gould Cozzens, *Guard of Honor,* 1948

> . . . were obsessed at this moment with the urgency of heading southeast —William L. Shirer, *The Rise and Fall of the Third Reich,* 1960

> . . . as soon as he suspects her of infidelity, he becomes morbidly obsessed by jealousy —Edmund Wilson, *Axel's Castle,* 1931

> . . . gamblers, obsessed by their own fictions of speculation —Thomas Wolfe, *You Can't Go Home Again,* 1940

Obsess has also been used infrequently with *of* or *on:*

> . . . too obsessed for our own good of the idea that our supposedly superior intelligence was all the insurance we needed —Norman Cousins, *Saturday Rev.,* 17 Jan. 1942

> The crop of Negro fiction written during the last decade is obsessed on the subject of race —Charles I. Glicksberg, *Western Rev.,* Winter 1949

obsolete The use of this word as a verb is called into question by a few recent commentators—a usage panelist in Harper 1985, Janis 1984, Copperud 1980. Copperud blames the verb on the American military, as have a few of our correspondents. But the OED exculpates the Pentagon: the functional shift of *obsolete* from adjective to verb was first pulled off in 1640. In the 19th century the verb was used by Fitzedward Hall 1873, among others. Modern use appears to be an American revival dating, our files indicate, from the late 1930s:

> For radio itself deliberately obsoletes today what it built yesterday —David Sarnoff, *Television,* 1936

These modern, lightweight Anchors have obsoleted all old style, "deadweight" equipment —advt., *Yachting,* April 1940

Things obsolete themselves more rapidly than at any time in our history —*Scientific American,* July 1944

In current use, it almost always appears in technical contexts:

One of these could easily develop some day into a reimaging process that would obsolete the ones we work with now —Philip E. Tobias, *Book Production Industry,* July 1967

... older cpu's whose speed and efficiency never were fully tapped before they were effectively obsoleted by their manufacturers —Edith Myers, *Datamation,* November 1977

The only losers are those who own the obsoleted capital —D. G. Soergel, *Wall Street Jour.,* 31 Dec. 1980

obtain 1. The transitive *obtain* is denigrated as pretentious for *get* by some of the same commentators who tell you that *get* is overused. But if you look in your dictionary, you will see that *obtain* does not mean simply "get"; it means "to gain or attain usually by planned action or effort." We think you will not be tempted very often to slip it in for plain *get.*
2. The intransitive *obtain* is described as literary by Safire 1984 (he cites Krapp 1927 and Nicholson 1957 in support) and viewed with distrust by Freeman 1983, who thinks *prevail* or *is/are still with us* might be better. This use of *obtain* looks like this in context:

... in rural areas where a degree of casual familiarity has always obtained —William Styron, *This Quiet Dust and Other Writings,* 1982

There's nothing wrong with being a little literary now and then.

obtrude *Obtrude* is used with a great many prepositions; those which occur most frequently are *in, into, on,* or *upon:*

... contemptuous of anyone who allows the past to obtrude in the present —Robert Craft, *Stravinsky,* 1972

It is interesting to note how progressive divergencies in pattern obtrude themselves in some species —J. Stevenson-Hamilton, *Wild Life in South Africa,* 1947

We have to wait until the seventeenth century for a real democratic movement, obtruding itself into the Civil War —A. J. P. Taylor, *New Statesman & Nation,* 29 Aug. 1953

... by otherwise obtruding his ego into the picture —Winthrop Sargeant, *New Yorker,* 5 Dec. 1953

... last summer he was again most painfully obtruded on my notice —Jane Austen, *Pride and Prejudice,* 1813

I'm not sure whether Miss Murdoch's novel needs that extra dimension of allusion, but it never obtrudes on the excitement —Derwent May, *Saturday Rev.,* January 1981

Phil stared at the sign with reproach, as though she thought it had ... no business obtruding itself upon her attention —Donald Barr Chidsey, *Panama Passage,* 1946

... a clergyman, committed to the religious point of view, but he obtrudes no dogma upon the reader —Gerald W. Johnson, *New Republic,* 8 Feb. 1954

Obtrude is also used with *before* and *between,* but these appear less often:

... obstacles and impediments will obtrude themselves before your gaze —*Selected Writings of Benjamin N. Cardozo,* ed. Margaret E. Hall, 1947

Whenever the mechanics of language obtrude between a poet and his experience —*Times Literary Supp.,* 22 Oct. 1971

obtuse Trouble is brewing for *obtuse.* This adjective has been used for about five centuries without causing a stir, but recent years have seen the development of a new sense, and voices of criticism are beginning to be heard. Its older senses are consistent with its derivation from the Latin *obtusus,* "dull, blunt." An obtuse angle is an angle that is not acute, and an obtuse person is a person who is not sharp—who has, in other words, a dull or insensitive mind:

... another point missed by the disarmingly honest but hopelessly obtuse Meneghini —Peter G. Davis, *N.Y. Times Book Rev.,* 21 Nov. 1982

Recently, however, *obtuse* has begun to be used in the sense "difficult to comprehend; unclear":

... they are now so obscure, so obtuse, so contradictory —Charles Price, *Esquire,* May 1977

His answer, often phrased in obtuse language, was in brief that a child learns by discrete stages —Alden Whitman, *N.Y. Times,* 17 Sept. 1980

... offered only an obtuse explanation. "I wanted to be more aggressive," he said, "but there was a situation, something I don't want to discuss, that dictated the approach we took. ..." —Dale Robertson, *Houston Post,* 3 Sept. 1984

This sense most likely arose from confusion with *obscure* and *abstruse.* The use has not yet become very common and is therefore not yet notorious, but its occurrence in a letter written by a U.S. general in 1983 did draw some unfriendly commentary from William Safire. If this sense becomes more widespread, the critical reaction to it will no doubt become more virulent. The use is well enough established to appear in some dictionaries, but if you are cautious about new words and meanings, you might want to avoid it.

obviate Bernstein 1958, 1965 and Follett 1966 seem to have invented the notion that *obviate* can mean only "make unnecessary," not "anticipate and prevent." They may have arrived at this conclusion by focusing too narrowly on the second part of the definition in Webster's Second. The editors of the OED, Webster's Second, Webster's Third, and Webster's Ninth New Collegiate Dictionary were unaware of any such limitation, and so were the writers on whose work they based their definitions. Notice how in many of the following examples the "prevent" sense of *obviate* is intended:

To obviate the tedium of repeating item (2) over and over again on hundreds of slips —*Historical Introduction, OED Supplement,* 1933

He looked at a person once ... and after that he remembered how they looked well enough to obviate another inspection —Tennessee Williams, *The Roman Spring of Mrs. Stone*, 1950

... robs a dealer of gems to obviate his being slaughtered by yeggs —S. J. Perelman, *New Yorker*, 3 Mar. 1951

... even in populations badly shattered by war most of these genetic ill effects could be obviated if monogamy were less of an ingrained human practice —W. C. Allee, *Cooperation Among Animals*, rev. ed., 1951

... its most sizable service is simply in obviating further, future demonstrations of how dull sex can be as a subject for a full evening —Robert Craft, *N.Y. Rev. of Books*, 6 Nov. 1969

... different in such a way as to obviate the second Russian Revolution of 1917 —George F. Kennan, *New Yorker*, 1 May 1971

... the description ... still seems serviceable enough to obviate any need for me to paraphrase my own prose —Jay Jacobs, *Gourmet*, March 1977

... they were plenty alarmed because they felt Mel's film might obviate a movie production of the play —Liz Smith, *New Orleans Times-Picayune*, 26 Sept. 1979

You are free to follow Bernstein and Follett and avoid the "prevent" sense, but many good writers do not.

Flesch 1964 recommends avoiding the word altogether because it "sounds pompous and academic." He suggests *do away with, cancel, prevent, forestall, blot out,* and *meet* as alternatives. While all of those words have merit, there are still times when many writers feel *obviate* is the better choice.

occasion 1. *Occasion* is often followed by *for* or *of;* the two prepositions seem to be in about equal use:

... a formula that has been the occasion for a considerable amount of misunderstanding —I. A. Richards, *Basic English and Its Uses*, 1943

His death in 1945 was not an occasion for revising a harsh general opinion —Christopher Sykes, *Encounter*, December 1954

The birthday, apparently, was merely the occasion, not the cause, of the guests' effusions —Lillian Ross, *New Yorker*, 24 May 1952

... one of life's minor absurdities and small occasions of anguish —Robert Kiely, *N.Y. Times Book Rev.*, 1 July 1979

Occasion also is followed quite frequently with *to* and the infinitive. In this construction *occasion* is typically preceded by the verb *have* or, once in a while, another verb such as *find* or *take:*

Einstein had the occasion one afternoon to call Mays —Al Silverman, *Saturday Rev.*, 23 Apr. 1955

... I had occasion to see an unusual number of movies —Lewis H. Lapham, *Harper's*, November 1971

... the Honourable Peter ... found occasion to get some conversation with Adrian alone —George Meredith, *The Ordeal of Richard Feverel*, 1859

... Lowell took occasion to describe the direction of his interest in American English usage —Jayne Crane Harder, *American Speech*, October 1954

2. Andy Rooney writes (*And More by Andy Rooney,* 1982) that he has to check his spelling of *occasion* to make sure he hasn't stuck two *s*'s in the word. Copperud 1980 also reports the double *s* misspelling, and our files have plenty of examples of *occasion* and *occasionally* with the otiose *s*. So check your spelling; if Andy Rooney can, so can you.

occupy When *occupy* is used with a preposition, *with* appears most frequently:

I hadn't really thought about it, so occupied had I been with all the arrangements —Graham Greene, *Travels with My Aunt*, 1969

He was occupied with turning human actions into poetry —T. S. Eliot, "Shakespeare and the Stoicism of Seneca," in *Selected Essays*, 1932

... you had to occupy yourself with that rudimentary light show, the NBC test pattern —Jan Hodenfield, *Rolling Stone*, 13 May 1971

... the irony of thanking a mother for occupying herself with the details of her own daughter's wedding —Edith Wharton, *The Old Maid*, 1924

Occupy by is found almost as often:

He occupied himself by taking long walks —Green Peyton, *San Antonio: City in the Sun*, 1946

The center of the house was occupied by a magnificent mahogany staircase —Robert Morss Lovett, *All Our Years*, 1948

Occupy also occurs with *in:*

... she occupied herself in social-service work — John Cheever, *The Wapshot Chronicle*, 1957

They occupy themselves in showing that America started in the gutter —Percy Holmes Boynton, quoted in Charles I. Glicksberg, *American Literary Criticism 1900–1950*, 1951

occur See TAKE PLACE, OCCUR.

octopus Do you know what the plural of *octopus* is? Three receive mention: *octopuses, octopodes, octopi.* But only *octopuses* and *octopi* are in use. The OED gives *octopodes* as the first plural (*octopuses* as the alternative), but the OED also enters *octopus* with double bars as a foreign word. The OED has only one plural example, for *octopuses,* dated 1884.

Octopi is attacked from time to time as improper, chiefly by those who know (or have been told) that a plural formed on the Greek would be *octopodes*. *Octopus,* however, is not directly imported from the Greek; it comes from New Latin, which took it from the Greek *oktopous*. *Octopi* is, however, irregularly formed—on analogy, we suppose, with the plurals of other Latin nouns of the second declension (like *alumnus*).

The history of these plurals in English shows *octopuses* the oldest, starting with the OED's 1884 example. *Octopi* first turned up in our files in 1922. The editors of Webster's Second had exactly the same number of citations for *octopi* and *octopuses,* and from about the same kinds of sources, so they included both, along with the OED's *octopodes*. The citations gathered for the books published after Webster's Second show *octopuses* slightly more popular than *octopi.* Several publications—*Time,* the *New York Times,* the *Times Literary Supplement,* and publications of the Smithsonian Institution, for instance—have used both plurals. Citations gathered since the publication of Webster's Ninth New Collegiate Dictionary (1983) show *octopuses* continuing to increase its edge over *octopi.*

So the evidence to date shows that *octopuses* is gaining in frequency of use, and that *octopi* is dropping back but is still a respectable second. *Octopodes* is a nonstarter: we have no evidence of its use in context. If neither of the live plurals is your cup of tea, you can always take the way out used by a timid writer of a ninth-grade text: "chitons, the squids and the octopus tribe."

-odd When used to indicate a quantity somewhat greater than a given round number, *odd* is usually preceded by a hyphen.

> . . . the past twenty-odd years —Alec Rackowe, *The Writer,* May 1953

> The three thousand-odd people who attended —*New Yorker,* 19 Sept. 1953

> . . . the 50-odd people she has interviewed —George P. Hunt, *Life,* 21 July 1967

> . . . the two-hundred-odd commercial stations — Stanley Gortikov, quoted in *Center Mag.,* September 1968

> . . . the 600-odd Scouts returned home —Dick Pryce, *Scouting,* January–February 1972

Unhyphenated examples do occur,

> . . . the 50 odd most popular U.S. stocks —*Wall Street Jour.,* 28 Oct. 1946

but they entail a greater risk of being misunderstood, and often with unintended humorous results.

> . . . disciplinary regulations which . . . must apply to the five hundred odd officers —James Gould Cozzens, *Guard of Honor,* 1948

> . . . forty-six of the eighty odd stories written by Poe —*British Book News,* May 1955

> . . . they sold four million odd records, more than the Beatles ever did in a year —Michael Thomas, *Rolling Stone,* 16 Mar. 1972

Our advice is to include the hyphen and so avoid possible ambiguity.

Copperud 1980 objects to *some* used before a number + *odd* as being redundant, but it seems idiomatic and not particularly bothersome to us, though it is clearly not required:

> . . . an enclave of some thirty-odd buildings —Russell Lynes, *Harper's,* November 1968

> . . . some 260-odd large and close-packed pages — John Crowe Ransom, *N.Y. Rev. of Books,* 23 Oct. 1970

In fact, we found fewer instances of such use in our files than we had expected. Here may be a clue to why this use with *some* seems so familiar: it occurs in both of our citations for *-odd* that are quotations from speech. In speech, where no hyphen is available to clearly distinguish this sense of *odd* from others, *some* takes on the job of the hyphen and acts as a sense marker to avoid misunderstanding. So in speech *some* + a number + *odd* is far from redundant. See also SOME 1.

of 1. *Of* is involved as a part of various subjects in this book. See, for instance, the compound prepositions ALONGSIDE OF, ALONGSIDE; INSIDE OF; OFF OF; OUTSIDE OF. It is also part of the construction discussed at DOUBLE GENITIVE.

2. *Of* for *'ve* or *have. Have* in a sentence like "I could have gone" rarely receives full stress and is consequently seldom pronounced \'hav\. In ordinary circumstances the *could have* would be pronounced \'kùd-əv\, with the accent on *could* and no accent on *have.* Thus in ordinary conversation *have,* unstressed, is pronounced the same as *of,* unstressed. When the unstressed *have* is spelled, it is usually spelled *'ve,* but children and others who are partly educated may equate the \əv\ with the spelling *of,* producing *could of* (and *should of, would of, ought to of, might of, may of, must of).*

We find that the *of* spelling of *have* (or *'ve*) occurs in two ways. First we find the naive use. Bernstein 1977 allows that a schoolchild cannot be blamed for *could of*—once. But the habit must be difficult to eradicate, because warnings against *could of* and its relatives are carried in most schoolbooks and college handbooks— Warriner 1986, Corder 1981, Scott, Foresman 1981, Macmillan 1982, Irmscher 1978, Prentice Hall 1978, Bell & Cohn 1980, Little, Brown 1980, 1986, among others—and in many general usage books—Harper 1975, 1985, Bernstein 1977, Janis 1984, Reader's Digest 1983, Johnson 1982, Shaw 1970, Freeman 1983, among others. And such warnings have been carried since MacCracken & Sandison 1917. In spite of the warnings, naive *of* can be found in print:

> . . . Our Store Hours Were Stated Incorrectly and Should of Read . . . —advt., quoted by William Safire, *N.Y. Times Mag.,* 8 June 1980

> This movie would of sunk (as would many others) if the male 'protagonist' was out bayoneting babies — letter to the editor, *Valley Advocate,* 5 Mar. 1980

The second use—more complicated—is deliberate use by writers. Writers use the spelling to create an unlettered persona:

> Dock Knowitall he was Good an' Rattled by this time, an' the mos' Heedless Observer could easy of seen he was in fer one o' the Sensations of a Life Time —Frank W. Sage, D.D.S., *Dental Digest,* November 1902

> I could of beat them easy with any kind of support —Ring Lardner, *You Know Me Al,* 1916

> . . . he must of thought I said it was the last bottle in the world —Ring Lardner, *The Big Town,* 1921

F. Scott Fitzgerald used the spelling to represent the speech of a woman who was not overeducated:

> "Everybody kept saying to me: 'Lucille, that man's 'way below you!' But if I hadn't met Chester, he'd of got me sure." —*The Great Gatsby,* 1925

Writers are still using it to transcribe fictional speech. Notice the contrast in the next example between the detective's *have* and the motel manager's *of*—perhaps the detective is supposed to be better educated.

Charlie took the bullet and rolled it around in his hand. "Could it have been there before they came?"

"Sure, it's possible," said Bellamy. "We always clean but I guess we could of missed it. I just don't think we did, that's all."
—Stephen Dobyns, *Saratoga Snapper,* 1986

It is also used to transcribe real speech:

That's about what he should of done, felt sorry for him because Pierce didn't know what was going on, and even if he had, he wouldn't of known what to do about it —Harry S. Truman, in Merle Miller, *Plain Speaking,* 1973

The OED Supplement dates the naive (or ignorant) use of *of* back to 1837. A century and a half of use have not made it respectable, and you had better avoid it in your own writing. You will, of course, have to decide whether you want to use *have* or the more conversational *'ve.* Deliberate use in fiction is a more difficult matter. It can be used as Ring Lardner used it—as part of the creation of a fictional persona. But if you use it, you must take care to be as consistent with it as he was. The OED Supplement has an example where an author uses *might have been* and then *might of been,* which can only leave the reader puzzling over the possible significance of the switch. What the purpose might be of using *of* for *'ve* in writing fictional dialogue is not clear, but obviously writers like it enough to keep using it. We do not see the purpose of using it in transcribing real speech, since the unstressed \əv\ can be transcribed just as faithfully with *'ve* as it is with *of.*

For *had of,* see PLUPLUPERFECT.

3. *Of* is used in a periphrastic version of the adverbial genitive (which see). The noun after *of* may be either singular or plural. The construction has a distinctly literary feel:

I walk out here of an afternoon, and hear the notes of the thrush —William Hazlitt, letter, February 1822

. . . settle down of an afternoon to compare audition notes —Kim Waller, *Town & Country,* September 1983

. . . will be like . . . sitting down of an evening with you —Robert Frost, letter, 10 Oct. 1920

I don't sleep well of nights, either —William Humphrey, *Sports Illustrated,* 14 Oct. 1985

of a On 2 April 1984 former shortstop Pee Wee Reese was asked (in front of a television camera) about the speech he would make when he was inducted into the Baseball Hall of Fame. "It won't be that long of a speech," said Pee Wee. Another former shortstop, Tony Kubek, on a nationally televised baseball broadcast (15 August 1987), remarked that some idea or other was "too radical of a theory." What have we here? Shortstop idiom? Not exactly. Golfers use it too:

. . . wouldn't be that difficult of a shot —Lee Trevino, golf telecast, 16 Nov. 1985

And newscasters use it:

How big of a carrier task force? —Jim Lehrer, television newscast, 24 Mar. 1986

And hosts of television cooking shows:

You can't get in here and make that big of a mess, can you? —Jeff Smith, "The Frugal Gourmet" (telecast), 14 Mar. 1987

And mayors:

I don't want to be considered too good of a loser — Edward Koch, quoted in *N.Y. Times,* 4 Oct. 1982

Even newspaper columnists will use it:

I don't care how good of a shape the economists say we're in —Erma Bombeck, *Springfield* (Mass.) *Union,* 16 Sept. 1976

What we have here is a fairly recent American idiom that has nearly a fixed form: *that* or *how* or *too,* or sometimes *as,* followed by an adjective, then *of a* and a noun. (In the rare instances where a plural noun is used, *a* is omitted.) Our evidence shows the idiom to be almost entirely oral; it is rare in print except in reported speech. The earliest examples we have seen so far are in the American Dialect Dictionary and date back to 1942 and 1943. It is undoubtedly at least somewhat older.

This current idiom is just one of a group of idioms that are characterized by the presence of *of a* as the link between a noun and some sort of preceding qualifier. Perhaps the oldest of these is the *kind of a* or *sort of a* construction, which is used by Shakespeare and is even older than that. It has been aspersed by usage commentators since 1779 (see KIND OF A, SORT OF A).

The newspaperman has the same kind of a job as the housewife, eat it and forget it, read it and forget it — Flannery O'Connor, letter, 16 Feb. 1963

Nouns other than *kind* and *sort* are also found in this construction:

There's some class of a leak above —Myles na gCopaleen (Flann O'Brien), *The Best of Myles,* 1968

Similar to these is the *giant of a man* idiom, which has not been aspersed, as far as we know. Like the *kind of a* idiom, it has a noun as its head:

. . . thanks to their idiot of a King's being Catholic —Henry Adams, letter, 22 Apr. 1859

Francis Lee Pratt, a writer of New England dialect stories in the late 19th century, used another similar idiom in which *first-rate* does the work of a noun. It was presumably current in New England at that time, because she used it several times.

. . . and Captain Ben makes a first-rate of a husband —"Captain Ben's Choice," in *Mark Twain's Library of Humor,* 1888

When *enough, more,* or *much* is used in place of the noun, the idiom is scarcely noticeable:

The show made enough of a hit for us to have to give a command performance —Alexander Woollcott, letter, 4 Dec. 1917

Instead, she's more of a mid-sized, no-nonsense cruiser —John Owens, *Boating,* January 1984

This is too much of a temptation to the editor — Ring Lardner, preface, *How to Write Short Stories,* 1924

A possible forerunner of the current idiom is an older one in which the head is *considerable.* The Dictionary of American Regional English has examples going back as far as 1766 and shows two forms of the construction: *considerable of a* and *a considerable of a.*

> A brick came through the window with a splintering crash, and gave me a considerable of a jolt in the back —Mark Twain, *Sketches Old and New,* 1875 (in DARE)

The examples in our files have the first *a* omitted:

> For a high toned agitator and Mayor of the Tombstone city water works it is considerable of a comedown —*Tombstone Epitaph,* ca. 1880, in Douglas D. Martin, *Tombstone's Epitaph,* 1951

> ... who at that time was considerable of a Socialist —*The Autobiography of William Allen White,* 1946

> ... that is considerable of an understatment —Rolfe Humphries, ed., introduction, *New Poems by American Poets,* 1953

> ... *The McGill News* apparently caused considerable of a furore by printing a "top secret" picture of the famous fence —*McGill News,* Spring 1954

> ... and it was quite evident that he fancied himself considerable of a sheik —Octavus Roy Cohen, in *Great Railroad Stories of the World,* ed. Samuel Moskowitz, 1954

We conclude that all is not known about these idioms. Whether they are all structurally related in fact or simply seem to be from the sharing of *of a* is uncertain. Of those forms that are American (or North American)—the present idiom, the *first-rate* one, the *considerable* one—only the *first-rate* version appears to be geographically limited. The others seem to be widespread.

The only sure thing is that when normative usage writers encounter these idioms their reaction is to condemn. Thus, we have had 200 years of condemnation of *kind of a* in spite of its literary use. MacCracken & Sandison 1917 condemned "rather of an athlete" and was dubious about "He isn't much of an athlete." And so it goes, right down to the current idiom:

> ... Is "honesty" too strong of a word? —advt., *N.Y. Times Mag.,* 10 Feb. 1980

Reader's Digest 1983 and Copperud 1980 condemn this as nonstandard and erroneous. But the only stricture on it suggested by our evidence is that it is a spoken idiom: you will not want to use it much in writing except of the personal kind.

of any See ANY 3.

of course *Of course* is commonly used in writing to qualify some statement of fact that the writer is sure most of the readers already know, but some may not, and others may need reminding of. It is added as a sort of courtesy, as if the unvarnished statement might insult the intelligence of the majority who can be expected to know.

> On the Continent and in England, soccer is, of course, the most popular mass sport —Joseph Wechsberg, *New Yorker,* 22 Jan. 1955

> ... but being Jewish she could not, of course, be accepted by a sorority —John Corry, *Harper's,* February 1971

> ... on the commercial networks, and of course these same programs can also be viewed on cable — Thomas Whiteside, *New Yorker,* 3 June 1985

A few commentators mention that some people dislike the use of *of course* for the purpose of one-upmanship when it is attached to some little-known fact. Its invidious use is well illustrated by this example:

> Your reviewer quotes me: "A certain Spanish bishop called Simancas ..." Thereupon he loftily observes: "Simancas, of course, was not a bishop, but a place." His *of course* is inimitable. He has *always* known all about Simancas, of course! —Wyndham Lewis, *Times Literary Supp.,* 16 Oct. 1948

It can be used less nastily:

> ... mentioned quite casually that, of course, quasars had been a pet interest of his because he and a colleague had discovered the first one —Tom Buckley, *N.Y. Times Mag.,* 12 Sept. 1976

A couple of other commentators object to its use to buttress unsubstantiated assertions; the example given is of this sort: "The administration, of course, is corrupt." Our files have no good examples of this use, which may be more common in oral discussions and in partisan publications than in ordinary edited prose.

off *Off* in the sense of "from" is disparaged in a few books: Opdyke 1939, Longman 1984, Trimmer & McCrimmon 1988. Mittins et al. 1970 put a sentence with "bought some tomatoes off" in their survey, and found it ranked very low in acceptability, but they were unable to find many commentators who mention it and were unable to discover any rationale for its disapproval. None of our sources provides any rationale either. The OED dates such use of the preposition from the middle of the 16th century, and adds "esp. with *take, buy, borrow, hire,* and the like." A handful of modern examples:

> ... so I took the bike off Joe and we worked this stunt —Ian Cross, *The God Boy,* 1973

> ... taking a long draw off a bottle of light brew — Glenn Lewis, *Houston Post,* 26 Aug. 1984

> ... I figured that if two could live on eighteen hundred dollars a year three could struggle along some way on the income off one hundred and fifty thousand dollars —Ring Lardner, *The Big Town,* 1921

> ... were hunted on foot as well as off a pony —Rex Hudson, *Shooting Times & Country Mag.,* 31 Mar. 1976

> ... eventually the government banned them off the radio stations —Michael Manley, quoted in *Jamaica Jour.,* March/June 1973

> ... videocassette recorders, with which they can record shows off their cable systems or off the networks —Thomas Whiteside, *New Yorker,* 3 June 1985

Some of the uses here were undoubtedly not even thought of by the critics. There is nothing wrong with *off* in the sense of "from," although it is perhaps more often a speech form than a written one and to many people it will suggest uneducated speech. So, while the objection may have no rational foundation, you should at least be aware that it exists.

For discussion of *off of* used in the same way and drawing the same criticism, see OFF OF.

offensive   When *offensive* is used with a prepositional-phrase complement, the preposition is almost always *to:*

> Yes; it is in two points offensive to me —Jane Austen, *Persuasion,* 1818

> ... it's offensive to a gentleman's feelings when his word isn't believed —Dorothy L. Sayers, *The Nine Tailors,* 1934

> ... it is far less offensive to modern taste than many other situations —T. S. Eliot, "Thomas Heywood," in *Selected Essays,* 1932

> This mannerism which has become so offensive to the friends of the Sperbers —Norman Mailer, *Advertisements for Myself,* 1959

off from   The OED notes that the adverb *off* is frequently used with *from* (as well as *of*—see OFF OF). The OED treats this combination as if it were entirely standard but shows fewer examples of it than of *off of.* Other examples can be found in the works of Jonson, Milton, Swift, Defoe, and Blake. A few commentators—MacCracken & Sandison 1917, Lincoln Library 1924, Jensen 1935, Little, Brown 1980, Heritage 1982—object to the *from* in *off from* as redundant (as they do to the *of* in *off of*) in contexts where *off* can stand alone as a preposition. Watt 1967 calls it rare. He may be right, as modern citations for *off from* are very hard to find.

In fact, we have none in our collection more recent than Melville's *Pierre* (1852):

> ... which no flannel, or thickest fur, or any fire then could keep off from me ...

The OED ends with a letter of Carlyle's (1871).

Other combinations of *off* and *from* have never been subject to criticism:

> Nor can China have taken with a light heart her decision to sheer off from the West and to side with Russia —Arnold J. Toynbee, *London Calling,* 18 Mar. 1954

> ... he cut himself off from friends and the public eye —*Newsweek,* 12 June 1967

An idiom considered standard by the OED and of apparently so little use now can hardly be a major worry. The OED notes a peculiarity of this idiom—it can be reversed:

> Surreptitiously Miss Thriplow slipped the opal ring from off the little finger of her right hand —Aldous Huxley, *Those Barren Leaves,* 1925

offhand, offhanded, offhandedly   *Offhand* has been in use as both an adjective and adverb for about 300 years. It is an older word and a shorter word than *offhanded* and *offhandedly,* and has therefore been preferred to one or both of them by a few usage commentators from the time of Utter 1916. About *offhanded* there is little to be said except that it is a standard word which was first recorded in 1835 and is used in much the same way as *offhand,* but is less common:

> ... with offhanded humor and the intimate ironies of Yiddish inflections —Lincoln Caplan, *Saturday Rev.,* 15 Oct. 1977

> ... an offhanded way with plot and structure — Richard Locke, *N.Y. Times Book Rev.,* 21 May 1978

The adverb *offhandedly,* however, is quite distinct from the adverb *offhand.* The most common adverbial use of *offhand* is as a sentence modifier which basically means "without premeditation or preparation":

> Offhand, this would not seem too far-fetched — *Commonweal,* 9 Oct. 1970

> Offhand, I'd say that there will be at least nine starters —Audax Minor, *New Yorker,* 5 June 1971

> ... but, offhand, this particular pair wouldn't have been my first choice —Max Lerner, *Saturday Rev.,* 29 May 1976

Offhandedly is never used in this way. It also differs from *offhand* in that it can modify adjectives (*offhand* cannot), it is sometimes modified by other adverbs (*offhand* never is), and it almost always means "casually" (*offhand* rarely does):

> As Kagan somewhat offhandedly sums up a portion of the findings —Anne Bernays, *Atlantic,* March 1970

> ... the off-handedly monotonous renderings of Auden —*Times Literary Supp.,* 16 July 1971

> ... imperturbably snobbish and offhandedly puncturing —John Simon, *New York,* 1 Nov. 1971

> ... said it so offhandedly that one would think there was nothing particularly spooky —Robert F. Jones, *Sports Illustrated,* 1 June 1981

Note that *offhand* could not be used idiomatically in any of these passages.

Summary: The adjective *offhanded* is a relatively uncommon synonym of *offhand.* It is standard and respectable, but can easily be replaced by the shorter word if you want it to. The adverb *offhandedly,* however, is common, useful, and distinct from the adverb *offhand.* If anyone tells you to replace *offhandedly* with *offhand,* pay no attention.

office   The turning of nouns into verbs is frequently condemned by commentators. One of these verbs created by functional shift is *office,* and it is condemned by Copperud 1980. Copperud also reports that Harper 1975 disapproves, though we have not been able to locate the passage. He further states that only Webster recognizes the use, and gives as an example a passive transitive use that is not recognized in either Webster's Second or Webster's Third, although both dictionaries recognize other senses of the verb.

This particular functional shift began in the 15th century, according to the OED, which also recognizes the verb. Shakespeare was not diffident about making a verb of *office.* Most of the OED senses are now obsolete, but the OED Supplement provides examples of the intransitive sense which is recorded in Webster's Third. It means "to have an office," or, followed by *with,* "to share an office." The OED Supplement marks the use *"U.S."* (we also have Canadian evidence) and dates it from 1892. Here are three recent examples (the first is Canadian):

> When I took my first teaching job at the University of Manitoba in 1949 I taught and officed in what was known as the old Broadway Buildings —James Reaney, preface, *Masks of Childhood,* 1972

Mr. Mardian spoke of a man who "officed in that same agency." —Israel Shenker, *N.Y. Times,* 11 Aug. 1973

. . . in some cases they office right in their homes — Arlene Rossen Cardozo, *Woman at Home,* 1976

The *office with* construction was the subject of a controversy at Louisiana State Universtiy in 1975; it is exactly the same construction as the entirely uncontroversial *room with.* Aside from this squabble and one other reported use, we have no evidence for this construction in our files. The OED Supplement has one, though, from 1936.

The passive transitive use criticized by Copperud does exist:

. . . historians who were apparently officed on an upper floor —Lillian Langseth-Chistensen, *Gourmet,* November 1979

This use is too rare at present for dictionary recognition.

officer The use of *officer* to mean "a member of a police force" has occasionally been criticized, chiefly on the theory that *officer* should only be applied to policemen and policewomen who have an officer's rank (as lieutenant or captain). This issue is now about a hundred years old.

It is no solecism to call a police constable an 'officer'. . . . A police-constable is a peace officer . . . and is therefore entitled to be styled an 'officer' —E. H. Marshall, *Notes & Queries,* 1888 (OED)

Peace officer has been used to mean "policeman" since at least 1714. *Police officer* was first recorded in this sense in 1806. Both terms continue to be used (*police officer* is especially common), and neither has been criticized:

. . . not a politician, but a highly respected peace officer —Harry S. Ashmore, *Center Mag.,* May 1968

The lowest-ranking police officer—the patrolman— has the greatest discretion —James Q. Wilson, *Harvard Today,* Autumn 1968

Officer by itself, however, still receives some unfavorable attention, although criticism of it is not widespread and tends now to be somewhat subdued. The principal use of *officer* in its "policeman" sense is as a respectful form of address, as in "Did I do something wrong, officer?" Evans 1957 considers this a "slight archaism" which is likely to be passing out of use. Bernstein 1965 says that "the feeling among the discriminating is that to speak of a policeman as an *officer* has a provincial flavor, much as has *counselor* for a lawyer. . . ." He also asserts that it is "worthwhile to preserve the distinction between ordinary cops and officers." Having given these opinions, however, he then admits that police departments themselves do not observe the distinction and that *officer* is sometimes the only suitable way to address a policeman. Copperud 1964 sees merit in the *patrolman–officer* distinction, but he notes that it is not supported by usage.

Contrary to the prediction of Evans, the "policeman" sense of *officer* is not falling into disuse. It continues to be common and is entirely standard. There may still be some people out there who dislike hearing a patrolman addressed as "officer," but you can be fairly sure that the patrolman will make no objection.

officiate Harper 1975, 1985 assures us that *officiate* is only an intransitive verb, but *officiate* has been used transitively since the 17th century. Some transitive uses are still alive:

Spencer, a master of ceremonies in Britain who has officiated some 700 royal occasions —Julie Gilbert, *Houston Post,* 27 Aug. 1984

And sports fans know that games, matches, and contests are officiated—often poorly. Let us assure you that *officiate* can be used transitively to mean "to carry out (an official duty or function)," "to serve as a leader or celibrant of (a ceremony)," or "to administer the rules of (a game or sport) esp. as a referee or umpire."

officious, official A handful of commentators (almost all British) and the Oxford American Dictionary warn against confusion of *officious* and *official.* Fowler 1926 started the tradition of having an entry for these words, but his point concerns their technical meanings in diplomacy rather than their potential for confusion in their ordinary meanings. We have no evidence of such confusion in our files. *Officious* was occasionally used as a synonym of *official* in previous centuries, but that sense of the word is now obsolete. *Official* has never been used to mean "officious." There may be no problem, in fact.

Officious in current English is essentially synonymous with *meddlesome.* Here are a few typical examples of current use:

. . . usually barges into things, officious and overconfident —Lloyd N. Jeffrey, *CEA Critic,* January 1971

. . . experienced educators and teachers—rather than officious bureaucrats —Harold Howe II, *Saturday Rev.,* 20 Nov. 1971

. . . the silence was shattered by the bustle and officious chatter —*Runner's World,* October 1980

off of *Off of* is an innocuous idiom—a compound preposition made of the adverb *off* and the preposition *of*—that has been in use since the 16th century:

CARDINAL. What art thou lame?
SIMPCOX.   Ay, God Almighty help me!
SUFFOLK. How cam'st thou so?
SIMPCOX.   A fall off of a tree.
WIFE. A plum tree, master
                —Shakespeare, *2 Henry VI,* 1592

Ayres 1881 seems to have been the first commentator to question the phrase. He objected to its use in "Give me a yard off of this piece of calico," calling the *of* "vulgarly superfluous." From Ayres the criticism found its way into MacCracken & Sandison 1917, the *Literary Digest* (10 June 1922), Lincoln Library 1924, Whipple 1924, *Century Collegiate Handbook* 1924, Powell 1925, Lurie 1927, Jensen 1935, and so on through a host of handbooks right up to Cook 1985 and Harper 1985. Ebbitt & Ebbitt 1982 notes the occurrence of *off of* in general writing; Bryant 1962 and Watt 1967 find it informal. Most of the rest follow Ayres and call the *of* redundant.

The OED notes that the adverb *off* occurs with *of* in many of its senses, with the note "formerly and still *dialectally,*" which is echoed in Bell & Cohn 1981: "Formerly in standard use but now dialectal." The comment is probably true of British English: the only British commentator to mention the construction (Phythian 1979) says that *off of* is common in some parts of England, and we also have a citation for it from a collection of Suffolk dialect.

Here are some live examples of how *off of* has been used. First a few older ones:

> ... to the Rose Tavern, and there got half a breast of mutton, off of the spit, and dined all alone —Samuel Pepys, diary, 18 May 1668

> ... he entered into a very narrow passage, which was about a furlong off of the porter's lodge —John Bunyan, *Pilgrim's Progress,* 1678

> I could not keep my Eyes off of her —Sir Richard Steele, *The Spectator,* No. 306, 1712 (OED)

A couple of more recent British examples:

> "... only for that there forty pound Mr. Noakes had off of me." —Dorothy L. Sayers, *Busman's Honeymoon,* 1937

> ... and he takes a big parcel of newspaper off of Tiger and opens it up —Richard Llewellyn, *None But the Lonely Heart,* 1943

These are all American:

> I judge the telephone company never made much money off of Mrs. Whitridge —Irvin S. Cobb, *Old Judge Priest,* 1915

> ... don't take your eye off of just what happened —Booth Tarkington, *Ramsey Milholland,* 1919

> "... Who the hell do you eat off of ... ?" —Ernest Hemingway, *To Have and Have Not,* 1937

> "... She figured Brunold had taken a walkout powder, so she was off of men." —Erle Stanley Gardner, *The Case of the Counterfeit Eye,* 1935

> ... they could do far worse than to strip their regional cloaks off of their minds —N.Y. Herald Tribune Book Rev., 16 Apr. 1939

> ... there were moments when, with several cars coming toward me, and two or three honking behind me, and a curved road ahead, I would take my foot off of everything and wail, "Where the hell am I?" — James Thurber, letter, August 1935

> ... I'd borrow two or three dollars off of the judge —Mark Twain, *Huckleberry Finn,* 1884 (*A Mark Twain Lexicon,* 1938)

> "... Eck knows all about them horses ... how much him and that Texas man aim to get for them, make off of them...." —William Faulkner, *Spotted Horses,* 1940

> ... the people lived off of Anise Slane's hoarded gold —Margaret Marchand, *Saturday Rev.,* 27 Apr. 1940

> ... had overstocked in July and were now living off of their fat —Time, 18 Dec. 1950

We sold our home in June and have been living off of our equity ever since —Vellar C. Plantz, *Forbes,* 1 Dec. 1970

She wore a necklace of every ear, nose and eye she had gouged off of men in fights —American Guide Series: Louisiana, 1941

'Did you take it off of his finger?' I asked —Robert Penn Warren, *Partisan Rev.,* Fall 1944

LaGuerre, who couldn't take his eyes off of it — *Time,* 10 June 1946

> ... he could give you a scolding that would burn the hide off of you —Harry S. Truman, quoted in Merle Miller, *Plain Speaking,* 1973

> ... would be much obliged if you would send them a copy that I get the 40% off of —Flannery O'Connor, letter, 24 May 1952

> ... maybe you do need to be involved, to get the edges beaten off of you a little every day —William Faulkner, 25 Feb. 1957, in *Faulkner in the University,* 1959

> "Well, it feels as though you were on a very hard and sharp horn, and you wish sincerely that you were off of it...." —Barnaby Conrad, *Matador,* 1952

> ... hoping to lure women off of their jobs — *Muhammad Speaks,* 31 May 1968

> ... forcing most other countries off of the gold standard —E. W. Cundiff, *Current History,* December 1951

> You can't make nearly as much money off of horse farmers as you can off tractor farmers —Draft Horse Jour., Autumn 1983

> "Sir, please get off of me." —Jay McInerney, *Bright Lights, Big City,* 1984

> This night glow is sunlight being reflected off of cosmic dust particles —N.Y. Times, 10 Mar. 1969

You can see that in American English *off of* is used in contexts ranging from uneducated (Huck Finn) to general. It still seems to be primarily a form used in speech: most of the citations from fiction represent fictional speech. It is an idiom that occurred naturally in the speech of William Faulkner, Flannery O'Connor, Harry S. Truman, and James Thurber, among others. If it is part of your personal idiom and you are not writing on an especially elevated plane, you have no reason to avoid *off of.*

offspring   *Offspring* functions both as a singular and as a plural:

> Given a cooperative offspring of course mother is the best placed person of all to stimulate her child's intellect —Times Literary Supp., 14 Nov. 1968

> ... others young enough to have been her own offspring —Peter Quennell, *N.Y. Times Book Rev.,* 10 Oct. 1976

Offsprings also has a long history of occasional use as an alternative plural:

> ... half a dozen male offsprings and a girl or two — Saki (H. H. Munro), *The Unbearable Bassington,* 1912

But our evidence indicates that the *-s* plural is now rarely used. As Copperud 1970, 1980 notes, some people consider it an error.

oftener, oftenest   Ayres 1881 approved these forms and disapproved *more often, most often.* Between him and Partridge 1942 someone must have taken the opposite view, because Partridge defends the inflected forms. So does Copperud 1980. Our recent evidence shows both forms in use, with *more often* and *most often* used about twice as often as their inflected equivalents.

of which   See WHOSE 1.

oh   See O, OH.

O.K., OK, okay   1. *Spelling.* The spellings *O.K., OK,* and *okay* are the predominant ones today. We find a few publishers that use *ok* and *o.k.,* but they are in the minority. We have a Canadian instance of *okeh,* the form preferred by Woodrow Wilson because he believed it to be a Choctaw word meaning "it is so."

There is little to choose in frequency between the first three forms at the present time. *Okay* may be slightly ahead of *O.K.* and *OK.* Some commentators—Reader's Digest 1983, for example—prefer *okay* because when used as a verb it has the advantage of taking regular inflections without apostrophes.

2. *O.K.* is used as an adjective, adverb, noun, and verb. It has been a bugbear of the college handbook from MacCracken & Sandison 1917 to Trimmer & McCrimmon 1988. You may safely infer from this that it is not okay to use *O.K.* in a freshman English paper. Flesch 1983 and Reader's Digest 1983 both point out that *O.K.* is widely used on a much higher level than the college handbooks and usage panels are willing to recognize. Flesch says that it has long been in standard use, not only in this country, but throughout the English-speaking world. The OED Supplement supports this view by showing examples of use in British English since the 1860s.

As an example of the high status of *O.K.,* Flesch cites William F. Buckley, Jr. Here are a few examples from our files:

> No OK comparison is too OK for the Hitchcock exegetes —Stanley Kauffmann, *Before My Eyes,* 1980

> All this has been okayed by the Hays Office, Good Housekeeping and the survivors of the Haymarket Riots —Groucho Marx, letter, 1945

> ... and feel O.K. about ourselves in transit —Jay McInerney, *N.Y. Times Book Rev.,* 24 Mar. 1985

> On April 4, the Fed OK'd an acquisition of a Columbus, Ohio thrift —*Wall Street Jour.,* 12 Apr. 1982

> ... he starts out with a couple of Ole and Lena jokes, which they like okay —Garrison Keillor, *Lake Wobegon Days,* 1985

> With the old school, it's OK, too —Mary McGrory, *Boston Globe,* 22 July 1984

> I infer that that would be okay with you fellows —John O'Hara, letter, 30 July 1956

> The sommelier looked particularly taken aback. But La Vanderbilt merely smiled sweetly, reasoning that it must be the OK thing to do —Callan, *Punch,* 6 Mar. 1974

> Every project has received Brooke Astor's personal okay —Arthur M. Schlesinger, Jr., *Architectural Digest,* May 1986

> ... constituting the first new viral vaccine okay by the FDA in a decade —*Science News,* 26 Dec. 1981

The inescapable conclusion is that the handbooks are looking backward and not at contemporary usage. *O.K.* (or *OK* or *okay*) is widely used on every level of speech and on all levels of writing except the stodgiest. Unless you are taking freshman English, you can use it freely.

old adage   We find the expression *old adage* called a tautology by Vizetelly 1922 because an adage is an old saying. He repeats his animadversion for the Lincoln Library in 1924. Theodore Bernstein calls *old adage* redundant in *Winners & Sinners* in 1962; he says the same thing in 1965; Copperud 1964, 1970, 1980 holds the same view; Harper 1975 calls it redundant and repeats the charge in 1985; Bremner 1980, Bryson 1984, and Kilpatrick 1984 come to the same conclusion. All of these commentators base their opinions on the fact that *adage* is defined in dictionaries as "an old saying."

Whence this definition? Johnson 1755 defines *adage* as "a maxim handed down from antiquity." Noah Webster's 1828 definition, "an old saying, which has obtained credit by long use," continued in Merriam-Webster dictionaries until 1934. Editors of Webster's Second noted a change in the way the word was being used, however, a change exemplified by this citation from the *Yale Review* (October 1917):

> It is an adage that the tired business man abets his wife in all. . . .

So the editors of Webster's Second snicked *old* out of the definition. At the time Webster's Third was edited, the definition was completely revised. It had become evident that an adage, while embodying some common observation, need not come down from antiquity:

> Some people forget the lovely adage that people who live in glass houses should undress in the dark — *Publishers Weekly,* 12 Aug. 1950

> ... what is meant by the adage, "an imperfect democracy is better than a perfect autocracy" — Lucius Garvin, *A Modern Introduction to Ethics,* 1953

> "A stock well bought is already half way to a profit", could be an adage exemplifying the wisdom of proper timing —pamphlet issued by Stock Trend Service, Inc., 1954

> The adage that the rise of civilization is the result of a series of intellectual minorities pitting themselves against the barbaric masses is open to question — Richard L. Russell, *N.Y. Times Mag.,* 23 Jan. 1955

It is also worth our notice that *old* has gone with *adage* since the word first came into English:

> He forgat the olde adage, saynge in tyme of peace provyde for warre —Edward Hall, *Chronicle (The Union of Two Noble and Illustre Families of Lancastre and York),* 1548 (OED)

> 'Much company, much knavery'—as true as that old adage 'Much courtesy, much subtlety.' —Thomas Nashe, *The Unfortunate Traveller,* 1594

So it is not surprising that *old* has continued to accompany *adage* both from force of habit and, in more recent use, to impute age to the adage, which may not be very old at all:

> ... racegoers remembered the old adage, "Second in the Trial, first in the Derby." After all, they'd seen it come true five times in sixteen years, which is quite enough to establish an adage —Audax Minor, *New Yorker,* 8 May 1954

Or the *old* may merely be factual:

> No saying was ever more true than the old adage that without his tools the workman is helpless —Thomas F. McNally, *Bulletin of the National Catholic Education Association,* August 1949

> Contrary to the old adage, practice won't make you perfect —Willie Mosconi, *Winning Pocket Billiards,* 1965

> . . . the old adage holds—what fools we mortals be —Irving Wallace, *The Plot,* 1967

> . . . the old adage "misery loves company" —Natalie Babbitt, *N.Y. Times Book Rev.,* 24 June 1979

Old adage is as old as *adage* itself in English. Usage writers who object to it on grounds of redundancy have not taken note of a change of meaning. Go ahead and use it where it seems apt to you.

old cliché, old maxim Copperud 1980 and Kilpatrick 1984 object to *old cliché* and Kilpatrick to *old maxim* on the same grounds that they object to *old adage.* The basic argument is set forth at OLD ADAGE. But *maxim* and *cliché* are not quite like *adage.* Neither is used particularly often with *old,* although both are occasionally, and *cliché* more commonly than *maxim.*

Cliché does have some tendency to attract intensifying modifiers that could be objected to as redundant, if some quibbler chose to do so. Among these (in our files) are *time-worn, familiar, tired, traditional,* and *overworked. Old* pops up more often than these do:

> I laughed too much at this old cliché, but she was certain I had never heard the joke before —Burl Ives, *Wayfaring Stranger,* 1952

> . . . as the old cliché has it —*Harper's,* May 1939

> . . . the old cliché that "to serve government is a privilege." —Vannevar Bush, *N.Y. Times Mag.,* 13 June 1954

Sometimes *venerable:*

> So firmly established is this venerable cliché — Ernest Newman, *N.Y. Times Book Rev.,* 27 Mar. 1955

Kilpatrick wonders why we can't have new clichés. Well, we have had them:

> The ancient gag of the B-picture director who announced, "The boss says, don't use any more old clichés, so we gotta think up some new clichés" — Craig Rice, quoted in *Saturday Rev.,* 18 Mar. 1950

Clichés also come in *modern* and *current.*

A maxim is most often a pithy expression of some rule of conduct or general principle and need not be old at all, so modification of *maxim* by *old* or *ancient* is not really open to the objection of redundancy.

> Our people would do well to recollect that ancient maxim of Frederick the Great —Henry Adams, letter, 10 July 1863

> There is an ancient maxim "Many receive advice, few profit by it" —Sara M. Jordan, *New England Jour. of Medicine,* 21 May 1953

> It is an old military maxim that no successful offensive can be launched except from a secure base — Vannevar Bush, *N.Y. Times Mag.,* 13 June 1954

> . . . the old Greek maxim that a large book is a great evil —Historical Introduction, OED Supplement, 1933

We conclude that there is no reason to object to *old* with *maxim* and little or none to object to *old* with *cliché.* We have chosen examples of a certain age to show that such use, if not as old as *old adage,* is not of particularly recent occurrence.

old-fashion, old-fashioned Copperud 1964 considers *old-fashion* an error for *old-fashioned.* A more objective view would be that it is an extremely rare variant. Both terms were first recorded in the 17th century, and both have been used by reputable writers, but *old-fashioned* seems always to have been far more common than *old-fashion.* In current English, *old-fashioned* is the usual, almost invariable choice. Most of the little recent evidence we have for *old-fashion* is from advertisements, in which it may have been chosen for its somewhat archaic quality or it may be a pronunciation spelling. The current tendency seems to be to spell it as two words:

> OLD FASHION CANDIES —label, Arlington Candy Co., ca. 1961

> THE GOOD OLD FASHION KIND —advt., *Early American Life,* August 1980

oldster *Oldster* was coined in the 19th century by analogy with *youngster.* Early citations typically include both words:

> Her eyes would play the Devil with the youngsters before long,—'and the oldsters too . . . ,' added the Major —Charles Dickens, *Dombey and Son,* 1848 (OED)

And current usage often has *oldster* and *youngster* keeping company still:

> Are you a youngster hunting around for something more permanent . . . ? An oldster searching for something less constricting . . . ? —Alan Green, *Saturday Rev.,* 26 Feb. 1972

> . . . occupy the youngsters so that the oldsters can pursue their own activities —*Town & Country,* January 1983

But *oldster* also frequently stands on its own:

> . . . the hospitality of a delightful oldster —Robert Trumbull, *N.Y. Times Book Rev.,* 21 Sept. 1975

> . . . an oldster's recalling his childhood as a "breaking boy" —Judith Crist, *Saturday Rev.,* 5 Mar. 1977

> . . . the respect youth feels for the oldsters who brought them their heritage —Ray Walters, *N.Y. Times Book Rev.,* 18 Dec. 1977

Such success as *oldster* has enjoyed can be attributed in part to the need writers and speakers feel for a word that refers to old people without disparaging connotations. The underlying problem is that the word *old* itself has such connotations in our culture, so that to call someone an "old man" or an "old woman" is to run the risk of giving offense. However, the use of *oldster* has remained limited primarily to writing in which the tone is somewhat humorous or jaunty. Usage commentators who have taken note of *oldster* include Evans 1957, who strongly criticizes it as a term of condescension, and Flesch 1964, who calls it "an ugly invention." It is nonetheless standard within its range of use.

omitted relative   For omission of the relative pronoun of a restrictive clause, see CONTACT CLAUSES.

on   1. *On, upon.* A sizable number of commentators recommend that you choose *on* when you have a choice between *on* and *upon. On* is certainly the more common word: the Brown University Corpus (Kučera & Francis 1967) shows it to be used more than thirteen times as often as *upon. Upon,* however, is far from rare; it ranks 205th in the list of the top 6000 words in frequency in that corpus. Clearly many writers do not choose to follow the handbooks' advice. Here are some fairly recent examples of *upon* at work:

> . . . a novel means of spacecraft propulsion based upon the extraction of energy from the electromagnetic field of the solar wind —Charles P. Sonett, *Science,* 8 Dec. 1972

> . . . of course that depends upon who is looking at each one —William Faulkner, 13 May 1957, in *Faulkner in the University,* 1959

> . . . these questions and others Barbara Walters can be depended upon to ask —Aristides, *American Scholar,* Winter 1981–1982

> Upon Seaver's arrival, several of his teammates acted like star-struck teenyboppers —Ron Fimrite, *Sports Illustrated,* 14 July 1986

> . . . economic assumptions agreed upon by business, labor and government —Felix G. Rohatyn, *The Twenty-Year Century,* 1983

2. See ONTO, ON TO.

on account of   1. *On account of* is commonly used as a compound preposition equivalent to *because of:*

> . . . partly on account of the violent attacks on their work —*Times Literary Supp.,* 18 Dec. 1969

It is especially likely in writing that has a conversational tone:

> At first I figure I am going to like Otash on account of the lingo he uses —Dan Greenburg, *N.Y. Times Book Rev.,* 10 Oct. 1976

> . . . lived in my house only on account of a pretty casual decision about real estate —Garrison Keillor, *Lake Wobegon Days,* 1985

On account of was first recorded in this use in 1792, and has long been established as standard in both British and American English. Usage commentators have no special fondness for it, but most of them give it at least grudging acceptance, if only because they regard it as the lesser of two evils (see section 2 below). Harper 1975, 1985, for example, describes it as "acceptable in speech." Our evidence shows that it is also common in writing, although certainly far less common than *because of.*
2. *On account of* is also sometimes used as a compound conjunction equivalent to *because.* This use of the phrase is limited almost entirely to dialectal and nonstandard speech. Its occasional occurrence in writing is

strictly for the purpose—often humorous—of imitating or evoking the quality of such speech:

> Scotsmen, we're told, are virile on account of they don't wear knickers under their kilts —Marje Proops, *Sunday Mirror* (London), 10 Nov. 1974

> . . . his feet are on the ground on account of no money remained for a pedestal —Garrison Keillor, *Lake Wobegon Days,* 1985

Several usage commentators take the conjunctive *on account of* seriously enough to condemn its use, but we suspect that such condemnation serves little purpose. The nonstandard nature of the phrase will be obvious to anyone who encounters it in reading.

on behalf of   See BEHALF.

one   1. The pronoun *one,* when it stands for a person, is usually the mark of a formal style. In such a context it may refer to a particular kind of individual or it may mean "anyone at all" or it may be used as a substitute for *I* or *me.* In the first two examples that follow, a particular kind of individual is referred to; in the third, the meaning seems to be "anyone at all":

> One might wish that the book consisted entirely of such fresh and surprising matter —John Updike, *New Yorker,* 24 May 1982

> In the next few years, one marched in Harlem and elsewhere . . . , went on sympathy marches for civil-rights workers who were killed . . . —Nora Sayre, *Esquire,* March 1970

> . . . he now seemed to have a new girl friend, the wife of a gangster who was lying in hospital after a shooting affray, a rather dangerous relationship one would have thought —Graham Greene, *Getting to Know the General,* 1984

The use of *one* in place of *I* or *me* (or *one's* in place of *my*) is chiefly British, and it has been objected to by some commentators—mostly American. In the first of these examples, the speaker has been asked if he considers himself an ecumenical person.

> Oh yes, very much so. I attended the World Council conferences in New Delhi and Uppsala, and am planning now to go to Nairobi; but it's not only a question of the official level, one's whole ministry has been along ecumenical lines —Donald Coggan, Archbishop of Canterbury, quoted in *The Economist,* 29 Mar. 1975

> I would reject a natural lawn even if it made sense in a garden like mine and wouldn't look . . . as though one were too slatternly to keep a garden decent —Eleanor Perenyi, *Green Thoughts,* 1983

In some cases like this, the use of *one* can broaden beyond *I.* In the first of the examples that follow, *one* can easily be taken to mean "you and I"; in the second, "I and others" may be intended:

> . . . I do not think him so very ill-looking as I did— at least one sees many worse —Jane Austen, *Mansfield Park,* 1814

> I'm watching this pretty carefully and I hope this issue will come up in the Lords and one may be able to speak about it —Donald Coggan, Archbishop of Canterbury, quoted in *The Economist,* 29 Mar. 1975

In some cases, the reader or the person being addressed is clearly one of the particular kind of individual being referred to, and in these cases, *one* comes close to meaning simply *you,* but even here, some broadening of view can be discerned. The following example is from a novel written in the second person, and *one* is clearly meant to be more inclusive than *you.*

> As long as one is at one's desk by ten-thirty, one is relatively safe. Somehow you manage to miss this banker's deadline at least once a week —Jay McInerney, *Bright Lights, Big City,* 1984

At least one book on writing (Trimble 1975) recommends avoiding *one* and using *you* when addressing the reader on the grounds that the printed page itself puts enough distance between reader and writer, and that it need not be increased by using more formality. E. B. White agrees, but sees a problem:

> As for me, I try to avoid the impersonal "one" but have discovered that it is like a face you keep encountering in the streets and can't always avoid bowing to —letter, 26 Sept. 1963

2. A question that comes up frequently in connection with *one* is what pronoun to use later in the sentence to refer to it. *He, they,* and *one* are all likely candidates, but which one do you choose? This choice has been a matter of contention since the 18th century.

It appears that the earliest solution was to use *he, him,* and *his* to refer back to a beginning *one.* Shakespeare did so; Bernstein 1971 and Freeman 1983 both give the same quotation from *As You Like It.* The OED has an example from the 15th century and says that use of *he* and *his* was usual. The practice was attacked by Baker 1770 and by Alford 1866; they both recommended the consistent employment of *one, one's,* and *oneself* after *one.* There has been a great deal of subsequent comment, and a divergence of usage. Since the second half of the 19th century, British usage has tended to follow the consistent use of *one.* American usage—and American commentators—are divided. British commentators assert that *one . . . he* is an American practice, yet some American commentators (Bernstein 1971 and Watt 1967, for instance) recommend following British practice. So Americans do it both ways:

> Besides, life is too short for one to waste his time reading any but our best writers —Thomas Meehan, *N.Y. Times Book Rev.,* 14 Aug. 1983

> If one were to take literally all the tales of market coups that one hears over lunch tables, one would be astonished at how often one is asked to split the check —*New Yorker,* 10 May 1982

> . . . one is always paid for one's sins —Flannery O'Connor, letter, 5 May 1956

> And one must be careful not to shoot himself —Stuart Chase, *The Tyranny of Words,* 1938

Sometimes you can even find *one . . . you:*

> When one is very old, as I am . . . your legs give in before your head does —George Bernard Shaw, quoted in *Time,* 21 Oct. 1946

The Harper 1975, 1985 panel split nearly evenly on the *one . . . one, one . . . he* question, and one panelist offered the suggestion that the use of *one . . . one* might be stimulated by the desire to avoid the male chauvinism of *one . . . he.* While some of the other panelists

pooh-poohed the idea, the consideration of gender apparently enters into the use of the sequence *one . . . they, their, them,* which, if overlooked by the handbooks, is not missed by the OED. The OED says that the plural pronouns "were formerly in general use on account of their indefiniteness of gender" but that the practice "is now considered ungrammatical." The ungrammaticality here is a violation of formal or grammatical number agreement, and the OED's view is based on the assumption that *they, their, them* can only be plural (for a discussion of this subject, see THEY, THEIR, THEM).

Use of *they, their, them* in singular reference to *one* dates back to the 17th century and Sir Kenelm Digby (in OED). Some more recent examples are these:

> . . . shut up in a nasty Scotch jail, where one cannot even get the dirt brushed off their clothes —Sir Walter Scott (in Bolinger 1980)

> One could not help coveting the privileges they enjoyed for their sisters —Miss M. B. Edwards, *A Winter with the Swallows,* 1867 (in Hodgson 1889)

> . . . one may escape the duty by demonstrating themselves to be a hopeless administrator —*Harvard-Radcliffe Parents Newsletter* (in *New Yorker,* 2 Dec. 1985)

> What does one do to get to the stage where they can mentally orchestrate like this? —Ted Greene, *Guitar Player,* August 1981

> If one sees themself in the characters depicted herein, it is strictly a figment of their own imagination —publisher's disclaimer, quoted in Simon 1980

This last example illustrates as well as any the pressures and influences that lead to statements being made with *one.* First, there is the felt need to make the statement formal and dignified. This may be reinforced generally by the handbooks and usage books, which encourage the use of formal diction. Further, there is an old prejudice against the indefinite *you,* still repeated in some books (Freeman 1983, for example). You would not expect such a disclaimer to be as breezy as "If you think you are one of the characters in this book, you are imagining things." So *one* must be used in the interest of dignity. But what of a string of *one's* in the British fashion? "If one sees oneself in the characters depicted herein, it is strictly a figment of one's own imagination." This is perhaps too starchy for American taste. And for a modern publisher, use of third-person singular masculine pronouns is out, lest sexual bias be alleged. This leaves the *his or her* formulas a possibility: "If one sees himself or herself in the characters depicted herein, it is strictly a figment of his or her own imagination." In light of these possibilities, the attraction of *they, their, them* is obvious.

By now you may agree with several commentators that the best way out of one of these situations is to throw the whole passage out and start over—maybe the old impersonal formulas like "any resemblance to persons living or dead is strictly coincidental" did have their uses. And you can see that for the American writer in these cases there is no simple solution: you just have to handle them in the way that sounds best to you.

See also ONE OF THOSE WHO and the various articles at AGREEMENT.

one another, one another's See EACH OTHER 1, 2.

one in (out of) See AGREEMENT, SUBJECT-VERB: ONE OR MORE, ONE IN (OUT OF) ——— 2.

one of the See ONE OF THOSE WHO.

one of the ... if not the Phythian 1979 discusses this example:

> The new National Theatre is one of the most imaginative, if not the most imaginative, buildings of our time.

The problem here, says Phythian (and his view of this construction is shared by Bernstein 1965, Harper 1975, 1985, Shaw 1975, 1987, and Copperud 1964, 1970, 1980), is that the part of the sentence outside the commas calls for the plural *buildings,* and the part inside the commas calls for the singular *building.* The sentence is therefore ungrammatical.

This construction is somewhat similar to *as good or better than* (which see) in that it contains a grammatical anomaly or discontinuity that is more likely to be troubling to usage commentators than to ordinary readers. It does not hinder understanding and is at worst a stylistic blemish. You can revise the problem away easily enough by moving the noun forward to follow the first adjective; most of your readers are not likely to be aware of the difference.

We do not have much evidence for the construction. It may be infrequent in edited prose, or it may simply be that this is not the sort of construction that readily catches the attention of those who read to collect citations for dictionaries. It is older, naturally, than the comment on it:

> ... a busy America is one of the great, if not the greatest, influences —James Forrestal, quoted in *Time,* 20 Jan. 1947

A bit of a curiosity, perhaps, is this example with a singular rather than a plural noun after the commas. This would be equally unsatisfactory to the commentators; it is probably due to the attraction of the closer phrase.

> For we are in the midst of one of the greatest, if not the greatest, crisis of our national history —Louis M. Hacker, *N.Y. Herald Tribune Book Rev.,* 2 Nov. 1941

one of those things See ONE OF THOSE WHO.

one of those who Under this heading we have gathered several similar constructions, all of which display the same disputed point of grammar. We begin with Kilpatrick 1984, who reproaches himself for having written this sentence:

> In Washington we encounter *to prioritize* all the time; it is one of those things that makes Washington unbearable.

For Kilpatrick the error is in *makes;* the theory that makes the verb culpable—a theory going all the way back to Baker 1770—says that the antecedent of *that,* which is the subject of *makes,* is *things* and therefore the verb should be plural: *make.*

Kilpatrick was duly chastened when his error was pointed out to him by a correspondent, but a year or so later he wrote:

> With the expulsion of the PLO from Lebanon, Mr. Reagan may have caught one of those tides in the affairs of men which, taken at the flood, leads on to fortune.

This time his wrist was slapped by William F. Buckley, Jr. In contrition, Mr. Kilpatrick turned to Follett 1966, where he found stern comments about writers who "fumble their handling of the phrase." But he was able to find solace in the comments of some members of the Harper 1975 usage panel, 22 percent of whom preferred the singular verb.

The trouble with the firm rule of Follett 1966 and Baker 1770 (as well as Bache 1869, Bernstein 1962, and Shaw 1987) is that it has no firm foundation of usage to support it: it is largely airy theory. The practice these writers would correct can be found in Old English as early as the 10th century. The usages of the past cannot be undone, and if the same mental processes that led to past usages are still in effect, the reformers are going to have a hard time. In this case the mental process involves the pull of notional agreement (see NOTIONAL AGREEMENT, NOTIONAL CONCORD). Kilpatrick, in paraphrasing Follett, puts it this way:

> By a mental shortcut, the *one* in whom we are interested jumps over the class ... and links itself to the defining words. ...

Or here it is put another way:

> Jespersen (*Grammar,* II, 181) suggests that the singular verb or pronoun is 'attracted' to *one.* Perhaps this is but saying in grammatical terminology what may be otherwise expressed by saying that the writer or speaker is more immediately concerned with *one* than with *those* —John S. Kenyon, *American Speech,* October 1951

So it is simply a matter of which is to be master—*one* or *those.* In Kilpatrick's sentences and in those of a great many other writers, it has been *one:*

> My worthy Friend Sir ROGER is one of those who is not only at Peace within himself, but beloved and esteemed by all about him —Joseph Addison, *The Spectator,* No. 122, 20 July 1711

> Waugh is not one of those who finds the modern world attractive —Randolph S. Churchill, *Book-of-the-Month-Club News,* December 1945

> ... he is one of the few serious young novelists who has tried to go directly toward the center of post-war experience —Irving Howe, *New Republic,* 10 Nov. 1958

> ... analysis of one of the greatest minds which has been concerned with economic matters in this century —John Perry Miller, *Yale Rev.,* Autumn 1954

> ... is one of the few people alive who still writes a letter as if the telephone had never been invented —John Mason Brown, *Encore,* July 1946

> ... one of those rare books which justifies the jacket blurb —Cleveland Amory, *N.Y. Times Book Rev.,* 28 Feb. 1954

> They would sail to the Caribbean on one of those ships that was your hotel while you were in port, and it had better be an English ship —John P. Marquand, *Point of No Return,* 1949

> ... one of those film buffs who has seen everything and understood nothing —John Gregory Dunne, quoted in Simon 1980

The primacy of *one* in the writer's mind may be signaled by pronoun reference, too:

> ... he is one of those that must lose his employment whenever the great shake comes —Jonathan Swift, *Journal to Stella* (in Jespersen 1909–49, vol. 2)

> About the Lourdes business. . . . I will not be taking any bath. I am one of those people who could die for his religion easier than take a bath for it —Flannery O'Connor, letter, 17 Dec. 1957

But do not think that *one* is always the master. An article in *The English Journal* in October 1951 reported a citation count (from 1531–1951) showing five plural verbs to one singular. The actual preponderance in favor of the plural verb may not be so great—certainly it is not in our files. But it is plain that *those* is often the master:

> I am one of those People who by the general Opinion of the World are counted both Infamous and Unhappy —Joseph Addison, *The Spectator*, No. 203, 1711 (in Kenyon, *American Speech*, October 1951)

> He is one of those kind of people who are always very much pleased with every thing —William Hazlitt, letter, 5 Nov. 1809

> Tom Sawyer's Aunt Polly was one of those people who are infatuated with patent medicines —Mark Twain, "A Dose of Pain Killer," in *Mark Twain's Library of Humor*, 1888

> I don't want you to think I'm one of those people who are always talking about their bodily ailments —Frank Sullivan, *A Rock in Every Snowball*, 1946

> The urge to revisit his childhood is surely one of the magnets that draw a man to Yankee Stadium —Red Smith, *Saturday Rev.*, 26 June 1976

> ... Alexis Korner is one of the few genuine lightweights who turn up on the album —John Chance, *Rolling Stone*, 6 Jan. 1972

> It is one of those bright ideas that do not come off — Newgate Callendar, *N.Y. Times Book Rev.*, 8 Feb. 1981

> ... wondered if he was to be one of those players who never realize their full potential —*Current Biography*, November 1966

> ... for he is one of those authors who seem to write almost in collusion with their audience —Anatole Broyard, *N.Y. Times Book Rev.*, 9 Mar. 1986

The plural notion may also be signaled by pronoun reference alone:

> ... one of the Englishmen who came to Ireland for a visit, married, and made Ireland their home —John O'Hara, letter, 18 Oct. 1959

So the choice of a singular or plural verb, and of the matching singular or plural pronoun (which the commentators pass over), is a matter of notional agreement: is *one* or *those* to be the master? We cannot trace the practice of Old English down to our time in an unbroken line of descent, but there is abundant evidence that *one* has controlled number in modern English sentences from Shakespeare to James J. Kilpatrick, and there is likewise abundant evidence that *those* has controlled

number in other sentences. Addison was not troubled by using both constructions. You need not be more diffident than Addison.

The best discussion we have seen of this subject is the one by John S. Kenyon in *American Speech,* October 1951, quoted above.

one or more   See AGREEMENT, SUBJECT-VERB: ONE OR MORE, ONE IN (OUT OF) ———— 1.

ongoing   The British appear to have a particular dislike for this adjective. Howard 1984 reports that "noble and eloquent voices" in the House of Lords have spoken out against *ongoing* during debates on "the decay of English," and Howard himself describes it as a vogue word. Several other British sources in our files reveal a similar attitude.

> The author's style is also marred by the ugly misuse of jargon words such as "ongoing" and "perceived" —Patricia Burnett, *Times Literary Supp.,* 16 Dec. 1983

And at least one British dictionary (Longman 1984) includes a usage note warning the wary writer that *ongoing* is "widely disliked as a cliché." The issue enjoys some currency among American commentators as well. Those who have mentioned *ongoing* disapprovingly include Flesch 1964, Harper 1975, 1985, Edwin Newman (in *Change,* April 1975), and E. B. White (cited by James Sledd in Greenbaum 1985).

Ongoing was first recorded as a noun in 1825 and as an adjective in 1877:

> This edition ... will be a steady on-going thing —J. Blackwood, letter, 15 Oct. 1877 (OED Supplement)

Written evidence of adjective use was scanty until the 1940s, when we collected 13 citations for it from such diverse sources as *New Republic, Religion in America, Guatemala News, The Psychology of Behavior Disorders,* and *The Scotsman.* It was in the 1950s, however, that *ongoing* really became a common word:

> ... the ongoing life of her college —Lynn White, Jr., *Atlantic,* January 1950

> ... the on-going work —*Friends Intelligencer,* 8 July 1950

> ... the on-going affairs of men —Claude C. Bowman, *American Sociological Rev.,* August 1950

> ... comes alive in the ongoing present —Jerome Nathanson, *John Dewey,* 1951

> ... ongoing automatically habitual activity —John O'Connor, *Jour. of Philosophy,* 3 Dec. 1953

> ... the ongoing Korean conflict —James C. Davies, *American Political Science Rev.,* December 1954

> ... ongoing programs for junior and senior high school youth —*American Child,* November 1955

> ... that ongoing, steady rhythm of community life —Arthur Miller, *Atlantic,* April 1956

> ... on-going cancer research —Elizabeth Ogg, *When a Family Faces Cancer,* 1959

The popularity of *ongoing* has continued unabated— and may even have grown somewhat—in the years since. Therein, of course, lies the problem. A new (or newly common) word that acquires great popularity is almost certain to be derided as a vogue word by those who watch over the language, especially when an older word, such as *continuing,* is available to be used in the same contexts. There also seems to be something about adjectives of the form preposition + participle that strikes sensitive ears as jargonistic (see UPCOMING). And it may be, in addition, that the particularly strong feelings against *ongoing* among the British have something to do with its first having come into widespread use in the U.S.

Be that as it may, *ongoing* has now been in common, reputable use for about 40 years. Unless you happen to be making a speech before the House of Lords, we see no compelling reason to avoid it.

on line   Do you stand *in* line or *on* line? Twenty-five years ago *on line* would have marked a writer or speaker as a New Yorker. Bryant 1962 describes it as a regionalism peculiar to New York City and the Hudson Valley. A number of later commentators have repeated her. More recent commentators such as Geoffrey Nunberg in Shopen & Williams 1980 and Safire 1982 attest to the continued use of *on line* in New York. But Evans 1962 says his correspondents report it from many parts of the country, and he assumes that it is a regionalism that is spreading into standard use. Copperud 1980 complains that New Yorkers are foisting their provincialisms on the rest of us.

Certainly *on line* has not replaced *in line,* and from our recent evidence it is not entirely clear whether *on line* is really spreading into other dialects, since so many of the national magazines in which we find it are themselves edited, and to some extent written, in New York. At the very least, however, *on line* is better known nationally than it used to be.

> ... hates waiting in lines —Robert R. Harris, *N.Y. Times Book Rev.,* 19 Dec. 1982

> Hundreds of them stand in line on campus to grab the 450 tickets passed out free of charge —Jorjanna Price, *Houston Post,* 30 Aug. 1984

> Hamden, Conn. (AP)—Many people get frustrated waiting on long lines at the Department of Motor Vehicles office —*Springfield* (Mass.) *Morning Union,* 3 Oct. 1985

> ... while waiting on line at our local movie theater —Joseph A. King, *Newsweek,* 14 Apr. 1986

> Just before leaving the stable or while waiting on line for inspection ... —P. Wynn Norman, *Chronicle of the Horse,* 11 May 1984

only   **1.** A correspondent wrote to us in 1986 complaining about the misplacement of the word *only* in contemporary writing and offering "a few examples taken mostly from recent news articles" with her corrections:

1. "Sara only comes to California under protest."
   It should read, "Sara comes to California only under protest."
2. "The flood only kills a few characters."
   It should read, "The flood kills only a few characters."
3. "He was only told about his real dad about four years ago."
   It should read, "He was told about his real dad only four years ago."

4. "I think we will only be pleased when the issue is finally resolved."
   It should read, "I think we will be pleased only when the issue is finally resolved."
5. "A foreigner can only drive a car for one year in England without taking a test."
   This should read, "A foreigner can drive a car for only one year in England without taking a test."
6. A quote from FBI Director William Webster on NBC "Today" show:
   "They only should be given when the situation is considered really serious."
   He should have said, "They should be given only when the situation is considered really serious."

We should begin by placing this issue in historical perspective.

> Thus it is commonly said, 'I *only* spake three words': when the intention of the speaker manifestly requires, 'I spake *only* three words.' —Lowth 1763

> Another blunder, of which the instances are innumerable, is the misplacing of the word *only.* Indeed, this is so common, so absolutely universal, one may almost say that "only" cannot be found in its proper place in any book within the whole range of English literature,—to say nothing of newspapers, magazines, and the various departments of spoken language —Gould 1867

> *only:* This word, whose correct position depends upon the intention of the author, is often misplaced —Vizetelly 1906

> *Only.* "He only had one." Say, He had only one, or, better, one only —Bierce 1909

> *only* Make sure you put it immediately before the word it actually modifies —Trimble 1975

> "Drink Budweiser only for five days.".... If this means we are to drink no water or beverage other than Bud for five days, it is correct. Otherwise *only* is misplaced —Simon 1980

> On the matter of the misplaced *only,* I am as crotchety as an old bear with a thorn in his paw, and I nurse a lasting grudge against Fowler and Follett because of their indifference —Kilpatrick 1984

We can see that this problem of the misplaced *only* has been around for over two centuries. We can also see that writers are held to misplace it with some frequency. And we will see from the following examples that the chief mistake is the placing of *only* between the subject and the verb or between the auxiliary verb and the main verb—common locations for many common adverbs.

Who are the writers who misplace *only?* Hall 1917 calls them "the standard authors," and cites 104 of them from the 17th through the 19th centuries. Here is a sampler:

> ... I will only add this in the defence of our present Writers —John Dryden, "Defence of the Epilogue," 1672

> ... follies that are only to be killed by a constant and assiduous culture —Joseph Addison, *The Spectator* (in Hall)

> Every other author may aspire to praise; the lexicographer can only hope to escape reproach —Samuel Johnson, *Preface to the Dictionary,* 1755

I shall only mention one particular of dress —Tobias Smollett, *Travels Through France and Italy,* 1766

I set out immediately, with my son, for London, and we only stopped a little by the way to view Stonehenge on Salisbury Plain —Benjamin Franklin, *Autobiography,* 1788

. . . but which through a stupid blunder . . . only did cost one American dollar and a half —Henry Adams, letter, 15–17 May 1859

He only does it to annoy,
Because he knows it teases
     —Lewis Carroll, *Alice in Wonderland,* 1865
     (in Cyrus Day, *Word Study,* December 1962)

We see cherubs by Raphael, whose baby-innocence could only have been nursed in Paradise —Nathaniel Hawthorne, *The Marble Faun,* 1860 (in Hall)

The perfect loveliness of a woman's countenance can only consist in the majestic peace which is founded in memory of happy and useful years —John Ruskin, *Sesame and Lilies,* 1865 (in Hall)

The endeavor to find the distinctions of Latin grammar in that of English has only resulted in grotesque errors —A. H. Sayce, *Encyclopædia Britannica,* 11th ed., 1910

I think that Stephen Spender was only attempting to enumerate oil and water colour pictures and not photographs —T. S. Eliot, letter, 16 Oct. 1963

I'll only stop to fetch the little calf —Robert Frost (in Day, *Word Study*)

We feel very badly about your only having one turkey —James Thurber, letter, Fall 1938

They only opened one bag and took the passports in and looked at them —Ernest Hemingway (in Day, *Word Study*)

. . . the critics and scholars (most of them) gave him high marks in Speech when he had only earned them in Observation —John O'Hara, letter, 17 Feb. 1959

I only got wine by roaring for it —Evelyn Waugh (in Burchfield 1981)

. . . that would only mean that a noble distinction, hard to replace, had been lost —I. A. Richards, *Confluence,* March 1954

He only planned to keep on going as far as each streetcar would take him —E. L. Doctorow, *Ragtime,* 1975

If writers from Dryden to Doctorow have ignored the rule that *only* must immediately precede the word it modifies, where did the rule come from? It seems to have originated with Bishop Lowth in 1763. It was not directed by Lowth at the placement of *only* (his mention of *only* is in a footnote), but is a rule for adverbs generally:

> The Adverb, as its name imports, is generally placed close or near to the word, which it modifies or affects; and its propriety and force depend on its position.

Baker 1770 censures the misplacement of *only* along with that of *not only, neither,* and *either;* there are, he says, "innumerable Instances" of their wrong placing.

Lindley Murray 1795 likewise is addressing a more general principle when he cites two instances of misplaced *only* (one of which is Baker's example). The narrowing of the rule to *only* must have taken place later, in the 19th or 20th centuries. But even many modern handbooks include words other than *only* in their discussions: Chambers 1985, for instance, mentions *even* with *only;* Scott, Foresman 1981 adds *almost, even, hardly, scarcely, just,* and *nearly.*

But why the disparity between rule and practice? The answer undoubtedly lies in the rule's foundation: it is based on the application of logical thinking to written English. The "misplacing" of *only* is caused by the operation of idiom in spoken English. Lowth's original objection to "I only spake three words" depends on his interpreting *only* to apply ambiguously to either *I* or to *spake,* an interpretation that would not be possible if the words were spoken. Prose was not written laboriously in the 18th century; careful and painstaking revision was, in the main, reserved for poetry. Thus, 18th-century prose was undoubtedly closer to spoken English than it appears from this distance. We know that Dr. Johnson, who habitually put such things off until the last minute, dashed off many of his prose works and never revised them. We should not be surprised, therefore, that many instances of "misplaced" *only* can be found in his prose works.

A rule based on logic that is applied to written English and does not take into account the natural idiom of speech will create thousands of "violations" as soon as it is formulated. This plainly has been the case with the rule for placing *only.*

If the grammarians and rhetoricians who preached strict adherence to the placement rule viewed noncompliance only as so much more incorrect English, the disparity between rule and practice was seen by others in a different light. One of the earliest to comment was Alford 1866:

> The adverb *only* in many sentences where strictly speaking it ought to follow the verb and to limit the objects of the verb, is in good English placed before the verb.

Goold Brown 1851 calls Lowth's criticism of "I only spake three words"—which he found with *spake* altered to *spoke* in a later grammar—hypercritical. Hall 1917 devotes six pages to the subject and lists 104 authors in over 400 passages in violation of the rule. But the most trenchant notice of the disparity is taken by Fowler 1926. He begins with a quotation and appends his opinion:

> I read the other day of a man who 'only died a week ago', as if he could have done anything else more striking or final; what was meant by the writer was that he 'died only a week ago'. There speaks one of those friends from whom the English language may well pray to be saved, one of those modern precisians who have more zeal than discretion, & wish to restrain liberty as such, regardless of whether it is harmfully or harmlessly exercised.

He continues:

> For *He only died a week ago* no better defence is perhaps possible than that it is the order that most people have always used & still use, & that, the risk of misunderstanding being chimerical, it is not worth while to depart from the natural. Remember that in speech there is not even the possibility of misunderstanding, because the intonation of *died* is entirely

different if it, & not *a week ago,* is qualified by *only;* & it is fair that a reader should be supposed capable of supplying the decisive intonation where there is no temptation to go wrong about it.

Fowler has his contemporary followers:

To quibble about the position of *only* when meaning is not at stake is to waste time —Perrin & Ebbitt 1972

The placement of *only* in a sentence is a matter of great concern to a few self-styled purists, but happily not for most speakers and writers.... The simple fact is that the "rule" about placing *only* next to the element modified is honored now more in the breach than in the observance. Especially in speech, the normal placement of *only* is before the verb and this must be considered to be a perfectly acceptable part of the American idiom —Harper 1985

The placement in speech is well attested:

... I once tried to buy such a pair, for myself: but only got the crushing reply that "slippers of *that* kind are *only* worn by *ladies*"! —Lewis Carroll, letter, 11 Nov. 1896

There was a young man, who had only worked there six weeks —William Benton, in Studs Terkel, *Hard Times,* 1970

He only got in three innings' work all spring —Dick Howser, quoted in *New Yorker,* 9 Dec. 1985

All these examples that run counter to the rule for what Fowler terms "orthodox" placement might lead you to suspect, as Harper 1985 does, that few people use the orthodox placement. Such is not the case, however. What has happened is that both parties to this dispute have been at pains to find examples that disagree with the rule; the prescribers present them for correction, and the rule's critics present them as evidence that the rule and usage do not match. No one—at least until comparatively recent times—has bothered to collect examples that adhere to the orthodox placement. Such examples do exist, abundantly:

The Endymion is now waiting only for orders, but may wait for them perhaps a month —Jane Austen, letter, 1 Nov. 1800

To many women marriage is only this —Mary Webb, *The Golden Arrow,* 1916

She looked at the body only enough to make sure that it was all over —Glenway Wescott, *Apartment in Athens,* 1945

... I can only try to explain what was in my mind — Christopher Fry, *Atlantic,* March 1953

There is no evil in the atom; only in men's souls — Adlai E. Stevenson, *Speeches,* ed. Richard Harrity, 1952

... I'd taken it only just in time —Christopher Isherwood, in *New World Writing,* 1952

... maybe we'd have only one more chance —William Faulkner, 25 Feb. 1957, in *Faulkner in the University,* 1959

He needed only to suffer —E. L. Doctorow, *Ragtime,* 1975

Indeed, we spent so little time in bed most of us had only one child —James Thurber, letter, 24 June 1959

But we can ultimately only guess about Davis — Robert Penn Warren, *Jefferson Davis Gets His Citizenship Back,* 1980

Bryant 1962 notes that the position of *only* with respect to the word or phrase it modifies is not fixed in standard English—especially not in speech—but in edited written English it is usually placed immediately before the word or words it modifies. She cites a study of magazines—presumably American—showing that 84 percent of the *only*s appeared in the orthodox position—a figure she speculates may be somewhat heightened by the strictures of textbook writers or the preferences of editors. An examination of the citations in the Merriam-Webster files made in 1982 reached a similar conclusion: in edited prose *only* tends to be placed immediately before the word or words it modifies.

Although no one has searched 18th-century literature for examples of the orthodox positioning of *only,* it seems reasonable to suppose that the orthodox positioning and the idiomatic speech positioning have both been in use all along, and that writers have used the orthodox positioning when it seemed useful to do so. Thus Jane Austen's use of it in 1800—in a letter.

So what rather looks like an increase in use of the orthodox positioning may be somewhat illusory if it has, as we conjecture, been in use all along (note that in some of the examples no other positioning is likely). Such increase may be due in part to the urging of the "rule" by editors and textbooks, but it is just as likely that it is due to the increased prestige of prose as a literary medium. Prose is certainly considered more worthy of revision and polishing than it was two centuries ago; the logical positioning of *only* is likely to be more desirable the less the prose resembles spontaneous speech. Our correspondent's examples are all drawn from journalism or speech; journalism is prose produced to a deadline—in just the way Samuel Johnson used to write. There is less time to revise such writing, and there is correspondingly greater likelihood that such a writer will use the natural idioms of speech.

To conclude, we offer these few summary observations. The position of *only* in standard spoken English is not fixed; ambiguity is prevented by clarifying stress and intonation. In literary English from the 17th century to the present, the placement of *only* according to the idiom of speech has been freely used; it is still used, especially in prose that keeps close to the rhythms of speech. In current edited prose—especially that for which ample time has been provided for revision—*only* tends to be used in the orthodox position—immediately before (or sometimes after) the word or words it modifies.

See also EVEN.

2. The conjunction *only,* for reasons not stated, is rejected by the usage panel of Heritage 1969, 1982 and is questioned in formal use by Longman 1984. It is called incorrect by Woolley & Scott 1926. Bache 1869 had censured it too, but his example, from a sign at an Albany, N.Y., trolley-car stop, is not very useful to generalize from. The OED dates use of *only* as a conjunction back to the 14th century. Goold Brown 1851 notes the use without comment; he even quotes a use from another grammarian without censure. Here are a few examples, arranged not by meaning, but by position in the sentence:

It is intended to stop all debate, like the previous question in the General Court. Only it don't — Oliver Wendell Holmes d. 1894, *The Autocrat of the Breakfast-Table,* 1858

... they were getting plenty of notice of German intentions and preparations. Only, they failed to heed them —William L. Shirer, *The Nightmare Years,* 1984

For, brethren, ye have been called unto liberty; only use not liberty for occasion to the flesh —Galatians 5:13 (AV), 1611

... they would have had an answer, only the old lady began rattling on —W. M. Thackeray, *History of Sam Titmarsh and the Great Hoggarty Diamond,* 1841 (in Jespersen 1917)

I should not have noticed this one only it happened to come alone —Sir Arthur Conan Doyle, *The Hound of the Baskervilles,* 1902 (in Jespersen)

I'd introduce you to her, only you'd win her —Jack London, *Martin Eden,* 1909 (in Jespersen)

Rhododendron time in Seattle is fairly spectacular, only I can't think when rhododendrons are in bloom —E. B. White, letter, 23 June 1946

You can ask Shakespeare to speak for himself, only he won't do it —Eric Bentley, *New Republic,* 5 May 1952

... they were right enough in a way, only they failed to understand that the choice had already been made —Irving Howe & Eliezer Greenberg, *New Republic,* 9 Aug. 1954

These uses are standard. It may be that because the conjunction is sometimes found in dialectal contexts, some may feel it is not standard. Particular contexts may be dialectal; the senses in which *only* is used are not:

"Only I'm an old man now I'd change his tune for him. I'd take the stick to his back...." —James Joyce, *Dubliners,* 1914

... he kept telling how he could catch them thieves easy, only the rheumatiz was so bad he couldn't walk —Vance Randolph, *Western Folklore,* January 1951

Oi should hev cut the hay today, only that wuz tew wet —A. O. D. Claxton, *The Suffolk Dialect of the 20th Century,* 1954

on the part of This common idiomatic phrase can often be replaced by a single preposition, such as *by* or *among,* and several commentators think—not surprisingly—that it should be. Its use is easily avoided by anyone who finds it awkward or needlessly wordy. Many writers apparently do not find it so:

After a proper resistance on the part of Mrs. Ferrars —Jane Austen, *Sense and Sensibility,* 1811

... evinces, on the part of the author, an utter and radical want of the adapting or constructive power —Edgar Allen Poe, "The Literati of New York City," 1846

It determined on the part of poor Giovanelli a further pious, a further candid, confidence —Henry James, *Daisy Miller,* 1879

... high standards of integrity and conduct on the part of all concerned —C. W. Caress, *American School Board Jour.,* March 1968

... increased willingness on the part of the parents to speak up —Jack J. Levine, *Columbia Forum,* Spring 1968

... ignorance on the part of many English teachers ... of the most elementary facts about the nature of language —Barnard 1979

onto, on to The preposition *onto,* which was originally spelled *on to,* was aspersed as a vulgarism or an unnecessary formation in the 19th century. Alford 1866 disapproved it, and so did Ayres 1881; other disapprovers are mentioned by Vizetelly 1906 and Bernstein 1971. As a two-word preposition, *on to* has been in use since the 16th century; perhaps it was not much used in the best-known literature, but several of its users who are quoted in the OED had at least minor literary reputations. Alford was probably unaware of its early use. Apparently he had many correspondents who defended the term, which suggests that it was then popular.

Part of the resistance to *on to* in British English can be attributed to its being even more popular in America, and no doubt some American resistance to it was based on a distaste for the usages of American humorists:

... and her shoes is red morocker, with gold spangles onto them —*Artemus Ward: His Book,* 1862

"... mam were feedin us brats onto mush and milk...." —George Washington Harris, "Rare Ripe Garden Seed," 1867, in *The Mirth of a Nation,* ed. Walter Blair & Raven I. McDavid, Jr., 1983

If these usages were typical of spoken 19th-century American English, it is perhaps not too surprising that the preposition was associated in some minds with a certain vulgarity. At any rate, *onto* has had some difficulty winning acceptance. Even now it meets some resistance in Great Britain, especially in the solid form *onto,* which seems to have been originally American.

In current American usage *onto* is usually interchangeable with *on* in the sense "to a position on":

... with the McCarthy news pushed over onto page 4 —James Thurber, letter, 1 June 1954

... the crowd was so excited that they ran out onto the field —Tip O'Neill with William Novak, *Man of the House,* 1987

... some tramp who had wandered onto the grounds —E. L. Doctorow, *Loon Lake,* 1979

In winter time he needs to shovel the snow from in front of his windows in order to see out; it gets so deep he can walk right onto the roof when the ice must be scraped off —Edward Hoagland, *Atlantic,* July 1971

Some commentators contrast *onto* with *on* in uses like these, especially with verbs like *run, wander, walk,* and *step,* as *walk on* the roof suggests something different from *walk onto* the roof.

Onto is also used for attachment:

> ... my father's Model T with the isinglass windows in side curtains that had to be buttoned onto the frame in bad weather —Russell Baker, *Growing Up,* 1982

Nearly every commentator from Alford to the present (and the OED as well) warns about not confusing the preposition *onto* with the adverb *on*—associated with a preceding verb—followed by the preposition *to:*

> Pass this on to MR. PAYNE and apprize Martin thereof —Charles Lamb, letter, undated (perhaps 1823)

> ... the decision to hold on to the price line —*Fortune,* December 1960 (in Bryant 1962)

A correspondent complains to us that this distinction is frequently not observed with *hold,* especially when the preposition follows its object:

> I'd given this company, a bank, all my money to hold onto for me until I needed it —*And More by Andy Rooney,* 1982

The distinction between the adverb followed by the preposition and the compound preposition is not as readily discernible with *hold* as it would be with some of the other verbs, such as *travel* or *go,* and it may be that the preposition *onto* will become established with *hold.*

In American English the preposition is regularly spelled *onto;* the open compound *on to* is still preferred by some British writers and publishers.

Onto also is used in a sense close to "aware of." This use is originally American, but the OED Supplement says it is now also used in British English:

> Alvarez is onto some kind of truth —Wilfrid Sheed, *The Good Word and Other Words,* 1978

onward, onwards As is noted by several commentators, *onward* serves both as an adjective ("an onward rush") and as an adverb ("rushing onward"); *onwards* is an adverb only ("from 1600 onwards"). Evans 1957 notes that *onward* is the preferred adverb in American English, and our evidence supports that observation. In British English, however, *onwards* is in common use, especially following a prepositional phrase beginning with *from:*

> ... was uniquely able from 1945 onwards —Sir James Mountford, *British Universities,* 1966

> ... dating from about 900 onwards —W. F. Bolton, *A Short History of Literary English,* 1967

> ... eighteenth-century art from the Goncourts onwards —*Times Literary Supp.,* 14 May 1970

ophthalmia, ophthalmologist See PHTH.

opine This verb has been used in English since the 15th century, and it certainly is not a rare word today, but not everyone is inclined to take it seriously. Several recent commentators have described it as a stilted word, appropriate only in facetious use, and it does have an undeniable tendency to turn up in humorous writing:

> "Even *good* moon cheese ain't worth the trouble," Joe opines. "Bottom's plumb out of the moon-cheese market." —Larry L. King, *Cosmopolitan,* November 1976

It also commonly serves to imply some disparagement of or disagreement with the opinion being reported:

> Many opine that a writer, and particularly a poet, for some reason, must love language —William Stafford, *Writing the Australian Crawl,* 1978

> "America is now a failure," he opines at one point —David Margolick, *N.Y. Times Book Rev.,* 23 Jan. 1983

More generally, it serves to emphasize that the opinion being reported is just that—an opinion:

> ... has recently opined that melting the ice cap "would not mean the end of human society." —Robert Claiborne, *Saturday Rev.,* 13 Nov. 1976

> "... They wanted to make a killing with a stock scheme to go public," opines Cousins —Lisa See, *Publishers Weekly,* 23 Sept. 1983

opportunity In American usage, *opportunity* is regularly used with *to* followed by an infinitive:

> ... it was a fine day and a good opportunity to enjoy the salt air —John Cheever, *The Wapshot Chronicle,* 1957

> He gave them every opportunity to escape —Saul Bellow, *Herzog,* 1964

> ... had hoped for an opportunity to start work on a novel —*Current Biography,* January 1966

Opportunity to seems to occur only infrequently in British English:

> ... offered new opportunities to these communities to enter an honourable and profitable profession — D. W. Brogan, *The English People,* 1943

American usage favors *opportunity for* followed by a noun phrase somewhat less frequently than it does *opportunity to* followed by an infinitive:

> ... offered unlimited opportunities for water transport —*American Guide Series: Rhode Island,* 1937

> ... opportunities for broad university reforms are endless —George W. Bonham, *Change,* March–April 1969

British usage of *opportunity for* with a noun phrase occurs only a little more often than does use with *to:*

> ... a present that can offer little except an opportunity for limited reparation —*Times Literary Supp.,* June 1969

Opportunity for followed by a gerund is found less frequently in both American and British usage than the constructions already mentioned:

> ... gave him an opportunity for thinking and writing —*Current Biography,* July 1965

> ... the street boy has not the same opportunities for working off his adventurous animal spirits —George Sampson, *English for the English,* 1921

Opportunity of occurs in both American and British usage. In fact, *opportunity of* followed by a gerund appears from our evidence to be the most common of these constructions in British usage. Although it still occurs in American English now and then, it was more frequent thirty years ago and before:

> He seldom loses an opportunity of dispraising the present, of showing his profound pessimism —*The Journals of Arnold Bennett,* ed. Frank Swinnerton, 1954

> ... have an opportunity of becoming acquainted only with his work as a teacher —*Times Literary Supp.,* 12 Jan. 1967

> ... he delayed accepting the opportunity of returning to the Washington *Post* —*Current Biography,* May 1965

> ... affords the lay reader the opportunity of entering into intellectual intimacy with Judge Learned Hand —Felix Frankfurter, *N.Y. Herald Tribune Book Rev.,* 18 May 1952

Opportunity of followed by a noun phrase is also found in both American and British English, but less often than the construction with the gerund:

> ... would give the priest moderator an opportunity of more frequent personal contact —Thomas F. Cribbin, *Bulletin of the National Catholic Education Association,* August 1949

> "This," I said, "would give us an opportunity of long-needed talks...." —Sir Winston Churchill, *Closing the Ring,* 1951

opposite Many commentators observe that *opposite* as an adjective is followed by either *to* or *from* ("They sat opposite to/from each other") and that *opposite* as a noun is followed by *of* ("His opinions are the opposite of hers"). With regard to the adjective, our evidence supports the observation entirely:

> ... in a direction opposite to that hypothesized —Robert F. Forston & Charles Urban Larson, *Jour. of Communication,* June 1968

> ... almost exactly opposite from me —John Hawkes, *Fiction,* vol. 1, no. 4, 1973

But our evidence for the noun is more equivocal. The usual preposition following the noun is unquestionably *of:*

> The overall tone ... is the opposite of scholarly —Norman Horrocks, *Library Jour.,* July 1966

> ... for legislation precisely the opposite of the Pastore bill —John Fischer, *Harper's,* December 1969

But *to* has also had some reputable use with the noun:

> ... he perversely accomplishes the opposite to what he presumably intended —*College English,* January 1945

> ... the opposite to the goal actually sought —Brian Crozier, *Interplay,* June/July 1969

There is no particular reason why this choice of preposition should be considered incorrect; it certainly does not violate idiom in any way. It is atypical, however.

opposition *Opposition,* when used with a preposition, is usually followed by *to:*

> ... was sometimes in active opposition to the school to which Laura gave her adherence —Archibald Marshall, *Anthony Dare,* 1923

> The early theater suffered the brunt of moral opposition to the arts —*American Guide Series: New York,* 1940

> ... was also in the vanguard of the opposition to a renewal of the demand for subsidies —C. Vann Woodward, *Reunion and Reaction,* 2d ed. rev., 1956

> ... he was in opposition to the Democratic majority —*Current Biography,* January 1968

Opposition also has been used—in a different relation and with paired objects—with *between* or *of;* they occur less frequently:

> ... Rousseau ... accepts the natural opposition between imagination and reason —Irving Babbitt, *The New Laokoon,* 1910

> ... the opposition between the complete classical form and the open ... blurred form of romantic poetry —René Wellek, in *Twentieth Century English,* ed. William S. Knickerbocker, 1946

> ... I propose ... to consider how the concrete educated thought of men has viewed this opposition of mechanism and organism —Alfred North Whitehead, *Science and the Modern World,* 1925

> ... he is seldom content to allow his opposition of separateness and union to work on a reader's feelings —E. K. Brown, *Rhythm in the Novel,* 1950

Opposition has also been used, but considerably less often, with *against:*

> ... maintains a steady opposition against the general proposal of the Committee —*Manchester Guardian Weekly,* 18 Dec. 1936

opt The verb *opt* has a modern, truncated quality that may make it seem like a recent invention, but in fact it is more than a hundred years old. It is derived from the French *opter* "to choose," and it was first used in English in a specifically French context—to report the choices of citizenship being made in the 1870s by inhabitants of Alsace-Lorraine, a formerly French territory that had been ceded to Germany by the Treaty of Frankfurt (written in French) in 1871:

> The Paris correspondent of the *Times* ... was allowed to speak of Alsatians *opting* between France and Germany —*The World,* 25 Apr. 1877 (OED)

> ... a native of Alsace-Lorraine, who had 'opted' to become a French subject —George Augustus Sala, *Paris Herself Again,* 1879 (OED)

From this use, *opt* developed the specific sense in English "to make a choice of citizenship":

> Poland, of course, contains a large number of German-speaking citizens in her new territories, and these have "opted" either to become or not to become Poles —*Manchester Guardian Weekly,* 30 Oct. 1925

> ... the Treaty of Versailles had given three years to Germans in Czechoslovakia who wished to opt for German citizenship —John Gunther, *Inside Europe,* rev. ed., 1940

Extended use of *opt* to mean simply "to make a choice" dates back to at least 1899, but it seems not to have become common until the 1950s. Its surge in popularity at that time may have owed much to the widespread use of *opt* in its original sense to describe the many decisions about citizenship and forms of government that confronted individuals and nations in the years following World War II:

> . . . the small state of Junagadh . . . has caused a turmoil by opting to join Pakistan —*The Economist,* 11 Oct. 1947

> . . . have shown that when the choice is real . . . Germans opt for the West —*Times Literary Supp., 3 Apr.* 1953

> Enemy prisoners who had opted for repatriation —*Time,* 3 Aug. 1953

> . . . estranged from a husband who had opted for the "People's Poland" —*Time,* 12 July 1954

The original sense of *opt* is now rare, but its connection with the current, general sense of the word is still discernible (if only barely) in the way that *opt* continues to be applied primarily to the choosing of a course of action:

> . . . persecuted vagabonds who have opted out of the universal regimentation —*Times Literary Supp.,* 25 Mar. 1965

> . . . adopt the view that most members of the [black middle] class opt out of the race —Charles V. Hamilton, *N.Y. Times Mag.,* 14 Apr. 1968

> . . . they opt for peaceful reform of American institutions —Robert E. Kavanaugh, *Psychology Today,* October 1968

> . . . the generals who held power opted for war — Albert H. Johnston, *Publishers Weekly,* 29 Dec. 1975

> Lars opts to decline medical services and to live out his last months in his own cottage —John Updike, *New Yorker,* 11 Jan. 1982

Its use in describing the selection of a material thing is relatively uncommon, although it does enjoy some popularity among fashion writers:

> . . . you can opt for short sleeves . . . or none at all — *New Yorker,* 20 Nov. 1965

> . . . opts for a leather-like polyester-coated cotton zip-front jacket —*Playboy,* September 1968

optimum In Latin the adjective *optimum* means "best," but as an English word it has acquired a more specific sense, "most favorable or best possible under given conditions." It was adopted as an English word in the late 19th century by scientific writers who used it, both as a noun and as an adjective, in describing conditions most favorable to the growth of an organism. Its principal use continues to be in scientific contexts, but it also turns up regularly now in general writing:

> . . . train himself to maintain his composure under less than optimum conditions —*Current Biography,* June 1965

> The optimum time for learning a particular thing is when the child begins to wonder about it —Barbara M. Rush, *Children's House,* vol. 4, no. 4, 1970

> . . . each person must discover the meaning . . . at an optimum moment in life —Barrett J. Mandel, *AAUP Bulletin,* September 1971

Several critics contend that *optimum* is often inappropriately used to mean simply "best," but they give no examples of such usage. Our own evidence shows that even when *optimum* can be replaced by *best* in a given context (as in the quotation above from Barbara M. Rush), the full sense of the adjective is actually "best possible" or "most favorable." *Optimum* is probably seldom used when the sense is simply "best," as it would be in "This is the optimum meal I've ever had." That is not to say, of course, that *optimum* can never be replaced by *best* in contexts in which both adjectives are possible. *Best* is a simpler word and a more straightforward one, but *optimum* also has its uses, and you need not regard it as a word to be strenuously avoided.

or See AGREEMENT, SUBJECT-VERB: COMPOUND SUBJECTS 2; EITHER 3, 4; NEITHER 2; NO 2.

-or, -our In words like *color* and *honor* the ending *-our* is standard in British English. The elimination of the *u* is largely the doing of Noah Webster's spellers and dictionaries. It has become one of the regular features that distinguishes British from American spelling.

oral See VERBAL, ORAL.

orate Many commentators have noted, and our evidence confirms, that this back-formation from the noun *oration* is usually used in a humorous or disparaging way to describe impassioned or pompous speech:

> . . . go around orating about Pure Southern Womanhood and making big talk that Atlanta, Georgia, or the State of Kentucky has the most beautiful women in the world —James Street, *Holiday,* October 1954

> An old man beside me was orating as to how anyone who lives to be 60 in New York deserves a medal — Alan Rich, *New York,* 26 Feb. 1973

Its straightforward use in the sense, "to make a speech," is rare, except in writing about the past, but it can be found:

> . . . the respected literary critic and staunch apologist for nationalism orating at the Federation of Ontario Naturalists —Valerie Miner, *Chatelaine,* June 1975

orchestrate Figurative use of the word *orchestrate* has drawn criticism from language commentators on the grounds that it is faddish or a cliché, or that its figurative use has strayed too far from the original musical sense. However, if use of the figurative sense, "to arrange or combine so as to achieve maximum effect," is a fad, it is a long-lived one, as this use is attested as early as 1883 and is almost as old as the literal use, which is attested only from 1880. Merriam-Webster's earliest evidence for the figurative sense comes almost exclusively from writings about painting:

> . . . Cottet, who combined in himself the romantic fire and feeling for orchestrated colour of Delacroix with the incisive realism . . . of Courbet —*Encyclopaedia Britannica,* 10th ed., 1902–1903

> Even as a symphony is in D or a sonata is in A, his pictures were orchestrated according to a tone — Arthur Jerome Eddy, *Recollections and Impressions of James A. McNeill Whistler,* 1903

> . . . lacquers in which the cold and lovely detail of fairy-land was not so much depicted as orchestrated —James Hilton, *Lost Horizon,* 1933

In the late 1940s, *orchestrate* started gaining wider use, at first in application to literature and then to other subjects:

> The rhythm and idiom of contemporary speech were orchestrated into the complex harmonies of *King Lear* and *The Tempest* —Robert Speaight, *Drama Since 1939,* 1947

> Their outmoded language was an expression of what was backward-glancing in his spirit. It pleased him by being out of date. It orchestrated his melancholy —John Mason Brown, *Saturday Rev.,* 24 July 1948

> Kanin knows how to orchestrate a gag by timing it shrewdly —Brooks Atkinson, quoted in *Current Biography 1953*

> . . . the "popular indignation" over the "affronts and insults to Spanish dignity" orchestrated . . . by the Falange newspapers —Frank Gorrell, *New Republic,* 22 Feb. 1954

By the 1970s and 80s, figurative use of *orchestrate* had indeed become quite common and had begun attracting criticism from the language commentators. Clearly, however, many good writers, including the authors of these passages, think the figurative use is quite acceptable:

> . . . moments later he is again on the phone, while his secretary orchestrates incoming and outgoing calls —John McPhee, *New Yorker,* 11 Sept. 1971

> A few days later, in orchestrated pursuance of a policy to suppress criticism of seven weeks of appeasement —William Safire, *N.Y. Times,* 27 Dec. 1979

> People are positioned; looks are orchestrated; gestures are timed —Stanley Kauffmann, *Before My Eyes,* 1980

> Any break at a line, any caesura, any surfacing of a natural syllable intonation—these are all a total of language-feel that the writer orchestrates according to what comes along in the act of composing —William Stafford, *Writing the Australian Crawl,* 1978

order See IN ORDER THAT; IN ORDER TO.

ordinance, ordnance A number of usage commentators trouble themselves to distinguish between these words, along the following lines. *Ordinance* has several meanings, the most common of which is "a law set forth by a governmental authority":

> . . . the nation's first planning and zoning ordinance to set up controls for a historic district —David Butwin, *Saturday Rev.,* 15 Apr. 1972

Ordnance is a military word which is etymologically related to *ordinance* (both are derived from the Middle French *ordenance,* "act of arranging") but is otherwise distinct from it. *Ordnance* can mean "artillery," "a service of the army in charge of combat supplies," or "military supplies for combat":

> . . . the danger from unexploded ordnance —Paul R. Ehrlich & John P. Holdren, *Saturday Rev.,* 4 Dec. 1971

Confusion of these similar words is rare, but not unheard of. The most likely mistake to be made is the substitution of the more common word, *ordinance,* for the less common *ordnance:*

> Early in 1944, Joe was drafted into the Army and trained in ordinance —*Guitar Player,* August 1981

organizations considered as collective nouns See AGREEMENT: ORGANIZATIONS CONSIDERED AS COLLECTIVE NOUNS.

Oriental See ASIAN, ASIATIC, ORIENTAL.

orientate *Orientate,* first attested in 1849 in the same issue of the same journal that first used *orientation,* has been under critical fire since 1945; the frequency of criticism seems to have increased in recent years. After you have weeded out the ill-considered or uninformed commentary, the criticism comes down to this: *orientate* is three letters and one syllable longer than *orient.* That would seem like a rather trivial concern, but the word seems to draw criticism for no better reason than that. You will have to decide for yourself how important that consideration is in your writing. Here are some examples from writers who obviously saw nothing wrong with *orientate:*

> What parting gift could give that friend protection,
> So orientated, his salvation needs
> The Bad Lands and the sinister direction?
>   —W. H. Auden, *New Republic,* 25 Nov. 1940

> When they come to London, colonials orientate themselves by Piccadilly Circus —Ngaio Marsh, *Death of a Peer,* 1940

> . . . the propaganda of the period has to orientate itself in relation to these landmarks —Aldous Huxley, *The Olive Tree,* 1937

> . . . a poet already strongly impelled, and already definitely orientated —F. R. Leavis, *New Bearings in English Poetry,* new ed., 1950

> . . . the behaviour of the suppliant is carefully orientated in respect to this mysterious undesirability — Margaret Mead, *Coming of Age in Samoa,* 1928

> She was only standing there to catch her nervous balance, to orientate herself —Tennessee Williams, *The Roman Spring of Mrs. Stone,* 1950

> In modern terms the modistae were theory orientated, and the adherents of classical literature and Priscian's grammar as it stood were data orientated —R. H. Robins, *A Short History of Linguistics,* 1967

> . . . France and Italy, where the conservatives tend to be clerically orientated —*Times Literary Supp.,* 26 Apr. 1974

> I don't want to suggest that Chinamen are less aesthetically orientated than I —Robert Morley, *Punch,* 25 Dec. 1974

> . . . the struggle in Greece to promote the classically-orientated Katharevousa —Randolph Quirk, *Style and Communication in the English Language,* 1982

We have omitted scientific and technical uses that would be beyond the purview of usage writers. You have probably noticed that most of the writers cited are British; *orientate* is much more frequently used in British English than it is in American. *Orient* is indeed shorter, and it seems to be the usual choice in American English.

originate   *Originate,* when used with a preposition, is most often used with *in:*

> The reports as presented in these meetings all originate in widely separated company departments — James K. Blake, *Dun's,* January 1954

> . . . television programs originating in Richmond — *NEA Jour.,* January 1965

> *Virginia Woolf: The Inward Voyage* shows signs of having originated in a doctoral dissertation — *Times Literary Supp.,* 30 July 1971

A little less often, *originate* is used with *from:*

> Originating from a commingling of Indians with runaway slaves, these people had fled . . . —*American Guide Series: Texas,* 1940

> . . . arranged for ten organ recitals originating from the Germanic Museum to be broadcast over CBS — *Current Biography 1950*

Originate is also used with *as, at, on, out of, outside of,* and *with:*

> The classical view is that the earth originated as a hot body —A. E. Benfield, *Scientific American Reader,* 1953

> The system originated at the end of World War I — *Current Biography 1950*

> . . . the concept of the separable soul has been originated on primitive "scientific" grounds —Weston La Barre, *The Human Animal,* 1954

> A poem does not originate out of an impulse to communicate —John Hall Wheelock, *N.Y. Times Book Rev.,* 23 May 1954

> . . . in the case of families that originated outside of North America —Ernst Mayr, *Wilson Bulletin,* March 1946

> Mr. Lowell . . . issued the invitation, but the idea had originated with Lawrence Henderson —Lucien Price, *Dialogues of Alfred North Whitehead,* 1954

or less   See LESS, FEWER.

or no   See NO 3.

or not   See WHETHER OR NOT.

or otherwise   See OTHERWISE.

other   **1.** For uses of *other* in *of any other*—in what is called false comparison—see ANY 3.
2. *Other . . . than, but, except.* A few commentators, mostly British (Partridge 1942, Longman 1984; our latest American commentator is Vizetelly 1906), insist on *than* and reject *but* or *except* after *other* as an adjective in constructions like these:

> . . . never looked on him in any other light than as my friend —Henry Fielding, *A Journey from This World to the Next,* 1743

> And great and heroic men have existed, who had no other information than by the printed page —Ralph Waldo Emerson, "The American Scholar," 1837

> . . . there can hardly be found any other criterion than normality —H. M. Parshley, translation of Simone de Beauvoir, *The Second Sex,* 1952

But, however, is idiomatic and fully standard in American English:

> No other creature but man seems to have just that constellation of capacities —Eric H. Lenneberg, *Biological Foundations of Language,* 1967

> He would have preferred any other job but that of G-3 —Norman Mailer, *The Naked and the Dead,* 1948

> . . . the U.S. had no other choice but to hold to its position —*Time,* 20 Sept. 1948

We have no evidence to suggest that *except* has ever been common in this construction, at least in writing, and we have no modern example except what Partridge offers from British journalism. This extract from the conversation of Jane Austen's Marianne Dashwood, however, continues to sound both idiomatic and modern:

> ". . . I have not known him long indeed, but I am much better acquainted with him, than I am with any other creature in the world, except yourself and mama. . . ." —*Sense and Sensibility,* 1811

This version of the construction may well be more common in speech than in writing, and it may occur in writing chiefly where it is motivated, as here, by the appearance of *than* nearby in the context.

other than   *Other* has a propensity for being used with *than.* The trouble is, as the OED shows, that *other* can be an adjective, a pronoun, or an adverb, and still be used with *than.* This flexibility has created a variety of *other than* constructions and the consequent bewilderment of usage commentators, beginning with Fowler 1926. The critics who follow Fowler more or less repeat, with varying degrees of expansiveness, his dictum that "*other than* should be registered as a phrase to be avoided." Writers have paid scant attention to this advice; *other than* is not avoided.

The grammatical problem that Fowler brought on himself was a result of not paying attention to the OED. Fowler approved *other* as an adjective; he disapproved it as an adverb, even though the OED recognized it. And he overlooked the fact that the OED also covers it as a pronoun. This oversight left him stumped when, damning uses he had decided were adverbial, he ran up against an example to which his adverbial analysis did not apply:

> Up to the very end no German field company would look with other than apprehension to meeting the 25th on even terms.

This *other* is the seventh sense of the OED's pronoun. It has been around for quite a while and is still current:

> I can not in honesty or self-respect do other than protest —Dewitt Clinton Poole, quoted in *Current Biography 1950*

> . . . the geographical scheme was introduced by other than Sumerians —Henry Lutz, in *Semitic and Oriental Studies,* ed. Walter J. Fischel, 1951 .

> . . . when the cue ball is frozen to the cushion and you face other than a straightaway shot —Willie Mosconi, *Winning Pocket Billiards,* 1965

Fowler was similarly perplexed when *other than* was followed by an adjective:

> But it is doubtful if any of the leaders . . . would have been other than dismayed and frightened at the idea —Gerald Carson, *New-England Galaxy,* Winter 1965

> . . . he always wondered how she could be other than happy —Robert Canzoneri, *McCalls's,* March 1971

When *other* is rather obviously an adjective or an adverb, the compound *other than* works much like a compound preposition meaning "besides" or "except":

> . . . a high-level dialogue, covering issues other than hostages —Oliver North, in *The Tower Commission Report,* 1987

> . . . discovering he has a lover other than her —Martin Tucker, *Commonweal,* 11 Apr. 1969

> . . . laborers in disciplines other than experimental science —Robert M. Hutchins, *Center Mag.,* January 1969

> Milton . . . is trying to do something quite other than Donne —F. R. Leavis, *Revaluation,* 1947

> . . . cannot be viewed other than with regret —*American Labor,* July 1968

> . . . openings other than doors were rare —Katharine Kuh, *Saturday Rev.,* 28 June 1969

> Nor shall I enter into details concerning the ensuing half-dozen nights, other than to say that promptly on the stroke of every midnight, the shade of Ernest appeared at the bedside of Ida May —Katherine Anne Porter, *Ladies' Home Jour.,* August 1971

This quasi-prepositional use is sometimes close in meaning to "apart from":

> Other than twisting and untwisting her hands, she sits perfectly still —Jim Jerome, *N.Y. Times Mag.,* 14 Jan. 1979

> Other than Chinese and Indian restaurants . . . I can only think of one place in London where you can get lunch —Margaret Costa, *Illustrated London News,* 31 Aug. 1968

In addition, you will sometimes find *other than that* used like *except that:*

> I do not recall in what territory it was, other than that it was west of Albuquerque —Agnes Morley Cleaveland, *No Life for a Lady,* 1941

All of these uses are standard English. It seems quite clear that the last word on the grammar of these phrases has not yet been written, but inability to analyze constructions in a satisfying way has never deterred writers from using them. There seems little point in changing *other than* to *except* or *besides* or *otherwise than* or *apart from* unless you think the change makes your sentence sound better. You surely need not avoid *other than* simply because usage writers are perplexed by its grammar.

otherwise   The problem here is that old devil grammar. The commentator with the problem is Fowler 1926, who, as Bernstein 1971 puts it, "worked himself into a thousand-word lather over what he deemed misuses of *otherwise.*" This time Fowler had not missed

something in the OED, as he had with *other than;* the construction upon which he intended mayhem was not really covered in the OED, having become established only at the end of the 19th century (the OED Supplement dates it from 1886). The problem, as Fowler saw it, was *or otherwise* tacked on after an adverb, adjective, or noun (or verb, the OED Supplement adds) to indicate its contrary. (In actual use *otherwise* may also indicate an indefinite alternative, not necessarily a contrary.)

Fowler decided that *otherwise* had to be an adverb and so rejected *or otherwise* when attached to an adjective or noun. Bernstein and Copperud 1970, 1980 point out that *otherwise* is an adjective in most dictionaries, and they dismiss Fowler's objections (repeated by Phythian 1979) as pendantry. They tend to accept his objections to *or otherwise* attached to a noun, however.

The difficulty with all this ratiocination is that *otherwise,* one of our oldest everyday words, is far too flexible to be confined in the rigid part-of-speech categories of Latin. An example:

> No record exists of an Indian maiden, beautiful or otherwise —*American Guide Series: Minnesota,* 1938

Our commentators would parse *otherwise* as an adjective here because it indicates the contrary of *beautiful.* But let us look at another implied contrary of an adjective—this one familiar from children's play:

> Here I come—ready or not.

Surely none of our commentators would reject *not* here because it is not an adjective. Nor would they argue that it must be an adjective because it is paired with *ready.*

But enough of these grammatical puzzles. Here are some examples in which *or otherwise* (or *and otherwise*) suggests a contrary:

> . . . certain people whose deeds, admirable or otherwise, entitle them to more public attention —John Fischer, *Harper's,* December 1971

> . . . the stability or otherwise of this resolved and obstinate war Government —Sir Winston Churchill, *The Unrelenting Struggle,* 1942

> . . . we are shown portraits, prints, and drawings, contemporary and otherwise —*Times Literary Supp.,* 27 Aug. 1971

> . . . this cluster of shops for visitors, barefoot and otherwise —*Southern Living,* July 1972

> . . . essays by 16 Hardy enthusiasts, scholarly and otherwise —Peter Gardner, *Saturday Rev.,* 21 Feb. 1976

> . . . endurance tests to prove their fitness or otherwise for the status of manhood —Francis Birtles, *Battle Fronts of Outback,* in *Wanderers in Australia,* ed. Colin Roderick, 1949

> . . . the principal's willingness or otherwise to give it —Freeman Wills Crofts, *The Loss of the 'Jane Vosper',* 1936

The phrases are not uncommonly linked with a noun used as an adjective:

> . . . personalities, show biz and otherwise —Daisy Maryles, *Publishers Weekly,* 5 July 1976

> He has his wardens confiscate the tackle of the fisherman, VIP or otherwise, who spins in a fly stream —Fitzhugh Turner, *Outdoor Life,* February 1972

... could be discussing their hits, baseball and otherwise —*People,* 22 Nov. 1976

Otherwise may also imply an unspecified alternative, rather than a simple contrary. One of these examples shows *otherwise* linked with an impeccable adverb and so meets even Fowlerian standards of acceptability.

... if vacancies happen by resignation or otherwise during the recess of the legislature of any State —*Constitution of the United States,* 1787

It was clear that an effort was being made to intimidate senators and so prevent any laws, punitive and otherwise, from being enacted —Oliver St. John Gogarty, *It Isn't This Time of Year At All!,* 1954

... for most travelers, European or otherwise —Robin Prestage, *Saturday Rev.,* 1 Jan. 1972

They also were too apathetic or inexperienced to set rules for themselves, either academically or otherwise —Edith Hollerman, *Change,* Summer 1971

These constructions are standard, every one.

ought   1. *Ought* is a little awkward to put into the negative. In writing, *ought not* is the usual form, and it may be followed by the bare infinitive or the infinitive with *to:*

... it ought not to be weighed in the balance —Henry L. Stimson, *New Republic,* 22 Nov. 1954

... we ought not be completely absorbed in the technique of the law —Harlan F. Stone, quoted in *Commonweal,* 7 June 1940

... though professors ought not shout —Neil Schaeffer, *College English,* February 1976

... ought they not ask for membership in the new U.N. Trusteeship Council? —*Time,* 17 Mar. 1947

We really ought not expect more than one or two theories a generation —Nehemiah Jordan, *Themes in Speculative Psychology,* 1968

But thousands of others ought not to be in prison at all —Karl Menninger, quoted in *Psychology Today,* February 1969

Although *ought not* is used in speech, it does seem a bit stuffy for everyday use. *Oughtn't* is one spoken substitute. In the U.S. it is regionally limited, being found most commonly in Midland and Southern areas of the Atlantic Seaboard and in parts of the Northern Midland area. It has somewhat limited use in writing, mostly in reported speech or light prose:

You oughtn't to have to trot up there every time somebody gets it into his head he wants to ask you something —William Ruckleshaus, quoted in *N.Y. Times Mag.,* 19 Aug. 1973

... that's why Communist China oughtn't to be used here —W. E. Chilton III, quoted in *U.P.I. Reporter,* 15 July 1971

Muriel thought she oughtn't to disturb Roy —George P. Elliot, *Esquire,* February 1972

... but he oughtn't to have left out the gambling —David Williams, *Punch,* 15 June 1966

Bryant 1962 explains *hadn't ought* as a survival of an old use of *ought* as a past participle. It is found only in speechlike prose, speech, and fictional speech:

... he hadn't ought to have shown my letter to you. (I use American, that lovely tongue.) —H. L. Mencken, letter, 4 Sep. 1911

... and she kind of whispers to me, "Say, you hadn't ought to kid the servants like that." —Sinclair Lewis, *The Man Who Knew Coolidge,* 1928

"But he hadn't ought to be telling lies about Cleve Pikestaff." —Hodding Carter, *Southwest Rev.,* Winter 1948

The British equivalent of the American *hadn't ought* is *didn't ought.* It is aspersed in one way or another in various British usage books. It seems to be a spoken form only, and a footnote in Quirk et al. 1985 suggests that it may be a dwindling form, since it was the least popular negative form in a test of British teenage informants. Here are a couple of older examples:

Dixon was promoted in 1948 to be ambassador in Prague. [British Foreign Secretary Ernest] Bevin later commented, "I didn't ought to have sent you to that awful place" —*Times Literary Supp.,* 29 Feb. 1968

"Don't talk to your mother like that, Herbert," she flared up. "You didn't ought to have brought a woman like that into my house. . . ." —W. Somerset Maugham, *Quartet,* 1949

2. Some commentators (Follett 1966, for example) insist on retaining *to* before the infinitive after *ought* in every instance; others (Evans 1957, for instance) say *to* is optional in negative statements. Bernstein 1971 criticizes both sides, saying the *to* is optional in either negative or positive statements when something intervenes between *ought* and the infinitive, and he provides two examples of positive statements. Quirk et al. 1985 reports that tests of young people in both Great Britain and the U.S. showed the omission of *to* widely acceptable in what he calls "nonassertive contexts." Our files have only a couple of examples of omitted *to* in positive contexts from written sources; they would seem to fit the description of "nonassertive." Here is one:

... find stronger rationalizations for why people ought better communicate —Allan G. Mottus, *Women's Wear Daily,* 27 Aug. 1973

Here is an example with the intervening matter mentioned by Bernstein:

They ought logically go first to the standing committee —*N.Y. Times,* 28 Dec. 1966

But in edited prose, retention of the *to* is usual:

... the standard against which men ought to be measured —Ward Just, *Atlantic,* October 1970

Things are different in negative contexts. If you look back at the examples in section 1, you will note that *to* was often omitted after *ought not,* but retained after *oughtn't* and the double modal forms. We cannot say that this evidence is definitive, but there seems to be a noticeable tendency to retain the *to* in the spoken forms (one of the *ought not to* examples is from speech, too). Quirk et al. 1985 says that *to* tends to be retained in assertive contexts.

3. *Hadn't ought* and *didn't ought* we have looked at above. In the U.S. *hadn't ought* is a geographical variant rather than a social variant. The positive forms *had* *ought* and *should ought,* however, are characteristic of uneducated speech. Bryant says that *had ought* is, like *hadn't ought,* a Northern form, but an uncultivated one:

> . . . and so they had ought to be quiet, for they have nothin' to fight about —Thomas Chandler Halliburton, *The Clockmaker,* 1837

Should ought is a favorite of Ring Lardner's characters:

> "They should only ought to of had one. . . ." —*You Know Me Al,* 1916

4. See HAD OUGHT, HADN'T OUGHT.

ought to of   The *of* here stands for *'ve* or *have.* See OF 2.

-our   See -OR, -OUR.

ours   The possessive pronoun *ours,* like the possessive pronouns *its, theirs,* and *yours,* is properly spelled without an apostrophe.

ourselves   See MYSELF.

out   See OUT OF, OUT.

out loud   *Out loud* was once widely decried as an error for *aloud,* and it is still sometimes described as a colloquialism to be avoided in formal writing. Its first recorded use was in the early 19th century:

> Lord Andover in the presence of Lord and Lady Suffolk and speaking *out loud* —Maria Edgeworth, letter, 1821 (OED Supplement)

Its heyday as an object of criticism came about a hundred years later, when American commentators such as MacCracken & Sandison 1917, Ball 1923, Woolley & Scott 1926, and Krapp 1927 routinely prescribed against it in their books. Its use continued to be common, however, and its notoriety eventually diminished. It now survives as a usage topic chiefly in composition textbooks for high school and college students.

Our abundant written evidence for *out loud* shows clearly that it is not a colloquialism. We would agree that *aloud* is more likely in solemn writing, but in general use the two terms are essentially interchangeable:

> She read it aloud to my classmates —Russell Baker, *Growing Up,* 1982

> He was reading my words out loud to the entire class —Russell Baker, *Growing Up,* 1982

> . . . being permitted to think aloud with friends and colleagues —Bruce Dearing, *CEA Forum,* April 1971

> . . . afraid to let themselves or others think out loud —Nehemiah Jordan, *Themes in Speculative Psychology,* 1968

A distinctive and exclusive use of *out loud* is in the idiom "for crying out loud!" It is also preferred to *aloud* following the verb *laugh:*

> . . . *Mazeppa* makes him laugh out loud —Robert Craft, *N.Y. Rev. of Books,* 25 Feb. 1971

> He laughed out loud —E. L. Doctorow, *Loon Lake,* 1979

out of, out   A few commentators observe that the *of* is superfluous most of the time, or sometimes—depending on whose opinion you are reading—when *out* is used with verbs of motion. The observation, however, is not especially useful, for *out* and *out of* are interchangeable only in a very few restricted contexts; *out* simply cannot be substituted for *out of* in most cases.

Out is used much more often as an adverb than as a preposition. When used as a preposition, it seems most often to go with *door* or *window:*

> We went out the door and got into the car —Paul Ernst, *Redbook,* March 1964

> . . . old budgetary guidelines have gone out the window —Jerry Edgerton, *Money,* March 1980

> . . . permits prevailing west breezes to carry warm greenhouse air out the door —Glenn Munson, *Blair & Ketchum's Country Jour.,* January 1980

> He stares out the window —John Corry, *Harper's,* February 1969

With *window, out of* is about equally common:

> . . . who stared blankly out of a window —Emmanuel Bernstein, *Psychology Today,* October 1968

> . . . upstairs his fat wife leaned out of the window — Bernard Malamud, *The Magic Barrel,* 1958

With nouns that designate places or things that can be thought of as containing or surrounding, *out of* is usual:

> You never need get out of your car —Eileene Cofield, *Ford Times,* November 1967

> I would have done anything to get out of that kitchen —William M. Clark, *New-England Galaxy,* Fall 1969

> A bathtub is, at best, a makeshift place to take a shower. It's hard to get into and out of gracefully — *And More by Andy Rooney,* 1982

> . . . the fellow who, before being ridden out of town on a rail, remarked that if it wasn't for the honor of the thing, he'd prefer to walk —Robert Bendiner, *N.Y. Times Mag.,* 13 June 1954

Out has been used this way, but it sounds not quite part of the mainstream:

> "Father! father!" exclaimed a piercing cry from out the mist —James Fenimore Cooper, *The Deerslayer,* 1841

> Dock Knowital he Snuck Out the room an' Disappeared —Frank W. Sage, D.D.S., *Dental Digest,* November 1902

> The woman came out the bath house —Flannery O'Connor, *Partisan Rev.,* February 1949

We conclude that *out* is much more likely to be an adverb than a preposition. The prepositional *out* has a narrow range of application. It can seldom be idiomatically substituted for *out of.*

outside of   **1.** Bernstein 1965 sees nothing wrong with *outside of* as a synonym for *outside,* but a whole string of commentators from Bierce 1909 to Shaw 1987 do see something wrong. The culprit is *of,* all two letters and one syllable of it. Our evidence suggests that writers and speakers retain the *of* when it sounds right to them, and drop it when it does not. You have the same choice. Here are a few who kept *of:*

> Well, as an old veteran sixth-grader, that question is I think outside of my province —William Faulkner, 11 Mar. 1957, in *Faulkner in the University,* 1959

> If you order it outside of Boston, however, the waiter is not likely to know what you're talking about —Safire 1982

> . . . a power of language rarely found outside of a legislative assembly —Leacock 1943

> "Yes. He's a fine one," Pop said.
> "Where did you get him?"
> "Just outside of camp."
> —Ernest Hemingway, *Green Hills of Africa,* 1935

> . . . under an appropriate finding you could authorize the CIA to sell arms to countries outside of the provisions of the laws —Oliver North, in *The Tower Commission Report,* 1987

> Most of the papers chosen had been written outside of class to meet regular assignments —James Sledd, in Greenbaum 1985

> . . . but I was relatively unknown outside of Capitol Hill —Tip O'Neill with William Novak, *Man of the House,* 1987

2. Bernstein 1965 disparages *outside of* in the sense of "except for" or "aside from," and so do several college handbooks from Woolley & Scott 1926 to Macmillan 1982. The usage is, however, quite respectable in ordinary writing.

> Really outside of Hume no one in English philosophy has quite the same magic —Harold J. Laski, letter, 11 Apr. 1920

> . . . Britain and France can buy all the supplies they want from us, outside of munitions —*New Republic,* 8 Mar. 1939

> Expressions of dissatisfaction with newspapers, outside of a few major centers and a relatively limited list of papers, are very widely heard —Erwin D. Canham, *Saturday Rev.,* 14 Feb. 1953

> . . . all fish and shellfish—outside of a few specimens such as abalone and octopus—are tender in their raw state —Thomas Mario, *Playboy,* September 1968

> . . . was given no preferential treatment, outside of being addressed as Ypsilotatos —*Current Biography,* April 1967

> Outside of a few politicians, I can't imagine anyone so stuffy that he wouldn't enjoy this —Noel Coppage, *Stereo Rev.,* September 1971

3. See INSIDE OF.

over The preposition *over* has a dozen senses in Webster's Ninth New Collegiate Dictionary. Nearly half of these were under attack in the late 19th and early 20th centuries, but most of this controversy has been forgotten by now. One use, however—*over* in the sense "more than"—has not been forgotten.

Disapproval of *over* "more than" is a hoary American newspaper tradition. It began with William Cullen Bryant's *Index Expurgatorius* of 1877, compiled when he was editor of the *New York Evening Post.* Bryant sim-

ply forbade *over* (and *above*) in this sense; he gave no reason. From Bryant the dictum passed to Bierce 1909. (Bryson 1984, Copperud 1970, 1980, and Bernstein 1971 suspect Bierce of originating the notion.) From Bierce *over* passed into almost all of the newspaper handbooks: we find it in Hyde 1926; George C. Bastien et al., *Editing the Day's News* (4th ed., 1956); and Bremner 1980. *Time* for 11 Oct. 1948 twitted the Detroit *Free Press* for disapproving the usage while the newspaper's motto is "On Guard for Over a Century"; New World 1988 mentions the stylebooks of the *Washington Post, Los Angeles Times* and the Associated Press.

Neither Bryant nor Bierce deigned to give any reason for disapproval, but later commentators have devised a few. Bremner, for instance, distinguishes between 30,000 dollars and 200 pounds, which are "collective quantity" and 10,000 people and 200 buildings, which are "countables"—*over* may be used with the first two but not the second two. Of the stylebooks cited in New World, one insists that *over* refers only to physical location, and another allows it for age but not for other numerical quantities. The limitation to physical position is also mentioned by Harper 1975, 1985 and Freeman 1983.

All of this rationalization seems tortured. *Over* in the sense of "more than" has been used in English since the 14th century. Here are some examples of *over* in the disputed sense. You will note they were not written by American newspaper reporters.

> . . . over 32,000 acres are under vineyards —*Encyclopædia Britannica,* 11th ed., 1910

> Johnson's biographical writings cover a period of over forty years —John Butt, *English Literature in the Mid-Eighteenth Century,* edited & completed by Geoffrey Carnall, 1979

> I have now a library of nearly 900 volumes, over 700 of which I wrote myself —Henry David Thoreau, journal, 30 Oct. 1853, quoted in *N.Y. Times Book Rev.,* 7 Nov. 1982

> . . . Mr. Kallman and I have been close friends for over thirty years —W. H. Auden, *Harper's,* March 1972

> "How old is M'Cola?" I asked Pop.
> "He must be over fifty," Pop said.
> —Ernest Hemingway, *Green Hills of Africa,* 1935

> And I counted over six hundred men come out of there —Harry S. Truman, quoted in Merle Miller, *Plain Speaking,* 1973

> . . . the phrase in question appeared over six hundred years earlier —W. F. Bolton, *A Short History of Literary English,* 1967

> I have been in show business man and boy for over forty years —Groucho Marx, letter, 5 Sept. 1951

> It has been almost twenty-two years since you were at "Shorelee" and it doesn't seem a day over seventeen —James Thurber, letter, 1 June 1954

> Over two hundred friends from my district came —Tip O'Neill with William Novak, *Man of the House,* 1987

There is no reason why you need to avoid this usage.

overall This word has become common only in the 20th century, and its newfound popularity has led to criticism from several commentators (such as Evans 1957, Gowers 1965, and Phythian 1979). Their basic objection is not to the word itself but to its overuse, especially as an adjective in place of such familiar words as *general, total, complete,* and *comprehensive.* It is, certainly, an extremely common word, and although all of its common uses are standard, you may well want to give some thought to its value or appropriateness in a particular context before you use it in your writing. It is not, however, a word to be shunned. Here are a few examples of its use, both as an adjective and as an adverb:

> Despite an overall cultural similarity, the various parts of West Pakistan are dominated by different communal groups —Rosanne Klass, *Saturday Rev.,* 5 Feb. 1972

> ... the overall effect of the book is numbing — Michael Kammen, *N.Y. Times Book Rev.,* 4 July 1976

> ... the overall temper, the general disposition of the writer —I. A. Richards, *Times Literary Supp.,* 7 July 1978

> The sale, overall, appeared to have been successful —*Antiques and the Arts Weekly,* 29 Oct. 1982

> Overall, we need to promote public awareness — Russ Peterson, *Audubon Mag.,* November 1982

overlook, oversee A glance in any dictionary will show that the verb *overlook* has many senses, including one in which it is synonymous with *supervise.* This sense dates back to 1532, but in current English it has become extremely rare—for obvious reasons:

> The operators "overlook" the machines —Anglo-American Council on Productivity, *Packaging,* 1950

Take away the quotation marks and most readers will get an impression of distracted operators neglecting or perhaps tripping over their machines, since "to fail to notice; ignore" has long been established as the principal sense of *overlook.* The "supervise" sense now survives almost solely in the noun *overlooker,* a chiefly British synonym of *foreman:*

> ... overlookers in metal manufacture and engineering —B. Benjamin & H. W. Haycocks, *The Analysis of Mortality and Other Actuarial Statistics,* 1970

> ... require an overlooker to take charge of our Fancy Yarn Department —advt., *Telegraph & Argus* (Bradford, Eng.), 4 June 1974

The history of *oversee* closely resembles that of *overlook,* except that the "supervise" sense is the one that has prevailed:

> ... a few aides who were to oversee the major departments —*New Yorker,* 12 May 1972

Oversee also once meant "to fail to notice; disregard":

> ... to oversee and wilfully neglect the gross advances made him by my wife —William Congreve, *The Way of the World,* 1700 (OED)

But that sense of the word is now obsolete.

overly Bache 1869 and Ayres 1881 succinctly insulted contemporaries who used this word, calling them vulgar and unschooled. Times have changed: modern critics

merely insult the word itself. Follett 1966, for example, claims that *overly* is useless, superfluous, and unharmonious and should be replaced by the prefix *over-.* Bryson 1984 adds that "when this becomes overinelegant ..., the alternative is to find another adverb: 'excessively' or 'unnecessarily' or even the admirably concise 'too'." You may not want to go to such lengths to avoid *overly,* and some modern commentators (Evans 1957, for example) would agree that there is no need to. We concur. In fact, in some cases none of the alternatives sounds as good as *overly.*

> ... a not overly clean tunic —Thomas B. Costain, *The Black Rose,* 1945

> ... the author of various not overly inspired books —Robert A. Hall, Jr., *A Short History of Italian Literature,* 1951

> ... make his otherwise overly comfortable life more interesting —Pauline Kael, *Harper's,* February 1969

Even when *over-, too, excessively,* or *unnecessarily* would be a successful substitute, the fact that a synonym is available does not mean that you have to use it. These writers used *overly:*

> ... has been too long an observer of human folly to be overly optimistic —Leland Stone, *N.Y. Herald Tribune Book Rev.,* 13 May 1945

> In trying to get too much in he sometimes gets overly vehement —Sidney Monas, *Hudson Rev.,* Autumn 1950

> ... so much playing is overly concerned with notes —Howard Klein, *N.Y. Times,* 7 Apr. 1966

> ... Russian leaders seemed overly suspicious — Norman Cousins, *Saturday Rev.,* 30 Oct. 1971

> ... an overly educated European newspaperman — Norman Mailer, *N.Y. Times Mag.,* 26 Sept. 1976

> ... an overly eager land developer —William Styron, *N.Y. Times Mag.,* 15 June 1980

Overly is not as commonly used in England as in the U.S., but according to the OED Supplement it is gaining ground there.

oversee See OVERLOOK, OVERSEE.

overview This is another recently popular word. Shakespeare used it in *Love's Labour's Lost* (1595), but its now common use in the sense "a general survey" dates only from the 1920s:

> Very few courses now give an over-view of any field —*Jour. of Home Economics,* October 1926

Overview first became popular in the field of education, but by the 1950s it had come into more widespread use. It now occurs commonly enough to attract occasional criticism as a vogue word (as in Harper 1975, 1985). Its most frequent use, according to our evidence, is in describing a written work:

> ... includes a brief and interesting overview of the development of geological thinking —Barbara Blau Chamberlain, *Smithsonian,* January 1972

> It offers, however, a readable overview of American intervention —Peter Winn, *N.Y. Times Book Rev.,* 9 May 1976

This article is a bit heavy on metallurgy, but gives an excellent overview —*Blair & Ketchum's Country Jour.,* April 1980

overwhelm When *overwhelm* is used in the passive voice or as an adjectival past participle, it is most often followed with *by; with* is also found sometimes:

> . . . we have not been overwhelmed by the air attack —Sir Winston Churchill, *The Unrelenting Struggle,* 1942

> . . . an irrational, heroic, mystic world, beset by treachery, overwhelmed by violence —William L. Shirer, *The Rise and Fall of the Third Reich,* 1960

> . . . Oxford's dreaming spires overwhelmed by factories —John Fischer, *Harper's,* July 1972

> . . . a village whose final fate was to be overwhelmed with drifting sand —Jacquetta & Christopher Hawkes, *Prehistoric Britain,* 1949

When some other form of *overwhelm* is used, *by* and *with* are also used. Occasionally, *in* is also found:

> Your letter overwhelms me a little by its affectionate generosity —Harold J. Laski, letter, 2 Apr. 1920

> The danger of historical parallels is their power to overwhelm the judgment with the pat and triumphant testimony of coincidence —Archibald MacLeish, *Saturday Rev.,* 9 Feb. 1946

> . . . overwhelming the viewer with a mass of detail —*Current Biography,* September 1967

> . . . a blast furnace burst, overwhelming some twenty men in a stream of molten metal —*Times Literary Supp.,* 30 July 1971

over with *Over with* has been cited as an error or as a colloquialism in usage handbooks throughout the 20th century. The critics typically regard the *with* as superfluous. Some advise using *over* by itself; others express a preference for *finished* or *ended.* Our evidence indicates that *over with* occurs primarily in speech and in writing that has the informal quality of speech. It serves especially to express a desire or determination to have something unpleasant done or finished as soon as possible:

> I will be real glad when this television thing is over with —Flannery O'Connor, letter, 18 May 1955

Its most characteristic use is with the verb *get:*

> We may both live to be sorry we didn't go through school . . . and get it over with —Robert Frost, letter, 26 May 1926

> . . . talked of the need "to get this over with, the best way we can." —Eric F. Goldman, *Harper's,* January 1969

> We want to tackle a problem and get it over with — Henry Huglin, *Center Mag.,* January/February 1970

> The Carter administration, no doubt, will now try to ignore the flap and get the renominations over with —*Wall Street Jour.,* 3 June 1980

Such usage is perfectly idiomatic and need not be avoided in an appropriate context.

owing to For some comments about the history of this preposition, which has frequently been prescribed by the commentators in place of *due to,* see the article on DUE TO.

P

pace This preposition was introduced into English from Latin in the 19th century. In Latin it had been part of various polite formulas such as *pace tua* "by your leave" and *pace Veneris* "if Venus will not be offended by my saying so." In English it serves a somewhat similar purpose, being used primarily as a courteous (the OED Supplement will also allow ironical) apology for introducing a contradictory opinion. It tends to be used in writing of the learned sort, and is almost always italicized—a useful practice, for it helps distinguish the Latinism from the much older English noun and verb *pace.*

Fowler 1926, 1965 takes a dim view of this word—a Latinism, he says, that English could have done very well without. He finds it not only misunderstood when used rightly, but also frequently used wrongly. The largest part of his discussion is given over to two lengthy examples, the authors of which believed *pace* to mean "according to." Our files have no examples of this misunderstanding.

Fowler also shows a Latinist's distaste for the extended application of the Latin word in English by the Latinless. The passage that Fowler picks out as an atrocious example uses *pace* before a noun designating not a person but something produced by a person. In spite of Fowler's distaste, this extension appears legitimate;

we have respectable examples of its use, although it is distinctly a minority usage:

> English writing on Godoy has not been limited, *pace* the translator's foreword, to one book published some 40 years ago —*Times Literary Supp.,* 13 Feb. 1953

> . . . if one admits—as I do (*pace* the doctrinaire eschatology of the old and new left) —Theodore Roszak, *The Making of a Counter Culture,* 1969

> . . . a volume which, *pace* the blurb, will be of much greater interest to the beginner than to the advanced student —*Times Literary Supp.,* 12 Feb. 1970

If you suspect that this use is not uncommon in the pages of the *Times Literary Supplement,* you are correct.

This brings us to another problem. What does this preposition mean when it is used, as it is most of the time, in front of a person's name, as, for instance, in this example?

> . . . an extremely mysterious figure whose date of birth is still, *pace* Miss Byrne, highly problematic — J. H. Plumb, *N.Y. Times Book Rev.,* 14 June 1981

The dictionaries are not especially helpful here. They generally content themselves with English renderings of what the Latin word would have meant in Latin: for instance "by the leave of; with the permission of; with all due respect to." The last of these seems the most relevant to English contexts; it can be put in the place of *pace* in the quotation from J. H. Plumb, for instance. But only Fowler, apparently, has concentrated on defining the word in English context. He says it means "despite someone's opinion."

Fowler has isolated the meaning of the chief use of *pace* better than the dictionary definers. Try his definition or these variations on it—"contrary to the opinion of, in spite of what _____ says"—in these mainstream examples:

> *Pace* Anita Loos, six out of ten prefer brunettes — *Time,* 1 Sept. 1947

> Another, *pace* Cassidy, blamed the influence on various foreign groups —H. L. Mencken, *The American Language, Supplement II,* 1948

> Their systems, *pace* Haldane, have burdened and bored the world —Oliver Wendell Holmes d. 1935, letter, 27 Aug. 1927

> His critical poise is manifested in (pace Mr Eliot) a lively ironic humour —F. R. Leavis, *The Common Pursuit,* 1952

> Life, *pace* Jeremy Bentham, is not exclusively utilitarian —*Times Literary Supp.,* 11 Nov. 1965

> *Pace* Mr. Morris, nobody is being *forced* to listen — Harold C. Schonberg, *N.Y. Times,* 7 Dec. 1975

> *Pace* my tormentor of 1938, it is most common in Michigan —Raven I. McDavid, Jr., *American Speech,* Spring–Summer 1977

> Easiness is a virtue in grammar, *pace* old-fashioned grammarians of the Holofernes school, who confused difficulty with depth —Howard 1984

Fowler's point about misuse was not entirely mistaken. Although the great preponderance of use is standard and clear, we do have in our files some few examples that show the author's unfamiliarity with how most writers use the word. In the first the author seems to have been uncertain; if he knew what he meant, he has not made it clear to us. In the second the preposition is put to use as a kind of deprecatory interjection; this use is not established. In the third the author seems to think *pace* is a French word.

> *Pace* Woody Allen, it is a true sleeper, a movie both of substantial flaw and surprise —Jay Cocks, *Time,* 27 Jan. 1975

> It is without question that the modernist novel centers in Joyce; but *pace,* Pound, it is not all Joyce — Herman Wouk, *Saturday Rev.,* 29 June 1974

> IBM could have bought Intel—*pacé* the Justice Department —Howard Banks et al., *Forbes,* 28 Feb. 1983

In conclusion, we may say that *pace* is generally confined to learned or at least somewhat elevated discourse. If you are not especially familiar with its use, you should probably avoid using it. If you do use it, we suggest that you stick to the majority usage and that you italicize the word. It is used most safely when you intend to express an opinion contrary to that expressed in some conspicuous way by another person.

pachyderm, pachydermatous A handful of critics complain about these words. Copperud 1964, 1970, 1980 and Flesch 1964 object to newspaper use of *pachyderm* as a synonym for *elephant;* Flesch mentions a report that it is hard to find a pachyderm parking space in Bangkok. Flesch has failed to note the appeal of the alliteration in his example. Copperud says that Fowler 1926, 1965 objects to *pachydermatous* as a synonym for *elephantine,* but he is a little off-target. Fowler actually mentions *pachydermatous* as a favorite of what he calls "polysyllabic humorists," who use it to mean "thick-skinned" as they use *terminological inexactitude* for "lie." He feels, understandably, that such attempts at humor are, well, elephantine and quickly grow tiresome.

There is really no problem with these words that a little restraint in using them will not eliminate. The chances are that you will be careful enough to avoid overkill. So go ahead and use *pachyderm* or *pachydermatous* if it suits your purpose. As you can see from the following examples, the purpose need not be dead serious.

> A mighty creature is the germ,
> Though smaller than the pachyderm.
> —Ogden Nash, "The Germ," reprinted in *Chains of Light* (8th grade textbook), 1982

> Mrs. Hammond rents her adorable pachyderm out to Republican party (naturally) clambakes —Leo Rosten, *Saturday Rev.,* 25 Jan. 1975

> . . . the halcyon days of the mat game in Cape Town when fans used to work themselves up into a frenzy over the antics of the cabbage-eared pachyderms — *Cape Times* (South Africa), 8 Dec. 1945

> . . . making one another laugh by sticking pins into venerable pachyderms like the royal family, the army, the Archbishop of Canterbury —Patrick Campbell, *Saturday Rev.,* 11 June 1977

> Let us, then, advise every book-lover to turn to Mr. Clive in preference to best sellers. You will do well to pass up those pachyderms —Owen Dudley Edwards, *N.Y. Times Book Rev.,* 1 Apr. 1973

If you look into your dictionary, you will discover that *pachyderm* is used of several animals besides the elephant. Among the better known of these are the hippopotamus and the rhinoceros. Considered together with the elephant, who most often parades under the name, these pachyderms suggest a certain bulk and solidity. Hence it is no surprise to see the term extended to professional wrestlers, certain hidebound institutions, and fat best-selling novels.

Next, some examples of the adjective from sources that range from the humorous to the entirely sober:

> . . . when P. G. Wodehouse wrote, on the subject of one of his sabre-toothed and pachydermatous aunts, 'A massive silence prevailed in the corner where the aunt sat' —Howard 1977

> . . . galumphs into a vein of pachydermatous verbalizing —G. Legman, *Rationale of the Dirty Joke,* 2d series, 1975

> . . . even in dealing with the most pachydermatous political systems, patient pressure is neither counterproductive nor futile —*The Economist,* 19 July 1985

One humorist, not especially polysyllabic, has even used the rarer *pachydermic:*

> Even ponderous pachydermic objects—like the automobile and refrigerator—were willing to wear out after a mere two or three years so that succeeding generations of automobiles and refrigerators could have their chances to browse in my bank account —Russell Baker, *N.Y. Times Mag.,* 21 Nov. 1976

paid   See PAY.

pair   1. *Plural: "pair," "pairs."* The usual plural is *pairs,* when there is no preceding number or indicator of number (as *several*):

> ... maturity is the ability to live with conflicting pairs of truths —Faubion Bowers, *Saturday Rev.,* 12 Feb. 1972

When a number or indicator of number precedes *pair,* either *pair* or *pairs* may be used:

> ... hung the pin-stripe suit with the two pair of pants —Wright Morris, *Real Losses, Imaginary Gains,* 1976

> ... six pair of blue jeans —Marcia Cohen, *N.Y. Times Mag.,* 2 Mar. 1975

> It had oarlocks for three pairs of oars —Frances H. Eliot, *New England Journeys,* 1953

> In a saucepan soak 2 pairs of sweetbreads —Evan Jones, *Gourmet,* February 1973

A few commentators—Harper 1985, Bremner 1980, Shaw 1987—disparage the plural form *pair* after a number. Our evidence shows that both *pair* and *pairs* are in reputable use in the U.S.
2. *Agreement. Pair* is one of those collective nouns that take a singular or plural verb according to notional agreement. If you are thinking of the individuals in the pair, you will use a plural verb:

> A pair of elephants were grazing near the camp — Alan Moorehead, *No Room in the Ark,* 1959, in Henry I. Christ, *Modern English in Action,* 1982

If you are thinking of the pair as a unit, you will use the singular:

> Genuine crocodile loafers. ... The handsome pair has a hand-sewn moccasin construction —catalog, *Trifles,* Fall 1987

3. *Pair of twins.* Among the minor matters that engage some usage writers is the expression *pair of twins.* Shaw 1987 and Bremner 1980 conclude that *pair of twins* should not be used unless four people are meant. Bernstein 1971 pooh-poohs this view: ". . . in ordinary, forgiveable usage *a pair of twins* is the customary phrase." Bernstein even finds the expression useful. It could sometimes be useful for clarification, perhaps. We have a snippet from a magazine in the Merriam-Webster files that refers to a doctor surrounded by 8 or 10 twins. How many people would that be? Unfortunately we do not have enough of the story to be able to tell for sure. *Pair of twins* appears to be a spoken usage; we have no evidence for it in print.

pajamas, pyjamas   Until the early 20th century, in the United States the spelling *pajamas* vied with the spelling *pyjamas.* However, *pajamas* is now the usual American spelling and *pyjamas* is the British:

> ... a silent, distrustful crowd of villagers gathered in their ragged black pajamas and wide conical hats — Darrell Berrigan, *Saturday Evening Post,* 12 Nov. 1955

> ... old women in black pajamas, hair pulled back — Peggy Seeger & Diane Alexander, *N.Y. Times,* 13 Apr. 1975

> ... the bed was turned back and a suit of remarkably brilliant pyjamas ... was laid out —Ngaio Marsh, *Colour Scheme,* 1943

> ... perhaps it was the colour of his pyjamas —Graham Greene, *Travels with My Aunt,* 1969

Exceptions, of course, can occur:

> The Professor in pyjamas was not an unpleasant sight —Willa Cather, *The Professor's House,* 1925

> ... a pair of puce pajamas newly laundered — Anthony Burgess, *MF,* 1971

Perhaps the biggest categorical exception occurs in contemporary American advertising, where the spelling *pyjamas* is found with some regularity, perhaps for snob appeal; even so, the spelling *pajamas* can be found in the same publications:

> Evening pyjamas made for us alone —advt., *Vogue,* June 1982

> ... silky black jersey hostess pyjamas —catalog, *Horchow,* July–August 1982

> ... takes Polyester Georgette into a tea length dress and evening pajamas —caption, *Vogue,* May 1985

palimpsest   In late classical and medieval times, the *Encyclopædia Britannica* tells us, parchment and vellum were both scarce and costly. These materials were sometimes recycled; books that had become neglected or outdated would be disassembled, the writing on them removed by various means, and the sheets used for writing new texts on. Later scholars discovered that the original texts on these reused sheets could be read and recovered; important texts of classical authors such as Cicero, Livy, and Plautus survive in palimpsests.
The word *palimpsest* for this sort of reused sheet of writing material came into English in the first quarter of the 19th century—just about the time, apparently, that scholars were beginning to recover old texts from them. The earliest citation in the OED is dated 1825; it mentions the pioneer in deciphering erased texts, Angelo Mai (spelled Mayo in the citation). The word had hardly been in the language twenty years before it began to be used figuratively.
Keeping in mind that an actual palimpsest is a piece of writing material that has been erased and written on again, we can understand many of the figurative uses of the word. Sometimes writing, erasing, and rewriting is the underlying idea:

> This was the first of a very long series of those bizarre 'revisions' and 'corrections' that, in the end, were to make the history of the revolution an almost illegible palimpsest —Isaac Deutscher, *Stalin,* 1949

> The traces of scholarly tradition are always present in the fictional context that employs them, present

"under erasure," as Derrida would suggest, making the text a palimpsest that both hides and reveals all its previous sources —Shari Benstock, *PMLA,* March 1983

Most often it is the notion of the layers that prevails:

The style he has invented for his purpose works on the principle of a palimpsest: one meaning, one set of images, is written over another —Edmund Wilson, *Axel's Castle,* 1931

. . . Canada, like any country, is a palimpsest, an overlay of classes and generations —Margaret Atwood, *N.Y. Times Book Rev.,* 10 Mar. 1985

He had become aware too that at any given moment the mind is a palimpsest of perceptions, conscious and unconscious —Arthur Mizener, *The Saddest Story,* 1971

We even find *palimpsest* stretched from layers written and layers seen to the realm of what is heard:

There is also the additional problem raised by the casting of Rod Steiger as Fields. . . . I find it hard to forget that this face and this voice are Steiger's, which gives me a kind of audiovisual palimpsest — John Simon, *New York,* 5 Apr. 1976

Today's pop record is a palimpsest of noninstrumental sounds —Richard R. Lingeman, *N.Y. Times Mag.,* 27 Nov. 1966

The palimpsest is clearly a metaphor with a strong appeal to the more intellectual sort of writer. The trouble with an appealing metaphor is that it can be slipped into a context where the reader has a hard time connecting the word to even its obvious figurative meaning:

The great difficulty for the reader is that Pilling's commentary is like a palimpsest; one needs the text open in front of one in order to follow his exposition —Phyllis Grosskurth, *Times Literary Supp.,* 28 Nov. 1981

But by the use of the "madwoman" and other palimpsests, they were able to refute and reinterpret his mandates —Valerie Miner, *Christian Science Monitor,* 11 Feb. 1980

Talking shaped our faces, turned them into palimpsests, mobile and restless, waiting to pounce —Anatole Broyard, *N.Y. Times Book Rev.,* 24 Jan. 1982

. . . a visitor can read the history of the city in the palimpsest of shop signs —Nancy Harmon Jenkins, *N.Y. Times Mag.,* 3 Nov. 1985

We suggest that if you are tempted to use this hard word, you keep the original palimpsest—written, erased, written over, with the older layer dimly visible under the newer—firmly in mind. You will be less likely to puzzle your readers if you do.

palpable   Fowler 1926 considers *palpable* a dead metaphor that can be brought to "angry life" by extended use. Krapp 1927 cautions that the word must be handled carefully, a sentiment echoed by Copperud 1970, 1980; Flesch 1964 thinks the word is bookish; Evans 1957 thinks *palpable lie* is no longer fresh. All of this cautionary exhortation seems belied by the fact that published writers who use the word—there seem to be plenty of them—have no particular difficulty with it.

The primary meaning is "capable of being touched or felt," a sense that is common in medical use:

The liver span was 18 cm, and the edge was palpable 8 cm below the right costal margin —Howard Wilson, M.D., et al., *JAMA,* 23 Feb. 1979

By the 15th century, *palpable* was being used figuratively, applied to what could be perceived by senses other than touch:

. . . Madame saw her smile at Lion. Hilda thought the smile was secret, but it was completely palpable to Madame —Rumer Godden, *A Candle for St. Jude,* 1948

As palpable and constant as the smell in the house —Jean Stafford, *New Yorker,* 7 Apr. 1951

. . . the sharp drafts of autumn are palpable in the cool air flowing down the mountain —Stephen Goodwin, *Prose,* Fall 1972

Further extension, from the physical senses to mental perception, took place in the 16th century:

This vulgar notion is, indeed, a palpable error — Matthew Arnold, *Essays in Criticism, First Series,* 1865

That, I tell him, is palpable nonsense —David Brudnoy, *National Rev.,* 17 Dec. 1971

. . . a modest but palpable good time —John Simon, *New York,* 26 Mar. 1973

. . . has sued directors for a "palpable break of fiduciary duty" in a class action suit —Maria Shao, *Wall Street Jour.,* 8 June 1981

. . . I had dashed off my own offering on "the jury system." It was a palpable plagiarism from Mark Twain —*The Autobiography of William Allen White,* 1946

No slander was too gross, no lie too palpable —Vernon Louis Parrington, *Main Currents in American Thought,* 1930

Figurative use is the predominant use in present-day English. Some writers signal the original sense of the word by overtly marking the figurative nature of their use:

". . . you seem to be able to touch beauty as though it were a palpable thing . . ." —W. Somerset Maugham, *The Moon and Sixpence,* 1919

In the expiring, diffused twilight . . . it was the immensity of space made visible—almost palpable —Joseph Conrad, *Chance,* 1913

. . . the strong constant smell of the pines was coming down on them with no wind behind it yet firm and hard as a hand almost, palpable against the moving body as water would have been —William Faulkner, *Intruder in the Dust,* 1948

. . . a profligate alcoholic whose hatred of his father is so fierce it is almost palpable —Edith Oliver, *New Yorker,* 1 May 1971

The moonlight seems palpable, a dense pure matrix in which is embedded curbstone and building alike —Walker Percy, *The Moviegoer,* 1961

There are, then, two ways to use *palpable* figuratively—with an overt signal, such as *seem* or *almost,* or without it, as most writers apparently prefer to do. If you use the word in ways like those of the writers quoted here, you are unlikely to go wrong.

panacea A panacea literally is a magical medicine that cures all ailments and figuratively is a magical solution that solves all problems. Since no such medicine and no such solution actually exist, the word *panacea* almost always occurs in negative constructions ("There is no panacea for these problems") or in contexts in which the writer is criticizing a single proposed or attempted solution to a broad array of problems as inadequate or simplistic:

> Oversight, the current panacea of liberal legislative mechanics, means very little if it is not part of a process that clearly involves large numbers of citizens —Marcus Raskin, *N.Y. Times Book Rev.,* 11 Apr. 1976

Panacea is also sometimes used to speak—usually in a deprecating way—of a simple, easy solution to a single problem. Such use may seem inconsistent with the word's "cure-all" denotation, but the underlying logic of it is usually evident: it implies that the problem (or, in literal applications, the ailment) is a complex and difficult one having many aspects which no single solution can, by itself, put right:

> Decentralization has been proposed as a panacea for this major problem —Albert Shanker, *N.Y. Times,* 9 Jan. 1969

> ... private involvement is not a panacea for the over-all problem of municipal recreation —Barry Tarshis, *New York,* 5 July 1971

> ... have concentrated on stimulation of demand as the panacea for economic stagnation —John Lenczowski, *Saturday Rev.,* 6 Jan. 1979

> ... the official panacea for managing social conflict at home was economic growth —Richard J. Barnet, *N.Y. Times Book Rev.,* 18 July 1982

Cases in which *panacea* has been used more broadly to mean "an easy and complete cure or solution," without the implication that the ailment or problem in question is especially complex, are rare, according to our evidence. Bernstein 1962, 1965 disapprovingly cites a passage from the *New York Times* in which the writer refers to a possible "panacea for mosquito bites." Other commentators who have criticized such usage include Evans 1957, Harper 1985, and Bryson 1984.

pander 1. *Pander, panderer.* Copperud 1980 says *panderer* is more common in the newspapers, but *pander* is the original noun. *Pander* is a 16th-century noun; *panderer* is a 19th-century word derived from the verb. Our files show no particular difference in frequency between the two nouns at the present time. Both are seen decidedly less often than the verb. Both nouns are also used in the figurative sense:

> ... at 50 he decided ... that he was nothing more than a pander to people who had nothing better to do with their time than read —E. L. Doctorow, *N.Y. Times Book Rev.,* 25 Aug. 1985

> Basically he was a panderer, out to seduce, or amuse, or thrill his public —Harold C. Schonberg, *N.Y. Times,* 2 Apr. 1972

2. The intransitive verb *pander* is regularly used with *to:*

> ... the public interest could be served without pandering to idle curiosity —E. Pendleton James, *Business Week,* 19 Apr. 1982

> ... which panders to the frustrated, inarticulate ambitions of the illiterate lower middle classes — Robert Pattison, *On Literacy,* 1982

> ... a mercenary who has used his brilliant gifts to pander to popular taste —Hubert Saal, *N.Y. Times Book Rev.,* 13 Mar. 1983

pants Ambrose Bierce was no man to mince words, and his opinion of *pants* was characteristically unequivocal: "vulgar exceedingly" he called it in 1909. He was not the first to think so:

> The thing named 'pants' in certain documents,
> A word not meant for gentlemen, but 'gents'
>   —Oliver Wendell Holmes d. 1894,
>   *Rhymed Lesson,* 1846 (OED)

Pants, originally short for *pantaloons,* is an Americanism that was first recorded in 1840. Its bad reputation as a vulgar synonym for *trousers* lasted nearly a century, but its increasingly common use eventually quieted the critics, and no one now disputes that *pants* is standard and respectable. Such criticism as is now heard is directed at the singular form *pant,* which has seen occasional use since at least the 1890s:

> They say: 'I have a pant that I can sell you' —H. A. Shands, *Some Peculiarities of Speech in Mississippi,* 1893 (OED Supplement)

> ... the perfect complement for a handsome blazer and trim belted pant —advt., *N.Y. Times Mag.,* 29 Feb. 1976

> ... exciting re-thinking on the new cropped pant — advt., *N.Y. Times,* 22 Sept. 1981

This use of *pant* is now common in clothing advertisements and catalogs but is otherwise rare.

The British have adopted *pants* from American English, but they use it primarily in a distinct sense, as a synonym for *underpants* or *drawers.* This is a distinction that Americans traveling in Great Britain may consider worth remembering.

paparazzo, paparazzi *Paparazzo,* usually seen in the form of its plural *paparazzi,* is a quite recent import from Italian. It usually refers to one of those free-lance photographers who are noted for their aggressive pursuit of celebrities:

> ... only a remote chance that gossip columnists or paparazzi will crash the parties in the hotel's private suites —*Newsweek,* 10 Jan. 1966

> ... used paparazzi tactics in order to snap candid pictures of reclusive celebrities —Patricia Bosworth, *Esquire,* May 1973

> It was like *paparazzi* photographing each other instead of the celebrities —Ronald Steel, *N.Y. Times Book Rev.,* 5 Aug. 1984

It should come as no surprise that a recent import from Italian suffers a certain amount of misspelling and has its plural taken as a singular. One wire service managed to do both at once:

> ... a self-styled "papparrazi" who claimed he had taken and sold thousands of photos —*Transcript-Telegram* (Holyoke, Mass), (UPI), 6 July 1972

Remember that the ending in *i* is the plural and that only the *z* is doubled. If you spell the word with two or three sets of double letters, you're in trouble.

See LATIN PLURALS for other plurals used as singulars.

paradigm   *Paradigm* is a learned word that has been in use since the 15th century. Its original meaning was "example, pattern." At the end of the 16th century grammarians appropriated the word and applied it to a pattern of inflected forms in a language, which were usually displayed in tabular form. Flesch 1964, Reader's Digest 1983, Janis 1984, and Barzun 1985 all note that *paradigm* has become a popular jargon word. These commentators were not the only ones who noticed the word:

> Every season there's a new word in vogue. There was a time when everything had to be *viable* or *relevant*. This year, the word is *paradigm*. The Left is "looking for a new paradigm," one hears. "The liberals have lost their paradigm." —Amanda Spake, *Mother Jones*, February/March 1980

The old sense has continued to flourish. Here we find it as "a typical example":

> The descriptions of Frankfurt as a paradigm of modern city life —Joseph P. Bauke, *Saturday Rev.*, 27 Nov. 1971

Here as "an outstanding or perfect example":

> Louis XIV, the paradigm of absolute monarchs — John Wilkinson, *Center Mag.*, March 1968

And as "a pattern of behavior":

> His logic is the familiar paradigm: If radicals take two steps forward, society will eventually take one —Robert Sklar, *The Progressive*, February 1967

> ... by the standards of the 1960s, the paradigm of revolution; the cadre was thoroughly committed, socially heterogeneous, and tragically ineffectual — Bernard F. Dick, *Saturday Rev.*, 18 Mar. 1972

It can even appear in place of *paragon:*

> It is the finest cigar in all the world. ... The photographic use we, at enormous self-sacrifice, have made of this paradigm of stogies is not to torment you with visions of the unobtainable —*Esquire*, September 1973

Such uses as these are, relatively speaking, paradigms of clarity when compared to the most active area of current popular jargonistic use—that of science. The father of the new use seems to be Thomas S. Kuhn, who, in the second edition of his influential *The Structure of Scientific Revolutions* (1973) admitted that in his first edition (1962) he had used *paradigm* at least 22 different ways. With such a diverse foundation, it is not surprising that the ways in which the scientific and theoretical writers throw the word around may sometimes puzzle us innocent bystanders. Here are a few examples. They share the broad central notion of "a theoretical framework":

> Western scientific medicine is undergoing a fundamental shift in basic beliefs and assumptions. ...

> This paradigm shift from reductionism to holism is altering the practice of medicine in America today —*Interface*, Fall 1979

> The psychophysical paradigm was a self-paced method of constant stimuli —Dennis M. Levi & Stanley Klein, *Nature*, 15 July 1982

> For example, the beginnings of some paradigms might be Aristotle's analysis of motion or Maxwell's mathematization of the electromagnetic field — Mary A. Meyer, *Physics Today*, June 1983

> ... they have used a research paradigm, that of intervention in a normal infant care context —M. J. Konner, *Science*, 19 Jan. 1973

> The adaptationist view bids fair to become the dominant paradigm within evolutionary biology and ecology —Stephen Rose, *N.Y. Times Book Rev.*, 8 May 1983

But we should not point at scientists alone. The literary critics have been known to throw the word about too:

> Genet, then, as the very paradigm of existentialist schizophrenia, embodied not only the mystic heart of Sartreian philosophy but the entire preoccupation with the dialectics of negation and illusion —John Killinger, *Jour. of Modern Literature*, 1st issue, 1970

parallel   **1.** It is not hard to misspell *parallel*, what with all those *l*'s congregating in strange ways. If it gives you trouble, you can try thinking of the two *l*'s in the middle as parallel lines cutting through the word. Better yet, keep a dictionary handy.
2. Prepositions that occur idiomatically after the adjective *parallel* are *to* and *with:*

> ... an undertaking which ran parallel to the more orthodox ... theorizing —*Times Literary Supp.*, 5 June 1969

> ... a form of expression that for many years ran parallel with his painting —*Current Biography*, April 1968

To seems to be preferred in mathematical writing:

> ... a plane parallel to the base of a cone —School Mathematics Study Group, *Geometry, Part II*, 1965

> ... with the line y = f(a) parallel to the x-axis — School Mathematics Study Group, *Calculus, Part I*, 1965

The noun *parallel* is idiomatically followed by *to, with*, and *between:*

> ... look for a parallel to the all-Brahms recital — Irving Kolodin, *Saturday Rev.*, 13 Nov. 1971

> To cite another parallel with Vietnam —Ronald P. Kriss, *Saturday Rev.*, 26 Feb. 1972

> The parallel between the treatment of blacks and women by our society —Ruth R. Hawkins, *Change*, November–December 1969

3. Simon 1980 finds fault with Joyce Carol Oates for having written "Nor do the parallels between the two American women become too aggressively pointed." According to Simon, "Parallels are lines that run side by side; in no sense can they be pointed." This is not a serious issue, but let us point out the obvious: *parallel* as used by Oates means "a comparison showing similarity," a sense of the word that is nearly four centuries old and has been recognized as standard in dictionaries since Samuel Johnson's time. In this sense, parallels can indeed be pointed.

parallelism   See FAULTY PARALLELISM; NOT ONLY . . . BUT ALSO.

parameter   Sometime in 1958 *New York Times* columnist James Reston included *parameter* in a list of baffling technical terms he did not like. The newspaper in June of that year reported the list had brought in a large number of protests from "scientific gentlemen," several of whom essayed to define the term for laypeople. A typical definition, said the *Times,* was this:

> A parameter is a point of the domain of a mapping, this domain frequently being an interval on the real line, and the range of the domain being a subset of Euclidean space of several dimensions or even of Hilbert space —9 June 1958

If that is what a parameter is, it is hard to disagree with this comment:

> *Parameter* is a mathematical term with a precise meaning which, it is safe to say, not one in ten of those who use it understands —Sir Bruce Fraser, in Gowers 1973

But by 1973 *parameter* was, in fact, much more than a mathematical term with a precise meaning. The spread of usage had begun much earlier, but unlike later usage spread, the earlier was done chiefly by people working in technical fields:

> In polyatomic molecules the nuclear configuration is described by several parameters, and variation of two parameters is sufficient to establish degeneracy —Francis Owen Rice & Edward Teller, *The Structure of Matter,* 1949

> The parameters (a 3% price change, and 10% growth change) were intentionally selected so that the growth effect on working capital retention would offset the price effect —Felix Kaufman & Alan Gleason, *Accounting Rev.,* October 1953

> The general picture of the carbon skeleton was thus provisionally defined by the three parameters mentioned above (aromaticity, ring condensation index and aromatic area) —P. H. Hermans, translation of D. W. Van Krevelen & J. Schuyer, *Coal Science,* 1957

> The satellite has light sensitive elements which alter the radio frequencies of the signals and the correlation between their durations and intermissions as soon as the temperature or other parameters of the satellite change —*Science,* 18 Oct. 1957

> There has been a good deal of monitoring of circulatory and respiratory parameters of native highlanders —*Nature,* 9 Aug. 1969

Even the spread to more general use was prefigured:

> . . . pondering the fact that the whole parameter of personal success bulks very small indeed in a world which is earnestly trying to find out whether the human race must necessarily destroy itself —John G. Jenkins, *Science,* 11 Jan. 1946

> . . . the space-fiction cosmos of fantasy, with . . . its invisibility, immortality and freedom from all other limiting parameters —Jonathan Norton Leonard, *Flight into Space,* 1953

If James Reston's list was the distant early warning of *parameter*'s creeping into more general use, usage writers were not quick to respond. No commentator seems to have noticed the term until the 1970s. If we take as the earliest of these Fraser in Gowers 1973, Newman 1974, and Nickles 1974, we will see that all three subscribe to the theory that *parameter* is a misused mathematical term, which, as noted earlier, is not an adequate description. Fraser and Nickles both put forward the notion that *parameter* is frequently used where *perimeter* is meant. Such confusion may occur in speech, but it is an odd observation to make of edited prose, for *perimeter* (before 1973) was quite rare in extended use, and whereas *parameter* in the criticized use is usually plural, *perimeter* in figurative use (before 1973) was usually singular. (The possible effect of *parameter*-avoidance on the figurative use of *perimeter* is discussed at PERIMETER.)

The use of *parameter* most likely to attract comment about misuse for *perimeter* is that in which it is used in the plural in the sense of "limits." Note that in the first two examples below *parameters* clearly means "limits," but *perimeter* or *perimeters* could not be used; in the second two you could force *perimeters* in, but other words such as *bounds* or *range* or *confines* would work as well or better.

> In the event that temperature levels exceed parameters, the system will warn the operator —*Datamation,* February 1976

> . . . [it] is clearly within the parameters of Yariv's simple formula that Mr. Kissinger would seek to concoct his own equation for bringing Israel and the P.L.O. together —Edward R. F. Sheehan, *N.Y. Times Mag.,* 8 Dec. 1974

> *The Teachings of Don Juan* and *Fire on the Moon* both fall within the parameters of science fiction as an attitude —Michael Baron, *Real Paper,* 3 Dec. 1975

> Eno's eccentric music doesn't stray beyond rock's accustomed borders so much as it innovates within those parameters —Charley Walters, *Rolling Stone,* 6 May 1976

You may also notice that things tend to be *within* parameters. This was not the idiom with *perimeter(s)* before the middle 1970s.

By the time that most of the usage commentators were coming down hard on *parameter,* the computer had established itself in the powerful position it now holds, where it can meddle with the lives of every one of us. With the computer came *parameter,* stronger than ever. It is unlikely to be dislodged until a swankier term comes along. Just look at the publications, largely general in nature, where it is entrenched:

> With these formulas in place, Grycz can change any parameter (book length, typesetting costs, royalty) and project the net impact on all costs automatically —Robyn Shotwell, *Publishers Weekly,* 5 Feb. 1982

> But a true novel is an extended piece of fiction: Length is clearly one of its parameters —Anthony Burgess, *N.Y. Times Book Rev.,* 5 Feb. 1984

For the technically oriented, this approach, among other parameters, involves careful consideration of the distance from the woofer to reflective surfaces — Henry Hunt, *Houston Post,* 26 Aug. 1984

. . . the infinite fantasies of the imagination, the divine and the wretched parameters of the human condition —Leo Rosten, *Harper's,* July 1972

. . . the . . . cliché expert, Dr. Arbuthnot, revealed the parameters of the new Presidentialese to the official translators —William Safire, *N.Y. Times,* 18 Nov. 1976

At the beginning of the planning process that generated the current options, the parameters were established not by the requirements of defending the nation but the requirements of reaching a strategic arms agreement —*Wall Street Jour.,* 31 Aug. 1981

. . . exploring the possibilities of sounds in space, revealing how one can transubstantiate one musical parameter into another —Jonathan Cott, *American Poetry Rev.,* vol. 3, no. 5, 1974

. . . the airlines compete vigorously in every other parameter of service including schedule frequency —Anthony Lewis, *N.Y. Times,* 8 Nov. 1976

The two basic parameters of the industry—production index and price index—also point up the flat state of the West German chemical economy —Dermot O'Sullivan, *Chemical & Engineering News,* 22 Feb. 1982

The adverse criticism of *parameter* took the wrong direction from the start, based as it was on outdated dictionary definitions ("a term in mathematics") and the assumption that *perimeter* must have been intended. More telling criticism, perhaps, would have been to point out that *parameter* was unnecessarily displacing such words as *factor* or *criterion.* But it is too late now. You need not use the word if you dislike it, naturally, but you will probably not be able to avoid seeing it, often used in ways that are less than illuminating:

Calm, powerful prose explores the parameters of reason and emotion, of growing up and growing old and how these mesh into a continuum of a life lived — *N.Y. Times Book Rev.,* 14 Nov. 1976

paramount *Paramount* is used as a sort of emphatic or superlative version of *first* or *important;* it designates what or who is preeminent or most important. A couple of commentators, Flesch 1964 and Evans 1957, worry about *paramount*'s being used as a mere synonym of *first* or *important.* There seems to be little need for worry, as there is no pattern of disputable use in our files. Flesch also thinks that *paramount* is pompous. All the same, *paramount* is available to you, if you need to use it, and should cause no concern. Here are a few typical uses:

. . . refused to kowtow to the new paramount Viking chief —John Geipel, *The Viking Legacy,* 1971

Honesty was for him so paramount a need that it overrode all considerations of natural and humane decorum —John Bayley, *N.Y. Rev. of Books,* 30 Dec. 1971

. . . the paramount, perhaps the only, consideration in preserving the marriage was the children — Joseph P. Lash, *McCall's,* October 1971

. . . dinner can range from 30 to as many as 250 guests. Under these circumstances, flexibility is paramount —Kristin K. Hubbard, *Harper's Bazaar,* July 1980

Harper 1985 believes *paramount* to be an uncomparable adjective—this bugaboo we discuss at ABSOLUTE ADJECTIVES.

paranoia, paranoiac, paranoid *Paranoia* and *paranoid* receive some attention from a couple of British commentators (Howard 1977, Phythian 1979) and one Canadian (Colter 1981), the upshot of which is that the popular use of these terms erodes the language and mocks serious mental illness. These criticisms are wrong on two points. First, the technical usage of the psychiatrist, psychologist, or other professional is not one whit impaired by the popular use. Second, it seems unlikely that a word that has developed so common an extended sense can sensibly be seen to mock serious mental illness any more than other words with common extended meanings, such as *insanity, lunacy,* or *madness.* The popular use is fully established in American English and recognized by American dictionaries; it is also defended and justified by Reader's Digest 1983. You need not give it a second thought. Here are a few examples:

Paranoia is not so much the belief that the FBI spies on citizens as it is the belief that the paranoid is the primary target of the spying —Hugh Drummond, M.D., *Mother Jones,* January 1980

. . . the deteriorating economy will probably add to the government's paranoia —*The Economist,* 1 Feb. 1975

. . . a form of cultural paranoia that saw affronts to that dignity everywhere —Joseph Epstein, *Commentary,* January 1972

There was a paranoia in Richard Nixon's White House —James M. Perry, *National Observer,* 7 July 1973

In adjective use, *paranoiac* is much less commonly used in the popular sense than *paranoid* is. Consequently it has rather a highbrow cachet:

. . . this rhetoric reaches paranoiac heights of scurrility and lunatic accusation: terror already stalks the land, the police are supporting groups of left-wing assassins —E. J. Hobsbawm, *N.Y. Rev. of Books,* 23 Sept. 1971

Single men in the Hamptons during the week are paranoiac about the intentions of the slim, tanned beauties —Linda Franke, *New York,* 5 July 1971

Paranoid is the common term. Here are some attributive examples:

. . . argued that the Soviet leaders had a paranoid view of the outside world —Richard J. Barnet, *Harper's,* November 1971

Its more paranoid supporters like to argue that it is the victim of repression —John Tebbel, *Saturday Rev.,* 13 Nov. 1971

. . . the Russians have moved what appears to be a permanent force of a million men up against the frontier with the result that both nations live in the paranoid shadow of war —Barbara Tuchman, *Harper's,* December 1972

... do stunning bits as, respectively, a mod minister, an up-from-poverty judge and a paranoid cop — Judith Crist, *New York,* 8 Feb. 1971

As a predicate adjective *paranoid* seems quite common in speech as well as print. It tends to be followed by *about, over,* and *of:*

He's kind of paranoid about his privacy —Patrick Anderson, *Cosmopolitan,* July 1976

... the star exploded, possibly paranoid about appearing as somewhat less than a totally "serious" person —Mary Reinholz, *Women's Wear Daily,* 19 Mar. 1979

One coach who seems to be particularly paranoid over long hair, pot, militant blacks and so forth — Dan Jenkins, *Sports Illustrated,* 14 Sept. 1970

... he was a little paranoid of landing in Havana — Jeanne Devries, *Avant Garde,* March 1970

paraphernalia *Paraphernalia* is a plural noun from medieval Latin for which there is no operative singular in English. The grammarian H. Poutsma in 1904 found its use with a singular verb (attested since 1788 in the OED) objectionable; three quarters of a century later the grammarian Randolph Quirk (*Style and Communication in the English Language,* 1982) expressed doubts that a native speaker of English, in spite of the insistence of dictionaries, would use it as a plural count noun. The evidence at this dictionary office falls somewhere between the two opinions.

We know from evidence that *paraphernalia* is used with both singular and plural verbs:

... the paraphernalia of Christianity is prophylactic against the taint —George Stade, *N.Y. Times Book Rev.,* 14 Jan. 1973

The paraphernalia of line fishing are found — Edward P. Lanning, *Peru Before the Incas,* 1967

Use with a plural verb does not in itself prove that a noun is a plural count noun, because many collective nouns, even though singular in form, can be used with plural verbs. But the next example seems to show a bona fide plural count noun:

... all those paraphernalia of women's lives — Judith Chernaik, *Saturday Rev.,* 6 Jan. 1973

Somewhat more often, however, the word seems to be perceived as a mass noun:

... every bit of transistorized paraphernalia gleams —Arlene Croce, in *The Film,* 1968

It's stuffed with every kind of oldfangled paraphernalia —*Playboy,* February 1981

Here we have notional agreement at work. Some feel *paraphernalia* is a plural count noun; some feel it is a singular mass noun. We cannot fault either use.

See LATIN PLURALS for other plurals used as singulars.

parenting Heritage 1982 contains a usage note informing us that the usage panel finds the verb *parent* unacceptable. This disapproval is misdirected. The transitive verb *parent* has existed since the 17th century, but it is not commonly used. You can occasionally see such examples as these:

The twins were parented, it is often held, by the Renaissance —*Times Literary Supp.,* 8 May 1948

... the ease with which I parented my own child — Brenda Maddox, *N.Y. Times Mag.,* 8 Aug. 1976

What the panelists were really objecting to is the noun *parenting,* a recent formation (1958) that has received decidedly mixed reviews in usage circles. The Harper 1985 panel rejected it, although a 39 percent minority found it to be a useful term. Copperud 1980 does not like it, but Safire 1982 finds it "a good new word." While reviews may be mixed, the word is being used with some frequency, perhaps because it says in one word what formerly had to be said in several. Here are some examples; you can make up your own mind as to its appropriateness.

In our most common parenting scenario, we instill ideals into our children, resent it when they challenge us for not living up to them, and then feel reassured when they give ideals up —Ellen Goodman, *Springfield* (Mass.) *Daily News,* 7 May 1980

The strategy for expanding the crane's population involves an ingenious system of surrogate parenting —*National Wildlife,* December 1982/January 1983

You will learn about marriage, parenting and caring for children —Frances Baynor Parnell et al., *Homemaking: Skills for Everyday Living,* 1981

Publishers call them parenting books, and new ones are born every month —Judith Appelbaum, *N.Y. Times Book Rev.,* 19 June 1983

If your child has this sort of parenting, he will grow up knowing that he is valuable —Anne Allen, *Sunday Mirror,* 4 June 1967

parlous That this old adjective, both a synonym and a derivative of *perilous,* has experienced a resurrection in the 20th century is a development noted with varying degrees of disapproval by Fowler 1926, Krapp 1927, and Evans 1957. By and large, the critics regard the word as an archaic affectation. It continues in fairly common use, however, occurring most frequently as a modifier of *state* and *times:*

... such being the parlous state of my nursery culture —Robert Craft, *Stravinsky,* 1972

... reflected the league's parlous state —Clive Gammon, *Sports Illustrated,* 5 Oct. 1981

... seem unaware of the parlous state of the world economy —Paul Lewis, *N.Y. Times Book Rev.,* 26 Dec. 1982

But these were parlous times —John Brooks, *New Yorker,* 20 Aug. 1973

... appropriate for these parlous economic times — Phyllis Feldkamp, *Christian Science Monitor,* 17 Sept. 1979

Yes, these are parlous times on Publishers Row — Ray Walters, *N.Y. Times Book Rev.,* 18 July 1982

Its use with other nouns is less common, but not rare:

Each one of these parlous, impatient maneuvers — Roger Angell, *New Yorker,* 10 May 1982

... the parlous pursuit of independence —Edward Boyer, *Fortune,* 5 Sept. 1983

... as the world became decidedly more unstable and parlous —R. Emmett Tyrrell, Jr., *American Spectator,* October 1984

parson Copperud 1970, 1980 is displeased with dictionaries because they do not reflect the opinion of Evans 1957 that in the U.S. the word *parson* is humorous or archaic and of Bernstein 1965 that it is provincial. This body of opinion seems to have been in circulation since Vizetelly 1906; he considered that *parson* detracted from the dignity of the office.

Vizetelly may have had in mind the common use of *parson* in the writings of 19th century American humorists. But dictionaries can't depend on a single area of usage for their treatment of a word. Dictionaries have to take into account such uses as these—not humorous, not rustic, not archaic, not provincial, not contemptuous:

> Bob Richards, the "pole-vaulting parson," has been awarded the Sullivan Trophy for 1951 —*My Weekly Reader,* 22 Feb. 1952

> And how, some too-often-exhorted parson is bound to ask, is all this to be done while pastor and church are expected to carry on a year-long, rounded program long ago laid down by the denomination? —*Christian Century,* 28 Oct. 1953

> The son of an impecunious Episcopal parson, he went to work at the age of fourteen —E. J. Kahn, Jr., *New Yorker,* 10 May 1952

Humorous use still exists too:

> India was always the parson among nations.
> "Oh, oh!" all the other nations would say when they saw India coming down the street. "Hide the guns under the table and get rid of the loaded dice. Here comes India." —Russell Baker, *N.Y. Times Mag.,* 9 June 1974

part 1. Bernstein 1965 notes that the intransitive verb *part* is followed by *from* or *with* and indeed this is true, so far as it goes. In contemporary usage, *part* is found more often with *with* than with *from,* and in almost all instances, means "give up":

> ... used to pay for an elector's right, whose owner was willing to part with his right to vote —E. H. Collis, *Lost Years,* 1948

> "... It's simply that he can't bear to part with a dime." —Hamilton Basso, *The View From Pompey's Head,* 1954

> ... in carrying on this war, the British may have to part with that control —Franklin D. Roosevelt, 12 Jan. 1940, business conference, in *Franklin D. Roosevelt's Own Story,* ed. Donald Day, 1951

> ... unwilling to part with favorite possessions —Gary E. McCalla, *Southern Living,* November 1971

Part from occurs less frequently. At one time, it was used for "relinquish" but in current usage it generally means "leave" or "separate":

> His precious bag, which he would by no means part from —George Eliot, *Life,* 1885

> The gold had to be left where it was. He parted from it philosophically —Geoffrey Household, *The Third Hour,* 1938

> I parted from McNeil at Victoria —Nevil Shute, *Most Secret,* 1945

> He parted from the British Army in 1946 —Barbara Campbell, *N.Y. Times,* 21 Jan. 1978

In the late 1800s, Ralph Olmsted Williams and Fitzedward Hall took issue with one another over the use of *part with* in the sense of "leave another person" (the discussion may be found in Williams 1897). Hall maintained that "so infrequent has it been for the last fifty years, more or less, that it must be ranked, as is 'never so,' among those second-rate archaisms which the best writers of recent times have generally avoided." Williams fired back with examples of this use of *part with* ranging from Shakespeare, Ann Radcliffe, and Jane Austen to Tennyson, Cardinal Newman, and Matthew Arnold, showing that the use was still prevalent at the time the two men were writing, at least in British English. On into the 20th century commentators continued to discuss *part with* (a person): MacCracken & Sandison 1917 notes its use but calls it rare; Krapp 1927 says that *part with* means "surrender, give up" and *part from* "leave"; and Weseen 1928 follows Krapp. One of the latest to enter an opinion is Chambers 1985, which notes that *part from* means "leave" and *part with* "to give up." Our evidence indicates that *part with* (a person) is not found in contemporary prose. *Part from* (a person) seems to be preferred.
2. See ON THE PART OF.

partake As an intransitive verb, *partake* may be followed by *in* or *of.* The use of *in* implies active participation in something:

> ... have imagined myself partaking in some incredible romance —*The Autobiography of William Butler Yeats,* 1953

> Of course, all the fine arts partake in this representative function —Scott Buchanan, "So Reason Can Rule," 1967

Of is also used in such contexts:

> ... their inability to partake of some of the activities —Walter E. Ditmars, *Who's Handicapped?,* 1954

Often, however, a less active role is implied by *of.* The underlying sense may be one of passive experience or simple sharing:

> ... he came while we were at dinner, and partook of our elegant entertainment —Jane Austen, letter, 1 Dec. 1798

Or the emphasis may be less on "sharing" than it is on "taking a portion or serving of," especially in contexts having to do with food and drink:

> Johnson then called for a bottle of port, of which Goldsmith and I partook, while our friend, now a water-drinker, sat by us —James Boswell, *Life of Samuel Johnson,* 1791

> Milk next meets with his refusal, and very soon he begins to refuse nearly everything; what he does accept he partakes of sparingly —Harry R. Litchfield, M.D. & Leon H. Dembo, M.D., *A Pediatric Manual for Mothers,* 1951

> Besides tea, a dainty sandwich, and cake, one could partake of coffee and a hot crisp waffle —Alice Herbert, *Yankee,* July 1968

A few critics from Vizetelly 1906 to Evans 1957 and Bernstein 1964 have argued that *partake* should be restricted to uses having to do with the shared behavior of two or more people, but they do not state their reasons for thinking so. All of the uses of *partake* in the above illustrations are old, well-established, and standard. Some critics simply consider *partake* inherently "overformal," "stilted," "bookish," or the like. Certainly a phrase like "partake of liquid refreshment" for "have a drink" would seem to merit those epithets, but the uses above do not strike us in the same way.

part and parcel   Although you will find this phrase denigrated in Copperud 1970, 1980, Shaw 1975, 1987, Evans 1957, and Bernstein 1965, critics seem not to understand its meaning or function very well. Evans believes the phrase is "now almost meaningless." Bernstein and Shaw consider it verbose and easily reducible to *part* in all occurrences.

Part and parcel dates back to the time of Henry VIII. It appears to have been originally a legal phrase, perhaps, as suggested by a 1441 citation from the Rolls of Parliament in the form *parcel and partie* (OED), which goes back to law French. The purpose of the phrase was emphasis, *part* having essentially its present meaning and *parcel* meaning a part that is integral with a whole. This emphatic, intentionally somewhat redundant use of *and parcel* survives in modern applications of the phrase. *Part and parcel* applies not to what is just a part of something, but to what is an integral or essential part of something. You cannot simply omit *and parcel*, as Bernstein counsels, without losing a shade of meaning. Here are some examples:

> Its phraseology has become part and parcel of our common tongue —John Livingston Lowes, *Essays in Appreciation,* 1936

> ... mannerisms that now seem old-fashioned but that were part and parcel of the virtuoso violin playing of the time —Winthrop Sargeant, *Saturday Rev.,* 4 Oct. 1975

> ... the Carolingian legends had become part and parcel of popular Italian folk poetry —Robert A. Hall, Jr., *A Short History of Italian Literature,* 1951

> ... these are practically flaunted as part and parcel of the secret war —Hanson W. Baldwin, *Saturday Rev.,* 6 Mar. 1976

> ... a will to succeed that is part and parcel of their religion —Robert Lindsey, *N.Y. Times Mag.,* 12 Jan. 1986

> ... his expressive freewheeling illustrations were part and parcel of his genius —Joseph Kastner, *Smithsonian,* September 1981

partial   1. *Partial* is used with the preposition *to* when it means "markedly fond of someone or something":

> "But if a woman is partial to a man, and does not endeavor to conceal it, he must find it out." —Jane Austen, *Pride and Prejudice,* 1813

> ... its large hearth, constructed for turf-fires, a fuel the captain was partial to in the winter season — Thomas Hardy, *The Return of the Native,* 1878

> We have become very partial to bean sprouts —Jean Stafford, *The Mountain Lion,* 1947

> Intellectuals have always been partial to grandiose ideas about themselves —Irving Howe, *Partisan Rev.,* January–February 1954

> ... a Countess who is admired by both the Composer and the Poet, but cannot decide to which she

is partial —Irving Kolodin, *Saturday Rev.,* 24 Apr. 1954

The OED traces this sense of *partial* to 1696; it labels the sense colloquial (in the standard descriptive way of dictionaries). In the early part of the 20th century, some American commentators also used the label *colloquial,* but in the pejorative sense. Recent commentators accept the use without quibble.

2. A few commentators, MacCracken & Sandison 1917, Shaw 1970, 1975, 1987, and Phythian 1979, mention this adjective. Phythian merely gives the three standard dictionary definitions; MacCracken & Sandison are concerned about possible confusion between the "biased" sense and the "incomplete" sense, and that seems to be Shaw's concern too. An unexpressed purpose of these entries is to refer to the dispute discussed at PARTIALLY, PARTLY.

partiality   *Partiality* is most often followed by the preposition *for:*

> "... I have a partiality for a man who isolates an issue and pleads to it. ..." —James Gould Cozzens, *Guard of Honor,* 1948

> "... I think that it was done by him unawares, his partiality for her was so great." —Robert Penn Warren, *All the King's Men,* 1946

> He has a partiality for suburban life —*Times Literary Supp.,* 29 May 1953

Occasionally, *partiality* has been used with *to* or *toward:*

> Our aversion to raw meat is understood, our partiality to fish ... appreciated —A. V. Davis, *Punch,* 6 July 1953

> Sometimes newcomers to the fleet were a bit annoyed over the skipper's partiality toward this absent-minded youth —Lloyd C. Douglas, *The Big Fisherman,* 1948

partially, partly   First, let us review a few facts. The adverb *partially* has been used in the sense "in some measure or degree" since the 15th century; the adverb *partly* has been used in the same sense since the 16th century. In this sense the adverbs are pretty much interchangeable, although there are uses in which you can distinguish between them if you want to, as we will see later. The adverb *partially* also has another sense, "with bias or favoritism; unfairly," that began to be used in the 16th century. This sense of *partially* is unattested since 1800 and is virtually obsolete.

Our controversy begins in 1870 with Richard Grant White. He was reading a book by Swinburne—whom he seems not to have cared much for—when he ran across the clause "If this view of the poem be wholly or partially correct." White found this to be impossible, for, he said, *partially* meant "with unjust or unreasonable bias." He based his opinion on the mistaken assumption that the adjective *partial* meant only "biased."

White's view was trenchantly attacked by Fitzedward Hall in books published in 1872 (*Recent Exemplifications of False Philology*) and 1873 (*Modern English*). In a footnote in the 1873 volume, Hall shows that *partially* in the sense attacked by White had been in use for a long time and that it had been used with increasing frequency during the 19th century. He gives quotations and appends a list of other authors who use the sense. (In addition, Hall finds *partially* more euphonious, and he attacks White's powers of reasoning.)

Bardeen 1883 quotes both White and Hall, but he is clearly more impressed with Hall's evidence. Ayres 1881, on the other hand, favors White's view, although he has obviously read Hall. His comment is, in its way, a classic example of one common stance of usage writers: "This use of the adverb *partially* is sanctioned by high authority, but that does not make it correct."

Partially for *partly* was put on William Cullen Bryant's *Index Expurgatorius,* compiled before 1877 for the *New York Evening Post,* and thus became part of American newspaper tradition. The proscription is repeated in Bierce 1909, Hyde 1926, and no doubt many others right up to Bernstein 1971 and Copperud 1980.

Vizetelly 1906 warns against *partially* on the grounds that it is ambiguous—an argument subsequently repeated many times, from Utter 1916 and F. K. Ball 1923 to Bernstein and Copperud. As a lexicographer, Vizetelly might have been expected to realize that the "biased" sense was obsolescent, but he did not.

Hall 1917 finds White's opinion repeated in two turn-of-the-century college rhetoric texts; Krapp 1927 considers *partly* simpler than *partially.*

With Fowler 1926 two new ingredients are added to the broth. He introduces the notion of *partially* as a long variant of *partly,* and he introduces a distinction in usage between the two. Since Fowler's distinction is frequently repeated (by Bremner 1980, Nickles 1974, Janis 1984, Strunk & White 1972, 1979, Sellers 1975, Bryson 1984, Heritage 1969, Longman 1984, and Chambers 1985), it is worth examining. Fowler says that *partly* (which he opposes to *wholly*) is better used to mean "as regards a part and not the whole," while *partially* (opposed to *completely*) is better used to mean "to a limited degree." Bryson 1984 puts this point most succinctly, equating *partially* with "incompletely" and *partly* with "in part."

Fowler's distinction is a clear and simple one. It is, however, wholly factitious, the words both having been in use in more complex patterns for 300 years or more when Fowler devised it. Although most of the examples provided by usage writers to illustrate it have been made up, it is not hard to find examples that follow its general outlines. Here, for instance, we find *partially* clearly used to mean "to a limited degree":

> . . . their ramble did not appear to have been more than partially agreeable —Jane Austen, *Mansfield Park,* 1814

> . . . steps were taken to furnish these partially trained forces with whatever equipment could be made available —George C. Marshall, *The United States at War,* 1943

> . . . but he has only partially succeeded in it —*Times Literary Supp.,* 16 Apr. 1970

> I'm partially drunk, by the way —James Joyce, *Ulysses,* 1922

> A sharp-featured face with a partially bald head — Norman Mailer, *The Naked and the Dead,* 1948

And here we find *partly* meaning "in part" with no hint of incompleteness or limited degree:

> . . . a Reprimand, which partly occasioned that Discourse of the Battle of the Books —Jonathan Swift, *A Tale of a Tub,* 1710

> . . . may at least partly explain their common genius —William Styron, *This Quiet Dust and Other Writings,* 1982

> . . . I knew, partly from experience and partly from instinct —Charlotte Brontë, *Jane Eyre,* 1848

The last example shows a construction, *partly x, partly y,* in which *partly* is very common and *partially* quite rare.

You can follow Fowler's distinction if you want to. But the distinction is transparent only in the clearest of contexts; more often writers seem to use the adverbs interchangeably:

> . . . her figure was partly enveloped in a shawl — Charlotte Brontë, *Jane Eyre,* 1848

> . . . her hat-brim partially shaded her face —Charlotte Brontë, *Jane Eyre,* 1848

> . . . female religious (partly clothed . . .) —James Joyce, *Ulysses,* 1922

> . . . a partially nude señorita, frail and lovely — James Joyce, *Ulysses,* 1922

> . . . it only partly explains his lack of interest —Richard Poirier, *A World Elsewhere,* 1966

> . . . scarcity of suitable screen material partially explains the trend —*Publishers Weekly,* 9 June 1951

Fowler added one more comment, sometimes repeated, that *partially* is overused. It is, however, used less often than *partly.*

From Fowler to the present time, little has changed; most commentators have been willing to repeat Fowler or some other earlier comment. A little originality was injected by a Harper 1975 usage panelist who reversed Fitzedward Hall; Hall had praised *partially* as more euphonious; the panelist said that *partly* sounds better.

Our evidence shows that there is some tendency toward differentiation, but it is far from completely established. *Partially* is used more often than *partly* to modify an adjective or past participle that names or suggests a process:

> The snow was partially melted —George Meredith, *The Ordeal of Richard Feverel,* 1859

> . . . killed and partially eaten —J. Stevenson-Hamilton, *Wild Life in South Africa,* 1947

> . . . a partially cleared grassy circle —John McNulty, *New Yorker,* 13 June 1953

> . . . partially concealed by a reddish beard —Gay Talese, *Harper's,* February 1969

> . . . a partially paid-for-car —Philip G. Schrag, *Columbia Forum,* Summer 1970

Partly, on the other hand, is used more often than *partially* before clauses and phrases offered by way of explanation:

> . . . it is also partly because Chaucer's English lies almost directly behind our own —W. F. Bolton, *A Short History of Literary English,* 1967

> Partly to reassure him, North invited Ghorbanifar to the United States —*The Tower Commission Report,* 1987

> Partly for this reason, the search . . . was not undertaken —Noam Chomsky, *Columbia Forum,* Spring 1968

These observations may indicate a trend, but only time will tell whether more differentiation or less will be the result. At the present time we have plenty of exceptions even to the general trend, and many more examples in which the context might elicit either word:

> . . . a new kind of revolt, which is only partly connected with the generation gap —Margaret Mead, *Barnard Alumnae,* Winter 1971

> He is trembling, partially from cold —Norman Mailer, *The Naked and the Dead,* 1948

> . . . while not convincing, is at least partly true —Edwin O. Reischauer, *N.Y. Times Book Rev.,* 23 May 1954

> . . . at least partially reversed the general trend —J. L. Dillard, *American Talk,* 1976

> . . . at least partly directed against herself —Irving Howe, *Harper's,* January 1972

Most native speakers of English will have no difficulty with these words. If you are a learner, we suggest that you follow either Fowler's distinction, insofar as possible, or the current general trends as illustrated here.

participate For the most part, *participate* is used with the preposition *in:*

> No one individual is ever familiar with the whole of the culture in which he participates —Ralph Linton, Foreword to Abram Kardiner, *The Individual and His Society,* 1939

> They participated, with a curious, restrained passion, in the speech made by the red-haired man —Christopher Isherwood, *The Berlin Stories,* 1946

> . . . Stalin himself was personally participating in the negotiations —William L. Shirer, *The Rise and Fall of the Third Reich,* 1960

> . . . the information they need to participate knowledgeably in public debates —Norman Cousins, *Saturday Rev.,* 25 June 1977

Occasionally, *participate* is followed by *with:*

> . . . we also participate with banks which in turn use their funds for part of the loans —*Nation's Business,* April 1954

And, in what appears to be a British usage, *participate* is followed by *on:*

> . . . an illegitimate child . . . had no right to participate on the intestacy of either of his parents —S. M. Cretney, *Principles of Family Law,* 1974

> . . . while participating on the Programme —*Weight Watchers,* 1975

participle 1. See DANGLING MODIFIERS; POSSESSIVE WITH GERUND.
2. *Participles as adjectives.* Both past and present participles can be used much like adjectives. A usage issue concerning the propriety of using *very* as a premodifier before a past participle in predicative position ("I am very tired") sprang up in the second half of the 19th century and has not yet entirely died down. The construction of *very* plus past participle has been in use since 1641, according to the OED. The thrust of the argument is that *very* cannot modify a verb and therefore should not modify its past participle; *very much* is prescribed. That the basis of the argument is illogical is pointed up

by the omission of the present participle from the discussion, a defect that is, shall we say, very disappointing. This issue is treated more fully at VERY 1.

particle transformation See UP, *adverb* 2.

particular *Particular* is considered an overused adjective by Copperud 1964, Fowler 1965, Phythian 1979, and Janis 1984. They are especially leery of its use following the demonstrative adjectives *this* and *that:*

> Students get into this particular category too —Margaret Mead, *Barnard Alumnae,* Winter 1971

> . . . had brought me to this particular point in space and time —Norman Cousins, *Saturday Rev.,* 30 Oct. 1971

> . . . to change the rules to fit that particular reality —William Johnson, *Sports Illustrated,* 15 July 1968

Particular adds a certain emphasis in these passages which the critics regard either as unnecessary or non-existent. Its omission in such cases, if you are of a mind to follow the critics' advice, is easy and painless. Note, however, that in some other cases, especially in negative constructions, *particular* after *this* or *that* has implications which go beyond simple emphasis:

> . . . discovered that Benítez was not guilty of that particular theft —*Current Biography,* January 1966

> . . . but I did not find this particular manual dull —Willoughby Newton, *Saturday Rev.,* 20 Nov. 1971

The implications are that Benítez was or may have been guilty of *other* thefts and that Newton did or might very well find *other* manuals dull. *Particular* can not be deleted from either passage without some loss of meaning.

partitive genitive See DOUBLE GENITIVE.

partly See PARTIALLY, PARTLY.

parts of speech By the time most of us have finished elementary school and high school, we have the notion that the parts of speech are immutable components of the language. But the truth is that the parts of speech are categories erected by grammarians for their convenient use in analyzing a language. The set used in teaching English grammar in schools—Roberts 1954 lists noun, pronoun, adjective, verb, adverb, preposition, conjunction, interjection—is actually the culmination of a long tradition going back at least to Dionysius Thrax (1st century B.C.), an Alexandrian grammarian.

His grammar—of Greek—had eight parts of speech: noun, pronoun, verb, participle, adverb, preposition, conjunction, and article. The Latin grammarian Priscian (around 500 A.D.) took over Dionysius Thrax's categories, but he replaced the article—there is none in Latin—with the interjection. Ben Jonson (before 1640) took Priscian's list right over for English and added the article as a ninth part of speech. Joseph Priestley (1761) seems to have been the first to come up with the modern list (the same as that of Roberts 1954); he ignored the article and substituted the adjective for the participle. Bishop Lowth 1762 used Priestley's list with Jonson's article added, and so did Lindley Murray 1795.

The Dionysius Thrax-Priscian-Jonson-Priestley connection represents what we may call the mainstream of part-of-speech theory. But it is instructive to remember that it took many years before the magic number of eight was reached. Greek grammatical theory as known from Plato had but two categories, corresponding approximately to subject and predicate or noun phrase and verb phrase. Aristotle added a third category for such odds and ends as the conjunction, article, and pronoun. A Roman grammarian named Varro, who was roughly contemporary with Dionysius Thrax, settled on a system of four categories for Latin: nouns—words with case inflections; verbs—words with tense forms; participles—words with both case inflections and tense forms; and the rest—conjunctions, adverbs—words with neither case inflections nor tense forms. Varro's analysis shows that grammarians then used inflectional endings as a major factor in deciding what categories were needed. The dependence on endings also explains the absence of the adjective from most of these early classifications. Latin adjectives had the same endings as nouns and were thus included in the noun category. This, in turn, explains the terms *noun substantive* and *noun adjective* that you may find in some older grammars and dictionaries.

Varro apparently was not imitated by later grammarians, but four-part systems of grammatical classification do appear from time to time. McKnight 1928 mentions a number of English thinkers of the late 17th century who rejected Latin as the basis for English grammar and who thought to develop a purely English grammar. One of these, a schoolmaster named A. Lane, published a book in 1700 which contained a four-part classification: substantive, adjective, verb, and particle (the last a handy category for everything else). The same categories were used by an 18th-century grammarian named Brightland, although he used different labels: names, qualities, affirmations, and (of course) particles. These grammarians seem not to have been very influential; the Latinists have held sway. A. Lane, incidentally, took credit for introducing the logical terms *subject, object,* and *predicate* into English grammar.

The parts of speech, then, are categories that grammarians over a considerable period of time have developed to help them in their analysis and description of a language. Since the 18th century, however, they have been commonly viewed as something rather more definite and fixed. If a more enlightened view of the subject had obtained all along, this book would be considerably thinner than it is. Many problems of usage result from grammarians trying to cram unruly English words into absolute Latin categories.

The famous eight parts of speech are simply holdovers from Latin used for convenience—few grammarians want to be faced with the task of devising an adequate set of descriptors for English. And for English, the parts of speech are not categories of words, but of functions. Many of our English words—*out, fan, hit, back, like,* for instance—can function as more than one part of speech. In Latin a word functions as only one part of speech (at least when you lump prepositions and conjunctions together as particles). If you remember that, in English, words function as parts of speech but are not themselves parts of speech, you will not be misled by people who insist that *like* is not a conjunction or that nouns cannot be used as verbs.

party   Copperud 1980 informs us that the use of *party* in the sense of "person" "comes from the jargon of the telephone service." In fact, the earliest complaint about this usage we are aware of comes from Dean Alford in 1866, ten years before Alexander Graham Bell patented the telephone. And the OED shows that the usage itself has been around since the 15th century. (The legal use of *party* goes back almost 200 more years.) Einstein 1985 similarly assures us that *party* was alive in the 17th century but fell into disuse and was reborn in the U.S. in the 1930s when many telephone subscribers had party lines. But if it was in disuse until the 1930s, why do we have commentators writing about the usage in 1866, 1869, 1870, 1873, 1878, 1881, 1906, and 1909? The telephone may have had some influence, though even that is doubtful, but it cannot have been the principal source of this use.

What, then, is all the fuss about? In a word: class. The most penetrating analysis seems to have been made by Fitzedward Hall back in the 1870s. *Party* for *person* was apparently in common and serious use in the 15th, 16th, and 17th centuries. Hall seems to imply that its use went into decline—perhaps in the 18th and early 19th centuries, although he has evidence from both periods—and when it revived it became common in the speech of the uneducated, the vulgar, the unwashed. In the United States it was associated (by such commentators as Richard Grant White 1870) with the speech of shopkeepers and tradesmen. The usage was one of those held to distinguish the socially superior from the socially inferior.

From our vantage point it is hard to tell if there really was a decline in ordinary use that made its appearance in the mouths of the vulgar more striking. The OED has enough 18th- and 19th-century examples to suggest that there was no decline in use; perhaps it was simply an increase in use by the less cultured that led editor Murray to add (as of 1905) "now shoppy, vulgar, or jocular." Such evidence as we have suggests that ordinary use continued until at least the middle of the 19th century:

> "I know he must have exerted himself very much, for I know the parties he had to move. . . . " —Jane Austen, *Mansfield Park,* 1814

> Now I would give a trifle to know, historically and authentically, who was the greatest fool that ever lived. . . . Marry, of the present breed, I think I could without much difficulty name you the party — Charles Lamb, "All Fools' Day," *Essays of Elia,* 1823

> . . . my travelling companions were very disagreeable individuals; these parties being a pair of squalid females and two equally unwelcome personages of the male sex —William Cullen Bryant, *Letters of a Traveller,* 1850

We are doubtful that ordinary use ever disappeared:

> . . . evidently recognizing in me a representative of the ancient parties he once so cunningly ruined — John Burroughs, *Wake-Robin,* 1871

> . . . he is a shameless and determined old party — Winston Churchill, *The Crisis,* 1901

> "Oh!" said the other party, while Densher said nothing —Henry James, *The Wings of the Dove,* 1902

The vulgar use that was objected to is probably exemplified by DeMorgan's apparently provincial Englishman and Flann O'Brien's garrulous Irishmen:

> . . . he thought he could ackomerdate him at that too. Anyhow, he knew a party as could! —William DeMorgan, *Joseph Vance,* 1906

> Now be damned but hadn't they a man in the tent there from the county Cork, a bloody dandy at the long jump, a man that had a name, a man that was known in the whole country. A party by the name of

Bagenal, the champion of all Ireland —Flann O'Brien, *At Swim-Two-Birds,* 1939

The brother gave a promise to a certain party not to leave town during the emergency —Myles na gCopaleen (Flann O'Brien), *The Best of Myles,* 1968

Alford 1866 was the first to censure this use in England (the good dean was a bit embarrassed by earlier use of the word in the Apocrypha and in Shakespeare) and Richard Grant White 1870 was the first in the U.S. It received frequent mention in subsequent 19th-century sources and in early 20th-century sources. It got into newspaper tradition through William Cullen Bryant's *Index Expurgatorius* compiled before 1877 for the *New York Evening Post* (he was unmindful of his own earlier use) and the contemporaneous "Don't List" of the *New York Herald.* It was warned against in reference books (we have noted the OED) and books on business correspondence (Whipple 1924, Powell 1925) and college handbooks (Ball 1923, *Century Collegiate Handbook* 1924). It can still be found in such sources.

The phone company did not come in for mention until after World War II. Our earliest example is Nicholson 1957; she specifically excuses telephone company use. Telephone company use—"your party is on the line," for instance—has, in fact, never been in question. It seems to have served only to buttress the ruminations of those commentators disinclined to look at the OED. Nor has legal use—whence this use seems to have sprung some 500 years ago—ever been questioned.

What about current use? The "jocular" use mentioned by the OED has clearly flourished; it is quite common in light, breezy writing and is applied especially to persons who have reached a certain age:

The matriarch is Ma Jukes, a friendly old party — Frank Sullivan, *A Rock in Every Snowball,* 1946

The Museum owns a photograph of an old party with a walrus mustache playing it —Robert Evett, *Smithsonian,* August 1970

. . . a six-foot, erect, florid party in his early eighties —Audax Minor, *New Yorker,* 17 July 1971

I, a respectable middle-aged party with long, tidy hair in a bun and a black dinner dress —Nika Hazelton, *N.Y. Times Book Rev.,* 11 Mar. 1973

Author Singer, a bossy old party of 79 —Brad Darrach, *People,* 12 Dec. 1983

It is used in more serious contexts when it clearly means "one of the persons involved":

. . . suggested that all three parties involved undergo psychological examinations —Eileen Hughes, *Ladies' Home Jour.,* September 1971

. . . a reversal of traditional roles . . . ; and *An American Romance* is one of the first novels to treat the complexities of such changing social patterns without demeaning either party —David Bellamy, *Saturday Rev.,* 29 Apr. 1978

. . . directed at all the participants in the conversation—the addressees and third parties alike —Herbert H. Clark & Thomas B. Carlson, *Language,* June 1982

. . . argues that their authors are merely reminding themselves of what they know already, rather than recreating it for a third party —Philip Larkin, *Required Writing,* 1983

In summary, the strictures on *party* in the sense of "person" are a 19th-century social commentary that has carried into the latter part of the 20th century purely by inertia. The use by the uneducated that occasioned the issue no longer seems to be a matter of comment among those who play the game of identifying social status by lexical item. Perhaps there never was very much to the issue. At any rate, the phone company is not to blame. Current use is as we have shown it and is completely standard.

pass away, pass on, pass   A few commentators wrinkle their noses at *pass away* and *pass on* as objectionable euphemisms for *die.* This attitude is perhaps a little unfair, being a strictly modern view of the use. In the past it has been, perhaps, just another word for *die.* *Pass* meaning "die" has been in the language since the 14th century; so has *pass away.* *Pass on* is a 19th-century term, and *pass away* was revived in the 19th century after some centuries of apparent disuse. We suspect that these phrases are rather more common in speech than in edited prose.

Of some minor interest is the survival of the intransitive *pass,* which had once been used by Chaucer, Shakespeare, and Tennyson, in some regional varieties of American English. Commentators have noticed its survival in Mississippi speech. We have a few journalistic examples:

Mrs. Nancy Mahala Flanagan . . . passed Sept. 18, 1984 —*Atlanta Constitution,* 19 Sept. 1984

. . . a short time before his passing at a ripe old age —Vincent Perry, *Dog World,* December 1981

. . . passed into eternal rest on Monday —*Houston Post,* 14 Sept. 1984

You probably will not have much reason to use *pass, pass away,* or *pass on* in most kinds of discursive prose, but if you need them, you can use them. They seem to be part of the mildly euphemistic usage of polite speech; they need not be avoided in such use.

passed, past   The thrust of the advice in all the handbooks and schoolbooks is that the unwary and unsophisticated student should not confuse the homophones *passed* (past tense and past participle of *pass*) and *past* (variously a noun, adjective, adverb, and preposition).

Passed and *past* are originally the same word; the adjective and preposition are derived from the past participle of the verb, and the noun and adverb are derived by functional shift from the adjective. The spelling *past* was at one time used for both the past tense and past participle:

I did not tell you how I past my time yesterday — Jonathan Swift, *Journal to Stella,* 25 Jan. 1711

. . . he was so much offended . . . that he past the latter part of his life in a state of hostility —Samuel Johnson, Preface to Johnson's edition of Shakespeare, 1765

He past; a soul of nobler tone —Alfred Lord Tennyson, *In Memoriam,* 1850 (OED)

The bitter cup is from him past —Jonathan Swift, "Ode to Dr. William Sancroft," 1692

I know what has past between you —Oliver Goldsmith, *She Stoops to Conquer,* 1773 (OED)

Our latest citations show no instances of the spelling *past* used for the past tense or past participle of the verb; *passed* is the only spelling in current use for these functions. *Past* is becoming archaic as a spelling for the verb's inflected forms. It is, of course, still used for the adjective, preposition, noun, and adverb. The recommended differentiation actually seems to have taken root in the language, in this case.

passel   Harper 1985 finds *passel* a useful and colorful word while Nickles 1974 denigrates it as a cracker-barrel term that should be avoided. With opinion thus divided, you can do as you please. Harper does warn against its use in formal contexts; our evidence shows it not used in highly formal situations.

Passel is by origin a pronunciation spelling of a dialectal pronunciation of *parcel*. In its current manifestation it is primarily an Americanism, but it exists both as a pronunciation and a spelling in British dialects too, and as a pronunciation spelling it can be found as long ago as the Paston letters of the middle 15th century.

Passel seems to have been fairly common in 19th-century American humor and fiction, mostly of the local-color variety, and occasionally popped up in British writing (at least once in Kipling, for instance). It began to creep into more general use in the 20th century. It got its biggest boost in the 1940s when such popular weekly magazines as *Time, Newsweek,* and the *Saturday Review* began using it. It continues to have wide nonregional use in similar publications. A few examples:

In a passel of trees —Carl Sandburg, *Smoke and Steel,* 1920

... returned growling and out of temper, with the news that the Federal Union was run by a passel of blockheads —James Thurber, "The Night the Bed Fell," from *My Life and Hard Times,* 1933

A passel of authors on the hoof —Bennett Cerf, *Saturday Rev.,* 5 Nov. 1949

... the passel of plain good folk with whom there is nothing wrong that a little extra brain and taste could not cure —John Simon, *New York,* 15 Feb. 1971

... I've met up with an unusually large passel of geese this year —Jean Stafford, *New Yorker,* 3 Dec. 1973

... Rousseau, Hobbes, Marx and a passel of other post-16th century thinkers —Ezra Bowen, *Time,* 6 May 1985

Although *passel* is most often used with count nouns, it is also used occasionally with mass nouns:

... it was quite a passel of legal tender —Dan Parker, *The ABC of Horse Racing,* 1947

... Alaskans, who want to make a passel of money tapping their natural resources —Jon Margolis, *Esquire,* March 1970

passive voice   1. A large number of commentators agree that sentences in which the verb is in the active voice are preferable to those in which the verb is in the passive voice. The passive has long been discouraged as the weaker form of expression. In spite of generations of textbooks, use of the passive has increased and, ironically, studies show the passive to be much more frequently used by the educated than by the uneducated.

The passive has its uses, as we shall see. Even grammarians and usage commentators find it useful, or perhaps subtly enticing. Joseph M. Williams caught these two specimens for exhibit in *College Composition and Communications,* May 1981:

Emphasis is often achieved by the use of verbs rather than nouns formed from them, and by the use of verbs in the active rather than in the passive voice —S. J. Reisman, ed., *A Style Manual for Technical Writers and Editors,* 1972

... the passive voice is wherever possible used in preference to the active —George Orwell, "Politics and the English Language," 1946

Orwell's dictum in the same essay is "Never use the passive where you can use the active."

Orwell's essay is interesting in another regard. Bryant 1962 reports three statistical studies of passive versus active sentences in various periodicals; the highest incidence of passive constructions was 13 percent. Orwell runs to a little over 20 percent in "Politics and the English Language." Clearly he found the construction useful in spite of his advice to avoid it as much as possible.

There is general agreement that the passive is useful when the receiver of the action is more important than the doer; Bryant's example is "The child was struck by the car." Orwell also uses the passive for this purpose in "Politics and the English Language":

... noun constructions are used instead of gerunds. ...

The range of verbs is further cut down. ...

... banal statements are given an appearance of profundity. ...

The passive is also useful when the doer is unknown, unimportant, or perhaps too obvious to be worth mentioning. Bryant exemplifies each of these with

The store was robbed last night.

Plows should not be kept in the garage.

Kennedy was elected president.

Orwell makes use of the passive in this way too:

People are imprisoned for years without trial, or shot in the back of the neck or sent to die of scurvy in Arctic lumber camps: this is called *elimination of unreliable elements.*

The passive with the unknown or unimportant doer is disapproved in some instances by quite a few commentators who consider it evasive. Copperud 1970 gives as an example of evasive use, "It is felt that your request must be denied." Whether this evasion is useful or not depends on your point of view: if it is your request that is denied, it is irritating not to know who denied you; if you are some poor functionary whose duty it is to inform people that their request has been denied, it may seem most helpful. Orwell in the passage just cited is generalizing rather than evading. The force of his statement would not be much strengthened by using the active with a general subject:

Totalitarian regimes imprison people for years without trial ... ; they call this *elimination of unreliable elements.*

Indeed, the absence of a named agent might be seen as part of the writer's point.

A few commentators find the passive useful in scientific writing (one even believes it to be necessary) because of the tone of detachment and impersonality that it helps establish.

The point, finally, is that sentences cast in the passive voice have their uses and are an important tool for the writer. Everyone agrees you should not lean too heavily on passive sentences and that you should especially avoid awkwardly constructed passives. The few statistical studies we have seen or heard of indicate that you are likely to use the active voice most of the time anyway.

2. Lounsbury 1908 devotes several pages to the problem of the passive followed by a retained object, as in "He was refused admittance" or "I was promised venison." This was an 18th- and 19th-century issue, apparently; no one questions the construction any more.

past   See PASSED, PAST.

past history   *Past history* is censured as a redundancy by several commentators, who point out that all history is in the past. The phrase seems to occur more often in speech than in writing, but its use in expository prose is not uncommon:

> . . . consider the past history of Yakutsk —Wendell Willkie, *One World,* 1943

> . . . a percentage of direct labor based on past history —Ralph E. Cross, *Dun's,* January 1954

> While most of the remanufactured engine may be new, the past history of its significant pieces . . . is unknown —Nicholas E. Silitch, *Private Pilot,* November 1988

Such usage is idiomatic. In fact, you might not want to delete *past* in the second example, as its use there helps signal which of the many senses of *history* the author intended. On the other hand, the *past* in the first and third examples probably could be omitted. Your use of *past history* is unlikely to be noticed or criticized by most readers, but if you share the commentators' enthusiasm for expunging redundancies, you will want to avoid it. See also REDUNDANCY.

pastiche   *Pastiche* is a word growing in popularity with reviewers. It is used in three ways: it is used of a work—it could be music, art, literature, or architecture—that is a deliberate imitation of the style of another person or of another time; it is used of a work that is made up of selections or bits and pieces of other works; and it is used of something that is a mixture of different, often disparate, things.

Here we have the first use:

> But his style, an overblown pastiche of 17th century prose, unsuited to the subject matter, spoils the account —Ted Morgan, *Saturday Rev.,* August 1979

This sense can be used attributively:

> Part of the book seems meant as pastiche Waugh, but most of it is just strainedly facetious —*Times Literary Supp.,* 7 July 1966

Here is the second use:

> *The good doctor* is a Neil Simon pastiche of Chekov stories, with a narrator who is Chekov himself —Judy Barbour, *Nation Rev.* (Melbourne), 1 May 1975

The third use is more broadly applied:

> A pleasant pastiche of political science and storytelling —*Playboy,* April 1984

> . . . the grand pastiche of nationalities that make up Australia —Edwards Park, *Smithsonian,* October 1982

Bryson 1984 worries that *pastiche* may be misused to mean "parody." Since the word in its first two senses may be used of something that is intended as parody, it is easy to see how the two meanings might converge. In the following two examples it is possible for the reader to think, at least, of *parody:*

> . . . a tiny gem, a perfect pastiche of the musicals of the twenties —Judith Crist, *New York,* 10 June 1972

> . . . written in a style that was almost a pastiche of George Moore —*Times Literary Supp.,* 23 Apr. 1971

Pastiche and *parody* are sometimes distinguished:

> . . . literate pastiche and respectful avoidance of parody were no substitute for Fleming's innate virtues —Philip Larkin, *Required Writing,* 1983

The third sense can be used pejoratively:

> . . . a pastiche of undirected elements that never forms a convincing whole —Iva Hellman, *People,* 21 July 1986

The commentators might better be more concerned about vague use:

> . . . even a dog who has been cruelly subjected to brain surgery is not entitled to speak like a pastiche of King Lear's monologues —Charles Nicol, *Saturday Rev.,* 4 Mar. 1978

past perfect   See PLUPLUPERFECT.

patient   In the senses "able or willing to bear" and "subject to," *patient* seems to be found most often with *of:*

> . . . the United States be patient of misrepresentations of its motives —*Current Biography 1948*

> . . . most scientific modern excavations are patient of chronological reassessment —*Times Literary Supp.,* 18 Dec. 1969

In the more common senses involving calmness and forbearance, *patient* is found with *with:*

> . . . I don't imagine that he would be very patient with dreams —Walter de la Mare, *Encounter,* December 1954

> He had been all too patient with her, too long —Herman Wouk, *Marjorie Morningstar,* 1955

In older literature we also find these senses of *patient* used with *toward, in, at,* and *under,* but we have no recent evidence for them, as it happens. They continue to sound idiomatic, however.

patron   *Patron* has been criticized as a fancy and inaccurate substitute for *customer* by commentators dating back to Richard Grant White 1870. This sense of *patron* apparently originated among merchants during the 19th century. Merchants in the 20th century have continued to use it, despite the repeated criticism, and it seems safe to say that merchants in the 21st century will use it as well. It also occurs regularly in expository writing, especially of a journalistic nature. As Evans 1957 notes, it tends to refer less often to the customers of shops than to the customers of restaurants, bars, hotels, theaters, and the like:

> ... selling flowers to the patrons of the luxurious hotels —*Current Biography,* November 1965

> ... in a quarrel with another patron at the Copacabana night club —*Current Biography,* February 1967

> Patrons are asked to make a note of the exit nearest to their seat —*Boston Symphony Orchestra Program,* 22 Oct. 1971

A person staying at a hotel or attending a performance is, in fact, unlikely to be called a customer (the most likely word for the hotel-stayer is probably *guest*), but *customer* is, of course, commonly used for a person being served in a restaurant or bar. *Patron* just sounds a little classier—or more pretentious, depending on the one you ask. It also more strongly implies a regular or frequent customer than does *customer* itself.

pavilion   Bremner 1980 points out there is properly only one *l* in this word. It is not infrequently given two, but that spelling must still be considered an error.

pawn off   This is a peculiar expression. None of the usual dictionaries of slang mentions it, and neither do any of the usual usage books except Harper 1985. *Pawn off* was called to Harper's attention by one of the usage panelists who sent in an advertisement from the *New Yorker:*

> We tell you this not because we are trying to pawn Countess Isserlyn [a cosmetic] off as a bargain.

This is easy enough to interpret: it must mean "palm off" or "pass off" or "fob off." It would appear to have originated by similarity of sound to *palm* in *palm off.* The OED thinks it erroneous for *palm,* but it may in fact be a dialectal variant.

The use has been around for quite a long time. The OED has an example of *pawn upon* with the same meaning from 1787 and an example of *pawn off* from the novelist Captain Frederick Marryat in 1832. We have found an earlier example from Scotland. According to one 18th-century student's notes, Adam Smith, perhaps best known for *The Wealth of Nations,* used the phrase *pawn upon* in a lecture given on 14 January 1763:

> The teller of wonderful or lamentable stories is disagreeable because he endeavours to pawn them upon us for true ones.

Our files first show *pawn off* as part of a list in a 1920 work on verb–adverb combinations in English. An editor for Webster's Third slipped it into a definition written in 1956 (it was revised). Our earliest example in context dates from 1955:

> I am not for a moment suggesting that our own dealers should pawn off inferior works by means of the same system —James Thrall Soby, *Saturday Rev.,* 5 Feb. 1955

It has subsequently turned up here and there, but not with great frequency:

> ... Manville pawns his wife off on Berlin so that he, Manville, is free to marry his offstage lover —*Current Biography,* January 1968

> ... the dumping grounds for what business cannot pawn off on more alert consumers —Ralph Nader, *Who Speaks for the Consumer?,* 1968

> ... I was still slightly shaken from the inverse cube law of gravity he'd pawned off on me last visit —Alan Lightman, *Science 84,* April 1984

This *pawn* (with *over*) seems to exist in Irish English too:

> ... a couple of musty sweet cakes that would be pawned over on him by some of the shopkeepers —Arnold Schrier, *Irish Digest,* March 1956

Pawn off has been lurking just below the threshold of dictionary recognition (except for the OED) for quite a long time. If we count the early *pawn upon,* it's been in at least limited use for 200 years.

pay   A few commentators (such as Watt 1967 and Bremner 1980) note that *paid* is the spelling for the past and past participle of *pay* except in the nautical *pay out,* where it is usually *payed.* The nautical spelling is sometimes used for the regular past tense, where it should not be:

> ... she payed—or actually bought breakfast—for Scott —*Springfield* (Mass.) *Morning Union,* 23 Apr. 1984

peace   See PIECE, PEACE.

peaceable, peaceful   Several commentators note a distinction between these words, the upshot of which is that *peaceable* means "disposed toward peace; preferring peace" and *peaceful* means "characterized by peace." Those are in fact the usual meanings of *peaceable* and *peaceful* in current English:

> But if labor's leaders were feeling peaceable toward the administration, it was the best-kept secret in town —Meg Greenfield, *The Reporter,* 2 June 1966

> ... would always have been as peaceful as a church social —John Kenneth Galbraith, *Saturday Rev.,* 6 Nov. 1971

However, *peaceable* and *peaceful* can also be properly used as synonyms, and they have been since the 14th century. The "characterized by peace" sense of *peaceable* and the "disposed toward peace" sense of *peaceful* are now relatively uncommon, but they are still standard, as a look in any good dictionary will show. Here are a few examples of their use, recent and not so recent:

> ... that through orderly, peaceable processes ... change would come —*Center Mag.,* November/December 1971

> ... assigned to a ladder company in remote and peaceable Staten Island —Tom Buckley, *N.Y. Times Book Rev.,* 3 Oct. 1976

> Congo natives are peaceful, and the drums often mean an invitation to a dance —Wallace W. Atwood & Helen Goss Thomas, *Visits in Other Lands* (textbook), 1950

> ... the modest man becomes bold, the shy confident, the lazy active, or the impetuous prudent and peaceful —W. M. Thackeray, *Vanity Fair,* 1848

peace officer   See OFFICER.

peak, peek, pique These homophones have a way of being muddled by nodding writers. Most of the examples we have seen involve the substitution of *peak* for one of the other two. James J. Kilpatrick both in his 1984 book and later newspaper columns has caught a number of these, including "a peak at the machines" where *peek* was wanted, and "peaked our curiosity" where *piqued* was wanted. We have a few too:

> . . . she could peak into the bedroom —*N.Y. Times,* 2 Sept. 1983 *(peek)*

> . . . peaking students' desire to learn —an elementary-school principal, 16 May 1983 *(piquing)*

A writer needs to keep the meaning in mind and match it to the correct spelling.

peculiar When *peculiar* is used to mean "characteristic of one only," it is usually followed by the preposition *to:*

> . . . a drowsy fervour of manner and tone which was quite peculiar to her —Thomas Hardy, *The Return of the Native,* 1878

> . . . the French woman, from very early times, has shown qualities peculiar to herself —Henry Adams, *Mont-Saint-Michel and Chartres,* 1904

> . . . the system shown has some aspects peculiar to service life —William H. Whyte, Jr., *Is Anybody Listening?,* 1952

> . . . they must be characters peculiar to *this* story and no other —Shirley Jackson, *The Writer,* January 1969

pedagogue 1. Bryson 1984 says that *pedagogue* means the same thing as *pedant.* Our evidence shows that it does not. Bryson's statement is a bit like saying *politician* means "crook." The categories may overlap in some cases, but the words do not have the same meaning. *Pedagogue* means "teacher"—whether a boring teacher or a fascinating one:

> McCracken was the essence of the pedagogue, his presentations to the President having the bloodless quality of professional lectures in Economics 100 — Rowland Evans, Jr. & Robert D. Novak, *Atlantic,* July 1971

> The ballet faculty, which included that most distinguished pedagogue from Paris, Madame Nova — Walter Terry, *Saturday Rev.,* 16 Oct. 1976

2. The spelling *pedagog,* which seems to have been born in the spelling reform movement of the late 19th century, is still sometimes used:

> . . . abdication of parent, priest, and pedagog —F. R. Buckley, *N.Y. Times,* 20 Nov. 1972

pedal, peddle Copperud 1980 and Bernstein 1962 both have found instances of the verb *peddle* used where *pedal* was meant. The OED has a late 19th century *peddler* for *pedaler.* This is mere carelessness.

peek See PEAK, PEEK, PIQUE.

penultimate Safire 1984 records the efforts of a correspondent who sent a couple of newspaper clippings in which *penultimate* was used in the sense of "ultimate, final, last." It may be tempting to some people to use

penultimate, which means "next-to-last," in this way. It has a more impressive look and sound than a mere *ultimate* or *final.* But it is not always easy to tell if *penultimate* is being used as an emphatic *ultimate.* It often requires extra-linguistic knowledge: you have to know if the penultimate whatever-it-is was in fact the last one or not. Or you have to persevere through enough context to find out whether or not the writer knows what is penultimate. Sometimes a writer provides a giveaway, though:

> Just as the first of these three novels begins with a missionary teacher . . . so the third and penultimate volume . . . —Nancy Wilson Ross, *Saturday Rev.,* 24 June 1972

You may be a bit suspicious of what a writer had in mind when you find *penultimate* modifying a plural:

> The penultimate days of the event —Benjamin DeMott, *American Scholar,* Winter 1962–1963

> . . . the penultimate decades of the century —Gerald Taylor, *Silver,* 2d ed., 1963

But most of the time, unless you have knowledge to the contrary, you have to assume writers know the meaning of the word:

> . . . regulations have cleared the penultimate hurdle and appear ready to become law —John Aloysius Farrell, *Sunday Denver Post,* 2 Sept. 1984

> . . . rises to a rare moment of lyric power in the novel's penultimate paragraph —Joyce Carol Oates, *N.Y. Times Book Rev.,* 3 Oct. 1982

If you remember the meaning of *penultimate,* it should give you no trouble.

people, persons The questioning of the use of *people* to mean *persons* began in the middle of the 19th century. Alford 1866 mentions a correspondent who wrote in to object to the expression *several people;* he said it ought always to be *several persons.* Alford was lukewarm to the proposal. Bardeen 1883 lists another 19th-century commentator, William Mathews, who in his *Words; Their Use and Abuse,* 1876, seems not to have objected to *many people.* Around the turn of the century things heated up. *People* for *persons* went on the "Don't List" of the *New York Herald* and thereafter became a staple of the journalistic usage writers (for instance, Bierce 1909, Hyde 1926, Bernstein 1962, 1965, 1971, Copperud 1964, 1970, 1980, Bremner 1980, Safire 1982, Kilpatrick 1984).

Our files contain some traces of what must have been a raging dispute on the subject in the pages of the *Washington* (D.C.) *Times* in 1915 and 1916. The chief figure in the dispute seems to have been an energetic letter writer named Francis de Sales Ryan, who peppered the paper with objections to usages such as a Funk & Wagnalls advertisement urging readers to "do what 1,500,000 other people are doing—read the Literary Digest." Ryan claimed to have the staffs of all other newspapers in Washington on his side, and he cited dictionaries liberally. He seems to have been willing to spar with such other newspaper readers as undertook to rebut him. The newspaper finally ran a large story (25 Feb. 1916) in which they invoked the authority of Dr. C. Alphonso Smith of the University of Virginia, who was billed as the "highest authority on precise word meaning in the United States," to defend the usage. Our records do not tell us whether this authority overmatched Mr. Ryan or not.

Like many controversial usages examined in this book, *people* managed to hold its place while the grounds of dispute shifted. At first *people* was objected to when the context gave any indication that the word was thought of as a plural—*several* and *many* were the disputed modifiers. Then followed the dispute about numerical designators—*1,500,000, a thousand,* etc. More recently the use of round numbers with *people* has been declared acceptable, but some still object to use with specific numbers, like *five* or *two*. Safire 1982 reports that an Associated Press style manual revised around 1980 prescribes *people* for all plural uses. Safire says this decision was greeted with joy by some people working in the *New York Times* newsroom, where the style manual still prescribed *persons* with specific numbers. Kilpatrick 1984 disagrees with the AP decision.

The dictionaries of the time seem to have provided fuel for the objections of Francis de Sales Ryan and other critics. The use of *people* with a preceding number seems to have been missed by the OED, Webster 1909, the Century, and Funk & Wagnalls. If the dictionaries missed the use, the grammarians did not. Poutsma 1904–26 cited Dickens ("A Christmas Carol") and *Punch*. Jespersen 1909–49 found the usage to be as old as Chaucer's "a thousand peple"; he cited as later examples Defoe, Dickens, Disraeli, and others. He also found the construction *one or two people* in Dickens and H. G. Wells.

It is reassuring, at least, to know that recent handbooks and style books will now allow you to use *people* as Chaucer did nearly 600 years ago or as Dickens did a century or more ago. Sometimes progress is slow. Here are modern examples of most of the originally disputed usages:

. . . many people who feel that the federal funds have not always been wisely spent —Lucy Eisenberg, *Harper's,* November 1971

More than 1,500 people . . . attended —Ron Fimrite, *Sports Illustrated,* 20 Mar. 1978

. . . equipped to seat six people comfortably —*Esquire,* April 1973

I told him I could give him a couple of people who would look after him —Ernest Hemingway, "Miss Mary's Lion," 1956

But what about *persons?* It has not vanished from these contexts. We find it chosen as an alternative where *people* has just been used:

Some 400,000 people, most of them young persons —*Current Biography,* June 1968

. . . program involving young people, led by persons in their own generation —John Cogley, *Center Mag.,* September–October 1972

. . . has peopled his story with real persons —Liz Smith, *New York,* 9 Feb. 1976

We find it used naturally where the older style books would require it:

. . . almost one million persons are today confined —Alan M. Dershowitz, *Psychology Today,* February 1969

. . . put 100,000 hard-core unemployed persons to work —Henry Ford II, *Michigan Business Rev.,* July 1968

. . . only three persons lost their lives —*Current Biography,* May 1966

And occasionally it is put in place of *people* by inattentive writers and editors, as in this example from *Winners & Sinners:*

Mike Curtis, who likes to hit persons hard, slammed his 232 pounds into . . . the Ram running back —*N.Y. Times,* 9 Nov. 1971

You can safely follow your ear in your choice of *people* or *persons* after a number—or simply use *people,* in accordance with the latest advisories.

per Bernstein 1971 traces opposition to the preposition *per* all the way back to William Cobbett in the early 19th century. Cobbett's objection was that *per* was not English and to most people was "a mystical sort of word." Later 19th-century commentators such as Ayres 1881 and Long 1888 omitted the mention of mysticism but disapproved *per* before English words. The same injunction appeared in Vizetelly 1906 and Bierce 1909, among others; it can be found as recently as Freeman 1983.

Bernstein's point is that *per* is no longer a mystical word, yet newspaper reporters and editors are still told to replace it with *a* or *an,* even in statistical and economic contexts where *per* is appropriate. Here we have a few of these typical contexts where *per* has slipped into print:

About 8–9 parts per million of nitrate in an infant's drinking water may interfere with hemoglobin function —Barry Commoner, *Columbia Forum,* Spring 1968

. . . contributions . . . will be made by sponsors who will pay per mile for distances covered —*Massachusetts Audubon News,* May–June 1971

. . . the average use per residential customer —*Annual Report, Union Electric Co.,* 1970

Dividends per share of Common Stock —*Annual Report, R. J. Reynolds Industries, Inc.,* 1970

He referred to the $29.75 bite (including city taxes) per concert ticket —J. Sebastian Sinisi, *Denver Post,* 1 Sept. 1984

The districts now pay $6.25 per student per year —*Saturday Rev.,* 14 Apr. 1973

What is the average number of sentences per paragraph? —Albert H. Marckwardt, *Introduction to the English Language,* 1942

Sports writing is frequently statistical also:

. . . during the last thirty-nine games he scored almost a goal per game —*Current Biography,* October 1966

. . . twenty-nine and one-half points and fifteen rebounds per game —*Current Biography,* July 1967

Both men gave career best performances in taking five wickets per piece as Notts. were dismissed in two hours 55 minutes for 94 —Terry Bowles, *Evening Post* (Nottingham, England), 13 July 1974

Probably no one needs to be reminded of *miles per hour, miles per gallon,* and such.

The demystification of *per* has gone so far that it can

be found in rather more literary contexts than you might expect:

> ... and on up to four more English writers per publishing season —Bernard DeVoto, *Harper's,* November 1952

> Complicating matters are two beautiful women, one per agent, and an assortment of double agents — Arthur Krystal, *N.Y. Times Book Rev.,* 18 Nov. 1984

> ... gives us as much serious fun per word as anyone around —George Stade, *N.Y. Times Book Rev.,* 6 Mar. 1983

Janis 1984 notes a use of *per* meaning "according to," often found in business correspondence in such expressions as "per your instructions" and sometimes preceded by *as* (see AS PER). This use he calls stilted. It is not limited to business correspondence. Here are four examples, none of which sound particularly stilted:

> Kesselring still believes that even after the failure to destroy the Russian ground forces (per his advice) ... Hitler could have changed the course of the war —A. J. Liebling, *New Yorker,* 26 Mar. 1955

> The computer then tells the printer where to print the address, per your instructions —Rex Nelsen, *Popular Computing,* March 1983

> Many of them were rowdy and wasted, per tradition —John Rockwell, *N.Y. Times,* 16 June 1976

> The Soviets, per custom, besieged the U.S. women with questions —Demmie Stathoplos, *Sports Illustrated,* 2 Aug. 1982

No commentator seems to question the use of *per* to mean "by the means or agency of":

> ... a narrator, opening the play, announces the plot; the voice is the voice of George Moore (per David Warrilow) —Edith Oliver, *New Yorker,* 28 June 1982

> ... a cavernous saloon, where, per his invitation, a rambunctious dairyman who insulted him, the brother of a man he killed ... , and a faro dealer ... await him with guns —Judith Crist, *Saturday Rev.,* 21 Aug. 1976

Also unmentioned by the critics is the adverbial use of *per,* which is essentially the preposition with its object understood:

> At $100 per, tickets ... are the most expensive in Broadway history —Andrea Chambers, *People,* 16 Nov. 1981

> ... tickets going at a bargain $3.50 per —*New York,* 13 Sept. 1971

Harper 1975, 1985 notes that when *per* is used, *each* is not necessary. We do not find this redundancy very often in print, but it does occur now and then. We have an educational report summarized in the *Springfield* (Mass.) *Union* (20 Mar. 1969) which recommends that school libraries "have 20 volumes per each student." Another curious item is from *Editor & Publisher* (11 Sept. 1976) where what appears to be an explanation of a grammatical test—perhaps from an advertisement— says "there is supposed to be only one error per a sentence." You should avoid such combinations.

The examples shown above represent most of the common standard uses of *per.* You will notice that reflexive substitution of *a* or *an* for *per,* recommended by some commentators, simply does not produce acceptable English in many instances. Bernstein is right: *per* is no longer a mystical word, and you need not worry about using it in contexts such as those we have illustrated.

peradventure Chances are you have never used this word and never will use it, but in case you feel the urge, be advised that Fowler 1926 and Krapp 1927 consider *peradventure* archaic and Flesch 1964 considers it pompous. As an adverb meaning "perhaps" it is certainly archaic (the most recent evidence of the adverb that we know of is from 1874), but as a noun it persists in occasional—very occasional—use, most often following the preposition *beyond:*

> Beyond peradventure, certainly, Chopin was a neurotic —James Lyons, *Boston Symphony Orchestra Program,* December 1970

> I know a surgeon who, having left the room, is certain, beyond peradventure of doubt, that his disembodied radiance lingers on —Richard Selzer, "Letter to a Young Surgeon," 1982, in *The Contemporary Essay,* ed. Donald Hall, 1984

As these citations show, the noun *peradventure* is understood somewhat differently by different writers. It can mean either "doubt" ("beyond peradventure") or "chance" ("beyond peradventure of doubt"). Whichever way the writer understands it, however, there is an excellent chance that some readers will not understand it at all. If you feel the need to use this word, you had better use it with caution.

perceive, perceived Kilpatrick 1984 and Safire 1986, two commentators who work in the political line as well as the language line, take up the subject of *perceive* and *perceived* as used in current political writing. Kilpatrick is at pains to defend his use in "how the American character is perceived in the Kremlin" from attack by an academic for whom *perceive* can only mean "to become aware of something as it really is." This is an interesting matter in which both disputants are partly in the right. Kilpatrick's use is in the mainstream of current political writing, and the professor's perception of the meaning is broadly true for older use of *perceive.* Dictionaries have let both down by not being quick enough to recognize the newer use, although the professor's disapproval would probably not have been affected by mere dictionary recognition.

The newer uses of *perceive* emphasize not external reality—"something that is readily observed"—but rather the mental conception or interpretation of what something really is, regardless of external reality. The use may have originated in psychology.

Let us compare the older and newer uses. First, two of the older ones:

> This was also pointed out twenty-five years ago by no less a critic than David Garnett, who clearly perceived the nature of my method —James Thurber, letter, 24 Oct. 1958

> If this person has really been inadequate for some time, his brighter subordinates probably perceive the fact before the front office does —Samuel Feinberg, *Women's Wear Daily,* 27 May 1975

Now some examples of the newer use:

> ... the key issue: what kind of threat is China *perceived* to be? —Stephen S. Rosenfeld, *Saturday Rev.,* 5 Feb. 1972

> No wonder his father is angered by his constant daydreaming. Jack Penfield perceives it as mental incompetence —E. L. Doctorow, *Loon Lake,* 1979

> ... Washington was perceived as tilting toward Pakistan —Geoffrey Godsell, *Christian Science Monitor,* 26 Oct. 1979

> In *The Anderson Tapes* the Mafia is perceived as an admired business corporation —Lewis H. Lapham, *Harper's,* November 1971

You can see the difference in emphasis—interpretation in the newer use, observation in the older. It is interesting that the newer use tends to be most often passive in construction. The past participle is in frequent use as an adjective, and it is the adjective that Safire mentions. He distinguishes his use of *felt* as an adjective from his use of *perceived.* Typical adjective uses of *perceived* look like this:

> ... real and perceived discrimination —John V. Lindsay, letter to the editor, *Harper's,* December 1971

> ... widening the perceived as well as real gap — Harry B. Ellis, *Christian Science Monitor,* 22 Oct. 1979

> Suppose the perceived network threat is eavesdropping or tapping —Jan Johnson, *Datamation,* 1 May 1984

> ... helpless victims of perceived injustice —Neil Hickey, *TV Guide,* 22 Dec. 1973

percent, per cent You can use either the one-word or the two-word form. Both are correct; the one-word form is more common in American use. *Per cent* used to be perceived as an abbreviation of *per centum* and was commonly styled as *per cent.,* with a period. The form with the period is old-fashioned and rarely seen anymore.

Percent can be followed by either a plural or singular verb. This is rather like notional agreement but it is usually more explicit: the noun related to *percent* frequently follows but sometimes precedes, and its number tends to determine that of the verb:

> ... 80 percent of family physicians do make them — Dodi Schultz, *Ladies' Home Jour.,* August 1971

> Of the ... inhabitants, 75 percent are of African descent —Esther Silver, *Essence,* November 1970

> ... 25 percent of the population was overweight — *Current Biography,* December 1967

One commentator complains that "a large percent" is vague; doubtless it is frequently intended to be so:

> ... might be able to pick up a large percent of the delegates with a modest percent of the votes —Ken Auletta, *New York,* 29 Mar. 1976

A number of handbooks dislike the appearance of the percent sign % in discursive prose.

percolator For pronunciation problems with this word, see NUCLEAR.

perfect "The phrases, *more perfect,* and *most perfect,* are improper," declared Lindley Murray in his *Grammar* of 1795, starting a hare that is being chased to this very day. For instance:

> *Perfect* is viewed by many careful writers as one of the uncomparable adjectives —Harper 1985

> *Perfect* has traditionally been considered an absolute term —Heritage 1982

> Many people feel that since things either are or are not perfect it is illogical to speak of *very* perfect or *more* perfect —Longman 1984

Copperud 1970 reports that the consensus of his usage authorities is that *perfect* may be freely compared, and the dictionaries cited above agree. But some commentators do not: Bernstein 1965, 1971 favors keeping *perfect* free from comparison, and Simon 1980 believes that *perfect* can have no superlative. Here is the background of this disagreement.

Evidence in the OED shows *perfect,* in one sense or another, has been used in the comparative and superlative since the 14th century; citations from the 14th century include Wycliffe, from the 16th Sir Thomas Elyot, Robert Greene, and Shakespeare, and from the 17th the King James Bible, Pepys, Locke, and Sir William Temple. Examples from the 18th century are numerous and include such authors as Addison, Swift, and Bolingbroke and such grammarians and rhetoricians as Hugh Blair, Campbell 1776, and Lowth 1762; Lindley Murray himself copied Blair's and Campbell's uses in his own grammar of 1795. For Americans, the most important 18th-century example is the Preamble to the U.S. Constitution: "in order to form a more perfect union."

How did Murray and the grammarians who followed him come to believe *perfect* should not be compared in spite of usage? They applied rigorous logic, or so they thought. Lowth and Priestley 1798 had already seen certain adjectives as having, to use Lowth's words, "in themselves a superlative signification" to which they thought it improper or illogical to add a superlative ending, although they recognized that such in fact was done (for a complete discussion, see ABSOLUTE ADJECTIVES). Lowth noticed *chiefest* and *extremest;* it was Murray who added *perfect* to the list. And, of course, once other grammarians (Goold Brown 1851 lists several, including Samuel Kirkham, whose book *English Grammar in Familiar Lectures,* 1st ed., 1823, with several subsequent editions, was rather widely used in the U.S.) had copied Murray, *perfect* became solidly ensconced in ever-growing lists of adjectives not to be compared. The opinions of the grammarians were repeated in handbooks, such as Ayres 1881, and thence passed on to our modern commentators.

And how is it that American grammarians and usage commentators have ignored the authority of the Constitution's example? Harper 1985 says that one rebuttal to the urging of the constitutional example is the argument that the usage of 1787 is not the same as today's. The argument, though a valid enough generalization in many respects, will not hold water in this case. The OED shows 19th-century examples, including one from Leigh Hunt; Merriam-Webster files have these in addition:

> ... man and the more perfect animals —John Stuart Mill, *A System of Logic,* 1843–1872

> ... made my reverie one of the perfectest things in the world —William Dean Howells, *Venetian Life,* enlarged ed., 1872

Their love had been as yet too perfect —Charles Kingsley, *Hereward the Wake,* 1866

That is one reason I like reading *older* novels—Scott's, Miss Austen's, Miss Edgeworth's, etc.—that the *English* is so perfect —Lewis Carroll, letter, 10 July 1892

. . . the stronger and more perfect parts of his music —John Burroughs, *Wake-Robin,* 1871

Twentieth-century examples are numerous. Here are a few:

. . . the perfectest herald of joy —James Branch Cabell, *The Rivet in Grandfather's Neck,* 1915

. . . creating a more perfect theocratic machinery —Vernon Louis Parrington, *Main Currents in American Thought,* 1930

I believe this passage contains the most perfect poetry yet written by any of the younger poets —C. Day Lewis, *A Hope for Poetry,* 3d ed., 1936

. . . utilizing the machine to make the world more perfect —Lewis Mumford, *Technics and Civilization,* 1934

. . . until we get absolutely perfect knowledge —Morris R. Cohen, *The Faith of a Liberal,* 1946

. . . some of the most perfect examples of early Colonial and Federalist architecture —John P. Marquand, *New England Journeys,* No. 2, 1954

. . . a more perfect rake has seldom existed —Nancy Mitford, *Atlantic,* May 1954

. . . the most perfect writer of my generation —Norman Mailer, *Advertisements for Myself,* 1959

. . . the most perfect Puck I have ever seen —Walter Terry, *N.Y. Herald Tribune,* 28 Jan. 1962

. . . the owner of a most perfect nose and huge, startled eyes —*Vogue,* September 1976

"*Perfect,* if taken in its strictest sense, must not be compared"—so said Goold Brown in 1851. Only one correction is necessary: *must not be* should read *is not.* "But this word," Goold Brown continues, "like many others which mean most in the positive, is often used with a certain latitude of meaning, which renders its comparison by the adverbs not altogether inadmissible; nor is it destitute of authority." The comparison of *perfect* has been in respectable use from the 14th century to the present; it has never been wrong, except in the imagination of Lindley Murray and those who repeat after him.

If we say, "This is *more perfect* than that," we do not mean that either is perfect without limitation, but that "this" has "more" of the qualities that go to make up perfection than "that"; it is *more nearly* perfect. Such usage has high literary authority —Fernald 1946

perfectly Both Harper 1985 and Heritage 1982 record that *perfectly* used as an intensive, as in

. . . knew perfectly well that *The Songs of Bilitis* were made 'out of the whole cloth' —Gilbert Highet, *The Classical Tradition,* 1949

is sometimes objected to but is very common. Such objection as we have found (Watt 1967, Partridge 1942)

is not very strong. We think you can use it without fear of criticism.

A curious side issue is raised by Mary Hiatt in *The Way Women Write* (1977), a study which finds *perfectly* typical of fiction written by women but not of fiction written by men. Our evidence, which is primarily from nonfiction, suggests that both men and women use the word:

It is perfectly possible to construct an "Arab case" and a "Jewish case," each having a high degree of plausibility —Noam Chomsky, *Columbia Forum,* Winter 1969

Why ship money to Switzerland, when it is perfectly safe back home? —William F. Buckley, Jr., *National Rev.,* 25 Aug. 1970

It was perfectly clear they were rebelling against bad treatment —Margaret Mead, *Barnard Alumnae,* Winter 1971

Annabel, the heroine, was having a perfectly rotten time —P. G. Wodehouse, *Something Fresh,* 1915

perimeter One of the most persistent criticisms of the word *parameter* has been that it is misused in place of *perimeter.* A typical example of the criticized sense of *parameter* is this:

. . . readers with earthier appetites will find *Chiaroscuro* well within the parameters of their crime fiction menus —Peter Plagens, *Art in America,* July 1986

The frequent assumption of those who criticize *parameter* is that *perimeter* is regularly used in this way, in a figurative sense meaning "limits" or "outer limits," and, in fact, such a sense was in use before 1973, when *parameter* critics began making their assumption. Let's consider a few examples of that use:

The most useful division is between criticism which attempts to bring to literature insights found outside its perimeter, and criticism which dives directly to the center of the literature and works outward to the perimeter —Wayne Shumaker, *Elements of Critical Theory,* 1952

. . . it had become a flexible philosophy . . . and its supernatural perimeter attracted many a young searcher for truth —William Manchester, *Disturber of the Peace,* 1951

. . . being aware, on the perimeter of his mind, of the rest of the court —John Creasy, *Alibi,* 1971

It was also, somewhat illogically, used in the plural:

The limits of the world have already been reached by exploration; . . . the "perimeters of the future" are already in sight —*Times Literary Supp.,* 27 July 1951

. . . he belongs among the pioneers of the conquering human spirit who dare beyond the perimeters of complacency into the uncharted wilderness —Robert Lindner, quoted in *N.Y. Times Book Rev.,* 31 Jan. 1954

The perimeters of his poetic estate are clearly defined by the seas on all sides and his refusal to cross them —Raymond Gardner, *The Guardian,* 13 Oct. 1971

As these examples are a goodly portion of all our figurative evidence earlier than 1973, we conclude that such was not at all a common use of *perimeter* then. We may note also that figurative use then was as often singular as plural; this contrasts with *parameter,* almost always plural in the criticized construction. And we find *within* commonly used with *parameters* (see also the examples at PARAMETER), but not with *perimeter.* On the basis of these features, then, we think it unlikely that the criticized use of *parameter* developed out of its substitution for the figurative sense of *perimeter.*

The mainstream figurative use of *perimeter*—now apparently somewhat more frequent in the plural than in the singular—has continued beyond 1973:

> . . . both extended the perimeters of the musical play —Goddard Lieberson, *Saturday Rev.,* 3 Apr. 1976

> . . . rethink the farce in terms of the new dimensions and perimeters —John Simon, *New York,* 30 Aug. 1976

> . . . a rich boy eager for experience beyond the perimeters of his sedate world —Frederic Morton, *N.Y. Times Book Rev.,* 7 Sept. 1980

> . . . because its fulfillment was possible within the perimeter of Soviet ideology —Stanley Kauffmann, *Before My Eyes,* 1980

But now we are finding *within perimeters* as well:

> Let us do good things within their own proper perimeters —James A. Michener, *N.Y. Times Book Rev.,* 27 Feb. 1977

> . . . within the perimeters of what is considered correct business attire —Diane Sustendal, *N.Y. Times Mag.,* 16 Sept. 1984

The use of *within* with *perimeters* is quite new. It may come simply as a carryover from the very frequent use of *within* with *parameters* or, conversely, it may result from people's consciously replacing *parameter* with what they are told is the "correct" word, yet unconsciously using the familiar preposition. In either case, we have an increase in the figurative use of *perimeter,* now sometimes the object of *within,* that has co-occurred with the increase of hostile criticism of *parameter.* This development may be entirely fortuitous, but it is hard to dismiss the possibility that the use of *perimeter* has been stimulated by either the use or the criticism of *parameter.*

period of time This phrase has been censured as a redundancy by Shaw 1987, Janis 1984, Copperud 1980, and Phythian 1979. The basis for objection is put this way by Shaw: "The word *period* conveys the idea of time. . . ." But consider these examples:

> The account of the loss of the ship makes a fitting period to a brave and hopeful voyage into a new world —Farley Mowat, *Westviking: The Ancient Norse in Greenland and North America,* 1965

> Most of the characters speak in rounded periods, often with a touch of malicious wit —Newgate Callendar, *N.Y. Times Book Rev.,* 19 Jan. 1986

The point is simple: *period* does not necessarily convey the idea of time. *Period* is a word of several senses— Webster's Ninth New Collegiate Dictionary defines over a dozen of them—and people who write *period of time* (or *period of years,* or other similar formulations) are

merely taking care that you do not miss their meaning, as in this fifth-grade text, for instance:

> What have you heard about rock music played for long periods of time? —H. Thompson Fillmer et al., *Patterns of Language,* Level E, 1977

Even accomplished writers will sometimes use more than a bare minimum of words to get the point across clearly:

> Over a period of thirty years the late Wilder Hobson and I played a name game —John O'Hara, *Holiday,* May 1967

When using such a phrase improves the clarity of your sentence, we think you can sensibly afford to ignore the criticism.

peripheral When the adjective *peripheral* is used with a preposition, the preposition is *to:*

> . . . the political issue has been seen as peripheral to the psychological and the stylistic —Helen Muchnic, *N.Y. Times Book Rev.,* 4 Mar. 1979

> The accumulation of art objects is peripheral to the activity of art —William Stafford, *Writing the Australian Crawl,* 1978

permeate *Permeate* is used with *by* or *with* about equally. When it is used with *by,* the verb is almost always in the passive; when *permeate* is followed by *with,* the verb may appear in either the active or the passive voice:

> The German philosophers were of the view that the universe was permeated by a similar spiritual activity —S. F. Mason, *Main Currents of Scientific Thought,* 1953

> . . . a language that was still permeated by the assumption that politics could *not* be an objective science —Irving Kristol, *Encounter,* December 1954

> . . . a general joylessness that permeates their lives with frustration —Stanley Kubrick, *Playboy,* September 1968

> . . . his stories are permeated with a sense of vague regret not far removed from fright —William Peden, *Saturday Rev.,* 11 Apr. 1953

Infrequently, *permeate* is used intransitively and may then be followed by *beyond:*

> . . . the influence of the Court permeates even beyond its technical jurisdiction —Felix Frankfurter, in *Aspects of American Government,* ed. Sydney D. Bailey, 1950

permissive, permissivism These are two of the words used by those who think they are defending English to belittle those who offer information on which opinions about language matters might be based more soundly. The use of either by a commentator is almost certainly a sign that a lexicographer, a linguist, or another writer on usage has trodden upon one of the commentator's cherished beliefs. The periphrastic equivalent of *permissive* is *anything goes.*

The last word on the issue of permissivism should have been (but was not and, sadly, will not be) that of

Bergen Evans, co-author of Evans 1957, in an address to the managing editors of the Associated Press:

> People often hurl at me the word *permissive.* They say, "You are permissive." What do you mean "permissive"? There are 300 million who speak this language. What am I do to? Club them all on the head? What have I got to do with it? I permit Niagara Falls to go over, too. I don't know what to do about it. I permit the Grand Canyon to remain just where it is. To talk about people being permissive of what 300 million people do every day—back of this is an incredibly arrogant assumption that we who have to do with observing and using speech in some way control it. We don't. The masses control speech. And all we do, ultimately, is follow on —"Editor's Choice—You Couldn't Do Woise," 1963

permit of   Copperud 1964, 1980 regards the *of* in *permit of* as superfluous, but he concedes that its use is standard. Like *admit of* and *allow of, permit of* is almost always used with an impersonal subject. Its sense is "to make possible," and its use in place of the transitive *permit* is especially appropriate in describing something that simply by its nature does or does not make something else possible:

> ... there are very few matters ... that do not permit of a difference of opinion —O. S. Nock, *The Railways of Britain,* 1947

> Enough ratings are to hand to permit of some definitive judgment —Jack Gould, *N.Y. Times,* 1 Dec. 1957

> ... wartime paper restrictions do not permit of my attempting to publish —C. L. Wrenn, *Word and Symbol,* 1967 (essay first published in 1943)

See also ADMIT 3; ALLOW 2.

pernickety, persnickety   When a correspondent in 1986 wants to know whether *pernickety* or *persnickety* is the preferred form of the word, you know you are hearing from someone with a long memory. From the mid-1940s to about 1961 a dispute about the propriety of *persnickety* was waged fitfully in the pages of newspapers and weekly newsmagazines.

The controversy seems to have had its origin in Webster's Second 1934. That book was the first Merriam-Webster to recognize the version with -*s*-, but it tucked the spelling away in the pearl section at the foot of the page—several pages away from *pernickety.* Apparently some of the objectors to *persnickety* failed to look closely at the pearl section and assumed that the -*s*-spelling was not to be found in the dictionary.

Pernickety was introduced into English by Scottish writers in the early 19th century. *Persnickety* is an Americanism, first attested in the early 20th century. It soon reached the public prints:

> This detachment caused him to be looked upon as slightly finicky, not to say persnickety —*American Mercury,* August 1926

> ... the second act ... should take one into *Florence's* persnickety home —*New Yorker,* 18 Dec. 1926

> ... The Atchison Globe ... thumbed a persnickety snoot at Emporia —*Emporia* (Kans.) *Gazette,* 10 May 1927

In recent use, *persnickety* is more common than *pernickety* in the United States; *pernickety* does have some American use, and it is the only form used in British English.

> An order of double lamb chops cooked medium-rare and served with a hot mint sauce pleased a persnickety guest —Caroline Bates, *Gourmet,* January 1979

> ... the iron deficient housewife and the persnickety feline —William Bayer & Ann Bayer, *N.Y. Times Book Rev.,* 26 Sept. 1976

> His writing, nevertheless, is greatly to be preferred to that of many people who are more pernickety in these matters —C. B. A. Behrens, *N.Y. Rev. of Books,* 3 Dec. 1970

> Pheasants have a reputation for being pernickety — David Stephen, *Scottish Field,* October 1973

> He made a point of being pernickety: he always used to say that dinner was to be at 8.14, while lunch must be at 1.11 —Sacheverell Sitwell, quoted in *The Listener,* 13 Dec. 1973

You can use whichever spelling you prefer.

perpetrate, perpetuate   Many handbooks on usage either state or imply that these two familiar words are frequently or occasionally confused, but actual examples of mistaken use are in extremely short supply. The error warned against is the use of *perpetrate,* "to commit (as a crime)," in place of *perpetuate,* "to cause to continue or to last." Copperud 1964 quotes a clear-cut instance of *perpetrator* used for *perpetuator,* and Kingsley Amis, in Michaels and Ricks 1980, quotes a news report in which *perpetuate* is obviously the word wanted, but *perpetrate* is the word used. We have no other hard evidence. Flesch 1964 quotes a passage in which *perpetrate* is used in a somewhat unusual way, but it is not clearly a mistake for *perpetuate,* and Flesch does not call it one.

This dearth of evidence suggests several possible conclusions: (1) the confusion described by the commentators does not really exist, and the few mistakes they have found are actually nothing more than typographical errors; (2) the confusion exists but is far less common than the commentators think it is; or (3) the confusion exists and is quite common, but we have somehow managed to overlook it. Any of those conclusions may be valid, but we are inclined to give both the commentators and ourselves something of a break by favoring the second.

perquisite, prerequisite   Shaw 1987 says these two words get their prefixes confused; the Oxford American Dictionary warns against confusion; Copperud 1980 distinguishes them. If you do not know the meaning of these words, you will find them plainly defined in any good dictionary. We have almost no evidence of the words' being interchanged in print; the OED says that *perquisite* is used erroneously for *prerequisite* but offers no examples, so we cannot say how far back possible confusion might go.

If you tend to mix up the spelling of the two words, here are a few clues to go by. First, if you want an adjective, it must be *prerequisite; perquisite* is a noun only. And the prepositions typically used with each word are different. *Perquisite* regularly takes *of:*

> It is one of the perquisites of membership —*PMLA,* March 1982

... the perquisites of his position—a chauffeured limousine, a chef —Tony Schwartz, *N.Y. Times Book Rev.,* 9 Dec. 1979

Prerequisite, on the other hand, usually takes *for* or *to:*

... has come to be nearly a prerequisite for leadership —Robert Pattison, *On Literacy,* 1982

... a prerequisite for graduation —James Cass, *Saturday Rev.,* 29 May 1976

... making unfair demands as a prerequisite to improved relations —Lynda Schuster, *Wall Street Jour.,* 3 Feb. 1982

... registration before an election is a prerequisite to casting a vote —*American Girl,* November 1952

Of is used, but somewhat less frequently:

... oratorical abilities—the first prerequisite, as he had always maintained, of a successful politician —William L. Shirer, *The Rise and Fall of the Third Reich,* 1960

persevere   *Persevere* is most often followed by *in:*

Up to this time he had persevered in his resolve not to invite her back —Thomas Hardy, *The Return of the Native,* 1878

This change was persevered in and afterward afforded the basis of President Jackson's assertion —*The Encyclopedia Americana,* 1943

... he may feel that to persevere in that suggestion would alienate Washington's already fluctuating affections—*New Statesman & Nation,* 19 Dec. 1953

In the retail motor-gasoline business, affiliates persevered in their efforts at greater selectivity —*Annual Report, Standard Oil Co.* (New Jersey), 1970

Persevere may sometimes be used with *with;* although it is found in American English, it seems more often to occur in British and Commonwealth English:

... a general exhortation to the young men and women of the country to persevere with their education —*Farmer's Weekly* (South Africa), 9 Dec. 1953

... many people would persevere with the Victorian conception of a schizophrenic culture —Robin Boyd, *Meanjin* (Australia), Autumn 1952

... his suggestion that they persevere with their medicine —A. J. Cronin, *The Citadel,* 1937

... the great Oxford English Dictionary, for instance, which no commercial publisher could have persevered with —John Russell, *N.Y. Times Book Rev.,* 16 Apr. 1978

persnickety   See PERNICKETY, PERSNICKETY.

person   1. See PEOPLE, PERSONS.
2. One of the more noticeable outgrowths of the concern about sexism in language during the 1970s and beyond has been the coinage of compound terms in which the terminal element *-man* (as in *draftsman*) and sometimes *-woman* (as in *chairwoman*) is replaced by *-person.* A few of those compounds were enthusiastically adopted by those endeavoring to be nonsexist: *chairperson, anchorperson, spokesperson,* for instance, are now well established. Critical opinion of such compounds in the press and in usage books has been chiefly negative and chiefly written by men. Perhaps the hostile attitude of commentators has helped winnow out the weakest of such proposed compounds, but the most useful have persevered in use widely enough to gain admission to dictionaries.

Bolinger 1980 observes that there is a tendency in actual use for the new compound, such as *chairperson* or *spokesperson,* to be applied chiefly to women, so that where once we had *spokesman–spokeswoman* we now begin to find *spokesman–spokesperson.* This tendency— and our files suggest it is only a tendency, not an accomplished fact—has also turned some women against some of the *-person* compounds. The disaffection of women with *chairperson* and *anchorperson* has probably furthered the development of *chair* and *anchor* as replacements for the compound forms, but we have not spotted a *spokes* yet.

Janis 1984 notes the effect of the employment ads on such usages. Many employers are zealous to avoid the suggestion of bias, and such compounds as *draftsperson* exist chiefly because of their frequency of use in the help-wanted pages. Janis also notes that many open compounds such as *delivery person* are also used. He thinks these should be avoided, but the peculiar requirements of the help-wanted pages are likely to keep many of them in use.

Unless you are constrained by particular circumstances, you are free to use or avoid compounds such as *spokesperson* as you wish. If you do choose to use them, we suggest that you check with a recent dictionary or two to be sure that the compound you have picked is in current use.

See also SEXISM.

persona   From the comments in Harper 1975, 1985, Reader's Digest 1983, Howard 1978, Gowers in Fowler 1965, and Copperud 1980, it is clear that the commentators are not completely familiar with this word. Reader's Digest says it originated in the psychological theory of Carl Gustav Jung and has passed into popular or extended use; the editors of Harper agree with a panelist who terms it "nouveau and faddistic"; Copperud calls it a fad to use *persona* where *person* will do and calls it a technical term in psychology; Gowers also notes that it is a Jungian term. Howard, on the other hand, identifies it as a technical term in literary criticism, and he dislikes its use as a substitute for *image* or *personality.* The commentators have gotten little guidance from dictionaries.

Much of this commentary is correct: there is popular use; *persona* is a term identified with the psychology of Jung; it is likewise a term considerably used in literary criticism. It seems to have been brought into English from Latin by Joseph Addison in 1704; he used it in its original Latin sense "an actor's mask," and he was writing about Roman actors. This etymologically primary meaning has subsequently been used in English context, but its users have often tended to treat *persona* as a Latin word, though Addison did not. Here is another writer who has used this sense as English:

... and, to employ a metaphor that has become fashionable in erudite circles, he appears to his readers in a persona and thus shows not a face but a mask, as though he were an actor in a drama presented to an audience in ancient Athens —Eric Partridge, *British and American English Since 1900,* 1951

No dictionary of which we are aware includes this sense as English; it is certainly of low frequency.

It was the sense of "mask" that appealed to Ezra Pound, who is one of the people responsible for enlarging the word's domain.

> Ever since he began printing his poems, Mr. Pound has played with the Latin word *persona. Persona,* etymologically, was something through which sounds were heard, and thus a mask. Actors used masks through which great thoughts and actions acquired voice. Mr. Pound's work has been to make *personae,* to become himself, as a poet, in this special sense a person through which what has most interested him in life and letters might be given voice — R. P. Blackmur, *The Double Agent,* 1935

Pound used the word as a title as early as 1909. It is from Pound's use and from criticism of Pound's work that *persona* acquired its use as a term in literary criticism.

According to a citation in the OED Supplement, some of the works of C. G. Jung had been translated into English by 1917. *Persona* was a term Jung used:

> I term the outer attitude, or outer character, the *persona,* the inner attitude I term the *anima,* or *soul* — *Psychological Types,* translated by H. G. Baynes, 1924

Jung's theories had many explicators in English. As the following examples show, each one seemed to give a little individual twist to Jung's notion:

> **persona** . . . That part of the conscious mind which comes into relation with the external world (Jung) — Richard H. Hutchings, M.D., *A Psychiatric Word Book,* 1939

> The persona is the agent responsible for the adaptation of the individual's inner constitution to the environmental world —*Times Literary Supp.,* 9 May 1942

> *Persona* is Jung's celebrated word for the mask that the ego wears before society —*Times Literary Supp.,* 12 May 1950

> A related concept is the "persona," which refers to the role played by the individual in society. . . . The persona is not a part of the true character but is firmly attached to it and acts as a sort of protection of the inner man —Gerald S. Blum, *Psychoanalytic Theories of Personality,* 1953

It is hard to tell just how close each of these explanations is to Jung's original notion, but it is worth noting that the concept appears to have become externalized: if Jung considered the *persona* an aspect of the individual's personality, it has become in the last two explanations a kind of separate entity acting as a protection or buffer. This view of the persona from the outside as a kind of independent entity—perhaps influenced by the original "mask" sense of the word—proved to be suggestive to writers.

It invaded the world of literary criticism, providing new life and new dimension to the Ezra Pound–centered use:

> You might call it a mask, or as Jung would say, a *persona* that soon had a life of its own —Malcolm Cowley, *New Republic,* 18 Mar. 1946

And it also started on an independent life of its own as a word for a person's public personality:

> A likeable personality, he seemed to me, quite without the arrogance I had been led to expect. But he

may have been giving his *persona* a night off —J. B. Priestley, *Irish Digest,* April 1955

> . . . his major work . . . is an appendage to his public persona rather than a great book —Anthony West, *New Yorker,* 10 Dec. 1955

> Few Englishmen have such an officially English persona —V. S. Pritchett, *N.Y. Times Mag.,* 21 Sept. 1958

> . . . the differences between the modern author's *persona* as conveyed to the public and his character as seen by his intimates —Frank Swinnerton, *Saturday Rev.,* 2 Mar. 1957

You may have noticed that each of the examples given so far has a certain amount of age—all of them are over 30. We have selected them to demonstrate that these uses are far from brand-new or "nouveau." What probably attracted the critics' attention is the frequency with which *persona* is currently used. The literary use is flourishing, as is the "public personality" use. We add two more recent examples of each:

> . . . one might argue the "I" of the poem is more often than not a *persona* created by the poet especially for the occasion —*Times Literary Supp.,* 25 Jan. 1974

> But even a lyric poem posits some self that is moved to utterance. The posited self of a lyric may be taken as purely fictional or as a shadowy persona of a literal self, the author —Robert Penn Warren, *Democracy and Poetry,* 1975

> Wayne and Cooper developed personae which they controlled and exhibited skillfully —Stanley Kauffmann, *Before My Eyes,* 1980

> . . . masked her frightful bouts of pain and debility with the glamorous, heavily made-up, in the end sybylline persona who sought to be entertaining — John Updike, *N.Y. Times Book Rev.,* 23 Feb. 1986

We caution you that these are only the most common uses of *persona.* There is a legal sense we have not mentioned. There are also other quite recent uses that leave us uncertain—they may only be temporary aberrations, or they may be new senses just developing. Only time will tell. One of these is a sense apparently meaning "inner or basic self," which is the polar opposite of Jung's sense. If it becomes well-established, use of *persona* might become a genuinely confusing matter. In the meantime we would suggest that you should probably confine your use of *persona* to the two currently popular uses.

personal 1. *Personal* is a word of frequent occurrence. While the critics will allow it to be occasionally useful, they generally tend to disparage its use as redundant or unnecessary, especially in the expressions *personal friend, personal opinion,* and *personal physician.* They are vague, if not downright silent, about where they find these uses. Do they find them in speech?

> . . . a criticism is after all a personal opinion, and any personal opinion on any work is valid because the work itself is only the writer's personal opinion on a situation —William Faulkner, 1 May 1958, in *Faulkner in the University,* 1959

If such uses are common in speech, our files have few instances of the criticized combinations from edited prose.

Personal friend might be useful, suggests one critic, if there were reason to distinguish business from professional friendship:

> If you ask the personal friends and associates of ... —*Ladies' Home Jour.,* October 1971

The two or three critics who sniff at *personal physician* miss the point: the phrase is used of the rich and powerful, who can afford to keep a physician available to them at need. The middle-class or poor person has no personal physician.

> One of his ancestors ... was the personal physician of Napoleon Bonaparte's brother —*Current Biography,* July 1965

A few critics will allow *personal* to be useful in emphasizing privacy or one's private life or possessions:

> ... an interesting minor poet whose personal story was deeply poignant —Irving Howe, *Harper's,* January 1972

> He doesn't believe in talking about himself; ... he thinks the personal side of his life is very much his —David Halberstam, *McCall's,* November 1971

> The Rachmaninoff No. 3 is generally considered the personal property of Vladimir Horowitz —Irving Kolodin, *Saturday Rev.,* 13 Nov. 1976

> ... pleasure and my own personal happiness ... are all I deem worth a hoot —George Jean Nathan, *Testament of a Critic,* 1931

It may be used to emphasize the individual personality:

> ... each practiced an extremely personal form of religious expression —Garson Kanin, *Cosmopolitan,* March 1972

> ... a dancer whose training and development is concentrated on the projection of a unique, personal style —Calvin Tomkins, *Saturday Rev.,* 29 Jan. 1972

> ... neither candidate had much personal appeal — Richard H. Rovere, *New Yorker,* 18 Nov. 1972

> She was big and strong and handsome, although without much personal force —Arlene Croce, *Harper's,* April 1971

It may emphasize firsthand participation:

> Like every journalist, I have personal memories of Nikita Khrushchev —Timothy Foote, *Harper's,* November 1971

In this use it often stresses what one does oneself as opposed to what one's agents or representatives do:

> ... was the personal choice of Secretary of Defense Robert S. McNamara —*Current Biography,* January 1965

> ... believed in the power of diplomacy, and personal diplomacy at that —Martin Mayer, *Cosmopolitan,* January 1972

In short, the censured uses of *personal* do not seem to be especially common in edited prose; and when they do appear, authors generally have a good reason for them. We think you need not be too concerned about the critics' censures as long as you have a good reason for using *personal.*

2. *Personal, personnel.* A surprisingly large number of books warn against confusing these two words. Such confusion would appear unlikely because they are pronounced differently and function as different parts of speech. It is possible that they both may be misspelled sometimes as *personel.*

personality There is no cult of *personality* among usage writers. Several find *personality* in the sense of "celebrity" or "notable" overused and at least mildly objectionable (Harper 1975, 1985, Shaw 1987, Bremner 1980). The Harper panel of 1985 is more hostile than the 1975 panel. Gowers in Fowler 1965 looks at the use rather more dispassionately; he says that personalities are much better paid than personages.

Harper believes the use to be recent, and Bremner says it came in with television. The new OED Supplement, however, dates it back to George Bernard Shaw in 1889. Virginia Woolf used it in 1919, carefully surrounding it with quotation marks to indicate she thought the use rather new. Widespread popular use perhaps began in the 1930s with "radio personalities." The alleged overuse is not reflected in our files. Here are two examples:

> ... the best tactic to hide the lockjaw of his shrinking genius was to become the personality of our time — Norman Mailer, *Advertisements for Myself,* 1959

> In general, nobody speaks out. Public personalities confide their fear in private —*The Economist,* 1 Feb. 1975

personally The objections raised to the use of *personally* approximate those made to *personal;* they are concentrated on a narrow spectrum of use, probably more oral than written, in which the use of *personally* (especially in conjunction with *I*) is called redundant, gratuitous, a meaningless emphasis, or the like. The use of *personally* with *I* in print seems rather to be the mark of an informal conversational style:

> To date I personally haven't seen a flake of snow — Robert Frost, letter, 25 Dec. 1912

> Personally I have found it a good scheme to not even sign my name to the story —Ring Lardner, Preface, *How to Write Short Stories,* 1924

> Personally, I am never happy when I am away from my beloved books —Myles na gCopaleen (Flann O'Brien), *The Best of Myles,* 1968

> Personally, I am most grateful to Mr. Hibben for his salvation of the gazelles —John Fischer, *Harper's,* October 1971

> Admittedly, these usages are not precisely parallel ... and I personally couldn't care less —Robert Claiborne, *Our Marvelous Native Tongue,* 1983

We suggest that you limit your use of this construction to such deliberately informal contexts; to use it in a passage of serious discussion may leave you open to criticism.

Personally is, however, used in serious contexts where it emphasizes personal contact, or the doing of something in person that might have been delegated, or the exclusion of considerations other than personal ones. Here are some examples of such uses:

> Palmer was at pains to get the oldest and most doddery doctors ... with whom he was personally on

friendly terms, to sign the death-certificates of the victims —*Times Literary Supp.,* 27 Aug. 1971

... would probably strike us as pleasant if we met him personally rather than in a movie —Hollis Alpert, *Saturday Rev.,* 10 Jan. 1970

... excellent on the problems of which he was personally in command —John Kenneth Galbraith, *Saturday Rev.,* 6 Nov. 1971

... which President Carter planned to tour personally to determine the extent of the devastation —Wayne King, *N.Y. Times,* 22 May 1980

... the idea that a customer would pay $200 more for a dangerous car that would deteriorate more rapidly being personally offensive —David Halberstam, *Harper's,* February 1971

It is also used to mean "as a person":

... with a look of being personally unusual —Ivy Compton-Burnett, *The Last and the First,* 1971

Sympathetic to New Deal purposes, he disliked the New Dealers personally —Edwin M. Yoder, Jr., *Harper's,* February 1971

personal pronouns Usage problems with personal pronouns are covered under the names of the individual pronouns. For discussions of the use of the nominative versus the objective case, see AS . . . AS 3; BETWEEN YOU AND I; HYPERCORRECTION; IT'S ME; THAN 1.

personnel   **1.** This word seems to have been introduced into English in its present meaning by John Stuart Mill in 1837; it is originally French, and as late as 1947 *The Times* of London was railing at "this alien collective." It was listed with parallel bars as a foreign term in Webster 1890 and in the OED in 1905, but was accepted as English in Webster 1909 and the 1933 OED Supplement. Sir Ernest Gowers still felt the need to defend the word against attack as an objectionable neologism in his 1965 revision of Fowler.

There has been some confusion about the number of the verb used with *personnel.* It appears to have been originally considered a singular, much like *staff,* but later became conceived of as one of those pesky collective nouns (like *committee*) that take a singular verb when thought of as a unit and a plural verb when thought of as a number of individuals.

From the use with a plural verb, *personnel* came to be viewed as a noun with a plural meaning "persons," or more precisely, "persons of a particular group." Around the end of World War II, this sense began to be used occasionally with a preceding number:

Japanese figures show they lost a total of 276,000 personnel —Chester W. Nimitz, *National Geographic,* June 1946

The bank's staff in August 1948 consisted of about 435 personnel —*Collier's Year Book,* 1949

... a land Army ... with a total strength of 34,400 personnel —*Statesman's Year-Book,* 1957

This use, which appears to be of American origin, has been disapproved by a number of commentators, such as Bernstein 1962, Harper 1975, 1985, and Longman 1984. Copperud 1964 defends it:

It is a puristic fiction that the word cannot be preceded by a number, although, since it is a plural, one

would not speak of *one personnel.* . . . Phrases like *three military personnel* are irreproachable and convenient.

Convenience does seem to be one of the reasons for the continuation of the usage. Here, for example, is part of a report on a bomb explosion in Melbourne, Australia:

Most of the injured, who included 12 police personnel, suffered cuts and abrasions from flying glass. A policewoman with burns covering 80 percent of her body was the only victim listed in serious condition —*International Herald Tribune* (UPI), 28 Mar. 1986

Here the reporter, by using *personnel,* avoided a possible uncertainty about the propriety of *12 police;* avoided *policemen,* which would have been inaccurate; avoided *police officers,* perhaps not used in Australia; and avoided *policemen and policewomen.* Convenience of expression may be noted in this next example, too:

College store retailers must have felt the lure of Boston's historic attractions because a record 1717 store personnel turned out for the four-day event —*Publishers Weekly,* 7 May 1982

The usage seems at present to be confined to journalistic publications and others in which statistics appear frequently.
2. See PERSONAL 2.

persons   See PEOPLE, PERSONS.

perspicacious, perspicacity, perspicuous, perspicuity   Fowler 1926 was perhaps wise in his approach to this subject: he lumped all of these hard words under the heading *perspic-* and avoided a lot of tedious spelling. In case you are uncertain, the pair with *a* go together and the pair with *u* go together. The purpose of Fowler's discussion, and that of Evans 1957, Krapp 1927, Copperud 1964, 1970, Phythian 1979, and Bryson 1984, is to point out confusion—the substitution of one or another of each pair for one or another of the other pair.

One easy way to keep out of trouble with these words is not to use them, of course, as they are never really required. Any good thesaurus will give you several alternatives for each. A more sensible, and surely bolder, approach is to check your desk dictionary before you use them. We say desk dictionary, not unabridged, because your desk dictionary has the present-day mainstream meanings. An unabridged dictionary has all the meanings, and that, as we shall see, is the problem.

According to the commentators, the chief mistake is substitution of *perspicuity* for *perspicacity* (it has been going on since 1662) and of *perspicuous* for *perspicacious.* The latter is a real problem for the commentators: *perspicuous* was used in the sense of *perspicacious* in 1584, two years before it was used in its current mainstream meaning (1586) and 56 years before *perspicacious* (1640) is attested in English at all.

The meanings we are concerned with, then, are "of acute discernment; keen" (you might even say "shrewd")—the chief modern meaning of *perspicacious*—and "acuteness of discernment or insight"—the chief modern meaning of *perspicacity.* With history in mind, we cannot call the use of *perspicuous* and *perspicuity* in these senses a mistake, or even a confusion. The adjective has priority, and although the noun does not, it is as likely to have been derived from the old sense of the adjective as it is from confusion with *perspicacity.*

We must point out, however, that the trend of development since the 16th and 17th centuries has been toward differentiation, with *perspicacious* and *perspicacity* used chiefly in the senses just given, and *perspicuous* and *perspicuity* used in the senses of "clear to the understanding; plain, lucid" and "clarity, lucidity." Here are some examples of mainstream use:

> ... she took some comfort in her perspicacity at having guessed his passion —Vita Sackville-West, *The Edwardians,* 1930

> ... triumph is itself fortuitous, and is therefore no great credit to his perspicacity —George F. Kennan, *New Yorker,* 1 May 1971

> The dictum of Ben Jonson . . . that "the chief virtue of style is perspicuity. . . ." —*Times Literary Supp.,* 18 Mar. 1944

> ... the problems that still confound us were formulated with remarkable clarity and perspicuity — Noam Chomsky, *Columbia Forum,* Spring 1968

> ... St. Augustine has some very perspicacious remarks on Plato —I. F. Stone, *N.Y. Times Mag.,* 22 Jan. 1978

> Being not only sane but perspicacious, General Grigorenko kept mum —Robert C. Tucker, *N.Y. Times Book Rev.,* 2 Jan. 1983

> One must be extremely exact, clear, and perspicuous in everything one says —Lord Chesterfield, *Letters to his Son,* 1774

> ... offering a perspicuous picture of the movement of empires —*Times Literary Supp.,* 12 Feb. 1970

These examples are in the mainstream. The use of *perspicuous* and *perspicuity* where *perspicacious* and *perspicacity* are expected has historical justification but may be seen as a mistake or may confuse your readers. We suggest that you stick to the mainstream uses or skip the words altogether.

persuade *Persuade* is most often used with *to* and an infinitive:

> ... persuading young people to make one of the sciences . . . their life's work —Russell H. Johnsen, *Scientific Monthly,* January 1954

> ... is deputed by the firm of lawyers to which he belongs to persuade her to resume her married life —Anthony Powell, *Punch,* 8 Apr. 1953

> ... his test is not so much what happened as what he believes he can persuade other people to believe — John Kenneth Galbraith, *Saturday Rev.,* 6 Nov. 1971

Occasionally *to* is followed by a noun:

> ... persuading the attention of the variable human mind to Divine objects —T. S. Eliot, "Lancelot Andrewes," in *Selected Essays,* 1932

> Persuaded to the hospital for examination and medications, he insisted on returning home —Larry L. King, *Harper's,* April 1971

Persuade occurs quite frequently with a clause:

> The reading of the card persuaded me that he was dead —James Joyce, *Dubliners,* 1914

> Slowly his anger grew. . . . He even persuaded himself that he felt jealousy —Edith Sitwell, *Fanfare for Elizabeth,* 1946

> ... the palpable effort of that book to persuade that Concord was a Brook Farm where no Hawthorne ever worked on a dung-hill —Alfred Kazin, *Partisan Rev.,* September–October 1940

It is somewhat less often used with *of, by,* or *into:*

> I doubted that my father was persuaded of approaching great comfortableness —Kenneth Roberts, *Oliver Wiswell,* 1946

> ... his anxiety to refute polemical over-simplifications and persuade the reader of his objectivity — Dennis H. Wrong, *Change,* April 1972

> ... I might be persuaded by your eloquence —Lewis H. Lapham, *Harper's,* January 1972

> ... films designed to persuade and convince by an appeal to emotions —*Report: Royal Commission on National Development in the Arts, Letters & Sciences, 1949–1951* (Ottawa, Canada)

> The speech . . . persuades us into accepting her surrender —T. S. Eliot, "Thomas Heywood," in *Selected Essays,* 1932

> ... persuading her (the car) into a truck after baffling the plans of the shunters for smashing her —George Bernard Shaw, letter, 19 Aug. 1912

And, to give you an idea of the wide assortment of prepositions used with *persuade,* here are examples of *as to, from, out of, with,* and *upon,* with which it is found occasionally:

> She could not persuade herself as to the advisability of her promise —Theodore Dreiser, *Sister Carrie,* 1900

> Pickets are then sent to the plant gates to persuade others from taking the places of the strikers —*New Republic,* 20 Jan. 1937

> ". . . This brother of yours would persuade me out of my senses, Miss Morland. . . ." —Jane Austen, *Northanger Abbey,* 1818

> ... to persuade the intelligence with reason rather than to overwhelm it with a profusion of detail — Walter Prescott Webb, *The Great Frontier,* 1952

> ... his ministers will clearly have difficulty in persuading it upon ordinary people —David Wood, *The Times* (London), 19 Nov. 1973

See also CONVINCE, PERSUADE.

persuasion Back in the 19th century writers like Dickens or Trollope commonly used *persuasion* to mean "religion"—either as a system of beliefs or as a group of people adhering to those beliefs. (The use actually goes back to the 16th and 17th centuries.) Thus a Roman Catholic might be referred to as "a person of the Catholic persuasion" or a Jew as "a person of the Hebrew persuasion." This use must have been so common as to invite parody; in 1866 Dean Alford was complaining that he had seen and heard "Jewish persuasion" and "Hebrew persuasion" so often he expected soon to encounter "an individual of the negro persuasion." So, from a word used to indicate a set of religious beliefs or believers, *persuasion* came to be used for any group or kind.

Fowler 1926 objected to such use as "worn-out humour" and Flesch 1964 thought it sounded "genteel and Victorian." Their reservations have been ignored by writers. The older religious sense is still alive:

> He is a vegetarian and a Hindu of the Kamakoti Pitam persuasion —*Current Biography,* September 1965

And the denigrated use is thriving:

> I have cooked hundreds of batches of chili and have eaten chilies of all makes and persuasions —Craig Claiborne, *N.Y. Times,* 5 Nov. 1980

> With the exception of three young men of Japanese persuasion, everyone in the hall is middle-aged — Robert Alan Aurthur, *Esquire,* April 1973

> . . . listen to fiddlers of every musical persuasion — Robert E. Tomasson, *N.Y. Times,* 25 May 1979

> . . . women's liberationists of various persuasions — Nancy Ryan, *Saturday Rev.,* 1 Apr. 1972

> . . . where no man had ever been beaten in one-on-one basketball by an opponent of the female persuasion —Joseph Honig, *N.Y. Times,* 6 Jan. 1980

pertinent *Pertinent* is usually used with *to* and a noun object:

> This is a play that she would like to see revived as she feels it is very pertinent to the present —*Current Biography,* June 1964

> This balance of contrasted emotion is in the dramatic situation to which the speech is pertinent —T. S. Eliot, "Tradition and the Individual Talent," 1917, in *American Harvest,* ed. Allen Tate & John Peale Bishop, 1942

> . . . the "digging up" of all facts and figures pertinent to the project —Axel Bruzelius, *Area Development,* July 1970

Sometimes *pertinent* is followed by *to* and an infinitive:

> . . . it is pertinent to take stock of the position and consider what it implies for the future —*The Economist,* 21 May 1953

Occasionally, *pertinent* has been followed by *as regards, for,* or *in:*

> This is especially pertinent as regards corporations that operated at less than optimum —C. E. Ferguson, *Southern Economic Jour.,* October 1952

> . . . although pertinent for some points of view, is irrelevant to our purpose here —George B. Hurff, *Social Aspects of Enterprise In the Large Corporation,* 1950

> . . . find a new instrument for the 1970s and '80s which will be more pertinent in achieving those still valid goals —Calvin H. Plimpton, *Amherst College Bulletin,* November 1968

peruse *Peruse* is a literary word. Marlowe and Shakespeare used it; so did Pope and Swift and Johnson, Wordsworth and Tennyson. In poetry it was a useful alternative to the monosyllabic *read.* But taste in literature has changed, and *peruse* is no longer used as frequently as it was in times past.

Early in the 20th century, when regular literary use of *peruse* began to wane, there arose the notion among American critics that the word should only be used in a narrow sense. Vizetelly 1906 seems to have been the earliest to propound this view:

> **peruse** should not be used when the simple *read* is meant. The former implies to read with care and attention and is almost synonymous with *scan,* which is to examine with critical care and in detail. A person is more apt to *read* than to *scan* or *peruse* the Bible.

Vizetelly was soon followed by F. H. Teall, a sometime Merriam editor, in a journal called *The Inland Printer.* Teall misquotes the definition of *peruse* in Webster's 1890 to make his point.

After these early warnings, *peruse* received mention in some handbooks of the 1920s—two of which Vizetelly had a hand in—and eventually came in for mention in more recent books, such as Evans 1957, Flesch 1964, Harper 1975, 1985, and Bryson 1984.

While we cannot be sure, it appears that this notion of the correct use of *peruse* was Vizetelly's own invention. It was certainly born in disregard of dictionary definitions of the word and in apparent ignorance of the literary traditions on which those dictionary definitions were based.

The sense that is criticized was defined by Samuel Johnson in his 1755 Dictionary simply as "To read." We know from the evidence that *peruse* was in Johnson's working vocabulary and that he was familiar with its use. It meant "to read" to him. Later lexicographers elaborated on Johnson's treatment. Webster, for instance, defined it in 1828 as "To read, or to read with attention." At least part of the reason for elaborating on Johnson's definition was probably the sense development of *read.* Johnson recognized three senses of *read;* his reviser, Archdeacon Todd, a half century later, doubled that number. No doubt Webster's addition at *peruse* was made partly to narrow the focus of *read* as a defining term.

James A. H. Murray, editing the word for the OED from an undoubtedly greater range of citational evidence than was available to either Johnson or Webster, framed a definition in three parts: "To read through or over; to read thoroughly or carefully; hence (loosely) to read." Most American dictionaries of the 20th century have taken the same approach.

Murray's three components can be considered as broad (to read), medium (to read through or over), and narrow (to read thoroughly or carefully). All three of these have coexisted at least since the time of Marlowe and Shakespeare; the broadness or narrowness is usually shown by the context. For instance here we find the narrow use being signaled:

> In meantime take this book; peruse it thoroughly
> And thou shalt turn thyself into what shape thou wilt
> —Christopher Marlowe, *Dr. Faustus,* 1604

> Have you with heed perused
> What I have written to you?
> —Shakespeare, *Coriolanus,* 1608

> Having carefully perused the Journals of both Houses —Edward Hyde, Earl of Clarendon, *A History of the Great Rebellion,* 1647 (OED)

> . . . especially let his Method of Phisick be diligently perused —George Herbert, *A Priest to the Temple,* 1652

> Let the Preface be attentively perused —James Boswell, *Life of Samuel Johnson,* 1791

. . . many books
Were skimmed, devoured, or studiously perused,
But with no settled plan
—William Wordsworth, *The Prelude,* 1805

By the same means the broad sense could be signaled:

Whatever is common is despised. Advertisements are now so numerous that they are very negligently perused —Samuel Johnson, *The Idler,* 20 Jan. 1759

I've even found myself idly perusing the Yellow Pages —Lesley Conger, *The Writer,* October 1968

Those of us who have been idly perusing the latest flock of holiday brochures —*The Guardian* (in Bryson)

The bulk of the evidence is not marked by the use of adverbial modifiers to point the reader in the narrow or the broad direction. Most of it, we would assume, falls into the middle range (read through or over):

Peruse this writing here, and thou shalt know
The treason that my haste forbids me show
—Shakespeare, *Richard II,* 1596

I have perused the note —Shakespeare, *The Taming of the Shrew,* 1594

Oh! Mr. Pamphlet, your servant. Have you perused my poems? —George Farquhar, *Love and a Bottle,* 1698

He only is the master who keeps the mind in pleasing captivity; whose pages are perused with eagerness, and in hope of new pleasure are perused again —Samuel Johnson, *Lives of the Poets,* 1783

. . . nor do we doubt but our reader, when he hath perused his story, will concur with us in allowing him that title —Henry Fielding, *Jonathan Wild,* 1743

Those who ne'er deigned their Bible to peruse
Would think it hard to be denied their news
—George Crabbe, *The Newspaper,* 1785 (in Lounsbury 1908)

. . . with heart how full Would he peruse these lines —William Wordsworth, *The Prelude,* 1805

. . . resolved instantly to peruse every line before she attempted to rest —Jane Austen, *Northanger Abbey,* 1818

I have a letter from William which you may peruse —Henry Adams, letter, 18 Aug. 1863

. . . take upon himself the painful labor of purchasing and perusing some of the cheap periodical prints which form the people's library of amusement —W. M. Thackeray, *The Paris Sketch Book,* 1840

I perused a number of public notices attached to the wall —Flann O'Brien, *At Swim-Two-Birds,* 1939

How depressing political allegory can be may be discovered by perusing Addison's *Trial of Count Tariff* —Bonamy Dobrée, *English Literature in the Early Eighteenth Century, 1700–1740,* 1959

You may have noticed by now that the plain word *read* can readily be substituted in any of these examples, even where the idea of "read through or over" is pretty obvious. Sometimes the suggestion of the broader sense is equally plain:

Both they and we, perusing o'er these notes,
May know wherefore we took the sacrament
—Shakespeare, *King John,* 1597

Or else, to shew their learned Labour, you
May backward be perus'd, like Hebrew
—Jonathan Swift, "George Nim-Dan-Dean Esq.," 1721

. . . but when I returned to Boston in 1733, I found this change had obtained favour, and was then become common, for I met with it often in perusing the newspapers —Benjamin Franklin, letter, 26 Dec. 1789

O the old books we shall peruse here! —Charles Lamb, letter, 18 Sept. 1827

I have also perused *But Gentlemen Marry Brunettes*—that nothing be lost —Oliver Wendell Holmes d. 1935, letter, 17 June 1928

Mr. Warburton then and thereforth seemed to lose his appetite for information. He ceased perusing the *Wall Street Journal* —James Purdy, *Cabot Wright Begins,* 1964

Sometimes the narrower sense is implied, too:

. . . I beg the favour that you will peruse the inclosed, and . . . correct the mistaken passages —Edmund Cave, letter, 15 July 1737

. . . having written scandalous speeches without license or approbation of those that ought to peruse and authorise the same —Vita Sackville-West, *Aphra Behn,* 1928

With Dickinson and his cohorts perusing it in the meantime with critical eyes —Claude G. Bowers, *The Young Jefferson, 1743–1789,* 1945

In conclusion we recommend that you reread the examples and see for yourself in how many Samuel Johnson's simple "read" definition would work perfectly well. There are likely to be only a few in which adding the adverbs used by later dictionary definers will enhance anyone's understanding of the passage. Vizetelly's strictures do not stand the test of being tried against actual usage by people familiar with the word. *Peruse* has not changed much since Shakespeare's time, but it is not a word we use very often any more. Therefore if you choose to use it, you are best advised to use it in a literary context.

peruser The strictures discussed just above at *peruse* are also occasionally applied to its derivative *peruser.*

. . . writers whose names . . . flashed like a red signal to the casual peruser of cartoons and ads —*N.Y. Times,* 17 Feb. 1985

That passage was censured in *Winners & Sinners,* 19 Apr. 1985:

Casual peruser is an oxymoron: *peruse* means inspect minutely, not browse.

The *Winners & Sinners* writer is wrong on two counts. First he has confused two senses of *peruse:* it is the "read" sense that should apply here, not the "examine" sense. And second, the notion that the "read" sense can only be narrowly applied is erroneous (see PERUSE). The usage of the *Times* reporter is not very different from that of a regular user of the words *peruse* and *peruser* some two centuries ago:

> ... those quotations which to careless or unskilful perusers appear only to repeat the same sense, will often exhibit, to a more accurate examiner, diversities of signification —Samuel Johnson, *Preface to the Dictionary,* 1755

Peruser is simply a harder or fancier word for *reader.*

pervert   *Pervert* is used with *into, to,* or *by:*

> ... those who pervert honest criticism into falsification of fact —Franklin D. Roosevelt, fireside chat, 28 Apr. 1942, in *Nothing to Fear,* ed. B. D. Zevin, 1946

> According to Sadat, Ali Sabri perverted it into an instrument that gave him personal control over large parts of the country —Joseph Kraft, *New Yorker,* 18 Sept. 1971

> ... those who pervert good words to careless misuse —Jacques Barzun, *Atlantic,* December 1953

> There is no possible way to prevent peaceful atoms from being perverted to warlike purposes —Morehead Patterson, quoted in *The Reporter,* 12 Jan. 1956

> The habit of perverting values by subordinating the eternal to the temporal —*Times Literary Supp.,* 23 May 1942

> They have perverted the concept of academic freedom by broadening its scope to include social action —Ronald Reagan, *Change,* July–August 1969

Somewhat less frequently, *pervert* is followed by *for, from,* or *with:*

> ... perverting justice for reactionary political ends —William L. Shirer, *The Rise and Fall of the Third Reich,* 1960

> ... were not only impeded but spoiled and perverted from their true nature —Robert A. Hall, Jr., *A Short History of Italian Literature,* 1951

> Luther protested against a Catholic Church that had ... perverted it [Scripture] with casuistry —Irving Babbitt, *The New Laokoon,* 1910

pessimistic   Copperud 1970, 1980 seems to argue that *pessimistic* should be applied to persons only, and should not be allowed to modify nonhuman or inanimate nouns; for this view he invokes the authority of dictionaries. What dictionaries he has been looking at we are uncertain, but *pessimistic* in our files is usually applied to nonhuman and inanimate nouns.

> ... the most ... relentless expression of the pessimistic view —Louis J. Halle, Jr., *Saturday Rev.,* 12 Apr. 1941

> "... Dr. Baines always takes a pessimistic view of everything...." —Dorothy L. Sayers, *The Nine Tailors,* 1934

> ... a really pessimistic winter for the farmers — Adrian Bell, *Silver Ley,* 1931

> ... muttering pessimistic prophecies —G. M. Trevelyan, *British History in the Nineteenth Century,* 1922

> ... wrapped in pessimistic gloom —Paul Elmer More, *Selected Shelburne Essays,* 1935

> No pessimistic policy about the future of America — Franklin D. Roosevelt, fireside chat, 29 Dec. 1940, in *Nothing to Fear,* ed. B. D. Zevin, 1946

> ... a series of pessimistic ... intelligence estimates —Peter Schrag, *Saturday Rev.,* 13 Nov. 1971

> ... his own pessimistic evaluation —Henry S. F. Cooper, Jr., *New Yorker,* 11 Nov. 1972

phase   See FAZE, PHASE, FEAZE, FEEZE.

phenomenon   **1.** The plural is *phenomena* or *phenomenons. Phenomena* is much more frequent at the present time, but *phenomenons* prevails in the sense "an exceptional or unusual person, thing, or occurrence." **2.** Perhaps we in the dictionary trade should get around to recognizing that *phenomena* is used as a singular. The OED dates the use as far back as 1576; the plural form *phenomenas* goes back to 1635, and among its 17th century users the OED numbers Robert Boyle, the famous chemist and physicist. It cannot be simply an illiteracy used by those ignorant of Latin and Greek; Robert Boyle undoubtedly knew more Latin and Greek than most of the subsequent commentators who have disparaged the form. Philip Howard, who seems to have some classical background, has this comment:

> It is a notable recent *phenomena* that one *criteria* of education in an influential *strata* of the community is to be good at criticizing what the *media* is saying about all this *data* on the decay of English. Instead of crying barbarism, it is more constructive to investigate why this should be happening. Fewer people know Latin and Greek these days, and accordingly there are fewer around to be pained by outrages upon their methods of word-formation. And, in any case, English grammar evolves with majestic disregard for the susceptibilities of classical scholars —*Weasel Words,* 1978

Evidence in our files for the singular *phenomena* goes back to the mid 1920s. The OED has a note that the form was found in the 18th and 19th centuries, but besides the 1576 citation they give only one 19th-century source. Hodgson 1889, who seems to be the first commentator to pick the subject up, also has a 19th-century example. We have some modern examples collected from print, and here are a few:

> ... this phenomena can be used —*Science,* 28 Apr. 1944

> ... the Borgia were, in modern terms, a media phenomena —*The Economist,* 23 Nov. 1974

> ... a fine analysis of this phenomena —*Publishers Weekly,* 31 May 1976

But the majority of our evidence comes from speech. It has been reported or recorded in the speech of university professors, U.S. Senators, poets, and literary critics as well as from the speech of well-known figures from the world of professional sports. In current American English, then, the singular *phenomena* is primarily a speech form—in the old days it would have been called colloquial—that is occasionally found in print other than reported speech. Its occurrence in print is not nearly as common as that of the plural *phenomena,* which we also have attested from speech.

A case can be made that the singular *phenomena,* now more than 400 years old, ought to be a recognized form. It is no more etymologically irregular than *stamina, agenda,* and *candelabra,* all of which are accepted as standard. It is—at least in current American English—primarily used in speech; it has nowhere near the sort of use in print that, say, *stamina* has. Until it gets more regular use in print, however, it must be recognized as a borderline form at best. You can be a pioneer, if you wish, but we do not recommend it.

There is, incidentally, some little evidence (1767, 1925, 1979) for a plural *phenomenae.* Since two of these three examples are misspelled quite apart from the *ae,* the form must be considered to be a long, long way from recognition. If you fancy the singular *phenomena,* you had better stick to *phenomenas* as a plural.

For other foreign plurals, see LATIN PLURALS.

phone   Prentice Hall 1978 and Bell & Cohn 1981 tell us in all seriousness that *phone* is colloquial and not to be used in formal writing. The ban on *phone* was announced by Emily Post back in 1927. It was one of a number of clipped forms—*auto* and *photo* were two others—that were viewed askance by linguistic etiquette books (such as MacCracken & Sandison 1917) in the early years of this century. In the same list with *phone,* Emily Post included *mints.* No usage writer has commented on that one.

If Emily Post's ideal Mrs. Worldly would never have said *phone* in 1927, she probably would say it today. You need not give its use in writing at any level a second thought, though the unclipped *telephone* is equally available if you prefer it.

phony, phoney 1.   *Phony* is an Americanism of obscure origin first attested in print in 1900. H. L. Mencken in *The American Language, Supplement II* (1948) suggests that *phony* is a legacy of the pitchmen who used to congregate around fairs and carnivals, but the earliest citation so far found is from *More Fables,* the sequel volume to the breezy *Fables in Slang* (1899) of the humorist George Ade. The word was entered in Webster 1909 as slang and so continued in Webster's Second 1934.

It has proved very popular, and has appeared more and more often in contexts that are not slangy. Such an appearance brought it to the notice of Bernstein 1965. He looked in Webster's Second, saw the *slang* label, and pronounced *phony* inappropriate in the context of the newspaper article he was reading. But Harper 1975, 1985 thinks it so widespread it must be considered acceptable at least in informal contexts, and Copperud 1970, 1980 opines that its "progress to standard seems to be beyond doubt."

The difference between the early status of *phony* and its status today can be shown by these examples, old and more recent.

> Now, this lawyer party must get away to-night or these grafters will hitch the horses to him on some phony charge —R. E. Beach, *The Spoilers,* 1906

> It is giving "phoney" advice to a base runner —Christy Mathewson, *Pitching in a Pinch,* 1912

> The tout's stock devices—the "bank-roll" game, the "phoney" ticket, the "jockey's cousin" —Henry M. Blossom, Jr., *Checkers,* before 1909

> ... he has a talent for exposing phonies which cannot but pacify the spirit of the late H. L. Mencken —Paul Fussell, *Los Angeles Times Book Rev.,* 25 Apr. 1971

> The idolatry of science in our age has insured that this phony knowledge be taken seriously —Sigmund Koch, *Psychology Today,* September 1969

> Vouchers issued in the United States for flights home often were found to be phony —Barbara Johnson, *Saturday Rev.,* 4 Mar. 1972

> *A Night Full of Rain,* in short, seems to me silly, boring, and phony. There is some nice pastel cinematography —Arthur M. Schlesinger, Jr., *Saturday Rev.,* 1 Apr. 1978

> ... his character is a ludicrous phoney —John Simon, in *The Film,* 1968

> ... as the years make ever more prominent its phoney operatics —*Times Literary Supp.,* 4 Jan. 1968

> ... who has amassed over 40 phoney degrees himself in five years of investigations —*The Economist,* 6 Sept. 1985

> ... the damage the Victorians had done in imposing a phoney tradition of gentility on the heroes —Ronald Hayman, *The Set-Up,* 1973

You will have noticed some British examples here. There seems to have been little fuss over the establishment of this Americanism in British English, although Foster 1968 does quote a disgruntled letter writer of 1955. Gowers in Fowler 1965 says that *phony* became widely known in the autumn of 1939 with the advent of the "Phoney War." The new OED Supplement has a British citation from 1935.

Commentators like Bernstein appear to have been a bit behindhand in their acceptance of *phony.* It looks standard to us.

2. Copperud 1980, who is primarily concerned with American use, says that while Fowler 1965 and the dictionaries recognize the spelling *phoney,* it is not used. This statement is not accurate.

Phoney is the first attested spelling; it is the one George Ade used. But *phony* was not far behind; our files contain a 1906 citation for the spelling and the old OED Supplement (1933) has one from 1904. Webster 1909 put the definition under *phony* and entered *phoney* as a variant; Webster's Second 1934 followed suit. American use has pretty much followed the Merriam-Webster entries.

Here is how the spellings stack up today. *Phoney* is the usual spelling in British English; *phony* is seldom found there (though we do have Australian evidence for it). Both *phony* and *phoney* are found in American English, but *phony* is the predominant form by quite a wide margin.

photo   Here is another survivor from Emily Post 1927 (see PHONE) and from the older commentators (such as MacCracken & Sandison 1917) still to be found, surprisingly, in handbooks like Bell & Cohn 1981 and Prentice Hall 1978. Sellers 1975 says that in Great Britain some people still regard it as a vulgarism.

Photo presents quite a different problem from *phone.* In general use, it has been elbowed aside by *picture* (and perhaps also by *snapshot*) so we do not find it in the regular, widespread, popular use that *phone* enjoys. We find it in schoolbooks, in catalogs, in advertisements, but not very frequently in ordinary prose like these examples:

> ... taking flash photos of indigent families —E. L. Doctorow, *Ragtime*, 1975

> ... isn't just a man who likes his photo all over his books —Herbert Gold, *Los Angeles Times Book Rev.*, 23 May 1971

It is often found attributively in such combinations as *photo emulsions, photo editor, photo enlargements, photo negatives.*

> ... the punchy West German photo weekly —*Time*, 25 Feb. 1985

In such use it is probably felt to be clearer than *picture* might be.

phth   When this cluster of consonants occurs in words such as in *diphtheria, diphthong,* or *naphtha,* the recommended pronunciation is with \fth\, but the most usual version is \pth\. The popular version may even be heard in the speech of specialists: our pronunciation files attest \\'dip-ˌthäŋ\ from linguists and \dip-'thir-ē-ə\ from distinguished doctors. *Ophthalmia* and *ophthalmologist,* being rarer words, are more likely to get \f\, but again we have heard \p\ versions even from physicians. (This last-named word presents another trap: we have instances of ophthalmologists and professors of medicine saying \ˌäf-thə-'mäl-ə-jəst\, skipping over the *l* before the *m.*)

pianist   One sometimes reads that musicians themselves say \\'pē-ə-nəst\; one sometimes hears, on the other hand, that this pronunciation, while posh, is prissy and obnoxious. In our own file of pronunciations, \pē-'an-əst\ seems to prevail among classical musicians and radio announcers, while some very unassuming people have been recorded as saying \\'pē-ə-nəst\. In any event, consensus has it that our pianist plays on a \pē-'an-ō\, not on a \pī-'an-ə\; and when he plays softly, he plays \pē-'än-ō\. Further, if he is accompanying a violinist, he is an \ə-'kəmp-ə-nəst\, not an \ə-'kəmp-ə-nē-əst\. For all that Dickens once wrote *accompanyist,* the accepted pronunciation matches the accepted spelling, *accompanist.*

piece, peace   A few schoolbooks and handbooks warn against confusing *piece* with *peace.* This would seem a schoolchild's error, but in fact adults in their less attentive moments do sometimes botch the two. We had a correspondent in 1985 who wondered whether *peace* or *piece* was the spelling to be used in "Speak now or forever hold your _____."
     Piece is also one of those *-ie-* words that get misspelled with *-ei-.* The old reminder for vowel order used to be "piece of pie." Our examples of the misspelling are old, but they are genuine. We suggest you take care with these homophones.

pinch-hit, pinch hitter   Objections to the use of *pinch-hit* and *pinch-hitter* in non-baseball contexts in the sense of "substitute" (verb and noun) have been expressed by Evans 1957, Bernstein 1958, 1965, Copperud 1964, and Harper 1975. The basis for this objection is that the pinch hitter is a player sent out to bat in the expectation that he will do better than the player for whom he is to hit. Whatever the merits of such a defi-

nition in the context of baseball, in non-baseball use it is the simple notion of substitution that prevails. The verb *pinch-hit* seems to be more often used than *pinch-hitter.* The terms are sometimes applied to inanimate subjects. Here are some typical examples:

> ... coordinates some of our photography sessions with food stylists, pinch-hits as a recipe editor —*Cuisine*, October 1984

> ... doing two or three jobs at once, even pinch-hitting for absent workers —Gene Bylinsky, *Fortune*, 1 June 1981

> Fruit butters are delicious with toast, popovers, biscuits, and can also pinch-hit when a last-minute dessert is needed —Beatrice H. Comas, *Christian Science Monitor*, 20 Sept. 1979

> Mr. Huston was brought in largely as a pinch hitter to help train Miss Hefner —Wendy L. Wall, *Wall Street Jour.*, 21 Feb. 1984

> ... the large number of singers Mr. Bing keeps around as pinch-hitters —Winthrop Sargeant, *New Yorker*, 29 Oct. 1966

A peculiarity of the non-baseball *pinch-hit* is the occasional occurrence of the past *pinch-hitted:*

> ... so Gordon and Sheila MacRae pinch-hitted for him at the first show —Cole Lesley, *Remembered Laughter: The Life of Noel Coward*, 1976

The 1985 Harper usage panel rather thumpingly rejected the notion that there is anything wrong with the non-baseball use of *pinch-hit.* Copperud 1970, 1980 says that the acceptance of *pinch hitter* as standard "seems beyond doubt." These folks are right.

pique   When the verb *pique* is used in passive constructions and is followed by a preposition, the preposition is usually *at* or *by.* Either preposition is possible when the meaning of *pique* is "to irritate":

> ... she had been piqued at my discovery of her in one of her most secret hiding-places —W. H. Hudson, *Green Mansions*, 1904

> The Swiss will be piqued at the U.S. because of the higher tariff —*Wall Street Jour.*, 30 July 1954

> ... he seemed piqued, too, by what he considered to be a premature disclosure of the plan —Trevor Armbrister, *Saturday Evening Post*, 12 Feb. 1966

> ... I think she was piqued ... by my victory —George P. Elliott, *Esquire*, March 1970

When *pique* means "to excite or arouse," the preposition of choice is *by:*

> One's interest is piqued but not captured by the chronicle of this weak-willed man —*N.Y. Times*, 25 May 1952

In an old sense, now much less often used, *pique* means "to pride" and is followed, like *pride,* by either *on* or *upon:*

> ... Mary, who piqued herself upon the solidity of her reflections —Jane Austen, *Pride and Prejudice*, 1813

> Horace Winterton piqued himself on this —Sylvia Townsend Warner, *New Yorker*, 8 Mar. 1952

See also PEAK, PEEK, PIQUE.

piteous, pitiable, pitiful   What *piteous, pitiable,* and *pitiful* have in common is that each of them is used to mean "arousing pity or compassion." The OED notes that in this sense, *piteous* first occurred around 1290, *pitiable* in 1456, and *pitiful* around 1450. While all three words are still used in this way, *piteous* seems to occur a little less often than *pitiable* or *pitiful:*

> ... the poor girl ... raved and ran hither and thither in hysteric insanity—a piteous sight —W. M. Thackeray, *Vanity Fair,* 1848

> ... no piteous cry or agonised entreaty, would make them even look at me —Bram Stoker, *Dracula,* 1897

> ... that piteous or compassionate wish to say, or at least to report officially, no evil of the dead —James Gould Cozzens, *Guard of Honor,* 1948

> Poverty, to be picturesque, should be rural. Suburban misery is as hideous as it is pitiable —Anthony Trollope, *The Macdermots of Ballycloran,* 1847

> ... Gatsby, a man who happened to have a lot of money but was not a rich man, was made so pitiable that there were those who loved him —John O'Hara, Introduction to an edition of *The Great Gatsby,* 1945

> He felt a tender pity for her, mixed with shame for having made her pitiable —Bernard Malamud, *The Assistant,* 1957

> ... most pitiful and moving of all, perhaps, was the pretense—people with naked terror in their eyes still whistling to keep up their courage —Thomas Wolfe, *Atlantic,* February 1947

> As a woman, she had to feel sorry for any girl, no matter what a pitiful, poor, pathetic creature she was —James T. Farrell, *What Time Collects,* 1964

> ... has arrived at the knowledge that man is the pitiful victim of a pointless joke —Archibald MacLeish, *Saturday Rev.,* 13 Nov. 1971

Pitiable and *pitiful* also share a second sense, "evoking mingled pity and contempt especially because of inadequacy." *Pitiful* is somewhat more frequent:

> The resorting to epithets ... is a pitiable display of intellectual impotence —Morris R. Cohen, *The Faith of a Liberal,* 1946

> ... revolutionary rhetoric nourishes resentments and self-deceptions that are worse than ludicrous or pitiable —Benjamin DeMott, *Atlantic,* March 1970

> The most important impediment to obtaining efficient administrative officials ... has been the pitiful wage scale —Harry S. Truman, *Message to Congress,* 6 Sept. 1945

> The man who after Eugene O'Neill was our best playwright—I say *was* because his later plays have been pitiful travesties of his beautiful early ones —Simon 1980

Although *piteous* is not often used in this sense, it does occur:

> In the club "library", a piteous collection of a couple of hundred dated, dog-eared Victorian popular editions —Benny Green, *Punch,* 27 Apr. 1976

place   **1.** Copperud 1970, 1980 notes that Fowler 1965 considers the expression *going places* questionable, while Bernstein 1965 and Evans 1957 consider it idiomatic. In American English *going places* has had two distinct uses. In one, *places* is either literal or nearly so; the sense is either to go to some unspecified place, or to go out on the town to some unspecified place or places. This use is often extended into *go places and do things.* We see little of this idiom in print these days, so it may be a bit passé. Perry Mason knew it, though:

> Mason took the list, nodded and said, "Come on, we're going places." He snapped on the ignition, slammed the car into gear, and started driving at high speed back towards Los Angeles —Erle Stanley Gardner, *The Case of the Stuttering Bishop,* 1936

The second *going places* means "to be on the way to success." This idiom is labeled *slang* in those dictionaries that look to older dictionaries or settled opinion for guidance. It seems to have been popular among the up-and-coming business community at one time, and was perhaps stigmatized as some sort of Babbitry. It may never have really been slang. It too is not so frequently met as it used to be, but it seems a bit more common than the literal sense. Some examples:

> ... a strong Malenkov man, destined to go places with his patron —Edmund Stevens, *This Is Russia,* 1950

> Keep your eye on Senator Kefauver; he's going places —Bennett Cerf, *Saturday Rev.,* 7 Apr. 1951

> But even that wasn't the beginning of the end for us. That happened when I started going places. He couldn't take it and I finally had to concentrate on my own good thing —Bette Davis, quoted in *Women's Wear Daily,* 5 Oct. 1976

2. The *place* in *going places* is a noun in adverbial function. Such idiomatic uses—which may be more common in American English than in British—have long troubled commentators. Vizetelly 1906, for instance, objects to *go places, go any place, go some place,* and *I can't find it any place.* Many others worry about *anyplace, someplace, noplace.* Bolinger 1980 observes that *place* is one of a small number of nouns that are idiomatically drawn into adverbial function. He lists *way, reason,* and *time* as three others; they are nouns closely associated with the adverbial questions *where, how, why,* and *when.* He constructs a frame, "That was the _____ he did it," in which the adverbially oriented nouns *place, way, reason,* and *time* will fit idiomatically, but such quasi-synonyms as *location, manner, motive,* and *occasion* will not. Here are a couple of other adverbial uses of *place:*

> ... middle-income people trapped with no place to go —Ruth Mooney, *Harper's,* April 1972

> "... one of the places this could go...." —Carol Bly, *Letters from the Country,* 1981

And presumably *place* is adverbial in this casually idiomatic replacement of *everywhere:*

> ... lots of sales, enthusiastic reviews all over the place —Newgate Callendar, *N.Y. Times Book Rev.,* 19 Dec. 1982

These uses are solidly established in American English. There never has been a reason to avoid them in general writing.

See also ANYPLACE; EVERYPLACE; NOPLACE; SOMEPLACE.

plan **1.** A few recent commentators—Harper 1985, Janis 1984, Copperud 1970, 1980, Bryson 1984—take note of various combinations of words with *plan* that can be considered redundant. These combinations tend to serve the purpose of narrowing the focus of the verb—the verb having more than one sense (although the commentators take no account of this very relevant consideration). Among such combinations are *plan ahead, plan in advance,* and, presumably, *plan out,* which is an old idiom.

It grieved Piet to see her beg, to see her plan ahead —John Updike, *Couples,* 1968

... I would take up my seven-page single-spaced typed outline, and see what I had planned ahead for the next day —Irving Wallace, *The Writer,* November 1968

You can use the automatic toll gates only if you have the exact change. That means to go through all of them without waiting in line at the manned gates, you have to plan in advance to have six quarters, two dimes and a nickel —*And More by Andy Rooney,* 1982

As he was ready to entertain himself with future pleasures, he had planned out a scheme of life in the country —Samuel Johnson, *Life of Savage,* 1744

... she was not yet incapable of planning out a day for herself —Elizabeth Bowen, *The Hotel,* 1927

... lesser towns like Silchester, which the Romans planned out in their rectangular fashion —G. M. Trevelyan, *A Shortened History of England,* 1942

The noun combinations of *future plans* and *advance plans* are also mentioned by the critics—they seem to be primarily spoken usages.
2. *Plan on, plan to. Plan on,* followed by the gerund, is a standard American idiom, according to Evans 1957 and Watt 1967. A few handbooks insist that in formal use it be replaced by *plan to* followed by the infinitive:

Always signal well in advance if you plan to slow down for a turn —Julie Candler, *Ford Truck Times,* Summer 1970

Give them away, or plan to take them with you —Anna Fisher Rush, *McCall's,* March 1971

Our evidence suggests that *plan on* is more often found in spoken than in written use; we have few printed examples.

I will be discharged from the service in early 1979 and plan on returning to the States —Russ Sherlock, *Cats Mag.,* December 1977

Plan on is also used with a noun object:

If you're having a luncheon, plan on cheese sandwiches with ... —radio broadcast, 4 Mar. 1975

playwright, playwrite The *-wright* in *playwright* is from an obsolete sense of *wright* that meant "maker" (in the formation of words such as *wheelwright, shipwright,* and *wainwright* it means "maker" or "worker in wood"). The potential for confusion with *write* is always lurking in *playwright,* though it finds its way into print less frequently than you might think—so infrequently that *playwrite* remains a misspelling.

A simplistic work about an idealistic black playwrite —*New York,* 3 Feb. 1975

When we move to verb and verbal use, though, the dormant tension between the two spellings and between the equally appropriate meanings of their second elements rises to the surface. A few usage commentators try to beat it back down again: "A playwright is engaged in playwriting," says Bremner 1980. "The chap who writes plays is a playwright, but ... he is engaged in *playwriting,* not *playwrighting,*" proclaims Bernstein 1977. In actual practice, *playwriting* and *playwrighting* are almost equally common:

... the art of playwriting —Frank M. Whiting, *An Introduction to the Theatre,* 1954

... most of my playwriting life —S. N. Behrman, *New Yorker,* 20 May 1972

... lecturing, playwriting, and lashing out at the pessimists —Kathleen Tynan, *N.Y. Times Book Rev.,* 18 Nov. 1979

To study playwrighting —William Saroyan, *Not Dying,* 1963

... an Obie Award for playwrighting —Glenna Sloan, *Language Arts,* November–December 1981

plead **1.** *Plead* belongs to the same class of verbs as *bleed, lead, speed, read,* and *feed,* and like them it has a past and past participle with a short vowel spelled *pled* or sometimes *plead.* Competing with the short-vowel form from the beginning was a regular form *pleaded.* Eventually *pleaded* came to predominate in mainstream British English, while *pled* retreated into Scottish and other dialectal use. Through Scottish immigration or some other means, *pled* reached America and became established here.

In the late 19th and early 20th centuries, *pled* was attacked by many American commentators—Bache 1869, Ayres 1881, Vizetelly 1906, Bierce 1909—perhaps because it was not in good British use. But MacCracken & Sandison 1917 said only that it was "not now usual," and by the time of Krapp 1927 and Lurie 1927 *pled* was seen as at least partly respectable. And in spite of occasional backward-looking by a commentator or two, it is fully respectable today. Both *pled* (or *plead*) and *pleaded* are in good use in the U.S. *Pled* seems still to be current in Scottish use. A few examples of the disputed form:

Both pled not guilty —Ernest McIntyre, *Glasgow Herald,* 12 June 1974

... a scene, for whose life I pled, vainly —Sinclair Lewis, "The Art of Dramatization," 1933

My mother pled with the girl's mother to allow her to let the dress down —Nancy Hale, *New Yorker,* 20 Nov. 1965

2. A few commentators are fond of pointing out that in the courtroom one must plead "guilty" or "not guilty" and that one may not plead "innocent." In life outside the courtroom, however, *plead innocent* is very common and perfectly respectable. *Plead innocent* is the usual phrase used on radio and television, undoubtedly because it cannot be misheard for *plead guilty.* Both forms can be found in newspaper accounts:

... pleaded innocent before Criminal Court Judge Jerome Kay —*Springfield* (Mass.) *Morning Union,* 13 May 1986

... pled not guilty and was found not guilty —*Monte Vista* (Colo.) *Jour.,* 18 Jan. 1973

please 1. At one time, the imperative *please* was quite regularly followed by *to* and an infinitive:

> "... Now tell me, Brandon, and pray do speak in answer to my questions, and please to forget you are dealing with a woman." —George Meredith, *The Ordeal of Richard Feverel,* 1859

> Please to thank the Lady. She is very gentle to care —Emily Dickinson, letter, 9 June 1866

However, by the beginning of the 20th century the usage was being questioned:

> Please To or Please? The imperative "please" may or may not be followed by "to" before an infinitive. Milton's "Heavenly stranger, please to taste these bounties" is of course more formal, less colloquial, than our everyday "Please taste this." —*Ladies' Home Jour.,* October 1901

Our evidence indicates that while this usage has not entirely disappeared in the U.S., it is more likely to be found in British English:

> "What I did was very bad. Please to forgive me, Shane." —Harry J. Boyle, *The Great Canadian Novel,* 1972

> "Please to shut up!" cried Syd Parks, endearing landlord of The Bull —Alan Coren, *Punch,* 3 Oct. 1973

Outside of this imperative use, *please* is occasionally found with *to* and an infinitive in both American and British English:

> ... I can easily find some one who will take care of you as long as you please to stay —George Bernard Shaw, *Cashel Byron's Profession,* 1886

> ... an able man, licensed by the times to do pretty much as he pleased, and pleasing to do some strange and lawless things —James H. Hanford, *N.Y. Herald Tribune Book Rev.,* 25 Apr. 1954

> This is not because I think that national governments will ever please to ratify them —W. Warren Wagar, *Center Mag.,* September 1968

2. When *please* is used in the passive voice or when it takes a direct object, it is often followed by *to* and an infinitive:

> "I'm always pleased to meet a new member of the Company." —James Jones, *From Here to Eternity,* 1951

> ... have ceased to lie to themselves, ceased the pretense we are pleased to label sanity —Richard Schickel, *Harper's,* April 1971

> ... it had pleased her to pay me out in this manner —W. H. Hudson, *Green Mansions,* 1904

> ... mindful of the state of life into which it had pleased the Prime Minister to call me —Noël Gilroy Annan, *ACLS Newsletter,* January–February 1969

Also found quite frequently with the passive *pleased* are prepositional phrases beginning with *with, about,* or *by,* and clauses:

> "... if you expect your family to be pleased with your marriage...." —Mary Austin, *Starry Adventure,* 1931

> He gets more pleased with himself with each new film —Arthur M. Schlesinger, Jr., *Saturday Rev.,* 1 Apr. 1978

> I am very much pleased about what you have done with the manuscript —Flannery O'Connor, letter, 3 Feb. 1949

> ... were more irked than pleased by these signs of progress —Virginia Douglas Dawson & Betty Douglas Wilson, *The Shape of Sunday,* 1952

> People in Britain are pleased that Sir Winston Churchill and Anthony Eden are meeting the President — Hugh Gaitskell, *N.Y. Times Mag.,* 27 June 1954

pleasing The adjective *pleasing,* when used with a preposition, is usually followed by *to* and a noun or by *to* and an infinitive:

> ... its streamlined shape is pleasing to the eye and appeals to the esthetic sense —Harry G. Armstrong, *Principles and Practice of Aviation Medicine,* 1939

> Clapp's Unitarian doctrines were pleasing to some of his old congregation —*American Guide Series: Louisiana,* 1941

> That is why the form (the short story) is so infinitely pleasing to work on —Margaret Shedd, *The Writer,* May 1968

pled See PLEAD 1.

plentitude A 1965 issue of *Winners & Sinners* and the Oxford American Dictionary maintain that *plentitude* is not the word; it is *plenitude. Plentitude* is a less frequent variation of *plenitude* formed under the influence of *plenty.* It has been around since 1615 (*plenitude* is a couple of centuries older) and seems to have been used more than once by Sir Walter Scott. It is used in the same sorts of contexts that *plenitude* is, but not as frequently. Here are a couple of samples:

> Like undertakers, they have a plentitude of gravity, a deficiency of true seriousness —Robert G. Hoyt, *Harper's,* October 1971

> ... it springs, not from fear and need, but from joy and plentitude —Eric Bentley, *New Republic,* 21 Mar. 1955

plenty *Plenty* is a short word with all the vigor of speech. As such it has long been a source of worry for those who concern themselves with purity and propriety of speech. The critics started on *plenty* back in the 18th century and have not stopped yet. Like some other long-lived controversies, this one has developed new grounds for objection as the old grounds have lost interest. We will take up four separate issues here.
1. *Predicate adjective.* The original objection to *plenty* was to its use as a predicate adjective. Samuel Johnson in his Dictionary of 1755 may have been the first to take a stand; he deemed *plenty* a noun substantive and he thought it used "barbarously" as an adjective meaning "plentiful." He gave two citations, however, one from the 16th-century writer Thomas Tusser and the other from Shakespeare. Shakespeare's line has subsequently been quoted often:

> If reasons were as plenty as blackberries, I would give no man a reason upon compulsion —*I Henry IV,* 1598

Joseph Priestley in his 1768 edition also deemed *plenty* a noun and noted its use where *plentiful* would have served; he did not especially disparage the use, but he did seem to consider it aberrant. Campbell 1776, however, is forthright: he calls it "so gross a vulgarism" that he would not have included it at all had he not "sometimes found it in works of considerable merit." Hall 1917 points out the contradictory nature of Campbell's statement.

The OED shows that the adjectival *plenty* had been in use since the 14th century. At the time Campbell was being outraged, the following writers were using *plenty* (both quotations are from the Century Dictionary):

> They seem formed for those countries where shrubs are plenty and water scarce —Oliver Goldsmith

> When labourers are plenty, their wages will be low —Benjamin Franklin

Nineteenth-century commentators kept *plenty* under comment. Fitzedward Hall 1873 listed it in his chapter on "Our Grandfathers' English," which seems to mean that he considered it to have passed from use. Ayres 1881 reprints the comments of Joseph Worcester's Dictionary (1859)—Worcester enters the adjective noting literary use and the opposition of Johnson and Campbell—and then advises using *plentiful* instead. Bardeen 1883 lists William Mathews (*Words; their Use and Abuse,* 1880) as also opposing *plenty.* The adverse comments were carried by numerous early 20th-century commentators too—Utter 1916, Vizetelly 1906, MacCracken & Sandison 1917, F. K. Ball 1923, Lincoln Library 1924, Hyde 1926, and Lurie 1927 among them. An exasperated editor working on Webster's Second wrote on one slip, "This is cheap pedantic Bosh."

And bosh it was. The evidence shows that the predicate adjective *plenty* was in respectable literary use at least through the 19th century, although it is not very common in the 20th. Hall 1917 and turn-of-the-century lexicographers thought the use had continued in speech; we are not sure about present use because our evidence is scanty and none of it very recent. Here are three older American examples:

> Their peculiar oaths were getting as plenty as pronouns —Richard Henry Dana, *Two Years Before the Mast,* 1840

> ... churches are plenty, graveyards are plenty, but morals and whisky are scarce —Mark Twain, *Innocents Abroad,* 1869 (OED Supplement)

> Bread is never too plenty in Indian households — Willa Cather, *Death Comes for the Archbishop,* 1927

2. *Attributive adjective.* Evans 1957 says that use of *plenty* before the noun it modifies—in a construction just like *plenty of* but with the *of* omitted—is a Scottish idiom. His observation is apparently based on the OED, where Murray shows just an example from Robert Louis Stevenson and a made-up example typical of current Scots. Fowler 1926, on the other hand, finds the construction similar to others in which a noun has come to be used as an attributive adjective with *of* omitted: "a little brandy," "a dozen apples." Fowler has perhaps made the better guess, for the construction was used by Robert Browning, not at all a Scot:

> One block, pure green as a pistachio-nut,
> There's plenty jasper somewhere in the world ...
> —"The Bishop Orders His Tomb at Saint Praxed's Church," 1855

Fowler opined that this construction was "still considered a solecism"; those American commentators who bother to mention the construction—Century Collegiate Handbook 1924, Watt 1967, Harper 1985, Reader's Digest 1983, Macmillan 1982, for instance—all find something wrong with it.

The evidence for this use of *plenty* is hard to characterize overall. Browning is certainly literary, and we do have some later literary use. Most use, however, would appear to be spoken. OED and OED Supplement evidence seems to show that the main use lies outside of standard British English; besides the OED Scots examples, the Supplement provides American, Irish, Australian, and Caribbean examples and a hint of African use via Graham Greene. Here are some examples from our files. The first is by an author from Trinidad:

> ... for when Indian people got married it was a big thing, plenty food and drink, plenty ceremony — Samuel Selvon, *A Brighter Sun,* 1952

> He is not only a Humorist but has got plenty money to show that he is —Will Rogers, *The Illiterate Digest,* 1924

> There's plenty wolves and catamounts
> Prowling in the wood.
> —*Collected Poems of Elinor Wylie,* 1932

> The answer to that was that if they did, he would immediately do something else, and find plenty reasons to support him —Maurice Hewlett, *Halfway House,* 1908

> ... Greek ships had plenty freight —U.S. Naval Institute, *Proceedings,* June 1938

> ... she would close up at 5 P.M. and leave plenty memos —Christopher Morley, *The Man Who Made Friends With Himself,* 1949

> There were plenty days when they didn't even eat — John Dos Passos, *Number One,* 1943

> After the arms program tapers off, there is plenty work to be done —*Time,* 5 Jan. 1953

But we have found little evidence in print recently, which leads us to suspect that the attributive adjective *plenty* is at present chiefly in spoken use.

3. *Adverb.* The OED dates adverbial use—more or less as an intensifier—to the 1840s. The OED notes that the adverb is in widespread British and American colloquial use. Fowler 1926 calls it "colloquial, but not literary, English." Some more recent commentators—Harper 1985, for instance—term the adverbial use "informal," while others—such as Readers' Digest 1983—consider it nonstandard. A few handbooks prescribe *very, quite,* or *fully* in place of *plenty,* but the prescription is not a remedy in every case—*plenty* can carry a notion of "more than enough" that the suggested replacements lack. The adverbial *plenty* has its own place and may not always be easily substituted for.

We know the adverbial *plenty* to be common in speech. It is also frequent in writing, although not in writing of the starchier sort. Here are numerous examples of use:

> It's already plenty hot for us in the kitchen without some dolt opening the oven doors —Colton H. Bridges, *Massachusetts Wildlife,* November–December 1975

... may not be rising quite as rapidly as other health costs, but it is going up plenty fast enough —*Changing Times,* May 1977

I've played under four managers in the big leagues, and each one was plenty smart —Ted Williams, *Saturday Evening Post,* 17 Apr. 1954

A couple of minutes later she came down looking plenty excited —Erle Stanley Gardner, *The Case of the Stuttering Bishop,* 1936

The Metropolitan Museum, already plenty big, is expanding —Bruce Kovner, *New York,* 7 Feb. 1972

Having practiced plenty in the interim —Peter Hellman, *N.Y. Times Mag.,* 22 Feb. 1976

... and they talk about them plenty —Evans 1962

... I am a lot better and plenty good enough for my purposes —E. B. White, letter, January 1945

The boat still averaged 71.9 mph—plenty fast enough —Bob Ottum, *Sports Illustrated,* 19 Nov. 1984

... a calm, thoughtful man of forty-five, who has got around plenty ... in belles-lettres —Bernard Kalb, *Saturday Rev.,* 9 May 1953

The drinks may have been soft, but ... the advertising claims were plenty hard —David M. Schwartz, *Smithsonian,* July 1986

The "young daughter" here was seventeen and plenty nubile —Timothy Crouse, *New Yorker,* 30 July 1984

Plenty peppery, this soup is filled with ... crabmeat —Jean Anderson, *Bon Appetit,* May 1983

4. *Used with "more."* Evans 1957 says that *plenty* may be followed by *more,* with or without a noun following *more,* wisely avoiding the trap of trying to categorize such use of *plenty* as belonging to one or another of the traditional parts of speech. Here is one of those annoyingly hard-to-classify constructions where something that may or may not follow the word in question presumably has a hand in determining its part of speech. Here are a couple of examples, for which we will let you pick your own part of speech:

... we have plenty more to say on the subject —*New Yorker,* 22 Nov. 1952

The accidental century surely has plenty more accidents in store —*Times Literary Supp.,* 31 Mar. 1966

The girl who'd been doing all the talking began to do plenty more —Walter Peters, in *The Best from Yank,* 1945

... on the *Intrepid*'s deck were plenty more combustibles —C. S. Forester, *The Barbary Pirates,* 1953

Conclusion: The use of *plenty* will always have its detractors among the usage commentators. It is too vigorous, too much like plain talk for the sort of writing they seem to prefer. Almost every use that *plenty* has has been questioned at one time or another; all the same, the uses that are still current are also standard, at least in relaxed surroundings. We think you should feel free to use *plenty* where it sounds right to you.

plethora 1. Sometimes the remarks of a usage commentator will alert the lexicographer to the development

of a new sense of a word, and sometimes they can remind the lexicographer that dictionary treatment has not been quite as perspicuous as it should have been. The complaint of Bryson 1984 that a plethora "is not merely a lot, it is an excessive amount" seems to indicate the latter problem. Lexicographers have tended to elect a lumping treatment of the common uses of the word (it has technical senses too), and "excessive amount" is the primary organizing notion. Reader's Digest 1983, however, descries two closely related but slightly different senses—"abundant supply" and "over-abundant supply"—which more accurately describe 20th-century usage. Perhaps we could combine the two in a definition something like "a large and often undesirable or hampering supply."

We can shed a bit more light on this matter by showing some examples of how the word has been used in the 20th century (it seems not to have been much used in nontechnical contexts earlier). First, here are some examples of the undesirable or hampering *plethora:*

> Organization chokes now and then on the plethora of detail —Wallace Stegner, *N.Y. Times Book Rev.,* 24 Feb. 1985

> ... a tendency to overdress his materials with a plethora of ornaments —Igor Kipnis, *Stereo Rev.,* October 1971

> ... one needs the patience of Job and the leisure of Sardanapalus to plough through the plethora of references —Dwight Macdonald, *New Yorker,* 29 Nov. 1952

These all connote excess. We could perhaps call this "the reviewer's *plethora.*" In the next two examples we see the undesirable or hampering *plethora* without any clear connotation of excess:

> ... the term began with a plethora of irritating duties —Harold J. Laski, letter, 29 Sept. 1917

> Early meetings experienced, as most early ones do, a dearth of good horses and a plethora of complaints —Red Smith, *Saturday Evening Post,* 29 June 1957

And we can sometimes find the notion of excess without a strong suggestion of undesirability or hampering:

> Callow, inexperienced, and unripe despite his plethora of wives —Irving Howe, *Harper's,* October 1970

Then we have the plain "abundance, profusion" sense of *plethora* in which there are connotations neither of excess nor of undesirability:

> ... Leonardo, with his plethora of talents —*Atlantic,* February 1939

> ... the dressing case on the rack above her head. It was a beautiful one, but abominably heavy. It had been given her in the days of lady's maids and a plethora of porters —Elizabeth Goudge, *Pilgrim's Inn,* 1948

> With a plethora of "colyumnists," as they were called in that period, the *World* printed two facing pages of editorials, commentary, and interpretive articles —Hillier Krieghbaum, *Saturday Rev.,* 13 Nov. 1971

> The ads for the six gadgets promise a plethora of benefits —*Consumer Reports,* November 1978

... he also dangles the names of a plethora of other suspected traitors —Edward Jay Epstein, *N.Y. Times Book Rev.*, 18 May 1980

Daily the world enters our homes through the newspapers, magazines, television, and a plethora of new books, to feed the natural curiosity of the young —Milton S. Eisenhower, *Johns Hopkins Mag.*, February 1966

This use is first attested in our files from the celebrated eleventh edition of the *Encyclopædia Britannica:*

> The decade between 1870 and 1880 may be termed the first Golden Age of yachting. . . . Of races there was a plethora; indeed no fewer than 400 matches took place in 1876, as against 63 matches in 1856 —*Encyclopædia Britannica*, 11th ed., vol. 28, 1911

Plethora, then, may connote an undesirable excess, an undesirably large supply but not an excess, an excess that is not necessarily or not greatly undesirable, and simply an abundant supply. All of these uses are well attested and standard.

2. *Plethora* is a singular noun with a plural *plethoras* that is seen only once in a while. It often occurs in the phrase *a plethora of* followed by a plural noun. When this unit governs the verb of a sentence, notional agreement holds sway. Writers who view the plethora as a lump use a singular verb; those who view it as a collection of discrete items use a plural verb:

> . . . the plethora of retellings which descends on the market —*Times Literary Supp.*, 22 Oct. 1971

> . . . a plethora of spurious Rodin drawings were glutting the market —Katharine Kuh, *Saturday Rev.*, 25 Dec. 1971

plunge   When *plunge* is used with a preposition, it is used most often with *into:*

> The death of an infant daughter had plunged her into the deepest melancholy —*Dictionary of American Biography*, 1928

> . . . Mr. Hawkins, snatching the receiver, plunged into a long conversation with some unknown person —Dorothy L. Sayers, *Murder Must Advertise*, 1933

> Beneath it is the dining room into which a mountain waterfall plunges —*American Guide Series: Oregon*, 1940

> After the introduction, Horowitz plunges elbow-deep into the first solo sections —Abram Chasins, *Saturday Rev.*, 26 Mar. 1955

> He plunged at once into the two reviews that I had recently written —Allen Tate, *Prose*, Fall 1971

Plunge is also frequently used with *in:*

> . . . bending over the dish-pan with her arms plunged in soapsuds —Ellen Glasgow, *Barren Ground*, 1925

> . . . he has ten years, more or less, in which to plunge his energy —John P. Frank, *N.Y. Times*, 3 Oct. 1954

> . . . a puritan of a different type, who regards most of us as pretty irrevocably plunged in illusion —Iris Murdoch, *The Fire and the Sun*, 1977

Less frequently, *plunge* is used with *through* or *to:*

> . . . rock-walled coulees through which a mighty river once plunged —*American Guide Series: Washington*, 1941

> The bears fare best who take a risk, such as . . . plunging through a populated area —Edward Hoagland, *Harper's*, February 1971

> . . . saboteurs stuck limpet mines on two gun-running yachts, plunging them to the harbor's bottom —*Newsweek*, 30 Dec. 1957

> We drove into the smoke, and visibility plunged to near zero —Fred Ward, *National Geographic*, January 1972

Plunge is also used with *beneath, down, for, on, over, toward,* or *towards:*

> . . . the road plunged beneath over-arching trees —Dorothy L. Sayers, *Murder Must Advertise*, 1933

> . . . the whole herd . . . plunged down the steep bank of Sugar River —Edmund Wilson, *New Yorker*, 5 June 1971

> Those who plunge for any uncomplicated view of society are bound to have trouble in understanding . . . natural law —Robert M. Hutchins, *Center Mag.*, November/December 1971

> . . . embezzling about $400,000 to plunge on the stock market —*Times-Picayune* (New Orleans), 6 May 1952

> . . . plunged headlong over the side of the boat —Elizabeth George Speare, *The Witch of Blackbird Pond*, 1958

> . . . showed the world was plunging toward destruction —Oscar Handlin, *The American People in the Twentieth Century*, 1954

> . . . as the Age of Reason plunged towards revolution —*Times Literary Supp.*, 12 Nov. 1954

plupluperfect   English abounds in surprising constructions. Various observers have commented on the fact that in speech the ordinary past tense *(ate)* often replaces the present perfect tense *(have eaten)* or the pluperfect or past perfect tense *(had eaten).* And we find other observers commenting on the fact that the pluperfect is—in speech again—often supplied with an extra auxiliary *(had have eaten).* A correspondent of the magazine *English Today* named Ian Watson wrote in April 1986 commenting on this use, which he dubbed *plupluperfect.* He quoted a British politician named Jim Prior who used the plupluperfect in a radio interview:

> If I had've been there. . . .

Subsequent correspondence in the same magazine showed that the construction was by no means new, having been traced by historical grammarians to the 15th century. The OED under *have,* definition 26, notes that in the 15th and 16th centuries there are many instances of a superfluous *had* or *have* in compound tenses. The editors give several examples, of which the most recent is dated 1768.

The present-day version of the construction seems usually to show *have* as the extra auxiliary. In speech this *have* tends to be unstressed and reduced, and in written representations of speech it comes out spelled '*ve, a,* or *of:* "if I had've been," "if I hadda been," "if I had of been." We have already seen an example of *'ve.* Paul Christophersen in *English Today,* October 1986, gives these examples of *a:*

> ... if we'd a left the blame tools at the dead tree we'd a got the money —Mark Twain, *Tom Sawyer,* 1876

> If we'd a-known that before, we'd not a-started out with you so early —John Galsworthy, *Strife,* 1909

We have these examples spelled *of:*

> "It was four o'clock in the morning then, and if we'd of raised the blinds we'd of seen daylight." —F. Scott Fitzgerald, *The Great Gatsby,* 1925

> "The army ain't got none like mine," says Daley. "I guess they wished they had of had...." —Ring Lardner, *The Big Town,* 1921

(The contraction *-'d* in the examples from Twain, Galsworthy, and Fitzgerald makes it impossible to be sure that these are not, rather, examples of *would have* and so not the true plupluperfect.)

Partridge 1942 points out that the construction is by no means confined to the illiterate, although the fictional examples presented so far are surely intended for characters of little education. Partridge cites an unnamed novel in which an educated character has these musings:

> "But then ... should I have been any more understanding if I hadn't have happened to have been there that afternoon...."

And Christophersen gives an example from a 1976 English examination paper:

> If the two had have been married, Criseyde would not have had to be exchanged for Antenor.

The construction would have to be judged nonstandard in ordinary written discourse, but we have no evidence that it ever occurs there, at least in the edited varieties.

Christophersen's article in *English Today* gives a historical account of the construction and two explanations of its origin that have been put forward. No one is really certain how the construction arose, and no one seems to have advanced a theory to account for its use. In its modern manifestation the plupluperfect seems to occur in the conditional clause of a hypothetical or counterfactual statement, so it may be related to the limitations of the modern subjunctive which, except for the verb *be,* is unmarked for tenses of past time. This construction, and the similar one with *would,* may simply represent an attempt by the speaker to impose a subjunctive marker on the standard past perfect.

So we have, on the one hand, a tendency to replace the pluperfect with the simple past and, on the other, a tendency to emphasize the pluperfect with an extra auxiliary or even to create a sort of pluperfect subjunctive. Who said English was plain and simple?

plurality See MAJORITY 4.

plurals Rules for the formation of plurals can be found in many dictionaries, handbooks, and style manuals, and we do not intend to summarize them all here. Several special aspects of plural formation, however, have received attention in a number of usage books, and we will note them briefly.
1. *Proper names.* Personal names, especially those ending in *-s,* seem to be the proper nouns most often mentioned in usage books. The standard way of pluralizing most problematic proper names is shown in this example:

> ... to think of these characters of fiction—from the Charlie McCarthys and the Mr. Chipses and Mrs. Minivers of the present hour—back to the Huck Finns and the Pickwicks —Leacock 1943

Use of an apostrophe to form the plural of a name like *Mr. Chips* is considered by many to be an error. (There is a fuller treatment of proper nouns in *Webster's Standard American Style Manual.*)
2. *Letters, numerals, symbols, and other oddities.* Older style recommended apostrophe plus *-s* to make the plurals of such things as *1, 1920,* and *&.* Newer style recommends just *-s.* Currently the older style and the newer style are used with about equal frequency. In the following example the author has chosen apostrophe plus *-s* to pluralize sounds spelled in ordinary letters:

> We sprinkle our speech with nonverbal sound effects, snorts and mm's, sighs and tsk's —Mitchell 1979

See also APOSTROPHE 3.

plus The little four-letter word *plus* has prompted quite a bit of commentary in recent times. The two uses exciting the most interest are, grammatically, conjunctive and adverbial. Even though not a few commentators have mixed these together, we will treat them separately for clarity's sake.
1. *Conjunctive use. Plus* used as a conjunction springs directly from its earlier use as a preposition. There are two somewhat differing conjunctive uses which spring from two senses of the preposition. The first of these is found in the familiar "two plus two makes four." In this use *plus* means the same as *and* but demonstrates its prepositional character by not affecting the number of the verb. With *plus* used this way, the singular verb seems to be the standard in mathematics; there may be difficulties when non-mathematicians get involved, and these are explored at TWO AND TWO.

But *plus* does not limit itself to mathematical contexts. It has slipped out into general use. Ordinarily this use is acceptably prepositional; sometimes the prepositional character is emphasized when *plus* occurs between two noun phrases governing a verb:

> Verb plus predicate complement is used with comparisons —*Language,* October–December 1943

> This plus the old bitterness of Berliners ... has made for a certain amount of ill-feeling —Walter Sullivan, *N.Y. Times,* 22 Mar. 1953

> The partition of Germany, plus the Cold War, has cut off markets —Percy W. Bidwell, *Yale Rev.,* June 1953

> ... but fantasy plus fantasy adds up —Phoebe-Lou Adams, *Atlantic,* February 1972

As *plus* in its signification of "and" crept into general use, the likelihood increased that it would begin to be used like *and.* The first flares calling attention to this use were sent up by Theodore Bernstein. In Bernstein 1962 he exhibits this example:

> This, plus a change in top management of the brewing company, are believed to be the factors responsible....

He took the plural verb used here to mean that *plus* was being used as a conjunction, just like *and.* Perrin & Ebbitt 1972 has a similar example, perhaps a bit earlier:

> The Smyth report, plus an idea and some knowledge of bureaucracy, were all I needed —Pat Frank, *Saturday Rev.,* 24 Dec. 1960

These examples show *plus* beginning to be apprehended as a conjunction between the parts of a compound subject of a sentence. It had in fact been used earlier as a conjunction in less obvious circumstances: in the two following examples, *plus* is a coordinating conjunction between adjectives and between prepositional phrases:

> ... a mere box-office success like *Kiss and Tell* and a box-office plus critical and artistic success like *Strange Interlude* —George Jean Nathan, *The Theatre Book of the Year, 1949–1950*

> For some years, the Morrisons have lived quietly in a modest house in Eltham, a London suburb, plus in a sliver of an apartment in an old-fashioned small hotel —Mollie Panter-Downes, *New Yorker,* 31 Mar. 1951

This older conjunctive use of *plus* seems, then, to have originated around 1950, and to be primarily a written use. It cannot be called nonstandard, but it does not seem to be especially common.

The prepositional *plus* has another sense that means "besides." It seems to be only a little older than the first conjunctive *plus:*

> And they swing awesomely. Plus which they avoid as much as possible using the Dixie standards that have been played to death —*Down Beat,* 20 Oct. 1950

> Also, there is that Major Douglas bug he swallowed. Plus his conviction that he has read American history —Archibald MacLeish, letter, 27 July 1943

Sometime in the 1960s this sense of *plus* began to turn up, primarily in speech, meaning "besides which" and introducing a clause rather than a noun or pronoun to which a clause is attached:

> "I'm not a mere producer," he announced proudly. "I take the stills, plus I play a part in the film...." —*New Yorker,* 23 July 1966

> This is a danger to youngsters going to and from school, plus it cuts off many areas of the community from fire protection —letter to the editor, *Salt Lake Tribune,* 5 Aug. 1968

> She'd give him some money, plus she'd go to bed with him —Robin Langston, quoted in Studs Terkel, *Hard Times,* 1970

This second, primarily spoken conjunctive *plus* appears to be rather more common than our earlier conjunctive use. But its areas of application, so far, are limited almost entirely to speech, advertising, and breezy prose:

> If you want to make a superinvestment plus you don't happen to be rich —radio commercial, 22 Aug. 1973

> ... can emulate any standard HASP multileaving workstation in RJE mode, plus it can operate as a host to other workstations —advt., *Datamation,* December 1982

> A fan gets to see new artists and new shows every year at Fan Fair, plus we get to see other fans —Loudilla Johnson, quoted in *People,* 27 June 1983

> ... once the hustling and shooting started up again, she couldn't manage without a nanny—plus there was the hefty expense —Robert Sawyer, *Metropolitan Home,* July 1984

This later conjunctive *plus* is much more prominent right now than the older one, and it has been the subject of considerable adverse comment. As a speech form it is impervious to such comment, but it shows no sign just now of elbowing its way into serious prose. You will probably not want to use it in writing except, perhaps, in your breeziest stuff.

2. *Adverbial use.* What we are calling the adverbial use of *plus* is in fact a third use of the conjunction. It is called adverbial by some commentators, however, probably because it is close in meaning to the adverb *besides.* It differs from the second conjunctive use primarily in being used to introduce a sentence rather than to connect two clauses. It too seems to date from the 1960s.

> I would have liked to have written that ad myself. Plus, this is a free country —letter to the editor, *Saturday Rev.,* 9 July 1966

> ... I am impelled to add my own pet peeve.... It is "Plus you get," for "In addition you receive" —letter to the editor, *Saturday Rev.,* 9 July 1966

This use of *plus* appears in the same sorts of places as the second conjunctive use—speech, advertising, and informal prose—but it seems to be a bit more respectable in that it is found more often in informal prose than the second conjunctive use is.

> Plus we have many college students who are eager to work with youth, but unable to find jobs —Leonard J. Collamore, quoted in *Springfield* (Mass.) *Union,* 7 July 1970

> Plus it's coming in with two times the level of sodium —George Cross, quoted in *New England Farmer,* November 1982

> Plus, I get upset about this book she's writing —Patrick Anderson, *Cosmopolitan,* July 1976

> Plus, the Polish stereotype is much nastier than the Irish stereotype —Sandra McCosh, *Maledicta,* Winter 1977

> You've got your comforts and you've got to be thankful for that these days, what with everything. Plus we like to plan a few improvements round the place —*Punch,* 14 Apr. 1976

> Unlike most of us, David doesn't rumple. Plus, he's too rich —Douglas S. Looney, *People,* 31 Jan. 1983

> Plus, he's relaxed enough to joke —Christopher Connelly, *Houston Post,* 2 Sept. 1984

To sum up, the first conjunctive *plus* has been in respectable use all along. The second conjunctive *plus* calls attention to itself, and it has little use in discursive prose. The third conjunctive or adverbial *plus* is a little more respectable than the second conjunction; you might want to use it occasionally in informal prose— many writers seem to do so these days. Neither of the latter two usages appears in formal surroundings.

p.m.   See A.M., P.M.

podium The definition of *lectern* in Webster's Second reads like this:

> **1.** A choir desk, or reading desk, in some churches, from which the lections, or Scripture Lessons, are chanted or read. **2.** A reading or writing desk; an escritoire. *Chiefly Scot.*

This definition seems to have prompted several letters enquiring about the correct term for whatever it was that an ordinary lay lecturer placed his or her notes on before addressing an audience. Slips in our files show that for Webster's Third the editor who worked on *lectern* was instructed in no uncertain terms to define it in such a way as to reflect actual usage of the word.

We do not know if newspaper writers baffled by the churchly definition of *lectern* were the first to use *podium* for the lectern of the ordinary lecturer or not. But they might have been. At any rate some newspaper writers did begin using *podium* in that sense (and so did some lecturers), and the Webster's Third definer of *podium*, finding journalistic evidence, included a definition of *podium* meaning "lectern." For this attention to duty, Webster's Third has been rebuked by a usage commentator or two. One wonders whether they have ever looked up *lectern* in Webster's Second, their favorite large dictionary.

The "lectern" sense of *podium* is a favorite bugbear of the journalistic commentators—Copperud 1964, 1970, 1980, Bernstein 1962, Kilpatrick 1984, and Harper 1985, for instance. Several make jokes about a *New York Times* example reading

> President Ayub, wearing a gray summer suit, white shirt and gray necktie, gripped the podium tightly as he answered questions —18 July 1961

by suggesting that the poor man must have been on hands and knees, or flat on his face.

What goes unmentioned by the commentators, however, is that the average reader has not been put off or misled one bit. When the article says that President Ayub gripped the podium, the reader instantly gets the correct picture without having to work past a vision of the man messing up his gray suit crawling around on the platform.

So what we have here is not really a usage problem at all—no one is confused or misled—but a usage writer's in-joke. You can laugh along with them or ignore the matter.

Our citations for the "lectern" sense of *podium* are not especially numerous—we have fewer genuine examples of use than we have of commentators expounding upon the subject—so the usage may be in large part oral. We do have some evidence that the usage is known to those who appear behind the thing:

> He stood at a big redwood lectern (he called it a podium) —Alastair Cooke, *Manchester Guardian Weekly,* 10 Mar. 1955

> Pounding the podium and talking loudly, Rover accused the judge —Judge Luther W. Youngdahl, *New Republic,* 1 Nov. 1954

The use is standard, though you may certainly prefer to use *lectern* (now with an appropriate definition in Webster's Third and its abridgments), especially if you fear your writing may otherwise become the object of someone's merriment.

poetess *Poetess,* Evans 1957 says, "emphasizes the sex of the writer when the sex is largely irrelevant."

That, of course, is a modern view. An 1873 citation in the OED informs us that Homer and Sappho were considered so preeminent among the ancients that Homer was referred to simply as "the poet" and Sappho as "the poetess." The word, as Reader's Digest 1983 observes (in recommending *poet*), has been associated with Sappho in English from 1593 to at least 1984:

> ... the Greek poetess Sappho —Helen C. Griffith, *Southern Accents,* September–October 1984

Copperud 1970, 1980 tells us that *poetess* has fallen into disuse; he is, without knowing it, repeating the opinion of Priestley in 1768, who pronounced it almost obsolete. Fitzedward Hall 1873, who dug out Priestley's comment, thought the word established.

Shaw 1987 observes that *poetess* and several other words ending in *-ess* were considered offensive "even before the women's lib movement." This is true, but the grounds on which they offended apparently had little to do with women's sensibilities. The attack seems to have been started by Edward S. Gould in 1867. His comments show him to have been offended by most compounds ending in *-ess,* which he seems to have considered neologisms (even though *poetess* has been in English since 1530). He had a number of other objections, none of them very concretely grounded, and thought we were in danger of being swamped with *-ess* coinages. Ayres 1881 quoted Gould with approbation and Bierce 1909 thought *poetess* "a foolish word." Richard Grant White 1870, on the other hand, found nothing especially objectionable about such words and considered the objections to be based on personal taste alone.

There is evidence that women have sometimes found the word objectionable. The OED has a 1748 citation from a Lady Luxborough, who calls *poetess* "a reproachful name," and in 1976 the scholar and teacher Helen Bevington was quoted in the *Saturday Review* as calling it "that mortifying word."

> ... the word "poetess," with all its suggestion of tepid and insipid achievement —Marguerite Ogden Wilkinson, *New Voices,* new ed., rev., 1921

> She is a poet (she hates to be called a poetess) — *Time,* 17 Jan. 1955

Simon 1980 suggests that *poetess* got this bad odor from its association with what he calls "female-ghetto poetry." We do find it used pejoratively now and then:

> Is there a Parson, much bemus'd in beer,
> A maudlin Poetess, a rhyming Peer
> —Alexander Pope, *An Epistle to Dr. Arbuthnot,* 1735

> I can't understand why birds like you & Wilson ... think Edna is a poetess. Let alone a poet —Archibald MacLeish, letter, 4 Oct. 1929

But genuine pejorative use does not appear to be frequent. If you want to condemn unmistakably, you can trot out better words:

> ... Eliza Cook, the pious Victorian poetastress — Howard 1983

Most of our evidence for *poetess* is neutral in tone. Some writers and reviewers seem to find it a handy way to identify sex and occupation in a single word:

> The story—half truth, half fiction—of a very minor London poetess of the eighteen-twenties —*New Yorker,* 29 Sept. 1951

... bizarre dialogue, in which a would-be poetess and a failed ballet dancer discuss "art" —James Campbell, *Time Literary Supp.*, 22 Aug. 1980

The slim, shy poetess —John Updike, *Bech Is Back*, 1982

Female Poems on Several Occasions by this unidentified poetess appeared in 1679 —James Sutherland, *English Literature of the Late Seventeenth Century*, 1969

Occasionally we find a writer who assumes that *poet* designates males only:

Among the poets and poetesses of the period —Donald C. Masters, *A Short History of Canada*, 1958

But in more cases it is used where there is no question about the sex of the writer:

Marianne Moore is just about the most accomplished poetess alive —*Time*, 10 Dec. 1951

We are fortunate that Thomas H. Johnson, the foremost modern authority on the Amherst poetess — publisher's note, *Emily Dickinson: Selected Letters*, 1986

Anne Morrow Lindbergh, a poetess, philosopher and novelist —Donald Robinson, *Ladies' Home Jour.*, January 1971

It looks to us as though *poetess* is still alive, in spite of opinions to the contrary, is still associated with Sappho, and is still found useful for any of several reasons by reviewers and other writers. It is offensive to some women writers, perhaps because of its association with second-rate writing. It seems in intention to be much more often neutral than pejorative. All the same, it does seem to be used at times when *poet* would work just as well.
See -ESS.

point in time   Bureaucracy makes an easy target for criticism of many kinds, not excluding criticism of English usage. Harper 1975, 1985, for instance, has a whole entry devoted to *bureaucratic barbarism*. Part of this entry reads

The tendency of bureaucrats to use two or three elaborate words or phrases when a simple word would suffice was never more in evidence than during the final months of the Nixon administration.... "At this (or that) point in time" became an instant cliché....

Point in time (sometimes *point of time*) was indeed brought forcefully to public attention during the Senate Watergate hearings in 1973 and 1974, but it had been in use a long time before that. Arthur M. Schlesinger, Jr., mentioned the phrase as frequent among State Department people in the 1960s:

... never said "at this time" but "at this point in time." —*A Thousand Days*, 1965 (in Nickles 1974)

But bureaucrats are hardly the only people to use the phrase. It has even been prescribed:

Do not use *period* for *point of time* —Long 1888

And usage commentators too have been known to use the phrase:

The first and obvious meaning is to put back to an earlier point of time —Harper 1975, 1985 (at *set back*)

A locus of moods, impulses, ideas, behaviors, external forces, etc., at a given point in time and space — Thomas H. Middleton, *Saturday Rev.*, 4 Sept. 1976

Other writers on language and grammar have found it useful:

The exact point in time has not yet been fixed — David Mellinkoff, *The Language of the Law*, 1963

The other tenses, called perfect tenses, refer to time in a more complex way. They place an action or a statement in some relation to a specified point in time —Battles et al. 1982

Reviewers and essayists use it:

All of these men felt ... that their life's work was, at each point in time, breaking against the shore of the moment —Donald Hall, *Goatfoot Milktongue Twinbird*, 1978

How can we wonder at an Englishman telling a darkling tale at this point in time —Celia Betsky, *Saturday Rev.*, 5 Apr. 1975

... a comprehensive history of Irish music, beginning about the third century A.D., a point in time some fourteen centuries before the earliest authentic example of notated Irish music —*Times Literary Supp.*, 19 Feb. 1971

Biographers use it:

At this point in time—1890—Independence was by no means the quaint little farming community — Margaret Truman, *Harry S. Truman*, 1972

One has a strange propensity to fix upon some point of time from whence a better course of life may begin —James Boswell, *Journal of a Tour to the Hebrides*, 1785

Not to mention historians and educators:

But it is not only the contemporary historian who may feel a twinge of self-doubt about his educational role at this point in time —Gordon Wright, *American Historical Rev.*, February 1976

Purists might raise their eyebrows at such an academic anomaly; but at this point of time we can appreciate how important was to be the role played by this degree —Sir James Mountford, *British Universities*, 1966

... little effect on what a person learns between any two points in time —*Annual Report, Educational Testing Service*, 1966–1967

Bureaucrats can be blamed for a lot of things, but they cannot reasonably be blamed for *point in* (or *of*) *time*. The Watergate hearings seem to have brought the phrase to the attention of the commentators; so far Shaw 1987, Harper 1975, 1985, Zinsser 1976, Phythian 1979, Janis 1984, Nickles 1974, and Little, Brown 1986 have had their say. *Point in time* is, frankly, the long way round; you can use it if you want it for rhythm or another stylistic reason. Otherwise, you will probably do as well with either *time* or *point* by itself.

point of view   Those commentators who bother with this term at all discuss varying aspects of it. For its relation to several words closely akin in meaning, see STANDPOINT and VIEWPOINT.

Gowers in Fowler 1965 thinks *point of view* is used in what he calls "clumsy periphrasis"; the examples he gives involve "from the point of view of a living wage" and "from the point of view of cleaning." Uses such as these that link *point of view* with something nonhuman seem to be the concern also of Nickles 1974 and Phythian 1979. But these constructions do not seem to be especially frequent. We find such uses as "from a maintenance point of view" and "from a security point of view" from time to time in trade publications. We do not find many similar constructions in publications of more general interest, although we do have this stunner:

> The coffee bars and restaurants have also impressed me from a design, decor, tariff and standard of food point of view —Carole Payne, *Thursday* (Auckland, N.Z.), 8 May 1975

But there seems little point in condemning uses like the following one:

> . . . not so much from the point of view of salary — K. M. Elisabeth Murray, *Caught in the Web of Words,* 1977

The rest of the criticism is on other grounds. Evans 1957 and Shaw 1975, 1987 seem to think *point of view* overused. Evans also does not like *point of view* preceded by an adjective because an adverb will say the same thing more briefly. Evans's judgment would probably put these examples under the ban:

> . . . though one may frown on the practice from the critical point of view —Simon 1980

> From an educational point of view, the four other institutions will backstop Hampshire's efforts —Calvin H. Plimpton, *Amherst College Bulletin,* November 1967

It is hard to see much wrong with uses like these. Simon could even claim with justice that the adverb would not be clear in his context. This is another case where what needs to be avoided is not the construction but overreliance on it.

police officer   See OFFICER.

politic, political   Chambers 1985 distinguishes between *politic* and *political.* Actually *politic* is the earlier adjective used in reference to government and politics. *Political* has now superseded it in this use, except in the phrase *body politic. Politic* is now usually used to suggest shrewdness or tact:

> A punch in the nose is about as direct a statement as you can make, but it is not always politic —Red Smith, *N.Y. Times,* 6 Oct. 1980

politics   *Politics* can take either a singular or a plural verb. When it means "a person's political opinions or sympathies," it is quite likely to be plural:

> Mr. Trumbo's politics were not mine —Richard Schickel, *Harper's,* March 1971

> . . . his somewhat doctrinaire radical politics offer a refreshing contrast —Gerald Jonas, *N.Y. Times Book Rev.,* 20 July 1975

Other senses may be either singular or plural:

> . . . politics is fully as sophisticated . . . as psychiatry —Arthur M. Schlesinger, Jr., *Saturday Rev.,* 7 Sept. 1974

> . . . Catholic politics in that period are one of Dr. Spadolini's special subjects —*Times Literary Supp.,* 16 July 1970

> Japanese politics on the surface also seems wild and confusing —Edwin O. Reischauer, *The Lamp,* Summer 1970

> . . . bedroom politics continue to be more tempestuous than national politics —N. Weber, *Harper's Weekly,* 23 Aug. 1976

Around the turn of the century there was considerable controversy on the subject, with Vizetelly 1906 and Bierce 1909 prescribing the singular verb. Newspapers who followed this line equated "politics are" with "molasses are." Utter 1916 and Webster 1909 said the choice could be either singular or plural; Hall 1917 found more instances of the plural than the singular in his literary sources. Today's approach is the more balanced one of Utter and Webster.

polyglot   Copperud 1980 objects to a use of *polyglot* as a noun that he found in this sentence:

> Most of the valley is a verdant and prosperous polyglot of cities.

What the writer quoted is driving at is not especially clear from the sentence as given without surrounding context. Copperud hazards a guess that it might mean "mixture." *Polyglot* does have a noun sense meaning "mixture"—it has been around since the 18th century—but for a long time the mixture was usually of something linguistic, if not languages, then nomenclature or terminology:

> Modifications in the transplanted nomenclatures immediately became necessary. . . . There resulted a polyglot of diagnostic labels and systems —George N. Raines, M.D., Foreword to *Diagnostic and Statistical Manual: Mental Disorders,* 1952

> . . . the language of electrophysiology is a polyglot drawn from all these disciplines —Robert Galambos, *Nerves and Muscles,* 1962

In the middle of this century we began to find uses in which the linguistic connection becomes tenuous indeed, and the notion of a heterogeneous mixture seems uppermost:

> . . . the polyglot of inferior courts that speckle the judicial map —*Our State and Local Government of New York,* 1954

> . . . the clapboard stalls of the countryside are loaded with a polyglot of twentieth century Continental luxuries —Paul Grimes, *N.Y. Times,* 4 June 1961

Sometimes the referent is clearly a diverse ethnic mixture, with its implication of many languages, and so the use is closer in spirit to the original sense:

> . . . Chicago's 43rd Ward, a polyglot —*Newsweek,* 23 Feb. 1959

> . . . America is the world's most cosmopolitan nation, a polyglot of all mankind —Robin Prestage, *Saturday Rev.,* 1 Jan. 1972

> Many of the new ethnic neighborhoods are polyglots, mixes of many nationalities —Nancy Harmon Jenkins, *N.Y. Times Mag.,* 3 Nov. 1985

An extension of the "mixture" sense of the noun *polyglot* to the notion of a diverse mixture of ethnic or national backgrounds seems to have been developing for some thirty or more years now. It is perhaps this sense that Copperud's author intended. It is not recorded in dictionaries yet, but it seems to be moving toward respectability.

ponder   When Simon 1980 looks askance at *ponder with* used in speech by an academic, we cannot be sure whether he is finding fault with the idiomatic use of *with* or whether he believes *ponder* is only a transitive verb. Since intrasitive use dates back to Shakespeare, we will assume the question is the idiom. The quoted *ponder with* may have been a nonce syntactic blend of *ponder* and *struggle with* or *wrestle with,* for we have no other examples of *ponder with* in our files. The prepositions usually used with *ponder* are *on* and *over:*

> . . . should ponder deeply on these aspects of imaginative writing —Leacock 1943

> . . . can help us to ponder on what Saint Augustine meant —Robert Penn Warren, *Democracy and Poetry,* 1975

> . . . pondered over God's greatness —Henry O. Taylor, *The Mediaeval Mind,* 4th ed., 1925

> . . . another interesting example to ponder over — Nehemiah Jordan, *Themes in Speculative Psychology,* 1968

Sometimes we find *about* or *upon:*

> . . . those who are disposed to ponder about the state —V. O. Key, Jr., *New Republic,* 10 Aug. 1953

> . . . the identity of him upon whom I had so often pondered —Osbert Sitwell, *Noble Essences,* 1950

poorly   Handbooks from MacCracken & Sandison 1917 to Macmillan 1982 have denigrated the adjective *poorly* used as a predicate adjective to indicate poor health; they call it provincial, colloquial, or dialectal. Since we cannot be sure what these folks mean by *colloquial* we pass over that label, but provincial or dialectal *poorly* is not. Reader's Digest 1983 calls it standard but not very formal, which is accurate. The statement in the Oxford American Dictionary that careful speakers say "feeling poor" is fiction. *Poor* used as a modifier of animate nouns to indicate health or physical condition is applied chiefly to domestic animals; it is applied to human beings chiefly in dialect.

The OED speculates that the adjective *poorly* developed from the use of the adverb after verbs like *look,* which is now a linking verb and takes an adjective complement, but which in the 17th and 18th centuries was commonly followed by an adverb. The OED has a 16th-century example of adverbial *poorly* after *look,* followed by obvious predicate adjective uses from the mid-18th century on.

Here are some examples:

> . . . poor little Cassy is grown extremely thin & looks poorly —Jane Austen, letter, 14 Oct. 1813

> She was still very poorly —Jane Austen, *Pride and Prejudice,* 1813

> . . . I cannot invite him to come when he pleases, in my present state. It vexes me to be so unfriendly, but I am very poorly —Charles Lamb, letter, 29 June 1829

> She was rather poorly or troubled in mind, he thought —Norman Douglas, *South Wind,* 1917

> She is poorly and has been debating for several weeks whether she should take a dose of calomel — Flannery O'Connor, letter, 11 Oct. 1958

> He lost a stone in weight and became even more poorly after catching a chill —David Frith, *The Sunday Times Mag.* (London), 12 May 1974

The combination *taken poorly* seems to be British:

> Elsie said quickly, "Well, Eddie . . . see, Mrs. Manning's been taken poorly, so . . ." —Nigel Balchin, *A Way Through the Wood,* 1951

> One of the nurses told me that Ma had been taken poorly —William Golding, *Free Fall,* 1959

pore, pour   Some confusion in the use—or, actually, the spelling—of these two verbs was first noted by Evans 1957. A brief discussion of the problem, such as it is, can now be found in many usage books. The mistake that occasionally occurs is that *pour* is used when less familiar *pore,* "to read or study attentively," is called for:

> . . . meet in small groups to pour over the management problems —*Contact,* April–May 1982

> . . . had been spent pouring over constantly revised lists —*Northeast Horseman,* June 1982

> . . . couples and families pouring over the racks of home viewing choices —*Sunday Denver Post,* 16 Sept. 1984

This mistaken use of *pour* is a recent development for which we have little evidence. It seems to be growing more common in less attentively edited publications, but its chances of ever becoming standard seem somewhat dim—if only because a phrase like "couples and families pouring over the racks" calls to mind such strange images, as of cascading couples and fluid families.

portentious   *Portentious* is an alteration of *portentous* that seems rather to show the effect of the adjective ending *-ious,* as in *pretentious,* than to be a true blend of *portentous* and *pretentious.* The earliest citations have the same meaning as the earliest sense of *portentous;* only the spelling has changed. The OED Supplement's earliest example, dated 1863, is spelled *portenteous* (the OED has a *portentuous* too); Archibald MacLeish in 1918 used the spelling *portentious* in a letter. Partridge 1942 notes that *portentious* "is seldom written but often uttered"; here too we see the apparent attraction of the *-ious* ending over *-ous.* Partridge notes a similar tendency with *presumptuous;* it is often pronounced, he says, as if it were spelled *presumptious.* A more familiar example of *-ious* for *-ous* is *grevious* (see GRIEVOUS, GRIEVOUSLY).

The sense development of *portentious* mirrors that of *portentous.* The first few examples in the OED Supplement relate to a portent, a sign of the future, the oldest sense of *portentous.* Here is one of our examples:

> . . . followed 177 days later by a second solar obscuration just as portentious —Herbert J. Spinden, *Annual Report, Smithsonian Institution,* 1948

The OED Supplement has a 1956 citation from the *Baltimore Sun* in which *portentious* has the second sense of *portentous*, "prodigious":

> . . . you witnessed a portentious enlargement of mankind's field of knowledge.

Our earliest printed citation is somewhat vague, but apparently reflects the third and newest sense of *portentous*, "self-consciously weighty; pompous":

> The recognized rules of procedure taught in all the best night schools hardly come in with their portentious beginnings, middles, and ends —*Saturday Rev.*, 21 Mar. 1925

Most of our recent evidence and of that in the OED Supplement is for this sense:

> . . . a portentious statement containing the whole truth about the meaning, or meaningless, of life —*The Times*, 29 Oct. 1958 (OED Supplement)

> An Italian send-up of the portentious I.Q. flummery —*John o' London's*, 15 Feb. 1962 (OED Supplement)

> . . . entails a pushing-off of the traditional and the historically well-accepted, even if the push causes distortions of history and misreadings of portentious social fact —Thomas J. Cottle, *Change*, Summer 1971

> . . . Samuel Johnson, who had something portentious to say on every topic —Ivan Sparkes, *Stagecoaches & Carriages*, 1975

Although *portentious* is still quite rare in print, it has already developed derivatives:

> . . . no soundtrack narrator portentiously telling us what we should be seeing, how we should feel —Vincent Canby, *N.Y. Times*, 4 Oct. 1967

> Portentiousness—a sense that something grave and grand, though incomprehensible, is nigh —Benjamin DeMott, *N.Y. Times Mag.*, 23 Mar. 1969

The OED Supplement seems to be the only dictionary so far to try to account for *portentious* and its offspring. We do not know if it will ever establish itself, but we do know that it occasionally appears in print. It is not a word that we recommend your using. See also PORTENTOUS.

portentous   *Portentous* has as its earliest sense "relating to or being a portent." It can be a more neutral adjective than the similar *ominous*, which has come to indicate only bad things to come. Here we have a few examples:

> . . . the dreadful omens and portentous sights and sounds in the air —Washington Irving, "The Legend of Sleepy Hollow," 1820

> . . . the stillness in the Ritz bar was strange and portentous —F. Scott Fitzgerald, "Babylon Revisited," 1931

> What seem trivial details to others may be portentous symbols to him —Harry Levin, *James Joyce*, 1941

Almost concurrently with its first use in the 16th century, *portentous* developed a second sense that in effect reflected a different point of view of the same phenomenon. If the earliest sense is focused on the portent, the second sense is focused on the observers and what they think of the event. This sense removes consideration of the future and concentrates on the thing or event itself; it means "eliciting amazement or wonder; prodigious, marvelous, monstrous."

> . . . the portentous strength of the Black Knight forced his way inward in despite of De Bracy and his followers —Sir Walter Scott, *Ivanhoe*, 1819

> . . . my books and files for the last two years are beginning to assume a portentous size —Henry Adams, letter, 6 Mar. 1863

> The Secretary of Agriculture was the owner of a portentous power: within discretion . . . he could raise support prices to 90% of parity whenever he thought it desirable —*Time*, 31 Oct. 1949

Floating somewhere between these two senses were various uses of the word in which the notion of grave consequences or of weightiness or importance were uppermost:

> The assassination in itself was easy, for Caesar would take no precautions. So portentous an intention could not be kept entirely secret —J. A. Froude, *Caesar*, 1879

> . . . when Mrs. Bridgetower was talking about any subject less portentous than the Oriental plottings in the Kremlin, she was apt to be heavily ironical —Robertson Davies, *Tempest-tost*, 1951

> . . . and still more must his future be considered, a problem too portentous to grasp —Marcia Davenport, *My Brother's Keeper*, 1954

An editor of Webster's Second noticed that this sort of use was quite often applied to people, their actions, and their manner, and wrote a third definition "grave, solemn, significant" which was later refined to get across the idea that it often means "affectedly solemn, pompous." In this sense, *portentous* is somewhat similar to *pretentious* in meaning; Burchfield 1981 disapproves the sense, and it is not entered in the OED Supplement. We are not quite sure when the new sense arose, but it was well attested before 1934:

> *A pause. They all look portentous; but they have nothing to say* —George Bernard Shaw, *Man and Superman* (stage direction), 1903

> He paused, softly portentous, where he stood, and so he met Rosanna's eyes —Henry James, *The Ivory Tower*, 1917

> . . . a parliamentary candidate, very properly got up for the job and with the portentous seriousness that comes from having a mission —Harold J. Laski, letter, 1 Nov. 1920

> Troop, Peter held, regarded all these things with a portentous solemnity —H. G. Wells, *Joan and Peter*, 1918

> They will turn off with a deprecating laugh any too portentous remark —Bertrand Russell, *The Scientific Outlook*, 1931

> . . . and then the portentous thought, when it comes, turns out to be one of the commonplaces of modern scientific philosophy —Edmund Wilson, *Axel's Castle*, 1931

This third sense has become fully established—helped no doubt by frequent use in *Time* and the *New Yorker* in the 1950s—and is still in frequent use, especially in criticism:

> To be portentous, one ought to be deeper than that —Mary McCarthy, *N.Y. Times Book Rev.,* 22 Apr. 1984

> . . . relatively free of the portentous air and slick packaging that characterize the big networks' news shows —Thomas Whiteside, *New Yorker,* 3 June 1985

portend sounds . . . portentous —Flesch 1964

portion Richard Grant White 1870 and Ayres 1881 claimed that *portion* was misused to mean "part"; Flesch 1964 objects to *portion* as a more formal synonym for *part;* Partridge 1942 wants to distinguish the two words. Whether these views are ultimately connected we do not know. Bernstein 1971 explodes the myth of misuse, however, noting that the sense meaning "part" has been in use since the 15th century. It is standard.

> . . . the portion of human experience that is most absent in the *Ariel* poems —Irving Howe, *Harper's,* January 1972

> . . . a portion of the Lao people has absorbed the heaviest aerial attack in history —Jonathan Mirsky, *N.Y. Times Book Rev.,* 20 May 1973

> In geometry, the term is used chiefly to denote a portion of a circle —Robert W. Marks, *The New Mathematics Dictionary and Handbook,* 1964

possessed When *possessed* is used as a form of the verb *possess* meaning "to make or be the owner," it is used with *of:*

> . . . this delicacy at least was possessed of one advantage —Osbert Sitwell, *Noble Essences,* 1950

> . . . Second Lieutenant Charles Carter, who . . . wrongfully possessed himself of Lieutenant Day's side arm —James Gould Cozzens, *Guard of Honor,* 1948

> . . . he finds himself possessed of an immense spiritual and physical loneliness —Hollis Alpert, *Saturday Rev.,* 27 Mar. 1954

When *possessed* is used as a past participle or an adjective meaning "influenced or controlled," it is used with *by:*

> Lawrence, then, possessed, or, if you care to put it the other way round, was possessed by, a gift—a gift to which he was unshakeably loyal —Aldous Huxley, *The Olive Tree,* 1937

> The scene was graceful and quietly amusing . . . sordid only if you were possessed by high morals — Peggy Bennett, *The Varmints,* 1947

> . . . a woman of remarkable energy and courage, possessed by a deep religious zeal —Peter Quennell, *N.Y. Times Book Rev.,* 29 Aug. 1954

Less frequently the adjective *possessed* is followed by *with:*

> . . . if Mr. Paul V. Carroll's priests were not so completely possessed with the idea of their immense

importance —Thomas Halton, *Irish Digest,* April 1955

> There must be over 10,000 itchy Americans who are possessed . . . with the ambition to make a *Jules and Jim* —Daniel Talbot, *Evergreen,* August 1967

possessive See APOSTROPHE 2, 4; DOUBLE GENITIVE; GENITIVE; POSSESSIVE WITH GERUND; PRONOUN WITH POSSESSIVE ANTECEDENT.

possessive with gerund The gerund, or verbal noun, in English is the present participle of a verb used as a noun. Since the end of the 17th century, and probably before—Hall 1917 found a couple of 15th century examples—a construction involving the gerund and a preceding pronoun or noun has infiltrated the written language from speech. Sometimes the pronoun or noun is in the possessive case:

> . . . in hopes of his being able to join me —Lewis Carroll, letter, 11 Mar. 1867

> I have consulted your father on the subject of your attending Mr. Godon's lectures —Thomas Jefferson, letter, 9 May 1809

> . . . in spite of . . . the company's not having any intention of issuing a new edition —Ian Ballantine, letter, 5 Aug. 1939

And sometimes the pronoun or noun is not in the possessive case:

> . . . however I suppose the music prevented any of it being heard —Lewis Carroll, letter, 11 Mar. 1867

> . . . I couldn't abide him being such a splendid man —Russell Baker, *Growing Up,* 1982

> . . . in spite of the book being out of print for many years —Ian Ballantine, letter, 5 Aug. 1939

The dates of these passages show you that one example of each construction comes from a single author in a single letter. One of the curious facts about this construction is that it is not at all uncommon for an author to use both forms and to use them close together.

From the middle of the 18th century to the present time, from George Harris's *Observations on the English Language* of 1752 to Harper 1985 and Cook 1985, grammarians and other commentators have been baffled by the construction. They cannot parse it, they cannot explain it, they cannot decide whether the possessive is correct or not. The earliest commentators, Harris and Lowth 1763, were distinctly hostile to the possessive case. Campbell 1776 thought the possessive ought not to be repudiated, Priestley in 1768 allowed either form, Murray 1795 favored the possessive, Noah Webster in *Dissertations on the English Language* (1789) prescribed the possessive as the true form of the idiom. But opposition to the possessive had not died; Goold Brown 1851 opposed it, and so, apparently, did some other 19th-century grammarians who objected to the possessive case being used with inanimate nouns.

The dispute (along with some undisputatious discussion) continued right on into the 20th century. Fowler 1926 was a notable proponent of the virtue, even the necessity, of the possessive. (He labeled nonuse of the possessive the *fused participle.*) Otto Jespersen's profusely illustrated *S.P.E. Tract 25* (1926) was intended to overpower some of Fowler's contentions with a volley of quotations from literature. Hall 1917 treated the subject extensively, too, with lists and charts based on his investigations of literature. And so it has gone, down to the present time.

A prominent feature of many discussions is the attempt to analyze the construction by means of traditional grammar, which, as it is still taught in most schools, is Latin grammar grafted onto English. Otto Jespersen has pointed out the problem with such an approach: the present participle in English has features of both noun and verb. Jespersen in *S.P.E. Tract 25* makes the point succinctly with "there is no resisting him" in which the adjective *no* shows *resisting* to be a noun and the objective *him* shows *resisting* to be a verb.

Almost the only really important information in the enormous amount of analysis and comment written about the construction is contained in Hall's lists and Jespersen's quotations. These demonstrate beyond a doubt what our few examples at the beginning showed: the same authors commonly use both constructions. From this fact it should be obvious that the selection of the possessive or the selection of the "fused participle" is simply not a matter of right and wrong. But why, you may ask, would Boswell, George Eliot, Dickens, or Thackeray use one form one time and the other form another time? The answer must lie in something akin to notional agreement.

The factors governing the choice between the possessive and the common (or objective or nominative) case in this construction appear to be rather complex. One of the factors appears to be a matter of what element is to be stressed.

She approves of this one's being a girl —Flannery O'Connor, letter, 8 May 1955

In this example the object of *approves of* is a noun phrase *this one's being a girl;* the whole phrase is the object and there is no particular emphasis intended for the pronoun *one.*

... but I can't see me letting Harold C. condense it —Flannery O'Connor, letter, 11 Dec. 1956

But in this second example additional emphasis is placed on the pronoun *me;* it serves as the direct object of the main verb and is followed by a complementizing phrase.

The same contrast can be found with nouns. In the first example below *weaning* seems to be the most important term; in the second the writer is thinking about the person:

... its episodes too neatly arranged to build to the quiet crescendo of the boy protagonist's weaning from his family —Tom Dowling, *San Francisco Examiner,* 19 Nov. 1985

I keep thinking of Don Castro not smoking on the maiden voyage of that goddam zeppelin —James Thurber, letter, 18 July 1952

There seem to be a number of other considerations that may militate against using the possessive in particular situations. For instance, the noun or pronoun may be of such a form that it resists the genitive form. Jespersen has many examples in which the noun or pronoun is followed by a modifying phrase that would make the genitive form moot. But even simple nouns and pronouns can resist the genitive:

... to find out what is responsible for my feet swelling —Flannery O'Connor, letter, 30 Apr. 1960

... I would certainly ... insist on you all coming here —William Faulkner, letter, 1959

A noun ending in *-s* or a plural noun ending in *-s* sounds like the genitive and is consequently likely to be unmarked by an apostrophe:

... without the parties having any choice —Samuel Johnson, in James Boswell, *Life of Samuel Johnson,* 1791

The Grants showing a disposition to be friendly and sociable, gave great satisfaction —Jane Austen, *Mansfield Park,* 1814

I was glad to hear of the bills being paid —Harry S. Truman, letter, 7 Sept. 1947

While our backing is far from conclusive, we do have much evidence of the possessive's not being used in speech of recent vintage:

... could have been a part of my background, my experience, without me knowing it —William Faulkner, 11 Mar. 1957, in *Faulkner in the University,* 1959

I'll miss Moe screaming at me —Dan Issel, quoted in *Springfield* (Mass.) *Daily News,* 23 Jan. 1985

... him getting that interception —Ronnie Lott, television interview, 29 Dec. 1984

... the possibility of him being there —radio newscast, 23 Oct. 1985

But in writing, even recent writing, the chances are that an ordinary personal pronoun will be in the possessive:

... thy being in London is such a mystery —George Farquhar, *Love and a Bottle,* 1698

... gave his consent to my returning again to Philadelphia —Benjamin Franklin, *Autobiography,* 1771

... hope this note may reach you in time to warn you of its coming —Lewis Carroll, letter, 5 Jan. 1867

... the possibility of my filling the vacancy —George Bernard Shaw, preface, *The Shaw-Terry Letters,* 1931

... a performance I wouldn't mind your seeing — Alexander Woollcott, letter, 1 Apr. 1940

You don't know how much I appreciated your going to all the trouble —Harry S. Truman, letter, 4 Oct. 1957

My story of Houdini ... begins with my meeting his widow —James Thurber, letter, 17 May 1961

... the danger of his dwindling into a employee — Gerald Weales, *Smithsonian,* December 1985

Let's recapitulate. This construction, both with and without the possessive, has been used in writing for about 300 years. Both forms have been used by standard authors. Both forms have been called incorrect, but neither is. Those observers who have examined real examples have reached the following general conclusions: 1. A personal pronoun before the gerund tends to be a possessive pronoun in writing (of course, with *her* you cannot tell the case). Fries 1940 found that the possessive predominated even in letters written by the less educated. 2. The accusative pronoun is used when it is meant to be emphasized. 3. In speech the possessive pronoun may not predominate, but available evidence is inconclusive. 4. Both possessive and common-case (uninflected) nouns, including proper nouns, are used before the gerund. Fries's evidence presented almost no possessive nouns, but our literary evidence shows plenty of possessives, and so does Jespersen's. It is clear, however, that the possessive case does not predominate with nouns to the extent it does with personal pronouns. 5. Complicating factors such as modifying phrases tend to militate against use of the possessive form. 6. Plurals and other nouns ending in -s also are often unmarked for the possessive inflection. 7. Many writers use both forms of the construction. Clearly there are times when one or the other sounds more euphonious, is clearer, or otherwise suits the purpose better.

We suspect that this is one of those idiomatic usages that seldom give the native speaker trouble. It will trouble learners of English much more. We can only advise learners that the possessive will almost always be safe for pronouns and will probably work most of the time with nouns. But in doubtful cases, you may need to consult a native speaker.

possibility When the likelihood of something is being considered, we usually refer to the possibility *of* its occurrence or existence:

> . . . a physiological study of the possibility of life on Mars —*Current Biography,* July 1966

> . . . the possibility of reversal is questionable — Arthur M. Gompf, *Johns Hopkins Mag.,* Summer 1971

When *possibility* is used in the plural with a meaning close to "opportunities," it is idiomatically followed by *for:*

> . . . additional possibilities for future growth —Leslie H. Warner, *Annual Report, General Telephone & Electronics,* 1970

> . . . discussing the possibilities for the exchange of students —John Coyne, *Change,* March 1973

possible 1. *Possible* is sometimes considered to be an absolute adjective. See ABSOLUTE ADJECTIVES.
2. *Possible, possibly.* Three or four commentators opine that *may* is redundant with *possible* or *possibly.* Our files show such use to be quite rare. Here are two examples to show you how utterly innocuous such co-occurrence is:

> The political future of Latin America may quite possibly hinge upon the success . . . —*Current Biography,* October 1964

> . . . to see what might possibly work —Noel Farmer, *Barnard Alumnae,* Winter 1971

What *possibly* does here is reinforce the modal, underlining its seriousness. There is nothing wrong with such use. The adverb may often be omitted without loss, but need not always be omitted.

pour See PORE, POUR.

practicable, practical *Practicable* has two basic senses, "feasible" and "usable." *Practical* has a much wider range of meaning, but the sense closest to those of *practicable* is "capable of being put into use, useful."

These two words form a popular topic among usage writers, who advise against confusing them. The real issue would seem to be whether *practicable* can be used to mean "practical," since the meaning of *practical* subsumes that of *practicable.* Judging from the evidence we have, writers by and large successfully distinguish between *practicable* and *practical* where necessary. Here is a representative sampling of *practicable* citations:

> What Henchard had written in the anguish of his dying was respected as far as practicable —Thomas Hardy, *The Mayor of Casterbridge,* 1886

> It was not practicable to remove all of this powder without destroying some of the uncorroded metal — *Jour. of Research,* November 1936

> . . . there was a practicable route up the southern side of Mount Everest —Eric Shipton, *Geographical Jour.,* June 1953

> This simple and thoroughly practicable reform will not begin to solve all the defects of the income tax —Milton Friedman, reprinted column, 1969

> Loudspeaker systems had sufficiently advanced by this time to make the wiring of large theaters practicable —Peter Andrews, *Saturday Rev.,* 12 Nov. 1977

> . . . some easy, practicable strategies for achieving harmony on the job —Denise Fortino, *Harper's Bazaar,* August 1980

Macmillan 1982 and others claim that *practicable* cannot be used to describe persons, and we have found this to be true, as might be expected from the definitions.

Some of our citations for *practicable* and *practical* supply a context in which either word could have been placed, and we must assume that each writer has chosen the word that correctly gets his specific meaning across. We also have a few citations in which the meaning of *practicable* has been confused or blurred.

> . . . translating the feasible into the practicable — Forest Woody Horton, *Information World,* May 1980

However, such uses are quite uncommon and have not established a new sense of *practicable,* so the distinction between *practicable* and *practical* remains valid.

practically *Practically* has a second sense meaning "almost, nearly, virtually" that Bierce 1909 decided was a misuse (even though it had been in the language since 1748). Jensen 1935 raised the same objection. More recently Copperud 1964, 1970, 1980, Shaw 1975, 1987, Janis 1984, Evans 1957, and Gowers in Fowler 1965 have agreed. So perhaps has the usage panel of Heritage 1969. We say "perhaps" because the panelists found one sentence illustrating the use acceptable, 51–49 percent, but found another sentence illustrating the same meaning unacceptable, 46–54 percent.

Now what is wrong with this sense? We are never given a clear explanation by any of these commentators; they simply see it as "loose" in relation to the original sense. The plain fact is, however, that a sense of a word that has been in everyday use for more than two centuries and comes naturally from the pens of reputable writers is entirely standard. Some examples follow:

> Under favorable conditions, practically everybody can be converted to practically anything —Aldous Huxley, *Brave New World Revisited,* 1958

Who's wearing pants? Practically everybody —Amy Vanderbilt, *Ladies' Home Jour.,* January 1971

... until Elizabeth's proclamation ... in 1599 practically killed historical painting in England —*Times Literary Supp.,* 18 Dec. 1969

... attracted practically no attention —John Fischer, *Harper's,* March 1971

practice, practise Here is what our files show about these words. The noun is almost always spelled *practice* in both British and American usage; we have British, Canadian, and American examples of *practise* as a noun, but not very many. The verb is regularly spelled *practise* in British usage; in American usage both *practice* and *practise* are used with considerable frequency.

precede, proceed Quite a few handbooks distinguish these words, lest you mix them up, but dictionaries do the job better. If you are in doubt, look in your dictionary. We believe, however, that problems with these words are more likely to be a matter of spelling than of semantics. Several books note that *precede* is occasionally misspelled *preceed.* This is true; we have several examples of the misspelling or typographical error. Be aware that this is a word prone to be misspelled. We have also seen *procede* a time or two.

precedence 1. *Precedence* is now usually followed by the preposition *over:*

Henry began by demanding precedence over Francis —Francis Hackett, *Henry the Eighth,* 1929

To give organizations precedence over persons is to subordinate ends to means —Aldous Huxley, *Brave New World Revisited,* 1958

New exigencies began to take precedence over freedom —*New Yorker,* 10 Apr. 1971

Although we have no very recent evidence for the combination, *precedence* has also been used with *of:*

... who hated her brother-in-law, and hated, still worse, his dead wife, who, as Queen-Dowager, had taken precedence of her —Edith Sitwell, *Fanfare for Elizabeth,* 1946

... although weapons must in some instances take precedence of exports —Vera Micheles Dean, *Harper's,* December 1952

2. *Precedence, precedent(s).* From Vizetelly 1920 to Ebbitt & Ebbitt 1982 and Harper 1985 usage writers have warned against confusing *precedence* with *precedent.* Such confusion is only likely among those who pronounce *precedence* like *precedents.*

The Ebbitts cite a student paper with a sentence beginning "Now that precedence has been set ..." where it was clear that *a precedent* was the meaning intended. The substitution of a mass noun for a count noun is most peculiar indeed, and the example is not an aberration—we ourselves have a little evidence of its occurrence in print:

... the United States Supreme Court where great precedence is going to be set —*Police,* September–October 1967

If all goes well—and there is no precedence in these latitudes that it will —*Saturday Rev.,* 10 May 1964

Words change their meanings in mysterious ways. We cannot tell if these examples mark the beginning of a genuine change in use or if they are simply isolated errors. Until that uncertainty is resolved, we recommend that you avoid the usage.

We do have a single example of *precedence* used as a count noun. It must be considered a mistake.

... this incident sets a precedence —*Westfield* (Mass.) *Evening News,* 27 Feb. 1985

precedent 1. When the adjective *precedent* is used with a preposition, the preposition is usually *to:*

Identification is a condition precedent to an inquest. It is a matter of law —Raymond Chandler, *The Simple Art of Murder,* 1950

... it most certainly is the condition precedent to any intelligent choice —Adlai E. Stevenson, *Speeches,* ed. Richard Harrity, 1952

Croce has claimed the right to 'spiritualise' this primal vivacity which he makes precedent—not in time but in the spirit—to the moral choice —Cecil Sprigge, *Benedetto Croce,* 1952

Occasionally, *precedent* has been used with *of:*

Therefore collective security is a condition precedent of all else —George Soule, *New Republic,* 14 June 1943

... a system ... that makes publication a condition precedent of advancement in a profession —*Times Literary Supp.,* 3 July 1969

From the evidence it appears that when the adjective is used postpositively, *condition* is very often the noun it follows.
2. When the noun *precedent* is used with a preposition, the preposition is most often *for:*

I do not think there is any historical precedent for Israel's extraordinary success —Denis Healey, *New Republic,* 3 Jan. 1955

... new editions, reset and arranged in a way for which there existed no precedent —*Times Literary Supp.,* 19 Feb. 1971

There were, to be sure, precedents for crime in the Old World countries from which these immigrants came —Joseph Epstein, *Commentary,* January 1972

Precedent is also used with *of,* though somewhat less frequently:

I shall hold you and your commanders criminally accountable under the rules and precedents of war — Douglas MacArthur, quoted in *Time,* 28 Aug. 1950

... the Republican Presidential contest of 1912, set an unhappy precedent of creative slander —Richard Reeves, *Harper's,* January 1972

Occasionally, *precedent* has been used with *against* or *to:*

... even in the Old Testament there is a dire precedent against registration —J. Carter Swaim, *Right and Wrong Ways to Use the Bible,* 1953

... the earlier discussions of his own ideas that were an essential precedent to the new concept —L. V. Berkner, *New Republic,* 12 June 1954

precipitate, precipitous Many people, including most usage commentators, are insistent about keeping these adjectives distinct. *Precipitate,* they say, means "headlong," "abrupt," or "rash"; *precipitous* means only "steep." Such a clear distinction does not exist absolutely in actual usage, although *precipitate,* which formerly was sometimes used to mean "steep," does now appear to be used only in the senses approved by the critics:

> ... the precipitate withdrawal of the United Nations Emergency Force —*Saturday Rev.,* 8 July 1967

> ... causing him to appear precipitate, out of control —Aaron Latham, *New York,* 17 Nov. 1975

> ... her precipitate flight from the scene of the accident —Peter Taylor, *The Old Forest and Other Stories,* 1985

And *precipitous* does usually mean "steep":

> ... one of the less precipitous trails —Morten Lund, *Ski,* November 1971

> Precipitous mountain watersheds laced with energetic, fast-falling streams —Matt Herron, *Smithsonian,* December 1982

The problem is that *precipitous* and *precipitously* are also commonly used in contexts which, according to the critics, require *precipitate* and *precipitately:*

> I had intended to see you before leaving but at the last moment we go rather precipitously —Robert Frost, letter, 1915

> ... struck up a precipitous flirtation —George Bernard Shaw, letter, 4 Sept. 1916

> Precipitous action, needless to say, has no place in wise security policy —Clinton P. Anderson, *New York Times Mag.,* 4 Sept. 1955

> Cardinal Cushing's precipitous withdrawal of support —*Commonweal,* 23 Feb. 1968

> ... has not made precipitous changes in social welfare policy —Frances Fox Piven, *Columbia Forum,* Summer 1970

> ... protection against precipitous action by the military and other agencies —Harvey Wheeler, *Center Mag.,* January/February 1971

> The black comedy ... is too precipitously introduced —John Simon, *New York,* 22 Nov. 1971

> ... in view of its precipitous demobilization — George F. Kennan, *Atlantic,* November 1982

> A mother can learn, perhaps, not to act precipitously —Carrie Carmichael, *N.Y. Times Book Rev.,* 25 Jan. 1987

The picture is further complicated by the common use of *precipitous* and *precipitously* in describing a sudden, sharp decline:

> ... a precipitous decline in the number of Jews in the Soviet Government —*Newsweek,* 1 Sept. 1958

> ... the performance ... fell precipitously as their dosage of marijuana increased —Solomon H. Snyder, *Psychology Today,* May 1971

> His fall from power was even more precipitous — Geoffrey C. Ward, *N.Y. Times Book Rev.,* 1 Aug. 1982

> ... the number of reported cases ... fell precipitously —Nan Robertson, *N.Y. Times Mag.,* 19 Sept. 1982

These are really just straightforward figurative applications of the word's literal sense, "steep," but their connotations of suddenness and abruptness bear an obvious resemblance to those of *precipitate.* Most commentators will allow this figurative usage. A few, however (such as Bryson 1984), insist that *precipitous* should only be used to describe physical characteristics ("a precipitous cliff"). Such reasoning may play a part in persuading some writers to use the adverb *precipitately* in place of *precipitously* when describing a steep decline:

> ... registration in Russian language courses dropped precipitately —William O. Douglas, *Freedom of the Mind,* 1962

> ... childbearing has dropped precipitately in the United States since the end of the baby boom —Didi Moore, *N.Y. Times Mag.,* 18 Jan. 1981

Many commentators would regard this use of *precipitately* as an error.

Actual usage, then, is far more complicated than the commentators would like it to be. The objective truth is that *precipitate* and *precipitous* are similar words whose uses have had a tendency to overlap for centuries. Dictionaries have always shown them to have synonymous senses; in 1755, for example, Samuel Johnson defined *precipitate* as "steeply falling," "headlong," and "hasty" and *precipitous* as "headlong; steep," "hasty," and "rash." Noah Webster's Dictionary of 1828 included much the same definitions as Johnson's, and our own dictionaries, from 1847 onward, have continued to show the two words to be standard as synonyms. That is not to say, however, that the distinction favored by the critics has no basis. Evidence in the OED shows that in the 19th century "steep" became the predominant sense of *precipitous,* with its other senses falling largely into disuse. Their revival in the early 20th century caught the attention of Fowler 1926, and the voices of criticism have been heard ever since. At this point, the criticized usage and the criticism itself are both alive and flourishing. So although almost all dictionaries show that *precipitous* has as one of its senses "precipitate" and are quite right to do so, you had better be prepared to defend yourself if you use it in that sense.

preclude When *preclude* is used with a preposition, it is usually *from:*

> ... a person is precluded from accepting legal assistance from a friend —E. Maitland Woolf, *Irish Digest,* March 1953

> Rover even attempted to preclude Lattimore's attorneys from opposing the affidavit of bias —Judge Luther W. Youngdahl, *New Republic,* 1 Nov. 1954

> ... the discrimination that still precludes Catholics from senior ... posts in civic and social life —Eric Bourne, *Christian Science Monitor,* 13 Sept. 1979

> ... the pains Disney often took to preclude his cartoons and live-action films from consideration as serious art —Daniel Menaker, *N.Y. Times Book Rev.,* 28 Nov. 1976

Occasionally, *preclude* has been used with *to:*

> But there were many doors that he didn't open. Whole sections seemed precluded to him —Arturo Vivante, *New Yorker,* 11 May 1963

> He is not . . . an equally good novelist, though of course nothing is precluded to a man of his abilities —Stanley Kauffmann, *N.Y. Times Book Rev.,* 4 Apr. 1976

In another relation *preclude* may be followed with *by:*

> Monotony was precluded by the use of decorative pieces, color, and light —*American Guide Series: Michigan,* 1941

precondition "A modish but tautologous Lit Crit synonym for condition" is the evaluation of *precondition* pronounced by Howard 1980. Bryson 1984 brings forth an example in which the *pre-* adds nothing: "three preconditions to be met before negotiations can begin." But it is (or should be) difficult to evaluate a usage on the basis of one example. On this side of the Atlantic, Safire 1986 worries about the word's redundancy.

Precondition had a literary beginning; it was introduced by Coleridge in 1825, and it was used by DeQuincey. But during the last forty years or so, it has been most frequently used in writing in social and political science and reporting on affairs of state, although it is by no means limited to such contexts. And it has a generous record of use, indicating that writers have found it a useful word.

If *precondition* were simply a tautologous synonym for *condition,* we should be able to use *condition* in its place wherever it occurs. But we cannot. For instance, we find *precondition* used with the preposition *to:*

> . . . a desire to obtain a favorable settlement of her dispute with Germany over the Saar Basin as a precondition to ratification of the EDC treaty —Omar N. Bradley, *Saturday Evening Post,* 10 Apr. 1951

> . . . what the Thais regarded as unacceptable preconditions to the conference —Denis Warner, *The Reporter,* 26 Mar. 1964

> . . . a necessary precondition to making the full emancipation of women a reality —Gerda Lerner, *Columbia Forum,* Fall 1970

Since we cannot put *condition* very comfortably into any of these examples, we must conclude that *condition* and *precondition* are not quite the same here.

We also find *precondition* with *of; condition* can also be used with *of,* so we should be able to substitute it without difficulty. See how many of these examples are unchanged by such substitution:

> Weakness invites aggression. Now and in the future, strength is the precondition of peace —Dean Acheson, quoted in *The Pattern of Responsibility,* ed. McGeorge Bundy, 1951

> The implication in such a pronouncement, emanating from the seat of government, is that religious faith is a *condition,* or even a *precondition,* of the democratic life —E. B. White, *New Yorker,* 18 Feb. 1956

> . . . the biological preconditions of human speech — Philip Morrison, *Scientific American,* February 1978

> . . . the classicizing sculptures . . . which were a precondition of the development of a classicizing style in painting —*Times Literary Supp.,* 22 Oct. 1971

Finally we have *precondition* with *for.* Again, *condition* would seem to be usable in the same constructions. Test them.

> . . . the precondition for woman's emancipation is the reform not of social institutions, but of . . . — Dwight Macdonald, *The Reporter,* 14 Apr. 1953

> . . . the precondition for existence at Daytop is truthfulness —Renata Adler, *New Yorker,* 15 Apr. 1967

> Let us then assume that crises are a necessary precondition for the emergence of novel theories — Thomas S. Kuhn, *The Structure of Scientific Revolutions,* 2d ed., 1973

> To insist on absolute answers as a precondition for any great undertaking is to deprive the future of its main source of intellectual energy —Norman Cousins, *Saturday Rev.,* 7 Aug. 1976

We think you will have found by now that *condition* does not satisfactorily replace *precondition* in many (if any) of the examples. The reason is simple: the *pre-* is not simply otiose. It focuses the mind of the reader (*condition* in *Webster's Ninth New Collegiate Dictionary* has 14 different senses) and emphasizes the notion of "before." If you are going to spell out the notion of "before" contextually, as the writer quoted by Bryson did, you certainly do not need *precondition.* But the authors quoted here let the *pre-* take care of that part of the message (and so did the rest of the authors in our file). From our evidence we judge that *precondition* is not usually used redundantly.

predestine *Predestine* is often followed by the preposition *to:*

> . . . for reasons which we cannot fathom, God predestines some to eternal life —Kenneth Scott Latourette, *A History of Christianity,* 1953

> Who would expect a godfather to give a child a name that would predestine it to become a cruel person? —Kurt Lewent, *Modern Language Notes,* March 1957

> Television is so beset by "new ideas"—generally predestined to disappear within weeks —Irving Kolodin, *Saturday Rev.,* 1 Nov. 1975

Predestine may also be used with *for:*

> . . . adherence to socialist principles seemed to predestine him for a leading position in communist Hungary —*Times Literary Supp.,* 18 Dec. 1969

> . . . to push the working class into the action for which history had predestined it —Alfred G. Meyer, *Marxism Since the Communist Manifesto,* 1961

predicate 1. The use of the verb *predicate* in the sense of "to base, found" with *on* or *upon* is an Americanism attested as early as 1766. George Washington used it. In the middle of the 19th century this use came under sharp attack either on the grounds of infidelity to its Latin roots (Richard Grant White 1870, Gould 1867) or simply as a misuse (Bache 1869, Ayres 1881). The use had, however, already been recorded by Webster 1864, and the use persisted. The issue might have died by the turn of the century (Vizetelly 1906 speaks of it only as a U.S. usage), but Bierce 1909 kept the issue alive and Bernstein 1958, 1965 brought it into mid-century. Aside from Bernstein, no recent critic objects to the usage— even the Heritage 1969 usage panel finds it acceptable. This may fairly be judged a dead issue now, to be found in Harper 1975, 1985, Bremner 1980, and Copperud 1970, 1980 only because Bernstein revived it. The OED Supplement shows that this sense of *predicate* has entered British usage too. Here are a few examples from our collection:

Such a community predicates its operation upon the containment of various egoistic drives —Reinhold Niebuhr, *Yale Rev.,* Spring 1951

The grants are predicated on need —Horace Sutton, *Saturday Rev.,* August 1978

... their political success is predicated on disaster — Michael Straight, *New Republic,* 22 Nov. 1954

2. Older senses of *predicate,* when used in constructions requiring a preposition, take *of:*

Many distinct ways in which a oneness predicated of the universe might make a difference —William James, *Pragmatism,* 1907

And if we predicate simplicity of Hopkins.... —F. R. Leavis, *The Common Pursuit,* 1952

3. Alford 1864, Hodgson 1889, and Partridge 1942 dislike a use of *predicate* in the sense of "predict." The OED marks the sense "erroneous," apparently on the basis of the word's etymology, which is discussed at some length by Hodgson. This use dates back to Henry Cockeram's 1623 dictionary of hard words. Cockeram seems to have given us the fitfully appearing *expediate* (which see) as well as such other sesquipedalian Latinisms as *effacination, nundination, repumicate,* and *succollation;* perhaps this *predicate* was also the result of such self-conscious latinizing. It does seem to have had some genuine use, but we have no recent evidence and the OED Supplement gives none, so such use as it has had may be subsiding. However, books as recent as Longman 1984 tender a warning against confusing *predicate* with *predict.*

predominate, predominately Copperud 1964 sounded the clarion: "*Predominately* is not necessarily an error, for it has found its way into the dictionary. Nonetheless, it is a rare bird, and you can lay ten to one the writer was aiming at *predominantly....* *Predominate* as an adjective ... is an error for *predominant.*" You may wonder what dictionaries Mr. Copperud looked at for the adjective he thought an error. Not Webster's Third, nor Webster's Second, nor Webster 1909, nor the OED, for *predominate* as an adjective can be found in all of them.

Copperud 1970 still finds himself alone in objecting to *predominate* as an adjective, but his call would soon be heeded; Harper 1975, Bernstein 1977, Bremner 1980, and Johnson 1982 all denounce the use. Bremner and Johnson insist that *predominate* is only a verb. Bernstein adds that even though it appears in a couple of dictionaries as an adjective, it is not fully established. A few college handbooks comment too. Bander 1978, Macmillan 1982, and Guth 1985 all say *predominate* is only a verb. Two other books, Watt 1967 and Perrin & Ebbitt 1972, recognize *predominate* as an adjective of some rarity, and recommend *predominant.*

We have only a couple of critics before Copperud 1964. John W. Clark, in *British & American English* (1951), called *predominate(ly)* illiterate and said it was partly the fault of second-rate newspapers. Before that MacCracken & Sandison 1917 called *predominate* "an apparently mistaken and rare form of *predominant.*" An editor of Webster's Second wrote "bosh" on the slip bearing that remark.

Here is what the dictionaries know that most of the usage writers do not. *Predominate* has been an adjective in English since the end of the 16th century; it antedates the verb by a few years. It is first attested, according to the OED, in 1591 in the writings of Thomas Nashe, Elizabethan man of letters and controversialist. *Predominant* is slightly older, first attested in 1576; it was used in 1592 by William Shakespeare, a better-known and more influential Elizabethan man of letters. Most subsequent literary and general use has followed Shakespeare's lead rather than Nashe's.

The OED marked *predominate* and *predominately* "Rare," and so did Webster 1909 and Webster's Second. The editors of Webster's Second had a little bit of 20th-century evidence, so they moved both words from the pearl section—the small type at the foot of the page— where they had been in 1909 to the main word list. Between Webster's Second and Webster's Third more evidence accumulated, primarily from technical sources.

Of predominate interest in chlorophylls are the locations of hydrogens which may be active in photoreduction —*Botanical Rev.,* December 1950

... the predominate gonadal sex in cases of true hermaphroditism —*JAMA,* 9 Feb. 1952

Throughout our analysis we attempt to conform to the predominate tendencies in the language — Eugene A. Nida, *Morphology,* 1946

Occasionally it could be found in general sources as well:

His strong belief that patriotism should be one of the predominate principles of religion —*American Guide Series: Minnesota,* 1938

Rieve's predominate strength is in New England — *New Republic,* 26 May 1952

The evidence for *predominately* from this period tended to be more general than technical:

... the population is predominately native-born white —*American Guide Series: Texas,* 1940

The poem gives a predominately creative expression —K. E. Cameron, *The Young Shelley,* 1950

Blue light, which stimulates the rods predominately —Charles H. Best & Norman B. Taylor, *The Physiological Basis of Medical Practice,* 5th ed., 1950

Our most recent evidence shows that *predominately* is being used somewhat more frequently than *predominate* but that neither is likely to threaten the preeminent position of *predominant* and *predominantly.* So the adjective *predominate* and its derivative *predominately* are in the 20th century what they were in the 17th, 18th, and 19th—less frequently used alternatives. Literary use has all along preferred the *-ant* form. But being less frequent does not make the *-ate* form wrong.

preface　**1.** *Noun. Preface* is usually used with *to:*

> . . . Wilson explained in his preface to *Axel's Castle* —*Current Biography,* January 1964

> . . . we know that our defeat and dismay may be the preface to our successors' victory —T. S. Eliot, "Francis Herbert Bradley," in *Selected Essays,* 1932

> This is not of course a complete political philosophy. . . . But it is a poet's preface to politics —Eric Bentley, in *Forms of Modern Fiction,* ed. William Van O'Connor, 1948

Preface also has some use with *for:*

> Jean-Paul Sartre . . . wrote the preface for her second novel —*Current Biography,* June 1966

2. *Verb. Preface* may be used with *with:*

> The brief poems with which he prefaced and followed 'Al Aaraaf' —Daniel Hoffman, *Poe Poe Poe Poe Poe Poe Poe,* 1972

> Her cousin prefaced his speech with a solemn bow —Jane Austen, *Pride and Prejudice,* 1813

> . . . prefaces each section of his book with mystical epigraphs —Paul Zweig, *Saturday Rev.,* August 1978

> They prefaced their skating with dinner in a Spanish restaurant —Aurelia Levi, *Discovery,* March 1954

Preface often is found with *by:*

> . . . a forebuilding carrying two circular tempiettos at its ends and prefaced by an open octagonal porch — John Summerson, *Heavenly Mansions,* 1948

> The chapters on the historians are prefaced by chapters on Aristotle and Homer —*Times Literary Supp.,* 29 Aug. 1955

> . . . the laws themselves should be prefaced by preambles of a "persuasive" sort —Glenn R. Morrow, *Philosophical Rev.,* April 1953

Infrequently, *preface* is followed by *to:*

> . . . a note prefaced to the score —Edward Sackville-West & Desmond Shawe-Taylor, *The Record Year,* 1952

prefer　*Prefer* is most often used in constructions that do not involve prepositions. However, when it is used to compare two things in the same sentence, the second, especially if it is a noun or pronoun, is usually introduced by *to:*

> Movement is always to be preferred to inaction — Norman Mailer, *Advertisements for Myself,* 1959

> . . . monarch butterflies, who prefer them to any other flower —Eleanor Perenyi, *Green Thoughts,* 1983

> . . . he prefers sweaters and slacks to suits —*Current Biography,* July 1965

Sometimes other prepositions are used. The OED notes *above* and *before* as being used formerly (George Washington used *before*). *Over* is occasionally used:

> . . . but who, nevertheless, are preferred over the A type or the D type —William J. Reilly, *Life Planning for College Students,* 1954

This construction is especially frequent in advertisements for products where doctors or housewives or members of some other group will be said to prefer one brand over all others.

Numerous commentators point out that when the two things compared are represented by infinitive phrases, there can arise a problem of too many *to*s: "prefers to eat to to starve." The solution hit upon by writers facing this problem has often been to use *rather than* in place of *to:*

> . . . prefer to leave rather than to subvert their values —Shelly Halpern, *Change,* November–December 1969

Rather than is also used when the *to* or even the whole infinitive is understood:

> . . . prefers to stand rather than sit —*Current Biography,* September 1964

> . . . preferred to preach in it rather than in his mother tongue —*Dictionary of American Biography,* 1936

Only rarely do we find the *rather* omitted before the *than:*

> . . . he would have preferred to fast than carry it — Margaret Drabble, *The Needle's Eye,* 1972

When the two things compared are expressed in gerunds (sometimes with the second *-ing* form deleted) we find both *to* and *rather than:*

> He preferred living like a Grecian, to dying like a Roman —J. W. Croker, 20 July 1815, in *The Croker Papers,* 1884 (OED)

> It seems we prefer reading magazines to books — John Barkham, *Saturday Rev.,* 13 Feb. 1954

> . . . the rich preferred spending rather than investing —*Times Literary Supp.,* 2 July 1971

Beginning at least as early as Vizetelly 1906 there has been criticism of constructions with *than* and *rather than.* The critics have been far from unanimous in their opinions. Some condemn both *than* and *rather than;* some recommend *rather than* and condemn *than;* none give reasons for their opinions. Plain *than* seems to have no defenders and to be rarely used (the only genuine example besides our own that we have seen is in Reader's Digest 1983). And, to be truthful, plain *than* does sound awkward, perhaps simply from its unfamiliarity. See also RATHER THAN 2.

preferable　*Preferable* is sometimes considered to be an absolute adjective, so that its use with *more* is regarded as incorrect (Fowler 1926 calls it "an inexcusable pleonasm"). Our written evidence for *more preferable* is scanty.

> . . . getting the word "hillbilly" taken off the label of his records, and therefore inspiring everyone else in the trade to replace it with the more preferable "country and western" —Bob Claypool, *Houston Post,* 8 Sept. 1984

See ABSOLUTE ADJECTIVES.

preference　*Preference* is often followed by *for:*

> . . . Lincoln ignored this opinion in preference for one of Attorney General Bates —*Dictionary of American History,* 1940

Spinoza's preference for democracy —Morris R. Cohen, *The Faith of a Liberal,* 1946

Does the answer have something to do with a preference for superpower diplomacy? —Leslie H. Gelb & Morton H. Halperin, *Harper's,* November 1971

Preference is used with *to* when the object of the preposition is the thing not preferred. When *preference* is used in this way, it is often preceded by *in:*

... he chose Kentucky politics in preference to national affairs —*Dictionary of American Biography,* 1928

... a happy narcotic shrub widely grown in preference to food —Hal Lehrman, *N.Y. Times Book Rev.,* 15 Aug. 1954

When the object names the area within which preference is expressed rather than the specific thing preferred or not, *preference* also occurs with *in, of,* and *regarding:*

A German dialect is spoken generally, and German preferences in food prevail —*American Guide Series: Michigan,* 1941

... those preferences of sexual selection that go by the name of "love" —Edmund Wilson, *A Piece of My Mind,* 1956

Everyone has certain *preferences* regarding clothes —John E. Brewton et al., *Using Good English* (textbook), 1962

pregnant   When *pregnant* is used with a preposition, it is usually *with:*

Every hour was pregnant with monotony and weariness —C. S. Forester, *The African Queen,* 1935

We can impart to youth the meaning of life and their part in making history. But the words must be pregnant with fulfillment —William O. Douglas, *Being an American,* 1948

... create situations as pregnant with danger as with promise —Richard H. Rovere, *New Yorker,* 25 July 1953

The new physics is pregnant with revelations for everyone interested in the cosmos —Timothy Ferris, *N.Y. Times Book Rev.,* 20 Nov. 1983

Pregnant also occurs, although less often and in varying relations, with *by, for, in,* and *of:*

This time she's pregnant by a cad who won't marry her —John McCarten, *New Yorker,* 13 May 1950

... to see that the present is pregnant for the future, rather than a revolt against the past —Malcolm Bradbury, *Times Literary Supp.,* 25 Apr. 1968

... one of the indelible performances of my operatic experience, as rich in reality as it is pregnant in overtones —Claudia Cassidy, *Europe—On the Aisle,* 1954

Its five component essays are as pregnant of ideas as the leitmotif is of thematic metamorphoses —*Times Literary Supp.,* 23 May 1968

prejudice, prejudiced   **1.** *Prejudice to.* Murray 1795 corrected a *prejudice to* to *prejudice against.* Oddly enough, Longman 1984 also carries a warning against

the use of *to.* We have no instances of *to* except in the occasionally encountered legal (or legalistic) phrase "without prejudice to." If the usage does exist, it may be primarily a spoken British use.

2. *Prejudice(d) against, in favor of, toward(s).* Given the generally negative meaning attached to *prejudice,* noun and verb, it is not surprising that the most frequently used preposition is *against:*

... some absurd prejudice against living on one's friends —Stella Gibbons, *Cold Comfort Farm,* 1932

... inner agreement with the prevailing prejudice against him —Eric Hoffer, *N.Y. Times Mag.,* 29 Nov. 1964

... the former middle-class prejudice against wearing second-hand clothing —Roy Lewis & Angus Maude, *The English Middle Classes,* 1950

In favor of is much less common. Some older commentators (Bache 1869, Ayres 1881, Vizetelly 1906) disapproved *prejudice* or *prejudiced* used this way, but no one disapproves any more.

... a definite prejudice in favor of low latitude living —William G. Byron, *Annals of the Association of American Geographers,* June 1952

Bander 1978 points out that *prejudice toward(s)* can be ambiguous, and indeed it can. Our few printed citations require quite a bit of context to make them clear, and we recommend that you avoid *toward(s).*

The verb (especially in the form of its past participle *prejudiced*) behaves just like the noun:

... is prejudiced against a lot of different kinds of people —Bob Beamon, quoted in *Sports Illustrated,* 15 July 1968

... no matter how prejudiced in favor of the men — Norman Mailer, *Harper's,* March 1971

prejudicial   Usually *prejudicial* is followed by *to:*

... these are rarely useful to scholarship and are almost always prejudicial to teaching —Robert A. Nisbet, *Psychology Today,* March 1971

... the Prince of Orange was revolving some great design prejudicial to his Majesty's service —John Lothrop Motley, *The Rise of the Dutch Republic,* 1898

... information they considered irrelevant or prejudicial to the student's employability —Harold Perkin, *Times Literary Supp.,* 19 Mar. 1970

However, *prejudicial* has been used with *of:*

His analysis was unfairly prejudicial of an administration superior to any previously known in the colony —*Australian Dictionary of Biography,* 1966

premier   Gowers in Fowler 1965 and Flesch 1964 object to *premier* in the sense of "first, foremost," a sense it has had in English since the 15th century. There are no serious grounds for objection to uses like the ones quoted, even if advertisers like to use it hyperbolically at times.

... and thus Davis was first linked with the statesman whose mantle as the premier champion of states' rights he eventually assumed —Robert Penn Warren, *Jefferson Davis Gets His Citizenship Back,* 1980

... the nation's premier women's colleges —Diane Ravitch, *N.Y. Times Book Rev.*, 28 Oct. 1984

... recognized today as the premier authority in this country on rhododendrons —Stephen Harvey, *Scottish Field*, July 1975

premiere The verb *premiere* is resoundingly rejected by the major usage panels, although most commentators take no notice of it and dictionaries treat it as standard. The panelists tend to regard it as jargon, in part because of its derivation from the noun *premiere*, which, in their opinion, makes it a noun misused as a verb, and in part because of its origins in the world of show business. It is also a fairly new word, although not as new as some might suppose. We first encountered it in 1933, and by the 1940s it had established itself in regular use as both a transitive and intransitive verb:

... the Paris Opéra plans to premiere an old work of Jean Cocteau and Arthur Honegger —*Modern Music*, November–December 1942

The latter two houses première foreign films —Parker Tyler, *Tomorrow*, March 1945

The night Crosby premiered —*Newsweek*, 28 Oct. 1946

... the new show premièred on June 26 —*Newsweek*, 2 Aug. 1948

Its use continues to be common today:

... Trollope will premiere on television in the midst of the latest squall in Anglo-American relations —Karl E. Meyer, *Saturday Rev.*, 22 Jan. 1977

... when the play was premièred in 1889 —Ronald Hayman, *Times Literary Supp.*, 28 Jan. 1983

Anyone determined to avoid it will find that it has no exact synonym. *Open* can sometimes be used in place of the intransitive *premiere*, but it less strongly denotes a "first ever" public performance than does the longer word, and in many cases it is simply unidiomatic. A television program or musical composition, for example, could not be said to "open." *Open* is also unidiomatic in transitive use—you could not say "The Paris Opéra plans to open an old work...." Of course, one may always replace *premiere* with a phrase, as in "... the new show was first performed on June 26" or "... Crosby performed for the first time on television ...," but the necessity of such revision seems dubious. The verb *premiere* may have deserved to be called "jargon" fifty years ago, but in current English it is just another available verb, and we recommend that you regard it as such.

premises, premisses *Premises* is normally construed as a plural, even when used in the singular sense, "a building or part of a building":

... a tenant may assign his lease or sublet the premises or any part of them —McKee Fisk & James C. Snapp, *Applied Business Law*, 8th ed., 1960

Usage commentators warn against treating *premises* in this sense as a singular, as by preceding it with the indefinite article *a:*

The IRS padlocked a premises and was ordered to pay rent as the occupant —*Wall Street Jour.*, 2 June 1971

Such usage has a certain logic to it, but it is too uncommon to be considered standard.

A related topic is the correctness of the spelling *premisses.* Various commentators have described this spelling either as an error or as a variant sometimes used by the British to distinguish the plural of the "presupposition" sense of *premise* ("one of the premisses of his argument") from the "building" sense of *premises* ("was asked to leave the premises"). What it is, in fact, is the plural of *premiss,* a spelling variant of *premise* that is common in British English:

... examine the premisses on which his opinions were based —Ian Jack, *English Literature 1815–1832,* 1963

What I object to is his basic premiss —John Higginbotham, *Times Literary Supp.,* 28 Dec. 1967

... was needlessly confused by the premiss that ... —B. C. Akehurst, *Tobacco,* 1968

... diameters, planets, terms, premisses —Howard 1977

Premiss is actually the original and etymologically more faithful spelling of this word, but it now survives only in Great Britain, and only in the senses of the word relating to logic and arguments. The spellings *premise* and *premises* are used for all senses in American English.

preoccupied *Preoccupied* is almost always used with *with:*

... it is always ... the individual will, with which the Romantic poet is preoccupied —Edmund Wilson, *Axel's Castle,* 1931

... the difficulties of being understood in a world that was preoccupied with standard reactions —Louis Auchincloss, *The Injustice Collectors,* 1950

... a society ever more preoccupied with leisure —William H. Whyte, Jr., *The Organization Man,* 1956

... his proof that God lives and is daily preoccupied with the virtues and faults of John Quincy Adams —Alfred Kazin, *N.Y. Rev. of Books,* 23 Oct. 1969

Although the verb almost always appears as a past participle when it is used with a preposition, once in a while an active use shows up:

The children form a secret society which preoccupies itself with dares —*Times Literary Supp.,* 22 Oct. 1971

Preoccupied may also be followed by *about* or *by:*

One has observed them so preoccupied about simultaneity of attack —Virgil Thomson, *The Musical Scene,* 1947

Ignorant of life and of nature, she was, he has also supposed, preoccupied by love —Carol Ohmann, *College English,* May 1971

preparatory 1. When used with a preposition, *preparatory* is followed by *to:*

... the transports were already taking in their cargoes preparatory to dropping down the Thames —W. M. Thackeray, *Vanity Fair,* 1848

Van Helsing is lying down, having a rest preparatory to his journey —Bram Stoker, *Dracula,* 1897

Webster however thought of his first dictionary as only preparatory to a larger work —*Dictionary of American Biography,* 1936

. . . studied law preparatory to being admitted to the state bar in 1898 —*The Americana Annual 1953*

2. A few commentators (Flesch 1964, Copperud 1964, 1970, 1980, Cook 1985) consider *preparatory to* pretentious or wordy for *before.* Not every writer is willing to be limited to *before* in every case, however. If the examples above are not enough, here are four more. We are not persuaded that they sound pretentious or even that they mean just what they would mean if *before* were used:

I sat it up on my desk for a while preparatory to rewrapping it —James Thurber, letter, 6 Sept. 1947

He stopped, put the gears into reverse and twisted around in his seat preparatory to backing up —E. L. Doctorow, *Ragtime,* 1975

For all I know, you are a spy, sent here by an alien race to study us, preparatory to invasion —Gore Vidal, "Visit to a Small Planet," 1955

. . . a few years ago when I was shipping off stuff to Cornell preparatory to dying —E. B. White, letter, 9 Jan. 1970

See also PREVIOUS TO; PRIOR TO.

preposition 1. See PREPOSITION AT END.
2. The idiomatic preference for one preposition or another after certain verbs, adjectives, and nouns has been a subject for worry by grammarians since the 18th century. Lowth 1762 and Murray 1795, for instance, think it important to correct the prepositions selected by earlier 18th-century writers. Many modern handbooks, too, devote space to the problem—Bernstein 1965, for instance, includes many idiomatic combinations, and most commentators mention at least a few. In this book such combinations are each treated separately, with copious examples of actual usage, the entry word being the verb, adjective, or noun. Our coverage of combinations with prepositions is quite extensive; however, some combinations were undoubtedly missed. For more nearly complete coverage, it may help to consult a specialized dictionary aimed specifically at learners of English.
3. There are a few problems with prepositions that receive the attention of various commentators. These usually involve compound prepositions which are idiomatic but are deemed redundant or wordy by some commentators. A related problem is what Copperud 1970, 1980 calls "piled-up prepositions." These seem to be the result of the juncture of two idiomatic expressions, and while no ordinary hearer or reader is puzzled by them, the commentators claim to be. One class of these involves the prepositions *between* and *from* used after *of* to emphasize the idea of a range or spread. For instance, your television weatherman might predict "temperatures of between 65 and 72 degrees." Those who wish for a purely rational language want to get rid of the *of,* but when it is gone the expression does not have the same idiomatic sound.

A somewhat similar apparent redundancy can be found in this sentence:

I sat it up on my desk —James Thurber, letter, 6 Sept. 1947

Here the *up* appears to be an unnecessary preposition, but it is in fact an adverb that goes with *sit;* again we have two idiomatic expressions occurring side by side to create a redundancy that is only apparent, not real. Many of the compound prepositions that come in for censure—*alongside of, off of, off from, prior to,* and so forth—consist of exactly the same components we find here in *up on:* an adverb and a preposition. (See ALONGSIDE OF, ALONGSIDE; OFF FROM; OFF OF; PRIOR TO.) Idiom and sound, not logical analysis, govern the use of these combinations—some of which are recognized as compound prepositions in dictionaries.

There are more complex combinations of prepositions that intrigue linguists but that commentators do not try to grapple with. These include long strings of prepositions, as in "What did you bring that book I didn't want to be read to out of up for?" (A scenario has been devised to explain that sentence.) Otto Jespersen (*Essentials of English Grammar,* 1933) apparently made sense when he used this string of prepositions and adverbs: "up till within about twenty years" (quoted in J. Miller, *Semantics and Syntax,* 1985).

Miller, in the book just cited, has several interesting examples of phrases introduced by prepositions that function in their entirety as noun phrases and are the objects of another preposition:

. . . children from on the estate and from off the estate —a BBC program, 20 Apr. 1976

We do not wish to impose plans from on top —*The Scotsman,* 7 Aug. 1976

. . . the Adjective Shift transformation . . . moves the adjective from after the noun to in front of the noun —from an examination paper

preposition at end The question of the correctness of a preposition at the end of a sentence or clause is one which has been under discussion for more than three centuries. As is not the case with some of the other long-lived topics examined in this book, recent commentators—at least since Fowler 1926—are unanimous in their rejection of the notion that ending a sentence with a preposition is an error or an offense against propriety. Fowler terms the idea a "cherished superstition." And not only do the commentators reject the notion, but actual usage supports their rejection. So if everybody who is in the know agrees, there's no problem, right? Wrong.

Thank you for your reply to my questions but I find it extremely difficult to trust an opinion on grammar prepared by someone who ends a sentence with a preposition.

This is part of a letter received by one of our editors who had answered some questions for the writer. Members of the never-end-a-sentence-with-a-preposition school are still with us and are not reluctant to make themselves known:

Some time ago I ended a column with the observation that sportscaster John Madden had better be respected "because he is too big to argue with." To my dismay, that sentence provoked at least a dozen reproachful letters saying that I had violated "one of the oldest rules" of good writing, and that I was providing a poor example to the young. Alas, I had ended a sentence with a preposition —Mary Pat Flaherty, *Pittsburgh Press,* 28 Apr. 1985

And, lest you think the true believers are made up only of the sort of people who write letters to the editor, a full twenty percent of the Harper 1975 usage panel—people who are professional writers—believed the preposition at the end was an error.

Where did this "cherished superstition" come from? It seems to have originated with the 17th-century English poet, playwright, and essayist John Dryden. In 1672 Dryden wrote a piece of criticism called "Defence of the Epilogue," the main purpose of which was to demonstrate that the English used by writers of Dryden's time was superior to that of an earlier generation of writers. The writers Dryden talks chiefly about are Shakespeare, Fletcher, and Jonson, and he chooses Jonson, who had the highest reputation of the three at the time, as the one from whom to take specific examples. The italic line is from Jonson's *Catiline* (1611); the comment on it is Dryden's:

> *The bodies that those souls were frighted from.*
> The Preposition in the end of the sentence; a common fault with him, and which I have but lately observ'd in my own writings.

Dryden at some time later in his career went back over his own works and revised the final prepositions he found. We cannot be sure how Dryden developed the idea that the terminal preposition was an error, but Latin is probably involved. The construction does not exist in Latin, and Dryden claimed to have composed some of his pieces in Latin and then translated them into English—apparently for greater elegance or propriety of expression.

Almost a century later Bishop Lowth 1762 dealt with the problem. He may have had the episcopal tongue partly in the cheek:

> This is an idiom, which our language is strongly inclined to: it prevails in common conversation, and suits very well with the familiar style in writing: but the placing of the preposition before the relative, is more graceful, as well as more perspicuous; and agrees much better with the solemn and elevated style.

Lowth's approach is quite reasonable; clearly he cannot be blamed (as he is by Bryson 1984) for an absolutist approach to the matter. Hall 1917 says that Hugh Blair, author of a widely used book on rhetoric published in 1783, gave wide vogue to the notion that the terminal preposition must be avoided. If Blair did, then he may have passed the notion on to Lindley Murray 1795. Murray confected his very popular grammar from the works of several predecessors, including Lowth and Blair. Murray was notoriously strait-laced: he quoted Lowth's statement, but where Lowth said "which our language is strongly inclined to," Murray wrote "to which our language is strongly inclined." Even a bishop could not put a preposition at the end of a clause and satisfy Murray.

To Blair and Murray we may add Noah Webster. According to Baron 1982, Webster in his 1784 grammar strongly disapproved the terminal preposition. So the 19th century began with three widely used, standard school texts formidably opposing the preposition at the end of the sentence. The topic entered the general consciousness through schoolteachers, and, as we have seen, it persists there still.

Perhaps the construction was relatively new in Dryden's time, and he was reacting, as many do, to some-

thing new and obtrusive. But he did pick one out of Ben Jonson, and Shakespeare had used it too:

> Thou hast no speculation in those eyes
> Which thou dost glare with
>
>   —*Macbeth,* 1606

We also have evidence that the postponed preposition was, in fact, a regular feature in some constructions in Old English. No feature of the language can be more firmly rooted than if it survives from Old English. Evidently the whole notion of its being wrong is Dryden's invention.

And what is curious is the fact that the first example Dryden picked to make his point about (the one quoted above) contains a construction in which the preposition must be put at the end—a relative clause introduced by *that.* Some recent commentators such as Burchfield 1981 have pointed out that there are a few constructions in which the postponed preposition is either mandatory or preferable. The restrictive clause introduced by *that* has required the postponing of the preposition since Old English. Here are some examples:

> Sure, this must be some very notable matter that he's so angry at —George Villiers, *The Rehearsal,* 1672

> "Now," thought he, "I see the dangers that Mistrust and Timorous were driven back by." —John Bunyan, *Pilgrim's Progress,* 1678

> Fanny could with difficulty give the smile that was here asked for —Jane Austen, *Mansfield Park,* 1814

> . . . owing to the restrictions of space that Mr. Belloc has contented himself with —*Times Literary Supp.,* 20 Feb. 1937

> . . . with whatever it is that good English is good for —James Sledd, in Greenbaum 1985

When the restrictive clause is a contact clause (with the relative pronoun omitted), the preposition also must come at the end:

> These were some of the placid blessings I promised myself the enjoyment of —Samuel Johnson, *The Idler,* 10 June 1758

> . . . the style I am speaking of —William Hazlitt, quoted in Bailey 1984

> . . . permission to use the title they wish for —Lewis Carroll, letter, 6 Feb. 1888

> The University is one most people have heard of — Robert Frost, letter, 20 Jan. 1936

> . . . to visit a guy I went to Ohio State with —James Thurber, letter, 1937

> . . . the race of men she's had to deal with —E. L. Doctorow, *Loon Lake,* 1979

> . . . something all of us can learn a thing or two from —Simon 1980

Clauses introduced by *what* require postponing the preposition:

> . . . the Court affecting what the Prince was fond of —Jonathan Swift, "A Proposal for Correcting, Improving and Ascertaining the English Tongue," 1712

> I know what you are thinking of —Jane Austen, *Mansfield Park,* 1814

"... no one would believe what she had to put up with." —James Stephens, *The Crock of Gold,* 1912

... what the small cars look like —*Young America Junior Reader,* 7 Mar. 1952

That's what the taxpayers provide our salaries and buildings for —John Summerskill, quoted in *Change,* October 1971

Wh- clauses in general tend to have the preposition at the end:

In this letter, which I am fond of —Lady Mary Wortley Montague, letter, 15 Aug. 1712

... the reception which this proposal met with —Henry Fielding, *Jonathan Wild,* 1743

... the man whom mamma gave a tremendous hiding to last spring —Henry Adams, letter, 9 Dec. 1860

... aspects of Army life which I delight in —Edward Weeks, *Atlantic,* December 1952

... people ... whom you would like to dine with —Archibald MacLeish, letter, 13 Sept. 1954

... a pitch which the New York batter ... swung at —E. L. Doctorow, *Ragtime,* 1975

Wh- questions usually have the preposition postponed:

... what does it shape up to? —Hermann J. Weigand, *PMLA,* June 1952

... What else are they for? —Trimble 1975

"And what are they made of?" Alice asked —Lewis Carroll, *Alice's Adventures in Wonderland,* 1865

Whom is that literature about? —Earl Shorris, *N.Y. Times Book Rev.,* 1 July 1984

Infinitive clauses have the preposition at the end:

He had enough money to settle down on —James Joyce, *Dubliners,* 1914

... should have had a paragraph all to himself to die in —Leacock 1943

The peculiarities of legal English are often used as a stick to beat the official with —Gowers 1948

... it is difficult to find a name for —Lionel Trilling, *Partisan Rev.,* September–October 1940

Burchfield also mentions two other constructions. One is the passive:

None of them ... has yet been heard of —*The Intimate Notebooks of George Jean Nathan,* 1932

The other is the exclamation: "What a shocking state you are in!" (Example from Burchfield). And here are a few assorted inversions, passives, and other constructions in which the terminal preposition is idiomatic:

He had however a blotted Copy by him ... , and this the Publishers were well aware of —Jonathan Swift, *A Tale of a Tub,* 1710

Albania, indeed, I have seen more of than any Englishman —Lord Byron, letter, 3 May 1810

... the Pretender had not gratified his enemies by getting himself put an end to —Henry Adams, letter, 3 Sept. 1863

They probably know which shelf everything is on in the refrigerator —*And More by Andy Rooney,* 1982

... shorts, size 36, which she spent the rest of the evening crawling in and out of —Russell Baker, *N.Y. Times Mag.,* 29 Jan. 1984

The preposition at the end has always been an idiomatic feature of English. It would be pointless to worry about the few who believe it is a mistake. You can avoid the construction but you do so at your peril, as our final two examples show:

... a certain cachet and authority on which others wished to capitalize on —Norman Blake, *The English Language in Medieval Literature,* 1977

I never stop worrying as to with whom she's kicking up her heels now —quoted in Barnard 1979

prerequisite, *noun*   **1.** The noun *prerequisite* is usually followed by *for* or *to* when it takes a preposition:

In other countries land reform is a prerequisite for democracy —Bruce Bliven, *New Republic,* 12 Nov. 1945

The prerequisite for graduate work ... is an undergraduate major in one of the departments concerned —*Bulletin of the University of Minnesota Graduate School,* 1952–1954

... declaring that the prerequisite for destroying fascism was a socialist revolution in England —Irving Howe, *Harper's,* 1969

The pictures ... were not notable for good draftsmanship—a prerequisite for surrealism —Anthony Burgess, *MF,* 1971

A general background of content in liberal arts courses is a necessary prerequisite to professional training —*Catalogue: The College of William & Mary,* April 1952

... he answered the questions put to him by the Senators as a prerequisite to his confirmation —*Current Biography 1949*

... strengthening the bulwarks of academic freedom that ... are an essential prerequisite to ... your glorious future —Albert L. Nickerson, *University of Chicago Round Table,* 24 Jan. 1954

Sometimes *prerequisite* is used with *of:*

... he possesses the prerequisite of an original poet—a percipience ... exact and exhilarating —C. Day Lewis, *A Hope for Poetry,* 3d ed., 1936

... the prerequisite of all German political parties, a daily newspaper in which to preach the party's gospels —William L. Shirer, *The Rise and Fall of the Third Reich,* 1960

2. See PERQUISITE, PREREQUISITE.

prerequisite, *adjective*   The adjective *prerequisite* is usually followed by *to* when it takes a preposition:

... the interaction of the opposite forces of attraction and repulsion was prerequisite to the existence of material objects —S. F. Mason, *Main Currents of Scientific Thought,* 1953

... contained most of the ingredients prerequisite to box-office success —*Current Biography,* May 1966

The ability to perform that slight distortion of all the elements in the world of a play . . . which is prerequisite to great farce . . . —T. S. Eliot, "Philip Massinger," in *Selected Essays,* 1932

present The verb *present* is most commonly found with *to* or *with,* the former marking the receiver and the latter the thing presented:

He had continually to be presenting to allies their supposed advantage —Hilaire Belloc, *Richelieu,* 1930

The nature of the tasks presented to school administrators and teachers —James B. Conant, *Slums and Suburbs,* 1961

. . . a mediocre man . . . whom, he thought, it would be positively humiliating to present to the Germans —William L. Shirer, *The Rise and Fall of the Third Reich,* 1960

. . . the new instrument with which Einstein has presented the mathematicians —W. R. Inge, *The Church in the World,* 1928

Both of these developments present us with the question: What are the potentialities of the human mind? —Margaret Mead, *The Lamp,* Summer 1963

There was something mildly debonair, he thought pleasantly, in presenting your wife with a rose — William Styron, *Lie Down in Darkness,* 1951

Present is also used with *as, at,* or *for:*

Reston presented himself and his staff as team players —Gay Talese, *Harper's,* January 1969

Some of the photographers . . . presented their cameras at the Generals on the balcony as if they had been highwaymen —Eric Linklater, *Private Angelo,* 1946

Though not yet of legal age to practise, he was presented for the bar by Judah P. Benjamin —*Dictionary of American Biography,* 1929

present incumbent Usage books are prone to get themselves into difficulty when their editors fail to think carefully enough about what they say. Consider this:

Since *incumbent* means one who holds office at the present time, *present incumbent* is redundant —Harper 1975, 1985

If that is what *incumbent* means, we should be able to substitute the definition for the word in typical contexts without a great strain on idiom and without significant change of meaning.

President Grant promptly appointed Bristow the first incumbent —*Dictionary of American Biography,* 1929

Was Bristow "the first holder of office at the present time"? That is hardly likely since Grant's action occurred more than five decades before this passage was written in the 1920s.

. . . Welles held that office longer than any previous incumbent —*Dictionary of American Biography,* 1936

Could Welles be the "previous holder of office at the present time"? That is clearly impossible.

In January 1841 he succeeded as locum and later as incumbent —*Australian Dictionary of Biography,* 1967

Can we say, in any conceivable sense, that he "succeeded . . . later as holder of office at the present time"?

An incumbent is, of course, only the holder of a benefice or an office; an incumbent can exist in the past, present, or future, just like a president, a press agent, or a usage writer. It is embarrassing to admit that a principal source of this problem resides in our own dictionaries; the *present* can be found in the definition in Webster 1909, and it was carried into Webster's Second unthinkingly. The definition was properly ridiculed in the *Houston Press* on 23 Feb. 1935. The Texas editorialist pointed out that other important dictionaries such as those of Oxford and Funk & Wagnalls had not fallen into the same error. An editor of Webster's Third fixed the mistake, but its influence may persist until usage commentators stop using Webster's Second.

The combination *present incumbent* is, then, not redundant, since *present* was erroneous in the definitions of Webster 1909 and Webster's Second. The combination has been in respectable use for a long time:

. . . and, though the present incumbent was somewhat of the Independent, yet he ordinarily preached sound doctrine —John Evelyn, *Diary,* ca. 1682

We promise to place qualifications on all elective and appointive offices as to honor, integrity and mentality, thus automatically disqualifying ninety-eight percent of the present incumbents —*The Intimate Notebooks of George Jean Nathan,* 1932

All that the present incumbent wants is an orderly transfer of authority —Harry S. Truman, diary, 15 Nov. 1952

Dick Bartleton, the present incumbent, is almost as liberal —Wyndham Lewis, *Rotting Hill,* 1951

. . . the present incumbent admirably fills the role — Eric Solomon, *New York,* 15 Dec. 1975

presently An ill-founded notion, of fairly recent origin, holds that there is something wrong with the sense of *presently* that means "at present, now." For instance, the Oxford American Dictionary says that careful writers avoid the sense; Shaw 1975 calls it "debatable and inaccurate"; Copperud 1970 cites four authorities who think *presently* would be best reserved to mean "before long." How these opinions came to be held is a moderately complex story which involves some history: the history of the word, of its treatment in dictionaries, and of its treatment by the usage commentators.

The "at present" sense of *presently* has been in use more or less continuously since 1485. According to the OED, it appears to have dropped out of literary English in the 17th century. It seems, however, to have continued in nonliterary use; the OED notes it as common in Scottish writers and "most other English dialects." Although 18th- and 19th-century citations are not numerous, the sense stayed in use. Thackeray knew it:

I have been thinking over our conversation of yesterday, and it has not improved the gaiety of the work on w[hich] I am presently busy —letter, 4 Mar. 1862

The sense became more common in the 20th century. The OED cites a 1901 Leeds newspaper; here are a few examples from our files:

I have no use for him presently —Lady Gregory, *Damer's Gold*, in *New Comedies*, 1913

. . . Professor Eric Walker—presently of the University of Capetown —*Times Literary Supp.*, 12 Sept. 1936

. . . for sheer theatrical ineptitude the once-esteemed Guild presently hasn't a rival this side of an Arkansas little theatre —George Jean Nathan, *Newsweek*, 10 Oct. 1938

. . . the diseases which presently afflict the South —*Saturday Rev.*, 28 Dec. 1940

When the presently available bacitracin is used —*JAMA*, 12 Mar. 1949

. . . is presently chief editor at Chappell —Herbert Warren Wind, *New Yorker*, 17 Nov. 1951

. . . the government departments which presently share in the maladministration of Eskimo affairs —John Nicol, *Canadian Forum*, June 1952

Lasser is presently fiddling around with ideas for a book —E. J. Kahn, Jr., *New Yorker*, 14 Mar. 1953

. . . but neither is presently able to engage in a sustained practical politics of its own —Irving Howe, *Partisan Rev.*, January–February 1954

Dictionary treatment of the "at present" sense has been somewhat spotty. Samuel Johnson, working with mostly literary material, had no citations for the sense more recent than the 16th and 17th centuries; he marked the sense obsolete. Noah Webster in 1828 followed Johnson and left it obsolete, as did Merriam-Webster dictionaries following Webster, right up through 1909. When the OED evidence for the sense became available in 1909, Webster 1909 had already been edited and the sense labeled *Obs.* The editors of the 1934 edition labeled the sense *Rare exc. dial.* and included the quotation from Lady Gregory above. The 1934 treatment brought us quite a bit of correspondence, some of it wondering if the quotation from Lady Gregory was meant to imply that the sense was of the Irish dialect, but most of it enclosing newspaper clippings and wondering why we thought it was rare. But most of our current evidence had been gathered after the book was published (the *dial.* was derived from the longer statement in the OED). Consequently in 1947 the entry was revised to show the sense as current; the sense has been treated as current in all our subsequent dictionaries.

There seems to have been no interest in the sense from a standpoint of linguistic propriety until the early 1950s. Our earliest evidence is a 1951 letter to the editor of the *Christian Science Monitor* in which the writer claims to find ambiguous the perfectly obvious sentence "The ship presently has a length of 600 feet." Theodore Bernstein appears to have been the first usage writer to take a position against the sense: in *Winners & Sinners* (3 Feb. 1954) he states "'Presently' means 'forthwith' or 'soon'; it does not mean 'at present.'" By 1958 when he collected his comments into a book, he softened the remark: "'Presently' should be reserved for the meaning 'forthwith' or 'soon'; it should not be diluted to take in also 'at present.'" (He would retreat farther in his 1965 and 1977 books.)

Once Bernstein had let the genie out of the bottle, there was no getting it back, and numerous usage commentators have come forward to condemn the use, generally on the ground that it can be ambiguous. This observation is buttressed with a context-free example made up for the purpose. In actual use, the word is almost never ambiguous. Quirk et al. 1985 note that when *presently* means "at present," it is used in modern contexts with the present tense of a verb. (Quirk finds this more common in American than British English.) When it is used to mean "before long," it tends to go with a verb accompanied by a modal auxiliary or with a verb in the past tense. Genuinely ambiguous uses are very hard to find.

If there is any restriction on the "at present" sense of *presently*, it is that it is used more often in business and political writing than in more literary or academic prose, but it is not infrequent in such writings either:

. . . the paradoxical and uncertain fame which Lévi-Strauss presently enjoys —*Times Literary Supp.*, 2 May 1968

Seven states of the Union presently maintain hanging as the maximum penalty for first-degree murder —Lamberts 1972

We close with a citation from a political writer:

The fastest-rising welfare cost is Medicaid, presently paid by the states and cities —William Safire, *Springfield* (Mass.) *Morning Union*, 29 Jan. 1982

In his *New York Times Magazine* column of 14 Dec. 1980, Safire recommended avoiding the word entirely because of its ambiguity.

Conclusion: the sense of *presently* meaning "at present" has been in more or less continuous standard use since 1485. The commentators who warn against its use do so without good reason. There is nothing wrong with it.

present writer   *The present writer* is a convention by which a reporter, reviewer, or author can put in personal observations or opinions without using the pronoun *I*. Copperud 1970, 1980, Bremner 1980, and Nickles 1974 express mild disapproval, but this is an innocuous convention.

It once fell to the lot of the present writer to have an extended conversation with a noted female author who had very decided opinions as to the character of the sex to which he had the fortune or misfortune to belong —Lounsbury 1908

The present writer once suggested to him . . . —F. Scott Fitzgerald, in *New Republic*, 22 Nov. 1954

The present writer too has wept over these —Virgil Thomson, *American Music Since 1910*, 1971

At last, the present writer, asked to say how he would go about it, . . . —Frederic G. Cassidy, Introduction to *Dictionary of American Regional English*, 1985

Such combinations as *present reviewer, present author*, and *present commentator* are also occasionally used.

preside   *Preside* is most commonly found with *over*:

. . . Marian Anderson . . . presided over an all-American musical program —Eric F. Goldman, *Harper's*, January 1969

... three judges are usually assigned to preside over the district court —Rev. Joseph N. Moody & Joseph F. X. McCarthy, *Man the Citizen,* 1957

... made one feel that the occasion was not a party over which he was presiding but a species of mixed smoker —Edmund Wilson, *Memoirs of Hecate County,* 1946

Vice-president Boucher presided, first over the bar and buffet, then over the business meeting —*Third Degree,* September 1947

It is not the nature of the Mayor or the men around him to preside over the dismemberment of their empire —Dan Cordtz, *New York,* 22 Nov. 1971

... Berlin was always a place presided over by the camera —Stephen Spender, *N.Y. Times Mag.,* 30 Oct. 1977

Somewhat less frequently, *preside* is used with *at:*

Ella presided at the punch bowl —William Styron, *Lie Down in Darkness,* 1951

... will preside at a Judgment Day, when the saved will be winnowed from the damned —Edmund Wilson, *A Piece of My Mind,* 1956

The two visible objects, the original and the copy, differ because that which ordered the work of art does not preside at the manufacture of the copy —Clive Bell, *Art,* 1914

As Council president, Impellitteri presided at its three or four meetings each month —*Current Biography 1951*

Preside is also sometimes used with *in:*

Carpetbaggers sat in every legislature, presided in every court, and ruled from every statehouse —Marshall Smelser & Harry W. Kirwin, *Conceived in Liberty,* 1955

... the mayor presides in council meetings in cities of Illinois —Frederic A. Ogg & P. Orman Ray, *Introduction to American Government,* 8th ed., 1945

prestigious It may come as a bit of a surprise to some readers to find that the only living sense of *prestigious* was aspersed by Follett 1966 and a panelist of Harper 1975 on the grounds of the word's etymological connection to *prestidigitation* and its early archaic sense relating to conjuring. The older sense has not been attested since the 1880s.

The current sense, as far as we know, was first used by Joseph Conrad in his novel *Chance* in 1913, in which he referred to "the prestigious or desirable things of the earth." How the word got from Conrad into American journalism we do not know, but here are our next two earliest citations:

... the most prestigious yearly salon of pictorial photography in America —*Carnegie Mag.,* March 1937

... starred in such prestigious successes as *Winterset* —*Time,* 3 Jan. 1938

Its frequent appearance in *Time* during the 1940s and 1950s undoubtedly helped popularize the new sense. It is in reputable use in spite of a few doubters—many of whom, according to Howard 1984, are the sort who write letters to newspapers pointing out that the sense is

not in the OED (the volume that includes the entry for *prestigious* was published in 1909).

... journalistic awards more respectable but less prestigious than the Pulitzers —Simon 1980

A recommendation from the Philological Society ... must be counted as one of Webster's more prestigious recommendations —E. Jennifer Monaghan, *A Common Heritage,* 1983

The change in the meaning of *prestigious* was influenced by a similar change in the meaning of *prestige* that took place in the 19th century.

presume See ASSUME, PRESUME.

presumptive, presumptuous Bryson 1984, Shaw 1975, 1987, the Oxford American Dictionary and Copperud 1970, 1980 warn us not to confuse *presumptive* with *presumptuous.* An old sense (1609) of *presumptive* does, in fact, mean "presumptuous." This sense, to judge from the example in Bryson 1984, is still found on rare occasions. It is not wrong, but it is rare enough to occasion surprise and perhaps confusion. We do not recommend your using it. Here are a couple of mainstream uses of the words:

The old indictment was now revised by the federal government to place him in a group of presumptive conspirators —Robert Penn Warren, *Jefferson Davis Gets His Citizenship Back,* 1980

I don't even claim that the book is wholly purified of the sins it rails against with such presumptuous authority —Zinsser 1976

This is a question you can easily settle by using your desk dictionary.

Copperud 1980 says also that *presumptuous* is sometimes misspelled *presumptious.* Actually, *presumptious* is an old spelling of the word; the OED has examples from about 1400 to 1815. Our files have examples from the 1940s and 1950s. It is, however, a rare spelling that is better avoided.

pretense, pretence The usual spelling in American English is *pretense;* the usual spelling in British English is *pretence.* American writers have also used *pretence,* but we have no really recent examples and most of what we have dates from the 1940s or earlier. *Pretense* is very rare in British usage. We have Canadian examples of both spellings.

pretty The adverb *pretty,* used as a down-toning qualifier like *somewhat* or *rather,* has been used in literary English since 1565. And, at the same time, it has been used in speech and informal writing such as letters. Why it is a subject of discussion in more than twenty of our usage sources is something of a mystery. The fuss seems to start with Vizetelly 1906, who finds that it "lacks elegance and definitiveness." Later criticism adds nothing more substantial to this original criticism; time and time again we are told that *pretty* is established but it is overworked or it is colloquial or it is informal, etc. But such remarks might equally be made of *cat* or *dog* or *take* or *set. Pretty* is, in fact, widely used on all levels of discourse. The following examples will make our point. First some from informal sources:

... his lady—a fine young Scotch lady, pretty handsome —Samuel Pepys, diary, 3 Oct. 1665

... which, thank my Stars, I can pretty well bear — Thomas Gray, letter, 15 July 1736

We supt with the Clarksons one night—Mrs. Clarkson pretty well. Mr. C. somewhat fidgety —Charles Lamb, letter, 26 June 1806

Have you seen it in any of the papers? ... It is a pretty good one —William Hazlitt, letter, January 1807

... a "northeast storm"—a little north of east, in case you are pretty definite —Emily Dickinson, letter, 8 June 1851

I feel pretty sure —Lewis Carroll, letter, 27 May 1879

... I am a pretty shrewd old boy for a countryman —Robert Frost, letter, 11 Oct. 1929

Mother, however, looks pretty well —E. B. White, letter, 17 Oct. 1935

I'm pretty sure you won't want to read all this — Archibald MacLeish, letter, 10 July 1956

... he did pretty well as a writer —William Faulkner, 20 May 1957, in *Faulkner in the University,* 1959

I'm watching this pretty carefully —Donald Coggan, Archbishop of Canterbury, quoted in *The Economist,* 29 Mar. 1975

Some from literature of several kinds and from literary journalism:

... the contents were pretty plain, I thought — George Farquhar, *The Constant Couple,* 1699

... served them pretty tolerably for a Devil —Jonathan Swift, *A Tale of a Tub,* 1710

... her inclination and strength for more were pretty well at an end —Jane Austen, *Mansfield Park,* 1814

". . . I suppose you know Paris pretty correctly. . . ." —Henry James, *The American,* 1877

I must have felt pretty weird by that time —F. Scott Fitzgerald, *The Great Gatsby,* 1925

Pretty soon the lawn begins to take heart —Frank Sullivan, *The Night the Old Nostalgia Burned Down,* 1953

My mother considered herself pretty well prepared in her kitchen and pantry for any emergency — Eudora Welty, in *The Contemporary Essay,* ed. Donald Hall, 1984

... I'm being responsible in a pretty reckless way — William Stafford, *Writing the Australian Crawl,* 1978

... even though their religious knowledge is often pretty exiguous —David Martin, *Times Literary Supp.,* 11 Dec. 1981

... seven more children, who were added pretty straight off the reel —Mollie Panter-Downes, *New Yorker,* 4 Nov. 1985

... I could pretty much go wherever I felt a story led —Roy Blount, Jr., *N.Y. Times Book Rev.,* 9 Mar. 1986

And some from miscellaneous other writings:

These colours were faint and dilute, unless the light was trajected obliquely; for by that means they became pretty vivid —Sir Isaac Newton, *Optics,* 1704 (in Johnson 1755)

The unification of these two forces ... is now pretty well accepted in the scientific community —James S. Trefil, *Science 81,* September 1981

It has been pretty regularly shunned —Lounsbury 1908

The word wed in all its forms as a substitute for marry, is pretty hard to bear —Bierce 1909

The first round of the battle was fought over standards of usage and was pretty well finished by the late thirties —James Sledd, *A Short Introduction to English Grammar,* 1959

... regards most of us as pretty irrevocably plunged in illusion —Iris Murdoch, *The Fire and the Sun,* 1977

The adverb *pretty* was entered in Johnson's 1755 Dictionary with eight quotations from the learned, pious, and elegant writers of the late 17th and early 18th centuries. It was acceptable to Samuel Johnson and it is acceptable today.

prevail   *Prevail* is most often used with *upon* when it means "to use persuasion successfully":

Knowing me to be under a promise that naught can prevail upon me to break —Rafael Sabatini, *Saint Martin's Summer,* 1924

... Harney prevailed upon the men in the sloop to sail up the river again —Marjory Stoneman Douglas, *The Everglades: River of Grass,* 1947

... the McCarthy advisers had been successful in prevailing upon the candidate —David Halberstam, *Harper's,* December 1968

Less frequently we find it with *on:*

... could Wickham be prevailed on to marry his daughter —Jane Austen, *Pride and Prejudice,* 1813

... the Mayor of Winsted ... prevailed on Army engineers to spend a quarter of a million dollars — John Hersey, *New Yorker,* 17 Sept. 1955

This sense of *prevail* is also used sometimes with *with:*

... 'I don't at all fear of prevailing with the young lady, if once I get her to the room.' —Fanny Burney, *Evelina,* 1778

... they must also formulate policy and try to make it prevail with Congress —John McDonald, *Fortune,* July 1954

In its other senses, *prevail* is found quite often with *over* and *against:*

... the rush of pity which always prevailed over every other sensation —Edith Wharton, *The Old Maid,* 1924

... no matter how many troublesome Montgomerys there may be on his team, in the end he will prevail over them —Max Ascoli, *The Reporter,* 12 Jan. 1956

Society may require that the squatter shall prevail over the swagman —William Power, *Yale Rev.,* Summer 1954

Not until the slain father returns from heaven . . . in the form of his own statue, does he prevail against his slayer —George Bernard Shaw, *Man and Superman,* 1903

. . . newly worked out moral truths can prevail against habit and prejudice —Robert M. Hutchins, *Center Mag.,* January 1968

prevent   *Prevent* is used in several constructions that have received comment. The first of these is *prevent* + a noun or pronoun + *from* + an *-ing* form of a verb. This construction is prescribed as correct by both American and British usage books and is in fact the most common American construction represented in our files.

It can't help you win, but it might prevent you from losing —Arthur Ashe, quoted in *Playboy,* May 1980

. . . to prevent the President from establishing a military dictatorship —Francis D. Wormuth, "The Vietnam War: The President versus the Constitution," 1968

. . . a slight defect in his spine prevented him from pursuing this ambition —*Current Biography,* July 1965

Then we have *prevent* + possessive pronoun or noun + *-ing.* This construction is also prescribed by the handbooks, but it is much less common in our files.

. . . never quite served to prevent your colliding with them —Jack Hulbert, *London Calling,* 9 Dec. 1954

. . . ill health prevented his resuming his duties —*Dictionary of American Biography,* 1936

And we have *prevent* + noun or objective pronoun + *-ing.* Evans 1957 finds this a standard construction, but several other commentators disapprove it, for example, Shaw 1975, 1987, who calls it substandard. It is nothing more than a specific instance of what H. W. Fowler called the "fused participle." For a general discussion of this problem, see POSSESSIVE WITH GERUND. Our files show the construction to be fairly uncommon in American English, but quite common in recent British usage:

. . . the edges of sharp instruments should be masked to prevent them injuring the staff —*Punch,* 17 Oct. 1973

. . . to insulate the ice-cream and prevent it melting —*Weekend,* 4 June 1968

. . . order his porters to prevent the speaker entering the building —Peter Wilby, *The Observer,* 19 May 1974

Prevent + an *-ing* form with no noun or pronoun turns up now and then:

. . . obliged to cling, to prevent being washed away —Captain Frederick Marryat, *Peter Simple,* 1834

To prevent being misled —Melissa Ludtke, *Sports Illustrated,* 10 Apr. 1978

Barzun 1985 catches himself starting to use *prevent* + object + *to* + infinitive and then decides that it is an impossible construction. It is perhaps not possible for most writers, but we do find it once in a great while:

. . . providing an excuse for preventing "foreign" blacks to settle in urban areas —*Times Literary Supp.,* 14 July 1966

There is nothing to prevent what Congress has done today to be undone tomorrow —Arthur Markewich, quoted in *Springfield* (Mass.) *Union,* 30 Mar. 1967

All of these constructions can be found in standard sources. The last two are the rarest and the last one the most awkward-sounding.

preventative, preventive   The critics have panned *preventative* for over a century, preferring its shorter synonym *preventive* in spite of the fact that both words have been around for over 300 years and both have had regular use by reputable writers. Here is the basic premise behind the objections: if two similar adjectives are derived from the same verb, then one of them must be in some way inferior to the other, and the likely culprit is the longer one. But the only real difference in status between these two words is that *preventative* is much less common than *preventive.* If you decide you like the sound of that extra syllable and are willing to brave possible criticism for it, you may take heart from the example set by these writers:

. . . send a preventative Medicine —Daniel Defoe, *A Journal of the Plague Year,* 1722 (OED)

Wearing flannel next the skin is the best cure for, and preventative of the Rheumatism I ever tried —George Washington, *Writings,* 1793 (OED)

The initiative for any *preventative* measures —Henry A. Wallace, *Commonweal,* 11 Aug. 1944

. . . a preventative-maintenance program —Oran I. Brown, *Book Production Industry,* September 1964

Fear is not a preventative of war —Frederic Wertham, *Johns Hopkins Mag.,* Summer 1971

. . . which may or may not be particularly instructive and most certainly not preventative —Michael Sturgin, *Chaucer Rev.,* Fall 1980

You may wonder how *preventative* came to be objected to. The earliest attack is in Bache 1869; he said that there was no such word. Bache's book was one of those used by Ayres 1881, who also criticized *preventative.* From Ayres it went to Vizetelly 1906, Bierce 1909, MacCracken & Sandison 1917, and Lurie 1927. Fowler 1926 picked it up too, and so it has gone right down to the 1980s. A couple of commentators—Evans 1962 and Watt 1967—realize that *preventative* is acceptable. Probably none of the recent objectors realizes that his opinion goes back to Bache 1869. But the moderns do not claim that *preventative* is nonexistent anymore; nowadays they say it is wrong because it is "irregularly formed." That is not so, of course. It is formed in just the same way as *authoritative* and *talkative,* words to which no one objects.

previous to   *Previous to,* which is a compound preposition, has been objected to by numerous commentators. The earliest line of attack began with Baker 1770, who descries an adverbial use of *previous* in the compound. He considers this "not good English." Ayres 1881, Bierce 1909, and MacCracken & Sandison 1917 all take the same line; they recommend *previously to* instead. But early 20th-century commentary becomes diffuse: Utter 1916 seems to approve either construction; Vizetelly 1906 prefers *prior to* to *previous to;* Lincoln Library 1924 approves both *previous to* and *previously to* in certain circumstances; F. K. Ball 1923 does not like either one (or *prior to* either) and suggests using *before* in place of all of them. An editor working on Webster's Second noted on the slip containing Ball's opinion, "Advice not supported by good usage."

Ball, however, seems to have anticipated many modern commentators. Partridge 1942 labels *previous to* "commercialese" and "verbose" and *previously to* "catachrestic." (He may have been unaware that earlier writers had prescribed *previously to.*) Janis 1984 and Copperud 1964, 1970, 1980 find *previous to* "pretentious." Cook 1985 and Little, Brown 1980, 1986 consider it wordy; Gowers in Fowler 1965 does not like it, but Fowler in the 1926 original found it idiomatic. Bernstein 1965 and Evans 1957 (who go unmentioned in Copperud's consensus) find *previous to* unobjectionable. The grammatical explanations that have been offered with these various prescriptions are considerably various themselves.

What about real usage? Our files show *previous to,* though in use since the 18th century, not occurring so frequently as to warrant the number of attacks that have been made upon it. It is perfectly plain that most writers find *before* more useful most of the time. *Previous to* and other compound prepositions (see, for instance, PREPARATORY 2 and PRIOR TO) are available for variety when you want them.

> ... and have answered both previous to leaving Cephalonia —Lord Byron, letter, 4 Mar. 1824

> ... the three months previous to that my wages had gone into making the first payment on a second hand Overland car —Will Rogers, *The Illiterate Digest,* 1924

Previously to, incidentally, did have some actual use during the 19th century but seems to have had very little since, although Partridge found a 1935 example. Here are a pair from the 19th century:

> I believe there must be a balance in my favour, as I did not draw a great deal previously to going —Lord Byron, letter, 1 May 1816

> ... business it was requisite he should settle in person, previously to his meditated departure from England —Charlotte Brontë, *Jane Eyre,* 1847

prewar   *Prewar* is used primarily as an adjective, but it is also sometimes used as an adverb:

> ... the smaller manufacturers who, pre-war, had to be content with crumbs —*Scientific American,* November 1944

> American railroads, which prewar received 9 per cent of the total steel —*Steel Facts,* October 1945

> ... more people can afford autos than prewar —*Time,* 28 Nov. 1949

> Pre-war it was considered bad manners to discuss food while the meal was in progress —Susan Deacon, *English Digest,* March 1953

> ... food output per person ... was only 2 per cent more than prewar —*Times Literary Supp.,* 5 Mar. 1970

The earliest record (in the OED Supplement) of this adverb is from 1920. It was criticized by Fowler 1926, but it has never caught on as a popular target among usage commentators. The probable reason is that it is too uncommon to attract much notice.

principal, principle   There is nothing that we can tell you about this spelling problem that innumerable handbooks (we have more than forty in our collection) and dictionaries from grammar-school level on up have not. But read it one more time: only *principal* is an adjective. *Principal* is also a noun, usually signifying either a person or money. *Principle* is only a noun, usually designating a law or rule. A quick check of any reputable dictionary will guide you in doubtful cases.

Ah, but even if you know the difference, it is still easy to goof by writing "the basic principal" or "their principle occupation." These errors seem to be the ones that are most common. And bear in mind that if you have a word processor, it will not help you here.

> I am even nervous about some words I should have mastered in grade school. I know when to use ... "principle" not "principal," but I always pause just an instant to make sure —*And More by Andy Rooney,* 1982

Perhaps we should imitate Andy Rooney's pause. It could be the pause that refreshes the memory.

principle of proximity   See AGREEMENT, SUBJECT-VERB: THE PRINCIPLE OF PROXIMITY.

prioritize   *Prioritize* is a jargon word used in various specialized fields such as the military, business, the social sciences, and data processing. Here are three actual uses of the word:

> ... some criteria to guide and prioritize our efforts —William A. McConnell, *American Documentation,* July 1968

> We're having a great deal of difficulty in prioritizing our interests —Adm. Thomas B. Hayward, quoted in U.S. Naval Institute, *Proceedings,* August 1982

> Women have difficulty prioritizing their roles — Georgia Witkin-Lanoil, Ph.D., quoted in *Vogue,* April 1984

We bring up the question of actual use because our files indicate that this word almost never appears in general publications except in the form of comment by watchdogs of the language, who note that the word is used by business managers, or politicians, or unnamed officials of one sort or another.

Our advice to you is simple. Jargon is the language by which specialists communicate with other specialists. Specialists do not much care what the general public thinks of the words they use. Unless you are working in a field where *prioritize* is commonly used, you will probably never need the word or need to worry about it. We have no persuasive evidence that *prioritize* is moving out of specialized jargon into widespread general use.

See -IZE 2.

prior to   "Stilted," "affected," "formal," "incongruous," "stiff," and "clumsy" are among the adjectives that have been used by commentators to describe the use of *prior to,* with "formal" being the most common label. *Before* is the generally preferred substitute, "except in contexts involving a connexion between the two events more essential than the simple time relation," says Fowler 1926. Follett 1966 makes the same point more briefly: "*prior to* carries with it the idea of necessary precedence." This restricted use of *prior to* turns up in the following examples:

> If guards are to be used, arrangements must exist prior to the emergency —Mary Margaret Hughes, *Security World,* May 1968

> . . . make it mandatory for every passenger to be fluoroscoped prior to boarding a plane —*American Labor,* September 1968

> . . . a high-precision device that permits accurate positioning of the patient prior to exposure to the actual treatment —*Annual Report, CIT Financial Corp.,* 1970

> . . . her appointment would be terminated as of September 29, unless prior to that time she requested a hearing —*AAUP Bulletin,* September 1971

> . . . if page makeup decisions are verified and approved prior to typesetting, proofreading of pages afterward becomes unnecessary —*Publishers Weekly,* 3 Dec. 1979

However, uses of *prior to* which emphasize the notion of anticipation are in the minority in the Merriam-Webster citation files. We find that *prior to* used simply as a synonym of *before* is more common. The phrase most often appears in rather formal contexts:

> Its main wing is believed to have been built prior to 1669 —*American Guide Series: N.Y. City,* 1939

> Prior to the hurricane of 1893 there was a thriving settlement here —*American Guide Series: Louisiana,* 1941

> Just prior to the beginning of the academic year — Edward M. Kennedy, *Massachusetts Teacher,* April 1965

> . . . prior to Grant's appointment as Commander-in-Chief, three other generals had occupied this post and each had failed —Ralph F. Lewis, *Arthur Young Jour.,* Autumn 1967

> . . . $424,340 was used prior to year-end to purchase 6,463 shares —*Annual Report, Owens-Illinois,* 1970

> Prior to 1776, the Church of England . . . was the established religion of Maryland —Asbury Smith, *Maryland Mag.,* Autumn 1971

> . . . in the centuries prior to their descent on Britain the tribes of north-west Germany were continuously on the move —D. J. V. Fisher, *The Anglo-Saxon Age,* 1973

Although Reader's Digest 1983 says *prior to* is "now accepted at all levels of usage," we lack citations which show its use in informal or personal contexts, where apparently it is avoided. The made-up examples of Krapp 1927 ("He always drinks a glass of milk prior to retiring") and Follett ("She twisted her ankle prior to getting home") seem not to be representative of actual usage. The evidence indicates that *prior to* does have formal connotations, but we do not agree with the commentators that *before* is always a better choice. In a formal or impersonal context *prior to* is perfectly appropriate.

See also PREPARATORY 2; PREVIOUS TO.

pristine *Pristine* is a 16th-century word meaning "belonging to the earliest state or period; original." In this sense it can be applied to what is not desirable as easily as to what is:

> . . . our friend, the Collector, had lost a great deal of his pristine timidity, and was now, especially when fortified with liquor, as talkative as might be —W. M. Thackeray, *Vanity Fair,* 1848

> . . . we have given up a lot of freedom: to knock our neighbor over the head, for instance; or more recently, to raise our children in pristine ignorance —Robert Hatch, *New Republic,* 1 Aug. 1949

> . . . what might be called a pristine vulgarity is largely outlawed —Louis Kronenberger, *American Scholar,* Winter 1951–1952

But it has long been a tendency of civilized people to admire a simpler and unsullied past. The supposition is that when things were in their oldest or original state, they were better:

> If a picture had darkened into an indistinct shadow through time and neglect, . . . she seemed to possess the faculty of seeing it in its pristine glory —Nathaniel Hawthorne, *The Marble Faun,* 1860

> It seems that once upon a time the universe was all tidy, with everything in its proper place, and that ever since it has been growing more and more disorderly, until nothing but a drastic spring-cleaning can restore it to its pristine order —Bertrand Russell, *The Scientific Outlook,* 1931

> . . . he gives his themes the pristine quality they must have had when they were the living substance of the cultures that produced them —Anthony West, *New Yorker,* 5 Dec. 1953

> . . . a heritage of pristine virtues to be restored and defended against modern sophistications —*Times Literary Supp.,* 4 May 1967

It is then but a small step to uses in which the notion of "unspoiled, uncorrupted, unpolluted" is primary and the notion of "original, earliest" is secondary:

> . . . in so far as men attain this emotional union they are merely reverting to a pristine felicity —Irving Babbitt, *The New Laokoon,* 1910

> The region was still naturally pristine, essentially unspoiled —Hervey Allen, *Bedford Village,* 1944

> Polynesian life was nicely pristine before the rush of European adventurers and missionaries —*Newsweek,* 7 May 1956

> No one could possibly have believed that . . . Niagara Falls could lose its pristine clearness and fume like brown smoke —Lord Ritchie-Calder, *Center Mag.,* May 1969

> . . . a number of pristine white communities accepted some token black residents —Gerald D. Suttles, *Annals of the Association of American Geographers,* December 1981

> Again, the Nishis of 1944 are introduced as pristine tribals "unaffected by any contact. . . ." —Nicholas J. Allen, *Times Literary Supp.,* 11 Feb. 1983

What is unspoiled or uncontaminated may connote the freshness and cleanness of something that has just been made:

> The pristine light and the loud singing reminded her of some ideal—some simple way of life —John Cheever, *New Yorker,* 16 Apr. 1955

> . . . the pristine freshness that the night air on Broadway has when one leaves the auditorium —Winthrop Sargeant, *New Yorker,* 25 Dec. 1955

> . . . the snow which is pristine powder —*Holiday,* February 1957

> The books had never been read. It was likely, from their stiff pristine condition, that they had not been opened since leaving the hands of the bookbinder —Ellery Queen, *Origin of Evil,* 1951

> One of the grubbiest little gardening books in my bookshelves is a first edition of *Simple Propagation.* . . . Now a pristine, enlarged third edition stands beside it —Tony Venison, *Country Life,* 8 Apr. 1976

> The architecture and the landscape work superbly here: the entire environment is so crisp and pristine it feels as if it could be within a computer —Paul Goldberger, *N.Y. Times,* 1 May 1980

The two extended senses have come under some critical fire, mostly from British commentators, ostensibly on the grounds of etymology. The OED Supplement, however, shows the extensions to have been of 20th-century American origin (our files contain no contradictory evidence), and it is quite likely the American origin that primarily disturbs the British commentators.

Our most recent evidence shows that the original sense and both its extensions are in current standard use on both sides of the Atlantic.

probe Bremner 1980, Copperud 1964, 1970, 1980, and Flesch 1964 all disapprove of *probe* used as a noun to mean "investigation" or a verb to mean "investigate"; the use, they assert, was born in newspaper headlines and ought not to extend beyond them. This theory of origin can be found in Utter 1916 and in an OED Supplement citation for 1903. However, both of these sources are referring only to the noun, and for the noun, the theory seems to be plausible—the OED has only one 19th-century figurative use of the noun that does not involve prodding. But figurative use of the verb to mean "to search into, look into," even "to interrogate," dates back to the middle of the 17th century. The newspapers in this instance merely took over a well-established sense for a somewhat specialized application.

The trouble with the criticism is that it takes no account of the widespread figurative uses of both verb and noun in kinds of writing other than headlines. Dictionaries have recognized these uses for a long time. Here is a sampling—first of the verb, then of the noun:

> . . . a citizens committee . . . which had been appointed to probe corruption in government —*Current Biography,* April 1967

> . . . went on to get his M.D. at Harvard while continuing to probe the minuscule world of the insect —Isaac Asimov, *Think,* May–June 1967

> . . . indefatigably probed the North Korean political climate —Howard L. Boorman, *N.Y. Times Book Rev.,* 22 Apr. 1973

> Republican analysts probe the Catholic vote —Richard Reeves, *Harper's,* January 1972

> . . . to probe into the basic objectives and methods of higher education —Jerome Evans, *Change,* September 1971

> . . . market analysts, always probing for what people would wish to buy —Martin Mayer, *Cosmopolitan,* February 1973

> . . . violinist . . . whose musical sensibility probes to the very depths of the work —Thor Eckert, Jr., *Christian Science Monitor,* 26 Oct. 1979

> . . . it is possible that unmanned spaceships will probe beyond the limits of the Solar System —Myron G. H. Ligda, in *Astronautics for Science Teachers,* ed. John G. Meitner, 1965

> . . . broadening the probe to cover construction labor and management practices —*Business Week,* 26 May 1975

> . . . the probe into the nursing home industry —radio newscast, 15 Aug. 1979

> Later that year in *A Sense of Loss,* he gave us a personality probe of those involved in the troubles that beset Northern Ireland —Judith Crist, *Saturday Rev.,* 16 Oct. 1976

> . . . a series of probes begun by NASA in 1961 to study the characteristics of the moon —*Current Biography,* February 1968

These uses are all perfectly standard.

proceed 1. See PRECEDE, PROCEED.
2. *Proceed, procedure.* Note the spelling. A few commentators point out that the verb is sometimes misspelled *procede* (using the ending of *precede*) and the noun is misspelled *proceedure.* We have examples of both misspellings, so one needs to be alert.
3. Janis 1984 and Copperud 1964, 1970, 1980 seem to believe that *proceed* can mean only "to go forward." Where this notion originated, we have no idea. Look at any good desk dictionary, or an unabridged dictionary, or the OED to see the variety of meanings this word can have.

procure This word is pompous (or pretentious) for *get,* say Flesch 1964, Copperud 1964, 1970, 1980, and Janis 1984. A better description of many uses would be *literary:*

> . . . felt grateful, as well she might, for the chance which had procured her such a friend —Jane Austen, *Northanger Abbey,* 1818

> Some gifted spirit on our side procured (probably by larceny) a length of mine fuse —H. G. Wells, *Mr. Britling Sees It Through,* 1916

It is also used for official procurement, especially of such things as armaments:

> . . . his program of building up the armed services and procuring arms for them —William L. Shirer, *The Rise and Fall of the Third Reich,* 1960

In less exalted contexts it suggests care and effort:

> . . . the task of procuring men for the openings now available —Archibald MacLeish, letter, 9 May 1917

She has the boss to dinner, ... procures the proper tennis, golf, and backgammon players for Harold's leisure hours —Lyn Tornabene, *Cosmopolitan,* April 1973

Procure is not an everyday substitute for *get* or *obtain,* but it has its uses and need not be consistently avoided.

prodigal 1. The adjective *prodigal* is frequently used with *of:*

... like a lovely woman graciously prodigal of her charm and beauty —W. Somerset Maugham, *The Moon and Sixpence,* 1919

Wildly prodigal of color, the new sun then sketched a wide band of throbbing red-gold —F. Van Wyck Mason, *Himalayan Assignment,* 1952

She had been prodigal of all her resources, money and energy and imaginative strategems —Katherine Anne Porter, *The Never-Ending Wrong,* 1977

Prodigal is also commonly followed by *with:*

He had always been prodigal with his whistle, tooting it for children's birthday parties —John Cheever, *The Wapshot Chronicle,* 1957

... excludes the debilitating habit of some state courts of being too prodigal with rehearing —Felix Frankfurter, in *Aspects of American Government,* ed. Sydney D. Bailey, 1950

It has also been used sometimes with *as to* or *in:*

Masterfully economical as to words, Mr. Saroyan is ... almost recklessly prodigal as to feeling —Elizabeth Bowen, *New Republic,* 9 Mar. 1953

Nor will posterity censure the present age for having been too prodigal in its applause of this great man —Joseph Wood Krutch, *Samuel Johnson,* 1944

2. Bryson 1984 and Harper 1975, 1985 say that many people think *prodigal* means "wandering" or "tending to stray" because they associate it with the New Testament parable of the prodigal son who, having received his inheritance, "took his journey into a far country, and there wasted his substance with riotous living" (Luke 15:13, AV). The son returned, repentant, and was welcomed back by his father, who killed the fatted calf in celebration.

Our files do not show the adjective being used to mean "wandering." The usage, if it exists, may be primarily oral, or perhaps the idea has been oversimplified in the usage books. The OED includes a sense under the noun *prodigal* that covers the many meanings the word can have when it is used in allusion to the parable. The examples there all reflect one aspect or another of the parable—especially that of the repentant sinner welcomed home—and not just the "wasteful" meaning of the adjective. We have some recent allusive examples, but all are for the noun or for the adjective in the compounds *prodigal son* and *prodigal daughter.*

... stared at the prodigal who had come home to her —Priscilla Johnson McMillan, excerpt in *Book Digest,* February 1978

... she was received into her mother's household as a prodigal daughter —John Updike, *N.Y. Times Book Rev.,* 23 Feb. 1986

I used it again on this visit home, leaving it behind as an offering at the bier from a prodigal son —Harry S. Ashmore, *Center Mag.,* May 1968

... had been dropped for six months, then returned, a prodigal son, to the BBC, all forgiven and forgotten —Janice Elliott, *Angels Falling,* 1969

These uses echo the parable and do not necessarily imply extravagance or wastefulness. Such use dates back to Shakespeare in 1596 and Ben Jonson in 1601 and, while apparently not especially common, would appear to be entirely legitimate. But it seems not to be the use Harper and Bryson are talking about.

productive When used with a preposition, *productive* is usually followed by *of:*

Their knowledge and methods were enormously productive of new weapons and devices of war —James Phinney Baxter 3d, *Scientists Against Time,* 1946

He is also aware that Congressional investigating committees have been productive of much good —Robert K. Carr, *N.Y. Times Book Rev.,* 27 Feb. 1955

... hunting in the neighborhood is nearly always productive of the permitted quota of game —*American Guide Series: Maine,* 1937

proficient *Proficient,* when used with a preposition, usually takes *in* or *at:*

... proficient in the art of self-defence —George Bernard Shaw, *Cashel Byron's Profession,* 1886

While in college he was proficient in mathematics and philosophy —*Dictionary of American Biography,* 1929

This captain must be an experienced person, trained and proficient in his job —F. Glen Nesbitt, *Sperryscope,* Fourth Quarter 1954

Jane began to type. It bored her, but she was fairly proficient at it —Rose Macaulay, *Potterism,* 1920

Occasionally *proficient* is used with *on:*

While he was a student he also became proficient on the guitar —*Current Biography,* July 1966

profit The verb *profit* is followed most often by *from* when it takes a prepositional-phrase complement:

Scholarship would profit greatly from a more painstaking examination of manuscripts —Eugene S. McCartney, *Recurrent Maladies in Scholarly Writing,* 1953

... his battle descriptions would sometimes have profited from consultation of the official records —Lynn Montross, *N.Y. Times Book Rev.,* 19 Sept. 1954

... both Hawthorne and Thoreau profited more from their acquaintanceship than has been generally allowed —Earle Labor, *CEA Critic,* January 1971

Almost as frequently, *profit* is used with *by:*

... their descendants, who profited by the industrial development —*American Guide Series: Michigan,* 1941

... whenever Miss Clark lets herself go her book profits by it —Sean O'Faolain, *Books of the Month,* April 1953

... should get as much liberal education as he can intellectually absorb and profit by —Cormac Philip, *CEA Critic,* November 1954

progressive passive   Jane Austen in a letter (8 Feb. 1807) wrote "Our Dressing-Table is constructing on the spot. . . ." If she were writing today she would say "Our dressing-table is being constructed on the spot. . . ." The verb phrase *is being constructed* is an example of what is referred to as the progressive passive—a passive verb construction that indicates an ongoing process. Today no one thinks twice about the progressive passive, but a century ago it was the source of considerable controversy.

The construction was widely apprehended as new in the 19th century and a number of 19th-century commentators—George Perkins Marsh 1859, Alford 1866, Richard Grant White 1870, for instance—objected to it. (Hall 1917 lists several other lesser-known grammarians too.) It was apparently just coming into widespread use in the early 19th century; White claimed that it started with Southey in 1795; Fitzedward Hall 1873 found examples from 1779. Hall, who called the construction the *imperfect passive,* wrote extensively on the subject, and his numerous examples seem to have turned the tide in favor of accepting the construction. Ayres 1881, for example, reprints an entire 10-page article by Hall. J. Lesslie Hall 1917 may have had the last word on the subject. He found examples from the 15th century and from the early 17th century; it was his opinion that this construction had been long available but did not come into common use until the later 18th century. Since Hall 1917, no one has had much to say about it. It is good to know that some old usage issues do fade away at last.

prohibit   A number of fairly recent books—Freeman 1983, Longman 1984, Copperud 1970, 1980—insist that *prohibit* should not be followed by *to* and an infinitive. This prohibitory admonition goes back through Partridge 1942 to Fowler 1926. The construction with *to* and the infinitive seems to be the original construction for *prohibit* in this particular sense. The earliest example in the OED is from Lord Berners, doing a little promotional work in the preface to his translation of Froissart's *Chronicles.* The doughty knight was explaining all the advantages that come from reading history; he notes how it makes young men equal to old men in prudence, and how it moves rulers and governors to do noble deeds, and so on and so on:

... and it prohibiteth reprovable persons to do mischievous deeds, for fear of infamy and shame — 1523

The OED, having no examples of this construction later than the middle of the 18th century, supposed the construction archaic. Actually it appears to be one of those banes of the lexicographer, the low-frequency item. It had not, in fact, quite disappeared:

... they are prohibited to add new names —H. C. Burdick, *Sales Promotion by Mail,* 1916

H. W. Fowler 1926 culled two examples from British newspapers. Taking the OED's *archaic* label to be an absolute, he decided that his modern examples must, therefore, be violations of idiom. Fowler himself must

have used the *prohibit from* followed by an *-ing* construction that he prescribed. This construction, which is the common one in present-day English, is only attested in the OED from about 1840.

... prohibiting anyone working for the commission from having any financial interest in a strip mining operation —Marion Edey, *Not Man Apart,* July 1971

... are prohibited from taking any job that involves contact or dealings with the government —Anthony Bailey, *New Yorker,* 20 Nov. 1971

Prohibit may also be followed by a noun or gerund direct object; no one has disputed these constructions:

... prohibited the employment of workers under 16 —*American Guide Series: North Carolina,* 1939

... family finances prohibited his going to college — *Current Biography 1953*

Prohibit from can also be followed by a noun:

... it should not be prohibited from prayer — George Bush, radio interview, 23 Aug. 1984

The dispute over the propriety of *prohibit to* followed by an infinitive boils down to this: it is the older idiom and if it has not fallen completely into disuse, it is certainly seldom used. *Prohibit from* followed by a gerund is the usual construction now.

prolegomenon, prolegomena   *Prolegomenon* is the singular and *prolegomena* the plural form of this scholarly word, which means "prefatory remarks" or, more specifically, "a formal essay or critical discussion serving to introduce and interpret an extended work." It is also used in a broader sense to refer generally to something that serves as an introduction.

As is the case with its much commoner brethren *criterion* and *phenomenon,* the irregular plural form of *prolegomenon* may be mistaken for a singular by some English speakers. Another complicating factor is the meaning of the word, which simultaneously encompasses a singular and a plural notion, as you can see from the definitions above. The dual nature of the word is attributable to the use of *Prolegomena* in the title of noteworthy scholarly and philosophical works, such as Friedrich August Wolf's *Prolegomena ad Homerum* (1795) and Immanuel Kant's *Prolegomena to Any Future Metaphysics Which Will Be Able to Come Forth as Science* (1783), which not unnaturally came to be referred to as Kant's *Prolegomena.* People then started to think of *prolegomena* as denoting both a single work and the remarks included in it. At the same time, many of these scholarly folk realized that *prolegomenon* was the singular form of the word.

As a result, we find that when the context gives no clue to the singular or plural number of the word, *prolegomenon* and *prolegomena* are used with about equal frequency. Some writers hark back to an earlier *Prolegomena,* others use *prolegomenon* to show that they recognize it as the singular form, and the rest probably just use the form they happen to know.

... it provides the best prolegomenon to *Comus* which any modern reader could have —T. S. Eliot, *Sewanee Rev.,* Spring 1948

... Mead has not presented us with a "metaphysic of time"; let us say, instead, that he has given us the prolegomenon to such a metaphysic —Maurice Natanson, *Jour. of Philosophy,* 3 Dec. 1953

... included the following passage in the prolegomenon to his treatise, *De Jure Belli ac Pacis,* written in 1625 —Jon M. Van Dyke, *Center Mag.,* July/August 1971

... a critical and exegetical edition ... with learned prolegomena, critical notes, and ample commentary —*Dictonary of American Biography,* 1928

... whose *Art of Spiritual Harmony,* written in 1910, is the prolegomena to what ... I am calling metaphysical painting —Herbert Read, *The Philosophy of Modern Art,* 1952

The book developed out of the prolegomena to a work on Shakespeare's dramatic structure —E. T. Sehrt, *Modern Language Notes,* November 1955

And while we do have citations in which *prolegomenon* is clearly construed as a singular and *prolegomena* is clearly construed as a plural, we also have a few examples in our files in which *prolegomena* is used in a singular construction.

Semiotic offers a challenge to philosophy; it is indeed a "prolegomena to any future philosophy," ... —Charles Morris, *Signs, Language, and Behavior,* 1946

... a valuable philosophical prolegomena to a sound theological understanding of the Christian faith —Theodore M. Greene, *Scientific Monthly,* May 1954

The book served as a stepping stone, or as Payne-Gaposchkin preferred to think of it, a prolegomena —Elske V. P. Smith, *Physics Today,* June 1980

We do not, by the way, have citations for *prolegomenon* used as a plural or for a plural form *prolegomenons.* This strengthens the argument that the use of *prolegomena* as a singular is not merely caused by confusion over a foreign ending but is influenced by the *Prolegomena* of past writers. So those who use *prolegomena* as a singular and are accused of ignorance may defend themselves on the grounds that they know too much rather than too little. Those who use *prolegomenon* as a singular and *prolegomena* as a plural will be immune from criticism. And those who come across the word and do not have the foggiest notion of what it means will have a lot of company.

For other foreign plurals, see LATIN PLURALS.

promise   Vizetelly 1906 objects to the verb *promise* in the sense of "assure." "A promise always implies futurity," he says. The same objection finds more recent voice in Shaw 1987 and Longman 1984.

The sense of *promise* under criticism here is pretty old—the OED dates it back to 1469. Shakespeare used it:

I do not like thy look, I promise thee —*Much Ado About Nothing,* 1599

The OED also has quotations from Addison, Fielding, and Thackeray. After Thackeray in 1862 there seems to be nothing. The OED suspected the sense to be archaic; so did the editors of Webster's Third. But Vizetelly must have seen or heard it somewhere, and so must Shaw and the editors of Longman 1984. But where?

The answer seems to be that the usage has receded into speech only. The OED examples are mostly of a colloquial nature—they represent speech, or are found in writing that has speechlike qualities. We have but a single modern example. It, too, is taken from speech, that of a small-town American school superintendent:

She has promised me that the father is not a student —in *People,* 17 Jan. 1983

It appears, then, that instead of being archaic, this use still exists to a certain extent in British and American speech. You can forget the notion that *promise* has to refer to the future. That consideration seems to have been invented by Vizetelly, and it certainly never bothered Shakespeare or Addison or Fielding or Thackeray. But note that this sense of *promise* is not used in current ordinary discursive prose.

prone, supine   Quite a few commentators insist on the distinction that *prone* means "face down" and *supine* means "face up." Harper 1975, for instance, says "It is impossible for a man to 'lie *prone* on his back.' *Prone* means 'face downward.' If he is lying on his back, he is *supine.*" The first part of that assertion is somewhat dubious, as we shall see.

John Simon's pun that "when it comes to learning good English, most people are prone to be supine" (Simon 1980) points to one of the influences operating on the meanings of these words: the chief uses of both *prone* and *supine* have nothing to do with physical position. *Prone* is used chiefly in the sense of "having a tendency or inclination," as in "prone to worry" or "accident-prone." *Supine* is used chiefly in the sense of "mentally or morally slack." The senses that relate to physical position, then, are secondary.

Supine itself also complicates the situation. It is a relatively rare word: in Merriam-Webster files *prone* is nearly five times as frequent as *supine* and in the Brown University Corpus (Kučera & Francis, 1967) there are 14 *prone*'s to a single *supine.* It is clearly a less well-known word, and it is more bookish or literary than *prone.*

A third factor is the use of *prone,* at least since the 18th century, with inanimate objects having no identifiable ventral surface, such as ancient towers or obelisks. In these uses *prone* contrasts with *upright* and simply means "lying flat"; the relative position on the ground is not a consideration:

The third (obelisk) which had also lain prone for a thousand years —Emil Ludwig, *The Nile,* 1937

I joyfully swish my feet through the prone golden autumn harvest of leaves —Michael P. O'Connor, *Irish Digest,* April 1955

A fourth factor is the pejorative overtones of the most frequently used sense of *supine.* One that is supine is usually looked down on in some fashion, as the Simon quotation suggests.

Given these four factors, it is not surprising that *prone* is used more loosely than some would wish in describing persons and objects having a discernible front and back.

Everybody seems to agree that *supine* means "lying face upward," but only a few writers actually use it in general or literary contexts:

Foxy, in a ... maternity swimsuit, lay supine on a smooth rock, eyes shut, smiling —John Updike, *Couples,* 1968

Prone is regularly distinguished from *supine* in medical and physiological writing, where the distinction is a very important one. *Prone* regularly means lying on one's belly to those who shoot guns and write about it, but *supine* appears to be unknown to them.

Outside these contexts, *prone* is sometimes used when the orientation of the body is uncertain, unknown, or unimportant:

> ... I caught sight of the large prone figure in bed — D. H. Lawrence, *The White Peacock,* 1911

> I too have been prone on my couch this week, a victim of the common cold —Flannery O'Connor, letter, 20 Mar. 1961

It is even sometimes used when a human being is clearly flat on the back:

> He lies prone, his face to the sky, his hat rolling to the wall —James Joyce, *Ulysses,* 1922

When you consider all these uses, it is clear that in relation to physical position *prone* most often means flat on one's belly, quite often means merely flat or prostrate, and less frequently flat on one's back. It is possible that the choice of *prone* in this third case may be influenced by a desire to avoid the notion of passiveness connoted by *supine;* while such might have been the case with James Joyce, it is probable that nothing more than the relative rarity of *supine* works against its selection in other instances.

If you are about to use *prone* to describe physical position, you are unimpeachably safe if an animate object is face down, or if you are describing an inanimate object. If your prone person or animal is belly up, you might incur the wrath of some critic. If that prospect displeases, you may want to use *flat* or *prostrate* instead. The expression "prone on one's back" is the one most likely to attract unfavorable notice.

If your main concern is getting across the point that whoever or whatever is described as prone is lying face down, you should supply some additional clue to that intention in the context, since *prone* can also refer to other positions. Your reader has no certain way of divining your distinction unless you reinforce it in the context.

See also PROSTRATE.

pronoun agreement See AGREEMENT, PRONOUN: NOUNS JOINED BY AND, OR.

pronounce When *pronounce* is used with a preposition, generally it is found with *on* or *upon*. Both Raub 1897 and Bernstein 1965 (neither of whom mention *pronounce upon*) prescribe *on* with a thing; Bernstein allows only *against* with a person. Although *pronounce on* usually has a thing as its object, at times it does have a person. *Pronounce upon* occurs more often in British English than in American English.

> "What would uncle Egmont have said of Lawrence Leffert's pronouncing on anybody's social position? . . ." —Edith Wharton, *The Age of Innocence,* 1920

> The Speaker was twice required to pronounce on the question of free speech —Guy Eden, *Punch,* 11 Mar. 1953

> . . . I found Sonia . . . pronouncing on various writers she knew —David Plante, *Difficult Women,* 1983

> Whatever he has pronounced himself upon—linguistics, genetics, . . . painting—his words have at once had the authority of holy writ —Malcolm Muggeridge, *Punch,* 11 Mar. 1953

> ... the United States, where the courts habitually pronounce upon the constitutionality of statutes — Frederic A. Ogg & Harold Zink, *Modern Foreign Governments,* 1949

> ... his desire to influence others, to pronounce upon questions ... of the day —Roy Jenkins, *The Times* (London), 19 Nov. 1973

Pronounce also occurs, though less frequently, with *in favor of* or its counterpart *against:*

> ... when civil war seemed inevitable he pronounced himself decidedly in favor of the Union —*Dictionary of American Biography,* 1929

> ... liberal platforms regularly pronounce in favor of more vigorous anti-trust enforcement —Carl Kaysen, *New Republic,* 22 Nov. 1954

> Receive it from me then: war and confusion
> In Caesar's name pronounce I 'gainst thee
> —Shakespeare, *Cymbeline,* 1610

> From his pinnacle of power . . . Nikita Krushchev . . . has pronounced against skyscrapers —Flora Lewis, *N. Y. Times Mag.,* 3 Apr. 1955

Pronounce is also found occasionally with *about:*

> ... when my friends pronounce responsibly about the values of creative work —William Stafford, *Writing the Australian Crawl,* 1978

Although these uses of *pronounce* with various prepositions are usually intransitive, uses with a reflexive pronoun as direct object are found, the examples from Muggeridge and Ryden above being typical.

pronouns 1. English pronouns seem to be the source of many vexing usage problems. A few will be touched on here, but most of the ones that have generated considerable comment are treated at their own places. We refer you then to BETWEEN YOU AND I; BUT; I; IT'S ME; ME; MYSELF; ONE OF THOSE WHO; THAN; THAT; THEY, THEIR, THEM; WHO, WHOM; YOU; and to the several articles at AGREEMENT, many of which treat questions about pronouns.

2. It is sometimes useful to remember that we have several kinds of pronouns. People reminded of pronouns may think only of the personal pronouns, in their nominative, objective, and possessive forms, and maybe the reflexive pronouns based on the personal pronouns. But we also have relative pronouns, demonstrative pronouns, and indefinite pronouns. There are also interrogative pronouns, if you wish, although these are really just some of the relative pronouns doing extra duty.

Remembering the variety of pronouns will help keep you from making generalizations like "Every pronoun necessarily has an antecedent" (Barzun 1985). Barzun's statement (which, to be fair, is made in the context of an example that lacks a needed antecedent) is an overgeneralization. Indefinite pronouns, for instance, do not require an antecedent.

3. One of the favorite pastimes of writers on usage is to find examples of pronouns that are in the objective case when they should be in the nominative, or are in the nominative when they should be in the objective. Sometimes a worried commentator will deduce from the frequency of such examples that the language is deteriorating or that illiteracy is about to overwhelm us or that our educational system is a complete failure. Beyond the likelihood that the educational system has failed to explain pronouns adequately to many people, the wor-

ries are without a sound basis. The use of object forms where subject forms belong, and vice versa, has been going on for hundreds of years.

It was, for instance, common in the 17th century to interchange the nominative and objective forms of the second person plural pronoun, *ye* and *you,* with the result that eventually the objective *you* replaced *ye* altogether. Interchange of nominative and objective forms of other pronouns was also anything but rare; Wyld 1920, for instance, gives this quotation from Sir John Suckling: "What have they to do with you and I?" You can find a good deal on the subject in historical grammars—Jespersen 1909–49, Henry Sweet's *A New English Grammar* (1892), and Wyld 1920, among others.

Quirk et al. 1985 notes that these interchanges of nominative and objective forms actually occur only in a limited number of constructions. The first of these is the use of the objective case where traditional normative grammar calls for the nominative after *be* or *as* and *than.* The rule calling for the nominative is based on analogy with Latin; the use of the objective comes from the influence of the rules of normal word order in English. In English, the nominative is required only in the subject position directly before the verb; the objective tends to be used everywhere else, as if the objective were the unmarked case form to be used everywhere there are no positive reasons for using the nominative. In this respect modern English is much like French. Besides those positions already mentioned, the objective form tends to be chosen in absolute and emphatic uses:

Who said that? Me.

Me—afraid of flying?

Better them than us —Don Baylor, quoted in *Springfield* (Mass.) *Daily News,* 13 Oct. 1986

There is no question that these constructions, and "It's me" and the rest, would never have been anything but unexceptionable had not our earliest grammarians been so heavily influenced by Latin.

We next come to two separate constructions involving coordination, usually with *and.* The first is characteristic of less educated English, or, as it is delicately put these days, non-mainstream varieties of English. This is the use of the objective case before the verb when the pronoun is coordinated with a noun or another pronoun:

Me and my baby goes back and sleeps the day — anonymous speaker, quoted in Walt Wolfram, *Appalachian Speech,* 1976

Quirk says that the objective pronoun can even occur in the position next to the verb. Wolfram notes that the objective pronoun does not occur by itself in subject position, only in combination with another noun or pronoun.

The second coordinated pairing—which one of our correspondents has named "the Someone and I syndrome"—occurs in rather more educated varieties of English. Here we find a nominative pronoun coordinated with a noun or another pronoun and occurring in the object position after a preposition or after a verb. *I* is the most common pronoun in such pairs, but others such as *he* and *she* are also found:

Now Margaret's curse is fall'n upon our heads,
When she exclaimed on Hastings, you, and I . . .
    —Shakespeare, *Richard III,* 1593

. . . invited my love and I —Lady Strafford, letter, 1734 (in Wyld 1920)

It must all light upon Heartfree and I —Sir John Vanbrugh, *The Provok'd Wife,* 1697 (OED)

. . . a most furious conflict between Sir W. Pen and I —Samuel Pepys, diary, 21 Feb. 1667

. . . the poet, like you and I, dear reader —W. H. Auden, quoted in *Time,* 2 Feb. 1948

Louise and I gave it to he and she last Christmas — James Thurber, quoting his cousin, letter, 25 June 1956

According to both he and Sam, my donkey act . . . had quite an effect —Oliver North, quoted in *The Tower Commission Report,* 1987

In this construction, *someone and I* is treated as a polite fixed unit, to be used either in subject or object position. Several recent commentators ascribe this usage to hypercorrection—the overly cautious use of the nominative pronoun because it is prescribed in such constructions as "It is I." (See HYPERCORRECTION.) But the early appearance of the construction, with such 16th- and 17th-century exemplars as Shakespeare, Suckling, Pepys, and Vanbrugh, antedates the teaching of English grammar. (For a modern and more linguistically oriented explanation of *someone and I,* see the brief treatment of Chomsky's analysis at BETWEEN YOU AND I.)

Another linkage that produces case confusion is the pronoun in apposition to a noun. This combination frequently produces objective forms in subject positions where the pronoun is emphasized:

Us Valley Girls have to endure a lot —letter to the editor, *People,* 13 Sept. 1982

It may be the influence of hypercorrection in avoiding the subjective *us girls* that leads to the nominative in apposition following a preposition:

At last—a sherry for we Amontillado connoisseurs —advt., quoted in Howard 1978

We ultimately commune with others of our own faith, and for we westerners, nature is an article out of another faith —Paul Gruchow, *Update* (Univ. of Minn.), October 1985

The last of the problem environments mentioned by Quirk et al. is the pronoun that seems to lie between two clauses; this pronoun is often drawn toward both the nominative and objective forms by reason of its different relationships to the preceding and following parts of the sentence. Usage is decidedly mixed:

It was she (her?) John criticized —in Quirk et al.

Everything comes to him who waits —English proverb

Just as the ideal of even-handed justice for all can be somewhat tilted toward he who can afford to argue the rightness of his case —*Globe and Mail* (Toronto), 8 Oct. 1982, quoted in Greenbaum 1985

I'm against whoever is in office —*And More by Andy Rooney,* 1982

They can't decide where to fight or who to salute — *N.Y. Times,* 20 Feb. 1987

But it were vain for you and I
In single fight our strength to try.
—William E. Aytoun, "Bothwell,"
1856 (in Alford 1866)

. . . the reporter whom Mr. Friendly said had been
given the secret plan —*N.Y. Times,* 17 Feb. 1987

Some of these examples follow the dictates of traditional
grammar, and others do not. But you can see how each
of them is tugged in two directions at once.

pronoun with possessive antecedent   Bernstein
1971 has an article under this heading in which he
quotes from three books a rule applying to the construction; stated most baldly it goes "a pronoun cannot take
as an antecedent a noun in the possessive case." Bernstein is not very impressed by the cogency of the rule,
and he is right not to be, but it can be found enunciated
in other handbooks—in Barzun 1985, Simon 1980, and
Ebbitt & Ebbitt 1982, for instance.

We have not discovered where this rule originated,
but it is likely to have been with one of those 18th-cen-
tury appliers of logic to language. We get a hint of this
sort of origin from Barzun:

. . . there can be no logical link between a proper
name in the possessive case and a personal pronoun.
"Wellington's victory at Waterloo made him the
greatest name in Europe" is all askew, because there
is in fact no person named for the *him* to refer to.

Right away you can see something missing from this
analysis. In the first place, you have no trouble understanding the sentence; if it is illogical, at least its meaning is as plain as day. Second, you can see that the whole
problem can easily be removed by changing *him* to *his*
and greatly increasing the elegance of the sentence. But
wait—isn't *his* a personal pronoun too? Yes, but at least
it's in the possessive case and matches *Wellington's.* It
must be all right for a possessive pronoun to refer to a
possessive noun, proper or not:

. . . Bob Tizzy . . . filed St. Boniface's nose smooth
with his face —W. M. Thackeray, *The Book of
Snobs,* 1846

Your daughter's feet are nearly ruined by her shoes
—Paula Fox, *A Servant's Tale,* 1984

Clearly the objection has to be to a pronoun in some
other case referring to a noun in the possessive case.
That can be viewed as illogical. But this sort of logic
(which is only Latin grammar in disguise) does little
more than impose an unnecessary burden on the writer.
When the reader clearly understands what is written,
what more logic is needed? The reader knows that Wellington is in the writer's mind even if, as Barzun contends, he is not technically there in the sentence. The
reader ignores the technicalities, understands, and reads
on. A kind of notional agreement has been in operation.
Bernstein quotes the first of his three sources to the
effect that the rule is little respected by writers. A little
looking around shows that indeed it is not:

It was Mr. Squeers's custom to call the boys together
and make a sort of report, after every half-yearly
visit to the metropolis, regarding the relations and
friends he had seen —Charles Dickens, *Nicholas
Nickleby,* 1839

. . . shaking Snooks's hand cordially, we rush on to
the pier, waving him a farewell —W. M. Thackeray,
The Book of Snobs, 1846

Strafford's enemies were in deadly earnest, because
while he lived they and all they strove for were in
jeopardy —G. M. Trevelyan, *A Shortened History of
England,* 1942

My father tried valiantly to wrest Pittsburgh Phil's
title from him —Frank Sullivan, *The Night the Old
Nostalgia Burned Down,* 1953

. . . played on Hull's mounting fear that he and his
men would be cut off —James MacGregor Burns,
The Vineyard of Liberty, 1981

I just hope the people who make up the President's
schedule don't arrange any more breakfast meetings
for him —*And More by Andy Rooney,* 1982

Ebbitt & Ebbitt 1982 has an example of the construction
in which the relative pronoun *who* refers to the possessive antecedent. The example is awkward indeed, to the
point of sounding rather implausible. Yet we have a
genuine example of the construction; it is old and similarly awkward-sounding, but still easily understandable.

I do not at all mean to detract from Garrick's merit,
who was a real genius in his way —Horace Walpole,
letter, 1 Feb. 1779

Bernstein says the rule can be ignored where it does
not interfere with sense. We agree. But we would not
recommend Walpole's construction, which sounds awkward to the modern ear.

propellant, propellent   The editors of the OED entered only the *-ent* spelling, but three quarters of their
citations were spelled *-ant.* The OED Supplement says
the *-ant* spelling is now the most common for both
adjective and noun. Our evidence shows that the word
is used primarily in technical contexts and is much
more often a noun than an adjective. The *-ant* spelling
predominates. Our most recent evidence for the *-ent*
spelling comes primarily from British sources.

prophecy, prophesy   A surprising amount of ink has
been used in a surprising number of handbooks to
inform everyone that *prophecy* is a noun and *prophesy*
is a verb—the very information carried in every dictionary. The common assertion is that the two words are
confused—an assertion our files cannot confirm, even
though we have a 1980 *prophecied* from the *Saturday
Review.* The particular objection seems to be to the use
of *prophesy* as a noun.

The OED shows that historically both spellings have
been used for both functions. Webster's Second recognizes *-cy* for the verb and *-sy* for the noun as infrequent
variants, and so does Webster's Third. Copperud 1970,
1980 reads this recognition as our considering the terms
interchangeable, but that is not the case. The variants
are clearly marked as to their secondary status. Webster's Ninth New Collegiate Dictionary omits the *-cy*
variant of the verb as too rare to warrant inclusion, but
the *-sy* variant of the noun is still there in its secondary
status. At this writing we have had no examples of the
-sy noun since 1967; it may well be omissible from
future desk dictionaries, although the unabridged will
still have to take account of it on historical grounds.

Most writers, then, follow the mainstream and use
prophecy as a noun, and *prophesy* as a verb.

prophesize   Bremner 1980 says this word does not
exist, but it does. It is, however, of such low frequency

in print that it is not eligible for entry even in an unabridged dictionary. We have examples so far from 1966 and 1981, and a local western Massachusetts newspaper not noted for elegant spelling essayed *prophecize* in 1974.

It seems likely that *prophesize* may be primarily a spoken use, perhaps based on a misinterpretation of the present, third singular form *prophesies*. One would suppose that if the confusion between *prophecy* and *prophesy* asserted by the handbooks really existed, *prophesize* would be better attested since it would sidestep the imputed noun–verb confusion.

prophesy   See PROPHECY, PROPHESY.

propitious   *Propitious* is usually used with *for* or *to*. *For* is often followed by a gerund; *to* is often followed by an infinitive.

> Flora's fine eyes, that were so observant, noticed how propitious was this moment for their entry —Stella Gibbons, *Cold Comfort Farm,* 1932

> . . . when the environment was propitious for expanding the role of science and research —Eli Ginzberg, *Columbia Forum,* Fall 1970

> . . . the time might now be propitious for seeking an amelioration of the religious situation —Norman Cousins, *Saturday Rev.,* 30 Oct. 1971

> . . . those journalists who asserted, some years ago, that logical positivism was propitious to fascism —Alfred Jules Ayer, *Encounter,* April 1955

> . . . the French decided that the moment was propitious to declare Viet Nam completely independent —*Time,* 27 Sept. 1954

> . . . felt that the time was propitious to come out into the open —*Collier's Year Book,* 1949

proportion   There are two issues involving *proportion*. The first of these is an American newspaper tradition that seems to have begun with Bierce 1909, and is carried on by Bernstein 1958, 1965, Bremner 1980, and Paul Fussell in the *New Republic* in 1979. This is an objection to *proportion* used in the sense of "size, dimension." It is often plural in this sense. The reason for the objection is said to be that *proportion* expresses a relationship and has nothing to do with size. The argument may seem logical, but it is controverted by usage. The word has been used in the disputed sense at least since the 17th century and in the 19th century was used in this sense by none other than the language precisian Walter Savage Landor.

The sense is, however, considered acceptable by several commentators and the usage panel of Heritage 1969; Bremner and Fussell are holdouts quite in the tradition of Bierce. The sense has been standard all along, but it does not make up a very large part of our evidence for *proportion*. Here are some examples:

> He was fired as a security risk. . . . The anonymity of his discharge gave it oracular proportions —John Cheever, *The Wapshot Chronicle,* 1957

> . . . if there had not been a civil rights movement, or at least not a movement of any proportion —Paul Potter, *Johns Hopkins Mag.,* October 1965

> Three communicable diseases, the CDC declared, posed an unexpected . . . threat of reaching epidemic

proportions —Dodi Schultz, *Ladies' Home Jour.,* August 1971

> . . . it is a symbol of considerable proportions both in the United States and in China —Stanley Karnow, *Saturday Rev.,* 11 Dec. 1976

> . . . hired . . . to disport her generous proportions around swimming pools —James Brady, *Saturday Rev.,* 30 Sept. 1978

The second issue was originally raised by Fowler 1926. He offers a long criticism of *proportion* in a sense meaning "share, part, portion"; his argument is based, apparently, on the same premise as Bierce's objection to the "size" sense—namely, that *proportion* properly expresses a relationship, a ratio. The reasoning is somewhat undermined by the OED, which shows the criticized meaning as the earliest sense in English. Later commentators—Partridge 1942, Flesch 1964, Copperud 1964, 1970, 1980—have repeated Fowler's objection while omitting his reasoning. This sense of the word has slightly more literary use than the first sense objected to.

> . . . traditionally gave their time and a good proportion of their possessions as a matter of course to those dependent upon them —Vita Sackville-West, *The Edwardians,* 1930

> About half the population of Port Anne, and a much higher proportion from the villages disappeared entirely —John Wyndham, *The Kraken Wakes,* 1953

> . . . the greater proportion of these terms have never been taken up by the literary language —John Geipel, *The Viking Legacy,* 1971

> . . . a far smaller proportion were willing to emigrate —Samuel Eliot Morison, *Oxford History of the American People,* 1965

> At the stroke of any midnight in the year a far larger proportion of the population is awake in the United States than in any other place on earth —John Lear, *Saturday Rev.,* 15 Apr. 1972

Both of these uses are entirely standard.

proportional, proportionate, proportionable   Dictionaries, Fowler 1926, and Copperud 1970, 1980 are in substantial agreement that *proportional* and *proportionate* mean the same thing. Copperud observes that *proportional* is the more common word, an observation confirmed by our citational evidence. *Proportional* is the more frequently used one in fixed technical combinations, such as *proportional counter, proportional dividers,* and *proportional representation.* Harper 1975, 1985 sets forth a distinction that "fastidious writers" are supposed to observe; it reserves *proportional* for situations involving a number of things and *proportionate* for only two things. The distinction is not confirmed by our evidence.

Proportionable is a rare word; Fowler mentions it, but no one else does. It has been seldom seen since the 19th century.

proposition   1. *Noun.* Sometime in the 1870s *proposition* acquired a new sense. It originated in the United States and was a sense of broad application, applied variously to contrivances, situations, enterprises, or even people that one had to deal with. About 40 years later the critics discovered the use (only a few years after dictionaries like Webster 1909 and the Century Dictionary's 1909 Supplement had entered it). Comment appears in Utter 1916, MacCracken & Sandison 1917, Whipple 1924, Hyde 1926, Lurie 1927, Krapp 1927, and others of the same period, all of it disapproving.

Proposition had been disapproved before. Ayres 1881 disapproved it in the sense of "proposal" (a sense that has been in use since the 14th century), and a number of later commentators—Powell 1925, for instance—continued his objection. Lincoln Library 1924 and Fowler 1926 rolled both objections into one, a compendious approach followed by such later commentators as Copperud 1970, 1980. An issue that had built up that much impetus by the 1920s was likely to survive, and this one has; it can be found in Bernstein 1962, 1965, Phythian 1979, Macmillan 1982, Watt 1967, and Shaw 1975, 1987, in addition to those already mentioned. Is the censure of 1916–1927 still justified? Recent dictionaries—Webster's Third, the OED Supplement—do not stigmatize the term. You can judge its status for yourself from these early and recent examples:

It looks like the biggest mining proposition on earth —Walter Church, quoted in *N.Y. Evening Sun,* 19 Mar. 1900

This here sleeping proposition is a lottery —Owen Wister, *The Virginian,* 1902

Now, it may occur to some that 33 different scientific bureaus under one head is rather a large proposition —*Congressional Record,* 26 Oct. 1921

... finding ... the valley a most fat and satisfying proposition in the way of garden produce —Mary Wiltshire, *Thursday's Child,* 1925

But marriage is a very complicated proposition —*U.S. Daily,* 23 Aug. 1925

He was absorbed in his own dexterity and in the proposition of trying to deceive a fish with a bird's feather and a bit of hair —John Cheever, *The Wapshot Chronicle,* 1957

The music hall is a worthless proposition economically —Paul Goldberger, *N.Y. Times,* 1 June 1979

... getting a smile from her is a tough proposition —Barry McDermott, *Sports Illustrated,* 18 Jan. 1982

Divorce ... is a buy-now-pay-later proposition —Gael Greene, *Cosmopolitan,* July 1972

Panjabi is a much more solid proposition than Rajasthani and we take it as our second example —W. B. Lockwood, *A Panorama of Indo-European Languages,* 1972

The other book ... is an altogether different proposition —Anatole Broyard, *N.Y. Times Book Rev.,* 24 Mar. 1985

This sense seems to have entered British usage from its hinterlands early in the 20th century (we have a 1903 citation from *Anglo-African Argus & Gold Coast Globe*) and to have become pretty well established by the middle 1920s (H. W. Fowler hated it). Nowadays it does not seem to be used in as many slangy contexts as it was fifty to seventy years ago; it is old hat to the writers of racy prose. We think the commentators could very well abandon their superannuated complaints; *proposition* is used in entirely respectable surroundings these days, even though it is not used in the most stately writing.

2. The verb *proposition* is even newer than the noun sense just discussed, apparently having originated in the 1920s. Its presence seems to have been noticed in the 1930s, although none of our books mentions it before Bernstein 1958. Bernstein saw it in the *New York Times,* apparently in its later and more specific sense of suggesting sexual intercourse, and was so flabbergasted he didn't believe his eyes: "There's no such verb," he said. By 1965 he admitted it was slang. It seems to have proved useful in this sense, and Copperud 1970, 1980 reports it as standard. It is certainly used without qualms:

... was arrested as part of a vice detail's sweep of the area after he allegedly propositioned an undercover policewoman —*Sports Illustrated,* 28 Jan. 1985

The older and more general use of the verb has not received much mention in the handbooks. This sense too seems to have become entirely respectable:

There hadn't been a box-office smash among them, and so the movie companies weren't propositioning Korty —Judith Crist, *New York,* 28 Jan. 1974

... an English publisher propositioned me to write a life of Sainte-Beuve —John Russell, *N.Y. Times Book Rev.,* 23 Feb. 1975

The last complainer about the verb *proposition* that we have seen was the British writer Honor Tracy (in *Encounter,* January 1975) who objected to *proposition* used in place of *propose.* If you test *propose* in the examples above, you will notice it does not fit comfortably.

prostrate Some commentators say that *prostrate* should be confined to the meaning "lying face down." This same issue is frequently raised about *prone* (see PRONE, SUPINE) but less often about *prostrate,* which is just as well since *prostrate* often simply means "lying down." Like *prone,* it is sometimes used of inanimate objects that have no faces to be up or down:

He clambered over half-visible rocks, fell over prostrate trees —Willa Cather, *Death Comes for the Archbishop,* 1927

When used to describe the position of a person, *prostrate* implies "face down" only when the person is prostrate in adoration or submission. Otherwise the direction the person faces is unimportant—even in medical sources where terminology is precise.

Prostrate in homage, on her face, silent —Gordon Bottomley, *King Lear's Wife,* 1915

... it requires the patient ... to assume the prostrate or horizontal position —Warren H. Cole & Robert Elman, *Textbook of General Surgery,* 6th ed., 1952

... not even more brandy could revive the prostrate form of the vanquished boy —J. A. Maxtone Graham, *Sports Illustrated,* 15 July 1968

protagonist Fowler 1926 first made *protagonist* a usage issue. It was he who brought in the Greek roots of which the word is composed to deride plural use of the word as absurd, and it was he who suggested the influence of *pro-* "in favor of" in the development of the sense meaning "proponent, advocate." Thus we have two main lines of dispute, right down to the present time.

The first of these two disputed uses is the longer-lived

one. Criticism of it is summed up reasonably succinctly here:

> Thus the worthy Irving Howe writes, on the front page of the *New York Times Book Review* (April 9, 1978), about "main protagonists." Now, the protagonist is the main actor in something and has, since Greek times, always been used in the singular. "Protagonists" is incorrect (unless you are referring to the protagonists of two or more dramas), and "main protagonists" (main main actors) is redundant to boot —Simon 1980

There are a few weaknesses in Simon's statement. To begin with, "always been used in the singular" is wrong: the earliest citation for the word in English is plural (it is from Dryden), and the OED editors are not certain whether Dryden was using the sense Simon says is acceptable (the original OED editor thought so) or the sense Simon says is incorrect (the Supplement editors think it is this sense). And Simon has overgeneralized; the limitation to a single protagonist is true of Greek drama, but it is not therefore necessarily true in English literary tradition, as the Supplement editors observe.

Now the evidence for *protagonist* in each of the two senses given in the OED is quite slight. The word, it seems, did not establish itself as one of frequent use in literature and journalism until the early 20th century, too late to come to the attention of the original OED editors (the volume containing *protagonist* was published in 1909). So when Fowler found a lot of examples in the 1920s, it is not surprising he failed to find similar uses well represented in the OED.

To understand how *protagonist* is used, we have to begin with 20th century use. So if in ancient Greek drama the protagonist was the main character, in a modern work with more than one main character, there might be more than one protagonist. This is no more than taking the central notion of a word and stretching it to meet new conditions.

> In the entire treatment of the theme there is a morning freshness that sorts well with the callow years of the protagonists —*The Nation*, 30 Sept. 1909

> ... the protagonists of "The Mysterious Stranger" are the boys —Van Wyck Brooks, *The Ordeal of Mark Twain*, 1920

> Burton Rascoe's forthcoming novel, "Gustibus," has a living person ... as its principal protagonist —*Emporia* (Kans.) *Gazette*, 30 June 1928

> The wicked world enters the scene as a protagonist —Francis Steegmuller, *N.Y. Times Book Rev.*, 11 Apr. 1954

> The end of the novel dissolves into a fantasia in which the narrator ... places the protagonists on trial —*Times Literary Supp.*, 14 Nov. 1968

> This water tank is the nemesis for all three of the story's protagonists —Anne Fremantle, *Commonweal*, 9 Oct. 1970

There is nothing inherently unreasonable so far—if a literary work (a Greek drama, say) has but one central character, it has but one protagonist; if there are several main characters, there are several protagonists.

Now let us suppose that we liken a real-life situation to a drama. Might not the central figure then be the protagonist? And if there were two central figures?

> ... William III. and Louis XIV., the protagonists in the struggle —*Encyclopædia Britannica*, 11th ed., 1910

> ... but they usually come from minor actors, and not till now have we seen the protagonists falling foul of each other as Roosevelt and Taft are doing —*The Nation*, 2 May 1912

> To everybody except the protagonists ... marriage is nothing but a nuisance —Jan Struther, *Mrs. Miniver*, 1940

> ... the memoirs of the political and military protagonists, Mr. Churchill, General Eisenhower, Lord Cunningham —*Times Literary Supp.*, 4 Jan. 1952

> The chief losers in all this are the two original protagonists—Britain and Persia —Andrew Shonfield, *London Calling*, 7 Oct. 1954

> Ostensibly, this great medical row was about the correct treatment of the ailing Fuhrer, and the protagonists in it were Dr. Theodor Morell, Hitler's physician, and Dr. Karl Brandt, his surgeon —Hugh Trevor-Roper, *American Scholar*, Winter 1981/1982

The unetymological sense "proponent, advocate, champion, supporter" was spotted by the OED in use as early as 1877. This sense is postulated to have been influenced by *pro-* "in favor of" because in many examples the context shows that the person or thing called *protagonist* is not necessarily the main one or a main one. This sense seems to have become established in the 1920s:

> ... Raymond Poincaré, bitter anti-German, determined anti-bolshevist, protagonist of strict enforcement of the Treaty of Versailles —*The Nation*, 25 Jan. 1922

> He is the protagonist of that great majority —H. L. Mencken, *Prejudices, 2d Series*, 1920

> The true university is the protagonist of liberty and tolerance —*Science*, 5 Mar. 1926

> ... Mr. Darwin, Evolution's best known protagonist —*America*, 16 July 1927

> The Greeks were the first intellectualists. In a world where the irrational had played the chief role, they came forward as the protagonists of the mind —Edith Hamilton, *The Greek Way to Western Civilization*, 1930

> Thoreau will be remembered ... as a protagonist of man against the state —Henry Seidel Canby, *Thoreau*, 1939

> He became a protagonist of the New Realism —Maxwell Geismar, *The Last of the Provincials*, 1947

> ... Sir Winston proclaimed himself a protagonist of high-level talks without agenda —*New Statesman & Nation*, 28 Nov. 1953

The loss of the notion of primacy is often signaled by the use of an adjective such as *chief* or *principal:*

> ... the chief protagonist of the Government in the Paris press —*Manchester Guardian Weekly*, 2 Sept. 1921

> Mrs. Sanger, Marie Stopes, Ettie Rout and Miss Bocker, the principal protagonists of birth-control —*The Bulletin* (Sydney, Australia), 2 Sept. 1926

. . . the Socialists, who are the leading protagonists of the "Anschluss" movement —*N.Y. Herald Tribune,* 13 Nov. 1927

Indeed he and Arnold Bennett were the chief protagonists in London of unusual evening shirts —Osbert Sitwell, *Noble Essences,* 1950

. . . the communist parties . . . became the chief protagonists of nationalism —John K. Fairbank, *New Republic,* 20 Jan. 1968

Historically, then, *protagonist* in English was first applied to Greek drama and then extended to English drama and English fiction. At first it was usually used only of a single leading character. In the late 19th century it was applied to the leading figure in a real-life situation, and also to a prominent supporter or champion of a cause. In the 20th century, the word became frequently used in the plural, to account for multiple leading characters, real and literary, and multiple proponents. Adjectives such as *main, chief,* and *principal* are used more frequently with the "proponent" sense than with the others. The OED Supplement has British evidence for the "proponent" sense as late as 1979, but we have little American evidence for it since the 1960s. The "proponent" sense may possibly be on the wane in American use.

These uses are all standard. The traditional bases for objection have been demolished by the evidence in the OED Supplement.

protect *Protect* is frequently found with *from* and a little less frequently (though still quite commonly) with *against:*

. . . the scanty vegetation was insufficient to protect the light soil from blustery winds —Ray Allen Billington, *Westward Expansion,* 1949

Mark, being deaf, is protected from her interference —John Cheever, *The Wapshot Chronicle,* 1957

He seemed to want to protect her from her worse self —Herman Wouk, *Marjorie Morningstar,* 1955

To protect against such an eventuality the treaty contains a safeguarding clause —*Encyclopaedia of the Social Sciences,* 1933

We feel that this step-by-step process is necessary to protect against duplicity —William R. Frye, *The Reporter,* 22 Sept. 1955

. . . citizens need to be protected against thieves and murderers —Alexander B. Smith & Harriet Pollack, *Saturday Rev.,* 4 Dec. 1971

Protect is also used frequently with *by* to express a different relation:

He blew hard on hands half protected by shabby woolen mittens —F. Van Wyck Mason, *The Winter at Valley Forge,* 1953

I thought it would only be fair to protect the readers of the magazine I was editing by describing my own biases —Nicolas H. Charney, *Saturday Rev.,* 11 Dec. 1971

Protect with appears less often but is not rare either:

. . . the mind does not shy away from anything, it does not protect itself with any illusion —I. A. Richards, quoted in F. R. Leavis, *The Common Pursuit,* 1952

. . . protecting unimportant secrets with mystifying ritual —Frederic L. Paxson, *Pre-War Years 1913–1917,* 1936

protest, *noun* The noun *protest* is most often used with *against:*

. . . resigned from the government in protest against the backstage maneuvering —*Current Biography,* September 1964

The Communists termed "absurd" the U.S. protests against Red fighter plane attacks —*Wall Street Jour.,* 30 July 1954

. . . this was a kind of strategic protest against her husband's double life —Van Wyck Brooks, *Saturday Rev.,* 6 Mar. 1954

Protest is also followed by *at:*

He was also associated with the work of UNESCO, but resigned in protest at the admission of Franco's Spain —*Current Biography,* January 1964

. . . an immediate storm of public protest at the proposed use of park land for great buildings —*Dictionary of American Biography,* 1929

Occasionally *protest* is found with *of* or *to:*

. . . resigned from the "Voice of America" program in protest of this Kaghan discharge by . . . the State Department's new security officer —T. R. B., *New Republic,* 8 June 1953

. . . have recalled their ambassadors in protest to the executions —radio news broadcast, 27 Sept. 1975

protest, *verb* *Protest,* when used with a preposition, usually appears with *against:*

He went here and there swearing and protesting against every delay —Sherwood Anderson, *Poor White,* 1920

. . . protesting with admirable chivalry against jesting at maiden ladies —Saxe Commins, *Saturday Rev.,* 1 Sept. 1945

. . . the number of people who were protesting against the morals of the time —Gilbert Seldes, *Saturday Rev.,* 13 Feb. 1954

In the next decades Cotter practised in various places and continued to protest against his dismissal —*Australian Dictionary of Biography,* 1966

Occasionally *protest* has appeared with *about, at,* or *over:*

I sent her off to her address in a taxi . . . : she protested about the expense —Edmund Wilson, *Memoirs of Hecate County,* 1946

He protested at the usury laws of 1829 —*Australian Dictionary of Biography,* 1966

He was protesting over losing his pilot's licence —*The Sun* (Melbourne), 14 Apr. 1975

While the use of intransitive *protest* with a preposition remains very common, this sense of *protest* used as a transitive verb without the preposition can be found about as often in the U.S. *Against* began to be omitted around the turn of the century—some have said in order to save space in newspaper headlines—and *protest* used alone has become established in American English. British English normally still uses *protest against.* Although some usage commentators have warned that confusion may arise if *against* is not used, our evidence shows that this has not been the case:

> She marched with the pickets, protesting atmospheric testing —Dick Kleiner, *Springfield* (Mass.) *Union,* 14 Mar. 1966

> . . . we who had originally contracted to distribute his books protested Gaige's hokus-pokus from the outset —Bennett Cerf, *Saturday Rev.,* 2 Jan. 1954

> It has become customary for the Soviet Union to protest the seating of the delegates of the National Government of China —Philip C. Jessup, *The Reporter,* 6 July 1954

> . . . she also became part of a politically oriented "gang of five" that protested Rostropovich —Martin Bernheimer, *N.Y. Times Book Rev.,* 23 Sept. 1984

protractor See INCOMPARABLE.

proved, proven A lot of ink has been devoted to questioning the propriety of *proven* versus *proved* since the controversy started in the 19th century (our earliest comment comes from 1829). *Proven* is historically the past participle of *preven,* in Middle English the usual spelling of what has become *prove. Proven* survived in and descends to us from Scottish English. It apparently first established itself in legal use and has been slowly working its way into literary and general use. Tennyson was one of its first frequent users in literature; he seems to have used it for metrical reasons.

Surveys thirty or forty years ago showed *proved* to be about four times as common as *proven.* But *proven* has caught up in the past twenty years; it is now just about as common as *proved* as part of a verb phrase; it is more common than *proved* when used as an attributive adjective. You can use whichever form you like.

> I should hate to see Ezra die ignominiously in that wretched place where he is for a crime which if proven couldn't have kept him all these years in prison —Robert Frost, letter, 24 June 1957

> That theory ordinarily would never have had a chance of being proven even in the Republican Senate —David A. Stockman, *Newsweek,* 28 Apr. 1986

> The Peace Corps has proven over the years that it can survive —Robert Shogan, *N.Y. Times Book Rev.,* 9 Feb. 1986

> But I had proved I could make money if I put my mind to it —James Thurber, letter, 27 Dec. 1952

> . . . his amazing recuperative powers having again proved themselves —Robert Craft, *Stravinsky,* 1972

> What artist had ever really proved a reliable guide to the meanings generated by his work? —Dan Hofstadter, *New Yorker,* 6 Jan. 1986

Although *proven* is more common as an attributive adjective, you can use *proved* too:

> Richard Cork, a proven authority on the first machine age in its relation to British art —John Russell, *N.Y. Times Book Rev.,* 2 June 1985

> . . . a perfect knowledge of their own past record and proved capabilities —Roger Angell, *New Yorker,* 9 Dec. 1985

Some writers use both:

> . . . where they were known, where what they were did not have to be proved —E. L. Doctorow, *Loon Lake,* 1979

> He had proven not the sturdiest member of the expedition —E. L. Doctorow, *Ragtime,* 1975

Both forms are standard now.

provide When *provide* is used intransitively, it is most often used with *for:*

> . . . provide for the common defense —*Constitution of the United States,* 1787

> And no sooner he's provided for than he turns on you —Joseph Conrad, *Chance,* 1913

> . . . an Automobile Accident Compensation Board would provide for strict liability —Samuel H. Hofstadter, *N.Y. Times Mag.,* 21 Feb. 1954

> The contract provided for increased wages, pensions, insurance —*Current Biography,* November 1965

When *provide* is used transitively to mean "to supply or make available," the recipient of the provision is frequently named in a prepositional phrase beginning with *for* or *to:*

> . . . a discontent which has provided fertile soil for the agitator —L. S. B. Leakey, *Mau Mau and the Kikuyu,* 1952

> A new Urban Service Corps providing public employment for unemployed youth —James B. Conant, *Slums and Suburbs,* 1961

> . . . it will provide nearly eleven-million units of electricity to people in rural areas —*London Calling,* 18 Feb. 1954

> Provide schools and teachers to all children and illiteracy goes down dramatically —Peter Rossi, *Trans-Action,* June 1967

But when *provide* is used transitively to mean "to make something available to," the thing being provided is usually named in a prepositional phrase introduced by *with:*

> The bereaved woman was provided with a collection of gruesome anecdotes —Ellen Glasgow, *Barren Ground,* 1925

> The route is well provided with signs —*American Guide Series: New Hampshire,* 1938

> . . . a collection of short stories, like a sketch-book, may provide him with an ideal form —*Times Literary Supp.,* 23 Apr. 1970

When *provide* is used transitively to mean "to stipulate," it is often followed by a clause:

> The next year the assembly provided that the fort be given to Abraham Wood for three years —*American Guide Series: Virginia,* 1941

> . . . the Mutual Security Treaty, which provides that in June, 1970, either party may give notice —William O. Douglas, *Center Mag.,* March 1969

Provide is also used both transitively and intransitively with *against:*

> ... but can Congress predict, and provide against, every emergency in which quick action might be essential? —Elmer Davis, *But We Were Born Free,* 1954

> ... a cushion must sometimes be provided against too sudden deflation —Thurman W. Arnold, *The Bottlenecks of Business,* 1940

provided, providing Both *provided* and *providing* are in standard use as conjunctions, either alone or in combination with *that.* Both have been in use for about the same amount of time: *provided that* in the OED dates from 1460, *providing that* from 1423; *provided* alone from 1600, *providing* from 1632. You can use whichever sounds better to you. Our evidence shows that *provided* is used more often than *providing* and that *provided* has the greater literary backing.

It is possible that the lead that *provided* has always had over *providing* has been increased by the dispute over *providing* that made its debut with Ayres 1881. Ayres decided—on his own, apparently—that *providing* was vulgar. Long 1888 prescribes *provided.* Vizetelly 1906 does the same, but he offers a reason, declaring that *providing* is not a conjunction. Of course *providing* has been a conjunction for about as long as *provided,* but facts sometimes seem hardly to matter in these disputes. The notion that *providing* is an error has entered the mainstream of American usage lore and in particular the world of pedagogy; Bernstein 1971 says that generations of schoolteachers have insisted on *provided* and proscribed *providing.* And commentators from Josephine Turck Baker 1927 and Lurie 1927 down to Follett 1966 and Freeman 1983 have also insisted.

Defenders of *providing* began to speak up fairly early. MacCracken & Sandison 1917 looked in the OED and found *providing* acceptable, though less frequent; Krapp 1927 also finds *providing* acceptable. Partridge 1942 says that "a certain writer errs" in saying that *providing* is misused for *provided.* The preponderance of recent opinion finds both words acceptable, and so do dictionaries. Such evenhanded treatment has caused culture shock:

> When I really succumbed to unprofessorial language was the day I found in a recent dictionary that *provided* and *providing* may be used interchangeably! What is left to teach? —Calvin T. Ryan, letter to the editor, *Word Study,* December 1955

The issue in British usage arose on different grounds. Fowler 1907, 1926, 1965 objects to *provided* used where *if* would do; no notice is taken of *providing.* Eventually cross-fertilization takes place, with Treble & Vallins 1937 picking up the American objection to *providing* and numerous American commentators picking up Fowler's objection to use of *provided* where *if* would do. The point they make is that *provided* (or *providing*) is the narrower, more precise word and that *if* should be used where the notion of stipulation or provision is not needed. Here are a handful of examples. *If* will fit idiomatically into any of them, but it will not always leave the meaning the same or seem an improvement.

> He would have offered better material for Dickens than Leigh Hunt or Landor, providing Dickens stuck to the text and curbed the spirit of caricature — *Times Literary Supp.,* 14 July 1950

> Already he was formulating the way he would let the news out, providing he decided not to keep it a secret —J. F. Powers, *Accent,* Winter 1946

> ... the spring shall see me there—provided I neither marry myself, nor unmarry any one else in the interval —Lord Byron, journal, 14 Nov. 1813

> ... there would be no reason to continue to hold him provided sensible arrangements for his care could be made —Archibald MacLeish, letter, 16 Oct. 1957

> "... I have nothing against mediocre people, provided I don't have to teach them anything." —John Updike, *Couples,* 1968

proximity See CLOSE PROXIMITY.

proximity, the principle of See AGREEMENT, SUBJECT-VERB: THE PRINCIPLE OF PROXIMITY.

publically *Publically* is an occasionally used variant spelling of *publicly.* It is either based on the obsolete *publical* or, more likely, simply on analogy with many other *-ically* adverbs. Chambers 1985 considers it a misspelling. It is not really a misspelling—it is recognized in dictionaries like Webster's Third and the OED Supplement. You can use it if you like, but we do not really recommend it, because it will look unfamiliar to many who encounter it.

punish *Punish* is found most often with *for* and an object that names the offense:

> ... with the terrible December wind punishing him for the ungodly hour —Larry L. King, *Harper's,* March 1969

> The gifted Don DeLillo is currently being punished for not writing "End Zone" again —Wilfrid Sheed, *N.Y. Times Book Rev.,* 3 June 1973

Less often *punish* is used with *by* or *with* and an object that names the punishment:

> ... the wife whom he loved ... who punished him with frenetic fits of "nerves" —Oscar Handlin, *Atlantic,* February 1955

> ... the United States showed an inclination to punish Argentina by breaking off relations —Richard W. Van Alstyne, *Current History,* March 1953

purebred See THOROUGHBRED, PUREBRED.

purge *Purge* is most often used with *of,* and the object names what is gotten rid of:

> ... whose minds were to be purged of all the natural decencies, of all the laboriously acquired inhibitions of traditional civilization —Aldous Huxley, *Brave New World,* 1932

> ... the room had never quite been purged of the bad taste of preceding generations —Edmund Wilson, *Memoirs of Hecate County,* 1946

> ... allowed even enemy aliens to purge themselves of the guilt of their emperors —Oscar Handlin, *The American People in the Twentieth Century,* 1954

> ... it is severely purged of those autobiographical elements often germane to first novels —Francine Du Plessix Gray, *N.Y. Times Book Rev.,* 15 July 1979

Less often, *purge* is found with *from,* and here the object may name either what is removed or the environment from which it is removed:

> Pure economics, purged from the nationalistic virus, would work for free trade and peace —Albert Gué-rard, *Education of a Humanist,* 1949

> . . . religious dogmas were purged from public education —Rexford G. Tugwell, *Center Mag.,* January/February 1973

> The players themselves have had a spring in Florida or Arizona to purge the talk of tax shelters from their conversations —Daniel Okrent, *N.Y. Times Book Rev.,* 3 May 1981

Purge is sometimes used with *by* to show means:

> . . . he (Antony) purged his levies by executing a number of soldiers whose loyalty he distrusted —John Buchan, *Augustus,* 1937

> . . . he was sentenced to jail for refusing to hand over certain spending records . . . but later purged the sentence by handing over the documents —Stephen J. Sansweet, *Wall Street Jour.,* 28 Oct. 1976

purist *Purist* is the most persistent of the many terms used to describe those people who concern themselves with "correct English" or "correct grammar." Among other epithets we find *tidier-up, precisian, schoolmarm, grammaticaster, word-worrier, prescriptivist, purifier, logic-chopper* (H. W. Fowler's word), *grammatical moralizer* (Otto Jespersen's term for H. W. Fowler), *usage-aster, usagist, usager,* and *linguistic Emily Post.* All of these seem at least faintly pejorative, some more than faintly so. Quinn 1980's *pop grammarian,* also pejorative, is a narrower term that applies chiefly to those commentators who have received wide dissemination through the popular media in the 1970s and 1980s. Ellsworth Barnard's (1979) *absolutist* is more neutral.

Perhaps many purists would prefer to call themselves "conservative"—a term probably borrowed from politics, but here misapplied, since purists are not interested in preserving the language as it is, but in reforming and correcting it to attain a nearer approach to perfection. In politics such an attitude might be characterized as "radical." Perhaps Thomas Love Peacock's term *perfectibilian* (used to describe a school of philosophical and social thought) would be reasonably descriptive.

The concern with the improvement, correction, and perfection of the existing language goes back to the 18th century, when the first influential grammars of English were written. There was current at that time a notion that a perfect language existed, at least in theory, and that reformation of the imperfect way existing language was used would lead to that perfection. The way in which reformation and correction were to be attained was through cerebration—one used reasoning and analogy (especially to Latin and sometimes to Greek—the only grammar taught then) to decide for oneself what must be right. How this usage tradition developed in grammars and books of opinion through the 18th century and down to our own day is sketched in the introductory essay to this book.

The purist is thus the recipient of a body of opinion concerned primarily with matters of propriety, taste, and personal preference, often elevated to the status of grammatical rules. Such opinion does not, in general, draw upon literature except to correct it. Shaw 1970 opines that "a purist seems to feel that man was made for language and refuses to acknowledge that language was not only made for man but that it is determined and shaped by his use—and nothing else."

Copperud 1970 points out that discussions can be found under the heading *Purist* in Bernstein 1965, Copperud 1964, and Evans 1957, and under *Purism and Pedantry* in Fowler 1965. He notes that the opinions expressed of purism are generally derogatory.

purport Fowler 1926 started this hare. He discovered "an ugly recent development" in the use of *purport:* it was being used in the passive and also with a personal subject. His disapproval has been repeated in Evans 1957, Bernstein 1962, 1965, Copperud 1970, Freeman 1983, Bryson 1984, and Longman 1984 (and by Gowers in Fowler 1965).

Fowler thinks the passive use new, because he can only find one example in the OED, dated 1897. It is actually a newer construction than Fowler thought; there are no examples of a true passive in the OED. What Fowler found was a participial adjective, used attributively; the usual pattern of a passive in English is *be* (or *get*) plus the past participle. The OED shows that in the 19th century *purport* was undergoing changes in its idiomatic construction: the *purporting* recommended by Fowler in place of *purported* dates only from 1879 itself; *purport* appears with a personal subject in one meaning in 1803 and in the meaning Fowler comments on only in 1884.

Purport came into English in the 16th century as a transitive verb with a noun or pronoun direct object, and by the very end of the 17th century could take a relative clause as object. In the 18th century it began to be followed by what some grammarians (for instance Quirk et al. 1985) call a "subjectless infinitive clause"—a clause with an understood subject in which the verb is an infinitive. The earliest example in the OED (1790) reads:

> This epistle purports to be written after St. Paul had been at Corinth —William Paley, *Horae Paulinae, or the Truth of the Scripture History of St. Paul Evinced*

Here are modern examples of the same construction:

> The regime adheres to a false philosophy which purports to offer freedom, security, and greater opportunity to mankind —Harry S. Truman, inaugural address, 20 Jan. 1949

> This book purports to be a history of American imperialism —Arthur M. Schlesinger, Jr., *Saturday Rev.,* 5 Feb. 1972

This construction, with the infinitive complement, has now almost monopolized the verb; although the older transitive uses with noun or pronoun or clause still turn up, they are fairly rare.

Now a transitive verb can be made passive; for every "Man bites dog" there can be a "Dog is bitten by man." *Purport,* however, gives us no evidence of real passive use. And the predominant modern construction, with the infinitive complement, cannot be made passive. In "this book purports to be," *purport* is more like a copula, or linking verb, than a transitive.

But what about examples like these?

> The second act brings the fairies with their military quartet to the castle, where each of the latter is set to woo the Beauty in what is whimsically purported to

be his native fashion —George Jean Nathan, *Theatre Arts,* March 1953

. . . Cantelli introduced to this country a symphony, in C major, that was unearthed in Cremona after the war and is purported to have been written by Mozart at the age of fourteen —Douglas Watt, *New Yorker,* 21 Mar. 1953

. . . a scene of what is purported to have been passionate revenge —Ray B. West, Jr., *Sewanee Rev.,* 1949

These examples, like a couple of examples near the end of Fowler's exegesis, look like passives: they consist of a form of *be* followed by a past participle. But like the active *purport* with the infinitive complement, this construction too lacks its reciprocal: it has no active counterpart in which the subject of the passive verb becomes the direct object of the active verb. Thus they are not true passives. *Is purported* means and functions the same as *purports.* Most likely they are what Quirk calls a pseudo-passive, in which the *be* is not an auxiliary verb but is a copula.

And we have two more constructions to look at, as represented by these examples:

. . . when I smoked a cigarette purported to contain hashish and fainted dead away after two puffs —*New Yorker,* 12 Feb. 1949

. . . an undated instruction of the same period purported to have been sent to the Soviet Military Attaché —O. Edmund Clubb, *Annals of the American Academy of Political and Social Science,* September 1951

. . . a theory, purporting to come from a critic of high repute, that is worth mentioning —F. R. Leavis, *Revaluation,* 1947

. . . found to be carrying forged documents purporting to prove that Dr. Merida's moustache was not his own —*Punch,* 12 Sept. 1945

In these, the past and present participles are used much like postpositive adjectives with an infinitive complement, somewhat like *pleased* in "I'm pleased to meet you." Fowler lumped similar past participles in with his disapproved passives; the present participle in the same construction received his blessing.

That is a heavy dose of grammar, but it shows us that the older (and not quite dead) transitive *purport* has largely been supplanted by an active construction in which the verb is most like a copula, a construction that looks passive but is not, and a pair of constructions in which participles are used much like adjectives. So the grammatical objections of Fowler and his repeaters to the passive are actually miscast: they criticize a usage that does not exist.

There is one further observation to be made about *purports/is purported.* If we say "This book purports to be," we imply that what is asserted is overt—somehow, perhaps in a subtitle or in the preface, the book declares itself openly. In "This book is purported to be," however, may reside a suggestion that someone other than the book's author has discovered this undeclared purpose. The two constructions are likely not to be synonymous; perhaps here was a distinction aborning that Fowler, defender of distinctions, overlooked.

Fowler's other objection is to the use of a personal subject with *purport.* For Fowler's generation the usage

was still fairly new (first attested in 1884); the OED called it rare. By Fowler's time it apparently was not so rare any more, and it is not at all rare today:

. . . the man who purports to offer a general discussion of political or military events —Malcolm Cowley, *New Republic,* 20 Mar. 1944

Most of the sequences in which Mr. Webb purports to be a Lothario of the silent screen are pretty funny —John McCarten, *New Yorker,* 2 Aug. 1952

. . . Vice President Nixon who with a smile, albeit somewhat wry, purports to welcome the Maine results —Griffing Bancroft, *New Republic,* 4 Oct. 1954

. . . they purported to be too far from the sources of power . . . to be sure of the exact causes —Richard H. Rovere, *New Yorker,* 6 Aug. 1955

. . . interviewed someone who purported to be a member of their studio audience —Whitney Balliett, *New Yorker,* 24 Sept. 1973

None purports to have found a link between the quantum world and that of gravitation —Timothy Ferris, *N.Y. Times Mag.,* 26 Sept. 1982

Summary: *Purport* is most commonly used in these constructions: (1) active verb (*purport, purports,* or past tense *purported*) + infinitive complement; (2) *be* + *purported* + infinitive complement; (3) noun + *purporting* + infinitive complement; (4) noun + *purported* + infinitive complement. In addition the transitive use—*purport* + noun or pronoun or relative clause—is occasionally found. Of these the active verb is by far the most common and most commonly appears with an inanimate subject. All of these constructions, including the relatively rare transitive, are established in standard English.

These constructions, which Fowler distrusted, have stood the test of time—they are more common now than they were before 1926. The objection to *is purported* on the basis of grammar and a "passive meaning" (Fowler, Evans) we have found to be baseless because the construction is not grammatically passive. We have also noted that the active verb and the *is purported* construction seem to carry different connotations: the active verb connoting an overt claim, and *is purported* tending to suggest that somebody unnamed and perhaps unknown thinks so. Thus,

. . . publication of what is purported to be a semi-autobiographical novel —*N.Y. Times,* 14 Aug. 1976

suggests that the semi-autobiographical quality is alleged by somebody other than the author or publisher and not advertised on the front cover.

purposefully, purposely, purposedly Distinguishing between *purposefully* and *purposely* is a concern of several fairly recent handbooks—Reader's Digest 1983, Harper 1975, 1985, Phythian 1979, Bryson 1984, Chambers 1985, Shaw 1987. It is not completely evident what the source of the sudden interest is; none of the commentators has brought forth a genuine example of confusion.

What is at work here may be the realization that the two adverbs can be used in similar situations. Here are a couple with *purposefully*:

. . . those who literally and often purposefully drank themselves to death —Herbert Hendin, *Columbia Forum,* Fall 1969

... at a New York address she has purposefully hidden from her father —Joshua Hammer, *People,* 27 Feb. 1984

In these contexts the writer might have used *purposely,* but with different meaning, for *purposely* is the simpler word, meaning merely "on purpose, not by accident," while *purposefully* is intended to suggest that the persons written about did what they did for a purpose, perhaps even with determination. Here we have *purposely* used in similar surroundings:

> If the Western Powers had selected their allies in the Lamarckian manner intelligently, purposely, and vitally —George Bernard Shaw, preface, *Back To Methuselah,* 1921

> De Gaulle purposely arrived last and spoke first — Stephen E. Ambrose, *Johns Hopkins Mag.,* April 1966

Cases like these illustrate that there are contexts which will allow either word, and there is probably little to be gained by second-guessing the writer. You should, however, be aware of the distinction when you go to use either one yourself.

Purposefully is often used to describe a manner of locomotion:

> ... as I stride purposefully toward the children's department —Carol Eisen Rinzler, *New York,* 1 Nov. 1971

> ... the people in green were scurrying about purposefully —E. L. Doctorow, *Loon Lake,* 1979

Purposely is not used in this way.

These next examples are of contexts in which there is little likelihood of interchange:

> His study should stimulate many teachers to think more purposefully about the books they use in the classroom —Janet Smith, *N.Y. Rev. of Books,* 2 Dec. 1971

> ... a basketball shoe covered, purposely, with graffiti —*Sports Illustrated,* 24 Feb. 1986

Purposedly is a rare synonym of *purposely* that turns up from time to time; it may perplex those with no access to an unabridged dictionary.

To sum up, then, there is no real evidence of widespread confusion of *purposefully* and *purposely,* but they are used in contexts where interchange is possible because the meaning of either word would make sense; in these contexts it is a good idea to remember the distinction between them—*purposefully* "for a purpose," *purposely* "on purpose." *Purposefully* and not *purposely* is used as an adverb to describe a style of performance.

pursuit   When followed by a preposition, *pursuit* is used with *of:*

> ... amassed a fortune in the pursuit of her profession —*American Guide Series: Louisiana,* 1941

> ... the real founders of the typically English middle-class pursuit of branch banking —Roy Lewis & Angus Maude, *The English Middle Classes,* 1950

> ... protesting against the acceptance by the church of the pursuit of wealth —D. W. Brogan, *The English People,* 1943

> ... in pursuit of his objective to bring to America every bird mentioned in Shakespeare —Morris Gilbert, *N.Y. Times Mag.,* 19 Sept. 1954

> Military action was not pursuit of a military solution but an argument by force that would bring Hanoi to an agreement —Barbara W. Tuchman, *N.Y. Times Book Rev.,* 11 Nov. 1979

> Several publishers are bringing out books on Iran, in hot pursuit of the headlines —Herbert Mitgang, *N.Y. Times Book Rev.,* 17 Feb. 1980

pyjamas   See PAJAMAS, PYJAMAS.

pyrrhic victory   Your dictionary will tell you what *pyrrhic victory* means: "a victory won at excessive cost." Bryson 1984 tells us that the phrase does not mean "a hollow victory." But when you stop to think about it, a victory won at *excessive* cost would indeed turn out to be hollow.

More important, perhaps, *pyrrhic* is a word to keep an eye on, for it is in the process of changing its behavior in the language to some extent. We find it quite frequently now as an independent adjective used after a linking verb:

> But the victory ... proves to be somewhat pyrrhic: in the process of winning the court battle, the teacher suffers "unrelenting torment" at the hands of colleagues and neighbors —Alan M. Dershowitz, *N.Y. Times Book Rev.,* 28 Nov. 1976

> But their victory may be only Pyrrhic if they do not push on —Jerome Karabel, *Change,* May 1972

> Even the victory of Kennedy supporters ... may have been Pyrrhic; for it intensified the hostility of the coalition and offended many of the Congressional elders —Tom Wicker, *N.Y. Times,* 7 Nov. 1976

It is even being attached to other nouns:

> It would be a Pyrrhic gesture to summarily put down Anton Chekhov because he comes from a distant time and place —Ed Bullins, *N.Y. Times,* 4 Feb. 1973

> ... the French breeders' pride has the Pyrrhic satisfaction that more and more of the best French products are being bought by foreigners —G. Y. Dryansky, *Town & Country,* July 1984

This instability may point to new senses emerging.

Q

qua This Latinate preposition means "in the capacity or character of; as." It is not a word that most people use or recognize, but several usage writers have paid some attention to it. Fowler 1926 devoted a column to discussing what he regarded as its correct use. He believed it should be restricted to cases in which "a person or thing spoken of can be regarded from more than one point of view or as the holder of various coexistent functions, & a statement about him (or it) is to be limited to him in one of these aspects," as in "He was a good husband and father, but, qua businessman, he was a failure." Fowler disapproved its use in other contexts where the less "precise" *as* would be adequate. Later critics such as Flesch 1964 and Copperud 1964 have not concerned themselves with such niceties—they have simply regarded *qua* as a pretentious substitute for *as*.

Our evidence shows that *qua* is in fact used in a distinctive way, but not the one prescribed by Fowler. Consider the following passages:

... will provide a key to any one poem *qua* poem — Louis MacNeice, *The Poetry of W. B. Yeats,* 1941

... the obsession with routine qua routine —Charles E. Silberman, *Atlantic,* July 1970

... not so much a question of voice qua voice — Harold C. Schonberg, *N.Y. Times,* 24 Jan. 1973

Not to teach students grammar qua grammar is as bad as teaching mathematics unmathematically — Simon 1980

... the role of scientist qua scientist —Philip Handler, *Science,* 6 June 1980

Killing Russians qua Russians —Thomas Powers, *Atlantic,* November 1982

Most of our citations for *qua* show it being used in just this way, between repetitions of a noun. It seems to function in such contexts as a somewhat more emphatic synonym of *as.* If *as* were used instead, italics might very well be employed to signal the added emphasis the voice would provide in speech ("... the role of scientist *as* scientist"). When *qua* is used, the italics are not necessary (although *qua* is, in fact, sometimes italicized by those to whom it seems not fully English).

Qua does not always occur between repeated nouns, but its use in other contexts is a good deal less common:

It cannot, qua film, have the scope of a long book — John Simon, *Esquire,* March 1974

Since its launching qua museum last August 3, it has played to capacity crowds —Hudson Bridges, *Gourmet,* December 1982

If you choose to use the preposition *qua* as it is now most often used, you stand a small chance of being criticized by a disciple of Fowler. If you use it only as Fowler recommended, you still stand some chance of being called pretentious. In neither case should you be greatly concerned. A better reason for avoiding it—if you want one—is that most readers will find it a strange and unfamiliar word. *As,* of course, will confuse no one.

quandary *Quandry* occasionally finds its way into print but is considered a misspelling of *quandary,* based on pronunciation.

... I still find myself in a quandry on this point — *Philosophical Rev.,* April 1953

Such is the quandry of justice Harry Blackmun — *N.Y. Times Mag.,* 20 Feb. 1983

quantum jump, quantum leap The phrase *quantum jump* (or *leap*) is derived from the world of physics, in which it has the meaning, "an abrupt transition (as of an electron, an atom, or a molecule) from one discrete energy state to another." Most people are more familiar with its extended use in the sense "an abrupt change, sudden increase, or dramatic advance." This sense was first recorded in 1955 (the original sense dates back to about 1926), and its use has been common since the 1960s:

Radioactive fall-out is the "third quantum jump" in the history of modern weapons. The first quantum jump, Dr. Lapp explained, was the A-bomb that shattered Hiroshima —*Science News Letter,* 19 Feb. 1955 (OED Supplement)

... a quantum jump in the number of men considered qualified for the bench —*Time,* 21 Feb. 1955

... the artistic quantum leap of our time —Donal Henahan, *N.Y. Times,* 7 July 1968

My views ... involve a quantum jump from conventional theory and policy —Neil H. Jacoby, *A Center Occasional Paper,* June 1969

... help China make a quantum leap to a more advanced level of industrial development —*Wall Street Jour.,* 29 Jan. 1979

... pushing science ahead by quantum leaps — Lynde McCormick, *Christian Science Monitor,* 18 Jan. 1980

Such usage has been criticized as voguish or jargonistic, but most recent commentary (as from Howard 1978, Bryson 1984, and Barzun 1985) attacks it primarily on logical grounds, pointing out that in physics, a quantum jump is actually a very small change, not a large or dramatic one. The critics regard *quantum jump* as a technical term misused by ignorant laymen. The argument is academic, since the criticized usage is now established as standard, but it seems worthwhile to point out that the idea originally underlying the extended sense was abruptness rather than largeness, and that this sense appears to have originated among scientists, not laymen. In any case, a quantum jump in physics may be small, but it is also significant. The extended sense is not quite as illogical as the commentators make it out to be.

quasi The pronunciation of *quasi,* which comes from a Latin form meaning "as if" and "as it were," perplexes many speakers. The clear front-runner in our file of attested pronunciations is \\ˈkwā-ˌzī\\ (rhyming with *day's eye*), a version not even mentioned in many discussions of this word, either as the pronunciation usually produced (but deprecated) or as the pronunciation to aim for. Following neck and neck at a respectful distance are \\'kwā-₁sī\\ and \\'kwä-zē\\ (rhyming with *may sigh* and *Ozzie*). Trotting along companionably behind these are \\'kwä-sē\\ and \\'kwä-₁zī\\, with \\'kwä-₁sī\\ and \\'kwä-zē\\ bringing up the rear. A rule of thumb might be to say \\'kwä-₁zī\\ if you want to sound like your neighbors, and \\'kwä-sē\\ if you want to sound like Caesar. All these pronunciations are in respectable use, however, and you might just prefer not to change the pronunciation you use now.

quasi-coordinators See AGREEMENT, SUBJECT-VERB: COMPOUND SUBJECTS 3; AS WELL AS.

query Several commentators, dating back to Partridge 1942, have distinguished between the nouns *query* and *inquiry,* noting that *query* refers to a single question, while *inquiry* can also refer to a series of questions or an investigation. The implication is that *query* is sometimes misused in place of *inquiry,* but only Bernstein 1965 gives an actual example of such misuse. Since our files contain no further examples of it, we assume that it is not a serious problem. Our evidence shows that *query* is used as the commentators say it should be:

> Because of his poor English, he had misunderstood the query —*Current Biography,* March 1968

> Answering various other queries from the audience —Mark Phillips, *Media & Methods,* September 1969

question 1. When *question* is followed by a preposition, it is usually *of:*

> ... poses the somber question of whether we are in for another war —*Time,* 15 Apr. 1946

> Nor does the question of length trouble a novelist — Bernard DeVoto, *The World of Fiction,* 1950

> A little honest thieving hurts no one, especially when it is a question of gold —Graham Greene, *Travels with My Aunt,* 1969

> There was the question of Jefferson Davis. In my shadowy understanding of history, I assumed that ... he was beyond reproach —Robert Penn Warren, *Jefferson Davis Gets His Citizenship Back,* 1980

> The question of whether it is appropriate for private U.S. banks to lend to foreign governments has yet to be debated —Felix G. Rohatyn, *The Twenty-Year Century,* 1983

Question is also used, but much less frequently, with *about* and *as to:*

> You've got to tell them the exact truth. There's really no question about it —Rose Macaulay, *Potterism,* 1920

> ... the procedures ... are not easy and there is considerable question as to their value —James B. Conant, *Slums and Suburbs,* 1961

2. Preceded by a qualifier like *no* or *little, question* is often followed by a clause introduced by *but that, but what,* or simply *that.* Reader's Digest 1983 prefers *that,* though acknowledging the other conjunctions. All are standard.

> There is no question but that there will be a general rise in wages in the next month or two —Edwin A. Lahey, *New Republic,* 1 Oct. 1945

> There is no question but that these changes shift the civilian-military balance —Townsend Hoopes, *Yale Rev.,* December 1953

> There can be no question but what the action taken ... did much to discourage future attempts to pick up cheap gains —Leland M. Goodrich, *Jour. of International Affairs,* Spring 1952

> There is no question but what the national nominating convention is a faithful expression of the genius of the American people —Wilfred E. Binkley, *New Republic,* 1 Mar. 1954

> ... there seemed little question that it would be able to count on government support —*Collier's Year Book,* 1949

Question may also be followed by a clause introduced by *whether* or *which:*

> This view begs the question whether literature is only or essentially art —Wayne Shumaker, *Elements of Critical Theory,* 1952

> The President and the Prime Minister were both accustomed to holding the centre of the stage. In a sense, what the "first summit" was about was the question which would up-stage the other —*Times Literary Supp.,* 9 Apr. 1970

questionnaire This word is sometimes misspelled with only one *n.*

quick, quickly Use of *quick* as an adverb dates back to about 1300. It has a highly respectable pedigree, having occurred in the works of such authors as Shakespeare and Milton:

> The latter quick up flew, and kickt the beam —*Paradise Lost,* 1667 (OED)

This adverb is still correct and is commonly used, but it is now more likely to be encountered in speech ("Come quick!") than in writing, except when the writing is deliberately informal or includes dialogue:

> "... You two learn so quick...." —Sinclair Lewis, *Babbitt,* 1922

> He shook his head. "You could take her a cup of coffee pretty quick...." —Walter Van Tilburg Clark, *Track Of The Cat,* 1949

> I ditched that quick enough, but one thought struck me about that dumb high school I go to —Paul Zindel, *Scholastic Voice,* 13 Apr. 1970

> With this guy I decided to end it quick —R. C. Padden, *Harper's,* February 1971

> ... I suppose the old lady was astounded at how quick I could get away on crutches —Flannery O'Connor, letter, 10 Nov. 1955

Its occurrence in less casual prose is relatively uncommon:

> What they carried was needed, tragically quick, at the blast furnaces —Stewart Holbrook, *N.Y. Herald Tribune Book Rev.,* 12 Jan. 1947

This lovely menace spreads unbelievably quick — Alan L. Otten, *Wall Street Jour.,* 19 June 1956

... he will probably die quicker —David Dempsey, *N.Y. Times Mag.,* 23 June 1974

The usual choice in such contexts—and the one recommended by usage commentators—is *quickly:*

A brilliant student, he moved quickly through his studies —*Current Biography,* March 1967

... he'd rise and walk quickly to Floral Hall — Edward Hoagland, *Harper's,* October 1970

Note that *quick* is also distinguished from *quickly* in that it almost always follows rather than precedes the verb it modifies ("They came quick," not "They quick came"; but "They came quickly" or "They quickly came").

See also FLAT ADVERBS.

quiet, quieten *Quieten,* a synonym of *quiet,* was considered a "superfluous word" by Fowler 1926, who found that "while good writers seem to avoid it, it is common in uneducated talk." Despite Fowler's objections, *quieten* has persisted in British English, where its use is now by no means limited to the uneducated or unskillful:

... making quietening gestures with both hands — William Golding, *Free Fall,* 1959

When, at last, Lord Snowdon had quietened us —V. S. Pritchett, *New Yorker,* 24 June 1985

... she thought Roberta was quietening down — Doris Lessing, *The Good Terrorist,* 1985

In American English, the verb used is *quiet:*

... quieted the air like a summer Sunday morning —Zelda Fitzgerald, *Ladies' Home Jour.,* January 1971

... because, as one camp leader said, "They never quieted down." —Alfred Lubrano, *Plain Dealer* (Cleveland, Ohio), 27 July 1985

quip Bremner 1980 and Copperud 1970, 1980 find fault with the way newspaper journalists use the verb *quip* to point out that some remark that looks dull in print sounded pretty funny at the time. This use is by no means limited to the daily papers:

This moving little speech is even more of a success than the music, which, after all, as I.S. quips, "was half-Tchaikovsky ... and half Rimsky-Korsakov ..." —Robert Craft, *Stravinsky,* 1972

In 1961, when Hirt estimated that he would clear about $200,000, he quipped, "I've already called off the elopement drills for my daughters." —*Current Biography,* February 1967

"We're just a small company," he quips —Alvin A. Butkus, *Dun's,* October 1971

"Just enough to put him on easy street," she quipped, to his relief —James Purdy, *Cabot Wright Begins,* 1964

You probably need to have been there.

quite A number of recent commentators notice that *quite* is used in two almost antithetical senses, one

approximately "fully, altogether, entirely" and the other approximately "to a considerable extent, moderately." In this respect, *quite* operates much like *rather* (see RATHER 2). There are actually three uses of *quite,* according to the OED and dictionaries that follow the OED analysis. The first use is a completive one originally used with verbs and participles to emphasize that an action is complete.

... an endeavour to recapture the treasure, which they were quite satisfied was hopeless —James Stephens, *The Crock of Gold,* 1912

He felt that the world he had loved had quite gone —Edmund Wilson, *N.Y. Times Book Rev.,* 20 July 1986

When used this way with adjectives and adverbs, *quite* emphasizes the fullest degree of the adjective or adverb. It functions as an intensive, emphasizing the meaning without changing it.

To-morrow I bury her, and then I shall be quite alone —Charles Lamb, letter, 12 May 1800

If you are quite sure you would have no use of them, I may as well destroy them —Lewis Carroll, letter, 21 June 1881

... bragged falsely of having made conquests of quite other girls —Renata Adler, *Pitch Dark,* 1983

From the intensive use a weaker, subtractive sense developed, a sense used not to intensify but to tone down. In the words of Fitzedward Hall 1873, it occupies "a place intermediate between 'altogether' and 'somewhat.'"

As I came home through the woods with my string of fish, trailing my pole, it being now quite dark, I caught a glimpse of a woodchuck stealing across my path —Henry David Thoreau, *Walden,* 1854

Thoreau's *quite* is exemplary: it brings the adjective up just short of its full power.

By all accounts the subtractive sense is the prevalent one in 20th-century English, but in many particular instances it is hard to be certain that the subtractive sense rather than the intensive sense is intended:

Her uncovered ears were quite white and very small —Aldous Huxley, *Those Barren Leaves,* 1925

... and the weather in the main has been quite good —E. B. White, letter, 3 Mar. 1965

You would think that the coexistence of these two uses would lead to problems of ambiguity and confusion, but in practice this seems not often to be the case. For although the lexicographer must try to determine the exact meaning of each occurrence of a word, the reader is under no such constraint. The distinction between the two senses is not always crucial to a general understanding of the sentence; when it is, the reader has the larger context for help. And the writer can always use a negative with *quite* when he or she wants to emphasize a falling just short:

In my opinion, my work ... ain't quite good enough —William Faulkner, 13 May 1957, in *Faulkner in the University,* 1959

He does not quite say that a propitious environment would create a population composed entirely of geniuses —John Butt, *English Literature in the Mid-Eighteenth Century,* edited & completed by Geoffrey Carnall, 1979

In the middle of the 19th century there was some reprehension of the use of *quite* before *a* and a noun— Bache 1869, Richard Grant White 1870, and Ayres 1881 all objected, for instance. There were two bases for objection: the commentators noticed that *quite* was not an intensive in the expressions, and they did not believe an adverb should modify a noun. Fitzedward Hall 1873 ignored the theoretical grammatical questions and was content to produce evidence that the idiom had been in use at least since the middle of the 18th century:

Quite a rake —Samuel Richardson, *Pamela,* 1740 (in Fitzedward Hall)

We decided, though, that he would be quite a swell guy sober —James Thurber, letter, April 1936

Irene Franey, a little older than I, was quite a beauty —John O'Hara, letter, 30 Dec. 1963

We have some British examples in which this *quite a* has a clearly intensive function:

. . . the crow that must have been shot quite a month before —Doreen Tovey, *Cats in the Belfry,* 1958

There are quite a dozen significant regional languages —W. B. Lockwood, *A Panorama of Indo-European Languages,* 1972

In these two examples *quite* means something like "every bit of, fully."
Quite is also used before *the:*

"He was quite the picture of a middle-aged businessman," recalls William O. Bourke —Faye Rice, *Fortune,* 24 Nov. 1986

I am quite the wrong person to write this foreword —Philip Larkin, *Required Writing,* 1983

These are established idioms, beyond cavil.

quiz Several critics feel that *quiz* is an informal word which, as Bernstein 1965 puts it, "is best restricted to the campus and the television screen." They particularly object to its use, both as a noun and as a verb, in reference to a formal investigation or examination, as in a criminal trial or by a legislative committee. Our evidence shows that such usage is extremely uncommon in running text (it may well occur more often in headlines, as the critics suggest). We have, in fact, only one bona fide citation for it:

. . . the investigation into RFC lending policies, . . . and currently the quiz on the extracurricular activities, if any, of Chairman Boyle of the Democratic National Committee —*Christian Science Monitor,* 10 Oct. 1951

We do have a few citations in which the verb *quiz* is used to describe close questioning in a police investigation, but not in a formal setting:

They quizzed the Forest Service lookouts in the area. Some suspicious facts emerged —Frank Cameron, *Saturday Evening Post,* 14 Aug. 1954

. . . he and Haquin went to quiz the crew of a patrol car who had radioed in the report —Michael Butterworth, *Cosmopolitan,* January 1972

Such usage is entirely consistent with the verb's established sense, "to question closely."

quondam See ERSTWHILE, QUONDAM, WHILOM.

quote 1. The noun *quote,* short for *quotation,* was first recorded in 1888:

Stodgy 'quotes' from the ancients? —*Pall Mall Gazette,* 12 Dec. 1888 (OED)

One of its chief early uses was in the world of publishing to denote a passage of favorable criticism quoted as advertisement for a book:

. . . three sentences that might have been framed specially to give the publisher an easy 'quote' —*Century Mag.,* February 1919

Its occurrence in general contexts was fairly rare until the 1940s, when we found it being used in a number of popular newspapers and magazines and very often without the distancing quotation marks of earlier years:

Miss Ross works with quotes from letters and diaries —Ernestine Evans, *N.Y. Herald Tribune Book Rev.,* 15 Oct. 1944

With a quote from the *Troy Times* —Ben Lucien Burman, *Saturday Rev.,* 28 Dec. 1946

. . . a distorted quote from a speech before the Congress of American-Soviet Friendship —*Atlantic,* August 1948

. . . riddles his opposition with a salvo of quotes — Richard E. Lauterbach, *New Republic,* 11 Apr. 1949

. . . some witty quotes picked from their own works —*Time,* 18 Apr. 1949

Its use since the 1940s has continued to be common and, for the most part, unremarkable. It occurs most often in writing that has a casual tone or, at least, is not highly formal:

It was mighty thoughtful of you to send me that quote from dear old Sam Adams's letter —James Thurber, letter, 3 Dec. 1958

. . . he said something to the effect that sex should be used sparingly, and refused to give Harcourt, Brace a quote for an ad —John O'Hara, letter, 9 Dec. 1961

To put quotes in the mouths of living people —Seymour Krim, *Evergreen,* August 1967

It started with quotes taken out of context —Suzette Haden Elgin, *English Jour.,* November 1976

. . . is obvious even before the quotes are collected —David Harris, *N.Y. Times Mag.,* 9 Mar. 1980

Only after the sweat has dried comes the quote — Wilfrid Sheed, *Harper's,* February 1984

This sense of *quote* has met with strong disapproval in some quarters. Such commentators as Bernstein 1965, Follett 1966, Shaw 1975, and Trimmer & McCrimmon 1988 have disparaged its use in writing, and the Heritage 1969, 1982 usage panel rejected it by a large majority. Some other critics, however, have taken a more tolerant view. Harper 1985, for example, accepts its use in writing that has "a conversational tone"; Bremner 1980 calls it "standard in the publishing business"; and The Right Handbook 1986 suggests that "probably only purists" insist on distinguishing between *quote* and *quotation.*

The noun *quote* is now widely used in standard if mostly casual writing, as the above quotations show, but there are still times when it seems more appropriate to choose *quotation* instead (as we have in writing this sentence). We recommend that you let your own judgment of the writing situation and your sense of idiom be your guide.

2. The noun *quote* is also used to mean "quotation mark," and it has also been criticized in this sense. Like the "quotation" sense, this "mark" sense is about 100 years old:

> The portion of this quotation which we have put within quotes —*Scottish Leader,* 2 Apr. 1891 (OED)

Its use in American English is well established:

> . . . quotes within quotes are often confusing, and unhinge the minds of thousands of poor copy-readers every year —H. L. Mencken, *The American Language, Supplement II,* 1948

The written contexts in which it appears are similar in tone to those in which the "quotation" sense of *quote* appears. Those critics who dislike the "quotation" sense tend naturally to dislike the "quotation mark" sense as well. Again, we recommend that you rely on your own judgment.

quoth   *Quoth* is the past tense of an obsolete verb *quethen.* It is used in the first and third persons and is regularly followed by its subject. It is archaic as a regular verb form and is used nowadays in special contexts, such as when a writer of historical fiction tries to recreate the speech and atmosphere of an earlier time. It is also sometimes used in modern contexts for humorous or arch effect or simply to catch attention:

> "That's all right, Dad," quoth he —Martin Mayer, *Esquire,* May 1974

> Then the mayor labored mightily and brought forth an "austerity" budget. Not good enough, quoth the bankers —Sidney Cohen, *Harper's Weekly,* 4 July 1975

R

rabbit, rarebit   See WELSH RABBIT, WELSH RAREBIT.

rack, wrack   The prescriptions of the critics are usually stated along the following lines: the verb *rack,* which is related to the noun designating an instrument of torture, properly means "strain" or "torment" and is the correct choice in *nerve-racking, rack one's brains,* and similar expressions; the verb *wrack* and noun *wrack,* on the other hand, are etymologically related to *wreck* and should therefore be used when wreckage or destruction is being described, as in *storm-wracked* and *wrack and ruin.*

The facts of actual usage are somewhat different. *Wrack* is commonly used as a verb synonymous with the figurative senses of *rack:*

> Perpetual longing perpetually denied was too wracking —Amy Lowell, *John Keats,* 1925

> . . . if a society is wracked with internal conflicts —Kenneth E. Boulding, *Center Mag.,* May/June 1971

> . . . a world wracked by change —Harrison E. Salisbury, *N.Y. Times Book Rev.,* 6 Nov. 1966

> . . . wracking his brain for the next day's copy —William Irvin, *Saturday Rev.,* 24 Dec. 1955

Nerve-wracking is an established variant of *nerve-racking:*

> . . . a business more nerve-wracking and exhausting than reading a newspaper —H. L. Mencken, *Prejudices: Second Series,* 1920

> . . . nerve-wracking period —John Gunther, *Inside Europe,* rev. ed., 1937

> . . . less nerve-wracking —Richard J. Barnet, *N.Y. Times Book Rev.,* 17 Oct. 1976

> . . . this nerve-wracking chapter in so many American lives —Arthur M. Schlesinger, Jr., *Saturday Rev.,* 6 Jan. 1979

The noun *rack* is sometimes used as a synonym of *wrack,* especially in the phrase *rack and ruin:*

> . . . the Bank was going to rack and ruin without him —Rudyard Kipling, *Plain Tales from the Hills,* 1888

> . . . let the business go to rack and ruin —*Punch,* 15 June 1966

Wrack (verb) meaning *rack* was first recorded in 1553, *rack* (noun) meaning *wrack* was first recorded in 1599. The tendency among modern commentators is to regard *rack and ruin* as acceptable, but to persist in regarding such usage as "he wracked his brain" as incorrect. Why one should be acceptable and the other unacceptable is not easily discerned. Probably the most sensible attitude would be to ignore the etymologies of *rack* and *wrack* (which, of course, is exactly what most people do) and regard them simply as spelling variants of one word. If you choose to toe the line drawn by the commentators, however, you will want to write *nerve-racking, rack one's brains, storm-wracked,* and for good measure *wrack and ruin.* Then you will have nothing to worry about being criticized for—except, of course, for using too many clichés.

racket, racquet   These spelling variants are both established in reputable use:

> . . . hoisted his racket to his shoulder like a baseball bat —John Updike, *Couples,* 1968

> . . . I grabbed a tennis racquet hanging in its press —E. L. Doctorow, *Loon Lake,* 1979

Racket is appreciably the more common of the two except when the reference is to the game racquets, which in American English is usually spelled as we have spelled it here:

> Racquets today is almost as aristocratic a game as court tennis —Dick Miller et al., *Town & Country,* May 1984

The British, however, prefer *rackets* for the name of the game:

> ... recorded the double in the ... tennis and rackets competitions at Manchester yesterday —*The Times* (London), 29 Oct. 1973

The British preference may be partly attributable to the opinions of such commentators as Partridge 1942 and Gowers in Fowler 1965, both of whom treat *racquet* as a spelling error. *Racquet* is, in fact, something of a strange hybrid, combining the English *racket* with the French *raquette*. But its use dates back to the early 19th century, and it has long been recognized as a standard variant in both British and American dictionaries.

railroad, railway There is no usage controversy involving *railroad* and *railway,* but several commentators have pointed out—and our evidence confirms— that *railway* is the word used in British English. The first of these examples is from a New Zealander:

> ... the railway waiting rooms came to be looked upon as dormitories —Frank Sargeson, *Once Is Enough,* 1973

> ... undermine subsidised railway systems —*The Economist,* 16 May 1986

Railroad and *railway* are both used in American English, and are essentially interchangeable. *Railroad* is considerably more common than *railway* in the U.S., except that *railway* is more likely to be used when the reference is to an actual set of tracks rather than a system of transportation:

> An ornate little car on an incline railway glides between the parking lot and the top level of the restaurant —Paul Showers, *N.Y. Times,* 10 Apr. 1977

raise, rear "I thought we *raise* plants & animals and *rear* children?" This query on a proof received from our typesetters in late 1985 is evidence of the hardiness of this old issue.

The Dictionary of American English says that *raise* used of children had some currency in British English at one time, but that it dropped out of use around 1800. It did not drop out of use in North America; the OED labels the sense *Now chiefly U.S.* The OED Supplement has a couple of recent British citations that associate *raise* with the United States, but almost all of the evidence from John Adams to the present is American.

The disappearance of the use in British English made the usage noticeable, and it was criticized as provincial as early as 1818. Bache 1869 quotes Dr. Alfred L. Elwyn, who published a book on Americanisms in 1859, to the effect that *raise* is a Southernism. Bache himself finds it "certainly no longer confined to the Southern States" but considers *rear* or *bring up* "the preferable expression." Vizetelly attacked *raise* in both his 1906 book and the Funk & Wagnalls dictionary. In the book he says it is "often misapplied to the bringing up of human beings. One *rears* cattle, *raises* chickens, but *brings up* children. *Rear,* meaning 'to nurture and train,' may also be used of children." Many subsequent commentators, and many, many schoolteachers, have followed his prescription, although *bring up* is fairly often overlooked.

Raise, however, never dropped out of use despite the disapproval, and most modern commentators recognize that it is perfectly standard American, although still apparently not used in Great Britain. A few commentators, such as Kilpatrick 1984 and Jacques Barzun (quoted in Safire 1986), still follow the Vizetelly line. But as these examples show, *raise* is both perfectly respectable and still very common in the Southern U.S.

> ... I was not trying to say, This is the sort of folks we raise in my part of Mississippi —William Faulkner, 15 May 1958, in *Faulkner in the University,* 1959

> I told my mother I'd changed my mind about wanting to succeed in the magazine business. "If you think I'm going to raise a good-for-nothing," she replied, "you've got another think coming." —Russell Baker, *Growing Up,* 1982

> Cousin Katie left me the house in Savannah I was raised in —Flannery O'Connor, letter, 15 Feb. 1959

> ... the town where I was born and raised —William Styron, *This Quiet Dust and Other Writings,* 1982

> Both parents are now more often engaged in active, day-to-day childraising —Elizabeth Janeway, in Harper 1985

> Raised poor in Tennessee by a religious mother — Geoffrey Wolff, *N.Y. Times Book Rev.,* 21 Nov. 1982

> ... she might at the same time be raising a family of her own —Peter Taylor, *The Old Forest and Other Stories,* 1985

> For Eliot, nonetheless, it was a very great advantage to have been raised in an atmosphere of evangelical piety —Irving Howe, *New Republic,* 18 Oct. 1954

> Every youngster as he grows up knows he was a darned sight smarter than his daddy was, and he has to get to be about forty before he finds out the old man was smart enough to raise him —Harry S. Truman, quoted in Merle Miller, *Plain Speaking,* 1973

Rear is still in common use too, and it varies freely with *raise* in the word-stock of some writers:

> She'd reared her children there —Russell Baker, *Growing Up,* 1982

> Born and reared in South Carolina —William Styron, *This Quiet Dust and Other Writings,* 1982

> ... where Macon's grandfather, a factory owner, reared his four grandchildren —John Updike, *New Yorker,* 28 Oct. 1985

> She reared the kids and kept the house clean — Edwards Park, *Smithsonian,* February 1986

> Barkley kept looking at him and wondering if the gentleman could have been reared in Egypt —Harry S. Truman, letter, 28 Jan. 1952

raise, rise **1.** *Verb.* It is an axiom of about twenty handbooks in our collection—mostly but not exclusively those aimed at a school and college audience— that *raise* is only transitive. A transitive *raise* and an intransitive *rise* make for a tidy world. Unfortunately the matter is a little more complicated than that. By and large *raise* and *rise* do form a transitive-intransitive pair; however, *raise* can also be an intransitive verb.

Intransitive *raise* has been objected to from as far back as Bache 1869, even though intransitive uses date to the 15th century in the works of Malory and Caxton. But it seems to have dropped out of mainstream British

English before the end of the 18th century; the historian David Hume—and he was a Scot—is the last (1761) literary figure quoted in the OED. It stayed alive, however, in dialectal use and in America:

> The Water having raised, . . . I could form no accurate judgment of the progress —George Washington, diary, 22 Sept. 1785 (in OED Supplement)

George Washington's use can still be found in American regional English:

> . . . and whenever there was much rain, and the river went to raising, I couldn't do my work —Elbert Herald, quoted in *Our Appalachia,* ed. Laurel Shackleford & Bill Weinberg, 1977

Our evidence shows four chief uses of the intransitive *raise*. They are not all regional, although the one which means "to get up out of bed" may be. It is found in the journals of Lewis and Clark in the early 19th century and also more recently:

> . . . Simon was beating the bottom of the dishpan with the spoon, hollering, "Raise up and get your four-o'clock coffee!" —William Faulkner, *Saturday Evening Post,* 5 Mar. 1955

There is also a use in which the intransitive is the semantic equivalent of a passive:

> He wants Britain's beet quota raising from 900,000 tons to 1,200,000 tons a year —*The Sun* (London), 22 Oct. 1974

> The flashlights momentarily converged on the dog, then raised —Erle Stanley Gardner, *The Case of the Negligent Nymph,* 1949

Another pattern finds *raise* used as if a reflexive pronoun object had been omitted from a transitive construction:

> At Bledsoe's defiance, he half raised from his seat and ejaculated, "The son of a bitch!" —Alexander Woollcott, letter, 23 Feb. 1933

> He periodically raised up on his elbows and fired —N.Y. Times, 24 Apr. 1970

> Uncle Jake was stirring unconsciously in the chair as he spoke, and I raised up from his lap and peered across the tablecloth into father's face —Peter Taylor, *The Old Forest and Other Stories,* 1985

And, finally, *raise* is simply used in place of various senses of *rise:*

> . . . perhaps it was the distraction of the drama which prevented him raising any higher on the moving staircase of public service —Laurence Irving, *Henry Irving: The Actor and His World,* 1952

> A blade [of a screwdriver] which tapers out from the tip . . . has a tendency to raise out of the slot —General Motors Corp., *ABC's of Hand Tools,* 1945

The intransitive *raise* was labeled *obsolete* in some older dictionaries, but it is still alive in dialectal use and in some at least sporadic general use. It is not incorrect nor illiterate. It seems rather to be a little-used survival from the past.

2. *Noun.* Vizetelly 1906 and others of similar vintage objected to the noun *raise* used in the sense "an increase in pay." *Rise,* which is still the usual word in British

English, was prescribed. The prescription survived long enough in some newspaper stylebooks to receive mention in Harper 1975, 1985. But *raise* is standard in this sense in America.

raising *Raising* is a term used by linguists for the idiomatic shifting of a subject or a negative from a subordinate clause to the "higher" clause it is dependent on (Bolinger 1980). The more important phenomenon, for usage writers (who do not use the term *raising*), is the one in which a negative is shifted.

Let's take an example:

> But I suppose I oughtn't to say that.

Does that seem a bit stiff and awkward? The most likely pattern in present-day English would show the negative shifted from *ought,* where it logically belongs, to the verb of the main clause:

> . . . but I don't suppose I ought to say that —Harry S. Truman, quoted in Merle Miller, *Plain Speaking,* 1973

Some of the most common expressions in which negative-raising is usual involve verbs like *think, suppose, believe,* and *seem.* The sentences "I don't think it will rain" and "I don't believe I'll go" were disapproved as solecisms by Vizetelly 1906. The objection was, of course, that the raised negatives are illogical. Illogical they may be, perhaps, but standard idioms nonetheless—especially in speech and relaxed writing. Flesch 1964 and Bolinger 1980 bother to defend them, so there evidently has been a fair amount of objection along Vizetelly's lines. Here are some examples of raising:

> I don't suppose there is much room to doubt that we will be actually at war before another fortnight is out —Archibald MacLeish, letter, 4 Feb. 1917

> I don't suppose there was a scarcer or more highly prized item in all of Belgium —*And More by Andy Rooney,* 1982

> "I don't suppose you remembered that bagel," Megan says —Jay McInerney, *Bright Lights, Big City,* 1984

> Well, I don't think the writer finds peace —William Faulkner, 13 Mar. 1958, in *Faulkner in the University,* 1959

> I don't think those things fall in the same category —Senator Lowell Weicker, radio interview, 28 Nov. 1975

> . . . he says that he doesn't think he's going to like "your chapter on editing" —James Thurber, letter, 3 Dec. 1958

> The roar of the traffic and continual street and building construction don't seem to faze the sidewalk cafe devotee —Barbara Gamarekian, *N.Y. Times,* 7 May 1978

> . . . for as he did not seem in the least to lessen his Affection to me, so neither did he lessen his Bounty —Daniel Defoe, *Moll Flanders,* 1722

> . . . I went up to New York to see Meyer Wolfshiem; I couldn't seem to reach him any other way —F. Scott Fitzgerald, *The Great Gatsby,* 1925

Never is also raised sometimes. Vizetelly 1906 complains of one example, and Phythian 1979 corrects "I never expected to find it" to "I expected never to find it." But the raised position has long been established:

> ... though 'Gondibert' never appears to have been popular —Samuel Johnson, *Life of Dryden,* 1783 (in Fitzedward Hall 1873)

Objections to idioms like *I don't think* or *can't seem* (unfavorably noticed from Schele de Vere 1872 to Shaw 1987) are a waste of good indignation; English idiom simply defies the dictates of abstract logic at some points, and this is one of them.
See also CAN'T SEEM.

raison d'être This French term, meaning literally "reason for being," is commonly used to refer to the fundamental purpose of something (or someone) or to an original and central cause or justification:

> When the seat of State government was removed to Annapolis in 1695, the town lost its raison d'être — James F. Waesche, *Maryland Mag.,* Autumn 1971

> ... the March of Dimes, having lost its raison d'être, switched from polio to arthritis —John L. Hess & Karen Hess, *The Taste of America,* 1977

Because its intrinsic Frenchness is so apparent, the term is sometimes written in italics:

> UNESCO's very *raison d'être*—the widening of man's cultural and scientific horizons —Katharine Kuh, *Saturday Rev.,* 24 Jan. 1976

Fowler 1926 cites as an error a passage in which *raison d'être* is used to mean simply "reason." Evans 1957 calls such use "an affectation" and also criticizes the use of *raison d'être* to mean "explanation." We have no evidence in our files for either of the criticized uses.

range Bernstein 1965 states flatly that *range* (presumably the verb) takes the prepositions *through, with, along,* or *between.* Why he chooses to specify those four is unclear. Our evidence shows that *range* is idiomatically followed by a great many prepositions—so many, in fact, that to list and illustrate all of them would serve no useful purpose. Suffice it to say that you need not agonize over the choice of prepositions following *range.*
It may be worth noting that by far the most common preposition to follow *range* is one not included in Bernstein's list, namely *from:*

> ... ranging from lock-pickers through photographers to psychiatrists —*Times Literary Supp.,* 2 July 1971

> ... ranging from a whisper to a bray —Susan Braudy, *Ms.,* March 1973

rarefy, rarify *Rarefy* is the usual spelling, but *rarify* has been in use as a variant since the 15th century. The earliest citations in the OED for this word, in fact, show it spelled with an *-i-*. Examples of the *-i-* spelling in standard, edited prose are extremely easy to come by:

> ... in an increasingly rarified atmosphere —Walter Millis, *Center Mag.,* January 1968

> ... by rarified philosophical speculation —*Times Literary Supp.,* 18 Dec. 1969

> ... how one rarified precedent may ... follow from another —David Riley, *The Washingtonian,* November 1970

> ... the rarified chambers of the museum —Susan Sidlauskas, *Vogue,* June 1982

> His suits are off the peg, and not a rarified peg — Diane Sustendal, *N.Y. Times Mag.,* 25 Mar. 1984

Nevertheless, *rarify* is widely regarded as a spelling error, so if you want to avoid possible criticism, however mild, we recommend that you choose the more common spelling, *rarefy.*

rarely ever *Rarely ever* is one of several intensive forms of the adverb *rarely.* Bryant 1962 calls it an established colloquial idiom, which agrees with our evidence. The idiom is possibly a telescoped form of *rarely if ever,* an intensified form of *rarely* that is more common in print, but the historical evidence is against this conjecture. OED evidence dates *rarely ever* from 1694; *rarely if ever* from 1756. *Rarely ever* is used in both British and American English:

> ... and the thieves are rarely ever caught —magistrate quoted in Ronald Blythe, *Akenfield,* 1969

> I rarely ever think about the past —Edmund Wilson, *New Yorker,* 12 June 1971

The longer intensive forms of *rarely* include *rarely if at all* (cited in Bryant), *rarely or never* (Bryant and OED), and *rarely if ever,* the best-attested version in our files. It is used with or without commas:

> In all the hullabaloo about Justice Douglas we rarely, if ever, told our readers ... —Theodore Bernstein, *Winners & Sinners,* 30 Apr. 1970

> ... says it rarely if ever sees a repeat shoplifting offender —Glynn Mapes, *Security World,* May 1968

The criticism of *rarely ever* takes some strange forms. One critic calls it "wordy, unidiomatic." How a 300-year-old idiom can be unidiomatic he does not say. As to wordiness, this critic suggests you replace *rarely ever* with *hardly ever, rarely, if ever,* or *rarely or never.*
Criticism of *rarely ever* can be ignored; Bryant has the right idea. In ordinary discursive prose, however, *rarely* is almost always used alone.

rarify See RAREFY, RARIFY.

rather 1. See HAD RATHER.
2. *Rather* is used both as a mild intensifier and as a mild de-emphasizer. The intensifier:

> He considers Pappy rather small potatoes —Harry S. Truman, diary, 10 Aug. 1945

The de-emphasizer:

> ... led a rather lonely but not altogether unhappy childhood —*Current Biography,* November 1965

In this respect *rather* operates much like *quite* (which see).
The use of *rather* in its diluting or softening function has drawn a smattering of criticism objecting to its use with words (usually adjectives) that are "warm" (Fowler 1926) or "strong, affirmative" (Copperud 1970). In spite of the comment in Copperud 1964, 1970, 1980, Fowler 1926, 1965, Follett 1966, and Janis 1984, we cannot find much basis for their objections; examples of the sort

they bring forth are hard to find in our files. Here are a few of our examples:

> ... in the late 1950's there came a rather dramatic swing in another direction —William G. Moulton, *NEA Jour.,* January 1965

> Delhi has had a problem with some rather ferocious monkeys —Peter Thomson, quoted in *Sports Illustrated,* 15 July 1968

> ... and an occasional quarrel ... was rather fun — Edward Seidensticker, *Low City, High City,* 1983

> ... would have looked down their aristocratic noses to see rather middle class men and women drinking sherry ... in their rooms —Suzanne Wilding, *Town & Country,* June 1976

> I read a little Samuel Pepys, rather like it —Renata Adler, *Pitch Dark,* 1983

> The other stories in this volume are rather more cheerful —*Times Literary Supp.,* 16 Apr. 1970

> I was becoming rather cross by this time —Graham Greene, *Travels with My Aunt,* 1969

> You write rather well and if you are interested I think I can get you a job as a cub reporter —Groucho Marx, undated letter to Goodman Ace, in *The Groucho Letters,* 1967

These examples are typical of our file on *rather* in its use as a softening qualifier, and they seem fully acceptable to us. It is hard to see what the problem is supposed to be.

3. *Rather a.* Phythian 1979 and Partridge 1942 offer some remarks on the proper employment of *rather a* before a noun. The concern here does not seem to be the old objection to *quite a,* some critics claiming it was improper for an adverb to qualify a noun, but to the retention of the word order with the adverb before the article when an adjective intervenes between *rather a* and the noun. Both Partridge and Phythian accept *rather a* with no adjective:

> ... it was rather a relief when the narcotics testimony ended —Richard Dougherty, *Atlantic,* February 1972

They prescribe *a rather* when an adjective intervenes:

> ... inside a rather larger plastic fish tank —Charles Baptist-Smith, *Observer Mag.,* 3 Feb. 1974

But we find that some writers retain the inverted order:

> ... the French could make rather a good counter-argument —Stephen E. Ambrose, *Johns Hopkins Mag.,* April 1966

> It was rather an unbelievable example of using excessive means —Hannah Arendt, *N.Y. Rev. of Books,* 18 Nov. 1971

> He is rather a worried participant in the custom — Richard Poirier, *A World Elsewhere,* 1966

The writers who keep the inverted order *rather a* in front of an adjective probably do so because they feel that the form is slightly more emphatic: "rather a good counter-argument" being felt to be stronger than "a rather good counter-argument." This, then, is not a matter of right and wrong; both orders are completely respectable. We suggest you make your choice with dis-

cretion; most of our examples follow the prescribed word order.

rather than   **1.** A knowledge of traditional grammar can lead the usage commentator astray. In the Latin grammar that traditional English grammar is based on, a word that is a conjunction can almost never be a preposition as well. English, however, is not bound by the limitations of Latin; many English words function as more than one part of speech. And English compound function words are especially slippery. It is often very hard to tell whether *as well as* or *other than* is working as a preposition or a conjunction or just as a combination of individual words. It is just this slipperiness that brings *rather than* up as a subject in Fowler 1926, 1965, Bremner 1980, Janis 1984, and Cook 1985. The question that puzzled Fowler was whether *rather than* always operated as a conjunction and thus had the same construction before as it had after, or whether it could also operate as a preposition and so connect dissimilar constructions.

We will not go into all of Fowler's thinking on this subject. We will simply point out that *rather than* does function like a preposition:

> Rather than being so quick to knock an attempt at change, Mr. Rustin should extend it the same leeway ... —Burrill L. Crohn, letter to the editor, *Harper's,* April 1970

> Rather than argue for the overthrow of the entire system, the Colonists realized ... that the basic values of British law were still valid —Daniel Sisson, *Center Mag.,* May 1969

> Is there any chance of spring publication, rather than waiting till fall? —E. B. White, letter, 28 Jan. 1942

In the most apparent prepositional use of *rather than,* it is followed by a gerund; in such use *rather than* frequently begins a sentence:

> Rather than permitting us to imagine ..., Lindblom forces us to consider ... —*N.Y. Times Book Rev.,* 19 Feb. 1978

But when parallel constructions appear on each side of *rather than,* it is functioning like a conjunction:

> ... implicating them, this time subtly rather than powerfully —J. I. M. Stewart, *Eight Modern Writers,* 1963

> ... speaking of her as a person rather than as an actress —*Current Biography,* September 1964

> ... for the sake of dramatic convenience rather than for motives that appeal to reason —John Butt, *English Literature in the Mid-Eighteenth Century,* edited & completed by Geoffrey Carnall, 1979

> ... they cause young people to think and reason rather than just sit and listen —Albert F. Eiss & Carolyn Mulford, *NEA Jour.,* November 1965

> ... I define the language by the literature in which it appears, rather than the literature by the language it employs —W. F. Bolton, *A Short History of Literary English,* 1967

We have met with the conjunctive use somewhat more often than the prepositional use; both are used in standard English.

2. Commentators from Partridge 1942 to Janis 1984 and Cook 1985 notice a curious construction in which a comparative that you would expect to be followed by *than* takes *rather than* instead. Here are two examples:

All this was new to him, his experience having made him more knowing about bookies rather than books —John Ferguson, *Death of Mr. Dodsley,* 1937 (in Partridge)

The group is more interested in the edible varieties and in experimenting with recipes rather than in pursuing rare specimens —*N.Y. Times,* 29 Dec. 1970 (in *Winners & Sinners,* 14 Jan. 1971)

Bernstein 1977 rejected these constructions on the basis of *rather's* etymology—it is the comparative of an obsolete adverb, but etymology is not really the point. The reason for the awkwardness of the sentences is that the *more* in each sentence leads the reader to expect the usual *than,* but *rather than* turns up in its place. The existence of such sentences (which we advise you to avoid) is good evidence that *rather than* is perceived as a unit by many writers. We lexicographers will, in time, have to recognize its existence.

For the controversy over *rather than* after *prefer,* see PREFER.

ravage, ravish Both of these verbs are ultimately derived from the same Middle French verb, *ravir,* but their fundamental meanings are distinct. *Ravage* has the basic sense "to plunder or destroy":

The war would ravage two particular reputations: Johnson's and McNamara's —David Halberstam, *Harper's,* February 1971

. . . as the coal company's power shovels ravage the land around them —H. L. Van Brunt, *Saturday Rev.,* 8 Apr. 1972

Ravish has three primary senses—"to seize and carry away":

The food was ravished by the semi-wild, emaciated cat —Dave Lee, *Cats Mag.,* July 1980

"to overcome with emotion (as joy or delight)":

Bellow is ravished by Alexandra's exotic . . . celebrity —Richard Stern, *N.Y. Times Mag.,* 21 Nov. 1976

and "to rape":

. . . brutally ravished her in a lower berth —*Time,* 3 Jan. 1955

As many commentators have noted, *ravage* and *ravish* are easily confused, although our evidence suggests that errors are rare in edited writing. We have only a few clear-cut examples:

. . . coming whenever he wanted to ravage her —James T. Farrell, *What Time Collects,* 1964

. . . a mountain torrent ravishes his potato field —*Saturday Rev.,* 29 Mar. 1952

If you feel uncertain about which word to use in a particular context, a quick look in the dictionary will clear things up.

It should be noted that *ravish* also has the rare sense "to plunder or rob."

. . . slaves and concubines ravished from the Pecos people —Willa Cather, *Death Comes for the Archbishop,* 1927

Buccaneer Henry Morgan, ravishing Panama of 400,000 pieces of eight in 1671 —*Time,* 24 Aug. 1953

Used in this sense, *ravish* resembles *ravage* closely enough that it may give the appearance of confusion even when none exists. That being so, you may well want to avoid this sense of *ravish.*

re This preposition was borrowed straight from Latin in the 18th century. It has some use in legal and business writing, but the usage books (for instance Harper 1975, 1985, Bernstein 1965, Flesch 1964, Copperud 1964, 1970, 1980, Irmscher 1976, Shaw 1975, 1987) tell everyone else to avoid it. Harper, for instance, calls it "pretentious in nonbusiness or nonlegal situations"; nonetheless, it is used in the book:

(He voted "no" re writing.) —Harper 1985

The evidence in our files shows that *re* is not a high-frequency word but has more general use than the usage writers suppose:

. . . fortunate or unfortunate enough to have something very like fanatical convictions re métier —Ezra Pound, *Polite Essays,* 1937

I have no idea what Don Regan knows or does not know re my private U.S. operation —Oliver North, quoted in *The Tower Commission Report,* 1987

. . . as low as you can get re fiction —Flannery O'Connor, letter, 31 May 1960

Snow, who has come back to rendezvous with Abbott and Angel re a new musical —Martin Levin, *N.Y. Times Book Rev.,* 24 June 1973

Call the Waterville Valley Resort Association . . . re inns and rental condominiums —Barbara Walder, *New York,* 15 Nov. 1976

It is only occasionally italicized in general contexts.

reaction There has been a considerable reaction against *reaction* used, as it often is in print and electronic journalism, as a sort of rough equivalent of *response, feeling,* or *opinion.* It usually turns up after something has been said, done, or produced:

. . . the critical reaction was no warmer than pessimistic rumor had predicted —*Current Biography,* April 1966

. . . the nature books . . . during the past three or four years have had a mixed reaction —Jude Bell, *N.Y. Times Book Rev.,* 19 Sept. 1976

On the two evening news shows I watched, Mr. Ford got as much time as a local crime story; one station even filmed the reaction in a downtown tavern —Karl E. Meyer, *Saturday Rev.,* 20 Mar. 1976

In no instance can I remember opposition Congressmen . . . ever having been brought into a studio for reaction following a news conference —Robert Goralski, *Johns Hopkins Mag.,* Spring 1971

. . . asking for comments and reaction to the black students' criticisms —*Bowdoin Alumnus,* January 1971

... but I feel that using the score from a movie for the celebration of the Lord's supper borders on the profane. What is your reaction? —Amy Vanderbilt, *Ladies' Home Jour.*, September 1971

More than half the critics say something to the effect that *reaction* is a scientific word and should not be used of people, an opinion that conveniently overlooks nearly two centuries of use as a political term in such expressions as "the forces of progress and reaction." *Reaction* has been used figuratively in various senses since Sir Thomas Browne in 1643. There is no reason to restrict its use to scientific contexts (in which, to be sure, it is frequently used), even if it becomes, at times, a tiresome cliché of the journalist. You can substitute some other word—*response, opinion, judgment, view,* or the like—if you think that *reaction* is overused. But the word has its own meaning and overtones, and it is not easily expendable in every circumstance.

Bremner 1980 and Bryson 1984 say that if you must use *reaction,* you should restrict its meaning to an immediate response to the event. This is eminently sensible advice, but we must observe that writers ignore it as often as they follow it.

read where See WHERE 2.

real The adverb *real,* which is used only as an intensifier, developed from a use of the adjective to modify compound noun phrases like *good turn.* By the 18th century the *real* was apprehended as an intensifier modifying *good* alone, and its independent use grew from then. It was a development that took place, apparently, outside of mainstream British English; the OED identifies it as chiefly Scottish and American, and we have some slight Irish evidence. It has been from the start primarily a spoken use.

Criticism of the adverbial *real* began as early as Ayres 1881, and it has not begun to drop off yet. Insofar as this criticism tells you that *real* is informal and more suitable to speech than to writing, it is fairly accurate. When it wanders from this line to insist that *real* is an adjective only, or that *real* is a substitute for *really,* it is wrong. It is potentially misleading to label *real* as an error for *really,* because *real* and *really* are not very often used in the same way. *Real* is a simple intensifier, more or less equivalent to *very;* it is used only with adjectives and adverbs. *Really* is a full-fledged adverb; it is only sometimes used in an intensive function, and even then is more likely to mean "truly, unquestionably" than simply "very." The handbook writer who set forth "My aunt is really ill" and "My aunt is real ill" as synonymous is mistaken. The difference can perhaps be suggested by this passage from an interview published in a University of Minnesota publication:

You work at writing for a couple of years and you get to feeling real sociable. By the end of a day spent sitting in a room with a typewriter, you're really ready to meet and greet and go hang out with your friends —Garrison Keillor, quoted in *Update* (Univ. of Minn.), Fall 1981

We should add here a word about speech and writing. While it is still true that *real* is more likely to be encountered in speech than in writing, we notice that it has spread considerably in general writing—primarily that of newspapers and magazines—as a part of an informal, conversational style.

A booth with a real different look was set up by a Los Gatos, Calif., shop —*Antiques and the Arts Weekly,* 3 Dec. 1982

... he didn't follow politics real closely —Larry Pressler, *People,* 12 July 1982

... plays a playwright who travels back in time. How? By closing his eyes and wishing real hard —David Sterritt, *Christian Science Monitor,* 18 Dec. 1980

Also, armadillos are real special to Texans —Wayne King, *N.Y. Times,* 7 Dec. 1982

We plan to do all of the above real soon —*Playboy,* August 1986

... who will see viewers real soon —Guy D. Garcia, *Time,* 29 Oct. 1984

... promising ourselves another visit real soon —Teresa Byrne-Dodge, *Houston Post Mag.,* 9 Sept. 1984

... with the stereo turned up real loud —Jack McCallum, *Sports Illustrated,* 3 Nov. 1986

On the first real warm day, you can sit on the back steps in your PJs —Garrison Keillor, *Lake Wobegon Days,* 1985

Although this is mainly an American usage, we do have just a bit of British evidence:

I'm having a real good time —Ellen Terry, letter, 7 Dec. 1896

The baddies were real bad, and the hero was intensely heroic —Benny Green, *Punch,* 4 May 1976

A real swish, swinging rally is in store at Great Brickhill on Saturday —*Bucks Standard* (Newport Pagnell, England), 20 Sept. 1974

Even some literary people are not averse to *real* in their letters:

He suffered everything but death—he is one they hung up by the heels, head downwards ... but stuck to his convictions like a hero—John Barker, a real manly fellow —Walt Whitman, letter, 9 June 1863

It's been real hot here —Flannery O'Connor, letter, 31 Oct. 1963

Men regard me as a real daft one —E. B. White, letter, 1 Nov. 1956

real facts See TRUE FACTS.

Realtor See JEWELRY.

rear See RAISE, REAR.

reason is because Bremner 1980 succinctly states two objections to *the reason is because:*

The grammatical reason for the error in "The reason he failed is because he didn't study" is that *the reason is* calls for a nounal clause: "The reason he failed is that he didn't study." The adverbial conjunction *because* is correct in "He failed because he didn't study."

A simpler reason is that *because* means "for the reason that" and therefore one would be saying,

"The reason he failed is for the reason that . . . ," which is as redundant as saying "The because is because."

Bremner's first objection is a 20th-century one; the second is older. The grammatical objection that *because* can only introduce an adverbial clause qualifying a verb and hence is wrong introducing a noun clause synonymous with *reason* was presumably erected to buttress the older objection, but who first formulated it we do not know. It is, however, mentioned in Fowler 1926, Utter 1916, and MacCracken & Sandison 1917.

Evans 1957 offers the best treatment of the grammatical question. He notes that *because* in most cases introduces a clause that qualifies a verb and is therefore said to be an adverbial conjunction. He also notes that some grammarians claim that *because* cannot be used in any other way and especially that it cannot introduce a noun clause. But Evans disagrees:

> *Because* may certainly introduce a noun clause that is joined to *it, this,* or *that* by some form of the verb *to be,* as in *if you are hungry it is because you didn't eat.* This has been standard English for centuries and the very grammarians who condemn the use of *because* in a noun clause do not hesitate to write *this is because.*

One of those objecting grammarians was H. W. Fowler, and he indeed did use *because* after *is* to introduce a noun clause:

> There is indeed no mystery about why people go wrong; it is because, if the thing had to be said without the use of the verb *like, would* & not *should* is the form to use —Fowler 1926, s.v. *like,* v.

And if *because* can refer to a pronoun like *it, this,* or *that,* Evans continues, there is no reason it should not refer to a noun like *reason.*

In other words, the grammatical objection has no basis in principle. It is erected ad hoc to rationalize dislike of *the reason is because* and is not invoked in other cases where *because* introduces a noun clause. But this has not prevented commentators from repeating the assertion or from defending it. In *American Speech,* February 1933, Fannye N. Cherry of the University of Texas established the standardness of *is because* by producing 31 citations of the construction from writers from Samuel Johnson to Robert Benchley; many well-known 19th-century writers such as Poe, Hawthorne, Thackeray, Hardy, Scott, and Stevenson were included. She also had examples of *the reason is because* from Bacon, Swift, and Addison.

So with the grammatical argument disposed of, the objectors must get along with the older charge of redundancy (as most of them do anyway). Bremner's summary is both succinct and apt, for he has used exactly the same test for redudancy that the original objector, Baker 1770, did: he defines *because* as "for the reason that" (Baker used "by Reason") and finds it redundant with the earlier *reason* in the sentence. Baker did not apply the term *redundant;* he merely said, "This Expression does not make Sense."

Any lexicographer can see the fault in that argument at once: *because* has been defined in such a way as to guarantee that it will be redundant or not make sense. Unless people actually write sentences like "The reason he failed is for the reason that . . ."—and in general they do not—there is no reason to assume that *because* has the meaning the critics assign it. Lexicographers have to define words *in situ,* not in the abstract, removed from context, and they know how easy it is to make hash of any sentence by deciding beforehand that a word in it means something other than what the author intended. If, instead, you grant that *because* can have the meaning "the fact that" or simply be equivalent to the conjunction *that,* the phrase *the reason is because* makes quite clear sense and is not redundant.

So we conclude that there is no sufficient basis for either the 18th-century or the 20th-century objection. But there still remains a question of the kind of writing in which the construction is used. Is it relatively rare in literary use and found primarily in dialectal use or in the speech of the uneducated? We think these examples will answer:

> The Reason was, because the *Religion* of the Heathen, consisted rather in Rites and Ceremonies —Francis Bacon, *Essays,* 1625

> . . . but Gad, the strongest reason is because I can't help it —John Dryden, *Marriage à-la-Mode,* 1673

> We may call them the weaker sex, but I think the true reason is because our Follies are stronger and our faults more prevailing —William Congreve, "Concerning Humour in Comedy," 1695

> The reason I tell you so is, because it was done by your parson —Jonathan Swift, *Journal to Stella,* 14 May 1711

> "You must know," says Will, "the reason is, because they consider every animal as a brother or sister in disguise. . . ." —Joseph Addison, *The Spectator,* 3 Apr. 1712 (in Cherry)

> The reason is because it is of more importance . . . that innocence should be protected than it is that guilt should be punished —John Adams, final argument in defense of the British soldiers involved in the Boston Massacre, 1770

> And the reason is, because language is not made either by Grammarians or Philosophers —Thomas Reid, *Essays on the Intellectual Power of Man,* 1785 (in Tucker 1967)

> If the fellow who wrote it seems to know more of my goings and comings than he could without complicity of mine, the reason is because he is a lovely old boy and quite took possession of me while I was in Boston —Robert Frost, letter, 22 Mar. 1915

> The reason every one now tries to avoid it, to deny that it is important, to make it seem vain to try to do it, is because it is so difficult —Ernest Hemingway, *Green Hills of Africa,* 1935

> One of the reasons so many found it difficult to understand Billy Mitchell was because the man was a stark realist —Eddie Rickenbacker, *Chicago Tribune Mag. of Books,* 28 Dec. 1952

> The only reason my appearances are rare (and this is something I don't usually disclose) is because nobody asks me oftener —Groucho Marx, letter, 22 Oct. 1951

> . . . they live in their own right, and the reason is because Sturt was not only *aware* but also because nature, thought and experience had made him compassionate —*Times Literary Supp.,* 13 July 1967

> The reason such a job won't be done again is simply because nobody can afford it —William Morris, *Col-*

lege Composition and Communication, October 1969

The reason the story has never been made into a film is because I won't sign a contract —E. B. White, letter, 28 Oct. 1969

One of the reasons Fulton is in such constant demand in all the media is because he is such a grafter —Paul Foster, *Scottish Field,* March 1975

... the reason for talking about his technique at all is because it was his means of producing that light —John Wain, *American Scholar,* Summer 1986

Except for Adams, these examples are all from written sources, a good many of them literary, with some letters and journals. The Dryden example was spoken by one of the heroes in the play. The phrase existed in 17th-century speech, and it exists in 20th-century speech:

... I think the reason anyone writes is because it's fun —William Faulkner, 30 May 1957, in *Faulkner in the University,* 1959

You may have noticed that in the 20th-century examples, *reason* is often separated from the *because* clause by intervening matter, sometimes quite long. In the older examples *reason* is more frequently found right next to *is because.*

Reason and *because* are sometimes found in constructions where they are linked by *than:*

... upon no wiser a Reason than because it is wondrous *Dark* —Jonathan Swift, *A Tale of A Tub,* 1710

I didnt want to be the one to direct you to the Gum Gatherer; but it is a favorite of mine if for no other reason than because it is the only poem that I know of that has found a way to speak poetically of chewing gum —Robert Frost, letter, 19 Feb. 1919

Occasionally, I write out what I have said in verse, and generally for no better reason than because I remember that I have written no verse for a long time —*The Autobiography of William Butler Yeats,* 1953

... for no other reason than because he's a tenor singer! —Ring Lardner, *How to Write Short Stories,* 1924

In this construction, too, *because* introduces a noun clause.

No treatment of *the reason is because* would be complete without mention of the doubly "redundant" *the reason why is because* (see also REASON WHY). It is more common in older sources (it seems to have been a favorite construction of Swift's) than newer ones but is certainly not yet extinct:

... the true reason why the country gentlemen are for a land-tax, and against a general excise, is, because they are fearful that if the latter be granted, they shall never get it down again —Samuel Pepys, diary, 5 Nov. 1666

And the reason why we are often louder than the players is, because we think we speak more wit —William Wycherly, *The Country Wife,* 1675

Now, the Reason why those Antient Writers treated this Subject only by Types and Figures, was, because they durst not make open Attacks —Jonathan Swift, *A Tale of A Tub,* 1710

And perhaps the reason why common Criticks are inclin'd to prefer a judicious and methodical Genius to a great and fruitful one, is, because they find it easier for themselves. ... —Alexander Pope, preface to translation of the *Iliad,* Book III, 1715

He saw that the reason why witchcraft was ridiculed was, because it was a phase of the miraculous —W. E. H. Lecky, *History of Rationalism in Europe,* 1865 (in Hodgson 1889)

The reason why all we novelists ... are abandoning novels and taking to writing motion-picture scenarii is because the latter are so infinitely the more simple —P. G. Wodehouse, *Something Fresh,* 1915

... one of the reasons why I am not particularly well read today is because I have spent so large a part of the last twenty years rereading Dickens and Jane Austen —Alexander Woollcott, letter, 15 Mar. 1932

The reason why his conclusion concerning Frege's argument seemed plausible at the time was because his propositional constituents are entities rather than the names of those entities —Ronald J. Butler, *Philosophical Rev.,* July 1954

... he clung to the literal truth of every word of the Bible, to the extent of believing that the reason why the Mastodons had become extinct ... was because they were too big to get into the Ark —*Times Literary Supp.,* 19 Sept. 1968

Practically everything that we have shown you so far is from writing, although there are three instances of fictitious speech (Dryden, Wycherly, Addison) and three of real speech (Adams, Faulkner, and Hemingway, who is quoting himself being interviewed). Bryant 1962 reports several studies showing *the reason is that*—the form prescribed by teachers of composition—occurs in edited prose about twice as often as *the reason is because;* the same studies show the proportion approximately reversed in speech. We have good evidence of the latter's currency in speech. In 1986 and 1987 we have recorded it from a counsel at the Iran-Contra hearings, a local newscaster, television actor Edward Woodward, and such sports figures as Lee Trevino, Henry Aaron, Jim Palmer, and Billy Martin. To these we can add the colleague who remarked of a newspaper story, "The reason she has a Mercedes is because her husband is an orthopedic surgeon."

A few points made earlier in passing should be underlined. You will note, as Bryant did also, that *the reason is because* occurs more often than not with words intervening between *reason* and *is because,* especially in the 20th-century evidence. You will also note that the evidence is heavily literary; *the reason is because* is not a locution avoided by writers. We suspect, however, that its use is often a matter of habit. We have multiple examples from Francis Bacon, Jonathan Swift, Alexander Woollcott, Ernest Hemingway, and Groucho Marx—not bad company for a writer.

In conclusion, the locution *the reason is because* has been attested in literary use for about three and a half centuries. It has been the subject of denigration for more than two centuries. Both the literary use and the disapproval will doubtless continue unabated. *Reason* and *because* seem to go together, probably, as Bryant remarks, because "the natural connective stressing the idea of reason is *because.*"

Our examination of the reasons for condemning the locution shows that they have little foundation, though this will not prevent their being repeated frequently by teachers of composition and usage commentators still to come. We are not advising you to use *the reason is because* just because many well-known writers have used it. If it is not your natural idiom, there is no reason for you to cultivate it. But if it is your natural idiom and you choose to continue with it, you will surely be in some very distinguished company.

reason why   *Reason why* is denounced as a redundancy by American Heritage 1969, 1982, Shaw 1970, 1975, 1987, and Prentice Hall 1978; it is defended by Evans 1957 and Bernstein 1971. Bernstein, in fact, finds instances when the *why* is required, and says that even when it is not required, it is never unidiomatic or wrong. Most other commentators who mention it are tolerant. Their tolerance is well taken, for many usage writers themselves use *reason why*. We have examples from Lounsbury 1908, Fowler 1926, Gowers 1948, Evans 1957, Phythian 1979, Johnson 1982, and Howard 1984.

The question of the propriety of *reason why* is an American one that originated in this century. We do not know who started it. Vizetelly 1906 mentions it, but only as an idiom; he later called it correct in a 1929 issue of the *Literary Digest*. Leonard included it on his 1932 survey of usage, where it was considered established, as it was again in Crisp's 1971 survey.

A contemporary author responding to Crisp's survey blamed the expression on Tennyson because of his line "Theirs not to reason why. . . ." A couple of commentators—Simon 1980 and Harper 1975, 1985—also give Tennyson some credit for propagating the phrase. But Tennyson—who used the verb *reason*, not the noun—could not have had more than a slight reinforcing effect: the locution dates back to 1225 and was well established long before Tennyson's time.

> The reason why a Poet is said, that hee ought to have all knowledges, is that . . . —Ben Jonson, *Timber: or, Discoveries,* before 1637

> I believe your Lordship will agree with me in the Reason, Why our Language is less Refined than those of Italy, Spain, or France —Jonathan Swift, *A Proposal for Correcting, Improving and Ascertaining the English Tongue,* 1712

> These observations will show the reason why the poem of *Hudibras* is almost forgotten —Samuel Johnson, *The Idler,* 2 June 1759

> . . . describing the reasons why any one should do so —Emily Dickinson, letter, 12 May 1842

> I see no reason why you should't be heard from — Henry Adams, letter, 18 Dec. 1863

> That is one reason why I like reading *older* novels — Lewis Carroll, letter, 10 July 1892

> . . . all reasons why he should avoid me —George Bernard Shaw, letter, 6 Sept. 1896

> . . . no good reason why you should publish a poem of mine of this length —Archibald MacLeish, letter, 21 Feb. 1926

> . . . several reasons why I should like to see it get back —James Thurber, letter, 19 Nov. 1946

> . . . this was one reason why Romanized Britain fell so easy a prey to the invader —G. M. Trevelyan, *A Shortened History of Britain,* 1942

> . . . one of the many reasons why the passage . . . throws into relief . . . —Henry James, *The Art of the Novel,* 1934

Reason why is still current:

> The reasons why a local conflict . . . could invoke a great world struggle —Charles S. Maier, *N.Y. Times Book Rev.,* 29 July 1984

> Fear of terrorist attacks is not the only reason why Americans are deciding to stay at home —*The Economist,* 26 Apr. 1986

Mary Vaiana Taylor's survey of university teaching assistants (*College English,* April 1974) discovered that 70 percent of them marked *reason why* as an error—making TAs more hostile to the phrase than even the Heritage usage panel. So if you are taking freshman English, you had perhaps best avoid offending with this usage. Anyone else can use *reason why* freely.

For a discussion of *reason why* followed by a linking verb and a clause introduced by *because,* see REASON IS BECAUSE.

receipt, recipe   The status of *receipt* as a synonym of *recipe* has been the cause of some uneasiness and confusion for decades:

> A perplexed correspondent asked Emily Post why it was that she used the word "receipt" instead of "recipe" in discussing cookery. Mrs. Post replied that "receipt" is a word of fashionable descent, used in this sense, so she preferred it to the more commercial "recipe" —Mrs. J. N. Cornelius, *Birmingham* (Ala.) *News,* 30 July 1937

A look in the OED doesn't give much support to the "fashionable" and "commercial" distinction made by Emily Post, but it does show that both *receipt* and *recipe* have been used in their synonymous sense for many centuries. Both words originally had to do with medicinal preparations rather than with food. *Receipt* is the older word, having as its first recorded use an occurrence in Chaucer's *Canterbury Tales* (ca. 1386). *Recipe* was first recorded as a noun in the 1500s. Both words had begun to be applied to cookery by about the middle of the 18th century. Thereafter *recipe* gradually took precedence over *receipt,* and it has long since established itself as the almost invariable word of choice. *Receipt* is now most familiar in the sense "a writing acknowledging the receiving of goods or money," a meaning that it has had since the 17th century. Its use as a synonym of *recipe* does still occur, and it is not incorrect, but it has a strongly old-fashioned quality, and its appearance in writing seems now almost always meant to evoke the past:

> . . . boiled cider applesauce, straight out of Grammie Bowles' blue receipt file —*Holiday,* November 1973

> . . . so she could follow a century-old Vermont "receipt" that called for cooking the whole fruit until it was tangy —Evan Jones, *N.Y. Times,* 6 Jan. 1982

receptive   When used with a preposition, *receptive* is now almost always followed by *to:*

> Now more than ever publishers will be forced to be receptive to bestseller books —James T. Farrell, in *New Directions,* 1946

> . . . he is just as receptive to constructive criticism as he is ready to give it —Chris Albertson, *Saturday Rev.,* 27 Nov. 1971

... Pasternak had been mildly receptive to the revolution —Irving Howe, *N.Y. Times Book Rev.*, 5 Feb. 1978

At one time *receptive* was quite commonly found with *of;* the OED quotes both Defoe and Coleridge, among other authors, for the use. *Receptive of* seems to have receded in contemporary writing, although it was not rare in the first half of the 20th century:

Robinson was, like the Wells he goes out of his way so often to praise, almost too receptive of new ideas —*Saturday Rev.*, 9 Jan. 1937

... expanding one's personality that it may become receptive of that inexplicable energy which guarantees personal power —Lloyd C. Douglas, *Doctor Hudson's Secret Journal*, 1939

Infrequently, *receptive* has been used with *for:*

... increase tension of the ear drum, making it more receptive for light sounds —*Saturday Rev.*, 9 Jan. 1937

recipe See RECEIPT, RECIPE.

recipient Fowler 1926 scornfully cites several instances of inflated journalistic prose in which someone is said to have been "the recipient of a presentation" or "the recipient of congratulations." Such self-conscious formality is perhaps less popular among journalists than it once was; we, at least, have collected no further evidence of *recipient* used in such a stiffly unnatural way. Its most familiar use in current English is to denote a person to whom something desirable, such as an award or a diploma, has been formally presented:

... is also the recipient of two honorary degrees — *Current Biography*, January 1967

... would an Englishman rather be the recipient of the Victoria Cross or ... —Herbert R. Mayes, *Saturday Rev.*, 4 Dec. 1971

The formality of the word is appropriate in these contexts.

reckon 1. When used with a preposition, *reckon* is most often followed by *with*, the phrase constituting an idiom meaning "to take into consideration":

... a brilliant book that will have to be reckoned with by all informed students of American society — Richard Hofstadter, *N.Y. Times Book Rev.*, 27 Feb. 1955

... have found Mormonism so fascinating or so provocative that they have been unable to resist the urge to reckon with it in print —Fawn Brodie, *Frontier*, December 1952

The assertion that man was always a killer ... must reckon with these many alternative possibilities — Lewis Mumford, *American Scholar*, Winter 1966–67

... the Communists were still a force to be reckoned with —Robert Shaplen, *New Yorker*, 24 Apr. 1971

Although *reckon* is also followed by *without*, meaning "to fail to consider," this usage is not nearly so prevalent as is *reckon with:*

But the Georgia legislature had reckoned without the speculators and their friends —Sidney Warren, *Current History*, February 1952

Miss Hope reckoned without the genius of Feuer and Martin —Henry Hewes, *Saturday Rev.*, 16 Oct. 1954

Reckon is sometimes used with *on:*

The King scarcely knew on what members of his own cabinet he could reckon —T. B. Macaulay, *The History of England*, vol. I, 1849

... a man of our own times and once again in the generations a man and a poet to reckon on — Edward Townsend Booth, *Saturday Rev.*, 4 Oct. 1947

Occasionally *reckon* is followed by *among, as, at, by, in,* or *upon:*

... he must be reckoned among the great mathematicians of our time —*Times Literary Supp.*, 21 May 1970

I pass to another field where the dominance of the method of sociology may be reckoned as assured — *Selected Writings of Benjamin N. Cardozo*, ed. Margaret E. Hall, 1947

These assets were reckoned at $1,250,000 —Marquis James, *The Texaco Story*, 1953

... each cutter's share ... was reckoned only by the number of days he had worked —Joel Aronoff, *Psychology Today*, January 1971

... RCA's productivity as reckoned in sales per employee —Edgar H. Griffiths, *Annual Report, RCA*, 1977

There are many things in which I think I shall be wiser if I come back, but do not reckon upon it — *The Letters of Rachel Henning, Written between 1853 and 1882*, 1952

In American English, *reckon* may be found with *to*, but only infrequently. In British English, *reckon* followed by *to* and the infinitive is quite common:

... despite his astonishing anticipations of the painting of the end of the nineteenth century, it seems better to reckon him to the old school —Frank Jewett Mather, Jr., *Modern Painting*, 1927

... up till then it had not reckoned to accept papers of living authors, even as gifts —Philip Larkin, *Required Writing*, 1983

... with gold in the $170 range, it is reckoned to be worthwhile having a look at the gold prospects — Leslie Parker, *Financial Times* (London), 17 Apr. 1974

... he reckons to spend about a year on a book — Anna Pavord, *Observer Mag.*, 14 Apr. 1974

In both American and British English, *reckon* is often followed by a clause:

"I reckon it would scare Senator Johns half to death...." —John Dos Passos, *Number One*, 1943

"... As for finishing the job, I reckon we'll all be there together...." —Richard Llewellyn, *A Few Flowers for Shiner*, 1950

He doubtless reckoned, as almost everyone here reckons, that it was a mite better to uphold the courts —Richard H. Rovere, *New Yorker*, 5 Oct. 1957

We reckon that we have been hired to get results —
The Bookseller, 18 May 1974

2. *"Reckon" in the sense of "suppose, think":*

... so I reckon Bernage is on very good foot when he goes to Spain —Jonathan Swift, *Journal to Stella,* 12 Feb. 1711

Howard 1977 notes this use of *reckon* as one of several standard 18th-century usages that survive in common use in British English but have dropped out of standard American use. Some examples from British English:

Our brickies reckon the house that Jack built in England would go up faster here —*8 O'Clock* (Auckland, N.Z.), 8 Feb. 1975

"If you reckon that paradise is a hamburger...." — William Nagle, *Nation Rev.* (Melbourne), 1 May 1975

... I reckon they pinched the money —John Fowles, *The Collector,* 1963

We used to reckon it upped a man's sex appeal at least 20 per cent —advt., *Sunday Times Mag.* (London), 7 Apr. 1974

Russia is one place Americans reckon they are unlikely to be victims of a terrorist attack —*The Economist,* 26 Apr. 1986

In American English this use is mostly dialectal; it may occasionally be used in informal or deliberately countrified contexts:

And I bought this one for $4.75. I was, oh I reckon, ten years old —William Faulkner, 7 Mar. 1957, in *Faulkner in the University,* 1959

I reckon I grew up under Roosevelt —Representative Claude Pepper, quoted in *People,* 21 June 1982

I reckon he doesn't like to feel surrounded by females —Flannery O'Connor, letter, 20 Sept. 1951

... we fairly reckoned you'd be with us on one of the weekends —John O'Hara, letter, March 1931

I reckon if anybody wears a double-breasted suit properly it's Doug Fairbanks —G. Bruce Boyer, *Town & Country,* March 1983

More Americans would use *I guess* where these people use *I reckon.*

recollect, remember   The distinction that can be made between these words is that *recollect* implies—or can imply—a conscious effort to recall something to the mind ("He tried to recollect the name of the street"), while *remember* more generally implies only having something available in one's memory ("He always remembered what she had said"). This distinction has been noted in dictionaries at least since Webster 1828, and in books on usage at least since Richard Grant White 1870. White regarded the use of *recollect* without connotations of conscious effort as an error, and a number of subsequent commentators (such as Vizetelly 1906, Bierce 1909, Fowler 1926, and Evans 1957) have more or less agreed with him. But the evidence shows that the distinction is not really a strong one. The "conscious effort" connotations of *recollect* certainly exist, and they come across clearly in some contexts:

"... tried to recollect how you looked, but I have never been able to recall a single feature." —Douglas

Southall Freeman, "General Lee at the Surrender," in *Worlds of Adventure* (textbook), ed. Matilda Bailey & Ullin Whitney Leavell, 1951

But for many writers the real distinguishing characteristic of *recollect* seems to be that it has a folksy quality suggestive of rustic speech:

"I don't recollect ever hearing anything foolish about Rebekah ..." —Ellen Glasgow, *Barren Ground,* 1925

I don't recollect ever once hearing any man of my family swear ..., so of course it didn't come natural to me —Gerald Warner Brace, *The Garretson Chronicle,* 1947

And *recollect* also occurs in contexts where it seems to be little more than a straightforward synonym of *remember:*

Thank you for recollecting my weakness —Emily Dickinson, letter, 1869

... I recollect very clearly that one day when I was out sailing it snowed —Frances H. Eliot, *New England Journeys,* 1953

In short, *recollect* has distinct shades of meaning that are apparent in some but not all of its uses. It is, fundamentally, a synonym of *remember,* and its use without connotations of conscious effort is not an error.

reconcile   Two prepositions are idiomatic after *reconcile*—*with* and *to:*

... to reconcile technology with human cussedness —Russell Lynes, *Harper's,* October 1968

... how could one reconcile this arrogant separatism with the goals of integration? —David Loye, *Psychology Today,* May 1971

... it temporarily reconciles us to that condition — Clifton Fadiman, *Center Mag.,* January/February 1971

Nothing can reconcile Nader to the time lag — Charles McCarry, *Saturday Rev.,* 12 Feb. 1972

Only *with* is possible when *reconcile* is being used as an intransitive verb:

... was estranged from her husband ... but has since reconciled with him —*Springfield* (Mass.) *Union,* 24 May 1968

recourse   See RESOURCE.

recrudescence   *Recrudescence* in its literal sense is a medical word denoting a renewed outbreak of a disease:

... prompt use of penicillin in streptococcic pharyngitis ... has eliminated recrudescences following such infections —*Therapeutic Notes,* Feburary 1951

In extended use, *recrudescence* typically describes a renewed occurrence or appearance of something objectionable:

... the recrudescence of violent nationalism in any European country —Walter Laqueur, *Commentary,* January 1972

It has also sometimes been used as a neutral term simply equivalent to *renewal* or *revival:*

> ... dates from this recrudescence of the Italian theatre —Sacheverell Sitwell, *The Dance of the Quick and the Dead,* 1936

> ... there has been a sharp recrudescence of interest in the Rogers mystique —H. Allen Smith, *Esquire,* May 1974

Such usage was first criticized in 1906 by the Fowler brothers, who argued that *recrudescence* should only be applied to the renewal of something unwelcome. H. W. Fowler repeated the criticism more strongly in 1926, and Eric Partridge noted and agreed with Fowler's opinion in 1942. Evans 1957, however, asserted that in American usage *recrudescence* was applicable to any renewed outbreak, "good or bad."

This issue is not an important one for most writers. *Recrudescence* is a fairly uncommon word, and most writers are unlikely to use it, either because they do not know it themselves or because they suspect that many of their readers will not know it. Our evidence suggests that *recrudescence* was in somewhat more common use during the first half of the century than it is now, and most of our examples of the disputed use are from that period. Those who now use the word in extended applications, according to our evidence, almost always use it in ways that would be approved by the Fowlers and by Partridge.

recur, recurrence, reoccur, reoccurrence Of these two pairs, *recur* and *recurrence* are by far the more common. A couple of commentators criticize *reoccur* and *reoccurrence* as unnecessary, but they are distinguishable in some ways from *recur* and *recurrence*. *Reoccur* and *reoccurrence* are the more basic words: they simply tell you that something happened again. *Recur* and especially *recurrence* can suggest a periodic or frequent repetition as well as the simpler notion.

> Castillo was removed from the game after the third because of a muscle pull on the right side of his neck. Twins trainer Dick Martin said it was a reoccurrence of a previous injury —Tom Yantz, *Hartford* (Conn.) *Courant,* 20 May 1983

In this example, *reoccurrence* merely says that the muscle pull had happened before; if the trainer had used *recurrence,* it could have suggested that the player had had the same injury more than once before. This does not quite mean, as one or two critics hold, that *reoccurrence* means one repetition only; it rather implies nothing about the number of repetitions, whereas *recurrence* is likely to.

But such niceties aside, most writers make do with *recur* and *recurrence:*

> There was a recurrence of this after the cataract operation —James Thurber, letter, 18 Dec. 1950

> ... institutions specifically created to prevent a recurrence of past fiscal problems —Felix G. Rohatyn, *The Twenty-Year Century,* 1983

> ... the motifs have become so numerous ... that the mind cannot hold them together. One can only enjoy them as they occur and recur —George Stade, *N.Y. Times Book Rev.,* 17 June 1979

redolent According to Follett 1966, *redolent with* has a bad odor. He calls it "almost as uncouth as *smells with*

would be." Bernstein 1965 says flatly that *redolent* takes the preposition *of.* And so it does:

> ... are delightfully well-regulated, clean, orderly and redolent of pleasure —Albert Goldman, *New York,* 24 July 1972

> ... the air was redolent of sawdust, paint, and coffee —David Dorsey, *New England Monthly,* March 1988

But it also takes the preposition *with,* as a look in the OED clearly shows. *Redolent of* is the older and more common idiom, but *redolent with* has been in use since the early 19th century and is certainly standard:

> The Grand Being entered his magnificent palace, redolent with fragrant perfumes —Henry Alabaster, *The Wheel of the Law,* 1871 (OED)

> ... a London working-class shopping district ... redolent with fried fish shops —C. S. Forester, *The African Queen,* 1935

> ... the atmosphere had been redolent with sympathies —Angus Wilson, *Such Darling Dodos,* 1950

> ... the image is redolent with keen, even if less than original, irony —John Simon, *New York,* 18 Oct. 1976

redundancy Have you ever felt that when you were talking to someone you were not being listened to? That your message was being misunderstood, or only partially understood? We have all had that experience, surely. It could be described as transmitting a message over a noisy channel—the noise in this instance being whatever it is in the mind of our listener that distracts attention from what we are saying. It is analogous to the problem of sending a message by radio or telephone through a lot of static.

Every language, it seems, has built-in mechanisms for helping the spoken message penetrate the noise. These mechanisms are called *redundancy,* a sense of the term perhaps borrowed from information science, the mathematical study of the transmission of electronic messages. A useful definition of *redundancy* can be found in Todd & Hancock 1986:

> In linguistics, it refers to data which may be unnecessary but which may help our understanding. In a phrase such as:
> *those two dogs*
> plurality is marked three times. Most speech contains redundancies and so we often understand utterances even if we miss part of what was said.

This redundancy is something that helps a speaker or a writer get a message across even when the hearer or reader has missed part of it through inattention or distraction. This, then, is a useful redundancy; it protects the message and it facilitates the reception of the information or the idea the speaker or writer is trying to communicate.

Repetition, in one way or another, is the most obvious form of useful redundancy; by repeating an idea or a whole message, the writer or speaker can ensure that the reader or hearer does not miss the point. But, as the information scientists point out, a price must be paid for this use of repetition. It is loss of transmission speed. If everything in the message were to be repeated, transmission speed would slow down to almost nothing. If the speaker repeats and repeats, communication is likely to be broken altogether; the hearer falls asleep or walks away. If the writer repeats and repeats, the reader closes the book.

This brings us to a second meaning of *redundancy* that Todd & Hancock mentions: the use of too many words, what we might call wordy redundancy. The whole question of redundancy for writers comes down to the identification of the fine line between useful redundancy and wordy redundancy. This is seldom a problem in conversation, unless you have the misfortune to be a long-winded bore, but it may be one for the public speaker. It is also not a problem for usage writers, almost all of whom fail to recognize that there is such a thing as useful redundancy, even though they employ it themselves.

Here are a number of examples of useful redundancy. We will depart from the usual style of our examples and italicize the redundancies. You will note that many of them involve adverbs and prepositions. There are also several examples with emphasizing adjectives.

> These five passages have not been picked *out* because they are especially bad. . . . I number them so that I can refer *back* to them —George Orwell, "Politics and the English Language," 1946

> . . . to see if the waters were abated from *off* the face of the ground —Genesis 8:8 (AV), 1611

> And both return *back* to their chairs —Shakespeare, *Richard II,* 1596

> . . . would also revert *back* to Panama —*Current Biography,* June 1968

> **concur** . . . has three *different* meanings —Harper 1985

> There is *also the additional* problem raised by the casting . . . —John Simon, *New York,* 5 Apr. 1976

> . . . are usually *unnecessary* padding in a sentence — Little, Brown 1986

> . . . marked for James the *final* end of his freedom — K. M. Elisabeth Murray, *Caught in the Web of Words,* 1977

> . . . one's *past* history was going to be removed — Norman Mailer, *Harper's,* March 1971

> . . . the process of starting *over again* —Leacock 1943

> . . . let us begin with a *true and authentic* story —W. M. Thackeray, *The Book of Snobs,* 1846

> . . . the unequal combat waged here nightly is replayed *again* —Robert E. Taylor, *Wall Street Jour.,* 11 Sept. 1980

> . . . it commands our attention so much that we are never necessitated to repeat the same thing *over a second time* —Adam Smith, lecture, 14 Jan. 1763, in *Lectures on Rhetoric and Belles Lettres,* ed. John M. Lothian, 1971

None of these redundancies impedes the flow of information, not even the last and longest (taken from speech, where longer redundancies are more useful than they are in writing). They all belong to our first type of redundancy—the useful—or if not positively useful, at least harmless. It is interesting that the handbooks quoted here (especially Harper 1985 and Little, Brown 1986) devote considerable space to the denunciation of

exactly these kinds of redundant combinations, as does the book written by John Simon (Simon 1980). And George Orwell, in the very article we have quoted, lays it down as a rule that we should cut all unnecesssary words out of our writing.

The notion that redundant words should be eliminated from writing goes back to the 18th century. Lindley Murray 1795 put it this way:

> The first rule for promoting the strength of a sentence, is, to prune it of all redundant words and members.

Murray may have taken this rule from one of his sources. It is not much different from Orwell's:

> If it is possible to cut a word out, always cut it out.

But it had been recognized by writers as early as Ben Jonson that too terse a style could be a fault, not a virtue:

> . . . the Language is thinne, flagging, poore, starv'd; scarce covering the bone, and shewes like stones in a sack. Some men to avoid Redundancy, runne into that; and while they strive to have no ill blood, or Juyce, they loose their good —*Timber: or, Discoveries,* before 1637

Some recent commentators too, such as Evans 1957 and Bailey 1984, warn against being too concise.

To repeat, there are two kinds of redundancy—the desirable kind of the linguist and the undesirable wordy kind. Much that is written in usage books about redundancy mistakes the first for the second. The usual pronouncements about *refer back, final result, collaborate together, continue on, end result, past history, general consensus, personal friend, off of,* and many, many more should therefore be taken with a large grain of salt. This is not to say that you *must* use the redundant forms, but you should feel free to judge for yourself where they may be useful to communication or may simply sound better than the shorter alternatives. Remember that the sound and rhythm of a sentence are important in transmitting your message through the noise:

> . . . inside a sentence the mere sound, the mere number of syllables used, is sometimes more important than the bare meaning of the words. In writing, as in conversation, an economical use of words is not always what we want —Evans 1957

See also WORDINESS.

refer   This verb is often used with *back:*

> . . . "Death in Venice" also refers back to Britten's earlier operas on nearly every page —Peter G. Davis, *N.Y. Times,* 13 Oct. 1974

Such usage has been the object of criticism at least since Krapp 1927 described it as "a crude pleonasm for *refer.*" Among recent commentators who have cited *refer back* for redundancy are Shaw 1975, Harper 1975, 1985, and Copperud 1980. Bernstein 1971, on the other hand, pooh-poohs such criticism, asserting that "The notion of *back* is not at all prominent or even necessarily present in the word *refer,* which has as its primary meaning to direct attention to." We think that Bernstein makes a good point. *Back* may seldom be necessary with *refer,* but the "backward" connotations of *refer* are usually not strong, and *back* can be useful in reinforcing them:

> Professor Dulles . . . has throughout referred back to the original sources —Owen Lattimore, *N.Y. Herald Tribune Book Rev.*, 2 June 1946

> They do not refer back to models in the reality we know —John W. Aldridge, *After the Lost Generation*, 1951

> I number them so that I can refer back to them when necessary —George Orwell, "Politics and the English Language," 1946

> I have to be careful with my own research. I put it down in black and white. People can refer back to it —John D. MacDonald, *TV Guide*, 24 Nov. 1979

If you tend to be especially sensitive to redundancy in writing, you may want to avoid *refer back* in your own. Many good writers find it useful, however.

referendums, referenda These two plurals are about equally represented in our files for the past thirty years. In the 1960s and 1970s, *referendums* was somewhat more common; in the 1980s *referenda* has a slight lead. Copperud 1980 thinks that *referenda* sounds affected, but there is nothing in our evidence to suggest that anyone else does.

No one seems to have any difficulty in recognizing *referenda* as a plural. For a list of foreign plurals which are sometimes used as singulars, see LATIN PLURALS.

reflexive pronouns For a discussion of the use of reflexive pronouns in place of nominative and especially objective forms, see MYSELF. See also HISSELF; THEIRSELVES; THEMSELF; YOURSELF, YOURSELVES.

refute *Refute* has two senses, both of which are in common use, but one of which is widely regarded as an error. Its original and uncontroversial sense is "to prove wrong; show to be false or erroneous":

> It is not necessary to refute such an argument point by point —Denis Goulet, *Center Mag.*, May 1969

> . . . his superior book . . . appears to refute that contention —*New Yorker*, 2 Oct. 1971

Its disputed sense is "to deny the truth or accuracy of":

> We refute these aspersions whether they come from our best friends or our worst foes —Sir Winston Churchill, address in House of Commons, 18 Jan. 1945, in *Voices of History 1945–46*, ed. Nathan Ausubel, 1946

> Prime Minister Michael Manley . . . yesterday again refuted allegations that Jamaica House interfered — *Jamaica Weekly Gleaner*, 13 Feb. 1974

This sense seems to have originated in the 20th century. Its common use has become apparent only in the past several decades, but criticism of it dates back as far as Utter 1916. Most usage commentators now routinely take note of it, and all that do consider it a mistake (the British, in particular, seem to feel strongly on this subject). It is, however, extremely common, and the contexts in which it occurs are standard. Its most frequent use is by journalists in reporting the emphatic denials issued by those accused of wrongdoing. Hardly a day now goes by, it seems, without one government official or another refuting a new set of allegations.

regard 1. *In regard to, with regard to, as regards, regarding.* There is a mixed bag of opinion about these, in which we can discern two main lines of commentary. The first of these apparently began with Quiller-Couch 1916, who condemned *as regards* and *with regard to* as circumlocutory and jargonistic. Many modern handbooks, especially the college variety, express a similar judgment, often extending it to *in regard to* and *regarding* as well. The critics prefer such alternatives as *about, on,* and *concerning,* and in many contexts you will no doubt find them preferable yourself. But remember that the matter of wordiness is entirely secondary to the matter of how your sentence sounds. When longer phrases suit the rhythm of a sentence better than short ones, the longer ones are a better choice.

The second line of comment goes back at least as far as MacCracken & Sandison 1917, where *in regards to* used in place of *in regard to* is cited as an error. The adherents to this line are also numerous, but they are almost all American (the one exception is Longman 1988). The issue in this case appears to be largely a social one. *In regards to* seems to be an expression heard chiefly from those who speak H. L. Mencken's "vulgate."

Most of our citations were taken from phone-in radio programs. We also have found it in a letter written to us and once in print by this noted practitioner of the vulgate:

> . . . maybe boys and gals who wants to take up writing as their life work would be benefited if some person like I was to give them a few hints in regards to the technic of the short story —Ring Lardner, preface, *How to Write Short Stories*, 1924

Our evidence suggests that *in regards to* is an oral use not found in edited prose.

In regard to, with regard to, as regards, and *regarding,* on the other hand, are all perfectly standard. Here are a few examples of the words at work:

> In regard to the work of an already famous or infamous author it decides . . . —Edgar Allan Poe, *The Literati*, 1850

> . . . conclusions I had reached with regard to Vietnam —Tip O'Neill with William Novak, *Man of the House*, 1987

> . . . adviser to Douglas of Cavers with regard to the annual distribution of alms —K. M. Elisabeth Murray, *Caught in the Web of Words*, 1977

> Indeed the similarity . . . is extraordinary, as regards the military methods of both sides —G. M. Trevelyan, *A Shortened History of England*, 1942

> As regards function, these centuries are those in which the ancient patterns of cumulative negation appear in the standard language —Strang 1970

> Regarding the four types of heart diseases . . . , the president of ABC said . . . —Winston Munnings, *Nassau* (Bahamas) *Guardian*, 3 Mar. 1984

> Miss Crawley was pleased at the notion of a gossip with her sister-in-law regarding the late Lady Crawley —W. M. Thackeray, *Vanity Fair*, 1848

2. A curious issue concerns the omission of *as* after *regard* in constructions where *as* would normally be expected ("was regarded a traitor" rather than "was regarded as a traitor"). This subject has troubled British commentators from Fowler 1907 to Longman 1988. It has penetrated one or two American books, perhaps because of its lengthy treatment by Fowler. The problem is this: *regard* is generally associated with verbs that take a direct object and a second complement introduced by a particle: *regard* (object) *as, describe* (object) *as, take* (object) *for, look upon* (object) *as,* and so forth. Since some time in the 19th century (the OED's earliest example is from 1836), *regard* has been showing some movement in the direction of complex transitive verbs like *think,* which take an object and a complement with no intervening particle. *Consider,* the verb prescribed by Fowler to replace *regard* in his numerous examples, is strongly linked with the complex transitive verbs (though it is also used with *as* like *regard,* a usage decried by some American commentators).

The fact that Fowler 1926 has more than twice as many examples as Fowler 1907 suggests that this use of *regard* had a burst of popularity around the turn of the century, which continued right up to 1926. As late as 1968 the grammarian Randolph Quirk (quoted in Strang 1970) said that it was "readily attested in everyday examples of speech and writing as well as in the vociferous complaints of purists." But, curiously enough, Quirk et al. 1985 calls *as* with *regard* obligatory and makes no mention of complex transitive use at all. It hardly seems possible that the construction disappeared completely between 1968 and 1985.

All of this British controversy is a bit puzzling to the American, as Copperud 1980 attests. The constructions that so exercised Fowler are rare in our files. Fowler's first objection was to *regard* with a complement introduced by an infinitive rather than *as:*

> "You perceive that even if this Jehovah is not God he is nevertheless regarded to be in the enjoyment of considerable powers...." —Henry Baerlein, *The House of the Fighting-Cocks,* 1880

That is our only example. Of the complex transitive we have a genuine American example (in the passive):

> ... treated in a manner calculated to make him feel that he is regarded a sinister figure —George F. Kennan, *New Republic,* 2 Feb. 1953

But this, too, is our only one. Either our editors have been missing this construction for the past half century, or it is relatively rare in American English.

We have no current British evidence, either, so we are not sure whether British use of complex transitive *regard* has dwindled. The silence of Quirk et al. 1985 might suggest that, but the notices in Longman 1984 and Longman 1988 suggest that it is still in use.

Objections to the use of *as* after other complex transitive verbs are noted at AS 5 and at CONSIDER 1.

regret When a preposition follows the noun *regret,* the usual choice is *for:*

> ... his bitter regrets for past happiness —T. S. Eliot, "Shakespeare and the Stoicism of Seneca," in *Selected Essays,* 1932

> ... regrets for past mistakes —*Times Literary Supp.,* 29 Apr. 1955

Note that in the Eliot citation "regrets for" means something like "regretful longings for," whereas in the second citation it means simply "regretful feelings for." The second citation illustrates the more common usage. Other prepositions that may occur after *regret* are *at* and

over, neither of which would be idiomatic with the "regretful longings" sense, but both of which are possible with the "regretful feelings" sense.

regretful, regrettable, regretfully, regrettably Fowler 1926 was the first to observe that *regretful* is sometimes confused with *regrettable.* Many later commentators have also felt the need to explain the distinction between these words, although the emphasis in recent years has shifted more to the use of the adverbs, *regretfully* and *regrettably.* Fowler cited three passages, apparently gleaned from newspapers, in which *regretful* was used to mean "causing regret" (which is the meaning of *regrettable*) rather than "feeling or showing regret." Strangely enough, we have no further evidence of *regretful* used in this way from any other source, including other usage writers, the OED, and our own citation files. If this use of *regretful* still occurs, it is apparently quite rare. The adverb *regretfully,* on the other hand, is beginning to show a tendency to be used as a synonym of *regrettably,* meaning "to a regrettable extent" or "in a manner that causes regret." Our first evidence of this use is from the mid-1960s, which is also when it was first criticized (by Flesch 1964 and Bernstein 1965). It is possible that this use owes something to the similar use of *hopefully* (which see), which underwent a boom in popularity a few years earlier. *Regretfully* has never approached *hopefully* in frequency of use, however. We have only a handful of citations for the disputed sense of *regretfully,* including the following:

> ... seems to have been their last, and regretfully lost, chance to talk with Jenny —Mabel F. Hale, *New-England Galaxy,* Winter 1965

> ... its regretfully pronounced tendency to obliterate distinctions —Maurice Friedberg, *Saturday Rev.,* 10 Jan. 1970

> ... we regretfully overlooked an announcement —Mort Reed, *Springfield* (Mass.) *Union,* 5 Aug. 1972

> Regretfully, that is no grounds for leniency towards him —*New Statesman,* 20 Aug. 1976 (OED Supplement)

Regrettably is still much the more common choice in such contexts:

> ... and shows, regrettably, that he is still under their influence —John Kenneth Galbraith, *Saturday Rev.,* 6 Nov. 1971

> None of my uncles, regrettably, was French —S. J. Perelman, *N.Y. Times Mag.,* 15 Jan. 1978

> ... which I regrettably missed —Simon 1980

Note that *regrettably* functions in these passages as a sentence modifier (see SENTENCE ADVERB), more or less equivalent to "I regret to say." *Regretfully* in the passage from *New Statesman* functions in the same way.

reign, rein The triumph of the automobile is revealed in our loss of awareness of words associated with the horse. *Rein* is a case in point. Once an everyday household word, it has been driven into relative obscurity by the automobile. Horse-lovers still know and use it, of course, as do jockeys and enthusiasts of horse racing and dressage. Several idiomatic expressions with *rein* continue in general use, but since the word is not nearly as common as it once was, writers and keyboarders tend to confuse it with its homophone *reign.* Copperud 1980 takes note of *in full reign* and *turn over the reigns.* Our files have *free reign* from *Harper's Bazaar* in 1981 and *People* in 1987, and *takes the reigns* from *TV Guide* in 1986. If you are not sure whether you want *rein* or *reign,* your dictionary will help you.

reiterate This verb has attracted commentary because it has a kind of built-in redundancy; there is a rarely used verb *iterate* (from the Latin *iterum,* "again") that itself means "to say or do again," so that it seems as if *reiterate* ought to mean something like "to re-say or re-do again," or "to say or do over and over." Bernstein 1962 disapproves its use in describing a first repetition (he favors *repeat* or *restate*), and Einstein 1985 agrees:

> If you've said something once and you now say it again, you aren't reiterating. You're iterating. From the third time on, you're reiterating.

But other commentators (such as Harper 1975, 1985 and Bryson 1984) recognize that no such nice distinction exists in actual usage. Both *iterate* and *reiterate* are used essentially as synonyms of *repeat,* with the chief distinction between them being that *reiterate* is the far more common word. *Reiterate* does, however, often convey the idea of many repetitions:

> ... by echoing the point ... Mr. Kaminsky had frequently reiterated with gallows humor —Judith Appelbaum, *N.Y. Times Book Rev.,* 12 Dec. 1982

> ... and repeatedly reiterates his views that the Supreme Court's ... decision was wrong —David Farrell, *Boston Globe,* 22 July 1984

> ... even such genuine affection grows numbing when reiterated more than 600 times —Geoffrey C. Ward, *N.Y. Times Book Rev.,* 7 Aug. 1983

But it frequently has no such connotations. Very often, it is instead distinguished from such common verbs as *repeat* and *restate* by connotations of forcefulness and emphasis:

> ... he reiterated his anti-war views even more forcefully —*Dictionary of American Biography,* 1936

> In his speech of acceptance Wilson reiterated his belief in "aggressive Americanism, international realism, and no compromise with communism." —*Current Biography 1953*

> This, I reiterate, *might* have happened —George F. Kennan, *New Yorker,* 1 May 1971

> To reiterate: a catch phrase is something to be both admired ... and avoided —Simon 1980

Iterate, on the other hand, is rarely used except in mathematical and technical writing:

> ... the functions obtained by iterating the operation of differentiation —School Mathematics Study Group, *Calculus, Part I,* 1965

Outside of such contexts, it is a decidedly bookish word:

> This ancient motif ... was classically iterated by Horace and later, in the last gasp of a noble and epicurean Roman culture, by Ausonius —J. O. Tate, *National Rev.,* 15 Nov. 1985

rejoice The next time something makes you feel like rejoicing, feel free to rejoice either *in* it or *at* it. *In* is the more common choice, but *at* is also idiomatic and far from rare:

> We do not, I suspect, rejoice in force more than other nations —Stringfellow Barr, *Center Mag.,* May 1968

> ... the young people who rejoice in such language —Franklin L. Ford, *Harvard Today,* Autumn 1968

> A layman can only rejoice at the legal subtlety and boldness —Robert Lekachman, *New Republic,* 29 Nov. 1954

Rejoice in is sometimes used to mean simply "have or possess":

> One of the characters ... rejoices in the name of Sherlock Feldman —Bennett Cerf, *Saturday Rev.,* 22 May 1954

> The higher parts of the mountains rejoice in an average annual rainfall of thirty inches —Oliver La Farge, *N.Y. Times Mag.,* 15 Aug. 1954

Another preposition that occasionally occurs after *rejoice* is *over:*

> I wish you to rejoice with me over the consummation of this great gift —Ira Remsen, quoted in *Johns Hopkins Mag.,* April 1966

relate The sense of intransitive *relate* that means "to have or establish a relationship, interact" seems to have had its origins in the jargon or shoptalk of psychology and sociology. It established itself in general use during the 1960s as something of a vogue word. It has received unflattering notice in Strunk & White 1972, 1979, Perrin & Ebbitt 1972, Ebbitt & Ebbitt 1982, Bremner 1985, and Harper 1975, 1985. A few of these find it a tad more tolerable when *relate* is followed by a *to* phrase. It occurs both without and with such a phrase:

> ... she herself had been the kind of child to grow up incapable of relating: insecure, cold, undeveloped, guilt-ridden —Margaret Drabble, *The Needle's Eye,* 1972

> "They (teen-age salespeople) know what you want and they can relate," says Karen Rascon as she thumbs through Contempo's racks —Bonnie Gangelhoff, *Houston Post,* 2 Sept. 1984

> "You can't just come in off the street and make them," Mr. [Bob] Raspanti said emphatically. "You have to understand the dough in order to relate to it." —*New Yorker,* 4 Oct. 1982

> I really don't relate to football like I do baseball —Joe Falls, *Sporting News,* 25 Oct. 1982

In this last example *relate* means roughly "respond favorably," a sense that has grown out of the popularized psychological one. The commentators—and you—may find these uses a bit tiresome, but they clearly are established in speech and in general writing.

relation 1. *Relation, relative.* It is not exactly clear why these words are to be found in so many usage books when almost the only useful things to be said about them are that they are synonymous in the sense "a person to whom one is related" and that they are frequently plural in that sense. But in the books they are, and have been, from Vizetelly 1906, Utter 1916, MacCracken & Sandison 1917, and Fowler 1926, right down to Harper

1985, Chambers 1985, Shaw 1987, and Longman 1988. The commentators have tended to disagree in minor ways about which is preferable. Evans 1957 and Bernstein 1962 believe *relation* to be rustic or bucolic; Simon 1980, however, thinks *relation* is U (for "upper-crust"); Fowler 1926, 1965 says *relation* is more common, but Copperud 1970, 1980 and Shaw say *relative* is more common. Perhaps we should all join Chambers 1985 and "justifiably conclude that such distinctions as [the critics] do discern are matters of personal whim...." One thing we can say with certainty is that both *relation* and *relative* are in common current use:

> I grew up in a house where the only regular guests were my relations. On a certain day, enormous families of relatives would visit us —Richard Rodriguez, in *The Bedford Reader,* ed. X. J. Kennedy & Dorothy M. Kennedy, 1985

2. *Relation* is usually used with *of* in the sense of "relative" and sometimes in other senses:

> ... a polar explorer and a relation of Butler's first wife —*Current Biography,* September 1964

> ... she stood in the relation of a chaperone and sponsor to Elfine —Stella Gibbons, *Cold Comfort Farm,* 1932

But *to* is more common with most senses and with most of the idiomatic expressions:

> While his relations to women were self-serving —Anatole Broyard, *N.Y. Times Book Rev.,* 9 May 1982

> He has expressed his views on Africa and its relation to the rest of the world —*Current Biography,* March 1966

> ... bears no relation to what I'm saying —Stephen Vizinczey, letter to the editor, *Times Literary Supp.,* 5 June 1969

> Stanza two presents her mind and body in relation to her soul —John T. Shawcross, *Hartford Studies in Literature,* vol. 2, no. 1, 1969

> ... their comfortable and complacent lives bear little relation to the ideology they proclaim —*Times Literary Supp.,* 7 Mar. 1968

In other senses, *with* and *between* (occasionally *among*) are used:

> ... their relation with their slaves rested on injustice and violence —Eugene D. Genovese, *N.Y. Times Book Rev.,* 20 July 1986

> Relations between the United States and Spain —*Current Biography,* November 1965

> ... the cultivation of relations among people for the improvement of society —Dale B. Harris, in *Automation, Education, and Human Values,* ed. W. W. Brickman & S. Lehrer, 1966

3. Bernstein 1965, Harper 1985, and Shaw 1987 discuss negative constructions with *relation.* They contend that if, for example, you want to say that your friend Murgatroyd is not related to the famous Murgatroyd, you should say that he or she is "no relation of the well-known Murgatroyd" rather than "no relation to the well-known M." This issue does not seem to come up very often; in fact, the only example our files have seen of the criticized construction in recent years is from a

1968 *Winners & Sinners* in which a writer for the *New York Times* is corrected for having written "He was no relation to Senator McCarthy...." Apparently this construction occurs more often in speech than in writing. *Of* may be insisted on in such a context because it is used in positive statements for this sense of relation, as illustrated in section 2 above. But *no relation to* is idiomatic with other senses of *relation,* and is not misleading with this one.

relative   See RELATION 1.

relatively   *Relatively* has been subjected to the same strictures as *comparatively* has been—namely, that it should not be used to modify an adjective when no comparison is stated or implied—and by essentially the same commentators. The first to state the proposition seems to have been Gowers 1948, who later added it to Fowler 1965. It also appears in Bernstein 1958, 1965, Evans 1957, Nickles 1974, Shaw 1975, Phythian 1979, Bryson 1984, and Heritage 1982.

The definition of *comparatively* in the OED might have given Gowers a basis for his assertion, even though he would have had to narrow it considerably (see COMPARATIVELY 1), but the OED definition at *relatively* makes no mention at all of comparisons, either stated or implied. The OED examples show that the usage Gowers dislikes has been established since the earliest uses of the adverb to modify adjectives.

In current practice, both uses of *relatively*—without an explicit comparison and with an explicit comparison—are common, and there is no valid reason for you to bother yourself about which way you use the word. Here are a few examples of both:

> I had a talk with Armstrong, who was looking quite spick and span in relatively new clothes —*The Journals of Arnold Bennett,* ed. Frank Swinnerton, 1954

> It apparently made relatively slow progress at the start, but after a couple of years it was in wide and indeed almost general use —H. L. Mencken, *The American Language, Supplement I,* 1945

> ... the springbuck, the blesbuck, and the black wildebeest, denizens of high, relatively bare, plateau country —J. Stevenson-Hamilton, *Wild Life in South Africa,* 1947

> ... grew up to be a tall blond youth—relatively unspoiled in spite of his wealth —William Styron, *Lie Down in Darkness,* 1951

> An atomic problem is not absolutely insoluble.... A problem is only relatively insoluble; insoluble with given tools —W. W. Sawyer, *Prelude to Mathematics,* 1955

> ... these two features are amongst the relatively few fundamental ones that distinguish our handling of words and sentences from that of 1611 —W. F. Bolton, *A Short History of Literary English,* 1967

> Yes, men were relatively fragile —Norman Mailer, *Harper's,* March 1971

> The relatively few American leaders who understood the military absurdity of this exercise were quickly cowed —Chester Bowles, *Saturday Rev.,* 6 Nov. 1971

> Those who are worried about their status discover in the use of textbook English a relatively easy way to

assert their superiority to the masses —Barnard 1979

By comparison the progress of Leonid Brezhnev . . . seems relatively modest —Geoffrey Hosking, *Times Literary Supp.,* 15 Aug. 1980

relative pronouns See THAT; WHAT; WHICH; WHO, WHOM; WHOSE.

relevant **1.** No one questions the use of *relevant* when it is an attributive adjective or when as a predicate adjective it is followed by a *to* phrase, as in this example:

It's simply that they are not relevant to my experience —James Baldwin, quoted in *N.Y. Times Book Rev.,* 27 May 1984

But sometime in the middle 1960s *relevant,* conspicuously used as a predicate adjective without a prepositional phrase, came to be rather a vogue word, especially among college students. What was happening was not so much the development of a new construction as the development of a new meaning much used in that construction. Here we have some examples:

I felt life was more relevant here; I figured the race struggle is treated more significantly here —Morris B. Abram, quoted in *Current Biography,* October 1965

In academic circles these days it is the fashion to be *relevant* —*Johns Hopkins Mag.,* December 1965

Great books are universally relevant and always contemporary —Mortimer J. Adler, *Playboy,* January 1966

They are demanding that colleges and universities be socially and morally relevant —Kenneth B. Clark, *American Scholar,* Winter 1966–1967

The relevance implicit in the adjective in these uses is political or (especially) social relevance. As the usage continued to be very common in the early 1970s, it began to attract some unfavorable attention and soon appeared for denigration in Strunk & White 1972, Harper 1975, and subsequent American handbooks. The usage has also crossed the Atlantic, and so has the criticism: Howard 1984 reports its being decried in the House of Lords.

The new sense has also been used in the more usual constructions, but these uses have not drawn fire from the critics:

. . . piously asserts the need for relevant social science on a giant scale —Irving Louis Horowitz & Lee Rainwater, *Trans-Action,* June 1967

Education is supposed to be relevant to contemporary issues —Robert M. Hutchins, *Center Mag.,* September 1968

. . . the importance of making the curriculum relevant to social issues —Philip G. Altbach, *The Progressive,* October 1969

Those who dislike the socially relevant *relevant* will be glad to know that its popular usage has dropped off considerably in recent years. It is, however, not defunct:

For all its scholarship, it is intensely relevant —H. Jack Geiger, *N.Y. Times Book Rev.,* 9 Jan. 1983

2. A number of commentators warn against the metathesized pronunciation and spelling *revelant.* It sometimes turns up in surprising places:

. . . furnishes references where revelant to *STC* —*Times Literary Supp.,* 15 Oct. 1964

See METATHESIS.

reliable Lounsbury 1908 commented that the controversy over *reliable* was then a century or more old (he did not say who started it, unfortunately) and showed no signs of dying out. The issue was etymology: since *reliable* means "able to be relied *on*" rather than "able to rely," it was held to have been improperly formed. Its critics were many. Lounsbury cited the English essayist Thomas De Quincey. The OED says that Worcester's 1860 dictionary objected to the formation. Alford 1866 condemned the word. Richard Grant White 1870 devoted seven pages to its denunciation; in these he found grounds for dismissing (to his own satisfaction) the defense based on analogy with such similarly formed words as *available, indispensable, laughable,* and *unaccountable.* (The analogical words were mentioned in Webster 1864.) *Reliable* was placed on William Cullen Bryant's 1877 *Index Expurgatorius.* In Great Britain it was commonly condemned as an Americanism, although De Quincey thought that Coleridge had coined it. Neither guess was right; *reliable* had been in sporadic use since the 16th century, but in frequent popular use only since the middle of the 19th. *Reliable* looks like another example of a usage issue brought on by a sudden increase in use.

In spite of Lounsbury's feeling that the issue would not die soon, it did. The last serious objector we have found is Bierce 1909. *Reliable* is mentioned in Utter 1916, but he only quotes the OED note and tells his readers they can use *trustworthy* as an alternative if they prefer. Hall 1917 gives an account of the controversy, but more recent references are hard to find. Why did a subject pursued with such vehemence for a century or so suddenly lose interest? Since its real cause was apparently the noticeable increase in use in the mid-19th century, it probably died because people simply got used to the word.

In any case, there is no usage problem with *reliable* anymore.

relish When the noun *relish* is followed by a preposition, the preposition may be either *of* or *for. For* is the more common choice:

. . . a certain relish for debate —Bell Gale Chevigny, *Village Voice,* 28 Feb. 1968

. . . the reader must have a relish for suspense — Catherine Meyer, *Harper's,* May 1971

But *of* is also standard:

She had tremendous earthy relish of concrete manifestations of place and people —Ruth Suckow, *College English,* March 1953

. . . a relish of the trivia of the private lives of public persons —J. H. Plumb, *Saturday Rev.,* 28 June 1969

remand Bernstein 1958, 1965 and Harper 1975, 1985 caution against what they consider the redundant use of *back* with *remand.* Their warnings may be unnecessary in this case; *remand back* seems hardly ever to occur. In fact, our files contain only a single instance of it:

He may be remanded back to prison for a little more penitence —Karl Menninger, *Avant-Garde,* May 1968

See also REDUNDANCY.

remediable, remedial Several commentators distinguish between these words, but only two of them—Follett 1966 and Copperud 1970, 1980—explicitly state that *remediable* and *remedial* are ever confused. Follett cites an instance in which *remedial,* which means "serving or intended as a remedy," is used in place of *remediable,* which means "capable of being remedied." Our files contain no other examples of such misuse. The OED shows that the original meaning of *remediable* was, in fact, "remedial," but the most recent evidence of *remediable* in this obsolete sense is from 1596. What we conclude from all of this is that these two words are rarely confused. Here are a few examples of typical current use:

He noted the various remedial proposals that have been made —*Center Mag.,* November 1969

. . . he had begun this remedial reading with the firmest male prejudice of them all —Norman Mailer, *Harper's,* March 1971

Happily, my problem was remediable —Carll Tucker, *Saturday Rev.,* 18 Mar. 1978

. . . at least partly remediable social wrongs —Irving Howe, *N.Y. Times Book Rev.,* 18 Apr. 1982

remedy When used with a preposition, *remedy* is often followed by *for:*

Work was generally deplored as too drastic a remedy for our unemployment —Cyril Connolly, *The Condemned Playground,* 1946

. . . she used to have only one remedy for every problem—a proper thrashing —André P. Brink, *Looking on Darkness,* 1974

. . . we applied the human remedy, the remedy my family had found in Saskatchewan for any unwanted life —Wallace Stegner, *Blair & Ketchum's Country Jour.,* December 1979

Less frequently, it is found with *against* or *to:*

. . . the people's remedy against the abuse of government —Morris R. Cohen, *The Faith of a Liberal,* 1946

. . . to wait with growing impatience for the remedies against tyranny —*Times Literary Supp.,* June 1969

. . . controls offer no real remedy to inflation, but merely serve as a tranquilizer —Leif H. Olson, quoted in *Barron's,* 8 May 1972

. . . endorsed the plan . . . as a remedy to the deep stagnation which engulfed Germany —Fritz Karl Mann, *Annals of the American Academy of Political and Social Science,* January 1950

remember See RECOLLECT, REMEMBER.

remind Two commentators (Bernstein 1965 and Copperud 1964, 1970, 1980) issue warnings against

what they consider to be intransitive uses of this transitive verb. Here is one of our few examples of the usage that they disapprove:

Your recent correspondence . . . reminds of a question —*Times Literary Supp.,* 11 Feb. 1983

This is better regarded as an absolute use of the verb than as a genuine intransitive; the direct object of *remind, me* in this case, is missing but understood. The OED labels such usage *elliptical* and illustrates it with two 19th-century citations. But the correct label— *intransitive, absolute,* or *elliptical*—is not really the issue. The commentators who object to the use of *remind* without an object do so because they find it unidiomatic, that is, because it does not sound right. Considering how rarely such usage occurs, we suspect that this feeling is shared by most other readers and writers.

remunerate, remuneration These undeniably formal words are sometimes cited as pretentious substitutes for such ordinary alternatives as *pay* and *payment.* Our evidence shows them to be most at home in writing that concerns serious financial matters, especially when large amounts of money—or other forms of compensation—are involved:

Marquand's post in the Ministry of Health is remunerated at the Cabinet rate . . . but does not carry with it a seat in the Cabinet —*Current Biography 1951*

. . . where a company's income is extracted very largely as directors' remuneration which is intended to equalize year by year the tax burden —J. M. Cope, *Business Taxation,* 1972

Copperud 1970, 1980 notes that *remunerate* is sometimes misspelled *renumerate.* We have an example of this error in our files:

. . . the highest renumerated corporate executive in the U.S. —*Town & Country,* March 1980

It is worth remembering that impressive words become far less impressive when misspelled.

render *Render* in the sense "to give a performance of" is pronounced "pretentious" by Copperud 1970, 1980 and "stilted" by Evans 1957. What they have in mind are such uses as "The Star-Spangled Banner will now be rendered by Miss Emily Brown," in which they would prefer the straightforward *sung.* And so may you, but note that *render* in this sense can also occur in contexts where it is neither pretentious nor stilted, as in this example:

When I first came home May 1 from the hospital I was hearing the celestial chorus—"Clementine" is what it renders when I am weak enough to hear it. Over & over. . . . The transfusion cut that out. Must come from not enough blood getting to the head — Flannery O'Connor, letter, 15 May 1964

renowned Copperud 1964, 1970, 1980 finds that *renown* is commonly misused as an adjective equivalent to *renowned.* We have a little evidence of this curious error in our files:

. . . a world-renown authority on peregrines —*Massachusetts Audubon News Letter,* April 1971

. . . the woven fibers are renown for their soft, silky texture —catalog, Britches of Georgetowne, Fall 1981

... a renown clinical psychologist —*Cats Mag.,* December 1985

Perhaps such usage occurs because the final *n* of *renown* is felt to be a participial ending, like the final *n* of *known* or *shown.* Perhaps the reason is more obscure. All we know for certain is that *renown* is not established as an adjective in standard English. Use *renowned* instead.

Copperud also mentions the misspellings *reknown* and *reknowned.* These are both attested in our files and should be avoided.

reoccur, reoccurrence   See RECUR, RECURRENCE, REOCCUR, REOCCURRENCE.

repast   Various commentators describe *repast* as stiff, pretentious, obsolescent, or quaint. A look at the evidence shows it to be a somewhat literary word of fairly low frequency that has lately begun to acquire some currency, probably because of the recent increase in writing about food. It also has some literary use, in modern stories as well as older novels. Here are a few examples from our files:

> ... Madame Foucault, who had herself served Sophia with her invalid's repast —Arnold Bennett, *The Old Wives' Tale,* 1908

> ... a splendid repast, with silver, crystal, damask, 3 roast goose —Ursula K. LeGuin, "The Rule of Names," in *Adventures for Readers* (8th grade text), ed. Egbert W. Nieman et al., 1979

> One of the most delectable meals I have sampled in a long while was a simple repast —Craig Claiborne, *N.Y. Times Mag.,* 20 Apr. 1986

repeat again   Jensen 1935, Copperud 1980, and Shaw 1987 consider *repeat again* redundant for *repeat.* But look at this example:

> A theme was repeated again and again. In the middle of frills, grace-notes, runs and catches it recurred with a strange, almost holy, solemnity —James Stephens, *The Crock of Gold,* 1912

This is a perfect example of useful redundancy, for a discussion of which see REDUNDANCY.

repel   See REPULSE, REPEL.

repetition   See REDUNDANCY.

replete   There is a sense of *replete* which some critics regard as nonexistent. The problem has to do with the use of *replete* as a synonym of *complete.* The OED, which treats this sense of *replete* as standard, shows that it has been used—although only rarely—since 1601, when it occurred in Shakespeare's *All's Well That Ends Well.* Its use has become more frequent in the 20th century, but it still is not especially common. The first to criticize it was Fowler 1926, whose opinion has been more or less repeated by such later commentators as Evans 1957 and Harper 1975, 1985. The distinction they draw between *replete* and *complete* begins from a valid observation, that *replete* normally indicates fullness or abundance. To describe a book as "complete with illustrations" is to simply say that it has illustrations, but to describe it as "replete with illustrations" is to say that it has illustrations in abundance. As far as the critics are concerned, that is where the story ends, but in fact *replete* is also sometimes used in standard

writing to mean "complete," as in the following passages:

> ... stylized landscape of Deep South farmland at sundown, replete with wheeling buzzards and eroding soil —*Time,* 19 Mar. 1945

> ... an elderly doctor replete with whiskers and a young wife who does not love him —*Newsweek,* 5 Mar. 1951

> ... preferred to come on ... with all the solemnity of the risen Christ, replete with white cotton pajamas, incense, and the stigmata of his legal persecutions —Theodore Roszak, *The Making of a Counter Culture,* 1969

> ... Mr. Gatien's new nightclub-cum-discotheque ... a former Episcopal church replete with altars and crucifixes —Laura Landro, *Wall Street Jour.,* 29 Nov. 1983

Replete may have been chosen by some of these writers because it has connotations of abundance and opulence even when its basic denotation is simply "complete."

replica   *Replica* is used in the fine arts with the narrow meaning of a copy or reproduction of a work of art made by or under the supervision of the original artist. Fowler 1926, 1965, Bernstein 1958, 1965, 1977, and Shaw 1975, 1987 believe this to be the only proper sense; Kilpatrick 1984 knows it is not but wishes it were. The evidence in the OED suggests, however, that the word has been applied loosely since the middle of the 19th century, when it was first introduced into English. In present-day use it more often refers to a reproduction of some artifact than to a work of art and frequently is used of a miniaturized copy. It is also used figuratively. Some examples:

> At the moment, a replica of the Mayflower—or, rather, what purports to be a replica, for nobody knows exactly what the ship looked like—is being built in England —E. J. Kahn, Jr., *New Yorker,* 1 Oct. 1955

> The Langley Research Center has designed, constructed, and tested a 1/5-scale replica model of the Saturn SA-1 launch vehicle —Harry L. Runyan & Robert W. Leonard, *Structures for Space Operations,* December 1962

> ... chemists learned how to make laboratory replicas of increasingly complex natural products — Barry Commoner, *New Yorker,* 2 Oct. 1971

> Bottex now sits beside the cathedral and paints replicas of "The Last Supper" for tourists. But he uses the visitor's face for the Judas —Caleb Pirtle III, *Southern Living,* November 1971

> ... building a bridge that was said to be an exact replica of one of the bridges that Caesar built across the Rhine —Merle Miller, *Plain Speaking,* 1973

> ... transforming some of the shore and lake country of southern Maine ... into replicas of suburban shopping malls —Morgan McGinley, *N.Y. Times,* 12 Aug. 1984

> Three musical shows, all rehearsing under the impression that they were replicas of "South Pacific," opened and folded in jig time —Groucho Marx, letter, 3 Oct. 1950

Intensifying adjectives such as *exact, authentic,* and *perfect* are sometimes used with *replica* to stress fidelity of detail. They are harmless, and at any rate are more common in advertising matter than in other contexts.

reprisal Bernstein 1965 notes that *reprisal* "takes preposition *for* (an act); *against* or *upon* (the perpetrator)," but actual usage is less clear-cut. The most common preposition following *reprisal* seems to be *against,* and while it is true that a reprisal is usually *against* a "perpetrator," we also have evidence for its occasional use when an "act" is involved:

> The seizure may have been a reprisal against the action of the Privy Council in London —Theodore Hsi-en Chen, *Current History,* November 1952

> In "All Quiet" waggish reprisals against non-coms were still possible —Frederic Morton, *Saturday Rev.,* 22 May 1954

> . . . any terrorist act by any Arab or Jew can properly be the occasion for a reprisal against any Jew or Arab —Noam Chomsky, *Columbia Forum,* Winter 1969

> . . . I think we can say that *Bech,* at least in part, represents a reprisal, and a healthy one, against the literary establishment —L. E. Sissman, *Atlantic,* August 1970

Upon seems to occur with *reprisal* very seldom now, but *on* does have some use. It occurs in the same contexts as *against,* but less frequently:

> . . . lest Mr. Raycie's mysterious faculty of hearing what was said behind his back should bring sudden reprisals on the venerable lady —Edith Wharton, *False Dawn,* 1924

> . . . had considered it a peculiarly unfortunate feature of Jackson's proposal for reprisal on French shipping —Francis D. Wormuth, "The Vietnam War: The President versus the Constitution," 1968

Reprisal is also used with *for* in the way noted by Bernstein:

> . . . in reprisal for maltreatment of an American naval lieutenant —Francis D. Wormuth, "The Vietnam War: The President versus the Constitution," 1968

And we also have one example of *reprisal* used with *to:*

> . . . U.S. goods are spontaneously boycotted by the population in reprisal to our increase of duties —S. J. Rundt, *Wall Street Jour.,* 2 Sept. 1954

repugnance When *repugnance* is used with a preposition, it is usually *to:*

> . . . her instinctive dignity and repugnance to any show of emotion —George Eliot, *Silas Marner,* 1861

> . . . a deep-seated repugnance to monopoly in almost any form —Neil J. Curry, *Atlantic,* December 1955

Other prepositions sometimes used with *repugnance* are *for, toward,* or *towards:*

> . . . they headed for a place prostrated by war which also shared their repugnance for arms —George Weller, *Saturday Evening Post,* 1 Sept. 1956

> . . . without at the same time restraining her repugnance toward the political philosophy of the Fascist

states —Maurice Halperin, *Foreign Affairs,* October 1940

> . . . having so far overcome his repugnance towards the language employed in their theoretical writings —*Times Literary Supp.,* 8 Oct. 1954

Repugnance was also once used with *against,* as the OED shows, but we have no evidence that such usage still occurs.

repulse, repel Quite a few commentators—Evans 1957, Bernstein 1962, 1965, Bremner 1980, Copperud 1970, 1980, Shaw 1975, 1987, Bryson 1984, Freeman 1983—insist on a distinction between the figurative uses of *repel* and *repulse.* What this distinction amounts to is disapproval of the sense of *repulse* that means "to cause repulsion in." Bernstein illustrates the desired distinction with this sentence:

> She repulsed the suitor because he repelled her.

Here *repulse* means basically "to drive off or turn away," which is its oldest sense (and which, incidentally, is also a sense of *repel*). *Repulse* is often used in this sense, as Bernstein suggests, and *repel* is often used to mean "to cause repulsion in":

> . . . she had learned to be on the watch and to repulse advances that were disagreeable —Ellen Glasgow, *Barren Ground,* 1925

> A teacher embittered by personal disappointment can hurt and repulse with corrosive wit the timid or groping student —Donald H. Morrison, *N.Y. Times Mag.,* 16 Oct. 1955

> . . . the inevitable promiscuity attached to a sexual search repelled him —Norman Mailer, *Harper's,* March 1971

> . . . he was personally repelled by some of the racial policies of the Metropolitan Club in Washington —Gay Talese, *Harper's,* January 1969

But *repulse* is also used like *repel,* as in these examples:

> . . . Malone sat trembling on the edge of the table, repulsed by his own weakness and distress —Carson McCullers, *Botteghe Oscure,* Quaderno XI, 1953

> Hoarding repulses Mr. Risolo, the barber —Philip Hawkins, *Wall Street Jour.,* 5 Oct. 1966

> People who had been repulsed by his wartime pamphleteering were eager to forget him —John W. Aldridge, *Saturday Rev.,* 7 Aug. 1976

The suggestion in Copperud and Evans that it is an error to associate *repulse* with *repulsion* has no foundation; both words are derived from the same Latin word, and there is no logical reason they should not share senses.

You will, of course, feel free to observe the distinction between *repulse* and *repel* urged by the commentators if you find it useful to do so. But it is one thing to observe the distinction yourself and another to insist that other people observe it too. The distinction itself does not seem to be an especially helpful one. The context in all our citations for *repulse* makes it clear which sense is being used. *Repel* is, however, far more common in the disputed sense than is *repulse.* The choice is yours.

request A number of British commentators, from Fowler 1926 to Longman 1988, and one American,

Bernstein 1958, 1965, have objected to the use of *for* after the verb *request*. Here is Bernstein's example:

> The President has requested Congress for both these powers —*N.Y. Times,* 28 Feb. 1957

The opinion of all the commentators is that this construction is based on analogy with *ask,* common in the same construction, and that it is unidiomatic (or incorrect). Another influence may be the noun *request,* which is common with *for:*

> ... the request for the release of Archbishop Slipyi —Norman Cousins, *Saturday Rev.,* 30 Oct. 1971

At any rate, the construction appears to be rare in print. We have only one example besides those given by Fowler and Bernstein:

> ... Prime Minister Attlee has requested President Truman for renewed American efforts —*Current History,* November 1951

Such usage should not be confused with the use of *request* with *for* in a construction like the following, in which *request* has an impersonal object:

> Indian officials requested the area for Indian families —*American Guide Series: Minnesota,* 1938

The impersonal object can also be followed by *of:*

> ... the machine could begin to request specific things of the child —*Johns Hopkins Mag.,* April 1966

resemblance When *resemblance* is followed by a preposition, the preposition is usually *to:*

> ... a resemblance to one of his own targets — Phoebe-Lou Adams, *Atlantic,* February 1972

> He bears little resemblance to the characters he has portrayed —Claire Safran, *Redbook,* July 1974

In another common construction, *between* follows *resemblance:*

> ... to discover any resemblance between the two situations —Edith Wharton, *The Age of Innocence,* 1920

> ... the resemblance between this correspondence and the epistolary novel —*Times Literary Supp.,* 19 Feb. 1971

Bernstein 1965 indicates that *resemblance* is also followed by *among,* and that seems not altogether implausible. We have, however, no evidence for *resemblance among.*

resentment *Resentment* is not very particular about the prepositions that follow it. We have evidence for more than a half-dozen, the most common of which are *at, of,* and *against:*

> She felt no resentment at this miscarriage of her preparations —John Cheever, *The Wapshot Chronicle,* 1957

> ... to gratify an old man's resentment of skepticism —Anthony Boucher, *Far and Away,* 1955

> ... resentment against other poets' prizes —Martin Green, *N.Y. Times Book Rev.,* 19 Dec. 1976

Other possibilities are *toward* (or *towards*) and, much less often, *over* and *for:*

> ... a great deal of children's resentment toward school in general —Bruno Bettelheim, *Ladies' Home Jour.,* September 1971

> ... French resentment over Secretary Dulles' recent speech —Roscoe Drummond, *Town Jour.,* January 1954

> ... not because of resentment for his hard youth — Sherwood Anderson, *Poor White,* 1920

reside *Reside,* in one of its senses, is a slightly formal-sounding word meaning "to live in a place as a legal residence"—or, put perhaps more simply, "to live officially." It is a word used in legal contexts, in rules, in constitutions (including the U.S. Constitution), and in other such writings. In more general works, it is used in books of brief biographies and similar works of reference. Usage writers have been disparaging it as highfalutin from Ayres 1881 to Longman 1988. Surely this misses the mark: the writers of biographical sketches and the like must use *live* over and over, and *reside* is an acceptable alternative once in a while. And, as Harper 1975, 1985 (the word's only defender) points out, it is useful in contrasting a place of residence with, for instance, a place of employment.

Here is how reference-book writers use *reside:*

> ... was born on March 31, 1912, in Chicago, where his brother and three sisters still reside —*Current Biography,* July 1967

> ... daughter of a wealthy English architect and builder residing in New York —*Dictionary of American Biography,* 1929

These uses are perfectly acceptable. And remember that you can use *reside* to elevate your style on purpose. Here it is used to add to a tone of solemn denunciation:

> "James," he said, "there is a particular place in hell, in fact its innermost heart, where reside for eternity the tormented souls of men of your sort. ..." —E. L. Doctorow, *Loon Lake,* 1979

resort See RESOURCE.

resource Fowler 1926 cites several sentences in which *resource* is mistakenly used in place of *recourse* and *resort* in such phrases as *have recourse to* and *in the last resort.* A few later commentators (Partridge 1942, Evans 1957, Copperud 1970, 1980, and Phythian 1979) have repeated Fowler's warnings against such misuse, and one recent British dictionary (Longman 1984) continues to describe it as "a common confusion." Our evidence, however, does not agree. We do have a few citations, most of them from the 19th century, in which *resource* is used when either *recourse* or *resort* seems possible, and perhaps preferable to modern ears:

> ... finally resolved that it could be the last resource, if her private inquiries ... were unfavourably answered —Jane Austen, *Pride and Prejudice,* 1813

But we have no clear-cut examples of mistaken use other than the ones cited by Fowler. We do not doubt that some confusion may still occur, but our lack of evidence strongly suggests that it is not at all common in edited prose. Current writers appear to have little trouble keeping *resource* distinct from *recourse* and *resort:*

> ... must now learn to function as a resource to her colleagues —Barbara Aiello, *N.Y. Times,* 25 Apr. 1976

> ... the idea of a library as a cultural resource persists —O. B. Hardison, Jr., *Entering the Maze,* 1981

> They dry well, too, I am told, without recourse to messy boxes of borax or gel —Eleanor Perenyi, *Green Thoughts,* 1983

> In the last resort, Hitler's sense of destiny was his doom —Terence Prittie, *N.Y. Times Book Rev.,* 26 Sept. 1976

respect   *Respect* occurs in a few idiomatic phrases that have been involved in one usage issue or another over the years. For instance, Bierce 1909 objected to *respect* in the sense "way, matter," which is used in such phrases as *in that respect.* Such phrases are, of course, perfectly standard:

> More representative in this respect was Lord Chesterfield —John Butt, *English Literature in the Mid-Eighteenth Century,* edited & completed by Geoffrey Carnall, 1979

> In one other respect Johnson proposed to improve upon his predecessors —John Butt, *English Literature in the Mid-Eighteenth Century,* edited & completed by Geoffrey Carnall, 1979

And Quiller-Couch 1916 objected to *in respect of* as jargonish. *Respect* occurs in three such phrases: *in respect of, in respect to,* and *with respect to.* For a discussion of these phrases, see IN RESPECT OF, IN RESPECT TO, WITH RESPECT TO.

respective, respectively   There is quite a bit of opinion about *respective* and *respectively* in print, and except for the early and unheeded recommendation of Bierce 1909 that *several* replace *respective,* it all concerns the familiar use of the two words in matching sets of things in the correct order.

> ... we will continue to use the conventional symbols NP, VP, AP, and PP for the maximal projections of N, V, A, and P, respectively —Noam Chomsky, *Knowledge of Language,* 1986

Respective and *respectively* also have a distributive function that assigns separate things to members of a group referred to by a plural noun:

> ... blows up an atomic energy plant during dedication ceremonies, respectively killing and injuring the daughters of two Supreme Court justices —*Publishers Weekly,* 17 June 1983

The gist of the commentary is that *respective* and *respectively* are often used where not strictly necessary (does Chomsky really need *respectively* to help you match *NP* with *N,* etc.?) and, even when correctly used, should be avoided because they tend to slow down the progress of the reader.

The points made by the critics are worth remembering, but so is the point that there are times when a writer wants to slow readers down to make sure they are paying attention. Chomsky's material does not look like easy going, and he may be inserting the *respectively* to

remind readers not to let their eyes glaze over in the midst of a bunch of symbolic representations. "Pay attention," he seems to say, "I'll be asking questions later." (Chomsky probably does need to prod; our excerpt above omits such additional symbols as *X, X',* and *X″.*)

The uses in the three examples that follow are all of the kind that would be called unnecessary by the commentators. The first two are harmless, mere reminders of individuality. The third is surely otiose, a classic example of omissible *respectively.*

> ... the ... result of this arrangement is, that such men as have female companions with them pass their time in prowling about the precincts of the "ladies' apartment"; while their respective ladies pop their heads first out of one door and then out of another —Fanny Kemble, *Journal of a Residence on a Georgian Plantation in 1838–1839,* 1863

> She analyzes CDs, stocks, bonds, options, mutual funds, U.S. Savings Bonds, tax-free investments, collectibles, and partnerships as to their suitability in an IRA. ... She also "forecasts" their respective suitability should the new tax law affect them —Steven J. Mayover, *Library Jour.,* August 1986

> ... a harshly funny and effective study of Nazi self-delusion and atrocity respectively, presenting them in terms of elaborate fantasy —*Times Literary Supp.,* 14 Nov. 1968

responsibility   A person is usually said to have a responsibility *for* something and *to* someone:

> The responsibility for engineering the line of cars which in 1908 evolved the immortal Model T — John Kenneth Galbraith, *N.Y. Times Book Rev.,* 28 Feb. 1954

> ... Joachim not only assumed personal responsibility for his future study but became his part-time teacher —*Current Biography,* February 1966

> A great soprano has a responsibility to her public — Robert Evett, *Atlantic,* September 1970

> ... Landau's piece, examining the fan's, and the journalist's responsibility to rock stars —Lawrence Dietz, *Los Angeles Times Book Rev.,* 23 May 1971

Responsibility is also frequently followed by *of,* which occurs in the same contexts as *for:*

> ... he determined to take upon his own shoulders the responsibility of organizing some amusements —Thomas Hardy, *The Mayor of Casterbridge,* 1886

> ... it laid the whole responsibility of the war upon Britain —*Manchester Guardian Weekly,* 27 Oct. 1939

> The banks had the responsibility of the amalgamation of industries —*The Autobiography of William Allen White,* 1946

Other prepositions that sometimes occur with *responsibility* include *about, in,* and *toward* (or *towards*):

> Things you've had to take responsibility about really should have been mine —Angus Wilson, *The Middle Age of Mrs. Eliot,* 1958

> ... federal responsibility in civil rights shifted from the Department of Justice to a broad government base —*Current Biography,* February 1965

Anthony Burton had once said that this was your responsibility toward society —John P. Marquand, *Atlantic,* November 1947

The idea that he has any responsibility towards Amy or should feel any affection for their son —*Times Literary Supp.,* 29 June 1967

responsible The use of *responsible* with reference to an impersonal noun (as in "The blizzard was responsible for three deaths") seems to have originated in American English sometime around the turn of the century. Its occurrence in American English is now common and entirely reputable:

> ... to discover the variables responsible for the occurrence of an event —Howard H. Kendler, *Basic Psychology,* 2d ed., 1968

> ... believe that racial discrimination was responsible —David M. Rafky, *Change,* October 1971

Some critics have argued that only a human being can be considered truly responsible—that is, answerable—and that *responsible* should therefore be used only of people. But that argument, which dates back to Bierce 1909, is now rarely heard in the U.S. The use of *responsible* with an impersonal subject is still occasionally criticized by British commentators (such as Sellers 1975), and doubtless there are still some American purists who regard it with disapproval, but no American commentator that we know of has found fault with it for more than thirty years.

restaurateur, restauranteur The word *restaurateur* was borrowed into English from French at the end of the 18th century. Several decades later, according to written evidence, *restaurant* was similarly borrowed. In the years since, *restaurant* has become an extremely common English word, but *restaurateur* has remained uncommon—or, at least, far less common than *restaurant.* This difference in frequency of use has given rise to the variant form *restauranteur,* pronounced and spelled with an *n.* Our first written evidence of *restauranteur* is from the 1920s:

> The individual restauranteur is helpless —*New Yorker,* 20 Feb. 1926

> Why should a restauranteur hold fast to his ancient traditions ... ? —*Harper's,* September 1926

In current English, *restauranteur* is quite common in speech and fairly common in writing:

> ... fellow Houston restauranteurs —Tom Curtis, *Inc. Mag.,* August 1982

> ... respected cooking teacher, cookbook author and restauranteur —*Publishers Weekly,* 17 Sept. 1982

Restaurateur is the usual written form, especially in writing that has passed under a copy editor's eye, but *restauranteur* is a standard secondary variant.

restive Richard Grant White 1870 seems to have been the first to make an issue of this word: "Restive means standing stubbornly still, not frisky, as some people seem to think it does." Ayres 1881 and Vizetelly 1906 noted a reply by Fitzedward Hall, who adduced proofs that the ordinary sense of *restive* had always been "unruly, intractable, refractory." Ayres even noted that the contemporary Webster 1864 carried a definition

"impatient, uneasy." There the matter seemed to rest, although Bierce 1909 grumbled. Fowler 1926 ignored the matter, and Krapp 1927 thought *restive* showed signs of passing out of use altogether, like its earlier form *restiff.* But the issue has flared up again among some recent commentators (Gowers in Fowler 1965, Follett 1966, Bernstein 1977, Phythian 1979), with the emphasis now on defending the sense "unruly, intractable" against the old Webster's sense, which has been reinterpreted as "restless."

The definition mentioned by Ayres reads in full: "Impatient under coercion, chastisement, or opposition; uneasy." This sense has become the most common one in present-day English. Since the dictionary in which it appears was published in 1864, the sense had been in use for more than a century when the latest set of critics began to denigrate it. Its connotations are not quite the same as those of *restless:*

> He did right to preach to women: men would not have listened to him. As it was, Miss Joy Blewins, and Mrs. M'Murphy, were restive —George Meredith, *The Ordeal of Richard Feverel,* 1859

> They were all becoming restive under the monotonous persistence of the missionary —Willa Cather, *Death Comes for the Archbishop,* 1927

> The audience was growing restive; there was some stamping of feet at the back —J. B. Priestley, *The Good Companions,* 1929

> We sat a restive hour after starting time and at nine o'clock a solitary man ... came before the curtain to ask us to bear with him five minutes longer —Robert Frost, letter, 10 Nov. 1920

The connotations here are more of impatience than of restlessness. Here are a few quite recent examples:

> ... the audience, restive after the long public hearing, repeatedly interrupted the council's discussions —Sue Lewis, *Denver Post,* 8 Sept. 1984

> ... were becoming increasingly restive with their economic lot —John F. Baker, *Publishers Weekly,* 12 Mar. 1982

> Now, the Sudan would prove susceptible to the message of a messiah, its people restive under Egypt's corrupt rule —John H. Waller, *Military History,* June 1985

Notice how easily the last example could have developed from this one two centuries earlier:

> ... your colonies become suspicious, restive, and untractable —Edmund Burke, (Speech on) *Conciliation with America,* 1775

The sense of "resisting control, balky" has not vanished in the 20th century, as a few commentators fear:

> The most comical sights in the parade were the mounted Navy and Air Force officers, who joggled along unhappily on their restive horses —Mollie Panter-Downes, *New Yorker,* 13 June 1953

> The United States also was finding its other allies increasingly restive. They were less inclined to follow the U.S. lead —*Newsweek,* 13 July 1953

> ... their minorities ... are becoming progressively more demonstrative and restive in their opposition —Claude A. Buss, *Wilson Library Bulletin,* November 1968

restrictive appositives   See APPOSITIVES.

reticent, reticence   *Reticent* has recently developed a new sense, and usage watchers are not keeping quiet about it. In its older, better established uses, *reticent* can mean "inclined to be silent":

> An extremely reticent man, Morris does not like to talk about his experience in personal terms —Helen Dudar, *N.Y. Times Mag.,* 30 Oct. 1977

or "restrained in expression or appearance":

> ... two or three rather reticent abstract paintings — Jay Jacobs, *Gourmet,* January 1979

In its disputed sense, *reticent* is synonymous with *reluctant* or *hesitant:*

> Bankers naturally are reticent to pay steep rates on deposits —William D. Hartley, *Wall Street Jour.,* 29 Dec. 1969

This sense may have developed in the following way. With *reticent* in its "inclined to be silent" sense, a person may be said to be "reticent about" a particular subject. With a slight extension of meaning, a person may be said to be "reticent about discussing" a particular subject, in which case *reticent* is being used essentially as a synonym of *hesitant,* but still in a context that relates specifically to speech. The next step would be the use of *reticent* with an infinitive, still relating to speech:

> ... its sponsors, not reticent to affirm their aspiration —*Annual Report of the Librarian of Congress,* 1952

> They were disturbed ... by my being reticent to talk about the collision —Peter Taylor, *The Old Forest and Other Stories,* 1985

Here *reticent* even more clearly means "hesitant" or "reluctant." In the final step, its associations with speech are entirely lost:

> ... bluefish are extremely reticent to strike surface poppers —Robert P. Lawton, *Massachusetts Wildlife,* May–June 1980

> "But I'm reticent," she said, "to use real shells in my work. . . ." —Angela Cummings, quoted in *Town & Country,* July 1981

> ... taxpayers have been reticent to put up the money —Connie Chung, television news broadcast, 24 Aug. 1985

The same extension of meaning has occurred with the noun *reticence:*

> Retailers' reticence to place Christmas orders until late in the season —Stanley H. Slom, *Wall Street Jour.,* 19 Sept. 1972

> ... criticized the reticence of West European governments to support American sanctions —*N.Y. Times,* 19 Mar. 1980

> Arafat's reticence to talk is understandable —Peter Carlson, *People,* 1 Aug. 1983

However this new sense developed, there is no denying that it is now well established in the language, and chances are that it will grow more common in years to come. There is also no denying, however, that many people, including several usage commentators, regard it

as an error. If you use it, do not be surprised to find yourself being corrected.

return back   This is another verb phrase that is sometimes cited (by Shaw 1987, for example) as redundant. *Back* is, of course, not needed with *return;* it is simply a little reinforcement that is occasionally added to make sure the reader or hearer does not miss the point. The combination is an old one:

> ... the bill must be sent to Murry, accepted by him, and then returned back —Jonathan Swift, *Journal to Stella,* 7 June 1711

> ... when that's done, 'twill be time to return back to the parlour fire-side, where we left my uncle *Toby* in the middle of his sentence —Laurence Sterne, *Tristram Shandy,* 1760

> ... I shall return back to Venice in a few days — Lord Byron, letter, 12 May 1817

See REDUNDANCY.

Rev.   See REVEREND, REV.

revel   Bernstein 1965 says that *revel* is used with the preposition *in,* and most of the time it is:

> ... revelling in its barber shop quavers —Eugene O'Neill, *The Great God Brown,* 1926

> ... I fairly revelled in reminiscent sympathy with him —Max Beerbohm, *Seven Men,* 1920

> ... a woman ... reveling in the violent surge of her blood —William Styron, *Lie Down in Darkness,* 1951

> ... it revels in name-calling —Daniels 1983

Once in a while *revel* can be found with *at, around, on,* or *with.* Of these only *at* is used like *in,* to connect the verb with the object of revelry.

> ... they reveled at his cockiness —A. H. Raskin, *N.Y. Times Mag.,* 7 Nov. 1976

> ... a brilliant scapegrace who had ... revelled around Europe for years —Herman Wouk, *Marjorie Morningstar,* 1955

> ... was revelling on the fat of the land in Philadelphia —Samuel Eliot Morison & Henry Steele Commager, *The Growth of the American Republic,* 3d ed., 1942

> ... a school teacher afraid life is passing her by, revels with Arthur O'Connell —*N.Y. Times Mag.,* 25 Dec. 1955

revenge   1. See AVENGE, REVENGE.
2. The noun *revenge* is often followed by *on, against,* or *for.* The first two of these prepositions mark the object of the revenge, the last its motive.

> ... an act of revenge on their greatness —David Denby, *Atlantic,* September 1971

> It often takes revenge on civilians —Max Clos, *N.Y. Times Mag.,* 10 Jan. 1965

> ... thirsting for revenge against his "friend and successor" —William L. Shirer, *The Rise and Fall of the Third Reich,* 1960

Is this some kind of revenge for what happened to your sister? —John Masters, *Fandango Rock,* 1959

Reverend, Rev. Concern over the proper use of *Reverend* and its abbreviation *Rev.* in addressing American Protestant clergymen goes back at least to Richard Grant White 1870; it has continued unabated in usage books, etiquette books, and the public prints ever since. The usual prescriptions can be easily summed up: *Reverend* is an adjective; it is not a title; it should be preceded by *the;* it should be followed by a surname or a title such as *Dr.* or *Mr.;* therefore, it is wrong to address a clergyman, as President Reagan did in 1981, as "Reverend Moomaw."

A few usage books, such as Reader's Digest 1983, Copperud 1980, and Harper 1975, 1985, acknowledge that these prescriptions do not reflect actual usage and that many American Protestant denominations do not follow them. (The prescriptions reflect primarily the practice of the Church of England and American Episcopalians.) The prescriptions have a couple of other weaknesses, for *Reverend* is in fact used as a title, and it is also used as a noun (and has been since the 17th century).

This is primarily an American problem because of history: the forms prescribed now did not come into use in England until the 18th century, and early English settlers in this country brought the older prevailing practice—in which *the* was omitted regularly and the surname omitted at least some of the time. So early American Protestant practice continued forms that later went out of style in England.

There seems to be considerably greater acceptance of such forms as "Reverend Moomaw" than most authorities recognize. The Harper usage panel, for instance, gave 50 percent acceptance to the omission of *the,* 45 percent acceptance to the omission of the surname, and 40 percent acceptance to *Reverend* by itself as a form of address. Reader's Digest says many churches freely use those forms.

If you are trying to be really careful, then, you will need to learn the preferred or accepted forms for the church in question, perhaps by, as Reader's Digest suggests, asking your own clergyman. In a pinch you can probably make do with the old prescribed forms.

The abbreviation *Rev.* is subjected to the same restrictions as *Reverend* by most of the usage books. But as these three examples show, heterodox usage is as well entrenched for the abbreviation as it is for *Reverend:*

Rev. John Hayes of Salem or Rev. W. Wolcott of this city will answer questions with regard to me —Robert Frost, letter, 11 Sept. 1897

... Rev. Harris was Chaplain for the Senate when I was V.P. —Harry S. Truman, diary, 8 Feb. 1948

The release of Rev. Jenco did little to mitigate their unhappiness —*The Tower Commission Report,* 1987

There is, clearly, acceptable usage other than that prescribed in most of the stylebooks, handbooks, and etiquette books. Again, this is really a matter of etiquette more than of linguistic propriety, and the preference of the clergy involved should be taken into account if it can be determined.

More detail will be found in Harper 1975, 1985. There are several pages of historical material on the subject in Mencken 1963 (abridged), and an extensive treatment appears in "Speaking of the Clergy" by Lillian M. Fein-

silver in *American Speech,* Summer 1983. (She even finds variation in the forms of addressing American Jewish clergy.)

revert Although *revert back* is frequently cited as a redundancy (see REDUNDANCY), its occurrence in edited writing is not rare:

... would also revert back to Panama after a specified time —*Current Biography,* June 1968

... international conflict reverted back to a struggle between whole systems —Stephen A. Garrett, *Center Mag.,* July/August 1971

A conversion is always imminent; one cannot revert back to a lower level of consciousness —Joyce Carol Oates, *Saturday Rev.,* November 1972

But our evidence does show that *revert* by itself occurs far more often:

... to revert to the discussion of tragedy for a moment —Richard Schickel, *Harper's,* March 1971

... with the land reverting to forests —Jack Swedberg, *Massachusetts Wildlife,* May–June 1976

... often revert to an earlier stage of their development —*Changing Times,* March 1980

review, revue *Review* has many meanings, but *revue* has only one: "a theatrical production consisting typically of satirical skits, songs, and dances." That also happens to be one of the meanings of *review:*

... American composer of many musical reviews —*The Dance Encyclopedia,* ed. Anatole Chujoy, 1949

His opportunity to appear in a Broadway musical review —*Current Biography 1953*

... the Shanghai Theatre ... with three blue films which were shown in the intervals of a nude review —Graham Greene, *Travels with My Aunt,* 1969

Review acquired this sense from *revue,* which was the name given these shows when they first became popular in Paris during the 19th century. The shows were —and often still are—intended to satirically review current events; hence the name *revue,* which is simply the French word for "review." Perhaps because of this etymological connection, usage commentators are generally tolerant toward the use of *review* as a synonym (or, if you prefer, a spelling variant) of *revue.* The only critics explicitly rejecting such use are Phythian 1979 and the Oxford American Dictionary. Others, such as Evans 1957 and Copperud 1964, consider *review* acceptable but prefer *revue.* So, apparently, do most writers and editors. Our evidence shows that *revue* is appreciably more common than *review* in this sense.

reward The usual idiom with this verb calls for your being rewarded *for* something done, *with* or sometimes *by* something desirable, and *by* an agent, which need not be human. Thus the *by* construction can either indicate the reward or its giver. Both *by* uses do not, of course, occur in the same sentence.

... rewarded them for outstanding work —Harry Levinson, *Think,* May–June 1967

... individuals who, while not technically public servants, are rewarded ... with public money for performing a public service —Roy Lewis & Angus Maude, *The English Middle Classes,* 1950

. . . made a mild pun involving Latin and was rewarded with an immediate laugh —Jacques Barzun, *Atlantic,* December 1953

. . . books whose theme was that if the poor are virtuous, they are always rewarded by wealth and honor —*Collier's Year Book,* 1949

. . . was never rewarded by the least glimpse of the celebrated Lady Paignton —J. D. Beresford, *Jacob Stahl,* 1911

. . . portrait painting applauded & rewarded by the rich & great —William Blake, Annotations to Sir Joshua Reynolds' *Works,* ca. 1808

. . . you will be well rewarded by a visit to the Marine Historical Association's unique museum —Dana Burnet, *New England Journeys,* No. 2, 1954

rhetoric In ancient times—in the days of Aristotle and before—rhetoric was simply the art of speaking and writing effectively, the art of persuasion. Rhetoric was a subject of study at least as early as the time of Socrates, when it was taught by itinerant teachers known as Sophists to any free male Athenian citizen who could afford it and who wanted to improve his powers of persuasion in the councils of the city-state.

Rhetoric continued to be a subject of study into the Middle Ages, which was when the word *rhetoric* came into English. The study of rhetoric had by then, of course, long recognized certain standard methods of embellishment in speech and writing, and the word *rhetoric* in English soon began to be applied to those methods too, as in this 20th-century example:

The Senate soon found that if he spoke with studied elegance in favour of a motion he meant that he wanted it voted against, and that if he spoke with studied elegance against it this meant that he wanted it passed; and that on the very few occasions when he spoke briefly and without any rhetoric he meant to be taken literally —Robert Graves, *I, Claudius,* 1934

So if *rhetoric* could refer to the heightening of speech by the application of traditional devices, it would be no great stretch to use it to refer to that heightening or those devices in a depreciatory way, as belonging more to form than to substance. Such use began in the 17th century, according to evidence in the OED. It was still occurring in the late 19th and early 20th centuries:

He owes his superiority to a resolution to look facts in the face, instead of being put off by flimsy rhetoric —Leslie Stephen, *History of English Thought in the 18th Century,* 1876

My brother Clarke uttered a larmoyant dissent that seemed to me more sentiment and rhetoric than reasoning —Oliver Wendell Holmes d. 1935, letter, 29 Mar. 1922

It looks like mere "rhetoric," certainly not "deeds and language such as men do use." It appears to us, in fact, forced and flagitious bombast —T. S. Eliot, "Ben Jonson," in *Selected Essays,* 1932

That passage, Sir, is not empty rhetoric —Virginia Woolf, *Three Guineas,* 1938

So far this use had not raised a single eyebrow. But then came the 1960s and its sometimes unruly and unkempt students demanding "relevance" and damning "rhetoric." *Rhetoric* became rather a vogue word, and commentators like Edwin Newman soon discovered it:

Still worse is the destruction of rhetoric. Rhetoric does not mean fustian, exaggeration, or grand and empty phrases. . . . Suddenly beloved of politicians and journalists, rhetoric is now used to mean something doubtful and not quite honest. . . . Its misapplication could hardly tell more than it does —Newman 1974

Newman obviously did not realize that his newly discovered misapplication had been recorded in dictionaries published well before he was born, such as the Century of 1897, Webster 1909, and the OED (the volume covering *R* was published in 1910). Other commentators who have largely repeated Newman's criticism include Bremner 1980, Kilpatrick 1984, and Harper 1975, 1985. Critical commentary in the newspapers has come from William Safire (*N.Y. Times Book Rev.,* 6 June 1976) and Andrew Knight, a British writer, who in the *New York Times* for 7 May 1978 asserted that Americans had changed the meaning of *rhetoric* by using it only pejoratively—a curious assertion since Evans 1957, before the deluge, commented that the pejorative sense was primarily British.

But you need not concern yourself greatly with this minor issue. The pristine old sense of *rhetoric* is still in respectable use, and so are the senses from which the depreciatory sense developed. Nothing has really happened except that the depreciatory sense has gained wider circulation than it used to have.

rhinoceros The plural of *rhinoceros* seems to have vexed a great many writers, to judge from the wide variety of plurals shown in the OED. The variety has boiled down to three in present-day use: *rhinoceroses,* the most common, and *rhinoceros* and *rhinoceri.* Rhinoceri has occasionally been disapproved (Evans 1957), apparently because of its irregular formation, but has been used at least occasionally since the end of the 18th century.

. . . the African giants—elephants, rhinoceroses, hippopotamuses —Barbara Ford, *Saturday Rev.,* 5 Aug. 1972

. . . land-based creatures that have since disappeared: elephants, buffalo, rhinoceros —Frederic V. Grunfeld, *The Reporter,* 14 July 1966

. . . the perissodactyls, dwindled to a few tapirs and myopic rhinoceri in my own era —John Updike, *New Yorker,* 14 Aug. 1971

rich When used with a preposition, *rich* is most often found with *in:*

. . . a dog rich in leisure and in meditation —Sinclair Lewis, *Babbitt,* 1922

. . . no nation is rich enough in diplomatic talent — Hans J. Morgenthau, *New Republic,* 18 Apr. 1955

. . . Beecham's "Capriccio Italien," if not so rich in sound, is richer in spirit —Irving Kolodin, *Saturday Rev.,* 26 June 1954

Retrospective wisdom (in which we're all rich) — Irving Howe, *N.Y. Times Book Rev.,* 7 Nov. 1976

It is also found less frequently with *with:*

> ... life ... in all its manifold complexity, rich with its unnoticed and unrecorded little happenings — Thomas Wolfe, *You Can't Go Home Again,* 1940

> Life for her was rich with promise. She was to see herself fulfilled —D. H. Lawrence, *Sons and Lovers,* 1913

rid   *Rid* is now almost always used with *of:*

> ... I set out to rid myself of a sneaky city prose style —Garrison Keillor, *New Yorker,* 18 Sept. 1971

> ... distinguished people who simply could not rid themselves of the notion that Europe was the home of the arts —Edmund Wilson, *A Piece of My Mind,* 1956

> ... had not yet completely rid itself of the stillness of night —Hamilton Basso, *The View from Pompey's Head,* 1954

The past participle is common in the idiomatic phrases *get rid of* and *be rid of:*

> ... a desire of serfs to get rid of the feudalism that has held them in a vise —William O. Douglas, *Saturday Rev.,* 23 Apr. 1955

> The liberals wished to get rid of sectarian injustices —Conor Cruise O'Brien, *N.Y. Rev. of Books,* 6 Nov. 1969

> ... were willing to sacrifice everything in order to be rid of slavery —Henry Seidel Canby, *Walt Whitman,* 1943

> ... desired nothing in the world so much as to be rid of us —Katherine Anne Porter, *The Never-Ending Wrong,* 1977

At one time *rid* was commonly used with *from,* but this combination now seldom occurs:

> ... the most effective combinations for ridding sandflies from houses —*Experiment Station Record,* August 1939

In this context, *rid* essentially means "to remove completely." The more likely construction in current English would be "ridding houses of sandflies," where *rid* means "to make free; relieve."

right   1. This old and homely adverb (many of its senses go back to the time of King Alfred the Great) has bothered commentators—primarily American commentators—for about a century and a half. A number of senses have been found objectionable—often for being Americanisms or colloquialisms. Among the uses criticized are those illustrated here:

> Michael was not going to strangle her right here — Daphne du Maurier, *Ladies' Home Jour.,* August 1971

> McCarthyism came right at the end of World War II —David Halberstam, *New Times,* 16 May 1975

> You can drive your car right through the area where the animals roam free —Polly Bradley, *Massachusetts Audubon,* June 1968

> ... right now there are people that are willing to accept compromise —William Faulkner, 16 May 1957, in *Faulkner in the University,* 1959

> I think I had better describe her right away —Vladimir Nabokov, *Lolita,* 1958

> He always went right ahead with his description of the violence he would do Uncle Andrew's assailant —Peter Taylor, *The Old Forest and Other Stories,* 1985

These uses are of course standard, and they are little disputed today, although Longman 1988 considers them more appropriate to speech than to writing, and Perrin & Ebbitt 1972 and Ebbitt & Ebbitt 1982 say they are common in general writing but not in formal writing. We agree with this last observation; we have plenty of written evidence for these uses of *right,* but the contexts in which they occur are not noticeably formal.

Much of the attention given to adverbial *right* has concerned its use as an intensifier. This intensive use is old, too; the OED dates it from about 1200. It has a long literary pedigree:

> I am right glad that he's so out of hope —Shakespeare, *The Tempest,* 1612

> ... those illustrious and right eloquent Pen-men, the Modern Travellers —Jonathan Swift, "A Discourse Concerning the Mechanical Operation of the Spirit," 1710

> Of his person and stature was the King
> A man right manly strong
>   —Dante Gabriel Rossetti (in Hall 1917)

In this country, for some reason, the spoken use of intensive *right* came to be a Southernism; it was attacked as a Southern corruption by a writer in the Boston *Pearl* in 1836 (cited in Thornton 1912). Hall 1917 names a number of turn-of-the-century grammarians and rhetoricians who identify it as provincial; several more recent handbooks call it colloquial or dialectal (especially Southern). American dialecticians identify it with Southern and Midland speech; Raven I. McDavid, Jr., in *PADS* (Publication of the American Dialect Society), April 1967, adds the Hudson Valley. Our latest British source, Longman 1988, calls it archaic or regional.

If intensive *right* can be identified as a regionalism in speech, it is less easy to pin down in writing. Hall mentions the problem; he is perplexed as to how the comments of the rhetoricians can be squared with his examples collected from such poets as Tennyson, Browning, Lowell, Rossetti, and Swinburne. He surmises that perhaps the literary use can be ascribed mostly to writers who are fond of archaizing.

Our evidence is different. We have, of course, a considerable amount of fictional speech, both dialectal and old-fashioned. And we have direct evidence from reported speech and from letters, presumably of people to whom Southern or Midland speech is native. The intensive *right* also appears in the discursive writing of these people.

> I did not feel right comfortable for some time afterward —Mark Twain, *Innocents Abroad,* 1869 (*A Mark Twain Lexicon,* 1938)

> It is right hard to understand what he says —Ellen Glasgow, *Barren Ground,* 1925

> He was a man for detail, and he did a right competent job of stage management —*The Autobiography of William Allen White,* 1946

It took a right smart bug to find a safe place to hide —Frank J. Taylor, *Saturday Evening Post,* 26 July 1958

I am right embarassed to think every story is the best —Flannery O'Connor, letter, 6 Mar. 1959

Again Hamilton, in the shining armor of his genius, rides right gallantly upon the scene —Claude G. Bowers, *Jefferson in Power,* 1936

I know I whine right regularly over things about our town that are no more —Celestine Sibley, *Atlanta Constitution,* 19 Sept. 1984

So far we have quoted people we either know or assume to have been born in the Southern and Midland speech areas. The following examples, however, appear to be anomalous from the geographical standpoint:

... a right merry letter it was too —Emily Dickinson, letter, 21 Oct. 1847

I should like right well to make a longer excursion on foot —Henry David Thoreau, *A Yankee in Canada,* 1866 (OED)

... enabled him to carry himself in right royal fashion —Jack London, *The Call of the Wild,* 1903

And, of course, *right* is sometimes used, like *ain't* and *allow as how,* in a deliberately casual or pseudo-dialectal style:

They are right pleased about it, too —*Changing Times,* February 1952

He moved nimbly among the delegates, chanting: "Peanuts, popcorn, chewing gum, cigars, cigarettes!" He did right well for a lad of 11 —*Newsweek,* 18 June 1956

... a defender of the language—you remember, he defended it right profitably in his earlier *Strictly Speaking* —William Cole, *Saturday Rev.,* 13 Nov. 1976

Oh no, they came out of the box right smartly —Paul Zimmerman, *Sports Illustrated,* 12 Nov. 1983

The usage is not unknown in British English, but more common, apparently, is an intensive adjective use approximately equivalent to the American's *real:*

You can get in a right muddle of commas when lists include phrases in apposition —Howard 1984

Clearly we do not know everything there is to know about the intensive *right.* That it is in some respects a regionalism is evident, but no simple label seems adequate to describe the range of its common use, or to account for its use outside that range by such writers as New England's Emily Dickinson and San Francisco's Jack London. In practical terms, if the intensive *right* is part of your native dialect, you should of course feel free to use it without qualm when it seems appropriate, even in writing. It has a long and honorable history and an impressive literary background, and our evidence shows that it is fairly common in current writing, especially in writing that has a light and informal style.

2. *Right, rightly.* See WRONG, WRONGLY.

ring, rang, rung   The usual past tense of *ring* is *rang:*

His voice rang around in the girdered heights of the gymnasium —Paul Horgan, *Ladies' Home Jour.,* January 1971

Josef rang for cold drinks —Irving Stone, *McCall's,* March 1971

The past participle of *ring* is *rung:*

... as many as 479,001,600 changes can be rung —Lois I. Woodville, *Christian Science Monitor,* 1 Oct. 1954

"... She told me that you'd rung her. ..." —*Sunday Mirror* (London), 3 Mar. 1968

Rung was also formerly in common use as an alternative past tense of *ring:*

The Heav'ns and all the Constellations rung —John Milton, *Paradise Lost,* 1667 (OED)

One with whose name the world rung —Benjamin Disraeli, *Venetia,* 1837 (OED)

But this use of *rung* is now extremely rare in writing. Dialect studies such as E. Bagby Atwood's *A Survey of Verb Forms in the Eastern United States* (1953) have found *rung* continuing in reputable spoken use as a past tense, especially in parts of New England. Atwood describes this use of *rung* as "old-fashioned," however.

rise   See RAISE, RISE.

rob   **1.** *Rob* is used most often with *of,* when a prepositional phrase follows:

"Yes, it was wonderful," she said, but robbed the phrase of its full effect by adding: "I didn't imagine I *could* be so glad to see him again. ..." —Aldous Huxley, *Point Counter Point,* 1928

"Remember, George, the Sons of Liberty have already robbed me of so much freedom that I can't risk losing more." —Kenneth Roberts, *Oliver Wiswell,* 1940

At funerals his mien of settled woe somehow robbed the chief mourners of their proper eminence —Robertson Davies, *Tempest-tost,* 1951

His friends say that the history profession robbed the stage of one of its most gifted mimes —C. Vann Woodward, *N.Y. Rev. of Books,* 3 Dec. 1970

Once in a great while, *rob* occurs with *from* (see section 2 below):

Concave surfaces are troublesome in that they tend to focus sound in some spots and rob sound energy from others —James F. Nickerson, *Education Digest,* March 1953

One red or green bulb ... will not rob color from your fish —Virginia Carlson, *All Pets,* July 1962

2. *Rob,* as used figuratively in the last two examples above, sometimes has as its object what is stolen, as *steal* would. This use is quite old, going back to the 13th century. It is not uncommon in earlier literature:

... They themselves contrive
To rob the Honey and subvert the Hive.
—John Dryden, *Virgil's Georgics,* 1697 (OED)

The OED describes the use as *now rare.* It is not, indeed, nearly as common as the other uses, and it is sometimes considered wrong, or archaic, by commentators no longer familiar with it. Bernstein 1958 and Harper 1975, 1985 associate the use with newspaper headlines. We have also collected evidence of it from news broadcasts and newspaper reports.

> . . . set it afire on Sunday, then robbed $100 after the clerk fled the flames —*Springfield* (Mass.) *Morning Union,* 24 Feb. 1986

This is not really a misuse, since it is a continuation of an old standard sense. Still, we find it occurring only in news reports. It does not appear to be used at present in other writing, except for the rare figurative use, and we cannot recommend its cultivation.

robbery See BURGLARY, ROBBERY.

rooftop Theodore Bernstein had a definite dislike for this word and recommended (in *The Careful Writer,* 1965, and elsewhere) that it always be replaced by either *housetop* or *roof.* No other commentator has expressed disapproval of it. It is not a new word (the OED has a citation for it from 1611), but it was an extremely rare one—at least in print—until about the middle of the 20th century, and it has only recently been entered in dictionaries. Its omission from dictionaries may have been what caused Bernstein to disapprove of it in the first place; however, it is now a common word, universally recognized as standard. Like *housetop,* it refers especially to the level surface of a flat roof:

> . . . loping over the rooftops to safety in a vacant lot —Charles Perry, *Rolling Stone,* 3 Aug. 1972

> . . . nesting on the gravelly rooftops of shopping complexes —Elizabeth Cary Pierson, *Blair & Ketchum's Country Jour.,* June 1980

Its most distinctive use is as an attributive adjective meaning "situated or taking place on a rooftop":

> . . . sitting two tables away in the rooftop nightclub —David Butwin, *Saturday Rev.,* 13 Nov. 1971

> . . . using a rooftop observatory to track the Apollo 13 spacecraft —Henry S. F. Cooper, Jr., *New Yorker,* 11 Nov. 1972

> . . . were handsomely refurbished and a rooftop indoor pool added —Linda Gwinn, *Town & Country,* April 1980

Note that neither *housetop* nor *roof* can be idiomatically substituted for *rooftop* in these three passages.

round, around See AROUND 2.

royal *we* See WE 1.

ruddy See BLOODY.

rules There exists in the folk memory a set of facetious grammatical rules that pop up in various places and in various forms from time to time. They are to be found in Harper 1985 and Einstein 1985, for example, and in each instance the rules are ascribed to some old newspaper editor of beloved memory. The order may change, the phraseology may vary, but the essential idea is always the same. The rules we show here are taken from an article by George W. Feinstein in *College English,* April 1960. We will give only the first fifteen of his twenty rules, because they are the ones that seem to turn up most often.

1. Each pronoun agrees with their antecedent.
2. Just between you and I, case is important.
3. Verbs has to agree with their subjects.
4. Watch out for irregular verbs which has crope into our language.
5. Don't use no double negatives.
6. A writer mustn't shift your point of view.
7. When dangling, don't use participles.
8. Join clauses good, like a conjunction should.
9. Don't write a run-on sentence you got to punctuate it.
10. About sentence fragments.
11. In letters themes reports articles and stuff like that we use commas to keep a string of items apart.
12. Don't use commas, which aren't necessary.
13. It's important to use apostrophe's right.
14. Don't abbrev.
15. Check to see if you any words out.

The beauty of rules like these is that almost anybody can come up with the same or similar ones and believe that they are original creations. Mr. Feinstein's set is the earliest we have found in print, but similar sets have undoubtedly been around for many years.

In the realm of language, *rule* is a word that the wise tend not to bandy about. Many observers from the 18th century to the present have pointed out the limitations of rules as a guide to good writing:

> Rules may obviate faults, but can never confer beauties —Samuel Johnson, *The Idler,* 19 May 1759

> I think the following rules will cover most cases: . . . (vi) Break any of these rules sooner than say anything outright barbarous —George Orwell, "Politics and the English Language," 1946

> We ought not to get so straitjacketed in "rules" that we sacrifice vigor and clarity to form —James J. Kilpatrick, *Portland Oregonian,* 2 Nov. 1985

run Funny things happen to our verbs. *Run* results from the coming together in Middle English of two older verbs, an intransitive *rinnan* and a causative *irnan.* The first of these produced the past *ran* and the second produced the past *run.* If everything had developed according to theory, we would now have, according to Lamberts 1972, a verb *rin* with a past singular *ran,* a past plural *run,* and a past participle *run* or *runnen,* in the same class of irregular verbs as *ring, swim,* and *begin.* But things went awry in early modern English: *run* replaced *rin* sometime around the 16th century (Lamberts says *rin* still survives in Scottish and Irish folk speech). So instead of developing into *rin, ran, run,* the verb developed into two patterns, *run, ran, run* and *run, run, run.* (If you look into the OED, you will see the full story is much more complex than this brief sketch reveals.)

In terms of current usage, the problem with this verb centers on the past *run.* It appears in literature from the 16th to the 19th centuries; Jespersen 1909–49 (volume 6) lists Shakespeare, Bunyan, Defoe, Swift, Fielding, and Goldsmith as using it. Modern dialectologists, such as Michael I. Miller (*American Speech,* Summer 1984), attest its currency in speech in both southern England and in parts of the U.S. But *ran* is now virtually the only form used in writing. Modern practice may be partly attributable to Johnson's Dictionary (1755), where only *ran* is listed for the past. Lowth 1762 attacked past *run,* and the tradition in school grammars ever since has been to insist on *ran.* Noah Webster 1828 gave *ran* or *run,* departing from Johnson, and his successors through 1909 followed suit. Webster's Second, however, called *run* dialectal, and Webster's Third calls it nonstandard. Miller feels this treatment misrepresents the usage of past *run,* and perhaps it does to some extent. But dictionaries find it hard to devise a short descriptor that will mean "used in speech in southern England and in the southern U.S. and New England, especially by older people, and used formerly in literature."

In any case, there is no denying that past *run* is now considered nonstandard by many people, if not by dialectologists. The surveys of Leonard 1932 and Crisp 1971 indicate as much. If it is part of your natural speech, you should not avoid it. But you will want to use *ran* in writing, as just about everyone now does.

run-on sentences See COMMA FAULT.

S

sacrilegious For obvious reasons, it is easy to misspell this word as *sacreligious.* One way to avoid the error is to remember that *religious* and *sacrilegious* are not etymologically related to each other. *Religious* is derived from the Latin word *religio,* meaning "reverence, religion," whereas *sacrilegious* is derived ultimately from the Latin combining form *sacr-,* meaning "sacred," and the verb *legere,* meaning "to steal." The Latin noun *sacrilegus* means "one who steals sacred things." It also may be helpful to remember that *sacrilegious* is the adjective formed from *sacrilege.*

Sahara, Sahara desert Because the Arabic word *sahara* (or *sahra*) means literally "desert," several commentators, notably Bernstein 1958, Bremner 1980, and Harper 1975, 1985, have criticized *Sahara desert* as a redundancy. If English and Arabic were one language, the critics might have a good argument, but the fact is that *Sahara* in English is no more a synonym for *desert* (except in figurative use) than are *Gobi* and *Mojave;* it is, instead, the specific name of a specific desert, one that is commonly and idiomatically called both "the Sahara" and "the Sahara desert." Some writers do make a point of omitting *desert* after *Sahara,* but many others do not, and there is no reason why you should feel compelled to.

> . . . so the Sahara desert had to form —David Attenborough, TV broadcast, 2 Nov. 1987

> The story within the story is set in the Sahara Desert —*Booklist,* 1 June 1982

It is interesting to note that the Mongolian word *gobi* means literally "waterless place," so that the same logic that finds redundancy in *Sahara desert* should also find it in *Gobi desert.* As far as we know, however, no one has ever called *Gobi desert* redundant.

For similar problems with words borrowed from foreign languages, see HOI POLLOI and SIERRA.

said All commentators agree that use of *said* as an adjective synonymous with *aforementioned* is appropriate only in legal and business contexts, and it is certainly true that it now appears far more commonly in those contexts than in any other:

> . . . fixed sinking fund requirements and final maturity amount on the said bonds —*Annual Report, Armco Steel Corp.,* 1970

> . . . an order rescinding the supplemental agreement referred to in said Note —*Annual Report, R. J. Reynolds Industries, Inc.,* 1970

Said has been favored in legal writing for centuries, but its use in general contexts was also unremarkable once:

> The said article is so very mild and sentimental — Lord Byron, letter, 22 Aug. 1813

> . . . attending them to their carriage after the said dinner visit —Jane Austen, *Mansfield Park,* 1814

> And so you don't agree with my view as to said photographer? —Lewis Carroll, letter, 1 Apr. 1887

Such usage still occurs, but the legalistic connotations of *said* have long been so familiar that those who employ it in other contexts typically do so for deliberate effect, often humorous:

> This petition sheweth that the best way of proving clearly that a man is not dead is by setting forth his manner of life, and, first, that he, the said W. Hazlitt, has regularly for the last month rang the bell at eleven at night —William Hazlitt, letter, 11 Jan. 1808

> He was also an extremely vain man who would keep said mustache at the proper rakish tilt with the aid of paper clips —Richard Freedman, *N.Y. Times Book Rev.,* 28 Mar. 1976

sake Fowler 1926 and Evans 1957 both regard the apostrophe as optional in *for goodness' sake, for conscience' sake,* and similar expressions in which the word preceding *sake* ends in an *s* or *z* sound. They both consider it incorrect to add an apostrophe plus *-s.* Our evidence indicates that the apostrophe is rarely omitted in such expressions, and that the apostrophe plus *-s* is only avoided when the \s\ sound is never added in speech, as when the expression is a fixed idiom (as *for goodness' sake* and *for conscience' sake* are), or when the word in question is multisyllabic (as in *for convenience' sake*) so that pronouncing the *-s* would be especially awkward. When the word is short and no fixed idiom is involved, the *-s* is likely to be pronounced and the apostrophe plus *-s* is likely to be written: *for peace's sake, for the human race's sake.*

salad days Shakespeare coined this term in *Antony and Cleopatra* (1607), wherein Cleopatra dismisses her former love of Caesar as having occurred in "My salad days, when I was green in judgment. . . ." Modern writers have taken up the figure of speech, and *salad days* is often now used to mean "a time of youthful inexperience":

> The Paris student is a notorious rebel in his salad days —James P. O'Donnell, *Saturday Evening Post,* 19 Jan. 1957

When a starlet was promoted to star, she immediately set about changing her image.... The salad days were never much remembered, certainly not talked about —*Esquire,* February 1976

In recent years, we have seen the development of a new sense of *salad days,* "an early flourishing period; heyday":

... a rundown pub that had seen its salad days at the turn of the century —Horace Sutton, *Saturday Rev.,* 30 Oct. 1971

... the way Coward himself in his salad days could sing them with an ... enormously insinuating phrasing —Alan Rich, *New York,* 19 Feb. 1973

Those were Sahl's salad days, when The New Yorker did a worshipful profile —Jean Shepherd, *N.Y. Times Book Rev.,* 3 Oct. 1976

A few usage commentators have taken note of *salad days,* and none of them have much cared for it. Fowler 1926 was inclined to think it was "fitter for parrots' than for human speech"; Evans 1957 found it "wilted." Bremner 1980 quotes Evans; Copperud 1980 believes the phrase is growing quaint and disused. These examples indicate otherwise:

Our reading life has its salad days, its autumnal times —William H. Gass, *N.Y. Times Book Rev.,* 1 Apr. 1984

... had not put together two good seasons since his salad days of 1972 and '73 —Mickey Herskowitz, *Golf Digest,* August 1983

same The use of *same* as a pronoun, often with *the,* has attracted criticism from many commentators, dating back to Vizetelly 1906. The use of *same* as a substitute for *it, this, that,* and *them* is typically described as unliterary business jargon, if not as an out-and-out error. But a look at the long history and current use of the pronoun *same* shows clearly that the judgment of the critics is undeservedly harsh. *Same* has been in continuous use as a pronoun since the 14th century. It was well known to the Shakespearean businessman:

And in the instant that I met with you
He had of me a chain. At five o'clock
I shall receive the money for the same.
 —Shakespeare, *The Comedy of Errors,* 1593

But its use has never been limited to the world of business. Here are some further examples, old and new, to counter the dismissal of pronominal *same* as mere jargon:

Each house shall keep a journal of *its* proceedings, and from time to time publish the same —*Constitution of the United States,* 1787

It then transpired that Old Crockford was a village, and, from the appearance of the team on the day of battle, the Old Crockfordians seemed to be composed exclusively of the riff-raff of same —P. G. Wodehouse, *Tales of St Austin's,* 1903

... mentioning the receipt of the same and stating that no great harm had been done by the delay — William Hazlitt, letter, 7 Apr. 1822

You are aware of the high hopes following Frost's and my visit to the now Attorney General last sum-

mer. You are aware of the higher hopes in Frost's mind following his repeat visit to same in November —Archibald MacLeish, letter, 18 Feb. 1958

You said you wanted a picture of me and I enclose same —Flannery O'Connor, letter, 16 Nov. 1961

... the letters he wrote were revealing and full of immense feeling and the joy of life and the terror of same —E. B. White, letter, 21 June 1967

The rich had clothes made by couturiers, tailors, or designers, and the masses wore knockoffs of same — Tom Wolfe, *Esquire,* December 1979

... have brought rejoicing to millions who have now seen opera live in their homes and who can look forward to more of the same next winter —Irving Kolodin, *Saturday Rev.,* 8 July 1978

... a dispute about the accommodations, or lack of same, for the team —Douglas S. Looney, *Sports Illustrated,* 31 Dec. 1979

He also discusses the wisdom, or lack of same, of candor —Genevieve Stuttaford, *Publishers Weekly,* 7 Sept. 1984

The pronoun *same* may sound wooden in an awkwardly written business letter, but in the hands of a competent writer it is often simply a mark of an informal style.

same as **1.** Several usage books, dating back to Krapp 1927, have warned against using *the same as* as an adverbial phrase in place of *as* or *just as* ("He acts the same as he used to" instead of " ... just as he used to"). No particular reasons are given for the warnings, but they are presumably attributable to the elliptical and somewhat informal quality of adverbial *the same as:*

Black folks have a right to hate white folks the same as white folks have a right to hate us —Dick Gregory, *Avant Garde,* January 1969

Writers were at each other's throats in the thirties the same as they are today —Granville Hicks, *American Scholar,* Summer 1966

As and *just as* are more common in writing than *the same as,* but *the same as* is not incorrect. Note that it is actually more flexible in its application than is *just as,* in that the *same* in the phrase can be qualified:

... function much the same as they did five hundred centuries ago —David R. Reuben, M.D., *McCall's,* March 1971

2. Another old controversy—a nearly dead issue now, though mentioned in Longman 1984—has to do with whether a clause following *same* should be introduced by *as* rather than *that.* Both are in fact in reputable use:

... decades to get the same amount of information as they are gathering —Thomas L. Barnett, quoted in *N.Y. Times,* 9 Aug. 1973

... much the same acclaim that welcomed the book —*Current Biography,* March 1968

sanatorium, sanitarium People used to write letters to newspapers—and to dictionary editors—about these two words, but the small controversy that once existed concerning their use has now died out. The argument favoring a distinction between them ran more or less as follows: *sanatorium* is derived from the Latin verb *san-*

are, meaning "to restore to health," and properly refers to an establishment set up for the treatment of disease or for the care of invalids; *sanitarium,* on the other hand, is derived from the Latin noun *sanitas,* meaning "health," and properly refers to an establishment set up for the preservation rather than the restoration of health—a health resort, in other words. The problem for those who favored this tidy etymological distinction was that it bore no relation to actual English usage. As is now generally conceded, *sanatorium* and *sanitarium* are synonymous words, used interchangeably. The only distinctions that can be made on the basis of the evidence in our files are that *sanatorium* is somewhat more likely to be used when the establishment referred to is specifically for the treatment of tuberculosis, and that *sanitarium*—possibly because of association with *sanity*—is somewhat more likely when the establishment is for the treatment of mental and emotional disorders.

sanguinary See BLOODY.

sans This French preposition meaning "without" was borrowed into English in the 14th century and occurs fairly commonly today, but it has never entirely lost its Frenchness. It might have passed into disuse long ago were it not for the influence of Shakespeare, who used it in many of his plays, most memorably in *As You Like It* (1600):

> Last scene of all,
> That ends this strange eventful history,
> Is second childishness and mere oblivion,
> Sans teeth, sans eyes, sans taste, sans everything.

Modern writers still occasionally echo this famous passage:

> I had forgotten . . . that this was wartime; sans Salts, sans fish, sans nets, sans sails, sans everything — Gladys Bronwyn Stern, *Trumpet Voluntary,* 1944

But *sans* also frequently occurs when no allusion to Shakespeare is being made. In its most typical use, its object is a regular noun rather than a pronoun or gerund, and the *a, an,* or *the* which would normally occur after *without* is dropped:

> Most rooms on Hotel Circle in Mission Valley, sans waterbed, go for just $12 —David Butwin, *Saturday Rev.,* 10 July 1971

> . . . was named as a special assistant to the President-elect, sans press title —David Wise, *Esquire,* May 1973

> Negotiations ensued and the ad finally did run, sans marijuana leaf —Laurel Leff, *Wall Street Jour.,* 4 June 1981

Because it still retains much of its foreign quality, *sans* often appears in italics. Even when it is in roman type, however, *sans* is an unusual word, one that calls attention to itself. It occurs much more commonly in writing than in speech, but if you do have occasion to say it, be advised that its usual pronunciation in English is \'sanz\.

sartorial *Sartorial* is a dressy word in more ways than one, and its use may elicit a few grumbles from those who scorn dressiness in language. Two such scorners among usage writers are Fowler 1926, who classes *sartorial* as "pedantic humor," and Flesch 1964, who

dismisses it as "fancy." Anyone determined to avoid its use, however, will have to contend with the fact that it has no synonym, fancy or plain. There are times when *sartorial* (or *sartorially*) is the only word that fits, and there are other times when a little dressiness may not be such a bad thing:

> . . . he observes the preparations of a sartorial dandy —Richard Poirier, *A World Elsewhere,* 1966

> I use the tie to push me over the edge when I am at my sartorial greatest —E. B. White, letter, 9 Jan. 1967

> Can anyone deny that the appeal of films about the Nazis is partly sartorial? —Anthony Burgess, *Saturday Rev.,* 23 June 1979

> . . . on the assumption that sartorial splendor can make up for the notoriously uncomfortable seating arrangements —Paul Hofmann, *N.Y. Times,* 4 May 1980

> . . . divide the delegates into groups sartorially, alcoholically, and conversationally —*New Yorker,* 18 July 1964

> He stands out sartorially, too —Martin Mayer, *N.Y. Times Mag.,* 7 Feb. 1965

> . . . a sartorially impressive figure —Robert Penn Warren, *Jefferson Davis Gets His Citizenship Back,* 1980

sated, satiated Both *sated* and *satiated* are idiomatically followed by *with:*

> . . . tend to be quickly sated with tales involving fame or wealth —Norman Cousins, *Saturday Rev.,* 24 June 1978

> . . . went and went again, never satiated with the theme —Robert Morss Lovett, *All Our Years,* 1948

satisfy

"Satisfied" is straying, is pushing into the place long filled properly by "convinced" or even the lowly "sure." The result is sometimes startling. For instance: "The man's family is satisfied that he was murdered." Of course that may be literally true, but the family did not mean to tell the world so —Alice Hamilton, M.D., *Atlantic,* September 1954

A look in the OED shows that *satisfy* has been used in a sense essentially synonymous with *convince* since at least 1520. (*Convince* itself was first recorded in this sense in 1606.) It has occurred in the works of such writers as Shakespeare, John Locke, Henry Fielding, Francis Bacon, Jane Austen, Thomas Macaulay, and Charles Lamb:

> Keeping them up till midnight . . . would, I am satisfied, in a medical point of view, prove the better caution —Charles Lamb, *The Essays of Elia,* 1823

Samuel Johnson duly recorded it as a standard sense in 1755, and so did Noah Webster in 1828. In the late 19th century, however, it had the misfortune of being noticed by Alfred Ayres, who was reported (in the *Inland Printer,* October 1899) to regard it as "unnecessary." 20th-century criticism has been sporadic. Whipple 1924 states flatly that *satisfy* "should not be used as a synonym for *convince.*" Evans 1957 concurs with that opinion, but Gowers in Fowler 1965 acknowledges the long history of the sense, limiting his criticism to what he regards as its overuse in contexts where its suggestion of contentment may seem inappropriate.

The "convince" sense of *satisfy* continues in fairly common use, and there is no doubt that it is entirely reputable. You may wish to avoid it in certain contexts, as Gowers recommends, but keep in mind that *satisfy* and *convince* have different connotations and are not always interchangeable. Such a sentence as "The man's family is satisfied that he was murdered" may seem ludicrous taken out of context, but making it "The man's family is convinced that he was murdered" results in a significant change in meaning. *Convinced* implies an utter certainty which may or may not have a sound basis ("All the evidence suggests an accident, but the man's family is convinced that he was murdered"). *Satisfied* emphasizes certainty less strongly; it implies a realization that doubts (or hopes) have been shown by the evidence to be unreasonable or groundless ("After seeing the evidence, the man's family is satisfied that he was murdered").

saturate   When *saturate* is followed by a preposition, the usual choice is *with:*

> . . . Soviet trading missions abroad were so saturated with intelligence agents . . . —Hedrick Smith, *Atlantic,* December 1974

> . . . have an easy time saturating the marketplace with their potboilers —Norman Cousins, *Saturday Rev.,* 24 June 1978

> . . . his books . . . are saturated with politics —Irving Howe, *N.Y. Times Book Rev.,* 24 Oct. 1982

Other prepositions that occasionally occur after *saturate* are *by* and *in:*

> . . . saturated by prejudice and emotion —William J. Reilly, *Life Planning for College Students,* 1954

> . . . children are so saturated by television —Michele Murray, *Children's House,* Summer 1970

> A moment ago, he was saturated in sunniness —Liz Smith, *Cosmopolitan,* May 1975

> . . . are they not . . . saturated in Christian cosmology? —John Updike, *N.Y. Times Book Rev.,* 23 May 1976

When the object of *saturate* is a reflexive pronoun, the preposition that follows is *in:*

> . . . saturated himself in literature about, and photographs of, Nijinsky —Walter Terry, *Saturday Rev.,* 13 Nov. 1976

> . . . will allow athletic types to saturate themselves in basketball, volleyball, and skating —Richard F. Shepard, *N.Y. Times,* 10 Dec. 1976

savant   *Savant* is not a remarkably common word, but it does have a wide range of applications. It can be used seriously to denote a person of great knowledge and brilliance:

> The volume demonstrates the savant's great learning, depth of understanding and ease of presentation —*British Book News,* December 1965

But it can also mean little more than "one who is in the know":

> It is this particular window . . . that industry savants believe holds the key to the fiscal future —Kenneth Turan, *TV Guide,* 20 July 1984

And it often has a strongly ironic—or even sarcastic—quality:

> . . . in reading, say, a book review by one of the apple-cheeked savants of the quarterlies or one of the pious gremlins who manufacture puns for *Time* —John Updike, in *Five Boyhoods,* ed. Martin Levin, 1962

This variability of tone and meaning seems to have played some part in provoking occasional criticism by usage commentators. Copperud 1964, for one, considers *savant* in many of its uses to be journalese.

Savant has recently developed a new sense that deserves to be noted. The term *idiot savant* has long been used in medical parlance to describe a person who is mentally deficient but exhibits great talent or brilliance in a particular field, such as music or mathematics. The term is not meant to be offensive in any way, but *idiot* is such a strongly derogatory word that its use in this term seems needlessly cruel to many people, and the tendency in recent years has been to use *savant* by itself:

> It is not even clear who qualifies as a savant, nor is it easy to tell the difference between a mentally retarded savant and an autistic savant —Richard Restak, *Science 82,* May 1982

saving, savings   *Savings* has several familiar uses. It occurs as a mass noun, plural in construction, with the sense "money put by (as in a bank)":

> Savings have a deflationary effect, since they cut down the amount of spending for consumer goods —Albert H. Sayer et al., *Economics in Our Democracy,* 1950

It is also used in this sense as an attributive adjective in such terms as *savings account* and *savings bank:*

> . . . fulfill the function of deposit and savings banks through their numerous branches —George J. Henry, *Forbes,* 1 Dec. 1970

These uses are straightforward and uncontroversial. The problems for *savings* arise when it is used as a singular noun with the sense "an act or instance of economizing" or "reduction in cost." We first recorded this use in the 1940s, and we have encountered it with increasing frequency in the decades since:

> . . . resulting in an *actual cash savings* on your taxes —*N.Y. Herald Tribune Book Rev.,* 15 Dec. 1946

> . . . would represent a savings of 183,000 miles a year —*Buffalo Courier Express,* 24 Apr. 1963

> . . . a savings which can be passed on to you —advt., *N.Y. Times Mag.,* 27 Sept. 1964

> . . . up to a 25 minute time savings on each inbound trip —John D. Caplan, *Annual Report, General Motors Corp.,* 1971

> . . . buy one now at a $275 savings —radio advt., 16 May 1974

A savings of space becomes a savings in money — Steve Lambert, *Apple Computer Publication,* July 1984

A few usage commentators (notably Bernstein 1965 and Safire 1986) are emphatic in disapproving this use of *savings,* and the usage panelists of Heritage 1969, 1982 and of Harper 1975, 1985 reject it in writing. Nevertheless, it is extremely common and has clearly established itself as idiomatic in American English. If you feel inclined to avoid it, you can always use *saving* instead:

> ... a saving of approximately $60,000,000 a year — *Current Biography,* January 1965

> ... can be purchased at a saving of up to 60% — Caleb Pirtle III, *Southern Living,* November 1971

A related concern is the use of *savings* in *daylight savings time.* The original term, and the usual term in writing, is *daylight saving time,* but *daylight savings time* (or often just *daylight savings*) is very common in speech, and it does occasionally make its way into print:

> ... upheld the validity of the Massachusetts daylight-savings time law —George W. Hervey & Reign S. Hadsell, *Inspection & Control of Weights & Measures in the USA,* May 1942

> He called this idea Daylight Savings Time —Joseph M. Oxenhorn et al., *Pathways in Science* (textbook), 1982

Usage commentators who take up this subject regard *daylight savings time* as an error.

say   The use of *say* for *said* in a narration, as in *says I,* is now and then pointed to as an error. There are two aspects of the problem: the use of the third person singular *says* with first and second person pronouns, and the use of the present where the past might be expected. Curme 1931 explains the first as a survival of older literary English. When the Northern *-s* was in the process of replacing the Southern *-th* ending in early Modern English, it was not limited to just the third person singular. (It had been used for all persons in Northern dialect.) The survival of this older form in the *says I* of the narrator is a mark of a conversational style of narration. It is used to identify the narrator's speech as distinct from the rest of the narrative and the speech of interlocutors. Curme has an example from one of Thackeray's less serious works. Here are a few from our own files:

> Why, says I, this is a little Nosegay of Conceits, a very Lump of Salt: Every Verse hath something in it that piques. ... Dear Mr. *Bickerstaff,* says he, shaking me by the Hand, every Body knows you to be a Judge of these Things —Joseph Addison, *The Tatler,* No. 163, 25 Apr. 1710

> But I was going to tell what husband said. He says to me, says he, "Silly." I says, says I, "What?" — Frances Miriam Whitcher, "Hezekiah Bedott," 1855, in *The Mirth of a Nation,* ed. Walter Blair & Raven I. McDavid, Jr., 1983

> Thin we wint up to each other. 'A Happy New Year,' says I. 'Th' same to you,' says he, 'an' manny iv thim,' he says. 'Ye have a brick in ye'er hand,' says I. 'I was thinkin' iv givin' ye a New Year's gift,' says he. 'Th' same to you, an' manny iv thim,' says I, fondlin' me own ammunition —Finley Peter Dunne, *Mr. Dooley in Peace and in War,* 1898

One of them in Texas fixed me with a seedy eye and said, "Miss O'Connor, what is your motivation in writing?" "Because I'm good at it," says I —Flannery O'Connor, letter, 24 Nov. 1962

The use of the present where the past might be expected appears to add a certain immediacy to the narration. Such usage is fine in a chatty, colloquial style, even though a bit iffy by modern grammatical standards. You will not, of course, use it in your high-powered, dead serious prose.

scan   The case of *scan* is a bit unusual. In the 20th century it has developed a new sense which—on the face of it—seems directly contradictory to one of its older senses, but almost no one seems to mind. The older sense is "to examine thoroughly and carefully." It was first recorded in about 1800, and continues in use today:

> Conscious of handwritings now, she scanned Eden's carefully —Herman Wouk, *Marjorie Morningstar,* 1955

The newer, and now more common, sense of *scan* is "to look over or glance through quickly," which was first recorded in the 1920s:

> ... he approached the letter boxes and quickly scanned the nameplates —Bernard Malamud, *Atlantic,* March 1973

> I scanned the story rapidly and felt a little better — Russell Baker, *Growing Up,* 1982

The contradiction in these uses of *scan* is not as extreme as it may appear. The fundamental, underlying sense in both cases is that the eyes are moving from point to point. They may be moving slowly and searchingly, carefully taking in every detail ("The lookout scanned the horizon"), or they may be moving quickly, looking only for points of particular interest ("He scanned the morning paper before breakfast"), but the idea of movement is always primary.

Criticism of *scan* in its "look over quickly" sense has been limited to British commentators, such as Partridge 1942 and Phythian 1979. British dictionaries, on the other hand, now treat this sense as standard. American commentators, including Evans 1957 and Bernstein 1971, note its apparent inconsistency with the older sense, but regard it as established and acceptable nevertheless. Heritage 1969 suggests that care should be taken to assure that the context makes clear which sense is intended. This is usually accomplished by the use of adverbs, such as *carefully, quickly,* and *rapidly* in the passages quoted above.

scarcely   1. *Scarce, scarcely.* Several commentators have disparaged as an affectation the use of the old flat adverb *scarce* in modern contexts where *scarcely* would also do. The flat adverb was once common:

> ... the gentlemen of the next age will scarce have learning enough to claim the benefit of the clergy — Thomas Shadwell, *The Virtuoso,* 1676

> ... allow his surgeon scarce time sufficient to dress his wound —Laurence Sterne, *Tristram Shandy,* 1759

But it is now relatively rare. The extent to which it is an affectation in a particular context can only be judged subjectively. These examples do not seem to be affected:

> Store money was predicated on handling the products of the community, something scarce any store does nowadays —John Gould, *Christian Science Monitor*, 19 Nov. 1976

> . . . I could scarce see the horses' tails —J. K. Milne, *Scottish Field*, April 1974

See FLAT ADVERBS.

2. *Scarcely* is lumped with *hardly* (which see) in quite a few usage books as a negative, and its use with a preceding negative is disparaged as a double negative. There are two points to be made concerning this issue. First, *scarcely* is not a negative. Obviously "I scarcely studied" and "I didn't study" do not mean the same thing; the second is a negative, the first only somewhat like a negative. Second, the criticized construction seems to be rare in present-day English. Here is a late 19th-century example:

> . . . it wa' n't scarcely fair to keep it all to myself — H. N. Westcott, "The Horse Trader," 1898, in *The Mirth of a Nation*, ed. Walter Blair & Raven I. McDavid, Jr., 1983

Our files do not hold recent examples of this sort of construction, even from reported or fictional speech, and we suspect that it is not nearly as common as similar constructions with *hardly,* for which we have abundant evidence.

On the other hand, *scarcely* is commonly followed by some sort of negative construction:

> . . . was scarcely unaware that a last great tribute to the world-famous composer could not fail to bring . . . a large number of visitors —Francis Steegmuller, *New Yorker*, 1 May 1971

> . . . there was scarcely an old family in New England which . . . did not profit from the slave trade —Chester Bowles, *N.Y. Times Mag.*, 7 Feb. 1954

> There is scarcely a peroration or passage . . . which does not contain a gibe —Richard M. Weaver, *The Ethics of Rhetoric*, 1953

No one objects to these standard constructions.

scarcely . . . than   The sequence *scarcely . . . when* is considered impeccable by all commentators:

> Scarcely had Ida May recovered . . . when she heard a loud, bumptious knocking at her door —Katherine Anne Porter, *Ladies' Home Jour.*, August 1971

> David had scarcely rung the bell when the door flew open —Agnes Sligh Turnbull, *The Gown of Glory*, 1951

This sequence means about the same as *no sooner . . . than.* The combining of *no sooner . . . than* with *scarcely . . . when* produces the syntactic blend *scarcely . . . than,* which has been denounced as an error since at least the 1880s (see SYNTACTIC BLEND). Hodgson 1889 has several examples, including these:

> Scarcely had she gone, than Clodius and several of his gay companions broke in upon him —Edward Bulwer-Lytton, *The Last Days of Pompeii*, 1834

> But, as it happened, scarcely had Phoebe's eyes rested again on the judge's countenance than all its

ugly sternness vanished —Nathaniel Hawthorne, *The House of the Seven Gables,* 1851

If the examples in Hodgson are a reliable guide, *scarcely . . . than* was quite common in the 19th century. (It had been noticed as early as Priestley 1798, in which an example from Smollett is given.) The 20th century appears to be another story. Fowler 1926 exhibits one example, and Bryant 1962 has another, taken from a 1940 *Reader's Digest.* Our files contain nothing further. It may be that a century of disapproval (the subject can be found in Longman 1988 and Trimmer & McCrimmon 1988) has had a discouraging effect, or it may be that the construction has simply fallen into disuse quite on its own. Whatever the reason, on the basis of our evidence it is hard to say that the sequence has ever really established itself but equally hard to say that it poses a significant problem for writers now.

See HARDLY . . . THAN for a similar syntactic blend.

scared   1. When used with a preposition, *scared* is most often followed by *of:*

> I am scared of rats —Graham Greene, *Another Mexico,* 1939

> He tells us as much about the Presidency as he does about the C.I.A., and he leaves me scared stiff of both —John le Carré, *N.Y. Times Book Rev.,* 14 Oct. 1979

> ". . . I think he was scared of what you'd say to him, that's why he took off." —John Updike, *New Yorker,* 28 Dec. 1981

It is also used quite commonly with *about, at,* and *by:*

> . . . a weak government allows bigger wage increases than it ought to; then it gets scared about them — *The Economist,* in *Atlas,* December 1969

> Many Democrats were scared stiff at the prospect of being out of step with the mood of the country — Tip O'Neill with William Novak, *Man of the House,* 1987

> . . . obviously scared by the prestige and the mass base the Communists built up during the war — Alfred Kazin, *Partisan Rev.,* May 1948

Scared is also followed by *to* and the infinitive:

> I ain't laughed so much since the time John Potter got on the bear's back without no knife, and rode him round like a hoss, and was scared to get off! — William C. Hall, "How Sally Hooter Got Snakebit," 1850, in *The Mirth of a Nation,* ed. Walter Blair & Raven I. McDavid, Jr., 1983

> What they said to him was that he was a country boy in the city, scared to go out on the street —Peter Taylor, *The Old Forest and Other Stories,* 1985

2. The combination *scared of* has been disparaged by a handful of commentators (Vizetelly 1906, Krapp 1927, Weseen 1928, Partridge 1942, and Freeman 1983), all of whom have recommended *afraid* in place of *scared.* The earlier examples and these that follow show that it is standard. It is more common in speech—real and fictional—and in casual and informal prose than it is in highly serious writing. It may have originated as an

Americanism (its exact origin is uncertain), but it is now used in both American and British English.

> ... I'd be as scared of snakes if we did it every night for a year —Ernest Hemingway, *Green Hills of Africa*, 1935

> ... the experienced Georgia Sothern, who doesn't look at all scared of anything —George Jean Nathan, *The Entertainment of a Nation*, 1942

> Americans seem less scared ... of some European countries than others —*The Economist*, 26 Apr. 1986

scarify *Scarify* is really two words, the older of which, first attested in 1541, has the basic meaning "to make scratches or cuts in." It has several literal applications:

> Some seeds ... may need special treatment, such as scarifying ... to make them more penetrable to water —C. H. Wadleigh, in *The Yearbook of Agriculture 1957: Soil*

> ... burning over or scarifying the ground, then planting seedlings —John J. Putnam, *National Geographic*, April 1974

> Men and women have been beautifying, scarifying and mutilating their bodies ... since the dawn of time —Matilda Traherne, *Times Literary Supp.*, 7 Mar. 1980

And it is sometimes used figuratively:

> ... this is the Nixon ... that Garry Wills (in his fascinating book) scarifies as a human being —William F. Buckley, Jr., *National Rev.*, 26 Jan. 1971

The newer *scarify*, with a meaning somewhere between "scare" and "terrify," was first recorded almost 200 years ago:

> ... I have little doubt but the Weomen and Children would be scarified out of part of their senses —A. Thomas, *Newfoundland Jour.*, 1794 (OED Supplement)

But the next evidence of its use dates from the end of the 19th century, and it is only in the past 50 years or so that this new *scarify* has begun to appear commonly in print. It is an inconspicuous word in some ways, because it occurs most often in the form of the present participle, *scarifying*, used as an adjective in contexts which sometimes fail to make its meaning clear. Our files contain enough clear-cut examples, however, to show that the newer *scarify* is now in widespread, standard use. Here are some of those examples:

> ... vivid snapshots of the Paris barricades ... and a few scarifying pictures of both sides' firing squads —*Times Literary Supp.*, 30 Sept. 1965

> ... with two bullet holes in his car and a scarifying tale to go with them —Peter Goldman, *Newsweek*, 15 July 1968

> ... the disquieting life style of rock groups and audiences—the hair, the costumes, the volume, scarifying hints of sexual liberation —Benjamin DeMott, *N.Y. Times Mag.*, 25 Aug. 1968

> ... dire, scarifying illustrations of what can happen to kids who have the habit —Arthur Knight, *Saturday Rev.*, 2 Oct. 1971

> It is scarifying in the opposite way from a nightmare —Paul Theroux, *N.Y. Times Book Rev.*, 16 Nov. 1975

> Read as a cautionary tale, it's pretty scarifying — Katha Pollitt, *N.Y. Times Book Rev.*, 21 May 1978

Most current usage commentators have said nothing about the new *scarify*, probably because they have not noticed it yet. Exceptions are Reader's Digest 1983 and the Oxford American Dictionary, both of which flatly reject it, saying in effect that there is no *scare* in *scarify*. Whether they like it or not, however, the *scare* is there, and it is probably there to stay. Several contemporary dictionaries now enter the new *scarify*, treating it as a standard homograph of the older word.

scenario *Scenario* first attracted attention as a vogue word in the late 1960s, not long after it had crept out of theater and visual arts parlance into use by politicians and government officials and by the journalists who report what politicians and governmental officials say and do. We first encountered it in 1967:

> His scenario for a settlement envisages the eventual reunification of Vietnam —Selig S. Harrison, *New Republic*, 25 Nov. 1967

> The oil industry, then, acts according to the classic Leninist scenario —Michael Harrington, *American Power in the Twentieth Century*, 1967

In these, the scenario is a sequence of events imagined, postulated, or projected. This is the primary new use of the word, and it is flourishing to the extent that Reader's Digest 1983 terms it "one of the unmistakable signature words of our period."

The early critics of *scenario* were journalists, but in due time the writers of usage books joined their ranks: Newman 1974, Howard 1977, Ebbitt & Ebbitt 1982, and Janis 1984 all comment unfavorably. Reader's Digest 1983 and Harper 1975, 1985 explain rather than condemn. Both of them notice a use that cropped up in the Watergate hearings, in which real people had to follow a sort of scripted sequence of events, like the actors in a movie. This use seems to be fairly uncommon, but it apparently had occurred before Watergate:

> The whole scenario is a recurrence of the one played out in 1960 when McNamara had to behave as if there were a "missile gap" to justify the campaign myth —Arthur Blaustein, *Harper's*, March 1969

If the verb *play out* is a clue to this use, we may also have it in the following example, although the context is not very clear:

> Ollie North put him in touch with us. He has 3 or 4 scenarios he would like to play out —William J. Casey, in *The Tower Commission Report*, 1987

The popularity of *scenario* has brought about a further spread (some might call it metastasis) of meaning. In these two examples from British and Australian English, it is close in meaning to *setting*:

> Nevertheless, Oxford is not an obvious scenario for dramatic confrontation —*Isis*, 19 Oct. 1974

> Stylish architect-designed concrete buildings dot the outback scenario —Gerald Frape, *Nation Rev.* (Melbourne), 17 Apr. 1975

In the next two examples, its meaning tends toward *scene:*

> When leadoff hitter Steve Sax singled in the first for Los Angeles, Carlton quickly picked him off, a scenario that would be repeated in the final game — Ron Fimrite, *Sports Illustrated,* 17 Oct. 1983

> John McHale, president of the Montreal Expos, said cocaine was the reason his team did not win its division championship in 1982. . . .
> "I don't think there's any doubt in '82 that whole scenario cost us a chance to win," McHale said — Murray Chass, *N.Y. Times,* 20 Aug. 1985

The most vigorous figurative sense, however, continues to be the original one:

> It is called Seven Tomorrows, and it offers seven possible scenarios for the 1980s and 1990s —James Atlas, *Atlantic,* October 1984

> Our whole budget plan, I told them, depended on the accuracy of "Rosy Scenario," the five-year economic forecast we had fashioned in February —David A. Stockman, *Newsweek,* 28 Apr. 1986

scene   The most recent extended senses of *scene* have been the object of some disparagement from usage commentators. Our files show that the vogue for these senses in the middle 1970s has fallen off considerably in the 1980s, but they are still found from time to time:

> . . . the local police are powerless to control the drug scene that flourishes in this part of the village —Kim Waller, *Town & Country,* September 1983

> "It's a bad scene all the way around," said Chauncy J. Medberry, former chairman of BankAmerica Corp. —Patrick Boyle, *Los Angeles Times,* 23 Sept. 1984

> But come here not for the food but the crowd, which is the ne plus ultra of the downtown scene —*Elle,* May 1986

As the vogue for these senses passes and they become a settled part of the vocabulary, they are likely to draw less critical attention. They are certainly standard in general writing.

sceptic   See SKEPTIC, SCEPTIC.

scotch   When Shakespeare wrote in *Macbeth,* "We have scotch'd the snake, not kill'd it," he was using *scotch* to mean "to disable by wounding," a sense of the verb that is now archaic. The current meaning of *scotch* is "to put an end to."

> But if the king's suspicions of Roger of Salisbury were justified, he did well to scotch the danger while he was still strong —Frank Barlow, *The Feudal Kingdom of England 1042–1216,* 3d ed., 1972

> In the process they scotch many a fable —Timothy Ferris, *N.Y. Times Book Rev.,* 31 July 1983

> The plan was scotched in the White House —*Business Week,* 5 Aug. 1985

> 'Hopefully' we can scotch this vulgarism —Stanley Kunitz, in Harper 1975

Fowler 1926 made the modern use of *scotch* an issue when he attributed it to the carelessness of journalists,

and a few recent commentators have shown the influence of Fowler by continuing to insist that the disused sense is the only correct one. Needless to say, the cause is lost. The current sense of *scotch* is unquestionably standard.

Scotch, Scottish, Scots   Chambers 1985, which, having been published in Scotland, would seem to be a reasonable source for accurate and up-to-date information on this subject, says that *Scottish* is the normal adjective:

> . . . people whose ancestry was Scottish —William Faulkner, 7 May 1957, in *Faulkner in the University,* 1959

> The revival of Scottish literature —John Butt, *English Literature in the Mid-Eighteenth Century,* edited & completed by Geoffrey Carnall, 1979

> In most Scottish schools —K. M. Elisabeth Murray, *Caught in the Web of Words,* 1977

Scotch is used chiefly in familiar compounds for well-known things like Scotch broth, Scotch whisky, Scotch salmon, the Scotch pine and the Scotch terrier. *Scots,* too, is restricted in application, referring mostly to law or language.

> But as a child he started writing down the Scots words and phrases —Howard 1984

These are essentially the usages preferred by the Scots, and these preferences have evolved over about the last century. Earlier usage is different, as the admirably detailed historical sketch in the OED shows. *Scotch,* which is rather disliked in Scotland except in such uses as those just mentioned, dates only from the end of the 16th century, but was the predominant adjective in the 18th and 19th centuries; it was used by such writers as Boswell, James Beattie, Robert Burns, and Sir Walter Scott. It was likewise used by more recent Scots, including James A. H. Murray, the OED editor; presumably some Scots still use it.

Non-Scottish use has never quite conformed to Scottish preferences. The English, many of whom have not been averse to needling the Scots, have kept on using *Scotch,* although Reader's Digest 1983 assures us that the politer ones use *Scottish.* In North America *Scotch* is the prevailing adjective, at least partly because the earlier immigrants to this continent from Scotland left that country when *Scotch* was still prevalent there.

> . . . Scotch rhetoricians —McKnight 1928

> . . . may have so infuriated the Scotch that they all reverted to oatmeal —Alexander Woollcott, letter, 22 Nov. 1935

> He said he was part Scotch, English and Gypsy — Groucho Marx, letter, 5 Sept. 1940

> My first two books were published in England by the Scotch and English —Robert Frost, letter, 26 July 1942

> . . . a difference of opinion as to who was superior. The Scotch believed, I have always thought rightly, that they were —John Kenneth Galbraith, *The Scotch,* 1964

If you live in the United Kingdom, you are aware of Scottish preferences. If you live in North America, you are likely to use *Scotch* automatically, especially when

Scottish susceptibilities are not a consideration. There is no harm, of course, in following the Scottish preferences—*Scottish* is, after all, the old word, and both *Scotch* and *Scots* are derived from it. There is another rule of thumb that works fairly well for the American who does not want to offend but does not know or want to know the finer points of Scottish practice: use *Scottish* for people and *Scotch* for things.

sculp, sculpt, sculpture   About half a century ago, dictionaries such as the OED and Webster's Second 1934 were calling the verbs *sculp* and *sculpt* "jocular" and "humorous." The evidence on which those labels were based must have been primarily oral, as written evidence from that period is scanty. It was not until the 1940s and 1950s that we began to find *sculp* and, in particular, *sculpt* in widespread written use, very little of which was humorous:

> . . . he has sculped more famous heads —*Time,* 27 Oct. 1941

> . . . Mussolini's sculpted horses —Irwin Shaw, *Yale Rev.,* Summer 1944

> . . . Brancusi once sculpted a wooden column of similar rhythm —Frederick J. Kiesler, *Partisan Rev.,* Winter 1946

> Moore, who sculpts and draws mostly figures —*Newsweek,* 11 Mar. 1946

> . . . sculpted works which themselves implied the conquest of space —*Horizon,* December 1946

> . . . was one of the fifty artists chosen . . . to paint or sculp her portrait —Robert Gibbings, *Trumpets from Montparnasse,* 1955

Citations such as these made it clear that the old labels were no longer appropriate, and they have since been dropped. *Sculp* and *sculpt* are now established as standard synonyms of *sculpture.* A few usage commentators, particularly Bernstein 1962, 1965, have regarded them with lingering disapproval, but most either ignore them or find them acceptable.

search   When used with a preposition, the noun *search* is usually followed by *for,* except in the phrase *in search of:*

> . . . the requisite search for knowledge —Robert A. Nisbet, *Psychology Today,* March 1971

> . . . the growers worked hard in search of new markets —A. V. Krebs, Jr., *Commonweal,* 9 Oct. 1970

Shaw 1970 states that *in search for* is also common, but that *in search of* is preferred. Our evidence indicates that *in search for* is rare in edited prose. We have only two examples of it, both from a single year:

> . . . while in search for a title for his first book of poems —*Time,* 15 Feb. 1954

> . . . not the businessman in search for orders or for the secrets of know-how —D. W. Brogan, *Saturday Rev.,* 17 Apr. 1954

seasonable, seasonal   Whereas *seasonable* means "suitable to the season" (seasonable temperatures, seasonable clothes), *seasonal* means "of or relating to a season; occurring in a particular season" (seasonal migration, seasonal employment). So say the usage writers,

and, according to our evidence, they speak the truth on this matter. We do have some evidence of *seasonable* being used where *seasonal* would be expected, but such usage is extremely rare. The OED Supplement has a few citations for this use (which it labels erroneous), and our own files provide two more:

> "Work in the General Motors plants here is seasonable at best," he went on —*N.Y. Times,* 12 Apr. 1937

> . . . the business is less seasonable than in most other countries —*An Exhibition of Swiss Books,* February, March, April 1953

This use of *seasonable* is nonstandard.

Seasonal is sometimes used to mean "seasonable" as well, but this use is also nonstandard. Although it occurs fairly commonly in television and radio weather reports, we have yet to encounter it in writing.

Also to be considered, however, are the words *unseasonable* and *unseasonal,* which, as it happens, are synonyms. *Unseasonable* is the more common word by far, and it means just what you would expect it to, "not seasonable." *Unseasonal,* however, seems never to have meant "not seasonal." All of our evidence shows *unseasonal* being used to mean "not seasonable," as in the following citations:

> . . . late spring frosts and unseasonal rains —*Time,* 10 Dec. 1945

> . . . adjourned happily into the unseasonal Long Island sunshine —*Time,* 17 Jan. 1949

> . . . in which to store potatoes, cotton, tobacco and the few unseasonal clothes —Max Steele, *Discovery,* March 1954

Make no mistake, however—*unseasonal* is a very rare word. Usage writers have not even noticed it. If they had, you can be sure they would have called it an error.

secondly   Used with some frequency in a series after *first* or *in the first place*—by Charles Lamb and Samuel Johnson, to name just two. See FIRSTLY.

secure   *Secure* in the sense "to obtain by effort; gain secure control or possession of" is recognized as legitimate by usage commentators (it has been around since the 18th century), but it makes some of them uneasy. Their concern is that it should not be used when a simple *get* or *obtain* would be more appropriate. Bernstein 1965 offers the following as an example of misuse: "He went to the store to secure a package of cigarettes." It is easy to see how a sentence like that might raise a few eyebrows, but we have no real evidence that *secure* is actually used when *get* or *buy* so obviously called for. In edited prose, at least, *secure* seems almost always to be used in ways that even usage commentators would find unobjectionable, with implications of effort or of lasting possession:

> He secured for the university library many outstanding private book collections —*Current Biography,* April 1966

> . . . the pressure to secure a job immediately after high school —Donald McDonald, *Center Mag.,* July/August 1970

> . . . who failed to secure the party's nomination for reëlection —William Edgett Smith, *New Yorker,* 30 Oct. 1971

He secured the use of an army parade grounds —E. L. Doctorow, *Ragtime,* 1975

see, seed, seen   The standard past tense of *see* is *saw.* American dialectologists say that the past forms *see* and *seed* are nonstandard and regionally restricted. Both of them were commonly used by the American dialect humorists of the 19th century, and *seed* was additionally listed as a Cockneyism as far back as 1807.

Seen as the past tense seems to be widespread but nonstandard. There are at least two explanations for its low status. Margaret Shaklee in Shopen & Williams 1980 says that it was a southern regionalism brought into the north and midwest around the end of the 19th century by southerners who migrated north looking for work. This explanation is given some support as to chronology by our earliest evidence for the correction of *seen,* in Vizetelly 1906. Mencken 1963 (abridged), on the other hand, associates *seen* with the immigration of the Irish to the United States in the 1840s. His explanation is supported by the English Dialect Dictionary, which calls past tense *seen* chiefly Irish. In either case we see that a regional speech characteristic has turned into a social rather than a regional marker.

Past *seen,* then, is a speech characteristic associated with the less educated and is used in writing chiefly to mark characters as being such. An example:

> We had a visitor the other day, an old man, who said he wouldn't go to Europe if they gave it to him. Said a feller went over there and set down on some steps he seen in front of a church . . . —Flannery O'Connor, letter, 1953

seeing, seeing as, seeing as how, seeing that
Seeing has long been used as a conjunction meaning "inasmuch as; in view of the fact that":

> They all wanted to know why—seeing I had the same genes as Tracy—I couldn't swim as fast as she could —Amy Caulkins, quoted in *Sports Illustrated,* 20 Apr. 1981

This conjunction has been in use since the 16th century, but it does not now appear very frequently in writing. It originally appeared as part of a compound in *seeing that,* which is still used, and it also appears in the compound forms *seeing as* and *seeing as how.*

Seeing as and *seeing as how* are chiefly spoken forms for which we have little written evidence. Both are attested in American and British English (*seeing as how* was noticed in debate in the House of Commons in 1961).

> "Well, seeing as I like your style," he said, "I think we might just be able to fit you in, mightn't we, Pauline?" —Alan Coren, *Punch,* 7 Apr. 1976

> . . . haven't paid her any profuse attention, seein' as the German girls never know what to make of it when a person takes any notice of them —Henry Adams, letter, 8 Nov. 1859

> Seeing as how the Governor was a co-sponsor of the original bill . . . , I've got a sneaking hunch he just might veto this —Jim Stoicheff, *Priest River* (Idaho) *Times,* 26 Jan. 1973

Seeing that is the best attested of all four forms in writing:

> It seems to me most strange that men should fear, Seeing that death, a necessary end

> Will come when it will come
> —Shakespeare, *Julius Caesar,* 1600

> . . . inappropriate, seeing that Campanella is only about thirty yards above sea-level —Norman Douglas, *Siren Land,* 1911

> Seeing that his brother . . . had resigned the Lord Lieutenancy without setting foot in Ireland, Frederick had really done well for himself —*Irish Digest,* May 1952

Seeing as how is aspersed in a few handbooks as nonstandard, but it seems rather to be simply a spoken form; we have no evidence that links it with the usage of the uneducated. It is possible that in American use it is geographically restricted, since our slender evidence suggests it may be a Northern form. The Dictionary of American Regional English will have the last word on that question.

seek   The verb *seek* is frequently used with *after* or *for.* *After* tends to occur most often with the past participle *sought* in an idiomatic passive, but active use also occurs. *For* is common with all tenses and voices.

> . . . he was much sought after on account of his wide reading —*Dictionary of American Biography,* 1929

> . . . Namath was the one collegiate player most sought after by professional teams —*Current Biography,* December 1966

> ". . . If the *effect* of his behaviour does not justify him with you, we had better not seek after the cause." —Jane Austen, *Northanger Abbey,* 1818

> These differences are by no means so evident to (or so sought for by) a majority of peoples of non-European origin —Weston La Barre, *The Human Animal,* 1954

> Now he learns to talk and thereby joins the Republic of Learning, a republic composed of men who seek for meaning —Stringfellow Barr, *Center Mag.,* March 1968

Seek is also commonly followed by *to* and an infinitive:

> We can seek to perpetuate the myths or to focus on the real issues —Leslie H. Gelb & Morton H. Halperin, *Harper's,* November 1971

seem   See CAN'T SEEM.

see where   *See where* is disparaged in many usage books, most of which identify it as a speech form. *Where* is also used to introduce clauses that are the objects of other verbs than *see.* See WHERE 2.

seldom ever, seldom if ever, seldom or ever, seldom or never   All of these idioms are intensive forms of *seldom* that have attracted a bit of attention from usage writers over the years (from the 1860s at least). The commentators are typically concerned with distinguishing between them or, alternatively, with reducing the field by rejecting one or two of them. Thus we find *seldom ever* criticized as redundant by one commentator, as self-contradictory by another (a contrary pair of opinions those are), and as absurd by a third. *Seldom or ever* is called meaningless or erroneous. The movement to oust *seldom or never,* however, died a-borning in the 19th century; Alford 1866 reports it but defends the phrase, and we hear no more of the complaint.

Let us see how these phrases are actually used. *Seldom ever,* according to the OED, has been around since about 1000; like it or not, it is a well-aged idiom. Since we have in our files more complaints about it than examples of its use in print, we conclude that it is more frequently a feature of speech than of writing. Here is one of our few written examples:

> ... consideration of curriculum is frequently postponed to some future date which seldom ever arrives —Dayton Benjamin, *American School Board Jour.,* June 1968

Seldom or ever is not attested until the 18th century. It is perhaps a blend of *seldom if ever* and *seldom or never.* This undated example is probably older than the first citation in the OED:

> We seldom or ever see those forsaken who trust in God —Francis Atterbury (in Raub 1897)

If we can trust the considerable list of examples compiled by Hodgson 1889, *seldom or ever* must have been quite common during the 19th century.

> Those who walk in their sleep have seldom or ever the most distant recollection that they have been dreaming —Sydney Smith, *Moral Philosophy,* 1850 (in Hodgson 1889)

> Seldom or ever could I detect any approach to a labial —Alexander Ellis, *Transactions of the Philological Society* (in Jespersen 1917)

We have no recent 20th-century examples, but we cannot say whether this version has dropped out of use entirely or has simply receded into speech.

Seldom or never is dated back to 1398. Francis Bacon used it, and it is still common in the 20th century:

> *Younger Brothers* are commonly Fortunate, but seldome or never, where the *Elder* are disinherited —Francis Bacon, *Essays,* 1625

> My interest is always in the subjective event, seldom or never in the objective event —H. L. Mencken, letter, 23 Apr. 1911

> ... elementary school, where home assignments are seldom or never given —Betty M. Shaw, *NEA Jour.,* February 1965

Seldom if ever presents us with a bit of a problem from the standpoint of using it with *seldom or never* to explain *seldom or ever* as a blended form. The OED does not happen to show any examples of it, so the earliest evidence of its use we have is Alford's comments of 1866. It is well attested in 20th-century use:

> ... words that seldom if ever appeared in the writings of those sophisticated enough to strive for what they regarded as standard form —Mathews 1931

> But the women at work in the shipyards and other war plants were seldom if ever called *ladies* —H. L. Mencken, *The American Language, Supplement I,* 1945

Our knowledge of these phrases is far from complete, but one thing that we can say with certainty now is that *seldom if ever* and *seldom or never* are the only ones commonly used in writing in the 20th century, and they are subject to no rational criticism.

self   Several commentators have disparaged *self* used like *myself* for *I* or *me.* Such use dates back to the 18th century, but we have little evidence of its occurrence in modern edited prose. Here is one example:

> Self and coworkers ... have shown that hornworms ... —B. C. Akehurst, *Tobacco,* 1968

This use of *self* is not an error, but it will not win you any awards as a prose stylist.

A good deal more attention has been paid to *myself* and other reflexive pronouns used in this way. See MYSELF.

self-confessed   *Self-confessed* has been regarded by a few critics as a tautological substitute for *confessed.* Note, however, that in typical usage the meaning of *self-confessed* is closer to *admitted* or *avowed* than it is to *confessed* and *confessed* will not always substitute for it comfortably:

> ... a man old enough to be my father, and a self-confessed master of English prose —Ernest Hemingway, "African Journal," 1956

> That was the fate of ... Eugene McCarthy, a self-confessed poet —E. L. Doctorow, *N.Y. Times,* 11 Apr. 1976

> A lifelong bachelor with a self-confessed taste for medals —Thomas Powers, *N.Y. Times Book Rev.,* 21 May 1978

> ... an engaging portrait of a self-confessed maverick —Mel Watkins, *N.Y. Times Book Rev.,* 7 Oct. 1979

> Warburg, a self-confessed "eccentric" and Anglophile —advt. flyer, Oxford University Press, June 1981

self-defeating   See COUNTERPRODUCTIVE, SELF-DEFEATING.

self-deprecating, self-deprecatory   These adjectives are apparently of quite recent formation. They are occasionally dragged into the dispute about *deprecate* and *depreciate,* to the obfuscation of that issue. The earliest citation we know of for *self-deprecatory* is included—without a date—in Fowler 1907, in which it is treated as a misuse of *deprecate:*

> In the present self-deprecatory mood in which the English people find themselves —*Spectator*

The Fowlers prescribed *self-depreciatory,* but *self-depreciatory* is a word that no one seems ever to have actually used.

About the time that *self-deprecatory* was first recorded, *deprecate* was beginning to be used in a new way (our earliest example is from 1898). This was a sense reflecting personal modesty: "to play down, undervalue, or discount one's own accomplishments." Since this use of the verb was always directed at the subject, the appropriate adjective related to it would be *self-deprecatory.*

Despite the Fowlers' disapproval, *self-deprecatory* has continued in reputable use, and it has recently been joined by the synonymous *self-deprecating,* which we first recorded in 1952. Here is an example or two of each:

> Some kind of embarrassment about her own intentions, though, has made her trim her novel with that

self-deprecating humour lady columnists in Sunday newspapers use to protect themselves —*Times Literary Supp.,* 2 Oct. 1969

... a short, unpretentious and self-deprecating account of the work he did —Doris Grumbach, *N.Y. Times Book Rev.,* 3 Feb. 1980

... cultivate a flat, unrhetorical style to convey a self-deprecatory impression —*Times Literary Supp.,* 14 Nov. 1968

... the indirect demonstration (under a veil of self-deprecatory remarks) of how right he was and how misguided were most others —Walter Mills, *Center Mag.,* March 1968

Of the two, *self-deprecating* appears to be the more frequently used.

See also DEPRECATE, DEPRECIATE; DEPRECATING, DEPRECATORY, DEPRECIATORY; SELF-DEPRECIATION, SELF-DEPRECATION.

self-depreciation, self-deprecation *Self-depreciation* is attested in our files as early as 1917. It appears at first to have indicated a lack of self-esteem:

... the self-depreciation that made him powerless before her mother's reproaches —*Hearst's Mag.,* March 1917

This sense has not been lost:

... an increase in group solidarity, a lessening of self-depreciation, a feeling of potential strength —Gerda Lerner, *Columbia Forum,* Fall 1970

The word is also used for a conscious downplaying or undervaluing of oneself, usually for the purpose of conveying a real or assumed modesty:

... owes her nationwide popularity largely to her mastery of satirical self-depreciation —*Current Biography,* July 1967

In this use, it is a noun clearly parallel to the adjectives *self-deprecating* and *self-deprecatory* (see SELF-DEPRECATING, SELF-DEPRECATORY).

In recent years—only since 1971 in our files—*self-deprecation* has sprung up as a synonymous rival to *self-depreciation.* It is used in the same ways:

One pollyannish anecdote after another illustrates each phase—anecdotes that will plunge any experienced mother into feelings of inadequacy and self-deprecation —Margaret O'Brien Steinfels, *N.Y. Times Book Rev.,* 7 Nov. 1976

... they use self-deprecation as a way of making themselves attractive, and it is as aggressive as ordinary boasting —David Denby, *Atlantic,* April 1971

He proved everything by his self-deprecation, his sighs, his lachrymose pauses —E. L. Doctorow, *Loon Lake,* 1979

... what's missing under Allen's highly salable self-deprecation, is any true sense of dissatisfaction — Stanley Kauffmann, *Before My Eyes,* 1980

Self-deprecation makes a better match with the adjectives *self-deprecating* and *self-deprecatory* than does the older *self-depreciation,* and it is not unlikely that it is the influence of the adjectives that has promoted the use of the newer word. While our evidence may not be conclu-sive, it is interesting to note that our citations for *self-depreciation* began to grow rarer just about the time that those for *self-deprecation* first appeared. It seems likely that the newer word will become the more common.

self-destruct   See DESTRUCT, SELF-DESTRUCT.

senior   See IMPLICIT COMPARATIVE.

senior citizen   The earliest evidence for *senior citizen* indicates that it originated as a politician's euphemism:

Mr. Downey had an inspiration to do something on behalf of what he calls, for campaign purposes, "our senior citizens" —*Time,* 24 Oct. 1938 (OED Supplement)

We do not know the outcome of Mr. Downey's campaign, but we do know that *senior citizen* eventually gained an established place in the vocabulary of English. We have no further evidence of its use until 1954, but by 1960 it had become a common term, and it remains common today.

Senior citizen has succeeded because people have felt a need for a term that refers to the elderly without any derogatory connotations. Those who dislike it, including many usage commentators, regard it as a well-meant but vapid euphemism at best. Like any euphemism that survives for many years, however, it has lost much of its euphemistic quality. Frequent and prolonged use has made *senior citizen* a familiar and unremarkable term for most people. It is especially common in the plural as a term for referring to elderly people in general or in a group:

... started construction last month on its first public housing development for senior citizens —*New Englander,* April 1962

... annual convention of the National League of Senior Citizens —*N.Y. Times,* 22 May 1962

... fulfilling the needs of many of our senior citizens by offering them a healthful, productive, and convivial life —Bill Davidson, *Saturday Evening Post,* 16 Jan. 1965

... running their own scheme to help senior citizens in their town —*Christian Science Monitor,* 22 Mar. 1965

... a group of senior citizens who had come ... for the morning show —*New Yorker,* 24 Dec. 1966

... about 25 percent of all the poverty is borne by our senior citizens —Leon H. Keyserling, *New Republic,* 18 Mar. 1967

Ninety senior citizens from Kansas City, Mo., will arrive in Boise tonight —*Idaho Daily Statesman,* 6 Aug. 1968

Its use in the singular to describe an individual is less common, but not rare:

... one more indignant senior citizen penning complaints about the universal decay of virtue —John Updike, *N.Y. Times Book Rev.,* 25 Nov. 1962

... maintains an active schedule as an insurance broker, unofficial historian and senior citizen —Stephen Dolley, *Westways,* September 1967

... Westmoreland, 70, a white-haired senior citizen —Linda Marx, *People,* 22 Oct. 1984

Critics who dislike *senior citizen* recommend that you use instead such words as *old, aged, elderly,* and *retired* to describe old, aged, elderly, and retired persons. Another possibility is the noun *senior,* used as a short form of *senior citizen:*

> Apartments for seniors that are within the modest budgets of people living on their social security payments —Eleanor Gurewitsch, *Christian Science Monitor,* 9 June 1977

> The seniors can count on the coffee hour to follow for genial, intelligent conversation —Carol Bly, *Letters from the Country,* 1981

> ... many striking examples of seniors who lead productive lives —*Booklist,* 1 June 1984

sensational *Sensational* was coined in the mid-19th century with the literal meaning "of or relating to sensation or the senses." The extended meanings it has since acquired essentially parallel those of the noun *sensation,* which has been used to mean "a state of excited interest or feeling" since at least 1779 and "a cause of excited interest or feeling" since at least 1864. That which is intended or which serves to create such interest or feeling soon came to be described as *sensational:*

> ... Stupendous sensational effect, never equalled on any stage —*The Times,* 11 Apr. 1864 (OED)

A further extension of meaning in the 20th century has given *sensational* the sense "exceedingly or unexpectedly excellent," without the implication of actually creating a sensation:

> ... he was sensational at the plate, with thirteen hits and a .406 average —*Current Biography,* May 1966

> The restaurants are all on a par, nothing too sensational in the way of cuisine —Walter Hackett, *Christian Science Monitor,* 1 Apr. 1980

These extended senses of *sensational* are often used in a somewhat hyperbolic way, and that has earned them the disapproval of several critics, particularly Evans 1957. No one disputes that they are standard English, however.

sensible In a range of senses having to do with awareness and sensitivity rather than good sense, *sensible* may take a prepositional phrase complement, usually beginning with *of:*

> "If my children are silly, I must hope to be always sensible of it." —Jane Austen, *Pride and Prejudice,* 1813

> "... For my part, though deeply sensible of its influence, I cannot seize it." —Nathaniel Hawthorne, *The Marble Faun,* 1860

> ... he had been to a certain extent sensible of having been noticed in a quiet manner by the father —Joseph Conrad, *Chance,* 1913

> ... Hooker, like Burke, is sensible of the force of circumstances —A. S. P. Woodhouse, *Philosophical Rev.,* October 1952

Sensible is used less often with *to:*

> ... quickly become sensible to slight changes of temperature —Samuel Eliot Morison, *Admiral of the Ocean Sea,* 1942

> Sensible to these favors, he resisted the temptation —Noel F. Busch, *My Unconsidered Judgment,* 1944

To judge from the evidence that has been collected for the Merriam-Webster files over the last thirty or forty years, *sensible* is now being used less often in these constructions than it formerly was.

sensitive When *sensitive* is complemented by a prepositional phrase, the preposition is often *to:*

> Madame Defarge being sensitive to cold, was wrapped in fur —Charles Dickens, *A Tale of Two Cities,* 1859

> Lawrence is as sensitive to falsity as the True Princess was to the pea —Eudora Welty, *Atlantic,* March 1949

> ... became sensitive to the rights and special needs of the handicapped —Ronald Reagan, *Abortion and the Conscience of the Nation,* 1984

The next most common preposition is *about,* followed by *of* and *on:*

> ... the Nationalist Government today is probably more sensitive about its face —Peggy Durdin, *N.Y. Times Mag.,* 23 Jan. 1955

> I'm sorry. I'm somewhat sensitive about it —Leonard Bernstein, *Atlantic,* April 1955

> ... be sensitive of the rights of the Opposition —Clement Atlee, Speech on the King's Address, 16 Aug. 1945, in *Voices of History 1945–46,* ed. Nathan Ausobel, 1946

> "... This affair is too damned serious to be sensitive on etiquette. ..." —Van Wyck Mason, *The Shanghai Bund Murders,* 1933

Very occasionally, *sensitive* has also been used with *as to, for, in,* or *over:*

> ... was sensitive as to its rights and jealous of its constitutional prerogatives —*Dictionary of American Biography,* 1928

> ... a little frightened, big-eyed and simple, sensitive for himself in a way that bordered on the humble —Francis Hackett, *Henry The Eighth,* 1929

> The Russians are notoriously sensitive in keeping all observers from their border areas —*New Republic,* 9 July 1951

> ... sensitive over the affliction of growing deafness —*Dictionary of American Biography,* 1929

sensual, sensuous *Sensuous* was coined by John Milton in 1641 in order to avoid "certain associations"—to use the OED's phrase—of the much older word *sensual. Sensuous* seems to have existed only in Milton's works until Coleridge unearthed it in the early 19th century. Once it had been set in circulation, it became used quite commonly, and since its meaning was not far removed from some meanings of *sensual,* it began after a time to attract attention in usage books, many of which now distinguish between the two words. The consensus of the commentators, from Vizetelly 1906 to the present, is that *sensuous* emphasizes aesthetic pleasure while *sensual* emphasizes gratification or indulgence of the physical appetites.

The distinction is true enough within one range of

meanings, and it is worth remembering. The difficulty is that both words have more than one sense, and they tend often to occur in contexts where the distinction between them is not as clear-cut as the commentators would like it to be. Here are a few examples showing typical uses of *sensual* and *sensuous,* in some of which the prescribed distinction is clear, but in others of which it is not clear at all:

> You or I will feel a poem sensuously: your Frenchman will receive sensuous pleasure from the fact that he has comprehended a poem intellectually —Archibald MacLeish, letter, March 1925

> You would not believe it Lucinda, but I was very sensual.
> I believe it.
> No, you're smiling. But I was, I really was. I lived in such an altered state that even the daylight sifting through a cloud would give me enormous shuddering response
> —E. L. Doctorow, *Loon Lake,* 1979

> Yet in the work of Ernest Hemingway our sharpest memories are of sensuous experiences—primarily visual, though also at times involving hearing and smell and taste and touch —Barnard 1979

> Having placed in my mouth sufficient bread for three minutes' chewing, I withdrew my powers of sensual perception and retired into the privacy of my mind —Flann O'Brien, *At Swim-Two-Birds,* 1939

> Both men said that all sensuous qualities are mere appearances that result from different arrangements of the atoms —Morris Kline, *Mathematics and the Search for Knowledge,* 1985

> . . . a fluffy zabaglione, that sensual blend of Marsala, egg yolks, and sugar —Geri Trotta, *Gourmet,* July 1982

> . . . the delicacy and sensuously creamy qualities of Italian sweets at their best —C. P. Reynolds, *Gourmet,* April 1982

> Refinishing furniture was a minor occupation but a major pleasure of Eliza's. She had a sensual feeling for wood, for its smooth unvarnished touch —Alice Adams, *Listening to Billie,* 1977

> As long as the beat people abandon themselves to all sensual satisfactions, on principle, you can't take them for anything but false mystics —Flannery O'Connor, letter, 21 June 1959

> It is her creed she is pronouncing, of feverish enjoyment, without distinction between sensuous delight and sensual pleasure —Mary McCarthy, *Occasional Prose,* 1985

If you feel doubt about which word to choose in a particular context, we recommend consulting a dictionary, particularly one which devotes itself to, or includes within its apparatus, discrimination of the meanings of closely related words.

sentence adjective   *Sentence adjective* is a term used in the OED Supplement to describe the use of *important* in constructions like this:

> More important, a majority of public school students come from a poverty subculture —Susan Jacoby, *Saturday Rev.,* 18 Nov. 1967

Quirk et al. 1985 indicates that sentence-modifying adjectives are quite a bit less common than adverbs in the same function. You can find the controversy over *(more) important* and *(more) importantly* at IMPORTANT 1.

See also SENTENCE ADVERB.

sentence adverb   The sentence adverb is an adverb or adverbial phrase that is connected with a whole sentence rather than with a single word or phrase in the sentence. Sentence adverbs are a common feature of present-day English, and they go by many names. You will find them called *dangling adverbs, floating adverbs, adverbial disjuncts,* and probably other things as well.

The chief virtue of the sentence adverb is its compactness: it permits the writer or speaker to express in a single word or short phrase what would otherwise take a much longer form. Consider this example:

> Luckily I never mentioned having asked —Henry Adams, letter, 23 Nov. 1859

That one *luckily* replaces some longer expression like "It's lucky for me that. . . ." Here is another one:

> Strictly, when *because of* is right, *due to* is wrong — Johnson 1982

Strictly could be replaced here by the popular *strictly speaking,* but that too is a variety of sentence adverb. If the adverb were not available, it would be necessary to write something like "From the standpoint of strict grammatical correctness. . . ." So you can see the appeal of the sentence adverb. Here are a couple more for you to try paraphrasing:

> Basically, you make an inference if you derive something unstated by using your ability to reason —Bailey 1984

> Phenomenologically, youth is a time of alternating estrangement and omnipotentiality —Kenneth Keniston, *American Scholar,* Autumn 1970

Some handbooks point out that conjunctive adverbs like *therefore, nevertheless,* and *however* can also be considered sentence adverbs because to the extent they are adverbial they modify clauses rather than any particular part of the clause.

One of the common uses of the sentence adverb is to express an attitude of the writer or speaker:

> Clearly we have found that violence is no answer — W. E. Brock, *AAUP Bulletin,* September 1969

> Strangely, people who write and think like that insist that they are champions of what they have named "humanistic" education —Mitchell 1979

> Hopefully, The Bluebird, when it is finished, will turn out to be a bluebird and not a turkey —Art Evans, *Edmonton Jour.,* 22 May 1975

> Curiously enough, I met Hartman for the first time last night —H. L. Mencken, letter, 24 Oct. 1924

> Luckily the strength of the piece did not depend upon him —Jane Austen, *Mansfield Park,* 1814

> Oddly, though, over the years *scan* also has developed an opposite meaning —Michael Gartner, *Advertising Age,* 17 Oct. 1985

> Amusingly, they had widely divergent attitudes toward corrections in their copy —Simon 1980

A great many of the adverbs used as attitudinal sentence adverbs are also used as adverbs of manner, as *frankly* is used here:

> He frankly admits his fondness for the wealth and fame —*Current Biography,* December 1965

This duality of function is one of the reasons advanced by commentators in objection to a few specific sentence adverbs (in particular, *hopefully,* which see). They also purport not to understand who is expressing the attitude, although in almost every instance it is perfectly plain that it is the writer or speaker.

Note that sentence-modifying adverbs do not necessarily stand first in a sentence:

> This is one of the words that turn up, predictably, in the sports pages —Harper 1985

> When Isaac Newton sat under a tree in the 17th century and was famously struck by a falling apple — Martin Hollis, *Invitation to Philosophy,* 1985

> Matters complicate, unsurprisingly —Stanley Kauffmann, *Before My Eyes,* 1980

separate, separately, separation   Note the spelling, especially the sequence *-par-*. The substitution *-per-* is well-attested:

> It is of singular use to *Princes,* if they take the Opinions of their *Counsell,* both Seperately, and Together —Francis Bacon, *Essays,* 1625

But Francis Bacon had the advantage of writing before the invention of spelling books. His spelling is no longer considered acceptable.

sequence of tenses   Although this is not a subject to stir strong feelings, a great deal has been written about it in usage books (Fowler 1926, 1965, Bernstein 1965, Bremner 1980, Copperud 1980, Cook 1985, and many college handbooks). One problem commonly discussed under this heading (there are others) concerns the tense of the verb in a subordinate clause pointing to present or future time. When the present or future tense is used without reference to the verb in the superordinate clause, we have what Roberts 1954 calls the "natural sequence of tenses," as in a sentence like "Novak said that she is going tomorrow." When the verb in the subordinate clause is made past to agree with the first verb, we have the "attracted sequence of tenses": "Novak said that she was going tomorrow." Roberts says that the attracted sequence is normal in what he calls "Choice" English. Most of the discussions in usage books relate to problems with the attracted sequence.

For instance, there is the problem of the "continuing or timeless fact"—as in "Crime doesn't pay." If we make this a subordinate clause with a main clause in the past tense, the commentators would have us follow natural sequence: "The Lone Ranger said that crime doesn't pay." Most writers probably do just that, but what of the earnest seeker after Choice English who makes it past? "The Lone Ranger said that crime didn't pay." We suspect that such usage in an ordinary context would pass unnoticed by the average reader: " . . . and then the Lone Ranger said that crime didn't pay, and he and Tonto rode off into the sunset."

This subject has been discussed in usage books since the 18th century. The evidence in Murray 1795 suggests that the early commentators were at great pains to correct such locutions as "The Lord hath given and the Lord hath taken away." We suggest you will be a lot happier if you simply do not worry about them.

See also WOULD HAVE.

service   Many commentators disparage the use of the verb *service* in contexts where *serve* is also possible. They favor restricting *service* to those senses which are uniquely its own, especially "to repair or provide maintenance for," as in "service a car." This verb is not an old one in any of its senses. Its first recorded use was by Robert Louis Stevenson:

> If I am to service ye the way that you propose, I'll lose my lifelihood —Robert Louis Stevenson, *Catriona,* 1893 (OED Supplement)

Stevenson used *service* in this one instance as a nonstandard synonym of *serve.* There is no further evidence of *service* as a verb until the 1920s, when the "repair or maintain" sense began to appear commonly in print:

> Here we serviced the ship, as we had been out two hours and forty-five minutes —*Aero Digest,* August 1924

H. L. Mencken, in *The American Language* (4th ed., 1936), says that this sense was first used around 1910, when "American garages began *servicing* cars." Almost certainly it was a new coinage, unrelated to Stevenson's *service.* Further written evidence of the "serve" sense did not appear until the 1940s:

> . . . any town serviced by Greyhound bus — *Esquire's Jazz Book,* ed. Paul E. Miller, 1944

> . . . the reduced-rate market now serviced by Sears Roebuck and Montgomery Ward —Victor Lebow, *Harper's,* July 1945

> Airports are so far from the cities they supposedly service —John Steinbeck, *Russian Journal,* 1948 (OED Supplement)

Critics such as Copperud 1964, Bernstein 1965, Gowers in Fowler 1965, Shaw 1975, Phythian 1979, Bryson 1984, and Janis 1984 would presumably have advised Steinbeck to use *serve* instead. Nevertheless, the disapproved sense of *service* continues to be fairly common:

> Some loan sharks service a neighborhood in the same fashion as a barber or shoe repairman —Donald R. Cressey, *Harper's,* February 1969

> . . . increased its ability to service customers —William F. May, *Annual Report, American Can Co.,* 1970

> . . . need not spend a good half of his time . . . servicing volunteers —Virginia H. Mathews, *Publishers Weekly,* 2 July 1973

> Many of those not in the energy business are also doing very nicely by servicing it —Tom Curtis, *Town & Country,* September 1979

> . . . they end up by servicing the richer countries at the expense of their own ability to innovate —Richard J. Barnet, *N.Y. Times Book Rev.,* 27 May 1984

set, sit   Originally *set* was the causative verb corresponding to the intransitive *sit* and meant "to cause to sit." But as early as the early 14th century *set* began to be used as an intransitive equivalent to *sit. Sit* itself, as if in retaliation, later took on the sense of "to cause to sit" from *set*. Given that these interchanges between the two words had several centuries' head start on the lexicographers, grammarians, and teachers who have since tried to disentangle them, it is a wonder that things are as relatively simple as they are today.

The intransitive sense of *set* meaning "to be seated" is at the present time considered dialectal or uneducated; it is in general a socially marked usage. This state of affairs must be considered a relative victory for schoolteachers and writers of school textbooks, even though they have failed to extinguish the usage. Dr. Johnson in his 1755 Dictionary said that *set* meaning "to sit" was "commonly used in conversation" and "though undoubtedly barbarous, is sometimes found in authors." Some other 18th-century commentators (including Webster in 1790) commented on the usage. Yet the OED quotes Thomas Jefferson using it in 1788:

> It is very possible that the President and the new Congress may be setting at New York.

Noah Webster, whose 1828 dictionary made heavy use of Johnson, simply omitted Johnson's sense, perhaps because Johnson's illustration, from Shakespeare's *Coriolanus* (1608), was for a specialized meaning of *set* (or *sit*) *down* having to do with laying a siege; or Webster may have thought it too improper for his dictionary. The battle was left to the teachers, textbooks, and handbooks. Textbooks, especially: Malmstrom 1964, which compares the findings of the linguistic atlases with textbooks, reports 170 textbooks that treat *set* and *sit* from nine different viewpoints.

The linguistic atlas researchers found *set* "to sit" in the speech of high school graduates and some college graduates in large areas along the Atlantic seaboard; these findings (along with British evidence) are the basis for calling the usage dialectal. It is presumably this oral use that Pyles 1979 notes as having been heard during the Army–McCarthy hearings in 1954:

> Actually, members of this Committee set in a semi-judicial capacity —Senator Charles E. Potter, Michigan

> You've let them set there and testify day after day — Senator John McClellan, Arkansas

But *set* "to sit" is also typical of less educated and more rural people. English writers of the 19th century— Dickens and Thackeray are cited in the OED—put *set* in the mouths of their more countrified and less educated characters. American writers have done the same:

> I seen then it wasn't so Offul Urgent about me agoin', after all, so I set still, not reely wantin' to Rile him —Frank W. Sage, D.D.S., *Dental Digest*, November 1902

> I had set next to him at so many Speakers Tables, at banquets —Will Rogers, *The Illiterate Digest,* 1924

> This is a great big yard with a whole lot of benches strewed round it, but you can't set on them in the daytime —Ring Lardner, *The Big Town,* 1921

> We had a visitor the other day, an old man, who said he wouldn't go to Europe if they gave it to him. Said a feller went over there and set down on some steps he seen in front of a church. Another feller came along and held out his hand. First one said, What for now? Feller holding out his hand said, Step rent — Flannery O'Connor, letter, 1953

A few other issues have been raised within the context of the general *set–sit* controversy. Bache 1869 has this entry in his chapter on the use of the wrong verb:

> *Set* is often used for *sit;* as, "*Set* down for a moment." The sun *sets*, but a human being *sits*. A hen is generally said to *set*, but she does not—she *sits*.

The question of whether a hen *sits* or *sets* has persisted longer than you might suppose—Jean Malmstrom found it in six of her 170 textbooks. In print, OED evidence shows *sit* to be some 500 years earlier than *set*— but we do not know how old the oral use of *set* might be. In any case, nowadays saying that a hen sets is considered standard.

Richard Grant White 1870 spent several pages etymologizing in order to rationalize why the sun sets, rather than sits. Few people since have been concerned about the sun setting.

Whether clothing *sets* or *sits* well was another issue around the turn of the century, commented upon again as recently as Evans 1961. As with the setting hen, OED evidence shows that clothes were sitting before they were setting, at least in print. But *set* is the usage of tailors; it appears no longer to be disputed.

Baker 1770 disapproved the transitive use of *sit:* "*I'll sit you down—He sat her down—They sat us down*— are not proper." The use is fully standard today:

> She sat me in a claw-foot tub and gave me a bath — E. L. Doctorow, *Loon Lake,* 1979

> I got Loretta on the train and sat her down by a stern-looking man —Flannery O'Connor, letter, July 1952

The transitive *sit* is, in fact, so standard that the original transitive *set* is felt to be dialectal in this use. The character speaking here is a Southerner:

> . . . I turned just as two men arrived at the table. "Set yourself down!" Red greeted them —E. L. Doctorow, *Loon Lake,* 1979

The origin of the intransitive *set* is explained by the OED editor Henry Bradley as developing naturally from reflexive and passive uses of the transitive. A stranger explanation, however, is offered by Paul Fussell, who in *The Boy Scout Handbook* (1982) asserts that unconscious inhibition causes *set* to replace *sit*, "lest," he says, "low excremental implications be inferred." Not plausible, perhaps, but entertainingly original.

In summary, *set* for *sit* is primarily a spoken use; it is considered dialectal or uneducated; it is generally not used in writing except to represent the speech of characters who would use it naturally. Some intransitive uses of *set* have become fully standard: the sun sets, a hen sets, and so do jelly, plaster and concrete; clothes may set or sit on the wearer. The transitive *sit* is also fully standard.

sewage, sewerage In their principal senses, *sewage* and *sewerage* are distinct words. *Sewage* refers to the refuse carried off by sewers:

> . . . will be used to remove phosphates from the sewage —*Annual Report, Allied Chemical Corp.,* 1970

Sewerage refers to the process of eliminating sewage:

> . . . attend to local needs such as . . . drainage and sewerage, street lighting, rubbish collection —Ministry of Foreign Affairs, *About New Zealand,* 1982

Or to a system of sewers:

> ... Fox Basin is treeless, roadless, without paint, without roofs, without sewerage —Josephine W. Johnson, *Jordanstown,* 1937

Both words were first recorded in these senses in 1834. The distinction in their meanings has never been strictly observed, however. It was also in 1834 that *sewage* was first used to mean "sewerage":

> The public have ... built more sewage within the same level and the same term of years —*Report of the Select Committee on Metropolitan Sewers,* 1834 (OED)

And it was not long afterward that *sewerage* was used to mean "sewage":

> Which forms a part of the street mud ... rather than of the sewerage —Henry Mayhew, *London Labour and the London Poor,* 1851 (OED)

No one claims that the distinction between *sewage* and *sewerage* is vitally important, but usage commentators, dating back to the 1880 revised edition of Gould 1867, tend naturally to think that it should be observed. Use of *sewage* to mean "sewerage" is not the issue; it was never common, and seems no longer to occur. The "sewage" sense of *sewerage* persisted into the 20th century, though it too may be receding now:

> ... poured a little social sewerage into his ears —George Meredith, *The Ordeal of Richard Feverel,* 1859

> ... purification of water and sewerage —*Science,* 6 Nov. 1936

> ... shocked even his fellow partisans by the sewerage he poured forth in a New Year's address —Claude G. Bowers, *Jefferson in Power,* 1936

Dictionaries have treated this sense of *sewerage* as standard since 1864, but the punctilious writer may wish to use *sewage* instead (assuming that the punctilious writer does not wish to avoid the subject altogether).

sexism   The women's movement has in recent years drawn considerable attention to the problems of masculine bias in the language. The issues here are social rather than linguistic, but like earlier social issues they will probably leave a mark on the language.

Ebbitt & Ebbitt 1982 sensibly points out that the hard choices in word selection with respect to sexism have to be made by middle-of-the-roaders; the partisans—the militant feminists and the entrenched elderly males—have already made up their minds and are seldom in doubt. The areas where the thoughtful in-betweener will want to be alert concern nouns and pronouns.

1. *Nouns.* Occupational titles that incorporate the word *man,* such as *fireman, policeman, salesman,* and *mailman,* are frequently replaced by gender-neutral terms such as *firefighter, police officer, sales representative,* and *letter carrier.* There are several influences at work here. One is that more women are now employed in many of these occupations than were formerly. Some changing of nomenclature has also been mandated by government agencies, and some by voluntary associations to which both men and women belong. It seems likely that many of the new terms will stick, especially if schoolchildren grow up familiar with them from their textbooks, in which nonsexist language has been mandated.

It should be noted that a few traditional female occupational designations are also in transition. *Stewardess,* for instance, is being replaced by *flight attendant.* Such changes are again attributable in part to the fact that both men and women are now commonly employed in jobs that were formerly reserved for one sex or the other. Harper 1985 lists some of the new occupational names taken from various sources. A few—like *private household cleaners* for *maids* and *servants*—look more like euphemisms to disguise menial jobs than new descriptors to avoid sexual bias.

Some years ago there was considerable interest in finding a substitute suffix for *-man* in a number of compounds like *spokesman, chairman, congressman,* and *draftsman.* The combining form *-one* was a failure; compounds like *chairone* simply looked too mysterious to be useful. The form *-person* has had more, but limited, success. Although loudly decried by some, such combinations as *spokesperson, chairperson,* and *anchorperson* have received wide enough currency to gain at least marginal dictionary recognition (see PERSON 2). *Draftsperson* can be found in the want ads. *Chairperson* and *anchorperson* are in competition with the simpler and equally neutral *chair* and *anchor.*

The *-person* compounds have also been somewhat retarded in their general adoption by some women who reject feminine and neutral forms for the older masculine forms, such as *chairman* and *spokesman.* And in some areas of endeavor, indeed, the existing masculine forms seem to be used simply as a matter of course; in women's basketball, for instance, no one seems chary of playing an aggressive man-to-man defense.

The status of nouns ending in *-ess* is an older but related topic. Their use was urged by at least one 19th-century feminist and disparaged by several 19th-century male commentators (they were particularly hard on *authoress* and *poetess*). In the 20th century, there has been some changing of positions. This subject is treated in more detail at -ESS.

2. *Pronouns.* The issue here concerns pronoun reference to an indefinite pronoun or singular noun used generically. Feminists have merely given new emphasis to an old problem (see the articles on pronoun reference at AGREEMENT, and THEY, THEIR, THEM 1) in attacking the routine use of the masculine singular pronoun in all instances. Handbooks examining the question of the generic masculine from a nonsexist point of view generally recommend several approaches to a solution. Let us make up an example to demonstrate those approaches:

> Each student must send his references with his application.

In order not to seem to exclude women, this could be revised using the old expedient *his or her:*

> Each student must send his or her references with his or her application.

If this seems wordy or "legalistic" (a term several commentators apply to *his or her*), you can try omitting the pronoun or substituting an article:

> Each student must send references with the application.

Another commonly suggested solution is to rephrase in the plural:

> Students must send their references with their applications.

Generally not recommended is the use of such obviously manufactured forms as *(s)he* and *his/her,* chiefly on the grounds that they are distracting. Not recommended on the same grounds is the alternation of masculine and feminine pronouns. A few authors have used the generic feminine pronoun ("Each student must send her references with her application"), but this too seems to be more distracting than useful.

The folk, of course, have had a solution to this impasse for many centuries—one of stunning simplicity: they simply use the plural pronouns *they, their, them.* The folk solution exists more commonly in speech than in writing, and is probably more acceptable in references to indefinite pronouns such as *anyone, someone,* and *everyone* than to generic nouns such as the *student* of our made-up example.

Since the 19th century, theorists have proposed remedying the lack of a gender-neutral singular pronoun with any number of invented forms, some of which make confections like *s/he* look almost sensible. There is a list of such forms at EPICENE PRONOUNS.

In conclusion, all we can offer as a general recommendation is that, being a thoughtful writer, you give some consideration to the question of careless or unconscious sexual bias in the language you use and, where you find it, seek a solution that makes sense in the immediate context.

shall, will *Shall* and *will* have attracted a great deal of attention from usage commentators. Let us begin with a clear expression of present-day American use:

> The old distinction between these words is no longer observed by most people. *Shall,* which was once considered the only correct form for the expression of the simple future in the first person, has been replaced by *will* in the speech and writing of most people.... In a few expressions *shall* is the only form ever used and so presents no usage problem: *Shall* we go? *Shall* I help you? To use *will* in these expressions would change the meaning. With the exception of these special uses, *will* is as correct as *shall* —Warriner 1986

And let us contrast that with the traditional rule, as expressed in a British usage book:

> In its simplest form, the rule governing the use of *shall* and *will* is as follows: to express a simple future tense, use *shall* with *I* or *we, will* with *you, he, they,* etc.; to express permission, obligation, determination, compulsion, etc., use *will* with *I* and *we, shall* elsewhere —Chambers 1985

Chambers goes on to note that there are "many exceptions" to this rule, especially in American, Scottish, and Irish English (as distinguished from the English of England itself).

The reason that things have come to this pass is history, or rather two histories—the history of the words and the history of the rules. Let us consider the words first, drawing heavily on Jespersen 1909–49 (vol. 4) and Strang 1970.

Shall and *will* were originally finite verbs and came only gradually into their present use as auxiliaries. *Will* originally carried the sense of volition, and *shall* that of obligation. Both, it appears, were used in Middle English to express future time. Jespersen and Strang point out that in the 14th century there were signs that *will* was beginning to prevail in this use—it does in Chaucer's works, for instance.

But *shall* received assistance about this same time from the schools and from John Wycliffe, a 14th-century religious reformer and one-time master of Balliol who instituted the first full English translation of the Bible. It was the practice of the schools to use *will* to translate Latin *volo; shall* had no exact Latin equivalent, so it was used to mark the future tense. The school practice was followed in the translated Bible. The twin influences of the English Bible and the school tradition seem to have had an effect on writing, particularly that of a solemn or serious sort. Strang suggests that this countervailing force saved *shall* in England from the relative extinction it has experienced as a future marker in the English of North America, Scotland, and Ireland.

The traditional rule given by Chambers was first set down in the 17th century by John Wallis, a bishop and a well-known mathematician. Wallis's grammar was written in Latin for the edification of foreigners; modern commentators assume it was a sort of learner's grammar, but Thomas De Quincey, in an 1839 article, described it as "patriotically designed as a polemic grammar against the errors of foreigners." Whether designed for instruction or reproof, Wallis's rules were probably simplified. Strang says they do not reflect the practice of the preceding century (although McKnight 1928 detects a tendency in their direction in Shakespeare's usage), and thinks they might have been closer to the actual usage of Wallis's own time than that of any other. A few randomly collected examples of 17th-century usage cast doubt even on that cautious assessment; sometimes usages match the rules and sometimes they do not. A good part of the problem is in interpretation— both of the terms used by the grammarians to make the distinctions and of the intentions of old writers. With this warning, here are some 17th-century examples:

> If a man will begin with certainties, he shall end in doubts —Francis Bacon, *The Advancement of Learning,* 1605

> For if it may please any to compare but the Lords Prayer in other languages, he shall finde as few Latine and borrowed forraine words in ours, as in any other whatsoever —William Camden, *The Languages,* 1605

> . . . I shall speak when I have spoken of the Passions —Thomas Hobbes, *Of Speech,* 1651

> But, it may be you will object that this was *Asper, Macilente,* or, *Carlo Buffone:* you shall, therefore, hear him speak in his own person —John Dryden, "Defence of the Epilogue," 1672

> . . . I hope I shall not be thought arrogant —John Dryden, "Defence of the Epilogue," 1672

> . . . I will only add this in defence of our present Writers —John Dryden, "Defence of the Epilogue," 1672

> "He that will have a May Pole shall have a May Pole." This is a maxim with them —William Congreve, "Concerning Humour in Comedy," 1695

> LOVELESS. Let me see his wound.
> SERRINGE. Then you shall dress it, sir; for if anybody looks upon it, I won't.
> —Sir John Vanbrugh, *The Relapse,* 1696

> . . . the two great Seminaries we have, are without comparison the *Greatest,* I won't say the *Best* in the World —Daniel Defoe, *Of Academies,* 1697

These examples seem to us to follow the theory sometimes and sometimes not. If the usage of Wallis's own century was not exactly uniform, you can well imagine that over time the rules came to match actual usage even less.

By the 18th century, grammarians were finding Wallis's rules too simple. Lowth 1762 added rules for interrogatives, and later grammarians elaborated even further. William Ward in 1765 put the rules into verse, presumably the better to memorize them. But William Cobbett 1823 did not bother with rules; he told his son, to whom his grammar was addressed, that the uses of the auxiliaries, "various as they are, are as well known to us all as the uses of our teeth and noses." He had nothing more to say about *shall* and *will,* relying instead on the native speaker's instinct. Such reliance was not uncommon in the 19th century. Alford 1864 commented that he never heard an Englishman who misused *shall* and *will* but had never heard an Irishman or Scotchman who did not misuse them sometimes. On this side of the Atlantic, Richard Grant White 1870 was employing the same method to distinguish the "correct" New England use from that of the provincial folk and immigrants (mostly Irish at that time). A somewhat similar attitude can be found in Fowler 1926, in which a distinction is made between those "to the manner born"—in this case, the English—and those not so lucky.

Fowler listed several pages of what he regarded as misuses culled from British newspapers, but his faith in the English English rules never wavered, perhaps because of his belief that the British press was controlled by Scots. Had he looked to literary rather than journalistic sources, however, he could have found plenty of variation among non-Scots:

> If you procure the young gentleman in the library to write out . . . , I will send to Mr. Prince the bookseller to pay him —Samuel Johnson, letter, 7 Aug. 1755

> If I come to live at Oxford, I shall take up my abode at Trinity —Samuel Johnson, 1754, quoted by Thomas Warton, in James Boswell, *Life of Samuel Johnson,* 1791

> I have no desire to return to England, nor shall I, unless compelled —Lord Byron, letter, 12 Nov. 1809

> I will write when I can —Lord Byron, letter, 12 Nov. 1809

> As plainly as I behold what happened, I will try to write it down —Charles Dickens, *David Copperfield,* 1850

> His French author I never saw, but have read fifty in the same strain, and shall read no more —Thomas Gray, letter, 18 Aug. 1758

> . . . as soon as I am settled there, I will propose a day for fetching my newest little friend —Lewis Carroll, letter, 1 July 1892

Notice how easily first person *will* slips in when it is part of a contraction:

> I'll send her book from Oxford —Lewis Carroll, letter, 9 June 1892

> Well, I won't talk about myself, it is not a healthy topic —Lewis Carroll, letter, 29 July 1885

Notice too that *will* and *would* can be used with second and third persons to give directions or to show determination:

> You will therefore retain the manuscript in your own care —Lord Byron, letter, 23 Aug. 1811

> . . . he would carve a fowl, which he did very ill favordly, because 'we did not know how indispensible it was for a Barrister to do all those sort of things well . . .' —Charles Lamb, letter, 24 May 1830

Fowler dismissed the use of *shall* and *will* in the same construction as "elegant variation." We have seen two or three examples of such usage from the 17th century already. Here is one from the 19th century:

> . . . I shall delay it till it can be made in person, and then I will shorten it as much as I can —Lord Byron, letter, 29 Feb. 1816

It is clear that even in the English of England there has always been some deviance from Wallis's (and Fowler's) norm.

In America, of course, there has been considerable straying from the Wallis rules. *Will* has by no means entirely supplanted *shall* for marking simple futurity, but *will* and *would* are certainly fully established as standard with the first person:

> I'm a poor Underdog;
> But tonight I will bark
> With the Great Overdog
> That romps through the dark.
>   —Robert Frost, "Canis Major," 1925

> I have no idea on what continent I will be in September —Alexander Woollcott, letter, 8 Jan. 1936

> We would all like it if the bards would make themselves plain, or we think we would —E. B. White, in *The Practical Cogitator,* ed. Charles P. Curtis, Jr. & Ferris Greenslet, 1945

> The mechanics . . . were perfect, I would say — Philip Hamburger, *New Yorker,* 12 Aug. 1950

> Tomorrow morning I will wake up in this first-class hotel suite . . . and I will appreciate its elegance — Tennessee Williams, *Story,* Spring 1948

> Tell Stan I have a textbook out, on English usage and style, and will send him a copy —E. B. White, letter, 16 June 1959

> . . . since I will be seeing you in a fortnight, we can then talk until the cows come home —Groucho Marx, letter, 16 Sept. 1960

> I know beforehand what I will not like about Jane later (she'll be too thin, of course. . . . What will I find to talk to her about? . . .) —Joseph Heller, *Something Happened,* 1974

As for *shall,* it has become a bit fashionable in recent years to disparage its use in American English. Its critics allow that it is entrenched in legal usage and in the questions mentioned at the beginning of the article, but in other uses they tend to regard it as affected or precious. Some allowance is made for the expression of determination or resolve, in which it is used with pronouns of all persons:

> I shall return —General Douglas MacArthur, on leaving the Philippines, 11 Mar. 1942

If we can succeed in persuading every man and woman, every nation to do their utmost, we shall master this famine —Herbert Hoover, quoted in *Time,* 27 May 1946

I can't approve of such goings on and I shall never approve it —Harry S. Truman, letter, 18 Aug. 1948

. . . those who frustrate communication and threaten identity by insisting that everybody else shall speak and write as they themselves do —James Sledd, in Greenbaum 1985

Shall and *should* are also used in more ordinary functions, however, by those Americans to whom they are natural (some of whom also use *will* and *would* in the same ways).

So I've sent Hopkins to Moscow and Davies to London. We shall see what we shall see —Harry S. Truman, diary, 22 May 1945

. . . I shall be in Washington for a few days —Alexander Woollcott, letter, 20 Oct. 1936

Perhaps I shall get down in January —Flannery O'Connor, letter, 15 Dec. 1948

We shall call *I, we, he, she,* and *they* the subject forms —Roberts 1962

I shall always remember two sentences he handed me —James Thurber, letter, 21 May 1954

. . . and "I did not think to tell them"—I should use in conversation without a second thought —Barnard 1979

There was one I shall never forget —Gerald Holland, *Atlantic,* May 1971

. . . I shall be embarrassed by the check —Archibald MacLeish, letter, March 1972

. . . I should love to settle myself uncomfortably into a chair by Josef Hoffmann but I can't afford it —William J. Gass, *N.Y. Times Book Rev.,* 3 Aug. 1986

Our conclusion is that the traditional rules about *shall* and *will* do not appear to have described real usage of these words very precisely at any time, although there is no question that they do describe the usage of some people some of the time and that they are more applicable in England than elsewhere. The historical tendency described by Strang toward the use of *will* only has developed further in America than in England, but not quite as far as the British writer Pamela Hansford Johnson suggests:

And then you suddenly find out, if you're an English writer, that no American really says "shall" and "should." —Pamela Hansford Johnson, quoted in *The Writer's Place,* ed. Peter Firchow, 1974

In current American English, *shall* and *should, will* and *would* are pretty much interchangeable, with the second pair more common. There is perhaps only one thing to concern the learner of English, and that is the business of questions mentioned by Warriner. Consider these two examples:

. . . shall I be compassionate or shall I be uncompassionate? —William Faulkner, 25 Feb. 1957, in *Faulkner in the University,* 1959

Shall we be relativists, and leave everybody's language alone . . . ? —James Sledd, *American Speech,* Fall 1978

Both of these ask for an opinion, a preference, a decision. What do we want to do? If *will* replaces *shall,* the meaning changes. A prediction is asked for. What is going to happen? *Shall* also occurs in an interjected question of fixed rhetorical form. No answer is expected, and *will* is simply not used:

He was 6 foot 2. I was somewhat shorter, shall I say, and from the city —Stephen A. Howard, quoted in Wallace Terry, *Bloods,* 1984

See also SHOULD, WOULD.

shambles *Shambles* is both an old word and a new one—old in that most of its senses had developed by the end of the 16th century, new in that the senses in which it is now commonly (and almost exclusively) used date only from the 1920s. In Old English, the word *scamul* (variously spelled) meant "a stool" and "a money changer's table." The Middle English derivative *shamel* had the additional meaning "a table for the exhibition of meat for sale," which in turn gave rise in the early 15th century to a use of the plural, eventually spelled *shambles,* with the meaning "a meat market." A further extension of meaning in the 16th century produced the sense "a slaughterhouse," from which quickly developed the figurative use of *shambles* to refer to a place of terrible slaughter or bloodshed. So far, so good. In our own century, however, yet another extension of meaning has taken place. Probably because a place of terrible slaughter, such as a battlefield or a besieged city, is also usually a place of great destruction and disorder, *shambles* has acquired the senses "a scene or state of great destruction" and "a scene or state of great disorder and confusion; a mess." These senses were first recorded in the 1920s, but they seem not to have become widespread until about the time of World War II. That was also when they were first criticized:

Once, I could have said "The room was a shambles," and would have been instantly understood to mean that the room was splashed with blood. . . . But now I have been robbed of that figure of speech by careless writers who have ignorantly understood the word to mean a place where the furniture has been wrecked —Ted Robinson, *Plain Dealer* (Cleveland, Ohio), July 1945

Other critics expressed similar dismay, but often in a tone of resignation, recognizing that the battle to keep the blood in *shambles* had already been lost. The new senses of *shambles* had actually turned a rare word into a common one (after all, rooms are messy much more often than they are "splashed with blood"). Most usage writers seem to have bowed to the inevitable, and dictionaries now routinely treat the new senses of *shambles* as standard. They are far and away the most common senses of the word:

Lawrence's story world is a shambles—a world just let go, like a sketchy housekeeper's un-straightened-up room —Eudora Welty, *Atlantic,* March 1949

The apartment was usually in disorder, except on the day the maid came in, when it became a shambles —S. J. Perelman, *New Yorker,* 23 Apr. 1955

. . . saved the evening from becoming an utter shambles —Robert Shaplen, *New Yorker,* 10 Nov. 1956

... tried to fool themselves into thinking that the Axis which they had forged ... was not also in shambles —William L. Shirer, *The Rise and Fall of the Third Reich,* 1960

Having described what a shambles the party system is in —Harry S. Ashmore, *Center Mag.,* September 1968

... the only hotel, a shambles of rotting wood —Lewis H. Lapham, *Harper's,* November 1971

Inflation, which has made a shambles of most homemakers' budgets —Frank J. Prial, *N.Y. Times,* 17 Apr. 1979

... a version of Romeo and Juliet that turns into a hilarious shambles —James Wolcott, *Atlantic,* September 1981

... the shambles of my high school French vocabulary —Stephen King, *Playboy,* January 1982

... had not the city itself been a shambles of torn-up streets —Eleanor Perenyi, *Atlantic,* February 1982

... the accident had reduced the reactor's inner workings to a shambles —Michael Gold, *Science,* October 1982

shame   The basic sense of the noun *shame* can be followed by *at* or *for;* you can feel shame *at* or *for* something, or you can feel shame *for* someone *at* something. *Over* and *about* also have some use following *shame:*

... shame at wanting or enjoying sex —Harriet La Barre, *Ladies' Home Jour.,* August 1971

... shame for having chosen to marry someone who falls short of their expectations —Elizabeth Janeway, *Atlantic,* March 1970

... he feeling shame for her at the unease with which she read —Norman Mailer, *Advertisements for Myself,* 1959

... shame over wasted time and talents —Elizabeth Janeway, *Atlantic,* March 1970

There is a shame about advertising yourself —Norman Mailer, *Advertisements for Myself,* 1959

shan't   *Shan't* is a standard contraction of *shall not.* It came into use sometime during the 17th century, along with such other negative contractions as *an't, don't, han't,* and *won't,* most of which displeased commentators in the 18th and 19th centuries, and some of which are still usage issues. *Shan't* began to appear in print in the 1660s, but not all at once. Thomas Shadwell used *shan't* in 1668, but the OED shows Dryden using *shan'not* that same year, and in 1673 Aphra Behn was still using *shall not I.* The forms *shan't,* which is still predominant, and *sha'n't* have both been used from the 17th century to the 20th. An occasional disciple of George Bernard Shaw may produce *shant.*

The few American commentators who mention *shan't* agree that it is more common in British English than in American English. Our evidence confirms their observation. Here are some American examples, two older and two newer.

I sha'n't apologize for the Whitmanesque —Robert Frost, letter, 19 Dec. 1911

I shan't pretend to be full of jollity —Alexander Woollcott, letter, 12 Jan. 1918

I shan't offer any training tips —Donald McCaig, *Blair & Ketchum's Country Jour.,* June 1984

... the next year in which outlays shan't exceed the receipts —Vermont Royster, *Wall Street Jour.,* 4 Aug. 1982

You might wonder if *shan't,* as a contraction from *shall,* follows the old rules about *shall* and *will.* About all we can say is that sometimes it does, and sometimes it does not. That is about all we can say for *shall* and *will,* too, to be truthful. See SHALL, WILL.

share   Safire 1986 wonders about a new use of *share* with the meaning "tell, tell about." In this use you share your insights, thoughts, reflections, experience, etc. with someone else. Safire prints the comments of several correspondents who dislike the new use, calling it, among other things, cloying, condescending, and gushy.

Such evidence as we have for the use associates it with some of our chief modern pieties—religion, education, and politics. One of Safire's correspondents suggests that its origin lies in pulpit English; the OED Supplement traces it back to the 1930s and the language of the religious movement known as Moral Rearmament, in which it referred to the open confession of sins. The comments of Safire's correspondents suggest that the new use is a sort of secularization of the religious sense. Here are a few examples from our files:

... a panel discussion in which visitors from other institutions shared the benefits of their own, related experience —Calvin H. Plimpton, *Amherst College Bulletin,* November 1967

... we all met together ... to share how the Happening had happened. Mostly we ended up sharing messages —Bud Church, *Media & Methods,* January 1970

When he finished reading it aloud to us, someone told him, "I certainly am glad you shared with us. I'd like to really thank you for sharing." —Carol Bly, *Letters from the Country,* 1981

... was on the telephone ... apparently sharing with a client the insight that the Saudis were seeking to maximize their profits —Leslie H. Gelb, *N.Y. Times Mag.,* 20 Apr. 1986

This use of *share* appears to occur more commonly in speech than in writing at the present time.

she   A few commentators take note of the conventional usage in which *she* and *her* are used to refer to certain things as if personified—nations, ships, mechanical devices, nature, and so forth. The origin of the practice is obscure. The OED has evidence from the 14th and 15th centuries, some of which is translated material, and it is not known if the gender markers in the original had any influence on the translators' practice. The conventions are still observed:

It was a good furnace all last winter ... ; it ran real quiet and when they turned up the thermostat early Sunday morning, she went from fifty to seventy in about an hour flat —Garrison Keillor, *Lake Wobegon Days,* 1985

In 1841 Steers designed the *William G. Hagstaff* for the Jersey pilots, and she regularly beat the New York boats —Robert H. Boyle, *Sports Illustrated,* 30 June 1986

England, therefore, was not so feudal as Gaul. But she was probably developing in the same direction —Frank Barlow, *The Feudal Kingdom of England, 1042–1216,* 3d ed., 1972

Nature has come through again—she always does — Stephen Jay Gould, *The Flamingo's Smile,* 1985

Copperud 1964, 1970, 1980 and Flesch 1964 prefer *it* when the reference is to a nation. Reader's Digest 1983 says that many women object to the feminine pronouns. To the extent that this is so, they seem to be viewed as relatively minor problems in comparison with other aspects of sexism in language. They are covered in Rosalie Maggio's *The Nonsexist Word Finder* (1987) by a single sentence that recommends avoiding them. Casey Miller and Kate Swift similarly prefer *it* to *she* in these uses in *The Handbook of Nonsexist Writing* (1980), but the four pages given to personification are unheated and end mildly with the sensible observation that "writers who use *it* to identify something inanimate are not tempted to rely on supposedly universal sex-linked characteristics to make their point."

See also SEXISM 2.

s/he, (s)he   These conspicuously created forms are among the more recent proposed solutions to the problem of the missing gender-neutral (but not quite so neutral as *it*) third person singular pronoun in English. They will probably not be the last of these suggestions (a list of some of the older ones can be found at EPICENE PRONOUNS). For the record, *s/he,* with its spiffy, high-tech virgule, is American; *(s)he,* with its dowdy, traditional parentheses, is British.

Unlike most of the earlier artificial pronouns, both *s/he* and *(s)he* have appeared in otherwise relatively commonplace prose. Frequent use so far, however, does seem to be limited chiefly to specialized journals (most of them in the fields of English language and linguistics). The readers of these journals obviously do not move their lips when they read; if they did, how would they pronounce *s/he* and *(s)he?* The unpronounceability of these invented forms is a major problem for anyone who advocates their use.

Here are a few of our examples for *s/he* and *(s)he,* in some of which you may detect a certain facetiousness:

Bowing to women's lib, the Service Employes Union replaces the pronoun "he" in its new steward's manual with the term "s/he" —*Wall Street Jour.,* 18 Dec. 1973

Your child's slothlike work habits make it hard to determine if s/he is learning or nesting —Judy Forman, *English Jour.,* October 1986

... assume that your mail will be delivered by a dumb, drunken, spaced-out, semi-illiterate substitute carrier. Can s/he figure out your address? —*Benedicta,* Fall 1982

Anybody with the time, literacy and access fee these days can get together with just about any piece of specialized knowledge s/he may need —Thomas Pynchon, *N.Y. Times Book Rev.,* 28 Oct. 1984

... who is willing to screw anything else on two legs provided (s)he is agreeable and above the legal age —Peter Lewis, *Times Literary Supp.,* 4 July 1980

See also SEXISM 2; THEY, THEIR, THEM 1.

sherbert, sherbet   We have had a few inquiries in recent years about the *sherbert* spelling of *sherbet,* which Merriam-Webster dictionaries recognize as a standard variant, but which many other people, it seems, regard as a misspelling. The basis for their opinion is that the second *r* is unetymological, the word being derived from Turkish or Persian words without it.

The word was imported into English—along with the drink it named—in the 17th century. Derived from an exotic language with an exotic alphabet, it naturally had numerous spellings as an English word. Among fourteen shown in the OED (for the 17th century) are *sherbet* and *sherbert,* the only two in use today (not counting *sorbet,* which came from the same source through Italian). *Sherbet* became the established spelling in the 18th century. *Sherbert* has staged its comeback in the 20th century, apparently; at least we have no 18th- or 19th-century evidence for it. Its resurgence seems to parallel the more widespread use of the word in a new sense, "a flavored ice," which is now far and away the usual sense in American English.

Curiously, our earliest evidence for *sherbert* is American, and our most recent evidence is heavily British. We leave you with two examples from British fiction. The first is English, and the compound terms are favorite sweets of schoolchildren. The second is Australian, and the *sherbert* there probably means "beer."

... Rose had promised either twopenny sherbert fountains with liquorice suckers, or sherbert dabs — Margaret Drabble, *The Needle's Eye,* 1972

We run down Bourke Street with McCarthy a balloon pumped up with sherberts —Barry Oakley, *A Salute to the Great McCarthy,* 1970

Sherbet is still the usual spelling. Probably more common than the *sherbert* spelling is the pronunciation it represents, \'shər-bərt\, which is also sometimes cited as an error, though it can be heard from educated speakers of English.

shibboleth   A story in the Bible tells how the pronunciation of the word *shibboleth* was used by the Gileadites to distinguish between the soldiers of their own army and those of their enemy, the Ephraimites, who were attempting to escape after being routed in battle. *Shibboleth* in the realm of grammar and usage denotes a word or a use of language that is supposed to distinguish the members of one group—usually the anointed, the educated, the elite—from another group—usually the illiterate, the uneducated, the rabble:

Still, "ain't" ... is the shibboleth that divides the saved from the damned —Barnard 1979

... another great Shibboleth of English syntax, the split infinitive —Howard 1984

It is apparently a fact that many of these traditional usages no longer work very well as shibboleths. Some of the people who devise aptitude tests for college-bound students have discovered that poor students were better at spotting many of the traditional shibboleths than good students were. Since the tests are supposed to help identify good students, those likely to be successful in college, the testers have removed many of the traditional shibboleths, including the famous split infinitive.

Longman 1988 notes that *shibboleth* has also become a rather derogatory term for some entrenched or mindlessly repeated dogma or opinion. That use of *shibboleth* looks like this:

> Of course, not everybody who calls himself or is called a Marxist or a Trotskyite subscribes to all (or any) of the relevant credos and shibboleths —Howard 1977

> . . . sees himself as an anarchist, a rebel, a one-man opposition party to fashionable shibboleths and slogans —Michael Billington, *N.Y. Times,* 17 Jan. 1982

shine *Shine* is a verb that has had competing strong and weak principal parts since the 16th century. Samuel Johnson in his 1755 Dictionary gave *shone* as the primary past tense and past participle with *shined* as the secondary past and past participle. He showed examples of *shined* from Spenser, Dryden, Pope, and the King James Bible. But a century later, Fitzedward Hall 1873 thought *shined* was then only used by the uneducated, although he noted that it had once been in more elevated use (he gave an example from Bishop Lowth). The OED (1914) more or less confirmed Hall's opinion, terming *shined* "now chiefly *dial*[ectal] and *arch*[aic]," but the OED also showed that *shined* was usual for the sense "polish," and its use in an American hunting sense was recorded.

Evans 1957, on the other hand, found *shined* to be standard—indeed, literary—in transitive uses generally, and not just in the "polish" sense. It seems clear, in fact, that *shined* has never lost currency in American English to the extent that it has in British English. Longman 1988, a British book, recognizes *shined* for the "polish" sense only, but *shined* is used more widely than that in American English.

We regularly find *shined* meaning "polished", of course:

> He was having his shoes shined —*And More by Andy Rooney,* 1982

We have only one example of *shone* in this sense, by a Trinidadian:

> . . . they shone the brass —Ismith Khan, *The Jumbie Bird,* 1974

American English also uses *shined* for the transitive sense "to direct the light of":

> . . . shined his flashlight into the den —Adele Conover, *Smithsonian,* April 1983

British English uses *shone:*

> . . . and shone his torch down to give him some light —Ann Bale, *Maratoto Gold,* 1971

Intransitive uses tend to be *shone* in both varieties:

> For the first time, light shone on a possibility —Russell Baker, *Growing Up,* 1982

> The long, toothy face, with the big ears on either side, simply shone with enthusiasm —Roald Dahl, *Someone Like You,* 1953

> . . . that hard fierce light of publicity which everybody hates shone on everything he did —William Faulkner, 16 May 1957, in *Faulkner in the University,* 1959

But we also occasionally find intransitive *shined* in American English:

> The California sun shined on the ninth annual . . . show —*Southwest Art,* July 1985

Notice both transitive and intransitive *shined* in this example:

> Elated researchers shined their lights around the hilly prairie dog towns . . . and reflections from ferret eyes shined back everywhere —Ian J. Strange, *Natural History,* February 1986

These uses of *shined* are standard in American English.

should, would

> I need not dwell here on the uses of *will, shall, may, might, should, would, can, could,* and *must:* which uses, various as they are, are as well known to us all as the uses of our teeth and our noses —Cobbett 1823

It is very tempting to adopt Cobbett's attitude and let *should* and *would* go, but they have unfortunately been dragged into the rules propounded originally in the 17th century for *shall* and *will.* We need not go into detail here (all you need to know is at SHALL, WILL), but it does seem worthwhile to point out the typical ways in which *should* and *would* are actually used.

The reason *should* and *would* are mentioned with *shall* and *will* is that they function as the past tenses of those verbs. They turn up in this function in the indirect reporting of speech:

> She banged on the door and said we should be late —Basil Boothroyd, *Punch,* 30 Oct. 1974

> . . . asked in a commanding voice if I wouldn't turn to my third choice —Warren Bennis, *Atlantic,* April 1971

No doubt the woman in the first example said, "We shall be late." An American describing this scene might not be so accurate as Boothroyd and might very well write *would* even though *shall* had been said. In the second example the speaker might have said either *will* (i.e., *won't* in this case) or *would,* which is often used in place of *will* because it is felt to be more polite.

In conditional sentences both *should* and *would* are used:

> . . . I should not be bothering you with this letter if I thought the trouble at all likely to end where it is today —Joseph Alsop, *N.Y. Times Mag.,* 14 Dec. 1975

> We . . . would be glad to have three or four more machines if you could send them to us —E. B. White, letter, 9 Aug. 1922

> If Eastbourne was only a mile off from Scarborough, I would come and see you tomorrow —Lewis Carroll, letter, 14 July 1877

> If Angel were as uncomplicated as he has often been read . . . *Tess* would be much less of a novel —Robert B. Heilman, *Southern Rev.,* April 1970

> . . . had we been continued in office we would have quickly overcome the depression —Herbert Hoover, quoted in *Time,* 5 May 1952

Would is used with pronouns of all persons to express habitual action:

> In the semicircular portico of the National Library we would meet every morning —Oliver St. John Gogarty, *It Isn't This Time of Year At All!,* 1954

He would eat hot soup and drink whiskey and sweat —Aristides, *American Scholar,* Winter 1981–1982

You are not the kind of guy who would be at a place like this at this time of the morning —Jay McInerney, *Bright Lights, Big City,* 1984

Would is also used as a finite verb to express a wish. It is used with or without a subject:

I would God you two were the tender apple blossom and could be shipped here in a sachet bag —James Thurber, letter, October 1936

It does not. Would that it did —Margaret Drabble, letter to the editor, *Times Literary Supp.,* 4 Oct. 1985

... would that I'd kept all my charts! —John Gardner, *N.Y. Times Book Rev.,* 30 Jan. 1983

Should is used in the sense of "ought to":

... the necessity of accomplishing something in less time than should truly be allowed for its doing — Ernest Hemingway, *Green Hills of Africa,* 1935

The third recommendation was that the fleet should be ordered to move north —Dean Acheson, quoted in Merle Miller, *Plain Speaking,* 1973

His French vocabulary was drawn from conversations with his mother and aunt, and should have been full of tenderness —Mavis Gallant, *New Yorker,* 8 July 1985

Should also has a few idiomatic uses all to itself:

My own feeling about this, if I may put it in slang, is "I should worry." —Leacock 1943

"He should live so long I'd make him such a price...." —Mordecai Richler, *The Apprenticeship of Duddy Kravitz,* 1959

Jimmy should be so lucky as to get liverwurst —Jean Gonick, *Northeast Mag.,* 13 Jan. 1985

The point to be remembered here is this: the uses of *should* and *would* are more varied than those of *shall* and *will,* and the traditional rules, shaky as they are for *shall* and *will,* tell us even less about *should* and *would.* And we have not even tried to examine all the uses of *should* and *would* (you can find these recorded in a good dictionary). Native speakers of English mostly handle these words with Cobbett's attitude—they do what comes naturally and do not worry. Learners have more of a problem, but they should follow the practice of native speakers and not become ensnared in artificial distinctions.

should of This is a transcription of the contracted form *should've* of *should have.* Sometimes it is used intentionally for a special effect—for instance, by Ring Lardner—but most writers will want *should have* or *should've.* See OF 2.

should ought See OUGHT 3.

show 1. *Show* has been used to mean "show up; appear" for many years:

'Gojar never shows by day,' explained Talbot —B. M. Croker, *Company's Servant,* 1907 (OED Supplement)

Well, Ralston showed about midnight —Ring Lardner, *The Big Town,* 1921

This sense of *show* began to appear commonly in print in the 1950s, and it has continued in regular use since then. It would not be at home in highly formal prose, but its use is not otherwise restricted:

... Mary seemed to be feeling better and I hoped the lion would show in the late afternoon —Ernest Hemingway, "Miss Mary's Lion," 1956

... those few Congressmen and Congressional aides who did show —Victor S. Navasky, *N.Y. Times Book Rev.,* 20 July 1975

Michaels had failed to show —Michael Katz, *N.Y. Times,* 13 Feb. 1983

... members of the U.S. squad had spoken of the fete without enthusiasm, and, indeed, none of them showed —Robert Sullivan, *Sports Illustrated,* 5 Mar. 1984

The only commentator to have criticized this use of *show* is Theodore Bernstein 1965, who describes it as "a sad casualism."

2. *Showed, shown.* The usual past participle of *show* is *shown:*

... the Vatican has shown itself ready —Irving R. Levine, *Atlantic,* September 1970

Showed can also be used as a past participle:

... had showed their willingness to compromise — *Book Previews,* November 1950

... there had never been a moment when he had showed any meanness of spirit —Mario Puzo, *The Sicilian,* 1984

Such usage is entirely correct; the past participle *shewed* dates from the 14th century, *showed* from the 15th. *Showed* occurs too frequently to be considered rare but is less common than *shown.* Usage commentators generally acknowledge that *showed* as a past participle is standard, but they recommend using *shown* instead.

3. *Shew, shewed, shewn.* The *e* variant of *show* has been less and less used since the 19th century. It is kept familiar through its use by George Bernard Shaw, Henry James, Ford Madox Ford, and other literary figures, as well as by its frequent appearance in older authors. Longman 1988 says it can still be found in British legal use, and we have an example from a 1969 publication on heraldry.

show up *Show up* in its chief transitive and intransitive senses has been labeled a colloquialism in college handbooks from Woolley & Scott 1926 and Jensen 1935 to Prentice Hall 1978 and Bell & Cohn 1981. The label is, it seems, a bit of a tradition in such works. The studies cited by Bryant 1962 find *show up* occurring frequently in informal writing and in speech. Our own evidence, however, shows wide use in general prose as well, and occasional use in more formal contexts. Some examples:

Demonstration plots of themselves have not had much effect on the countryside. Inevitably they show up the inefficiency and lack of knowledge of the average farmer and so arouse a certain amount of opposition —John M. Mogey, *Rural Life in Northern Ireland,* 1947

Xenophon has been shown up for what he is or rather for what he is not —George Cawkwell, introduction to Xenophon's *A History of My Times,* 1979

The good thing about the intelligent anti-intellectual is that he scents with appropriate alarm the dangers of committing himself to abstract attitudes that a later or rougher or rounder experience would show up —Robert Fitzgerald, *New Republic,* 25 Apr. 1949

. . . American ships showed up now and then to continue the blockade —C. S. Forester, *The Barbary Pirates,* 1953

They start to show up about mid-May, and the 'run' is on until around June 20 —Alan Villiers, *London Calling,* 15 Apr. 1954

The problems began to show up last January — *Forbes,* 1 Dec. 1970

. . . you could show up on registration day without advance notice —Tom Wicker, *Change,* September 1971

And it had also shown up the extent to which both the ACTU and employer groups practise tokenism —*Nation Rev.* (Melbourne), 24 Apr. 1975

shrink   According to our evidence, in written use the usual past tense of *shrink* is *shrank:*

. . . he shrank from forcing the decision —Henry F. Graff, *N.Y. Times Book Rev.,* 20 May 1979

Families shrank partly because . . . —Christopher Jencks, *N.Y. Times Book Rev.,* 10 Apr. 1983

Shrunk also occurs as the past tense of *shrink.* In fact, in linguistic surveys conducted in the eastern and midwestern U.S. several decades ago more than 80 percent of the people polled used *shrunk* in preference to *shrank.* The past tense *shrunk* is undoubtedly standard, but we have relatively little evidence of its use in writing:

The Suez shutdown shrunk U.S. Middle East oil imports by one-third —*Newsweek,* 3 Dec. 1956

. . . I shrunk self-consciously in my seat —Stringfellow Barr, *Center Mag.,* May 1968

Shrunk and *shrunken* are both used as the past participle of *shrink. Shrunk* is the usual choice when the participle is functioning as a verb:

. . . the lake has shrunk to a mirage of shimmering blue —William Kittredge, *Fiction,* vol. 1, no. 3, 1973

Or had they only shrunk? —Wilfrid Sheed, *The Good Word and Other Words,* 1978

Shrunken is the usual choice when the participle is functioning as an adjective:

. . . a somewhat shrunken functionary, barely worth a book —Wilfrid Sheed, *The Good Word and Other Words,* 1978

. . . a frail and shrunken fragment of the old dream —Mavis Gallant, *N.Y. Times Book Rev.,* 11 May 1983

shroud   The verb *shroud* is occasionally found in literal use:

. . . he washed the bodies of the Muslim dead and shrouded them for burial —V. S. Naipaul, *Among the Believers,* 1981

More often *shroud* is used figuratively:

The depression that shrouds all of her fiction is original in its mood, unlike anything else being written —Elizabeth Hardwick, *N.Y. Times Book Rev.,* 13 May 1973

The origins of the teddy bear, like those of life itself, are shrouded in controversy —Catherine Calvert, *Town & Country,* December 1982

. . . the full extent of the damage to American intelligence resulting from the mishaps is shrouded in secrecy —Peter Ackroyd, *N.Y. Times Book Rev.,* 13 July 1986

These figurative uses are, of course, standard, but the particular phrases *shrouded in fog* and *shrouded in secrecy* are sometimes disparaged as clichés (as in Copperud 1980 and Longman 1988).

shy   A person can be said to be shy *of* or *about* doing something:

". . . Mr. Fox could not be afraid of Dr. Johnson; yet he certainly was very shy of saying any thing in Dr. Johnson's presence." —Edward Gibbon, quoted in James Boswell, *The Life of Samuel Johnson,* 1791

. . . one may well be rather shy of reverting to topics that are not, perhaps, yet exhausted —F. R. Leavis, *Revaluation,* 1947

. . . I should have been more shy about questioning such a suggestion —F. R. Leavis, *The Common Pursuit,* 1952

Miss Mori did not, as expected, produce printed furs. However, she wasn't shy about lavender or mauve dyed minks —Angela Taylor, *N.Y. Times,* 17 May 1980

Shy can also be followed by *to* and the infinitive:

Authors even then were not shy to take liberties with the English language —*Times Literary Supp.,* 2 Oct. 1969

Although shy to call himself a collector, Mr. Coady means business about handcrafted furniture —Stephen Drucker, *N.Y. Times,* 21 Oct. 1982

When *shy* has the sense "showing a lack" or "short," it is followed by *of:*

. . . a fat man shy of natural quickness —Larry L. King, *New Times,* 21 Feb. 1975

The entire tree is just shy of eight feet tall —*Early American Life,* August 1980

sibling   *Sibling* is to *brother* and *sister* more or less as *spouse* is to *husband* and *wife:* a formal word that is sometimes useful in contexts where either of the sexually specific words would be inappropriate. *Sibling* most often occurs in scientific writing:

. . . the genetic changes undergone by one or both siblings during the period of separation —Peter Matthiessen, *New Yorker,* 27 May 1967

... how dependent these children are on their parents or siblings —Jerome L. Singer, *Psychology Today,* April 1968

It sometimes shows up in general writing as well:

... a small fee to reward the older sibling for serving as a sitter —Letty Cottin Pogrebin, *Ladies' Home Jour.,* September 1971

In recent years figurative uses have become increasingly popular:

Pocket Books is a sibling of Simon & Schuster's many divisions —Ray Walters, *N.Y. Times Book Rev.,* 14 Oct. 1979

The sun has its starry sibling: Alpha Centauri — Philip Morrison, *Scientific American,* February 1978

sic *Sic,* usually enclosed in brackets, is a word editors use in the reproduction of someone else's speech or writing to indicate that an unexpected form exactly reproduces the original and is not a copier's mistake. In the three typical uses here, *sic* is used to show a word spoken with an extra syllable, an unusual spelling, and a misspelling.

"I'm a conservationalist [sic]," she replies —Judy Klemesrud, *N.Y. Times,* 1 Dec. 1974

... the Phenix [sic] Society —Albert H. Johnston, *Publishers Weekly,* 6 Feb. 1978

... we beleive [sic] it to be worth the risk —*The Tower Commission Report,* 1987

Several commentators remind us that it is bad manners to use a [*sic*] to needlessly call attention to someone's error or to deride the language of a less educated person.

Sierra The literal meaning of *sierra* in Spanish is "saw," from which arose its extended sense, "a jagged mountain range." This sense has some use in English as well as in Spanish:

... invasions that have taken place in the Peruvian sierra in recent years —Norman Gall, *N.Y. Rev. of Books,* 20 May 1971

But *sierra* is far less well-known to most English speakers as a generic noun than as a part of the proper names of several mountain ranges—especially, for Americans, the Sierra Nevada of eastern California, also commonly known as the Sierra Nevada range, the Sierra Nevada mountains, the Sierra mountains, the Sierra Nevadas, the Sierras, and the Sierra. This plurality of names leads to a familiar problem: the same people who find redundancy in *Sahara desert* (because *sahara* means "desert" in Arabic) are also likely to find it in *Sierra Nevada range, Sierra Nevada mountains,* and *Sierra mountains.* In addition, some critics have objected to *the Sierras,* arguing that *sierras* can only mean "the mountain ranges" since the singular *sierra* denotes an entire range rather than a single mountain. What this means in practical terms is that if you want to be absolutely sure of offending no one, you will have to write either *the Sierra Nevada* or *the Sierra* when referring to the Sierra Nevada mountains. If, on the other hand, you can accept the idea that the *Sierra* of *Sierra Nevada* is actually a proper name, not a generic noun, and that English and Spanish are two different languages, you

will feel entitled to refer to those mountains in whatever way seems natural and idiomatic to you.

See also SAHARA, SAHARA DESERT.

sight See CITE, SITE, SIGHT.

similar 1. *Similar* is sometimes used as an adverb:

A sponge bath is taken similar to the way you wash your face —Margil Vanderhoff, *Clothes, Clues, and Careers,* 1981

Such usage is extremely rare in written English and is regarded as an error. It can easily be avoided, either by substituting *similarly* or by rearranging the parts of the sentence to make it read more smoothly: "Taking a sponge bath is similar to washing your face."
2. One thing is said to be similar in some way *to* another, and two or more things are said to be similar *in* some respect. Some critics have apparently seen *as* used after *similar,* because they mention it as an error to be avoided, but our files do not contain a single example of *similar . . . as.*
3. *Similar* is not normally a word of great precision. To describe two things as "similar" is to say only that they resemble each other in some way, which may or may not be specified. The degree of resemblance may be great or slight, but usually, when *similar* is used by itself without a modifying adverb such as *very,* a moderate degree of resemblance is implied. A few commentators have therefore looked with disfavor on the occasional use of *similar* to mean "the same" or "corresponding":

No two animal habitats are exactly similar —W. H. Dowdeswell, *Animal Ecology,* 2d ed., 1959

I told Pope John that Chairman Khrushchev had expressed almost similar sentiments —Norman Cousins, *Saturday Rev.,* 30 Oct. 1971

... casualties for the year to date are running little more than half the number in the similar 1970 period —Rowena Wyant, *Dun's,* October 1971

Such usage is not especially common, but it has a long history and is undoubtedly standard. The observations made by Noah Webster in his 1828 Dictionary are still accurate today:

Similar may signify exactly alike, or having a general likeness, a likeness in the principal points. Things perfectly *similar* in their nature, must be of the same essence, or homogeneous; but we generally understand *similar* to denote a likeness that is not perfect.

4. For pronunciation problems with this word, see NUCLEAR.

simple reason This phrase has attracted surprisingly strong criticism from several commentators (Bernstein 1958, 1965, Copperud 1970, 1980, and Shaw 1975, 1987), who regard it as verbose and patronizing. Because it is a phrase whose meaning is self-explanatory (and therefore not a candidate for dictionary entry), we have gathered little evidence of its use over the years, but we suspect that it occurs commonly in speech and fairly often in writing. Here is one example:

He said he wouldn't publish John Gould Fletcher's book for two simple reasons: first because it wouldn't sell and second because he hated the kind of thing Fletcher wrote —Robert Frost, letter, 10 Mar. 1924

It seems clear that *simple reason* can, in fact, have a certain mildly hostile or patronizing tone, although in written use the hostility is probably more often directed toward a third party (as in the above quotation) than toward the reader. The question of verbosity specifically concerns the phrase *for the simple reason that,* which, the critics observe, can be replaced by the single word *because.* But if a writer or speaker wants to express a little irritation, *for the simple reason that* does it better than *because.* If, for example, you hate to fish and someone keeps asking you why you won't go fishing, you might finally say, "For the simple reason that standing knee-deep in water and being eaten alive by mosquitoes is not my idea of a good time." Your ideas about fishing might be wrong, but your use of the language would not be.

simplistic   *Simplistic* is usually a denigrating word that means "oversimplified." However, it is occasionally used with the neutral meaning "simple," a fact that causes some prescriptivists to start prescribing. There may, we must concede, be some cause for complaint here, for, although *simplistic* clearly means "simple" in a few of the citations we have, in other citations the meaning is not so straightforward, and the use is potentially confusing:

> Despite much current oratory, there are no simplistic solutions —Robert C. Weaver, *Michigan Business Rev.,* July 1968

> . . . the question cannot be simplistically or in any sense definitively answered now —Malcolm Boyd, *N.Y. Times Book Rev.,* 16 Apr. 1967

> . . . to show variety of Hindu thought from simplistic tales to sophisticated speculations —Callie Kingsbury, *English Jour.,* January 1975

> . . . the simplistic murals . . . still circumnavigated the upper reaches of a dining room distinguished by the mellowness of its patina —Jay Jacobs, *Gourmet,* April 1980

Many people who think of *simplistic* as a word with negative connotations, as they are probably entitled to from the dominant use, will be taken aback by such neutral uses and may even misunderstand them.

Shaw 1975 and Ebbitt & Ebbitt 1982 call *simplistic* a vogue word, and indeed the bulk of our evidence for *simplistic* is from the past two decades. We see no reason to disdain a word just because other people happen to find it useful, but we do counsel using this one as a pejorative rather than a neutrally descriptive term.

simultaneous   The use of *simultaneous* as an adverb was called "a common, if mild, solecism" by Bernstein 1965 and was unanimously disapproved by the Heritage 1969 usage panel. Bernstein may have encountered such use primarily in speech, for we have not found it to be common in writing. Our files contain only a single example of the adverbial *simultaneous:*

> Simultaneous with the paring of the news, space-wasting typographic practices should be eliminated —Robert C. Nicholson, *Linotype News,* Fall 1951

Standard English requires *simultaneously* in this context.

since   **1.** If you have already read many articles in this book, you will have noticed times change and language habits with them. Not long ago a correspondent wrote

to us inquiring if it is "incorrect to begin a sentence with *because.*" He admitted to preferring to replace *because* with *since* whenever possible. His attitude represents quite a turnabout; Bernstein 1971 and Copperud 1970, 1980 point out that at one time there was a notion current that *since* could not be used as a causal conjunction. Our old books do not shed much light on this notion; Utter 1916 does, however, censure "Since I am sleepy, I will go to bed" on the grounds that in the sentence *since* means simply "because" and not "in view of the fact that." Sellers 1975, the work of a British newspaperman, censures *since* for *because* as an unacceptable Americanism. We are not sure whether this is simply an idiosyncrasy or whether British newspapermen traditionally reject the usage of Shakespeare; Bernstein 1971, an American newspaperman, quotes two instances from Shakespeare:

> Since mine own doors refuse to entertain me, I'll knock elsewhere —*The Comedy of Errors,* 1593

> Since it is as it is, mend it for your own good —*Othello,* 1605

Another American newspaperman, Kilpatrick 1984, prefers *because,* "a fine, honest conjunction; . . . it puts on no airs; it cannot be misunderstood." He lists some sentences in which the use of *since* is ambiguous:

> In a second term, Carter might have moved the course of government toward the left, but since Reagan won the election the nation's political movement has been toward the right instead —*Washington Star*

Freeman 1983 notes that *because* is more emphatic, and Johnson 1982 notes that *since* is less emphatic. A. S. Hornby, in *A Guide to Patterns and Usage in English* (1954), makes the additional point that *since* calls more attention to the cause than *as* (see AS 1).

Clearly *since* can be used to mean "because," though it may be a bit less emphatic than *because.* It can, however, cause readers to stumble if both its causal and temporal senses are meaningful in the same context. It is not necessarily preferable to *because,* as our correspondent perhaps hoped we would tell him.

2. *Since, ago.* There are three different issues concerning *since* and *ago,* all of them pretty ancient. First we have the flat condemnation of *since* meaning "ago"; it appears in Bierce 1909, and a usage note in Webster 1909 testifying to the dislike of some critics suggests there were others besides Bierce. But the editors of Webster's Second deleted the 1909 note, and there seems to have been no basis for the objection. The sense is old, going back, according to the OED, to about 1489; Shakespeare used it, and many subsequent authors, including this well-known American of some years since:

> I received, some time since, your *Dissertations on the English Language* —Benjamin Franklin, letter to Noah Webster, 26 Dec. 1789

This particular usage appears to be rather uncommon, and perhaps old-fashioned sounding, in current American English. It still is active in British English. It has currency in both British and American English in the phrase *long since:*

> I should have done it long since —Veronica Milligan, *Observer Mag.,* 18 Nov. 1973

> . . . I have long since learned to divide them into two classes —John Barkham, *Saturday Rev.,* 13 Feb. 1954

Note that this is interchangeable with *long ago* when the present perfect tense is used:

> . . . would long ago have retired him —*Current Biography,* July 1964

But with other past tenses, *long ago* tends to be used rather than *long since:*

> Moscow long ago had to accept the Yugoslav heresy —Arthur M. Schlesinger, Jr., *Harper's,* March 1969

The affinity of *since* for the present perfect tense is also noted in Bryson 1984 and Bernstein 1965 (among others); they extend their observations beyond the adverbial use discussed above to the preposition. This is a sentence typical of the ones they would correct:

> . . . he was associate editor of the *Journal* . . . , a post he fills again since 1947 —*Current Biography 1949*

Both Bryson and Bernstein would emend *fills* to read *has filled;* the sentence does read more smoothly with the present perfect, which is in fact the usual choice.

The second issue also concerns the same meaning. Here the use is not condemned, but instead the commentators limit *since* to time recently past and *ago* to time long past. Among these commentators were Vizetelly 1906, the synonymist of Webster 1909 (John Livingston Lowes), Whipple 1924, and Lurie 1927. Utter disagreed. The issue appears to have died.

Fowler 1926 resurrected the third issue in objecting to the tautology of employing *ago* and *since* in the same sentence:

> It is barely 150 years ago since it was introduced — example in Fowler 1926

His objection goes back to Baker 1770 ("*It is three years ago since his Father died.*—These Expressions don't make sense. . . .") and has been repeated as recently as Freeman 1983. Fowler calls the mistake very common, but the Merriam-Webster files do not bear that out, having added but a single example since Fowler was published:

> It is just a hundred years ago since there was published in Britain a famous report —Professor K. C. Wheare, *London Calling,* 16 Sept. 1954

Since this too is British, it is possible that the usage itself is chiefly British. *Ago* is certainly expendable in these examples, but its inclusion does not seem to be a problem of great moment.

sine qua non   The literal meaning of this Latin phrase is "without which not." It serves in English as a noun referring to something absolutely indispensable or essential, in which use it has drawn occasional criticism from usage commentators. Evans 1957, for example, considers it a cliché. Our evidence shows that its written use is common:

> . . . the tall ships seem to be the sine qua non of celebrations these days —Lawrence Van Gelder, *N.Y. Times,* 9 May 1982

> . . . where fastidious editing is the sine qua non of staying in business —Arthur Plotnik, *Publishers Weekly,* 29 Oct. 1982

It occurs in speech much less frequently, perhaps because many people feel unsure about how to pronounce it. The usual pronunciations in American English are \ˌsin-i-ˌkwä-ˈnän\ and \ˌsin-i-ˌkwä-ˈnōn\.

sing   Usage commentators dating back to Richard Grant White 1870 have agreed that *sang* is the usual past tense of sing. White regarded the past tense *sung* as an error, and a few more recent commentators have taken the same line, but most recognize that both *sang* and *sung* have had reputable use as the past tense of *sing.*

In current English, the past tense *sung* is not so much wrong as simply old-fashioned. Samuel Johnson in his 1755 Dictionary listed the past tense as *sung* or *sang,* but over the intervening two centuries, *sang* has come to predominate. Here are a few older examples with *sung:*

> Mrs. Bland sung it in boy's clothes the first time I heard it —Charles Lamb, letter, 2 Jan. 1810

> . . . Huldy was just like a bee: she always sung when she was workin —Harriet Beecher Stowe, "The Minister's Housekeeper," 1871, in *The Mirth of a Nation,* ed. Walter Blair & Raven I. McDavid, Jr., 1983

> Once M'Cola, in the dark . . . sung out a stream of what sounded like curses —Ernest Hemingway, *Green Hills of Africa,* 1935

sink   Both *sank* and *sunk* are used for the past tense of *sink. Sank* is used more often, but *sunk* is neither rare nor dialectal as a past tense, though it is usually a past participle.

> He sank himself word by word into the literature — Robert Penn Warren, *Jefferson Davis Gets His Citizenship Back,* 1980

> Then I sunk back never again to blaze perhaps — Robert Frost, letter, 8 July 1935

> . . . when I saw that program listing my heart sank —Edith Oliver, *New Yorker,* 20 Nov. 1971

> . . . the squall that sunk the Pride of Baltimore —M. Murray, *Science News,* 2 Aug. 1986

sit   See SET, SIT.

site   See CITE, SITE, SIGHT.

situated   Watt 1967 finds *situated* often used as padding, and *Winners & Sinners,* 21 Apr. 1988, elaborates upon the same theme. Here are two examples from the latter publication:

> . . . the centers are often situated in poor neighborhoods —*N.Y. Times,* 8 Mar. 1988

> The hall is situated on the college's campus —*N.Y. Times,* 21 Mar. 1988

The *Winners & Sinners* editor says that *situated* should have been omitted from both of these because it adds no information. But the question that should be asked is not whether the word can be omitted but whether the sentence is improved by dropping the word. Some writers' ears for English prose will tell them immediately that in those examples something more readily stressed than a preposition is needed in the place where *situated* appears. In the first example either *often* or *in* has to receive more stress than it deserves if *situated* is removed, and *on* gets too much in the second. Here is a similar *situated* from an essay; we doubt that the author would view with much favor a suggestion that he strike the word.

> The city, situated above the rapids and its clumps of vivid green islands . . . —William Styron, *This Quiet Dust and Other Writings,* 1982

Situated is certainly omissible in some contexts, but in others it serves a useful purpose. Remember: you need not delete words unless deletion improves the sentence.

situation The *situation* situation is a major concern in British usage circles, but not so much a cause for comment by Americans. Criticism of *situation,* particularly as it occurs in phrases like *emergency situation* and *strike situation* used in place of *emergency* and *strike,* appears to be a sort of post-World War II tradition in Britain; the topic begins with Gowers 1948 and receives more space in each of his succeeding editions (1954 and 1973); it is found in Fowler 1965 (which Gowers edited), Phythian 1979, Burchfield 1981, Bryson 1984, and Longman 1988; it is discussed by J. Enoch Powell in Michaels & Ricks 1980 and by Robert F. Ilson in Greenbaum 1985. The criticized uses of *situation* have also been satirized in the British magazine *Private Eye,* in which particularly bad examples have appeared in a regular column headed "Ongoing Situations." (The phrase *ongoing situation,* for which we have almost no evidence, is especially notorious among the British, who apparently regard it as the quintessence of bureaucratic jargon. They also dislike *ongoing* by itself. See ONGOING.)

Most of what little American comment there has been on *situation* can be found in college handbooks, in which it is typically dismissed as padding. The American criticism presumably derives from Gowers (by way of Fowler 1965), but the jargonistic *strike situation* usage is generally not mentioned by the Americans; they simply treat *situation* as an overused word. The jargonistic usage appears, in fact, to be rare in American English. Here is a tongue-in-cheek sentence from a British commentator to give you a better idea of its quality:

> Clearly 'clearly' is in an ongoing perspicuity situation as a transparently vacuous vogue word —Howard 1980

Ilson in Greenbaum 1985 comments thoughtfully on two compounds—*crisis situation* and *no-win situation*—listed as objectionable by Burchfield. Ilson points out that a crisis situation is likely not to be quite the same as a crisis, and that *no-win situation* is a short way to express a fairly complex idea. These combinations are both found in American English:

> . . . the family doctor, . . . now being recast in a modern role as a specialist in comprehensive, continuing medicine, with as much emphasis on prevention as on crisis situations —Dodi Schultz, *Ladies' Home Jour.,* August 1971

> . . . the ingenious Mr. Jeffries juggles his plot so that the murderer is faced with a no-win situation — Newgate Callendar, *N.Y. Times Book Rev.,* 8 Jan. 1984

Neither of these combinations has attracted much criticism from American commentators. *No-win situation,* in particular, is established as a common idiom and is inoffensive to American ears. Other American uses of *situation* with a noun attributive modifier seem also to differ somewhat from those disliked by the British:

> Not necessarily the man for a heart-to-heart, but indispensable in a party situation —Jay McInerney, *Bright Lights, Big City,* 1984

> . . . to get the hostage situation out of the way — Charles Allen, quoted in *The Tower Commission Report,* 1987

We conclude that the British use of *situation,* especially in official jargon, is a bit different from American use. The jargon of the bureaucrat, the educator, and the social scientist is, in any case, rather of an eddy along the mainstream of English. Its faults and virtues are essentially unchanging, and it seems to have little effect on general usage. *Situation* is one of those vague words that is useful when precision is not wanted. No doubt it can be and is used unnecessarily, but in American English, at least, there seems to be no reason to go out of your way to avoid it.

skeptic, sceptic *Skeptic* and related words *(skeptical, skepticism)* are usually spelled in American English with a *k:*

> . . . I am a skeptic about mystical experiences —William Styron, *This Quiet Dust and Other Writings,* 1982

In British English, these words are spelled with a *c:*

> I have been perhaps unduly sceptical —Graham Greene, *Getting to Know the General,* 1984

H. W. Fowler noted this distinction in 1926 and expressed a preference for the American spelling, on the grounds that it more accurately and unequivocally represents the pronunciation of these words. (In most words beginning *sce-,* such as *scepter* and *scene,* the *c* is not pronounced.) His opinion on this matter has, however, had no apparent effect on British spelling.

skirt Bernstein 1965 cites *skirt around* as a redundancy to be avoided, inasmuch as *skirt* by itself means "to go around." According to our evidence, the verb *skirt* occurs only occasionally with *around* (or, in British use, with *round*) in edited writing, but it is certainly standard. Here are a few examples:

> . . . the doctor may think it unwise and even irresponsible to add desolation to pain; and so he skirts around the truth —Norman Cousins, *Saturday Rev.,* 1 Oct. 1977

> Mr. Heilman's book skirts around the edges of the question —Arthur Hertzberg, *N.Y. Times Book Rev.,* 3 Feb. 1985

> He obviously wanted me to comment on the Harvard trouble . . . , and I was not less eager to avoid it, so we skirted round each other amusingly —Harold J. Laski, letter, 3 July 1922

> . . . by omission only, never by distortion, or by supple skirting round ugly truth —*Times Literary Supp.,* 1 June 1940

See REDUNDANCY.

slate As a verb, *slate* has very different meanings in American and British English. In American English it commonly means "to schedule or designate":

... the place was up for sale and slated to be converted into a run-of-the-mill hospital —E. J. Kahn, Jr., *New Yorker,* 4 Apr. 1953

... how many employees are slated to be taken off the payroll —Maria Shao & Bill Paul, *Wall Street Jour.,* 28 June 1982

... on Monday he's slated to appear in Kansas City —Curry Kirkpatrick, *Sports Illustrated,* 14 Feb. 1983

The meaning of the British *slate* is "to criticize severely":

... she slated me like a fishwife for being a lazy slacker —Richard Hull, *The Murder of My Aunt,* 1934

... a national weekly transport magazine which slates the use of the word "Transit" as an "Americanism" —*Evening Gazette* (Middlesbrough, England), 31 May 1974

The American *slate* and the British *slate* are two entirely different words. The American verb is derived from the familiar noun *slate,* while the British verb is thought to be derived from the little-used verb *slat,* which has among its senses "to hurl or throw smartly" and "to strike or pummel." The British *slate* dates from the early 19th century; the American *slate* was first recorded in 1904. Copperud 1970, 1980 notes that the American verb has been "often criticized in journalism," partly because it is thought to be a misuse of the British verb; however, Copperud himself dismisses such criticism, and no other commentator has repeated it.

slave In literal use, the noun *slave* usually takes *of,* when it needs a prepositional-phrase complement.

... a Nazi-ruled Europe ... whose people would be made slaves of the German master race —William L. Shirer, *The Rise and Fall of the Third Reich,* 1960

Of also occurs with *slave* in figurative use, but *to* is more common:

... much too functional as an accompaniment for a visual medium of which it is the slave —Otis L. Guernsey, Jr., *N.Y. Herald Tribune Book Rev.,* 7 Nov. 1954

All his life he had been a slave to the land —Ellen Glasgow, *Barren Ground,* 1925

... a habitual bird-watcher, a canoe addict, and a slave to the camping-out habit —Dwight Macdonald, *New Yorker,* 18 July 1953

slay The surviving and normal past tense of *slay* is *slew* (for an inkling of the huge variety of alternatives that once was, see the OED), and the past participle *slain.*

... he slew twenty-nine adversaries in his lifetime —Robert Penn Warren, *Jefferson Davis Gets His Citizenship Back,* 1980

... the Japanese swordsmen who are indifferent to getting slain —Flannery O'Connor, letter, 25 Nov. 1960

There is also a regular form *slayed.* It is sparsely attested as a dialectal form in the American Dialect Dictionary. Roberts 1954 and Longman 1988 note, and our evidence confirms, that it is usual with the showbiz sense

"to be a great hit with" (stodgily defined in dictionaries as "overwhelm"):

... it turns out *Harold and Maude* just slayed 'em in Japan —Ruth Gordon, quoted in *People,* 13 Oct. 1980

Slayed as the past tense for the "kill" sense seems to occur occasionally in speech. The professional wrestler Hulk Hogan, for one large example, used it while doing a little pre-fight boasting for publicity in 1985 or 1986: "You're a dragon, Piper ... and you're gonna be slayed." It is also sparsely attested in print. A 1962 children's book of Greek myths had "Cadmus easily slayed it," and *slayed* was used in a prominent headline in an advertisement run in several national magazines in 1985. But *slayed* cannot be considered established in such use. Whether it eventually becomes established remains to be seen.

slow, slowly The controversy over whether *slow* is a proper adverb seems to have come in with the automobile, which brought with it the "GO SLOW" and "DRIVE SLOW" signs. We find comment on the subject as far back as MacCracken & Sandison 1917, in which we are told that conservative signmakers prefer *slowly* but that *slow* is gaining ground. The automotive aspect of the question is still sometimes mentioned:

The adverb *slow* is used mainly by highway police, who order us to *go slow.* Careful writers prefer the adverb *slowly* —Oxford American Dictionary 1980

But restriction of adverbial *slow* to the vocabulary of policemen is simply uninformed. *Slow* is an old adverb, and it has had many users other than highway police:

... but, O, methinks, how slow
This old moon wanes!
—Shakespeare, *Midsummer Night's Dream,* 1596

I pray you have a continent forbearance till the speed of his rage goes slower —Shakespeare, *King Lear,* 1606

Faith this letter goes on but slow; it is a week old — Jonathan Swift, *Journal to Stella,* 16 Feb. 1711

Twice I have walked out with Miss Goldsmid & her friend Mrs. Naylor.... But Lord! Lord! how slow they walk —Edward Lear, letter, 16 Feb. 1862

The war moves slow if it moves at all —Robert Frost, letter, 7 Mar. 1944

He drives slower, staring ahead for the slightest clues of road —Garrison Keillor, *Lake Wobegon Days,* 1985

God the Master Mechanic died slow, with many a confusing deathbed word —John Updike, *New Yorker,* 30 Dec. 1985

Slow, however, has a rather restricted range of application. Except in exclamatory expressions ("... how slow they walk"), *slow* regularly follows the verb it modifies, and the verb is regularly one of action or motion. *Slowly* is more generally applicable. It can precede the verb:

... a test, it is true, which can only be slowly and cautiously applied —T. S. Eliot, "Tradition and the Individual Talent," 1917, in *American Harvest,* ed. Allen Tate & John Peale Bishop, 1942

It was almost as if something ... were slowly circling the tent —Arthur C. Clarke, *Boy's Life,* August 1967

It can follow the same sort of verbs *slow* can:

> ... because, she said, I drove too slowly —David Plante, *Difficult Women,* 1983

> ... I tried to walk as slowly as I could —Ernest Hemingway, *Green Hills of Africa,* 1935

It can follow verbs with which *slow* would not be idiomatic, and appear in contexts where *slow* would not be idiomatic for other reasons:

> ... the leadership turned slowly toward bombing as a means of striking back —David Halberstam, *Harper's,* February 1971

> ... grain by grain, as the pigeon said when he picked up the bushel of corn slowly —Edward Lear, letter, 29 May 1862

> ... I did an abrupt about-face ... and started walking slowly away —James Jones, *Harper's,* February 1971

Slowly also modifies participial adjectives:

> ... the slowly accumulated intimacy on which Mrs. Wharton places such redeeming value —Richard Poirier, *A World Elsewhere,* 1966

> ... stares gravely out over lines of slowly moving cars —Irwin Shaw, *Harper's,* September 1970

Slow is not used with past participles, but it can form compounds (usually hyphenated) with some present participles, including *moving:*

> ... slow-moving shell-encrusted survivors from an earlier epoch —John Fischer, *Harper's,* February 1971

Slow and *slowly* should really present no usage problem. They each have their proper place, and good writers keep them there.

See also FLAT ADVERBS.

smell 1. Longman 1988 notes, and our evidence confirms, that in British English either *smelt* or *smelled* may be used as the past tense of this verb, while *smelled* is usual in the U.S.:

> I smelt the sooty reek of the oil flames —Benedict Allen, *Who Goes Out in the Midday Sun?,* 1986

> "... I smelt beer on the breath of a young lad...." —Frank Palmer, *Daily Mirror* (London), 21 Nov. 1974

> ... even the noblest in the land must have smelled a long way off —Hunter Davies, *Sunday Times Mag.* (London), 14 Apr. 1974

> I turned toward her and smelled that she'd brushed her teeth —John Irving, *The Hotel New Hampshire,* 1981

> As a boxing contest and as vaudeville, it smelled — Red Smith, *N.Y. Times,* 4 Oct. 1976

2. The question of whether the intransitive *smell* must be followed by an adjective or whether it may be followed by an adverb is discussed by a few commentators. *Smell* is one of those verbs, linking verbs often, that are used with both adjectives and adverbs. When a writer is describing the quality of a smell, an adjective is usual:

> What's in a name? That which we call a rose
> By any other name would smell as sweet
>   —Shakespeare, *Romeo and Juliet,* 1595

> ... the soil of America smelled so good to them — Russell Lord, *Behold Our Land,* 1938

> On this score, Dante and Milton ... don't smell neutral to us —Peter Viereck, *New Republic,* 7 June 1954

> ... the smaller places usually smelt so awful that you wouldn't have noticed the preparation of a complete Tandoori meal —Barry Took, *Punch,* 13 Jan. 1976

But *smell* can also be used with an adverb of manner. Longman 1988 points out that adverbs are more likely to be used when *smell* means "stink":

> Abdullah wrinkled the edge of his flat nose and shook his head. They really smelled abominably — Ernest Hemingway, *Green Hills of Africa,* 1935

> ... with the coming of hot weather the jars had begun to smell noticeably —John Barth, *The Floating Opera,* 1956

Smell is also frequently followed by a prepositional phrase introduced by *of.* In this construction, an adverb of manner is quite common:

> ... the novel smells faintly of the Hollywood atmosphere is which it was composed —*Time,* 22 Sept. 1974

> ... smelt very powerfully of the fish they spent most of their lives catching —John Davies, *Annabel,* July 1974

> ... who smelled quite as richly of class privilege as their British counterparts —John Le Carré, *N.Y. Times Book Rev.,* 14 Oct. 1979

sneak, snuck *Sneak* is a word of mysterious origin. It first turns up in Shakespeare:

> Sneak not away, sir; for the friar and you must have a word —*Measure for Measure,* 1605

It seems to have no sure antecedents. There is a possible source in Old English—a verb *snīcan,* of similar meaning. But Old English strong verbs of the class that *snīcan* belongs to came into modern English with *-ike* (as *strike* from *strīcan*), and there is no evidence extant in Middle English to connect *sneak* with *snīcan.* The original past and past participle of *sneak* were regular, *sneaked.* But sometime in the late 19th century a variant irregular form, *snuck,* began to appear in the United States.

> ... an' den snuck home —*The Lantern* (New Orleans), 17 Dec. 1887

The *Lantern* citation is the earliest yet uncovered. The American Dialect Society turned up a few examples from around the turn of the century. The earliest printed citation in the Merriam-Webster files dates from 1902:

> Dock Knowital he Snuck Out the room an' Disappeared —Frank W. Sage, D.D.S., *Dental Digest,* November 1902

A decade later, *snuck* appeared in the stories of Ring Lardner:

> ... I snuck off down the street and got something to eat —Ring Lardner, *You Know Me Al,* 1916

While Lardner's characters used *snuck,* those of this older contemporary O. Henry used *sneaked:*

> I knew what it meant; so I climbed down and sneaked a five dollar bill into the hand of a man with a German silver star on his lapel —O. Henry, *The Gentle Grafter,* 1908

From these sparse pieces of evidence it appears that the few authors who had heard *snuck* considered it typical of the speech of rural and not overly educated Americans and they used it in generally humorous contexts.

The members of the American Dialect Society who began collecting examples early in this century clearly assumed *snuck* to be a dialectal form. Novelists did too. From the 1930s on, *snuck* turns up in novels set in such various places as Tennessee, Ohio, and New England, often around the Civil War period. From the evidence we now have, use of *snuck* in a mid-19th-century setting would appear to be anachronistic.

Eventually *snuck* began to appear in contexts with a different purpose—not representing the comical speech of a bumpkin or the supposed dialect of a fictional character in the past, but in journalistic prose where it seems to be used for a lightening or humorous effect:

> ... photographers snuck up and took pictures of the inventor sound asleep and snoring in the middle of the day —*N.Y. Herald Tribune Book Rev.,* 22 Jan. 1939

> ... I attended a fashion show the other day. I snuck in like a sneak —Vincent X. Flaherty, *Los Angeles Examiner,* 6 Apr. 1952

From such uses, it shortly began to appear in other kinds of contexts:

> A wry smile snuck across Johnny's freckles, as his straight blond hair blew in the soft tradewind —*Boy's Life,* June 1953

> He snuck the Hearst collection away from Macy's, you know —an unnamed Gimbel's executive, quoted in *New Yorker,* 17 Feb. 1951

> ... I really hammed it up. I snuck an extra blanket under my bedspread, making sure I'd sweat plenty —William Goldman, *Temple of Gold,* 1957

Since the 1950s, *snuck* has appeared with increasing frequency in newspapers and magazines, primarily in straightforward contexts without humorous overtones. Two language surveys in the 1970s, one in Canada and one in the United States, revealed the use of *snuck* to be widespread—not restricted geographically—and to be more common among younger informants. If we assume that the younger informants will continue to use it as they grow older, it would seem that *snuck* stands a good chance to become the dominant form of the past and past participle. The results of these surveys corroborate the evidence in the Merriam-Webster files.

But where does *snuck* come from? We don't know; it is as mysterious as the origin of *sneak* itself. The only evidence that we have suggests *snuck* is a late 19th-century North American innovation. One theory suggests it may have been a survival in some obscure northern English or Scottish dialect brought here by settlers. It is tempting to trace it from Old English *snīcan;* Old English *strīcan* of the same class of strong verbs gave us *strike* and *struck;* there is at least one surviving instance of Middle English *snike* (pronounced \\'snē-kə\\), around 1240, which is clearly derived from *snīcan.* But no evidence survives to connect either *sneak* or *snuck* conclusively to *snīcan* and *snike.* It is a long time from 1240 to 1887.

Usage commentators were slow to discover *snuck.* Krapp 1927 noted a dialectal past and past participle *snuk,* which suggests he had not seen the word in print (he evidently did not read Ring Lardner). There seems to be no other comment until the 1970s when a few critics (Shaw 1970, Bernstein 1977, Harper 1976) offer remarks indicating they were aware of the way the word was being used in Ring Lardner's time.

In summary we can say that in about a century *snuck* has gone from an obscure and probably dialectal variant of the past and past participle to a standard, widely used variant that is about as common as the older *sneaked.* Some evidence suggests it may become the predominant form in North American English. Occurrence in British English is rare but not unknown. Perhaps there is no better illustration of the rise of *snuck* to respectability than a comparison of Dr. Sage's 1902 use quoted early in this article with more recent ones:

> *Entitlements* is a word that snuck into the political lexicon with few considering what it meant —*Wall Street Jour.,* 27 Mar. 1981

> ... half the programme was unfortunately devoted to a penetrating interview with the star, which is obviously how the programme snuck into the arts slot —Bart Mills, *The Listener,* 30 Jan. 1975

> When I was a teenager, I snuck off to the movies as often as possible. I would come out of some heady piece of derring-do and walk down the prosaic streets of my home town, quite altered by what I had just seen, fantasizing myself thoroughly into one of the characters —Robert MacNeil, Presentation Address at the James E. Scripps Award Ceremony, Detroit, 30 Apr. 1981

> But, again, Ruddock has snuck his unexpected and modern signature into these rooms —Carol Vogel, *N.Y. Times Mag..* 15 Apr. 1984

so, *adverb*   The use of *so* as an intensifier has been subject to criticism in usage books since at least Mac-Cracken & Sandison 1917. Here is a succinct version of the usual warning:

> Avoid, in writing, the use of *so* as an intensifier: "so good"; "so warm"; "so delightful." —Strunk & White 1959

But some commentators (notably Bryant 1962) have observed that the usage of intensive *so,* considered in its full range, is not quite as simple as these examples suggest. *So* is regularly used as an indefinite adverb of degree with the degree indicated by a following clause:

> ... and so frightened Mark Twain that he died — James Thurber, letter, 2 May 1946

> It had gone so simply and easily that he thought it might be worthless —Ernest Hemingway, "An African Betrayal," *Sports Illustrated,* 5 May 1986

When there is no following clause, *so* becomes more of an intensifier. Nevertheless, it may sometimes be rooted in material that went before in the context:

> However, after all, it seems to me contrary to reason to suppose that Napoleon is going to do so crazy a thing —Henry Adams, letter, 13 Mar. 1859

> I cannot be so patient with the White House —David A. Stockman, *Newsweek,* 28 Apr. 1986

> I don't know why it got on my nerves so —Peter Taylor, *The Old Forest and Other Stories,* 1985

And in another intensive use—never criticized—*so* indicates a definite degree that is implied rather than specified:

> Many thanks for sending me so truly welcome a piece of news —Lewis Carroll, letter, 17 June 1893

> The cephalopod eye is an example of a remarkable evolutionary parallel because it is so like the eye of a vertebrate and there is no evidence of a common ancestor —Sarah Fraser Robbins, *Massachusetts Audubon,* June 1968

> ... the kind of sterile over-ingenuity which afflicts so many academic efforts —*Times Literary Supp.,* 2 Oct. 1969

This use is frequently found in negative contexts:

> ... the word ballet was not so well known then —G. B. L. Wilson, *Dance News,* May 1982

> ... he has not been so successful —Herbert Brown, *American Literature,* May 1944

> What we are not so keen on is getting the truth —Anthony Quinton, *N.Y. Times Book Rev.,* 15 July 1984

The criticized use of the intensive *so* occurs when it means "to a large and indefinite extent or degree" and functions much like *very, exceedingly,* or *extremely.* In general, the written contexts in which this *so* appears are informal; since the use is common in speech, it naturally gravitates to contexts that are close to speech. A few commentators call it a feminine use, and we do, of course, have evidence of its use by women:

> ... how am I to read these books? What is the right way to get about it? They are so many and so various. My appetite is so fitful and so capricious —Virginia Woolf, "How Should One Read a Book?" 1926, in *Yale Review Anthology,* 1942

Robin Lakoff, in *Language and Woman's Place* (1975), agrees that this intensive *so* is more common in women's language than men's, "though certainly men can use it." Indeed, they can and do:

> ... on the ground under the shelf were little orange and magnolia trees. It looked so pretty —Mark Twain, letter, 1 June 1857

> ... she chose a little red one from high on the vine, wiped it on her dress, and bit off half of it. It was so good, and then the bright sunshine made her sneeze —Garrison Keillor, *Lake Wobegon Days,* 1985

> Mother will be so happy to know of the use to which you put Kenny's words —Archibald MacLeish, letter, 28 Apr. 1919

> Mother, I was so glad to get a letter from Jeff this morning, enclosing one from George dated June 1st. It was so good to see his handwriting once more —Walt Whitman, letter, 10 June 1864

> I'm so excited about the trip, and the prospect of being able to buy a Ford phaeton of my very own —John O'Hara, letter, 4 June 1934

> ... I'm dreadfully sorry to hear about all the pains and colds and everything, it is so discouraging —E. B. White, letter, 4 Feb. 1942

> I appreciate your sending the sporting magazines and the Book Reviews ever so much —Ernest Hemingway, letter, 20 Mar. 1925

> This is me, Winston Churchill, speaking himself to you, and I am so glad to be able to thank you in this remarkable way —quoted in *Time,* 1 Apr. 1946

We can see that men writers are not afraid of the usage, at least in their letters, where they can be themselves.

Clearly the intensive *so* is well established (the OED traces it back to Old English), and in spite of the adjurations of the commentators it is not avoided in speech or in informal writing. In its less noticeable varieties it can even appear in more formally edited prose. You may, however, want to avoid its baldest form—where it modifies an otherwise unadorned adjective ("The scenery was *so* beautiful!")—in your most serious writing.

so, *conjunction*   Except for the repeated complaint in schoolbooks and college handbooks that *so* is overused as a connective, opinion about conjunctional *so* is divided. Some critics tell us that *so that* should be used instead of *so* in both clauses of result and clauses of purpose; others think *so* is all right to introduce clauses of result but *so that* should be used for clauses of purpose; and still others find *so* all right in both uses but *so that* more formal.

One thing shown clearly by the evidence is that *so* predominates in speech, especially, it appears, in uneducated speech. Fries 1941 found *so* to be six times more frequent in his corpus of uneducated speech than in his educated one; this may be related to the "*so*-habit" referred to by Bryant 1962—the habit of using *so* indiscriminately as a connective in narrative, as children are supposed to be fond of doing.

In spite of what the usage books say about *so that* being the more appropriate in formal prose, however, we do not find much difference in level of formality between *so* and *so that* in our most recently collected evidence. You can judge their relative formality in the following examples (in which you will also note that the clause introduced by *so* may be a separate sentence). First, clauses of result:

> Rarely here is one more than a few miles from a great brackish tideland stream ... , so that what is specifically Southern becomes commingled with the waterborne, the maritime —William Styron, *This Quiet Dust and Other Writings,* 1980

> It was a convention of each periodical that the work was directed by a projector ... whose imaginary personality was adopted by each contributor. So Boswell's essays were written by The Hypochondriack —John Butt, *English Literature in the Mid-Eighteenth Century,* edited & completed by Geoffrey Carnall, 1979

One of the actors fumbled every line and kept saying "Balls," so that fifteen speeches ended with this word —James Thurber, letter, Summer 1950

"Realistic" politicians have prided themselves on understanding that "the people" are concerned only with . . . bread-and-butter issues—taxes, inflation, and the like. So they have been frequently surprised —Elizabeth Drew, *New Yorker,* 3 May 1982

And clauses of purpose:

. . . some overtures to be made to what were described as more moderate elements within the Iranian Government, and it was related to establishing a relationship so that we would have some influence in the future —Edwin Meese 3d, quoted in *The Tower Commission Report,* 1987

. . . about to lose his fight to save his "Garden of Eden" from city officials who want to bulldoze it so low-income housing can be constructed —*New Yorker,* 8 July 1985

Just be sure you've got the guts. So that if you have to steal or take a sap to someone's head for a meal, you'll be able to —E. L. Doctorow, *Loon Lake,* 1979

. . . and half the citizens don't know or care where they were born just so they can get somewhere fast —Robert Penn Warren, *Jefferson Davis Gets His Citizenship Back,* 1980

It may not be amiss to point out that conjunctive *so* can also introduce clauses other than clauses of purpose and result:

I shall write to Mary as soon as I have time, so I hope she won't be impatient —Henry Adams, letter, 18 Jan. 1859

Robert Lowell has said he will recommend me for the Guggenheim, so if it is not too late to add a name, I would appreciate. . . . —Flannery O'Connor, letter, 14 Nov. 1948

The American League East is a demanding division, I said, but with their pitching the O's could not lose many games in a row. . . . And so the season has started, and Baltimore, at this writing, is at four and twelve, and dead last —Roger Angell, *New Yorker,* 7 May 1984

. . . could get baskets full of horror stories about teaching. So who would they surprise? —Ken Donelson, *English Jour.,* November 1982

If you have outgrown the "*so*-habit," there does not seem to be much reason for you to fret over the choice between *so* and *so that.* We do not have the perspective yet to know whether *so* is moving up the scale of formality, or whether *so that* is becoming less formal and sliding down toward *so.* In either case, we see little difference between *so* and *so that* in level of formality at present.

so . . . as   See AS . . . AS 1.

so as to   Because the *so as* of *so as to* is omissible in some contexts ("We left early [so as] to beat the traffic"), it has sometimes been called redundant (as in Copperud 1970, 1980). On the other hand, Longman 1984 and Freeman 1983 suggest *so as to* as a possible replacement

for conjunctive *so.* Where the critics are at odds in this way, you must follow your ear. If a sentence sounds better to you without *so as,* omit it; if it sounds better with *so as,* keep it. And note that some contexts positively require *so as* or an equivalent like *in order:*

. . . he carefully slipped off his shoes before climbing atop a university police car so as not to damage campus property —Richard Stengel, *Time,* 15 Oct. 1984

so-called   Several commentators find fault with using quotation marks to enclose a term or terms following *so-called,* as in "you and your so-called 'friends.'" Their advice is to omit either the quotation marks or the *so-called:* "you and your so-called friends" or "you and your 'friends.'" Our evidence shows that in edited writing quotation marks are in fact more often than not omitted after *so-called:*

In so-called real life . . . —John Bainbridge, *Gourmet,* November 1982

The so-called gender gap . . . —Nancy J. Walker, *N.Y. Times Book Rev.,* 11 Mar. 1984

These so-called Watergate Babies . . . —Tip O'Neill with William Novak, *Man of the House,* 1987

But their use is not at all rare:

. . . the so-called "cold war liberals" . . . —Alden Whitman, *Saturday Rev.,* 18 Mar. 1978

. . . their so-called "news value" . . . —Orville Schell, *N.Y. Times Book Rev.,* 11 May 1983

. . . the so-called "Fifth Generation" of computers . . . —Paul Delany, *N.Y. Times Book Rev.,* 18 Mar. 1984

The use of quotation marks following *so-called* is not an error, but they are just as easily and sensibly omitted.

so don't I   The use of contracted *not* following *so* in a way that does not affect the positive meaning of the statement ("so don't I," "so aren't they") is a curious idiom that appears to be confined to the Northeast and is most frequently heard in New England. It is hard to find in print, being mostly used in speech, but here are a couple of examples:

This expression is akin to the old jocular negative in the following piece of dialogue:
"I wish I had an orange."
"So don't I."
Here again, the speaker means a strong "So do I." —Horace Reynolds, *N.Y. Times Book Rev.,* 28 Jan. 1962

We are victims and so aren't the consumers who will have to pay higher prices to recoup the losses of shoplifting —businessman quoted in *Springfield* (Mass.) *Morning Union,* 1 Feb. 1980

It is one of the curiosities of English that a negative can sometimes mean the same thing as a positive. For a synonymous pair of positive and negative phrases that have occasioned considerable comment, see COULD CARE LESS, COULDN'T CARE LESS.

so far as   See AS FAR AS, SO FAR AS.

solicitous It is possible to be solicitous *about, for,* or *of* something:

> . . . as if he were shy and solicitous about it, and wanted to protect it from us —Edmund Wilson, *Axel's Castle,* 1931

> Contracts . . . are the objects about which the constitution is solicitous —John Marshall, *Dartmouth College* v. *Woodward,* 1819

> . . . what naturalist with a microscope in his pocket, what scholar solicitous for the changing shapes of language —Virginia Woolf, *The Second Common Reader,* 1932

> . . . no one solicitous for the future of American culture —Jacques Barzun, *Saturday Rev.,* 9 Mar. 1940

> . . . if only Pamela would try to be a little less solicitous of my welfare —Roald Dahl, *Someone Like You,* 1953

> . . . parents solicitous of the moral welfare of their progeny —George Jean Nathan, *Encyclopaedia of the Theatre,* 1940

Much less commonly, *solicitous* is followed by *toward:*

> For its part, the All England made sincere attempts to be more solicitous toward its athletic minions — Frank Deford, *Sports Illustrated,* 12 July 1982

And it has had some use with *to* and the infinitive:

> . . . an opinion which he had seemed solicitous to give —Jane Austen, *Persuasion,* 1818

> . . . Middleton is solicitous to please his audience — T. S. Eliot, "Thomas Middleton," in *Selected Essays,* 1932

solon *Solon,* the name of a wise lawgiver of ancient Athens, has been used figuratively as an English word for many centuries, but it has never been remarkably common or widespread. Most of its figurative uses have had a strongly ironic quality, although the word has also been used in referring seriously to a wise statesman. Its greatest popularity has been among 20th-century American journalists, who have employed it as an occasional—and often sneering—synonym for *legislator:*

> The act that emerged from Congress was highly touted by the Solons, but honest Harry Truman denounced it for what it was, "a sham" —Harry Caudill, *N.Y. Rev. of Books,* 2 Dec. 1971

> . . . many of the solons still had . . . rotgut whiskey fueling their affection for education —Bill Hornby, *Sunday Denver Post,* 30 Sept. 1984

The word is now rarely capitalized.

Solon in its current use has been criticized as journalese by several commentators. Perhaps a better reason to avoid it is that fewer people nowadays are knowledgeable on the subject of wise Athenians, and the word *solon* itself is uncommon enough that many readers are apt to find it baffling.

so long as See AS LONG AS, SO LONG AS.

solution When used with a preposition, *solution* is usually followed by *of* or *to:*

> . . . the solution of the mystery of existence —Sherwood Anderson, *Poor White,* 1920

> . . . the intervention of government for the solution of problems that cannot be solved by private enterprise —*Current Biography,* July 1967

> . . . has tried to find a peaceful solution to the Cyprus crisis —*Current Biography,* September 1964

> . . . presumably his solution to the problem will carry some weight —J. D. O'Hara, *Saturday Rev.,* 20 May 1972

Occasionally *solution* is followed by *for:*

> . . . the population [was] too backward for political independence to be considered as a current solution for their problems —*Collier's Year Book,* 1949

some, *adjective* Like the adverb (see SOME, *adverb* 3), adjective *some* is used as an intensive, but its appearance usually draws no stronger reprobation from the commentators who notice it (for example, Shaw 1975, 1987, Little, Brown 1980) than the label colloquial or informal. It is, in fact, always found in casual surroundings and more often in speech than in writing of any kind. Here are a few examples:

> You'd be some kind of hitter if you took a wider stance —Willie Mays, quoted in *Sporting News,* 26 Mar. 1966

> MacLeish looks a little like Doctor Devol, and he is some smooth poet —E. B. White, letter, 31 Jan. 1942

> . . . that was some sustained drive —Arnold Dean, radio broadcast of football game, 21 Sept. 1974

> . . . it had taken her some doing to get it —Liz Smith, *Cosmopolitan,* February 1972

In the 19th century the intensive adjective was used as a predicate adjective (as in "He was some in a fight"), to judge from the examples in Thornton 1912. *Considerable* and other adjectives were used in the same way. We have no recent examples showing *some* in this construction.

some, *pronoun* The indefinite pronoun *some* is governed by notional agreement and may take either a singular or plural verb. *Some of* followed by a plural noun or pronoun takes a plural verb:

> . . . demonstrated that some of the new particles were slow to decay —*Current Biography,* February 1966

> And some of them are saying that . . . —Margaret Mead, *Barnard Alumnae,* Winter 1971

When a singular mass or collective noun follows *some of,* a singular verb is usual:

> Some of the biggest news in knits this year is being made at home —Nora O'Leary, *Ladies' Home Jour.,* August 1971

> Some of the office staff was there —E. L. Doctorow, *Ragtime,* 1975

When *some* stands by itself, the source of the notional agreement will be only in the writer's mind or in more distant context, but it will still prevail. This *some* usually takes a plural verb when it means "some people":

> It may be, as some argue, that . . . —Amos Elon, *New Yorker,* 29 July 1985

Some feel we are not treating other people in the world fairly —W. E. Brock, *AAUP Bulletin,* September 1969

The use of a singular verb with this sense, as in a recent newspaper headline which read "Should Meals Be Included in Education Budget? Some Thinks So," is distinctly odd-sounding. But when *some* stands for part of a mass, a singular verb is usual:

The text . . . is rather uneven. Much is summary and factual. . . . Some has undertones of . . . —*Times Literary Supp.,* 24 Nov. 1966

See also AGREEMENT, INDEFINITE PRONOUNS; NOTIONAL AGREEMENT, NOTIONAL CONCORD.

some, *adverb* **1.** When *some* is used to modify a number, it has the force of *about* and is almost always tacked onto a round number:

. . . would by now have collected some $500 billion from the tax —Felix G. Rohatyn, *The Twenty-Year Century,* 1983

. . . ordered the slaughter of some 20,000 of his brother's followers in Rome —Robert Payne, *Saturday Rev.,* 18 Mar. 1972

There has been occasional objection (Bernstein 1958, 1965, 1977, Copperud 1970, 1980) to *some* used with numbers that are not approximate. Such usage seems to take two forms. First, with dates: since years and centuries are equivalent more or less to round numbers, *some* usually retains its meaning of "about":

Some fifteen years ago, a gentleman representing an exclusive and expensive special-editions club came to the office —James Thurber, letter, August 1947

. . . a point in time some fourteen centuries before the earliest authentic example —*Times Literary Supp.,* 19 Feb. 1971

The second example also suggests the second use of *some* with numbers that are not approximate: as a mild intensifier, used as if to elicit "Wow! That many?" from the reader. Bernstein has a perfect example:

Some 35,683 attended the races at Aqueduct —Bernstein 1958, 1965

And here is one from our own files:

An expert parachutist, he has some 115 jumps to his credit —*Current Biography,* July 1965

Some is certainly omissible in such contexts, but it does provide an emphasis which would otherwise be lacking. It is also good to keep in mind that a unit that seems quite precise to you may not be so precise to someone accustomed to smaller units. It would be overfastidious, for instance, to object to *some*—meaning "about"—in a context like this one:

. . . had, collectively, improved the boat's upwind speed by some six seconds a mile in winds of 18 knots and up —Sarah Ballard, *Sports Illustrated,* 26 Jan. 1987

See also -ODD.

2. A favorite with usage writers for more than a century has been the subject of the use of *some* in the sense "somewhat." It can be found in such early works as Bache 1869, Ayres 1881, Compton 1898, Vizetelly 1906,

and Bierce 1909, and in recent books like Trimmer & McCrimmon 1988, Shaw 1987, Warriner 1986, and Little, Brown 1986. Evidence in the OED suggests that the usage has two sources. As the modifier of a comparative ("some better"), it seems to have belonged originally to Scots or northern English dialect. As the postpositive modifier of a verb ("has grown some"), it is apparently not dialectal. Both uses were imported to America from Great Britain, and the outbreak of comment in the later 19th century was apparently in reaction to popular 19th-century spoken American usage.

Commentary on this subject has varied little over the years. The repeated prescription has been to use *somewhat* in place of *some,* which was called dialectal and provincial in Vizetelly 1906 but has more recently been labeled informal, colloquial, or nonstandard. The basic prescription is, however, more than a little oversimplified. The only use in which *somewhat* is virtually certain to substitute smoothly is the one where *some* precedes a comparative:

She does feel some better, and is able to take short walks —E. B. White, letter, 14 Feb. 1963

Our most recent evidence includes very few examples of this construction in writing, in spite of its being mentioned in almost every usage book since Bache 1869.

And our recent evidence shows that *some* following the verb is the usual construction. When *some* is itself followed by *more,* you certainly would not want to use *somewhat* instead:

Here in Newport, both Southern Cross and Courageous practiced some more —William N. Wallace, *N.Y. Times,* 10 Sept. 1974

But in what is by far the most common construction in our evidence *some* stands alone after the verb. It can sometimes be replaced by *somewhat,* but it also occurs commonly in contexts where *somewhat* is not idiomatic:

But I've been brooding some about it —E. B. White, letter, 4 Feb. 1942

She wept some, and tried to retract —William Faulkner, "Centaur in Brass," in *The Collected Stories of William Faulkner,* 1950

I know him some, not well —*And More by Andy Rooney,* 1982

But even to get to be anemic looking, Hershiser had to fill out some —Bruce Newman, *Sports Illustrated,* 5 May 1986

To know that she is often compared to Maria Callas helps some —Joseph Mathewson, *Horizon,* May 1985

. . . was slowing down some, now that he'd reached middle age —Andrew H. Malcolm, *N.Y. Times Mag.,* 23 Mar. 1986

He also helped out some at Ben & Jerry's —Calvin Trillin, *New Yorker,* 8 July 1985

She may be oversimplifying some —Jay Cocks, *Time,* 19 Mar. 1984

The evidence shows, in short, that the adverbial *some,* in the senses "in some degree; to some extent; a little; somewhat," is a well-established American idiom. It is freely used in edited prose in the 1980s, although it seems not to be found in prose of the highest formality. You need not (and sometimes cannot) automatically replace it with *somewhat* when it is used in constructions like those illustrated above.

It is worth mention in passing that we have no current evidence for the downtoning *some* used in front of an adjective, as in the 1817 "His clothes were some bloody" recorded in Thornton 1912.

3. There is also an intensive adverbial *some,* best known, perhaps, in the combinations *going some* and *go some:*

> I still retain my pure English, even when I lose my temper, which is going some —Kenneth McGaffey, *The Sorrows of a Show Girl,* 1908 (in A Dictionary of Americanisms 1951)

> Well, her sister's about twict as good-lookin' as her, and that's going some —Ring Lardner, "Alibi Ike," in *How to Write Short Stories,* 1924

> ... will have to go some to surpass the April program —Robert J. Armbruster, *Johns Hopkins Mag.,* June 1970

This sense is attested as modifying a following adjective, too. Our most recent examples associate it with the state of Maine:

> I knew one thing: With that eye he looked some funny —Oscar Cronk, Jr. (identified as a Maine trapper), quoted in *Sports Illustrated,* 24 Jan. 1983

> "This place is some nice," I begin —A. G. Mojtabai, *Autumn* (novel set in Maine), 1982

> The salmon preparation ... was, in the argot of Maine and Long Island lobstermen, some good —Jay Jacobs, *Gourmet,* April 1985

Earlier it had use outside of Maine:

> Husky young fellow, nice voice, steady, clear eyes, kinda proud, I thought, an' some handsome —Zane Grey, *Desert Gold,* 1913

M. H. Scargill, in *A Short History of Canadian English* (1977), mentions *some hot* "really hot" as existing in Canadian English. Editors of the Dictionary of American Regional English tell us that this use is currently attested in Hawaii, Texas, and New Jersey, as well as Maine (and elsewhere in northern New England). It also exists in British dialect. It looks to us like a form that was once rather widespread but has survived in speech only in scattered places.

somebody, someone   **1.** *Somebody* and *someone* are two of those curious indefinite pronouns that take a singular verb but are often referred to by the plural pronouns *they, their,* and *them.* A number of commentators are on record as insisting on grounds of logical consistency that singular pronouns be used. The governing principle in the choice of pronouns is notional agreement, and when the speaker or writer has more than one person in mind, or a very indefinite somebody, the plural pronoun tends to be used:

> "Somebody told me they thought he killed a man once." —F. Scott Fitzgerald, *The Great Gatsby,* 1925

> "... Someone hated him so much that they don't want anything he possessed to remain." —Margery Allingham, *Death of a Ghost,* 1934

> You talk to someone like Dore Schary, and they say, 'Miss Cornell, wouldn't you be interested in making a picture?' —Katherine Cornell, quoted in *Time,* 20 Apr. 1953

> ... instantly, the minute somebody opens their mouth —Robert A. Hall, Jr., *Leave Your Language Alone,* 1950

> ... if he finds someone who needs help ... he should tell them where they can get it or offer to pass on their name —*Times Literary Supp.,* 4 Apr. 1968

> ... too nice a man to decline when someone says they want him to show up at one of their functions so they can honor him —*And More by Andy Rooney,* 1982

> Then someone suggested knocking off early and getting some beer and they even offered to chip in for a bottle of Chivas Regal for Manny —Joseph Wambaugh, *Lines and Shadows,* 1984

You will note that in some of these examples the choice of *they, their, them* contrasts usefully with another pronoun which is third person singular.

When a singular pronoun (usually masculine, occasionally feminine) is used to refer to *somebody* or *someone,* the speaker or writer often seems to have someone specific in mind (or in Alice's case, in sight):

> "I see somebody now!" she exclaimed at last. "But he's coming very slowly...." —Lewis Carroll, *Through the Looking-Glass,* 1871

> ... till somebody happened to note it as the only case he had met ... —Henry James, "The Turn of the Screw," 1898

> ... it was a bit risky to bring him home as eventualities might possibly ensue (somebody having a temper of her own sometimes) —James Joyce, *Ulysses,* 1922

But the singular pronoun is also used when the *someone* or *somebody* is not specific:

> If someone doesn't carry any money, the chances are he's loaded. I'm not sure about rich women, but I know rich men don't usually have a nickel with them —*And More by Andy Rooney,* 1982

See also AGREEMENT: INDEFINITE PRONOUNS; NOTIONAL AGREEMENT, NOTIONAL CONCORD; THEY, THEIR, THEM.

2. Copperud 1980 has a curious note to the effect that it is a superstition that *someone* is preferable to *somebody,* and a similar notion is mentioned in Shaw 1987. *Somebody* and *someone* are of the same age, according to the OED, and when the OED came out, *somebody* was much better attested. In the 20th century, however, *someone* has come on strong, and we seem to have slightly more evidence now for *someone* than for *somebody.* But both, of course, are equally standard; use whichever one you think sounds better in a given context.

somebody else's   See ELSE.

some . . . -odd   See -ODD.

someone   See SOMEBODY, SOMEONE.

someplace   *Someplace* is like *anyplace,* an adverb that has become standard in American English during the 20th century. A few commentators continue to call it an informal word and to discourage its written use in favor of *somewhere,* but our evidence shows that *someplace* has been common in general and even academic writing since at least the 1940s:

> They were going someplace together —Adria Locke Langley, *A Lion Is in the Streets,* 1945

> ... which we fear because someplace therein lurks a terror, the beast, which we cannot see —William Van O'Connor, *Sense and Sensibility in Modern Poetry,* 1948

> ... on the day of the happening they are supposed to chronicle he was someplace else —A. J. Liebling, *New Yorker,* 24 June 1950

> ... not so much a way to get someplace or a means to an end —Eugene Jennings, *Psychology Today,* July 1970

> Is it really better someplace else? —*And More by Andy Rooney,* 1982

See also ANYPLACE; EVERYPLACE; NOPLACE.

something The adverb *something,* synonymous with *somewhat,* is now something less of an adverb than it once was. In previous centuries, it was used in ways that made its adverbial nature unmistakable:

> There is one Bill ordered to be brought in of a something new nature —Andrew Marvell, letter, 1666 (OED)

> I shall be something relieved of a load of sorrow which oppressed me —Thomas Holcroft, *Tales of the Castle,* 1785 (OED)

> "Answer for thyself, Friar," said King Richard, something sternly —Sir Walter Scott, *Ivanhoe,* 1819

Now, however, it prefers to keep a low profile. The OED notes that it "chiefly survives in contexts which admit of the word being felt as a noun." Here are some examples of typical current use:

> ... have to pay nonresidence entrance fees, averaging something over $300 —Frank J. Taylor, *Saturday Evening Post,* 24 May 1958

> The argument goes something like this —Robert M. Gorrell, in *The College Teaching of English,* ed. John C. Gerber, 1965

> The critical response ... was something less than enthusiastic —*Current Biography,* May 1966

> Something more than two centuries later —Gorham Munson, *Southern Rev.,* April 1970

Another, stranger, use of the adverb *something* is as an intensive modifying an adjective such as *awful, fierce,* and *terrible,* when the adjective is being used adverbially. A confusing description, perhaps, but here is an example of what we are talking about:

> ... they cried and took on something terrible until I removed my wig —Bob Hope, *Saturday Evening Post,* 10 Apr. 1951

The main function of *something* in such a context seems to be to give adverbial force to the adjective, so that "something terrible" is really just another way of saying "terribly." This use of *something* is rare in writing.

sometime 1. The adverb is written as a single word: "He arrived sometime last night." A phrase combining the adjective *some* and the noun *time* is written as two words: "He needed some time to think"; "We haven't seen them for some time." The difference is easy to see in these examples, but it is not always so clear. Consider the sentence "He arrived some time ago." The difference between *sometime last night* and *some time ago* may not be instantly apparent, since both phrases have an adverbial function. In *some time ago,* however, *some* and *time* still function within the phrase itself as an adjective and a noun, like *five* and *minutes* in the phrase *five minutes ago.* An easy way to tell if *some* and *time* should be written as one word or two in most contexts is to insert *quite* before *some* and see if the passage still makes sense. If it does, *some* and *time* should be written separately: "We haven't seen them for quite some time"; "He arrived quite some time ago." If it does not (as in "He arrived quite sometime last night"), *sometime* is the correct choice.

2. The adjective *sometime* has two meanings, the older of which is "former":

> ... a sometime Communist ... refuses to say whether he is a Communist now —*National Rev.,* 30 June 1970

> ... a sometime English professor turned administrator —Bruce Dearing, *CEA Forum,* April 1971

In its newer sense, *sometime* is essentially equivalent to *occasional.* This sense was first attested in the 1930s. It appears to have originated in the southern U.S., but in recent decades it has worked its way into the mainstream of American English:

> The philosopher and sometime poet took seriously the commonplace that "man is a rational animal" — Richard A. Macksey, *Johns Hopkins Mag.,* Spring 1968

> ... was a sometime participant in the international activities of Dada after the First World War —Roger Shattuck, *N.Y. Rev. of Books,* 12 Mar. 1970

> ... I am an inveterate browser and a sometime buyer of small objects —Claire Berman, *New York,* 1 Nov. 1971

> It is for this sometime shrillness of tone that one criticizes Mr. Brackman —Edmund Fuller, *Wall Street Jour.,* 8 Sept. 1980

> The City Fathers of Beverly Hills, in their sometime wisdom, recently banned sightseeing buses —Oscar Millard, *N.Y. Times,* 19 Feb. 1984

> ... was the confidant, adviser and sometime agent of Presidents from Franklin D. Roosevelt to Lyndon B. Johnson —William V. Shannon, *N.Y. Times Book Rev.,* 28 Oct. 1984

It often occurs in the phrase *a sometime thing,* where its meaning may tend toward "unreliable" or "transient":

> But a counter culture is a sometime thing —Todd Gitlin, *Psychology Today,* January 1970

> ... communication between Wellman workers and the union was truly a sometime thing —Irving Kahan, *Harper's,* February 1971

> ... feel that the health care in pro football is a sometime thing —William Barry Furlong, *N.Y. Times Mag.,* 30 Nov. 1980

It turned out in later years that Mr. Frank's liberalism was no sometime thing —Suzanne Garment, *Wall Street Jour.,* 27 Feb. 1981

This newer sense of *sometime* has only recently begun to show up in dictionaries. Although there is—or should be—no question about its being standard English, you still stand a small chance of being criticized if you use it. Most usage handbooks make no mention of it, but a majority of the Heritage 1982 panel finds it unacceptable.

someway, someways   The adverb *someway,* synonymous with *somehow,* is recognized by dictionaries as standard in American English, but its standing among usage commentators is less certain. Evans 1957 called it standard, but a significant majority (85 percent) of the Heritage 1969 panel found it unacceptable in writing that was not "deliberately informal." What our evidence shows is that *someway* occurs at all levels of writing, but is not especially common at any of them. It sometimes shows up in representations of dialectal speech:

"Well! P'raps it's best to have it over with, Lime, but someway I feel kind o' scary about it." —Hamlin Garland, *Prairie Folks,* rev. ed., 1899

I hate the hawks eatin' the quail, but I don't someway mind the 'coons eatin' the grapes —Marjorie Kinnan Rawlings, *The Yearling,* 1938 (OED Supplement)

But it also appears in much more formal contexts:

Some way her books, which gave out that same energy and delight, passed away when her body perished —*Autobiography of William Allen White,* 1946

Someway, somehow, we must let the peoples of the world know that. We must reach behind the façade of ministers and cabinets and commissions —William O. Douglas, *Being an American,* 1948

The variant *someways* is rare. Its use in writing is limited to representations of speech:

"Oh, it's a good morning. I someways like a day just like this. . . ." —Elizabeth Madox Roberts, *My Heart and My Flesh,* 1927

somewhat   See SOME, *adverb* 2.

somewheres   *Somewheres* is, like *anywheres* and *nowheres,* a dialectal Americanism that is not used in standard writing. Its written use is limited almost entirely to dialogue:

"I reckon . . . it's somewheres along the end of March. . . ." —Zane Grey, *Desert Gold,* 1913

A police man come and said, . . . you all git on somewheres else so I won't have to run you in —Robert Penn Warren, in *New Directions,* 1947

"Oughta be a lamp somewheres around the place. . . ." —Burt Arthur, *The Buckaroo,* 1947

See also ANYWHERES; NOWHERES.

sooner   See NO SOONER.

sort, sort of, sort of a   See KIND 1; KIND OF, SORT OF; KIND OF A, SORT OF A.

so that   See SO, *conjunction.*

sound out   This phrasal verb is commonly used to mean "to seek the views or intentions of":

When they sounded out their parents on the matter —R. Gilbert Culter, Jr., *NEA Jour.,* December 1964

Selznick asked Kay Brown to sound out Tallulah Bankhead . . . on whether she would play Belle Watling, the Atlanta madam —Gavin Lambert, *Atlantic,* February 1973

. . . should tour the Middle East . . . to sound out the region's leaders —Stanley Karnow, *N.Y. Times Mag.,* 15 Jan. 1978

Several commentators, beginning with Partridge 1942, have criticized the *out* as unnecessary, noting that *sound* by itself conveys the same meaning.

He sounded Butler on this subject, asking what he would think of an English living —Sir Walter Scott, *The Heart of Midlothian,* 1818 (OED)

However, our evidence shows that *sound out* is now the prevalent idiom, and its acceptability is not subject to serious question.

sparing   *Sparing* is generally followed by *in* or *of* when it is complemented by a prepositional phrase:

The English, for instance, are sparing in their use of it —David Abercrombie, *English Language Teaching,* October–December 1954

. . . again the music critics were sparing in their praise —*Current Biography,* February 1966

He was lavish of encouragement, sparing of negation —Samuel Hopkins Adams, *Incredible Era,* 1939

Miss Foley's foreword . . . is notably sparing of generalizations —Milton Crane, *Saturday Rev.,* 5 Sept. 1953

Occasionally, *sparing* is found with *with:*

Unfortunately, however, Ellison is too sparing with this gift of characterization —*American Mercury,* June 1952

spate   The literal meaning of *spate* is "flood," a sense of the word that now persists chiefly in British English, especially in the phrase *in spate:*

. . . swept through our village like a river in spate —Alison Bruce, *Over 21* (London), September 1974

Americans are primarily familiar with the word in its common figurative senses, most of which can be broadly defined together as "a notably large number or amount appearing or occurring suddenly or within a brief time":

. . . a spate of technical studies in the early 60s —Ivar Berg, *Change,* September 1971

. . . the spate of periodicals released in the last two or three years —Berry Gargal Richards, *Library Jour.,* 15 Dec. 1975

The current spate of books on language usage —Anatole Broyard, *N.Y. Times Book Rev.,* 22 Mar. 1981

This figurative *spate* is not a perfect reflection of the literal *spate*. To speak of a "spate of periodicals" is not the same as to speak of a flood or torrent of periodicals. *Flood* and *torrent* in their figurative uses suggest an overwhelming quantity; *spate* is appreciably less forceful. Several usage commentators have argued that since *spate* means "flood" literally it should also mean "flood" figuratively. According to our evidence, however, it almost never does.

spay, spayed, spade, spaded *Spay* is a transitive verb meaning "to remove the ovaries of (a female animal)." Its most familiar use is in the form of the past participle, *spayed:*

> ... their jittery spayed terrier —John Updike, *Couples,* 1968

> ... found in spayed females —Susan L. Mathews, *Cats Mag.,* September 1984

A synonymous verb is *spade,* which was first recorded in 1611, and which undoubtedly originated from a misunderstanding of *spayed.* The OED labels *spade* obsolete as a synonym of *spay,* but we find that its use is now fairly common (quite possibly, its modern use represents a recoinage—or re-misunderstanding—rather than a continued use of the old verb). It is, however, restricted almost entirely to speech. Our only modern written evidence is from classified advertisements:

> LOST German shepard [sic] spaded dog —classified advt., *Springfield* (Mass.) *Union,* 30 June 1953

Spade also sometimes appears as a misspelling of *spayed:*

> OLD ENGLISH Sheep Dog, spade —classified advt., *Denver Post,* 20 Sept. 1984

special, specially, especial, especially These words are etymologically the same, so they might be expected to be synonymous. That they are essentially synonymous is at least historically true, but in present-day English they are not synonymous very often. When they are, it is usually *special* and *specially* that are used like *especial* and *especially* rather than the other way around.

Special is the older and more widely used of the adjectives. It has all the fixed phrases, like *special delivery, special effects,* and *special interest,* and all the euphemistic uses, like *special needs, special education,* and *special children. Especial,* as the less usual word, is therefore somewhat more emphatic:

> ... dissected in minute detail but with especial glee —Tony Palmer, *Observer Mag.,* 16 Dec. 1973

> *For the Union Dead* carried on the styles of *Life Studies,* with especial success in the title poem — Donald Hall, *Goatfoot Milktongue Twinbird,* 1978

Special would not work as well in either of those contexts. But a present-day writer would most likely use *special* for Jane Austen's *especial* here:

> ... I must wait till there is an especial assembly for the representation of younger sons —*Mansfield Park,* 1814

The adverbs, however, are much different. While *especially* is apparently much the more common word in general, *specially* has typical uses that *especially* lacks:

> ... treats his friends very specially —Samuel G. Freedman, *N.Y. Times Mag.,* 21 Apr. 1985

> The plants have been specially selected to associate well —Roy Hay, *The Times* (London), 17 Nov. 1973

> The breeder who has a range of specially constructed kennels —Roy Genders, *Greyhounds,* 1960

Especially would not be used in any of those contexts. It typically is found in constructions like the following:

> ... even thereafter the older use survived, especially in fixed phrases like 'I know not' —W. F. Bolton, *A Short History of Literary English,* 1967

> It is an especially British condition, I think —Jan Morris, *N.Y. Times Mag.,* 2 Feb. 1975

> ... seems to have been built especially for developmental research —Gary Blonston, *Science 84,* March 1984

Specially is sometimes used in the same constructions. It has a somewhat more informal quality:

> ... the history of the American South, specially that of the state of Virginia —Douglas Tallack, *British Book News,* April 1984

> ... euphemism, which is an effort to make something sound specially nice —Robert M. Adams, *N.Y. Times Book Rev.,* 31 Mar. 1985

> An appropriate bread is baked specially for the dinner —Caroline Bates, *Gourmet,* October 1981

Specially seems to be a stronger competitor of *especially* in the construction of the third example—modifying a preceding verb—than in those of the first two. It is much less likely to be used in constructions like these:

> Especially did she disagree with the observation that social stability is not a precondition for the writing of a novel —Norman Cousins, *Saturday Rev.,* 24 June 1978

> ... there was nothing especially radical in the notion —Stanley Karnow, *N.Y. Times Mag.,* 15 Jan. 1978

species, specie The word *species* has the same form both in the singular and the plural:

> ... it ranks as a new species —Norman Myers, *Natural History,* February 1985

> There are about thirty thousand species of spiders throughout the world —Katherine W. Moseley, *Massachusetts Audubon,* June 1971

That final *s* looks like a plural ending, however, and it fools some people into thinking that the singular form must be *specie.* This is scarcely a modern corruption, as the OED's first record of *specie* as the singular of *species* is from 1711. In total, the OED includes half a dozen citations for the singular *specie* from the 18th and 19th centuries. Our own files provide a number of 20th-century examples, including the following:

> Though one specie, called by us the red phalarope — I. W. Russell, *N.Y. Times Book Rev.,* 19 Apr. 1953

> ... some new specie appears that is difficult to classify —John P. Marquand, *New England Journeys,* 1953

> In this race specie is paired in mind-contact with alien specie —Barbara A. Bannon, *Publishers Weekly,* 11 Apr. 1980

The evidence we have accumulated in recent decades gives some indication that this use of *specie* is becoming more common, but it is not yet sufficiently widespread to be considered standard, and perhaps it never will be. The standard use of *specie* in current English is as a noun meaning "money in coin":

> With a limited amount of specie in the country, . . . the American monetary system was uniquely ill-qualified to cope with financial "panics" —Martin Mayer, *The Bankers,* 1974

> . . . where money was necessary and specie scarce —Arthur M. Schlesinger, Jr., *The Age of Jackson,* 1945

> United States silver purchases drained out much specie from China —David Nelson Rowe, *Modern China,* 1959

spell Not long ago one of our correspondents asking for information used these words in her letter:

> . . . how words with variant spellings will be spelt in our publication.

This gave us some recent evidence that *spelt,* which is much more common in British English, is still occasionally used in American English. Here are two British examples:

> . . . culture is spelt with a small "c" —Michael Watkins, *The Guardian,* 27 Oct. 1973

> Misspelt names bring newspapers into disrepute. They should be spelt out, spelt back, and re-checked —Sellers 1975

Americans generally use *spelled:*

> These jolly buccaneers knew that rum spelled "gold" —Marilyn Kaytor, *American Way,* December 1971

> The ability to convert a field goal spelled the difference —*Sporting News,* 27 Dec. 1972

> For the next seven hours, several planes spelled each other —Michael McRae, *Outside,* December 1985

Longman 1988 notes that British writers also prefer *spelled* for the sense "to relieve for a time."

spelling Ernest Hemingway, in a letter to F. Scott Fitzgerald, made this remark in his first paragraph:

> You write a swell letter. Glad somebody spells worse than I do —24 Dec. 1925

Fitzgerald was notorious for his bad spelling, although one of his editors says in his defense that his spelling seemed worse than it really was because he consistently misspelled certain words. Hemingway, on the other hand, was an inconsistent misspeller; he could spell a word both right and wrong in the same letter.

It does not seem the least bit strange to talk about someone's misspelling words. We do it all the time, and quite a few usage commentators have been fond of belittling their correspondents (the ones who disagree with them) and others on the basis of bad spelling. But bad spelling is a flimsy basis for belittling anyone; you can see that the literary reputations of Fitzgerald and Hemingway have not suffered noticeably by their personal difficulties with English orthography. Nor is it easy to think of any writer who made a considerable reputation on the basis of slick spelling alone.

Wilson 1987 makes the interesting observation that "spelling is mostly a neuromuscular skill in the development of which practice helps, but for which certain innate equipment is the main requirement." In this respect it is rather like swinging a golf club, hitting a tennis ball, or playing the guitar. You know you can improve by practice, but somehow you suspect that Nancy Lopez will putt better, Ivan Lendl will serve better, and Andres Segovia will play better than you, no matter how much practicing you do. Aptitude for spelling is no more evenly distributed in the population than is aptitude for golf, tennis, or guitar. We all have to make the best of the ability we have. Those whose innate ability to spell is not especially high can take heart by remembering that there are various devices—dictionaries, spelling books, and latterly computer chips, for instance—that can be far more useful to a bad speller than a new putter is to a bad golfer.

The idea of bad spelling is a relatively new one. If Ben Jonson had corresponded familiarly with William Shakespeare, he would not have made the sort of wisecrack that Hemingway made to Fitzgerald. In Shakespeare's time there were no rules for spelling English, a situation which troubled some reformers. Thomas Smith, John Hart, and William Bullokar, from about the mid-1560s to the 1580s, separately published works advocating phonetic spelling systems. The advocacy of such systems probably represented some reaction to the Latin-based tinkering with English spelling that was going on at about the same time, in which a number of words were remodeled according to their real or supposed ultimate classical source. Many of these tinkerings have come down to us. For instance, *avance* became *advance; faucon, falcon; parfit, perfect; dette, debt; doutte, doubt; vittles, victuals;* and *savacion, salvation* (these particular examples are drawn from McKnight 1928 and Strang 1970). Some of these tinkerings were downright erroneous: the *s* in *island,* for one, has no business being there; the word is not related to *isle* (from early French) but comes from Old English *igland* or *iegland.* The *c* in *scissors* and *scythe* is a similar intruder. But we live with them all today.

The conventional spelling of today was arrived at only gradually. The two primary influences in its development were printers and dictionaries. Printers began the trend toward consistency, if not regularization, in the 17th century—earlier printers had been anything but an influence in that direction because they often varied the spelling of words to justify (that is, to space evenly) their lines. The invention of more varied spacing material later made that dodge unnecessary. There followed a trend toward normalization, to some extent based on the spellings used in the King James Bible. When large dictionaries became available in the 18th century, printers had another authority to follow, and the trend toward uniformity increased.

Greater uniformity of spelling meant that the number of acceptable variant spellings was greatly reduced. But more survive in dictionaries than many people realize. Their recognition is not as consistent as you might expect, but lexicographers have no simple objective test by which to judge the acceptability of a variant spelling. Almost any reasonable spelling will be found to have some historical precedent, given the history of our present-day spelling; what is given dictionary recognition, therefore, is often a matter of precedent in earlier editions and individual decisions made by editors. Extraneous factors—such as the number of pages available for a given edition—may also complicate editorial decisions. So some inconsistency is to be expected. Let us look at a few specific cases.

How about *vocal chords?* Do you consider that a misspelling? The original spelling of the second part was *cord.* But *cord* has Latin and Greek forebears, and sometime in the past one of those etymological tinkerers stuck an *h* into it to show the connection with Latin and Greek. The spelling *chord* thus became the scholarly spelling. It was used in mathematics and music—and still is. It was also used in medicine for anatomical structures: hence *spinal chord, vocal chord.* In American English the old *cord* is now used anatomically, but there is still some lingering use of *chord* in British technical publications, and quite a lot in popular American writing. Is it incorrect?

When *confident* came into English from French, it had but one spelling as both a noun and an adjective. In the 18th century the variant spellings *confidant* and *confidante* for the noun were invented. They proved to be useful, for they distinguished the parts of speech. Today the handbooks tell us that the original and etymologically correct *confident* is an error for the noun.

Momento is an unetymological spelling of *memento,* probably influenced by English *moment.* The first dictionary to recognize it as a variant was Webster's Third in 1961. Its inclusion there was an individual editorial decision, but subsequent events seem to have justified the decision: the OED Supplement has now recognized the spelling, citing George Eliot and Dylan Thomas in support. Our archives have recently yielded an early example in an 1853 letter written by Chauncey A. Goodrich, the first editor in chief of Merriam-Webster dictionaries.

Of course recognition of a variant spelling like *momento* by any number of dictionaries does not force you to use it. But stop and think a moment. If you reject *momento* as a misspelling, on what grounds do you base your objection? Certainly it is unetymological, but so is *confidante,* so is *island,* so is *scissors.* A better basis for deciding whether to use or reject a variant spelling is prevalent current use; most people spell it *memento.*

Our present-day spelling, then, is a mishmash of archaism, reform, error, and accident, and it is unsurprising that not everyone who is heir to the tradition can handle it perfectly. Even so, with all the aids available to the poor speller, including electronic spelling-checkers, you might think there would be very few misspellings found in print.

But the opposite is true, to judge from ordinary observation and from published comment. There seem to be several factors bearing on this. First, there seems to be a noticeably smaller population of proofreaders and copy editors in the publishing business than there once was. Taking the place of proofreaders in some cases is the electronic device for checking spelling. Most such devices are very good at finding mechanical errors: if you intend "sly as a fox" but instead keyboard in "sgy as a ofx," the machine will catch the errors. But if you enter "shy as a fox" or "sly as a box," the chances are the machine will not find anything wrong, for both *shy* and *box* are real words. It has been conjectured, perhaps without basis, that overreliance on such machines may account for the frequency with which garbled homophones—*they're* for *their, reign* for *rein, tow* for *toe, diffuse* for *defuse, sight* for *site,* and so forth—can be found in print, not infrequently in rather tony publications.

An additional consideration has been suggested by Robert Burchfield, editor of the OED Supplement. In an interview published in the *Boston Sunday Globe* (12 May 1985), he observed that in our age of electronic communication numbers are more important than words. On a flight plan or airline reservation, if the dates

and numbers are correct, a misspelled word or two does not matter. Burchfield suggests that we may be going back to a time, like that of Shakespeare, when spelling was not a matter of prime importance. If he is right, you will be finding even more funny spellings in your newspapers, magazines, and books. We hope you do not find too many in this book (although "shy as a fox" almost got in).

Many of the words that commentators feel to be frequently misspelled are separate entries in this book. See also SPELLING REFORM.

spelling reform The inadequacies of English spelling were apparent to some observers as early as the middle of the 16th century—long before our present traditional but inconsistent system was established. Three such observers were Thomas Smith, John Hart, and William Bullokar. Each of them was interested in phonetics and was aware that there were more sounds in English than there were letters in the alphabet—then counted as 24 letters, with *i* and *j* and *u* and *v* being used as variant forms rather than as one distinct vowel and one distinct consonant. And each of them devised an extended alphabet to remedy the problem, at least one of which, Hart's, was made into printing type, with books being printed from it. All of the new alphabets were failures, but one radical suggestion from both Smith and Hart—that *i* and *u* be used exclusively as vowels and *j* and *v* as consonants—did bear fruit after a couple of centuries.

The hope of these early reformers was to institute a more phonetic system of spelling. (Bullokar was a teacher, and he may have been the first to go on record with the complaint that it was hard to teach children to read with the current method of spelling. The same complaint resulted in the Initial Teaching Alphabet of the mid-20th century). The hope of almost every subsequent spelling reformer has been the same: to bring the spelling of English more in line with its pronunciation.

Opposing the reformers have been those who have felt that a strictly phonetic system would obscure the etymological background of words. Jonathan Swift, for one, in 1712 criticized the "foolish Opinion . . . that we ought to spell exactly as we speak." The conflict of opposing sets of reformers and etymology preservers in the end produced almost no change of a theoretical sort in English spelling.

Probably the most successful spelling reformer was Noah Webster. His reading books, spellers, and dictionaries from about 1787 through 1828 succeeded in instituting most of the major systematic differences between American and British spelling. That we spell *honor, music,* and *theater* the way we do is largely his achievement. Webster was not initially a spelling reformer; he had written in 1783 disapproving of several proposals for reformed spelling—the subject was much in the air after the end of the Revolutionary War—and objecting in particular to dropping the *u* in *honour.* But in 1786 he met Benjamin Franklin, an ardent spelling reformer (Franklin, too, devised an improved alphabet). Franklin seems to have won Webster over to the side of reform, for by 1787 Webster was directing his printer to use the spellings *honor, music,* and *theater,* then usually spelled *honour, musick,* and *theatre.*

The reformed Webster was an adherent of phonetic spelling, although his system was not as radical as several proposed by such contemporaries as Franklin, because he more or less restricted himself to the regular alphabet. It is interesting to note that where he can be said to have been successful—as in the three words above—the spellings he promoted were not outright inventions, but alternative forms that had been in occasional use all along (*honor,* for instance, is used in Thomas Heywood's *A Woman Killed with Kindness,* published in 1607). His more phonetic innovations, such as *iz* (for *is*), *improovment, yeer, ritten,* and *reezon,* did not catch on at all. Although Webster put what we might call his simplified spellings—*honor, music, ax, plow*—in his dictionaries, he forebore from including his phonetic inventions. This was probably no more than a matter of good business, as there was considerable controversy about the reformed spellings.

Although phonetic systems and new alphabets—some of them very elaborate—continued to be proposed during the 19th century (and are still being proposed today), the next high tide of spelling reform concerned itself less with the implementation of a whole system of spelling than with the simplification, chiefly through the omission of silent letters, of the spelling of particular words. This movement, which was better organized and better financed than previous ones, began in the 1880s and lasted into the first decades of the 20th century. It involved leading scholars, writers, journalists, lexicographers, and politicians on both sides of the Atlantic, and several professional organizations as well. Around the turn of the century the participants in this crusade had high hopes of success; books were written predicting adoption of the lists of simplified spellings, and some newspapers and some of the writers associated with the movement actually began using the new forms. President Theodore Roosevelt was convinced of the rightness of the movement, and in 1906 he issued an executive order directing the Government Printing Office to use a list of 300 simplified spellings suggested by the Simplified Spelling Board. But the GPO resisted, and eventually the order was withdrawn.

In spite of the involvement and approval of many prominent figures (including Mark Twain), the simplified spelling movement eventually petered out, leaving behind only a handful of accepted forms—*catalog, analog, tho, thru*—which have had varying degrees of success. The *Chicago Tribune* adopted many simplified spellings and stuck with them longer than anyone else, but finally threw in the towel in 1975.

So four hundred years and more of proposals for spelling reform have left a few tracks in our spelling, but have had no systematic effect at all. You can see two obvious reasons for the failure. First, if a phonetic spelling scheme were adopted, we would be further from a consistent spelling than we are now, for the language is not pronounced consistently. The more accurate the phonetic system, the more varied would be the resulting spellings. Our present system has at least the virtue of having one traditional spelling that can serve as the visual equivalent of any number of variant pronunciations. The second reason is the considerable investment in time and effort every literate user of English has made in learning the present system. Few of us would be willing to throw that away and learn a new system, no matter how efficient it was.

spell out This phrasal verb has been commonly used since the 1940s in the sense "to make plain." Its newness and its popularity have occasionally attracted some relatively mild criticism:

Only the man possessed of "savvy" and "know-how" "spells out" when he explains, "briefs" when he supplies facts and "pinpoints" when he determines something exactly —Thomas Pyles, *N.Y. Times Mag.,* 15 June 1958

Bernstein 1958, 1965 considered *spell out* to be overused, and he also found it to be redundant in such constructions as "spell out the details." Complaints about overuse are no longer heard, but the charge of redundancy has been repeated in Heritage 1969 and Harper 1975, 1985. The assumption is that *spell out* by itself strongly implies an explanation or enumeration of details. Our evidence shows, however, that it is usually far less suggestive of details than of clear presentation. To "spell out the details" or "spell out in detail" is simply to explain the details in a clear and unmistakable way.

... elsewhere in these five amendments this principle is spelled out in detail —Dwight Macdonald, *New Yorker,* 11 July 1953

... never spelled out their legal theories in any detail —Jon M. Van Dyke, *Center Mag.,* July/August 1971

... the contract should spell out full details of the loan —Sylvia Porter, *Ladies' Home Jour.,* August 1971

spill In American English the usual past tense and past participle of *spill* is *spilled:*

Gasoline lines spilled onto freeways —*N.Y. Times,* 12 May 1979

... could sop up 1,000 barrels of spilled oil —*Dun's,* October 1971

The variant *spilt* is common in British English, especially as the past participle:

... too much blood has been spilt —*Times Literary Supp.,* 28 May 1971

Far more American blood has been spilt in Asia — Alistair Buchan, *The Listener,* 13 Dec. 1973

When the past participle is used as an attributive adjective (as in the proverb, "There's no use crying over spilt milk"), *spilt* also occurs occasionally in American English:

... began wondering where all the spilt oil went — Warren R. Young, *Smithsonian,* November 1970

spiral The verb *spiral* can describe either upward or downward movement:

Costs are spiraling (at about double the rate of the rise in general cost of living . . .) —*Carnegie Quarterly,* Summer 1970

A leaf spiraled to the ground —Michelle Willette, *Cat Fancy,* May–June 1973

The figurative use of *spiral* in the sense "to rise steadily" has attracted occasional criticism from those who feel that the word more properly connotes a downward path or that it at least requires an accompanying adverb, such as *up* or *upward,* to make its meaning clear. But such criticism is not widespread. Our evidence shows that the "upward" connotations of *spiral* are now well enough established, especially when the subject is money, that an accompanying adverb, while certainly possible, is not usually necessary:

... in a year of spiralling commodity inflation —*The Economist,* 1 Feb. 1975

... to bring their spiraling costs in line —*Wall Street Jour.,* 8 Nov. 1983

... was sensibly designed to check spiraling salaries —Jerry Kirshenbaum, *Sports Illustrated,* 21 Nov. 1983

spit The common verb *spit* has as its past tense and past participle either *spat* or *spit.* The British prefer *spat,* but both forms are widespread in American English:

I spit the beer out, and with it came a long, thin brown roach —Dennis Smith, *Report from Engine Co. 82,* 1972

... the Jamaican mountains that were spit from the sea —Caleb Pirtle III, *Southern Living,* November 1971

A computer spat out this list in June —*Fortune,* 7 Sept. 1981

... I'd have thought she'd inwardly cursed or spat —Kenneth Roberts, *Oliver Wiswell,* 1940

Nonstandard variants are *spitted* and *spitten:*

... like someone had spitten tobacco into it —Dave Godfrey, in *Canadian Short Stories, Second Series,* ed. Robert Weaver, 1968

In the helicopter one of [them] spitted in this lieutenant's face —Richard J. Ford III, quoted in Wallace Terry, *Bloods,* 1984

The unrelated verb *spit* meaning "to skewer or impale on a spit" consistently becomes *spitted* in the past tense and past participle:

Juma cooked the birds spitted on a stick —Ernest Hemingway, "An African Betrayal," in *Sports Illustrated,* 5 May 1986

The lamb ... is spitted off to the side of the fire and turned regularly —Ann Ingerson, *New England Farmer,* April 1984

spitting image The original phrase was *spit and image,* derived from the use of *spit* to mean "the exact likeness." This sense of *spit,* first recorded in 1825, still occurs in British English:

... was eight months old, bonny and amiable, the dead spit of his father —Mollie Chappell, *Annabel,* May 1974

The phrase *spit and image* dates from the late 19th century. *Spitting image* was first recorded in 1901. (Other variants, now rare, are *spitten image* and *splitting image.*) *Spitting image* was once commonly cited as an error, in dictionaries and elsewhere, but, as Copperud 1970, 1980 notes, it has now established itself as the usual form:

... the spitting image of her mom —Nancy Anderson, *US,* 28 Mar. 1983

I could swear it's the spitting image of the house I saw —David M. Schwartz, *Smithsonian,* November 1985

Spit and image may continue in occasional use, but our evidence suggests that it is extremely rare. Our most recent evidence for it is from a British writer:

Bert was the spit-and-image of his father —Alan Sillitoe, *Saturday Night and Sunday Morning,* 1958

split infinitive *Split infinitive* is the name given to a syntactical construction in which an adverbial modifier comes between *to* and the infinitive itself. The term is first attested in 1897, when the construction had already been under discussion for about half a century. It is quite possible that the enduring popularity of the split infinitive as a subject is due to its catchy name. Even Ambrose Bierce thought so:

Condemnation of the split infinitive is now pretty general, but it is only recently that any one seems to have thought of it. Our forefathers and we elder writers of this generation used it freely and without shame—perhaps because it had not a name, and our crime could not be pointed out without too much explanation —Bierce 1909

But the term is actually a misnomer, as *to* is only an appurtenance of the infinitive, which is the uninflected form of the verb. In many constructions the infinitive is used alone or with some other word such as *and* preceding it. Native speakers do not really split infinitives, unless it is in the slangy construction in which an expletive is infixed between the syllables of a word, as in "He said to re(expletive)invent the wheel if we have to."

The traditional split infinitive is most fully treated in Curme 1931. Curme summarizes earlier investigations of the construction, such as an article by Fitzedward Hall in *The American Journal of Philology* in 1893 and a long discussion in Lounsbury 1908. Fitzedward Hall dated the construction back to the 14th century in *Sir Gawain and the Green Knight* and provided examples from each succeeding century. Lounsbury added more, and J. L. Hall 1917 still more. Curme reprints many of these along with a number from his own collection of 20th-century examples. It might not be amiss to add here further and more recent 20th-century evidence.

In a quarter of an hour the movement began to noticeably slacken —James Stephens, *The Crock of Gold,* 1912

But I would come back to where it pleased me to live; to really live —Ernest Hemingway, *Green Hills of Africa,* 1935

... feels itself competent to fruitfully reformulate the basic problems of man —Paul Radin, *Kenyon Rev.,* Summer 1949

... floor-sweepers were too easily replaced to ever form into such a craft union —Howard Fast, in *The Aspirin Age 1919–1941,* ed. Isabel Leighton, 1949

And then when the time came to really bury the silver, it was too late —*The Collected Stories of William Faulkner,* 1950

... I got a brief note from [Harold] Ross splitting an infinitive as follows: "Tell Sayre to damn well and soon return those proofs." —James Thurber, letter, 13 Dec. 1950

Our moral incapacity to satisfactorily cope with the complex problems —E. M. Adams, *Jour. of Philosophy,* 13 Sept. 1951

But the primary objective of the sisters was to somehow propel their sons into the Presbyterian ministry —St. Clair McKelway, *New Yorker,* 18 May 1957

Further to complicate matters and to cautiously avoid splitting an infinitive ... —John O'Hara, letter, 7 June 1958

But how to actually move children or adolescents toward this goal —Barnard 1979

. . . the government's ability to meet its promises to simultaneously cut taxes, increase defense spending and balance the budget —Kenneth H. Bacon, *Wall Street Jour.*, 5 Feb. 1981

Many of the out-of-towners who came for the event apparently felt that there was no time like the present to really dress —John Duka, *N.Y. Times,* 27 Sept. 1983

Yet here it works, serving to metaphorically foreshadow Edgar's eventual deliverance —Tom Dowling, *San Francisco Examiner,* 19 Nov. 1985

We will not attempt to summarize all of Curme's discussion here, but one important point—often mentioned as well by other commentators—can be conveniently shown by illustration:

. . . the authorities would be required correctly to anticipate their requirements for at least ten days ahead —W. Manning Dacey, *The British Banking Mechanism,* 1951

In the sequence "required correctly to anticipate" the adverb *correctly* can be construed as modifying either *required* or *to anticipate.* In spoken English there would be no ambiguity, and if the author had certainly intended *correctly* to mean "as they should be" he could have made that clear by setting the adverb off with commas. But as it appears on the printed page, there is just a slight opportunity for doubt. The sequence "required to correctly anticipate" would remove that doubt, without changing the intended meaning of the sentence. The adverb can also be placed after *anticipate,* but doing this would have the effect of emphasizing the adverb rather than the verb. Had the author intended *correctly* to be the focus, he probably would have written "required to anticipate their requirements correctly." Some commentators have advised routinely repairing split infinitives by placing the adverb after the infinitive, but note that this has the effect of altering the emphasis of the sentence.

There has always been a question about how frequently the split infinitive construction occurs. Hall 1917 found it used by many authors but only occasionally. He found the construction common only in Browning. Curme, however, says flatly that the construction is common—he seems to have collected more evidence than anyone else—and shows it to be frequent in Mark Twain, Thomas Hardy, and Rudyard Kipling as well as Browning.

The one thing we know for certain about the frequency of the split infinitive is that it noticeably increased in the 19th century. Although Lounsbury said he had seen the construction mentioned in a few late 18th-century reviews, he gave no particulars, and no one else has found a mention of the construction before 1840 or 1850. The first of our commentators to mention it is Alford 1866, who was shocked to discover that such a construction existed. It was subsequently condemned by several of his contemporaries, including Bache 1869 and Hodgson 1889.

Sometime between Alford's book and the end of the century, the split infinitive seems to have established itself in that subculture of usage existing in the popular press and in folk belief. Almost every commentator from the turn of the century on, in the course of giving a more measured opinion, has said that the split infinitive is roundly condemned by grammarians, or, sometimes, by purists. Its firm establishment in the popular mind was illustrated by Lounsbury from a biography written by Andrew Lang and published in 1890. In the book Lang recounts an incident from the negotiations between the United States and Great Britain over a treaty settling the *Alabama* claims and other matters. Instructions to the British negotiators from the government in London permitted them to make concessions on such matters as fishing rights and reparations, but enjoined them under no circumstances to accept an adverb between *to* and the infinitive in the treaty. Lang approved the intransigence.

Lounsbury quoted another piece by Lang in which he facetiously suggests that anyone who aspires to be a bad writer should split as many infinitives as possible. Doing that probably would produce bad writing, as the evidence shows that the split infinitive is not a construction that is in constant demand. The consensus in the 20th century, however, seems to be that awkward avoidance of the split infinitive has produced more bad writing than use of it.

Critical opinion as expressed in usage books appears to have settled on a wary compromise. The commentators recognize that there is nothing grammatically wrong with the split infinitive, but they are loath to abandon a subject that is so dear to the public at large. Therefore, they tell us to avoid split infinitives except when splitting one improves clarity. Since improved clarity is very often the purpose and result of using a split infinitive, the advice does not amount to much. The upshot is that you can split them when you need to.

To repeat, the objection to the split infinitive has never had a rational basis. The original cause for complaint was probably awareness of a relatively sudden marked increase in use of the construction, perhaps combined with the knowledge that in those more elegant languages, Latin and Greek, the infinitive is never split—because it is a single word distinguished by its ending rather than by an introductory particle. Even though it goes back to the 14th century, the split infinitive was relatively rare until the 19th. The reason for the increase in split infinitives, Curme tells us, is simply the increase in the number of sentences with clauses (as Curme calls them) introduced by *to*-infinitives.

One word of warning. In some sentences—particularly ones where the infinitive comes after a copula and particularly ones with a negative like *never* or *not*—the infinitive is customarily not split. Here are two examples:

Molee's quest for a perfect replacement for English seems never to have ended —Baron 1982

. . . human qualities that even the most zealous military officer must possess if he is effectively to command men —William Styron, *This Quiet Dust and Other Writings,* 1982

From these two examples you might reasonably conclude that such placement does give some emphasis to the adverb.

The split infinitive, as several commentators remark, seems never to have been common in the speech of the less educated. Its use is pretty much confined to users of standard English and to literary contexts.

spoil, spoiled, spoilt In American English *spoiled* is usual for both verbal and adjectival use, although we have some evidence for *spoilt* as an adjective. In British

English both *spoiled* and *spoilt* are used. Longman 1988 says *spoilt* and *spoiled* are equally common in British use, but our files show more British evidence for *spoilt* than for *spoiled.*

> ... so spoiled that we never knew how to leave —David Halberstam, *New Times,* 16 May 1975

> ... spoiled rotten and considerably less than innocent —Newgate Callendar, *N.Y. Times Book Rev.,* 6 Feb. 1983

> ... behave like a spoilt hysteric —*Time,* 5 Mar. 1984

> ... spoiled Notre Dame's unbeaten season —*Oxford Companion to Sports and Games,* ed. John Arlott, 1975

> This comedy, although it is spoilt in places by some childish farce —James Sutherland, *English Literature of the Late Seventeenth Century,* 1969

> You have hitherto been a spoiled child —William Hazlitt, letter, March 1822

> ... a crowd of spoilt, ungrateful children —Ann Lovell, *Annabel,* June 1974

> ... grew up into a stuttering, spoilt brat —Harold Beaver, *Times Literary Supp.,* 4 July 1980

spokesperson See PERSON 2.

spoonful This word has two plural forms: *spoonfuls* and *spoonsful. Spoonfuls* is by far the more common of the two and is the form preferred by usage commentators. See -FUL.

spouse The advantage that *spouse* has over *wife* and *husband* is that it is not limited to a particular sex. This makes it a useful word in special contexts where the person referred to may be either male or female, as in legal documents and income tax forms. Its use outside such contexts has been advised against by several commentators, who generally regard it as too formal a word to be used in ordinary speech and writing for anything other than pseudo-elegant humor. Our evidence essentially supports the observations and opinions of the critics. *Spouse* is certainly not a word that occurs normally in casual speech, and in writing it seems to occur primarily when the writer is being deliberately coy or facetious or when its formality or lack of specific sexual reference makes it an appropriate choice:

> If his spouse can digest all this pertinent information and dish it out later when he needs it most —Land Kaderli, *Saturday Evening Post,* 3 July 1954

> Religion was not his faith; it was his spouse, and he loved it ... passionately —*Time,* 27 Dec. 1954

> ... when either parent buys a first-class or coach airplane ticket, the accompanying spouse and children under 25 years travel at greatly reduced rates —Paul J. C. Friedlander, *N.Y. Times,* 6 Nov. 1955

Sometimes, too, neither *wife* nor *husband* seems to be an appropriate choice:

> Anthony Sullivan, a 33-year-old Australian, clasped the hand of his spouse, Richard F. Adams, 28, of Los Angeles —Grace Lichtenstein, *N.Y. Times,* 27 Apr. 1975

spring The past tense of the verb *spring* can be either *sprang* or *sprung. Sprang* is the more common form, but *sprung* is not at all rare:

> The parents sprang into action —Susan Edmiston, *Woman's Day,* October 1971

> Dufour ... sprung up the rocks like a cat —Jeremy Bernstein, *N.Y. Times Mag.,* 28 May 1978

> ... none of these problems sprung into being overnight —Norman Cousins, *Saturday Rev.,* June 1980

> Self-help computer clubs sprung up around the country —Paul Freiberger, *Infoworld,* 28 Nov. 1983

Sprung also serves as the past participle of *spring:*

> The new Avery Fisher Hall, which has sprung from the skeleton of the old one —Harold C. Schonberg, *N.Y. Times,* 20 Oct. 1976

squeeze, squoze When the President of the United States uses a dialectal past tense of a verb at a news conference, people notice. Ronald Reagan in August 1985 was commenting on a small skin cancer that had been removed from his nose. He had thought it a pimple:

> I picked at it and I squoze it and so forth and messed myself up a little.

This use puzzled syndicated columnist James J. Kilpatrick, who wrote that he had never encountered it before. He might have found it in Harper 1975, 1985, where it is called substandard.

Squoze is apparently the most common of a number of dialectal variants of the past tense of *squeeze.* It is attested in both British and American dialect: the OED Supplement shows it in American English since 1844. Our most recent evidence apart from President Reagan happens to associate it with orange-growing areas, but older evidence shows *squoze* to be more widespread.

The form used in writing is consistently *squeezed. Squoze,* so far, is oral and dialectal. Both *squoze* and *squozen* are sparsely attested as dialectal past participles.

squinting modifier, squinting construction The squinting modifier resides chiefly in college-level handbooks. The term is used of an adverb or phrase that stands between two sentence elements and can be taken to modify either what precedes or what follows. Let us construct an example:

> To laugh often can be embarrassing.

In our made-up example, *often* can be construed as modifying either *laugh* or *can be embarrassing.* But you can see right away that we are in learners' territory—most of us would have written *can often be* if we had intended *often* to go with the second part. Here is perhaps a better example, sent to us by a correspondent from Korea:

> The store that had the big sale recently went bankrupt.

Here *recently* can be interpreted as modifying either the preceding or following part. But the content of the sentence suggests it is a learner's sentence; a native speaker would not be likely to convey the information in such a flat and unspecific manner.

The examples of the squinting modifier shown in college handbooks are comparable to the two we have used here, and they seem about as likely to occur in actual writing. This degree of improbability, along with the dearth of examples in our own files, suggests to us that the squinting modifier is more of a theoretical possibility—with, it must be admitted, a catchy title—than a real problem. It would seem most likely to occur when a split infinitive is being carefully avoided by putting the would-be splitting adverb ahead of the infinitive, as in

> ... authorities would be required correctly to anticipate their requirements —W. Manning Dacey, *The British Banking Mechanism,* 1951

stadium   Some people, mindful of the Latin origins of *stadium,* prefer to give it a Latin plural, *stadia,* while others are content to treat it as a normal English word with a normal English plural, *stadiums.* Both plural forms are standard and correct. *Stadiums* is especially likely to occur when the word is being used in its most familiar sense:

> ... addressing huge audiences—some of them in stadiums —*N.Y. Times Book Rev.,* 11 Apr. 1982

> ... into new, spacious, plastic-turfed stadiums —Bill James, *Sports Illustrated,* 6 Sept. 1982

Stadia is much less common than *stadiums* in this sense, particularly in speech, but we do have substantial evidence of its written use:

> ... operators of many stadia about the country — Melvin Durslag, *TV Guide,* 11 Oct. 1969

> ... heard in political circles these days almost as much as in football stadia —Neil Amdur, *N.Y. Times,* 7 Nov. 1970

Most of the other, less common senses of *stadium,* such as "an ancient Greek unit of length," hark back more clearly to the classical origins of the word and are usually pluralized as *stadia:*

> At the same time in Alexandria, 5,000 stadia distant —Alan Lightman, *Science 82,* March 1982

For other foreign plurals, see LATIN PLURALS.

staffer   *Staffer* appears to be one of those words about which most language-watchers have no particular opinion until they are asked for one, whereupon they discover within themselves a deep-seated dislike which has previously been lying dormant. Most usage writers have taken no notice of *staffer,* but when a panelist in Harper 1975 expressed his irritation with it, a poll of the other panelists revealed that 77 percent of them shared his feelings. What is wrong with *staffer?* First and foremost, it is relatively new. Our earliest evidence of its use is from 1941:

> The British legation staffers and Minister Rendel — *Time,* 24 Mar. 1941

The second strike against it is that it seems to have originated or been popularized in *Time* magazine, which gives it a certain jargonistic stigma in the eyes of some people. The third strike, related to the second, is that it has always been a word used chiefly—and used frequently—by journalists. A good reason is that journalists, unlike the rest of us, are frequently called upon to report the actions or statements of people who are members of a staff:

> ... an LBJ staffer materialized to get Sam into his formal attire —Larry L. King, *Harper's,* April 1970

> ... in the words of one staffer at last night's session —George S. Wills, *Johns Hopkins Mag.,* Fall 1971

> Many staffers were indignant about parts of the Thurber book —E. B. White, letter 24 May 1973

> At the FCC, staffers are rounding up data —Richard K. Doan, *TV Guide,* 22 Dec. 1973

> ... I erred in blaming a former Special Prosecutor staffer —William Safire, *N.Y. Times,* 8 Nov. 1976

> ... staffers already are beginning to study various acquisition prospects —*Business Week,* 11 May 1981

> ... uses revealing chunks of internal A.E.C. documents ... and leaks from A.E.C. staffers —Edward Zuckerman, *N.Y. Times Book Rev.,* 31 Oct. 1982

Staffer is certainly not an indispensable word, even for journalists. Anyone determined to avoid its use can easily do so by replacing it with such terms as *staff member, official,* and *employee.* It is, however, a word that many writers obviously find handy, and there is no reason to suppose that its popularity will diminish soon.

stage   *Stage* is an old verb, but until the 20th century it was primarily a theatrical one, with such meanings as "to represent on the stage" and "to produce (as a play) on a stage." It has now developed several extended uses, and these have been occasionally criticized since at least the 1920s:

> One may perhaps express a pious wish that some check might be imposed upon the journalistic use of the verb *stage.* ... Every newspaper reader must have noticed the frequency with which the word is now used to describe every sort of occurrence, from a street row to a wedding —George B. Ives, *Text, Type, and Style,* 1921

The sporadic criticism has had no apparent effect on the word's popularity.

> ... young separatists stage a sit-down to draw public attention to their demands —*Saturday Evening Post,* 10 Oct. 1964

> ... a group of P.L.C. supporters staged a demonstration in front of Gallagher's office —David Boroff, *N.Y. Times Mag.,* 28 Mar. 1965

> ... when he staged his most recent bid for re-election —*Current Biography,* December 1967

> ... before the Catawba could stage a comeback — Brian McGinty, *Early American Life,* February 1980

stamp   See STOMP, STAMP.

stanch, staunch   Fowler 1926 observed that the verb is usually spelled *stanch* and the adjective *staunch.* That observation still holds true today. The verb and adjective are both derived from the Old French *estancher,* meaning "to stop the flow of; stanch." The two spelling variants have been in reputable use for centuries, and they are standard both for the verb and for the adjective. *Stanch* is the much more common spelling of the verb:

> ... the icy cold ... had stanched the flow of blood —Brock Brower, *Holiday,* February 1966

> ... some evidence this has stanched the outward flow —William K. Stevens, *N.Y. Times,* 1 Mar. 1978

. . . has stanched a dangerous cash hemorrhage —
Ralph E. Winter, *Wall Street Jour.,* 11 Aug. 1981

But *staunch* is not rare:

. . . in an attempt to staunch the flow of oil —*Nature,*
15 Feb. 1969

Proposition 10 may staunch the wounds —*Wall
Street Jour.,* 27 May 1980

For the adjective, *staunch* is by far the more common
spelling, but *stanch* is also in widespread use:

. . . animal lovers who have been zoos' staunchest
supporters —Jon Luoma, *Audubon Mag.,* November 1982

. . . even now many programmers are staunch holdouts —Steve Olson, *Science 84,* January/February
1984

. . . once was a stanch ally of the West —Karl E.
Meyer, *The Reporter,* 6 July 1954

. . . a stanch foe of the Vietnam war —Philip B. Kur-
land, *N.Y. Times Book Rev.,* 14 Oct. 1973

standard, standard English *Standard English* is of
necessity defined in somewhat general terms in dictionaries. We would like to point out three of its characteristics from the definition in Webster's Ninth New
Collegiate Dictionary. It is "substantially uniform,"
"well-established" in the "speech and writing of the educated," and "widely recognized as acceptable." There is
room for a lot of variation within those limits, with the
result that there can be substantial disagreement about
the propriety of perfectly standard words and
constructions.

It is quite common for usage commentators to use
standard English in a highly personal way to stand for
the particular brand of English that they are expounding. We need only one example to make the point:

At about. This wordy phrase should be avoided in
standard English —Shaw 1970

Now compare Shaw's opinion with this use of *at about:*

Two of your stories, "The Boarding-House" and "A
Little Cloud" are in the May Smart Set; I am having
two copies of the number sent to you by this post.
We were unable to take more because the American
publisher of "Dubliners", Mr. B. W. Huebsch, of 225
Fifth Avenue, New York, planned to bring out the
book at about this time —H. L. Mencken, letter to
James Joyce, 20 Apr. 1915

Mencken's letter is plainly written in standard English,
so we conclude that Shaw's *standard English* has a very
personal meaning.

We can use Mencken's letter to make another point.
Standard English is the language of business, literature,
and journalism. It has evolved over the centuries as the
means by which speakers of diverse dialects of English
can communicate effectively with each other. It is an
economic necessity in a world where English is the most
widely recognized language and is not likely to disappear any time soon, whatever reports of its death may
come your way.

See also NONSTANDARD; SUBSTANDARD.

standpoint *Standpoint* came into English in the first
half of the 19th century as a translation of or a coinage

on the model of German *standpunkt.* American commentators began to disparage it as early as Richard
Grant White 1870. It was subsequently criticized in William Cullen Bryant's 1877 *Index Expurgatorius,* Ayres
1881, Long 1888, Vizetelly 1906, and Bierce 1909. What
was the problem?

Richard Grant White recognized but dismissed the
connection with the German word; he rejected *standpoint* on the basis of a rule for English compounds that
he seems to have devised on his own. Compounds like
washtub, cookstove, and *standpoint* are ill formed, he
says. Their initial element should be a participle. But
even *standing point,* he concludes, is inferior to *point of
view.* Bryant, Ayres, Vizetelly, and Bierce offered no reasons for their disapproval. Long 1888 did, though, saying "*Point of view* is preferable to *standpoint;* as the latter expression is logically absurd; one cannot stand on a
point." The weakness of that argument has been pointed
out by Bernstein 1971, who tartly observes that many a
West Point cadet would be interested to learn that it is
impossible to stand on a point.

The real problem with *standpoint,* of course, was simply that it was a new and popular word. As it has continued to be popular but has gradually died out, the old
antagonism toward it has gradually died out. There may
still be a few editors with long memories who dislike
standpoint, but its place in standard English has long
been established, and usage commentators now generally ignore it altogether. Here are a few examples of its
use:

From this standpoint the drama may be said to have
begun —G. K. Chesterton, reprinted in *The Pocket
Book of Father Brown,* 1946

. . . depends a great deal on the standpoint from
which one regards it —Robert M. Coates, *New
Yorker,* 16 Dec. 1950

. . . a success from the standpoint of free speech and
the protection of dissent —Herbert L. Packer, *N.Y.
Rev. of Books,* 6 Nov. 1969

. . . to find a standpoint from which to view all societies —*Times Literary Supp.,* 27 July 1967

See also POINT OF VIEW; VIEWPOINT.

stanza See VERSE, STANZA.

state Commentators dating back to Richard Grant
White 1870 have repeatedly condemned what they
regard as the pretentious misuse of *state* in place of *say.*
The frequent criticism suggests that the problem is
widespread, but our files actually contain little evidence
of this use of *state.* Most commonly, *state* is used to
imply a formal, precise, or emphatic declaration or
report:

. . . being able to state clearly a technological prob-
lem or define a technological need —Hubert H.
Humphrey, in *Automation, Education and Human
Values,* ed. W. W. Brickman & S. Lehrer, 1966

Richard Nixon, who had often stated he would never
be the first American President to lose a war —
Goodman Ace, *Saturday Rev.,* 20 Nov. 1971

Say is a far more common and widely applied word. It
is the word that is normally used in reporting ordinary
remarks ("He said he'd be a little late" seems more natural than "He stated he'd be a little late"). *State* can,

however, be appropriately used where *say* might be expected as a way to underscore the emphatic nature of what might otherwise seem to be an ordinary remark:

> "I like you, Alice," he stated. "You are a really sincere person. . . ." —Doris Lessing, *The Good Terrorist,* 1985

state of the art   Here is another term from technical literature that has moved into the general consciousness and into general use. Although it is not as well known to or as widely disliked by the critics as *parameter* or *interface* (which see), it is beginning to attract the disapproval of some, including Copperud 1980 and the Harper 1985 usage panel. Janis 1984 notes its popularity in advertising.

In general use *state of the art* more often functions as a hyphenated adjective than as a noun. As a general adjective it is not much more than a flossy version of *up-to-date* with pleasant overtones of technical know-how. One Harper panelist opined—apparently seriously—that *state-of-the-art* is less precise than *up-to-date.* Here are a few general uses of the adjective:

> This large Tudor-styled kitchen includes all-ash cabinetry, abundant shelf space, a full state-of-the-art appliance package —*Houston Post,* 2 Sept. 1984

> . . . have added a fresh and pastoral touch to the rooms of the Barbizon . . . as well as a state-of-the-art urban spa —Jennifer Kramer, *Town & Country,* September 1984

> . . . providing 20th-century creature comforts such as state-of-the-art plumbing —Marylin Bender, *N.Y. Times,* 15 July 1984

> . . . that spring scale over there is not exactly state of the art —Jacqueline Mallorca, *Jour. of Gastronomy,* Summer 1984

Occasionally it is pure buzzword:

> The speech was state-of-the-art Sam: tough, smart and calm —Nancy Cooper, *Newsweek,* 27 Oct. 1986

Use as a noun is less common in general prose, but it does turn up now and then:

> . . . stinted nothing that would make his Comanche Trace horse breeding farm the state of the art — Hugh Best, *Town & Country,* June 1983

As a popularized technical term *state of the art* is probably close enough to ordinary language that it is not too mysterious for ready apprehension. It would seem unlikely to produce the sort of mumbo-jumbo that a determined operator can produce from *parameter* and similar words. But it is a good idea to remember that a reader has the right to be suspicious of what you may be trying to hide behind bright and shiny terminology.

stationary, stationery   The adjective that means "not moving" is *stationary;* the noun that means "paper for writing letters" is *stationery.* These two words look like prime candidates for being misspelled, but our evidence shows that they rarely are, at least in edited prose. The usual advice for remembering the distinction is to associate the *er* in *stationery* with the *er* in *letter* or *paper.*

statistic   The singular *statistic* is derived from *statistics,* which in its oldest sense refers to a field of study,

like *economics,* and which is itself often construed as a singular:

> To reach a better understanding of how statistics functions, and of its limitations, weaknesses and dangers —Darrell Huff, *Think,* January 1963

This sense of *statistics* dates back to the late 18th century. The earliest recorded use of *statistics* as a plural occurred not long afterward:

> . . . the few who love statistics for the sake of what they indicate —Harriet Martineau, *Society in America,* 1837 (OED)

Statistics here denotes not a field of study, but numerical data that have been collected for study. Derivation of the singular *statistic* from this plural use was almost inevitable.

> There is not a statistic wanting. It is as succinct as an invoice —Mark Twain, *A Tramp Abroad,* 1880 (OED Supplement)

Statistic has at times been criticized (as by Follett 1966) on the theory that if there is no plural word *statistics,* there can be no singular *statistic.* However, the plural *statistics* does exist and has for more than 150 years. The singular *statistic* is now completely standard.

staunch   See STANCH, STAUNCH.

stave   The verb meaning "to break or crush inward" has as its past tense and past participle either *staved* or *stove.* It usually takes the adverb *in:*

> . . . that had stove in the planks of the wheelhouse — Alistair MacLean, *Saturday Evening Post,* 23 Sept. 1956

> . . . a massive gold-processing plant . . . , its peaked front all staved in —James Traub, *Smithsonian,* November 1984

The earliest evidence for *stove* shows it appearing in nautical contexts ("a stove boat"), but our evidence shows that it now occurs commonly in general contexts as well:

> . . . he clambered over the stockade wall and stove in the jail door —Howard Troyer, *Antioch Rev.,* Summer 1948

> Theaters were stampeded, limousines were ripped and rent and stove in —Michael Thomas, *Rolling Stone,* 16 Mar. 1972

On the basis of our evidence, it appears that *stave off,* meaning "to ward or fend off," regularly becomes *staved off* in the past tense:

> . . . noncommissioned officer who staved off a German attack near the Siegfried Line —*Current Biography,* October 1966

> . . . it staved off its possible demise by signing a new labor contract —*Wall Street Jour.,* 18 Dec. 1981

still and all   This adverbial phrase is not well-loved by several critics who regard its last two words as illogical and superfluous—mere excess baggage adding nothing to the meaning of *still.* Its frequent appearance in print is a fairly recent development, but the phrase itself is not new: the OED Supplement includes a citation for it from 1829, and it was doubtless in spoken use for some time before that. In the past it has been regarded as dialectal, but it is clearly standard today. The attractions it holds for the writers who use it are probably that it is less formal than the starchy *nevertheless* and less abrupt than the monosyllabic *still.* It has, in other words, a casual, conversational quality which is consistent with the informal tone of much modern prose:

> Still and all . . . Fishberg could indubitably whip up a musicale that would receive better notices than any other large-scale family jamboree in town —Andy Logan, *New Yorker,* 29 Oct. 1949

> Still and all, Alice would never have become a queen without her aid —Elizabeth Janeway, *Leaving Home,* 1953

> Still and all, the Goldwater people attached some value to his support —Richard H. Rovere, *New Yorker,* 25 July 1964

> Still and all, if you are cagy, you can leave town with plenty of cash in your jeans —George V. Higgins, *Boston Globe Mag.,* 18 Nov. 1979

> But, still and all, Monaco remains a jewel of a play-ground —Barry Tarshis, *Town & Country,* April 1980

> Nowadays I recognize the bad-spell-of-weather joke as a bad joke. Still and all, Miss Laney had a point —Gordon Grindstaff, *Christian Science Monitor,* 27 July 1981

> Still and all, there is no manual or handbook for the creation of a perfect translation —Gregory Rabassa, *American Scholar,* Winter 1974/75

stimulant, stimulus In scientific usage, a clear distinction is made between these words. A stimulant is an agent (such as a drug) that increases the functional activity of an organism or any of its parts; a stimulus is something (such as an environmental change) that produces a reaction in living tissue. Amphetamines and caffeine are stimulants; bright light is a stimulus that causes the pupils of the eyes to contract. In general usage, however, this distinction is not so strictly observed. Both words are used to describe something that rouses or excites to activity or that provides motivation for change or progress. *Stimulus* is much more common in this use than *stimulant:*

> . . . as a stimulus to change in the interpretation or rejection of Marxist ideas —*Times Literary Supp.,* 5 Mar. 1970

> . . . the President's program contains virtually no fiscal stimulus —Robert Lekachman, *Dun's,* October 1971

> . . . would probably be the strongest stimulus to West European unity —Anatole Shub, *Harper's,* January 1972

But *stimulant* also occurs:

> Aid . . . can only be a stimulant. The main growth has to come out of the resources of the poor countries themselves —Peter F. Drucker, *Harper's,* December 1968

> . . . this book may serve as a stimulant to revaluation —Robert Pattison, *On Literacy,* 1982

This use of *stimulant* is not highly controversial, but an assortment of commentators, dating back to Vizetelly 1906, have disapproved of it. Our evidence indicates that it is relatively uncommon but nonetheless standard.

stink, stank, stunk Both *stank* and *stunk* are used as the past tense of *stink. Stank* is more common in edited prose. Both are standard:

> . . . Arthur Levitt thought the idea stank —Byron Klapper, *Wall Street Jour.,* 15 Dec. 1975

> . . . will tell you that in 1979 business stank —Marc Kirkeby, *Rolling Stone,* 24 July 1980

> . . . although I stunk at algebra, Zock pushed me through —William Goldman, *Temple of Gold,* 1957

When the verb is followed by *of,* the past tense is almost invariably *stank:*

> The room stank of cigar smoke —Walter Wager, *Telefon,* 1975

> . . . for whom both stank of corruption —Peter Schjeldahl, *N.Y. Times Book Rev.,* 15 Feb. 1976

The past participle of *stink* is always *stunk.*

stomp, stamp *Stomp* originated in American English as a dialectal variant of *stamp,* first recorded in the early 19th century. The passing years have seen it gain steadily in respectability. Its status in current English is that of a standard synonym of *stamp* in several of its senses, all having to do, literally or figuratively, with bringing the foot down heavily:

> . . . she angrily stomped out of the office —*Current Biography,* December 1966

> . . . resist the temptation to stomp on him when he's down —Norman Cousins, *Saturday Rev.,* 14 Oct. 1978

> . . . I heard the horses stomping in the stable —E. L. Doctorow, *Loon Lake,* 1979

> On national television, he stomped a folding chair and verbally abused players —Alexander Wolff, *Sports Illustrated,* 3 Feb. 1986

These uses of *stomp* are generally uncontroversial, although their somewhat informal quality attracts occasional comment. *Stomp* is most likely to be criticized when it occurs in such a phrase as *stomp one's feet.* The usage panels of Heritage 1969 and Heritage 1982 reject this use of *stomp* in favor of *stamp* by a large majority, but this use has much the same quality as the other uses of *stomp,* and its occurrence in edited writing is just as common:

> . . . while I stood there stomping my feet against the cold —John McNulty, *New Yorker,* 24 Jan. 1953

> Moses LaMarr . . . stomped his foot and opened his mouth wide as an alligator —Truman Capote, *New Yorker,* 27 Oct. 1956

> . . . a way of stomping one's foot on the ground and saying, "Enough! . . ." —Carll Tucker, *Saturday Rev.,* 29 Apr. 1978

> . . . an enclosed vestibule where people stomp their boots in winter —Andrew H. Malcolm, *N.Y. Times Mag.,* 23 Mar. 1986

The Heritage dictionaries also note that *stamp* rather than *stomp* is the verb used with *out* for the figurative sense "eliminate entirely" (as in "stamp out poverty"). Our evidence confirms this observation:

> ... to stamp out some of the potent and concrete conditions behind it, such as race prejudice —Frederic Wertham, *Johns Hopkins Mag.*, Summer 1971

> ... was able to stamp out addiction in five years —Horace Sutton, *Saturday Rev.*, 17 Mar. 1979

stop The use of *stop* to mean "stay" was much criticized in the late 19th and early 20th centuries. An early critic was Bache 1869, whose remarks are typical:

> *To stop* is to bring progress to an abrupt termination. ... A man cannot stop for a week or a day. If he *stops*, he *stays*, until his journey, or his locomotion of whatever sort, is resumed.

The usage Bache was objecting to specifically was in such a sentence as "He is stopping at the hotel for a week." Note that while *stop* does mean "stay" in such a sentence, it usually also implies a temporary break or pause in a journey. A slightly different use of *stop* is in a phrase such as *stopping at home*, in which *stop* has the sense "to remain" with no implication of a pause or break. This use of *stop* was cited as a Briticism by Richard Grant White 1870 (he also considered *stopping at a hotel* to be British). Later commentators, including Gould 1867, Vizetelly 1906, Bierce 1909, and Weseen 1928, concerned themselves mainly with the *stopping at a hotel* usage, which they faulted for the same reasons as Bache.

Questions about the propriety of *stop* for *stay* have persisted only among the British. Longman 1984 reports that "careful writers" prefer *staying at a hotel*, confining *stop* to short breaks only ("stop for lunch"). No American commentator addresses this subject, and the criticized usage is fairly common in American English:

> ... when he was in New York he usually stopped at the Windsor House —John Kobler, *New Yorker*, 25 Feb. 1956

> ... the Manila Hotel, a favorite stopping place for musicians —Robert Jacobson, *Saturday Rev.*, 30 Oct. 1971

The use of *stop* that was noted by Richard Grant White has continued in informal British English:

> "... I wasn't going to stop in bed, in retreat, all my life...." —Ford Madox Ford, *The Last Post*, 1928

> Oh, all right, you can stop till I'm dressed if you like —Vita Sackville-West, *The Edwardians*, 1930

> Will playing football make a German more Nazi or stopping at home make him less so? —*Manchester Guardian Weekly*, 15 June 1945

> "You must not sleep alone at Hampstead," said Godfrey. "Call on Lisa Brooke and ask her to stop with you for a few days...." —Muriel Spark, *Memento Mori*, 1959

In American English, the word used in these contexts would be *stay*.

straight, strait A few commentators, most of them British, warn against the confusion of *straight* and *strait*. Actual confusion seems unlikely, since the words are

used in rather different senses, but they are homophones and hence can be muddled in spelling. We have no actual examples of confusion in our files. If you are in doubt, check your dictionary.

straitened The adjective that means "distressed" or "deprived" ("straitened circumstances") is actually the past participle of the verb *straiten* and has no relation to either *straight* or *straighten*. Despite that fact, the spelling error is still fairly easy to make in a moment of inattention:

> ... in the Chinese farmer's straightened circumstances —*N.Y. Times Book Rev.*, 12 Dec. 1948

> ... living perhaps in some straightened home or lonely cottage —*Time*, 8 Oct. 1951

straitjacket, straitlaced, straightjacket, straightlaced The original and still the usual spellings are *straitjacket* and *straitlaced*:

> ... this would put a straitjacket on industrial progress —*Times Literary Supp.*, 23 June 1972

> ... he's inclined to be rather straitlaced —Rosemary Brown, *Ladies' Home Jour.*, September 1971

But *straightjacket* and *straightlaced* are also in common use:

> ... loosening a few strings of the economic straightjacket —John Fischer, *Harper's*, July 1972

> ... showed up at a straight-laced ... church —Dennis Farney, *Wall Street Jour.*, 12 Nov. 1981

The *straight-* spellings originated as errors, and they are still regarded as errors by many people. Because of their common occurrence in reputable publications, however, they are recognized as standard variants in almost all current dictionaries.

strata, stratum *Strata* is a Latin plural with ambitions to become an English singular. The Latin *stratum*, which means literally "something spread or laid down," was first used in English at the end of the 16th century. As an English word it has become common in several senses, all of which share the basic meaning "layer" or "level." The Latin plural has been retained as the usual plural in English:

> ... the strata of dried oceans rise up to remind you of the planet's age —Richard Rhodes, *Harper's*, November 1970

> ... an omnibus organization that attracted all strata of society —Michael T. Kaufman, *N.Y. Times Mag.*, 23 Mar. 1980

A variant plural, *stratums*, is rare in writing:

> ... must learn to move in the various stratums of society —Lou Richter, *Annual Report, Peace Officers Training School*, August 1952

In addition to its plural use, *strata* has seen occasional use as a singular since the 18th century. The OED labeled the singular *strata* obsolete in 1917, but it has since been resurrected (if, indeed, it ever disappeared entirely). It occurs most often in the sense "a social level":

> There was a strata of Paris which mere criticism of books fails to get hold of —Ezra Pound, *Polite Essays*, 1937

A single strata in the black world —Robert Deane Pharr, *Library Jour.,* October 1968

. . . they represent a strata that is often viewed with derision by intellectuals —Harvey G. Cox, *N.Y. Times Book Rev.,* 22 Feb. 1976

Its plural is *stratas:*

. . . in each of these very distinct worlds different stratas exist —Patricia Johnson, *N.Y. Times,* 11 Mar. 1973

The island has obvious stratas of society —Ronald Faux, *Scottish Field,* January 1974

Our evidence does not show the singular *strata* to be common, but it does seem to be persistent. Usage commentators, by and large, will not tolerate it. Continued use may eventually elevate it to the standard status of *agenda* and *candelabra,* but its current status is something less than that, and you are well advised to avoid it. When the sense is singular, use *stratum;* when plural, *strata.*

For other foreign plurals, see LATIN PLURALS.

strike, struck, stricken *Struck* is the past tense of *strike* ("The clock struck twelve"), and in most contexts it also functions as its past participle ("The tree was struck by lightning"). The alternative participle *stricken* is used when *strike* has the sense "to afflict suddenly":

. . . was stricken with ileitis in June 1956 —*Current Biography,* April 1968

. . . with so much devilry having stricken the life of Mrs. MacNeil —Keith S. Felton, *Los Angeles Times Book Rev.,* 23 May 1971

It is also common for the sense "to cancel or delete":

. . . have certain of their remarks modified or stricken from the record —Andy Logan, *New Yorker,* 30 Oct. 1971

. . . the term "false alarm" has been stricken from the vocabulary —*Harper's,* June 1972

And *stricken* has several familiar adjectival uses as well:

With several stricken faces looking at him —Nancy Milford, *Harper's,* January 1969

. . . blew up two 100,000-barrel oil storage tanks. . . . The two stricken tanks were 15 per cent full —Lawrence Mosher, *National Observer,* 28 Apr. 1973

Other uses of *stricken* are rare, and they tend to have an unidiomatic ring:

I am still stricken by McComb's and Mangin's classic City Hall and its calm exterior —Gilbert Millstein, *N.Y. Times Mag.,* 30 Nov. 1975

strive *Strive* is most often followed by *to* and the infinitive:

. . . they strove to establish the sense of their identity —Oscar Handlin, *The American People in the Twentieth Century,* 1954

. . . perhaps it is for them that he has so rigorously strived "to be exact" —John Irving, *N.Y. Times Book Rev.,* 12 Aug. 1979

. . . the limitations of background that, subconsciously rather than consciously perhaps, he had

striven to overcome —Norman Cousins, *Saturday Rev.,* 6 Apr. 1974

Once in a while, *to* is followed by a noun object:

. . . women have either borne the moral burden, or shared it, or striven, through the self-love Trilling denies them, to the autonomous condition that might redeem the earth —Carolyn Heilbrun, *Saturday Rev.,* 29 Jan. 1972

Strive is also frequently used with *for:*

With all his will Venters strove for calmness —Zane Grey, *Riders of the Purple Sage,* 1912

. . . each national group, striving for greater freedom, has the support of its neighbors —Henry C. Atyeo, *Current History,* November 1952

We have strived for reform of the chaotic and unworkable welfare system —John Gardner, *Common Cause,* 9 Jan. 1973

Other prepositions used with *strive* include *after, against, at, in, into, toward, towards, with,* and *within:*

. . . apartments that have exceeded mere functionalism and now strive after taste —Anthony Austin, *N.Y. Times Mag.,* 9 Mar. 1980

". . . Though we strive against butchers, let us not wet our hands in butchery. . . ." —Irwin Shaw, *The Young Lions,* 1948

. . . he strove at his seemingly endless task —*American Guide Series: Texas,* 1940

The San Francisco 49ers and Oakland Raiders have striven mightily in football, without success —*Springfield* (Mass.) *Union,* 23 Oct. 1972

. . . the farmers roll from their bunks, strive into their jeans, and fall out for morning roll-call —*Century Mag.,* April 1919

. . . two sentences which state beautifully what many educators have been striving toward —Sim O. Wilde, Jr., *Center Mag.,* May 1969

. . . some curious region where the spirit strives towards an unseen God —Virginia Woolf, *The Second Common Reader,* 1932

. . . a figure that had striven with the generations who found Chicago a swamp mudhole and saw it made into an audacious metropolis —*Dictionary of American Biography,* 1936

He guessed at the grief and perplexity that must strive within her —Anne Douglas Sedgwick, *The Little French Girl,* 1924

subject 1. *Noun.* When the noun *subject* is followed by a preposition, it is usually *of:*

. . . it's our fighting men . . . that make the proper subject of American fiction —James Purdy, *Cabot Wright Begins,* 1964

. . . the exercise of power is the great subject of history —*Times Literary Supp.,* June 1969

. . . became a subject of violent controversy —William L. Shirer, *The Rise and Fall of the Third Reich,* 1960

Subject is sometimes also used with *for:*

> The subject for Milton's "Paradise Lost" is, as Bradley says, the fall of man —John Dewey, *Art as Experience,* 1934

> It was so long since the sculptress had regarded sex as anything but a subject for conversation —Angus Wilson, *Anglo-Saxon Attitudes,* 1956

When *subject* is used to mean "victim," it has also been used with *to:*

> ... one would never have guessed that William James was the subject to a heart ailment —Sidney Lovett, *Yale Rev.,* Summer 1954

2. *Adjective.* The adjective *subject* is usually used with *to:*

> ... the party convicted [after impeachment] shall, nevertheless, be liable and subject to indictment, trial, judgment, and punishment —*Constitution of the United States,* 1787

> Paul was rather a delicate boy, subject to bronchitis —D. H. Lawrence, *Sons and Lovers,* 1913

> ... they proved that the society is no longer as subject to that "relentless tide of ups and downs" which Marx was among the first to chart —Michael Harrington, *Center Mag.,* September 1969

3. *Verb.* The verb *subject* is usually used with *to:*

> My partners in St. Louis have been subjected to several attempts to stop the flight —Charles A. Lindbergh, *The Spirit of St. Louis,* 1953

> ... she had never subjected herself to the discipline of continuousness —John Cheever, *The Wapshot Chronicle,* 1957

> He writes of them in their own right, without attempting to subject them to general concepts —*Times Literary Supp.,* 26 Mar. 1970

> Uncle Harold was often subjected to these small humiliations —Russell Baker, *Growing Up,* 1982

subjective genitive   See GENITIVE 1.

subject-verb agreement   See the several articles at AGREEMENT, SUBJECT-VERB.

subjunctive

> Fading into the sunset, probably forever, is that splendid old mood we have known as the subjunctive —Richard L. Tobin, *Righting Words,* May/June 1988

Another writer, it seems, has discovered the disappearing subjunctive; observers of the language have been reading obsequies for the subjunctive for a century or more. As long ago as 1907 the brothers Fowler were quoting "an experienced word-actuary" who put the subjunctive's life expectancy at a generation. The word-actuary was Henry Bradley, one of the OED editors, and he made the statement in a book, *The Making of English,* published in 1904.

But even Bradley was not breaking new ground. Ayres 1881 paraphrased three unnamed grammarians who thought the subjunctive more or less defunct. One of them was probably William Dwight Whitney, who is quoted in Finegan 1980 as remarking in an 1877 grammar that "the subjunctive, as a separate mode, is almost lost and out of mind in our language." Even earlier, at the end of the 18th century, Noah Webster was either regretting or welcoming the loss of the subjunctive (he took different views in different works). And even before that Priestley—we assume from our 1798 edition that it was in his 1768 book—observed that the subjunctive (he called it *conjunctive,* after the practice of Samuel Johnson) was "much neglected by many of our best writers." The 18th-century grammarians had barely discovered the subjunctive, so apparently it was in decline as soon as it was recognized. The historical grammarians show that it has, in fact, been in decline since Old English, when the modal auxiliaries began to take over some of its functions.

But the subjunctive has not disappeared. H. L. Mencken, who had declared the subjunctive "virtually extinct in the vulgar tongue" in *The American Language* (4th ed., 1936), commented in his second supplement (1948):

> On higher levels, of course, the subjunctive shows more life, and there is ground for questioning the conclusion of Bradley, Krapp, Vizetelly, Fowler and other authorities that it is on its way out.

Mencken made the distinction between the written and spoken language that many other commentators have overlooked. Our evidence, mostly written, bears out Mencken's observation.

The subjunctive in modern English is, however, an all but invisible verb form. Its chief characteristic for most verbs is a lack of inflection, and so it is only noticeable when it turns up in a context calling for an inflection. The present subjunctive of the verb *think,* for instance, is *think,* and you really only notice that it is a subjunctive when it appears with a subject that would ordinarily require *thinks.* The verb whose subjunctive forms are most noticeable is *be,* with *be* in the present, which contrasts with all the indicative forms *(am, are, is),* and *were* in the past, which frequently (as we shall see) contrasts with *was.* It is this latter contrast, especially in various conditional clauses, that has stirred the most controversy. We will come to that problem in due course, but first let us take note of two uncontroversial uses of the subjunctive which are seldom considered in notices of its death.

The subjunctive is preserved like a fossil in a number of fixed formulas—*so be it, be that as it may, Heaven forbid, come what may, suffice it to say,* and so forth— that are used every day without much thought about their peculiarity. An example or two of some others:

> I write entirely by smell as it were —Flannery O'Connor, letter, 19 Feb. 1956

> ... willing to make digressions and, if need be, to get nowhere —Leacock 1943

> "... and far be it from me to throw any fanciful impediment in the way...." —Jane Austen, *Mansfield Park,* 1814

> ... the randomness and drift, the sheer, as it were, deadness —Wilfrid Sheed, *The Good Word and Other Words,* 1978

These phrases excite no controversy.

Also uncontroversial is the so-called mandative subjunctive—a highfalutin term for the subjunctive found in the common parliamentary formula "I move that the meeting be adjourned." This subjunctive occurs in clauses following such verbs as *ask, demand, recommend, suggest, insist* and such phrases as *it is advisable* and *it is necessary.*

> ... it was recommended that the President not inform Congress —Edwin Meese 3d, quoted in *The Tower Commission Report,* 1987

> The author suggested that buildings be found that are near high-voltage power lines —Jon M. Van Dyke, *Center Mag.,* July/August 1970

> What she found led her to recommend ... that thalidomide be barred from the market —*Current Biography,* March 1966

> ... when to recommend that a student seek help —Nancy S. Prichard, *College Composition and Communication,* February 1970

> Mrs. Clark suggested that the class learn some simple first-aid and health rules —Matilda Bailey et al., *Our English Language,* 3d ed., 1963 (6th-grade text)

This use of the subjunctive is regular. Todd & Hancock 1986 notes that these sentences are of a rather formal structure.

The controversial uses of the subjunctive occur with verbs of wishing and in contrary-to-fact conditional clauses, almost always in contexts involving the contrast of the subjunctive *were* with the indicative *was.* Here are some examples of the subjunctive in such contexts:

> I wish there weren't stones in my boots, so I do, and I wish to God I had a cup of tea and a fresh egg —James Stephens, *The Crock of Gold,* 1912

> ... although I wish that Ralph Mooney's sweet-and-sad singing steel guitar were a bit more up-front —Tony Glover, *Rolling Stone,* 18 July 1974

> If I were younger and could see anything at all I would appear or let someone make a film —James Thurber, letter, 15 Aug. 1959

> ... brings it down gently on the driver's shoulder, as if he were bestowing knighthood —Jay McInerney, *Bright Lights, Big City,* 1984

> ... minutely scrutinizes the novels along with the writer, as though she were inviting us to watch her take an extremely rare watch to pieces and put it together again —Mollie Panter-Downes, *New Yorker,* 4 Nov. 1985

> Today it is snowing here & were I not confined to my bed taking two-toned pills I would be painting a snow scene —Flannery O'Connor, letter, March 1960

> Were a war to break out —Kosta Tsipsis, *Discover,* April 1987

From these examples it can be seen that the subjunctive is likely to be found after the verb *wish* (and perhaps in other expressions of a wish), after *if, as if,* and *as though,* and at the beginning of a clause or sentence stating something contrary to fact or hypothetical. Hall 1917 and Jespersen 1909–49 (vol. 4) observe that *was* began to compete with *were* in these contexts sometime around the end of the 16th century (Jespersen's earliest example is from Christopher Marlowe's *Hero and Leander,* published in 1598, five years after Marlowe's death). The next earliest examples are from the second half of

the 17th century, however, so we may hazard a guess that *was* did not become frequent in this use until around the end of the 17th century—beginning, say, with Defoe (Jespersen cites examples from Defoe and other early 18th-century writers such as Swift and Addison). Jespersen hazards no guess as to why *was* began to compete with the older *were,* other than to note that in some contexts *was* is more emphatic. Such an emphatic *was* can be illustrated, with a bit of scene-setting, by a few lines from George Farquhar's *The Inconstant* (1702). Captain Duretete has designs upon a young lady named Bisarre who had adopted a pose of being absorbed in the study of philosophy. Duretete is sure he can win her by philosophical argument and bribes her maid for admittance to her rooms in order to talk. The maid secretes him behind a screen. But when Bisarre comes in and sees no one around, she drops her philosophical pose, throws down her book, and calls for music.

> BISARRE. Come wench, let's be free; call in the fiddle, there's nobody near us.
>   Enter Fiddler.
> CAPTAIN DURETETE [aside]. Would to the Lord there was not!

But most of the examples, in Jespersen and elsewhere, are not notably emphatic:

> I wish my cold hand was in the warmest place about you —Jonathan Swift, *Journal to Stella,* 5 Feb. 1711

> I wish H. was not quite so fat —Lord Byron, letter, 8 Dec. 1811

> I wish it was Elinor and I seeing you about now instead of them two irresponsible wastrels our son and daughter —Robert Frost, letter, 1 Nov. 1927

> I wish I was six feet tall and I wouldn't mind if I was handsome —*And More by Andy Rooney,* 1982

Was is likewise common in unemphatic contexts after *if, as if,* and *as though:*

> If Eastbourne was only a mile off from Scarborough, I would come and see you tomorrow —Lewis Carroll, letter, 14 July 1877

> The situation in the Middle East ... might be very different if there was an international left with a strong base —Noam Chomsky, *Columbia Forum,* Winter 1969

> Why do I grin when I see her, as if I was delighted? —W. M. Thackeray, *The Book of Snobs,* 1846

> ... and the women can all carry me in their arms as though I was a baby —Henry Adams, letter, 9 Oct. 1890

It may seem that *was* is crowding out subjunctive *were* in informal contexts, such as the letters and journals among our examples here. But not necessarily:

> ... if you were allowed to cut your finger with it, once a week —Lewis Carroll, letter, 23 Jan. 1862

> If I were ten years younger I might have tackled one of these assignments —Groucho Marx, letter, 5 July 1961

> ... I should feel as if I were flirting with my aunt —Henry Adams, letter, 23 Nov. 1859

Jespersen observes that subjunctive *were* is least likely to be displaced in the constructions without a conjunction in which it begins a clause or sentence. But even here he found a few examples with *was,* like this one:

> Was I Diogenes, I would not move out of a kilderkin into a hogshead —Charles Lamb, letter, 29 Mar. 1809

One of the curiosities of the *was–were* competition is the tendency of many writers to use both, often very close together, even in the same sentence. The tendency was noted as early as the 18th century (by Priestley 1798) and Jespersen has numerous examples. Here are a couple we have found:

> ... and all staring, gravely, as if it were a funeral, at me as if I was the coffin —Henry Adams, letter, 15 May 1859

> I wish I was a dog and Ronald Reagan were a Jelly Bean tree —Reinhold Aman, *Maledicta,* Summer/ Winter 1982

It should be remarked that *if* and *as if* do not always introduce an unreal condition and therefore *if* and *as if* do not necessarily call for a subjunctive:

> If he was to marry the queen, the power of the nobles was such that he would have first to gain their approbation —John Butt, *English Literature in the Mid-Eighteenth Century,* edited & completed by Geoffrey Carnall, 1979

> ... Freud felt as if he was being observed; raising his eyes he found some children staring down at him — E. L. Doctorow, *Ragtime,* 1975

> ... asked Dick if there was any way that he could get us to meet before the 3 Nov. meeting —Oliver North, quoted in *The Tower Commission Report,* 1987

Sometimes the subjunctive *were* is actually used when there is no unreal or hypothetical condition; it is probably triggered somewhat automatically by a preceding *if:*

> He was asked if he were apprehensive —*N.Y. Times,* 16 Jan. 1972

> I do not even know if she *were* actually a War Widow —Richard Cobb, *Still Life,* 1983

> It could have been then; if it weren't, it was certainly the next day —Donald Regan, testifying at the Iran-Contra hearings, 1987

This use is considered hypercorrect by those who notice it; it would be safe to say, however, that very few notice it.

To repeat, we do not really know why, three or four hundred years ago, *was* began to compete with the older subjunctive *were* in wishes and hypothetical and other unreal statements. It simply happened. The success that the indicative form has had since then has probably been abetted by the near invisibility of the subjunctive. We do not have any distinctive subjunctive forms in modern English; every one we can identify as a subjunctive is simply an indicative form doing double duty. The subjunctive as an entity, then, has very little support in the grammar, and much of the time the subjunctive and indicative are identical:

> And here in Missouri we don't charge our kinfolks with fees like we would do if they were strangers —

Luther Burrus, quoted in Merle Miller, *Plain Speaking,* 1973

Little wonder, then, that the subjunctive has so little impact on the general consciousness.

But the old forms die hard. If it is generally true, as commentators have been saying for a century, that the subjunctive is dying out of the common speech (as distinct from writing), there are still signs that it is not yet extinct. A colleague reports hearing this subjunctive in the chatter of two children on a Chicago subway train:

> If I were fat like you, I wouldn't. . . .

And clearly the subjunctive is not gone from writing, no matter how many commentators say that it is not as common now as it was a century ago. You will doubtless find many uses for it in your own writing, whether you are aware of them or not.

See also IF 3.

subsequent, subsequently, subsequent to Some relatively mild criticism has been directed at these terms by a few commentators who regard them as little more than stuffy substitutes for such words as *following, later,* and *after.* It is certainly true that informality is not their strong point:

> As subsequent sections of this memorandum seek to make plain, this kind of multiple activity is not necessarily incompatible with good teaching —Hazen Foundation Committee on Undergraduate Teaching, *The Importance of Teaching,* 1968

> ... this notification was subsequently rescinded through a compromise that gave Dr. Gibbs a temporary research assignment —*AAUP Bulletin,* December 1967

> My acquaintance with him was subsequent to the heart affliction, which must have necessarily precluded bodily exercise —Sidney Lovett, *Yale Rev.,* Summer 1954

Our evidence indicates that use of these terms is generally restricted to writing in which one is deliberately aiming at a formal tone, as in the above examples. They are unlikely to be used in casual speech and writing; it is hard to imagine anyone saying, "I'll give you a call subsequent to dinner." Formality is not their only distinctive feature, however. To describe something as "later" is usually just to establish its relative place in time, but to describe it as "subsequent" may also imply that it not only follows but in some way grows out of or is otherwise closely connected with what precedes it:

> ... the reviews we saw were favorable and looked forward to the subsequent books in the series —Leo Bergson & Robert McMahon, *The Writer,* October 1968

> The report, and its authors' subsequent prodding, moved the faculty last spring to agree —Larry Van Dyne, *Change,* November–December 1969

substandard The label *substandard* is widely used in usage books. In dictionaries—and in this book—it signifies no more than that the word or construction so labeled is normally used within a speech community by a group other than the one with prestige. This tends to suggest use by the least educated. Hence *substandard* contrasts with *nonstandard* (which see), which is applied to words and constructions that are not characteristic of the usage of educated native speakers but may be employed by them at times—for example, a strictly local term or a slang expression. In much writing about usage, however, *substandard* tends to mean only that the word or construction so labeled does not accord with the commentator's own notions of good English.

substitute In its oldest and still most common transitive sense, *substitute* means "to put or use in place of another":

> ... echoes of a more spontaneous life before the Puritan middle class had substituted asceticism for beauty ... —Vernon Louis Parrington, *Main Currents in American Thought,* 1930

> Such logic encourages the state to substitute its vision ... for the religious views of the Amish —Stephen Arons, *Saturday Rev.,* 15 Jan. 1972

However, the OED shows that *substitute* has also been used since the 17th century to mean "to take the place of; replace":

> Good brandy was being substituted by vile whiskey —Catherine C. Hopley, *Life in the South,* 1863 (OED)

The OED said in 1915 that this use was "now regarded as incorrect." Fowler 1926 was strong in his objection to this newer sense, which he found to be increasingly common and which he regarded as a serious threat to the older meaning of the word. Fowler illustrated the "corruption," as he called it, with a full twenty quotations, presumably culled from British periodicals. Several later commentators have repeated Fowler's criticism. Bernstein 1965, for one, describes the use of *substitute* to mean "replace" as "a common solecism." The volume of the OED Supplement published in 1986 calls this use of *substitute* incorrect.

Despite this criticism, there is ample evidence showing *substitute* being used in this sense in standard writing on both sides of the Atlantic:

> ... left all the horses, which he substituted with mules —*Dictionary of American History,* 1940

> ... names like *Jane* are always substituted by the pronoun *she* —Robert A. Hall, Jr., *American Speech,* October 1951

> ... at least substitute conjecture with facts —Maurice Friedberg, *Saturday Rev.,* 4 Dec. 1971

> ... concludes that British Rail's proposals to compensate ... at rates of four, five, and six per cent. are inadequate and substitutes them with levels of five, 7½, and 10 per cent. —*Daily Telegraph,* 25 July 1974 (OED Supplement)

> ... first-rate criminals were substituted by hi-jackers, hostage-takers, and other blackmailers —George Mikes, *Punch,* 1 Jan. 1975

> ... the pungent pines ... have been substituted by filling stations, Pizza Huts, and shoddy motels — Suzanne Wilding, *Town & Country,* August 1976

Given its use in general, and even sometimes scholarly, writing and its presence in the language for more than 300 years, we see no reason to dismiss this use of *substitute* as an error, and it has been recognized as standard in Merriam-Webster dictionaries since Webster's Second (1934). On the other hand, it is the less common

sense of the word, and to some ears it will seem less than idiomatic.

Faced with this potential for a negative reaction, you may want to avoid this sense of *substitute,* but worries about confused meaning need not concern you. The choice of preposition almost always makes the meaning clear. The older sense of *substitute* is used with *for* ("substitute a new version for the old one"); the "replace" sense is used with *by* or *with* ("substitute the old version with (or by) a new one").

succeed A person may fail *to do* something or succeed *in doing* it:

> ... the little man had succeeded in disturbing the boy —Roald Dahl, *Someone Like You,* 1953

> ... may well succeed in carrying the day —*Times Literary Supp.,* 19 Feb. 1970

Fowler 1926 cited as an error a passage in which *succeed* was followed by an infinitive rather than by *in* plus a gerund. A few later commentators have also observed that the infinitive after *succeed* is not idiomatic. Our evidence supports that observation. Aside from the Fowler citation, we have encountered only a single example of *succeed* followed by an infinitive:

> Only a few individuals succeed now to enter and to climb these ladders —Pitirim A. Sorokin, *Society, Culture, and Personality: Their Structure and Dynamics,* 1947

such 1. *Pronoun.* There has been much discussion of *such* as a pronoun. Most commentators agree only in criticizing it; otherwise, their comments are divergent. One calls it formal, another informal if not substandard, another stilted, another literary. Some just call it wrong:

> May one say, correctly, "Of *such* I want no part"? Not in the opinion of most authorities. In that example, *such* is acting as a pronoun, a part of speech to which it does not belong, even though the Bible says "... of such is the kingdom of God." —Freeman 1983

But the OED shows that *such* has been a pronoun since the time of King Alfred the Great, more than 900 years ago. It is still in use, and it is used in standard English, no matter how the commentators label it. Many of its uses are actually uncontroversial. It is most likely to attract criticism when it occurs in contexts where it can be replaced by common alternatives like *it, them, this,* and *these,* as in a sentence such as "If you retained a receipt, please enclose such." *Such* may not be the best-chosen word in such a context, but it is not an error. To give you a better idea of the respectability and range of pronominal *such,* here is a sampling of usage:

> ... Suffer little children to come unto me, and forbid them not: for of such is the Kingdom of God —Luke 18:16 (AV), 1611

> Edmund did not wonder that such should be his father's feelings —Jane Austen, *Mansfield Park,* 1814

> ... my last two books have been clipbooks, and I have been hoping that before publishing another such I could produce an Original Work —E. B. White, letter, 19 Aug. 1940

> ... the wives will be free to have their say to such as Lord Redmayne —*The Times* (London), 16 Apr. 1974

She was looking for ... an unfamiliar movement, one that was out of place in her world. Had she seen such, she would have disappeared back into the burrow —Lawrence Wishner, *Smithsonian,* October 1982

Locke envisaged clean and decent residential training centres. Few such existed —*Times Literary Supp.,* 5 Mar. 1970

... a token nonacademic or two; one such was Courtenay Stone —Steve Lohr, *N.Y. Times,* 12 Mar. 1980

He can make statements without worrying about the wrath of club owners because none such employ him —Pete Axthelm, *New York,* 30 Aug. 1971

The use of *such* to begin a sentence was criticized as far back as Murray 1795 (and probably further back, as Murray was not markedly original). It is rarely criticized now, however, and it is, of course, entirely standard:

Such was the degree of my emotional disturbance that I walked down to the centre of the town without adverting to my surroundings —Flann O'Brien, *At Swim-Two-Birds,* 1939

Such are the harsh facts, and no new formulas, however ingenious, no theoretical legerdemain, can make them disappear —Walter Laqueur, *Commentary,* January 1972

Such is often followed by a clause that explains or expands. The clause is usually introduced by *as:*

... were such as made him seem not even quite an Englishman —Edmund Wilson, *New Yorker,* 18 Sept. 1971

... standards of decency and standards of truth (such as survive) —Robert M. Adams, *Bad Mouth,* 1977

... an easy lack of fearsomeness such as is weirdly charming —Christopher Ricks, *N.Y. Rev. of Books,* 9 Mar. 1972

If the clause following *such* shows a result, it is usually introduced by *that:*

... a container such that when rations were dropped from airplanes to ground troops there would be no breaking or crumbling of Saltines —Renata Adler, *Pitch Dark,* 1983

... Anderson's medical knowledge is such that it's surprising to learn she's never worked in a hospital —*Publishers Weekly,* 24 May 1985

Such is also used as part of a tag that suggests an indefinite number of the same sort; the common forms are *and such, or such,* and *or some such.* These uses of *such* seem to attract a fair amount of criticism, but our evidence shows them to be respectable:

Does anything, even Freud's work, belong with Plato and Homer, Shakespeare, Milton and such? —Diana Trilling, *N.Y. Times Book Rev.,* 3 June 1979

She had heard Baptists and such call their minister a *preacher* —George P. Elliott, *Esquire,* February 1972

When the story begins, fourteen daughters of doctors, bankers, lawyers, and such are graduating from the local Female College —Mona Simpson, *Vogue,* July 1984

... excellent Alsatian wine (the noble Riesling, the flowery Gewürztraminer, or such) —Colman Andrews, *Metropolitan Home,* November 1983

... by a calculus of his own devising, the letters in the word "love" added up to sixteen, or fifty-four, or some such —*New Yorker,* 19 Mar. 1984

Evans 1957 observes that in speech some of the pronominal uses of *such*—not the tag lines—tend to be replaced by other pronouns or by other constructions. In other words, *such* as a pronoun tends to be more likely in writing than in speech. The example "one such was Courtenay Stone" would probably come out in speech as something like "one of them was Courtenay Stone" or "Courtenay Stone was one of those." You do not have to replace pronominal *such* in writing, but you will probably use it less often in talking. It is the greater frequency of *such* in writing that leads some commentators to feel that it is formal or even stilted.

2. *Adjective, adverb.* The adjective *such* regularly qualifies a noncount noun or a plural count noun:

... clergymen who advocated such recognition —*Current Biography,* November 1967

... such equity in earnings exceeded dividends —*Annual Report, Texaco Inc.,* 1970

The National Cancer Institute hopes to find more such plants —Catherine Caufield, *New Yorker,* 14 Jan. 1985

It was on such nights that they liked to lollygag —Joseph Wambaugh, *Lines and Shadows,* 1984

Before a singular count noun, idiom usually requires that the indefinite article follow *such:*

... said that he never remembered such a severe winter as this —Jane Austen, letter, 17 Jan. 1809

... I never see such a performance but that ... —Sherwood Anderson, quoted in *New Yorker,* 12 Nov. 1984

The article is normally omitted when *such* is preceded by another modifier:

... called "Marxism and the Developing World", or some such title —*Times Literary Supp.,* 5 Mar. 1970

... the first such painting he did —Tex Maule, *Sports Illustrated,* 29 July 1968

No such agreement previously existed —Naomi F. Levin, *Barnard Alumnae,* Winter 1971

Several similar but distinguishable uses of *such* have drawn criticism since Priestly in 1768. Ayres 1881 cited "I have never before seen such a large ox," which he felt was equivalent to "I have never before seen an ox such large." He argued that "such a large ox" should be "so large an ox." The notion that *such* is somehow being misused for *so,* as Priestly and Ayres thought, was repeated by several later commentators (Bierce 1909, for one). Fowler 1926 was lukewarm in his assessment of it, however, and no one now seems to take it very seriously. The OED shows that the criticized usage dates back to the 16th century and has occurred in the works of Shakespeare, Addison, Scott, and Dickens. It is, of course, irreproachably standard:

... but such a dismal Sight I never saw —Daniel Defoe, *Robinson Crusoe,* 1719

... condolences and consolations are such common and such useless things, that the omission of them is no great crime —Samuel Johnson, letter (in Hall 1917)

The quotation from Jane Austen in the preceding paragraph also exemplifies this construction.

The focus of critical attention has shifted in the 20th century to the use of *such* as an intensive, as in "He's such a nice boy." The difference between this use of *such* and the use criticized by Ayres is that in "I have never before seen such a large ox" there is an implied comparison—". . . such a large ox [as that one]." In "He's such a nice boy" there is no comparison; the meaning is simply "He's a very nice boy." This intensive use of *such* has been criticized at least since Weseen 1928, in which it was said to be "commonly called" the feminine *such*. Most recent criticism has been in college handbooks, in which it is typically described as too informal for writing. Our evidence confirms that written use of the purely intensive *such* is relatively rare, but several citations given in Bryant 1962 show that it can appropriately occur in writing that is not notably informal. Here are two of Bryant's examples:

He went to work for the future, showing in the process how terribly he had needed the language he launched; he had such a great deal to say —*Atlantic,* October 1953

And yet Henri Michaux himself is such a deceptively gentle, gracious man . . . ; perhaps this merely proves that his catharsis is effective —Justin O'Brien, *Saturday Rev.,* 26 Mar. 1949

As Bryant notes, these uses of *such* are standard.

such as See AS 6; LIKE, SUCH AS.

suffer A few sources of usage comment, Copperud 1970, 1980 and Heritage 1969 among them, say that *suffer* should be used with *from* rather than *with* when referring to a condition of health. Longman 1984 says "One *suffers from* a disease . . . but *suffer with* is often used where actual pain is involved. . . ." The evidence in our files shows that *suffer* is almost always used with *from:*

. . . deeply disappointed that we were not suffering from bubonic plague —Roald Dahl, *Someone Like You,* 1953

. . . by which diet he controls a duodenal ulcer from which he suffers —*Current Biography,* September 1953

The ladies wore their evening gowns, revealing lovely shoulders and bosoms not suffering from undernourishment —Upton Sinclair, *Presidential Mission,* 1947

. . . far too many of them suffer from nervous or heart disabilities —Hanson W. Baldwin, *Harper's,* April 1941

In fact, we have very little evidence from written sources of *suffer* ever being used with *with,* no matter what the meaning. That it is essentially an idiom of speech is perhaps sufficiently clear from this example:

Can't sleep a wink at night for crying;
All my worries get renewed
And I suffer with those all night blues
—Gertrude (Ma) Rainey, "Those All Night Blues," recorded December 1923

suitable The usual preposition after *suitable* is *for:*

. . . subjects regarded as suitable for college work — James B. Conant, *Slums and Suburbs,* 1961

. . . more suitable for a boy than a girl —*Current Biography,* October 1967

To is also used, but less commonly:

Apparently no words were suitable to this strange pilgrimage —Lloyd C. Douglas, *The Big Fisherman,* 1948

. . . arable land . . . suitable to vegetables and flowers —Marion Wilhelm, *Americas,* July 1954

superior See IMPLICIT COMPARATIVE; INFERIOR, SUPERIOR.

superlative of two The notion, so beloved of modern commentators, that the superlative degree should not be used of only two seems to have had its origin in the 18th century. Joseph Priestley was one of the earliest to express it (Leonard 1929 cites a 1769 edition), but he only gave one example of the superlative of two and concluded, "This is a very pardonable oversight." Campbell 1776 was the next to take it up. He did so speculatively, allowing both "the weaker of the two" and "the weakest of the two," but preferring the comparative to the superlative on "the most general principles of analogy," which principles he did not explain. Lindley Murray 1795 took his discussion of the superlative straight from Campbell, but in later editions he eliminated any element of doubt. "The weaker of the two" became "the regular mode of expression, because there are only two things compared." Campbell's speculation had become a rule.

Evidently Murray's formulation of the question was picked up by a great many grammarians in the 19th century. Goold Brown 1851 provided a long list of them, side by side with examples of the superlative of two drawn from their own works. The rule did not impress Goold Brown:

The common assertion of the grammarians, that the superlative degree is not applicable to *two* objects, is not only unsupported by any reason in the nature of things, but is contradicted in practice by almost every man who affirms it.

But Goold Brown's opinion seems to have had no influence on the school books, and both grammarians and rhetoricians clung steadfastly for a time to Murray's rule. Around the turn of the century, according to Hall 1917, the attitude of some grammarians at higher levels of speculation began to soften—one Scottish grammarian even advocated abolishing the comparative of two as a useless impediment. But the rhetoricians of the time were holding fast. The same division of opinion exists today. The grammarians are more latitudinarian: even school grammars allow the superlative of two in everyday or informal circumstances. The hard-line commentators of today, however, continue to insist that the superlative of two is an out-and-out error.

Two things should be noted about the rule. First, as Lamberts 1972 points out, it makes no difference from the standpoint of communication whether you use the comparative or the superlative of two. No one will misunderstand you if you say "She is the older of the two" or if you say "She is the oldest of the two." The rule serves no useful purpose at all. It is therefore a perfect shibboleth, serving no practical function except to separate those who observe the rule from those who do not.

The second thing is that the rule clearly has never reflected actual usage. From the examples collected by Otto Jespersen and other historical investigators, it is plain that many of our best writers have used either the comparative or superlative of two, as suited their fancy at the time. Among the writers who found the superlative appropriate for two are—from the compilations of Hall and Jespersen—Shakespeare, Milton, Defoe, Addison, Goldsmith, Dr. Johnson, Chesterfield, Austen, Byron, Scott, Irving, Hawthorne, Thackeray, Disraeli, Ruskin, Emerson, and Stevenson; Curme 1931 and Lamberts add Thoreau and James Russell Lowell to the list. There is clearly a strong literary tradition for the practice. Here are some examples from our collection:

Here am I brought to a very pretty dilemma; I must commit murder or commit matrimony! Which is best, now? —George Farquhar, *The Constant Couple,* 1699

However, I was condemned to be beheaded, or burnt, as the king pleased; and he was graciously pleased, from the great remains of his love, to choose the mildest sentence —Henry Fielding, *A Journey from This World to the Next,* 1743

We cannot agree as to which is the eldest of the two Miss Plumbtrees —Jane Austen, letter, 31 May 1811

She and her sister had had pretty good situations as ladies' maids. . . . Many a time I have seen the eldest of them. . . . —Elizabeth Gaskell, *Cranford,* 1853

dinghy, dingey. The first is best —Fowler 1926

Crane wrote two fine stories. *The Open Boat* and *The Blue Hotel.* The last one is the best —Ernest Hemingway, *Green Hills of Africa,* 1935

. . . there was once a contest between Athena and the god Poseidon for the possession of the Acropolis. Athena came off best —H. D. F. Kitto, *The Greeks,* rev. ed., 1957

It is not rare to find the comparative and superlative cheek by jowl:

. . . or, if one be alive and the other dead, it is usually the latter that is the handsomest —Thomas Gray, letter, 22 Feb. 1747

Warburton has the most general, most scholastic learning; Lowth is the more correct scholar. I do not know which of them calls names best —Samuel Johnson, quoted in James Boswell, *Life of Samuel Johnson,* 1791

. . . got to admit that each party is worse than the other. The one that's out always looks the best — Will Rogers, *The Illiterate Digest,* 1924

. . . it usually turns out that not the better man but the least tired man wins —Aristides, *American Scholar,* Autumn 1981

It seems clear from our experience in gathering examples of the superlative of two for this book that they are plentiful and can be readily found by anyone who is interested enough to look for them.

We conclude that the superlative of two is alive and well in current English. The construction goes back at least to the time of Shakespeare and has a considerable

history of literary use. The rule requiring the comparative has a dubious basis in theory and no basis in practice, and it serves no useful communicative purpose whatsoever. Because it does have a fair number of devoted adherents, however, you may well want to follow it in your most dignified or elevated writing.

In speech, we recommend that you simply follow your instincts—the native speaker is not likely to go wrong. There are more traps for the learner, however. If you are a learner you must look out for the fixed phrases: it is always *lower lip* and *best foot forward.* It is always the comparative in a construction with *than* following: "I am taller than Jim." The superlative seems to be most likely when the judgment, measurement, or characteristic denoted by the adjective or adverb is the primary point being considered. Thus Fowler's "the first is best." He is not interested in comparing the two spellings as such; he is recommending that you use the first one.

supersede, supercede *Supercede* has a long history of occasional use as a spelling variant of *supersede;* or, to put it another way, people have been misspelling *supersede* for centuries. It all depends on your point of view. Both spellings can be etymologically justified: the original Latin verb was spelled *supersedere,* but the derivative verb in Old French, by way of which the word came into English, was first spelled *superceder* and only later *superseder,* according to the OED. The earliest record of this word in English (1491) shows it spelled with a *c.* Most other early citations, however, are for the *s* spelling, and there is no doubt that the *s* spelling has always been the dominant one in English. *Supersede* continues to be widely regarded—not just by usage commentators—as the only correct spelling of this word. *Supercede,* on the other hand, continues to turn up regularly in standard, edited prose:

. . . is in some ways superceding other forms — Annette Michelson, *Evergreen,* August 1967

. . . existing programs . . . were superceded by programs that channeled funds directly into inner-city neighborhoods —Frances Fox Piven, *Columbia Forum,* Summer 1970

They were superceded early in the twentieth century by publicly owned corporations —Webster Schott, *Saturday Rev.,* 29 Apr. 1978

. . . does not intend his book to supercede professional treatment —Genevieve Stuttaford, *Publishers Weekly,* 2 Apr. 1979

. . . had been superceded by more modern values — Eric Foner, *N.Y. Times Book Rev.,* 23 May 1982

supine See PRONE, SUPINE.

supportive *Supportive* has occasionally been criticized as jargon. It is an old adjective, dating back to the 16th century, but it was rarely used until recently. Its current popularity seems to be an outgrowth of its use in modern medical and psychological circles:

. . . a very withdrawn young woman who might have been expected to require some more supportive type of therapy —*Psychological Abstracts,* March 1948

Combined with appropriate surgical measures and supportive treatment . . . —*Therapeutic Notes,* January 1951

Current usage shows a wide range of applications:

> ... a new rotary kiln and supportive equipment is under construction —*Annual Report, Pfizer,* 1970

> And the final impression left by their work isn't supportive of optimism —Benjamin DeMott, *Saturday Rev.,* October 1972

> ... the overarching, interlocking, and mutually supportive structures of science, technology, and big organizations —Robert Penn Warren, *Democracy and Poetry,* 1975

> ... they need understanding, supportive husbands —Anita Shreve, *N.Y. Times Mag.,* 21 Nov. 1982

It is a common and obviously useful word, but it does tend to turn up on occasion in the type of prose that is likely to provoke a sneer:

> The above positions also require progressive leadership skills. Selected candidates will find a highly supportive atmosphere, geared towards growth and career enrichment.... Ample parking available —advt., *N.Y. Times,* 19 Sept. 1982

supposed to   *Supposed to* is indistinguishable in speech from *suppose to*—the *d* is not pronounced. For this reason the unwary sometimes omit it in writing as well. Many commentators warn against this error, and we imagine that its occurrence in casual writing is not rare, but we have only one example of it from a published source:

> "He's suppose to make us respect our city's Finest...." —*Media & Methods,* November 1968

Even here, it is likely that the *d* was deliberately omitted to suggest nonstandard speech (somewhat pointlessly, since, as noted above, *suppose to* and *supposed to* sound alike when spoken).

See also USED TO, USE TO.

supreme   *Supreme* is sometimes considered to be an absolute adjective. See ABSOLUTE ADJECTIVES.

surcease   This word still occurs fairly often as a fancy or old-fashioned synonym of *cessation* or *respite:*

> ... sensed the national desire for a surcease of anxiety —James D. Barber, *Center Mag.,* January/February 1971

> Girls don't help, although an amateurish singer ... offers him surcease briefly —Hollis Alpert, *Saturday Rev.,* 3 July 1971

> They offer surcease from the battering of the sun —Roger G. Kennedy, *Smithsonian,* November 1982

It is also sometimes used as a verb, although not as commonly as in centuries past:

> There is a general surceasing of education as a means of producing cultured men and women —Jeanne L. Noble, in *Threshold 1965, Ball State University,* September 1965

Several usage commentators, dating back to Fowler 1926, have found *surcease* to be archaic as both noun and verb and have discouraged its use as an affectation. We certainly do not consider *surcease* to be archaic as a noun, and it is probably not archaic as a verb either, although verb use is very rare.

sure, surely   The adverbs *sure* and *surely* are both reasonably old; *surely* is about a century earlier than *sure.* The OED evidence of early use shows both words occurring in the same senses, but over the centuries they have diverged. For instance, one of the chief uses of *surely* is persuasive; it is used with a statement that the speaker or writer is trying to get the hearer or reader to agree with. As recently as the 18th century, both adverbs could be used in this way:

> Surely nothing is more reproachful to a being endowed with reason, than to resign its powers to the influence of the air —Samuel Johnson, *The Idler,* 24 June 1758

> ... the most undeserving people in the world must sure have the vanity to wish somebody had a regard for them —Thomas Gray, letter, 20 Dec. 1735

And both adverbs were also once used in the sense "without doubt, certainly," as by John Milton:

> ... but he shall surely be put to death —*Eikonoklastes,* 1649

> God sure esteems the growth and completing of one virtuous person —*Areopagitica,* 1644

But during the 19th and 20th centuries the use of adverbial *sure* dropped off in mainstream British English, except in a few fixed phrases like *sure enough* and *as sure as. Sure* continued in use in the outlying forms of English, such as Scottish English, Irish English, and American English. In Irish English, *sure* and *surely* seem to have remained more or less interchangeable into the 20th century. Here is James Stephens, for instance:

> "I never ate cheese," said Seumas. "Is it good?"
> "Surely it is," replied Pan
>   —*The Crock of Gold,* 1912

> "Let me sit here for a while and play with the little dog, sir," said she, "sure the roads do be lonesome...." —*The Crock of Gold,* 1912

In American English adverbial *sure* came under attack around the end of the 19th century (the earliest criticism we have found is in Schele de Vere 1872) and continued into the early 20th century, when Vizetelly 1906 and Bierce 1909 spearheaded the attack. The assault has continued vigorously in the years since, especially in schoolbooks and college handbooks.

But the long-continued attack on *sure* has not driven it out of use; to the contrary, adverbial *sure* is probably now better established in speech and in general writing than ever. Its uses are, however, clearly differentiated from those of *surely. Sure* is used in less formal contexts, on the whole, than *surely.* It is used as a simple intensifier—mostly (at least in our recent evidence) as an intensifier of verbs rather than adjectives:

> A Time gal phoned me to see if I still stuck to a quote of mine she found in the Time clips.... I told her I sure did stick to it —James Thurber, letter, 9 July 1959

> You ought to write an article on Iris Murdoch.... I sure wish you would —Flannery O'Connor, letter, 27 May 1961

> ... on condition that I did not mention religion or sex. That sure cramped my style —A. S. Neill, *Neill! Neill! Orange Peel!,* 1972

I can never know how much I bored her, but, be certain, she sure amused me —Norman Mailer, *N.Y. Times Mag.,* 18 Apr. 1982

Sure is used in affirmation:

Q. Do you just take it from what you read?
A. Sure, you can get a lot of it. That's a very good way to learn the craft of writing —William Faulkner, 6 May 1957, in *Faulkner in the University,* 1959

Sure, it's escape music, and what's wrong with that? —Nat Hentoff, *Cosmopolitan,* April 1976

As a strong intensifier, *sure* is used when the writer or speaker expects the reader or hearer to agree:

'Images' sure don't *reflect!* —George Wald, in Harper 1975, 1985

Well, he's sure not following out your orders, if that's the case —John Erlichman, 17 Apr. 1973, quoted in *The Presidential Transcripts,* 1974

Scientists are really careful when digging the bones out of the ground, but the bandits sure aren't —Sallie Luther, *Ranger Rick,* April 1985

The Iranians sure have a way of bringing out the worst in us —Meg Greenfield, *Newsweek,* 29 Dec. 1986

And *sure* is regularly used in the same phrases that survive in British English—*sure enough, as sure as, sure as:*

. . . I said, 'That son of a bitch is gonna run against me,' and sure enough I was right —Harry S. Truman, quoted in Merle Miller, *Plain Speaking,* 1973

I knew it was for me as sure as I knew my own face in the mirror —E. L. Doctorow, *Loon Lake,* 1979

It's a moot point whether politicians are less venal than in Twain's day. But they're sure as the devil more intrusive —Alan Abelson, *Barron's,* 8 May 1972

But we all looked like that. I sure as hell did —Maurice Sendak, *N.Y. Times Book Rev.,* 8 May 1983

Surely, in American English, tends to be used in somewhat more elevated styles than *sure.* It too can be used as an intensive:

I surely don't want to leave the impression that I had an unhappy childhood —Edward C. Welsh, quoted in *Current Biography,* January 1967

I don't want you to get the wrong impression and I'm surely not talking about a sick cat or kitten — Susie Page, *Cats Mag.,* October 1983

Surely is less positive, more diffident, or more neutral than *sure.* Its use suggests that the writer or speaker is not altogether confident that the reader or hearer will agree; the tone may be speculative or hopeful or persuasive:

This kind of derogatory remark, if persisted in by one or both parties to a marriage, will surely lead to divorce —James Thurber, *Thurber Country,* 1953

. . . it would surely be possible, within a few years, to program a computer to construct a grammar from a large corpus of data —Noam Chomsky, *Columbia Forum,* Spring 1968

. . . the worst sort of empty rant, all the more so because Wolfe himself surely knew better —William Styron, *This Quiet Dust and Other Writings,* 1982

But surely a book on the avant-garde cannot be so conventional in philosophy —Karl Shapiro, *Los Angeles Times Book Rev.,* 15 Apr. 1971

As my reader has surely heard if he is tuned in to literary events —Mary McCarthy, *Occasional Prose,* 1985

Webster's 10th Collegiate surely will include it — James J. Kilpatrick, *Mayville* (Ky.) *Ledger-Independent,* 25 Aug. 1984

Surely if they have any real bona fides they can get a visa in Tehran —Robert C. McFarlane, quoted in *The Tower Commission Report,* 1987

In present-day American English, then, adverbial *sure* and *surely* are not used in quite the same contexts or for quite the same purposes, even though they share the same meanings.

sure and   For constructions like *be sure and,* see TRY AND.

surely   See SURE, SURELY.

surprised   The prepositions that occur after *surprised* are *at* and *by. By* is the choice when *surprised* means "taken unawares":

At dawn the household was surprised by a sudden Indian attack —*American Guide Series: New Hampshire,* 1938

Both *at* and *by* are possible when *surprised* means "struck with wonder" or "taken aback":

I am surprised at this evidence —Eric Larrabee, *CEA Critic,* October 1954

. . . have been myself continually surprised . . . by the abrupt and vast changes that I have seen —S. P. B. Mais, *The English Scene To-day,* 2d ed., 1949

surround   Such expressions as "surrounded on three sides" may be criticized (as by Bryson 1984 and Kilpatrick 1984) on the grounds that *surround* means "to enclose completely." But the criticism is less common than the expressions themselves:

. . . with two or three steps surrounding it on three sides —Edna St. Vincent Millay, *Aria Da Capo,* 1921

When the level of the water was raised, it was surrounded on two sides —R. W. Hatch, *New England Journeys,* 1953

. . . was surrounded on three sides by great fir trees —John Reed, *New Republic,* 22 Nov. 1954

. . . a good-sized barn, surrounded on three sides by woods —John Fischer, *Harper's,* January 1969

We have no evidence that anything has ever been described as "surrounded on one side," which would be a neat trick.
    The same critics who dislike "surrounded on three sides" also dislike "surrounded on all sides," "completely surrounded," and similar expressions, which

they regard as redundant. Here again, the criticized expressions are common in standard writing:

> ... at the bottom of the neck, which it entirely surrounds —Oliver Goldsmith, *A History of the Earth and Animated Nature,* 1774 (OED)

> The earth on which we live is ... surrounded by stars on all sides —J. Norman Lockyer, *Elementary Lessons in Astronomy,* 1868 (OED)

> ... square white columns completely surround it —*American Guide Series: Louisiana,* 1941

suspected 1. The problem with *suspected* is the same as the problem with *accused*—it sometimes occurs with nouns like *murderer* and *criminal:*

> ... those prisoners who are suspected war criminals —Robert H. Jackson, Report to the President, 7 June 1945, in *Voices of History 1945–1946,* ed. Nathan Ausubel, 1946

> ... a suspected dope peddler in California —*The Americana Annual 1953*

A suspected dope peddler is, of course, a person who is suspected of being a dope peddler, not a dope peddler who happens to be suspected of something. The use of *suspected* in this way is entirely idiomatic and does not appear to be a serious source of confusion, but it is apparently troubling to those who try to analyze idioms logically, and it has been cited with disapproval by the same critics who dislike the similar use of *accused* (which see).

2. When used with a preposition, *suspected* ordinarily takes *of:*

> ... expel from the Army all officers suspected of complicity in the plot against him —William L. Shirer, *The Rise and Fall of the Third Reich,* 1960

> ... spent with the bravado of a man who suspected himself of infallibility —Israel Shenker, *Smithsonian,* September 1979

> ... no one had hitherto suspected him of statecraft —John Buchan, *Augustus,* 1937

> Sweeping down and surrounding a South Vietnamese village suspected of aiding ... the Vietcong —Senator Ernest Gruening & Herbert W. Beaser, in *A Center Occasional Paper,* June 1968

suspicion An issue about which there is some comment but no real controversy is the use of *suspicion* as a verb meaning "to suspect." The OED includes an early 17th-century citation for this verb, but the next most recent evidence of its use dates from about 1820, and the OED Supplement notes that the first citation is probably "a fortuitous occurrence unrelated to later uses." In modern English the verb *suspicion* has been chiefly a feature of uneducated or dialectal speech. It occurs in writing primarily in representations or imitations of such speech:

> Anybody would suspicion us that saw us —Mark Twain, *Tom Sawyer,* 1876

> Everybody knowed them Newton boys wasn't no 'count and was rustling cattle, but nobody would have suspicioned them of killing a man —J. Frank Dobie, *Coronado's Children,* 1931

> Our nineteen-year-old son, which he's home from Yale ... and don't suspicion that his folks are rifting —S. J. Perelman, *New Yorker,* 5 Jan. 1946 (OED Supplement)

It does not appear in formal writing.

sustain *Sustain* is an old verb with many senses, most of which have been in use for centuries. Among them is the sense "to suffer or undergo," as in "sustain an injury" and "sustain losses," which was first attested in the early 1400s. Samuel Johnson included this sense without stigma in his dictionary, illustrating its use with quotations from Shakespeare and Milton. Noah Webster also regarded it as a standard sense, and it continues to be treated as one in current dictionaries. Usage commentators, however, have found various reasons for disliking it.

The first critic to take note of *sustain* seems to have been Dean Alford 1866, who regarded the "suffer" sense as an example of the "diluted English" favored by journalists. Like most of its later critics, Alford seems unaware that this sense has a long history of reputable use. His regarding it as a recent corruption suggests that it may well have come into more widespread use by way of newspapers during the 19th century. Part of what caught his attention was the use of this sense of *sustain* with a specific injury, such as "a fracture," as its direct object. He implied that such use was ludicrous to anyone acquainted with the "proper" senses of *sustain,* such as "to bear up under" and "to give support to":

> Men never break their legs, but they always *"sustain a fracture"* of them; a phrase which suggests to one the idea of the poor man with both hands holding up the broken limb to keep it straight.

The 20th-century critics of the "suffer" sense of *sustain* have, like Alford, generally regarded it as illogical and pretentious journalese. Bierce 1909 observed that "he sustained a broken neck" should be understood as meaning "that although his neck was broken he did not yield to the mischance." Fowler 1926 was aware of the history of this sense and did not consider it erroneous, but he recommended avoiding it anyway, both because it seemed excessively formal to him and because he felt that its use tended to weaken "the other meaning in which [*sustain*] is valuable, viz to bear up against...." Krapp 1927 saw it as a feature of "crudely ambitious writing." Partridge 1942 limited his censure to its use with such specific direct objects as *fracture* and *broken leg,* regarding "sustain injuries" as formal but acceptable. Among more recent critics, Flesch 1964 has dismissed it as "pompous," and Bernstein (in *Winners & Sinners,* 25 June 1958) has called it "a flossy synonym for *'receive'* or *'suffer.'"*

The criticism, however, has not been universal by any means. The Heritage 1969 panel found the "suffer" sense of *sustain* acceptable by a slight majority, and Copperud 1964 referred to its critics as "those who have never looked up the word." Most very recent commentators have nothing to say on the subject, and their silence strongly suggests that the controversy concerning this time-honored sense may be gradually dying out. The sense itself, meanwhile, continues to be alive and well:

> ... the company sustained operating losses totalling more than $30 million —Richard A. Lester, *New Republic,* 27 June 1955

... decorated with the Purple Heart for injuries he sustained on Okinawa —*Current Biography,* November 1967

... mentioned the "neglect and destruction" Jerusalem had sustained "during its more-or-less recent history" —Katharine Kuh, *Saturday Rev.,* 24 Jan. 1976

... estimates that some 77,000 persons a year sustain bruises, cuts ... —*Consumer Reports,* September 1980

... in December 1980 Howe sustained a grisly injury —Jack Falla, *Sports Illustrated,* 17 Jan. 1983

swap, swop   *Swap* is the usual spelling in American English, and, according to British dictionaries, it is also preferred in British English (the OED Supplement says that it is "recommended"). But in Fowler 1965, Sir Ernest Gowers finds that *swop* "is probably now commoner" than *swap,* and he undoubtedly bases his opinion on British usage. *Swop* is extremely rare in American English, but we have substantial evidence of its use by British writers:

... it was to swop yarns about murder —Philip Collins, *Times Literary Supp.,* 20 Nov. 1981

... just swopping old cigarette cards and comics — *This England,* Autumn 1983

In 1918, the editors of the OED considered *swap* slang or colloquial. Several usage commentators in the years since have taken a similar view and have discouraged the use of *swap* in writing. Our evidence clearly shows, however, that the OED's assessment is no longer valid. *Swap* is a common word, both as a verb and as a noun, and its use in all but the most formal writing is now unremarkable:

... proposed a swap of immunity from prosecution in exchange for possibly self-incriminating information —*N.Y. Times,* 14 Nov. 1954

Always trading and swapping to hold the line — David Halberstam, *Harper's,* February 1971

... Miles swapped its potentially profitable land for a thirty-acre tract —E. J. Kahn, Jr., *New Yorker,* 10 Apr. 1971

... would swap their stake in the joint venture for stock in the electronics company —*Dun's,* October 1971

... child swapping was commonly practiced between households of equal social standing —Jane Wilson, *N.Y. Times Book Rev.,* 1 July 1973

... was acquired from the Yankees in a minor-league-level swap last year —Roger Angell, *New Yorker,* 29 Nov. 1982

swell   This verb has two past participles in standard usage—*swelled* and *swollen.* The principal distinction that can be made between them is that *swollen* is the one used frequently as an attributive adjective:

... does not have to kowtow to some swollen bureaucracy —Ted Williams, *Massachusetts Wildlife,* November–December 1975

... battle of avarice and swollen ego —Anson Mount, *Playboy,* August 1977

Swelled is used attributively only in the idiom *swelled head,* as far as our citations indicate:

... where isolation too often breeds swelled heads in legislators and administrators —*Round Table,* March 1939

Otherwise, the two forms are more or less interchangeable, although, as Longman 1984 notes, *swollen* is more likely in describing a harmful or undesirable swelling:

... your face feeling unwashed and swollen from the intermittent sleep you got —William Styron, *Lie Down in Darkness,* 1951

The area becomes inflamed and swollen —Claude A. Villee et al., *General Zoology,* 3d ed., 1968

... his vanity had swollen to monstrous proportions —Malcolm Muggeridge, *Esquire,* December 1971

Swelled also occurs in such contexts:

Their feet had swelled up with infection —Raymond A. Sokolov, *Fading Feast,* 1981

But more often *swelled* tends to be used in a neutral or positive way, especially in describing an increase in numbers:

From 105 attorneys ... , the firm has now swelled to 120 —Paul Hoffman, *New York,* 26 Apr. 1971

... the ranks were swelled by more than 200,000 — Seymour M. Lipset & Everett C. Ladd, Jr., *Change,* May–June 1971

... the student body has swelled to 500 —Hank Hersch, *Sports Illustrated,* 19 Nov. 1986

swim, swam, swum   In current English, the standard past tense of *swim* is *swam,* and the standard past participle is *swum:*

... the moon swam palely in the pale blue daylight sky —Graham Greene, *Travels with My Aunt,* 1969

... and we have swum naked in cold country ponds —John Cheever, *N.Y. Times Book Rev.,* 28 Aug. 1983

Evidence in the OED shows that *swam* was also once in reputable use as a past participle:

Who, being shipwrecked, had swam naked to land —Samuel Johnson, *The Rambler,* 1750 (OED)

The messengers ... had swam across the Elbe and the Moldau —Thomas Carlyle, *German Romance,* 1827 (OED)

However, we have no 20th-century evidence of such use in writing. More complex is the history of *swum* in the past tense, as in these lines by Tennyson:

Who turn'd half-round to Psyche as she sprang
To meet it, with an eye that swum in thanks
—Alfred, Lord Tennyson, *The Princess,* 1847
(OED)

Additional written evidence is hard to come by, but dialect studies have shown that *swum* as the past of *swim* was common in certain areas of the U.S.—particularly New England—until fairly recently. E. Bagby Atwood, in *A Survey of Verb Forms in the Eastern*

United States (1953), noted that *swum* then appeared to be passing into disuse:

> What is particularly striking is the extent to which *swum* is being replaced by *swam*. In N. Eng. I count 57 communities where usage is clearly divided between the two forms; in 48 of these the more old-fashioned informant uses *swum,* the more modern *swam.*

Whatever its present status in speech, *swum* has never been commonly used in writing as the past tense of *swim.* Our files contain only a single 20th-century example of such use:

> He swum from the ship and was thrown up on the Welsh coast rocks —Cledwyn Hughes, *A Wanderer in North Wales,* 1949

swop   See SWAP, SWOP.

syndrome Reader's Digest 1983 and a few British commentators—Gowers 1973, Howard 1977, Phythian 1979, and Longman 1988—note that the figurative use of the medical term *syndrome* has gotten a bit out of hand and suggest that it is overused. Most of the British commentators are especially displeased when the word is used with the verb *suffer;* since a syndrome is not a disease, they say, *suffer* is the wrong verb.

Our evidence shows that *syndrome* is in fact a very common word these days. We do not find it used extremely often with *suffer,* but "suffer from the x syndrome" does seem to be one recurrent pattern of metaphorical use. The following examples constitute a typical sampling of our evidence:

> This second book suffers from a mild case of sequel syndrome. It simply does not rise to the same heights as the first —Aaron Latham, *N.Y. Times Book Rev.,* 27 Nov. 1983

> Now, I am not advocating messianic leadership. I think the Moses syndrome has run its course for us —Orde Coombs, *Harper's,* January 1972

> ... the whole accusation-and-guilt syndrome that had plagued the marriage —Cyra McFadden, *The Serial,* 1977

> ... although it did present opponents of the 'best-seller' syndrome with a ready opportunity —*British Book News,* June 1974

> ... there's that rare and wonderful film that does transmit a feeling of joy, a pure pleasure syndrome —Judith Crist, *New York,* 5 Mar. 1973

> It's the old Marilyn Monroe syndrome. Nobody takes a pretty girl seriously —Farrah Fawcett-Majors, quoted in *People,* 3 Jan. 1977

> ... the need for constantly increasing profits, as we discussed earlier—the result of the price/earnings syndrome among analysts, investors and corporate

> management —Ray Brady, quoted in *Dun's,* October 1971

> ... the author's quest plunges you into the Sancho Panza syndrome —*Times Literary Supp.,* 3 Nov. 1966

> Following the book-reviewer's syndrome, I searched for errors and omissions —A. J. Dessler, *Science,* 5 Apr. 1968

syntactic blend A syntactic blend is an unconscious combination of two (or perhaps more) phrases to produce a new one, such as *equally as good* from *just as good* and *equally good* (example from Bolinger 1980). A few syntactic blends recur often enough to become the subject of discussion in usage books (including the present one)—*equally as, accused with, hardly ... than, scarcely ... than,* for instance—and some may eventually become well enough established to be counted as idioms. A few are probably conscious combinations used as slang.

But most syntactic blends are accidents of speech and are probably not repeated except by chance. Gerald Cohen, who produces the journal *Comments on Etymology,* has been presenting lists of syntactic blends on a regular basis since 1975; his number 3–4 of 1981 contains almost a hundred of them, a great many taken from people talking on television. The bulk of these—several are rather humorous—would be more accurately described as malapropisms. Some of Cohen's examples include *bet your bottom boots,* from *bet your boots* and *bet your bottom dollar; couldn't give a damn less,* from *couldn't care less* and *don't give a damn;* and *out of skelter,* from *out of kilter* and *helter-skelter.*

Once in a while such blends will crop up in print. Here are a few we have found:

> Just wait to you hear Shlomo Mintz

This is probably *wait till you hear* and *can't wait to hear.*

> ... though perhaps not quite to the degree as was believed at the time

This seems to be *to the degree that* and *to such a degree as.*

> Quite a lot of more falling bodies

This must be from *quite a lot of* and *a lot more of.*

> ... probably alongside with the legends which the author has tried to destroy

This seems to be from *along with* and *alongside (of).*

> He induced Georgia Tech guard Bruce Dalrymple into picking up two quick fouls

This is likely a blend of *induce to* and *entice into.*

Part of Gerald Cohen's interest in syntactic blends stems from the fact that current theories of language do not account for them very well. So keep an ear and eye open for syntactic blends. They can show you how the language works when it is not hitting on all cylinders.

See also MALAPROPISM; MIXED METAPHOR.

T

tablespoonful, teaspoonful   These words are usually pluralized *tablespoonfuls* and *teaspoonfuls,* although *tablespoonsful* and *teaspoonsful* also occur as uncommon variants. Most people successfully avoid having to choose between these plurals by using the plurals *tablespoons* and *teaspoons* instead.

See -FUL.

take   **1.** For a discussion of point of view in relation to the use of *bring* and *take,* see BRING 1.
2. *Take,* a verb of Scandanavian origin, is a model strong verb with a past tense *took* and a past participle *taken.* Lamberts 1972 notes that there has long been some leveling of the past and past participle—going back at least to the 16th century. Mencken 1963 notes the same in his discussion of the vulgate, and *taken* as a past and *took* as a past participle are apparently not rare in the folk speech of many areas.

> He hesitated a second and then he taken that whiskey glass and put it up to his face —William Wister Haines, *High Tension,* 1938

> . . . leaving their half-took drinks behind —Flann O'Brien, *At-Swim-Two-Birds,* 1939

> Old Eagle had done already took off —William Faulkner, *Saturday Evening Post,* 5 Mar. 1955

In ordinary prose, of course, the standard forms are used.
3. At the end of the 19th century, the use of *take* with food and drink was considered less than refined by a number of American commentators; Ayres 1881, Long 1888, Compton 1898, and Vizetelly 1906 all aspersed it. But like many an issue, this one has died out and is forgotten by present-day writers.

> . . . crewmen can take their meals with their families —Sarah Ballard, *Sports Illustrated,* 10 Nov. 1986

> Yes, you can take tea with Edith Wharton, or at least with the actress who portrays her —*Elle,* June 1986

> . . . only the former hustle industriously by taking power breakfasts —David Berlinski, *Black Mischief,* 1986

take and   *Take and* is used in essentially an intensive function before another verb in much the same way as *go and* (as in "Go and leave me if you want to"). Our evidence of the construction is not as full as we would like, but what we have suggests that it was quite common in the 19th century. Mark Twain used it often:

> ". . . Well, when pap's full, you might take and belt him over the head with a church and you couldn't phase him. . . ." —*Tom Sawyer,* 1876

> So she took and dusted us both with the hickry — *Huckleberry Finn,* 1884

It persists in 20th-century American English, too:

> Homer was courting a second time to get him a good wife and a home-keeper for his children, when he took and fell off the church-house roof —Maristan Chapman, *The Happy Mountain,* 1928

> You might as well take and trim the rim off an old soft hat —William Carlos Williams, *Life Along the Passaic River,* 1938

And it also occurs in Irish English:

> Look at Matt Finn, the coffin-maker, put his hand on a cage the circus brought, and the lion took and tore it —Lady Gregory, *The Full Moon,* in *New Comedies,* 1913

Wentworth's American Dialect Dictionary carries a report that *take and* was "exceedingly common" in the mid-1930s. Our recent evidence of it in print is slight, but we suppose that the criticism of *take and* in Shaw 1975, 1987 and Prentice Hall 1978 attests to its continued vitality in speech. The OED Supplement includes an example from a 1977 novel.

Take and is one of those speech constructions that mark the language of the common people—H. L. Mencken's "vulgate." Its primary use in writing is to re-create that speech. It does not occur in ordinary prose.

See also GO AND.

take exception to   See EXCEPTION.

take place, occur   A few commentators, dating back to Vizetelly 1906, have wanted to restrict *take place* to events and actions that are planned, as in "The wedding ceremony will take place on Friday afternoon," and to restrict *occur* to those things that happen by chance, as in "The accident occurred at a busy intersection." The problem with this neat distinction is the same as with so many other distinctions promulgated by usage writers: it tries to elevate a tendency into a rule. It is true, in general, that planned ceremonies and events are much more often said to take place than to occur:

> When the gala première of *Vanessa* took place at the Metropolitan Opera House —*Current Biography,* November 1965

> If an arraignment is to take place, find out where and when —Myron Brenton, *McCall's,* March 1971

And it seems to be true as well that accidents are more often said to occur than to take place:

> . . . accidents occur while boys and girls are riding bicycles —*My Weekly Reader,* 18 Jan. 1952

But no simple rule of usage follows from these general observations. In much speech and writing, planned events also occur, and accidents also take place:

> His ordination occurred on Apr. 9, 1872 —*Dictionary of American Biography,* 1929

> A series of conferences . . . occurred during the six-week period —*AAUP Bulletin,* December 1967

> . . . the explosion took place in the evening, when most of the miners had already left —Laurence Learner, *Harper's,* December 1971

And *take place* is extremely common in contexts that have nothing to do with planned events or accidents:

... the intensity of the artistic process, the pressure, so to speak, under which the fusion takes place —T. S. Eliot, "Tradition and the Individual Talent," in *Selected Essays,* 1932

... to study the physiological and psychological changes taking place —*Current Biography,* December 1966

... that so much human misery could take place amid scenes of such exquisite beauty —Roland Gelatt, *Saturday Rev.,* 21 June 1969

She did not remember what had taken place under the hypnosis —Irving Stone, *McCall's,* March 1971

... for even now a miracle might take place — Daphne du Maurier, *Ladies' Home Jour.,* September 1971

In short, *take place* and *occur* are synonymous. The distinction promoted by the commentators is not made out of whole cloth, but it does ignore the variety of uses to which these words are put. There is no reason to consider the use of *occur* with planned events or *take place* with unplanned events to be an error.

talented

I regret to see that vile and barbarous vocable *talented,* stealing out of the newspapers into the leading reviews and most respectable publications of the day —Samuel Taylor Coleridge, *Table-Talk,* 8 July 1832 (OED)

It may seem hard to believe now, but *talented* was in fact once regarded by more than a few people as "vile and barbarous." Their objection to it was based on the mistaken notion that an adjective could not properly be formed by adding *-ed* to a noun. *Talented* was unacceptable as an adjective, in this view, because there was no such verb as *talent;* according to Bierce 1909, "If Nature did not talent a person the person is not talented." It follows from the same reasoning that if nature did not wing a bird, a bird is not winged. The fact is that many English adjectives have been formed by adding *-ed* to a noun; for example, *bigoted, crested, dogged, moneyed, skilled, spotted,* and *tenured.* The criticism of *talented* was entirely groundless, and its inadequacy was recognized by such commentators as Fitzedward Hall 1873, Hodgson 1881, and Utter 1916. The issue died a quiet death in the early 20th century.

taps Although its form is plural, the noun *taps,* referring to the military bugle call, usually takes a singular verb:

... will face the casket and execute the hand salute ... while taps is being sounded —*Dept. of the Army Field Manual,* June 1950

Bernstein 1965 states flatly that the verb should be plural, but his opinion is not supported by other commentators, by dictionaries, or by actual usage.

target Several commentators have aimed their guns at the figurative use of *target* to mean "an objective or goal to be achieved." This sense of *target* seems to have originated in World War II. Its most characteristic use relates to industrial production:

The 1942 production targets set by the government home timber production department were exceeded —*Britannica Book of the Year 1944*

... the failure of plants to reach their target —John Baker White, *Atlantic,* April 1949

... the production of cloth, cement, sugar and coal has exceeded the targets —Adlai E. Stevenson, *Look,* 14 July 1953

Production targets had to be cut back again and again —*Newsweek,* 11 Jan. 1954

Another familiar use is with reference to a specific time or date at or by which something is to be done:

... the target date for the invasion of France (Operation Overlord) was set at May 1, 1944 —Franklin D. Roosevelt, 25 May 1943, in *Franklin D. Roosevelt's Own Story,* ed. Donald Day, 1951

When the project is completed—1976 is the target date —Bruce Kovner, *New York,* 7 Feb. 1972

Criticism of *target* in this figurative sense originated in England, and the issue has continued to be primarily a British one. In the 1948 edition of *Plain Words,* Sir Ernest Gowers quoted at length a London *Times* editorial in which the new use of *target* was drolly ridiculed. The basis of the criticism was—and still is—that it only makes metaphorical sense to speak of hitting or missing a target, not of reaching, exceeding, or achieving one. The extent to which this argument has been accepted and repeated in Great Britain is due in part to the considerable influence of Gowers, and in part to the stream of witticisms the subject has inspired (many of which date back to the original *Times* editorial). More than one commentator has noted, for example, how curious it is that when a production target is doubled it doesn't become twice as easy to hit, as you might expect, but twice as hard. This sort of thing makes for entertaining usage books and helps to keep the issue alive.

Despite the repeated criticism, however, the use of *target* to mean "an objective or goal to be achieved" has continued unabated. As Evans 1957 has noted, it occurs somewhat more frequently in Great Britain than in the U.S. (another reason for the more widespread criticism among the British), but its occurrence in American English is not at all uncommon. The critics continue to regard the figurative *target* as, at best, a needless synonym for *goal* or *objective,* but it is distinguished from those words in at least one important respect: it almost always refers to a specific quantity or time. A shoelace company that has a *goal* of increasing production may have as its production *target* 760,000 shoelaces a month. It is this connotation of specificity that makes the figurative *target* a distinct and useful word and assures that its widespread use will continue.

tautology Although a few commentators treat *tautology* as a term to be distinguished from *pleonasm,* most American commentators use both of them as synonyms for *redundancy.* They are referring, in general, to things that are discussed at REDUNDANCY.

tax When the verb *tax* means "charge, accuse," it is idiomatically followed by *with:*

... suddenly taxed the little clergyman with being the sole author —H. L. Morrow, *Irish Digest,* November 1953

... but they will not be taxed with sin —Eugene Kennedy, *N.Y. Times Mag.,* 5 Aug. 1979

The less common sense "censure" is followed by *for:*

... taxes science for being unable ... to give us moral directives —Bernard Rosenberg, *American Scholar,* Spring 1953

... one would not tax a man for such becoming modesty —Richard Schickel, *Harper's,* April 1971

teach The transitive verb *teach,* in its various senses, can have many objects. It is possible to teach a student, teach a lesson, teach a class, teach a subject, and teach school. All of these uses of *teach* are venerable. The only one to have excited any critical comment is "to teach school," which was first recorded in 1686. It originated in British English, but the OED notes that it is "now *dial.* and *U.S.*" In American English it is common and standard:

... she taught school at Van Wert for five years — *The Americana Annual 1953*

... and is now teaching school in New York —William Pennell Rock, *Center Mag.,* November/December 1971

teaspoonful See TABLESPOONFUL, TEASPOONFUL.

telecast, televise Bergen Evans was a man with considerable experience of the world of television, and Evans 1957 notes a distinction in the meaning of these words:

[*Telecast*] means to broadcast by television. *Televise,* on the other hand, means to record by means of television apparatus and to broadcast what is so recorded.

In other words, the idea of broadcasting is secondary in *televise* to the idea of photographing (we would now say "videotaping") by means of a television camera. This distinction in meaning has, in fact, been observed in the past:

Models being televised in the afternoon before the show went on. Station WNBQ telecasted on Monday, July 18, a complete showing of nine models — *Fur News,* September 1949

But it is doubtful that anyone observes it now. Both *telecast* and *televise* now usually mean "to broadcast by television":

... the network decided to telecast only the first, as a one-time special —Carey Winfrey, *N.Y. Times,* 17 Aug. 1980

... when presentation of the Tony awards was televised, an audience estimated at 40,000,000 people saw her perform —*Current Biography,* April 1968

The great expense in televising programs coast to coast —Les Brown, *Saturday Rev.,* 16 Sept. 1978

Televise has been used with this meaning since it was first coined, as one of our earliest citations for it shows:

... the usual broadcast sounds are received first and then the radio announcer will say, "We shall now televise the face of our next singer. ..." —*Science and Invention,* October 1928

A dictionary editor who read this citation in 1930 wrote on it "Fairly rare and I think ephemeral," which shows, in case anyone was wondering, that lexicographers have no special standing as prophets.

temblor, tremblor, trembler A synonym for *earthquake, temblor* owes its existence as an English word in part to the presence of a large Hispanic population in the southwestern U.S. and in part to the activities of the San Andreas Fault. It is taken directly from Spanish, in which its literal meaning is "trembling." It became established as an English word in the early 20th century, when it was widely used in reports of California earthquakes, including the one that nearly destroyed San Francisco in 1906. It has never been a common word, however. The tendency among some speakers and writers unfamiliar with Spanish has been to make it more recognizably English by inserting an *r* after the initial *t,* and sometimes also by changing the *o* to an *e:*

... registered 7.3 on the Richter Scale—classifying as a major tremblor —*N.Y. Times* (UPI), 1 Dec. 1975

... the storms, floods, dust and tremblors that somehow conditioned their lives —Kathryn Livingston, *Town & Country,* November 1980

... shattered show business traditions like a point eight [sic] trembler on the San Andreas fault —Ralph J. Gleason, *Rolling Stone,* 26 Oct. 1972

... there are some 500 earthquakes in California each year. Most are minor tremblers —Brad Knickerbocker, *Christian Science Monitor,* 30 Jan. 1980

Temblor is still the usual spelling, however, and is still regarded by many people as the only correct one, though the variants are recognized by very large dictionaries such as Webster's Third.

temperature A few critics have gotten hot under the collar about the use of *temperature* to mean "fever," as in "You look like you're running a temperature." This sense of *temperature* is extremely common in speech but rare in writing. Its first use is recorded in the OED as from near the end of the 19th century. This sense of *temperature* has an illogical quality which some people are bound to find irritating (Gowers in Fowler 1965 calls it "absurd" and "foolish") and some others are bound to find appealing. Most people, of course, will not give it a second thought in their speech and will not think to use it in writing.

tenant, tenet Kilpatrick 1984 cites a newspaper article in which *tenant,* "occupant, land-holder," is mistakenly used in place of *tenet,* "principle, doctrine." This does not seem to be a common error, at least in published prose, but we find an example of it now and then:

One of the ancient tenants of the Buddist [sic] belief is, "He who sits still, wins" —*Police,* January/February 1968

Bolinger 1980 has seen the same error; he associates it with jargonistic writing. Here is his example:

Indeed this has been stated as an explicit tenant by Chomsky —Charles Goodwin, "The Interactive Construction of the Sentence Within the Turn at Talk in Natural Conversation," 1975

You will probably never make this mistake with *tenant,* but if you think you might, remember that *tenant* and *occupant* both end in *-ant.*

tend   The use of *tend* as an intransitive verb meaning "to pay attention; attend" is standard in American English:

> We should tend to our business—which is to teach the young —Milton Friedman, reprinted column, 1969

> He suggested that Russia and the United States might work out their problems separately and the United Nations could tend to what was left — Eugene J. McCarthy, *Center Mag.,* March/April 1971

> . . . tends to the worldwide oil empire his late father built up —Susan Sheehan, *McCall's,* October 1971

> . . . the administrations have tended to the more general matters of institutional survival —George W. Bonham, *Change,* April 1972

This sense of *tend* is extremely old, dating back to the 14th century. It originated as a short form of *attend,* as did the transitive *tend* of "tend the fire" and "tend the sick." The intransitive *tend* appears to have fallen out of written use in the 1600s, but it survived in spoken dialect thereafter and has experienced an impressive revival in writing during the past 100 years. Evidence from the late 19th and early 20th centuries shows it being used by such authors as Mark Twain, William Faulkner, and Margaret Mitchell in written representations of southern U.S. speech. It also occasionally occurred in ordinary, straightforward writing, where it was noted and criticized by Fowler 1926. Recent decades have seen a gradual increase in its respectability, and it now occurs regularly in standard contexts. The usual advice of current usage commentators is that it should be strictly limited to informal writing. That advice does not appear to be widely followed.

tendency   A tendency may be either *to* or *toward* (or *towards*) something:

> . . . an endearing tendency to wild exaggeration — *Times Literary Supp.,* 22 Oct. 1971

> . . . Arlene, with her tendency toward guile —Edith-Jane Bahr, *Ladies' Home Jour.,* October 1971

> . . . a tendency towards maintaining the status quo —Calvin H. Plimpton, *Amherst College Bulletin,* November 1967

In medical writing, *to* is preferred:

> . . . a family in which there is a tendency to diabetes —Morris Fishbein, *The Popular Medical Encyclopedia,* 1946

tendinitis, tendonitis   The common health problem that keeps runners from running and pitchers from pitching can be spelled either *tendinitis* or *tendonitis.* Both spellings are common, and both are used in medical circles:

> It is unusual for the pain of supraspinatus tendinitis to persist for as long as five years —John L. Skosey, *JAMA,* 4 Jan. 1980

> . . . disorders such as rheumatoid arthritis, carpal tunnel syndrome, bursitis, and tendonitis —Norman L. Gottlieb, M.D. et al., *JAMA,* 18 Apr. 1980

tenet   See TENANT, TENET.

tenses   See SEQUENCE OF TENSES.

terminal preposition   See PREPOSITION AT END.

terminate   *Terminate,* a long word, has been criticized now and again as an overused substitute for *end,* a short one. Nevertheless, writers seem to find *terminate* a useful word. When both words are possible in a particular context, *terminate* is more likely to be used if the ending described has an official or a legal nature:

> If the insured wishes to terminate his insurance coverage, he may surrender his policy —Nelda W. Roueche, *Business Mathematics,* 1969

> . . . the Congressional vote to terminate action in Cambodia —Barbara W. Tuchman, *N.Y. Times Book Rev.,* 11 Nov. 1979

> The anthropology department . . . voted to terminate his candidacy for the Ph.D. —Richard Bernstein, *N.Y. Times Book Rev.,* 30 Oct. 1983

terms   See IN TERMS OF.

terrible, terribly   Much of the terror has gone out of these words. The oldest sense of *terrible,* "causing terror or dread; terrifying," is now relatively rare:

> . . . the main cat qualities he had were his laziness and his short, terrible speed —Ernest Hemingway, "African Journal," 1956

More commonly, *terrible* implies not so much terror as great distress or suffering:

> . . . during those five terrible days of war —*New Yorker,* 17 June 1967

> . . . came to me on that terrible day in 1963 —Mrs. Medgar Evers, *Ladies' Home Jour.,* September 1971

It also commonly means "extremely severe":

> . . . corporations have overcome these terrible handicaps —Arnold J. Toynbee, in Arnold J. Toynbee et al., "Will Businessmen Unite the World?" 1971

These uses of *terrible* are uncontroversial. But its frequent use in the sense "extremely bad" is often cited as a colloquialism, or at least as something to be avoided in formal writing. This sense has long been established in ordinary speech, and our evidence shows that its occurrence in ordinary writing is also now common:

> . . . though the book is hard to classify, it is not hard to evaluate. It is terrible —Dwight Macdonald, *New Yorker,* 22 May 1954

> Some were bad, some were good, and some were terrible —Robert M. Coates, *New Yorker,* 7 Jan. 1956

> . . . the terrible thing about a television set is that you can have no interaction with it —S. I. Hayakawa, *ETC,* June 1968

> The boasting about it is terrible —Russell Baker, *N.Y. Times Mag.,* 19 Aug. 1973

> As could easily have been predicted, the song is terrible —Newman 1974

The contexts in which this sense of *terrible* occurs could not be called formal, but neither are they remarkably informal. They have the conversational tone that is characteristic of much modern writing.

The adverb *terribly* is an issue primarily because of its use as an intensive equivalent to *very* or *extremely.* Such usage dates back to the 19th century. The critics feel, again, that the intensive *terribly* is inappropriate in formal writing, and the evidence shows, again, that it occurs commonly in ordinary discursive prose, though not in the more solemn kinds of writing:

> But Mrs. Rigg is terribly nice, and I was glad to be there —E. B. White, letter, 4 Feb. 1942

> . . . a rather good old-fashioned provincial newspaper, dignified but terribly stodgy —W. H. Auden, *New Yorker,* 12 July 1952

> . . . extremely bright children who have become terribly restless —Irving Howe, *Harper's,* February 1971

> They were, in the main, extremely talented, terribly hard workers —John Chancellor, *N.Y. Times Book Rev.,* 27 May 1984

See also AWFUL, AWFULLY.

than 1. A dispute over whether *than* is a preposition or a conjunction has been going on now for more than two centuries. It is one portion of the price we pay for the 18th-century assumption that the parts of speech of Latin and Greek are readily applicable to English, an assumption that continues to gain uncritical acceptance to this day.

There were two sides to the question right from the beginning. Lowth 1762 held *than* to be a conjunction, and the case of a following pronoun to be determined by its relation to a verb understood. Thus, "thou art wiser than I [am]" and "you love him more than [you love] me." Since the second construction is fairly infrequent, Lowth's analysis was essentially a prescription for *than* plus the nominative. Priestley, at least as early as the 1769 edition cited by Leonard 1929, considered *than* a preposition and thought the objective case proper. He suspected that others' preference for the nominative was based not on English, but on a dubious analogy with Latin. Campbell 1776, however, followed Lowth, and expressed some surprise at Priestley's views. He granted Priestley the "colloquial dialect" for which he—Campbell—had very little use indeed. Lindley Murray 1795 also followed Lowth, and so have most grammarians since.

Lowth's prescription for the nominative had one important exception: he held *than whom* to be correct. His explanation for this single exception—that *who* has reference only to its antecedent and not to an understood verb or preposition—is grammatically unimpressive, but the real reason may have been the authority of Milton's use of *than whom* in *Paradise Lost* (1667), which he quotes:

> Which when Beëlzebub perceived—than whom, Satan except, none higher sat—with grave Aspect he rose. . . .

(Milton, however, did not originate *than whom;* the OED and Hall 1917 have earlier examples.) Lindley Murray accepted Lowth's defense of *than whom,* as have many succeeding generations of grammarians and commentators. As a result, the consensus of the critics has reached these inconsistent conclusions: *than* is a conjunction and in ordinary comparisons must be followed by the nominative case of the pronoun, but *than whom* is standard—although some later commentators allow it to be clumsy.

It is hard to avoid the conclusion, however, that if *than whom* is indeed standard, *than* must be a preposition as well as a conjunction. And if it is indeed a preposition, explaining that when it is thought of as a conjunction, clauses or substantives in the nominative case follow it, and when it is thought of as a preposition, the objective case is used. Ward's explanation covered actual usage perfectly, but it was probably too commonsensical—not sufficiently absolutist—to prevail. As far as we know, Ward had no followers, although Hall 1917 cites one or two late-19th-century grammarians who employed the same line of reasoning.

Than has been a conjunction since Old English, but it has only been a preposition since the 16th century. From the 16th century on, writers have used it as a preposition when it suited their fancy. Shakespeare did:

> A man no mightier than thyself or me
> In personal action, yet prodigious grown
> And fearful, as these strange eruptions are.
>   —*Julius Caesar,* 1600

So the preposition had some two centuries of at least occasional use behind it before the 18th-century grammarians began their wrangling. Here are a few 18th-century examples:

> For thou art a girl as much brighter than her As he was a poet sublimer than me
>   —Matthew Prior, "Better Answer," 1718 (OED)

> And, though by Heaven's severe Decree She suffers hourly more than me . . .
>   —Jonathan Swift, "To Stella, Visiting Me in Sickness," 1720

> No man had ever more discernment than him, in finding out the ridiculous —Samuel Johnson, *A Dissertation on the Greek Comedy* (in Hall 1873)

> A woman does not complain that her brother, who is younger than her, gets their common father's estate —James Boswell, *Life of Samuel Johnson,* 1791 (in Jespersen 1909–49, vol. 7)

And here are some more recent examples, a few of them from speech but others from writing of several kinds:

> Though he was thirty years or so older than us, he tolerated our company —Oliver St. John Gogarty, *It Isn't This Time of Year At All!,* 1954

> Our consul general here is a Columbus man named Streeper, about two years younger than me —James Thurber, letter, 1 June 1954

> Why should a man be better than me because he's richer than me —William Faulkner, 7 Mar. 1957, in *Faulkner in the University,* 1959

> . . . Mr. Ballast, whose aim is to bring down the captain, or get higher than him —Richard R. Lingeman, *N.Y. Times Mag.,* 10 July 1966

Macmillan was nine or ten years older than me —
Lord Butler of Saffron Waldon, BBC interview, 8
Aug. 1966

. . . but I was a better Senator McCarthy than him —
Garrison Keillor, *Lake Wobegon Days,* 1985

LoPresti, who was a few years older than me —Tip
O'Neill with William Novak, *Man of the House,*
1987

The *than whom* construction, against which only
Baker 1770 seems to have objected, has continued
beyond Milton's time:

The King of Dikes, than whom no Sluice of Mud
With deeper Sable blots the Silver Flood
—Alexander Pope, *The Dunciad,* 1728

I was on Montmartre not long ago with my dear
Walter Duranty, than whom no one can have a
warmer spot in my foolish heart —Alexander Woollcott, letter, 5 Sept. 1918

T. S. Eliot, than whom nobody could have been
more insularly English —Anthony Burgess, *Saturday Rev.,* 28 Apr. 1979

And reflexive pronouns (see MYSELF) have also been
used after *than:*

. . . a man who we know was last year no better than
ourselves —Samuel Johnson, quoted in James
Boswell, *Life of Samuel Johnson,* 1791

. . . Mr. Rushworth could hardly be more impatient
for the marriage than herself —Jane Austen, *Mansfield Park,* 1814

The conjunction, however, is more common than the
preposition, at least in print, and is not at all uncommon
even in such informal contexts as letters:

. . . you will be able to determine better than I —William Hazlitt, letter, 30 Aug. 1805

. . . so you are no better off than I —Emily Dickinson, letter, 6 Nov. 1847

Nearly three years older than I —Henry Adams, letter, 23 Nov. 1859

. . . someone else who can take it less seriously than
I —Robert Frost, letter, 2 Feb. 1920

. . . there were profounder asses in the world than we
—*The Intimate Notebooks of George Jean Nathan,*
1932

. . . he is twenty years younger than I —John O'Hara,
letter, 8 Nov. 1962

. . . Uncle Etch's oldest son, much older than I —
Russell Baker, *Growing Up,* 1982

. . . others might be affected even more than he —
Garrison Keillor, *Lake Wobegon Days,* 1985

Even Lowth's conjunction with the objective turns up
once in a while:

My experience is larger, and my comment says more
about me than them —James Baldwin, quoted in
N.Y. Times Book Rev., 27 May 1984

To conclude: William Ward had it right in 1765.
Than is both a preposition and a conjunction. In spite
of much opinion to the contrary, the preposition has

never been wrong. In current usage *than* is more often a
conjunction than a preposition; *than whom* is pretty
much limited to writing; *me* after the preposition is
more common than the other objective-case pronouns;
and the preposition is more common in speech than in
edited prose. You have the same choice Shakespeare
did—you can use *than* either way. But the closer your
writing is to speech, the more likely you are to choose
the preposition.
2. There are a number of syntactic blends involving
than, some of which are separately treated in this book:
see AS GOOD OR BETTER THAN; HARDLY . . . THAN; SCARCELY
. . . THAN. Priestley 1798 has an example of *scarcely . . .
than* from Smollett, which makes that construction
older than it would appear from OED evidence. Harper
1985 mentions a couple of instances of *twice as many
. . . than,* which would seem to be compounded of *more
. . . than* and *twice as many . . . as.* We have also found
this construction with *much:*

. . . twice as much office space is being built this year
in the suburbs around New York City than in Manhattan —*N.Y. Times,* 27 July 1985

See SYNTACTIC BLEND.
3. *Than, then.* A number of handbooks are at pains to
point out that *than* and *then* are different words. This is
simply a spelling problem, of course. Actually, *then* was
occasionally used as a variant spelling of *than* in centuries past:

. . . there are fewe Universities that have lesse faultes
then Oxford —John Lyly, *Euphues. The Anatomy of
Wit,* 1578

Our composition must bee more accurate in the
beginning and end, then in the midst —Ben Jonson,
Timber: or, Discoveries, before 1637

This spelling is no longer acceptable.

than any See ANY 3.

thankfully The adverb *thankfully,* used as a sentence
modifier ("Thankfully, it didn't rain"), is at once less
popular and less unpopular than the sentence-modifying
hopefully ("Hopefully, it won't rain"). Its use is sufficiently common to have drawn some critical attention,
but not so common as to have attracted the kind of sustained and vitriolic abuse that has been heaped on *hopefully* for the past quarter century.
Our earliest evidence for the sentence-modifying
thankfully is from 1963, which is about the time when
hopefully was beginning to become an infamous word
among language watchers.

Thankfully, the publishers have reproduced many of
the canvases in detail —*Saturday Rev.,* 16 Feb. 1963

Such usage was noted and criticized in 1966 by Wilson
Follett, who offered it as an example of how "the rotten
apple will corrupt the barrel"—that is, how the use of
hopefully will encourage similar use of other adverbs.
Later critics (such as Copperud 1970, Harper 1975, and
Phythian 1979) have taken a similar view but have generally kept their criticism of *thankfully* brief, more or
less as an adjunct to their extensive criticism of *hopefully.* It is safe to assume, in fact, that anyone who dislikes *hopefully* will also dislike *thankfully,* but because
of its somewhat less obtrusive presence and its status as
a side issue to the main controversy, *thankfully* is less
likely to be criticized than *hopefully.* As far as actual

usage is concerned, our evidence shows that the sentence-modifying *thankfully* occurs fairly widely in both British and American general writing in contexts that are entirely reputable:

> Garton, thankfully, is perfectly English —*The Observer*, 6 Jan. 1974

> ... though thankfully this was not apparent in the streets —Richard Gordon, *Punch*, 1 May 1974

> Thankfully, the "practice" section is much more useful —Florence Carlson & David Shroyer, *English Jour.*, March 1977

> Greek art, thankfully, is not obsessed by either death-demons or ghosts —John Boardman, *Times Literary Supp.*, 25 Jan. 1980

> ... unnecessary moralizing, which Mr. Auletta has thankfully outgrown —Bob Kuttner, *N.Y. Times Book Rev.*, 10 Aug. 1980

> ... the odor had thankfully diminished —Michael Baughman, *Sports Illustrated*, 22 Nov. 1982

> Which means, thankfully, that the hype is about to end —Jeff Jarvis, *People*, 30 July 1984

> Thankfully, those opinions are advanced with graceful prose —Ken Auletta, *N.Y. Times Book Rev.*, 28 July 1985

For more detailed consideration of sentence-modifying adverbs, see HOPEFULLY and SENTENCE ADVERB.

thanking you in advance Many commentators strongly denigrate the use of this phrase in correspondence, finding in it such faults as triteness, a presumption that the favor being asked will be done, and an implication that the writer will not take the trouble to express appreciation later when the favor actually *has* been done. The writers who use it, we suspect, are really just trying to be polite, but its reputation is bad enough to make it a poor choice for politeness. Inoffensive alternatives are not hard to come by; for example, "Any help that you may give me will be appreciated" or simply "Your help will be appreciated."

thanks to The commentators who have passed judgment on this prepositional phrase agree that it is standard, which is a reasonable assessment in light of the fact that it has been in reputable use since at least the 18th century. Its use in current English is common and is subject to no restrictions with regard to formality. As the commentators (notably Bernstein 1965) point out, it can apply to negative as well as to positive and neutral causes:

> He wears thick telescope-lens glasses, thanks to a painful eye operation after a car crash —Robert Windeler, *Stereo Rev.*, October 1971

> ... never got caught in ideological quicksand, thanks largely to the maturity of its organizers —John Egerton, *Change*, May 1972

> True, thanks to the telephone, ordinary people write less than they did —Mary McCarthy, *Occasional Prose*, 1985

than whom See THAN 1.

that 1. *"That," "which" introducing restrictive and nonrestrictive clauses. That* is our oldest relative pronoun. According to McKnight 1928 *that* was prevalent in early Middle English, *which* began to be used as a relative pronoun in the 14th century, and *who* and *whom* in the 15th. *That* was used not only to introduce restrictive clauses, but also nonrestrictive ones:

> Fleance his son, that keeps him company —Shakespeare, *Macbeth*, 1606

By the early 17th century, *which* and *that* were being used pretty much interchangeably. Evans 1957 quotes this passage from the Authorized (King James) Version (1611) of the Bible:

> Render therefore unto Caesar the things which are Caesar's; and unto God the things that are God's.

During the later 17th century, Evans tells us, *that* fell into disuse, at least in literary English. It went into such an eclipse that its reappearance in the early 18th century was noticed and satirized by Joseph Addison in *The Spectator* (30 May 1711) in a piece entitled "Humble Petition of *Who* and *Which* against the upstart Jack Sprat *That*." *That* had returned, and although it could still be used to introduce a nonrestrictive clause,

> Age, that lessens the enjoyment of life, increases our desire of living —Oliver Goldsmith (quoted in Lurie 1927)

this function was much reduced. Its nonrestrictive function continued to diminish, and although it was still so used in 19th-century literature, by the early 20th century such use seemed anomalous enough that Fowler 1907 singled out these examples (and others) for censure:

> And with my own little stock of money besides, that Mrs. Hoggarty's card-parties had lessened by a good five-and-twenty shillings, I calculated ... —Thackeray

> How to keep the proper balance between these two testy old wranglers, that rarely pull the right way together, is as much ... —George Meredith

> As to dictionaries of the present day, that swell every few years by the thousand items, the presence of a word in one of them shows merely ... —Richard Grant White

The brothers Fowler may have been prompted to find nonrestrictive *that* anomalous by the opinions some grammarians expressed around the turn of the century. Hall 1917 cited several of these, who seem to have felt that nonrestrictive *that* had always been rare or had become so lately. Hall thought the grammarians had not looked very hard at English literature; he did, and listed some 115 authors who used nonrestrictive *that* (in some 1100 passages). About half of his authors are from the 19th century. Hall made one important point that no one else seems to: poets are the heaviest users of nonrestrictive *that*. The reason is fairly obvious: *that* flourishes in unstressed positions where *which* will not fit comfortably. Grammarians and usage commentators tend to look at prose. It may well be that the historical tendency of *that* to be less often used in introducing nonrestrictive clauses has always been more marked in prose than in poetry and speech. At any rate, Virginia McDavid in *American Speech* (Spring–Summer 1977) reports a study showing *that* to introduce only restrictive clauses in mid-20th-century edited prose.

The finding of 1977 should satisfy you if you are writing prose. No one seems to have considered poetry since

Hall in 1917. The nonrestrictive *that* is not entirely dead, however; Evans 1957 hinted at its continuing use, but his two unidentified examples may be from poetry (or even older prose). We do find the use occasionally in represented speech and in speechlike prose (as, for instance, a chatty letter not intended for publication):

> "I mean little Sid Mercer, that rides for me. He's the duke of them all when he lays off the liquor. . . ." —Ring Lardner, *The Big Town,* 1921

> ". . . Take while I'm in an offering mood. I'm not the Red Cross that you can call at any emergency." —Mordecai Richler, *The Apprenticeship of Duddy Kravitz,* 1959

> When I was in the hospital even the nurses' aides that didn't have sense enough to do anything but empty the ice-water were full of that chatter —Flannery O'Connor, letter, April 1956

And in January 1969 Theodore Bernstein in *Winners & Sinners* took time to censure two instances of nonrestrictive *that* that had appeared in the *New York Times* earlier in the month. He said that he had not had to mention such a use for years. The evidence seems to indicate, however, that nonrestrictive *that* is still natural to some people, even though it is not used in edited prose.

The examples Fowler 1907 gives of nonrestrictive *that* show that commentators and grammarians were then well aware of its diminishing range. And if *that* was being confined to introducing restrictive clauses, might it not be useful (as well as symmetrical) to confine *which* to nonrestrictive clauses? The Fowler brothers thought so, as perhaps some of their predecessors had: Ayres 1881 corrected a *which* to a *that* in a restrictive clause, observing that such is the practice of "our most idiomatic writers." Bierce 1909 made a similar correction. Fowler 1926 put the proposition succinctly:

> . . . if writers would agree to regard *that* as the defining relative pronoun, & *which* as the non-defining, there would be much gain both in lucidity & in ease. Some there are who follow this principle now; but it would be idle to pretend that it is the practice either of most or of the best writers.

Evans 1957 responds: "What is not the practice of most, or of the best, is not part of our common language."

Evans's commonsensical observation did not occur to, or did not impress, most subsequent usage writers, who remember only Fowler's first sentence. The general recommendation of the majority is to follow Fowler's wish, although many of them hedge the recommendation round with exceptions, caveats, and appeals to euphony or formality.

But *which* is as firmly entrenched in its restrictive function as in its nonrestrictive one. Joseph M. Williams in *College Composition and Communications* (May 1981) points out that even some of those who recommend using *that* instead of *which* in restrictive function use *which* themselves unawares. For instance, Jacques Barzun, in *Simple & Direct* (1975), says this in the middle of one page:

> In conclusion, I recommend using *that* with defining clauses, except when stylistic reasons interpose. [The stylistic reasons discussed refer to a succession of *that*s.]

And this to open the first paragraph on the next page:

> Next is a typical situation which a practiced writer corrects "for style" virtually by reflex action: . . .

Williams also cites the discussion of *which* and *that* from Strunk & White 1959, which recommends "which-hunting," and then quotes White's own usage:

> . . . the premature expiration of a pig is, I soon discovered, a departure which the community marks solemnly on its calendar —E. B. White, "Death of a Pig"

If the discussions in many of the handbooks are complex and burdened with exceptions, the facts of usage are quite simple. Virginia McDavid's 1977 study shows that about 75 percent of the instances of *which* in edited prose introduce restrictive clauses; about 25 percent, nonrestrictive ones.

We conclude that at the end of the 20th century, the usage of *which* and *that*—at least in prose—has pretty much settled down. You can use either *which* or *that* to introduce a restrictive clause—the grounds for your choice should be stylistic—and *which* to introduce a nonrestrictive clause. A number of commentators raise the additional question of the relative formality of *that* and *which*. If you read many of them, you will find their observations contradictory. Formality does not seem to be much of a consideration in the choice of *that* or *which*.

2. *"That," "which," "who"—what may they refer to?* *That* is our most general relative pronoun, as well as our oldest. It was regularly used to refer to persons as well as to things in earlier literature:

> Ah, great God that art so good —*Noah's Flood,* prob. written before 1425, in *Everyman and Medieval Miracle Plays,* ed. A. C. Cawley, 1959 (spelling modernized)

> By heaven, I'll make a ghost of him that lets me —Shakespeare, *Hamlet,* 1601

When *that* came back into literary use around the beginning of the 18th century after falling out of favor during the 17th, it was noticed with some disapproval (see section 1 above) by such writers as Joseph Addison. Jespersen 1905 points out that the expressed preference for *who* and *which* may have come partly from their conforming to the Latin relative pronouns (*that* having no Latin correlative). Jespersen also notes that when Addison edited *The Spectator* to appear in book form, he changed many of his own uses of *that* to *who* or *which*. The 18th century also marks the first appearance of works devoted to the correction of English usage; some, naturally, discussed relative pronouns. McKnight 1928 cites an anonymous 1752 *Observations upon the English Language* (George Harris wrote it, says Leonard 1929), which condemned the use of *that* and prescribed *who* as "the only proper Word to be used in Relation to Persons and Animals" and *which* "in Relation to Things." It may be that some carryover from the 18th-century general dislike of *that* has produced the apparently common, yet unfounded, notion that *that* may be used to refer only to things. Bernstein 1971 and Simon 1980 mention receiving letters objecting to the use of *that* in reference to persons. The notion persists: we have heard of a professor of political science in California whose class stylesheet (in 1984) insisted *that* could only refer to things, and William Safire in the *New York Times Magazine* (8 June 1980) panned an ad beginning "We seek a managing editor that can. . . ." *That* has applied to persons since its 18th-century revival just as it did before its 17th-century eclipse. Evans 1957 records an 1885 translation of the Bible that began "The Lord's Prayer" with

> Our Father that art in heaven

using the same *that* used in Wycliffe's version of 1389. A few other examples:

> In a letter dated Aug. 16, 1776, Horace Walpole wrote the Countess of Upper Ossory, "This world is a comedy to those that think, a tragedy to those that feel." One might add, "And a put-on to those that neither think nor feel. . . ." —Vincent Canby, *N.Y. Times,* 27 June 1976

> . . . being filled with one of my rolls, gave the other two to a woman and her child that came down the river in the boat with us —Benjamin Franklin, *Autobiography,* 1788

> The woman who kissed him and—pinched his poke—was the lady that's known as Lou —Robert W. Service, "The Shooting of Dan McGrew," 1907

> "Is it my prisoner that's gone?" said Shawn in a deep voice —James Stephens, *The Crock of Gold,* 1912

> Ben Lucien Burman: "I would like to unmirandize any person that uses the word. . . ." —Harper 1985

In the past *which* was also used of persons as well as things:

> Our Father which art in heaven —Matthew 6:9 (AV), 1611

> Caroline, Anna, and I have just been devouring some cold souse, and it would be difficult to say which enjoyed it most —Jane Austen, letter, 14 Jan. 1796

It has now been replaced by *who* and *that* in this function, and is usually limited to things:

> . . . listening to language which his actions contradicted —Jane Austen, *Mansfield Park,* 1814

> . . . that curious access of tenderness which may bring tears to the eyes —C. E. Montague, *A Writer's Notes on His Trade,* 1930

> . . . that voice which was such a strange amalgam of fog and frog —William Styron, *This Quiet Dust and Other Writings,* 1982

Which may still be used of one considered somewhat less than human:

> A banshee which has long stationed itself outside my office, and who devilishly calls Pell "Mel" —Safire 1984

Which may also be used of persons in conscious echoing of an older style:

> Beware of the scribes, which love to go in long clothing, and love salutations in the marketplaces — Howard 1980 (echoing Luke 20:46 (AV), 1611)

Who and *whom* are not very controversial, save in relation to their case forms (see WHO, WHOM 1). The prescription of our anonymous 18th-century critic that *who* "is the only proper word to be used in Relation to Persons and Animals" seems fairly descriptive of actual use of *who:*

> Our Father who art in heaven —Matthew 6:9 (RSV), 1946

> . . . a strapping, loud woman named Doris, whom Ronda Ray fervently called a slut —John Irving, *The Hotel New Hampshire,* 1981

> . . . the old goat who I found expiring —Daniel Defoe, *Robinson Crusoe,* 1719

> . . . snapshots she had taken . . . of the hamster who had died —John Updike, *Couples,* 1968

> Tonto is his cat, whom he walks on a leash —Stanley Kauffmann, *Before My Eyes,* 1980

Who also refers to words for entities that consist of people:

> There is a very good literary society whom it would be well worth while to know —Henry Adams, letter, 23 Nov. 1859

> Texaco, who is proud to present. . . . —cited in Simon 1980

Summary: In current usage, *that* refers to persons or things, *which* chiefly to things and rarely to subhuman entities, *who* chiefly to persons and sometimes to animals. *That* is definitely standard when used of persons. Because *that* has no genitive form or construction, *of which* or *whose* must be substituted for it in contexts that call for the genitive. See WHOSE 1.

3. *Omission of "that."* See CONTACT CLAUSE.

4. *"That" repeated. That* is sometimes unnecessarily doubled, Copperud 1970 tells us; it happens when an interrupting element delays the rest of the clause. Watt 1967 concurs: "Because *that* is such a natural, unobtrusive connective, a writer sometimes forgets that he has used it. . . ." Robert Baker made the same discovery back in 1770, citing this sentence:

> I expected that, when I told him the News, that he would be more surprised at it than he really was.

"This is nonsense," says Baker bluntly. However, he does excuse the practice when enough words intervene "that it may be supposed the Reader or Hearer has so far forgot it." To illustrate this circumstance, Baker proceeds to devise a sentence in which nine typeset lines come between his first *that* and his second. Our suggestion would be that if you have really written your way into such an involved sentence that the reader may have forgotten your first *that,* you ought to start over again.

5. *"That" as an adverb.* Sometime in the second half of the 19th century the propriety of *that* as an adverb was called into question. Hall 1917 cites Alford 1866 as calling it "quite indefensible." Vizetelly 1906 calls it "wholly inexcusable" and "an unpardonable vulgarism." The condemnation is repeated in various handbooks and grammars from the turn of the century through the 1920s and 1930s. Although Bryant 1962 and Harper 1975, 1985 find this use standard, Freeman 1983 says, "*That* is also made to serve as an adverb where it cannot function as one." He goes on to call the adverbial *that* "wrongly employed for *very* or *so*" (interestingly, he doesn't like *very* or *so* either).

Prentice Hall 1978 labels adverbial *that* colloquial and gives two example sentences: "She's that poor she can't buy food" and "I didn't like the book that much." These two examples are really different uses. In Prentice

Hall's first sentence *that* qualifies an adjective completed by a clause. Hall 1917 cites "I am *that* sick I can hardly stand up" as a common locution in his part of Virginia. The American Dialect Dictionary cites many examples from various parts of the country, including one from Edith Wharton, in a novel set in New England, one from an Uncle Remus story, and one from a 1941 radio broadcast of Lowell Thomas. The OED dates this adverbial use from the 15th century and labels its survival Scottish and dialectal. Webster's Third labels it dialectal, Bryant 1962 colloquial.

The second use of *that* as an adverb is much more common and widespread. The OED dates it back to the 17th century; Thomas Jefferson and Harriet Beecher Stowe, among others, are cited. The OED identifies the adverb as being used chiefly with adjectives to express quantity and ascribes its use in preference to *so* to its being more precise. Usually the amount or degree which *that* refers to is specified earlier in the text:

It is a hot day, in rare truth, when boys devote themselves principally to conversation and this day was that hot —Booth Tarkington, *Penrod,* 1914

The Altgeld Gardens project is now considered unpoliceable. Before the Cabrini Green project became that bad, headquarters saturated the area — Gail Sheehy, *McCall's,* March 1971

. . . makes pronouncements about corruption in the courts, ambitious judges, plea-bargainings for the rich, lock-up pens for the poor. The only stereotype left out is police brutality, it's that clichéd a novel — Genevieve Stuttaford, *Publishers Weekly,* 11 Aug. 1975

That *that* and *so* are not readily interchangeable as adverbs is demonstrated by Bolinger 1980, who shows that it is possible to say of a 4-year-old "I didn't realize she was that old," where the substitution of *so* would be unnatural or even nonsensical since *so old* connotes considerable advancement in years.

The most common current use, however, is in negative statements in which *that* is reduced more or less to an intensifier:

They may be imagined as ignorant, if you like, but not *that* ignorant —*New Freeman,* 29 Mar. 1930

He said to Ratliff: "This town aint that big. Why hasn't Flem caught them?" —William Faulkner, *The Town,* 1957

. . . I often forget myself and remind them of their futures as parents. It is not that easy —Thomas J. Cottle, *Saturday Rev.,* 1 Feb. 1969

The movie *is* different, but not *that* different —Pauline Kael, in *The Film,* 1968

McNamara was rather casual about it at first. He did not think that they were that close to a treaty — David Halberstam, *Harper's,* February 1971

This use in negative constructions is frequently found with the intensifier *all* added. See ALL THAT.

Summary: *that* has essentially two adverbial uses, both of some longevity. In the first of these, it modifies an adjective that is followed by a clause. This use seems to be chiefly dialectal. In the second, *that* modifies an adjective (or occasionally an adverb). In positive constructions this *that* cannot usually be replaced by *so.* In negative constructions, *that* is closer to being a simple

intensifier. Both aspects of the second use are standard in general prose.

See also THIS 3.

6. For the use of pronominal *that* to refer to preceding ideas, topics, sentences, or paragraphs, see THIS 1.

that there See THIS HERE, THAT THERE.

thee See THOU.

their **1.** *Their, there, they're.* It is not unusual to see these common words misspelled in casual writing. Haste and inattention to detail probably have more to do with most such errors than does actual confusion about which word is which. However, for the record, *their* is a possessive pronoun ("Their house is down the street"); *there* has various uses as an adjective ("that man there"), a noun ("take it from there"), a pronoun ("There shall come a time"), and, chiefly, an adverb ("stop right there"); and *they're* is a contraction of *they are* ("They're coming tomorrow").
2. See THEY, THEIR, THEM.

theirs Like *its, ours,* and *yours, theirs* is spelled without an apostrophe in present-day English. Editors and proofreaders are undoubtedly well aware of this fact, but in casual writing the apostrophe can sneak in fairly easily, and it sometimes even succeeds in making its way into print:

. . . Exxon gas stations have the best I've seen and their's is free —letter to the editor, *Harper's Weekly,* 1 Dec. 1975

theirselves *Theirselves* is, like *hisself,* a logically formed pronoun of impressive age that now occurs only in substandard speech and representations thereof. In form it is analogous to *myself, yourself, herself,* and *ourselves,* but logic and analogy are as nothing compared to usage, and usage decrees that the word favored in standard English is *themselves.* In centuries past, *theirselves* did appear from time to time in reputable writing:

They aver that they theirselves have been no less scandalized than I myself —J. Morgan, *A Complete History of Algiers,* 1728 (OED)

But the only writing it now shows up in is imitative of rustic speech:

They was talking and bawling amongst theirselves, but . . . the ones I heard was more scairt than hurt — William Wister Haines, *High Tension,* 1938

See also HISSELF.

them **1.** See IT'S ME; THEY, THEIR, THEM.
2. *Demonstrative pronoun.*

A century ago New York Mayor "Boss" Tweed, smarting from Thomas Nast's cartoons, exclaimed, "I don't care what they print about me, but stop them damn cartoons!" —Peter Bates, *Bostonia Mag.,* March 1984

Boss Tweed's *them* is a demonstrative pronoun with a mysterious history. In its modern form, it is attested only since the end of the 16th century. But many observers have been tantalized by the possibility that modern English *them* is a survival of Old English *ðǣm (thǣm),* the masculine and neuter dative of the definite article. The theory is an attractive one, but it has one serious defect—the missing Middle English link. All examples of *them* found in Middle English so far are of the personal pronoun, not the demonstrative. In Middle English the Old English dative seems to have weakened and the final -*m* become -*n* or simply disappeared. If there was a demonstrative *them* that survived in Middle English, it has not been discovered yet. So our attractive theory must be set aside for the present. (For another word with a missing Middle English link, see the discussion of *snuck* at SNEAK, SNUCK.)

From the early examples in the OED and in Jespersen 1909–49 (vol. 2), it would appear that demonstrative *them* enjoyed about a century of unnoticed use. Many of its early occurrences were in works of piety, of which John Bunyan's *Grace Abounding to the Chief of Sinners* (1660) is probably the closest approach to literature. There seem to have been no truly literary uses of the word until the 19th century, when it began to occur in fictitious speech.

The demonstrative *them* seems to have first attracted commentary at about the beginning of the 19th century (it was criticized in Lindley Murray's *English Grammar* at that time, although we do not know for certain in which edition the criticism first appeared). H. L. Mencken in *The American Language, Supplement II* (1948), mentions its being denounced as a barbarism by the Reverend Adiel Sherwood, who included a glossary in his 1827 "Gazetteer of the State of Georgia." James C. Stalker in Greenbaum 1985 cites Thomas Harvey's *Practical Grammar of the English Language* (1868) as warning against it. It was mentioned in Bache 1869, and from that point on it has come in for regular criticism in schoolbooks.

Perhaps because of the efforts of two centuries worth of schoolmasters, the demonstrative *them* is now largely restricted to the speech of the uneducated and to the familiar speech of others. It has been in use for about four centuries, and has still not reached respectability. In writing, then, you can expect to find it in the same places you would find words of similar status: in reported speech, in fictitious speech (especially of little-educated characters), and, especially in the 20th century, in the familiar usage of educated people when they are being humorous. Here are some of our examples:

> ... and then father had bid him bring up them two bits of board, for he could not nohow do without them —Jane Austen, *Mansfield Park,* 1814

> I butts in then and said Don't worry, Cobb. You won't have to run because we have got a catcher who can hold them third strikes —Ring Lardner, *You Know Me Al,* 1916

> ... he bars the doctors. He'd die roarin' before he'd let them boys put a finger on him —Myles na gCopaleen (Flann O'Brien), *The Best of Myles,* 1968

> Can I afford to let Etta clean up those dishes in the sink and get them biscuits baked...? —Robert Bench-ley, *The Benchley Round Up,* 1954

> She never really had liked them big droopy things —Garrison Keillor, *Lake Wobegon Days,* 1985

> You mustn't fake articles any more. Not even in details. Them's orders —Robert Frost, letter, 18 Mar. 1913

> I aim to read Cicero, Caesar, Tacitus and any other of them boys that I can think of —Flannery O'Con-nor, letter, 7 Apr. 1956

> You remember Chesterton's slogan—"My mother, drunk or sober!" Well, them's my sentiments toward you, old thing —Alexander Woollcott, letter, 15 Nov. 1920

themself   According to the OED, *themself* was the normal form of the third person plural reflexive pronoun until about 1540, when it was superseded by *themselfs* and, ultimately, *themselves.* The OED says that *themself* "disappeared" by about 1570, but we do have a little recent evidence of its use:

> ... they think that they're seeing probably pieces of themself —actor speaking on the "Today" television program, 9 Feb. 1983

This may be nothing more than an awkward slip of the tongue, but one recent use seems to have been intentional. A restaurant chain several years ago encouraged its customers to appraise the service they had been given by filling out a card on which several questions were asked, including "Did the server introduce themself by name?" *Themself* seems to have been deliberately chosen as a gender-neutral singular reflexive pronoun, taking the place of *himself or herself.* This use of *themself* is similar to the use of *they, their,* and *them* in reference to singular terms (see THEY, THEIR, THEM). Such use of *they, their,* and *them* is old and well established, but this use is not.

then   **1.** Some controversial issues never quite get off the ground. The use of *then* as an adjective was criticized by Baker in the 18th century, and Follett has expressed some reservations about it in the 20th, but the consensus among the few other commentators who have taken note of it is that the adjective *then* is a useful and concise word. It is an old one, certainly, first recorded in 1584. Among the authors who have used it are Johnson, Boswell, Coleridge, Poe, Tennyson, and Henry James. It continues in widespread use today:

> ... went to Wales to tutor the daughter of the then Chancellor of the Exchequer —Elizabeth Janeway, *Cosmopolitan,* February 1972

> ... the university's then president —*Sports Illus-trated,* 27 Sept. 1982

There is some tendency in recent years to attach *then* to the word it modifies by means of a hyphen:

> ... aimed at Reagan, the then-Governor of Califor-nia —Jess Nierenberg, *Maledicta 1983*

But it is still usually treated as a separate adjective:

> ... to the then prominent engraver, John Farley —Barry Moser, *Publishers Weekly,* 6 July 1984

> ... the then editor of the Merriam dictionaries —Harper 1985

See also NOW.
2. See THAN 3.

thence   See FROM WHENCE, FROM THENCE, FROM HENCE.

theorize   As an intransitive verb, *theorize* is usually used with *about:*

> ... a great mass of theorising about adolescence is flooding the book shops —Margaret Mead, *Coming of Age in Samoa,* 1928

Sheed theorized about, and deplored, what he called a "Guiness Book of World Records" approach to book reviewing —John Leonard, *N.Y. Times Book Rev.*, 10 June 1973

It also occurs with *on:*

There are few subjects on which people, informed or less informed, are more willing to theorize than the history of Russia —*Times Literary Supp.*, 22 Oct. 1971

there Strang 1970 points out that King Alfred, back in the 9th century, could write a sentence (in Old English, of course) "So few of them were." In Old English such a sentence is both meaningful and complete, but it leaves us uncomfortable in modern English. Either some kind of complement is needed to complete the thought—a predicate adjective, perhaps—or a so-called "dummy" or anticipatory subject, *there,* is needed to help make the word order idiomatic: "There were so few of them."

The use of *there* (and of *it,* which is similarly used) as a dummy subject has long been established in the language. It first came under examination by the 18th-century rhetoricians and grammarians who busied themselves with trying to rationalize the language to their own taste. At least one of them appears to have come across *there* as a dummy subject and to have decided that it was a weak way to begin a sentence. We assume this because the topic turned up in Lindley Murray 1795, which was patched together out of the work of a number of predecessors. Murray termed this use "an expletive," and he mildly disapproved it except where it gave "a small degree of emphasis." But in another section of Murray's own book we find this:

There is often a peculiar neatness, in beginning a sentence with the conjunctive form of the verb.

You can see how insidious the dummy subject is. Even its critics can easily fail to notice it in their own works.

The topics written about by Murray and his predecessors have often had long lives, and *there* is no exception. Bernstein 1971 and Copperud 1970, 1980 tell us that at one time sentences beginning with *there* were frequently criticized as weak (recent evidence is that such criticism is still widespread today). Both dismiss the complaint, citing frequent use in literature and the several necessary functions of the construction. Both warn, however, against using too many sentences beginning with *there.*

In an article appearing in *Written Communication* for July 1988, Thomas N. Huckin and Linda Hutz Pesante investigate the use of *there* as dummy subject, calling it "existential *there.*" They decided to test the common handbook warning not to begin sentences with *there* against a 100,000-word sample of good writing by what they call "expert" writers. Their survey found the construction very common; the expert writers obviously paid no attention to the handbook prohibition. They found *there* sentences used for four chief purposes: to assert existence, to present new information, to introduce topics, and to summarize. Clearly, then, *there* sentences are often highly useful, and they seem to occur with roughly the same frequency at all levels of discourse. Huckin and Pesante conclude that there is no empirical justification for a handbook rule prohibiting them.

Huckin and Pesante further suggest sensibly that genuine overuse of *there*-sentences may reflect some fault—such as making too many shifts of topic—that should

be dealt with in terms of the entire piece of writing rather than individual sentences. The construction itself is impeccable, however.

See also THEIR 1; THERE IS, THERE ARE.

therefor, therefore *Therefor* and *therefore* were originally variant spellings of the same adverb. Each came eventually to have a distinct meaning and a distinct pronunciation, however, and they are now regarded as separate words. *Therefor,* which is pronounced with the principal stress on the second syllable, almost always means "for that" or "in return for that." It is not a word that is now commonly used, except, perhaps, by accountants:

. . . so far as they relate to accountancy and to managerial responsibility therefor —*Jour. of Accountancy,* April 1940

. . . the amount of refunds, if any, which may be requested will not be material, and no provision has been made therefor in the financial statements —*Annual Report, General American Transportation Co.,* 1952

. . . any expenditure or liability incurred therefor which creates an asset —Wayne K. Goettsche, *Arthur Young Jour.,* Autumn, 1967

Therefore is pronounced with the principal stress on the first syllable. It is, of course, an extremely common word, whose basic meaning is "for that reason; consequently":

. . . providing a constantly renewed source of food for the larger forms of marine life, which therefore abound —Edward P. Lanning, *Peru Before the Incas,* 1967

Therefor has also been occasionally used as a synonym of *therefore:*

. . . it would not, therefor, be a morpheme —Dwight L. Bolinger, *Word,* April 1948

. . . the frog test for pregnancy is probably therefor based on the excess of the luteinizing hormones — *Biological Abstracts,* January 1943

When used in this way, *therefor* is pronounced in the same way as *therefore.* Most readers will undoubtedly regard it simply as a misspelling or typographical error, and it seems safer to keep the two words distinct in spelling.

there is, there are When *there* is a "dummy" or anticipatory subject, the number of the verb is determined by the number of the true subject following:

There is no more grasping man within the four walls of the world —Lady Gregory, *Damers Gold,* in *New Comedies,* 1913

"There are whiskers on it," said he soberly —James Stephens, *The Crock of Gold,* 1912

Simple enough, isn't it? A singular verb followed by a singular noun, a plural verb followed by a plural noun. That is the way things are supposed to work and often do, but there are complications.

For instance, when a compound subject follows the verb and the first element is singular, we find mixed usage—the verb may either be singular or plural. Jespersen 1909–49 (vol. 2) explains the singular verb as a case of attraction of the verb to the first subject, and illustrates it with this from Shakespeare:

> There comes an old man, and his three sons —*As You Like It,* 1600

Perrin & Ebbitt 1972 also suggests that many writers feel the plural verb is awkward before a singular noun, and Bryant 1962 cites studies that show the singular verb is much more common in standard English. (You can see by the first of the following examples that clauses beginning with *here,* though less frequent than ones beginning with *there,* follow the same principles.)

> . . . for here is a Noun, and a Pronoun representing it —Bishop Lowth (in Leonard 1929)

> So long as there's rain and salamanders on Henry Street, Winston will be there too —Elizabeth Frey, *Springfield* (Mass.) *Morning Union,* 1 Apr. 1987

Some writers, however, follow formal agreement and use a plural verb:

> . . . there were perplexity and agitation —Jane Austen, *Mansfield Park,* 1814

> . . . where there were a white beach and an amusement park —John Cheever, *The Wapshot Chronicle,* 1957

We also find mixed usage when a collective noun that is the formal subject is followed by a prepositional phrase with a plural noun as the object. A correspondent in 1984 complained of the lack of agreement in this sentence:

> There's been a lot of highway traffic problems.

The verb in a construction like this is governed by notional agreement. When the speaker or writer has the collective in mind, a singular verb is used:

> There is a handful of other caves —*Geographical Mag.,* May 1984

> . . . she suddenly perceives, feels, that there is an extraordinary number of handsome young men —Alice Adams, *Listening to Billie,* 1977

And when the plural noun is in mind, a plural verb is used:

> . . . there are a new variety of potatoes —unidentified woman on television, 9 Feb. 1983

> . . . there were a passel of Italian movie producers shooting Westerns in the Israeli desert —Daniel B. Drooz, *N.Y. Times,* 1 July 1973

Harder to explain, perhaps, is a long-standing propensity for *there is* or *there's* in every case, even when the following subject is clearly plural and there are no complications to cloud our minds. Jespersen finds the same construction in Danish, Russian, and Italian, and dates it back in English to the 15th century. It certainly has been common:

> Honey, and milk, and sugar: there is three —Shakespeare, *Love's Labour's Lost,* 1595

> How many is there of 'em, Scrub? —George Farquhar, *The Beaux Stratagem,* 1707

> . . . but there is in nature, I fear, too many tendencies to envy and jealousy —Charles Lamb, letter, 13 June 1797

> A lottery where there is a hundred thousand blanks to one prize —Daniel Defoe, *Moll Flanders,* 1722

> There was forty acres in bluegrass —Harry S. Truman, quoted in Merle Miller, *Plain Speaking,* 1973

> . . . if there's several ways you can use something before or after the verb, we'll use two sample sentences —Stuart Berg Flexner, quoted in *Righting Words,* July/August 1987

Some of these can be variously explained away. For instance, Harry Truman no doubt thought of the forty acres as a parcel (he referred to them with *it* later in the sentence), and there are quite a few words between *there is* and *tendencies* in the Lamb quotation. The latter brings us to Jespersen's shrewd theory that *there is* or *there's* is often out—in speech or on paper—before the whole sentence is formulated. Early choice of the verb before the number of the subject is actually decided would also explain the occasional instance of the plural verb with a singular subject:

> There were one group you did not mention —Daniel Schorr, speaking on television, 27 Jan. 1981

Jespersen notes that the invariable singular occurs mostly in the colloquial style—speech and speechlike prose—and is generally avoided in the literary style. That observation accords with our evidence. In the more complex constructions, you are best guided by your own sense of what sounds right in the particular context to avoid awkwardness and maintain the smooth flow of the sentence.

the same as   See SAME AS 1.

these kind of, these sort of   See KIND 1.

the way   See WAY, *noun.*

they   **1.** For *they* used to refer to a singular noun or pronoun, see THEY, THEIR, THEM.
2. *They* used as an indefinite subject is sometimes objected to, primarily on the assumption that every pronoun should have an antecedent. Lamberts 1972 calls that assumption shaky, as indeed it is, since many pronouns do not require antecedents. Perrin & Ebbitt 1972 reports that indefinite *they* occurs in all varieties of usage. It is standard. Here is a sample of its uses:

> In Lagos, they were sleeping in the streets —John Updike, *Bech Is Back,* 1982

> In seventh grade they were always assigning you to write about things like farm produce —Russell Baker, *Growing Up,* 1982

> They're tearing down a nine-story building just outside my office window —*And More by Andy Rooney,* 1982

> They say Freddy plays only when he wants to — Sparky Anderson, quoted in *Springfield* (Mass.) *Morning Union,* 10 Jan. 1985

> They say he kept a whore in the White House, but I don't suppose I ought to say that —Harry S. Truman, quoted in Merle Miller, *Plain Speaking,* 1973

3. *They* as a pronunciation spelling of *there* goes back as far as 1799 (the earliest occurrence we have seen is in a citation for *an't* in the Dictionary of American English).

In this century it has been used chiefly to represent dialectal or uneducated speech:

> They's also a ballroom and a couple card rooms —Ring Lardner, *The Big Town,* 1921

they, their, them   The question of the propriety of using *they, their, them* to refer to indefinite pronouns and singular nouns has two aspects that are distinct but often overlap. Both relate to perceived gaps in the language. The first, and most often discussed, is this:

> One most annoying gap in English vocabulary is that created by the lack of a third person singular pronoun that does not state explicitly the sex of the person or persons referred to —Chambers 1985

The missing pronoun, in other words, would be a common-gender or common-sex (Otto Jespersen's term) third person singular pronoun. The second aspect of the question is glanced at in Chambers's use of "person or persons"—it is what Jespersen 1909–49 (vol. 2) refers to as a lack of common number or neutral number, a form of number that is neither definitely singular nor definitely plural. Jespersen says that "the lack of a common-number (and common-sex) pronoun leads to the frequent use of *they* and *their* in referring to an indefinite pronoun (or similar expression) in the singular." We shall examine these problematic aspects of the use of *they, their, them* separately.

1. *Common-gender pronoun.* Although the lack of a common-gender third person singular pronoun has received much attention in recent years from those concerned with women's issues, the problem, as felt by writers, is much older; the plural pronouns have been pressed into use to supply the missing form since Middle English:

> And whoso fyndeth hym out of swich blame,
> They wol come up . . .
> —Chaucer, "The Pardoner's Prologue,"
> ca. 1395 (in Jespersen)

The use of the plural pronouns to refer to indefinite pronouns—*anyone, each, everyone, nobody, somebody,* etc.—results from the concurrence of two forces: notional agreement (the indefinite pronouns are usually plural in implication) and the lack of sexual identification that indefinite pronouns share with *they, their, them.* You will find many examples of this reference at the entries in this book under AGREEMENT and at those for the individual indefinite pronouns. We add only a few examples here:

> . . . every one prepared themselves —George Pettie, *A Petite Pallace of Pettie his Pleasure,* 1576 (in McKnight 1928)

> And every one to rest themselves betake —Shakespeare, *The Rape of Lucrece,* 1594

> . . . if ye from your hearts forgive not every one his brother their trespasses —Matthew 18:35 (AV), 1611

> Nobody here seems to look into an Author, ancient or modern, if they can avoid it —Lord Byron, letter, 12 Nov. 1805

> I would have everybody marry if they can do it properly —Jane Austen, *Mansfield Park,* 1814

> Everyone in the building is in a constant process of evaluating and criticizing their institution —Roger Angell, *Holiday,* November 1953

> . . . it is too hideous for anyone in their senses to buy —W. H. Auden, *Encounter,* February 1955

> . . . the detachment and sympathy of someone approaching their own death —Alan Moorehead, *The Blue Nile,* 1962

> Each designs to get sole possession of the treasure, but they only succeed in killing one another —Sir Paul Harvey, *The Oxford Companion to English Literature,* 4th ed., 1967

The relative pronoun *who* is also unmarked as to sex, and the plural pronoun is used in reference to it:

> Who makes you their confidant? —Jane Austen, *Emma,* 1815 (in Jespersen)

> . . . who ever thought of sparing their grandmother worry? —Edith Wharton, *The Age of Innocence,* 1920

> . . . Al Haig declared, "I'm *appalled* by this proceeding. I'm wondering who thinks they are the Secretary of Defense around here." —David A. Stockman, *Newsweek,* 28 Apr. 1986

A second kind of reference connects *they, their, them* to singular nouns that can apply to either sex or to noun phrases that apply to both sexes. Again, we can see that the practice has a long history:

> Every servant in their maysters lyverey —Lord Berners, translation of Froissart's *Chronicles,* 1523 (in McKnight)

> . . . every fool can do as they're bid —Jonathan Swift, *Polite Conversation,* 1738 (in Jespersen)

> Every person . . . now recovered their liberty —Oliver Goldsmith, *The History of England,* 1771 (OED)

> A person can't help their birth —W. M. Thackeray, *Vanity Fair,* 1848 (OED)

> . . . unless a person takes a deal of exercise, they may soon eat more than does them good —Herbert Spencer, *Autobiography,* 1904 (in Jespersen)

> It was a surprise to me to note how quickly the native . . . learned how to work on the land in the more modern way and I watched them doing all kinds of work —R. Bates, *Paper & Print,* Summer 1951

> We can only know an actual person by observing their [sic] behaviour in a variety of different situations —George Orwell, as quoted by Edward Crankshaw, *Times Literary Supp.,* 26 Dec. 1980

> The consumer is very careful with what they're spending —Eugene Glazer, on *Wall Street Week* (television), 10 Dec. 1982

> I had to decide: Is this person being irrational or is he right? Of course, they were often right —Robert Burchfield, in *U.S. News & World Report,* 11 Aug. 1986

As most commentators note, the traditional pronoun for each of these cases is the masculine third person singular, *he, his, him.* This tradition goes back to the 18th-century grammarians, who boxed themselves into the position by first deciding that the indefinite pronouns must always be singular. They then had to decide between the masculine and feminine singular pronouns for use in reference to the indefinites, and they chose the masculine (they were, of course, all men). Naturally there is plenty of evidence for the masculine pronoun used in this way:

> A person can thus learn to swim up to the limits imposed by his ... physique —Leacock 1943

> Nobody attains reality for my mother until he eats —Flannery O'Connor, letter, 28 June 1956

> Now, a writer is entitled to have Roget on his desk —Barzun 1985

> ... everyone allegedly being entitled to his ignorance —Simon 1980

> The client benefits by getting his well drilled at a guaranteed cost —*Annual Report, Global Marine Inc.,* 1982

> In my book, everyone has his book, everyone blows his nose, and everybody goes his way —Kilpatrick 1984

But the insistence on the masculine singular has its limitations. Sometimes its results are downright silly:

> ... everyone will be able to decide for himself whether or not to have an abortion —Albert Bleumenthal, N.Y. State Assembly (cited in Longman 1984)

Reader's Digest 1983 also points out that the masculine pronoun is awkward at best used in reference to antecedents of both sexes:

> She and Louis had a game—who could find the ugliest photograph of himself —Joseph P. Lash, *Eleanor and Franklin* (in Reader's Digest)

> ... the ideal that every boy and girl should be so equipped that he shall not be handicapped in his struggle for social progress —C. C. Fries, *American English Grammar,* 1940 (in Reader's Digest)

It is an arguable point whether a phrase like "every boy and girl" is singular or plural. But note how much more natural and sensible the plural pronoun sounds:

> ... the liberty of every father and mother to educate their children as they desire —Robert A. Taft, quoted in *Time,* 20 Sept. 1948

Some commentators recommend *he or she, his or her, him or her* to avoid the sex bias of the masculine and the presumed solecism of the plural. Bolinger 1980 points out that this solution, too, is old, going back to the 18th century, but that many commentators are also hostile to the forms as unwieldy (see HE, HE OR SHE). Even the *he or she* formula can lead the unwary into trouble, as in this instance where it is used to refer to a plural pronoun:

> Those who have been paid for the oil on his or her property —Lucia Mouat, *Christian Science Monitor,* 4 Aug. 1983 (cited by Allan Metcalf, *American Speech,* Fall 1984)

One more point needs to be made. Simon 1980 writes:

> ... I bristle at Miller and Swift's advocacy of *they, their,* etc., as singular pronouns because "reputable writers and speakers" have used them with indefinite antecedents. ... But the lapses of great ones do not make a wrong right. ...

The examples here of the "great ones" from Chaucer to the present are not lapses. They are uses following a normal pattern in English that was established four centuries before the 18th-century grammarians invented the solecism. The plural pronoun is one solution devised by native speakers of English to a grammatical problem inherent in that language—and it is by no means the worst solution.

We must remember that the English pronoun system is not fixed. Several centuries ago the objective plural *you* drove the nominative and objective singulars *thou* and *thee* and the nominative plural *ye* out of general use. It appears to have happened for social reasons, not linguistic reasons (see YOU 3). *They, their, them* have been used continuously in singular reference for about six centuries, and have been disparaged in such use for about two centuries. Now the influence of social forces is making their use even more attractive. Thomas Pyles (*Modern Language Notes,* December 1955) sums up their position: "The use of *they, their,* and *them* as singular relative pronouns of indeterminate gender has long been perfectly well established, even in formal contexts." Evans 1957 agrees; Reader's Digest 1983 agrees; Chambers 1985 agrees. So do we. But remember that in this case (unlike the case of *you*) you have a choice: you can use the plural pronouns when they seem natural and you can use the singular pronouns when they seem natural.

2. *Common-number pronoun.* The examples involving nouns like *person, human being,* and *fool* cited in the preceding section might have equally well been set down here, because they illustrate the use of *they, their, them* to refer to singular nouns used in such a way that the singular stands for and includes any or all. Examples of this use are very old, and they include many cases where sex is perfectly obvious:

> The righteous man ... that taketh not their life in vain —*Pearl,* ca. 1380 (spelling modernized)

> There's not a man I meet but doth salute me
> As if I were their well-acquainted friend
> —Shakespeare, *The Comedy of Errors,* 1593

> 'Tis meet that some more audience than a mother,
> Since nature makes them partial, should o'erhear
> The speech
> —Shakespeare, *Hamlet,* 1601

> No man goes to battle to be killed.—But they do get killed —George Bernard Shaw, *Three Plays for Puritans,* 1901 (in Jespersen)

> The GI in Britain feels that the papers ... are ungrateful for their "sacrifices" and contemptuous of their society and country —Jean Rikhoff Hills, *New Republic,* 23 Aug. 1954

We even find *they, their, them* used in reference to inanimate nouns (although we have no literary evidence for this practice):

> Do you wear a chain belt? If not, you may be out of the run of fashion in Ireland, for they are gaining a widespread popularity —*Irish Digest,* July 1953

> Your usual store should have their Autumn stocks in now —advt., *Punch,* 30 Sept. 1953

> Oh, we have an argument now and then, but they never carry over —Lessa Nanney, quoted in *Bluegrass Unlimited,* February 1981

In addition, we find *they, their, them* used in reference to singular nouns modified by a distributive (such as *every*) which imparts a notional plurality:

> . . . every man went to their lodging —Lord Berners, translation of Froissart's *Chronicles,* 1523 (in McKnight)

> . . . every president should assemble their companies —Archbishop Parker, letter, 8 May 1545 (OED)

> . . . every horse had been groomed with as much rigour as if they belonged to a private gentleman — Thomas De Quincey, *The English Mail Coach,* 1849 (in McKnight)

They, their, them are used in both literature and general writing to refer to singular nouns, when those nouns have some notion of plurality about them. All the cases in this section, and a good many of those in the first section, illustrate this operation of notional agreement. Look again at the example from Shaw above. It would be a violation of English idiom to use a singular pronoun in the second sentence (But he does get killed) on the assumption that because *no man* is singular in form and governs a singular verb, it must take a singular pronoun in reference. Notional agreement is in control, and its dictates must be followed.

3. For other usage questions with *they,* see THEY 2, 3.

they're   See THEIR 1.

thing   As a look in any dictionary will show, *thing* is a word having many uses and many senses. Its occurrence is common at all levels of usage, but it turns up especially often in speech and in writing that has something of the casual quality of speech:

> Culture is really the thing here—it's bigger than surfing —E. B. White, letter, 3 Mar. 1965

> . . . the diplomatic thing to do in Europe is give the natives a piece of the action —Neil McInnes, *Barron's,* 10 Apr. 1972

> The thing is, I'm not just another American being snotty about English poetry —Donald Hall, *Goatfoot Milktongue Twinbird,* 1978

> . . . that old thing about raising the standard of cooking in Britain —Kingsley Amis, *Times Literary Supp.,* 15 July 1983

Several commentators have noticed that it is often easy to revise *thing* out of a sentence, as by replacing it with a more specific word. Sometimes it can be dropped altogether: for example, instead of writing, "The first thing he told me was . . ." you could simply write, "First he told me . . ." But should you? The answer to that question really depends upon considerations of tone and rhythm. Good writers are directed in such matters by their ear—their sense of what sounds right in a particular context. We recommend that you let your ear tell you when and when not to use *thing.*

think   The use of *think* with *to* and an infinitive (as in "We didn't think to ask him") was called an illiteracy by Fowler 1926, but it has now won general acceptance. Evans 1957 found the construction to be standard in American English when the sense of *think* was "remember" but archaic when the sense was "plan" or "expect."

Our evidence shows, however, that *think to* meaning "expect or intend to" continues in good use:

> . . . and I thought to succeed as they did, and as rapidly —*The Autobiography of William Butler Yeats,* 1953

> Or else the writer thinks to succeed by piling up an accumulation of details —Leacock 1943

> . . . has done what few people who write for the screen think to do —Pauline Kael, *New Yorker,* 2 Oct. 1971

> Martin thinks to make a case for Whitman as a model —Robert Boyers, *Times Literary Supp.,* 30 May 1980

See also BELIEVE, THINK.

thinking man   *Thinking man* and similar expressions are sometimes used as a way of discouraging disagreement:

> Equally, no thinking person can fail to recognize the individual and, even, the occasional corporate courage and wisdom —letter to the editor, *Center Mag.,* May/June 1971

The implication—that anyone who disagrees with what the writer is asserting must be an idiot—is bound to cause a certain amount of irritation, especially among the disagreers. Fowler 1926 and Flesch 1964 have criticized such usage for that reason. Note, however, that the adjective *thinking* and the expression *thinking man* have other uses which are entirely inoffensive:

> . . . tried his hand at a magazine for the thinking public —Henry Ladd Smith, *New Republic,* 22 Nov. 1954

> . . . to produce thinking citizens —*Change,* May–June 1969

> Mr. Ustinov is a thinking man with a satiric mind —Haskel Frankel, *Saturday Rev.,* 13 Nov. 1971

> . . . he is a thinking man's spy—reflective, historically aware —Michael Malone, *N.Y. Times Book Rev.,* 12 Jan. 1986

this   **1.** *Pronoun.* The use of pronominal *this* (and *that, which,* and *it* as well) to refer broadly to a preceding idea, topic, sentence, or paragraph, was under severe attack in usage books years ago. Follett 1966 seems to have been one of the last to criticize it. Nowadays the usage, which is often convenient, is considered quite respectable. College handbooks still include this subject (see Little, Brown 1980 and Macmillan 1982, for example), but they are now content with simply advising the student writer to make the reference clear. Here are some examples of the usage:

> It is not just that he was selling arms to Iran in order to retrieve American hostages, even as he swore to do no business with terrorists and bombed Colonel Qaddafi, but that he can see no inconsistency in this —*The Economist,* 6 Mar. 1987

> But language is the expression of the human psyche, and this is something that nobody has yet been able, except in the crudest way, to measure —Barnard 1979

I decided a good idea might be to drive along the road in the car, watching for kudu, and hunt any likely-looking clearings. We went back to the car and did this —Ernest Hemingway, *Green Hills of Africa,* 1935

The question whether we would not accept the issues as real breaks down into two questions: Would we be upset if it were proved that the environment in which an animal grew up changed the hereditary endowment which it passed on to its offspring? and: Did Kammerer's experiments look like proving that? —*Times Literary Supp.,* 22 Oct. 1971

. . . some courses that might have only the charm of novelty were still to the good in a subject so hagridden by obsolete tradition as English, and most of the new courses were an improvement on the old ones— all of which implies that we do have acceptable standards of judgment —Herbert J. Muller, *The Uses of English,* 1967

It was a lesson to me—in temperament, in point of view; I went with his mood, tried even to outdo him, in the hope of spurring him to outdo himself. I only mention it because I did it so well that it led to extraordinary consequences —Joseph Conrad & Ford Madox Ford, *The Inheritors,* 1900

Now that *this* is no longer an issue when referring to a preceding clause or sentence, a few commentators have switched their objections to *this* when it refers to a preceding noun and another pronoun could possibly be used instead. The underlying reason for the criticism in this case is probably that the construction is more typical of speech than writing.

And I listened to him talk for a half hour or so . . . to evaluate what kind of person this was —Robert C. McFarlane, quoted in *The Tower Commission Report,* 1987

. . . an old man . . . sent I am sure by the Lord to be a plague to the penwomen. This was a poet, and he had his poems in a paper bag —Flannery O'Connor, letter, 9 Aug. 1957

The use of constructions typical of speech is not a particularly heinous fault in writing, however, unless you are aiming to produce highly formal prose.
See also WHICH 2.

2. *Adjective.* It is not uncommon in speech for *this* to be used for emphasis in place of the indefinite article, as in "This guy said to me. . . ." Use of the emphatic *this* in writing has sometimes been discouraged (as in Heritage 1982), but our evidence shows that it is neither rare nor inappropriate in writing of a conversational tone. You can get a good sense of its quality from these examples:

From the beginning of the show, Stanley makes a real pain in the neck of himself as this farmer who wants a ride in an airplane —Alan Loncto, quoted in *New Yorker,* 27 Aug. 1984

Strange, even to me, that I haven't become a cynic after all I've been through, that I am still this sucker for the Land of Opportunity —Philip Roth, *Atlantic,* April 1981

. . . is comic-book stuff that reads as though he snapped it off on a free afternoon with his favorite word processor. There's this retired C.I.A. hit man —Newgate Callendar, *N.Y. Times Book Rev.,* 10 Apr. 1983

He pictured himself as this hard, lonely man —Wilfrid Sheed, *People Will Always Be Kind,* 1973

See also THIS HERE, THAT THERE.

3. *Adverb.* MacCracken & Sandison 1917 noted frequent objection to *this* as a sort of adverbial intensifier, as in "We didn't expect to wait this long," but judged such usage to be acceptable, even if somewhat informal. It seems hard now to understand why anybody would object to such an innocuous use, but Longman 1984 tells us that it still has its critics. We feel that you may safely ignore them. The adverbial *this* is certainly standard; it can turn up even in a consciously literary style:

All of my neighbors who cherish French poodles owe their interest in them to Booth Tarkington's various accounts of his dear Gamin, this many years dust in some such apple orchard as your own —Alexander Woollcott, letter, 1 Aug. 1935

See also THAT 5.

this here, that there The frequency with which admonitions against the use of *this here* and *that there* are included in handbooks on writing suggests that students everywhere are composing essays in some sort of backwoods idiom: "Well, now, this here Captain Ahab fella gets hisself all riled up agin that there whale. . . ." For all we know they might be, but our evidence from published sources shows that writers in general have no need to be told that *this here* and *that there* are something less than standard English. The use of *here* and *there* for emphasis following a demonstrative adjective is a characteristic of dialectal and uneducated speech. It does not occur in writing except when such speech is being recorded, evoked, or imitated:

Brush, brush, brush, that there brush kept on swearing through its teeth, proper savage, it was —Richard Llewellyn, *None But the Lonely Heart,* 1943

"My back's nearbout broke and I ain't able to do another lick. This here kitchen looks like a hog sty." —Margaret Long, *Louisville Saturday,* 1950

. . . and he said, "Say, mister, ain't this here number we're headin' for that house full o' junk . . . ?" — Marcia Davenport, *My Brother's Keeper,* 1954

See also THIS 2.

thither See HITHER 1.

thitherto See HITHERTO.

tho *Tho* has seen occasional use as a spelling variant of *though* for many centuries:

For tho' we allow every man something of his own and a peculiar Humour —William Congreve, "Concerning Humour in Comedy," 1695

Attempts by 19th and 20th century spelling reformers to encourage the use of *tho* have not met with widespread success, but in its heyday *tho* did appear in some widely circulated periodicals:

Even tho this was said partly in earnest —*Better Homes and Gardens,* August 1946

. . . tho the average speed dictated by its rule makes the drivers go fast enough —*Road and Track,* December 1951

Its current use is confined chiefly to advertisements and some technical journals:

> Tho nothing so colorful is really anticipated — David Hellyer, *Industrial Research/Development,* April 1979

For more information about the history and current status of simplified spellings, see SPELLING REFORM; THRU.

thoroughbred, purebred   These words are synonymous in their basic sense, "bred from the best blood through a long line." Used in this sense, both words are applicable to domestic animals of any species:

> ... on dangerous ground in showing thoroughbred dogs in their sales messages —Vance Packard, *The Hidden Persuaders,* 1957

> ... the showcase division, housing the purebred cattle —Kurt Markus, *Western Horseman,* May 1980

Horse breeders make a definite distinction between *thoroughbred* and *purebred,* however. *Thoroughbred* refers specifically to a breed of horses directly descended from three Arabian stallions who were bred with English mares in the late 17th and early 18th centuries. *Purebred* is used in describing pure-blooded horses of other breeds. This distinction exists whether the words are used as adjectives or nouns:

> We currently have seven mares (five purebreds and two Thoroughbreds) —Joan McKenna et al., *Chronicle of the Horse,* 18 Nov. 1983

Many people in the horse-breeding business therefore consider it incorrect to speak of "thoroughbred dogs," "thoroughbred hogs," or "thoroughbred anything" other than horses belonging to the Thoroughbred breed. People outside the horse-breeding business do not necessarily agree:

> A purebred rabbit.... is sometimes also called a *thoroughbred* —Bob Bennett, *The T.F.H. Book of Pet Rabbits,* 1982

But *thoroughbred* does have such strong associations with horses in the public mind (perhaps because of Thoroughbred racing) that its use in describing animals of other species is now relatively uncommon.

those kind of, those sort of   See KIND 1.

thou   *Thou* was once the common form of the second person singular pronoun. In other words, it was once normal to address another person as "thou." In the period of Middle English, however, *thou* (and the related forms *thee, thy,* and *thine*) was gradually replaced by the plural *you* (and *your*), first in addressing a person of high social rank (as in "your majesty") and later in addressing a social equal. *Thou* was used only in speaking to a person of inferior social position, such as a servant, and it was eventually superseded by *you* even in this use. In Modern English, *thou* has been most familiar as a formal alternative to *you* in prayers and poetry:

> Thou still unravag'd bride of quietness,
> Thou foster-child of silence and slow time
>   —John Keats, "Ode on a Grecian Urn," 1819

Thou has also persisted in more general use in some dialects—most notably, perhaps, in the language of the Friends (that is, the Quakers). An interesting feature of

some dialectal usage, including that of the Friends, is that the accusative form *thee* ("I shall teach thee") occurs in place of the nominative *thou* ("Thou shalt learn from me") and is used with verbs inflected in the third person singular, so that instead of saying, "Thou hast forgotten" a Friend will say, "Thee has forgotten."

> I remember in court when they were going to indict a Norwegian Quaker ... his wife said, "Simon, thee must go to jail." —Harry Terrell, quoted in Studs Terkel, *Hard Times,* 1970

Exactly how this nominative use of *thee* developed is not known.

though   See ALTHOUGH, THOUGH.

thrill   As an intransitive verb meaning "to become thrilled," *thrill* is idiomatically followed by either *at* or *to:*

> Alice thrilled at the suggestion —Patrick J. Costello, *Irish Digest,* April 1954

> ... was taken to it by two maiden aunts who, I dare say, thrilled to it —John Simon, *New York,* 30 Aug. 1971

thronged   *Thronged* is usually used with *with:*

> ... his mind must have been thronged with feelings of being unwanted —John Cheever, *New Yorker,* 26 Sept. 1953

> ... on a cold Sunday, when the galleries were thronged with out-of-towners —Jean Stafford, *Children Are Bored on Sunday,* 1953

> ... my head became thronged with ideas for books —Edmund Wilson, *New Yorker,* 5 June 1971

Sometimes it occurs with *by:*

> ... always much covered by newspapers and television, and thronged by over two hundred thousand visitors —Libby Purves, *British Airways High Life,* May 1982

> Thronged in season by hunters and fishermen — *American Guide Series: California,* 1939

through   The use of *through* as an adjective meaning "finished" was disparaged by many American commentators in the early 20th century. Krapp 1927, for example, described it as "colloquial and children's English." The "finished" sense of *through* was still fairly new at the time, having originated in American English during the late 1800s:

> He ... scrawled a dash underneath. 'There! I'm through!' he said —*Scribner's Mag.,* May 1887 (OED Supplement)

What may be most noteworthy about the criticism of *through* in this sense is that it did not last. Nicholson 1957 and Gowers in Fowler 1965 persist in describing this sense as colloquial, but most commentators have abandoned the subject altogether, and both American and British dictionaries now routinely treat the "finished" sense as standard. Its two principal applications in current English are in describing the completion of an activity:

> ... the hour when he expected to be through with his day's writing —Irving Wallace, *The Writer,* November 1968

And in describing a person who is washed-up:

> ... he had believed the 1950s would bring him to greatness. Now they were almost at an end and he was through —Paul Nelson, *Rolling Stone,* 14 Sept. 1972

See also DONE 1; FINISHED.

thru   A high-school English teacher wrote to us not long ago about the spelling *thru,* which she had apparently met with in a school memorandum and which she found in some way offensive. She wanted to know our reason for treating *thru* as an unstigmatized variant of *through* in Webster's Ninth New Collegiate Dictionary.

Thru has received only a little attention from usage writers (Watt 1967 calls it unacceptable in formal writing and Janis 1984 thinks it nonstandard but handy at times). The OED shows that it dates back to the 14th century, but our modern use is due primarily to the spelling reform movement of the late 19th and early 20th centuries (see SPELLING REFORM).

Thru was on the first list of reformed spellings issued by the American Philological Association in 1876 and on the list issued by the National Education Association in 1898, as well as on the lists published by the Simplified Spelling Board in the early 20th century. It was also one of the reformed spellings used by the *Chicago Tribune* from 1935 to 1975. In the heyday of the reformed spelling movement *thru* was widely used in newspapers and magazines:

> Experience has shown thru ever re-occurring instances —*Catholic School Jour.,* March 1927

> ... to look at the universe thru their eyes —W. S. Phillips, *Three Boys in the Indian Hills,* in *Publishers Weekly,* 2 Nov. 1918

> ... borrowed thru a public library —*Library Jour.,* 1 Dec. 1925

> ... this stem went thru vegetation —*American Botanist,* August 1923

> Poisonous tides from the mother's blood swept thru my foetal heart —*JAMA,* 14 Aug. 1926

> ... pressed on thru the novel —*The Bookman,* September 1925

> ... young men at college pay their way thru school by playing in amateur dance orchestras —*Music Trade News,* June 1926

It could even be found now and then in literary surroundings:

> They were sick of winters; but they tried
> To ponder thru the window at the snow
> —Stanley Burnshaw, "Waiting in Winter," in
>   *Anthology of Magazine Verse for 1926,*
>   ed. William Stanley Braithwaite, 1926

> They clasp their hands and pray,
> And the sun shines brightly on them thru the
>   stripped Autumn vines
>   —Amy Lowell, "The Cornucopia of Red and
>   Green Comfits," in Marguerite Ogden
>   Wilkinson, *New Voices,* new ed., rev., 1921

As the organized interest in spelling reform waned, however, the use of *thru* in publications also shrank, although in the 1940s it could still be found in such periodicals as *Better Homes and Gardens* and the *New Republic.* We have evidence that the NEA was still using *thru* in their publications as late as 1944, even though they had withdrawn their endorsement of the reformed spelling movement in 1921.

Moreover, our evidence shows that *thru* is still in use, primarily in technical journals, and in places like catalogs and programs where compactness is a virtue. We have no recent evidence of its use in literature, and very little evidence of its use in any kind of book. *Thru* is showing some signs of vitality in combination: we are beginning to find examples like *feedthru* and *thruput* (*thruway,* of course, is well-established). It undoubtedly continues to flourish as a spelling of convenience in letters and notes:

> After we got thru our conversation —Harry S. Truman, appointment sheet, 19 May 1945

> ... leaves ... with the sun coming thru them —Randall Jarrell, letter, 6 May 1952

Thru is a simplified form that did not fight its way into respectable usage from below, like *alright,* but was imposed from above by educators, reformers, and philologists. It has never been less than standard, but it remains a distant second choice in print. In the Brown University million-word corpus, which is composed of edited English texts published in 1961, there are 969 examples of *through* to just 10 of *thru* (Kučera & Francis 1967). It is an available spelling, but not many writers avail themselves of it when they are writing for publication.

See also THO.

thrust   Several figurative uses of the noun *thrust* have become widespread during the past few decades and have therefore drawn some critical attention. Two new senses of the word that have become particularly popular are "the essential point or meaning":

> I shall attempt to give the thrust of the argument — James R. Newman, *New Republic,* 12 July 1947

> I agree with the thrust of the lengthy section he devotes to the estrangement between whites and Negroes —Eli Ginzberg, *Saturday Rev.,* 12 Feb. 1966

> ... where the main thrust of his book lies —Stanley Hoffmann, *N.Y. Times Book Rev.,* 3 July 1983

And "the principal concern or objective":

> The thrust of *Essence* is to create a sense of self-awareness and pride —Pamela Howard, *Saturday Rev.,* 8 Jan. 1972

> The thrust is to recapitalize these subsidiary companies to provide greater financial flexibility — *Annual Report, Continental Group,* 1981

> Touting mayhem has been the principal promotional thrust of wrestling and Roller Derby —Bil Gilbert, *Sports Illustrated,* 31 Jan. 1983

The popularity of *thrust* in figurative use presumably owes something to its vigorous and forceful connotations. Those who dislike it, on the other hand, are inclined to regard it as nothing more than pretentious jargon. Usage commentators who have expressed or implied such an opinion include Strunk & White 1972, 1979, Newman 1974, and Mitchell 1979. Despite their objections, however, the figurative uses of *thrust* continue to be common, and they are likely here to stay.

thusly Few words have a worse reputation among the arbiters of correct usage than *thusly*. Bernstein 1965 is relatively kind in his characterization of it: he calls it "superfluous." Most other critics have shown less leniency, typically describing it as nonstandard or illiterate. The *Oxford American Dictionary* states flatly that "*thusly* as a substitute for *thus* is always incorrect."

The first recorded use of *thusly* is from 1865:

> It happened, as J. Billings would say, 'thusly' —*Harper's,* December 1865 (OED Supplement)

The "J. Billings" referred to is undoubtedly Josh Billings (real name, Henry Wheeler Shaw), an American humorist who became famous after the Civil War for his illogical, ungrammatical, and misspelled comic essays. The *Harper's* citation suggests that *thusly* was either coined by Billings for comic effect or was used by him in imitation of actual rustic speech. Other sources in our file indicate—although without substantiating evidence—that the word originated with Artemus Ward (real name, Charles Farrar Browne), another popular American humorist of the 19th century. It seems clear, in any case, that *thusly* as originally used was not a word to be taken seriously.

The process by which *thusly* arose from its comic origins to an established, if not exalted, place in the vocabulary of English is not easily traced. There are a few citations from the late 1800s which show the word being used in what seems to be a straightforward way, but written evidence through the early decades of the 20th century is scanty. The first usage commentator to take note of it was Krapp 1927, who called it "facetious." H. L. Mencken, in *The American Language, Supplement II* (1948), also regarded *thusly* as a chiefly humorous word, although he noted an instance of its serious use in the *Congressional Record* in 1943. Citational evidence from the late 1940s and early 1950s shows that *thusly* was beginning then to appear more frequently in standard writing. In current English, *thusly* is probably still more likely to occur in speech than in writing, but its written use is by no means rare.

One reason *thusly* has gradually been able to gain a secure foothold in the language is undoubtedly that it is used primarily in ways that are, to some degree, distinct from the principal uses of *thus*. As in the original *Harper's* citation, *thusly* almost always follows the verb it modifies:

> I have the vision of a little old man . . . who gives himself silent chuckles by seating people thusly —William F. Buckley, Jr., *Esquire,* September 1974

> After addressing his rod thusly, Charlie Bowman began to walk —Douglas Chadwick, *Blair & Ketchums Country Jour.,* August 1981

Its most frequent use is as an introductory word preceding a quotation or other passage set off by a colon:

> . . . the syllogism would apparently turn thusly: The United Nations is the sole bulwark of world peace. There can't be a United Nations with the Soviet Union —Vermont Royster, *Wall Street Jour.,* 7 Dec. 1964

> He also defends Chaplin's routine use of the camera and even those locomotive wheels, the former thusly: "Chaplin . . . obviously believes that. . . ." —Dwight Macdonald, *Esquire,* April 1965

> . . . introduced him to a colleague thusly: "This is George Foreman. . . ." —William Nack, *Sports Illustrated,* 22 Sept. 1980

> He was answered thusly by NOW head Eleanor Smeal: "The letter. . . ." —Daniel Seligman, *Fortune,* 10 Aug. 1981

> . . . one of Harbaugh's plays was described thusly: "Harbaugh, under a heavy rush. . . ." —Rick Telander, *Sports Illustrated,* 22 Sept. 1986

Of course, it is also possible to use *thus* in this way:

> The experimental psychologist generalizes thus: "Interest in religion. . . ." —F. Ernest Johnson, *Annals of the American Academy of Political and Social Science,* March 1953

But such use, while not rare, is relatively uncommon in modern English. *Thusly* appears to be appreciably more common than *thus* when the adverb follows the verb and precedes a colon (more common than either is a phrase such as "in this way"). On the other hand, *thusly* is rarely used in contexts where *thus* would normally be expected. When such use does occur, *thusly* may indeed seem badly out of place:

> The white silent majority has been readied to hate the press as the author of Black ticker-tape radicalism. Thusly Nixon's slaughter program for the poor and Black . . . —Leon Forrest, *Muhammad Speaks,* 16 Feb. 1973

> . . . should occupy no more than 4000 cubic inches and thusly fit into a standard large suitcase —Gene Miller with Barbara Mackle, *Ladies' Home Jour.,* May 1971

What these facts indicate is that, whatever its origins, *thusly* is not now merely an ignorant or comic substitute for *thus:* it is a distinct adverb that is used in a distinct way in standard speech and writing. Knowledge of the subtleties of its use may give you the courage to face down its critics, but if discretion, prudence, or faintheartedness compels you to shun it (or if you just dislike it), our advice is not to replace it automatically with *thus* but to consider instead a more natural-sounding phrase such as "in this way" or "as follows."

thyself See MYSELF.

tight, tightly *Tight* is usually an adjective, but it is also commonly used as an adverb. Some of its adverbial uses overlap with those of *tightly:*

> "Hold him tight," said the sergeant —James Stephens, *The Crock of Gold,* 1912

> Liz had closed her apartment tight —Van Siller, *Cosmopolitan,* March 1972

> "My baby," she said, holding Marilee tightly —Paul Horgan, *Ladies' Home Jour.,* January 1971

> . . . houses and shops which survived plundering are still closed tightly —*Time,* 2 Sept. 1946

By and large, however, the two words are used in distinct ways. *Tight* almost always follows the verb it modifies. It occurs especially in such idioms as *freeze tight, sit tight,* and *sleep tight,* as well as with such verbs as *hold, close, squeeze,* and *shut. Tightly* is a somewhat more common word which is used both before and after the verb or participle it modifies:

> . . . a tightly woven cycle of mutually dependent events —Barry Commoner, *Columbia Forum,* Spring 1968

His argument is tightly reasoned —John Fischer, *Harper's,* March 1971

... that green baseball cap clamped tightly on his head —Caleb Pirtle III, *Southern Living,* June 1972

... thinking that is focused tightly on human problems —*Christian Science Monitor,* 13 Feb. 1980

See also FLAT ADVERBS.

till, until, 'til   *Till* and *until* are both venerable words, and are both highly respectable. The notion that *till* is a short form of *until* is erroneous: *till* is actually the older word, dating back to at least the 9th century. *Until* was first recorded around 1200. The relative status of these words in current usage is discussed briefly in most handbooks. Both are invariably found to be acceptable, but *until* is often said to have a somewhat more formal quality than *till,* and to be the more likely choice at the beginning of a sentence or clause. In general, our evidence supports those observations. Note, however, that *till,* although less common than *until,* can still be perfectly at home in highly serious writing and at the beginning of a sentence:

... initiate change instead of responding to pressures, or waiting till revolution has destroyed the seam of its structure —Calvin H. Plimpton, *Amherst College Bulletin,* November 1967

... the outsider's role that had always been his, and that he would play with mounting intensity till he died —Walter Kendrick, *N.Y. Times Book Rev.,* 3 Apr. 1983

Till she got through, he would have to hide his face —Conrad Richter, *The Trees,* 1940

Till recently, the only important structure in Philadelphia was the PSFS Building —Lewis Mumford, *New Yorker,* 26 May 1956

The other subject of concern to usage commentators is the status of *'til,* a form that has been variously described as "correct in standard English" (Shaw 1970), "absurd" (Simon 1980), "poetic" (Corder 1981), "superfluous" (Bernstein 1971), and "acceptable only in informal writing" (Harper 1975, 1985). What *'til* is, unarguably, is a variant spelling of *till* used by writers who do not know that *till* is a complete, unabbreviated word in its own right. Use of *'til* is undoubtedly common in casual writing, and it does turn up in edited prose on occasion:

... the overemphasis placed upon its limitations has 'til now managed to inhibit its needed expansion — George N. Torrey & Richard P. Finn, *Massachusetts Teacher,* January 1965

But if you are writing for publication, you will do well to spell it *till.*

time period   This phrase has been cited for redundancy by several commentators.

Direct information about Freud's life during this fruitful time period has been scarce —John Dollard, *N.Y. Herald Tribune Book Rev.,* 23 May 1954

Like most redundant phrases, this one is idiomatic. You can easily avoid it, if you are inclined to, by deleting either word. See also POINT IN TIME.

times

... but now I am resolved to drink ten times less than before —Jonathan Swift, *Journal to Stella,* 30 July 1711

This is the *times* that tries men's souls. Such commentators as Evans 1957, Bernstein 1962, Copperud 1970, and Kilpatrick 1984 have argued that *times* should not be used in comparing that which is less (as in size, frequency, distance, or strength) to that which is greater. The essence of their argument is that since *times* has to do with multiplication it should only be used in comparing the greater to the smaller (as in "ten times as many" or "three times as strong"). Instead of saying "ten times less," "three times closer," and "five times fainter," you should say "one-tenth as much," "one-third as far," and "one-fifth as bright." So goes the argument. It has, undoubtedly, a certain mathematical logic to it, and it may therefore seem intimidatingly persuasive to the nonmathematical (among whose ranks we may safely expect to find most usage commentators). There is a good reason for rejecting it, however. It is that mathematics and language are two different things: attempting to apply mathematical logic to the study and understanding of language is, in fact, illogical (and usually unproductive into the bargain). The question to be asked concerning such a construction as *ten times less* is not whether it makes sense mathematically, but whether it makes sense linguistically—that is, whether people understand what it means. The answer to that question is obviously yes. *Times* has now been used in such constructions for about 300 years, and there is no evidence to suggest that it has ever been misunderstood.

Men who had ten or twenty times less to remember —W. E. Gladstone, *Gleanings of Past Years,* 1879 (OED)

... said that present day anesthetics are seven times less toxic than cocaine —*Chicago Sunday Tribune,* 23 Feb. 1947

... sensitive to lights hundreds of times weaker than the lights they could respond to initially —Howard H. Kendler, *Basic Psychology,* 2d ed., 1968

... found that it was 1,000 times less abundant than ATP —Ira Pastan, *Scientific American,* August 1972

... they are almost a thousand times smaller — Roger Lewin, *Saturday Rev.,* 26 Jan. 1974

But the controversy does not end there. Many of the commentators who object to *times less* also object—for an entirely different reason—to *times more.* The argument in this case is that *times more* (or *times larger, times stronger, times brighter,* etc.) is ambiguous, so that "He has five times more money than you" can be misunderstood as meaning "He has six times as much money as you." It is, in fact, possible to misunderstand *times more* in this way, but it takes a good deal of effort. If you have $100, five times that is $500, which means that "five times more than $100" can mean (the commentators claim) "$500 more than $100," which equals "$600," which equals "six times as much as $100." The commentators regard this as a serious ambiguity, and they advise you to avoid it by always saying "times as much" instead of "times more." Here again, it seems that they are paying homage to mathematics at the expense of language. The fact is that "five times more" and "five times as much" are idiomatic phrases which have—and are understood to have—exactly the same meaning. The "ambiguity" of *times more* is imaginary: in the world of actual speech and writing, the meaning of *times more* is clear and unequivocal. It is an idiom that has existed in our language for more than four centuries, and there is no real reason to avoid its use.

This might you reade, and ten times more
In the Bible
—Robert Crowley, *Pleasure and Payne,* 1551 (OED)

... tho' it be five times larger than the other —Joseph Addison, *The Spectator,* 1712 (OED)

... as much as 10 times more quickly —David Hamilton, *New Scientist,* 13 Feb. 1969

... faces the mirror three times more often —Gordon G. Gallup, Jr., *Psychology Today,* March 1971

... approximately thirty-five times more active —Lawrence Locke, *The Lamp,* Summer 1971

For *times* in formulas like *two times two,* see TWO AND TWO.

tinker   When used with a preposition, *tinker* is most often found with *with:*

... loved to tinker with what he considered infelicities in Keats's poems —Amy Lowell, *John Keats,* 1925

Parliaments and synods may tinker as much as they please with their codes and creeds —George Bernard Shaw, *Man and Superman,* 1903

... ingenious mechanics and engineers who tinkered with motor-propelled vehicles —Arthur M. Schlesinger, Jr., *The Reporter,* 30 Mar. 1954

... some psychologists are tinkering with a test of a sense of humor —William H. Whyte, Jr., *The Organization Man,* 1956

... employing scientists to tinker with people's genes —*Times Literary Supp.,* 22 Oct. 1971

He was still tinkering with the engine when recess ended —Russell Baker, *Growing Up,* 1982

A number of usage books of the early 20th century, beginning with Fowler 1907, prescribed *tinker at,* treating *tinker with* as an error based on faulty analogy with *tamper with.* The earliest evidence of *tinker with* in the OED, however, is from 1658, while *tinker at* is not attested until the 19th century. It may be that *tinker at* was the usual idiom at one time, but it now occurs extremely infrequently. Our files contain only a few examples of it, the most recent of which is from 1958.

He began to tinker at the wound in rather a clumsy way —Stephen Crane, *The Red Badge of Courage,* 1895

... of course, I was always tinkering at verse —*The Autobiography of William Allen White,* 1946

... has risen to become a full-fledged artist from being a five-year-old child tinkering at the piano —*International Musician,* July 1958

tirade   See HARANGUE, TIRADE.

tired   The usual preposition after *tired* is *of:*

... the mood of the media seemed against him, tired of him —Gay Talese, *Harper's,* January 1969

I'm tired of being squashed in with other people —Marjorie Holmes, *Woman's Day,* October 1971

Much less commonly, *with* follows *tired:*

The tourist tired with *Baedeker* and his latter-day substitutes may turn ... —*Times Literary Supp.,* 2 Mar. 1967

Both *of* and *with* are standard. *With* never occurs when the object of the preposition is a gerund, as in the Holmes example.

to   1. The use of *to* in place of *at* has occasionally been cited as an error by American commentators since Ayres 1881. The issue primarily involves the use of *to* following a form of the verb *to be,* as in "She was to church yesterday." Such usage occurs only in nonstandard idiom when the verb is in the past tense, *was* or *were.*

We was to the breakfast-table a talkin' it over —Marietta Holley, "A Pleasure Exertion," in *Mark Twain's Library of Humor,* 1888

Ayres also considered *to* erroneous following the present perfect tense of *to be,* "She has been to church." Such usage is now recognized as standard, however, and is actually quite distinct from the "was to church" construction. The verb *be* in "She has been to church" is almost synonymous with *go,* although its connotations are somewhat different: "She has gone to church" may mean that she is still there, but "She has been to church" strongly suggests that she is there no longer. The essential point, in any case, is that *to* does not mean "at" when it follows *has been, have been,* or *had been,* and it is not at all erroneous:

I have been to the mountaintop —Martin Luther King, speech, 1968

2. It is unlikely that anyone reading this book needs help in distinguishing *to, too,* and *two,* but these words are often inadvertently misspelled, and you may want to keep an especially sharp eye out for possible errors when you proofread your own (or anyone else's) writing. Mistakes can be embarrassing:

The Needlenose tape shows the wreckage of that one two —*Pleasure Boating,* February 1984

to a degree   See DEGREE.

to all intents and purposes   Any idiomatic phrase consisting of five words and eight syllables is asking for trouble, and this one has gotten it, from Evans 1957, Phythian 1979, Copperud 1980, and Janis 1984. It is an old phrase, apparently originating in the language of 16th-century English law, where it was *to all intents, constructions, and purposes.* It has taken various forms throughout its history, including *to all intents, to all intent and purpose,* and *for all intents and purposes,* but *to all intents and purposes* has long been established as the most common one:

Most of the essential policies ... were, to all intents and purposes, those of a British colonial premier —H. L. Mencken, *Prejudices: Second Series,* 1920

... now he is to all intents and purposes a classic — Leonard Unger, *Sewanee Rev.,* Summer 1979

His courteous response was, to all intents and purposes, no response —Philip Roth, *N.Y. Times Book Rev.,* 15 Feb. 1976

The critics have predictably called it wordy and hackneyed, but, as these quotations show, it is used without ill effect by excellent writers, and there is no compelling reason to avoid it. If you prefer a shorter alternative, however, the best one is usually *in effect.*

together *Together* is sometimes cited as a redundancy when it occurs following such verbs as *join, gather, assemble,* and *connect.* See REDUNDANCY.

together with A number of books, including Bryson 1984, Heritage 1982, and Guth 1985, insist that *together with* is not equivalent to *and,* so that when *together with* tacks on another noun to a singular noun that is the subject of a sentence, the verb remains singular, as in this example:

The Corporation, together with Noranda Mines Limited, holds approximately 60% voting control — *Annual Report, The Mead Corp.,* 1970

This is acceptable theory, and it usually works where the segment introduced by *together with* is clearly perceived as parenthetical. When it is not so perceived, as Scott, Foresman 1981 points out, usage is mixed.

The only examples of additive *together with* that bear on this question are ones where the noun to which it is attached is singular and the verb is in the present or present perfect tense; in all others agreement does not reveal itself. As you might expect, revealing examples are not especially numerous, but what we have suggests that the dominant practice is probably the prescribed one.

We are, however, quite sure that a singular verb obtains with a singular noun subject when the *together with* segment begins the sentence or clause:

Together with the local Audubon Society it has rescued.... —John Fischer, *Harper's,* January 1969

See also AGREEMENT, SUBJECT-VERB: COMPOUND SUBJECTS 3.

token The idiomatic phrase *by the same token* has been the object of sporadic criticism, sometimes because it is thought to lack a clear meaning and to be imprecisely used, and sometimes because it is thought to be archaic. Archaic it certainly is not. The evidence in our files shows clearly that *by the same token* occurs commonly and idiomatically in current English. Its meaning can, however, be somewhat hard to pin down. In general it serves as a kind of loose connective between statements that have some logical association that is expected to be clear to the reader. Its meaning is usually close to "for the same reason," "at the same time," or "in the same way":

... the artist has mysteriously been hybridized with the criminal or the antisocial figure. By the same token ... crime has become obsessional in our society as a form of artistic expression —Marshall McLuhan, *American Scholar,* Spring 1966

We are so self-conscious ... that we not only generate critical prophesies, but by the same token defy them or undo them by discussing and examining

them to death —Robert Coles, *Trans-Action,* May 1968

New York was the pleasure capital.... But by the same token it was unreal, a mirage, and distinctly treacherous —Alfred Kazin, *Harper's,* December 1968

No serious objection can be made to these uses of the phrase. What you may want to avoid, however, is relying too heavily on *by the same token* to connect statements whose logical association may not be immediately clear:

Physicians dominate medical licensing and examining boards. By the same token, a leading intellectual is a person whom other leading intellectuals consider a leading intellectual —*Change,* March 1972

tolerance, tolerant The noun *tolerance* may be followed by any of several prepositions. *Tolerance of* usually means "willingness to tolerate":

... has acquired a tolerance of viewpoints not his own —Milton S. Eisenhower, *Johns Hopkins Mag.,* February 1966

... there is no tolerance of dissent —William G. Mather, in *Automation, Education and Human Values,* ed. W. W. Brickman & S. Lehrer, 1966

Tolerance to is most likely to occur in scientific contexts, where it has the meaning "ability to tolerate":

... what happens when a person becomes addicted to heroin is that his tolerance to the drug is increased —*Nature,* 14 Apr. 1972

... is said to have had a low tolerance to alcohol — John Corry, *N.Y. Times,* 27 Mar. 1976

A plant that possesses only tolerance to insect attack —A. N. Kishaba & G. R. Manglitz, *Jour. of Economic Entomology,* June 1965

Tolerance of is also sometimes used to mean "ability," and *tolerance to* is sometimes used to mean "willingness." *Tolerance for* is commonly used to mean both "willingness" and "ability":

... the society's decreasing tolerance for hardship — Richard Todd, *Atlantic,* September 1970

... was treated with equal tolerance for his blunders —Samuel Hopkins Adams, *Incredible Era,* 1939

... the dosage has to be increased later, as a tolerance for the drug is built up —S. S. Tomkins, ed., *Contemporary Psychopathology,* 1943

... his body develops a *tolerance* for the drug — James H. Otto & Albert Towle, *Modern Biology,* 1973

An uncommon variant, *tolerance toward* (or *towards*) is used only to mean "willingness":

... he should develop ... tolerance toward the opinions of others —*Bates College Bulletin,* 1 Jan. 1952

The adjective *tolerant* is most often followed by *of:*

... could be argued that the chronic smoker is tolerant of marijuana —Solomon H. Snyder, *Psychology Today,* May 1971

... he seemed more tolerant of them than some of the other local men —Edward Hoagland, *Harper's,* October 1970

Tolerant to is limited to scientific contexts:

Mice that were rendered tolerant to denatured DNA —*Science,* 5 Oct. 1973

Tolerant is never followed by *for. Toward* occurs about as frequently after *tolerant* as it does after *tolerance:*

... he had grown more tolerant toward literature —Robertson Davies, *Tempest-tost,* 1951

tome   In its original sense, *tome* is a synonym for *volume;* that is, "a book forming part of a larger work." The use in which *tome* has become established as a familiar word, however, is as a synonym for *book,* with strong connotations of great size or highly detailed—often ponderous—scholarship:

I waded conscientiously through many formidable tomes —W. Somerset Maugham, *The Summing Up,* 1938

The authors' opinions make it livelier than the ordinary academic tome —Rod Nordell, *Christian Science Monitor,* 5 Sept. 1957

In these days of overpadded tomes —Maria Lenhart, *Christian Science Monitor,* 10 Sept. 1979

... the fatty tomes that clog the literary mainstream —John Updike, *New Yorker,* 11 Jan. 1982

Used without regard for these connotations, *tome* sometimes draws the charge that it is pretentious or a bit of journalistic cant. The "ponderous" connotations of *tome* seem to have developed in the 19th century, but the word has been used as a synonym for *book* since at least 1573. Although it now usually serves to express criticism, it is also still used on occasion as a term of praise:

... I am one of the fortunate few in this country who has the time to wear each copy of this sturdy tome to tatters before the next update becomes available —Bill James, *Inside Sports,* August 1982

... lucky children receive tomes, not toys, as gifts — Anna Marie & Cullen Murphy, *Smithsonian,* November 1984

too   1. *Too* is like *very*—an adverb used only to modify adjectives ("too large") and other adverbs ("too far"). When a verb is being modified, an additional adverb, such as *much,* is required ("You talk too much"). The use of *too* in modifying the past participles of verbs ("We were too interested to leave") is analogous to the use of *very* with past participles, and though relatively few commentators have taken note of it, it raises similar questions. For a discussion of the aspects of such usage, and the opinions concerning it, see VERY 1.
2. *Too,* meaning "also," sometimes occurs at the beginning of a sentence:

Too, the Dutch emerged from the oil crisis with their heads high —Gordon F. Sander, *N.Y. Times Mag.,* 22 Aug. 1976

Too, it probably calls for the same kind of gas as today's small cars —Charles E. Dole, *Christian Science Monitor,* 29 Apr. 1980

Too, the agencies have increasingly pushed banks into the market —Susan Lee, *Wall Street Jour.,* 11 July 1983

Too, there's a certain magic surrounding Gable — Douglas S. Looney, *Sports Illustrated,* 18 July 1984

Moreover, besides, in addition, and *also* are more common in such contexts, but *too* is not incorrect. The OED indicated in 1913 that *too* was "rarely, now never, used at the beginning of a clause," but the OED Supplement shows that such usage has been revived in the 20th century, originally in American English but now in British English as well. No grammatical objection can be made to it, and the practice is clearly standard. Whatever problems it causes have to do with idiom—which is to say that, because of its relative rarity, it sounds peculiar to some people. Several usage handbooks therefore discourage the use of *too* at the beginning of a sentence. We suggest that the best guide in matters such as this is your own sense of idiom.
3. For *too* meaning "very," see NOT TOO.

toothsome   *Toothsome* can mean "delicious":

... fudgy chocolate cake, toothsome walnut pie — Florence Fabricant, *N.Y. Times,* 18 July 1980

Or "attractive":

... to coax his toothsome secretary into a close relationship —John McCarten, *New Yorker,* 4 Jan. 1964

Recently, this old adjective has been showing signs of developing an additional sense, "toothy." William Safire criticized its use in this sense by a *Newsweek* writer in 1982. We first saw it in 1975:

John Tunney, California's toothsome junior senator, is said to be trying to grim up his image. Tunney denies it, but word has it that he has hired a speech therapist, solely to teach him how to smile without flashing a mouthful of what appear to be some 65 teeth —*New York,* 11 Aug. 1975

Further evidence has been slow in coming, however, and it is clear that the "toothy" sense of *toothsome* still falls far short of being established.

top   *Top* has been used as an adjective for many centuries, and no one denies that its adjectival uses are established and reputable. Bernstein 1965, however, considers it overused by journalists in its sense "chief, leading." This sense of *top* was first recorded in 1647 and has been in regular use since then, but the widespread popularity it now enjoys dates only from the 1940s. Its most common use is in describing a group, especially one having power or influence:

... only top personnel in the key companies were given basic information —James Phinney Baxter 3d, *Atlantic,* September 1946

The White House has ordered top military officials to abolish every duplicating activity —*Newsweek,* 4 Nov. 1946

... in the offices of all other top editors —Gay Talese, *Harper's,* January 1969

Lovett and one of his top deputies —David Halberstam, *Harper's,* February 1971

Its use in describing an individual is most likely when the person referred to is a member of such a group:

> A top Tory announced yesterday that he was quitting —*Daily Mirror* (London), 24 Oct. 1974

Overuse is, of course, a matter of individual judgment, and neither Fowler 1926 nor Evans 1957, both of which enter *top,* makes this charge. Beyond doubt it is in very frequent use. If you see the word as Bernstein does, you will find many alternatives—*highest, foremost, leading, principal, most important,* and so forth—but none as short. If not, you will be in the company of most of the top commentators, it seems.

tormented   The preposition that usually occurs after *tormented* is *by:*

> ... was also obviously tormented by doubts and misgivings —Thomas Wolfe, *You Can't Go Home Again,* 1940

> ... at times tormented by voluptuous visions — Rebecca West, *The Thinking Reed,* 1936

> ... tormented by a lust for the pleasures and knowledge of this world —Robert E. Herzstein, *N.Y. University Bulletin,* Spring 1967

With is also used after *tormented,* but much less commonly than *by:*

> ... though tormented with a bitter sense of failure — Jerome Stone, *Saturday Rev.,* 8 Jan. 1955

> ... tormented with hunger and thirst —Nevil Shute, *Most Secret,* 1945

tortuous, torturous   Commentators routinely warn against confusing these two words. The distinction to be made between them is that *tortuous* means chiefly "winding or twisted" and that *torturous* means "causing torture; excruciating." The main concern of the critics is that *torturous* should not be used in place of *tortuous* in such phrases as *a tortuous path.* Our evidence shows that such usage is rare in edited prose, but the offending *torturous* does sneak into print from time to time, and we suspect that it occurs fairly often in casual writing and speech. In some contexts *torturous* may appear to be taking the place of *tortuous* even when its intended meaning is actually "causing torture":

> Ahead of the racers lay 1,946 miles of torturous mountain roads —*Time,* 1 Dec. 1952

Torturous may mean "twisting" here or it may mean "causing torture" or it may mean both. In any case, the writer might have done better to choose another adjective (perhaps *murderous* or *harrowing*), if only to avoid the appearance of confusion.

One problem with trying to keep *tortuous* and *torturous* distinct is that they are close relatives. Both words are derived ultimately from the Latin *tortus,* participle of the verb meaning "twist," and both words have strong ties with *torture,* which itself can describe not only torment but also twisting or distortion (as in "tortured reasoning"). *Tortuous* is, in general, a far more common word than *torturous.* It is especially common in extended uses, in most of which it can be defined either as "exceedingly complex or involved" or "deviously indirect or tricky":

> ... pursued a tortuous policy in his testimony, disclosing this piece of evidence and withholding that —Rebecca West, *Atlantic,* June 1952

> ... tortuous intrigues had at last brought him to the highest office —William L. Shirer, *The Rise and Fall of the Third Reich,* 1960

> ... the ways of the Legislature are slow and tortuous —John Deedy, *Commonweal,* 30 Jan. 1970

> I wish I did not find this explanation so tortuous — Mary Gordon, *Saturday Rev.,* 14 Apr. 1979

But extreme complexity can sometimes be a kind of torture, and *tortuous,* while its denotation may be "twisted" or "complex," does in some contexts have connotations of torment as well:

> ... the tortuous procedures that make up our criminal-justice system —John Sansing, *The Washingtonian,* October 1978

Likewise *torturous* can have connotations of extreme— or excruciating—complexity:

> ... today's dazzling landscape of higher education, with its vast mushroom fields of crowded campuses, its torturous selection processes, its maniacal pressures on the tender young —Tom Wicker, *Change,* September 1971

> ... This May Be The Most Torturous Puzzle You've Ever Grappled With —advt., *New Yorker,* 31 Mar. 1986

What this means is that the two words can and do appear in similar contexts. Our evidence shows, however, that the basic distinction in their meanings favored by the critics, especially as it relates to such phrases as *a tortuous path,* is in fact observed by most writers. Here are a few more examples of *tortuous* and *torturous* in their distinct senses:

> The river follows a tortuous course —A. H. J. Prins, *The Coastal Tribes of the North-Eastern Bantu,* 1952

> Weary and depressed after his torturous afternoon —Paul Zimmerman, *Sports Illustrated,* 31 Jan. 1983

> ... on the tortuous, corkscrew roads —Ronald Sullivan, *N.Y. Times,* 8 Jan. 1984

> ... found the strength and courage to survive torturous inquisitions —*Booklist,* 1 Nov. 1984

total, totally   Admonitions against the tautological use of *total* and *totally* in such phrases as "total annihilation" and "totally destroyed" can be found in a few books on usage. *Total* and *totally* can usually be omitted from such phrases without a loss of meaning, but it should be noted that their omission will almost always result in a loss of emphasis. Consideration of rhythm and idiom should also be taken into account.

> Thirty-five pounds of explosives ensured its total destruction —*Current Biography,* January 1966

> ... the bank was gutted by fire and totally destroyed —*Scholastic Voice,* 13 Apr. 1970

> ... as though nothing less than total annihilation would satisfy my rage —Sally Kempton, *Esquire,* July 1970

It is not at all clear that these passages would be improved by the omission of *total* and *totally.*

to the manner (manor) born   See MANNER.

toward, towards Many commentators have observed that *toward* is the more common choice in American English, while the preference in British English is for *towards.* Our evidence confirms that such is indeed the case. Both words are commonly used in the U.S., but *toward* is undoubtedly prevalent:

> ... looked down across sloping cornfields toward a small village —Russell Baker, *Growing Up,* 1982

> His later development ... was toward the occult —Arthur Miller, *N.Y. Times Book Rev.,* 6 Jan. 1985

> There is a tendency towards informality —Calvin H. Plimpton, *Amherst College Bulletin,* November 1967

The British strongly favor *towards:*

> ... a new tool towards the shaping of its own destiny —E. H. Gombrich, quoted in *British Book News,* November 1982

> ... edging slowly towards social democracy —Graham Greene, *Getting to Know the General,* 1984

At one time some critics (as Ayres 1881) preferred *toward* because they believed the *-s* of *towards* had died away. Letters from our correspondents sometimes seem to be seeking some semantic basis for a differentiation between these forms, but there is none.

to wit *To wit* has occasionally been criticized as an inappropriately legalistic synonym for *namely.* There is no denying that this adverbial phrase is most at home in legal writing:

> Thereafter when the transactions occurred forming the basis of this claim, to-wit, the giving of the treasurer's checks ... —*Banking Law Jour.,* May 1940

Its past occurrences in general writing have not been rare, but our recent evidence (or lack of evidence) suggests that its use may now be diminishing. It is most likely to occur, and seems most appropriate, in writing that has a notably formal tone:

> We need not engage in deceit to deal with what is human, to wit, erring —Robert T. Blackburn, *AAUP Bulletin,* December 1967

track, tract Confusion of these words is warned against by Copperud 1980. We find some evidence of it in our files:

> SCCAP skirted those obstacles by buying tracks of undeveloped land —*New Spirit,* October 1979

This may be simply a typographical error. For the record, however, the word called for in this context is *tract,* "an area of land."

tragedy In the world of literature, a tragedy is a highly serious work that typically describes the downfall of a great or heroic figure. Several commentators, with the literary sense in mind, have disapproved extended uses of *tragedy* to describe real events or circumstances of a somewhat less than earthshaking nature. The use most likely to be criticized is in such contexts as the following:

> It was the tragedy of American architecture that the way pointed out by Richardson, Sullivan, and Wright was long obscured —*American Guide Series: New York,* 1940

> The tragedy of marriage is not that it fails to assure woman the promised happiness —H. M. Parshley, translation of Simone de Beauvoir, *The Second Sex,* 1952

> It would be a genuine tragedy if liberals lost all sense of proportion —*Commonweal,* 11 Apr. 1969

The meaning of *tragedy* in such contexts is "something to be deeply regretted; a great misfortune." This sense of the word is common and well-established, but it can at times have a needlessly hyperbolic quality. We recommend that you use it thoughtfully.

transcendent, transcendental Some distinctions between these adjectives have been noted by several commentators, the primary one being that *transcendent* is preferred in the sense "surpassing" (as in "an issue of transcendent importance"). Our evidence supports this distinction, although it should be noted that *transcendental* is not incorrect when used to mean "surpassing":

> ... produced a series of objects of transcendental monstrosity —Osbert Lancaster, *All Done From Memory,* 1953

> ... or at least ordinariness, especially when carried to such transcendental levels —Peter Stansky, *Saturday Rev.,* 20 Jan. 1973

It has had this sense since the 18th century. Its primary senses, however, relate to philosophy and especially metaphysics, and its otherworldly associations may now be especially strong because of the attention given in recent years to transcendental meditation.

transmute When this somewhat bookish verb is followed by a preposition, the preposition is almost always *into:*

> ... took the national anguish ... and transmuted it into wildly successful comedy —Richard Grenier, *Cosmopolitan,* October 1976

> ... Melville transmutes the lowly fact ... into a meditation on mankind —John Updike, *New Yorker,* 10 May 1982

A much less common preposition after *transmute* is *to:*

> ... such a star transmutes lighter elements to heavier ones —Dietrick E. Thomsen, *Science News,* 10 Aug. 1985

transpire The use of *transpire* to mean "to come to pass, occur, happen" has been disparaged since at least 1870. Some of its critics have rather shortchanged this interesting word, saying that *transpire* can mean only "to leak out, become known." They pass over its earlier technical senses, which we still find in use, most often in botanical contexts.

Transpire was born as a technical word in the 17th century. In its literal senses, *transpire* describes the passing of a vapor through the pores of a membrane, such as the surface of a leaf. The word began to be used figuratively sometime in the first half of the century (the earliest figurative citation in the OED is from 1741). Samuel Johnson's 1755 Dictionary is the first to record the new sense, albeit disapprovingly. Johnson defined the sense as "To escape from secrecy to notice" and appended this comment: "a sense lately innovated from *France,* without necessity." He gave no example of its use. In James Boswell's *Life of Samuel Johnson* (1791), the Earl of Marchmont tells Boswell that Johnson's dislike of *transpire* was actually owing to its having first been used by Lord Bolingbroke, with whom Johnson had deep political differences. This use by Bolingbroke has not yet been discovered, but it might explain Johnson's comment about the sense's French origin. The sense was current for the corresponding French verb in the early 18th century, and Bolingbroke lived in exile in France from 1715 to 1725. Here are a few examples of its use in English:

... certainly, it would be next to a miracle that a fact of this kind should be known to a whole parish, and not transpire any farther —Henry Fielding, *Tom Jones*, 1749

No more news has transpired of that Wanderer —Charles Lamb, letter, 1 Feb. 1806

... it had just transpired that he had left gaming debts behind him to a very considerable amount —Jane Austen, *Pride and Prejudice*, 1813

... some circumstance has transpired which leads to a belief that the persons ... are in some way connected with the prisoner for some sinister purpose —anonymous broadside, 1842, in *Curiosities of Street Literature*, 1871

To be perfectly frank with you I am one of the most notable craftsmen of my time. That will transpire presently —Robert Frost, letter, 4 July 1913

Manning had a long interview with Pius IX ... Precisely what passed on that occasion never transpired —Lytton Strachey, *Eminent Victorians*, 1918

This particular use is no longer very common, according to our evidence. In present-day general English *transpire* most often occurs in an impersonal construction with *it*. The construction may have developed from uses like Jane Austen's above. In this impersonal construction *it transpired* ranges in meaning from "it was learned" to "it turned out." Here are several examples:

It transpired afterwards that Miss Maitland had had no intention of giving Ernest in charge —Samuel Butler, *The Way of All Flesh*, 1903

It then transpired that Old Crockford was a village and, from the appearance of the team on the day of battle, the Old Crockfordians seemed to be composed exclusively of the riff-raff of same —P. G. Wodehouse, *Tales of St Austin's*, 1903

It transpired after a confused five minutes that the man had heard Gatsby's name around his office —F. Scott Fitzgerald, *The Great Gatsby*, 1925

... but when they get there, it transpires that this is not the point of departure of their ship —James Thurber, *Thurber Country*, 1953

But in the end it transpired that the allusion was characteristically to an Edwardian popular song —Foster 1968

... said at the time that he took no fees from the cereal makers. But it transpired that he did receive retainers from them —John L. Hess, *Saturday Rev.*, August 1978

... therefore it was not resented by anybody when it transpired that indeed they did —William F. Buckley, Jr., quoted in *Harper's*, January 1986

The newest sense of *transpire*, "to take place; occur; happen," originated obscurely, probably in the late 18th century. Noah Webster in his 1828 Dictionary was the first to record the new meaning, which may be of American origin. It seems likely that it developed by misinterpretation of the earlier figurative sense in ambiguous contexts. For instance, the Dictionary of Americanisms and the OED Supplement both give this quotation as the first example of the new sense:

There is nothing new transpired since I wrote you last —Abigail Adams, letter, 31 July 1775

With just this much context given, however, the example is ambiguous: *transpired* might mean "has come out" or "has happened." Ambiguous examples are not hard to find. Here are two more:

I long to see you once more, to clasp you in my arms & to tell you of many things which have transpired since we parted —Emily Dickinson, letter, 8 Sept. 1846

... denied that anything had transpired that would jeopardize Walker's NCAA eligibility —Jerry Kirshenbaum, *Sports Illustrated*, 28 Feb. 1983

We think it not unlikely that the new sense came from people's hearing *transpire* in ambiguous contexts, taking it to mean "happen," and then using it to mean "happen." At any rate, *transpire* was clearly used to mean "happen" as early as 1804 in a fugitive publication from Hartford, Connecticut.

It is fitting that this early example of the "happen" sense was probably journalistic, for it was journalistic use that after some sixty years resulted in controversy. The first two critics were Richard Grant White 1870 and John Stuart Mill in *A System of Logic* (whether first in the 1866 or the 1872 edition we do not know). The "happen" sense of *transpire* came to the attention of each through its use in newspapers. White devoted four pages to his critique of this sense, but in the end he produced only three examples of it, while quoting twice as many examples of the sense he approved. White's most flamboyant example is this one, from an unidentified paper:

The police drill will transpire under shelter to-day in consequence of the moist atmosphere prevailing.

Mill contented himself with dismissing the new sense as a vulgarism, but White characteristically buttressed his opinion by reference to etymology, the upshot of which was that there is no logical connection between either the Latin roots of *transpire* ("breathe" and "across") or its literal English sense and its use to mean "happen." Many subsequent commentators have also based their criticism on etymology. Others have stressed more what they see as the pretentiousness of *transpire* in its disapproved sense.

The etymological argument against the use of *transpire* to mean "happen" can be dismissed along with many other such arguments. That this sense arose out of confusion seems undeniable, but the confusion that produced it occurred about 200 years ago. Modern writers and speakers who use *transpire* to mean "happen" are not confused about the meaning of the word; they know perfectly well that in current English "happen" is one of its established senses. The process by which it acquired this sense in the distant past is irrelevant; acquire the sense it did, and it now has it for good, or at least for the forseeable future. Anyone who tries seriously to claim in the late 20th century that *transpire* does not mean "happen" is obviously talking nonsense.

As for the charge of pretentiousness, there is no denying that *transpire* is a somewhat formal word, and like any formal word it can be used pretentiously (as in the passage about the police drill cited by Richard Grant White). But formal words can also be used appropriately, in contexts where a certain formality is called for. Our evidence for *transpire* meaning "happen" shows that its use is sometimes pretentious and sometimes not. Sometimes the pretentiousness is deliberately employed for comic effect. You can judge the range of use from this sampling:

Few changes—hardly any—have transpired among his ship's company —Charles Dickens, *Dombey and Son*, 1848 (OED)

All memorable events, I should say, transpire in morning time and in a morning atmosphere —Henry David Thoreau, *Walden*, 1854

... the first incidents of the origin of the fire which all told did not occupy more than five minutes in transpiring —*Tombstone Epitaph*, ca. 1880, in Douglas D. Martin, *Tombstone's Epitaph*, 1951

This here finish joke of Jaybird's transpires one evenin as the cook's startin in to rustle some chuck —Alfred Henry Lewis, "Jaybird Bob's Last Joke," 1897, in *The Mirth of a Nation*, ed. Walter Blair & Raven I. McDavid, Jr., 1983

All sorts of delays transpired in the work —*N.Y. Times*, 20 Nov. 1899

... if the project will shape into the building of a great American army to meet whatever may transpire —Archibald MacLeish, letter, 4 Feb. 1917

The stage, of course, was the dream. All that transpired there is now a memory —Charles A. Lindbergh, *The Spirit of St. Louis*, 1953

... most agreed that I gave an honest account of what transpired —James A. Michener, *Saturday Rev.*, 1 May 1954

Stage three, flirtation, depends on individuals, but a great deal of it transpires in airplanes —Robert Craft, *Stravinsky*, 1972

I did not learn much of what transpired until the next day —William L. Shirer, *The Nightmare Years*, 1984

... his faithful report of what transpired amounts to the proverbial smoking gun —David A. Stockman, *Newsweek*, 28 Apr. 1986

... documents which are often conflicting and occasionally far from what we believe transpired —*The Tower Commission Report*, 1987

It should be noted in passing that *transpire* is also a formal word in its uncontroversial sense, "to become known or apparent," and that its use in this sense can also at times seem pretentious.

In summary, *transpire* has two uses in general publications today. It is used in an impersonal construction, usually *it transpired that*, which means approximately "it turned out that" or "it developed that." And it is used to mean "to take place, occur, happen." In both uses it is a somewhat formal word that can sometimes

seem pretentious. In both uses it is firmly established as standard. The use of *transpire* to mean "happen" has attracted criticism for more than a century and will perhaps continue to attract criticism for many years to come, but it is extremely common, can be found in the works of excellent writers, and is in no sense an error.

tread See TROD.

treat When used as an intransitive verb meaning "negotiate," *treat* is idiomatically followed by *with*:

... to provide France with a competent representative to treat with President Eisenhower —Lansing Warren, *N.Y. Times*, 7 June 1953

... a Sioux Indian coming to treat with yet another cavalry general —Lewis H. Lapham, *Harper's*, May 1971

In less typical constructions, this sense of *treat* is followed by *for* and *on*:

... delegates were reported as leaving Berlin to treat for an armistice —Elizabeth Madox Roberts, *He Sent Forth a Raven*, 1935

... the commissioners sent to Hartford to treat on the Connecticut boundary —*Dictionary of American Biography*, 1936

When used to mean "to deal with a matter in writing," *treat* is followed by *of*:

Mr. Robson treats of Kipling's middle rather than late stories —*Times Literary Supp.*, 2 Apr. 1964

The first volume ... treated of the seminal thinkers —Theodore M. Avery, Jr., *Library Jour.*, 1 Apr. 1966

Several critics have called the use of *on* or *with* after this sense of *treat* an error. There is no evidence of such usage in the Merriam-Webster files. If it occurs, it probably represents a mental blending of *treat* with such combinations as *expound on* or *deal with*.

treble See TRIPLE, TREBLE.

trek *Trek* is derived ultimately from the Middle Dutch verb *trecken*, "to pull, haul, migrate." The English word was borrowed in the 19th century from the Boers of South Africa. As used by the Boers, *trek* referred specifically to large-scale migrations over land by means of ox-drawn wagons. That was also its original reference in English, both as a noun and as a verb, but in the 20th century it has come to be used more broadly. A few critics, mindful of its etymology, have regarded the extended uses of *trek* with disapproval, arguing that it should only be used to speak of journeys that are particularly arduous or long and that are undertaken on a large scale.

In actual usage, *trek* always retains at least some suggestion of its original meaning. It commonly describes movement on foot or by other means over land, especially when the going is slow or the movement has—or is being hyperbolically treated as if it has—a migratory or expeditionary nature:

... usually requires a considerable trek through mountains, forests or swamplands —Bert Reichert, *Ford Times*, February 1968

... twice a year trekking down to Bloomingdale's — Carol Eisen Rinzler, *New York*, 1 Nov. 1971

Over 100,000 people . . . have trekked through the museum in the past year —Thomas Fleming, *Cosmopolitan,* July 1972

Kraft's wife and children . . . trek up to the farmhouse to see what they can do —Paul L. Berman, *N.Y. Times Book Rev.,* 1 July 1979

. . . thousands of prospectors trekked north on the Alaska Gold Rush —Maria Wilhelm, *People,* 30 Aug. 1982

Even when the movement described is not necessarily over land, the "migratory or expeditionary" connotations of *trek* often make it the word of choice:

. . . they went on a trek to New Orleans in search of people to record —Charlie Gillett, *Rolling Stone,* 3 Feb. 1972

Pioneer 11 . . . completed a two-year trek to Jupiter in December —James S. Kunen, *New Times,* 4 Apr. 1975

. . . the usual stream of radical Arab leaders trekking to Moscow —Elliott House, *Wall Street Jour.,* 3 June 1981

Critics such as Evans 1957 and Gowers in Fowler 1965 object to such usage in part because they feel that *trek* is being used when a more general word such as *go, travel,* or *journey* would be more appropriate. No doubt a more general word could be substituted for *trek* in any of the above examples, but it is unlikely that the writers who chose *trek* would agree that such substitution represents a change for the better. *Trek* has distinct connotations of its own which make it a useful and popular word. There is no need to consciously avoid it, and our considerable evidence of its use indicates that most writers do not feel such a need either.

tremblor, trembler See TEMBLOR, TREMBLOR, TREMBLER.

tribute Fowler 1926 first took note of the peculiar use of *tribute* meaning "a proof of" or "a testament to" that occurs in the phrase *a tribute to:*

The skill with which English "county society" took in the newcomers was a tribute to its political good sense —D. W. Brogan, *The English People,* 1943

The building was a considerable tribute to human ingenuity —John Cheever, *The Wapshot Chronicle,* 1957

That which is being proved or demonstrated is usually praiseworthy, but not necessarily:

The chorus girls, hand-picked by Busby Berkeley, are a tribute to his apparently failing eyesight —John Simon, *New York,* 15 Feb. 1971

Fowler was critical of this use of *tribute.* His opinion was more or less repeated by Edmund Wilson in *The Bit Between My Teeth* (1963), but this is not a popular issue among modern commentators; almost all of them ignore it entirely. Current dictionaries that cover this use of *tribute* treat it as standard.

trigger The transitive verb *trigger* is a relatively new word. We first encountered it in 1916:

. . . blows the ionized gas through the hole in the disk to the other terminal, thus triggering off the spark — *Scientific American,* 29 Aug. 1916

Its widespread use dates only from the 1940s, when it began to appear in a variety of publications:

Libido . . . is not triggered by the glands, but by the brain —*Time,* 28 Apr. 1941

. . . that the alpha particle serves only to trigger off the nuclear disintegration —J. D. Stranathan, *The Particles of Modern Physics,* 1942

Then Pearl Harbor triggered the mass migration to the west coast shipyards —*N.Y. Herald Tribune,* 21 Nov. 1943

Its use became even more common in the 1950s, and it has continued to be extremely popular in the decades since:

. . . it triggered a complex and very public chain of events —Tom Wolfe, in *The Contemporary Essay,* ed. Donald Hall, 1984

. . . could have triggered a potentially disastrous run on deposits —Julie Salamon, *Wall Street Jour.,* 18 Dec. 1981

. . . appears that such movements have indeed triggered large earthquakes —W. Thatcher, *Nature,* 8 Sept. 1982

The split with the Johnsons was triggered by Mr. Johnson's belief —Garrison Keillor, *Lake Wobegon Days,* 1985

Usage commentators agree that *trigger* is a reputable verb, but several of them consider it overused, and they recommend giving preference to such alternatives as *start, cause, initiate, produce,* and *begin* (to name a few). *Trigger* does, however, have distinct connotations that make it an especially appropriate choice in many cases: it typically implies an immediate effect or reaction, usually an unintended or undesirable one. These useful connotations will doubtless assure its continuing popularity. We see no need to make a special point of avoiding its use.

triple, treble Some distinctions in the use of these two basically synonymous words have been discussed by several commentators, beginning with Fowler 1926. He observed that *treble* was the more common verb and noun, that *triple* was the more common adjective, and that, as an adjective, *treble* was more likely to mean "multiplied by three" and *triple* to mean "having three parts or elements." His observations, of course, were primarily based on British usage. Later American commentators, such as Evans 1957 and Shaw 1975, have found that *triple* is much more common in the U.S. than *treble* in all their synonymous senses. Our evidence indicates that *triple* is in fact the usual choice in American English, except that the verb *treble* is sometimes favored by business writers, and the adjective *treble* is common in the legal term *treble damages:*

Profits of this larger volume group have more than trebled in the same period —H. J. Nelson, *Barron's,* 10 Apr. 1972

. . . the $66 billion used to purchase stocks . . . could instead have more than trebled our acquisition of new . . . equipment —Alfred E. Kahn, *N.Y. Times Book Rev.,* 12 Dec. 1982

The bill would allow victims to sue for treble damages —*Women's Wear Daily,* 2 Apr. 1973

... is seeking $1.05 billion from the defendants, or treble damages, for alleged violations — *Wall Street Jour.,* 26 Nov. 1982

Treble also occurs—and is certainly standard—in general writing, but *triple* predominates. Excluding the musical senses of *treble* and the baseball sense of *triple,* neither word is commonly used as a noun.

triumphal, triumphant Fowler 1926 observes a distinction in the meanings of these words, and a few later commentators have followed suit. The distinction has been variously stated, but the basic idea is that *triumphal* should be used with the meaning "ceremonially celebrating or commemorating a victory," as in "a triumphal procession" and "a triumphal arch," and that *triumphant* should be used in all other cases, as with the meanings "having triumphed" ("a triumphant army"), "rejoicing for victory" ("a triumphant shout"), and "notably successful" ("a triumphant performance"). By and large, that is exactly how *triumphal* and *triumphant* are in fact used, except that *triumphal* occasionally occurs when *triumphant* might be expected:

> ... two certainties remain after last night's triumphal success —Virgil Thomson, *The Musical Scene,* 1947

> ... during the Toronto Symphony's triumphal visit to London —*Current Biography,* February 1968

Such usage was first recorded in 1513, but it seems never to have been common. *Triumphant* was also used as a synonym for *triumphal* in previous centuries:

> ... captives bound to a triumphant car —Shakespeare, *Henry VI,* 1592

But that sense of *triumphant* is now archaic.

trivia *Trivia* is much like *data*—an English word that has the form of the Latin plural that is its source but that is used as both a plural and a singular noun. The Latin singular *trivium* means literally "crossroads." The process by which the plural form *trivia* has acquired the English sense "unimportant facts or matters" is somewhat obscure, but there is no doubt that association with *trivial* has played a large part in it (*trivial* is derived from the Latin *trivialis,* meaning "commonplace"). *Trivia* was first used in this sense in the early 20th century:

> ... induces them to publish trivia of a peculiarly ephemeral character —*N.Y. Times,* 26 Dec. 1927

Such usage drew some early criticism on etymological grounds, but the small controversy concerning it never caught on among usage commentators. Follett 1966 lists resistance to the "trifles" sense of *trivia* as a "lost cause." A more persistent issue has been the use of *trivia* as a singular mass noun, as in "all this trivia" rather than "all these trivia." Commentators who regard the singular use of *trivia* as unacceptable include Bernstein 1965, Bryson 1984, and Barzun 1985. Our evidence shows, however, that the singular and plural uses of *trivia* are about equally common in reputable writing:

> ... such trivia comes as a welcome diversion —Trevor Armbrister, *Saturday Evening Post,* 12 Feb. 1966

> This is *trivia,* however —*Times Literary Supp.,* 3 Mar. 1966

> ... took careful notes on all this zany trivia —William V. Bower, *N.Y. Times Book Rev.,* 14 Sept. 1975

> ... as much trouble with the trivia of the past as with those of the present —Lois E. Bueler, *Saturday Rev.,* 30 Oct. 1971

> Trivia go alongside gloom in Cukor's book —*Punch,* 23 Dec. 1975

> ... even the trivia in his life deserve our attention — Robert Sherrill, *N.Y. Times Book Rev.,* 13 May 1979

Current dictionaries recognize that the singular use of *trivia* is now standard. For other foreign plurals used as singulars, see LATIN PLURALS.

trod *Trod* usually occurs as the past tense and past participle of *tread:*

> ... where he trod too often on the forbidden grass of his conservative committee —*Times Literary Supp.,* 2 May 1968

> ... steps which, according to tradition, were trod upon by Christ —Irving R. Levine, *Atlantic,* September 1970

But *trod* also has a long history of use as a verb in its own right. The OED says the verb *trod* is obsolete except in dialectal use and defines it both as a transitive verb meaning "track" and as an intransitive verb meaning "to pursue a path." The OED's transitive sense, first attested in 1225, seems no longer to be used except in Scottish dialect. The intransitive sense, which might also be defined simply as "tread," is a much later development, not recorded until 1909. It occurs chiefly in dialectal American speech, but it also occasionally finds its way onto the printed page:

> ... they were almost trodding on your correspondent's toes —*Springfield* (Mass.) *Daily News,* 15 Nov. 1961

> ... visitors have been coming in increasing numbers to trod down Main Street —Elizabeth Van Steenwyk, *Ford Times,* November 1967

A related transitive *trod* also sometimes appears in print. Like the intransitive *trod,* it is used both literally and figuratively:

> The eccentric is forced, therefore, to trod a lonely way —Martin Gardner, *In the Name of Science,* 1952

> ... we saw one horse with wagon ... trodding the cobbled yard —John A. Murray, *Grace Log,* Winter 1967–1968

> ... the crooked road so many of the city's youth seemed destined to trod —Caleb Pirtle III, *Southern Living,* December 1971

It is not certain whether the use of *trod* in place of *tread* grew out of the older "track" sense of *trod* or developed instead from the past and past participle *trod.* Critics such as Harper 1985 and Copperud 1980 take the latter view and regard it simply as a mistake. It is, in either case, very much a minority usage.

trooper, trouper A state policeman who can be counted on to do his job when the going gets rough is not only a good trooper (that is, a good state policeman), he is also a good trouper. *Trouper* is used figuratively to describe a person who carries on gamely through good times and bad. Such use owes its origin to the theatrical world of the 19th century, when *troupe* was first used in English to mean "a company of performers" and *trouper* to mean "a member of a troupe." In the 20th century, *trouper* has come to be applied to anyone who recognizes that the show must go on:

> Gary Hart came to Houston Thursday in the role of the good Democratic trouper . . . chipping in a good word or two on behalf of Walter Mondale, the man who edged him out for the Democratic presidential nomination —Jim Simmon, *Houston Post,* 7 Sept. 1984

Trooper is a more common word than *trouper,* with various meanings that relate primarily to the military and the police. The two words are pronounced alike, of course, and are close etymological relatives (both derived ultimately from the Middle French *troupe,* meaning "company, herd"). It is not surprising that the more familiar *trooper* is sometimes used in place of *trouper:*

> . . . real troopers in cultured places have turned out to be pills in the wild —John Heminway, *Town & Country,* July 1983

This use of *trooper* is treated as standard in the OED Supplement, wherein *trooper* is entered as a secondary spelling variant of *trouper.* However, this use of *trooper* is not entered in Merriam-Webster dictionaries, and usage writers who take up this subject consider it an error.

truculent This adjective is ultimately derived from the Latin *trux,* meaning "fierce, savage." Its oldest use is in fact as a synonym of *savage:*

> His aspect . . . was fierce, truculent, and fearful —Edward Topsell, *The Historie of Foure-Footed Beastes,* 1607 (OED)

In current usage, however, it has lost much of its etymological fierceness. It now chiefly serves to describe speech or writing that is notably harsh or a person who is notably self-assertive and belligerent:

> . . . his book has a more objective atmosphere than its famed, truculent predecessor —Robert S. Allen, *Saturday Rev.,* 21 June 1947

> . . . written with vigor and truculent eloquence —Orville Prescott, *N.Y. Times Book Rev.,* 6 June 1954

> Though truculent at times he seemed strangely on the defensive —William L. Shirer, *The Rise and Fall of the Third Reich,* 1960

> . . . I had become a truculent, moody husband —Winthrop Sargeant, *In Spite of Myself,* 1970

The "harsh" sense of *truculent* was first recorded in 1850; the "belligerent, surly" sense is a development of the 20th century.

The extended meanings of *truculent* have met with little resistance from usage commentators. Partridge 1942 and Evans 1957 are mainly concerned that *truculent* should not be used to mean "base, mercenary," a sense that is cited as an error in the OED and that seems not to have been used since the 19th century, and even then it was rare. Partridge also considers the "surly" sense an error. The most interesting commentary on *truculent* has been from Theodore Bernstein. In *Watch Your Language* (1958), Bernstein quotes and criticizes a passage

from the *New York Times* in which *truculent* is used to mean "belligerent." In *The Careful Writer* (1965), he quotes the same passage, but this time with complete approval, finding that the "savage" sense of *truculent* is now rarely seen and that the "belligerent" sense is well-established and useful. He also notes that dictionaries do not record the "belligerent" sense, an erroneous observation repeated by Copperud 1970, 1980. The "belligerent" sense of *truculent* has, in fact, been entered in Merriam-Webster dictionaries since the publication of Webster's Third in 1961. Most other dictionaries now also include this sense.

true When *true* means "faithful," it is followed by *to:*

> . . . reaps all the advantage there is in being true to a particular piece of earth —Mark Van Doren, *N.Y. Times Book Rev.,* 21 Mar. 1954

> True to form, I store it in the icebox, ready for unexpected guests —M. F. K. Fisher, *New Yorker,* 26 Apr. 1969

In other senses, *true* occurs commonly with *for* or *of:*

> . . . black men are more likely to hold the doctorate than black women in the sample, and the same is true for whites —David M. Rafky, *Change,* October 1971

> . . . it is not an age when the same event can be said to be true for faith but untrue for science —W. R. Inge, *The Church in the World,* 1928

> This, I shall maintain, is necessarily true of any form of externality —Bertrand Russell, *Foundations of Geometry,* 1897

> . . . even this, it seems, was truer of the Ivy League schools than of most others —Richard H. Rovere, *New Yorker,* 18 Nov. 1972

true facts The phrase *true facts* is cited as a redundancy by many commentators, who argue that all facts are, by definition, true. Against this argument it may be pointed out that many statements that are presented as facts turn out on closer examination to be less than entirely true. The phrase *true facts,* like *real facts* and *actual facts,* serves to emphasize that the truth of the facts in question is beyond doubt. *True facts* is especially likely to occur, and is most appropriately used, when there is reason to be suspicious of some of the "facts":

> I flung it aside after fifty pages and laid hold of *Mrs. Phillips,* where I expected to find at least probable, if not true, facts —Lady Mary Wortley Montagu, letter, 16 Feb. 1752

> ". . . We'd begun to get some true facts. We didn't have any real idea how many people were sick. . . . But we did have the number of deaths. . . . The rumors hadn't come close to it. . . ." —*New Yorker,* 30 Sept. 1950

> It's only now that the true facts are coming out, almost a hundred years, and it's a pity it took so long —Harry S. Truman, in Merle Miller, *Plain Speaking,* 1973

trust The prepositions *in* and *to* both occur after the verb *trust:*

> . . . hope for the best, and trust in God —Sydney Smith, *Lady Holland's Memoir,* 1855

Some of them, trusting to common sense —Aldous Huxley, *The Olive Tree,* 1937

The noun *trust* is usually followed by *in:*

> ... do not confuse trust in the students with sentimentality about them —Charles E. Silberman, *Atlantic,* August 1970

trustee, trusty   Evans 1957 and Copperud 1964 observe the distinction between these nouns: *trustee* denotes someone to whom property is legally committed in trust (or, more broadly, someone who has been entrusted with something); *trusty* denotes a prisoner who is considered trustworthy and is given special privileges. This distinction is real and is observed by most writers, but *trustee* does turn up from time to time in the "trustworthy prisoner" sense:

> Judson Kaines had been a trustee, a favorite of the warden's —James Clark Moloney, *Psychiatry,* February 1945

> "Sorry, bud," the trustee grinned relishingly.... "But we don't issue no campaign hats here...." —James Jones, *From Here to Eternity,* 1951

> The city government used trustee convicts from State Prison Camp 22 —*N.Y. Times,* 28 Aug. 1967

This use of *trustee* is logical and consistent with the normal use of the suffix *-ee* to mean "a recipient or beneficiary," but it is not common, and people who pride themselves on their spelling will undoubtedly call it an error. We recommend that you use *trusty* instead.

Note that the noun *trusty* is pronounced both \'trəs-tē\ and \ˌtrəs-'tē\. The pronunciation with the primary stress on the second syllable is analogous to the *trustee* spelling, but it occurs much more commonly than the spelling and, so far as we know, has never been criticized.

try and   The use of *try and* in contexts where *try to* would be possible has been subject to criticism since the 19th century. The issue continues to enjoy great popularity, although a number of usage commentators, including Fowler 1926, Evans 1957, and Follett 1966, are on record as recognizing that *try and* is an established standard idiom. Copperud 1980 remarks about one complicated attempt to differentiate between *try and* and *try to,* "This proves nothing but the lengths to which the wrongheaded will go to make nonexistent points."

The basis for objecting to *try and* is usually the notion that *try* is to be followed by the infinitive combined with the assumption that an infinitive requires *to.* This is the same mistaken assumption that has caused so much trouble over the so-called split infinitive (which see). In spite of what these critics believe, however, infinitives are used in many constructions without *to,* and some of those constructions use *and.*

The use of *and* between two verbs where *to* might be expected (*to* would seem unlikely in some of the constructions) is an old one in English. The OED has examples back to the 16th century; the Middle English Dictionary has examples as far back as the 13th. The verbs most often used in this construction in past centuries were *begin, go, take,* and *come*—the last three of which are still so used. *Try* did not appear as *try and* until the 17th century, when our familiar sense of the word was first established. Interestingly, the earliest example for the "make an attempt" sense in the OED involves the

try and construction, so *try and* may actually be older than *try to.*

The oldest example of *try to* in the OED, in fact, is an inverted construction:

> To repair his Strength he tries —John Dryden, *Virgil's Georgics,* 1697

Try and could not be used in an inverted construction. *Try and,* in fact, is not capable of much in the way of variation; it is almost always used in the fixed form *try and* followed by an infinitive. If you inflect *try,* insert an adverb, or invert the construction, you will use *try to.* (It may be noteworthy that the earliest criticism of *try and* we have seen is by a reviewer for *Routledge's Magazine,* October 1864, in a review reprinted in Moon 1865. The reviewer ridicules Dean Alford's use of *try and* in a magazine article by inflecting it to *tries and,* which he finds, of course, impossible.) In the next example, notice how Herbert Read has had to switch constructions in order to use *trying:*

> ... to try and keep it alive by State patronage is like trying to keep the dodo alive in a zoo —Herbert Read, *The Philosophy of Modern Art,* 1952

And Henry Adams, not averse to *try and* (as a later example will demonstrate), has to use *try to* when he slips in an adverb:

> ... I like the girls and try always to be polite —Henry Adams, letter, 7 June 1859

A negative may precede *try and,* but if a negative follows *try, to* is used:

> ... when you are on your moorings, don't try and get into her —Peter Heaton, *Cruising,* 1952

> Not to try and keep either a diary or careful income tax records —*And More by Andy Rooney,* 1982

> Try not to take her out shopping —nurse quoted in *McCall's,* March 1971

These restrictions give native speakers no problem whatever, but if you are a learner of English, you will want to keep them in mind.

A popular misconception among those who disparage *try and* is that the construction has only recently become widespread:

> "I'll try and see" is now universal in the spoken language, and is now spreading into print —Patrick Brogan, *Encounter,* February 1975

But *try and* has actually been common in print for about a century and a half, as the following garland of examples amply shows. You will observe that most of the examples are not from highly formal styles; many are from speech and fictional speech and from familiar letters:

> Now I will try and write of something else —Jane Austen, letter, 29 Jan. 1813

> 'Stand aside, my dear,' replied Squeers. 'We'll try and find out.' —Charles Dickens, *Nicholas Nickleby,* 1839

> The unfortunate creature has a child still every year, and her constant hypocrisy is to try and make her girls believe that their father is a respectable man —W. M. Thackeray, *The Book of Snobs,* 1846

"I am going to try and tack it with a kiss, sister,— there! ..." —Herman Melville, *Pierre,* 1852

... to try and soften his father's anger —George Eliot, *Silas Marner,* 1861 (in Hall 1917)

Do try and send me a little news —Henry Adams, letter, 18 Dec. 1863

"O, go 'long with you, Tom, before you aggravate me again. And you try and see if you can't be a good boy, for once...." —Mark Twain, *Tom Sawyer,* 1876

We are getting rather mixed. The situation entangled. Let's try and comb it out —W. S. Gilbert, *The Gondoliers,* 1889

If gentlemen sold their things, he was to try and get them to sell to him —Samuel Butler, *The Way of All Flesh,* 1903

... the best method to use in giving out these hints is to try and describe my own personal procedure — Ring Lardner, preface, *How to Write Short Stories,* 1924

... it induced *e.g.* Hobbes to try and make political science a geometry —Harold J. Laski, letter, 1 Mar. 1925

"... Come on there, try and sit still a minute and answer my question...." —F. Scott Fitzgerald, *The Great Gatsby,* 1925

I'm going to try and see him today —E. B. White, letter, August 1936

"I'll try and push this thing through in my own way." —Morley Callaghan, *The Loved and the Lost,* 1951

... they have lost the will to try and live better — Enid Bagnold, *Harper's,* August 1952

I am glad of the opportunity to try and get this point cleared up —William Empson, *Essays in Criticism,* July 1953

Try and read Scribe and you will be bored —Eric Bentley, *New Republic,* 23 May 1955

As long as there are empty seats at baseball and basketball games, it seems only sensible to try and fill them —Pete Axthelm, *New York,* 30 Aug. 1971

He always dressed rapidly, so as to try and conserve his night warmth till the sun rose —Doris Lessing, reprinted in *Literature Lives* (9th grade text), ed. Hanna Beate Haupt et al., 1975

... and Issy who has to try and outwit his own electronic burglar alarm system when he wants to raid the refrigerator in the middle of the night —David Lodge, *Times Literary Supp.,* 26 Sept. 1980

Let every reader try and remember this —Jonathan Spence, *N.Y. Times Book Rev.,* 4 Oct. 1987

These examples show that *try and* has been socially acceptable for these two centuries but that it is not used in an elevated style.

Quite a few commentators lump *try and* with other constructions in which *and* replaces a possible *to.* *Go and* (which see) is the oldest of these, dating back to the 13th century. It has always been respectable in speech and casual writing:

But I sought after George Psalmanazar the most. I used to go and sit with him at an alehouse in the city —Samuel Johnson, quoted in James Boswell, *Life of Samuel Johnson,* 1791

There! I may now finish my letter and go and hang myself —Jane Austen, letter, 24 Dec. 1798

I must go and see him again —Lord Byron, journal entry, 1 Dec. 1813

When you are puzzled, go and tell your puzzle to your Heavenly Father —Lewis Carroll, letter, 26 Dec. 1889

I have been leaving Franconia, New Hampshire ... to go and live in South Shaftsbury, Vermont —Robert Frost, letter, 10 Oct. 1920

Unlike *try and, go and* can be inflected, as in these constructions:

... and he went and sat on a stone —Kay Cicellis, *Encounter,* March 1955

I went and saw the Allen Brothers in a free concert —Rick Stacy, quoted in *Bluegrass Unlimited,* July 1982

Come and is also old, and equally respectable:

... desired I would come and see her —Jonathan Swift, *Journal to Stella,* 2 Feb. 1711

I was meditating to come and see you —Charles Lamb, letter, 4 Mar. 1830

... I would come and see you tomorrow —Lewis Carroll, letter, 14 July 1877

Be sure and is also frequently encountered:

And be sure and get tested for sheep blast —James Thurber, letter, 1937

Be sure and wear gloves —Kenneth A. Henderson, *Handbook of American Mountaineering,* 1942

You've got to get every Protestant in this outfit to be sure and be there at that mass —Harry S. Truman, quoted in Merle Miller, *Plain Speaking,* 1973

There are a few other verbs that turn up with *and* where *to* could have been used:

He didn't have to stop and think about his answer —Elmer Davis, *But We Were Born Free,* 1954

And you can tell your daddy that someday I'll be President of this country. You watch and see —Lyndon B. Johnson, quoted in Sam Houston Johnson, *My Brother Lyndon,* 1970

If you want to write, start and write down your thoughts —Leacock 1943

About the only thing that can be held against any of these combinations is that they seem to be more typical of speech than of high-toned writing—and that is hardly a sin. The judgment of *try and* in Fowler 1926 remains eminently sensible today:

It is an idiom that should be not discountenanced, but used when it comes natural.

tubercular, tuberculous The cause of tuberculosis was not discovered until Robert Koch isolated the tubercle bacillus in 1882. Before that time, *tubercular* and *tuberculous* were used more or less interchangeably to describe both the nodular lesions (tubercles) characteristic of several diseases and the diseases themselves. After 1882, however, *tuberculous* began to be limited in scientific application to lesions and diseases caused specifically by the tubercle bacillus. Similar lesions and diseases having a different cause were to be described as *tubercular*. The National Tuberculosis Association passed a resolution calling for the distinction to be observed "in the interests of clearness and uniformity of nomenclature" in 1906, and the NTA was energetic in promoting the distinction afterward. It apparently did so fairly successfully in medical circles, but its attempts to influence general usage met with predictable failure. In current English, a person suffering from tuberculosis is likely to be described by his doctor as tuberculous and by his friends as tubercular. In general, *tubercular* is a more common word than *tuberculous*. Its usual meaning is "of, relating to, or affected with tuberculosis":

　. . . the care of crippled children and tubercular patients —*Britannica Book of the Year 1944*

　. . . featuring Miss Fonda as a tubercular young lady —*Current Biography,* July 1964

　. . . for he was tubercular all his life —John Wain, *N.Y. Times Book Rev.,* 20 July 1980

It is also sometimes used as a noun meaning "a person affected with tuberculosis":

　. . . a grisly novelette about a tubercular who marries to escape a domineering mama —*Time,* 12 May 1952

　It banned tuberculars and mental patients —Judith & Neil Morgan, *Town & Country,* August 1979

Tuberculous occasionally occurs in general contexts:

　. . . found the tuberculous rich coming again to the magic mountain —*Time,* 8 Nov. 1948

But it is most likely to occur in medical writing:

　. . . the technique of radically excising tuberculous lungs —George Day, in *Modern Treatment Year Book 1951,* ed. Cecil Wakeley

　. . . indicates the presence of tuberculous lesions containing living tubercle bacilli —*JAMA,* 25 Feb. 1956

A distinction in the meanings of *tubercular* and *tuberculous* is observed by doctors but not by their patients. Unless you happen to be writing an article for a medical journal, you need not worry about which word to use.

tummy *Tummy* originated as baby talk for *stomach,* and it is still primarily a word used by children. Its use by adults, when not addressing children or meaning to be humorous, can often seem excessively coy (Evans 1957 goes further and describes it as "simply disgusting"). The most common written use of *tummy* in American English seems to be in advertisements for women's undergarments:

　Pull-on girdles of nylon power net, made with reinforced tummy panel —advt., *N.Y. Times,* 17 June 1956

It also occurs now in the phrase *tummy tuck,* which denotes a form of plastic surgery more technically known as an abdominal plasty:

　. . . a physician who had once been known as "The Tummy Tuck King of Palm Beach" —Calvin Trillin, *Uncivil Liberties,* 1982

Use of *tummy* among the British appears to be somewhat more common, but it has much the same quality as in American English:

　. . . who stands head, shoulders, and tummy button above the low altitude flyers of the Flat —John Trickett, *The Sun* (London), 20 Nov. 1974

　. . . getting up after a tummy bug to keep the date — Doreen Taylor, *Scottish Field,* July 1975

turbid, turgid Some words seem to have been specially created to encourage the use of dictionaries. *Turbid* and *turgid* are two such words. Not only do they look alike and sound alike, but they tend to be used in similar ways. Compounding the difficulty is their unfamiliarity: few people other than scientists and book reviewers have frequent occasion to describe anything as "turbid" or "turgid." All things considered, it is not surprising that these two words are sometimes confused. The distinction in their literal senses is that *turbid* means "muddy, clouded," and *turgid* means "swollen, distended." A turbid stream is a muddy stream; a turgid stream is a swollen, flooded stream. In their figurative senses, *turbid* means "unclear, confused, obscure," and *turgid* means "overblown, grandiloquent." Turbid prose is obscure prose; turgid prose is grandiloquent prose. Of course, a flooded stream is often muddy, and grandiloquence and obscurity often cohabit in the same writing. Thus, it is sometimes difficult to tell exactly what is meant by *turbid* and *turgid:*

　. . . they seem to share a certain turbid homogeneity of thought and phrase which perhaps explains their popularity —Wilfrid Sheed, *The Good Word and Other Words,* 1978

　. . . the Pentagon study is long, the documents turgid, and the summer had already begun —Peter Schrag, *Saturday Rev.,* 13 Nov. 1971

Chances are excellent that *turbid* and *turgid* are being used in their time-honored senses in these passages, but the context does not make their meanings obvious. Sometimes one word is clearly being used when the other is called for. The tendency is to replace *turbid* with *turgid,* which is relatively the more common word:

　The background is laid in the murky, turgid England of Roger Bacon —*Time,* 29 Oct. 1945

　The turgid water is pumped over the top of the bed. The water percolates through the bed, and the solids are retained in the sand —*McGraw-Hill Encyclopedia of Science & Technology,* 1960

The best way to avoid such mishaps is to keep a dictionary handy.

two and two Several people have written to us in recent years to ask whether the common arithmetical formulas *two and two, two times two, two plus two,* and the like, take singular or plural verbs. The question is an old one that has been examined by at least four commentators. Alford 1866 preferred the singular verb for abstract arithmetic ("two and two is four"), but allowed the plural for concrete instances ("two apples and two apples are four apples"). Evans 1957 found the singular verb to be more common but the plural to also have occasional use. More recently, Harper 1975, 1985 says the singular is preferred and only grudgingly admits the plural at the insistence of "some linguists." Copperud 1980, however, says that singular and plural verbs are equally frequent.

Historical grammarians have looked into the problem too. Poutsma 1904–26 thinks the singular more logical, but finds more examples of the plural. Jespersen 1909–49 (vol. 2) finds mixed usage.

Here is what we find. The two most mathematically inclined members of our editorial staff differ in their practice, offering modest confirmation of Copperud's statement. But a survey of recent American math texts in our library reveals universal use of the singular, as here:

> What number plus nine equals fifteen? —Edwina Deans et al., *Basic Mathematics,* Book D, 1977

> 36 plus 12 times n is 48 —Max A. Sabel et al., *Essentials of Mathematics,* Book 1, 1977

None of these books, however, use the common formula with *and.* Older literature, on the other hand, runs heavily to the plural verb with *and,* especially when the verb is *make:*

> We do in our Consciences believe two and two make four —Joseph Addison, *The Spectator,* No. 126, 1711 (OED)

> It is very possible that two and two make four —Thomas Gray, letter, 27 Oct. 1736

> O Ireland! O my country! ... when will you acknowledge that two and two make four ... ? —W. M. Thackeray, *The Book of Snobs,* 1846

> How much do one and one make? —Robert Frost, letter, 26 Mar. 1915

Charles Lamb, however, used the singular:

> Reason is only counting, two and two makes four — letter, 1830

We conclude that unless you are writing a mathematics text, you have the option to use either a singular or a plural verb. The plural is more likely with *and* than with other constructions, although our evidence of plural use in print now shows its age.

tycoon   This appealing word is derived from the Japanese *taikun,* another name for a shogun, a military governor. Its use in English appears to have begun in the world of 19th-century American politics, where it referred to a powerful leader (Abraham Lincoln in particular). The now familiar use of *tycoon* to mean "a business magnate" dates from the 1920s, when it appeared in *Time* magazine. *Time* claims credit for it, and the earliest citation for it supports that claim:

> Fred W. Fitch, 56, rich hair-tonic tycoon —*Time,* 14 June 1926 (OED Supplement)

Other early citations are also from *Time.*

The figurative *tycoon* has been labeled "colloquial" and "informal" by dictionaries and usage commentators in the past, but those labels are no longer valid, unless they are taken to mean that it is a word more at home in general writing than in scholarly discourse. It is a standard word that occurs commonly in writing of no special informality:

> These are some aspects of a situation that has been disturbing not only the book trade but also magazine publishers and newspaper tycoons —Malcolm Cowley, *New Republic,* 22 Nov. 1954

> ... business leaders today bear little resemblance to the buccaneers and tycoons of fifty years ago —Daniel Bell, *Commentary,* April 1948

Its association with the era of the '20s and '30s remains strong, so that its use to describe a current figure often implies—with a touch of irony, perhaps—comparison with the vastly wealthy and powerful businessmen of that earlier time:

> Lunch-time there is inclined to be a Big Business affair, but we just ignored the tycoons and concentrated on very nice veal escalopes —Alison Mitchell, *Scottish Field,* October 1973

> It is now the Pacific Union Club, inhabited by latter-day tycoons —Horace Sutton, *Saturday Rev.,* 20 Jan. 1980

type, -type, type of   Objection has been made to the use of *type* in the sense of "sort" as an attributive modifier of another noun, as in this example:

> ... the one big impression I got was that the game hasn't changed. It's the same as it was when I played. I see the same type pitchers, the same type hitters — Ted Williams & John Underwood, *The Science of Hitting,* 1971

The concern is an American one that seems to have first surfaced in the 1950s. The gist of the objection appears to be that *type* is a noun and should not be used as an adjective. The usual suggestion is to use *type of* instead of *type* alone. Attributive nouns (such as *apple* in *apple pie*) are a commonplace in English, however, and there is no grammatical reason why *type* should not be used attributively. It may be that the criticism actually has some more subtle basis. Paul Fussell, in *The Boy Scout Handbook* (1982), hints at a social stigma; he asserts that this usage is a lower-class one. Copperud 1980 takes the same view, seeing the locution as characteristic of the "lower East Side or the Bronx." Other factors contributing to the dislike of attributive *type* are its apparent origin in speech—it is mentioned as a spoken form by Evans 1957 and Bryant 1962—and its association with business, technical, and advertising usage.

Our evidence suggests that the usage has not established itself strongly in edited prose. It turns up occasionally in trade publications, but only seldom in more general writing. A sample:

> ... many breeders both new and old are searching for a smaller, meaty type rabbit —Rusty Schultz, *Rabbits,* September–October 1986

> ... reported to be interested in this type product — Richard C. Sizemore, *Women's Wear Daily,* 14 Jan. 1974

> ... the Supervisor in charge of this type office — Arthur S. Aubry, Jr., *Police,* January–February 1968

> ... a nagging sensation of do-gooder type guilt — Orson Bean, *National Rev.,* 23 Feb. 1971

Examples from speech—and one letter—show a wider spread of usage:

> You should see a diagram of the latest type incendiary —Randall Jarrell, letter, August 1945

> Says Fabergé president Richard Barrie, "We think Margaux really epitomizes today's young woman . . . she's an all-round type lady. . . ." —Gregg Kilday, *Cosmopolitan,* November 1976

> After an NSC meeting or an NSC type meeting . . . , a few of us were asked to gather in the Oval Office —Edwin Meese 3d, quoted in *The Tower Commission Report,* 1987

> I do a warm-up about local Buffalo things, and there's a champagne party afterward. It's really a family-type thing —Mark Russell, quoted in *TV Guide,* 23 June 1978

Notice the hyphen in the last example. Mark Russell obviously did not pronounce it; a writer or editor put it in. For some mysterious reason this hyphen removes much of the stigma from the usage: any number of commentators excuse the hyphenated use in technical contexts, and Copperud says it is "verging on respectability" in other contexts as well. A few examples:

> . . . to expose, disrupt, misdirect, discredit and otherwise neutralize the activities of black nationalists, hate-type organizations —J. Edgar Hoover, quoted in *N.Y. Times,* 30 Aug. 1974

> . . . a field jacket-type parka would have cost in the neighborhood of $250 —Kent Mitchell, *Atlanta Constitution,* 19 Sept. 1984

> . . . judicial-type decisions made by Government departments —A. H. Hanson & Malcolm Walles, *Governing Britain,* 1970

> One of my trenchcoat-type coats has two buttons missing —*And More by Andy Rooney,* 1982

Type is frequently used to make compound modifiers as needed in this way. It is fairly common with technical terms:

> . . . tetracycline-type antibiotic —*Annual Report, Pfizer,* 1970

> It's not practical to shrink this conveyor-type dishwasher down —William H. Dennler, quoted in *General Electric Investor,* Winter 1970

And many writers attach *-type* to proper names:

> . . . an adult Western with an Othello-type plot —*Current Biography,* June 1965

> . . . Goon-type funny voices —Peter Davalle, *Annabel,* May 1975

> . . . the plot is based on an Eric Ambler-type device —Fraser Sutherland, *Books in Canada,* June–July 1974

While a majority of commentators prescribe *type of* in place of attributive *type,* a minority—mostly college handbooks—disparage *type of* as frequently unnecessary. *Type of* is, indeed, deadwood in some uses. Here are a couple of examples where it could have been cut with no loss:

> . . . is all business—in a friendly type of way —Julie Gilbert, *Houston Post,* 3 Sept. 1984

> The most flagrant type of misuse is to say something like: 'They *decimated* almost half the enemy.' —Howard 1977

U

ultimate analysis See ANALYSIS.

unaware, unawares *Unaware* is common as an adjective and uncommon as an adverb. The usual adverb is *unawares.* Either adverb is most likely to occur following *catch:*

> . . . catching unaware the American press —Frederic L. Paxson, *Pre-War Years 1913–1917,* 1936

> It is fun to catch another unawares —Edith Sitwell, *Fanfare for Elizabeth,* 1946

The adverbs *unaware* and *unawares* both date from the 16th century, and both are standard.

unbeknown, unbeknownst The history of *unbeknown* and *unbeknownst* is relatively straightforward. *Unbeknown* was first recorded in 1636, *unbeknownst* in 1849 (exactly how the *-st* came to be added is not understood). The OED labeled *unbeknownst* colloquial and dialectal, but the OED Supplement notes that it is "now of much wider currency than in the 19th. cent." According to our evidence, in fact, both *unbeknown* and *unbeknownst* are now in widespread standard use and have

been for many years. *Unbeknownst* is the more common form:

> . . . had fetched them unbeknownst to the Western ocean —Conrad Richter, *The Trees,* 1940

> . . . unbeknownst to the procurement agent —*Atlantic,* December 1951

> . . . who unbeknownst to us had shifted his position —*New Yorker,* 13 Mar. 1954

> . . . had been doing this unbeknown to Harriet —Elizabeth Taylor, *A Game of Hide-and-Seek,* 1951

> Unbeknown to me —Frank Deford, *Sports Illustrated,* 1 Apr. 1974

In contrast with the fairly simple history of the words themselves, the history of opinions about them is rather a tangle. The first contributor to the general confusion was Bache 1869, who noted that "Unbeknown is obsolete in good usage" (he did not mention *unbeknownst*). Bache's opinion is not supported by the evidence in the OED, which includes 19th-century citations for *unbeknown* from Charles Dickens and A. E. Housman, among others. Vizetelly 1906, however, called *unbe-*

known "a vulgar provincialism used chiefly in the form *unbeknownst.*" MacCracken & Sandison in 1917 made no mention of *unbeknown* but dismissed *unbeknownst* as a "provincial error for *without (my) knowledge.*" In 1926, Fowler observed that both forms were "out of use except in dialect or uneducated speech." Krapp called them "humorous, colloquial, and dialectal" in 1927. Jensen in 1935 called *unbeknownst* "vulgar and dialectal for *unbeknown, unknown,*" which presumably indicates that he found nothing wrong with *unbeknown.* Evans 1957 noted that "neither of these words occurs in natural speech today." And so on. The latest to put in his two cents worth is John Simon 1980, who returns to Jensen's position by saying flatly that *unbeknownst* is "a vulgarism for 'unbeknown.'"

Almost the only thing—besides hostility to one or both words—that these varied opinions have in common is that, at least with regard to current usage, they are all incorrect. A few more examples should be adequate to show that both *unbeknown* and *unbeknownst* are now standard, and that neither is limited to the spoken language:

... unbeknownst to the jewel thieves —Cornelia Otis Skinner, *New Yorker,* 27 Oct. 1951

... unbeknown to their staffs —Anthony Bailey, *New Yorker,* 29 Oct. 1973

... unbeknown, undoubtedly, to the corporations' stockholders —Elizabeth Drew, *New Yorker,* 6 Dec. 1982

... unbeknownst to the teachers —Richard T. Schaefer, *Sociology,* 1983

... unbeknown to most historians —Paul Kennedy, *Times Literary Supp.,* 28 May 1982

... quite unbeknownst to her —E. B. White, *New Yorker,* 7 Apr. 1956

Unbeknownst to them —Garrison Keillor, *Lake Wobegon Days,* 1985

unbend, unbending A curiosity of the language that has caught the attention of several commentators is that the verb *unbend* means "to become less stiff; relax" but the adjective *unbending* means "stiff; unyielding." The verb in its oldest sense has to do with releasing the tension of a flexed bow by loosening its string. In current English it is most often used to indicate the relaxing of a formal or reticent manner:

... an office party where everyone unbends —Frederick Laws, *London Calling,* 22 Dec. 1955

... he unbends just enough in his love scenes —Andy Meisler, *TV Guide,* 25 June 1982

Unbend is also sometimes used to mean "straighten":

I rub my hands together briefly, bend and unbend my fingers —Aristides, *American Scholar,* Autumn 1981

The adjective is, of course, an unrelated word, akin to the sense of *bend* meaning "to make concessions; compromise":

... that fierce, unbending will which later would carry him so far —William L. Shirer, *The Rise and Fall of the Third Reich,* 1960

The rules ... were strict and unbending —John F. Henahan, *Saturday Rev.,* 29 July 1967

We have no evidence that these similar but distinct words have ever caused confusion. If you were to write such a sentence as "He was an unbending man who refused to unbend," you might indeed cause a few readers to scratch their heads; but, if you were to write such a sentence, that is probably just what you would be trying to do.

uncomparable adjectives See ABSOLUTE ADJECTIVES.

underhanded, underhand *Underhanded* was strongly criticized in the 19th century as a vulgarism for *underhand.* Its most severe critic seems to have been Gould 1870:

This "word" is formed by adding to the adjective *underhand* a participial termination; but the addition still leaves the word an adjective, without in the least modifying the sense of the true word. There is no verb *to* underhand, and no noun *an* underhand, from which such a compound could be made. The addition of *ed,* therefore, renders the word a mere vulgarism. ...

Gould noted with some surprise that dictionaries entered *underhanded* as a reputable word. "But," he wrote, "the indorsement is not strong enough to make the word good. It is no better than *leniency, jeopardize,* etc."

Almost everyone would now agree that *underhanded* is no better—and no worse—than *leniency* and *jeopardize,* which is to say that it is a perfectly good word. The 19th-century criticism has enjoyed little popularity in the 20th century, and no commentator since Partridge 1942 has repeated it. *Underhanded* continues to be used commonly as both an adjective and an adverb. As an adjective meaning "marked by secrecy and deception," it has almost entirely replaced *underhand* in American English:

... his old propensity for underhanded tactics against political opponents —Norman Cousins, *Saturday Rev.,* 20 Aug. 1977

The British, however, continue to use *underhand* in this sense:

... as unquieting and ambivalent and underhand in intention as he found them —Margaret Drabble, *The Needle's Eye,* 1972

When a method of throwing or striking a ball is being described, the adjective is almost always *underhand* ("an underhand toss"), but the adverb can be either *underhand* or *underhanded:*

... wants Chamberlain to shoot his free throws underhanded —Phil Elderkin, *Sporting News,* 26 Mar. 1966

... a lawn-tennis player served either underhand or shoulder high —Louis Kronenberger, *N.Y. Times Mag.,* 6 May 1973

underprivileged This word was called "illiterate" by Lord Conesford, an English baron with strong opinions:

A privilege is a special advantage which one person has over another. ... An underprivileged person must mean a person who has not enough privilege—a person, that is to say, who has not enough advantage over his neighbor. To pretend that you are in favor of equality before the law and then to use a word which complains that there is not enough inequality seems to me to exceed the stupidity limit —Lord Conesford, *Saturday Evening Post,* 13 July 1957

Conesford regarded *underprivileged* as an example of "American pretentious illiteracy." Perhaps he discussed the matter with Sir Ernest Gowers. In Fowler 1965 Gowers used the same reasoning as Conesford to criticize *underprivileged.* However impressively stated, that reasoning is specious. It can just as easily be argued that *underprivileged* is a perfectly logical word. The citizens of a country have fundamental rights and privileges by virtue of their citizenship. A citizen who, because of social or economic conditions, is denied certain of those rights and privileges can therefore logically be called an "underprivileged" person. In any case, a word is not necessarily equal to the sum of its parts. The facts about *underprivileged* are these: its first recorded use was in an 1896 edition of the *Princetonian;* evidence of its more widespread use, as in newspapers, dates from the mid-1920s; by the 1950s it had become a common word, and it continues to be one today, recognized as standard in both American and British dictionaries. Some people undoubtedly dislike it, regarding it as a euphemism for *poor.* It often implies more than simple poverty, however, and sometimes poverty does not enter into it at all:

> ... protest against suffering by a special underprivileged group—women —Natalie Shainess, M.D., *Psychology Today,* May 1970

> If you are one of the millions of Smiths, Thompsons, or Williamses, you are in the underprivileged part of the alphabet —John E. Gibson, *Catholic Digest,* December 1968

under the circumstances   See CIRCUMSTANCES.

under way, under weigh   This is an old issue, and possibly a dead one. The original expression is *under way,* probably adapted from the Dutch *onderweg,* "on the way." It is, of course, a nautical expression describing a vessel that is moving through the water or is not lying at anchor or aground. The first written record of *under way* is from 1743. *Under weigh* first appeared in print not long afterward, in 1777. No doubt the substitution of *weigh* for *way* was influenced by the use of the verb *weigh* to mean "lift" in "weigh anchor." Neither *under way* nor *under weigh* makes much literal sense, but *under weigh* at least has the advantage of looking nautical, and there seems to be some logic, however obscure, in saying that a ship that has weighed anchor is under weigh. For whatever reason, many prominent authors in the past have preferred *under weigh* to *under way:*

> "... The bark that wafts us hence will be under weigh ere we can reach the port." —Sir Walter Scott, *Ivanhoe,* 1819

> She got under weigh with very little fuss —Richard Henry Dana, *Two Years Before the Mast,* 1840 (OED)

> ... no profane songs would be allowed on board the Pequod, particularly in getting under weigh —Herman Melville, *Moby Dick,* 1851 (in Reader's Digest 1983)

The first commentator to call such usage a mistake was Bache 1869. His 20th-century brethren have also

favored *under way,* although several acknowledge that *under weigh* has a history of respectable use. The OED treats both *under way* and *under weigh* as standard. Our evidence indicates, however, that *under weigh* is now extremely rare, much more so than during the 19th century. Katherine Anne Porter used it in *Harper's* in 1950 (thereby provoking two letters to the editor, one pro and one con), but we have no evidence of its use since then. Chances are that it has fallen into disuse chiefly because *under way* has come to be used so widely in general contexts (as in "The meeting got under way at noon") that *way* is now firmly established in most people's minds as the correct word, whether one is speaking of oceangoing vessels or political campaigns. *Under weigh,* it seems, has never been used except in nautical contexts.

There is an increasing tendency in recent years to write *under way* as a solid word, *underway:*

> Work is already underway on a new East River tunnel —Bruce Kovner, *New York,* 7 Feb. 1972

> ... the constitutional conference now underway in London —Gary Thatcher, *Christian Science Monitor,* 12 Sept. 1979

> Already the day was well underway —Nathaniel Tripp, *Blair & Ketchum's Country Jour.,* June 1980

It is quite possible that this solid form will eventually predominate over the two-word form, but for the time being *under way* is still somewhat more common.

underwhelm   Some mystery surrounds the coinage of *underwhelm.* Several sources cite the playwright George S. Kaufman as its originator, but other sources suggest other possibilities, and Red Smith is quoted in Harper 1975, 1985 as having the impression that he coined the word himself. Chances are, in fact, that the word was coined by more than one inventive writer. Our earliest record of it is from the *New Yorker* in 1944, when it was used by Howard Brubaker in the form of the participial adjective *underwhelming.* We first found it used as a transitive verb in 1949:

> And Dr. James B. Conant's recent effort to find a cause for hope ... leaves me, in the words of Abner Dean, utterly underwhelmed —Philip Wylie, letter to the editor, *Atlantic,* April 1949

But it was not until the mid 1960s that we began to see it with any frequency. Its use became increasingly common in the 1970s and continues to be common today:

> ... feeling quite underwhelmed at the thought of what Roy Strong and Liberty's could produce —Kenneth Robinson, *Punch,* 2 Sept. 1975

> ... the actual numbers were underwhelming —David Shaw, *TV Guide,* 7 Sept. 1984

> ... a psychology book that had left me underwhelmed —Susan Brownmiller, *N.Y. Times Book Rev.,* 12 Jan. 1986

Underwhelm is certainly an innocuous word. It serves as a mildly humorous way of describing something unimpressive, and its common use has so far been largely uncontroversial. The only criticism that we know of is by the Harper usage panelists, who find it unacceptable by a large majority, essentially because they see it as a joke that is no longer funny. Several of the panelists regard its popularity as a fad, but over 40 years of increasing use strongly suggests that *underwhelm* is here to stay.

undoubtedly See DOUBTLESS, NO DOUBT, UNDOUBT-EDLY.

undue, unduly The meaning of *undue* is somewhat variable. At times it means simply "not called for; not necessary or appropriate":

... show undue panic at the thought —Norman Mailer, *Harper's,* March 1971

... has placed an undue hardship on students —Lee Maxwell, *Junior College Jour.,* November 1970

More often, however, its meaning is closer to "inappropriately excessive or immoderate":

... writes with almost undue ease and dash —*New Yorker,* 20 Nov. 1971

... to take undue profits out of war —Franklin D. Roosevelt, speech to Congress, 1944, in *Nothing to Fear,* ed. B. D. Zevin, 1946

... the danger of undue emphasis on the Soviet or Communist angle —Rodger Swearingen, *Current History,* July 1952

Sometimes, however, the notion of inappropriateness is almost entirely lost, so that *undue* serves essentially as a synonym of *excessive* or *great:*

... the problem of undue population growth in the developing world —Bernard Berelson, *Science,* 7 Feb. 1969

This same variation in meaning is apparent in the adverb *unduly,* which is sometimes used to mean "excessively" or "extremely":

In amyloid disease the kidney is unduly firm —*Special Pathology and Therapeutics of the Diseases of Domestic Animals,* ed. J. Russell Grieg et al., 5th ed., 1949

... it was unduly irritating to have to wait —Norman Mailer, *Harper's,* November 1968

Because of these variations in meaning, *undue* and *unduly* have occasionally appeared in contexts where they might seem to be redundant:

... said that there was no reason for undue alarm — *Farmer's Weekly* (South Africa), 18 Nov. 1953

... we have no reason to be unduly apprehensive — James B. Conant, *Atlantic,* May 1946

Many critics regard such usage as tantamount to saying "there was no reason for alarm for which there was no reason." What these two sentences actually mean, of course, is that there was no reason for great alarm or for inappropriately excessive alarm, and that we have no reason to be excessively apprehensive. The critics either fail to recognize the meanings of *undue* and *unduly* in such contexts, or they believe that it is incorrect to use *undue* and *unduly* with these meanings.

In any case, as an intelligent writer you should be aware that such usage is liable to be criticized. You may then, according to your disposition, either avoid the usage or disregard the criticism, on the perfectly legitimate grounds that the criticized senses are well established.

uneatable See INEDIBLE, UNEATABLE.

unequal *Unequal* is idiomatically followed by *to:*

Perhaps it is of the very essence of gratitude that it should feel itself unequal to the task —Ralph Barton Perry, *Atlantic,* October 1946

... they too have proved unequal to controlling the Mekong —*The Lamp,* Summer 1963

... we are unequal to the task —Peter F. Drucker, *Harper's,* January 1972

Fowler 1926 encountered at least one instance of *for* used in place of *to,* and he cited it as an error. A few later critics have followed suit, but this appears to be a non-issue; aside from the single citation in Fowler, we have no evidence of *for* used with *unequal.* Fowler also regarded the use of an infinitive after *unequal* as incorrect. Such usage is extremely rare in modern English, but it has sound historical backing:

... made her feel how unequal she was to encounter Charlotte's observation —Jane Austen, *Pride and Prejudice,* 1813

Unequal ... to arrange his own thoughts into suitable expressions —Sir Walter Scott, *Old Mortality,* 1816 (OED)

unequivocably, unequivocally The standard word is *unequivocally:*

... went on to state unequivocally that no other author had collaborated on the work —Gay Talese, *Harper's,* January 1969

... should speak out more unequivocally than it has —Samuel Krislov, *AAUP Bulletin,* September 1970

The nonstandard equivalent that sometimes shows up in reputable writing is *unequivocably:*

... holds unequivocably that the war is the greatest blunder that we have ever stumbled into —Claude A. Buss, *Wilson Library Bulletin,* November 1968

The results ... unequivocably demonstrate the demise of fatalism —Edwin S. Shneidman, *Psychology Today,* June 1971

unexceptionable, unexceptional Commentators beginning with Fowler have made the following distinction: *unexceptionable* means "not open to objection or criticism," as in "a man of unexceptionable character"; *unexceptional* means "not out of the ordinary; not exceptional," as in "The appetizer was excellent but the rest of the meal was unexceptional." The use of *unexceptional* to mean "not open to objection or criticism; unexceptionable" is regarded by all as incorrect.

The first recorded use of *unexceptional* was in 1775, when Madame D'Arblay (Fanny Burney) wrote "She bears an unexceptional character." The meaning of *unexceptional* here, as defined in the OED, is "unexceptionable." The OED includes two other citations for this sense of *unexceptional,* one from 1806 and one from 1877, when it was used by W. S. Gilbert in *Foggerty's Fairy.* The OED treats this sense as standard. The "not out of the ordinary" sense of *unexceptional* is not, strangely enough, entered in the OED or its Supplements. Since the OED does show, however, that the adjective *exceptional* was first used at about the middle of the 19th century, it seems safe to conclude that *unexceptional* was not used to mean "not exceptional" until some time after that. In other words, the "incorrect" sense of *unexceptional* is more than 75 years older than its "correct" sense.

In current usage, however, *unexceptional* nearly always means what the critics say it should mean:

> . . . his thoughts . . . are realistically stated, but unexceptional —Henry J. Steck, *Library Jour.,* 15 Jan. 1966

> . . . moments and details in routine days of mostly unexceptional lives —Robert Kiely, *N.Y. Times Book Rev.,* 1 July 1979

> . . . make unexceptional pizza all but irresistible —Gwen Kinkead, *Fortune,* 26 July 1982

> . . . unexceptional intellect, limited education and incompatible social background —Robert Craft, *N.Y. Times Book Rev.,* 29 Apr. 1984

The stigmatized sense of the word—that is, its original sense—is now extremely rare:

> . . . it was only the unexceptional work of the aircraft and engine manufacturers . . . which enabled the Expedition to take place that spring —*World Today,* September 1934

> Although they were both in good health and of unexceptional figure, Tony and Brenda were on a diet —Evelyn Waugh, *A Handful of Dust,* 1934

The exact meaning of *unexceptional* in the Evelyn Waugh quotation is questionable, but the context seems to call for "not open to criticism" rather than "not exceptional."

Unexceptionable is an older word, first attested in 1664. Typical current usage is illustrated by the following citations:

> . . . can be stipulated in terms rational men should find unexceptionable —Harry S. Ashmore, *Center Mag.,* May 1968

> . . . is an entirely legitimate and unexceptionable principle —Charles Yost, *Saturday Rev.,* 3 Apr. 1976

> And Engel's principal thesis . . . is, if unoriginal, unexceptionable —Benjamin DeMott, *N.Y. Times Book Rev.,* 10 Oct. 1976

Although *unexceptionable* can sometimes be a highly complimentary word, it is normally a term of lukewarm praise. *Unexceptional,* on the other hand, is normally a term of lukewarm criticism. The use of *unexceptional* in its original sense as a synonym for *unexceptionable* has been almost entirely superseded by its use as the negative of *exceptional.* The distinction favored by the critics is in this case observed by almost all writers.

See also EXCEPTIONABLE, EXCEPTIONAL.

unhuman, inhuman *Inhuman* is the older of these two words and by far the more common. Both were originally used to mean "lacking pity, kindness, or mercy"—*inhuman* in the 15th century and *unhuman* in the middle of the 16th. That sense of *inhuman* is still in frequent use, but since the late 1800s *unhuman* has primarily served simply as the negative of *human:*

> . . . the bodies looked as limp and unhuman as bags of grain —Norman Mailer, *The Naked and the Dead,* 1948

Inhuman is also used to mean "not human" with no implication of moral judgment. It is, in fact, more common in this sense than *unhuman:*

> . . . saw a strangeness in the daylight, and loved inhuman nature —John Updike, *N.Y. Times Book Rev.,* 14 Nov. 1976

> The Black Knight's voice was purposely made inhuman —John D. Tierney, *Science 81,* March 1981

> . . . a timeless and abiding (and inhuman) reality reasserts itself in the surrounding wilderness —Joyce Carol Oates, *N.Y. Times Book Rev.,* 13 Feb. 1983

uninterest See DISINTEREST, DISINTERESTEDNESS, UNINTEREST.

uninterested See DISINTERESTED, UNINTERESTED.

unique The law has been laid down time and time again: *unique* is an absolute adjective (see ABSOLUTE ADJECTIVES); it cannot be modified by such adverbs of degree as *more, most, somewhat,* and *very;* a thing is either unique or it isn't. These observations are accepted as gospel by many people, and no one who adheres to them is likely to be persuaded not to, but let it be noted anyway that they are not entirely true.

The French word *unique* was first borrowed into English in the early 17th century with two senses, "being the only one; sole" and "having no like or equal." For a long time it was an extremely rare word. The OED indicates that it was reacquired in its second sense from the French in the late 18th century, but it was still usually regarded as foreign and was still rarely used. Henry Todd entered it as a foreign word in his 1818 edition of Johnson's Dictionary, characterizing it as "affected and useless." Not until about the middle of the 19th century did *unique* come into widespread use and acceptance as a genuinely English word.

Words that are in widespread use have a natural tendency to take on extended meanings. In the case of *unique,* it was natural that a word used to describe something that was unlike anything else should also come to be used more broadly to describe something that was, simply, unusual or rare. A similar extension of meaning has occurred with *singular.* It should come as no surprise, therefore, that *unique* began to be used more broadly at almost exactly the time that it became a common word:

> A very unique child, thought I —Charlotte Brontë (in Fowler 1907)

> You will not wonder at these minute details, knowing how unique a thing an interview with Royalty is to me —Lewis Carroll, letter, 18 Dec. 1860

> . . . these summer guests found themselves defrauded of their uniquest recreations —*Harper's,* April 1885 (OED)

It was not long, however, before such usage began to be criticized.

The first commentator to notice that *unique* was being used in new ways was Richard Grant White. According to Bardeen 1883, White objected to the use of *unique* to mean "beautiful" (perhaps he understood "very unique" as "very beautiful"). Loud and persistent voices of protest were not raised until after the turn of the century. Vizetelly 1906 and Bierce 1909 were among the first to make the now familiar observation that there can be no degrees of uniqueness. Fowler 1907 also broached this subject. The Fowlers feared that *unique* might go the way of *singular,* that its correct meaning might be weakened and ultimately lost because of its common misuse by the careless. Variations on this theme have been repeated throughout the century. Actual usage of *unique,* meanwhile, seems to have changed little.

In current English, *unique* has four principal senses, the least common of which is its original sense, "being the only one; sole, single":

> "But what about your wife typing it out? I can't walk away with a unique copy. Suppose I lost it? . . ." — Kingsley Amis, *Antaeus,* Spring 1975

> The other misconception held man to be the unique toolmaker among animals —*Current Biography,* November 1967

Fowler 1926 disliked this use of *unique,* and Evans 1957 asserted that *unique* "can no longer be used in this sense." No other commentator has taken note of it.

The use of *unique* approved by the critics is its second sense, "having no like or equal":

> . . . thought that each of us from childhood on contains an ideal likeness of love that is unique —Paul Horgan, *Ladies' Home Jour.,* January 1971

> . . . is unique in the history of English art: who is there to match him . . . ? —Robert Halsband, *Saturday Rev.,* 18 Dec. 1971

> . . . he could stare at the flames, each one new, violent, unique —Robert Coover, *Harper's,* January 1972

> . . . is one of the rarest of all birds on the writing scene today—in fact he may well be unique —John F. Baker, *Publishers Weekly,* 24 May 1976

> . . . a one-time phenomenon, unique in its time — James A. Michener, *N.Y. Times Book Rev.,* 27 Feb. 1977

Use of this sense is widespread and shows no sign of dying out. As several commentators have noted, *unique* in this sense can be modified by such adverbs as *almost, nearly,* and *practically:*

> . . . a curious, almost unique turn of affairs —Roger Angell, *New Yorker,* 15 Aug. 1983

In a related and equally common sense, *unique* is used with *to* and has the meaning "distinctively characteristic; peculiar":

> . . . this is not a condition unique to California — Ronald Reagan, quoted in *Change,* September 1971

> . . . counts the ridges and whorls . . . which are unique to each print —Francesca Lunzer, *Forbes,* 18 June 1984

Fowler also disliked this use of *unique,* although he stopped short of calling it incorrect. Howard 1980 takes exception to it as well.

The controversial sense of *unique* can be variously defined. It sometimes equals *unusual,* sometimes *rare,* and sometimes *distinctive.* It can sometimes be interpreted not as a separate sense at all, but simply as the second sense, "having no like or equal," with a slightly different emphasis: that which is unique stands apart from all other things, that which is very unique stands

far apart from all other things. Usually this sense implies not only standing apart but also standing above—that is, having unusual excellence—and is therefore highly popular among the writers of advertising copy (doubtless one reason why the critics are hostile to it):

> A very unique ball point pen —advt., *Wall Street Jour.,* 21 May 1975

> . . . our ingredients are too unique to copy —advt., *Town & Country,* July 1980

But copywriters are by no means the only ones to make use of this sense:

> . . . nothing quite so unique in literature as these solemn admonitory poems —Edith Hamilton, *The Greek Way to Western Civilization,* 1930

> The more we study him, the less unique he seems — Harry Levin, *James Joyce,* 1941

> . . . the most unique of all these hills —Donald A. Whiting, *Ford Times,* February 1968

> She's the most unique person I ever met —Arthur Miller, quoted in *Theatre Arts,* November 1956

> . . . the most unique contribution ever submitted for publication —*Dun's,* October 1971

> . . . this rather unique situation —*Morgan Horse,* April 1983

> He was the most unique of men —Frank Deford, *Sports Illustrated,* 30 Apr. 1984

> An extremely unique enzyme —Richard Fitzhugh, *US,* 10 Sept. 1984

> . . . opts for a more unique approach —Tom Kessler, *Houston Post,* 16 Sept. 1984

> . . . one of the most unique organizations in pro football —Paul Henniger, *Los Angeles Times,* 8 Sept. 1984

This sense is most noticeable when it occurs with a modifying adverb, as in the above quotations, but its use without a modifier is equally common:

> . . . the unique camaraderie of career servicemen — Malcolm S. Forbes, *Forbes,* 1 Dec. 1970

> . . . is in a unique position to evaluate them both — *Times Literary Supp.,* 22 Oct. 1971

> The town . . . is mainly a collection of unique antique shops —*Southern Living,* November 1971

> . . . provided us with a unique opportunity and challenge —Chester Bowles, *Saturday Rev.,* 6 Nov. 1971

> . . . a unique breed of woman—independent, daring, cool-headed —Margaret Cronin Fisk, *Cosmopolitan,* October 1976

> Those who sell gourmet foods say buyers must be convinced that the products are unique and high-quality but not intimidating —Janet Guyon, *Wall Street Jour.,* 6 May 1982

> . . . his unique combination of touch and power led to tournament wins in Madrid —Barry Lorge, *Sport,* September 1983

What, then, is the intelligent writer to make of *unique?* The evidence allows several definite conclusions. Those who insist that *unique* cannot be modified by such adverbs as *more, most,* and *very* are clearly wrong: our evidence shows that it can be and frequently is modified by such adverbs. Those who believe that the use of such modifiers threatens to weaken (or has already weakened) the "having no like or equal" sense of *unique* are also wrong: our evidence shows that the "having no like or equal" sense is flourishing. And those who regard the use of *unique* to mean "unusual" or "distinctive" as a modern corruption are emphatically wrong: *unique* has been used with those meanings for well over a hundred years. Should you therefore use the disputed sense of *unique* with utter disregard for possible criticism? Should you shake the hand of the nearest usage commentator and tell him that you find his books "extremely unique"? Maybe not. The reasons people have for disliking such usage may not be especially sound, but they are cherished nonetheless, and they are widely promoted. There is no denying that many good writers and editors strongly disapprove of *unique* in its "unusual" sense, even though it is indisputably well established in general prose. Perhaps you might try being one who knows enough about its bad reputation to avoid it but who also knows enough about its actual history not to sneer at those who use it.

Note, by the way, that if you are revising a passage in which *unique* is modified by an adverb of degree, the way to do it is not to delete the adverb, but to replace *unique* with an uncontroversial synonym, such as *unusual* or *distinctive.* Deleting the adverb can result in nonsense; for example, a newspaper story several years ago included a reference to "two of the unique rooms anywhere in sports." Presumably an overzealous editor deleted *most* before *unique,* failing to notice that doing so effectively turned the sentence into gibberish. The sensible revision would have been to change *unique* to *unusual:* "two of the most unusual rooms anywhere in sports."

United States In current American usage, *United States* takes a singular verb when it is the subject of a sentence. (Our meager British evidence shows the plural verb preferred.) But the verb was always plural once:

> I think it a great misfortune that the United States are in the department of the former —Thomas Jefferson, letter, 30 Jan. 1787

Sometime between 1787 and now *United States* went from being considered a plural noun to being considered a singular one. Obviously during those two centuries the perception of the United States as a single entity established itself. Do we have any idea when?

We have theories but no conclusive evidence. The first is from an undated and unidentified newspaper clipping in which General John W. Foster, who was Secretary of State under Benjamin Harrison, replies to criticism of his use of the singular in a book he published in 1900. According to Foster, Andrew Jackson was the first president to adopt the singular, and every president from Lincoln to McKinley regularly used it. Two more recent commentators, W. V. Quine, *Quiddities,* 1987, and Gary Wills, *Lincoln at Gettysburg,* 1992, point to the Civil War as the time when plural use gave way to singular, Wills pinpointing the Gettysburg address.

These are interesting theories, but they are hard to prove. We don't know what Andrew Jackson used, but his second vice president and successor, Martin Van Buren, wrote in his autobiography (around 1854):

> ... the dignity and immense power that the United States have acquired since that day ...

And if Lincoln changed the outlook (and usage) of most Americans, he didn't change his own usage:

> ... the United States must hold themselves at liberty to increase their naval armament upon the lakes — annual message to Congress, December 1864

And it seems likely that those who grew up using the plural didn't change:

> ... the United States inherit by far their most precious possession —Walt Whitman, *North American Rev.,* vol. 141, 1885, reprinted in Bolton & Crystal 1969

Actual usage seems to have been most markedly changing around the turn of the century, when General Foster's singular was questioned and commentators like Bierce 1909 (against the singular) and Utter 1916 (noting the increasing use of the singular) were writing. About the only vestige of plural use we have left today is the expression "these United States." See also AMERICA, AMERICAN.

unless and until Criticized by many commentators as wordy and redundant, this somewhat legalistic-sounding phrase seems to occur rarely in edited prose. It serves, when used, to give added emphasis to a conditional statement when a simple *unless* or *until* is felt to be inadequate.

unlike The use of *unlike* as a conjunction is less common than the conjunctive use of *like* and has drawn less criticism. The conjunctive *unlike* almost always introduces a prepositional phrase. Its meaning is "not as" or "as is not the case":

> Unlike in Europe, it has invariably taken a crisis to stir us to action in Asia —Robert Shaplen, *The Reporter,* 16 Feb. 1954

> Well, I am glad to note that in Mr. Owens's book, unlike in Mr. Mehegan's, *graceless* is still a pejorative —Simon 1980

> Unlike with office buildings there's no need for a lot of ductwork in hotels —Gene Dallaire, *Civil Engineering,* January 1983

Such usage may be criticized, but similar use of *like* is probably more apt to be singled out as a mistake because *as* is established—and preferred by many—as an alternative to *like* in such contexts. There is no negative form of *as* to substitute for *unlike;* it can only be replaced by a phrase.

Sometimes the preposition following the conjunctive *unlike* is inadvertently dropped, with results like the following:

> ... unlike most boats the rounded end is the front —W. E. Swinton, *The Corridor of Life,* 1948

> So many fine men were outside the charmed circle that, unlike most colleges, there was no disgrace in not being a "club man" —John Reed, *New Republic,* 22 Nov. 1954

Such constructions, sometimes known as false comparisons, are best avoided.

See also FALSE COMPARISON; LIKE, AS, AS IF 1.

unprecedented The OED notes that this word has been "in frequent use from *c* 1760." That fact goes against the grain of some people who feel that there are very few things in this world that are truly novel. Their suspicion—or belief—is that *unprecedented* is often used when some such word as *unusual* or *remarkable* would be more accurate. Actual examples of such usage are extremely hard to come by, however. Our evidence indicates that writers who use the word *unprecedented* are aware of its meaning and choose it because it says what they want it to say; namely, that the thing being described is, in their view, without precedent:

> ... the number of women seeking employment will be unprecedented —Ruth R. Hawkins, *Change,* November–December 1969

> ... was accorded the unprecedented honor, for an Irishman, of being named captain of the British Walker Cup team —Herbert Warren Wind, *New Yorker,* 10 Apr. 1971

> ... a new level of civilization, unprecedented in man's history —Harrison Brown, *Saturday Rev.,* 25 Dec. 1971

> ... disclosure of secrets on a grand, even unprecedented scale —Renata Adler, *N.Y. Times Book Rev.,* 16 Dec. 1979

unreadable See ILLEGIBLE, UNREADABLE.

unsanitary, insanitary These synonyms were both coined at about the same time: *unsanitary* was first recorded in 1871, *insanitary* in 1874. In the early part of this century, the notion that *unsanitary* was "not a word" existed in the minds of some people. Their reasons for thinking so (as stated in letters to the editors of newspapers in which *unsanitary* had appeared) were somewhat variable, but they typically pointed out that *unsanitary* was not in the dictionary while *insanitary* was. In fact, both words were first entered in Webster 1909, but one was easier to find than the other. Because the prefix *in-* can have more than one meaning, *insanitary* was entered with a full definition. The meaning of *unsanitary* is self-evident, however, and for that reason it was not given a definition but was included instead in a list of self-explanatory words, printed in small type as a means of saving space.

People still sometimes express uncertainty about which of these words is the "correct" one, but nobody seems to be writing letters to the editor about it anymore. They are both correct, they are both common, and they are both used in the same way:

> ... in crowded, impoverished, and frightfully unsanitary slums —James B. Conant, *Slums and Suburbs,* 1961

> ... unsanitary conditions, high prices for bad meat —Richard M. Levine, *Harper's,* March 1969

> ... were stored under insanitary conditions —*Consumer Reports,* September 1967

> Acres of moldy, insanitary buildings —Lewis Mumford, *New Yorker,* 23 Oct. 1954

unsatisfied See DISSATISFIED, UNSATISFIED.

unseasonable, unseasonal See SEASONABLE, SEASONAL.

unthinkable This unremarkable adjective became a usage topic when H. W. Fowler turned his attention to it in 1926, devoting a full page and a half to a detailed and literal-minded critique of its various uses. Fowler believed that the word should be—and eventually would be—restricted to "its severely limited philosophic sense"; that is, "incapable of being perceived or apprehended by the mind." He considered all of its other, much more common uses, with such meanings as "preposterous," "entirely unacceptable," and "out of the question," to be mistaken.

Later commentators seem to have been at something of a loss to understand just why it was that Fowler felt so strongly about *unthinkable.* Only a few have seen a need to address the subject, and most of those who do acknowledge that the uses Fowler objected to are, by and large, established and above reproach. Follett 1966, who is not ordinarily notable for his liberality in such matters, goes so far as to attribute the criticism of *unthinkable* to "fussy literalism." The criticism can still be heard on occasion, but its validity is even more dubious now than it was in 1926. All of the uses objected to by Fowler occur frequently in standard writing:

> The idea of a coalition between the present-day Conservative and Labour leaders is also unthinkable —*Times Literary Supp.,* 30 July 1971

> It was unthinkable for a respectable girl simply to come to America by herself —Tom Wolfe, *New York,* 27 Sept. 1971

> ... it is unthinkable that the President could return American troops to the ground war —Richard H. Rovere, *New Yorker,* 18 Nov. 1972

> Government leaders no longer regard nuclear war as unthinkable —Norman Cousins, *Saturday Rev.,* 7 Feb. 1976

> As for raising the price at the gasoline pump, ... that is evidently unthinkable —Anthony Lewis, *N.Y. Times,* 1 Nov. 1979

> This was hardly a farm by modern standards, but it was land that could be used, and it was unthinkable that we would not use it —Wendell Berry, in *The Contemporary Essay,* ed. Donald Hall, 1984

until See TILL, UNTIL, 'TIL; UNLESS AND UNTIL.

untimely "When is death timely?" asks Flesch 1964, implying that the use of *untimely* to modify *death* and *end* is often inappropriate. The fact is, however, that the meaning of *untimely* in "an untimely death" is "premature" rather than "not timely." Why not use *premature,* then? Probably because *untimely,* more than *premature,* suggests the writer's sense of regret over an early death, especially when a person with particularly admirable qualities or talents has died:

> ... the wild and exquisitely gifted young writers who come to an untimely end through passion —Cyril Connolly, *The Condemned Playground,* 1946

> ... the apparent waste involved in the untimely death of virtuous and capable men —Milton Millhauser, *Hartford Studies in Literature,* vol. 1, no. 1, 1969

Untimely is also used as an adverb, with the same connotations of regret that are implicit in its adjectival use:

> . . . the poet Dylan Thomas, who died untimely a few months ago at the age of thirty-nine —Gerald Bullett, *London Calling,* 17 June 1954

up, *adverb* **1.** As any learner of the language is bound to know, *up* is in frequent use in English as an idiomatic particle after many verbs. Besides its function in forming such idiomatic verbs as *bring up, wind up,* and *hold up,* it serves as a completive and intensive particle in such combinations as *burn up, end up,* and *hurry up,* and as a directional particle in such combinations as *climb up* and *rise up.*

It is the intensive, completive, and directional uses that the commentators turn their attention to, and their conclusion generally is that *up* is not necessary. Here is a typical voice:

> Of course, when *up* is unnecessary, it belongs nowhere, not even in informal usage. For instance, it is meaningless in "Let's *divide up* the profits" and in "Anna will *make up* the bed." It is redundant in *end up, finish up, hurry up, join up,* and *pay up.* It does not belong in "His son *signed up* with the Marines," and it is surplusage in "The minister *opened up* the sermon with a parable." —Freeman 1983

But let us examine the idea of omitting *up* from such sentences from the standpoint of what we gain by the omission. If you punch a typewriter or word processor keyboard, you see the gain instantly: two letters and one space saved. And if you are speaking, you will save perhaps a twentieth of a second.

The fact of the matter is that the uses of *up* aspersed by the critics are a deeply rooted part of ordinary, everyday, conversational English. These uses are idiomatic, they are natural, and they are not governed by careful calculations performed in the privacy of the study. And it is useful to remember that the closer your writing is to the natural rhythms of speech, the less likely you are to produce jargon, gibberish, or awkward and stilted prose. You may often omit *up,* but you certainly do not have to in order to write well:

> But the thing comes just in time to counteract some furious attacks at home. All the patriots are stirred up —H. L. Mencken, letter, 20 Dec. 1919

> Never worry because I will always fix things up — Ernest Hemingway, letter, 11 Mar. 1929

> If I had known about that I would have had something ready and would have practiced up before your arrival —E. B. White, letter, 15 Oct. 1964

> The heaviest tractor cultivators may be used for bursting up unploughed land —*Fream's Elements of Agriculture,* ed. D. H. Robinson, 15th ed., 1975

> . . . was out of the house and into the street, where people were starting up cars to go to work —Doris Lessing, *The Good Terrorist,* 1985

We suggest that you let *up* fall where it naturally will and not become obsessed with revising it away.

Freeman 1983 is not alone—the same ideas can be found in Harper 1985, Bryson 1984, Kilpatrick 1984, Scott, Foresman 1981, and others all the way back to Jensen 1935 and MacCracken & Sandison 1917. Bryson

is interesting because he contradicts his own advice in the very act of giving it.

> But in a sentence such as 'He climbed up the ladder', the *up* does nothing but take up space.

2. One of the grammatical processes identified by modern linguists is called the particle transformation, and it describes the behavior of particles like *up* in transitive two-word verbs like *stick up* or *hold up.* The particle transformation specifies that when the direct object of the verb, say, *hold up,* is a noun, the particle *up* can either stay with the verb ("The gunman held up the cashier") or follow the direct object ("The gunman held the cashier up"). When the direct object is a pronoun, the particle regularly follows the direct object ("The gunman held her up"). Another way to state the matter is that when the direct object is a noun the movement is optional, but when it is a pronoun it is obligatory. The particle transformation rule describes actual idiomatic usage quite well.

Trimmer & McCrimmon 1988 and Freeman 1983, on the other hand, find the construction awkward in which the particle *up* follows a noun as direct object (they do not mention pronouns). Freeman even pretends that "The gunman held the cashier up" means that he picked her up and waved her in the air. Note, however, that the sentence can also be understood in that way—with a serious effort—when it is written "The gunman held up the cashier." Of course, it is only possible to make this interpretation because the sentence is removed from context. Taken out of context, the sentence could also be interpreted to mean that the gunman delayed the cashier.

You, however, will be writing sentences in context, so the putative ambiguity of "held the cashier up" is unlikely to be a consideration. What you will want to consider is how the sentence sounds; you will not need to exercise your option over the transformation on any other basis.

up, *verb* **1.** *Up* as a verb meaning "raise" or "increase" is considered dubious in writing but acceptable in speech by the Harper 1975, 1985 usage panel; Janis 1984 calls it informal; Copperud 1980 reports that it is treated as standard in two out of three dictionaries. Our evidence shows that it is certainly standard, but not especially formal:

> . . . to up the number of women on state boards and commissions from 11 to 20 percent —Lorraine Davis, *Vogue,* March 1984

> . . . we have upped the ante on autobiographical revelation —Philip Lopate, *N.Y. Times Book Rev.,* 18 Nov. 1984

> . . . other scientists' measurements of seismic events led Gulliver to up the estimated intensity of an earthquake wave in areas with a low water table — *Science News,* 11 Apr. 1987

2. Some usage books and schoolbooks view the phrase *up and* with the same distaste they direct at *take and, go and,* and *try and* (which see). *Up and* is no bucolic idiom redolent of our frontier past, however; it is current on both sides of the Atlantic, and is used in general publications, often by writers of more than ordinary sophistication. It, too, is not highly formal.

> . . . a young woman had upped and offed with the family chauffeur —Dr. James Hemming, *Good Housekeeping* (London), February 1976

You up and run away from home —Alan Coren, *Punch,* 12 Mar. 1975

. . . suddenly upped and won three more major championships —Frank Deford, *Sports Illustrated,* 19 Sept. 1983

. . . I think all biographers subconsciously hope their man will up and die, clearing the boards and making everything a whole lot simpler —E. B. White, letter, 20 Sept. 1968

upcoming One way to form an adjective in English is to invert a verb + preposition combination. An event that is going on thereby becomes an ongoing event. A train that is coming on becomes an oncoming train. And an election that is coming up becomes an upcoming election.

The adjective *upcoming* was formed in just the same way—and is used in just the same way—as *oncoming, forthcoming, incoming,* and *outgoing.* It differs from them in only one respect: it is relatively new. It was coined in the early 1940s and did not come into frequent use until after World War II. By the 1950s it had established itself as a common word, and it continues to be one today. It has sometimes been used as a predicate adjective:

Before I could determine what cotillions were upcoming . . . my attention was impaled on a singular advertisement —S. J. Perelman, *New Yorker,* 12 Dec. 1953

But its use as an attributive adjective is much more common:

This will make some sizable "bunching" for the upcoming holidays —Bosley Crowther, *N.Y. Times,* 15 Dec. 1957

. . . hoping for chill weather to greet the upcoming hunting season —David Butwin, *Saturday Rev.,* 20 Nov. 1971

. . . the aims, objectives and reasons for the upcoming fight —Jane O'Reilly, *New York,* 26 Feb. 1973

. . . and the results of the upcoming rocket reflight — J. R. Hickey et al., *Science,* 18 Apr. 1980

Upcoming has been denigrated as "journalese" by a few commentators, who recommend substituting *coming, forthcoming,* or *approaching* in its place. It does in fact occur most often in journalistic use, but that is hardly surprising considering that journalists are frequently called upon to write about events, occasions, and ceremonies that are coming up. There is really no particular reason to dislike the word, aside from its newness and its common use, and most commentators take no notice of it. Among those that do, disapproval appears to be centered in New York publishing circles. It may owe something to the word's fairly frequent use in *Time* magazine:

. . . a world where eminent people are "famed" and their associates are "staffers," where the future is always "upcoming" and someone is forever "firing off" a note. Nobody in *Time* has merely sent a note or a memo or a telegram in years —Zinsser 1976

Some years ago a newspaper publisher fired off a memo to his staff saying, "If I see the word 'upcoming' once more, I'm going to be downcoming and the

person responsible will be outgoing." —Edwin McDowell, *N.Y. Times,* 29 June 1983

Upcoming is a standard and reputable word, recognized as such by current dictionaries. Disapproval of it has never been especially widespread, and recent evidence suggests that it is becoming less so. You have little to worry about if you choose to use *upcoming.*

See also ONGOING.

upon See ON 1.

up until Since the meaning of *up until* is the same as that of *until* by itself, Bernstein 1965, Phythian 1979, and Freeman 1983 recommend omitting the *up.* We recommend instead that you regard *up until* as an idiomatic phrase which occurs naturally and appropriately in speech and in casual writing.

. . . a privilege that up until Stark took over Willard had guarded jealously —James Jones, *From Here to Eternity,* 1951

. . . I had been protected all my life, up until the day he was killed —Myrlie Evers, quoted in *Essence,* November 1970

Up until now I've been waiting until I decided to turn in my old car —*And More by Andy Rooney,* 1982

Let your own writerly judgment determine whether *up* should stay or go in a particular context.

upward, upwards The adjective is *upward:*

She shifted her bill to a slightly upward angle —Josephine & Gilbert Fernandez, *Massachusetts Audubon,* June 1968

The adverb may be either *upward* or, less commonly, *upwards.* Both are standard:

. . . the electric door groans and rattles upward — Frank Conroy, *Harper's,* November 1970

. . . its small flame will flicker upward —Laurence Leamer, *Harper's,* December 1971

Theater ideas are absorbed upwards —Stuart W. Little, *New York,* 24 Apr. 1972

Both *upward* and *upwards* are used with *of* to mean "more than; in excess of." *Upwards of* is considerably more common than *upward of:*

. . . that an ostensibly sane adult would pay upwards of 2,000 recession dollars for a glorified calculator — Curt Suplee, *Smithsonian,* April 1983

. . . had won upwards of $7 million but had squandered that fortune —William Nack, *Sports Illustrated,* 23 July 1984

. . . ranging from about $35 for the smallest frying pan to upward of $150 for a large covered casserole —Cara Greenberg, *Metropolitan Home,* December 1983

Such usage, which was first recorded in the early 18th century, was disliked by Alfred Ayres in 1881 and by Ambrose Bierce in 1909, but is now recognized as perfectly reputable. What little controversy there is has to do with the use of *upwards of* (and *upward of*) to mean "a little less than; about; approximately." Clear-cut examples of such usage are extremely hard to find. In fact, the exact meaning of *upwards of* is often difficult to pin down:

> ... now estimated that the average candidate for Congress needs upwards of a hundred thousand dollars for an effective race, and in the more populous states this sum is not unusual in a contest for the state legislature —Harry S. Ashmore, *Center Mag.,* January 1969

Does the writer mean "more than a hundred thousand dollars"? Perhaps, but the later reference to "this sum" (that is, a hundred thousand dollars) suggests that the meaning of *upwards of* in this case may be closer to "approximately" or "as much as and possibly more than." Certainly *upwards of* is less unequivocal than *more than.* What can be said definitely is that *upwards of* almost always occurs before an amount that the writer regards as impressively high. On those extremely rare occasions when it occurs before an amount that is not so regarded, some such definition as "approximately" seems to be called for:

> He outlined upwards of a thousand words by means of which, he maintained, almost anything could be expressed —*Selected Writings of Louise Pound,* 1949

us Like the other personal pronouns, *us* turns up in contexts where the schoolbooks have long said it does not belong. As might be expected, it occurs after the verb *be:*

> This is this year, and we are us —Paul Horgan, *Ladies' Home Jour.,* January 1971

And it is common in an emphatic position at the beginning of a statement:

> Us kids at Concord school in Mr. Thompson's reading class are studying dictionaries —letter from a schoolgirl in Pennsylvania, March 1980

> ... a sense of departmental loyalty: us against them —Jay McInerney, *Bright Lights, Big City,* 1984

A little harder to explain are the other appearances in subject position:

> This is not what us journalists call a "happy beat" — Hunter S. Thompson, *Rolling Stone,* 2 Mar. 1972

> ... wherein us romantics are supposed to accept Ava Gardner as Omar Sharif's royal mama —Judith Crist, *TV Guide,* 27 July 1973

These vexing usages and kindred problems concerning personal pronouns are discussed and illustrated at various places in this book. We suggest that you start with IT'S ME and PRONOUNS. These will lead you to other points of interest.

usage It is inevitable, we suppose, that a number of usage commentators comment on the word *usage.* What they say, by and large, is that *usage* should not be employed simply as a synonym of *use* in contexts like "the use/usage of public lands" and "increased use/usage of electricity." This issue seems to have originated with Gowers 1954, whose comments are typical:

> *Usage* does not mean *use;* it means either a manner of use (e.g. rough usage) or a habitual practice creating a standard (e.g. modern English usage).

A look in almost any dictionary shows, however, that *usage* does indeed mean "act of using or being used; use; employment." Evidence in the OED establishes that *usage* has had this sense since the 14th century. It has occurred in the works of such writers as Geoffrey Chaucer, Joseph Priestley, and Alfred, Lord Tennyson. Here are some 20th-century examples from our own files:

> ... his blue eyes dimmed with time and usage — Claude G. Bowers, *The Young Jefferson 1743–1789,* 1945

> The book you sent back for more signs and marks of usage, having now been through another campaign, looks to me in as ideal a condition for your purposes as you could expect —Robert Frost, letter, 4 Aug. 1953

> Usage of the "Cyclopedia" reveals few serious gaps —Wayne Hartwell, *Saturday Rev.,* 20 Mar. 1954

> ... ending credit card usage altogether —Guy Halverson, *Christian Science Monitor,* 10 Apr. 1980

> ... a squat, ladder-back chair whose short legs had the look of being worn away through long usage — Peter Taylor, *The Old Forest and Other Stories,* 1985

It is accurate to say that *use* is more common than *usage* in this sense, but it is not at all accurate to say that *usage* in this sense is therefore an error. *Usage* meaning "use" is standard English.

usage levels See LEVELS OF USAGE.

used to, use to *Use* was once commonly employed as an intransitive verb meaning "to be in the habit or custom; be wont":

> I did this night give the waterman who uses to carry me 10s. —Samuel Pepys, diary, 24 Mar. 1667

> The English then useing to let grow on their upperlip large Mustachio's —John Milton, *The History of Britain,* 1670 (OED)

> He does not use to be the last on these occasions — George Lillo, *London Merchant,* 1731

But this sense of *use* now occurs only in the past tense with *to:*

> ... the passion this issue used to ignite in the State Department —Henry Brandon, *Atlantic,* March 1970

Used to is extremely common in both speech and writing. Such problems as arise with it have to do basically with the *d* of *used.* Because the *d* is not pronounced, *used to* is indistinguishable in speech from *use to.* It may be, in fact, that many people actually say *use to* rather than *used to*—that is, the word they have in mind is *use* rather than *used* ("We use to be good friends")—but since the pronunciations are essentially identical, it makes no difference. In writing, however, *use to* in place of *used to* is an error.

The problem becomes a little trickier in constructions with *did.* The form considered correct following *did,* at least in American English, is *use to.* Just as we say "Did he want to?" rather than "Did he wanted to?," so we say "Did he use to?" rather than "Did he used to?" Here again, it may be that some people actually say "did ... used to," but the question is moot in speech. Only in writing does it become an issue. Our evidence shows that most writers do remember to drop the *d* of *used* following *did:*

> "Didn't he use to go with Laura?" she asked —Irwin Shaw, *The Young Lions,* 1948

> ". . . It didn't use to be like that." —James Jones, *From Here to Eternity,* 1951

> I believe Polk did use to be a town —Eudora Welty, *The Ponder Heart,* 1954

> Didn't half-mast use to represent mourning? —Lois Long, *New Yorker,* 21 Oct. 1967

But the spelling "did . . . used to" does sometimes find its way into print:

> "Did you used to walk with them?" he asked Concetta —Constantine FitzGibbon, *The Holiday,* 1953

> He told me, "Today orchestras announce auditions, which they didn't used to do. . . ." —James Lincoln Collier, *Village Voice,* 28 Feb. 1968

In American English, such usage is considered an error, but some British commentators find it acceptable. Chambers 1985 finds that in questions the phrases "Did he use to . . ." and "Did he used to . . ." are both "unexceptionable." Longman 1988, discussing the various negative forms of *used to* (which include *used not to* and *usedn't to,* both rare in American English), asserts that "the commoner negative . . . has become *They didn't use to* or (perhaps better) *They didn't used to.*" Quirk et al. 1985, however, says that the spelling *did . . . used to* is often regarded as nonstandard on both sides of the Atlantic. In American English, according to our evidence, the usual and correct form is *didn't use to.*

See also SUPPOSED TO.

used to could Admonitions against the use of this phrase have appeared in a few books on usage. The OED Supplement describes it as "a common phrase in certain dialects of England and in the United States. . . ." In American English, its use is a characteristic of Southern speech. The linguist Raven I. McDavid, Jr., observed in 1963 (in his abridgement of Mencken's *The American Language*) that in his experience *used to could* (or *use to could,* as he wrote it) was not limited to those of little education but was common in the casual speech of educated Southerners. It does not occur in writing except when used for deliberate effect:

> . . . we'll no longer be able to read good prose like we used to could —James Thurber, letter, 15 Aug. 1959

Similar but less common is the dialectal phrase *used to was:*

> . . . got to talking about . . . how much better off they used to was —Mark Twain, *Huckleberry Finn,* 1884 (*A Mark Twain Lexicon,* 1938)

Used to by itself has also had some dialectal use as an abverb synonymous with *formerly* or *once:*

> Used to Pa wouldn't a done a thing like this —Jesse Stuart, *Men of the Mountains,* 1941 (American Dialect Dictionary)

useful Something is said to be useful *to* somebody:

> Information and guidelines . . . are most useful to the beginner —Bill Scott, *Media & Materials,* February 1970

> . . . literary criticism, useful to all of us who remember the books of our childhood —Clara Claiborne Park, *Saturday Rev.,* December 1978

When the way in which something is useful is being described, either *in* or *for* may be used:

> . . . the book is useful in recording the details of several rare editions —*Times Literary Supp.,* 2 Oct. 1970

> . . . a low-power . . . microscope will be found useful for examining material such as the larger insect larvae —W. H. Dowdeswell, *Animal Ecology,* 2d ed., 1959

> It was then we found our sea-slugs useful for turning on our opponent —Gerald Durrell, *My Family and Other Animals,* 1956

utilize Usage writers dislike *utilize* because they regard it as a needlessly wordy and pretentious substitute for *use.* They generally recommend either that it be disdained altogether or that it be used (not utilized) only when it has the meaning "to turn to practical use or account." That is, in fact, almost invariably the meaning of *utilize* in actual usage:

> Scientific knowledge, for example, is developing exponentially—faster perhaps than our culture can . . . utilize it wisely —Milton S. Eisenhower, *Johns Hopkins Mag.,* February 1966

> . . . suggesting novel ways of utilizing Barnard's facilities —Jamienne Studley, *Barnard Alumnae,* Winter 1971

> . . . women who want to work at jobs that utilize their full potential —Bella S. Abzug, *Saturday Rev.,* 7 Aug. 1976

Use could certainly be substituted for *utilize* in any of these passages, but not without some loss of connotation. *Utilize* is a distinct word having distinct implications. More than *use,* it suggests a deliberate decision or effort to employ something (or someone) for a practical purpose. Its greatest sins are that it has two more syllables than *use* and that it ends with the dreaded *-ize.* It is a common word, nevertheless, and every indication is that it will continue to be one.

V

vacuity, vacuousness Some commentators have made a distinction between *vacuity* and *vacuousness.* Evans 1957 prefers *vacuousness* for descriptions of facial expressions. Fowler 1926 regards *vacuousness* as an acceptable alternative in such cases, but notes that in other contexts *vacuity* is "the usual word." Our evidence shows that *vacuity* is by far the commoner term, regardless of meaning. *Vacuousness* is rarely used but occurs in the same kinds of contexts as *vacuity.*

vagary *Vagary* is rather an odd word, in that the ending -*ary*, which certainly looks like a suffix, does not go back to Latin -*arius (-arium, -aria),* as in *apothecary, seminary,* and hundreds of other words. Rather the word appears to have been born as an unusual use of the Latin infinitive *vagari* "to wander." The second *a* is long in the Latin sourceword, and the traditional pronunciation \və-'ger-ē\ accords with this fact. But the usual pronunciation now in America, and the one currently recommended in England, is \'vā-gə-rē\.

variant spellings See MILLENNIUM; SPELLING.

various *Various* is sometimes used as a pronoun, usually followed by *of:*

> . . . various of these weeds also are poisonous to livestock —Wendell H. Camp, in *The Scientists Look at Our World,* 1952

> Various of the men, then Clark, and finally Lewis fell ill —Bernard De Voto, *Minority Report,* 1940, in *The Practical Cogitator,* ed. Charles P. Curtis, Jr. & Ferris Greenslet, 1945

This use was first cited in Bartlett's *Dictionary of Americanisms* (4th ed., 1877), which included a quotation from a correspondent in the *New York Times:* "I talked for an hour with various of them." The OED made no mention of this use in 1916, but by 1926 it was widespread enough for Fowler to warn against it:

> ANALOGY has lately been playing tricks with the word & persuading many people that they can turn it at will, as *several, few, many, divers, certain, some,* & other words are turned, from an adjective into a pronoun. . . . To write *various of them* &c. is no better than to write *different of them, diverse of them,* or *numerous* or *innumerable of them.*

Later commentators have echoed Fowler's sentiments. Their objections do not make it clear why *various* should necessarily be classed with adjectives like *different* rather than with those like *several.* Presumably the critics either fail to recognize that the pronoun *various* is derived from the sense of the adjective meaning "of an indefinite number greater than one" (as in "We stopped at various towns along the way"), or they regard this sense of the adjective as nonstandard (for more on this subject, see VARIOUS DIFFERENT). In either case, their objections seem open to challenge.

Be that as it may, those objections exist. If you use the pronoun *various,* you should be aware that many people will regard it as a mistake.

See also NUMEROUS.

various and sundry This is a common fixed phrase which has been criticized as a redundancy. It need not be despised as such, but if you like your prose to be lean, you will probably want to avoid it.

various different This phrase has been criticized as redundant by those who do not recognize that its meaning is "a number of different," not "different different." Other critics have contended that it is incorrect to use *various* in this way to mean "of an indefinite number greater than one." Such use is actually well-established and is certainly standard:

> The boy dreamed of saving the various nickels which he earned by hours of lawn-mowing —Sinclair Lewis, Introduction to *Four Days on the Webutuck River,* 1925

> . . . the various press representatives were forced to share a single radio teletypewriter —*Current Biography,* December 1964

Even so, you may wish to steer clear of *various different.* Its meaning notwithstanding, it has the appearance of redundancy, and our evidence shows that it rarely occurs in edited prose.

vary One thing or group of things is said to vary *from* another:

> . . . the relative spaces allotted vary greatly from the norm —*Philosophical Rev.,* October 1953

> . . . these numbers vary inversely . . . from the corresponding given numbers —Ethel L. Grove et al., *Basic Mathematics,* Book 1, 1961

When a range of variation is being described, *vary* is followed by a prepositional phrase beginning with either *from* or *between. From* is more common:

> . . . his weight varies from about 138 to 145 pounds —*Current Biography,* July 1965

> . . . webs that vary from the loosely tangled web of the house spider to the work of art of the garden spider —Katherine W. Moseley, *Massachusetts Audubon,* June 1971

> The temperature . . . varies between 120 and 140 degrees Fahrenheit —Gerald S. Craig & Margaret Oldroyd Hyde, *New Ideas in Science,* 1950

vastly The use of *vastly* to mean "to a great degree" in contexts not involving measurement or comparison has been criticized as an affectation, especially in British English. Such use is common and idiomatic in American English:

> The soil is a vastly complex ecosystem —Barry Commoner, *Columbia Forum,* Spring 1968

> I am aware that I have vastly oversimplified some of the most complicated questions —Richard Neuhaus, *Harper's,* October 1971

Affectation or not, it also occurs in British English:

... because the existence of God would make them vastly probable —Stephen Clark, *Times Literary Supp.,* 25 Jan. 1980

... is vastly insulted when used as a common convict —A. E. Rodway, *Essays in Criticism,* July 1953

vast majority   See MAJORITY 3.

vehement   See VEHICLE.

vehicle   For a long time, dictionaries recommended sounding the \h\ in *vehicle,* and similarly in *vehement.* But we have evidence back to the early 17th century that the \h\ was often dropped in these words. *Annihilate* \ə-'nī-ə-ˌlāt\ also shows this dropping of \h\ when it would fall after the stress and between vowels. The resulting vocalic hiatus (two vowels occurring next to each other without a consonant in between) is often simplified to a single vowel: again, we have early evidence for two-syllable pronunciations \'vē-kəl\ and \'vē-mənt\. A similar simplification may be observed in the very common current American pronunciations of *diamond* and *diaper:* \'dī-mənd\ and \'dī-pər\.

Today, the usual (and the recommended) pronunciation of *vehicle* is without \h\: \'vē-ə-kəl\ or \'vē-ˌik-əl\. In the United States, a pronunciation with \h\ is also widespread: \'vē-hik-əl\ or \'vē-ˌhik-əl\. It is considered especially characteristic of the South, though it is not universal there and may also be heard throughout the rest of the country. For reasons that are not entirely clear, \'vē-ˌhik-əl\ suffers from an unjust stigma as a yokel's pronunciation. Various suggestions have been put forward for the tenacity of the \h\: influence of the spelling, of the adjective *vehicular* where \h\ is normally sounded, and of the special cadences of Armed Services speech.

We are also warned, in usage sources, against giving primary stress to the second syllable of *vehicle.* This pronunciation is far less common than any of the variants with initial stress. Our pronunciation files include only three citations for \(ˈ)vē-'hik-əl\, although one of them is from a university president.

See also H.

venal, venial   *Venal,* which means "open to or characterized by corruption," is sometimes confused with *venial,* which means "pardonable":

I'm a ... sinner! Venal, mortal, carnal, major, minor—however you want to call it —Hunter S. Thompson, *Fear and Loathing in Las Vegas,* 1972

... the venial, inefficient trading community —Peter Forster, *London Calling,* 17 Mar. 1955

These mistakes are not common in edited writing, but they are easily made in a moment of inattention.

verbal, oral   The first definition of *verbal* in Johnson's Dictionary (1755) is "Spoken; not written." Noah Webster also made this the first sense in his *American Dictionary of the English Language* (1828): "Spoken; expressed to the ear in words; not written; as a *verbal* message; a *verbal* contract, *verbal* testimony." The earliest citation for this sense of *verbal* in the OED dates from 1591. (The earliest citation for the synonymous sense of *oral,* on the other hand, is from 1628.) There is no indication from Johnson, Webster, or the OED that

this sense of *verbal* is anything other than standard English.

Why, then, has it been singled out for criticism by commentators on usage? The trouble seems to have started in the late 19th century. Hodgson 1881, who knew the etymologies of *verbal* (from Latin *verbum* "word") and *oral* (from Latin *os* "mouth"), declared that the correct meaning of *verbal* was "couched in words" (which is, in fact, one of the many senses of *verbal,* first attested in 1530). Hodgson dismissed the "spoken rather than written" sense as a "blunder," albeit a common one made by "writers of standing" such as Anthony Trollope, Henry Kingsley, and Henry Fielding:

The captain returned a verbal answer to a long letter —Henry Fielding, *Journal of a Voyage to Lisbon,* 1755

He might also have added Samuel Pepys, Jonathan Swift, and Charles Dickens:

"I would not consent to your being charged with any written answer, but perhaps you will take a verbal one?" —Charles Dickens, *A Tale of Two Cities,* 1859

Since Hodgson's time, disapproval of this sense of *verbal* has been widespread among usage commentators, most of whom clearly regard it as a recent development. Some commentators now concede that it is standard, but nearly all express a preference for *oral,* arguing that the multiple meanings of *verbal* could cause confusion. The truth is that the context almost always makes the meaning clear, and the only serious confusion appears to be in the minds of the commentators themselves. Simon 1980 postulates that the use of *verbal* to mean "oral" may have become widespread "because *oral* also designates nonspeaking functions of the mouth, as in *oral hygiene* or *oral sex,* and so begets the ignorant assumption that the spoken word must be covered by that other adjective, *verbal.*" Samuel Johnson and Noah Webster would probably have been surprised by such reasoning.

The use of *verbal* to mean "spoken rather than written" occurs commonly and unambiguously with such words as *agreement, commitment,* and *contract.* Very often it is contrasted with the adjective *written* in contexts that make its meaning unmistakable:

... I found the word in constant written and verbal use by my American colleagues —Sir St. Vincent Troubridge, *American Speech,* October 1946

... far fewer written, recorded discussions, far more private, verbal discussions —Warren Bennis, *Saturday Rev.,* 6 Mar. 1976

The adverb *verbally* is also extremely common in this sense:

Stalin boggled at a treaty clause setting a date for Soviet evacuation ... , but agreed verbally to have all troops out in three months —*Time,* 3 Sept. 1945

... have already expressed to me in a letter (as well as verbally) their desire to produce a faithful adaptation —E. B. White, letter, 24 May 1967

Whilst Bode was able to communicate verbally his feelings ... , he failed when it came to putting pen to paper —*Times Literary Supp.,* 2 May 1968

... but Freeman says she'd already verbally accepted a CNN offer —*TV Guide,* 31 May 1985

There is no ambiguity in these passages. Of course, if you do see a chance of ambiguity in a particular context, you can always use *oral* instead. But do not let anyone tell you that the use of *verbal* to mean "oral" is a recent corruption of the language. That idea is a popular myth, nothing more.

verbal nouns See POSSESSIVE WITH GERUND.

verbiage *Verbiage* in its original and usual sense denotes an excess of words. It is similar to *wordiness*, except that it stresses more the superfluous words themselves than the quality that produces them; that is, a writer with a fondness for *verbiage* might be accused of *wordiness*.

> One cannot spin such an easy brocade of verbiage in nonfiction of this caliber —Edward Hoagland, *N.Y. Times Book Rev.*, 17 Oct. 1982

> ... designed to decode the verbiage of experts —Judith Appelbaum, *N.Y. Times Book Rev.*, 9 Jan. 1983

> As an artist, I find much of the verbiage of art commentators insufferable —Gertrude Myrrh Reagan, letter to the editor, *Science News*, 17 May 1986

Verbiage has also been used since the early 19th century as a synonym of *wording* or *diction*:

> The language of the dialogue is as familiar as the verbiage of the parlour fireside —*The New British Theatre*, 1814 (OED)

> In musical verbiage a phrase is a portion of a melody that is performed without a pause —Albert E. Weir, *The Piano*, 1940

> ... the kid-glove verbiage of diplomacy —Frank Abbott Magruder, *National Governments and International Relations*, 1950

Such usage is treated as standard in the OED and in many current dictionaries, including our own, but some people continue to regard it as an error, insisting that *verbiage* should always imply excess. Those same people are also likely to find fault with such phrases as *excess verbiage* and *excessive verbiage*, in which they detect redundancy. The evidence shows, however, that the meaning of *verbiage* is often underscored in standard writing by an appropriate adjective:

> ... Aunt Phoebe's imagination, her florid verbiage —H. G. Wells, *Joan and Peter*, 1918

> ... serving them without excess verbiage —Edwin Way Teale, *N.Y. Herald Tribune Book Rev.*, 12 Dec. 1948

> ... not just of words but of excess verbiage running into the billions of tons —Thomas H. Middleton, *Saturday Rev.*, 15 Oct. 1977

> ... the windy verbiage he seems to love —Grace-Anne Andreassi DeCandido, *N.Y. Times Book Rev.*, 13 Feb. 1983

verbified nouns See NOUNS AS VERBS.

veritable The adjective *veritable* has raised the hackles of some commentators—most notably Fowler 1926, who found nothing at all to like about it:

> ... its appearance in a description has always the effect of taking down the reader's interest a peg or

two, both as being a FORMAL WORD, & as the now familiar herald of a strained top note.

Such criticism seems excessive for so inoffensive a word. It is clear, in any case, that the assertions made in 1926 (and repeated by Gowers in Fowler 1965) do not hold true today. Far from being a "formal word," *veritable* is now most often used to stress the aptness of a metaphor in contexts having a somewhat humorous tone:

> The delay this time was two hours and 13 minutes, as a veritable monsoon swept across the Busch Stadium carpet, transforming it into another Great Lake —Ron Fimrite, *Sports Illustrated*, 1 Nov. 1982

> ... he was a man who twitched with sociability, whose conversation was a veritable memo pad of given names, connections, ties, appointments —Mary McCarthy, *Partisan Rev.*, February 1948

> ... a philanthropist advertised ... that he would pay a penny each for toads delivered to him alive. ... The toad fancier turned out to be a veritable mother lode for a couple of hundred boys —Ted Smiley, *Sports Illustrated*, 8 Nov. 1982

> The Fat Man was a veritable Iron Mike with a fungo bat. He could pound the ball —Joe Piscopo, *Inside Sports*, March 1982

Veritable is perfectly at home in such contexts. It poses no apparent threat to the reader's interest.

The use of *veritable* in its literal sense, "actual," occurs less commonly, but it too seems unobjectionable:

> The only guts that are mentioned in this story are the veritable entrails of fish —Mark Schorer, *New Republic*, 6 Oct. 1952

verse, stanza In prosody, *verse* means "a line of metrical writing," *stanza* means "a division of a poem consisting of a series of lines arranged together in a usually recurrent pattern of meter and rhyme." In the great world outside of prosody, *verse* is often used to mean "stanza," especially with reference to the lyrics of a song. Use of *verse* to mean "a line of metrical writing" is rare in general prose; the word of choice for most people is, simply, *line*.

very 1. *"Very" and the past participle.* Fitzedward Hall 1873 cited a Professor Maximilian Muller as asserting that expressions like "very pleased" and "very delighted" were Americanisms. Hall refuted the assertion, quoting "very concerned" from 1760 and other similar 18th- and 19th-century examples, all British. Hall's comments are the earliest that we know of in which interest is expressed in the combination of *very* with an adjective formed from a past participle. By the time of Vizetelly 1906, the question had become one of propriety; making exception for those participles established as adjectives, he found that "it is now thought more grammatical to interpose an adverb between the participle" and *very*. Similar advice has since appeared in many usage books. The adverb most often recommended was and is *much*.

The reasoning involved in this issue is easy enough to follow. *Very* by itself does not modify verbs, and therefore it cannot modify the past participle of a verb. The crux of the matter, then, is whether the past participle is simply a participle or whether it is an adjective. On this point many commentators are uncertain.

Fowler 1926 sets down four criteria for determining whether *very* can be used before a given participle. The first is the consideration of whether the participle has become an established adjective, a judgment which would seem to be highly subjective. The other three criteria are supposed to help in cases where the participle is not an established adjective. If the participle is being used attributively rather than predicatively ("a very worried expression" rather than "he was very worried"), it is functioning as an adjective and can be modified by *very.* If the noun or pronoun modified by the participle names "the person or thing on which the verbal action is exercised" rather than some aspect or feature of that person or thing ("he was very worried" rather than "his expression was very worried"), then the participle is functioning as a verb and requires *much.* And finally, if the "verbal character" of the participle is "betrayed" by a preposition such as *by* ("very worried by what he had heard"), *much* is again required. So says Fowler.

Where Fowler's ratiocination goes astray becomes evident when we consider the distinguishing criteria for adjectives given in Quirk et al. 1985. Quirk identifies four criteria for adjectives: attributive use, predicative use after the verb *seem,* premodification by *very,* and comparison. Quirk knows that not every adjective meets all four criteria, but some combination of them will usually serve to distinguish an adjective from an adverb or a participle.

The problem for the critics, then, is that they are trying to pass judgment on the propriety of what is, in fact, a distinguishing characteristic of the adjective as opposed to the participle—premodification by *very.* Copperud 1970, 1980, Evans 1957, and Flesch 1964, who would allow *very* wherever it does not offend the ear, are on the right track. And time has made Fowler wrong: his examples of *very annoyed* and *very concerned* do not illustrate misuses of *very* but are in fact evidence that *annoyed* and *concerned* are moving or have moved into adjective function.

The movement of past participles into adjective function—based on evidence of premodification by *very*—began in the 17th century; the OED has examples from 1641 on. It is a continuing process. The *annoyed* and *concerned* that, when used with *very,* bothered Fowler sound unexceptionable today. Participles that sound awkward with *very* today may sound fine in another generation.

You can see for yourself how well established Fowler's offending *annoyed* is as an adjective by testing it in sample sentences by Quirk's criteria. Attributive use:

She gave me an annoyed look.

Predicative use with *seem:*

She seems rather annoyed by the delay.

Premodification by *very:*

Rather annoyed? I'd say she's very annoyed.

Comparison:

She's growing more annoyed by the minute.

You can try similar test sentences for doubtful participles if you like—it can even be fun sometimes—but for practical purposes you are going to have to trust your ear.

Two other points are worth bearing in mind. First, a prepositional phrase with *by* marking an agent can be an indicator of verbal force:

She was annoyed by the panhandler.

When this agent is animate, it is a good indicator that the participle is still a participle, and you would not use *very* as a modifier. But if the agent is not animate, the participle may be an adjective:

She was very annoyed by your behavior.

Second, many participial adjectives do not take *very* and do not compare because their meaning is such that they are not what Quirk calls "gradable": they are seldom used in senses that admit of degrees. We have seen that *annoyed* admits of degrees; but such participles as *deceased, defeated,* and *performed* do not. Occasionally, however, participles that are seldom used in a gradable way can be used with *very* as a stylistic device:

... other very famous, very rich, and/or very titled people who live here —Lawrence B. Eisenberg, *Cosmopolitan,* February 1978

She offered me a chair in her green-and-white, very decorated office —Sally Quinn, *We're Going to Make You a Star,* 1975

Very much can be similarly used:

The girl in the center was still very much undressed and screamed when she saw the MPs —Walter Peters, in *The Best from Yank,* 1945

Premodification by *very* is an "explicit indication" (Quirk) that a participle has achieved adjective status. If *very* sounds all right before a participle to you, that participle is an adjective for your purposes. But since the participle-into-adjective process is still going on, you will have to accept the fact that what is a participial adjective to you may only be a participle to someone else, and vice versa. We leave you with a few typical examples:

She seemed very attached to her husband —Josephine W. Johnson, *Virginia Quarterly Rev.,* Spring 1939

Authors are not very interested in this problem —C. H. Rolph, *Times Literary Supp.,* 9 Mar. 1967

Now, I won't be satisfied, in fact I'll be very dissatisfied, if you are not one of the sponsors —Robert Frost, letter, 20 Jan. 1947

I am very pleased to know that I can get a quart of mouse milk for under ten dollars —E. B. White, letter, 10 Nov. 1966

2. From the numerous warnings in usage books against overuse or even any use of *very* in writing, you might think that no writer of reputation would actually use "this colorless, exhausted word" (McMahan & Day 1980) as an intensifier. But, of course, many writers do:

The Philosopher was very hungry, and he looked about on all sides to see if there was anything he might eat —James Stephens, *The Crock of Gold,* 1912

David had worked very hard for four days —Ernest Hemingway, "An African Betrayal," in *Sports Illustrated,* 5 May 1986

The hero is a computer expert with a very pregnant wife —Newgate Callendar, *N.Y. Times Book Rev.,* 18 Dec. 1983

It's going to be very interesting, you think, to look at these many objects from olden days —Garrison Keillor, *Lake Wobegon Days,* 1985

... very representative of Washington this winter. It is a seething turmoil of glumness —Russell Baker, *N.Y. Times Mag.,* 15 Feb. 1976

The important thing is to consider carefully how you use the intensifier. It is even possible to achieve emphasis by using a string of *very*s, as in this example:

It was a day of very white clouds, and very blue skies, and very dark green spruces —E. B. White, letter, 27 June 1922

But you are more likely to make effective use of the word if you use it—or any intensifier—sparingly in your writing. Use it where it will count the most.

vest An abstract possession, such as a power or right, is vested *in* a person or institution, but a person or institution is vested *with* an abstract possession. Both these uses of the transitive verb *vest* are common and correct:

The United States Constitution vested all harbor rights and responsibilities in the Federal Government —*Dictionary of American History,* 1940

The framers of the system of 1875 intended to vest the President with some measure of independent power —Ernest Barker, *Essays on Government,* 1945

via The English preposition *via* was taken directly from Latin in the late 18th century. It was used to mean "by way of; by a route passing through," as in "We traveled from Boston to Philadelphia via New York City." It continued to be used only in this way throughout the 19th century and into the 20th, during which time it was, according to available evidence, invariably printed in italics, an indication that those who used it still regarded it primarily as a Latin word. In the 1920s and 30s, however, changes began to occur: *via* began to appear in regular roman rather than in italic type, its use became more widespread, and it began to take on extended meanings. All of these changes indicate that *via* was working its way into the mainstream of English. It was being used increasingly by people who were not conscious of—or who were indifferent to—its Latin roots.

Before long those who *were* conscious of its Latin roots took unfavorable notice of the new trend. The use of *via* to indicate the means of travel rather than the route taken, as in "We went to Chicago via train," was called "wrong, very wrong, misleadingly wrong" by Partridge 1942. *Via* was also being used to mean "by means of" or "through the medium of" in contexts having nothing to do with travel:

... advertising via the screen —*Harper's,* March 1935

... to sugar-coat music for them via story-telling is to imply that music is a bitter pill —*Saturday Rev.,* 25 Dec. 1939

Despite the protests of the few, these new uses of *via* caught on quickly with the many. Their popularity remains unabated today. Many modern commentators presumably find them inoffensive, since they make no mention of *via* in their books, but voices of criticism are still often raised (as in Bernstein 1965, Copperud 1970, 1980, Nickles 1974, and Bryson 1984). If you use *via* in any but its original sense, you still run the risk

of ruffling a few feathers, but you will be in good company:

... a deer can't move anywhere in this community without having its whereabouts flashed via the grapevine —E. B. White, *New Yorker,* 24 Dec. 1955

I want to thank the officials and judges of the American Book Awards via whom this honor has come to me —John Updike, quoted in *Publishers Weekly,* 14 May 1982

... he was never able to rid himself of the thought that suicide via jumping from the nineteenth floor was a religious act —Norman Mailer, *Harper's,* March 1971

viable This adjective, which literally means "capable of living" (as in "a viable fetus"), has been much criticized as a vogue word that is imprecisely used in place of such established alternatives as *workable* and *practical*. It is not a new word; the OED shows that it has been used in both literal and figurative senses since the middle of the 19th century. Its use, however, has become common only in recent decades. Our evidence shows that its rise in popularity began in the 1940s:

... the chances of a viable international order — Max Lerner, *New Republic,* 7 July 1941

A viable society is one in which those who have qualified themselves to see indicate the goals to be aimed at —Aldous Huxley, *The Perennial Philosophy,* 1945

... the restoration of truly viable peacetime conditions —*Commonweal,* 31 May 1946

By the 1950s it had become a common word—common enough to attract unfavorable attention:

The last word on our list, *viable,* is threatening to become as fashionable among intellectuals and their camp-followers as are *ambivalent* and *dichotomy* — Ben Ray Redman, *Saturday Rev.,* 2 Mar. 1957

Commentators who have criticized *viable* in the years since include Flesch 1964, Gowers in Fowler 1965, Newman 1974, Harper 1975, 1985, Phythian 1979, and Bryson 1984, among others. The repeated criticism has had no apparent effect on the word's popularity:

Is it possible that feminist concerns ... are no longer viable as subjects for serious fiction? —Joyce Carol Oates, *N.Y. Times Book Rev.,* 21 Nov. 1976

... the ability to plan and finance a viable presidential campaign —Carll Tucker, *Saturday Rev.,* 21 July 1979

If ... performing arts and cultural programs on TV become commercially viable —Peter Caranicas, *Saturday Rev.,* January 1981

... that the new league, slimmed down to 16, would be more viable —Clive Gammon, *Sports Illustrated,* 5 Oct. 1981

... NASA worked out a viable relationship with J.P.L. and Cal Tech —Henry S. F. Cooper, Jr., *N.Y. Times Book Rev.,* 9 Jan. 1983

Dictionaries recognize these uses of *viable* as standard, and so should you, but you may also want to approach this word with some caution. The voluminous evidence that we have collected testifies to its being a heavily used—and some would say overused—word. Misgivings about this word may be particularly in order with respect to its use in the phrase *viable alternative,* as this phrase, innocuous as in itself it really is, is so frequently used that it is sure to strike some readers or listeners as a cliché.

vice, vise In American English, the "moral fault" is spelled *vice* while the "clamping tool" is spelled *vise.* In British English, *vice* is the preferred spelling for both the fault and the tool.

victual This word, which is pronounced \\\'vit-²l\\, provides a good example of the confusion that can result from artificial tampering with the language. It was originally borrowed from Middle French in the 14th century as *vitaille* (with many variant spellings). The present spelling resulted from the efforts of 16th-century grammarians to restore the word to a form more closely resembling its Latin ancestor, *victualia.* They succeeded in establishing the new spelling, but the old pronunciation remained unchanged. The result was yet another English word whose spelling and pronunciation have little in common—just what the language did not need.

The noun *victual* is almost always used in the plural. It is now widely regarded as a rustic or homely synonym for *food:*

> ... encourage the ... townspeople and their mountain neighbors to swap victuals for tickets —Jerry H. Simpson, Jr., *Southern Living,* July 1972

> ... I was putting away a heaping plate of down-home victuals —Tom Wicker, *N.Y. Times,* 24 Dec. 1976

> The clamor of soup being slurped testified ... to the enjoyment of the victuals —George Feifer, *Cosmopolitan,* February 1972

The variant *vittles* also occurs in such contexts. It is standard, and it is admirably consistent with the word's pronunciation, but it is less common than *victuals:*

> ... "Ma, are ye goin' to let all the vittles get cold?" —Ruth Suckow, "A Rural Community," in *Mid Country,* ed. Lowry C. Wimberly, 1945

> "Well, I'll declare," Martha put in.... "I don't see how you city folks live on such scanty vittles." — *Southern Literary Messenger,* September 1940

Vittles seems to occur most often in representations or transcriptions of rustic speech, where the Latinate *victuals* appears out of place.

Victual is also used as a verb, usually meaning either "to supply with food" or "to lay in provisions." The verb does not have the rustic connotations of the noun:

> ... his cart and two horses lost in the king's service while victualling the castle —article from *Irish Echo,* reprinted in *Irish Digest,* November 1953

> ... American whalers who victualled at the port — *Australian Dictionary of Biography,* 1966

vie *Vie* is typically used with the prepositions *with* and *for:* competitors vie *with* each other *for* something desired. Using *against* rather than *with* in such a context has been called a mistake, although similar verbs, such as *compete* and *fight,* may be followed by either preposition, and although the meaning of *with* in "vie with" is actually "against." In truth, the only good reason for

not using *against* with *vie* is, simply, that almost no one does so, at least in print. Our files include only a single citation (from 1944) for *vie against,* compared with more than 50 for *vie with.* Here are a few examples of the common prepositions:

> ... we have lately been vying with the Russians in an ostrich-like and naïve absurdity —Edmund Wilson, *A Piece of My Mind,* 1956

> Welsh literature vies with Irish in antiquity —Simeon Potter, *Language in the Modern World,* 1960

> ... hosts of other social and civilian programs are vying for the federal budget dollar —*Forbes,* 1 Dec. 1970

> Diverse objects, both contemporary and antique, vie for attention —Monica Meenan, *Town & Country,* July 1980

view The phrase *with a view* usually takes the preposition *to:*

> ... treating patients ... with a view to bringing about benefit, if not cure —Morris Fishbein, *The Popular Medical Encyclopedia,* 1946

> ... began acquiring Monhegan's wildlands ... with a view to preserving them in their natural state — Eleanor Sterling, *Yankee,* July 1968

Alternative prepositions are *toward* and *of,* both of which occur much less frequently than *to:*

> ... studying the structure of the Federal Government, with a view toward reorganizing the executive branch —*Current Biography 1947*

> ... prompted the boy to turn back ... with a view of asking Miss Eustacia Vye to let her servant accompany him home —Thomas Hardy, *The Return of the Native,* 1878

When the phrase is *with the view* rather than *with a view,* *of* is almost invariably the preposition that follows:

> ... accepted a second term as governor with the view of winning the United States senatorship —*Dictionary of American Biography,* 1928

The OED treats *with a view of* (for which the earliest evidence is from 1723), *with a view to* (1728), and *with the view of* (1827) as standard phrases. Fowler's preference in 1926 was for *with a view to,* although he also found *with the view of* acceptable. He considered *with a view of* to be a mistake, but it is not clear why he thought so. (*With a view toward* is not mentioned in the OED or in Fowler.)

Some later commentators have followed Fowler's lead in prescribing against *with a view of,* but this is not an issue that stirs deep feelings. One reason for the lack of vehemence in this case may be that, as our evidence shows, the favored phrase *(with a view to)* is also the one most commonly used. The other phrases should not be sneered at, however; although uncommon, they are standard variants with a long history of use.

Fowler also disliked the use of the infinitive following *with a view to,* as in "with a view to preserve" rather than "... to preserving" or "... to preservation." His opinion may have had some effect in this case; although the OED includes several earlier citations for this use, our files contain not a single 20th-century example of it.

viewpoint A few critical brickbats have been directed at *viewpoint* since it was coined in the mid-19th century, but it has never been subjected to a full-scale assault. Most modern commentators who take note of this word regard it as a useful alternative to *point of view*. Simon 1980 is almost alone when he says "centuries of sound tradition have hallowed *point of view* as preferable to the Teutonism *viewpoint*." The evidence does not support him. The OED does include a single 18th-century citation for *point of view* (a gloss from Chambers' *Cyclopaedia*, 1727–41), but the first evidence showing its actual use in running text is from the early 19th century (in Coleridge's periodical *The Friend*, 1809–10), not all that long before *viewpoint* was first used (1856). It appears to us that *viewpoint* and *point of view* are about equally hallowed. In any case, they are both certainly standard:

> ... it probably produces more variety of age and viewpoint —Kingman Brewster, Jr., *Yale University: Report of President 1967–68*

> Like print reporting—a magazine article or a newspaper analysis—"Teddy" [a television program] had a viewpoint —Richard Reeves, *Panorama*, February 1980

> ... the points of view represented seem almost impossibly diverse —Alan Anderson, *Saturday Rev.*, 6 Nov. 1973

> Her point-of-view and how, or if, it differs from the viewpoints of others —Susan Jacoby, *N.Y. Times Book Rev.*, 10 Oct. 1982

See also POINT OF VIEW; STANDPOINT.

view with alarm *View with alarm* is sometimes called a cliché that is a typical bit of political bombast, but the most conspicuous thing about the phrase may be its elusiveness. William Safire mentions it in *Safire's Political Dictionary* (1978) but has no examples of its use, and H. L. Mencken (*The American Language, Supplement I*, 1945) notes that it is missing from the Dictionary of American English and the Dictionary of Americanisms.

Our first evidence of the phrase is from 1926. Our later evidence shows that it can be used straightforwardly and unbombastically:

> Liebling views with alarm the trend toward fewer newspapers —*Time*, 10 Nov. 1947

> Mr. Krutch is not alone in viewing with alarm the growing use of scientific techniques in the study of man —Ernest Nagel, *New Republic*, 28 June 1954

But its present status as a cliché may be discouraging writers from using *view with alarm;* we have very little current evidence for it.

vigilant When *vigilant* is used with a preposition, the choice is most often *against, in,* or *to:*

> ... we should be eternally vigilant against attempts to check the expression of opinions that we loathe —Oliver Wendell Holmes d. 1935, *Abrams et al. v. United States*, 1919

> All of us ... must be vigilant in preserving our birthright —Adlai E. Stevenson, *Speeches*, ed. Richard Harrity, 1952

> We must be eternally vigilant to prevent that —Peter P. Muirhead, quoted in *Change*, October 1971

Occasionally, *vigilant* may be followed by *about* or *for:*

> ... has always been cannily vigilant about the moneys coming in —Robert Lewis Taylor, *New Yorker*, 28 Apr. 1956

> The saints at table, ever vigilant for propriety, are uneasy —William Laurence Sullivan, *Epigrams and Criticisms in Miniature*, 1936

violoncello It is logical to suppose that the beginning of this word is spelled like *violin*, and in fact the spelling *violincello* has turned up in respectable surroundings on occasion:

> Mr. Skimpole could play on the piano and the violincello —Charles Dickens, *Bleak House*, 1852 (OED)

Nevertheless, the original and accepted spelling is *violoncello*. The reason for the difference is that *violin* is derived from *violino*, "little viola," while *violoncello* is derived from *violone*, "big viola." You can commit that distinction to memory if you like, or you can do what most people do (as Copperud 1970, 1980 points out) and just use *cello* instead.

virtual subject See LET 2.

virus *Virus* has occasionally been used to mean "a virus infection":

> ... has recovered from a virus which confined her to home for several days —*Springfield* (Mass.) *Daily News*, 21 May 1954

> If cancer is a virus —Pat McGrady & Murray Morgan, *Saturday Evening Post*, 9 May 1964

This sense of *virus* is analogous to the sense of *bug* meaning "a disease caused by a germ." It is not especially common in print but seems common enough in speech. In any case, it is not likely to occur on the pages of a medical journal. The only usage commentator to take note of it is Bernstein 1965, who dislikes it.

vis-à-vis The literal meaning of *vis-à-vis* in French is "face to face," and it has had some use in English (as in French) as a preposition meaning "face to face with":

> His master dived down to him, leaving me *vis-à-vis* the ruffianly bitch —Emily Brontë, *Wuthering Heights*, 1847 (OED)

But *vis-à-vis* is far more familiar in its two extended senses, "in relation to" and "in comparison with," both of which it also has in French, and both of which have been in use in English since the 18th century. They now occur fairly commonly in writing, to which they impart something of a continental tone:

> ... the idea that the proper role of the press, vis-a-vis government, lies in an adversary relationship —Moll Ivins, *Change*, March 1972

> ... the division and the decline of Europe vis-a-vis the two superpowers —*Wall Street Jour.*, 6 Jan. 1982

> A standoff will have been achieved vis-à-vis the Russians —Mary McCarthy, *N.Y. Times Book Rev.*, 9 Feb. 1986

> ... the militia called Amal ..., which still stands for moderation vis-à-vis more militant Shiites —Mary

Catherine Bateson, *N.Y. Times Book Rev.,* 25 May 1986

These uses of *vis-à-vis* are largely uncontroversial (although Follett 1966 insists that *vis-à-vis* should only be used "with a clear sense" of its literal meaning).

It now appears that a slight further extension of meaning is creating the additional sense "with regard to; concerning":

It is true that between 1930 and 1933, many papers were neutral vis-à-vis Nazism —Walter Laqueur, *N.Y. Times Book Rev.,* 20 June 1982

Bernstein 1965 cites such usage as an error, and our evidence shows it to be relatively rare. It does not, however, represent a radical shift in meaning from the established sense "in relation to."

vise See VICE, VISE.

visit, visit with A few British critics unfamiliar with American idiom have misunderstood the phrase *visit with* as a needlessly wordy alternative to *visit.* Most Americans, however, will instantly recognize that to "visit with someone" is not the same as to "visit someone." "Visit with" is actually a typical American use of *visit* as an intransitive verb meaning "chat" or "converse." This sense of *visit* seems to have originated in the Southern U.S. during the late 19th century. It is often, but not always, followed by *with:*

We visited with him for two hours —*The Autobiography of William Allen White,* 1946

Chances are you've visited with your neighbors often about what should be done in Washington today —*Successful Farming,* December 1953

I know a village full of bees,
 And gardens lit by canna torches,
Where all the streets are named for trees
 And people visit on their porches
  —Phyllis McGinley, *New Yorker,* 4 Aug. 1951

As the last quotation shows especially well, this intransitive *visit* often carries connotations of friendship and neighborliness. To say that you "visited with" someone usually implies not only that you conversed, but that you went a bit out of your way for the sake of some friendly talk.

visitation A few commentators are concerned that *visitation* should not be used interchangeably with *visit.* They would be reassured to see our citational evidence, which confirms that the two words, although basically synonymous, are used in distinct ways. *Visit* is, of course, the more general and widely applicable word. *Visitation* normally connotes a visit that is in some way out of the ordinary, as in having a formal or official nature or a supernatural dimension, or as in representing a kind of benefaction:

The Dalai Lama continued his unprecedented visitation of his followers and friends in England yesterday —Philip Howard, *The Times* (London), 24 Oct. 1973

When the assessor arrives on his annual visitation —Jonathan Evan Maslow, *Saturday Rev.,* 16 Sept. 1978

The nun was as elated as if she had had a blessed visitation. It *was* a visitation. A glow suffused her heart —Harry Hervey, *Barracoon,* 1950

. . . the rare visitations of evening grosbeaks and bluebirds that make one feel, quite unjustifiably, like one of the chosen —Eleanor Perenyi, *Green Thoughts,* 1983

Visit would be possible in any of the above passages, but it lacks the connotations that make the longer word especially apt there. *Visitation* also has several distinct uses for which *visit* is not possible:

The town suffered severely from a visitation of the plague in the 17th century —*The Encyclopedia Americana,* 1943

Spreading the use of the parks by having more visitation in spring and fall —Robert Cahn, *Christian Science Monitor,* 15 May 1968

. . . said she would help her own adopted children seek their biological parents when they reach the age of majority. But she objected to visitation rights before that time —Nadine Brozan, *N.Y. Times,* 23 Jan. 1978

Use of a room in the funeral home for a three-hour "visitation" costs about $370 —David Black, *Harper's,* September 1985

visual *Visual* is sometimes used to mean "visible":

. . . finding a visual equivalent for feelings which enrich experience —Michael Kitson, *Encounter,* February 1955

This sense of *visual* is not new. It was used in 1756 by Edmund Burke, who wrote of "visual beauty" and "perceptions and judgments on visual objects." Such usage is standard but uncommon. It is most likely to occur in contexts where the writer is distinguishing that which can be seen from that which is perceived by the other senses—contexts, in other words, where the emphasis is on the sense of vision rather than the specific object of vision. It does not occur in contexts such as "The horizon became visible as the fog cleared" or "His distress was clearly visible."

vittles See VICTUAL.

viva voce See HYPERFOREIGNISMS.

vocal chords, vocal cords See CHORD, CORD.

voice The use of *voice* as a verb meaning "to express in words" (as in "voice a complaint") has attracted sporadic criticism for many years. Hall 1917 noted that it was "sometimes condemned by writers on usage" but was also recognized as standard in dictionaries and had occurred in the works of good writers dating all the way to Sir Francis Bacon. He added, however, " . . . it is true that it is a 'pet word' with a certain class of speakers not recognized as authorities." More recent commentary has come from Flesch 1964, who finds the verb "pompous," and Copperud 1980, who feels that "there is no question that *voiced objections, voiced praise* are wordy and indirect for *objected, praised.*" What our evidence shows is that *voice* has distinct connotations that make it a useful and appropriate verb in many contexts. It usually implies not simply expressing something, but expressing it publicly or openly:

> . . . he is not ashamed to voice his dismay at British mismanagement —*Time,* 4 Dec. 1950

> Norris' book . . . was eagerly accepted by the young naturalists of the time as a manifesto voicing their aesthetic creed —Charles I. Glicksberg, *American Literary Criticism 1900–1950,* 1951

> . . . part of a new proposal voiced by Ellen Sulzberger Straus, a leader in the volunteer movement — *McCall's,* March 1971

> The response was usually sour; teachers voiced anger at having been deceived —Joseph Pilcher et al., *People,* 20 Dec. 1982

The OED notes that *voice* in this sense has been common since the late 19th century in both England and the U.S.

void   When the adjective *void* is followed by a preposition, the preposition is *of:*

> . . . a drama which . . . is really void of sexual interest —George Bernard Shaw, preface to *Man and Superman,* 1903

> . . . a force directly opposed to him and void of love —Norman Mailer, *Harper's,* March 1971

The OED includes two citations showing *void* used with *in,* but we have no modern evidence of such use.

vulnerable   Derived from the Latin verb *vulnerare* "to wound," *vulnerable* originally meant "capable of being physically wounded." It is now rarely used with that meaning, but it continues to thrive in modern English because of the popularity of its figurative, extended senses. When used figuratively, *vulnerable* is often followed by the preposition *to:*

> ". . . you're less vulnerable to whatever horrors happen in life." —Herman Wouk, *Marjorie Morningstar,* 1955

> This timetable was, of course, terribly vulnerable to bad weather —John Kenneth Galbraith, *The Scotch,* 1964

> . . . those institutions most vulnerable to government pressure —Daniel P. Moynihan, *Atlantic,* August 1968

W

wait on, wait upon   The use of *wait on* (sometimes *wait upon*) to mean "wait for," as in "We waited on him but he never came," has been attracting criticism for one reason or another for well over a century. H. L. Mencken in *The American Language, Supplement I* (1945) reports that an unidentified writer using the name Aristarcus attacked Noah Webster in a series of articles published in 1801, part of the argument of which concerned some real or imaginary Americanisms, including *wait on* for *wait for.* There seems to be no connection, however, between the attack on Webster, which was apparently politically motivated, and the criticism of *wait on* that can be found in many 20th-century usage books. Frederic G. Cassidy, chief editor of the Dictionary of American Regional English, is quoted in Safire 1980 as placing the start of the modern objection somewhere around the middle of the 19th century.

Cassidy also discusses the geographical distribution of *wait on.* Basing his comments on materials collected for the DARE, he divides the U.S. into a Northern *wait for* area and a Southern *wait on* area. Dialectal studies conducted earlier broadly confirm the generalization, which can be interpreted to suggest that the objection to *wait on* is at least in part a matter of northern prejudice, the chief pedagogical publishers being located mainly in the north. Cassidy ascribes the present distribution of *wait for* and *wait on* to a standoff between "Southern conservatism and Northern schoolmarming."

On the other side of the Atlantic, Foster 1968 records a resurgence in the use of *wait on* in the British press during the 1950s and especially the 1960s. He ascribes the revival to American influence.

The written record, so far as we have collected it, shows that the *wait on* question is even more complicated than the preceding remarks would suggest. The OED records fifteen geographically unrestricted meanings for *wait on,* plus a couple of Scotticisms. Most of the senses of *wait on* are marked as obsolete in the OED, but several have survived, including the familiar "serve" sense, and the sense "to call on, pay a visit to." A sense "to accompany, go along with, escort," which is quite old, seems from OED and Dictionary of American English evidence to have survived at least into the 1880s. It can be found in the works of Shakespeare, Evelyn, Congreve, Defoe, Cleland, and Washington Irving, among others. The Dictionary of American English and the American Dialect Dictionary both record an American specialization of the "call on" sense: "to pay court to." The OED further notes a use frequent in the King James Bible:

> Say not thou, I will recompense evil; but wait on the Lord, and he shall save thee —Proverbs 20:22 (AV), 1611

The OED definitions that equate to various uses of *wait for* are all attested in the second half of the 17th century (Milton and Bunyan are among those cited). Lack of 18th- and 19th-century evidence undoubtedly led the editor, Henry Bradley, to mark them obsolete. Because the uses began to crop up again in the middle of the 19th century, however, it is unlikely that they had vanished altogether; they must have survived beyond the watchful eye of dictionary editors. The earliest American example in the ADD is dated 1852, but you will recall that *wait on* came up in the 1801 attack on Webster, so it had clearly survived in this country. It had survived in England, too:

> . . . no groups of idle or of busy reapers could here stand waiting on the guidance of a master, for there was no farm here —Thomas Carlyle, *The Life of John Sterling,* 1851

Carlyle probably learned the phrase from usage prevalent north of Hadrian's Wall. It seems not improbable that the post–World War II revival in British English resulted as much from latent native memory as from American stimulation. Here, for instance, it crops up in a work by an Australian author:

> . . . I ventured to observe that "Foote's trick of waiting on a laugh was old. . . ." —Hugh McCrae, *Story-Book Only,* 1948

This citation is from a group of anecdotes written in imitation or parody of Boswell's *Life of Samuel Johnson,* and we do not know whether McCrae used *wait on* naturally, thought it was an 18th-century literary use (something it was not, in fact), or used it as a bit of theater terminology. In any case, examples of *wait on* from other parts of the Commonwealth are not hard to find:

> They all began drifting off. Mac waited on Bob and me —A. P. Gaskell, "The Big Game," in *New Zealand Short Stories,* ed. D. M. Davin, 1953

> But he wouldn't burn it tonight, because we were waiting on Johnny.
> 'Is there any sign of him?' said Mammie, when Daddy came in again —Michael McCaverty, "Pigeons," in *The Best British Short Stories 1936,* ed. Edward J. O'Brien

> . . . courtship is unduly prolonged and marriage has to wait on the price of the wedding —John D. Sheridan, *Irish Digest,* February 1955

> Even the ceiling looked as if it was waiting on something —Richard Llewellyn, *None But the Lonely Heart,* 1943

> The fridge I'd been waiting on 12 months was delivered within two days of your notification —letter, *Sunday Post* (Glasgow), 19 July 1964

This quick survey takes in a fair number of varieties of British English and drops us back in Scotland where we began with Carlyle. It is really not surprising, then, that *wait on* has reappeared in mainstream British English.

> But this should not wait on private capital which is especially hard to find in a drought-stricken land — Lord Rennell, *Geographical Jour.,* September 1953

> . . . hours spent in line waiting on eightpence-worth of beef —Leslie Eytle, *London Calling,* 25 Feb. 1954

> . . . negotiation at Geneva must wait upon disengagement in Syria —*The Economist,* 2 Feb. 1974

> We have done our best to give the crops a good start and now we must wait on Nature —*Country Life,* 9 May 1947

The ADD shows that *wait on* for *wait for* was once fairly widespread in American use. The bulk of the material is Southern and Midland, but here and there bits of northern evidence are seen. Edith Wharton's *Ethan Frome* (1911) is cited, for example; it is set in western Massachusetts. If recent evidence from speech shows *wait on* to be predominantly Southern and Midland, the evidence from printed sources since around World War II does not appear to be so limited. Here is a sampling:

> An adequate answer to these questions must wait on the survey I have mentioned —James B. Conant,

Report of the President of Harvard University to the Board of Overseers, 1940–1941

> But settlement of the big problems still waited on Russia —*Time,* 6 Nov. 1944

> While waiting on events to shape the answer . . . — Samuel Lubell, *Saturday Rev.,* 27 Dec. 1952

> . . . pictures, which once had to wait upon the slow processes of wood engraving —Frank Luther Mott, *The News in America,* 1952

> . . . the rest must wait on public realization, acceptance, and support —Bernard DeVoto, *Harper's,* August 1952

> For two days I've been waiting on weather. A general storm area hovers over the Rocky Mountains — Charles A. Lindbergh, *The Spirit of St. Louis,* 1953

> I couldn't make out from your letter whether Harper was waiting on me for approval —E. B. White, letter, 14 May 1954

> The funeral would not wait upon a man's ability to pay for it —Oscar Handlin, *The American People in the Twentieth Century,* 1954

> . . . they've been waiting on a new novel from him for over six years —Hamilton Basso, *The View from Pompey's Head,* 1954

> I don't want to undertake something you don't want me to undertake. I therefore wait upon your word — Archibald MacLeish, letter, September 1955

> . . . problems whose solutions have long waited upon the coordinated worldwide scale of the IGY effort — *Newsweek,* 9 July 1956

> . . . there was another one waiting on me when I got back —Flannery O'Connor, letter, 5 May 1956

> . . . the staggering bill that waited on them at the white commissary downtown —Maya Angelou, in *Exploring Literature,* ed. Louise Grindstaff et al., 1981

> She sat in the back of the store, her pencil over a ledger, while he stood and waited on children to make up their minds —Eudora Welty, in *The Contemporary Essay,* ed. Donald Hall, 1984

> A true measure of Borg's achievement, however, must wait on a comparison with other individual sports and sportsmen —Curry Kirkpatrick, *Sports Illustrated,* 16 July 1979

> . . . the boredom of the black Africans sitting there, waiting on the whims of a colonial bureaucracy — Vincent Canby, *N.Y. Times,* 23 Jan. 1983

> . . . doesn't care to sit around waiting on a House that's virtually paralyzed —Glenn A. Briere, *Springfield* (Mass.) *Sunday Republican,* 8 Apr. 1984

Note that the meaning of *wait on* (and *wait upon*) varies in these passages. The use of *wait on* that is most often singled out for criticism in usage books occurs when it is clearly equivalent to *wait for* in the sense "await; await the arrival, appearance, or occurrence of," as in Flannery O'Connor's ". . . there was another one waiting on me when I got back." This is the use of *wait on* that appears to be most strongly identified with the South and Midland, and that is probably least likely to occur in general writing outside those areas. The other uses of *wait on* illustrated above are also more or less equivalent to *wait for,* but they suggest other meanings; such as "to wait in deference to or because of" or "to be dependent on." These uses of *wait on* have not attracted the attention of usage commentators, even though many of them insist that *wait on* should only be used to mean "to serve" in writing.

We conclude that *wait on* for *wait for* cannot be accurately characterized as dialectal, colloquial, regional, or substandard; on the contrary, it is found in standard and widely circulated sources. If it has been the mission of Northern teachers to stamp out *wait on,* they have failed in more places than just the South. *Wait for* continues to be more common, as it has been since the 18th century, especially in the North and especially when its meaning is clearly "to await." But there is nothing intrinsically wrong with *wait on* or its occasional variant *wait upon.* If the use of *wait on* is natural to you, there is certainly no need to avoid it.

waive, wave The usual meaning of *waive* is "to relinquish" or "to refrain from enforcing," as in "to waive a right" or "to waive a rule." It is also sometimes used in a sense synonymous with *wave:*

> ... concrete troubles and evils remain. They are not magically waived out of existence —John Dewey, *Reconstruction in Philosophy,* 1920

> He would waive the whole business aside —Oliver St. John Gogarty, *It Isn't This Time of Year at All!,* 1954

> ... said "no,"
> And waived them off
> —Edgar Lee Masters, "Finding of the Body," *Domesday Book,* 1920

This sense of *waive* was first attested in 1832. It undoubtedly arose from confusion with *wave,* and it is widely regarded as an error. The prudent thing to do is to use *wave* instead.

wake, waken We had a phone call not long ago from a concerned grandmother who was disturbed by her grandson's use of the past participle *woken.* She knew only *waked* and was surprised to find that *woken* was recognized as legitimate in the dictionary. *Wake* is a verb whose usage has changed in this century, and it will probably continue to change for some time to come. *Waken* is included here only by way of contrast: its principal parts are regular—*wakened, wakening*—and have not changed at all.

The ferment noticeable in the past and past participle of *wake* comes from its origin. In the beginning there were two separate verbs, one intransitive with irregular principal parts and the other causative or transitive with regular principal parts. These coalesced in Middle English, and our modern muddle of inflected forms is the result.

The OED tells us that the strong forms *woke* and *woken* are not found in Shakespeare, the 1611 Bible, or Milton's verse. The strong forms were in use by other writers around the same time, but Samuel Pepys used the weak forms:

> But, Lord! the mirth which it caused to me, to be waked in the night by their snoring round about me —diary, 1 Oct. 1665

Woken was described as perhaps "obsolescent" in the OED in 1921; Fowler 1926 thought *woke* and *woken*

both rare. But both forms, *woke* especially as the past tense, have undergone a revival in the 20th century, and are at the present time the dominant forms.

For the past tense, *woke* is usual:

> The porter woke by himself —James Thurber, letter, 4 Sept. 1944

> ... he woke once with the moonlight on his face — Ernest Hemingway, "An African Betrayal," in *Sports Illustrated,* 5 May 1986

> Every morning you woke to the smell of bread from the bakery downstairs —Jay McInerney, *Bright Lights, Big City,* 1984

> ... I woke to hear the clickety-clack of the wheels — Anthony Bailey, *New Yorker,* 29 July 1985

Waked was more common formerly than it is now, but it has not disappeared from use:

> My *Republican* was borrowed before I waked — Emily Dickinson, letter, August 1884

> ... and only just waked up in time to dress for breakfast —*New Yorker,* 28 Nov. 1970

For the past participle, *woken* is the predominant form in British English:

> I have just been woken up from my summer sleep by the first rugger practices —Robert Graves, letter, 11 Sept. 1918

> In the mornings he was woken by his butler —Julian Huxley, *Memories,* 1970

> ... one night he was woken by someone coming into the bedroom —Graham Greene, *Getting to Know the General,* 1984

In American English *woken* and *waked* are both used for the past participle:

> Woken by a flashlight held close to her face —*New Yorker,* 9 Aug. 1982

> ... he had woken them, clearing his throat —John Updike, *Playboy,* 1 Jan. 1982

> ... I knew this was one time he would not mind being woken up —Harrison E. Salisbury, *N.Y. Times Mag.,* 17 Apr. 1983

> During the night he has waked up sweating —Mary McCarthy, *Occasional Prose,* 1985

> ... is waked this morning by the whistling of the 7:18 —John Cheever, *The Wapshot Chronicle,* 1957

> ... she had been waked up out of that bed every morning —Dianne Benedict, *Atlantic,* February 1982

Woke as the past participle is less frequent:

> ... it must have woke him up —Ted Williams & John Underwood, *The Science of Hitting,* 1971

See also AWAKE, AWAKEN.

wangle, wrangle *Wangle* and *wrangle* are easily distinguished in most of their uses. *Wangle* has the basic sense, "to accomplish something in a scheming or indirect way," while *wrangle* basically means "to argue or engage in controversy." Thus, one wangles out of difficulties, for example, and the opposing sides in a labor dispute wrangle over a new contract. The distinction in most cases is clear, but not when the two verbs occur in such contexts as the following:

> . . . he had to wangle independent financing —Hollis Alpert, *Saturday Rev.,* 16 Nov. 1974

> The big "execs" were worried about how to wrangle more money and prestige from the new democratic order —Bill AuCoin, *Redneck,* 1977

> . . . delivering luxury yachts to distant ports and wangling . . . cushy deals —Ray Kennedy, *Sports Illustrated,* 14 May 1984

> Rebuked by Mayor Koch in his attempt to wrangle a multimillion tax abatement and zoning exemptions —*Newsweek,* 29 June 1987

This may look like a simple case of one verb being confused for the other, but the matter is not quite as straightforward as that. Both *wangle* and *wrangle* appear to have developed the sense "to obtain" independently. The OED shows that *wrangle* was used to mean "to obtain by wrangling" (that is, by arguing or bargaining) as far back as 1624:

> We wrangled out of the King ten quarters of Corne for a copper Kettell —Captain John Smith, *The Generall Historie of Virginia,* 1624 (OED)

Wangle, a newer verb of American origin, has been used in the sense "to obtain by wangling" (that is, by slyly using one's influence or powers of persuasion) since at least the early 20th century:

> . . . and when in home waters had 'wangled' a few days' leave —*Bulletin,* 28 Dec. 1917 (OED)

The "obtain" sense of *wrangle* was labeled "obsolete or rare" by the OED in 1928, but recent decades have seen its renewed use is due in part to the success of *wangle* in its own "obtain" sense— and may in fact be mainly the result of confusion about which word is which. Nevertheless, the "obtain" sense of *wrangle* is established in reputable use, and is treated as standard by current dictionaries. The "obtain" sense of *wangle* is also standard, of course, and is appreciably more common than that of *wrangle.*

want Several informal idioms with *want* are commonly cited with disapproval in usage handbooks. The most frequent admonitions are against the use of such a construction as "I want for you to do this" instead of "I want you to do this." This "want for" construction appears to be limited to informal speech; we have found no evidence of it in published sources. It should not be confused with the use of *want for* to mean "lack," which is standard:

> The museum will never want for relics of Lewes' colorful history —Jay Dugan, *Ford Times,* March 1955

> No one in the movie wants for anything but love —Pauline Kael, *New Yorker,* 3 Feb. 1973

Also standard, as Heritage 1982 points out, are such constructions as "What I want is for you to do this" and "I want very much for you to do this," in which the clause introduced by *for* does not follow immediately after *want:*

> . . . she very much wanted, we all did, for him to succeed —Mary Jane Truman, quoted in Merle Miller, *Plain Speaking,* 1973

A related issue concerns the use of *want* with a clause introduced by *that* as its object:

> They wanted that the debts due them should be paid, or payable, in gold —Mark Sullivan, *Our Times,* vol. 6, 1935

Again, such usage appears to be limited almost entirely to speech. The normal written construction would be "They wanted the debts due them to be paid. . . ." As with the "want for" construction, however, the use of *want* with a *that* clause is standard when the clause does not immediately follow the verb; for example, "What they wanted was that the debts due them should be paid. . . ."

Want is sometimes used as a virtual synonym of *ought:*

> You want to be very careful what you say about such music —Claudia Cassidy, *Europe—On the Aisle,* 1954

> You want to buy three yards of each color material selected —Robert J. Pearcy, *Cats Mag.,* January 1982

> . . . you want to have a large, impressive bandage —James Gorman, *People,* 21 Mar. 1983

The informality of such usage has attracted frequent commentary, dating back at least to Ball 1923. The usual judgment has been that it is best avoided in writing. In informal writing, however, it is neither uncommon nor inappropriate.

See also WANT IN, WANT OUT.

want in, want out The use of *want* in the elliptical sense "to desire to come, go, or be" (as in "the cat wants in") is generally regarded by usage commentators as a colloquialism to be avoided in writing. The OED indicated in 1921 that such usage was then chiefly a characteristic of Scottish, Northern Irish, and American speech. It was first attested in 1844, and it has been repeatedly discouraged in American usage books at least since MacCracken & Sandison 1917. Its popularity in the U.S. seems to have formerly been somewhat localized, being confined primarily to the Midwest and to the Appalachians, but it has grown increasingly widespread over the years and is no longer strongly associated with any particular region.

The elliptical *want* is especially common in the phrases *want in* and *want out,* both of which now occur frequently not only in speech but also in writing. Written use tends to be figurative:

> Mr. Davis, who now wants in again, has been advised that he has a good prospect of becoming naturalized in 1952 —*New Yorker,* 14 Oct. 1950

> Some others prefer not to join; some want in, but have not yet been admitted —Joe Alex Morris, *Saturday Evening Post,* 15 May 1954

> . . . it is recognized that the President wants out and the Joint Chiefs of Staff and Senator Knowland want in —Richard H. Rovere, *New Yorker,* 26 Feb. 1955

> Cypriots . . . want out of the Commonwealth —*Time,* 11 July 1955

> . . . some students are astonished at Aviation's rules and regulations, and want out —Peter Janssen, *N.Y. Times Mag.,* 7 Dec. 1975

But he wanted out, and we agreed to take care of him —Daniel P. Moynihan, *N.Y. Times Book Rev.,* 17 Feb. 1985

The informal quality of *want in* and *want out* is evident, but that informality can be useful in expressing a sense of urgency or determination that may not be communicated as well by a more formal alternative. The same holds true for other uses of *want* in its elliptical sense:

... airline pilots all wanted back in the Air Force — *Newsweek,* 20 Dec. 1948

... will want off at the second floor —Bill Harrison, *Saturday Evening Post,* 11 Dec. 1954

ESPN badly wants into the NFL —William Taaffe, *Sports Illustrated,* 29 Sept. 1986

warn Use of *warn* as an intransitive verb is common and widespread, although it is actually a fairly recent development. It seems to have originated in American English in the early 20th century. American dictionaries have recognized the intransitive *warn* as standard for many years, but several prominent British dictionaries continue to omit it, suggesting that it may occur less commonly in British than in American English. (On the other hand, Sir Ernest Gowers noted in his 1965 revision of Fowler that "intransitive use ... is now common in journalism.") Few commentators have warned against its use. Those who have would revise the preceding sentence so that *warned* has a direct object, making it something like "Few commentators have warned their readers against its use." Such revision is unnecessary and may even be awkward or misleading in contexts where the warning is directed generally rather than to a specific individual or group:

... which warns of the approach of spring —Mary Austin, *Starry Adventure,* 1931

But he warns against what he thinks might well turn out to be a fatal illusion —Alain Locke, *Key Reporter,* Autumn 1951

Often in the years that followed, Gottwald warned against the rising tide of Fascist parties —*Current Biography 1948*

wary *Wary* is often followed by *of:*

... we should be wary of the sensational book on a scientific subject —Charles E. Kellogg, in *The Wonderful World of Books,* ed. Alfred Stefferud, 1952

The rector was a large man and ... not at all wary of clerical black —John Cheever, *New Yorker,* 16 Apr. 1955

He did, however, seem wary of reporters —Trevor Armbrister, *Saturday Evening Post,* 12 Feb. 1966

A less common preposition following *wary* is *in.* It obviously could not be used in any of the above quotations, but it does occur when a cautious or hesitant approach toward *doing* something is described or advocated:

... leads the student to be wary in giving his trust to the professor —W. David Maxwell, *AAUP Bulletin,* September 1969

... let us be very wary in introducing it into education —Robert Ennis, in *Invitational Conference on Testing Problems,* 1 Nov. 1969

Of could certainly be used in such contexts, but its use would result in a slight change of meaning. To be wary *in* doing something is to do something warily, while to be wary *of* doing something is usually to avoid doing it at all:

... potential black enrollees are wary of entering institutions where they will be isolated —Francis X. Cannon, *Change,* September 1971

You should also be wary of choosing an insurer solely on the basis of low rates —Charles A. Cerami, *Woman's Day,* October 1971

Another possible preposition after *wary* is *about.* It occurs in the same contexts as *of,* but less often:

... the liberal is increasingly wary about the process of centralizing power —Eric F. Goldman, *The Reporter,* 23 June 1953

was, were See SUBJUNCTIVE; YOU WAS.

watershed Back in 1926, H. W. Fowler had this to say about the correct use of *watershed:*

The original meaning of the word ... was the line of high land dividing the waters that flow in one direction from those that flow in the other. The older of us were taught that this was its meaning, & that the senses river-basin & area of collection & drainage-slope were mere ignorant guesses due to confusion with the familiar word *shed.*

Fowler noted sadly that the "mistaken senses" had "found acceptance [even] with those who could appreciate the risks of ambiguity," but they certainly had not found acceptance with him. "The old sense should be restored & rigidly maintained," he wrote.

Fifty-eight years later, James J. Kilpatrick had some thoughts of his own about *watershed,* specifically concerning its widespread figurative use to mean "a dividing point or line":

Properly speaking, a *watershed* is not a single point or a sharp line; it is a whole region or area in which water drains in a particular direction. ... If we are determined to use clichés, let us use clichés with some feeling for accuracy. ...

Indeed. It looks to a Fowlerian as if Kilpatrick has committed a howling blunder, but perhaps his mistake about what *watershed* means, "properly speaking," is not all that blameworthy. The physical sense of *watershed* that Kilpatrick knows is, in fact, far more common, at least in American English, than the older sense prescribed by Fowler. The older sense is still treated as the principal one in British dictionaries, but in American English Fowler's "line of high land" is known as a *waterparting* or *divide.* Most Americans, if they stopped to think about it, would probably be struck as Kilpatrick was by the apparent disparity between the literal sense and the figurative sense of *watershed.*

Watershed seems to have originated as a translation of the German word *wasserscheide,* with which it is synonymous in its oldest sense. The earliest evidence for *watershed* in the OED is from 1803. The senses to which Fowler objected began to appear in print several decades later—the "drainage-slope" sense in 1839 and the "river-basin" sense in 1874. By the end of the 19th century, the "river-basin" sense was firmly established in American English; it was entered as the first sense of *watershed* in Webster 1890.

Our earliest evidence for the figurative use of *watershed* is from the 1920s:

> ... follows a narrow path, a kind of "watershed" between biography and bibliography —D. B. Updike, *Printing Types,* 1922

> ... the quality of the expected settlement is best expressed in Mr. Chamberlain's phrase that it will be "a real watershed between peace and war...." —*Manchester Guardian Weekly,* 16 Oct. 1925

The quotation from Sir Austen Chamberlain perfectly illustrates the sense of *watershed* that is now so popular among politicians and journalists. We have sporadic evidence for this sense throughout the 1930s and 1940s, but it seems not to have caught on in a big way until about 1950. It is now far and away the most common sense of the word:

> ... looks more and more like one of history's great watersheds —Stewart Alsop, *Saturday Evening Post,* 30 May 1964

> ... may turn out a watershed in the way people look at China —Ross Terrill, *Atlantic,* November 1971

> ... we may be experiencing a watershed phenomenon, a historic ideological turning point —Robert Lewis Shayon, *Saturday Rev.,* 27 Nov. 1971

> ... to understand why evolution was such a watershed in the history of ideas —Stephen Jay Gould, *Natural History,* October 1984

> ... a sociological as well as a scientific watershed in astronomy —Wallace Tucker, *Sky and Telescope,* April 1985

When Sir Ernest Gowers revised Fowler's *Modern English Usage* in 1965, he concluded the discussion of *watershed* by noting hopefully that "the figurative use of watershed now in journalistic favor may help to preserve its proper meaning." However, the widespread figurative use of *watershed* has shown no sign of reviving its "proper meaning," at least in American English. We cannot be certain, but it appears likely that many of the people who now use *watershed* in its figurative sense have little idea what the word originally meant.

wave See WAIVE, WAVE.

wax The verb *wax,* in the sense "to grow or become," is uncommon enough in present-day English for some writers to feel a little uncertain about how to use it. Copperud 1980 cites a passage in which "TV commentators" are said to have "waxed authoritatively." We have evidence in our files of a similar error:

> ... he does not wax enthusiastically over combining rock and symphonic music —*Philharmonic Hall,* December 1970

Standard English requires "wax enthusiastic," just as it requires "become enthusiastic." The reason for the confusion is presumably that such phrases as *wax authoritative* and *wax enthusiastic* normally relate to speech or writing, so that *wax enthusiastic* is almost equivalent in meaning to *speak enthusiastically.* Writers who follow *wax* with an adverb apparently understand it as meaning "to speak or hold forth," but that meaning is not established. For the phrase *wax wroth,* see WRATH, WRATHFUL, WROTH.

way, *noun* The noun *way* has a sense that means approximately "manner, method." Woolley & Scott 1926 notice and disapprove uses of this sense in which what they think are necessary parts of the structure of the sentence are omitted. Here are a couple of examples to which we have added in brackets the parts Woolley & Scott would prefer to be included:

> I never write [in] that way —John O'Hara, letter, 11 Oct. 1956

> The way [in which] the virtue of the purest is corrupted here is wonderful —Henry Adams, letter, 9 Feb. 1859

The objection seems to be to the use of the noun as if it were an adverb. But worse than that, *way*—as *the way*—can be used in constructions in which even more words are left out:

> How do girls learn to smile [in] the way [in which *or* that] they do? —G. A. Birmingham, *Found Money,* 1923

Woolley & Scott recognize this use of *way* as a conjunction; their preferred revision replaces *the way* with *as.*

The OED includes the adverbial uses Woolley & Scott object to; they date back as far as the 14th century. But coverage of the conjunction appears to be missing. The OED Supplement adds a conjunction, but it is Irish, and it means approximately "so that":

> ... adroitly donning his wet hat the way he could raise it for politeness —Flann O'Brien, *At Swim-Two-Birds,* 1939

The Irish use can be found in Webster's Third also, but the only connection it bears to the use in the G. A. Birmingham example is that both are conjunctions (Webster's Third does not recognize the latter use though it recognizes a third conjunctional use that we will come to below). Here are a few more examples later than Birmingham:

> ... makes orange juice the way Helen wants it — James Thurber, letter, 6 Oct. 1937

> Her dialogue reads the way a conversation overheard in a restaurant sounds —Jane O'Reilly, *N.Y. Times Book Rev.,* 1 Apr. 1973

> ... I'm not making lasagna or Caesar salads the way I used to, but I'm stir-frying up a storm —*And More by Andy Rooney,* 1982

> His mother had been a scrubwoman, and he wasn't going to let these ladies suffer the way she had —Tip O'Neill with William Novak, *Man of the House,* 1987

Perhaps you noticed the fact that you could easily use the disputed conjunction *like* in place of *the way* in these examples. Perrin & Ebbitt 1972 noticed it; they say that this use of *the way* provides an escape from the choice between *like* and *as.* James Thurber used this escape route many times in his writing.

The usage surveys of Leonard in 1932 and Crisp in 1971 both found no objection to this use of *the way* in American English; the people surveyed considered it established. Mittins 1970 and Longman 1984, however, report resistance to it in Great Britain. We do not know how common the construction is in British English.

The way is used in a couple of other meanings. It can

mean "in view of the manner in which"—the other sense to be found in Webster's Third:

> ... he was nervous being around them the way they carried their rifles —Garrison Keillor, *Lake Wobegon Days,* 1985

It can also mean "how," especially in fixed phrases:

> That's the way the cookie crumbles —Goodman Ace, *Saturday Rev.,* 16 Oct. 1976

> This is the way it goes with writers: they resent you to the degree that they depend on you —Jay McInerney, *Bright Lights, Big City,* 1984

If you are an American, you can feel safe using conjunctive *the way* in any of these three senses in writing of a casual tone; you may also find it a useful way to get around the *like* and *as* controversy. The dictionaries will eventually catch up with you and Thurber and the rest.

way, *adverb* *Way* was first used as an adverb way back in the 13th century. An apheteic form of *away*—that is, a form created by the dropping of a short, unaccented vowel—it was used only occasionally until the 1800s. The now familiar use of *way* to mean "by a long distance or great amount; far"—as an intensifier, actually—was first recorded in 1849. This use quickly became established in American English and was eventually adopted by the British as well. It continues to be extremely common both in speech and writing:

> ... in his place—and that's way, way down —William H. Whyte, Jr., *Saturday Rev.,* 21 Nov. 1953

> ... is above cost, but abroad it goes for from thirty-five to fifty cents, which is way below —Dwight Macdonald, *New Yorker,* 3 Dec. 1955

> ... are way off base —Robert Shaplen, *New Yorker,* 27 Feb. 1954

> ... are way ahead of the faculties of almost all other nations —Kingman Brewster, Jr., *Yale University: Report of President 1967–68*

> ... falls way short of what might have been done —William Bundy, *Saturday Rev.,* 10 June 1978

> ... the market ... was way down —William F. Buckley, Jr., *New Yorker,* 31 Jan. 1983

> ... moved way beyond any claims —Christopher Butler, *After The Wake,* 1980

The similar use of *way* to mean "all the way" also originated in the 19th century. It occurs primarily in American English:

> ... was new way back in 1880 —Lewis Mumford, *New Yorker,* 26 Sept. 1953

> ... way out near the end of a scarcely travelled byroad —Robert M. Coates, *New Yorker,* 20 Oct. 1951

Usage commentators in the early 20th century tended to view the adverbial *way* with disfavor, but in recent decades it has won general acceptance. It was formerly written with an apostrophe, *'way,* but such styling is no longer very common.

See also WAYS.

ways *Ways* has been used as a synonym of *way* in such expressions as "a long ways off" since at least 1588. The OED includes citations for this use from Henry Fielding, Lord Byron, and Stephen Crane, among others. In this century, it has been called different things by different critics (Ambrose Bierce, for one, called it "surprising"), but the usual label is something like "colloquial" or "informal." It occurs widely, however, and is by no means limited to the spoken language:

> We went inland a ways —H. L. Mountzoures, *New Yorker,* 30 Oct. 1971

> ... the downturn still has a ways to go —Alan Abelson, *Barron's,* 24 July 1972

> ... a short ways outside of Greenfield —Peter Marshall, *Massachusetts Wildlife,* September–October 1969

> Casey's idea of fund-raising was quite a ways from mine —Wilfrid Sheed, *People Will Always Be Kind,* 1973

> ... still a long ways from a solution —Raymond W. Murray, *Man's Unknown Ancestors,* 1943

> ... any wholesale hacking away at production facilities ... seems a ways away —*Business Week,* 2 Feb. 1981

Such usage is standard in American English. In British English, on the other hand, it appears to have died out (the British dictionaries which enter *ways* now label it "North American"). Its occurrence in writing is still frowned upon by a number of commentators. *Way,* of course, occurs more commonly, and without any stigma.

we **1.** The use of *we* to mean "I" is very old in English. The OED dates such use by sovereigns, sometimes called the "royal *we,*" back to the time of Beowulf, and includes citations from Henry VI, James I, and Charles I. A famous example of the royal *we* is Queen Victoria's "We are not amused."

Just as old—or perhaps a bit older—is the use known nowadays as the "editorial *we,*" which the OED also traces back to before 1000. The editorial *we* gets its name from its use in newspaper editorials, in which it is meant to imply that a collective rather than an individual opinion is being expressed. More generally, it typically serves to give a less personal tone to the writing in which it occurs. (Its use for this purpose in academic papers is noted by Robin Lakoff in *Language and Women's Place,* 1975; she terms it the "academic-authorial *we.*") Its occasional use in casual prose tends to have something of a playful quality, perhaps with overtones of the royal *we:*

> It is just as well I didn't sign this letter ... , for in the interval since I wrote the last paragraphs, we have had a flood of letters ... , entirely restoring our good humor —Alexander Woollcott, letter, October 1917

The casual editorial *we* is well known to readers of the *New Yorker* magazine, in which it was long ago adopted as a stylistic mannerism. A good idea of its quality can be gained from the following examples, taken from a single issue:

> ... the following Sunday evening, we called him up and asked if we might talk with him —*New Yorker,* 2 May 1988

An hour later, when we were in the front seat of a cab heading crosstown and Matt and his cello were riding in the back, we turned around and asked if he could tell us about his instrument —*New Yorker,* 2 May 1988

We couldn't resist asking His Royal Highness what he thought of the architectural pronunciamentos of his cousin Prince Charles —*New Yorker,* 2 May 1988

We can also indicate that the speaker or writer identifies himself or herself with a group (in this example, referred to by a generic singular, *architect*):

... his view of how an architect works is more romantic than accurate. He thinks we jump out of bed in the morning and design any pretty building that happens to enter our heads —The Duke of Gloucester, quoted in *New Yorker,* 2 May 1988

There are in addition a couple of oral uses of *we*—not much found in writing—that receive occasional mention by commentators. These are characterized by Perrin & Ebbitt 1972 as "the kindergarten *we* (We won't lose our mittens, will we?)" and "the hospital *we* (How are we feeling this morning?)".

These various uses of *we* should not be cause for concern. Consider that the *New Yorker* has been using *we* for a half century or better, and making it sound sophisticated. All you really need worry about is its appropriateness to the piece you are writing; there is nothing wrong in the *we* itself.

2. The OED, with typical thoroughness, devotes a whole numbered sense of *we* to its uses in place of *us;* the earliest example comes from the dawn of the 16th century. The OED assures us that *we* for *us* is now heard only from the uneducated. It is certainly to be found in the speech of the fictional uneducated:

What makes we New Yorkers sore is to think they should try and wish a law like that on us —Ring Lardner, *The Big Town,* 1921

But we also have some evidence of its use by the educated. The writer of the next example is noted on our citation as the literary editor of a prestigious British newspaper:

... at that time in the faculty of English was J. R. R. Tolkien; he was equally at the disposal of we cadets —Anthony Curtis, *British Book News,* June 1977

Note that in these examples *we* turns up hard by an appositive ("we New Yorkers"). Most of our evidence for the accusative *we* shows it occurring with appositives.

In some dialects of English, *we* has captured even more ground. A calypso by Lord Kitchener has this line, quoted in the *Trinidad Guardian,* 29 Jan. 1975: "Give we back we stadium." It will probably be quite some time before mainstream American and British English reach that level of caselessness.

wean A peculiar extension in the meaning of *wean* has occurred in the 20th century. The word means, in its literal sense, "to accustom (a child) to take food other than by nursing," and, in an established figurative sense, "to detach from a cause of dependence or preoccupation":

Despite gallant efforts to wean the populace from the tube —Carll Tucker, *Saturday Rev.,* 15 Sept. 1979

Increasingly common, however, is the use of *wean* as a figurative synonym of *raise* or *rear.* Our earliest evidence of this use is from the letters of Fred Allen:

Babies are being weaned on aspirin to fortify them for the economic headaches they will certainly face —Fred Allen, letter, 6 May 1931

You are too late to stunt Figgi's growth. He should have been weaned on black coffee —Fred Allen, letter, 11 Dec. 1933

No doubt other people besides Allen were using *wean* in this way in the 1930s (and perhaps earlier), but, curiously, we have no further evidence of such usage until 1958:

Boswell, who happens to come from a line of English coach builders and who was weaned on timber, so to speak —Ernest O. Hauser, *Saturday Evening Post,* 9 Aug. 1958

The new use of *wean* was noticed and criticized by Bernstein 1965, but we did not begin to encounter it with any frequency in print until the 1970s. We now find it occurring in a wide range of publications:

... I was carefully weaned on G. A. Henty —Glen Frankfurter, *Books in Canada,* October 1972

... a handsome Conservative MP who can be said to have been weaned in the television studios — Hardcastle, *Punch,* 2 Oct. 1974

... Parisians, weaned on truffles and sauces —Ted Burke, *Town & Country,* June 1976

... State Department veterans weaned on the notion that good will can be measured in dollars given away —*Wall Street Jour.,* 27 Aug. 1982

Musicians weaned on the free jazz of the sixties — Gary Giddins, *Atlantic,* November 1982

Weaned on the microcomputer, ... these pubescent youngsters have been hailed ... —Frank Rose, *Science 82,* November 1982

... speak as if they were weaned on Twinings English Breakfast Tea —Jay McInerney, *Bright Lights, Big City,* 1984

... a writer weaned on the short story —*N.Y. Times Book Rev.,* 17 Mar. 1985

Exactly how this use of *wean* originated is hard to say. It may be that such a phrase as "weaned on timber" was meant to suggest that timber was the form of nourishment, figuratively speaking, which took the place of nursing when the child was weaned. Or perhaps it was a simple case of confusion about the meaning of *wean.* The question is now academic, in any case, since it is apparent that the new sense of *wean* has established an independent existence for itself, apart from the literal meaning of the word. Its eventual appearance in dictionaries is just a matter of time, if its use continues at its current rate. It has not yet acquired the status of a full-blooded usage controversy, but that too may be just a matter of time.

weave When *weave* is used in its literal senses ("weave cloth," "weave a basket"), its usual past tense and past participle are *wove* and *woven:*

... people who wove their homespun clothes — *American Guide Series: North Carolina,* 1939

The nest was woven of grass tucked into a slight depression —Dr. Henry Marion Hall, *Massachusetts Audubon,* June 1968

The same inflected forms are normally used in straightforward figurative applications of *weave:*

... Thomson wove together folk dances, waltzes, marches ... , and original tunes —*Current Biography,* October 1966

... values and perceptions long woven into the fabric of society —Osborn Elliot, *One Nation Divisible* (published speech), November 1969

But when *weave* describes a winding course of movement ("weave down the field"), the form that usually serves as both its past tense and past participle is *weaved:*

The men ... weaved through the grass —Norman Mailer, *The Naked and the Dead,* 1948

... Russian and U.S. delegates ... have weaved through a maze of procedural and technical arguments —*Time,* 17 Mar. 1947

These observations are not hard and fast rules by any means, but they do reflect the practice usual among current writers.

wed *Wed* is an old Anglo-Saxon word that has been largely displaced in its literal sense by *marry,* a word derived from French. The literal sense of *wed* is now most likely to occur in special contexts, including popular songs ("Oh, how we danced on the night we were wed") and in the marriage ceremony itself:

With this Ring I thee wed —*The Book of Common Prayer,* 1789

As has been noted by several commentators, the literal sense of *wed* is also used in newspaper headlines, where its brevity gives it an advantage over *marry.* Its use in general contexts is relatively uncommon, but it does occur:

... a tendency for young people to wed earlier — Elizabeth Ogg, *When a Family Faces Stress,* 1963

So I finished the manuscript and wedded an ornithologist —Priscilla Bailey, *Massachusetts Audubon,* June 1968

In July 1942 Grant wed Woolworth heiress Barbara Hutton —*Current Biography,* November 1965

The past and past participle of *wed* is usually *wedded,* but the form *wed* occurs as a secondary variant. The OED called this variant dialectal in 1926, but the evidence no longer supports that label. *Wed* is used in standard speech and writing as a past and past participle of the literal sense of *wed* (as in the above quotation from *Current Biography*) and of its much more common figurative senses:

It may seem ... that we are wed to our test tubes — Peter Benchley, in *Cosmopolitan,* July 1974

... choose mates in marriage who would also be wed to The Times —Gay Talese, *Harper's,* January 1969

... a program in which dancing and skating are inextricably wed —Chip Greenwood, *Rolling Stone,* 7 Feb. 1980

weep The past tense and past participle of *weep* is *wept:*

... when winter wept its damp upon the panes — Virginia Woolf, *Between the Acts,* 1941

... how you had mourned for me, and wept for me —Charles Dickens, *Bleak House,* 1853 (OED)

A variant form, *weeped,* shows up once in a great while in reputable writing:

All the way in she weeped and wailed —Flannery O'Connor, letter, 24 Feb. 1962

He talked of how his brother ... had weeped over his loss —Michael Goodwin, *N.Y. Times,* 4 Oct. 1982

Weeped, however, is far too rare to be judged a standard variant. Use *wept.*

weird *Weird* is one of a number of words that give the lie to the old chant, "*i* before *e* except after *c* or when sounded as *a,* as in *neighbor* and *weigh.*" There is no *c* in *weird,* and no *a* sound either, but the *e* comes before the *i* just the same. Other words that break the "rule" are *either, neither, foreign, forfeit, height, leisure, seize,* and *seizure.*

For a discussion of the vagaries of English spelling, see SPELLING.

welch See WELSH, WELCH.

well 1. There are those who will criticize your "do good" and your "feel badly," but you are safe no matter how you use *well. Well* has been both an adjective and an adverb since the time of King Alfred the Great, and you can use it with impunity after a linking verb:

... I imagined it might be well to publish the articles —Benjamin Franklin, *Autobiography,* 1788

It is not well to say "the fact affords a reasonable presumption" —Bierce 1909

We had a very neat chaise from Devises; it looked almost as well as a gentleman's —Jane Austen, letter, 5 May 1801

... if I couldn't think well of Clara, I'd turn my mind from her —E. L. Doctorow, *Loon Lake,* 1979

... it is well to preserve a distinction —Harper 1985

See also GOOD; FEEL BAD, FEEL BADLY.
2. Well, what about that prefatory *well* that so many of us put in front of sentences? It must have been given some unfriendly attention in the mid-19th century, for Alford 1866 discusses what he calls "prefatory particles," and after examination decides that they are "by no means to be proscribed." He thinks they are all right in conversation, that is; he does not recommend their use in writing. Woolley & Scott 1926 calls this *well* "a colloquialism, not proper in a formal context." That is essentially what Dean Alford was saying. Phythian 1979 would have us eschew prefatory *well* altogether.

This *well* also goes back to the time of King Alfred the Great. The OED's evidence shows *well* used in conversation and in various not especially formal writings. We find it being used often by American literati in their letters:

The large things in the book—well I won't name them —Robert Frost, letter, 7 Dec. 1916

Well, I have been living at the front with the infantry —Alexander Woollcott, letter, 6 July 1918

Well, anyway, we got to New Orleans for the Mardi Gras —Ring Lardner, letter, 23 Feb. 1926

Well, what happened was this —Archibald MacLeish, letter, 11 Mar. 1929

Well good evening Mr. G. —Ernest Hemingway, letter, 15 July 1934

Well, I love my country and I like to live free —E. B. White, letter, 4 Feb. 1942

Well, I took out my jimmy pipe and my Persian slipper —John O'Hara, letter, 1 Dec. 1948

Well, I didn't expect you to like it much —Conrad Aiken, letter, 13 Aug. 1969

And we find it occasionally in general prose that is cast in a casual style:

I was very, well, conscientious about this mission —Alan Coren, *Punch,* 18 May 1976

Well, this reader would have liked to know more —J. Max Bond, Jr., *Natural History,* October 1981

Well, for one thing, oil prices . . . have started rising again —Lindley H. Clark, Jr., *Wall Street Jour.,* 26 Jan. 1987

well-nigh The adjective *well-nigh* has been variously called "antique" (Fowler 1926, 1965), "a cliché" (Partridge 1942), "rustic or comic" (Evans 1957), and "medieval" (Flesch 1964). None of these characterizations is given much support by the evidence in our files. *Well-nigh* is a fairly common word, which in general appears to be nothing but a perfectly good synonym for *nearly:*

The attractions . . . are well-nigh irresistible —Norton E. Long & Nena Groskind, *Change,* May 1972

. . . the pressures for conformity . . . have been well-nigh overwhelming —Martin Kilson, *N.Y. Times Mag.,* 2 Sept. 1973

The resultant recording is well-nigh perfect — Thomas Heinitz, *Saturday Rev.,* 24 Apr. 1954

. . . the evidence is well-nigh unimpeachable —Morris Fishbein, *The Popular Medical Encyclopedia,* 1946

. . . was actually a well-nigh total edulcoration of the novel —John Simon, *Atlantic,* April 1982

welsh, welch The proper noun and the proper adjective which refer to the people, things, and language of Wales are almost always spelled *Welsh. Welch* is an established but uncommon variant. The verb meaning "to avoid payment" or "to break one's word" is also usually spelled *welsh,* but the variant *welch* is widely used. Whatever its spelling, the verb is typically followed by *on:*

. . . the Devil has never tried to welsh on a deal — Peter Andrews, *N.Y. Times Book Rev.,* 1 Aug. 1982

. . . did not want Linda to think that he'd welsh on a promise —Mordecai Richler, *The Apprenticeship of Duddy Kravitz,* 1959

. . . would accuse the networks of welshing on some vital public responsibility —Ron Powers, *Inside Sports,* August 1982

. . . state officials welched on the deal —John Fischer, *Harper's,* December 1970

The townspeople have not welched on their agreement —Cyril E. Bryant, *Christian Herald,* December 1969

The etymology of the verb has never been conclusively established, but some connection with *Welsh* seems probable.

Welsh rabbit, Welsh rarebit The dish that goes by the name *Welsh rabbit* or *Welsh rarebit* has no rabbit in it, is not especially rare, and may not even be originally Welsh (one of the sources in our files identifies it as "a very old Italian dish"). It consists essentially of melted cheese with a few well-chosen additions (such as beer, mustard, and red pepper) served over toast or crackers. The name *Welsh rabbit* was first given to this humble dish during or some time before the early 18th century, presumably by the same kind of wag as those who later gave the name *Cape Cod turkey* to codfish and *Arkansas T-bone* to bacon. The earliest written evidence for *Welsh rabbit* is from 1725. When Francis Grose defined *Welsh rabbit* in *A Classical Dictionary of the Vulgar Tongue* in 1785, he mistakenly indicated that *rabbit* was a corruption of "rare bit." It is not certain that this erroneous idea originated with Grose, or even that his book had much to do with spreading it, but before long *Welsh rarebit* had become established as a synonym of *Welsh rabbit. Welsh rarebit*—sometimes shortened to just *rarebit*—is now the more common name, although *Welsh rabbit* is also frequently used. Neither term is likely to occur very often outside of cookbooks and menus, except in discussions about which name is the correct one.

what As a relative pronoun, *what* is quite old, apparently having been introduced into Old English on analogy with some uses of *quod* in Latin; in the 13th century it appeared in natural English idiom. Its chief survival in writing is in the combination *but what,* which is discussed at BUT 5. As a plain relative, meaning "who, that, which," *what* has largely dropped out of mainstream English and has retreated to mostly oral use in rural areas. Our present evidence shows that relative *what* survives in the United States primarily in Midland and Southern speech areas and is used chiefly by the little educated. It was once in frequent use by dialect humorists:

"Well, when we got there I went to the basket what had the vittles in it. . . ." —William C. Hall, "How Sally Hooter Got Snakebit," 1850, in *The Mirth of a Nation,* ed. Walter Blair & Raven I. McDavid, Jr., 1983

. . . Miss Watson, what's the sourest old Maid in the city —Frank W. Sage, D.D.S., *Dental Digest,* November 1902

And it still crops up in print in quoted speech, sometimes in fixed phrases:

You're looking at a man what ain't straining — George C. Wallace, quoted in *N.Y. Times,* 30 Mar. 1975

. . . dance with the ones what brung me —Representative Philip Gramm, quoted in *People,* 24 Jan. 1983

It also occurs, of course, in fictional dialogue:

"... Boy, the guy what thought it up sure was a smart one...." —Garrison Keillor, *Lake Wobegon Days,* 1985

what-clauses See AGREEMENT, SUBJECT-VERB: WHAT-CLAUSES.

whatever 1. Our evidence suggests that few people nowadays have occasion to write such a sentence as "Whatever did you mean by that?" However, if you do find yourself writing such a sentence, you may wonder whether or not you should insert a space between the *what* and the *ever.* Fowler 1926 was certain that the space should be there, and the OED also indicates that *whatever* is "more properly written as two words" in such contexts. The reasoning behind that opinion is straightforward: the *ever* was originally an intensive adverb added to such a sentence as "What did you mean by that?" in order to emphasize the bewilderment of the questioner (compare the adverbial phrase *in the world* in "What in the world did you mean by that?"). Those who favor keeping *what* and *ever* separate in such sentences believe that the *ever* is still properly regarded as a distinct word. The tendency to make the two words into one is strong, however, if only because the single word *whatever* is so common in its other, uncontroversial uses ("do whatever you want," "use whatever means are necessary," "no help whatever," etc.). The OED shows that *whatever* was being treated by some writers as an interrogative pronoun synonymous with *what* as far back as the 14th century. Current practice is hard to determine because this use of *whatever* (or of *what ever*) rarely occurs in writing, being limited entirely to questions that are far more likely to be spoken than written. The issue is, therefore, almost entirely academic. Nevertheless, a few recent commentators have expressed a strong preference for the two-word treatment (most do not address the subject), while almost all dictionaries now recognize the interrogative *whatever* as standard.

These general observations also hold true for such analogous terms as *however* ("However will we get there?"), *whenever* ("Whenever will they leave?"), and *wherever* ("Wherever did you put it?").
2. Fowler 1926 also warned against following *whatever* with *that,* as in "He dismisses whatever arguments that have been made against him." In such a sentence, *whatever* is being used as a synonym for *any.* There is some historical precedent for such usage, and we suspect that its occurrence in speech may be fairly common, but our evidence shows that it is extremely rare in edited writing. We think you would be well advised to omit *that.*
3. In recent decades, *whatever* has come to be widely used in the sense "whatever else might be mentioned; whatnot." This use of *whatever* occurs at the end of a series and is usually preceded by *or:*

. . . you drive along in comfort until you find your buffalo or rhinoceros or whatever —Alan Moorehead, *New Yorker,* 8 June 1957

. . . their current stocks of beer, toothpaste, or whatever —A. J. Liebling, *New Yorker,* 12 Jan. 1957

. . . we are always asking: Can I marry the girl I love? Can I sell my house? or whatever —W. H. Auden, *Columbia Forum,* Winter 1970

Sometimes the *or* is dropped:

. . . to provide baby-sitting, housekeeping, whatever —Gail Sheehy, *McCall's,* March 1971

. . . a play, a film, a series of paintings, whatever — Henry Bromell, *Change,* November 1971

This use of *whatever* has an obvious informal quality, and its popularity might be expected to raise a few hackles, but it has so far attracted little criticism. Howard 1980, in fact, finds that "the new use evidently fills a need and can, on occasions, be charming as well as useful."

when, where A substantial number of recent usage books and schoolbooks object to the use of *is when* or *is where* in framing definitions, which use is often described as childish or immature. Bryant 1962 finds the objection to be founded on the theory that it is improper to have a clause introduced by *where* or *when* follow the verb *be.* The usual argument runs that such clauses are adverbial and either a noun construction is needed after *be* or a verb (such as *occur*) that can take an adverb clause. (For another usage problem that is argued similarly, see REASON IS BECAUSE.) Bryant's cited studies show, however, that *when* and *where* clauses are commonly used after *be* in standard writing:

Midnight . . . is when the hydrogen war starts — Thomas K. Finletter, *New Republic,* 21 Feb. 1955

Experiences were many. Perhaps the most exciting was when the driving, sleety snowstorms came on winter nights —Willa Cather, *The Old Beauty,* 1948 (in Bryant)

Another exception is when you are writing for a specific market —Clement Wood, *Poets' Handbook,* 1940

He wanted the tree to be where he could enjoy it — *New Yorker,* 21 Dec. 1957 (in Bryant)

And that is where you come in —John O'Hara, letter, 23 June 1959

. . . Harlem was where the action was —Ishmael Reed, *N.Y. Times Book Rev.,* 29 Aug. 1976

This is where I say that I don't believe in scientists —James Thurber, letter, 6 Oct. 1937

. . . it's not smug to point out that anguish is where some artists need to live —Stanley Kauffmann, *Saturday Rev.,* 1 Nov. 1975

Recent commentators do not object to standard uses like these, even though they fall into the area covered by the general rule. Their objection is to definitions. These are harder to find in print, but they turn up once in a while:

Cop-out is when you duck an issue and refuse to face up to your thing —Ruth Nathan, *Plain Dealer* (Cleveland, Ohio), 22 Dec. 1968

What is humor? Humor is when you laugh —Earl Rovit, *American Scholar,* Spring 1967

Home is where you check your hat —*New Yorker,* 26 Oct. 1957 (in Bryant)

This issue appears to have had its origin in Goold Brown 1851, in which both the general principle and its specific application to definitions were laid down:

> Note VI.—The adverb *when, while,* or *where,* is not fit to follow the verb *is* in a definition, or to introduce a clause taken substantively; because it expresses identity, not of being, but of time or place. . . .

Early 20th-century handbooks—MacCracken & Sandison 1917, Ball 1923, Woolley & Scott 1926, Jensen 1935, for instance—carried a version of Goold Brown's general rule, but the objected-to constructions were almost always definitions. As we have already noted, few recent commentators bother with the general principle at all, which is just as well—there never has been any factual basis for it.

Leonard 1929 tells us that the *is when, is where* definition was freely utilized throughout the 18th century, and he gives short examples from the grammarians Greenwood (who originally published in 1711) and Lowth (who originally published in 1762). The evidence provided by Goold Brown bears out Leonard's observation. It includes a list of forty or so definitions drawn from grammar books, the bulk of which were originally published in the 18th century. Here are two of Goold Brown's examples:

> A Solecism is when the rules of Syntax are transgressed —Alexander Adam, *Latin and English Grammar,* 1772

> A Proper Diphthong is where both the Vowels are sounded together; as *oi* in *Voice* —A. Fischer, *Grammar,* 1753

It might be noted that Goold Brown's examples contain many more definitions with *is when* than with *is where.*

The 18th-century grammarians and their 19th-century imitators clearly found nothing wrong with *is when* and *is where* definitions. On the contrary, they must have thought them effective. But things seem to have changed after Goold Brown. A modern grammarian would not be caught dead writing such a definition, even though Bryant demonstrates that the *is when* definition sometimes can be both more compendious and more understandable than one framed to avoid *is when.* The dearth of printed examples leads her to conclude that *is when* definitions are knowingly avoided in writing, although they are common in speech. It may be that they sound too unsophisticated (or "childish," as the commentators would say) for written use. Our most recent examples are from speech, like this one:

> I've always said that power is when people think you have power —Tip O'Neill with William Novak, *Man of the House,* 1987

For whatever reason, it is no longer possible for grammarians and lexicographers to use the handy and understandable *is when* definition. This was regretted years ago by one of our colleagues during work on a dictionary intended for the elementary grades. You, too, will probably want to avoid *is when* definitions in your writing. The other *is where, is when* constructions are normal and standard. *Where* and *when* have been heading clauses used as nouns since Old English. Do not be afraid of either when it sounds right. For another branch of this tree, see WHERE 2.

when and if   See IF AND WHEN.

whence   See FROM WHENCE, FROM THENCE, FROM HENCE.

whenever   See WHATEVER 1.

where   1. See WHERE . . . AT.
2. A number of schoolbooks and college handbooks are concerned about the use of *where* in the sense "that" after the verbs *see* and *read.* The schoolbooks prohibit the use; the college handbooks find it informal. The use they describe appears to be more common in speech than in writing, but it is not rare in writing by any means:

> But I cannot see where the neurotic laboratory rats have served to deepen or enlarge our understanding of human behavior —Leslie A. White, *The Science of Culture,* 1949

> The music got on her nerves, and he could see where it would —John Cheever, *The Brigadier and the Golf Widow,* 1964

> You read where Pres. Reagan supports a move to repeal the 22nd Amendment, which limits the president to two four-year terms? —Herb Caen, *San Francisco Chronicle,* 5 Aug. 1986

The construction gets quite a bit of use in fictional dialogue as well:

> I have nothing against Mr. Jones personally, but I can't see where he's fitted to be President —Frank Sullivan, *A Rock in Every Snowball,* 1946

> Well, Al old pal I suppose you seen in the paper where I been sold to the White Sox —Ring Lardner, *You Know Me Al,* 1916

> He . . . cackled maliciously, "I suppose you saw where Forward Press folded up. . . ." —James A. Michener, *The Fires of Spring,* 1949

The issue as presented in the handbooks and schoolbooks is rather oversimplified. The criticized use is but one facet of a longstanding use of *where* to introduce noun clauses that serve as the objects of verbs. (This use—and similar use of *when*—has also occasionally been criticized; see WHEN, WHERE.) During the last two or three hundred years this use has become much more restricted than it once was, and *where* now introduces object clauses after only a few verbs such as *find, forget,* and *remember* as well as *see, read, tell,* and so forth. *Where* also often introduces a clause that modifies a noun, serving as an approximate equivalent to *in which:*

> I think mine is the case, where when they ask an egg, they get a scorpion —Emily Dickinson, letter, Autumn 1853

> I saw a Picture in the Paper last summer where the Prince was on one of his Horses and its name was Will Rogers —Will Rogers, *The Illiterate Digest,* 1924

> The other plays . . . where the director's name had been left off the screen I hadn't wondered why. I had understood —Goodman Ace, *Saturday Rev.,* 1 May 1954

> . . . the kind of dampness which puts out a cigarette after the third puff, the kind where you leave a pair of sneaks beside your bed at night, and in the morning you have to dump them before putting them on —E. B. White, letter, 11 July 1945

There are floor boards 14 inches wide, two fireplaces where you can bake bread in the ovens —Randall Jarrell, letter, 19 May 1952

. . . the sturdy admonishment addressed 'To the Principal and Professors of the University of St. Andrews, on their superb treat to Dr. Johnson', where the vigour and vulgarity of the vernacular enhance the abuse —John Butt, *English Literature in the Mid-Eighteenth Century,* edited & completed by Geoffrey Carnall, 1979

Another use of *where* is to introduce clauses that are the objects of prepositions.

But we kept that horse and gentled him to where I finally rode him —William Faulkner, 7 Mar. 1957, in *Faulkner in the University,* 1959

Strang 1970, citing Daniel Defoe, says that this construction came into use around the beginning of the 18th century.

What we have shown here is a sample of the ways in which *where* introduces noun clauses. The criticism of one aspect of such use in the handbooks is legitimate only insofar as it draws your attention, as do most of our examples, to the fact that this use is typically found in less formal kinds of writing.

whereabouts   The final *-s* in the noun *whereabouts* may look like a plural ending, but it isn't one. The noun is derived from the adverb *whereabouts,* and the *-s* is actually an adverbial suffix—one that also occurs in such words as *hereabouts, thereabouts,* and *towards.* The adverbial origins of that final *-s* have persuaded a few critics that the noun *whereabouts* should only be construed as singular, but the apparently plural form of the word seems to cry out for a plural verb.

The suspect's whereabouts is unknown.

The suspect's whereabouts are unknown.

Which would you say? Our evidence suggests that you are more likely to say "are" than "is." Either way, you are conforming to standard usage:

. . . his whereabouts was known only to his personal staff —*Fortune,* February 1954

. . . its exact whereabouts usually remains a secret guarded by hunters —*Our Appalachia,* ed. Laurel Shackelford & Bill Weinberg, 1977

His whereabouts are kept secret —*Manchester Guardian Weekly,* 20 Nov. 1936

Miss Watkins's whereabouts were established — Lewis Funke, *N.Y. Times,* 28 Jan. 1973

. . . its whereabouts remain elusive —Natalie Babbitt, *N.Y. Times Book Rev.,* 8 July 1973

where . . . at   The use of *at* following *where* was first noted in 1859 by Bartlett, who observed in his *Dictionary of Americanisms* that it was "often used superfluously in the South and West, as in the question 'Where is he *at?*'" Such usage first drew the attention of critics at the turn of the century, and they have routinely prescribed against it since. Although fairly common in speech, this construction rarely occurred in writing until the 1960s, when the idiomatic phrases *where it's at* and

where one is at came into widespread use by jazz and rock musicians, hippies, and others:

Harvey and I are going through this dynamic right now and it's kinda where I'm at —Cyra McFadden, *The Serial,* 1977

. . . grab them by the collar and tell them where it's at —Paul Mazursky, quoted in *Christian Science Monitor,* 22 Aug. 1980

. . . they realized vocals were where it's at —Charles M. Young, *Rolling Stone,* 29 Nov. 1979

. . . make sure you know just exactly where it's at — Hunter S. Thompson, *Rolling Stone,* 6 Jan. 1972

. . . naive to assume that if we all . . . find out where our heads are at, a social order will somehow result —Dr. Gordon K. Davies, *Emory and Henry Alumnus,* Summer 1980

. . . to develop in his readers a gut feeling for where modern biology is at —Gunther S. Stent, *N.Y. Times Book Rev.,* 8 Sept. 1974

These phrases continue to be used today, although they have some of the passé quality of old slang. They are most likely to occur when the language and attitudes of the 1960s and early 1970s are being deliberately evoked or mimicked. Other than in these phrases, *at* almost never occurs after *where* in writing from standard sources. See also AT.

whereby, wherein   Criticized by several commentators as archaic or excessively formal, these words continue nevertheless to be in widespread use as conjunctions in general as well as in more elevated prose:

. . . substituting a system whereby the federal government would return tax money to the states —*Current Biography,* October 1967

. . . a program whereby foreign-service officers will serve —David FitzHugh, *Saturday Rev.,* 18 Oct. 1975

. . . find approaches whereby they can learn —Dr. Jeanne Chall, *The Instructor,* March 1968

. . . chivalric fable wherein the heroine suffers and dies —John Seelye, *New York,* 15 Feb. 1971

. . . another book . . . wherein so many pronouns do (or attempt) the work of so few appositives —David J. Dwyer, *Commonweal,* 22 Aug. 1969

. . . a poetic style wherein . . . he can be the gregarious flirt —Richard Poirier, *A World Elsewhere,* 1966

. . . saw the rooms wherein and the devices whereby the enemies of Hitler were killed —Ben Hibbs, *Boy's Life,* September 1965

As an interrogative adverb (as in Shakespeare's "Whereby hangs a tale, sir?"), *whereby* is obsolete. *Wherein* continues to be used as an interrogative adverb, but only rarely:

Wherein lies the difference? —Louise M. Rosenblatt, in *The Promise of English: NCTE Distinguished Lectures,* 1970

wherefore   When Juliet asks, "O Romeo, Romeo! wherefore art thou Romeo?" she is not trying to find out if her true love is hiding in the bushes beneath her window. *Wherefore* means "why," not "where." Some confusion on this score seems to have resulted from the frequent use of this famous line in popular entertainment. A humorous takeoff on the balcony scene, for example, might feature a nearsighted Juliet squinting searchingly into the darkness as she asks wherefore her Romeo art (to which he might reply, "I'm right down here, Julie baby").

Another reason for the confusion is that *wherefore* is now rarely used, except as a noun meaning "reason":

> ... good to know the whys, hows, and wherefores of what you are seeing —Elin Schoen, *American Way,* December 1971

> ... the whys and wherefores of automated sound mixing —Michael Lydon, *N.Y. Times Book Rev.,* 23 May 1976

> ... questioning the whys and wherefores of disciplinary action —Noel McInnis, *Change,* January–February 1971

Note that *why* also means "reason" in such contexts, so that the alliterative phrase *whys and wherefores* could, it seems, be called redundant. In truth, however, to know the whys and wherefores is not simply to know the reasons, but to know *all* the reasons. The seemingly redundant phrase has an added meaning of its own.

wherein See WHEREBY, WHEREIN.

wherever See WHATEVER 1.

wherewithal Sometimes criticized as a fancy substitute for *means* or *resources,* this noun usually refers to substantial amounts of money—money that is often either lacking or hard to come by:

> We would guarantee not to be expensive guests, because through lack of wherewithal, we have forgotten how to spend money —John O'Hara, letter, December 1932

> ... the few competitors who did have the wherewithal to move from country to country —William Johnson, *Sports Illustrated,* 15 July 1968

> ... the club had never had the wherewithal to maintain it in first-class condition —Herbert Warren Wind, *New Yorker,* 10 Apr. 1971

But *wherewithal* can refer to other resources as well:

> The palm's juice is the staple of the people's diet and its leaves, leafstalks, and trunks provide the wherewithal for their housing —Rita Campon, *Natural History,* December 1985

> A force of thirty-six tourists but he doubted they had the wherewithal to hold up a gas station —Garrison Keillor, *Lake Wobegon Days,* 1985

whether See IF 1.

whether or not Numerous commentators have pointed out that *or not* is not always necessary after *whether,* as in "We don't know whether or not they'll come." They naturally recommend that *or not* should be omitted whenever possible, on the usual assumption that fewer words make better prose. It should be noted, however, that this use of *or not* is more than 300 years

old and is common among educated speakers and writers. It is, in short, perfectly good, idiomatic English:

> ... will you go and see it and tell me whether they murder it or not —George Bernard Shaw, letter, 28 Nov. 1895

> ... never knew whether or not to insert the names of his parents —John Updike, *Couples,* 1968

> ... determines whether or not a patient will be accepted —Joanne Nadol, *Johns Hopkins Mag.,* Summer 1971

> ... Mr. Truman turned to the general and asked whether or not he was satisfied —Dean Acheson, quoted in Merle Miller, *Plain Speaking,* 1973

> ... trying to determine whether or not she is wearing a bra —Jay McInerney, *Bright Lights, Big City,* 1984

> I don't know whether or not you are a writer of gobbledygook —Bailey 1984

The option of omitting *or not* only exists when the clause introduced by *whether* serves as the subject of the sentence or as the object of a preposition or verb, as in the above quotations. When the clause has an adverbial function, *or not* must be retained:

> Whether or not one agrees with Vidal's judgments, there are some trenchant formulations —Simon 1980

> ... adhere to some kind of ... methodology, whether or not it works —Daniels 1983

Of course, the simplest way to determine whether the *or not* can be omitted is to see if the sentence still makes sense without it.

An alternative to *whether or not* is *whether or no,* which is discussed at NO 3.

which **1.** For a discussion of *which* in restrictive and nonrestrictive clauses, and of what it, along with *who* and *that,* may refer to, see THAT 1, 2.

2. The use of *which* to refer to a whole sentence or clause, or as the OED puts it, to a fact, circumstance, or statement, was at one time considered a mistake. Thus Lurie 1927 could take Charles Reade and Charles Dickens to task for such use. The argument was, of course, that *which* should refer to a specific antecedent. But even Lurie had to admit that the authorities did not all disapprove the use, and almost all modern commentators find it acceptable. Some of them (Barnard 1979, Bernstein 1958, 1965, 1971, and Copperud 1970, 1980, for instance) warn against the possibility of ambiguity when it is uncertain whether the *which* refers to a preceding clause or to a noun at the end of it. Their ambiguous examples are, for the most part, not very ambiguous, but the clarity of the reference is an important consideration that you need to keep in mind. Here are a few examples of the construction:

> It was decided ... that the hotel glass should be returned to me, which it was —James Thurber, letter, 6 Oct. 1937

> We are to be at Astley's to-night, which I am glad of —Jane Austen, letter, August 1796

> ... but nobody really wanted to hear him speak. They wanted to see him grin and show his teeth, which he did —Harry S. Truman, quoted in Merle Miller, *Plain Speaking,* 1973

"I don't want to be a teacher," Father said quietly, which meant he was angry again —John Irving, *The Hotel New Hampshire,* 1981

You don't want to be talking to this bald girl, or even listening to her, which is all you are doing —Jay McInerney, *Bright Lights, Big City,* 1984

The cultural positioning of a work of art is often helpful, but, which is too often forgotten, it is quite distinct from esthetic judgment —Stanley Kauffmann, *Before My Eyes,* 1980

See also THIS 1.

while The earliest meanings of *while*—"during the time that," "as long as"—are temporal, but senses unrelated to time have been established in English since Shakespeare's time. American commentators decided that such use was questionable early in the 20th century, and they have continued to express doubts about it in the years since. Here are a few examples:

While it looks innocent enough, the white sand is a cause of miners' silicosis —Laurence Leamer, *Harper's,* December 1971

The hit shows are always sold out, and while there may be an occasional gem being ignored, most of what's left is third rate —*And More by Andy Rooney,* 1982

While Hume was very far from disparaging the ancients, . . . he was happy to live in eighteenth-century Britain —John Butt, *English Literature in the Mid-Eighteenth Century,* edited & completed by Geoffrey Carnall, 1979

. . . seemed to have been over-cleaned in restoration, while other pictures, which were gummy and dark, seemed to need restoration —Sanford Schwartz, *New Yorker,* 16 Sept. 1985

The mostly British *whilst* is also used in this way:

It is generally agreed that almost all of these alternative theories are excluded by the albeit meagre, experimental data, whilst none has the aesthetic appeal of Einstein's theory —P. C. W. Davis, *Space and Time in the Modern Universe,* 1977

The second part of the report deals with the detailed treatment of fences, railings, paths, and the like; whilst the final section puts forward ideas for the redevelopment of Quayside —*Book Exchange,* June 1974

These uses are established and standard. They are also extremely common. Bryant 1962 cites a study that shows *while* meaning "whereas" to be just as common as *whereas.*

A number of commentators raise the specter of ambiguity with respect to nontemporal uses of *while.* It is not very difficult to work up a sentence in which *while* can be understood in more than one way. If you happen to write such a sentence, you should certainly revise it. But you will notice that the examples above offer no ambiguity, and they are typical of the citations in our collection. Ambiguity is not an inherent problem in these uses of *while.*

whilom See ERSTWHILE, QUONDAM, WHILOM.

whiskey, whisky The spelling *whiskey* is used by Irish and American distillers; *whisky* is preferred by

their counterparts in Britain and Canada. Both spellings are used by Americans in general contexts (that is, other than on the label of a bottle of rye or bourbon), but *whiskey* is more common:

. . . he had been arrested and tried for making whiskey —William Faulkner, *Knight's Gambit,* 1949

. . . walking to the filing cabinet for the hidden whiskey —James Jones, *From Here To Eternity,* 1951

. . . produced bootleg whisky —Nicholas Pileggi, *New York,* 24 July 1972

. . . a glass of whiskey beside the typewriter —Arthur M. Schlesinger, Jr., *Saturday Rev.,* 29 Oct. 1977

Some writers make a point of omitting the *e* when referring specifically to whiskey distilled in Britain (that is, Scotland) or Canada.

whither See HITHER 1.

who, whom 1. It may seem that the use of these interrogative and relative pronouns should be simple enough: *who* is the nominative ("Who is it?") and *whom* is the objective ("the man whom we had met"). As is generally recognized, however, there is a certain disparity between the way *who* and *whom* are supposed to be used and the way they are actually used. Let us begin with a little lesson in Shakespeare.

LAUNCE. Can nothing speak? Master, shall I strike?
PROTEUS. Who wouldst thou strike?
LAUNCE. Nothing.
—*The Two Gentlemen of Verona,* 1595

BOYET. Now, madam, summon up your dearest spirits.
Consider who the King your father sends,
To whom he sends, and what's his embassy
—*Love's Labour's Lost,* 1595

MACBETH. . . . For certain friends that are both his and mine,
Whose loves I may not drop, but wail his fall
Who I myself struck down.
—*Macbeth,* 1606

ALBANY. Run, run, O, run!
EDGAR. To who, my lord? Who has the office?
—*King Lear,* 1606

POLONIUS. . . . I'll speak to him again.—What do you read, my lord?
HAMLET. Words, words, words.
POLONIUS. What is the matter, my lord?
HAMLET. Between who?
POLONIUS. I mean, the matter that you read, my lord.
—*Hamlet,* 1601

IAGO. Not this hour, Lieutenant; 'tis not yet ten o'th'clock. Our general cast us thus early for the love of his Desdemona; who let us not therefore blame.
—*Othello,* 1605

These examples have been chosen to show that Shakespeare was not at all averse to using *who* in places where the strict grammarians—who were still a century and a half away when Shakespeare wrote—would prescribe *whom.* They show, in addition, that he sometimes used both *who* and *whom* in the fashion later to be prescribed. Shakespeare's use does not in fact appear to be substantially different from present-day use; *who* for *whom* is most usual at the beginning of an utterance ("Who wouldst thou strike?"), but it sometimes occurs after a preposition or verb ("To who, my lord?"). And it should be noted that most of the speakers represented here are from the upper orders of society; these speakers are not louts or clowns. Nor was Shakespeare an innovator with these uses. Flesch 1983 notes that *who* had been substituted for *whom* in constructions like these as far back as the 14th century.

The anomaly of finding both *who* and *whom* used for objective functions did not escape the attention of the 18th-century grammarians. Lowth 1762 came out foursquare for strict construction, insisting on (for example) "Whom is this for?" rather than "Who is this for?" Only the considerable prestige of Milton's *Paradise Lost* dented Lowth's orthodoxy; he allowed *than whom* as an exception (see THAN 1). Priestley, at least as early as the 1769 edition cited by Leonard 1929, disagreed with Lowth, favoring "Who is this for?" as the more natural way of speaking. Leonard mentions several other grammarians of the age, each disagreeing with one point or another urged by some other grammarian, or introducing some new analogy. Noah Webster managed to write himself, through successive editions and works, from Lowth's position around to Priestley's.

The 19th-century grammarians seem not to have added anything of substance to the dispute. But Richard Grant White 1870 did sound a new note when he predicted the demise of *whom:*

One of the pronoun cases is visibly disappearing — the objective case *whom.*

Since White's solemn pronouncement, quite a few commentators have made the same observation. Here is a sampling:

Whom is fast vanishing from Standard American — Mencken, *The American Language,* 1936

If . . . we lose the accusative case *whom*—and we are in great danger of losing it —Simon 1980

Whom is dying out in England, where "Whom did you see?" sounds affected —Anthony Burgess, *N.Y. Times Book Rev.,* 20 July 1980

The first question that needs to be asked, then, is whether *whom* is truly in danger of disappearing. The answer depends on where you look and listen. *Whom* seems to be rare in ordinary speech, which is what Mencken and Burgess were paying attention to. But it does not seem to be disappearing from written English. It is worth pointing out, though we will not take the space to illustrate at length, that the Merriam-Webster files are rich in examples of the prescribed uses of *whom.* Beyond that, persistence of *whom* in constructions such as "a person whom everybody admits is successful"— where in fact normative grammar prescribes *who*—gave Fowler 1926 considerable concern. He found an abundance of evidence in British newspapers and feared the use might become a "sturdy indefensible." Dwight L. Bolinger voiced the same fear:

Yet recent instances in print seem to show that this ultra-correct use of *whom* is increasing, and that it may, alas, establish itself some day just as *than whom* even now compels acceptance —*Words,* September 1941

Bryant 1962 devotes some space to these constructions, which she calls "hypercorrect" and in which she says *whom* is "mistakenly" used as the subject.

Jespersen 1909–49 (vol. 3) has a fairly long treatment of the "hypercorrect" *whom.* After discussing Fowler's interpretation, he goes on to list a large number of examples and to examine in some detail the reasons for the use of *whom.* His judgment is quite the opposite of Fowler's; he concludes that *whom* is natural and correct in such constructions and that *who* represents either the historical trend of avoiding *whom* or is the result of schoolmastering.

It is distinctly possible, then, that subject *whom* need not be hypercorrect. Let us return to Shakespeare, before hypercorrectness or even simple correctness was a concern, for some examples:

PROSPERO. . . . They now are in my pow'r;
And in these fits I leave them, while I visit
Young Ferdinand, whom they suppose is drown'd,
And his and mine lov'd darling.
——*The Tempest,* 1612

TIMON. . . . Spare not the babe
Whose dimpled smiles from fools exhaust their mercy.
Think it a bastard whom the oracle
Hath doubtfully pronounc'd thy throat shall cut,
And mince it sans remorse.
——*Timon of Athens,* 1608

BASTARD. . . . And others more, going to seek the grave
Of Arthur, whom they say is kill'd to-night
On your suggestion.
——*King John,* 1597

HELENA. . . . But such a one, thy vassal, whom I know
Is free for me to ask, thee to bestow.
——*All's Well That Ends Well,* 1603

ELBOW. My wife, sir, whom I detest before heaven and your honour—
ESCALUS. How? thy wife?
ELBOW. Ay, sir; whom I thank heaven is an honest woman.
——*Measure for Measure,* 1605

Here we find the "hypercorrect" construction a century and a half before Bishop Lowth prescribes what is correct. The grammatical point at issue can be illustrated by Elbow's two *whom*s. In the first, "My wife . . . whom I detest," the relative pronoun is the object of *I detest.* But in ". . . whom I thank heaven is an honest woman," the *I thank heaven* is parenthetical, and the relative is actually the subject of *is an honest woman.* The two constructions are otherwise similar, however, and *whom* has been produced for both. According to Jespersen, it is something about the tightness of such constructions that elicits *whom.* When the parenthetical insertion is clearly set off by a pause or a pause is indicated by punctuation, *who* then becomes much more likely than *whom.* Jespersen has numerous examples, of which we append two here:

MARK ANTONY. . . . I should do Brutus wrong, and Cassius wrong,
Who, you all know, are honourable men.
——Shakespeare, *Julius Caesar,* 1600

There was one H———, who, I learned in after days, was seen expiating some maturer offence in the hulks ——Charles Lamb, *Essays of Elia,* 1823

When *who* is affixed without pause to the parenthetical insertion, Jespersen calls on the historical trend away from *whom* and the effect of schoolmastering for explanation. Again he provides examples, including Fielding, from before schoolmastering, and Dickens, after schoolmastering. He also notes that some writers have used both *who* and *whom* as subject—Benjamin Franklin and James Boswell among them.

To repeat, our evidence shows that present-day uses of *who* and *whom* are in kind just about the same as they were in Shakespeare's day. What sets us apart from Shakespeare is greater self-consciousness: the 18th-century grammarians have intervened and given us two sets of critics to watch our *who*s and *whom*s—the strict constructionists following Lowth and the loose constructionists following Priestley and the later Webster. Self-consciousness turns up at least as early as Dickens:

'Think of who?' inquired Mrs. Squeers; who (as she often remarked) was no grammarian, thank God — *Nicholas Nickleby*, 1839

And later:

"It's not what you know," we say, "but who you know." And I don't mean "whom." —W. Allen, *Western Folklore*, January 1954

"By whom?" I said. When I was serious my English was good —Robert B. Parker, *The Widening Gyre*, 1983

And sometimes self-consciousness becomes an unfortunate self-doubt:

Mr. Beeston said he was asked to step down, although it is not known exactly who or whom asked him —*Redding* (Conn.) *Pilot*, in *New Yorker*, 31 May 1982

But this greater self-consciousness appears to have changed actual usage very little. The following examples show just about the same kinds of uses found in Shakespeare:

I should like to help him, but hardly know who to apply to —Henry Adams, letter, 8 Nov. 1859

They become leaders. It doesn't matter who they lead —Ernest Hemingway, *Green Hills of Africa*, 1935

And he said, Well, haven't you got any opinion at all about them? and I said, About who? —William Faulkner, 18 May 1957, in *Faulkner in the University*, 1959

. . . which social group we identify with . . . , and who we are talking to —Margaret Shaklee, in Shopen & Williams 1980

So who would they surprise? —Ken Donelson, *English Jour.*, November 1982

. . . his three cousins from Minneapolis . . . who he left because he was nervous being around them — Garrison Keillor, *Lake Wobegon Days*, 1985

Let tomorrow's people decide who they want to be their President —William Safire, *N.Y. Times Mag.*, 11 Oct. 1987

. . . a very timid but forthright recruit whom he hoped would prove to be a crack salesman —Bennett Cerf, *This Week Mag.*, 19 July 1953

Colombo, 48 years old, whom law enforcement officials have said is the head of a Mafia family in Brooklyn —*N.Y. Times*, 5 July 1971

"My roommate and I sat up half the night talking about it," said one student, whom, I suspect, has never before read anything he wasn't forced to — John Medelman, *Esquire*, January 1974 (this *whom* is contrary to Jespersen's theory.)

In preparing to make a speech, the speaker gives some thought to whom his audience is —Linda Costigan Lederman, *New Dimensions*, 1977

. . . the Blair family, whom Safire says were the Kennedys of their time —Trish Todd, *Publishers Weekly*, 29 May 1987

All that remains to be said is that objective *who* and nominative *whom* are much less commonly met in print than nominative *who* and objective *whom*. In speech, you rarely need to worry about either one. In writing, however, you may choose to be a bit more punctilious, unless you are writing loose and easy, speechlike prose. Our files show that objective *whom* is in no danger of extinction, at least in writing.

2. For a discussion of *who (whom), that*, and *which* in reference to persons or things, see THAT 2.

who else's See ELSE.

whoever, whomever These words are much less common than *who* and *whom*, and the problems of case attendant upon them are not substantially different in kind from those that beset *who* and *whom*. For a discussion of such problems, see WHO, WHOM 1.

whole Barzun 1985 carries a warning against the phrase *in whole or in part*, which he declares should be avoided because you would not say *in whole* by itself. The OED shows, however, that *in whole or in part*, sometimes with the order reversed, has been in standard use since the middle of the 16th century. There is no need to shy away from it now.

whom See WHO, WHOM.

who's, whose See WHOSE 2.

whose **1.** *Whose, of which.* The misinformation that passes for gospel wisdom about English usage is sometimes astounding. A correspondent in 1986 wanted us to help him choose between two sentences containing *of which*; he had used *of which* to refer to the word *house*, he said, and had not used *whose* because it is "not formal." Not formal! Look at these passages:

I could a tale unfold whose lightest word
Would harrow up thy soul . . .
    —Shakespeare, *Hamlet*, 1601

. . . a land whose stones are iron, and out of whose hills thou mayest dig brass —Deuteronomy 8:9 (AV), 1611

Of man's first disobedience, and the fruit
Of that forbidden tree, whose mortal taste
Brought death into the World . . .
    —Milton, *Paradise Lost*, 1667

Relentless walls! whose darksome round contains
Repentant sighs, and voluntary pains
    —Alexander Pope, "Eloisa to Abelard," 1717

. . . Past and Future be the wings
On whose support harmoniously conjoined
Moves the great spirit of human knowledge . . .
    —William Wordsworth, *The Prelude*, 1805

It would be hard to find passages surpassing these in formality and solemnity.

Since English is not blessed with a genitive form for *that* or *which, whose*—originally the genitive of *what* and *who*—has been used to supply the missing forms since sometime in the 14th century. No one seems to have thought the use worthy of notice until the 18th century. Lowth 1762 mentioned it somewhat equivocally in a footnote, disapproving its use in passages from Dryden and Addison, but apparently not objecting to such use in "the higher Poetry, which loves to consider everything as bearing a personal character." He cites the lines from *Paradise Lost* quoted above as the example of higher poetry. Priestley in 1768 is also equivocal:

The word *whose* begins likewise to be restricted to persons, but it is not done so generally but that good writers, and even in prose, use it when speaking of things. I do not think, however, that the construction is generally pleasing.

Lindley Murray 1795 is similarly of two minds, noting the use with seeming approval—"By the use of this license, one word is substituted for three"—in one place and then reprinting Priestley's opinion verbatim in another.

After Lowth and Priestley had let the genie of disapproval out of the bottle, however tentatively, there was no putting it back. Leonard 1929 lists several other 18th-century grammarians in disapproval (including Noah Webster in 1798); Goold Brown 1851 carries the list into the 19th century, noting especially one T. O. Churchill (1823) as pronouncing "this practice is now discountenanced by all correct writers." Even Henry Bradley in the OED says that *whose* is "usually replaced by *of which*, except where the latter would produce an intolerably clumsy form."

Goold Brown, after citing various opinions as to the propriety of *whose*, many hedged round with exceptions for personification and solemn poetry, observes: "Grammarians would perhaps differ less, if they read more." Indeed. Hall 1917 read and, somewhat to his surprise, found *whose* used of inanimate things in some 140 authors, in more than 1,000 passages, from the 15th century to the early 20th. Once again we find the peculiar situation of usage commentary: the grammarians are very attentive to one another's opinions, and the standard authors pay them no attention at all. (See, for another example, the history of the controversy over the placement of *only*, at ONLY 1.)

The force that has always worked against acceptance of *whose* used of inanimate things is its inevitable association with *who*. The force that has always worked in its favor was suggested by Murray: it provides not only a shorter but a smoother and more graceful transition than the alternative "the ... of which." Its common occurrence in poetry undoubtedly owes more to its graceful quality than to any supposed love of personification among poets. In prose as well, the value of gracefulness (or, at least, the value of avoiding awkwardness) is generally recognized by good writers. As a result, this is one disputed usage that is perhaps more likely to occur in the works of good writers than bad ones:

... villages and farms whose inhabitants reflect the various cultures —Norman Douglas, *Siren Land,* 1911

... house in one of whose rooms was a striker wounded by Adkin's men —Sinclair Lewis, *Cheap and Contented Labor,* 1929

... a world whose values were becoming totally materialist —Stephen Spender, *New Republic,* 20 July 1953

... a wonderful book ... whose author is the German poet Rainer Maria Rilke —e e cummings, *New Republic,* 2 Nov. 1953

... that quality whose absence from the English middle-class mind was so deplored —Steven Marcus, *Partisan Rev.,* January–February 1954

... a precaution whose necessity was demonstrated a while back —Lewis Mumford, *New Yorker,* 6 Apr. 1957

... a word whose sources have been explained and reexplained over the centuries —Baron 1986

I can see its lights through my window, whose sash rattles —John Updike, *New Yorker,* 23 Jan. 1989

In the last half of the 20th century we find the subject of *whose* and *of which* discussed in most of the current books; not one of them finds *whose* anything but standard. But what about our correspondent? We have to wonder where he got the notion that *whose* is not formal. And this also gives us pause: the Leonard usage survey of 1932 found *whose* to be considered established by the group of respondents as a whole, but when Crisp replicated the survey in 1971, *whose* was rated disputable by the group as a whole. In *College English* in 1974 Mary Vaiana Taylor published (in an article aptly titled "The Folklore of Usage") the results of some surveys she had conducted; her survey of college and university teaching assistants showed that 67 percent of them would mark *whose* wrong in a student's paper. The specter of the 18th-century grammarian is still loose in the land.

The notion that *whose* may not properly be used of anything except persons is a superstition; it has been used by innumerable standard authors from Wycliffe to Updike, and is entirely standard as an alternative to *of which the* in all varieties of discourse.

2. *Whose, who's.* Nearly every handbook right down to the level of the fifth grade or so is at pains to distinguish *whose*, possessive pronoun, from *who's*, contraction of *who is, who has*. In spite of Bishop Lowth's glossing of *whose* as *who's* in 1762, no one today is supposed to confuse the two. Since they are pronounced the same, however, people do muddle them.

Teaching Reading and Writing Skills: Whose Responsible —brochure for a New England educational conference, reprinted in *New Yorker,* 21 Mar. 1983

... somebody else whose got nine jillion dollars —*Town & Country,* May 1976

When others are called for cross-checking, who's timing is always right? —advt., cited in Simon 1980

These are errors of inattention, of course, and to be avoided.

whys and wherefores See WHEREFORE.

widow, widower When a married man dies, is he survived by his widow or by his wife? This is not a question that many people ask themselves, but it has some importance for the writers of obituaries. The few commentators who have passed judgment on this matter favor *wife* over *widow,* possibly because it is considered redundant to identify a woman as a widow when the death of her husband has already been established, or because using *widow* somehow seems to imply that the woman was a widow even before her husband's death. In any case, a review of current practice in various newspapers shows that both *wife* and *widow* are used (some papers favor one, some favor the other, some use both). *Wife* is the more common choice.

Another question that is of concern chiefly to journalists is whether or not it is correct to write "Mrs. Nancy Smith, widow of the late George Smith." Several commentators, including Bernstein 1965 and Copperud 1970, 1980, have criticized this use of *the late* as redundant. Redundant it may be, but it is also idiomatic English. *The late* actually functions as a sort of title of respect in such contexts (see LATE).

It is worth noting that no such questions are likely to arise when the person who has died is the wife rather than the husband. A woman is never said to be "survived by her widower." If the woman who has died was a particularly noteworthy person, her surviving husband may be identified as "widower of the late . . . ," but "husband of the late . . ." is probably more likely. *Widower* is a less common word than *widow* and, unlike *widow,* it is rarely preceded by a possessive or followed by *of.* Two reasons for the differences in usage are that husbands are not normally identified by reference to their wives and that wives usually outlive their husbands. Those who are angered by the first reason may take some solace from the second.

will See SHALL, WILL.

win The use of *win* as a noun synonymous with *victory* was first recorded in 1862. Like *victory,* it occurs commonly in contexts having to do with sports and politics:

> . . . paced the freshman team to ten wins out of fourteen games —*Current Biography,* July 1965

> . . . has improved his record by a win a season since 1967 —*Sports Illustrated,* 21 Sept. 1970

> . . . can't afford anything but a thumping win . . . in that primary —Hunter S. Thompson, *Rolling Stone,* 3 Feb. 1972

> . . . an outright Communist win cannot be entirely discounted —*The Economist,* 4 Apr. 1953

> Political consultants, he says, do not have the high percentage of wins that they claim —Robert Sherrill, *N.Y. Times Book Rev.,* 27 Dec. 1981

This use of *win* has been viewed with disfavor by only a few critics. Bernstein 1965 calls it a "needless casualism" and would limit it to the sports pages, where presumably it is all right to be casual. Bernstein's opinion is not shared by many, however, and it is not reflected by actual usage.

-wise Despite its recent notoriety, *-wise* is no Johnny-come-lately combining form. It has been quietly used for centuries to mean "in the manner of" (as in *crabwise* and *fanwise*) and "in the position or direction of" (as in *slantwise* and *clockwise*). These uses of *-wise* are not controversial, but they have given birth to a controversial offspring. Since at least the late 1930s, *-wise* has been used to mean "with regard to; in respect of." Presum-

ably this new use developed mainly from the "in the manner of" sense of *-wise,* which has often been tacked onto nouns to form convenient nonce words:

> . . . his hands clasped Buddha-wise before him — Celestine Sibley, *Saturday Evening Post,* 27 Dec. 1958

Such adaptability is also one of the most noteworthy features of *-wise* meaning "with regard to." Our earliest evidence for the new sense of *-wise* is from 1938, when *Fortune* magazine was using it in the word *percentagewise:*

> . . . industrial sales remained more or less level percentagewise —*Fortune,* February 1938

> Percentagewise, the overhead costs plus profits for manufacturing industries went up —*Fortune,* March 1938

Other uses soon followed, in *Fortune* and elsewhere:

> Vacationwise, the most exceptional characteristic of these prosperous people is that they can come and go pretty much as they like —*Fortune,* January 1939

> . . . morale-wise it was a great victory —*Time,* 29 May 1944

> Mapwise, Arno looks like an old physiology picture of an amoeba —*National Geographic,* September 1945

> . . . this kind of nationalist boasting is highly important propaganda-wise —John Gunther, *Behind the Curtain,* 1949

> . . . to hold the party together and to make it effective election-wise —John Steinbeck, *New Republic,* 5 Jan. 1953

The rapid success of the new *-wise* is easily explained: it provided a simpler and shorter way to say things. Its use quickly became popular among many writers, including a fair number in the field of business, where its conciseness may have been felt to suggest a brisk, efficient, and businesslike manner:

> . . . to put that firm in a favorable competitive position, not only pricewise but also volumewise and qualitywise —Carl E. Borklund, *Manual for Technicians,* 1951

> Most expenses were higher dollarwise than in 1951 —*Annual Report, Jewel Tea Co.,* 1952

> Earnings-wise, the C. & O. is not exceptional among U.S. railroads —*Time,* 15 Mar. 1954

The new *-wise* began to come in for criticism during the late 1950s, after it had been in use for about 20 years, and commentators have been nearly universal in their deprecation of it since. Although its use has never been limited to a single group, it has come to be widely identified—and derided—as a characteristic of businessmen's jargon. Many writers have made fun of its use:

> I too think Fortune is in good shape organization-wise though understaffed as always good-writer-wise —Archibald MacLeish, letter, 20 July 1938

> This has been the summer of the great discontent and widespread confusion, weatherwise, healthwise, and otherwisewise —E. B. White, letter, 4 Sept. 1959

Gentle, nonaggressive and stoned out of his mind, he'd struck Kate as slightly off balance yin-and-yang-wise —Cyra McFadden, *The Serial,* 1977

Nevertheless, it continues to be in fairly common use, especially in speech. It has established itself as a homely and workmanlike combining form, not much favored by those who aim for elegance and gracefulness in their writing. It continues to be used almost exclusively for the formation of nonce words.

wish   *Wish* is commonly used as a transitive verb meaning "to want" or "to desire," often with an infinitive as its object:

> I do not wish to pay for tears anywhere but upon the stage —Robert Louis Stevenson, *Virginibus Puerisque and Other Papers,* 1881

> It is not that they wish to pretend that they are busy —Oliver St. John Gogarty, *It Isn't This Time of Year at All!,* 1954

> We may wish to cajole him, plead with him, try to change his tastes —Milton Friedman, reprinted column, 1969

In another typical construction, the object is a proper name or personal pronoun followed by an infinitive:

> I wished Foster to go away —Robert McAlmon, *There Was a Rustle of Black Silk Stockings,* 1963

> I wish you to rejoice with me —Ira Remsen, quoted in *Johns Hopkins Mag.,* April 1966

These uses of *wish* are not controversial, although two commentators (Flesch 1964 and Janis 1984) find them somewhat affected and express a general preference for *want.* The real point of dispute is whether the transitive *wish* should be used with a simple noun object. Several commentators have criticized such usage as a genteelism, typically offering some such sentence as "Do you wish some more coffee?" as an example of what not to say. The OED, which shows that the use of *wish* with a simple noun object dates back to Old English, called it dialectal in 1933, but our evidence does not support that label:

> ... in days when not to have property, if one wished it, was almost a certain sign of shiftlessness —Van Wyck Brooks, *The Flowering of New England, 1815–1865,* rev. ed., 1946

> ... a majority of employees wished a union shop — *Current Biography 1948*

> When a visitor ... wishes a license to operate a rented car —Bert Pierce, *N.Y. Times,* 14 Mar. 1954

Wish is certainly far less common than *want* or *desire* in such contexts, but it is also certainly standard.

with   *With* used to join two nouns (as what Quirk et al. 1985 calls a quasi-coordinator) has attracted some attention among usage commentators. A few maintain that a singular noun coordinated with another singular noun by *with* should take a singular verb; others, quoting authoritative works on syntax, believe either a singular or plural verb may be used, depending on notional agreement. Surveyed opinion (Leonard 1932, Crisp 1971) holds the use of a plural verb to be disputable.

Here is one example of such use:

> Pichon was, indeed, glowering. He with Roosevelt were the representatives of republics —Mark Sullivan, *Our Times,* vol. 4, 1932

For more on this topic, see AGREEMENT, SUBJECT-VERB: COMPOUND SUBJECTS 3.

with a view, with the view   See VIEW.

without   The use of *without* as a conjunction meaning "unless" was once perfectly respectable:

> A very reverent body. Ay, such a one as a man may not speak of without he say 'sir-reverence' —Shakespeare, *The Comedy of Errors,* 1593

> That any laud to me thereof should grow,
> Without my plumes from others' wings I take
> —Sir Philip Sidney, *Astrophel and Stella,* 1591

By the 18th century, however, it had fallen far enough from grace for Samuel Johnson to note in his 1755 Dictionary that it was "not in use." (The 1798 edition of Johnson's Dictionary says "not in use, except in conversation.") Noah Webster, who argued unpersuasively that this *without* was actually a preposition rather than a conjunction, also noted in his Dictionary (1828) that "This use of *without,* is nearly superseded by *unless* and *except,* among good writers and speakers; but is common in popular discourse or parlance." Although evidence in the OED (including quotations from Tennyson and the elder Oliver Wendell Holmes) shows that both Johnson and Webster were somewhat premature in their observations on the conjunctive *without,* it is clear that they were essentially correct in noting its lack of written use. Since the late 19th century, this conjunction has occurred rarely in print except in representations of uneducated or dialectal speech:

> You don't know about me without you have read a book by the name of *The Adventures of Tom Sawyer* —Mark Twain, *Huckleberry Finn,* 1884

> "... There ain't none in the oil-shed, that I do know—without there might be a bit in the wash'us—but it'll have been there a long time," she concluded dubiously —Dorothy L. Sayers, *Busman's Honeymoon,* 1937

> "Doctor'll be here soon, without the snow holds him up ..." —H. E. Bates, *Selected Stories,* 1957

See also AGAINST 1.

without hardly   See HARDLY.

with regard to   See REGARD 1.

with respect to   See IN RESPECT OF, IN RESPECT TO, WITH RESPECT TO.

with the exception of   This phrase is commonly used as a synonym for *except* or *except for:*

> ... accepted by the legislatures of all the territories concerned with the exception of British Guiana and the Virgin Islands —*The Americana Annual 1953*

> ... with the exception of cases of deliberate, premeditated theft —Glynn Mapes, *Security World,* May 1968

An emphatic adjective is sometimes added before *exception:*

> He was a very bad influence over all his friends, with the single exception of myself —Oscar Wilde, *The Picture of Dorian Gray,* 1891

This is a venerable phrase, first attested in the early 17th century, when it was written *with exception of.* In recent years it has been criticized by some for wordiness, but it continues to be in good use. You should avoid it only if you count yourself among those who believe that you can never be too terse.

See also EXCEPTION.

with the hope of, with the hope that   See HOPE 2.

witness   An assortment of critics, beginning with Richard Grant White 1870, have had unkind things to say about the use of *witness* to mean "see." White noted that such usage occurred "with absurd effect," and he offered the following as an example: "'I declare,' an enthusiastic son of Columbia says, as he gazes upon New York harbor, 'this is the most splendid bay I ever witnessed.'" White explained that it is only correct to speak of witnessing an act, not a thing, such as a harbor or a mountain range or "a poodle dog." The same opinion has been expressed in this century by Bernstein 1965: "What is *witnessed* is an event, an occurrence, an action, perhaps even a situation, but not either a 'thing' or a person." Our evidence agrees with Bernstein's observation. The usage that he and White object to almost never occurs, at least in written English.

A few other commentators have taken a different tack by criticizing the use of *witness* in contexts where the notions of testifying or acting as a legal witness to a particular act or occurrence are not involved, as in "Almost 50,000 spectators were on hand to witness the game." This is in fact one of the most common uses of the transitive verb *witness:*

> ... the merchants had flocked thither ... to taste of all the luscious feasts and witness the lavish entertainments —F. Scott Fitzgerald, "May Day," 1920

> ... the most bitter scene I had ever witnessed —Katherine Anne Porter, *The Never-Ending Wrong,* 1977

> I went to the ceremony at noon ... and there witnessed a scene which Germany had not seen since 1914 —William L. Shirer, *The Rise and Fall of the Third Reich,* 1960

> ... have not been in a church for other than architectural reasons or to witness a marriage or funeral —John Kenneth Galbraith, *The Scotch,* 1964

This use of *witness* is old and well established. The OED shows that it first occurred in the 16th century. It is unquestionably standard English and is treated as such in dictionaries.

woman   See LADY.

wont   As an adjective, *wont* means "accustomed" or "inclined." It occurs only as a predicate adjective, and it is almost always followed by an infinitive:

> ... the appearance of one before whom all her doubts were wont to be laid —Jane Austen, *Mansfield Park,* 1814

> ... presumably they take it seriously, as children are wont to do —Thomas H. Middleton, *Saturday Rev.,* 19 Mar. 1977

> ... where the candidates, their managers, and various ranking journalists are wont to gather —Hunter S. Thompson, *Rolling Stone,* 16 Mar. 1972

As a noun meaning "habitual way of doing," *wont* occurs most often in phrases beginning "as is ..." or "as was ...":

> ... saying as is his wont that the *literary* scholars don't know anything anyway —Louis Marder, *CEA Critic,* May 1971

> ... but as was his wont, he stated his opinion in bold and provocative language —George Clark Sellery, *The Renaissance,* 1950

2. Confusion of *wont* with *won't* has been warned against on occasion, but we have no evidence that such confusion has ever actually occurred, even though authors like William Faulkner and George Bernard Shaw may choose to omit the apostrophe. See WON'T.

won't   *Won't* is one of the most irregular looking of the negative contractions that came into popular use during the 17th century and into print around the 1660s (others include *an't, han't, don't,* and *shan't*). *Won't* was shortened from earlier *wonnot,* which in turn was formed from *woll* (or *wol*), a variant form of *will,* and *not.* It appeared in various forms in Restoration comedies:

> No, no, that won't do —Thomas Shadwell, *The Sullen Lovers,* 1668

> We'll thrust you out, if you wo'not —William Wycherly, *The Country Wife,* 1675

> But wo't thou really marry her? —Aphra Behn, *The Dutch Lover,* 1673

> Why, you wont baulk the Frollick? —William Congreve, *The Double-Dealer,* 1694

Won't was among the contracted and truncated forms that Joseph Addison attacked in *The Spectator* on 4 August 1711. It seems to have been under something of a cloud, as far as the right-thinkers were concerned, for more than a century afterward. This did not, of course, interfere with its employment, and it was common enough to enjoy the distinction of being damned in the same breath as *ain't* in an address delivered before the Newburyport (Mass.) Female High School in December 1846, as reported by Shirley Brice Heath in Shopen & Williams 1980. The speaker termed both "absolutely vulgar." How *won't* eventually escaped the odium that still clings to *ain't* is a mystery, but today it is entirely acceptable.

A few modern writers—William Faulkner and George Bernard Shaw come readily to mind—have followed the example of Congreve and omitted the apostrophe, but by far the usual styling in current English is to retain it.

See also AIN'T.

wood, woods   Both *wood* and its plural *woods* are used to refer to a forested area. The singular *wood* usually denotes a delineated area of medium size, larger than a grove and smaller than a forest:

> Walking the other day in an old hemlock wood —John Burroughs, *Wake-Robin,* 1871

... a cornfield, a field of oats, a wood —John Bartlow Martin, *Saturday Evening Post,* 22 June 1957

... discovers her in a wood close at hand —Edgar Allan Poe, *The Literati,* 1850

The plural *woods* is also sometimes used with this meaning, in which case it is usually (though not always) construed as singular:

... had moved out of a woods and onto a frozen road —James A. Michener, *The Bridges at Toko-Ri,* 1953

... a woods where deer sometimes graze —John Mariani, *Town & Country,* June 1981

The path to the marsh leads through a woods —John P. Wiley, Jr., *Smithsonian,* September 1983

Whose woods these are I think I know....
The woods are lovely, dark and deep
     —Robert Frost, *New Hampshire,* 1923

More commonly, the plural *woods* refers to the forest generally, without the suggestion of a delineated area that is implicit in the singular *wood:*

... went back to the woods without saying a word
... and that was the last the women saw of them for a week —Conrad Richter, *The Trees,* 1940

When used in this way, *woods* is construed as plural:

The woods decay, the woods decay and fall —Alfred, Lord Tennyson, "Tithonus," 1860

wordiness You might tend to think or opine that *wordiness* would refer to the use and/or utilization of many more extra words, terms, phrases, and locutions than are absolutely required, needed, or necessary for writing, saying, or otherwise expressing your ideas, thoughts, theses, or opinions. In theory it is. In practice, it is not. Usage writers are nearly unanimous in condemning as wordy the ordinary, short, idiomatic phrases of spoken discourse, such as *climb up, as to, consensus of opinion, for free, have got to, meet up with, refer back, what for, able to, would like to, who is, advance planning, ask a question, at about, continue on, but that, but what, the field of, where . . . at, first began, off of,* and *inside of,* to name a few. Many commentators are also pretty severe on the old formal phrases of business correspondence and on long formulas like *in view of the fact that, somewhere in the neighborhood of,* and *the question as to whether,* which are sometimes used to rescue a writer from a desperate construction. Nearly all of the commentators would heartily subscribe to Professor Strunk's Rule 13 (see Strunk & White 1959): "Omit needless words."

In actual practice, of course, writers—even usage writers—do not omit all needless words (unless perhaps, they are composing a telegram). Examples of needless words are easy to find in usage books:

... remember that *due to the fact that* is a wordy way of saying the short and simple word *since* —Shaw 1970

What does "the short and simple word" add to the statement?

Certain other *in* phrases are nothing but padding and can be omitted entirely —Little, Brown 1986

Couldn't this be boiled down to "Other *in* phrases may simply be omitted"? And here is Bernstein 1965 on *climb up:*

But here we have tautology aggravated by wastefulness. The writer who values terseness will usually omit the *up.*

The writer who really values terseness could omit everything but the last three words.

But this is too easy a game to be helpful. What we see in these examples are writers who have warmed to their subject and who are trying to make their point, heedless of their own prescriptions. No good writer writes to rule. James Sledd has demonstrated persuasively (in Greenbaum 1985) that E. B. White contravened his own rules of composition in the very act of composing Strunk & White 1959.

The fact is that what seem to be needless words to one writer may not seem so needless to another. We can illustrate this by taking a look at the chapter on jargon in Sir Arthur Quiller Couch's *On the Art of Writing,* a book published in 1916. Sir Arthur's treatment of the subject is not quite what a modern commentator's would be—in fact much of his comment deals with many of the expressions that modern critics consider wordy. In the course of his discussion, Sir Arthur addresses the question of the value of the concrete term versus the abstract term. He produces these two examples for comparison:

In large bodies the circulation of power must be less vigorous at the extremities. Nature has said it. The Turk cannot govern Ægypt and Arabia and Curdistan as he governs Thrace; nor has he the same dominion in Crimea and Algiers which he has in Brusa and Smyrna. Despotism itself is obliged to truck and huckster. The Sultan gets such obedience as he can. He governs with a loose rein, that he may govern at all; and the whole of the force and vigour of his authority in his centre is derived from a prudent relaxation in all his borders —Edmund Burke, *On Conciliation with America*

In all the despotisms of the East, it has been observed that the further any part of the empire is removed from the capital, the more do its inhabitants enjoy some sort of rights and privileges: the more inefficacious is the power of the monarch; and the more feeble and easily decayed is the organisation of the government —Lord Brougham, *Inquiry into the Policy of the European Powers*

As Sir Arthur observes, Lord Brougham "has transferred Burke's thought to his own page." Sir Arthur much prefers Burke's version for its concreteness; "will you not also perceive," he says, "how pitiably, by dissolving Burke's vivid particulars into smooth generalities, he has enervated its hold on the mind?"

But the current group of critics and commentators concerned with wordiness would have to differ if they were true to their principle—Lord Brougham says it more concisely. He uses one sentence while Burke needs five. Why isn't Brougham better?

Simply, briefer is not always better. There are reasons for the different ways in which Burke and Brougham handled the subject. Burke was writing a speech for listeners. Brougham was writing a book for readers. Sir Arthur thought the version intended for listeners more effective, despite its lack of brevity. To make his point effectively, Burke used some repetition, some redundancy, and perhaps one or two of those little particles that the handbooks so often call wordy but that occur so naturally in speech.

Conciseness is a virtue in writing, but it is not the only virtue. If you use the forms that are natural to speech, you will often get your point across better—or at least more easily. The conscious avoidance of the natural expressions of speech can sometimes lead you to stray into jargon (see JARGON).

See also REDUNDANCY.

wordy See WORDINESS.

worsen This is an old verb, recorded as far back as the 13th century, but its written use was relatively uncommon until the 1800s. The OED has an interesting note: "The word is common in dialect ... and was reintroduced to literature *c* 1800–1830 (by writers like Southey and De Quincey) as a racy vernacular substitute for *deteriorate* and the like." It is hard now to think of *worsen* as ever having been "racy." Its written use in the 20th century has been common and entirely reputable, but a few people have had lingering qualms about it:

> ... yesterday's editorial on "Salonica" states: "At this point the Austrian situation began to worsen."
> Now, the writer ain't got no Webster's unabridged handy, and that little word "worsen" rather grated on his unaccustomed ear —letter to the editor, *N.Y. Tribune,* 19 Dec. 1915

Its only critic among usage commentators, however, appears to have been Krapp 1927, who considered it "much too rare to be counted customary good English." Fowler 1926, on the other hand, recognized it as a standard verb, and none of the few recent commentators who have addressed the subject has disagreed. Copperud 1970, 1980 indicates that it still has some critics, but he himself is not one of them. Neither should you be. *Worsen* is, in fact, an ordinary, unexciting word, having long ago cast off the last vestiges of its former raciness:

> Such a "solution" ... can only worsen the situation —*Times Literary Supp.,* 2 Oct. 1969

> ... these odds could worsen quickly —Vance Bourjaily, *Harper's,* March 1972

worser See DOUBLE COMPARISON.

worst comes to worst The idiomatic phrase *if worst comes to worst* has many variants. It was first recorded in 1597 as *if the worst come to the worst.* Its meaning then, as now, was "if the worst that can possibly happen does happen." As is the case with many idioms, the phrase seems nonsensical if its parts are examined individually. Presumably it was the desire to make the phrase more logical that gave rise to the variant *if the worse comes to the worst,* which was first recorded in 1719, when it was used (in the past tense) by Daniel Defoe in *Robinson Crusoe.* In the centuries since, this peculiar phrase has shown a stubborn unwillingness to settle into a fixed form:

> ... will of course eventually, and if worst comes to worst, come to the aid of France —*New Republic,* 17 Nov. 1937

> ... if worse comes to the worst, the author can himself arrange for it —H. M. Silver, *PMLA,* February 1952

> If worst came to worst I could always get by —James Norman Hall, *Atlantic,* October 1952

> If worse came to worst she could telephone Nick —Daphne du Maurier, *Ladies' Home Jour.,* August 1971

> Still, if the worst came to the worst —Jere H. Wheelwright, Jr., *The Strong Room,* 1948

> "... wanted to see her once more, if worst should come to worst...." —Charles Bracelen Flood, *Omnibook,* June 1954

The forms which are most commonly used are *if worst comes to worst* and *if worse comes to worst.* There are those who regard the form having *worse* as incorrect, but its use is too widespread and well established for it to be regarded as anything other than standard. Use of *if worse comes to worse* is considerably less common, at least in print. The definite articles are now omitted more often than not.

worst way The adverbial phrase *the worst way* originated in American speech during the 19th century. It is basically equivalent to *very much,* but it has forceful connotations all its own. To want something very much is not quite the same as to want it the worst way. *The worst way,* now often used with *in,* typically implies an intense, almost desperate or childlike longing:

> ... he wanted to be a football star in the worst way —*Time,* 13 Aug. 1956

> She knew I wanted a guitar in the worst way —Wynn Fay, quoted in *Valley Advocate,* 19 Sept. 1979

The use of this phrase in writing has occasionally been discouraged in handbooks on usage, dating back to MacCracken & Sandison 1917. Our evidence shows that its written use is rare and is limited to contexts having an informal or conversational tone.

worthwhile This adjective originated as a two-word phrase, *worth while,* which was essentially a short way of saying "worth one's while" and which functioned strictly as a predicate adjective (as in "the experience was worth while"). In the early 20th century, it first began to appear as an attributive adjective, in which use it was hyphenated (as in "a worth-while experience"). For a number of years the customary practice seems to have been to hyphenate the compound when using it attributively and to treat it as two words when using it predicatively. Eventually the hyphenated form was largely superseded by the solid form, *worthwhile,* which became so well-established in time that it grew to be the favored form even in the predicate ("The experience was worthwhile"). In current English, the hyphenated and two-word forms are still sometimes used and are not at all incorrect:

> ... identifying himself as a worth-while citizen —Virgil M. Rogers, in *Automation, Education and Human Values,* ed. W. W. Brickman & S. Lehrer, 1966

> ... it is still worth while to say ... —Nehemiah Jordan, *Themes in Speculative Psychology,* 1968

But the solid form is now the usual choice in all contexts:

> ... speaks only when he has something worthwhile to contribute —*Current Biography,* July 1964

It's a worthwhile addition to the small but growing documentation —Ross Russell, *N.Y. Times Book Rev.,* 24 Oct. 1976

Worthwhile has become such a common word that it has attracted some unfavorable attention. Fowler 1926 devoted a great deal of space to a discussion of what he considered to be errors in its use (or actually in the use of *worth while* as a phrase), but more recent commentary has tended to be less specific; the usual complaint is that *worthwhile* is an overused and imprecise word (E. B. White describes it as "emaciated" in Strunk & White 1972). The complaint is not without justice, it seems to us, but you should not banish *worthwhile* from your vocabulary on that account. Its vagueness is often useful when a general term of approbation is needed. Just keep in mind that a more specific adjective can sometimes be a more appropriate choice.

would   See SHALL, WILL; SHOULD, WOULD.

would have   The use of *would have* in place of *had* in the protasis of a conditional sentence (as in "If they would have come earlier, we could have left on time") has been cited as an error in books on usage since at least 1924 (Garland Greever & Easley S. Jones, *The Century Collegiate Handbook*). Such usage appears to be a characteristic of informal speech, in which it may often occur in a contracted form ("If they'd have come earlier . . ."). Our evidence indicates that it does not occur in standard writing that finds its way into print, but it is notorious in student writing and therefore a staple of college handbooks even today.

See also PLUPLUPERFECT.

would of   This phrase is a transcription of the contracted form *would've* of *would have*. It is sometimes used intentionally—for instance, by Ring Lardner. Except for very special purposes you will want *would have* or *would've*. See OF 2.

would rather   See HAD RATHER.

wrack   See RACK, WRACK.

wrangle   See WANGLE, WRANGLE.

wrath, wrathful, wroth   These related words have had overlapping uses in centuries past, but they are now easily distinguished. *Wrath* is the noun:

. . . would call down bureaucratic wrath on the fledgling systems analysis office —I. F. Stone, *N.Y. Rev. of Books,* 11 Mar. 1971

Wrathful is the usual adjective:

. . . in an effort to appease wrathful farmers —*N.Y. Times,* 1 Nov. 1986

And *wroth* is an adjective synonymous with *wrathful* that now rarely occurs except in the phrase *wax wroth,* which normally serves as a playful or deprecating way of saying "grow angry":

. . . the India-haters who get their kicks by waxing wroth over what most of us take for granted — Joseph Kraft, *St. Louis Post-Dispatch,* 27 Dec. 1971

Fowler 1926 proposed as a further distinction that *wrathful* be considered the attributive adjective (as in "a wrathful God") and *wroth* the predicative adjective (as in "God was wroth"), but this distinction is not

observed. *Wrathful* is the usual choice regardless of its position in the sentence:

Then he became wrathful in a dry legal fashion — Agatha Christie, *Sad Cypress,* 1940

Fowler also preferred \'rōth\ (rhyming with *both*) as the pronunciation of *wroth,* but the pronunciation now favored in both American and British English is \'rŏth\ (rhyming with *cloth*).

wreak, wreck   Havoc is usually said to be wreaked:

Nor is this feisty crew beyond wreaking havoc among themselves —James Atlas, *N.Y. Times Book Rev.,* 13 Sept. 1981

But it is sometimes said to be wrecked:

. . . the isolationists wrecked their havoc by boldly asserting that economic and military assistance were two entirely different and separate things —*New Republic,* 10 Sept. 1951

Wreak havoc is the original expression and is regarded by many people as the only correct one. Those same people regard \'rēk\ as the only correct pronunciation of *wreak,* but \'rek\ also occurs as a secondary variant (of course, it is not always possible to determine whether the person saying \'rek\ would write *wreak* or *wreck*). The meaning of the word in this context is "to bring about; cause." Several factors contribute to the tendency to substitute *wreck* for *wreak:* the fact that *wreak* is an unfamiliar word in general, whereas *wreck* is quite common; the fact that when havoc is wreaked, the result may be a wreck, so the verb *wreck* appears to go naturally with *havoc;* and, perhaps, the fact that *wreak* \'rēk\ is a homophone for the common verb *reek* means that for some people the phrase *wreak havoc* smells a little fishy.

Other verbs are also used with *havoc,* of course; they include *create, play, raise,* and, occasionally, *work:*

One agency in particular which is working havoc in the minds of many —Lounsbury 1908

. . . had begun to work havoc in the orthodox communities of Connecticut —Lois Bailey Wills, *New-England Galaxy,* Winter 1965

In the past tense, *work havoc* becomes either *worked havoc* or, more commonly, *wrought havoc:*

. . . had worked havoc with his sea communications —John Buchan, *Augustus,* 1937

. . . the havoc that was wrought by the war of 1914 —W. Bridges-Adams, *The British Theatre,* rev. ed., 1946

. . . they wrought havoc during the hours in between —Grace Metalious, *Peyton Place,* 1956

Usage commentators, who seem to be unfamiliar with the *work havoc* variant, regard *wrought* simply as an erroneous substitute for *wreaked,* and they issue stern warnings against its use. It is not an error, but you may want to take the fact that some people mistakenly think that it is into account in deciding whether or not to use it.

If these various points of contention have you feeling overwrought, you can avoid the whole issue by calling *wreak havoc* a cliché and dismissing it contemptuously from your vocabulary. You are well advised, in any case, to steer clear of *wreck havoc.*

write The standard surviving principal parts are past tense *wrote* and past participle *written*. Lamberts 1972 notes that *write* and *bite* are in the same class, but when their old four-part inflection was reduced to our modern three-part one, *write* kept its singular preterite *wrote*, with plural *writ* dwindling into dialectal use, while *bite* kept the plural preterite *bit*.

For the past participle, *wrote* was acceptable well into the 18th century:

> ... he had wrote to hinder it on some pretence or other —Thomas Gray, letter, 12 Sept. 1756

But it has long since dropped out of mainstream use. Another old past participle, *writ*, probably derived from the even older *ywritte*, is kept alive by the phrase *writ large* and by writers who use it when being deliberately or playfully literary or dialectal:

> For two months, dear Bang, I have rotted a dry rot. I have read nothing, writ nothing, dreamed nothing —Archibald MacLeish, letter, 30 July 1915

> Write me what you want writ in them and I will write it —Flannery O'Connor, letter, 1 Mar. 1960

> (And, yes, Little Eva, the foregoing sentence was writ deliberate.) —Kilpatrick 1984

write-up This noun originated among American journalists in the late 19th century. As its use became common, it attracted the disapproval of such American commentators as Krapp 1927, who considered it "colloquial, verging on low colloquial," and Weseen 1928, who described it as "journalistic cant." The common use continued, however, and the criticism did not. The only recent critic to take note of *write-up* is Shaw 1975, 1987, who allows that it is standard but considers it trite. Our evidence shows that *write-up* continues to be primarily a jounalist's word. It does not occur in highly formal writing.

> ... a monthly newsletter containing brief write-ups on books of general interest —Judith Appelbaum, *N.Y. Times Book Rev.,* 23 Oct. 1983

> ... earned him a write-up in The Salt Lake City Tribune last January —Robert L. Miller, *Sports Illustrated,* 3 Sept. 1984

wrong, wrongly *Wrong* is a versatile word. It can be used as an adjective, noun, or verb, and as an adverb synonymous with *wrongly*. Some commentators have observed that *wrong* is preferred to *wrongly* when the adverb occurs after the verb it modifies, while *wrongly* is used when the adverb precedes the verb. This observation accords with usage in most respects, but it leaves out several important complications.

The adverb *wrong* occurs most frequently with the verbs *do, get, have,* and especially *go*. With each of these verbs it forms set phrases in which *wrongly* cannot be idiomatically substituted:

> ... falls under suspicion as the man who did her wrong —*Time,* 17 Apr. 1950

> Don't get me wrong. I like Mr. Eberhart —Richard Bennett Hovey, *New Republic,* 16 Nov. 1953

> When the people go wrong it is not from selfishness or materialism —A. J. P. Taylor, *Saturday Rev.,* 11 Dec. 1954

Wrong is also used with other verbs. It usually follows immediately after the verb, often at the end of a sentence or clause:

> The worst that can happen is that his instinct fails and he pushes wrong —Jeremy Larner, *Harper's,* April 1971

> After all, one could guess wrong —Stan Sauerhaft, *Dun's,* March 1972

> The costs had been figured wrong —Martin Mayer, *Change,* March 1972

> ... and if you choose wrong, you may lose your honor —Jeremy Larner, *Harper's,* April 1971

Wrongly occurs in such contexts, but it is less common than *wrong*.

When the adverb precedes the verb or participle that is being modified, *wrongly* is indeed the only possible choice:

> ... they are often wrongly accused of being politically biased —Robert B. Binswanger & Alan Winslow, *Change,* July–August 1969

> ... this phrase is wrongly attributed to his broadcast on June 18 —*Times Literary Supp.,* 14 May 1970

> ... restored him to a position which has wrongly been denied him —Maurice Edelman, *Books of the Month,* April 1953

Note, however, that even if these sentences are rewritten so that the verbs come before the adverbs, it is still necessary to use *wrongly*. You could not say "often accused wrong of being," "is attributed wrong to his broadcast," or "a position which has been denied him wrong." *Wrongly* is often the adverb of choice regardless of whether it precedes or follows the verb:

> ... tends to harm many people by stigmatizing them wrongly as addicts —David W. Maurer & Victor H. Vogel, *Narcotics and Narcotic Addiction,* 1954

> ... he has sometimes applied this subtle rhythmic resource of the French style quite wrongly —Bernard Jacobson, *Stereo Rev.,* October 1971

The best way to choose between *wrong* and *wrongly* is to rely on your own grasp of English idiom. The one that *sounds* correct *is* correct. If they both sound correct, then either one may be used.

These general observations also hold true for the analogous adverbs *right* and *rightly*.

wroth See WRATH, WRATHFUL, WROTH.

X Y Z

Xmas *Xmas* has been used as a short form of *Christmas* since the 16th century. The *X* is derived from the Greek letter chi (X), which is the first letter in Χριστος, "Christos." *X, Xp,* and *Xt,* all derived from the Greek name, have been used to stand for *Christ-* in other words besides *Xmas.* There is evidence in the OED and the OED Supplement for *Xpen* (1485), *Xpian* (1598), and *Xtian* (1845, 1915, 1940), all meaning "Christian," and for *Xpofer* (1573), "Christopher," *Xstened* (1685–86), "christened," and *Xtianity* (1634, 1811, 1966), "Christianity." Most of the recent evidence for these words comes from the letters of educated Englishmen who know their Greek. *Xmas* also has shown a tendency to turn up in the letters of the well-educated:

> . . . but if you won't come here before Xmas, I very much fear we shall not meet *here* at all —Lord Byron, letter, 9 Sept. 1811

> . . . which I hope to get published before Xmas —Lewis Carroll, letter, 10 June 1864

> I expect about Xmas a visit —Oliver Wendell Holmes d. 1935, letter, 11 Oct. 1923

By and large, however, *Xmas* is limited in current usage to advertisements, headlines, and banners, where its brevity is an advantage. When read aloud, it is pronounced either \ˈkris-məs\ or \ˈek-sməs\. Some people dislike it because it displaces the *Christ-* in *Christmas.* Its association with the world of advertising has also done nothing for its reputation.

yclept This peculiar-looking word is actually the past participle of the archaic verb *clepe,* which means "to call or name." Its strange spelling gives it a certain appeal, as does the fact that many people have no idea what it means, and the occasional writer still enjoys using it as a playful synonym of *called* or *named:*

> These folks include the gargantuan Neanderthal proprietor, yclept Thor —Judith Crist, *Saturday Rev.,* 29 May 1976

> . . . a monstrous big sloop, yclept the Concorde —William F. Buckley, Jr., *N.Y. Times Mag.,* 9 Oct. 1983

If you are willing to risk puzzling your readers, you may find some use for *yclept* yourself. But before you start singing about "A Boy Yclept Sue," be warned that Fowler classed *yclept* as "worn-out humor" back in 1926, and several subsequent commentators (Evans 1957, Flesch 1964, and Bernstein 1965) have also failed to be amused.

ye, *pronoun* *Ye* was originally the nominative form of the second person plural pronoun. It contrasted with *you,* the oblique (accusative and dative) form. Around the middle of the 16th century the contrast began to break down, and the two forms became interchangeable. Wyld 1920 says that in the 16th century nominative *you* was much more frequent than *ye* as an accusative or dative. But in the 17th century *ye* was much more often found in object positions:

> All of ye —Thomas Shadwell, *The Sullen Lovers,* 1668

> . . . I'll be judge between ye —Aphra Behn, *The Dutch Lover,* 1673

> . . . what think you now, of a fellow that can eat and drink ye a whole louis-d'or at a sitting? —George Farquhar, *The Inconstant,* 1702

It was also used in a reduced form—just a representation of the vowel, tacked to the end of another word:

> Paints de'e say? —William Congreve, *The Double Dealer,* 1694

> Hark'ee, Oriana —George Farquhar, *The Inconstant,* 1702

Attached to the end of words like *hark* and *thank,* a remnant of *ye* has survived in various spellings. *Ye* by itself has survived, too, primarily as a dialectal variant of *you:*

> '. . . I'll tell ye,' I says —H. N. Westcott, "The Horse Trader," 1898, in *The Mirth of a Nation,* ed. Walter Blair & Raven I. McDavid, Jr., 1983

> ". . . every damn man of ye. . . ." —James Stephens, *The Crock of Gold,* 1912

> . . . if a man is going to pay you he'll pay ye without too much dunning —Dock Franklin, quoted in *Our Appalachia,* ed. Laurel Shackelford & Bill Weinberg, 1977

> Straight man [at a Scottish music-hall performance]: "Why didn't ye cut him doun?" —Israel Shenker, *N.Y. Times,* 20 Oct. 1974

Strang 1970 points out, in addition, that in the 18th century, as *you* took over as the usual second person pronoun in all functions, *ye* continued in elevated literary use. Undoubtedly some of the elevated use was liturgical and ceremonial, and this too survives:

> Hark ye, O, King Solomon, and all ye who hear me —*Adoptive Rite Ritual—Eastern Star,* rev. ed., 1952

And, of course, *ye* survives in deliberate archaizing, as in fiction set in the past:

> ". . .Ye followed him secret-like, eh? Maybe he took ye for a spy from the Customs. . . ." —Max Peacock, *King's Rogue,* 1947

> "Ye are idle, ye are idle," the Pharaoh reproved them —Joseph Heller, *God Knows,* 1984

See also YOU 3.

ye, *article* Students of English spelling are aware that part of its oddity derives from the fact that the earliest printers were working with manuscripts in which the spelling at least in part represented pronunciations that were no longer in use. These printers had brought their technology to England from the continent. The types they had—black letter, roman, italic—were European types, whose letters of the alphabet were those in general European use. Not in use on the continent were some of the runic characters still being used in Middle English. One such was the thorn (Þ), a character somewhat resembling a *p*, which stood for what the continental alphabets less efficiently spelled *th*.

In 14th-century manuscripts, some scribes were writing a form of the thorn that was all but indistinguishable in shape from the letter *y*, and one of its most common uses was in the short forms of *the, that, they, them,* and the like, that the scribes used to save themselves writer's cramp. Early printers set these abbreviated forms as they found them, so that the short *the* would appear in print as, say, *y^e*, and *that* as *y^t*.

So this early rendition of scribal *the* has given us the alternate form *ye*, typically used nowadays because of its conspicuous, antiquarian flavor with *olde* in the quaint-sounding names of various business establishments ("Ye Olde Antique Shoppe").

It would seem that few things could be less important than a disquisition upon the pronunciation of antiquarian *ye*, but a fair number of commentators have troubled themselves to remark upon the subject, and they have disagreed. Some have insisted that *ye* should be pronounced like *the*, others have noted and accepted that its far more common pronunciation is \yē\. This is not a matter to be taken seriously. We think you can safely judge for yourself how *ye* is to be pronounced in such facetious uses as still occur:

> You are in ye olde desperate straits —Kathy Crafts & Brenda Hauther, *Surviving the Undergraduate Jungle,* 1976

> . . . when ye olde faithful hoste, Alistair Cooke, introduces the author —Arthur Unger, *Christian Science Monitor,* 19 Nov. 1980

yearn People who yearn usually yearn *for* something:

> He yearned for a drink —William Styron, *Lie Down in Darkness,* 1951

> . . . the man yearns for companionship —Daphne du Maurier, *Ladies' Home Jour.,* August 1971

Less common prepositions following *yearn* are *after, toward* (or *towards*), and *over:*

> . . . who yearned after the social and economic setup of the nineteenth century —*Collier's Year Book,* 1949

> He yearns toward the European grand-prix circuits —*Newsweek,* 22 Mar. 1954

> . . . and the new . . . hand-sewing machines the Indian women yearned over —Marjory Stoneman Douglas, *The Everglades: River of Grass,* 1947

yet The use of *yet* with a verb in the plain past tense with *did* ("Did he leave yet?" rather than "Has he left yet?") has sometimes been criticized. Shaw 1975, 1987 calls such use nonstandard; Longman 1984 says that it does not occur "except in informal American English." Such use is common and unobjectionable in ordinary speech. Its occurrence in writing, according to our evidence, is rare. Here is one example:

> But he didn't see it even yet —Lincoln Steffens, "A Prince and a Cowboy," in *Chains of Light* (8th-grade textbook), ed. Theodore Clymer, 1982

Such use is not limited to American English. Here we find it in the dialogue of an Irish play:

> Did Mr. Mineog come yet, John? —Lady Gregory, *Coats,* in *New Comedies,* 1913

you 1. You may have noticed that the editors of this book have often used *you* in addressing you, the reader, directly. Our reason for doing so is well described in this comment:

> Bernstein and Copperud agree that the use of you to address the reader . . . conduces to informality and directness —Copperud 1970

Quite a number of commentators also remark that you can use *one* instead of *you* when you want to be more formal, distant, and impersonal. They sensibly warn, however, that you should be careful not to mix the formal *one* with the more informal *you*. One pays one's money and takes one's choice, as it were.

2. *Indefinite "you."* Related to the use of *you* to address the reader directly is the use of *you* to address no one in particular—in indefinite reference. Such use has apparently been something of a bugbear to college composition teachers. In Woolley & Scott 1926, the indefinite *you* received top billing under the *Misuses of Pronouns* heading, ranking ahead of the indefinite *they* and the use of *it* without an antecedent. Recent college handbooks still mention it, although its status has been downgraded (Prentice Hall 1988, for instance, runs *they* and *it* ahead of *you*). Woolley & Scott prescribed either *one* or the passive voice. Both of these prescriptions have provided grist for other usage writers: some American writers find *one* sniffishly British (see ONE 1) and a goodly number object to the passive (see PASSIVE VOICE). More recent writers are perhaps aware of dissatisfaction with the easy solutions of the past, and are therefore somewhat more willing to accept the indefinite *you*. They all stress its informality, however.

> And so every Southern household when they bought books they bought Scott. That was because you got more words for your money, maybe —William Faulkner, 13 May 1957, in *Faulkner in the University,* 1959

> You can be the most important congressman in the country, but you had better not forget the people back home —Tip O'Neill with William Novak, *Man of the House,* 1987

> How much domestic spending did you have to cut to get a balanced budget in 1984 after the tax cut and defense increase? —David A. Stockman, *Newsweek,* 28 Apr. 1986

> You drive through the average city or even the average village these days, and the houses are so close together . . . that there's no place for the kids to play but in the street —*And More by Andy Rooney,* 1982

> After the forward pass was legalized, in 1906, the most versatile backs were triple threats: you didn't know whether they would run, pass, or kick the ball —Herbert Warren Wind, *New Yorker,* 18 Jan. 1982

You in these examples is not directed at the reader, but the informal effect is similar; it is rather more like listening to someone talk than reading a formal exposition.

Perrin & Ebbitt 1972 says that *you* is more common than *one* in general writing and that it is not rare even in formal writing. There is good literary precedent for the usage: the OED has examples from Bacon, Swift, and Ruskin. And a recent editor of the 14th-century poem *Pearl* has found the usage there. But many of the handbook writers and the composition teachers brought up on them are still chary of *you.*

The direct, intimate effect of *you* is also cultivated by writers of fiction, autobiography, and fictionalized autobiography who are looking for the immediacy of talk:

> In seventh grade they were always assigning you to write about things like farm produce —Russell Baker, *Growing Up,* 1982

> ... I was as happy as you are after you have been with a woman that you really love —Ernest Hemingway, *Green Hills of Africa,* 1935

> You went for the small things, the molded metal car models that would fit in your palm, you watched the lady in her green smock —E. L. Doctorow, *Loon Lake,* 1979

3. The history of the pronoun *you* provides a good example of the effect social forces can have on the language. *You* began as the accusative and dative form of the second person plural pronoun. The nominative plural was *ye.* The form used to address one person in centuries past was *thou* (*thee* was the accusative and dative form of the singular).

As far back as the 14th century, the plural forms *ye* and *you* began to be used to address one person—usually a superior—as a mark of deference and respect. Curme 1931 conjectures that this use may be related to the use of the first-person plural *we* by sovereigns: Jespersen 1909–49 (vol. 2) lays it to French politeness at work in Middle English. However it began, the use of the polite plural gradually grew: Strang 1970 points out that such a use once begun must grow, since people would rather be polite than risk giving offense in cases of doubt. So as the use of the plural increased, the singular became the special use, the limited form. By about the beginning of the 17th century, *thou* and *thee* marked an intimate or personal relationship, or a superior to inferior relationship (Evans 1962 quotes the prosecutor of Sir Walter Raleigh using *thou* in deliberate disrespect).

Then by about the middle of the 16th century the contrast in function between *ye* and *you* began breaking down. Henry Sweet, in his *New English Grammar* (1892), attributed part of the breakdown to sound: there seems to have been a tendency to push *ye* into uses that matched the rhyming *thee* and *you* into those that matched the rhyming (then) *thou.* Ben Jonson's early-17th-century Grammar listed *you* and *ye* as simple variants, while *thou* and *thee* retained their traditional functions. Wyld 1920 observes that the first Queen Elizabeth seems to have used only *you* in writing; a user of her prestige must surely have given *you* a boost. Wyld also says that in 16th-century usage there was much more use of *you* as a nominative than of *ye* as an accusative or dative—in other words, *you* was expanding its range at the expense of *ye.* This process has continued, although *ye* has not disappeared entirely (see YE, *pronoun*).

The displacement of the singular pronouns did not go entirely unnoticed. In 1660 George Fox published an attack on those who used *you* as a singular, but it had no effect at all. Fox couched his attack in grammatical terms, but as Marckwardt 1958 points out, Fox was the leader of the Quakers, and there were political and reli-

gious motives behind his remarks. The Quakers believed in equality and disapproved *you* as an acknowledgment of one's betters.

The loss of a singular pronoun for everyday use was noticed in the common speech and gave rise to various remedies. The first was to make the distinction between singular *you* and plural *you* by verb agreement; *you was* for the singular continued in polite if informal use well into the 18th century before it lost respectability (see YOU WAS). Special plural forms were later contrived to hold *you* chiefly to singular use; these include such formations as *you-all* (see YOU-ALL), *you-uns, yez,* and *youse.* None of these save *you-all* has enjoyed much success, or at least much prestige.

So the simple social drive of good manners has in a few centuries completely remade the second person pronoun. No doubt the social pressures of today will work changes in the language as well. (For examples of changes that may be taking place, see PERSON 2 and THEY, THEIR, THEM 1.) The chances are, however, that most changes they bring about will not be rapid.

you-all   The debate over *you-all* (and its contraction, *y'all*) has to do with whether Southerners use it strictly as a plural of *you* or sometimes use it as a singular as well. An entertaining history of the dispute, which dates back to the end of the 19th century, can be found in H. L. Mencken, *The American Language, Supplement II* (1948). In brief, Southerners themselves have for the most part insisted that *you-all* is only a plural and that its use as a singular occurs only among Northerners doing a poor imitation of Southern speech, while contentious Northerners and a few renegade Southerners have argued that singular use is not unheard of among Southerners themselves. Just about everyone agrees, at least, that *you-all* does usually function as a plural. Even when only one person is being addressed, *you-all* normally implies the inclusion of another or others whom the single person is understood to represent; for example, "When will you-all be coming by?," addressed to a single person, means "When will you and [a person or persons unnamed] be coming by?" However, the evidence, most of which is testimonial, does indicate that *you-all* has also been used as a singular in the South, although such usage is certainly atypical and is not regarded with approval by a great many Southerners. The Northerner attempting to write Southern dialogue or imitate Southern speech would do well to restrict *you-all* to plural use.

> "Hello, honey-chile," he said when the operator answered. "Think you-all could get me the Courier editorial office?"
> "You know," said the operator, "down here we can always spot Yankees by the way they use 'you-all' in the singular."
> —Arthur Gordon, *Reprisal,* 1950

you know   The repeated use of *you know* as a filler in hesitant speech is a great source of irritation to many people, including most usage commentators. It is typically seen as a characteristic of the speech of relatively inarticulate young people, such as athletes being interviewed on television, and it is easily parodied: "Well, you know, I was, you know, lookin' for the ball out over the plate, you know, and I just, you know, went with it." The threat to the language posed by such post-game hemming and hawing does not appear to be, shall we say, major-league, but its capacity to grate on sensitive nerves is obviously considerable.

Note that *you know* is not a problem in writing. The phrase is actually quite old, being attested in the OED as early as the 16th century, and its use in informal writing, as in a letter, can be perfectly appropriate:

> You know, I've been sitting here with my dreadful pipe, trying to get straightened out —E. B. White, letter, April 1922

> You know Plato virtually says himself two thousand years before Freud that . . . —Robert Frost, letter, 5 July 1925

> I'm sure he'd like to see you. He's a pretty lonely guy you know —Archibald MacLeish, letter, June 1934

> We farmers are always behind, you know —E. B. White, letter, 28 Jan. 1942

You know suggests a certain intimacy and mutual understanding in such contexts. Its occurrence in casual speech is also blameless, of course, except when it occurs three or four times in a sentence. Then it is apt to become annoying.
See also FILLERS.

your, you're 1. The possessive pronoun is *your:* "Your spelling is atrocious." The contraction of *you are* is *you're:* "You're an atrocious speller."
2. In addition to functioning as a possessive pronoun, *your* is often used without any particular meaning, more or less as an equivalent to *the.* Such usage is quite old: it was first recorded in the 16th century and can be found in Shakespeare's *A Midsummer Night's Dream* and *Hamlet.* In modern idiom, it frequently occurs with such adjectives as *average, standard, ordinary, usual,* and *basic:*

> . . . sets him apart from your average professor of art history —James Breckenridge, *N.Y. Times Book Rev.,* 24 Feb. 1980

> . . . a father compared to whom your average eunuch is a model of virility —John Simon, *New York,* 9 Feb. 1976

> . . . is not your ordinary college —Malcolm Scully, *The Chronicle,* 28 Oct. 1975

> . . . your usual Bake-Off contestant —Nora Ephron, *Esquire,* July 1973

> . . . your basic historical pageant —Alan Rich, *New York,* 15 Mar. 1976

> Your basic returning boomerang —Stephen S. Hall, *Smithsonian,* June 1984

Bishop Lowth objected to such usage in the 18th century, and Roy Copperud has objected to it in the 20th. Other usage commentors seem not to have had much to say about it. As the examples above indicate, it is right at home in casual prose but is not found in notably elevated written discourse.

yours It is true that the *-s* in *yours* is a genitive ending, and it is true that the genitive *-s* is normally preceded by an apostrophe, but it is not true that there is an apostrophe in *yours.* Do not be too hard on yourself if you mistakenly include one, however. It could happen to almost anyone:

> . . . if you will do your's by repeating the French Grammar —Jane Austen, letter, 12 Nov. 1800

> Believe me, Mr. Terry, your's Truly —Lord Byron, letter, 12 Nov. 1805

> Your's of the 28th. ult. came to hand by our last post —Thomas Jefferson, letter, 9 May 1809

Actually, *your's* was standard in the 18th century, and it was an acceptable variant in the early 19th century, although it was appreciably less common than *yours.* In the late 20th century, however, *yours* is the only acceptable form.
See also HERS.

yourself, yourselves The use of the reflexive pronouns *yourself,* singular, and *yourselves,* plural, in constructions where they are not reflexive or intensive has been criticized since at least the time of MacCracken & Sandison 1917, chiefly by the same commentators who have attacked *myself.* The criticism has been somewhat perfunctory for the most part. Nothing particularly baneful has been seen in either *yourself* or *yourselves,* and in general the unpleasant name-calling of the *myself* issue has not been repeated (see MYSELF).
The most insightful commentary about these pronouns can be found in Jespersen 1909–49 (vol. 2) and Evans 1957. Both point out that *yourself* and *yourselves* preserve the distinction between singular and plural that has been lost from *you,* and they further suggest that *yourself* and *yourselves* are sometimes used in place of *you* for the purpose of making number explicit.
The OED shows *yourself* in uses neither reflexive nor emphatic from the 15th century on; the same uses for *yourselves,* a less common word, start in the 16th century. Here are some examples of ours:

> I remark a considerable payment made to yourself on this Third of December —Robert Browning, *Pippa Passes,* 1841

> I have read you; that is a favour few authors can boast of having received from me besides yourself— Samuel Johnson, *The Idler,* 10 June 1758

> . . . I shall be as much benefited by it as yourselves —Jane Austen, *Sense and Sensibility,* 1811

> Has it not been industriously circulated by yourselves? —Jane Austen, *Pride and Prejudice,* 1813

> This vizard is a spark, and has a genius that makes her worthy of yourself, Dorimant —George Etherege, *The Man of Mode,* 1676

> In our days there is scarcely an instance of a learned or unlearned man who has written gracefully, excepting your friend Goldsmith and (if your modesty will admit my approaches) yourself —Walter Savage Landor, *Imaginary Conversations,* 1848

> Don't let him know she liked them best,
>   For this must ever be
> A secret, kept from all the rest,
>   Between yourself and me.
>   —Lewis Carroll, "She's All
>   My Fancy Painted Him," ca. 1854

> Get me some good left-handers like yourself and Robinson —Robert Frost, letter, 23 Jan. 1921

> In all this I look to nothing but the happiness of yourself, Mr. Randolph, and the dear children — Thomas Jefferson, letter, 27 Feb. 1809

Those who, like yourself, know what they are about —Walter W. Skeat, letter, in K. M. Elisabeth Murray, *Caught in the Web of Words,* 1977

. . . you once told me about sighting a sea serpent—either yourself or a friend of yours saw it —James Thurber, letter, 4 Aug. 1955

The respectability of these uses is obviously above reproach. Evans finds them acceptable but is doubtful of their literary standing. We think these examples show a modest connection with literary usage.

you was As *you* gradually lost its use as a second-person plural pronoun and came to serve as both a singular and a plural, various expedients had to be developed to make the distinction that the pronoun had lost. One obvious way to distinguish between singular and plural is by means of the verb, and Strang 1970 tells us that in the 17th and 18th centuries it was a common practice to use the singular verb with *you* when addressing just one person. But as early as Swift's time, Strang reports, *you was* was pretty much restricted to informal and nonliterary uses, as in correspondence. Here are a few examples from 18th-century letters, the first of which, from *The Spectator,* is supposed to have been written by the butler of Sir Roger de Coverly at the time of his master's death:

Knowing that you was my old Master's good Friend, I could not forbear sending you the melancholy News —Joseph Addison, *The Spectator,* 23 Oct. 1712

I am just now as well, as when you was here —Alexander Pope, letter to Swift (in Lowth 1762)

. . . which you was so good as to send me —Sir Alexander Dick, letter to Samuel Johnson, 17 Feb. 1777

Even these innocuous uses were censured by Lowth 1762. Producing examples from the letters of Pope, Bolingbroke, and Richard Bentley, Lowth called the usage "an enormous solecism." Other grammarians followed. A few seem to have disagreed, and Noah Webster argued on both sides at different times. Yet by the 19th century, *you was* had been relegated to the speech of the uneducated, where it is still to be found.

zeal One may either have zeal *for doing* something or zeal *to do* something:

Wilson's zeal for converting the world to American virtues —Milton Viorst, *Interplay,* February 1969

. . . has allowed his zeal for overlooking no one to lead him into being inconclusive —*Saturday Rev.,* 19 Dec. 1953

In its zeal to protect itself from liability —John C. Burton, *Arthur Young Jour.,* Winter/Spring 1971

. . . and genuine zeal to throw off colonialism —Jon Stewart, *Mother Jones,* June 1979

Where the object is a noun rather than a verbal, *for* is the usual preposition after *zeal:*

. . . confessed that Chinese youth lack zeal for the Revolution —Alex Campbell, *New Republic,* 2 Apr. 1966

. . . there was no widespread zeal for the idea —Ben Harte, *The Lamp,* Spring 1972

zealous **1.** See JEALOUS 1.
2. When it is followed by a preposition, *zealous* usually occurs with *for:*

. . . its industry, eager for markets, and its bankers, zealous for investments, developed new techniques of economic imperialism —Allan Nevins & Henry Steele Commager, *The Pocket History of the U.S.,* 1942

Lewis, zealous even to bigotry for the doctrines of the Church of Rome —T. B. Macaulay, *The History of England,* vol. I, 1849

It has occasionally occurred with *about:*

. . . those who are more zealous about the triumph of their righteous cause —Morris R. Cohen, *The Faith of a Liberal,* 1946

And it also occurs with *to* plus an infinitive:

. . . Swinburne stops thinking just at the moment when we are most zealous to go on —T. S. Eliot, *The Sacred Wood,* 1920

zoology The traditional and recommended pronunciation of this word is \zō-ˈäl-ə-jē\. Gowers in Fowler 1965 calls \zü-ˈäl-ə-jē\ a "very common vulgarism," due probably to the influence of *zoo.* Another possible reason for the rise of this variant is the fact that, in relaxed speech, the first pronunciation tends to come out as \zə-ˈwäl-ə-jē\, which could easily be apprehended as a reduced or relaxed form of \zü-ˈäl-ə-jē\. (A similar interplay between stressed and unstressed versions of a single word led historically to the differentiation of *of* and *off.*)

An analogous state of affairs obtains for *zoological:* traditionally \ˌzō-ə-ˈläj-i-kəl\, now also \ˌzü-ə-ˈläj-i-kəl\.

Condemnation of the newer variant is sociolinguistically problematic, since the people to whom one might be inclined to allow the last word, namely zoologists themselves, not uncommonly use the \zü-\ version. We even find the traditional disyllabic \ˌzō-ə-\ being reduced in the speech of scientists to a monosyllabic \ˌzü-\. Our pronunciation files show these bargain-basement variants for a couple of fifty-dollar words: *zoonoses* pronounced \ˌzü-ˈnō-ˌsēz\ by a university veterinarian, and *zooxanthellae* turned to \ˌzü-ˌzan-ˈthel-ē\ in the mouth of a biologist.

zoom There are those who claim that it is incorrect to speak of "zooming along the highway" or "zooming down a hill." This strange idea owes its origin to the use of *zoom* in aeronautics, where it means, in simple terms, "to climb rapidly and steeply." Pointing to the aeronautical use, such critics as Evans 1957 and Bernstein 1965 have contended that it is not possible to zoom in any direction but up.

But the origins of *zoom* actually have nothing to do with aeronautics. The word is onomatopoeic, like *zap, zing,* and *zip.* The earliest evidence of its use can be found in the first (1933) Supplement to the OED:

The crystal went zooming into the fence-corner —*Century Mag.,* 1886

Zoom here apparently suggests the sound of something moving at a high speed. Other early citations for *zoom* have to do with sounds produced by bees and by musical instruments. The aeronautics sense of *zoom,* which of course did not originate until the early 20th century, apparently developed from the older, onomatopoeic sense, and it was no doubt responsible for making *zoom* a much more common word than it had been. But the onomatopoeic sense has never gone out of use. It has persisted especially in describing something or someone moving at great speed, regardless of direction:

... trade winds that zoom down across Hawaii from northern seas —advt., *National Geographic,* June 1924

... two of the 143 roaring racers zoomed off the road —*Time,* 18 Apr. 1938

... zooming sixty-five yards to a touchdown —*Kansas City Star,* 2 Jan. 1943

... Bold Ruler went zooming along alone, passing the six-furlong pole —Audax Minor, *New Yorker,* 22 June 1957

... a rocket sled zooming on rails down an incline —*Science News Letter,* 19 Dec. 1964

My brakes could not hold the added weight perfectly, and down the hill I zoomed —Neville H. Bremer et al., *Skills in Spelling* (6th-grade textbook), 1976

... she zoomed recklessly down ski slopes —*People,* 3 Jan. 1983

Its connotations of great speed have also led to the common use of *zoom* in describing rapid flight that is not necessarily upward. Such usage is of course inconsistent with the specifically aeronautical sense and is therefore relatively susceptible to criticism, but the evidence shows that it is established in standard writing:

... peels off, zooming down in a 60-degree power dive —Byron Kennerly, *Harper's,* July 1941

... government planes zoomed down to bomb tanks and strafe street fighters —*Time,* 1 Aug. 1949

The plane zooms past them, zoom!, and silent guns fire and that whole gang falls dead —Garrison Keillor, *Lake Wobegon Days,* 1985

Zooming low over the Queen Mary ... , each airplane emits a long vapor trail —Dennis Meredith, *Air and Space/Smithsonian,* August/September 1986

The "upward" connotations of *zoom* are also strongly established. They have given rise, so to speak, to the common use of *zoom* in the figurative sense "to increase rapidly":

... his fee for professional services has zoomed —Arthur Knight & Hollis Alpert, *Playboy,* December 1971

The popularity of her novels has zoomed —Ray Walters, *N.Y. Times Book Rev.,* 6 Nov. 1977

The rent zoomed up to eighty-seven dollars —Tip O'Neill with William Novak, *Man of the House,* 1987

And *zoom* is also commonly used in optics and photography, without connotations of either speed or upward movement:

... focus first at the highest power and then zoom to whatever lower power you may want —*Consumer Reports,* November 1971

... when the KTTV camera zoomed in on George and Crazy Ed —Joe Eszterhas, *Rolling Stone,* 14 Sept. 1972

Clearly, the aeronautics sense of *zoom* is but one of many, all of which are standard.

Bibliography

This list consists primarily of works—books of commentary on English usage, grammars, college handbooks, dictionaries, and a few miscellaneous items—that have been referred to in the body and front matter of the present book.

A few additional works have also been included even though they are not referred to specifically elsewhere in the book. Some were consulted for general orientation during the course of work; others are simply important books on such topics as the history of English and the American variety of the language that are of general interest.

A uniform style is followed throughout this bibliography, except that no attempt is made to give a publisher for books published before 1900.

Cross-references leading to appropriate entries in the bibliography are supplied when text references to a work do not match the name or title under which the work is listed here or when an editor's name may be more familiar than the title of a work.

Alford, Henry. 1866. *A Plea for the Queen's English.* London and New York.

Algeo, John. 1977. "Grammatical Usage: Modern Shibboleths." In *James B. McMillan: Essays in Linguistics by His Friends and Colleagues.* Ed. James C. Raymond and I. Willis Russell. University: Univ. of Alabama Press.

———. 1983. "Usage." In *Needed Research in American English.* Publication of the American Dialect Society No. 71.

American Dialect Dictionary. See Wentworth, Harold.

American Heritage Dictionary of the English Language. 1969. Ed. William Morris. Boston: Houghton Mifflin.

American Heritage Dictionary of the English Language. 1982. 2d College ed. Boston: Houghton Mifflin.

Ayres, Alfred. 1881. *The Verbalist.* New York.

[Bache, Richard Meade.] 1869. *Vulgarisms and Other Errors of Speech.* 2d ed. Philadelphia.

Bailey, Edward P., Jr. 1984. *Writing Clearly: A Contemporary Approach.* Columbus: Charles E. Merrill.

Baker, Josephine Turck. 1927. *The Correct Word: How to Use It.* Evanston, Ill.: Correct English.

[Baker, Robert.] 1770. *Reflections on the English Language.* London.

———. 1779. *Remarks on the English Language.* London.

Baker, Sheridan. 1981. *The Practical Stylist.* 5th ed. New York: Harper and Row.

———. 1984. *The Complete Stylist and Handbook.* 3d ed. New York: Harper and Row.

Ball, F. K. 1923. *Constructive English.* Boston: Ginn.

Bander, Robert G. 1978. *American English Rhetoric.* 2d ed. New York: Holt, Rinehart & Winston.

Bardeen, C. W. 1883. *Verbal Pitfalls.* Syracuse.

Barnard, Ellsworth. 1979. *English for Everybody.* Amherst, Mass.: Dinosaur.

Baron, Dennis E. 1982. *Grammar and Good Taste.* New Haven: Yale Univ. Press.

———. 1986. *Grammar and Gender.* New Haven: Yale Univ. Press.

Barzun, Jacques. 1985. *Simple & Direct.* Rev. ed. New York: Harper and Row.

Battles, H. K., et al. 1982. *Words and Sentences,* Book 2. Lexington, Mass.: Ginn.

Baugh, Albert C., and Thomas A. Cable. 1978. *A History of the English Language.* 3d ed. Englewood Cliffs, N.J.: Prentice Hall.

Belanoff, Pat, et al. 1986. *The Right Handbook.* Upper Montclair, N.J.: Boynton/Cook.

Bell, James K., and Adrian A. Cohn. 1981. *Bell & Cohn's Handbook of Grammar, Style, and Usage.* 3d ed. New York: Macmillan.

Bernstein, Theodore. 1958. *Watch Your Language.* Great Neck, N.Y.: Channel.

———. 1962. *More Language That Needs Watching.* Manhasset, N.Y.: Channel.

———. 1965. *The Careful Writer.* New York: Atheneum.

———. 1971. *Miss Thistlebottom's Hobgoblins.* New York: Farrar, Straus and Giroux.

———. 1977. *Do's, Don'ts & Maybes of English Usage.* New York: Times Books.

Bierce, Ambrose. 1909. *Write It Right.* New York: Union Library Assoc., 1937.

Bolinger, Dwight L. 1980. *Language—The Loaded Weapon.* London: Longman.

Bolton, W. F. 1966. *The English Language.* Cambridge, England: Cambridge Univ. Press.

Bolton, W. F., and D. Crystal. 1969. *The English Language.* Vol. 2. Cambridge, England: Cambridge Univ. Press.

Bremner, John B. 1980. *Words on Words.* New York: Columbia Univ. Press.

Bridges, Robert. 1919. *On English Homophones.* S.P.E. (Society for Pure English): Tract No. 2. London: Oxford Univ. Press.

Brown, Goold. 1851. *The Grammar of English Grammars.* New York.

Brown, Ivor. 1945. *A Word in Your Ear and Just Another Word.* New York: E. P. Dutton.

Brown University Corpus. *See* Kučera, Henry; Francis, W. Nelson.

Bryant, Margaret M. 1962. *Current American Usage.* New York: Funk & Wagnalls.

Bryant, William Cullen. 1877. *Index Expurgatorius.* Reprinted in Bernstein 1971.

Bryson, Bill. 1984. *The Facts on File Dictionary of Troublesome Words.* New York: Facts on File.

Building English Skills. Orange Level (9th grade). 1982. Rev. ed. Ed. Joy Littell et al. Evanston, Ill.: McDougal, Littell.

Burchfield, Robert. 1981. *The Spoken Word.* New York: Oxford Univ. Press.

Campbell, George. 1776. *The Philosophy of Rhetoric.* Edinburgh.

Canby, Henry Seidel, and John B. Opdyke. 1918. *Good English.* New York: Macmillan.

Century Collegiate Handbook. See Greever, Garland.

Century Dictionary. 1889–91. Ed. William Dwight Whitney. New York.

Chambers Pocket Guide to Good English. 1985. Ed. George W. Davidson. Edinburgh: W & R Chambers.

Clark, Thomas L., et al. 1981. *Language: Structure And Use.* Glenview, Ill.: Scott, Foresman.

Cobbett, William. 1823. *A Grammar of the English Language.* Oxford.

Colter, Rob. 1981. *Grammar to Go.* Rev. ed. Toronto: Anansi.

Compton, Alfred G. 1898. *Some Common Errors of Speech.* New York.

Cook, Claire Kehrwald. 1985. *Line by Line.* Boston: Houghton Mifflin.

Copperud, Roy H. 1960. *Words on Paper.* New York: Hawthorn.

————. 1964. *Webster's Dictionary of Usage and Style.* New York: Avenal.

————. 1970. *American Usage: The Consensus.* New York: Van Nostrand Reinhold.

————. 1980. *American Usage and Style: The Consensus.* New York: Van Nostrand Reinhold.

Corder, Jim W. 1981. *Handbook of Current English.* 6th ed. Glenview, Ill.: Scott, Foresman.

Creswell, Thomas J. 1974. *Usage in Dictionaries and Dictionaries of Usage.* Diss. U. of Chicago. Publication of the American Dialect Society Nos. 63–64. 1975.

Crisp, Raymond Dwight. 1971. *Changes in Attitudes Toward English Usage.* Diss. U. of Illinois. Ann Arbor: University Microfilms International, 1980. 72–12,126.

Curme, George O. 1931. *Syntax.* Boston: D. C. Heath. Vol. 3 of *A Grammar of the English Language.* 2 vols. 1931–1935.

————. 1935. *Parts of Speech and Accidence.* Boston: D. C. Heath. Vol. 2 of *A Grammar of the English Language.* 2 vols. 1931–1935.

Daniels, Harvey A. 1983. *Famous Last Words.* Carbondale, Ill.: Southern Illinois. Univ. Press.

A Dictionary of American English. 1938–44. Ed. Sir William A. Craigie and James R. Hulbert. 4 vols. Chicago: Univ. of Chicago Press.

A Dictionary of Americanisms. 1951. Ed. Mitford M. Mathews. 2 vols. Chicago: Univ. of Chicago Press.

Dictionary of American Regional English. 1985– . Vol. 1 Ed. Frederic G. Cassidy, Vol. 2 Ed. Frederic G. Cassidy and Joan Houston Hall. Cambridge, Mass.: Harvard Univ. Press.

Dillard, J. L. 1976. *American Talk.* New York: Random House.

Ebbitt, Wilma R., and David R. Ebbitt. 1982. *Writer's Guide and Index to English.* 7th ed. Glenview, Ill.: Scott, Foresman.

Einstein, Charles. 1985. *How to Communicate.* New York: McGraw-Hill.

Evans, Bergen. 1962. *Comfortable Words.* New York: Random House.

Evans, Bergen, and Cornelia Evans. 1957. *A Dictionary of Contemporary American Usage.* New York: Random House.

Fennell, Francis L. 1980. *Writing Now: A College Handbook.* Chicago: Science Research Associates, Inc.

Fernald, James C. 1946. *English Grammar Simplified.* New York: Funk and Wagnalls.

Finegan, Edward. 1980. *Attitudes toward English Usage.* New York: Teachers College Press.

Flesch, Rudolf. 1964. *The ABC of Style.* New York: Harper and Row.

————. 1983. *Lite English.* New York: Crown.

Follett, Wilson. 1966. *Modern American Usage.* Ed. and completed by Jacques Barzun. New York: Hill and Wang.

Foster, Brian. 1968. *The Changing English Language.* London: Macmillan.

Fowler, Henry W. 1926. *A Dictionary of Modern English Usage.* Oxford: Clarendon Press.

————. 1965. *A Dictionary of Modern English Usage.* 2d ed. Ed. Sir Ernest Gowers. Oxford: Clarendon Press.

Fowler, Henry W., and Francis George Fowler. 1907. *The King's English.* Oxford: Clarendon Press.

Francis, W. Nelson. 1958. *The Structure of American English.* New York: Ronald.

Francis, W. Nelson, and Henry Kučera. 1982. *Frequency Analysis of English Usage.* Boston: Houghton Mifflin.

Freeman, Morton S. 1983. *A Treasury for Word Lovers.* Philadelphia: ISI Press.

Fries, Charles Carpenter. 1927. *The Teaching of the English Language.* New York: Thomas Nelson.

————. 1940. *American English Grammar.* New York: D. Appleton-Century.

Funk & Wagnalls New Standard Dictionary of the English Language. 1913.

Goldstein, Miriam B. 1966. *The Teaching of Language in Our Schools.* Urbana, Ill.: National Council of Teachers of English.

Goold Brown. *See* Brown, Goold.

Gould, Edward S. 1867. *Good English.* New York.

Gowers, Sir Ernest. 1948. *Plain Words.* London: His Majesty's Stationery Office.

————. 1954. *Complete Plain Words.* London: Her Majesty's Stationery Office. Reprinted 1962 as *Plain Words: Their ABC.* New York: Alfred A. Knopf.

————. 1973. *Complete Plain Words.* Ed. Sir Bruce Fraser. 2d ed. London: Her Majesty's Stationery Office.

Greenbaum, Sidney. 1984. "Good English." Inaugural Lecture. University College London. 14 March.

————, ed. 1985. *The English Language Today.* Oxford: Pergamon Press.

Greenbaum, Sidney, and Janet Whitcut. 1988. *Longman Guide to English Usage.* Harlow, Eng.: Longman.

Greenough, James B., and George L. Kittredge. 1901. *Words and Their Ways in English Speech.* New York: Macmillan.

Greever, Garland, and Easley S. Jones. 1924. *The Century Collegiate Handbook.* New York: Century.

Guth, Hans P. 1980. *American English Today.* 3d ed. New York: McGraw-Hill.

————. 1985. *New English Handbook.* 2d ed. Belmont, Calif.: Wadsworth.

Hall, Fitzedward. 1872. *Recent Exemplifications of False Philology.* New York.

————. 1873. *Modern English.* New York.

Hall, J. Lesslie. 1917. *English Usage.* Chicago: Scott, Foresman.

Harper Dictionary of Contemporary Usage. See Morris, William.

Heritage. *See American Heritage Dictionary of the English Language.*

Hiatt, Mary. 1977. *The Way Women Write.* New York: Teachers College Press.

Hill, Adams Sherman. 1895. *The Principles of Rhetoric.* New York.

Hill, Archibald A. 1979. "Bad Words, Good Words, Misused Words." In *Studies in English Linguistics.* Ed. Sidney Greenbaum et al. London: Longman.

————. 1965. "The Tainted Ain't Once More." *College English* Jan.: 298–303.

Himstreet, William C., and Wayne Murlin Baty. 1977. *Business Communications.* 5th ed. Belmont, Calif.: Wadsworth.

Hodges, John C., and Mary E. Whitten. 1984. *The Harbrace College Handbook.* 9th ed. New York: Harcourt Brace Jovanovich.

Hodgson, William B. 1889. *Errors in the Use of English.* Edinburgh.

Howard, Philip. 1977. *New Words for Old.* New York: Oxford Univ. Press.

————. 1978. *Weasel Words.* New York: Oxford Univ. Press.

————. 1980. *Words Fail Me.* New York: Oxford Univ. Press.

————. 1983. *A Word in Your Ear.* New York: Oxford Univ. Press.

————. 1984. *The State of the Language.* New York: Oxford Univ. Press.

Hyde, G. M. 1926. *Handbook for Newspaper Workers.* Enlarged ed. New York: Appleton.

Irmscher, William F. 1976. *The Holt Guide to English.* 2d ed. New York: Holt, Rinehart and Winston.

Janis, J. Harold. 1984. *Modern Business Language and Usage in Dictionary Form.* Garden City, N.Y.: Doubleday.

Jensen, Dana O., et al. 1935. *Modern Composition and Rhetoric.* Boston: Houghton Mifflin.

Jespersen, Otto. 1909–49. *A Modern Grammar on Historical Principles.* 7 vols. Heidelberg: Carl Winter.

————. 1917. *Negation in English and Other Languages.* Copenhagen: Ejnar Munksgaard.

————. 1924. *Philosophy of Grammar.* New York: Holt.

————. 1946. *Mankind, Nation and Individual.* Bloomington, Ind.: Indiana Univ. Press.

————. 1948. *Growth and Structure of the English Language.* 9th ed. New York: Macmillan.

Johnson, Edward D. 1982. *The Handbook of Good English.* New York: Facts on File.

Johnson, Samuel. 1755. *A Dictionary of the English Language.* London.

Jonson, Ben. 1640. *The English Grammar.* London. Ed. with introduction and notes by Alice V. Waite. New York: Sturgis and Walton, 1909.

Joos, Martin. 1967. *The Five Clocks.* New York: Harcourt Brace Jovanovich.

Kilpatrick, James J. 1984. *The Writer's Art.* Kansas City: Andrews, McMeel & Parker.

Krapp, George Philip. 1909. *Modern English: Its Growth and Present Use.* New York: Scribners.

————. 1925. *The English Language in America.* 2 vols. New York: Ungar, 1960.

————. 1927. *A Comprehensive Guide to Good English.* Chicago: Rand McNally.

Kučera, Henry, and W. Nelson Francis. 1967. *Computational Analysis of Present-Day American English.* Providence, R.I.: Brown Univ. Press.

Kurath, Hans. *See Middle English Dictionary.*

Lakoff, Robin. 1975. *Language and Woman's Place.* New York: Harper and Row.

Lamberts, J. J. 1972. *A Short Introduction to English Usage.* New York: McGraw-Hill.

Language 8. 1981. Ginn Language Program. Lexington, Mass.: Ginn.

Language: Structure and Use. See Clark, Thomas L.

Leacock, Stephen. 1943. *How to Write.* New York: Dodd, Mead.

Leonard, Sterling A. 1929. *The Doctrine of Correctness in English Usage, 1700–1800.* Madison: University of Wisconsin Studies in Language and Literature: No. 25.

————. 1932. *Current English Usage.* English Monograph No. 1. Chicago: National Council of Teachers of English.

The Lincoln Library of Essential Information. 1924. Buffalo, N.Y.: Frontier Press.

Lindley Murray. *See* Murray, Lindley.

The Little, Brown Handbook. 1980. Ed. H. Ramsey Fowler et al. Boston: Little, Brown.

The Little, Brown Handbook. 1986. Ed. H. Ramsey Fowler et al. 3d ed. Boston: Little, Brown.

Long, J. H. 1888. *Slips of Tongue and Pen.* New York.

Longman Dictionary of the English Language. 1984. London: Longman.

Longman Guide to English Usage. See Greenbaum, Sidney.

Lounsbury, Thomas R. 1908. *The Standard of Usage in English.* New York: Harper.

Lowth, Robert. 1762. *A Short Introduction to English Grammar.* London.

————. 1763. *A Short Introduction to English Grammar.* 2d ed., corrected. London.

————. 1775. *A Short Introduction to English Grammar.* Philadelphia.

Lurie, Charles N. 1927. *How to Say It.* New York: G. P. Putnam's.

Lynes, Russell. 1970. "Usage, precise and otherwise." *Harper's* April: 6 +.

MacCracken, H. N., and Helen E. Sandison. 1917. *Manual of Good English.* New York: Macmillan.

McKnight, George H. 1928. *Modern English in the Making.* New York: Appleton.

McMahan, Elizabeth, and Susan Day. 1980. *The Writer's Rhetoric and Handbook.* New York: McGraw-Hill.

————. 1984. *The Writer's Rhetoric and Handbook.* 2d ed. New York: McGraw-Hill.

The Macmillan Handbook of English. 1982. Ed. Robert F. Willson, Jr., et al. 7th ed. New York: Macmillan.

Maggio, Rosalie. 1987. *The Nonsexist Word Finder.* Phoenix: Oryx.

Malmstrom, Jean. 1964. "Linguistics Atlas Findings *vs.* Textbook Pronouncements on Current American Usage." In Harold Allen, ed. *Readings in Applied English Linguistics.* New York: Appleton-Century-Crofts.

Marckwardt, Albert H. 1958. *American English.* New York: Oxford Univ. Press.

Marckwardt, Albert H., and Fred Walcott. 1938. *Facts About Current English Usage.* New York: Appleton-Century.

A Mark Twain Lexicon. See Ramsay, Robert L.

Marsh, George Perkins. 1859. *Lectures on the English Language.* New York.

Martin, Phyllis. 1977. *Word Watcher's Handbook.* New York: David McKay.

Mathews, Mitford M. 1931. *The Beginnings of American English.* Chicago: Univ. of Chicago Press.

Matthews, Brander. 1901. *Parts of Speech.* New York: Charles Scribner's.

Mencken, H. L. 1919. *The American Language.* New York: Knopf.

————. 1936. *The American Language*. 4th ed. New York: Knopf.

————. 1945. *The American Language, Supplement I*. New York: Knopf.

————. 1948. *The American Language, Supplement II*. New York: Knopf.

————. 1963. *The American Language*. 4th ed. and two supplements. Abridged by Raven I. McDavid. New York: Knopf.

Michaels, Leonard, and Christopher Ricks, eds. 1980. *The State of the Language*. Berkeley: Univ. of California Press.

Middle English Dictionary. 1954– . Ed. Hans Kurath et al. Ann Arbor, Mich.: Univ. of Michigan Press.

Miller, Casey, and Kate Smith. 1976. *Words and Women*. Garden City, N.Y.: Doubleday.

————. 1980. *The Handbook of Nonsexist Writing*. New York: Lippincott.

Mitchell, Richard. 1979. *Less Than Words Can Say*. Boston: Little, Brown.

Mittins, W. H., et al. 1970. *Attitudes to English Usage*. London: Oxford Univ. Press.

Montgomery, Michael, and John Stratton. 1981. *The Writer's Hotline Handbook*. New York: New American Library.

Moon, George Washington. 1865. *The Dean's English*. 4th ed. New York.

Morris, William, and Mary Morris. 1975. *Harper Dictionary of Contemporary Usage*. New York: Harper and Row.

————. 1985. *Harper Dictionary of Contemporary Usage*. 2d ed. New York: Harper and Row.

Murray, Lindley. 1795. *English Grammar Adapted to the Different Classes of Learners*. York.

————. 1847. *English Grammar, Adapted to the Different Classes of Learners*. 55th ed. London.

Newman, Edwin. 1974. *Strictly Speaking*. Indianapolis: Bobbs-Merrill.

Nicholson, Margaret. 1957. *A Dictionary of American-English Usage*. New York: Oxford Univ. Press.

Nickles, Harry G. 1974. *Dictionary of Do's and Don'ts for Writers and Speakers*. New York: Greenwich House.

Opdyke, John B. 1935. *Get It Right*. New York: Funk and Wagnalls.

————. 1939. *Don't Say It*. New York: Funk and Wagnalls.

Oxford American Dictionary. 1980. New York: Oxford Univ.Press.

Oxford English Dictionary. 1884–1933. Ed. James A. H. Murray et al. 13 vols. Oxford: Clarendon.

Oxford English Dictionary, Supplement. 1972–1986. Ed. Robert W. Burchfield. 4 vols. Oxford: Clarendon.

Partridge, Eric. 1942. *Usage and Abusage*. New York: Harper.

Perrin, Porter G., and Wilma R. Ebbitt. 1972. *Writer's Guide and Index to English*. 5th ed. Glenview, Ill.: Scott, Foresman.

Phythian, B. A. 1979. *A Concise Dictionary of Correct English*. Totowa, N.J.: Littlefield, Adams.

Pooley, Robert C. 1974. *The Teaching of English Usage*. Urbana, Ill.: National Council of Teachers of English.

Post, Emily. 1927. *Etiquette*. New and enlarged ed. New York: Funk and Wagnalls.

————. 1945. *Etiquette*. New ed. New York: Funk and Wagnalls.

Poutsma, H. 1904–26. *A Grammar of Late Modern English*. Groningen, Netherlands: P. Noordhoff.

Powell, John A. 1925. *How to Write Business Letters*. Chicago: Univ. of Chicago Press.

Prentice Hall Handbook for Writers. 1978. Ed. Glenn Leggett et al. 7th ed. Englewood Cliffs, N.J.: Prentice Hall.

Prentice Hall Handbook for Writers. 1988. Ed. Glenn Leggett et al. 10th ed. Englewood Cliffs, N.J.: Prentice Hall.

Priestley, Joseph. 1761. *The Rudiments of English Grammar*. London.

————. 1798. *The Rudiments of English Grammar*. A New Edition Corrected. London.

Pyles, Thomas. 1952. *Words and Ways of American English*. New York: Random House.

————. 1979. *Selected Essays on English Usage*. Ed. John Algeo. Gainesville, Fla.: Univ. of Florida Presses.

————. 1982. *Origin and Development of the English Language*. 3d ed. New York: Harcourt Brace Jovanovich.

Pyles, Thomas, and John Algeo. 1970. *English*. New York: Harcourt, Brace and World.

Quiller-Couch, Sir Arthur. 1916. *On the Art of Writing*. New York: G. P. Putnam's.

Quinn, Jim. 1980. *American Tongue and Cheek*. New York: Pantheon.

Quirk, Randolph, et al. 1985. *A Comprehensive Grammar of the English Language*. London: Longman.

Ramsay, Robert L., and Frances Guthrie Emerson. 1938. *A Mark Twain Lexicon*. University of Missouri Studies: Vol. 13, No. 1. Columbia, Mo.: University of Missouri.

Randall, Bernice. 1988. *Webster's New World Guide to Current American Usage*. New York: Simon & Schuster.

The Random House Dictionary of the English Language. 1966. Ed. Jess Stein. New York: Random House.

The Random House Dictionary of the English Language. 1987. 2d ed. Ed. Stuart Berg Flexner. New York: Random House.

Raub, Robert N. 1897. *Helps in the Use of Good English*. Philadelphia.

Reader's Digest. *See Success with Words*.

Richard Grant White. *See* White, Richard Grant.

The Right Handbook. *See* Belanoff, Pat.

Roberts, Paul. 1954. *Understanding Grammar*. New York: Harper and Row.

————. 1962. *English Sentences*. New York: Harcourt, Brace and World.

Safire, William. 1980. *On Language*. New York: Times Books.

————. 1982. *What's the Good Word?* New York: Times Books.

————. 1984. *I Stand Corrected*. New York: Times Books.

————. 1986. *Take My Word for It*. New York: Times Books.

————. 1988. *You Could Look It Up*. New York: Times Books.

Scargill, M. H., et al. 1974. *Modern Canadian English Usage*. Toronto: McClelland and Stuart.

Schele de Vere, M. 1872. *Americanisms: The English of the New World*. New York.

Scott, Foresman. *See* Clark, Thomas L.

Sellers, Leslie. 1975. *Keeping Up the Style*. London: Pitman.

Shaw, Harry. 1970. *Errors in English*. 2d ed. New York: Barnes and Noble.

————. 1975. *Dictionary of Problem Words and Expressions*. New York: McGraw-Hill.

————. 1987. *Dictionary of Problem Words and Expressions.* Rev. ed. New York: McGraw-Hill.

Shopen, Timothy, and Joseph M. Williams. 1980. *Standards and Dialects in English.* Cambridge, Mass.: Winthrop.

Simon, John. 1980. *Paradigms Lost: Reflections on Literacy and Its Decline.* New York: Clarkson N. Potter.

Sledd, James. 1959. *A Short Introduction to English Grammar.* Chicago: Scott, Foresman.

Sledd, James, and Wilma R. Ebbitt, ed. 1962. *Dictionaries and THAT Dictionary.* Chicago: Scott, Foresman.

Strang, Barbara M. H. 1970. *A History of English.* London: Methuen.

Strunk, William F., Jr., and E. B. White. 1959. *The Elements of Style.* New York: Macmillan.

————. 1972. *The Elements of Style.* 2d ed. New York: Macmillan.

————. 1979. *The Elements of Style.* 3d ed. New York: Macmillan.

Success with Words. 1983. Ed. Peter Davies. Pleasantville, N.Y.: Reader's Digest Association.

Sundby, Bertil, et al. 1991. *A Dictionary of English Normative Grammar 1700–1800.* Amsterdam: John Benjamins.

Swan, Michael. 1980. *Practical English Usage.* Oxford: Oxford Univ. Press.

Sweet, Henry. 1892–98. *A New English Grammar.* 2 vols. Oxford.

Thornton, Richard H. 1912. *An American Glossary.* Vols. 1 and 2. London: St. Francis.

————. 1939. *An American Glossary.* Vol. 3. Ed. Louise Hanley. Madison, Wisc.: American Dialect Society.

Todd, Loreto, and Ian Hancock. 1986. *International English Usage.* London: Croom Helm.

Treble, H. A., and G. H. Vallins. 1937. *An A.B.C. of English Usage.* New York: Oxford Univ. Press.

Trimble, John R. 1975. *Writing with Style.* Englewood Cliffs, N.J.: Prentice Hall.

Trimmer, Joseph F., and James M. McCrimmon. 1988. *Writing with a Purpose.* 9th ed. Boston: Houghton Mifflin.

Tucker, Susie I. 1967. *Protean Shape: A Study in Eighteenth-Century Vocabulary and Usage.* London: Athlone Press.

Utter, Robert Palfrey. 1916. *Everyday Words and Their Uses.* New York: Harper.

Venolia, Jan. 1982. *Write Right!* Berkeley, Calif.: Ten Speed Press.

Vere, M. Schele de. *See* Schele de Vere, M.

Visser, F. T. 1963–73. *An Historical Syntax of the English Language.* 4 vols. Leiden, Netherlands: Brill.

Vizetelly, Frank. 1906. *A Desk-Book of Errors in English.* New York: Funk and Wagnalls.

————. 1920. *Mend Your Speech.* New York: Funk and Wagnalls.

————. 1922. *S.O.S.: Slips of Speech.* New York: Funk and Wagnalls.

Warriner, John E. 1986. *English Grammar and Composition: Complete Course.* Orlando, Fla.: Harcourt Brace Jovanovich.

Watt, William. 1967. *A Short Guide to English Usage.* Cleveland: World.

Webster, Noah. 1800. *A Grammatical Institute of the English Language. . . . Part Second. Containing a Plain and Comprehensive Grammar. . . .* 6th Connecticut ed. Hartford.

————. 1806. *A Compendious Dictionary of the English Language.* Hartford.

————. 1828. *An American Dictionary of the English Language.* New York.

————. 1841. *An American Dictionary of the English Language.* Rev. ed. New York.

————. 1847. *An American Dictionary of the English Language.* Ed. Chauncey Goodrich. Rev. and enlarged. Springfield, Mass.

————. 1864. *An American Dictionary of the English Language.* Ed. Noah Porter. Royal Quarto ed. Springfield, Mass.

Webster's International Dictionary. 1890. Ed. Noah Porter. Springfield, Mass.

Webster's New Dictionary of Synonyms. 1968. Springfield, Mass.: G. & C. Merriam.

Webster's New International Dictionary. 1909. Ed. William Torrey Harris. Springfield, Mass.: G. & C. Merriam.

Webster's New International Dictionary. 1934. Ed. William Allan Neilson. 2d ed. Springfield Mass.: G. & C. Merriam.

Webster's New World Dictionary. 1980. Ed. David B. Guralnik. 2d College ed. New York: Simon and Schuster.

Webster's New World Guide to Current American Usage. See Randall, Bernice.

Webster's Ninth New Collegiate Dictionary. 1983. Ed. Frederick C. Mish. Springfield, Mass.: Merriam-Webster.

Webster's Standard American Style Manual. 1985. Springfield, Mass.: Merriam-Webster.

Webster's Third New International Dictionary. 1961. Ed. Philip B. Gove. Springfield, Mass.: G. & C. Merriam.

Wentworth, Harold. 1944. *American Dialect Dictionary.* New York: Thomas Y. Crowell.

Weseen, Maurice H. 1928. *Crowell's Dictionary of English Grammar.* New York: Thomas Y. Crowell.

Whipple, T. H. Bailey. 1924. *Principles of Business Writing.* East Pittsburgh, Pa.: Westinghouse Technical Night School Press.

White, Richard Grant. 1870. *Words and Their Uses, Past and Present.* New York.

Whitford, Robert C., and James R. Foster. 1937. *American Standards of Writing.* New York: Farrar & Rinehart.

Williams, Ralph Olmstead. 1897. *Some Questions of Good English.* New York.

Wilson, Kenneth G. 1987. *Van Winkle's Return.* Hanover, N.H.: Published for the Univ. of Conn. by the Univ. Presses of New England.

Winners & Sinners: A Bulletin of Second-Guessing Issued Occasionally from the Newsroom of the New York Times. 1951– .

Woolley, Edwin C. 1920. *Handbook of Composition.* Rev. ed. Boston: D. C. Heath.

Woolley, Edwin C., and Franklin W. Scott. 1926. *New Handbook of Composition.* Boston: D. C. Heath.

Wyld, H. C. 1920. *A History of Modern Colloquial English.* London: T. Allen Unwin.

Zinsser, William. 1976. *On Writing Well.* New York: Harper and Row.